Pocket Oxford German Dictionary

Fourth Edition

German ----> English
English ----> German

Chief Editors
M. Clark
O. Thyen

OXFORD
UNIVERSITY PRESS

OXFORD
UNIVERSITY PRESS

Great Clarendon Street, Oxford OX2 6DP

Oxford University Press is a department of the University of Oxford.
It furthers the University's objective of excellence in research, scholarship,
and education by publishing worldwide in

Oxford New York

Auckland Cape Town Dar es Salaam Hong Kong Karachi
Kuala Lumpur Madrid Melbourne Mexico City Nairobi
New Delhi Shanghai Taipei Toronto

With offices in

Argentina Austria Brazil Chile Czech Republic France Greece
Guatemala Hungary Italy Japan Poland Portugal Singapore
South Korea Switzerland Thailand Turkey Ukraine Vietnam

Oxford is a registered trade mark of Oxford University Press
in the UK and in certain other countries

Published in the United States
by Oxford University Press Inc., New York

© Oxford University Press and Bibliographisches Institut & F. A. Brockhaus AG
1992, 1997, 2000, 2003, 2006
© Oxford University Press 2008, 2009

The moral rights of the author have been asserted
Database right Oxford University Press (maker)

First edition 1992
Revised edition 1997
Second edition 2000
Revised 2003
Third edition 2006
Revised 2008
Fourth edition 2009

British Library Cataloguing in Publication Data
Data available

Library of Congress Cataloging in Publication Data
Data available

Designed by Information Design Unit, Newport Pagnell
Typeset in Nimrod, Arial and Meta by Asiatype, Inc.
Printed in Great Britain by Clays Ltd, St Ives plc

ISBN 978-0-19-956076-9

3

7664794177912211

Preface

Words added to this edition of the *Pocket Oxford German Dictionary* have for the first time been garnered from Oxford's brand-new Languages Tracker programme, which monitors up-to-the-minute German writing and records changes in the language as they happen.

The *Pocket* combines the authority of the *Oxford German Dictionary* with the convenience of a small format and quick-access layout and is thus the ideal reference tool for all those requiring quick and reliable translations on the spot. It provides clear guidance on selecting the most appropriate translation, numerous examples to help with problems of usage and construction, and precise information on grammar, style, and pronunciation. All grammatical terms used are explained in a glossary at the back.

Additional help is provided by a centre supplement on life and culture in German-speaking countries, with a calendar of festivals and an A–Z of cultural institutions and practices, as well as a guide to letter-writing and a list of text-message abbreviations. There is also a succinct German grammar appendix, accompanied by sections on irregular verbs and numbers.

Reforms to the spelling of German ratified by the governments of Germany, Austria, and Switzerland have been fully incorporated, and former spellings are still included, marked as such, with cross-references to the modern forms when necessary. All the major spelling changes are also described in the introductory pages.

Designed to meet the needs of a wide range of users, from the student at intermediate level or above to the enthusiastic traveller and business professional, the *Pocket Oxford German Dictionary* is an invaluable resource for learners of modern, idiomatic German.

Editors and contributors

Editors

Michael Clark
Olaf Thyen
Werner Scholze-Stubenrecht
Magdalena Seubel
Bernadette Mohan
Robin Sawers
Gunhild Prowe

For the Fourth Edition

Maurice Waite

Data input

Susan Wilkin
Anne McConnell
Anna Cotgreave

A–Z of German culture Calendar of traditions, festivals, and holidays

Ella Associates
Valerie Grundy
Eva Vennebusch
Neil Morris
Roswitha Morris
Penelope Isaac
Michael Deicke

Summary of German Grammar

Nicholas Rollin
Marie-Louise Wasmeier

Inhalt / Contents

Erläuterungen zum deutsch-englischen Text / Key to German-English Entries

Stichwort •———— **Bịld·schirm** *der* (Ferns., Informationst.) screen
Headword

Bịldschirm-: ∼**gerät** *das* VDU; visual • Kompositablock.
display unit; ∼**schoner** *der;* ∼∼s, ∼∼   Eine Tilde ersetzt
(DV) screen saver   jeweils den
                                                        gemeinsamen

Die Aussprache- •——— **Blues** /blu:s/ *der;* ∼, ∼: blues *pl.*   ersten Bestandteil
angaben (in IPA-   der Komposita
Lautschrift) stehen   Compound block
unmittelbar hinter   with a swung dash
dem Stichwort   representing the
(s.S.xvi)   first element of
Pronunciation is   each compound
shown in IPA
immediately after the **dar|bieten** (geh.) *unr. tr. V.* (aufführen, •—— Ein senkrechter
headword (see p. xvi) vortragen) perform; ...   Strich nach dem
                                                   ersten Bestandteil
                                                   eines zusammen-
Ein unter einen •——— **darüber** *Adv.* (a) over it/them; ∼ **stehen**   gesetzten Verbs
Vokal gesetzter (fig.) be above such things   zeigt an, dass es
waagerechter Strich   sich um eine unfeste
zeigt die Länge des   Zusammensetzung
Vokals und in   handelt
mehrsilbigen   A vertical bar
Wörtern zugleich   indicates that a
die Betonung der   compound verb is
betreffenden Silbe   separable
an
An underline indicates
a long vowel, stressed **darụm** *Adv.* (a) [a]round it/them; ... • Ein unter einen
in words of more than   Vokal gesetzter
one syllable   Punkt zeigt die
                                                   Kürze des Vokals
                                                   und in mehrsilbigen
                                                   Wörtern zugleich
Ein hochgestellter •——— **dạss**, **dạß* *Konj.* (a) that; ...   die Betonung
Stern vor einem   der betreffenden
Stichwort zeigt an,   Silbe an
dass es sich um eine   An underdot
alte, nicht mehr   indicates a short
gültige Schreibung   vowel, stressed in
handelt   words of more than
An asterisk indicates   one syllable
an old spelling

                        Erst·aufführung *die* première •—— Kompositionsfuge
Grammatische •——— **erstklassig** [1] *Adj.* first-class   Dot marking the
Gliederungspunkte [2] *adv.* superbly   juncture of the
und Wortartangaben   elements of a
Grammatical   compound
categories
and parts of speech

· ·

Die Formen des •——— **Falter** *der;* ~s, ~ (Nacht~) moth; (Tag~)
Genitivs und des butterfly
Plurals eines
Substantivs **fliehen** /'fliːən/ *unr. itr. V.; mit sein* flee ———• **Der Hinweis** *mit sein*
Genitive and plural (vor + *Dat.* from); ... **zeigt an, dass das**
forms of a noun **betreffende Verb die**
  Perfekttempora mit
  dem Hilfsverb *sein*
Unregelmäßige •——— **fromm**; ~er *od.* **frömmer,** ~st... *od.* **bildet**
Steigerungsformen **frömmst...** 1 *Adj.* pious, devout ⟨*person*⟩; *mit sein* indicates that
eines Adjektivs a verb is conjugated
Irregular comparative with the auxiliary verb
and superlative forms *sein* in its perfect
of an adjective tenses

  Gehässigkeit *die;* ~, ~en (a) (Wesen) ——• **Semantische**
   spitefulness **Gliederungspunkte**
   (b) (Äußerung) spiteful remark **und Bedeutungs-**
Stilistische •——— **indikatoren**
Kennzeichnungen **happig** *Adj.* (ugs.) ~e Preise fancy prices Sense categories and
Style labels (coll.) indicators

  Haube *die;* ~, ~n (a) bonnet; (einer
   Krankenschwester) cap
   (b) (Kfz-W.) bonnet (Brit.); hood (Amer.) ——• **Angaben zur**
Bereichsangaben • **heuer** *Adv.* (südd., österr., schweiz.) this year **räumlichen**
Subject labels   **Zuordnung**
  Icon /'aiːkən/ *das;* ~s, ~s (DV) icon Regional labels
  Immun·schwäche *die* (Med.)
   immunodeficiency; immune deficiency

  knallen 1 *itr. V.* (a) ⟨*shot*⟩ ring out; ——• **Kollokatoren**
   ⟨*firework*⟩ go bang; ⟨*cork*⟩ pop; ⟨*door*⟩ slam; **(Wörter, mit denen**
   ⟨*whip, rifle*⟩ crack; ... **zusammen das**
  knapp 1 *Adj.* (a) meagre; narrow ⟨*victory,* **Stichwort häufig**
   lead⟩; narrow, bare ⟨*majority*⟩; ... **vorkommt) als Hilfe**
  zur Auswahl der für
Beispiele (jeweils • **machen** 1 *tr. V.* (a) make; **aus Plastik/** **den jeweiligen**
mit einer Tilde an **Holz** *usw.* **gemacht** made of plastic/wood *etc.;* **Kontext passenden**
Stelle des **sich** (*Dat.*) **etw.** ~ **lassen** have sth. made; ... **Übersetzung**
Stichworts) Collocators (words
Examples (with often used with the
a swung dash headword) shown to
representing the help select the correct
headword) translation for each
  context

  Omi *die;* ~, ~s ▶ OMA ——• **Ein Pfeil verweist**
  auf ein bedeutungs-
Mit *s. auch* **wird** • **Samstag** *der;* ~[e]s, ~e Saturday; *s. auch* **gleiches anderes**
auf ein Stichwort DIENSTAG **Stichwort**
verwiesen, unter An arrow directs the
dem noch user to another
zusätzliche headword with the
Informationen same meaning
zu finden sind
s. auch directs the
user to another
headword where
additional information
can be found

Key to English-German Entries /
Erläuterungen zum englisch-deutschen Text

Headword •——— **barber** /'bɑːbə(r)/ n. [Herren]friseur, der;
Stichwort   ~'s shop (Brit.) Friseursalon, der
barbiturate /bɑːˈbɪtjʊrət/ n. (Chem.)
Barbiturat, das

bar: ~ chart n. Stabdiagramm, das; •——— **Compound block**
~ **code** n. Strichcode, der   **with a swung dash**
representing the
first element of each
Each phrasal verb •— **bear²** ① v.t., bore /bɔː(r)/, borne /bɔːn/ ...   **compound**
is entered on a new   ■ **bear 'out** v.t. (fig.) bestätigen ⟨Bericht,   Kompositablock. Eine
line immediately   Erklärung⟩; ~ sb. out jmdm. Recht geben   Tilde ersetzt jeweils
following the entry   ■ **'bear with** v.t. Nachsicht haben mit   den gemeinsamen
for the first element   ersten Bestandteil der
Die *Phrasal Verbs*   Komposita
folgen, jedes auf einer
neuen Zeile, direkt auf
den Eintrag zu ihrem
Grundverb   **bemused** /bɪˈmjuːzd/ adj. verwirrt   •——— **Pronunciation**
shown in IPA
(see p. xviii).
Ausspracheangaben
Stress mark, •——————   (in IPA-Lautschrift)
showing stress on   **'bin liner** n. Müllbeutel, der   (s. S. xviii)
the following
syllable
Betonungszeichen vor   **cart** /kɑːt/ ① n. Wagen, der   •——— **Grammatical**
der betonten Silbe   ② v.t. (coll.) schleppen   **categories**
and parts of speech
Grammatische
Irregular tenses •—   **choose** /tʃuːz/ ① v.t., chose /tʃəʊz/,   Gliederungspunkte
of a verb   chosen /'tʃəʊzn/ (a) wählen   und Wortartangaben
Unregelmäßige
Verbformen
dub /dʌb/ v.t., -bb- (Cinemat.) synchronisieren   ——— **Doubling of a final**
consonant of a verb
before -ed or -ing
Verdoppelung des
Endkonsonanten
Irregular •——————   **good** /gʊd/ ① adj., better /'betə(r)/, best   eines Verbs vor -ed
comparative and   /best/ (a) gut; günstig ⟨Gelegenheit,   oder -ing
superlative forms   Angebot⟩; ...
of an adjective
Unregelmäßige
Steigerungsformen   **groom** /gruːm, grʊm/ ① n. (a) (stable boy)   •——— **Sense categories**
eines Adjektivs   Stallbursche, der   **and sense**
(b) (bride~) Bräutigam, der   **indicators**
Semantische
Gliederungspunkte
Subject labels •———   **HTML** abbr. (Comp.) =**hypertext markup**   und Bedeutungs-
Bereichsangaben   **language** HTML   indikatoren
immobilizer /ɪˈməʊbɪlaɪzə(r)/ n. (Motor Veh.)
Wegfahrsperre, die

Key to English-German entries

· ·

Style labels •————
Stilistische
Kennzeichnungen

'jam-packed *adj.* (coll.) knallvoll (ugs.),
proppenvoll (ugs.) (with von)

loch /lɒx, lɒk/ *n.* (Scot.) See, *der*
Medicare /'medɪkeə(r)/ *n.* (Amer.)
[*bundes*]*staatliches*
Krankenversicherungssystem für Personen
über 65 Jahre

————• **Regional labels**
Angaben zur
räumlichen
Zuordnung

Collocators •————
(words often used
with the headword)
shown to help select
the correct transla-
tion for each context.
Kollokatoren (Wörter,
mit denen zusammen
das Stichwort häufig
vorkommt) als Hilfe
zur Auswahl der für
den jeweiligen Kontext
passenden
Übersetzung

oppress /ə'pres/ *v.t.* unterdrücken; (fig.)
‹*Gefühl:*› bedrücken
oppressive /ə'presɪv/ *adj.* repressiv; (fig.)
bedrückend ‹*Ängste, Atmosphäre*›; (hot and
close) drückend ‹*Wetter, Klima, Tag*›

price /praɪs/ *n.* (lit. or fig.) Preis, *der;* **at a**
~ **of** zum Preis von; **what is the** ~ **of this?**
was kostet das?; **at/not at any** ~: um jeden/
keinen Preis

————• **Examples (with a**
swung dash
representing the
headword)
Beispiele (jeweils mit
einer Tilde an Stelle
des Stichworts)

An arrow directs •————
the user to another
headword with the
same meaning
Ein Pfeil verweist auf
ein bedeutungs-
gleiches anderes
Stichwort

sitcom /'sɪtkɒm/ (coll.) ▶ SITUATION COMEDY

Sunday /'sʌndeɪ, 'sʌndɪ/ *n.* Sonntag, *der;*
~ **opening** die sonntägliche Öffnung;
~ **trading** sonntägliche Ladenöffnung; *see*
also FRIDAY

————• ***see also* directs the**
user to another
headword where
additional
information can be
found
Mit *see also* wird auf
ein Stichwort
verwiesen, unter dem
noch zusätzliche
Informationen zu
finden sind

German spellings in this dictionary

German spellings in this dictionary are in accordance with the reforms ratified by the governments of Germany, Austria, and Switzerland in July 1996 and in force since August 1998. Key points of the reforms are summarized below.

To help the user who may not yet be familiar with the reforms, the German-English section of the dictionary gives both the new spellings and the old versions which became 'invalid' in 2005. The old spellings are marked with an asterisk and are cross-referred where necessary to the new. For example, the translations of the compound verb *wiedererkennen* will no longer be found at this headword, since under the new spelling rules the word vanishes from the language. Instead they are covered by two phrases at the entry for *wieder: jemanden/etwas wieder erkennen* (in the form *jmdn./etw. ~ erkennen*) and *er war kaum wieder zu erkennen* (in the form *er war kaum ~ zu erkennen*). Similarly, the translations of the adjective previously written *belemmert* will be found at the new entry for the headword *belämmert*.

In a number of cases, however, implementing the new spelling rules has meant that just some, but not all, uses of a word have had to be transferred from one entry to another. In these cases the headword is not marked with an asterisk, but the entry is provided

with a cross-reference to where the transferred information is now to be found. So, for example, the user who consults the entry for *leid* looking for a translation of the phrase previously written *jemandem leid tun* will find a cross-reference to the entry for the noun *Leid*, since according to the new spelling rules the word is written with a capital *L* in this expression. The headword *leid* itself is not marked with an asterisk, since it continues to exist in its own right as an adjective.

The following summary lists the most important changes:

1 The ß character The ß character, which is generally replaced in Switzerland by a double s, is retained in Germany and Austria, but is now only written after a long vowel (as in Fuß, Füße) and after a diphthong (as in Strauß, Sträuße).

Fluß, Baß, keß, läßt, Nußknacker become: *Fluss, Bass, kess, lässt, Nussknacker*

2 Nominalized adjectives Nominalized adjectives are written with a capital, even in set phrases.

sein Schäfchen ins trockene bringen, im trüben fischen, im allgemeinen become: *sein Schäfchen ins Trockene bringen, im Trüben fischen, im Allgemeinen*

3 Words from the same word family In certain cases the spelling of words belonging to the same family has been made uniform.

numerieren, überschwenglich become: *nummerieren* (like Nummer), *überschwänglich* (being related to Überschwang)

4 The same consonant three times in a row When the same consonant occurs three times in a row in compounds, all three are written, even when a vowel follows.

Brennessel, Schiffahrt become: *Brennnessel, Schifffahrt* (exceptions are dennoch, Drittel, Mittag)

5 Verb, adjective, and participle compounds
Verb, adjective, and participle compounds are written as two words more frequently than previously.

spazierengehen, radfahren, ernstgemeint, erdölexportierend become: *spazieren gehen, Rad fahren, ernst gemeint, Erdöl exportierend*

6 Compounds containing numbers in figures Compounds containing numbers in figures are now written with a hyphen.

24karätig, 8pfünder become: *24-karätig, 8-Pfünder*

7 The division of words containing st st is treated like a normal combination of consonants and is no longer indivisible.

Ha-stig, Ki-ste become: *has-tig, Kis-te*

8 The division of words containing ck The combination ck is not divided and goes on to the next line.

Bäk-ker, schik-ken become: *Bä-cker, schi-cken*

9 The division of foreign words Compound foreign words which are hardly recognized as such today may be divided by syllables, without regard to their original components.

He-li-ko-pter (from the Greek *helix* and *pteron*) may also be written: *He-li-kop-ter*

10 The comma before und Where two complete clauses are connected by *und,* a comma is no longer obligatory.

Karl war in Schwierigkeiten, und niemand konnte ihm helfen. may also be written: *Karl war in Schwierigkeiten und niemand konnte ihm helfen.*

11 The comma with infinitives and participles Even longer clauses containing an infinitive or participle do not have to be divided off with a comma.

Er begann sofort, das neue Buch zu lesen. Ungläubig den Kopf schüttelnd, verließ er das Zimmer. may also be written: *Er begann sofort das neue Buch zu lesen. Ungläubig den Kopf schüttelnd verließ er das Zimmer.*

Abkürzungen / Abbreviations

anderes, andere	a.	other, others		chemisch	chem.	chemical
ähnliches, ähnliche	ä.	similar		Kindersprache	child lang.	child language
Abkürzung	abbr.	abbreviation		christlich	christl.	Christian
Abkürzung	Abk.	abbreviation		Kinematographie	Cinemat.	Cinematography
absolut	abs.	absolute		umgangssprachlich	coll.	colloquial
adjektivisch	adj.	adjective, adjectival		Kollektivum	collect.	collective
Adjektiv	Adj.	adjective		Kombination	comb.	combination
Verwaltungssprache	Admin.	Administration, Administrative		Handel, Handels-	Commerc.	Commerce, Commercial
adverbial	adv.	adverb, adverbial		elektronische Datenverarbeitung	Comp.	Computing
Adverb	Adv.	adverb		Komparativ, komparativ	compar.	comparative
Flugwesen	Aeronaut.	Aeronautics		Konditional, konditional	condit.	conditional
Landwirtschaft	Agric.	Agriculture				
Akkusativ	Akk.	accusative		Konjunktion	conj.	conjunction
Amerika	Amer.	American, America		Dativ	Dat.	dative
amerikanisch	amerik.	American		Deutsche Demokratische Republik	DDR	German Democratic Republic
Amtssprache	Amtsspr.	official language				
Anatomie	Anat.	Anatomy		bestimmt	def.	definite
Anthropologie	Anthrop.	Anthropology		Deklination	Dekl.	declension
veraltet	arch.	archaic		Demonstrativpronomen	Demonstrativpron.	demonstrative pronoun
Archäologie	Archaeol.	Archaeology				
Architektur	Archit.	Architecture		Zahnmedizin	Dent.	Dentistry
Artikel	art.	article		abwertend	derog.	derogatory
Astrologie	Astrol.	Astrology		das heißt	d. h.	that is [to say]
Astronomie	Astron.	Astronomy		Dialekt	dial.	dialect
Raumfahrt	Astronaut.	Astronautics		dichterisch	dichter.	poetic
Altes Testament	A. T.	Old Testament		Damenschneiderei	Dressm.	Dressmaking
attributiv	attr., attrib.	attributive		Druckwesen	Druckw.	Printing
Australien	Austral.	Australian, Australia		deutsch	dt.	German
Bauwesen	Bauw.	Construction		Datenverarbeitung	DV	Data Processing
Bergmannssprache	Bergmannsspr.	Mining		kirchlich	Eccl.	Ecclesiastical
besonders	bes.	especially		Ökologie	Ecol.	Ecology
Bezeichnung	Bez.	name		Ökonomik	Econ.	Economics
biblisch	bibl.	biblical		Bildungswesen	Educ.	Education
Biologie	Biol.	Biology		ehemals, ehemalig	ehem.	former, formerly
Buchführung	Bookk.	Bookkeeping		Eisenbahn	Eisenb.	Railways
Börsenwesen	Börsenw.	Stock Market		Elektrizität	Electr.	Electricity
Botanik	Bot.	Botany		Elektrotechnik	Elektrot.	Electrical Engineering
Bundesrepublik Deutschland	BRD	Federal Republic of Germany				
britisch, Großbritannien	Brit.	British, Britain		elektrisch	elektr.	electrical
				elliptisch	ellipt.	elliptical
britisch	brit.	British		emphatisch	emphat.	emphatic
Bruchzahl	Bruchz.	fraction		besonders	esp.	especially
Buchführung	Buchf.	Bookkeeping		etwas	etw.	something
Buchwesen	Buchw.	Book Trade		euphemistisch	euphem.	euphemistic
Chemie	Chem.	Chemistry		evangelisch	ev.	Evangelical
				ausdrückend	expr.	expressing

fachsprachlich	**fachspr.**	technical	Kindersprache	**Kinderspr.**	child language
familiär	**fam.**	familiar	Kochkunst	**Kochk.**	Cookery
feminin	**fem.**	feminine	Komparativ	**Komp.**	comparative
Fernsehen	**Ferns.**	Television	Konjunktion	**Konj.**	conjunction
Fernsprechwesen	**Fernspr.**	Telephony	landschaftlich	**landsch.**	regional
figurativ	**fig.**	figurative	Landwirtschaft	**Landw.**	Agriculture
Finanzwesen	**Finanzw.**	Finance	Linguistik	**Ling.**	Linguistics
Flugwesen	**Flugw.**	Aeronautics	wortwörtlich	**lit.**	literal
Fußball	**Footb.**	Football	Literatur	**Lit.**	Literature
Forstwesen	**Forstw.**	Forestry	Literaturwissen-	**Literaturw.**	Literary Studies
Fotografie	**Fot.**	Photography	schaft		
Gastronomie	**Gastr.**	Gastronomy	Luftfahrt	**Luftf.**	Aeronautics
gehoben	**geh.**	elevated	mittelalterlich	**ma.**	medieval
Genitiv	**Gen.**	genitive	Mittelalter	**MA.**	Middle Ages
Geographie	**Geog.**	Geography	marxistisch	**marx.**	Marxist
Geologie	**Geol.**	Geology	maskulin	**masc.**	masculine
Geometrie	**Geom.**	Geometry	Mathematik	**Math.**	Mathematics
Handarbeit	**Handarb.**	Handicraft	Maschinenbau	**Mech.**	Mechanical
Heraldik	**Her.**	Heraldry		**Engin.**	Engineering
Hilfsverb	**Hilfsv.**	auxiliary verb	Medizin	**Med.**	Medicine
historisch	**hist.**	historical	Meereskunde	**Meeresk.**	Oceanography
Geschichte,	**Hist.**	History, historical	Meteorologie	**Met.**	Meteorology
historisch			Metallurgie	**Metall.**	Metallurgy
Hochschulwesen	**Hoch-**	Higher Education	Metallbearbeitung	**Metall-**	Metalwork
	schulw.			**bearb.**	
Gartenbau	**Hort.**	Horticulture	Metallbearbeitung	**Metalw.**	Metalwork
Imperativ,	**imper.**	imperative	Meteorologie	**Meteorol.**	Meteorology
imperativisch			Militär	**Mil., Milit.**	Military
unpersönlich	**impers.**	impersonal	modifizierend	**mod.**	modifying
unbestimmt	**indef.**	indefinite	Modalverb	**Modalv.**	modal verb
Indefinitpronomen	**Indefinit-**	indefinite	Kraftfahrzeug-	**Motor Veh.**	Motor Vehicles
	pron.	pronoun	wesen		
indeklinabel	**indekl.**	indeclinable	Musik	**Mus.**	Music
Indikativ	**Indik.**	indicative	Mythologie	**Mythol.**	Mythology
Infinitiv	**Inf.**	infinitive	Substantiv	**n.**	noun
Interjektion	**Interj., int.**	interjection	Seemannssprache	**Naut.**	Nautical
interrogativ	**interrog.**	interrogative	negativ	**neg.**	negative
intransitiv	**intr.**	intransitive	Nominativ	**Nom.**	nominative
irisch, Irland	**Ir.**	Irish, Ireland	norddeutsch	**nordd.**	North German
ironisch	**iron.**	ironical	nordostdeutsch	**nordostd.**	North-East
Jägersprache	**Jägerspr.**	Hunting			German
jemand	**jmd.**	somebody	Substantive	**ns.**	nouns
jemandem	**jmdm.**	somebody		*(English)*	
jemanden	**jmdn.**	somebody	nationalsozialis-	**ns.**	National
jemandes	**jmds.**	somebody's	tisch	*(Deutsch)*	Socialist
scherzhaft	**joc.**	jocular	Neues Testament	**N. T.**	New Testament
Journalismus	**Journ.**	Journalism	Kernphysik	**Nucl. Phys.**	Nuclear Physics
Jugendsprache	**Jugend-**	young people's	ohne; oben	**o.**	without; above
	spr.	language	Objekt	**obj.**	object
juristisch	**jur.**	legal	oder	**od.**	or
Kardinalzahl	**Kardinalz.**	cardinal number	Ordinalzahl	**Ordinalz.**	ordinal number
katholisch	**kath.**	Catholic	Ornithologie	**Ornith.**	Ornithology
Kaufmanns-	**Kauf-**	Business	österreichisch	**österr.**	Austrian
sprache	**mannsspr.**		Papierdeutsch	**Papierdt.**	officialese
Kraftfahrzeug-	**Kfz-W.**	Motor Vehicles	Parlament	**Parl.**	Parliament
wesen			Partizip	**Part.**	participle

Passiv	pass.	passive
Perfekt	Perf.	perfect
Person	Pers.	person
Philosophie	Philos.	Philosophy
Fotografie	Photog.	Photography
Phrase(n)	phr(s).	phrase(s)
Physik	Phys.	Physics
Physiologie	Physiol.	Physiology
Plural	Pl., pl.	plural
Plusquamperfekt	Plusq.	pluperfect
dichterisch	poet.	poetical
Politik	Polit.	Politics
possessiv, Possessiv-	poss.	possessive
nachgestellt	postpos.	postpositive
Postwesen	Postw.	Post Office
zweites Partizip	p.p.	past participle
prädikativ	präd.	predicative
Präposition	Präp.	preposition
Präsens	Präs.	present
Präteritum	Prät.	preterite
prädikativ	pred.	predicative
Präfix	pref.	prefix
Präposition	prep.	preposition
Präsens	pres.	present
erstes Partizip	pres. p.	present participle
Eigenname	pr. n.	proper noun
Pronomen	Pron., pron.	pronoun
sprichwörtlich	prov.	proverbial
Psychologie	Psych.	Psychology
Präteritum	p.t.	past tense
Warenzeichen	®	Registered Trade Mark
Eisenbahn	Railw.	Railways
Raumfahrt	Raumf.	Space Travel
römisch-katholische Kirche	RC Ch.	Roman Catholic Church
Rechtssprache	Rechtsspr.	legal terminology
Rechtswesen	Rechtsw.	Law
reflexiv	refl.	reflexive
regelmäßig	regelm.	regular
relativ	rel.	relative
Religion	Rel.	Religion
Relativpronomen	Relativ-pron.	relative pronoun
römisch	röm.	Roman
römisch-katholisch	röm-kath.	Roman Catholic
Rundfunk	Rundf.	Radio
siehe	s.	see
Seite	S.	page
jemand	sb.	somebody
Schule	Sch.	School
scherzhaft	scherzh.	jocular
Schülersprache	Schüler-spr.	school slang
schweizerisch	schweiz.	Swiss
Wissenschaft	Sci.	Science
schottisch	Scot.	Scottish, Scotland
Schulwesen	Schulw.	School System
Seemannssprache	Seemanns-spr.	Nautical
Seewesen	Seew.	Maritime Affairs
Singular	Sg., sing.	singular
salopp	sl.	slang
siehe oben	s. o.	see above
Soziologie	Sociol.	Sociology
Soldatensprache	Soldaten-spr.	army slang
Soziologie	Soziol.	Sociology
spöttisch	spött.	derisive
Sprichwort	Spr.	proverb
Sprachwissenschaft	Sprachw.	Linguistics
Börsenwesen	St. Exch.	Stock Exchange
Steuerwesen	Steuerw.	Taxation
etwas	sth.	something
Studentensprache	Studen-tenspr.	student slang
siehe unten	s. u.	see below
Subjekt	Subj.	subject
substantivisch; substantiviert	subst.	nominal; nominalized
Substantiv	Subst.	noun
süddeutsch	südd.	South German
südwestdeutsch	südwestd.	South-West German
Suffix	suf.	suffix
Superlativ	Sup., superl.	superlative
Landvermessung	Surv.	Surveying
Symbol	symb.	symbol
fachsprachlich	tech.	technical
Fernsprechwesen	Teleph.	Telephony
Fernsehen	Telev.	Television
Textilwesen	Textilw.	Textiles
Theologie	Theol.	Theology
Tiermedizin	Tiermed.	Veterinary Medicine
transitiv	tr.	transitive
Trennung	Trenn.	division
und	u.	and
und Ähnliches	u. Ä.	and similar
umgangssprachlich	ugs.	colloquial
unbestimmt	unbest.	indefinite
Universität	Univ.	University
unpersönlich	unpers.	impersonal
unregelmäßig	unr.	irregular
gewöhnlich	usu.	usually
und so weiter	usw.	et cetera
von	v.	of
Verb	V.	verb
Hilfsverb	v. aux.	auxiliary verb

veraltet; veraltend	**veralt.**	obsolete; obsolescent		transitives und intransitives Verb	**v. t. & i.**	transitive and intransitive verb
Verhaltensforschung	**Verhaltensf.**	Behavioural Research		vulgär	**vulg.**	vulgar
verhüllend	**verhüll.**	euphemistic		Werbesprache	**Werbespr.**	advertising jargon
Verkehrswesen	**Verkehrsw.**	Transport		westdeutsch	**westd.**	western German
Versicherungswesen	**Versicherungsw.**	Insurance		Wirtschaft	**Wirtsch.**	Commerce and Industry
Tiermedizin	**Vet. Med.**	Veterinary Medicine		Wissenschaft	**Wissensch.**	Science
vergleiche	**vgl.**	compare		Warenzeichen	ⓦ	Registered Trade Mark
intransitives Verb	**v. i.**	intransitive verb		Zahnmedizin	**Zahnmed.**	Dentistry
Verkleinerungsform	**Vkl.**	diminutive		zum Beispiel	**z. B.**	for example
				Zeitungswesen	**Zeitungsw.**	Newspaper Industry
Völkerkunde	**Völkerk.**	Ethnology				
volkstümlich	**volkst.**	popular, vernacular		Zoologie	**Zool.**	Zoology
				Zusammensetzung	**Zus.**	compound
reflexives Verb	**v. refl.**	reflexive verb		Zusammenschreibung	**Zusschr.**	writing as one word
transitives Verb	**v. t.**	transitive verb				

Als Markenzeichen geschützte Wörter / Note on Proprietary Status

Namen und Kennzeichen, die als Marken bekannt sind und entsprechenden Schutz genießen, sind durch die Zeichen ® oder ⓦ gekennzeichnet. Handelsnamen ohne Markencharakter sind nicht gekennzeichnet. Aus dem Fehlen der Zeichen ® oder ⓦ darf im Einzelfall nicht geschlossen werden, dass ein Name oder Zeichen frei ist. Eine Haftung für ein etwaiges Fehlen der Zeichen ® oder ⓦ wird ausgeschlossen.

This dictionary includes some words which have, or are asserted to have, proprietary status as trade marks or otherwise. Their inclusion does not imply that they have acquired for legal purposes a non-proprietary or general significance, nor any other judgement concerning their legal status. In cases where the editorial staff have some evidence that a word has proprietary status, this is indicated in the entry for that word by the abbreviation ® or ⓦ, but no judgement concerning the legal status of such words is made or implied thereby.

Phonetic symbols used in transcriptions of German words

Phonetic information given in the German-English section

The pronunciation of German is largely regular, and phonetic transcriptions have only been given where additional help is needed. In all other cases only the position of the stressed syllable and the length of the vowel in that syllable are shown: a long vowel is indicated by an underline, e.g. **Maß**, a short vowel by a dot placed underneath, e.g. **Masse**.

a	*hat*	hat
aː	*Bahn*	baːn
ɐ	*Ober*	'oːbɐ
ɐ̯	*Uhr*	uːɐ̯
ã	*Ensemble*	ã'sãːbl̩
ãː	*Abonnement*	abɔnə'mãː
ai	*weit*	vait
au	*Haut*	haut
b	*Ball*	bal
ç	*ich*	ɪç
d	*dann*	dan
dʒ	*Gin*	dʒɪn
e	*egal*	e'gaːl
eː	*Beet*	beːt
ɛ	*mästen*	'mɛstn̩
ɛː	*wählen*	'vɛːlən
ɛ̃	*Mannequin*	'manəkɛ̃
ɛ̃ː	*Cousin*	ku'zɛ̃ː
ə	*Nase*	'naːzə
f	*Faß*	fas
g	*Gast*	gast
h	*hat*	hat
i	*vital*	vi'taːl
iː	*viel*	fiːl
i̯	*Studie*	'ʃtuːdi̯ə
ɪ	*Birke*	'bɪrkə
j	*ja*	jaː
k	*kalt*	kalt
l	*Last*	last
l̩	*Nabel*	'naːbl̩

Phonetics used in transcriptions of German

m	*Mast*	mast	|		Glottal stop, e.g. *beachten* /bə|axtn̩/
n	*Naht*	na:t			
n̩	*baden*	'ba:dn̩	:		Length sign, indicating that the preceding vowel is long, e.g. *Chrom* /kro:m/
ŋ	*lang*	laŋ			
o	*Moral*	mo'ra:l			
o:	*Boot*	bo:t	~		Indicates a nasal vowel, e.g. *Fond* /fõ:/
o̜	*loyal*	lo̜a'ja:l			
õ	*Fondue*	fõ'dy:	'		Stress mark, immediately preceding a stressed syllable, e.g. *Ballon* /ba'lɔn/
õ:	*Fond*	fõ:			
ɔ	*Post*	pɔst			
ø	*Ökonom*	øko'no:m			
ø:	*Öl*	ø:l			
œ	*göttlich*	'gœtlɪç			
œ̃	*Parfum*	par'fœ̃:			
ɔy	*Heu*	hɔy			
p	*Pakt*	pakt			
pf	*Pfahl*	pfa:l			
r	*Rast*	rast			
s	*Hast*	hast			
ʃ	*schal*	ʃa:l			
t	*Tal*	ta:l			
ts	*Zahl*	tsa:l			
tʃ	*Matsch*	matʃ			
u	*kulant*	ku'lant			
u:	*Hut*	hu:t			
u̜	*aktuell*	ak'tu̜ɛl			
ʊ	*Pult*	pʊlt			
v	*was*	vas			
x	*Bach*	bax			
y	*Physik*	fy'zi:k			
y:	*Rübe*	'ry:bə			
ỹ	*Nuance*	'nỹã:sə			
ʏ	*Fülle*	'fʏlə			
z	*Hase*	'ha:zə			
ʒ	*Genie*	ʒe'ni:			

Die für das Englische verwendeten Zeichen der Lautschrift

ɑ	*barb*	bɑ:b		p	*pet*	pet
ã:	*séance*	'seɪɑ̃s		r	*rat*	ræt
æ	*fat*	fæt		s	*sip*	sɪp
æ̃	*lingerie*	'læ̃ʒərɪ		ʃ	*ship*	ʃɪp
aɪ	*fine*	faɪn		t	*tip*	tɪp
aʊ	*now*	naʊ		tʃ	*chin*	tʃɪn
b	*bat*	bæt		θ	*thin*	θɪn
d	*dog*	dɒg		ð	*the*	ðə
dʒ	*jam*	dʒæm		u:	*boot*	bu:t
e	*met*	met		ʊ	*book*	bʊk
eɪ	*fate*	feɪt		ʊə	*tourist*	'tʊərɪst
eə	*fairy*	'feərɪ		ʌ	*dug*	dʌg
əʊ	*goat*	gəʊt		v	*van*	væn
ə	*ago*	ə'gəʊ		w	*win*	wɪn
ɜ:	*fur*	fɜ:(r)		x	*loch*	lɒx
f	*fat*	fæt		z	*zip*	zɪp
g	*good*	gʊd		ʒ	*vision*	'vɪʒn
h	*hat*	hæt		:	Längezeichen, bezeichnet Länge des unmittelbar davor stehenden Vokals, z. B. *boot* /bu:t/	
ɪ	*bit, lately*	bɪt, 'leɪtlɪ				
ɪə	*nearly*	'nɪəlɪ				
i:	*meet*	mi:t		'	Betonung, steht unmittelbar vor einer betonten Silbe, z. B. *ago* /ə'gəʊ/	
j	*yet*	jet				
k	*kit*	kɪt				
l	*lot*	lɒt		(r)	Ein „r" in runden Klammern wird nur gesprochen, wenn im Textzusammenhang ein Vokal unmittelbar folgt, z. B. *pare* /peə(r)/; *pare away* /peər ə'weɪ/	
m	*mat*	mæt				
n	*not*	nɒt				
ŋ	*sing*	sɪŋ				
ɒ	*got*	gɒt				
ɔ:	*paw*	pɔ:				
ɔɪ	*boil*	bɔɪl				

a, A /a:/ *das;* ~, ~ **(a)** (Buchstabe) a/A; **das A und O** (fig.) the essential thing/things (*Gen.* for); **von A bis Z** (fig. ugs.) from beginning to end
(b) (Musik) [key of] A

a *Abk.* = **Ar**

à /a/ *Präp. mit Nom., Akk.* (Kaufmannsspr.) **zehn Marken à 0,56 Euro** ten stamps at 0.56 euros each

A *Abk.* = **Autobahn** ≈ M

Aal *der;* ~[e]s, ~e eel; ~ **grün** (Kochk.) green eels; stewed eels

aalen *refl. V.* (ugs.) stretch out

aal·glatt (abwertend) [1] *Adj.* slippery; ~ **sein** be as slippery as an eel
[2] *adv.* smoothly

Aas *das;* ~es, ~e *od.* **Äser (a)** *Pl.* ~e carrion *no art.;* (Kadaver) [rotting] carcass
(b) *Pl.* **Äser** (salopp abwertend) swine; (anerkennend) devil

ab [1] *Präp. mit Dat.* **(a)** from; **ab 1980** as from 1980; **ab Werk** (Kaufmannsspr.) ex works; **ab Frankfurt fliegen** fly from Frankfurt
(b) ([Rang]folge) from … on[wards]; **ab 20 Euro** from 20 euros [upwards]
[2] *Adv.* **(a)** (weg) off; away; **ab sein** (ugs.: sich [von etw.] gelöst haben) have come off [sth.]
(b) (ugs.: Aufforderung) off; away; **ab nach Hause** get off home
(c) Gewehr ab! (milit. Kommando) order arms!
(d) ab und zu *od.* an now and then

ab|ändern *tr. V.* alter; amend ⟨text⟩

Ab·änderung *die* alteration; (eines Textes) amendment

ab|arbeiten *tr. V.* work for ⟨meal⟩; work off ⟨debt, amount⟩

Ab·art *die* variety

ab·artig *Adj.* deviant; abnormal

Ab·artigkeit *die;* ~, ~en abnormality; deviancy

Abb. *Abk.* = **Abbildung** Fig.

Ab·bau *der* **(a)** dismantling; (von Zelten, Lagern) striking
(b) ▶ ABBAUEN C: cutback (*Gen.* in); pruning; reduction
(c) (Bergbau) mining; (von Stein) quarrying

ab|bauen *tr. V.* **(a)** dismantle; strike ⟨tent, camp⟩
(b) (beseitigen) gradually remove; break down ⟨prejudices, inhibitions⟩
(c) (verringern) cut back ⟨staff⟩; prune ⟨jobs⟩; reduce ⟨wages⟩
(d) (Bergbau) mine; quarry ⟨stone⟩

ab|beißen [1] *unr. tr. V.* bite off
[2] *unr. itr. V.* have a bite

ab|bekommen *unr. tr. V.* **(a)** get
(b) einen Schlag/ein paar Kratzer ~: get hit/get a few scratches; **etwas** ~ (getroffen werden) be hit; (verletzt werden) be hurt
(c) (los-, herunterbekommen) get ⟨paint, lid, chain⟩ off

ab|berufen *unr. tr. V.* recall ⟨ambassador, envoy⟩ (aus, von from)

ab|bestellen *tr. V.* cancel

ab|bezahlen *tr. V.* pay off

ab|biegen *unr. itr. V.; mit sein* turn off; **links/rechts** ~: turn [off] left/right

Abbieger *der;* ~s, ~, **Abbiegerin** *die;* ~, ~nen (Verkehrsw.) motorist/cyclist/car *etc.* turning off

Ab·bild *das* (eines Menschen) likeness; (eines Gegenstandes) copy; (fig.) portrayal

ab|bilden *tr. V.* copy; reproduce ⟨object, picture⟩; depict ⟨person, landscape⟩; (fig.) portray

Abbildung *die* illustration

ab|binden *unr. tr. V.* **(a)** (losbinden) untie; undo
(b) (abschnüren) put a tourniquet on ⟨artery, arm, leg, etc.⟩; tie ⟨umbilical cord⟩

ab|blasen *unr. tr. V.* (ugs.) call off

ab|blättern *itr. V.; mit sein* flake off

ab|blenden *tr., itr. V.* black out; dip (Brit.), dim (Amer.) ⟨headlights⟩; **bei Gegenverkehr frühzeitig** ~: dip *or* (Amer.) dim one's headlights promptly when there is oncoming traffic

ab|blitzen *itr. V.; mit sein* (ugs.) **sie ließ alle Verehrer** ~: she gave all her admirers the brush-off

ab|brausen *tr. V.* ▶ ABDUSCHEN

ab|brechen [1] *unr. tr. V.* **(a)** break off; break ⟨needle, pencil⟩
(b) (zerlegen) strike ⟨tent, camp⟩
(c) (abreißen) demolish, pull down ⟨building⟩
(d) (beenden) break off ⟨negotiations, [diplomatic] relations, discussion, activity⟩; (vorzeitig) cut short ⟨conversation, holiday, activity⟩
(e) (DV) cancel
[2] *unr. itr. V.* **(a)** *mit sein* break [off]
(b) (aufhören) break off

ab|bremsen [1] *tr. V.* **(a)** brake
(b) retard ⟨motion⟩
[2] *itr. V.* brake

ab|brennen [1] *unr. itr. V.; mit sein* **(a)** be burned down; **das Haus ist abgebrannt** the house has burned down
(b) ⟨fuse⟩ burn away; ⟨candle⟩ burn down
[2] *unr. tr. V.* **(a)** let off ⟨firework⟩
(b) burn down ⟨building⟩

ạb|bringen *unr. tr. V.* **jmdn. davon ~, etw. zu tun** dissuade sb. from doing sth.; **jmdn. vom Kurs ~:** make sb. change course

ạb|bröckeln *itr. V.; mit sein* (auch fig.) crumble away

Ạb·bruch *der* **(a)** (Abriss) demolition; pulling down **(b)** (Beendigung) breaking-off; (einer Schwangerschaft) termination **(c) einer Sache** (*Dat.*) **[keinen] ~ tun** do [no] harm to sth.

ạb|buchen *tr. V.* ⟨*bank*⟩ debit (**von** to); ⟨*creditor*⟩ claim by direct debit (**von** to); **etw. ~ lassen** (durch die Bank) pay sth. by standing order; (durch Gläubiger) pay sth. by direct debit

ạb|bügeln *tr. V.* (ugs.) reject, brush aside ⟨*warning, question, criticism*⟩; rebuff ⟨*person*⟩

ạb|bürsten *tr. V.* **(a)** brush off **(b)** (säubern) brush ⟨*garment*⟩

ạb|büßen *tr. V.* serve [out] ⟨*prison sentence*⟩

Ạbc /a(ː)beˑ(ː)'tseː/ *das; ~* (auch fig.) ABC

Ạbc-Schütze *der,* **Ạbc-Schützin** *die* child just starting school

ạb|dampfen *itr. V.; mit sein* (ugs.: abfahren) set off

ạb|danken *itr. V.* ⟨*ruler*⟩ abdicate; ⟨*government, minister*⟩ resign

Ạbdankung *die; ~, ~en* ▸ ABDANKEN: abdication; resignation

ạb|decken *tr. V.* **(a)** open up; ⟨*gale*⟩ take the roof/roofs off ⟨*house*⟩, take the tiles off ⟨*roof*⟩ **(b)** (herunternehmen, -reißen) take off **(c)** (abräumen) clear ⟨*table*⟩; clear away ⟨*dishes*⟩ **(d)** (schützen) cover ⟨*person*⟩

ạb|dichten *tr. V.* seal

ạb|drängen *tr. V.* push away

ạb|drehen ① *tr. V.* **(a)** (ausschalten) turn off; **den Hahn ~** (fig.) turn off the supply **(b)** (abtrennen) twist off ② *itr. V.; meist mit sein* turn off

Ạb·druck *der; Pl.* **Abdrücke** mark; (Fuß~) footprint; (Wachs~) impression; (Gips~) cast

ạb|drücken ① *itr. V.* pull the trigger; shoot ② *tr. V.* (zudrücken) constrict

ạb|dunkeln *tr. V.* darken ⟨*room*⟩; dim ⟨*light*⟩

ạb|duschen *tr. V.* **sich/jmdn. [warm] ~:** take/give sb. a [hot] shower

ạb|düsen *itr. V.* (ugs.) zoom off

*abend ▸ ABEND

Ạbend *der; ~s, ~e* evening; **guten ~!** good evening; **am [frühen/späten] ~:** [early/late] in the evening; **heute/morgen/gestern ~:** this/tomorrow/yesterday evening; **zu**

~ essen have dinner; (allgemeiner) have one's evening meal; **ein bunter ~:** a social [evening]

ạbend-, Ạbend-: **~akademie** *die* evening school; **~anzug** *der* evening suit; **~blatt** *das* evening [news]paper; **~brot** *das* supper; **~dämmerung** *die* [evening] twilight; **~essen** *das* dinner; **~füllend** *Adj.* occupying a whole evening *postpos., not pred.;* **ein ~füllendes Programm** a full evening's programme; **~gymnasium** *das* night school, evening classes *pl.* (leading to the 'Abitur'); **~kasse** *die* box office (*open on the evening of the performance*); **~kleid** *das* evening dress; **~kurs[us]** *der* evening class

Ạbend·land *das;* **~[e]s** West

ạbendlich *Adj.* evening; ⟨*quiet, coolness*⟩ of the evening

Ạbend-: **~mahl** *das* (Rel.) Communion; (N.T.) Last Supper; **~programm** *das* evening programmes *pl.;* **~rot** *das* red glow of the sunset sky

ạbends *Adv.* in the evenings; **um sechs Uhr ~:** at six o'clock in the evening

Ạbend-: **~schule** *die* night school; **~sonne** *die* evening sun; **~stern** *der* evening star; **~stunde** *die* evening hour; **in den frühen/späten ~stunden** early/late in the evening; **~vorstellung** *die* evening performance; **~zeitung** *die* ▸ ~BLATT

Abenteuer *das;* **~s, ~** **(a)** (auch fig.) adventure **(b)** (Unternehmen) venture **(c)** (Liebesaffäre) affair

abenteuerlich *Adj.* **(a)** (riskant) risky **(b)** (bizarr) bizarre

Abenteuer-: **~lust** *die* thirst for adventure; **~roman** *der* adventure novel; **~urlaub** *der* adventure holiday

Abenteurer *der;* **~s, ~:** adventurer

Abenteurerin *die; ~, ~nen* adventuress

aber ① *Konj.* but ② *Partikel* **~ ja/nein!** why, yes/no! **~ natürlich!** but of course!; **du bist ~ groß!** aren't you tall!

Ạber·glaube[n] *der* superstition

ạber·gläubisch *Adj.* superstitious

ạbermals *Adv.* once again; once more

Abf. *Abk.* = **Abfahrt** dep.

ạb|fahren ① *unr. itr. V.; mit sein* **(a)** (wegfahren) leave; **wo fährt der Zug nach Paris ab?** where does the Paris train leave from? **(b)** (hinunterfahren) drive down; (Skisport) ski down **(c)** (salopp: sich begeistern) **auf jmdn./etw. [voll] ~:** be mad about sb./sth. **(d)** (salopp: abgewiesen werden) **jmdn. ~ lassen** tell sb. where he/she can go (sl.) ② *unr. tr. V.* **(a)** (abtransportieren) take away **(b)** (abnutzen) wear out; **abgefahrene Reifen** worn tyres

Ab·fahrt *die* **(a)** departure
(b) (Skisport) descent; (Strecke) run
Abfahrts-: ∼**lauf** *der* (Skisport) downhill [racing]; ∼**läufer** *der*, ∼**läuferin** *die* (Skisport) downhill racer; ∼**rennen** *das* (Skisport) downhill [racing]; ∼**zeit** *die* time of departure; departure time
Ab·fall *der* (Küchen∼ o. Ä.) rubbish, (Amer.) trash *no indef. art., no pl.;* (Fleisch∼) offal *no indef. art., no pl.;* (Industrie∼) waste *no indef. art.;* (auf der Straße) litter *no indef. art., no pl.*
Abfall-: ∼**beseitigung** *die* refuse disposal; (industriell) waste disposal; ∼**eimer** *der* rubbish bin; trash can (Amer.); (auf der Straße) litter bin; trash can (Amer.)
ab|fallen *unr. itr. V.; mit sein* **(a)** fall off
(b) (abschüssig sein) ⟨*land, road, etc.*⟩ drop away, slope
(c) (übrigbleiben) be left [over]; **für dich wird [dabei] auch etwas** ∼: you'll get something out of it too
(d) von jmdm. ∼: leave sb.; **vom Glauben** ∼: desert the faith
ab·fällig ⓵ *Adj.* disparaging
⓶ *adv.* **sich** ∼ **über jmdn. äußern** make disparaging remarks about sb.
Abfall-: ∼**produkt** *das* (auch fig.) by-product; (Sekundärstoff) secondary product; ∼**vermeidung** *die* waste avoidance
ab|fangen *unr. tr. V.* **(a)** catch; intercept ⟨*agent, message, aircraft*⟩
(b) repel ⟨*charge, assault*⟩; ward off ⟨*blow, attack*⟩
ab|färben *itr. V.* **(a)** ⟨*colour, garment, etc.*⟩ run
(b) auf jmdn./etw. ∼ (fig.) rub off on sb./sth.
ab|fassen *tr. V.* write ⟨*report, letter, etc.*⟩; draw up ⟨*will*⟩
ab|fegen *tr. V.* **(a)** brush off; **etw. von etw.** ∼: brush sth. off sth.
(b) (säubern) **etw.** ∼: brush sth. clean
ab|feiern *tr. V.* use up ⟨*excess hours worked*⟩ (by taking time off)
ab|fertigen *tr. V.* dispatch ⟨*mail*⟩; deal with ⟨*applicant*⟩; handle ⟨*passengers*⟩; serve ⟨*customer*⟩; clear ⟨*ship*⟩ for sailing; clear ⟨*aircraft*⟩ for take-off; clear ⟨*lorry*⟩ for departure
ab|feuern *tr. V.* fire
ab|finden ⓵ *unr. tr. V.* **jmdn. mit etw.** ∼: compensate sb. with sth.; **seine Gläubiger** ∼: settle with one's creditors
⓶ *unr. refl. V.* **sich** ∼: resign oneself; **sich** ∼ **mit** come to terms with; learn to live with ⟨*noise, heat*⟩
Abfindung *die;* ∼, ∼**en** settlement; **eine** ∼ **in Höhe von … zahlen** make a settlement of …
Abfindungs·summe *die* ▸ ABFINDUNG
ab|flauen *itr. V.; mit sein* die down; subside; ⟨*interest, conversation*⟩ flag; ⟨*business*⟩ become slack; ⟨*noise*⟩ abate
ab|fliegen *unr. itr. V.; mit sein* leave

ab|fließen *unr. itr. V.; mit sein* flow off
Ab·flug *der* departure
Abflug·zeit *die* departure time
Ab·fluss, *****Ab·fluß** *der* drain; (Rohr) drainpipe; (für Abwasser) waste pipe
Ab·folge *die* sequence; **die** ∼ **der Jahreszeiten** the cycle of the seasons
ab|fotografieren *tr. V.* take pictures of
ab|fragen *tr. V.* test; **jmdn. od. jmdm. die Vokabeln** ∼: test sb. on his/her vocabulary
Abfuhr *die;* ∼, ∼**en (a)** removal
(b) jmdm. eine ∼ **erteilen** (fig. ugs.) rebuff sb.
ab|führen ⓵ *tr. V.* **(a)** (nach Festnahme) take away
(b) (zahlen) pay out
(c) (abbringen) take away
⓶ *itr. V.* (für Stuhlgang sorgen) be a laxative
Abführ·mittel *das* laxative
ab|füllen *tr. V.* (in Flaschen) bottle; (in Dosen) can
Ab·gabe *die* **(a)** handing in; (eines Briefes, Pakets, Telegramms) delivery; (eines Gesuchs, Antrags) submission
(b) (Steuer, Gebühr) tax; (auf Produkte) duty
(c) (Ausstrahlung) release; emission
(d) (Sport: Abspiel) pass
Ab·gang *der* **(a)** leaving; departure; (Abfahrt) departure; (Theater) exit
(b) (jmd., der ausscheidet) departure; (Schule) leaver
(c) (bes. Amtsspr.: Todesfall) death
(d) (Turnen) dismount
Ab·gas *das* exhaust
Abgas·katalysator *der* (Kfz-W.) catalytic converter
abgearbeitet *Adj.* work-worn ⟨*hands*⟩
ab|geben ⓵ *unr. tr. V.* **(a)** (aushändigen) hand over; deliver ⟨*letter, parcel, telegram*⟩; hand in, submit ⟨*application*⟩; hand in ⟨*school work*⟩; **den Mantel in der Garderobe** ∼: leave one's coat in the cloakroom
(b) auch itr. jmdm. [etwas] von etw. ∼: let sb. have some of sth.
(c) (abfeuern) fire
⓶ *unr. refl. V.* **sich mit jmdm./etw.** ∼: spend time on sb./sth.; (geringschätzig) waste one's time on sb./sth.
ab·gebrannt *Adj.* (ugs.) broke (coll.)
abgebrüht *Adj.* (ugs.) hardened
ab·gedroschen *Adj.* (ugs.) hackneyed
ab·gegriffen *Adj.* battered
ab|gehen *unr. itr. V.; mit sein* **(a)** (sich entfernen) leave; (Theater) exit
(b) (ausscheiden) leave
(c) (abfahren) ⟨*train, ship, bus*⟩ leave, depart
(d) (abgeschickt werden) ⟨*message, letter*⟩ be sent [off]
(e) (abzweigen) branch off
(f) (sich lösen) come off
abgehetzt *Adj.* exhausted
ab·gelegen *Adj.* remote; (einsam) isolated; out-of-the-way ⟨*district*⟩

ạbgemagert *Adj.* emaciated; wasted

ạb·geneigt *Adj.* averse (*Dat.* to); **[nicht]** ~ **sein, etw. zu tun** [not] be averse to doing sth.

Ạbgeordnete *der/die; adj. Dekl.* member [of parliament]; (z.B. in Frankreich) deputy

ạb·gerissen *Adj.* ragged

ạb·geschieden *Adj.* secluded; (abgelegen) isolated

ạb·geschlagen *Adj.* (Sport) [well] beaten

ạb·geschlossen *Adj.* secluded

ạb·geschnitten *Adj.* isolated; **von der Außenwelt** ~: cut off from the outside world

ạb·gesehen *Adv.* ~ **von** apart from; ~ **davon, dass** ... apart from the fact that ...

ạb·gespannt *Adj.* weary; exhausted

ạb·gestanden *Adj.* flat

ạb·gestorben *Adj.* dead ⟨branch, tree⟩; numb ⟨fingers, legs, etc.⟩

ạb·getreten *Adj.* worn down

ạbgewetzt *Adj.* well-worn; battered ⟨case etc.⟩

ạb|gewöhnen *tr. V.;* jmdm. etw. ~: make sb. give up sth.; **sich** (*Dat.*) etw. ~: give up sth.

ạb|gießen *unr. tr. V.* pour away ⟨liquid⟩; drain ⟨potatoes⟩

ạbgöttisch *Adj.* idolatrous

ạb|grenzen *tr. V.* (a) bound; **etw. gegen od. von etw.** ~: separate sth. from sth. (b) (unterscheiden) distinguish

Ạb·grund *der* abyss; chasm; (Abhang) precipice

ạb|hacken *tr. V.* chop off; **jmdm. die Hand usw.** ~: chop sb.'s hand *etc.* off

ạb|haken *tr. V.* tick off; check off (Amer.)

ạb|halten *unr. V.* (a) jmdn./etw. [von jmdm./etw.] ~: keep sb./sth. off [sb./sth.] (b) jmdn. davon ~, etw. zu tun stop sb. doing sth. (c) (durchführen) hold ⟨elections, meeting, referendum⟩

ạb|handeln *tr. V.* (a) jmdm. etw. ~: do a deal with sb. for sth. (b) (darstellen) handle

abhạnden *Adv.* ~ **kommen** get lost; go astray; **etw. kommt jmdm.** ~: sb. loses sth.

Ạb·handlung *die* treatise (über + *Akk.* on)

Ạb·hang *der* slope; incline

ạb|hängen¹ *unr. itr. V.* **von jmdm./etw.** ~: depend on sb./sth.

ạb|hängen² ① *tr. V.* (a) take down (b) (abkuppeln) uncouple (c) (ugs.) shake off ⟨pursuer, competitor⟩. ② *itr. V.* (den Hörer auflegen) hang up

abhängig *Adj.* dependent (**von** on); (süchtig) addicted (**von** to); **von jmdm./etw.** ~ **sein** depend on sb./sth.

Ạbhängige *der/die; adj. Dekl.* (Rechtspr.) dependant; (Untergebene) subordinate

Abhängigkeit *die;* ~, ~en dependence; (Sucht) addiction

Abhängigkeits·verhältnis *das* relationship of dependence (**zu** on)

ạb|härten *tr. V.* harden

ạb|hauen ① *unr. tr. V.* (a) *Prät.* **haute ab** knock off (b) *Prät.* **hieb** (geh.) *od.* **haute ab** (mit Schwert, Axt usw.) chop off ② *unr. itr. V.; mit sein; Prät.* **haute ab** (salopp) beat it (coll.)

ạb|heben ① *unr. tr. V.* (a) lift off ⟨lid, cover, etc.⟩; **[den Hörer]** ~: answer [the telephone] (b) (von einem Konto) withdraw ⟨money⟩ ② *unr. itr. V.* ⟨balloon⟩ rise; ⟨aircraft, bird⟩ take off; ⟨rocket⟩ lift off ③ *unr. refl. V.* stand out (**von** against)

ạb|heften *tr. V.* file

ạb|hetzen *refl. V.* rush [around]; *s. auch* ABGEHETZT

Ạb·hilfe *die* action to improve matters; ~ **schaffen** put things right

ạb|holen *tr. V.* collect, pick up ⟨parcel, book, tickets, etc.⟩; pick up ⟨person⟩

ạb|hören *tr. V.* (a) jmdm. *od.* jmdn. Vokabeln ~: test sb.'s vocabulary [orally]; **das Einmaleins** ~: ask questions on the multiplication tables (b) tap ⟨telephone conversation, telephone⟩; bug (coll.) ⟨conversation, premises⟩; jmdn. ~: tap sb.'s telephone

ạbhör·sicher *Adj.* bug-proof (coll.); tap-proof ⟨telephone⟩

Ạbi *das;* ~s, ~s (Schülerspr.), **Abitur** *das;* ~s, ~e Abitur (school-leaving examination at grammar school needed for entry to higher education); ≈ A levels (Brit.)

Abiturient *der;* ~en, ~en, **Abiturientin** *die;* ~, ~nen sb. who is taking/has passed the 'Abitur'

ạb|jagen *tr. V.* jmdm. etw. ~: finally get sth. away from sb.

Abk. *Abk.* = **Abkürzung** abbr.

ạb|kapseln *tr. V.* encapsulate; **sich gegen die Umwelt** ~ (fig.) isolate oneself from one's surroundings

ạb|kaufen *tr. V.* jmdm. etw. ~: buy sth. from sb.

Ạb·klatsch *der* (abwertend) pale imitation; poor copy

ạb|klopfen *tr. V.* (a) knock off (b) (säubern) knock the dirt/snow/crumbs *etc.* off (c) (untersuchen) tap

ạb|knallen *tr. V.* (salopp) shoot down; gun down

ạb|knicken ① *tr. V.* snap off ② *itr. V.; mit sein* snap

ạb|kochen *tr. V.* boil

ạb|kommen *unr. itr. V.; mit sein* (a) **vom Weg** ~: lose one's way; **vom Kurs** ~: go off

---
*alte Schreibung – vgl. Hinweis auf S. x

course; **von der Fahrbahn** ~: leave the road;
vom Thema ~: stray from the topic
(b) von einem Plan ~: abandon a plan
Ab·kommen *das;* ~s, ~: agreement
abkömmlich *Adj.* free; available
ab|können *unr. tr. V.* (nordd.: mögen) stand;
(vertragen) take
ab|kratzen ⟨1⟩ *tr. V.* **(a)** (mit den Fingern)
scratch off; (mit einem Werkzeug) scrape off
(b) (säubern) scrape [clean]
⟨2⟩ *itr. V.; mit sein* (derb) snuff it (sl.)
ab|kriegen *tr. V.* (ugs.) ▶ ABBEKOMMEN
ab|kühlen ⟨1⟩ *tr. V.* cool down
⟨2⟩ *itr., refl. V.; itr. meist mit sein* cool down
Ab·kühlung *die* cooling
ab|kupfern *tr. V.* (ugs.) copy mechanically
(bei from)
ab|kürzen *tr., itr. V.* **(a)** (räumlich) shorten;
den Weg ~: take a shorter route
(b) (zeitlich) cut short
(c) (kürzer schreiben) abbreviate (**mit** to)
Abkürzung *die* **(a)** (Weg) short cut
(b) (Wort) abbreviation
ab|küssen *tr. V.* cover with kisses
ab|laden *unr. tr., itr. V.* unload
Ab·lage *die* **(a)** storage place
(b) (Raum) storage room
(c) (Bürow.) filing
ab|lagern *tr. V.* deposit
ab|lassen ⟨1⟩ *unr. tr. V.* let out (**aus** of); let
off ⟨*steam*⟩
⟨2⟩ *unr. itr. V.* **(a) von jmdm./etw.** ~: leave
sb./sth. alone
(b) von etw. ~ (etw. aufgeben) give sth. up
Ab·lauf *der* **(a)** (Verlauf) course; (einer
Veranstaltung) passing off
(b) (Ende) **nach** ~ **eines Jahres** after a year;
nach ~ **einer Frist** at the end of a period of
time
ab|laufen *unr. itr. V.; mit sein* **(a)** flow
away; (aus einem Behälter) run out
(b) (verlaufen) pass off
(c) ⟨*alarm clock*⟩ run down; ⟨*parking meter*⟩
expire
(d) ⟨*period, contract, passport*⟩ expire
ab|lecken *tr. V.* **(a)** lick off
(b) (säubern) lick clean
ab|legen ⟨1⟩ *tr. V.* **(a)** lay *or* put down
(b) (Bürow.) file
(c) stop wearing ⟨*clothes*⟩
(d) give up ⟨*habit*⟩; lose ⟨*shyness*⟩
(e) swear ⟨*oath*⟩; sit ⟨*examination*⟩; make
⟨*confession*⟩
⟨2⟩ *tr., itr. V.* take off; **möchten Sie** ~? would
you like to take your coat off?
⟨3⟩ *itr. V.* **[vom Kai]** ~: cast off
Ableger *der;* ~s, ~: layer; (Steckling) cutting
ab|lehnen *tr. V.* **(a)** decline; decline, turn
down ⟨*money, invitation, position*⟩; reject
⟨*suggestion, applicant*⟩
(b) (missbilligen) disapprove of
Ablehnung *die;* ~, ~en **(a)** rejection
(b) (Missbilligung) disapproval

ab|leiten *tr. V.* **(a)** divert
(b) (herleiten) **etw. aus/von etw.** ~: derive
sth. from sth.
Ab·leitung *die* derivation
ab|lenken *tr. V.* **(a)** deflect
(b) jmdn. von etw. ~: distract sb. from sth.
(c) (zerstreuen) divert; **sich** ~: amuse oneself
Ab·lenkung *die* ▶ ABLENKEN: deflection;
distraction; diversion
Ablenkungs·manöver *das*
diversion[ary tactic]
ab|lesen *unr. tr. V.* **(a)** read ⟨*speech,
lecture*⟩; **werden Sie frei sprechen oder** ~?
will you be talking from notes or reading
your speech?
(b) read ⟨*gas meter, thermometer, etc.*⟩;
check ⟨*time, speed, temperature*⟩
(c) (erkennen) see
ab|lichten *tr. V.* **(a)** (fotokopieren) photocopy
(b) (fotografieren) take a photograph of
Ab·lichtung *die* **(a)** (das Fotografieren)
photographing; (das Fotokopieren)
photocopying
(b) (Fotokopie) photocopy
ab|liefern *tr., itr. V.* hand in; deliver
⟨*goods*⟩
ab|lösen ⟨1⟩ *tr. V.* **(a) etw. [von etw.]** ~: get
sth. off [sth.]
(b) jmdn. ~: relieve sb.; **sich** *od.* **einander**
~: take turns
⟨2⟩ *refl. V.* **sich [von etw.]** ~: come off [sth.]
Ab·lösung *die* (eines Postens) changing;
ich schicke Ihnen jemanden zur ~: I'll send
someone to relieve you
ab|machen *tr. V.* **(a)** (ugs.) take off; take
down ⟨*sign, rope*⟩
(b) (vereinbaren) agree
Abmachung *die;* ~, ~en agreement
ab|magern *itr. V.; mit sein* become thin;
(absichtlich) slim
Abmagerungs·kur *die* reducing diet
ab|marschieren *itr. V.; mit sein* depart;
(Milit.) march off
ab|melden *tr. V.* **(a) sich/jmdn.** ~: report
that one/sb. is leaving
(b) (Umzug melden) *notify the authorities that
one is moving from an address*
(c) ein Auto ~: cancel a car's registration
(d) (DV) ▶ AUSLOGGEN
Ab·meldung *die* **(a)** (beim Weggehen) report
that one is leaving
(b) (beim Umzug) *registration of a move with
the authorities at one's old address*
(c) ~ **eines Autos** cancellation of a car's
registration
Ab·messung *die* (Dimension) dimension;
measurement
ab|montieren *tr. V.* take off ⟨*part*⟩;
dismantle ⟨*machine, equipment*⟩
ab|mühen *refl. V.* toil; **sie mühte sich mit
dem schweren Koffer ab** she struggled with
the heavy suitcase
ab|murksen *tr. V.* (salopp) do in (sl.)

a

Abnahme *die;* ~, ~n **(a)** (das Entfernen) removal
(b) (Verminderung) decrease
ab|nehmen ① *unr. tr. V.* **(a)** (entfernen) take off; take down ‹*picture, curtain, lamp*›
(b) jmdm. den Koffer ~: take sb.'s suitcase; jmdm. eine Arbeit ~: save sb. a job
(c) jmdm. ein Versprechen/einen Eid ~: make sb. give a promise/swear an oath
(d) (prüfen) inspect and approve; test and pass ‹*vehicle*›
(e) jmdm. etw. ~ (wegnehmen) take sth. off sb.
(f) (beim Telefon) answer ‹*telephone*›; pick up ‹*receiver*›
(g) (Handarb.) decrease
(h) das nehme ich dir/ihm *usw.* nicht ab I won't buy that (coll.)
② *unr. itr. V.* **(a)** (Gewicht verlieren) lose weight
(b) (sich verringern) decrease; drop; ‹*attention, interest*› flag; ‹*brightness*› diminish; **wir haben** ~**den Mond** there is a waning moon
(c) (beim Telefon) answer the telephone
Ab·neigung *die* dislike (**gegen** for)
ab|nutzen, (landsch.:) **ab|nützen** *tr., refl. V.* wear out; **abgenutzt** worn
Abonnement /abɔnə'mãː/ *das;* ~s, ~s subscription (*Gen.* to)
Abonnent *der;* ~en, ~en, **Abonnentin** *die;* ~, ~nen subscriber (+ *Gen.* to); (Theater, Oper) season ticket holder
abonnieren *tr. V.* subscribe to
Ab·ordnung *die* delegation
ab|packen *tr. V.* pack; wrap ‹*bread*›; **abgepacktes Obst/abgepackte Fleischportionen** packaged fruit/pieces of meat
ab|passen *tr. V.* **(a)** (abwarten) wait for
(b) (aufhalten) catch
ab|pausen *tr. V.* trace
ab|pfeifen (Sport) ① *itr. V.* blow the whistle
② *tr. V.* [blow the whistle to] stop
Ab·pfiff *der* (Sport) final whistle; (Halbzeit~) half-time whistle
ab|pflücken *tr. V.* pick
ab|plagen *refl. V.* slave away
ab|prallen *itr. V.; mit sein* rebound; ‹*bullet, missile*› ricochet
Ab·produkt *das* waste product
ab|puffern *tr. V.* offset; offset, cushion ‹*effect*›
ab|putzen *tr. V.* (ugs.); **(a)** wipe off
(b) (säubern) wipe; **jmdm./sich das Gesicht** ~: clean sb.'s/one's face
ab|quälen *refl. V.* **sich [mit etw.]** ~: struggle [with sth.]
ab|rackern *refl. V.* (ugs.) flog oneself to death (coll.)
ab|rasieren *tr. V.* shave off

ab|raten *unr. itr. V.* jmdm. von etw. ~: advise sb. against sth.
ab|räumen *tr. V.* **(a)** clear away
(b) (leer machen) clear ‹*table*›
ab|rechnen ① *itr. V.* cash up; **mit jmdm.** ~ (fig.) call sb. to account
② *tr. V.* **die Kasse** ~: reckon up the till; **seine Spesen** ~: claim one's expenses
Ab·rechnung *die* **(a)** cashing up *no art.;* (Aufstellung) statement
(b) (fig.: Vergeltung) reckoning
Ab·rede *die* **(a)** arrangement; agreement
(b) **etw. in** ~ **stellen** deny sth.
ab|regen *refl. V.* (ugs.) calm down; **reg dich ab!** cool it! (coll.); calm down!
ab|reiben *unr. tr. V.* **(a)** rub off
(b) (säubern) rub
Ab·reise *die* departure (**nach** for); **bei meiner** ~: when I left/leave
ab|reisen *itr. V.; mit sein* leave (**nach** for)
ab|reißen ① *unr. tr. V.* **(a)** tear off; tear down ‹*poster, notice*›; pull off ‹*button*›
(b) (niederreißen) demolish, pull down ‹*building*›
② *unr. itr. V.; mit sein* **(a)** fly off; ‹*shoelace*› break off
(b) (aufhören) come to an end; ‹*connection, contact*› be broken off
ab|richten *tr. V.* train
Ab·riss, *Ab·riß *der* **(a)** ▶ ABREISSEN 1B: demolition; pulling down
(b) (knappe Darstellung) outline
ab|rollen ① *tr. V.* unwind
② *itr. V.; mit sein* unwind [itself]
ab|rücken ① *tr. V.* (wegschieben) move away
② *itr. V.; mit sein* move away
Ab·ruf *der:* **auf** ~: on call; (DV) in retrievable form
ab|rufen *unr. tr. V.* summon; call
ab|runden *tr. V.* **(a)** (auch fig.) round off
(b) round ‹*figure*› up/down (**auf** + **Akk.** to); **etw. nach oben/unten** ~: round sth. up/down
abrupt ① *Adj.* abrupt
② *adv.* abruptly
ab|rüsten *itr., tr. V.* disarm
Ab·rüstung *die;* ~: disarmament
ab|rutschen *itr. V.; mit sein* **(a)** slip
(b) (nach unten rutschen) slide down
Abs. *Abk.* **(a)** = **Absender;**
(b) = **Absatz**
ABS *Abk.* = **Antiblockiersystem** ABS
Ab·sage *die* (auf eine Einladung) refusal; (auf eine Bewerbung) rejection
ab|sagen ① *tr. V.* cancel; withdraw ‹*participation*›
② *itr. V.* jmdm. ~: tell sb. one cannot come
ab|sägen *tr. V.* saw off
Ab·satz *der* **(a)** (am Schuh) heel
(b) (Textunterbrechung) break
(c) (Textabschnitt) paragraph
(d) (Kaufmannsspr.) sales *pl.*

---

absatz-, Absatz-: ∼**chance** *die* (Kaufmannsspr.) sales prospect; ∼**förderung** *die* (Kaufmannsspr.) sales promotion; ∼**markt** *der* (Kaufmannsspr.) market; ∼**steigerung** *die* (Kaufmannsspr.) increase in sales

ab|saufen *unr. itr. V.; mit sein* (ugs.) ⟨*engine, car*⟩ flood

ab|saugen *tr. V.* (a) suck away
(b) (säubern) hoover (Brit.)

ab|schaben *tr. V.* (a) scrape off
(b) (säubern) scrape [clean]

ab|schaffen *tr. V.* (a) (beseitigen) abolish ⟨*capital punishment, regulation, customs duty, institution*⟩; repeal ⟨*law*⟩; put an end to ⟨*injustice, abuse*⟩
(b) (weggeben) get rid of

Ab·schaffung *die* abolition; (von Gesetzen) repeal; (von Unrecht, Missstand) ending

ab|schalten *tr., itr. V.* switch off; shut down ⟨*power station*⟩

abschätzig ⟨1⟩ *Adj.* derogatory
⟨2⟩ *adv.* derogatorily

Ab·scheu *der;* ∼s detestation; abhorrence

abscheulich ⟨1⟩ *Adj.* (a) disgusting ⟨*smell, taste*⟩; repulsive ⟨*sight*⟩
(b) (verwerflich) disgraceful ⟨*behaviour*⟩; abominable ⟨*crime*⟩
⟨2⟩ *adv.* disgracefully

ab|schicken *tr. V.* send [off]

ab|schieben *unr. tr. V.* (a) push away
(b) (abwälzen) shift ⟨*responsibility, blame*⟩
(c) (außer Landes bringen); deport

Ab·schiebung *die* (Rechtsw.) deportation

Abschiebungs-haft *die* (Rechtsw.) detention prior to deportation

Abschied *der;* ∼[e]s, ∼e parting (von from); farewell (von to); ∼ nehmen take one's leave (von of)

Abschieds-: ∼**brief** *der* farewell letter; ∼**geschenk** *das* parting gift; ∼**gruß** *der* goodbye; farewell

ab|schießen *unr. tr. V.* (a) shoot down ⟨*aeroplane*⟩
(b) fire ⟨*arrow*⟩; launch ⟨*spacecraft*⟩
(c) (töten) take

ab|schirmen *tr. V.* (a) (schützen) shield
(b) (fernhalten) screen off ⟨*light, radiation*⟩

ab|schlachten *tr. V.* slaughter

Ab·schlag *der* (a) (Kaufmannsspr.) discount
(b) (Teilzahlung) interim payment; (Vorschuss) advance
(c) (Fußball) goalkeeper's kick out

ab|schlagen ⟨1⟩ *unr. tr. V.* (a) knock off; (mit dem Beil, Schwert usw.) chop off
(b) (ablehnen) refuse
(c) (abwehren) beat off
⟨2⟩ *unr. itr. V.* (Fußball) kick the ball out

ab|schleifen *unr. tr. V.* (von Holz) sand off; (von Metall, Glas usw.) grind off

Abschlepp-dienst *der* breakdown recovery service; tow[ing] service (Amer.)

ab|schleppen tow away; take ⟨*ship*⟩ in tow; **ein Auto zur Werkstatt** ∼: tow a car to the garage

Abschlepp: ∼**seil** *das* tow rope; (aus Draht) towing cable; ∼**stange** *die* tow bar; ∼**wagen** *der* breakdown vehicle; tow truck (Amer.); (der Polizei) tow-away vehicle

ab|schließen ⟨1⟩ *unr. tr. V.* (a) auch itr. (zuschließen) lock ⟨*door, gate, cupboard*⟩; lock [up] ⟨*house, flat, room, park*⟩
(b) (verschließen) seal; **etw. luftdicht** ∼: seal sth. hermetically
(c) (begrenzen) border
(d) (zum Abschluss bringen) conclude; **sein Studium** ∼: finish one's studies; **Bewerber mit abgeschlossenem Universitätsstudium** applicants with a degree
(e) (vereinbaren) strike ⟨*bargain, deal*⟩; make ⟨*purchase*⟩; enter into ⟨*agreement*⟩
⟨2⟩ *unr. itr. V.* (aufhören, enden) end; ∼**d sagte er** ...: in conclusion he said ...

Ab·schluss, **Ab·schluß der*
(a) (Verschluss) seal
(b) (Beendigung) conclusion; end
(c) (eines Geschäfts, Vertrags) conclusion

Abschluss-, *Abschluß-: ∼**ball** *der* final dance; ∼**prüfung** *die* (a) (Schulw.) leaving *or* (Amer.) final examination; (Hochschulw.) final examination; finals *pl.;*
(b) (Wirtsch.) audit

ab|schmecken *tr. V.* (a) (kosten) taste; try
(b) (würzen) season

ab|schmieren *tr. V.* (Technik) grease

ab|schminken *tr. V.* jmdn./sich ∼: remove sb.'s/one's make-up

ab|schmirgeln *tr. V.* rub off with emery; (mit Sandpapier) sand off

ab|schnallen *tr. V.* unfasten

ab|schneiden ⟨1⟩ *unr. tr. V.* (a) (auch fig.: isolieren) cut off; cut down ⟨*sth. hanging*⟩; **etw. von etw.** ∼: cut sth. off sth.; **sich** (*Dat.*) **eine Scheibe Brot** ∼: cut oneself a slice of bread
(b) (kürzer schneiden) cut
(c) **jmdm. den Weg** ∼: take a short cut to get ahead of sb.
⟨2⟩ *unr. itr. V.* **bei etw. gut/schlecht** ∼: do well/badly in sth.

Ab·schnitt *der* (a) (Kapitel) section
(b) (Zeitspanne) phase
(c) (Teil eines Formulars) [detachable] portion

ab|schrauben *tr. V.* unscrew [and remove]

ab|schrecken *tr. V.* (a) deter
(b) (fernhalten) scare off
(c) (Kochk.) pour cold water over

Abschreckung *die;* ∼, ∼**en** deterrence; (Mittel zur Abschreckung) deterrent

ab|schreiben ⟨1⟩ *unr. tr. V.* (a) copy out; **etw. bei** *od.* **von jmdm.** ∼ (in der Schule) copy sth. off sb.; (als Plagiator) plagiarize sth. from sb. ⋯⋮

(b) (Wirtsch.) amortize
2 *unr. itr. V.* **bei** *od.* **von jmdm.** ~ (in der Schule) copy off sb.; (als Plagiator) copy from sb.
Ab·schreibung *die* (Wirtsch.) amortization
Ab·schrift *die* copy
ab|schürfen *tr. V.* graze
Ab·schuss, *⟨*Ab·schuß *der* **(a)** (eines Flugzeugs) shooting down
   (b) (von Geschossen) firing; (eines Raumschiffs) launching
abschüssig *Adj.* downward sloping ⟨*land*⟩
ab|schütteln *tr. V.* shake off; (herunterschütteln) shake down
ab|schwächen **1** *tr. V.* **(a)** (mildern) tone down ⟨*statement, criticism*⟩
   (b) (verringern) lessen ⟨*effect, impression*⟩; cushion ⟨*blow, impact*⟩
   2 *refl. V.* ⟨*interest, demand*⟩ wane
Abschwächung *die;* ~ **(a)** (Milderung) toning down
   (b) (eines Aufpralls, Stoßes usw.) cushioning
ab|schweifen *itr. V.; mit sein* digress
Abschweifung *die;* ~, ~en digression
ab|schwören *unr. itr. V.* **dem Teufel/ seinem Glauben** ~: renounce the Devil/ one's faith; **dem Alkohol/Laster** ~: forswear alcohol/vice
absehbar *Adj.* foreseeable; **in** ~**er Zeit** within the foreseeable future
ab|sehen **1** *unr. tr. V.* **(a)** (voraussehen) predict; foresee ⟨*event*⟩
   (b) es auf etw. (Akk.) abgesehen haben be after sth.; **er hat es darauf abgesehen, uns zu ärgern** he's out to annoy us; **der Chef hat es auf ihn abgesehen** the boss has got it in for him
   2 *unr. itr. V.* **(a) von etw.** ~ (etw. nicht beachten) leave aside sth.; *s. auch* ABGESEHEN
   (b) von etw. ~ (auf etw. verzichten) refrain from sth.
ab|seilen **1** *tr. V.* lower [with a rope]
   2 *refl. V.* (Bergsteigen) abseil
***ab|sein** ▸ AB 2A
abseits **1** *Präp. mit Gen.* away from
   2 *Adv.* **(a)** far away
   (b) (Ballspiele) ~ **sein** *od.* **stehen** be offside
Abseits *das;* ~, ~: **das war ein klares** ~: that was clearly offside
ab|senden *unr. od. regelm. tr. V.* dispatch
Ab·sender *der,* **Ab·senderin** *die;* ~, ~**nen** sender; (Anschrift) sender's address
ab|setzen **1** *tr. V.* **(a)** take off ⟨*hat, glasses, etc.*⟩
   (b) (hinstellen) put down ⟨*bag, suitcase*⟩
   (c) (aussteigen lassen) **jmdn.** ~ (im öffentlichen Verkehr) put sb. down; let sb. out (Amer.); (im privaten Verkehr) drop sb. [off]
   (d) remove ⟨*chancellor, judge*⟩ from office; depose ⟨*king, emperor*⟩
   2 *refl. V.* **(a)** (sich ablagern) be deposited
   (b) (flüchten) get away

Absetzung *die;* ~, ~en ▸ ABSETZEN 1D: removal; deposition
ab|sichern **1** *tr. V.* make safe
   2 *refl. V.* safeguard oneself
Ab·sicht *die* intention; **etw. mit** ~ **tun** do sth. intentionally; **etw. ohne** *od.* **nicht mit** ~ **tun** do sth. unintentionally
ab·sichtlich **1** *Adj.* intentional; deliberate
   2 *adv.* intentionally; deliberately
ab|sinken *unr. itr. V.; mit sein* sink
absolut *Adj.* absolute
Absolutismus *der;* ~ (hist.) absolutism *no art.*
Absolvent /ˈˈvɛnt/ *der;* ~en, ~en, **Absolventin** *die;* ~, ~nen (einer Schule) one who has taken the leaving *or* (Amer.) final examination; (einer Akademie) graduate
absolvieren *tr. V.* complete
Absolvierung *die;* ~: completion
ab·sonderlich *Adj.* strange; odd
ab|sondern **1** *tr. V.* exude; (Physiol.) secrete
   2 *refl. V.* isolate oneself
absorbieren *tr. V.* absorb
ab|speisen *tr. V.* **jmdn. mit etw.** ~: fob sb. off with sth.
abspenstig *Adj.* **jmdm. etw.** ~ **machen** get sb. to part with sth.
ab|sperren *tr. V.* seal off; close off
Ab·spiel *das* (Ballspiele) passing
ab|spielen **1** *tr. V.* **(a)** play ⟨*record, tape*⟩
   (b) vom Blatt ~: ⟨*piece of music*⟩ play at sight
   (c) (Ballspiele) pass
   2 *refl. V.* take place
Ab·sprache *die* arrangement; **eine** ~ **treffen** make an arrangement
ab|sprechen *unr. tr. V.* **(a) jmdm. etw.** ~: deny that sb. has sth.
   (b) (vereinbaren) arrange
ab|springen *unr. itr. V.; mit sein* jump off; (herunterspringen) jump down; **vom Fahrrad** ~: jump off one's bicycle
Ab·sprung *der* take-off; (das Herunterspringen) jump
ab|spülen **1** *tr. V.* **(a)** wash off
   (b) (reinigen) rinse off; **sich** *(Dat.)* **die Hände** *usw.* ~: rinse one's hands *etc.;* **das Geschirr** ~ (bes. südd.) wash the dishes
   2 *itr. V.* (bes. südd.) wash up
ab|stammen *itr. V.* be descended (**von** from)
Abstammung *die;* ~, ~en descent
Ab·stand *der* **(a)** distance; **in 20 Meter** ~: at a distance of 20 metres
   (b) (Unterschied) gap
ab|stauben *tr., itr. V.* dust
Abstecher *der;* ~s, ~: side trip
ab|stehen *unr. itr. V.* stand up; ⟨*hair*⟩ stick out; ~**de Ohren** protruding ears

Ab·steige *die;* ~, ~n (ugs. abwertend) cheap and crummy hotel (coll. derog.)

ab|steigen *unr. itr. V.; mit sein* **(a)** [**vom Pferd/Fahrrad**] ~: get off [one's horse/bicycle]
(b) (abwärts gehen) go down

ab|stellen *tr. V.* **(a)** put down
(b) (unterbringen) put; (parken) park
(c) (ausschalten, abdrehen) turn off
(d) (unterbinden) put a stop to

Abstell-: ~**kammer** *die,* ~**raum** *der* lumber room

ab|stempeln *tr. V.* **(a)** frank ⟨*letter*⟩; cancel ⟨*stamp*⟩
(b) (fig.) label, brand (**zu, als** as)

ab|sterben *unr. itr. V.; mit sein*
(a) [gradually] die
(b) (gefühllos werden) go numb

Abstieg *der;* ~[e]s, ~e **(a)** descent
(b) (Niedergang) decline

ab|stimmen ① *itr. V.* vote (**über** + Akk. on)
② *tr. V.* etw. mit jmdm. ~: discuss and agree on sth. with sb.

Ab·stimmung *die* **(a)** vote; **während der** ~: during the voting
(b) (Absprache) agreement

abstinent /apstiˈnɛnt/ *Adj.* teetotal;
~ **sein** be a teetotaller

Abstinenz *die;* ~: teetotalism

Abstinenzler *der;* ~s, ~,
Abstinenzlerin *die;* ~, ~nen teetotaller

ab|stoppen ① *tr. V.* halt; stop; check ⟨*advance*⟩
② *itr. V.* come to a halt; ⟨*person*⟩ stop

Ab·stoß *der* (Fußball) goal kick

ab|stoßen *unr. tr. V.* **(a)** push off
(b) (be schädigen) chip ⟨*crockery, paintwork, plaster*⟩
(c) (verkaufen) sell off
(d) (anwidern) repel; put off

abstoßend *Adj.* repulsive

abstrakt /apˈstrakt/ *Adj.* abstract

ab|streifen *tr. V.* pull off; strip off ⟨*berries*⟩; **die Asche [von der Zigarette/Zigarre]** ~: remove the ash [from one's cigarette/cigar]

ab|streiten *unr. tr. V.* deny

Ab·strich *der* **(a)** (Med.) swab; **einen** ~ **machen** take a swab
(b) (Streichung, Kürzung) cut; ~**e machen** make cuts (**an** + Dat. in)

ab|stumpfen *itr. V.; mit sein* **jmd. stumpft ab** (wird unsensibel) sb.'s mind becomes deadened

Ab·sturz *der* fall; (eines Flugzeugs) crash

ab|stürzen *itr. V.; mit sein* fall; ⟨*aircraft, pilot, passenger*⟩ crash

Absturz·ursache *die* cause of the crash

ab|stützen ① *refl. V.* support oneself (**mit** on, **an** + Dat. against)
② *tr. V.* support

ab|suchen *tr. V.* search (**nach** for)

absurd *Adj.* absurd

absurderweise *Adv.* absurdly enough

Absurdität *die;* ~, ~en absurdity; (Ungereimtheit) inconsistency

Abszess, *Abszeß *der;* Abszesses, Abszesse **(a)** (Med.) abscess
(b) (Geschwür) ulcer

Abszisse *die;* ~, ~n (Math.) abscissa

Abt *der;* ~[e]s, Äbte abbot

Abt. *Abk.* = Abteilung

ab|tasten *tr. V.* etw. ~: feel sth. all over

ab|tauen ① *itr. V.; mit sein* (eis-/schneefrei werden) become clear of ice/snow; ⟨*refrigerator*⟩ defrost
② *tr. V.* melt; thaw; defrost ⟨*refrigerator*⟩

Abtei *die;* ~, ~en abbey

Abteil *das;* ~[e]s, ~e compartment

Ab·teilung *die* department

Abteilungs·leiter *der,*
Abteilungs·leiterin *die* head of department

ab|tippen *tr. V.* (ugs.) type out

Äbtissin *die;* ~, ~nen abbess

ab|tönen *tr. V.* tint

ab|töten *tr. V.* destroy ⟨*parasites, germs*⟩; deaden ⟨*nerve, feeling*⟩

ab|tragen *unr. tr. V.* (abnutzen) wear out; **abgetragen** well worn

abträglich *Adj.* (geh.) **einer Sache** (Dat.) ~ **sein** be detrimental to sth.

Ab·transport *der ▶* ABTRANSPORTIEREN: taking away; removal

ab|transportieren *tr. V.* take away; remove ⟨*dead, injured*⟩

ab|treiben ① *unr. tr. V.* **(a)** carry away; **jmdn./ein Schiff vom Kurs** ~: drive sb./a ship off course
(b) abort ⟨*foetus*⟩; **ein Kind** ~ **lassen** have an abortion
② *unr. itr. V.; mit sein* be carried away; ⟨*ship*⟩ be driven off course

Abtreibung *die;* ~, ~en abortion

ab|trennen *tr. V.* detach

ab|treten ① *unr. tr. V.* **(a) sich** (Dat.) **die Füße/Schuhe** ~: wipe one's feet
(b) jmdm. etw. ~: let sb. have sth.
② *unr. itr. V.; mit sein* **(a)** (Theater) exit; (fig.) make one's exit
(b) (zurücktreten) step down; ⟨*monarch*⟩ abdicate

Abtreter *der;* ~s, ~: doormat

ab|trocknen *tr. V.* dry; **sich** (Dat.) **die Hände/die Tränen** ~: dry one's hands/tears

ab|tropfen *itr. V.; mit sein* drip off

abtrünnig *Adj.* (einer Partei) renegade; (einer Religion, Sekte) apostate; **der Kirche/dem Glauben** ~ **werden** desert the Church/the faith

ab|tun *unr. tr. V.* dismiss

ab|wägen *unr. od. regelm. tr., itr. V.* weigh up; **abgewogen** carefully weighted; balanced ⟨*judgement*⟩

ab|wählen *tr. V.* vote out; drop ⟨*school subject*⟩

ab|wandeln *tr. V.* adapt

ab|wandern *itr. V.; mit sein* migrate; (in ein anderes Land) emigrate

Abwanderung *die* migration; (in ein anderes Land) emigration

Ab·wandlung *die* adaptation

Ab·wärme *die* (Technik) waste heat

ab|warten ① *itr. V.* wait; **sie warteten ab** they awaited events; **warte ab!** wait and see; (als Drohung) just you wait! ② *tr. V.* wait for

abwärts *Adv.* downwards; (bergab) downhill; **den Fluss ~:** downstream

Abwärts·trend *der* downward trend

Abwasch *der; ~[e]s* washing-up (Brit.); washing dishes (Amer.); **den ~ machen** do the washing-up/wash the dishes

abwaschbar *Adj.* washable

ab|waschen ① *unr. tr. V.* (a) wash off (b) (reinigen) wash down; wash [up] ⟨*dishes*⟩ ② *unr. itr. V.* wash up (Brit.); wash the dishes (Amer.)

Ab·wasser *das; Pl.* Abwässer sewage

Abwasser: **~aufbereitung** *die;* **~~:** sewage treatment; **~kanal** *der* sewer

ab|watschen *tr. V.* (ugs.) lambaste (coll.)

ab|wechseln *refl., itr. V.* alternate; **wir wechselten uns ab** we took turns

abwechselnd *Adv.* alternately

Abwechslung *die; ~, ~en* variety; (Wechsel) change; **zur ~:** for a change

Ab·weg *der:* **auf ~e kommen** *od.* **geraten** go astray

abwegig erroneous; false ⟨*suspicion*⟩

Ab·wehr *die;* **~** (a) repulsion; (von Schlägen) fending off; (Sport) clearance; clearing (Amer.) (b) (Sport: Hintermannschaft) defence

ab|wehren *tr. V.* (a) repulse; fend off ⟨*blow*⟩; (Sport) clear ⟨*ball, shot*⟩ (b) avert ⟨*danger, consequences*⟩

Abwehr: **~kraft** *die* power of resistance; **~spieler** *der,* **~spielerin** *die* (Sport) defender

ab|weichen *unr. itr. V.; mit sein* (a) deviate (b) (sich unterscheiden) differ

Abweichung *die; ~, ~en* (a) deviation (b) (Unterschied) difference

ab|weisen *unr. tr. V.* turn away; turn down ⟨*applicant, suitor*⟩

abweisend *Adj.* cold ⟨*look, tone of voice*⟩; **in ~em Ton** coldly

Ab·weisung *die:* ▸ ABWEISEN: turning away; turning down

ab|wenden ① *unr. od. regelm. tr. V.* (a) turn away (b) *nur regelm.* (verhindern) avert ② *unr. od. regelm. refl. V.* turn away

*old spelling – see note on page x

ab|werben *unr. tr. V.* lure away

ab|werfen ① *unr. tr. V.* (a) drop; throw off ⟨*clothing*⟩; jettison ⟨*ballast*⟩; throw ⟨*rider*⟩ (b) (ins Spielfeld werfen) throw out ⟨*ball*⟩ (c) (einbringen) bring in; **Profit ~:** make a profit ② *unr. itr. V.* (Sport) throw the ball out

ab|werten *tr., unr. itr. V.* devalue

abwertend *Adj.* derogatory ⟨*term*⟩

Ab·wertung *die* devaluation

abwesend *Adj.* absent

Abwesenheit *die; ~:* absence

ab|wickeln *tr. V.* (a) unwind (b) (erledigen) deal with ⟨*case*⟩; do ⟨*business*⟩

Abwicklung *die; ~, ~en* ▸ ABWICKELN B: dealing (Gen. with); doing

ab|wiegen *unr. tr. V.* weigh out; weigh ⟨*single item*⟩

ab|wimmeln *tr. V.* (ugs.) get rid of

ab|winken *itr. V.* uninteressiert **~:** wave it/them aside uninterestedly; **Skat dreschen bis zum Abwinken** (ugs.) play skat till you can't stand any more (coll.); **Champagner bis zum Abwinken** (ugs.) more champagne than you can drink

ab|wischen *tr. V.* (a) wipe away (b) (säubern) wipe

Ab·wurf *der* (a) dropping; (von Ballast) jettisoning (b) **beim ~ stolperte der Torwart** the goalkeeper stumbled as he threw the ball out

ab|zahlen *tr. V.* pay off ⟨*debt, loan*⟩

ab|zählen *tr. V.* count

Ab·zahlung *die* paying off; **etw. auf ~ kaufen/verkaufen** buy/sell sth. on easy terms

Ab·zeichen *das* emblem; (Anstecknadel, Plakette) badge

ab|zeichnen ① *tr. V.* (a) (kopieren) copy (b) (signieren) initial ② *refl. V.* stand out; (fig.) begin to emerge

Abzieh·bild *das* transfer

ab|ziehen ① *unr. tr. V.* (a) pull off; peel off ⟨*skin*⟩; strip ⟨*bed*⟩ (b) (Fot.) make a print/prints of (c) (Milit., auch fig.) withdraw (d) (subtrahieren) subtract; take away; (abrechnen) deduct ② *unr. itr. V.; mit sein* (a) (sich verflüchtigen) escape (b) (Milit.) withdraw

Abzocke *die; ~, ~n* (salopp) rip-off (coll.)

Abzocker *der; ~s, ~* (salopp) rip-off merchant (coll.)

Abzockerei *die; ~, ~en* (salopp) profiteering *no pl.;* **das ist reine ~:** that's a complete rip-off (coll.)

Abzockerin *die; ~, ~nen* ▸ ABZOCKER

Ab·zug *der* (a) (an einer Schusswaffe) trigger

(b) (Fot.) print
(c) (Verminderung) deduction
abzüglich *Präp. mit Gen.* (Kaufmannsspr.) less
ab|zweigen ① *itr. V.; mit sein* branch off ② *tr. V.* put aside
Abzweigung *die;* ∼, ∼en turn-off; (Gabelung) fork
ach *Interj.* **(a)** (betroffen, mitleidig) oh [dear]
(b) (bedauernd, unwirsch) oh
(c) (klagend) ah
(d) (erstaunt) oh; ∼, **wirklich?** no, really?; ∼, **der!** oh, him!
(e) ∼ **so!** oh, I see; ∼ **was** *od.* **wo!** of course not
Achat *der;* ∼[e]s, ∼e (Min.) agate
Achse *die;* ∼, ∼n **(a)** (Rad∼) axle
(b) (Dreh∼, Math., Astron.) axis
Achsel *die;* ∼, ∼n (Schulter) shoulder; (∼höhle) armpit
Achsel-: ∼**haare** *Pl.* armpit hair *sing.;* ∼**höhle** *die* armpit
acht¹ *Kardinalz.* eight; **um** ∼ **[Uhr]** at eight [o'clock]; **um halb** ∼: at half past seven; **drei viertel** ∼, **Viertel vor** ∼: [a] quarter to eight; **es steht** ∼ **zu** ∼/∼ **zu zwei** (Sport) the score is eight all/eight to two
acht²: sie waren zu ∼: there were eight of them
Acht¹ *die;* ∼, ∼en **(a)** eight
(b) (Figur) figure eight
(c) (Verbiegung) buckle; **mein Rad hat eine** ∼: my wheel is buckled
Acht²: etw. außer ∼ **lassen** disregard sth.; **sich in** ∼ **nehmen** be careful; **sich vor jmdm./etw. in** ∼ **nehmen** be wary of sb./sth.; **auf jmdn./etw.** ∼ **geben** take care of sb./sth.; ∼ **geben** be careful
acht... *Ordinalz.* eighth; **der** ∼**e September** the eighth of September; **München, [den] 8. Mai 1984** Munich, 8 May 1984
Achte *der/die; adj. Dekl.* eighth
acht-, Acht-: ∼**eck** *das* octagon; ∼**eckig** *Adj.* octagonal; ∼**einhalb** *Bruchz.* eight and a half
achtel *Bruchz.* eighth
Achtel *das* (schweiz. meist *der*); ∼s, ∼: eighth
Achtel·note *die* (Musik) quaver
achten ① *tr. V.* respect ② *itr. V.* auf etw. (*Akk.*) ∼: pay heed to sth.
achtens *Adv.* eighthly
Achterbahn *die* roller coaster
acht·fach *Vervielfältigungsz.* eightfold; **die** ∼**fache Menge** eight times the quantity; ∼**fach vergrößert/verkleinert** magnified/reduced eight times; **das Achtfache kosten** cost eight times as much
*acht|geben ▸ ACHT²
acht-: ∼**hundert** *Kardinalz.* eight hundred; ∼**jährig** *Adj.* (8 Jahre alt) eight-year-old *attrib.;* eight years old *pred.;* (8 Jahre

dauernd) eight-year *attrib.;* ∼**köpfig** *Adj.* ⟨family, committee⟩ of eight
acht·los ① *Adj.* heedless ② *adv.* heedlessly
Achtlosigkeit *die;* ∼: heedlessness
acht-: ∼**mal** *Adv.* eight times; ∼**spurig** *Adj.* eight-lane ⟨road⟩; eight-track ⟨cassette⟩; ∼**stellig** *Adj.* eight-figure *attrib.;* ∼**stellig sein** have eight figures; ∼**stimmig** ① *Adj.* eight-part *attrib.;* ② *adv.* in eight parts; ∼**stöckig** *Adj.* eight-storey *attrib.;* ∼**tägig** *Adj.* (8 Tage alt) eight-day-old *attrib.;* (8 Tage dauernd) eight-day[-long] *attrib.;* ∼**tausend** *Kardinalz.* eight thousand; ∼**teilig** *Adj.* eight-piece ⟨tea service, tool set, etc.⟩; eight-part ⟨series, serial⟩
Achtung *die;* ∼ **(a)** respect (**vor** + *Dat.,* **Gen.** for)
(b) ∼! watch out!; ∼, **fertig, los!** on your marks, get set, go!
acht·zehn *Kardinalz.* eighteen; **18 Uhr 33** 6.33p.m.; (auf der 24-Stunden-Uhr) 1833
achtzehn·jährig *Adj.* (18 Jahre alt) eighteen-year-old *attrib.;* eighteen years old *pred.;* (18 Jahre dauernd) eighteen-year *attrib.*
achtzig *Kardinalz.* eighty; **[mit]** ∼ **[km/h] fahren** drive at *or* (coll.) do eighty [k.p.h.]; **über/etwa** ∼ **[Jahre alt] sein** be over/about eighty [years old]; **mit** ∼ **[Jahren]** at eighty [years of age]
achtzig·jährig *Adj.* (80 Jahre alt) eighty-year-old *attrib.;* eighty years old *pred.;* (80 Jahre dauernd) eighty-year *attrib.*
ächzen *itr. V.* groan
Acker *der;* ∼s, **Äcker** field
Acker-: ∼**bau** *der* arable farming; ∼**land** *das* farmland
Act /ɛkt/ *der;* ∼s, ∼s (Jargon) act
A.D. *Abk.* = **Anno Domini** AD
ADAC *Abk.* = **Allgemeiner Deutscher Automobilclub**
Adams·apfel *der* (ugs.) Adam's apple
adäquat /atǀɛˈkvaːt/ *Adj.* appropriate (*Dat.* to); suitable (*Dat.* for)
addieren ① *tr. V.* add [up] ② *itr. V.* add
Addition *die;* ∼, ∼en addition
ade *Interj.* (veralt., landsch.) farewell (dated) bye (coll.); **jmdm.** ∼ *od.* **Ade sagen** bid farewell to sb.
Adel *der;* ∼s nobility; **der niedere/hohe** ∼: the lesser nobility/the aristocracy
adelig ▸ ADLIG
Adelige ▸ ADLIGE
adeln *tr. V.* jmdn. ∼: give sb. a title; (in den hohen Adel erheben) raise sb. to the peerage
Adels-: ∼**geschlecht** *das,* ∼**haus** *das* noble family; ∼**stand** *der* nobility; (hoher Adel) nobility; ∼**titel** *der* title of nobility
Ader *die;* ∼, ∼n **(a)** blood vessel
(b) (Anlage, Begabung) streak ⋯⋙

(c) (Bot., Geol.) vein
(d) (Elektrot.) core
adieu /a'diø:/ *Interj.* (veralt.) adieu
adipös /adi'pø:s/ *Adj.* (Med.) **(a)** (fetthaltig)
adipose 〈*tissue, abdomen*〉
(b) (fettleibig) obese 〈*child, adult*〉
Adjektiv *das;* ~s, ~e (Sprachw.) adjective
Adjutant *der;* ~en, ~en, **Adjutantin**
die; ~, ~nen adjutant
Adler *der;* ~s, ~: eagle
adlig *Adj.* noble; ~ sein be a noble
[man/woman]
Adlige *der/die; adj. Dekl.* noble [man/
woman]
Admiral *der;* ~s, ~e *od.* Admiräle admiral
adoptieren *tr. V.* adopt
Adoption *die;* ~, ~en adoption
Adoptiv-: ~**eltern** *Pl.* adoptive parents;
~**kind** *das* adopted child; ~**mutter** *die;*
Pl. ~mütter adoptive mother; ~**sohn** *der*
adoptive *or* adopted son; ~**tochter** *die*
adoptive *or* adopted daughter; ~**vater** *der*
adoptive father
Adressat *der;* ~en, ~en, **Adressatin**
die; ~, ~nen addressee
Adress·buch, *Adreß·buch *das*
directory
Adresse *die;* ~, ~n address; **bei jmdm. an**
die falsche ~ kommen *od.* **geraten** (fig. ugs.)
come to the wrong address (fig.)
adressieren *tr. V.* address
adrett ①*Adj.* smart
② *adv.* smartly
adult /a'dʊlt/ *Adj.* (Biol., Genetik) adult
Advent /at'vɛnt/ *der;* ~s **(a)** (Advent
(b) (Adventssonntag) Sunday in Advent
Advents-: ~**kalender** *der* Advent
calendar; ~**kranz** *der: garland of evergreens*
with four candles for the Sundays in Advent
Adverb /at'vɛrp/ *das;* ~s, ~ien (Sprachw.)
adverb
adverbial (Sprachw.) ①*Adj.* adverbial
② *adv.* adverbially
Advokat /atvo'ka:t/ *der;* ~en, ~en,
Advokatin *die;* ~, ~nen (österr., schweiz.,
sonst veralt.) lawyer; advocate (arch.)
Aero- /aero- *od.* ɛ:ro-: / ~**gramm** *das*
air[mail] letter; ~**sol** *das;* ~~s, ~~e
aerosol
Affäre *die;* ~, ~n affair; **sich aus der**
~ **ziehen** (ugs.) get out of it
Affe *der;* ~n, ~n **(a)** monkey; (Menschen~)
ape
(b) (salopp) (dummer Kerl) oaf; clot (Brit. coll.);
(Geck) dandy
Affekt *der;* ~[e]s, ~e emotion; **im ~:** in the
heat of the moment
affektiert (abwertend) ①*Adj.* affected
② *adv.* affectedly
Affen·theater *das* (salopp) farce

Afghane /af'ga:nə/ *der;* ~n, ~n **(a)** Afghan
(b) (Hund) Afghan hound
Afghanin *die;* ~, ~nen Afghan
afghanisch *Adj.* Afghan
Afghanistan /af'ga:nɪsta:n/ *(das);* ~s
Afghanistan
Afrika *(das);* ~s Africa
Afrikaner *der;* ~s, ~, **Afrikanerin** *die;*
~, ~nen African
afrikanisch *Adj.* African
After *der;* ~s, ~: anus
AG *Abk.* **(a)** = **Aktiengesellschaft**
PLC (Brit.); Ltd. (private company) (Brit.); Inc.
(Amer.)
(b) = **Arbeitsgemeinschaft**
Agent *der;* ~en, ~en, **Agentin** *die;* ~,
~nen agent
Agentur *die;* ~, ~en agency
Agentur·bericht *der,*
Agentur·meldung *die* agency report
Aggregat *das;* ~[e]s, ~e (Technik) unit;
(Elektrot.) set
Aggregat·zustand *der* (Chemie) state
Aggression *die;* ~, ~en aggression
aggressiv ①*Adj.* aggressive
② *adv.* aggressively
Aggressivität *die;* ~: aggressiveness
Aggressor *der;* ~s, ~en, **Aggressorin**
die; ~, ~nen aggressor
Agitation *die;* ~: agitation
agitieren *itr. V.* agitate
Agrar·land *das* agrarian country
Ägypten *(das);* ~s Egypt
Ägypter *der;* ~s, ~, **Ägypterin** *die;* ~,
~nen Egyptian
ägyptisch *Adj.* Egyptian
ah *Interj.* (verwundert) oh; (freudig, genießerisch)
ah; (verstehend) oh; ah
äh /ɛ(:)/ *Interj.* **(a)** (angeekelt) ugh
(b) (stotternd) er; hum
aha /a'ha(:)/ *Interj.* (verstehend) oh[, I see];
(triumphierend) aha
ähm /ɛ:m/ *Interj.* er; erm
Ahn *der;* ~[e]s, *od.* ~en, ~en (geh.), **Ahne**
der; ~n, ~n forebear; ancestor
ähneln *itr. V.* jmdm. ~: resemble *or* be like
sb.; jmdm. sehr/wenig ~: strongly resemble
or be very like sb./bear little resemblance
to sb.; einer Sache (*Dat.*) ~: be similar to
sth.; be like sth.; sich (*Dat.*) ~: resemble one
another; be alike
ahnen *tr. V.* **(a)** (im Voraus fühlen) have a
premonition of
(b) (vermuten) suspect; das konnte ich doch
nicht ~! I had no way of knowing that
Ahnin *die;* ~, ~nen ▶ AHN
ähnlich ①*Adj.* similar; jmdm. ~ sein be
like sb.; ~ wie like
② *adv.* similarly; 〈*answer, react*〉 in a
similar way
③ *Präp. mit Dat.* like

---

*alte Schreibung – vgl. Hinweis auf S. x

Ähnlichkeit *die;* ~, ~**en** similarity; **mit jmdm.** ~ **haben** be like sb.

Ahnung *die;* ~, ~**en** (a) (Vorgefühl) premonition
(b) (ugs.: Kenntnisse) knowledge; **von etw.**
[viel] ~ **haben** know [a lot] about sth.; **keine** ~**!** [I've] no idea

ahnungs·los *Adj.* (nichts ahnend) unsuspecting; (naiv, unwissend) naïve

Ahnungslosigkeit *die;* ~ (Naivität, Unschuld) naïvety; innocence; (Unwissenheit) naïvety

ahoi *Interj.* (Seemannsspr.) ahoy

Ahorn /'aːhɔrn/ *der;* ~**s**, ~**e** maple

Ähre *die;* ~, ~**n** ear

Aids /eːts/ *das;* ~: Aids

Aids-: ~**kranke** *der/die* person suffering from Aids; ~**test** *der* Aids test

Airbag /'ɛːɐ̯bɛk/ *der;* ~**s**, ~**s** (Kfz.-W.) air bag

Akademie *die;* ~, ~**n** academy; (Bergbau, Forstw., Bauw.) school; college

Akademiker *der;* ~**s**, ~,
Akademikerin *die;* ~, ~**nen**
[university/college] graduate

akademisch ① *Adj.* academic
② *adv.* academically

Akazie /a'kaːtsi̯ə/ *die;* ~, ~**n** acacia

akklimatisieren *refl. V.* become *or* get acclimatized

Akkord *der;* ~**[e]s**, ~**e** (a) (Musik) chord
(b) (Wirtsch.) (Arbeit) piecework; (Lohn) piecework pay *no indef. art., no pl.;* (Satz) piece rate

Akkordeon *das;* ~**s**, ~**s** accordion

Akku *der;* ~**s**, ~**s** (ugs.), **Akkumulator** *der;* ~**s**, ~**en** accumulator (Brit.); storage battery

akkurat ① *Adj.* meticulous
② *adv.* meticulously

Akkusativ *der;* ~**s**, ~**e** (Sprachw.) accusative [case]

Akkusativ·objekt *das* (Sprachw.) accusative *or* direct object

Akku·schrauber *der* cordless screwdriver

Akne *die;* ~, ~**n** (Med.) acne

Akribie /akri'biː/ *die;* ~ (geh.) meticulousness; meticulous precision

akribisch /a'kriːbɪʃ/ ① *Adj.* meticulous; meticulously precise
② *adv.* meticulously; with meticulous precision

Akrobat *der;* ~**en**, ~**en** acrobat

Akrobatik *die;* ~: acrobatics *pl.*

Akrobatin *die;* ~, ~**nen** acrobat

akrobatisch *Adj.* acrobatic

Akt *der;* ~**[e]s**, ~**e** (a) (auch Theater, Zirkus-, Varieteeakt) act
(b) (Zeremonie) ceremony
(c) (Geschlechtsakt) sexual act

(d) (Kunst) nude

Akt-: ~**aufnahme** *die* nude photograph; ~**bild** *das* nude [picture]

Akte *die;* ~, ~**n** file

Akten-: ~**deckel** *der* folder; ~**koffer** *der* attaché case; ~**mappe** *die* briefcase; ~**notiz** *die* note [for the files]; ~**ordner** *der* file; ~**tasche** *die* briefcase; ~**zeichen** *das* reference

Akteur /ak'tøːɐ̯/ *der;* ~**s**, ~**e**, **Akteurin** *die;* ~, ~**nen** person involved

Akt·foto *das* nude photo

Aktie /'aktsi̯ə/ *die;* ~, ~**n** (Wirtsch.) share; ~**n** shares (Brit.); stock (Amer.); **die** ~**n fallen/steigen** share *or* stock prices are falling/rising

Aktien-: ~**gesellschaft** *die* joint stock company; ~**kapital** *das* share capital; ~**mehrheit** *die* majority shareholding (Gen. in); ~**paket** *das* block of shares

Aktion *die;* ~, ~**en** (a) action *no indef. art.;* (militärisch) operation
(b) (Kampagne) campaign

Aktionär *der;* ~**s**, ~**e**, **Aktionärin** *die;* ~, ~**nen** shareholder

aktiv ① *Adj.* (a) active
(b) (Milit.) serving *attrib.* ⟨officer, soldier⟩
② *adv.* actively

Aktiv *das;* ~**s**, ~**e** (Sprachw.) active

Aktive *der/die; adj. Dekl.* (Sport) participant

aktivieren *tr. V.* (a) mobilize ⟨party members, group, class, etc.⟩; **den Kreislauf** ~: stimulate the circulation
(b) (DV) activate

Aktivität *die;* ~, ~**en** activity

Akt·modell *das* nude model

aktualisieren *tr. V.* update

Aktualität *die;* ~, ~**en**
(a) (Gegenwartsbezug) relevance [to the present]
(b) (von Nachrichten usw.) topicality

aktuell *Adj.* topical; (gegenwärtig) current; (neu) up-to-the-minute; **eine** ~**e Sendung** (Ferns., Rundf.) a [news and] current affairs programme

Akupunktur *die;* ~, ~**en** (Med.) acupuncture

Akustik *die;* ~ (a) (Lehre vom Schall) acoustics *sing., no art.*
(b) (Schallverhältnisse) acoustics *pl.*

akustisch ① *Adj.* acoustic
② *adv.* acoustically

akut *Adj.* (auch Med.) acute; pressing, urgent ⟨question, issue⟩

AKW *Abk.* = **Atomkraftwerk**

Akzent *der;* ~**[e]s**, ~**e** (a) (Sprachw.) (Betonung) stress; (Betonungszeichen) accent
(b) (Sprachmelodie, Aussprache) accent

akzeptabel ① *Adj.* acceptable
② *adv.* acceptably

akzeptieren *tr. V.* accept

à la /ala/ (Gastr., ugs.) à la

a

Alabaster *der;* ~s, ~: alabaster

à la carte /ala'kart/ (Gastr.) à la carte

Alarm *der;* ~[e]s, ~e alarm; (Flieger~) air-raid warning; ~ **geben**/(fig. ugs.) **schlagen** raise the alarm; **blinder** ~: false alarm

alarm-, Alarm-: ~**anlage** *die* alarm system; ~**bereit** *Adj.* on alert *postpos.;* ~**bereitschaft** *die* alert

alarmieren *tr. V.* (a) alarm
(b) (zu Hilfe rufen) call [out] ‹*doctor, police, fire brigade, etc.*›

Alarm-: ~**sirene** *die* warning siren; ~**stufe** *die* alert stage

Albaner *der;* ~s, ~, **Albanerin** *die;* ~, ~nen Albanian

Albanien /al'ba:niən/ (*das*); ~s Albania

albanisch *Adj.* Albanian

Albatros *der;* ~, ~se (Zool.) albatross

Alben ▶ ALBUM

albern *Adj.* (a) silly; **sich** ~ **benehmen** act silly
(b) (ugs.: nebensächlich) silly; stupid

Albernheit *die;* ~, ~en silliness

Albino *der;* ~s, ~s albino

Alb·traum *der* nightmare

Album *das;* ~s, Alben album

Alcopop /'alkopɔp/ *der od. das;* ~s, ~s alcopop

Alge *die;* ~, ~n alga

Algebra /*österr.:* al'ge:bra/ *die;* ~: algebra

Algerien /al'ge:riən/ (*das*); ~s Algeria

Algerier *der;* ~s, ~, **Algerierin** *die;* ~, ~nen Algerian

algerisch *Adj.* Algerian

alias *Adv.* alias

Alibi *das;* ~s, ~s alibi

Alkohol *der;* ~s, ~e alcohol

alkohol-, Alkohol-: ~**abhängig** *Adj.* dependent on alcohol *postpos.;* ~**abhängigkeit** *die* dependence on alcohol; alcohol dependence; ~**ein·fluss**, **~**ein·fluß** *der,* ~**ein·wirkung** *die* influence of alcohol *or* drink; **unter** ~**einfluss** *od.* ~**einwirkung [stehen] [be]** under the influence of alcohol *or* drink; ~**fahne** *die* smell of alcohol [on one's breath]; **eine** ~**fahne haben** smell of alcohol; ~**frei** *Adj.* non-alcoholic

Alkoholiker *der;* ~s, ~, **Alkoholikerin** *die;* ~, ~nen alcoholic

alkoholisch *Adj.* alcoholic

Alkoholismus *der;* ~: alcoholism *no art.*

alkohol-, Alkohol-: ~**konsum** *der* consumption of alcohol; ~**missbrauch**, **~**mißbrauch** *der* alcohol abuse; ~**sucht** *die* alcohol addiction; alcoholism; ~**süchtig** *Adj.* addicted to alcohol *postpos.;* alcoholic; ~**süchtige** *der/die; adj. Dekl.* alcoholic; ~**sünder** *der,* ~**sünderin** *die* (ugs.) drunk[en] driver;

*old spelling – see note on page x

~**vergiftung** *die* alcohol[ic] poisoning

all *Indefinitpron. u. unbest. Zahlw.* **1** *attr.* (ganz, gesamt...) all; ~**es andere/Weitere/ Übrige** everything else; ~**es Schöne** everything *or* all that is beautiful; ~**es Gute!** all the best!; **wir/ihr/sie** ~**e** all of us/you/them; ~**e Anwesenden** all those present; ~**e Bewohner der Stadt** all the inhabitants of the town; ~**e Jahre wieder** every year; ~**e fünf Minuten/Meter** every five minutes/metres; **Bücher** ~**er Art** all kinds of books; **in** ~**er Ruhe** in peace and quiet
2 *allein stehend* (a) ~**e** all; ~**e, die ...:** all those who ...
(b) ~**es** (auf Sachen bezogen) everything; (auf Personen bezogen) everybody; **das** ~**es** all that; **trotz** ~**em** in spite of everything; ~**es in** ~**em** all in all; **vor** ~**em** above all; **das ist** ~**es** that's all *or* (coll.) it; **ist das** ~**es?** is that all *or* (coll.) it?; ~**es mal herhören!** (ugs.) listen everybody!; ~**es aussteigen!** (ugs.) everyone out!; (vom Schaffner gesagt) all change!

All *das;* ~s ▶ WELTALL

alle *Adj.* ~ **sein** be all gone; ~ **werden** run out

alle-dem *Pron.* **trotz** ~: in spite of *or* despite all that

Allee *die;* ~, ~n avenue

allein **1** *Adj.* (a) (für sich) alone; on one's/its own; by oneself/itself; **ganz** ~: all on one's/its own
(b) (einsam) alone
2 *adv.* (ohne Hilfe) by oneself/itself; on one's/its own; **etw.** ~ **tun** do sth. oneself; **von** ~ (ugs.) by oneself/itself
3 *Adv.* (a) (geh.: ausschließlich) alone
(b) [schon] ~ **der Gedanke, [schon] der Gedanke** ~: the mere thought [of it]

alleine (ugs.) ▶ ALLEIN 1A, 2, 3B

allein-, Allein-: **~**erziehend** *Adj.* single ‹*mother, father, parent*›; ~**erziehende** *der/die; adj. Dekl.* single parent; ~**gang** *der* (fig.) independent initiative; **im** ~**gang** off one's own bat

alleinig *Adj.* sole

allein·stehend *Adj.* ‹*person*› living alone; (ledig) single ‹*person*›

Alleinstehende *der/die; adj. Dekl.* person living alone; (Ledige[r]) single person

alle-mal *Adv.* (ugs.) any time (coll.); **was der kann, das kann ich doch** ~: anything he can do, I can do too; *s. auch* EIN[1] 1

allen·falls *Adv.* (a) (höchstens) at [the] most
(b) (bestenfalls) at best

aller-: ~**dings** *Adv.* (a) (einschränkend) though; **es stimmt** ~**dings, dass ...:** it's true though that ...; (b) (zustimmend) [yes,] certainly; **das war** ~**dings Pech** that was bad luck, to be sure; ~**erst...** *Adj.* (a) very first; **der/die/das** ~**erste** the very first;
(b) (best...) very best

allergen (Med.) **1** *Adj.* allergenic
2 *adv.* ~ **wirken** have an allergenic effect
Allergen /alɛr'geːn/ *das;* ~s, ~e (Med.) allergen
Allergie *die;* ~, ~n (Med.) allergy
allergisch **1** *Adj.* (Med.) allergic (**gegen** to)
2 *adv.* **auf etw.** (*Akk.*) ~ **reagieren** have an allergic reaction to sth.
aller-, Aller-: ~**größt...** *Adj.* utmost ‹*trouble, care, etc.*›; biggest ‹*car, house, town, etc.*› of all; tallest ‹*person*› of all; **am** ~**größten sein** be [the] biggest/tallest of all; ~**hand** *indekl. Adj.* (ugs.) **(a)** *attr.* all kinds *or* sorts of; **(b)** *allein stehend* all kinds *or* sorts of things; **das ist** ~**hand** (viel) that's a lot; **das ist ja** ~**hand!** that's just not on! (Brit. coll.); ~**heiligen** *das;* ~~s (bes. kath. Kirche) All Saints' Day; ~**herzlichst** **1** *Adj.* warmest ‹*thanks, greetings, congratulations*›; most cordial ‹*reception, welcome, invitation*›; **2** most warmly; ~**höchst...** **1** *Adj.* highest ‹*building, tree, etc.*› of all; **2** *adv.* **am** ~**höchsten** ‹*fly, jump, etc.*› the highest of all; ~**höchstens** *Adv.* at the very most
allerlei *indekl. Adj.* all kinds *or* sorts of; *allein stehend* all kinds *or* sorts of things
Allerlei *das;* ~s, ~s (Gemisch) pot-pourri; (Durcheinander) jumble
aller-: ~**letzt...** *Adj.* **(a)** very last; **(b)** (ugs. abwertend) most dreadful (coll.); **das ist das Allerletzte** that is the absolute limit; ~**liebst...** **1** *Adj.* most favourite; **es wäre mir am** ~**liebsten** *od.* **das Allerliebste, wenn** ...: I should like it best of all if ...; **2** *adv.* **etw. am** ~**liebsten tun** like doing sth. best of all; ~**meist...** **1** *Indefinitpron. u. unbest. Zahlw.* by far the most *attrib.;* **das** ~**meiste/am** ~**meisten** most of all/by far the most; **2** *Adv.* **am** ~**meisten** most of all; ~**mindest...** *Adj.* slightest; least; **das** ~**mindeste** the very least; ~**nächst...** **1** *Adj.* very nearest *attrib.;* (Reihenfolge ausdrückend) very next *attrib.;* **2** *adv.* **am** ~**nächsten** nearest of all; ~**neu[e]st...** *Adj.* very latest *attrib.;* **das Allerneu[e]ste** the very latest; ~**schlimmst...** *Adj.* very worst *attrib.;* ~**schönst...** **1** *Adj.* most beautiful *attrib.;* loveliest *attrib.;* (angenehmst...) very nicest *attrib.;* **2** *adv.* **er singt am** ~**schönsten** his singing is the most beautiful of all; ~**seits** *Adv.* **guten Morgen** ~**seits!** good morning everyone
Allerwelts-: ~**gesicht** *das* nondescript face; ~**wort** *das* hackneyed word
allerwenigst... **1** *Adj.* lest ... of all; *Pl.* fewest ... of all
2 *adv.* **am** ~**wenigsten** least of all
alle·samt *Indefinitpron. u. unbest. Zahlw.* (ugs.) all [of you/us/them]; **wir** ~: we all
Alles·kleber *der* all-purpose adhesive
all·gemein **1** *Adj.* general; universal ‹*conscription, suffrage*›; **im** ~**en Interesse** in the common interest; **im Allgemein,** **~en*

in general
2 *adv.* **(a)** generally; (ausnahmslos) universally; **es ist** ~ **bekannt, dass** ...: it is common knowledge that ...
(b) (unverbindlich) ‹*write, talk, discuss*› in general terms
Allgemein-: ~**befinden** *das* (Med.) general state of health; ~**bildung** *die* general education
Allgemeinheit *die;* ~ **(a)** generality **(b)** *die* ~: the general public
Allgemein-: ~**medizin** *die* general medicine; ~**wohl** *das* public good
All·heilmittel *das* (auch fig.) cure-all; panacea
Alligator *der;* ~s, ~en alligator
Alliierte *der; adj. Dekl.* ally; **die** ~**n** the Allies
all-: ~**jährlich** **1** *Adj.* annual; yearly; **2** *adv.* annually; every year; ~**mächtig** *Adj.* all-powerful
all·mählich **1** *Adj.* gradual
2 *adv.* gradually
3 *Adv.* **wir sollten** ~ **gehen** it's time we got going
all-, All-: ~**morgendlich** **1** *Adj.* regular morning; **2** *adv.* every morning; ~**rad·antrieb** *der* (Kfz-W.) all-wheel drive; ~**rad·fahrzeug** *das* four-by-four; ~**seitig** **1** *Adj.* general; all-round, (Amer.) all-around *attrib.;* **2** *adv.* generally; ~**seits** *Adv.* on all sides; ~**tag** *der* **(a)** (Werktag) weekday; **(b)** (Einerlei) daily routine; **der graue** ~: the dull routine of everyday life; ~**täglich** *Adj.* ordinary ‹*face, person, appearance, etc.*›; everyday ‹*topic, event, sight*›; commonplace ‹*remark*›; **ein nicht** ~**täglicher Anblick** a sight one doesn't see every day; ~**tags** *Adv.* [on] weekdays
Alltags- everyday *attrib.;* of everyday life *postpos., not pred.;* ~**pflicht** daily duty
allzu *Adv.* all too; ~ **bald/früh** all too soon/early; ~ **lange/oft/sehr** too long/often/much; ~ **viel** too much; **nicht** ~ **viele** not too many
*allzu·bald *usw.* ▸ ALLZU
Alm *die;* ~, ~en mountain pasture; Alpine pasture
Alm·hütte *die* Alpine hut
Almosen *das;* ~s, ~: alms *pl.*
Aloe vera /'aːloe 'veːra/ *die;* ~~, ~~s aloe vera
Alp *die;* ~, ~en (bes. schweiz.) ▸ ALM
Alpaka *das;* ~s, ~s alpaca
Alpen *Pl. die* ~: the Alps
Alpen-: ~**rose** *die* rhododendron; ~**veilchen** *das* cyclamen
Alpha *das;* ~[s], ~[s] alpha
Alphabet *das;* ~[e]s, ~e alphabet
alphabetisch **1** *Adj.* alphabetical
2 *adv.* alphabetically

Alp·horn *das* alpenhorn

alpin *Adj.* Alpine

Alpinist *der;* ~en, ~en, **Alpinistin** *die;*
~, ~nen Alpinist

Alp·traum ▸ ALBTRAUM

als *Konj.* **(a)** (zeitlich) when; damals, ~: [in
the days] when; gerade ~: just as
(b) (kausal) um so mehr, ~: all the more
since *or* in that
(c) *Vergleichspartikel* größer/älter/mehr/
weniger ~: bigger/older/more/less than;
anders ~ wir sein/leben be different/live
differently from us; so viel/so weit
~ möglich as much/as far as possible; so
bald/schnell ~ möglich as soon/as quickly
as possible; ~ [wenn *od.* ob] (+ Konjunktiv II)
as if; as though; ~ ob ich das nicht wüsste!
as if I didn't know
(d) ~ Rentner/Arzt as a pensioner/a doctor;
sich ~ wahr/Lüge erweisen prove to be
true/a lie

also 1 *Adv.* so; therefore
2 *Partikel* **(a)** (das heißt) that is
(b) (nach Unterbrechung) well [then]
(c) (verstärkend) na ~! there you are[, you
see]; ~ schön well all right then

alt, älter, ältest... *Adj.* **(a)** old; Alt
und Jung old and young; seine ~en Eltern
his aged parents; wie ~ bist du? how old
are you?; mein älterer/ältester Bruder my
elder/eldest brother
(b) (nicht mehr frisch) old; ~es Brot stale bread
(c) (vom letzten Jahr) old; ~e Äpfel/Kartoffeln
last year's apples/potatoes
(d) (langjährig) long-standing ⟨*acquaintance*⟩
(e) (antik, klassisch) ancient
(f) (vertraut) old familiar ⟨*streets, sights, etc.*⟩;
ganz der/die Alte sein be just the same

Alt¹ *der;* ~s, ~e (Musik) alto; (Frauenstimme)
contralto; (im Chor) contraltos *pl.*

Alt² *das;* ~[s], ~: *top fermented, dark beer*

Altar *der;* ~[e]s, Altäre altar

alt-, Alt-: ~**bau·wohnung** *die* flat (Brit.)
or (Amer.) apartment in an old building;
~**bekannt** *Adj.* well-known; ~**bier** *das*
▸ ALT²

Alte *der/die; adj. Dekl.* **(a)** (alter Mensch) old
man/woman; *Pl.* old people
(b) (salopp) (Vater, Ehemann) old man (coll.);
(Mutter, Ehefrau) old woman (coll.); (Chef)
governor (coll.); (Chefin) boss (coll.); die ~n
(Eltern) my/his *etc.* old man and old woman
(coll.)
(c) *Pl.* (Tiereltern) parents

alt·ehrwürdig *Adj.* (geh.) venerable; time-
honoured ⟨*customs*⟩

Alt·englisch *das* Old English

Alten-: ~**pfleger** *der,* ~**pflegerin** *die*
geriatric nurse; ~**tages·stätte** *die* old
people's day centre

Alter *das;* ~s, ~: age; (hohes ~) old age;

im ~: in one's old age; im ~ von at the age of

älter 1 ▸ ALT
2 *Adj.* (nicht mehr jung) elderly

altern *itr. V.; mit sein* age

alters-, Alters-: ~**beschwerden**
Pl. complaints of old age; ~**genosse**
der, ~**genossin** *die* contemporary;
person/child of the same age; meine
~genossen my contemporaries; people of
my age; ~**gruppe** *die* age group; ~**heim**
das old people's home; old-age home (Amer.);
~**rente** *die* old-age pension; ~**ruhe·geld**
das retirement pension; ~**schwach**
Adj. old and infirm ⟨*person*⟩; old and
weak ⟨*animal*⟩; ~**schwäche** *die* (bei
Menschen) [old] age and infirmity; (bei Tieren)
[old] age and weakness; ~**starrsinn**
der obstinacy of old age; ~**stufe** *die* age;
~**unterschied** *der* age difference;
~**versorgung** *die* provision for one's old
age; (System) pension scheme

Altertum *das;* ~s antiquity *no art.*

Älteste *der/die; adj. Dekl.* **(a)** (Dorf-, Vereins-,
Kirchenälteste usw.) elder
(b) (Sohn, Tochter) eldest

alt-, Alt-: ~**glas** *das* waste glass;
(Flaschen) empty bottles; ~**glas·behälter**
der bottle bank; ~**griechisch**
das classical *or* ancient Greek;
~**hochdeutsch** *das* Old High German;
~**klug;** ~kluger, ~klugst... 1 *Adj.*
precocious; 2 *adv.* precociously; ~**last**
die (Ökologie) old, improperly disposed of
harmful waste; (fig.) inherited problem

ältlich *Adj.* rather elderly

alt-, Alt-: ~**metall** *das* scrap metal;
~**modisch** 1 *Adj.* old-fashioned;
2 *adv.* in an old-fashioned way;
~**papier** *das* waste paper; ~**rosa**
Adj. old rose; ~**stadt** *die* old [part of
the] town; ~**waren·händler** *der,*
~**waren·händlerin** *die* second-hand
dealer

Alu *das;* ~s (ugs.) aluminium

Alu·folie *die* aluminium foil

Aluminium *das;* ~s aluminium;
aluminum (Amer.)

Alzheimer /'altshaɪmɐ/ *der;* ~s (ugs.),
Alzheimer *die;* ~ (ugs.) Alzheimer's

am *Präp. + Art.* **(a)** = an dem;
(b) Frankfurt am Main Frankfurt on [the]
Main; am Marktplatz on the market square;
am Meer/Fluss by the sea/on *or* by the river;
am Anfang/Ende at the beginning/end;
am 19. November on 19 November; am
schnellsten laufen run [the] fastest; am
Verwelken sein be wilting

Amalgam *das;* ~s, ~e (Chemie, auch fig.)
amalgam

Amalgam·füllung *die* (Zahnmed.)
amalgam filling

Amateur /ama'tøːɐ/ *der;* ~s, ~e,
Amateurin *die;* ~, ~nen amateur

---

*alte Schreibung – vgl. Hinweis auf S. x

Amazonas der; ~: Amazon

Amboss, *Amboß der; ~es, ~e anvil

ambulant (Med.) [1] Adj. outpatient attrib.; [2] adv. jmdn. ~ behandeln give sb. outpatient treatment

Ambulanz die; ~, ~en (a) (in Kliniken) outpatient[s'] department (b) (Krankenwagen) ambulance

Ameise die; ~, ~n ant

Ameisen-: ~bär der anteater; ~haufen der anthill

amen Adv. amen

Amen das; ~s, ~: Amen

Amerika (das); ~s America

Amerikaner der; ~s, ~ (a) American (b) (Gebäck) small, flat iced cake

Amerikanerin die; ~, ~nen American

amerikanisch Adj. American

Amino·säure die (Chemie) amino acid

Ammann der; ~[e]s, Ammänner (schweiz.) (Gemeinde-, Bezirksamman) ≈ mayor; (Landamman) cantonal president

Amme die; ~, ~n wet nurse

Amnestie /amnɛs'tiː/ die; ~, ~n amnesty

amnestieren tr. V. grant an amnesty to

Amöbe die; ~, ~n (Biol.) amoeba

Amok der: ~ laufen run amok

Amok·läufer der madman

Amok·läuferin die madwoman

Ampel die; ~, ~n (a) (Verkehrsw.) traffic lights pl. (b) (für Pflanzen) hanging flowerpot

Amphibie /am'fiːbiə/ die; ~, ~n (Zool.) amphibian

Amphibien·fahrzeug das amphibious vehicle

Amphi·theater das amphitheatre

Ampulle die; ~, ~n (Med.) ampoule

Amputation die; ~, ~en (Med.) amputation

amputieren tr. V. amputate

Amsel die; ~, ~n blackbird

Amt das; ~[e]s, Ämter (a) (Stellung) post; position; (hohes politisches od. kirchliches ~) office; **im ~ sein** be in office (b) (Aufgabe) task; job (c) (Behörde) office (d) (Fernsprechvermittlung) exchange

amtieren itr. V. (a) hold office (b) (vorübergehend) act (**als** as)

amtlich [1] Adj. official; (ugs.: sicher) definite [2] adv. officially

Amt·mann der; Pl. ...männer od. ...leute, **Amt·männin** die; ~, ~nen senior civil servant

Amts-: ~anmaßung die (Rechtsw.) unauthorized assumption of authority; ~arzt der, ~ärztin die medical officer; ~eid der oath of office; ~gericht das local or district court; ~geschäfte Pl. official duties; ~handlung die official act or duty;

~leitung die (Fernspr.) exchange line

Amulett das; ~[e]s, ~e amulet; charm

amüsant [1] Adj. entertaining; amusing [2] adv. in an entertaining or amusing way

amüsieren [1] refl. V. (a) (sich vergnügen) enjoy oneself; **sich mit jmdm. ~:** have fun or a good time with sb. (b) (belustigt sein) be amused; **sich über** jmdn./etw. ~: find sb./sth. funny [2] tr. V. amuse

an [1] Präp. mit Dat. (a) (räumlich) at; (auf) on; **Frankfurt an der Oder** Frankfurt on [the] Oder; **Tür an Tür** next door to one another; **an ... vorbei** past (b) (zeitlich) on; **an jedem Sonntag** every Sunday; **an Ostern** (bes. südd.) at Easter (c) **arm/reich an Vitaminen** low/rich in vitamins; **jmdn. an etw. erkennen** recognize sb. by sth.; **an etw. leiden** suffer from sth.; **an einer Krankheit sterben** die of a disease (d) **an [und für] sich** actually [2] Präp. mit Akk. (a) to; (auf, gegen) on (b) **an etw./jmdn. glauben** believe in sth./sb.; **an etw. denken** think of sth.; **sich an etw. erinnern** remember sth. [3] Adv. (a) (Verkehrsw.) **Köln an: 9.15** arriving Cologne 09.15 (b) (ugs.: in Betrieb) on; **die Waschmaschine/ der Fernseher/das Licht/das Gas ist an** the washing machine/television/light/gas is on (c) (ugs.: ungefähr) around; about; **an [die] 2 000 Euro** around or about 2,000 euros

Anabolikum das; ~s, Anabolika (Med.) anabolic steroid

analog [1] Adj. (a) (gleichartig) analogous; ~ [zu] diesem Fall analogous to this case (b) (Technik, DV) analogue [2] adv. (a) (gleichartig) analogously (b) (Technik, DV) ⟨display, reproduce⟩ in analogue form

Analog-: ~rechner der (DV) analogue computer; ~uhr die analogue clock; (Armbanduhr) analogue watch

Analphabet der; ~en, ~en, **Analphabetin** die; ~, ~nen illiterate [person]; ~ sein be illiterate

Analphabetentum das; ~s illiteracy

Analphabetismus der; ~: illiteracy

Analyse die; ~, ~n analysis

analysieren tr. V. analyse

Analyst der; ~en, ~en, **Analystin,** die; ~, ~nen (Börsenw.) analyst

analytisch [1] Adj. analytical [2] adv. analytically

Ananas die; ~, ~ od. ~se pineapple

Anarchie die; ~, ~n anarchy

Anarchist der; ~en, ~en, **Anarchistin** die; ~, ~nen anarchist

Anästhesie die; ~, ~n (Med.) anaesthesia

anästhesieren tr. V. (Med.) anaesthetize

Anästhesist der; ~en, ~en, **Anästhesistin** die; ~, ~nen (Med.) anaesthetist

Anatomie *die;* ~, ~n anatomy
anatomisch *Adj.* anatomical
an|bahnen ☐1 *tr. V.* initiate ⟨*negotiations, talks, process, etc.*⟩; develop ⟨*relationship, connection*⟩
 ☐2 *refl. V.* ⟨*development*⟩ be in the offing; ⟨*friendship, relationship*⟩ start to develop
an|bändeln *itr. V.* mit jmdm. ~ (ugs.) get off with sb. (Brit. coll.); pick sb. up
An·bau *der; Pl.* ~ten (a) building
 (b) (Gebäude) extension
 (c) (das Anpflanzen) growing
an|bauen ☐1 *tr. V.* (a) build on
 (b) (anpflanzen) grow
 ☐2 *itr. V.* (das Haus vergrößern) build an extension
an·bei *Adv.* (Amtsspr.) herewith; **Rückporto** ~: return postage enclosed
an|beißen ☐1 *unr. tr. V.* bite into; take a bite of
 ☐2 *unr. itr. V.* (auch fig. ugs.) bite
an|belangen *tr. V.* was mich/dies *usw.* anbelangt as far as I am/this matter is *etc.* concerned
an|beten *tr. V.* (auch fig.) worship
An·betracht *der:* in ~ einer Sache (*Gen.*) in view of the
an|betreffen *unr. tr. V.* ▶ ANBELANGEN
an|betteln *tr. V.* jmdn. ~: beg from sb.; jmdn. um etw. ~: beg sb. for sth.
Anbetung *die;* ~, ~en (auch fig.) worship
an|biedern *refl. V.* sich [bei jmdm.] ~: curry favour [with sb.]
an|bieten ☐1 *unr. tr. V.* offer; jmdm. etw. ~: offer sb. sth.
 ☐2 *unr. refl. V.* (a) offer one's services; sich ~, etw. zu tun offer to do sth.
 (b) (fig.) ⟨*possibility, solution*⟩ suggest itself
An·bieter *der*, **An·bieterin** *die* (Wirtsch.) supplier
an|binden *unr. tr. V.* tie [up] (an + *Dat. od. Akk.* to); tie up, moor ⟨*boat*⟩ (an + *Dat. od. Akk.* to); tether ⟨*animal*⟩ (an + *Dat. od. Akk.* to)
an|blasen *unr. tr. V.* (a) blow at
 (b) (anfachen) blow on
An·blick *der* sight
an|blicken *tr. V.* look at
an|blinzeln *tr. V.* (a) blink at
 (b) (zuzwinkern) wink at
an|brechen ☐1 *unr. tr. V.* (a) crack
 (b) (öffnen) open
 (c) (zu verbrauchen beginnen) break into ⟨*supplies, reserves*⟩
 ☐2 *unr. itr. V.; mit sein* (geh.: beginnen) ⟨*dawn, day*⟩ break; ⟨*age, epoch*⟩ dawn
an|brennen ☐1 *unr. tr. V.* (anzünden) light
 ☐2 *unr. itr. V.; mit sein* burn
an|bringen *unr. tr. V.* (a) (befestigen) put up ⟨*sign, aerial, curtain, plaque*⟩ (an + *Dat.* on)

(b) (äußern) make ⟨*request, complaint, comment*⟩
(c) (zeigen) demonstrate ⟨*knowledge, experience*⟩
(d) (ugs.: herbeibringen) bring
An·bruch *der* (geh.: Beginn) dawn[ing]; **der** ~ des Tages daybreak
an|brüllen *tr. V.* (ugs.) bellow at
Andacht *die;* ~, ~en (a) (Sammlung) rapt attention; (im Gebet) silent worship *or* prayer
 (b) (Gottesdienst) prayers *pl.*
andächtig ☐1 *Adj.* rapt; (ins Gebet versunken) devout
 ☐2 *adv.* with rapt attention; (ins Gebet versunken) devoutly
an|dauern *itr. V.* ⟨*negotiations*⟩ continue, go on; ⟨*weather, rain*⟩ last
andauernd ☐1 *Adj.* continual; constant
 ☐2 *adv.* continually; constantly
Anden *Pl. die* ~: the Andes
An·denken *das;* ~s, ~ (a) memory; **zum** ~ an jmdn./etw. to remind you/us *etc.* of sb./sth.
 (b) (Erinnerungsstück) memento; (Reise~) souvenir
ander... *Indefinitpron.* ☐1 *attr.* (a) other; ein ~er/eine ~e/ein ~es another; das Kleid gefällt mir nicht, haben Sie noch ~e/ein ~es? I don't like that dress, do you have any others/another?; jemand ~er *od.* ~es someone else; (in Fragen) anyone else; niemand ~er *od.* ~es nobody else; etwas ~es something else; (in Fragen) anything else; nichts ~es nothing else; not anything else
 (b) (verschieden) different
 ☐2 *allein stehend* ein ~r/eine ~e: another [one]; nicht drängeln, einer nach dem ~n don't push, one after the other; ein ~er/eine ~e/ein ~es another [one]; ein[e]s nach dem ~[e]n first things first; ich will weder das eine noch das ~e I don't want either
anderen·falls *Adv.* otherwise
anderer·seits *Adv.* on the other hand
ander·mal *Adv.* ein ~: another time
ändern ☐1 *tr. V.* change; alter; alter ⟨*garment*⟩; change ⟨*person*⟩
 ☐2 *refl. V.* change
andern·falls *Adv.* otherwise
anders *Adv.* (a) (verschieden) ⟨*think, act, feel, do*⟩ differently (als from *or* (esp. Brit) to); ⟨*be, look, sound, taste*⟩ different (als from *or* (esp. Brit.) to); es war alles ganz ~: it was all quite different
 (b) (sonst) else; niemand ~: nobody else; jemand ~: someone else; (in Fragen) anyone else
anders-, Anders-: ~artig *Adj.* different; ~farbig *Adj.* different-coloured *attrib.;* of a different colour *postpos.;* ~gläubige *der/die* person of a different religion; ~herum *Adv.* the other way round *or* (Amer.) around; ~herum gehen/

fahren go/drive round or (Amer.) around the other way; **∼wo** Adv. (ugs.) elsewhere; **∼woher** Adv. (ugs.) from somewhere else; **∼wohin** Adv. (ugs.) somewhere else

andert·halb Bruchz. one and a half; **∼ Stunden** an hour and a half

Änderung die; ∼, ∼en change (Gen. in); alteration (Gen. to)

Änderungs·schneiderei die tailor's [that does alterations]

anderweitig ① Adj. other ② adv. in another way

an|deuten ① tr. V. **(a)** (zu verstehen geben) hint
(b) (nicht vollständig ausführen) outline; (kurz erwähnen) indicate ② refl. V. be indicated

An·deutung die hint

An·drang der crowd; (Gedränge) crush

andre... ▶ ANDER...

an|drehen tr. V. **(a)** (einschalten) turn on
(b) jmdm. etw. ∼ (ugs.) palm sb. off with sth.

andrer·seits Adv. on the other hand

an|drohen tr. V. jmdm. etw. ∼: threaten sb. with sth

An·drohung die threat

an|drücken tr. V. press down

an|ecken itr. V.; mit sein bei jmdm. ∼ (fig. ugs.) rub sb. [up (Brit.)] the wrong way

an|eignen refl. V. **(a)** appropriate
(b) (lernen) acquire; learn

an-einander Adv. (zusammen) together; (nebeneinander) next to each other; next to one another; ∼ **denken** think of each other or one another; ∼ **vorbeigehen** pass each other or one another

***aneinander|denken** usw.
  ▶ ANEINANDER

Anekdote die; ∼, ∼n anecdote

an|ekeln tr. V. disgust

Anemone die; ∼, ∼n anemone

an|erkennen unr. tr. V. **(a)** recognize ⟨country, record, verdict, qualification, document⟩; acknowledge ⟨debt⟩; accept ⟨demand, bill, conditions, rules⟩; allow ⟨claim, goal⟩
(b) (nicht leugnen) acknowledge
(c) (würdigen) appreciate; respect ⟨viewpoint, opinion⟩; **ein ∼der Blick** an appreciative look

anerkennens·wert Adj. commendable

Anerkennung die; ∼, ∼en
  ▶ ANERKENNEN: **(a)** recognition; acknowledgement; acceptance; allowance
(b) acknowledgement
(c) appreciation; respect (Gen. for)

an|fachen tr. V. fan; (fig.) arouse ⟨anger, curiosity, enthusiasm⟩; inflame ⟨passion⟩; stir up ⟨hatred⟩; inspire ⟨hope⟩; ferment ⟨discord, war⟩

an|fahren ① unr. tr. V. **(a)** run into; hit
(b) (herbeifahren) deliver

(c) (ansteuern) stop at ⟨village etc.⟩; ⟨ship⟩ put in at ⟨port⟩
(d) (zurechtweisen) shout at
② unr. itr. V.; mit sein **(a)** (starten) start off
(b) angefahren kommen come driving/ riding up

An·fahrt die **(a)** (das Anfahren) journey
(b) (Weg) approach

Anfahrts·skizze die map showing directions

An·fall der attack; (epileptischer ∼, fig.) fit; **einen ∼ bekommen** od. (ugs.) **kriegen** have an attack/a fit

an|fallen ① unr. tr. V. attack
② unr. itr V.; mit sein ⟨costs⟩ be incurred; ⟨interest⟩ accrue; ⟨work⟩ come up

an·fällig Adj. ⟨person⟩ with a delicate constitution; ⟨machine⟩ susceptible to faults; **gegen** od. **für etw. ∼ sein** be susceptible to sth.

An·fang der beginning; start; (erster Abschnitt) beginning; **am** od. **zu ∼:** at first; **von ∼ an** from the outset; ∼ **1984**/der Woche usw. at the beginning of 1984/of the week etc.

an|fangen ① unr. itr. V. **(a)** begin; start; **mit etw. ∼:** start [on] sth.; ∼, **etw. zu tun** start to do sth.
(b) (zu sprechen anfangen) begin; **von etw. ∼:** start on about sth.
(c) (eine Stelle antreten) start
② unr. tr. V. **(a)** begin; start; (anbrechen) start
(b) (machen) do

An·fänger der; ∼s, ∼, **An·fängerin** die; ∼, ∼nen beginner

anfänglich Adj. initial

anfangs Adv. at first; initially

Anfangs-: ∼**buchstabe** der initial [letter]; ∼**stadium** das initial stage

an|fassen ① tr. V. **(a)** (fassen, halten) take hold of
(b) (berühren) touch
(c) jmdn. ∼ (an der Hand nehmen) take sb.'s hand
(d) (angehen) tackle ⟨problem, task, etc.⟩
(e) (behandeln) treat ⟨person⟩
② itr. V. **[mit]** ∼: lend a hand

anfechtbar Adj.; ▶ ANFECHTEN A: disputable; contestable; challengeable

an|fechten unr. tr. V. **(a)** dispute ⟨statement, contract⟩; contest ⟨will⟩; challenge ⟨decision, law, opinion⟩
(b) (beunruhigen) trouble

an|fertigen tr. V. make

an|feuchten tr. V. moisten ⟨lips, stamp⟩; dampen ⟨ironing, cloth, etc.⟩

an|feuern tr. V. spur on

an|fixen tr. V. (Drogenjargon) **jmdn. ∼:** get sb. shooting up for the first time (sl.); **von etw. angefixt sein** (fig.) be hooked on sth. (coll.)

an|flehen *tr. V.* beseech; implore
an|fliegen ① *unr. itr. V.; mit sein* fly in;
angeflogen kommen come flying in; **gegen**
den Wind ∼: fly into the wind
② *unr. tr. V.* fly to ⟨*city, country, airport*⟩
An·flug *der* (a) approach
(b) (Hauch) hint
(c) (Anwandlung) fit; **in einem** ∼ **von**
Großzügigkeit in a fit of generosity
an|fordern *tr. V.* ask for; order ⟨*goods,*
materials⟩; send for ⟨*ambulance*⟩
An·forderung *die* (a) (das Anfordern)
request (*Gen.* for)
(b) (Anspruch) demand
An·frage *die* inquiry; (Parl.) question
an|fragen *itr. V.* inquire; ask
an|freunden *refl. V.* become friends
an|fügen *tr. V.* add
an|fühlen *refl. V.* feel
an|führen *tr. V.* (a) lead
(b) (zitieren) quote
(c) (nennen) give ⟨*example, reason, details,*
proof⟩
(d) (ugs.: hereinlegen) have on (Brit. coll.); dupe
An·führer *der,* **An·führerin** *die* leader;
(Rädelsführer) ringleader
An·führung *die* (a) (das Zitieren, Zitat)
quotation
(b) (Nennung) giving
Anführungs-: ∼**strich** *der,*
∼**zeichen** *das* quotation mark
An·gabe *die* (a) (das Mitteilen) giving
(b) (Information) piece of information; ∼n
information *sing.*
(c) (Ballspiele) service; serve
an|geben ① *unr. tr. V.* (a) give ⟨*reason*⟩;
declare ⟨*income, dutiable goods*⟩; name
⟨*witness*⟩
(b) (bestimmen) set ⟨*course, direction*⟩; **den**
Takt ∼: keep time
② *unr. itr. V.* (a) (prahlen) boast; brag; (sich
angeberisch benehmen) show off
(b) (Ballspiele) serve
Angeber *der;* ∼s, ∼: braggart
Angeberei *die;* ∼: showing-off
Angeberin *die;* ∼, ∼nen ▸ Angeber
angeblich ① *Adj.* alleged
② *adv.* supposedly; allegedly
an·geboren *Adj.* innate ⟨*characteristic*⟩;
congenital ⟨*disease*⟩
An·gebot *das* (a) offer
(b) (Wirtsch.) supply; (Sortiment) range; ∼ **und**
Nachfrage supply and demand
(c) (Kaufmannsspr.: Sonder∼) [special] offer; **im**
∼: on [special] offer; ∼ **der Woche** bargain
of the week
an·gebracht *Adj.* appropriate
an·gegriffen *Adj.* weakened ⟨*health,*
stomach⟩; strained ⟨*nerves, voice*⟩
angeheitert *Adj.* tipsy

an|gehen ① *unr. itr. V.; mit sein*
(a) ⟨*radio, light, heating*⟩ come on; ⟨*fire*⟩ catch
(b) (anwachsen, wachsen) ⟨*plant*⟩ take root
(c) **es mag noch** ∼: it's [just about]
acceptable
(d) **gegen etw./jmdn.** ∼: fight sth./sb.
② *unr. tr. V.* (a) (angreifen) attack
(b) (in Angriff nehmen) tackle ⟨*problem,*
difficulty⟩; take ⟨*fence, bend*⟩
(c) (bitten) ask (**um** for)
(d) (betreffen) concern; **das geht dich nichts**
an it's none of your business
angehend *Adj.* budding; (zukünftig)
prospective
an|gehören *itr. V.* jmdm./einer Sache
∼: belong to sb./sth.; **der Regierung/einer**
Familie ∼: be a member of the government/
a family
an·gehörig *Adj.* belonging (*Dat.* to)
Angehörige *der/die; adj. Dekl.*
(a) (Verwandte) relative; relation
(b) (Mitglied) member
Angeklagte *der/die; adj. Dekl.* accused;
defendant
Angel *die;* ∼, ∼n (a) fishing rod
(b) (Tür∼, Fenster∼ usw.) hinge; **etw. aus den**
∼n heben (fig.) turn sth. upside down
An·gelegenheit *die* matter; (Aufgabe,
Problem) affair
Angel·haken *der* fish hook
angeln ① *tr. V.* (zu fangen suchen) fish for;
(fangen) catch
② *itr. V.* angle; fish
Angel·rute *die* fishing rod
Angel·sachse *der,* **Angel·sächsin** *die*
Anglo-Saxon
Angel·schnur *die* fishing line
an·gemessen *Adj.* appropriate;
reasonable, fair ⟨*price, fee*⟩
an·genehm ① *Adj.* pleasant; ∼**e Reise/**
Ruhe! [have a] pleasant journey/have a good
rest; **[sehr]** ∼! delighted to meet you
② *adv.* pleasantly
an·gesehen *Adj.* respected
angesichts *Präp. mit Gen.* (geh.) (a) in
the face of
(b) (fig.: in Anbetracht) in view of
an·gespannt *Adj.* (a) close ⟨*attention*⟩;
taut ⟨*nerves*⟩
(b) tense ⟨*situation*⟩; tight ⟨*market, economic*
situation⟩
an·gestellt *Adj.* **bei jmdm.** ∼ **sein** be
employed by sb.; work for sb.
Angestellte *der/die; adj. Dekl.* [salaried]
employee
Angestellten·gewerkschaft *die*
white-collar union
an·getan *Adj.* **von jmdm./etw.** ∼ **sein** be
taken with sb./sth.
an·getrunken *Adj.* [slightly] drunk
an·gewiesen *Adj.* **auf jmdn./etw.** ∼ **sein**
have to rely on sb./sth.

---

*alte Schreibung – vgl. Hinweis auf S. x

an|gewöhnen *tr. V.* jmdm. etw. ~: get sb. used to sth.; jmdm. ~, etw. zu tun get sb. used to doing sth.; **sich** (*Dat.*) etw. ~: get into the habit of sth.; **[es] sich** (*Dat.*) ~, etw. zu tun get into the habit of doing sth.

An-gewohnheit *die* habit

an|gleichen ① *unr. tr. V.* etw. einer Sache (*Dat.*) od. an etw. (*Akk.*) ~: bring sth. into line with sth.
② *unr. refl. V.* sich jmdm./einer Sache od. an jmdn./etw. ~: become like sb./sth.

An-gleichung *die:* die ~ der Löhne an die Preise bringing wages into line with prices

Angler *der;* ~s, ~, **Anglerin** *die;* ~, ~nen angler

Anglikaner *der;* ~s, ~, **Anglikanerin** *die;* ~, ~nen Anglican

anglikanisch *Adj.* Anglican

Anglistik *die;* ~: English studies *pl., no art.*

Angola (*das*); ~s Angola

Angora-: ~**katze** *die* angora cat; ~**wolle** *die* angora [wool]

an|greifen ① *unr. tr. V.* (a) (auch fig.) attack
(b) (schwächen) affect ⟨*health, heart, stomach, intestine, voice*⟩; weaken ⟨*person*⟩
② *unr. itr. V.* (auch fig.) attack

Angreifer *der;* ~s, ~, **Angreiferin** *die;* ~, ~nen (auch fig.) attacker

An-griff *der* (a) attack; **zum** ~ **blasen** (auch fig.) sound the attack
(b) **etw. in** ~ **nehmen** tackle sth.

angst *Adj.* jmdm. ist/wird [es] ~ [und bange] sb. is/becomes frightened

Angst *die;* ~, **Ängste** (a) (Furcht) fear; ~ **bekommen** od. (ugs.) **kriegen** become frightened; ~ **haben** be frightened (**vor** + *Dat.* of)
(b) (Sorge) anxiety; ~ **haben** be anxious (**um** about); **keine** ~, **ich vergesse es schon nicht!** don't worry, I won't forget [it]!

ängstigen ① *tr. V.* frighten; (beunruhigen) worry
② *refl. V.* be frightened; (sich sorgen) worry

ängstlich ① *Adj.* anxious
② *adv.* anxiously

Ängstlichkeit *die;* ~: timidity

an|gucken *tr. V.* (ugs.) look at; **sich** (*Dat.*) etw./jmdn. ~: have a look at sth./sb.

an|gurten *tr. V.* strap in; **sich** ~: put on one's seat belt

an|haben *unr. tr. V.* (a) (ugs.: am Körper tragen) have on
(b) jmdm./einer Sache etwas ~ **können** be able to harm sb./sth.

an|halten ① *unr. tr. V.* (a) stop
(b) (auffordern) urge
② *unr. itr. V.* (a) stop
(b) (andauern) go on; last

anhaltend ① *Adj.* constant; continuous
② *adv.* constantly; continuously

An-halter *der* hitch-hiker; **per** ~ **fahren**

hitch[-hike]

An-halterin *die* hitch-hiker

Anhalts-punkt *der* clue (**für** to); (für eine Vermutung) grounds *pl.*

an-hand ① *Präp. mit Gen.* with the help of
② *Adv.* ~ **von** with the help of

An-hang *der* (a) (Buchw.) appendix
(b) (Anhängerschaft) following
(c) (Verwandtschaft) family

an|hängen ① *tr. V.* (a) hang up (**an** + *Akk.* on)
(b) (ankuppeln) couple on (**an** + *Akk.* to); hitch up ⟨*trailer*⟩ (**an** + *Akk.* to)
(c) (anfügen) add (**an** + *Akk.* to)
(d) (ugs.: zuschreiben, anlasten) jmdm. etw. ~ blame sb. for sth.; blame sth. on sb.; **er will mir nur was** ~ he just wants to pin something on me
② *refl. V.* (a) hang on (**an** + *Akk.* to)
(b) (ugs.: sich anschließen) **sich [an jmdn.** od. **bei jmdm.]** ~: tag along [with sb.]

An-hänger *der* (a) (Mensch) supporter
(b) (Wagen) trailer
(c) (Schmuckstück) pendant
(d) (Schildchen) tag

Anhängerin *die;* ~, ~nen ▶ ANHÄNGER A

Anhängerschaft *die;* ~, ~en supporters *pl.*

anhänglich *Adj.* devoted ⟨*dog, friend*⟩

Anhänglichkeit *die;* ~: devotion

an|hauchen *tr. V.* breathe on ⟨*mirror, glasses*⟩; blow on ⟨*fingers, hands*⟩

an|häufen *tr. V.* accumulate

Anhäufung *die* accumulation

an|heben *unr. tr. V.* (a) lift [up]
(b) (erhöhen) raise ⟨*prices, wages, etc.*⟩

an|heften *tr. V.* attach ⟨*label, list*⟩; put up ⟨*sign, notice*⟩

anheim (geh.): **[es] jmdm.** ~ **stellen, etw. zu tun** leave it to sb. to do sth.

*anheim|stellen ▶ ANHEIM

An-hieb *der:* **auf** ~ (ugs.) straight off

an|himmeln *tr. V.* worship

An-höhe *die* rise

an|hören ① *tr. V.* listen to; **sich** (*Dat.*) jmdn./etw. ~: listen to sb./sth.
② *refl. V.* sound

animieren *tr. V.* encourage

Anis *der;* ~es aniseed

Ank. *Abk.* = **Ankunft** arr.

An-kauf *der* purchase

an|kaufen *tr. V.* purchase; buy

Anker *der;* ~s, ~ anchor; **vor** ~ **gehen/liegen** drop anchor/lie at anchor; ~ **werfen** drop anchor

ankern *itr. V.* (a) anchor
(b) (vor Anker liegen) be anchored

Anker-platz *der* anchorage

An-klage *die* (a) charge; **unter** ~ **stehen** have been charged (**wegen** with)
(b) (~vertretung) prosecution

Anklage·bank *die; Pl.* **Anklagebänke**
dock; **auf der ~ sitzen** (auch fig.) be in the
dock

an|klagen *tr. V.* **(a)** (Rechtsw.) charge (*Gen.,*
wegen with); accuse
(b) (geh.: beschuldigen) accuse

An·kläger *der,* **An·klägerin** *die*
prosecutor

an|klammern 1 *tr. V.* peg (Brit.), pin
(Amer.) ⟨*clothes, washing*⟩ up; clip ⟨*sheet etc.*⟩;
(mit Heftklammern) staple ⟨*sheet etc.*⟩
2 *refl. V.* **sich an jmdn./etw. ~:** cling to
sb./sth.

An·klang *der:* [bei jmdm.] **~ finden** meet
with [sb.'s] approval

an|kleben 1 *tr. V.* stick up ⟨*poster, etc.*⟩
2 *itr. V.; mit sein* stick

an|kleiden *tr. V.* (geh.) dress; **sich ~:** dress

an|klicken *tr. V.* (DV) click on

an|klopfen *itr. V.* knock

an|knüpfen 1 *tr. V.* **(a)** tie on (**an** + *Akk.*
to)
(b) (beginnen) start up ⟨*conversation*⟩;
establish ⟨*relations, business links*⟩; form
⟨*relationship*⟩
2 *itr. V.* **an etw.** (*Akk.*) **~:** take sth. up; **ich
knüpfe dort an, wo …** I'll pick up where …

an|kommen *unr. itr. V.; mit sein*
(a) (eintreffen) arrive; **seid ihr gut
angekommen?** did you arrive safely?
(b) [bei jmdm.] [gut] **~** (fig. ugs.) go down
[very] well [with sb.]
(c) gegen jmdn./etw. ~: be able to deal with
sb./fight sth.
(d) *unpers.* **es kommt auf jmdn./etw. an**
(jmd./etw. ist ausschlaggebend) it depends on
sb./sth.; **es kommt auf etw.** (*Akk.*) **an** (etw. ist
wichtig) sth. matters (*Dat.* to); **es kommt** [ganz]
darauf an *od.* **drauf an** (ugs.) it [all] depends
(e) *unpers.* **es darauf** *od.* **drauf ~ lassen**
(ugs.) chance it; **es auf etw.** (*Akk.*) **~ lassen**
[be prepared to] risk sth.

an|koppeln 1 *tr. V.* couple ⟨*carriage*⟩ up;
hitch ⟨*trailer*⟩ up; dock ⟨*spacecraft*⟩
2 *itr. V.* ⟨*spacecraft*⟩ dock

an|kreuzen *tr. V.* mark with a cross

an|kündigen 1 *tr. V.* announce
2 *refl. V.* announce itself

An·kündigung *die* announcement

Ankunft *die; ~,* Ankünfte arrival; „**~**"
'arrivals'

Ankunfts-: **~halle** *die* arrival[s] hall;
~tafel *die* arrivals board

an|kuppeln *tr. V.* ▶ ANKOPPELN 1

an|kurbeln *tr. V.* **(a)** crank [up]
(b) (fig.) boost ⟨*economy, production, etc.*⟩

Anl. *Abk.* = **Anlage** encl.

an|lächeln *tr. V.* smile at

an|lachen 1 *tr. V.* smile at
2 *refl. V.* **sich** (*Dat.*) **jmdn. ~** (ugs.) get off
with sb. (Brit. coll.); pick sb. up

An·lage *die* **(a)** (das Anlegen) (einer Kartei)
establishment; (eines Parks, Gartens usw.)
laying out; (eines Parkplatzes, Stausees)
construction
(b) (Grünanlage) park; (um ein Schloss usw.
herum) grounds *pl.*
(c) (Einrichtung) facilities *pl.;* **militärische ~n**
military installations
(d) (Werk) plant
(e) (Musikanlage usw.) system
(f) (Geldanlage) investment
(g) (Konzeption) conception; (Struktur)
structure
(h) (Veranlagung) aptitude; (Neigung) tendency
(i) (Beilage zu einem Brief) enclosure

Anlage-: **~berater** *der,* **~beraterin**
die investment advisor; **~kapital** *das*
investment capital

Anlass, *Anlaß *der;* Anlasses, Anlässe
(a) cause (**zu** for); **etw. zum ~ nehmen, etw.
zu tun** take sth. as an opportunity to do sth.;
aus aktuellem ~: because of current events
(b) (Gelegenheit) occasion

an|lassen 1 *unr. tr. V.* **(a)** leave ⟨*light,
radio, heating, etc.*⟩ on; leave ⟨*engine*⟩
running; leave ⟨*candle*⟩ burning
(b) keep ⟨*coat, gloves, etc.*⟩ on
(c) (in Gang setzen) start [up]
2 *unr. refl. V.* **sich gut/schlecht ~:** get off
to a good/bad start

Anlasser *der;* **~s,** **~:** starter

an·lässlich, *an·läßlich *Präp. mit Gen.*
on the occasion of

An·lauf *der* **(a)** run-up; [mehr] **~ nehmen**
take [more of] a run-up
(b) (Versuch) attempt; **beim** *od.* **im ersten/
dritten ~:** at the first/third attempt

an|laufen 1 *unr. itr. V.; mit sein*
(a) angelaufen kommen come running
along; (auf einen zu) come running up
(b) gegen jmdn./etw. ~: run at sb./sth.
(c) (Anlauf nehmen) take a run-up
(d) (zu laufen beginnen) ⟨*engine*⟩ start [up]; (fig.)
⟨*film*⟩ open; ⟨*production, campaign, search*⟩
start
(e) rot/dunkel *usw.* **~:** go or turn red/dark
etc.
(f) (beschlagen) mist up
2 *unr. tr. V.* put in at ⟨*port*⟩

an|legen 1 *tr. V.* **(a)** put *or* lay ⟨*domino,
card*⟩ [down] (**an** + *Akk.* next to); place,
position ⟨*ruler, protractor*⟩ (**an** + *Akk.* on);
put ⟨*ladder*⟩ up (**an** + *Akk.* against)
(b) die Flügel/Ohren ~: close its wings/lay
its ears back; **die Arme ~:** put one's arms to
one's sides
(c) (geh.: anziehen, umlegen) don
(d) (schaffen, erstellen) lay out ⟨*town, garden,
plantation, street*⟩; start ⟨*file, album*⟩;
compile ⟨*statistics, index*⟩
(e) (investieren) invest
(f) (ausgeben) spend (**für** on)
(g) es darauf ~, etw. zu tun be determined
to do sth.

---

*old spelling – see note on page x

2 *itr. V.* **(a)** (landen) moor
(b) (Kartenspiele) lay a card/cards
(c) (Domino) play [a domino/dominoes]
(d) (zielen) aim (**auf** + *Akk.* at)
3 *refl. V.* **sich mit jmdn.** ∼: pick an
argument with sb.
Anlege-: ∼**platz** *der* berth; ∼**steg** *der*
jetty
an|lehnen 1 *tr. V.* **(a)** lean (**an** + *Akk. od.*
Dat. against)
(b) leave ⟨door, window⟩ slightly open
2 *refl. V.* **sich [an jmdn.** *od.* **jmdm./etw.]**
∼: lean [on sb./against sth.]
Anlehnung *die:* **in** ∼ **an** (+ *Akk.*) in
imitation of; following
Anleihe *die;* ∼, ∼**n** (Finanzw.) bond
an|leiten *tr. V.* instruct
An·leitung *die* instructions *pl.*
an|lernen *tr. V.* train
an|liegen *unr. itr. V.* **(a)** ⟨pullover etc.⟩ fit
tightly
(b) (ugs.: vorliegen) be on
An·liegen *das;* ∼**s,** ∼ (Bitte) request;
(Angelegenheit) matter
anliegend *Adj.* **(a)** (angrenzend) adjacent
(b) (beiliegend) enclosed
Anlieger *der;* ∼**s,** ∼, **Anliegerin** *die;* ∼,
∼**nen** resident; „∼ **frei** 'access only'
an|locken *tr. V.* attract ⟨customers,
tourists, etc.⟩; lure ⟨bird, animal⟩
an|lügen *tr. V.* lie to
an|machen *tr. V.* **(a)** put ⟨light, radio,
heating⟩ on; light ⟨fire⟩
(b) mix ⟨cement, plaster, paint, etc.⟩; dress
⟨salad⟩
(c) (ugs.: ansprechen) ⟨woman, girl⟩ give
⟨man, boy⟩ the come-on (coll.); ⟨man, boy⟩
chat ⟨woman, girl⟩ up (Brit. coll.)
(d) (ugs.: begeistern, erregen) get ⟨audience etc.⟩
going; **das macht mich ungeheuer/nicht an**
it really turns me on (coll.)/does nothing for
me (coll.)
(e) (provozieren) **mach mich nicht an!** leave
me alone!
an|malen *tr. V.* paint
an|maßen *refl. V.* **sich** (*Dat.*) **etw.** ∼: claim
sth. [for oneself]
an·maßend 1 *Adj.* presumptuous;
(arrogant) arrogant
2 *adv.* presumptuously; (arrogant)
arrogantly
Anmaßung *die;* ∼, ∼**en** presumption;
(Arroganz) arrogance
Anmelde·formular *das* **(a)** application
form
(b) (einer Meldebehörde) registration form
an|melden *tr. V.* 1 **(a)** (als Teilnehmer)
enrol (**zu** for); **sich** ∼: enrol (**zu** for)
(b) (melden, anzeigen) license ⟨radio,
television⟩; apply for ⟨patent⟩; register
⟨domicile, change of address, car, trade
mark⟩; **sich** ∼: register one's new address
(c) (ankündigen) announce; **sind Sie**

angemeldet? do you have an appointment?;
sich beim Arzt ∼: make an appointment to
see the doctor
(d) (geltend machen) express ⟨reservation,
doubt, wish⟩; put forward ⟨demand⟩
2 *refl. V.* (DV) log on
An·meldung *die* **(a)** (zur Teilnahme)
enrolment
(b) ▸ ANMELDEN B: licensing; application
(*Gen.* for); registration
(c) (Ankündigung) announcement; (beim Arzt,
Rechtsanwalt usw.) making an appointment
an|merken *tr. V.* **(a)** jmdm. seinen Ärger/
seine Verlegenheit *usw.* ∼: notice that sb. is
annoyed/embarrassed *etc.;* **man merkt ihm
[nicht] an, dass er krank ist** you can[not]
tell that he is ill; **sich nichts** ∼ **lassen** not
let it show
(b) (geh.: bemerken) note
Anmerkung *die;* ∼, ∼**en (a)** (Fußnote) note
(b) (geh.: Bemerkung) comment
an|motzen *tr. V.* (ugs.) swear at
Anmut *die;* ∼ (geh.) grace
an·mutig (geh.) 1 *Adj.* graceful ⟨girl,
movement, dance⟩; charming, delightful
⟨girl, smile, picture, landscape⟩
2 *adv.* ⟨move, dance⟩ gracefully; ⟨smile,
greet⟩ charmingly
an|nähen *tr. V.* sew on
an|nähern 1 *refl. V.* get closer (*Dat.* to
sth)
2 *tr. V.* bring closer (*Dat.* to)
annähernd 1 *Adv.* almost; (ungefähr)
approximately
2 *adj.* approximate
Annahme *die;* ∼, ∼**n (a)** (das Annehmen)
acceptance
(b) (Vermutung) assumption; **in der** ∼,
dass ...: on the assumption that ...
annehmbar 1 *Adj.* **(a)** acceptable
(b) (recht gut) reasonable
2 *adv.* reasonably [well]
an|nehmen 1 *unr. tr. V.* **(a)** accept; take;
accept ⟨alms, invitation, condition, help⟩;
take ⟨food, telephone call⟩; accept, take up
⟨offer, challenge⟩
(b) (Sport) take ⟨ball, pass, etc.⟩
(c) (billigen) approve
(d) (aufnehmen) take on ⟨worker, patient,
pupil⟩
(e) (hinnehmen) accept ⟨fate, verdict,
punishment⟩
(f) (adoptieren) adopt
(g) (haften lassen) take ⟨dye, ink⟩
(h) (sich aneignen) adopt ⟨habit, mannerism,
name, attitude⟩
(i) (bekommen) take on ⟨look, appearance,
form, dimension⟩
(j) (vermuten, voraussetzen) assume;
angenommen, [dass] ...: assuming [that] ...
2 *unr. refl. V.* (geh.) **sich jmds./einer Sache**
∼: look after sb./sth.
Annehmlichkeit *die;* ∼, ∼**en** comfort;
(Vorteil) advantage

annektieren *tr. V.* annex

Annektierung *die;* ~, ~en, **Annexion** *die;* ~, ~en annexation

Annonce /aˈnõːsə/ *die;* ~, ~n advertisement; advert (Brit. coll.)

annoncieren *itr. V.* advertise

annullieren *tr. V.* annul

Annullierung *die;* ~, ~en annulment

anonym 1 *Adj.* anonymous
2 *adv.* anonymously

Anonymität *die;* ~: anonymity

Anorak *der;* ~s, ~s anorak

an|ordnen *tr. V.* (a) (arrangieren) arrange
(b) (befehlen) order

An·ordnung *die* ▶ ANORDNEN:
(a) arrangement
(b) order

anorektisch /anˌoˈrɛktiʃ/ *Adj.* anorexic

Anorexie /anˌorɛˈksiː/ *die;* ~ (Med.) anorexia

an·organisch *Adj.* inorganic

an|packen 1 *tr. V.* (a) (ugs.: anfassen) grab hold of
(b) (angehen) tackle
2 *itr. V.* [mit] ~ (ugs.: mithelfen) lend a hand

an|passen 1 *tr. V.* (a) (passend machen) fit
(b) (abstimmen) suit (*Dat.* to)
2 *refl. V.* adapt [oneself] (*Dat.* to); ⟨*animal*⟩ adapt

Anpassung *die;* ~, ~en adaptation (an + *Akk.* to)

anpassungs·fähig *Adj.* adaptable

an|pfeifen 1 *unr. tr. V.* **das Spiel/die zweite Halbzeit** ~: blow the whistle to start the game/the second half
2 *unr. itr. V.* blow the whistle

An·pfiff *der* (a) (Sport) whistle for the start of play
(b) (salopp: Zurechtweisung) bawling-out (coll.)

an|pflanzen *tr. V.* (a) plant
(b) (anbauen) grow

an|pöbeln *tr. V.* (ugs.) abuse

an|prangern *tr. V.* denounce (**als** as)

an|preisen *unr. tr. V.* extol

An·probe *die* fitting

an|probieren *tr. V.* try on

an|rechnen *tr. V.* (a) count
(b) jmdm. etw. ~ (in Rechnung stellen) charge sb. for sth.

An·recht *das* right; **ein** ~ **auf etw.** (*Akk.*) **haben** be entitled to sth.

An·rede *die* form of address

an|reden *tr. V.* address

an|regen *tr. V.* (a) stimulate ⟨*imagination, digestion*⟩; whet ⟨*appetite*⟩
(b) (ermuntern) prompt; (vorschlagen) propose

anregend *Adj.* stimulating

An·regung *die* (a) ▶ ANREGEN A: stimulation; whetting

(b) (Denkanstoß) stimulus
(c) (Vorschlag) proposal

an|reichern 1 *tr. V.* enrich
2 *refl. V.* accumulate

An·reise *die* journey [there/here]

an|reisen *itr. V.; mit sein* travel there/here; **mit der Bahn** ~: go/come by train

An·reiz *der* incentive

an|rempeln *tr. V.* barge into; (absichtlich) jostle

Anrichte *die;* ~, ~n sideboard

an|richten *tr. V.* (a) arrange ⟨*food*⟩; (servieren) serve
(b) cause ⟨*disaster, confusion, devastation, etc.*⟩

anrüchig *Adj.* (a) disreputable
(b) (unanständig) indecent

an|rücken *itr. V.; mit sein* ⟨*troops*⟩ advance; ⟨*firemen, police*⟩ move in

An·ruf *der* call

Anruf·beantworter *der;* ~s, ~: [telephone] answering machine

an|rufen *unr. tr. V.* (a) call or shout to ⟨*friend, passer-by*⟩; call ⟨*sleeping person*⟩
(b) (geh.: angehen, bitten) appeal to ⟨*person, court*⟩ (**um** for); call upon ⟨*God*⟩
(c) *auch itr.* (telefonisch ~) call

Anrufer *der;* ~s, ~, **Anruferin** *die;* ~, ~nen caller

an|rühren *tr. V.* (a) touch
(b) (bereiten) mix

ans *Präp. + Art.* (a) = **an das;**
(b) **sich** ~ **Arbeiten machen** set to work

An·sage *die* announcement

an|sagen *tr. V.* (a) announce
(b) (Kartenspiele) bid

Ansager *der;* ~s, ~, **Ansagerin** *die;* ~, ~nen (Radio, Fernsehen) announcer

an|sammeln 1 *tr. V.* accumulate; amass ⟨*riches, treasure*⟩
2 *refl. V.* accumulate; (fig.) ⟨*anger, excitement*⟩ build up

An·sammlung *die* (a) collection
(b) (Auflauf) crowd

ansässig *Adj.* resident

An·satz *der* (erstes Zeichen, Beginn) beginnings *pl.*

an|schaffen *tr. V.* [**sich** (*Dat.*)] **etw.** ~ get [oneself] sth.

An·schaffung *die* purchase

an|schalten *tr. V.* switch on

an|schauen *tr. V.* (bes. südd., österr., schweiz.) ▶ ANSEHEN

anschaulich 1 *Adj.* vivid
2 *adv.* vividly

Anschauung *die;* ~, ~en
(a) (Wahrnehmung) experience
(b) (Auffassung) view

An·schein *der* appearance; **allem** *od.* **dem** ~ **nach** to all appearances

an·scheinend *Adv.* apparently

an|schieben *unr. tr. V.* push ⟨*vehicle*⟩

an|schlagen *unr. tr. V.* shoot and wound

An·schlag *der* (a) (Bekanntmachung) notice; (Plakat) poster
  (b) (Attentat) assassination attempt; (auf ein Gebäude, einen Zug usw.) attack
  (c) (Texterfassung) keystroke
  (d) mit dem Gewehr im ∼: with rifle/rifles levelled

an|schlagen *unr. tr. V.* **(a)** put up, ⟨*notice, announcement, message*⟩ (**an** + *Akk.* on)
  (b) (beschädigen) chip

an|schließen ① *unr. tr. V.* **(a)** connect (**an** + *Akk. od. Dat.* to); connect up ⟨*electrical device*⟩
  (b) (festschließen) lock, secure (**an** + *Dat. od. Akk.* to)
  ② *unr. refl. V.* **sich jmdm./einer Sache ∼:** join sb./sth.

An·schluss, *An·schluß *der* connection; **kein ∼ unter dieser Nummer** number unobtainable

Anschluss, *Anschluß: ∼kabel *das* connecting cable *or* (esp. Brit.) lead; **∼zug** *der* connecting train

an|schnallen *tr. V.* put on ⟨*skis, skates*⟩; **sich ∼** (im Auto) put on one's seat belt; (im Flugzeug) fasten one's seat belt

an|schrauben *tr. V.* screw on (**an** + *Akk.* to)

An·schreiben *das* covering letter

an|schreien *unr. tr. V.* shout at

An·schrift *die* address

An·schub *der;* ∼**[e]s,** ∼**e** impetus, stimulus (**zu** for)

Anschuldigung *die;* ∼**,** ∼**en** accusation

an|schwärzen *tr. V.* (ugs.) **jmdn. ∼** (in Misskredit bringen) blacken sb.'s name; (schlecht machen) run sb. down (**bei** to); (denunzieren) inform *or* (Brit. sl.) grass on sb. (**bei** to)

an|schwellen *unr. itr. V.; mit sein*
  (a) swell [up]; (fig.) swell; ⟨*water, river*⟩ rise
  (b) (lauter werden) grow louder; ⟨*noise*⟩ rise

an|schwemmen *tr. V.* wash ashore

an|sehen *unr. tr. V.* **(a)** look at; watch ⟨*television programme*⟩; see ⟨*play, film*⟩; **jmdn. groß/böse ∼:** stare at sb./give sb. an angry look; **hübsch** *usw.* **anzusehen sein** be pretty *etc.* to look at; **sieh [mal] [einer] an!** (ugs.) well, I never! (coll.)
  (b) (erkennen) **man sieht ihm sein Alter nicht an** he does not look his age; **man sieht ihr die Strapazen an** she's showing the strain
  (c) (zusehen bei) **etw. [mit] ∼:** watch sth.; **das kann man doch nicht [mit] ∼:** I/you can't just stand by and watch that

Ansehen *das;* ∼**s** [high] standing

an·sehnlich *Adj.* **(a)** (beträchtlich) considerable
  (b) (gut aussehend, stattlich) handsome

*an|sein ▸ AN 3B

an|setzen *tr. V.* **(a)** (in die richtige Stellung bringen) position ⟨*ladder, jack, drill, saw*⟩

(b) (anfügen) attach, put on (**an** + *Akk. od. Dat.* to)
  (c) (festlegen) fix ⟨*meeting etc.*⟩ (**für, auf** + *Akk.* for); fix, set ⟨*deadline, date, price*⟩
  (d) (veranschlagen) estimate
  (e) (anrühren) mix

An·sicht *die* **(a)** (Meinung) opinion; view; **meiner ∼ nach** in my opinion *or* view
  (b) (Bild) view

Ansichts·karte *die* picture postcard

an|spannen *tr. V.* **(a)** harness ⟨*horse etc.*⟩ (**an** + *Akk.* to); yoke up ⟨*oxen*⟩ (**an** + *Akk.* to); hitch up ⟨*carriage, cart, etc.*⟩ (**an** + *Akk.* to)
  (b) (anstrengen) strain

An·spannung *die* strain

an|spielen *itr. V.* **auf jmdn./etw. ∼:** allude to sb./sth.

Anspielung *die;* ∼**,** ∼**en** allusion (**auf** + *Akk.* to); (verächtlich, böse) insinuation (**auf** + *Akk.* about)

Ansporn *der;* ∼**[e]s,** ∼**e** incentive

an|spornen *tr. V.* spur on

An·sprache *die* speech; address

an|sprechen ① *unr. tr. V.* **(a)** speak to
  (b) (gefallen) appeal to
  ② *unr. itr. V.* (reagieren) respond (**auf** + *Akk.* to)

ansprechend ① *Adj.* attractive; attractive, appealing ⟨*personality*⟩
  ② *adv.* attractively

Ansprech·partner *der,*
  Ansprech·partnerin *die* contact

an|springen ① *unr. itr. V.; mit sein* ⟨*car, engine*⟩ start
  ② *unr. tr. V.* jump up at

An·spruch *der* **(a)** claim; (Forderung) demand; **[keine] Ansprüche stellen** make [no] demands; **in ∼ nehmen** take advantage of ⟨*offer*⟩; exercise ⟨*right*⟩; take up ⟨*time*⟩; **[einen] ∼/keinen ∼ auf etw.** (*Akk.*) **haben** be/not be entitled to sth.
  (b) (Anrecht) right

an·spruchs-: ∼los ① *Adj.* **(a)** (genügsam) undemanding; **(b)** (schlicht) unpretentious;
  ② *adv.* **(a)** (genügsam) undemandingly; ⟨*live*⟩ modestly; **(b)** (schlicht) unpretentiously;
  ∼voll *Adj.* discriminating ⟨*reader, audience, gourmet*⟩; (schwierig) demanding; ambitious ⟨*subject*⟩

an|spucken *tr. V.* spit at

Anstalt *die;* ∼**,** ∼**en** institution

An·stand *der* decency

anständig ① *Adj.* decent; (ehrbar) respectable
  ② *adv.* decently; (ordentlich) properly

an|starren *tr. V.* stare at

an·statt *Konj.* **∼ zu arbeiten/∼, dass er arbeitet** instead of working

an|stecken ① *tr. V.* **(a)** pin on ⟨*badge, brooch*⟩; put on ⟨*ring*⟩
  (b) (infizieren, auch fig.) infect
  ② *itr. V.* be infectious   ···⋗

ansteckend *Adj.* infectious; (durch
Berührung) contagious
Ansteckung *die;* ∼, ∼**en** infection; (durch
Berührung) contagion
Ansteckungs-gefahr *die* risk *or* danger
of infection
an|stehen *unr. itr. V.* (Schlange stehen)
queue [up], (Amer.) stand in line (**nach** for)
an-stelle 1 *Präp. mit Gen.* instead of
2 *Adv.* ∼ **von** instead of
an|stellen 1 *refl. V.* queue [up], (Amer.)
stand in line (**nach** for)
2 *tr. V.* (a) (aufdrehen) turn on
(b) (einschalten) switch on
(c) (einstellen) employ
An-stellung *die* (a) employment
(b) (Stellung) job
Anstieg *der;* ∼[e]s rise, increase (+ *Gen.* in)
an|stiften *tr. V.* incite
An-stifter *der,* **An-stifterin** *die* instigator
An-stiftung *die* incitement
an|stimmen *tr. V.* start singing ⟨song⟩;
start playing ⟨piece of music⟩; **ein Geschrei**
∼: start shouting
An-stoß *der* (a) stimulus (**zu** for); **den**
[**ersten**] ∼ **zu etw. geben** initiate sth.
(b) ∼ **erregen** cause offence (**bei** to); [**keinen**]
∼ **an etw.** (*Dat.*) **nehmen** [not] object to sth.
an|stoßen 1 *unr. itr. V.* (a) *mit sein* **an**
etw. (*Akk.*) ∼: bump into sth.
(b) [**mit den Gläsern**] ∼: clink glasses; **auf**
jmdn./etw. ∼: drink to sb./sth.
2 *unr. tr. V.* **jmdn./etw.** ∼: give sb./sth. a
push; **jmdn. aus Versehen** ∼: knock into sb.
inadvertently
anstößig 1 *Adj.* offensive
2 *adv.* offensively
an|strahlen *tr. V.* (a) illuminate; (mit
Scheinwerfer) floodlight
(b) (anblicken) beam at
an|streben *tr. V.* (geh.) aspire to; (mit großer
Anstrengung) strive for
an|streichen *unr. tr. V.* (a) paint
(b) (markieren) mark
an|strengen 1 *refl. V.* make an effort;
sich mehr/sehr ∼: make more of an effort/a
great effort
2 *tr. V.* strain ⟨eyes, ears, voice⟩; be a strain
on ⟨person⟩; **seine Fantasie** ∼: exercise
one's imagination
anstrengend *Adj.* (körperlich) strenuous;
(geistig) demanding
Anstrengung *die;* ∼, ∼**en** (a) effort;
große ∼**en machen, etw. zu tun** make every
effort to do sth.
(b) (Strapaze) strain
An-strich *der* paint
An-sturm *der* rush (**auf** + *Akk.* to); (auf
Banken, Waren) run (**auf** + *Akk.* on)
Antarktika (*das*) ∼s Antarctica

Antarktis *die;* ∼: Antarctic
antarktisch *Adj.* Antarctic
An-teil *der* share (**an** + *Dat.* of); ∼ **an etw.**
(*Dat.*) **nehmen** take an interest in sth.
An-teilnahme *die;* ∼ (a) interest (**an**
+ *Dat.* in)
(b) (Mitgefühl) sympathy (**an** + *Dat.* with)
Antenne *die;* ∼, ∼**n** aerial; antenna (Amer.)
Anthrax /'antraks/ *der;* ∼ (Med.) anthrax
anthrazit *Adj.* anthracite[-grey]
anthrazit-grau *Adj.* anthracite-grey
anti-, Anti- anti-
Anti-alkoholiker *der,*
Anti-alkoholikerin *die* teetotaller
Antibiotikum *das;* ∼s, Antibiotika (Med.)
antibiotic
anti-, Anti-: ∼**blockier-system**
das (Kfz-W.) anti-lock braking system;
∼**faschist** *der,* ∼**faschistin** *die* anti-
fascist; ∼**faschistisch** *Adj.* anti-fascist
antik *Adj.* (a) classical
(b) (aus vergangenen Zeiten) antique ⟨furniture,
fittings, etc.⟩
Antike *die;* ∼: classical antiquity *no art.*
Antilope *die;* ∼, ∼**n** antelope
Antipathie *die;* ∼, ∼**n** antipathy
Antiquariat antiquarian bookshop/
department; (mit neueren gebrauchten Büchern)
second-hand bookshop/department
Antiquität *die;* ∼, ∼**en** antique
Antiviren-software *die* (DV) anti-virus
software
Antlitz *das;* ∼**es**, ∼**e** (dichter., geh.)
countenance (literary); face
Antrag *der;* ∼[e]s, Anträge (a) application
(**auf** + *Akk.* for); **einen** ∼ **stellen** make an
application
(b) (Formular) application form
Antrags-formular *das* application form
an|treffen *unr. tr. V.* find; (zufällig) come
across
an|treiben *unr. tr. V.* (a) drive ⟨animals,
column of prisoners⟩ on *or* along; (fig.) urge
(b) (in Bewegung setzen) drive; power ⟨ship,
aircraft⟩
an|treten 1 *unr. itr. V.; mit sein* (a) form
up; (in Linie) line up; (Milit.) fall in
(b) (sich stellen) meet one's opponent; (als
Mannschaft) line up; **gegen jmdn.** ∼: meet
sb./line up against sb.
2 *unr. tr. V.* start ⟨job, apprenticeship⟩;
take up ⟨position, appointment⟩; set out on
⟨journey⟩; begin ⟨prison sentence⟩; come into
⟨inheritance⟩
An-trieb *der* drive
An-tritt *der:* **vor** ∼ **Ihres Urlaubs** before
you go on holiday (Brit.) *or* (Amer.) vacation;
vor ∼ **der Reise** before setting out on the
journey
an|tun *unr. tr. V.* (a) **jmdm. ein Leid**
∼: hurt sb.; **jmdm. etwas Böses/ein Unrecht**
∼: do sb. harm/an injustice

(b) jmd./etw. **hat es** jmdm. **angetan** sb. was taken with sb./sth.; *s. auch* ANGETAN

Antwort *die;* ~, ~**en (a)** answer; reply; **er gab mir keine** ~: he didn't answer [me] *or* reply
(b) (Reaktion) response

antworten *itr. V.* **(a)** answer; reply; **auf etw.** (*Akk.*) ~: answer sth.; reply to sth.; jmdm. ~: answer sb.; reply to sb.
(b) (reagieren) respond (**auf** + *Akk.* to)

Antwort-schein *der:* internationaler ~ (Postw.) international reply coupon

an|vertrauen ① *tr. V.* jmdm. etw. ~: entrust sb. with sth.; (fig.: mitteilen) confide sth. to sb.
② *refl. V.* **sich** jmdm./**einer Sache** ~: put one's trust in sb./sth.; **sich** jmdm. ~ (fig.: sich jmdm. mitteilen) confide in sb.

an|wachsen *unr. itr. V.; mit sein* **(a)** grow on
(b) (Wurzeln schlagen) take root
(c) (zunehmen) grow

Anwalt *der;* ~**[e]s,** Anwälte, **Anwältin** *die;* ~, ~**nen (a)** (Rechtsanwalt, -anwältin) lawyer; solicitor (Brit.); attorney (Amer.); (vor Gericht) barrister (Brit.); attorney[-at-law] (Amer.); advocate (Scot.)
(b) (Fürsprecher) advocate

An-wärter *der,* **An-wärterin** *die* candidate (**auf** + *Akk.* for); (Sport) contender (**auf** + *Akk.* for)

an|weisen *unr. tr. V.* instruct

An-weisung *die* instruction

an|wenden *unr.* (*auch regelm.*) *tr. V.* use, employ ⟨*process, trick, method, violence, force*⟩; use ⟨*medicine, money, time*⟩; apply ⟨*rule, paragraph, proverb, etc.*⟩ (**auf** + *Akk.* to)

Anwender *der;* ~s, ~ (DV) user

anwenderfreundlich *Adj.* (bes. DV) user-friendly

Anwenderin *die;* ~, ~nen (DV) user

An-wendung *die* **(a)** ▶ ANWENDEN: use; employment; application
(b) (DV) application

An-wesen *das* property

anwesend *Adj.* present (**bei** at); **die** Anwesenden those present

Anwesenheit *die;* ~: presence

an|widern *tr. V.* nauseate

Anwohner *der;* ~, ~nen, **Anwohnerin** *die;* ~, ~nen resident; **Parken nur für** ~ residents-only parking

An-zahl *die;* ~: number; **eine ganze** ~: a whole lot

an|zahlen *tr. V.* put down ⟨*sum*⟩ as a deposit (**auf** + *Akk.* on); (bei Ratenzahlung) make a down payment of ⟨*sum*⟩ (**auf** + *Akk.* on)

An-zahlung *die* deposit; (bei Ratenzahlung) down payment

An-zeichen *das* sign; indication

Anzeige *die;* ~, ~n **(a)** (Straf~) report
(b) (Inserat) advertisement
(c) (eines Instruments) display

an|zeigen *tr. V.* **(a)** (Strafanzeige erstatten) jmdn./etw. ~: report sb./sth. to the police/the authorities
(b) (zeigen) show; indicate; show ⟨*time, date*⟩
(c) (DV) display

Anzeigen-: ~**blatt** *das* advertiser; ~**teil** *der* advertisement section *or* pages *pl.*

an|ziehen *unr. tr. V.* **(a)** (auch fig.) attract
(b) draw up ⟨*knees, feet, etc.*⟩
(c) tighten ⟨*rope, wire, screw, knot, belt, etc.*⟩; put on ⟨*handbrake*⟩
(d) (ankleiden) dress; **sich** ~: get dressed
(e) (anlegen) put on ⟨*clothes*⟩

anziehend *Adj.* attractive

An-ziehung *die* attraction

Anziehungs-kraft *die* attractive force; (fig.) attraction

An-zug *der* **(a)** suit
(b) **im** ~ **sein** ⟨*storm*⟩ be approaching; ⟨*fever, illness*⟩ be coming on; ⟨*enemy*⟩ be advancing

anzüglich ① *Adj.* insinuating ⟨*remark, question*⟩
② *adv.* in an insinuating way

Anzüglichkeit *die;* ~, ~**en (a)** (Art) insinuating nature
(b) (Bemerkung) insinuating remark

an|zünden *tr. V.* light; set fire to ⟨*building etc.*⟩

an|zweifeln *tr. V.* doubt; question

apart ① *Adj.* individual *attrib.;*
② *adv.* in an individual style

Apartheid *die;* ~: apartheid *no art.*

Apartheit *die;* ~: individuality

Apartment *das;* ~s, ~s studio flat (Brit.); studio apartment (Amer.)

Apartment-haus *das* block of studio flats (Brit.) *or* (Amer.) studio apartments

Apathie *die;* ~, ~n apathy

apathisch ① *Adj.* apathetic
② *adv.* apathetically

Aperitif /aperi'ti:f/ *der;* ~s, ~s aperitif

Apfel *der;* ~s, Äpfel apple

Apfel-: ~**baum** *der* apple tree; ~**kuchen** *der* apple cake; (mit Äpfeln belegt) apple flan; ~**mus** *das* apple purée; ~**saft** *der* apple juice; ~**saft-schorle** *die* apple juice with mineral water

Apfelsine *die;* ~, ~n orange

Apfel-: ~**strudel** *der* apfelstrudel; ~**wein** *der* cider

Apostel *der;* ~s, ~: apostle

Apotheke *die;* ~, ~n **(a)** chemist's [shop] (Brit.); drugstore (Amer.)
(b) (Hausapotheke) medicine cabinet; (Reise-, Bordapotheke) first-aid kit ⋯⋙

a

Apotheker der; ~s, ~, **Apothekerin** die; ~, ~nen [dispensing] chemist (Brit.); druggist

App. Abk. = **Apparat** ext.

Apparat der; ~[e]s, ~e (a) apparatus no pl.; (Haushaltsgerät) appliance; (kleiner) gadget (b) (Radio) radio; (Fernseher) television; (kamera) camera (c) (Telefon) telephone; (Nebenstelle) extension; **am** ~! speaking! (d) (Personen und Hilfsmittel) organization; (Verwaltungsapparat) system

Apparate-medizin die (oft abwertend) high-technology medicine

Appartement /apartə'mã:, (schweiz. auch:) -'mɛnt/ das; ~s, ~s (schweiz. auch: ~e) (a) ▶ APARTMENT (b) (Hotelsuite) suite

Appell der; ~s, ~e (a) appeal (**zu** for, **an** + Akk. to) (b) (Milit.) muster; (Anwesenheits~) roll-call

appellieren itr. V. appeal (**an** + Akk. to)

Appetit der; ~[e]s, ~e appetite (**auf** + Akk. for); **guten** ~! enjoy your meal!

appetitlich Adj. (a) appetizing (b) (sauber, ansprechend) attractive and hygienic

Appetit·losigkeit die; ~: lack of appetite

applaudieren itr. V. applaud

Applaus der; ~es, ~e applause

Aprikose die; ~, ~n apricot

April der; ~[s], ~e April; **der** ~: April

apropos /apro'po:/ Adv. apropos; by the way; incidentally

Aquädukt der od. das; ~[e]s, ~e aqueduct

Aquaplaning das; ~s aquaplaning

Aquarell das; ~s, ~e watercolour [painting]

Aquarium das; ~s, Aquarien aquarium

Äquator der; ~s equator

Ar das od. der; ~s, ~e are

Ära die; ~, Ären era

Araber der; ~s, ~, **Araberin** die; ~, ~nen Arab

Arabien /a'ra:biən/ (das); ~s Arabia

arabisch Adj. Arabian; Arabic ⟨language, numeral, literature, etc.⟩

Arbeit die; ~, ~en (a) work no indef. art.; **vor/nach der** ~ (ugs.) before/after work (b) (Produkt, Werk) work (c) (Aufgabe) job (d) (Klassenarbeit) test

arbeiten ⊡ itr. V. work ⊡ tr. V. (herstellen) make

Arbeiter der; ~s, ~, **Arbeiterin** die; ~, ~nen worker; (Bau~, Land~) labourer

Arbeiter-: ~**kind** das working-class child; ~**klasse** die working class[es pl.]

Arbeiterschaft die; ~: workers pl.

Arbeit·geber der; ~s, ~: employer

Arbeitgeber·anteil der employer's contribution

Arbeitgeberin die; ~, ~nen employer

Arbeitgeber·verband der employers' association or organization

Arbeitnehmer der; ~s, ~: employee

Arbeitnehmer·anteil der employee's contribution

Arbeitnehmerin die; ~, ~nen employee

arbeits-, Arbeits-: ~**amt** das job centre (Brit.); ~**anfang** der starting time [at work]; ~**bedingungen** Pl. working conditions; ~**beginn** der ▶ ~ANFANG; ~**belastung** die workload; ~**beschaffungs·maßnahme** die job-creation measure; ~**erlaubnis** die work permit; ~**fähig** Adj. fit for work postpos.; (grundsätzlich) able to work postpos.; ~**gang** der operation; ~**genehmigung** die work permit; ~**gericht** das industrial tribunal; ~**kollege** der, ~**kollegin** die (bei Arbeitern) workmate (Brit.); fellow worker; (bei Angestellten, Beamten) colleague; ~**kraft** die (a) capacity for work; (b) (Mensch) worker; ~**last** die burden of work; ~**leben** das (a) (Berufstätigkeit) working life; (b) (Arbeitswelt) world of work; working life no art.; ~**los** Adj. unemployed; ~**los melden** sign on [for the dole] (coll.); ~**lose** der/die/adj. Dekl. unemployed person/man/woman etc.; **die** ~**losen** the unemployed; ~**losengeld** das (full-rate) earnings-related unemployment benefit; ~**losenhilfe** die (a) (Geld) reduced-rate unemployment benefit; (b) (Institution) reduced-rate unemployment benefit system; ~**losigkeit** die; ~~: unemployment no indef. art.; ~**mangel** der lack of work; ~**markt** der labour market; ~**platz** der (a) (Platz im Betrieb) workplace; **am** ~**platz** at one's workplace; (b) (~stätte) place of work; **den** ~**platz wechseln** change one's place of work; (c) (~verhältnis) job; ~**platz·abbau** der reduction in the number of jobs; ~**scheu** Adj. work-shy; ~**tag** der working day; ~**teilung** die division of labour; ~**suchende** der/die/adj. Dekl. person/man/woman looking for work; **die** ~**suchenden** those looking for work; ~**unfähig** Adj. unfit for work postpos.; (grundsätzlich) unable to work postpos.; ~**unfähigkeit** die ▶ ~UNFÄHIG: inability to work; unfitness for work; ~**unfall** der industrial accident; **er hatte einen** ~**unfall** he had an accident at work; ~**vermittlung** die (a) (Tätigkeit) arranging employment; (b) (Stelle) employment exchange; job centre (Brit.); (Firma) employment agency; ~**vertrag** der contract of employment; ~**zeit** die working hours pl.; **die tägliche** ~**zeit** the working day; ~**zeit·konto** das flexitime work record; ~**zimmer** das study

Archäologe *der;* ~n, ~n archaeologist
Archäologie *die;* ~: archaeology *no art.*
Archäologin *die;* ~, ~nen archaeologist
archäologisch *Adj.* archaeological
Arche *die;* ~, ~n ark; **die** ~ **Noah** Noah's Ark
Architekt *der;* ~en, ~en, **Architektin** *die;* ~, ~nen architect
Architektur *die;* ~ architecture
Archiv *das;* ~s, ~e archives *pl.;* archive
Ären ▶ ÄRA
Arena *die;* ~, Arenen arena; (Stierkampf~, Manege) ring
arg, ärger, ärgst... (geh., landsch.)
  1 *Adj.* **(a)** (schlimm) bad; **im Argen liegen** be in a sorry state
  (b) (unangenehm groß, stark) severe ⟨*pain, hunger, shock, disappointment*⟩; serious ⟨*error, dilemma*⟩; extreme ⟨*embarrassment*⟩; gross ⟨*exaggeration, injustice*⟩
  2 *adv.* (äußerst, sehr) extremely
Ärger *der;* ~s **(a)** annoyance
  (b) (Unannehmlichkeiten) trouble; ~ **bekommen** get into trouble
ärgerlich **1** *Adj.* **(a)** annoyed
  (b) (Ärger erregend) annoying
  2 *adv.* **(a)** with annoyance
  (b) (Ärger erregend) annoyingly
ärgern **1** *tr. V.* **(a)** annoy
  (b) (reizen) tease
  2 *refl. V.* **sich [über jmdn./etw.]** ~: be/get annoyed [at sb./about sth.]
Ärgernis *das;* ~ses, ~se annoyance; (etw. Anstößiges) nuisance
arg-, Arg-: ~**list** *die* deceit; (Heimtücke) malice; ~**listig** *Adj.* deceitful; (heimtückisch) malicious; ~**los** **1** *Adj.* unsuspecting;
  2 *adv.* unsuspectingly; ~**losigkeit** *die;* ~~: unsuspecting nature
ärgst... ▶ ARG
Argument *das;* ~[e]s, ~e argument
Argumentation *die;* ~, ~en argumentation
argumentieren *itr. V.* argue
Argwohn *der;* ~[e]s suspicion
argwöhnisch (geh.) **1** *Adj.* suspicious
  2 *adv.* suspiciously
Arie /'aːrɪə/ *die;* ~, ~n aria
arisch *Adj.* (Völkerk., Sprachw., ns.) Aryan
Aristokrat *der;* ~en, ~en aristocrat
Aristokratie *die;* ~, ~n aristocracy
Aristokratin *die;* ~, ~nen aristocrat
aristokratisch **1** *Adj.* aristocratic
  2 *adv.* aristocratically
arithmetisch **1** *Adj.* arithmetical
  2 *adv.* arithmetically
Arkade *die;* ~, ~n arcade
Arktis *die;* ~: Arctic
arktisch *Adj.* Arctic; (fig.) arctic
arm, ärmer, ärmst... *Adj.* poor; **Arm und Reich** (veralt.) rich and poor [alike];

~ **an Nährstoffen** poor in nutrients; **der/die Ärmste** *od.* **Arme** the poor man/boy/woman/ girl
Arm *der;* ~[e]s, ~e arm; jmdm. **[mit etw.]** **unter die** ~**e greifen** help sb. out [with sth.]; **ein Hemd mit halbem** ~: a short-sleeved shirt
Armaturen-brett *das* instrument panel; (im Kfz) dashboard
Arm-: ~**band** *das* bracelet; (Uhr~) strap; ~**band-uhr** *die* wristwatch
Armee *die;* ~, ~n (auch fig.) army
Ärmel *der;* ~s, ~: sleeve; **[sich (Dat.)] etw. aus dem** ~ **schütteln** (ugs.) produce sth. just like that
Ärmel-kanal *der;* ~s [English] Channel
ärmer ▶ ARM
ärmlich **1** *Adj.* cheap ⟨*clothing*⟩; shabby ⟨*flat, office*⟩; meagre ⟨*meal*⟩
  2 *adv.* cheaply ⟨*furnished, dressed*⟩
Arm-reif *der* armlet
arm-selig *Adj.* **(a)** miserable; pathetic ⟨*result, figure*⟩; meagre ⟨*meal, food*⟩; paltry ⟨*return, salary, sum, fee*⟩
  (b) (abwertend: erbärmlich) miserable
ärmst... ▶ ARM
Armut *die;* ~: poverty
Armuts-: ~**falle** *die* poverty trap; ~**grenze** *die* (Soziol.) poverty line
Aroma *das;* ~s, Aromen (Duft) aroma; (Geschmack) flavour
aromatisch *Adj.* aromatic; distinctive ⟨*taste*⟩; ~ **duften** give off an aromatic fragrance
arrangieren /arãˈziːrən/ **1** *tr. V.* (geh., Musik) arrange
  2 *refl. V.* **sich** ~: adapt; **sich mit jmdm.** ~: come to an accommodation with sb.
Arrest *der;* ~[e]s, ~e detention
arrogant **1** *Adj.* arrogant
  2 *adv.* arrogantly
Arroganz *die;* ~ arrogance
Arsch *der;* ~[e]s, Ärsche (derb) **(a)** arse (Brit. coarse); ass (Amer. sl.); **leck mich am** ~! (fig.) piss off (sl.); **im** ~ **sein** (fig.) be buggered (coarse)
  (b) (widerlicher Mensch) arsehole (Brit. coarse); asshole (Amer. coarse.)
Arsch-loch *das* (derb) ▶ ARSCH B
Art *die;* ~, ~en **(a)** kind; sort; **Bücher aller** ~: all kinds *or* sorts of books; **[so] eine** ~ ...: a sort of ...; **aus der** ~ **schlagen** not be true to type; (in einer Familie) be different from all the rest of the family
  (b) (Biol.) species
  (c) (Wesen) nature; (Verhaltensweise) way; (gutes Benehmen) behaviour; **die feine englische** ~ (ugs.) the proper way to behave
  (d) (Weise) way; **auf diese** ~: in this way; ~ **und Weise** way; (Kochk.) manner; **nach** ~ **des Hauses** à la maison; **nach Schweizer** ~: Swiss style ⋯⋗

arten-, Arten-: ~**barriere** die,
~**grenze** die (Biol.) species barrier;
~**reich** Adj. (Biol.) species-rich;
~**reichtum** der (Biol.) species-richness;
~**schutz** der protection of species; species
protection
Arterie /arˈteːriə/ die; ~, ~n artery
artig Adj. well-behaved; **sei** ~: be a good
boy/girl/dog etc.
Artikel der; ~s, ~ (a) article
(b) (Ware) item
Artillerie die; ~, ~n artillery
Artischocke die; ~, ~n artichoke
Artist der; ~en, ~en, **Artistin** die; ~,
~nen [variety/circus] performer
Arznei die; ~, ~en (veralt.),
Arznei‑mittel das medicine
Arzt der; ~es, Ärzte, **Ärztin** die; ~, ~nen
doctor
Arzthelferin die doctor's receptionist
ärztlich ① Adj. medical; **auf** ~**e**
Verordnung on doctor's orders
② adv. **sich** ~ **behandeln lassen** have
medical treatment
****As** ▶ Ass
Asbest der; ~[e]s, ~e asbestos
Asche die; ~, ~n ash[es pl.]; (sterbliche
Reste) ashes pl.
Aschen-: ~**becher** der ashtray;
~**brödel** das; ~~s, ~~ (auch fig.)
Cinderella
Ascher‑mittwoch der Ash Wednesday
Äser ▶ Aas
Asiat der; ~en, ~en, **Asiatin** die; ~,
~nen Asian
asiatisch Adj. Asian
Asien /ˈaːziən/ (das); ~s Asia
Askese die; ~: asceticism
Asket der; ~en, ~en, **Asketin** die; ~,
~nen ascetic
asketisch ① Adj. ascetic
② adv. ascetically
asozial ① Adj. asocial; (gegen die
Gesellschaft gerichtet) antisocial
② adv. asocially
Aspekt der; ~[e]s, ~e aspect
Asphalt der; ~[e]s, ~e asphalt
Aspik der (österr. auch das); ~s, ~e aspic
aß 1. u. 3. Pers. Sg. Prät. v. essen
Ass das; ~es, ~e ace
Assistent der; ~en, ~en, **Assistentin**
die; ~, ~nen assistant
Ast der; ~[e]s, Äste branch; **sich** (Dat.)
einen ~ **lachen** (ugs.) split one's sides [with
laughter]
Aster die; ~, ~n aster; (Herbstaster)
Michaelmas daisy
ästhetisch ① Adj. aesthetic
② adv. aesthetically

*old spelling – see note on page x

Asthma das; ~s asthma
ast‑rein ① Adj. (ugs.) (in Ordnung) on the
level (coll.); (echt) genuine; (salopp: prima, toll)
fantastic (coll.); great (coll.)
② adv. (salopp: prima) fantastically (coll.)
Astrologe der; ~n, ~n astrologer
Astrologie die; ~: astrology no art.
Astrologin die; ~, ~nen astrologer
Astronaut der; ~en, ~en, **Astronautin**
die; ~, ~nen astronaut
Astronom der; ~en, ~en astronomer
Astronomie die; ~: astronomy no art.
Astronomin die; ~, ~nen astronomer
astronomisch Adj. astronomical
Asyl das; ~s, ~e (a) asylum
(b) (Obdachlosenheim) hostel
Asylant der; ~en, ~en, **Asylantin** die;
~, ~nen asylum seeker
Asylanten‑heim das asylum seekers'
hostel
Asyl-: ~**antrag** der application
for asylum; ~**bewerber** der,
~**bewerberin** die person seeking
[political] asylum; ~**bewerber‑heim**
das ▶ asylantenheim; ~**gesetz** das
asylum law[s pl.]; ~**missbrauch,**
*~**mißbrauch** der misuse of asylum;
~**recht** das (Rechtsw.) (a) right of
[political] asylum; (b) (eines Staates) right to
grant [political] asylum; ~**werber** der;
~~s, ~~, ~**werberin** die; ~~, ~~nen
(österr.) ▶ bewerber
Atelier /atəˈlieː/ das; ~s, ~s studio
Atem der; ~s breath; **außer** ~ **sein/geraten**
be/get out of breath
atem-, Atem-: ~**beraubend** ① Adj.
breathtaking; ② adv. breathtakingly; ~**los**
① Adj. breathless; ② adv. breathlessly;
~**pause** die breathing space; ~**zug** der
breath
Atheismus der; ~: atheism no art.
Atheist der; ~en, ~en, **Atheistin** die; ~,
~nen atheist
atheistisch ① Adj. atheistic
② adv. atheistically
Athen (das); ~s Athens
Äther der; ~s, ~: ether
Äthiopien /ɛˈt?ioːpiən/ (das); ~s Ethiopia
Athlet der; ~en, ~en (a) (Sportler) athlete
(b) (ugs.: kräftiger Mann) muscleman
Athletin die; ~, ~nen athlete
athletisch Adj. athletic
Atlanten ▶ atlas
Atlantik der; ~s Atlantic
atlantisch Adj. Atlantic; **der Atlantische**
Ozean the Atlantic Ocean
Atlas der; ~ od. ~ses, Atlanten od. ~se
atlas
atmen itr., tr. V. breathe
Atmosphäre /atmoˈsfɛːrə/ die; ~, ~n
(auch fig.) atmosphere

Atmung *die;* ~: breathing

Atom *das;* ~s, ~e atom

atomar *Adj.* atomic; (Atomwaffen betreffend) nuclear

atom-, Atom-: ~**ausstieg** *der* abandonment of nuclear power; ~**bombe** *die* atom bomb; ~**energie** *die* nuclear energy *no indef. art.;* ~**kern** *der* atomic nucleus; ~**kraft** *die* nuclear power *no indef. art.;* ~**kraftwerk** *das* nuclear power station; ~**krieg** *der* nuclear war; ~**müll** *der* nuclear waste; ~**physik** *die* nuclear physics *sing., no art.;* ~**pilz** *der* mushroom cloud; ~**reaktor** *der* nuclear reactor; ~**strom** *der* (ugs.) electricity generated by nuclear power; ~**waffe** *die* nuclear weapon; ~**waffen·frei** *Adj.* nuclear-free; ~**waffen·test** *der* nuclear [weapons] test; ~**zeit·alter** *das* nuclear age

Attacke *die;* ~, ~n (auch Med.) attack (**auf** + *Akk.* on)

Attentat *das;* ~[e]s, ~e assassination attempt; (erfolgreich) assassination

Attentäter *der;* ~s, ~, **Attentäterin** *die;* ~, ~nen would-be assassin; (erfolgreich) assassin

Attest *das;* ~[e]s, ~e medical certificate

Attraktion *die;* ~, ~en attraction

attraktiv ① *Adj.* attractive
② *adv.* attractively

Attraktivität *die;* ~: attractiveness

Attrappe *die;* ~, ~n dummy

Attribut *das;* ~[e]s, ~e attribute

At-Zeichen /'ɛt-/ *das* (DV) at sign

ätzen ① *tr. V.* etch
② *itr. V.* corrode

ätzend ① *Adj.* corrosive; (fig.) caustic ⟨*wit, remark, criticism*⟩; pungent ⟨*smell*⟩
② *adv.* caustically ⟨*ironic, critical*⟩

au *Interj.* (a) (bei Schmerz) ouch
(b) (bei Überraschung, Begeisterung) oh

Aubergine /obɛrˈʒiːnə/ *die;* ~, ~n aubergine (Brit.); eggplant

auch ① *Adv.* (a) as well; too; also; **Klaus war** ~ **dabei** Klaus was there as well *or* too; Klaus was also there; **Ich gehe jetzt. – Ich** ~: I'm going now – So am I; **Mir ist warm. – Mir** ~: I feel warm – So do I; **das weiß ich** ~ **nicht** I don't know either
(b) (sogar, selbst) even; ~ **wenn, wenn** ~: even if
② *Partikel* (a) etwas anderes habe ich ~ **nicht erwartet** I never expected anything else; **nun hör aber** ~ **zu!** now listen!
(b) **bist du dir** ~ **im Klaren, was das bedeutet?** are you sure you understand what that means?; **bist du** ~ **glücklich?** are you truly happy?; **lügst du** ~ **nicht?** you're not lying, are you?
(c) **wo ...**/**wer ...**/**was ...** *usw.* ~: wherever/whoever/whatever *etc.* ...; **wie dem** ~ **sei** however that may be

(d) **mag er** ~ **noch so klug sein** no matter how clever he is

Audienz *die;* ~, ~en audience

Auditorium *das;* ~s, Auditorien
(a) (Hörsaal) auditorium
(b) (Zuhörerschaft) audience

auf ① *Präp. mit Dat.* (a) on; ~ **See** at sea; ~ **dem Baum** in the tree; ~ **der Erde** on earth; ~ **der Welt** in the world; ~ **der Straße** in the street
(b) at ⟨*post office, town, hall, police station*⟩; ~ **seinem Zimmer** (ugs.) in his room; **Geld** ~ **der Bank haben** have money in the bank; ~ **der Schule/Uni** at school/university
(c) at ⟨*party, wedding*⟩; on ⟨*course, trip, walk, holiday, tour*⟩
② *Präp. mit Akk.* (a) on; ~ **einen Berg steigen** climb up a mountain; ~ **die Straße gehen** go [out] into the street
(b) ~ **die Schule/Uni gehen** go to school/university; ~ **einen Lehrgang gehen** go on a course
(c) ~ **10 km [Entfernung]** for [a distance of] 10 km; **wir näherten uns der Hütte [bis]** ~ **30 m** we approached to within 30m of the hut
(d) ~ **Jahre [hinaus]** for years [to come]; **etw.** ~ **nächsten Mittwoch verschieben** postpone sth. until next Wednesday; **die Nacht von Sonntag** ~ **Montag** Sunday night; **das fällt** ~ **einen Montag** it falls on a Monday
(e) ~ **diese Art und Weise** in this way; ~ **Deutsch** in German; ~ **das Sorgfältigste** (geh.) most carefully
(f) ~ **Wunsch** on request; ~ **meine Bitte** at my request; ~ **Befehl** on command
(g) **ein Teelöffel** ~ **einen Liter Wasser** one teaspoon to one litre of water; ~ **die Sekunde/den Millimeter [genau]** [precise] to the second/millimetre; ~ **deine Gesundheit!** your health; ~ **bald/morgen!** (bes. südd.) see you soon/tomorrow
③ *Adv.* (a) (aufgerichtet, aufgestanden) up; ~! (steh/steht auf!) up you get!
(b) **sie waren längst** ~ **und davon** they had made off long before
(c) ~! (bes. südd.: los) come on; ~ **gehts** off we go; ~ **ins Schwimmbad!** come on, off to the swimming pool!
(d) ~ **und ab** (hin und her) up and down; to and fro
(e) **Helm/Hut/Brille** ~! helmet/hat/glasses on!
(f) (ugs.: geöffnet, offen) open; **Fenster/Mund** ~! open the window/your mouth!

auf|atmen *itr. V.* breathe a sigh of relief

auf|bahren *tr. V.* lay out; **aufgebahrt sein** lie in state

Auf·bau *der;* ~[e]s, ~ten (a) building
(b) (Struktur) structure
(c) *Pl.* (Schiffbau) superstructure *sing.*

auf|bauen *tr. V.* (a) erect ⟨*hut, kiosk, podium*⟩; set up ⟨*equipment, train set*⟩; build ⟨*house, bridge*⟩; put up ⟨*tent*⟩
(b) (hinstellen, arrangieren) lay *or* set out ⋯⊱

⟨food, presents, etc.⟩
(c) (fig.: schaffen) build ⟨state, economy, etc.⟩;
build up ⟨business, organization, army, spy
network⟩
(d) (fig.: strukturieren) structure
auf|bäumen refl. V. rear up; **sich gegen
jmdn./etw.** ~ (fig.) rise up against sb./sth.
auf|bessern tr. V. improve; increase
⟨pension, wages, etc.⟩
auf|bewahren tr. V. keep; **etw. kühl**
~: store sth. in a cool place
Auf·bewahrung die keeping
auf|bieten unr. tr. V. exert ⟨strength,
energy, will power, influence, authority⟩;
call on ⟨skill, wit, powers of persuasion or
eloquence⟩
auf|blasen unr. tr. V. blow up; inflate
auf|bleiben unr. itr. V.; mit sein
(a) (geöffnet bleiben) stay open
(b) (nicht zu Bett gehen) stay up
auf|blenden itr. V. switch to full beam
auf|blicken itr. V. **(a)** look up; (kurz)
glance up
(b) zu jmdm. ~ (fig.) look up to sb.
auf|blühen itr. V.; mit sein **(a)** come into
bloom; ⟨bud⟩ open
(b) (fig.: aufleben) blossom [out]
auf|brauchen tr. V. use up
auf|brechen 1 unr. tr. V. break open
⟨lock, safe, box, crate, etc.⟩; break into ⟨car⟩;
force [open] ⟨door⟩
2 unr. itr. V.; mit sein **(a)** ⟨bud⟩ open; ⟨ice
[sheet], surface, ground⟩ break up; ⟨wound⟩
open
(b) (losgehen, -fahren) set off
auf|bringen unr. tr. V. **(a)** find; raise
⟨money⟩; (fig.) summon [up] ⟨strength,
energy, courage⟩; find ⟨patience⟩
(b) (kreieren) start ⟨fashion, custom, rumour⟩;
introduce ⟨slogan, theory⟩
(c) jmdn. ~: make sb. angry
(d) jmdn. gegen jmdn./etw. ~: set sb.
against sb./sth.
Auf·bruch der departure
auf|brühen tr. V. brew [up]
auf|decken tr. V. **(a)** uncover
(b) (Kartenspiele) show
(c) (fig.) reveal; uncover; (enthüllen) expose
auf|drängen 1 tr. V. **jmdm. etw.** ~: force
sth. on sb.
2 refl. V. **sich jmdm.** ~: force oneself on sb.
auf|drehen tr. V. **(a)** unscrew ⟨bottle cap,
nut⟩; undo ⟨screw⟩; turn on ⟨tap, gas, water⟩;
open ⟨valve, bottle, vice⟩
(b) (ugs.) turn up ⟨radio, record player, etc.⟩
auf·dringlich 1 Adj. pushy (coll.)
⟨person⟩; (fig.) insistent ⟨music,
advertisement⟩; pungent ⟨perfume, smell⟩;
loud ⟨colour, wallpaper⟩
2 adv. ⟨behave⟩ pushily (coll.)
Aufdringlichkeit die; ~ ▶ AUFDRINGLICH:

pushiness (coll.); insistent manner;
pungency
auf·einạnder Adv. **(a)** on top of one
another; ~ **prallen** crash into one another;
collide; (fig.) ⟨opinions⟩ clash; ~ **treffen** (fig.)
meet
(b) ~ **folgen** follow one another; ~**folgend**
successive
Aufeinạnder·folge die sequence; **in
rascher** ~ in rapid or quick succession
*aufeinạnder|folgen usw.
▶ AUFEINANDER
Aufenthalt der; ~[e]s, ~e **(a)** stay
(b) (Fahrtunterbrechung) stop
Aufenthalts-: ~**erlaubnis** die
residence permit; ~**raum** der (in einer
Schule o. Ä.) common room (Brit.); (in einer
Jugendherberge) day room; (in einem Betrieb o. Ä.)
recreation room
auf|essen unr. tr. (auch itr.) V. eat up
auf|fahren 1 unr. itr. V.; mit sein **(a) auf
ein anderes Fahrzeug** ~ (aufprallen) drive
into the back of another vehicle
(b) auf den Vordermann zu dicht ~: drive
too close to the car in front
(c) (vorfahren) drive up
(d) (in Stellung gehen) move up [into position]
2 unr. tr. V. **(a)** (in Stellung bringen) move up
(b) (ugs.: auftischen) serve up
Auf·fahrt die **(a)** drive up
(b) (Weg) drive
(c) (Autobahnauffahrt) slip road (Brit.); access
road (Amer.)
(d) (schweiz.) ▶ HIMMELFAHRT
Auffahr·unfall der rear-end collision
auf|fallen unr. itr. V.; mit sein stand out;
jmdm. fällt etw. auf sb. notices sth.
auffallend 1 Adj. conspicuous;
(eindrucksvoll, bemerkenswert) striking
2 adv. conspicuously; (eindrucksvoll,
bemerkenswert) strikingly
auf·fällig 1 Adj. conspicuous; garish
⟨colour⟩
2 adv. conspicuously
auf|fangen unr. tr. V. **(a)** catch
(b) (aufnehmen, sammeln) collect
Auffang·lager das reception camp
auf|fassen tr. V. grasp; **etw. als etw.**
~: regard sth. as sth.; **etw. persönlich/falsch**
~: take sth. personally/misunderstand sth.
Auf·fassung die (Ansicht) view; (Begriff)
conception; **der** ~ **sein, dass ...:** take the
view that ...
auffindbar Adj. findable
auf|finden unr. tr. V. find
auf|fordern tr. V. **jmdn.** ~, **etw. zu tun** call
upon sb. to do sth.; (einladen, ermuntern) ask
sb. to do sth.; **jmdn. [zum Tanz]** ~: ask sb.
to dance
Auf·forderung die request; (nachdrücklicher)
demand; (Einladung, Ermunterung) invitation
auf|forsten 1 tr. V. afforest; (wieder ~)
reforest; **einen Wald** ~: restock a forest

2 *itr. V.* establish woods; (wieder ~)
reestablish the woods

Aufforstung *die;* ~, ~en afforestation;
(Wieder~) reforestation; **die** ~ **der Wälder**
restocking the forests

auf|fressen *unr. tr. V.* (auch fig.) eat up

auf|frischen 1 *tr. V.* freshen up;
brighten up ⟨*colour, paintwork*⟩; renovate
⟨*polish, furniture*⟩; (restaurieren) restore
⟨*tapestry, fresco, etc.*⟩; (fig.) revive ⟨*old
memories*⟩; renew ⟨*acquaintance,
friendship*⟩; **seine Englischkenntnisse**
~: brush up one's [knowledge of] English
2 *itr. V.; auch mit sein* ⟨*wind*⟩ freshen

auf|führen 1 *tr. V.* (a) put on ⟨*film*⟩; stage
⟨*play, ballet, opera*⟩; perform ⟨*piece of music*⟩
(b) (auflisten) list
2 *refl. V.* behave

Auf·führung *die* performance

Auf·gabe *die* (a) task
(b) (fig.: Zweck, Funktion) function
(c) (Schulw.) (Übung) exercise; (Prüfungs~)
question; (Haus~) ▶ HAUSAUFGABE
(d) (Rechen~, Mathematik~) problem
(e) (Kapitulation) retirement; (im Schach)
resignation; **jmdn. zur** ~ **zwingen** force sb.
to retire/resign
(f) (das Aufgeben a) giving up
(g) (einer Postsendung) posting (Brit.); mailing
(Amer.); (eines Telegramms) handing in; (einer
Bestellung, einer Annonce) placing
(h) (von Gepäck) checking in

Aufgaben-: ~**bereich** *der,* ~**gebiet**
das area of responsibility

Auf·gang *der* (a) (eines Gestirns) rising
(b) (Treppe) stairs *pl.;* staircase; stairway;
(in einem Bahnhof, zu einer Galerie, einer Tribüne)
steps *pl.*

auf|geben 1 *unr. tr. V.* (a) give up; (Sport)
retire from ⟨*race, competition*⟩
(b) (übergeben, übermitteln) post (Brit.), mail
⟨*letter, parcel*⟩; hand in, (telefonisch) phone
in ⟨*telegram*⟩; place ⟨*advertisement, order*⟩;
check ⟨*luggage, baggage*⟩ in
(c) (Schulw.: als Hausaufgabe) set (Brit.); assign
(Amer.)
(d) jmdm. ein Rätsel ~: set (Brit.) *or* (Amer.)
assign sb. a puzzle
2 *unr. itr. V.* give up; (im Sport) retire; (im
Schach) resign

Auf·gebot *das* (a) contingent; **ein
gewaltiges** ~ **an Polizisten/Fahrzeugen/
Material** a huge force of police/array of
vehicles/materials
(b) (zur Heirat) notice of an/the intended
marriage; (kirchlich) banns *pl.*

auf|gehen *unr. itr. V.; mit sein* (a) rise
(b) (sich öffnen [lassen]) ⟨*door, parachute,
wound*⟩ open; ⟨*stage curtain*⟩ go up; ⟨*knot,
button, zip, bandage, shoelace, stitching*⟩
come undone; ⟨*boil, pimple, blister*⟩ burst;
⟨*flower, bud*⟩ open [up]
(c) (keimen) come up
(d) (aufgetrieben werden) ⟨*dough, cake*⟩ rise

(e) (Math.) ⟨*calculation*⟩ work out; ⟨*equation*⟩
come out
(f) etw. **geht jmdm. auf** sb. realizes sth.

auf|geilen *tr. V.* (salopp) jmdn. **[mit/durch
etw.]** ~: get sb. randy [with sth.]; **sich [an
etw.** (*Dat.*)] ~: get randy [with sth.]; (fig.) get
worked up [about sth.]

aufgeklärt *Adj.* enlightened; ~ **sein**
(sexualkundlich) know the facts of life

auf·gelegt *Adj.* **gut/schlecht** *usw.* ~ **sein**
be in a good/bad *etc.* mood; **zu etw.** ~ **sein** be
in the mood for sth.

auf·gelöst *Adj.* distraught ⟨*person*⟩

aufgeregt 1 *Adj.* excited; (nervös,
beunruhigt) agitated
2 *adv.* excitedly; (nervös, beunruhigt) agitatedly

auf·geschlossen *Adj.* open-minded
(**gegenüber** as regards, about); (interessiert,
empfänglich) receptive (*Dat.,* **für** to);
(zugänglich) approachable

Auf·geschlossenheit *die*
▶ AUFGESCHLOSSEN: open-mindedness;
receptiveness; approachableness

aufgeweckt *Adj.* bright

Aufgewecktheit *die;* ~: brightness

auf|gießen *unr. tr. V.* make ⟨*coffee, tea*⟩

auf|gliedern *tr. V.* subdivide, break down
(**in** + *Akk.* into)

Auf·gliederung *die* subdivision;
breakdown

auf|greifen *unr. tr. V.* pick up

aufgrund *Präp. mit Gen.* on the basis *or*
strength of; (wegen) because of

auf|haben (ugs.) 1 *unr. tr. V.* (a) (aufgesetzt
haben) have on
(b) (geöffnet haben) have ⟨*zip*⟩ undone; have
⟨*door, window, jacket, blouse*⟩ open
2 *unr. itr. V.* ⟨*shop, office*⟩ be open

auf|halsen *tr. V.* (ugs.) jmdm./sich etw.
~: saddle sb./oneself with sth.; **sich** (*Dat.*)
etw. ~ **lassen** get oneself saddled with sth.

auf|halten 1 *unr. tr. V.* (a) halt
(b) (stören) hold up
(c) (ugs.: geöffnet halten) hold ⟨*sack, door, etc.*⟩
open; **die Augen [und Ohren]** ~: keep one's
eyes [and ears] open
2 *unr. refl. V.* (a) stay
(b) **sich mit jmdm./etw.** ~: spend [a long]
time on sb./sth.

auf|hängen 1 *tr. V.* (a) hang up; hang
⟨*picture, curtains*⟩
(b) (erhängen) hang
2 *refl. V.* hang oneself

Aufhänger *der;* ~s, ~: loop

auf|heben *unr. tr. V.* (a) pick up
(b) (aufbewahren) keep
(c) (abschaffen) abolish; repeal ⟨*law*⟩; rescind
⟨*order, instruction*⟩; cancel ⟨*contract*⟩; lift
⟨*ban, prohibition*⟩
(d) (ausgleichen) cancel out; neutralize ⟨*effect*⟩

Aufheben *das;* ~s: **viel** ~**[s]/kein** ~ **von
jmdm./etw. machen** make a great fuss/not
make any fuss about sb./sth.

Aufhebungs·vertrag *der* agreement to terminate a/the contract

auf|heitern ⟦1⟧ *tr. V.* cheer up
⟦2⟧ *refl. V.* ⟨*weather*⟩ brighten up

Aufheiterung *die;* ~, ~**en** (a) (des Wetters) bright period
(b) (Erheiterung) cheering up

auf|hetzen *tr. V.* incite

auf|holen ⟦1⟧ *tr. V.* make up ⟨*time, delay*⟩; pull back ⟨*lead*⟩
⟦2⟧ *itr. V.* catch up; ⟨*athlete, competitor*⟩ make up ground

auf|horchen *itr. V.* prick up one's ears

auf|hören *itr. V.* stop; [damit] ~, etw. zu tun stop doing sth.

auf|kaufen *tr. V.* buy up

auf|klappen *tr. V.* open, fold open ⟨*chair, table*⟩; open [up] ⟨*suitcase, trunk*⟩; open ⟨*book, knife*⟩

auf|klären ⟦1⟧ *tr. V.* (a) clear up ⟨*matter, mystery, question, misunderstanding, error, confusion*⟩; solve ⟨*crime, problem*⟩; explain ⟨*event, incident, cause*⟩; resolve ⟨*contradiction, disagreement*⟩
(b) (unterrichten) enlighten; ein Kind ~ (sexualkundlich) tell a child the facts of life
⟦2⟧ *refl. V.* (a) ⟨*misunderstanding, mystery*⟩ be cleared up
(b) ⟨*weather*⟩ brighten [up]; ⟨*sky*⟩ brighten

Auf·klärung *die* ▶ AUFKLÄREN 1:
(a) clearing up; solution; explanation; resolution
(b) enlightenment; die ~ der Kinder (über Sexualität) telling the children the facts of life

auf|kleben *tr. V.* stick on; (mit Kleister) paste on

Auf·kleber *der* sticker

auf|knöpfen *tr. V.* unbutton; undo

auf|kochen ⟦1⟧ *tr. V.* bring to the boil
⟦2⟧ *itr. V.; mit sein* come to the boil

auf|kommen *unr. itr. V.; mit sein*
(a) ⟨*wind*⟩ spring up; ⟨*storm, gale*⟩ blow up; ⟨*fog*⟩ come down; ⟨*rumour*⟩ start; ⟨*suspicion, doubt, feeling*⟩ arise; ⟨*fashion, style, invention*⟩ come in; ⟨*boredom*⟩ set in; ⟨*mood, atmosphere*⟩ develop
(b) ~ für (bezahlen) bear ⟨*costs*⟩; pay for ⟨*damage*⟩; pay ⟨*expenses*⟩; be liable for ⟨*debts*⟩; stand ⟨*loss*⟩
(c) ~ für (Verantwortung tragen für) be responsible for

auf|krempeln *tr. V.* roll up

Auflade·karte *die* top-up card

auf|laden ⟦1⟧ *unr. tr. V.* (a) load (auf + Akk. on [to])
(b) jmdm. etw. ~ (ugs.) load sb. with sth.; (fig.) saddle sb. with sth.
(c) charge [up] ⟨*battery*⟩
⟦2⟧ *unr. refl. V.* ⟨*battery*⟩ charge

Auf·lage *die* (a) (Buchw.) edition
(b) (Verpflichtung) condition

---

*old spelling – see note on page x

auflagen·stark *Adj.* high-circulation ⟨*newspaper, magazine*⟩

auf|lassen *unr. tr. V.* (ugs.) (a) leave ⟨*door, window, jacket, etc.*⟩ open
(b) keep on ⟨*hat, glasses, etc.*⟩

auf|lauern *itr. V.* jmdm. ~: lie in wait for sb.

Auf·lauf *der* (a) (Menschen~) crowd
(b) (Speise) soufflé

auf|leben *itr. V.; mit sein* revive; (fig.: wieder munter werden) come to life

auf|legen ⟦1⟧ *tr. V.* (a) put on; den Hörer ~: put down the receiver
(b) (Buchw.) publish
⟦2⟧ *itr. V.* (den Hörer auflegen) hang up

auf|lehnen *refl. V.* rebel

Auflehnung *die;* ~, ~**en** rebellion

auf|leuchten *itr. V.; auch mit sein* light up; (für kurze Zeit) flash

auf|lockern *tr. V.* (a) loosen; break up ⟨*soil*⟩
(b) (fig.) introduce some variety into ⟨*landscape, lesson, lecture*⟩; relieve ⟨*pattern, façade*⟩; make ⟨*mood, atmosphere, evening*⟩ more relaxed

Auf·lockerung *die* (a) ▶ AUFLOCKERN A: loosening; breaking up
(b) zur ~ der Stimmung/des Abends to make the mood/evening more relaxed

auf|lösen ⟦1⟧ *tr. V.* dissolve; resolve ⟨*difficulty, contradiction*⟩; solve ⟨*puzzle, equation*⟩; break off ⟨*engagement*⟩; cancel ⟨*arrangement, contract, agreement*⟩; dissolve ⟨*organization*⟩
⟦2⟧ *refl. V.* dissolve (in + Akk. into); ⟨*parliament*⟩ dissolve itself; ⟨*crowd, demonstration*⟩ break up; ⟨*fog, mist*⟩ lift; (fig.) ⟨*empire, social order*⟩ disintegrate

Auf·lösung *die* (a) ▶ AUFLÖSEN 1: dissolving; resolution; solution; breaking off; cancellation; dissolution
(b) ▶ AUFLÖSEN 2: dissolving; breaking up lifting; disintegration

auf|machen ⟦1⟧ *tr. V.* (a) open; undo ⟨*button, knot*⟩
(b) (ugs.: eröffnen) open [up] ⟨*shop, business, etc.*⟩
⟦2⟧ *itr. V.* (a) ⟨*shop, office, etc.*⟩ open
(b) (ugs.: die Tür öffnen) open the door; jmdm. ~: open the door to sb.
(c) (ugs.: eröffnet werden) ⟨*shop, business*⟩ open [up]

Aufmachung *die;* ~, ~**en** presentation; (Kleidung) get-up

Aufmarsch·gebiet *das* (Milit.) deployment area

auf|marschieren *itr. V.; mit sein* assemble; (heranmarschieren) march up; Truppen sind an der Grenze aufmarschiert troops were deployed along the border

aufmerksam ⟦1⟧ *Adj.* (a) attentive; sharp ⟨*eyes*⟩; jmdn. auf jmdn./etw. ~ machen draw

sb.'s attention to sb./sth.; **auf jmdn./etw.**
~ **werden** become aware of sb./sth.;
~ **werden** notice
(b) (höflich) attentive
⟨2⟩ *adv.* attentively
Aufmerksamkeit *die;* ~, ~**en**
(a) attention
(b) (Höflichkeit) attentiveness
(c) (Geschenk) small gift
auf|motzen *tr. V.* (ugs.) tart up (Brit. coll.);
doll up (coll.)
auf|muntern *tr. V.* **(a)** cheer up
(b) (beleben) liven up
(c) (ermutigen) encourage
Aufmunterung *die;* ~ ▶ AUFMUNTERN:
cheering up; livening up; encouragement
Aufnahme *die;* ~, ~**n (a)** ▶ AUFNEHMEN B:
opening; establishment; taking up
(b) (Empfang) reception
(c) ▶ AUFNEHMEN D: admission (**in** + *Akk.*
into)
(d) (Einschließung) inclusion
(e) (Finanzw.) raising
(f) (Aufzeichnung) taking down; (von Personalien,
eines Diktats) taking [down]
(g) ▶ AUFNEHMEN K: taking: photographing;
filming
(h) (Bild) shot
(i) (das Aufnehmen auf Tonträger, das
Aufgenommene) recording
(j) (Anklang) reception; response (*Gen.* to)
(k) (Einverleibung, Absorption) absorption
aufnahme-, Aufnahme-: ~**antrag**
der application for membership; ~**fähig**
Adj. receptive (**für** to); **ich bin nicht**
mehr ~**fähig** I can't take any more in;
~**fähigkeit** *die* receptivity (**für** to); ability
to take things in; ~**land** *das* host country
auf|nehmen *unr. V.* **(a)** (aufheben) pick
up; (fig.) take up ⟨*idea, theme, etc.*⟩; **es mit**
jmdm./etw. ~**/nicht** ~ **können** (fig.) be a/no
match for sb./sth.
(b) (beginnen mit) open ⟨*negotiations,*
talks⟩; establish ⟨*relations, contacts*⟩; take
up ⟨*studies, activity, occupation*⟩; start
⟨*production, investigation*⟩
(c) (empfangen) receive; (beherbergen) take in
(d) (beitreten lassen) admit (**in** + *Akk.* to)
(e) (einschließen, verzeichnen) include
(f) (erfassen) take in ⟨*impressions,*
information, etc.⟩
(g) (absorbieren) absorb
(h) (Finanzw.) raise ⟨*mortgage, money, loan*⟩
(i) (reagieren auf) receive
(j) (aufschreiben) take down; take [down]
⟨*dictation, particulars*⟩
(k) (fotografieren) take ⟨*picture*⟩; photograph,
take a photograph of ⟨*scene, subject*⟩; (filmen)
film
(l) (auf Tonträger) record
(m) (auf Videoband) videotape; video
auf|opfern *refl. V.* devote oneself
sacrificingly (**für** to)
aufopfernd ⟨1⟩ *Adj.* self-sacrificing

⟨2⟩ *adv.* self-sacrificingly
auf|passen *itr. V.* **(a)** watch out;
(konzentriert sein) pay attention; **pass mal auf!**
(ugs.: hör mal zu!) now listen
(b) auf jmdn./etw. ~: keep an eye on sb./sth.
auf|platzen *itr. V.; mit sein* burst open;
⟨*seam, cushion*⟩ split open; ⟨*wound*⟩ open up
Auf·prall *der;* ~**[e]s,** ~**e** impact
auf|prallen *itr. V.; mit sein* **auf etw.** (*Akk.*)
~: hit sth.
Auf·preis *der* additional charge
auf|pumpen *tr. V.* pump up
auf|putschen *tr. V.* stimulate; arouse
⟨*passions, urge*⟩
Aufputsch·mittel *das* stimulant
auf|räumen *tr., itr. V.* clear up
Aufräumungs·arbeiten *Pl.* clearance
work *sing.*
auf·recht ⟨1⟩ *Adj.* (auch fig.) upright
⟨2⟩ *adv.* ⟨*walk, sit, hold oneself*⟩ straight
aufrecht|erhalten *unr. tr. V.* maintain;
keep up ⟨*deception, fiction, contact, custom*⟩
auf|regen ⟨1⟩ *tr. V.* excite; (ärgern) annoy;
irritate; (beunruhigen) agitate
⟨2⟩ *refl. V.* get worked up (**über** + *Akk.* about)
Auf·regung *die* excitement *no pl.;*
(Beunruhigung) agitation *no pl.;* **jmdn. in**
~ **versetzen** make sb. excited/agitated
auf|reißen ⟨1⟩ *unr. tr. V.* **(a)** (öffnen) tear
open; wrench open ⟨*drawer*⟩; fling open
⟨*door, window*⟩; **die Augen/den Mund**
~: open one's eyes/mouth wide
(b) (beschädigen) tear open; tear ⟨*clothes*⟩;
break up ⟨*road, soil*⟩
⟨2⟩ *itr. V.; mit sein* ⟨*clothes*⟩ tear; ⟨*seam*⟩
split; ⟨*wound*⟩ open; ⟨*cloud*⟩ break up
auf|reizen *tr. V.* excite
auf·reizend ⟨1⟩ *Adj.* provocative
⟨2⟩ *adv.* provocatively
auf|richten ⟨1⟩ *tr. V.* erect; put up; **den**
Oberkörper ~: raise one's upper body; **jmdn.**
[wieder] ~ (fig.) give fresh heart to sb.
⟨2⟩ *refl. V.* stand up [straight]; **sich an**
jmdm./etw. [wieder] ~ (fig.) take heart from
sb./sth.
auf·richtig ⟨1⟩ *Adj.* sincere
⟨2⟩ *adv.* sincerely
Auf·richtigkeit *die* sincerity
auf|rücken *itr. V.; mit sein* move up
Auf·ruf *der* **(a)** call
(b) (Appell) appeal (**an** + *Akk.* to)
auf|rufen *unr. tr. V.* **(a)** call
(b) jmdn. ~, **etw. zu tun** call upon sb. to do sth.
(c) (Rechtsw.) appeal for ⟨*witnesses*⟩
Aufruhr *der;* ~**s,** ~**e (a)** (Widerstand) rebellion
(b) (Erregung) turmoil
aufrührerisch *Adj.* inflammatory
auf|rüsten *tr., itr. V.* **(a)** arm; **wieder**
~: rearm
(b) (DV) upgrade
Auf·rüstung *die* armament

aufs *Präp. + Art.* = **auf das**

auf|sagen *tr. V.* recite

auf|sammeln *tr. V.* gather up

aufsässig ① *Adj.* recalcitrant
② *adv.* recalcitrantly

Aufsässigkeit *die;* ~, ~**en**
(a) recalcitrance
(b) (Handlung) piece of recalcitrance

Auf·satz *der* (Text) essay

auf|saugen *unr. (auch regelm.) tr. V.* soak up; (fig.) absorb

auf|schieben *unr. tr. V.* postpone

Auf·schlag *der* (a) (Aufprall) impact
(b) (Preis~) surcharge
(c) (Ärmel~) cuff; (Hosen~) turn-up; (Revers) lapel
(d) (Tennis usw.) serve

auf|schlagen ① *unr. itr. V.* (a) *mit sein* **auf etw.** *(Dat. od. Akk.)* ~: hit sth.
(b) (teurer werden) ⟨price, rent, costs⟩ go up
(c) (Tennis usw.) serve
② *unr. tr. V.* (a) (öffnen) crack ⟨nut, egg⟩ [open]; knock a hole in ⟨ice⟩; **sich** *(Dat.)* **das Knie/den Kopf** ~: cut one's knee/head
(b) open ⟨book, newspaper, one's eyes⟩; **schlagt Seite 15 auf!** turn to page 15
(c) turn up ⟨collar, sleeve, trouser leg⟩
(d) (aufbauen) set up ⟨camp⟩; pitch ⟨tent⟩; put up ⟨bed, hut, scaffolding⟩
(e) **5% auf etw.** *(Akk.)* ~: put 5% on sth.

auf|schließen ① *unr. tr. V.* unlock
② *unr. itr. V.* **[jmdm.]** ~: unlock the door/gate *etc.* [for sb.]

Auf·schluss, *****Auf·schluß** *der* information *no pl.*

auf|schneiden ① *unr. tr. V.* (a) cut open
(b) (zerteilen) cut
② *unr. itr. V.* (ugs.: prahlen) boast (**mit** about)

Auf·schneider *der,* **Auf·schneiderin** *die* (ugs. abwertend) boaster; braggart

Auf·schnitt *der* [assorted] cold meats *pl.*/cheeses *pl.*

auf|schnüren *tr. V.* undo

auf|schrauben *tr. V.* unscrew; unscrew the top of ⟨bottle, jar, etc.⟩

Auf·schrei *der* cry; (stärker) yell; (schriller) scream; **ein** ~ **der Empörung** *od.* **Entrüstung** (fig.) an outcry

auf|schreiben *unr. tr. V.* write down; **[sich** *(Dat.)*] **etw.** ~: make a note of sth.

auf|schreien *unr. itr. V.* cry out; (stärker) yell out; (schrill) scream

Auf·schrift *die* inscription

Auf·schub *der* postponement; **die Sache duldet keinen** ~: the matter brooks no delay

Auf·schwung *der* upturn (*Gen.* in)

Aufsehen *das;* ~**s** stir; **[großes]** ~ **erregen** cause a [great] stir

Auf·seher *der,* **Auf·seherin** *die;* ~, ~**nen** (im Gefängnis) warder (Brit.); [prison]

guard (Amer.); (im Park) park-keeper; (im Museum, auf dem Parkplatz) attendant; (auf einem Gut, Sklavenaufseher) overseer

*auf|sein ▶ AUF 3A, B, F

auf|setzen ① *tr. V.* (a) put on
(b) (verfassen) draw up ⟨text⟩
② *refl. V.* sit up

Auf·sicht *die* supervision; (bei Prüfungen) invigilation (Brit.); proctoring (Amer.)

auf|spielen ① *refl. V.* (ugs. abwertend: angeben) put on airs; **sich vor jmdm.** ~: show off in front of sb.
② *itr. V.* (a) (musizieren) play; **zum Tanz** ~: play dance music
(b) (Sport) **groß/eindrucksvoll** ~: give a fine/impressive display

auf|springen *unr. itr. V.; mit sein*
(a) jump up
(b) (hinaufspringen) jump on (**auf** + *Akk.* to)
(c) (rissig werden) crack

auf|stacheln *tr. V.* incite

Auf·stand *der* rebellion

auf·ständisch *Adj.* rebellious

auf|stehen *unr. itr. V.; mit sein* stand up; (aus dem Liegen) get up

auf|steigen *unr. itr. V.; mit sein* (a) (auf ein Fahrzeug) get on; **auf etw.** *(Akk.)* ~: get on [to] sth.
(b) (bergan steigen) climb
(c) (hochsteigen) ⟨sap, smoke, mist⟩ rise
(d) (beruflich, gesellschaftlich) rise (**zu** to); **zum Direktor** ~: rise to be manager

auf|stellen ① *tr. V.* (a) put up (**auf** + *Akk.* on); set up ⟨skittles⟩; (postieren) post
(b) (aufrecht hinstellen) stand up
(c) (Sport) select, pick ⟨team, player⟩
(d) (bilden) put together ⟨team of experts⟩; raise ⟨army⟩
(e) (nominieren) nominate; put up
② *refl. V.* position oneself

Auf·stellung *die* (a) ▶ AUFSTELLEN 1A: putting up; setting up; posting
(b) ▶ AUFSTELLEN B: standing up
(c) ▶ AUFSTELLEN C: selection; picking
(d) ▶ AUFSTELLEN D: putting together; raising
(e) (Nominierung) nomination

Aufstieg *der;* ~**[e]s,** ~**e** (a) climb
(b) ▶ AUFSTEIGEN D: rise

auf|stoßen ① *unr. tr. V.* push open
② *unr. itr. V.* belch; ⟨baby⟩ bring up wind

Auf·strich *der* spread

auf|stützen ① *tr. V.* rest ⟨one's arms etc.⟩
② *refl. V.* support oneself; **die Arme auf etw.** *(Akk. od. Dat.)* ~: rest one's arms on sth.

auf|suchen *tr. V.* call on; go to ⟨doctor⟩

Auf·takt *der* (a) (fig.) start
(b) (Musik) upbeat

auf|tauchen *itr. V.; mit sein* (a) surface
(b) (sichtbar werden) appear

auf|tauen ① *tr. V.* thaw
② *itr. V.; mit sein* (auch fig.) thaw

---

auf|teilen *tr. V.* **(a)** divide [up]
(b) (verteilen) share out

Auftrag *der;* ~[e]s, **Aufträge**
(a) instructions *pl.;* **in jmds.** ~ (*Dat.*) on sb.'s instructions; (für jmdn.) on behalf of sb
(b) (Bestellung) order; (bei Künstlern, Architekten usw.) commission
(c) (Mission) task; (Aufgabe) job

auf|tragen *unr. V.* **(a) jmdm.** ~, **etw. zu tun** instruct sb. to do sth.
(b) (aufstreichen) put on ⟨*paint, make-up, etc.*⟩

Auftrag·geber *der;* ~s, ~,
Auftrag·geberin *die;* ~, ~nen client

auftrags-, Auftrags-: ~**buch** *das*
(Kaufmannsspr.) order book; ~**killer** *der,*
~**killerin** *die* contract killer

auf|treten *unr. itr. V.; mit sein* **(a)** tread
(b) (sich benehmen) behave
(c) (eine Vorstellung geben) appear; **als Zeuge/ Kläger** ~: appear as a witness/a plaintiff
(d) (auftauchen) ⟨*problem, difficulty, difference of opinion*⟩ arise; ⟨*symptom, danger, pest*⟩ appear

Auftreten *das;* ~s (Benehmen) manner

Auf·trieb *der* **(a)** (Physik) (statischer ~) buoyancy; (dynamischer ~) lift
(b) (fig.) impetus; **das hat ihm** ~/neuen ~ **gegeben** that has given him a lift/given him new impetus

Auf·tritt *der* **(a)** (Vorstellung) appearance
(b) (Theater: das Auftreten) entrance; (Szene) scene

auf|tun *unr. refl. V.* (geh.) open; (fig.) open up

auf|wachen *itr. V.; mit sein* wake up, awaken (**aus** from); (aus Ohnmacht, Narkose) come round (**aus** from)

auf|wachsen *unr. itr. V.; mit sein* grow up

Auf·wand *der;* ~[e]s cost; expense

aufwändig ▶ AUFWENDIG

Aufwands·entschädigung *die* expense allowance

auf|wärmen ① *tr. V.* heat *or* warm up ⟨*food*⟩
② *refl. V.* warm oneself up

aufwärts *Adv.* upwards

Aufwärts·trend *der* upward trend

auf|wecken *tr. V.* wake [up]; waken

auf|weichen ① *tr. V.* soften
② *itr. V.; mit sein* become soft; soften up

auf|wenden *unr.* (*auch regelm.*) *tr. V.* use ⟨*skill, influence*⟩; expend ⟨*energy, resources*⟩; spend ⟨*money, time*⟩; **viel Geld/seine ganze Freizeit für etw.** ~ spend a great deal of money/all one's spare time on sth.

auf·wendig ① *Adj.* lavish; (kostspielig) costly; expensive
② *adv.* lavishly; (kostspielig) expensively

Auf·wendung *die* **(a)** ▶ AUFWENDEN: using; expenditure; spending; **unter** ~ **von etw.** by using/expending/spending sth.
(b) *Pl.* (Kosten) expenditure *sing.*

auf|wiegeln *tr. V.* incite; stir up

auf|wirbeln *tr. V.* swirl up

auf|wischen *tr. V.* **(a)** wipe *or* mop up
(b) (säubern) wipe ⟨*floor*⟩; (mit Wasser) wash ⟨*floor*⟩

auf|zählen *tr. V.* list

Auf·zählung *die* **(a)** listing
(b) (Liste) list

auf|zeichnen *tr. V.* **(a)** record
(b) (zeichnen) draw

Auf·zeichnung *die* record; (Film-, Tonaufzeichnung) recording; ~en (Notizen) notes

auf|ziehen ① *unr. tr. V.* **(a)** pull open ⟨*drawer*⟩; open, draw [back] ⟨*curtains*⟩; undo ⟨*zip*⟩
(b) wind up ⟨*clock, toy, etc.*⟩.
② *unr. itr. V.; mit sein* come up; ⟨*clouds, storm*⟩ gather

Auf·zucht *die* raising; rearing

Aufzucht·station *die* animal rescue centre

Auf·zug *der* **(a)** (Lift) lift (Brit.); elevator (Amer.)
(b) (abwertend: Aufmachung) get-up
(c) (Theater: Akt) act

Aug·apfel *der* eyeball

Auge *das;* ~s, ~n eye; **gute/schlechte** ~n **haben** have good/poor eyesight; **auf einem** ~ **blind** blind in one eye; **da wird er** ~n **machen** (fig. ugs.) his eyes will pop out of his head; **ich traute meinen** ~n **nicht** (ugs.) I couldn't believe my eyes; **ein** ~ *od.* **beide** ~n **zudrücken** (fig.) turn a blind eye; **jmdn./etw. nicht aus den** ~n **lassen** not take one's eyes off sb./sth.; **ins** ~ **gehen** (fig. ugs.) end in disaster; **unter vier** ~n (fig.) in private

augen-, Augen-: ~**arzt** *der,*
~**ärztin** *die* eye specialist; ~**blick** /*auch:* --'-/ *der* ▶ MOMENT[1]; ~**blicklich** /*auch:* --'--/ ① *Adj.* **(a)** (sofortig) immediate;
(b) (gegenwärtig) present; ② *adv.* **(a)** (sofort) at once; **(b)** (zurzeit) at the moment;
~**braue** *die* eyebrow; ~**farbe** *die* colour of one's eyes; ~**klinik** *die* eye hospital; ~**kontakt** *der* eye contact; ~**lid** *das* eyelid; ~**maß** *das:* **ein gutes/schlechtes** ~**maß haben** have a good eye/no eye for distances; ~**merk** *das:* **sein** ~**merk auf jmdn./etw. richten** *od.* **lenken** give one's attention to sb./sth.; ~**optiker** *der,*
~**optikerin** *die* ophthalmic optician

Augen·schein *der* (geh.) **(a)** (Eindruck) appearance; **dem** ~ **nach** by all appearances
(b) (Betrachtung) inspection; **jmdn./etw. in** ~ **nehmen** have a close look at sb./sth.; give sb./sth. a close inspection

augen·scheinlich (geh.) ① *Adj.* (scheinbar) apparent; evident; (sichtbar) obvious; evident
② *adv.* (scheinbar) apparently; evidently; (sichtbar) obviously; evidently ····⊹

augen-, Augen-: ∼**weide** die feast
for the eyes; ∼**zeuge** der, ∼**zeugin** die
eyewitness; ∼**zwinkernd** ⟨1⟩ Adj. tacit
⟨agreement⟩; ⟨2⟩ adv. with a wink

August der; ∼[e]s od. ∼, ∼e August

Auktion die; ∼, ∼en auction

Aula die; ∼, Aulen od. ∼s hall

Aupair /o'pɛːr/ das; ∼s, ∼s au pair

aus ⟨1⟩ Präp. mit Dat. **(a)** (aus dem Inneren
von) out of
(b) (Herkunft, Quelle, Ausgangspunkt angebend,
auch zeitlich) from; ∼ **Spanien/Köln** usw. from
Spain/Cologne etc.
(c) ∼ **der Mode/Übung sein** be out of
fashion/training
(d) (Grund, Ursache angebend) out of; **etw.**
∼ **Erfahrung wissen** know sth. from
experience; ∼ **Versehen** by mistake
(e) (bestehend ∼) of; (hergestellt ∼) made of;
∼ **etw. bestehen** consist of sth.
(f) ∼ **ihm ist ein guter Arzt geworden** he
made a good doctor
⟨2⟩ Adv. **(a)** (ugs.: vorbei) over; **wann ist
die Vorstellung** ∼? what time does the
performance end?; **die Schule ist** ∼ school is
out; ∼ **jetzt!** that's enough
(b) (ausgeschaltet) off; (erloschen) out
(c) **vom Fenster/obersten Stockwerk**
∼: from the window/top storey; **von mir** ∼
(ugs.) if you like; **von sich** (Dat.) ∼: of one's
own accord

aus|atmen itr., tr. V. breathe out

aus|baden tr. V. (ugs.) carry or take the
can for (Brit. coll.); take the rap for (coll.)

Aus·bau der; ∼[e]s **(a)** (Erweiterung) extension
(b) (Ausgestaltung) conversion (**zu** into)

aus|bauen tr. V. **(a)** (demontieren) remove
(**aus** from)
(b) (erweitern) extend

Aus·beute die yield

aus|beuten tr. V. exploit

Ausbeutung die; ∼, ∼en exploitation

aus|bilden tr. V. **(a)** train
(b) (entwickeln) develop

Aus·bildung die **(a)** training
(b) (Entwicklung) development

Aus·blick der view (**auf** + Akk. of)

aus|brechen unr. itr. V.; mit sein
(a) break out (**aus** of); (fig.) break free (**aus**
from)
(b) **jmdm. bricht der Schweiß aus** sb. breaks
into a sweat
(c) ⟨volcano⟩ erupt
(d) (beginnen) break out; ⟨crisis⟩ break
(e) **in Gelächter/Weinen** ∼: burst out
laughing/crying; **in Beifall/Tränen** ∼: burst
into applause/tears

aus|breiten ⟨1⟩ tr. V. spread; spread
[out] ⟨map, cloth, sheet, etc.⟩; open out ⟨fan,
newspaper⟩; (nebeneinander legen) spread out
⟨2⟩ refl. V. spread

Aus·bruch der **(a)** (Flucht) escape (**aus** from)
(b) (Beginn) outbreak
(c) (Gefühlsausbruch) outburst
(d) (eines Vulkans) eruption

aus|brüten tr. V. hatch out; (im Brutkasten)
incubate

aus|bürsten tr. V. brush out ⟨dust, dirt⟩
(**aus** of); brush ⟨clothes, upholstery, etc.⟩

aus|chillen itr. V. (salopp) chill out (coll.)

Aus·dauer die stamina

aus·dauernd Adj. with stamina postpos.

Ausdauer·training das stamina
training

aus|dehnen ⟨1⟩ tr. V. **(a)** stretch; (fig.)
extend (**auf** + Akk. to)
(b) (zeitlich) prolong
⟨2⟩ refl. V. expand; (zeitlich) go on

Aus·dehnung die expansion; (fig.)
extension; (zeitlich) prolongation

aus|denken unr. refl. V. **sich** (Dat.) **etw.**
∼: think sth. up

aus|diskutieren tr. V. **etw.** ∼: discuss
sth. fully or thoroughly

Aus·druck der; Pl. **Ausdrücke** expression;
(Terminus) term; **etw. zum** ∼ **bringen** express
sth.

aus|drucken tr. V. (Nachrichtenw., DV)
print out

aus|drücken ⟨1⟩ tr. V. **(a)** (auspressen)
squeeze ⟨juice⟩ out; squeeze [out] ⟨lemon,
grape, orange, etc.⟩; squeeze out ⟨sponge⟩;
squeeze ⟨boil, pimple⟩
(b) stub out ⟨cigarette⟩
(c) (mitteilen) express
⟨2⟩ refl. V. **(a)** express oneself
(b) (offenbar werden) be expressed

ausdrücklich /od. ˈ-ˈ-/ ⟨1⟩ Adj. express
attrib. ⟨command, wish, etc.⟩; explicit
⟨reservation⟩
⟨2⟩ adv. expressly; ⟨mention⟩ explicitly

ausdrucks-: ∼**los** ⟨1⟩ Adj.
expressionless; ⟨2⟩ adv. expressionlessly;
∼**voll** ⟨1⟩ Adj. expressive; ⟨2⟩ adv.
expressively

aus·einander Adv. **(a)** (voneinander
getrennt) apart; **etw.** ∼ **schreiben** write sth.
as separate words; ∼ **brechen** break up;
etw. ∼ **brechen** break sth. up; ∼ **gehen**
part; ⟨crowd⟩ disperse; ⟨opinions, views⟩
differ; **zwei Dinge** ∼ **halten** (unterscheiden)
distinguish between two things; **ich kann
die beiden Brüder nicht** ∼ **halten** I cannot
tell the two brothers apart; **etw.** ∼ **nehmen**
take sth. apart
(b) **jmdm. etw.** ∼ **setzen** explain sth. to sb.;
sich mit jmdm. ∼ **setzen** have it out with
sb.; **sich mit etw.** ∼ **setzen** concern oneself
with sth.

*****auseinander|brechen** usw.
▶ AUSEINANDER

Auseinandersetzung die; ∼, ∼en
(a) (Streit) argument
(b) (Kampfhandlung) clash

---

*old spelling – see note on page x

Aus·fahrt *die* exit

Aus·fall *der* **(a)** (das Nichtstattfinden) cancellation
(b) (Einbuße, Verlust) loss
(c) (eines Motors) failure; (einer Maschine, eines Autos) breakdown

aus|fallen *unr. itr. V.; mit sein* **(a)** fall out
(b) (nicht stattfinden) be cancelled; **etw.** ~ **lassen** cancel sth.
(c) (ausscheiden) drop out
(d) (nicht mehr funktionieren) ⟨*engine, brakes, signal*⟩ fail; ⟨*machine, car*⟩ break down
(e) (ein bestimmtes Ergebnis zeigen) turn out

ausfallend *Adj.* **[gegen jmdn.]** ~ **sein/ werden** be/become abusive [towards sb.]

Ausfall·straße *die* main road out of the/a town/city

aus·findig *Adv.* **jmdn./etw.** ~ **machen** find sb./sth.

Aus·flug *der* outing

Ausflügler *der;* ~s, ~, **Ausflüglerin** *die;* ~, ~**nen** day tripper; excursionist (Amer.)

Ausflugs-: ~**dampfer** *der* pleasure steamer; ~**lokal** *das* restaurant/café catering for [day] trippers; ~**verkehr** *der* (am Wochenende) weekend holiday traffic; (an Feiertagen) holiday traffic

aus|fragen *tr. V.* **jmdn.** ~: question sb., ask sb. questions (**nach, über** + *Akk.* about)

aus|fransen *itr. V.; mit sein* fray

Aus·fuhr *die;* ~, ~**en** ▶ EXPORT

aus|führen *tr. V.* **(a)** (ausgehen mit) take ⟨*person*⟩ out
(b) (spazieren führen) take ⟨*person, animal*⟩ for a walk
(c) (exportieren) export
(d) (durchführen) carry out; (Sport) take ⟨*penalty, free kick, corner*⟩

ausführlich /*auch:* '--'--/ **1** *Adj.* detailed; full
2 *adv.* in detail

Ausfuhr·sperre *die* ▶ AUSFUHRVERBOT

Aus·führung *die* (Durchführung) carrying out; (Sport) taking

Ausfuhr·verbot *das* (Wirtsch.) export embargo

aus|füllen *tr. V.* **(a)** fill; fill in ⟨*form, crossword puzzle*⟩
(b) (beanspruchen, einnehmen) take up ⟨*space*⟩

Aus·gabe *die* **(a)** giving out; (von Essen) serving
(b) (Geldausgabe) item of expenditure; ~**n** expenditure *sing.* (**für** on)
(c) (Edition) edition
(d) (DV) output

Ausgabe·gerät *das* (DV) output device

Aus·gang *der* **(a)** (Erlaubnis zum Ausgehen) time off; (von Soldaten) leave
(b) (Tür ins Freie) exit (*Gen.* from)
(c) (Anat.) outlet
(d) (Ende) end; (eines Romans, Films usw.) ending

(e) (Ergebnis) outcome; (eines Wettbewerbs) result; **ein Unfall mit tödlichem** ~: an accident with fatal consequences

Ausgangs-: ~**punkt** *der* starting point; ~**sperre** *die* (bes. Milit.) (für Zivilisten) curfew; (für Soldaten) confinement to barracks; **[eine]** ~**sperre verhängen** impose a curfew/confine the soldiers/regiment etc. to barracks

aus|geben *unr. tr. V.* **(a)** give out; serve ⟨*food, drinks*⟩
(b) (verbrauchen) spend ⟨*money*⟩ (**für** on)

ausgebucht *Adj.* booked up

ausgedehnt *Adj.* extensive

aus·gefallen *Adj.* unusual

Ausgeflippte *der/die; adj. Dekl.* (salopp) dropout (coll.)

ausgeglichen *Adj.* balanced; well-balanced ⟨*person*⟩; equable ⟨*climate*⟩

aus|gehen *unr. itr. V.; mit sein* **(a)** go out
(b) (fast aufgebraucht sein) run out
(c) (enden) end; **gut/schlecht** ~: turn out well/badly; ⟨*story, film*⟩ end happily/ unhappily
(d) von jmdm./etw. ~: come from sb./sth.
(e) von etw. ~ (etw. zugrunde legen) take sth. as one's starting point; (etw. annehmen) assume sth.

aus·gelassen **1** *Adj.* exuberant ⟨*mood, person*⟩; lively ⟨*party, celebration*⟩; (wild) boisterous
2 *adv.* exuberantly; (wild) boisterously

aus·gemacht *Adj.* **(a)** (beschlossen) agreed; **es ist [eine]** ~**e Sache, dass ...** it is an accepted fact that ...
(b) (vollkommen) complete; complete, utter ⟨*nonsense*⟩; **eine** ~**e Dummheit** downright stupidity

aus·genommen *Konj.* except

ausgeprägt *Adj.* marked

ausgerechnet *Adv.* (ugs.) ~ **heute/ morgen** today/tomorrow of all days; ~ **hier** here of all places; ~ **Sie** you of all people

aus·geschlossen *Adj.* **das ist** ~: that is out of the question

aus·geschnitten *Adj.* low-cut ⟨*dress, blouse, etc.*⟩

aus·gesprochen **1** *Adj.* definite, marked ⟨*preference, inclination, resemblance*⟩; pronounced ⟨*dislike*⟩; marked ⟨*contrast*⟩; ~**es Pech/Glück haben** be decidedly unlucky/lucky; **ein** ~**es Talent für etw.** a definite talent for sth.; **ein** ~**er Gegner von etw. sein** be a strong opponent of sth.
2 *adv.* (besonders) decidedly; downright ⟨*stupid, ridiculous, ugly*⟩

aus·gestorben *Adj.* **[wie]** ~: deserted

aus·gewogen *Adj.* (ausgeglichen) balanced; [well-]balanced ⟨*personality*⟩

Aus·gewogenheit *die;* ~: balance

ausgezeichnet /*od.* '--'--/ **1** *Adj.* excellent; outstanding ⟨*expert*⟩
2 *adv.* excellently

ausgiebig ① *Adj.* substantial ⟨*meal*⟩
② *adv.* ⟨*profit*⟩ handsomely; ⟨*read*⟩
extensively; **von etw.** ∼ **Gebrauch machen**
make full use of sth.

aus|gießen *unr. tr. V.* **(a)** pour out **(aus** of)
(b) (leeren) empty

Ausgleich *der;* ∼**[e]s,** ∼**e**
(a) ▸ AUSGLEICHEN A: evening out;
reconciliation
(b) (Schadensersatz) compensation; **als** *od.*
zum ∼ **für etw.** to make up for sth.

aus|gleichen *unr. tr. V.* **(a)** even
out; reconcile ⟨*differences of opinions,
contradictions*⟩
(b) compensate for ⟨*damage*⟩; make up for
⟨*misfortune, lack*⟩; **etw. durch etw.** ∼: make
up for sth. with sth.; **sich** ∼: balance out;
(sich gegenseitig aufheben) cancel each other out

aus|graben *unr. tr. V.* dig up; (Archäol.)
excavate

Aus·grabung *die* (Archäol.) excavation

Aus·guss, *Aus·guß *der* sink

aus|halten *unr. tr. V.* stand; bear; endure;
withstand ⟨*attack, load, pressure, test, wear
and tear*⟩; **er konnte es zu Hause nicht mehr**
∼: he couldn't stand it at home any more;
es ist nicht zum Aushalten it is unbearable

aus|handeln *tr. V.* negotiate

aus|händigen *tr. V.* hand over

Aus·hang *der* notice; **einen** ∼ **machen** put
up a notice

aus|heben *unr. tr. V.* dig out ⟨*earth etc.*⟩;
dig ⟨*trench, grave, etc.*⟩

aus|helfen *unr. itr. V.* help out; **jmdm.**
∼: help sb. out **(mit, bei** with)

Aus·hilfe *die* **(a)** (das Aushelfen) help
(b) ▸ AUSHILFSKRAFT

aushilfs-, Aushilfs-: ∼**kraft** *die*
temporary worker; (in Läden, Gaststätten)
temporary assistant; (Sekretärin) temporary
secretary; temp (coll.); ∼**lehrer** *der,*
∼**lehrerin,** *die* supply teacher; ∼**weise**
adv. on a temporary basis

aus|holen *itr. V.* **[mit dem Arm]** ∼: draw
back one's arm; (zum Schlag) raise one's arm

aus|kennen *unr. refl. V.* (an einem Ort usw.)
know one's way around; (in einem Fach, einer
Angelegenheit usw.) know what's what; **sie
kennt sich in dieser Stadt aus** she knows her
way around the town; **sich [gut] mit/in etw.**
(*Dat.*) ∼: know [a lot] about sth.

Aus·klang *der* (geh.) end; **zum** ∼ **des
Festes** to end *or* close the festival

aus|kleiden *tr. V.* (geh.) undress; **sich**
∼: undress

aus|klingen *unr. itr. V.; mit sein* end

aus|klopfen *tr. V.* **(a)** beat out **(aus** + *Dat.*
of)
(b) (säubern) beat ⟨*carpet*⟩; knock ⟨*pipe*⟩ out

aus|kochen *tr. V.* boil; (keimfrei machen)
sterilize ⟨*instruments etc.*⟩ [in boiling water]

---

*alte Schreibung – vgl. Hinweis auf S. x

aus|kommen *unr. itr. V.; mit sein*
(a) manage (mit on)
(b) mit jmdm. [gut] ∼: get on [well] with sb.

Auskommen *das;* ∼**s** livelihood

Auskunft *die;* ∼, **Auskünfte** **(a)** piece of
information; **Auskünfte** information *sing.*;
[jmdm. über etw. (*Akk.*)**]** ∼ **geben** give [sb.]
information [about sth.]
(b) (Stelle) information desk/counter/office/
centre *etc.*; (Fernspr.) directory enquiries
no art. (Brit.); directory information *no art.*
(Amer.)

Auskunftei *die;* ∼, ∼**en** private detective
agency; (Kredit∼) credit reference agency

Auskunfts-: ∼**büro** *das* information
office; enquiry office (Brit.); ∼**schalter**
der information counter; ∼**stelle** *die*
information office

aus|kungeln *tr. V.* (ugs.) reach by
wheeling and dealing

aus|kurieren *tr. V.* heal ⟨*wound*⟩
[completely]

aus|lachen *tr. V.* laugh at

aus|laden *unr. tr. V.* unload ⟨*goods etc.*⟩

Aus·lage *die* **(a)** *Pl.* (Unkosten) expenses
(b) (ausgestellte Ware) item on display; ∼**n**
goods on display

aus|lagern *tr. V.* **(a)** remove ⟨*art
treasures*⟩ for safe-keeping
(b) relocate ⟨*firm, activity*⟩ **(nach** to); (an
einen externen Dienstleister) outsource ⟨*function,
activity*⟩

Aus·land *das* foreign countries *pl.;* **im/ins**
∼: abroad; **aus dem** ∼: from abroad

Ausländer *der;* ∼**s,** ∼, **Ausländerin**
die; ∼, ∼**nen** foreigner

ausländer·feindlich *Adj.* hostile to
foreigners *postpos.*

ausländisch *Adj.* foreign

Auslands-: ∼**aufenthalt** *der* stay
abroad; ∼**einsatz** *der* (Milit.) overseas
deployment; ∼**gespräch** *das* (Fernspr.)
international call; ∼**korrespondent**
der, ∼**korrespondentin** *die* foreign
correspondent; ∼**reise** *die* trip abroad

aus|lassen *unr. tr. V.* **(a)** (weglassen) leave
out
(b) (versäumen) miss ⟨*opportunity, chance,
etc.*⟩

Auslauf *der* **(a)** keinen/zu wenig ∼ haben
have no/too little chance to run around
outside
(b) (Raum) space to run around in

aus|laufen *unr. itr. V.; mit sein* **(a)** run
out **(aus** of)
(b) (leer laufen) empty; ⟨*egg*⟩ run out
(c) (in See stechen) sail **(nach** for)
(d) (erlöschen) ⟨*contract, agreement, etc.*⟩ run
out

Aus·läufer *der* **(a)** (Geogr.) foothill
usu. in pl.
(b) (Met.) ⟨*eines Hochs*⟩ ridge; ⟨*eines Tiefs*⟩
trough

aus|legen *tr. V.* **(a)** (hinlegen) lay out; display ⟨*goods, exhibits*⟩
(b) etw. mit Fliesen/Teppichboden ~: tile/ carpet sth.
(c) (leihen) lend
(d) (interpretieren) interpret; **etw. falsch** ~: misinterpret sth.

Auslegung *die;* ~, ~en interpretation

aus|leihen *unr. tr. V.* ▶ LEIHEN

aus|liefern *tr. V.* **(a)** jmdm. etw. *od.* etw. an jmdn. ~: hand sth. over to sb.
(b) *auch itr.* (Kaufmannsspr.: liefern) deliver

Aus·lieferung *die* **(a)** (Übergabe) handing over; (an ein Land) extradition; **jmds.** ~ **fordern** demand that sb. be handed over/extradited
(b) (Kaufmannsspr.: Lieferung) delivery

Auslieferungs-: ~**antrag** *der* application for extradition; ~**lager** *das* (Wirtsch.) distribution centre

aus|loggen *refl. V.* (DV) log off *or* out

aus|löschen *tr. V.* **(a)** extinguish
(b) (beseitigen) erase ⟨*drawing, writing*⟩

aus|losen *tr. V.* etw. ~: draw lots for sth.

aus|lösen *tr. V.* **(a)** trigger ⟨*mechanism, device, alarm, etc.*⟩; release ⟨*camera shutter*⟩
(b) provoke ⟨*discussion, anger, laughter, reaction, outrage, heart attack*⟩; cause ⟨*sorrow, horror, surprise, disappointment, panic, war*⟩; excite, arouse ⟨*interest, enthusiasm*⟩

Auslöser *der;* ~s, ~ (Fot.) shutter release

aus|machen *tr. V.* **(a)** (ugs.) put out ⟨*light, fire, cigarette, candle*⟩; switch off ⟨*television, radio, hi-fi*⟩; turn off ⟨*gas*⟩
(b) (vereinbaren) agree [on]; ~, **dass** ...: agree that ...
(c) (auszeichnen, kennzeichnen) make up
(d) wenig/nichts/viel ~: make little/no/a great difference
(e) das macht mir nichts aus I don't mind

Aus·maß *das* **(a)** (Größe) size
(b) (Grad) extent

aus|messen *unr. tr. V.* measure up

Aus·nahme *die;* ~, ~n exception; **mit** ~ **von** with the exception of; **bei jmdm. eine** ~ **machen** make an exception in sb.'s case

Ausnahme-: ~**erscheinung** *die* exceptional phenomenon; ~**zustand** *der* state of emergency

ausnahms-: ~**los** 1 *Adj.* unanimous ⟨*approval, agreement*⟩; 2 *adv.* without exception; ~**weise** *Adv.* by way of an exception; **Dürfen wir mitkommen? – Ausnahmsweise [ja]** May we come too? – Yes, just this once

aus|nehmen *unr. tr. V.* **(a)** gut ⟨*fish, rabbit, chicken*⟩
(b) (ausschließen von) exclude; (gesondert behandeln) make an exception of

aus|nüchtern *tr., itr., refl. V.* sober up

Ausnüchterung *die;* ~, ~en sobering up; **jmdm. zur** ~ **auf die Wache bringen** take sb. to the [police] station to sober up

Ausnüchterungs·zelle *die* drying-out cell

aus|nutzen, (bes. südd., österr.)
aus|nützen *tr. V.* **(a)** take advantage of
(b) (ausbeuten) exploit

Aus·nutzung *die,* (bes. südd., österr.)
Aus·nützung *die;* ~: use; (Ausbeutung) exploitation; **unter voller** ~ **einer Sache** (*Gen.*) making full use of sth.

aus|packen 1 *tr., itr. V.* unpack; (auswickeln) unwrap
2 *itr. V.* (ugs.) (Geheimnisse verraten) talk (coll.); squeal (sl.)

aus|pressen *tr. V.* squeeze out ⟨*juice*⟩; squeeze ⟨*orange, lemon*⟩; (keltern) press ⟨*grapes etc.*⟩

aus|probieren *tr. V.* try out

Aus-puff *der* exhaust

Auspuffgase *Pl.* exhaust fumes *pl.*

aus|radieren *tr. V.* rub out; erase

aus|rangieren *tr. V.* (ugs.) throw out; discard; scrap ⟨*vehicle, machine*⟩; **ausrangierte Fahrzeuge** scrap vehicles

aus|rasten *itr. V.; mit sein* (Technik) disengage; **er rastete aus, es rastete bei ihm aus** (fig. salopp) something snapped in him

aus|rauben *tr. V.* rob

aus|räuchern *tr. V.* (auch fig.) smoke out; fumigate ⟨*room*⟩

aus|räumen 1 *tr. V.* **(a)** clear out **(aus of)**
(b) (fig.) clear up; dispel ⟨*prejudice, suspicion, misgivings*⟩
2 *itr. V.* clear everything out

aus|rechnen *tr. V.* work out; **das kannst du dir leicht** ~ (ugs.) you can easily work that out [for yourself]

Aus-rede *die* excuse

aus|reden 1 *itr. V.* finish [speaking]
2 *tr. V.* jmdm. etw. ~: talk sb. out of sth.

aus|reichen *itr. V.* be enough *or* sufficient (**zu** for)

ausreichend 1 *Adj.* sufficient; enough; (als Note) fair
2 *adv.* sufficiently

Aus-reise *die:* jmdm. die ~ **verweigern** refuse sb. permission to leave [the/a country]; **vor/bei der** ~: before/when leaving the country

Ausreise·antrag *der* application to leave the country; application for an exit visa

aus|reißen 1 *unr. tr. V.* tear out; pull out ⟨*plants, weeds*⟩
2 *unr. itr. V.; mit sein* **(a)** (sich lösen) come off
(b) (ugs.: weglaufen) run away (*Dat.* from)

aus|renken *tr. V.* dislocate

aus|richten *tr. V.* **(a)** jmdm. etw. ~: tell sb. sth.
(b) (einheitlich anordnen) line up
(c) (erreichen) achieve

aus|rollen *tr. V.* roll out

aus|rotten tr. V. eradicate

Aus-ruf der cry

aus|rufen unr. tr. V. (a) call out; „Schön!"
rief er aus 'Lovely', he exclaimed
(b) (offiziell verkünden) proclaim; declare ‹state
of emergency›
(c) (zum Kauf anbieten) cry

Ausrufe-zeichen das exclamation mark

aus|ruhen refl., itr. V. have a rest; [sich]
ein wenig/richtig ~: rest a little/have a good
rest; **ausgeruht sein** be rested

aus|rüsten tr. V. equip

Aus-rüstung die (a) equipping
(b) (Gegenstände) equipment no pl.

Ausrüstungs-gegenstand der item
of equipment

aus|rutschen itr. V.; mit sein slip

aus|säen tr. (auch itr.) V. (auch fig.) sow

Aus-sage die statement

aussage-, Aussage-: ~kraft
die meaningfulness; (Ausdruckskraft)
expressiveness; ~kräftig Adj.
meaningful; (ausdruckskräftig) expressive

aus|sagen 1 tr. V. (a) say
(b) (vor Gericht, vor der Polizei) state; (unter Eid)
testify
2 itr. V. make a statement; (unter Eid) testify

aus|saugen regelm. (geh. auch unr.) tr. V.
(a) suck out (aus of); (leer saugen) suck dry
(b) (fig.: ausbeuten) jmdn./etw. ~: bleed
sb./sth. [white]; jmdn. bis aufs Blut od. Mark
~: bleed sb. white

aus|schaben tr. V. (a) scrape out
(b) (Med.) remove; (mit der Kürette) curette

aus|schalten tr. V. (a) switch or turn off
(b) (fig.) eliminate; exclude ‹emotion,
influence›; dismiss ‹doubt, objection›; shut
out ‹feeling, thought›

Aus-schank der; ~[e]s serving

Aus-schau die: nach jmdm./etw. ~ halten
keep a lookout for sb./sth.

aus|schauen itr. V. nach jmdm./etw.
~: look out for sb./sth.

aus|scheiden 1 unr. itr. V.; mit sein
(a) aus etw. ~: leave sth.; aus dem Amt
~: leave office
(b) (Sport) be eliminated
(c) diese Möglichkeit/dieser Kandidat
scheidet aus this possibility/candidate has
to be ruled out
2 unr. tr. V. (Physiol.) excrete ‹waste›;
eliminate, expel ‹poison›; exude ‹sweat›

Aus-scheidung die (a) (Physiol.)
▶ AUSSCHEIDEN 2: excretion; elimination;
expulsion; exudation; ~en (Ausgeschiedenes)
excreta
(b) (Sport) qualifier

aus|schenken tr. V. serve

aus|scheren itr. V.; mit sein pull out

aus|schildern tr. V. signpost

aus|schimpfen tr. V. jmdn. ~: tell sb. off

aus|schlachten tr. V. (a) (ugs.: brauchbare
Teile ausbauen aus) cannibalize ‹machine,
vehicle›; break ‹vehicle› for spares
(b) (ugs. abwertend: ausnutzen) exploit; etw.
politisch ~: make political capital out of sth.

aus|schlafen 1 unr. itr., refl. V. have a
good sleep
2 unr. tr. V. seinen Rausch ~: sleep off the
effects of alcohol

Aus-schlag der (a) (Hautausschlag) rash
(b) (eines Zeigers, einer Waage) deflection; (eines
Pendels) swing; den ~ geben (fig.) tip the
scales (fig.)

aus|schlagen 1 unr. tr. V. (a) knock out
(b) (ablehnen) turn down
2 unr. itr. V. (a) ‹horse› kick
(b) ‹needle, pointer› be deflected, swing
(c) (sprießen) come out [in bud]

ausschlag-gebend Adj. decisive

aus|schließen unr. tr. V. (a) (ausstoßen)
expel (aus from)
(b) (nicht teilnehmen lassen) exclude (aus from)
(c) (fig.) rule out ‹possibility›; jeden Irrtum
~: rule out all possibility of error
(d) (aussperren) lock out

aus-schließlich /od. '-'--, -'--/ 1 Adj.
exclusive
2 Adv. exclusively
3 Präp. mit Gen. excluding

Ausschließlichkeit die;
~: exclusiveness

Aus-schluss, *Aus-schluß der
exclusion (von from); (aus einer Gemeinschaft)
expulsion (aus from); unter ~ der
Öffentlichkeit with the public excluded;
(Rechtsw.) in camera

aus|schmücken tr. V. deck out

aus|schneiden unr. tr. V. cut out; (DV)
cut

Aus-schnitt der (a) (Zeitungsausschnitt)
cutting; clipping
(b) (Halsausschnitt) neck; ein tiefer ~: a
plunging neckline
(c) (Teil) part; (eines Textes) excerpt; (eines
Films) clip; (Bildausschnitt) detail

aus|schreiben unr. tr. V. (a) (nicht
abgekürzt schreiben) etw. ~: write sth. out in
full
(b) (ausstellen) make out ‹cheque, invoice,
receipt›
(c) (bekannt geben) call ‹election, meeting›;
advertise ‹flat, job›; put ‹supply order etc.›
out to tender

Aus-schreibung die ▶ AUSSCHREIBEN C:
calling; advertisement; invitation to tender

Ausschreitungen Pl. acts of violence

Aus-schuss, *Aus-schuß der
committee

aus|schütten tr. V. tip out ‹water, sand,
coal, etc.›; (ausleeren) empty ‹bucket, bowl,
container›

---

ausschweifend ① Adj. wild ⟨imagination, emotion, hope, desire, orgy⟩; extravagant ⟨idea⟩; riotous, wild ⟨enjoyment⟩; dissolute ⟨life, person⟩ ② adv. ~ leben lead a dissolute life

Ausschweifung die; ~, ~en (im Genießen) dissolution

aus|sehen unr. itr. V. look ⟨wie like⟩; **so siehst du aus!** (ugs.) that's what you think!

Aussehen das; ~s appearance

***aus|sein** unr. itr. V.; mit sein; nur im Inf. und Part. zusammengeschrieben **(a)** ⟨play, film, war⟩ be over; **wann ist die Vorstellung aus?** what time does the performance end?; **die Schule ist aus** school is out **(b)** ⟨fire, candle, etc.⟩ be out **(c)** ⟨radio, light, etc.⟩ be off

außen Adv. outside; **die Vase ist ~ bemalt** the vase is painted on the outside; **das Fenster geht nach ~ auf** the window opens outwards; **von ~:** from the outside

außen-, Außen-: ~**dienst** der: im ~dienst sein od. arbeiten, ~dienst machen od. haben be working out of the office; ⟨salesman⟩ be on the road; ~**handel** der foreign trade no art.; ~**handels·bilanz** die balance of trade; ~**minister** der, ~**ministerin** die Foreign Minister; ~**ministerium** das Foreign Ministry; ~**politik** die foreign politics sing.; ~**politisch** ① Adj. ⟨question⟩ relating to foreign policy; ② adv. as regards foreign policy; ~**seite** die outside

Außenseiter der; ~s, ~, **Außenseiterin** die; ~, ~nen outsider

Außen: ~**spiegel** der exterior mirror; ~**stände** Pl. outstanding debts or accounts; ~**wand** die external or outside wall; ~**welt** die outside world

außer ① Präp. mit Dat. **(a)** (abgesehen von) apart from; aside from (Amer.) **(b)** (außerhalb von) out of; ~ **sich sein** be beside oneself (vor + Dat. with) **(c)** (zusätzlich zu) in addition to ② Präp. mit Akk. ~ **sich geraten** become beside oneself (vor + Dat. with) ③ Konj. except

äußer... Adj. outer; outside ⟨pocket⟩; outlying ⟨district, area⟩; external ⟨injury, form, circumstances, cause, force⟩; outward ⟨appearance, similarity, effect, etc.⟩; foreign ⟨affairs⟩

außer·dem /auch: --'-/ Adv. as well; (überdies) besides

Äußere das; Adj. Dekl. [outward] appearance

außer-: ~**ehelich** ① Adj. extra-marital; illegitimate ⟨child, birth⟩; ② adv. outside marriage; ~**gewöhnlich** ① Adj. **(a)** unusual; **(b)** (das Gewohnte übertreffend) exceptional; ② adv. **(a)** unusually; **(b)** (sehr) exceptionally; ~**halb** Präp. mit Gen. outside

äußerlich ① Adj. external ⟨use, injury⟩; outward ⟨appearance, calm, similarity, etc.⟩

② adv.: s. Adj.: externally; outwardly

Äußerlichkeit die; ~, ~en formality; (Unwesentliches) minor point

äußern ① tr. V. express, voice ⟨opinion, view, criticism, reservations, disapproval, doubt⟩; express ⟨wish⟩; voice ⟨suspicion⟩ ② refl. V. **(a)** sich über etw. (Akk.) ~: give one's view on sth. **(b)** ⟨illness⟩ manifest itself (in + Dat., durch in)

außer-: ~**ordentlich** ① Adj. **(a)** extraordinary; **(b)** (das Gewohnte übertreffend) exceptional; ② adv. (sehr) exceptionally; extremely ⟨pleased, relieved⟩; ~**schulisch** Adj. outside the school postpos.

äußerst Adv. extremely

äußerst... Adj. **(a)** extreme **(b)** (letztmöglich) latest possible ⟨date, deadline⟩; (höchst...) highest ⟨price⟩; (niedrigst...) lowest ⟨price⟩ **(c)** (schlimmst...) worst

außerstande Adv. ~ sein, etw. zu tun (nicht befähigt) be unable to do sth.; (nicht in der Lage) not be in a position to do sth.

Äußerung die; ~, ~en comment

aus|setzen ① tr. V. **(a)** expose (Dat. to); **Belastungen ausgesetzt sein** be subject to strains **(b)** (sich selbst überlassen) abandon ⟨baby, animal⟩; (auf einer einsamen Insel) maroon **(c)** an jmdm./etw. etwas auszusetzen haben find fault with sb./sth. ② itr. V. **(a)** (aufhören) stop; ⟨engine, machine⟩ cut out **(b)** (pausieren) ⟨player⟩ miss a turn; **mit der Arbeit/dem Training [ein paar Wochen] ~:** stop work/training [for a few weeks]

Aus·sicht die **(a)** view (auf + Akk. of) **(b)** (fig.) prospect; ~ **auf etw.** (Akk.) **haben, etw. in ~ haben** have the prospect of sth.

aussichts-, Aussichts-: ~**los** ① Adj. hopeless; ② adv. hopelessly; ~**losigkeit** die; ~~: hopelessness; ~**punkt** der vantage point; ~**reich** Adj. promising; ~**turm** der lookout tower

Aus·siedler der (Auswanderer) emigrant; (Evakuierter) evacuee; (Umsiedler) resettled person

Aussiedler·heim das resettlement hostel (for German nationals and ethnic Germans from Eastern europe)

Aussiedlerin, die ▶ AUSSIEDLER

aus|sortieren tr. V. sort out

aus|spannen itr. V. take or have a break

aus|sparen tr. V. leave ⟨line etc.⟩ blank; (fig.) leave out; omit

Aussparung die; ~, ~en **(a)** (das Aussparen) leaving blank **(b)** (Stelle) gap

aus|sperren ① tr. V. lock out; shut ⟨animal⟩ out ② itr. V. lock the workforce out ⋯⟶

Aus·sperrung *die* lockout

aus|spielen *tr. V.* **(a)** *auch itr.* (Kartenspiel) lead

(b) jmdn./etw. gegen jmdn./etw. ~: play sb./sth. off against sb./sth.

Aus·sprache *die* **(a)** pronunciation
(b) (Gespräch) discussion

aus|sprechen ① *unr. tr. V.*
(a) pronounce
(b) (ausdrücken) express; voice ⟨suspicion, request⟩
② *unr. refl. V.* **(a)** sich lobend/missbilligend *usw.* über jmdn./etw. ~: speak highly/disapprovingly of *etc.* sb./sth.
(b) (offen sprechen) say what's on one's mind; sich bei jmdm. ~: have a heart-to-heart talk with sb.
(c) (Strittiges klären) talk things out (**mit** with)
③ *unr. itr. V.* (zu Ende sprechen) finish [speaking]

Aus·spruch *der* remark

aus|spucken ① *itr. V.* spit
② *tr. V.* spit out

aus|spülen *tr. V.* rinse out

Aus·stand *der* strike

aus|statten /ˈaʊsʃtatn̩/ *tr. V.* provide (**mit** with); (mit Gerät) equip; (mit Möbeln, Teppichen, Gardinen usw.) furnish

Ausstattung *die;* ~, ~en
(a) ▶ AUSSTATTEN provision; equipping; furnishing
(b) (Ausrüstung) equipment; (Innenausstattung eines Autos) trim
(c) (Einrichtung) furnishings *pl.*

aus|stehen ① *unr. itr. V.* noch ~ ⟨debt⟩ be outstanding; ⟨decision⟩ be still to be taken; ⟨solution⟩ be still to be found
② *unr. tr. V.* ich kann ihn/das nicht ~: I can't stand him/it

aus|steigen *unr. itr. V.;* **(a)** *mit sein* get out; (aus einem Zug, Bus) get off
(b) (ugs.: sich nicht mehr beteiligen) ~ aus opt out of; give up ⟨show business, job⟩; leave ⟨project⟩
(c) (ugs.: der Gesellschaft den Rücken kehren) drop out

Aussteiger *der;* ~s, ~, **Aussteigerin** *die;* ~, ~nen (ugs.) dropout (coll.)

aus|stellen *tr. V.* **(a)** put on display; display; (im Museum, auf einer Messe) exhibit
(b) (ausfertigen) make out ⟨cheque, prescription, receipt, bill⟩; issue ⟨visa, passport, certificate⟩; einen Scheck auf jmdn. ~: make out a cheque to sb.
(c) (ugs.: ausschalten) switch off ⟨cooker, radio, heating, engine⟩

Aus·stellung *die* **(a)** exhibition
(b) ▶ AUSSTELLEN B: making out; issuing

Ausstellungs-: ~**gelände** *das* exhibition site; ~**katalog** *der* exhibition catalogue

aus|sterben *unr. itr. V.; mit sein* die out; ⟨species⟩ become extinct; vom Aussterben bedroht sein be threatened with extinction

Aus·steuer *die* trousseau (consisting mainly of household linen)

Ausstieg *der:* ~[e]s, ~e **(a)** exit
(b) (ugs.) opting out (**aus** of); der ~ aus einem Projekt/aus der Atomenergie leaving a project/abandoning nuclear energy

aus|stopfen *tr. V.* stuff

Aus·stoß *der* (Wirtsch.) output

aus|stoßen *unr. tr. V.* **(a)** expel; give off, emit ⟨gas, fumes, smoke⟩
(b) give ⟨cry, whistle, laugh, sigh, etc.⟩; let out ⟨cry, scream, yell⟩; utter ⟨curse, threat, etc.⟩

aus|strahlen ① *tr. V.* **(a)** (auch fig.) radiate; ⟨lamp⟩ give out ⟨light⟩
(b) (Rundf., Ferns.) broadcast
② *itr. V.* **(a)** radiate; ⟨light⟩ be given out; (fig.) ⟨pain⟩ spread
(b) auf jmdn./etw. ~ (fig.) communicate itself to sb./influence sth.

Aus·strahlung *die* (fig.) charisma

aus|strecken ① *tr. V.* stretch out; put out ⟨feelers⟩
② *refl. V.* stretch out

aus|streichen *unr. tr. V.* cross out

aus|strömen *itr. V.; mit sein* pour out; ⟨gas, steam⟩ escape

aus|suchen *tr. V.* choose; pick

Aus·tausch *der* **(a)** exchange; im ~ für od. gegen in exchange for
(b) (das Ersetzen) replacement (**gegen** with)

aus|tauschen *tr. V.* **(a)** exchange (**gegen** for)
(b) (ersetzen) replace (**gegen** with)

Austausch-: ~**motor** *der* replacement engine; ~**schüler** *der,* ~**schülerin** *die* exchange pupil *or* student

aus|teilen *tr. V.* distribute (**an** + Akk. to); (aushändigen) hand out ⟨books, post, etc.⟩ (**an** + Akk. to); give ⟨orders⟩; deal [out] ⟨cards⟩; give out ⟨marks, grades⟩; serve ⟨food etc.⟩

Auster *die;* ~, ~n oyster

aus|tragen *unr. tr. V.* **(a)** deliver ⟨newspapers, post⟩
(b) ⟨pregnant woman⟩ carry ⟨child⟩ to full term; (nicht abtreiben) have ⟨child⟩
(c) (ausfechten) settle ⟨conflict, differences⟩; fight out ⟨battle⟩

Australien /aʊsˈtraːli̯ən/ ⟨das⟩ ~s Australia

Australier *der;* ~s, ~, **Australierin** *die;* ~, ~nen Australian

australisch *Adj.* Australian

aus|treiben *unr. tr. V.* **(a)** exorcize, cast out ⟨evil spirit, demon⟩
(b) jmdm. etw. ~: cure sb. of sth.

aus|treten ① *unr. tr. V.* **(a)** tread out ⟨spark, cigarette end⟩; trample out ⟨fire⟩
(b) (bahnen) tread out ⟨path⟩

---

*alte Schreibung – vgl. Hinweis auf S. x

(c) wear out ⟨*shoes*⟩
2 *unr. itr. V.; mit sein* **(a)** (ugs.: zur Toilette gehen) pay a call (coll.)
(b) aus etw. ~ (ausscheiden) leave sth.

aus|trinken *tr. V.* drink up ⟨*drink*⟩; finish ⟨*glass, cup, etc.*⟩

Aus·tritt *der* leaving

aus|trocknen **1** *tr. V.* dry out; dry up ⟨*river bed, marsh*⟩
2 *itr. V.; mit sein* dry out; ⟨*river bed, pond, etc.*⟩ dry up; ⟨*skin, hair*⟩ become dry

aus|üben *tr. V.* practise ⟨*art, craft*⟩; follow ⟨*profession*⟩; carry on ⟨*trade*⟩; do ⟨*job*⟩; hold ⟨*office*⟩; wield ⟨*power, right, control*⟩

Aus·verkauf *der* sale

ausverkauft *Adj.* sold out

Aus·wahl *die* **(a)** choice
(b) (Sortiment) range; **viel/wenig ~ haben** have a wide/limited selection (**an** + *Dat.*, **von** of)

aus|wählen *tr. V.* choose (**aus** from)

Aus·wanderer *der,* **Aus·wanderin** *die* emigrant

aus|wandern *itr. V.; mit sein* emigrate

Aus·wanderung *die* emigration

auswärtig *Adj.* **(a)** non-local
(b) (das Ausland betreffend) foreign

auswärts *Adv.* **(a)** (nach außen) outwards
(b) (nicht zu Hause) ⟨*sleep*⟩ away from home; **~ essen** eat out
(c) (nicht am Ort) in another town; (Sport) away

Auswärts·spiel *das* (Sport) away match

aus|waschen *unr. tr. V.* wash out

aus|wechseln *tr. V.* **(a)** change (**gegen** + *Akk.* for)
(b) (ersetzen) replace (**gegen** with); (Sport) substitute ⟨*player*⟩

Aus·weg *der* way out (**aus** of)

ausweg·los **1** *Adj.* hopeless
2 *adv.* hopelessly

Ausweglosigkeit *die; ~:* hopelessness

aus|weichen *unr. itr. V.; mit sein* get out of the way (*Dat.* of); (Platz machen) make way (*Dat.* for); **einem Schlag/Angriff ~:** dodge a blow/evade an attack; **dem Feind ~:** avoid [contact with] the enemy; **einer Frage ~:** evade a question; **eine ~de Antwort** an evasive answer

Ausweich·manöver *das* evasive manœuvre

aus|weinen *refl. V.* have a good cry; **sie hat sich bei mir darüber ausgeweint** (ugs.) she had a good cry on my shoulder about it

Ausweis *der; ~es, ~e* card; (Personalausweis) identity card

aus|weisen **1** *unr. tr. V.* **(a)** expel (**aus** from)
(b) jmdn. als etw. ~: show that sb. is/was sth.
2 *unr. refl. V.* prove *or* establish one's identity [by showing one's papers]; **können Sie sich ~?** do you have any means of

identification?

Ausweis·papiere *Pl.* identity papers

Aus·weisung *die* expulsion (**aus** from)

aus|weiten *tr. V.* stretch

aus·wendig *Adv.* **etw. ~ können/lernen** know/learn sth. [off] by heart

aus|werfen *unr. tr. V.* **(a)** cast ⟨*net, anchor, rope, line, etc.*⟩
(b) (herausschleudern) throw out ⟨*sparks*⟩; ⟨*volcano*⟩ eject, spew out ⟨*lava, ash, etc.*⟩; eject ⟨*cartridge case*⟩

aus|werten *tr. V.* analyse and evaluate

Aus·wertung *die* analysis and evaluation

aus|wildern *tr. V.* (bes. Jägerspr.) return ⟨*animal*⟩ to the wild

aus|wirken *refl. V.* have an effect (**auf** + *Akk.* on); **sich günstig ~:** have a favourable effect

Aus·wirkung *die* effect (**auf** + *Akk.* on)

Aus·wuchs *der* **(a)** (Wucherung) growth; excrescence (Med., Bot.)
(b) (fig.) unhealthy product; (Exzess) excess

aus|wuchten *tr. V.* (Technik) **die Räder ~:** balance the wheels

aus|zahlen **1** *tr. V.* **(a)** pay out ⟨*money*⟩
(b) pay off ⟨*employee, worker*⟩; buy out ⟨*business partner*⟩
2 *refl. V.* pay

aus|zählen *tr. V.* **(a)** count [up] ⟨*votes etc.*⟩
(b) (Boxen) count out

aus|zeichnen *tr. V.* **(a)** (mit einem Preisschild) mark
(b) (ehren) honour

Aus·zeichnung *die* **(a)** (von Waren) marking
(b) (Ehrung) honouring; (Orden) decoration; (Preis) award

Auszieh·couch *die* sofa bed

aus|ziehen **1** *unr. tr. V.* **(a)** pull out ⟨*couch*⟩; extend ⟨*table, tripod, etc.*⟩
(b) (ablegen) take off ⟨*clothes*⟩
(c) (entkleiden) undress; **sich ~:** get undressed
2 *unr. itr. V.; mit sein* move out (**aus** of)

Auszubildende *der/die; adj. Dekl.* (bes. Amtsspr.) trainee; (im Handwerk) apprentice

Aus·zug *der* **(a)** (das Ausziehen) move
(b) (Bankw.) statement
(c) (Textpassage) extract

auszugs·weise *Adv.* in extracts *or* excerpts; **etw. ~ lesen** read extracts from sth.

authentisch *Adj.* authentic

Autismus /au'tɪsmʊs/ *der; ~* (Med.) autism

Autist *der; ~en, ~en,* **Autistin** *die; ~, ~nen* autistic

autistisch *Adj.* (Med.) autistic

Auto *das; ~s, ~s* car; automobile (Amer.); **~ fahren** drive; (mitfahren) go in the car

auto-, Auto-: ~bahn *die* motorway (Brit.); expressway (Amer.); **~biografie** /-----'-/ *die* autobiography; ····⟩

~biografisch /----'--/ *Adj.*
autobiographical; **~bombe** *die* car bomb;
~bus *der* ▶ Bus; **~dieb** *der,* **~diebin**
die car thief; **~fähre** *die* car ferry;
~fahren *das;* ~~s driving; motoring;
~fahrer *der,* **~fahrerin** *die* [car]
driver; **~fahrt** *die* drive; **~gramm** /--'-/
das; ~~s, ~~e autograph; **~händler**
der, **~händlerin** *die* car dealer;
~immun·erkrankung *die* autoimmune
disease; **~kino** *das* drive-in cinema
Automat *der;* ~en, ~en **(a)** (Verkaufs~)
[vending] machine; (Spiel~) slot machine
(b) (in der Produktion) robot
Automatik *die;* ~, ~en automatic control
mechanism; (Getriebeautomatik) automatic
transmission
automatisch (auch fig.) **1** *Adj.* automatic
2 *adv.* automatically
automatisieren *tr. V.* automate
Automatisierung *die;* ~, ~en
automation
auto-, Auto-: **~mobil** /---'-/ *das;* ~~s,
~~e (geh.) motor car; automobile (Amer.);
~nom /--'-/ **1** *Adj.* autonomous; **2** *adv.*
autonomously; **~nomie** /---'-/ *die;* ~~,
~~n autonomy; **~nummer** *die* [car]
registration number; **~pilot** *der* (Flugw.)
autopilot
Autopsie /autɔ'psi:/ *die;* ~, ~n post

mortem [examination]
Autor *der;* ~s, ~en author
Auto-: **~radio** *das* car radio; **~reifen**
der car tyre; **~reise·zug** *der* Motorail
train (Brit.); auto train (Amer.); **~reparatur**
die car repair; repair to the/a car
Autorin *die;* ~, ~nen authoress; author
autoritär *Adj.* authoritarian
Autoritarismus /autorita'rɪsmʊs/ *der;* ~
authoritarianism
Autorität *die;* ~, ~en authority
Auto-: **~schalter** *der* drive-in
counter; **~schlange** *die* queue of cars;
~schlüssel *der* car key; **~skooter**
/-sku:tɐ/ *der;* ~~s, ~~: dodgem; bumper
car; **~stopp** *der* hitch-hiking; per
~stopp fahren, ~stopp machen hitch-
hike; **~telefon** *das* car telephone; **~tür**
die car door; **~unfall** *der* car accident;
~vermietung *die* car rental firm;
~verwerter *der,* **~verwerterin**
die car breaker; **~verwertung** *die* car
breaker's [yard]; **~wäsche** *die* car wash;
~werkstatt *die* garage
Avocado /avo'ka:do/ *die;* ~, ~s avocado
[pear]
Axt *die;* ~, Äxte axe
Azalee /atsa'le:ə/ *die;* ~, ~n azalea
Azubi *der;* ~s, ~s/*die;* ~, ~s (ugs.)
▶ AUSZUBILDENDE

Bb

b, B /be:/ *das;* ~, ~ **(a)** (Buchstabe) b/B
(b) (Musik) [key of] B flat
B *Abk.* = **Bundesstraße** ≈ A (Brit.)
Baby /'be:bi/ *das;* ~s, ~s baby
Baby·sitter /'be:bisɪtɐ/ *der;* ~s, ~;
Baby·sitterin *die;* ~, ~: babysitter
Bach *der;* ~[e]s, Bäche **(a)** stream; brook
(b) (Rinnsal) stream [of water]
Back·blech *das* baking sheet
Back·bord *das* (Seew., Luftf.) port [side]
Backe *die;* ~, ~n cheek
backen **1** *unr. itr. V.* bake
2 *unr. tr. V.* **(a)** bake
(b) (bes. südd.) ▶ BRATEN
Backen·zahn *der* molar
Bäcker *der;* ~s, ~: baker; **er ist ~:** he is a
baker; **zum/beim ~:** to the/at the baker's
Bäckerei *die;* ~, ~en baker's [shop]
Bäckerin *die;* ~, ~nen baker
Back-: **~fisch** *der* fried fish (*in*

breadcrumbs); **~form** *die* baking tin (Brit.);
baking pan (Amer.); **~hähnchen** *das,*
~hendl *das* (österr.), **~huhn** *das* fried
chicken (*in breadcrumbs*); **~ofen** *der* oven;
~pulver *das* baking powder; **~stein**
der brick; **~waren** *Pl.* bread, cakes, and
pastries
Bad *das;* ~[e]s, Bäder **(a)** bath; (das
Schwimmen) swim; (im Meer usw.) bathe; **ein
~ nehmen** (geh.) take a bath; (schwimmen) go
for a swim; (im Meer usw.) bathe
(b) (Badezimmer) bathroom; **ein Zimmer mit
~:** a room with [private] bath
(c) (Schwimm~) [swimming] pool
(d) (Heil~) spa; (See~) [seaside] resort
Bade-: **~anzug** *der* bathing costume;
~hose *die* bathing trunks *pl.;* **~mantel**
der dressing gown; bathrobe; **~meister**
der, **~meisterin** *die* swimming-pool
attendant; **~mütze** *die* bathing cap
baden **1** *itr. V.* **(a)** have a bath
(b) (schwimmen) bathe; **~ gehen** go for a bathe
2 *tr. V.* bath ⟨*child, patient, etc.*⟩; bathe
⟨*wound, eye, etc.*⟩

---
*old spelling – see note on page x

Baden-Württemberg (*das*); ∼s Baden-Württemberg

Bäder ▸ BAD

Bade-: ∼**strand** *der* bathing beach; ∼**tuch** *das; Pl.* ∼**tücher** bath towel; ∼**wanne** *die* bath[tub]; ∼**wasser** *das* bath water; ∼**zimmer** *das* bathroom

Badminton *das;* ∼s badminton

Bagatelle *die;* ∼, ∼n trifle

Bagger *der;* ∼s, ∼: excavator; (Schwimmbagger) dredger

Bagger-see *der* flooded gravel pit

Bahn *die;* ∼, ∼en (a) (Weg) path (b) (Route) path; (eines Geschosses) trajectory (c) (Sport) track; (für Pferderennen) course (Brit.); track (Amer.); (für einzelne Teilnehmer) lane; (Kegel∼) alley; (Bowling∼) lane (d) (Eisen∼) railways *pl.;* railroad (Amer.); (Zug) train; **jmdn. zur** ∼ **bringen** take sb. to the station; **[mit der]** ∼ **fahren** go by train (e) (Straßen∼) tram; streetcar (Amer.)

bahn-, Bahn-: ∼**beamte** *der,* ∼**beamtin** *die* railway *or* (Amer.) railroad official; ∼**brechend** *Adj.* pioneering; ∼**brecher** *der,* ∼**brecherin** *die;* ∼∼, ∼∼nen pioneer; ∼**bus** *der* railway bus; ∼**damm** *der* railway embankment

bahnen *tr. V.* clear ⟨way, path⟩; **jmdm./ einer Sache einen Weg** ∼ (fig.) pave the way for sb./sth.

Bahn-: ∼**fahrt** *die* train journey; ∼**hof** *der* [railway *or* (Amer.) railroad] station; ∼**reise** *die* train journey; ∼**schranke** *die* level crossing (Brit.) *or* (Amer.) grade crossing barrier/gate; ∼**steig** *der;* ∼∼[e]s, ∼∼e [station] platform; ∼**übergang** *der* level crossing (Brit.); grade crossing (Amer.); ∼**verbindung** *die* train connection

Bahre *die;* ∼, ∼n (a) (Trage) stretcher (b) (Totenbahre) bier

Baiser /bɛˈzeː/ *das;* ∼s, ∼s meringue

Bajonett *das;* ∼[e]s, ∼e bayonet

Bakterie /bakˈteːri̯ə/ *die;* ∼, ∼n bacterium

Balance /baˈlãsə/ *die;* ∼, ∼n balance

balancieren *itr., tr. V.; itr. mit sein* balance

bald *Adv.* (a) soon; (leicht, rasch) quickly; easily; **wirds** ∼? get a move on, will you; **bis** ∼**!** see you soon (b) (ugs.: fast) almost

Baldrian /ˈbaldriaːn/ *der;* ∼s, ∼e valerian

Balkan /ˈbalkaːn/ *der;* ∼s: **der** ∼: the Balkans *pl.;* (Gebirge) the Balkan Mountains *pl.* **auf dem** ∼: in the Balkans

Balken *der;* ∼s, ∼: beam

Balken-diagramm *das* (DV) bar chart

Balkon /balˈkɔŋ, balˈkoːn/ *der;* ∼s, ∼s /balˈkɔŋs/ *od.* ∼e /balˈkoːnə/ (a) balcony (b) (im Theater, Kino) circle

Ball *der;* ∼[e]s, Bälle (a) ball; ∼ **spielen** play ball

(b) (Fest) ball

Ballade *die;* ∼, ∼n ballad

Ballast *der;* ∼[e]s, ∼e ballast

Ballast-stoffe *Pl.* (Med.) roughage *sing.*

ballen [1] *tr. V.* clench ⟨fist⟩ [2] *refl. V.* ⟨fist⟩ clench

Ballen *der;* ∼s, ∼ (a) (Packen) bale (b) (Hand-, Fußballen) ball

Ballerina *die;* ∼, Ballerinen ballerina

Ballett *das;* ∼[e]s, ∼e ballet

Ballett-: ∼**schuh** *der* ballet shoe; ∼**schule** *die* ballet school; ∼**tänzer** *der,* ∼**tänzerin** *die* ballet dancer

Ball-: ∼**junge** *der* ballboy; ∼**kleid** *das* ball gown

Ballon /baˈlɔŋ/ *der;* ∼s, ∼s balloon

Ball-: ∼**saal** *der* ballroom; ∼**spiel** *das* ball game; ∼**spielen** *das;* ∼∼s playing ball *no art.*

Ballungs-gebiet *das* conurbation

Balsam *der;* ∼s, ∼e balsam; (fig.) balm

Balte *der;* ∼n, ∼n, **Baltin** *die;* ∼, ∼nen Balt

Baltikum *das;* ∼s Baltic States *pl.*

baltisch *Adj.* Baltic

Bambus *der;* ∼ *od.* ∼ses, ∼se bamboo

banal *Adj.* (a) banal (b) (gewöhnlich) commonplace

Banane *die;* ∼, ∼n banana

Banause *der;* ∼n, ∼n, **Banausin** *die;* ∼, ∼nen (abwertend) philistine

band *1. u. 3. Pers. Sg. Prät. v.* BINDEN

Band[1] *das;* ∼[e]s, Bänder (a) ribbon; (Haar∼, Hut∼) band; (Schürzen∼) string (b) (Klebe∼, Isolier∼, Ton∼ usw.) tape; **etw. auf** ∼ ⟨*Akk.*⟩ **aufnehmen** tape[-record] sth. (c) ▸ FÖRDERBAND (d) ▸ FLIESSBAND (e) **am laufenden** ∼ (ugs.) nonstop (f) (Anat.) ligament

Band[2] *der;* ∼[e]s, Bände /ˈbɛndə/ volume

Band[3] /bɛnt/ *die;* ∼, ∼s band; (Beat∼, Rock∼ usw.) group

Bande[1] *die;* ∼, ∼n (a) gang (b) (ugs.: Gruppe) mob (coll.)

Bande[2] *die;* ∼, ∼n (Sport) [perimeter] barrier; (mit Reklame) billboards *pl.;* (Billard) cushion

Banden-: ∼**krieg** *der* gang war; ∼**werbung** *die:* advertising on hoardings around the perimeter of a football pitch etc.

Bänder ▸ BAND[1]

Bänder-: ∼**riss**, ***∼**riß** *der* (Med.) torn ligament; ∼**zerrung** *die* (Med.) pulled ligament

bändigen *tr. V.* tame ⟨animal⟩; control ⟨person, anger, urge⟩

Bandit *der;* ∼en, ∼en bandit

Band-scheibe *die* [intervertebral] disc

bang, bange; banger, bangst... od. bänger, bängst...: [1] *Adj.* afraid; ⋯⟫

scared; (besorgt) anxious; **mir ist/wurde**
~ **[zumute]** I am/became scared
② *adv.* anxiously
bangen *itr. V.* be anxious
Bank¹ *die;* ~, **Bänke** bench; (mit Lehne)
bench seat; (Kirchen~) pew; **etw. auf die
lange** ~ **schieben** (ugs.) put sth. off
Bank² *die;* ~, ~**en** bank
Bankett¹ *das;* ~**[e]s,** ~**e** banquet
Bankett² *das;* ~**[e]s,** ~**e** (an Straßen)
shoulder; (unbefestigt) verge
Bank·geheimnis *das* (Wirtsch.) bankers'
duty to maintain confidentiality
Bankier /baŋ'kie:/ *der;* ~**s,** ~**s** banker
Bank-: ~**kauffrau** *die,* ~**kaufmann**
der [qualified] bank/building society/stock
market clerk; ~**konto** *das* bank account;
~**leit·zahl** *die* [bank] sort code; ~**note**
die banknote; bill (Amer.); ~**raub** *der* bank
robbery; ~**räuber** *der,* ~**räuberin** *die*
bank robber
bankrott *Adj.* bankrupt; **Bankrott** *od.*
*~ **gehen** go bankrupt
Bankrott *der;* ~**[e]s,** ~**e** bankruptcy;
~ **machen** go bankrupt; *s. auch* BANKROTT
Bankrott·erklärung *die* declaration of
bankruptcy; (fig.) declaration of [one's own]
failure
Bank-: ~**überfall** *der* bank raid;
~**verbindung** *die* particulars of one's
bank account; ~**wesen** *das* banking
system
Bann *der;* ~**[e]s** (fig. geh.) spell
bar ① *Adj.* cash
② *adv.* in cash; **etw. [in]** ~ **bezahlen** pay for
sth. in cash; pay cash for sth.
Bar *die;* ~, ~**s** bar
Bär *der;* ~**en,** ~**en** bear
Baracke *die;* ~, ~**n** hut
Barbar *der;* ~**en,** ~**en** barbarian
Barbarei *die;* ~, ~**en** (a) (Rohheit)
barbarity
(b) (Kulturlosigkeit) barbarism *no indef. art.*
Barbarin *die;* ~, ~**nen** barbarian
barbarisch ① *Adj.* (a) (roh) barbarous
(b) (unzivilisiert) barbaric
② *adv.* (a) (roh) barbarously
(b) (unzivilisiert) barbarically
Bar·code *der* bar code
Bar·dame *die* barmaid
bären-, Bären-: ~**dienst** *der;* jmdm.
einen ~**dienst erweisen** do sb. a disservice;
~**hunger** *der* (ugs.) einen ~**hunger
haben/kriegen** be famished (coll.) *or* starving
(coll.)/get famished (coll.) *or* ravenous (coll.);
~**markt** *der* (Börsenw.) bear market;
~**stark** *Adj.* as strong as an ox *postpos.*
Barett *das;* ~**[e]s,** ~**e** (eines Geistlichen)
biretta; (eines Richters, Professors) cap;
(Baskenmütze) beret

bar·fuß *indekl. Adj.; nicht attr.* barefooted;
~ **herumlaufen/gehen** run about/go barefoot
barg *1. u. 3. Pers. Sg. Prät. v.* BERGEN
bar-, Bar-: ~**geld** *das* cash; ~**geld·los**
Adj. cashless; ~**hocker** *der* bar stool
Bariton /'ba(:)ritɔn/ *der;* ~**s,** ~**e** baritone
Barkasse *die;* ~, ~**n** launch
barmherzig (geh.) ① *Adj.* merciful
② *adv.* mercifully
Barmherzigkeit *die;* ~ (geh.) mercy
Barock *das od. der;* ~**[s] (a)** baroque
(b) (Zeit) baroque age
Baro·meter *das* barometer
Baron *der;* ~**s,** ~**e** baron; (als Anrede) **[Herr]**
~: ≈ my lord
Baronin *die;* ~, ~**nen** baroness; (als Anrede)
[Frau] ~: ≈ my Lady
Barren *der;* ~**s,** ~ (a) (Gold~, Silber~ usw.)
bar
(b) (Turngerät) parallel bars *pl.*
Barriere /ba'riɛ:rə/ *die;* ~, ~**n** (auch fig.)
barrier
Barrikade *die;* ~, ~**n** barricade
barsch ① *Adj.* curt
② *adv.* curtly
Barsch *der;* ~**[e]s,** ~**e** perch
barst *1. u. 3. Pers. Sg. Prät. v.* BERSTEN
Bart *der;* ~**[e]s,** **Bärte (a)** beard;
(Oberlippen~, Schnurr~) moustache
(b) (von Katzen, Mäusen, Robben) whiskers *pl.*
(c) (am Schlüssel) bit
Barten·wal *der* (Zool.) whalebone whale
bärtig *Adj.* bearded
Bart·wuchs *der* growth of beard
Bar-: ~**zahlung** *die* cash payment;
~**zahlungs·rabatt** *der* cash discount
Basalt *der;* ~**[e]s,** ~**e** basalt
Basar *der;* ~**s,** ~**e** bazaar
Basis *die;* ~, **Basen (a)** (Grundlage) basis
(b) (Math., Archit., Milit.) base
Baske *der;* ~**n,** ~**n** Basque
Basken-: ~**land** *das* Basque region;
~**mütze** *die* beret
Basket·ball /'ba(:)skɛt-/ *der* basketball
Baskin *die;* ~, ~**nen** Basque
Bass, *Baß *der;* **Basses, Bässe** (Musik)
(a) bass
(b) (Instrument) double bass
Bassin /ba'sɛ̃:/ *das;* ~**s,** ~**s** (Schwimmbecken)
pool; (im Garten) pond
Bassist *der;* ~**en,** ~**en** (Musik) (a) (Sänger)
bass
(b) (Instrumentalist) double-bass player;
bassist; (in einer Rockband) bass guitarist
Bassistin *die;* ~, ~**nen** ▶ BASSIST B
Bast *der;* ~**[e]s,** ~**e** bast; (Raffia~) raffia
basta *Interj.* (ugs.) that's enough; **und damit**
~! and that's that!
Bastelei *die;* ~, ~**en; (a)** (Gegenstand) piece
of handicraft work
(b) (ugs.: das Basteln) handicraft work

**alte Schreibung – vgl. Hinweis auf S. x

basteln ① *tr. V.* make
② *itr. V.* make things [with one's hands]
Bastion *die;* ~, ~en bastion
bat *1. u. 3. Pers. Sg. Prät. v.* BITTEN
Bataillon /batal'joːn/ *das;* ~s, ~e (Milit.)
  battalion
Batik *der;* ~s, ~en *od. die;* ~, ~en batik
Batist *der;* ~[e]s, ~e batiste
Batterie *die;* ~, ~n battery
batterie-, Batterie-: ~**betrieb** *der*
  battery operation; ~**betrieben** *Adj.*
  battery-operated; ~**huhn** *das* battery
  chicken; (Henne) battery hen
Batzen *der;* ~s, ~ (ugs.) (a) (Klumpen) lump
  (b) (Menge) pile (coll.)
Bau¹ *der;* ~[e]s, ~ten (a) (Errichtung)
  building; im ~ sein be under construction
  (b) (Gebäude) building
  (c) auf dem ~ arbeiten (Bauarbeiter sein) be in
  the building trade
  (d) (Struktur) structure
Bau² *der;* ~[e]s, ~e (Kaninchenbau) burrow;
  hole; (Fuchsbau) earth
Bau·arbeiten *Pl.* building work *sing.*
Bauch *der;* ~[e]s, Bäuche (auch fig.: von
  Schiffen, Flugzeugen) belly
bauchig *Adj.* bulbous
Bauch-: ~**laden** *der* vendor's
  tray; ~**landung** *die* belly landing;
  ~**nabel** *der* (ugs.) belly button (coll.);
  ~**nabel·piercing** *das* belly-button
  piercing; (Schmuck) belly button stud;
  navel stud; ~**redner** *der,* ~**rednerin**
  die ventriloquist; ~**schmerzen** *Pl.*
  stomach ache *sing.;* ~**speichel·drüse**
  die pancreas; ~**tanz** *der* belly dance;
  ~**tänzerin** *die* belly dancer; ~**weh** *das*
  (ugs.) tummy ache (coll.); stomach ache
Bau·denkmal *das* architectural
  monument
bauen ① *tr. V.* build
  ② *itr. V.* (a) build; wir wollen ~: we want to
  build a house; (bauen lassen) we want to have
  a house built
  (b) auf jmdn./etw. ~ (fig.) rely on sb./sth.
Bauer¹ *der;* ~n, ~n (a) farmer; (mit
  niedrigem sozialem Status) peasant
  (b) (Schachfigur) pawn
  (c) (Kartenspiele) ▶ BUBE
Bauer² *das od. der;* ~s, ~: [bird]cage
Bäuerin *die;* ~, ~nen (a) ▶ BAUER¹ A:
  [lady] farmer; peasant [woman]
  (b) (Frau eines Bauern) farmer's wife
bäuerlich *Adj.* farming *attrib.;* (ländlich)
  rural
Bauern-: ~**haus** *das* farmhouse; ~**hof**
  der farm; ~**markt** *der* farmer's market
bau-, Bau-: ~**fällig** *Adj.* ramshackle;
  unsafe ⟨roof, ceiling⟩; ~**fälligkeit** *die*
  bad state of dilapidation; badly dilapidated
  state; ~**herr** *der,* ~**herrin** *die* client
  (*for whom a house etc. is being built*);

~**jahr** *das* year of construction; (bei
  Autos) year of manufacture; ~**kasten**
  der construction set; (mit Holzklötzen) box
  of bricks; ~**kasten·system** *das* unit
  construction system; ~**klotz** *der* building
  brick; ~**kran** *der* construction crane
baulich *Adj.* structural
Baum *der;* ~[e]s, Bäume tree
Bau-: ~**markt** *der* (Kaufhaus) DIY
  hypermarket; ~**maschine** *die* piece
  of construction plant *or* machinery;
  ~**maschinen** construction plant *sing. or*
  machinery
Bäumchen *das;* ~s, ~ small tree
Bau·meister *der* (hist.) [architect and]
  master builder
baumeln *itr. V.* (ugs.) dangle (an + *Dat.*
  from)
Baum-: ~**schule** *die* tree nursery;
  ~**stamm** *die* tree trunk; ~**sterben** *das;*
  ~s, ~~: dying-off of trees; ~**stumpf**
  der tree stump; ~**wolle** *die* cotton
Bau·platz *der* site for building
bäurisch (abwertend) ① *Adj.* boorish
  ② *adv.* boorishly
Bau·satz *der* kit
Bausch *der;* ~[e]s, ~e *od.* Bäusche
  (a) (Watte~) a wad
  (b) etw. in ~ und Bogen verwerfen/
  verdammen reject/condemn sth. wholesale
bauschen ① *tr. V.* billow ⟨sail, curtains,
  etc.⟩
  ② *refl. V.* ⟨dress, sleeve⟩ puff out; (ungewollt)
  bunch up; (im Wind) ⟨curtain, flag, etc.⟩ billow
  [out]
bauschig *Adj.* puffed ⟨dress⟩; baggy
  ⟨trousers⟩
bau-, Bau-: ~**sparen** *itr. V.; nur
  Inf. gebr.* save with a building society;
  ~**sparkasse** *die* ≈ building society;
  ~**stein** *der* (a) building stone;
  (b) (Bestandteil) element; (Elektronik, DV)
  module; (c) (~klotz) building brick;
  ~**stelle** *die* building site; (beim Straßenbau)
  roadworks *pl.;* ~**stoff** *der* building
  material; ~**teil** *das* component
Bauten *Pl.:* ▶ BAU
Bau-: ~**unternehmer** *der,*
  ~**unternehmerin** *die* building
  contractor; ~**weise** *die* method of
  construction; ~**werk** *das* building; (Brücke,
  Staudamm) structure; ~**wirtschaft** *die*
  building *or* construction industry
Bayer *der;* ~n, ~n **Bayerin** *die;* ~, ~nen
  Bavarian
bay[e]risch *Adj.* Bavarian
Bayern (*das*) ~s Bavaria
Bazille *die;* ~, ~n (ugs.) ▶ BAZILLUS A
Bazillus *der;* ~, Bazillen (a) bacillus
  (b) (fig.) cancer
Bd. *Abk.* = **Band** Vol.
beabsichtigen *tr. V.* intend

beachten *tr. V.* (a) follow ⟨*rule, regulations, instruction*⟩; heed, follow ⟨*advice*⟩; obey ⟨*traffic signs*⟩; observe ⟨*formalities*⟩
(b) (berücksichtigen) take account of; (achten auf) pay attention to

beachtlich ⟦1⟧ *Adj.* considerable
⟦2⟧ *adv.* considerably

Beachtung *die;* ∼ (a) ▸ BEACHTEN A: following; heeding; obeying
(b) (Berücksichtigung) consideration
(c) (Aufmerksamkeit) attention

Beach·volleyball /'bi:tʃ-/ *der* beach volleyball

Beamte *der; adj. Dekl.* official; (Staats∼) [permanent] civil servant; (Kommunal∼) [established] local government officer; (Polizei∼) [police] officer

Beamtin *die;* ∼, ∼**nen** ▸ BEAMTE

beängstigend *Adj.* worrying

beanspruchen *tr. V.* (a) claim; etw. ∼ **können** be entitled to expect sth.
(b) (ausnutzen) make use of ⟨*person, equipment*⟩; take advantage of ⟨*hospitality, services*⟩
(c) (erfordern) demand ⟨*energy, attention, stamina*⟩; take up ⟨*time, space, etc.*⟩

Beanspruchung *die;* ∼, ∼**en** demands *pl.* (*Gen.* on); **die ∼ durch den Beruf** the demands of his/her job

beanstanden *tr. V.* take exception to; (sich beklagen über) complain about

Beanstandung *die;* ∼, ∼**en** complaint

beantragen *tr. V.* apply for

beantworten *tr. V.* answer; reply to ⟨*letter*⟩; return ⟨*greeting*⟩

bearbeiten *tr. V.* (a) deal with; handle ⟨*case*⟩
(b) edit ⟨*text, document*⟩
(c) (adaptieren) adapt (**für** for)

Bearbeitung *die;* ∼, ∼**en** (a) **die ∼ eines Antrags/eines Falles** *usw.* dealing with an application/handling a case *etc.*
(b) (Adaption) adaptation

beaufsichtigen *tr. V.* supervise; look after ⟨*child*⟩

beauftragen *tr. V.* entrust

bebauen *tr. V.* build on; develop

bebaut *Adj.* **ein [dicht] ∼es Gebiet** a densely built-up area; **ein ∼es Gelände** a developed site

Bebauung *die;* ∼, ∼**en** (a) development
(b) (Gebäude) buildings *pl.*

beben *itr. V.* shake

Beben *das;* ∼**s**, ∼: ▸ ERDBEBEN

bebildern *tr. V.* illustrate

Bebilderung *die;* ∼, ∼**en** illustrations *pl.*

Becher *der;* ∼**s**, ∼ (Glas∼, Porzellan∼) glass; tumbler; (Plastik∼) beaker; cup; (Eis∼)

(aus Glas, Metall) sundae dish; (aus Pappe) tub; (Joghurt∼) carton

Becken *das;* ∼**s**, ∼ (a) (Wasch∼) basin; (Abwasch∼) sink; (Toiletten∼) pan
(b) (Anat.) pelvis
(c) *Pl.* (Musik) cymbals

bedacht *Adj.* **auf etw.** (*Akk.*) ∼ **sein** be intent on sth.

bedächtig ⟦1⟧ *Adj.* (a) deliberate; measured ⟨*steps, stride, speech*⟩
(b) (besonnen) thoughtful; well-considered ⟨*words*⟩
⟦2⟧ *adv.* (a) deliberately
(b) (besonnen) thoughtfully

bedanken *refl. V.* say thank you; **sich bei jmdm.** [**für etw.**] ∼: thank sb. [for sth.]

Bedarf *der;* ∼[**e**]**s** need (**an** + *Dat.* of); requirement (**an** + *Dat.* for); (Bedarfsmenge) needs *pl.;* requirements *pl.;* **bei ∼:** if required

bedauerlich *Adj.* regrettable

bedauerlicher·weise *Adv.* regrettably

bedauern *tr., itr. V.* (a) feel sorry for; **sie lässt sich gerne ∼:** she likes being pitied
(b) (schade finden) regret; **ich bedaure sehr, dass …:** I am very sorry that …

Bedauern *das;* ∼**s** regret; **zu meinem ∼:** to my regret

bedauerns·wert *Adj.* (geh.) unfortunate ⟨*person*⟩

bedecken *tr. V.* cover

bedeckt *Adj.* overcast ⟨*sky*⟩

bedenken *unr. V.* (a) consider
(b) (beachten) take into consideration

Bedenken *das;* ∼**s**, ∼ reservation (**gegen** about); **ohne ∼:** without hesitation

bedenken·los ⟦1⟧ *Adj.* unhesitating; (skrupellos) unscrupulous
⟦2⟧ *adv.* without hesitation; (skrupellos) unscrupulously

bedenklich ⟦1⟧ *Adj.* (a) dubious ⟨*methods, transactions, etc.*⟩
(b) (bedrohlich) alarming
⟦2⟧ *adv.* alarmingly

Bedenk·zeit *die* time for reflection

bedeuten *tr. V.* (a) mean; **was soll das ∼?** what does that mean?
(b) (sein) represent; **das bedeutet ein Wagnis** that is being really daring

bedeutend ⟦1⟧ *Adj.* (a) significant; important
(b) (groß) substantial; considerable ⟨*success*⟩
⟦2⟧ *adv.* considerably

Bedeutung *die;* ∼, ∼**en** (a) meaning
(b) (Wichtigkeit) importance

bedeutungs-: ∼**los** *Adj.* insignificant; ∼**voll** ⟦1⟧ *Adj.* (a) significant; (b) (viel sagend) meaningful; meaning ⟨*look*⟩; ⟦2⟧ *adv.* meaningfully

bedienen ⟦1⟧ *tr. V.* (a) serve; **werden Sie schon bedient?** are you being served?
(b) (handhaben) operate ⟨*machine*⟩
⟦2⟧ *itr. V.* serve

---

*old spelling – see note on page x

3 *refl. V.* help oneself; **sich selbst** ~ (im Geschäft, Restaurant usw.) serve oneself
Bedienstete *der/die; adj. Dekl.* (Amtsspr.) employee
Bedienung *die;* ~, ~en **(a)** (das Bedienen) service; ~ **inbegriffen** service included **(b)** (das Handhaben) operation **(c)** (Servierer[in]) waiter/waitress
Bedienungs·anleitung *die* operating instructions *pl.*
bedingen *tr. V.* cause
Bedingung *die;* ~, ~en condition; **unter der** ~, **dass** ...: on condition that ...
bedingungs·los *Adj.* unconditional
bedrängen *tr. V.* **(a)** besiege ⟨*town, fortress, person*⟩; put ⟨*opposing player*⟩ under pressure **(b)** (belästigen) pester
Bedrängnis *die;* ~, ~se (geh.) (innere Not) distress; (wirtschaftliche Not) [great] difficulties *pl.;* **in** ~ **geraten/sein** get into/be in great difficulties *pl.*
bedrohen *tr. V.* threaten; **bedrohte Arten** endangered species
bedrohlich **1** *Adj.* (Unheil verkündend) ominous; (gefährlich) dangerous **2** *adv.* (Unheil verkündend) ominously; (gefährlich) dangerously
Bedrohlichkeit *die;* ~: dangerousness; (einer Krankheit usw.) dangerous nature
Bedrohung *die* threat (*Gen.* to)
bedrucken *tr. V.* print
bedrücken *tr. V.* depress
Beduine *der;* ~n, ~n, **Beduinin** *die;* ~, ~nen Bed[o]uin
bedürfen *unr. itr. V.* jmds./einer Sache ~ (geh.) require *or* need sb./sth.
Bedürfnis *das;* ~ses, ~se need (nach for); **das** ~ **haben, etw. zu tun** feel a need to do sth.
bedürfnislos *Adj.* ⟨*person*⟩ with few [material] needs; modest, simple ⟨*life*⟩; ~ **sein** have few [material] needs
Bedürfnislosigkeit *die;* ~: lack of [material] needs
bedürftig *Adj.* needy
Beef·steak /'bi:f-/ *das* [beef]steak; **deutsches** ~: ≈ beefburger
beehren *tr. V.* (geh.) honour
beeiden *tr. V.* ~, **dass** ...: swear [on oath] that ...; **eine Aussage** ~: swear to the truth of a statement
beeilen *refl. V.* hurry [up (coll.)]
beeindrucken *tr. V.* impress
beeindruckend *Adj.* impressive
beeinflussen *tr. V.* influence
Beeinflussung *die;* ~, ~en influencing
beeinträchtigen *tr. V.* restrict ⟨*sights, freedom*⟩; detract from ⟨*pleasure, enjoyment, value*⟩; spoil ⟨*appetite, good humour*⟩; impair ⟨*quality, reactions, efficiency, vision, hearing*⟩; damage, harm ⟨*sales, reputation*⟩

Beeinträchtigung *die;* ~, ~en
▶ BEEINTRÄCHTIGEN: restriction; detracting (+ *Gen.* from); spoiling; impairment; damage (*Gen.* to)
beenden, beendigen *tr. V.* **(a)** end; finish ⟨*piece of work etc.*⟩; complete ⟨*studies*⟩ **(b)** (DV) quit ⟨*program*⟩
beengen *tr. V.* hinder, restrict ⟨*movements*⟩; (fig.) restrict ⟨*freedom [of action]*⟩; **beengt wohnen** live in cramped surroundings *or* conditions; **sich beengt fühlen** feel cramped
beerben *tr. V.* jmdn. ~: inherit sb.'s estate
beerdigen *tr. V.* bury
Beerdigung *die;* ~, ~en burial; (Trauerfeier) funeral
Beerdigungs·institut *das* [firm *sing.* of] undertakers *pl.*
Beere *die;* ~, ~n berry
Beet *das;* ~[e]s, ~e (Blumenbeet) bed; (Gemüsebeet) plot
befahrbar *Adj.* passable
befahren *unr. tr. V.* **(a)** drive on ⟨*road*⟩; drive across ⟨*bridge*⟩; use ⟨*railway line*⟩; **die Straße ist stark/wenig** ~: the road is heavily/little used; **eine stark** ~**e Straße** a busy road **(b)** sail ⟨*sea*⟩; navigate, sail up/down ⟨*river, canal*⟩
befallen *unr. tr. V.* **(a)** overcome; ⟨*misfortune*⟩ befall; **von Panik/Angst** ~ **werden** be seized with panic/fear **(b)** ⟨*pests*⟩ attack
befangen **1** *Adj.* **(a)** self-conscious ⟨*person*⟩ **(b)** (voreingenommen) biased **2** *adv.* self-consciously
Befangenheit *die;* ~ **(a)** self-consciousness **(b)** (Voreingenommenheit) bias
befassen *refl. V.* **sich mit etw.** ~: occupy oneself with sth.; ⟨*article, book*⟩ deal with sth.; (etw. studieren) study sth.
Befehl *der;* ~[e]s, ~e **(a)** order **(b)** **den** ~ **über jmdn./etw. haben** be in command of sb./sth.
befehlen **1** *unr. tr., itr. V.* order; (Milit.) order; **man befahl ihm zu warten** he was told to wait **2** *unr. itr. V.* **über jmdn./etw.** ~: have command of *or* be in command of sb./sth.
Befehls·haber *der;* ~s, ~ (Milit.) commander
befestigen *tr. V.* **(a)** fix; **etw. an der Wand** ~: fix sth. to the wall **(b)** (haltbar machen) stabilize ⟨*bank, embankment*⟩; make up ⟨*road, path, etc.*⟩ **(c)** (sichern) fortify ⟨*town etc.*⟩; strengthen ⟨*border*⟩
Befestigung *die;* ~, ~en **(a)** fixing **(b)** (Milit.) fortification
befeuchten *tr. V.* moisten; damp ⟨*hair, cloth*⟩

befiehlst, befiehlt 2., 3. Pers. Sg.
Präsens v. BEFEHLEN

befinden unr. refl. V. be

Befinden das; ~s health; (eines Patienten)
condition

befindlich Adj.(a) to be found postpos.;
das in der Kasse ~e Geld the money in
the till
(b) (in einem Zustand) **die im Bau ~en
Häuser** the houses [which are/were] under
construction

Befindlichkeit die; ~, ~en (geh.) state

beflecken tr. V. stain

befohlen 2. Part. v. BEFEHLEN

befolgen tr. V. follow, obey ⟨instruction,
grammatical rule⟩; obey, comply with ⟨law,
regulation⟩; follow ⟨advice, suggestion⟩

Befolgung die; ~ ▶ BEFOLGEN: following;
obedience (Gen. to); compliance (Gen. with)

befördern tr. V. (a) carry; transport
(b) (aufrücken lassen) promote

Beförderung die; ~, ~en (a) carriage;
transport; (von Personen) transport
(b) (das Aufrückenlassen) promotion

befragen tr. V. (a) question (über + Akk.
about)
(b) (konsultieren) ask

Befragung die; ~, ~en (a) questioning
(b) (Konsultation) consultation
(c) (Umfrage) opinion poll

befreien ⒈ tr. V. (a) free; liberate
⟨country, people⟩ (von from)
(b) (freistellen) exempt (von from)
(c) jmdn. von Schmerzen ~: free sb. of pain
⒉ refl. V. free oneself (von from)

Befreier der, **Befreierin** die; ~, ~nen
liberator

Befreiung die; ~ (a) ▶ BEFREIEN 1A:
freeing; liberation
(b) (Freistellung) exemption
(c) die ~ von Schmerzen release from pain

befremden tr. V. jmdn. ~: put sb. off

Befremden das; ~s surprise and
displeasure

befremdlich (geh.) ⒈ Adj. strange; odd
⒉ adv. strangely

befreunden refl. V. ▶ ANFREUNDEN; [gut
od. eng] befreundet sein be [good or close]
friends (mit with)

befriedigen tr. V. (a) satisfy; gratify
⟨lust⟩
(b) (ausfüllen) ⟨job, occupation, etc.⟩ fulfil
(c) (sexuell) satisfy; **sich [selbst]
~**: masturbate

befriedigend ⒈ Adj. satisfactory
⒉ adv. satisfactorily

Befriedigung die; ~ (a) ▶ BEFRIEDIGEN A:
satisfaction; gratification
(b) (Genugtuung) satisfaction

---

*alte Schreibung – vgl. Hinweis auf S. x

befristet Adj. temporary ⟨visa⟩; fixed-term
⟨ban, contract⟩

befruchten tr. V. fertilize ⟨egg⟩; pollinate
⟨flower⟩; impregnate ⟨female⟩; **ein Tier
künstlich ~**: artificially inseminate an
animal

Befruchtung die; ~, ~en ▶ BEFRUCHTEN:
fertilization; pollination; impregnation;
künstliche ~: artificial insemination

Befugnis die; ~, ~se authority

befühlen tr. V. feel

Befund der (bes. Med.) result[s pl.]

befürchten tr. V. fear; **ich befürchte,
dass …**: I am afraid that …

befürworten tr. V. support

begabt Adj. talented; gifted; **hoch ~**:
highly talented or gifted

Begabung die; ~, ~en talent; gift

begann 1. u. 3. Pers. Sg. Prät. v. BEGINNEN

begatten tr. V. mate with; ⟨man⟩ copulate
with; **sich ~**: mate; ⟨persons⟩ copulate

Begattung die; ~, ~en mating; (bei
Menschen) copulation

begeben unr. refl. V. (geh.) proceed; make
one's way; go; **sich zu Bett ~**: retire to bed;
sich an die Arbeit ~: commence work

Begebenheit die; ~, ~en (geh.) event;
occurrence

begegnen itr. V.; mit sein jmdm. ~: meet
sb.; **sich** (Dat.) ~: meet [each other]

Begegnung die; ~, ~en (a) meeting
(b) (Sport) match

begehen unr. tr. V. (a) commit ⟨crime,
adultery, indiscretion, sin, suicide, faux-pas,
etc.⟩; make ⟨mistake⟩; **eine [furchtbare]
Dummheit ~**: do something [really] stupid
(b) (geh.: feiern) celebrate

begehren tr. V. desire

begehrens-wert Adj. desirable

begehrlich ⒈ Adj. greedy
⒉ adv. greedily

begehrt Adj. much sought-after

begeistern ⒈ tr. V. jmdn. [für etw.]
~: fire sb. with enthusiasm [for sth.]
⒉ refl. V. get enthusiastic (für about)

begeisternd Adj. rousing

begeistert ⒈ Adj. enthusiastic (von
about)
⒉ adv. enthusiastically

Begeisterung die; ~: enthusiasm

begeisterungs-, Begeisterungs-:
~fähig Adj. ⟨children, people, etc.⟩ who
are able to get enthusiastic or are capable
of enthusiasm; **~fähigkeit** die capacity
for enthusiasm; **~sturm** der storm of
enthusiastic applause

Begierde die; ~, ~n desire (nach for)

begierig ⒈ Adj. eager
⒉ adv. eagerly

begießen unr. tr. V. water ⟨plants⟩

Beginn *der;* ~[e]s beginning; [gleich] zu ~: [right] at the beginning

beginnen ① *unr. itr. V.* start; begin; **mit dem Bau** ~: start *or* begin building; **dort beginnt der Wald** the forest starts there ② *unr. tr. V.* start; begin; start ⟨*argument*⟩; ~, **etw. zu tun** start to do sth.

beglaubigen *tr. V.* certify

Beglaubigung *die;* ~, ~en certification

begleichen *unr. tr. V.* settle ⟨*bill, debt*⟩; pay ⟨*sum*⟩

Begleit-brief *der* covering *or* accompanying letter

begleiten *tr. V.* accompany; **jmdn. nach Hause** ~: see sb. home

Begleiter *der;* ~s, ~, **Begleiterin** *die;* ~, ~nen companion; (zum Schutz) escort; (Führer[in]) guide

Begleitung *die;* ~, ~en (a) **er bot uns seine** ~ **an** he offered to accompany us; **in** ~ **eines Erwachsenen** accompanied by an adult (b) (Musik) accompaniment

beglückwünschen *tr. V.* congratulate (zu on)

begnadet *Adj.* (geh.) divinely gifted

begnadigen *tr. V.* pardon; reprieve

Begnadigung *die;* ~, ~en reprieving; (Straferlass) pardon; reprieve

begnügen *refl. V.* content oneself

Begonie /be'go:nɪə/ *die;* ~, ~n begonia

begonnen 2. *Part. v.* BEGINNEN

begraben *unr. tr. V.* bury

Begräbnis *das;* ~ses, ~se burial; (~feier) funeral

begreifen ① *unr. tr. V.* understand; **er konnte nicht** ~, **was geschehen war** he could not grasp what had happened ② *itr. V.* understand; **schnell** *od.* **leicht/ langsam** *od.* **schwer** ~: be quick/slow on the uptake

begreiflich *Adj.* understandable

begrenzen *tr. V.* limit, restrict (**auf** + *Akk.* to)

Begriff *der* (a) concept; (Terminus) term (b) (Auffassung) idea; **sich** ⟨*Dat.*⟩ **keinen** ~ **von etw. machen können** not be able to imagine sth.; **ein/kein** ~ **sein** be/not be well known (c) **im** ~ **sein** *od.* **stehen, etw. zu tun** be about to do sth.

begriffs-stutzig *Adj.* (abwertend) obtuse

Begriffsstutzigkeit *die;* ~ (abwertend) obtuseness

begründen *tr. V.* (a) give reasons for (b) (gründen) found; establish ⟨*fame, reputation*⟩

Begründer *der;* ~s, ~, **Begründerin** *die;* ~, ~nen founder

begründet *Adj.* well-founded; reasonable ⟨*demand, objection, complaint*⟩

Begründung *die;* ~, ~en reason[s]; **mit der** ~, **dass** …: on the grounds that …

begrüßen *tr. V.* (a) greet; ⟨*hostess, host*⟩ welcome (b) (fig.) welcome

Begrüßung *die;* ~, ~en greeting; (von Gästen) welcoming; (Zeremonie) welcome (*Gen.* for)

begünstigen *tr. V.* favour

Begünstigung *die;* ~: favouring

begutachten *tr. V.* (a) examine and report on (b) (ugs.) have a look at

Begutachtung *die;* ~, ~en examination

begütert *Adj.* wealthy

begütigen *tr. V.* placate

behaart *Adj.* hairy; **stark** ~ **sein** be covered with hair; **stark** ~**e Beine** very hairy legs

behäbig ① *Adj.* slow and ponderous ② *adv.* slowly and ponderously

behagen *itr. V.* **etw. behagt jmdm.** sb. likes sth.

Behagen *das;* ~s pleasure

behaglich ① *Adj.* comfortable ② *adv.* comfortably

Behaglichkeit *die;* ~: comfortableness

behalten *unr. tr. V.* (a) keep; **etw. für sich** ~: keep sth. to oneself (b) (zurück~) be left with ⟨*scar, defect, etc.*⟩ (c) (sich merken) remember

Behälter *der;* ~s, ~ container; (für Abfälle) receptacle

behämmert *Adj.* (salopp) ▶ BEKLOPPT

behänd, behände ① *Adj.* (geschickt) deft; (flink) nimble ② *adv. s. Adj.:* deftly; nimbly

behandeln *tr. V.* (auch Med.) treat; handle ⟨*matter, machine, device*⟩; deal with ⟨*subject, question etc.*⟩

Behandlung *die;* ~, ~en treatment

behängen *tr. V.* hang

beharren *itr. V.* **auf etw.** (*Dat.*) ~ (etw. nicht aufgeben) persist in sth.; (auf etw. bestehen) insist on sth.

beharrlich ① *Adj.* dogged ② *adv.* doggedly

Beharrlichkeit *die;* ~: doggedness

behauen *unr. tr. V.* hew

behaupten ① *tr. V.* (a) maintain; assert; ~, **jmd. zu sein/etw. zu wissen** claim to be sb./know sth.; **man behauptet** *od.* **es wird behauptet, dass** …: it is said *or* claimed that … (b) (verteidigen) maintain ⟨*position*⟩; retain ⟨*record*⟩ ② *refl. V.* (a) assert oneself; (nicht untergehen) hold one's ground; (dableiben) survive (b) (Sport) win through

Behauptung *die;* ~, ~en assertion

Behausung *die;* ~, ~en dwelling

beheben *unr. tr. V.* remove ⟨*danger, difficulty*⟩; repair ⟨*damage*⟩; remedy ⟨*abuse, defect*⟩ ┈┈>

Behebung *die;* ~, ~en ▸ BEHEBEN: removal; repair; remedying

beheimatet *Adj.* an einem Ort/in einem Land *usw.* ~ **sein** be native to a place/to a country *etc.*

beheizbar *Adj.* heatable; **eine** ~**e Heckscheibe** a heated rear window

beheizen *tr. V.* heat

behelfen *unr. refl. V.* make do

behelfs·mäßig ① *Adj.* makeshift ② *adv.* in a makeshift way

behelligen *tr. V.* bother; (zudringlich werden gegen) pester

***behend, *behende** ▸ BEHÄND, BEHÄNDE

beherbergen *tr. V.* accommodate

beherrschen ① *tr. V.* (a) control; rule ⟨*country, people*⟩
(b) (meistern) control ⟨*vehicle, animal*⟩; be in control of ⟨*situation*⟩
(c) (bestimmen, dominieren) dominate ⟨*townscape, landscape, discussions*⟩
(d) (zügeln) control ⟨*feelings*⟩; control, curb ⟨*impatience*⟩
(e) (gut können) have mastered ⟨*instrument, trade*⟩; have a good command of ⟨*language*⟩
② *refl. V.* control oneself

beherrscht ① *Adj.* self-controlled ② with self-control

Beherrschung *die;* ~ (a) control; (eines Volks, Landes *usw.*) rule
(b) (das Meistern) control
(c) (Beherrschtheit) self-control
(d) (das Können) mastery

beherzigen *tr. V.* take ⟨*sth.*⟩ to heart

beherzt ① *Adj.* spirited ② *adv.* spiritedly

behilflich *Adj.* [jmdm.] ~ **sein** help [sb.] (bei with)

behindern *tr. V.* (a) hinder; impede ⟨*movement*⟩; hold up ⟨*traffic*⟩
(b) (Sport, Verkehrsw.) obstruct

behindert *Adj.* handicapped

Behinderte *der/die; adj. Dekl.* handicapped person; **die** ~**n** the handicapped; **WC für** ~: toilet for disabled persons

Behinderten-: ~**sport** *der* disabled sport; ~**sportler** *der* disabled sportsman; ~**sportlerin** *die* disabled sportswoman

Behinderung *die;* ~, ~en (a) hindrance
(b) (Sport, Verkehrsw.) obstruction
(c) (Gebrechen) handicap

Behörde *die;* ~, ~n authority; (Amt, Abteilung) department

behördlich ① *Adj.* official ② *adv.* officially

behüten *tr. V.* protect (vor + *Dat.* from); (bewachen) guard

behutsam ① *Adj.* careful
② *adv.* carefully

bei *Präp. mit Dat.* (a) (nahe) near; (dicht an, neben) by; **wer steht da** ~ **ihm?** who is standing there with him?; **etw.** ~ **sich haben** have sth. with *or* on one; **sich** ~ **jmdm. entschuldigen** apologize to sb.
(b) (unter) among; **war heute ein Brief für mich** ~ **der Post?** was there a letter for me in the post today?
(c) (an) by; **jmdn.** ~ **der Hand nehmen** take sb. by the hand
(d) (im Wohn-/Lebens-/Arbeitsbereich von); ~ **uns tut man das nicht** we don't do that; ~ **mir [zu Hause]** at my house; ~ **uns um die Ecke/gegenüber** round the corner from us/opposite us; ~ **seinen Eltern leben** live with one's parents; **wir sind** ~ **ihr eingeladen** we have been invited to her house; **wir treffen uns** ~ **uns/Peter** we'll meet at our/Peter's place; ~ **uns in der Firma** in our company; ~ **Schmidt** (auf Briefen) c/o Schmidt; ~ **einer Firma sein** be with a company; ~ **jmdm./einem Verlag arbeiten** work for sb./a publishing house
(e) (im Bereich eines Vorgangs) at; ~ **einer Hochzeit/einem Empfang** *usw.* be at a wedding/reception *etc.;* ~ **einem Unfall** in an accident
(f) (im Werk von) ~ **Goethe** in Goethe
(g) (im Falle von) in the case of; **wie** ~ **den Römern** as with the Romans; ~ **der Hauskatze** in the domestic cat
(h) (modal) ~ **Tag/Nacht** by day/night; ~ **Tageslicht** by daylight; ~ **Nebel** in fog
(i) (im Falle des Auftretens von) „~ **Nässe Schleudergefahr"** 'slippery when wet'
(j) (angesichts) with; ~ **dieser Hitze** in this heat; ~ **deinen guten Augen/ihrem Talent** with your good eyesight/her talent
(k) (trotz) ~ **all seinem Engagement/seinen Bemühungen** in spite of *or* despite *or* for all his commitment/efforts

bei||behalten *unr. tr. V.* keep; retain; keep up ⟨*custom, habit*⟩; keep to ⟨*course, method*⟩; preserve, maintain ⟨*way of life; attitude*⟩

bei||bringen *unr. tr. V.* (a) jmdm. etw. ~: teach sb. sth.
(b) (ugs.: mitteilen) jmdm. ~, dass …: break it to sb. that …
(c) (zufügen) jmdm./sich etw. ~: inflict sth. on sb./oneself

Beichte *die;* ~, ~n confession *no def. art.*

beichten ① *itr. V.* confess ② *tr. V.* (auch fig.) confess

Beicht-: ~**stuhl** *der* confessional; ~**vater** *der* father confessor

beid… *Indefinitpron. u. Zahlw.* ① *Pl.* ~**e** both; (der/die/das eine oder der/die/das andere) either *sing.;* **die** ~**en** the two; **die/seine** ~**en Brüder** the/his two brothers; **die** ~**en ersten Strophen** the first two verses; **kennst du die** ~**en?** do you know those two?; **alle** ~**e** both of us/you/them; **ihr/euch** ~**e** you two; **ihr/euch** ~**e nicht** neither of you; **wir/uns** ~**e** the two of us/both of us; **er hat** ~**e Eltern**

---
*old spelling – see note on page x

verloren he has lost both [his] parents; **mit ∼en Händen** with both hands; **ich habe ∼e gekannt** I knew both of them; **einer/eins von ∼en** one of the two; **keiner/keins von ∼en** neither [of them]

2 *Neutr. Sg.; ∼es* both *pl.;* (das eine oder das andere) either; **∼es ist möglich** either is possible; **ich glaube ∼es/∼es nicht** I believe both things/neither thing; **das ist ∼es nicht richtig** neither of those is correct

beiderlei *indekl. Adj.* **∼ Geschlechts** of both sexes

beider·seits 1 *Präp. mit Gen.* on both sides of
2 *Adv.* on both sides

bei·einander *Adv.* together; **∼ Trost suchen** seek comfort from each other

Bei·fahrer *der,* **Bei·fahrerin** *die*
(a) passenger
(b) (berufsmäßig) co-driver; (im LKW) driver's mate

Beifahrer·sitz *der* passenger seat; (eines Motorrads) pillion

Bei·fall *der* (a) applause
(b) (Zustimmung) approval

bei·fällig 1 *Adj.* approving
2 *adv.* approvingly

Bei·fang *der* (Fischerei) by-catch

beige /beːʃ/ *Adj.* beige

Beige /beːʃ/ *das; ∼, ∼ od.* (ugs.) *∼s* beige

Bei·geschmack *der:* **einen bitteren** *usw.* **∼ haben** have a slightly bitter *etc.* taste [to it]

Bei·hilfe *die* (a) aid; (Zuschuss) allowance
(b) (Rechtsw.: Mithilfe) aiding and abetting

bei·kommen *unr. itr. V.; mit sein*
(a) (gewachsen sein) **jmdm. ∼:** get the better of sb.
(b) (bewältigen) **den Schwierigkeiten/der Unruhe/jmds. Sturheit ∼:** overcome the difficulties/deal with the unrest/cope with sb.'s obstinacy

Beil *das; ∼[e]s, ∼e* axe; (kleiner) hatchet

Bei·lage *die* (a) (Zeitungs∼) supplement
(b) (zu Speisen) side dish; (Gemüse) vegetables *pl.*

bei·läufig 1 *Adj.* casual
2 *adv.* casually

bei·legen *tr. V.* (a) enclose
(b) (schlichten) settle ⟨*dispute etc.*⟩

Bei·leid *das* sympathy; **[mein] herzliches** *od.* **aufrichtiges ∼!** please accept my sincere condolences

bei·liegen *unr. itr. V.* **einem Brief ∼:** be enclosed with a letter

bei·liegend *Adj.* enclosed; **∼ senden wir …:** please find enclosed …

beim *Präp. + Art.* (a) = bei dem;
(b) **∼ Film sein** be in films
(c) **er will ∼ Arbeiten nicht gestört werden** he doesn't want to be disturbed when working; **∼ Duschen sein** be taking a shower

bei‖messen *unr. tr. V.* attach

Bein *das; ∼[e]s, ∼e* leg; **jmdm. ein ∼ stellen** trip sb.; (fig.) put *or* throw a spanner *or* (Amer.) a monkey wrench in sb.'s works; **wieder auf den ∼en sein** be back on one's feet again

bei·nah[e] *Adv.* almost

Bei·name *der* epithet

Bein·bruch *der:* **das ist [doch] kein ∼** (ugs.) it's not the end of the world

beinhalten *tr. V.* (Papierdt.) involve

-beinig *adj.* -legged

bei‖pflichten *itr. V.* agree (*Dat.* with)

beirren *tr. V.* **sich durch nichts/von niemandem ∼ lassen** not be deterred by anything/anybody

beisammen *Adv.* together

beisammen‖haben *unr. tr. V.* (a) have got together
(b) **er hat [sie] nicht alle beisammen** (ugs.) he's not all there (coll.)

Beisammen·sein *das* get-together

Bei·schlaf *der* sexual intercourse

Bei·sein *das:* **in jmds. ∼:** in the presence of sb. *or* in sb.'s presence

bei·seite *Adv.* aside

Beis[e]l *das; ∼s, ∼ od. ∼n* (österr.) pub (Brit.); bar (Amer.)

bei‖setzen *tr. V.* lay to rest; inter ⟨*ashes*⟩

Bei·setzung *die; ∼, ∼en* funeral; burial

Bei·spiel *das* example (**für** of); **zum ∼:** for example; **mit gutem ∼ vorangehen** set a good example

beispielhaft *Adj.* exemplary

beispiel·los *Adj.* unparalleled

beispiels·weise *Adv.* for example

beißen 1 *unr. tr., itr. V.* (auch fig.) bite
2 *unr. refl. V.* (ugs.) ⟨*colours, clothes*⟩ clash

beißend *Adj.* biting ⟨*cold*⟩; acrid ⟨*smoke, fumes*⟩; sharp ⟨*frost*⟩

Beiß·zange *die* ▶ KNEIFZANGE

Bei·stand *der* (geh.: Hilfe) aid

bei‖stehen *unr. itr. V.* **jmdm. ∼:** aid sb.

bei‖steuern *tr. V.* contribute

Beitrag *der; ∼[e]s, Beiträge* contribution; (Versicherungsbeitrag) premium; (Mitgliedsbeitrag) subscription

bei‖tragen *unr. tr. V., itr. V.* contribute (**zu** to)

bei‖treten *unr. itr. V.; mit sein* join ⟨*union, club, etc.*⟩; **einem Abkommen/Pakt ∼:** accede to ⟨*pact, agreement*⟩

Bei·tritt (a) *der* joining
(b) (zur EU) accession (**zu** to)

Bei·wagen *der* sidecar

Bei·werk *das* accessories *pl.*

bei‖wohnen *itr. V.* **einer Sache** (*Dat.*) **∼** (geh.) be present at sth.

Beize *die; ∼, ∼n* (Holzbearb.) [wood]stain

beizeiten *Adv.* in good time

beizen *tr. V.* (Holzbearb.) stain
bejahen /bə'jaːən/ *tr. V.* **(a)** *auch itr.*
answer ⟨*sth.*⟩ in the affirmative
(b) (gutheißen) approve of; **das Leben** ~: have
a positive *or* an affirmative attitude to life
Bejahung *die;* ~, ~**en (a)** affirmative
reply
(b) (das Gutheißen) approval
bejammern *tr. V.* lament
bejubeln *tr. V.* cheer; acclaim
bekämpfen *tr. V.* **(a)** fight against
(b) combat ⟨*disease, epidemic, pest,
unemployment, crime, etc.*⟩
Bekämpfung *die;* ~ **(a)** fight (*Gen.*
against)
(b) ▶ BEKÄMPFEN B: combating
bekannt *Adj.* **(a)** well-known; **etw.**
~ **geben** announce sth.; **etw.** ~ **machen**
announce sth.; (der Öffentlichkeit) make
sth. public; ~ **werden** become known;
es ist nichts davon ~: nothing is known
concerning it
(b) jmd./etw. **ist jmdm.** ~: sb. knows
sb./sth.; **Darf ich** ~ **machen? Meine Eltern**
may I introduce my parents?
Bekannte *der/die; adj. Dekl.* acquaintance
Bekannt·gabe *die;* ~: announcement
***bekannt|geben** ▶ BEKANNT A
bekanntlich *Adv.* as is well known; **etw.**
ist ~ **der Fall** sth. is known to be the case
***bekannt|machen** ▶ BEKANNT A
Bekannt·machung *die;* ~, ~**en**
announcement
Bekanntschaft *die;* ~, ~**en**
acquaintance
***bekannt|werden** ▶ BEKANNT A
bekehren ① *tr. V.* convert
② *refl. V.* become converted
Bekehrung *die;* ~, ~**en** (auch fig.)
conversion (zu to)
bekennen ① *unr. tr. V.* **(a)** confess; ~,
dass ... admit that ...
(b) (Rel.) profess
② *refl. V.* **sich zum Islam** ~: profess Islam;
sich zu Buddha ~: profess one's faith in
Buddha; **sich zu seiner Schuld** ~: confess
one's guilt; **sich schuldig/nicht schuldig**
~: confess/not confess one's guilt; (vor
Gericht) plead guilty/not guilty
Bekenntnis *das;* ~**ses**, ~**se**
(a) confession
(b) (Eintreten) **ein** ~ **zum Frieden** a
declaration for peace
(c) (Konfession) denomination
bekiffen *refl. V.* (ugs.) get stoned (sl.)
bekifft *Adj.* (ugs.) stoned
beklagen ① *tr. V.* (geh.) **(a)** (betrauern)
mourn
(b) (bedauern) lament
② *refl. V.* complain

bekleckern *tr. V.* (ugs.) **etw./sich [mit
Soße** *usw.*] ~: drop *or* spill sauce *etc.* down
sth./oneself
bekleiden *tr. V.* **(a)** clothe; **mit etw.
bekleidet sein** be wearing sth.
(b) (geh.: innehaben) occupy ⟨*office, position*⟩
Bekleidung *die;* ~, ~**en** clothing; clothes
pl.
beklemmend *Adj.* oppressive
Beklemmung *die;* ~, ~**en** oppressive
feeling
beklommen *Adj.* uneasy; (stärker)
apprehensive
bekloppt *Adj.* (salopp) barmy (Brit. coll.);
loony (coll.)
beknackt *Adj.* (salopp) lousy (coll.); **ein** ~**er
Typ** a berk (Brit. coll.); a jerk (coll.)
beknien *tr. V.* (ugs.) beg
bekommen ① *unr. tr. V.* **(a)** get; get,
receive ⟨*money, letter, reply, news, orders*⟩;
(erreichen) catch ⟨*train, bus, flight*⟩; **was**
~ **Sie?** (im Geschäft) can I help you?; (im
Lokal, Restaurant) what would you like?;
was ~ **Sie [dafür]?** how much is that?;
Hunger/Durst ~: get hungry/thirsty;
Angst/Mut ~: become frightened/take
heart; **er bekommt einen Bart** he's growing
a beard; **sie bekommt eine Brust** her breasts
are developing; **Zähne** ~: ⟨*baby*⟩ teethe; **sie
bekommt ein Kind** she's expecting a baby
(b) etw. **durch die Tür/ins Auto** ~: get sth.
through the door/into the car
② *unr. V.; in der Funktion eines Hilfsverbs
zur Umschreibung des Passivs* get; **etw.
geschenkt** ~: get [given] sth. *or* be given
sth. as a present
③ *unr. itr. V.; mit sein* **jmdm. gut** ~: do sb.
good; **jmdm. [gut]** ~: ⟨*food, medicine*⟩ agree
with sb.; **wohl bekomms!** your [very good]
health!
bekömmlich *Adj.* easily digestible
beköstigen *tr. V.* cater for
bekräftigen *tr. V.* reinforce ⟨*statement*⟩;
reaffirm ⟨*promise*⟩
bekreuzigen *refl. V.* (kath. Kirche) cross
oneself
bekriegen *tr. V.* wage war on; (fig.) fight;
sich ~: be at war; (fig.) fight
bekümmern *tr. V.* **jmdm.** ~: cause sb.
worry
bekümmert *Adj.* worried; (stärker)
distressed
bekunden *tr. V.* express
belächeln *tr. V.* smile [pityingly/
tolerantly *etc.*] at
beladen *unr. tr. V.* load ⟨*ship*⟩; load [up]
⟨*car, wagon*⟩; load up ⟨*horse, donkey*⟩
Belag *der;* ~**[e]s, Beläge (a)** coating
(b) (Fußbodenbelag) covering; (Straßenbelag)
surface; (Bremsbelag) lining
(c) (von Kuchen, Scheibe Brot usw.) topping; (von
Sandwiches) filling
belagern *tr. V.* (auch fig.) besiege

Belagerung *die;* ∼, ∼en siege; (fig.) besieging

Belang *der;* ∼[e]s, ∼e **(a)** von/ohne ∼ sein be of importance/of no importance **(b)** *Pl.* (Interessen) interests

belangen *tr. V.* (Rechtsw.) sue; (strafrechtlich) prosecute

belang·los *Adj.* (trivial) trivial; (unerheblich) of no importance (**für** for)

Belanglosigkeit *die;* ∼, ∼en unimportance; (Trivialität) triviality

belassen *unr. tr. V.* leave

belastbar *Adj.* tough, resilient ⟨*person*⟩; **seelisch/körperlich** ∼ **sein** be emotionally/ physically tough *or* resilient; be able to stand emotional/physical stress; **ein** ∼**er Mitarbeiter** an employee who can work under pressure

Belastbarkeit *die;* ∼, ∼n toughness; resilience; (von Mitarbeitern) ability to work under pressure

belasten *tr. V.* **(a)** etw. ∼: put sth. under strain; (durch Gewicht) put weight on sth. **(b)** (beeinträchtigen) pollute ⟨*atmosphere*⟩; put pressure on ⟨*environment*⟩ **(c)** (in Anspruch nehmen) burden (**mit** with) **(d)** jmdn. ∼ ⟨*responsibility, guilt*⟩ weigh upon sb.; ⟨*thought*⟩ weigh upon sb.'s mind **(e)** (Rechtsw.) incriminate **(f)** (Geldw.) jmds. **Konto mit 100 Euro** ∼: debit sb.'s account with 100 euros

belästigen *tr. V.* bother; (sehr aufdringlich) pester; (sexuell) molest

Belästigung *die* ▸ BELÄSTIGEN: bothering; pestering; molestation

Belastung *die;* ∼, ∼en **(a)** strain; (das Belasten) straining; (durch Gewicht) loading; (Last) load **(b) die** ∼ **der Atmosphäre/Umwelt durch Schadstoffe** the pollution of the atmosphere by harmful substances/the pressure on the environment caused by harmful substances **(c)** (Bürde, Sorge) burden

Belastungs-: ∼**-EKG** *das* (Med.) electrocardiogram after effort; ∼**zeuge** *der,* ∼**zeugin** *die* (Rechtsw.) witness for the prosecution

belaufen *unr. refl. V.* sich auf ... (*Akk.*) ∼: come to ...

belauschen *tr. V.* eavesdrop on

beleben ① *tr. V.* enliven; stimulate ⟨*economy*⟩ ② *refl. V.* ⟨*market, economic activity*⟩ revive, pick up

belebend ① *Adj.* invigorating ② *adv.* ∼ **wirken** have an invigorating effect

belebt *Adj.* busy ⟨*street, crossing, town, etc.*⟩

Beleg *der;* ∼[e]s, ∼e (Beweisstück) piece of [supporting] documentary evidence; (Quittung) receipt

belegen *tr. V.* **(a)** (Milit.: beschießen) bombard; (mit Bomben) attack

(b) (mit Belag versehen) cover ⟨*floor*⟩ (**mit** with); fill ⟨*flan base, sandwich*⟩; top ⟨*open sandwich*⟩; **eine Scheibe Brot mit Käse** ∼: put some cheese on a slice of bread **(c)** (in Besitz nehmen) occupy ⟨*seat, room, etc.*⟩ **(d)** (Hochschulw.) enrol for ⟨*seminar, lecture course*⟩ **(e)** **den ersten/letzten Platz** ∼ (Sport) take first place/come last **(f)** (nachweisen) prove; give a reference for ⟨*quotation*⟩

Belegschaft *die;* ∼, ∼en staff

belegt *Adj.* **(a) ein** ∼**es Brot** an open *or* (Amer.) openface sandwich; (zugeklappt) a sandwich; **ein** ∼**es Brötchen** a roll with topping; an open-face roll (Amer.); (zugeklappt) a filled roll; a sandwich roll (Amer.) **(b)** (mit Belag bedeckt) furred ⟨*tongue, tonsils*⟩ **(c)** (heiser) husky ⟨*voice*⟩ **(d)** (nicht mehr frei) ⟨*room, flat*⟩ occupied

belehren *tr. V.* teach; instruct; (aufklären) enlighten; (informieren) inform; **ich lasse micht gern** ∼: I'm quite willing to believe otherwise

Belehrung *die;* ∼, ∼en instruction; (Zurechtweisung) lecture

beleibt *Adj.* (geh.) portly

beleidigen *tr. V.* insult

beleidigt *Adj.* insulted; (gekränkt) offended

Beleidigung *die;* ∼, ∼en **(a)** insult **(b)** (Rechtsw.) (schriftlich) libel; (mündlich) slander

belesen *Adj.* well-read

beleuchten *tr. V.* light up; light ⟨*stairs, room, street, etc.*⟩

Beleuchtung *die;* ∼, ∼en lighting; (Anstrahlung) illumination

beleumdet *Adj.* **übel/gut** ∼ **sein** have a bad/good reputation

Belgien /'bɛlgiən/ (*das*) ∼s Belgium

Belgier *der;* ∼s, ∼, **Belgierin** *die;* ∼, ∼nen Belgian

belgisch *Adj.* Belgian

belichten *tr. V.* (Fot.) expose; *itr.* **richtig/falsch/kurz** ∼: use the right/wrong exposure/a short exposure time

Belichtung *die* (Fot.) exposure

Belieben *das;* ∼s: **nach** ∼: just as you/they *etc.* like

beliebig ① *Adj.* any ② *adv.* as you like/he likes *etc.;* ∼ **lange/ viele** as long/many as you like/he likes *etc.*

beliebt *Adj.* popular; favourite *attrib.*

Beliebtheit *die;* ∼: popularity

beliefern *tr. V.* supply

bellen *itr. V.* bark

Belletristik /bɛle'trɪstɪk/ *die;* ∼: belles-lettres *pl.*

belohnen *tr. V.* reward ⟨*person, thing*⟩

Belohnung *die;* ∼, ∼en reward

belüften *tr. V.* ventilate

Belüftung *die* ventilation

belügen *unr. tr. V.* lie to

belustigen *tr. V.* amuse

Belustigung *die;* ∼, ∼en amusement

bemächtigen *refl. V.* sich jmds./einer Sache ∼ (geh.) seize sb./sth.

bemalen *tr. V.* paint; (verzieren) decorate

bemängeln *tr. V.* find fault with

bemerkbar *Adj.* sich ∼ machen attract attention [to oneself]; (erkennbar werden) become apparent; (spürbar werden) make itself felt

bemerken *tr. V.* (a) (wahrnehmen) notice; ich wurde nicht bemerkt I was unobserved (b) (äußern) remark

bemerkenswert ① *Adj.* remarkable ② *adv.* remarkably

Bemerkung *die;* ∼, ∼en (a) (Äußerung) remark; comment (b) (Notiz) note; (Anmerkung) comment

bemitleiden *tr. V.* pity; feel sorry for

bemitleidens·wert *Adj.* pitiable

bemogeln *tr. V.* (ugs.) cheat; diddle (Brit. coll.)

bemühen *refl. V.* make an effort; sich ∼, etw. zu tun endeavour to do sth.; sich um etw. ∼: try to obtain sth.; sich um eine Stelle ∼: try to get a job; sich um jmdn. ∼ (kümmern) seek to help sb.

Bemühung *die;* ∼, ∼en effort

benachbart *Adj.* neighbouring *attrib.*

benachrichtigen *tr. V.* notify (von of)

Benachrichtigung *die;* ∼, ∼en notification

benachteiligen *tr. V.* put at a disadvantage; (diskriminieren) discriminate against; die sozial benachteiligten Schichten the underprivileged classes

Benachteiligte *der/die; adj. Dekl.* disadvantaged person; die ∼n the disadvantaged; those at a disadvantage; die sozial ∼n the underprivileged; the socially deprived

benehmen *unr. refl. V.* behave

Benehmen *das;* ∼s behaviour; kein ∼ haben have no manners *pl.*

beneiden *tr. V.* envy; jmdn. um etw. ∼: envy sb. sth.

beneidens·wert *Adj.* enviable

Benelux·länder *Pl.* Benelux countries

benennen *unr. tr. V.* name

Bengel *der;* ∼s, ∼ *od.* (nordd.) ∼s (a) (abwertend: junger Bursche) young rascal (b) (fam.: kleiner Junge) little lad

benommen *Adj.* dazed; (durch Fieber, Alkohol) muzzy

benoten *tr. V.* mark (Brit.); grade (Amer.); einen Test mit „gut" ∼: mark a test 'good' (Brit.); assign a grade of 'good' to a test (Amer.)

benötigen *tr. V.* need; require

benutzen *tr. V.* use

Benutzer *der;* ∼s, ∼: user

benutzer·freundlich *Adj.* user-friendly

Benutzerin *die;* ∼, ∼nen user

Benutzer·name *der* (DV) user name

Benutzung *die;* ∼: use

Benzin *das;* ∼s petrol (Brit.); gasoline (Amer.); gas (Amer. coll.); (Wasch∼) benzine

Benzol *das;* ∼s, ∼e (Chemie) benzene

beobachten *tr. V.* observe; watch

Beobachter *der;* ∼s, ∼, **Beobachterin** *die;* ∼, ∼nen observer

Beobachtung *die;* ∼, ∼en observation

bepacken *tr. V.* load

bepfänden *tr. V.* charge a deposit on ⟨bottle etc.⟩

bepflanzen *tr. V.* plant

bequem ① *Adj.* (a) comfortable (b) (abwertend: träge) idle ② *adv.* (a) comfortably (b) (leicht) easily

bequemen *refl. V.* sich dazu ∼, etw. zu tun (geh.) condescend to do sth.

Bequemlichkeit *die;* ∼ (a) comfort (b) (Trägheit) idleness

berappen *tr., itr. V.* (ugs.) ▶ BLECHEN

beraten ① *unr. tr. V.* (a) advise; jmdn. gut/schlecht ∼: give sb. good/bad advice (b) (besprechen) discuss ⟨plan, matter⟩ ② *unr. itr. V.* über etw. (Akk.) ∼: discuss sth. ③ *unr. refl. V.* sich mit jmdm. ∼, ob ...: discuss with sb. whether ...

Berater *der;* ∼s, ∼, **Beraterin** *die;* ∼, ∼nen adviser

beratschlagen ① *tr. V.* discuss ② *itr. V.* über etw. (Akk.) ∼: discuss sth.

Beratung *die;* ∼, ∼en (a) advice *no indef. art.;* (durch Arzt, Rechtsanwalt) consultation (b) (Besprechung) discussion

berauben *tr. V.* (auch fig.) rob (Gen. of)

berauschen (geh.) ① *tr. V.* (auch fig.) intoxicate ② *refl. V.* become intoxicated (an + Dat. with)

Berber *der;* ∼s, ∼ (a) Berber (b) (Teppich) Berber carpet/rug (c) (Nichtsesshafter) tramp

Berberin *die;* ∼, ∼nen ▶ BERBER A, C

berechenbar *Adj.* calculable; predictable ⟨behaviour⟩

Berechenbarkeit *die;* ∼: calculability; (des Verhaltens) predictability

berechnen *tr. V.* (a) (auch fig.) calculate; predict ⟨behaviour, consequences⟩ (b) (anrechnen) charge; jmdm. 10 Euro für etw. *od.* jmdm. etw. mit 10 Euro ∼: charge sb. 10 euros for sth.; jmdm. zu viel ∼: overcharge sb.

Berechnung *die;* ∼, ∼en (a) calculation (b) (Eigennutz) [calculating] self-interest

---

berechtigen *tr. V.* entitle; *itr.* **die Karte berechtigt zum Eintritt** the ticket entitles the bearer to admission

berechtigt *Adj.* **(a)** (gerechtfertigt) justified **(b)** (befugt) authorized

Berechtigung *die;* ~, ~en **(a)** (Befugnis) entitlement; (Recht) right **(b)** (Rechtmäßigkeit) legitimacy

bereden *tr. V.* **(a)** (besprechen) discuss **(b)** jmdn. ~, etw. zu tun talk sb. into doing sth.

beredsam *Adj.* eloquent

Beredsamkeit *die;* ~: eloquence

beredt *Adj.* (auch fig.) eloquent

Bereich *der;* ~[e]s, ~e area; **im privaten/ staatlichen** ~: in the private/public sector

bereichern *refl. V.* get rich

Bereicherung *die;* ~, ~en **(a)** money-making **(b)** (Nutzen) valuable acquisition

bereifen *tr. V.* put tyres on ⟨*car*⟩; put a tyre on ⟨*wheel*⟩

Bereifung *die;* ~, ~en [set *sing.* of] tyres *pl.*

bereinigen *tr. V.* clear up ⟨*misunderstanding*⟩; settle, resolve ⟨*dispute*⟩

bereisen *tr. V.* travel around *or* about; travel through ⟨*towns*⟩; (beruflich) ⟨*representative etc.*⟩ cover ⟨*area*⟩; **fremde Länder** ~: travel in foreign countries

bereit *Adj.* ready; ~ **sein, etw. zu tun** be ready *or* willing to do sth.

bereiten *tr. V.* **(a)** prepare; make ⟨*tea, coffee*⟩ **(b)** (verursachen) cause ⟨*trouble, sorrow, difficulty, etc.*⟩

bereit-: ~|**halten** *unr. tr. V.* have ready; ~|**legen** *tr. V.* lay out ready; ~|**liegen** *unr. itr. V.* be ready

bereits *Adv.* already

Bereitschaft *die;* ~: readiness; willingness

Bereitschafts·dienst *der;* ~ **haben** ⟨*doctor, nurse*⟩ be on call; ⟨*policeman, fireman*⟩ be on standby duty; ⟨*chemist's*⟩ be on rota duty ⟨*for dispensing outside normal hours*⟩

bereit-: ~|**stehen** *unr. itr. V.* be ready; ~|**stellen** *tr. V.* place ready; get ready ⟨*food, drinks*⟩; ready, make ⟨*money, funds*⟩ available; ~**willig** ① *Adj.* willing. ② *adv.* readily

Bereitwilligkeit *die;* ~: willingness

bereuen ① *tr. V.* regret ② *itr. V.* be sorry; (Rel.) repent

Berg *der;* ~[e]s, ~e **(a)** hill; (im Hochgebirge) mountain **(b)** (Haufen) huge pile; (von Akten, Abfall auch) mountain

berg-, Berg-: ~**ab** /-'-/ *Adv.* downhill; ~**auf** /-'-/ *Adv.* uphill; ~**bahn** *die* mountain railway; (Seilbahn) mountain

cableway; ~**bau** *der* mining

bergen *unr. tr. V.* **(a)** rescue, save ⟨*person*⟩; salvage ⟨*ship, cargo, belongings*⟩ **(b)** (geh.: enthalten) hold

Berg-: ~**führer** *der,* ~**führerin** *die;* ~~, ~~**nen** mountain guide; ~**hütte** *die* mountain hut

bergig *Adj.* hilly; (mit hohen Bergen) mountainous

Berg-: ~**kette** *die* range *or* chain of mountains; mountain range *or* chain; ~**kristall** *der* rock crystal; ~**land** *das* hilly country *no indef. art;* (mit hohen Bergen) mountainous country *no indef. art.;* ~**mann** *der; Pl.* ~**leute** miner; ~**station** *die* top station; ~**steigen** *das;* ~~**s** mountaineering *no art.;* ~**steiger** *der,* ~**steigerin** *die;* ~~, ~~**nen** mountaineer

Bergung *die;* ~, ~en **(a)** rescue **(b)** (von Schiffen, Gut) salvaging

Berg-: ~**wacht** *die* mountain rescue service; ~**werk** *das* mine

Bericht *der;* ~[e]s, ~e report

berichten *tr., itr. V.* report

Bericht-: ~**erstatter** *der;* ~~**s**, ~~, ~**erstatterin** *die;* ~~, ~~**nen** reporter; ~**erstattung** *die* reporting *no indef. art.*

berichtigen *tr. V.* correct

Berichtigung *die;* ~, ~en correction

berieseln *tr. V.* **(a)** (bewässern) irrigate **(b)** sich ständig mit Musik ~ **lassen** (ugs. abwertend) constantly have music on in the background

Berlin *(das);* ~**s** Berlin

Berliner ① *indekl. Adj.* Berlin ② *der;* ~**s**, ~: **(a)** Berliner **(b)** (Gebäck) [jam (Brit.) *or* (Amer.) jelly] doughnut

Berlinerin *die;* ~, ~**nen** Berliner

berlinisch *Adj.* Berlin *attrib.*

Bern *(das);* ~**s** Bern[e]

Bernhardiner *der;* ~**s**, ~: St. Bernard [dog]

Bern·stein *der* amber

bersten *unr. itr. V.; mit sein* (geh.) ⟨*ice*⟩ break up; ⟨*glass*⟩ shatter [into pieces]; ⟨*wall*⟩ crack up

berüchtigt *Adj.* notorious (**wegen** for); (verrufen) disreputable

berücksichtigen *tr. V.* take into account; consider ⟨*applicant, application, suggestion*⟩

Berücksichtigung *die;* ~: **bei** ~ **aller Umstände** taking all the circumstances into account

Beruf *der;* ~[e]s, ~e occupation; (akademischer) profession; (handwerklicher) trade; **was sind Sie von** ~? what do you do for a living?

berufen¹ ① *unr. tr. V.* **(a)** (einsetzen) appoint ····>

(b) berufe es nicht! (ugs.) don't speak too soon!
[2] *unr. refl. V.* **sich auf etw.** (*Akk.*) ∼: refer to sth.; **sich auf jmdn.** ∼: quote *or* mention sb.'s name

berufen² *Adj.* **(a)** competent; **aus** ∼**em Munde** from somebody qualified to speak **(b) sich dazu** ∼ **fühlen, etw. zu tun** feel called to do sth.

beruflich [1] *Adj.* vocational ⟨*training etc.*⟩; (bei akademischen Berufen) professional ⟨*training etc.*⟩
[2] *adv.* ∼ **erfolgreich sein** be successful in one's career; **sich** ∼ **weiterbilden** undertake further job training

berufs-, Berufs-: ∼**akademie** *die* vocational college; ∼**ausbildung** *die* vocational training; ∼**aussichten** *Pl.* job prospects (*in a particular profession etc.*); ∼**berater** *der,* ∼**beraterin** *die* vocational adviser; ∼**beratung** *die* vocational guidance; ∼**bild** *das* outline of a/the profession/trade as a career; ∼**erfahrung** *die* [professional] experience; ∼**geheimnis** *das* professional secret; (Schweigepflicht) professional secrecy; ∼**krankheit** *die* occupational disease; ∼**leben** *das* working life; ∼**schule** *die* vocational school; ∼**soldat** *der,* ∼**soldatin** *die* regular soldier; ∼**sportler** *der* professional sportsman; ∼**sportlerin** *die* professional sportswoman; ∼**tätig** *Adj.* working *attrib.;* ∼**tätige** *der/die; adj. Dekl.* working person; ∼**tätige** *Pl.* working people; ∼**verkehr** *der* rush hour traffic

Berufung *die;* ∼, ∼**en (a)** (für ein Amt) offer of an appointment (**auf, in, an** + *Akk.* to) **(b)** (innerer Auftrag) vocation **(c)** (das Sichberufen) **unter** ∼ (*Dat.*) **auf jmdn./etw.** referring *or* with reference to sb./sth. **(d)** (Rechtsw.: Einspruch) appeal; ∼ **einlegen** lodge an appeal

beruhen *itr. V.* **auf etw.** (*Dat.*) ∼: be based on sth.; **etw. auf sich** ∼ **lassen** let sth. rest

beruhigen /bə'ruːɪɡn/ [1] *tr. V.* calm [down]; pacify ⟨*child, baby*⟩; salve ⟨*conscience*⟩; (trösten) soothe; (von einer Sorge befreien) reassure
[2] *refl. V.* ⟨*person*⟩ calm down; ⟨*sea*⟩ become calm

Beruhigung *die;* ∼ ▶ BERUHIGEN 1: calming [down]; pacifying; salving; soothing; reassurance

Beruhigungs-mittel *das* tranquillizer

berühmt *Adj.* famous

berühmt-berüchtigt *Adj.* notorious

Berühmtheit *die;* ∼, ∼**en (a)** (Ruhm) fame **(b)** (Mensch) celebrity

berühren *tr. V.* **(a)** touch; (fig.) touch on ⟨*topic, issue. etc.*⟩; **sich** ∼: touch

(b) (beeindrucken) affect; **das berührt mich nicht** it's a matter of indifference to me

Berührung *die;* ∼, ∼**en** touch; **mit jmdm./etw. in** ∼ (*Akk.*) **kommen** (auch fig.) come into contact with sb./sth.

besagen *tr. V.* say; (bedeuten) mean

besänftigen *tr. V.* calm [down]; pacify; calm, soothe ⟨*temper*⟩

Besatz *der;* ∼**es,** Besätze (Borte) trimming *no indef. art.*

Besatzung *die;* ∼, ∼**en (a)** (Mannschaft) crew
(b) (Milit.: Verteidigungstruppe) garrison **(c)** (Milit.: Okkupationstruppen) occupying forces *pl.*

Besatzungs-: ∼**macht** *die* occupying power; ∼**zone** *die* occupied zone

besaufen *unr. refl. V.* (salopp) get canned (Brit. sl.) *or* bombed (Amer. sl.)

Besäufnis *das;* ∼**ses,** ∼**se** (salopp) booze-up (Brit. coll.): blast (Amer. coll.)

beschädigen *tr. V.* damage

Beschädigung *die;* ∼, ∼**en (a)** damaging **(b)** (Schaden) damage

beschaffen¹ *tr. V.* obtain, get (*Dat.* for)

beschaffen² *Adj.* **so** ∼ **sein, dass ...:** be such that ...

Beschaffenheit *die;* ∼: properties *pl.*

Beschaffung *die;* ∼: ▶ BESCHAFFEN¹: obtaining; getting

beschäftigen [1] *refl. V.* occupy oneself; **sich viel mit Musik/den Kindern** ∼: devote a great deal of one's time to music/the children; **sehr beschäftigt sein** be very busy
[2] *tr. V.* **(a)** (geistig in Anspruch nehmen) **jmdn.** ∼: preoccupy sb.
(b) (angestellt haben) employ ⟨*workers, staff*⟩ **(c)** (zu tun geben) occupy; **jmdn. mit etw.** ∼: give sb. sth. to occupy him/her

Beschäftigte *der/die; adj. Dekl.* employee

Beschäftigung *die;* ∼, ∼**en (a)** (Tätigkeit) activity
(b) (Anstellung, Stelle) job **(c)** (mit einer Frage, einem Problem) consideration (**mit** of); (Studium) study (**mit** of) **(d)** (von Arbeitskräften) employment

beschämen *tr. V.* shame

beschämend [1] *Adj.* **(a)** (schändlich) shameful
(b) (demütigend) humiliating [2] *adv.* shamefully

beschämt *Adj.* ashamed

Beschämung *die;* ∼: shame

beschatten *tr. V.* **(a)** (geh.) shade **(b)** (überwachen) shadow

beschaulich [1] *Adj.* peaceful ⟨*life, manner, etc.*⟩ [2] *adv.* peacefully

Beschaulichkeit *die;* ∼: peacefulness

Bescheid *der;* ∼**[e]s,** ∼**e (a)** (Auskunft) information; (Antwort) answer; reply; **jmdm.**

~ **geben** *od.* **sagen[, ob …]** let sb. know or tell sb. [whether …]; **sage bitte im Hotel** ~, **dass** …: please let the hotel know that …; **[über etw.** (*Akk.*)] ~ **wissen** know [about sth.]

(b) (Entscheidung) decision

bescheiden[1] [1] *unr. tr. V.* jmdn./etw. **abschlägig** ~: turn sb./sth. down
[2] *unr. refl. V.* (geh.) be content

bescheiden[2] [1] *Adj.* modest
[2] *adv.* modestly

Bescheidenheit *die;* ~: modesty

bescheinigen *tr. V.* confirm ‹sth.› in writing

Bescheinigung *die;* ~, ~en written confirmation *no indef. art.;* (Schein, Attest) certificate

bescheißen *unr. tr. V.* (derb) jmdn. ~: rip sb. off (coll.); screw sb. (coarse)

beschenken *tr. V.* give ‹sb.› a present/presents

bescheren *tr. V.* jmdn. [mit etw.] ~: give sb. [sth. as] a Christmas present/Christmas presents

Bescherung *die;* ~, ~en **(a)** (zu Weihnachten) giving out of the Christmas presents
(b) das ist ja eine schöne ~ (ugs.) this is a pretty kettle of fish

bescheuert *Adj.* (salopp) **(a)** (verrückt) barmy (Brit. coll.); nuts (coll.)
(b) (unangenehm) stupid ‹task, party, etc.›

beschichten *tr. V.* (Technik) coat

Beschichtung *die;* ~, ~en (Technik) coating

beschießen *unr. tr. V.* fire at; (mit Artillerie) bombard

beschimpfen *tr. V.* abuse; swear at

Beschimpfung *die;* ~, ~en insult; ~en abuse *sing.;* insults

beschissen *Adj.* (derb) lousy (coll.); shitty (coarse)

Beschlag *der;* ~[e]s, **Beschläge (a)** fitting
(b) jmdn./etw. mit ~ belegen *od.* in ~ nehmen monopolize sb./sth.

beschlagen[1] [1] *unr. tr. V.* shoe ‹horse›
[2] *unr. itr. V.; mit sein* ‹window› mist up (Brit.), fog up (Amer.); (durch Dampf) steam up

beschlagen[2] *Adj.* knowledgeable

Beschlagnahme *die;* ~, ~n confiscation

beschlagnahmen *tr. V.* confiscate

Beschlagnahmung *die;* ~, ~en
▶ BESCHLAGNAHME

beschleunigen [1] *tr. V.* accelerate; speed up ‹work, delivery›; quicken ‹pace, step[s], pulse›
[2] *refl. V.* ‹heart rate› increase; ‹pulse› quicken
[3] *itr. V.* ‹driver, car, etc.› accelerate

Beschleunigung *die;* ~, ~en
▶ BESCHLEUNIGEN 1: acceleration; speeding

up; quickening

beschließen *unr. tr. V.* **(a)** decide; pass ‹law›; ~, etw. zu tun decide *or* resolve to do sth.
(b) (beenden) end

Beschluss, *Beschluß *der;* **Beschlusses, Beschlüsse** decision; (gemeinsam gefasst) resolution; **einen** ~ **fassen** come to a decision/pass a resolution

beschluss-fähig, *beschluß-fähig *Adj.* quorate

Beschluss-fähigkeit, *Beschluß-fähigkeit *die* presence of a quorum

beschmieren *tr. V.* etw./sich ~: get sth./oneself in a mess

beschmutzen *tr. V.* make ‹sth.› dirty

beschneiden *unr. tr. V.* **(a)** cut ‹hedge›; prune ‹bush›; cut back ‹tree›; **einem Vogel die Flügel** ~: clip a bird's wings
(b) (Med., Rel.) circumcise

Beschneidung *die;* ~, ~en
(a) ▶ BESCHNEIDEN A: cutting; pruning; cutting back
(b) (Med., Rel.) circumcision

beschnüffeln *tr. V.* sniff at

beschönigen *tr. V.* gloss over

beschränken [1] *tr. V.* restrict (**auf** + *Akk.* to)
[2] *refl. V.* sich auf etw. (*Akk.*) ~: restrict oneself to sth.

beschränkt [1] *Adj.* **(a)** (dumm) dull-witted
(b) (engstirnig) narrow-minded
[2] *adv.* narrow-mindedly

Beschränktheit *die;* ~: **(a)** (Dummheit) lack of intelligence
(b) (Engstirnigkeit) narrow-mindedness

Beschränkung *die;* ~, ~en restriction

beschreiben *unr. tr. V.* **(a)** write on; (voll schreiben) write ‹page, side, etc.›
(b) (darstellen) describe

Beschreibung *die;* ~, ~en description

beschriften *tr. V.* label; inscribe ‹stone›; letter ‹sign, label, etc.›; (mit Adresse) address

beschuldigen *tr. V.* accuse (*Gen.* of)

Beschuldigte *der/die; adj. Dekl.* accused

Beschuldigung *die;* ~, ~en accusation

beschummeln *tr. V.* (ugs.) cheat; diddle (Brit. coll.)

Beschuss, *Beschuß *der;* Beschusses fire; [heftig *od.* stark] unter ~ geraten/stehen *od.* liegen (auch fig.) come/be under [heavy] fire

beschützen *tr. V.* protect (**vor** + *Dat.* from)

Beschützer *der;* ~s, ~,
Beschützerin *die;* ~, ~nen protector

Beschwerde *die;* ~, ~n **(a)** complaint (gegen, über + *Akk.* about)
(b) *Pl.* (Schmerz) pain *sing.;* (Leiden) trouble *sing.*

b

beschweren 1 *refl. V.* complain (über + *Akk.*, wegen about); **sich bei jmdm.** ∼: complain to sb.
2 *tr. V.* weight down

beschwerlich *Adj.* arduous; (ermüdend) exhausting

beschwichtigen *tr. V.* pacify; mollify ⟨anger etc.⟩

Beschwichtigung *die;* ∼, ∼en pacification; (des Zorns usw.) mollification

beschwingt *Adj.* lively

beschwipst *Adj.* (ugs.) tipsy

beschwören *unr. tr. V.* (a) swear to; ∼, **dass …:** swear that …; **eine Aussage** ∼: swear a statement on oath
(b) charm ⟨snake⟩
(c) (erscheinen lassen) invoke ⟨spirit⟩
(d) (bitten) implore

Beschwörung *die;* ∼, ∼en
(a) (Zauberspruch) spell; incantation
(b) ▶ BESCHWÖREN C: invoking
(c) (Bitte) entreaty

beseitigen *tr. V.* remove; eliminate ⟨error, difficulty⟩; dispose of ⟨rubbish⟩

Beseitigung *die;* ∼: ▶ BESEITIGEN: removal; elimination; disposal

Besen *der;* ∼s, ∼ broom; **ich fress einen** ∼, **wenn das stimmt** (salopp) I'll eat my hat if that's right (coll.); **neue** ∼ **kehren gut** (Spr.) a new broom sweeps clean (prov.)

besessen *Adj.* (a) possessed
(b) (fig.) obsessive ⟨gambler⟩; **von einer Idee** ∼ **sein** be obsessed with an idea

Besessenheit *die;* ∼ (a) possession
(b) obsessiveness

besetzen *tr. V.* (a) (mit Pelz, Spitzen) edge; trim; **mit Perlen besetzt** set with pearls
(b) (belegen; auch Milit.: erobern) occupy
(c) (vergeben) fill ⟨post, position, role, etc.⟩

besetzt *Adj.* occupied; ⟨table, seat⟩ taken *pred.;* (gefüllt) full; (Fernspr.) engaged; busy (Amer.)

Besetzung *die;* ∼, ∼en (a) (einer Stellung) filling
(b) (Film, Theater usw.) cast
(c) (Eroberung) occupation

besichtigen *tr. V.* see ⟨sights⟩; see the sights of ⟨town⟩; view ⟨house etc. for sale⟩

Besichtigung *die;* ∼, ∼en: **zur** ∼ **der Stadt/des Schlosses/der Wohnung** to see the sights of the town/to see the castle/to view the flat

besiedeln *tr. V.* settle

besiedelt *Adj.* **dicht/dünn** ∼: densely/thinly populated

besiegen *tr. V.* defeat

besinnen *unr. refl. V.* (a) think it over
(b) **sich [auf jmdn./etw.]** ∼: remember [sb./sth.]

Besinnung *die;* ∼: consciousness; **die**

∼ **verlieren** faint; **[wieder] zur** ∼ **kommen** regain consciousness

besinnungs·los 1 *Adj.* unconscious
2 *adv.* mindlessly

Besinnungslosigkeit *die;* ∼: unconsciousness *no art.*

Besitz *der* (a) property
(b) (das Besitzen) possession; **im** ∼ **einer Sache** (Gen.) **sein** be in possession of sth.

Besitz·anspruch *der* claim to ownership

besitzen *unr. tr. V.* own; have ⟨quality, talent, etc.⟩; (nachdrücklicher) possess

Besitzer *der;* ∼s, ∼, **Besitzerin** *die;* ∼, ∼nen owner

besoffen *Adj.* (salopp) canned (Brit. sl.); bombed (Amer. sl.)

Besoffene *der/die/adj. Dekl.* (salopp) drunk

besohlen *tr. V.* sole; **neu** ∼: resole

besonder… *Adj.* special; **ein** ∼**es Ereignis** an unusual *or* a special event; **keine** ∼**e Leistung** no great achievement

Besonderheit *die;* ∼, ∼en special feature; (Eigenart) peculiarity

besonders 1 *Adv.* particularly
2 *Adj.; nicht attr.; nur verneint* (ugs.) **nicht** ∼ **sein** be nothing special

besonnen 1 *Adj.* prudent
2 *adv.* prudently

Besonnenheit *die;* ∼: prudence

besorgen *tr. V.* (a) get; (kaufen) buy
(b) (erledigen) take care of

Besorgnis *die;* ∼, ∼se concern

besorgt 1 *Adj.* concerned (**um** about)
2 *adv.* with concern

Besorgung *die;* ∼, ∼en purchase

bespitzeln *tr. V.* spy on

besprechen *unr. tr. V.* discuss; (rezensieren) review

Besprechung *die;* ∼, ∼en discussion; (Konferenz) meeting; (Rezension) review

bespritzen *tr. V.* (a) splash; (mit einem Wasserstrahl) spray
(b) (beschmutzen) bespatter

besprühen *tr. V.* spray

besser 1 *Adj.* (a) better; **umso** ∼: so much the better
(b) (sozial höher gestellt) superior
2 *adv.* **[immer] alles** ∼ **wissen** always know better; **es** ∼ **haben** be better off; **es geht ihr** ∼: she feels better; ∼ **gesagt** to be [more] precise
3 *Adv.* (lieber) **das lässt du** ∼ **sein** *od.* (ugs.) **bleiben** you'd better not do that

*besser|gehen ▶ BESSER 2

bessern 1 *refl. V.* improve; ⟨person⟩ mend one's ways
2 *tr. V.* improve; reform ⟨criminal⟩

Besserung *die;* ∼, ∼en recovery; **gute** ∼! get well soon

best… 1 *Adj.* (a) best; **bei** ∼**er Gesundheit/Laune sein** be in the best of

---

Bestand ···⋮ Bestimmtheit ·····

health/spirits *pl.;* im ∼en Falle at best;
in den ∼en Jahren, im ∼en Alter in one's
prime; ∼e Grüße an … (*Akk.*) best wishes
to …; mit den ∼en Grüßen *od.* **Wünschen**
with best wishes; (als Briefschluss) ≈ yours
sincerely
  (b) es ist *od.* wäre das Beste, wenn …: it
would be best if …; der/die/das nächste
Beste …: the first … one comes across; einen
Witz zum Besten geben entertain [those
present] with a joke; das Beste vom Besten
the very best; sein Bestes tun do one's best;
zu deinem Besten for your benefit
  ② *adv.* am ∼en best
  ③ *Adv.* am ∼en fährst du mit dem Zug it
would be best for you to go by train
Bestand *der;* ∼, **Bestände (a)** existence,
(Fort∼) continued existence
  (b) (Vorrat) stock (an + *Dat.* of)
bestanden *Adj.* von *od.* mit etw. ∼ sein
have sth. growing on it; mit Tannen ∼e
Hügel fir-covered hills
beständig ① *Adj.* **(a)** constant
  (b) (gleich bleibend) constant; steadfast
⟨*person*⟩; settled ⟨*weather*⟩
  (c) (widerstandsfähig) resistant (gegen) to)
  ② *adv.* constantly
Beständigkeit *die;* ∼ **(a)** steadfastness
  (b) (Widerstandsfähigkeit) resistance (gegen) to)
Bestand·teil *der* component
bestärken *tr. V.* confirm
bestätigen ① *tr. V.* confirm; endorse
⟨*document*⟩; acknowledge ⟨*receipt*⟩
  ② *refl. V.* be confirmed; ⟨*rumour*⟩ prove to
be true
Bestätigung *die;* ∼, ∼en confirmation;
(des Empfangs) acknowledgement; (schriftlich)
letter of confirmation
bestatten *tr. V.* (geh.) inter (formal); bury
Bestattung *die;* ∼, ∼en (geh.) interment
(formal); burial; (Feierlichkeit) funeral
Bestattungs-: ∼**institut** *das,*
∼**unternehmen** *das* [firm of]
undertakers *pl.* or funeral directors *pl.;*
funeral parlor (Amer.)
bestäuben *tr. V.* **(a)** dust
  (b) (Biol.) pollinate
bestaunen *tr. V.* marvel at
bestechen *unr. tr. V.* bribe
bestechlich *Adj.* corruptible; open to
bribery *postpos.*
Bestechung *die;* ∼, ∼en bribery *no*
indef. art.
Bestechungs-: ∼**geld** *das* bribe;
∼**versuch** *der* attempted bribery
Besteck *das;* ∼[e]s, ∼e cutlery setting;
(ugs.: Gesamtheit der Bestecke) cutlery
bestehen ① *unr. itr. V.* **(a)** exist; es
besteht [die] Aussicht/Gefahr, dass …: there
is a prospect/danger that …; noch besteht
die Hoffnung, dass …: there is still hope
that …; ∼ bleiben remain; ⟨*regulation*⟩
remain in force

  (b) (fortdauern) survive; last
  (c) aus etw. ∼: consist of sth.; (hergestellt sein)
be made of sth.
  (d) auf etw. (*Dat.*) ∼: insist on sth.
  ② *unr. tr. V.* pass ⟨*test, examination*⟩
Bestehen *das;* ∼s existence; die
Firma feiert ihr 10 jähriges ∼: the firm is
celebrating its tenth anniversary
***bestehen|bleiben** ▶ BESTEHEN 1A
bestehend *Adj.* existing; current
⟨*conditions*⟩
bestehlen *unr. tr. V.* rob
besteigen *unr. tr. V.* **(a)** climb; mount
⟨*horse, bicycle*⟩; ascend ⟨*throne*⟩
  (b) board ⟨*ship, aircraft*⟩; get on ⟨*bus, train*⟩
Besteigung *die;* ∼, ∼en ascent
bestellen *tr. V.* **(a)** *auch itr.* order (bei
from); würden Sie mir bitte ein Taxi ∼?
would you order me a taxi?
  (b) (reservieren lassen) reserve ⟨*tickets, table*⟩
  (c) jmdn. [für 10 Uhr] zu sich ∼: ask sb. to
go/come to see one [at 10 o'clock]
  (d) (ausrichten) jmdm. etw. ∼: tell sb. sth.;
bestell deinem Mann schöne Grüße von mir
give your husband my regards
Bestellung *die;* ∼, ∼en **(a)** order
  (b) (Reservierung) reservation
besten·falls *Adv.* at best
bestens *Adv.* extremely well
besteuern *tr. V.* tax
bestialisch ① *Adj.* **(a)** bestial
  (b) (ugs.: schrecklich) ghastly (coll.)
  ② *adv.* **(a)** in a bestial manner
  (b) (ugs.: schrecklich) awfully (coll.)
Bestialität *die;* ∼: bestiality
besticken *tr. V.* embroider
Bestie /'bɛstiə/ *die;* ∼, ∼en beast
bestimmen ① *tr. V.* **(a)** (festsetzen) decide
on; fix ⟨*price, time, etc.*⟩
  (b) (vorsehen) intend; das ist für dich
bestimmt that is meant for you
  (c) (identifizieren) identify; determine ⟨*age,*
position⟩; define ⟨*meaning*⟩
  (d) (prägen) determine the character of
  ② *itr. V.* **(a)** make the decisions
  (b) über jmdn. ∼: tell sb. what to do; [frei]
über etw. (*Akk.*) ∼: do as one wishes with
sth.
bestimmend ① *Adj.* decisive
  ② *adv.* decisively
bestimmt ① *Adj.* **(a)** (speziell) particular;
(gewiss) certain; (genau) definite
  (b) (festgelegt) fixed; given ⟨*quantity*⟩
  (c) (Sprachw.) definite ⟨*article etc.*⟩
  (d) (entschieden) firm
  ② *adv.* **(a)** (deutlich) clearly; (genau) precisely
  (b) (entschieden) firmly
  ③ *Adv.* for certain; du weißt es doch [ganz]
∼ noch I'm sure you must remember it; ich
habe das ∼ liegen gelassen I must have left
it behind
Bestimmtheit *die;* ∼: firmness; (im
Auftreten) decisiveness ···⋮

Bestimmung *die;* ~, ~en **(a)** (das Festsetzen) fixing
(b) (Vorschrift) regulation
(c) (Zweck) purpose
(d) ▶ BESTIMMEN 1c: identification; determination; definition
(e) (Sprachw.) modifier; **adverbiale ~:** adverbial qualification
best·möglich *Adj.* best possible
bestrafen *tr. V.* punish (**für, wegen** for); **es wird mit Gefängnis bestraft** it is punishable by imprisonment
Bestrafung *die;* ~, ~en punishment
bestrahlen *tr. V.* **(a)** illuminate; floodlight ⟨*building*⟩
(b) (Med.) treat ⟨*tumour, part of body*⟩ using radiotherapy
Bestrahlung *die;* ~, ~en (Med.) radiation [treatment] *no indef. art.*
Bestreben *das;* ~s endeavour[s *pl.*]
bestrebt *Adj.:* ~ **sein, etw. zu tun** endeavour to do sth.
Bestrebung *die;* ~, ~en effort; (Versuch) attempt
bestreichen *unr. tr. V.* **A mit B ~:** spread B on A
bestreiten *unr. tr. V.* **(a)** dispute; (leugnen) deny
(b) (finanzieren) finance ⟨*studies*⟩; pay for ⟨*studies, sb.'s keep*⟩; meet ⟨*costs, expenses*⟩
(c) (gestalten) carry ⟨*programme, conversation, etc.*⟩
bestreuen *tr. V.* sprinkle
Bestseller /ˈbɛstzɛlɐ/ *der;* ~s, ~: bestseller
bestürzend *Adj.* disturbing; (erschreckend) alarming
bestürzt 1 *Adj.* dismayed
2 *adv.* with dismay
Bestürzung *die;* ~: dismay
Besuch *der;* ~[e]s, ~e **(a)** visit (*Gen.,* **bei** to); **ein ~ bei jmdm.** a visit to sb.; (kurz) a call on sb.
(b) (Teilnahme) attendance (*Gen.* at)
(c) (Gast) visitor; (Gäste) visitors *pl.;* ~ **haben** have visitors/a visitor
besuchen *tr. V.* **(a)** visit; (weniger formell) go to see ⟨*person*⟩; go to ⟨*exhibition, theatre, museum, etc.*⟩; (zur Besichtigung) go to see ⟨*church, exhibition, etc.*⟩
(b) die Schule/Universität ~: go to school/university
Besucher *der;* ~s, ~, **Besucherin** *die;* ~, ~nen visitor
Besuchs-: ~**erlaubnis** *die* visiting permit; ~**zeit** *die* visiting time *or* hours *pl.;* **es ist keine ~zeit** it is not visiting time
besucht *Adj.* **gut/schlecht ~:** well/poorly attended ⟨*lecture, performance, etc.*⟩; much/little frequented ⟨*restaurant etc.*⟩
Beta·blocker /-blɔkɐ/ *der;* ~s, ~ (Med.)

betablocker
betagt *Adj.* (geh.) elderly
betasten *tr. V.* feel [with one's fingers]
betätigen 1 *refl. V.* occupy oneself; **sich politisch/körperlich ~:** engage in political/physical activity
2 *tr. V.* operate ⟨*lever, switch, flush, etc.*⟩; apply ⟨*brake*⟩
Betätigung *die;* ~, ~en: **(a)** activity
(b) ▶ BETÄTIGEN 2: operation; application
betäuben *tr. V.* **(a)** (Med.) anaesthetize; deaden ⟨*nerve*⟩; **jmdn. örtlich ~:** give sb. a local anaesthetic
(b) (unterdrücken) deaden ⟨*pain*⟩; still ⟨*unease, fear*⟩
(c) (benommen machen) daze; (mit einem Schlag) stun
Betäubung *die;* ~, ~en: **(a)** (Med.) anaesthetization; (Narkose) anaesthesia
(b) (Benommenheit) daze
Betäubungs·mittel *das* narcotic; (Med.) anaesthetic
beteiligen 1 *refl. V.* take part (**an** + *Dat.* in)
2 *tr. V.* **jmdn. [mit 10%] an etw.** (*Dat.*) ~: give sb. a [10%] share of sth.
beteiligt *Adj.* **(a)** involved (**an** + *Dat.* in)
(b) (finanziell) **an einem Unternehmen/am Gewinn ~ sein** have a share in a business/in the profit
Beteiligte *der/die; adj. Dekl.* person involved
Beteiligung *die;* ~, ~en **(a)** participation (**an** + *Dat.* in)
(b) (Anteil) share (**an** + *Dat.* in)
beten 1 *itr. V.* pray (**für, um** for)
2 *tr. V.* say ⟨*prayer*⟩
beteuern *tr. V.* affirm; protest ⟨*one's innocence*⟩
Beteuerung *die;* ~, ~en ▶ BETEUERN: affirmation; protestation
Beton /beˈtɔŋ, bes. österr.: beˈtoːn/ *der;* ~s, ~s /-ɔŋs/ *od.* (bes. österr.:) ~e /-oːnə/ concrete
Beton·burg *die* (ugs., meist abwertend) concrete monstrosity (derog.)
betonen *tr. V.* **(a)** stress ⟨*word, syllable*⟩
(b) (hervorheben) emphasize
betonieren *tr. V.* concrete; surface ⟨*road etc.*⟩ with concrete
betont 1 *Adj.* **(a)** stressed
(b) (bewusst) studied
2 *adv.* studiedly
Betonung *die;* ~, ~en **(a)** stressing
(b) (Akzent) stress; (Intonation) intonation
(c) (Hervorhebung) emphasis
betören *tr. V.* (geh.) captivate
betr. *Abk.* = **betreffs, betrifft** re
Betr. *Abk.* = **Betreff** re
Betracht: **jmdn./etw. in ~ ziehen** consider sb./sth.; **jmdn./etw. außer ~ lassen** disregard sb./sth.

betrachten *tr. V.* (a) look at
(b) jmdn./etw. als etw. ~: regard sb./sth. as
sth.
(c) (beurteilen) consider

Betrachter *der;* ~s, ~, **Betrachterin**
die; ~, ~nen observer

beträchtlich ① *Adj.* considerable
② *adv.* considerably

Betrachtung *die;* ~, ~en
(a) contemplation; (Untersuchung)
examination
(b) (Überlegung) reflection

Betrachtungs·weise *die* way of
looking at things; (Standpunkt) point of view

Betrag *der;* ~[e]s, Beträge amount;
„~ dankend erhalten" 'received with
thanks'

betragen ① *unr. itr. V.* be; (bei
Geldsummen) come to; amount to
② *unr. refl. V.* behave

Betragen *das;* ~s behaviour

Betreff *der;* ~[e]s, ~e (im Brief) heading

betreffen *unr. tr. V.* concern; ⟨new rule,
change, etc.⟩ affect

betreffend *Adj.* concerning; der ~e
Sachbearbeiter the person dealing with
this matter; in dem ~en Fall in the case in
question

betreffs *Präp. mit Gen.* (Amtsspr.,
Kaufmannsspr.) concerning

betreiben *unr. tr. V.* (a) proceed with,
(energisch) press ahead with ⟨task, case, etc.⟩;
pursue ⟨policy, studies⟩; carry on ⟨trade⟩; go
in for ⟨sport⟩
(b) run ⟨business, shop⟩
(c) (in Betrieb halten) operate

betreten[1] *unr. tr. V.* (hineintreten in) enter;
(treten auf) step on to; (begehen) walk on
⟨carpet, grass, etc.⟩; „Betreten verboten"
'Keep off'; (kein Eintritt) 'Keep out'

betreten[2] ① *Adj.* embarrassed
② *adv.* with embarrassment

betreuen *tr. V.* look after; care for
⟨invalid⟩; supervise ⟨youth group⟩; see to the
needs of ⟨tourists, sportsmen⟩

Betreuung *die;* ~: care *no indef. art.*

Betrieb *der;* ~[e]s, ~e (a) business; (Firma)
firm
(b) (das In-Funktion-Sein) operation; außer
~ sein not operate; (wegen Störung) be out
of order; in/außer ~ setzen start up/stop
⟨machine etc.⟩
(c) (ugs.: Treiben) bustle; (Verkehr) traffic; es
herrscht großer ~, es ist viel ~: it's very
busy

betrieblich *Adj.* firm's; company

Betriebs-: ~angehörige
der/die employee; ~anleitung *die,*
~anweisung *die* operating instructions
pl.; ~ausflug *der* staff outing; ~ferien
Pl. firm's annual close-down *sing.;*
„Wegen ~ferien geschlossen" 'closed for
annual holidays'; ~klima *das* working

atmosphere; ~prüfer *der,* ~prüferin
die auditor; ~rat *der* (a) works committee;
(b) (Person) member of a/the works
committee; ~rätin *die* ▶ BETRIEBSRAT B;
~system *das* (DV) operating system;
~versammlung *die* meeting of
the workforce; ~wirt *der,* ~wirtin
die graduate in business management;
~wirtschaft *die* business management

betrinken *unr. refl. V.* get drunk

betroffen ① *Adj.* upset; (bestürzt)
dismayed
② *adv.* in dismay

Betroffenheit *die;* ~: dismay

betrüblich *Adj.* gloomy

betrübt ① *Adj.* sad; gloomy ⟨face etc.⟩
② sadly; (schwermütig) gloomily

Betrug *der;* ~[e]s deception; (Delikt) fraud

betrügen ① *unr. tr. V.* deceive; be
unfaithful to ⟨husband, wife⟩; (Rechtsw.)
defraud; (beim Spielen) cheat; jmdn. um 100
Euro ~: cheat *or* (coll.) do sb. out of 100
euros; (arglistig) swindle sb. out of 100 euros
② *unr. itr. V.* cheat; (bei Geschäften) swindle
people

Betrüger *der;* ~s, ~: swindler;
(Hochstapler) conman (coll.); (beim Spielen) cheat

Betrügerei *die;* ~, ~en deception;
(beim Spielen usw.) cheating; (bei Geschäften)
swindling

Betrügerin *die;* ~, ~nen swindler; (beim
Spielen) cheat

betrunken *Adj.* drunken *attrib.;* drunk
pred.

Betrunkene *der/die; adj. Dekl.* drunk

Bett *das;* ~[e]s, ~en (a) bed; ins *od.* zu
~ gehen go to bed; die Kinder ins ~ bringen
put the children to bed
(b) (Feder~) duvet

Bett-: ~bezug *der* duvet cover;
~decke *die* blanket; (gesteppt) quilt

Bettelei *die;* ~, ~en begging *no art.*

betteln *itr. V.* beg (um for)

bettlägerig *Adj.* bedridden

Bett·laken *das* sheet

Bett·lektüre *die* bedtime reading *no
indef. art.*

Bettler *der;* ~s, ~, **Bettlerin** *die;* ~,
~nen beggar

bett-, Bett-: ~reif *Adj.* (ugs.) ready
for bed *pred.;* ~ruhe *die* bed rest;
~schwere *die;* die nötige *od.* notwendige
~schwere haben (ugs.) be ready for one's
bed; ~tuch *das; Pl.* ~tücher sheet;
~wäsche *die* bedlinen; ~zeug *das* (ugs.)
bedclothes *pl.*

betucht *Adj.* (ugs.) well-heeled (coll.);
well-off

betupfen *tr. V.* dab

Beuge *die;* ~, ~n (Turnen) bend

beugen ① *tr. V.* (a) bend; bow ⟨head⟩
(b) (Sprachw.: flektieren) inflect ⟨word⟩ ⋯⋙

b

2 *refl. V.* **(a)** bend over; **sich nach vorn/hinten** ~: bend forwards/bend over backwards; **sich aus dem Fenster** ~: lean out of the window
(b) (sich fügen) give way
Beugung *die;* ~, ~**en** (Sprachw.) inflexion
Beule *die;* ~, ~**n** bump; (Vertiefung) dent
beulen *itr. V.* bulge
beunruhigen *tr., refl. V.* worry
beurlauben *tr. V.* **(a)** jmdn. **[für zwei Tage]** ~: give sb. [two days'] leave of absence
(b) (suspendieren) suspend
beurteilen *tr. V.* judge; assess ⟨*situation etc.*⟩
Beurteilung *die;* ~, ~**en** **(a)** judgement; (einer Lage usw.) assessment
(b) (Gutachten) assessment
Beute *die;* ~, ~**n** **(a)** (Gestohlenes) haul; loot *no indef. art.*
(b) (von Raubtieren) prey; (eines Jägers) bag
Beute·kunst *die* looted art
Beutel *der;* ~**s**, ~ bag; (kleiner, für Tabak usw.) pouch
bevölkern *tr. V.* populate
Bevölkerung *die;* ~, ~**en** population; (Volk) people
Bevölkerungs-: ~**dichte** *die* population density; ~**explosion** *die* population explosion; ~**zunahme** *die,* ~**zuwachs** *der* increase in population
bevollmächtigen *tr. V.* authorize
Bevollmächtigte *der/die; adj. Dekl.* authorized representative
bevor *Konj.* before; ~ **du nicht unterschrieben hast** until you have signed
bevor·munden *tr. V.* jmdn. ~: impose one's will on sb.; **sie wollen sich nicht länger** ~ **lassen** they do not want to be dictated to any longer
bevor|stehen *unr. itr. V.* be near; **unmittelbar** ~: be imminent; **jmdm. steht etw. bevor** sth. is in store for sb.
bevorstehend *Adj.* forthcoming; **unmittelbar** ~: imminent
bevorzugen *tr. V.* **(a)** (vorziehen) prefer (vor + *Dat.* to)
(b) (begünstigen) favour; give preference *or* preferential treatment to (vor + *Dat.* over)
bevorzugt **1** *Adj.* favoured; (privilegiert) privileged; preferential ⟨*treatment*⟩
2 *adv.* jmdn. ~ **behandeln** give sb. preferential treatment
Bevorzugung *die;* ~, ~**en** (Begünstigung) preferential treatment
bewachen *tr. V.* guard; **bewachter Parkplatz** car park with an attendant
Bewacher *der;* ~**s**, ~, **Bewacherin** *die;* ~, ~**nen** guard
Bewachung *die;* ~, ~**en** guarding

bewaffnen **1** *tr. V.* arm
2 *refl. V.* (auch fig.) arm oneself (**mit** with)
bewaffnet *Adj.* armed; **bis an die Zähne** ~: armed to the teeth
Bewaffnung *die;* ~, ~**en** **(a)** arming
(b) (Waffen) weapons *pl.*
bewahren *tr. V.* **(a)** protect (**vor** + *Dat.* from)
(b) (erhalten) **seine Fassung** ~: retain one's composure; **Stillschweigen** ~: remain silent
bewähren *refl. V.* prove oneself/itself
bewährt *Adj.* proven ⟨*method, design, etc.*⟩; well-tried ⟨*recipe, cure*⟩; reliable ⟨*worker*⟩
Bewährung *die;* ~, ~**en** (Rechtsw.) probation
Bewährungs-: ~**frist** *die* (Rechtsw.) period of probation; ~**helfer** *der,* ~**helferin** *die* probation officer; ~**zeit** *die* (Rechtsw.) probation period
bewaldet *Adj.* wooded
bewältigen *tr. V.* cope with; overcome ⟨*difficulty, problem*⟩; cover ⟨*distance*⟩
Bewältigung *die;* ~, ~**en** ▶ BEWÄLTIGEN: coping with; overcoming; covering
bewandert *Adj.* well-versed
Bewandtnis *die;* ~, ~**se:** **mit etw. hat es [seine eigene/besondere** ~: there's a [special] story behind sth.
bewässern *tr. V.* irrigate
Bewässerung *die;* ~, ~**en** irrigation
bewegen¹ **1** *tr. V.* **(a)** move
(b) (ergreifen) move
(c) (innerlich beschäftigen) preoccupy
2 *refl. V.* move
bewegen² *unr. tr. V.* jmdn. **dazu** ~, **etw. zu tun** ⟨*thing*⟩ induce sb. to do sth.; ⟨*person*⟩ prevail upon sb. to do sth.
Beweg·grund *der* motive
beweglich *Adj.* **(a)** movable; moving ⟨*target*⟩
(b) (rege) agile ⟨*mind*⟩
bewegt *Adj.* eventful; (unruhig) turbulent
Bewegung *die;* ~, ~**en** **(a)** movement; (bes. Technik, Physik) motion
(b) (körperliche ~) exercise
(c) (Ergriffenheit) emotion
(d) (Bestreben, Gruppe) movement
Bewegungs·freiheit *die* freedom of movement
bewegungslos *Adj.* motionless
Bewegungslosigkeit *die;* ~: motionlessness
beweiden *tr. V.* (Landw.) **(a)** graze the grass in ⟨*garden etc.*⟩
(b) (als Weide nutzen) use ⟨*meadow etc.*⟩ as pasture
Beweis *der;* ~**es**, ~**e** proof (*Gen.,* **für** of); **belastende** ~**e** incriminating evidence
beweisbar *Adj.* provable
beweisen *unr. tr. V.* prove
Beweis-: ~**material** *das* evidence; ~**mittel** *das* (Rechtsw.) form of evidence;

∼stück *das* piece of evidence; ∼stücke evidence *sing.*

bewẹnden *unr. V.* es bei *od.* mit etw. ∼ lassen content oneself with sth.

bewẹrben *unr. refl. V.* apply (**bei** to, **um** for)

Bewẹrber *der;* ∼s, ∼, **Bewẹrberin** *die;* ∼, ∼nen applicant

Bewẹrbung *die* application

Bewẹrbungs-: ∼**bogen** *der* application form; ∼**mappe** *die* job application portfolio; ∼**schreiben** *das* letter of application; ∼**unterlagen** *Pl.* documents in support of an/the application

bewẹrfen *unr. tr. V.* jmdn./etw. mit etw. ∼: throw sth. at sb./sth.

bewẹrkstelligen *tr. V.* pull off, manage ⟨deal, sale, etc.⟩; es ∼, etw. zu tun contrive *or* manage to do sth.

bewẹrten *tr. V.* assess; rate; (dem Geldwert nach) value (**mit** at)

Bewẹrtung *die;* ∼, ∼en assessment; (dem Geldwert nach) valuation

bewịlligen *tr. V.* grant

Bewịlligung *die;* ∼, ∼en granting

bewịrken *tr. V.* bring about; cause

bewịrten *tr. V.* feed; jmdn. mit etw. ∼: serve sb. sth.

bewịrtschaften *tr. V.* **(a)** manage ⟨estate, farm, restaurant, business, etc.⟩ **(b)** farm ⟨fields, land⟩

Bewịrtung *die;* ∼, ∼en provision of food and drink

bewog *1. u. 3. Pers. Sg. Prät. v.* BEWEGEN[2]

bewohnbar *Adj.* habitable

bewohnen *tr. V.* inhabit, live in ⟨house, area⟩; live in ⟨room, flat⟩

Bewohner *der;* ∼s, ∼, **Bewohnerin** *die;* ∼, ∼nen (eines Hauses, einer Wohnung) occupant; (einer Stadt, eines Gebietes) inhabitant

bewohnt *Adj.* occupied ⟨house etc.⟩; inhabited ⟨area⟩

bewölken *refl. V.* cloud over; become overcast

bewölkt *Adj.* cloudy; overcast

Bewölkung *die;* ∼, ∼en cloud [cover]

Bewụnderer *der;* ∼s, ∼, **Bewụnderin** *die;* ∼, ∼nen admirer

bewụndern *tr. V.* admire (**wegen, für** for)

bewụnderns·wert [1] *Adj.* admirable [2] *adv.* admirably

Bewụnderung *die;* ∼: admiration

bewụsst, *bewụßt [1] *Adj.* conscious ⟨reaction, behaviour, etc.⟩; (absichtlich) deliberate ⟨lie, deception, attack, etc.⟩; etw. ist/wird jmdm. ∼: sb. is/becomes aware of sth.; sb. realizes sth.; **sich** (*Dat.*) **einer Sache** (*Gen.*) ∼ **sein/werden** be/become aware of something [2] *adv.* consciously; (absichtlich) deliberately

bewụsst·los, *bewụßt·los *Adj.* unconscious

Bewụsstlosigkeit, *Bewụßtlosigkeit *die;* ∼: unconsciousness

Bewụsst·sein, *Bewụßt·sein *das* **(a)** consciousness; das ∼ verlieren/wiedererlangen lose/regain consciousness; bei vollem ∼ sein be fully conscious **(b)** (deutliches Wissen) awareness

bewụsstseins-, *bewụßtseins-, Bewụsstseins-, *Bewụßtseins-: ∼**erweiternd** mind-expanding; psychedelic; ∼**erweiterung** *die* expansion of consciousness; ∼**trübung** *die* clouding *or* dimming of consciousness; ∼**veränderung** *die* change of awareness *or* outlook

bezahlbar *Adj.* affordable

bezahlen [1] *tr. V.* pay ⟨person, bill, taxes, rent, amount⟩; pay for ⟨goods etc.⟩; **das macht sich bezahlt** it pays off [2] *itr. V.* pay; **Herr Ober, ich möchte** ∼ *od.* **bitte** ∼: waiter, the bill *or* (Amer.) check please

Bezahl·fernsehen *das* pay television; pay TV

Bezahlung *die;* ∼, ∼en payment; (Lohn, Gehalt) pay

bezaubernd [1] *Adj.* enchanting [2] *adv.* enchantingly

bezeichnen *tr. V.* **(a)** jmdn./sich/etw. als etw. ∼: call sb./oneself/sth. sth. **(b)** (Name, Wort sein für) denote

bezeichnend *Adj.* characteristic (**für** of)

Bezeichnung *die;* ∼, ∼en **(a)** marking; (Angabe durch Zeichen) indication **(b)** (Name) name

bezeugen *tr. V.* testify to

bezịchtigen *tr. V.* accuse

beziehen [1] *unr. tr. V.* **(a)** cover ⟨seat, cushion, etc.⟩; **die Betten frisch** ∼: put clean sheets on the beds **(b)** (einziehen in) move into ⟨house, office⟩ **(c)** (Milit.) take up ⟨position, post⟩ **(d)** (erhalten) obtain ⟨goods⟩; take ⟨newspaper⟩; draw ⟨pension, salary⟩ **(e)** (in Beziehung setzen) apply (**auf** + *Akk.* to) [2] *unr. refl. V.* **(a)** es/der Himmel bezieht sich it/the sky is clouding over *or* becoming overcast **(b)** sich auf jmdn./etw. ∼ (sich berufen auf) ⟨person, letter, etc.⟩ refer to sb./sth.; (betreffen) ⟨question, statement, etc.⟩ relate to sb./sth.; **wir** ∼ **uns auf Ihr Schreiben vom 28. 8.** with reference to your letter of 28 August

Beziehung *die;* ∼, ∼en **(a)** relation; (Zusammenhang) connection (**zu** with); **zwischen A und B besteht keine/eine** ∼: there is no/a connection between A and B **(b)** (Freundschaft, Liebes∼) relationship **(c)** (Hinsicht) respect; **in mancher** ∼: in many respects ⋯⋗

beziehungs·weise *Konj.* and ... respectively; (oder) or

beziffern *tr. V.* estimate (**auf** + *Akk.* at); **den Schaden auf 3 000 Euro** ~: estimate the damage at 3,000 euros

Bezirk *der;* ~**[e]s,** ~**e** district

*bezug ▸ BEZUG D

Bezug *der* **(a)** (für Kissen usw.) cover; (für Polstermöbel) loose cover; slip cover (Amer.); (für Betten) duvet cover; (für Kopfkissen) pillowcase **(b)** (Erwerb) obtaining; (Kauf) purchase; ~ **einer Zeitung** taking a newspaper **(c)** *Pl.* salary *sing.* **(d)** (Papierdt.) **mit** *od.* **unter** ~ **auf etw.** (*Akk.*) with reference to sth.; **in** ~ **auf jmdn./etw.** regarding sb./sth.; ~ **nehmend auf unser Telex** with reference to our telex

bezüglich *Präp. mit Gen.* regarding

bezwecken *tr. V.* aim to achieve

bezweifeln *tr. V.* doubt

bezwingen *unr. tr. V.* conquer ⟨*enemy, mountain, pain, etc.*⟩; defeat ⟨*opponent*⟩; capture ⟨*fortress*⟩

BH /beː'haː/ *der;* ~**[s],** ~**[s]** *Abk.* = **Büstenhalter** bra; **BH-Träger** bra strap

Biathlon /'biːatlɔn/ *das;* ~**s,** ~**s** (Sport) biathlon

Bibel *die;* ~, ~**n** (auch fig.) Bible

Biber *der;* ~**s,** ~: beaver

Bibliographie *die;* ~, ~**n** bibliography

bibliographisch *Adj.* bibliographical

Bibliothek *die;* ~, ~**en** library

Bibliothekar *der;* ~**s,** ~**e,** **Bibliothekarin** *die;* ~, ~**nen** librarian

biblisch *Adj.* biblical

Bidet /bi'deː/ *das;* ~**s,** ~**s** bidet

bieder *Adj.* unsophisticated; (langweilig) stolid; (treuherzig) trusting

biegen ① *unr. tr. V.* bend ② *unr. refl. V.* bend; (nachgeben) give ③ *unr. itr. V.; mit sein* turn

biegsam *Adj.* flexible; pliable ⟨*material*⟩

Biegsamkeit *die;* ~ ▸ BIEGSAM: flexibility; pliability

Biegung *die;* ~, ~**en** bend

Biene *die;* ~, ~**n** bee

Bienen-: ~**honig** *der* bees' honey; ~**königin** *die* queen bee; ~**korb** *der* straw hive; ~**stock** *der* beehive

Bier *das;* ~**[e]s,** ~**e** beer

Bier-: ~**bauch** *der* (ugs. spött.) beer belly; ~**brauerei** *die* brewery; ~**deckel** *der* beer mat; ~**dose** *die* beer can; ~**fass,** *~**faß** *das* beer barrel; ~**flasche** *die* beer bottle; ~**garten** *der* beer garden; ~**glas** *das* beer glass; ~**kasten** *der* beer crate; ~**trinker** *der,* ~**trinkerin** *die* beer drinker; ~**zelt** *das* beer tent

Biest *das;* ~**[e]s,** ~**er** (ugs. abwertend)

(a) (Tier, Gegenstand) wretched thing **(b)** (Mensch) wretch

bieten ① *unr. tr. V.* **(a)** offer; put on ⟨*programme etc.*⟩; provide ⟨*shelter, guarantee, etc.*⟩ **(b)** **ein schreckliches Bild** ~: present a terrible picture; **einen prächtigen Anblick** ~: be a splendid sight ② *unr. refl. V.* **sich jmdm.** ~: present itself to sb. ③ *unr. itr. V.* bid

Bigamie *die;* ~: bigamy *no def. art.*

Bigamist *der;* ~**en,** ~**en,** **Bigamistin** *die;* ~, ~**nen** bigamist

biken /baikn̩/ *itr. V.; mit sein* (Jargon) cycle

Biker /'baikɐ/ *der;* ~**s,** ~**s** (Jargon) biker

Bikerin *die;* ~, ~**nen** (Jargon) [female] biker

Bikini *der;* ~**s,** ~**s** bikini

Bikini-: ~**höschen** *das* bikini bottom; ~**oberteil** *das* bikini top

Bilanz *die;* ~, ~**en** **(a)** balance sheet **(b)** (Ergebnis) outcome; ~ **ziehen** take stock

Bild *das;* ~**[e]s,** ~**er** **(a)** picture **(b)** (Anblick) sight **(c)** (Metapher) image

bilden ① *tr. V.* **(a)** form (**aus** from); (modellieren) mould (**aus** from); **eine Gasse** ~: make a path; **sich** (*Dat.*) **ein Urteil** ~: form an opinion **(b)** (ansammeln) build up ⟨*fund, capital*⟩ **(c)** (darstellen) be ⟨*exception etc.*⟩ **(d)** (erziehen) educate ② *refl. V.* **(a)** form **(b)** (lernen) educate oneself

bildend *Adj.* **(a)** **die** ~**e Kunst, die** ~**en Künste** the plastic arts *pl.* (*including painting and architecture*) **(b)** (belehrend) educational

Bilder-: ~**buch** *das* picture book (*for children*); ~**geschichte** *die* picture story; ~**rahmen** *der* picture frame; ~**rätsel** *das* picture puzzle; (Rebus) rebus

bild-, Bild-: ~**hauer** *der* sculptor; ~**hauerin** *die;* ~, ~~**nen** sculptress; ~**hübsch** *Adj.* really lovely; stunningly beautiful ⟨*girl*⟩

bildlich ① *Adj.* pictorial; (übertragen) figurative ② *adv.* pictorially; (übertragen) figuratively

Bildnis /'bɪltnɪs/ *das;* ~**ses,** ~**se** portrait

Bild-: ~punkt *der* (DV) picture element; pixel; ~**qualität** *die* picture quality; ~**redakteur** *der,* ~**redakteurin** *die* picture editor; ~**röhre** *die* (Ferns.) picture tube

Bild·schirm *der* (Ferns., Informationst.) screen

Bildschirm-: ~**gerät** *das* VDU; visual display unit; ~**schoner** *der;* ~~**s,** ~~ (DV) screen saver

bild-, Bild-: ~**schön** *Adj.* really lovely; stunningly beautiful ⟨*girl, woman*⟩; ~**telefon** *das* video telephone

---

Bildung *die;* ~, ~**en (a)** (Erziehung) education; (Kultur) culture **(b)** (das Formen) formation

Bildungs-: ~**lücke** *die* gap in one's education; ~**minister** *der,* ~**ministerin** *die* minister of education; ≈ Secretary of State for Education (Brit.); ~**wesen** *das* education system; das ~wesen education

Bild·unterschrift *die* caption

Billard /'bɪljart, *österr.:* bi'ja:ɐ̯/ *das;* ~s, ~e billiards

Billard-: ~**kugel** *die* billiard ball; ~**stock** *der* billiard cue; ~**tisch** *der* billiard table

Billett /bɪl'jɛt/ *das;* ~[e]s, ~e *od.* ~s (schweiz., veralt.) ticket

Billiarde *die;* ~, ~n thousand million million; quadrillion (Amer.)

billig [1] *Adj.* **(a)** cheap **(b)** (abwertend: primitiv) cheap ‹*trick*›; feeble ‹*excuse*› [2] *adv.* cheaply

Billig·angebot *das* special *or* cut-price offer

billigen *tr. V.* approve

Billig-: ~**flieger** *der* (ugs.) budget airline; ~**flug** *der* cheap flight; ~**flug·linie** *die* budget airline; ~**lohn·land** *das* low-wage country

Billigung *die;* ~: approval

Billion *die;* ~, ~en trillion; million million

bimmeln *itr. V.* (ugs.) ring

bin *1. Pers. Sg. Präsens v.* SEIN[1]

binär *Adj.* binary

Binde *die;* ~, ~n **(a)** (Verband) bandage; (Augenbinde) blindfold **(b)** (Armbinde) armband

Binde-: ~**gewebe** *das* (Anat.) connective tissue; ~**haut** *die* (Anat.) conjunctiva

binden [1] *unr. tr. V.* **(a)** (auch fig.) tie; knot ‹*tie*›; make up ‹*wreath, bouquet*›; **jmdn. an sich** (*Akk.*) ~ (fig.) make sb. dependent on one **(b)** (fesseln, festhalten, zusammenhalten, fig.: verpflichten, Buchw.) bind **(c)** (Kochk.: legieren) thicken ‹*sauce*› [2] *unr. refl. V.* tie oneself down

Binder *der;* ~s, ~ tie

Binde·strich *der* hyphen

Bind·faden *der* string

Bindung *die;* ~, ~en **(a)** (Beziehung) relationship (**an** + *Akk.* to) **(b)** (Verbundenheit) attachment (**an** + *Akk.* to) **(c)** (Ski~) binding

binnen *Präp. mit Dat. od.* (geh.) *Gen.* within

Binnenmarkt *der* (Wirtsch.) domestic *or* home market; **europäischer** ~: internal European market

Binsen·weisheit *die* truism

Bio- (ugs.) organic ‹*farmer, garden, vegetables, etc.*›

bio-, Bio-: ~**abfall** *der* biowaste; ~**brennstoff** *der* biofuel; ~**chemie** *die* biochemistry; ~**graf** *der;* ~~en, ~~en biographer; ~**grafie** *die;* ~~, ~~n biography; ~**grafin** *die;* ~~, ~~nen biographer; ~**grafisch** *Adj.* biographical; ~**kraftstoff** *der* (Kfz.-W.) biofuel; ~**loge** *der;* ~~n, ~~n biologist; ~**logie** *die;* ~~: biology *no art.;* ~**login** *der;* ~~, ~~nen biologist; ~**logisch** *Adj.* **(a)** biological; **(b)** (natürlich) natural ‹*medicine, cosmetic, etc.*›; ~**masse** *die* biomass; ~**metrisch** [1] *Adj.* biometric; [2] *adv.* biometrically; ~**müll** *der* biowaste; ~**sprit** *der* (ugs.) (Benzin) biofuel; ~**technologie** *die* biotechnology; ~**terrorismus** *der* bioterrorism; ~**top** *der od. das;* ~~s, ~~e (Biol.) biotope; ~**waffe** *die* biological weapon

bipolar /bipo'la:ɐ̯/ *Adj.* ~e Störung (Psych. Med.) bipolar disorder

Birke *die;* ~, ~n birch [tree]; (Holz) birch[wood]

Birma (*das*) ~s Burma

Birn·baum *der* pear tree

Birne *die;* ~, ~n **(a)** pear **(b)** (Glühlampe) [light]bulb **(c)** (salopp: Kopf) nut (coll.)

bis [1] *Präp. mit Akk.* **(a)** (zeitlich) until; till; (die ganze Zeit über und bis zu einem bestimmten Zeitpunkt) up until; up till; (nicht später als) by **(b)** (räumlich) to; **dieser Zug fährt nur** ~ **Offenburg** this train only goes as far as Offenburg; ~ **5 000 Euro** up to 5,000 euros **(c)** ~ **auf** (einschließlich) down to; (mit Ausnahme von) except for [2] *Adv.* ~ **zu 6 Personen** up to six people [3] *Konj.* **(a)** (nebenordnend) to **(b)** (unterordnend) until; till; (österr.: sobald) when

Bisam·ratte *die* muskrat

Bischof *der;* ~s, Bischöfe, **Bischöfin** *die;* ~, ~nen bishop

bischöflich *Adj.* episcopal

bi·sexuell [1] *Adj.* bisexual [2] *adv.* bisexually

bis·her *Adv.* up to now; (aber jetzt nicht mehr) until now; till now

bisherig *Adj.* (vorherig) previous; (momentan) present

Biskaya /bɪs'ka:ja/ *die;* ~: the Bay of Biscay

Biskuit /bɪs'kvi:t/ *das od. der;* ~[e]s, ~s *od.* ~e **(a)** sponge biscuit **(b)** (~teig) sponge

bis·lang *Adv.:* ▸ BISHER

Bison *der;* ~s, ~s bison

Biss, *Biß *der;* Bisses, Bisse bite

bisschen, *bißchen *indekl.* *Indefinitpron.* **(a)** *adj.* **ein** ~ **Geld/Wasser** a bit of *or* a little money/a drop of *or* a little water; **ein/kein** ~ **Angst haben** be a bit/not a bit frightened ⋯▸

(b) *adv.* **ein/kein** ~: a bit *or* a little/not a *or* one bit
(c) *subst.* **ein** ~: a bit; a little; (bei Flüssigkeiten) a drop; a little; **das/kein** ~: the little [bit]/not a *or* one bit
Bissen *der;* ~s, ~: mouthful
bissig ⊡ *Adj.* **(a)** ~ **sein** ⟨dog⟩ bite; **ein** ~**er Hund** a dog that bites; „**Vorsicht,** ~**er Hund**" 'beware of the dog'
(b) cutting ⟨remark, tone, etc.⟩
⊡ *adv.* ⟨say⟩ cuttingly
Biss·wunde, *Biß·wunde *die* bite
bist 2. *Pers. Sg. Präsens v.* SEIN¹
Bistum /'bɪstuːm/ *das;* ~s, Bistümer bishopric; diocese
bis·weilen *Adv.* (geh.) from time to time
Bit /bɪt/ *das;* ~s, ~[s] (DV) bit
bitte ⊡ *Adv.* please
⊡ *Interj.* **(a)** (Bitte, Aufforderung) please; **zwei Tassen Tee,** ~: two cups of tea, please; ~**[, nehmen Sie doch Platz]!** do take a seat; **Noch eine Tasse Tee? – [Ja]** ~**!** Another cup of tea? – Yes, please
(b) (Aufforderung, etw. entgegenzunehmen) ~ **[schön od. sehr]!** there you are!
(c) (Ausdruck des Einverständnisses) ~ **[gern]!** certainly; of course; **Entschuldigung! – Bitte!** [I'm] sorry! – That's all right!
(d) ~ **[schön od. sehr]!** (im Laden, Lokal) yes, please?
(e) [wie] ~**?** (Nachfrage) sorry
(f) Vielen Dank! – Bitte [schön od. sehr] Many thanks! – Not at all *or* you're welcome
Bitte *die;* ~, ~**n** request; (inständig) plea
bitten *unr. tr. V.* **(a)** *auch itr.* ask **(um for)**; **darf ich Sie um Feuer/ein Glas Wasser** ~**?** could I ask you for a light/a glass of water, please?
(b) (einladen) ask
bitter ⊡ *Adj.* **(a)** bitter; plain ⟨chocolate⟩
(b) (fig.) (verbittert) bitter
(c) (schmerzlich) bitter, painful, hard ⟨loss⟩; hard ⟨time, fate, etc.⟩; dire ⟨need⟩; desperate ⟨poverty⟩; grievous ⟨injustice, harm⟩
⊡ *adv.* (sehr stark) desperately; ⟨regret⟩ bitterly
bitter-: ~**böse** ⊡ *Adj.* furious; ⊡ *adv.* furiously; ~**kalt** *Adj.* bitterly cold
bitterlich ⊡ *Adj.* slightly bitter ⟨taste⟩
⊡ *adv.* (heftig) ⟨cry, complain, etc.⟩ bitterly
bitter-süß *Adj.* (auch fig.) bitter-sweet
Bitt·steller *der;* ~s, ~, **Bitt·stellerin** *die;* ~, ~**nen** petitioner
Biwak *das;* ~s, ~s (bes. Milit., Bergsteigen) bivouac
bizarr ⊡ *Adj.* bizarre
⊡ *adv.* bizarrely
Bizeps *der;* ~[es], ~**e** biceps
Blähung *die;* ~, ~**en** flatulence *no art., no pl.*
Blamage /bla'maːʒə/ *die;* ~, ~**n** disgrace

blamieren ⊡ *tr. V.* disgrace
⊡ *refl. V.* disgrace oneself; (sich lächerlich machen) make a fool of oneself
blank *Adj.* shiny
Blanko-: ~**scheck** *der* (auch fig.) blank cheque; ~**vollmacht** *die* (auch fig.) carte blanche
Bläschen /'blɛːsçən/ *das;* ~s, ~
(a) [small] bubble
(b) (in der Haut) [small] blister
Blase *die;* ~, ~**n (a)** bubble
(b) (in der Haut) blister
(c) (Harn~) bladder
Blasebalg *der;* ~s, Blasebälge bellows *pl.*
blasen ⊡ *unr. itr. V.* blow
⊡ *unr. tr. V.* **(a)** blow
(b) (spielen) play ⟨musical instrument, tune, melody, etc.⟩
Bläser *der;* ~s, ~, **Bläserin** *die;* ~, ~**nen** (Musik) wind player
blasiert (abwertend) ⊡ *Adj.* blasé
⊡ *adv.* in a blasé way
Blas-: ~**instrument** *das* wind instrument; ~**kapelle** *die* brass band; ~**musik** *die* brass-band music
Blasphemie /blasfe'miː/ *die;* ~, ~**n** blasphemy
Blas·rohr *das* blowpipe
blass, *blaß ⊡ *Adj.* pale
⊡ *adv.* palely
Blässe *die;* ~: paleness
Blatt *das;* ~[e]s, Blätter **(a)** (von Pflanzen) leaf
(b) (Papier) sheet
(c) (Buchseite usw.) page; **etw. vom** ~ **spielen** sight-read sth.
(d) (Zeitung) paper
(e) (Spielkarten) hand
(f) (am Werkzeug, Ruder) blade
Blättchen *das;* ~s, ~ **(a)** (von Pflanzen) [small] leaf
(b) (Papier) [small] sheet
blättern *itr. V.* **in einem Buch** ~: leaf through a book
Blätter·teig *der* puff pastry
Blatt-: ~**gold** *das* gold leaf; ~**grün** *das* chlorophyll; ~**laus** *die* aphid; ~**salat** *der* green salad; ~**spinat** *der* leaf spinach
blau *Adj.* blue; **en** ~**er Fleck** a bruise; ~ **sein** (fig. ugs.) be tight (coll.); **das Blaue vom Himmel herunterlügen** (ugs.) lie like anything
Blau *das;* ~s, ~ *od.* (ugs.:) ~s blue
blau-, Blau-: ~**äugig** *Adj.* **(a)** blue-eyed; **(b)** (naiv) naive; ~**beere** *die* bilberry; ~**grau** *Adj.* blue-grey; ~**grün** *Adj.* blue-green
bläulich *Adj.* bluish
blau-, Blau-: ~**licht** *das* flashing blue light; ~**|machen** *itr. V.* (ugs.) skip work; ~**mann** *der; Pl.* ~**männer** (ugs.) boiler suit; ~**säure** *die* (Chemie) prussic acid;

~**stichig** Adj. (Fot.) with a blue cast postpos., not pred.; ~**stichig sein** have a blue cast

Blazer /'ble:ze/ der; ~s, ~: blazer

Blech das; ~[e]s, ~e (a) sheet metal; (Stück Blech) metal sheet (b) (Back~) [baking] tray

Blech-: ~**bläser** der, ~**bläserin** die brass player; die ~**bläser** (im Orchester) the brass [section] sing.; ~**büchse** die, ~**dose** die tin

blechen tr., itr. V. (ugs.) cough up (coll.)

blechern ① Adj. (metallisch klingend) tinny ⟨sound, voice⟩ ② adv. tinnily

Blech-: ~**musik** die (abwertend) brass-band music; ~**napf** der metal bowl

Blechner der; ~s, ~, **Blechnerin** die; ~, ~nen (südd.) ▶ KLEMPNER

Blech-: ~**schaden** der (Kfz-W.) damage no indef. art. to the bodywork; ~**trommel** die tin drum

blecken tr. V. **die Zähne** ~: bare one's/its teeth

Blei das; ~[e]s, ~e lead

Bleibe die; ~, ~n place to stay

bleiben unr. itr. V.; mit sein (a) stay; remain; ~ **Sie bitte am Apparat** hold the line please; **wo bleibt er so lange?** where has he got to?; **auf dem Weg** ~: keep to the path; **sitzen** ~: stay or remain sitting down or seated; **bei etw.** ~ (fig.: an etw. festhalten) keep to sth. (b) (übrig bleiben) be left; remain (c) etw. ~ **lassen** give sth. a miss

bleibend Adj. lasting; permanent ⟨damage⟩

*****bleiben|lassen** ▶ BLEIBEN C

bleich Adj. pale

bleichen[1] tr. V. bleach

bleichen[2] regelm., veralt. auch unr. itr. V. become bleached

blei-, Blei-: ~**frei** Adj. unleaded ⟨fuel⟩; ~**kristall** das lead crystal; ~**kugel** die lead ball; (Geschoss) lead bullet; ~**schwer** Adj. heavy as lead postpos.; ~**stift** der pencil; **mit** ~**stift** in pencil; ~**stift-spitzer** der pencil sharpener

Blende die; ~, ~n (a) (Lichtschutz) shade; (am Fenster) blind (b) (Optik, Film, Fot.) diaphragm; (Blendenzahl) aperture setting

blenden ① tr. V. (a) (auch fig.) dazzle (b) (blind machen) blind ② itr. V. ⟨light⟩ be dazzling

blendend ① Adj. **es geht mir** ~: I feel wonderfully well ② adv. **wir haben uns** ~ **amüsiert** we had a marvellous time

blich 1. u. 3. Pers. Sg. Prät. v. BLEICHEN[2]

Blick der; ~[e]s, ~e (a) look; (flüchtig) glance

(b) (Ausdruck) look in one's eyes; **mit misstrauischem** ~: with a suspicious look in one's eye (c) (Aussicht) view; **ein Zimmer mit** ~ **aufs Meer** a room with a sea view (d) (Urteil[skraft]) eye

blicken ① itr. V. look; (flüchtig) glance ② tr. V. **sich** ~ **lassen** put in an appearance

Blick-: ~**fang** der eye-catcher; **als** ~**fang dienen** serve to catch the eye; ~**feld** das field of vision; ~**kontakt** der eye contact; ~**punkt** der view; ~**winkel** der (a) angle of vision; (b) (fig.) point of view; viewpoint

blieb 1. u. 3. Pers. Sg. Prät. v. BLEIBEN

blies 1. u. 3. Pers. Sg. Prät. v. BLASEN

blind ① Adj. (a) (auch fig.) blind; ~ **werden** go blind (b) (trübe) clouded ⟨glass⟩ (c) **ein** ~**er Passagier** a stowaway (d) ~**er Alarm** a false alarm ② adv. (a) (ohne hinzusehen) without looking; (wahllos) blindly (b) (unkritisch) ⟨trust⟩ implicitly; ⟨obey⟩ blindly

Blind-: ~**bewerbung** die unsolicited application; ~**darm** der (a) caecum; (b) (volkst.: Wurmfortsatz) appendix

Blinde der/die/adj. Dekl. blind person; blind man/woman; **die** ~n the blind

Blinde-kuh: ~ **spielen** play blind man's buff

Blinden-: ~**hund** der guide dog; ~**schrift** die Braille

Blindheit die; ~ (auch fig.) blindness

blindlings Adv. blindly; ⟨trust⟩ implicitly

blind-, Blind-: ~**probe** die blind tasting; ~**schleiche** die; ~~, ~~n slowworm; ~**wütig** ① Adj. raging ⟨anger, hatred, fury, etc.⟩; wild ⟨rage⟩; ② adv. in a blind rage

blinken ① itr. V. (a) ⟨light, glass, crystal⟩ flash; ⟨star⟩ twinkle; ⟨metal, fish⟩ gleam (b) (Verkehrsw.) indicate ② tr. V. flash

Blinker der; ~s, ~: indicator [light]

Blink-: ~**licht** das (a) flashing light; (b) ▶ BLINKER; ~**zeichen** das flashlight signal

blinzeln itr. V. blink; (mit einem Auge, um ein Zeichen zu geben) wink

Blitz der; ~es, ~e (a) lightning no indef. art.; **ein** ~: a flash of lightning; **[schnell] wie der** ~: like lightning (b) (Blitzlicht) flash

blitz-, Blitz-: ~**ab-leiter** der lightning conductor; ~**artig** ① Adj. lightning; ② adv. like lightning; ⟨disappear⟩ in a flash; ~**blank** Adj. (ugs.) ~**blank [geputzt]** sparkling clean; brightly polished ⟨shoes⟩

blitzeblank ▶ BLITZBLANK

blitzen itr. V. (a) unpers. **es blitzte** (einmal) there was a flash of lightning; (mehrmals) there was lightning ····>

(b) (glänzen) ⟨*light, glass, crystal*⟩ flash; ⟨*metal*⟩ gleam

blitz-, Blitz-: ~**gerät** das flash [unit]; ~**licht** das flash[light]; ~**schnell** ① *Adj.* lightning *attrib.*; ~**schnell sein** be like lightning; ② *adv.* like lightning; ⟨*disappear*⟩ in a flash; ~**start** der lightning start

Block der; ~[e]s, Blöcke od. ~s **(a)** Pl. nur Blöcke (Brocken) block

(b) (Wohnblock) block

(c) Pl. nur **Blöcke** (Gruppierung von politischen Kräften, Staaten) bloc

(d) (Schreibblock) pad

Blockade die; ~, ~n blockade

Block-: ~**flöte** die recorder; ~**haus** das, ~**hütte** die log cabin

blockieren tr. V. block; jam ⟨*telephone line*⟩; halt ⟨*traffic*⟩; lock ⟨*wheel, machine, etc.*⟩

Block·schrift die block capitals pl.

blöd[e] (ugs.) ① *Adj.* **(a)** (dumm) stupid; idiotic (coll.)

(b) (unangenehm) stupid

② *adv.* stupidly; idiotically (coll.)

Blödelei die; ~, ~en silly joke

blödeln itr. V. make silly jokes

Blödheit die; ~, ~en stupidity

blöd-, Blöd-: ~**mann** der; Pl. ~**männer** (salopp) stupid idiot (coll.); ~**sinn** der (ugs.) nonsense; **mach doch keinen** ~**sinn!** don't be stupid; ~**sinnig** (ugs.) ① *Adj.* idiotic (coll.); ② *adv.* idiotically (coll.)

blöken itr. V. ⟨*sheep*⟩ bleat; ⟨*cattle*⟩ low

blond *Adj.* fair-haired, blond ⟨*man, race*⟩; blonde ⟨*woman*⟩; blond/blonde, fair ⟨*hair*⟩

Blondchen das; ~s, ~ (ugs. abwertend) blonde bimbo (coll.)

Blondine die; ~, ~n blonde

bloß ① *Adj.* **(a)** (nackt) naked

(b) (nichts als) mere ⟨*words, promises, triviality, suspicion, etc.*⟩; der ~e Gedanke daran the mere thought of it

② *Adv.* (ugs.: nur) only

③ *Partikel* **was hast du dir** ~ **dabei gedacht?** what on earth were you thinking of?

Blöße die; ~: **sich** (*Dat.*) **eine/keine** ~ **geben** show a/not show any weakness

bloß|stellen tr. V. show up; expose ⟨*swindler, criminal, etc.*⟩

Blouson /blu'zõ:/ das od. der; ~s, ~s blouson

blubbern itr. V. (ugs.) bubble

Bluejeans /'blu:dʒi:ns/ Pl. od. die; ~, ~: [blue] jeans pl.

Blues /blu:s/ der; ~, ~: blues pl.

Bluff der; ~s, ~s bluff

bluffen tr., itr. V. bluff

blühen itr. V. **(a)** ⟨*plant*⟩ flower, be in flower or bloom; ⟨*flower*⟩ be in bloom,

be out; ⟨*tree*⟩ be in blossom; ~**de Gärten** gardens full of flowers

(b) (florieren) thrive

(c) (ugs.: bevorstehen) jmdm. ~: be in store for sb.; **das kann dir auch noch** ~: the same could happen to you

blühend *Adj.* **(a)** (frisch, gesund) glowing ⟨*colour, complexion, etc.*⟩; radiant ⟨*health*⟩

(b) (übertrieben) vivid ⟨*imagination*⟩

Blümchen das; ~s, ~: [little] flower

Blume die; ~, ~n **(a)** flower

(b) (des Weines) bouquet

(c) (des Biers) head

blumen-, Blumen-: ~**beet** das flower bed; ~**erde** die potting compost; ~**geschäft** das florist's; ~**geschmückt** *Adj.* flower-bedecked; adorned with flowers *postpos.*; ~**kasten** der flower box; (vor einem Fenster) window box; ~**kohl** der cauliflower; ~**strauß** der; Pl. ~**sträuße** bunch of flowers; (Bukett) bouquet of flowers; ~**topf** der flowerpot; ~**vase** die [flower] vase; ~**zwiebel** die bulb

Bluse die; ~, ~n blouse

Blut das; ~[e]s blood

blut-, Blut-: ~**arm** *Adj.* (Med.) anaemic; ~**armut** die (Med.) anaemia; ~**bad** das bloodbath; ~**bahn** die bloodstream; ~**bank** die; Pl. ~~**en** (Med.) blood bank; ~**befleckt** *Adj.* bloodstained; ~**beschmiert** *Adj.* smeared with blood *postpos.*; ~**buche** die copper beech; ~**druck** der; Pl. ~**drücke** blood pressure

Blüte die; ~, ~n **(a)** flower; bloom; (eines Baums) blossom; ~**n treiben** flower; ⟨*tree*⟩ blossom

(b) (das Blühen) flowering; (Baumblüte) blossoming

Blut·egel der; ~s, ~: leech

bluten itr. V. bleed **(aus** from)

blüten-, Blüten-: ~**blatt** das petal; ~**honig** der blossom honey; ~**staub** der pollen; ~**weiß** *Adj.* sparkling white

Bluter der; ~s, ~, **Bluterin** die; ~, ~nen (Med.) haemophiliac

Blut·erguss, *Blut·erguß der haematoma; (blauer Fleck) bruise

Bluter·krankheit die haemophilia no art.

Blut-: ~**fleck[en]** der bloodstain; ~**gefäß** das (Anat.) blood vessel; ~**gerinnsel** das; ~~**s, ~~** blood clot; ~**gruppe** die blood group; ~**hochdruck** der high blood pressure; ~**hund** der bloodhound

blutig (a) bloody; jmdn. ~ **schlagen** beat sb. to a pulp

(b) (fig. ugs.: völlig) complete ⟨*beginner, layman, etc.*⟩

blut-, Blut-: ~**jung** *Adj.* very young; ~**konserve** die container of stored blood; ~**konserven** stored blood; ~**körperchen**

---

*alte Schreibung – vgl. Hinweis auf S. x

das; ~~s, ~~: blood corpuscle; **rote/weiße** ~**körperchen** red/white corpuscles; ~**krebs** *der* leukaemia; ~**kreislauf** *der* blood circulation; ~**lache** *die* pool of blood; ~**leer** *Adj.* bloodless; ~**leere** *die* restricted blood supply; ~**orange** *die* blood orange; ~**plasma** *das* (Physiol.) blood plasma; ~**probe** *die* (a) (~entnahme, ~untersuchung) blood test; (b) (kleine ~menge) blood sample; ~**rache** *die* blood revenge; ~**rot** *Adj.* blood-red; ~**rünstig** ⟨1⟩ *Adj.* bloodthirsty; ⟨2⟩ *adv.* bloodthirstily; ~**schande** *die* incest; ~**spende** *die* (das Spenden) giving *no indef. art.* of blood; (~menge) blood donation; ~**spender** *der;* ~**spenderin** *die* blood donor; ~**spur** *die* trail of blood; ~**stillend** *Adj.* styptic

bluts-, Bluts-: ~**tropfen** *der* drop of blood; ~**verwandt** *Adj.* related by blood *postpos.;* ~**verwandtschaft** *die* blood relationship

Blut-: ~**tat** *die* (geh.) bloody deed; ~**transfusion** *die* blood transfusion; ~**übertragung** *die* blood transfusion

Blutung *die;* ~, ~en (a) bleeding *no indef. art., no pl.* (b) (Regelblutung) period

blut-, Blut-: ~**unterlaufen** *Adj.* suffused with blood *postpos.;* bloodshot ⟨eyes⟩; ~**vergießen** *das;* ~~s bloodshed; ~**vergiftung** *die* blood poisoning *no indef. art., no pl.;* ~**wurst** *die* black pudding; ~**zucker-spiegel** *der* (Physiol.) blood-sugar level

Bö *die;* ~, ~en gust [of wind]

boarden /'bɔːdn̩/ ⟨1⟩ *itr. V.* (a) (Flugw.) board (b) *mit sein* (snowboarden) snowboard. ⟨2⟩ *tr. V.* (Seew. Jargon) board [and inspect] ⟨vessel⟩

Bob *der;* ~, ~s bob[sleigh]

Bob-: ~**bahn** *die* bob[sleigh] run; ~**fahrer** *der,* ~**fahrerin** *die* bobber

Bock¹ *der;* ~[e]s, Böcke (a) (Reh~, Kaninchen~) buck; (Ziegen~) billy goat; he-goat; (Schafs~) ram; **einen/keinen** ~ **auf** etw. (*Akk.*) **haben** (ugs.) fancy/not fancy sth.; **einen/keinen** ~ **haben, etw. zu tun** (ugs.) fancy/not fancy doing sth. (b) (Gestell) trestle (c) (Turngerät) buck

Bock² *das;* ~s (Bier) bock [beer]

Bock·bier *das* bock [beer]

bocken *itr. V.* refuse to go on; (vor einer Hürde) refuse; (sich aufbäumen) buck

bockig ⟨1⟩ *Adj.* stubborn and awkward ⟨2⟩ *adv.* stubbornly [and awkwardly]

Bocks·horn *das:* **sich ins** ~ **jagen lassen** (ugs.) let oneself be browbeaten

Bock-: ~**springen** *das;* ~~s (Turnen) vaulting [over the buck]; ~**wurst** *die* bockwurst

Boden *der;* ~s, Böden (a) (Erd~) ground; (Fuß~) floor; **am** ~ **zerstört [sein]** (ugs.) [be]

shattered (coll.); **bleiben wir doch auf dem** ~ **der Tatsachen** (fig.) let's stick to the facts (b) (unterste Fläche) bottom; (Torten~) base (c) (Dach~, Heu~) loft

boden-, Boden-: ~**belag** *der* floor-covering; ~**ertrag** *der* crop yield; ~**fläche** *die* land area; ~**frost** *der* ground frost; ~**kammer** *die* attic; ~**los** *Adj.* (a) bottomless; (b) (ugs.: unerhört) incredible ⟨foolishness, meanness, etc.⟩; ~**nebel** *der* ground fog/mist; ~**satz** *der* sediment; ~**schätze** *Pl.* mineral resources

Boden·see *der;* ~s Lake Constance

boden-, Boden-: ~**ständig** *Adj.* indigenous ⟨culture, population, etc.⟩; ~**turnen** *das* floor exercises *pl.;* ~**welle** *die* bump

Bodybuilding /ˈbɔdibɪldɪŋ/ *das;* ~s bodybuilding *no art.*

Böe *die;* ~, ~n ► Bö

bog *1. u. 3. Pers. Sg. Prät. v.* BIEGEN

Bogen *der;* ~s, ~, (südd., österr.:) Bögen (a) curve; (Math.) arc (b) (Archit.) arch (c) (Waffe, Musik: Geigen~ usw.) bow (d) (Papier~) sheet

bogen-, Bogen-: ~**fenster** *das* arched window; ~**förmig** *Adj.* arched; ~**schießen** *das;* ~~s archery *no art.*

Boheme /boˈeːm/ *die;* ~: bohemian society

Bohemien /boeˈmiɛ̃:/ *der;* ~s, ~s bohemian

Bohle *die;* ~, ~n [thick] plank

Böhnchen *das;* ~s, ~: [small] bean

Bohne *die;* ~, ~n bean; **nicht die** ~ (ugs.) not one little bit

Bohnen-: ~**eintopf** *der* bean stew; ~**kaffee** *der* real coffee; ~**kraut** *das* savory; ~**stange** *die* (auch ugs.: Mensch) beanpole; ~**stroh** *das:* **dumm wie** ~**stroh** (ugs.) as thick as two short planks (coll.); ~**suppe** *die* bean soup

bohnern *tr., itr. V.* polish

Bohner·wachs *das* floor polish

bohren ⟨1⟩ *tr. V.* (a) bore; (mit Bohrer, Bohrmaschine) drill ⟨hole⟩; sink ⟨well, shaft, pole, post etc.⟩ (**in** + *Akk.* into) (b) (bearbeiten) drill ⟨wood, concrete, etc.⟩ (c) (drücken in) poke (**in** + *Akk.* in[to]) ⟨2⟩ *itr. V.* (a) drill; **in der Nase** ~: pick one's nose; **nach Öl/Wasser** *usw.* ~: drill for oil/water *etc.* (b) (ugs.: drängen, fragen) keep on ⟨3⟩ *refl. V.* bore its way

bohrend *Adj.* (a) gnawing ⟨pain, hunger, remorse⟩ (b) (hartnäckig) piercing ⟨look etc.⟩; probing ⟨question⟩

Bohrer *der;* ~s, ~ drill

Bohr-: ~**hammer** *der* hammer drill; ~**insel** *die* drilling rig; ···⊹

∼maschine die drill; **∼schrauber** der power drill/screwdriver; **∼turm** der derrick

Bohrung die; ∼, ∼en drill hole

böig Adj. gusty

Boiler /'bɔylɐ/ der; ∼s, ∼: water heater

Boje die; ∼, ∼n buoy

Bolivien /bo'li:vi̯ən/ (das); ∼s Bolivia

Böller·schuss, ***Böller·schuß** der gun salute

Boll·werk das bulwark; (fig.) bulwark; bastion; stronghold

Bolschewik der; ∼en, ∼i, (abwertend:) ∼en, **Bolschewikin** die; ∼, ∼nen Bolshevik

Bolschewismus der; ∼: Bolshevism no art.

Bolschewist der; ∼en, ∼en, **Bolschewistin** die; ∼, ∼nen Bolshevist

bolschewistisch Adj. Bolshevik

bolzen (ugs.) itr. V. kick the ball about

Bolzen der; ∼s, ∼: bolt

bombardieren tr. V. (a) bomb (b) (fig. ugs.) bombard

Bombardierung die; ∼, ∼en (a) (Milit.) bombing (b) (fig. ugs.) bombardment

bombastisch ① Adj. bombastic ② adv. bombastically

Bombe die; ∼, ∼n bomb

bomben-, Bomben-: ∼angriff der bomb attack; ∼anschlag der bomb attack; ∼attentat das bomb attack; ∼drohung die bomb threat; ∼erfolg der (ugs.) smash hit (coll.); ∼fest Adj. (ugs.: unveränderbar) dead certain; ∼fest stehen be dead certain; be a dead cert (Brit. coll.); ∼form die (ugs.) top form; ∼sicher Adj. (ugs.: gewiss) dead certain; **das ist eine ∼sichere Sache** that's dead certain; that's a dead cert (Brit. coll.) or a sure thing (Amer.); ∼stimmung die (ugs.) tremendous or fantastic atmosphere (coll.); ∼trichter der bomb crater

Bomber der; ∼s, ∼: bomber

Bon /bɔŋ/ der; ∼s, ∼s (a) voucher; coupon (b) (Kassenzettel) receipt

Bonbon /bɔŋ'bɔŋ/ der od. (österr. nur) das; ∼s, ∼s sweet (Brit.); candy (Amer.); (fig.) treat

bongen tr. V. (ugs.) ring up; **gebongt sein** (ugs.) be fine; **ist gebongt!** (ugs.) fine!

Bongo das; ∼[s], ∼s od. die; ∼, ∼s bongo [drum]

Bonmot /bõ'mo:/ das; ∼s, ∼s bon mot

Bonze der; ∼n, ∼n bigwig (coll.)

boolesch /'bu:lʃ/ Adj. (Math., DV) Boolean

Boom /bu:m/ der; ∼s, ∼s boom

Boot das; ∼[e]s, ∼e boat

Boots-: ∼fahrt die boat trip; ∼haus das boathouse; ∼steg der landing stage;

∼verleih der boat hire

Bord[1] das; ∼[e]s, ∼e shelf

Bord[2] der; ∼[e]s, ∼e (eines Schiffes) side; **an ∼:** on board; **über ∼:** overboard

Bordell das; ∼s, ∼e brothel

Bord-stein der kerb

Bordüre die; ∼, ∼n edging

borgen tr. V.: ▶ LEIHEN

Borke die; ∼, ∼n bark

Borken-käfer der bark beetle

borniert ① Adj. bigoted ② adv. in a bigoted way

Börse die; ∼, ∼n stock market; (Gebäude) stock exchange

Börsen-: ∼krach der stock market crash; ∼makler der stockbroker

Borste die; ∼, ∼n bristle

borstig Adj. bristly

Borte die; ∼, ∼n braiding no indef. art.; edging no indef. art.

bös ▶ BÖSE

bös-artig ① Adj. (a) (heimtückisch) malicious ⟨person, remark, etc.⟩; vicious ⟨animal⟩ (b) (Med.) malignant ② adv. maliciously

Bös-artigkeit die; ∼ (a) maliciousness; (von Tieren) viciousness (b) (Med.) malignancy

Böschung die; ∼, ∼en embankment

böse ① Adj. (a) wicked; evil (b) (übel) bad ⟨times, illness, dream, etc.⟩; nasty ⟨experience, affair, situation, trick, surprise, etc.⟩ (c) (ugs.) (wütend) mad (coll.); (verärgert) cross (coll.) (d) (fam.: ungezogen) naughty (e) (ugs.: arg) terrible (coll.) ⟨pain, fall, shock, disappointment, storm, etc.⟩ ② adv. (a) (übel) ⟨end⟩ badly; **es war doch nicht ∼ gemeint** I didn't mean it nastily (b) (ugs.) (wütend) angrily; (verärgert) crossly (coll.) (c) (ugs.: sehr) terribly (coll.)

boshaft ① Adj. malicious ② adv. maliciously

Boshaftigkeit die; ∼, ∼en (a) maliciousness (b) (Bemerkung) malicious remark

Bosheit die; ∼, ∼en (a) malice (b) (Bemerkung) malicious remark

Boss, ***Boß** der; Bosses, Bosse (ugs.) boss (coll.)

bös-willig ① Adj. malicious; wilful ⟨desertion⟩ ② adv. maliciously; wilfully ⟨desert⟩

Bös-willigkeit die; ∼: malice; maliciousness

bot 1. u. 3. Pers. Sg. Prät. v. BIETEN

Botanik die; ∼: botany no art.

botanisch ① Adj. botanical ② adv. botanically

Bötchen *das;* ~s, ~: little boat

Bote *der;* ~n, ~n (a) messenger
  (b) (Laufbursche) errand boy

Botin *die;* ~, ~nen ▶ BOTE: (a) messenger
  (b) errand girl

Botschaft *die;* ~, ~en (a) message
  (b) (diplomatische Vertretung) embassy

Botschafter *der;* ~s, ~,
  Botschafterin *die;* ~, ~nen
  ambassador

Böttcher *der;* ~s, ~, **Böttcherin** *die;*
  ~, ~nen cooper

Bottich *der;* ~s, ~e tub

Bouillon /bul'jɔŋ/ *die;* ~, ~s bouillon

Boulevard /bulə'vaːɐ̯/ *der;* ~s, ~s
  boulevard

Boulevard-: ~**blatt** *das*
  ▶ BOULEVARDZEITUNG; ~**presse** *die*
  (abwertend) popular press; ~**stück** *das*
  (Theater) boulevard drama; ~**zeitung** *die*
  (abwertend) popular rag (derog.); tabloid

Bourgeoisie /burʒoa'ziː/ *die;* ~, ~n
  bourgeoisie

Boutique /bu'tiːk/ *die;* ~, ~s *od.* ~n
  boutique

Bowle /'boːlə/ *die;* ~, ~n punch *(made of
  wine, champagne, sugar, and fruit or spices)*

bowlen /'boːlən/ *itr. V.* bowl

Bowling /'boːlɪŋ/ *das;* ~s, ~s [tenpin]
  bowling

Bowling-bahn *die* bowling alley

Box *die;* ~, ~en (a) box
  (b) (Lautsprecher) speaker
  (c) (Pferdebox) [loose] box
  (d) (Motorsport) pit

boxen ⊡ *itr. V.* box; **gegen jmdn.** ~: fight
  sb.; box [against] sb.
  ⊡ *tr. V.* punch

Boxen-stopp *der* (Motorsport) pit stop

Boxer *der;* ~s, ~ (Sportler, Hund) boxer

Boxerin *die;* ~, ~nen boxer

Box-: ~**handschuh** *der* boxing glove;
  ~**kampf** *der* boxing match; (im Streit) fist
  fight; ~**ring** *der* boxing ring; ~**sport** *der*
  boxing *no art.*

Boy /bɔy/ *der;* ~s, ~s servant; (im Hotel)
  pageboy

Boykott /bɔy'kɔt/ *der;* ~[e]s, ~s boycott

boykottieren *tr. V.* boycott

brach[1] *1. u. 3. Pers. Sg. Prät. v.* BRECHEN

brach[2] *Adj.* fallow; (auf Dauer) uncultivated

Brachial-gewalt *die* brute force

Brach-land *das* fallow [land]; (auf Dauer)
  uncultivated land

brach|liegen *unr. itr. V.* (auch fig.) lie
  fallow; (auf Dauer) lie waste

brachte *1. u. 3. Pers. Sg. Prät. v.* BRINGEN

Branche /'brãːʃə/ *die;* ~, ~n [branch of]
  industry

Branchen-: ~**führer** *der,* ~**führerin**
  die (Wirtsch.) market[-sector] leader; (einer

Industrie) industry leader; ~**verzeichnis**
  das classified directory; (Telefonbuch) Yellow
  Pages ® *pl.*

Brand *der;* ~[e]s, Brände fire; **beim** ~ **der
  Scheune** when the barn caught fire; **etw. in**
  ~ **stecken** set fire to sth.

Brand-anschlag *der* arson attack (**auf**
  + *Akk.* on)

branden *itr. V.* (geh.) break

Branden-burg (*das*); ~s Brandenburg

brand-, Brand-: ~**fall** *der* fire; **im** ~**fall/
  für den** ~**fall** in case of fire; ~**marken**
  tr. V. brand *‹person›*; denounce *‹thing›*;
  ~**neu** *Adj.* (ugs.) brand-new; ~**salbe**
  die ointment for burns; ~**schaden** *der*
  fire damage *no pl., no indef. art.;* ~**stelle**
  die burn; ~**stifter** *der,* ~**stifterin** *die*
  arsonist; ~**stiftung** *die* arson

Brandung *die;* ~, ~en surf

Brand-wunde *die* burn

brannte *1. u. 3. Pers. Sg. Prät. v.* BRENNEN

Brannt-wein *der* spirits *pl.;* (Sorte) spirit

Brasilianer *der;* ~s, ~, **Brasilianerin**
  die; ~, ~nen Brazilian

brasilianisch *Adj.* Brazilian

Brasilien /bra'ziːliən/ (*das*); ~s Brazil

brät *3. Pers. Sg. Präsens v.* BRATEN

Brat-apfel *der* baked apple

braten *unr. tr., itr. V.* fry; (im Backofen) roast

Braten *der;* ~s, ~ (a) joint
  (b) roast [meat] *no indef. art.*

Braten-: ~**saft** *der* meat juice[s *pl.*];
  ~**soße** *die* gravy

Brat-: ~**fett** *das* [cooking] fat; ~**fisch**
  der fried fish; ~**hähnchen** *das,* (südd.,
  österr.) ~**hendl** *das* roast chicken; (gegrillt)
  broiled chicken; ~**hering** *der* fried
  herring; ~**kartoffeln** *Pl.* fried potatoes;
  home fries (Amer.); ~**pfanne** *die* frying
  pan; ~**spieß** *der* spit; ~**wurst** *die*
  [fried/grilled] sausage

Brauch *der;* ~[e]s, Bräuche custom

brauchbar *Adj.* useful; (benutzbar) usable;
  wearable *‹clothes›*

brauchen ⊡ *tr. V.* (a) (benötigen) need
  (b) (aufwenden müssen) **mit dem Auto braucht
  er zehn Minuten** it takes him ten minutes by
  car; **wie lange brauchst du dafür?** how long
  will it take you?; (im Allgemeinen) how long
  does it take you?
  (c) (benutzen, gebrauchen) use; **ich könnte es
  gut** ~: I could do with it
  ⊡ *mod. V.;2. Part* brauchen: need; **du
  brauchst nicht zu helfen** there is no need [for
  you] to help; **du brauchst doch nicht gleich
  zu weinen** there's no need to start crying

Brauchtum /'brauxtuːm/ *das;* ~s,
  Brauchtümer custom

Braue *die;* ~, ~n [eye]brow

brauen *tr. V.* brew

Brauerei *die;* ~, ~en brewery

braun *Adj.* brown; ~ **werden** ····⊱

b

(sonnengebräunt) get a tan; **~ gebrannt** [sun]-tanned

Braun *das;* ~s, ~, (ugs.) ~s brown

Braun-bär *der* brown bear

Bräune *die;* ~: [sun]tan

bräunen *tr. V.* **(a)** tan; **sich ~:** get a tan **(b)** (Kochk.) brown

braun-, Braun-: *~**gebrannt** ▶ BRAUN; ~**kohle** *die* brown coal; lignite

bräunlich *Adj.* brownish

Bräunung *die;* ~, ~en browning

Braus ▶ SAUS

Brause *die;* ~, ~n **(a)** fizzy drink; (~pulver) sherbet **(b)** (veralt.: Dusche) shower

brausen ① *itr. V.* **(a)** ⟨wind, water, etc.⟩ roar **(b)** (sich schnell bewegen) race **(c)** *auch refl.:* ▶ DUSCHEN 1 ② *tr. V.* ▶ DUSCHEN 2

Brause-: ~**pulver** *das* sherbet; ~**tablette** *die* effervescent tablet

Braut *die;* ~, Bräute bride

Bräutigam *der;* ~s, ~e [bride]groom

Braut-: ~**jungfer** *die* bridesmaid; ~**kleid** *das* wedding dress; ~**paar** *das* bride and groom

brav ① *Adj.* **(a)** (artig) good **(b)** (redlich) honest ② *adv.* **nun iss schön ~ deine Suppe** be a good boy/girl and eat up your soup

bravo /'braːvo/ *Interj.* bravo

Bravo *das;* ~s, ~s cheer

Bravo-ruf *der* cheer

BRD *Abk.* = **Bundesrepublik Deutschland** FRG

Brech-: ~**bohne** *die* green bean; ~**eisen** *das* crowbar

brechen ① *unr. tr. V.* **(a)** break; **sich** (*Dat.*) **den Arm/das Genick ~:** break one's arm/neck **(b)** (ablenken) break ⟨waves⟩; refract ⟨light⟩ **(c)** (bezwingen) overcome ⟨resistance⟩; break ⟨will, silence, record, blockade, etc.⟩ **(d)** (nicht einhalten) break ⟨agreement, contract, promise, the law, etc.⟩ **(e)** (ugs.: erbrechen) bring up ② *unr. itr. V.* **(a)** *mit sein* break; **brechend voll sein** be full to bursting **(b)** **mit jmdm. ~:** break with sb. **(c)** *mit sein* **durch etw. ~:** break through sth. **(d)** (ugs.: sich erbrechen) throw up ③ *unr. refl. V.* ⟨waves etc.⟩ break; ⟨rays etc.⟩ be refracted

Brecher *der;* ~s, ~: breaker

Brech-: ~**mittel** *das* emetic; ~**reiz** *der* nausea; ~**stange** *die* crowbar

Bredouille /breˈdʊljə/ *die;* ~, ~n (ugs.) **in der ~ sein** *od.* **sitzen** be in real trouble; **in die ~ kommen** get into real trouble

Brei *der;* ~[e]s, ~e (Hafer~) porridge (Brit.), oatmeal (Amer.) *no indef. art.;* (Reis~) rice pudding; (Grieß~) semolina *no indef. art.*

breiig *Adj.* mushy

breit ① *Adj.* **(a)** wide; broad, wide ⟨hips, face, shoulders, forehead, etc.⟩; **etw. ~er machen** widen sth.; **die Beine ~ machen** open one's legs; **ein 5 cm ~er Saum** a hem 5 cm wide **(b)** (groß) **die ~e Masse** the general public **(c)** **sich ~ machen** take up room; (sich ausbreiten) be spreading ② *adv.* **~ gebaut** sturdily built

Breit-: ~**band** *das* (DV) broadband; ~**band·anschluss** *der* (DV) broadband connection

breit·beinig ① *Adj.* rolling ⟨gait⟩ ② *adv.* with one's legs apart

Breite *die;* ~, ~n **(a)** ▶ BREIT 1A: width; breadth **(b)** (Geogr.) latitude

breiten (geh.) *tr., refl. V.* spread

Breiten-: ~**grad** *der* degree of latitude; parallel (~kreis); ~**kreis** *der* parallel

breit-, Breit-: *~**|machen** ▶ BREIT 1C; ~**schult[e]rig** *Adj.* broad-shouldered; ~**seite** *die* long side; (eines Schiffes) side; ~**|treten** *unr. tr. V.* (ugs. abwertend) go on about; ~**wand** *die* (Kino) big screen

Bremen (*das;*) ~s Bremen

Brems-: ~**backe** *die* brake shoe; ~**belag** *der* brake lining

Bremse¹ *die;* ~, ~n brake

Bremse² *die;* ~, ~n (Insekt) horsefly

bremsen *tr. V.* **(a)** *auch itr.* brake **(b)** (fig.) slow down ⟨rate, development, production, etc.⟩; restrict ⟨imports etc.⟩

Brems-: ~**klotz** *der* brake pad; ~**licht** *das* brake light; ~**pedal** *das* brake pedal; ~**spur** *die* skid mark; ~**weg** *der* braking distance; ~**zug** *der* brake cable

brenn·bar *Adj.* combustible

brennen ① *unr. itr. V.* **(a)** burn; ⟨house etc.⟩ be on fire; **schnell/leicht ~:** catch fire quickly/easily; **es brennt!** fire! **(b)** (glühen) be alight **(c)** (leuchten) be on; **das Licht ~ lassen** leave the light on **(d)** **die Sonne brannte** the sun was burning down **(e)** (schmerzen) ⟨wound etc.⟩ sting; ⟨feet etc.⟩ be sore **(f)** **darauf ~, etw. zu tun** be dying to do sth. ② *unr. tr. V.* **(a)** burn ⟨hole, pattern, etc.⟩; **einem Tier ein Zeichen ins Fell ~:** brand an animal **(b)** (mit Hitze behandeln) fire ⟨porcelain etc.⟩; distil ⟨spirits⟩ **(c)** (rösten) roast ⟨coffee beans, almonds, etc.⟩

brennend ① *Adj.* (auch fig.) burning; lighted ⟨cigarette⟩; urgent ⟨topic⟩ ② *adv.* **es interessiert mich ~, ob ...:** I'm dying to know whether ...

---

*alte Schreibung – vgl. Hinweis auf S. x

Brenner der; ~s, ~: burner
Brennerei die; ~, ~en distillery
*Brennnessel die; ~, ~n ▶ BRENNNESSEL
Brenn-: ~**glas** das burning glass; ~**holz** das firewood; ~**material** das fuel; ~**nessel** die stinging nettle; ~**ofen** der kiln; ~**punkt** der focus; ~**spiritus** der methylated spirits pl.; ~**stoff** der fuel; ~**stoff-zelle** die fuel cell; ~**weite** die (Optik) focal length
brenzlig Adj. (a) ⟨smell, taste, etc.⟩ of burning not pred.
(b) (ugs.: gefährlich) dicey (coll.)
Bresche die; ~, ~n gap; breach; [für jmdn.] in die ~ springen stand in [for sb.]
Brett das; ~[e]s, ~er (a) board; (lang und dick) plank; (Diele) floorboard; **schwarzes** ~: noticeboard; **ein** ~ **vor dem Kopf haben** (fig. ugs.) be thick
(b) Pl. (Ski) skis
Bretter-: ~**wand** die wooden partition; ~**zaun** der wooden fence
Brett-spiel das board game
Brezel die; ~, ~n pretzel
Bridge /brɪtʃ/ das; ~: bridge
Brief der; ~[e]s, ~e letter
Brief-: ~**beschwerer** der; ~~s, ~~: paperweight; ~**block** der; Pl. ~~s od. ~**blöcke** writing pad; ~**bogen** der sheet of writing paper; ~**freund** der, ~**freundin** die penfriend; pen pal (coll.); ~**freundschaft** die penfriendship; ~**geheimnis** das privacy of the post; ~**karte** die correspondence card; ~**kasten** der (a) postbox; (b) (privat) letter box; ~**kopf** der (a) letter heading; (b) (aufgedruckt) letterhead; ~**kuvert** das (veralt.) ▶ ~UMSCHLAG
brieflich ① Adj. written
② adv. by letter
Brief-marke die [postage] stamp
Briefmarken-: ~**album** das stamp album; ~**sammler** der, ~**sammlerin** die stamp collector; ~**sammlung** die stamp collection
Brief-: ~**öffner** der letter-opener; ~**papier** das writing paper; ~**partner** der, ~**partnerin** die penfriend; ~**schreiber** der, ~**schreiberin** die [letter-]writer; ~**tasche** die wallet; ~**taube** die carrier pigeon; ~**träger** der postman; letter-carrier (Amer.); ~**trägerin** die postwoman; [female] letter-carrier (Amer.); ~**umschlag** der envelope; ~**waage** die letter scales pl.; ~**wahl** die postal vote; ~**wechsel** der correspondence
Bries das; ~es, ~e (Kochk.) sweetbreads pl.
briet 1. u. 3. Pers. Sg. Prät. v. BRATEN
Brigade die; ~, ~n (Milit.) brigade
Brikett das; ~s, ~s briquette
brillant /brɪl'jant/ ① Adj. brilliant
② adv. brilliantly

Brillant der; ~en, ~en brilliant
Brillant-: ~**ring** der (brilliant-cut) diamond ring; ~**schmuck** der (brilliant-cut) diamond jewellery
Brillanz /brɪl'jants/ die; ~: brilliance
Brille die; ~, ~n (a) glasses pl.; spectacles pl.; **eine** ~: a pair of glasses or spectacles; **eine** ~ **tragen** wear glasses or spectacles
(b) (ugs.: Klosettbrille) [lavatory] seat
Brillen-: ~**etui** das, ~**futteral** das glasses case; spectacle case; ~**glas** das [spectacle] lens; ~**schlange** die spectacled cobra; ~**träger** der, ~**trägerin** die person who wears glasses; ~**träger/-trägerin sein** wear glasses
Brimborium das; ~s (ugs. abwertend) hoo-ha (coll.)
bringen unr. tr. V. (a) (her~) bring; (hin~) take; **jmdm. Glück/Unglück** ~: bring sb. [good] luck/bad luck; **jmdm. eine Nachricht** ~: bring sb. news
(b) (begleiten) take; **jmdn. nach Hause/zum Bahnhof** ~: take sb. home/to the station
(c) **es zu etwas/nichts** ~: get somewhere/ get nowhere
(d) **jmdn. ins Gefängnis** ~ ⟨crime, misdeed⟩ land sb. in gaol; **jmdn. wieder auf den rechten Weg** ~ (fig.) get sb. back on the straight and narrow; **jmdn. zum Lachen/zur Verzweiflung** ~: make sb. laugh/drive sb. to despair; **jmdn. dazu** ~, **etw. zu tun** get sb. to do sth.; **etw. hinter sich** ~ (ugs.) get sth. over and done with
(e) **jmdn. um seinen Besitz** ~: do sb. out of his property
(f) (präsentieren) present; (veröffentlichen) publish; (senden) broadcast
(g) **ein Opfer** ~: make a sacrifice
(h) **einen großen Gewinn/hohe Zinsen** ~: make a large profit/earn high interest
(i) **das bringt es mit sich, dass …:** that means that …
(j) (verursachen) cause
brisant Adj. explosive
Brisanz die; ~: explosiveness
Brise die; ~, ~n breeze
Britannien (das); ~s Britain; (hist.) Britannia
Brite der; ~n, ~n Briton; **die** ~n the British; **er ist [kein]** ~: he is [not] British
Britin die; ~, ~nen Briton; British girl/woman
britisch Adj. British; **die Britischen Inseln** the British Isles
bröckelig Adj. crumbly
bröckeln ① itr. V. (a) crumble
(b) mit sein **von der Wand** ~: crumble away from the wall
② tr. V. crumble
Brocken der; ~s, ~ (von Brot) hunk; (von Fleisch) chunk; (von Lehm, Kohle, Erde) lump; **ein paar** ~ **Englisch** (fig.) a smattering of English

brodeln itr. V. bubble
Broiler /'brɔylɐ/ der; ~s, ~ (regional)
▶ BRATHÄHNCHEN
Brok̲at der; ~[e]s, ~e brocade
Brokkoli der; ~s, ~[s] broccoli
Brom·beere die blackberry
Bronchie /'brɔnçiə/ die; ~, ~n bronchial
tube
Bronch̲itis die; ~, bronchitis
Bronze /'brõ:sə/ die; ~: bronze
Bronze-: ~**medaille** die bronze medal;
~**zeit** die Bronze Age
Brosche die; ~, ~n brooch
Broschu̲re die; ~, ~n booklet
Brösel der; ~s, ~: breadcrumb
brös̲elig Adj. crumbly
bröseln itr. V. crumble
Brot das; ~[e]s, ~e bread no pl., no indef.
art.; (Laib) loaf [of bread]; (Scheibe) slice [of
bread]
Brot-: ~**aufstrich** der spread; ~**belag**
der topping; (im zusammengeklappten Brot) filling
Brötchen das; ~s, ~: roll
Brot-: ~**erwerb** der way to earn a living;
~**korb** der bread basket; ~**laib** der loaf
[of bread]; ~**messer** das bread knife;
~**rinde** die [bread] crust; ~**zeit** die
(südd.) **(a)** (Pause) [tea/coffee/lunch] break;
(b) (Vesper) snack; (Vesperbrot) sandwiches pl.
Browser /'braʊzɐ/ der; ~s, ~ (DV)
browser
Bruch der; ~[e]s, Brüche **(a)** break; **in die
Brüche gehen** (zerbrechen) get broken; (fig.)
break up
(b) (Med.: Knochen~) fracture; break
(c) (Med.: Eingeweide~) hernia
(d) (fig.) (eines Versprechens) breaking; (eines
Abkommens, Gesetzes) violation
(e) (Math.) fraction
brüchig Adj. **(a)** brittle ⟨rock, brickwork⟩
(b) (fig.) crumbling ⟨relationship, marriage,
etc.⟩
Bruch-: ~**landung** die crash-landing;
~**rechnen** das fractions pl.; ~**strich**
der fraction line; ~**stück** das fragment;
~**teil** der fraction; **im** ~**teil einer Sekunde**
in a split second
Brücke die; ~, ~n **(a)** (auch:
Kommandobrücke, Zahnmed., Bodenturnen, Ringen)
bridge
(b) (Landungsbrücke) gangway
(c) (Teppich) rug
Brücken-: ~**bogen** der arch [of a/the
bridge]; ~**geländer** das parapet; ~**kopf**
der (Milit., auch fig.) bridgehead
Bruder der; ~s, Brüder brother
Brüderchen das; ~s, ~: little brother
brüderlich 1 Adj. brotherly
2 adv. in a brotherly way
Brüderlichkeit die; ~: brotherliness

*old spelling – see note on page x

Brüderschaft die; ~: [mit jmdm.]
~ **trinken** drink to close friendship [with
sb.] (agreeing to use the familiar 'du' form)
Brühe die; ~, ~n **(a)** stock; (als Suppe) clear
soup
(b) (ugs. abwertend) (Getränk) muck;
(verschmutztes Wasser) filthy water
brühen tr. V. **(a)** blanch
(b) (ugs.) brew; make ⟨tea⟩; make ⟨coffee⟩
brüh-, Brüh-: ~**warm** Adj. etw. ~**warm
weitererzählen** (ugs.) pass sth. on straight
away; ~**würfel** der stock cube
brüllen 1 itr. V. **(a)** ⟨bull, cow, etc.⟩ bellow;
⟨lion, tiger, etc.⟩ roar
(b) (ugs.) (schreien) roar; (weinen) howl
2 tr. V. yell
Brüller der; ~s, ~ (ugs.) **(a)** (etw. sehr
Komisches) scream (coll.)
(b) (Erfolg) hit
brummen tr., itr. V. **(a)** ⟨insect⟩ buzz;
⟨bear⟩ growl; ⟨engine etc.⟩ drone
(b) (unmelodisch singen) drone
(c) (mürrisch sprechen) mumble
Brummer der; ~s, ~ (ugs.) **(a)** (Fliege)
bluebottle
(b) (LKW) heavy lorry (Brit.) or truck
brummig Adj. (ugs.) grumpy
Brumm-: ~**kreisel** der humming top;
~**schädel** der (ugs.) thick head
brünett Adj. dark-haired ⟨person⟩; dark
⟨hair⟩
Brünette die; ~, ~n brunette
Brunnen der; ~s, ~ **(a)** well
(b) (Springbrunnen) fountain
Brunnen·kresse die watercress
Brunst die; ~, Brünste (von männlichen Tieren)
rut; (von weiblichen Tieren) heat
Brunst·zeit die (bei männlichen Tieren)
rutting season; (bei weiblichen Tieren) [season
of] heat
brüsk 1 Adj. brusque
2 adv. brusquely
brüskieren tr. V. offend; (stärker) insult;
(schneiden) snub
Brüssel (das); ~s Brussels
Brust die; ~, Brüste **(a)** chest
(b) (der Frau) breast
(c) (Hähnchen~) breast; (Rinder~) brisket
(d) (Brustschwimmen) breaststroke
brüsten refl. V. **sich mit etw.** ~: boast
about sth.
brust-, Brust-: ~**kasten** (ugs.) chest;
~**korb** der (Anat.) thorax (Anat.); ~**krebs**
der breast cancer; ~**schwimmen** unr.
itr. V.; nur im Inf. do [the] breaststroke;
~**schwimmen** das breaststroke;
~**tasche** die breast pocket
Brüstung die; ~, ~en parapet; (Balkon~)
balustrade
Brust·warze die nipple
Brut die; ~, ~en **(a)** brooding
(b) (Jungtiere, auch fig. scherzh.: Kinder) brood

brutal ┄┊┄ Bühne ┄┄┄

brutal 1 *Adj.* brutal; violent ⟨*attack, programme, etc.*⟩; brute ⟨*force, strength*⟩
  2 *adv.* brutally
Brutalität *die;* ~, ~**en (a)** brutality
  (b) (Handlung) act of brutality
brüten *itr. V.* **(a)** brood
  (b) (grübeln) ponder (**über** + *Dat.* over);
  brütend: ~ **heiß:** (ugs.) boiling hot
Brüter *der;* ~**s,** ~ (Kernphysik) breeder
Brut-: ~**kasten** *der* incubator;
  ~**reaktor** *der* (Kernphysik) breeder reactor;
  ~**stätte** *die* (auch fig.) breeding ground
brutto *Adv.* gross
Brutto-: ~**einkommen** *das*
  gross income; ~**gehalt** *das* gross
  salary; ~**lohn** *der* gross wage;
  ~**sozialprodukt** *das* (Wirtsch.) gross
  national product
brutzeln 1 *itr. V.* sizzle
  2 *tr. V.* (ugs.) fry [up]
BSE /beɛs'eː/ *die;* ~: BSE
Bub *der;* ~**en,** ~**en** (südd., österr., schweiz.)
  boy; lad
Bube *der;* ~**n,** ~**n** (Kartenspiele) jack; knave
Bubi *der;* ~**s,** ~**s (a)** [little] boy *or* lad
  (b) (salopp: Schnösel) young lad
Buch *das;* ~**[e]s,** Bücher (Dreh~)
  script; **über etw.** (*Akk.*) ~ **führen** keep a
  record of sth.
Buch-: ~**besprechung** *die* book
  review; ~**binder** *der,* ~**binderin** *die;*
  ~~, ~~**nen** bookbinder; ~**druck** *der*
  letterpress printing
Buche *die;* ~, ~**n (a)** beech [tree]
  (b) (Holz) beech[wood]
Buch·ecker *die;* ~, ~**n** beech nut
buchen *tr. V.* **(a)** enter
  (b) (vorbestellen) book
Bücher·brett *das* bookshelf
Bücherei *die;* ~, ~**en** library
Bücher-: ~**regal** *das* bookshelves
  pl.; ~**schrank** *der* bookcase;
  ~**verbrennung** *die* burning of books;
  ~**wurm** *der* (scherzh.) bookworm
Buch-: ~**fink** *der* chaffinch; ~**führung**
  die bookkeeping; ~**halter** *der,*
  ~**halterin** *die* bookkeeper; ~**haltung**
  die **(a)** accountancy; **(b)** (Abteilung)
  accounts department; ~**händler**
  der, ~**händlerin** *die* bookseller;
  ~**handlung** *die* bookshop; ~**klub**
  der book club; ~**laden** *der; Pl.* ~läden
  ▶ ~HANDLUNG; ~**messe** *die* book fair;
  ~**rücken** *der* spine
Buchs·baum /'buks-/ *der* box [tree]
Buchse /'buksə/ *die;* ~, ~**n (a)** (Elektrot.)
  socket
  (b) (Technik) bush
Büchse /'bʏksə/ *die;* ~, ~**n (a)** tin
  (b) (ugs.: Sammel~) [collecting] box
  (c) (Gewehr) rifle; (Schrot~) shotgun
Büchsen- ▶ DOSEN-

Buchstabe *der;* ~**ns,** ~**n** letter; (Druckw.)
  character; **ein großer/kleiner** ~: a capital
  [letter]/small letter
buchstabieren *tr. V.* spell
buchstäblich *Adv.* literally
Bucht *die;* ~, ~**en** bay
Buchung *die;* ~, ~**en (a)** entry
  (b) (Vorbestellung) booking
Buckel *der;* ~**s,** ~ **(a)** hump; **einen**
  ~ **machen** ⟨*cat*⟩ arch its back; ⟨*person*⟩
  hunch one's shoulders
  (b) (ugs.: Rücken) back; **rutsch mir den**
  ~ **runter!** (salopp) get lost! (coll.)
buckeln *itr. V.* (ugs.) bow and scrape; **vor**
  jmdm. ~: kowtow to sb.
bücken *refl. V.* bend down
bucklig *Adj.* hunchbacked
Bucklige *der/die; adj. Dekl.* hunchback
Bückling[1] *der;* ~**s,** ~**e** (ugs. scherzh.:
  Verbeugung) bow
Bückling[2] *der;* ~**s,** ~**e** (Hering) bloater
buddeln *itr., tr. V.* (ugs.) dig
Buddha /'buda/ *der;* ~**s,** ~**s** Buddha
Buddhismus *der;* ~: Buddhism *no art.*
Buddhist *der;* ~**en,** ~**en, Buddhistin**
  die; ~, ~**nen** Buddhist
buddhistisch *Adj.* Buddhist *attrib.*
Bude *die;* ~, ~**n (a)** kiosk; (Markt~) stall;
  (Jahrmarkts~) booth
  (b) (Bau~) hut
  (c) (ugs.) (Haus) dump (coll.); (Zimmer) room;
  digs *pl.* (Brit. coll.)
Budget /by'dʒeː/ *das;* ~**s,** ~**s** budget
Büfett *das;* ~**[e]s,** ~**s** *od.* ~**e (a)** sideboard
  (b) (Schanktisch) bar
  (c) (Verkaufstisch) counter
  (d) kaltes ~: cold buffet
Büffel *der;* ~**s,** ~: buffalo
büffeln (ugs.) 1 *itr. V.* swot (Brit. coll.); cram
  2 *tr. V.* swot up (Brit. coll.); cram
Buffet /by'feː/ *das;* ~**s,** ~**s** ▶ BÜFETT
Bug *der;* ~**[e]s,** ~**e** *u.* **Büge** bow
Bügel *der;* ~**s,** ~ **(a)** (Kleider~) hanger
  (b) (Brillen~) earpiece
  (c) (an einer Tasche, Geldbörse) frame
bügel-, Bügel-: ~**brett** *das* ironing
  board; ~**eisen** *das* iron; ~**falte** *die*
  [trouser] crease; ~**frei** *Adj.* non-iron
bügeln *tr., itr. V.* iron
bugsieren /bʊ'ksiːrən/ *tr. V.* (ugs.) shift;
  manœuvre; steer ⟨*person*⟩
buh *Interj.* boo
Buh *das;* ~**s,** ~**s** (ugs.) boo
buhen *itr. V.* (ugs.) boo
buhlen *itr. V.* (geh. abwertend) **um jmds.**
  Gunst ~: court sb.'s favour
Buh·mann *der* whipping boy
Buhne /'buːnə/ *die;* ~, ~**n** groyne
Bühne *die;* ~, ~**n (a)** stage; **ein Stück auf**
  die ~ **bringen** put on *or* stage a play
  (b) (Theater) theatre ┄┄┊

bühnen-, Bühnen-: ~**arbeiter**
der, ~**arbeiterin** *die* stagehand;
~**ausstattung** *die* stage set; ~**bild**
das [stage] set; ~**bildner** *der;* ~~**s,** ~~,
~**bildnerin** *die;* ~~, ~~**nen** stage
designer; ~**reif** *Adj. ⟨play etc.⟩* ready for
the stage; ⟨*imitation etc.*⟩ worthy of the
stage; dramatic ⟨*entrance etc.*⟩

Buh-ruf *der* boo

buk *1. u. 3. Pers. Sg. Prät. v.* BACKEN

Bukett *das;* ~**s,** ~**s** *od.* ~**e** (geh.) bouquet

Bulette *die;* ~, ~**n** (bes. berl.) rissole

Bulgare *der;* ~**n,** ~**n** Bulgarian

Bulgarien /bʊl'gaːri̯ən/ *(das);* ~**s** Bulgaria

Bulgarin *die;* ~, ~**nen** Bulgarian

bulgarisch *Adj.* Bulgarian

Bull-: ~**auge** *das* circular porthole;
~**dogge** *die* bulldog; ~**dozer** /-doːzɐ/
der; ~~**s,** ~~: bulldozer

Bulle *der;* ~**n,** ~**n** (a) bull
(b) (salopp: Polizist) cop (coll.)

Bullen-: ~**hitze** *die* (ugs.) sweltering *or*
boiling heat; ~**markt** *der* (Börsenw.) bull
market

Bulletin /byl'tɛ̃/ *das;* ~**s,** ~**s** bulletin

bullig ① *Adj.* (a) beefy ⟨*person,
appearance, etc.*⟩; chunky ⟨*car*⟩
(b) (drückend) sweltering ⟨*heat*⟩
② *adv.* ~ **heiß** boiling hot

Bull-terrier *der* bull terrier

bum *Interj.* bang

Bumerang *der;* ~**s,** ~**e** *od.* ~**s** boomerang

Bummel *der;* ~**s,** ~ (a) stroll (**durch**
around)
(b) (durch Lokale) pub crawl (coll.)

Bummelei *die;* ~, ~**en** (ugs.) (a) dawdling
(b) (Faulenzerei) loafing about

bummelig (ugs.) ① *Adj.* (a) slow
(b) (nachlässig) slipshod
② *adv.* (a) slowly
(b) (nachlässig) in a slipshod way

bummeln *itr. V.* (a) *mit sein* stroll (**durch**
around); **durch die Kneipen** ~: go on a pub
crawl (Brit. coll.)
(b) (trödeln) dawdle
(c) (faulenzen) laze about

bums *Interj.* bang

Bums *der;* ~**es,** ~**e** (ugs.) bang; (dumpfer)
thud

bumsen *itr. V.* (ugs.) (a) bang; (dumpfer)
thump; *unpers.* **es bumste ganz furchtbar**
there was a terrible bang/thud
(b) *mit sein* (stoßen) bang

Bund¹ *der;* ~**[e]s, Bünde** (a) (Vereinigung)
association; (Bündnis, Pakt) alliance
(b) (föderativer Staat) federation
(c) (an Röcken, Hosen) waistband

Bund² *das;* ~**[e]s,** ~**e** bunch

Bündchen *das;* ~**s,** ~ band

Bündel *das;* ~**s,** ~ bundle

bündeln *tr. V.* bundle up ⟨*newspapers, old
clothes, rags, etc.*⟩; tie ⟨*banknotes etc.*⟩ into
bundles/a bundle; tie ⟨*flowers, radishes,
carrots, etc.*⟩ into bunches/a bunch; sheave
⟨*straw, hay, etc.*⟩

Bundes- federal; (in Namen, Titeln) Federal

bundes-, Bundes-: ~**bürger** *der,*
~**bürgerin** *die* (veralt.) West German
citizen; ~**deutsch** *Adj.* (veralt.) West
German; ~**ebene** *die:* **auf** ~**ebene** at
federal *or* national level; ~**gerichtshof**
der Federal Supreme Court; ~**kabinett**
das Federal Cabinet; ~**kanzler** *der*
(a) Federal Chancellor; (b) (schweiz.)
Chancellor of the Confederation; ~**land**
das [federal] state; (österr.) province; ~**liga**
die national division; ~**minister** *der,*
~**ministerin** *die* Federal Minister;
~**ministerium** *das* Federal Ministry;
~**politisch** ① *Adj.* relating to Federal
politics *postpos.*; ⟨*key figure*⟩ in Federal
politics; ② *adv.* in Federal politics;
~**präsident** *der,* ~**präsidentin**
die (a) [Federal] President; (b) (schweiz.)
President of the Confederation; ~**rat** *der*
Bundesrat; ~**regierung** *die* Federal
Government; ~**republik** *die* federal
republic; **die** ~**republik Deutschland** The
Federal Republic of Germany; ~**straße**
die federal highway; ≈ A road (Brit.); ~**tag**
der Bundestag

Bundestags-: ~**abgeordnete**
der/die member of parliament; member
of the Bundestag; ~**präsident** *der,*
~**präsidentin** *die* President of the
Bundestag; ~**wahl** *die* parliamentary *or*
general election

bundes-, Bundes-: ~**trainer**
der, ~**trainerin** *die* national team
manager; ~**verfassungs-gericht**
das Federal Constitutional Court;
~**verwaltungs-gericht** *das* Supreme
Administrative Court; ~**wehr** *die*
[Federal] Armed Forces *pl.*; ~**weit** *Adj.,
adv.* nationwide

Bund-: ~**falten** *Pl.* pleats;
~**falten-hose** *die* pleat[ed]-front trousers
pl.; ~**hose** *die* knee breeches

bündig ① *Adj.* (a) succinct
(b) (schlüssig) conclusive
② *adv.* (a) succinctly
(b) (schlüssig) conclusively

Bündnis *das;* ~**ses,** ~**se** alliance

Bungalow /'bʊŋgalo/ *der;* ~**s,** ~**s** bungalow

Bunker *der;* ~**s,** ~ (a) bunker
(b) (Luftschutzbunker) air-raid shelter

bunt ① *Adj.* (a) colourful; (farbig) coloured;
~**e Farben/Kleidung** bright colours/brightly
coloured clothes
(b) (fig.) varied ⟨*programme etc.*⟩
② *adv.* (a) colourfully; ~ **bemalt** brightly
painted
(b) (fig.) **ein** ~ **gemischtes Programm** a
varied programme

---

*alte Schreibung – vgl. Hinweis auf S. x

bunt-, Bunt-: *∼**bemalt** ▸ BUNT 2A;
∼**papier** *das* coloured paper; ∼**specht**
der spotted woodpecker; ∼**stift** *der*
coloured pencil/crayon

Bürde *die;* ∼, ∼n (geh.) weight; load

Burg *die;* ∼, ∼en (a) castle
(b) (Strand∼) wall of sand

Bürge *der;* ∼n, ∼n guarantor

bürgen *itr. V.* (a) für jmdn./etw. ∼: vouch
for sb./sth.
(b) (fig.) guarantee

Bürger *der;* ∼s, ∼, **Bürgerin** *die;* ∼,
∼nen citizen

Bürger-: ∼**initiative** *die* citizens' action
group; ∼**krieg** *der* civil war

bürgerlich *Adj.* (a) (staats∼) civil ⟨rights,
marriage, etc.⟩; civic ⟨duties⟩
(b) (dem Bürgertum zugehörig) middle-class; **die**
∼**e Küche** good plain cooking
(c) (Polit.) non-socialist; (nicht marxistisch) non-
Marxist

bürger-, Bürger-: ∼**meister** *der,*
∼**meisterin** *die* mayor; ∼**nah** *Adj.*
which/who reflects the general public's
interests *postpos., not pred.;* ∼**pflicht** *die*
duty as a citizen; ∼**steig** *der;* ∼∼s, ∼∼e
pavement (Brit.); sidewalk (Amer.)

Bürgertum /'--tu:m/ *das;* ∼s (a) middle
class
(b) (Großbürgertum) bourgeoisie

Bürgin *die;* ∼, ∼nen ▸ BÜRGE

Bürgschaft *die;* ∼, ∼en (a) guarantee
(b) (Betrag) penalty

burgunder·farben *Adj.* burgundy [red]

Burka /'bʊrka/ *die;* ∼, ∼s burka

Büro *das;* ∼s, ∼s office

Büro-: ∼**angestellte** *der/die* office
worker; ∼**artikel** *der* item of office
equipment; ∼**haus** *das* office block;
∼**klammer** *die* paper clip; ∼**kraft** *die*
clerical worker

Bürokrat *der;* ∼en, ∼en bureaucrat

Bürokratie *die;* ∼, ∼n bureaucracy

Bürokratin *die;* ∼, ∼nen bureaucrat

bürokratisch 1 *Adj.* bureaucratic
2 *adv.* bureaucratically

Büro-: ∼**stunden** *Pl.* office hours;
∼**technik** *die* office technology

Bürschchen /'bʏrʃçən/ *das;* ∼, ∼: little
fellow

Bursche *der;* ∼n, ∼n (a) boy; lad
(b) (abwertend: Kerl) guy (coll.)

burschikos 1 *Adj.* (a) sporty ⟨look,
clothes⟩; [tom]boyish ⟨behaviour, girl,
haircut⟩
(b) (ungezwungen) casual ⟨comment,
behaviour, etc.⟩
2 *adv.* (a) [tom]boyishly
(b) (ungezwungen) in a colloquial way

Bürste *die;* ∼, ∼n brush

bürsten *tr. V.* brush

Bus *der;* ∼ses, ∼se bus

Bus·bahnhof *der* bus station

Busch *der;* ∼[e]s, Büsche bush; **auf den
∼ klopfen** (fig. ugs.) sound things out

Büschel *das;* ∼s, ∼: tuft; (von Heu, Stroh)
handful

Busen *der;* ∼s, ∼ bust

Bus-: ∼**fahrer** *der,* ∼**fahrerin** *die* bus
driver; ∼**haltestelle** *die* bus stop

Business /'bɪznɪs/ *das;* ∼ (a) (abwertend:
vom Profitdenken bestimmtes Geschäft) business;
(Handel) trade
(b) (Geschäftsleben) business

Bus·linie *die* bus route

Bussard *der;* ∼s, ∼e buzzard

Buße *die;* ∼, ∼n (Rel.) penance *no art.*

büßen 1 *tr. V.* (a) atone for
(b) (fig.) pay for
2 *itr. V.* (a) für etw. ∼: atone for sth.
(b) (fig.) pay

Buß·geld *das* (Rechtsw.) fine

Buß- und Bettag *der* (ev. Kirche) Day of
Prayer and Repentance (*Wednesday eleven
days before the first Sunday in Advent*)

Büsten·halter *der* bra; brassière (formal)

Butan·gas *das* butane gas

Butt *der;* ∼[e]s, ∼e flounder; butt

Bütten·papier *das* handmade paper (*with
deckle edge*)

Butter *die;* ∼: butter; **es ist alles in ∼** (ugs.)
everything's fine

butter-, Butter-: ∼**berg** *der*
(ugs.) butter mountain; ∼**blume** *die*
(Sumpfdotterblume) marsh marigold;
(Hahnenfuß) buttercup; ∼**brot** *das* slice of
bread and butter; (zugeklappt) sandwich;
∼**creme** *die* buttercream; ∼**milch** *die*
buttermilk; ∼**weich** *Adj.* beautifully soft

b. w. *Abk.* = **bitte wenden** p.t.o.

Bypass /'baipɑs/ *der;* ∼es, Bypässe (Med.)
bypass

Byte /bait/ *das;* ∼s, ∼[s] (DV) byte

bzw. *Abk.* = **beziehungsweise**

Cc

c, C /tse:/ *das;* ~, ~: **(a)** (Buchstabe) c/C
(b) (Musik) [key of] C

C *Abk.* = **Celsius** C

ca. *Abk.* = **cirka** c.

Cache /kɛʃ/ *der;* ~, ~s (DV) cache

Café *das;* ~s, ~s café

Cafeteria *die;* ~, ~s cafeteria

cal *Abk.* = **[Gramm]kalorie** cal.

Callboy /'kɔːlbɔɪ/ *der;* ~s, ~s call-boy

Callgirl /'kɔːlgəːl/ *das;* ~s, ~s call girl

Camp /kɛmp/ *das;* ~s, ~s camp

campen *itr. V.* camp

Camping *das;* ~s camping

Camping-: ~**bus** *der* motor caravan;
camper; ~**kocher** *der* camping stove;
~**platz** *der* campsite; campground (Amer.)

Canasta *das;* ~s canasta

Cannabis /'kanabɪs/ *der;* ~: cannabis

Cantilever·bremse /'kæntiliːvɐ-/ *die*
cantilever brake

Caravan /'ka(ː)ravan/ *der;* ~s, ~s
(Wohnwagen) caravan; trailer (Amer.)

carven /'kaːvn̩/ *itr. V.*; *mit sein* (Skifahren)
carve

Carving·ski *der* carving ski

Cashflow /kæʃ'floʊ/ *der;* ~s (Wirtsch.)
[gross] cash flow

Castor-: ~**behälter** *der* Castor
container; Castor cask; ~**transport** *der*
Castor transport

Catcher /'kɛtʃɐ/ *der;* ~s, ~, **Catcherin**
die; ~, ~nen all-in wrestler

Cayenne·pfeffer /ka'jɛn-/ *der* cayenne
[pepper]

CD /tse:'de:/ *die;* ~, ~s CD

CD-Brenner *der;* ~s, ~ (DV) CD burner;
CD writer

CD-ROM /tsede'rɔm/ *die;* ~, ~[s] (DV)
CD-ROM

CD-ROM-Laufwerk *das* (DV) CD-ROM
drive

CD-Spieler /tse:'de:-/ *der* compact disc
player

CDU *Abk.* = **Christlich-
Demokratische Union
[Deutschlands]** [German] Christian
Democratic Party

C-Dur /'tse:-/ *das* C major

Cellist /tʃɛ'lɪst/ *der;* ~en, ~en, **Cellistin**
die; ~, ~nen cellist

Cello /'tʃɛlo/ *das;* ~s, ~s *od.* **Celli** cello

Celsius: 20 Grad ~: 20 degrees Celsius *or*
centigrade

Cembalo /'tʃɛmbalo/ *das;* ~s, ~s *od.*
Cembali harpsichord

Cent *der* ~[s], ~[s] cent, 50 ~ 50 cents

Champagner /ʃam'panjɐ/ *der;* ~s, ~
champagne (from Champagne)

Champignon /'ʃampɪnjɔn/ *der;* ~s, ~s
mushroom

Chance /'ʃãːsə/ *die;* ~, ~n **(a)** chance
(b) *Pl.* (Aussichten) prospects; **[bei jmdm]** ~n
haben stand a chance [with sb.]

Chancen·gleichheit *die* (Soziol.)
equality *no art.* of opportunity

chancen·los *Adj.* with no chance
postpos.; ~ **sein** have no chance

Chaos /'k...*/ *das;* ~: chaos *no art.*

Chaot /ka'oːt/ *der;* ~en, ~en, **Chaotin**
die; ~, ~nen **(a)** (Politik) anarchist (trying to
undermine society)
(b) (salopp: unordentlicher Mensch) **ein
[furchtbarer]** ~ **sein** be [terribly]
disorganized

chaotisch ① *Adj.* chaotic
② *adv.* chaotically; **es geht** ~ **zu** there is
chaos

Charakter /ka...*/ *der;* ~s, ~e /...'teːrə/
character

charakterisieren *tr. V.* characterize

charakteristisch *Adj.* characteristic
(für of)

charakterlich ① *Adj.* character *attrib.*
② *adv.* in [respect of] character

charakter·los *Adj.* unprincipled;
(niederträchtig) despicable; (labil) spineless

Charisma /'çaːrɪsma/ *das;* ~s, **Charismen**
charisma

charismatisch /çarɪs'maːtɪʃ/ *Adj.*
charismatic

charmant /ʃar'mant/ ① *Adj.* charming
② *adv.* charmingly

Charme /ʃarm/ *der;* ~s charm

Charter- /'tʃartɐ-/: ~**flug** *der* charter
flight; ~**maschine** *die* chartered aircraft

Charts /tʃarts/ *Pl.* charts

Chassis /ʃa'siː/ *das;* ~ /ʃa'siː(s),/ ~
/ʃa'siːs/ chassis

Chat /tʃɛt/ *der* (DV Jargon) chat

Chatroom /'tʃɛtruːm/ *der;* ~s, ~s (DV
Jargon) chatroom

chatten /'tʃɛtn̩/ *itr. V.* (DV Jargon) chat

Chauffeur /ʃɔ'føːɐ/ *der;* ~s, ~e,
Chauffeurin /ʃɔ'føːrɪn/ *die;* ~, ~nen
driver; (privat angestellt) chauffeur

checken /'tʃɛkn̩/ *tr. V.* **(a)** (bes. Technik: kontrollieren) check; examine **(b)** (salopp: begreifen) twig (coll.); (bemerken) spot; **ich habe das noch nicht gecheckt** I haven't got it yet

Check-liste *die* checklist; (Passagierliste) passenger list

Check-up /tʃɛk|'ap/ *der od. das;* ~[s], ~s check-up

Chef /ʃɛf/ *der;* ~s, ~s, **Chefin** /'ʃɛfɪn/ *die;* ~, ~nen (Leiter[in]) head; (der Polizei, des Generalstabs) chief; (einer Partei, Bande) leader; (Vorgesetzte[r]) superior; boss (coll.)

Chef-: ~**koch** *der,* ~**köchin** *die* chef; head cook; ~**sekretärin** *die* director's secretary

Chemie *die;* ~ **(a)** chemistry *no art.* **(b)** (ugs.: Chemikalien) chemicals *pl.*

Chemikalie /çemi'ka:liə/ *die;* ~, ~n chemical

Chemiker *der;* ~s, ~, **Chemikerin** *die;* ~, ~nen (graduate) chemist

chemisch [1] *Adj.* chemical [2] *adv.* chemically

Chemo-therapie *die* (Med.) chemotherapy

Chicorée /'ʃikore/ *der;* ~s *od. die;* ~: chicory

Chiffon /'ʃɪfõ/ *der;* ~s, ~s chiffon

Chiffre /'ʃɪfrə/ *die;* ~, ~n **(a)** (Zeichen) symbol **(b)** (Geheimzeichen) cipher **(c)** (in Annoncen) box number

Chile /'tʃi:le, 'çi:lə/ (*das*); ~s Chile

Chilene /tʃi'le:nə, çi'le:nə/ *der;* ~n, ~n, **Chilenin** *die;* ~, ~nen Chilean

chilenisch *Adj.* Chilean

Chili /'tʃi:li/ *der;* ~s, ~es **(a)** *Pl.* (Schoten) chillies **(b)** (Gewürz) chilli [powder]

chillen /'tʃɪlən/ *itr. V.* (Jugendspr.) chill out (coll.)

China (*das*); ~s China

Chinese *der;* ~n, ~n, **Chinesin** *die;* ~, ~nen Chinese

chinesisch *Adj.* Chinese

Chip /tʃɪp/ *der;* ~s, ~s **(a)** (Spielmarke) chip **(b)** (Kartoffel~) [potato] crisp (Brit.) *or* (Amer.) chip **(c)** (Elektronik) [micro]chip

Chip-karte *die* smart card

Chirurg *der;* ~en, ~en surgeon

Chirurgie *die;* ~, ~n **(a)** surgery *no art.* **(b)** (Abteilung) surgical department; (Station) surgical ward

Chirurgin *die;* ~, ~nen surgeon

chirurgisch [1] *Adj.* surgical [2] *adv.* surgically; by surgery

Chlor /k.../ *das;* ~s chlorine

Chloroform /k.../ *das;* ~s chloroform

Chlorophyll /k.../ *das;* ~s chlorophyll

Cholera *die;* ~: cholera

cholerisch *Adj.* irascible; choleric ‹*temperament*›

Cholesterin *das;* ~s cholesterol

Chor *der;* ~[e]s, Chöre /'kø:rə/ (auch Archit.) choir; (in Oper, Sinfonie, Theater; Komposition) chorus; **im** ~ **rufen** shout in chorus

Choral *der;* ~s, Choräle (Kirchenlied) chorale

Choreograph /koreo'gra:f/ *der;* ~en, ~en choreographer

Choreographie *die;* ~, ~n choreography

Choreographin *die;* ~, ~nen choreographer

choreographisch *Adj.* choreographic

Chose /'ʃo:zə/ *die;* ~, ~n (ugs.) stuff; **die ganze** ~: the whole lot (coll.) *or* (coll.) shoot

Chow-Chow /tʃau 'tʃau/ *der;* ~s, ~s chow

Christ /k.../ *der;* ~en, ~en Christian

Christ-: ~**baum** *der* (bes. südd.) Christmas tree; ~**demokrat** *der,* ~**demokratin** *die* (Politik) Christian Democrat

Christenheit *die;* ~: Christendom *no art.*

Christentum *das;* ~s Christianity *no art.;* (Glaube) Christian faith

Christin *die;* ~, ~nen Christian

Christ-kind *das* Christ-child (*as bringer of Christmas gifts*)

christlich [1] *Adj.* Christian [2] *adv.* in a [truly] Christian spirit

Christ-: ~**messe** *die* (kath. Rel.) Christmas Mass; ~**mette** *die;* ~~, ~~n (kath. Rel.) Christmas Mass; (ev. Rel.) midnight service [on Christmas Eve]; ~**rose** *die* Christmas rose; ~**stollen** *der* stollen; [German] Christmas loaf (*with candied fruit, almonds, etc.*)

Christus (*der*); ~ *od.* Christi Christ

Chrom /k.../ *das;* ~s chromium

Chromosom /k.../ *das;* ~s, ~en (Biol.) chromosome

Chromosomen-satz *der* (Biol.) chromosome set

Chronik /k.../ *die;* ~, ~en chronicle

chronisch *Adj.* chronic

Chrysantheme /k.../ *die;* ~, ~n chrysanthemum

City /'sɪti/ *die;* ~, ~s city centre

clean /kli:n/ *Adj.* (ugs.) clean (coll.); ~ **werden** come off drugs

clever /'klɛvɐ/ [1] *Adj.* (raffiniert) shrewd; (intelligent, geschickt) clever [2] *adv.: s. Adj.:* shrewdly; cleverly

Clique /'klɪkə/ *die;* ~, ~n **(a)** (abwertend) clique **(b)** (Freundeskreis) set; (größere Gruppe) crowd (coll.)

Clown /klaun/ *der;* ~s, ~s, **Clownin** /'klaunɪn/ *die;* ~, ~nen clown

Club /klap/ *der* ~s, ~s (Diskothek) club; disco

Clubber /'klabɐ/ *der* clubber; disco-goer

Clubbing /'klabɪŋ/ *das* (Besuch von Discos) clubbing; **clubbing gehen** go clubbing

cm *Abk.* = **Zentimeter** cm.

Co. *Abk.* = **Compagnie** Co.

CO₂: ~-**Ausgleich** *der* carbon offsetting; ~-**Bilanz** *die* carbon footprint; ~-**Handel** *der* carbon trading; ~-**neutral** ① *Adj.* carbon-neutral; ② *adv.* in a carbon-neutral way; ~-**Steuer** *der* carbon tax

Coach /koʊtʃ/ *der;* ~s, ~s (Sport) coach; (bes. Fußball: Trainer) manager

coachen /'koʊtʃn/ *tr., itr. V.* (Sport) coach; (Trainer sein) manage

Cockpit *das;* ~s, ~s cockpit

Cocktail /'kɔkteɪl/ *der;* ~s, ~s cocktail

Cognac Ⓦ /'kɔnjak/ *der;* ~s, ~s Cognac

Cola /'ko:la/ *das;* ~s, ~s *od. die;* ~, ~s (ugs.) Coke ®

Color- (Fot.) colour ⟨film, slide, etc.⟩

Colt Ⓦ *der;* ~s, ~s Colt ® [revolver]

Comeback /kam'bɛk/ *das;* ~s, ~s comeback; **ein** ~ **feiern** stage a comeback

Comic·heft *das* comic

Computer /kɔm'pju:tɐ/ *der;* ~s, ~: computer

computer·gestützt *Adj.* computer-aided; computer-assisted

computerisieren *tr. V.* computerize ⟨data, system⟩; (aufbereiten) make ⟨data⟩ computer-compatible

computer-, Computer-: ~**raum** *der* computer rooom; ~**spiel** *das* computer

game ~**unterstützt** *Adj.* computer-aided; computer-assisted

Container /kɔn'te:nɐ/ *der;* ~s, ~: container; (für Müll) [refuse] skip

cool /ku:l/ (ugs.) ① *Adj.* cool; ~ **bleiben** keep one's cool (coll.) ② *adv.* coolly (coll.)

Cord *der;* ~[e]s, ~e *od.* ~s cord; (~samt) corduroy

Corned Beef /'kɔ:nd'bi:f/ *das;* ~s corned beef

Couch /kaʊtʃ/ *die,* (schweiz. auch:) *der;* ~, ~es sofa

Coup /ku:/ *der;* ~s, ~s coup

Coupon /ku'põ/ *der;* ~s, ~s coupon; voucher

Courage /ku'ra:ʒə/ *die;* ~ (ugs.) courage

Cousin /ku'zɛ̃:/ *der;* ~s, ~s, **Cousine** *die;* ~, ~n cousin

Cover /'kavɐ/ *das;* ~s, ~s **(a)** (von Illustrierten) cover **(b)** (von Schallplatten) sleeve

covern /'kavɐn/ *tr. V.* cover ⟨song, record⟩

Cowboy /'kaʊbɔy/ *der;* ~s, ~s cowboy

Creme /kre:m/ *die;* ~, ~s, (schweiz.:) ~n cream

CSU *Abk.* = **Christlich-Soziale Union** CSU

CT (Med.) *Abk.* = **Computertomographie** CT

Curry /'kɔri/ *das;* ~s, ~s curry powder

Curry·wurst *die: sliced fried sausage sprinkled with curry powder and served with ketchup*

Cursor /'kɔ:sə/ *der;* ~s, ~s (DV) cursor

Cyberspace /'saɪbɐspe:s/ *der;* ~ (DV) cyberspace

Dd

d, D /de:/ *das;* ~, ~ **(a)** (Buchstabe) d/D **(b)** (Musik) [key of] D

D *Abk.* = **Damen**

da ① *Adv.* **(a)** (dort) there; **da draußen/ drinnen/drüben/unten** out/in/over/down there; **da, wo** where **(b)** (hier) here **(c)** (zeitlich) then; (in dem Augenblick) at that moment **(d)** (deshalb) **der Zug war schon weg, da habe ich den Bus genommen** the train had already gone, so I took the bus **(e)** (ugs.: in diesem Fall) **da kann man nichts machen** there's nothing one can do about it

(f) da sein (existieren) exist; (übrig sein) be left; (anwesend sein) be about or around; (im Haus, zu Hause sein) be in; (zu sprechen sein) be available; (angekommen, eingetroffen sein) have arrived; (fig.) ⟨case⟩ have occurred; ⟨moment⟩ have arrived; ⟨situation⟩ have arisen; **ich bin gleich wieder da** I'll be right or straight back ② *Konj.* (weil) as; since

da·bei *Adv.* **(a)** with it/him/her/them; **nahe** ~: close by; ~ **sein** (anwesend sein) be there; be present (**bei** at); (teilnehmen) take part (**bei** in) **(b)** (währenddessen) at the same time; (bei diesem Anlass) then; on that occasion; **die** ~ **entstehenden Kosten** the expense involved; **[gerade]** ∼ **sein, etw. zu tun** be just doing sth.

(c) (außerdem) ∼ **[auch]** what is more

(d) (hinsichtlich dessen) about it/them; **was hast du dir denn** ∼ **gedacht?** what 'were you thinking of?

dabei-: ∼|**bleiben** *unr. itr. V.; mit sein* stay there; be there; ∼|**haben** *unr. tr. V.* have with one; ***∼|**sein** ▸ DABEI A, B; ∼|**stehen** *unr. itr. V.* stand there

da|bleiben *unr. itr. V.; mit sein* stay there; (hier bleiben) stay here

Dach *das;* ∼**[e]s, Dächer** roof

Dach-: ∼**antenne** *die* roof aerial; ∼**boden** *der* loft; **auf dem** ∼**boden** in the loft; ∼**decker** /-dɛkɐ/ *der;* ∼∼**s,** ∼∼, ∼**deckerin** *die;* ∼∼, ∼∼**nen** roofer; ∼**fenster** *das* skylight; (∼gaube) dormer window; ∼**garten** *der* roof garden; ∼**gaube** *die* dormer window; ∼**gepäckträger** *der* (Kfz-W.) roof rack; ∼**geschoss,** ***∼**geschoß** *das* attic [storey]; ∼**kammer** *die* attic [room]; ∼**luke** *die* skylight; ∼**pappe** *die* roofing felt; ∼**rinne** *die* gutter

Dachs /daks/ *der;* ∼**es,** ∼**e** badger

Dach·stuhl *der* roof truss

dachte *1. u. 3. Pers. Sg. Prät. v.* DENKEN

Dach-: ∼**terrasse** *die* roof terrace; ∼**wohnung** *die* attic flat (Brit.) or (Amer.) apartment; ∼**ziegel** *der* roof tile; ∼**zimmer** *das* attic room

Dackel *der;* ∼**s,** ∼: dachshund

da·durch *Adv.* **(a)** through it/them **(b)** (durch diesen Umstand) as a result; (durch dieses Mittel) by this [means]

da·für *Adv.* **(a)** for it/them; ∼**, dass** ... (wenn man berücksichtigt, dass) considering that ...; (damit) so that ...; ∼ **sorgen [, dass** ...**]** see to it [that ...] **(b)** ∼ **sein** be in favour [of it]; **ein Beispiel** ∼ **ist** ...: an example of this is ... **(c)** (als Gegenleistung) in return [for it]; (beim Tausch) in exchange; (stattdessen) instead **(d) etwas/nichts** ∼ **können** be/not be responsible

***da**für|können** ▸ DAFÜR D

dagegen *Adv.* **(a)** against it/them; **etwas** ∼ **haben** have sth. against it; **ich habe nichts** ∼: I've no objection; ∼ **sein** be against it **(b)** (im Vergleich dazu) by or in comparison

da·heim *Adv.* (bes. südd., österr., schweiz.) **(a)** (zu Hause) at home; (nach Präp.) home **(b)** (in der Heimat) [back] home

da·her *Adv.* **(a)** from there **(b)** (durch diesen Umstand) hence **(c)** (deshalb) therefore; so

daher|kommen *unr. itr. V.* come along

da·hin (a) there **(b)** (fig.) ∼ **musste es kommen** it had to come to that **(c) bis** ∼: to there; (zeitlich) until then **(d)** ∼ **sein** be or have gone

(e) (in diesem Sinne) ∼ **[gehend], dass** ...: to the effect that ...

da·hinten *Adv.* over there

da·hinter *Adv.* behind it/them; (folgend) after it/them

Dahlie /ˈdaːli̯ə/ *die;* ∼, ∼**n** dahlia

da-: ∼|**lassen** *unr. tr. V.* (ugs.) leave [there]; (hier lassen) leave here; ∼|**liegen** *unr. itr. V.* lie there

dalli *Adv.* (ugs.) **[**∼**]!** get a move on!

damalig *Adj.* at that or the time *postpos.*

damals *Adv.* at that time

Damast *der;* ∼**[e]s,** ∼**e** damask

Dame *die;* ∼, ∼**n (a)** (Frau) lady **(b)** (Schach, Kartenspiele) queen **(c)** (Spiel) draughts (Brit.); checkers (Amer.)

Damen-: ∼**binde** *die* sanitary towel (Brit.) or (Amer.) napkin; ∼**friseur** *der,* ∼**friseurin** *die* ladies' hairdresser; ∼**rad** *das* lady's bicycle; ∼**toilette** *die* ladies' toilet

da·mit ① *Adv.* **(a)** with it/them **(b)** (gleichzeitig) with that **(c)** (daher) thus ② *Konj.* so that

dämlich (ugs. abwertend) ① *Adj.* stupid ② *adv.* stupidly

Damm *der;* ∼**[e]s, Dämme** embankment; levee (Amer.); (Deich) dike; (Stau∼) dam

dämmern *itr. V.* **es dämmert** (morgens) it is getting light; (abends) it is getting dark

Dämmerung *die;* ∼, ∼**en (a)** (Abend∼) twilight; dusk **(b)** (Morgen∼) dawn

Dämon *der;* ∼**s,** ∼**en** /dɛˈmoːnən/ demon

dämonisch *Adj.* demonic

dämonisieren *tr. V.* demonize; portray as a demon/demons

Dampf *der;* ∼**[e]s, Dämpfe** steam *no pl., no indef. art.*

Dampf·bügel·eisen *das* steam iron

dampfen *itr. V.* steam (**vor** + *Dat.* with)

dämpfen *tr. V.* **(a)** (garen) steam 〈fish, vegetables, potatoes〉 **(b)** (mildern) muffle 〈sound〉; cushion, absorb 〈blow, impact, shock〉

Dampfer *der;* ∼**s,** ∼: steamer

Dampf-: ∼**kochtopf** *der* pressure cooker; ∼**maschine** *die* steam engine; ∼**nudel** *die* (südd., Kochk.) steamed yeast dumpling; ∼**walze** *die* steamroller

da·nach *Adv.* **(a)** (zeitlich) after it/that; then **(b)** (räumlich) after it/them **(c)** (entsprechend) in accordance with it/them

Däne *der;* ∼**n,** ∼**n** Dane

da·neben *Adv.* **(a)** beside him/her/it/them *etc.* **(b)** (im Vergleich dazu) in comparison

daneben-: ∼|**benehmen** *unr. refl. V.* (ugs.) blot one's copybook (coll.); ∼|**gehen** *unr. itr. V.; mit sein* miss [the target]; ∼|**schießen** *unr. itr. V.* miss [the target]

Dänemark (das); ~s Denmark
Dänin die; ~, ~nen Dane; Danish woman/girl
dänisch Adj. Danish
dank Präp. mit Dat. u. Gen. thanks to
Dank der; ~[e]s thanks pl.; **mit [vielem od. bestem] ~** zurück thanks for the loan; (bes. geschrieben) returned with thanks!; **vielen/besten/herzlichen ~!** thank you very much
dankbar ①Adj. grateful; (anerkennend) appreciative ‹child, audience, etc.›; **[jmdm.] für etw. ~ sein** be grateful [to sb.] for sth. ②adv. gratefully
Dankbarkeit die; ~: gratitude
danke Höflichkeitsformel thank you; (ablehnend) no, thank you; **~ schön/sehr/vielmals** thank you very much
danken ①itr. V. (Dank aussprechen) thank; **ich danke Ihnen vielmals** thank you very much; **na, ich danke!** (ugs.) no, 'thank you! ②tr. V. **[aber bitte,] nichts zu ~:** don't mention it
Danke-schön das; ~s thank-you
dann Adv. (a) then; **was ~?** what happens then?; **noch drei Tage, ~ ist Ostern** another three days and it will be Easter; **bis ~:** see you then; **~ und wann** now and then
(b) (in diesem Falle) then; in that case; **~ will ich nicht weiter stören** in that case I won't disturb you any further; **[na,] ~ eben nicht!** in that case, forget it!; **nur ~, wenn ...:** only if ...
daran /da'ran/ Adv. (a) (an dieser/diese Stelle, an diesem/diesen Gegenstand) on it/them; **dicht ~:** close to it/them; **nahe ~ sein, etw. zu tun** be on the point of doing sth.
(b) (hinsichtlich dieser Sache) about it/them; **~ ist nichts zu machen** there's nothing one can do about it; **kein Wort ~ ist wahr** not a word of it is true; **mir liegt viel ~:** it means a lot to me
(c) **ich wäre beinahe ~ erstickt** I almost choked on it; **er ist ~ gestorben** he died of it
daran|setzen tr. V. devote ‹energy etc.› to it; summon up ‹ambition›; set it; (aufs Spiel setzen) risk ‹one's life, one's honour› for it
darauf Adv. (a) on it/them; (oben ~) on top of it/them
(b) **er hat ~ geschossen** he shot at it/them (c) (danach) after that; **ein Jahr ~/kurz ~ starb er** he died a year later/shortly afterwards; **~ folgend** following
darauf-: *~folgend ▸ DARAUF C; ~hin /--'-/ Adv. (a) thereupon; (b) (unter diesem Gesichtspunkt) with a view to this/that
daraus Adv. (a) from it/them; out of it/them (b) **mach dir nichts ~:** don't worry about it; **was ist ~ geworden?** what has become of it?
dar|bieten (geh.) unr. tr. V. (aufführen, vortragen) perform; **es wurden Gedichte und Lieder dargeboten** a recital of poems and songs was presented
Darbietung die; ~, ~en (geh.)
(a) presentation
(b) (Aufführung) performance; (beim Varieté usw.) act
darf 1. u. 3. Pers. Sg. Präsens v. DÜRFEN
darfst 2. Pers. Sg. Präsens v. DÜRFEN
darin Adv. (a) in it/them
(b) (in dieser Hinsicht) in that respect
dar|legen tr. V. explain; set forth ‹reasons, facts›
Darlehen das; ~s, ~: loan; **ein ~ aufnehmen** get or raise a loan; **jmdm. ein ~ gewähren** give or grant sb. a loan
Darm der; ~[e]s, Därme intestines pl.; bowels pl.
dar|stellen tr. V. (a) depict; portray; **etw. grafisch ~:** present sth. graphically
(b) (verkörpern) play; act
(c) (schildern) describe ‹person, incident, etc.›; present ‹matter, argument›
(d) (sein, bedeuten) represent
Darsteller der; ~s, ~: actor
Darstellerin die; ~, ~nen actress
Darstellung die (a) representation; (Schilderung) portrayal; (Bild) picture; **grafische/schematische ~:** diagram; (Graph) graph
(b) (Beschreibung, Bericht) description; account
(c) (einer Theaterrolle) interpretation; **seine ~ des Mephisto** his portrayal or interpretation of Mephisto
darüber Adv. (a) over it/them; **~ stehen** (fig.) be above such things
(b) **~ hinaus** in addition [to that]; (noch obendrein) what is more
(c) (über dieser/diese Angelegenheit) about it/them
(d) (über diese Grenze, dieses Maß hinaus) over [that]
*darüber|stehen ▸ DARÜBER A
darum Adv. (a) [a]round it/them
(b) (diesbezüglich) **ich sorge mich ~:** I worry about it
(c) /'--/ (deswegen) for that reason
darunter Adv. (a) (unter dem Genannten/das Genannte) under it/them
(b) (unter dieser Grenze, diesem Maß) less; **Bewerber im Alter von 40 Jahren und ~:** applicants aged 40 and under
das ① best. Art. Nom. u. Akk. the ② Demonstrativpron. (a) attr. **das Kind war es** it was 'that child
(b) allein stehend **das [da]** that one; **das [hier]** this one [here]
③Relativpron. (Mensch) who; that; (Sache, Tier) which; that
*da|sein ▸ DA 1F
Da-sein das existence
Daseins-berechtigung die right to exist; **das findet darin** od. **dadurch seine ~:** this justifies its existence

da|sitzen *unr. itr. V.* sit there

dasjenige ► DERJENIGE

dass, *daß *Konj.* (a) that; entschuldigen Sie bitte, ~ ich mich verspätet habe please forgive me for being late; ich verstehe nicht, ~ sie ihn geheiratet hat I don't understand why she married him
(b) (nach Pronominaladverben o. Ä.) [the fact] that; das liegt daran, ~ du nicht aufgepasst hast that comes from your not paying attention
(c) (im Konsekutivsatz) that; [so]~: so that
(d) (im Finalsatz) so that
(e) (im Ausruf) ~ mir das passieren musste! why did it have to [go and] happen to me!

dasselbe ► DERSELBE

da|stehen *unr. itr. V.* (a) stand there
(b) (fig.) gut ~: be in a good position; [ganz] allein ~: be [all] alone in the world

Datei /da'tai/ *die;* ~, ~en data file

Datei-name (DV) *der* file name

Daten 1 ► DATUM
2 *Pl.* data

Daten-: ~**autobahn** *die* (DV) data highway; ~**bank** *die; Pl.* ~~-en data bank; ~**erfassung** *die* data collection *or* capture; ~**schutz** *der* data protection *no def. art.;* ~**träger** *der* data carrier; ~**verarbeitung** *die* data processing *no def. art.*

datieren *tr. V.* date

Dativ *der;* ~s, ~e (Sprachw.) dative [case]

Dativ-objekt *das* (Sprachw.) indirect object

Dattel *die;* ~, ~n date

Dattel-palme *die* date palm

Datum *das;* ~s, Daten date

Dauer *die;* ~ (a) length; für die ~ eines Jahres *od.* von einem Jahr for a period of one year
(b) (Fortbestehen) von ~ sein last [long]; auf die ~: in the long run; auf ~: permanently

dauer-, Dauer-: ~**auftrag** *der* (Bankw.) standing order; ~**haft** 1 *Adj.*
(a) [long-]lasting ‹peace, friendship, etc.›;
(b) (haltbar) durable; 2 *adv.* lastingly;
~**karte** *die* season ticket; ~**lauf** *der* jogging *no art.;* ein ~lauf a jog

dauern *itr. V.* last; ‹job etc.› take; einen Moment, es dauert nicht lange just a minute, it won't take long

dauernd 1 *Adj.*constant ‹noise, interruptions, etc.›; 2 *adv.* constantly; er kommt ~ zu spät he keeps on arriving late

Dauer-: ~**regen** *der* continuous rain; ~**stellung** *die* permanent position; ~**welle** *die* perm; ~**wurst** *die* smoked sausage (*with good keeping properties, esp. salami*); ~**zustand** *der* permanent state [of affairs]; zum ~zustand werden become permanent *or* a permanent state

Daumen *der;* ~s, ~: thumb

Daune *die;* ~, ~n down [feather]; ~n down *sing.*

davon *Adv.* (a) (von dieser Stelle entfernt, weg) from it/them; (von dort) from there; (mit Entfernungsangabe) away [from it/them]
(b) (hinsichtlich dieser Sache) about it/them
(c) (durch diese Angelegenheit verursacht) by it/them; das kommt ~! (ugs.) [there you are,] that's what happens
(d) ich hätte gern ein halbes Pfund ~: I would like half a pound of that/those
(e) ~ kann man nicht leben you can't live on that

davon-: ~|**fahren** *unr. itr. V.; mit sein* leave; (mit dem Auto) drive off; (mit dem Fahrrad, Motorrad) ride off; ~|**kommen** *unr. itr. V.; mit sein* get away; ~|**laufen** *unr. itr. V.; mit sein* run away; ~|**tragen** *unr. tr. V.*
(a) carry away; take away ‹rubbish›;
(b) (geh.: erringen) gain ‹a victory, fame›;
(c) (geh.: sich zuziehen) receive ‹injuries›

da-vor *Adv.* (a) in front of it/them;
~ liegen/stehen *usw.* lie/stand *etc.* in front of it/them
(b) (zeitlich) before [it/them]

*davor|liegen *usw.* ► DAVOR A

Dax *der;* ~: Dax [index]

da-zu *Adv.* (a) (zusätzlich zu dieser Sache) with it/them; (gleichzeitig) at the same time; (außerdem) what is more
(b) (diesbezüglich) about it/them
(c) (zu diesem Zweck) for it
(d) (zu diesem Ergebnis) to it; ~ reicht unser Geld nicht we haven't enough money for that

dazu-: ~|**geben** *unr. tr. V.* add;
~|**gehören** *tr. V.* belong to it/them;
~|**kommen** *unr. itr. V.; mit sein*
(a) (hinkommen) arrive; (b) (hinzukommen) kommt noch etwas dazu? is there anything else [you would like]?; ~ kommt, dass ... (fig.) what's more, ...; on top of that ...;
~|**rechnen** *tr. V.* add on; ~|**tun** *unr. tr. V.* (ugs.) add

da-zwischen *Adv.* in between; between them; (darunter) among them

dazwischen-: ~|**kommen** *unr. itr. V.; mit sein* (a) mit dem Finger ~kommen get one's finger caught [in it]; (b) (es verhindern) prevent it; es ist mir etwas ~gekommen I had problems; ~|**reden** *itr. V.* interrupt

DDR *Abk.* = **Deutsche Demokratische Republik** GDR; East Germany

Deal /di:l/ *der od. das;* ~s, ~s (salopp) deal

dealen /'di:lən/ *itr. V.* (ugs.) push drugs; mit LSD ~: push LSD

Dealer *der;* ~s, ~, **Dealerin** *die;* ~, ~nen (ugs.) pusher

Debatte *die;* ~, ~n debate (über + *Akk.* on); zur ~ stehen be under discussion

Debit-karte /'de:bɪt-/ *die* (Finanzw.) debit card

Debüt /de'by:/ *das;* ~s, ~s debut

Deck *das;* ~[e]s, ~s deck

Deck·bett *das* ▶ OBERBETT

Decke *die;* ~, ~n (a) (Tisch~) tablecloth
(b) (Woll~, Pferde~, fig.) blanket; (Reise~) rug
(c) (Zimmer~) ceiling

Deckel *der;* ~s, ~ (a) lid; (auf Flaschen,
Gläsern usw.) top; (Schacht~, Uhr~, Buch~ usw.)
cover
(b) (Bier~) beer mat

decken ☐ *tr. V.* (a) etw. über etw. (*Akk.*)
~: spread sth. over sth.
(b) roof ⟨*house*⟩; cover ⟨*roof*⟩
(c) **den Tisch** ~: lay the table
(d) (schützen; Finanzw., Versicherungsw.) cover
(e) (befriedigen) meet ⟨*need, demand*⟩
☐ *itr. V.* (den Tisch decken) lay the table

Deck·mantel *der* cover

Deckung *die;* ~, ~en (a) (Schutz; auch fig.)
cover (esp. Mil.); (Boxen) guard; (bes. Fußball)
defence; **in** ~ **gehen** take cover
(b) (Befriedigung) meeting
(c) (Finanzw., Versicherungsw.) cover[ing]

deckungs·gleich *Adj.* (Geom.) congruent

defekt *Adj.* defective; faulty; ~ **sein** have
a defect; be faulty; (nicht funktionieren) not be
working

Defekt *der;* ~[e]s, ~e defect, fault (**an**
+ *Dat.* in)

defensiv ☐ *Adj.* defensive
☐ *adv.* defensively

Defensive *die;* ~, ~n defensive; **in der**
~: on the defensive; **die** ~ (Sport) defensive
play

definieren *tr. V.* define

Definition *die;* ~, ~en definition

definitiv ☐ *Adj.* definitive
☐ *adv.* finally

Defizit *das;* ~s, ~e (a) deficit
(b) (Mangel) deficiency

deformieren *tr. V.* (a) (verformen) distort
(b) (entstellen) deform (also fig.)

deftig *Adj.* (ugs.) (a) [good] solid *attrib.*
⟨*meal etc.*⟩; [nice] big ⟨*sausage etc.*⟩
(b) (derb) crude, coarse ⟨*joke, speech, etc.*⟩

Degen *der;* ~s, ~ (a) (Waffe) [light] sword
(b) (Fechtsport) épée

degradieren *tr. V.* demote

Degradierung *die;* ~, ~en (a) (im Rang)
demotion
(b) (Herabwürdigung) degradation; reduction
(**zu** to the level of)

dehnbar *Adj.* (a) (elastisch) ⟨*material etc.*⟩
that stretches *not pred.;* elastic ⟨*waistband
etc.*⟩
(b) (fig.: vage) elastic; **das ist ein** ~**er Begriff**
it's a loose concept

Dehnbarkeit *die;* ~: elasticity

dehnen *tr., refl. V.* stretch

Deich *der;* ~[e]s, ~e dike

Deichsel /'daiksl/ *die;* ~, ~n shaft

deichseln *tr. V.* (ugs.) fix

dein *Possessivpron.* your; **viele Grüße von**
~**em Emil** with best wishes, yours Emil; **das
Buch dort, ist das** ~**[e]s?** that book over
there, is it yours?; **du und die Deinen** (geh.)
you and yours

deiner *Gen. des Personalpronomens* **du**
(geh.) of you

deiner·seits *Adv.* (von deiner Seite) on your
part; (auf deiner Seite) for your part

deinet·wegen *Adv.* because of you; (für
dich) on your behalf; (dir zuliebe) for your sake

Dekade /de'ka:də/ *die;* ~, ~n decade

dekadent *Adj.* decadent

Dekadenz *die;* ~: decadence

deklamieren *tr., itr. V.* recite

Deklination *die;* ~, ~en (Sprachw.)
declension

deklinieren *tr. V.* (Sprachw.) decline

dekodieren *tr. V.* (fachspr.) decode

Dekolleté /dekɔl'te:/ *das;* ~s, ~s
low[-cut] neckline; décolletage

Dekor *das;* ~s, ~s *od.* ~e decoration;
(Muster) pattern

Dekorateur /dekora'tø:ɐ̯/ *der;* ~s,
~e, **Dekorateurin** *die;* ~, ~nen
(Schaufenster~) window dresser; (von
Innenräumen) interior designer

Dekoration *die;* ~, ~en decorations *pl.;*
(Schaufenster~) window display

dekorativ ☐ *Adj.* decorative
☐ *adv.* decoratively

dekorieren *tr. V.* decorate ⟨*room etc.*⟩;
dress ⟨*shop window*⟩

Deko·stoff *der* furnishing fabric

Dekret *das;* ~[e]s, ~e decree

Delegation *die;* ~, ~en delegation

delegieren *tr. V.* (a) send as a delegate/as
delegates
(b) delegate ⟨*task etc.*⟩ (**an** + *Akk.* to)

Delegierte *der/die; adj. Dekl.* delegate

Delfin ▶ DELPHIN

delikat *Adj.* (a) delicious; (fein) delicate
⟨*bouquet, aroma*⟩
(b) (heikel) delicate

Delikatesse *die;* ~, ~n delicacy

Delikt *das;* ~[e]s, ~e offence

Delinquent *der;* ~en, ~en,
Delinquentin *die;* ~, ~nen offender

Delirium *das;* ~s, Delirien delirium

Delle *die;* ~, ~n (ugs.) dent

Delphin *der;* ~s, ~e dolphin

dem ☐ *best. Art., Dat. Sg. v.* DER¹ 1 *u.* DAS 1:
to the; (nach Präp.) the
☐ *Demonstrativpron., Dat. Sg. v.* DER¹ 2 *u.*
DAS 2: (a) *attr.* that; **gib es dem Mann** give it
to 'that man
(b) *allein stehend* **gib es nicht dem, sondern
dem da!** don't give it to him, give it to that

---

*alte Schreibung – vgl. Hinweis auf S. x

man/child *etc.*
3 *Relativpron., Dat. Sg. v.* DER¹ 3 *u.* DAS 3 (Person) that/whom; (Sache) that/which; **der Mann/das Kind, dem ich das Geld gab** the man/the child I gave the money to
Demagoge *der;* ~n, ~n, **Demagogin** *die;* ~, ~nen demagogue
demagogisch *Adj.* demagogic
Dementi *das;* ~s, ~s denial
dementieren **1** *tr. V.* deny **2** *itr. V.* deny it
dem-: ~**entsprechend** **1** *Adj.* appropriate; **2** *adv.* accordingly; (vor Adjektiven) correspondingly; ~**gemäß** *Adv.* (a) (infolgedessen) consequently; (b) (entsprechend) accordingly; ~**jenigen** ▸ DERJENIGE; ~**nach** *Adv.* therefore; ~**nächst** *Adv.* shortly
Demo *die;* ~, ~s (ugs.) demo; **auf der** ~: at the demo
Demokrat *der;* ~en, ~en democrat; (Parteimitglied) Democrat
Demokratie *die;* ~, ~n democracy
Demokratin *die;* ~, ~nen ▸ DEMOKRAT
demokratisch **1** *Adj.* democratic **2** *adv.* democratically
demokratisieren *tr. V.* democratize
demolieren *tr. V.* wreck; smash up ⟨furniture⟩
Demonstrant *der;* ~en, ~en, **Demonstrantin** *die;* ~, ~nen demonstrator
Demonstration *die;* ~, ~en demonstration (**für** in support of, **gegen** against)
demonstrativ **1** *Adj.* (a) pointed (b) (Sprachw.) demonstrative **2** *adv.* pointedly
Demonstrativ·pronomen *das* (Sprachw.) demonstrative pronoun
demonstrieren **1** *itr. V.* demonstrate (**für** in support of, **gegen** against) **2** *tr. V.* demonstrate
dem·selben ▸ DERSELBE
Demut *die;* ~: humility
demütig **1** *Adj.* humble **2** *adv.* humbly
demütigen **1** *tr. V.* humiliate **2** *refl. V.* humble oneself
Demütigung *die;* ~, ~en humiliation
dem·zufolge *Adv.* consequently
den¹ **1** *best. Art., Akk. Sg. v.* DER¹ 1: the **2** *Demonstrativpron., Akk. Sg. v.* DER¹ 2: (a) *attr.* that; **ich meine den Mann** I mean 'that man (b) *allein stehend* **ich meine den [da]** I mean 'that one **3** *Relativpron., Akk. Sg. v.* DER¹ 3 (Person) that/whom; (Sache) that/which; **der Mann, den ich gesehen habe** the man that I saw
den² **1** *best. Art., Dat. Pl. v.* DER¹ 1, DIE¹ 1, DAS 1: the

2 *Demonstrativpron. Dat. Pl. v.* DER¹ 2A, DIE¹ 2A, DAS 2A: those
denen **1** *Demonstrativpron., Dat. Pl. v.* DER¹ 2B, DIE¹ 2B, DAS 2B them; **gib es** ~, **nicht den anderen** give it to 'them, not to the others **2** *Relativpron., Dat. Pl. v.* DER¹ 3, DIE¹ 3, DAS 3 (Personen) that/whom; (Sachen) that/which; **die Menschen,** ~ **wir Geld gegeben haben** the people to whom we gave money; **die Tiere,** ~ **er geholfen hat** the animals that he helped
denjenigen ▸ DERJENIGE
denkbar **1** *Adj.* conceivable **2** *adv.* (sehr, äußerst) extremely
Denke *die;* ~, ~n (ugs.) way of thinking
denken **1** *unr. itr. V.* think (**an** + *Akk.* of, **über** + *Akk.* about); **wie denkst du darüber?** what do you think about it?; what's your opinion of it?; **schlecht von jmdm.** ~: think badly of sb.; **denk daran, dass …/zu …:** don't forget that …/to …; **ich denke nicht daran!** no way!; not on your life!; **ich denke nicht daran, das zu tun** I've no intention of doing that **2** *unr. tr. V.* think; **wer hätte das gedacht?** who would have thought it?; **eine gedachte Linie** an imaginary line **3** *unr. refl. V.* (a) (sich vorstellen) imagine (b) **sich** (*Dat.*) **bei etw. etwas** ~: mean something by sth.; **ich habe mir nichts [Böses] dabei gedacht** I didn't mean any harm [by it]
Denken *das;* ~s thinking; (Denkweise) thought
Denker *der;* ~s, ~, **Denkerin** *die;* ~, ~nen thinker
denk-, Denk-: ~**fabrik** *die* think tank; ~**faul** *Adj.* mentally lazy; ~**fehler** *der* flaw in one's reasoning; ~**mal** *das; Pl.* ~**mäler** *od.* ~**male** monument; memorial; **jmdm. ein** ~**mal errichten** *od.* **setzen** erect *or* put up a memorial to sb.
Denkmal[s]·schutz *der* protection of historic monuments; **unter** ~ **stehen/stellen** be/put under a preservation order
denk-, Denk-: ~**pause** *die* pause for thought; ~**sport·aufgabe** *die* brain teaser; ~**vermögen** *das* ability to think [creatively]; ~**würdig** *Adj.* memorable; ~**zettel** *der* lesson
denn **1** *Konj.* (a) (kausal) for; because (b) (geh.: als) than **2** *Adv.* **es sei** ~, …: unless … **3** *Partikel* (in Fragesätzen) **wie geht es dir** ~? tell me, how are you?; **wie heißt du** ~? tell me your name; **warum** ~ **nicht?** why ever not?
dennoch *Adv.* nevertheless
denselben ▸ DERSELBE
Denunziant *der;* ~en, ~en, **Denunziantin** *die;* ~, ~nen informer; grass (sl.) ····❯

denunzieren *tr. V.* denounce; (bei der Polizei) inform against; grass on (sl.) (**bei** to)

Deo *das;* ~s, ~s, **Deodorant** *das;* ~s, ~s (auch:) ~e deodorant

Deo·spray *das* deodorant spray

Deponie *die;* ~, ~n tip (Brit.); dump

deponieren *tr. V.* put; (im Safe o. Ä.) deposit

Deportation *die;* ~, ~en transportation; (ins Ausland) deportation

deportieren *tr. V.* transport; (ins Ausland) deport

Deportierte *der/die; adj. Dekl.* transportee; (ins Ausland) deportee

Depot /de'po:/ *das;* ~s, ~s (a) depot; (Lagerhaus) warehouse; (für Möbel usw.) depository; (im Freien, für Munition o. Ä.) dump; (in einer Bank) strongroom; safe deposit (b) (hinterlegte Wertgegenstände) deposits *pl.*

Depp *der;* ~en (auch:) ~s, ~en (auch:) ~e (bes. südd., österr., schweiz. abwertend) ▶ DUMMKOPF

Depression *die;* ~, ~en depression

depressiv [1] *Adj.* depressive
[2] *adv.* ~ veranlagt sein have a tendency towards depression

deprimieren *tr. V.* depress

deprimierend *Adj.* depressing

deprimiert [1] *Adj.* depressed
[2] *adv.* dejectedly

der[1] [1] *best. Art. Nom.* the; **der Tod** death; **der „Faust"** 'Faust'; **der Bodensee/Mount Everest** Lake Constance/Mount Everest; **der Iran/Sudan** Iran/the Sudan; **der Mensch/Mann ist …**: man is …/men are …
[2] *Demonstrativpron.* (a) *attr.* that; **der Mann war es** it was 'that man
(b) *allein stehend* he; **der war es** it was 'him; **der [da]** (Person) that man/boy; (Sache) that one; **der [hier]** (Person) this man/boy; (Sache) this one
[3] *Relativpron.* (Person) who/that; (Sache) which/that; **der Mann, der da drüben entlanggeht** the man walking along over there
[4] *Relativ- u. Demonstrativpron.* the one who

der² [1] *best. Art.* (a) *Gen. Sg. v.* DIE[1] 1: **der Hut der Frau** the woman's hat; **der Henkel der Tasse** the handle of the cup
(b) *Dat. Sg. v.* DIE[1] 1 to the; (nach Präp.) the
(c) *Gen. Pl. v.* DER[1] 1, DIE[1] 1, DAS 1: **das Haus der Freunde** our/their *etc.* friends' house; **das Bellen der Hunde** the barking of the dogs
[2] *Demonstrativpron.* (a) *Gen. Sg. v.* DIE[1] 2: of the; of that
(b) *Dat. Sg. v.* DIE[1] 2 *attr.* **der Frau [da/hier] gehört es** it belongs to that woman there/this woman here
(c) *Gen. Pl. v.* DER[1] 2A, DIE[1] 2A, DAS 2A: of those

[3] *Relativpron.; Dat. Sg. v.* DIE[1] 3: **die Frau, der ich es gegeben habe** the woman I gave it to; **die Katze, der er einen Tritt gab** the cat [that] he kicked

der·art *Adv.* so; **es hat lange nicht mehr ~ geregnet** it hasn't rained as hard as that for a long time; **sie hat ~ geschrien, dass …**: she screamed so much that …

der·artig [1] *Adj.* such
[2] *adv.* ▶ DERART

derb [1] *Adj.* (a) tough ‹*material*›; stout, ‹*shoes*›
(b) (kraftvoll, deftig) earthy ‹*scenes, humour*›
[2] *adv.* (a) strongly ‹*made, woven, etc.*›
(b) (kraftvoll, deftig) earthily

deren [1] *Relativpron.* (a) *Gen. Sg. v.* DIE[1] 3 (Personen) whose; (Sachen) of which
(b) *Gen. Pl. v.* DER[1] 3, DIE[1] 3, DAS 3 (Personen) whose; (Sachen) **Maßnahmen, ~ Folgen wir noch nicht absehen können** measures, the consequences of which we cannot yet foresee
[2] *Demonstrativpron.* (a) *Gen. Sg. v.* DIE[1] 2: **meine Tante, ihre Freundin und ~ Hund** my aunt, her friend and her dog
(b) *Gen. Pl. v.* DER[1] 2, DIE[1] 2, DAS 2: **meine Verwandten und ~ Kinder** my relatives and their children

derent-: ~wegen *Adv.* [1] *relativ* (Personen) because of whom; (Sachen) because of which; [2] *demonstrativ* because of them; ~willen *Adv.* um ~willen (Personen) for whose sake; (Sachen) for the sake of which

derer *Demonstrativpron.; Gen. Pl. v.* DER[1] 2, DIE[1] 2, DAS 2 of those

der·gleichen *indekl. Demonstrativpron.* (a) *attr.* such; like that *postpos., not pred.*
(b) *allein stehend* that sort of thing

Derivat *das;* ~[e]s, ~e derivative

der·jenige, die·jenige, das·jenige *Demonstrativpron.* (a) *attr.* that; *Pl.* those
(b) *allein stehend* that one; *Pl.* those

derlei *indekl. Demonstrativpron.:* ▶ DERGLEICHEN

der·maßen *Adv.* ~ schön *usw.*, **dass …**: so beautiful *etc.* that …

derselbe, dieselbe, dasselbe *Demonstrativpron.* (a) *attr.* the same
(b) *allein stehend* the same one; *Pl.* the same people; **er sagt immer dasselbe** he always says the same thing; **noch einmal dasselbe, bitte** (ugs.) [the] same again please

der·zeit *Adv.* at present

der·zeitig *Adj.* present; current

des [1] *best. Art.; Gen. Sg. v.* DER[1] 1, DAS 1: **die Mütze des Jungen** the boy's cap; **das Klingeln des Telefons** the ringing of the telephone
[2] *Demonstrativpron.; Gen. Sg. v.* DER[1] 2, DAS 2: **er ist der Sohn des Mannes, der …**: he's the son of the man who …

Deserteur /dezɛr'tø:ɐ̯/ *der;* ~s, ~e, **Deserteurin** /dezɛr'tø:rɪn/ *die;* ~, ~nen deserter

---
*old spelling – see note on page x

desertieren *itr. V.; mit sein* desert

des·gleichen *Adv.* likewise; **er ist Arzt,** ∼ **sein Sohn** he is a doctor, as is his son

des·halb *Adv.* for that reason; ∼ **bin ich zu dir gekommen** that is why I came to you

Design /di'zain/ *das;* ∼**s,** ∼**s** design

Designer /di'zainɐ/ *der;* ∼**s,** ∼, **Designerin** *die;* ∼, ∼**nen** designer

Designer·droge /-'----/ *die;* ∼, ∼**n** designer drug

Desinfektion *die;* ∼, ∼**nen** disinfection

Desinfektions·mittel *das* disinfectant

desinfizieren *tr. V.* disinfect

Desinteresse *das;* ∼**s** lack of interest

Desktop /'dɛsktɔp/ *der;* ∼**s,** ∼**s** (DV) desktop

Despot /dɛs'po:t/ *der;* ∼**en,** ∼**en,** **Despotin** *die;* ∼, ∼**nen** despot; (fig. abwertend) tyrant

despotisch [1] *Adj.* despotic
[2] *adv.* despotically

des·selben ▸ DERSELBE

dessen [1] *Relativpron.; Gen. Sg. v.* DER[1] 3, DAS 3 *attr.* (Person) whose; (Sache) of which
[2] *Demonstrativpron.; Gen. Sg. v.* DER[1] 2, DAS 2: **mein Onkel, sein Sohn und** ∼ **Hund** my uncle, his son, and 'his dog

Dessert /dɛ'se:ɐ̯/ *das;* ∼**s,** ∼**s** dessert

Destille *die;* ∼, ∼**n** distillery

destillieren *tr. V.* (Chemie) distil

desto *Konj., vor Komp.* **je eher,** ∼ **besser** the sooner the better

des·wegen *Adv.* ▸ DESHALB

Detail /de'tai̯/ *das;* ∼**s,** ∼**s** detail

detailliert [1] *Adj.* detailed
[2] *adv.* in detail; **sehr** ∼: in great detail

Detektiv *der;* ∼**s,** ∼**e, Detektivin** *die;* ∼, ∼**nen** [private] detective

Detonation *die;* ∼, ∼**en** detonation; explosion

detonieren *itr. V.; mit sein* detonate; explode

Deut **keinen** ∼: not one bit

deuten [1] *itr. V.* point; **[mit dem Finger] auf jmdn./etw.** ∼: point [one's finger] at sb./sth.
[2] *tr. V.* interpret

deutlich [1] *Adj.* clear
[2] *adv.* clearly

Deutlichkeit *die;* ∼ (a) clarity
(b) (Eindeutigkeit) clearness

deutsch [1] *Adj.* German; **Deutsche Mark** Deutschmark; German mark
[2] *adv.* **Deutsch sprechen/schreiben** speak/write German

Deutsch *das;* ∼**[s]** German; **gutes/fließend** ∼ **sprechen** speak good/fluent German; **auf** *od.* **in** ∼: in German; **auf [gut]** ∼ (ugs.) in plain English

Deutsche[1] *der/die; adj. Dekl.* German; **er ist** ∼**r** he is German

Deutsche[2] *das; adj. Dekl.* **das** ∼: German; **aus dem** ∼**n/ins** ∼ **übersetzen** translate from/into German

Deutschland (*das*) ∼**s** Germany

deutsch-, Deutsch-: ∼**lehrer** *der,* ∼**lehrerin** *die* German teacher; ∼**sprachig** *Adj.* (a) German-speaking; (b) German-language *attrib.;* ∼**unterricht** *der* German teaching; (Unterrichtsstunde) German lesson

Deutung *die;* ∼, ∼**en** interpretation

Devise *die;* ∼, ∼**n** motto

Devisen *Pl.* foreign currency *sing.*

Devisen-: ∼**börse** *die* foreign exchange market; ∼**kurs** *der* exchange rate; rate of exchange

Dezember *der;* ∼**s,** ∼: December

dezent [1] *Adj.* quiet ‹colour, pattern, suit›; subdued ‹lighting, music›
[2] *adv.* discreetly; ‹dress› unostentatiously

dezimal *Adj.* decimal

Dezimal-: ∼**system** *das* decimal system; ∼**zahl** *die* decimal [number]

dezimieren *tr. V.* decimate

DG *Abk.* = **Dachgeschoss**

dgl. *Abk.* = **dergleichen, desgleichen**

d. h. *Abk.* = **das heißt** i.e.

Di. *Abk.* = **Dienstag** Tue[s].

Dia *das;* ∼**s,** ∼**s** slide

Diabetes *der;* ∼: diabetes

Diabetiker *der;* ∼**s,** ∼, **Diabetikerin** *die;* ∼, ∼**nen** diabetic

Diagnose /dia'gno:zə/ *die;* ∼, ∼**n** diagnosis

diagonal [1] *Adj.* diagonal
[2] *adv.* diagonally

Diagonale *die;* ∼, ∼**n** diagonal

Diagramm *das* graph; (von Gegenständen) diagram

Dialekt *der;* ∼**[e]s,** ∼**e** dialect

Dialog *der;* ∼**[e]s,** ∼**e** dialogue

Dialog·fenster *das* (DV) dialogue box

Dialyse /dia'ly:zə/ *die;* ∼, ∼**n** (Physik, Chemie, Med.) dialysis

Diamant *der;* ∼**en,** ∼**en** diamond

***diät** ▸ DIÄT

Diät *die;* ∼, ∼**en** diet; **eine** ∼ **einhalten** keep to a diet; ∼ **essen** be on a diet; ∼ **kochen** cook according to a/one's diet

Diäten *Pl.* [parliamentary] allowance *sing.*

dich [1] *Akk. von* DU you
[2] *Akk. des Reflexivpron. der 2. Pers. Sg.* yourself

dicht [1] *Adj.* (a) thick; dense ‹forest, hedge, crowd›; heavy, dense ‹traffic›
(b) (undurchlässig) (für Luft) airtight; (für Wasser) watertight
[2] *adv.* (a) densely ‹populated, wooded›; ∼ **bebaut** heavily built up
(b) (undurchlässig) tightly
(c) *mit Präp.* (nahe) ∼ **neben** right next to

*dicht·bebaut ▸ DICHT 2A

Dichte *die;* ~ (Physik, fig.) density

dichten [1] *itr. V.* write poetry
[2] *tr. V.* (verfassen) write; compose

Dichter *der;* ~s, ~: poet; (Schriftsteller) writer; author

Dichterin *die;* ~, ~nen poet[ess]; (Schriftstellerin) writer; author[ess]

dichterisch *Adj.* poetic; (schriftstellerisch) literary

dicht|machen *tr., itr. V.* (ugs.) shut; (endgültig) shut down

Dichtung[1] *die;* ~, ~en seal; (am Hahn usw.) washer; (am Vergaser, Zylinder usw.) gasket

Dichtung[2] *die;* ~, ~en (a) work of literature; (in Versform) poetic work; poem
(b) (Dichtkunst) literature; (in Versform) poetry

dick [1] *Adj.* (a) thick; stout ⟨tree⟩; fat ⟨person, legs, etc.⟩; swollen ⟨cheek, ankle, tonsils, etc.⟩; ~ **werden** get fat; **5 cm ~ sein** be 5 cm thick
(b) (ugs.: groß) big ⟨mistake⟩; hefty, (coll.) fat ⟨salary⟩
[2] *adv.* thickly; **etw.** ~ **unterstreichen** underline sth. heavily; **sich** ~ **anziehen** wrap up warm[ly]; **etw. 5 cm ~ schneiden** cut sth. 5 cm. thick; ~ **geschwollen** (ugs.) badly swollen

Dicke[1] *die;* ~: thickness; (von Menschen, Körperteilen) fatness

Dicke[2] *der/die; adj. Dekl.* (ugs.) fatty (coll.)

dick·fellig (ugs.) *Adj.* thick-skinned

Dickfelligkeit *die;* ~ (ugs.) insensitivity

Dickicht /'dɪkɪçt/ *das;* ~[e]s, ~e thicket

dick-, Dick-: ~**kopf** *der* (ugs.) mule (coll.); **ein** ~**kopf sein** be stubborn as a mule; **einen** ~**kopf haben** be pigheaded; ~**köpfig** *Adj.* (ugs.) pigheaded; ~**macher** *der* (ugs.) fattening food; ~**milch** *die* sour milk

die[1] [1] *best. Art. Nom.* the; **die Helga** (ugs.) Helga; **die Frau/Menschheit** women *pl.*/mankind
[2] *Demonstrativpron.* (a) *attr.* **die Frau war es** it was 'that woman
(b) *allein stehend* she; **die war es** it was 'her; **die [da]** (Person) that woman/girl; (Sache) that one
[3] *Relativpron. Nom.* (Person) who; that; (Sache, Tier) which; that
[4] *Relativ- u. Demonstrativpron.* the one who

die[2] [1] *best. Art.* (a) *Akk. Sg. v.* DIE[1] 1 the; **ich sah die Frau** I saw the women
(b) *Nom. u. Akk. Pl. v.* DER[1] 1, DIE[1] 1, DAS 1: the
[2] *Demonstrativpron. Nom. u. Akk. Pl. v.* DER[1] 1, DIE[1] 1, DAS 1: *attr.* **ich meine die Männer, die ...** I mean those men who ...; *allein stehend* **ich meine die [da]** I mean 'them
[3] *Relativpron.* (a) *Akk. Sg. v.* DIE[1] 3 (Person) who; (Sache) that

(b) *Nom. u. Akk. Pl. v.* DER[1] 3, DIE[1] 3, DAS 3 (Personen) whom; (Sachen) which; **die Männer, die ich gesehen habe** the men I saw

Dieb *der;* ~[e]s, ~e thief

Diebin *die;* ~, ~nen [woman] thief

diebisch [1] *Adj.* (a) thieving
(b) (verstohlen) mischievous
[2] *adv.* mischievously

Diebstahl *der;* ~[e]s, Diebstähle theft

die·jenige ▸ DERJENIGE

Diele *die;* ~, ~n hall[way]

dienen *itr. V.* serve; **womit kann ich** ~? what can I do for you?

Diener *der;* ~s, ~: servant; **einen** ~ **machen** (ugs.) bow; make a bow

Dienerin *die;* ~, ~nen maid; servant

dienlich *Adj.* helpful

Dienst *der;* ~[e]s, ~e (a) (Tätigkeit) work; (von Soldaten, Polizeibeamten, Krankenhauspersonal usw.) duty; **seinen** ~ **antreten** start work/go on duty; ~ **haben** be at work/on duty; ⟨doctor⟩ be on call; ⟨chemist⟩ be open
(b) (Arbeitsverhältnis) post; **Major außer** ~: retired major
(c) (Tätigkeitsbereich) service; *s. auch* ÖFFENTLICH
(d) (Hilfe) service

Diens·tag *der* Tuesday; **am** ~: on Tuesday; ~, **der 1. Juni** Tuesday, 1 June; **er kommt** ~: he is coming on Tuesday; **ab nächsten** ~: from next Tuesday [onwards]; ~ **in einer Woche** a week on Tuesday; ~ **vor einer Woche** a week last Tuesday

diens·tags *Adv.* on Tuesday[s]

dienst-, Dienst-: ~**bereit** *Adj.* ⟨chemist⟩ open *pred.*; ⟨doctor⟩ on call; ⟨dentist⟩ on duty; ~**bote** *der,* ~**botin** *die* servant; ~**eifrig** *Adj.* zealous; ~**frei** *Adj.* free ⟨time⟩; ~**geheimnis** *das* (a) professional secret; (im Staatsdienst) official secret; (b) professional secrecy; (im Staatsdienst) official secrecy; ~**grad** *der* (Milit.) rank; ~**leister** *der;* ~~s, ~~, ~**leisterin** *die;* ~~, ~~nen (Firma, auch DV) service provider; ~**leistung** *die* (auch Wirtsch.) service

Dienstleistungs-: ~**branche** *die* (Wirtsch.) (a) service industry; (b) ▸ ~SEKTOR; ~**sektor** *der* (Wirtsch.) service sector

dienstlich [1] *Adj.* business ⟨call⟩; (im Staatsdienst) official ⟨letter, call, etc.⟩
[2] *adv.* on business; (im Staatsdienst) on official business

Dienst-: ~**reise** *die* business trip; ~**stelle** *die* office; ~**wagen** *der* official car; (Geschäftswagen) company car; ~**weg** *der* official channels *pl.;* ~**zeit** *die* (a) period of service; (b) (tägliche Arbeitszeit) working hours *pl.*

dies ▸ DIESER

dies·bezüglich *adv.* regarding this

diese ▸ DIESER

Diesel *der;* ~s, ~: diesel
die·selbe ▶ DERSELBE
Diesel·motor *der* diesel engine
dieser, diese, dieses, dies
Demonstrativpron. (a) *attr.* this; *Pl.* these
(b) *allein stehend* this one; *Pl.* these; **dies**
alles all this; **dies und das,** (geh.) **dieses und**
jenes this and that
diesig *Adj.* hazy
dies-: ~**mal** *Adv.* this time; ~**seits**
[1] *Präp. mit Gen.* on this side of; [2] *Adv.*
~**seits von** on this side of
Dietrich *der;* ~s, ~e picklock
diffamieren *tr. V.* defame
Diffamierung *die;* ~, ~en defamation
Differential *usw.* ▶ DIFFERENZIAL *usw.*
Differenz *die;* ~, ~en difference;
(Meinungsverschiedenheit) difference [of
opinion]
Differenzial /dɪfərɛnˈts̩ iaːl/ *das;* ~s, ~e
(a) (Math.) differential
(b) (Technik) differential [gear]
Differenzial·rechnung *die* (Math.)
differential calculus
differenziert *Adj.* complex; subtly
differentiated ‹*methods, colours*›;
sophisticated ‹*taste*›
diffus [1] *Adj.* (a) (Physik, Chemie) diffuse
(b) (geh.) vague; vague and confused ‹*idea,*
statement, etc.›
[2] *adv.* in a vague and confused way
digital (DV) [1] *Adj.* digital
[2] *adv.* digitally
Digital- digital ‹*clock, display, etc.*›
Digital·fernsehen *das* digital television
digitalisieren *tr. V.* (DV) digitalize
Digital-: ~**kamera** *die* digital camera;
~**radio** *das* digital radio
Diktat *das;* ~[e]s, ~e dictation
Diktator *der;* ~s, ~en, **Diktatorin** *die;*
~, ~nen dictator
diktatorisch [1] *Adj.* dictatorial
[2] *adv.* dictatorially
Diktatur *die;* ~, ~en dictatorship
diktieren *tr. V.* dictate
Diktier·gerät *das* dictating machine
Dilemma *das;* ~s, ~s dilemma
Dilettant /dilɛˈtant/ *der;* ~en, ~en,
Dilettantin *die;* ~, ~nen dilettante
dilettantisch [1] *Adj.* dilettante;
amateurish
[2] *adv.* amateurishly
Dill *der;* ~[e]s, ~e dill
Dimension *die;* ~, ~en (Physik, fig.)
dimension
DIN /diːn/ *Abk.* = **Deutsche**
Industrie-Norm[en] *German*
Industrial Standard[s]*;* DIN; **DIN-A4-Format**
A4
Ding¹ *das;* ~[e]s, ~e (a) thing
(b) **nach Lage der** ~**e** the way things are;

persönliche/private ~e personal/private
matters; **ein** ~ **der Unmöglichkeit sein** be
quite impossible; **vor allen** ~**en** above all
(c) **guter** ~**e sein** (geh.) be in good spirits
Ding² *das;* ~[e]s, ~er (ugs.) thing; **das ist ja**
ein ~! that's really something
Dinkel *der;* ~s, ~ (Landw.) spelt
Dino *der;* ~s, ~s (ugs.) dinosaur
Dino·saurier *der;* ~s, ~: dinosaur
Diode *die;* ~, ~n (Elektrot.) diode
Dioden·rücklicht *das* LED rear light
Dioxin *das;* ~s (Chemie) dioxin
Diözese *die;* ~, ~n diocese
Dipl.-Ing. *Abk.* = **Diplomingenieur**
academically qualified engineer
Diplom *das;* ~s, ~e ≈ [first] degree (*in*
a scientific or technical subject); (für einen
Handwerksberuf) diploma
Diplom- qualified
Diplomat *der;* ~en, ~en, **Diplomatin**
die; ~, ~nen diplomat
diplomatisch [1] *Adj.* diplomatic
[2] *adv.* diplomatically
dir [1] *Dat. von* DU to you; (nach Präp.) you;
Freunde von ~: friends of yours
[2] *Dat. des Reflexivpron. der 2. Pers. Sg.*
yourself
direkt [1] *Adj.* direct
[2] *adv.* straight; directly; **etw.** ~ **übertragen**
broadcast sth. live
Direkt·flug *der* direct flight
Direktion *die;* ~, ~en management;
(Büroräume) managers' offices *pl.*
Direktor *der;* ~s, ~en, **Direktorin** *die;*
~, ~nen director; (einer Schule) headmaster/
headmistress; (einer Strafanstalt) governor;
(einer Abteilung) manager
Direkt·übertragung *die* live broadcast
Dirigent *der;* ~en, ~en, **Dirigentin** *die;*
~, ~nen conductor
dirigieren *tr. V.* (a) *auch itr.* conduct
(b) (führen) steer
Disc·jockey /ˈdɪskdʒɔke/ *der* disc jockey
Disco /ˈdɪskoː/ *die;* ~, ~s disco
Disk /dɪsk/ *die;* ~, ~s disc
Diskette *die;* ~, ~n (DV) floppy disk
Disketten·laufwerk *das* (DV)
[floppy-]disk drive
Diskont·satz *der* (Finanzw.) discount rate
Diskothek *die;* ~, ~en discothèque
Diskrepanz *die;* ~, ~en discrepancy
diskret [1] *Adj.* (vertraulich) confidential;
(taktvoll) discreet; tactful
[2] *adv.* (vertraulich) confidentially; (taktvoll)
discreetly; tactfully
Diskretion *die;* ~ (a) (Verschwiegenheit, Takt)
discretion
(b) (Unaufdringlichkeit) discreetness
diskriminieren *tr. V.* discriminate
against ⋯>

Diskriminierung *die;* ~, ~en discrimination

Diskussion *die;* ~, ~en discussion; **zur** ~ **stehen** be under discussion

Diskussions-: **~beitrag** *der* contribution to a/the discussion; **~leiter** *der* chair[man] [of the discussion]; **~leiterin** *die* chair[woman] [of the discussion]

diskutieren ① *itr. V.* über etw. (*Akk.*) ~: discuss sth. ② *tr. V.* discuss

Disqualifikation *die;* ~, ~en (auch Sport) disqualification

disqualifizieren *tr. V.* disqualify

Distanz *die;* ~, ~en (auch fig.) distance

distanzieren *refl. V.* sich von jmdm./etw. ~ (fig.) dissociate oneself from sb./sth.

distanziert *Adj.* reserved

Distel *die;* ~, ~n thistle

Distel-fink *der* goldfinch

Disziplin *die;* ~, ~en discipline; (Selbstbeherrschung) [self-]discipline

disziplinieren ① *tr. V.* discipline ② *refl. V.* discipline oneself

diszipliniert ① *Adj.* well-disciplined; (beherrscht) disciplined ② *adv.* in a well-disciplined way; (beherrscht) in a disciplined way

divers... /di'vɛrs.../ *Adj.* various; (mehrer...) several

Dividende /divi'dɛndə/ *die;* ~, ~n (Wirtsch.) dividend

dividieren *tr. V.* divide

Division *die;* ~, ~en (auch Milit.) division

DM *Abk.* = **Deutsche Mark** DM

D-Mark /'deː-/ *die* Deutschmark

DNA *die;* ~, ~[s] DNA

DNS *Abk.* (Chemie)
= **Desoxyribonukleinsäure** DNA

Do. *Abk.* = **Donnerstag** Thur[s].

doch ① *Konj.* but ② *Adv.* **(a)** (jedoch) but **(b)** (dennoch) all the same; still **(c)** (geh.: nämlich) **wusste er** ~, **dass ...**: because he knew that ... **(d)** (entgegen allen gegenteiligen Behauptungen, Annahmen) **er war also** ~ **der Mörder!** so he 'was the murderer! **(e)** (ohnehin) in any case ③ *Interj.* **Das stimmt nicht. – Doch!** That's not right. – [Oh] yes it is!; **Hast du keinen Hunger? – Doch!** Aren't you hungry? – Yes [I am]! ④ *Partikel* **(a)** (Ungeduld ausdrückend) **pass** ~ **auf!** [oh] do be careful!; **das ist** ~ **nicht zu glauben** that's just incredible **(b)** (Zweifel ausdrückend) **du hast** ~ **meinen Brief erhalten?** you did get my letter, didn't you?

(c) (Überraschung ausdrückend) **das ist** ~ **Karl!** there's Karl!
(d) (verstärkt Bejahung/Verneinung ausdrückend) **gewiss/sicher** ~: [why] certainly; of course; **ja** ~: [yes,] all right; **nicht** ~! (abwehrend) [no,] don't!
(e) (Wunsch verstärkend) **wäre es** ~ ...: if only it were ...

Docht *der;* ~[e]s, ~e wick

Dock *das;* ~s, ~s dock

Dogge *die;* ~, ~n: [deutsche] ~: Great Dane

Dogma *das;* ~s, Dogmen (auch fig.) dogma

dogmatisch (Theol., auch fig.) *Adj.* dogmatic

Dohle *die;* ~, ~n jackdaw

Doktor *der;* ~s, ~en (auch ugs.: Arzt) doctor; (Titel) Doctor

Doktor-arbeit *die* doctoral thesis

Doktor-grad *der* doctorate; doctor's degree

Doktorin *die;* ~, ~nen ▶ DOKTOR

Doktor-titel *der* title of doctor

Doktrin *die;* ~, ~en doctrine

Dokument *das;* ~[e]s, ~e document

Dokumentar-: **~bericht** *der* documentary report; **~film** *der* documentary [film]

Dokumentation *die;* ~, ~en
(a) documentation
(b) (Bericht) documentary report

dokumentieren *tr. V.* **(a)** document; (fig.) demonstrate
(b) (festhalten) record

Dolch *der;* ~[e]s, ~e dagger

Dolde *die;* ~, ~n (Bot.) umbel

doll (bes. nordd., salopp) ① *Adj.*
(a) (ungewöhnlich) incredible
(b) (großartig) great (coll.) ② *adv.* **(a)** (großartig) fantastically [well] (coll.)
(b) (sehr) ⟨hurt⟩ dreadfully (coll.), like mad

Dollar *der;* ~s, ~s dollar; **zwei** ~: two dollars

dolmetschen *itr. V.* act as interpreter

Dolmetscher *der;* ~s, ~, **Dolmetscherin** *die;* ~, ~nen interpreter

Dom *der;* ~[e]s, ~e cathedral

dominieren *itr. V.* dominate

dominikanisch *Adj.* Dominican; **die Dominikanische Republik** the Dominican Republic

Domino *das;* ~s, ~s (Spiel) dominoes *sing.*

Domizil *das;* ~s, ~e (geh.) domicile; residence

Dom-pfaff *der;* ~en *od.* ~s, ~en (Zool.) bullfinch

Dompteur /dɔmp'tøːɐ/ *der;* ~s, ~e, **Dompteurin** /dɔmp'tøːrɪn/ *die;* ~, ~nen, **Dompteuse** /dɔmp'tøːzə/ *die;* ~, ~n tamer

Donau *die;* ~: Danube

Donner *der;* ~s, ~: thunder

donnern *itr. V.* **(a)** (*unpers.*) thunder **(b)** (fig.) thunder; ⟨*engine*⟩ roar

Donners·tag *der* Thursday; *s. auch* DIENSTAG

donnerstags *Adv.* on Thursday[s]; *s. auch* DIENSTAGS

Donner·wetter *das* (ugs.) **(a)** (Krach) row **(b)** /'--'--/ **zum ~ [noch einmal]!** damn it!; **~!** my word

doof (ugs.) ⟨1⟩ *Adj.* stupid; dumb (coll.) ⟨2⟩ *adv.* stupidly

Doping /'do:pɪŋ/ *das;* ~s (Sport) taking drugs

Doping·kontrolle *die* (Sport) drug[s] test

Doppel *das,* ~s, ~ **(a)** (Kopie) duplicate; copy **(b)** (Sport) doubles *sing. or pl.*

doppel-, Doppel-: ~**bett** *das* double bed; ~**bock** *das* extra-strong bock beer; ~**decker** *der;* ~~s, ~~: biplane; ~**deutig** /-dəytɪç/ ⟨1⟩ *Adj.* **(a)** ambiguous; **(b)** (anzüglich) suggestive; ⟨2⟩ *adv.* **(a)** ambiguously; **(b)** (anzüglich) suggestively; ~**fenster** *das* double-glazed window; ~**gänger** *der;* ~~s, ~~, ~**gängerin** *die;* ~~, ~~nen double; ~**haus** *das* pair of semi-detached houses; ~**haus·hälfte** *die* semi[-detached] house]; ~**kinn** *das* double chin; ~**klick** *der;* ~~s, ~~s (DV) double click; ~**moral** *die* double standards *pl.;* ~**pass,** ***~**paß** *der* (ugs.) der ~pass dual nationality *no art.;* ~**punkt** *der* colon; ~**stunde** *die* double period

doppelt ⟨1⟩ *Adj.* double; **die** ~**e Menge** twice the quantity; **mit** ~**er Kraft arbeiten** work with twice as much energy ⟨2⟩ *adv.* ~ **so groß/alt wie ...:** twice as large/old as ...; **sich** ~ **anstrengen** try twice as hard

Doppelte *das; adj. Dekl.* **das** ~ **bezahlen** pay twice as much; pay double

Doppel-: ~**tür** *die* double door; ~**zentner** *der* 100 kilograms; ~**zimmer** *das* double room

Dorf *das;* ~[e]s, Dörfer village; **auf dem** ~: in the country

Dorf-: ~**bewohner** *der,* ~**bewohnerin** *die* villager; ~**depp** *der* (bes. südd., österr.) village idiot; ~**trottel** *der* village idiot

Dorn *der;* ~[e]s, ~en thorn; **jmdm. ein** ~ **im Auge sein** annoy sb. intensely

dornig *Adj.* thorny

Dorn·röschen (*das*) the Sleeping Beauty

dörren *tr. V.* dry

Dörr-: ~**fleisch** *das* (südd.) lean bacon; ~**obst** *das* dried fruit

Dorsch *der;* ~[e]s, ~e cod

dort *Adv.* there; ~ **bleiben** stay there; *s. auch* DA 1A

dort-: ***~**|bleiben** ▶ DORT; ~**her** *Adv.* **[von]** ~her from there; ~**hin** *Adv.* there

dortig *Adj.* there

Dose *die;* ~, ~n **(a)** (Blech~) tin; (Pillen~) box; (Zucker~) bowl **(b)** (Konserven~) can; tin (Brit.); (Bier~) can

dösen *itr. V.* (ugs.) doze

Dosen-: ~**bier** *das* canned beer; ~**milch** *die* canned *or* (Brit.) tinned milk; ~**öffner** *der* can-opener; tin-opener (Brit.); ~**pfand** *das* deposit on [drinks] cans

dosieren *tr. V.* etw. ~: measure out the required dose of sth.

Dosierung *die;* ~, ~en **(a)** measuring out; (das Zuführen) administering; (fig.) dispensing **(b)** ▶ DOSIS

Dosis *die;* ~, Dosen dose

Dossier /dɔ'sie:/ *das,* (veraltet:) *der;* ~s, ~s dossier

Dotcom /'dɔtkɔm/ *das;* ~s, ~s dot-com [company]

Dotter *der od. das;* ~s, ~: yolk

Dotter·blume *die* marsh marigold

doubeln /'du:b|n/ *tr. V.* stand in for ⟨*actor*⟩; use a stand-in for ⟨*scene*⟩; **sich** ~ **lassen** use *or* have a stand-in

Dozent *der;* ~en, ~en, **Dozentin** *die;* ~, ~nen lecturer (**für** in)

dpa *Abk. =* **Deutsche Presse-Agentur** German Press Agency

Dr. *Abk. =* **Doktor** Dr

Drache *der;* ~n, ~n (Myth.) dragon

Drachen *der;* ~s, ~ **(a)** kite **(b)** (Fluggerät) hang-glider

Dragee, Dragée /dra'ʒe:/ *das;* ~s, ~s dragee

Draht *der;* ~[e]s, Drähte **(a)** wire **(b)** (Leitung) wire; (Telefonleitung) line; wire **(c)** (Telefonverbindung) line

draht-, Draht-: ~**los** (Nachrichtenw.) ⟨1⟩ *Adj.* wireless; ⟨2⟩ *adv.* etw. ~**los** telegrafieren/übermitteln radio sth.; ~**seil** *das* [steel] cable; ~**seil·bahn** *die* cable railway; ~**zieher** *der;* ~~s, ~~, ~**zieherin** *die;* ~~, ~~nen (fig.) wire puller

drall *Adj.* strapping ⟨*girl*⟩; full, rounded ⟨*cheeks, face, bottom*⟩

Drama *das;* ~s, Dramen drama; (fig., ugs.) disaster

Dramatiker *der;* ~s, ~, **Dramatikerin** *die;* ~, ~nen dramatist

dramatisch ⟨1⟩ *Adj.* dramatic ⟨2⟩ *adv.* dramatically

dramatisieren *tr. V.* dramatize

dramaturgisch *adj.* dramaturgical

dran *Adv.* (ugs.) **(a)** häng das Schild ~**!** put the sign up! **(b)** arm ~ **sein** be in a bad way; **gut/schlecht** ~ **sein** be well off/badly off; **früh/spät** ~ **sein** be early/late; **ich bin** ~ **:** it's my turn

dran|bleiben *unr. itr. V.; mit sein* (ugs.) (am Telefon) hang on (coll.)

drang *1. u. 3. Pers. Sg. Prät. v.* DRINGEN

Drạng *der;* ∼[e]s, Dränge urge

drạ̈nge *1. u. 3. Pers. Sg. Konjunktiv II v.*
DRINGEN

drạ̈ngeln (ugs.) 1 *itr. V.* (a) push [and
shove]
(b) (auf jmdn. einreden) go on (coll.)
2 *tr. V.* (a) push; shove
(b) (einreden auf) go on at (coll.)
3 *refl. V.* **sich nach vorn** ∼: push one's way
to the front

drạ̈ngen 1 *itr. V.* (a) push
(b) die Zeit drängt time is pressing
2 *tr. V.* (a) push
(b) (antreiben) press; urge
3 *refl. V.* crowd

drangsalie̱ren *tr. V.* (quälen) torment;
(plagen) plague

drạn-: ∼|**halten** *unr. refl. V.* (ugs.) get a
move on (coll.); ∼|**kommen** *unr. itr. V.;*
mit sein (ugs.) have one's turn; ∼|**nehmen**
unr. tr. V. (ugs.) (beim Friseur usw.) see to; (beim
Arzt) see

drạstisch 1 *Adj.* drastic ⟨*measure,*
means⟩
2 *adv.* drastically; ⟨*punish*⟩ severely

drauf *Adv.* (ugs.) on it

drauf-, Drauf-: ∼**gänger** *der;* ∼∼s,
∼∼, ∼**gängerin** *die;* ∼∼, ∼∼nen
daredevil; ∼**gängerisch** *Adj.* daring;
∼|**gehen** *unr. itr. V.; mit sein* (ugs.)
(a) (umkommen) kick the bucket (coll.);
(b) (verbraucht werden) go (für on); ∼|**zahlen**
(ugs.) 1 *tr. V.* noch etwas/50 Euro ∼**zahlen**
fork out (coll.) *or* pay a bit more/an extra 50
euros; 2 *itr. V.* (Unkosten haben) ich zahle
dabei noch ∼: it's costing me money

drau̱ßen *Adv.* outside; hier/da ∼: out here/
there; von/nach ∼: from outside/outside

Drẹck *der;* ∼[e]s (a) (ugs.) dirt; (sehr viel)
filth; (Schlamm) mud
(b) (salopp abwertend: Angelegenheit) **mach**
deinen ∼ **allein** do it yourself; **das geht dich**
einen [feuchten] ∼ **an** (salopp) none of your
damned business (coll.)
(c) (salopp abwertend: Zeug) junk *no indef. art.*

Drẹck·arbeit *die* (auch fig.) dirty work *no*
*indef. art., no pl./*dirty job

drẹckig 1 *Adj.* (a) (ugs., auch fig.) dirty;
(sehr schmutzig) filthy
(b) (salopp: unverschämt) cheeky
2 *adv.* (a) es geht ihm ∼ (ugs.) he's in a bad
way
(b) (salopp: unverschämt) cheekily

Dreck-: ∼**sau** *die,* ∼**schwein** *das* (derb)
filthy swine

Dreh *der;* ∼s, ∼s (ugs.) (a) den
∼ **heraushaben** have [got] the knack
(b) [so] um den ∼: about that

Dreh-: ∼**arbeiten** *Pl.* (Film) shooting
sing. (zu of); ∼**bank** *die; Pl.* ∼bänke lathe;
∼**buch** *das* screenplay; [film] script

alte Schreibung – vgl. Hinweis auf S. x

dre̱hen 1 *tr. V.* (a) turn
(b) (formen) twist ⟨*rope, thread*⟩; roll
⟨*cigarette*⟩
(c) (Film) shoot ⟨*scene*⟩; film ⟨*report*⟩; make
⟨*film*⟩
2 *itr. V.* (a) ⟨*car*⟩ turn; ⟨*wind*⟩ change
(b) an etw. (*Dat.*) ∼: turn sth.
(c) (Film) shoot; film
3 *refl. V.* (a) turn
(b) (ugs.: zum Gegenstand haben) **sich um etw.**
∼: be about sth.

Dreh-: ∼**kreuz** *das* turnstile; (Flugw.) hub;
∼**orgel** *die* barrel organ; ∼**ort** *der* (Film)
location; ∼**restaurant** *das* revolving
restaurant; ∼**stuhl** *der* swivel chair; ∼**tür**
die revolving door

Dre̱hung *die;* ∼, ∼en turn; (um einen
Mittelpunkt) revolution

Dreh-: ∼**zahl** *die* revolutions *or* (coll.) revs
(*esp. per minute*); ∼**zahl-messer** *der;*
∼∼s, ∼∼: revolution counter; rev counter
(coll.); tachometer

drei *Kardinalz.* three;

Drei *die;* ∼, ∼en three; **eine** ∼ **schreiben**
(Schulw.) get a C

drei-, Drei-: ∼**eck** *das;* (Geom.) triangle;
∼**eckig** *Adj.* triangular; ∼**ein·halb**
Bruchz. three and a half

Dreier *der;* ∼s, ∼ (ugs.) three

dreierlei *indekl. Adj.* (a) *attr.* three kinds
or sorts of; three different
(b) *subst.* three [different] things

drei-, Drei-: ∼**fach** *Vervielfältigungsz.*
triple; die ∼fache Menge three times the
amount; ∼**fache** *das; adj. Dekl.* das
∼fache kosten cost three times as much;
das ∼fache von 3 ist 9 three times three
is nine; ∼**faltigkeit** *die;* ∼∼ (christl. Rel.)
Trinity; ∼**hundert** *Kardinalz.* three
hundred; ∼**jährig** *Adj.* (3 Jahre alt) three-
year-old *attrib.;* (3 Jahre dauernd) three-year
attrib.; ∼**kampf** *der* (Sport) triathlon;
∼**klang** *der* triad; ∼**köpfig** *Adj.* ⟨*family,*
crew⟩ of three; ∼**mal** *Adv.* three times;
∼**malig** *Adj.* eine ∼malige Wiederholung
three repeats

drein (ugs.) ▶ DAREIN

drein-: ∼|**blicken,** ∼|**schauen** *itr. V.*
look

drei-, Drei-: ∼**rad** *das* tricycle; ∼**satz**
der rule of three; ∼**seitig** *Adj.* three-sided
⟨*figure*⟩; three-page ⟨*letter, leaflet, etc.*⟩

dreißig *Kardinalz.* thirty; *s. auch* ACHTZIG

dreißigjährig *Adj.* (30 Jahre alt) thirty-
year-old *attrib.;* (30 Jahre dauernd) thirty-year
attrib.

dreißigst... *Ordinalz.* thirtieth

Dreißigstel *das;* ∼s, ∼: thirtieth

dreist 1 *Adj.* brazen; barefaced ⟨*lie*⟩
2 *adv.* brazenly

drei-stellig *Adj.* three-figure *attrib.*

Dreistigkeit *die;* ∼, ∼en (a) brazenness
(b) (Handlung) brazen act

drei-, Drei-: ∼**tausend** *Kardinalz.*
three thousand; ∼**teilig** *Adj.* three-part
attrib.; three-piece attrib. ⟨suit⟩; *∼**viertel**
▶ VIERTEL; ∼**viertel-stunde** /--'--/ *die*
three-quarters of an hour; ∼**viertel-takt**
/-'---/ *der* three-four time; ∼**zehn**
Kardinalz. thirteen; *s. auch* ACHTZEHN

Dresche *die;* ∼ (salopp) walloping (coll.);
thrashing

dreschen [1] *unr. tr. V.* **(a)** thresh
(b) (salopp: schlagen) wallop (coll.); thrash
[2] *unr. itr. V.* thresh

dressieren *tr. V.* train ⟨*animal*⟩

Dressur *die;* ∼, ∼**en** training

Drill *der;* ∼[e]s drilling; (Milit.) drill

drillen *tr. V.* (auch Milit.) drill

Drilling *der;* ∼s, ∼e triplet

drin *Adv.* (ugs.) **(a)** in it
(b) ▶ DRINNEN

dringen *unr. itr. V.* **(a)** *mit sein* durch/in
etw. ∼: penetrate sth.
(b) *mit sein* in jmdn. ∼ (geh.) press sb.
(c) auf etw. (*Akk.*) ∼: insist upon sth.

dringend [1] *Adj.* urgent; strong
⟨*suspicion, advice*⟩
[2] *adv.* urgently; ⟨*advise, suspect*⟩ strongly;
∼ erforderlich essential

dringlich [1] *Adj.* urgent
[2] *adv.* urgently

Dringlichkeit *die;* ∼: urgency

drinnen *Adv.* inside; (im Haus) indoors;
inside

dritt *in* wir waren zu ∼: there were three
of us

dritt... *Ordinalz.* third

Drittel *das,* (schweiz. meist *der*); ∼s, ∼: third

dritteln *tr. V.* split *or* divide three ways

drittens *Adv.* thirdly

DRK *Abk.* = **Deutsches Rotes**
Kreuz German Red Cross

Dr. med. *Abk.* = **doctor medicinae**
MD

droben *Adv.* (südd., österr., sonst geh.) up
there

Droge *die;* ∼, ∼n drug

drogen-, Drogen-: ∼**abhängig**
Adj. addicted to drugs *postpos.;*
∼**abhängige** *der*/*die; adj. Dekl.* drug
addict; ∼**abhängigkeit** *die* drug
addiction; ∼**beratungs-stelle** *die* drug
advice centre; ∼**gefährdet** *Adj.* at risk
from drugs *postpos.;* ∼**handel** *der* drug
trafficking; ∼**konsum** *der* drug-taking;
∼**konsument** *der,* ∼**konsumentin**
die drug user; ∼**missbrauch,**
*∼**mißbrauch** *der* drug abuse;
∼**rausch** *der* [state of] drug intoxication;
etw. im ∼rausch tun do sth. while under
the influence of drugs *or* while [high (coll.)]
on drugs; ∼**süchtig** *Adj.* ▶ ∼ABHÄNGIG;
∼**szene** *die* drug scene

Drogerie *die;* ∼, ∼n chemist's [shop] (Brit.);

drugstore (Amer.)

Drogist *der;* ∼en, ∼en, **Drogistin** *die;* ∼,
∼nen chemist (Brit.); druggist (Amer.)

drohen *itr., mod. V.* threaten; (bevorstehen)
be threatening; jmdm. droht etw. sb. is
threatened with sth.

drohend *Adj.* threatening; (bevorstehend)
impending

Drohne *die;* ∼, ∼n drone

dröhnen *itr. V.* boom; ⟨*machine*⟩ roar

Drohung *die;* ∼, ∼en threat

drollig [1] *Adj.* funny; comical; (niedlich)
sweet; cute (Amer.)
[2] *adv.: s. Adj.:* comically; sweetly; cutely
(Amer.)

Dromedar *das;* ∼s, ∼e dromedary

Drops *der od. das;* ∼, ∼: fruit *or* (Brit.) acid
drop

drosch *1. u. 3. Pers. Sg. Prät. v.* DRESCHEN

Drossel *die;* ∼, ∼n thrush

drosseln *tr. V.* **(a)** turn down ⟨*heating, air
conditioning*⟩; throttle back ⟨*engine*⟩
(b) (herabsetzen) reduce

Dr. phil. *Abk.* = **doctor philosophiae**
Dr

drüben *Adv.* dort *od.* da ∼: over there;
∼ auf der anderen Seite over on the other
side

Druck¹ *der;* ∼[e]s, Drücke **(a)** (auch fig.)
pressure
(b) ein ∼ auf den Knopf a touch of the
button

Druck² *der;* ∼[e]s, ∼e **(a)** printing; in
∼ gehen go to press
(b) (Produkt) print

Druck-buchstabe *der* printed letter

drucken *tr., itr. V.* print

drücken [1] *tr. V.* **(a)** press; press, push
⟨*button*⟩; squeeze ⟨*juice, pus*⟩ **(aus** out of);
jmdm. die Hand ∼: squeeze sb.'s hand
(b) (liebkosen) jmdn. ∼: hug [and squeeze] sb.
(c) ⟨*shoe etc.*⟩ pinch
(d) (herabsetzen) push down ⟨*price, rate*⟩;
depress ⟨*sales*⟩; bring down ⟨*standard*⟩
[2] *itr. V.* **(a)** press; auf den Knopf ∼: press
or push the button; „bitte ∼": 'push'
(b) (Druck verursachen) ⟨*shoe etc.*⟩ pinch
[3] *refl. V.* (ugs.: sich entziehen) shirk; sich vor
etw. (*Dat.*) ∼: get out of sth.

drückend *Adj.* **(a)** heavy ⟨*debt, taxes*⟩;
serious ⟨*worries*⟩; grinding ⟨*poverty*⟩
(b) (schwül) oppressive

Drucker *der;* ∼s, ∼: printer

Druckerei *die;* ∼, ∼en printing works;
(Firma) printing house; printer's

Druckerin *die;* ∼, ∼nen printer

druck-, Druck-: ∼**fehler** *der* misprint;
printer's error; ∼**knopf** *der* press stud
(Brit.); snap fastener; ∼**luft** *die* compressed
air; ∼**mittel** *das* means of bringing
pressure to bear (**gegenüber** on); ∼**reif**
[1] *Adj.* ready for publication; (∼**fertig**) ····⟩

ready for press; ⟨2⟩ *adv.* ⟨*speak*⟩ in a polished manner; ~**sache** *die* (Postw.) printed matter; ~**schrift** *die* (a) printed writing; (b) (Schriftart) type[face]; (c) (Schriftwerk) pamphlet

drum *Adv.* (ugs.) (a) ▶ DARUM (b) [a]round; **alles** *od.* **das [ganze] Drum und Dran** (bei einer Mahlzeit) all the trimmings; (bei einer Feierlichkeit) all the palaver that goes with it (coll.)

Drum·herum *das;* ~s everything that goes/went with it

drunter *Adv.* (ugs.) underneath; **es** *od.* **alles geht ~ und drüber** everything is topsy-turvy

Drüse *die;* ~, ~n gland

Dschihad /dʒiˈhaːt/ *der;* ~[s] jihad;

Dschihad-Kämpfer *der* jihadi

Dschungel /ˈdʒʊŋl̩/ *der;* ~s, ~ (auch fig.) jungle

dt. *Abk.* = **deutsch** G.

Dtzd. *Abk.* = **Dutzend** doz.

du *Personalpron.; 2. Pers. Sg. Nom.* you; **Du zueinander sagen** use the familiar form in addressing one another; *s. auch* (*Gen.*) DEINER, (*Dat.*) DIR, (*Akk.*) DICH

Dübel *der;* ~s, ~: plug

ducken ⟨1⟩ *refl. V.* duck ⟨2⟩ *itr. V.* (fig. abwertend) humble oneself (**vor** + *Dat.* before)

Duckmäuser *der;* ~s, ~, **Duckmäuserin** *die;* ~, ~nen (abwertend) moral coward

Duckmäusertum *das;* ~s (abwertend) moral cowardice

Dudel·sack *der* bagpipes *pl.*

Duell *das;* ~s, ~e duel

duellieren *refl. V.* fight a duel

Duett *das;* ~[e]s, ~e (Musik) duet; **im ~ singen** sing a duet

Duft *der;* ~[e]s, Düfte scent; (von Parfüm, Blumen) scent; fragrance; (von Kaffee usw.) aroma

duften *itr. V.* smell (**nach** of)

dulden *tr. V.* tolerate; put up with

duldsam ⟨1⟩ *Adj.* tolerant (**gegen** towards) ⟨2⟩ *adv.* tolerantly

Duma *die;* die ~: the Duma

dumm, dümmer, dümmst... ⟨1⟩ *Adj.* (a) stupid (b) (unvernünftig) foolish (c) (ugs.: töricht, albern) idiotic; silly (d) (ugs.: unangenehm) nasty ⟨*feeling*⟩; annoying ⟨*habit*⟩; **das wird mir jetzt zu ~** (ugs.) I've had enough of it ⟨2⟩ *adv.* (ugs.) idiotically

Dumme *der/die; adj. Dekl.* fool; **der/die ~ sein** (ugs.) be the loser

dummer·weise *Adv.* (a) unfortunately; (ärgerlicherweise) annoyingly (b) (törichterweise) foolishly

Dummheit *die;* ~, ~en (a) stupidity (b) (unkluge Handlung) stupid thing

Dumm·kopf *der* (ugs.) nitwit (coll.)

dumpf ⟨1⟩ *Adj.* (a) dull ⟨*thud, rumble of thunder*⟩; muffled ⟨*sound, thump*⟩ (b) (muffig) musty (c) (stumpfsinnig) dull ⟨2⟩ *adv.* (a) ⟨*echo*⟩ hollowly (b) (stumpfsinnig) apathetically

Dumping /ˈdampɪŋ/ *das;* ~s (Wirtsch.) dumping

Dumping·preis *der* dumping price

Düne *die;* ~, ~n dune

düngen ⟨1⟩ *tr. V.* fertilize ⟨*soil, lawn*⟩; spread fertilizer on ⟨*field*⟩; scatter fertilizer around ⟨*plants*⟩ ⟨2⟩ *itr. V.* **gut ~** ⟨*substance*⟩ be a good fertilizer

Dünger *der;* ~s, ~: fertilizer

dunkel ⟨1⟩ *Adj.* (auch fig.) dark; (tief) deep ⟨*voice, note*⟩; (undeutlich) vague ⟨2⟩ *adv.* (a) (tief) ⟨*speak*⟩ in a deep voice (b) (undeutlich) vaguely

Dünkel *der;* ~s (geh.) arrogance; (Einbildung) conceit[edness]

dunkel-: ~**blond** *Adj.* light brown ⟨*hair*⟩; ⟨*person*⟩ with light brown hair; ~**häutig** *Adj.* dark-skinned

Dunkelheit *die;* ~: darkness

Dunkel·kammer *die* darkroom

dunkeln *itr. V.* (*unpers.*) **es dunkelt** (geh.) it is growing dark

Dunkel·ziffer *die* number of unrecorded cases

dünn ⟨1⟩ *Adj.* thin; slim ⟨*book*⟩; fine ⟨*stocking*⟩; watery ⟨*coffee, tea, beer*⟩ ⟨2⟩ *adv.* thinly ⟨*sliced, populated*⟩; lightly ⟨*dressed*⟩

Dunst *der;* ~[e]s, Dünste (a) haze; (Nebel) mist (b) (Geruch) smell

dünsten *tr. V.* steam ⟨*fish, vegetables*⟩; braise ⟨*meat*⟩; stew ⟨*fruit*⟩

dunstig *Adj.* hazy

Duo *das;* ~s, ~s (Musik) duet; (fig. scherzh.) duo; pair

Duplikat *das;* ~[e]s, ~e duplicate

duplizieren *tr. V.* duplicate

Dur *das;* ~ (Musik) major [key]

durch ⟨1⟩ *Präp. mit Akk.* (a) (räumlich) through (b) (modal) by; ~ **Boten** by courier; **zehn [geteilt]** ~ **zwei** ten divided by two ⟨2⟩ *Adv.* (a) (hin~) **das ganze Jahr** ~: throughout the whole year (b) (ugs.: vorbei) **es war 3 Uhr** ~: it was gone 3 o'clock (c) ~ **und** ~ **nass/überzeugt** wet through [and through]/completely *or* totally convinced (d) **[durch etw.]** ~ **sein** be through [sth.] (e) ~ **sein** (abgefahren sein) ⟨*train, bus, etc.*⟩ have gone

---

*old spelling – see note on page x

(f) ~ **sein** (fertig sein) have finished; **durch etw.** ~ **sein** have got through sth.

(g) ~ **sein** ⟨*cheese*⟩ be ripe; ⟨*meat*⟩ be well done

durch|arbeiten 1 *tr. V.* work through 2 *itr. V.* work through; **die Nacht** ~: work through the night

durch-aus *Adv.* absolutely; perfectly, quite ⟨*correct, possible, understandable*⟩; **das ist** ~ **richtig** that is entirely right; ~ **nicht** by no means

durch|beißen *unr. tr. V.* bite through

durch|blättern *tr. V.* leaf through

Durch-blick *der* (ugs.) **den [absoluten]** ~ **haben** know [exactly] what's going on

durch|blicken *itr. V.* **(a)** look through; **durch etw.** ~: look through sth.

(b) ~ **lassen, dass** .../**wie** ...: hint that .../at how ...

Durch-blutung *die* flow of blood (+ *Gen.* to); [blood] circulation

Durchblutungs-störung *die* disturbance of the blood supply

durch|bohren¹ *tr. V.* drill through ⟨*wall, plank*⟩; drill ⟨*hole*⟩

durch-bohren² *tr. V.* pierce

durch|brechen¹ 1 *unr. tr. V.* **etw.** ~: break sth. in two 2 *unr. itr. V.; mit sein* **(a)** break in two

(b) (hervorkommen) ⟨*sun*⟩ break through

(c) (einbrechen) fall through ⟨*ice, floor, etc.*⟩

durch-brechen² *unr. tr. V.* break through

durch|brennen *unr. itr. V.; mit sein* **(a)** ⟨*heating coil, lightbulb*⟩ burn out; ⟨*fuse*⟩ blow

(b) (ugs.: weglaufen) (von zu Hause) run away; (mit der Kasse, mit dem Geliebten/der Geliebten) run off

durch|bringen *unr. tr. V.* get through; (bei Wahlen) **jmdn.** ~: get sb. elected; **seine Familie/sich** ~: support one's family/oneself

Durch-bruch *der* (fig.) breakthrough

durch-dacht *Adj.* **ein wenig/gut** ~**er Plan** a badly/well thought-out plan; **nicht [genügend]** ~ **sein** not be sufficiently well thought-out

durch|drehen 1 *tr. V.* put ⟨*meat*⟩ through the mincer *or* (Amer.) grinder 2 *itr. V.* **auch mit sein** (ugs.) crack up (coll.)

durch|dringen¹ *unr. itr. V.; mit sein* ⟨*rain, sun*⟩ come through

durch-dringen² *unr. tr. V.* penetrate; **jmdn.** ~ ⟨*idea*⟩ take hold of sb. [completely]

durch-einander *Adv.* ~ **bringen** (+ *Akk.*) (in Unordnung bringen) get ⟨*room, flat*⟩ into a mess; get ⟨*papers, file*⟩ into a muddle; muddle up ⟨*papers, file*⟩; (verwirren) confuse; (verwechseln) confuse ⟨*names, etc*⟩; get ⟨*names etc.*⟩ mixed up; ~ **sein** ⟨*papers, desk, etc.*⟩ be in a muddle; (verwirrt sein) be confused; (aufgeregt sein) be flustered

Durcheinander *das;* ~**s (a)** muddle; mess

(b) (Wirrwarr) confusion

***durcheinander|bringen**
▸ DURCHEINANDER

durch|exerzieren *tr. V.* (ugs.) go through, practise ⟨*rules, multiplication tables*⟩; rehearse ⟨*situation*⟩

durch|fahren *unr. itr. V.; mit sein*
(a) [durch etw.] ~: drive through [sth.]
(b) (nicht anhalten) go straight through; (mit dem Auto) drive straight through; **der Zug fährt [in H.] durch** the train doesn't stop [at H.]

Durch-fahrt *die* **(a)** „~ **verboten**" 'no entry except for access'; **auf der** ~ **sein** be passing through

(b) (Weg) thoroughfare; „**bitte [die]** ~ **freihalten**" 'please do not obstruct'

Durch-fall *der* diarrhoea *no art.*

durch|fallen *unr. itr. V.; mit sein* **(a)** fall through

(b) (ugs.: nicht bestehen) fail

durch|finden *unr. refl. V.* find one's way through

durchführbar *Adj.* practicable

Durchführbarkeit *die;* ~: practicability;

durch|führen 1 *tr. V.* carry out; put into effect ⟨*decision, programme*⟩; perform ⟨*operation*⟩; hold ⟨*meeting, election, examination*⟩ 2 *itr. V.* **durch etw./unter etw.** (*Dat.*) ~ ⟨*track, road*⟩ go through/under sth.

Durch-führung *die* carrying out; (einer Operation) performing; (einer Versammlung, Wahl, Prüfung) holding; (eines Wettbewerbs) staging

Durch-gang *der* **(a)** passage[way]; „**kein** ~", „~ **verboten**" 'no thoroughfare'

(b) (Phase) stage; (einer Versuchsreihe) run; (Sport, Wahlen) round

Durchgangs-: ~**straße** *die* through road; ~**verkehr** *der* through traffic

durch|geben *unr. tr. V.* announce ⟨*news*⟩; give ⟨*results, weather report*⟩; **eine Meldung im Radio/Fernsehen** ~ make an announcement on the radio/on television

durch-gefroren *Adj.* frozen stiff; chilled to the bone

durch|gehen 1 *unr. itr. V.; mit sein*
(a) [durch etw.] ~: go *or* walk through [sth.]
(b) (hindurchdringen) [durch etw.] ~: ⟨*rain, water*⟩ come through [sth.]
(c) (direkt zum Ziel führen) ⟨*train etc.*⟩ go [right] through (bis to); ⟨*flight*⟩ go direct
(d) (andauern) go on (bis zu until)
(e) (hingenommen werden) ⟨*discrepancy*⟩ be tolerated; ⟨*mistake, discourtesy*⟩ be allowed to pass; **jmdm. etw.** ~ **lassen** let sb. get away with sth.
(f) ⟨*horse*⟩ bolt
2 *unr. tr. V.; mit sein* go through ⟨*newspaper, text*⟩

durch-gehend 1 *Adj.* **(a)** continuous ⟨*line, pattern, etc.*⟩; constantly recurring ⟨*motif*⟩ ⋯⟫

(b) (direkt) through *attrib.* ⟨*train, carriage*⟩; direct ⟨*flight, connection*⟩
[2] *adv.* ~ **geöffnet haben/bleiben** be/stay open all day
durchgeknallt *Adj.* (ugs.) crazy
durch·geschwitzt *Adj.* ⟨*person*⟩ soaked *or* bathed in sweat; ⟨*clothes*⟩ soaked with sweat; sweat-soaked *attrib.* ⟨*clothes*⟩
durch|greifen *unr. itr. V.* [hart] ~: take drastic measures *or* steps
durch|halten [1] *unr. itr. V.* hold out; (bei einer schwierigen Aufgabe) see it through
[2] *unr. tr. V.* stand
durch|hängen *unr. itr. V.* sag
durch|kämmen *tr. V.* **(a)** comb ⟨*hair*⟩ through
(b) (durchsuchen) comb ⟨*area etc.*⟩
durch|kommen *unr. itr. V.; mit sein*
(a) come through; (mit Mühe) get through
(b) (ugs.: beim Telefonieren) get through
(c) (durchgehen, -fahren usw.) **durch etw.** ~: come through sth.
(d) (ugs.: überleben) pull through
durch|kreuzen[1] *tr. V.* cross out
durch·kreuzen[2] *tr. V.* (vereiteln) frustrate
durch|lassen *unr. tr. V.* **(a)** jmdn. [durch etw.] ~: let sb. through [sth.]
(b) (durchlässig sein) let ⟨*light, water, etc.*⟩ through
durchlässig *Adj.* permeable; (porös) porous; (undicht) leaky; ⟨*raincoat, shoe*⟩ that lets in water
Durch·lauf *der* (Sport, DV) run
durch|laufen[1] [1] *unr. itr. V.; mit sein*
(a) [durch etw.] ~: run through [sth.]; (durchrinnen) trickle through [sth.]
(b) (passieren) ⟨*runners*⟩ run *or* pass through
(c) (ohne Pause laufen) run without stopping
[2] *unr. tr. V.* go through ⟨*soles*⟩
durch·laufen[2] *unr. tr. V.* go through ⟨*phase, stage*⟩
durchlaufend [1] *Adj.* continuous
[2] *adv.* ⟨*numbered, marked*⟩ in sequence
durch|lesen *unr. tr. V.* **etw.** [ganz] ~: read sth. [all the way] through
durch·leuchten *tr. V.* x-ray; (fig.) investigate ⟨*case, matter, problem, etc.*⟩ thoroughly
durch·löchern *tr. V.* make holes in
durch|machen (ugs.) [1] *tr. V.*
(a) undergo ⟨*change*⟩; complete ⟨*training course*⟩; go through ⟨*stage, phase*⟩; serve ⟨*apprenticeship*⟩
(b) (erleiden) go through
(c) (durcharbeiten) work through ⟨*lunch break etc.*⟩
[2] *itr. V.* (durcharbeiten) work [right] through; (durchfeiern) celebrate all night/day etc.; keep going all night/day *etc.*
Durchmesser *der;* ~s, ~: diameter
durch|nehmen *unr. tr. V.* (Schulw.:

behandeln) do
durch|pauken *tr. V.* (ugs.) force through ⟨*law, regulation, etc.*⟩
durch|peitschen *tr. V.* (ugs. abwertend) railroad ⟨*law, application, etc.*⟩ through
durch|probieren *tr. V.* taste ⟨*wines, cakes, etc.*⟩ one after another
durch·queren *tr. V.* cross; travel across ⟨*country*⟩; ⟨*train*⟩ go through ⟨*country*⟩
durch|rechnen *tr. V.* calculate ⟨*costs etc.*⟩ [down to the last penny]; check ⟨*bill*⟩ thoroughly
Durch·reise *die* journey through
durch|reisen *itr. V.; mit sein* travel through
Durchreise·visum *das* transit visa
durch|reißen [1] *unr. tr. V.* **etw.** ~: tear sth. in two *or* in half
[2] *unr. itr. V.; mit sein* ⟨*fabric, garment*⟩ rip, tear; ⟨*thread, rope*⟩ snap [in two]
durch|rosten *itr. V.; mit sein* rust through
durchs *Präp. + Art.* **= durch das**
Durch·sage *die* announcement; (an eine bestimmte Person) message
durchschaubar *Adj.* transparent; **leicht** ~: easy to see through
durch·schauen *tr. V.* see through ⟨*person, plan, etc.*⟩; see ⟨*situation*⟩ clearly
durch|schlafen *unr. itr. V.* sleep [right] through
Durch·schlag *der* **(a)** (Kopie) carbon [copy]
(b) (Küchengerät) strainer
durch|schlagen *unr. tr. V.* **etw.** ~: chop sth. in two
durchschlagend *Adj.* resounding ⟨*success*⟩; decisive ⟨*effect, measures*⟩; conclusive ⟨*evidence*⟩
durch|schneiden *unr. tr. V.* cut through ⟨*thread, cable*⟩; cut ⟨*ribbon, sheet of paper*⟩ in two; cut ⟨*throat, umbilical cord*⟩; **etw. in der Mitte** ~: cut sth. in half
Durch·schnitt *der* average; **im** ~: on average; **über/unter dem** ~ **liegen** be above/below average
durchschnittlich [1] *Adj.* **(a)** *nicht präd.* average ⟨*growth, performance, output*⟩
(b) (ugs.: nicht außergewöhnlich) ordinary ⟨*life, person, etc.*⟩
(c) (mittelmäßig) modest; ordinary ⟨*appearance*⟩
[2] *adv.* ⟨*earn etc.*⟩ on [an] average; ~ **groß** of average height
Durchschnitts-: ~**alter** *das* average age; ~**geschwindigkeit** *die* average speed; ~**mensch** *der* average person; (Alltagsmensch) ordinary person; ~**temperatur** *die* average temperature; ~**wert** *der* average *or* mean value
Durch·schrift *die* carbon [copy]
durch|sehen [1] *unr. itr. V.* [durch etw.]

---
*alte Schreibung – vgl. Hinweis auf S. x

~: look through [sth.]
2 *unr. tr. V.* look through

durch|sein ▸ DURCH 2 D-G

durch|setzen 1 *tr. V.* carry through; achieve ⟨*objective*⟩; enforce ⟨*demand, claim*⟩
2 *refl. V.* assert oneself; ⟨*idea etc.*⟩ find *or* gain acceptance

Durch·sicht *die:* nach ~ der Unterlagen after looking *or* checking through the documents

durchsichtig *Adj.* (auch fig.) transparent

durch|sprechen *unr. tr. V.* talk ⟨*matter etc.*⟩ over; discuss ⟨*matter etc.*⟩ thoroughly

durch|stehen *unr. tr. V.* stand ⟨*pace, boring job*⟩; come through ⟨*difficult situation*⟩; get over ⟨*illness*⟩

durch|stellen *tr. V.* put ⟨*call*⟩ through (**in** + *Akk.*, **auf** + *Akk.* to)

durch|streichen *unr. tr. V.* cross out; (in Formularen) delete

durch·suchen *tr. V.* search (**nach** for); search, scour ⟨*area*⟩ (**nach** for)

Durchsuchung *die;* ~, ~en search

durch|treten *unr. tr. V.* press ⟨*clutch pedal, brake pedal*⟩ right down

durchtrieben (abwertend) 1 *Adj.* crafty; sly
2 *adv.* craftily; slyly

durch·wachsen *Adj.* ~er Speck streaky bacon

Durch·wahl *die* (a) direct dialling; **mein Apparat hat keine** ~: I don't have an outside line
(b) ▸ DURCHWAHLNUMMER

durch|wählen *itr. V.* (a) dial direct
(b) (bei Nebenstellenanlagen) dial straight through

Durchwahl·nummer *die* number of the/one's direct line

durch|zählen *tr. V.* count; count up

durch|ziehen 1 *unr. tr. V.* jmdn./etw. [durch etw.] ~: pull sb./sth. through [sth.]; ein Gummiband [durch etw.] ~: draw an elastic through [sth.]
2 *unr. itr. V.; mit sein* pass through; ⟨*soldiers*⟩ march through

Durch·zug *der* draught

dürfen 1 *unr. Modalverb; 2. Part.* dürfen:
(a) etw. tun ~: be allowed to do sth.; **darf ich rauchen?** may I smoke?; **was darf es sein?** can I help you?

(b) *Konjunktiv II + Inf.* das dürfte der Grund sein that is probably the reason
2 *unr. tr., itr. V.* er hat nicht gedurft he was not allowed to

durfte *1. u. 3. Pers. Sg. Prät. v.* DÜRFEN

dürfte *1. u. 3. Pers. Sg. Konjunktiv II v.* DÜRFEN

dürr *Adj.* (a) withered; arid, barren ⟨*ground, earth*⟩
(b) (mager) scrawny

Dürre *die;* ~, ~n drought

Durst *der;* ~[e]s thirst; ~ haben be thirsty; **ich habe ~ auf ein Bier** I could just drink a beer

durstig *Adj.* thirsty

durst-, Durst-: ~löscher *der* thirst-quencher; ~stillend *Adj.* thirst-quenching; ~strecke *die* lean period *or* time

Dusche *die;* ~, ~n shower

duschen *itr., refl. V.* have a shower

Düse *die;* ~, ~n (Technik) nozzle; (eines Vergasers) jet

Düsen-: ~flugzeug *das* jet aircraft; ~motor *der* jet engine

düster 1 *Adj.* (a) dark; gloomy; dim ⟨*light*⟩
(b) (fig.) gloomy; sombre ⟨*colour, music*⟩
2 *adv.* (fig.) gloomily

Dutzend *das;* ~s, ~e dozen; **zwei** ~: two dozen

dutzend·weise *Adv.* in [their] dozens (coll.)

duzen *tr. V.* call ⟨*sb.*⟩ 'du' (*the familiar form of address*)

Duz·freund *der,* **Duz·freundin** *die* good friend (*whom one addresses with 'du'*)

DV *Abk.* = **Datenverarbeitung** DP

DVD *die;* ~, ~s DVD

DVD-: ~Brenner *der* (DV) DVD burner; DVD writer; ~-Laufwerk *das* (DV) DVD drive; ~-Recorder, DVD-Rekorder *der* DVD recorder; ~-Spieler *der* DVD player

dynamisch 1 *Adj.* (auch fig.) dynamic
2 *adv.* dynamically

Dynamit *das;* ~s dynamite

Dynamo *der;* ~s, ~s dynamo

Dynastie *die;* ~, ~n dynasty

D-Zug /'de:-/ *der* express train

Ee

e, E /e:/ *das; ~, ~* **(a)** (Buchstabe) e/E
(b) (Musik) [key of] E

Ebbe *die; ~, ~n* ebb tide; (Zustand) low tide;
es ist ~: the tide is out

eben ⊡ *Adj.* **(a)** flat
(b) (glatt) level
⊡ *adv.* **(a)** (gerade jetzt) just
(b) (kurz) [for] a moment

Ebene *die, ~, ~n* **(a)** plain; **in der ~:** on
the plain
(b) (Geom., Physik) plane
(c) (fig.) level

eben·falls *Adv.* likewise; as well; **danke,
~:** thank you, [and] [the] same to you

Eben·holz *das* ebony

eben·so *Adv.* **(a)** *mit Adjektiven, Adverbien*
just as; **ich mag Erdbeeren ~ gern [wie...]**
I like strawberries just as much [as ...];
~ gern würde ich an den Strand gehen
I would just as soon go to the beach; **~ gut**
just as well
(b) *mit Verben* in exactly the same way

ebenso·gern *usw.* ▶ EBENSO A

Eber *der; ~s, ~:* boar

Eber·esche *die* rowan; mountain ash

ebnen *tr. V.* level ⟨*ground*⟩

Echo *das; ~s, ~s* echo

echt ⊡ *Adj.* **(a)** genuine; real ⟨*love,
friendship*⟩
(b) (typisch) real, typical
⊡ *adv.* **(a)** (ugs. verstärkend) really
(b) (typisch) typically

Eck *das; ~s, ~e* (südd., österr.:) ⟩~e corner

Eck-: **~ball** *der* (Sport) corner [kick/hit/
throw]; **einen ~ball treten** take a corner;
~bank *die; Pl.* **~bänke** corner seat

Ecke *die; ~, ~n* corner; **an der ~:** on *or* at
the corner; **um die ~:** round the corner

eckig *Adj.* square; angular

Eck·zahn *der* canine tooth

edel *Adj.* **(a)** thoroughbred ⟨*horse*⟩; species
⟨*rose*⟩
(b) (großmütig) noble[-minded], high-minded
⟨*person*⟩; noble ⟨*thought, gesture, feelings,
deed*⟩; honourable ⟨*motive*⟩

Edel-: **~metall** *das* precious metal;
~nutte *die* (salopp) high-class tart (sl.);
~pilz·käse *der* blue[-veined] cheese;
~stahl *der* stainless steel; **~stein** *der*
precious stone; gem[stone]

Edition *die; ~, ~en* edition

Edutainment /ɛdju'teɪnmənt/ *das; ~s*
edutainment

EDV *Abk.* = **elektronische
Datenverarbeitung** EDP

EEG *Abk.*
= **Elektroenzephalogramm** EEG;
ein EEG machen lassen have an EEG

Efeu *der; ~s* ivy

Effekt *der; ~[e]s, ~e* effect

effekt·voll *Adj.* effective; dramatic ⟨*pause,
gesture, entrance*⟩

EG *Abk.* **(a)** (EU) = **Europäische
Gemeinschaft[en]** EC
(b) = **Erdgeschoss**

egal *Adj.* (ugs.: einerlei) **es ist jmdm. ~:** it's
all the same to sb.; **[ganz] ~, wie/wer** *usw.*
...: no matter how/who *etc.* ...

Egge *die; ~, ~n* harrow

E-Gitarre *die* electric guitar

Egoist *der; ~en, ~en,* **Egoistin** *die; ~,
~nen* egoist

egoistisch ⊡ *Adj.* egoistic[al]
⊡ *adv.* egoistically

Egomane /ego'ma:nə/ *der; ~n, ~n,*
Egomanin *die; ~, ~nen* egomaniac

ehe *Konj.* before

Ehe *die; ~, ~n* marriage

Ehe-: **~bett** *das* marriage bed; (Doppelbett)
double bed; **~bruch** *der* adultery; **~frau**
die wife; (verheiratete Frau) married woman;
~krach *der* (ugs.) row; **~leute** *Pl.*
married couple

ehelich *Adj.* marital; matrimonial;
conjugal ⟨*rights, duties*⟩; legitimate ⟨*child*⟩

ehemalig *Adj.* former

ehe-, Ehe-: **~mann** *der; Pl.* **~männer**
husband; (verheirateter Mann) married
man; **~mündig** *Adj.* (Rechtsspr.) of
marriageable age *postpos.*; **~mündig sein** be
of marriageable age *or* of an age to marry;
~mündigkeit *die* (Rechtsspr.) being of
marriageable age; **~paar** *das* married
couple

eher *Adv.* **(a)** (früher) earlier; sooner
(b) (lieber) rather; sooner

Ehe-: **~ring** *der* wedding ring;
~scheidung *die* divorce; **~vertrag** *der*
(Rechtsw.) marriage contract

Ehre *die; ~, ~n* honour; **jmdm. ~ antun** pay
tribute to sb.

ehren *tr. V.* **(a)** honour; **Sehr geehrter Herr
Müller!/Sehr geehrte Frau Müller!** Dear Herr
Müller/Dear Frau Müller
(b) (Ehre machen) **deine Hilfsbereitschaft ehrt
dich** your willingness to help does you credit

ehren-, Ehren-: **~amt** *das* honorary
position *or* post; **~amtlich** ⊡ *Adj.*

---

honorary ⟨*position, membership*⟩; voluntary ⟨*help, worker*⟩; **2** *adv.* in an honorary capacity; (freiwillig) on a voluntary basis

ehrenhaft *Adj.* honourable

ehren-, Ehren-: ∼**rührig** *Adj.* defamatory ⟨*allegations*⟩; ∼**sache** *die: das ist* ∼**sache** that is a point of honour; ∼**sache!** you can count on me!; ∼**voll** *Adj.* honourable; ∼**wert** *Adj.* (geh.) worthy; ∼**wort** *das; Pl.* ∼∼**e:** ∼**wort** [!/?] word of honour [!/?]

ehrerbietig *Adj.* (geh.) respectful

Ehr·furcht *die* reverence (**vor** + *Dat.* for)

ehrfürchtig *Adj.* reverent

ehr-, Ehr-: ∼**gefühl** *das* sense of honour; ∼**geiz** *der* ambition; ∼**geizig** *Adj.* ambitious

ehrlich *Adj.* honest; genuine ⟨*concern, desire, admiration*⟩; upright ⟨*character*⟩

Ehrlichkeit *die;* ∼ ▸ EHRLICH: honesty; genuineness; uprightness

ehr·los *Adj.* dishonourable

Ehrung *die;* ∼, ∼**en: die** ∼ **der Preisträger** the prize-giving (Brit.) *or* (Amer.) awards ceremony; **bei der** ∼ **der Sieger** when the winners were awarded their medals/ trophies

ehr·würdig *Adj.* venerable

Ei *das;* ∼**[e]s,** ∼**er** egg

Eiche *die;* ∼, ∼**n** oak [tree]; (Holz) oak [wood]

Eichel *die;* ∼, ∼**n** acorn

eichen *tr. V.* calibrate ⟨*measuring instrument, thermometer*⟩; standardize ⟨*weights, measures, containers, products*⟩; adjust ⟨*weighing scales*⟩

Eich·hörnchen *das* squirrel

Eid *der;* ∼**[e]s,** ∼**e** oath

Eidechse /'aidɛksə/ *die;* ∼, ∼**n** lizard

eides·stattlich *Adj.* (Rechtsw.) **eine** ∼**e Erklärung** a statutory declaration

Ei·dotter *der od. das* egg yolk

Eier-: ∼**becher** *der* eggcup; ∼**kuchen** *der* pancake; (Omelett) omelette; ∼**likör** *der* egg flip; ∼**stock** *der* (Physiol., Zool.) ovary; ∼**uhr** *die* egg timer

Eifer *der;* ∼**s** eagerness

Eifer·sucht *die* jealousy (**auf** + *Akk.* of)

eifer·süchtig *Adj.* jealous (**auf** + *Akk.* of)

eifrig *Adj.* eager

Ei·gelb *das;* ∼**[e]s,** ∼**e** egg yolk

eigen *Adj.* own; (selbstständig) separate

eigen-, Eigen-: ∼**art** *die* (Wesensart) particular nature; (Zug) peculiarity; **eine** ∼**art dieser Stadt** one of the characteristic features of this city; ∼**artig** *Adj.* peculiar; strange; odd; ∼**artigerweise** *Adv.* strangely [enough]; oddly [enough]; ∼**artigkeit** *die* peculiarity; strangeness; oddness; ∼**brötelei** *die;* ∼∼, ∼∼**en** taking an [unduly] independent line; ∼**brötler** *der;* ∼∼**s,** ∼∼, ∼**brötlerin**

die; ∼∼, ∼∼**nen** loner; lone wolf; ∼**dynamik** *die* inherent dynamism; ∼**händig** **1** *Adj.* personal ⟨*signature*⟩; holographic ⟨*will, document*⟩; **2** *adv.* ⟨*present, sign*⟩ personally; ∼**heim** *das* house of one's own

Eigenheit *die;* ∼, ∼**en** peculiarity

eigen-, Eigen-: ∼**initiative** *die* initiative of one's own; ∼**lob** *das* self-praise; ∼**mächtig** *Adj.* unauthorized; ∼**name** *der* proper name; ∼**nützig** *Adj.* self-seeking; selfish ⟨*motive*⟩

eigens *Adv.* specially

Eigenschaft *die;* ∼, ∼**en** quality; characteristic; (von Sachen, Stoffen) property

Eigenschafts·wort *das; Pl.* **Eigenschaftswörter** adjective

eigen-, Eigen-: ∼**sinn** *der* obstinacy; ∼**sinnig** *Adj.* obstinate; ∼**ständig** *Adj.* independent; ∼**ständigkeit** *die;* ∼∼: independence

eigentlich **1** *Adj.* (wirklich) actual; real; (wahr) true; (ursprünglich) original **2** *Adv.* actually **3** *Partikel* **wie spät ist es** ∼**?** tell me, what time is it?; **was willst du** ∼**?** what exactly do you want?

Eigen·tor *das* (Ballspiele, fig.) own goal

Eigentum *das;* ∼**s** property; (einschließlich Geld usw.) assets *pl.*

Eigentümer *der;* ∼**s,** ∼: owner; (Hotel∼, Geschäfts∼) proprietor

Eigentümerin *die;* ∼, ∼**nen** owner; (Hotel∼, Geschäfts∼) proprietress; proprietor

Eigentums·wohnung *die* owner-occupied flat (Brit.); condominium apartment (Amer.)

eigen-, Eigen-: ∼**vorsorge** private [pension] provision; ∼**willig** *Adj.* self-willed

eignen *refl. V.* be suitable

Eigner *der;* ∼**s,** ∼, **Eignerin** *die;* ∼, ∼**nen** owner

Eignung *die;* ∼: suitability; **seine** ∼ **zum Fliegen** his aptitude for flying

Eignungs-: ∼**prüfung** *die,* ∼**test** *der* aptitude test

Eil-: ∼**bote** *der,* ∼**botin** *die* special messenger; „**durch** *od.* **per** ∼**boten**" (veralt.) 'express'; ∼**brief** *der* express letter

Eile *die;* ∼: hurry; **in** ∼ **sein** be in a hurry

eilen *itr. V.* (a) *mit sein* hurry; (besonders schnell) rush (b) (dringend sein) be urgent; „**eilt!**" 'urgent'

eilig **1** *Adj.* (a) hurried; **es** ∼ **haben** be in a hurry (b) (dringend) urgent **2** *adv.* hurriedly

Eil·zug *der* semi-fast train

Eimer *der;* ∼**s,** ∼: bucket; (Milch∼) pail; (Abfall∼) bin; **ein** ∼ **[voll] Wasser** a bucket of water; **im** ∼ **sein** (salopp) be up the spout (coll.)

ein¹ ☐1☐ *Kardinalz.* one; ~ für alle Mal,
**~ für allemal once and for all
☐2☐ *unbest. Art.* a/an
☐3☐ *Indefinitpron.* ▶ IRGENDEIN A; *s. auch*
EINER

ein² (elliptisch) ~ – **aus** (an Schaltern) on – off

Einakter *der;* ~s, ~: one-act play

einander *reziprokes Pron.; Dat. u. Akk.*
(geh.) each other; one another

ein|arbeiten *tr. V.* train 〈*employee*〉

ein-armig *Adj.* one-armed

ein|äschern *tr. V.* cremate

ein|atmen *tr., itr. V.* breathe in

ein-äugig *Adj.* one-eyed

Ein-bahn-straße *die* one-way street

Ein-band *der; Pl.* **Einbände** binding

Ein-bau *der; Pl.* ~ten fitting; (eines Motors)
installation

ein|bauen *tr. V.* build in, fit; install
〈*engine, motor*〉

Einbau-küche *die* fitted kitchen

ein-beinig *Adj.* one-legged

ein|berufen *unr. tr. V.* summon; call

Ein-berufung *die* (a) (das Einberufen)
calling
(b) (zur Wehrpflicht) call-up; conscription;
draft (Amer.)

Einbett-zimmer *das* single room

ein|beziehen *unr. tr. V.* include

ein|biegen *unr. itr. V.; mit sein* turn

ein|bilden *refl. V.* (a) sich (*Dat.*) etw.
~: imagine sth.
(b) (ugs.) sich (*Dat.*) etwas ~: be conceited
(auf + *Akk.* about)

Ein-bildung *die* (a) imagination
(b) (falsche Vorstellung) fantasy
(c) (Hochmut) conceitedness

ein|binden *unr. tr. V.* bind 〈*book*〉; etw.
neu ~: rebind sth.

ein|blenden *tr. V.* (Rundf., Ferns., Film)
insert

Ein-blick *der* (a) view; ~ in etw. (*Akk.*)
haben be able to see into sth.
(b) (Durchsicht) jmdm. ~ in etw. (*Akk.*)
gewähren allow sb. to look at *or* examine sth.
(c) (Kenntnis) insight

ein|brechen *unr. itr. V.* (a) *mit haben od.
sein* break in; **in eine Bank ~:** break into a
bank; **bei jmdm. ~:** burgle sb.
(b) *mit sein* (einstürzen) 〈*roof, ceiling*〉 cave in
(c) *mit sein* (durchbrechen) fall through

Einbrecher *der;* ~s, ~, **Einbrecherin**
die; ~, ~nen burglar

ein|bringen *unr. tr. V.* (a) bring in
〈*harvest*〉
(b) (verschaffen) Gewinn/Zinsen ~: yield
a profit/bring in interest; jmdm. Ruhm
~: bring sb. fame
(c) (Parl.: vorlegen) introduce 〈*bill*〉
(d) invest 〈*capital, money*〉

Ein-bruch *der* (a) burglary; **ein ~ in eine
Bank** a break-in at a bank
(b) (das Einstürzen) collapse

einbürgern ☐1☐ *tr. V.* naturalize
☐2☐ *refl. V.* 〈*custom, practice*〉 become
established; 〈*person, plant, animal*〉 become
naturalized

Einbürgerung *die;* ~, ~en naturalization

Ein-buße *die* loss

ein|büßen *tr. V.* lose; (durch eigene Schuld)
forfeit

ein|checken *tr., itr. V.* (Flugw.) check in

ein|cremen *tr. V.* put cream on 〈*hands
etc.*〉; sich ~: put cream on

ein|dämmen *tr. V.* (fig.) check; stem

ein|decken ☐1☐ *refl. V.* stock up
☐2☐ *tr. V.* (ugs.: überhäufen) jmdn. mit Arbeit
~: swamp sb. with work

Eindecker *der;* ~s, ~ (Flugw.) monoplane

eindeutig *Adj.* clear

Eindeutigkeit *die;* ~, ~en clarity

ein|dringen *unr. itr. V.; mit sein* in etw.
(*Akk.*) ~: penetrate into sth.; 〈*bullet*〉 pierce
sth.; (allmählich) 〈*water, sand, etc.*〉 seep into
sth.

ein-dringlich *Adj.* urgent; impressive
〈*voice*〉; forceful, powerful 〈*words*〉

Eindringling *der;* ~s, ~e intruder

Ein-druck *der; Pl.* **Eindrücke** impression

ein|drücken *tr. V.* smash in 〈*mudguard,
bumper*〉; stave in 〈*side of ship*〉; smash 〈*pier,
column, support*〉; break 〈*window*〉; crush
〈*ribs*〉; flatten 〈*nose*〉

eindrucks-voll ☐1☐ *Adj.* impressive
☐2☐ *adv.* impressively

eine ▶ EIN¹

ein|ebnen *tr. V.* level

eineiig /'ain|aiɪç/ *Adj.* identical 〈*twins*〉

ein-ein-halb *Bruchz.* one and a half;
~ **Stunden** an hour and a half

Eineltern-familie *die* single-parent family

ein|engen *tr. V.* (a) jmdn. ~: restrict sb.'s
movement[s]
(b) (fig.) restrict

einer, eine, eines, eins *Indefinitpron.*
(man) one; (jemand) someone; somebody;
(fragend, verneint) anyone; anybody; **kaum
einer** hardly anybody; **ein[e]s ist sicher** one
thing is for sure

Einer *der;* ~s, ~ (a) (Math.) unit
(b) (Sport) single sculler; **im ~:** in the single
sculls

einerlei *Adj.* ~, **ob/wo/wer** *usw.* no matter
whether/where/who *etc.;* **es ist ~:** it makes
no difference

Einerlei *das;* ~s monotony

einerseits *Adv.* on the one hand

ein-fach ☐1☐ *Adj.* (a) simple
(b) (nicht mehrfach) single 〈*knot, ticket, journey*〉
☐2☐ *Partikel* simply; just

Einfachheit *die;* ~: simplicity

ein|fädeln ① *tr. V.* thread (**in** + *Akk.* into)
② *refl. V.* (Verkehrsw.) filter in

ein|fahren ① *unr. itr. V.; mit sein* come in; ⟨*train*⟩ pull in; **in den Bahnhof** ∼: pull into the station
② *unr. tr. V.* **(a)** bring in ⟨*harvest*⟩
(b) (beschädigen) knock down ⟨*wall*⟩; smash in ⟨*mudguard*⟩

Ein·fahrt *die* **(a)** (das Hineinfahren) entry; **Vorsicht bei der** ∼ **des Zuges!** stand clear [of the edge of the platform], the train is approaching
(b) (Zufahrt) entrance; (Autobahn∼) slip road; „**keine** ∼" 'no entry'

Ein·fall *der* **(a)** (Idee) idea
(b) (Licht∼) incidence (Optics)

ein|fallen *unr. itr. V.; mit sein* **(a)** jmdm. ∼: occur to sb.; **was fällt dir denn ein!** what do you think you're doing?
(b) (in Erinnerung kommen) **ihr Name fällt mir nicht ein** I cannot think of her name; **plötzlich fiel ihr ein, dass ...:** suddenly she remembered that ...
(c) (von Licht) come in

einfalls-, Einfalls-: ∼**los** *Adj.* unimaginative; lacking in ideas; ∼**losigkeit** *die;* ∼∼: unimaginativeness; lack of ideas; ∼**reich** *Adj.* imaginative; full of ideas; ∼**reichtum** *der* imaginativeness; wealth of ideas; ∼**tor** *das* gateway

Einfalt *die;* ∼: simpleness; simple-mindedness

einfältig *Adj.* simple; naïve; naïve ⟨*remarks*⟩

Ein·familien·haus *das* house (as opposed to block of flats etc.)

ein|fangen *unr. tr. V.* catch

ein|fassen *tr. V.* border; edge; frame ⟨*picture*⟩; set ⟨*gem*⟩; edge ⟨*grave, lawn, etc.*⟩

Ein·fassung *die* ▸ EINFASSEN: border; edging; frame; setting

ein|fetten *tr. V.* grease; dubbin ⟨*leather*⟩; **sich** (*Dat.*) **die Haut/Hände** ∼: rub cream into one's skin/hands

ein|finden *unr. refl. V.* arrive; (sich treffen) meet; ⟨*crowd*⟩ gather

ein|fliegen *unr. tr. V.* fly in

ein|flößen *tr. V.* **(a)** jmdm. **Tee** ∼: pour tea into sb.'s mouth
(b) (fig.) jmdm. **Angst** ∼: put fear into sb.

Ein·fluss, *Ein·fluß *der* influence

einfluss-, *einfluß-, Einfluss-, *Einfluß-: ∼**bereich** *der* sphere of influence; ∼**nahme,** *die;* ∼∼: exertion of influence (**auf** + *Akk.* on); ∼**reich** *Adj.* influential

ein·förmig *Adj.* monotonous

ein|frieren ① *unr. itr. V.; mit sein* freeze; ⟨*pipes*⟩ freeze up
② *unr. tr. V.* **(a)** deep-freeze ⟨*food*⟩
(b) (fig.) freeze

ein|fügen *tr. V.* **(a)** fit in; **etw. in etw.** (*Akk.*) ∼: fit sth. into sth.

(b) (DV) insert; paste

ein|fühlen *refl. V.* **sich in jmdn.** ∼: empathize with sb.

einfühlsam *Adj.* understanding

Ein·fühlung *die;* ∼: empathy (**in** + *Akk.* with)

Ein·fuhr *die;* ∼, ∼**en** ▸ IMPORT

ein|führen *tr. V.* **(a)** (als Neuerung) introduce ⟨*fashion, method, technology*⟩
(b) (importieren) import

Einfuhr-: ∼**sperre** *die,* ∼**stopp** *der* embargo *or* ban on imports

Ein·führung *die* introduction

Einfuhr·verbot *das* ▸ ∼SPERRE

Ein·gabe *die* **(a)** (Gesuch) petition; (Beschwerde) complaint
(b) (DV) input

Eingabe-: ∼**gerät** *das* (DV) input device; ∼**taste** *die* (DV) enter key

Ein·gang *der* entrance; „**kein** ∼" 'no entry'

ein·gängig *Adj.* catchy

eingangs *Adv.* at the beginning *or* start

Eingangs-: ∼**halle** *die* entrance hall; (eines Hotels, Theaters) foyer; ∼**tür** *die* (von Kaufhaus, Hotel usw.) [entrance] door; (von Wohnung, Haus usw.) front door

ein|geben *unr. tr. V.* (DV) feed in; **etw. in den Computer** ∼: feed sth. into the computer

ein·gebildet *Adj.* **(a)** imaginary ⟨*illness*⟩
(b) (arrogant) conceited

Eingeborene *der/die; adj. Dekl.* (veralt.) native

ein·gefahren *Adj.* long-established; deep-rooted ⟨*prejudice*⟩; **sich auf** od. **in** ∼**en Bahnen** od. **Gleisen bewegen** go on in the same old way

ein|gehen ① *unr. itr. V.; mit sein*
(a) arrive
(b) (fig.) **in die Geschichte** ∼: go down in history
(c) (schrumpfen) shrink
(d) **auf eine Frage** ∼**/nicht** ∼: go into *or* deal with/ignore a question; **auf jmdn.** ∼: be responsive to sb.; **auf jmdn. nicht** ∼: ignore sb.'s wishes
② *unr. tr. V.* enter into ⟨*contract, matrimony*⟩; take ⟨*risk*⟩; accept ⟨*obligation*⟩

eingehend *Adj.* detailed

Ein·gemachte *das; adj. Dekl.* preserved fruit/vegetables

ein|gemeinden *tr. V.* incorporate ⟨*village*⟩ (**in** + *Akk.,* **nach** into)

ein·geschnappt *Adj.* (ugs.) huffy

Ein·geständnis *das* confession; admission

ein|gestehen *unr. tr. V.* admit

Eingeweide *das;* ∼**s,** ∼: entrails *pl.;* innards *pl.*

ein|gewöhnen *refl. V.* get used to one's new surroundings

ein|gießen *unr. tr., itr. V.* pour in

ein|gliedern tr. V. integrate (in + Akk. into); incorporate ⟨village, company⟩ (in + Akk. into); (einordnen) include (in + Akk. in)

Ein-gliederung die ▶ EINGLIEDERN: integration; incorporation; inclusion

ein|graben unr. tr. V. bury (in + Akk. in); sink ⟨pile, pipe⟩ (in + Akk. into)

ein|gravieren tr. V. engrave (in + Akk. on)

ein|greifen unr. itr. V. intervene (in + Akk. in)

Ein-griff der (a) intervention (in + Akk. in) (b) (Med.) operation

ein|haken ① tr. V. (a) (mit Haken befestigen) fasten
(b) sich ∼: link arms
② refl. V. sich bei jmdm. ∼: link arms with sb.

Ein-halt der: jmdm./einer Sache ∼ gebieten od. tun (geh.) halt sb./sth.

ein|halten ① unr. tr. V. keep ⟨appointment⟩; meet ⟨deadline, commitments⟩; keep to ⟨diet, speed limit, agreement⟩; observe ⟨regulation⟩
② unr. itr. V. (geh.) stop

ein-heimisch Adj. native; home attrib. ⟨team⟩

Einheimische der/die; adj. Dekl. local

Einheit die; ∼, ∼en unity

einheitlich ① Adj. unified; (unterschiedslos) uniform ⟨dress⟩; standard ⟨procedure, practice⟩
② adv. ∼ gekleidet sein be dressed the same

einhellig ① Adj. unanimous
② adv. unanimously

ein|holen ① tr. V. (a) catch up with ⟨person, vehicle⟩
(b) make up ⟨arrears, time⟩
② itr. V. (ugs.) ▶ EINKAUFEN 1

ein-hundert Kardinalz. ▶ HUNDERT

einig Adj. sich (Dat.) ∼ sein be agreed; sich (Dat.) ∼ werden reach agreement

einig... Indefinitpron. u. unbest. Zahlwort some; ∼e wenige a few; ∼e Hundert several hundred

einigen ① tr. V. unite
② refl. V. reach an agreement

einigermaßen Adv. somewhat

Einigkeit die; ∼ (a) unity
(b) (Übereinstimmung) agreement

ein-jährig Adj. (ein Jahr alt) one-year-old attrib.; one year old pred.; (ein Jahr dauernd) one-year attrib.

Ein-kauf der (a) Einkäufe machen do some shopping
(b) (eingekaufte Ware) purchase
(c) (Abteilung) purchasing department

ein|kaufen ① itr. V. shop; ∼ gehen go shopping
② tr. V. buy; purchase

Ein-käufer der, **Ein-käuferin** die buyer; purchaser

Einkaufs-: ∼**bummel** der [leisurely] shopping expedition; ∼**liste** die shopping list; ∼**preis** der (Kaufmannsspr.) wholesale price; ∼**tasche** die shopping bag; ∼**tüte** die shopping bag; ∼**zentrum** das shopping centre; ∼**zettel** der shopping list

ein|kehren itr. V.; mit sein stop; in einem Wirtshaus ∼: stop at an inn

ein|klammern tr. V. etw. ∼: put sth. in brackets; bracket sth.

Ein-klang der harmony; in od. im ∼ stehen accord

ein|kleben tr. V. stick in

ein|kleiden tr. V. clothe

ein|klemmen tr. V. (a) (quetschen) catch
(b) (fest einfügen) clamp

ein|kochen tr. V. preserve ⟨fruit etc.⟩

Einkommen das; ∼s, ∼: income

Einkommen·steuer die income tax

ein|kreisen tr. V. (a) etw. ∼: put a circle round sth.
(b) (umzingeln) surround

Einkünfte Pl. income sing.; feste ∼: a regular income

ein|laden¹ unr. tr. V. load ⟨goods⟩

ein|laden² unr. tr. V. invite ⟨person⟩ (zu for)

einladend Adj. inviting

Ein-ladung die invitation

Ein-lage die (a) (in Brief) enclosure
(b) (Kochk.) vegetables, dumplings, etc. added to a clear soup
(c) (Schuh∼) arch support
(d) (Programm∼) interlude

ein|lagern tr. V. store; lay in ⟨stores⟩

Einlass, *Einlaß der; Einlasses, Einlässe admission

ein|lassen unr. tr. V. (a) (hereinlassen) admit; let in
(b) (einfüllen) run ⟨water⟩

Ein-lauf der (Med.) enema

ein|laufen ① unr. itr. V.; mit sein
(a) ⟨ship⟩ come in
(b) (kleiner werden) shrink
② unr. tr. V. wear in ⟨shoes⟩

ein|leben refl. V. settle down

ein|legen tr. V. (a) load ⟨film⟩; engage ⟨gear⟩
(b) (Kochk.) pickle

ein|leiten tr. V. (a) introduce
(b) induce ⟨birth⟩
(c) lead in; etw. in etw. (Akk.) ∼: lead sth. into sth.

Ein-leitung die (a) introduction
(b) (einer Geburt) induction

ein|leuchten itr. V. jmdm. ∼: be clear to sb.

einleuchtend Adj. plausible

ein|liefern tr. V. take ⟨letter, person⟩ (bei, in + Akk. to)

---

*old spelling – see note on page x

Einlieger·wohnung *die* ≈ granny flat

ein|lösen *tr. V.* cash ⟨cheque⟩

ein|machen *tr. V.* preserve ⟨fruit etc.⟩; (in Gläser) bottle

einmal ⟨1⟩ *Adv.* (a) once; **noch** ∼ **so groß [wie]** twice as big [as]; **etw. noch** ∼ **tun** do sth. again

(b) /'-'-/ (später) one day; (früher) once; **es war** ∼ ...: once upon a time there was ...

⟨2⟩ *Partikel* **nicht** ∼: not even; **wieder** ∼: yet again

Einmal·eins *das;* ∼: [multiplication] tables *pl.*

einmalig ⟨1⟩ *Adj.* (a) unique; one-off ⟨payment, purchase⟩

(b) (ugs.) fantastic (coll.)

⟨2⟩ *adv.* (ugs.) really fantastically (coll.)

Ein·marsch *der* (a) entry

(b) (Besetzung) invasion (**in** + *Akk.* of)

ein|marschieren *itr. V.; mit sein* march in

ein|massieren *tr. V.* massage *or* rub in

ein|mauern *tr. V.* (a) immure ⟨prisoner, traitor⟩; wall in ⟨relic, treasure⟩

(b) (ins Mauerwerk einfügen) **etw. in die Wand** *usw.* ∼: set sth. into the wall *etc.*

ein|mischen *refl. V.* interfere (**in** + *Akk.* in)

ein|motten *tr. V.* **etw.** ∼: put sth. into mothballs; (fig.) mothball

Ein·mündung *die* (von Straßen) junction

einmütig ⟨1⟩ *Adj.* unanimous

⟨2⟩ *adv.* unanimously

ein|nähen *tr. V.* sew in

Einnahme *die;* ∼, ∼**n** (a) income; (Staats∼) revenue; (Kassen∼) takings *pl.*

(b) (von Arzneimitteln) taking

(c) (einer Stadt, Burg) taking

Einnahme·quelle *die* source of income; (des Staates) source of revenue

ein|nehmen *unr. tr. V.* (a) take; (verdienen) earn

(b) (ausfüllen) take up ⟨amount of room⟩

(c) (beeinflussen) **jmdn. für sich** ∼: win sb. over

einnehmend *Adj.* winning ⟨manner⟩; **ein** ∼**es Wesen haben** (scherzh.) take everything one can get

Ein·öde *die* barren waste

ein|ölen *tr. V.* (a) (mit Öl einreiben) **sich/ jmdn.** ∼: put *or* rub oil on oneself/sb.

(b) (ölen) oil

ein|ordnen ⟨1⟩ *tr. V.* arrange; put in order

⟨2⟩ *refl. V.* (a) (Verkehrsw.) get into the correct lane; "∼„ 'get in lane'

(b) (sich einfügen) fit in

ein|packen ⟨1⟩ *tr. V.* pack (**in** + *Akk.* in); (einwickeln) wrap [up]

⟨2⟩ *itr. V.* (ugs.) **er kann** ∼: he's had it (coll.)

ein|parken *tr., itr. V.* park

ein|pflanzen *tr. V.* (a) plant

(b) (Med., fig.) implant

ein|prägen *tr. V.* (a) stamp (**in** + *Akk.* into, on)

(b) (fig.) **sich** (*Dat.*) **etw.** ∼: memorize sth.; **jmdm. etw.** ∼: impress sth. on sb.

einprägsam *Adj.* easily remembered

ein|pudern *tr. V.* powder; **sich** (*Dat.*) **das Gesicht** ∼: powder one's face

ein|rahmen *tr. V.* frame

ein|räumen *tr. V.* (a) put away

(b) (füllen) **seinen Schrank** ∼: put one's things away in one's cupboard; **ein Zimmer** ∼: put the furniture into a room

(c) (zugestehen) admit

ein|reden ⟨1⟩ *tr. V.* **jmdm. etw.** ∼: talk sb. into believing sth.; **sich** (*Dat.*) ∼, **dass** ...: persuade oneself that ...

⟨2⟩ *itr. V.* **auf jmdn.** ∼: talk insistently to sb.

ein|regnen *refl. V.; unpers.* **es hat sich eingeregnet** it's begun to rain steadily

ein|reiben *unr. tr. V.* rub ⟨substance⟩ in; **etw. mit Öl** ∼: rub oil into sth.

ein|reichen *tr. V.* submit; lodge ⟨complaint⟩; tender ⟨resignation⟩

ein|reihen ⟨1⟩ *refl. V.* **sich in etw.** (*Akk.*) ∼: join sth.

⟨2⟩ *tr. V.* **jmdn. in eine Kategorie** ∼: place sb. in a category

Einreiher *der;* ∼**s**, ∼: single-breasted suit/jacket

Ein·reise *die* entry

Einreise·erlaubnis *die* entry permit

ein|reisen *itr. V.; mit sein* enter; **nach Schweden** ∼: enter Sweden

ein|reißen ⟨1⟩ *unr. tr. V.* (a) pull down ⟨building⟩

(b) (einen Riss machen in) tear; rip

⟨2⟩ *unr. itr. V.; mit sein* tear; rip

ein|renken *tr. V.* (a) (Med.) set

(b) (ugs.: bereinigen) sort out

ein|richten ⟨1⟩ *refl. V.* **sich schön** ∼: furnish one's home beautifully; **sich häuslich** ∼: make oneself at home

⟨2⟩ *tr. V.* furnish ⟨flat, house⟩; fit out ⟨shop⟩; equip ⟨laboratory⟩

Ein·richtung *die* (a) furnishing

(b) (Mobiliar) furnishings *pl.*

ein|rollen ⟨1⟩ *tr. V.* roll up ⟨carpet etc.⟩; put ⟨hair⟩ in curlers

⟨2⟩ *itr. V.; mit sein* roll in

ein|rosten *itr. V.; mit sein* go rusty

ein|rücken ⟨1⟩ *itr. V.; mit sein* (einmarschieren) move in

⟨2⟩ *tr. V.* indent ⟨line, heading, etc.⟩

eins ⟨1⟩ *Kardinalz.* one; **es ist** ∼: it is one o'clock; ∼ **zu null** one-nil; ∼ **zu** ∼: one all; „∼, **zwei, drei!"** 'ready, steady, go'

⟨2⟩ *Adj.* **mir ist alles** ∼: it's all the same to me

⟨3⟩ *Indefinitpron.* ▶ IRGENDEIN A

Eins *die;* ∼, ∼**en** (a) one

(b) (Schulnote) one; A

einsam *Adj.* (a) lonely ⟨person, decision⟩

(b) (einzeln) solitary ⟨tree, wanderer⟩

(c) (abgelegen) isolated

(d) (menschenleer) deserted ⋯⟶

Einsamkeit *die;* ~ **(a)** loneliness
(b) (Alleinsein) solitude
(c) (Abgeschiedenheit) isolation
ein|sammeln *tr. V.* **(a)** (auflesen) pick up; gather up
(b) (sich aushändigen lassen) collect in; collect ⟨*tickets*⟩
Ein·satz *der* **(a)** (aus Stoff) inset; (in Kochtopf, Nähkasten usw.) compartment
(b) (Betrag) stake
(c) (Gebrauch) use; (von Truppen) deployment
Einsatz-: ~**befehl** *der* order to go into action; den ~**befehl haben** have operational command; ~**leiter** *der,* ~**leiterin** *die* head of operations; ~**wagen** *der* (der Polizei) police car; (der Feuerwehr) fire engine; (Notarztwagen) ambulance
ein|saugen *unr.* (*auch regelm.*) *tr. V.* suck in; breathe [in] ⟨*fresh air*⟩
ein|schalten ① *tr. V.* **(a)** switch on ⟨*radio, TV, electricity, etc.*⟩
(b) (fig.) call in ⟨*press, police, expert, etc.*⟩
② *refl. V.* **(a)** switch [itself] on
(b) (eingreifen) intervene (in + *Akk.* in)
Einschalt·quote *die* (Rundf.) listening figures *pl.;* (Ferns.) viewing figures *pl.*
ein|schärfen *tr. V.* jmdm. etw. ~: impress sth. [up]on sb.
ein|schätzen *tr. V.* judge ⟨*person*⟩; assess ⟨*situation, income, damages*⟩; (schätzen) estimate
Ein·schätzung *die* ▸ EINSCHÄTZEN: judging; assessment; estimation
ein|schenken *tr., itr. V.* **(a)** (eingießen) pour [out]; jmdm. etw. ~: pour out sth. for sb.
(b) (füllen) fill [up] ⟨*glass, cup*⟩
ein|scheren *itr. V.; mit sein* **auf eine Fahrspur** ~: get *or* move into a lane
ein|schicken *tr. V.* send in
ein|schieben *unr. tr. V.* **(a)** push in
(b) (einfügen) insert; put on ⟨*trains, buses*⟩
ein|schiffen *tr., refl. V.* embark
einschl. *Abk.* = **einschließlich** incl.
ein|schlafen *unr. itr. V.; mit sein* **(a)** fall asleep
(b) (verhüll.: sterben) pass away
(c) (gefühllos werden) go to sleep
ein|schläfern *tr. V.* **(a)** jmdn. ~: send sb. to sleep, (betäuben) put sb. to sleep
(b) (schmerzlos töten) **ein Tier** ~: put an animal to sleep
einschläfernd ① *Adj.* soporific
② *adv.* ~ **wirken** have a soporific effect
ein|schlagen ① *unr. tr. V.* **(a)** knock in
(b) (zertrümmern) smash [in]
(c) (einwickeln) wrap up ⟨*present*⟩; cover ⟨*book*⟩
② *unr. itr. V.* **(a)** ⟨*bomb*⟩ land; ⟨*lightning*⟩ strike
(b) auf jmdn./etw. ~: rain blows on sb./sth.
einschlägig ① *Adj.* specialist ⟨*journal,*

shop*⟩*; relevant ⟨*literature, passage*⟩
② *adv.* **er ist** ~ **vorbestraft** he has previous convictions for a similar offence/similar offences
ein|schleichen *unr. refl. V.* steal in
ein|schließen *unr. tr. V.* **(a)** etw. in etw. (*Dat.*) ~: lock sth. up [in sth.]; jmdn./sich ~: lock sb./oneself in
(b) (umgeben) surround
einschließlich ① *Präp. mit Gen.* including; ~ **der Unkosten** including expenses
② *adv.* **bis** ~ **30. Juni** up to and including 30 June
ein|schmeicheln *refl. V.* **sich bei jmdm.** ~: ingratiate oneself with sb.
ein|schmuggeln *tr. V.* smuggle in
ein|schneiden *unr. tr. V.* **(a)** make a cut in
(b) (einritzen) carve
einschneidend *Adj.* drastic
ein|schneien *itr. V.; mit sein* get snowed in
Ein·schnitt *der* cut
ein|schränken ① *tr. V.* **(a)** reduce, curb ⟨*expenditure, consumption*⟩
(b) (einengen) limit; restrict; jmdn. in seinen Rechten ~: limit *or* restrict sb.'s rights
② *refl. V.* economize
Einschränkung *die;* ~, ~**en**
(a) restriction; limitation
(b) (Vorbehalt) reservation
ein|schrauben *tr. V.* screw in
ein|schreiben *unr. tr. V.* **(a)** (Postw.) register ⟨*letter*⟩
(b) (eintragen) **sich/jmdn.** ~: enter one's/sb.'s name
Ein·schreiben *das* (Postw.) registered letter; **per** ~: by registered mail
ein|schreiten *unr. itr. V.* intervene
ein|schrumpfen *itr. V.; mit sein* shrivel up; (fig.) dwindle
ein|schüchtern *tr. V.* intimidate
ein|schulen *tr. V.* **eingeschult werden** start school
ein|sehen *unr. tr. V.* **(a)** (überblicken) see into
(b) (prüfend lesen) look at
(c) (erkennen) realize
(d) (begreifen) see
ein|seifen *tr. V.* lather
ein·seitig ① *Adj.* **(a)** on one side *postpos.*
(b) (tendenziös) one-sided
② *adv.* **(a)** on one side
(b) (tendenziös) one-sidedly
ein|senden *unr. tr. V.* (*auch regelm.*) send [in]
Ein·sender *der,* **Ein·senderin** *die;* ~, ~**nen** sender; (bei einem Preisausschreiben) entrant
Einsende·schluss,
Einsende·schluß *der* closing date

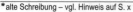
*alte Schreibung – vgl. Hinweis auf S. x

ein|setzen ① *tr. V.* **(a)** (hineinsetzen) put in
(b) put on ⟨*special train etc.*⟩
(c) (ernennen) appoint
(d) (in Aktion treten lassen) use
(e) (aufs Spiel setzen) stake ⟨*money*⟩
(f) (riskieren) risk
② *itr. V.* begin; ⟨*storm*⟩ break
③ *refl. V.* (sich engagieren) **ich werde mich
dafür ~, dass ...**: I shall do what I can to
see that ...; **sich nicht genug ~**: ⟨*pupil*⟩ be
lacking application; ⟨*minister*⟩ be lacking in
commitment
Ein·sicht *die* **(a)** view (**in** + *Akk.* into)
(b) (Einblick) **~ in die Akten nehmen** take *or*
have a look at the files
(c) (Erkenntnis) insight
einsichtig *Adj.* **(a)** (verständnisvoll)
understanding
(b) (verständlich) comprehensible
Ein·siedler *der,* **Ein·siedlerin** *die*
hermit
ein·silbig *Adj.* **(a)** monosyllabic ⟨*word*⟩
(b) (fig.) taciturn ⟨*person*⟩
Einsilbigkeit *die;* ~ (fig.) taciturnity
ein|sinken *unr. itr. V.* sink in
ein|sitzen *unr. itr. V.* (Rechtsw.) serve a
prison sentence; **er sitzt für drei Jahre ein**
he is serving three years *or* a three-year
sentence
Einsitzer *der;* ~s, ~: single-seater
einsitzig *Adj.* single-seater *attrib.*
ein|spannen *tr. V.* harness ⟨*horse*⟩; put in
⟨*paper*⟩: fix ⟨*fabric*⟩; clamp ⟨*work*⟩
ein|sparen *tr. V.* save
Einsparung *die;* ~, ~en saving (**an** + *Dat.*
in); ~**en an Kosten/Energie/Material** savings
or economies in costs/energy/materials
ein|speichern *tr. V.* (DV) feed in; input
ein|speisen *tr. V.* (Technik, DV) feed in
ein|sperren *tr. V.* lock up
einsprachig *Adj.* monolingual
ein|springen *unr. itr. V.;* mit sein stand
in; (aushelfen) step in and help out
ein|spritzen *tr. V.* inject; **jmdm. etw.
~**: inject sb. with sth.
Einspritz·motor *der* fuel-injection engine
Ein·spruch *der* objection (**gegen** to)
einspurig ① *Adj.* single-track ⟨*road*⟩
② *adv.* **die Autobahn ist nur ~ befahrbar**
only one lane of the motorway is open
einst *Adv.* (geh.) once
ein|stampfen *tr. V.* pulp ⟨*books*⟩
Ein·stand *der:* **seinen ~ geben** celebrate
starting a new job
ein|stecken *tr. V.* **(a)** put in
(b) (mitnehmen) put ⟨*sth.*⟩ in one's pocket/bag
etc.
ein|stehen *unr. itr. V.* **für jmdn. ~**: vouch
for sb.; **für etw. ~**: take responsibility for
sth.
ein|steigen *unr. itr. V.;* mit sein **(a)** (in ein
Fahrzeug) get in; **in ein Auto ~**: get into a car;

in den Bus ~: get on the bus
(b) (eindringen) climb in
einstellbar *Adj.* adjustable
ein|stellen ① *tr. V.* **(a)** (einordnen) put
away ⟨*books etc.*⟩
(b) (unterstellen) put in ⟨*car, bicycle*⟩
(c) (beschäftigen) take on ⟨*workers*⟩
(d) (regulieren) adjust
(e) (beenden) stop; call off ⟨*search, strike*⟩
(f) (Sport) equal ⟨*record*⟩
② *refl. V.* **(a)** arrive
(b) ⟨*pain, worry*⟩ begin; ⟨*success*⟩ come;
⟨*symptoms, consequences*⟩ appear
(c) **sich auf etw.** (*Akk.*) **~**: prepare oneself
for sth.; **sich schnell auf neue Situationen
~**: adjust quickly to new situations
ein·stellig *Adj.* single-figure *attrib.*
Ein·stellung *die* **(a)** (von Arbeitskräften)
employment
(b) (Regulierung) adjustment
(c) (Beendigung) stopping
(d) (Sport) **die ~ eines Rekordes** the
equalling of a record
(e) (Ansicht) attitude; **ihre politische/religiöse
~**: her political/religious views *pl.*
(f) (Film) take
Ein·stich *der* **(a)** insertion
(b) (~stelle) puncture; prick
Ein·stieg *der;* ~[e]s, ~e (Eingang) entrance;
(Tür) door/doors; **„kein ~"** 'exit only'
Einstiegs·droge *die* come-on drug
ein|stimmen ① *itr. V.* join in
② *tr. V.* **jmdn. auf etw.** (*Akk.*) **~**: get sb. in
the [right] mood for sth.
einstimmig ① *Adj.* **(a)** (Musik) for one
voice
(b) (einmütig) unanimous ⟨*decision, vote*⟩
② *adv.* **(a)** (Musik) in unison
(b) (einmütig) unanimously
ein·stöckig *Adj.* single-storey *attrib.*
ein|stöpseln *tr. V.* plug in ⟨*telephone,
electrical device*⟩
Ein·strahlung *die* irradiation; (Sonnen~)
insolation
ein|streichen *unr. tr. V.* (ugs.: für sich
behalten) pocket ⟨*money, winnings, etc.*⟩; (ugs.
abwertend) rake in (coll.) ⟨*money, profits, etc.*⟩
ein|studieren *tr. V.* rehearse
ein|stufen *tr. V.* classify; categorize
ein·stündig *Adj.* one-hour *attrib.*
ein|stürmen *itr. V.* **mit Fragen auf jmdn.
~**: besiege sb. with questions
Ein·sturz *der* collapse
ein|stürzen *itr. V.;* mit sein collapse
einst·weilen *Adv.* for the time being
eintägig *Adj.* one-day *attrib.*
Eintags·fliege *die* (Zool.) mayfly; (fig. ugs.)
seven-day wonder
ein|tauchen ① *tr. V.* dip; (untertauchen)
immerse
② *itr. V.;* mit sein dive in; ⟨*submarine*⟩ dive
ein|tauschen *tr. V.* exchange (**gegen** for)

ein·tausend *Kardinalz.:* ▶ TAUSEND
ein|teilen *tr. V.* (a) divide up; classify ⟨*plants, species*⟩
(b) (disponieren, verplanen) organize
einteilig *Adj.* one-piece
ein|tippen *tr. V.* (in die Kasse) register; (in einen Rechner) key in
eintönig ⟨1⟩ *Adj.* monotonous
⟨2⟩ *adv.* monotonously
Eintönigkeit *die;* ∼: monotony
Ein·topf *der* stew
Ein·tracht *die* harmony
ein·trächtig *Adj.* harmonious
Eintrag *der;* ∼[e]s, Einträge entry
ein|tragen *unr. tr. V.* (a) enter
(b) (Amtsspr.) register
einträglich *Adj.* lucrative
ein|treffen *unr. itr. V.; mit sein* (a) arrive
(b) (verwirklicht werden) come true
ein|treiben *unr. tr. V.* collect ⟨*taxes, debts*⟩; (durch Gerichtsverfahren) recover ⟨*debts, money*⟩
Eintreibung *die;* ∼, ∼en (von Steuern, Schulden) collection; (durch Gerichtsverfahren) recovery
ein|treten ⟨1⟩ *unr. itr. V.; mit sein*
(a) enter; bitte, treten Sie ein! please come in
(b) (Mitglied werden) in einen Verein/einen Orden ∼: join a club/enter a religious order
(c) (Raumfahrt) enter
⟨2⟩ *unr. tr. V.* kick in ⟨*door, window, etc.*⟩
ein|trichtern *tr. V.* (salopp) jmdm. etw. ∼: drum sth. into sb.
Ein·tritt *der* (a) entry; entrance; vor dem ∼ in die Verhandlungen (fig.) before entering into negotiations
(b) (Beitritt) der ∼ in einen Verein/einen Orden joining a club/entering a religious order
(c) (von Raketen) entry
(d) (Zugang, Eintrittsgeld) admission
(e) (Beginn) onset; ∼ der Dunkelheit nightfall
Eintritts-: ∼geld *das* admission fee; ∼karte *die* admission ticket; ∼preis *der* admission charge
ein|trocknen *itr. V.; mit sein* dry; ⟨*water, toothpaste*⟩ dry up; ⟨*leather*⟩ dry out; ⟨*berry, fruit*⟩ shrivel
ein|üben *tr. V.* practise
Ein·vernehmen *das;* ∼s harmony; (Übereinstimmung) agreement
ein·vernehmlich (Amtsspr.) ⟨1⟩ *Adv.* conjointly
⟨2⟩ *adj.* conjoint
einverstanden *Adj.* ∼ sein agree; mit jmdm./etw. ∼ sein approve of sb./sth.
Ein·verständnis *das* consent (zu to)
Ein·waage *die* (Kaufmannsspr.) contents *pl.*
ein|wachsen *unr. itr. V.; mit sein* grow into the flesh; eingewachsen ingrown ⟨*toenail*⟩

---

*old spelling – see note on page x

Einwand *der;* ∼[e]s, Einwände objection (gegen to)
Ein·wanderer *der*, **Ein·wanderin** *die* immigrant
ein|wandern *itr. V.; mit sein* immigrate (in + Akk. into)
Ein·wanderung *die* immigration
Einwanderungs-: ∼behörde *die* immigration authorities *pl.*; ∼land *das* country of immigration
einwand·frei ⟨1⟩ *Adj.* flawless; impeccable ⟨*behaviour*⟩; indisputable ⟨*proof*⟩
⟨2⟩ *adv.* flawlessly; ⟨*behave*⟩ impeccably; ⟨*prove*⟩ beyond question
ein|wechseln *tr. V.* (a) change ⟨*money*⟩
(b) (Sport) substitute ⟨*player*⟩
ein|wecken *tr. V.* preserve; bottle
Ein·weg-: ∼flasche *die* non-returnable bottle; ∼pfand *das* deposit on a/the disposable container; ∼spritze *die* disposable [hypodermic] syringe; ∼verpackung *die* disposable container
ein|weichen *tr. V.* soak
ein|weihen *tr. V.* open [officially] ⟨*bridge, road*⟩; dedicate ⟨*monument*⟩
Einweihung *die;* ∼, ∼en ▶ EINWEIHEN: [official] opening; dedication
ein|weisen *unr. tr. V.* (a) (in eine Tätigkeit) introduce
(b) (in ein Amt) install
ein|wenden *unr. (auch regelm.) tr. V.* dagegen lässt sich vieles ∼: there is a lot to be said against that
ein|werfen *unr. tr. V.* (a) mail ⟨*letter*⟩; insert ⟨*coin*⟩
(b) smash ⟨*window*⟩
(c) throw in ⟨*ball*⟩
(d) (bemerken, sagen) throw in ⟨*remark*⟩
ein|wickeln *tr. V.* wrap [up]
ein|willigen *itr. V.* agree (in + Akk. to)
Einwilligung *die;* ∼, ∼en agreement
ein|winken *tr. V.* (Verkehrsw.) guide in ⟨*aircraft, car*⟩
ein|wirken (a) (beeinflussen) auf jmdn. ∼: influence sb.
(b) (eine Wirkung ausüben) have an effect (auf + Akk. on)
Ein·wirkung *die* (Einfluss) influence; (Wirkung) effect
Einwohner *der;* ∼s, ∼, **Einwohnerin** *die;* ∼, ∼nen inhabitant
Einwohner·zahl *die* population
Ein·wurf *der* (a) insertion; (von Briefen) mailing
(b) (Ballspiele) throw-in
(c) (Bemerkung) interjection
Ein·zahl *die* singular
ein|zahlen *tr. V.* pay in; Geld auf ein Konto ∼: pay money into an account
Ein·zahlung *die* payment
ein|zäunen *tr. V.* fence in; enclose

Einzäunung *die;* ~, ~en fencing-in
ein|zeichnen *tr. V.* draw or mark in
einzeilig *Adj.* one-line *attrib.*
Einzel *das;* ~s, ~ (Sport) singles *pl.*
Einzel-: ~**bett** *das* single bed; ~**fall** *der* (a) particular case; (b) (Ausnahme) isolated case; ~**gänger** *der;* ~~s, ~~, ~**gängerin** *die;* ~~, ~~nen loner; ~**haft** *die* solitary confinement;
Einzel·handel *der* retail trade
Einzelhandels·preis *der* retail price
Einzel·händler *der,* ~**händlerin** *die* retailer
Einzelheit *die;* ~, ~en (a) detail
(b) (einzelner Umstand) particular
Einzel·kind *das* only child
Einzeller *der;* ~s, ~ (Biol.) unicellular organism
einzeln *Adj.* (a) (für sich allein) individual
(b) (allein stehend) solitary ⟨building, tree⟩; single ⟨lady, gentleman⟩
(c) ~e (wenige) a few; (einige) some
(d) *substantivisch* der/jeder **Einzelne** the/each individual; **Einzelnes** (manches) some things *pl.*; **das Einzelne** the particular
Einzel-: ~**preis** *der* individual price; ~**teil** *das* individual part; ~**zelle** *die* single cell; ~**zimmer** *das* single room
ein|ziehen [1] *unr. tr. V.* (a) put in; thread in ⟨tape, elastic⟩
(b) (einholen) haul in ⟨net⟩
(c) (einatmen) breathe in ⟨scent, fresh air⟩; inhale ⟨smoke⟩
(d) (einberufen) call up ⟨recruits⟩
(e) (beitreiben) collect
[2] *unr. itr. V.; mit sein* (a) ⟨liquid⟩ soak in
(b) (einkehren) enter
(c) (in eine Wohnung) move in
einzig [1] *Adj.* only; **kein** ~**es Wort** not a single word
[2] *adv.* (a) *intensivierend bei Adj.* extraordinarily
(b) (ausschließlich) only; **das** ~ **Wahre** the only thing
einzig·artig [1] *Adj.* unique
[2] *adv.* uniquely
Einzigartigkeit *die,* **Einzigkeit** *die* uniqueness
Ein·zug *der* (a) entry (**in** + *Akk.* into)
(b) (in eine Wohnung) move
Einzugs·bereich *der* catchment area
Eis *das;* ~es (a) ice; ~ **laufen** ice-skate
(b) (Speise~) ice cream; **ein** ~ **am Stiel** an ice lolly (Brit.) *or* (Amer.) ice pop
Eis-: ~**bahn** *die* ice rink; ~**bär** *der* polar bear; ~**becher** *der* ice cream sundae; ~**bein** *das* (Kochk.) knuckle of pork; ~**berg** *der* iceberg; ~**beutel** *der* ice bag; ~**blume** *die* frost flower; ~**bombe** *die* (Gastr.) bombe glacée; ~**brecher** *der* ice-breaker; ~**café** *das* ice cream parlour
Ei·schnee *der* stiffly beaten egg white

Eis·diele *die* ice cream parlour
Eisen *das;* ~s, ~: iron
Eisen·bahn *die* (a) railway; railroad (Amer.); **mit der** ~ **fahren** go by train
(b) (Bahnstrecke) railway line; railroad track (Amer.)
Eisenbahn·abteil *das* railway *or* (Amer.) railroad compartment
Eisenbahner *der;* ~s, ~: railwayman; railway worker; railroader (Amer.)
Eisenbahnerin *die;* ~, ~nen railway worker
Eisenbahn·unglück *das* train crash
Eisen-: ~**erz** *das* iron ore; ~**kette** *die* iron chain; ~**ring** *der* iron ring; ~**stange** *die* iron bar; ~**waren** *Pl.* ironmongery *sing.;* ~**zeit** *die* Iron Age
eisern [1] *Adj.* (auch fig.) iron
[2] *adv.* resolutely; ⟨save, train⟩ with iron determination; ~ **durchgreifen** take drastic measures
eis-, Eis-: ~**fach** *das* freezing compartment; ~**frei** *Adj.* ice-free; ~**gekühlt** *Adj.* iced; ~**glatt** *Adj.* (a) icy ⟨road⟩; (b) /'-'-/ (ugs.) ⟨floor, steps⟩ as slippery as ice; ~**glätte** *die* black ice; ~**hockey** *das* ice hockey
eisig [1] *Adj.* (a) icy ⟨wind, cold⟩; icy [cold] ⟨water⟩
(b) (fig.) frosty
[2] *adv.* (a) ~ **kalt sein** be icy cold
(b) (fig.) ⟨smile⟩ frostily
*****eisig·kalt** *Adj.* ▶ EISKALT 1A
eis-, Eis-: ~**kaffee** *der* iced coffee; ~**kalt** [1] *Adj.* (a) ice-cold ⟨drink⟩; freezing cold ⟨weather⟩; (b) (gefühllos) icy; ice-cold ⟨look⟩; [2] *adv.* **es lief mir** ~**kalt über den Rücken** a cold shiver went down my spine; ~**kunst·lauf** *der* figure skating; ~**kunst·läufer** *der,* ~**kunst·läuferin** *die* figure skater; ~**lauf** *der* ice skating; *~~*|**laufen** ▶ EIS A; ~**laufen** *das;* ~~s ice skating; ~**läufer** *der,* ~**läuferin** *die* ice skater
Ei·sprung *der* (Physiol.) ovulation
Eis-: ~**regen** *der* sleet; ~**schrank** *der* refrigerator; ~**sport** *der* ice sports *pl.;* ~**tanz** *der* (Sport) ice dancing; ~**tee** *der* iced tea; ~**waffel** *die* [ice cream] wafer; ~**wein** *der: wine made from grapes frozen on the vine;* ~**würfel** *der* ice cube; ~**zapfen** *der* icicle; ~**zeit** *die* ice age
eitel *Adj.* vain
Eitelkeit *die;* ~, ~en vanity
Eiter *der;* ~s pus
eitern *itr. V.* suppurate
eitrig *Adj.* suppurating
Ei·weiß *das;* ~es, ~e (a) egg white
(b) (Protein) protein
eiweiß-: ~**arm** *Adj.* low-protein *attrib.;* low in protein *postpos.;* ~**reich** *Adj.* high-protein *attrib.;* rich in protein *postpos.*

e

Ejakulation *die;* ~, ~en (Physiol.)
ejaculation

Ekel[1] *der;* ~s revulsion; [einen] ~ vor etw.
(*Dat.*) haben have a revulsion for sth.

Ekel[2] *das;* ~s, ~ (ugs. abwertend) horror; **er
ist ein [altes]** ~: he is quite obnoxious

ekelhaft *Adj.* revolting ⟨*sight*⟩; horrible
⟨*weather, person*⟩

ekeln [1] *refl. V.* be disgusted; **sich vor etw.**
(*Dat.*) ~: find sth. repulsive
[2] *tr., itr. V.* (*unpers.*) **es ekelt mich** *od.* **mir
ekelt davor** I find it revolting

eklig *Adj.* (a) ▶ EKELHAFT
(b) (ugs.: gemein) nasty

Ekstase /ɛk'staːzə/ *die;* ~, ~n ecstasy

Ekzem *das;* ~s, ~e (Med.) eczema

Elan *der;* ~s zest; vigour

elastisch *Adj.* elasticated ⟨*material*⟩;
springy ⟨*surface*⟩; supple ⟨*person, body*⟩

Elastizität *die;* ~: elasticity; (Federkraft)
springiness; (Geschmeidigkeit) suppleness

Elch *der;* ~[e]s, ~e elk; (in Nordamerika) moose

Elefant *der;* ~en, ~en elephant

elegant [1] *Adj.* elegant
[2] *adv.* elegantly

Eleganz *die;* ~: elegance

elektrifizieren *tr. V.* electrify

Elektrifizierung *die;* ~, ~en
electrification

Elektriker *der;* ~s, ~, **Elektrikerin**
die; ~, ~nen electrician

elektrisch [1] *Adj.* electric; electrical
⟨*resistance, wiring, system*⟩
[2] *adv.* ~ **kochen** cook with electricity;
~ **geladen sein** be electrically charged

elektrisieren [1] *tr. V.* (Med.) treat using
electricity
[2] *refl. V.* get an electric shock

Elektrizität *die;* ~ electricity

Elektrizitäts·werk *das* power station

elektro-, Elektro-: ~**artikel**
der electrical appliance; ~**auto** *das*
electric car; ~**gerät** *das* electrical
appliance; ~**geschäft** *das* electrical
shop *or* (Amer.) store; ~**herd** *der* electric
cooker; ~**magnet** *der* electromagnet;
~**magnetisch** [1] *Adj.* electromagnetic;
[2] *adv.* electromagnetically; ~**mobil**
das; ~~s, ~~e electric car; ~**motor** *der*
electric motor

Elektron *das;* ~s, ~en /-'troːnən/ electron

Elektronen-: ~**[ge]hirn** *das* (ugs.)
electronic brain (coll.); ~**hülle** *die* electron
shell; ~**rechner** *der* electronic computer

Elektronik *die;* ~ (a) electronics *sing.*,
no *art.*
(b) (Teile) electronics *pl.*

Elektronik·schrott *der* scrapped
electrical appliances *pl.*

elektronisch [1] *Adj.* electronic

[2] *adv.* electronically

elektro-, Elektro-: ~**rasierer** *der*
electric shaver; ~**smog** *der* (Jargon)
electronic smog; ~**statisch** [1] *Adj.*
electrostatic; [2] *adv.* electrostatically;
~**technik** *die* electrical engineering *no
art.;* ~**techniker** *der,* ~**technikerin**
die (a) electronics engineer; (b) (Elektriker)
electrician

Element *das;* ~[e]s, ~e element

elementar *Adj.* (a) (grundlegend)
fundamental
(b) (einfach) elementary ⟨*knowledge*⟩
(c) (naturhaft) elemental ⟨*force*⟩

Elementar·teilchen *das* (Physik)
elementary particle

elend *Adj.* wretched; miserable

Elend *das;* ~s misery

Elends-: ~**quartier** *das* slum [dwelling];
~**viertel** *das* slum area

elf *Kardinalz.* eleven

Elf *die;* ~, ~en (a) eleven
(b) (Sport) team; side

Elfe *die;* ~, ~n fairy

Elfen·bein *das* ivory

Elfenbein-: ~**schnitzerei** *die* ivory
carving; ~**turm** *der* (fig.) ivory tower

Elf·meter *der* (Fußball) penalty; **einen**
~ **schießen** take a penalty

Elfmeter·schießen *das;* ~s (Fußball)
durch ~: by *or* on penalties

eliminieren *tr. V.* eliminate

elitär *adj.* élitist; **ein** ~**es Bewusstsein an**
élite-awareness

Elite *die;* ~, ~n élite

Elite·truppe *die* (Milit.) élite *or* crack force

Ell·bogen *der; Pl.* ~: elbow

Elle *die;* ~, ~n (a) (Anat.) ulna
(b) (frühere Längeneinheit) cubit
(c) (veralt.: Maßstock) ≈ yardstick

Ellen·bogen *der; Pl.* ~: ▶ ELLBOGEN

Ellipse *die;* ~, ~n ellipse

Elsass, *****Elsaß *das;* ~ *od.* **Elsasses**
Alsace

Elster *die;* ~, ~n magpie

elterlich *Adj.* parental

Eltern *Pl.* parents *pl.*

eltern-, Eltern-: ~**abend** *der* (Schulw.)
parents' evening; ~**bei·rat** *der* (Schulw.)
parents' association; ~**haus** *das* home;
~**los** *Adj.* orphaned; ~**teil** *der* parent;
~**zeit** *die* [period of] parental leave

Email /e'maːj/ *das;* ~s, ~s, **Emaille**
/e'maljə/ *die;* ~, ~n enamel

E-Mail /'iːmeɪl/ *die;* ~, ~s (DV) email

Emanzipation *die;* ~, ~en emancipation

emanzipieren *refl. V.* emancipate

emanzipiert *Adj.* emancipated;
emancipated, liberated ⟨*woman*⟩

Embargo *das;* ~s, ~s embargo

Emblem *das;* ~s, ~e emblem

Ẹmbryo *der;* ~s, ~nen /-y'o:nən/ *od.* ~s embryo

Embryonenforschung *die* embryo research

Emigrạnt *der;* ~en, ~en, **Emigrạntin** *die;* ~, ~nen emigrant; (Flüchtling) emigré

Emigration *die;* ~, ~en (das Emigrieren) emigration

emigrieren *itr. V.; mit sein* emigrate

Emission (a) (Physik, Ökologie) emission (b) (Ausgabe [von Briefmarken, Wertpapieren]) issue

emissiọns-, Emissiọns-: ~**arm** *Adj.* low-emission; ~ **sein** be low in emissions; ~**handel** *der* emissions trading

Emotion *die;* ~, ~en emotion

emotionạl [1] *Adj.* emotional; emotive ⟨*topic, question*⟩ [2] *adv.* emotionally

Empfạng *der;* ~[e]s, Empfänge reception; (Entgegennahme) receipt

empfạngen *unr. tr. V.* receive

Empfänger *der;* ~s, ~ (a) recipient; (eines Briefes) addressee (b) (Empfangsgerät) receiver

Empfängerin *die;* ~, ~nen ▶ EMPFÄNGER A

empfänglich *Adj.* (a) receptive (**für** to) (b) (beeinflussbar) susceptible

Empfänglichkeit *die;* ~ (a) (Zugänglichkeit) receptivity, receptiveness (für to) (b) (Beeinflussbarkeit) susceptibility (für to)

Empfängnis *die;* ~: conception

Empfängnis·verhütung *die* contraception

empfạngs-, Empfạngs-: ~**berechtigt** *Adj.* authorized to receive payment/goods *postpos.;* ~**chef** *der* head receptionist; ~**dame** *die* receptionist; ~**halle** *die* reception lobby

empfehlen [1] *unr. tr. V.* recommend [2] *unr. refl. V.* (a) take one's leave (b) *unpers.* es empfiehlt sich, ... zu ...: it's advisable to ...

empfehlens·wert *Adj.* (a) to be recommended *postpos.;* recommendable (b) (ratsam) advisable

Empfehlung *die;* ~, ~en (a) recommendation (b) (Empfehlungsschreiben) letter of recommendation

empfiehl *Imperativ Sg. v.* EMPFEHLEN

empfiehlst *2. Pers. Sg. Präsens v.* EMPFEHLEN

empfiehlt *3. Pers. Sg. Präsens v.* EMPFEHLEN

empfịnden *unr. tr. V.* (a) (wahrnehmen) feel (b) (auffassen) etw. als Beleidigung ~: feel sth. to be an insult

Empfịnden *das;* ~s feeling; **für mein** *od.* **nach meinem** ~: to my mind

empfịndlich [1] *Adj.* (a) sensitive; fast ⟨*film*⟩ (b) (leicht beleidigt) sensitive (c) (anfällig) zart und ~: delicate (d) (spürbar) severe ⟨*punishment, shortage*⟩ [2] *adv.* ~ **auf etw.** (*Akk.*) **reagieren** (sensibel) be susceptible to sth.; (beleidigt) react oversensitively to sth.

Empfịndlichkeit *die;* ~, ~en ▶ EMPFINDLICH: sensitivity; severity; (eines Films) speed

empfịndsam *Adj.* sensitive ⟨*nature*⟩

Empfịndung *die;* ~, ~en (Gefühl) feeling

empfịng *1. u. 3. Pers. Sg. Prät. v.* EMPFANGEN

empfọhlen [1] *2. Part. v.* EMPFEHLEN [2] *Adj.* recommended

empịrisch [1] *Adj.* empirical [2] *adv.* empirically

empọr *Adv.* (geh.) upwards

Empọre *die;* ~, ~n gallery

empören [1] *tr. V.* fill with indignation; outrage [2] *refl. V.* become indignant *or* outraged

empörend *Adj.* outrageous

empört *Adj.* outraged

Empörung *die;* ~, ~en outrage

ẹmsig [1] *Adj.* industrious ⟨*person*⟩; bustling ⟨*activity*⟩ [2] *adv.* industriously

Emu *der;* ~s, ~s (Zool.) emu

Ẹnde *das;* ~s, ~n end; am ~ der Straße/Stadt at the end of the road/town; am/bis/gegen ~ des Monats at/by/towards the end of the month; ~ April at the end of April; zu ~ sein ⟨*patience, war*⟩ be at an end; ⟨*school*⟩ be over; ⟨*film, game*⟩ have finished; ~ gut, alles gut all's well that ends well (prov.)

Ẹnd·effekt *der* im ~: in the end; in the final analysis

ẹnden *itr. V.* (a) end; ⟨*programme*⟩ finish (b) in der Gosse ~: end up in the gutter; (dort sterben) die in the gutter

ẹnd-, Ẹnd-: ~**ergebnis** *das* final result; ~**gültig** [1] *Adj.* final ⟨*consent, decision*⟩; conclusive ⟨*evidence*⟩; [2] *adv.* das ist ~gültig vorbei that's all over and done with; sich ~gültig trennen separate for good; ~**haltestelle** *die* terminus; ~**kampf** *der* (Sport) final; (Milit.) final battle; ~**kunde** *der,* ~**kundin** *die* consumer; ~**lauf** *der* (Sport) final

ẹndlich [1] *Adv.* (a) (nach langer Zeit) at last (b) (schließlich) in the end [2] *Adj.* finite

ẹnd-, Ẹnd-: ~**los** [1] *Adj.* (a) (ohne Ende) infinite; (ringförmig) continuous; (b) (nicht enden wollend) endless; interminable ⟨*speech*⟩; [2] *adv.* ~los lange dauern be interminably long; ~**lösung** *die* (ns. verhüll.) Final Solution (*to the Jewish question*); ~**resultat** *das* final result; ~**runde** ⋯⋗

e

die (Sport) final; ~**spiel** *das* (Sport) final;
~**spurt** *der* (bes. Leichtathletik) final spurt;
~**stadium** *das* final stage; (Med.) terminal
stage; ~**station** *die* terminus; ~**summe**
die [sum] total

Endung *die;* ~, ~en (Sprachw.) ending

End-: ~**verbraucher** *der,*
~**verbraucherin** *die* (Wirtsch.) consumer;
~**ziffer** *die* final number; **das Los mit der**
~**ziffer** **4** the coupon with a number ending
in 4

Energie *die;* ~, ~n energy

energie-, Energie-: ~**bewusst,**
*~**bewußt** Adj.* energy-conscious; ~**mix**
der mix of energy sources; ~**politik** *die*
energy policy; ~**quelle** *die* energy source;
~**spar·lampe** *die* energy-saving lamp;
~**verbrauch** *der* energy consumption;
~**versorgung** *die* energy supply;
~**wirtschaft** *die* energy sector

energisch ① *Adj.* (a) energetic ⟨*person*⟩;
firm ⟨*action*⟩
(b) forceful ⟨*voice, words*⟩
② *adv.* (a) energetically; ~ **durchgreifen**
take drastic action
(b) ⟨*reject, say*⟩ forcefully; ⟨*stress*⟩
emphatically; ⟨*deny*⟩ strenuously

eng /ɛŋ/ ① *Adj.* (a) (schmal) narrow
(b) (dicht) close ⟨*writing*⟩
(c) (fest anliegend) close-fitting
(d) (beschränkt) narrow
(e) (nahe) close ⟨*friend*⟩
② *adv.* (a) (dicht) ~ [**zusammen**] **sitzen**/
stehen sit/stand close together
(b) (fest anliegend) ~ **anliegen**/**sitzen** fit closely
(c) (beschränkt) **etw. zu** ~ **auslegen** interpret
sth. too narrowly
(d) (nahe) closely

Engagement /ãgaʒə'mã:/ *das;* ~s, ~s
(a) (Einsatz) involvement; **sein** ~ **für etw.** his
commitment to sth.; **sein** ~ **gegen etw.** his
committed stand against sth.
(b) (eines Künstlers) engagement

engagiert *Adj.* committed ⟨*literature,*
film, director⟩; **politisch**/**sozial** ~ **sein** be
politically/socially committed *or* involved

Engagiertheit *die;* ~: commitment;
involvement

Enge *die;* ~, ~n confinement

Engel *der;* ~s, ~: angel

eng·herzig *Adj.* petty

England (*das*) ~s England

Engländer *der;* ~s, ~: Englishman/
English boy; **er ist** ~: he is English; **die**
~: the English

Engländerin *die;* ~, ~nen
Englishwoman/English girl; **sie ist** ~: she
is English

englisch ① *Adj.* English; **die** ~**e Sprache**/
Literatur the English language/English
literature

② *adv.* ~ **sprechen** speak English

Englisch *das;* ~[s] English

englisch-, Englisch-: ~**lehrer**
der, ~**lehrerin** *die* English teacher;
~**sprachig** *Adj.* (a) English-language
⟨*book, magazine*⟩; (b) (Englisch sprechend)
English-speaking ⟨*population, country*⟩;
~**unterricht** *der* English teaching;
(Unterrichtsstunde) English lesson

Eng·pass, *****Eng·paß** *der* (a) defile
(b) (fig.) bottleneck

eng·stirnig *Adj.* narrow-minded

Enkel *der;* ~s, ~: grandson

Enkelin *die;* ~, ~nen granddaughter

Enkel·kind *das* grandchild

enorm ① *Adj.* enormous ⟨*sum, costs*⟩;
tremendous (coll.) ⟨*effort*⟩; immense ⟨*strain*⟩
② *adv.* tremendously (coll.)

Ensemble /ã'sã:bl/ *das;* ~, ~s ensemble;
(Theater~) company

entarten *itr. V.; mit sein* degenerate

entbehren *tr. V.* (verzichten auf) do without

entbehrlich *Adj.* dispensable

Entbehrung *die;* ~, ~en privation

entbinden ① *unr. tr. V.* (a) **jmdn. von**
einem Versprechen ~: release sb. from a
promise; **seines Amtes** *od.* **von seinem Amt**
entbunden werden be relieved of [one's]
office
(b) **jmdn.** ~ (Med.) deliver sb.'s baby
② *unr. itr. V.* give birth

Entbindung *die* (Med.) delivery

Entbindungs·station *die* maternity ward

entblößen ① *refl. V.* take one's clothes
off; ⟨*exhibitionist*⟩ expose oneself
② *tr. V.* uncover ⟨*one's arm etc.*⟩

entdecken *tr. V.* (a) discover
(b) (ausfindig machen) **jmdn.** ~: find sb.; **etw.**
~: find *or* discover sth.

Entdecker *der;* ~s, ~, **Entdeckerin**
die; ~, ~nen discoverer

Entdeckung *die;* ~, ~en discovery

Ente *die;* ~, ~n duck

entehren *tr. V.* dishonour; ~**d** degrading

enteignen *tr. V.* expropriate

Enteignung *die;* ~, ~en expropriation

enterben *tr. V.* disinherit

entern *tr., itr. V.* board ⟨*ship*⟩

Enter·taste /'ɛntɐ-/ *die* (DV) enter key

entfachen *tr. V.* (geh.) (a) kindle, light
⟨*fire*⟩
(b) (fig.) provoke ⟨*quarrel, argument*⟩;
arouse ⟨*passion, enthusiasm*⟩

entfallen *unr. itr. V.; mit sein* (a) (aus dem
Gedächtnis) **es ist mir** ~: it escapes me
(b) (zugeteilt werden) **auf jmdn.**/**etw.** ~: be
allotted to sb./sth.
(c) (wegfallen) lapse

entfalten ① *tr. V.* (a) open [up]; unfold
⟨*map etc.*⟩
(b) (fig.) display ⟨*ability, talent*⟩

*****old spelling – see note on page x

2 *refl. V.* **(a)** open [up]
(b) (fig.) ⟨*personality, talent, etc.*⟩ develop
Entfaltung *die;* ~, ~en (fig.)
(a) (Entwicklung) development
(b) ▸ ENTFALTEN 1B: display
entfernen **1** *tr. V.* remove; take out
⟨*tonsils etc.*⟩
2 *refl. V.* go away
entfernt **1** *Adj.* **(a)** (fern) remote; **das ist
od. liegt weit** ~ **von der Stadt** it is a long
way from the town; **10 km/zwei Stunden**
~: 10 km/two hours away
(b) slight ⟨*acquaintance*⟩; distant ⟨*relation*⟩;
slight ⟨*resemblance*⟩
2 *adv.* **(a)** (fern) remotely
(b) slightly ⟨*acquainted*⟩; distantly ⟨*related*⟩
Entfernung *die;* ~, ~en **(a)** (Abstand)
distance
(b) (das Beseitigen) removal
entfesseln *tr. V.* unleash
entflammen **1** *tr. V.* arouse ⟨*enthusiasm
etc*⟩
2 *itr. V.; mit sein* flare up
entfliehen *unr. itr. V.; mit sein* escape;
jmdm. ~: escape from sb.
entfremden **1** *tr. V.* **(a)** etw. seinem
Zweck ~: use sth. for a different purpose
(b) (Philos., Soziol.) entfremdet alienated
2 *refl. V.* **sich jmdm./einer Sache** ~:
become estranged from sb./unfamiliar with
sth.
Entfremdung *die;* ~, ~en alienation;
estrangement
entführen *tr. V.* kidnap ⟨*child etc.*⟩; hijack
⟨*plane, lorry, etc.*⟩
Entführer *der,* **Entführerin** *die*
▸ ENTFÜHREN: kidnapper; hijacker
Entführung *die* ▸ ENTFÜHREN: kidnapping;
hijacking
entgegen **1** *Adv.* towards
2 *Präp. mit Dat.* ~ **meinem Wunsch**
against my wishes; ~ **dem Befehl** contrary
to orders
entgegen-, Entgegen-: ~|**bringen**
unr. tr. V. (fig.) show ⟨*love, understanding*⟩;
~|**fahren** *unr. itr. V.; mit sein* **jmdm.**
~**fahren** come/go to meet sb.; ~|**gehen**
unr. itr. V.; mit sein **(a)** jmdm. ~**gehen**
go to meet sb.; **(b)** (fig.) be heading for
⟨*catastrophe, hard times*⟩; ~|**gesetzt**
1 *Adj.* **(a)** (umgekehrt) opposite ⟨*end,
direction*⟩; **(b)** (gegensätzlich) opposing;
2 *adv.* **genau** ~**gesetzt handeln/denken** do/
think exactly the opposite; ~|**kommen**
unr. itr. V.; mit sein jmdm. ~**kommen**
come to meet sb.; (Zugeständnisse machen) be
accommodating towards sb.; ~|**kommen**
das; ~~s cooperation; (Zugeständnis)
concession; ~|**kommend** *Adj.* obliging;
~|**nehmen** *unr. tr. V.* receive; ~|**treten**
unr. itr. V.; mit sein go/come up to; (fig.)
stand up to ⟨*difficulties*⟩
entgegnen *tr. V.* retort; reply

entgehen *unr. itr. V.; mit sein*
(a) (entkommen) escape
(b) jmdm. entgeht etw. sb. misses sth.
entgeistert *Adj.* dumbfounded
Entgelt *das;* ~[e]s, ~e payment; fee
entgiften *tr. V.* decontaminate ⟨*substance
etc.*⟩; detoxicate ⟨*body etc.*⟩
entgleisen *itr. V.; mit sein* **(a)** be derailed
(b) (fig.) make a/some faux pas
entgräten *tr. V.* fillet
enthaaren *tr. V.* remove hair from
Enthaarungs-mittel *das* hair remover
enthalten¹ **1** *unr. tr. V.* contain
2 *unr. refl. V.* **sich einer Sache** (Gen.)
~: abstain from sth.; **sich der Stimme**
~: abstain
enthalten² *Adj.* **in etw.** (*Dat.*) ~ **sein** be
contained in sth.; **das ist im Preis** ~: that is
included in the price
enthaltsam **1** *Adj.* abstemious; (sexuell)
abstinent
2 *adv.* ~ **leben** live in abstinence
Enthaltsamkeit *die;* ~: abstinence
Enthaltung *die;* ~, ~en abstention
enthaupten *tr. V.* (geh.) behead
enthäuten *tr. V.* skin
entheben *unr. tr. V.* (geh.) relieve
enthemmt *Adj.* uninhibited
enthüllen *tr. V.* unveil ⟨*monument etc.*⟩;
reveal ⟨*face, truth, secret*⟩
Enthüllung *die;* ~, ~en ▸ ENTHÜLLEN:
unveiling; revelation
Enthusiasmus /ɛntuˈzɪasmʊs/ *der;*
~: enthusiasm
Enthusiast *der;* ~en, ~en,
Enthusiastin *die;* ~, ~nen enthusiast
enthusiastisch **1** *Adj.* enthusiastic
2 *adv.* enthusiastically
entkalken *tr. V.* decalcify
entkleiden *tr. V.* (geh.) **(a)** undress
(b) (berauben) strip
entkommen *unr. itr. V.; mit sein* escape
entkoppeln *tr. V.* **(a)** decouple ⟨*systems*⟩
(b) (isolieren) isolate (acoustically)
entkorken *tr. V.* uncork ⟨*bottle*⟩
entkräften *tr. V.* **(a)** weaken; **völlig**
~: exhaust
(b) (fig.) refute ⟨*argument etc.*⟩
Entkräftung *die;* ~, ~en **(a)** debility;
völlige ~: exhaustion
(b) (fig.) refutation
entladen **1** *unr. tr. V.* unload
2 *unr. refl. V.* **(a)** ⟨*storm*⟩ break
(b) (fig.) ⟨*anger etc.*⟩ erupt; ⟨*aggression etc.*⟩
be released
entlang **1** *Präp. mit Akk. u. Dat.* along
2 *Adv.* along; **hier/dort** ~, **bitte!** this/that
way please!
entlang-: ~|**fahren** *unr. itr. V.; mit sein*
(a) drive along; **(b)** (streichen) go
along; ~|**gehen** *unr. itr. V.; mit sein* ⋯❯

⟨*person*⟩ go *or* walk along; ∼|**laufen**
unr. itr. V.; mit sein **(a)** walk/run along;
(b) (verlaufen) go *or* run along
entlarven *tr. V.* expose
entlassen *unr. tr. V.* **(a)** (aus dem Gefängnis)
release; (aus dem Krankenhaus, der Armee)
discharge
(b) (aus einem Arbeitsverhältnis) dismiss; (wegen
Arbeitsmangels) make redundant (Brit.); lay off
Entlassung *die;* ∼, ∼en ▶ ENTLASSEN:
release; discharge; dismissal; redundancy
(Brit.); laying off
entlasten *tr. V.* **(a)** relieve
(b) (Rechtsw.) exonerate ⟨*defendant*⟩
Entlastung *die;* ∼, ∼en **(a)** relief
(b) (Rechtsw.) exoneration; defence
entlaufen *unr. itr. V.; mit sein* run
away; **ein** ∼**er Sträfling/Sklave** an escaped
convict/a runaway slave
entlausen *tr. V.* delouse
entledigen *refl. V.* **sich jmds./einer Sache**
(*Gen.*) ∼ (geh.) rid oneself of sb./sth.
entleeren *tr. V.* empty; evacuate ⟨*bowels,
bladder*⟩
entlegen *Adj.* remote
entleihen *unr. tr. V.* borrow
entlocken *tr. V.* (geh.) **jmdm. etw.** ∼: elicit
sth. from sb.
entlohnen *tr. V.* pay
Entlohnung *die;* ∼, ∼en payment; (Lohn)
pay
entlüften *tr. V.* ventilate
Entlüfter *der;* ∼s, ∼: ventilator
entmachten *tr. V.* deprive of power
entmilitarisieren *tr. V.* demilitarize
entmündigen *tr. V.* incapacitate
Entmündigung *die;* ∼, ∼en
incapacitation
entmutigen *tr. V.* discourage
Entnahme *die;* ∼, ∼n (von Wasser)
drawing; (von Blut) extraction
Entnazifizierung *die;* ∼, ∼en
denazification
entnehmen *unr. tr. V.* **(a)** etw. [einer
Sache (*Dat.*)] ∼: take sth. [from sth.]
(b) (ersehen aus) gather (*Dat.* from)
entnervend *Adj.* nerve-racking
entnervt *Adj.* ∼ **sein** be worn down; have
reached *or* be at the end of one's tether; **er
gab** ∼ **auf** he had reached the end of his
tether and gave up
entpuppen *refl. V.* **sich als etw./jmd.**
∼: turn out to be sth./sb.
entrahmen *tr. V.* skim ⟨*milk*⟩
entreißen *unr. tr. V.* **jmdm. etw.** ∼: snatch
sth. from sb.
entrichten *tr. V.* (Amtsspr.) pay ⟨*fee*⟩
entrümpeln *tr. V.* clear out
Entrümpelung *die;* ∼, ∼en clear-out

entrüsten ① *refl. V.* **sich** [**über etw.**
(*Akk.*)] ∼: be indignant [at *or* about sth.]
② *tr. V.* (empören) **jmdn.** ∼: make sb.
indignant
Entrüstung *die;* ∼, ∼en indignation (**über**
+ *Akk.* at, about)
Entsafter *der;* ∼s, ∼: juice extractor
entsagen *itr. V.* **einer Sache** (*Dat.*) ∼
(geh.) renounce sth.
Entsagung *die;* ∼, ∼en (geh.)
renunciation
entschädigen *tr. V.* compensate (**für** for);
jmdn. für etw. ∼ (fig.) make up for sth.
Entschädigung *die;* ∼, ∼en
compensation
entschärfen *tr. V.* defuse; tone down
⟨*discussion, criticism*⟩
entscheiden ① *unr. refl. V.* **(a)** decide
(b) (*unpers.*) **morgen entscheidet es sich,
ob** ...: I/we/you will know tomorrow
whether ...
② *unr. itr. V.* **über etw.** (*Akk.*) ∼: settle sth.
③ *unr. tr. V.* decide on ⟨*dispute*⟩; decide
⟨*outcome, result*⟩
entscheidend ① *Adj.* crucial; decisive
⟨*action*⟩
② *adv.* **jmdn./etw.** ∼ **beeinflussen** have a
decisive influence on sb./sth.
Entscheidung *die;* ∼, ∼en decision
entschieden ① *Adj.* **(a)** (entschlossen)
determined; resolute
(b) (eindeutig) definite
② *adv.* resolutely; **das geht** ∼ **zu weit** that
is going much too far
Entschiedenheit *die;* ∼: decisiveness;
etw. mit ∼ **behaupten/verneinen** state/deny
sth. categorically; **etw. mit** ∼ **fordern**
demand sth. emphatically
entschlafen *unr. itr. V.; mit sein* pass away
entschließen *unr. refl. V.* decide
Entschließung *die;* ∼, ∼en resolution
entschlossen *Adj.* determined
Entschlossenheit *die;*
∼: determination
Entschluss, *Entschluß *der;*
Entschlusses, Entschlüsse decision
entschlüsseln *tr. V.* decipher
entschuldigen ① *refl. V.* apologize
② *tr. V.* (auch *itr.*) V. excuse ⟨*person*⟩; **sich
∼ lassen** ask to be excused; ∼ **Sie [bitte]!**
(bei Fragen, Bitten) excuse me; (bedauernd) I'm
sorry
Entschuldigung *die;* ∼, ∼en **(a)** apology
(b) (Grund) excuse
(c) (Höflichkeitsformel) ∼! (bei Fragen, Bitten)
excuse me; (bedauernd) [I'm] sorry
entschwinden *unr. itr. V.; mit sein* (geh.)
disappear; vanish
entsetzen ① *refl. V.* be horrified
② *tr. V.* horrify; **über etw.** (*Akk.*) **entsetzt
sein** be horrified by sth.
Entsetzen *das;* ∼s horror

---

*alte Schreibung – vgl. Hinweis auf S. x

entsetzlich ① *Adj.* **(a)** horrible ‹*accident, crime, etc.*›
(b) (ugs.: stark) terrible ‹*thirst, hunger*›
② *adv.* terribly (coll.)
entsinnen *unr. refl. V.* **sich jmds./einer Sache** ~: remember sb./sth.
entsorgen *tr. V.* (Amtsspr., Wirtsch.) dispose of ‹*waste etc.*›
Entsorgung *die;* ~, ~en (Amtsspr., Wirtsch.) waste disposal
entspannen ① *tr. V.* relax
② *refl. V.* **(a)** ‹*person*› relax
(b) (fig.) ‹*situation, tension*› ease
Entspannung *die;* ~ **(a)** relaxation
(b) (politisch) easing of tension; détente
Entspannungs-politik *die* policy of détente
entsprechen *unr. itr. V.*
(a) (übereinstimmen mit) **einer Sache** (*Dat.*) ~: correspond to sth.; **der Wahrheit/den Tatsachen** ~: be in accordance with the truth/the facts
(b) (nachkommen) **einem Wunsch** ~: comply with a request; **den Anforderungen** ~: meet the requirements
entsprechend ① *Adj.*
(a) corresponding; (angemessen) appropriate
(b) (dem~) in accordance *postpos.*
② *adv.* **(a)** (angemessen) appropriately
(b) (dem~) accordingly
③ *Präp. mit Dat.* in accordance with
entspringen *unr. itr. V.; mit sein*
(a) ‹*river*› rise
(b) (entstehen aus) **einer Sache** (*Dat.*) ~: spring from sth.
entstehen *unr. itr. V.; mit sein*
(a) originate; ‹*quarrel, friendship, etc.*› arise
(b) (gebildet werden) be formed (**aus** from, **durch** by)
(c) (sich ergeben) occur; (als Folge) result
Entstehung *die;* ~: origin
entsteinen *tr. V.* stone
entstellen *tr. V.* **(a)** disfigure
(b) (verfälschen) distort ‹*text, facts*›
Entstellung *die;* ~, ~en
(a) disfigurement
(b) (Verfälschung) distortion
entstören *tr. V.* (Elektrot.) suppress ‹*engine, electrical appliance*›
Entstörungs-stelle *die* fault repair service
enttarnen *tr. V.* uncover
enttäuschen *tr. V.* disappoint
enttäuschend *Adj.* disappointing
enttäuscht *Adj.* disappointed; dashed ‹*hopes*›
Enttäuschung *die;* ~, ~en disappointment
entwachsen *unr. itr. V.; mit sein* **einer Sache** (*Dat.*) ~: grow out of sth.
entwaffnen *tr. V.* (auch fig.) disarm
entwaffnend *Adj.* disarming

entwarnen *itr. V.* sound the all-clear
Entwarnung *die;* ~, ~en all-clear
entwässern *tr. V.* drain
Entwässerung *die;* ~, ~en drainage
entweder *Konj.:* ~ ... **oder** either ... or
entweichen *unr. itr. V.; mit sein* escape
entwenden *tr. V.* (geh.) purloin
entwerfen *unr. tr. V.* design ‹*furniture, dress*›; draft ‹*novel etc.*›; draw up ‹*plans etc.*›
entwerten *tr. V.* **(a)** cancel ‹*ticket, postage stamp*›
(b) devalue ‹*currency*›
Entwerter *der;* ~s, ~: ticket-cancelling machine
entwickeln ① *refl. V.* develop
② *tr. V.* produce ‹*vapour, smell*›; display ‹*ability, characteristic*›; develop ‹*equipment, photograph, film*›; elaborate ‹*theory, ideas*›
Entwicklung *die;* ~, ~en
(a) development; (von Dämpfen usw.) production; **in der** ~ **sein** ‹*young person*› be adolescent
(b) (Darlegung) elaboration
(c) (Fot.) developing
Entwicklungs-: ~**helfer** *der,* ~**helferin** *die* development aid worker; ~**hilfe** *die* [development] aid; ~**land** *das* developing country; ~**politik** *die* development aid policy
entwirren *tr. V.* disentangle
entwischen *itr. V.; mit sein* (ugs.) get away
entwöhnen *tr. V.* wean
entwürdigend *Adj.* degrading
Entwurf *der;* ~, **Entwürfe (a)** design
(b) (Konzept) draft
entwurzeln *tr. V.* uproot
entziehen ① *unr. tr. V.* **(a)** take away
(b) (nicht zugestehen) withdraw
② *unr. refl. V.* **sich seinen Pflichten** (*Dat.*) ~: evade one's duty; **das entzieht sich meiner Kontrolle** that is beyond my control
Entziehung *die;* ~, ~en **(a)** withdrawal
(b) (Entziehungskur) withdrawal treatment *no indef. art.*
entziffern *tr. V.* decipher
entzückend *Adj.* delightful
entzückt *Adj.* delighted
Entzug *der;* ~[e]s withdrawal
Entzugs-erscheinung *die* withdrawal symptom
entzündbar *Adj.* [in]flammable
entzünden ① *tr. V.* light ‹*fire*›; strike ‹*match*›
② *refl. V.* **(a)** ignite
(b) (anschwellen) become inflamed
entzündlich *Adj.* **(a)** [in]flammable ‹*substance*›
(b) (Med.) inflammatory
Entzündung *die;* ~, ~en inflammation
entzwei *Adj.* (geh.) in pieces
entzweien *refl. V.* fall out ⋯▷

entzweigehen unr. itr. V.; mit sein (geh.) break

Enzian der; ~s, ~e gentian

Enzyklika die; ~, Enzykliken encyclical

Enzyklopädie die; ~, ~n encyclopaedia

enzyklopädisch Adj. encyclopaedic

Epen ▶ Epos

Epidemie die; ~, ~n epidemic

epigonal Adj. (geh.) ▶ EPIGONENHAFT

Epigone der; ~n, ~n (geh.) imitator

epigonenhaft Adj. (geh.) imitative; unoriginal

Epigonin die; ~, ~nen ▶ EPIGONE

Epik /'e:pɪk/ die; ~ (Literaturw.) epic poetry

Epilepsie die; ~, ~n (Med.) epilepsy no art.

Epileptiker der; ~s, ~, **Epileptikerin** die; ~, ~nen epileptic

epileptisch Adj. epileptic

episch Adj. epic

Episode die; ~, ~n episode

Epoche die; ~, ~n epoch

Epos /'e:pɔs/ das; ~, Epen epic [poem]; epos

er Personalpron. 3. Pers. Sg. Nom. Mask. he; (betont) him; (bei Dingen/Tieren) it; s. auch IHM; IHN; SEINER

erachten tr. V. (geh.) consider; etw. als od. für seine Pflicht ~: consider sth. [to be] one's duty

erarbeiten tr. V. work for

Erb·anlage die hereditary disposition

erbarmen refl. V. (geh.) take pity (Gen. on)

Erbarmen das; ~s pity

erbärmlich ① Adj. (a) (elend) wretched (b) (unzulänglich) pathetic (c) (abwertend: gemein) mean; wretched (d) (sehr groß) terrible ⟨hunger, fear, etc.⟩ ② adv. terribly

erbauen ① tr. V. (a) build (b) (geh.: erheben) uplift ② refl. V. sich an etw. (Dat.) ~: be uplifted by sth.

Erbauer der; ~s, ~, **Erbauerin** die; ~, ~nen architect

Erbe¹ das; ~s (a) inheritance (b) (Vermächtnis) legacy

Erbe² der; ~n ~n heir

erben tr. (auch itr.) V. inherit

erbetteln tr. V. get by begging

erbeuten tr. V. carry off, get away with ⟨valuables, prey, etc.⟩; capture ⟨enemy plane, tank, etc.⟩

Erb-: ~**faktor** der hereditary factor; ~**folge** die succession; ~**gut** das (Biol.) genetic make-up

Erbin die; ~, ~nen heiress

erbitten unr. tr. V. (geh.) request

erbittern tr. V. enrage

erbittert ① Adj. bitter

② adv. ~ kämpfen wage a bitter struggle

Erb·krankheit die hereditary disease

erblassen itr. V.; mit sein (geh.) turn pale; blanch (literary)

erbleichen itr. V.; mit sein (geh.) ▶ ERBLASSEN

erblich Adj. hereditary ⟨title, disease⟩

erblicken tr. V. (geh.) catch sight of; (fig.) see

erblinden itr. V.; mit sein lose one's sight

erblühen itr. V.; mit sein (geh.) bloom; blossom

Erb·masse die (Biol.) genetic make-up

erbost Adj. furious

erbrechen ① unr. tr. V. bring up ⟨food⟩ ② unr. itr., refl. V. vomit

Erbrechen das; ~s vomiting

erbringen unr. tr. V. produce

Erbschaft die; ~, ~en inheritance

Erbschaft[s]·steuer die estate or death duties pl.

Erb-: ~**schleicher** der; ~s, ~ (abwertend) legacy hunter; ~**schleicherei** die; ~~, ~~en (abwertend) legacy hunting; ~**schleicherin** die; ~~, ~~nen ▶ ~SCHLEICHER

Erbse die; ~, ~n pea

Erb-: ~**stück** das heirloom; ~**sünde** die original sin; ~**teil** das share of an/the inheritance

Erd-: ~**achse** die earth's axis; ~**anziehung** die earth's gravitational pull; ~**apfel** der (bes. österr.) ▶ KARTOFFEL; ~**atmosphäre** die earth's atmosphere; ~**beben** das earthquake; ~**beere** die strawberry; ~**boden** der ground; earth; etw. dem ~boden gleichmachen raze sth. to the ground

Erde die; ~, ~n (a) (Erdreich) soil; earth (b) (fester Boden) ground (c) (Welt) earth; world (d) (Planet) Earth

erdenklich Adj. conceivable

Erd-: ~**gas** das natural gas; ~**geschoss**, *~**geschoß** das ground floor; first floor (Amer.); ~**kugel** die terrestrial globe; earth; ~**kunde** die geography; ~**magnetismus** der terrestrial magnetism; ~**nuss**, *~**nuß** die peanut; ~**oberfläche** die earth's surface; ~**öl** das oil; ~öl exportierende Länder oil-exporting countries

erdöl-, Erdöl-: *~**exportierend** ▶ ERDÖL; ~**gewinnung** die oil production; ~**leitung** die oil pipeline

erdrosseln tr. V. strangle

erdrücken tr. V. (a) crush (b) (fig.: belasten) overwhelm

erdrückend Adj. overwhelming; oppressive ⟨heat, silence⟩

Erd-: ~**rutsch** der landslide; ~**rutsch·sieg** der (Politik) landslide victory; ~**teil** der continent

---

*old spelling – see note on page x

erdulden *tr. V.* endure ⟨*sorrow, misfortune*⟩; tolerate ⟨*insults*⟩; (über sich ergehen lassen) undergo

Erd-: ∼**umdrehung** *die* rotation of the earth; ∼**umlauf·bahn** *die* orbit [of the earth]

ereifern *refl. V.* get excited

ereignen *refl. V.* happen; ⟨*accident, mishap*⟩ occur

Ereignis *das;* ∼**ses,** ∼**se** event; occurrence

ereignis·reich *Adj.* eventful

Eremit *der;* ∼**en,** ∼**en, Eremitin** *die;* ∼**, ** ∼**nen** hermit

ererbt *Adj.* inherited

erfahren[1] *unr. tr. V.* **(a)** find out; learn; (hören) hear
(b) (geh.: erleben) experience; (erleiden) suffer

erfahren[2] *Adj.* experienced

Erfahrung *die;* ∼**, ** ∼**en** experience; ∼**en** sammeln gain experience *sing.;* **etw. in** ∼ **bringen** discover sth.

erfahrungs·gemäß *Adv.* in our/my experience

erfassen *tr. V.* **(a)** (mitreißen) catch
(b) (begreifen) grasp ⟨*situation, etc.*⟩
(c) (registrieren) record

Erfassung *die;* ∼**, ** ∼**en** registration

erfinden *unr. tr. V.* invent; **das ist alles erfunden** it is pure fabrication

Erfinder *der;* ∼**s,** ∼**, Erfinderin** *die;* ∼**, ** ∼**nen** **(a)** inventor
(b) (Urheber) creator

erfinderisch *Adj.* inventive; (schlau) resourceful

Erfindung *die;* ∼**, ** ∼**en** invention

erflehen *tr. V.* (geh.) beg

Erfolg *der;* ∼**[e]s,** ∼**e** success; **keinen** ∼ **haben** be unsuccessful

erfolgen *itr. V.; mit sein* take place; occur; **es erfolgte keine Reaktion** there was no reaction

erfolg-, Erfolg-: ∼**los** [1] *Adj.* unsuccessful; [2] *adv.* unsuccessfully; ∼**losigkeit** *die;* ∼∼: lack of success; ∼**reich** [1] *Adj.* successful; [2] *adv.* successfully

Erfolgs·erlebnis *das* feeling of achievement

erfolg·versprechend *Adj.* promising

erforderlich *Adj.* required; necessary

erfordern *tr. V.* require; demand

erforschen *tr. V.* discover ⟨*facts, causes, etc.*⟩; explore ⟨*country*⟩

Erforschung *die;* ∼ research (+ *Gen.* into); (eines Landes usw.) exploration

erfreuen [1] *tr. V.* please
[2] *refl. V.* **sich an etw.** (*Dat.*) ∼: take pleasure in sth.

erfreulich *Adj.* pleasant

erfreulicherweise *Adv.* happily

erfrieren [1] *unr. itr. V.; mit sein* freeze to death; ⟨*plant, harvest, etc.*⟩ be damaged by frost
[2] *unr. refl. V.* **sich** (*Dat.*) **die Finger** ∼: get frostbite in one's fingers

Erfrierung *die;* ∼**, ** ∼**en** frostbite *no pl.;* ∼**en an den Händen/Füßen** frostbitten hands/feet

erfrischen [1] *tr.* (*auch itr.*) *V.* refresh
[2] *refl. V.* freshen oneself up

erfrischend (auch fig.) *Adj.* refreshing

Erfrischung *die;* ∼**, ** ∼**en** (auch fig.) refreshment

Erfrischungs-: ∼**getränk** *das* soft drink; ∼**raum** *der* refreshment room; ∼**tuch** *das; Pl.* ∼**tücher** tissue wipe; towelette

erfüllen [1] *tr. V.* grant ⟨*wish, request*⟩; fulfil ⟨*contract*⟩; carry out ⟨*duty*⟩; meet ⟨*condition*⟩
[2] *refl. V.* ⟨*wish*⟩ come true

Erfüllung *die;* **in** ∼ **gehen** come true

erfunden *Adj.* fictional ⟨*story*⟩

ergänzen *tr. V.* **(a)** (vervollständigen) complete; (erweitern) add to
(b) (hinzufügen) add ⟨*remark*⟩

Ergänzung *die;* ∼**, ** ∼**en**
(a) (Vervollständigung) completion; (Erweiterung) enlargement
(b) (Zusatz) addition; (zu einem Gesetz) amendment

ergattern *tr. V.* (ugs.) manage to grab

ergaunern *tr. V.* get by underhand means

ergeben[1] [1] *unr. refl. V.* **(a) sich in etw.** (*Akk.*) ∼: submit to sth.
(b) (kapitulieren) surrender (*Dat.* to)
(c) (folgen, entstehen) arise (**aus** from)
[2] *unr. tr. V.* result in

ergeben[2] *Adj.* **(a)** (zugeneigt) devoted
(b) (resignierend) **mit** ∼**er Miene** with an expression of resignation

Ergebnis *das;* ∼**ses,** ∼**se** result

ergebnis·los *Adj.* fruitless

ergehen *unr. refl. V.* **sich in etw.** (*Dat.*) ∼: indulge in sth.

ergiebig *Adj.* rich ⟨*deposits, resources*⟩; fertile ⟨*topic*⟩

Ergiebigkeit *die;* ∼ ▶ ERGIEBIG: richness; fertility

ergonomisch [1] *Adj.* ergonomic
[2] *adv.* ergonomically

ergötzen (geh.) [1] *tr. V.* enthrall
[2] *refl. V.* **sich an etw.** (*Dat.*) ∼: be delighted by sth.

ergrauen *itr. V.; mit sein* go grey

ergreifen *unr. tr. V.* **(a)** (greifen) grab
(b) (festnehmen) catch ⟨*thief etc.*⟩
(c) (fig.: erfassen) seize
(d) (fig.: aufnehmen) take up ⟨*career*⟩; take ⟨*initiative, opportunity*⟩
(e) (fig.: bewegen) move

ergreifend *Adj.* moving   ···⟩

ergriffen *Adj.* moved
Ergriffenheit *die;* ~: **voller** ~: deeply moved
ergründen *tr. V.* ascertain; discover ⟨*cause*⟩
Erguss, *Erguß *der* (geh. abwertend) outburst; **ein poetischer** ~: a poetic outpouring
erhaben *Adj.* solemn ⟨*moment*⟩; awe-inspiring ⟨*sight*⟩; sublime ⟨*beauty*⟩; **über** etw. (*Akk.*) ~ **sein** be above sth.
Erhalt *der;* ~ (Amtsdt.) receipt
erhalten *unr. tr. V.* **(a)** receive ⟨*letter, news, gift*⟩; be given ⟨*order*⟩; get ⟨*good mark, impression*⟩
(b) (bewahren) preserve ⟨*town, building*⟩
erhältlich *Adj.* obtainable
Erhaltung *die;* ~: preservation; (des Friedens) maintenance
erhängen *tr. V.* hang
erhärten *tr. V.* strengthen ⟨*suspicion, assumption*⟩; substantiate ⟨*claim*⟩
erheben ① *unr. tr. V.* **(a)** raise
(b) (verlangen) levy ⟨*tax*⟩; charge ⟨*fee*⟩
② *unr. refl. V.* **(a)** rise
(b) (rebellieren) rise up (**gegen** against)
erhebend *Adj.* uplifting
erheblich ① *Adj.* considerable
② *adv.* considerably
Erhebung *die;* ~, ~en **(a)** (Anhöhe) elevation
(b) (Aufstand) uprising
(c) (Umfrage) survey
(d) (Einziehen) (von Steuern) levying; (von Gebühren) charging
erheitern *tr. V.* jmdn. ~: cheer sb. up
Erheiterung *die;* ~, ~en amusement
erhellen *tr. V.* light up
erhitzen ① *tr. V.* heat ⟨*liquid*⟩; jmdn. ~: make sb. hot
② *refl. V.* heat up; ⟨*person*⟩ become hot
erhoffen *tr. V.* **sich** (*Dat.*) **viel/wenig von** etw. ~: expect a lot/little from sth.
erhöhen ① *tr. V.* increase ⟨*prices, productivity, etc.*⟩
② *refl. V.* ⟨*rent, prices*⟩ rise
Erhöhung *die;* ~, ~en increase (*Gen.* in)
erholen *refl. V.* (auch fig.) recover (**von** from); (sich ausruhen) have a rest
erholsam *Adj.* restful
Erholung *die;* ~: ▶ ERHOLEN: recovery; rest; ~ **brauchen** need a rest
erholungs-bedürftig *Adj.* in need of a rest *postpos.*
Erholungs-urlaub *der* holiday for convalescence
erhören *tr. V.* (geh.) hear
Erika *die;* ~, ~s *od.* **Eriken** (Bot.) erica
erinnern ① *refl. V.* **sich an** jmdn./etw. ~: remember sb./sth.; **sich [daran]** ~, **dass** …: remember *or* recall that …
② *tr. V.* jmdn. **an** etw./jmdn. ~: remind sb.

of sth./sb.
Erinnerung *die;* ~, ~en memory (**an** + *Akk.* of); etw. **[noch gut] in** ~ **haben** [still] remember sth. [well]; **zur** ~ **an** jmdn./etw. in memory of sb./sth.
Erinnerungs-lücke *die* gap in one's memory
erjagen *tr. V.* **(a)** catch
(b) (gewinnen) win ⟨*fame*⟩; make ⟨*money, fortune*⟩
erkalten *tr. V.; mit sein* cool
erkälten *refl. V.* catch cold
Erkältung *die;* ~, ~en cold
Erkältungs-krankheit *die* cold
erkämpfen *tr. V.* win; **den Sieg** ~: gain a victory
erkaufen *tr. V.* **(a)** (durch Opfer) win
(b) (durch Geld) buy
erkennbar *Adj.* recognizable; (sichtbar) visible
erkennen *unr. tr. V.* **(a)** recognize
(b) (deutlich sehen) make out
erkenntlich *Adj.* **(a)** **sich [für etw.]** ~ **zeigen** show one's appreciation for sth.
(b) ▶ ERKENNBAR
Erkenntnis *die;* ~, ~se discovery; **zu der** ~ **kommen, dass** …: come to the realization that …
Erkennungs-: ~**melodie** *die* (einer Sendung) theme music; (eines Senders) signature tune; ~**zeichen** *das* sign [to recognize sb. by]
Erker *der;* ~s, ~: bay window
Erker-fenster *das* bay window
erklärbar *Adj.* explicable
erklären ① *tr. V.* **(a)** explain
(b) (mitteilen) state; declare
(c) jmdn. **für tot** ~: pronounce someone dead; jmdn. **zu etw.** ~: name sb. as sth
② *refl. V.* **sich einverstanden/bereit** ~: declare oneself [to be] in agreement/willing
erklärlich *Adj.* understandable
erklärt *Adj.* declared
Erklärung *die;* ~, ~en **(a)** (Darlegung) explanation
(b) (Mitteilung) statement
erklimmen *unr. tr. V.* (geh.) climb
erklingen *unr. itr. V.; mit sein* ring out
erkranken *itr. V.; mit sein* become ill (**an** + *Dat.* with); **schwer erkrankt sein** be seriously ill
Erkrankung *die;* ~, ~en illness; (eines Körperteils) disease
erkunden *tr. V.* reconnoitre ⟨*terrain*⟩
erkundigen *refl. V.* **sich nach** jmdm./etw. ~: ask after sb./enquire about sth.
Erkundigung *die;* ~, ~en enquiry
Erkundung *die;* ~, ~en (meist Milit.) reconnaissance

Erkundungs-: ∼**fahrt** *die* exploratory trip; ∼**flug** *der* reconnaissance flight

erlahmen *itr. V.; mit sein* tire; ⟨*strength*⟩ flag

erlangen *tr. V.* gain; obtain ⟨*credit, visa*⟩; reach ⟨*age*⟩

Erlass, *Erlaß *der;* Erlasses, Erlasse decree

erlassen *unr. tr. V.* **(a)** enact ⟨*law*⟩; declare ⟨*amnesty*⟩; issue ⟨*warrant*⟩ **(b)** (verzichten auf) remit ⟨*sentence*⟩

erlauben [1] *tr. V.* **(a)** allow **(b)** (ermöglichen) permit [2] *refl. V.* sich (*Dat.*) etw. ∼: permit oneself sth.

Erlaubnis *die;* ∼, ∼se permission; (Schriftstück) permit

erläutern *tr. V.* explain; comment on ⟨*picture etc.*⟩; annotate ⟨*text*⟩

Erläuterung *die* explanation

Erle *die;* ∼, ∼n alder

erleben *tr. V.* experience; **etwas Schreckliches** ∼: have a terrible experience; **er wird das nächste Jahr nicht mehr** ∼: he won't see next year; **du kannst was** ∼! (ugs.) you won't know what's hit you!

Erlebnis *das;* ∼ses, ∼se experience

erledigen [1] *tr. V.* deal with ⟨*task*⟩; settle ⟨*matter*⟩; **ich muss noch einige Dinge erledigen** I must see to a few things; **sie hat alles pünktlich erledigt** she got everything done on time [2] *refl. V.* ⟨*matter, problem*⟩ resolve itself; **vieles erledigt sich von selbst** a lot of things sort them'selves out

erledigt *Adj.* closed ⟨*case*⟩; (ugs.) worn out ⟨*person*⟩

erlegen *tr. V.* shoot ⟨*animal*⟩

erleichtern *tr. V.* **(a)** make easier **(b)** (befreien) relieve

Erleichterung *die;* ∼, ∼en **(a)** zur ∼ der **Arbeit** to make the work easier **(b)** (Befreiung) relief **(c)** (Verbesserung, Milderung) alleviation

erleiden *unr. tr. V.* suffer

erlernbar *Adj.* learnable

erlernen *tr. V.* learn

erlesen *Adj.* superior ⟨*wine*⟩; choice ⟨*dish*⟩

erleuchten *tr. V.* **(a)** light **(b)** (geh.: mit Klarheit erfüllen) inspire

Erleuchtung *die;* ∼, ∼en inspiration

erliegen *unr. itr. V.* succumb (*Dat.* to); **einem Irrtum** ∼: be misled; **einer Krankheit** (*Dat.*) ∼: die from an illness

erlogen *Adj.* made up

Erlös *der;* ∼es, ∼e proceeds *pl.*

erlöschen *unr. itr. V.; mit sein* ⟨*fire*⟩ go out; **ein erloschener Vulkan** an extinct volcano

erlösen *tr. V.* save, rescue (**von** from)

Erlöser *der;* ∼s, ∼ **(a)** saviour **(b)** (christl. Rel.) redeemer

Erlöserin *die;* ∼, ∼nen ▶ ERLÖSER A

Erlösung *die;* ∼, ∼en release (**von** from)

ermächtigen *tr. V.* authorize

Ermächtigung *die;* ∼, ∼en authorization

ermahnen *tr. V.* admonish; tell (coll.); (warnen) warn

Ermahnung *die;* ∼, ∼en admonition; (Warnung) warning

Ermang[e]lung *die;* ∼: in ∼ (+ *Gen.*) (geh.) in the absence of

ermäßigen *tr. V.* reduce

Ermäßigung *die;* ∼, ∼en reduction

ermatten (geh.) [1] *itr. V.; mit sein* become exhausted [2] *tr. V.* exhaust, tire

ermessen *unr. tr. V.* estimate, gauge

Ermessen *das;* ∼s estimation

ermitteln [1] *tr. V.* ascertain ⟨*facts*⟩; discover ⟨*culprit, address*⟩; establish ⟨*identity, origin*⟩; decide ⟨*winner*⟩; calculate ⟨*quota, rates, data*⟩ [2] *itr. V.* (Rechtsw.) investigate

Ermittlung *die;* ∼, ∼en **(a)** (das Ermitteln) ▶ ERMITTELN: ascertainment; discovery; establishment **(b)** (Untersuchung) investigation

ermöglichen *tr. V.* enable

ermorden *tr. V.* murder

Ermordung *die;* ∼, ∼en murder

ermüden [1] *itr. V.; mit sein* tire [2] *tr. V.* tire; make tired

ermüdend *Adj.* tiring

Ermüdung *die;* ∼, ∼en tiredness

ermuntern *tr. V.* encourage

ermunternd *Adj.* encouraging

ermutigen *tr. V.* encourage

Ermutigung *die;* ∼, ∼en encouragement

ernähren [1] *tr. V.* **(a)** feed ⟨*young, child*⟩ **(b)** (unterhalten) keep ⟨*family, wife*⟩ [2] *refl. V.* feed oneself

Ernährer *der;* ∼s, ∼, **Ernährerin** *die;* ∼, ∼nen breadwinner

Ernährung *die;* ∼: feeding; (Nahrung) diet

Ernährungs·wissenschaft *die* dietetics *sing., no art.*

ernennen *unr. tr. V.* appoint

Ernennung *die* appointment (**zu** as)

erneuerbar *Adj.* renewable; ∼**e Energien** renewable sources of energy

erneuern *tr. V.* **(a)** replace **(b)** (wiederherstellen) renovate ⟨*roof, building*⟩; (fig.) thoroughly reform ⟨*system*⟩

Erneuerung *die;* ∼, ∼en **(a)** replacement **(b)** (Wiederherstellung) renovation

erneut [1] *Adj.* renewed [2] *adv.* once again

erniedrigen *tr. V.* humiliate

Erniedrigung *die;* ∼, ∼en humiliation

ernst [1] *Adj.* **(a)** serious **(b)** (aufrichtig) genuine ⟨*intention, offer*⟩ ⋯⟩

(c) (gefahrvoll) serious ⟨*injury*⟩; grave ⟨*situation*⟩
2 *adv.* seriously; jmdn./etw. ~ nehmen take sb./sth. seriously; ~ gemeint serious; sincere ⟨*wish*⟩
Ernst *der;* ~[e]s **(a)** seriousness; **das ist mein [voller] ~:** I mean that [quite] seriously; **etw. im ~ meinen** mean sth. seriously
(b) (Wirklichkeit) **daraus wurde [blutiger/ bitterer] ~:** it became [deadly] serious; **der ~ des Lebens** the serious side of life
ernst-, Ernst-: ~**fall** *der:* im ~fall when the real thing happens; ***~**gemeint** ► ERNST 2; ~**haft** 1 *Adj.* serious; 2 *adv.* seriously; ~**haftigkeit** *die;* ~~: seriousness
ernstlich 1 *Adj.* **(a)** serious
(b) (aufrichtig) genuine ⟨*wish*⟩
2 *adv.* **(a)** seriously
(b) (aufrichtig) genuinely ⟨*sorry, repentant*⟩
Ernte *die;* ~, ~n **(a)** harvest
(b) (Ertrag) crop; **die ~ einbringen** bring in the harvest
Ernte·dank·fest *das* harvest festival
ernten *tr. V.* harvest
ernüchtern *tr. V.* sober up; (fig.) bring down to earth; ~d sobering
Ernüchterung *die;* ~, ~en (fig.) disillusionment
Eroberer *der;* ~s, ~, **Eroberin** *die;* ~, ~nen conqueror
erobern *tr. V.* **(a)** conquer; take ⟨*town, fortress*⟩
(b) seize ⟨*power*⟩
Eroberung *die;* ~, ~en conquest; (einer Stadt, Festung) taking
eröffnen *tr. V.* **(a)** open; start ⟨*business, practice*⟩
(b) (mitteilen) jmdm. etw. ~: reveal sth. to sb.
(c) ein Testament ~: read a will
Eröffnung *die;* ~, ~en **(a)** opening; (einer Sitzung) start
(b) (Mitteilung) revelation
(c) (Testaments~) reading
erogen *Adj.* erogenous ⟨*zone*⟩
erörtern *tr. V.* discuss
Erörterung *die;* ~, ~en discussion
Eros·Center *das* [licensed] brothel; eros centre
Erosion *die;* ~, ~en erosion
Erotik *die;* ~: eroticism
erotisch *Adj.* erotic
Erpel *der;* ~s, ~: drake
erpicht *Adj.* in auf etw. (*Akk.*) ~ sein be keen on sth.
erpressbar, *erpreßbar *Adj.* blackmailable; susceptible to blackmail *postpos.*
Erpressbarkeit, *Erpreßbarkeit *die;* ~: susceptibility to blackmail

erpressen *tr. V.* **(a)** (nötigen) blackmail
(b) (erlangen) extort ⟨*money etc.*⟩
Erpresser *der;* ~s, ~, **Erpresserin** *die;* ~, ~nen blackmailer
Erpressung *die;* ~, ~en blackmail *no indef. art.;* (von Geld, Geständnis) extortion
Erpressungs·versuch *der* blackmail attempt
erproben *tr. V.* test ⟨*medicine*⟩ (an + *Akk.* on)
Erprobung *die;* ~, ~en testing
erquickend *Adj.* (geh.) refreshing
erraten *unr. tr. V.* guess
errechnen *tr. V.* calculate
erregen 1 *tr. V.* **(a)** annoy
(b) (sexuell) arouse
(c) (verursachen) arouse
2 *refl. V.* get excited
erregend *Adj.* exciting; (sexuell) arousing
Erreger *der;* ~s, ~ (Med.) pathogen
erregt *Adj.* excited; (sexuell) aroused
Erregung *die;* ~, ~en excitement
erreichbar *Adj.* **(a)** within reach *postpos.*
(b) der Ort ist mit dem Zug ~: the place can be reached by train
erreichen *tr. V.* **(a)** reach; **den Zug ~:** catch the train; **er ist telefonisch zu ~:** he can be contacted by telephone
(b) (durchsetzen) achieve ⟨*goal, aim*⟩
errichten *tr. V.* **(a)** build ⟨*house, bridge, etc.*⟩
(b) (aufstellen) erect
erringen *unr. tr. V.* gain ⟨*victory*⟩; reach ⟨*first etc. place*⟩
erröten *itr. V.; mit sein* blush
Errungenschaft *die;* ~, ~en achievement
Ersatz *der;* ~es **(a)** replacement
(b) (Entschädigung) compensation
Ersatz-: ~**frau** *die* replacement; (Sport) substitute; ~**kasse** *die* private health insurance company; ~**mann** *der; Pl.* ~**männer** *od.* ~**leute** *die* replacement; (Sport) substitute; ~**rad** *das* spare wheel; ~**reifen** *der* spare tyre; ~**spieler** *der,* ~**spielerin** *die* (Sport) substitute [player]; ~**teil** *das* (bes. Technik) spare part; spare (Brit.)
ersaufen *unr. itr. V.; mit sein* (salopp) drown
ersäufen *tr. V.* drown
erschaffen *unr. tr. V.* create
Erschaffung *die* creation
erschaudern *itr. V.; mit sein* (geh.) shudder (**bei** at)
erscheinen *unr. itr. V.; mit sein* ⟨*book*⟩ published
Erscheinung *die;* ~, ~en **(a)** (Vorgang) phenomenon
(b) (äußere Gestalt) appearance
(c) (Vision) apparition; **eine ~ haben** see a vision

**old spelling – see note on page x

Erscheinungs-: ∼**bild** *das* appearance; ∼**form** *die* manifestation; ∼**weise** *die* die ∼**weise einer Zeitung** the frequency of publication of a newspaper; **wöchentliche/ monatliche** ∼**weise** weekly/monthly publication

erschießen *unr. tr. V.* shoot dead

Erschießung *die;* ∼, ∼**en** shooting

erschlaffen *itr. V.; mit sein* ⟨*muscle, limb*⟩ become limp; ⟨*skin*⟩ grow slack

erschlagen[1] *unr. tr. V.* strike dead; kill

erschlagen[2] *Adj.* (ugs.) **(a)** (erschöpft) worn out **(b)** (verblüfft) **wie** ∼ **sein** be flabbergasted (coll.) *or* thunderstruck

erschließen *unr. tr. V.* develop ⟨*area, building land*⟩; tap ⟨*resources*⟩

erschöpfen *tr. V.* exhaust

erschöpfend *Adj.* exhaustive

erschöpft *Adj.* exhausted

Erschöpfung *die;* ∼, ∼**en** exhaustion

Erschöpfungs-zustand *der* state of exhaustion

erschrecken[1] *unr. itr. V.; mit sein* be startled; **vor etw.** (*Dat.*) **od. über etw.** (*Akk.*) ∼: be startled by sth.

erschrecken[2] *tr. V.* frighten; scare

erschrecken[3] *unr. od. regelm. refl. V.* get a fright

erschreckend *Adj.* alarming

erschrocken [1] *2. Part. v.* ERSCHRECKEN[1] [2] *Adj.* frightened

erschüttern *tr. V.* (auch fig.) shake

erschütternd *Adj.* deeply distressing; deeply shocking ⟨*conditions*⟩

Erschütterung *die;* ∼, ∼**en** **(a)** vibration; (der Erde) tremor **(b)** (Ergriffenheit) shock; (Trauer) distress

erschweren *tr. V.* **etw.** ∼: make sth. more difficult

erschwerend [1] *Adj.* complicating ⟨*factor*⟩ [2] *adv.* **es kommt** ∼ **hinzu, dass er …:** to make matters worse he …

Erschwernis *die;* ∼, ∼**se** difficulty

erschwinglich *Adj.* reasonable

ersehen *unr. tr. V.* see; **aus etw. zu** ∼ **sein** be evident from sth.

ersetzen *tr. V.* **(a)** replace ⟨*durch* by⟩ **(b)** (erstatten) reimburse ⟨*expenses*⟩; **jmdm. einen Schaden** ∼: compensate sb. for damages

Ersetzung *die;* ∼, ∼**en** (von Kosten usw.) reimbursement; **die** ∼ **von Schäden** compensation for damage

ersichtlich *Adj.* apparent

ersinnen *unr. tr. V.* (geh.) devise

erspähen *tr. V.* (geh.) espy ⟨literary⟩; catch sight of

ersparen *tr. V.* save

Ersparnis *die;* ∼, ∼**se** saving

ersprießlich *Adj.* (geh.) fruitful ⟨*contacts, collaboration*⟩

erst [1] *Adv.* **(a)** (zu∼) first; ∼ **einmal** first [of all] **(b)** (nicht eher als) **eben** ∼: only just; ∼ **nächste Woche** not until next week; **er war** ∼ **zufrieden, als …:** he was not satisfied until … **(c)** (nicht mehr als) only [2] *Partikel* **so was lese ich gar nicht** ∼: I don't even start reading that sort of stuff

erst… *Ordinalz.* **(a)** first; **etw. das** ∼**e Mal tun** do sth. for the first time; **am Ersten [des Monats]** on the first [of the month]; **als Erster/Erste etw. tun** be the first to do sth. **(b)** (best…) **das** ∼**e Hotel** the best hotel; **der/die Erste [der Klasse]** the top boy/girl [of the class]

erstarren *itr. V.; mit sein* ⟨*jelly, plaster*⟩ set; ⟨*limbs, fingers*⟩ grow stiff

erstatten *tr. V.* **(a)** reimburse ⟨*expenses*⟩ **(b) Anzeige gegen jmdn.** ∼: report sb. [to the police]

Erstattung *die;* ∼, ∼**en** (von Kosten) reimbursement

Erst-aufführung *die* première

erstaunen *tr. V.* astonish

Erstaunen *das;* ∼**s** astonishment

erstaunlich [1] *Adj.* astonishing [2] *adv.* astonishingly

erstaunlicher-weise *Adv.* astonishingly *or* amazingly [enough]

erstaunt *Adj.* astonished; amazed

Erst-ausgabe *die* first edition

erstechen *unr. tr. V.* stab [to death]

erstehen (geh.) [1] *unr. tr. V.* (kaufen) purchase [2] *unr. itr. V.; mit sein* ⟨*difficulties, problems*⟩ arise

ersteigen *unr. tr. V.* climb

ersteigern *tr. V.* buy [at an auction]

erstellen *tr. V.* (Papierdt.) **(a)** (bauen) build **(b)** (anfertigen) make ⟨*assessment*⟩; draw up ⟨*plan, report, list*⟩

***erste-mal** ▸ MAL[1]

***ersten-mal** ▸ MAL[1]

erstens *Adv.* firstly; in the first place

erster… *Adj.* the former

erst-geboren *Adj.* first-born

ersticken [1] *itr. V.; mit sein* suffocate; (sich verschlucken) choke [2] *tr. V.* **(a)** (töten) suffocate **(b)** smother ⟨*flames*⟩

erstklassig [1] *Adj.* first-class [2] *adv.* superbly

erstmals *Adv.* for the first time

erstrangig *Adj.* **(a)** first-class **(b)** (vordringlich) of top priority *postpos.*

erstreben *tr. V.* strive for

erstrebens-wert *Adj.* ⟨*ideals etc.*⟩ worth striving for; desirable ⟨*situation*⟩

erstrecken *refl. V.* (a) (sich ausdehnen)
stretch
(b) (dauern) **sich über 10 Jahre** ~: carry on
for 10 years
Erst·stimme *die* first vote
erstürmen *tr. V.* take by storm
ersuchen *tr. V.* (geh.) ask; **jmdn.** ~, **etw. zu
tun** request sb. to do sth.
ertappen *tr. V.* catch ‹*thief, burglar*›
erteilen *tr. V.* give ‹*advice, information*›;
give, grant ‹*permission*›
Erteilung *die;* ~, ~en giving; (einer
Genehmigung) granting
ertönen *itr. V.; mit sein* sound
Ertrag *der;* ~[e]s, Erträge (a) yield
(b) (Gewinn) return
ertragen *unr. tr. V.* bear
erträglich *Adj.* tolerable; bearable ‹*pain*›
ertrag·reich *Adj.* lucrative ‹*business*›;
productive ‹*land, soil*›
ertränken *tr. V.* drown
ertrinken *unr. itr. V.; mit sein* be drowned;
drown
erübrigen ① *tr. V.* spare ‹*money, time*›
② *refl. V.* be unnecessary
erwachen *itr. V.; mit sein* (geh.) awake
Erwachen *das;* ~s (auch fig.) awakening
erwachsen¹ *unr. itr. V.; mit sein* (a) grow
(aus out of) ‹*rumour*› spread
(b) (sich ergeben) ‹*difficulties, tasks*› arise
erwachsen² *Adj.* grown-up *attrib.;*
~ sein be grown up
Erwachsene *der/die; adj. Dekl.* adult;
grown-up
erwägen *unr. tr. V.* consider
Erwägung *die;* ~, ~en consideration; **etw.
in** ~ **ziehen** take sth. into consideration
erwählen *tr. V.* (geh.) choose
erwähnen *tr. V.* mention
erwähnens·wert *Adj.* worth mentioning
postpos.
Erwähnung *die;* ~, ~en mention
erwärmen ① *tr. V.* heat
② *refl. V.* (warm werden) ‹*air, water*› warm up
Erwärmung *die;* ~: **eine** ~ **der
Luft/des Wassers** an increase in air/water
temperature; **bei** ~ **der Flüssigkeit** when the
liquid is heated
erwarten *tr. V.* expect; **jmdn. am Bahnhof**
~: wait for sb. at the station
Erwartung *die;* ~, ~en expectation
erwartungs-: ~**gemäß** *Adv.* as
expected; ~**voll** *Adj.* expectant
erwecken *tr. V.* (a) (auf~) wake
(b) (erregen) arouse ‹*longing, pity*›
erweichen *tr. V.* soften
erweisen ① *unr. tr. V.* (a) prove
(b) (bezeigen) **jmdm. Achtung** ~: show
respect to sb.

---
*alte Schreibung – vgl. Hinweis auf S. x

② *unr. refl. V.* **sich als etw.** ~: prove to be
sth.
erweitern ① *tr. V.* widen ‹*river, road*›;
expand ‹*library, business*›; enlarge
‹*collection*›; dilate ‹*pupil, blood vessel*›
② *refl. V.* ‹*road, river*› widen; ‹*pupil, blood
vessel*› dilate
Erweiterung *die;* ~, ~en ► ERWEITERN:
widening; expansion; enlargement; dilation
Erwerb *der;* ~[e]s (a) (Aneignung) acquisition
(b) (Kauf) purchase
erwerben *unr. tr. V.* (a) (verdienen) earn
(b) (sich aneignen) gain
(c) (kaufen) acquire
erwerbs-, Erwerbs-: ~**fähig** *Adj.*
capable of gainful employment *postpos.;* able
to work *postpos.;* ~**fähigkeit** *die* ability
to work; ~**los** *Adj.:* ► ARBEITSLOS; ~**lose**
der/die; adj. Dekl.: ► ARBEITSLOSE; ~**tätig**
Adj. gainfully employed; ~**unfähig** *Adj.*
incapable of gainful employment *postpos.;*
unable to work *postpos.*
Erwerbung *die* acquisition; (Gekauftes)
purchase
erwidern *tr. V.* (a) reply
(b) (reagieren auf) return ‹*greeting, visit*›;
reciprocate ‹*sb.'s feelings*›
Erwiderung *die;* ~, ~en (a) reply (auf
+ *Akk.* to)
(b) ► ERWIDERN B: return; reciprocation
erwiesen *Adj.* proved; proven ‹*fact*›
erwiesener·maßen *Adv.* as has been
proved
erwirken *tr. V.* obtain
erwirtschaften *tr. V.* **etw.** ~: obtain sth.
by careful management
erwischen *tr. V.* (ugs.) (a) catch ‹*culprit,
train, bus*›
(b) (greifen) grab
(c) (bekommen) manage to get
(d) (*unpers.*) **es hat ihn erwischt** (ugs.) (er ist
tot) he's bought it (sl.); (er ist krank) he's got it;
(er ist verletzt) he's been hurt; (scherzh.: er ist
verliebt) he's got it bad (coll.)
erwünscht *Adj.* wanted
erwürgen *tr. V.* strangle
Erz /ɛrts *od.* eːɐ̯ts/ *das;* ~es, ~e ore
erzählen *tr. V.* (*auch itr.*) *V.* tell ‹*joke, story*›;
jmdm. etw. ~: tell sb. sth.
Erzähler *der,* **Erzählerin** *die* storyteller;
(Autor[in]) writer [of stories]; narrative writer
Erzählung *die;* ~, ~en narration; (Bericht)
account; (Literaturw.) story
Erz-: ~**bischof** *der* archbishop;
~**bistum** *das,* ~**diözese** *die*
archbishopric; archdiocese; ~**engel** *der*
archangel
erzeugen *tr. V.* produce; generate
‹*electricity*›
Erzeuger *der;* ~s, ~ (Vater) father
Erzeugnis *das;* ~ses, ~se product

Erzeugung *die;* ~, ~en (von Lebensmitteln usw.) production; (von Industriewaren) manufacture; (Strom~) generation

Erz·feind *der,* **Erz·feindin** *die* arch enemy

erziehen *unr. tr. V.* bring up; (in der Schule) educate; **ein Kind zu Sauberkeit und Ordnung** ~: bring a child up to be clean and tidy

Erzieher *der;* ~s, ~, **Erzieherin** *die;* ~, ~nen educator; (Pädagoge) educationalist; (Lehrer) teacher

Erziehung *die;* ~, ~en upbringing; (Schul~) education

Erziehungs-: ~**berechtigte** *der/die; adj. Dekl.* parent or [legal] guardian; ~**urlaub** *der* child-rearing leave

erzielen *tr. V.* reach ⟨*agreement, compromise, speed*⟩; achieve ⟨*result, effect*⟩; make ⟨*profit*⟩; obtain ⟨*price*⟩

erzürnen (geh.) *tr. V.* anger; (stärker) incense

erzwingen *unr. tr. V.* force

es *Personalpron.; 3. Pers. Sg. Nom. u. Akk. Neutr.* **(a)** (*s. auch Gen.* **seiner**; *Dat.* **ihm**) (Sache) it; (weibliche Person) she/her; (männliche Person) he/him
(b) *ohne Bezug auf ein bestimmtes Subst., mit unpers. konstruierten Verben, als formales Satzglied* it; **ich bin es** it's me; **wir sind traurig, ihr seid es auch** we are sad, and so are you; **es sei denn, [dass]** ...: unless ...; **es ist genug!** that's enough; **es hat geklopft** there was a knock; **es klingelt** someone is ringing; **es wird schöner** the weather is improving; **es geht ihm gut/schlecht** he is well/unwell; **es wird gelacht** there is laughter; **es lässt sich aushalten** it is bearable; **er hat es gut** he has it good; **er meinte es gut** he meant well

Esche *die;* ~, ~n (Bot.) ash

Esel *der;* ~s, ~ **(a)** donkey; ass **(b)** (ugs.: Dummkopf) ass (coll.)

Esels-: ~**brücke** *die* (ugs.) mnemonic; ~**ohr** *das* (ugs.: umgeknickte Stelle) dog-ear

Eskalation *die;* ~, ~en escalation

eskalieren *tr., itr. V.* escalate

Eskapade /ɛska'paːdə/ *die;* ~, ~n escapade; (Seitensprung) amorous adventure

Eskimo *der;* ~[s], ~[s] Eskimo

Eskimo·frau *die* Eskimo woman

Eskorte *die;* ~, ~n escort

eskortieren *tr. V.* escort

Espe *die;* ~, ~n aspen

Essay /'ɛse/ *der od. das;* ~s, ~s essay

essbar, *eßbar *Adj.* edible; **nicht** ~: inedible

essen *unr. tr., itr. V.* eat; **etw. gern** ~: like sth.; **sich satt** ~: eat one's fill; **gut** ~: have a good meal; **(immer)** eat well; ~ **gehen** go out for a meal

Essen *das;* ~s, ~ (Mahlzeit) meal; (Speise) food; **[das]** ~ **machen/kochen** get/cook the meal

Essen[s]-: ~**marke** *die* meal ticket; ~**zeit** *die* mealtime

Essenz *die;* ~, ~en essence

Esser *der;* ~s, ~, **Esserin** *die;* ~, ~nen: **er ist ein schlechter Esser** he has a poor appetite

Essig *der;* ~s, ~e vinegar

Essig·gurke *die* pickled gherkin

Ess-, *Eß-: ~**kastanie** *die* sweet chestnut; ~**löffel** *der* (Suppenlöffel) soup spoon; (für Nach-, Vorspeise) dessert spoon; ~**stäbchen** *das* chopstick; ~**teller** *der* dinner plate; ~**tisch** *der* dining table; ~**waren** *Pl.* food *sing.;* ~**zimmer** *das* dining room

Establishment /ɪs'tɛblɪʃmənt/ *das;* ~s, ~s Establishment

Este *der;* ~n, ~n, **Estin** *die;* ~, ~nen Estonian

Est·land (*das*); ~s Estonia

Estragon /'ɛstragɔn/ *der;* ~s tarragon

Estrich /'ɛstrɪç/ *der;* ~s, ~e composition floor

Eszett /ɛs'tsɛt/ *das;* ~, ~ [the letter] ß

etablieren *tr. V.* establish; set up

etabliert *Adj.* established

Etablissement /etablɪs(ə)'mãː/ *das;* ~s, ~s establishment

Etage /e'taːʒə/ *die;* ~, ~n floor; storey

Etappe *die;* ~, ~n stage

Etat /e'taː/ *der;* ~s, ~s budget

etepetete /eːtəpe'teːtə/ *Adj.* (ugs.) fussy; finicky

Ethik *die;* ~, ~en **(a)** ethics *sing.* **(b)** (sittliche Normen) ethics *pl.*

ethisch *Adj.* ethical

ethnisch ① *Adj.* ethnic; ~**e Säuberung** ethnic cleansing ② *adv.* ethnically

Etikett *das;* ~[e]s, ~en *od.* ~e *od.* ~s label

Etikette *die;* ~, ~n etiquette

Etiketten·schwindel *der* (abwertend) playing with names

etikettieren *tr. V.* label

etlich... *Indefinitpron. u. unbest. Zahlwort: Sg.* quite a lot of; *Pl.* quite a few

Etüde *die;* ~, ~n (Musik) étude

Etui /ɛt'viː/ *das;* ~s, ~s case

etwa ① *Adv.* **(a)** (ungefähr) about; ~ **so groß wie** ...: about as large as ...; ~ **so** roughly like this **(b)** (beispielsweise) for example ② *Partikel* **störe ich** ~? am I disturbing you at all?

etwaig... /'ɛtva(ː)ɪg.../ *Adj.* possible

etwas *Indefinitpron.* **(a)** something; (fragend, verneinend) anything; **irgend**~: something **(b)** (Bedeutsames) **aus ihm wird** ~: he'll make something of himself **(c)** (ein Teil) some; (fragend, verneinend) ⋯⋗

any; ~ **von dem Geld** some of the money
(d) (ein wenig) a little; ~ **lauter/besser** a little
louder/better
Etymologie *die;* ~, ~n etymology
EU *Abk.* = **Europäische Union** EU
euch 1 *Dat. u. Akk. Pl. des Personalpron.*
ihr you
2 *Dat. u. Akk. Pl. des Reflexivpron. der 2.*
Pers. Pl. yourselves
euer[1] *Possessivpron.* your; **Grüße von**
eu[e]rer Helga/eu[e]rem Hans Best wishes,
Yours, Helga/Hans
euer[2] *Gen. des Personalpron.* **ihr** (geh.) **wir**
werden ~ **gedenken** we will remember you
Eule *die;* ~, ~n owl; ~**n nach Athen tragen**
carry coals to Newcastle
Eunuch *der;* ~**en**, ~**en** eunuch
Euphorie *die;* ~, ~n (bes. Med., Psych.)
euphoria
euphorisch (bes. Med., Psych.) 1 *Adj.*
euphoric
2 *adv.* euphorically
eure ▶ EUER[1]
eurer·seits ▶ DEINERSEITS
euret·wegen *Adv.* ▶ DEINETWEGEN
Euro *der;* ~[s], ~[s] euro; **50** ~: 50 euros
Eurocheque /'ɔyroʃɛk/ *der;* ~s, ~s
Eurocheque
Europa (*das*); ~s Europe
Europäer *der;* ~s, ~, **Europäerin** *die;*
~, ~**nen** European
europäisch *Adj.* European; **die**
Europäische Union the European Union
Europa-: ~**meister** *der,*
~**meisterin** *die* (Sport) European
champion; ~**meisterschaft** *die* (Sport)
(a) (Wettbewerb) European Championship;
(b) (Sieg) European title; ~**parlament**
das European Parliament; ~**pokal** *der*
(Sport) European cup; ~**rat** *der* Council
of Europe; ~**straße** *die* European long-
distance road
euro-, Euro-: ~**scheck** *der*
▶ EUROCHEQUE; ~**skeptisch** *Adj.*
Eurosceptic; ~**zone** *die* eurozone
Euter *das od. der;* ~s, ~: udder
ev. *Abk.* = **evangelisch** ev.
e.V., E.V. *Abk.* = **eingetragener**
Verein
evakuieren /evaku'iːrən/ *tr. V.* evacuate
Evakuierung *die;* ~, ~en evacuation
evangelisch /evaŋ'geːlɪʃ/ *Adj.* Protestant
Evangelium *das;* ~s, Evangelien **(a)** (auch
fig.) gospel
(b) (christl. Rel.) Gospel
Event /i'vɛnt/ *der od. das;* ~s, ~s event
Eventualität /evɛntuali'tɛːt/ *die;* ~, ~en
eventuality; contingency
eventuell 1 *Adj.* possible
2 *adv.* possibly; perhaps

---

*old spelling – see note on page x

Evolution /evolu'tsi̯oːn/ *die;* ~, ~en
evolution
evtl. *Abk.* = **eventuell**
EWG *Abk.* = **Europäische**
Wirtschaftsgemeinschaft EEC
ewig 1 *Adj.* eternal; (abwertend) never-ending
2 *adv.* eternally; for ever
Ewig·gestrige *der/die; adj. Dekl.*
(abwertend) **ein** ~**r sein** be an old reactionary
Ewigkeit *die;* ~, ~en **(a)** eternity
(b) (ugs.) **es dauert eine** ~: it takes ages (coll.)
ex *Adv.* (ugs.) **etw. ex trinken** drink sth. down
in one (coll.)
Ex- (vor Personenbez.: vormalig) ex-
exakt *Adj.* exact; precise
Exaktheit *die;* ~: precision; exactness
Examen *das;* ~s, ~ *od.* Examina
examination
exekutieren *tr. V.* **(a)** execute
(b) (österr.) ▶ PFÄNDEN
Exekution *die;* ~, ~en **(a)** execution
(b) (österr.) ▶ PFÄNDUNG
Exekutive *die;* ~, ~n (Rechtsw., Politik)
executive
Exempel *das;* ~s, ~: example
Exemplar *das;* ~s, ~e specimen; (Buch,
Zeitung usw.) copy
exemplarisch *Adj.* exemplary
exerzieren *tr., itr. V.* drill
Exhibitionist *der;* ~en, ~en,
Exhibitionistin *die;* ~, ~nen (Psych., fig.)
exhibitionist
exhibitionistisch (Psych.) 1 *Adj.*
exhibitionist
2 *adv.* **er ist** ~ **veranlagt** he has
exhibitionist tendencies
Exil *das;* ~s, ~e exile
exiliert *Adj.* exiled
Exil-regierung *die* government in exile
existentiell ▶ EXISTENZIELL
Existenz *die;* ~, ~en **(a)** existence
(b) (Lebensgrundlage) livelihood
(c) (Mensch) character
Existenz·grundlage *die* basis of one's
livelihood
existenziell *Adj.* existential; **in etw.**
(*Dat.*) **eine** ~**e Bedrohung sehen** see in sth.
a threat to one's existence
Existenz-: ~**kampf** *der* struggle for
existence; ~**minimum** *das* subsistence
level
existieren *itr. V.* exist
Exitus *der;* ~ (Med.) death
exkl. *Abk.* = **exklusiv[e]** excl.
exklusiv 1 *Adj.* exclusive
2 *adv.* exclusively
exklusive *Präp.* + *Gen.* exclusive of
Exklusiv·vertrag *der* exclusive contract
Exkommunikation *die;* ~, ~en
excommunication
Exkursion *die;* ~, ~en study trip

exotisch [1] *Adj.* exotic
[2] *adv.* exotically
expandieren *tr., itr. V.* expand
Expansion *die; ~, ~en* expansion
Expedition *die; ~, ~en* expedition
Experiment *das; ~[e]s, ~e* experiment
experimentell [1] *Adj.* experimental
[2] *adv.* experimentally
experimentieren *itr. V.* experiment
Experte *der; ~n, ~n,* **Expertin** *die; ~, ~nen* expert (für in)
Experten-system *das* (DV) expert system
explizit [1] *Adj.* explicit
[2] *adv.* ⟨describe, define⟩ explicitly
explodieren *itr. V.; mit sein* (auch fig.) explode; ⟨costs⟩ rocket
Explosion *die; ~, ~en* explosion
explosiv [1] *Adj.* (auch fig.) explosive
[2] *adv.* explosively
Exponent *der; ~en, ~en* (Math.) exponent
exponiert *Adj.* exposed
Export¹ *der; ~[e]s, ~e* export
Export² *das; ~s, ~e* (Bier) export; **zwei ~:** two export
Export-: **~artikel** *der* export; **~bier** *das* export beer
Exporteur /ɛkspɔr'tøːɐ̯/ *der; ~s, ~e,* **Exporteurin** *die; ~, ~nen* (Wirtsch.) exporter
Export-: **~firma** *die* exporter; **~handel** *der* export trade
exportieren *tr., itr. V.* export
Express-gut, *Expreß-gut *das* express freight
Expressionismus *der; ~:* expressionism *no art.*
expressionistisch *Adj.* expressionist
exquisit [1] *Adj.* exquisite
[2] *adv.* exquisitely
extern *Adj.* external

extra *Adv.* **(a)** (gesondert) ⟨pay⟩ separately
(b) (zusätzlich, besonders) extra
(c) (eigens) especially
Extra *das; ~s, ~s* extra
Extra-blatt *das* special edition
Extrakt *der; ~[e]s, ~e* extract
extra-terrestrisch *Adj.* (Astron.) extraterrestrial
extravagant /-va'gant/ *Adj.* flamboyant; flamboyantly furnished ⟨flat⟩
Extravaganz /-va'gants/ *die; ~, ~en*
(a) flamboyance
(b) *Pl.* **seine ~en** his flamboyance *sing.*
extravertiert /-vɛr'tiːɐ̯t/ *Adj.* (Psych.) extrovert[ed]
Extravertiertheit *die; ~* (Psych.) extroversion
Extra-wurst *die* (fig. ugs.) **eine ~ bekommen** get special treatment *or* special favours
extrem *Adj.* extreme
Extrem *das; ~s, ~e* extreme
Extrem-fall *der* extreme case
Extremismus *der; ~:* extremism
Extremist *der; ~en, ~en,* **Extremistin** *die; ~, ~nen* extremist
extremistisch *Adj.* extremist
Extremität /ɛkstremi'tɛːt/ *die; ~, ~en*
(a) extremity
(b) (das Extremsein) extremeness
Extrem-: **~sportart** *die* extreme sport; **~wert** *der* (Math.) extremum
Exzellenz *die; ~, ~en* Excellency
Exzentriker *der; ~s, ~,* **Exzentrikerin** *die; ~, ~nen* eccentric
exzentrisch [1] *Adj.* eccentric
[2] *adv.* eccentrically
Exzess, *Exzeß *der; Exzesses, Exzesse* excess
exzessiv /ɛkstsɛ'siːf/ [1] *Adj.* excessive
[2] *adv.* excessively

Ff

f, F /ɛf/ *das; ~, ~* **(a)** (Buchstabe) f/F
(b) (Musik) [key of] F
f. *Abk.* = **folgend** f.
Fa. *Abk.* = **Firma**
Fabel *die; ~, ~n* fable; (Kern einer Handlung) plot
fabelhaft [1] *Adj.* (ugs.: großartig) fantastic (coll.)
[2] *adv.* (ugs.) fantastically (coll.)
Fabrik *die; ~, ~en* factory
Fabrikant *der; ~en, ~en* manufacturer

Fabrikat *das; ~[e]s, ~e* product; (Marke) make
Fabrikation *die; ~:* production
Fabrikations-fehler *der* manufacturing fault; factory fault
Fabrik-: **~besitzer** *der,* **~besitzerin** *die* factory owner; **~direktor** *der,* **~direktorin** *die* works manager
fabrizieren *tr. V.* (ugs. abwertend) knock together (coll.)
fabulieren *itr. V.* invent stories; spin yarns

Fach *das;* ~[e]s, **Fächer (a)** compartment; (für Post) pigeonhole **(b)** (Studien~, Unterrichts~) subject; (Wissensgebiet) field; (Berufszweig) trade; **ein Mann vom** ~: an expert

Fach-: ~**arbeiter** *der,* ~**arbeiterin** *die* skilled worker; ~**arzt** *der,* ~**ärztin** *die* specialist (für in); ~**bereich** *der* (Hochschulw.) faculty; school; (in der Schule) department

fächer·übergreifend *Adj:*
▸ FACHÜBERGREIFEND

Fach-: ~**frau** *die* expert; ~**geschäft** *das* specialist shop; ~**hochschule** *die* college (*offering courses in a special subject*)

fachlich *Adj.* specialist ⟨*knowledge, work*⟩; technical ⟨*problem, explanation, experience*⟩

fach-, Fach-: ~**mann** *der;* *Pl.* ~**männer** *od.* ~**leute** expert; ~**terminus** *der* specialist/technical term; ~**übergreifend** ⟨1⟩ *Adj.* interdisciplinary ⟨*teaching*⟩; ⟨2⟩ *adv.* ⟨*think, argue*⟩ along interdisciplinary lines; ⟨*teach*⟩ using interdisciplinary methods; ~**werk** *das* (Bauweise) half-timbered construction; ~**werk·haus** *das* half-timbered house; ~**zeitschrift** *die* specialist/technical journal

Fackel *die;* ~, ~n torch

fade *Adj.* insipid; **ein** ~**r Beigeschmack** (fig.) a flat aftertaste

Faden *der;* ~s, **Fäden** thread; **ein** ~: a piece of thread

faden·scheinig *Adj.* threadbare; flimsy ⟨*excuse*⟩

Fagott *das;* ~[e]s, ~e bassoon

fähig *Adj.* **(a)** (begabt) able; capable **(b) zu etw.** ~ **sein** be capable of sth.

Fähigkeit *die;* ~, ~en **(a)** ability; capability; **geistige** ~**en** intellectual faculties **(b)** (Imstandesein) ability (**zu** to)

fahl *Adj.* pale; pallid; wan ⟨*light*⟩

fahnden *itr. V.* search (**nach** for)

Fahndung *die;* ~, ~en search

Fahne *die;* ~, ~n flag

Fahr·bahn *die* carriageway

Fähr·betrieb *der* ferry service; (von mehreren Fähren) ferry services *pl.*

Fähre *die;* ~, ~n ferry

fahren ⟨1⟩ *unr. itr. V.; mit sein* **(a)** (als Fahrzeuglenker) drive; (mit dem Fahrrad, Motorrad usw.) ride **(b)** (als Mitfahrer; mit öffentlichem Verkehrsmittel) go (**mit** by); (mit dem Aufzug/der Rolltreppe/der Seilbahn) take the lift (Brit.) *or* (Amer.) elevator/ escalator/cable car; (per Anhalter) hitch-hike **(c)** (reisen) go; **in Urlaub** ~: go on holiday **(d)** (los~) go; leave **(e)** ⟨*motor vehicle, train, lift, cable car*⟩ go; ⟨*ship*⟩ sail; **mein Auto fährt nicht** my car won't go

(f) (verkehren) ⟨*train etc.*⟩ run **(g)** etw. ~ **lassen** (loslassen) let sth. go; (fig.: aufgeben) abandon sth. ⟨2⟩ *unr. tr. V.* **(a)** (fortbewegen) drive ⟨*car, lorry, train, etc.*⟩; ride ⟨*bicycle, motorcycle*⟩ **(b) 50/80 km/h** ~: do 50/80 k.p.h.; **hier muss man 50 km/h** ~: you've got to keep to 50 k.p.h. here; sail ⟨*boat*⟩; **Auto** ~: drive [a car]; **Kahn** *od.* **Boot/Kanu** ~: go boating/ canoeing; **Ski** ~: ski; **U-Bahn** ~: ride on the underground (Brit.) *or* (Amer.) subway **(c)** (befördern) take

Fahrenheit: 70 Grad ~: 70 degrees Fahrenheit

*fahren|lassen ▸ FAHREN 1G

Fahrer *der;* ~s, ~: driver

Fahrerflucht *die:* **wegen** ~: for failing to stop after [being involved in] an accident; ~ **begehen** fail to stop after [being involved in] an accident

Fahrerin *die;* ~, ~nen driver

Fahr-: ~**gast** *der* passenger; ~**geld** *das* fare

fahrig *Adj.* nervous

fahr-, Fahr-: ~**karte** *die* ticket; ~**karten·automat** *der* ticket machine; ~**karten·schalter** *der* ticket window; ~**lässig** ⟨1⟩ *Adj.* negligent ⟨*behaviour*⟩; ~**lässige Tötung/Körperverletzung** (Rechtsw.) causing death/injury through [culpable] negligence; ⟨2⟩ *adv.* negligently; ~**lehrer** *der,* ~**lehrerin** *die* driving instructor

Fähr·mann *der;* *Pl.* **Fährmänner** *od.* **Fährleute** ferryman

fahr-, Fahr-: ~**plan** *der* timetable; schedule (Amer.); ~**plan·mäßig** ⟨1⟩ *Adj.* scheduled ⟨*departure, arrival*⟩; ⟨2⟩ *adv.* ⟨*depart, arrive*⟩ according to schedule, on time; ~**preis** *der* fare; ~**prüfung** *die* driving test; ~**rad** *das* bicycle; cycle; **mit dem** ~**rad fahren** cycle; ride a bicycle; ~**rad·kurier** *der,* ~**rad·kurierin** *die* bicycle *or* bike messenger; bicycle *or* bike courier; ~**rad·ständer** *der* bicycle rack; ~**schein** *der* ticket; ~**schein·automat** *der* ticket machine; ~**schein·entwerter** *der* ticket cancelling machine; ~**schule** *die* driving school; ~**spur** *die* traffic lane

fährst 2. *Pers. Sg. Präsens v.* FAHREN

Fahr-: ~**stuhl** *der* lift (Brit.); elevator (Amer.); (für Lasten) hoist; ~**stunde** *die* driving lesson

Fahrt *die;* ~, ~en **(a)** journey; **freie** ~ **haben** have a clear run; (Schiffsreise) voyage; (kurze Reise, Ausflug) trip **(b)** (Geschwindigkeit) **in voller** ~: at full speed

fährt 3. *Pers. Sg. Präsens v.* FAHREN

Fährte *die* trail; **jmds.** ~ **verfolgen** track sb.

Fahrt·kosten *Pl.* (für öffentliche Verkehrsmittel) fare/fares; (für Autoreisen) travel costs

Fahr·treppe *die* escalator

---
*alte Schreibung – vgl. Hinweis auf S. x

Fahrt·richtung *die* direction; **in** ~ **parken** park in the direction of the traffic; **die** ~ **ändern** change direction

fahr·tüchtig *Adj.* ⟨*driver*⟩ fit to drive; ⟨*vehicle*⟩ roadworthy

Fahrt-: ~**wind** *der* airflow; ~**ziel** *das* destination

Fahr-: ~**wasser** *das* shipping channel; fairway; **in ein gefährliches** ~**wasser geraten** (fig.) get on to dangerous ground; ~**werk** *das* (Flugw.) undercarriage; ~**zeit** *die* travelling time; ~**zeug** *das* vehicle; (Luft~) aircraft; (Wasser~) vessel; ~**zeug·papiere** *Pl.* vehicle documents *pl.*

fair /fɛːɐ̯/ [1] *Adj.* fair (**gegen** to)
[2] *adv.* fairly

Fäkalien /fɛːˈkaːliən/ *Pl.* faeces *pl.*

Fakten ▶ FAKTUM

faktisch [1] *Adj.* real; actual
[2] *adv.* **das bedeutet** ~ ...: it means in effect ...

Faktor *der;* ~**s,** ~**en** (auch Math.) factor

Faktum *das;* ~**s, Fakten** fact

Fakultät *die;* ~, ~**en** (Hochschulw.) faculty

Falke *der;* ~**n,** ~**n** (auch Politik fig.) hawk

Fall *der;* ~**[e]s, Fälle (a)** (Sturz) fall; **zu** ~ **kommen** have a fall; **jmdn. zu** ~ **bringen** (fig.) bring about sb.'s downfall
(b) (das Fallen) descent; **der freie** ~: free fall
(c) (Ereignis; Rechtsw., Med., Grammatik) case; (zu erwartender Umstand) eventuality; **es ist [nicht] der** ~: it is [not] the case; **gesetzt den** ~: assuming; **auf jeden** ~, **in jedem** ~, **auf alle Fälle** in any case; **auf keinen** ~: on no account

Falle *die;* ~, ~**n** (auch fig.) trap

fallen *unr. itr. V.; mit sein* **(a)** fall; **jmdn./ etw.** ~ **lassen** drop sb./sth.
(b) (hin~, stürzen) fall [over]; **über einen Stein** ~: trip over a stone
(c) ⟨*prices, light, glance, choice*⟩ fall; ⟨*temperature, water level*⟩ fall, drop; ⟨*fever*⟩ subside; ⟨*shot*⟩ be fired
(d) (im Kampf sterben) die; fall (literary)

fällen *tr. V.* **(a)** fell ⟨*tree, timber*⟩
(b) ein Urteil ~ ⟨*judge*⟩ pass sentence; ⟨*jury*⟩ return a verdict

***fallen|lassen** ▶ FALLEN A

fällig *Adj.* due

Fall·obst *das* windfalls *pl.*

Fallout /fɔːlˈlaʊt/ *der;* ~**s,** ~**s** (Kernphysik) fallout

falls *Konj.* **(a)** (wenn) if
(b) (für den Fall, dass) in case

Fall·schirm *der* parachute; **mit dem** ~ **abspringen** (im Notfall) parachute out; (als Sport) make a [parachute] jump

falsch [1] *Adj.* **(a)** (unecht, imitiert) false ⟨*teeth, plait*⟩; imitation ⟨*jewellery*⟩
(b) (gefälscht) forged; assumed ⟨*name*⟩
(c) (irrig, fehlerhaft) wrong
[2] *adv.* wrongly; **die Uhr geht** ~: the clock is wrong

fälschen *tr. V.* forge

Fälscher *der;* ~**s,** ~, **Fälscherin** *die;* ~, ~**nen** forger

Falschgeld *das* counterfeit money

fälschlich [1] *Adj.* false
[2] *adv.* falsely

Falsch·meldung *die* false report

Fälschung *die;* ~, ~**en** fake

Falt·blatt *das* leaflet; (in Zeitungen, Zeitschriften, Büchern) insert

Falte *die;* ~, ~**n (a)** crease
(b) (im Stoff) fold; (mit scharfer Kante) pleat
(c) (Haut~) wrinkle

falten [1] *tr. V.* fold; **die Hände** ~: fold one's hands
[2] *refl. V.* (auch Geol.) fold; ⟨*skin*⟩ become wrinkled

Falten·rock *der* pleated skirt

Falter *der;* ~**s,** ~, (Nacht~) moth; (Tag~) butterfly

faltig (a) *Adj.* ⟨*clothes*⟩ gathered [in folds]; wrinkled ⟨*skin, hands*⟩
(b) (zerknittert) creased

-fältig *Adj., adv.* -fold

Falt·rad *das* folding bicycle

Falz *der;* ~**es,** ~**e** fold

falzen *tr. V.* fold; seam

familiär *Adj.* **(a)** family ⟨*problems, worries*⟩
(b) (zwanglos) familiar; informal

Familie /faˈmiːliə/ *die;* ~, ~**n** family; ~ **Meyer** the Meyer family

familien-, Familien-: ~**angehörige** *der/die* member of the family; ~**feier** *die* family party; ~**freundlich** [1] *Adj.* family-friendly; [2] *adv.* in a family-friendly way; ~**grab** *das* family grave; ~**leben** *das* family life; ~**name** *der* surname; ~**planung** *die* family planning *no art.*; ~**stand** *der* marital status; ~**vater** *der:* ~**vater sein** be the father of a family; **ein guter** ~**vater** a good husband and father

Fan /fɛn/ *der;* ~**s,** ~**s** fan

Fanatiker *der;* ~**s,** ~, **Fanatikerin** *die;* ~, ~**nen** fanatic; (religiös) fanatic; zealot

fanatisch [1] *Adj.* fanatical
[2] *adv.* fanatically

fanatisieren *tr. V.* rouse to fanaticism; **der fanatisierte Mob** the fanatically excited mob

fand *1. u. 3. Pers. Sg. Prät. v.* FINDEN

Fanfare *die;* ~, ~**n** (Signal) fanfare

Fang *der;* ~**[e]s, Fänge (a)** (Tier~) trapping; (von Fischen) catching
(b) (Beute) bag; (von Fischen) catch

fangen [1] *unr. tr. V.* catch; capture ⟨*fugitive etc.*⟩; **jmdn./ein Tier gefangen halten** hold sb. prisoner/keep an animal in captivity; **jmdn. gefangen nehmen** take sb. prisoner
[2] *unr. refl. V.* **(a)** (in eine Falle geraten) be caught
(b) (wieder in die normale Lage kommen) ⋯▶

sich [gerade] noch ~: [just] manage to steady oneself

Fang·frage *die* catch question

Fantasie *die;* ~, ~n (a) imagination (b) (Produkt der ~) fantasy

fantasie·los ⒈ *Adj.* unimaginative ⒉ *adv.* unimaginatively

Fantasielosigkeit *die;* ~: lack of imagination; (Eintönigkeit) dullness

fantasieren *itr. V.* (a) indulge in fantasies, fantasize (**von** about) (b) (Med.: irrereden) talk deliriously

fantasievoll ⒈ *Adj.* imaginative ⒉ *adv.* imaginatively

fantastisch ⒈ *Adj.* (a) fantastic; ⟨*idea*⟩ divorced from reality (b) (ugs.: großartig) fantastic (coll.) ⒉ *adv.* (ugs.) fantastically (coll.)

Farb-: ~**bild** *das* (Foto) colour photo; ~**dia** *das* colour slide; ~**drucker** *der* (DV) colour printer

Farbe *die;* ~, ~n (a) colour (b) (für Textilien) dye; (zum Malen, Anstreichen) paint; ~**n mischen/auftragen** mix/apply paint

farb·echt *Adj.* colour-fast

färben ⒈ *tr. V.* dye ⒉ *refl. V.* change colour; **sich schwarz/rot** *usw.* ~: turn black/red *etc.* ⒊ *itr. V.* (ugs.: ab~) ⟨*material, blouse etc.*⟩ run

-farben *Adj.* coloured

farben-, Farben-: ~**blind** *Adj.* colour-blind; ~**froh** *Adj.* colourful; ~**pracht** *die* colourful splendour; ~**prächtig** *Adj.* vibrant with colour *postpos.*

Farb-: ~**fernsehen** *das* colour television; ~**fernseher** *der* (ugs.) colour telly (coll.) *or* television; ~**film** *der* colour film; ~**foto** *das* colour photo

farbig ⒈ *Adj.* (a) coloured (b) (bunt, auch fig.) colourful ⒉ *adv.* colourfully

-farbig *Adj.* -coloured

Farbige *der/die; adj. Dekl.* coloured man/woman; *Pl.* coloured people

farblich ⒈ *Adj.* in colour *postpos.;* as regards colour *postpos.* ⒉ *adv.* **etw.** ~ **abstimmen** match sth. in colour

farb-, Farb-: ~**los** *Adj.* (auch fig.) colourless; clear ⟨*varnish*⟩; neutral ⟨*shoe polish*⟩; ~**losigkeit** *die;* ~~ (auch fig.) colourlessness; ~**stift** *der* coloured pencil; ~**stoff** *der* (a) (Med., Biol.) pigment; (b) (für Textilien) dye; (c) (für Lebensmittel) colouring; ~**ton** *der; Pl.* ~**töne** shade; ~**tupfen,** ~**tupfer** *der* spot of colour

Färbung *die;* ~, ~en colouring

Farn *der;* ~[e]s, ~e, **Farn·kraut** *das* fern

Fasan *der;* ~[e]s, ~e[n] pheasant

Fasching *der;* ~s, ~e *od.* ~s [pre-Lent] carnival

Faschismus *der;* ~: fascism *no art.*

Faschist *der;* ~en, ~en, **Faschistin** *die;* ~, ~nen fascist

faschistisch *Adj.* fascist

faseln *itr. V.* (ugs. abwertend) drivel

Faser *die;* ~, ~n fibre

fasern *itr. V.* fray

Fass, *Faß *das;* **Fasses, Fässer** barrel; (Öl~) drum; (kleines Bier~) keg; (kleines Sherry~ usw.) cask; **Bier vom** ~: draught beer; **ein** ~ **ohne Boden** an endless drain on sb.'s resources

Fassade *die;* ~, ~n façade

fassbar, *faßbar *Adj.* (a) tangible ⟨*results*⟩ (b) (verständlich) comprehensible

Fass·bier, *Faß·bier *das* draught beer; beer on draught

fassen ⒈ *tr. V.* (a) (greifen) grasp; take hold of (b) (festnehmen) catch ⟨*thief, culprit*⟩ (c) (aufnehmen können) ⟨*hall, tank*⟩ hold (d) (begreifen) **ich kann es nicht** ~: I cannot take it in (e) **einen Entschluss** ~: make *or* take a decision ⒉ *itr. V.* (greifen) **nach etw.** ~: reach for sth.; **in etw.** (*Akk.*) ~: put one's hand in sth.

fasslich, *faßlich *Adj.* comprehensible

Fasson /fa'sõ:/ *die;* ~, ~s style; shape

Fassung *die;* ~, ~en (a) (Form) version (b) (Selbstbeherrschung) composure; **die** ~ **bewahren** keep one's composure; **die** ~ **verlieren** lose one's self-control; **jmdn. aus der** ~ **bringen** upset sb. (c) (für Glühlampen) holder

fassungs·los *Adj.* stunned

fast *Adv.* almost; nearly; ~ **nie** hardly ever

fasten *itr. V.* fast

Fast·nacht *die* carnival; ~ **feiern** celebrate Shrovetide *or* the carnival

Fastnachts-: ~**brauch** *der* Shrovetide custom; ~**dienstag** *der* Shrove Tuesday; ~**zug** *der* carnival procession

faszinieren *tr. V.* fascinate

faszinierend ⒈ *Adj.* fascinating ⒉ *adv.* fascinatingly

fatal *Adj.* (a) (peinlich, misslich) awkward (b) (verhängnisvoll) fatal

fauchen *itr. V.* ⟨*cat*⟩ hiss; ⟨*tiger, person*⟩ snarl

faul *Adj.* (a) (verdorben) rotten; bad ⟨*food, tooth*⟩; foul ⟨*water, air*⟩ (b) (träge) lazy

Fäule *die;* ~: foulness

faulen *itr. V.; meist mit sein* rot; ⟨*water*⟩ go foul; ⟨*meat, fish*⟩ go off

faulenzen *itr. V.* laze about; loaf about (derog.)

Faulenzer *der;* ~s, ~, **Faulenzerin** *die;* ~, ~nen idler; lazybones *sing.* (coll.)
Faulheit *die;* ~: laziness
faulig *Adj.* stagnating ⟨*water*⟩; ~ schmecken/riechen taste/smell off
Fäulnis *die;* ~: rottenness
Faul-: ~**pelz** *der* (fam.) lazybones *sing.* (coll.); ~**tier** *das* (a) (Zool.) sloth; (b) (ugs.: Faulenzer[in]) ▶ ~PELZ
Fauna *die;* ~, **Faunen** (Zool.) fauna
Faust *die;* ~, **Fäuste** fist; **eine ~ machen** clench one's fist; **das passt wie die ~ aufs Auge** (ugs.) (passt nicht) that clashes horribly; (passt) that matches perfectly; **auf eigene ~:** on one's own initiative
Fäustchen *das;* ~s, ~: **sich** (*Dat.*) **ins ~ lachen** laugh up one's sleeve
faust·dick *Adj.* as thick as a man's fist *postpos.;* (fig.) barefaced ⟨*lie*⟩
Fäustling *der;* ~s, ~e mitten
Faust·regel *die* rule of thumb
Favorit /favo'ri:t/ *der;* ~en, ~en, **Favoritin** *die;* ~, ~nen favourite
Fax *das;* ~, ~[e] fax
Fax·anschluss, ***Fax·anschluß** *der* fax line
faxen *tr. V.* fax
Faxen *Pl.* (ugs.) fooling around
Fax-: ~**gerät** *das* fax machine; ~**nachricht** *der* fax message; ~**nummer** *die* fax number
Fazit *das;* ~s, ~s *od.* ~e result
FCKW *Abk.* = **Fluorchlorkohlenwasserstoff** CFC
FCKW-frei *Adj.* CFC-free
FDP, F.D.P. *Abk.* = **Freie Demokratische Partei**
Feature /'fi:tʃɐ/ *das;* ~s, ~s (Rundf., Fers., Zeitungsw.) feature
Februar *der;* ~[s], ~e February
fechten *unr. itr., tr. V.* fence
Fechter *der;* ~s, ~, **Fechterin** *die;* ~, ~nen fencer
Feder *die;* ~, ~n (a) (Vogel~) feather (b) (zum Schreiben) nib (c) (Technik) spring
feder-, Feder-: ~**ball** *der* (a) (Spiel) badminton; (b) (Ball) shuttlecock; ~**bett** *das* duvet (Brit.); stuffed quilt (Amer.); ~**führend** *Adj.* in charge *postpos.;* ~**gabel** *die* (am Fahrrad) suspension forks *pl.;* ~**halter** *der* fountain pen; ~**leicht** *Adj.* ⟨person⟩ as light as a feather; featherweight ⟨object⟩; ~**lesen** *das:* **nicht viel ~lesen[s] mit jmdm./etw. machen** give sb./sth. short shrift
federn ① *itr. V.* ⟨springboard, floor, etc.⟩ be springy ② *tr. V.* (mit einer Federung versehen) spring; **das Bett ist gut gefedert** the bed is well-sprung

Federung *die;* ~, ~en (Kfz-W.) suspension
Fee *die;* ~, ~n fairy
Feedback /'fi:dbæk/ *das;* ~s, ~s feedback
Fege-feuer *das* purgatory
fegen ① *tr. V.* (a) (bes. nordd.: säubern) sweep (b) (schnell entfernen) brush ② *itr. V.* sweep up
Fehde *die;* ~, ~n feud
Fehde·hand·schuh *der* **jmdm. den ~ hinwerfen** throw down the gauntlet to sb.
fehl *Adv.* **~ am Platz[e] sein** be out of place
Fehl·anzeige *die:* ~**!** (ugs.) no chance! (coll.)
fehlen *itr. V.* (a) (nicht vorhanden sein) **ihm fehlt das Geld** he has no money (b) (ausbleiben) be absent (c) (verschwunden sein) be missing; **in der Kasse fehlt Geld** money is missing from the till (d) (vermisst werden) **er/das wird mir ~:** I shall miss him/that (e) (erforderlich sein) be needed; **ihm ~ noch zwei Punkte zum Sieg** he needs only two points to win; **es fehlte nicht viel, und ich wäre eingeschlafen** I all but fell asleep (f) *unpers.* (mangeln) **es fehlt an Lehrern** there is a lack of teachers (g) (krank sein) **was fehlt Ihnen?** what seems to be the matter?; **fehlt dir etwas?** is there something wrong?
Fehl-: ~**entscheidung** *die* wrong decision; ~**entwicklung** *die* abortive development
Fehler *der;* ~s, ~ (a) (Irrtum) mistake; error; (Sport) fault (b) (schlechte Eigenschaft) fault
fehler·frei *Adj.* faultless
fehlerhaft *Adj.* faulty; defective; imperfect ⟨pronunciation⟩
Fehler·quelle *die* source of error
fehl-, Fehl-: ~**geburt** *die* miscarriage; ~**investition** *die* (bes. Wirtsch.) bad investment; ~**planung** *die* [piece of] bad planning *no art.;* ~**schlag** *der* failure; ~|**schlagen** *unr. itr. V.; mit sein* fail; ~**start** *der* (Leichtathletik) false start; ~**tritt** *der* (fig. geh.) slip; ~**urteil** *das* (a) (Rechtsw.) **ein ~urteil fällen** ⟨jury⟩ return a wrong verdict; ⟨judge⟩ pass a wrong judgement; (b) (falsche Beurteilung) error of judgement; ~**verhalten** *das* (fehlerhaftes Verhalten) incorrect conduct; ~**zündung** *die* (Technik) misfire
Feier *die;* ~, ~n (a) (Veranstaltung) party; (aus festlichem Anlass) celebration (b) (Zeremonie) ceremony
Feier-abend *der* (Arbeitsschluss) finishing time; **nach ~:** after work; **~ machen** finish work
feierlich ① *Adj.* ceremonial ⟨act etc.⟩; solemn ⟨silence⟩ ② *adv.* solemnly; ceremoniously ⋯▷

Feierlichkeit *die;* ~, ~en (a) solemnity
(b) (Veranstaltung) celebration

feiern 1 *tr. V.* (a) celebrate ⟨*birthday,
wedding, etc.*⟩
(b) acclaim ⟨*artist, sportsman, etc.*⟩
2 *itr. V.* celebrate

Feier·tag *der* holiday; **ein gesetzlicher/
kirchlicher** ~: a public holiday/religious
festival

feig[e] 1 *Adj.* cowardly
2 *adv.* in a cowardly way

Feige *die;* ~, ~n fig

Feigheit *die;* ~: cowardice

Feigling *der;* ~s, ~e coward

Feile *die;* ~, ~n file

feilen *tr., itr. V.* file

feilschen *itr. V.* haggle (**um** over)

fein 1 *Adj.* (a) fine; finely-ground ⟨*flour*⟩;
finely-granulated ⟨*sugar*⟩
(b) (hochwertig) high-quality ⟨*fruit, soap, etc.*⟩;
fine ⟨*silver, gold, etc.*⟩; fancy ⟨*cakes, pastries,
etc.*⟩
(c) (ugs.: erfreulich) great (coll.)
(d) **sich** ~ **machen** (ugs.) dress up
2 *adv.* ~ [**he**]**raus sein** (ugs.) be sitting
pretty (coll.)

Feind *der;* ~[e]s, ~e, **Feindin** *die;* ~,
~nen enemy

feindlich 1 *Adj.* (a) hostile
(b) (Milit.) enemy ⟨*attack, activity*⟩
2 *adv.* in a hostile manner

Feindschaft *die;* ~, ~en enmity

feind·selig *Adj.* hostile

Feind·seligkeit *die;* ~, ~en hostility;
~en (Milit.) hostilities

Feinheit *die;* ~, ~en (a) fineness; delicacy
(b) (Nuance) subtlety

fein-, Fein-: ~**kost·geschäft** *das*
delicatessen; **~*|**machen** ▸ FEIN 1D;
~**schmecker** *der;* ~~s, ~~,
~**schmeckerin** *die;* ~~, ~~nen
gourmet; ~**sinnig** *Adj.* sensitive and
subtle; ~**staub** *der* particulates *pl.;*
~**waschmittel** *das* mild detergent

feist *Adj.* (meist abwertend) fat

Feld *das;* ~[e]s, ~er (a) field
(b) (Sport: Spiel~) pitch; field
(c) (auf Formularen) box; space; (auf Brettspielen)
space; (auf dem Schachbrett) square
(d) (Tätigkeitsbereich) field; sphere

Feld-: ~**herr** *der* (veralt.) commander;
~**marschall** *der* Field Marshal; ~**salat**
der corn salad; ~**stecher** *der;* ~~s, ~~
binoculars *pl.;* ~**versuch** *der* (Wissensch.)
field experiment; ~**webel** *der;* ~~s, ~~
(Milit.) sergeant; ~**weg** *der* path; track;
~**zug** *der* (Milit., fig.) campaign

Felge *die;* ~, ~n [wheel] rim

Fell *das;* ~[e]s, ~e (a) (Haarkleid) fur; (Pferde~,
Hunde~, Katzen~) coat; (Schaf~) fleece

(b) (Material) fur
(c) (abgezogen) hide; **ein dickes** ~ **haben**
(ugs.) be thick-skinned

Fels *der;* ~en, ~en rock

Felsen *der;* ~s, ~: rock; (an der Steilküste) cliff

felsen-, Felsen-: ~**fest** *Adj.* firm;
unshakeable ⟨*opinion, belief*⟩; ~**küste** *die*
rocky coast *or* coastline

felsig *Adj.* rocky

Fels-: ~**spalte** *die* crevice [in the rock];
~**wand** *die* rock face

feminin *Adj.* feminine

Feminismus *der;* ~: feminism *no art.*

Feminist *der;* ~en, ~en, **Feministin**
die; ~, ~nen feminist

Fenchel *der;* ~s fennel

Fenster *das;* ~s, ~: window

Fenster-: ~**bank** *die; Pl.* ~bänke
window sill; ~**laden** *der* [window] shutter;
~**leder** *das* wash leather; ~**platz** *der*
window seat; ~**putzer** *der;* ~~s, ~~,
~**putzerin** *die;* ~~, ~~nen window
cleaner; ~**rahmen** *der* window frame;
~**scheibe** *die* window pane

Ferien /'feːriən/ *Pl.* holiday[s *pl.*] (Brit.);
vacation (Amer.); **in die** ~ **fahren** go on
holiday/vacation; ~ **haben** have a *or* be on
holiday/vacation

Ferien-: ~**arbeit** *die* vacation work;
eine ~**arbeit** a vacation job; ~**haus**
das holiday house (Brit.); vacation house
(Amer.); ~**job** *der* vacation job; ~**ort**
der holiday resort (Brit.); vacation resort
(Amer.); ~**paradies** *das* holiday[maker's]
paradise (Brit.); vacationer['s] paradise
(Amer.); ~**wohnung** *die* holiday flat *or*
apartment (Brit.); vacation apartment (Amer.)

Ferkel *das;* ~s, ~: piglet

fern 1 *Adj.* distant; **jmdn./etw.** ~ **halten**
keep sb./sth. away
2 *adv.* ~ **von der Heimat** far from home
3 *Präp. mit Dat.* (geh.) far [away] from

fern-, Fern-: ~**bedienung** *die* remote
control; ~|**bleiben** *unr. itr. V.; mit sein*
(geh.) stay away

Ferne *die;* ~, ~n distance

ferner *Adv.* furthermore

fern-, Fern-: ~**fahrer** *der,* ~**fahrerin**
die long-distance lorry driver (Brit.) *or*
(Amer.) trucker; ~**flug** *der* long-distance *or*
long-haul flight; ~**gelenkt** *Adj.* remote-
controlled; ~**gespräch** *das* long-distance
call; ~**gesteuert** *Adj.* ▸ ~GELENKT;
~**glas** *das* binoculars *pl.;* *~|**halten**
▸ FERN 1; ~**heizung** *die* district
heating system; ~**lenkung** *die* remote
control; ~**licht** *das* (Kfz-W.) full beam;
~**melde·amt** *das* telephone exchange;
~**ost:** **in/aus/nach** ~**ost** in/from/to the
Far East; ~**rohr** *das* telescope; ~**ruf** *der*
telephone number; ~**schreiben** *das*
telex [message]; ~**schreiber** *der* telex
[machine]

---

*alte Schreibung – vgl. Hinweis auf S. x

Fernseh-: ~**ansprache** die television address; (Brit.) or (Amer.) antenna; ~**antenne** die television aerial (Brit.) or (Amer.) antenna; ~**apparat** der television [set]; ~**bericht** der television report

fern|sehen unr. itr. V. watch television

Fern·sehen das; ~s television; im ~: on television

Fern·seher der; ~s, ~ (ugs.) telly (Brit. coll.); TV

Fernseh-: ~**gebühren** Pl. television licence fee; ~**gerät** das television [set]; ~**journalist** der, ~**journalistin** die television reporter; ~**kanal** der television channel; ~**nachrichten** Pl. television news; ~**programm** das (a) (Sendungen) television programmes pl.; (b) (Kanal) television channel; (c) (Blatt, Programmheft) television [programme] guide; ~**publikum** das viewing public; ~**sender** der television transmitter; ~**sendung** die television programme; ~**serie** die television series; ~**spiel** das television play; ~**star** der television star; ~**studio** das television studio; ~**zuschauer** der, ~**zuschauerin** die television viewer

Fern·sicht die (Aussicht) view; (gute Sicht) visibility

Fern·sprecher der telephone

Fernsprech-: ~**gebühren** Pl. telephone charges; ~**teilnehmer** der, ~**teilnehmerin** die telephone subscriber; telephone customer (Amer.)

Fern-: ~**steuerung** die (Technik) remote control; ~**straße** die major road; ~**studium** das correspondence course; ≈ Open University course (Brit.); ~**unterricht** der correspondence courses pl.; ~**verkehr** der long-distance traffic; ~**zug** der long-distance train

Ferse die; ~, ~n heel

fertig Adj. (a) finished ⟨manuscript, picture, etc.⟩; das Essen ist ~: lunch/dinner etc. is ready; [mit etw.] ~ sein/werden have finished/finish [sth.]; etw. ~ machen finish sth.
(b) (bereit, verfügbar) ready (zu, für for)
(c) (ugs.: erschöpft) shattered (coll.); jmdn. ~ machen (erschöpfen) wear sb. out; (schikanieren) wear sb. down; (deprimieren) get sb. down
(d) etw. ~ bekommen od. bringen od. (ugs.) kriegen manage sth; etw. ~ stellen complete sth.

fertig-, Fertig-: ~**bau** der; Pl. ~~ten prefabricated building; ~**bauweise** die prefabricated construction; prefabrication; *~|**bringen** ▶ FERTIG D

fertigen tr. V. make

Fertig-: ~**gericht** das ready-to-serve meal; ~**haus** das prefabricated house; prefab (coll.)

Fertigkeit die; ~, ~en skill

fertig-, Fertig-: *~|**machen** ▶ FERTIG A, C; *~|**stellen** ▶ FERTIG D; ~**stellung** die completion

Fertigung die; ~: production; manufacture

Fessel die; ~, ~n fetter; shackle; (Kette) chain

fesseln tr. V. (a) tie up; ans Bett/ans Haus/an den Rollstuhl gefesselt sein (fig.) be confined to [one's] bed/tied to the house/confined to a wheelchair
(b) (faszinieren) ⟨book⟩ grip; ⟨work, person⟩ fascinate

fesselnd [1] Adj. compelling
[2] adv. compellingly

fest [1] Adj. (a) (nicht flüssig od. gasförmig) solid
(b) firm ⟨bandage⟩; sound ⟨sleep⟩; sturdy ⟨shoes⟩; strong ⟨fabric⟩; solid ⟨house, shell⟩; steady ⟨voice⟩; der ~en Überzeugung sein, dass …: be of the firm opinion that …
(c) (dauernd) permanent ⟨address⟩; fixed ⟨income⟩
[2] adv. (a) ⟨tie, grip⟩ tight[ly]
(b) (ugs. auch ~e) ⟨work⟩ with a will; ⟨eat⟩ heartily; ⟨sleep⟩ soundly
(c) ⟨believe, be convinced⟩ firmly; sich auf jmdn./etw. ~ verlassen rely one hundred per cent on sb./sth.
(d) (endgültig) firmly; etw. ~ vereinbaren come to a firm arrangement about sth.
(e) (auf Dauer) permanently; ~ befreundet sein be close friends; (als Paar) be going steady

Fest das; ~[e]s, ~e (a) celebration; (Party) party
(b) (Feiertag) festival; frohes ~! happy Christmas/Easter!

fest-, Fest-: ~**akt** der ceremony; ~|**binden** unr. tr. V. tie [up]; ~|**bleiben** unr. itr. V.; mit sein stand firm; ~**essen** das banquet; ~|**fahren** unr. itr., refl. V. (itr. V. mit sein) get stuck; (fig.) get bogged down; ~|**halten** [1] unr. tr. V. (a) (halten, packen) hold on to; (b) (nicht weiterleiten) withhold ⟨letter, parcel, etc.⟩; (c) (verhaftet haben) hold, detain ⟨suspect⟩; [2] unr. refl. V. sich an jmdm./etw. ~halten hold on to sb./sth.

festigen [1] tr. V. strengthen; consolidate ⟨position⟩
[2] refl. V. ⟨friendship, ties⟩ become stronger

Festival /'fɛstival/ das; ~s, ~s festival

fest-, Fest-: ~|**kleben** tr., itr. V.; mit sein stick (an + Dat. to); ~**land** das (Kontinent) continent; (im Gegensatz zu den Inseln) mainland; ~|**legen** tr. V. (a) fix ⟨time, deadline, price⟩; arrange ⟨programme⟩; (b) (verpflichten) sich [auf etw. (Akk.)] ~legen [lassen] commit oneself [to sth.]; jmdn. [auf etw. (Akk.)] ~legen tie sb. down [to sth.]

festlich [1] Adj. festive ⟨atmosphere⟩; formal ⟨dress⟩
[2] adv. festively; formally

fest-, Fest-: ~|**machen** tr. V. (a) (befestigen) fix; (b) (fest vereinbaren) arrange ⟨meeting etc.⟩; ~|**nageln** tr. V. ⋯⋗

(a) (befestigen) nail **(an** + *Dat.* to); **(b)** (ugs.: festlegen) jmdn. **[auf etw.** (*Akk.*)] **~nageln** tie sb. down [to sth.]; **~nahme** *die;* ~~, ~~n arrest; **bei seiner** ~nahme when he was/is arrested; **~nehmen** *unr. tr. V.* arrest; **~platte** *die* (DV) fixed disk; **~rede** *die* speech; **~|schnallen** *tr. V.* tie (an + *Dat.* to); **~|sitzen** *unr. itr. V.* be stuck; **~|stehen** *unr. itr. V.* ⟨*order, appointment, etc.*⟩ have been fixed; ⟨*decision*⟩ be definite; ⟨*fact*⟩ be certain; **~|stellen** *tr. V.* **(a)** establish ⟨*identity, age, facts*⟩; **(b)** (wahrnehmen) detect; diagnose ⟨*illness*⟩; **~stellung** *die* **(a)** establishment; **(b)** (Wahrnehmung) realization; **die ~stellung machen, dass ...**: realize that ...

Fẹst·tag *der* holiday; (Ehrentag) special day

Fẹstung *die;* ~, **~en** fortress

fẹst-, Fẹst-: **~zeit** *die* holiday (Brit.) *or* (Amer.) vacation [period]; **~zelt** *das* marquee; **~|ziehen** *unr. tr. V.* pull tight

Fẹte *die;* ~, **~n** (ugs.) party

fẹtt ① *Adj.* **(a)** fatty ⟨*food*⟩; **~er Speck** fat bacon
(b) (sehr dick) fat
(c) (Druckw.) bold
② *adv.* **(a)** **~ essen** eat fatty foods
(b) **~ gedruckt** bold

Fẹtt *das;* ~[e]s, **~e** fat; **~ ansetzen** ⟨*animal*⟩ fatten up; ⟨*person*⟩ put on weight

fẹtt-, Fẹtt-: **~absaugung** *die* liposuction; **~arm** *Adj.* low-fat ⟨*food*⟩; low in fat *pred.;* **~auge** *das* speck of fat; **~creme** *die* enriched [skim] cream; **~druck** *der* bold type; **~fleck[en]** *der* grease mark; **~gedruckt* ▸ FETT 2B; **~gehalt** *der* fat content

fẹttig *Adj.* greasy

fẹtt-, Fẹtt-: **~leibig** *Adj.* obese; **~leibigkeit** *die;* ~~: obesity; **~näpfchen** *das:* **ins ~näpfchen treten** (scherzh.) put one's foot in it; **~polster** *das* subcutaneous fat *no indef. art.;* fat pad; **~reich** *Adj.* high-fat; **~säure** *die* (Chemie) fatty acid; **~wanst** *der* (salopp abwertend) fatso (coll.)

Fẹtus *der;* ~ *od.* **~ses, ~se** *od.* **Fẹten** (Med.) foetus

Fẹtzen *der;* ~s, ~: scrap

feucht *Adj.* damp; humid ⟨*climate*⟩

feucht·fröhlich *Adj.* (ugs. scherzh.) merry ⟨*company*⟩; boozy (coll.) ⟨*evening*⟩

Feuchtigkeit *die* moisture

Feuchtigkeits·creme *die* (Kosmetik) moisturizing cream; moisturizer

feucht-: **~kalt** *Adj.* cold and damp; **~warm** *Adj.* muggy

feudal *Adj.* **(a)** feudal ⟨*system*⟩
(b) aristocratic ⟨*regiment etc.*⟩
(c) (ugs.: vornehm) plush ⟨*hotel etc.*⟩

Feuer *das;* ~s, ~ **(a)** fire; **jmdm. ~ geben** give sb. a light
(b) (Brand) fire; blaze; **~! fire!**
(c) (Milit.) **das ~ einstellen** cease fire

feuer-, Feuer-: **~alarm** *der* fire alarm; **~eifer** *der* enthusiasm; zest; **~fest** *Adj.* heat-resistant ⟨*dish, plate*⟩; fireproof ⟨*material*⟩; **~gefährlich** *Adj.* [in]flammable; **~holz** *das* firewood; **~leiter** *die* (bei Häusern) fire escape; (beim ~wehrauto) [fireman's] ladder; **~löscher** *der;* ~s, ~: fire extinguisher; **~melder** *der;* ~s, ~: fire alarm

feuern ① *tr. V.* **(a)** (ugs.: entlassen) fire (coll.); sack (coll.)
(b) (ugs.: schleudern, werfen) fling
② *itr. V.* (Milit.) fire **(auf** + *Akk.* at)

feuer-, Feuer-: **~rot** *Adj.* fiery red; **~schlucker** *der,* **~schluckerin** *die;* ~~, ~~nen fire-eater; **~sirene** *die* fire siren; **~stein** *der* flint; **~versicherung** *die* fire insurance; **~waffe** *die* firearm; **~wehr** *die;* ~~, ~~en fire service; **~wehr·auto** *das* fire engine; **~wehr·mann** *der; Pl.* **~männer** *od.* **~leute** fireman; **~wehr·wagen** *der* fire engine; **~werk** *das* firework display; (~werkskörper) fireworks *pl.;* **~werks·körper** *der* firework; **~zeug** *das* lighter

Feuilleton /fœjə'tõː/ *das;* ~s, **~s** arts section

feurig *Adj.* fiery

ff. *Abk.* = **folgende [Seiten]** ff.

Ffm. *Abk.* = **Frankfurt am Main**

Fiaker /'fi̯akɐ/ *der;* ~s, ~ (österr.) cab

Fiasko *das;* ~s, **~s** fiasco

Fibel *die;* ~, **~n** reader; primer

ficht /fɪçt/ *Imperativ Sg. u. 3. Pers. Sg. Präsens v.* FECHTEN

Fichte *die;* ~, **~n** spruce

ficken *tr., itr. V.* (vulg.) fuck (coarse)

fick[e]rig *Adj.* (landsch.: nervös) nervous

fidel *Adj.* (ugs.) jolly

Fieber *das;* ~s [high] temperature; (über 38°C) fever; **~ haben** have a [high] temperature/a fever; **bei jmdm. ~ messen** take sb.'s temperature

fieber·frei *Adj.* ⟨*person*⟩ free from fever

fieberhaft *Adj.* feverish

fieberig *Adj.* feverish

fiebern *itr. V.* have a temperature

Fieber·thermometer *das* [clinical] thermometer

fiebrig *Adj.* feverish

Fiedel *die;* ~, **~n** (veralt., scherzh.) fiddle

fiel *1. u. 3. Pers. Sg. Prät. v.* FALLEN

fiepen *itr. V.* ⟨*dog*⟩ whimper; ⟨*bird*⟩ cheep

fies ① *Adj.* (ugs.) nasty ⟨*person, character*⟩
② *adv.* in a nasty way

Figur *die;* ~, **~en (a)** (einer Frau) figure; (eines Mannes) physique;
(b) (Bildwerk) figure

**old spelling – see note on page x

(c) (geometrisches Gebilde) shape
(d) (Spielstein) piece
(e) (Persönlichkeit) figure
(f) (literarische Gestalt) character
fiktiv *Adj.* fictitious
Filet /fi'le:/ *das;* ~s, ~s fillet
Filiale *die;* ~, ~n branch
Filigran *das;* ~s, ~e filigree
Film *der;* ~[e]s, ~e (a) (Fot.) film
(b) (Kino~) film; movie (Amer. coll.)
Filme·macher *der,* **Filme·macherin**
die film-maker
filmen *tr., itr. V.* film
Film-: ~**festival** *das* film festival;
~**festspiele** *Pl.* film festival *sing.;*
~**industrie** *die* film industry;
~**kamera** *die* film camera;
(Schmalfilmkamera) cine camera; ~**kunst**
die cinematic art; ~**musik** *die* film
music; (eines einzelnen ~s) theme music;
~**plakat** *das* film poster; ~**produzent**
der, ~**produzentin** *die* film producer;
~**regisseur** *der,* ~**regisseurin** *die*
film director; ~**schauspieler** *der,*
~**schauspielerin** *die* film actor; ~**star**
der film star
Filter *der;* ~s, ~: filter
filtern *tr. V.* filter
Filter-: ~**papier** *das* filter paper;
~**zigarette** *die* [filter-]tipped cigarette
Filz *der;* ~es, ~e felt
filzen *tr. V.* (ugs.: durchsuchen) search ⟨room,
car, etc.⟩; frisk ⟨person⟩
Filz·stift *der* felt-tip pen
Fimmel *der;* ~s, ~: einen ~ für etw. haben
(ugs. abwertend) have a thing about sth. (coll.)
Finale *das;* ~s, ~[s] (a) (Sport) final
(b) finale
Finalist *der;* ~en, ~en, **Finalistin** *die;*
~, ~nen (Sport) finalist
Finanz *die;* ~: finance *no art.*
Finanz-: ~**amt** *das* (a) (Behörde) ≈
Inland Revenue; **(b)** (Gebäude) tax office;
~**beamte** *der,* ~**beamtin** *die* tax officer
Finanzen *Pl.* finances
finanziell /finan'tsi̯ɛl/ *Adj.* financial
finanzieren *tr. V.* finance
Finanzierung *die;* ~, ~en financing
finanz-, Finanz-: ~**kraft** *die* financial
strength; ~**kräftig** *Adj.* financially
powerful; ~**lage** *die* financial situation;
~**minister** *der,* ~**ministerin** *die*
minister of finance; ~**politik** *die* (des
Staates, eines Unternehmens) financial policy;
(allgemeine) politics of finance
Findel·kind *das* foundling
finden *unr. tr. V.* (a) find
(b) Freunde ~: make friends
(c) (einschätzen, beurteilen) **etw. gut/richtig**
~: think sth. is good/right; **wie ~ Sie dieses
Bild?** what do you think of this painting?
Finder *der;* ~s, ~: finder

Finder·lohn *der* reward [for finding sth.]
findig *Adj.* resourceful
Findling *der;* ~s, ~e (a) (Findelkind)
foundling
(b) (Geol.) erratic block
fing *1. u. 3. Pers. Sg. Prät. v.* FANGEN
Finger *der;* ~s, ~: finger; **lange ~ machen**
(ugs.) get itchy fingers
Finger-: ~**abdruck** *der* fingerprint;
~**fertigkeit** *die* dexterity;
~**handschuh** *der* glove [with fingers];
~**hut** *der* thimble; ~**kuppe** *die* fingertip
fingern *itr. V.* fiddle; **an etw.** (*Dat.*)
~: fiddle with sth.; **nach etw.** ~: fumble
[around] for sth.
Finger-: ~**nagel** *der* fingernail;
~**spitze** *die* fingertip;
~**spitzen·gefühl** *das* feeling
fingieren *tr. V.* fake; **ein fingierter Name** a
false name
Fink *der;* ~en, ~en finch
Finne *der;* ~n, ~n, **Finnin** *die;* ~, ~nen
Finn
finnisch *Adj.* Finnish
Finnland (*das*); ~s Finland
finster ① *Adj.* dark; dimly-lit ⟨*pub, district*⟩
② *adv.* jmdn. ~ ansehen give sb. a black look
Finsternis *die;* ~, ~se darkness; (auch
bibl., fig.) dark
Finte *die;* ~, ~n trick; **jmdn. durch eine
~ täuschen** deceive sb. by trickery
Firlefanz *der;* ~es (ugs. abwertend) frippery;
trumpery
firm *Adj.* **in etw.** (*Dat.*) ~ **sein** be well up
in sth.
Firma *die;* ~, Firmen firm; company
Firmen-: ~**inhaber** *der,* ~**inhaberin**
die owner of the/a company; ~**schild** *das*
company's name plate; ~**zeichen** *das*
trademark
Firmung *die;* ~, ~en confirmation
First *der;* ~[e]s, ~e ridge
Fisch *der;* ~[e]s, ~e (a) fish; [**fünf**] ~e
fangen catch [five] fish; **kleine** ~e (fig.) small
fry
(b) (Astrol.) **die** ~e Pisces; **er ist [ein]** ~: he is
a Piscean
fischen ① *tr. V.* (a) fish for
(b) (ugs.) **etw. aus etw.** ~: fish sth. out of sth.
② *itr. V.* fish; **nach etw.** ~: fish for sth.
Fischer *der;* ~s, ~: fisherman
Fischer-: ~**boot** *das* fishing boat;
~**dorf** *das* fishing village
Fischerei *die;* ~: fishing
Fischerin *die;* ~, ~nen fisherwoman
Fisch-: ~**fang** *der;* **vom** ~**fang leben**
make a/one's living by fishing; **auf**
~**fang gehen** go fishing; ~**geschäft**
das fishmonger's [shop] (Brit.); fish store
(Amer.); ~**grät[en]·muster** *das* (Textilw.)
herringbone pattern; ~**industrie**
die fishing industry; ~**konserve** *die* ···❖

canned fish; ~**kutter** *der* fishing trawler;
~**stäbchen** *das* (Kochk.) fish finger;
~**sterben** *das* death of the fish
Fiskus *der;* ~, Fisken *od.* ~se Government
(*as managing the State finances*)
Fitness·zentrum *das* fitness centre
Fittich *der;* ~[e]s, ~e (dichter.) wing
fix [1] *Adj.* (ugs.) quick; **ein** ~**er Bursche** a
bright lad; ~ **und fertig** quite finished; (völlig
erschöpft) completely shattered (coll.)
[2] *adv.* (ugs.) quickly; **mach** ~**!** hurry up!
fixen *itr. V.* (Drogenjargon) fix (sl.)
Fixer *der;* ~s, ~, **Fixerin** *die;* ~, ~nen
(Drogenjargon) fixer
fixieren *tr. V.* (a) fix one's gaze on; jmdn.
scharf ~: gaze sharply at sb.
(b) (geh.: schriftlich niederlegen) take down
Fix·stern *der* (Astron.) fixed star
Fjord /fjɔrt/ *der;* ~[e]s, ~e fiord
FKK /ɛf ka: 'ka:/ *Abk.*
= **Freikörperkultur** nudism *no art.;*
naturism *no art.*
FKK-Strand *der* nudist beach
flach *Adj.* (a) flat
(b) (niedrig) low
(c) (nicht tief) shallow ⟨water, dish⟩
Fläche *die;* ~, ~n (a) area
(b) (Ober~) surface
(c) (Geom.) area; (einer dreidimensionalen Figur)
side
Flächen-: ~**inhalt** *der* area; ~**maß**
das unit of square measure; ~**staat** *der*
territorial state
flach, Flach-: ~|**fallen** *itr. V.; mit*
sein (ugs.) ⟨trip⟩ fall through; ⟨event⟩ be
cancelled; ~**land** *das* lowland
Flachs *der;* ~es flax
flachsen *itr. V.* mit jmdm. ~ (ugs.) joke
with sb.
Flach·zange *die* flat tongs *pl.*
flackern *itr. V.* flicker
Fladen *der;* ~s, ~: *flat, round unleavened*
cake made with oat or barley flour
Flagge *die;* ~, ~n flag
flaggen *itr. V.* put out the flags
flambieren *tr. V.* (Kochk.) flambé
Flamme *die;* ~, ~n (a) flame
(b) (Brennstelle) burner
Flanell *der;* ~s, ~e flannel
flanieren *itr. V.; mit Richtungsangabe mit*
sein stroll
Flanke *die;* ~, ~n (a) (Weiche) flank
(b) (Ballspiele: Vorlage) centre
(c) (Teil des Spielfeldes) wing
Flasche *die;* ~, ~n bottle; **eine** ~ **Wein** a
bottle of wine; **dem Kind die** ~ **geben** feed
the baby
Flaschen-: ~**bier** *das* bottled beer;
~**öffner** *der* bottle-opener; ~**post** *die*
message in a/the bottle; ~**zug** *der* block

and tackle
flatterhaft *Adj.* fickle
flattern *itr. V.; mit Richtungsangabe mit*
sein flutter
flau *Adj.* (a) slack ⟨breeze⟩
(b) (leicht übel) queasy ⟨feeling⟩
Flaum *der;* ~[e]s fuzz
Flausch *der;* ~[e]s, ~e brushed wool
flauschig *Adj.* fluffy
Flause *die;* ~, ~n; *meist Pl.* (ugs.) **er hat nur**
~**n im Kopf** he can never think of anything
sensible
Flaute *die;* ~, ~n (a) (Seemannsspr.) calm
(b) (Kaufmannsspr.) fall[-off] in trade
Flechte *die;* ~, ~n (a) (Bot.) lichen
(b) (Med.) eczema
flechten *unr. tr. V.* plait ⟨hair⟩; weave
⟨basket, mat⟩
Fleck *der;* ~[e]s, ~e (a) stain
(b) (andersfarbige Stelle) patch
flecken *itr. V.* stain
flecken·los [1] *Adj.* spotless
[2] *adv.* spotlessly
Fleck·entferner *der* stain *or* spot remover
fleckig *Adj.* stained; blotchy ⟨face, skin⟩
Fleder·maus *die* bat
Flegel *der;* ~s, ~ (abwertend) lout
Flegelei *die;* ~, ~en (abwertend) loutish
behaviour
flegelhaft *Adj.* (abwertend) loutish
flegeln *refl. V.* (abwertend) **sich auf ein Sofa/**
in einen Sessel ~: flop on to a sofa/into an
armchair
flehen /'fle:ən/ *itr. V.* plead (**um** for)
Fleisch *das;* ~[e]s (a) flesh; ~ **fressend**
(Biol.) carnivorous
(b) (Nahrungsmittel) meat
Fleisch·brühe *die* bouillon; consommé
Fleischer *der;* ~s, ~: butcher
Fleischerei *die;* ~, ~en butcher's shop
fleisch·fressend *Adj.* carnivorous
Fleisch·fresser *der* (Biol.) carnivore
fleischig *Adj.* plump ⟨hands, face⟩; fleshy
⟨leaf, fruit⟩
Fleisch-: ~**käse** *der;* ~~s, ~~: meat
loaf; ~**klößchen** *das;* ~~s, ~~: small
meat ball; ~**pastete** *die* (Kochk.)
pâté; ~**salat** *der* (Kochk.) meat salad;
~**vergiftung** *die* food poisoning [from
meat]; ~**waren** *Pl.* meat products; ~**wolf**
der mincer; ~**wunde** *die* flesh wound;
~**wurst** *die* pork sausage
Fleiß *der;* ~es hard work; (Eigenschaft)
diligence
fleißig [1] *Adj.* hard-working
[2] *adv.* hard; ~ **lernen** learn as much as one
can
flennen *itr. V.* (ugs.) blubber
fletschen *tr., itr. V.* **die Zähne** *od.* **mit den**
Zähnen ~: bare one's teeth
Fleurop ⓦ /'flɔyrɔp/ *die* Interflora ®

---

*alte Schreibung – vgl. Hinweis auf S. x

flexibel ⏺1⏺ *Adj.* flexible
⏺2⏺ *adv.* flexibly
flicht *Imperativ Sg. u. 3. Pers. Sg. Präsens*
v. FLECHTEN
flicken *tr. V.* mend; repair ⟨*engine, cable*⟩
Flicken *der;* ∼s, ∼: patch
Flick-: ∼**werk** *das* (abwertend) botched-up
job; ∼**zeug** *das* repair kit
Flieder *der;* ∼s, ∼: lilac
Fliege *die;* ∼, ∼n (a) fly
(b) (Schleife) bow tie
fliegen ⏺1⏺ *unr. itr. V.; mit sein* (a) fly
(b) (ugs.: fallen) **vom Pferd/Fahrrad** ∼: fall off
a/the horse/bicycle
(c) (ugs.: entlassen werden) get the sack (coll.);
von der Schule ∼: be chucked out [of the
school] (coll.)
⏺2⏺ *unr. tr. V.* fly
Fliegen-: ∼**draht** *der* fly screen;
∼**fenster** *das* wire-mesh window;
∼**gewicht** *das* (Schwerathletik) flyweight;
∼**pilz** *der* fly agaric
Flieger *der;* ∼s, ∼: pilot
Flieger-alarm *der* air-raid warning
Fliegerin *die;* ∼, ∼nen pilot
fliegerisch *Adj.* aeronautical
fliehen /'fli:ən/ *unr. itr. V.; mit sein* flee
(**vor** + *Dat.* from); (aus dem Gefängnis usw.)
escape (**aus** from); **ins Ausland/über die**
Grenze ∼: flee the country/escape over the
border
Flieh·kraft *die* (Physik) centrifugal force
Fliese *die;* ∼, ∼n tile
Fließ·band *das* conveyor belt; **am**
∼ **arbeiten** *od.* (ugs.) **stehen** work on the
assembly line
fließen *unr. itr. V.; mit sein* flow; ∼**des**
Wasser running water; **eine Sprache** ∼**d**
sprechen speak a language fluently
Flimmer·kasten *der,* **Flimmer·kiste**
die (ugs.) telly (coll.); box (coll.)
flimmern *itr. V.* shimmer
flink ⏺1⏺ *Adj.* nimble ⟨*fingers*⟩; sharp ⟨*eyes*⟩;
quick ⟨*hands*⟩
⏺2⏺ *adv.* quickly
Flinkheit *die;* ∼ ▶ FLINK 1: nimbleness;
sharpness; quickness
Flinte *die;* ∼, ∼n shotgun; **die** ∼ **ins Korn**
werfen (fig.) throw in the towel
Flirt *der;* ∼s, ∼s flirtation
flirten *itr. V.* flirt
Flittchen *das;* ∼s, ∼ (ugs. abwertend) floozie
Flitter *der;* ∼s frippery; trumpery
Flitter·wochen *Pl.* honeymoon *sing.*
flitzen *itr. V.; mit sein* (ugs.) shoot; dart
Flitzer *der;* ∼s, ∼ (ugs.) sporty job (coll.)
floaten /'floʊtn̩/ *tr., itr. V.* (Wirtsch.) float
flocht *1. u. 3. Pers. Sg. Prät. v.* FLECHTEN
Flocke *die;* ∼, ∼n (a) flake
(b) (Staub∼) piece of fluff
flockig *Adj.* fluffy

flog *1. u. 3. Pers. Sg. Prät. v.* FLIEGEN
floh *1. u. 3. Pers. Sg. Prät. v.* FLIEHEN
Floh *der;* ∼[e]s, **Flöhe** flea
Floh-: ∼**markt** *der* flea market; ∼**zirkus**
der flea circus
Flora *die;* ∼, **Floren** flora
Florett *das;* ∼[e]s, ∼e foil
florieren *itr. V.* flourish
Florist *der;* ∼en, ∼en, **Floristin** *die;* ∼,
∼nen [qualified] flower arranger
Floskel *die;* ∼, ∼n cliché
floss *1. u. 3. Pers. Sg. Prät. v.* FLIESSEN
Floß *das;* ∼es, **Flöße** raft
Flosse *die;* ∼, ∼n (a) (Zool., Flugw.) fin
(b) (zum Tauchen) flipper
flößen *tr., itr. V.* float
Flößer *der;* ∼s, ∼: raftsman
Flößerin *die;* ∼, ∼nen raftswoman
Flöte *die;* ∼, ∼n flute; (Block∼) recorder
flöten ⏺1⏺ *itr. V.* ⟨*bird*⟩ flute; ∼ **gehen** (ugs.)
⟨*money*⟩ go down the drain; ⟨*time*⟩ be wasted
⏺2⏺ *tr. V.* whistle
*****flöten|gehen** ▶ FLÖTEN 1
flott ⏺1⏺ *Adj.* (a) (schwungvoll) lively
(b) (schick) smart
⏺2⏺ *adv.* ⟨*work*⟩ quickly; ⟨*dance, write*⟩ in a
lively manner; ⟨*be dressed*⟩ smartly
Flotte *die;* ∼, ∼n fleet
flott|machen *tr. V.* refloat ⟨*ship*⟩; get
⟨*car*⟩ back on the road
Flöz *das;* ∼es, ∼e (Bergbau) seam
Fluch *der;* ∼[e]s, **Flüche** curse; oath
fluchen *itr. V.* curse; swear
Flucht *die;* ∼: flight
flucht·artig ⏺1⏺ *Adj.* hurried; hasty
⏺2⏺ *adv.* hurriedly; hastily
flüchten ⏺1⏺ *itr. V.; mit sein* **vor jmdm./etw.**
∼: flee from sb./sth.; **vor der Polizei** ∼: run
away from the police
⏺2⏺ *refl. V.* take refuge
Flucht-: ∼**fahrzeug** *das* getaway
vehicle; ∼**helfer** *der,* ∼**helferin** *die*
person who aids/aided an/the escape;
∼**hilfe** *die* aiding an escape
flüchtig ⏺1⏺ *Adj.* (a) fugitive
(b) cursory; superficial ⟨*insight*⟩
⏺2⏺ *adv.* (a) (oberflächlich) cursorily
(b) (eilig) hurriedly
Flüchtigkeit *die;* ∼, ∼en cursoriness
Flüchtigkeits-fehler *der* slip
Flüchtling *der;* ∼s, ∼e refugee
Flüchtlings-: ∼**elend** *das* hardship
among refugees; ∼**hilfe** *die* refugee relief;
(Organisation) refugee relief agency; ∼**lager**
das refugee camp; ∼**treck** *der* long stream
of refugees
Flucht·weg *der* escape route
Flug *der;* ∼[e]s, **Flüge** flight
Flug-: ∼**bahn** *die* trajectory; ∼**blatt** *das*
pamphlet; leaflet

Flügel *der;* ~s, ~ (a) wing
(b) (Klavier) grand piano
Flügel·mutter *die; Pl.* ~n wing nut
Flug·gast *der* [air] passenger
flügge *Adj.* fully-fledged
Flug-: ~**gesellschaft** *die* airline;
~**hafen** *der* airport; ~**hafen·steuer**
die airport tax; ~**linie** *die* (a) (Strecke) air
route; (b) (Gesellschaft) airline; ~**lotse**
der, ~**lotsin** *die* air traffic controller;
~**platz** *der* airfield; ~**schein** *der* air
ticket; ~**schreiber** *der* flight recorder;
~**verbindung** *die* air connection;
~**verkehr** *der* air traffic
Flug·zeug *das* aeroplane (Brit.); airplane
(Amer.); aircraft
Flugzeug-: ~**absturz** *der* plane crash;
~**entführer** *der,* ~**entführerin** *die*
[aircraft] hijacker; ~**entführung** *die*
[aircraft] hijack[ing]; ~**katastrophe** *die*
air disaster; ~**träger** *der* aircraft carrier
Flunder *die;* ~, ~n flounder
flunkern *itr. V.* tell stories
Fluor *das;* ~s (Chemie) fluorine
Fluor·chlor·kohlen·wasserstoff *der*
(Chemie) chlorofluorocarbon
Flur¹ *der;* ~[e]s, ~e (Korridor) corridor;
(Diele) [entrance] hall; **im/auf dem** ~: in the
corridor/hall
Flur² *die;* ~, ~en farmland *no indef. art.*
Fluss, *Fluß* *der;* Flusses, Flüsse river;
(fließende Bewegung) flow
fluss-, *fluß-*, Fluss-, *Fluß-*:
~**ab[wärts]** *Adv.* downstream;
~**auf[wärts]** *Adv.* upstream; ~**bett** *das*
river bed
Flüsschen, *Flüßchen* *das;* ~s,
~: small river
Fluss·diagramm *das* (DV, Arbeitswiss.)
flow chart
flüssig ① *Adj.* (a) liquid
(b) (fließend, geläufig) fluent
(c) **einen Betrag** ~ **machen** make a sum of
money available
② *adv.* ⟨write, speak⟩ fluently
Flüssig·gas *das* liquid gas
Flüssigkeit *die;* ~, ~en (a) liquid; (auch
Gas) fluid
(b) (Geläufigkeit) fluency
Flüssig·kristall·anzeige *die* (Technik)
liquid crystal display
***flüssig|machen** ▸ FLÜSSIG 1C
Fluss·pferd, *Fluß·pferd* *das*
hippopotamus
flüstern *itr., tr. V.* whisper
Flut *die;* ~, ~en (a) tide
(b) (geh.: Wassermasse) flood
fluten *itr. V.; mit sein* (geh.) flood
Flut·licht *das* floodlight
focht *1. u. 3. Pers. Sg. Prät. v.* FECHTEN

*old spelling – see note on page x

Föderalismus *der;* ~: federalism *no art.*
föderalistisch *Adj.* federalist
Fohlen *das;* ~s, ~: foal
Föhn *der;* ~[e]s, ~e (a) föhn
(b) (Haartrockner) hair-drier
föhnen *tr. V.* blow-dry
Folge *die;* ~, ~n (a) (Auswirkung)
consequence; (Ergebnis) consequence; result
(b) (Aufeinander~) succession;
(zusammengehörend) sequence
(c) (Fortsetzung) (einer Sendung) episode; (eines
Romans) instalment
Folge·erscheinung *die* consequence
folgen *itr. V.; mit sein* follow; **jmdm. im
Amt/in der Regierung** ~: succeed sb. in
office/in government; **auf etw.** (*Akk.*)
~: follow sth.; **aus etw.** ~: follow from sth.
folgend *Adj.* following; **der/die/das
Folgende** the next in order; **im Folgenden**
od. **in Folgendem** in [the course of] the
following discussion/passage *etc.*
folgendermaßen *Adv.* as follows; (so) in
the following way
folge·richtig ① *Adj.* logical; consistent
⟨behaviour, action⟩
② *adv.* logically; ⟨act, behave⟩ consistently
Folge·richtigkeit *die* (einer Entscheidung,
Schlussfolgerung) logicality; (eines Verhaltens,
einer Handlung) consistency
folgern ① *tr. V.* etw. aus etw. ~: infer sth.
from sth.
② *itr. V.* richtig ~: draw a/the correct
conclusion
Folgerung *die;* ~, ~en conclusion
Folge·schaden *der* (a) damaging
after-effects
(b) (Versicherungsw.) consequential damage
folglich *Adv.* consequently
folgsam ① *Adj.* obedient
② *adv.* obediently
Folgsamkeit *die;* ~: obedience
Folie /'fo:liə/ *die;* ~, ~n (Metall~) foil;
(Plastik~) film
Folklore *die;* ~ (a) folklore
(b) (Musik) folk music
folkloristisch ① *Adj.* folkloric
② *adv.* in a folkloric way
Folter *die;* ~, ~n torture; **jmdn. auf die**
~ **spannen** (fig.) keep sb. in an agony of
suspense
Folterer *der;* ~s, ~, **Folterin** *die;* ~,
~nen torturer
foltern *tr. V.* torture; (fig.) torment
Folterung *die;* ~, ~en torture
Fön ⓌZ *der;* ~[e]s, ~e hairdrier
Fond /fõː/ *der;* ~s, ~s (geh.) back
Fonds /fõː/ *der;* ~ /fõː(s):/ ~ /fõːs/ fund
Fondue /fõˈdyː/ *die;* ~, ~s *od. das;* ~s, ~s
(Kochk.) fondue

*****fönen** ▸ FÖHNEN

Fontäne *die;* ∼, ∼n jet; (Springbrunnen) fountain

forcieren /fɔr'siːrən/ *tr. V.* step up ⟨*production*⟩; intensify ⟨*efforts*⟩; push forward ⟨*developments*⟩

Förderer *der;* ∼s, ∼: patron

Förderin *die;* ∼, ∼nen patroness

fordern *tr. V.* (a) demand
(b) (in Anspruch nehmen) make demands on

fördern *tr. V.* (a) promote; patronize, support ⟨*artist, art*⟩; further ⟨*investigation*⟩; foster ⟨*talent, tendency*⟩; improve ⟨*appetite*⟩; aid ⟨*digestion, sleep*⟩
(b) (Bergbau, Technik) mine ⟨*coal, ore*⟩; extract ⟨*oil*⟩

Forderung *die;* ∼, ∼en (a) demand
(b) (Kaufmannsspr.) claim (**an** + *Akk.* against)

Förderung *die;* ∼, ∼en (a) ▶ FÖRDERN A: promotion; patronage; support; furthering; fostering; improvement; aiding
(b) (Bergbau, Technik) output; (das Fördern) mining; (von Erdöl) extraction

Forelle *die;* ∼, ∼n trout

Forensik /fo'rɛnzɪk/ *die;* ∼ forensic science; forensics *sing.*

Form *die;* ∼, ∼en (a) shape; **in** ∼ **von Tabletten** in the form of tablets
(b) (bes. Sport: Verfassung) form; **in** ∼ **sein** be on form
(c) (vorgeformtes Modell) mould; (Back∼) baking tin
(d) (Darstellungs∼, Umgangs∼) form

formal ① *Adj.* formal
② *adv.* formally

formalisieren *tr. V.* formalize

Formalität *die;* ∼, ∼en formality

Format *das;* ∼[e]s, ∼e (a) size; (Buch∼, Papier∼, Bild∼) format
(b) (Persönlichkeit) stature

formatieren *tr. V.* (DV) format

formbar *Adj.* malleable

Form-: ∼**blatt** *das* form; ∼**brief** *der* form letter

Formel *die;* ∼, ∼n formula

formell *Adj.* formal

formen *tr. V.* (a) (gestalten) form; shape
(b) (bilden, prägen) mould, form ⟨*character, personality*⟩

Form·fehler *der* irregularity

formieren *tr., refl. V.* form

förmlich ① *Adj.* (a) formal
(b) (regelrecht) positive
② *adv.* (a) formally
(b) (geradezu) **sich** ∼ **fürchten** be really afraid

form·los *Adj.* (a) informal
(b) (gestaltlos) shapeless

Form·sache *die* formality

Formular *das;* ∼s, ∼e form

formulieren *tr. V.* formulate

Formulierung *die;* ∼, ∼en (a) (das Formulieren) formulation; (eines Entwurfes, Gesetzes) drafting
(b) (formulierter Text) formulation

form·vollendet ① *Adj.* perfectly executed ⟨*pirouette, bow, etc.*⟩; ⟨*poem*⟩ perfect in form
② *adv.* faultlessly

forsch *Adj.* forceful

forschen *itr. V.* (a) **nach** jmdm./etw. ∼: search *or* look for sb./sth.
(b) (als Wissenschaftler) research

Forscher *der;* ∼s, **Forscherin** *die;* ∼, ∼nen researcher

Forschung *die;* ∼, ∼en research

Forschungs-: ∼**reaktor** *der* research reactor; ∼**reisende** *der/die* explorer

Forst *der;* ∼[e]s, ∼e[n] forest

Förster *der;* ∼s, ∼, **Försterin** *die;* ∼, ∼nen forest warden

Forst·wirtschaft *die* forestry

Forsythie /fɔr'zyːtsiə/ *die;* ∼, ∼n forsythia

fort *Adv.* (a) ▶ WEG
(b) (weiter) **und so** ∼: and so on

fort-, Fort-: ∼**an** /-'-/ *Adv.* from now/then on; ∼**bestand** *der* continuation; (eines Staates) continued existence; ∼|**bewegen** ① *tr. V.* move; shift; ② *refl. V.* move [along]; ∼|**bilden** *tr. V.* **sich/jmdn.** ∼**bilden** continue one's/sb.'s education; ∼**bildung** *die* further education; (beruflich) further training; ∼**bildungs-kurs** *der* further education course; (beruflich) training course; ∼|**bleiben** *unr. itr. V.; mit sein* fail to come; ∼|**bringen** *unr. tr. V.:* ▶ WEGBRINGEN; ∼**dauer** *die* continuation; ∼|**dauern** *itr. V.* continue; ∼|**fahren** ① *unr. itr. V.* (a) *mit sein* leave; (b) *auch mit sein* (weitermachen) continue; go on; ② *unr. tr. V.* drive away; ∼|**führen** *tr. V.* (a) lead away; (b) (fortsetzen) continue; ∼**gang** *der* (a) departure (**aus** from); (b) (Weiterentwicklung) progress; ∼|**gehen** *unr. itr. V.; mit sein* leave; **geh** ∼! go away!; ∼**geschritten** *Adj.* advanced; ∼**geschrittene** *der/die; adj. Dekl.* advanced student/player; ∼|**kommen** *unr. itr. V.; mit sein* ▶ WEGKOMMEN A, B; ∼|**laufen** *unr. itr. V.; mit sein* (a) ▶ WEGLAUFEN; (b) (sich ∼setzen) continue; ∼**laufend** ① *Adj.* continuous; ② *adv.* continuously; ∼|**pflanzen** *refl. V.* (a) reproduce [oneself/itself]; (b) (sich verbreiten) ⟨*idea, mood*⟩ spread; ⟨*sound, light*⟩ travel; ∼**pflanzung** *die;* ∼∼: reproduction; ∼|**schaffen** *tr. V.* take away; ∼|**schreiben** *unr. tr. V.* update; (in die Zukunft) project forward; ∼**schreibung** *die* updating; (in die Zukunft) forward projection; ∼|**schreiten** *unr. itr. V.; mit sein* ⟨*process*⟩ continue; ⟨*time*⟩ move on; ∼**schritt** *der* progress; ∼**schritte** progress *sing.*; **ein** ∼**schritt** a step forward; ∼**schrittlich** ① *Adj.* progressive;
② *adv.* progressively; ⋯▸

∼**schrittlichkeit** *die;* ∼∼:
progressiveness; ∼|**setzen** ① *tr. V.*
continue; ② *refl. V.* continue; ∼**setzung**
die; ∼∼, ∼∼en **(a)** (das ∼setzen)
continuation; **(b)** (anschließender Teil)
instalment; ∼**setzungs·roman** *der*
serial; serialized novel; ∼|**während**
① *Adj. nicht präd.* continual; ② *adv.*
continually; ∼|**werfen** *unr. tr. V.*:
▶ WEGWERFEN
fossil *Adj.* fossilized; fossil *attrib.*
Foto *das;* ∼s, ∼s photo; ∼s **machen** take
photos
Foto-: ∼**album** *das* photo album;
∼**apparat** *der* camera
fotogen *Adj.* photogenic
Foto·graf *der;* ∼en, ∼en photographer
Fotografie *die;* ∼, ∼n **(a)** photography
no art.
(b) (Lichtbild) photograph
fotografieren *tr. V.* photograph; take a
photograph/photographs of
Fotografin *die;* ∼, ∼nen photographer
foto-, Foto-: ∼**kopie** *die* photocopy;
∼**kopieren** *tr., itr. V.* photocopy;
∼**kopierer** *der* photocopier
Foto: ∼**labor** *das* photographic
laboratory; ∼**modell** *das* photographic
model
Foul /fau̯l/ *das;* ∼s, ∼s (Sport) foul (an
+ *Dat.* on)
Foul·spiel /ˈfau̯l-/ *das* foul
Foyer /foaˈjeː/ *das;* ∼s, ∼s foyer
FPÖ *Abk.* = **Freiheitliche Partei
Österreichs**
Fr. *Abk.* **(a)** = **Franken** SFr.
(b) = **Frau;**
(c) = **Freitag** Fri.
Fracht *die;* ∼, ∼en (Schiffs∼, Luft∼) cargo;
freight; (Bahn∼, LKW-∼) goods *pl.;* freight
Fracht·brief *der* consignment note;
waybill
Frachter *der;* ∼s, ∼: freighter
Fracht-: ∼**gut** *das* slow freight; slow
goods *pl.;* ∼**schiff** *das* cargo ship
Frack *der;* ∼[e]s, Fräcke tails *pl.;* evening
dress
Frage *die;* ∼, ∼n question; (Angelegenheit)
issue; in ∼: ▶ INFRAGE
Fragebogen *der* questionnaire; (Formular)
form
fragen ① *tr., itr. V.* **(a)** ask
(b) (sich erkundigen) nach etw. ∼: ask *or*
inquire about sth.
(c) (nachfragen) ask for
② *refl.* sich ∼, ob ...: wonder whether ...
Frage·zeichen *das* question mark
fraglich *Adj.* **(a)** doubtful
(b) (betreffend) in question *postpos.;* relevant
Fragment *das;* ∼[e]s, ∼e fragment

---
*alte Schreibung – vgl. Hinweis auf S. x

frag·würdig *Adj.* **(a)** questionable
(b) (zwielichtig) dubious
Fragwürdigkeit *die;* ∼, ∼en
(a) questionableness
(b) (Zwielichtigkeit) dubiousness
Fraktion *die;* ∼, ∼en parliamentary party;
(mit zwei Parteien) parliamentary coalition
Fraktions- (Parl.): ∼**führer** *der,*
∼**führerin** *die* leader of the parliamentary
party/coalition; ∼**zwang** *der* obligation to
vote in accordance with party policy
frank *Adv.* ∼ **und frei** frankly and openly;
openly and honestly
Franken *der;* ∼s ∼: [Swiss] franc
Frankfurter *die;* ∼, ∼ (Wurst) frankfurter
frankieren *tr. V.* frank
Frank·reich (*das*); ∼s France
Franse *die;* ∼, ∼n strand [of a/the fringe]
Franzose *der;* ∼n, ∼n Frenchman; **er ist**
∼: he is French; **die** ∼n the French
Französin *die;* ∼, ∼nen Frenchwoman
französisch *Adj.* French
Französisch *das;* ∼[s] French
Fräse *die;* ∼, ∼n (für Holz) moulding
machine; (für Metall) milling machine
fraß *1. u. 3. Pers. Sg. Prät. v.* FRESSEN
Fraß *der;* ∼es (derb) muck
Fratze *die;* ∼, ∼n **(a)** hideous face
(b) (ugs.: Grimasse) grimace
Frau *die;* ∼, ∼en **(a)** woman
(b) (Ehe∼) wife
(c) (Titel, Anrede) ∼ **Schulze** Mrs Schulze;
(in Briefen) **Sehr geehrte** ∼ **Schulze** Dear
Madam; (bei persönlicher Bekanntschaft) Dear
Mrs/Miss/Ms Schulze
Frauen-: ∼**arzt** *der,* ∼**ärztin** *die*
gynaecologist; ∼**bewegung** *die* women's
movement; ∼**emanzipation** *die* female
emancipation; women's emancipation;
∼**gefängnis** *das* women's prison;
∼**gruppe** *die* women's group; ∼**haus**
das battered wives' refuge; ∼**klinik**
die gynaecological hospital *or* clinic;
∼**misshandlung,** *∼**mißhandlung**
die abuse of women; ∼**recht** *das*
women's right; ∼**rechtlerin** *die;* ∼∼,
∼∼nen feminist; Women's Libber (coll.);
∼**zeitschrift** *die* women's magazine;
∼**zimmer** *das* (abwertend) female
Fräulein *das;* ∼s, ∼ (*ugs.* ∼s) **(a)** (junges
∼) young lady; (ältliches ∼) spinster
(b) (Titel, Anrede) ∼ **Mayer/Schulte** Miss
Mayer/Schulte
fraulich ① *Adj.* feminine
② *adv.* in a feminine way
Frauschaft *die;* ∼, ∼en (bes. Sport)
women's team
frech ① *Adj.* **(a)** impertinent; cheeky;
barefaced ⟨lie⟩
(b) (keck, kess) saucy
② *adv.* impertinently; cheekily

Frech·dachs der (ugs., meist scherzh.) cheeky little thing

Frechheit die; ∼, ∼en **(a)** impertinence; cheek

(b) (Äußerung) impertinent or cheeky remark

frei ⓵ Adj. **(a)** (unabhängig) free

(b) (nicht angestellt) freelance

(c) (ungezwungen) free and easy

(d) (nicht mehr in Haft) free

(e) (offen) open; **im Freien sitzen/übernachten** sit out of doors/spend the night in the open; **ständig im Freien übernachten** sleep rough

(f) (unbesetzt) vacant; free

(g) (kostenlos) free ⟨food, admission⟩

(h) (verfügbar) spare; free ⟨time⟩

⓶ adv. freely

frei-, Frei-: ∼**bad** das open-air swimming pool; ∼|**bekommen** ⓵ unr. itr. V. (ugs.) get time off; ⓶ unr. tr. V. jmdn./etw. ∼**bekommen** get sb./sth. released; ∼**beruflich** ⓵ Adj. self-employed; freelance; ⟨doctor, lawyer⟩ in private practice; ⓶ adv. ∼**beruflich tätig sein/arbeiten** work freelance/practise privately; ∼**betrag** der (Steuerw.) [tax] allowance; ∼**bier** das free beer

Freier der; ∼s, ∼ (veralt.) suitor

frei-, Frei-: ∼**exemplar** das (Buch) free copy; (Zeitung) free issue; ∼**frau** die baroness; ∼**gabe** die release; ∼|**geben** unr. tr. V. release; ∼**gebig** Adj. generous; open-handed; ∼**gebigkeit** die; ∼∼: generosity; open-handedness; ∼**gehege** das outdoor enclosure; ∼**gepäck** das baggage allowance; ∼**hafen** der free port; ∼|**halten** unr. tr. V. **(a)** treat; **(b)** (offen halten) keep ⟨entrance, roadway⟩ clear; **Einfahrt** ∼**halten!** no parking in front of entrance; ∼**handels·zone** die free-trade zone; ∼**händig** adv. ⟨cycle⟩ without holding on

Freiheit die; ∼, ∼en **(a)** freedom; ∼**, Gleichheit, Brüderlichkeit** Liberty, Equality, Fraternity

(b) (Vorrecht) freedom; privilege

freiheitlich ⓵ Adj. liberal ⟨philosophy, conscience⟩; ∼ **und demokratisch** free and democratic

⓶ adv. liberally

Freiheits-: ∼**beraubung** die (jur.) wrongful detention; ∼**strafe** die (Rechtsw.) term of imprisonment; prison sentence

frei-, Frei-: ∼**herr** der baron; ∼**karte** die complimentary ticket; ∼|**kaufen** tr. V. ransom ⟨hostage⟩; buy the freedom of ⟨slave⟩; ∼|**kommen** unr. itr. V. **aus dem Gefängnis** ∼**kommen** be released from prison; ∼**körper·kultur** die nudism no art.; naturism no art.; ∼**land** das open ground; ∼|**lassen** unr. tr. V. set free; release; ∼|**legen** tr. V. uncover

freilich Adv. of course

Frei·licht-: ∼**bühne** die, ∼**theater**

das open-air theatre

frei-, Frei-: ∼|**machen** ⓵ refl. V. (ugs.: frei nehmen) take time off; ⓶ tr. V. (Postw.) frank; **etw. mit 0,56 Euro** ∼**machen** put a 56-cent stamp on sth.; ∼**marke** die postage stamp; ∼**mütig** ⓵ Adj. candid; frank; ⓶ adv. candidly; frankly; ∼**mütigkeit** die; ∼∼: candidness; frankness; ∼**schaffend** Adj. freelance; ∼**schärler** der; ∼∼s, ∼∼, ∼**schärlerin** die; ∼∼, ∼∼nen irregular [soldier]; ∼|**schwimmen** unr. refl. V. **sich** ∼**schwimmen** pass the 15-minute swimming test; ∼**sprech·anlage, sprech·einrichtung** die hands-free kit; ∼|**sprechen** unr. tr. V. **(a)** (Rechtsw.) acquit; **(b)** (für unschuldig erklären) exonerate (von from); ∼**spruch** der (Rechtsw.) acquittal; ∼|**stellen** tr. V. **(a)** jmdm. etw. ∼**stellen** leave sth. up to sb.; **(b)** (befreien) release ⟨person⟩; **jmdn. vom Wehrdienst** ∼**stellen** exempt sb. from military service; ∼**stoß** der (Fußball) free kick

Frei·tag der Friday; s. auch **DIENSTAG** usw.

freitags Adv. on Friday[s]; s. auch

DIENSTAG

frei-, Frei-: ∼**tod** der (verhüll.) suicide no art.; ∼**treppe** die [flight of] steps; ∼**übung** die; meist Pl. (Sport) keep-fit exercise; ∼**wild** das fair game; ∼**willig** ⓵ Adj. voluntary ⟨decision⟩; optional ⟨subject⟩; ⓶ adv. voluntarily; **sich** ∼**willig melden** volunteer; ∼**willige** der/die; adj. Dekl. volunteer; ∼**zeichen** das ringing tone;

Frei·zeit die spare time

Freizeit-: ∼**beschäftigung** die hobby; leisure pursuit; ∼**gestaltung** die (Soziol., Päd.) leisure activity; ∼**park** der amusement park

frei-, Frei-: ∼**zügig** Adj. **(a)** generous; **(b)** (gewagt, unmoralisch) risqué ⟨remark, film, dress⟩; ∼**zügigkeit** die; ∼∼ **(a)** generosity; **(b)** (freie Wahl des Wohnsitzes) freedom of domicile

fremd Adj. **(a)** foreign

(b) (nicht eigen) other people's; of others postpos.

(c) (unbekannt) strange

fremd-, Fremd-: ∼**arbeiter** der, ∼**arbeiterin** die (veralt., schweiz.) foreign worker; ∼**artig** Adj. strange

Fremde¹ der/die; adj. Dekl. **(a)** stranger

(b) (Ausländer) foreigner

Fremde² die; ∼ (geh.) **die** ∼: foreign parts pl.

fremden-, Fremden-: ∼**feindlich** Adj. xenophobic; hostile to strangers/foreigners postpos.; ∼**feindlichkeit** die xenophobia; hostility towards foreigners; ∼**führer** der, ∼**führerin** die tourist guide; ∼**hass,** *∼**haß** der xenophobia; hatred of foreigners; ∼**verkehr** der tourism no art.; ∼**zimmer** das room ⸱⸱⸱⸽

fremd-, Fremd-: ∼|**gehen** *unr. itr. V.;
mit sein (ugs.) be unfaithful; ∼**herrschaft**
die foreign domination; ∼**ländisch** *Adj.*
foreign; (exotisch) exotic

Fremdling *der;* ∼s, ∼e (veralt.) stranger

fremd-, Fremd-: ∼**sprache**
die foreign language;
∼**sprachen·assistent** *der,*
∼**sprachen·assistentin** *die* foreign-
language assistant; ∼**sprachig** *Adj.*
bilingual/multilingual *(staff, secretary)*;
foreign *(literature)*; foreign-language
(edition, teaching); ∼**sprachlich** *Adj.*
foreign-language *(teaching)*; foreign *(word)*;
∼**wort** *das; Pl.* ∼wörter foreign word

frenetisch 1 *Adj.* frenetic
2 *adv.* frenetically

Frequenz *die;* ∼, ∼en (Physik) frequency;
(Med.: Puls∼) rate

Fressalien /frɛˈsaliən/ *Pl.* (ugs. scherzh.)
grub (coll.)

Fresse *die;* ∼, ∼n (derb) (a) (Mund) gob (sl.)
(b) (Gesicht) mug (coll.)

fressen 1 *unr. tr. V.* (a) *(animal)* eat; (sich
ernähren von) feed on
(b) (ugs.: verschlingen) swallow up *(money,
time, distance)*; drink *(petrol)*
(c) (zerstören) eat away
(d) (derb: von Menschen) guzzle
2 *unr. itr. V.* (von Tieren) feed; (derb: von
Menschen) stuff one's face (sl.)

Fressen *das;* ∼s (a) (für Hunde, Katzen usw.)
food; (für Vieh) feed
(b) (derb: Essen) grub (coll.)

Fresserei *die;* ∼, ∼en (derb) guzzling

Freude *die;* ∼, ∼n joy; (Vergnügen) pleasure;
∼ an etw. *(Dat.)* haben take pleasure in sth.

Freuden-: ∼**fest** *das* celebration; **ein**
∼**fest feiern** hold a celebration; ∼**haus** *das*
house of pleasure; ∼**tag** *der* happy day

freudestrahlend *Adj.* beaming with joy;

freudig *Adj.* joyful; joyous *(heart)*;
delightful *(surprise)*;

freud·los *Adj.* joyless;

freuen 1 *refl. V.* be glad (über + *Akk.*
about); (froh sein) be happy; **sich auf etw.**
(Akk.) ∼: look forward to sth.
2 *tr. V.* please; **es freut mich, dass ...** I am
pleased *or* glad that ...; **das hat ihn sehr
gefreut** he was very pleased about it

Freund *der;* ∼es, ∼e (a) friend
(b) (Verehrer, Geliebter) boyfriend

Freundes·kreis *der* circle of friends; **im
engen** ∼: among close friends

Freundin *die;* ∼, ∼nen (a) friend
(b) (Geliebte) girlfriend; (älter) lady friend

freundlich 1 *Adj.* (a) kind *(face)*;
friendly *(reception)*;
(b) (angenehm) pleasant
(c) (freundschaftlich) friendly
2 *adv.* **jmdn.** ∼ **danken** thank sb. kindly

Freundlichkeit *die;* ∼: kindness

Freundschaft *die;* ∼, ∼en friendship;
mit jmdm. ∼ **schließen** make friends with sb.

freundschaftlich 1 *Adj.* friendly
2 *adv.* in a friendly way

Frevel /ˈfreːfl̩/ *der;* ∼s, ∼ (geh., veralt.)
crime; outrage

frevelhaft (geh.) 1 *Adj.* wicked *(deed,
rebellion, person)*; criminal *(stupidity)*
2 *adv.* wickedly

Friede *der;* ∼ns, ∼n (älter, geh.) ▶ FRIEDEN

Frieden *der;* ∼s, ∼: peace

Friedens-: ∼**abkommen** *das* peace
agreement; (Friedensvertrag) peace treaty;
∼**bewegung** *die* peace movement;
∼**bruch** *der* violation of the peace;
∼**forschung** *die* peace studies *pl., no
art.;* ∼**konferenz** *die* peace conference;
∼**nobelpreis** *der* Nobel Peace Prize;
∼**pfeife** *die* pipe of peace; ∼**richter**
der, ∼**richterin** *die: lay magistrate
dealing with minor offences;* ≈ Justice
of the Peace; ∼**taube** *die* dove of
peace; ∼**verhandlungen** *Pl.* peace
negotiations; ∼**vertrag** *der* peace treaty;
∼**zeiten** *Pl.* peacetime *sing.*

fried·fertig *Adj.* peaceable *(person,
character)*

Fried·fertigkeit *die;* ∼: peaceableness

Fried·hof *der* cemetery; (Kirchhof) graveyard

friedlich 1 *Adj.* peaceful
2 *adv.* peacefully

Friedlichkeit *die;* ∼: peacefulness

fried·liebend *Adj.* peace-loving

frieren *unr. itr. V.* (a) be *or* feel cold
(b) *mit sein* (gefrieren) freeze

Frikadelle *die;* ∼, ∼n rissole

frisch 1 *Adj.* fresh; new-laid *(egg)*; clean
(linen, underwear); wet *(paint)*
2 *adv.* freshly

Frische *die;* ∼ freshness; **geistige**
∼: mental alertness; **körperliche**
∼: physical fitness

Frisch-: ∼**fleisch** *das* fresh meat;
∼**halte·beutel** *der* airtight bag; ∼**luft**
die fresh air; ∼**milch** *die* fresh milk

Friseur /friˈzøːɐ/ *der;* ∼s, ∼e, **Friseuse**
/friˈzøːzə/ *die;* ∼, ∼n hairdresser

frisieren *tr. V.* **jmdn./sich** ∼: do sb.'s/one's
hair; **sich** ∼ **lassen** have one's hair done

friss, *friß *Imperativ Sg. v.* FRESSEN

frisst, *frißt 2. u. 3. Pers. Sg. Präsens v.
FRESSEN

Frist *die;* ∼, ∼en (a) time; period; **die**
∼ **verlängern** extend the deadline
(b) (begrenzter Aufschub) extension

frist-: ∼**gemäß,** ∼**gerecht** *Adj.,
adv.* within the specified time *postpos.;*
(bei Anmeldung usw.) before the closing date
postpos.; ∼**los** 1 *Adj.* instant; 2 *adv.*
without notice

Frisur *die;* ∼, ∼en hairstyle

---

*old spelling – see note on page x

fritieren *tr. V.* deep-fry

frivol /fri'vo:l/ *Adj.* **(a)** (schamlos) suggestive ⟨*remark, picture, etc.*⟩; risqué ⟨*joke*⟩; earthy ⟨*man*⟩; flighty ⟨*woman*⟩
(b) (leichtfertig) frivolous

froh *Adj.* **(a)** (happy; cheerful ⟨*person, mood*⟩; good ⟨*news*⟩
(b) (ugs.: erleichtert) pleased, glad (**über** + *Akk.* about)

fröhlich *Adj.* cheerful; happy

Fröhlichkeit *die;* ∼: cheerfulness; (eines Festes, einer Feier) gaiety

Froh-: ∼**natur** *die* cheerful person; ∼**sinn** *der* cheerfulness; gaiety

fromm; ∼**er** *od.* **frömmer,** ∼**st...** *od.* **frömmst...** ① *Adj.* pious, devout ⟨*person*⟩; devout ⟨*Christian*⟩
② *adv.* piously

Frömmigkeit *die;* ∼: piety; devoutness

Fron·leichnam /fro:n-/ ⟨*das*⟩; ∼**s** [the feast of] Corpus Christi

Front *die;* ∼, ∼**en (a)** (Gebäude∼) front; façade
(b) (Kampfgebiet) front [line]

frontal ① *Adj.* head-on ⟨*collision*⟩; frontal ⟨*attack*⟩
② *adv.* ⟨*collide*⟩ head-on; ⟨*attack*⟩ from the front

Front·antrieb *der* (Kfz-W.) front-wheel drive

fror *1. u. 3. Pers. Sg. Prät. v.* **FRIEREN**

Frosch *der;* ∼**[e]s, Frösche** frog

Frosch-: ∼**mann** *der; Pl.* ∼**männer** frogman; ∼**perspektive** *die* worm's-eye view; ∼**schenkel** *der* frog's leg

Frost *der;* ∼**[e]s, Fröste** frost

Frostbeule *die* chilblain

frösteln *itr. V.* feel chilly

Frost·grenze *die* (Met.) 0° C isotherm; (Geol.) frost line

frostig ① *Adj.* (auch fig.) frosty
② *adv.* frostily

Frostigkeit *die;* ∼: frostiness

Frost-: ∼**schaden** *der* frost damage; ∼**schutz·mittel** *das* **(a)** frost protection agent; **(b)** (Kfz-W.) antifreeze

Frottee *das* u. *der;* ∼**s,** ∼**s** terry towelling

Frottee·handtuch *das* terry towel

frottieren *tr. V.* rub; towel

frotzeln ① *tr. V.* tease
② *itr. V.* **über jmdn./etw.** ∼: make fun of sb./sth.

Frucht *die;* ∼, **Früchte** fruit

frucht·bar *Adj.* fertile; fruitful ⟨*work, idea, etc.*⟩

Fruchtbarkeit *die;* ∼: fertility; fruitfulness

Frucht·becher *der* fruit sundae

fruchten *tr. V.* **nichts** ∼: be no use

fruchtig *Adj.* fruity

frucht·los *Adj.* fruitless, vain ⟨*efforts*⟩

Frucht·losigkeit *die;* ∼∼: fruitlessness

Frucht-: ∼**saft** *der* fruit juice; ∼**wasser** *das; Pl.* ∼**wässer** (Anat.) amniotic fluid; waters *pl.* (coll.)

früh ① *Adj.* **(a)** early
(b) (vorzeitig) premature
② *adv.* early; **heute** ∼: this morning

früh·auf: **von** ∼ from early childhood on[wards]

Frühaufsteher *der;* ∼**s,** ∼,
Frühaufsteherin *die;* ∼, ∼**nen** early riser

Frühe *die;* ∼: **in aller** ∼: at the crack of dawn

früher ① *Adj., nicht präd.* **(a)** (vergangen) earlier; former
(b) (ehemalig) former ⟨*owner, occupant, friend*⟩
② *adv.* formerly; ∼ **war er ganz anders** he used to be quite different

Früh·erkennung *die* (Med.) early recognition

frühestens *Adv.* at the earliest

Früh·geburt *die* **(a)** premature birth
(b) (Kind) premature baby

Früh·jahr *das* spring

Frühjahrsmüdigkeit *die* springtime tiredness

Frühling *der;* ∼**s,** ∼**e** spring

Frühlings·anfang *der* first day of spring

früh-, Früh-: ∼**reif** *Adj.* precocious ⟨*child*⟩; ∼**schoppen** *der* morning drink; (um Mittag) lunchtime drink; ∼**sport** *der* early-morning exercise

Früh·stück *das;* ∼**s,** ∼**e** breakfast

frühstücken *itr. V.* have breakfast

Frühstücks-: ∼**fernsehen** *das* breakfast television; ∼**pause** *die* morning break; coffee break

früh-, Früh-: ∼**warn·system** *das* early warning system; ∼**zeitig** ① *Adj.* early; (vorzeitig) premature; ② *adv.* early; (vorzeitig) prematurely

Frustration *die;* ∼, ∼**en** (Psych.) frustration

frustrieren *tr. V.* frustrate

Fuchs *der;* ∼**es, Füchse** fox

fuchsen *tr. V.* annoy; vex

fuchs·teufels·wild *Adj.* (ugs.) livid (coll.)

Fuchtel *die;* ∼: **unter jmds.** ∼ (ugs.) under sb.'s thumb

fuchteln *itr. V.* (ugs.) **mit etw.** ∼: wave sth. about

Fuder *das;* ∼**s,** ∼: cartload

Fuge¹ *die;* ∼, ∼**n** joint; (Zwischenraum) gap

Fuge² *die;* ∼, ∼**n** (Musik) fugue

fügen ① *tr. V.* place; set; **etw zu etw.** ∼ (fig.) add sth. to sth.
② *refl. V.* **(a)** (sich ein∼) **sich in etw.** (*Akk.*) ∼: fit into sth.
(b) (gehorchen) **sich** ∼: fall into line   ⋯⋗

fügsam *Adj.* obedient

fühlbar *Adj.* noticeable

fühlen ⓵ *tr., itr. V.* feel
⓶ *refl. V.* **sich krank** ∼: feel sick

Fühler *der;* ∼s, ∼: feeler; antenna

Fühlungnahme *die;* ∼: initial contact

fuhr *1. u. 3. Pers. Sg. Prät. v.* FAHREN

Fuhre *die;* ∼, ∼n load

führen ⓵ *tr. V.* **(a)** lead; **jmdn. durch ein Haus/eine Stadt** ∼: show sb. around a house/town; **durch das Programm führt [Sie] Klaus Frank** Klaus Frank will present the programme
(b) (verkaufen) stock, sell ⟨*goods*⟩
(c) (durch∼) **Gespräche/Verhandlungen** ∼: hold conversations/negotiations; **eine glückliche Ehe** ∼: be happily married
(d) (leiten) manage, run ⟨*company, business, pub, etc.*⟩; lead ⟨*party, country*⟩; command ⟨*regiment*⟩
(e) (Amtsspr.) drive ⟨*train, motor, vehicle*⟩
(f) (als Kennzeichnung, Bezeichnung haben) bear; **einen Titel/Künstlernamen** ∼: have a title/use a stage name
(g) (angelegt haben) keep ⟨*diary, list, file*⟩
(h) (registrieren) **jmdn. in einer Liste/Kartei** ∼: have sb. on a list/on file
(i) (tragen) **etw. bei** *od.* **mit sich** ∼: have sth. on one; **eine Waffe/einen Ausweis bei sich** ∼: carry a weapon/a pass
⓶ *itr. V.* **(a)** lead
(b) (an der Spitze liegen) lead; be ahead

führend *Adj.* leading; high-ranking ⟨*official*⟩; prominent ⟨*position*⟩

Führer *der;* ∼s, ∼ **(a)** (Leiter) leader
(b) (Fremdenführer, Buch) guide

Führerin *die;* ∼, ∼nen ▶ FÜHRER

führer-, Führer-: ∼**los** ⓵ *Adj.* leaderless; (ohne Lenker) driverless ⟨*car*⟩; ⓶ *adv.* ▶ 1: without a leader; without a driver; ∼**schein** *der* driving licence (Brit.); driver's license (Amer.); ∼**schein-entzug** *der* disqualification from driving; driving ban

Führung *die;* ∼, ∼en **(a)** ▶ FÜHREN 1D: management; running; leadership; command
(b) (Fremdenführung) guided tour
(c) (führende Position) lead

Führungs-: ∼**kraft** *die* manager; ∼**spitze** *die* (Politik) top leadership; (im Betrieb) top management; ∼**zeugnis** *das: document issued by police certifying that holder has no criminal record*

Fuhr-: ∼**unternehmer** *der,* ∼**unternehmerin** *die* haulage contractor; ∼**werk** *das* cart

Fülle *die;* ∼ **(a)** wealth; abundance
(b) (Körper∼) corpulence

füllen ⓵ *tr. V.* **(a)** fill; (Kochk.) stuff
(b) (fig.) fill in ⟨*gap, time*⟩
⓶ *refl. V.* (voll werden) fill [up]

Füller *der;* ∼s, ∼ (ugs.) [fountain] pen

Füll·federhalter *der* fountain pen

füllig *Adj.* corpulent, portly ⟨*person*⟩; ample ⟨*figure, bosom*⟩

Füllung *die;* ∼, ∼en stuffing; (Kochk.; Zahnmed.) filling; (in Schokolade) centre

fummeln *itr. V.* (ugs.) **(a)** (fingern) fiddle
(b) (erotisch) pet

Fund *der;* ∼[e]s, ∼e (auch Archäol.) find

Fundament *das;* ∼[e]s, ∼e **(a)** (Bauw.) foundations *pl.*
(b) (Basis) base; basis

fundamental *Adj.* fundamental

Fundamentalismus *der;* ∼: fundamentalism

Fundamentalist *der;* ∼en, ∼en, **Fundamentalistin** *die;* ∼, ∼nen fundamentalist

Fund-: ∼**büro** *das* lost property office (Brit.); lost and found office (Amer.); ∼**grube** *die* treasure house

fundieren *tr. V.* underpin

fündig *Adj.* ∼ **sein** yield something; ∼ **werden** make a find; (bei Bohrungen) make a strike

Fund·ort *der* place *or* site where sth. is/was found

fünf *Kardinalz.* five

Fünf *die;* ∼, ∼en five; (Schulnote) E

fünf-, Fünf-: ∼**eck** *das;* pentagon; ∼**fach** *Vervielfältigungsz.* fivefold; ∼**fache** *das; adj. Dekl.* five times as much; ∼**hundert** *Kardinalz.* five hundred; ∼**kampf** *der* (Sport) pentathlon

Fünfling *der;* ∼s, ∼e quintuplet; quin (coll.)

fünf-: ∼**mal** *Adv.* five times; ∼**stellig** *Adj.* five-figure

fünft... *Ordinalz.* fifth

Fünf·tagewoche *die* five-day [working] week

fünf·tausend *Kardinalz.* five thousand

fünftel *Bruchz.* fifth

Fünftel *das* (schweiz. meist *der*); ∼s, ∼: fifth

fünftens *Adv.* fifthly

fünf·zehn *Kardinalz.* fifteen

fünfzig *Kardinalz.* fifty

Fünfzig *die;* ∼: fifty

Fünfzig·cent·stück *das* fifty-cent piece

fünfziger *indekl. Adj.* **die Fünfzigerjahre** the fifties

Fünfziger *der;* ∼s, ∼ **(a)** (ugs.) fifty-cent piece/fifty-euro note *etc.*
(b) (50-Jähriger) fifty-year-old

Fünfzig·euro·schein *der* fifty-euro note

fünfzigst... *Ordinalz.* fiftieth

fungieren *itr. V.* **als etw.** ∼ ⟨*person*⟩ act as sth.; ⟨*word etc.*⟩ function as sth.

Funk *der;* ∼s radio

Funk·ausstellung *die* radio and television exhibition

Funke der; ~ns, ~n (auch fig.) spark

funkeln itr. V. ⟨light, star⟩ twinkle; ⟨gold, diamonds⟩ glitter; ⟨eyes⟩ blaze

funken tr. V. radio; ⟨transmitter⟩ broadcast

Funker der; ~s, ~, **Funkerin** die; ~, ~nen radio operator

Funk-: ~**gerät** das radio set; (tragbar) walkie-talkie; ~**haus** das broadcasting centre; ~**kolleg** das radio-based [adult education] course; ~**sprech·gerät** das radiophone; (tragbar) walkie-talkie; ~**spruch** der radio signal; (Nachricht) radio message; ~**station** die, ~**stelle** die radio station; ~**stille** die radio silence; ~**streife** die [police] radio patrol; ~**taxi** das radio taxi; ~**telefon** das radio-telephone

Funktion die; ~, ~en function

Funktionär der; ~s, ~e official; functionary

funktionieren itr. V. work; function

funktions·tüchtig Adj. working; sound ⟨organ⟩

Funk-: ~**turm** der radio tower; ~**verbindung** die radio contact

Funzel die; ~, ~n (ugs.) useless light

für Präp. mit Akk. for; etw. ~ ungültig erklären declare sth. invalid; s. auch WAS 1

Furche die; ~, ~n (a) furrow (b) (Wagenspur) rut

Furcht die; ~: fear; ~ vor jmdm./etw. haben fear sb./sth.

furchtbar ① Adj. (a) dreadful (b) (ugs.: unangenehm) terrible (coll.) ② adv. (ugs.) terribly (coll.)

fürchten ① refl. V. sich [vor jmdm./etw.] ~: be afraid or frightened [of sb./sth.] ② tr. V. be afraid of; ich fürchte, [dass] …: I'm afraid [that] …

fürchterlich Adj., adv. ▶ FURCHTBAR

furcht·los ① Adj. fearless ② adv. fearlessly

furchtsam ① Adj. timid ② adv. timidly

für·einander Adv. for one another; for each other

Furie /ˈfuːriə/ die; ~, ~n Fury

Furnier das; ~s, ~e veneer

Für·sorge die; ~ (a) care (b) (veralt.: Sozialhilfe) welfare (c) (veralt.: Sozialamt) social services pl.

für·sorglich ① Adj. considerate ② adv. considerately

Für·sprache die support

Für·sprecher der, **Für·sprecherin** die advocate

Fürst der; ~en, ~en prince

Fürstentum das; ~s, Fürstentümer principality

Fürstin die; ~, ~nen princess

fürstlich ① Adj. (a) royal

(b) (fig.: üppig) lavish ② adv. lavishly

Furt die; ~, ~en ford

Furunkel der od. das; ~s, ~: boil; furuncle

Für·wort das; Pl. -wörter pronoun

Furz der; ~es, Fürze (derb) fart (coarse); einen ~ lassen let off a fart; jeder ~ (fig.) the slightest thing

furzen itr. V. (derb) fart (coarse)

Fusion die; ~, ~en amalgamation; (von Konzernen) merger

fusionieren itr. V. merge

Fuß der; ~es, Füße foot; (einer Lampe, Säule) base; (von Möbeln) leg; zu ~ gehen go on foot; walk; bei ~! heel!; (fig.) auf freiem ~ sein be at large; auf großem ~ leben live in great style

Fuß·ball der (a) (Ballspiel) [Association] football (b) (Ball) football

Fußballer der; ~s, ~, **Fußballerin** die; ~, ~nen footballer

Fußball-: ~**platz** der football ground; (Spielfeld) football pitch; ~**spiel** das (a) football match; (b) (Sportart) football no art.; ~**spieler** der, ~**spielerin** die football player

Fuß·boden der floor

Fußboden·heizung die underfloor heating

fußen itr. V. auf etw. (Dat.) ~: be based on sth.

Fuß·ende das foot

Fußgänger der; ~s, ~, **Fußgängerin** die; ~, ~nen pedestrian

Fußgänger-: ~**brücke** die footbridge; ~**übergang** der, ~**überweg** der pedestrian crossing; ~**unterführung** die pedestrian subway; ~**zone** die pedestrian precinct

Fuß-: ~**nagel** der toenail; ~**note** die footnote; ~**stapfen** der; ~~s, ~~: footprint; ~**tritt** der kick; ~**volk** das (a) (hist.) footmen pl.; (b) (abwertend: Untergeordnete) lower ranks pl.; ~**weg** der footpath

futsch Adj. (salopp) ~ sein have gone for a burton (Brit. coll.)

Futter[1] das; ~s (Tiernahrung) feed; (für Pferde, Kühe) fodder

Futter[2] das; ~s, ~ (von Kleidungsstücken usw.) lining

Futteral das; ~s, ~e case

Futter·mittel das animal food

füttern[1] tr. V. feed

füttern[2] tr. V. (mit Futter[2] ausstatten) line

Futter·pflanze die fodder plant; forage plant

Fütterung die; ~, ~en feeding

Futur das; ~s, ~e (Sprachw.) future [tense]

Fuzzi der; ~s, ~s (salopp) bozo (sl.)

Gg

g, G /ge:/ *das;* ~, ~ **(a)** (Buchstabe) g/G
   (b) (Musik) [key of] G
g *Abk.* **(a)** = **Gramm** g
   (b) = **Groschen**
gab *1. u. 3. Pers. Sg. Prät. v.* GEBEN
Gabe *die;* ~, ~n **(a)** (geh.: Geschenk, Talent) gift
   (b) (Almosen, Spende) alms *pl.*
Gabel *die;* ~, ~n fork; (Telefon~) cradle
gabeln *refl. V.* fork
Gabel-: ~**schlüssel** *der* flat spanner;
   ~**stapler** *der;* ~~s, ~~: forklift truck
Gabelung *die;* ~, ~en fork
Gaben·tisch *der* gift table
gackern *itr. V.* **(a)** cluck
   (b) (ugs.: lachen) cackle
gaffen *itr. V.* (abwertend) gape; gawp (coll.)
Gaffer *der;* ~s, ~, **Gafferin** *die;* ~,
   ~nen gaper; starer
Gag /gɛk/ *der;* ~s, ~s **(a)** (Theater, Film) gag
   (b) (Besonderheit) gimmick
Gage /'ga:ʒə/ *die;* ~, ~n salary; (für einzelnen Auftritt) fee
gähnen *itr. V.* (auch fig.) yawn
Gala /'ga:la, *auch* 'gala/ *die;* ~: formal dress
galant ① *Adj.* gallant; (amourös) amorous
   ② *adv.* gallantly
Gala·vorstellung *die* gala performance
Galeere *die;* ~, ~n galley
Galerie *die;* ~, ~n gallery
Galgen *der* gallows *sing.*
Galgen-: ~**frist** *die* reprieve; ~**humor** *der* gallows humour
Galle *die;* ~, ~n **(a)** (Gallenblase) gall [bladder]
   (b) (Sekret) (bei Tieren) gall; (bei Menschen) bile
Galopp *der;* ~s, ~s *od.* ~e gallop
galoppieren *itr. V.; meist mit sein* gallop
galt *1. u. 3. Pers. Sg. Prät. v.* GELTEN
galvanisch /gal'va:nɪʃ/ *Adj.* galvanic
Gamasche *die;* ~, ~n gaiter; (bis zum Knöchel reichend) spat
Gambe *die;* ~, ~n (Musik) viola da gamba
Gamma·strahlen *Pl.* (Physik, Med.) gamma rays
gammelig *Adj.* (ugs.) **(a)** bad; rotten
   (b) (unordentlich) scruffy
gammeln *itr. V.* **(a)** (ugs.) go off
   (b) (nichts tun) loaf around; bum around (Amer. coll.)
Gammler *der;* ~s, ~, **Gammlerin** *die;*

~, ~nen (ugs.) dropout (coll.)
Gämse *die;* ~, ~n chamois
gäng: ~ und gäbe sein be quite usual
Gang *der;* ~[e]s, Gänge **(a)** walk; gait
   (b) (Besorgung) errand
   (c) (Verlauf) course
   (d) (Technik) gear
   (e) (Flur) (in Zügen, Gebäuden usw.) corridor;
   (Verbindungs~) passage[way]; (im Theater, Kino, Flugzeug) aisle
   (f) (Kochk.) course
gangbar *Adj.* passable; (fig.) practicable
Gängel·band *das:* jmdn. am ~ führen keep sb. in leading reins
gängeln *tr. V.* (ugs.) jmdn. ~: boss sb. around
gang·genau *Adj.* accurate
Gang·genauigkeit *die* accuracy
gängig *Adj.* **(a)** (üblich) common; (aktuell) current
   (b) (leicht verkäuflich) popular
Gang·schaltung *die* (Technik) gear system; (Art) gear change
Gangway /'gæŋweɪ/ *die;* ~, ~s gangway
Ganove /ga'no:və/ *der;* ~n, ~n (ugs. abwertend) crook (coll.)
Gans *die;* ~, Gänse goose
Gänse-: ~**blümchen** *das* daisy;
   ~**braten** *der* roast goose; ~**füßchen**
   das; ~~s, ~~ (ugs.) ▶ ANFÜHRUNGSZEICHEN;
   ~**haut** *die* (fig.) gooseflesh; goose pimples
   pl.; ~**marsch** im ~marsch in single *or* Indian file
Gänserich *der;* ~s, ~e gander
ganz ① *Adj.* **(a)** (gesamt) whole; entire; den
   ~en Tag/das ~e Jahr all day/year
   (b) (ugs.: alle) die ~en Kinder/Leute/Gläser
   usw. all the children/people/glasses *etc.*
   (c) (vollständig) whole
   (d) (ugs.: ziemlich [groß]) eine ~e Menge/ein
   ~er Haufen quite a lot/quite a pile
   (e) (ugs.: unversehrt) intact; etw. wieder
   ~ machen mend sth.
   ② *adv.* quite
Ganze *das; adj. Dekl.* **(a)** whole
   (b) (alles) das ~: the whole thing
gänzlich *Adv.* entirely
ganz-: ~**tägig** ① *Adj.* all-day; eine
   ~tägige Arbeit a full-time job; ② *adv.* all
   day; ~**tags** *Adv.* ~ arbeiten work full-time
Ganztags-: ~**schule** *die* all-day school;
   (System) all-day schooling *no art.;* ~**stelle**
   die full-time job
gar¹ *Adj.* cooked; done *pred.*
gar² *Partikel* **(a)** (überhaupt) ~ nicht [wahr]
   not [true] at all; ~ nichts nothing at

all; ~ **niemand** od. **keiner** nobody at all;
~ **keines** not a single one; ~ **kein Geld** no
money at all
(b) (südd., österr., schweiz.: verstärkend) ~ **zu**
only too
(c) (geh.: sogar) even

Garage /ga'ra:ʒə/ die; ~, ~n garage

Garagen-: ~**firma** die garage startup;
~**wagen** der garaged car

Garant der; ~en, ~en guarantor

Garantie die; ~, ~n guarantee

Garantie-frist die guarantee period

garantieren ① tr. V. guarantee
② itr. V. **für etw.** ~: guarantee sth.

garantiert Adv. (ugs.) **wir kommen** ~ **zu
spät** we're dead certain to arrive late (coll.)

Garantie-schein der guarantee
[certificate]

Garantin die; ~, ~nen guarantor

Garaus /'ga:ʀlaus/ jmdm. **den** ~ **machen**
do sb. in (coll.)

Garbe die; ~, ~n **(a)** sheaf
(b) (Geschoss~) burst of fire

Garde die; ~, ~n guard

Garderobe die; ~, ~n **(a)** wardrobe;
clothes pl.
(b) (Flur~) coat rack
(c) (im Theater usw.) cloakroom; checkroom
(Amer.)

Garderoben-frau die cloakroom or
(Amer.) checkroom attendant

Gardine die; ~, ~n **(a)** net curtain
(b) (landsch., veralt.) curtain

Gardinen-: ~**predigt** die (ugs.) telling-
off (coll.); (einer Ehefrau zu ihrem Mann) curtain
lecture; ~**stange** die curtain rail

garen tr., itr. V. cook

gären regelm. (auch unr.) itr. V. ferment;
(fig.) seethe

Garn das; ~[e]s, ~e **(a)** thread; (Näh~)
cotton
(b) (Seew.) yarn

Garnele die; ~, ~n shrimp

garnieren tr. V. **(a)** decorate
(b) (Gastr.) garnish

Garnison die; ~, ~en garrison

Garnitur die; ~, ~en **(a)** set; (Wäsche) set of
[matching] underwear; (Möbel) suite
(b) (ugs.) **die erste/zweite** ~: the first/
second-rate people pl.

garstig Adj. nasty; bad ⟨behaviour⟩

Garstigkeit die; ~, ~en **(a)** nastiness
(b) (Handlung) piece of nastiness

Gärtchen das; ~s, ~: little garden

Garten der; ~s, Gärten garden

Garten-: ~**abfall** der garden waste;
~**abfälle** garden waste; ~**arbeit** die
gardening; ~**bau** der horticulture; ~**fest**
das garden party; ~**haus** das summer
house; ~**laube** die summerhouse; garden
house; ~**lokal** das beer garden; (Restaurant)
open-air café; ~**schau** die horticultural

show; ~**wirtschaft** die ▶ ~LOKAL;
~**zwerg** der **(a)** garden gnome; **(b)** (salopp
abwertend) little runt

Gärtner der; ~s, ~: gardener

Gärtnerei die; ~, ~en nursery

Gärtnerin die; ~, ~nen gardener

Gärung die; ~, ~en fermentation

Gas das; ~es, ~e **(a)** gas
(b) (Treibstoff) petrol (Brit.); gasoline (Amer.);
gas (Amer. coll.); ~ **wegnehmen** take one's
foot off the accelerator; ~ **geben** accelerate;
put one's foot down (coll.)

gas-, Gas-: ~**flasche** die gas cylinder;
(für einen Herd, Ofen) gas bottle; ~**förmig**
Adj. gaseous; ~**hahn** der gas tap; ~**herd**
der gas cooker; ~**kammer** die gas
chamber; ~**leitung** die gas pipe; (Hauptrohr)
gas main; ~**maske** die gas mask;
~**pedal** das accelerator [pedal]; gas pedal
(Amer.); ~**pistole** die pistol that fires gas
cartridges

Gasse die; ~, ~n lane; (österr.) street

Gassen-junge der (abwertend) street
urchin

Gast der; ~[e]s, Gäste **(a)** guest
(b) (Besucher eines Lokals) patron
(c) (Besucher) visitor

Gast-: ~**arbeiter** der, ~**arbeiterin**
die immigrant or guest worker; ~**dozent**
der, ~**dozentin** die (Hochschulw.) visiting
lecturer

Gäste-: ~**buch** das guest book; ~**haus**
das guest house; ~**zimmer** das (privat)
guest room; spare room; (im Hotel) room

gast-, Gast-: ~**freundlich** Adj.
hospitable; ~**freundlichkeit** die,
~**freundschaft** die hospitality;
~**geber** der host; ~**geberin** die hostess;
~**haus** das, ~**hof** der inn

gastieren itr. V. give a guest performance

gastlich Adj. hospitable

Gastlichkeit die; ~: hospitality

Gast-professor der,
Gast-professorin die visiting professor

Gastronom der; ~en, ~en restaurateur

Gastronomie die; ~: catering no art.;
(Gaststättengewerbe) restaurant trade

Gastronomin die; ~, ~nen restaurateur

Gast-: ~**spiel** das guest performance;
~**stätte** die public house; (Speiselokal)
restaurant; ~**wirt** der publican; landlord;
(eines Restaurants) [restaurant] proprietor;
(Pächter) restaurant manager; ~**wirtin** die
▶ ~WIRT: publican; landlady; [restaurant]
proprietress or owner; restaurant
manageress; ~**wirtschaft** die ▶ ~STÄTTE

Gas-: ~**vergiftung** die gas poisoning no
indef. art.; ~**versorgung** die gas supply;
~**werk** das gasworks sing.; ~**zähler** der
gas meter

Gatte der; ~n, ~n husband

Gatter *das;* ~s, ~ **(a)** (Zaun) fence; (Lattenzaun) fence; paling
(b) (Tor) gate
Gattin *die;* ~, ~nen (geh.) wife
Gattung *die;* ~, ~en **(a)** kind; sort; (Kunst~) genre; form
(b) (Biol.) genus
GAU *der;* ~s, ~s *Abk.* = **größter anzunehmender Unfall** MCA; maximum credible accident
Gaudi *das;* ~s (bayr., österr.) *die;* ~ (ugs.) bit of fun
Gaukler *der;* ~s, ~, **Gauklerin** *die;* ~, ~nen **(a)** (veralt.: Taschenspieler[in]) itinerant entertainer
(b) (geh.: Betrüger[in]) charlatan
Gaul *der;* ~[e]s, Gäule nag (derog.)
Gaumen *der;* ~s, ~: palate
Gauner *der;* ~s, ~ (abwertend) crook (coll.); rogue
Gaunerei *die;* ~, ~en swindle
Gaunerin *die;* ~, ~nen ▶ GAUNER
Gauner·sprache *die* thieves' cant *or* Latin
Gaze /'ga:zə/ *die;* ~, ~n gauze
geachtet *Adj.* respected
Geäst *das;* ~[e]s branches *pl.*
geb. *Abk.* **(a)** = **geboren;**
(b) = **geborene**
Gebäck *das;* ~[e]s, ~e cakes and pastries *pl.;* (Kekse) biscuits *pl.;* (Törtchen) tarts *pl.*
gebacken 2. *Part. v.* BACKEN
Gebälk *das;* ~[e]s, ~e beams *pl.;* (Dach~) rafters *pl.*
gebar 1. u. 3. *Pers. Sg. Prät. v.* GEBÄREN
Gebärde *die;* ~, ~n gesture
gebärden *refl. V.* behave
gebären *unr. tr. V.* bear; give birth to; *s. auch* GEBOREN
gebär·fähig *Adj.* Frauen im ~fähigen Alter women of child-bearing age.
Gebär·mutter *die; Pl.* Gebär·mütter womb
Gebäude *das;* ~s, ~ **(a)** building
(b) (Gefüge) structure
gebaut *Adj.* gut ~ sein have a good figure
Gebein *das;* ~[e]s, ~e *Pl.* (geh.) bones *pl.;* (sterbliche Reste) [mortal] remains
Gebell *das;* ~[e]s barking; (der Jagdhunde) baying
geben 1 *unr. tr. V.* give; jmdm. die Hand ~: shake sb.'s hand; ~ Sie mir bitte Herrn N. please put me through to Mr N.; Unterricht ~: teach; eins plus eins gibt zwei two and one is *or* makes two; etw. von sich ~: utter sth.
2 *unr. tr. V.* (unpers.) es gibt there is/are; heute gibts Fisch we're having fish today; morgen gibt es Schnee it'll snow tomorrow
3 *unr. itr. V.* **(a)** (Karten austeilen) deal
(b) (Sport: aufschlagen) serve

4 *unr. refl. V.* **(a)** sich [natürlich/steif] ~: act *or* behave [naturally/stiffly]
(b) das gibt sich noch it will get better
Gebet *das;* ~[e]s, ~e prayer
gebeten 2. *Part. v.* BITTEN
Gebets-: ~mühle *die* prayer wheel; ~teppich *der* (islam. Rel.) prayer mat
gebiert 3. *Pers. Sg. Präsens v.* GEBÄREN
Gebiet *das;* ~[e]s, ~e region; area; (Staats~) territory; (Bereich, Fach) field
gebieten (geh.) **(a)** command; order
(b) (erfordern) demand
Gebieter *der;* ~s, ~ (veralt.) master
Gebieterin *die;* ~, ~nen (veralt.) mistress
gebieterisch (geh.) *Adj.* imperious; (herrisch) domineering; peremptory ⟨tone⟩
Gebiets·anspruch *der* territorial claim
Gebilde *das;* ~s, ~: object; (Bauwerk) structure
gebildet *Adj.* educated
Gebimmel *das;* ~s (ugs.) ringing; (von kleinen Glocken) tinkling
Gebirge *das;* ~s, ~: mountain range; im ~: in the mountains
gebirgig *Adj.* mountainous
Gebiss, *Gebiß *das;* Gebisses, Gebisse
(a) set of teeth; teeth *pl.*
(b) (Zahnersatz) denture; plate (coll.); (für beide Kiefer) dentures *pl.*
gebissen 2. *Part. v.* BEISSEN
geblasen 2. *Part. v.* BLASEN
geblichen 2. *Part. v.* BLEICHEN
geblümt *Adj.* flowered
Geblüt *das;* ~[e]s (geh.) blood
gebogen 2. *Part. v.* BIEGEN
geboren 1 2. *Part. v.* GEBÄREN
2 *Adj.* blind/taub ~ sein be born blind/deaf; Frau Anna Schmitz ~e Meyer Mrs Anna Schmitz née Meyer
geborgen 1 2. *Part. v.* BERGEN
2 *Adj.* safe; secure
Geborgenheit *die;* ~: security
geborsten 2. *Part. v.* BERSTEN
gebot 1. u. 3. *Pers. Sg. Prät. v.* GEBIETEN
Gebot *das;* ~[e]s, ~e **(a)** (Grundsatz) precept; die Zehn ~e (Rel.) the Ten Commandments
(b) (Vorschrift) regulation
geboten 1 2. *Part. v.* BIETEN, GEBIETEN
2 *Adj.* (ratsam) advisable; (notwendig) necessary
Gebr. *Abk.* = **Gebrüder** Bros.
gebracht 2. *Part. v.* BRINGEN
gebrannt 2. *Part. v.* BRENNEN
gebraten 2. *Part. v.* BRATEN
Gebrauch *der* **(a)** use
(b) (Brauch) custom
gebrauchen *tr. V.* use
gebräuchlich *Adj.* **(a)** normal; customary
(b) (häufig) common

**alte Schreibung – vgl. Hinweis auf S. x

gebrauchs-, Gebrauchs-: ~**anweisung** *die* instructions *pl.* [for use]; ~**fertig** *Adj.* ready for use *pred.;* ~**gegenstand** *der* item of practical use; ~**wert** *der* utility value

gebraucht *Adj.* second-hand; used ‹*car*›

Gebraucht·wagen *der* used car

Gebrechen *das;* ~**s,** ~ (geh.) affliction

gebrechlich *Adj.* infirm

Gebrechlichkeit *die;* ~: infirmity

gebrochen ① 2. *Part. v.* BRECHEN
② *Adj.* ~es Englisch/Deutsch broken English/German
③ *adv.* ~ **Deutsch sprechen** speak broken German

Gebrüder *Pl.:* **die** ~ **Meyer** Meyer Brothers

Gebrüll *das;* ~[e]s roaring

Gebrumm *das;* ~[e]s (von Bären) growling; (von Flugzeugen, Bienen) droning; (von Insekten) buzz[ing]

gebückt *Adj.* **in** ~**er Haltung** bending forward

Gebühr *die;* ~, ~**en** charge; (Maut) toll; (Anwalts~) fee

gebühren (geh.) *itr. V.* **jmdm. gebührt Achtung** *usw.* sb. deserves respect *etc.*

Gebühren·anzeiger *der* (Fernspr.) telephone meter

gebührend ① *Adj.* fitting
② *adv.* fittingly

gebühren-, Gebühren-: ~**ermäßigung** *die* reduction of charges/fees; ~**frei** ① *Adj.* free of charge *pred.;* ② *adv.* free of charge; ~**pflichtig** *Adj.* **eine** ~**pflichtige Verwarnung** a fine and a caution; ~**vignette** *die* [Swiss] motorway fee sticker

gebunden ① 2. *Part. v.* BINDEN
② *Adj.* (verpflichtet) bound

Geburt *die;* ~, ~**en** birth

Geburten-: ~**kontrolle** *die* birth control; ~**rate** *die* birth rate; ~**ziffer** *die* birth rate

gebürtig *Adj.* **ein** ~**er Schwabe** a Swabian by birth

Geburts-: ~**anzeige** *die* birth announcement; ~**datum** *das* date of birth; ~**haus** *das:* **das** ~**haus Beethovens** the house where Beethoven was born; Beethoven's birthplace; ~**helfer** *der,* ~**helferin** *die* (Arzt, Ärztin) obstetrician; ~**hilfe** *die* (Med.) obstetrics *sing.;* (von einer Hebamme) midwifery; ~**ort** *der* place of birth; ~**stadt** *die* native town/city; ~**tag** *der* birthday; **jmdm. zum** ~**tag gratulieren** wish sb. many happy returns of the day; ~**ur·kunde** *die* birth certificate

Gebüsch *das;* ~[e]s, ~**e** bushes *pl.*

gedacht 2. *Part. v.* DENKEN, GEDENKEN

Gedächtnis *das;* ~**ses,** ~**se (a)** memory
(b) (Andenken) memory

Gedächtnis-: ~**lücke** *die* gap in one's memory; ~**schwund** *der* loss of memory

gedämpft *Adj.* subdued ‹*mood*›; subdued, soft ‹*light*›; muffled ‹*sound*›

Gedanke *der;* ~**ns,** ~**n (a)** thought; **der** ~ **an etw.** (*Akk.*) the thought of sth.
(b) *Pl.* (Meinung) ideas
(c) (Einfall) idea

gedanken-, Gedanken-: ~**gang** *der* train of thought; ~**gut** *das* thought; **christliches** ~**gut** Christian thought; **staatszersetzendes** ~**gut** subversive ideas *pl.;* ~**los** ① *Adj.* unconsidered; (zerstreut) absent-minded; ② *adv.* without thinking; (zerstreut) absent-mindedly; ~**losigkeit** *die;* ~~ (Zerstreutheit) absent-mindedness; (Unüberlegtheit) lack of thought; ~**strich** *der* dash; ~**verloren** *Adv.* lost in thought; ~**voll** ① *Adj.* pensive; ② *adv.* pensively

gedanklich ① *Adj.* intellectual
② *adv.* intellectually

Gedärm *das;* ~[e]s, ~**e** intestines *pl.;* bowels *pl.,* (eines Tieres) entrails *pl.*

Gedeck *das;* ~[e]s, ~**e (a)** place setting; cover
(b) (Menü) set meal
(c) (Getränk) drink [with a cover charge]

gedeihen *unr. itr. V.; mit sein* **(a)** thrive; (wirtschaftlich) flourish; prosper
(b) (fortschreiten) progress

gedenken *unr. itr. V.* **(a)** **jmds./einer Sache** ~ (geh.) remember sb./sth.; (in einer Feier) commemorate sb./sth.
(b) **etw. zu tun** ~: intend to do *or* doing sth.

Gedenk·stätte *die* memorial

Gedicht *das;* ~[e]s, ~**e** poem

gediegen ① *Adj.* solid ‹*furniture*›; sound ‹*piece of work*›
② *adv.* ~ **gebaut/verarbeitet** solidly built/made

gedieh 1. u. 3. *Pers. Sg. Prät. v.* GEDEIHEN

gediehen 2. *Part. v.* GEDEIHEN

Gedränge *das;* ~**s (a)** pushing and shoving; (Menge) crush; crowd
(b) **ins** ~ **kommen** *od.* **geraten** get into difficulties

gedroschen 2. *Part. v.* DRESCHEN

gedrungen ① 2. *Part. v.* DRINGEN
② *Adj.* stocky; thickset

Geduld *die;* ~: patience

gedulden *refl. V.* be patient; ~ **Sie sich bitte ein paar Minuten** please be so good as to wait a few minutes

geduldig ① *Adj.* patient
② *adv.* patiently

Gedulds-: ~**probe** *die* trial of one's patience; ~**spiel** *das* puzzle

gedurft 2. *Part. v.* DÜRFEN

geeignet *Adj.* suitable; (richtig) right

Gefahr *die;* ~, ~**en (a)** danger; (Bedrohung) danger; threat (**für** to); **bei** ~: in case of emergency

g

(b) (Risiko) risk; **auf eigene** ∼: at one's own risk

gefährden *tr. V.* endanger; jeopardize ⟨*enterprise, success, position, etc.*⟩

gefährdet *Adj.* ⟨*people, adolescents, etc.*⟩ at risk *postpos.*

Gefährdung *die;* ∼, ∼**en (a)** endangering; (eines Unternehmens, einer Position usw.) jeopardizing
(b) (Gefahr) threat (+ *Gen.* to)

gefahren *2. Part. v.* FAHREN

gefährlich ① *Adj.* dangerous; (gewagt) risky
② *adv.* dangerously

gefahr·los ① *Adj.* safe
② *adv.* safely

Gefährt *das;* ∼**[e]s,** ∼**e** (geh.) vehicle

Gefährte *der;* ∼**n,** ∼**n, Gefährtin** *die;* ∼, ∼**nen** (geh.) companion; (Ehemann/Ehefrau) partner in life

Gefälle *das;* ∼**s,** ∼: slope; incline; (einer Straße) gradient

gefallen[1] *unr. itr. V.* **(a) das gefällt mir [gut]** I like it [a lot]
(b) sich (*Dat.*) **etw.** ∼ **lassen** put up with sth.

gefallen[2] *2. Part. v.* FALLEN, GEFALLEN

Gefallen[1] *der;* ∼**s,** ∼: favour

Gefallen[2] *das;* ∼**s** pleasure

Gefallene *der; adj. Dekl.* soldier killed in action; **die** ∼**n** the fallen

Gefälle·strecke *die* incline

gefällig ① *Adj.* **(a)** obliging; helpful
(b) (anziehend) pleasing; agreeable ⟨*programme, behaviour*⟩
② *adv.* pleasingly; agreeably

Gefälligkeit *die;* ∼, ∼**en** favour

gefälligst *Adv.* (ugs.) kindly

gefangen *2. Part. v.* FANGEN

Gefangene *der/die; adj. Dekl.* prisoner

gefangen-: *∗*∼**|halten,** *∗*∼**|nehmen**
▶ FANGEN 1

Gefangenschaft *die;* ∼, ∼**en** captivity

Gefängnis *das;* ∼**ses,** ∼**se (a)** prison; gaol
(b) (Strafe) imprisonment

Gefängnis-: ∼**strafe** *die* prison sentence; ∼**wärter** *der,* ∼**wärterin** *die* [prison] warder

Gefasel *das;* ∼**s** (ugs. abwertend) twaddle (coll.); drivel (derog.)

Gefäß *das;* ∼**es,** ∼**e (a)** vessel; container
(b) (Anat.) vessel

gefasst, *∗***gefaßt** *Adj.* **(a)** calm; composed
(b) in auf etw. (*Akk.*) **[nicht]** ∼ **sein** [not] be prepared for sth.

Gefecht *das;* ∼**[e]s,** ∼**e** battle

Gefieder *das;* ∼**s,** ∼: plumage; feathers *pl.*

gefiedert *Adj.* feathered

geflissentlich ① *Adj.* deliberate
② *adv.* deliberately

geflochten *2. Part. v.* FLECHTEN

geflogen *2. Part. v.* FLIEGEN

geflohen *2. Part. v.* FLIEHEN

geflossen *2. Part. v.* FLIESSEN

Geflügel *das;* ∼**s** poultry

Geflügel·schere *die* poultry shears *pl.*

geflügelt *Adj.* winged ⟨*insect, seed*⟩; **ein** ∼**es Wort** (fig.) a standard *or* familiar quotation

gefochten *2. Part. v.* FECHTEN

Gefolge *das;* ∼**s,** ∼: entourage

Gefolgschaft *die;* ∼, ∼**en:** jmdm. ∼ **leisten** obey *or* follow sb.; give one's allegiance to sb.; **jmdm. die** ∼ **verweigern** refuse to obey *or* follow sb.; refuse to give sb. one's allegiance

gefragt *Adj.* in great demand *postpos.;* sought-after

gefräßig *Adj.* (abwertend) greedy

Gefreite *der; adj. Dekl.* (Milit.) lance corporal (Brit.); private first class (Amer.); (Marine) able seaman; (Luftw.) aircraftman first class (Brit.); airman third class (Amer.)

gefressen *2. Part. v.* FRESSEN

gefrieren *unr. itr. V.; mit sein* freeze

gefrier-, Gefrier-: ∼**fach** *das* freezing compartment; ∼**punkt** *der* freezing point; ∼**schrank** *der* freezer; ∼**|trocknen** *tr. V.; meist im Inf. u. 2. Part.* freeze-dry; ∼**truhe** *die* [chest] freezer

gefroren *2. Part. v.* FRIEREN, GEFRIEREN

gefrustet *Adj.* (ugs.) frustrated

Gefüge *das;* ∼**s,** ∼: structure

gefügig *Adj.* compliant; docile ⟨*animal*⟩

Gefühl *das;* ∼**s,** ∼**e (a)** sensation; feeling
(b) (Gemütsverfassung) feeling

gefühl·los *Adj.* **(a)** numb
(b) (herzlos, kalt) unfeeling

gefühls-, Gefühls-: ∼**betont** *Adj.* emotional; ∼**duselei** *die;* ∼∼ (ugs. abwertend) mawkishness; ∼**mäßig** *Adj.* emotional ⟨*reaction*⟩; ⟨*action*⟩ based on emotion; ∼**regung** *die* emotion

gefühl·voll ① *Adj.* sensitive; (ausdrucksvoll) expressive
② *adv.* sensitively; expressively

gefüllt *2. Part. v.* FÜLLEN

gefunden *2. Part. v.* FINDEN

Gegacker *das;* ∼**s (a)** (dauerndes Gackern) cackling
(b) (ugs.: Kichern) giggling

gegangen *2. Part. v.* GEHEN

gegeben *2. Part. v.* GEBEN

gegebenen·falls *Adv.* should the occasion arise

gegen *Präp. mit Akk.* **(a)** against; ∼ **etw. stoßen** knock into sth.; **ein Mittel** ∼ **Krebs** a cure for cancer; ∼ **die Abmachung** contrary

to the agreement
(b) ～ **Abend/Morgen** towards evening/
dawn; ～ **vier Uhr** around 4 o'clock
(c) (im Vergleich zu) compared with
(d) (im Ausgleich für) for; ～ **Quittung** against a
receipt
Gegen-: ～**angriff** der counter-attack;
～**argument** das counter-argument;
～**besuch** der return visit
Gegend die; ～, ～**en (a)** area
(b) (Körperregion) region
Gegen-: ～**darstellung** die: **eine**
～**darstellung [der Sache]** an account [of
the matter] from an opposing point of view;
～**druck** der counter pressure
gegen·einander Adv. against each other
or one another
gegen-, Gegen-: ～**gewicht** das
counterweight; **ein** ～**gewicht zu** od. **gegen**
etw. bilden (fig.) counterbalance sth.;
～**gift** das antidote; ～**kandidat** der,
～**kandidatin** die opposing candidate;
rival candidate; ～**leistung** die service in
return; ～**mittel** das (gegen Gift) antidote;
(gegen Krankheit) remedy; ～**partei** die
opposing side; other side; (Sport) opposing
side or team; ～**probe** die cross-check;
～**satz** der **(a)** (Gegenteil) opposite; **im**
～**satz zu** in contrast to or with; unlike;
(b) (Widerspruch) conflict; ～**sätzlich** Adj.
conflicting; ～**schlag** der counterstroke;
zum ～**schlag ausholen** prepare to
counter-attack or strike back; ～**seite**
die **(a)** (einer Straße, eines Flusses usw.) other
side; far side; **(b)** ▶ ～PARTEI; ～**seitig**
[1] Adj. (wechselseitig) mutual; [2] adv. **sich**
～**seitig helfen/überbieten** help/outdo each
other or one another; ～**seitigkeit** die;
～～: reciprocity; **auf** ～**seitigkeit** (Dat.)
beruhen be mutual; ～**spieler** der,
～**spielerin** die opponent; (Sport) opposite
number
Gegen·stand der object; (Thema) subject;
topic
gegenständlich Adj. (Kunst)
representational; (Philos.) objective
gegenstands·los Adj. **(a)** (hinfällig)
invalid
(b) (grundlos, unbegründet) unfounded
⟨accusation, complaint, jealousy⟩; baseless
⟨fear⟩
gegen-, Gegen-: ～**stimme** die vote
against; **ohne** ～**stimme** unanimously;
～**stück** das companion piece; (fig.)
counterpart; ～**teil** das opposite; **im** ～**teil**
on the contrary; ～**teilig** Adj. opposite;
contrary; ～**tor** das (Sport) goal for the other
side
gegen·über Präp. mit Dat. **(a)** opposite
(b) (in Bezug auf) ～ **jmdm.** od. **jmdm.**
～ **freundlich sein** be kind to sb.
(c) (im Vergleich zu) compared with
gegenüber-, Gegenüber-:
～|**stehen** unr. itr. V. **(a)** jmdm./einer

Sache ～**stehen** stand facing sb./sth.;
(fig.) face sb./sth.; **(b)** jmdm./einer Sache
feindlich/wohlwollend ～**stehen** be ill/well
disposed towards sb./sth.; ～|**stellen**
tr. V. confront; ～**stellung** die
(a) confrontation; **(b)** (Vergleich) comparison;
(c) (zur Identifizierung) identification parade;
～|**treten** unr. itr. V.; mit sein jmdm./einer
Sache ～**treten** (auch fig.) face sb./sth.
Gegen·verkehr der oncoming traffic
Gegenwart die; ～ **(a)** present
(b) (Anwesenheit) presence
(c) (Grammatik) present [tense]
gegenwärtig [1] Adj. present
[2] adv. at present; at the moment
Gegen-: ～**wehr** die resistance; ～**wert**
der equivalent; ～**wind** der head wind;
～**zug** der (Brettspiele, fig.) countermove
gegessen 2. Part. v. ESSEN
geglichen 2. Part. v. GLEICHEN
geglitten 2. Part. v. GLEITEN
Gegner der; ～s, ～, **Gegnerin** die; ～,
～**nen (a)** adversary; opponent
(b) (Sport) opponent
gegnerisch Adj. opposing; opponents'
⟨goal⟩
Gegnerschaft die; ～ (Einstellung)
hostility; antagonism
gegolten 2. Part. v. GELTEN
gegoren 2. Part. v. GÄREN
gegossen 2. Part. v. GIESSEN
gegriffen 2. Part. v. GREIFEN
Gehabe das; ～s (abwertend) affected
behaviour; **ihr wichtigtuerisches** ～: her
pompous behaviour
gehabt Adj. (ugs.: schon da gewesen) same old
(coll.); usual; **wie** ～: as before
Gehalt¹ der; ～[e]s, ～e **(a)** meaning
(b) (Anteil) content
Gehalt² das, (österr. auch: der) ～[e]s,
Gehälter salary
gehalten 2. Part. v. HALTEN
Gehalts-: ～**abrechnung** die salary
statement; payslip; ～**empfänger** der,
～**empfängerin** die salary earner;
～**erhöhung** die salary increase;
～**zettel** der salary slip
gehalt·voll Adj. nutritious ⟨food⟩; ⟨novel,
speech⟩ rich in substance
gehässig Adj. (abwertend) spiteful
Gehässigkeit die; ～, ～**en (a)** (Wesen)
spitefulness
(b) (Äußerung) spiteful remark
gehauen 2. Part. v. HAUEN
gehäuft Adj. **ein** ～**er Teelöffel/Esslöffel** a
heaped teaspoon/tablespoon
Gehäuse das; ～s, ～ (einer Maschine)
casing; housing; (einer Kamera, Uhr) case
geh·behindert Adj. able to walk only
with difficulty postpos.; disabled
Gehege das; ～s, ～ **(a)** (Jägerspr.)
preserve; **jmdm. ins** ～ **kommen** (fig.) ⋯⟩

poach on sb.'s preserve; **sich** (*Dat.*)
[gegenseitig] ins ∼ **kommen** (fig.) encroach
on each other's territory
(b) (im Zoo) enclosure
geheim ① *Adj.* **(a)** secret; **etw.** ∼ **halten**
keep sth. secret
(b) (mysteriös) mysterious
② *adv.* ∼ **abstimmen** vote by secret ballot
geheim-, Geheim-: ∼**agent** *der,*
∼**agentin** *die* secret agent; ∼**dienst** *der*
secret service; *∼|**halten** ▸ GEHEIM 1A
Geheimnis *das;* ∼**ses,** ∼**se** secret
Geheimnis·tuerei *die;* ∼ (ugs.)
secretiveness
geheimnis·voll *Adj.* mysterious
Geheim·nummer *die* **(a)** (Bankw.)
personal identification number; PIN
(b) (Telefonnummer) ex-directory number;
unlisted number (Amer.)
Geheim·zahl *die* ▸ GEHEIMNUMMER A
Geheiß *das:* **auf jmds.** ∼ (geh.) at sb.'s
behest
gehen ① *unr. itr. V.; mit sein* **(a)** walk; go;
über die Straße ∼: cross the street
(b) (sich irgendwohin begeben) go
(c) (regelmäßig besuchen) attend
(d) (weg∼) go; leave
(e) (in Funktion sein) work; **meine Uhr geht
falsch** my watch is wrong
(f) (möglich sein) **ja, das geht** yes, I/we can
manage that; **das geht nicht** that can't be
done
(g) (ugs.: gerade noch angehen) **Hast du gut
geschlafen? – Es geht** Did you sleep well?
– Not too bad
(h) (sich entwickeln) **der Laden/das Geschäft
geht gut/gar nicht** the shop/business is
doing well/not doing well at all; **es ist gut
gegangen** it turned out well
(i) (*unpers.*) **wie geht es dir?** How are you?;
jmdm. geht es gut/schlecht (gesundheitlich)
sb. is well/not well; (geschäftlich) sb. is doing
well/badly
(j) (*unpers.*) (sich um etw. handeln); **worum geht
es hier?** what is this all about?
(k) sich ∼ **lassen** (sich nicht beherrschen) lose
control of oneself; (sich vernachlässigen) let
oneself go
(l) (ein Liebespaar sein) **mit jmdm.** ∼: go out
with sb.
② *unr. tr. V.* (zurücklegen) **10 km** ∼: walk
10 km
*g**ehen**|**lassen** ▸ GEHEN 1K
geheuer *Adj.* **(a)** **in diesem Gebäude ist es
nicht** ∼: this building is eerie
(b) **ihr war doch nicht [ganz]** ∼: she felt [a
little] uneasy
(c) **die Sache ist [mir] nicht ganz** ∼: [I feel]
there's something odd about this business
Gehilfe *der;* ∼**n,** ∼**n, Gehilfin** *die;* ∼,
∼**nen** assistant
Gehirn *das;* ∼**[e]s,** ∼**e** brain

Gehirn-: ∼**erschütterung** *die*
concussion; ∼**schlag** *der* stroke;
∼**wäsche** *die* brainwashing *no indef. art.*
gehoben ① 2. *Part. v.* HEBEN
② *Adj.* **(a)** higher; senior ⟨*position*⟩
(b) (gewählt) elevated, refined
geholfen 2. *Part. v.* HELFEN
Gehör *das;* ∼**[e]s** [sense of] hearing; **[etw.]
nach dem** ∼ **singen/spielen** sing/play [sth.]
by ear; **das absolute** ∼ (Musik) absolute pitch
gehorchen *itr. V.* jmdm. ∼: obey sb.
gehören ① *itr. V.* **(a)** jmdm. ∼: belong
to sb.
(b) (Teil eines Ganzen sein) **zu jmds. Freunden/
Aufgaben** ∼: be one of sb.'s friends/part of
sb.'s duties
(c) (passend sein) **dein Roller gehört nicht in
die Küche!** your scooter does not belong in
the kitchen!
(d) (nötig sein) **es hat viel Fleiß dazu gehört**
it took a lot of hard work; **dazu gehört sehr
viel** that takes a lot
② *refl. V.* (sich schicken) be fitting; **es
gehört sich [nicht], ... zu ...**: it is [not] good
manners to ...
gehörig ① *Adj.* **(a)** proper
(b) (ugs.: beträchtlich) **ein** ∼**er Schrecken/eine**
∼**e Portion Mut** a good fright/a good deal of
courage
② *adv.* (ugs.: beträchtlich) ∼ **essen/trinken**
eat/drink heartily
gehorsam *Adj.* obedient
Gehorsam *der;* ∼**s** obedience
Geh·steig *der;* ∼**[e]s,** ∼**e** pavement (Brit.);
sidewalk (Amer.)
Geht·nicht·mehr *das:* **bis zum** ∼ (salopp)
ad nauseam
Gehupe *das;* ∼**s** honking; hooting
Geier *der;* ∼**s,** ∼: vulture
Geige *die;* ∼, ∼**n** violin
Geiger *der;* ∼**s,** ∼, **Geigerin** *die;* ∼,
∼**nen** violin player; violinist
Geiger·zähler *der* (Physik) Geiger counter
geil *Adj.* **(a)** (oft abwertend: sexuell erregt)
randy; horny (sl.); (lüstern) lecherous
(b) (Jugendspr.) great (coll.); fabulous (coll.)
Geilheit *die;* ∼ ▸ GEIL A randiness;
horniness (sl.); lecherousness
Geisel *die;* ∼, ∼**n** hostage
Geisel-: ∼**nahme** *die;* ∼∼, ∼∼**n** taking
of hostages; ∼**nehmer** *der;* ∼∼**s,** ∼∼,
∼**nehmerin** *die;* ∼∼, ∼∼**nen** terrorist/
guerrilla *etc.* holding the hostages
Geißel *die;* ∼, ∼**n** (hist., auch fig.) scourge
Geist *der;* ∼**[e]s,** ∼**er (a)** (Verstand) mind
(b) (Scharfsinn) wit
(c) (innere Einstellung) spirit
(d) (denkender Mensch) mind; intellect; **ein
großer/kleiner** ∼: a great mind/a person of
limited intellect
(e) (überirdisches Wesen) spirit; **der Heilige** ∼
(christl. Rel.) the Holy Ghost *or* Spirit
(f) (Gespenst) ghost

Geister-: ~**bahn** *die* ghost train;
~**fahrer** *der;* ~**fahrerin** *die: person
driving on the wrong side of the road or the
wrong carriageway*

geisterhaft *Adj.* ghostly; eerie
⟨*atmosphere*⟩

Geister·hand *die:* **wie von** *od.* **durch** ~: as
if by an invisible hand

geistes-, Geistes-: ~**abwesend**
⏢1⏢ *Adj.* absent-minded; ⏢2⏢ *adv.* absent-
mindedly; ~**blitz** *der* (ugs.) brainwave;
~**gegenwart** *die* presence of mind;
~**gegenwärtig** ⏢1⏢ *Adj.* quick-
witted; ⏢2⏢ *adv.* with great presence
of mind; ~**krank** *Adj.* mentally ill;
~**krankheit** *die* mental illness;
~**wissenschaften** *Pl.* arts;
humanities; ~**wissenschaftler** *der,*
~**wissenschaftlerin** *die* arts scholar;
scholar in the humanities; ~**zustand** *der*
mental state

geistig ⏢1⏢ *Adj.* **(a)** intellectual; (Psych.)
mental
(b) alcoholic ⟨*drinks*⟩
⏢2⏢ *adv.* intellectually; (Psych.) mentally

geistlich *Adj.* sacred ⟨*song, music*⟩;
religious ⟨*order, book, writings*⟩

Geistliche *der; adj. Dekl.* clergyman

geist-, Geist-: ~**los** *Adj.* dim-witted;
(trivial) trivial; ~**losigkeit** *die;* ~~: dim-
wittedness; (Trivialität) triviality; ~**reich**
⏢1⏢ *Adj.* witty; (klug) clever; ⏢2⏢ *adv.:* wittily;
cleverly; ~**tötend** *Adj.* soul-destroying
⟨*work, job*⟩; stupefyingly boring ⟨*chatter,
drivel*⟩

Geiz *der;* ~**es** meanness; (Knauserigkeit)
miserliness

geizen *itr. V.* be mean

Geiz·hals *der* (abwertend) skinflint

geizig *Adj.* mean; (knauserig) miserly

gekannt *2. Part. v.* KENNEN

Gekicher *das;* ~**s** giggling

geklungen *2. Part. v.* KLINGEN

geknickt *Adj.* (ugs.) dejected

gekniffen *2. Part. v.* KNEIFEN

gekommen *2. Part. v.* KOMMEN

gekonnt ⏢1⏢ *2. Part. v.* KÖNNEN
⏢2⏢ *Adj.* accomplished; (hervorragend ausgeführt)
masterly

gekrochen *2. Part. v.* KRIECHEN

gekünstelt ⏢1⏢ *Adj.* artificial
⏢2⏢ *adv.* **er lächelte** ~: he gave a forced smile

Gelächter *das;* ~**s,** ~: laughter

geladen *2. Part. v.* LADEN

Gelände *das;* ~**s,** ~ **(a)** (Landschaft)
ground; terrain
(b) (Grundstück) site; (von Schule, Krankenhaus
usw.) grounds *pl.*

Geländer *das;* ~**s,** ~: banisters *pl.;*
handrail; (am Balkon, an einer Brücke)

railing[s *pl.*]; (aus Stein) parapet

gelang *3. Pers. Sg. Prät. v.* GELINGEN

gelangen *itr. V.; mit sein* **an etw.** (Akk.)/**zu
etw.** ~: reach sth.; (fig.) **zu Ansehen** ~: gain
esteem

gelassen ⏢1⏢ *2. Part. v.* LASSEN
⏢2⏢ *Adj.* calm; (gefasst) composed

Gelassenheit *die;* ~: calmness;
(Gefasstheit) composure

Gelatine /ʒela'ti:nə/ *die;* ~: gelatine

gelaufen *2. Part. v.* LAUFEN

geläufig *Adj.* (vertraut) common ⟨*expression,
concept*⟩

gelaunt *Adj.* **gut** ~: cheerful; **schlecht**
~: bad-tempered; **gut/schlecht** ~ **sein** be in
a good/bad mood

gelb *Adj.* yellow

Gelb *das;* ~**s,** ~ *od.* (ugs.) ~**s** yellow

gelblich *Adj.* yellowish; yellowed ⟨*paper*⟩;
sallow ⟨*skin*⟩

Gelb·sucht *die* (Med.) jaundice

Geld *das;* ~**es,** ~**er** money; **großes**
~: large denominations *pl.;* **kleines/bares**
~: change/cash

geld-, Geld-: ~**automat** *der* cash
dispenser; ~**beutel** *der* (bes. südd.)
purse; ~**börse** *die* purse; ~**buße** *die*
fine; ~**gier** *die* avarice; ~**gierig** *Adj.*
avaricious; ~**haus** *das,* ~**institut**
das financial institution; ~**karte**
die cash card; ~**mangel** *der* lack of
money; ~**mittel** *Pl.* financial resources;
~**preis** *der* cash prize; ~**rück·gabe**
die **(a)** ~**rückgabe verlangen** ask for one's
money back; **Anspruch auf** ~**rückgabe
haben** be entitled to one's money back;
(b) (eines Automaten) coin return; ~**schein**
der banknote; bill (Amer.); ~**schrank** *der*
safe; ~**schwierigkeiten** *Pl.* financial
difficulties *or* straits; ~**spende** *die*
donation; contribution; ~**strafe** *die*
fine; ~**stück** *das* coin; ~**wechsel** *der*
exchanging of money; „~**wechsel**" 'bureau
de change'

Gelee /ʒe'le:/ *der od. das;* ~**s,** ~**s** jelly

gelegen ⏢1⏢ *2. Part. v.* LIEGEN
⏢2⏢ *Adj.* (passend) convenient

Gelegenheit *die;* ~, ~**en** opportunity;
(Anlass) occasion

Gelegenheits-: ~**arbeit** *die* casual
work; ~**kauf** *der* bargain

gelegentlich ⏢1⏢ *Adj.* occasional
⏢2⏢ *adv.* occasionally

gelehrig *Adj.* ⟨*child*⟩ who is quick to learn;
⟨*animal*⟩ that is quick to learn

gelehrt *Adj.* learned

Gelehrte *der/die; adj. Dekl.* scholar

Geleit *das;* ~[e]s, ~**e** (geh.) **sie bot uns ihr**
~ **an** she offered to accompany us

geleiten *tr. V.* (geh.) escort

Geleit·schutz *der* (Milit.) escort

Gelenk *das;* ~[e]s, ~**e** joint ····⟩

gelenkig ☐1 *Adj.* agile ⟨*person*⟩; supple ⟨*limb*⟩
☐2 *adv.* agilely
Gelenkigkeit *die;* ~: agility; (von Gliedmaßen) suppleness
gelernt *Adj.* qualified
gelesen 2. *Part. v.* LESEN
Geliebte *der/die; adj. Dekl.* lover/mistress
geliefert *Adj.:* ~ **sein** (salopp) have had it (coll.)
geliehen 2. *Part. v.* LEIHEN
gelind[e] ☐1 *Adj.* mild
☐2 *adv.* mildly; ~**e gesagt** to put it mildly
gelingen *unr. itr. V.; mit sein* succeed
Gelingen *das;* ~s success
gelitten 2. *Part. v.* LEIDEN
gellen *itr. V.* **(a)** (hell schallen) ring out
(b) (nachhallen) ring
geloben *tr. V.* (geh.) vow; **das Gelobte Land** the Promised Land
gelogen 2. *Part. v.* LÜGEN
gelöst *Adj.* relaxed
gelten ☐1 *unr. itr. V.* **(a)** (gültig sein) be valid; ⟨*banknote, coin*⟩ be legal tender; ⟨*law etc.*⟩ be in force
(b) (angesehen werden) **als etw.** ~: be regarded as sth.
(c) (+ *Dat.*) (bestimmt sein für) be directed at
☐2 *unr. tr. V.* **(a)** (wert sein) **sein Wort gilt viel/wenig** his word carries a lot of/little weight
(b) *unpers.* **es gilt, etw. zu tun** it is essential to do sth.
geltend: **etw.** ~ **machen** assert sth.
Geltung *die;* ~ **(a)** validity; **für jmdn.** ~ **haben** apply to sb.
(b) (Wirkung) recognition; **zur** ~ **kommen** show to [its best] advantage
Geltungs·bedürfnis *das* need for recognition
gelungen ☐1 2. *Part. v.* GELINGEN
☐2 *Adj.* **(a)** (ugs.: spaßig) priceless
(b) (ansprechend) inspired
gemächlich /gə'mɛ(ː)çlɪç/ ☐1 *Adj.* leisurely
☐2 *adv.* in a leisurely manner
Gemächlichkeit *die;* ~: leisureliness
gemacht: **ein** ~**er Mann sein** (ugs.) be a made man
Gemahl *der;* ~s, ~e (geh.) consort; husband
Gemahlin *die;* ~, ~nen (geh.) consort; wife
Gemälde *das;* ~s, ~: painting
gemäß *Präp. + Dat.* in accordance with
gemäßigt *Adj.* moderate; qualified ⟨*optimism*⟩; temperate ⟨*climate*⟩
Gemecker[e] *das;* ~s **(a)** (von Schafen, Ziegen) bleating
(b) (ugs. abwertend: Nörgelei) griping (coll.); grousing (coll.); moaning

gemein ☐1 *Adj.* **(a)** vulgar ⟨*joke, expression*⟩; nasty ⟨*person*⟩
(b) (niederträchtig) mean; dirty ⟨*lie*⟩; mean ⟨*trick*⟩
☐2 *adv.* in a mean *or* nasty way
Gemeinde *die;* ~, ~n **(a)** municipality; (Bewohner) community
(b) (Pfarr~) parish
(c) (versammelte Gottesdienstteilnehmer) congregation
Gemeinde-: ~**rat** *der* **(a)** (Gremium) local council; **(b)** (Mitglied) local councillor; ~**rätin** *die* local councillor; ~**schwester** *die* district nurse; ~**verwaltung** *die* local administration
gemein·gefährlich *Adj.* dangerous to the public
Gemein·gut *das* (geh.) common property
Gemeinheit *die;* ~, ~en **(a)** meanness
(b) (Handlung) mean trick
gemein·nützig *Adj.* serving the public good *postpos., not pred.;* (wohltätig) charitable
gemeinsam ☐1 *Adj.* **(a)** common ⟨*interests, characteristics*⟩; mutual ⟨*acquaintance, friend*⟩; joint ⟨*property, account*⟩; shared ⟨*experience*⟩; ~**e Interessen/Merkmale haben** have interests/ characteristics in common
(b) (miteinander unternommen) joint; **viel Gemeinsames haben** have a lot in common
☐2 *adv.* together
Gemeinsamkeit *die;* ~, ~en common feature
Gemeinschaft *die;* ~, ~en
(a) community
(b) (Verbundenheit) coexistence
gemeinschaftlich ▶ GEMEINSAM
gemein·verständlich *Adj.* generally comprehensible
Gemein·wohl *das* public good
gemessen ☐1 2. *Part. v.* MESSEN
☐2 *Adj.* (würdevoll) measured ⟨*steps, tones, language*⟩; deliberate ⟨*words, manner of speaking*⟩
Gemetzel *das;* ~s, ~: massacre
gemieden 2. *Part. v.* MEIDEN
Gemisch *das;* ~[e]s, ~e mixture (**aus**, **von** of)
gemocht 2. *Part. v.* MÖGEN
gemolken 2. *Part. v.* MELKEN
Gemse ▶ GÄMSE
Gemurmel *das;* ~s murmuring
***Gemüse** *das;* ~s, ~: vegetables *pl.*
gemusst, * **gemußt** 2. *Part. v.* MÜSSEN
Gemüt *das;* ~[e]s, ~er **(a)** nature
(b) (Empfindungsvermögen) heart
(c) (Mensch) soul
gemütlich ☐1 *Adj.* snug; cosy; (bequem) comfortable; (ungezwungen) informal
☐2 *adv.* cosily; (bequem) comfortably; ~ **beisammensitzen** sit pleasantly together

---

Gemütlichkeit *die;* ~: snugness; (Zwanglosigkeit) informality

gemüts-, Gemüts-: ~**krank** *Adj.* (Med., Psych.) emotionally disturbed; ~**mensch** *der* (ugs.) even-tempered person

gemüt·voll *Adj.* warm-hearted; (empfindsam) sentimental

Gen *das;* ~s, ~e (Biol.) gene

Gen- GM ⟨*maize, rape etc.*⟩

genannt 2. *Part. v.* NENNEN

genas 1. *u.* 3. *Pers. Sg. Prät. v.* GENESEN

genau ⟨1⟩ *Adj.* (a) (exakt) exact; precise (b) (sorgfältig, gründlich) meticulous, ⟨*person*⟩; careful ⟨*study*⟩ ⟨2⟩ *adv.* (a) exactly; precisely; ~ **um 8⁰⁰** at 8 o'clock precisely (b) (gerade, eben) just (c) (als Verstärkung) just (d) (als Zustimmung) exactly; precisely (e) (sorgfältig) ~ **arbeiten/etw.** ~ **durchdenken** work/think sth. out meticulously; ~ **genommen** strictly speaking

****genau·genommen** ▸ GENAU 2E

Genauigkeit *die;* ~ (a) (Exaktheit) exactness; precision; (einer Waage) accuracy (b) (Sorgfalt) meticulousness

genau·so *Adv.* (a) *mit Adjektiven* just as (b) *mit Verben* in exactly the same way; (in demselben Maße) just as much

genaustens *Adv.* etw. ~ **durchdenken/ beachten** think sth. out/observe sth. most meticulously

Gendarm /ʒanˈdarm/ *der;* ~en, ~en (österr., sonst veralt.) village *or* local policeman *or* constable

Gendarmerie /ʒandarməˈriː/ *die;* ~, ~n (österr., sonst veralt.) village *or* local constabulary

genehm *Adj.* jmdm. ~ **sein** (geh.) (jmdm. passen) be convenient to sb.; (jmdm. angenehm sein) be acceptable to sb.

genehmigen *tr. V.* approve ⟨*plan, alterations, application*⟩; authorize ⟨*stay*⟩; grant ⟨*request*⟩; give permission for ⟨*demonstration*⟩; **sich** (*Dat.*) **etw.** ~ (ugs.) treat oneself to sth.

Genehmigung *die;* ~, ~en (a) ▸ GENEHMIGEN; approval; authorization; granting; permission (*Gen.* for) (b) (Schriftstück) permit; (Lizenz) licence

geneigt *Adj.* **in** ~ **sein, etw. zu tun** be inclined to do sth.

General *der;* ~s, ~e *od.* Generäle general

General-: ~**direktor** *der* chairman; president (Amer.); ~**direktorin** *die* chairwoman; president (Amer.)

generalisieren *tr., itr. V.* generalize

Generalisierung *die;* ~, ~en generalization

general-, General-: ~**probe** *die*

(auch fig.) dress rehearsal; ~**streik** *der* general strike; ~**überholen** *tr. V.; nur im Inf. und 2. Part. gebr.* (bes. Technik) etw. ~**überholen** give sth. a general overhaul; ~**vertreter** *der,* ~**vertreterin** *die* general representative; ~**vollmacht** *die* (Rechtsw.) full *or* unlimited power of attorney

Generation *die;* ~, ~en generation

Generations·konflikt *der* generation gap

Generator *der;* ~s, ~en generator

generell ⟨1⟩ *Adj.* general ⟨2⟩ *adv.* generally

genervt *Adj.* annoyed

genesen *unr. itr. V.; mit sein* (geh.) recover

Genesung *die;* ~, ~en (geh.) recovery

genetisch (Biol.) *Adj.* genetic

Genf (*das*); ~s Geneva

Genfer ⟨1⟩ *der;* ~, ~: Genevese ⟨2⟩ *Adj.* Genevese; **der** ~ See Lake Geneva

Genferin *die;* ~, ~nen Genevese

Gen·forschung *die* (Biol.) genetic research

genial *Adj.* brilliant

Genialität *die;* ~: genius

Genick *das;* ~[e]s, ~e back *or* nape of the neck

Genie /ʒeˈniː/ *das;* ~s, ~s genius

genieren /ʒeˈniːrən/ *refl. V.* be embarrassed

genießbar *Adj.* (essbar) edible; (trinkbar) drinkable; **er ist heute nicht** ~ (fig. ugs.) he is unbearable today

genießen *unr. tr. V.* enjoy

Genießer *der;* ~s, ~, **Genießerin** *die;* ~, ~nen: **er ist ein richtiger Genießer** he is a regular 'bon viveur'; **sie ist eine stille Genießerin** she enjoys life [to the full] in her own quiet way

genießerisch ⟨1⟩ *Adj.* appreciative ⟨2⟩ *adv.* appreciatively; ⟨*drink, eat*⟩ with relish

Genitale *das;* ~s, **Genitalien** /geniˈtaːliən/, **Genital·organ** *das* genital organ

Genitiv *der;* ~s, ~e (Sprachw.) genitive [case]

Gen·manipulation *die* genetic manipulation

gen·manipuliert *Adj.* genetically engineered; genetically manipulated

Genom /geˈnoːm/ *das;* ~s, ~e (Biol.) genome

genommen 2. *Part. v.* NEHMEN

genoss, *genoß 1. *u.* 3. *Pers. Sg. Prät. v.* GENIESSEN

Genosse *der;* ~n, ~n comrade

genossen 2. *Part. v.* GENIESSEN

Genossenschaft *die;* ~, ~en cooperative ⋯⟩

Genossin *die;* ~, ~nen comrade
gen-, Gen-: ~**technik** *die* genetic
engineering *no art.;* ~**technisch** 1 *Adj.*
genetic engineering ⟨*techniques, research
etc.*⟩; ⟨*research, developments etc.*⟩ in genetic
engineering; 2 *adv.* by genetic engineering;
~**technisch verändert** genetically altered
or modified; altered *or* modified by genetic
engineering; ~**technologie** *die* genetic
engineering *no art.;* ~**test** *der* genetic test;
genetic testing *no art.*
genug *Adv.* enough
genügen *itr. V.* **(a)** be enough
(b) einer Sache (*Dat.*) ~: satisfy sth.
genügend 1 *Adj.* **(a)** enough
(b) (befriedigend) satisfactory
2 *adv.* enough
genügsam *Adj.* modest
Genugtuung /-tuːʊŋ/ *die;* ~, ~en
satisfaction
Genus *das;* ~, Genera (Sprachw.) gender
Genuss, *Genuß *der;* Genusses,
Genüsse **(a)** consumption
(b) (Wohlbehagen) etw. mit ~ essen/lesen eat
sth. with relish/enjoy reading sth.
genüsslich, *genüßlich *Adv.* ⟨*eat,
drink*⟩ with relish
gen·verändert *Adj.* genetically modified
Geograph *der;* ~en, ~en geographer
Geographie *die;* ~: geography *no art.*
Geographin *die;* ~, ~nen geographer
geographisch *Adj.* geographic[al]
Geologe *der;* ~n, ~n geologist
Geologie *die;* ~: geology *no art.*
Geologin *die;* ~, ~nen geologist
geologisch *Adj.* geological
Geometrie *die;* ~: geometry *no art.*
geometrisch *Adj.* geometric[al]
Gepäck *das;* ~[e]s luggage (Brit.); baggage
(Amer.); (am Flughafen) baggage
Gepäck-: ~**annahme** *die* **(a)** checking
in the luggage/baggage; **(b)** (Schalter)
[in-counter of the] luggage office (Brit.) *or*
baggage office (Amer.); (zur Aufbewahrung)
[in-counter of the] left-luggage office (Brit.)
or checkroom (Amer.); (am Flughafen) baggage
check-in; ~**aufbewahrung** *die* left-
luggage office (Brit.); checkroom (Amer.);
(Schließfächer) luggage lockers (Brit.); baggage
lockers (Amer.); ~**ausgabe** *die* [out-
counter of the] luggage office (Brit.) *or* (Amer.)
baggage office; (zur Aufbewahrung) [out-counter
of the] left-luggage office (Brit.) *or* (Amer.)
checkroom; (am Flughafen) baggage reclaim;
~**kontrolle** *die* baggage check; ~**netz**
das luggage rack (Brit.); baggage rack
(Amer.); ~**schalter** *der* ▸ ~ANNAHME B;
~**schein** *der* luggage ticket (Brit.); baggage
check (Amer.); ~**träger** *der* **(a)** porter;
(b) (am Fahrrad) carrier; rack

---

*alte Schreibung – vgl. Hinweis auf S. x

Gepard *der;* ~s, ~e cheetah; hunting
leopard
gepfeffert *Adj.* (ugs.) steep (coll.) ⟨*price,
rent, etc.*⟩
Gepfeife *das;* ~s (ugs. abwertend)
[continuous, tuneless] whistling
gepfiffen 2. *Part. v.* PFEIFEN
gepflegt *Adj.* **(a)** well-groomed; spruce
⟨*appearance*⟩; neat ⟨*clothing*⟩
(b) (hochwertig) choice ⟨*food, drink*⟩
Gepflogenheit *die;* ~, ~en (geh.) custom;
(Gewohnheit) habit
Geplapper *das;* ~s (ugs., oft abwertend)
prattling
geplättet *Adj.* (salopp) flabbergasted
Gepolter *das;* ~s clatter
gepriesen 2. *Part. v.* PREISEN
Gequake *das;* ~s (ugs.) croaking; (von
Enten) quacking
Gequäke *das;* ~s (ugs.) bawling
gequält *Adj.* forced ⟨*smile, gaiety*⟩; pained
⟨*expression*⟩
gequollen 2. *Part. v.* QUELLEN
gerade 1 *Adj.* **(a)** straight; etw. ~ biegen
bend sth. straight; straighten sth. [out];
~ stehen stand up straight
(b) (nicht schief) upright
(c) (aufrichtig) forthright; direct
(d) (Math.) even ⟨*number*⟩
2 *Adv.* just; (direkt) right
Gerade *die;* ~, ~n; *auch adj. Dekl.* (Geom.)
straight line
gerade-: ~**aus** *Adv.* straight ahead;
~|**biegen** *unr. tr. V.* (ugs.: bereinigen)
straighten out; ~**heraus** /----'-/ (ugs.)
Adv. etw. ~heraus sagen say sth. straight
out; ~**so** *Adv.* ~so groß/lang wie ...: just
as big/long as ...; ~|**stehen** *unr. itr. V.*
(fig.: einstehen) **für** etw. ~stehen accept
responsibility for sth.; ~**zu** *Adv.* really;
(beinahe) almost
gerad-, Gerad-: ~**linig** 1 *Adj.*
(a) straight; direct, lineal ⟨*descent,
descendant*⟩; **(b)** (aufrichtig) straightforward;
2 *adv.* **(a)** ~linig verlaufen run in a
straight line; **(b)** (aufrichtig) ~linig handeln/
denken be straightforward; ~**linigkeit**
die; ~~ **(a)** straightness; **(b)** (Aufrichtigkeit)
straightforwardness
gerammelt *Adv.* ~ voll (ugs.) [jam-]
packed (coll.); packed out (coll.)
Geranie /geˈraːni̯ə/ *die;* ~, ~n geranium
gerann 3. *Pers. Sg. Prät. v.* GERINNEN
gerannt 2. *Part. v.* RENNEN
gerät 3. *Pers. Sg. Präsens v.* GERATEN[1]
Gerät *das;* ~[e]s, ~e **(a)** piece of
equipment; (Fernseher, Radio) set; (Garten~)
tool
(b) (Turnen) piece of apparatus
geraten[1] *unr. itr. V.; mit sein* **(a)** (gelangen)
get
(b) (werden) turn out; (gut ~) turn out well

geraten² [1] 2. *Part. v.* RATEN, GERATEN¹
[2] *Adj.* advisable

Geratewohl: aufs ~ (ugs.) ⟨*select*⟩ at random; **wir fuhren aufs** ~ **los** (ugs.) we went for a drive just to see where we ended up

geraum *Adj.* (geh.) considerable

geräumig *Adj.* spacious ⟨*room*⟩; roomy ⟨*cupboard etc.*⟩

Geräusch *das;* ~[e]s, ~e sound; (unerwünscht) noise

geräusch-, Geräusch-: ~**arm** [1] *Adj.* quiet; [2] *adv.* quietly; ~**los** [1] *Adj.* silent; [2] *adv.* (a) silently; (b) (fig. ugs.) without [any] fuss; ~**pegel** *der* noise level; ~**voll** *Adj.* noisy

gerben *tr. V.* tan ⟨*hides, skins*⟩

gerecht [1] *Adj.* just; (unparteiisch) fair [2] *adv.* justly

gerechtfertigt *Adj.* justified

Gerechtigkeit *die;* ~: justice

Gerechtigkeits-sinn *der* sense of justice

Gerede *das;* ~s (abwertend) (a) (ugs.) talk (b) (Klatsch) gossip

geregelt *Adj.* regular, steady ⟨*job*⟩

gereizt *Adj.* irritable

Gericht¹ *das;* ~[e]s, ~e court; (Richter) bench; (Gebäude) court [house]; **das Jüngste** ~ (Rel.) the Last Judgement

Gericht² *das;* ~[e]s, ~e dish

gerichtlich [1] *Adj.* judicial; legal ⟨*proceedings*⟩ [2] *adv.* jmdn. ~ **verfolgen** take sb. to court

Gerichts-: ~**hof** *der* Court of Justice; ~**kosten** *Pl.* legal costs; ~**saal** *der* courtroom; ~**verfahren** *das* legal proceedings *pl.;* **ein** ~**verfahren einleiten** institute legal or court proceedings; **ohne** ~**verfahren** without trial; ~**vollzieher** *der;* ~~s, ~~, ~**vollzieherin** *die;* ~~, ~~**nen** bailiff

gerieben 2. *Part. v.* REIBEN

geriffelt *Adj.* corrugated ⟨*surface, sheet metal*⟩; fluted ⟨*column*⟩; ribbed ⟨*glass*⟩

gering *Adj.* (a) low; little ⟨*value*⟩; small ⟨*quantity, amount*⟩; short ⟨*distance, time*⟩ (b) (unbedeutend) slight; minor ⟨*role*⟩; **nicht im Geringsten** not in the slightest or least; **jmdn./etw.** ~ **achten** *od.* **schätzen** have a low opinion of or think very little of sb./sth.; **den Erfolg/Reichtümer** ~ **achten** *od.* **schätzen** set little store by success/riches

geringfügig [1] *Adj.* slight; minor ⟨*alteration, injury*⟩; trivial ⟨*amount, detail*⟩ [2] *adv.* slightly

Geringfügigkeit *die;* ~, ~en triviality

gering|schätzen ▸ GERING B

geringschätzig *Adj.* disdainful; disparaging ⟨*remark*⟩

gerinnen *unr. itr. V.; mit sein* ⟨*blood*⟩ clot; ⟨*milk*⟩ curdle

Gerippe *das;* ~s, ~: skeleton

gerippt *Adj.* ribbed; fluted ⟨*glass, column*⟩

gerissen [1] 2. *Part. v.* REISSEN [2] *Adj.* (ugs.) crafty

geritten 2. *Part. v.* REITEN

geritzt *Adj.* (salopp) etw. ist ~: sth. is [all] settled; ist ~! will do! (coll.)

Germane *der;* ~n, ~n, **Germanin** *die;* ~, ~nen (hist.) ancient German; Teuton

germanisch *Adj.* (auch fig.) Germanic; Teutonic

Germanistik *die;* ~: German studies *pl.*, *no art.*

gern[e]; lieber, am liebsten *Adv.* (a) etw. ~ tun like or enjoy doing sth.; **er spielt lieber Tennis als Golf** he prefers playing tennis to golf; etw. ~/am liebsten essen like sth./like sth. best; **ja, ~/aber** ~: yes, of course; certainly! (b) (durchaus) **das glaube ich** ~: I can well believe that

gerochen 2. *Part. v.* RIECHEN

Geröll *das;* ~s, ~e debris; (größer) boulders *pl.*

geronnen 2. *Part. v.* RINNEN, GERINNEN

Gerste *die;* ~: barley

Gersten-korn *das* (Med.) sty

Gerte *die;* ~, ~n switch

Geruch *der;* ~[e]s, Gerüche smell; (von Blumen) scent

Gerücht *das;* ~[e]s, ~e rumour

gerufen 2. *Part. v.* RUFEN

geruhsam [1] *Adj.* peaceful; leisurely ⟨*stroll*⟩ [2] *adv.* leisurely; quietly

Geruhsamkeit *die;* ~: peacefulness; (eines Spaziergangs) leisureliness

Gerümpel *das;* ~s junk

gerungen 2. *Part. v.* RINGEN

Gerüst *das;* ~[e]s, ~e scaffolding *no pl., no indef. art.*

gesamt *Adj.* whole; entire

gesamt-, Gesamt-: ~**deutsch** *Adj.* all-German; ~**eindruck** *der* general impression

Gesamtheit *die;* **die** ~ **der Bevölkerung** the entire population

Gesamt-: ~**schule** *die* comprehensive [school]; ~**werk** *das* œuvre; (Bücher) complete works *pl.*

gesandt 2. *Part. v.* SENDEN

Gesandte *der/die; adj. Dekl.* envoy

Gesandtschaft *die;* ~, ~en legation

Gesang *der;* ~[e]s, Gesänge (a) singing (b) (Lied) song

Gesang-: ~**buch** *das* hymn book; ~**verein** *der* choral society

Gesäß *das;* ~es, ~e backside; buttocks *pl.*

geschaffen 2. *Part. v.* SCHAFFEN 1

Geschäft *das;* ~[e]s, ~e (a) business; (Transaktion) [business] deal; **mit jmdm.** ~**e/ein** ~ **machen** do business with ····>

sb./strike a bargain *or* do a deal with sb.; **ein gutes ~ machen** make a good profit
(b) (Laden) shop; store (Amer.)
Geschäfte·macher *der*,
Geschäfte·macherin *die* (abwertend) profit-seeker
geschäftig *Adj.* bustling
geschäftlich 1 *Adj.* business *attrib.*
2 *adv.* on business
geschäfts-, Geschäfts-:
~bedingungen *Pl.* terms [and conditions] of trade; **~brief** *der* business letter; **~frau** *die* businesswoman; **~freund** *der*, **~freundin** *die* business associate; **~führer** *der* manager; (Vereinswesen) secretary; **~führerin** *die* ▶ ~FÜHRER: manageress; secretary; **~führung** *die* management; **~gebaren** *das* business *no art.*; business practices *pl.*; **~inhaber** *der*, **~inhaberin** *die* owner of the/a business; **~jahr** *das* financial year; **~kosten** *Pl.* auf ~kosten on expenses; **~lage** *die* [business] position; **~leitung** *die* ▶ ~FÜHRUNG; **~leute** ▶ ~MANN; **~mann** *der*; *Pl.* ~leute businessman; **~ordnung** *die* standing orders *pl.*; (im Parlament) [rules *pl.* of] procedure; **~partner** *der*, **~partnerin** *die* business partner; **~reise** *die* business trip; **~schluss** *der* closing time; **~stelle** *die* branch; (einer Partei, eines Vereins) office; **~straße** *die* shopping street; **~tüchtig** *Adj.* able, ⟨businessman, landlord, etc.⟩; **~viertel** *das* business quarter; (Einkaufszentrum) shopping district; **~wagen** *der* company car; **~zeit** *die* business hours *pl.*; (im Büro) office hours *pl.*
geschah 3. *Pers. Sg. Prät. v.* GESCHEHEN
geschehen *unr. itr. V.; mit sein* happen; occur; (ausgeführt werden) be done; **jmdm. geschieht etw.** sth. happens to sb.
gescheit *Adj.* **(a)** (intelligent) clever
(b) (ugs.: vernünftig) sensible
Gescheitheit *die;* ~: cleverness
Geschenk *das;* ~[e]s, ~e present; gift
Geschenk-: **~artikel** *der* gift; **~packung** *die* gift pack
Geschichte *die;* ~, ~n **(a)** history
(b) (Erzählung) story
geschichtlich *Adj.* **(a)** historical
(b) (bedeutungsvoll) historic
Geschichts-: **~atlas** *der* historical atlas; **~buch** *das* history book
Geschick[1] *das;* ~[e]s, ~e (geh.) fate
Geschick[2] *das;* ~[e]s skill
Geschicklichkeit *die;* ~: skilfulness; skill
geschickt 1 *Adj.* **(a)** skilful
(b) (klug) clever; adroit
2 *adv.* **(a)** (gewandt) skilfully
(b) (klug) cleverly; adroitly

geschieden 2. *Part. v.* SCHEIDEN
geschienen 2. *Part. v.* SCHEINEN
Geschirr *das;* ~[e]s, ~e **(a)** crockery; (benutzt) dishes *pl.*
(b) (für Zugtier) harness
Geschirr-: **~spül·maschine** *die* dishwasher; **~spülmittel** *das* washing-up liquid; **~tuch** *das; Pl.* ~tücher tea towel; dish towel (Amer.)
geschissen 2. *Part. v.* SCHEISSEN
geschlafen 2. *Part. v.* SCHLAFEN
geschlagen 2. *Part. v.* SCHLAGEN
Geschlecht *das;* ~[e]s, ~er **(a)** sex
(b) (Generation) generation
(c) (Sippe) family
(d) (Sprachw.) gender
geschlechtlich *Adj.* sexual
geschlechts-, Geschlechts-:
~akt *der* sex[ual] act; **~chromosom** *das* (Biol.) sex chromosome; **~krank** *Adj.* ⟨person⟩ suffering from VD; **~krankheit** *die* venereal disease; **~organ** *das* sex[ual] organ; genital organ; **~teil** *das* genitals *pl.*; **~verkehr** *der* sexual intercourse; **~wort** *das* ▶ ARTIKEL A
geschlichen 2. *Part. v.* SCHLEICHEN
geschliffen 1 2. *Part. v.* SCHLEIFEN
2 *Adj.* polished
geschlossen 1 2. *Part. v.* SCHLIESSEN
2 *Adj.* united ⟨action, front⟩; unified ⟨procedure⟩; **eine ~e Ortschaft** a built-up area
Geschlossenheit *die;* ~: unity
geschlungen 2. *Part. v.* SCHLINGEN
Geschmack *der;* ~[e]s, Geschmäcke taste
geschmacklos 1 *Adj.* tasteless
2 *adv.* tastelessly
Geschmacklosigkeit *die;* ~, ~en lack of [good] taste; bad taste; (Äußerung) tasteless remark
Geschmack[s]·sache *die:* **das ist ~:** that is a question *or* matter of taste
geschmack·voll 1 *Adj.* tasteful
2 *adv.* tastefully
Geschmatze *das;* ~s (ugs. abwertend) smacking one's lips *no art.*; (beim Essen) noisy eating *no art.*
Geschmeide *das;* ~s, ~ (geh.) jewellery *no pl.*
geschmeidig 1 *Adj.* **(a)** sleek ⟨hair, fur⟩; soft ⟨leather, boots, skin⟩
(b) (gelenkig) supple ⟨fingers⟩; lithe ⟨body, movement, person⟩
2 *adv.* (gelenkig) agilely
Geschmeidigkeit *die;*
~: ▶ GESCHMEIDIG 1: sleekness; suppleness; softness; litheness
geschmissen 2. *Part. v.* SCHMEISSEN
geschmolzen 2. *Part. v.* SCHMELZEN
Geschmuse *das;* ~s (ugs.) cuddling; (eines Pärchens) kissing and cuddling

---

*old spelling – see note on page x

Geschnetzelte *das; adj. Dekl.: small, thin slices of meat [cooked in sauce]*
geschnitten *2. Part. v.* SCHNEIDEN
geschoben *2. Part. v.* SCHIEBEN
geschollen *2. Part. v.* SCHALLEN
gescholten *2. Part. v.* SCHELTEN
Geschöpf *das;* ~[e]s, ~e creature
geschoren *2. Part. v.* SCHEREN
Geschoss¹, *Geschoß *das;* Geschosses, Geschosse projectile; (Kugel) bullet; (Rakete) missile
Geschoss², *Geschoß *das;* Geschosses, Geschosse floor; storey
geschossen *2. Part. v.* SCHIESSEN
geschraubt *Adj.* (ugs.) stilted
Geschrei *das;* ~s (a) shouting; (von Verletzten, Tieren) screaming; screams *pl.* (b) (ugs. fig.) fuss
geschrieben *2. Part. v.* SCHREIBEN
geschrie[e]n *2. Part. v.* SCHREIEN
geschritten *2. Part. v.* SCHREITEN
geschunden *2. Part. v.* SCHINDEN
Geschütz *das;* ~es, ~e [big] gun
Geschütz·feuer *das* artillery fire; shell fire
geschützt *Adj.* (a) sheltered (b) (unter Naturschutz) protected (c) ~er Geschlechtsverkehr sex with a condom
Geschwader *das;* ~s, ~ (Marine) squadron; (Luftwaffe) wing (Brit.); group (Amer.)
Geschwätz *das;* ~es (ugs. abwertend) prattling; (Klatsch) gossip
geschwätzig *Adj.* (abwertend) talkative
geschweige *Konj.* ~ [denn] let alone; never mind
geschwiegen *2. Part. v.* SCHWEIGEN
geschwind (bes. südd.) **1** *Adj.* swift; quick **2** *adv.* swiftly; quickly
Geschwindigkeit *die;* ~, ~en speed
Geschwindigkeits-: ~**begrenzung** *die,* ~**beschränkung** *die* speed limit
Geschwister *Pl.* brothers and sisters
geschwollen **1** *2. Part. v.* SCHWELLEN **2** *Adj.* (a) swollen (b) (fig. abwertend) pompous **3** *adv.* pompously
geschwommen *2. Part. v.* SCHWIMMEN
geschworen *2. Part. v.* SCHWÖREN
Geschworene *der/die; adj. Dekl.* juror
Geschwulst *die;* ~, Geschwülste tumour
geschwunden *2. Part. v.* SCHWINDEN
geschwungen **1** *2. Part. v.* SCHWINGEN **2** *Adj.* curved
Geschwür *das;* ~s, ~e ulcer; (Furunkel) boil
gesehen *2. Part v.* SEHEN
Geseire *das;* ~s (ugs.) drivel
Geselle *der;* ~n, ~n journeyman; (Kerl) fellow

gesellen *refl. V.* sich zu jmdm. ~: join sb.
gesellig *Adj.* sociable; ein ~er Abend/~es Beisammensein a convivial evening/a friendly get-together
Geselligkeit *die;* ~: die ~ lieben enjoy [good] company
Gesellin *die;* ~, ~nen journeyman; journeywoman (rare)
Gesellschaft *die;* ~, ~en (a) society (b) (Veranstaltung) party (c) (Kreis von Menschen) group of people (d) (Wirtschaft) company
Gesellschafter *der;* ~s, ~ (a) ein guter ~ sein be good company (b) (Wirtsch.) partner; (Teilhaber) shareholder
Gesellschafterin *die;* ~, ~nen (a) [lady] companion (b) (Wirtsch.) partner; (Teilhaberin) shareholder
gesellschaftlich *Adj.* social
gesellschafts-, Gesellschafts-: ~**fähig** *Adj.* (auch fig.) socially acceptable; ~**ordnung** *die* social order; ~**reise** *die* group tour; ~**schicht** *die* stratum of society; ~**spiel** *das* party game
gesessen *2. Part. v.* SITZEN
Gesetz *das;* ~es, ~e (a) law; (geschrieben) statute (b) (Regel) rule
gesetz-, Gesetz-: ~**buch** *das* statute book; ~**gebend** *Adj.* legislative; ~**geber** *der* legislator; (Organ) legislature; ~**gebung** *die;* ~: legislation
gesetzlich **1** *Adj.* legal; statutory ⟨holiday⟩; lawful ⟨heir, claim⟩ **2** *adv.* legally
gesetz-, Gesetz-: ~**los** *Adj.* lawless; ~**losigkeit** *die;* ~~: lawlessness; ~**mäßig** **1** *Adj.* (a) law-governed; ~**mäßig sein** be governed by *or* obey a [natural] law/[natural] laws; (b) (gesetzlich) legal; (rechtmäßig) lawful; **2** *adv.* in accordance with a [natural] law/[natural] laws; ~**mäßigkeit** *die* (a) conformity to a [natural] law/[natural] laws; (b) (Gesetzlichkeit) legality; (Rechtmäßigkeit) lawfulness
gesetzt *Adj.* staid
Gesetztheit *die;* ~: staidness
gesetz·widrig *Adj.* illegal; unlawful
Gesetz·widrigkeit *die* illegality; unlawfulness
Gesicht *das;* ~[e]s, ~er face; (fig.) das ~ einer Stadt the appearance of a town
Gesichts-: ~**ausdruck** *der* expression; look; ~**creme** *die* face cream; ~**punkt** *der* point of view; ~**wasser** *das* face lotion; ~**züge** *Pl.* features
Gesindel *das;* ~s (abwertend) rabble
gesinnt *Adj.* christlich/sozial ~ [sein] [be] Christian-minded/public-spirited; jmdm. freundlich ~ sein be well-disposed towards sb. ⋯⋗

Gesinnung *die;* ~, ~en [basic] convictions *pl.;* [fundamental] beliefs *pl.*
gesinnungs-, Gesinnungs-: ~los (abwertend) *Adj.* unprincipled; ~wandel *der* change of attitude
gesittet *Adj.* well-behaved; well-mannered
gesogen 2. *Part. v.* SAUGEN
gesondert ① *Adj.* separate ② *adv.* separately
gesonnen *Adj.* ~ sein, etw. zu tun feel disposed to do sth.
gesotten 2. *Part. v.* SIEDEN
Gespann *das;* ~[e]s, ~e (a) (Zugtiere) team (b) (Wagen) horse and carriage (c) (Menschen) couple; pair
gespannt *Adj.* (a) eager; rapt ‹*attention*›; ~ zuhören listen with rapt attention (b) tense ‹*situation, atmosphere*›; strained ‹*relationships*›
Gespenst *das;* ~[e]s, ~er (a) ghost (b) (geh.: Gefahr) spectre
gespenstig, gespenstisch *Adj.* ghostly; eerie ‹*building, atmosphere*›
gespie[e]n 2. *Part. v.* SPEIEN
gesponnen 2. *Part. v.* SPINNEN
Gespött *das;* ~[e]s mockery; ridicule
Gespräch *das;* ~[e]s, ~e conversation; (Diskussion) discussion; (Telefon~) call (**mit** to)
gesprächig *Adj.* talkative
Gesprächs-: ~partner *der,* ~partnerin *die:* wer war dein ~partner/ deine ~partnerin? who were you talking to?; ~stoff *der* topics *pl.* of conversation; ~thema *das* topic of conversation
gesprochen 2. *Part. v.* SPRECHEN
gesprossen 2. *Part. v.* SPRIESSEN
gesprungen 2. *Part. v.* SPRINGEN
Gespür *das;* ~s feel
gest. *Abk.* = **gestorben** d.
Gestalt *die;* ~, ~en (a) build (b) (Mensch, Persönlichkeit) figure (c) (in der Dichtung) character (d) (Form) form
gestalten *tr. V.* fashion; lay out ‹*public gardens*›; shape ‹*character, personality*›; arrange ‹*party, conference, etc.*›
Gestaltung *die;* ~, ~en ▶ GESTALTEN: fashioning; laying out; arranging
gestand 1. u. 3. Pers. Sg. Prät. v. GESTEHEN
gestanden ① 2. *Part. v.* STEHEN, GESTEHEN ② *Adj.* ein ~er Mann a grown man; ein ~er Parlamentarier an experienced *or* seasoned parliamentarian
geständig *Adj.:* ~ sein have confessed
Geständnis *das;* ~ses, ~se confession
Gestank *der;* ~[e]s (abwertend) stench; stink

Gestapo *die;* ~ (ns.) Gestapo
gestatten ① *tr., itr. V.* permit; allow; ~ Sie, dass ich ...: may I ...? ② *refl. V.* sich (*Dat.*) etw. ~: allow oneself sth.
Geste /'gɛstə, 'geːstə/ *die;* ~, ~n (auch fig.) gesture
Gesteck *das;* ~[e]s, ~e flower arrangement
gestehen *tr., itr. V.* confess
Gestein *das;* ~[e]s, ~e rock
Gestell *das;* ~[e]s, ~e (a) (für Weinflaschen) rack; (zum Wäschetrocknen) horse (b) (Unterbau) frame
gestern *Adv.* yesterday
gestiegen 2. *Part. v.* STEIGEN
gestikulieren *itr. V.* gesticulate
Gestirn *das;* ~[e]s, ~e star
gestochen ① 2. *Part. v.* STECHEN ② *Adj.* extremely neat ‹*handwriting*›
gestohlen 2. *Part. v.* STEHLEN
Gestöhne *das;* ~s groaning
gestorben 2. *Part. v.* STERBEN
gestoßen 2. *Part. v.* STOSSEN
Gestrampel *das;* ~s (ugs.) kicking about; (beim Radfahren) pedalling
Gesträuch *das;* ~[e]s, ~e shrubbery; bushes *pl.*
gestreift *Adj.* striped
gestrichen ① 2. *Part. v.* STREICHEN ② *Adj.* level ‹*measure*›
gestrig *Adj.* yesterday's
gestritten 2. *Part. v.* STREITEN
Gestrüpp *das;* ~[e]s, ~e undergrowth
gestunken 2. *Part. v.* STINKEN
Gestüt *das;* ~[e]s, ~e stud [farm]
Gesuch *das;* ~[e]s, ~e request (**um** for); (Antrag) application (**um** for)
gesucht *Adj.* (a) [much] sought-after (b) (gekünstelt) laboured
gesund; gesünder, *seltener:* ~er, gesündest..., *seltener:* ~est... *Adj.* healthy; wieder ~ werden get better; bleib ~! look after yourself!
gesunden *itr. V.; mit sein* ‹*person*› recover, get well, regain one's health
Gesundheit *die;* ~: health; ~! (ugs.) bless you!
gesundheitlich ① *Adj.; nicht präd.* ~e Betreuung health care; sein ~er Zustand [the state of] his health ② *adv.* wie geht es Ihnen ~? how are you?
gesundheits-, Gesundheits-: ~amt *das* [local] public health department; ~gefährdend *Adj.* ~gefährdend sein be a danger to health; ~gefährdende Bakterien/Produkte bacteria that are a danger to health/products that are a health risk; ~gefährdung *die* risk to health; ~minister *der,* ~ministerin *die* minister of health; Health Secretary

(Brit.); ~**schädlich** Adj. detrimental to [one's] health postpos.; ~**system** das health-care system; ~**vorsorge** die health care; ~**zeugnis** das certificate of health; ~**zustand** der state of health

gesungen 2. Part. v. SINGEN

gesunken 2. Part. v. SINKEN

getan 2. Part. v. TUN

Getier das; ~[e]s (geh.) animals pl.

Getöse das; ~s [thunderous] roar; (von vielen Menschen) din

getragen 2. Part. v. TRAGEN

Getränk das; ~[e]s, ~e drink; beverage (formal)

getrauen refl. V. dare

Getreide das; ~s grain

Getreide-: ~**anbau** der growing of cereals; ~**handel** der corn trade

getrennt ① Adj. separate
② adv. ⟨pay⟩ separately; ⟨sleep⟩ in separate rooms

getreten 2. Part. v. TRETEN

getreu ① Adj. (geh.) exact; faithful ⟨image⟩
② adv. (geh.) ⟨report, describe⟩ faithfully

Getriebe das; ~s, ~: gears pl.; (in einer Maschine) gear system

getrieben 2. Part. v. TREIBEN

getroffen 2. Part. v. TREFFEN, TRIEFEN

getrogen 2. Part. v. TRÜGEN

getrost ① Adj. confident
② adv. confidently; **du kannst es mir** ~ **glauben** you can take my word for it

getrunken 2. Part. v. TRINKEN

Getto das; ~s, ~s ghetto

Getue das; ~s (ugs. abwertend) fuss (**um** about)

Getümmel das; ~s tumult

geübt Adj. accomplished; practised ⟨eye, ear⟩

Gewächs das; ~es, ~e plant

gewachsen ① 2. Part. v. WACHSEN
② in jmdm./einer Sache ~ sein be a match for sb./be equal to sth.

gewagt Adj. daring; (gefährlich) risky; (fast anstößig) risqué ⟨joke etc.⟩

gewählt ① Adj. refined
② adv. in a refined manner

Gewähr die; ~: guarantee; **keine** ~ **übernehmen** be unable to guarantee sth.

gewähren tr. V. grant; give ⟨pleasure, joy⟩

gewähr·leisten tr. V. guarantee

Gewahrsam der; ~s (a) (Obhut) safe-keeping
(b) (Haft) custody

Gewährs·mann der; Pl. ~**männer** od. ~**leute**, **Gewährs·person** die informant; source

Gewalt die; ~, ~en (a) power
(b) (Willkür) force
(c) (körperliche Kraft) force; violence

gewalt-, Gewalt-: ~**akt** der act of

violence; ~**anwendung** die use of force or violence; ~**bereit** Adj. ⟨person⟩ prone to violence; ⟨group, organization⟩ prepared to resort to or use violence; ~**bereitschaft** die: ▶ ~BEREIT: propensity to violence; willingness to resort to or use violence

Gewalten·teilung die separation of powers

gewaltig ① Adj. (a) (immens) huge
(b) (imponierend) mighty, huge, massive ⟨building etc⟩; monumental ⟨literary work etc.⟩
② adv. (ugs.) very much

gewalt·los ① Adj. non-violent
② adv. without violence

Gewalt·losigkeit die; ~: non-violence

gewaltsam ① Adj. forcible ⟨expulsion⟩; enforced ⟨separation⟩; violent ⟨death⟩
② adv. forcibly

gewalt·tätig Adj. violent

Gewalt·tätigkeit die (a) (gewalttätige Art) violence
(b) ▶ ~AKT

Gewand das; ~[e]s, Gewänder (geh.) robe; gown

gewandt ① 2. Part. v. WENDEN
② Adj. skilful; (körperlich) agile
③ adv. skilfully; (körperlich) agilely

Gewandtheit die; ~: ▶ GEWANDT 2: skill; skilfulness; agility

gewann 1. u. 3. Pers. Sg. Prät. v. GEWINNEN

gewaschen 2. Part. v. WASCHEN

Gewässer das; ~s, ~: stretch of water

Gewebe das; ~s, ~ (a) (Stoff) fabric
(b) (Med., Biol.) tissue

Gewehr das; ~[e]s, ~e rifle; (Schrot~) shotgun

Geweih das; ~[e]s, ~e antlers pl.

Gewerbe das; ~s, ~: business; (Handel, Handwerk) trade

Gewerbe-: ~**freiheit** die right to carry on a business or trade; ~**ordnung** die laws pl. governing trade and industry; ~**schein** der licence to carry on a business or trade; ~**treibende** der/die; adj. Dekl. tradesman/tradeswoman; ~**zweig** der branch of trade

gewerblich ① Adj. commercial; business attrib.; (industriell) industrial
② adv. ~ tätig sein work

gewerbs·mäßig Adj. professional

Gewerkschaft die; ~, ~en trade union

Gewerkschaft[l]er der; ~s, ~, **Gewerkschaft[l]erin** die; ~, ~nen trade unionist

gewerkschaftlich ① Adj. [trade] union attrib.
② adv. ~ **organisiert sein** belong to a [trade] union

Gewerkschafts·funktionär der, **Gewerkschafts·funktionärin** die [trade] union official

gewesen 2. Part. v. SEIN[1]

gewichen 2. Part. v. WEICHEN

Gewicht das; ~[e]s, ~e (auch fig.) weight; [nicht] ins ~ fallen be of [no] consequence

Gewicht·heben das; ~s weightlifting

gewichtig Adj. weighty

Gewichts·klasse die (Sport) weight [division or class]

gewieft Adj. (ugs.) cunning

gewiesen 2. Part. v. WEISEN

gewillt Adj. in [nicht] ~ sein, etw. zu tun be [un]willing to do sth.

Gewimmel das; ~s throng; (von Insekten) teeming mass

Gewinde das; ~s, ~ (Technik) thread

Gewinn der; ~[e]s, ~e (a) profit
(b) (Preis einer Lotterie) prize; (beim Spiel) winnings pl.
(c) (Sieg) win

Gewinn·beteiligung die (Wirtsch.) profit sharing; (Betrag) profit-sharing bonus

gewinn·bringend Adj. lucrative

gewinnen [1] unr. tr. V. win; gain ‹time, influence, validity, etc.›
[2] unr. itr. V. win (bei at)

gewinnend Adj. winning

Gewinner der; ~s, ~, **Gewinnerin** die; ~, ~nen winner

Gewinn-: ~**quote** die share of prize money; ~**spanne** die profit margin; ~**sucht** die greed for profit

Gewinnung die; ~ (a) (von Kohle, Erz usw.) mining; extraction; (von Öl) recovery; (von Metall aus Erz) extraction
(b) (Erzeugung) production

Gewinn·zahl die winning number

Gewirr das; ~[e]s (a) tangle
(b) (Durcheinander) **ein** ~ **von Ästen** a maze of branches

gewiss, *****gewiß** [1] Adj. certain
[2] adv. certainly

Gewissen das; ~s, ~: conscience

gewissenhaft [1] Adj. conscientious
[2] adv. conscientiously

gewissen·los Adj. unscrupulous

Gewissens·bisse Pl. pangs of conscience

gewissermaßen Adv. (sozusagen) as it were; (in gewissem Sinne) to a certain extent

Gewissheit, *****Gewißheit** die; ~, ~en certainty

Gewitter das; ~s, ~: thunderstorm

Gewitter·wolke die thundercloud

gewittrig Adj. thundery

gewitzt Adj. shrewd

gewoben 2. Part. v. WEBEN[1]

gewogen [1] 2. Part. v. WIEGEN[1]
[2] Adj. (geh.) well disposed (+ Dat. towards)

gewöhnen [1] tr. V. jmdn. an jmdn./etw.

~: get sb. used to sb./sth.; accustom sb. to sb./sth.
[2] refl. V. **sich an jmdn./etw.** ~: get used or get accustomed to sb./sth.; accustom oneself to sb./sth.

Gewohnheit die; ~, ~en habit

gewohnheits-, Gewohnheits-: ~**mäßig** [1] Adj. habitual ‹drinker etc.›; automatic ‹reaction etc.›; [2] adv. (regelmäßig) habitually; ~**mensch** der creature of habit; ~**tier** das (scherzh.) creature of habit; ~**trinker** der, ~**trinkerin** die habitual drinker; ~**verbrecher** der, ~**verbrecherin** die (Rechtsw.) habitual criminal

gewöhnlich [1] Adj. (a) normal; ordinary
(b) (gewohnt, üblich) usual
(c) (abwertend: ordinär) common
[2] adv. (a) [für] ~: usually; **wie** ~: as usual
(b) (abwertend: ordinär) in a common way

gewohnt Adj. (a) usual
(b) etw. (Akk.) ~ **sein** be used to sth.

Gewölbe das; ~s, ~: vault

gewonnen 2. Part. v. GEWINNEN

geworben 2. Part. v. WERBEN

geworfen 2. Part. v. WERFEN

gewrungen 2. Part. v. WRINGEN

Gewühl das; ~[e]s milling crowd

gewunden 2. Part. v. WINDEN

Gewürz das; ~es, ~e spice; (würzende Zutat) seasoning

Gewürz-: ~**gurke** die pickled gherkin; ~**nelke** die clove

gewusst, *****gewußt** 2. Part. v. WISSEN

gez. Abk. = **gezeichnet** sgd.

Gezeit die; ~, ~en tide

Gezerre das; ~s wrangling

gezielt [1] Adj. specific ‹questions, measures, etc.›; deliberate ‹insult, indiscretion›; well-directed ‹advertising campaign›
[2] adv. ‹proceed, act› purposefully

geziemen (geh. veralt.) [1] itr. V. jmdm. [nicht] ~: [ill] befit sb
[2] refl. V. be proper; **sich für jmdn.** ~: befit sb.

geziert [1] Adj. (abwertend) affected
[2] adv. (abwertend) affectedly

gezogen 2. Part. v. ZIEHEN

Gezwitscher das; ~s twittering

gezwungen [1] 2. Part. v. ZWINGEN
[2] Adj. forced

gezwungenermaßen Adv. of necessity

gib Imperativ Sg. Präsens v. GEBEN

gibst 2. Pers. Sg. Präsens v. GEBEN

gibt 3. Pers. Sg. Präsens v. GEBEN

Gicht die; ~: gout

Giebel der; ~s, ~: gable

Gier die; ~: greed (**nach** for)

*****old spelling – see note on page x

gierig 1 *Adj.* greedy
2 *adv.* greedily
gießen 1 *unr. tr. V.* **(a)** pour (**in** + *Akk.*
into, **über** + *Akk.* over)
(b) (verschütten) spill (**über** + *Akk.* over)
(c) (begießen) water
2 *unpers.* (ugs.) pour [with rain]
Gießer *der;* ~s, ~: caster
Gießerei *die;* ~, ~en foundry
Gießerin *die;* ~, ~nen caster
Gift *das;* ~[e]s, ~e poison; (Schlangen~)
venom
gift·grün *Adj.* garish green
giftig *Adj.* poisonous; venomous ⟨snake⟩;
toxic, poisonous ⟨substance, gas, chemical⟩;
(fig.) venomous
Gift-: ~**mord** *der* [murder by] poisoning;
~**mörder** *der,* ~**mörderin** *die*
poisoner; ~**müll** *der* toxic waste; ~**pilz**
der poisonous mushroom; [poisonous]
toadstool; ~**schlange** *die* venomous
snake; ~**schrank** *der* poison cabinet *or*
cupboard; ~**stachel** *der* poisonous sting;
~**zahn** *der* poison fang
Gigant *der;* ~en, ~en giant
gigantisch *Adj.* gigantic
Gilde *die;* ~, ~n (hist.) guild
gilt 3. *Pers. Sg. Präsens v.* GELTEN
Gimpel *der;* ~s, ~: bullfinch
Gin /dʒɪn/ *der;* ~s, ~s gin
ging 1. u. 3. *Pers. Sg. Prät. v.* GEHEN
Ginster *der;* ~s, ~: broom
Gipfel *der;* ~s, ~: peak; (höchster Punkt des
Berges) summit; (fig.) height
Gipfel·konferenz *die* summit conference
gipfeln *itr. V.* **in** etw. (*Dat.*) ~: culminate
in sth.
Gipfel·treffen *das* summit meeting
Gips *der;* ~es, ~e plaster; gypsum (Chem.)
Gips·abdruck *der* plaster cast
gipsen *tr. V.* plaster; put ⟨leg, arm, etc.⟩ in
plaster
Gips·verband *der* plaster cast
Giraffe *die;* ~, ~n giraffe
Girlande *die;* ~, ~n festoon
Giro /'ʒiːro/ *das;* ~s, ~s, *österr. auch* Giri
(Finanzw.) giro
Giro·konto *das* (Finanzw.) current account
gis, Gis *das;* ~, ~ (Musik) G sharp
Gischt *der;* ~[e]s, ~e *od.* die; ~, ~en spray
Gitarre *die;* ~, ~n guitar
Gitarrist *der;* ~en, ~en, **Gitarristin** *die;*
~, ~nen guitarist
Gitter *das;* ~s, ~: bars *pl.;* (vor Fenster-,
Türöffnungen) grille; (in der Straßendecke, im
Fußboden) grating; (Geländer) railing[s *pl.*]
Gitter·fenster *das* barred window
Glacé·hand·schuh /gla'seː.../ *der* kid
glove
Gladiole *die;* ~, ~n gladiolus
Glanz *der;* ~es **(a)** (von Licht, Sternen, Augen)

brightness; (von Haar, Metall, Perlen, Leder usw.)
lustre; sheen
(b) (der Jugend, Schönheit) radiance; (des Adels
usw.) splendour
glänzen *itr. V.* **(a)** (Glanz ausstrahlen) shine;
⟨hair, metal, etc.⟩ gleam; ⟨elbows, trousers,
etc.⟩ be shiny
(b) (Bewunderung erregen) shine (**bei** at)
glänzend (ugs.) 1 *Adj.* shining;
gleaming ⟨hair, metal, etc.⟩; shiny ⟨elbows,
trousers, etc.⟩
(b) (bewundernswert) brilliant; splendid
⟨references, marks, results, etc.⟩
2 *adv.* ~ **mit** jmdm. auskommen get on
very well with sb.; **es geht mir/uns** ~:
I am/we are very well
glanz-, Glanz-: ~**leistung** *die* (auch
iron.) brilliant performance; ~**los** *Adj.*
dull; lacklustre; ~**nummer** *die* star turn;
~**voll** 1 *Adj.* brilliant; sparkling ⟨variety
number⟩; 2 *adv.* brilliantly
Glas *das;* ~es, Gläser **(a)** glass
(b) (Trinkgefäß) glass; **zwei** ~ *od.* Gläser Wein
two glasses of wine
(c) (Behälter) jar
Glas: ~**bläser** *der,* **Glas·bläserin** *die*
glass-blower
Gläschen *das;* ~s, ~ **(a)** [little] glass
(b) (kleines Gefäß) [little] [glass] jar
Glas·container *der* bottle bank
Glaser *der;* ~s, ~, **Glaserin** *die;* ~,
~nen glazier
gläsern *Adj.* glass
Glas·faser *die* glass fibre
glasieren *tr. V.* **(a)** glaze
(b) (Kochk.) ice; glaze ⟨meat⟩
glasig *Adj.* **(a)** glassy
(b) (Kochk.) transparent
Glas·malerei *die* stained glass
Glasur *die;* ~, ~en **(a)** glaze
(b) (Kochk.) icing; (auf Fleisch) glaze
glatt 1 *Adj.* **(a)** smooth; (rutschig) slippery
(b) (ugs.: offensichtlich) downright ⟨lie⟩;
outright ⟨deception, fraud⟩; flat ⟨refusal⟩
2 *adv.* **(a)** smoothly; ~ **gehen** (ugs.) go
smoothly
(b) (ugs.: rückhaltlos) jmdm. etw. ~ **ins Gesicht**
sagen tell sb. sth. straight to his/her face;
⟨reject, deny⟩ flatly
Glätte *die;* ~: smoothness; (Rutschigkeit)
slipperiness
Glatt·eis *das* glaze; ice; (auf der Straße)
black ice
glätten *tr. V.* smooth out ⟨piece of paper,
etc.⟩; smooth [down] ⟨feathers, fur, etc.⟩;
plane ⟨wood etc.⟩
glatt-: ***~|**gehen** ► GLATT 2A; ~**weg**
Adv. (ugs.) etw. ~**weg ablehnen/ignorieren**
turn sth. down flat/simply ignore sth.;
das ist ~**weg erlogen/erfunden** that's a
downright lie/that's pure invention
Glatze *die;* ~, ~n bald head; **eine**
~ **haben/bekommen** be/go bald

Glaube *der;* ~ns faith (an + *Akk.* in);
(Überzeugung, Meinung) belief (an + *Akk.* in)

glauben ① *tr. V.* **(a)** (meinen) think
(b) (für wahr halten) believe; **das glaube ich
dir nicht** I don't believe you; **das glaubst
du doch selbst nicht!** [surely] you can't
be serious; **sie glaubt ihm jedes Wort** she
believes every word he says; **ob du es
glaubst oder nicht ...** believe it or not ...; **das
ist doch kaum zu** ~ (ugs.) it's incredible
② *itr. V.* believe (an + *Akk.* in)

Glaubens-: ~**bekenntnis** *das* creed;
~**freiheit** *die* religious freedom; ~**krieg**
der religious war; ~**sache** *die* (ugs.)
matter of faith *or* belief

glaubhaft ① *Adj.* credible
② *adv.* convincingly

gläubig ① *Adj.* devout; (vertrauensvoll)
trusting
② *adv.* devoutly; (vertrauensvoll) trustingly

Gläubige *der/die; adj. Dekl.* believer

Gläubiger *der;* ~s, ~: creditor

glaub·würdig ① *Adj.* credible
② *adv.* convincingly

Glaubwürdigkeit *die;* ~: credibility

gleich ① *Adj.* **(a)** (identisch, von derselben
Art) same; ~ **bleiben** remain the same;
⟨*speed, temperature, etc.*⟩ remain constant;
~ **bleibend** constant, steady ⟨*temperature,
speed, etc.*⟩; ⟨~*berechtigt,* ~*wertig,* Math.⟩ equal
(b) (ugs.: gleichgültig) **es ist mir völlig** *od.* **ganz
~: I couldn't care less (coll.); **ganz ~, **wer
anruft, ...**: no matter who calls, ...;
② *adv.* **(a)** (übereinstimmend) ~ **groß/alt** *usw.*
sein be the same height/age *etc.;* ~ **gut/
schlecht** *usw.* equally good/bad etc.
(b) (in derselben Weise) ~ **aufgebaut/gekleidet**
having the same structure/wearing
identical clothes
(c) (sofort) at once; straight away; (bald) in a
moment
(d) (räumlich) right; just; ~ **rechts/links**
immediately on the right/left

gleich-, Gleich-: ~**alt[e]rig**
/-alt(ə)rɪç/ *Adj.* of the same age (mit
as); ~**artig** ① *Adj.* of the same kind
postpos. (+ *Dat.* as); (sehr ähnlich) very
similar (+ *Dat.* to); ② *adv.* in the same
way; ~**berechtigt** *Adj.* having equal
rights *postpos.;* ~**berechtigte Partner** equal
partners; ~**berechtigung** *die* equal
rights *pl.;* ***~**|bleiben,** ~**bleibend**
▶ GLEICH 1A

gleichen *unr. itr. V.* jmdm./einer Sache
~: be like *or* resemble sb./sth.;

gleichermaßen *Adv.* equally

gleich-, Gleich-: ~**falls** *Adv.*
(auch) also; (ebenfalls) likewise; **danke
~falls!** thank you, [and] the same to
you; ~**förmig** ① *Adj.* **(a)** (einheitlich)
uniform; **(b)** (monoton) monotonous; ② *adv.*
(a) (einheitlich) uniformly; **(b)** (monoton)

monotonously; ~**geschlechtlich** *Adj.*
homosexual; ~**gewicht** *das* balance;
~**gewichts·störung** *die* disturbance
of one's sense of balance; ~**gültig** ① *Adj.*
indifferent (**gegenüber** towards); (belanglos)
trivial; **das ist mir** ~**gültig:** it's a matter of
indifference to me; ② *adv.* indifferently;
~**gültigkeit** *die* indifference (**gegenüber**
towards)

Gleichheit *die;* ~, ~en **(a)** identity;
(Ähnlichkeit) similarity
(b) (gleiche Rechte) equality

Gleichheits·zeichen *das* equals sign

gleich-, Gleich-: ~**|kommen**
unr. itr. V.; mit sein **(a)** (entsprechen) be
tantamount to; **(b)** (die gleiche Leistung
erreichen) jmdm./einer Sache [an etw.
(*Dat.*)] ~**kommen** equal sb./sth. [in
sth.]; ~**|machen** *tr. V.* make equal;
~**macherei** *die;* ~~, ~~en (abwertend)
levelling down (derog.); egalitarianism;
~**mäßig** ① *Adj.* regular ⟨*interval,
rhythm*⟩; uniform ⟨*acceleration,
distribution*⟩; even ⟨*heat*⟩; ② *adv.* ⟨*breathe*⟩
regularly; **etw.** ~**mäßig verteilen/auftragen**
distribute sth. equally/apply sth. evenly;
~**mut** *der* equanimity; ~**mütig** ① *Adj.*
calm; composed; ② *adv.* with equanimity;
calmly; ~**namig** *Adj.*(a) of the same
name *postpos.;* **(b)** (Math.) ~**namige Brüche**
fractions with a common denominator;
Brüche ~**namig machen** reduce fractions to
a common denominator

Gleichnis *das;* ~ses, ~se (Allegorie)
allegory; (Parabel) parable

gleichsam *Adv.* (geh.) as it were

gleich-, Gleich-: ~**|schalten** *tr. V.*
force into line; ~**schenk[e]lig** *Adj.* (Math.)
isosceles; ~**schritt** *der* marching in step;
~**seitig** *Adj.* (Math.) equilateral; ~**|setzen**
tr. V. equate; ~**|stellen** *tr. V.* equate;
~**strom** *der* (Elektrot.) direct current

Gleichung *die;* ~, ~en equation

gleich-: ~**wertig** *Adj.* of the same
value *postpos.;* ~**wohl** /-'-- *od.* '--/
Adv. nevertheless; ~**zeitig** ① *Adj.*
simultaneous; ② *adv.* at the same time

Gleis *das;* ~es, ~e track; (Bahnsteig)
platform; (einzelne Schiene) rail

gleiten *unr. itr. V.; mit sein* glide; ⟨*hand*⟩
slide

Gleit-: ~**flug** *der* glide; ~**schirm** *der*
paraglider; ~**zeit** *die* flexitime; flexible
working hours *pl.*

Gletscher *der;* ~s, ~: glacier

Gletscher·spalte *die* crevasse

glich *1. u. 3. Pers. Sg. Prät. v.* GLEICHEN

Glied *das;* ~[e]s, ~er **(a)** limb; (Finger~,
Zehen~) joint
(b) (Ketten~, auch fig.) link
(c) (Teil eines Ganzen) section; (Mitglied)
member

---
*alte Schreibung – vgl. Hinweis auf S. x

gliedern ☐1 *tr. V.* structure; organize ⟨*thoughts*⟩
  ☐2 *refl. V.* **sich in Gruppen/Abschnitte** *usw.*
  ~: be divided into groups/sections *etc.*
Gliederung *die;* ~, ~**en** structure
Glied-: ~**maße** /-maːsə/ *die;* ~, ~n limb;
  ~**satz** *der* (Sprachw.) subordinate clause
glimmen *unr. od. regelm. itr. V.* glow
Glimm·stängel, *Glimm·stengel *der*
  (ugs. scherzh.) fag (coll.); ciggy (coll.)
glimpflich ☐1 *Adj.* (a) **der Unfall nahm ein**
  ~**es Ende** the accident turned out not to be
  too serious
  (b) (mild) lenient ⟨*sentence, punishment*⟩
  ☐2 *adv.* (a) (ohne Schaden) ~ **davonkommen**
  get off lightly
  (b) (mild) leniently
glitschig *Adj.* (ugs.) slippery
glitt *1. u. 3. Pers. Sg. Prät. v.* GLEITEN
glitzern *itr. V.* ⟨*star*⟩ twinkle; ⟨*diamond,*
  decorations⟩ sparkle; ⟨*snow, eyes, tears*⟩
  glisten
global ☐1 *Adj.* (a) global; worldwide
  (b) (umfassend) all-round ⟨*education*⟩; overall
  ⟨*control, planning, etc.*⟩
  (c) (allgemein) general
  ☐2 *adv.* (a) worldwide
  (b) (umfassend) in overall terms
  (c) (allgemein) in general terms
globalisieren *tr. V.* globalize
Globalisierung *die;* ~, ~**en**
  globalization
Globen ▶ GLOBUS
Globetrotter *der;* ~**s**, ~: globetrotter
Globus *der;* ~ *od.* ~**ses**, **Globen** globe
Glöckchen *das;* ~**s**, ~: [little] bell
Glocke *die;* ~, ~**n** bell
Glocken-: ~**blume** *die* (Bot.) campanula;
  ~**rock** *der* widely flared skirt; ~**spiel**
  das **(a)** carillon; (mit einer Uhr gekoppelt auch)
  chimes *pl.;* **(b)** (Instrument) glockenspiel
glomm *1. u. 3. Pers. Sg. Prät. v.* GLIMMEN
Glorien·schein /ˈgloːriən-/ *der* glory; (um
  den Kopf, fig.) halo
glorifizieren *tr. V.* glorify
Glorifizierung *die;* ~, ~**en** glorification
glor·reich ☐1 *Adj.* glorious
  ☐2 *adv.* gloriously
Glossar *das;* ~**s**, ~**e** glossary
Glosse *die;* ~, ~**n** commentary; (spöttische
  Bemerkung) sneering comment
Glotze *die;* ~, ~**n** (salopp) box (coll.); goggle-
  box (Brit. coll.)
glotzen *itr. V.* (abwertend) goggle; gawp (coll.)
Glotz·kiste *die* (salopp) box (coll.); goggle-
  box (Brit. coll.)
Glück *das;* ~**[e]s (a)** luck; **[es ist] ein** ~,
  dass ...: it's lucky that ...; **[kein]** ~ **haben**
  be [un]lucky; **viel** ~**!** [the] best of luck!; **zum**
  ~ *od.* **zu meinem/seinem** *usw.* ~: luckily *or*
  fortunately [for me/him *etc.*]
  (b) happiness

Glucke *die;* ~, ~**n** brood hen
glücken *itr. V.; mit sein* succeed; **etw. glückt**
  jmdm. sb. is successful with sth.
gluckern *itr. V.* gurgle; glug
glücklich ☐1 *Adj.* (a) happy (über + *Akk.*
  about)
  (b) (erfolgreich) lucky ⟨*winner*⟩; successful
  ⟨*outcome*⟩; safe ⟨*journey*⟩
  (c) (vorteilhaft) fortunate
  ☐2 *adv.* (a) (erfolgreich) successfully
  (b) (vorteilhaft, zufrieden) happily ⟨*chosen,*
  married⟩
glücklicher·weise *Adv.* fortunately;
  luckily
glück·selig ☐1 *Adj.* blissfully happy
  ☐2 *adv.* blissfully
Glück·seligkeit *die;* ~: bliss
glucksen *itr. V.* (a) ▶ GLUCKERN
  (b) (lachen) chuckle
Glücks-: ~**klee** *der* four-leaf clover;
  ~**pfennig** *der* lucky penny; ~**pilz** *der*
  (ugs.) lucky devil (coll.)
Glück[s]·sache *die:* **das ist** ~: it's a
  matter of luck
Glücks·spiel *das* game of chance
glück·strahlend *Adj.* radiantly happy
Glücks·zahl *die* lucky number
Glück·wunsch *der* congratulations
  pl.; **herzlichen** ~ **zum Geburtstag!** happy
  birthday!
Glüh·birne *die* lightbulb
glühen *itr. V.* glow
glühend ☐1 *Adj.* red-hot ⟨*metal etc.*⟩;
  blazing ⟨*heat*⟩; ardent ⟨*admirer etc.*⟩;
  passionate ⟨*words, letter, etc.*⟩
  ☐2 *adv.* ⟨*love*⟩ passionately; ⟨*admire*⟩
  ardently; ~ **heiß** blazing hot
Glüh-: ~**wein** *der* mulled wine;
  ~**würmchen** *das;* ~~**s**, ~~ (ugs.)
  (weiblich) glow-worm; (männlich) firefly
Glut *die;* ~, ~**en (a)** embers *pl.*
  (b) (geh.: Leidenschaft) passion
glut·rot *Adj.* fiery red
Glyzerin *das;* ~**s** glycerine
GmbH *Abk.* = **Gesellschaft mit**
  beschränkter Haftung ≈ plc, PLC
Gnade *die;* ~, ~**n** (Gunst) favour; (Rel.)
  grace; (Milde) mercy
gnaden-, Gnaden-: ~**brot** *das:*
  jmdm./einem Tier das ~**brot geben** keep
  sb./an animal in his/her/its old age; ~**frist**
  die reprieve; ~**gesuch** *das* plea for
  clemency; ~**los** (auch fig.) ☐1 *Adj.* merciless;
  ☐2 *adv.* mercilessly; ~**losigkeit**
  die; ~: mercilessness; ~**schuss**,
  *~**schuß** *der* coup de grâce ⟨*by shooting*⟩
gnädig *Adj.* gracious; (glimpflich) lenient
  ⟨*sentence etc.*⟩
Gnom *der;* ~**en**, ~**en** gnome
Gockel *der;* ~**s**, ~ (bes. südd., sonst ugs.
  scherzh.) cock
Gold *das;* ~**[e]s** gold ⋯⋰

Gọld·barren der gold bar
gọlden ⊡ Adj. (aus Gold) gold; (herrlich)
golden ⟨days, memories, etc.⟩
⊡ adv. like gold
Gọld-: ∼**fisch** der goldfish; ∼**füllung**
die gold filling; ∼**grube** die (auch fig.) gold
mine; ∼**hamster** der golden hamster
goldig Adj. sweet
gọld-, Gọld-: ∼**richtig** (ugs.) Adj.
absolutely right; ∼**schmied** der,
∼**schmiedin** die goldsmith; ∼**schnitt**
der gilt; ∼**währung** die (Wirtsch.) currency
tied to the gold standard
Gọlf¹ der; ∼[e]s, ∼e gulf
Gọlf² das; ∼s (Sport) golf
Gọlf-: ∼**platz** der golf course;
∼**schläger** der golf club; ∼**spieler** der,
∼**spielerin** die golfer; ∼**strom** der Gulf
Stream
Gondel die; ∼, ∼n gondola
gondeln itr. V.; mit sein (ugs.) **(a)** (mit einem
Boot) cruise
(b) (reisen) travel around
(c) (herumfahren) cruise around
Gong der; ∼s, ∼s gong
gongen itr. V. es hat gegongt the gong has
sounded
gönnen tr. V. jmdm. etw. ∼: not begrudge
sb. sth.; **sich/jmdm. etw.** ∼: allow oneself/sb.
sth.
Gönner der; ∼s, ∼: patron
gönnerhaft (abwertend) Adj. patronizing
Gönnerin die; ∼, ∼nen patroness
gor 3. Pers. Sg. Prät. v. GÄREN
Göre die; ∼, ∼n (nordd., oft abwertend) kid
(coll.)
Gorịlla der; ∼s, ∼s gorilla
goss, *goß 1. u. 3. Pers. Sg. Prät. v. GIESSEN
Gọsse die; ∼, ∼n gutter
Gọtik die; ∼ (Stil) Gothic [style]; (Epoche)
Gothic period
gọtisch Adj. Gothic
Gọtt der; ∼es, Götter **(a)** God; grüß [dich]
∼! (landsch.) hello!; **um** ∼**es Willen** (bei
Erschrecken) for God's sake; (bei einer Bitte) for
heaven's sake
(b) (übermenschliches Wesen) god
Gọttes-: ∼**dienst** der service; ∼**haus**
das (geh.) house of God; ∼**lästerung** die
blasphemy
Gọttheit die; ∼, ∼en deity
Göttin die; ∼, ∼nen goddess
göttlich ⊡ Adj. (auch fig.) divine
⊡ adv. divinely
gott-, Gọtt-: ∼**lob** adv. thank goodness;
∼**los** ⊡ Adj. **(a)** ungodly ⟨life etc.⟩;
impious ⟨words, speech, etc.⟩; **(b)** (Gott
leugnend) godless ⟨theory etc.⟩; ⊡ adv.
(verwerflich) irreverently; ∼**vater** der God
the Father; ∼**verlassen** Adj. (ugs.: abseits)

*old spelling – see note on page x

godforsaken; ∼**vertrauen** das trust in
God
Götze der; ∼n, ∼n (auch fig.) idol
Götzen-: ∼**bild** das idol; ∼**diener** der
idolater; ∼**dienerin** die idolatress
Gouverneur /guvɛrˈnøːɐ̯/ der; ∼s, ∼e
governor
Grab das; ∼[e]s, Gräber grave; **das**
Heilige ∼: the Holy Sepulchre; **das** ∼ **des**
Unbekannten Soldaten the tomb of the
Unknown Warrior
graben unr. tr., itr. V. dig
Graben der; ∼s, Gräben ditch; (Schützen∼)
trench; (Festungs∼) moat
Grab-: ∼**hügel** der grave mound;
∼**kammer** die burial chamber; ∼**mal**
das; Pl. ∼mäler, geh. ∼male monument;
∼**schändung** die desecration of a/the
grave/of [the] graves
grabschen ⊡ tr. V. grab; snatch
⊡ itr. V. **nach etw.** ∼: grab at sth.
gräbst 2. Pers. Sg. Präsens v. GRABEN
Grab·stein der gravestone
gräbt 3. Pers. Sg. Präsens v. GRABEN
Grabung die; ∼, ∼en (bes. Archäol.)
excavation
Grạcht die; ∼, ∼en canal
Grad der; ∼[e]s, ∼e degree; (Milit.) rank
grade (ugs.) ▶ GERADE
Grad·messer der gauge, yardstick (**für** of)
graduẹll ⊡ Adj. gradual; slight ⟨difference
etc.⟩
⊡ adv. gradually; ⟨different⟩ in degree
graduiert Adj. graduate; **ein** ∼**er Ingenieur**
an engineering graduate
Graf der; ∼en, ∼en count; (britischer ∼) earl
Graffịto der od. das; ∼[s], Graffịti **(a)** (Kunst)
graffito
(b) Pl. (Kritzelei) graffiti
Grafịk die; ∼, ∼en graphic art[s pl.];
(Kunstwerk) graphic; (Druck) print
Grafịker der; ∼s, ∼, **Grafịkerin** die;
∼, ∼nen [graphic] designer; (Künstler[in])
graphic artist
Gräfịn die; ∼, ∼nen countess
grafịsch ⊡ Adj. graphic
⊡ adv. graphically
Grafschaft die; ∼, ∼en **(a)** count's land;
(in Großbritannien) earldom
(b) (Verwaltungsbezirk) county
Gram der; ∼[e]s (geh.) grief; sorrow
grämen ⊡ tr. V. grieve
⊡ refl. V. grieve (**über** + Akk., **um** over)
Grạmm das; ∼s, ∼e gram
Grammạtik die; ∼, ∼en grammar
grammạtisch ⊡ Adj. grammatical
⊡ adv. grammatically
Grammophọn Ⓦ das; ∼s, ∼e
gramophone; phonograph (Amer.)
Granạt der; ∼[e]s, ∼e (Schmuckstein) garnet
Granạt·apfel der pomegranate

Granate *die;* ∼, ∼n shell; (Hand∼) grenade

Granat·feuer *das* shellfire *no pl., no indef. art.*

grandios [1] *Adj.* magnificent
  [2] *adv.* magnificently

Granit *der;* ∼s, ∼e granite

grantig (südd., österr. ugs.) [1] *Adj.* bad-tempered
  [2] *adv.* bad-temperedly

Grapefruit /'greːpfruːt/ *die;* ∼, ∼s grapefruit

Graph *der;* ∼en, ∼en (Math., Naturw.) graph

Graphik *usw.:* ▶ GRAFIK *usw.*

Graphit *der;* ∼s, ∼e graphite

Gras *das;* ∼es, Gräser (a) grass; **über etw.** (*Akk.*) ∼ **wachsen lassen** (ugs.) let the dust settle on sth.
  (b) (Drogenjargon) grass (sl.)

grasen *itr. V.* graze

Gras-: ∼**halm** *der* blade of grass; ∼**land** *das* grassland; ∼**narbe** *die* turf

grässlich, *gräßlich [1] *Adj.*
  (a) (abscheulich) horrible; terrible ⟨*accident*⟩
  (b) (ugs.: unangenehm) dreadful (coll.)
  (c) (ugs.: sehr stark) terrible (coll.)
  [2] *adv.* **(a)** (abscheulich) horribly; terribly
  (b) (ugs.: unangenehm) terribly (coll.)
  (c) (ugs.: sehr) terribly (coll.)

Grässlichkeit, *Gräßlichkeit *die;* ∼, ∼en **(a)** (Abscheulichkeit) horribleness; (eines Unfalls) terribleness
  (b) (unangenehme Art) dreadfulness (coll.)

Grat *der;* ∼[e]s, ∼e ridge

Gräte *die;* ∼, ∼n [fish] bone

Gratifikation *die;* ∼, ∼en bonus

gratinieren *tr. V.* (Gastr.) brown [the top of]; **gratinierter Blumenkohl** cauliflower au gratin

gratis *Adv.* free [of charge]; gratis

Gratis-: ∼**aktie** *die* (Börsenw.) bonus share; ∼**muster** *das,* ∼**probe** *die* free sample

Grätsche *die;* ∼, ∼n (Turnen) straddle; (Sprung) straddle vault

Gratulant *der;* ∼en, ∼en, **Gratulantin** *die;* ∼, ∼nen well-wisher

Gratulation *die;* ∼, ∼en congratulations *pl.*

gratulieren *itr. V.* jmdm. ∼: congratulate sb.; **jmdm. zum Geburtstag** ∼: wish sb. many happy returns [of the day]

Grat·wanderung *die* ridge walk; (fig.) balancing act

grau *Adj.* grey; (trostlos) dreary; drab; ∼ **meliert** greying ⟨*hair*⟩

Gräuel *der;* ∼s, ∼ **(a)** etw./jmd. ist jmdm. ein ∼: sb. loathes *or* detests sth./sb.
  (b) (geh.) (∼tat) atrocity

Gräuel·tat *die* atrocity

grauen¹ *itr. V.* (geh.) **der Morgen/der Tag graut** morning/day is breaking

grauen² *itr. V.* (*unpers.*) **ihm graut [es] davor/vor ihr** he dreads [the thought of] it/he's terrified of her

Grauen *das;* ∼s, ∼: horror (**vor** + *Dat.* of)

grauen·haft [1] *Adj.* horrifying; (ugs.: sehr unangenehm) terrible (coll.)
  [2] *adv.* horrifyingly; (ugs.: sehr unangenehm) terribly (coll.)

grauhaarig *Adj.* grey-haired

gräulich [1] *Adj.* **(a)** horrifying
  (b) (unangenehm) awful
  [2] *adv.* **(a)** horrifyingly
  (b) (unangenehm) terribly

***grau·meliert** ▶ GRAU

Graupe *die;* ∼, ∼n **(a)** grain of pearl barley
  (b) *Pl.* (Gericht) pearl barley *sing.*

Graupel *die;* ∼, ∼n soft hail pellet; ∼n soft hail; graupel

graupeln *itr. V.* (*unpers.*) **es graupelt** there's soft hail falling

grausam [1] *Adj.* **(a)** cruel
  (b) (furchtbar) terrible; dreadful
  [2] *adv.* **(a)** cruelly
  (b) (furchtbar) terribly, dreadfully

Grausamkeit *die;* ∼, ∼en **(a)** cruelty
  (b) (Handlung) act of cruelty

grausen [1] *tr., itr. V.* (*unpers.*) **es grauste ihm** *od.* **ihn davor/vor ihr** he dreaded it/he was terrified of her
  [2] *refl. V.* **sich vor etw./jmdm.** ∼: dread sth./be terrified of sth.

Grausen *das;* ∼s horror

grausig *Adj., adv.* ▶ GRAUENHAFT

gravieren *tr. V.* engrave

gravierend *Adj.* serious, grave

Gravierung *die;* ∼, ∼en engraving

Gravitation *die;* ∼ (Physik, Astron.) gravitation

Gravur /graˈvuːɐ̯/ *die;* ∼, ∼en engraving

Grazie /ˈgraːtsiə/ *die;* ∼, ∼n **(a)** (Anmut) gracefulness
  (b) (Myth.) Grace

greif·bar [1] *Adj.* **(a)** in ∼er Nähe (fig.) within reach; **der Urlaub ist in** ∼**e Nähe gerückt** (fig.) the holiday is just coming up [now]
  (b) (deutlich) tangible; concrete
  (c) (ugs.: verfügbar) available
  [2] *adv.* ∼ **nahe** (fig.) within reach

greifen [1] *unr. tr. V.* **(a)** (ergreifen) take hold of; grasp; (rasch ∼) seize
  (b) (fangen) catch
  [2] *unr. itr. V.* **(a)** in/unter/hinter etw./sich (*Akk.*) ∼: reach into/under/behind sth./one; **nach etw.** ∼: reach for sth.; (hastig) make a grab for sth.
  (b) (Technik) grip

Greis *der;* ∼es, ∼e old man

Greisin *die;* ∼, ∼nen old woman

grell [1] *Adj.* **(a)** (hell) glaring, ⟨*light, sun, etc.*⟩
  (b) (auffallend) garish ⟨*colour etc.*⟩; loud ····⟩

g

⟨*dress, pattern, etc.*⟩
(c) (schrill) shrill, ⟨*cry, voice, etc.*⟩
② *adv.* (a) (hell) with glaring brightness
(b) (auffallend) **gegen** *od.* **von etw.**
~ **abstechen** contrast sharply with sth.
(c) (schrill) shrilly
Gremium *das;* ~s, **Gremien** committee
Grenze *die;* ~, ~n (a) boundary; (Staats~)
border; (gedachte Trennungslinie) borderline
(b) (fig.) limit
grenzen *itr. V.* **an etw.** (*Akk.*) ~: border
[on] sth.
grenzen·los ① *Adj.* boundless; (fig.)
boundless, unbounded ⟨*joy, wonder,
jealousy, grief, etc.*⟩; unlimited ⟨*wealth,
power*⟩; limitless ⟨*patience, ambition*⟩;
extreme ⟨*tiredness, anger, foolishness*⟩
② *adv.* endlessly; (fig.) beyond all measure
Grenzen·losigkeit *die;*
~: boundlessness
Grenz-: ~**gänger** *der;* ~~s, ~~,
~**gängerin** *die;* ~~, ~~nen [regular]
commuter across the border *or* frontier;
~**konflikt** *der* border *or* frontier
conflict; ~**land** *das* border *or* frontier
area; ~**posten** *der* border *or* frontier
guard; ~**stein** *der* boundary stone;
~**übergang** *der* border crossing-point;
~**übertritt** *der* crossing of the border; **der
ungesetzliche** ~**übertritt** crossing the border
illegally; ~**verkehr** *der* [cross-]border
traffic
Gretchen·frage *die* crucial question;
sixty-four-thousand-dollar question (coll.)
*__Greuel__ ▶ GRÄUEL
*__Greueltat__ ▶ GRÄUELTAT
*__Greulich__ ▶ GRÄULICH
Grieche *der;* ~n, ~n Greek
Griechen·land (*das*); ~s Greece
Griechin *die;* ~, ~nen Greek
griechisch ① *Adj.* Greek
② *adv.* ⟨*speak, write*⟩ in Greek
Griechisch *das;* ~[s] Greek *no art.*
griesgrämig ① *Adj.* grumpy
② *adv.* in a grumpy manner
Grieß *der;* ~es, ~e semolina
Grieß·brei *der* semolina
griff *1. u. 3. Pers. Sg. Prät. v.* GREIFEN
Griff *der;* ~[e]s, ~e (a) grip; grasp
(b) (Knauf, Henkel) handle
griff·bereit *Adj.* ready to hand *postpos.*
Griffel *der;* ~s, ~: slate pencil
griffig *Adj.* (a) (handlich) handy
(b) (gut greifend) that grips well *postpos., not
pred.;* non-slip ⟨*surface, floor*⟩
Grill *der;* ~s, ~s grill; (Rost) barbecue
Grille *die;* ~, ~n (a) cricket
(b) (sonderbarer Einfall) whim
grillen ① *tr. V.* grill
② *itr. V.* **im Garten** ~: have a barbecue in

the garden
Grill·platz *der* barbecue area
Grimasse *die;* ~, ~n grimace
grimmig ① *Adj.* furious ⟨*person*⟩; grim
⟨*expression*⟩
② *adv.* grimly
grinsen *itr. V.* grin; (höhnisch) smirk
Grippe *die;* ~, ~n (a) influenza; flu (coll.)
(b) (volkst.: Erkältung) cold
Grips *der;* ~es brains *pl.*
grob ① *Adj.* (a) coarse; thick ⟨*wire*⟩; rough
⟨*work*⟩
(b) (ungefähr) rough
(c) (schwerwiegend) gross; flagrant ⟨*lie*⟩
(d) (barsch) rude
② *adv.* (a) coarsely
(b) (ungefähr) roughly
(c) (schwerwiegend) grossly
(d) (barsch) rudely
Grobheit *die;* ~, ~en (a) rudeness
(b) (Äußerung) rude remark
Grobian *der;* ~[e]s, ~e lout
Grog *der;* ~s, ~s grog
groggy *Adj.* (a) (Boxen) groggy
(b) (ugs.: erschöpft) whacked [out] (coll.); all in
(coll.)
grölen ① *tr. V.* (ugs. abwertend) bawl [out];
roar, howl ⟨*approval*⟩
② *itr. V.* bawl
Groll *der;* ~[e]s (geh.) rancour
grollen *itr. V.* (geh.) (a) [mit] jmdm. ~: bear
a grudge against sb.
(b) ⟨*thunder*⟩ rumble
Grönland (*das*); ~s Greenland
Gros /gro:/ *das;* ~ /gro:s/, ~ /gro:s/ bulk
Groschen *der;* ~s, ~ (a) (österreichische
Münze) groschen
(b) (ugs.: Zehnpfennigstück) ten-pfennig piece;
(fig.) penny; cent (Amer.)
groß; größer, größt... ① *Adj.* (a) big, large;
great ⟨*length, width, height*⟩; tall ⟨*person*⟩;
wide ⟨*selection*⟩; 1m² ~: 1m² in area; **im
Großen und Ganzen** by and large
(b) (älter) big ⟨*brother, sister*⟩; (erwachsen)
grown-up
(c) (lange dauernd) long, lengthy
(d) intense ⟨*heat, cold*⟩; high ⟨*speed*⟩; great,
major ⟨*event, artist, work*⟩
② *adv.* (ugs.: besonders) greatly;
~ **geschrieben werden** (ugs.) be stressed;
s. auch GROSSSCHREIBEN
groß-, Groß-: ~**abnehmer** *der*,
~**abnehmerin** *die* bulk buyer
or purchaser; ~**aktionär** *der*,
~**aktionärin** *die* (Wirtsch.) principal
or major shareholder; ~**artig**
① *Adj.* magnificent; splendid; ② *adv.*
magnificently; splendidly; ~**auftrag** *der*
(Wirtsch.) large order
Großbritannien (*das*); ~s the United
Kingdom; [Great] Britain
Groß·buchstabe *der* capital [letter]

g

Größe *die;* ~, ~n size; (Höhe, Körper~) height; (fig.) greatness; **die ~ der Katastrophe** the [full] extent of the catastrophe

Groß·eltern *Pl.* grandparents

Größen·ordnung *die* order [of magnitude]; **in einer ~ von einer Milliarde Euro** in the order of a thousand million *or* a billion euros

großen·teils *Adv.* largely; for the most part

Größen·wahn *der* delusions *pl.* of grandeur

größer ▸ GROSS

Groß-: ~**fahndung** *die* large-scale search; ~**familie** *die* (Soziol.) extended family; (mehrere Kleinfamilien) composite family; ~**handel** *der* wholesale trade; ~**händler** *der,* ~**händlerin** *die* wholesaler; ~**industrielle** *der/die; adj. Dekl.* big industrialist

Grossist *der;* ~en, ~en, **Grossistin** *die;* ~, ~nen (Kaufmannsspr.) wholesaler

groß-, Groß-: ~**macht** *die* great power; ~**maul** *das* (ugs. abwertend) bigmouth (coll.); ~**mut** *die;* ~~: generosity; ~**mütig** *Adj.* generous; ~**mutter** *die; Pl.* ~mütter grandmother; ~**rechner** *der* (DV) mainframe [computer]; ~**reinemachen** *das;* ~~s (ugs.) thorough cleaning; ~|**schreiben** *unr. tr. V.* write ⟨word⟩ with a capital; *s. auch* GROSS 2; ~**spurig** (abwertend) [1] *Adj.* boastful; (hochtrabend) pretentious; [2] *adv.* boastfully; (hochtrabend) pretentiously; ~**stadt** *die* city; large town; ~**städter** *der,* ~**städterin** *die* city-dweller

größt... ▸ GROSS

Groß·teil *der* (a) (Hauptteil) major part (b) (nicht unerheblicher Teil) large part

größten·teils *Adv.* for the most part

größt·möglich *Adj.* greatest possible

groß-, Groß-: ~|**tun** *unr. itr. V.* boast; ~**unternehmen** *das* (Wirtsch.) large-scale enterprise; big concern; ~**vater** *der* grandfather; ~**verbraucher** *der,* ~**verbraucherin** *die* bulk *or* large consumer; ~|**ziehen** *unr. tr. V.* bring up; raise; rear ⟨animal⟩; ~**zügig** [1] *Adj.* generous; grand and spacious ⟨building, garden, etc.⟩; [2] *adv.* generously; ~**zügigkeit** *die;* ~~: generosity

grotesk [1] *Adj.* grotesque [2] *adv.* grotesquely

Grotte *die;* ~, ~n grotto

grub *1. u. 3. Pers. Sg. Prät. v.* GRABEN

Grübchen *das;* ~s, ~: dimple

Grube *die;* ~, ~n pit; (Bergbau) mine

grübeln *itr. V.* ponder (über + *Dat.* on, over)

Gruben·arbeiter *der,* **Gruben·arbeiterin** *die* miner; mineworker

grüezi *Interj.* (schweiz.) hallo

Gruft *die;* ~, Grüfte vault; (in einer Kirche) crypt

grün *Adj.* green

Grün *das;* ~s, ~ *od.* (ugs.) ~s (a) green (b) (Pflanzen) greenery

Grün·anlage *die* green space; (Park) park

Grund *der;* ~[e]s, Gründe (a) ground; (eines Gewässers) bottom; **im ~e [genommen]** basically (b) (Ursache, Veranlassung) reason; **auf ~:** ▸ AUFGRUND

Grund-: ~**besitz** *der* (a) (Eigentum an Land) ownership of land; (b) (Land) land; ~**buch** *das* land register

gründen [1] *tr. V.* (a) found; set up, establish ⟨business⟩; start [up] ⟨club⟩ (b) (aufbauen) base ⟨plan, theory, etc.⟩ (auf + *Akk.* on) [2] *itr. V.* auf *od.* in etw. (*Dat.*) ~: be based on sth. [3] *refl. V.* sich auf etw. (*Akk.*) ~: be based on sth.

Gründer *der;* ~s, ~, **Gründerin** *die;* ~, ~nen founder

Grund·erwerb[s]·steuer *die* (Steuerw.) land transfer tax

Grund·gesetz *das* Basic Law

grundieren *tr. V.* prime

Grundierung *die;* ~, ~en (a) (das Grundieren) priming (b) (erster Anstrich) priming coat

grund-, Grund-: ~**kenntnis** *die* basic knowledge *no pl.* (in + *Dat.* of); ~**lage** *die* basis; foundation

Grundlagen·forschung *die* basic research

grund·legend [1] *Adj.* fundamental, basic (für to); seminal ⟨idea, work⟩ [2] *adv.* fundamentally

gründlich [1] *Adj.* thorough [2] *adv.* thoroughly

Gründlichkeit *die;* ~: thoroughness

grund·los [1] *Adj.* groundless [2] *adv.* sich ~ aufregen/ängstigen be needlessly agitated/alarmed

Grund·nahrungsmittel *das* basic food[stuff]

Grün·donnerstag *der* Maundy Thursday

Grund-: ~**ordnung** *die* basic fundamental [constitutional] order; ~**prinzip** *das* fundamental principle; ~**recht** *das* basic *or* constitutional right; ~**riss,** *~**riß** *der* (a) (Bauw.) [ground] plan; (b) (Leitfaden) outline; ~**satz** *der* principle

grund·sätzlich [1] *Adj.* (a) fundamental ⟨difference, question, etc.⟩ (b) (aus Prinzip) ⟨opponent etc.⟩ on principle (c) (allgemein) ⟨agreement etc.⟩ in principle [2] *adv.* (a) fundamentally ⋯⟶

(b) (aus Prinzip) on principle
(c) (allgemein) in principle
Grund-: ∼**schule** *die* primary
school; ∼**stein** *der* foundation stone;
∼**stein·legung** *die;* ∼∼, ∼∼en laying
of the foundation stone; ∼**stück** *das* plot
[of land]
Gründung *die;* ∼, ∼en ▶ GRÜNDEN 1A:
foundation; setting up; establishing;
starting [up]
Grund-: ∼**wasser** *das* (Geol.) ground
water; ∼**wortschatz** *der* (Sprachw.) basic
vocabulary; ∼**zug** *der* essential feature
Grüne¹ *das; adj. Dekl.* green; **im** ∼**n/ins**
∼: [out] in/into the country
Grüne² *der/die; adj. Dekl.* (Politik) member of
the Green Party; **die** ∼**n** the Greens
Grün-: ∼**fläche** *die* green space; (im Park)
lawn; ∼**gürtel** *der* green belt; ∼**land**
das (Landw.) (Wiese) meadow land; (Weide)
pastureland; ∼**pflanze** *die* foliage plant;
∼**schnabel** *der* (abwertend) [young]
whippersnapper; (Neuling) greenhorn;
∼**span** *der* verdigris; ∼**streifen** *der*
central reservation (*grassed and often with
trees and bushes*)
grunzen *tr., itr. V.* grunt
Gruppe *die;* ∼, ∼n **(a)** group
(b) (Klassifizierung) class; category
Gruppen-: ∼**druck** *der* group pressure;
∼**dynamik** *die* (Sozialpsych.) group
dynamics *sing., no art.;* ∼**leiter** *der,*
∼**leiterin** *die* group leader; ∼**reise** *die*
(Touristik) group travel *no pl., no art.;* **eine**
∼**reise nach London machen** travel to
London with a group; ∼**sieg** *der* (Sport) top
place in the group
gruppieren 1 *tr. V.* arrange
2 *refl. V.* form a group/groups
Gruppierung *die;* ∼, ∼en grouping
Grusel *der;* ∼s horror
gruselig *Adj.* eerie; creepy
gruseln 1 *tr., itr. V.* (unpers.) **es gruselt
jmdn.** *od.* **jmdm.** sb.'s flesh creeps
2 *refl. V.* be frightened
Gruß *der;* ∼es, Grüße **(a)** greeting; (Milit.)
salute
(b) (im Brief) **mit herzlichen Grüßen** [with]
best wishes; **mit bestem** ∼**/freundlichen
Grüßen** yours sincerely
grüßen 1 *tr. V.* **(a)** greet; (Milit.) salute
(b) (Grüße senden) **grüße deine Eltern [ganz
herzlich] von mir** please give your parents
my [kindest] regards; **grüß dich!** (ugs.) hello
or (coll.) hi [there]!
2 *itr. V.* say hello; (Milit.) salute
Grütze *die;* ∼, ∼n groats *pl.;* **rote** ∼: red
fruit pudding (*made with fruit juice, fruit
and cornflour, etc.*)
Guave /guˈaːvə/ *die;* ∼, ∼n guava

gucken *itr. V.* (ugs.) **(a)** look; (heimlich) peep
(b) (hervorsehen) stick out
(c) (dreinschauen) look
Guck·loch *das* spyhole
Guerilla /geˈrɪlja/ *die;* ∼, ∼s guerrilla
war; (Einheit) guerrilla unit
Gulasch /ˈɡʊlaʃ, ˈɡuːlaʃ/ *das od. der;*
∼[e]s, ∼e *od.* ∼s goulash
Gulden *der;* ∼s, ∼: guilder
gültig *Adj.* valid; current ‹*note, coin*›
Gültigkeit *die;* ∼: validity; ∼ **haben/
erlangen** be/become valid
Gummi *der od. das;* ∼s, ∼[s] rubber
Gummi-: ∼**band** *das* rubber *or* elastic
band; (in Kleidung) elastic *no indef. art.;*
∼**bärchen** *das;* ∼∼s, ∼∼: jelly baby;
∼**baum** *der* rubber plant
gummieren *tr. V.* gum
Gummi-: ∼**handschuh** *der* rubber
glove; ∼**knüppel** *der* [rubber] truncheon;
∼**sohle** *die* rubber sole; ∼**stiefel** *der*
rubber boot; (für Regenwetter) wellington
[boot] (Brit.)
Gunst *die;* ∼ **(a)** favour; goodwill
(b) zu ∼**en** ▶ ZUGUNSTEN
günstig 1 *Adj.* favourable; propitious
‹*sign*›; auspicious ‹*moment*›; beneficial
‹*influence*›; good
2 *adv.* favourably; **etw.** ∼ **beeinflussen**
have *or* exert a beneficial influence on sth.
günstig[st]en·falls *Adv.* at best
Gurgel *die;* ∼, ∼n throat; **jmdm. die**
∼ **zudrücken** throttle sb.
gurgeln *itr. V.* gargle
Gurke *die;* ∼, ∼n cucumber; (eingelegt)
gherkin
gurren *itr. V.* (auch fig.) coo
Gurt *der;* ∼[e]s, ∼e strap; (im Auto, Flugzeug)
[seat] belt
Gürtel *der;* ∼s, ∼: belt
Gürtel-: ∼**linie** *die* waist[line]; **das war
ein Schlag unter die** ∼**linie** (fig. ugs.) that was
hitting below the belt (fig. coll.); ∼**reifen** *der*
radial[-ply] tyre
Gurt·straffer *der;* ∼s, ∼ (Kfz.-W.)
[seat-]belt tensioner
Guru *der;* ∼s, ∼s guru
GUS *Abk.* = **Gemeinschaft
Unabhängiger Staaten** CIS
Guss, *Guß *der;* Gusses, Güsse **(a)** (das
Gießen) casting
(b) (ugs.: Regenschauer) downpour
Guss·eisen, *Guß·eisen *das* cast iron
guss·eisern, *guß·eisern *Adj.* cast
iron
gut; besser, best... 1 *Adj.* good; fine
‹*wine*›; **ein** ∼**es neues Jahr** a happy new
year; ∼ **tun** do good; **mir ist nicht** ∼: I'm not
feeling well; ∼ **aussehend** good-looking;
∼**en Appetit!** enjoy your lunch/dinner *etc.*!;
eine ∼**e Stunde [von hier]** a good hour [from
here]

⟨2⟩ *adv.* **(a)** well; ~ **gemeint** well-meant; **so ~ wie nichts** next to nothing
(b) (mühelos) easily; *s. auch* BESSER, BEST…
Gut *das;* ~[e]s, **Güter (a)** property; (Besitztum, auch fig.) possession
(b) (landwirtschaftlicher Grundbesitz) estate
(c) (Fracht~, Ware) item; **Güter** goods; (Fracht~) freight *sing.;* goods (Brit.)
gut-, Gut-: ~**achten** *das;* ~~s, ~~: [expert's] report; ~**artig** *Adj.*
(a) good-natured; **(b)** (nicht gefährlich) benign; ~**artigkeit** *die* **(a)** good nature; goodnaturedness; **(b)** (Ungefährlichkeit) benignity; **~***aussehend** ▶ GUT 1; ~**bürgerlich** *Adj.* good middle-class; ~**bürgerliche Küche** good plain cooking; ~**dünken** *das;* ~~s discretion
Güte *die;* ~: goodness; kindness; (Qualität) quality
Gute-nacht-kuss, *Gute-nacht-kuß *der* goodnight kiss
Güter-: ~**abfertigung** *die* **(a)** (Abfertigung von Waren) dispatch of freight *or* (Brit.) goods; **(b)** (Annahmestelle) freight *or* (Brit.) goods office; ~**bahnhof** *der* freight depot; goods station (Brit.); ~**wagen** *der* goods wagon (Brit.); freight car (Amer.); ~**zug** *der* goods train (Brit.); freight train (Amer.)
gut-, Gut-: **~***|gehen** ▶ GEHEN H, I;

~*gelaunt** ▶ GELAUNT; **~***gemeint** ▶ GUT 2A; ~**gläubig** *Adj.* innocently trusting; ~**haben** *das;* ~~s, ~~: credit balance; ~**|heißen** *unr. tr. V.* approve of; ~**herzig** *Adj.* kind-hearted
gütig ⟨1⟩ *Adj.* kindly
⟨2⟩ *adv.* ~ **lächeln** give a kindly smile
gütlich *Adj.* amicable
gut-, Gut-: ~**|machen** *tr. V.* make good ⟨damage⟩; put right ⟨omission, mistake, etc.⟩; ~**mütig** *Adj.* good-natured; ~**mütigkeit** *die;* ~~: good nature
Guts-besitzer *der,* **Guts-besitzerin** *die* owner of a/the estate; landowner
gut-, Gut-: ~**schein** *der* voucher, coupon (für, auf + *Akk.* for); ~**|schreiben** *unr. tr. V.* credit; ~**schrift** *die* credit
Guts-hof *der* estate; manor
gut-, Gut-: **~***|tun** ▶ GUT 1; ~**willig** ⟨1⟩ *Adj.* willing; (entgegenkommend) obliging; ⟨2⟩ *adv.* etw. ~**willig herausgeben/versprechen** hand sth. over voluntarily/promise sth. willingly
Gymnasium *das;* ~s, **Gymnasien** ≈ grammar school
Gymnastik *die;* ~: physical exercises *pl.;* (Turnen) gymnastics *sing.*
Gynäkologe *der;* ~n, ~n, **Gynäkologin** *die;* ~, ~nen gynaecologist

Hh

h, H /ha:/ *das;* ~, ~(a) (Buchstabe) h/H
(b) (Musik) [key of] B
h *Abk.* **(a)** = **Uhr** hrs
(b) = **Stunde** hr[s]
H *Abk.* **(a)** = **Herren;**
(b) = **Haltestelle**
ha¹ /ha(:)/ *Interj.* **(a)** (Überraschung) ah
(b) (Triumph) aha
ha² *Abk.* = **Hektar** ha
Haar *das;* ~[e]s, ~e hair; **blonde** ~**e** *od.* **blondes** ~ **haben** have fair hair; (fig.) ~**e auf den Zähnen haben** (ugs. scherzh.) be a tough customer; **um ein** ~ (ugs.) very nearly
Haar-: ~**ausfall** *der* hair loss; ~**bürste** *die* hairbrush; ~**büschel** *das* tuft of hair
haaren *itr. V.* moult
Haares-breite *die;* **um** ~: by a hair's breadth
haar-, Haar-: ~**festiger** *der;* ~s, ~: setting lotion; ~**genau** (ugs.) ⟨1⟩ *Adj.* exact; ⟨2⟩ *adv.* exactly

haarig *Adj.* hairy
haar-, Haar-: ~**klemme** *die* hairgrip; ~**nadel** *die* hairpin; ~**nadel-kurve** *die* hairpin bend; ~**schnitt** *der* haircut; (modisch) hairstyle; ~**spalterei** *die;* ~~, ~~en (abwertend) hair-splitting; **das ist doch** ~**spalterei** that's splitting hairs; ~**spange** *die* hairslide; ~**sträubend** *Adj.* **(a)** (grauenhaft) hair-raising; **(b)** (empörend) outrageous; shocking; ~**teil** *das* hairpiece; ~**waschmittel** *das* shampoo; ~**wasser** *das* hair lotion
Habe *die;* ~ (geh.) possessions *pl.*
haben ⟨1⟩ *unr. tr. V.* have; have got; **heute** ~ **wir schönes Wetter** the weather is fine today; **es gut/schlecht/schwer** ~: have it good (coll.)/have a bad time [of it]/have a difficult time; **du hast zu gehorchen** you must obey; **das Jahr hat 12 Monate** there are 12 months in a year
⟨2⟩ *refl. V.* (ugs.: sich aufregen) make a fuss
⟨3⟩ *Hilfsverb* have; **ich habe/hatte ihn eben gesehen** I've/I'd just seen him; **er hat es gewusst** he knew it   ····⟩

4 *mod. V.* du hast zu gehorchen you must obey; er hat sich nicht einzumischen he's not to interfere

Haben *das;* ~s, ~ (Kaufmannsspr.) credit

Habe·nichts *der;* ~, ~e pauper

Haben-: ~**seite** *die* (Kaufmannsspr.) credit side; ~**zinsen** *Pl.* interest *sing.* on deposits

Hab·gier *die* (abwertend) greed

hab·gierig **1** *Adj.* (abwertend) greedy **2** *adv.* greedily

Habicht *der;* ~s, ~e hawk

Hab-: ~**seligkeiten** *Pl.* [meagre] belongings; ~**sucht** *die;* (abwertend) greed; avarice

Hachse *die;* ~, ~n (südd.) knuckle

Hack *das;* ~s (ugs., bes. nordd.) mince

Hack·braten *der* meat loaf

Hacke[1] *die;* ~, ~n hoe; (Pickel) pick[axe]

Hacke[2] *die;* ~, ~n (bes. nordd. u. md.) heel

hacken **1** *itr. V.* **(a)** hoe **(b)** (picken) peck **2** *tr. V.* **(a)** hoe ⟨*garden, flower bed, etc.*⟩ **(b)** (zerkleinern) chop; chop [up] ⟨*meat, vegetables, etc.*⟩

Hacker *der;* ~s, ~, **Hackerin** *die;* ~, ~nen (DV-Jargon) hacker

hacke·zu *Adj.* (salopp) paralytic [drunk] (coll.)

Hack·fleisch *das* minced meat; mince

Häcksel *der od. das;* ~s (Landw.) chaff

hadern *itr. V.* (geh.) **mit etw.** ~: be at odds with sth.

Hafen *der;* ~s, Häfen harbour; port

Hafen-: ~**arbeiter** *der,* ~**arbeiterin** *die* dock worker; docker; ~**kneipe** *die* dockland pub (Brit.) *or* (Amer.) bar; ~**rundfahrt** *die* trip round the harbour; ~**stadt** *die* port; ~**viertel** *das* dock area

Hafer *der;* ~s oats *pl.*

Hafer-: ~**brei** *der* porridge; ~**flocken** *Pl.* porridge oats

Haff *das;* ~[e]s, ~s *od.* ~e lagoon

-haft *Adj., adv.* -like

Haft *die;* ~ **(a)** (Gewahrsam) custody; (aus politischen Gründen) detention **(b)** (Freiheitsstrafe) imprisonment

haftbar *Adj.* (bes. Rechtsspr.) **für etw.** ~ **sein** be liable for sth.

Haft·befehl *der* (Rechtsw.) warrant [of arrest]

haften[1] *itr. V.* stick (sich festsetzen) ⟨*smell, dirt, etc.*⟩; cling (**an** + *Dat.* to); ~ **bleiben** stick; (**an/auf** + *Dat.* to); ⟨*smell, smoke*⟩ cling (**an/auf** + *Dat.* to); (ugs.: im Gedächtnis bleiben) stick

haften[2] *itr. V.* **für jmdn./etw.** ~: be responsible for sb./liable for sth.; (Rechtsw., Wirtsch.) be liable

*****haften|bleiben** ▶ HAFTEN[1]

Häftling *der;* ~s, ~e prisoner

Haft·pflicht *die* liability (**für** for)

Haftpflicht·versicherung *die* personal liability insurance; (für Autofahrer) third party insurance

Haft-: ~**prüfung** *die* (Rechtsw.) review of a/the remand in custody; ~**schale** *die* contact lens; ~**strafe** *die* (Rechtsspr. veralt.) prison sentence

Haftung *die;* ~, ~en liability; **Gesellschaft mit [un]beschränkter** ~: [un]limited [liability] company

Hagebutte *die;* ~, ~n **(a)** (Frucht) rose hip **(b)** (ugs.: Heckenrose) dog rose

Hagel *der;* ~s, ~ (auch fig.) hail

hageln *itr., tr. V.* (unpers.) hail

Hagel-: ~**schaden** *der* damage *no pl.* caused by hail; ~**schauer** *der* [short] hailstorm; ~**schlag** *der* hail

hager *Adj.* gaunt

haha /ha'ha(:)/ *Interj.* ha ha

Häher *der;* ~s, ~: jay

Hahn[1] *der;* ~[e]s, Hähne cock; (Wetter~) weathercock

Hahn[2] *der;* ~[e]s, Hähne, *fachspr.:* ~en **(a)** (tap; faucet (Amer.) **(b)** (bei Waffen) hammer

Hähnchen *das;* ~s, ~: chicken

Hahnen·fuß *der* buttercup

Hai *der;* ~s, ~e shark

Häkchen *das;* ~s, ~ **(a)** [small] hook **(b)** (Zeichen) mark; (beim Abhaken) tick

häkeln *tr., itr. V.* crochet

Häkel·nadel *die* crochet hook

haken **1** *tr. V.* hook (**an** + *Akk.* on to) **2** *itr. V.* (klemmen) be stuck

Haken *der;* ~s, ~ **(a)** hook **(b)** (Zeichen) tick **(c)** (ugs.: Schwierigkeit) catch **(d)** (Boxen) hook

haken-, Haken-: ~**förmig** **1** *Adj.* hooked; hook-shaped; **2** *adv.* ~**förmig gebogen** hooked; hook-shaped; ~**kreuz** *das* swastika; ~**nase** *die* hooked nose; hook nose

halb **1** *Adj. u. Bruchz.* half; **eine** ~**e Stunde/ein** ~**er Meter** half an hour/a metre; **zum** ~**en Preis** [at] half price; ~ **Europa/die** ~**e Welt** half of Europe/half the world; **es ist** ~ **eins** it's half past twelve; **die** ~**e Wahrheit** half [of] the truth; **[noch] ein** ~**es Kind sein** be hardly more than a child **2** *adv.* ~ **voll/leer** half-full/-empty; ~ **offen** half-open; ~ **angezogen** half dressed; ~ **links/rechts** (Fußball) ⟨*play*⟩ [at] inside left/right

Halb·dunkel *das* semi-darkness

Halbe *der od. die; adj. Dekl.* (ugs.) half litre (*of beer etc.*)

Halb·edelstein *der* (veralt.) semi-precious stone

halber *Präp. mit Gen.; nachgestellt* (wegen) on account of; (um ... willen) for the sake of

halb-, Halb-: ~**finale** *das* (Sport) semi-final; ~**gar** *Adj.* half-cooked;

~**gefror[e]ne** *das; adj. Dekl.* soft ice cream

Halbheit *die;* ~, ~**en** (abwertend) half measure

halbieren *tr. V.* cut/tear ⟨*object*⟩ in half; halve ⟨*amount, number*⟩

halb-, Halb-: ~**insel** *die* peninsula; ~**jahr** *das* six months *pl.*; half year; ~**jährlich** [1] *Adj.* six-monthly; [2] *adv.* every six months; ~**kreis** *der* semicircle; ~**kugel** *die* hemisphere; ~**lang** *Adj.* mid-length ⟨*hair*⟩; mid-calf length ⟨*coat, dress, etc.*⟩; ~**links** /-'-/ *Adv.* (Fußball) ⟨*play*⟩ [at] inside left; ~**mast** *Adv.* at half-mast; ~**mond** *der* (a) (Mond) half-moon; (b) (Figur) crescent; ***~**offen** *Adj.:* ▸ HALB 2; ~**pension** *die* half-board; ~**rechts** /-'-/ *Adv.* (Fußball) ⟨*play*⟩ [at] inside right; ~**schlaf** *der* light sleep; **im** ~**schlaf liegen** be half asleep; doze; ~**schuh** *der* shoe; ~**starke** *der; adj. Dekl.* (ugs. abwertend) [young] hooligan

halb·tags *Adv.* ⟨*work*⟩ part-time; (morgens/nachmittags) ⟨*work*⟩ [in the] mornings/afternoons;

Halbtags-: ~**arbeit** *die,* ~**beschäftigung** *die* part-time job; (morgens/nachmittags) morning/afternoon job; ~**schule** *die* half-day school; ~**stelle** *die* part-time job; (morgens/nachmittags) morning/afternoon job

halb-, Halb-: ***~**voll** *Adj.:* ▸ HALB 2; ~**wegs** *Adv.* to some extent; ~**wüchsig** /-vy:ksɪç/ *Adj.* adolescent; ~**wüchsige** *der/die; adj. Dekl.* adolescent; ~**zeit** *die* (bes. Fußball) (a) half; (b) (Pause) half-time; ~**zeit·pause** *die* (Sport) half-time

Halde *die;* ~, ~**n** (Bergbau) slag heap

half *1. u. 3. Pers. Sg. Prät. v.* HELFEN

Hälfte *die;* ~, ~**n** (a) half (b) (ugs.: Teil) part

Halfter[1] *der od. das;* ~**s,** ~: halter

Halfter[2] *die;* ~, ~**n;** *auch das;* ~**s,** ~: holster

Hall *der;* ~**[e]s,** ~**e** (a) (geh.) reverberation (b) (Echo) echo

Halle *die;* ~, ~**n** hall; (Fabrik~) shed; (Hotel~, Theater~) foyer

hallen *itr. V.* (a) reverberate; ⟨*shot, bell, cry*⟩ ring out (b) (widerhallen) echo

Hallen- indoor ⟨*swimming pool, handball*⟩

Hallig *die;* ~, ~**en** small low island (*particularly one of those off Schleswig-Holstein*)

hallo *Interj.* hello

Hallo *das;* ~**s,** ~**s** cheering

Halluzination *die;* ~, ~**en** hallucination

Halm *der;* ~**[e]s,** ~**e** stalk; stem

Hals *der;* ~**es,** **Hälse** neck; (Kehle) throat; ~ **über Kopf** (ugs.) in a rush

hals-, Hals-: ~**ab·schneider** *der,* ~**ab·schneiderin** *die* (ugs. abwertend) shark; ~**band** *das* (für Tiere) collar; ~**bruch** *der:* ▸ ~- UND BEINBRUCH; ~**entzündung** *die* inflammation of the throat; ~**kette** *die* necklace; ~**-Nasen-Ohren-Arzt** *der,* ~**-Nasen-Ohren-Ärztin** *die* ear, nose, and throat specialist; ~**schlagader** *die* carotid [artery]; ~**schmerzen** *Pl.* sore throat *sing.;* ~**starrig** *Adj.* (abwertend) stubborn; obstinate; ~**tuch** *das; Pl.* ~**tücher** cravat; (des Cowboys) neckerchief; ~**- und Beinbruch** *Interj.* (scherzh.) good luck; ~**weh** *das* (ugs.) ▸ ~SCHMERZEN

halt *Interj.* stop

Halt *der;* ~**[e]s,** ~**e** (a) hold (b) (Stopp) stop; ~ **machen** stop

haltbar *Adj.* (a) ~ **sein** ⟨*food*⟩ keep [well]; ~ **bis 5. 3.** use by 5 March (b) (nicht verschleißend) hard-wearing ⟨*material, clothes*⟩ (c) (aufrechtzuerhalten) tenable ⟨*hypothesis etc.*⟩

Haltbarkeit *die;* ~ (Strapazierfähigkeit) durability

Halte·bucht *die* (Verkehrsw.) lay-by (Brit.); turnout (Amer.)

halten [1] *unr. tr. V.* (a) (auch Milit.) hold; **die Hand vor den Mund** ~: put one's hand in front of one's mouth (b) (Ballspiele) save ⟨*shot, penalty, etc.*⟩ (c) (bewahren) keep; (beibehalten, aufrechterhalten) keep up ⟨*speed etc.*⟩; maintain ⟨*temperature, equilibrium*⟩ (d) (erfüllen) keep; **sein Wort/ein Versprechen** ~: keep one's word/a promise (e) (besitzen, beschäftigen, beziehen) keep ⟨*chickens etc.*⟩; take ⟨*newspaper, magazine, etc.*⟩ (f) (einschätzen) **jmdn. für reich/ehrlich** ~: think sb. is rich/honest; **viel von jmdm.** ~: think a lot of sb. (g) (ab~, veranstalten) give, ⟨*speech, lecture*⟩ [2] *unr. itr. V.* (a) (stehen bleiben) stop (b) (unverändert, an seinem Platz bleiben) last (c) (Sport) save (d) (beistehen) **zu jmdm.** ~: stand by sb. [3] *unr. refl. V.* (a) (sich durchsetzen, behaupten) **wir werden uns/die Stadt wird sich nicht länger** ~ **können** we/the town won't be able to hold out much longer (b) (sich bewähren) **sich gut** ~: do well (c) (unverändert bleiben) ⟨*weather, flowers, etc.*⟩ last; ⟨*milk, meat, etc.*⟩ keep (d) (Körperhaltung haben) **sich schlecht/gerade** ~: hold oneself badly/straight (e) (bleiben) **sich auf den Beinen/im Sattel** ~: stay on one's feet/in the saddle; **sich links/rechts** ~: keep [to the] left/right; **sich an etw.** *(Akk.)* ~: keep to sth.

Halte·punkt *der* stop

Halter *der;* ~**s,** ~ (a) (Fahrzeug~) keeper (b) (Tier~) owner (c) (Vorrichtung) holder ⋯⟶

h

Halterin *die;* ~, ~nen **(a)** ▸ HALTER A: keeper
(b) ▸ HALTER B: owner
Halterung *die;* ~, ~en support
Halte-: ~**stelle** *die* stop; ~**verbot** *das* **(a)** („~verbot" 'no stopping'; **hier ist** ~verbot this is a no-stopping zone; **(b)** (Stelle) no-stopping zone; ~**verbots-schild** *das* no-stopping sign
-haltig, (österr.) **-hältig:** vitamin~/silber~ *usw.* containing vitamins/silver *etc.* postpos., not pred.; vitamin~ sein contain vitamins
halt-, Halt-: ~**los** *Adj.* **(a)** (labil) ~los sein be a weak character; **ein** ~**loser Mensch** a weak character; **(b)** (unbegründet) unfounded; ~**losigkeit** *die;* ~~ **(a)** (Labilität) weakness of character; **(b)** (mangelnde Begründung) unfoundedness; **~|machen* ▸ HALT B
Haltung *die;* ~, ~en **(a)** (Körper~) posture
(b) (Pose) manner
(c) (Einstellung) attitude
(d) (Fassung) composure
Halunke *der;* ~n, ~n scoundrel; villain
Hamburger *der;* ~s, ~ (Frikadelle) hamburger
hämisch ⒈ *Adj.* malicious
⒉ *adv.* maliciously
Hammel *der;* ~s, ~ **(a)** wether
(b) (Fleisch) mutton
Hammel·fleisch *das* mutton
Hammer *der;* ~s, Hämmer **(a)** hammer; (Holz~) mallet; ~ **und Sichel** hammer and sickle
(b) (Technik) ram
hammer·mäßig (Jugendspr.) ⒈ *Adj.* fantastic (coll.); awesome (coll.) ⟨*music, film*⟩
⒉ *adv.* ⟨*play etc.*⟩ fantastically well (coll.)
hämmern *itr., tr. V.* hammer
Hämorrhoiden /hɛmɔro'iːdn̩/ *Pl.* (Med.) haemorrhoids; piles
Hampel·mann *der* **(a)** jumping jack
(b) (ugs. abwertend) puppet
hampeln *itr. V.* (ugs.) jump about
Hamster *der;* ~s, ~: hamster
hamstern *tr., itr. V.* **(a)** (horten) hoard
(b) (Lebensmittel tauschen) barter goods for [food]
Hand *die;* ~, Hände hand; **eine** ~ **voll** a handful; jmdm. **die** ~ **geben** shake sb.'s hand; ~ **und Fuß/weder** ~ **noch Fuß haben** (ugs.) make sense/no sense; **alle** *od.* **beide Hände damit voll haben, etw. zu tun** (ugs.) have one's hands full doing sth.; **die Hände in den Schoß legen** sit back and do nothing; **etw. aus der** ~ **geben** let sth. out of one's hands; ~ **in** ~ **arbeiten** work hand in hand; **etw. zur** ~ **haben** have sth. handy; **zu Händen [von] Herrn Müller** attention Herr Müller; **unter der** ~ (fig.) on the quiet

---

*old spelling – see note on page x

Hand-: ~**arbeit** *die* **(a)** handicraft; etw. in ~arbeit herstellen make sth. by hand; **(b)** (Gegenstand) handmade article; **(c)** (Nadelarbeit) [piece of] needlework; ~**ball** *der* handball; ~**besen** *der* brush; ~**betrieb** *der* manual operation; ~**bewegung** *die* **(a)** movement of the hand; **(b)** (Geste) gesture; ~**bremse** *die* handbrake; ~**buch** *das* handbook; (technisches ~buch) manual
Händchen *das;* ~s, ~: [little] hand
Hände ▸ HAND
Hände-: ~**druck** *der;* *Pl.* ~drücke handshake; ~**klatschen** *das;* ~~s clapping
Handel *der;* ~s trade; ~ **treiben** trade; ~ **treibend** trading ⟨*nation*⟩
handeln ⒈ *itr. V.* **(a)** trade; deal
(b) (feilschen) haggle
(c) (agieren) act
(d) (sich verhalten) behave
(e) von etw. *od.* **über etw.** (*Akk.*) ~ ⟨*book, film, etc.*⟩ be about *or* deal with sth.
⒉ *refl. V.* (*unpers.*) **es handelt sich um …:** it is a matter of …; **(es dreht sich um)** it's about …
handels-, Handels-: ~**abkommen** *das* trade agreement; ~**bank** *die; Pl.* ~~en merchant bank; ~**bilanz** *die* **(a)** (eines Betriebes) balance sheet; **(b)** (eines Staates) balance of trade; ~**einig,** ~**eins:** mit jmdm. ~einig *od.* ~eins werden/sein agree/have agreed terms with sb.; ~**flotte** *die* merchant fleet; ~**gesellschaft** *die* company; ~**kammer** *die:* ▸ INDUSTRIE- UND HANDELSKAMMER; ~**klasse** *die* grade; ~**marine** *die* merchant navy; ~**partner** *der,* ~**partnerin** *die* trading partner; ~**register** *das* register of companies; ~**schiff** *das* merchant ship; ~**schule** *die* commercial college; ~**straße** *die* (hist.) trade route; ~**üblich** *Adj.* ~übliche Praktiken/Größen standard business practices/standard [commercial] sizes; ~**unternehmen** *das* trading concern; ~**vertreter** *der,* ~**vertreterin** *die* [sales] representative; travelling salesman/saleswoman; ~**vertretung** *die* trade mission; ~**zentrum** *das* trading centre
hände·ringend *Adv.* (ugs.: dringend) ⟨*need*⟩ urgently; ⟨*search for sb./sth.*⟩ desperately
hand-, Hand-: ~**feger** *der* brush; ~**fest** *Adj.* **(a)** robust; sturdy; **(b)** substantial ⟨*meal etc.*⟩; **(c)** solid ⟨*proof*⟩; concrete ⟨*suggestion*⟩; complete ⟨*lie*⟩; well-founded ⟨*argument*⟩; ~**fläche** *die* palm [of one's/the hand]; flat of one's/the hand; ~**gas** *das* (Kfz-W.) hand throttle; ~**gearbeitet** *Adj.* handmade; ~**gelenk** *das* wrist; ~**gemenge** *das* fight; ~**gepäck** *das* hand baggage; ~**geschrieben** *Adj.* handwritten; ~**granate** *die* hand grenade; ~**greiflich** *Adj.* **(a)** (tätlich) ~greiflich werden start using one's fists; **(b)** tangible

⟨*success, advantage, proof, etc.*⟩; palpable
⟨*contradiction, error*⟩; obvious ⟨*fact*⟩;
  ∼griff *der* (a) mit einem **∼griff/wenigen**
  ∼griffen in one movement/without much
  trouble; (schnell) in no time at all/next to no
  time; (b) (am Koffer, an einem Werkzeug) handle;
  ∼habe *die;* **∼∼,** **∼∼n: eine [rechtliche]**
  ∼habe [gegen jmdn.] a legal handle [against
  sb.]; **∼haben** *tr. V.* (a) handle; operate
  ⟨*device, machine*⟩; (b) (praktizieren) implement
  ⟨*law etc.*⟩; **∼habung** *die;* **∼∼,** **∼∼en**
  (a) handling; (eines Gerätes, einer Maschine)
  operation; (b) (Durchführung) implementation
Handheld /'hɛnthɛlt/ *das;* ∼s, ∼s (DV)
  handheld [device]
Handikap /'hɛndikɛp/ *das;* ∼s, ∼s (auch
  Sport) handicap
handikapen /'hɛndikɛpn/ *tr. V.* handicap
Hand-: **∼käse** *der* (landsch.) *small,
  hand-formed curd cheese;* **∼koffer** *der*
  [small] suitcase; **∼kuss,** ***∼kuß** der* kiss
  on sb.'s hand; **∼langer** *der;* ∼∼s, ∼∼,
  ∼langerin *die;* ∼∼, ∼∼nen (ungelernter
  Arbeiter) labourer; (abwertend) lackey; **∼lauf**
  der handrail
Händler *der;* ∼s, ∼, **Händlerin** *die;* ∼,
  ∼nen trader
handlich *Adj.* handy; easily carried
  ⟨*parcel, suitcase*⟩; easily portable ⟨*television,
  camera*⟩
Handlung *die;* ∼, ∼en (a) (Vorgehen)
  action; (Tat) act
  (b) (Fabel) plot
handlungs-, Handlungs-: **∼arm**
  Adj. short on action *pred.;* **∼fähig** *Adj.*
  able to act *pred.;* working *attrib.* ⟨*majority*⟩;
  ∼freiheit *die* freedom of action;
  ∼reisende *der/die* ▸ HANDELSVERTRETER;
  ∼weise *die* conduct
hand-, Hand-: **∼puppe** *die* glove *or*
  hand puppet; **∼schelle** *die* handcuff;
  ∼schlag *der* handshake; **∼schrift**
  die handwriting; **∼schriftlich** ① *Adj.*
  handwritten; ② *adv.* by hand; **∼schuh**
  der glove; **∼schuh·fach** *das* glove
  compartment; **∼signiert** *Adj.* signed;
  ∼spiegel *der* hand mirror; **∼stand**
  der (Turnen) handstand; **∼tasche** *die*
  handbag; **∼tuch** *das; Pl.* -tücher towel;
  ∼umdrehen: im **∼umdrehen** in no time
  at all; **∼verlesen** *Adj.* hand-picked;
  ***∼voll** ▸ HAND; **∼wäsche** *die* washing
  by hand
Hand·werk *das* craft; (als Beruf) trade; **sein
  ∼ kennen** *od.* **verstehen/beherrschen** know
  one's job
Handwerker *der;* ∼s, ∼: tradesman
Handwerkerin *die;* ∼, ∼nen
  tradeswoman
handwerklich *Adj.* **ein ∼er Beruf** a
  [skilled] trade
Handwerks·zeug *das* tools *pl.*
Handy /'hɛndi/ *das;* ∼s, ∼s mobile [phone]

Handy·nummer *die* mobile number
Hand·zeichen *das* sign [with one's hand];
  (eines Autofahrers) hand signal; (Abstimmung)
  show of hands
Hanf *der;* ∼[e]s hemp
Hang *der;* ∼[e]s, **Hänge** slope; (Neigung)
  tendency
Hänge-: **∼brücke** *die* suspension
  bridge; **∼lampe** *die* pendant light;
  ∼matte *die* hammock
hängen[1] *unr. itr. V.; südd., österr., schweiz.
  mit sein* hang (**an** + *Dat.* from); (an einem
  Fahrzeug) be hitched (**an** + *Dat.* to); **[mit der
  Ärmel** *usw.* **an/in etw.** (*Dat.*) **∼ bleiben** get
  one's sleeve *etc.* caught on/in sth.; **∼ bleiben**
  (ugs.: haften) stick (**an/auf** + *Dat.*) to; (ugs.:
  verweilen) get stuck (coll.)
hängen[2] ① *tr. V.* (a) hang (**in/über**
  + *Akk.*) in/over; **an/auf** + *Akk.* on)
  (b) (befestigen) hitch up (**an** + *Akk.* to); couple
  on ⟨*railway carriage, etc.*⟩ (**an** + *Akk.* to)
  ② *refl. V.* (a) **sich an etw.** (*Akk.*) **∼:** hang on
  to sth.
  (b) (sich festsetzen) cling (**an** + *Akk.* to)
***hängen|bleiben** ▸ HÄNGEN[1]
hängend *Adj.* hanging
Hänge·schrank *der* wall cupboard
Hang·lage *die* hillside location
Hansaplast Ⓦ *das;* ∼[e]s sticking
  plaster; Elastoplast ®
hänseln *tr. V.* tease
Hanse·stadt *die* Hanseatic city
Hantel *die;* ∼, ∼n (Sport) (kurz) dumb-bell;
  (lang) barbell
hantieren *itr. V.* be busy
Häppchen *das;* ∼s, ∼ (a) [small] morsel
  (b) (Appetithappen) canapé
Happen *der;* ∼s, ∼: morsel
happig *Adj.* (ugs.) **∼e Preise** fancy prices
  (coll.)
Happyend, Happy-End /'hɛpi'|ɛnt/
  das; ∼[s], ∼s happy ending
Hardware /'ha:dwɛə/ *die;* ∼, ∼s (DV)
  hardware
Harfe *die;* ∼, ∼n harp
Harke *die;* ∼, ∼n rake
harken *tr. V.* rake
harm·los ① *Adj.* (a) (ungefährlich) harmless;
  slight ⟨*injury, cold, etc.*⟩; mild ⟨*illness*⟩; safe
  ⟨*medicine, bend, road, etc.*⟩
  (b) (arglos) innocent; harmless ⟨*fun, pastime,
  etc.*⟩
  ② *adv.* (a) (ungefährlich) harmlessly
  (b) (arglos) innocently
Harmlosigkeit *die;* ∼ (a) (Ungefährlichkeit)
  harmlessness; (einer Krankheit) mildness;
  (eines Medikamentes) safety
  (b) (Arglosigkeit, harmloses Verhalten) innocence
Harmonie *die;* ∼, ∼n (auch fig.) harmony
harmonieren *itr. V.* (a) harmonize
  (b) (miteinander auskommen) get on well

Harmonika *die;* ∼, ∼s *od.* Harmoniken
harmonica
harmonisch ① *Adj.* harmonious; (Musik)
harmonic
② *adv.* harmoniously; (Musik) harmonically
harmonisieren *tr. V.* coordinate; **etw. mit
etw.** ∼ (Wirtsch.) bring sth. into line with sth.
Harmonisierung *die;* ∼, ∼en (Wirtsch.)
harmonization
Harmonium *das;* ∼s, Harmonien
harmonium
Harn *der;* ∼[e]s, ∼e (Med.) urine
Harn-blase *die* bladder
Harnisch *der;* ∼s, ∼e armour
Harpune *die;* ∼, ∼n harpoon
harpunieren *tr. V.* harpoon
harren *itr. V.* (geh.) **jmds./einer Sache** *od.*
auf jmdn./etw. ∼: await sb./sth.
harsch ① *Adj.* (a) (vereist) crusted
(b) (barsch) harsh
② *adv.* harshly
Harsch *der;* ∼[e]s crusted snow
hart; härter, härtest… ① *Adj.* (a) hard;
∼ **gekocht** hard-boiled ⟨egg⟩
(b) tough ⟨situation, job⟩; harsh ⟨reality,
truth⟩
(c) (streng) harsh ⟨penalty, punishment,
judgement⟩; tough ⟨measure, law, course⟩
(d) (rau) rough ⟨game, opponent⟩
② *adv.* hard chair; (a) (mühevoll) ⟨work⟩
hard
(b) (streng) harshly
(c) (nahe) close (**an** + *Dat.* to)
Härte *die;* ∼, ∼n (a) (auch Physik) hardness
(b) (Widerstandsfähigkeit) toughness
(c) (schwere Belastung) hardship
(d) (Strenge) harshness
(e) (Heftigkeit) (eines Aufpralls usw.) force; (eines
Streits) violence
(f) (Rauheit) roughness
Härte-fall *der* (a) case of hardship
(b) (ugs.: Person) hardship case
härten *tr., itr. V.* harden
härter ▸ HART
härtest… ▸ HART
hart-, Hart-: *∗∼gekocht* ▸ HART 1A;
∼**geld** *das* coins *pl.;* ∼**gummi** *das* hard
rubber; ∼**herzig** ① *Adj.* hard-hearted;
② *adv.* hard-heartedly; ∼**herzigkeit** *die;*
∼∼: hard-heartedness; ∼**käse** *der* hard
cheese; ∼**näckig** ① *Adj.* (a) (eigensinnig)
obstinate; stubborn; (b) (ausdauernd)
dogged; ② *adv.* (a) (eigensinnig) obstinately;
stubbornly; (b) (ausdauernd) doggedly;
∼**näckigkeit** *die;* ∼∼ (a) (Eigensinn)
obstinacy; stubbornness; (b) (Ausdauer)
doggedness
Härtung *die;* ∼, ∼en hardening; (von Stahl
auch) tempering
Hart·wurst *die* dry sausage

∗alte Schreibung – vgl. Hinweis auf S. x

Harz *das;* ∼es, ∼e resin
Harzer Käse *der;* ∼ ∼s, ∼ ∼: Harz
[Mountain] cheese
Haschee (Kochk.) *das;* ∼s, ∼s hash
haschen[1] *tr. V.* (veralt.) catch
haschen[2] *itr. V.* (ugs.) smoke [hash] (coll.)
Häschen /ˈhɛːsçən/ *das;* ∼, ∼s bunny
Haschisch *das od. der;* ∼[s] hashish
Haschisch-rausch *der;* [state of]
hashish intoxication; **etw. im** *od.* **bei einem**
∼**rausch tun** do sth. while under the effects
of hashish *or* while [high (coll.)] on hashish
Hase *der;* ∼n, ∼n (a) hare
(b) (landsch.) ▸ KANINCHEN
Hasel·nuss, ∗Hasel·nuß *die* hazelnut
Hasen-: ∼**fuß** *der* (spöttisch abwertend)
coward; chicken (coll.); ∼**scharte** *die*
(Med.) harelip
Haspel *die;* ∼, ∼n (Technik) (für Garn) reel;
(für ein Seil, Kabel) drum
Hass, ∗Haß *der;* Hasses hatred (**auf**
+ *Akk.,* **gegen** of, for)
hassen *tr., itr. V.* hate
hass·erfüllt, ∗haß·erfüllt *Adj.* filled
with hatred *postpos.*
hässlich, ∗häßlich ① *Adj.* (a) ugly
(b) (gemein) nasty
(c) (unangenehm) awful ⟨weather, cold,
situation, etc.⟩
② *adv.* (a) ⟨dress⟩ unattractively
(b) (gemein) nastily
Hässlichkeit, ∗Häßlichkeit *die;* ∼,
∼en (a) (Aussehen) ugliness
(b) (Gesinnung) nastiness
hast *2. Pers. Sg. Präsens v.* HABEN
Hast *die;* ∼: haste
hasten *itr. V.; mit sein* hurry
hastig ① *Adj.* hasty; hurried
② *adv.* hastily; hurriedly
hat *3. Pers. Sg. Präsens v.* HABEN
hätscheln *tr. V.* caress
hatschi *Interj.* atishoo
hatte *1. u. 3. Pers. Sg. Prät. v.* HABEN
hätte *1. u. 3. Pers. Sg. Konjunktiv II v.*
HABEN
Haube *die;* ∼, ∼n (a) bonnet; (einer
Krankenschwester) cap
(b) (Kfz-W.) bonnet (Brit.); hood (Amer.)
Hauch *der;* ∼[e]s, ∼e (geh.) (a) (Atem, auch
fig.) breath
(b) (Luftzug) breath of wind
(c) (leichter Duft) delicate smell
(d) (dünne Schicht) [gossamer-]thin layer
hauch·dünn *Adj.* gossamer-thin
⟨material, dress⟩; wafer-thin ⟨layer, slice,
majority⟩
hauchen *itr. V.* breathe (**gegen, auf** + *Akk.*
on)
Haue *die;* ∼, ∼n (a) (südd., österr.: Hacke) hoe
(b) (ugs.: Prügel) a hiding (coll.)

hauen ⓵ *unr. tr. V.* **(a)** (ugs.: schlagen) belt; clobber (coll.)
(b) (ugs.: auf einen Körperteil) belt (coll.); hit
(c) (herstellen) carve ⟨*figure, statue, etc.*⟩ (in + *Akk.* in)
⓶ *unr. itr. V.* **(a)** (ugs.: prügeln) **er haut immer gleich** he's quick to hit out
(b) (auf einen Körperteil) belt (coll.); hit
(c) (ugs.: auf/gegen etw. schlagen) thump
⓷ *unr. refl. V.* (ugs.: sich prügeln) have a punch-up (coll.)
Hauer *der;* ~**s**, ~ (Jägerspr.) tusk; (fig.) fang
Haufen *der;* ~**s**, ~: heap; pile; (Gruppe) bunch (coll.)
häufen ⓵ *tr. V.* heap, pile (**auf** + *Akk.* on to); (aufheben) hoard ⟨*money, supplies*⟩
⓶ *refl. V.* (sich mehren) pile up
häufig ⓵ *Adj.* frequent
⓶ *adv.* frequently; often
Häufigkeit *die;* ~, ~**en** frequency
Häufung *die;* ~, ~**en** increasing frequency
Haupt *das;* ~**[e]s**, **Häupter** (geh., auch fig.) head
haupt-, Haupt-: ~**bahnhof** *der* main station; ~**beruflich** ⓵ *Adj.* **seine** ~**berufliche Tätigkeit** his main occupation; ⓶ *adv.* **er ist** ~**beruflich als Elektriker tätig** his main occupation is that of electrician; ~**darsteller** *der* (Theater, Film) male lead; ~**darstellerin** *die* (Theater, Film) female lead; ~**eingang** *der* main entrance; ~**einschalt·zeit** *die* peak *or* prime viewing time; ~**fach** *das* major; ~**figur** *die* main character; ~**film** *der* main feature; ~**gang** *der* main corridor; **(b)** ▸ ~GERICHT; ~**gebäude** *das* main building; ~**gericht** *das* main course; ~**gewinn** *der* first prize
Häuptling *der;* ~**s**, ~**e** chief[tain]
haupt-, Haupt-: ~**mahlzeit** *die* main meal; ~**mann** *der; Pl.* ~**leute** (Milit.) captain; ~**person** *die* central figure; ~**postamt** *das* main post office; ~**quartier** *das* (Milit., auch fig.) headquarters *sing. or pl.;* ~**reise·zeit** *die* high season; peak [holiday] season; ~**rolle** *die* main role; lead; **die** ~**rolle spielen** (fig.) play the leading role; ~**sache** *die* main thing; ~**sächlich** ⓵ *Adv.* mainly; principally; ⓶ *Adj.; nicht präd.* main; principal; ~**saison** *die* high season; ~**satz** *der* main clause; (allein stehend) sentence; ~**schalter** *der* (Elektrot.) mains switch; ~**schlagader** *die* aorta; ~**schul·abschluss**, ***~**schul·abschluß** *der* ≈ secondary school leaving certificate; ~**schule** *die* ≈ secondary modern school; ~**schüler** *der*, ~**schülerin** *die* ≈ secondary modern school pupil; ~**sitz** *der* head office; headquarters *pl.;* ~**stadt** *die* capital [city]; ~**städtisch** *Adj.* metropolitan; ~**straße** *die* main street; ~**thema** *das* main topic *or* theme; (Musik) main theme;

~**verkehr** *der* bulk of the traffic
Hauptverkehrs-: ~**straße** *die* main road; ~**zeit** *die* rush hour
Haupt-: ~**versammlung** *die* (Wirtsch.) shareholders' meeting; ~**wache** *die* main police station; ~**wort** *das* (Sprachw.) noun
hau ruck *Interj.* heave[-ho]
Haus *das;* ~**es**, **Häuser (a)** house; (Amts-, Firmengebäude usw.) building; (Heim) home; **nach** ~**e** home; **zu** ~**e** at home; **das erste** ~ **am Platze** the best hotel in the town
(b) ~ **halten** be economical
haus-, Haus-: ~**angestellte** *der/die* domestic servant; ~**apotheke** *die* medicine cabinet; ~**arbeit** *die* housework; (Schulw.) homework; ~**arrest** *der* house arrest; ~**arzt** *der*, ~**ärztin** *die* family doctor; ~**aufgabe** *die* homework; ~**backen** ⓵ *Adj.* plain; unadventurous ⟨*clothes*⟩; ⓶ *adv.* ⟨*dress*⟩ unadventurously; ~**besetzer** *der;* ~**s**, ~, ~**besetzerin** *die;* ~, ~**nen** squatter; ~**besitzer** *der* houseowner; (Vermieter) landlord; ~**besitzerin** *die* houseowner; (Vermieterin) landlady; ~**besuch** *der* house call; ~**boot** *das* houseboat
Häuschen /ˈhɔʏsçən/ *das;* ~**s**, ~: small house; **aus dem** ~ **sein** (ugs.) be over the moon (coll.)
hausen *itr. V.* **(a)** (ugs. abwertend) live
(b) (Verwüstungen anrichten) **[furchtbar]** ~: wreak havoc
Häuser·block *der* block [of houses]
haus-, Haus-: ~**flur** *der* hall[way]; (im Obergeschoss) landing; ~**frau** *die* housewife; ~**freund** *der* **(a)** friend of the family; **(b)** (verhüll.: Liebhaber) man friend (euphem.); ~**freundin** *die* friend of the family; ~**friedens·bruch** *der* (Rechtsw.) trespass; ~**gebrauch** *der* domestic use; **das reicht für den** ~**gebrauch** (ugs.) it's good enough to get by (coll.); ~**geburt** *die* home birth; ~**gehilfin** *die* [home] help; ~**gemacht** *Adj.* home-made
Haus·halt *der* **(a)** household
(b) (Arbeit im ~) housekeeping; **jmdm. den** ~ **führen** keep house for sb.
(c) (Politik) budget
*~**haus|halten** ▸ HAUS B
Haushälterin *die;* ~, ~**nen** housekeeper
Haushalts-: ~**artikel** *der* household article; ~**debatte** *die* (Politik) budget debate; ~**geld** *das* housekeeping money; ~**jahr** *das* financial year; ~**kasse** *die* housekeeping money; ~**plan** *der* budget; ~**waren** *Pl.* household goods
haus-, Haus-: ~**herr** *der* **(a)** (Familienoberhaupt) head of the household; **(b)** (als Gastgeber) host; **(c)** (Rechtsspr.) (Eigentümer) owner; (Mieter) occupier; ~**herrin** *die* ▸ ~HERR A; **(b)** ▸ ~HERR B; ~**hoch** ⓵ *Adj.* as high as a house; (fig.) overwhelming; ⓶ *adv.* (fig.) ~**hoch gewinnen** win hands down

hausieren *itr. V.* [mit etw.] ~: hawk [sth.]; peddle [sth.]; „Hausieren verboten" 'no hawkers'

Hausierer *der;* ~s, ~, **Hausiererin** *die;* ~, ~nen pedlar; hawker

häuslich *Adj.* **(a)** domestic **(b)** (das Zuhause liebend) home-loving

Hausmacher·art *die:* nach ~: home-made-style *attrib.*

Haus·mann *der: man who stays at home and does the housework;* (Ehemann) househusband

Hausmanns·kost *die* plain cooking

Haus-: ~**marke** *die* **(a)** house wine; **(b)** (ugs.: bevorzugtes Getränk) favourite tipple (coll.); ~**meister** *der,* ~**meisterin** *die* caretaker; ~**mittel** *das* household remedy; ~**musik** *die* music at home; ~**nummer** *die* house number; ~**ordnung** *die* house rules *pl.;* ~**putz** *der* spring-clean; (regelmäßig) clean-out

Haus·rat *der* household goods *pl.*

Hausrat·versicherung *die* [household or home] contents insurance

Haus-: ~**schlüssel** *der* front-door key; house key; ~**schuh** *der* slipper; ~**segen** *der:* bei ihnen hängt der ~**segen** schief (ugs. scherzh.) they've been having a row

Haussuchung *die;* ~, ~en house search

Haussuchungs·befehl *der* search warrant

Haus-: ~**telefon** *das* internal telephone; ~**tier** *das* **(a)** pet; **(b)** (Nutztier) domestic animal; ~**tür** *die* front door; ~**verbot** *das* ban on entering the house/pub/restaurant etc.; ~**verwalter** *der,* ~**verwalterin** *die* manager [of the block]; ~**wirt** *der* landlord; ~**wirtin** *die* landlady; ~**wirtschaft** *die* domestic science and home economics; ~**zelt** *das* ridge tent

Haut *die;* ~, Häute skin; aus der ~ fahren (ugs.) go up the wall (coll.)

Haut-: ~**arzt** *der,* ~**ärztin** *die* skin specialist; ~**ausschlag** *der* [skin] rash

häuten ①*tr. V.* skin; flay ②*refl. V.* shed its skin/their skins

haut-, Haut-: ~**eng** *Adj.* skintight; ~**farbe** *die* [skin] colour; ~**krankheit** *die* skin disease; ~**krebs** *der* skin cancer

Häutung *die;* ~, ~en **(a)** ▶ HÄUTEN 1: skinning; flaying **(b)** (das Sichhäuten) eine Eidechse bei der ~: a lizard shedding its skin

Haxe *die;* ~, ~n ▶ HACHSE

he *Interj.* (ugs.) hey

Heb·amme *die* midwife

Hebel *der;* ~s, ~: lever

heben *unr. tr. V.* **(a)** lift; raise ⟨baton, camera, glass⟩ **(b)** (verbessern) raise ⟨standard, level⟩;

---

increase ⟨turnover, self-confidence⟩; improve ⟨mood⟩; enhance ⟨standing⟩; boost ⟨morale⟩

hecheln¹ *itr. V.* (ugs. abwertend) gossip

hecheln² *itr. V.* pant [for breath]

Hecht *der;* ~[e]s, ~e pike

Hecht·sprung *der* **(a)** (Turnen) Hecht vault **(b)** (Schwimmen) racing dive; (vom Sprungturm) pike-dive

Heck *das;* ~[e]s, ~e od. ~s stern; (Flugzeug~) tail; (Auto~) rear

Heck·antrieb *der* (Kfz-W.) rear-wheel drive

Hecke *die;* ~, ~n **(a)** hedge **(b)** (wild wachsend) thicket

Hecken-: ~**rose** *die* dogrose; ~**schütze** *der,* ~**schützin** *die* sniper

Heck·scheibe *die* rear window

Heer *das;* ~[e]s, ~e armed forces *pl.;* (für den Landkrieg, fig.) army

Hefe *die;* ~, ~n yeast

Hefe·teig *der* yeast dough

Heft¹ *das;* ~[e]s, ~e (geh.) haft; handle

Heft² *das;* ~[e]s, ~e **(a)** (bes. Schule) exercise book **(b)** (Nummer einer Zeitschrift) issue

Heftchen *das;* ~s, ~: book [of tickets/stamps etc.]

heften ① *tr. V.* **(a)** (mit einer Nadel) pin; (mit einer Klammer) clip; (mit Klebstoff) stick **(b)** (Schneiderei) tack **(c)** (Buchbinderei) stitch; (mit Klammern) staple ② *refl. V.* sich an jmds. Fersen (*Akk.*) ~: stick hard on sb.'s heels

Hefter *der;* ~s, ~: [loose-leaf] file

heftig ① *Adj.* violent; heavy ⟨rain, shower, blow⟩; severe ⟨pain⟩; ⟨person⟩ with a violent temper ② *adv.* ⟨rain, snow, breathe⟩ heavily; ⟨hit⟩ hard; ⟨quarrel⟩ violently

Heftigkeit *die;* ~: ▶ HEFTIG 1: violence; heaviness; severity

Heft-: ~**klammer** staple; ~**pflaster** *das* sticking plaster; ~**zwecke** *die* ▶ REISSZWECKE

hegen *tr. V.* **(a)** (bes. Forstw., Jagdw.) look after, tend **(b)** (geh.: umsorgen) look after **(c)** (fig.) feel ⟨contempt, hatred, mistrust⟩; cherish ⟨hope, wish, desire⟩; harbour ⟨grudge, suspicion⟩

Hehl *der od. das:* kein[en] ~ aus etw. machen make no secret of sth.

Hehler *der;* ~s, ~: receiver [of stolen goods]

Hehlerei *die;* ~, ~en (Rechtsw.) receiving [stolen goods] *no art.*

Hehlerin *die;* ~, ~nen ▶ HEHLER

Heide¹ *der;* ~n, ~n heathen

Heide² *die;* ~, ~n heath; (Landschaft) heathland

Heide-: ~**kraut** *das* heather; ~**land** *das* moorland; heathland

Heidel·beere *die* bilberry

Heidin *die;* ~, ~nen heathen

heidnisch *Adj.* heathen

heikel *Adj.* **(a)** (schwierig) delicate, ticklish ⟨*matter, subject*⟩; ticklish tricky ⟨*problem, question, situation*⟩ **(b)** (wählerisch) fussy (**in Bezug auf** + *Akk.* about)

heil *Adj.* (nicht entzwei) in one piece; **wieder** ~ **sein** ⟨*injured part*⟩ have healed [up]

Heil *das;* ~s **(a)** (Wohlergehen) benefit **(b)** (Rel.) salvation

Heiland *der;* ~[e]s, ~e Saviour

Heil·anstalt *die* (Anstalt für Kranke od. Süchtige) sanatorium; (psychiatrische Klinik) mental hospital

heilbar *Adj.* curable

Heil·butt *der* halibut

heilen ① *tr. V.* cure; heal ⟨*wound*⟩ ② *itr. V.; mit sein* ⟨*wound*⟩ heal [up]; ⟨*fracture*⟩ mend

heil·froh *Adj.* very glad

heilig *Adj.* **(a)** holy; **die Heiligen Drei Könige** the Three Kings *or* Wise Men; the Magi; **die Heilige Schrift** the Holy Scriptures *pl.;* **der Heilige Abend** Christmas Eve **(b)** (geh.: unantastbar) sacred ⟨*right, tradition, cause, etc.*⟩

Heilig·abend *der* Christmas Eve

Heilige *der/die; adj. Dekl.* saint

heiligen *tr. V.* keep ⟨*tradition, Sabbath, etc.*⟩; **der Zweck heiligt die Mittel** the end justifies the means

Heiligen·schein *der* gloriole; (um den Kopf) halo

Heiligkeit *die;* ~: holiness

Heiligtum *das;* ~s, **Heiligtümer** shrine

Heil-: ~**kraut** *das* medicinal herb; ~**mittel** *das* (auch fig.) remedy (**gegen** for); (Medikament) medicament; ~**praktiker** *der,* ~**praktikerin** *die* non-medical practitioner

heilsam *Adj.* salutary

Heils·armee *die* Salvation Army

Heilung *die;* ~, ~en (einer Wunde) healing; (von Krankheit, Kranken) curing

Heim *das;* ~[e]s, ~e **(a)** (Zuhause) home **(b)** (Anstalt, Alters~) home; (für Obdachlose) hostel

Heim·arbeit *die* outwork

Heimat *die;* ~, ~en **(a)** (Ort) home; home town/village; (Land) home; homeland **(b)** (Ursprungsland) natural habitat

Heimat-: ~**kunde** *die* local history, geography, and natural history; ~**land** *das* native land; (fig.) home

heimatlich *Adj.* native ⟨*dialect*⟩; nostalgic ⟨*emotions*⟩

heimat-, Heimat-: ~**los** *Adj.* homeless; ~**museum** *das* museum of local history; ~**ort** *der* home town/village; ~**stadt** *die* home town; ~**vertriebene**

der/die; adj. Dekl. expellee [from his/her homeland]

heim-, Heim-: ~**bringen** *unr. tr. V.* **(a)** jmdn. ~: take *or.* see sb. home; **(b)** bring home; ~**computer** *der* home computer; ~**fahren** ① *unr. itr. V.; mit sein* drive home; ② *unr. tr. V.* drive home; ~**fahrt** *die* journey home; (mit dem Auto) drive home; ~**gehen** *unr. itr. V.; mit sein* go home

heimisch *Adj.* (einheimisch) indigenous, native ⟨*plants, animals, etc.*⟩ (**in** + *Dat.* to); domestic ⟨*industry*⟩; **sich ~ fühlen** feel at home; ~ **werden** [**in** (+ *Dat.*)] settle in[to]

heim-, Heim-: ~**kehr** *die;* ~~: return home; homecoming; ~**kehren** *itr. V.; mit sein* return home (**aus** from); ~**kommen** *unr. itr. V.; mit sein* come home

heimlich ① *Adj.* secret ② *adv.* secretly

Heimlichkeit *die;* ~, ~en secret

heim-, Heim-: ~**reise** *die* journey home; ~**spiel** *das* (Sport) home match *or* game; ~**suchen** *tr. V.* ⟨*storm, earthquake, epidemic*⟩ strike; ⟨*disease*⟩ afflict; ⟨*nightmares, doubts*⟩ plague; ~**suchung** *die;* ~~, ~~en affliction; visitation; ~**tückisch** ① *Adj.* (bösartig) malicious; (fig.) insidious ⟨*disease*⟩; ② *adv.* maliciously; ~**wärts** *Adv.* (nach Hause zu) home; (in Richtung Heimat) homeward[s]; ~**weg** *der* way home; ~**weh** *das* homesickness; ~**weh haben** be homesick (**nach** for); ~**zahlen** *tr. V.* jmdm. etw. ~**zahlen** pay sb. back for sth.

Heinzel·männchen *das* brownie

Heirat *die;* ~, ~en marriage

heiraten ① *itr. V.* get married ② *tr. V.* marry

Heirats-: ~**antrag** *der:* jmdm. einen ~**antrag machen** propose to sb.; ~**anzeige** *die* announcement of a/the forthcoming marriage; ~**schwindler** *der,* ~**schwindlerin** *die: person who makes a spurious offer of marriage for purposes of fraud*

heiser ① *Adj.* hoarse ② *adv.* in a hoarse voice

Heiserkeit *die;* ~: hoarseness

heiß ① *Adj.* hot; **jmdm. ist ~:** sb. feels hot; **etw. ~ machen** heat sth. up; heated ⟨*debate, argument*⟩; fierce ⟨*fight, battle*⟩; ardent ⟨*wish, love*⟩; **ein ~es Thema** a controversial subject ② *adv.* ⟨*fight*⟩ fiercely; ⟨*love*⟩ dearly; ⟨*long*⟩ fervently

heißen *unr. itr. V.* (den Namen tragen) be called; (bedeuten) mean; (lauten) ⟨*saying*⟩ go; (unpers.) **es heißt, dass ...:** they say that ...; **in dem Artikel heißt es ...:** in the article it says that ...

Heiß·luft *die* hot air

Heißluft·backofen *der* fan oven

heiter *Adj.* cheerful, happy ⟨*person, nature*⟩; happy, merry ⟨*laughter*⟩; fine ⟨*weather, day*⟩

Heiterkeit *die;* ~ (a) (Frohsinn) cheerfulness
(b) (Belustigung) merriment

heizbar *Adj.* heated

Heiz·decke *die* electric blanket

heizen ① *itr. V.* have the heating on ② *tr. V.* heat ⟨*room etc.*⟩

Heizer *der;* ~s, ~, **Heizerin** *die;* ~, ~nen stoker

Heiz-: ~**kissen** *das* heating pad; ~**körper** *der* radiator; ~**ofen** *der* stove; heater; ~**platte** *die* hotplate

Heizung *die;* ~, ~en (a) [central] heating *no pl., no indef. art.*
(b) (ugs.: Heizkörper) radiator

Hektar *das od. der;* ~s, ~e hectare

Hektik *die;* ~: hectic rush; (des Lebens) hectic pace

hektisch *Adj.* hectic

Held *der;* ~en, ~en hero

heldenhaft ① *Adj.* heroic ② *adv.* heroically

Heldentum *das;* ~s heroism

Heldin *die;* ~, ~nen heroine

helfen *unr. itr. V.* help; jmdm. [bei etw.] ~: help sb. [with sth.]; (*unpers.*) **es hilft nichts** it's no use *or* good

Helfer *der;* ~s, ~, **Helferin** *die;* ~, ~nen helper; (Mitarbeiter[in]) assistant; (eines Verbrechens) accomplice

Helikopter *der;* ~s, ~: helicopter

hell ① *Adj.* (a) (von Licht erfüllt) light; well-lit ⟨*stairs*⟩
(b) (klar) bright ⟨*day, sky, etc.*⟩
(c) (viel Licht spendend) bright ⟨*light, lamp, star, etc.*⟩
(d) (blass) light ⟨*colour*⟩; fair ⟨*skin, hair*⟩; light-coloured ⟨*clothes*⟩
(e) (akustisch) high, clear ⟨*sound, voice*⟩; ringing ⟨*laugh*⟩
(f) (klug) bright
(g) (ugs.: absolut) sheer, utter ⟨*madness, foolishness, despair*⟩
② *adv.* brightly

hell-: ~**blau** *Adj.* light blue; ~**blond** *Adj.* very fair; light blonde

Helle *das; adj. Dekl.* ≈ lager

Heller *der;* ~s, ~: heller; **bis auf den letzten** ~/**bis auf** ~ **und Pfennig** (ugs.) down to the last penny *or* (Amer.) cent

hell-: ~**grün** *Adj.* light green; ~**häutig** *Adj.* fair-skinned

Helligkeit *die;* ~, ~en (auch Physik) brightness

hell-, Hell-: ~**rot** *Adj.* light red; ~**sehen** *unr. itr. V.; nur im Inf.* ~**sehen können** have second sight; ~**seher** *der,*

~**seherin** *die* clairvoyant; ~**wach** *Adj.* wide awake

Helm *der;* ~[e]s, ~e helmet

Hemd *das;* ~[e]s, ~en shirt; (Unterhemd) [under]vest; undershirt

Hemds·ärmel *der* shirtsleeve

hemmen *tr. V.* (a) (verlangsamen) slow [down]
(b) (aufhalten) check; stem ⟨*flow*⟩
(c) (beeinträchtigen) hinder

Hemmung *die;* ~, ~en (a) (Gehemmtheit) inhibition
(b) (Bedenken) scruple

hemmungs·los ① *Adj.* unrestrained ② *adv.* unrestrainedly

Hendl *das;* ~s, ~[n] (bayr., österr.) chicken; (Brathähnchen) [roast] chicken

Hengst *der;* ~[e]s, ~e (Pferd) stallion

Henkel *der;* ~s, ~: handle

Henker *der;* ~s, ~: hangman; (Scharfrichter, auch fig.) executioner

Henne *die;* ~, ~n hen

her /heːɐ̯/ *Adv.* ~ **damit** give it to me; give it here (coll.); **vom Fenster** ~: from the window; **wo ist er** ~? where is he from?; **von ihrer Kindheit** ~: since childhood; **von der Konzeption** ~: as far as the basic design is concerned; **hinter jmdm.** (ugs.)/**etw.** ~ **sein** be after sb./sth.; **einen Monat/lange** ~ **sein** be a month/a long time ago; **es ist lange** ~, **dass wir…**: it is a long time since we…

herab *Adv.* down; **von oben** ~ (fig.) condescendingly

herab-: ~|**hängen** *unr. itr. V.* hang [down] (**von** from); ~**hängende Schultern** drooping shoulders; ~|**lassen** ① *unr. tr. V.* let down; lower; ② *unr. refl. V.* (iron.: bereit sein) **sich** ~**lassen, etw. zu tun** condescend to do sth.; ~**lassend** ① *Adj.* condescending; patronizing (**zu** towards); ② *adv.* condescendingly; patronizingly; ~|**sehen** *unr. itr. V.* **auf jmdn.** ~**sehen** look down on sb.; ~|**setzen** *tr. V.* (a) reduce; (b) (abwerten) belittle

heran *Adv.* **an etw.** (*Akk.*) ~: right up to sth.

heran-, Heran-: ~|**bilden** *tr. V.* train [up]; (auf die Schule, Universität) educate; ~|**bringen** *unr. tr. V.* (a) bring [up] (**an** + *Akk.*, **zu** to); (b) (vertraut machen) **jmdn. an etw.** (*Akk.*) ~**bringen** introduce sb. to sth.; ~|**fahren** *unr. itr. V.; mit sein* drive up (**an** + *Akk.* to); ~|**kommen** *unr. itr. V.; mit sein* **an etw.** (*Akk.*) ~**kommen** come near to sth.; (erreichen) reach sth.; (erwerben) obtain sth.; ~|**reifen** *itr. V.; mit sein* ⟨*fruit, crops*⟩ ripen; **zur Frau** ~**reifen** mature into a woman; ~|**treten** *unr. itr. V.; mit sein* (sich wenden) **an jmdn.** ~**treten** approach sb.; ~|**wachsen** *unr. itr. V.; mit sein* grow up; ~**wachsende** *der/die; adj. Dekl.* young person; ~|**ziehen** *unr. tr. V.* pull over; pull up ⟨*chair*⟩; **etw. zu sich ∼ziehen** pull sth. towards one

herauf *Adv.* up

herauf-: ∼|**beschwören** *tr. V.*
(a) (verursachen) cause ⟨*disaster, war, crisis*⟩; **(b)** (erinnern) evoke ⟨*memories etc.*⟩; ∼|**kommen** *unr. itr. V.; mit sein* (nach oben kommen) come up; ∼|**setzen** *tr. V.* increase, put up ⟨*prices, rents, interest rates, etc.*⟩

heraus *Adv.* ∼ **aus den Federn!/dem Bett!** rise and shine!/out of bed!

heraus-, Heraus-: ∼|**bekommen** *unr. tr. V.* **(a)** (entfernen) get out **(aus** of); **(b)** (ugs.: lösen) work out ⟨*problem, answer, etc.*⟩; solve ⟨*puzzle*⟩ **(c)** (ermitteln) find out; **(d)** (als Wechselgeld bekommen) **5 Euro ∼bekommen** get back 5 euros change; **ich bekomme noch 5 Euro ∼:** I still have 5 euros [change] to come; ∼|**bringen** *unr. tr. V.* **(a)** (nach außen bringen) bring out **(aus** of); **(b)** (nach draußen begleiten) show out; **(c)** (veröffentlichen) bring out; (aufführen) put on, stage ⟨*play*⟩; screen ⟨*film*⟩; **(d)** (auf den Markt bringen) bring out; **(e)** (populär machen) make widely known; ∼|**fahren** ① *unr. itr. V.; mit sein* **(a)** (nach außen fahren) **aus etw. ∼fahren** drive/ride out of sth.; **(b)** (fahrend herauskommen) come out; ② *unr. tr. V.* **den Wagen [aus dem Hof] ∼fahren** drive the car out [of the yard]; **jmdn. ∼fahren** drive sb. out **(zu** to); ∼|**finden** ① *unr. tr. V.* find out; trace ⟨*fault*⟩; ② *unr. itr. V.* find one's way out **(aus** of); ∼|**fordern** ① *tr. V.* **(a)** (auch Sport) challenge; **(b)** (heraufbeschwören) provoke ⟨*person, resistance, etc.*⟩; invite ⟨*criticism*⟩; court ⟨*danger*⟩; ② *itr. V.* **zu etw. ∼fordern** provoke sth.; ∼**forderung** *die* (auch Sport) challenge; (Provokation) provocation; ∼|**geben** ① *unr. tr. V.* **(a)** (aushändigen) hand over ⟨*property, person, hostage, etc.*⟩; (zurückgeben) give back; **(b)** (als Wechselgeld zurückgeben) **5 Euro/zu viel ∼geben** give 5 euros/too much change; **(c)** (veröffentlichen) publish; **(d)** issue ⟨*stamp, coin, etc.*⟩; ② *unr. itr. V.* give change; ∼**geber** *der;* ∼**∼s,** ∼**∼,** ∼**geberin** *die;* ∼**∼,** ∼**∼nen** publisher; (Redakteur[in]) editor; ∼|**gehen** *unr. itr. V.; mit sein* **(a)** go out **(aus** of); **(b)** (sich entfernen lassen) ⟨*stain etc.*⟩ come out; ∼|**halten** *unr. refl. V.* keep out; ∼|**hängen** *tr. V.* hang out **(aus** of); ∼|**helfen** *unr. itr. V.* **jmdm. ∼helfen** (auch fig.) help sb. out **(aus** of); ∼|**holen** *tr. V.* **(a)** (nach außen holen) bring out; **(b)** (ugs.: erwirken) win ⟨*wage increase, advantage, etc.*⟩; ∼|**kommen** *unr. itr. V.; mit sein* **(a)** come out **(aus** of); **(b)** (erscheinen; ugs.: auf den Markt kommen, bekannt werden) come out; ∼|**nehmen** *unr. tr. V.* **(a)** take out **(aus** of); **(b)** (ugs.: entfernen) take out ⟨*appendix, tonsils, tooth, etc.*⟩; ∼|**reden** *refl. V.* (ugs.) talk one's way out **(aus** of); ∼|**reißen** *unr. tr. V.* **(a)** tear out **(aus** of); pull up ⟨*plant*⟩; **(b)** (aus der Umgebung, der Arbeit)

tear away **(aus** from); **die Krankheit hat ihn aus der Arbeit ∼gerissen** the illness has interrupted his work; **(c)** (Mängel ausgleichen) **den zunächst etwas langweiligen Abend ∼reißen:** rescue what had been rather a boring evening; **die Eins im Aufsatz reißt die Drei im Diktat heraus** the A for the essay makes up for the C in the dictation; ∼|**rutschen** *itr. V.; mit sein* (ugs.) ⟨*remark etc.*⟩ slip out; ∼|**stellen** *refl. V.* **es stellte sich ∼, dass ...:** it turned out that ...; ∼|**suchen** *tr. V.* pick out; look out ⟨*file*⟩

herb *Adj.* [slightly] sharp ⟨*taste*⟩; dry ⟨*wine*⟩; [slightly] sharp ⟨*smell, perfume*⟩; bitter ⟨*disappointment*⟩; severe ⟨*face, features*⟩; austere ⟨*beauty*⟩; harsh ⟨*words, criticism*⟩

herbei-: ∼|**eilen** *itr. V.; mit sein* hurry over; ∼|**laufen** *unr. itr. V.; mit sein* come running up

Herberge *die;* ∼, ∼**n** (veralt.: Gasthaus) inn

Herbergs-: ∼**mutter** *die; Pl.* ∼**mütter,** ∼**vater** *der* warden [of the/a youth hostel]

her|bringen *unr. tr. V.* **etw. ∼:** bring sth. [here]

Herbst *der;* ∼**[e]s,** ∼**e** autumn; fall (Amer.); *s. auch* FRÜHLING

Herbst·anfang *der* beginning of autumn

herbstlich *Adj.* autumn *attrib.;* autumnal

Herd *der;* ∼**[e]s,** ∼**e** cooker; (fig.) centre (*of disturbance/rebellion*)

Herde *die;* ∼, ∼**n** herd

Herd·platte *die* hot-plate

herein-: ∼|**bitten** *unr. tr. V.* **jmdn. ∼ bitten** ask *or* invite sb. in; ∼|**brechen** *unr. itr. V.; mit sein* (geh.) ⟨*night, evening, dusk*⟩ fall; ⟨*winter*⟩ set in; ⟨*storm*⟩ strike, break; ∼|**bringen** *unr. tr. V.* bring in; ∼|**fallen** *unr. itr. V.; mit sein* (ugs.) be taken for a ride (coll.); be done (coll.); ∼|**kommen** *unr. itr. V.; mit sein* come in; ∼|**lassen** *unr. tr. V.* let in; ∼|**legen** *tr. V.* (ugs.) **jmdn. ∼legen** take sb. for a ride (coll.) **(mit, bei** with); ∼|**platzen** *itr. V.; mit sein* (ugs.) burst in; ∼|**schneien** *unr. itr. V.; mit sein* (ugs.) turn up out of the blue (coll.)

her-, Her-: ∼**fahrt** *die* journey here; ∼|**fallen** *unr. itr. V.; mit sein* **über jmdn. ∼fallen** attack sb.; (gierig zu essen beginnen) **über etw.** (*Akk.*) ∼**fallen** fall upon sth.; ∼**gang** *der:* **der ∼gang der Ereignisse** the sequence of events; ∼|**geben** *unr. tr. V.* hand over; (weggeben) give away; ∼|**gehen** *unr. itr. V.; mit sein* **neben/vor/hinter jmdm. ∼gehen** walk along beside/in front of/behind sb.; ∼|**haben** *unr. tr. V.* (ugs.) **wo hat er/sie das ∼?** where did he/she get that from?; ∼|**halten** *unr. V.* ∼**halten müssen [für jmdn./etw.]** be the one to suffer [for sb./sth.]; ∼|**hören** *itr. V.* listen

Hering *der;* ∼**s,** ∼**e (a)** herring **(b)** (Zeltpflock) peg ⋯⟶

her-: ~|**kommen** *unr. itr. V.; mit
sein* come here; ~**kömmlich** *Adj.*
conventional; traditional ‹*custom*›
Herkunft *die;* ~, **Herkünfte** origin
Herkunfts·land *das* country of origin
her-: ~|**laufen** *unr. itr. V.; mit sein*
vor/hinter/neben jmdm. ~**laufen** run [along]
in front of/behind/alongside sb.; (nachlaufen)
hinter jmdm. ~**laufen** run after sb.; (fig.)
chase sb. up; ~|**leiten** *tr., refl. V.* derive
(**aus, von** from); ~|**machen** (ugs.) *refl. V.*
sich über etw. (*Akk.*) ~**machen** get stuck
into sth. (coll.)
Hermelin *der;* ~s, ~e (Pelz) ermine
hermetisch 1 *Adj.* hermetic
2 *adv.* hermetically
Heroin *das;* ~s heroin
Heroin·sucht *die* heroin addiction
heroin·süchtig *Adj.* addicted to heroin
postpos.
Herr *der;* ~n, ~en (a) (Mann) gentleman
(b) (Titel, Anrede) ~ **Schulze** Mr Schulze; **Sehr
geehrter** ~ **Schulze!** Dear Sir; (bei persönlicher
Bekanntschaft) Dear Mr Schulze; **meine** ~**en**
gentlemen
(c) (Gebieter) master
herren-, Herren-: ~**ausstatter**
der [gentle]men's outfitter; ~**los** *Adj.*
abandoned ‹*car, luggage*›; stray ‹*dog, cat*›;
~**salon** *der* men's hairdressing salon;
~**schuh** *der* man's shoe; ~**schuhe** men's
shoes; ~**toilette** *die* [gentle]men's toilet
Herr·gott *der;* ~s: der [liebe]/unser ~: the
Lord [God]; God
Herrgotts·frühe *die* in aller ~: at the
crack of dawn
her|richten *tr. V.* (bereitmachen) get ‹*room,
refreshments, etc.*› ready; arrange ‹*table*›; (in
Ordnung bringen) renovate
Herrin *die;* ~, ~en mistress
herrisch 1 *Adj.* overbearing; imperious
2 *adv.* imperiously
herrlich 1 *Adj.* marvellous; magnificent
‹*view, clothes*›
2 *adv.* marvellously
Herrlichkeit *die;* ~, ~en (a) (Schönheit)
magnificence; splendour
(b) (herrliche Sache) marvellous thing
Herrschaft *die;* ~, ~en (a) rule; (Macht)
power
(b) *Pl.* (Damen u. Herren) ladies and gentlemen
herrschen *itr. V.* rule; ‹*monarch*› reign,
rule; **draußen** ~ **30° Kälte** it's 30° below
outside
Herrscher *der;* ~s, ~, **Herrscherin**
die; ~, ~nen ruler
herrsch-, Herrsch-: ~**sucht**
die thirst for power; (herrisches Wesen)
domineering nature; ~**süchtig** *Adj.*
domineering

---

*old spelling – see note on page x

her-: ~|**rühren** *itr. V.* von jmdm./etw.
~rühren come from sb./stem from sth.;
*~|**sein** ▶ HER; ~|**stellen** *tr. V.* produce;
manufacture; make
Hersteller *der;* ~s, ~, **Herstellerin**
die; ~, ~nen producer
Her·stellung *die* production; manufacture
herüber *Adv.* over
herum *Adv.* um … ~ (Richtung) round;
(Anordnung) around; **um Weihnachten**
~: around Christmas; ~ **sein** (ugs.: vergangen
sein, vorüber sein) have passed
herum-: ~|**ärgern** *refl. V.* (ugs.) **sich mit
jmdm./etw.** ~**ärgern** keep getting annoyed
with sb./sth.; ~|**drehen** 1 *tr. V.* (ugs.)
turn ‹*key*›; turn over ‹*coin, mattress, hand,
etc.*›; 2 *refl. V.* turn [a]round; ~|**fahren**
(ugs.) 1 *unr. itr. V.; mit sein* (sich plötzlich
herumdrehen) spin round; 2 *unr. tr. V.* jmdn.
[**in der Stadt**] ~**fahren** drive sb. around
the town; ~|**führen** 1 *tr. V.* jmdn. [**in
der Stadt**] ~**führen** show sb. around the
town; 2 *itr. V.* **um etw.** ~**führen** ‹*road etc.*›
go round sth.; ~|**gehen** *unr. itr. V.; mit
sein* (vergehen) pass; **um etw.** ~**gehen** go
round sth.; **etw.** ~**gehen lassen** circulate
sth.; pass; ~|**kommandieren** (ugs.)
1 *tr. V.* jmdn. ~**kommandieren** boss (coll.)
or order sb. around *or* about; 2 *itr. V.*
boss (coll.) *or* order people around *or*
about; ~|**kommen** *unr. itr. V.; mit sein*
(ugs.) (a) (vermeiden können) **um etw.** [**nicht**]
~**kommen** [not] be able to get out of sth.;
(b) (viel reisen) get around *or* about; **in der
Welt** ~**kommen** see a lot of the world;
~|**laufen** *unr. itr. V.; mit sein* (a) walk/
(schneller) run around *or* about; **um etw.**
~**laufen** go round sth.; (b) (gekleidet sein) **wie
ein Hippie** ~**laufen** go about looking like
a hippie; ~|**lungern** *itr. V.* (salopp) loaf
around; ~|**schlagen** *unr. refl. V.* (ugs.)
sich mit Problemen/Einwänden ~**schlagen**
grapple with problems/battle against
objections; *~|**sein** ▶ HERUM; ~|**sitzen**
unr. itr. V. (ugs.) sit around *or* about;
~|**sprechen** *unr. refl. V.* get around
or about; ~|**stöbern** *itr. V.* (ugs.) keep
rummaging around *or* about (**in** + *Dat.* in);
~|**treiben** *unr. refl. V.* (ugs. abwertend) **sich
auf den Straßen/in Discos** ~**treiben** hang
around the streets/in discos; **sich in der Welt**
~**treiben** roam about the world
herunter *Adv.* (a) (nach unten) down;
[**körperlich**] ~ **sein** be in poor health
(b) (weg von) ~ (von) (fort) off; ~ **vom Sofa!**
[get] off the sofa!
herunter-: ~|**bringen** *unr. tr. V.* bring
down; ~|**fallen** *unr. itr. V.; mit sein* fall
down; **vom Tisch/Stuhl** ~**fallen** fall off
the table/chair; ~|**gehen** *unr. itr. V.;
mit sein* (a) come down; (b) (niedriger
werden) ‹*temperature*› drop; ‹*prices*› come
down, fall; ~**gekommen** 1 *2. Part.
v.* ~KOMMEN; 2 *Adj.* poor ‹*health*›;
dilapidated ‹*building*›; run-down ‹*area*›;

down and out ‹person›; ∼|**handeln** tr. V.
(ugs.) **einen Preis** ∼handeln beat down a
price; ∼|**hängen** unr. itr. V. hang down;
∼|**hauen** unr. tr. V. (ugs.) jmdm. eine
∼hauen give sb. a clout round the ear
(coll.); ∼|**kommen** unr. itr. V.; mit sein
(a) come down; **(b)** (ugs.: verfallen) go to
the dogs (coll.); ∼|**laden** unr. tr. V. (DV)
download; ∼|**lassen** unr. tr. V. lower;
∼|**schlucken** tr. V. swallow; *∼|**sein**
▶ HERUNTER A; ∼|**spielen** tr. V. (ugs.) play
down
hervor Adv. aus … ∼: out of
hervor-: ∼|**heben** unr. tr. V. stress;
∼**ragend** ⒈ Adj. outstanding[ly good];
⒉ adv. ∼ragend geschult outstanding
well trained; ∼ragend spielen/arbeiten
play/work outstandingly well; ∼|**tun** unr.
refl. V. distinguish oneself; (wichtig tun) show
off
Herz das; ∼ens, ∼en heart; (Kartenspiel)
hearts pl.; von ∼en kommen come from the
heart; **ein** ∼ **für die Armen haben** feel for
the poor; **ein** ∼ **für Kinder haben** have a love
of children; **schweren** ∼ens with a heavy
heart; **etw. auf dem** ∼en **haben** have sth.
on one's mind; **es nicht übers** ∼ **bringen,
etw. zu tun** not have the heart to do sth.;
sich (Dat.) **etw. zu** ∼en **nehmen** take sth.
to heart
Herz-: ∼**an·fall** der heart attack;
∼**beschwerden** Pl. heart trouble sing.
herzens-, Herzens-: ∼**gut** /'--'-/ Adj.
kind-hearted; ∼**lust** die: nach ∼lust to
one's heart's content
herzhaft ⒈ Adj. hearty; (nahrhaft) hearty
‹meal›; (von kräftigem Geschmack) tasty
⒉ adv. heartily; (nahrhaft) **er isst gern** ∼: he
likes to have a hearty meal
her|ziehen unr. itr. V.; mit sein od. haben
(ugs.) **über jmdn./etw.** ∼: run sb./sth. down
herzig ⒈ Adj. sweet; delightful
⒉ adv. sweetly; delightfully
herz-, Herz-: ∼**infarkt** der heart attack;
∼**klappen·fehler** der (Med.) valvular
defect or insufficiency; ∼**klopfen** das;
∼∼s: jmd. hat ∼klopfen sb.'s heart is
pounding; ∼**krank** Adj. ‹person› with
a heart condition; ∼**kranz·gefäß** das
coronary vessel
herzlich ⒈ Adj. warm ‹smile, reception›;
kind ‹words, regards›; (ehrlich gemeint)
sincere; ∼**en Dank** many thanks
⒉ adv. warmly; (ehrlich gemeint) sincerely;
‹congratulate› heartily; ∼ **wenig** very or
(coll.) precious little
Herzlichkeit die; ∼: warmth; kindness;
(Aufrichtigkeit) sincerity
herz·los ⒈ Adj. heartless
⒉ adv. heartlessly
Herzog der; ∼s, Herzöge duke
Herzogin die; ∼, ∼nen duchess
Herz·rhythmus·störung die (Med.)

disturbance of the heart or cardiac rhythm
herz-, Herz-: ∼**schlag** der
heartbeat; (Herzversagen) heart failure;
∼**schmerz** der pain in the region
of the heart; ∼**schrittmacher**
der (Anat., Med.) [cardiac] pacemaker;
∼**transplantation** die (Med.) heart
transplantation; ∼**zerreißend** ⒈ Adj.
heart-rending; ⒉ adv. heart-rendingly
Hessen (das); ∼s Hesse
hetero·sexuell Adj. heterosexual
Hetze die; ∼ **(a)** [mad] rush
(b) (abwertend) smear campaign
hetzen ⒈ tr. V. **(a)** hunt
(b) (antreiben) rush
⒉ itr. V. **(a)** (in großer Eile sein) rush
(b) mit sein (hasten) rush; (rennen) dash; race
Hetz-: ∼**kampagne** die (abwertend)
smear campaign; (gegen eine Minderheit)
hate campaign; ∼**rede** die (abwertend)
inflammatory speech
Heu das; ∼[e]s hay
Heuchelei die; ∼: hypocrisy
heucheln ⒈ itr. V. be a hypocrite
⒉ tr. V. feign
Heuchler der; ∼s, ∼, **Heuchlerin** die;
∼, ∼nen hypocrite
heuchlerisch ⒈ Adj. hypocritical
⒉ adv. hypocritically
heuer Adv. (südd., österr., schweiz.) this year
Heuer die; ∼, ∼n (Seemannsspr.) pay; wages
pl.
Heu·ernte die **(a)** hay harvest
(b) (Ertrag) hay crop
heulen itr. V. **(a)** howl; ‹siren etc.› wail
(b) (ugs.: weinen) howl; bawl
Heurige der; adj. Dekl. (bes. österr.)
(a) (Wein) new wine
(b) (Weinlokal) inn with new wine on tap
Heu-: ∼**schnupfen** der hay fever;
∼**schrecke** die grasshopper
heute Adv. today; ∼ **früh** early this
morning; ∼ **Morgen/Abend** this morning/
evening; ∼ **Mittag** [at] midday today;
∼ **Nacht** tonight; (letzte Nacht) last night;
∼ **in einer Woche** a week [from] today;
today week; ∼ **vor einer Woche** a week ago
today
heutig Adj. **(a)** (von diesem Tag) today's; der
∼e Tag today
(b) (gegenwärtig) today's; of today postpos.; in
der ∼en Zeit nowadays
heut·zu·tage Adv. nowadays
Hexe die; ∼, ∼n witch
hexen itr. V. work magic
Hexen·schuss, *Hexen·schuß der
lumbago no indef. art.
Hexerei die; ∼, ∼en witchcraft; (von
Kunststücken usw.) magic
Hickhack das od. der; ∼s, ∼s (ugs.)
squabbling; bickering
hieb 1. u. 3. Pers. Sg. Prät. v. HAUEN ⸱⸱⸱⧕

Hieb *der;* ~[e]s, ~e **(a)** (Schlag) blow; (mit der Peitsche) lash
(b) *Pl.* (ugs.: Prügel) hiding *sing.*
hieb·fest *Adj.*: hieb- und stichfest watertight; cast-iron
hielt *1. u. 3. Pers. Sg. Prät. v.* HALTEN
hier *Adv.* **(a)** here; [von] ~ oben/unten [from] up/down here
(b) (jetzt) now; **von** ~ **an** from now on
hieran *Adv.* here; **sich** ~ **festhalten** hold on to this; (fig.) **im Anschluss** ~: immediately after this
Hierarchie /hierar'çi:/ *die;* ~, ~n hierarchy
hierauf *Adv.* **(a)** on here; (darauf) on this; **wir werden** ~ **zurückkommen** we'll come back to this
(b) (danach) after that; then
(c) (infolgedessen) whereupon
hieraus *Adv.* out of here; (aus dieser Tatsache, Quelle) from this
hier-: ~|**behalten** *unr. tr. V.* jmdn./etw. ~behalten: keep sb./sth. here; ~|**bei** *Adv.* **(a)** (bei dieser Gelegenheit) **Diese Übung ist sehr schwierig. Man kann sich** ~**bei leicht verletzen.** This exercise is very difficult. You can easily injure yourself doing it; **(b)** (bei der erwähnten Sache) here; ~|**bleiben** *unr. itr. V.; mit sein* stay here; ~**durch** *Adv.* through here; (aufgrund dieser Sache) because of this; ~**für** *Adv.* for this
hier·her *Adv.* here; **ich gehe bis** ~ **und nicht weiter** I'm going this far and no further; ~**gehören** belong here; (hierfür wichtig sein) be relevant [here]; ~**kommen** *mit sein* come here
hier·hin *Adv.* here; **bis** ~: up to here
hier-: ~**in** *Adv.* **(a)** (räumlich) in here; **(b)** in this; ~**mit** *Adv.* with this/these; ~**mit ist der Fall erledigt** that puts an end to the matter; ~**nach** *Adv.* (anschließend) after that
Hieroglyphe /hiero.../ *die;* ~, ~n hieroglyph
hier-: ***~**sein** ▸ HIER A; ~**über** *Adv.* **(a)** (über dem Erwähnten) above here; (über das Erwähnte) over here; **(b)** (das Erwähnte betreffend) about this/these; ~**von** *Adv.* of this/these; ~**zu** *Adv.* with this; (hinsichtlich dieser Sache) about this; ~**zu gehört/gehören** ...: this includes/these include; ~**zu reicht mein Geld nicht** I haven't got enough money for that; ~**zu·lande** *Adv.* [here] in this country
hiesig *Adj.* local
hieß *1. u. 3. Pers. Sg. Prät. v.* HEISSEN
Hi-Fi-Anlage /'haifi./ *die* hi-fi system
high /hai/ *Adj.* (ugs.) high (coll.)
Hightech-, High-Tech- /'hai'tɛk-/ high-tech
Hijab *der* hijab

Hilfe *die;* ~, ~n **(a)** help; (für Notleidende) aid; relief; **zu** ~! help!
(b) (Hilfskraft) help; (im Geschäft) assistant
Hilfe-: ~**leistung** *die* help; ~**ruf** *der* cry for help; ~**stellung** *die* (Turnen) jmdm. ~**stellung geben** act as spotter for sb.
hilflos ① *Adj.* helpless
② *adv.* helplessly
Hilflosigkeit *die;* ~ helplessness
hilfs-, Hilfs-: ~**bedürftig** *Adj.*
(a) (schwach) in need of help *postpos.*;
(b) (notleidend) in need; needy; ~**bereit** *Adj.* helpful; ~**bereitschaft** *die* helpfulness; ~**gelder** *Pl.* aid money *sing.*; ~**kraft** *die* assistant; ~**mittel** *das* aid; ~**organisation** *die* aid *or* relief organization; ~**programm** *das* aid *or* relief programme; ~**verb** *das,* (Sprachw.) auxiliary [verb]; ~**werk** *das* aid agency
Himalaja *der;* ~[s]: der/im ~: the/in the Himalayas *pl.*
Him·beere *die* raspberry
Himmel *der;* ~s, ~ sky; (Rel.) heaven; ~ **noch [ein]mal!** for Heaven's sake!
himmel-, Himmel-: ~**bett** *das* four-poster bed; ~**blau** *Adj.* sky-blue; clear blue ⟨eyes⟩; ~**fahrt** *die* (Rel.) **(a)** Christi/Mariä ~fahrt: the Ascension of Christ/the Assumption of the Virgin Mary; **(b)** (Festtag) [Christi] ~: Ascension Day *no art.*
Himmels-: ~**richtung** *die* point of the compass; ~**schlüsselchen** *das;* ~~s, ~~: cowslip
himmel·weit *Adj.* enormous, vast ⟨difference⟩
himmlisch *Adj.* (auch fig.) heavenly
hin *Adv.* **(a)** (räumlich) **zur Straße** ~ **liegen** face the road
(b) (zeitlich) **gegen Mittag** ~: towards midday
(c) (in Verbindungen) **nach außen** ~: outwardly; **auf meinen Rat** ~: on my advice; **auf seine Bitte** ~: at his request
(d) (in Wortpaaren) ~ **und zurück** there and back; **einmal Köln** ~ **und zurück** a return [ticket] to Cologne; ~ **und her** to and fro; back and forth; ~ **und wieder** [every] now and then
(e) ~ **sein** (ugs.: verloren sein); be gone; (ugs.: nicht mehr brauchbar sein); have had it (coll.); ⟨car⟩ be a write-off; (salopp: tot sein) have snuffed it (sl.); **von jmdm./etw. ganz** ~ **sein** (ugs.: hingerissen sein) be mad about sb./bowled over by sth.
hinab *Adv.* ▸ HINUNTER
hinab- ▸ HINUNTER-
hinauf *Adv.* up; **bis** ~ **zu** up to
hinauf-: ~|**fahren** *unr. itr. V.; mit sein* go up; (im Auto) drive up; (mit einem Motorrad) ride up; ~|**gehen** *unr. itr. V.; mit sein* **(a)** (nach oben gehen) go up; **(b)** (nach oben führen) lead up; **(c)** (ugs.: steigen) ⟨prices, taxes, etc.⟩ go up; rise; ~|**klettern** *itr. V.; mit sein* climb up; ~|**steigen** *unr. itr. V.; mit sein* climb up;

~|**ziehen** 1 *unr. tr. V.* pull up; 2 *unr. itr. V.; mit sein* move up; 3 *unr. refl. V.* (sich erstrecken) stretch up

hinaus *Adv.* (a) (räumlich) out
(b) (zeitlich) **auf Jahre** ~: for years to come
(c) (etw. überschreitend) **über etw.** (*Akk.*) ~: in addition to sth.
(d) über etw. (*Akk.*) ~ **sein** be past sth.

hinaus-: ~|**bringen** *unr. itr. V.* jmdn./ etw. ~bringen see sb. out/take sth. out (**aus** of); ~|**fahren** 1 *unr. itr. V.; mit sein* aus etw. ~fahren (mit dem Auto) drive out of sth.; (mit dem Zweirad) ride out of sth.; ⟨*car, bus*⟩ go out of sth.; ⟨*train*⟩ pull out of sth.; **zum Flugplatz** ~fahren drive out to the airport; 2 *unr. tr. V.* jmdn./etw. ~fahren drive sb./take sth. out; ~|**fallen** *unr. itr. V.; mit sein* fall out (**aus** of); ~|**finden** *unr. itr. V.* find one's way out (**aus** of); ~|**gehen** *unr. itr. V.; mit sein* (a) go out (**aus** of); (b) (gerichtet sein) **das Zimmer geht zum Garten/nach Westen** ~: the room looks out on to the garden/faces west; ~|**kommen** *unr. itr. V.; mit sein* come out (**aus** of); ~|**laufen** *unr. itr. V.; mit sein* (a) run out (**aus** of); (b) (als Ergebnis haben) **auf etw.** (*Akk.*) ~laufen lead to sth.; ~|**sehen** *unr. itr. V.* look out; **zum Fenster** ~sehen look out of the window; ***~|**sein** ▸ HINAUS D; ~|**tragen** *unr. tr. V.* jmdn./etw. ~tragen carry sb./sth. out; ~|**werfen** *unr. tr. V.* (auch ugs. fig.) throw out (**aus** of); ~|**ziehen** 1 *unr. tr. V.* (a) (nach draußen ziehen) jmdn./etw. ~ziehen pull sb./sth. out (**aus** of); tow ⟨*ship*⟩ out; (b) (verzögern) put off; delay; 2 *unr. refl. V.* be delayed; ~|**zögern** 1 *tr. V.* delay; 2 *refl. V.* be delayed

hin-, Hin-: ~|**blick** *der:* im *od.* in ~blick auf etw. (*Akk.*) (wegen) in view of; (hinsichtlich) with regard to; ~|**bringen** *unr. tr. V.* jmdn./etw. ~bringen take sb./sth. [there]; ~|**denken** *unr. itr. V.* wo denkst du hin? (ugs.) whatever are you thinking of?

hinderlich *Adj.* ~ sein get in the way
hindern *tr. V.* (a) (abhalten) jmdn. ~: stop sb. (**an** + *Dat.* from)
(b) (behindern) hinder
Hindernis *das;* ~ses, ~se obstacle
hin|deuten *itr. V.* (a) auf jmdn./etw. *od.* zu jmdm./etw. ~: point to sb./sth.
(b) auf etw. (*Akk.*) ~ (fig.) point to sth.
Hindu *der;* ~[s], ~[s] Hindu
Hinduismus *der;* ~ Hinduism *no art.*
hin·durch *Adv.* (a) (räumlich) **durch den Wald** ~: through the wood
(b) (zeitlich) **das ganze Jahr** ~: throughout the year
hinein *Adv.* (a) (räumlich) in; **in etw.** (*Akk.*) ~: into sth.
(b) (zeitlich) **bis in den Morgen/tief in die Nacht** ~: till morning/far into the night
hinein-: ~|**bringen** *unr. tr. V.* take in; ~|**fahren** (mit dem Auto) drive in; (mit dem Zweirad) ride in; **in etw.** (*Akk.*) ~fahren

drive/ride into sth.; ~|**fallen** *unr. itr. V.; mit sein* fall in; **in etw.** (*Akk.*) ~fallen fall into sth.; ~|**gehen** *unr. itr. V.; mit sein* go in; **in etw.** (*Akk.*) ~gehen go into sth.; ~|**gucken** *itr. V.* (ugs.) look in; **in etw.** (*Akk.*) ~gucken look in[to] sth.; ~|**kommen** *unr. itr. V.; mit sein* (a) come in; **in etw.** (*Akk.*) ~kommen come into sth.; (b) (gelangen, auch fig.) get in; **in etw.** (*Akk.*) ~kommen get into sth.; ~|**reden** *itr. V.* jmdm. in seine Angelegenheiten/ Entscheidungen *usw.* ~reden interfere in sb.'s affairs/decisions *etc.*; ~|**sehen** *unr. itr. V.* look in; **in etw.** (*Akk.*) ~sehen look into sth.; ~|**versetzen** *refl. V.* sich in jmdn. *od.* jmds. Lage ~versetzen put oneself in sb.'s position; ~|**ziehen** *unr. tr. V.* (a) pull *or* draw in; etw./jmdn. **in etw.** (*Akk.*) ~ziehen pull *or* draw sth./sb. into sth.; (b) (verwickeln) jmdn. in eine Angelegenheit/ einen Streit/Skandal ~ziehen drag sb. into an affair/a dispute/scandal

hin-, Hin-: ~|**fahren** 1 *unr. itr. V.; mit sein* go there; 2 *unr. tr. V.* jmdn. ~fahren drive sb. there; ~|**fahrt** *die* journey there; (Seereise) voyage out; ~|**fallen** *unr. itr. V.; mit sein* (a) fall over; (b) jmdm. fällt etw. ~: sb. drops sth.; etw. ~fallen lassen drop sth.; ~**fällig** *Adj.* (a) infirm; frail; (b) (ungültig) invalid; ~|**fliegen** *unr. itr. V.; mit sein* fly there; ~**flug** *der* outward flight

hing 1. u. 3. Pers. Sg. Prät. v. HÄNGEN
Hin·gabe *die;* ~: devotion; (Eifer) dedication
Hingebung *die;* ~ devotion
hingebungs·voll 1 *Adj.* devoted
2 *adv.* devotedly; with devotion; ⟨*listen*⟩ with rapt attention; ⟨*dance, play*⟩ with abandon
hin·gegen *Konj., Adv.* (jedoch) however; (andererseits) on the other hand
hin-, Hin-: ~|**gehen** *unr. itr. V.; mit sein* (a) go [there]; **zu** jmdm./etw. ~gehen go to sb./sth.; (b) (verstreichen) ⟨*time*⟩ go by; ~|**halten** *unr. tr. V.* (a) hold out; (b) (warten lassen) jmdn. ~halten keep sb. waiting; ~**halte·taktik** *die* delaying tactics *pl.*; ~|**hören** *itr. V.* listen

hinken /'hɪŋkn̩/ *itr. V.* (a) walk with a limp
(b) *mit sein* (hinkend gehen) limp
hin-, Hin-: ~|**kommen** *unr. itr. V.; mit sein* (a) get there; (b) (an einen Ort gehören) go; belong; (c) (ugs.: stimmen) be right; ~**länglich** 1 *Adj.* sufficient; (angemessen) adequate; 2 *adv.* sufficiently; (angemessen) adequately; ~|**legen** 1 *tr. V.* put; (weglegen) put down; 2 *refl. V.* lie down; ~**reichend** 1 *Adj.* sufficient; (angemessen) adequate; 2 *adv.* sufficiently; (angemessen) adequately; ~**reise** *die* journey there; (mit dem Schiff) voyage out; ~**reißend** *Adj.* enchanting ⟨*person, picture, view*⟩; captivating ⟨*speaker, play*⟩; ~|**richten** *tr. V.* execute; ~**richtung** *die* execution

Hinrichtungs·kommando *das* firing squad

hin-, Hin-: ~|**sehen** *unr. itr. V.* look; ***~|**sein** ▶ HIN E; ~|**setzen** 1 *tr. V.* put; 2 *refl. V.* sit down; ~**sicht** *die* in gewisser ~sicht in a way/in some respects *or* ways; in jeder ~sicht in every respect; in finanzieller ~sicht financially; ~**sichtlich** *Präp. mit Gen.* (Amtsspr.) with regard to; (in Anbetracht) in view of; ~|**stellen** 1 *tr. V.* put; put up ⟨building⟩; (absetzen) put down; 2 *refl. V.* stand

hinten *Adv.* at the back; sich ~ anstellen join the back of the queue (Brit.) *or* (Amer.) line; weiter ~: further back; (in einem Buch) further on; die Adresse steht ~ auf dem Brief the address is on the back of the envelope; nach ~ hinaus liegen/gehen be at the back; die anderen sind ganz weit ~: the others are a long way back

hinter 1 *Präp. mit Dat.* behind; (nach) after; 3 km ~ der Grenze 3 km beyond the frontier; eine Prüfung ~ sich haben (fig.) have got an examination over [and done] with; viele Enttäuschungen/eine Krankheit ~ sich haben have experienced many disappointments/have got over an illness 2 *Präp. mit Akk.* behind

hinter... *Adj.; nicht präd.* back

hinter-, Hinter-: ~**einander** *Adv.* (a) (räumlich) one behind the other; (b) (zeitlich) one after another *or* the other; ~**gedanke** *der* ulterior motive; ~**gehen** /-'--/ *unr. tr. V.* deceive; ~**grund** *der* background; ~**grund·bericht** *der* background report; ~**gründig** 1 *Adj.* enigmatic; 2 *adv.* enigmatically; ~**grund·information** *die* item *or* piece of background information; ~**grundinformationen** [items *or* pieces of] background information *sing.*; ~**halt** *der* ambush; ~**hältig** 1 *Adj.* underhand; 2 *adv.* in an underhand manner; ~**her** *Adv.* (räumlich) behind; (nachher) afterwards; ~**hof** *der* courtyard; ~**land** *das* hinterland (Milit.) back area; ~**lassen** /--'-/ *unr. tr. V.* leave; ~**legen** /--'-/ *tr. V.* deposit (bei with); ~**list** *die* guile; deceit; ~**listig** *Adj.* deceitful; ~**mann** *der* (a) person behind; (b) (Gewährsmann) [secret] informant

Hintern *der;* ~s, ~ (ugs.) backside; bottom

hinter-, Hinter-: ~**rad** *das* rear wheel; ~**sinn** *der* deeper meaning; ~**sinnig** *Adj.* ⟨remark, story, etc.⟩ with a deeper meaning; ~**teil** *das* backside; behind; ~**treffen** *das* (ugs.): ins ~treffen geraten *od.* kommen fall behind; ~**treiben** /--'-/ *unr. tr. V.* foil ⟨plan⟩; prevent ⟨marriage, promotion⟩; block ⟨law, investigation, reform⟩; ~**treppe** *die* back stairs *pl.*; ~**tür** *die* back door; ~**wäldler** *der;* ~~s, ~~ (spött.) backwoodsman; ~**wäldlerin**

die; ~~, ~~nen backwoodswoman; ~**wäldlerisch** *Adj.* (spött.) backwoods *attrib.* ⟨views, attitudes, manners, etc.⟩

hinüber *Adv.* over; across

Hin- und Rück·fahrt *die* journey there and back; round trip (Amer.)

hinunter *Adv.* down

hinunter-: ~|**fahren** 1 *unr. itr. V.;* mit sein go down; (mit dem Auto) drive down; (mit dem Fahrrad) ride down; 2 *unr. tr. V.* jmdn./ein Auto/eine Ladung ~fahren drive sb. down/drive a car down/take a load down; ~|**gehen** *unr. itr. V.; mit sein* go down; ⟨aircraft⟩ descend; ~|**klettern** *itr. V.; mit sein* climb down; ~|**reichen** 1 *tr. V.* hand down; 2 *itr. V.* (sich bis hinunter erstrecken) reach down (bis auf + Akk. to)

hin·weg *Adv.* (a) (geh.) ~ mit dir! away with you! (b) über etw. ~: over sth.

Hin·weg *der* way there

hinweg-: ~|**gehen** *unr. itr. V.; mit sein* über etw. ~gehen pass over sth.; ~|**kommen** *unr. itr. V.; mit sein* über etw. (Akk.) ~kommen get over sth.; ~|**setzen** *refl. V.* sich über etw. (Akk.) ~setzen ignore sth.

Hinweis /'hɪnvaɪs/ *der;* ~es, ~e hint; unter ~ auf (+ Akk.) with reference to

hin-: ~|**weisen** 1 *unr. itr. V.* auf jmdn./etw. ~weisen point to sb./sth.; 2 *unr. tr. V.* jmdn. auf etw. (Akk.) ~weisen point sth. out to sb.; ~**weisend** *Adj.* (Grammatik) demonstrative; ~|**werfen** *unr. tr. V.* throw down; ~|**ziehen** 1 *unr. itr. V.* pull, draw (zu to, towards); 2 *unr. itr. V.; mit sein* (umziehen) move there; wo ist sie ~gezogen? where did she move to?; 3 *unr. refl. V.* (a) (sich erstrecken) drag on (über + Akk. for); (b) (sich verzögern) be delayed

hinzu-: ~|**fügen** *tr. V.* add; ~|**kommen** *unr. itr. V.; mit sein* (a) come along; (b) (hinzugefügt werden) zu etw. ~kommen be added to sth.; es kommt noch ~, dass ... (fig.) there is also the fact that ...; ~|**tun** *unr. tr. V.* (ugs.) add

Hiobs·botschaft *die* bad news

Hirn *das;* ~[e]s, ~e (a) brain (b) (Speise; ugs.: Verstand) brains *pl.*

hirn·tot *Adj.* brain-dead

Hirsch *der;* ~[e]s, ~e deer; (Rothirsch) red deer; (männlicher Rothirsch) stag; (Speise) venison

Hirse *die;* ~, ~n millet

Hirt *der;* ~en, **Hirte** *der;* ~n, ~n herdsman; (Schaf~) shepherd

Hirtin *die;* ~, ~nen shepherdess

hissen *tr. V.* hoist

historisch *Adj.* (a) historical (b) (geschichtlich bedeutungsvoll) historic

Hit *der;* ~[s], ~s (ugs.) hit

Hitler·jugend *die* Hitler Youth

Hit·parade *die* hit parade

**old spelling – see note on page x

Hitze *die;* ~: heat

hitze-, Hitze-: ~**beständig** *Adj.* heat-resistant; ~**frei** *Adj.* ~**frei haben** have the rest of the day off [school/work] because of excessively hot weather; ~**periode** *die* hot spell; spell *or* period of hot weather; ~**welle** *die* heat wave

hitzig *Adj.* (a) hot-tempered (b) (erregt) heated ⟨*discussion etc.*⟩

hitz-, Hitz-: ~**kopf** *der* hothead; ~**köpfig** *Adj.* hot-headed; ~**schlag** *der* heatstroke

HIV-: ~**-Anti·kör·per** *der* HIV antibody; ~**-Infektion** *die* HIV infection; ~**-infiziert** *Adj.* HIV-infected; ~**-kontaminiert** *Adj.* HIV-contaminated; ~**-positiv** *Adj.* HIV-positive; ~**-Test** *der* HIV test; ~**-verseucht** *Adj.* HIV-contaminated

hl *Abk.* = Hektoliter hl

H-Milch *die;* ~ long-life *or* UHT milk

HNO-Arzt *der,* **HNO-Ärztin** *die* ENT specialist

hob *1. u. 3. Pers. Sg. Prät. v.* HEBEN

Hobby *das;* ~s, ~s hobby

Hobel *der;* ~s, ~ (a) plane (b) (Küchengerät) [vegetable] slicer

Hobel·bank *die; Pl.* **Hobel·bänke** woodworker's bench

hobeln *tr., itr. V.* (a) plane (b) (schneiden) slice

hoch; höher, höchst... ⟨**1**⟩ *Adj.* high; tall ⟨*tree, mast*⟩; long ⟨*grass*⟩; deep ⟨*snow, water*⟩; heavy ⟨*fine*⟩; large ⟨*sum, amount*⟩; severe, extensive ⟨*damage*⟩; senior ⟨*official, officer, post*⟩; high-level ⟨*diplomacy, politics*⟩; **höchste Gefahr** extreme danger; **es ist höchste Zeit, dass ...**: it is high time that ...; **das hohe C** top C; **vier ~ zwei** (Math.) four to the power [of] two; four squared ⟨**2**⟩ *adv.* (in großer Höhe) high; (nach oben) up; (zahlenmäßig viel, sehr) highly; **~ begabt** highly gifted; **~ empfindlich** highly sensitive ⟨*instrument, device, material, etc.*⟩; fast ⟨*film*⟩; extremely delicate ⟨*fabric*⟩; **~ gestellt** ⟨*person*⟩ in a high position; important ⟨*person*⟩; **~ verschuldet/versichert** heavily in debt/insured for a large sum [of money]; **etw. ~ und heilig versprechen** promise sth. faithfully

Hoch *das;* ~s, ~s (a) (Hochruf) **ein [dreifaches] ~ auf jmdn. ausbringen** give three cheers for sb. (b) (Met.) high

Hoch·achtung *die* great respect

hochachtungs·voll *Adv.* (Briefschluss) yours faithfully

hoch-, Hoch-: ~**aktuell** *Adj.* highly topical; ~**amt** *das* (kath. Rel.) high mass; ~**|arbeiten** *refl. V.* work one's way up; ~**begabt** *Adj.* highly gifted; ~**betagt** *Adj.* aged; ~**betrieb** *der* (ugs.) **es herrschte ~betrieb im Geschäft** the shop

was at its busiest; ~**blüte** *die* golden age; ~**burg** *die* stronghold; ~**deutsch** *Adj.* High German; ~**deutsch** *das,* ~**deutsche** *das* High German; ~**druck** *der; Pl.* ~**drücke** (Physik, Met.) high pressure; *****empfindlich** ▸ HOCH 2; ~**|fahren** *unr. itr. V.; mit sein* (a) (ugs.) go up; (mit dem Auto) drive up; (mit dem Fahrrad, Motorrad) ride up; (b) (auffahren) start up; **aus dem Sessel ~fahren** start [up] from one's chair; (c) (aufbrausen) flare up; (d) (DV) start [up]; boot [up]; ~**finanz** *die;* ~~: high finance; ~**fliegend** *Adj.* ambitious; ~**form** *die* top form; ~**gebirge** *das* [high] mountains *pl.;* ~**gefühl** *das* [feeling of] elation; ~**|gehen** *unr. itr. V.; mit sein* (ugs.) go up; (zornig werden) blow one's top (coll.); explode; (explodieren) ⟨*bomb, mine*⟩ go off; ~**genuss**, *****~**genuß** *der:* **ein ~genuss sein** be a real delight; ~**geschlossen** *Adj.* high-necked ⟨*dress*⟩; *****~**gestellt** ▸ HOCH 2; ~**glanz** *der:* **etw. auf ~glanz bringen** give sth. a high polish; (fig.) make sth. spick and span; ~**gradig** ⟨**1**⟩ *Adj.* extreme; ⟨**2**⟩ *adv.* extremely; ~**|halten** *unr. tr. V.* hold up; ~**haus** *das* high-rise building; ~**|heben** *unr. tr. V.* lift up; raise ⟨*arm, leg, hand*⟩; ~**interessant** *Adj.* extremely interesting; ~**kant** *Adv.* (ugs.): **jmdn. ~kant hinauswerfen** chuck sb. out (coll.); throw sb. out on his/her ear (coll.); ~**|kommen** *unr. itr. V.; mit sein* (ugs.) come up; (vorwärts kommen) get on; ~**konjunktur** *die* (Wirtsch.) boom; **auf dem Automarkt herrscht ~konjunktur** the car market is booming; ~**|krempeln** *tr. V.* roll up; ~**|laden** *unr. tr. V.* (DV) upload; ~**land** *das* highlands *Pl.;* ~**|leben** *itr. V.* **jmdn./etw. ~leben lassen** cheer sb./sth.; **er lebe ~!** three cheers for him; ~**leistungs·sport** *der* top-level sport; ~**modern** *Adj.* ultra-modern; ~**mut** *der* arrogance; ~**mütig** *Adj.* arrogant; ~**näsig** *Adj.* (abwertend) stuck-up; ~**|nehmen** *unr. tr. V.* (ugs.: verspotten) **jmdn. ~nehmen** pull sb.'s leg; ~**ofen** *der* blast furnace; ~**prozentig** *Adj.* high-proof ⟨*spirits*⟩; ~**|rechnen** project; ~**rechnung** *die* (Statistik) projection; ~**ruf** *der* cheer; ~**saison** *die* (ugs.) high season; ~**|schlagen** ⟨**1**⟩ *unr. tr. V.* turn up ⟨*collar, brim*⟩; ⟨**2**⟩ *unr. itr. V.; mit sein* ⟨*water, waves*⟩ surge up; ⟨*flames*⟩ leap up; ~**schule** *die* college; (Universität) university; ~**|scrollen** (DV) *itr. u. tr. V.* scroll up

Hoch·see·fischerei *die* deep-sea fishing no art.

hoch-, Hoch-: ~**sitz** *der* (Jägerspr.) raised hide; ~**sommer** *der* high summer; ~**spannung** *die* (Elektrot.) high voltage; ~**|spielen** *tr. V.* blow up

höchst *Adv.* extremely; most

höchst... ▸ HOCH

Hoch·stapler /-ʃtaːplɐ/ *der;* ~s, ~: confidence trickster; conman (coll.); (Aufschneider) fraud

höchsten·falls *Adv.* at [the] most *or* the outside; at the very most

höchstens *Adv.* at most; (bestenfalls) at best

Höchst-: ∼**fall** *der:* im ∼**fall** at [the] most; ∼**form** *die* (bes. Sport) peak form; ∼**geschwindigkeit** *die* top speed; (Geschwindigkeitsbegrenzung) speed limit

Hoch·stimmung *die* high spirits *pl.*

höchst-, Höchst-: ∼**leistung** *die* supreme performance; (Ergebnis) supreme achievement; ∼**maß** *das:* ein ∼**maß an etw.** (*Dat.*) a very high degree of sth.; ∼**persönlich** ⓵ *Adj.* personal; ⓶ *adv.* in person; ∼**temperatur** *die* maximum *or* highest temperature; ∼**wahrscheinlich** *Adv.* very probably; ∼**wert** *der* maximum value

hoch-, Hoch-: ∼**tour** *die:* auf ∼**touren** laufen run at full speed; (intensiv betrieben werden) be in full swing; ∼**trabend** (abwertend) ⓵ *Adj.* high-flown; ⓶ *adv.* in a high-flown manner; ∼|**treiben** *unr. tr. V.* force up ⟨*prices etc.*⟩; ∼**verrat** *der* high treason; ∼**wasser** *das* (Flut) high tide; (Überschwemmung) flood; ∼**wertig** *Adj.* high-quality ⟨*goods*⟩; highly nutritious ⟨*food*⟩; ∼**würden** *der;* ∼∼[s] (veralt.) Reverend Father

Hoch·zeit *die;* ∼, ∼en wedding

Hochzeits-: ∼**feier** *die* wedding; ∼**nacht** *die* wedding night; ∼**reise** *die* honeymoon [trip]

Hocke *die;* ∼, ∼n (a) (Körperhaltung) squat; crouch (b) (Turnen) squat vault

hocken ⓵ *itr. V.* (a) *mit haben od.* (*südd.*) *sein* squat; crouch (b) *mit haben od.* (*südd.*) *sein* (ugs.: sich aufhalten) sit around ⓶ *refl. V.* crouch down

Hocker *der;* ∼s, ∼: stool

Höcker *der;* ∼s, ∼: hump; (auf der Nase) bump; (auf dem Schnabel) knob

Hockey /'hɔki/ *das;* ∼s hockey

Hoden *der;* ∼s, ∼: testicle

Hoden·bruch *der* (Med.) scrotal hernia

Hof *der;* ∼[e]s, Höfe (a) courtyard; (Schul∼) playground; (Gefängnis∼) [prison] yard (b) (Bauern∼) farm (c) (Herrscher, Hofstaat) court

Hof·dame *die* lady of the court; (Begleiterin der Königin) lady-in-waiting

hof·fähig *Adj.* presentable at court *pred.*

hoffen ⓵ *tr. V.* hope ⓶ *itr. V.* hope; **auf etw.** (*Akk.*) ∼: hope for sth.; (Vertrauen setzen auf) **auf jmdn./etw.** ∼: put one's faith in sb./sth.

hoffentlich *Adv.* hopefully; ∼! let's hope so

Hoffnung *die;* ∼, ∼en hope

hoffnungs-, Hoffnungs-: ∼**los** ⓵ *Adj.* hopeless; despairing ⟨*person*⟩; ⓶ *adv.* hopelessly; ∼**losigkeit** *die;* ∼∼: despair; (der Lage) hopelessness; ∼**voll** ⓵ *Adj.* (a) hopeful; full of hope *pred.;* (b) (erfolgversprechend) promising; ⓶ *adv.* (a) full of hope; (b) (erfolgversprechend) promisingly

höflich ⓵ *Adj.* polite ⓶ *adv.* politely

Höflichkeit *die;* ∼: politeness

hoh... ▶ HOCH

Höhe /'hø:ə/ *die;* ∼, ∼n height; etw. in die ∼ heben lift sth. up; **das ist ja die** ∼! (fig. ugs.) that's the limit!

Hoheit *die;* ∼, ∼en sovereignty (**über** + *Akk.* over); **Seine/Ihre** ∼: His/Your Highness

Hoheits-: ∼**gebiet** *das* [sovereign] territory; ∼**gewässer** *das* territorial waters

Höhen-: ∼**angst** *die* fear of heights; ∼**flug** *der* (fig.) flight; ∼**lage** *die* altitude; ∼**luft** *die* mountain air; ∼**messer** *der* altimeter; ∼**sonne** *die* (Med.) sun lamp; ∼**unterschied** *der* difference in altitude; ∼**zug** *der* (Geogr.) range of hills; (Bergkette) range of mountains; mountain range

Höhe·punkt *der* high point; (einer Veranstaltung) high spot; highlight; (einer Laufbahn, des Ruhms) peak; pinnacle; (Orgasmus; eines Stückes) climax

höher /'hø:ɐ/ ▶ HOCH

hohl *Adj.* hollow

Höhle *die;* ∼, ∼n (a) cave; (größer) cavern (b) (Tierbau) lair

Hohl-: ∼**maß** *das* measure of capacity; ∼**raum** *der* cavity; [hollow] space; ∼**spiegel** *der* concave mirror

Hohn *der;* ∼[e]s scorn; derision

höhnen (geh.) *itr. V.* jeer

höhnisch ⓵ *Adj.* scornful ⓶ *adv.* scornfully

Hokuspokus *der;* ∼: hocus-pocus; (abwertend: Drum und Dran) fuss

hold *Adj.* (dichter. veralt.) fair; lovely; lovely ⟨*sight, smile*⟩

holen ⓵ *tr. V.* (a) fetch; get (b) (ab∼) fetch (c) (ugs.: erlangen) get ⟨*prize etc.*⟩; carry off ⟨*medal, trophy, etc.*⟩ ⓶ *refl. V.* (ugs.: sich zuziehen) catch; **sich** (*Dat.*) **[beim Baden] einen Schnupfen** ∼: catch a cold [swimming]

Holland (*das*); ∼s Holland

Holländer *der;* ∼s, ∼: Dutchman

Holländerin *die;* ∼, ∼nen Dutchwoman

holländisch *Adj.* Dutch

Hölle *die;* ∼, ∼n hell *no art.*

Höllen·lärm *der* (ugs.) diabolical noise *or* row (coll.)

---

höllisch 1 *Adj.* **(a)** infernal; ⟨*spirits, torments*⟩ of hell
(b) (ugs.: sehr groß) tremendous (coll.)
2 *adv.* (ugs.: sehr) hellishly (coll.)
Holm *der;* ∼[e]s, ∼e (Turnen) bar
Holocaust *der;* ∼[s] Holocaust
holpern *itr. V. mit sein* (fahren) jolt; bump
holprig *Adj.* **(a)** bumpy; rough
(b) (stockend) halting ⟨*speech*⟩; clumsy ⟨*verses, style, language, etc.*⟩
Holunder *der;* ∼s, ∼: elder
Holz *das;* ∼es, Hölzer wood; (Bau∼, Tischler∼) timber; wood
Holz-: ∼**bein** *das* wooden leg; ∼**bläser** *der,* **Holz·bläserin** *die* woodwind player
hölzern *Adj.* (auch fig.) wooden
holz-, Holz-: ∼**fäller** *der;* ∼∼s, ∼∼: woodcutter; lumberjack (Amer.); ∼**frei** *Adj.* wood-free ⟨*paper*⟩
holzig *Adj.* woody
Holz-: ∼**klotz** *der* block of wood; (als Spielzeug) wooden block; ∼**kohle** *die* charcoal; ∼**kopf** *der* (salopp abwertend) blockhead; ∼**pantoffel** *der* clog; ∼**scheit** *das* piece of wood; (Brenn∼) piece of firewood; ∼**schnitt** *der* **(a)** (Technik) woodcutting *no art.;* **(b)** (Blatt) woodcut; ∼**schuh** *der* clog; ∼**stoß** *der* pile of wood; ∼**weg** *der:* auf dem ∼weg sein be on the wrong track (fig.); ∼**wolle** *die* wood wool; ∼**wurm** *der* woodworm
Home-: ∼**banking** /'hoʊmbɛŋkɪŋ/ *das;* ∼∼s home banking; ∼**page** /'hoʊmpeɪdʒ/ *die;* ∼∼, ∼∼s (DV) home page
homogen *Adj.* homogeneous
homöopathisch *Adj.* homoeopathic
Homo·sexualität *die;* ∼: homosexuality
homo·sexuell 1 *Adj.* homosexual
2 *adv.* ∼ veranlagt sein have homosexual tendencies
Honig *der;* ∼s, ∼e honey
Honig·kuchen *der* honey cake
Honig·wabe *die* honeycomb
Honorar *das;* ∼s, ∼e fee; (Autoren∼) royalty
Honoratioren /honora'tsi̯oːrən/ *Pl.* notabilities
honorieren *tr. V.* **(a)** jmdn. ∼: pay sb. [a/his/her fee]
(b) (würdigen) appreciate; (belohnen) reward
Hopfen *der;* ∼s, ∼: hop; bei ihm ist ∼ und Malz verloren (ugs.) he's a hopeless case
hopp *Interj.* quick; look sharp
hoppeln *itr. V.; mit sein* hop; (über + *Akk.* across, over)
hoppla *Interj.* oops; whoops
hopsen *itr. V.; mit sein* (ugs.) (springen) jump; (hüpfen) ⟨*animal*⟩ hop; ⟨*child*⟩ skip; ⟨*ball*⟩ bounce
Hopser *der;* ∼s, ∼ (ugs.) [little] jump
Hör·apparat *der* hearing aid

hörbar 1 *Adj.* audible
2 *adv.* audibly; (geräuschvoll) noisily
Hör·buch *das* audiobook
horchen *itr. V.* listen (auf + *Akk.* to); (heimlich zuhören) eavesdrop
Horde *die;* ∼, ∼n horde; (von Halbstarken) mob
hören 1 *tr. V.* hear; (anhören) listen to
2 *itr. V.* hear; (zuhören) listen; auf jmdn./ jmds. Rat ∼: listen to sb./sb.'s advice
Hören·sagen *das:* vom ∼: from hearsay
Hörer *der;* ∼s, ∼ **(a)** listener
(b) (Telefon∼) receiver
Hörerin *die;* ∼, ∼nen listener
Hörerschaft *die;* ∼, ∼en audience
Hör-: ∼**fehler** *der* **(a)** das war ein ∼fehler he/she *etc.* misheard; **(b)** (Schwerhörigkeit) hearing defect; ∼**funk** *der* radio; im ∼funk on the radio; ∼**funk·sendung** *die* radio programme; ∼**gerät** *das* hearing aid
hörig *Adj.:* jmdm. ∼ sein be submissively dependent on sb.; (sexuell) be sexually enslaved to sb.
Horizont *der;* ∼[e]s, ∼e (auch Geol., fig.) horizon
horizontal 1 *Adj.* horizontal
2 *adv.* horizontally
Horizontale *die;* ∼, ∼n **(a)** (Linie) horizontal line
(b) (Lage) die ∼: the horizontal
Hormon *das;* ∼s, ∼e hormone
Horn *das;* ∼[e]s, Hörner horn
Hörnchen *das;* ∼s, ∼ (Gebäck) croissant
Horn·haut *die* **(a)** callus; hard skin *no indef. art.*
(b) (am Auge) cornea
Hornisse *die;* ∼, ∼n hornet
Horoskop *das;* ∼s, ∼e horoscope
horrend *Adj.* shocking (coll.), horrendous (coll.) ⟨*price*⟩; colossal (coll.) ⟨*sum, amount, rent*⟩
Hör·rohr *das* stethoscope
Horror *der;* ∼s horror
Horror-: ∼**film** *der* horror film; ∼**roman** *der* horror novel
Hör-: ∼**saal** *der* lecture theatre *or* hall; ∼**spiel** *das* radio play
Horst *der;* ∼[e]s, ∼e eyrie
Hort *der;* ∼[e]s, ∼e ▸ KINDERHORT
horten *tr. V.* hoard; stockpile ⟨*raw materials*⟩
Hortensie /hɔr'tɛnzi̯ə/ *die;* ∼, ∼n hydrangea
Hör·weite *die:* in/außer ∼weite in/out of earshot
Höschen /'høːsçən/ *das;* ∼s, ∼: trousers *pl.;* pair of trousers; (kurzes ∼) shorts *pl.;* pair of shorts
Hose *die;* ∼, ∼n **(a)** trousers *pl.;* pants *pl.* (Amer.); (Unter∼) pants *pl.;* (Freizeit∼) slacks *pl.;* (Bund∼) breeches *pl.;* (Reit∼) ···❯

riding breeches *pl.;* **eine** ∼: a pair of trousers/pants/slacks *etc.*
(b) (fig.) **die** ∼**n anhaben** (ugs.) wear the trousers; **die** ∼**n runterlassen** (salopp) come clean (coll.); **in die** ∼**[n] gehen** (salopp) be a [complete] flop (coll.); **es ist tote** ∼ (Jugendspr.) there's nothing doing (coll.)

Hosen-: ∼**anzug** *der* trouser suit (Brit.); pant suit; ∼**matz** *der;* ∼∼**es,** ∼∼**e** *od.* ∼**mätze** (ugs. scherzh.) toddler; ∼**rock** *der* culottes *pl.;* ∼**tasche** *die* trouser pocket; pants pocket (Amer.); ∼**träger** *Pl.* braces; suspenders (Amer.); pair of braces/suspenders

Hospital *das;* ∼**s,** ∼**e** *od.* **Hospitäler** hospital

Hospiz *das;* ∼**es,** ∼**e** hospice

Hostie /'hɔstiə/ *die;* ∼, ∼**n** (christl. Rel.) host

Hotel *das;* ∼, ∼**s** hotel

Hotel·bar *die* hotel bar

Hotel garni /- gar'ni:/ *das;* ∼ ∼, ∼**s** ∼**s** /- gar'ni:/ bed-and-breakfast hotel

Hotelier /hotɛ'lje:/ *der;* ∼**s,** ∼**s** hotelier

Hotline /'hɔtlaɪn/ *die;* ∼, ∼**s** hotline

hüben *Adv.* over here

hübsch ⬚**1** *Adj.* pretty; nice ⟨*area, flat, voice, tune, etc.*⟩; nice-looking ⟨*boy, person*⟩; **ein** ∼**es Sümmchen** (ugs.) a tidy sum (coll.); a nice little sum; **das ist eine** ∼**e Geschichte** (ugs. iron.) this is a fine *or* pretty kettle of fish (coll.)
⬚**2** *adv.* prettily; (ugs.: sehr) ∼ **kalt** perishing cold

Hub·schrauber *der;* ∼**s,** ∼: helicopter

Hubschrauber·lande·platz *der* heliport; (kleiner) helicopter pad; landing pad

huckepack *Adv.* jmdn. ∼ **tragen** (ugs.) give sb. a piggyback

hudeln *itr. V.* (bes. südd., österr.) be sloppy **(bei in)**

Huf *der;* ∼**[e]s,** ∼**e** hoof

huf-, Huf-: ∼**eisen** *das* horseshoe; ∼**eisen·förmig** ⬚**1** *Adj.* horseshoe-shaped; ⬚**2** *adv.* in [the shape of] a horseshoe; ∼**schmied** *der* farrier

Hüfte *die;* ∼, ∼**n** hip

Hüft-: ∼**gelenk** *das* (Anat.) hip joint; ∼**gürtel** *der* girdle

Hügel *der;* ∼**s,** ∼ hill

hügelig *Adj.* hilly

Huhn *das;* ∼**[e]s,** **Hühner** chicken; (Henne) chicken; hen

Hühnchen *das;* ∼**s,** ∼: small chicken; **mit** jmdm. [noch] ein ∼ zu rupfen haben (ugs.) [still] have a bone to pick with sb.

Hühner-: ∼**auge** *das* (am Fuß) corn; ∼**brühe** *die* chicken broth

hui /hui/ *Interj.* whoosh

huldigen *itr. V.* jmdm. ∼: pay tribute to sb.

Huldigung *die;* ∼, ∼**en** tribute

Hülle *die;* ∼, ∼**n** cover

hüllen *tr. V.* (geh.) wrap

Hülse *die;* ∼, ∼**n** (a) case
(b) (Bot.) pod

Hülsen·frucht *die* (a) (Frucht) fruit of a leguminous plant; **Hülsenfrüchte** pulse *sing.*
(b) (Pflanze) legume; leguminous plant

human *Adj.* humane

Humanismus *der;* ∼: humanism; (Epoche) Humanism *no art.*

humanitär *Adj.* humanitarian

Humbug *der;* ∼**s** (ugs.) humbug

Hummel *die;* ∼, ∼**n** bumble-bee

Hummer *der;* ∼**s,** ∼: lobster

Humor *der;* ∼**s** humour; (Sinn für ∼) sense of humour; **den** ∼ **nicht verlieren** remain good-humoured

Humorist *der;* ∼**en,** ∼**en, Humoristin** *die;* ∼, ∼**nen** (a) (Autor[in]) humorist
(b) (Vortragskünstler[in]) comedian

humoristisch *Adj.* humorous

humor-: ∼**los** *Adj.* humourless; ∼**losigkeit** *die;* ∼∼: humourlessness; lack of humour; ∼**voll** *Adj.* humorous

humpeln *itr. V.* (a) auch mit sein walk with a limp
(b) *mit sein* (sich ∼d fortbewegen) limp

Hund *der;* ∼**es,** ∼**e** (a) dog; **auf den** ∼ **kommen** (ugs.) go to the dogs (coll.); **vor die** ∼**e gehen** (ugs.) go to the dogs (coll.); (sterben) kick the bucket (coll.)
(b) (abwertend) bastard (sl.)

hunde-, Hunde-: ∼**elend** *Adj.* (ugs.) [really] wretched *or* awful; ∼**hütte** *die* [dog] kennel; ∼**kuchen** *der* dog biscuit; ∼**müde** *Adj.* (ugs.) dog-tired; ∼**rasse** *die* breed of dog

hundert *Kardinalz.* (a) a *or* one hundred
(b) (ugs.: viele) hundreds of

Hundert¹ *das;* ∼**s,** ∼**e** hundred

Hundert² *die;* ∼, ∼**en** hundred

Hunderter *der;* ∼**s,** ∼ (ugs.) hundred-euro/-dollar *etc.* note

Hundert·euro·schein *der* hundred-euro note

hundert·mal *Adv.* a hundred times; **auch wenn du dich** ∼ **beschwerst** (ugs.) however much you complain

Hundert·meter·lauf *der* (Leichtathletik) hundred metres *sing.*

hundert·prozentig ⬚**1** *Adj.*
(a) [one-]hundred per cent *attrib.*
(b) (ugs.: völlig) a hundred per cent
(c) (ugs.: ganz sicher) absolutely reliable
⬚**2** *adv.* (ugs.) **ich bin nicht** ∼ **sicher** I'm not a hundred per cent sure

hundertst... /'hʊndɛtst.../ *Ordinalz.* hundredth

hundertstel /'hʊndɛtstl/ *Bruchz.* hundredth

Hundertstel *das* (schweiz. meist *der*); ∼**s,** ∼: hundredth

---

* old spelling – see note on page x

hundert·tausend *Kardinalz.* a *or* one hundred thousand

Hunde-: ∼**scheiße** *die* (derb) dog shit (coarse); ∼**steuer** *die* dog licence fee; ∼**zwinger** *der* dog run

Hündin *die;* ∼, ∼**nen** bitch

Hüne *der;* ∼**n**, ∼**n** giant

Hünen·grab *das* megalithic tomb; (Hügelgrab) barrow

Hunger *der;* ∼**s (a)** ∼ bekommen/haben get/be hungry
(b) (geh.: Verlangen) hunger; (nach Ruhm, Macht) craving

Hunger·kur *die* starvation diet

hungern *itr. V.* go hungry; starve; **nach etw.** ∼: (fig.) hunger for sth.

Hungers·not *die* famine

Hunger-: ∼**streik** *der* hunger strike; ∼**tuch** *das:* am ∼**tuch nagen** (ugs. scherzh.) be on the breadline

hungrig *Adj.* (auch geh. fig.) hungry (**nach** for)

Hupe *die;* ∼, ∼**n** horn

hupen *itr. V.* sound one's horn; **dreimal** ∼: hoot three times

hüpfen *itr. V.; mit sein* hop; ⟨*ball*⟩ bounce

Hürde *die;* ∼, ∼**n** hurdle

Hürden·lauf *der* (Leichtathletik) hurdling; (Wettbewerb) hurdles *pl.*

Hure *die;* ∼, ∼**n** (abwertend) whore

huren *itr. V.* (abwertend) whore

hurra *Interj.* hurray; hurrah; ∼/**Hurra schreien** cheer

Hurra *das;* ∼**s**, ∼**s** cheer

hurtig ⬚1⬚ *Adj.* rapid
⬚2⬚ *adv.* quickly

huschen *itr. V.; mit sein* (lautlos u. leichtfüßig) ⟨*person*⟩ steal; (lautlos u. schnell) dart; ⟨*mouse, lizard, etc.*⟩ dart; ⟨*smile*⟩ flit; ⟨*light*⟩ flash; ⟨*shadow*⟩ slide quickly

hüsteln *itr. V.* give a slight cough

husten ⬚1⬚ *itr. V.* cough; (Husten haben) have a cough
⬚2⬚ *tr. V.* cough up ⟨*blood, phlegm*⟩

Husten *der;* ∼**s**, ∼: cough

Husten-: ∼**anfall** *der* coughing fit; fit of coughing; ∼**bonbon** *das* cough drop; ∼**reiz** *der* tickling in the throat; ∼**saft** *der* cough syrup; cough mixture; ∼**tropfen** *Pl.* cough drops

Hut¹ *der;* ∼**es**, **Hüte** hat; (fig.) **da geht einem/mir der** ∼ **hoch** (ugs.) it makes you/me mad (coll.); **das kann er sich** (*Dat.*)

an den ∼ **stecken** (ugs. abwertend) he can keep it (coll.)

Hut² *die;* ∼ (geh.) keeping; care; **auf der** ∼ **sein** be on one's guard

hüten ⬚1⬚ *tr. V.* look after; tend ⟨*sheep, cattle, etc.*⟩
⬚2⬚ *refl. V.* be on one's guard

Hut·schnur *die:* **das geht mir über die** ∼ (ugs.) that's going too far

Hütte *die;* ∼, ∼**n (a)** hut; (ärmliches Haus) shack; hut
(b) (Eisen∼) iron [and steel] works *sing.* or *pl.*
(c) (Jagd∼) [hunting] lodge

Hütten-: ∼**käse** *der* cottage cheese; ∼**schuh** *der* slipper sock

Hyäne *die;* ∼, ∼**n** hyena

Hyazinthe *die;* ∼, ∼**n** hyacinth

Hydrant *der;* ∼**en**, ∼**en** hydrant

Hydrat *das;* ∼**[e]s**, ∼**e** (Chemie) hydrate

Hydraulik *die;* ∼ (Technik) **(a)** (Theorie) hydraulics *sing., no art.*
(b) (Vorrichtungen) hydraulics *pl.*

hydraulisch (Technik) ⬚1⬚ *Adj.* hydraulic
⬚2⬚ *adv.* hydraulically

Hydro·kultur *die* (Gartenbau) hydroponics *sing.*

Hygiene *die;* ∼ **(a)** (Gesundheitspflege) health care
(b) (Sauberkeit) hygiene

hygienisch ⬚1⬚ *Adj.* hygienic
⬚2⬚ *adv.* hygienically

Hymne /'hʏmnə/ *die;* ∼, ∼**n** hymn; (National∼) national anthem

hyper·aktiv /'hy:pɐ-/ ⬚1⬚ *Adj.* hyperactive
⬚2⬚ *adv.* hyperactively

Hypnose *die;* ∼, ∼**n** hypnosis

hypnotisieren *tr. V.* hypnotize

Hypochonder /hypo'xɔndɐ/ *der;* ∼**s**, ∼, **Hypochonderin** *die;* ∼, ∼**nen** hypochondriac

hypochondrisch *Adj.* hypochondriac

Hypotenuse *die;* ∼, ∼**n** (Math.) hypotenuse

Hypothek *die;* ∼, ∼**en** (Bankw.) mortgage; (fig.) burden

Hypothese *die;* ∼, ∼**n** hypothesis

hypothetisch ⬚1⬚ *Adj.* hypothetical
⬚2⬚ *adv.* hypothetically

Hysterie *die;* ∼, ∼**n** hysteria

hysterisch ⬚1⬚ *Adj.* hysterical
⬚2⬚ *adv.* hysterically

Ii

i, I /iː/ *das;* ~, ~ i/I; **das Tüpfelchen** *od.* **der Punkt auf dem** ~ (fig.) the final touch

i *Interj.* ugh; **i bewahre, i wo** (ugs.) [good] heavens, no!

i.A. *Abk.* = **im Auftrag[e]** p.p.

IC *Abk.* = **Intercity** IC

ICE *Abk.* = **Intercityexpress[zug]** ICE

ich *Personalpron.; 1. Pers. Sg. Nom.* I; **immer** ~ (ugs.) [it's] always me; ~ **nicht** not me; **Menschen wie du und** ~: people like you and me; *s. auch* (*Gen.*) MEINER, (*Dat.*) MIR, (*Akk.*) MICH

Ich *das;* ~[s], ~[s] (a) self (b) (Psych.) ego

Ichform *die* first person

Icon /'aɪkən/ *das;* ~s, ~s (DV) icon

ideal 1 *Adj.* ideal 2 *adv.* ideally

Ideal *das;* ~s, ~e ideal

Ideal-: ~**bild** *das* ideal; ~**fall** *der* ideal case; ~**gewicht** *das* ideal weight

idealisieren *tr. V.* idealize

Idealismus *der;* ~ (auch Philos.) idealism

Idealist *der;* ~en, ~en, **Idealistin** *die;* ~, ~nen idealist

idealistisch (auch Philos.) 1 *Adj.* idealistic 2 *adv.* idealistically

Idee *die;* ~, ~n (a) idea (b) (ein bisschen) **eine** ~: a shade; **eine** ~ **[Salz/Pfeffer]** a touch [of salt/pepper]

ideell *Adj.* non-material; (geistig-seelisch) spiritual

ideen-los *Adj.* [completely] lacking in ideas *postpos.*

Identifikation /idɛntifika'tsi̯oːn/ *die;* ~, ~en (auch Psych.) identification

identifizieren 1 *tr. V.* identify 2 *refl. V.* (auch Psych.) **sich mit jmdm./etw.** ~: identify with sb./sth.

identisch *Adj.* identical

Identität *die;* ~: identity

Identitäts-: ~**diebstahl** *der* identity theft; ~**krise** *die* identity crisis

Ideologe *der;* ~n, ~n ideologue

Ideologie *die;* ~, ~n /-iːən/ ideology

Ideologin *die;* ~, ~nen ideologue

ideologisch 1 *Adj.* ideological 2 *adv.* ideologically

Idiot *der;* ~en, ~en (auch ugs. abwertend) idiot

---

idioten-, Idioten-: ~**hügel** *der* (ugs. scherzh.) nursery slope; ~**sicher** *Adj.* (ugs. scherzh.) foolproof

Idiotie *die;* ~, ~n /-iːən/ (a) idiocy (b) (ugs. abwertend: Dummheit) madness

Idiotin *die;* ~, ~nen (auch ugs. abwertend) idiot

idiotisch 1 *Adj.* (a) (Psych.) severely subnormal (b) (ugs. abwertend) idiotic 2 *adv.* (auch ugs. abwertend) idiotically

Idol *das;* ~s, ~e (auch bild. Kunst) idol

Idyll *das;* ~s, ~e idyll

Idylle *die;* ~, ~n idyll

idyllisch *Adj.* idyllic

Igel *der;* ~s, ~: hedgehog

Iglu *der od. das;* ~s, ~s igloo

Ignoranz /igno'rants/ *die;* ~: ignorance

ignorieren *tr. V.* ignore

ihm *Dat. von* ER, ES: (bei männlichen Personen) him; (bei weiblichen Personen) her; (bei Dingen, Tieren) it; **gib es** ~: give it to him; give him it; **Freunde von** ~: friends of his

ihn *Akk. von* ER (bei männlichen Personen) him; (bei Dingen, Tieren) it

ihnen *Dat. von* SIE, *Pl.* them; **gib es** ~: give it to them; give them it; **Freunde von** ~: friends of theirs

Ihnen *Dat. von* SIE you; **ich habe es** ~ **gegeben** I gave it to you; **Freunde von** ~: friends of yours

ihr¹ /iːɐ̯/ *Dat. von* SIE, *Sg.* (bei Personen) her; (bei Dingen, Tieren) it

ihr² *Personalpron.; 2. Pers. Pl. Nom.* you

ihr³ *Possessivpron.* (a) *Sg.* (einer Person) her; (eines Tieres, einer Sache) its (b) *Pl.* their

Ihr *Possessivpron.* (Anrede) your; ~ **Hans Meier** (Briefschluss) yours, Hans Meier; **welcher Mantel ist** ~**er?** which coat is yours?

ihrer (a) *Gen. von* SIE, *Sg.* (geh.) **wir gedachten** ~: we remembered her (b) *Gen. von* SIE, *Pl.* (geh.) **wir werden** ~ **gedenken** we will remember them; **es waren** ~ **zwölf** there were twelve of them

Ihrer *Gen. von* SIE (geh.) **wir werden** ~ **gedenken** we will remember you

ihrerseits *Adv.* for her/their part; (von ihr/ihnen) on her/their part

Ihrerseits *Adv.:* ▶ DEINERSEITS

ihres·gleichen *indekl. Pron.* people *pl.* like her/them; (abwertend) the likes of her/them

Ihres·gleichen *indekl. Pron.* people *pl.* like you; (abwertend) the likes of you

ihret·wegen *Adv.:* ▸ MEINETWEGEN: because of her/them; for her/their sake; about her/them; as far as she is/they are concerned

Ihret·wegen *Adv.:* ▸ DEINETWEGEN

Ikone *die;* ∼, ∼n icon

illegal ⓵ *Adj.* illegal
⓶ *adv.* illegally

Illegalität *die;* ∼, ∼en illegality

illegitim *Adj.* (geh.) illegitimate

illuminieren *tr. V.* illuminate

Illusion *die;* ∼, ∼en illusion

illusorisch *Adj.* illusory; (zwecklos) pointless

Illustration *die;* ∼, ∼en illustration

illustrieren *tr. V.* illustrate

Illustrierte *die; adj.* ▸ *Dekl.* magazine

Iltis *der;* ∼ses, ∼se polecat; (Pelz) fitch

im *Präp. + Art.* (a) = in dem;
(b) (räumlich) in the; **im Theater** at the theatre; **im Fernsehen** on television; **im Bett** in bed
(c) (zeitlich) **im Mai** in May; **im letzten Jahr** last year; **im Alter von** … at the age of …
(d) (Verlauf) etw. **im Sitzen tun** do sth. [while] sitting down; **im Gehen sein** be going

Image /'ɪmɪtʃ/ *das;* ∼[s], ∼s image

imaginär *Adj.* (geh., Math.) imaginary

Imbiss, *Imbiß *der;* Imbisses, Imbisse
(a) (kleine Mahlzeit) snack
(b) ▸ IMBISSSTUBE

Imbiss·stube, *Imbiß·stube *die* café

Imitation *die;* ∼, ∼en imitation

imitieren *tr. V.* imitate

Imker *der;* ∼s, ∼, **Imkerin** *die;* ∼, ∼nen bee-keeper

Immatrikulation *die;* ∼, ∼en (Hochschulw.) registration

immatrikulieren *tr., refl. V.* (Hochschulw.) register

immer *Adv.* (a) always; **schon** ∼: always; ∼ **wieder** time and time again; ∼, **wenn** every time that
(b) immer + *Komp.:* ∼ **dunkler** darker and darker; ∼ **mehr** more and more
(c) (ugs.: jeweils) ∼ **drei Stufen auf einmal** three steps at a time
(d) (auch) **wo/wer/wann/wie [auch]** ∼: wherever/whoever/whenever/however
(e) (verstärkend) ∼ **noch, noch** ∼: still
(f) (ugs.: bei Aufforderung) ∼ **geradeaus!** keep [going] straight on

immer-, Immer-: ∼**fort** *Adv.* all the time; ∼**grün** *Adj.* evergreen; ∼**grün** *das* periwinkle; ∼**hin** *Adv.* (a) (wenigstens) at any rate; (b) (trotz allem) all the same; (c) (schließlich) after all; ∼**zu** *Adv.* (ugs.) the whole time

Immigrant *der;* ∼en, ∼en,
Immigrantin *die;* ∼, ∼nen immigrant

Immigration *die;* ∼, ∼en immigration

immigrieren *itr. V.; mit sein* immigrate

Immobilien *Pl.* property *sing.;* real estate *sing.*

immun (a) (Med., fig.) immune (**gegen** to)
(b) (Rechtsspr.) ∼ **sein** have immunity

Immunität *die;* ∼, ∼en (a) (Med.) immunity (**gegen** to)
(b) (Rechtsspr.) immunity (**gegen** from)

Immun-: ∼**schwäche** *die* (Med.) immunodeficiency; immune deficiency; ∼**therapie** *die* (Med.) immunotherapy; immune therapy

Imperativ *der;* ∼s, ∼e (a) (Sprachw.) imperative
(b) (Philos.) **[kategorischer] ∼:** [categorical] imperative

Imperfekt *das;* ∼s, ∼e (Sprachw.) imperfect [tense]

Imperialismus *der;* ∼: imperialism *no art.*

imperialistisch *Adj.* imperialistic

Imperium *das;* ∼s, Imperien (hist., fig.) empire

impfen *tr. V.* vaccinate; inoculate

Impf-: ∼**pass, *∼paß** *der* vaccination certificate; ∼**stoff** *der* vaccine

Impfung *die;* ∼, ∼en vaccination

implantieren *tr. V.* (Med.) implant

imponieren *itr. V.* impress

imponierend ⓵ *Adj.* impressive
⓶ *adv.* impressively

Imponier·gehabe *das* (Verhaltensf.) display; (fig.) showing off

Import *der;* ∼[e]s, ∼e import

Importeur /ɪmpɔr'tøːɐ̯/ *der;* ∼s, ∼e,
Importeurin *die;* ∼, ∼nen importer

importieren *tr., itr. V.* import

imposant ⓵ *Adj.* imposing; impressive ⟨*achievement*⟩
⓶ *adv.* imposingly

impotent *Adj.* impotent

Impotenz *die;* ∼: impotence

imprägnieren *tr. V.* impregnate; (wasserdicht machen) waterproof

Improvisation *die;* ∼, ∼en improvisation

improvisieren *tr., itr. V.* improvise

Impuls *der;* ∼es, ∼e stimulus; (innere Regung) impulse

impulsiv ⓵ *Adj.* impulsive
⓶ *adv.* impulsively

imstande *Adv.* ∼ **sein, etw. zu tun** be able to do sth.

in¹ ⓵ *Präp. mit Dat.* (auf die Frage: wo?/ wann?/wie?) in; **er hat** ∼ **Tübingen studiert** he studied at Tübingen; *s. auch* IM
⓶ *Präp. mit Akk.* (auf die Frage: wohin?) into; *s. auch* INS

in² *Adj.:* ∼ **sein** (ugs.) be in

In·anspruchnahme *die;* ∼, ∼n (starke Belastung) demands *pl.*

In·begriff der quintessence
inbegriffen Adj. included
In·betrieb·nahme die; ~, ~n,
In·betrieb·setzung die; ~, ~n
bringing into service
In·brunst die; ~ (geh.) fervour; (der Liebe)
ardour
in·brünstig (geh.) 1 Adj. fervent; ardent
⟨love⟩
2 adv. fervently; ⟨love⟩ ardently
in·dem Konj. (a) (während) while; (gerade
als) as
(b) (dadurch, dass) ~ man etw. tut by doing
sth.
Inder der; ~s, ~, **Inderin** die; ~, ~nen
Indian
in·dessen 1 Konj. (geh.) (a) (während)
while
(b) (wohingegen) whereas
2 Adv. (a) (inzwischen) meanwhile; in the
mean time
(b) (jedoch) however
Index der; ~ od. ~es, ~e od. Indizes (a) Pl.
~e od. Indizes (Register) index
(b) Pl. ~e (kath. Kirche) Index
Indianer der; ~s, ~: [American] Indian
Indianer·häuptling der Indian chief
Indianerin die; ~, ~nen [American]
Indian
indianisch Adj. Indian
Indien /'ɪndiən/ (das); ~s India
in·different Adj. indifferent
Indikativ der; ~s, ~e /-i:və/ (Sprachw.)
indicative [mood]
Indikator der; ~s, ~en (auch Chemie,
Technik) indicator
in·direkt 1 Adj. indirect
2 adv. indirectly
indisch Adj. Indian
in·diskret Adj. indiscreet
In·diskretion die; ~, ~en indiscretion
Individualist der; ~en, ~en,
Individualistin die; ~, ~nen (geh.)
individualist
Individualität die; ~, ~en (geh.)
(a) individuality
(b) (Persönlichkeit) personality
individuell 1 Adj. individual; private
⟨property, vehicle, etc.⟩
2 adv. individually
Individuum das; ~s, Individuen (auch
Chemie, Biol.) individual
Indiz das; ~es, ~ien (a) (Rechtsw.)
piece of circumstantial evidence; ~ien
circumstantial evidence sing.
(b) (Anzeichen) sign (für of)
Indizes ▸ INDEX
Indizien·beweis der (Rechtsw.) piece of
circumstantial evidence; ~e circumstantial
evidence sing.

indoktrinieren tr. V. indoctrinate
Indonesien /ɪndo'ne:ziən/ (das); ~s
Indonesia
Indonesier der; ~s, ~, **Indonesierin**
die; ~, ~nen Indonesian
indonesisch Adj. Indonesian
industrialisieren tr. V. industrialize
Industrialisierung die;
~: industrialization
Industrie die; ~, ~n industry
Industrie-: ~betrieb der industrial
firm; ~gebiet das industrial area;
~kauffrau die, ~kaufmann der:
person with three years' business training
employed on the business side of an
industrial company
industriell 1 Adj. industrial
2 adv. industrially
Industrielle der/die; adj. Dekl.
industrialist
Industrie-: ~staat der industrial
nation; ~stadt die industrial town
Industrie- und Handels·kammer
die Chamber of Industry and Commerce
Industriezweig der branch of industry
in·einander Adv. ~ greifen mesh together
(lit. or fig); ~ verliebt sein be in love with
each other or one another; ~ verschlungene
Ornamente intertwined decorations
*ineinander|greifen ▸ INEINANDER
infam 1 Adj. disgraceful
2 adv. disgracefully
Infanterie die; ~, ~n (Milit.) infantry
infantil (Psych., Med., sonst abwertend) 1 Adj.
infantile
2 adv. in an infantile way
Infarkt der; ~[e]s, ~e (Med.) infarction
Infekt der; ~[e]s, ~e (Med.) infection
Infektion die; ~, ~en (Med.)
(a) (Ansteckung) infection
(b) (ugs.: Entzündung) inflammation
Infektions-: ~gefahr die (Med.) risk
of infection; ~herd der (Med.) seat of
the/an infection; ~krankheit die (Med.)
infectious disease
Inferno das; ~s (geh.) inferno
Infinitiv der; ~s, ~e (Sprachw.) infinitive
infizieren 1 tr. V. infect
2 refl. V. become infected; sich bei jmdm.
~: be infected by sb.
in flagranti Adv. (geh.) in flagrante
[delicto]
Inflation die; ~, ~en (Wirtsch.) inflation;
(Zeit der ~) period of inflation
inflationär Adj. inflationary
Inflations·rate die inflation rate; rate of
inflation
in·folge 1 Präp. + Gen. as a result of
2 Adv. ~ von etw. (Dat.) as a result of sth.
infolge·dessen Adv. consequently

Informatik *die;* ~: computer science *no art.*

Informatiker *der;* ~s, ~,
Informatikerin *die;* ~, ~nen computer scientist

Information *die;* ~, ~en (a) information *no pl., no indef. art.* (**über** + *Akk.* about, on); **eine** ~: [a piece of] information
(b) (Büro) information bureau; (Stand) information desk

Informations-: ~**büro** *das* information bureau *or* office; ~**freiheit** *die* freedom of information; ~**material** *das* informational literature; ~**quelle** *die* source of information; ~**vielfalt** *die* variety of information

informativ *Adj.* informative

informieren [1] *tr. V.* inform (**über** + *Akk.* about)
[2] *refl. V.* inform oneself, find out (**über** + *Akk.* about)

in·frage: ~ **kommen** be possible; **das kommt nicht** ~ (ugs.) that is out of the question

Infra·rot *das* (Physik) infra-red radiation

Infra·struktur *die* infrastructure

Infusion *die;* ~, ~en (Med.) infusion

Ing. *Abk.* = **Ingenieur**

In·gebrauch·nahme *die;* ~, ~n: **vor** ~ **des Geräts** before operating the appliance

Ingenieur /ɪnʒe'niøːɐ̯/ *der;* ~s, ~e,
Ingenieurin *die;* ~, ~nen [qualified] engineer

Ingwer *der;* ~s, ~: ginger

Inhaber *der;* ~s, ~, **Inhaberin** *die;* ~, ~nen (a) holder
(b) (Besitzer) owner

inhaftieren *tr. V.* take into custody; detain

Inhaftierung *die;* ~, ~en detention

inhalieren *tr. V.* inhale

Inhalt *der;* ~[e]s, ~e (a) contents *pl.*
(b) (einer Geschichte usw.) content
(c) (bes. Math.) (Flächen~) area; (Raum~) volume

inhaltlich [1] *Adj.* **an** ~**en Gesichtspunkten gemessen** from the point of view of content
[2] *adv.* ~ **ist der Aufsatz gut** the essay is good as regards content; ~ **übereinstimmen** be the same in content

Inhalts-: ~**angabe** *die* summary [of contents]; synopsis; (eines Films, Dramas) synopsis; ~**verzeichnis** *das* table of contents; (auf einem Paket) list of contents

in·human *Adj.* (a) (unmenschlich) inhuman
(b) (rücksichtslos) inhumane

Initiale *die;* ~, ~n initial [letter]

Initiative *die;* ~, ~n initiative

Initiator *der;* ~s, ~en, **Initiatorin** *die;* ~, ~nen initiator; (einer Organisation) founder

Injektion *die;* ~, ~en (Med.) injection

injizieren *tr. V.* (Med.) inject

Inkarnation *die;* ~, ~en incarnation

inkl. *Abk.* = **inklusive** incl.

inklusive /ɪnklu'ziːvə/ [1] *Präp.* + *Gen.* (bes. Kaufmannsspr.) including
[2] *Adv.* inclusive

inkognito *Adv.* (geh.) incognito

in·kompetent *Adj.* incompetent

In·kompetenz *die* incompetence

in·konsequent [1] *Adj.* inconsistent
[2] *adv.* inconsistently

In·konsequenz *die* inconsistency

in·korrekt [1] *Adj.* incorrect
[2] *adv.* incorrectly

In·korrektheit *die;* ~, ~en
(a) (Fehlerhaftigkeit) incorrectness
(b) (Fehler) mistake

In·kraft·treten *das;* ~s: **mit** [dem] ~ **des Gesetzes** when the law comes/came into force

Inkubations·zeit *die;* ~, ~en (Med.) incubation period

In·land *das* (a) **im** ~: at home
(b) (Binnenland) interior; inland; **im/ins** ~: inland

inländisch *Adj.* domestic; home-produced ⟨goods⟩

Inlands-: ~**markt** *der* domestic market; ~**porto** *das* inland postage

in·mitten [1] *Präp.* + *Gen.* (geh.) in the midst of
[2] *Adv.* ~ **von** in the midst of

inne|haben *unr. tr. V.* hold, occupy ⟨position⟩; hold ⟨office⟩

innen *Adv.* inside; (auf/an der Innenseite) on the inside

innen-, Innen-: ~**architekt** *der,* ~**architektin** *die* interior designer; ~**aufnahme** *die* (Fot.) indoor photo[graph]; (Film) interior shot; ~**einrichtung** *die* furnishings *pl.;* ~**hof** *der* inner courtyard; ~**leben** *das* (a) [inner] thoughts and feelings *pl.;* (b) (oft scherzh.: Ausstattung) inside; ~**minister** *der,* ~**ministerin** *die* Minister of the Interior; ≈ Home Secretary (Brit.); ≈ Secretary of the Interior (Amer.); ~**ministerium** *das* Ministry of the Interior; ≈ Home Office (Brit.); ≈ Department of the Interior (Amer.); ~**politik** *die* (eines Staates) home affairs *pl.;* (einer Regierung) domestic policy/policies *pl.;* ~**politisch** ▸ ~POLITIK: [1] *Adj.* ~**politische Fragen** matters of domestic policy; [2] *adv.* as regards home affairs/ domestic policy; ~**stadt** *die* town centre; downtown (Amer.); (einer Großstadt) city centre

inner... *Adj.* inner; (inländisch; Med.) internal; inside ⟨pocket, lane⟩

Innere *das; adj. Dekl.* inside; (eines Gebäudes, Wagens, Schiffes) interior; inside; (eines Landes) interior

Innereien *Pl.* entrails; (Kochk.) offal *sing.* ⋯⋗

inner·halb ① *Präp.* + *Gen.* **(a)** within; ∼ **der Familie/Partei** (fig.) within the family/party
(b) (binnen) within; ∼ **einer Woche** within a week
② *Adv.* **(a)** ∼ **von** within
(b) (im Verlauf) ∼ **von zwei Jahren** within two years
innerlich ① *Adj.* inner
② *adv.* inwardly
innerst... *Adj.* innermost
Innerste *das; adj. Dekl.* innermost being
inne|wohnen *itr. V.* (geh.) etw. wohnt jmdm./einer Sache ∼: sb./sth. possesses sth.
innig ① *Adj.* deep ⟨*affection, sympathy*⟩; fervent ⟨*wish*⟩; intimate ⟨*friendship*⟩; **mein** ∼**ster Dank** my sincerest thanks
② *adv.* ⟨*love*⟩ with all one's heart
Innigkeit *die;* ∼: depth; (einer Beziehung) intimacy
innovativ *Adj.* innovative
Innung /'ɪnʊŋ/ *die;* ∼, ∼**en** [trade] guild
in·offiziell ① *Adj.* unofficial
② *adv.* unofficially
in puncto as regards
ins *Präp.* + *Art.* **(a)** = in das
(b) (räumlich) to the; ∼ **Bett gehen** go to bed
(c) ∼ **Schlendern geraten** go into a skid
Insasse *der;* ∼**n**, ∼**n**, **Insassin** *die;* ∼, ∼**nen** **(a)** (Fahrgast) passenger
(b) (Bewohner[in]) inmate
ins·besond[e]re *Adv.* particularly; in particular
In·schrift *die* inscription
Insekt /ɪn'zɛkt/ *das;* ∼**s**, ∼**en** insect
Insel *die;* ∼, ∼**n** island
Insel-: ∼**bewohner** *der*, ∼**bewohnerin** *die* islander; ∼**gruppe** *die* group of islands; ∼**staat** *die* island state; ∼**welt** *die* islands *pl.*
Inserat *das;* ∼**[e]s**, ∼**e** advertisement (*in a newspaper*)
Inserent *der;* ∼**en**, ∼**en**, **Inserentin** *die;* ∼, ∼**nen** advertiser
inserieren *itr. V.* advertise
ins·geheim *Adv.* secretly
ins·gesamt *Adv.* in all; altogether; (alles in allem) all in all
insofern ① *Adv.* /ɪn'zo:fɛrn/ (in dieser Hinsicht) to this extent; ∼ **als** in so far as
② *Konj.* /ɪnzo'fɛrn/ (falls) provided [that]
Insolvenz·verfahren *das* insolvency proceedings *pl.*
insoweit ① *adv.* /ɪn'zo:vaɪt/ ▸ INSOFERN 1
② *Konj.* /ɪnzo'vaɪt/ ▸ INSOFERN 2
in spe /ɪn 'spe:/ future *attrib.;* **mein Schwiegersohn** ∼ ∼: my future son-in-law
Inspektion *die;* ∼, ∼**en** inspection; (Kfz-W.) service
Inspiration *die;* ∼, ∼**en** inspiration

inspirieren *tr. V.* inspire
inspizieren *tr. V.* inspect
Installateur /ɪnstala'tø:ɐ̯/ *der;* ∼**s**, ∼**e**, **Installateurin** *die;* ∼, ∼**nen** plumber; (Gas∼) [gas] fitter; (Heizungs∼) heating engineer; (Elektro∼) electrician
Installation *die;* ∼, ∼**en** installation; (Rohre) plumbing *no pl.*
installieren *tr. V.* install
in·stand *Adv.* etw. ist gut/schlecht ∼: sth. is in good/poor condition; **etw.** ∼ **halten** keep sth. in good condition; **etw.** ∼ **setzen/ bringen** repair sth.
Instand·haltung *die* maintenance
in·ständig ① *Adj.* urgent
② *adv.* urgently
Instand·setzung *die;* ∼, ∼**en** repair; (Renovierung) renovation
Instanz /ɪn'stants/ *die;* ∼, ∼**en** **(a)** authority
(b) (Rechtsw.) **[die] erste/zweite/dritte** ∼: the court of original jurisdiction/the appeal court/the court of final appeal; **durch alle** ∼**en gehen** go through all the courts
Instinkt /ɪn'stɪŋkt/ *der;* ∼**[e]s**, ∼**e** instinct
instinktiv ① *Adj.* instinctive
② *adv.* instinctively
Institut /ɪnstɪ'tu:t/ *das;* ∼**[e]s**, ∼**e** institute
Institution *die;* ∼, ∼**en** (auch fig.) institution
Instruktion /ɪnstrʊk'tsi̯o:n/ *die;* ∼, ∼**en** instruction
Instrument /ɪnstru'mɛnt/ *das;* ∼**[e]s**, ∼**e** instrument
instrumental (Musik) ① *Adj.* instrumental
② *adv.* instrumentally
Insulin *das;* ∼**s** insulin
inszenieren *tr. V.* stage; put on; (Regie führen bei) direct; (fig.) (einfädeln) engineer; (organisieren) stage
Inszenierung *die;* ∼, ∼**en** staging; (Regie) direction; (Aufführung) production
intakt *Adj.* **(a)** (unbeschädigt) intact
(b) (funktionsfähig) in [proper] working order *postpos.;* healthy ⟨*economy*⟩
integer *Adj.* **eine integre Persönlichkeit** a person of integrity; ∼ **sein** be a person of integrity
Integral *das;* ∼**s**, ∼**e** (Math.) integral
Integration *die;* ∼, ∼**en** (auch Math.) integration
integrieren *tr. V.* integrate
Intellekt *der;* ∼**[e]s** intellect
intellektuell *Adj.* intellectual
Intellektuelle *der/die; adj. Dekl.* intellectual
intelligent ① *Adj.* intelligent
② *adv.* intelligently
Intelligenz *die;* ∼, ∼**en** **(a)** intelligence
(b) (Gesamtheit der Intellektuellen) intelligentsia

Intelligenz-quotient der intelligence quotient

Intendant der; ~en, ~en, **Intendantin** die; ~, ~nen (Theater) manager and artistic director; (Fernseh~, Rundfunk~) director general

Intensität die; ~: intensity

intensiv ① Adj. (gründlich) intensive ⟨kräftig⟩ intense
② adv. intensively

intensivieren tr. V. intensify; increase ⟨exports⟩; strengthen ⟨connections⟩

Intensiv-station die intensive-care unit

interaktiv Adj. interactive

Intercityzug der inter-city train

interessant ① Adj. interesting
② adv. ~ schreiben write in an interesting way

interessanterweise Adv. interestingly enough

Interesse das; ~s, ~n interest; ~ an jmdm./etw. haben be interested in sb./sth.

interesse-halber Adv. out of interest

Interessen-gebiet das field of interest

Interessent der; ~en, ~en, **Interessentin** die; ~, ~nen interested person; (möglicher Käufer/mögliche Käuferin) potential buyer

Interessen-verband der [organized] interest group

Interessen-vertretung die
(a) representation
(b) (Vertreter von Interessen) representative body

interessieren ① refl. V. sich für jmdn./etw. ~: be interested in sb./sth.
② tr. V. interest; das interessiert mich nicht I'm not interested [in it]

interessiert Adj. interested (an + Dat. in)

Interjektion die; ~, ~en (Sprachw.) interjection

Inter-: ~kontinental-rakete die (Milit.) intercontinental ballistic missile; ~mezzo das; ~~s, ~~s od. ~mezzi (Theat., Musik) intermezzo; (fig.) interlude; intermezzo

intern ① Adj. internal
② adv. internally

Internat das; ~[e]s, ~e boarding school

inter-, Inter-: ~national ① Adj. international; ② adv. internationally; ~nationale die; ~, ~n (a) International; Internationale; (b) (Lied) Internationale

Internats-: ~schule die boarding school; ~schüler der, ~schülerin die boarding school pupil; boarder

Internet /'ɪntɐnɛt/ das; ~s Internet; im ~: on the Internet

internet, Internet: ~anbieter der, ~anbieterin die (DV) Internet provider; ~anschluss der, *~anschluß der (DV) Internet connection; connection to the Internet; einen ~anschluss haben be

connected to the Internet; ~fähig Adj. (DV) Internet-capable; Internet-enabled; ~seite die (DV) Internet page; eb page

internieren tr. V. (Milit.) intern

Internierung die; ~, ~en internment

Internist der; ~en, ~en, **Internistin** die; ~, ~nen (Med.) internist

Interpol die; ~: Interpol no art.

Interpret der; ~en, ~en interpreter ⟨of music, text, events, etc.⟩

Interpretation die; ~, ~en interpretation ⟨of music, text, events, etc.⟩

interpretieren tr. V. interpret ⟨music, texts, events, etc.⟩

Interpretin die; ~, ~nen ▶ INTERPRET

Interpunktion die; ~ (Sprachw.) punctuation

Intervall /ɪntɐ'val/ das; ~s, ~e (Musik, Math.) interval

intervenieren itr. V. (geh., Politik) intervene

Intervention die; ~, ~en (geh., Politik) intervention; (Protest) representations pl.

Interview /ɪntɐ'vjuː/ das; ~s, ~s interview

interviewen /ɪntɐ'vjuːən/ tr. V. interview

Interviewer der; ~s, ~, **Interviewerin** die; ~, ~nen interviewer

intialisieren tr. V. (DV) initialize

intim ① Adj. intimate
② adv. ~ befreundet sein be intimate friends

Intimität die; ~, ~en intimacy

Intim-: ~partner der, ~partnerin die intimate partner; sexual partner; ~sphäre die private life

in-tolerant Adj. intolerant

In-toleranz die intolerance (gegenüber of)

Intonation die; ~, ~en intonation

Intranet das ~s, ~s (DV) Intranet

in-transitiv ① Adj. (Sprachw.) intransitive
② adv. intransitively

intravenös (Med.) ① Adj. intravenous
② adv. intravenously

Intrige die; ~, ~n intrigue

Intuition die; ~, ~en intuition

intuitiv ① Adj. intuitive
② adv. intuitively

intus: etw. ~ haben (ugs.) (begriffen haben) have got sth. into one's head; (gegessen od. getrunken haben) have put sth. away (coll.)

Invalide der; adj. Dekl. invalid

Invasion die; ~, ~en invasion

Inventar das; ~s, ~e (einer Firma) fittings and equipment pl.; (eines Hauses, Büros) furnishings and fittings pl.

inventarisieren tr. V. inventory; draw up or make an inventory of

Inventur die; ~, ~en stock-taking

investieren tr., itr. V. (auch fig.) invest (in + Akk. in) ⋯⋗

Investition *die;* ~, ~en investment
Investitions-güter *Pl.* (Wirtsch.) capital goods
Investor *der;* ~s, ~en /-'to:rən/, **Investorin** *die;* ~, ~nen (Wirtsch.) investor
in·wie·fern *Adv.* in what way; (bis zu welchem Grade) to what extent
in·wie·weit *Adv.* to what extent
In·zahlung·nahme *die;* ~, ~n part exchange; trade in (Amer.)
Inzest *der;* ~[e]s, ~e incest
In·zucht *die;* ~: inbreeding
in·zwischen *Adv.* (a) (seither) in the meantime; since [then]
  (b) (bis zu einem Zeitpunkt) (in der Gegenwart) by now; (in der Vergangenheit/Zukunft) by then
  (c) (währenddessen) meanwhile
IOK *Abk.* Internationales Olympisches Komitee IOC
Ion /i:n/ *das;* ~s, ~en (Physik, Chemie) ion
ionisieren *tr. V.* (Physik, Chemie) ionize
Iono·sphäre *die* ionosphere
Irak *(das);* ~s *od. der;* ~[s] Iraq
Iraker *der;* ~s, ~, **Irakerin** *die;* ~, ~nen Iraqi
irakisch Iraqi
Irak·krieg *der* Iraq War
Iran *(das);* ~s *od. der;* ~[s] Iran
Iraner *der;* ~s, ~, **Iranerin** *die;* ~, ~nen Iranian
iranisch *Adj.* Iranian
irden *Adj.* earthen[ware]
irdisch *Adj.* (a) earthly; worldly ⟨*goods, pleasures, possessions*⟩
  (b) (zur Erde gehörig) terrestrial; *das* ~e Leben life on earth
Ire *der;* ~n, ~n Irishman
irgend *Adv.* (a) ~ so ein Politiker (ugs.) some politician [or other]; ~ so etwas something like that
  (b) (irgendwie) wenn ~ möglich if at all possible
irgend-: ~**ein** *Indefinitpron.* (a) *attr.* some; (fragend, verneinend) any; (b) *subst.* ~einer/~eine someone; somebody; (fragend, verneinend) anyone; anybody; ~eines *od.* (ugs.) ~eins any one; ~**einmal** *Adv.* sometime; ~**etwas** something; (fragend, verneinend) anything; ~**jemand** *Indefinitpron.* someone; somebody; (fragend, vereinend) anyone; anybody; ~**wann** *Adv.* [at] some time [or other]; (zu jeder beliebigen Zeit) [at] any time; ~**was** *Indefinitpron.* (ugs.) something [or other]; (fragend, verneinend) anything; ~**welch** *Indefinitpron.* some; (fragend, verneinend) any; ~**wer** *Indefinitpron.* (ugs.) somebody or other (coll.); (fragend, verneinend) anyone; anybody; ~**wie** *Adv.* somehow; ~**wo** *Adv.*

somewhere; (fragend, verneinend) anywhere; ~**woher** *Adv.* from somewhere; (fragend, verneinend) from anywhere; ~**wohin** *Adv.* somewhere; (fragend, verneinend) anywhere
Irin *die;* ~, ~nen Irishwoman
Iris *die;* ~, ~ (Bot., Anat.) iris
irisch *Adj.* Irish
Irland *(das);* ~s Ireland
Ironie *die;* ~, ~n irony
ironisch ⓵ *Adj.* ironic; ironical
  ⓶ *adv.* ironically
ir·rational ⓵ *Adj.* irrational
  ⓶ *adv.* irrationally
irre ⓵ *Adj.* (a) insane
  (b) (salopp: faszinierend) amazing (coll.)
  ⓶ *adv.* (salopp) terribly (coll.)
Irre *der/die; adj. Dekl.* madman/madwoman; lunatic; (fig.) lunatic
irre-, Irre-: ~|**führen** *tr. V.* mislead; (täuschen) deceive; ~**führung** *die:* eine bewusste ~**führung** a deliberate attempt to mislead; ~**führung der Öffentlichkeit** misleading the public
ir·relevant *Adj.* irrelevant (**für** to)
irre|machen *tr. V.* disconcert; put off
irren ⓵ *refl. V.* be mistaken; **Sie haben sich in der Nummer geirrt** you've got the wrong number
  ⓶ *itr. V.* (a) da ~ **Sie** you are wrong there
  (b) *mit sein* (ziellos umherstreifen) wander
Irren-: ~**anstalt** *die* (veralt. abwertend) mental home; ~**haus** *das* (abwertend) [lunatic] asylum
ir·reparabel *Adj.* irreparable
Irr·fahrt *die* wandering
irriger·weise *Adv.* mistakenly
Irritation *die;* ~, ~en irritation
irritieren *tr., itr. V.* (a) (verwirren) put off
  (b) (stören) disturb
irr-, Irr-: ~**licht** *das* will o' the wisp; ~**sinn** *der* (a) insanity; madness; (b) (ugs. abwertend) lunacy; ~**sinnig** ⓵ *Adj.* (a) (geistig gestört) insane; mad; (absurd) idiotic; (b) (ugs.: extrem) terrible (coll.); terrific (coll.) ⟨*speed, heat, cold*⟩; ⓶ *adv.* (ugs.) terribly (coll.)
Irrtum *der;* ~s, Irrtümer mistake; ~! wrong!; **im** ~ **sein** be wrong *or* mistaken
irrtümlich ⓵ *Adj.* incorrect
  ⓶ *adv.* by mistake
Irr·weg *der* error; **diese Methode hat sich als** ~ **erwiesen** this method has proved to be wrong
Ischias *der od. das od.* (Med.) *die;* ~: sciatica
Islam /ɪs'la:m *od.* 'ɪslam/ *der;* ~[s] Islam
islamisch *Adj.* Islamic
Islamismus *der;* ~: Islamic fundamentalism; Islamism
Islamist *der;* ~en, ~en, **Islamistin** *die;* ~, ~nen Islamic fundamentalist; Islamist

islamistisch *Adj.* Islamic fundamentalist; Islamist

Island *(das);* ~s Iceland

Isländer *der;* ~s, ~, **Isländerin** *die;* ~, ~nen Icelander

isländisch *Adj.* Icelandic

Isolation *die;* ~, ~en ► ISOLIERUNG

Isolator *der;* ~s, ~en insulator

Isolier·band *das* insulating tape

isolieren *tr. V.* (a) isolate
(b) (Technik) insulate ⟨*wiring, wall, etc.*⟩; lag ⟨*boilers, pipes, etc.*⟩

Isolier·station *die* (Med.) isolation ward

Isolierung *die;* ~, ~en (a) isolation
(b) (Technik) ► ISOLIEREN B: insulation; lagging

Isotop *das;* ~s, ~e isotope

Israel /'ɪsraeːl/ *(das);* ~s Israel

Israeli *der;* ~[s], ~[s]/*die;* ~, ~[s] Israeli

israelisch *Adj.* Israeli

Israelit *der;* ~en, ~en, **Israelitin** *die;* ~, ~nen Israelite

israelitisch *Adj.* Israelite

iss, *iß *Imperativ Sg. v.* ESSEN

isst, *ißt *2. u. 3. Pers. Sg. Präsens v.* ESSEN

ist *3. Pers. Sg. Präsens v.* SEIN

Italien /i'taːliən/ *(das);* ~s Italy

Italiener *der;* ~s, ~, **Italienerin** *die;* ~, ~nen Italian

italienisch *Adj.* Italian

I-Tüpfel[chen] *das;* ~s, ~: final touch; bis aufs [letzte] ~: down to the last detail

i.V. *Abk.* = **in Vertretung**

Jj

• •

j, J /jɔt, *österr.:* jeː/ *das;* ~, ~: j/J

ja [1] *Interj.* yes; (nachgestellt: nicht wahr?) won't you/doesn't it *etc.?*
[2] *Partikel* Sie wissen ja, dass …: you know, of course, that …; da seid ihr ja! there you are!

Ja *das;* ~[s], ~[s] yes; mit ~ stimmen vote yes

Jacht *die;* ~, ~en yacht

Jacke *die;* ~, ~n jacket; (gestrickt) cardigan

Jacken·kleid *das* dress and jacket combination

Jacket·krone /'dʒɛkɪt-/ *die* (Zahnmed.) jacket crown

Jackett /ʒa'kɛt/ *das;* ~s, ~s jacket

Jade *die;* ~: jade

Jagd *die;* ~, ~en (a) die ~: shooting; hunting; auf die ~ gehen go hunting/shooting
(b) (Veranstaltung) shoot; (Hetzjagd) hunt
(c) (Verfolgung) hunt; (Verfolgungsjagd) chase; auf jmdn./etw. ~ machen hunt for sb./sth.

Jagd-: ~**beute** *die* bag; kill; ~**bomber** *der* (Luftwaffe) fighter-bomber; ~**flieger** *der,* ~**fliegerin** *die* (Luftwaffe) fighter pilot; ~**flugzeug** *das* (Luftwaffe) fighter aircraft; ~**gewehr** *das* sporting gun; ~**horn** *das* hunting horn; ~**hund** *der* gun dog; ~**hütte** *die* shooting box; ~**revier** *das* preserve; shoot; ~**schein** *der* game licence; ~**wurst** *die* chasseur sausage; ~**zeit** *die* open season

jagen [1] *tr. V.* (a) hunt ⟨*game, fugitive, criminal, etc.*⟩; shoot ⟨*game, game birds*⟩; (hetzen) chase ⟨*fugitive, criminal, etc.*⟩
(b) (treiben) drive; jmdn. aus dem Haus

~: throw sb. out of the house
[2] *itr. V.* (die Jagd ausüben) go shooting *or* hunting

Jäger *der;* ~s, ~: (a) hunter
(b) (Milit.) rifleman
(c) (Soldatenspr.: Jagdflugzeug) fighter

Jäger·hut *der* huntsman's hat

Jägerin *die;* ~, ~nen huntress

Jäger-: ~**latein** *das* (scherzh.) [hunter's] tall story/stories; das ist das reinste ~latein that's all wild exaggeration; ~**rock** *der* hunting jacket; ~**schnitzel** *das* (Kochk.) escalope chasseur

Jaguar *der;* ~s, ~e jaguar

jäh [1] *Adj.* (geh.) (a) sudden; abrupt ⟨*change, movement, stop*⟩; sudden, sharp ⟨*pain*⟩
(b) (steil) steep; precipitous
[2] *adv.* (a) ⟨*change*⟩ abruptly
(b) (steil) ⟨*fall, drop*⟩ steeply

jählings *Adv.* (geh.) (a) (plötzlich) ⟨*change, end, stop*⟩ suddenly, abruptly; ⟨*die*⟩ suddenly
(b) (steil) steeply

Jahr *das;* ~[e]s, ~e year; ein halbes ~: six months; im ~[e] 1908 in [the year] 1908; er ist zwanzig ~e [alt] he is twenty years old; Kinder bis zu zwölf ~en children up to the age of twelve; zwischen den ~en between Christmas and the New Year

jahr·aus *Adv.* ~, jahrein year in, year out

jahre·lang [1] *Adj.* [many] years of; long-standing ⟨*feud, friendship*⟩
[2] *adv.* for [many] years

jähren *refl. V.* heute jährt sich zum zehnten Mal, dass …: it is ten years ago today that … ⋯⟩

Jahres-: ~**bilanz** die (Wirtsch., Kaufmannsspr.) annual balance [of accounts]; (Dokument) annual balance sheet; ~**einkommen** das annual income; ~**ende** das end of the year; ~**frist**: in od. innerhalb od. binnen ~frist within [a period of] a or one year; ~**hälfte** die: die erste/zweite ~hälfte the first/second half or six months of the year; ~**karte** die yearly season ticket; ~**tag** der anniversary; ~**umsatz** der annual turnover; ~**urlaub** der annual holiday or (formal) leave or (Amer.) vacation; ~**wechsel** der turn of the year; zum ~wechsel die besten Wünsche best wishes for the New Year; ~**zahl** die date; ~**zeit** die season

Jahr·gang der (a) (Altersklasse) year; der ~ 1900 those born in 1900 (b) (eines Weines) vintage (c) (einer Zeitschrift) set [of issues] for a/the year

Jahr·hundert das century

Jahrhundert·wende die turn of the century

-jährig (a) (… Jahre alt) ein elfjähriges Kind an eleven-year-old child (b) (… Jahre dauernd) … year's/years'; nach vierjähriger Vorbereitung after four years' preparation; mit dreijähriger Verspätung three years late

jährlich ① Adj.; annual; yearly ② adv. annually; yearly; zweimal ~: twice a year

Jahr-: ~**markt** der fair; funfair; ~**tausend** das thousand years; millennium; ~**tausend·wende** die turn of the millennium; ~**zehnt** das decade

jahrzehnte·lang ① Adj.; nicht präd. decades of ⟨practice, experience, etc.⟩ ② adv. for decades

Jäh·zorn der violent anger

jäh·zornig ① Adj. violent-tempered ② adv. in a blind rage

ja·ja Part. (ugs.) (a) (seufzend) ~[, so ist das Leben] oh well[, that's life] (b) (ungeduldig) ~[, ich komme schon]! all right, all right[, I'm coming!]

Jalousie /ʒalu'zi:/ die; ~, ~n Venetian blind

Jamaika (das); -s Jamaica

Jamaikaner der; ~s, ~, **Jamaikanerin** die; ~, ~nen Jamaican

Jammer der; ~s [mournful] wailing; (Elend) misery

jämmerlich ① Adj. (a) pitiful (b) wretched ⟨appearance, existence, etc.⟩; paltry, meagre ⟨quantity⟩ ② adv. pitifully

jammern itr. V. wail; (sich beklagen) moan

*alte Schreibung – vgl. Hinweis auf S. x

jammer·schade Adj. (ugs.) es ist ~, dass …: it's a crying shame that …; es ist ~ um ihn it's a great pity about him

Janker der; ~s, ~ (südd., österr.) Alpine jacket

Januar der; ~[s], ~e January

Japan (das); ~s Japan

Japaner der; ~s, ~, **Japanerin** die; ~, ~nen Japanese

japanisch Adj. Japanese

japsen itr. V. (ugs.) pant

Jargon /jar'gõ:/ der; ~s, ~s jargon

Jasmin der; ~s, ~e jasmine

Ja·stimme die yes-vote

jäten tr., itr. V. weed; Unkraut ~: weed

Jauche die; ~, ~n liquid manure

Jauche·grube die liquid-manure reservoir

jauchzen itr. V. cheer; vor Freude ~: shout for joy

Jauchzer der; ~s, ~: cry of delight

jaulen itr. V. howl

Jause die; ~, ~n (österr.) (a) snack; eine ~ machen have a snack (b) (Nachmittagskaffee) [afternoon] tea

ja·wohl Part. certainly

Ja·wort das consent; jmdm. das ~ geben consent to marry sb.

Jazz /dʒæz od. dʒɛs od. jats/ der; ~: jazz

jazzen /'dʒɛsn̩ od. 'jatsn̩/ itr. V. play jazz

Jazzer /'dʒɛsɐ od. 'jatsɐ/ der; ~s, ~, **Jazzerin** die; ~, ~nen jazz musician

Jazz-: ~**keller** der jazz cellar; ~**tanz** der jazz dance

je¹ ① Adv. (a) (jemals) ever; mehr/besser denn je more/better than ever (b) (jeweils) je zehn Personen ten people at a time; sie kosten je 30 Euro they cost 30 euros each (c) (entsprechend) je nach Gewicht according to weight ② Präp. mit Akk. per; for each ③ Konj. je länger, je lieber the longer the better; je nachdem it all depends

je² Interj. ach je, wie schade! oh dear, what a shame!

Jeans /dʒi:nz/ Pl. od. die; ~, ~: jeans pl.; denims pl.

jede ▸ JEDER

jeden·falls Adv. (a) in any case (b) (zumindest) at any rate

jeder, jede, jedes Indefinitpron. u. unbest. Zahlwort ① attr. (a) (alle) every (b) (alle einzeln) each (c) (jeglicher) all ② allein stehend (a) (alle) everyone; everybody (b) (alle einzeln) jedes der Kinder each of the children

jeder-: ~**mann** Indefinitpron. everyone; everybody; ~**zeit** Adv. [at] any time

jedes ▶ JEDER
*jedes·mal ▶ MAL¹
je·doch *Konj., Adv.* however
je·her /*od.* '-'-/ *Adv.* seit *od.* von ∼: always; since time immemorial
jemals *Adv.* ever
jemand *Indefinitpron.* someone; somebody; (fragend, verneinend) anyone; anybody
Jemen (*das*); ∼s *od.* der; ∼[s] Yemen
jener, jene, jenes *Demonstrativpron.* (geh.) **1** *attr.* that; (im Pl.) those **2** *allein stehend* that one; (im Pl.) those
jenseits **1** *Präp. mit Gen.* on the other side of; (in größerer Entfernung) beyond **2** *Adv.* on the other side; ∼ **von** on the other side of
Jenseits *das;* ∼: hereafter; beyond
Jersey¹ /'dʒøːɐ̯zi/ *der;* ∼[s], ∼s (Textilind.) jersey
Jersey² *das;* ∼s, ∼s (Sport: Trikot) jersey
Jesus (*der*); Jesu Jesus
Jet /dʒɛt/ *der;* ∼[s], ∼s jet; **mit einem** ∼ **fliegen/reisen** fly/travel by jet
jetzig *Adj.* current
jetzt *Adv.* **(a)** just now; **bis** ∼: up to now; **bis** ∼ **noch nicht** not yet; **von** ∼ **an** *od.* **ab** from now on[wards]; **erst** ∼ *od.* ∼ **erst** only just; **schon** ∼: already **(b)** (heutzutage) now; nowadays
jeweilig *Adj.* **(a)** (in einem bestimmten Fall) particular **(b)** (zu einer bestimmten Zeit) current; of the time *postpos., not pred.* **(c)** (zugehörig, zugewiesen) respective
jeweils *Adv.* **(a)** (jedesmal) ∼ **am ersten/ letzten Mittwoch des Monats** on the first/last Wednesday of each month **(b)** (zur Zeit) at the time
Jg. *Abk.* = **Jahrgang**
Jh. *Abk.* = **Jahrhundert** c.
JH *Abk.* = **Jugendherberge**
jiddisch /'jɪdɪʃ/ *Adj.* Yiddish
Job /dʒɔp/ *der;* ∼s, ∼s (ugs.; auch DV) job
jobben /dʒɔbn̩/ *itr. V.* (ugs.) do a job/jobs
Job-: ∼**killer** *der* destroyer of jobs; ∼**sharing** /'-ʃɛərɪŋ/ *das;* ∼s ∼s jobsharing
Joch *das;* ∼[e]s, ∼e yoke
Jockei, Jockey /'dʒɔke *od.* 'dʒɔki/ *der;* ∼s, ∼s jockey
Jod *das;* ∼[e]s iodine
jodeln *itr., tr. V.* yodel
jod·haltig *Adj.* iodiferous
Joga *der od. das;* ∼[s] yoga
joggen /'dʒɔgn̩/ *itr. V.; mit Richtungsangabe mit* sein jog
Jogging·anzug *der* jogging suit
Joghurt /'joːgʊrt/ *der od. das;* ∼[s], ∼[s] yoghurt
Joghurt·becher *der* yoghurt pot (Brit.) *or* (Amer.) container
Johannis·beere *die* currant; rote/

weiße/schwarze ∼ redcurrants/white currants/blackcurrants
johlen *itr. V.* yell; (vor Wut) howl
Joint /dʒɔɪnt/ *der;* ∼s, ∼s (ugs.) joint (sl.)
Jolle *die;* ∼, ∼n keel-centreboard yawl
Jongleur /ʒɔŋ'løːɐ̯/ *der;* ∼s, ∼e, **Jongleurin** *die;* ∼, ∼nen juggler
jonglieren *tr., itr. V.* juggle
Joppe *die;* ∼, ∼n heavy jacket
Jordanien (*das*); ∼s Jordan
Jordanier *der;* ∼s, ∼, **Jordanierin** *die;* ∼, ∼nen Jordanian
jordanisch *Adj.* Jordanian
Jot *das;* ∼, ∼: j, J
Journalismus *der;* /ʒʊr'/ ∼: journalism *no art.*
Journalist *der;* ∼en, ∼en, **Journalistin** *die;* ∼, ∼nen journalist
journalistisch **1** *Adj.;* journalistic; **eine** ∼**e Ausbildung** a training in journalism **2** *adv.* journalistically; ∼ **tätig sein** be a journalist
Joystick /'dʒɔystik/ *der;* ∼s, ∼s (DV) joystick
jr. *Abk.* = **junior** Jr.
Jubel *der;* ∼s rejoicing; jubilation; (laut) cheering
Jubel·jahr *das* jubilee; **alle** ∼**e [einmal]** once in a blue moon
jubeln *itr. V.* cheer; **über etw.** (*Akk.*) ∼: rejoice over sth.
Jubilar *der;* ∼s, ∼e man celebrating his anniversary/birthday
Jubilarin *die;* ∼, ∼nen woman celebrating her anniversary/birthday
Jubiläum *das;* ∼s, Jubiläen anniversary; (eines Monarchen) jubilee
jubilieren *itr. V.* (geh.) jubilate (literary); rejoice
juchzen *itr. V.* (ugs.) shout with glee
jucken **1** *tr., itr. V.* **(a)** **mir juckt die Haut** I itch; **es juckt mich hier** I've got an itch here **(b)** (Juckreiz verursachen) irritate **2** *tr. V.* (reizen, verlocken) **es juckt mich, das zu tun** I am itching to do it **3** *refl. V.* (ugs.: sich kratzen) scratch
Juck·reiz *der* itch
Jude *der;* ∼n, ∼n Jew
Juden: ∼**hass, ***∼**haß** *der* anti-Semitism; hatred of [the] Jews; ∼**stern** *der* (ns.) Star of David
Judentum *das;* ∼s **(a)** (Volk) Jewry; Jews *pl.* **(b)** (Kultur u. Religion) Judaism
Juden·verfolgung *die* persecution of [the] Jews
Jüdin *die;* ∼, ∼nen Jewess
jüdisch *Adj.* Jewish
Judo *das;* ∼[s] judo *no art.*
Jugend *die;* ∼ **(a)** youth **(b)** (Jugendliche) young people ⋯⊱

jugend-, Jugend-: ∼**amt** *das* youth office *(agency responsible for education and welfare of young people)*; ∼**arbeitslosigkeit** *die* youth unemployment; ∼**arrest** *der* detention in a community home; ∼**bewegung** *die* (hist.) [German] youth Movement; ∼**buch** *das* book for young people; ∼**frei** *Adj.* ⟨*film, book, etc.*⟩ suitable for persons under 18; **nicht** ∼**frei** ⟨*film*⟩ not U-certificate *pred.*; ∼**gefährdend** *Adj.* liable to have an undesirable influence on the moral development of young people *postpos.*; ∼**heim** *das* youth centre; ∼**herberge** *die* youth hostel; ∼**klub** *der* youth club; ∼**kriminalität** *die* juvenile delinquency; ∼**kultur** *die* youth culture

jugendlich *Adj.* (a) young ⟨*offender, customer, etc.*⟩ (b) (für Jugendliche charakteristisch) youthful

Jugendliche *der/die; adj. Dekl.* young person; **die** ∼**n** the young people

Jugend-: ∼**liebe** *die* sweetheart of one's youth; ∼**schutz** *der* protection of young people; ∼**schutz-gesetz** *das* laws *pl.* protecting young people; ∼**sprache** *die* young people's language *no art.*; ∼**stil** *der* art nouveau; (in Deutschland) Jugendstil; ∼**strafanstalt** *die* detention centre; ∼**strafe** *die* youth custody sentence; ∼**sünde** *die* youthful folly; ∼**zeit** *die* youth; ∼**zentrum** *das* youth centre

Jugo·slawe *der* Yugoslav

Jugo·slawien (*das*); ∼**s** Yugoslavia

Jugo·slawin *die* Yugoslav

jugo·slawisch *Adj.* Yugoslav[ian]

Juli1 *der;* ∼[s], ∼s ▶ JULI

Juli *der;* ∼[s], ∼s July; *s. auch* APRIL

jung *Adj.;* jünger, jüngst... (a) young; new ⟨*project, undertaking, sport, marriage, etc.*⟩ (b) (letzt...) recent; **in jüngster Zeit** recently

Junge1 *der;* ∼n, ∼n *od.* (ugs.) Jung[en]s boy

Junge2 *das; adj. Dekl.* **ein** ∼**s** one of the young; ∼ **kriegen** give birth to young

jungen *itr. V.* give birth; ⟨*cat*⟩ have kittens; ⟨*dog*⟩ have pups

jungenhaft *Adj.* boyish

jünger *Adj.* youngish; **sie ist noch** ∼: she is still quite young; *s. auch* JUNG

Jünger *der;* ∼s, ∼, **Jüngerin** *die;* ∼, ∼**nen** follower

Jungfer *die;* ∼, ∼n (abwertend: ältere ledige Frau) spinster

Jungfern·fahrt *die* maiden voyage

Jungfern·häutchen *das;* ∼s, ∼: hymen

Jung·frau *die* (a) virgin (b) (Astrol.) Virgo

jung·fräulich *Adj.* (geh., auch fig.) virgin

Jung·geselle *der* bachelor

Jung·gesellin *die* bachelor girl

Jüngling *der;* ∼s, ∼e (geh., spött.) youth; boy

jüngst *Adv.* (geh.) recently

jüngst... ▶ JUNG

Jüngste *der/die; adj. Dekl.* youngest [one]

Jung-: ∼**verheiratete** *der/die; adj. Dekl.,* young married man/woman; **die** ∼**verheirateten** the newly-weds; ∼**wähler** *der,* ∼**wählerin** *die* first-time voter

Juni *der;* ∼[s], ∼s June; *s. auch* APRIL

junior *indekl. Adj.; nach Personennamen* junior

Junior *der;* ∼s, ∼en (a) (oft scherzh.) junior (joc.) (b) (Kaufmannsspr.) junior partner

Junior-: ∼**chef** *der* owner's *or* (coll.) boss's son; ∼**chefin** *die* owner's *or* (coll.) boss's daughter

Juno *der;* ∼[s], ∼s ▶ JUNI

Junta /'xʊnta/ *die;* ∼, Junten junta

Jura law *sing.;* ∼ **studieren** read Law

Jurist *der;* ∼en, ∼en, **Juristin** *die;* ∼, ∼nen lawyer; jurist

juristisch *Adj.* legal

Jury /ʒy'riː/ *die;* ∼, ∼s (a) (Preisrichter) panel [of judges]; jury (b) (Sachverständige) panel [of experts]

just *Adv.* (veralt., noch scherzh.) just; ∼ **in diesem Augenblick** just at that moment; at that very moment

justieren *tr. V.* adjust

Justierung *die;* ∼, ∼en adjustment

Justiz *die;* ∼: justice; (Behörden) judiciary

Justiz-: ∼**irrtum** *der* miscarriage of justice; ∼**minister** *der,* ∼**ministerin** *die* Minister of Justice; ∼**ministerium** *das* Ministry of Justice; ∼**mord** *der* judicial murder; ∼**vollzugs·anstalt** *die* (Amtsspr.) penal institution (formal); prison

Jute *die;* ∼: jute

Jütland (*das*); ∼s Jutland

Juwel *das od. der;* ∼s, ∼en piece of jewellery; (Edelstein) jewel

Juwelier /juvə'liːɐ̯/ *der;* ∼s jeweller

Juwelier·geschäft *das* jeweller's shop

Jux *der;* ∼es, ∼e (ugs.) joke

---

*old spelling – see note on page x

Kk

k, K /ka:/ *das;* ~, ~: k/K
Kabarętt *das;* ~s, ~s *od.* ~e (a) satirical revue
(b) (Ensemble) cabaret act
Kabarettist *der;* ~en, ~en,
Kabarettistin *die;* ~, ~nen revue performer
kabarettistisch *Adj.* [satirical] revue *attrib.;* ~e Szenen scenes in the style of a [satirical] revue
kąbbeln *refl. V.* (ugs.) bicker (**mit** with)
Kabel *das;* ~s, ~: cable; (für kleineres Gerät) flex
Kabel·fernsehen *das* cable television
Kabeljau *der;* ~s, ~e *od.* ~s cod
kabellos ⬚1 *Adj.* wireless
⬚2 *adv.* ⟨*communicate*⟩ in wireless format; ⟨*install*⟩ without wires
kabeln *tr., itr. V.* (veralt.) cable
Kabine *die;* ~, ~n (a) cabin
(b) (Umkleideraum, abgeteilter Raum) cubicle
(c) (einer Seilbahn) [cable] car
Kabinętt *das;* ~s, ~e Cabinet
Kabrio *das;* ~s, ~s, **Kabriolętt** *das;* ~s, ~s convertible
Kąchel *die;* ~, ~n [glazed] tile
kącheln *tr. V.* tile
Kąchel·ofen *der* tiled stove
Kącke *die;* ~ (derb; auch fig.) shit (coarse); crap (coarse)
kącken *itr. V.* (derb) shit (coarse); crap (coarse)
Kadaver *der;* ~s, ~: carcass
Kader *der od.* (schweiz.) *das;* ~s, ~ (a) cadre
(b) (Sport) squad
Käfer *der;* ~s, ~: beetle
Kąff *das;* ~s, ~s *od.* **Käffer** (ugs. abwertend) dump (coll.)
Kaffee /'kafe *od.* (österr.) ka'fe:/ *der;* ~s, ~s
(a) coffee
(b) (Nachmittags~) afternoon coffee;
~ trinken have afternoon coffee
Kąffee-: ~**kanne** *die* coffee pot; ~**kränzchen** *das* (veralt.)
(a) (Zusammentreffen) coffee afternoon;
(b) (Gruppe) coffee circle; ~**maschine** *die* coffee maker; ~**mühle** *die* coffee grinder;
~**satz** *der* coffee grounds *pl.;* ~**tante** *die* (ugs. scherzh.) coffee addict
Käfig *der;* ~s, ~e cage
kạhl *Adj.* (a) (ohne Haare) bald; **jmdn.**
~ **scheren** shave sb.'s head
(b) (ohne Grün, schmucklos) bare; **etw.**
~ **fressen** strip sth. bare

kạhl-, Kạhl-: *~|**fressen**
▶ KAHL B; ~**köpfig** *Adj.* bald[-headed];
*~|**scheren** ▶ KAHL A; ~**schlag** *der*
(a) clear-felling *no indef. art.;* (b) (Waldfläche) clear-felled area
Kạhn *der;* ~[e]s, Kähne (a) (Ruder~) rowing boat; (Stech~) punt
(b) (Lastschiff) barge
Kai *der;* ~s, ~s quay
Kaiser *der;* ~s, ~: emperor
Kaiserin *die;* ~, ~nen empress
Kaiser-: ~**krone** *die* imperial crown;
~**reich** *das* empire; ~**schnitt** *der* Caesarean section; ~**wetter** *das* (scherzh.) glorious, sunny weather (*for an event*)
Kajüte *die;* ~, ~n (Seemannsspr.) cabin
Kakao /ka'kau/ *der;* ~s, ~s cocoa;
jmdn./etw. durch den ~ ziehen (ugs.) make fun of sb./sth.
Kakerlak *der;* ~s *od.* ~en, ~en cockroach
Kąktus *der;* ~, Kaktеen cactus
Kalauer *der;* ~s, ~: corny joke (coll.);
(Wortspiel) atrocious *or* (coll.) corny pun
Kạlb *das;* ~[e]s, Kälber (a) calf
(b) (ugs.: ~fleisch) veal
kạlben *itr. V.* calve
Kạlb·fleisch *das* veal
Kạlbs-: ~**braten** *der* (Kochk.) roast veal *no indef. art.;* (Gericht) roast of veal; ~**leder** *das* calfskin; ~**schnitzel** *das* veal cutlet
Kalender *der;* ~s, ~: calendar; (Taschen~) diary
Kalender-: ~**jahr** *das* calendar year;
~**monat** *der* calendar month
Kalesche *die;* ~, ~n (hist.) barouche
Kali *das;* ~s, ~s potash
Kaliber *das;* ~s, ~: (a) (Technik, Waffenkunde) calibre
(b) (ugs., oft abwertend) sort; kind
Kalifornien /kali'fɔrniən/ (*das*); ~s California
Kalium (Chemie) *das;* ~s potassium
Kạlk *der;* ~[e]s, ~e calcium carbonate;
(Baustoff) lime; quicklime
kạlken *tr. V.* whitewash
Kạlk-: ~**mangel** *der* calcium deficiency;
~**stein** *der* limestone
Kalkül *das od.* **der;** ~s, ~e (geh.) calculation
Kalkulation *die;* ~, ~en (auch Wirtsch.) calculation
kalkulieren *tr. V.* calculate ⟨*cost, price*⟩;
cost ⟨*product, article*⟩
Kalorie *die;* ~, ~n calorie ····⟩

kalorien-, Kalorien-: ∼**arm** [1] *Adj.*
low-calorie *attrib.;* ∼**arm sein** be low in
calories; [2] *adv.* ∼**arm kochen** cook low-
calorie meals; ∼**gehalt** *der* calorie content
kalt; kälter, kältest… [1] *Adj.* cold; frosty
⟨*atmosphere, smile*⟩; ∼ **bleiben** (fig.) remain
unmoved; **jmdn.** ∼ **lassen** (ugs.) leave sb.
unmoved; (nicht interessieren) leave sb. cold
(coll.)
[2] *adv.* **(a)** ∼ **duschen** have a cold shower
Getränke/Sekt ∼ **stellen** cool drinks/chill
champagne
(b) (nüchtern) coldly
(c) (abweisend, unfreundlich) frostily
kalt-, Kalt-: ***∼|**bleiben** ▶ KALT 1;
∼**blütig** [1] *Adj.* **(a)** cool-headed;
(b) (abwertend: skrupellos) cold-blooded;
[2] *adv.* **(a)** coolly; **(b)** (abwertend: skrupellos)
cold-bloodedly; ∼**blütigkeit** *die;*
∼∼: ▶ ∼BLÜTIG: cool-headedness;
cold-bloodedness
Kälte *die;* ∼ cold; (fig.) coldness
Kälte-: ∼**einbruch** *der* (Met.) sudden
onset of cold weather; ∼**grad** *der* degree
of frost
kälter ▶ KALT
kältest… ▶ KALT
Kälte-welle *die* cold spell
kalt-, Kalt-: ∼**gepresst,** ***∼**gepreßt**
Adj. cold-pressed; ∼**herzig** *Adj.*
cold-hearted; ***∼**lächelnd** *Adv.* (ugs.
abwertend) **etw.** ∼**lächelnd tun** take callous
pleasure in doing sth.; ***∼|**lassen**
▶ KALT 1; ∼|**machen** *tr. V.* (salopp) **jmdn.**
∼**machen** do sb. in (sl.); ∼**miete** *die* rent
exclusive of heating; ∼**schale** *die: cold
sweet soup made with fruit, beer, wine, or
milk;* ∼**schnäuzig** (ugs.) [1] *Adj.* cold
and insensitive; (frech) insolent; [2] *adv.*
coldly and insensitively; (frech) insolently;
∼|**stellen** *tr. V.* (ugs.) **jmdn.** ∼**stellen** put
sb. out of the way (coll. joc.)
kam *1. u. 3. Pers. Prät. v.* KOMMEN
Kambodscha *(das);* ∼s Cambodia
käme *1. u. 3. Pers. Konjunktiv II v.* KOMMEN
Kamel *das;* ∼s, ∼e camel
Kamera *die;* ∼, ∼s camera
Kamerad *der;* ∼en, ∼en, **Kameradin**
die; ∼, ∼nen companion; (Freund[in]) friend;
(Mitschüler[in]) mate; (Soldat[in]) comrade; (Sport)
teammate
Kameradschaft *die;* ∼: comradeship
kameradschaftlich [1] *Adj.* comradely
[2] *adv.* in a comradely way
Kamera-: ∼**frau** *die* camerawoman;
∼**mann** *der Pl.;* ∼**männer** *od.* ∼**leute**
cameraman; ∼**team** *das* camera crew
Kamerun /'kaməru:n/ *(das);* ∼s
Cameroon; the Cameroons *pl.*
Kamille *die;* ∼, ∼n camomile
Kamin *der, schweiz.: das;* ∼s, ∼e fireplace

Kamin-feger *der,* **Kamin-fegerin** *die*
(bes. südd.) ▶ SCHORNSTEINFEGER
Kamm *der;* ∼[e]s, Kämme **(a)** comb
(b) (bei Hühnern usw.) comb
(c) (Gebirgs∼) ridge
kämmen *tr. V.* comb
Kammer *die;* ∼, ∼n **(a)** storeroom
(b) (Biol., Med., Technik, Waffenkunde) chamber
(c) (Parl.) chamber
Kammer-: ∼**diener** *der* (veralt.) valet;
∼**jäger** *der,* ∼**jägerin** *die* pest controller;
∼**musik** *die* chamber music; ∼**sänger**
der, ∼**sängerin** *die: title awarded to
singer of outstanding merit;* ∼**zofe** *die*
(veralt.) lady's maid
Kamm-garn *das* worsted
Kampagne /kam'panjə/ *die;* ∼, ∼n
campaign
Kampf *der;* ∼[e]s, Kämpfe **(a)** (militärisch)
battle (um für)
(b) (zwischen persönlichen Gegnern) fight; (fig.)
struggle
(c) (Wett∼) contest; (Boxen) contest; bout
(d) (Einsatz aller Mittel) fight (um, für for; gegen
against)
kampf-, Kampf-: ∼**abstimmung** *die*
(Politik) crucial vote; ∼**bereit** *Adj.* ready to
fight *postpos.;* ⟨*army, troops*⟩ ready for battle
kämpfen *itr. V.* **(a)** fight
(b) (Sport: sich messen) ⟨*team*⟩ play; ⟨*wrestler,
boxer*⟩ fight
Kampfer *der;* ∼s camphor
Kämpfer *der;* ∼s, ∼, **Kämpferin** *die;* ∼,
∼nen fighter
kampf-, Kampf-: ∼**fähig** *Adj.*
⟨*troops*⟩ fit for action; ⟨*boxer etc.*⟩ fit to
fight; ∼**handlungen** *Pl.* fighting *sing.;*
∼**hubschrauber** *der* (Milit.) helicopter
gunship; ∼**preis** *der* (Wirtsch.) cut price;
∼**richter** *der,* ∼**richterin** *die* (Sport)
judge; ∼**unfähig** *Adj.* ⟨*troops*⟩ unfit for
action; ⟨*boxer etc.*⟩ unfit to fight
kampieren *itr. V.* camp
Kanada *(das);* ∼s Canada
Kanadier /ka'na:diɐ/ *der;* ∼s, ∼,
Kanadierin *die;* ∼, ∼nen Canadian
kanadisch *Adj.* Canadian
Kanal *der;* ∼s, Kanäle **(a)** canal
(b) (Geogr.) **der** ∼: the [English] Channel
(c) (für Abwässer) sewer
(d) (zur Entwässerung, Bewässerung) channel;
(Graben) ditch
(e) (Rundf., Ferns., Weg der Information) channel
Kanalisation *die;* ∼, ∼en sewerage
system; sewers *pl.*
kanalisieren *tr. V.* **(a)** (lenken) channel
⟨*energies, goods, etc.*⟩
(b) (schiffbar machen) canalize
Kanal-tunnel *der* Channel Tunnel
Kanaren *Pl.* Canaries
Kanarien-vogel /ka'na:riən-/ *der* canary
Kanarische Inseln *Pl.* Canary Islands

***alte Schreibung – vgl. Hinweis auf S. x

Kandare *die;* ~, ~n curb bit; jmdn. an die ~ nehmen (fig.) take sb. in hand

Kandidat *der;* ~en, ~en, **Kandidatin** *die;* ~, ~nen **(a)** candidate **(b)** (beim Quiz usw.) contestant

Kandidatur *die;* ~, ~en candidature (auf + *Akk.* for)

kandidieren *itr. V.* stand [as a candidate] (für for)

kandieren *tr. V.* candy; **kandiert** crystallized ‹orange, petal›; glacé ‹cherry, pear›; candied ‹peel›

Kandis *der;* ~, **Kandis-zucker** *der* rock candy

Känguru, *Känguruh *das;* ~s, ~s kangaroo

Kaninchen *das;* ~s, ~: rabbit

Kanister *der;* ~s, ~: can; [metal/plastic] container

kann *1. u. 3. Pers. Sg. Präsens v.* KÖNNEN

Kännchen *das;* ~s, ~: [small] pot; (für Milch) [small] jug

Kanne *die;* ~, ~n **(a)** pot; (für Milch, Wein, Wasser) jug **(b)** (Henkel~) can; (für Milch) pail; (beim Melken) churn

kannst *2. Pers. Sg. Präsens v.* KÖNNEN

kannte *1. u. 3. Pers. Sg. Prät. v.* KENNEN

Kanon *der;* ~s, ~s canon

Kanone *die;* ~, ~n cannon; (fig. ugs.: Könner) ace

Kantate *die;* ~, ~n (Musik) cantata

Kante *die;* ~, ~n edge

kantig *Adj.* square-cut ‹timber, stone›; rough-edged ‹rock›; angular ‹face›; square ‹chin›

Kantine *die;* ~, ~n canteen

Kanton *der;* ~s, ~e canton

kantonal [1] *Adj.* cantonal [2] *adv.* on a cantonal basis

Kantor *der;* ~s, ~en choirmaster and organist

Kantorin *die;* ~, ~nen choirmistress and organist

Kanu *das;* ~s, ~s canoe

Kanüle *die;* ~, ~n (Med.) cannula

Kanzel *die;* ~, ~n **(a)** pulpit **(b)** (Flugw.) cockpit

Kanzlei *die;* ~, ~en **(a)** (veralt.: Büro) office **(b)** (Anwalts~) chambers *pl.* (*of barrister*); office (*of lawyer*)

Kanzler *der;* ~s, ~ chancellor

Kap *das;* ~s, ~s cape

Kapazität *die;* ~, ~en **(a)** capacity **(b)** (Experte) expert

Kapelle *die;* ~, ~n **(a)** (Archit.) chapel **(b)** (Musik~) band; [light] orchestra

Kapell-meister *der,*
Kapell-meisterin *die* bandmaster/ -mistress; (im Orchester) conductor; (im Theater usw.) musical director

Kaper *die;* ~, ~n caper *usu. in pl.*

kapern *tr. V.* **(a)** (hist.) capture **(b)** (ugs.) jmdn. [für etw.] ~: rope sb. in[to sth.]

kapieren (ugs.) [1] *tr. V.* (ugs.) get (coll.) [2] *itr. V.* **kapiert?** got it? (coll.)

Kapital *das;* ~s, ~e od. ~ien **(a)** capital **(b)** (fig.) asset

Kapital-anlage *die* (Wirtsch.) capital investment

Kapitalismus *der;* ~: capitalism *no art.*

Kapitalist *der;* ~en, ~en, **Kapitalistin** *die;* ~, ~nen capitalist

kapitalistisch *Adj.* capitalistic

Kapital-verbrechen *das* serious offence; (mit Todesstrafe bedroht) capital offence

Kapitän *der;* ~s, ~e, **Kapitänin** *die;* ~, ~nen captain

Kapitel *das;* ~s, ~: chapter

Kapitulation *die;* ~, ~en surrender; capitulation; **seine ~ erklären** admit defeat

kapitulieren *itr. V.* **(a)** surrender; capitulate **(b)** (fig.: aufgeben) give up; **vor etw.** (*Dat.*) ~: give up in the face of sth.

Kaplan *der;* ~s, Kapläne (kath. Kirche) chaplain; (Hilfsgeistlicher) curate

Kappe *die;* ~, ~n cap

kappen *tr. V.* **(a)** (Seemannsspr.) cut **(b)** (beschneiden) cut back ‹hedge etc.›; (abschneiden) cut off ‹branches etc.›

Käppi *das;* ~s, ~s garrison cap

Kapsel *die;* ~, ~n capsule

Kapstadt (*das*) ~s Cape Town

kaputt *Adj.* **(a)** broken; **das Telefon ist ~:** the phone is not working **(b)** (ugs.: erschöpft) shattered (coll.)

kaputt-: ~|**gehen** *unr. itr. V.; mit sein* (ugs.) (entzweigehen) break; ‹machine› break down, (coll.) pack up; ‹lightbulb› go; (zerbrechen) be smashed; ~|**lachen** *refl. V.* (ugs.) kill oneself [laughing] (coll.); ~|**machen** (ugs.) [1] *tr. V.* break; spoil ‹sth. made with effort›; ruin ‹clothes, furniture, etc.›; finish ‹person› off; [2] *refl. V.* wear oneself out

Kapuze *die;* ~, ~n hood; (bei Mönchen) cowl; hood

Kapuziner *der;* ~s, ~: Capuchin [friar]

Karabiner *der;* ~s, ~: carbine

Karaffe *die;* ~, ~n carafe; (mit Glasstöpsel) decanter

Karambolage /karambo'la:ʒə/ *die;* ~, ~n (ugs.) crash; collision

*Karamel *usw.* ▶ KARAMELL *usw.*

Karamell *der* (schweiz.: *das*); ~s caramel

Karamell-bonbon *der od. das* caramel [toffee]

Karaoke *das;* ~[s] karaoke

Karat *das;* ~[e]s, ~e carat

Karate *das;* ~[s] karate

Karawane *die;* ~, ~n caravan

Kardinal *der;* ~s, **Kardinäle** (kath. Kirche) cardinal

Kardinal-: ~**fehler** *der* cardinal error; ~**tugend** *die* cardinal virtue; ~**zahl** *die* cardinal [number]

Karenz *die;* ~, ~en, **Karenz·zeit** *die* waiting period

Kar·freitag *der* Good Friday

karg ⒈ *Adj.* meagre ⟨*wages etc.*⟩; frugal ⟨*meal etc.*⟩; poor ⟨*light, accommodation*⟩; (wenig fruchtbar) barren
  ⒉ *adv.* ~ **bemessen sein** ⟨*helping*⟩ be mingy (Brit. coll.); ⟨*supply*⟩ be scanty; ~ **leben** live frugally

kärglich ⒈ *Adj.* meagre, poor ⟨*wages etc.*⟩; poor ⟨*light*⟩; frugal ⟨*meal*⟩; scanty ⟨*supply*⟩
  ⒉ *adv.* poorly ⟨*lit, paid, rewarded*⟩

karibisch *Adj.* Caribbean

kariert *Adj.* check, checked ⟨*material, pattern*⟩; check ⟨*jacket etc.*⟩; squared ⟨*paper*⟩

Karies /'ka:ri̯ɛs/ *die;* ~: caries

Karikatur *die;* ~, ~en cartoon; (Porträt) caricature

Karikaturist *der;* ~en, ~en, **Karikaturistin** *die;* ~, ~nen cartoonist; (Porträtist) caricaturist

karikieren *tr. V.* caricature

kariös *Adj.* (Zahnmed.) carious

karitativ *Adj.* charitable

Karl /karl/ (*der*) Charles; ~ **der Große** Charlemagne

Karneval /'karnəval/ *der;* ~s, ~e *od.* ~s carnival; ~ **feiern** join in the carnival festivities

karnevalistisch *Adj.* carnival *attrib.*

Karnevals-: ~**kostüm** *das* carnival costume; ~**verein** *der* carnival society; ~**zug** *der* carnival procession

Karnickel *das;* ~s, ~ (landsch.) rabbit

Kärnten (*das*); ~s Carinthia

Karo *das;* ~s, ~s (a) square; (auf der Spitze stehend) diamond
  (b) (Karomuster) check
  (c) (Kartenspiel: Farbe) diamonds *pl.*
  (d) (Kartenspiel: Karte) diamond

Karosse *die;* ~, ~n [state] coach

Karosserie *die;* ~, ~n bodywork

Karotte *die;* ~, ~n small carrot

Karpaten *Pl.* Carpathians; Carpathian Mountains

Karpfen *der;* ~s, ~: carp

Karre *die;* ~, ~n (bes. nordd.) (a) ▶ KARREN
  (b) (abwertend: Fahrzeug) [old] heap (coll.)

Karree *das;* ~s, ~s: ums ~ **gehen/fahren** walk/drive round the block

karren *tr. V.* (a) cart
  (b) (salopp: mit einem Auto) run (coll.)

Karren *der;* ~s, ~ (bes. südd., österr.) cart;

(zweirädrig) barrow

Karriere /ka'ri̯e:rə/ *die;* ~, ~n career; ~ **machen** make a [successful] career for oneself

Kärrner·arbeit *die* donkey work

Kar·samstag *der* Easter Saturday

Karte *die;* ~, ~n card; (Speise~) menu; (Fahr~, Flug~, Eintritts~) ticket; (Land~) map; **alles auf eine ~ setzen** stake everything on one chance

Kartei *die;* ~, ~en card file

Kartei-: ~**karte** *die* file card; ~**kasten** *der* file-card box

Kartell *das;* ~s, ~e (Wirtsch., Politik) cartel

Kartell-: ~**amt** *das:* government body concerned with the control and supervision of cartels; ≈ Monopolies and Mergers Commission (Brit.); ~**gesetz** *das* law relating to cartels; ≈ monopolies law (Brit.)

Karten-: ~**haus** *das* house of cards; ~**spiel** *das* (a) (Spiel mit Karten) card game; (b) (Satz Spielkarten) pack *or* (Amer.) deck [of cards]; ~**telefon** *das* cardphone; ~**vorverkauf** *der* advance booking

Kartoffel *die;* ~, ~n potato

Kartoffel-: ~**brei** *der* mashed potatoes *pl.;* mash (coll.); ~**chips** *Pl.* [potato] crisps (Brit.) *or* (Amer.) chips; ~**käfer** *der* Colorado beetle; ~**kloß** *der* potato dumpling; ~**puffer** *der* potato pancake (*made from grated raw potatoes*); ~**püree** *das:* ▶ ~BREI

Karton /kar'tɔŋ/ *der;* ~s, ~s (a) (Pappe) card[board]
  (b) (Schachtel) cardboard box

Karussell *das;* ~s, ~s *od.* ~e merry-go-round; carousel (Amer.); (kleineres) roundabout

Kar·woche *die* Holy Week

karzinogen *Adj.* (Med.) carcinogenic

Karzinom *das;* ~s, ~e (Med.) carcinoma

kaschieren *tr. V.* conceal; hide; disguise ⟨*fault*⟩

Kaschmir¹ (*das*); ~s Kashmir

Kaschmir² *der;* ~s, ~e (Textilw.) cashmere

Käse *der;* ~s, ~: cheese; (ugs. abwertend: Unsinn) rubbish

Käse-: ~**blatt** *das* (salopp abwertend) rag; ~**glocke** *die* cheese dome

Kaserne *die;* ~, ~n barracks *sing. or pl.*

käse·weiß *Adj.* (ugs.) [as] white as a sheet

käsig *Adj.* (ugs.) pasty; pale

Kasino *das;* ~s, ~s (a) (Spiel~) casino
  (b) (Offiziers~) [officers'] mess
  (c) (Speiseraum) canteen

Kasko·versicherung *die* (Voll~) comprehensive insurance; (Teil~) *insurance against theft, fire, or act of God*

Kasper *der;* ~s, ~: ≈ Punch; (fig. ugs.) clown

Kasperl *das;* ~s, ~[n] (österr.), **Kasperle** *das od.* der; ~s, ~: ▶ KASPER

---

*old spelling – see note on page x

Kasper-: ~**puppe** *die* ≈ Punch and Judy puppet; ~**theater** *das* ≈ Punch and Judy show; (Puppenbühne) ≈ Punch and Judy theatre

Kasse *die;* ~, ~**n (a)** cash box; (Registrier~) till **(b)** (Ort zum Bezahlen) cash desk; (im Supermarkt) checkout; (in einer Bank) counter **(c)** (Kassenraum) cashier's office **(d)** (Theater~, Kino~) box office

Kasseler *das;* ~**s** smoked loin of pork

Kassen-: ~**arzt** *der,* ~**ärztin** *die: doctor who treats members of a health insurance schemes;* ~**bon** *der* sales slip; receipt; ~**lage** *die* financial situation; **die** ~**lage der Firma** the state of the company's finances; **nach** ~**lage** as finances allow/allowed; **eine Rentenpolitik nach** ~**lage** a pensions policy dependent on what finances will allow; ~**patient** *der,* ~**patientin** *die: patient who is a member of a health insurance scheme;* ~**wart** *der;* ~~**s**, ~~**e,** ~**wartin** *die;* ~~, ~~**nen** treasurer; ~**zettel** *der:* ▶ ~BON

Kassette *die;* ~, ~**n (a)** box; case **(b)** (mit Büchern, Schallplatten) boxed set; (Tonband~, Film~) cassette

Kassetten-: ~**deck** *das* cassette deck; ~**recorder,** ~**rekorder** *der;* ~~**s,** ~~: cassette recorder

kassieren **1** *tr. V.* **(a)** collect **(b)** (ugs.: wegnehmen) confiscate; take away ‹*driving licence*› **2** *itr. V.* **bei jmdm.** ~: give sb. his/her bill *or* (Amer.) check; (ohne Rechnung) settle up with sb.; **darf ich bei Ihnen** ~? would you like your bill?/can I settle up with you?

Kassierer *der;* ~**s,** ~, **Kassiererin** *die;* ~, ~**nen** cashier; (bei einem Verein) treasurer

Kastanie /kas'ta:niə/ *die;* ~, ~**n** chestnut

kastanien-braun *Adj.* chestnut

Kästchen *das;* ~**s,** ~ **(a)** small box **(b)** (vorgedrucktes Quadrat) square; (auf Fragebögen) box

Kaste *die;* ~, ~**n** caste

kasteien *refl. V.* **(a)** (als Bußübung) chastise oneself **(b)** (sich Entbehrungen auferlegen) deny oneself

Kasteiung *die;* ~, ~**en (a)** (als Bußübung) self-chastisement **(b)** (Auferlegung von Entbehrungen) self-denial

Kastell *das;* ~**s,** ~**e (a)** (hist.: röm. Lager) fort **(b)** (Burg) castle

Kasten *der;* ~~**s,** **Kästen (a)** box; (für Flaschen) crate **(b)** (ugs.: Briefkasten) postbox **(c)** (ugs. abwertend) (Gebäude) barracks *sing. or pl.;* (Auto) heap (coll.); (fig. ugs.) **etw. auf dem** ~ **haben** have got it up top (coll.)

Kasten-brot *das* tin [loaf]

Kastration /kastra'tsjo:n/ *die;* ~, ~**en** castration

kastrieren *tr. V.* castrate

Kat *der;* ~**s,** ~**s** (ugs.) ▶ KATALYSATOR B

Katalog *der;* ~**[e]s,** ~**e** (auch fig.) catalogue

katalogisieren *tr. V.* catalogue

Katalysator *der;* ~**s,** ~**en (a)** (Chemie, fig.) catalyst **(b)** (Kfz-W.) catalytic converter

Katamaran *der od. das;* ~**s,** ~**e** catamaran

katapultieren *tr. V.* (auch fig.) catapult; eject ‹*pilot*›

Katarrh /ka'tar/ *der;* ~**s,** ~**e** (Med.) catarrh

katastrophal /katastro'fa:l/ **1** *Adj.* disastrous; (stärker) catastrophic **2** *adv.* disastrously; (stärker) catastrophically

Katastrophe /katas'tro:fə/ *die;* ~, ~**n** (Unglück) disaster; (stärker, auch Literaturw.) catastrophe

Katastrophen-: ~**alarm** *der* disaster alert; ~**gebiet** *das* disaster area; ~**schutz** *der* (Organisation) emergency services *pl.;* (Maßnahmen) disaster procedures *pl.*

Kategorie *die;* ~, ~**n** category

kategorisch **1** *Adj.* categorical **2** *adv.* categorically

Kater *der;* ~**s,** ~ **(a)** tomcat **(b)** (ugs.) hangover

Kathedrale *die;* ~, ~**n** cathedral

Katholik *der;* ~**en,** ~**en, Katholikin** *die;* ~, ~**nen** [Roman] Catholic

katholisch *Adj.* [Roman] Catholic

Katholizismus *der;* ~: [Roman] Catholicism *no art.*

Katz *die* ~ **und Maus [mit jmdm.] spielen** (ugs.) play cat and mouse [with sb.]; **für die** ~ **sein** (salopp) be a waste of time

Kätzchen *das;* ~**s,** ~ **(a)** little cat; pussy; (junge Katze) kitten **(b)** *meist Pl.* catkin

Katze *die;* ~, ~**n** cat

katzen-, Katzen-: ~**auge** *das* reflector; Cat's-eye ®; ~**jammer** *der* **(a)** (Kater) hangover; **(b)** (fig.) mood of depression; ~**musik** *die* (ugs. abwertend) terrible row (coll.); ~**sprung** *der* stone's throw; ~**wäsche** *die* (ugs.) ~**wäsche machen** have a lick and a promise (coll.)

Kauderwelsch *das;* ~**[s]** gibberish *no indef. art.*

kauen *tr., itr. V.* chew; **[die] Nägel** ~: bite one's nails

kauern *itr., refl. V.* crouch [down]; (ängstlich) cower

Kauf *der;* ~**[e]s, Käufe (a)** (das Kaufen) buying; purchasing (formal) **(b)** (das Gekaufte) purchase

kaufen **1** *tr. V.* buy; purchase **2** *itr. V.* (einkaufen) shop

Käufer *der;* ~**s,** ~, **Käuferin** *die;* ~, ~**nen** buyer; purchaser (formal)

Kauf-: ~**frau** *die* (Geschäftsfrau) businesswoman; (Händlerin) trader; ⸱⸱⸱⸱▸

~**haus** *das* department store; ~**kraft**
die (Wirtsch.) **(a)** (Wert des Geldes) purchasing
power; **(b)** (Zahlungsfähigkeit) spending power
käuflich ① *Adj.* **(a)** for sale *postpos.*
(b) (bestechlich) venal; ~ **sein** be easily
bought
② *adv.* etw. ~ **erwerben/erstehen** purchase
sth.
Kauf·mann *der; Pl.* **Ka̲ufleute**
(a) (Geschäftsmann) businessman; (Händler)
trader
(b) (Besitzer) shopkeeper; (eines
Lebensmittelladens) grocer
kaufmännisch *Adj.* commercial;
business *attrib.*
Kauf-: ~**preis** *der* purchase price;
~**vertrag** *der* contract of sale; (beim
Hauskauf) title deed
Kau·gummi *der od. das;* ~**s**, ~**s** chewing
gum
Ka̲ukasus *der;* ~: the Caucasus
Ka̲ulquappe *die;* ~, ~**n** tadpole
kaum *Adv.* hardly; scarcely; ~ **hatte er**
Platz genommen, als ...: no sooner had he
sat down than ...
kausal *Adj.* (geh., Sprachw.) causal
Kau·tabak *der* chewing tobacco
Kautio̲n *die;* ~, ~**en** **(a)** (bei Freilassung eines
Gefangenen) bail
(b) (beim Mieten einer Wohnung) deposit
Ka̲utschuk *der;* ~**s**, ~**e** rubber
Ka̲uz *der;* ~**es**, **Ka̲uze** **(a)** (Wald~) tawny
owl; (Stein~) little owl
(b) (Sonderling) strange fellow; oddball (coll.)
Kavalier /kava'liːɐ̯/ *der;* ~**s**, ~**e**
gentleman
Kavaliers·delikt *das* trifling offence
Kavalleri̲e /kavalə'riː/ *die;* ~, ~**n** (Milit.
hist.) cavalry
Kavalleri̲st *der;* ~**en**, ~**en** cavalryman
Kaviar /'kaːvi̯ar/ *der;* ~**s**, ~**e** caviare
kcal *Abk.* = **Kilo[gramm]kalorie** kcal
ke̲ck ① *Adj.* **(a)** cheeky; saucy (Brit.)
(b) (veralt.: verwegen) bold
(c) (flott) jaunty, pert ‹hat etc.›
② *adv.* **(a)** cheekily; saucily (Brit.)
(b) (veralt.: verwegen) boldly
(c) (flott) jauntily
Ke̲ckheit *die;* ~, ~**en** **(a)** cheek; sauce
(Brit.)
(b) (veralt.: Kühnheit) boldness
Ke̲gel *der;* ~**s**, ~ **(a)** cone
(b) (Spielfigur) skittle; (beim Bowling) pin
Ke̲gel-: ~**bahn** *die* skittle alley;
~**förmig** *Adj.* conical
kegeln ① *itr. V.* play skittles *or* ninepins
② *tr. V.* **eine Partie** ~: play a game of
skittles *or* ninepins; **eine Neun** ~: score a
nine
Ke̲hle *die;* ~, ~**n** throat

---

* alte Schreibung – vgl. Hinweis auf S. x

Ke̲hl·kopf *der* (Anat.) larynx
Ke̲hlkopf·krebs *der* (Med.) cancer of the
larynx
Ke̲hre *die;* ~, ~**n** sharp bend
ke̲hren[1] ① *tr. V.* turn
② *refl. V.* turn
ke̲hren[2] ① *itr. V.* (bes. südd.) sweep; do the
sweeping
② *tr. V.* sweep; (mit einem Handfeger) brush
Ke̲hricht *der od. das;* ~**s** (schweiz.: Müll)
refuse; garbage (Amer.)
Ke̲hr·seite *die* **(a)** back; (einer Münze,
Medaille) reverse; (scherzh.) (Gesäß) backside
(b) (nachteiliger Aspekt) drawback;
disadvantage
ke̲hrt|machen *itr. V.* (ugs.) turn [round
and go] back
ke̲ifen *itr. V.* (abwertend) nag
Ke̲il *der;* ~**[e]s**, ~**e** **(a)** (zum Spalten) wedge
(b) (zum Festklemmen) chock; (unter einer Tür)
wedge
ke̲ilen *refl. V.* (ugs.: sich prügeln) fight; scrap
Ke̲iler *der;* ~**s**, ~ (Jägerspr.) wild boar
Keilerei̲ *die;* ~, ~**en** (ugs.) punch-up (coll.);
fight
Ke̲il-: ~**riemen** *der* (Technik) V-belt;
~**schrift** *die* cuneiform script
Ke̲im *der;* ~**[e]s**, ~**e** (Bot.) shoot; (Biol.)
embryo
Ke̲im-: ~**bahn** *die* (Biol.) germ line;
~**drüse** *die* (Zool., Med.) gonad
ke̲imen *itr. V.* germinate; (fig.) ‹hope› stir
ke̲im-, Ke̲im-: ~**frei** *Adj.* germ-free;
sterile; ~**zelle** *die* nucleus
ke̲in *Indefinitpron.* **(a)** no
(b) (ugs.: nicht ganz; nicht einmal) less than
ke̲in... *Indefinitpron.* ~**er**/~**e** nobody; no
one; ~**s von beiden** neither [of them]
ke̲inerlei *indekl. Adj.* no ... what[so]ever
ke̲ines-: ~**falls** *Adv.* on no account;
~**wegs** *Adv.* by no means
ke̲in·mal *Adv.* not [even] once
Ke̲ks *der;* ~ *od.* ~**es**, ~ *od.* ~**e** biscuit
(Brit.); cookie (Amer.)
Ke̲lch *der;* ~**[e]s**, ~**e** goblet; (Rel.) chalice
Ke̲lle *die;* ~, ~**n (a)** ladle
(b) (Signalstab) signalling disc
(c) (Maurer~) trowel
Ke̲ller *der;* ~**s**, ~: cellar; (~geschoss)
basement
Ke̲ller·assel *die;* ~, ~**n** woodlouse
Kellerei̲ *die;* ~, ~**en** winery; (Kellerräume)
[wine] cellars *pl.*
Ke̲ller: ~**geschoss**, *~**geschoß** *das*
basement; ~**wohnung** *die* basement flat
(Brit.) *or* (Amer.) apartment
Ke̲llner *der;* ~**s**, ~: waiter
Ke̲llnerin *die;* ~, ~**nen** waitress
ke̲llnern *itr. V.* (ugs.) work as a waiter/
waitress
Ke̲lte *der;* ~**n**, ~**n** Celt

Kelter *die;* ~, ~n winepress
keltern *tr. V.* press ‹*grapes etc.*›
Kelt in *die;* ~, ~nen Celt
keltisch *Adj.* Celtic
Kenia (*das*); ~s Kenya
Kenianer *der;* ~s, ~, **Kenianerin** *die;*
~, ~nen Kenyan
kennen *unr. tr. V.* know; jmdn./etw.
~ lernen get to know sb./sth.; jmdn.
~ lernen (jmdm. erstmals begegnen) meet sb.;
jmdn. als etw. ~ lernen come to know sb.
as sth.
***kennen|lernen** ▸ KENNEN
Kenner *der;* ~s, ~: expert (+ *Gen.* on); (von
Wein, Speisen) connoisseur
Kenner·blick *der* expert eye; mit ~: with
an expert eye
Kennerin *die;* ~, ~nen ▸ KENNER
Kenn·marke *die* [police] identification
badge; ≈ [police] warrant card *or* (Amer.)
ID card
kenntlich *Adj.:* ~ sein be recognizable (**an**
by); etw./jmdn. ~ **machen** mark sth./make
sb. [easily] identifiable
Kenntnis *die;* ~, ~se knowledge
Kenntnisnahme *die;* ~ (Papierdt.) nach
~ der Akten after giving the documents
my/his *etc.* attention
kenntnis·reich *Adj.* well-informed;
knowledgeable
kenn-, Kenn-: ~**wort** *das; Pl.*
~wörter code word; (Parole) password;
code word; (Erkennungszeichen)
badge; (auf einem Behälter, einer Ware usw.)
label; (am Fahrzeug) registration number;
~**zeichnen** *tr. V.* (a) mark; label; mark
‹*way*›; (b) (charakterisieren) characterize;
~**zeichnend** *Adj.* typical, characteristic
(für of)
kentern *itr. V. mit sein* capsize
Keramik *die;* ~, ~en ceramics *pl.;* pottery;
(Gegenstand) piece of pottery
Kerbe *die;* ~, ~n notch
Kerbel *der;* ~s chervil
Kerb·holz *das:* etwas auf dem ~ haben
(ugs.) have done a job (sl.)
Kerker *der;* ~s, ~ (hist.) dungeons *pl.;*
(einzelne Zelle) dungeon
Kerl *der;* ~s, ~e (*nordd., md. auch:* ~s)
(ugs.) fellow (coll.); bloke (Brit. coll.)
Kern *der;* ~[e]s, ~e pip; (von Steinobst) stone;
(von Nüssen usw.) kernel; (Atom~) nucleus;
(fig.) der ~ **einer Sache** the heart of a matter;
der harte ~: the hard core
kern-, Kern-: ~**energie** *die* nuclear
energy *no art.;* ~**gehäuse** *das* core;
~**geschäft** *das* core business;
~**gesund** *Adj.* fit as a fiddle *pred.*
kernig *Adj.* earthy ‹*language*›; forceful
‹*speech*›; pithy ‹*saying*›
kern-, Kern-: ~**kraft** *die* nuclear power;

~**kraftwerk** *das* nuclear power station
or plant; ~**los** *Adj.* seedless; ~**obst** *das*
pomaceous fruit; ~**physik** *die* nuclear
physics *sing., no art.;* ~**reaktor** *der*
nuclear reactor; ~**seife** *die* washing
soap; ~**spaltung** *die* (Physik) nuclear
fission *no art.;* ~**spin-tomographie**
/'kɛrnspɪntomografi:/ *die;* ~~ (Med.)
[nuclear] magnetic resonance imaging;
~**waffe** *die* nuclear weapon; ~**zeit** *die*
core time
Kerze *die;* ~, ~n candle
kerzen-, Kerzen-: ~**gerade,** (ugs.)
~**grade** ⬚1⬚ *Adj.* dead straight; ⬚2⬚ *adv.*
bolt upright; ~**halter** *der* candle holder;
~**leuchter** *der* candlestick; ~**licht** *das*
the light of a candle/of candles; bei ~licht
by candlelight
kess, *keß ⬚1⬚ *Adj.* (a) pert; jaunty ‹*hat,
dress, etc.*›
(b) (frech) cheeky
⬚2⬚ *adv.* (a) (flott) jauntily
(b) (frech) cheekily
Kessel *der;* ~s, ~ (a) kettle; (zum Kochen)
pot; (Wasch~) copper
(b) (Berg~) basin-shaped valley
(c) (Milit.) encircled area
Kessel-: ~**stein** *der* scale; ~**treiben**
das (Hetzkampagne) witch-hunt
Kette *die;* ~, ~n chain; (Hals~) necklace;
(von Ereignissen) string
ketten *tr. V.* chain (an + *Akk.* to)
Ketten-: ~**hund** *der* guard dog (*kept
on a chain*); ~**rauchen** *das;* ~~s
chain-smoking *no art.;* ~**raucher** *der,*
~**raucherin** *die* chain-smoker; ~**säge**
die chain saw; ~**schaltung** *die* derailleur
gears *pl.*
Ketzer *der;* ~s, ~ (auch fig.) heretic
Ketzerei *die;* ~, ~en (auch fig.) heresy
Ketzerin *die;* ~, ~nen ▸ KETZER
keuchen *itr. V.* gasp for breath
Keuch·husten *der* whooping cough *no
art.*
Keule *die;* ~, ~n (a) club
(b) (Kochk.) leg
keusch ⬚1⬚ *Adj.* chaste
⬚2⬚ *adv.* ~ **leben** lead a chaste life
Keuschheit *die;* ~: chastity
Kfz *Abk.* = **Kraftfahrzeug**
kg *Abk.* = **Kilogramm** kg
KG *Abk.* = **Kommanditgesellschaft**
kichern *itr. V.* giggle
kicken (ugs.) ⬚1⬚ *itr. V.* play football
⬚2⬚ *tr. V.* kick
kidnappen /'kɪtnɛpn/ *tr. V.* kidnap
Kidnapper *der;* ~s, ~, **Kidnapperin**
die; ~, ~nen kidnapper
Kiebitz *der;* ~es, ~e lapwing; peewit
Kiefer[1] *der;* ~s, ~: jaw; (~knochen)
jawbone
Kiefer[2] *die;* ~, ~n pine[tree]

Kiefer·höhle *die* (Anat.) maxillary sinus
Kiefern·holz *das* pine [wood]
Kiel *der;* ~[e]s, ~e keel
kiel·holen *tr. V.* (Seemannsspr.) keelhaul
⟨*person*⟩
Kiel·wasser *das* wake
Kieme *die;* ~, ~n gill
Kien *der;* ~[e]s resinous wood
Kies *der;* ~es, ~e gravel; (auf dem Strand)
shingle
Kiesel *der;* ~s, ~: pebble
Kiesel·stein *der* pebble
Kies-: ~**grube** *die* gravel pit; ~**weg** *der*
gravel path
kiffen *itr. V.* (ugs.) smoke pot (sl.) *or* grass
(sl.)
Kiffer *der;* ~s, ~, **Kifferin** *die;* ~, ~nen
(ugs.) pothead (sl.)
kikeriki /kikəri'kiː/ *Interj.* (Kinderspr.) cock-
a-doodle-doo
Killer *der;* ~s, ~, **Killerin** *die;* ~, ~nen
(salopp) killer; (gegen Bezahlung) hit man
Kilo *das;* ~s, ~[s] kilo
Kilo·gramm *das* kilogram
Kilometer *der;* ~s, ~: kilometre
kilometer-, Kilometer-: ~**lang**
⟨1⟩ *Adj.* miles long *pred.;* ⟨2⟩ *adv.* for miles
[and miles]; ~**stand** *der* mileage reading
Kilowatt·stunde *die* (Physik; bes. Elektrot.)
kilowatt-hour
Kimme *die;* ~, ~n sighting notch
Kimono *der;* ~s, ~s kimono
Kind *das;* ~[e]s, ~er (a) child; ein
~ erwarten be expecting
(b) [~er,] ~er! my goodness!
Kinder-: ~**arzt** *der,* ~**ärztin** *die*
paediatrician; ~**betreuung** *die* child
care; ~**bett** *das* cot; (für größeres Kind)
child's bed; ~**dorf** *das* children's village
Kinderei *die;* ~, ~en childishness *no
indef. art., no pl.*
kinder-, Kinder-: ~**erziehung** *die*
bringing up of children; ~**feindlich** *Adj.*
hostile to children *pred.;* ~**freibetrag**
der (Steuerw.) child [tax] allowance;
~**freundlich** *Adj.* fond of children *pred.;*
⟨*town, resort*⟩ which caters for children;
⟨*planning, policy*⟩ which caters for the needs
of children; ~**garten** *der* nursery school;
~**gärtnerin** *die* nusery-school teacher;
~**geld** *das* child benefit; ~**heilkunde**
die paediatrics *sing., no art.;* ~**hort** *der* day
home for schoolchildren; ~**krankheit**
die **(a)** (Infektionskrankheit) children's disease
or illness; **(b)** (fig.: Anfangsschwierigkeiten)
teething troubles; ~**krippe** *die* crèche;
day nursey; ~**lähmung** *die* poliomyelitis;
~**leicht** (ugs.) childishly simple; dead
easy; **das ist** ~**leicht** it's kid's stuff (coll.); it's
child's play; ~**lieb** *Adj.* fond of children

pred.; ~**los** *Adj.* childless; ~**reich** *Adj.*
with many children *postpos., not pred.;*
~**sterblichkeit** *die* child mortality;
~**stube** *die* eine gute/schlechte ~stube
gehabt haben have been well/badly brought
up; ~**tages·heim** *das,* ~**tages·stätte**
die day nursery; crèche ~**teller** *der* (auf
der Speisekarte) children's menu; ~**wagen**
der pram (Brit.); baby carriage (Amer.);
(Sportwagen) pushchair (Brit.); stroller (Amer.)
Kindes-: ~**alter** *das* childhood;
~**misshandlung,** *~**mißhandlung**
die (Rechtsw.) child abuse
Kindheit *die;* ~: childhood
kindisch ⟨1⟩ *Adj.* childish, infantile; naïve
⟨*ideas*⟩
⟨2⟩ *adv.* childishly
kindlich ⟨1⟩ *Adj.* childlike
⟨2⟩ *adv.* ⟨*behave*⟩ in a childlike way
Kinkerlitzchen *Pl.* (ugs.) trifles
Kinn *das;* ~[e]s, ~e chin
Kinn-: ~**haken** *der* hook to the chin;
~**lade** *die* jaw
Kino *das;* ~s, ~s cinema (Brit.); movie
theater (Amer.)
Kino-: ~**gänger** *der;* ~~s, ~~,
~**gängerin** *die;* ~~, ~~nen cinema-
goer (Brit.); movie-goer (Amer.); ~**karte** *die*
cinema ticket (Brit.); movie ticket (Amer.)
Kiosk *der;* ~[e]s, ~e kiosk
Kippe¹ *die;* ~, ~n (ugs.) cigarette end;
dog-end (coll.)
Kippe² *die;* ~, ~n **(a)** (Bergmannsspr.) slag
heap
(b) etw. steht auf der ~ (fig.) it's touch and
go with sth.; (etw. ist noch nicht entschieden) sth.
hangs in the balance
kippen ⟨1⟩ *tr. V.* **(a)** tip [up]
(b) (ausschütten) tip [out]
(c) (ugs.: trinken) knock back (coll.); einen
~: have a quick one (coll.) *or* a drink
⟨2⟩ *itr. V.; mit sein* tip over; ⟨*top-heavy
object*⟩ topple over; ⟨*person*⟩ topple; ⟨*boat*⟩
overturn; ⟨*car*⟩ roll over
Kipp-: ~**fenster** *das* horizontally
pivoted window; ~**schalter** *der* tumbler
switch
Kirche *die;* ~, ~n church; **in die** ~ **gehen**
go to church
Kirchen-: ~**fest** *das* church festival;
~**lied** *das* hymn; ~**musik** *die* church
music; ~**steuer** *die* church tax
Kirch-: ~**gänger** *der;* ~~s, ~~,
~**gängerin** *die;* ~~, ~~nen churchgoer;
~**hof** *der* (veralt.) churchyard
kirchlich ⟨1⟩ *Adj.* ecclesiastical; church
attrib. ⟨*wedding, funeral*⟩
⟨2⟩ *adv.* ~ getraut/begraben werden have a
church wedding/funeral
Kirch-: ~**turm** *der* [church] steeple;
(ohne Turmspitze) church tower; ~**weih** *die;*
~~, ~~en fair (held on the anniversary of the
consecration of a church)

---

*old spelling – see note on page x

Kirmes *die;* ~, **Kirmessen** (bes. md., niederd.)
▶ KIRCHWEIH

Kirsch·baum *der* cherry [tree]

Kirsche *die;* ~, ~n cherry

Kirsch-: ~**torte** *die* cherry gateau; (mit Tortenboden) cherry flan; ~**wasser** *das; Pl.* ~**wässer** kirsch

Kissen *das;* ~s, ~: cushion; (Kopf~) pillow

Kiste *die;* ~, ~n box; (Truhe) chest; (Latten~) crate

Kita *die;* ~, ~s day nursery; crèche

Kitsch *der;* ~[e]s kitsch

kitschig *Adj.* kitschy

Kitt *der;* ~[e]s, ~e putty; (für Porzellan, Kacheln usw.) cement

Kittchen *das;* ~s, ~ (ugs.) clink (sl.)

Kittel *der;* ~s, ~ (a) overall; (eines Arztes usw.) white coat
(b) (hemdartige Bluse) smock

kitten *tr. V.* cement [together]

Kitz *das;* ~es, ~e (Reh~) fawn; (Ziegen~, Gämsen~) kid

kitzeln *tr., itr. V.* tickle

kitzlig *Adj.* (auch fig.) ticklish

KKW *Abk.* = **Kernkraftwerk**

Klacks *der;* ~es, ~e (ugs.) dollop (coll.); (~ Senf) dab; etw. ist nur ein ~ [für jmdn.] (fig.) sth. is no trouble at all [for sb.]

Kladde *die;* ~, ~n rough book

Kladderadatsch *der;* ~[e]s, ~e (ugs.) unholy mess (coll.)

klaffen *itr. V.* yawn; ⟨hole, wound⟩ gape

kläffen *itr. V.* (abwertend) yap

Kläffer *der;* ~s, ~ (ugs. abwertend) yapping dog; yapper

Klafter *der od. das;* ~s, ~ (Raummaß für Holz) cord

Klage *die;* ~, ~n (a) (Äußerung der Trauer) lament
(b) (Beschwerde) complaint
(c) (Rechtsw.) action; (im Strafrecht) charge

klagen ①*itr. V.* (a) (geh.: jammern) wail; (stöhnend) moan
(b) (sich beschweren) complain (über + *Akk.* about)
(c) (bei Gericht) take legal action
②*tr. V.* jmdm. sein Leid/seine Not ~: pour out one's sorrows *pl.*/troubles *pl.*

Kläger *der;* ~s, ~, **Klägerin** *die;* ~, ~nen (im Zivilrecht) plaintiff; (im Strafrecht) prosecuting party; (bei einer Scheidung) petitioner

kläglich *Adj.* (a) (Mitleid erregend) pitiful
(b) (minderwertig) pathetic
(c) (erbärmlich) despicable ⟨behaviour, role, compromise⟩; pathetic ⟨result, defeat⟩

Klamauk *der;* ~s (ugs. abwertend) fuss; (Lärm, Krach) row (coll.)

klamm *Adj.* (a) (feucht) cold and damp
(b) (steif) numb

Klammer *die;* ~, ~n (Wäsche~) peg; (Haar~) [hair]grip; (Zahn~) brace; (Büro~) paper clip; (Heft~) staple; (Schriftzeichen) bracket

klammern ①*refl. V.* sich an jmdn./etw. ~ (auch fig.) cling to sb./sth.
②*tr. V.* (a) eine Wunde ~: close a wound with a clip/clips
(b) (mit einer Büroklammer) clip; (mit einer Heftmaschine) staple; (mit Wäscheklammern) peg

Klamotten *Pl.* (salopp) (Kleidung) gear *sing.* (coll.); (Kram) stuff *sing.*

Klampfe *die;* ~, ~n (volkst.: Gitarre) guitar

klang *1. u. 3. Pers. Sg. Prät. v.* KLINGEN

Klang *der;* ~[e]s, **Klänge (a)** (Ton) sound
(b) (~farbe) tone

Klapp·bett *das* folding bed

Klappe *die;* ~, ~n **(a)** [hinged] lid; (am LKW) tailgate; (seitlich) side gate; (am Kombiwagen) back; (am Ofen) [drop-]door
(b) (an Musikinstrumenten) key; (an einer Trompete) valve
(c) (Filmjargon) clapperboard
(d) (salopp: Mund) trap (sl.)

klappen ①*tr. V.* nach oben/unten ~: turn up/down ⟨collar, hat brim⟩; lift up/put down ⟨lid⟩; nach vorne/hinten ~: tilt forward/back ⟨seat⟩
②*itr. V.* (a) ⟨door, shutter⟩ bang
(b) (stoßen) bang
(c) (ugs.: gelingen) work out all right

klapperig *Adj.* rickety

klappern *itr. V.* (a) rattle
(b) (ein Klappern erzeugen) make a clatter

Klapper·schlange *die* rattlesnake

Klapp·fahrrad *das* folding bicycle

klapprig *Adj.* rickety

Klapp-: ~**sitz** *der* tip-up seat; ~**stuhl** *der* folding chair

Klaps *der;* ~es, ~e (ugs.) smack; slap

Klaps·mühle *die* (salopp) loony bin (sl.)

klar ①*Adj.* (a) clear; straight ⟨question, answer⟩; sich (*Dat.*) über etw. (*Akk.*) ~ werden realize sth.; jmdm. ~ werden become clear to sb.; sich (*Dat.*) über etw. (*Akk.*) im Klaren sein realize sth.; etw. ~ machen (ugs.) make sth. clear
(b) (fertig) ready
②*adv.* clearly; ~ sehen understand the matter

Klär·anlage *die* sewage treatment plant

Klare *der;* ~n, ~n schnapps

klären ①*tr. V.* (a) settle ⟨question, issue, matter⟩; clarify ⟨situation⟩; clear up ⟨case, affair, misunderstanding⟩
(b) (reinigen) purify; treat ⟨effluent, sewage⟩
②*refl. V.* (a) ⟨situation⟩ become clear; ⟨question, issue, matter⟩ be settled
(b) (rein werden) ⟨liquid, sky⟩ clear; ⟨weather⟩ clear [up]

klar|gehen *unr. itr. V.; mit sein* (ugs.) go OK (coll.)

Klarheit *die;* ~: clarity; sich (*Dat.*) über etw. (*Akk.*) ~ verschaffen clarify sth.

Klarinẹtte die; ∼, ∼n clarinet

klar-: ∼|**machen** tr. V. (Seemannsspr.) get ready

klaro Adj., Interj. (ugs.) of course; it goes without saying; ∼, dass …: it goes without saying that …

*klar|sehen ▸ KLAR 2

Klarsicht·folie die transparent film

klar|stellen tr. V. clear up; clarify

Klar·text der (auch DV) clear text; im ∼text (fig.) in plain language

Klärung die; ∼, ∼en (a) clarification
(b) (Reinigung) purification; (von Abwässern) treatment

*klar|werden ▸ KLAR 1A

Klär·werk das sewage works sing. or pl.

klasse (ugs.) [1] indekl. Adj. great (coll.)
[2] adv. marvellously

Klasse die; ∼, ∼n (a) (Schul∼) class; (Raum) classroom; (Stufe) year; grade (Amer.)
(b) (Sport) league; (Boxen) division
(c) (Fahrzeug∼, Boots∼, Qualitätsstufe) class; das ist einsame od. ganz große ∼! (ugs.) that's [just] great (coll.) or marvellous!

klassen-, Klassen-: ∼**arbeit** die (Schulw.) [written] class test; ∼**buch** das (Schulw.) book recording details of pupils' attendance, and of topics covered in each lesson; ≈ [class] register; ∼**fahrt** die (Schulw.) class outing; ∼**gesellschaft** die (Soziol.) class society; ∼**kampf** der (marx.) class struggle; ∼**lehrer** der, ∼**lehrerin** die (Schulw.) class teacher; ∼**los** Adj. (Soziol.) classless; ∼**sprecher** der, ∼**sprecherin** die (Schulw.) class spokesman; ∼**treffen** das (Schulw.) class reunion; ∼**ziel** das (Schulw.) required standard (for pupils in a particular class); ∼**zimmer** das (Schulw.) classroom

klassifizieren tr. V. classify (als as)

Klassifizierung die; ∼, ∼en classification

Klạssik die; ∼ (a) (Antike) classical antiquity no art.
(b) (Zeit kultureller Höchstleistung) classical period

Klạssiker der; ∼s, ∼, **Klạssikerin** die; ∼, ∼nen classical writer/composer

klạssisch Adj. classical; (vollendet, zeitlos; auch iron.) classic

Klassizịsmus der; ∼: classicism

Klạtsch der; ∼[e]s, ∼e (a) (ugs. abwertend) gossip
(b) (Geräusch) smack

Klạtsch·base die (ugs. abwertend) gossip

klạtschen itr. V. (a) auch mit sein ⟨waves, wet sails⟩ slap
(b) (mit den Händen; applaudieren) clap
(c) (schlagen) slap
(d) (ugs. abwertend: reden) gossip (über + Akk. about)

klạtschhaft Adj. gossipy; fond of gossip pred.

klạtsch-, Klạtsch-: ∼**mohn** der corn poppy; ∼**nass,** *∼**naß** Adj. (ugs.) sopping wet; dripping wet ⟨hair⟩; ∼**spalte** die (ugs. abwertend) gossip column

Klaue die; ∼, ∼n (a) claw; (von Raubvögeln) talon; (salopp: Hand) mitt (coll.)
(b) (salopp abwertend: Schrift) scrawl

klauen (ugs.) [1] tr. V. pinch (coll.); jmdm. etw. ∼: pinch sth. from sb.
[2] itr. V. pinch (coll.) things

Klause die; ∼, ∼n hermitage; (Klosterzelle) cell

Klausel die; ∼, ∼n clause; (Bedingung) condition; (Vorbehalt) proviso

Klausur die; ∼, ∼en [examination] paper; (Examen) examination; eine ∼ schreiben take a[n examination] paper/an examination

Klausur-: ∼**arbeit** die [examination] paper; ∼**tagung** die private meeting

Klavier /kla'viːɐ̯/ das; ∼s, ∼e piano

Klebe·folie die adhesive film

kleben [1] itr. V. (a) stick (an + Dat. to)
(b) (ugs.: klebrig sein) be sticky (von, vor + Dat. with)
[2] tr. V. (a) (befestigen) stick; (mit Klebstoff) glue; jmdm. eine ∼ (salopp) belt sb. one (coll.)
(b) (reparieren) stick or glue ⟨vase etc.⟩ back together

Kleber der; ∼s, ∼: adhesive; glue

klebrig Adj. sticky

Kleb-: ∼**stoff** der adhesive; glue; ∼**streifen** der adhesive or sticky tape

kleckern (ugs.) itr. V. make a mess

Klẹcks der; ∼es, ∼e (a) stain; (nicht aufgesogen) blob; (Tintenfleck) [ink] blot
(b) (ugs.: kleine Menge) spot; (von Senf, Mayonnaise) dab

klẹcksen itr. V. (a) make a stain/stains; (mit Tinte) make a blot/blots; ⟨pen⟩ blot
(b) (ugs. abwertend: schlecht malen) daub

Klee der; ∼s clover

Klee·blatt das cloverleaf

Kleid das; ∼es, ∼er (a) dress
(b) Pl. (Kleidung) clothes

kleiden [1] refl. V. dress
[2] tr. V. (a) dress
(b) (jmdm. stehen) suit

Kleider-: ∼**bügel** der clothes hanger; coat hanger; ∼**bürste** die clothes brush; ∼**haken** der coat hook; ∼**schrank** der wardrobe; ∼**spende** die donation of [second-hand] clothes or clothing; ∼**ständer** der coat stand

kleidsam Adj. becoming

Kleidung die; ∼: clothes pl.

Kleidungs·stück das garment

klein [1] Adj. (a) little; small; er ist ∼er als ich he is shorter than me; etw. ∼ schneiden cut sth. into small pieces; Zwiebeln ∼ schneiden/hacken chop up onions [small]
(b) (jung) little; von ∼ auf from an early age

(c) (von kurzer Dauer) little, short ⟨while⟩; short ⟨walk, break, holiday⟩; brief ⟨moment⟩ **(d)** (von geringer Menge) small; low ⟨price⟩; **∼es Geld haben** have some [small] change **(e)** (von geringem Ausmaß) small ⟨party, gift⟩; scant ⟨attention⟩; slight ⟨cold, indisposition, mistake, irregularity⟩; minor ⟨event, error⟩ **(f)** (unbedeutend) lowly ⟨employee⟩; minor ⟨official⟩; **∼ anfangen** (ugs.) start off in a small way

2 adv. **die Heizung ∼/∼er einstellen** turn the heating down low/lower; **ein Wort ∼ schreiben** write a word with a small initial letter

klein-, Klein-: ∼aktionär der, **∼aktionärin** die (Wirtsch.) small shareholder; **∼anzeige** die (Zeitungsw.) small or classified advertisement; **∼asien** (das) Asia Minor; **∼buchstabe** der small letter; **∼bürger** der, **∼bürgerin** die lower middle-class person; (abwertend: Spießbürger) petit bourgeois; **∼bürgerlich** Adj. **(a)** (das Kleinbürgertum betreffend) lower middle-class; **(b)** (abwertend: spießbürgerlich) petit bourgeois

Kleine¹ der; adj. Dekl. **(a)** (kleiner Junge) little boy

(b) (ugs. Anrede) little man

Kleine² die; adj. Dekl. **(a)** (kleines Mädchen) little girl

(b) (ugs. Anrede) love; (abwertend) little madam

klein-, Klein-: ∼familie die (Soziol.) nuclear family; **∼geld** das [small] change; **∼gläubig** Adj. sceptical

Kleinigkeit die; ∼, **∼en** small thing; (Einzelheit) [small] detail; **ich habe noch eine ∼ zu erledigen** I still have a small matter to attend to; **eine ∼ essen** have a [small] bite to eat; **eine ∼ für jmdn. sein** be no trouble for sb.

klein-, Klein-: ∼kind das small child; **∼kram** der (ugs.) odds and ends pl.; (unbedeutende Dinge) trivial matters pl.; **∼kredit** der (Bankw.) personal loan ⟨repayable within two years⟩; **∼|kriegen** tr. V. (ugs.) **(a)** (zerkleinern) crush [to pieces]; **(b)** (zerstören) smash; break; **(c)** (aufbrauchen) get through; **(d)** jmdn. **∼kriegen** get sb. down (coll.); (durch Drohungen) intimidate sb.; (gefügig machen) bring sb. into line; **∼kunst** die cabaret; **∼laut** **1** Adj. subdued; (verlegen) sheepish; **2** adv. in a subdued fashion; (verlegen) sheepishly

kleinlich (abwertend) **1** Adj. pernickety; (ohne Großzügigkeit) mean; (engstirnig) small-minded; petty

2 adv. meticulously

Kleinod das; ∼[e]s, ∼e od. ∼ien (geh.) **(a)** (Schmuckstück) piece of jewellery; (Edelstein) jewel

(b) (Kostbarkeit) gem

klein-, Klein-: ∼|rechnen tr. V. undercalculate; *∼|schneiden ▶ KLEIN 1A; **∼stadt** die small town;

∼städter der, **∼städterin** die small-town dweller

Kleinste der/die/das; adj. Dekl. youngest boy/girl/child

klein|stellen tr. V. turn down [low]

Klein·wagen der small car

Kleister der; ∼s, ∼: paste

Klementine die; ∼, ∼n clementine

Klemme die; ∼, ∼n clip; **in der ∼ sein** od. **sitzen** (ugs.) be in a fix (coll.)

klemmen **1** tr. V. **(a)** (befestigen) tuck; stick (coll.)

(b) (quetschen) **sich** (Dat.) **den Fuß/die Hand ∼:** get one's foot/hand caught or trapped **2** refl. V. **sich hinter etw.** (Akk.) **∼** (fig. ugs.) put some hard work into sth.

3 itr. V. ⟨door, drawer, etc.⟩ stick

Klempner der; ∼s, ∼, **Klempnerin** die; ∼, ∼nen tinsmith; (Installateur[in]) plumber

Kleptomanie die; ∼ (Psych.) kleptomania no art.

klerikal Adj. (auch abwertend) clerical; church ⟨property⟩

Klerus der; ∼: clergy

Klette die; ∼, ∼n bur; (Pflanze) burdock

klettern itr. V.; mit sein (auch fig.) climb; **auf einen Baum ∼:** climb a tree

Kletter·pflanze die creeper; (Bot.) climbing plant; climber

Klett·verschluss, *Klett·verschluß der Velcro ® fastening

klicken itr. V. click

Klient der; ∼en, ∼en, **Klientin** die; ∼, ∼nen client

Klima das; ∼s, ∼s od. **Klimate** climate

Klima·anlage die air conditioning no indef. art.

klimatisch Adj. climatic

klimatisieren tr. V. air-condition

Klima-: ∼wandel der climate change; **∼wechsel** der climate change; (Med.) change of climate

Klimm·zug der (Turnen) pull-up

klimpern **1** itr. V. jingle

2 tr. V. (ugs. abwertend) plunk out ⟨tune etc.⟩

Klinge die; ∼, ∼n blade

Klingel die; ∼, ∼n bell

Klingel-: ∼beutel der offertory bag; collection bag; **∼knopf** der bell push

klingeln itr. V. ring; ⟨alarm clock⟩ go off; **es klingelt** (an der Tür) there is a ring at the door; (Telefon) the telephone is ringing

Klingel·ton der ringtone

klingen unr. itr. V. sound; **die Glocken klangen** the bells were ringing

Klinik die; ∼, ∼en hospital; (spezialisiert) clinic

Klinke die; ∼, ∼n door handle

Klinker der; ∼s, ∼: [Dutch] clinker

klipp Adv. **∼ und klar** (ugs.) quite plainly

Klippe die; ∼, ∼n rock

klirren itr. V. clink; ⟨weapons in fight⟩ clash; ⟨window pane⟩ rattle; ⟨chains, spurs⟩ rattle; ⟨harness⟩ jingle

Klischee das; ~s, ~s cliché

klitsch·nass, *klitsch·naß Adj. (ugs.) sopping wet; (tropfnass) dripping wet

klitze·klein Adj. (ugs.) teeny[-weeny] (coll.)

Klo das; ~s, ~s (ugs.) loo (Brit. coll.); john (Amer. coll.)

Kloake die; ~, ~n cesspit; (Kanal) sewer

klobig Adj. heavy and clumsy[-looking] ⟨shoes, furniture⟩; bulky ⟨figure⟩; (plump) clumsy

Klon der; ~s, ~e (Biol.) clone

klonen tr. V. clone

Klo·papier das (ugs.) loo paper (Brit. coll.); toilet paper

klopfen ⟨1⟩ itr. V. (a) (schlagen) knock (b) (pulsieren) ⟨heart⟩ beat; ⟨pulse⟩ throb ⟨2⟩ tr. V. beat ⟨carpet⟩

Klöppel der; ~s, ~ (Glocken~) clapper

klöppeln tr., itr. V. [etw.] ~: make [sth. in] pillow lace

Klops der; ~es, ~e (nordostd.) meat ball

Klosett das; ~s, ~s od. ~e lavatory

Kloß der; ~es, Klöße dumpling; (Fleisch~) meat ball

Kloster das; ~s, Klöster (Mönchs~) monastery; (Nonnen~) convent

Klotz der; ~es, Klötze block [of wood]; (Stück eines Baumstamms) log

Klub der; ~s, ~s club

Klub·sessel der club chair

Kluft[1] die; ~, ~en (ugs.) gear (coll.); (Uniform) garb

Kluft[2] die; ~, Klüfte (veralt.) (Spalte) cleft; (im Gletscher) crevasse; (Abgrund) chasm; (fig.) gulf

klug; klüger, klügst... Adj. clever; bright ⟨child, pupil⟩; intelligent ⟨eyes⟩; (vernünftig) wise; sound ⟨advice⟩; (geschickt) shrewd ⟨politician, negotiator, question⟩; astute ⟨businessman⟩

Klugheit die; ~ ▶ KLUG: cleverness; brightness; intelligence; wisdom; soundness; shrewdness; astuteness

klumpen itr. V. go lumpy

Klumpen der; ~s, ~: lump; **ein ~ Gold** a gold nugget

km Abk. = **Kilometer** km.

knabbern ⟨1⟩ tr. V. nibble ⟨2⟩ itr. V. **an etw.** (Dat.) ~: nibble [at] sth.

Knabe der; ~n, ~n (geh. veralt./südd., österr., schweiz.) boy; (ugs.: Bursche) chap (coll.)

knabenhaft ⟨1⟩ Adj. boyish ⟨2⟩ adv. boyishly

Knäcke·brot das crispbread; (Scheibe) slice of crispbread

knacken ⟨1⟩ itr. V. (a) ⟨bed, floor, etc.⟩ creak

(b) mit sein (ugs.: zerbrechen) snap; ⟨window⟩ crack

⟨2⟩ tr. V. (a) crack ⟨nut, shell⟩ (b) (salopp: aufbrechen) crack ⟨safe⟩ [open]; break into ⟨car, bank, etc.⟩

knackig Adj. (a) crisp (b) (ugs.: attraktiv) delectable

Knacks der; ~es, ~e (ugs.) crack; (fig.: Defekt) **einen ~ bekommen** ⟨person⟩ have a breakdown; ⟨health⟩ suffer

Knall der; ~[e]s, ~e bang

knallen ⟨1⟩ itr. V. (a) ⟨shot⟩ ring out; ⟨firework⟩ go bang; ⟨cork⟩ pop; ⟨door⟩ slam; ⟨whip, rifle⟩ crack; **mit der Tür ~:** slam the door

(b) (ugs.: schießen) shoot, fire (**auf** + Akk. at) (c) (Ballspiele ugs.) **aufs Tor ~:** belt the ball/puck at the goal (coll.) ⟨2⟩ tr. V. (a) (ugs.) slam down; (werfen) sling (coll.)

(b) (ugs.: schlagen) **jmdm. eine ~** (salopp) belt sb. one (coll.)

knall-: ~hart (ugs.) ⟨1⟩ Adj. very tough ⟨demands, measures, etc.⟩; ⟨person⟩ as hard as nails; ⟨2⟩ adv. brutally; **gegen etw. ~hart vorgehen** take very tough action against sth.; **~rot** Adj. bright or vivid red; **sie wurde ~rot** she turned as red as a beetroot

knapp ⟨1⟩ Adj. (a) meagre; narrow ⟨victory, lead⟩; narrow, bare ⟨majority⟩; **die Vorräte wurden ~:** supplies ran short; **vor einer ~en Stunde** just under an hour ago

(b) (eng) tight-fitting ⟨garment⟩; (zu eng) tight ⟨garment⟩

(c) (kurz) terse ⟨reply, greeting⟩; succinct ⟨description, account, report⟩ ⟨2⟩ adv. (a) **~ bemessen sein** be meagre, ⟨time⟩ be limited; **~ gewinnen/verlieren** win/lose narrowly; **er ist ~ fünfzig** he is just this side of fifty

(b) (eng) **~ sitzen** fit tightly; (zu eng) be a tight fit

(c) (kurz) ⟨reply⟩ tersely; ⟨describe, summarize⟩ succinctly

Knappheit die; ~ (a) (Mangel) shortage (**an** + Dat. of)

(b) (Kürze) (einer Antwort, eines Grußes) terseness; (einer Beschreibung, eines Berichts) succinctness

Knarre die; ~, ~n (salopp: Gewehr) shooting iron (coll.)

knarren itr. V. creak

Knast der; ~[e]s, Knäste od. ~e (ugs.) (a) (Strafe) bird (sl.); time (b) (Gefängnis) clink (sl.); prison

Knatsch der; ~[e]s (ugs.: Ärger) trouble

knattern itr. V. clatter; ⟨sail⟩ flap; ⟨radio⟩ crackle

Knäuel der od. das; ~s, ~ ball; (wirres ~) tangle

Knauf der; ~[e]s, Knäufe knob; (eines Schwertes, Dolches) pommel

---

*old spelling – see note on page x

knauserig *Adj.* (ugs. abwertend) stingy; tight-fisted

knausern *itr. V.* (ugs. abwertend) be stingy; skimp

knautschen (ugs.) **1** *tr. V.* crumple; crease ‹*dress*›
2 *itr. V.* ‹*dress, material*› crease

Knebel *der;* ∼s, ∼ (a) gag
(b) (Griff) toggle

knebeln *tr. V.* gag

Knecht *der;* ∼[e]s, ∼e farm labourer

knechten *tr. V.* (geh.) reduce to slavery; enslave; (unterdrücken) oppress

Knechtschaft *die;* ∼, ∼en (geh.) bondage; slavery

kneifen **1** *unr. tr., itr. V.* pinch
2 *unr. itr. V.* (a) ‹*clothes*› be too tight
(b) (ugs.: sich drücken) chicken (coll.) out (**vor** + *Dat.* of)

Kneif·zange *die* pincers *pl.*

Kneipe *die;* ∼, ∼n (ugs.) pub (Brit. coll.); bar (Amer.)

Kneipen·tour *die* (ugs.) pub crawl

kneippen *itr. V.* (ugs.) take a Kneipp cure

Kneipp·kur *die* Kneipp cure

kneten *tr. V.* (a) (bearbeiten) knead ‹*dough, muscles*›; work ‹*clay*›
(b) (formen) model ‹*figure*›

Knet·masse *die* Plasticine ®

Knick *der;* ∼[e]s, ∼e sharp bend; (Falz) crease

knicken **1** *tr. V.* (a) (brechen) snap
(b) (falten) crease ‹*page, paper, etc.*›
2 *itr. V.; mit sein* snap

knick[e]rig *Adj.* (ugs. abwertend) stingy

Knick[e]rigkeit *die;* ∼ (ugs. abwertend) stinginess

Knicks *der;* ∼es, ∼e curtsy

knicksen *itr. V.* curtsy (**vor** + *Dat.* to)

Knie *das;* ∼s, ∼ /'kni:(ə)/ (a) knee
(b) (Biegung) sharp bend

knie-, Knie-: ∼**beuge** *die* knee bend; ∼**bund·hose** *die* knee breeches *pl.*; ∼**fall** *der:* einen ∼fall tun *od.* machen (auch fig.) go down on one's knees (**vor** + *Dat.* before); ∼**kehle** *die* hollow of the knee

knien /'kni:(ə)n/ **1** *itr. V.* kneel
2 *refl. V.* kneel [down]

Knie-: ∼**scheibe** *die* kneecap; ∼**strumpf** *der* knee-length sock

Kniff *der;* ∼[e]s, ∼e (a) pinch
(b) (Falte) crease
(c) (Kunstgriff) trick

knipsen *tr. V.* (a) (entwerten) clip; punch
(b) (fotografieren) take a snap[shot] of

Knirps *der;* ∼es, ∼e (a) ⓦ Taschenschirm) telescopic umbrella
(b) (ugs.: Junge) nipper (coll.)

knirschen *itr. V.* crunch; **mit den Zähnen** ∼: grind one's teeth

knistern *itr. V.* rustle; ‹*wood, fire*› crackle

knittern *tr., itr. V.* crease; crumple

knobeln *itr. V.* (mit Würfeln) play dice

Knob·lauch *der* garlic

Knoblauch·zehe *die* clove of garlic

Knöchel *der;* ∼s, ∼: ankle; (am Finger) knuckle

Knochen *der;* ∼s, ∼: bone

knochen-, Knochen-: ∼**bau** *der* bone structure; ∼**bruch** *der* fracture; ∼**hart** *Adj.* (ugs.) rock-hard; ∼**mark** *das* bone marrow

knochig *Adj.* bony

Knödel *der;* ∼s, ∼ (bes. südd., österr.) dumpling

Knöllchen *das;* ∼s, ∼ (ugs.: Strafzettel) [parking] ticket

Knolle *die;* ∼, ∼n tuber

Knopf *der;* ∼[e]s, Knöpfe button; (Knauf) knob

knöpfen *tr. V.* button [up]

Knopf·loch *das* buttonhole

Knorpel *der;* ∼s, ∼ (Anat.) cartilage; (im Steak o. Ä.) gristle

knorrig *Adj.* gnarled

Knospe *die;* ∼, ∼n bud

knospen *itr. V.* bud

knoten *tr. V.* knot

Knoten *der;* ∼s, ∼: knot; (Haartracht) bun; knot; (Med.) lump

Knoten·punkt *der* junction; intersection

Know-how /noʊ'haʊ/ *das;* ∼[s] know-how

knuffen *tr. V.* poke

Knüller *der;* ∼s, ∼ (ugs.) sensation; (Angebot, Verkaufsartikel) sensational offer

knüpfen *tr. V.* (a) tie (**an** + *Akk.* to); **Bedingungen an etw.** (*Akk.*) ∼: attach conditions to sth.
(b) (durch Knoten herstellen) knot; make ‹*net*›

Knüppel *der;* ∼s, ∼ cudgel; (Polizei∼) truncheon

knüppel-, Knüppel-: ∼**dick** *Adv.* (ugs.) **es kam** ∼dick it was one disaster after the other; ∼**schaltung** *die* (Kfz-W.) floor [-type] gear change

knurren *itr. V.* (a) ‹*animal*› growl; (wütend) snarl; (fig.) ‹*stomach*› rumble
(b) (murren) grumble (**über** + *Akk.* about)

knusprig *Adj.* crisp; crusty ‹*bread, roll*›

knutschen (ugs.) **1** *tr. V.* smooch with (coll.); (sexuell berühren) pet; **sich** ∼: smooch (coll.)/pet
2 *itr. V.* smooch (coll.); (sich sexuell berühren) pet

k. o. /ka:'|o:/ *Adj.* (a) (Boxen) **jmdn. k. o schlagen** knock sb. out
(b) (ugs.: übermüdet) all in (coll.)

koalieren *itr. V.* (Politik) form a coalition (**mit** with)

Koalition *die;* ∼, ∼en coalition

Koax·kabel *das* (Technik Jargon) coax [cable]; coaxial cable

Kobalt *das;* ~s (Chemie) cobalt
Kobold *der;* ~[e]s, ~e goblin
Kobra *die;* ~, ~s cobra
Koch *der;* ~[e]s, **Köche** cook; (Küchenchef) chef
Koch·buch *das* cookery book (Brit.); cookbook (Amer.)
kochen [1] *tr. V.* (a) boil; (zubereiten) cook ⟨*meal*⟩; make ⟨*purée, jam*⟩; **Tee** ~: make some tea
(b) (waschen) boil
[2] *itr. V.* (a) (Speisen zubereiten) cook
(b) (sieden) ⟨*water, milk, etc.*⟩ boil
Kocher *der;* ~s, ~ [small] stove; (Kochplatte) hotplate
Köcher *der;* ~s, ~ (für Pfeile) quiver
Koch·feld *das* ceramic hob
Köchin *die;* ~, ~nen cook
Koch-: ~**löffel** *der* wooden spoon; ~**nische** *die* kitchenette; ~**salz** *das* common salt; ~**topf** *der* [cooking] pot; ~**wäsche** *die* washing that is to be boiled
Köder *der;* ~s, ~: bait
ködern *tr. V.* lure
Koffein *das;* ~s caffeine
koffein·frei *Adj.* decaffeinated
Koffer *der;* ~s, ~: [suit]case
Koffer-: ~**kuli** *der* luggage trolley; ~**radio** *das* portable radio; ~**raum** *der* boot (Brit.); trunk (Amer.)
Kognak /'kɔnjak/ *der;* ~s, ~s brandy; *s. auch* COGNAC
Kohl *der;* ~[e]s (a) cabbage
(b) (ugs. abwertend: Unsinn) rubbish; rot (coll.)
Kohl·dampf *der* (salopp) ~ **haben** be ravenously hungry
Kohle *die;* ~, ~n (a) coal
(b) (salopp: Geld) dough (coll.)
Kohle·hydrat ▶ KOHLENHYDRAT
kohlen[1] *itr. V.* smoulder; ⟨*wick*⟩ smoke
kohlen[2] *itr. V.* (fam.) (lügen) tell fibs; (übertreiben) exaggerate
Kohlen-: ~**dioxid,** ~**dioxyd** /--'---/ *das* (Chemie) carbon dioxide; ~**grube** *die* coal mine; ~**händler** *der,* ~**händlerin** *die* coal merchant; ~**hydrat** *das* (Chemie) carbohydrate; ~**monoxid,** ~**monoxyd** /--'---/ *das* (Chemie) carbon monoxide; ~**säure** *die* (Chemie) carbon dioxide; carbonic acid; ~**stoff** *der* carbon
Kohle·papier *das* carbon paper
Köhler *der;* ~s, ~: charcoal burner
Kohle·zeichnung *die* charcoal drawing
Kohl-: ~**kopf** *der* [head of] cabbage; ~**rübe** *die* swede
Koitus *der;* ~, **Koitus** (geh.) sexual intercourse; coitus (formal)
Koje *die;* ~, ~n (a) (Seemannsspr.) bunk; berth

(b) (Ausstellungsstand) stand
(c) (ugs. scherzh.: Bett) bed
Kokain *das;* ~s cocaine
kokett [1] *Adj.* coquettish
[2] *adv.* coquettishly
kokettieren *itr. V.* mit etw. ~: make much play with sth.
Kokos·nuss, ***Kokos·nuß** *die* coconut
Koks *der;* ~es coke
Kolben *der;* ~s, ~ (a) (Technik) piston
(b) (Chemie: Glas~) flask
(c) (Teil des Gewehrs) butt
Kolchose /kɔl'çoːzə/ *die;* ~, ~n kolkhoz; Soviet collective farm
Kolibri *der;* ~s, ~s hummingbird
Kolik *die;* ~, ~en colic
Kollaborateur /kɔlabora'tøːɐ̯/ *der;* ~s, ~e, **Kollaborateurin** *die;* ~, ~nen collaborator
Kollaps *der;* ~es, ~e collapse
Kolleg *das;* ~s, ~s lecture
Kollege *der;* ~n, ~n colleague
kollegial [1] *Adj.* helpful and considerate
[2] *adv.* ⟨*act etc.*⟩ like a good colleague/good colleagues
Kollegin *die;* ~, ~nen colleague
Kollegium *das;* ~s, **Kollegien** (a) (Gruppe) group; (unmittelbar zusammenarbeitend) team
(b) (Lehrkörper) [teaching] staff
Kollekte *die;* ~, ~n collection
Kollektion *die;* ~, ~en collection; (Sortiment) range
kollektiv [1] *Adj.* collective
[2] *adv.* collectively
kollidieren *itr. V.* (a) *mit sein* collide
(b) (fig.) conflict
Kollier /kɔ'lieː/ *das;* ~s, ~s necklace
Kollision *die;* ~, ~en collision
Köln *(das);* ~s Cologne
Kölner [1] *indekl. Adj.* Cologne *attrib.;* (in Köln) in Cologne *postpos., not pred;* ⟨*suburb, archbishop, mayor, speciality*⟩ of Cologne
[2] *der;* ~s, ~: inhabitant of Cologne; (von Geburt) native of Cologne
Kölnerin *die;* ~, ~nen ▶ KÖLNER 2
Kolonialisierung *die;* ~, ~en colonialization
Kolonialismus *der;* ~: colonialism *no art.*
Kolonie *die;* ~, ~n colony
kolonisieren *tr. V.* colonize
Kolonisierung *die;* ~, ~en colonization
Kolonne *die;* ~, ~n column
Koloss, ***Koloß** *der;* **Kolosses, Kolosse** (auch fig. ugs.) giant
kolossal [1] *Adj.* (a) colossal; gigantic
(b) (ugs.: sehr groß) tremendous (coll.); incredible (coll.) ⟨*rubbish, nonsense*⟩
[2] *adv.* (ugs.) tremendously (coll.)
Kolumbianer *der;* ~s, ~,
Kolumbianerin *die;* ~, ~nen Colombian

***alte Schreibung – vgl. Hinweis auf S. x

Kolumbien /ko'lʊmbiən/ (*das*); ~s
Colombia

Koma /'ko:ma/ *das;* ~s, ~s *od.* ~ta (Med.)
coma

Komasaufen *das* binge-drinking

Kombination *die;* ~, ~en
(a) combination
(b) (gedankliche Verknüpfung) deduction; piece
of reasoning
(c) (Kleidungsstücke) ensemble; suit; (Herren~)
suit

kombinieren ① *tr. V.* combine
② *itr. V.* deduce; reason

Kombi-: ~**wagen** *der* estate [car];
station wagon (Amer.); ~**zange** *die*
combination pliers *pl.*

Komet *der;* ~en, ~en comet

Komfort /kɔm'foːɐ̯/ *der;* ~s comfort

komfortabel ① *Adj.* comfortable
② *adv.* comfortably

Komik *die;* ~: comic effect; (komisches
Element) comic element

Komiker *der;* ~s, ~, **Komikerin** *die* ~,
~en (a) (Vortragskünstler[in]) comedian
(b) (Darsteller[in]) comic actor

komisch *Adj.* (a) comical; funny
(b) (seltsam) funny

Komitee *das;* ~s, ~s committee

Komma *das;* ~s, ~s *od.* ~ta comma;
(Math.) decimal point; **zwei** ~ **acht** two point
eight

Kommandant *der;* ~en, ~en (Milit.)
commanding officer

Kommandeur /kɔman'døːɐ̯/ *der;* ~s, ~e
(Milit.) ▶ KOMMANDANT

kommandieren ① *tr. V.* (a) command;
be in command of; order ‹*retreat, advance*›
(b) (ugs.) jmdn. ~: boss sb. about (coll.)
② *itr. V.* (ugs.) boss people about (coll.)

Kommandit·gesellschaft *die* (Wirtsch.)
limited partnership

Kommando *das;* ~s, ~s command

Komma·stelle *die* decimal place; **auf
die** ~ **[genau]** [correct] to the last decimal
place; (fig.) ‹*know, calculate*› with complete
accuracy

kommen *unr. itr. V.; mit sein* (a) come;
angelaufen ~: come running along; (auf jmdn.
zu) come running up
(b) (gelangen, geraten) get; **unter ein Auto** ~:
be knocked down by a car; **wie kommst du
darauf?** what gives you that idea?
(c) ~ **lassen** (bestellen) order ‹*taxi*›; **den Arzt/
die Polizei** ~ **lassen** send for a doctor/the
police
(d) (aufgenommen werden) **zur Schule/aufs
Gymnasium** ~: start school/grammar school
(e) (auftauchen) ‹*seeds, plants*› come up;
‹*buds, flowers*› come out; ‹*teeth*› come
through
(f) (seinen festen Platz haben) go; belong; **in die
Schublade**~: go *or* belong in the drawer;
(seinen Platz erhalten) **in die Mannschaft** ~: get

into the team; **auf den ersten Platz** ~: go
into first place
(g) (Gelegenheit haben) **dazu** ~, **etw. zu tun** get
round to doing sth.
(h) (sich ereignen) come about; **wie kommt es,
dass …**: how is it that …; how come that …
(coll.)
(i) (etw. erlangen) **zu Geld** ~: become wealthy;
zu Erfolg/Ruhm *usw.* ~: gain success/fame
etc.

kommend *Adj.* (a) (folgend) next; **in den
~en Jahren** in years to come
(b) (mit großer Zukunft) **der** ~**e Mann/Meister**
the coming man/future champion

Kommentar *der;* ~s, ~e commentary;
(Stellungnahme) comment; **kein** ~**!** no
comment!

Kommentator *der;* ~s, ~en,
Kommentatorin *die;* ~, ~nen
commentator

kommentieren *tr. V.* (a) (erläutern)
furnish with a commentary ‹*text, work*›
(b) (Stellung nehmen zu) comment on

kommerziell ① *Adj.* commercial
② *adv.* commercially

Kommiss, *Kommiß *der;* Kommisses
(Soldatenspr.) army

Kommissar *der;* ~s, ~e,
Kommissarin *die;* ~, ~nen (a) (Beamter/
Beamtin der Polizei) detective superintendent
(b) (staatlicher Beauftragter/staatliche Beauftragte)
commissioner

Kommission *die;* ~, ~en (a) (Gremium)
committee; (Prüfungs~) commission
(b) **etw. in** ~ **nehmen/haben/geben** (Wirtsch.)
take/have sth. on commission/give sth. to a
dealer for sale on commission

Kommode *die;* ~, ~n chest of drawers

kommunal *Adj.* local; (bei einer städtischen
Gemeinde) municipal; local

Kommunal·wahl *die* local [government]
elections *pl.*

Kommunikation *die;* ~, ~en (Sprachw.,
Soziol.) communication

Kommunion *die;* ~, ~en (kath. Kirche)
[Holy] Communion

Kommuniqué /kɔmyni'keː/ *das;* ~s, ~s
communiqué

Kommunismus *der;* ~: communism

Kommunist *der;* ~en, ~en,
Kommunistin *die;* ~, ~nen communist

kommunistisch ① *Adj.* communist
② *adv.* Communist-‹*influenced, led, ruled,
etc.*›

kommunizieren *itr. V.* (a) (geh.)
communicate
(b) (kath. Kirche) receive [Holy] Communion

Komödiant *der;* ~en, ~en,
Komödiantin *die;* ~, ~nen (veralt.)
actor/actress; player; (abwertend: Heuchler[in])
play-actor

Komödie /ko'møːdiə/ *die;* ~, ~n comedy;
(Theater) comedy theatre

Kompagnon /kɔmpan'jõ:/ *der;* ~s, ~s
(Wirtsch.) partner; associate

kompakt *Adj.* solid

Kompanie *die;* ~, ~n company

Komparativ *der;* ~s, ~e (Sprachw.)
comparative

Kompass, *Kompaß *der;* Kompasses,
Kompasse compass

kompatibel *Adj.* (Nachrichtenw., Sprachw.)
compatible

Kompatibilität *die;* ~, ~en compatibility

Kompensation *die;* ~, ~en (Wirtsch.,
Physik, geh.) compensation

kompensieren *tr. V.* etw. mit etw. *od.*
durch etw. ~: compensate for sth. by sth.

kompetent *Adj.* competent

Kompetenz *die;* ~, ~en competence; (bes.
Rechtsw.) authority

komplett ☐ *Adj.* complete
☐ *adv.* fully ⟨*furnished, equipped*⟩; (ugs.:
ganz und gar) completely

komplettieren *tr. V.* complete

Komplett·preis *der* all-inclusive price

komplex *Adj.* complex

Komplex *der;* ~es, ~e (auch Psych.)
complex

Komplexität *die;* ~: complexity

Komplikation *die;* ~, ~en (auch Med.)
complication

Kompliment *das;* ~[e]s, ~e compliment

Komplize *der;* ~n, ~n (abwertend)
accomplice

komplizieren *tr. V.* complicate

kompliziert ☐ *Adj.* complicated
☐ *adv.* ~ aufgebaut sein have a
complicated *or* complex structure

Kompliziertheit *die;* ~: complexity;
complicatedness

Komplizin *die;* ~, ~nen ▸ KOMPLIZE

Komplott *das;* ~[e]s, ~e plot; conspiracy

komponieren *tr., itr. V.* compose

Komponist *der;* ~en, ~en,
Komponistin *die;* ~, ~nen composer

Komposition *die;* ~, ~en composition

Kompost *der;* ~[e]s, ~e, compost

Kompost·haufen *der* compost heap

kompostierbar *Adj.* compostable

kompostieren *tr. V.* compost

Kompott *das;* ~[e]s, ~e stewed fruit;
compote

Kompresse *die;* ~, ~n (Med.)
(a) (Umschlag) [wet] compress
(b) (Mull) [gauze] pad

Kompression *die;* ~, ~en (Physik, Technik,
Med., DV) compression

Kompressor *der;* ~s, ~en (Technik)
compressor

komprimieren *tr. V.* (auch Physik, Technik,
DV) compress

Kompromiss, *Kompromiß *der;*
Kompromisses, Kompromisse compromise

**kompromiss-, *kompromiß-,
Kompromiss-, *Kompromiß-:**
~**bereit** *Adj.* willing to compromise *pred.*;
~**los** ☐ *Adj.* uncompromising; ☐ *adv.*
uncompromisingly; ~**vorschlag** *der*
compromise proposal

kompromittieren *tr. V.* compromise

Kondensation *die;* ~, ~en (Physik,
Chemie) condensation

Kondensator *der;* ~s, ~en (Elektrot.)
capacitor

kondensieren *tr., itr. V. itr. auch mit sein*
(Physik, Chemie) condense

Kondens-: ~**milch** *die* condensed
milk; ~**streifen** *der* condensation trail;
~**wasser** *das* condensation

Kondition *die;* ~, ~en condition; eine
gute/schlechte ~ haben be/not be in good
condition *or* shape; keine ~ haben be out of
condition; (fig.) have no stamina

Konditional·satz *der* (Sprachw.)
conditional clause

Konditions·training *das* fitness
training

Konditor *der;* ~s, ~en pastry cook

Konditorei *die;* ~, ~en cake shop; (Lokal)
café

kondolieren *itr. V.* offer one's
condolences; jmdm. [zu jmds. Tod] ~: offer
one's condolences to sb. [on sb.'s death]

Kondom *das od. der;* ~s, ~e condom

Konfekt *das;* ~[e]s (a) confectionery;
sweets *pl.* (Brit.); candies *pl.* (Amer.)
(b) (bes. südd., österr., schweiz.: Teegebäck)
[small] fancy biscuits *pl.* (Brit.) *or* (Amer.)
cookies *pl.*

Konfektion *die;* ~, ~en ready-made
garments *pl.*

Konferenz *die;* ~, ~en conference;
(Besprechung) meeting

konferieren *itr. V.* confer (über + *Akk.*
on, about)

Konfession *die;* ~, ~en denomination

konfessionell ☐ *Adj.* denominational
☐ *adv.* as regards denomination;
~ [un]gebunden sein have [no]
denominational ties

Konfetti *das;* ~[s] confetti

Konfirmand *der;* ~en, ~en,
Konfirmandin *die;* ~, ~nen (ev. Rel.)
confirmand

Konfirmation *die;* ~, ~en (ev. Rel.)
confirmation

konfirmieren *tr. V.* (ev. Rel.) confirm

konfiszieren *tr. V.* (bes. Rechtsw.)
confiscate

Konfitüre *die;* ~, ~n jam

Konflikt *der;* ~[e]s, ~e conflict

Konföderation *die;* ~, ~en
confederation

---

*old spelling – see note on page x

konform *Adj.* concurring *attrib.;* ~ **gehen** be in agreement
Konformismus *der;* ~: conformism
Konformist *der;* ~en, ~en,
Konformistin *die;* ~, ~: conformist
konformistisch ① *Adj.* conformist
② *adv.* in a conformist way
Konfrontation *die;* ~, ~en confrontation
konfrontieren *tr. V.* confront
konfus ① *Adj.* confused
② *adv.* in a confused fashion
Kongo[1] *der;* ~[s] (Fluss) Congo
Kongo[2] *(das);* ~s *od.* der; ~[s] (Staat) the Congo
Kongress, Kongreß *der;* Kongresses, Kongresse congress; conference; **der** ~ (USA): Congress
Kongress·halle, *Kongreß·halle *die* conference hall
König *der;* ~s, ~e king
Königin *die;* ~, ~nen queen
königlich ① *Adj.* (a) royal
(b) (vornehm) regal
(c) (reichlich) princely ⟨*gift, salary, wage*⟩
② *adv.* ⟨*pay*⟩ handsomely; (ugs.: außerordentlich) ⟨*enjoy oneself*⟩ immensely (coll.)
König·reich *das* kingdom
Königs·haus *das* royal house
Königtum *das;* ~s, Königtümer
(a) (Monarchie) monarchy
(b) (veralt.: Reich) kingdom
Konjugation *die;* ~, ~en (Sprachw.) conjugation
konjugieren *tr. V.* (Sprachw.) conjugate
Konjunktion *die;* ~, ~en (Sprachw.) conjunction
Konjunktiv *der;* ~s, ~e (Sprachw.) subjunctive
Konjunktur *die;* ~, ~en (Wirtsch.)
(a) (wirtschaftliche Lage) [level of] economic activity; economy; (Tendenz) economic trend
(b) (Hoch~) boom; (Aufschwung) upturn [in the economy]
konjunkturell *Adj.* economic
Konjunktur·politik *die* (Wirtsch.) measures *pl.* aimed at avoiding violent fluctuations in the economy
konkav (Optik) ① *Adj.* concave
② *adv.* concavely
konkret ① *Adj.* concrete
② *adv.* in concrete terms
konkretisieren *tr. V.* etw. ~: put sth. in concrete terms
Konkurrent *der;* ~en, ~en,
Konkurrentin *die;* ~, ~nen (Sport, Wirtsch.) competitor
Konkurrenz *die;* ~, ~en (Sport, Wirtsch.) competition
konkurrenz-, Konkurrenz-:
~**fähig** *Adj.* competitive; ~**kampf** *der*

competition; (zwischen zwei Menschen) rivalry
konkurrieren *itr. V.* compete
Konkurs *der;* ~es, ~e (a) (Bankrott) bankruptcy; ~ **machen** *od.* in ~ **gehen** go bankrupt
(b) (gerichtliches Verfahren) bankruptcy proceedings *pl.*
können ① *unr. Modalverb; 2. Part.* **können: (a)** be able to; **er kann gut reden/ tanzen** he is a good talker/dancer; **ich kann nicht schlafen** I cannot *or* (coll.) can't sleep; **kann das explodieren?** could it explode?; **man kann nie wissen** you never know; **es kann sein, dass …:** it could be that …; **kann ich Ihnen helfen?** can I help you?
(b) (Grund haben) **du kannst ganz ruhig sein** you don't have to worry; **das kann man wohl sagen!** you could well say that
(c) (dürfen) **kann ich gehen?** can I go?; ~ **wir mit[kommen]?** can we come too?
② *unr. tr. V.* (beherrschen) know ⟨*language*⟩; be able to play ⟨*game*⟩; **sie kann das [gut]** she can do that [well]; **etw./ nichts für etw.** ~: be/not be responsible for sth.
③ *unr. itr. V.* (a) (fähig sein) **er kann nicht anders** there's nothing else he can do; (es ist seine Art) he can't help it (coll.)
(b) (Zeit haben) **ich kann heute nicht** I can't today (coll.)
(c) (ugs.: Kraft haben) **kannst du noch [weiter]?** can you go on?
(d) (ugs.: umgehen ~) **[gut] mit jmdm.** ~: get on [well] with sb.
Können *das;* ~s ability
Könner *der;* ~s, ~, **Könnerin** *die;* ~, ~nen expert
konnte *1. u. 3. Pers. Sg. Prät. v.* KÖNNEN
könnte *1. u. 3. Pers. Sg. Konjunktiv II v.* KÖNNEN
Konsens·gespräch *das* (Politik) discussion aimed at reaching a consensus
konsequent ① *Adj.* consistent; (folgerichtig) logical
② *adv.* consistently; (folgerichtig) logically
Konsequenz *die;* ~, ~en (a) (Folge) consequence
(b) (Unbeirrbarkeit) determination
konservativ ① *Adj.* conservative
② *adv.* conservatively
Konservative *der/die; adj. Dekl.* conservative
Konservatorium *das;* ~s, Konservatorien conservatoire; conservatory (Amer.)
Konserve *die;* ~, ~n (a) (Büchse) can; tin (Brit.)
(b) (konservierte Lebensmittel) preserved food; (in Dosen) canned *or* (Brit.) tinned food
Konserven-: ~**büchse** *die*, ~**dose** *die* can; tin (Brit.)
konservieren *tr. V.* preserve; conserve ⟨*work of art*⟩ ····⫶

k

Konservierung *die;* ~, ~en preservation
Konservierungs·mittel *das*
preservative
konsolidieren *tr. V.* consolidate
Konsolidierung *die;* ~, ~en (Festigung)
consolidation
Konsonant *der;* ~en, ~en consonant
Konsortium *das;* ~s, Konsortien (Wirtsch.)
consortium
konspirativ /kɔnspira'ti:f/ *Adj.*
conspiratorial
konstant /kɔn'stant/ ① *Adj.* (a) constant
(b) (beharrlich) persistent
② *adv.* (a) constantly
(b) (beharrlich) persistently
Konstellation /kɔnstɛla'tsi̯oːn/ *die;* ~,
~en (a) (von Parteien usw.) grouping; (von
Umständen) combination
(b) (Astron., Astrol.) constellation
konstituieren /kɔnstitu'iːrən/ ① *tr. V.*
(gründen) constitute; set up
② *refl. V.* be constituted
Konstitution /kɔnstitu'tsi̯oːn/ *die;* ~,
~en constitution
konstruieren /kɔnstru'iːrən/ *tr. V.*
(a) (entwerfen) design
(b) (aufbauen, Geom., Sprachw.) construct
(c) (abwertend) fabricate
Konstrukteur /kɔnstrʊk'tøːɐ̯/ *der;* ~s,
~e, **Konstrukteurin** *die;* ~, ~nen
designer; design engineer
Konstruktion /kɔnstrʊk'tsi̯oːn/
die; ~, ~en (a) (Aufbau, Geom., Sprachw.)
construction; (das Entwerfen) designing
(b) (Entwurf) design; (Bau) construction
konstruktiv ① *Adj.* constructive
② *adv.* constructively
Konsul *der;* ~s, ~n (Dipl., hist.) consul
Konsulat *das;* ~[e]s, ~e (Dipl., hist.)
consulate
Konsulin *die;* ~, ~nen ► Konsul
konsultieren *tr. V.* (auch fig.) consult
Konsum *der;* ~s consumption
Konsument *der;* ~en, ~en,
Konsumentin *die;* ~, ~nen consumer
Konsum·gesellschaft *die* consumer
society
konsumieren *tr. V.* consume
Kontakt *der;* ~[e]s, ~e contact; mit *od.* zu
jmdm. ~ haben/halten be/remain in contact
with sb.
kontakt-, Kontakt-: ~**freudig**
Adj. sociable; ~**linse** *die* contact lens;
~**los** *Adj.* contactless; ~**mann** *der;*
Pl.: ~männer *od.* ~leute (Agent) contact;
~**person** *die* (Med.) contact
Kontamination *die;* ~, ~en
contamination
kontaminieren *tr. V.* contaminate
Konten ► Konto

kontern *tr., itr. V.* (Boxen, auch fig.) counter;
(Ballspiele) counter-attack
Konter·revolution *die* counter-
revolution
Kontinent *der;* ~[e]s, ~e continent
kontinental *Adj.* continental
Kontingent *das;* ~[e]s, ~e quota
kontinuierlich ① *Adj.* steady
② *adv.* steadily
Kontinuität *die;* ~: continuity
Konto *das;* ~s, Konten *od.* Konti account;
ein laufendes ~: a current account
Konto-: ~**auszug** *der* (Bankw.) [bank]
statement; ~**bewegung** *die* transaction;
~**nummer** *die* account number
Kontor *das;* ~s, ~e branch; (einer Reederei)
office
Konto·stand *der* (Bankw.) balance; state of
an/one's account
kontra ① *Präp. mit Akk.* (Rechtsspr., auch
fig.) versus
② *Adv.* against
Kontra *das;* ~s, ~s (Kartenspiele) double;
jmdm. ~ geben (fig. ugs.) flatly contradict sb.
Kontrahent *der;* ~en, ~en,
Kontrahentin *die;* ~, ~nen adversary;
opponent
konträr *Adj.* contrary; opposite
Kontrast *der;* ~[e]s, ~e contrast
Kontroll·abschnitt *der* stub
Kontrolle *die;* ~, ~n (a) (Überwachung)
surveillance
(b) (Überprüfung) check; (bei Waren, bei
Lebensmitteln) inspection
(c) (Herrschaft) control; die ~ über etw. (Akk.)
verlieren lose control of sth.
Kontrolleur /kɔntrɔ'løːɐ̯/ *der;* ~s, ~e,
Kontrolleurin *die;* ~, ~nen inspector
Kontroll·gang *der* tour of inspection;
(eines Nachtwächters) round; (eines Polizisten)
patrol
kontrollieren *tr. V.* (a) (überwachen)
check; monitor
(b) (überprüfen) check; inspect ⟨goods, food⟩
(c) (beherrschen) control
Kontrollturm *der* control tower
kontrovers ① *Adj.* conflicting; (strittig)
controversial
② *adv.* sich ~ zu etw. äußern express
conflicting opinions on sth.
Kontroverse /kɔntro'vɛrzə/ *die;* ~, ~n
controversy (um, über + Akk. about)
Kontur *die;* ~, ~en contour; outline
Konvention /kɔnvɛn'tsi̯oːn/ *die;* ~, ~en
convention
konventionell ① *Adj.* (a) conventional
(b) (förmlich) formal
② *adv.* (a) conventionally
(b) (förmlich) formally
Konversation /kɔnvɛrza'tsi̯oːn/ *die;* ~,
~en conversation

---

*alte Schreibung – vgl. Hinweis auf S. x

Konversations·lexikon *das* encyclopaedia

konvertieren ① *itr. V.; auch mit sein* (Rel.) be converted
② *tr. V.* (Wirtsch., DV) convert

konvex /kɔn'vɛks/ (Optik) ① *Adj.* convex
② *adv.* convexly

Konvoi /kɔn'vɔy/ *der;* ~s, ~s (bes. Milit.) convoy

Konzentration *die;* ~, ~en concentration

Konzentrations-: ~**fähigkeit** *die* ability to concentrate; ~**lager** *das* (bes. ns.) concentration camp

konzentrieren *refl., tr. V.* concentrate; sich auf etw. (*Akk.*) ~: concentrate on sth.

konzentriert ① *Adj.* concentrated
② *adv.* with concentration

Konzept *das;* ~[e]s, ~e (a) [rough] draft
(b) (Programm) programme; (Plan) plan

Konzern *der;* ~[e]s, ~e (Wirtsch.) group [of companies]

Konzert *das;* ~[e]s, ~e (a) (Komposition) concerto
(b) (Veranstaltung) concert

Konzert·saal *der* concert hall

Konzession *die;* ~, ~en (a) (Amtsspr.) licence
(b) (Zugeständnis) concession

Konzil *das;* ~s, ~e od. ~ien (kath. Kirche) council

konzipieren *tr. V.* draft; design ⟨*device, car, etc.*⟩

Kooperation *die;* ~, ~en cooperation *no indef. art.*

kooperativ ① *Adj.* cooperative
② *adv.* cooperatively

kooperieren *tr. V.* cooperate

Koordinate *die;* ~, ~n coordinate

Koordinaten·system *das* (Math.) system of coordinates

koordinieren *tr. V.* coordinate

Kopenhagen (*das*) ~s Copenhagen

Kopf *der;* ~[e]s, Köpfe (a) head; ein ~ Salat a lettuce; ~ an ~: shoulder to shoulder; (im Wettlauf) neck and neck; (fig.) ~ stehen (ugs.: überrascht sein) be bowled over; **nicht wissen, wo einem der ~ steht** not know whether one is coming or going; ~ hoch! chin up!; den ~ hängen lassen become disheartened
(b) (Person) person; **ein kluger/fähiger ~ sein** be a clever/able man/woman; pro ~: per head; **die führenden Köpfe der Wirtschaft** the leading minds in the field of economics
(c) (Wille) seinen ~ durchsetzen make sb. do what one wants
(d) (Verstand) mind; head; sich (*Dat.*) den ~ zerbrechen (ugs.) rack one's brains (**über** + *Akk.* over)

Kopf-: ~**bahnhof** *der* terminal station; ~**bedeckung** *die* headgear; **ohne** ~**bedeckung** without anything on one's head

Köpfchen *das;* ~s, ~: brains *pl.;* ~ **muss man haben** you've got to have it up here (coll.)

köpfen *tr. V.* (a) decapitate; (hinrichten) behead
(b) (Fußball) head

kopf-, Kopf-: ~**ende** *das* head end; ~**haut** *die* [skin of the] scalp; ~**hörer** *der* headphones *pl.;* ~**kissen** *das* pillow; ~**lastig** *Adj.* down by the head *pred.;* ~**los** ① *Adj.* rash; (in Panik) panic-stricken; ② *adv.* rashly; ~**los davonrennen** flee in panic; ~**rechnen** *itr. V.; nur im Inf. gebr.* do mental arithmetic; ~**rechnen** *das* mental arithmetic; ~**salat** *der* head lettuce; ~**schmerz** *der* headache; ~**schmerzen haben** have a headache *sing.;* ~**sprung** *der* header; ~**stand** *der* headstand; **~|***stehen** ▸ Kopf A; ~**stein·pflaster** *das* cobblestones *pl.;* ~**tuch** *das; Pl.* ~tücher headscarf; ~**weh** *das* (ugs.) headache; ~**weh haben** have a headache; ~**zerbrechen** *das;* ~s: etw. bereitet *od.* macht jmdm. ~zerbrechen *das* has to rack his/her brains about sth.; (etw. macht jmdm. Sorgen) sth. is a worry to sb.

Kopie *die;* ~, ~n copy; (Durchschrift) carbon copy; (Fotokopie) photocopy; (Fot., Film) print

kopieren *tr. V.* copy; (fotokopieren) photocopy; (Fot., Film) print

Kopierer *der;* ~s, ~: [photo]copier

Kopier·gerät *das* photocopier

Kopilot *der;* ~en, ~en, **Kopilotin** *die;* ~, ~nen (Flugw.) co-pilot

Koppel[1] *das;* ~s, ~, österr.: die; ~, ~n (Gürtel) [leather] belt (*as part of a uniform*)

Koppel[2] *die;* ~, ~n paddock

koppeln *tr. V.* couple (**an** + *Akk.* to); dock ⟨*spacecraft*⟩

Koppelung ▸ KOPPLUNG

Kopplung *die;* ~, ~en coupling; (Raumf.) docking

kopulieren *itr. V.* copulate

Koralle *die;* ~, ~n coral

Koran *der;* ~s, ~e Koran

Korb *der;* ~es, Körbe (a) basket
(b) jmdm. einen ~ geben turn sb. down

Korb·ball *der* netball

Kord *der;* ~[e]s (a) corduroy; cord
(b) ▸ KORDSAMT

Kordel *die;* ~, ~n cord

Kord·samt *der* cord velvet

Korea (*das*); ~s Korea

Koreaner *der;* ~s, ~, **Koreanerin** *die;* ~, ~nen Korean

koreanisch *Adj.* Korean

Korinthe *die;* ~, ~n currant

Kork *der;* ~s, ~e cork

Korken *der;* ~s, ~: cork

Korken·zieher *der;* ~s, ~: corkscrew

Korn[1] *das;* ~[e]s, Körner (a) (Frucht) grain; (Getreide~) grain [of corn]; (Pfeffer~) corn ┄┅▸

(b) *o. Pl.* (Getreide) corn; grain
(c) (Salz~, Sand~) grain; (Hagel~) stone
Korn² *der;* ~[e]s, ~ (ugs.) corn schnapps;
corn liquor (Amer.)
Korn·blume *die* cornflower
Körnchen *das;* ~s, ~: tiny grain; (von
Sand usw.) [tiny] grain; granule
Körner ▶ KORN
Korn·feld *das* cornfield
körnig *Adj.* granular
Korona *die;* ~, Koronen crowd (coll.)
Körper *der;* ~s, ~: body
körper-, Körper-: ~**bau** *der*
physique; ~**behindert** *Adj.* physically
handicapped; ~**behinderte**
der/die physically handicapped person;
~**behinderte** *Pl.* physically handicapped
people; ~**geruch** *der* body odour; BO
(coll.); ~**größe** *die* height
körperlich ① *Adj.* physical
② *adv.* physically
Körper·pflege *die* body care *no art.*
Körperschaft[s]·steuer *die* (Steuerw.)
corporation tax
Körper-: ~**spray** *der od. das* deodorant
spray; ~**teil** *der* part of the/one's body;
~**verletzung** *die* (Rechtsw.) bodily harm
no indef. art.
Korps /koːɐ̯/ *das;* ~ /koːɐ̯(s),/ ~ /koːɐ̯s/
(a) (Milit.) corps
(b) (Studentenverbindung) student duelling
society
korpulent *Adj.* corpulent
korrekt ① *Adj.* correct
② *adv.* correctly
korrekter·weise *Adv.* to be [strictly]
correct
Korrektheit *die;* ~: correctness
Korrektor *der;* ~s, ~en /-'toːrən/,
Korrektorin *die;* ~, ~nen proof-reader
Korrektur *die;* ~, ~en correction
Korrespondent *der;* ~en, ~en,
Korrespondentin *die;* ~, ~nen
correspondent
Korrespondenz *die;* ~, ~en
correspondence
korrespondieren *itr. V.* correspond
(mit with)
Korridor *der;* ~s, ~e corridor
korrigieren *tr. V.* correct; revise ⟨opinion,
view⟩
korrodieren *tr., itr. V.* (itr. mit sein) (bes.
Chemie, Geol.) corrode
Korrosion *die;* ~, ~en (auch Geol., Med.)
corrosion
korrosions-, Korrosions-:
~**beständig** *Adj.,* ~**fest** *Adj.* corrosion-
resistant; ~**schutz** *der* protection against
corrosion
korrupt *Adj.* corrupt

Korruption *die;* ~, ~en corruption
Korsett *das;* ~s, ~s *od.* ~e corset
Korsika (*das*); ~s Corsica
Kortison *das;* ~s (Med.) cortisone
koscher *Adj.* kosher
Kose-: ~**form** *die* familiar form;
~**name** *der* pet name
Kosinus *der;* ~, ~ *od.* ~se (Math.) cosine
Kosmetik *die;* ~ **(a)** beauty culture *no art.*
(b) (fig.) cosmetic procedures *pl.*
Kosmetikerin *die;* ~, ~nen cosmetician;
beautician
Kosmetikum *das;* ~s, Kosmetika
cosmetic
kosmetisch ① *Adj.* (auch fig.) cosmetic
② *adv.* jmdn. ~ beraten give sb. advice on
beauty care; **sich** ~ **behandeln lassen** have
beauty treatment
kosmisch *Adj.* cosmic ⟨ray, dust, etc.⟩;
space ⟨age, station, research, etc.⟩; meteoric
⟨iron⟩
Kosmos *der;* ~: cosmos
Kost *die;* ~: food; ~ **und Logis** board and
lodging
kostbar ① *Adj.* valuable; precious ⟨time⟩
② *adv.* expensively ⟨dressed⟩; luxuriously
⟨decorated⟩
Kostbarkeit *die;* ~, ~en **(a)** (Sache)
treasure
(b) (Eigenschaft) value
kosten¹ ① *tr. V.* taste; try
② *itr. V.* (probieren) have a taste
kosten² *tr. V.* **(a)** cost
(b) (erfordern) take; cost ⟨lives⟩
Kosten *Pl.* cost *sing.;* costs; (Auslagen)
expenses; (Rechtsw.) costs; **auf jmds.** ~: at
sb.'s expense
kosten-, Kosten-: ~**deckend** *Adj.*
that covers/cover [one's] costs *postpos., not
pred.;* ~**erstattung** *die* reimbursement
of costs; ~**los** ① *Adj.* free; ② *adv.* free
of charge; ~**pflichtig** (Rechtsw.) ① *Adj.*
eine ~pflichtige Verwarnung a fine and
a caution; ② *adv.* eine Klage ~pflichtig
abweisen dismiss a case with costs; ein
Auto ~pflichtig abschleppen tow a car
away at the owner's expense; ~**punkt** *der*
(ugs.) ~punkt? how much is it/are they?;
~punkt 25 Euro it costs/they cost 25 euros;
~**schub** *der* cost inflation; price increases
pl.; ~**stelle** *die* (Wirtsch.) cost centre;
~**vor·anschlag** *der* estimate
Kost·gänger *der;* ~s, ~,
Kost·gängerin *die;* ~, ~nen (veralt.)
boarder
köstlich ① *Adj.* delicious; (unterhaltsam)
delightful
② *adv.* ⟨taste⟩ delicious; **sich** ~ **amüsieren/
unterhalten** enjoy oneself enormously (coll.)
Köstlichkeit *die;* ~, ~en (Sache) delicacy
Kost·probe *die;* ~, ~n taste
kost·spielig *Adj.* costly

k

---
*old spelling – see note on page x

Kostüm *das;* ~s, ~e **(a)** suit
  (b) (Theater~, Verkleidung) costume
kostümieren *tr. V.* dress up
Kot *der;* ~[e]s, ~e excrement
Kotangens *der;* ~, ~ (Math.) cotangent
Kotelett /kɔt'lɛt/ *das;* ~s, ~s chop; (vom Nacken) cutlet
Koteletten *Pl.* side whiskers
Köter *der;* ~s, ~ (abwertend) cur
Kot·flügel *der* (Kfz-W.) wing
kotzen *itr. V.* (derb) puke (coarse)
KP *Abk.* = **Kommunistische Partei** CP
Krabbe *die;* ~, ~n **(a)** (Zool.) crab
  (b) (ugs.: Garnele) shrimp; (größer) prawn
krabbeln ① *itr. V.; mit sein* crawl
  ② *tr. V.* (ugs.: kraulen) tickle
Krach *der;* ~[e]s, Kräche **(a)** (Lärm) noise; row
  (b) (lautes Geräusch) crash
  (c) (ugs.: Streit) row
krachen ① *itr. V.* **(a)** (Krach auslösen) ⟨thunder⟩ crash; ⟨shot⟩ ring out
  (b) *mit sein* (ugs.: bersten) ⟨ice⟩ crack; ⟨bed⟩ collapse
  (c) *mit sein* (ugs.: mit Krach auftreffen) crash
  ② *refl. V.* (ugs.) row (coll.)
krächzen *itr. V.* ⟨raven, crow⟩ caw; ⟨parrot⟩ squawk; ⟨person⟩ croak
kraft *Präp. + Gen.* (Amtsspr.) ~ **[meines]** Amtes by virtue of my office; ~ Gesetzes by law
Kraft *die;* ~, Kräfte strength; (Wirksamkeit) power; (Physik) force; (Arbeits~) employee; **mit letzter** ~: with one's last ounce of strength; **aus eigener** ~: by one's own efforts; **mit vereinten Kräften werden wir …**: if we join forces *or* combine our efforts we will …; **außer** ~ **setzen** repeal ⟨law⟩; countermand ⟨order⟩; **außer** ~ **sein/treten** no longer be/cease to be in force; **in** ~ **treten/sein/bleiben** come into/be in/remain in force
Kraft-: ~**aufwand** *der* effort; ~**brühe** *die* strong meat broth; ~**fahrer** *der*, ~**fahrerin** *die* driver; motorist
Kraft·fahrzeug *das* motor vehicle
Kraftfahrzeug-: ~**brief** *der* vehicle registration document; logbook (Brit.); ~**schein** *der* vehicle registration document; ~**steuer** *die* vehicle tax
kräftig ① *Adj.* strong; vigorous ⟨plant, shoot⟩; powerful, hefty ⟨blow, kick, etc.⟩; nourishing ⟨soup, bread, meal, etc.⟩
  ② *adv.* powerfully ⟨built⟩; ⟨rain, snow⟩ heavily; ⟨eat⟩ heartily
kräftigen *tr. V.* ⟨holiday, air, etc.⟩ invigorate; ⟨food etc.⟩ fortify
kraft-, Kraft-: ~**meier** *der;* ~~s, ~~ (ugs.: abwertend) muscleman; ~**probe** *die* trial of strength; ~**rad** *das* (Amtsspr.) motorcycle; ~**stoff** *der* (Kfz-W.) fuel; ~**stoff·verbrauch** *der* fuel

consumption; ~**voll** ① *Adj.* powerful;
  ② *adv.* powerfully; ~**wagen** *der* motor vehicle; ~**werk** *das* power station
Kragen *der;* ~s, ~, (südd., österr. u. schweiz. auch:) Krägen collar
Kragen·weite *die* collar size
Krähe /'krɛ:ə/ *die;* ~, ~n crow
krähen *itr. V.* (auch fig.) crow
Krähen·füße *Pl.* (ugs.) crow's feet
krakeelen *itr. V.* (ugs.) kick up a row (coll.)
krakeln *tr., itr. V.* (ugs.) scrawl
kraklig *Adj.* (ugs. abwertend) scrawly
Kralle *die;* ~, ~n claw
krallen ① *refl. V.* **sich an etw.** (Akk.) ~ ⟨cat⟩ dig its claws into sth.; ⟨person⟩ clutch sth. [tightly]
  ② *tr. V.* (fest greifen) **die Finger in/um etw.** (Akk.) ~: dig one's fingers into sth./clutch sth. [tightly] with one's fingers
Kram *der;* ~[e]s (ugs.) **(a)** stuff; (Gerümpel) junk
  (b) (Angelegenheit) affair
kramen ① *itr. V.* **in etw.** (Dat.) ~: rummage about in sth.
  ② *tr. V.* (ugs.) **etw. aus etw.** ~: fish (coll.) sth. out of sth.
Krämer *der;* ~s, ~, **Krämerin** *die;* ~, ~nen grocer
Kram·laden *der* (ugs. abwertend) junk shop
Krampf *der;* ~[e]s, Krämpfe **(a)** cramp; (Zuckung) spasm
  (b) painful strain; (sinnloses Tun) senseless waste of effort
Krampf·ader *die* varicose vein
krampfhaft ① *Adj.* convulsive; (verbissen) desperate
  ② *adv.* convulsively; (verbissen) desperately
Kran *der;* ~[e]s, Kräne **(a)** crane
  (b) (südwestd.: Wasserhahn) tap; faucet (Amer.)
Kranich *der;* ~s, ~e crane
krank; kränker, kränkst… *Adj.* ill *usu. pred.*; sick; bad ⟨leg, tooth⟩; diseased ⟨plant, organ⟩; (fig.) ailing ⟨economy, business⟩; ~ **werden** be taken ill
Kranke *der/die; adj. Dekl.* sick man/woman; (Patient) patient
kränkeln *itr. V.* be in poor health
kränken *tr. V.* jmdn. ~: hurt sb. *or* sb.'s feelings
Kranken-: ~**geld** *das* sickness benefit; ~**gymnastik** *die* remedial *or* medical gymnastics *sing.;* physiotherapy; ~**gymnastin** *die;* ~~, ~~nen remedial gymnast; medical gymnast; physiotherapist; ~**haus** *das* hospital; ~**kasse** *die* health insurance scheme; (Körperschaft) health insurance institution; (privat) health insurance company; ~**pfleger** *der* male nurse; ~**schein** *der* health insurance certificate; ~**schwester** *die* nurse; ~**versicherung** *die* **(a)** (Versicherung) health insurance; **(b)** (Unternehmen) ····⦂

health insurance company; **∼wagen** der ambulance

kränker ▶ KRANK

krank|feiern itr. V. (ugs.) skive off work (coll.) [pretending to be ill]

krankhaft ① Adj. pathological; morbid ⟨growth, state, swelling, etc.⟩
② adv. pathologically; morbidly ⟨swollen, sensitive⟩

Krankheit die; ∼, ∼en (a) illness; (bestimmte Art, von Pflanzen, Organen) disease (b) (Zeit des Krankseins) illness

Krankheits·erreger der pathogen

kränklich Adj. ailing

krank|schreiben tr. V. give ⟨person⟩ a medical certificate

kränkst... ▶ KRANK

Kränkung die; ∼, ∼en: eine ∼: an injury to one's/sb.'s feelings

Kranz der; ∼es, Kränze wreath; garland; (auf einem Grab usw.) wreath

Kränzchen das; ∼s, ∼: coffee circle; coffee klatch (Amer.)

Krapfen der; ∼s, ∼: doughnut

krass, *kraß ① Adj. blatant ⟨case⟩; flagrant ⟨injustice⟩; stark ⟨contrast⟩; complete ⟨contradiction⟩; sharp ⟨difference⟩; out-and-out ⟨egoist⟩
② adv. sich ∼ ausdrücken put sth. bluntly; sich von etw. ∼ unterscheiden be in stark contrast to sth.

Krater der; ∼s, ∼: crater

Kratz·bürste die (ugs. scherzh.) prickly so-and-so

kratzen ① tr. V. scratch; (entfernen) scrape
② itr. V. (a) scratch (b) (jucken) itch

Kratzer der; ∼s, ∼ (ugs.) scratch

kratzig Adj. itchy ⟨material⟩

Kraul das; ∼s (Sport) crawl

kraulen¹ ① itr. V. do the crawl
② tr. V.; auch mit sein eine Strecke ∼: cover a distance using the crawl

kraulen² tr. V. jmdm. das Kinn ∼: tickle sb. under the chin; jmdn. in den Haaren ∼: run one's fingers through sb.'s hair

kraus Adj. creased ⟨skirt etc.⟩; frizzy ⟨hair⟩

Krause die; ∼, ∼n (Kragen) ruff; (am Ärmel) ruffle

kräuseln ① tr. V. ruffle ⟨water, surface⟩; gather ⟨material etc.⟩; frizz ⟨hair⟩
② refl. V. ⟨hair⟩ go frizzy; ⟨water⟩ ripple; ⟨smoke⟩ curl up

Kraut das; ∼[e]s, Kräuter (a) herb (b) (bes. südd., österr.: Kohl) cabbage

Kraut·salat der coleslaw

Krawall der; ∼s, ∼e (a) riot (b) (ugs.: Lärm) row (coll.)

Krawatte die; ∼, ∼n tie

kraxeln itr. V.; mit sein (bes. südd., österr.

ugs.) climb; (mit Mühe) clamber

kreativ ① Adj. creative
② adv. ∼ veranlagt sein have a creative bent

Kreativität die; ∼: creativity

Kreatur die; ∼, ∼en creature

Krebs der; ∼es, ∼e (a) crustacean; (Fluss∼) crayfish; (Krabbe) crab (b) (Krankheit) cancer (c) (Astrol.) Cancer; the Crab

krebs-, Krebs-: ∼erregend, ∼erzeugend Adj. carcinogenic; ∼forschung die cancer research; ∼geschwulst die cancerous growth or tumour; ∼geschwür das (volkst.) cancerous ulcer; (fig. geh.) cancer; ∼krank Adj. ∼krank sein have cancer; ∼rot Adj. as red as a lobster postpos.

Kredit der; ∼[e]s, ∼e credit; (Darlehen) loan

kredit-, Kredit-: ∼institut das credit institution; ∼karte die credit card; mit ∼karte bezahlen pay by credit card; ∼klemme die credit crunch; ∼nehmer der; ∼∼s, ∼∼, ∼nehmerin die; ∼∼, ∼∼nen borrower; ∼würdig Adj. (Finanzw.) creditworthy

Kreide die; ∼, ∼n chalk

kreide·bleich Adj. as white as a sheet postpos.

Kreide·felsen der chalk cliff

kreieren /kreˈiːrən/ tr. V. create

Kreis der; ∼es, ∼e circle; (Verwaltungsbezirk) district; (Wahl∼) ward

Kreis·bahn die orbit

kreischen itr. V. screech; ⟨door⟩ creak

Kreisel der; ∼s, ∼ (Kinderspielzeug) top; (ugs.: Kreisverkehr) roundabout

kreisen itr. V.; auch mit sein ⟨planet⟩ revolve ⟨um around⟩; ⟨satellite etc.⟩ orbit; ⟨aircraft, bird⟩ circle

kreis-, Kreis-: ∼förmig Adj. circular; ∼lauf der (Physiol.) circulation; (der Natur, des Lebens usw.) cycle; ∼lauf·störungen Pl. (Med.) circulatory trouble sing.; ∼rund Adj. [perfectly] round; ∼säge die circular saw

Kreiß·saal der (Med.) delivery room

Kreis-: ∼stadt die chief town of a/the district; ∼verkehr der roundabout

Krem die; ∼, ∼s ▶ CREME

Krematorium das; ∼s, Krematorien crematorium

Krempe die; ∼, ∼n brim

Krempel der; ∼s (ugs. abwertend) stuff; (Gerümpel) junk

krepieren itr. V.; mit sein (salopp) ⟨person⟩ snuff it (sl.)

Krepp der; ∼s, ∼s od. ∼e crêpe

***Kreppapier** das, **Krepp·papier** das crêpe paper

Kresse die; ∼, ∼n (Bot.) cress

Kreta (das); ∼s Crete

Kreuz *das;* ~**es,** ~**e (a)** cross; (Kreuzzeichen) sign of the cross
(b) (Teil des Rückens) small of the back; **jmdn. aufs** ~ **legen** (salopp) take sb. for a ride (coll.)
(c) (Kartenspiel) (Farbe) clubs *pl.;* (Karte) club
(d) (Autobahn) interchange
(e) (Musik) sharp
kreuzen ⏹1 *tr. V.* (auch Biol.) cross
⏹2 *refl. V.* **(a)** (überschneiden) cross
(b) (zuwiderlaufen) clash (**mit** with)
⏹3 *itr. V.; mit haben od. sein* (fahren) cruise
Kreuz-: ~**fahrer** *der* (hist.) crusader; ~**fahrt** *die* cruise; ~**feuer** *das* (Milit., auch fig.) crossfire; ~**gang** *der* cloister
kreuzigen *tr. V.* crucify
Kreuzigung *die;* ~, ~**en** crucifixion
Kreuz-: ~**otter** *die* adder; [common] viper; ~**ritter** *der* (hist.) crusader; ~**schlitz·schraube** *die* Phillips screw ®; ~**schmerzen** *Pl.* pain *sing.* in the small of the back; ~**spinne** *die* cross spider; garden spider
Kreuzung *die;* ~, ~**en (a)** crossroads *sing.*
(b) (Biol.) crossing; cross-breeding; (Ergebnis) cross
kreuz-, Kreuz-: ~**verhör** *das* cross-examination; ~**weise** *adv.* crosswise; ~**wort·rätsel** *das* crossword [puzzle]; ~**zug** *der* (hist., fig.) crusade
kribbelig *Adj.* (ugs.) (vor Ungeduld) fidgety; (nervös) edgy
kribbeln *itr. V.* (jucken) tickle; (prickeln) tingle
kriechen *unr. itr. V.* **(a)** *mit sein* ⟨insect, baby⟩ crawl; ⟨plant⟩ creep; ⟨person, animal⟩ creep, crawl
(b) *auch mit sein* (fig. abwertend) crawl (**vor** + *Dat.* to)
Kriecher *der;* ~**s,** ~, **Kriecherin** *die;* ~, ~**nen** (abwertend) crawler
Kriech·spur *die* (Verkehrsw.) crawler lane
Krieg *der;* ~**[e]s,** ~**e** war; ~ **führend** warring; belligerent
kriegen *tr. V.* (ugs.) get; (erreichen) catch ⟨train, bus, etc.⟩
Krieger *der;* ~**s,** ~, **Kriegerin** *die;* ~, ~**nen** warrior
kriegerisch *Adj.* **(a)** (kampflustig) warlike
(b) (militärisch) military; **eine** ~**e Auseinandersetzung** an armed conflict
*****krieg·führend** ▶ KRIEG
kriegs-, Kriegs-: ~**beil** *das* tomahawk; **das** ~**beil begraben** (scherzh.) bury the hatchet; ~**bemalung** *die* (Völkerk.) warpaint; ~**beschädigt** *Adj.* war-disabled; ~**beschädigte** *der/die; adj. Dekl.* war invalid; ~**dienst** *der* **(a)** (im Krieg) active service;
(b) (Wehrdienst) military service; **den** ~**dienst verweigern** be a conscientious objector; ~**dienst·verweigerer** *der* conscientious objector; ~**ende** *das* end of the war; **bei/vor** ~**ende** at/before the end

of the war; ~**erklärung** *die* declaration of war; ~**gefangene** *der* prisoner of war; POW; ~**gefangenschaft** *die* captivity; ~**opfer** *das* war victim; ~**schiff** *das* warship; ~**verbrechen** *das* (Rechtsw.) war crime; ~**verbrecher** *der,* ~**verbrecherin** *die* war criminal; ~**waise** *die* war orphan
Krimi *der;* ~**[s],** ~**[s]** (ugs.) crime thriller
Kriminal·beamte *der,*
Kriminal·beamtin *die* [plain-clothes] detective
kriminalisieren *tr. V.* **jmdn.** ~: make sb. turn to crime
kriminalistisch ⏹1 *Adj.* ⟨methods, practice⟩ of criminalistics; ⟨abilities⟩ in the field of criminalistics
⏹2 *adv.* ⟨proceed etc.⟩ using the methods of criminalistics
Kriminalität *die;* ~: crime *no art.*
Kriminal-: ~**polizei** *die* criminal investigation department; ~**roman** *der* crime novel; (mit Detektiv als Held) detective novel
kriminell ⏹1 *Adj.* criminal
⏹2 *adv.* ~ **veranlagt sein** have criminal tendencies; ~ **handeln** act illegally
Kriminelle *der/die; adj. Dekl.* criminal
Krimskrams *der;* ~**[es]** (ugs.) stuff
Kringel *der;* ~**s,** ~ (Kreis) [small] ring; (Kritzelei) round squiggle; (Gebäck) [ring-shaped] biscuit
kringeln *refl. V.* curl [up]; ⟨hair⟩ go curly; **sich** ~ **[vor Lachen]** (ugs.) kill oneself [laughing] (coll.)
Kripo *die;* ~ (ugs.) **die** ~: ≈ the CID
Krippe *die;* ~, ~**n (a)** (Futtertrog) manger; crib
(b) (Weihnachts~) model of a nativity scene
(c) (Kinder~) crèche
Krise *die;* ~, ~**n** (auch Med.) crisis
kriseln *itr. V.* (unpers.) **es kriselt in ihrer Ehe/in der Partei** their marriage is in trouble/the party is in a state of crisis
Krisen-: ~**gebiet** *das* crisis area; ~**herd** *der* trouble spot
Kristall[1] /krɪsˈtal/ *der;* ~**s,** ~**e** crystal
Kristall[2] *das;* ~**s** crystal *no indef. art.*
Kristallisation *die;* ~, ~**en** (bes. Chemie) crystallization
kristallisieren *itr. V.* (bes. Chemie) crystallize
Kriterium *das;* ~**s, Kriterien** criterion
Kritik *die;* ~, ~**en (a)** criticism *no indef. art.* (**an** + *Dat.* of); **an jmdm./etw.** ~ **üben** criticize sb./sth.
(b) (Besprechung) review
Kritiker *der;* ~**s,** ~, **Kritikerin** *die;* ~, ~**nen** critic
kritik·los ⏹1 *Adj.* uncritical
⏹2 *adv.* uncritically
kritisch ⏹1 *Adj.* critical   ····⋗

2 *adv.* critically

kritisieren *tr. V.* criticize; review ⟨*book, play, etc.*⟩

kritzeln 1 *itr. V.* (schreiben) scribble; (zeichnen) doodle

2 *tr. V.* scribble

Kroatien /kro'a:tsiən/ (*das*); ~s Croatia

kroatisch *Adj.* Croatian

kroch *1. u. 3. Pers. Sg. Prät. v.* KRIECHEN

Krokant *der;* ~s praline

Krokette *die;* ~, ~n (Kochk.) croquette

Krokodil *das;* ~s, ~e crocodile

Krokodils·tränen *Pl.* (ugs.) crocodile tears

Krokus *der;* ~, ~ *od.* ~se crocus

Krone *die;* ~, ~n crown; (eines Baumes) top; crown; (einer Welle) crest; **die ~ der Schöpfung** the pride of creation

krönen *tr. V.* (auch fig.) crown

Kronen·korken *der* crown cork

Kron-: ~**juwelen** *Pl.* the crown jewels; ~**leuchter** *der* chandelier; ~**prinz** *der* crown prince; ~**prinzessin** *die* crown princess

Krönung *die;* ~, ~en coronation; (fig.) culmination

Kron·zeuge *der,* **Kron·zeugin** *die* (Rechtsw.) person who turns Queen's/King's evidence; **als ~ auftreten** turn Queen's/King's evidence

Kropf *der;* ~[e]s, Kröpfe (Med.) goitre

Kröte *die;* ~, ~n (a) toad

(b) *Pl.* (salopp: Geld) **ein paar/eine ganze Menge ~n verdienen** earn a few bob (Brit. coll.)/a fair old whack (coll.)

Krücke *die;* ~, ~n crutch

Krück·stock *der* walking stick

Krug *der;* ~[e]s, Krüge jug; (größer) pitcher; (Bier~) mug

Krume *die;* ~, ~n crumb

Krümel *der;* ~s, ~: crumb

krümeln *itr. V.* (a) crumble

(b) (Krümel machen) make crumbs

krumm 1 *Adj.* (a) bent ⟨*nail, back*⟩; crooked ⟨*stick, branch, etc.*⟩; bandy ⟨*legs*⟩; **sich über etw. (Akk.) ~ lachen** (ugs.) fall about laughing over sth.

(b) (ugs.: unrechtmäßig) crooked

(c) **etw. ~ nehmen** (ugs.) take sth. the wrong way

2 *adv.* crookedly

krümmen 1 *tr. V.* bend

2 *refl. V.* (a) (sich winden) writhe

(b) (krumm verlaufen) ⟨*road, path, river*⟩ bend

krumm-: **~*|**lachen** ▸ KRUMM 1A; **~*|**nehmen** ▸ KRUMM 1C

Krümmung *die;* ~, ~en bend

Krüppel *der;* ~s, ~: cripple

Kruste *die;* ~, ~n crust; (vom Braten) crisp

**old spelling – see note on page x

Kruzifix *das;* ~es, ~e crucifix

Krypta *die;* ~, Krypten (Archit.) crypt

Kuba (*das*); ~s Cuba

Kubaner *der;* ~s, ~, **Kubanerin** *die;* ~, ~nen Cuban

Kübel *der;* ~s, ~: pail

Kubik- cubic ⟨*metre, foot, etc.*⟩

Küche *die;* ~, ~n kitchen; (Einrichtung) kitchen furniture *no indef. art.;* (Kochk.) cooking; cuisine; **kalte/warme ~:** cold/hot food

Kuchen *der;* ~s, ~: cake; (Obst~) flan; (Torte) gateau

Küchen-: ~**abfälle** *Pl.* kitchen scraps; ~**chef** *der,* ~**chefin** *die* chef

Küchen-: ~**form** *die* cake tin; ~**gabel** *die* pastry fork

Küchen-: ~**gerät** *das* kitchen utensil; (als Kollektivum) kitchen utensils *pl.;* ~**maschine** *die* food processor; ~**meister** *der,* ~**meisterin** *die* chef; ~**messer** *das* kitchen knife; ~**schabe** *die* cockroach; ~**schrank** *der* kitchen cupboard; ~**tisch** *der* kitchen table

Kuckuck *der;* ~s, ~e (a) cuckoo; **zum ~ [noch mal]!** (salopp) for crying out loud! (coll.)

(b) (scherzh.: Pfandsiegel) bailiff's seal (*placed on distrained goods*)

Kuckucks·uhr *die* cuckoo clock

Kufe *die;* ~, ~n runner; (von Flugzeugen, Hubschraubern) skid

Kugel *die;* ~, ~n (a) ball; (Geom.) sphere; (Kegeln) bowl; (beim Kugelstoßen) shot

(b) (ugs.: Geschoss) bullet

Kugel·lager *das* (Technik) ball bearing

kugeln 1 *tr. V.* roll

2 *refl. V.* **sich [vor Lachen] ~** (ugs.) double *or* roll up [laughing]

kugel-, Kugel-: ~**rund** /-'-/ *Adj.* round as a ball *postpos.;* (scherzh.: dick) rotund; tubby; ~**schreiber** *der* ball pen; Biro ®; ~**sicher** *Adj.* bulletproof; ~**stoßen** *das;* ~~s shot[-put]; (Disziplin) putting the shot *no art.*

Kuh *die;* ~, Kühe cow

Kuh-: ~**fladen** *der* cowpat; ~**handel** *der* (ugs. abwertend) shady horse-trading *no indef. art.;* **ein ~handel** a bit of shady horse-trading; ~**haut** *die:* **das geht auf keine ~haut** (fig. salopp) it's absolutely staggering

kühl 1 *Adj.* cool; **etw. ~ lagern** keep sth. in a cool place

2 *adv.* coolly

Kuhle *die;* ~, ~n (ugs.) hollow

Kühle *die;* ~: coolness

kühlen 1 *tr. V.* cool; chill ⟨*wine*⟩; refrigerate ⟨*food*⟩

2 *itr. V.* ⟨*cold compress, ointment, breeze, etc.*⟩ have a cooling effect

Kühler *der;* ~s, ~ (a) (am Auto) radiator; (Kühlerhaube) bonnet (Brit.); hood (Amer.)

(b) (Sekt~) ice bucket

Kühler·haube *die* bonnet (Brit.); hood (Amer.)

Kühl-: ~**fach** *das* frozen food compartment; ~**haus** *das* cold store; ~**raum** *der* cold store; cold-storage room; ~**schrank** *der* refrigerator; fridge (Brit. coll.); icebox (Amer.); ~**truhe** *die* [chest] freezer; (im Lebensmittelgeschäft) freezer [cabinet]

Kühlung *die;* ~, ~en cooling; (Vorrichtung) cooling system; (für Lebensmittel) refrigeration system

Kühl·wasser *das* cooling water

kühn [1] *Adj.* bold; (dreist) audacious [2] *adv.* boldly; (gewagt) daringly; (dreist) audaciously

Kühnheit *die;* ~: boldness; (Gewagtheit) daringness; (Dreistigkeit) audacity

Kuh·stall *der* cowshed

Küken *das;* ~s, ~: chick

kulant *Adj.* obliging; fair ‹*terms*›

Kulanz *die;* ~: willingness to oblige

Kuli *der;* ~s, ~s **(a)** coolie **(b)** (ugs.) ballpoint; Biro ®

kulinarisch *Adj.* culinary

Kulisse *die;* ~, ~n piece of scenery; flat; (Hintergrund) backdrop; **die** ~**n** the scenery *sing.;* **hinter den** ~**n** (fig.) behind the scenes

kullern (ugs.) *itr. V. mit sein* roll

Kult *der;* ~[e]s, ~e (auch fig.) cult

Kult·film *der* cult film

kultivieren *tr. V.* (auch fig.) cultivate

kultiviert [1] *Adj.* cultured; (vornehm) refined [2] *adv.* in a cultured manner; (vornehm) in a refined manner

Kultur *die;* ~, ~en **(a)** culture; (kultivierte Lebensart) refinement; **ein Mensch von** ~: a cultured person **(b)** (Zivilisation, Lebensform) civilization

Kultur-: ~**abkommen** *das* cultural agreement; ~**austausch** *der* cultural exchange; ~**beutel** *der* sponge bag (Brit.); toilet bag

kulturell [1] *Adj.* cultural [2] *adv.* culturally

Kultur-: ~**film** *der* documentary film; ~**geschichte** *die* history of civilization; (einer bestimmten Kultur) cultural history; ~**politik** *die* cultural and educational policy

Kultus·minister *der,*
Kultus·ministerin *die* minister for education and cultural affairs

Kümmel *der;* ~s, ~: caraway [seed]; (Branntwein) kümmel

Kummer *der;* ~s sorrow; grief; (Ärger, Sorgen) trouble; ~ **um od. über jmdn.** grief for sb.; **jmdm.** ~ **machen** give sb. trouble

kümmerlich *Adj.* **(a)** (schwächlich) puny; stunted ‹*vegetation, plants*›

(b) (ärmlich) wretched; miserable **(c)** (abwertend: gering) miserable; meagre ‹*knowledge, leftovers*›

kümmern [1] *refl. V.* **(a)** sich um jmdn./ etw. ~: take care of sb./sth. **(b)** (sich befassen mit) **sich nicht um Politik** ~: not be interested in politics [2] *tr. V.* concern

Kumpan *der;* ~s, ~e, **Kumpanin** *die;* ~, ~nen (ugs.) **(a)** pal (coll.); buddy (coll.) **(b)** (abwertend: Mittäter[in]) accomplice

Kumpel *der;* ~s, ~ **(a)** (Bergmannsspr.) miner **(b)** (salopp: Kamerad) pal (coll.); buddy (coll.)

Kumulus·wolke *die* (Met.) cumulus cloud

kündbar *Adj.* terminable ‹*contract*›; redeemable ‹*loan, mortgage*›

Kunde[1] *der;* ~n, ~n customer; (eines Architekten-, Anwaltbüros, einer Versicherung usw.) client

Kunde[2] *die;* ~ (geh.) tidings *pl.* (literary)

Kunden·dienst *der* service to customers; (Wartung) after-sales service

Kundgebung *die;* ~, ~en rally

kundig *Adj.* (kenntnisreich) knowledgeable; (sachverständig) expert

kündigen [1] *tr. V.* cancel ‹*subscription, membership*›; terminate ‹*contract, agreement*›; **seine Stellung** ~: hand in one's notice (**bei** to) [2] *unr. itr. V.* **(a)** (ein Mietverhältnis beenden) ‹*tenant*› give notice; **jmdm.** ~ ‹*landlord*› give sb. notice to quit; **zum 1. Juli** ~: give notice for 1 July **(b)** (ein Arbeitsverhältnis beenden) ‹*employee*› hand in one's notice (**bei** to); **jmdm.** ~ ‹*employer*› give sb. his/her notice

Kündigung *die;* ~, ~en **(a)** (der Mitgliedschaft, eines Abonnements) cancellation; (eines Vertrags) termination **(b)** (eines Arbeitsverhältnisses) **jmdm. die** ~ **aussprechen** give sb. his/her notice

Kündigungs-: ~**frist** *die* period of notice; ~**schutz** *der* protection against wrongful dismissal

Kundin *die;* ~, ~nen customer/client

Kundschaft *die;* ~, ~en ▶ KUNDE[1]: customers *pl.;* clientele

Kundschafter *der;* ~s, ~,
Kundschafterin *die;* ~, ~nen scout

kund|tun (geh.) *unr. tr. V.* announce

künftig [1] *Adj.* future [2] *adv.* in future

Kunst *die;* ~, Künste **(a)** art; **die bildende** ~, **die bildenden Künste** the plastic arts *pl.;* **die schönen Künste** [the] fine arts **(b)** (das Können) skill; (die ärztliche ~: medical skill; **das ist keine** ~! (ugs.) there's nothing 'to it

kunst-, Kunst-: ~**ausstellung** *die* art exhibition; ~**buch** *das* art book; ~**druck** *der; Pl.* ~~**e (a)** [fine] art print; **(b)** (Druckw.) fine-art printing; ···⫶

~**erzieher** der, ~**erzieherin** die art teacher; ~**faser** die synthetic fibre; ~**führer** der guide to cultural and artistic monuments [of an/the area]; ~**genuss**, *~**genuß** der enjoyment of art; (Ereignis) artistic treat; ~**gerecht** ⓵ Adj. expert; ⓶ adv. expertly; ~**geschichte** die art history; ~**geschichtlich** ⓵ Adj. art historical ⟨studies, evidence, expertise⟩; ⟨work⟩ on art history; ⓶ adv. ~ **geschichtlich interessiert/versiert** interested/well versed in art history; ~**gewerbe** das arts and crafts pl.; ~**griff** der trick; dodge; ~**halle** die art gallery; ~**händler** der, ~**händlerin** die [fine-]art dealer; ~**handwerk** das craftwork; ~**kritiker** der, ~**kritikerin** die art critic; ~**leder** imitation leather

Künstler der; ~s, ~, **Künstlerin** die; ~, ~nen (a) artist; (Zirkus~, Varietee~) artiste (b) (Könner) genius (in + Dat. at)

künstlerisch ⓵ Adj. artistic ⓶ adv. artistically

Künstler·name der stage name

künstlich ⓵ Adj. (a) artificial (b) (gezwungen) forced ⟨laugh, cheerfulness, etc.⟩ ⓶ adv. artificially

kunst-, Kunst-: ~**licht** das artificial light; ~**los** Adj. plain; ~**postkarte** die art postcard; ~**saal** der art room; ~**sammler** der, ~**sammlerin** die art collector; ~**sammlung** die art collection; ~**schatz** der art treasure; ~**stoff** der synthetic material; plastic; ~**stück** das trick; **das ist kein** ~**stück** (ugs.) it's no great feat; ~**turnen** das gymnastics sing.; ~**voll** ⓵ Adj. ornate and artistic; (kompliziert) elaborate; ⓶ adv. (a) ornately or elaborately and artistically; (b) (geschickt) skilfully; ~**werk** das work of art

kunter·bunt ⓵ Adj. multi-coloured; (abwechslungsreich) varied; (ungeordnet) jumbled ⟨confusion, muddle, etc.⟩ ⓶ adv. ⟨painted, printed⟩ in many colours; ~ **durcheinander sein** be higgledy-piggledy

Kupfer das; ~s (a) copper (b) (~geschirr) copperware; (~geld) coppers pl.

Kupfer-: ~**geld** das coppers pl.; ~**stich** der (a) copperplate engraving no art.; (b) (Blatt) copperplate print or engraving

Kuppe die; ~, ~n (a) [rounded] hilltop (b) (Finger~) tip; end

Kuppel die; ~, ~n dome; (kleiner) cupola

Kuppelei die; ~: procuring

kuppeln itr. V. operate the clutch

Kupplung ▶ KUPPLUNG

Kuppler der; ~s, ~: procurer

Kupplerin die; ~, ~nen procuress

Kupplung die; ~, ~en (a) (Kfz-W.) clutch

(b) (Technik: Vorrichtung zum Verbinden) coupling

Kur die; ~, ~en [health] cure; (ohne Aufenthalt im Badeort) course of treatment

Kür die; ~, ~en (Eiskunstlauf) free programme; (Turnen) optional exercises pl.

Kurbel die; ~, ~n crank [handle]; (an Spieldosen, Grammophonen) winder; (an einem Brunnen) [winding] handle

kurbeln tr. V. etw. nach oben/unten ~: wind sth. up/down

Kurbel·welle die (Technik) crankshaft

Kürbis der; ~ses, ~se pumpkin

Kurde der; ~n, ~n, **Kurdin** die; ~, ~nen Kurd

kurdisch Adj. Kurdish

Kur-: ~**fürst** der (hist.) Elector; ~**gast** der visitor to a/the spa; (Patient) patient at a/the spa

Kurier der; ~s, ~e courier

kurieren tr. V. (auch fig.) cure (**von** of)

Kurierin die; ~, ~nen ▶ KURIER

kurios ⓵ Adj. curious ⓶ adv. curiously; strangely; oddly

Kuriosität die; ~, ~en (a) strangeness (b) (Gegenstand) curiosity; curio

Kur-: ~**konzert** das concert [at a spa]; ~**ort** der spa; ~**pfuscher** der, ~**pfuscherin** die (ugs. abwertend) quack

Kurs der; ~es, ~e (a) (Richtung) course; **ein harter/weicher** ~ (fig.) a hard/soft line (b) (von Wertpapieren) price; (von Devisen) exchange rate; **der** ~ **des Dollars** the dollar rate (c) (Lehrgang) course; (Teilnehmer) class

Kürschner der; ~s, ~, **Kürschnerin** die; ~, ~nen furrier

kursieren itr. V.; auch mit sein circulate

Kurs·teilnehmer der, **Kurs·teilnehmerin** die course participant

Kursus der; ~, Kurse ▶ KURS

Kurs·wagen der (Eisenb.) through carriage

Kur·taxe die; visitors' tax (at a spa)

Kurve die; ~, ~n (a) (einer Straße) bend (b) (Geom.) curve (c) (in der Statistik, Temperatur~ usw.) graph

kurven itr. V.; mit sein (a) ⟨aircraft⟩ circle; ⟨tanks etc.⟩ circle [round] (b) (ugs.: fahren) drive around

kurven·reich Adj. winding; twisting

kurz; kürzer, kürzest... ⓵ Adj. short; (zeitlich; knapp) short, brief; quick ⟨look⟩ ⓶ adv. (a) (zeitlich) briefly; (knapp) ~ **gesagt** in a word (b) (wenig) just; ~ **vor/hinter der Kreuzung** just before/past the crossroads; ~ **vor/nach Pfingsten** just before/after Whitsun

kurz-, Kurz-: ~**arbeit** die short-time working; ~**ärm[e]lig** Adj. short-sleeved

Kürze die; ~ (a) shortness (b) (geringe Dauer) shortness; brevity; **in**

---

*alte Schreibung – vgl. Hinweis auf S. x

~: shortly

(c) (Knappheit) brevity

Kürzel *das;* ~s, ~: shorthand symbol

kürzen *tr. V.* shorten; abridge ⟨*article, book*⟩; cut ⟨*pension, budget*⟩

kürzer ▸ KURZ

kürzer·hand *Adv.* without more ado

kürzest... ▸ KURZ

kurz-, Kurz-: ~**fristig** ☐1 *Adj.* **(a)** ⟨*refusal, resignation, etc.*⟩ at short notice; **(b)** (für kurze Zeit) short-term; ☐2 *adv.* **(a)** at short notice; **(b)** (für kurze Zeit) for a short time; (auf kurze Sicht) in the short term; (in kurzer Zeit) without delay; ~**geschichte** *die* short story; ~**haar·frisur** *die* bob; bobbed hairstyle; ~**lebig** *Adj.* (auch fig.) short-lived; ~**lebigkeit** *die;* ~~: short-livedness

kürzlich *Adv.* recently; not long ago

kurz-, Kurz-: ~**meldung** *die* brief report; (während einer anderen Sendung) news flash; ~**parker** *der;* ~~s, ~~, ~**parkerin** *die;* ~~, ~~nen short-stay (Brit.) *or* short-term parker; ~**schluss,** ***~**schluß** *der* (Elektrot.) short circuit; ~**sichtig** (auch fig.) ☐1 *Adj.* short-sighted; ☐2 *adv.* short-sightedly; ~**sichtigkeit** *die;* ~~ (auch fig.) short-sightedness

Kurzstrecken·rakete *die* short-range missile

Kürzung *die;* ~, ~en cut

kurz-, Kurz-: ~**waren** *Pl.* haberdashery *sing.* (Brit.); notions (Amer.); ~**weilig** *Adj.* entertaining; ~**welle** *die* (Physik, Rundf.) short wave; ~**zeitig** ☐1 *Adj.* brief; ☐2 *adv.* briefly

kuschelig *Adj.* cosy

kuscheln *refl. V.* sich an jmdn. ~: snuggle up to sb.

Kuschel·tier *das* cuddly toy

kuschen *itr. V.* knuckle under (**vor** + *Dat.* to)

Kusine *die;* ~, ~n ▸ COUSINE

Kuss, *Kuß *der;* Kusses, Küsse kiss

kuss·echt, *kuß·echt *Adj.* kissproof

küssen *tr., itr. V.* kiss

Kuss·hand, *Kuß·hand *die:* jmdm. eine ~ zuwerfen blow sb. a kiss; mit ~ (ugs.) gladly

Küste *die;* ~, ~n coast

Küsten-: ~**linie** *die* coastline; ~**wache** *die* coastguard [service]

Küster *der;* ~s, ~, **Küsterin** *die;* ~, ~nen sexton

Kutsche *die;* ~, ~n coach

Kutscher *der;* ~s, ~, **Kutscherin** *die;* ~, ~nen coach driver

kutschieren ☐1 *itr. V.; mit sein* drive, ride [in a coach] ☐2 *tr. V.* jmdn. ~: drive sb. [in a coach]

Kutte *die;* ~, ~n [monk's/nun's] habit

Kutter *der;* ~s, ~: cutter

Kuvert /ku'veːɐ̯/ *das;* ~s, ~s envelope; (geh.: Gedeck) cover

Kuwait /ku'vaɪt/ *(das);* ~s Kuwait

Kybernetik *die;* ~: cybernetics *sing.*

Kybernetiker *der;* ~s, ~, **Kybernetikerin** *die;* ~, ~nen cybernetician; cyberneticist

kybernetisch *Adj.* cybernetic

KZ *Abk.* = **Konzentrationslager**

KZ-Häftling *der,* **KZler** *der;* ~s, ~, **KZlerin** *die;* ~, ~nen concentration-camp prisoner

Ll

l, L /ɛl/ *das;* ~, ~: l/L

l *Abk.* = **Liter** l.

Lab *das;* ~[e]s, ~e rennet

labberig *Adj.* (ugs. abwertend) **(a)** (fade) wishy-washy; ~ schmecken taste of nothing **(b)** (weich) floppy, limp ⟨*material*⟩; floppy ⟨*trousers, dress, etc.*⟩

laben (geh.) ☐1 *tr. V.* jmdn. ~: give sb. refreshment ☐2 *refl. V.* refresh oneself (**an** + *Dat.,* **mit** with)

labern *itr. V.* (ugs. abwertend) rabbit (Brit. coll.) *or* babble on

labil *Adj.* **(a)** (Med.) delicate ⟨*constitution, health*⟩; poor ⟨*circulation*⟩ **(b)** (auch Psych.) unstable ⟨*person, character, situation, etc.*⟩

Labor *das;* ~s, ~s, *auch:* ~e laboratory

Laboratorium *das;* ~s, Laboratorien laboratory

Labor·test *der* laboratory test (**an** + *Dat.* of; **auf** + *Akk.* for)

Labyrinth *das;* ~[e]s, ~e maze; labyrinth

Lache¹ *die;* ~, ~n (ugs.) laugh

Lache² /'la(ː)xə/ *die;* ~, ~n puddle; (von Blut, Öl) pool

lächeln *itr. V.* smile (**über** + *Akk.* at)

Lächeln *das;* ~s smile

lachen ☐1 *itr. V.* laugh (**über** + *Akk.* at) ☐2 *tr. V.* **was gibt es denn zu ~?** what's so funny? ⋯⟫

Lachen *das;* ~s laughter; **ein lautes** ~: a loud laugh

lächerlich ① *Adj.* ridiculous; ludicrous ⟨*argument, statement*⟩ ② *adv.* ridiculously

Lächerlichkeit *die;* ~: ridiculousness; (von Argumenten, Behauptungen usw.) ludicrousness

lachhaft *Adj.* ridiculous

Lachs *der;* ~es, ~e salmon

Lack *der;* ~[e]s, ~e varnish; (für Metall, Lackarbeiten) lacquer

lackieren *tr. V.* varnish; spray ⟨*car*⟩

Lack·leder *das* patent leather

Lade *die;* ~, ~n (landsch.) drawer

Lade-hemmung *die* jam

laden[1] ① *unr. tr. V.* load; (Physik) charge ② *unr. itr. V.* load [up]

laden[2] *unr. tr. V.* **(a)** (Rechtsspr.) summon **(b)** (geh.: einladen) invite

Laden *der;* ~s, Läden **(a)** shop; store (Amer.); **der** ~ **läuft** (ugs.) business is good **(b)** (Fensterladen) shutter

Laden-: ~**dieb** *der,* ~**diebin** *die* shoplifter; ~**diebstahl** *der* shoplifting; ~**schluss,** **~***schluß** *der* shop or (Amer.) store closing time; ~**tisch** *der* [shop] counter

Lade-: ~**rampe** *die* loading ramp; ~**raum** *der* (beim Auto) luggage space; (beim Flugzeug, Schiff) hold; (bei LKWs) payload space; ~**station** *die* (Elektrot.) charging unit; charger; charging station

lädieren *tr. V.* damage

lädst *2. Pers. Sg. Präsens v.* LADEN

lädt *3. Pers. Sg. Präsens v.* LADEN

Ladung *die;* ~, ~en **(a)** (Schiffs~, Flugzeug~) cargo; (eines LKW) load **(b)** (beim Sprengen, Schießen; Physik) charge **(c)** (Rechtsspr.: Vor~) summons *sing.*

lag *1. u. 3. Pers. Sg. Prät. v.* LIEGEN

Lage *die;* ~, ~n **(a)** situation; **eine gute** ~ **haben** be well situated **(b)** (Art des Liegens) position **(c)** (Situation) situation

Lage·plan *der* map of the area

Lager *das;* ~s, ~ **(a)** camp **(b)** storeroom; (in Geschäften, Betrieben) stockroom **(c)** (Warenbestand) stock

Lager-: ~**bestand** *der* (Wirtsch.) stock; **den** ~**bestand aufnehmen** do a stocktake; ~**feuer** *das* campfire; ~**halle** *die* warehouse

lagern ① *tr. V.* **(a)** store **(b)** (hinlegen) lay down ② *itr. V.* **(a)** camp **(b)** (liegen) lie; ⟨*foodstuffs, medicines, etc.*⟩ be kept

Lager-: ~**platz** *der* campsite; ~**raum**

---

storeroom; (im Geschäft, Betrieb) stockroom

Lagerung *die;* ~, ~en storage

Lagune *die;* ~, ~n lagoon

lahm *Adj.* **(a)** (gelähmt) lame; (ugs.: unbeweglich) stiff **(b)** (ugs.: unzureichend) lame ⟨*excuse, explanation, etc.*⟩ **(c)** (ugs. abwertend: matt) dreary

lahmen *itr. V.* be lame

lähmen *tr. V.* paralyse; (fig.) paralyse ⟨*economy, industry*⟩; bring ⟨*traffic*⟩ to a standstill

Lähmung *die;* ~, ~en paralysis; (fig.) (der Wirtschaft, Industrie) paralysis; **zu einer** ~ **des Verkehrs führen** bring traffic to a standstill

Laib *der;* ~[e]s, ~e loaf; **ein [halber]** ~ **Brot** [half] a loaf of bread

Laich *der;* ~[e]s, ~e spawn

laichen *itr. V.* spawn

Laie *der;* ~n, ~n (Mann) layman; (Frau) laywoman

Lakai *der;* ~en, ~en lackey; liveried footman

Lake *die;* ~, ~n brine

Laken *das;* ~s, ~ (bes. nordd.) sheet

Lakritze *die;* ~, ~n liquorice

lallen *tr., itr. V.* ⟨*baby*⟩ babble; ⟨*drunk/ drowsy person*⟩ mumble

Lamelle *die;* ~, ~n (einer Jalousie) slat; (eines Heizkörpers) rib

lamentieren *itr. V.* (ugs.) moan (**über** + *Akk.* about)

Lametta *das;* ~s lametta

Lamm *das;* ~[e]s, Lämmer lamb

lamm-, Lamm-: ~**fell** *das* lambskin; ~**fleisch** *das* lamb; ~**fromm** ① *Adj.* ⟨*person*⟩ as meek as a [little] lamb; ② *adv.* ⟨*answer*⟩ like a lamb

Lämpchen *das;* ~s, ~: small or little light; **ein rotes** ~: a little red light

Lampe *die;* ~, ~n light; (Tisch~, Öl~, Signal~) lamp

Lampen-: ~**fieber** *das* stage fright; ~**schirm** *der* [lamp]shade

Lampion /lam'piͻŋ/ *der;* ~s, ~s Chinese lantern

Land *das;* ~es, Länder *od.* (veralt.) ~e **(a)** land *no indef. art.;* (dörfliche Gegend) country *no indef. art.;* **an** ~: ashore; **auf dem** ~ **wohnen** live in the country **(b)** (Staat) country; **hier zu** ~e [here] in this country **(c)** (Bundesland) Land; state; (österr.) province

Land-: ~**arbeiter** *der,* ~**arbeiterin** *die* agricultural worker; farm worker; ~**bevölkerung** *die* rural population

Lande-: ~**anflug** *der* (Flugw.) [landing] approach; ~**bahn** *die* (Flugw.) [landing] runway; ~**erlaubnis** *die* (Flugw.) permission to land *no art.*

landen ① *itr. V.; mit sein* **(a)** land; (ankommen) arrive

**old spelling – see note on page x

(b) (ugs.: gelangen) land up
2 *tr. V.* **(a)** land ⟨*aircraft, troops, passengers, fish, etc.*⟩
(b) (ugs.: zustande bringen) pull off ⟨*victory, coup*⟩; have ⟨*smash hit*⟩
Ländereien *Pl.* estates
Länder-: ∼**kampf** *der* (Sport) international match; ∼**spiel** *das* (Sport) international [match]
Landes-: ∼**innere** *das* interior [of the country]; ∼**kunde** *die* regional studies *pl., no art.;* ∼**regierung** *die* government of a/the Land/province; ∼**sprache** *die* language of the country
Lande·steg *der* landing stage; jetty
Landes-: ∼**tracht** *die* national costume *or* dress; ∼**verrat** *der* (Rechtsw.) treason; ∼**währung** *die* currency of a/the country
land-, Land-: ∼**flucht** *die* migration from the land *or* countryside [to the towns]; ∼**friedens·bruch** *der* (Rechtsw.) breach of the peace; ∼**gewinnung** *die* reclamation of land; ∼**haus** *das* country house; ∼**karte** *die* map; ∼**kreis** *der* district; ∼**läufig** *Adj.* widely accepted
ländlich *Adj.* rural; country *attrib.* ⟨*life*⟩
Land-: ∼**luft** *die* country air; ∼**mine** *die* land mine; ∼**plage** *die* (fig.) pest; nuisance; ∼**ratte** *die* (ugs.) landlubber
Landschaft *die;* ∼, ∼en landscape; (ländliche Gegend) countryside
landschaftlich **1** *Adj.* regional
2 *adv.* ∼ herrlich gelegen sein be in a glorious natural setting; **die Umgebung der Stadt ist** ∼ **sehr schön** the town is in *or* has a beautiful natural setting
Land·schul·heim *das* ▸ SCHULLANDHEIM
Lands-: ∼**mann** *der; Pl.* ∼**leute** fellow countryman; compatriot; ∼**männin** *die;* ∼∼, ∼∼**nen** fellow countrywoman; compatriot
Land-: ∼**straße** *die* country road; (im Gegensatz zur Autobahn) ordinary road; ∼**streicher** *der;* ∼∼s, ∼∼, ∼**streicherin** *die;* ∼∼, ∼∼**nen** tramp; ∼**strich** *der* area; ∼**tag** *der* Landtag; state parliament; (österr.) provincial parliament
Landung *die;* ∼, ∼en landing
Landungs·brücke *die* [floating] landing stage
land-, Land-: ∼**weg** *der* overland route; **auf dem** ∼**weg** overland; ∼**wirt** *der,* ∼**wirtin** *die* farmer; ∼**wirtschaft** *die* agriculture *no art.;* farming *no art.;* ∼**wirtschaftlich** **1** *Adj.* agricultural; **2** *adv.* ∼**wirtschaftlich genutzt werden** be used for agricultural purposes; ∼**zunge** *die* (Geogr.) tongue of land
lang; länger, längst... **1** *Adj.* long; (ugs.: groß) tall
2 *adv.* [for] a long time; **eine Sekunde/ mehrere Stunden** ∼: for a second/several hours

lang-: ∼**ärm[e]lig** *Adj.* long-sleeved; ∼**atmig** **1** *Adj.* long-winded; **2** *adv.* long-windedly; ⟨*relate*⟩ at great length
lange; länger, am längsten *Adv.* **(a)** a long time; **bist du schon** ∼ **hier?** have you been here long?
(b) (bei weitem) **ich bin noch** ∼ **nicht fertig** I'm nowhere near finished; **hierist es** ∼ **nicht so schön** it isn't nearly as nice here
Länge *die;* ∼, ∼n length; (Geogr.) longitude
langen (ugs.) **1** *itr. V.* **(a)** be enough
(b) (greifen) reach **(in +** *Akk.* into; **auf +** *Akk.* on to; **nach for)**
2 *tr. V.* **jmdm. eine** ∼ (ugs.) give sb. a clout [around the ear] (coll.)
Längen·grad *der* (Geogr.) degree of longitude
länger **1** ▸ LANG, LANGE
2 *Adj.* **seit** ∼**er Zeit** for quite some time
Lange·weile *die;* ∼ *od.* Langenweile boredom; ∼ **haben** be bored
lang-, Lang-: ∼**fristig** **1** *Adj.* long-term; long-dated ⟨*loan*⟩; **2** *adv.* on a long-term basis; ∼**jährig** *Adj.* ⟨*customer, friend*⟩ of many years' standing; long-standing ⟨*friendship*⟩; ∼**jährige Erfahrung** many years of experience; ∼**lauf** *der* (Skisport) cross-country; ∼**lebig** *Adj.* long-lived ⟨*animals, organisms*⟩; durable ⟨*goods, materials*⟩
länglich *Adj.* oblong
lang-, Lang-: ∼**mut** *die;* ∼∼: forbearance; ∼**mütig** *Adj.* forbearing; ∼**mütigkeit** *die;* ∼∼: forbearance
längs **1** *Präp. +* Gen. *od.* (selten) Dat. along
2 *Adv.*lengthways
Längs·achse *die* longitudinal axis
langsam **1** *Adj.* slow
2 *adv.* **(a)** slowly; ∼, **aber sicher** (ugs.) slowly but surely
(b) (allmählich) gradually
Lang-: ∼**schläfer** *der,* ∼**schläferin** *die* late riser; ∼**spiel·platte** *die* long-playing record; LP
Längs·schnitt *der* longitudinal section
längst *Adv.* **(a)** (schon lange) a long time ago
(b) (bei weitem) **hier ist es** ∼ **nicht so schön** it isn't nearly as nice here
längst... ▸ LANG
längstens *Adv.* (ugs.) (höchstens) at [the] most; (spätestens) at the latest
Languste *die;* ∼, ∼n spiny lobster
lang-, Lang-: ∼**weilen** **1** *tr. V.* bore; **2** *refl. V.* be bored; ∼**weilig** **1** *Adj.* boring; dull ⟨*place*⟩; **2** *adv.* boringly; ∼**welle** *die* (Physik, Rundf.) long wave; ∼**wierig** *Adj.* lengthy; prolonged ⟨*search*⟩
Lanze *die;* ∼, ∼n lance; (zum Werfen) spear
Laos (*das*); Laos' Laos
Laote *der;* ∼n, ∼n, **Laotin** *die;* ∼, ∼nen Laotian
lapidar **1** *Adj.* (kurz, aber wirkungsvoll) succinct; (knapp) terse ····⟩

2 *adv.* succinctly/tersely

Lappalie /la'pa:li̯ə/ *die;* ~, ~n trifle

Lappe *der;* ~n, ~n Lapp

Lappen *der;* ~s, ~: cloth; (Fetzen) rag; (Wasch~) flannel

Lappin *die;* ~, ~nen Lapp

läppisch *Adj.* silly

Lapp·land (*das*) Lapland

Laptop *der;* ~s, ~s (DV) laptop

Lärche *die;* ~, ~n larch

Lärm *der;* ~[e]s noise; (Krach) din; row (coll.)

Lärm·belästigung *die* disturbance caused by noise

lärmen *itr. V.* make a noise *or* (coll.) row

Lärm-: ~**pegel** *der* noise level; ~**schutz** *der* (a) protection against noise; (b) (Vorrichtung) noise barrier; noise *or* sound insulation *no indef. art.;* ~**schutz·wand** *die* sound-insulating wall

Larve *die;* ~, ~n grub; larva

las *1. u. 3. Pers. Sg. Prät. v.* LESEN

lasch **1** *Adj.* limp ⟨handshake⟩; feeble ⟨action, measure⟩; lax ⟨upbringing⟩ **2** *adv. s. Adj.:* limply; feebly; laxly

Lasche *die;* ~, ~n (Gürtel~) loop; (eines Briefumschlags) flap; (Schuh~) tongue

Laser /'leɪzɐ/ *der;* ~s, ~ (Physik) laser

Laser-: ~**drucker** *der* (DV) laser printer; ~**pointer** ~~s, ~~ *der* (DV) laser pointer

lass, *laß *Imperativ Sg. v.* LASSEN

lassen **1** *unr. tr. V.* (a) *mit Inf. + Akk.* (2. *Part.* lassen) (veranlassen) **etw. tun/ machen/bauen/waschen** ~: have *or* get sth. done/made/built/washed; **jmdn. warten** ~: keep sb. waiting; **jmdn. grüßen** ~: send one's regards to sb.; **jmdn. kommen/rufen** ~: send for sb.
(b) *mit Inf. + Akk.* (2.*Part.* lassen) (erlauben) **jmdn. etw. tun** ~: let sb. do sth.; allow sb. to do sth.
(c) (belassen) **jmdn. in Frieden** ~: leave sb. in peace
(d) (hinein~/heraus~) let *or* allow (**in** + *Akk.* into, **aus** out of)
(e) (unterlassen) stop
(f) (zurück~; bleiben~) leave
(g) (überlassen) **jmdm. etw.** ~: let sb. have sth.
(h) (als Aufforderung) **lass/lasst uns gehen/ fahren!** let's go!
(i) (verlieren) lose; (ausgeben) spend **2** *unr. refl. V.* **die Tür lässt sich leicht öffnen** the door opens easily; **das lässt sich nicht beweisen** it can't be proved **3** *unr. tr. V.* (a) (ugs.) **Lass mal. Ich mache das schon** Leave it. I'll do it
(b) (veranlassen) **ich lasse bitten** would you ask him/her/them to come in

lässig **1** *Adj.* casual **2** *adv.* casually

lässt, *läßt *3. Pers. Sg. Präsens v.* LASSEN

Last *die;* ~, ~en load; (Gewicht) weight; (Bürde) burden

lasten *itr. V.* be a burden; **auf jmdm./etw.** ~: weigh heavily [up]on sb./sth.

Laster¹ *der;* ~s, ~ (ugs.: Lkw) truck; lorry (Brit.)

Laster² *das;* ~s, ~: vice

lasterhaft *Adj.* (abwertend) depraved

lästern **1** *itr. V.* (abwertend) **über jmdn./etw.** ~: make malicious remarks about sb./sth. **2** *tr. V.* (veralt.) blaspheme against

lästig *Adj.* tiresome; troublesome ⟨illness, cough, etc.⟩

Last-: ~**schrift** *die* debit; ~**wagen** *der* truck; lorry (Brit.)

Lasur *die;* ~, ~en varnish; (farbig) glaze

Latein *das;* ~s Latin

Latein·amerika (*das*) Latin America

lateinisch *Adj.* Latin

latent *Adj.* latent

Laterne *die;* ~, ~n (a) (Leuchte) lamp; lantern (Naut.)
(b) (Straßen~) street light

Laternen·pfahl *der* lamp post

Latrine *die;* ~, ~n latrine

latschen *itr. V.; mit sein* (salopp) trudge; (schlurfend) slouch

Latschen *der;* ~s, ~ (ugs.) old worn-out shoe/slipper

Latte *die;* ~, ~n (a) lath; (Zaun~) pale
(b) (Sport: Quer~ des Tores) [cross]bar
(c) (Leichtathletik) bar

Latten-: ~**rost** *der* (auf dem Boden) duckboards *pl.;* (eines Bettes) slatted frame ~**zaun** *der* paling fence

Latz *der;* ~es, Lätze bib

Lätzchen *das;* ~s, ~: bib

lau *Adj.* tepid, lukewarm ⟨water etc.⟩; mild ⟨wind, air, evening, etc.⟩

Laub *das;* ~[e]s leaves *pl.;* **dichtes** ~: thick foliage

Laub·baum *der* broad-leaved tree

Laube *die;* ~, ~n summer house; (überdeckter Sitzplatz) bower; arbour

Laub-: ~**frosch** *der* tree frog; ~**säge** *die* fretsaw; ~**wald** *der* deciduous wood/forest

Lauch *der;* ~[e]s (Porree) leek

Lauer *die;* ~: **auf der** ~ **liegen** *od.* **sein** (ugs.) (jmdm. auflauern) lie in wait

lauern *itr. V.* (auch fig.) lurk

Lauf *der;* ~[e]s, Läufe (a) running
(b) (Sport: Wettrennen) heat
(c) (Ver~) course; **im** ~[e] **der Zeit** in the course of time; **im** ~[e] **der Jahre/des Tages** over the years/during the day
(d) (von Schusswaffen) barrel

Lauf·bahn *die* (a) (Werdegang) career
(b) (Leichtathletik) running track

Lauf·band *das* conveyer belt; (für Personen)

moving pavement; travelator; moving sidewalk (Amer.); (im Fitnesscenter) treadmill

laufen [1] *unr. itr. V.; mit sein* **(a)** run; (beim Eislauf) skate; (beim Ski∼) ski; (gehen) go; (zu Fuß gehen) walk; **in** *(Akk.)*/**gegen etw. ∼:** walk into sth.; **dauernd zum Arzt ∼** (ugs.) keep running to the doctor **(b)** (im Gang sein) ⟨*machine*⟩ be running; ⟨*radio, television, etc.*⟩ be on; (funktionieren) ⟨*machine*⟩ run; ⟨*radio, television, etc.*⟩ work **(c)** (gelten) ⟨*contract, agreement, engagement, etc.*⟩ run **(d)** (gespielt werden) ⟨*programme, play, etc.*⟩ be on
[2] *unr. tr. u. itr. V.* **(a)** *mit sein* (zurücklegen) (zu Fuß) walk; (rennen) run **(b)** *mit sein* (erzielen) **einen Rekord ∼:** set up a record **(c)** *mit haben od. sein* **Ski/Schlittschuh/ Rollschuh ∼:** ski/skate/roller-skate

laufend [1] *Adj.* **(a)** (ständig) regular ⟨*interest, income*⟩; recurring ⟨*costs*⟩ **(b)** (gegenwärtig) current ⟨*issue, year, month, etc.*⟩
[2] *adv.* constantly; ⟨*increase*⟩ steadily

Läufer *der;* ∼**s,** ∼ **(a)** (Sport) runner; (Handball; Fußball veralt.) halfback **(b)** (Teppich) ⟨*long narrow*⟩ carpet

Läuferin *die;* ∼, ∼**nen** ▶ LÄUFER A

Lauf·feuer *das* brush fire; **wie ein ∼:** like wildfire

Lauf-: ∼**masche** *die* ladder; ∼**pass,** *∗*∼**paß** *der:* **er hat seiner Freundin den** ∼**pass gegeben** (ugs.) he finished with his girlfriend (coll.); ∼**schritt** *der:* **im** ∼**schritt, marsch, marsch!** at the double, quick march!

läufst *2. Pers. Sg. Präsens v.* LAUFEN

Lauf·stall *der* playpen

läuft *3. Pers. Sg. Präsens v.* LAUFEN

Laufwerk *das* (Technik) mechanism; (DV) drive

Lauge *die;* ∼, ∼**n (a)** soapy water **(b)** (Chemie) alkaline solution

Laugen·brezel *die* (südd.) pretzel

Laune *die;* ∼, ∼**n** mood

launenhaft *Adj.* temperamental; (unberechenbar) capricious

launig witty

launisch *Adj.:* ▶ LAUNENHAFT

Laus *die;* ∼, **Läuse** louse

Laus·bub *der* little rascal

Lausch·aktion *die,* **Lausch·angriff** *der* bugging operation (coll.)

lauschen *itr. V.* **(a)** (horchen) listen **(b)** (zuhören) listen [attentively]

Lauscher *der;* ∼**s,** ∼, **Lauscherin** *die;* ∼, ∼**nen** eavesdropper

lauschig *Adj.* cosy, snug ⟨*corner*⟩

lausig [1] *Adj.* (ugs.) **(a)** (abwertend: unangenehm, schäbig) lousy (coll.); rotten (coll.) **(b)** (sehr groß) perishing (Brit. coll.), freezing

⟨*cold*⟩; terrible (coll.) ⟨*heat*⟩
[2] *adv.* terribly (coll.)

laut¹ [1] *Adj.* loud; (geräuschvoll) noisy
[2] *adv.* loudly; (geräuschvoll) noisily

laut² *Präp. + Gen. od. Dat.* (Amtsspr.) according to

Laut *der;* ∼**[e]s,** ∼**e** sound

Laute *die;* ∼, ∼**n** lute

lauten *itr. V.* ⟨*answer, instruction, slogan*⟩ be, run; ⟨*letter, passage, etc.*⟩ read, go; ⟨*law*⟩ state

läuten [1] *tr., itr. V.* ring; ⟨*alarm clock*⟩ go off
[2] *itr. V.* (bes. südd.: klingeln) ring; **es läutete** the bell rang *or* went (**zu** for)

lauter¹ *Adj.* (geh.) honourable ⟨*person, intentions, etc.*⟩; honest ⟨*truth*⟩

lauter² *indekl. Adj.* nothing but; sheer ⟨*nonsense, joy, etc.*⟩

läutern *tr. V.* (geh.) reform ⟨*character*⟩; purify ⟨*soul*⟩

Läuterung *die;* ∼, ∼**en** (geh.) reformation; (der Seele) purification

laut·hals *Adv.* at the top of one's voice; ∼ **lachen** roar with laughter

lautlich [1] *Adj.* phonetic
[2] *adv.* phonetically

laut-, Laut-: ∼**los** [1] *Adj.* silent; soundless; (wortlos) silent; [2] *adv.* silently; soundlessly; ∼**schrift** *die* (Phon.) phonetic alphabet; (Umschrift) phonetic transcription; ∼**sprecher** *der* loudspeaker; (einer Stereoanlage usw.) speaker; ∼**stark** [1] *Adj.* loud; vociferous, loud ⟨*protest*⟩; [2] *adv.* loudly; ⟨*protest*⟩ vociferously; ∼**stärke** *die* volume

lau·warm *Adj.* lukewarm

Lava *die;* ∼, **Laven** (Geol.) lava

Lavendel *der;* ∼**s,** ∼: lavender

Lawine *die;* ∼, ∼**n** (auch fig.) avalanche; **eine** ∼ **von Protesten** (fig.) a storm of protest

Lawinen·gefahr *die* danger of avalanches

lax [1] *Adj.* lax
[2] *adv.* laxly

Laxheit *die;* ∼: laxness; laxity

Layout /ˈleːˀaʊt/ *das;* ∼**s,** ∼**s** (Druckw., Elektronik) layout

Lazarett *das;* ∼**[e]s,** ∼**e** military hospital

Lead·sänger /ˈliːt-/ *der,* **Lead·sängerin** *die* lead singer

leasen /ˈliːzn̩/ *tr. V.* rent; (für längere Zeit mieten) lease ⟨*car etc.*⟩

leben *itr. V.* live; (lebendig sein) be alive; **leb[e] wohl!** farewell!; **von seiner Rente/seinem Gehalt ∼:** live on one's pension/salary

Leben *das;* ∼**s,** ∼ **(a)** life; **das ∼:** life; **sich** *(Dat.)* **das ∼ nehmen** take one's [own] life; **am** ∼ **sein/bleiben** be/stay alive; **ums** ∼ **kommen** lose one's life **(b)** (Betriebsamkeit) **auf dem Markt** ⋯⟩

herrschte ein reges ~: the market was bustling with activity; **das ~ auf der Straße** the comings and goings in the street
lebend *Adj.* living; live ‹*animal*›
lebendig 1 *Adj.* living; (lebhaft) lively 2 *adv.* (lebhaft) in a lively way
Lebendigkeit *die;* ~: liveliness
lebens-, Lebens-: ~**abend** *der* (geh.) evening of one's life (literary); ~**art** *die* (a) way of life; (b) (Umgangsformen) manners *pl.;* ~**aufgabe** *die* life's work; ~**bejahend** *Adj.* ‹*person*› with a positive attitude to life; ~**bereich** *der* area of life; ~**dauer** *die* lifespan; ~**ende** *das* end [of one's life]; ~**erinnerungen** *Pl.* memories of one's life; (aufgezeichnet) memoirs; ~**erwartung** *die* life expectancy; ~**fähig** *Adj.* (auch fig.) viable; ~**freude** *die* zest for life; ~**froh** *Adj.* full of zest for life *postpos.;* ~**gefahr** *die* mortal danger; „Achtung, ~**gefahr!**" 'danger'; ~**gefährlich** 1 *Adj.* highly dangerous; critical ‹*injury*›; 2 *adv.* critically ‹*injured, ill*›; ~**gefährte** *der,* ~**gefährtin** *die* (geh.) companion through life (literary); ~**geister** *Pl.* jmds. ~geister [wieder] wecken put new life into sb.; ~**groß** *Adj.* life-size; ~**größe** *die:* eine Statue in ~größe a life-size statue
Lebens·haltung *die* cost of living
Lebenshaltungs-: ~**index** *der* (Wirtsch.) cost-of-living index; ~**kosten** *Pl.* cost of living *sing.*
lebens-, Lebens-: ~**jahr** *das* year of [one's] life; ~**kraft** *die* vitality; ~**künstler** *der,* ~**künstlerin** *die:* ein [echter/wahrer] ~künstler a person who always knows how to make the best of things; ~**lage** *die* situation [in life]; ~**lang** 1 *Adj.* lifelong; 2 *adv.* all one's life; ~**länglich** 1 *Adj.* ~länglicher Freiheitsentzug life imprisonment; 2 *adv.* jmdn. ~länglich gefangen halten keep sb. imprisoned for life; ~**lauf** *der* curriculum vitae; c.v.; ~**licht** *das* (geh.) flame of life (literary); jmdm. das ~licht ausblasen *od.* auspusten (ugs.) send sb. to kingdom come (coll.); ~**lustig** *Adj.* ‹*person*› full of the joys of life
Lebens·mittel *das* food[stuff]; ~ *Pl.* food *sing.*
Lebensmittel-: ~**abteilung** *die* food department; ~**geschäft** *das* food shop; ~**vergiftung** *die* food poisoning
lebens-, Lebens- : ~**müde** *Adj.* weary of life *pred.;* ~**notwendig** *Adj.* essential; ~**raum** *der* (a) (Umkreis) lebensraum; (b) (Biol.) ▶ Вютор; ~**retter** *der,* ~**retterin** *die* rescuer; ~**standard** *der* standard of living; ~**unterhalt** *der:* seinen ~unterhalt verdienen/bestreiten earn one's living/support oneself;

~**versicherung** *die* life insurance; ~**wandel** *der* way of life; ~**weg** *der* [journey through] life; ~**weise** *die* way of life; ~**zeichen** *das* sign of life; ~**zeit** *die* life[span]; **auf ~zeit** for life
Leber *die;* ~, ~n liver
Leber-: ~**fleck** *der* liver spot; ~**käse** *der: meat loaf made with mincemeat, [minced liver,] eggs, and spices;* ~**tran** *der* fish-liver oil; (des Kabeljaus) cod-liver oil; ~**wurst** *die* liver sausage; ~**zirrhose** *die* (Med.) cirrhosis of the liver
Lebe-: ~**wesen** *das* living being; ~**wohl** /--'-/ *das;* ~~-[e]s, ~~ *od.* ~~e (geh.) farewell
lebhaft 1 *Adj.* (a) lively; busy ‹*traffic*›; brisk ‹*business*›
(b) (deutlich) vivid ‹*idea, picture, etc.*›
(c) (kräftig) bright ‹*colour*›; vigorous ‹*applause, opposition*›.
2 *adv.* (a) in a lively way
(b) (deutlich) vividly
(c) (kräftig) brightly ‹*coloured*›
leb-, Leb-: ~**kuchen** *der* ≈ gingerbread; ~**los** *Adj.* lifeless; ~**zeiten** *Pl.* **bei** *od.* **zu** jmds. ~zeiten during sb.'s lifetime
lechzen *itr. V.* (geh.) **nach einem Trunk ~:** long for a drink; **nach Rache** *usw.* **~:** thirst for revenge *etc.*
leck *Adj.* leaky; ~ **sein** leak
Leck *das;* ~[e]s, ~s leak
lecken[1] 1 *tr. V.* lick
2 *itr. V.* **an etw.** (*Dat.*) **~:** lick sth.
lecken[2] *itr. V.* (leck sein) leak
lecker *Adj.* tasty ‹*meal*›; delicious ‹*cake etc.*›; good ‹*smell, taste*›
Lecker·bissen *der* delicacy; **ein musikalischer ~** (fig.) a musical treat
Leckerei *die;* ~, ~en (ugs.) dainty; (Süßigkeit) sweet [meat]
led. *Abk.* = **ledig**
Leder *das;* ~s, ~: leather
Leder-: ~**handschuh** *der* leather glove; ~**hose** *die* leather shorts *pl.;* lederhosen *pl.;* (lang) leather trousers; ~**jacke** *die* leather jacket; ~**riemen** *der* [leather] strap; ~**waren** *Pl.* leather goods
ledig *Adj.* single; **eine ~e Mutter** an unmarried mother
Ledige *der/die; adj. Dekl.* single person
lediglich *Adv.* merely
leer *Adj.* empty; clean ‹*sheet of paper*›; ~ **stehend** empty, unoccupied
Leere *die;* ~ (auch fig.) emptiness
leeren *tr., refl. V.* empty
leer-, Leer-: ~**gefegt** *Adj.* deserted ‹*street, town*›; **wie ~gefegt** deserted; ~**lauf** *der* **im ~lauf den Berg hinunterfahren** ‹*driver*› coast down the hill in neutral; ‹*cyclist*› freewheel down the hill; **~**stehend** ▶ LEER; ~**taste** *die* space bar

Leerung *die;* ∼, ∼en emptying; (von Briefkästen) collection

Lefze *die;* ∼, ∼n lip

legal ⁌1⁍ *Adj.* legal
⁌2⁍ *adv.* legally

legalisieren *tr. V.* legalize

Legalisierung *die;* ∼, ∼en legalization

Legalität *die;* ∼: legality

legen ⁌1⁍ *tr. V.* (a) lay [down]
(b) (verlegen) lay ⟨*pipe, cable, carpet, tiles, etc.*⟩
⁌2⁍ *tr., itr. V.* ⟨*hen*⟩ lay
⁌3⁍ *refl. V.* (a) lie down
(b) (nachlassen) die down; abate; ⟨*enthusiasm*⟩ wear off, subside

legendär *Adj.* legendary

Legende *die;* ∼, ∼n legend

leger /le'ʒeːɐ̯/ ⁌1⁍ *Adj.* casual
⁌2⁍ *adv.* casually

legieren *tr. V.* alloy

Legierung *die;* ∼, ∼en alloy

Legislative *die;* ∼, ∼n (Politik) legislature

Legislatur·periode *die* legislative period

legitim *Adj.* legitimate

Legitimation *die;* ∼, ∼en
(a) legitimation
(b) (Ausweis) proof of identity

legitimieren ⁌1⁍ *tr. V.* (a) (rechtfertigen) justify
(b) (bevollmächtigen) authorize
(c) (für legitim erklären) legitimize ⟨*child, relationship*⟩
⁌2⁍ *refl. V.* show proof of one's identity

Legitimität *die;* ∼: legitimacy

Lehm *der;* ∼s loam; (Ton) clay

Lehne *die;* ∼, ∼n (Rücken∼) back; (Arm∼) arm

lehnen ⁌1⁍ *tr., refl. V.* lean (an + *Akk.*, gegen against)
⁌2⁍ *itr. V.* be leaning (an + *Dat.* against)

Lehn-: ∼**stuhl** *der* armchair; ∼**wort** *das; Pl.* ∼wörter loanword

Lehr-: ∼**auftrag** *der* lectureship; ∼**buch** *das* textbook

Lehre *die;* ∼, ∼n (a) apprenticeship
(b) (Weltanschauung) doctrine
(c) (Theorie, Wissenschaft) theory
(d) (Erfahrung) lesson

lehren *tr., itr. V.* teach

Lehrer *der;* ∼s, ∼ (auch fig.) teacher; (Ausbilder) instructor

Lehrer-: ∼**ausbildung** *die* teacher training *no art.;* ∼**ausflug** *die* staff outing

Lehrerin *die;* ∼, ∼nen teacher

Lehrer-: ∼**kollegium** *das* teaching staff; faculty (Amer.); ∼**konferenz** *das* staff meeting; ∼**zimmer** *das* staffroom

Lehr-: ∼**gang** *der* course (für, in + *Dat.* in); ∼**jahr** *das* year as an apprentice; ∼**körper** *der* (Amtsspr.) teaching staff; faculty (Amer.)

Lehrling *der;* ∼s, ∼e apprentice; (in kaufmännischen Berufen) trainee

lehr-, Lehr-: ∼**plan** *der* (Schulw.) syllabus; (Gesamtlehrgang) curriculum; ∼**reich** *Adj.* informative; ∼**stelle** *die* apprenticeship; (in kaufmännischen Berufen) trainee post; ∼**stoff** *der* (Schulw.) syllabus

Leib *der;* ∼[e]s, ∼er (geh.) body; mit ∼ und Seele Arzt/Krankenschwester *usw.* sein be a dedicated doctor/nurse *etc.;* mit ∼ und Seele dabei sein put one's whole heart into it

Leibes-: ∼**übungen** *Pl.* (Schulw.) physical education *sing.;* PE; ∼**visitation** *die;* ∼∼, ∼∼en body search

Leib·gericht *das* favourite dish

leibhaftig *Adj.* in person *postpos.;* (echt) real

leiblich *Adj.* physical ⟨*well-being*⟩; (blutsverwandt) real

Leib-: ∼**schmerzen** *Pl.* abdominal pain *sing.;* ∼**wächter** *der,* ∼**wächterin** *die* bodyguard

Leiche *die;* ∼, ∼n [dead] body; corpse

Leichen *der* hearse

leichen-, Leichen-: ∼**blass,** *∗*∼**blaß** *Adj.* deathly pale; ∼**schau·haus** *das* morgue; ∼**wagen** *der* hearse

Leichnam *der;* ∼s, ∼e (geh.) body

leicht ⁌1⁍ *Adj.* light; lightweight ⟨*suit, material*⟩; easy ⟨*task, question, job, etc.*⟩; slight ⟨*accent, illness, wound, doubt, etc.*⟩; mild ⟨*cigar, cigarette*⟩; ∼ fallen be easy; das fällt mir ∼: it's easy for me; jmdm./sich etw. ∼ machen make sth. easy for sb./oneself; etw. ∼ nehmen make light of sth.
⁌2⁍ *adv.* lightly ⟨*built*⟩; (einfach, schnell, spielend) easily; (geringfügig) slightly; ∼ verletzt slightly injured

leicht-, Leicht-: ∼**athletik** *die* [track and field] athletics *sing.;* *∗*∼**fallen** ▶ LEICHT 1; ∼**fertig** ⁌1⁍ *Adj.* careless ⟨*behaviour, person*⟩; rash ⟨*promise*⟩; ill-considered, slapdash ⟨*plan*⟩; ⁌2⁍ *adv.* carelessly; ∼**gläubig** *Adj.* gullible

Leichtigkeit *die;* ∼ (geringes Gewicht) lightness; (Mühelosigkeit) ease

leicht-, Leicht-: *∗*∼|**machen** ▶ LEICHT 1; *∗*∼|**nehmen** ▶ LEICHT 1; ∼**sinn** *der* carelessness *no indef. art.;* (mit Gefahr verbunden) recklessness *no indef. art.;* ∼**sinnig** ⁌1⁍ *Adj.* careless; (sich, andere gefährdend) reckless; (fahrlässig) negligent; ⁌2⁍ *adv.* carelessly; (gefährlich) recklessly; ⟨*promise*⟩ rashly; ∼**sinniger·weise** *Adv.* carelessly; (gefährlicherweise) recklessly; ⟨*promise*⟩ rashly; *∗*∼**verletzt** ▶ LEICHT 2

leid *Adj.* etw./jmdn. ∼ sein/werden (ugs.) be/get fed up with sth./sb. (coll.); *s. auch* LEID²

Leid¹ *das;* ∼[e]s (a) (Schmerz) suffering; (Kummer) grief; sorrow
(b) (Unrecht) wrong; (Böses) harm ⋯⟶

Leid²: es tut mir ∼, [dass]...: I'm sorry [that]...; **er tut mir** ∼: I feel sorry for him

leiden ① *unr. itr. V.* suffer (**an, unter** + *Dat.* from)

② *unr. tr. V.* (a) jmdn. [gut] ∼ **können** *od.* **mögen** like sb.

(b) (geh.: ertragen müssen) suffer ⟨*hunger, thirst, etc.*⟩

Leiden *das;* ∼s, ∼ (a) (Krankheit) illness; (Gebrechen) complaint

(b) (Qual) suffering

leidend *Adj.* (a) (krank) ailing

(b) (schmerzvoll) strained ⟨*voice*⟩; martyred ⟨*expression*⟩

Leidenschaft *die;* ∼, ∼en passion (**zu, für** for)

leidenschaftlich ① *Adj.* passionate; vehement ⟨*protest*⟩

② *adv.* passionately; (eifrig) dedicatedly; **etw.** ∼ **gern tun** adore doing sth.

Leidens·genosse *der,*

Leidens·genossin *die* fellow sufferer

leider *Adv.* unfortunately

leidig *Adj.* tiresome

leidlich *Adj.* reasonable

Leid·tragende *der/die; adj. Dekl.* victim

Leier *die;* ∼, ∼n lyre

leihen *unr. tr. V.* (a) jmdm. etw. ∼: lend sb. sth.

(b) (entleihen) borrow

Leih-: ∼**gabe** *die* loan (*Gen.* from); ∼**gebühr** *die* hire *or* (Amer.) rental charge; (bei Büchern) borrowing fee; ∼**haus** *das* pawnbroker's; pawnshop; ∼**mutter** *die; Pl.* ∼mütter surrogate mother; ∼**wagen** *der* hire *or* (Amer.) rental car

Leim *der;* ∼[e]s glue

leimen *tr. V.* glue (**an** + *Akk.* to)

Leine *die;* ∼, ∼n rope; (Wäsche∼, Angel∼) line; (Hunde∼) lead (esp. Brit.); leash; ∼ **ziehen** (ugs.) clear off

leinen *Adj.* linen ⟨*tablecloth, sheet, etc.*⟩

Leinen *das;* ∼s (a) (Gewebe) linen

(b) (Buchw.) cloth

Leinen·band *der* cloth-bound volume

Lein·wand *die* (a) linen; (grob) canvas

(b) (des Malers) canvas

(c) (für Filme und Dias) screen

leise ① *Adj.* (a) quiet; soft ⟨*steps, music, etc.*⟩

(b) (leicht) faint; slight; slight, gentle ⟨*touch*⟩

② *adv.* (a) quietly

(b) (leicht; kaum merklich) slightly; ⟨*touch, rain*⟩ gently

Leiste *die;* ∼, ∼n strip; (Holz∼) batten; (profiliert) moulding

leisten ① *tr. V.* do ⟨*work*⟩; (schaffen) achieve ⟨*a lot, nothing*⟩; jmdm. **Hilfe** ∼: help sb.

② *refl. V.* (ugs.) **sich** (*Dat.*) **etw.** ∼: treat

oneself to sth.; **sich** (*Dat.*) **etw. [nicht]** ∼ **können** [not] be able to afford sth.

Leisten·bruch *der* rupture

Leistung *die;* ∼, ∼en (a) (Qualität bzw. Quantität der Arbeit) performance

(b) (Errungenschaft) achievement; (im Sport) performance

(c) (Leistungsvermögen, Physik: Arbeits∼) power

(d) (Zahlung, Zuwendung) payment; (Versicherungsw.) benefit

(e) (Dienst∼) service

leistungs-, Leistungs-: ∼**druck** *der* (bei Arbeitnehmern) pressure to work harder; (bei Sportlern, Schülern) pressure to achieve *or* to do well; ∼**fähig** *Adj.* capable ⟨*person*⟩; (körperlich) able-bodied; ∼**gesellschaft** *die* competitive society; ∼**prinzip** *das* competitive principle; ∼**sport** *der* competitive sport *no art.*

Leit·artikel *der* (Zeitungsw.) leading article; leader

leiten *tr. V.* (a) (anführen) lead; head; be head of ⟨*school*⟩; (verantwortlich sein für) be in charge of ⟨*project, expedition, etc.*⟩; manage ⟨*factory, enterprise*⟩; (den Vorsitz führen bei) chair; conduct ⟨*orchestra, choir*⟩; ∼**der Angestellter** manager

(b) (begleiten, führen) lead

(c) (lenken) direct; route ⟨*traffic*⟩; (um∼) divert

Leiter¹ *der;* ∼s, ∼: leader; (einer Abteilung) head; (eines Instituts) director; (einer Schule) head teacher; headmaster (Brit.); principal (esp. Amer.); (Vorsitzender) chair[man]

Leiter² *die;* ∼, ∼n ladder

Leiterin *die;* ∼, ∼nen ▶ LEITER¹; (einer Schule) head teacher; headmistress (Brit.); principal (esp. Amer.)

Leit-: ∼**motiv** *das* (Musik, Literaturw., fig.) (a) leitmotiv; (b) (Leitgedanke) dominant *or* central theme; ∼**planke** *die* crash barrier; guardrail (Amer.)

Leitung *die;* ∼, ∼en (a) ▶ LEITEN A: leading; heading; being in charge; management; chairing

(b) (einer Expedition usw.) leadership; (Verantwortung für) responsibility (*Gen.* for); (eines Betriebes, Unternehmens) management; (einer Sitzung, Diskussion) chairmanship

(c) (leitende Personen) management; (einer Schule) head and senior staff

(d) (Rohr∼) pipe; (Haupt∼) main

(e) (Draht, Kabel) cable; (für ein Gerät) lead

(f) (Telefon∼) line

Leitungs·wasser *das* tap water

Leit·zins[satz] *der* (Finanzw.) discount rate; ≈ base rate

Lektion /lɛk'tsio:n/ *die;* ∼, ∼en lesson

Lektor *der;* ∼s, ∼en (a) (Hochschulw.) *junior university teacher in charge of practical or supplementary classes etc.*

(b) (im Verlag) [publisher's] editor

Lektüre *die;* ∼, ∼n (a) reading

(b) (Lesestoff) reading [matter]

---

*alte Schreibung – vgl. Hinweis auf S. x

Lẹnde *die;* ∼, ∼n loin
Lẹnden-: ∼**gegend** *die* loins *pl.;* lumbar
region (Anat.); ∼**schurz** *der* loincloth;
∼**wirbel** *der* (Anat.) lumbar vertebra
lẹnken *tr. V.* **(a)** *auch itr.* steer; be at the
controls of ⟨*aircraft*⟩; guide ⟨*missile*⟩; (fahren)
drive ⟨*car etc.*⟩
(b) direct ⟨*thoughts etc.*⟩ (auf + *Akk.* to);
turn ⟨*attention*⟩ (auf + *Akk.* to)
(c) (kontrollieren) control ⟨*person, press,
economy*⟩; govern ⟨*state*⟩
Lẹnker *der;* ∼s, ∼ **(a)** handlebars *pl.*
(b) (Fahrer) driver
Lẹnkerin *die;* ∼, ∼nen ▶ LENKER B
Lẹnk-: ∼**rad** *das* steering wheel;
∼**rad·schloss,** ***∼**rad·schloß** *das*
(Kfz-W.) steering [wheel] lock; ∼**stange** *die*
handlebars *pl.*
Lẹnz *der;* ∼es, ∼e (dichter. veralt.) spring
Leopạrd *der;* ∼en, ∼en leopard
Lẹpra *die;* ∼: leprosy *no art.*
Lẹrche *die;* ∼, ∼n lark
lẹrnen [1] *itr. V.* study; (als Lehrling) train
[2] *tr. V.* learn (aus from)
lẹsbar *Adj.* legible; (klar) lucid ⟨*style*⟩;
(verständlich) comprehensible
Lẹsbe *die;* ∼, ∼n (ugs.) lesbian
Lesbierin /'lɛsbiərın/ *die;* ∼, ∼nen
lesbian
lẹsbisch *Adj.* Lesbian
Lese-: ∼**brille** *die* reading glasses *pl.;*
∼**buch** *das* reader
lesen[1] *unr. tr., itr. V.* read
lesen[2] *unr. tr. V.* **(a)** pick ⟨*grapes, berries,
fruit*⟩; gather ⟨*firewood*⟩; **Ähren** ∼: glean
[ears of corn]
(b) (aussondern) pick over
Leser *der;* ∼s, ∼ reader
Leserbrief *der* reader's letter; ∼e readers'
letters; „∼e" (Zeitungsrubrik) 'Letters to the
editor'
Leserin *die;* ∼, ∼nen reader
Leserkreis *der* readership
leserlich [1] *Adj.* legible
[2] *adv.* legibly
Lese·zeichen *das* bookmark
Lesung *die;* ∼, ∼en reading
Lẹtte *der;* ∼n, ∼n, **Lẹttin** *die;* ∼, ∼nen
Latvian
lẹttisch *Adj.* Latvian; Lettish ⟨*language*⟩
Lẹtt·land (*das*); ∼s Latvia
Lẹtzt: zu guter ∼: in the end
lẹtzt... *Adj.* last; ∼en Endes in the end;
(äußerst...) ultimate; (neuest...) latest ⟨*news*⟩
***lẹtzte·mal:** ▶ MAL[1]
***lẹtzten·mal:** ▶ MAL[1]
lẹtzter... *Adj.* latter
lẹtztlich *Adv.* ultimately; in the end
Leucht·diode *die* light-emitting diode;
LED

Leuchte *die;* ∼, ∼n light
leuchten *itr. V.* **(a)** ⟨*moon, sun, star, etc.*⟩
be shining; ⟨*fire, face*⟩ glow
(b) shine a/the light; jmdm. ∼: light the way
for sb.
leuchtend *Adj.* **(a)** shining ⟨*eyes*⟩;
brilliant ⟨*colours*⟩; bright ⟨*blue, red, etc.*⟩
(b) (großartig) shining ⟨*example*⟩
Leuchter *der;* ∼s, ∼: candelabrum; (für
eine Kerze) candlestick
Leucht-: ∼**farbe** *die* luminous paint;
∼**kugel** *die* flare; ∼**reklame** *die* neon
sign; ∼**stoff·lampe** *die* fluorescent
light *or* lamp; ∼**turm** *der* lighthouse;
∼**ziffer·blatt** *das* luminous dial
leugnen [1] *tr. V.* deny
[2] *itr. V.* deny it
Leukämie *die;* ∼, ∼n (Med.) leukaemia
Leumund *der;* ∼[e]s (geh.) reputation
Leute *Pl.* people; die reichen/alten ∼: the
rich/the old
Leutnant *der;* ∼s, ∼s second lieutenant
leut·selig [1] *Adj.* affable
[2] *adv.* affably
Lẹxikon *das;* ∼s, Lẹxika *od.* Lẹxiken
encyclopaedia (*Gen.,* für of)
Libanese *der;* ∼n, ∼n, **Libanesin** *die;*
∼, ∼nen Lebanese
Libanon (*das*) *od. der;* ∼s Lebanon
Libẹlle *die;* ∼, ∼n dragonfly
liberal [1] *Adj.* liberal
[2] *adv.* liberally
Liberale *der/die; adj. Dekl.* liberal
liberalisieren *tr. V.* liberalize; relax
⟨*import controls*⟩
Libero *der;* ∼s, ∼s (Fußball) sweeper
Libyen (*das*); ∼s Libya
libysch *Adj.* Libyan
lịcht *Adj.* **(a)** light
(b) (dünn bewachsen) sparse; thin
Lịcht *das;* ∼[e]s, ∼er **(a)** light
(b) (elektrisches) light
(c) *Pl. auch* ∼e (Kerze) candle
lịcht-, Lịcht-: ∼**bild** *das* [small]
photograph ⟨*for passport etc.*⟩;
∼**empfindlich** *Adj.* sensitive to light
lịchten[1] [1] *tr. V.* thin out ⟨*trees etc.*⟩
[2] *refl. V.* ⟨*trees*⟩ thin out; ⟨*hair*⟩ grow thin;
⟨*fog, mist*⟩ lift
lịchten[2] *tr. V.* (Seemannsspr.) **den/die Anker**
∼: weigh anchor
lịchterloh [1] *Adj.* blazing ⟨*fire*⟩; leaping
⟨*flames*⟩
[2] *adv.* ∼ **brennen** be blazing fiercely
Lịchter·meer *das* sea of lights
Lịcht-: ∼**hupe** *die* headlight flasher;
∼**jahr** *das* (Astron.) light year; ∼**kegel**
der beam; ∼**maschine** *die* (Kfz-W.)
(mit Gleichstrom) dynamo; (mit Wechselstrom)
alternator; generator (esp. Amer.);
∼**reklame** *die* neon sign; ∼**schalter**
der light switch; ∼**schranke** *die* ⋯⋯⟩

photoelectric beam; **~schutz·faktor** der protection factor (against sunburn)

Lichtung die; ~, ~en clearing

Lid das; ~[e]s, ~er eyelid

lieb ① Adj. (a) (liebevoll) kind ⟨words, gesture⟩
(b) (liebenswert) likeable; nice; (stärker) lovable ⟨child, girl, pet⟩; ~ **aussehen** look sweet or (Amer.) cute
(c) (artig) good ⟨child, dog⟩
(d) (geschätzt) dear; **sein liebstes Spielzeug** his favourite toy; **~er Hans/~e Else!** (am Briefanfang) dear Hans/Else
(e) (angenehm) welcome; **es wäre mir** ~/**~er, wenn** ...: I should be glad/should prefer it if ...
(f) jmdn. ~ **haben** love sb.; (gern haben) be fond of sb.
② adv. (a) (liebenswert) kindly
(b) (artig) nicely

Liebe die; ~, ~n (a) love; ~ **zu jmdm./zu etw.** love for sb./of sth.; **aus ~ [zu jmdm.]** for love [of sb.]; **tu mir die ~ und** ...: do me a favour and ...; **mit ~:** lovingly; with loving care
(b) (ugs.: geliebter Mensch) love

Liebelei die; ~, ~en flirtation

lieben ① tr. V. (a) jmdn. ~: love sb.; (sexuell) make love to sb.; **sich ~:** be in love; (sexuell) make love
(b) etw. ~: be fond of sth.; (stärker) love sth.
② itr. V. be in love

liebend Adv. etw. ~ **gern tun** [simply] love doing sth.

liebens·würdig Adj. kind; charming ⟨smile⟩

lieber Adv. (a) ▶ GERN
(b) better; **lass das ~:** better not do that

Liebes-: **~brief** der love letter; **~paar** das courting couple; **~roman** der romantic novel

liebe·voll ① Adj. loving attrib. ⟨care⟩; affectionate ⟨embrace, gesture, person⟩
② adv. lovingly; affectionately; (mit Sorgfalt) lovingly

*****lieb|haben** ▶ LIEB 1F

Liebhaber der; ~s, ~ (a) lover
(b) (Interessierter, Anhänger) enthusiast (Gen. for); (Sammler) collector

Liebhaberei die; ~, ~: hobby

Liebhaberin die; ~, ~nen ▶ LIEBHABER

lieblich ① Adj. charming; (angenehm) sweet ⟨scent, sound⟩
② adv. sweetly; (angenehm) pleasingly

Liebling der; ~s, ~e (bes. als Anrede) darling; (bevorzugte Person) favourite

Lieblings- favourite

lieb·los ① Adj. loveless
② adv. (a) without affection
(b) (ohne Sorgfalt) without proper care

liebsten: am ~: ▶ GERN

─────────────
*old spelling – see note on page x

Liechtenstein (das); ~s Liechtenstein

Lied das; ~[e]s, ~er song

liederlich Adj. slovenly; messy ⟨hairstyle, person⟩

Lieder-: **~macher** der; ~~s, ~~, **~macherin** die; ~~, ~~nen singer-songwriter

lief 1. u. 3. Pers. Sg. Prät. v. LAUFEN

Lieferant der; ~en, ~en, **Lieferantin** die; ~, ~nen supplier

lieferbar Adj. available; (vorrätig) in stock

Liefer·bedingungen Pl. terms of delivery

liefern tr. V. (a) (bringen) deliver (an + Akk. to); (zur Verfügung stellen) supply
(b) (hervorbringen) produce; provide ⟨eggs, honey, examples, raw material, etc.⟩

Liefer-: **~schein** der delivery note; **~termin** der delivery date

Lieferung die; ~, ~en delivery

Liefer-: **~wagen** der [delivery] van; **~zeit** die delivery time

Liege die; ~, ~n daybed; (zum Ausklappen) bed settee; (als Gartenmöbel) sunlounger

liegen unr. itr. V. lie; ⟨person⟩ be lying down; (sich befinden) be; ⟨object⟩ be [lying]; ⟨town, house, etc.⟩ be [situated]; **im Bett ~:** lie in bed; ~ **bleiben** (liegen gelassen werden) stay; be left; (vergessen werden) be left behind; (unerledigt bleiben) be left undone; (nicht aufstehen) stay [lying]; **[im Bett] ~ bleiben** stay in bed; **etw. ~ lassen** leave sth.; (vergessen) leave sth. [behind]; (unerledigt lassen) leave sth. undone; **einen Brief ~ lassen** (nicht abschicken) leave a letter unposted; (nicht öffnen) leave a letter unopened; **das liegt an ihm** od. **bei ihm** it is up to him; (ist seine Schuld) it is his fault; **es liegt mir nicht** it doesn't suit me; (es spricht mich nicht an) it doesn't appeal to me; (ich mag es nicht) I don't like it; **daran liegt ihm viel/wenig/nichts** he sets great/little/no store by that

liegen-: *~|**bleiben** ▶ LIEGEN; *~|**lassen** ▶ LIEGEN

Liege-: **~stuhl** der deckchair; **~stütz** der; ~~es, ~~e press-up; **~wagen** der couchette car; **~wiese** die sunbathing lawn

lieh 1. u. 3. Pers. Sg. Prät. v. LEIHEN

lies Imperativ Sg. v. LESEN

ließ 1. u. 3. Pers. Sg. Prät. v. LASSEN

liest 3. Pers. Sg. Präsens v. LESEN

Lift der; ~[e]s, ~e od. ~s (a) lift (Brit.); elevator (Amer.)
(b) Pl.: ~e (Ski~, Sessel~) lift

Liga die; ~, Ligen league; (Sport) division

Likör der; ~s, ~e liqueur

lila indekl. Adj. mauve; (dunkel~) purple

Lila das; ~s od. (ugs.) ~s mauve; (Dunkel~) purple

Lilie /'li:li̯ə/ die; ~, ~n lily

Liliputaner *der;* ~s, ~, **Liliputanerin** *die;* ~, ~nen dwarf

Limit *das;* ~s, ~s limit

Limo *die, auch: das;* ~, ~[s] (ugs.) fizzy drink

Limonade *die;* ~, ~n fizzy drink; (Zitronen~) lemonade

Limousine *die;* ~, ~n [large] saloon (Brit.) or (Amer.) sedan

Linde *die;* ~, ~n lime [tree]

lindern *tr. V.* relieve ⟨*suffering, pain*⟩; slake ⟨*thirst*⟩

Lineal *das;* ~s, ~e ruler

Linie /'li:niə/ *die;* ~, ~n line; (Verkehrsstrecke) route; **die ~ 12** (Verkehrsw.) the number 12; **auf die [schlanke] ~ achten** (ugs. scherzh.) watch one's figure; **auf der ganzen ~** (fig.) all along the line

linien-, Linien-: ~**bus** *der* regular bus; ~**flug** *der* scheduled flight; ~**richter** *der,* ~**richterin** *die* (Fußball usw.) linesman; (Tennis) line judge; (Rugby) touch judge; ~**treu** [1] *Adj.* loyal to the party line *postpos.;* [2] *adv.* ⟨*act*⟩ in accordance with the party line

linieren, liniieren *tr. V.* rule

link... *Adj.* (a) left (b) (innen, nicht sichtbar) wrong, reverse ⟨*side*⟩ (c) (in der Politik) left-wing

linkisch [1] *Adj.* awkward [2] *adv.* awkwardly

links *Adv.* on the left; (Politik) on the left wing

links-, Links-: ~**abbieger** *der,* ~**abbiegerin** *die* (Verkehrsw.) motorist/ cyclist/car *etc.* turning left; ~**außen** *der;* ~~, ~~ (Ballspiele) left wing; outside left; ~**extremist** *der,* ~**extremistin** *die* (Politik) left-wing extremist; ~**händer** *der;* ~~s, ~~, ~**händerin** *die;* ~~, ~~nen left-hander; ~**kurve** *die* left-hand bend; ~**radikal** (Politik) [1] *Adj.* radical left-wing; [2] *adv.* **eine ~radikal orientierte Gruppe** a group with a radical left-wing orientation; ~**radikale** *der/die* left-wing radical; ~**radikalismus** *der* left-wing radicalism; ~**verkehr** *der* driving *no art.* on the left

Linoleum *das;* ~s linoleum; lino

Linse *die;* ~, ~n (a) (Bot., Kochk.) lentil (b) (Med., Optik) lens

Lippe *die;* ~, ~n lip

Lippen·stift *der* lipstick

liquid *Adj.* (Wirtsch.) liquid ⟨*funds, resources*⟩; solvent ⟨*business*⟩

liquidieren (verhüll.: töten; Wirtsch.) liquidate

lispeln *itr. V.* lisp

Lissabon (*das*); ~s Lisbon

List *die;* ~, ~en (a) [cunning] trick (b) (listige Art) cunning

Liste *die;* ~, ~n list; **schwarze ~:** blacklist

listig [1] *Adj.* cunning; crafty

[2] *adv.* cunningly; craftily

Litauen (*das*); ~s Lithuania

Litauer *der;* ~s, ~, **Litauerin** *die;* ~, ~nen Lithuanian

litauisch *Adj.* Lithuanian

Liter *der, auch: das;* ~s, ~: litre

literarisch *Adj.* literary

Literatur *die;* ~, ~en literature

Literatur-: ~**geschichte** *die* literary history; history of literature; ~**verzeichnis** *das* list of references

liter·weise *Adv.* by the litre; in litres

Litfaß·säule *die* advertising column

Lithografie, Lithographie *die;* ~, ~n (Druck) lithograph

litt *1. u. 3. Pers. Sg. Prät. v.* LEIDEN

Litze *die;* ~, ~n braid

live /laif/ (Rundf., Ferns.); [1] *Adj.* live [2] *adv.* live; **in dieser Sendung wird nur ~ gesungen** in this programme all the singing is live

Live-: ~**sendung, *~-Sendung** *die* (Rundf., Ferns.) live programme; ~**übertragung** *die* live transmission

Lizenz *die;* ~, ~en licence

Lizenz·gebühr *die* licence fee; (Verlagsw.) royalty

Lkw, LKW /ɛlka:'ve:/ *der;* ~[s], ~[s] *Abk.* = **Lastkraftwagen** truck; lorry (Brit.)

Lob *das;* ~[e]s, ~e praise *no indef. art.*

Lobby /'lɔbi/ *die;* ~, ~s *od.* **Lobbies** lobby

loben *tr. V.* praise

lobens·wert [1] *Adj.* praiseworthy; laudable; commendable [2] *adv.* laudably; commendably

löblich *Adj.* commendable

Lob·lied *das* song of praise

Loch *das;* ~[e]s, **Löcher** hole

lochen *tr. V.* punch holes/a hole in; punch ⟨*ticket*⟩

Locher *der;* ~s, ~: punch

löcherig *Adj.* full of holes *pred.*

Locke *die;* ~, ~n curl

locken *tr. V.* (a) lure (b) (reizen) tempt

Locken·wickler *der* [hair] curler

locker [1] *Adj.* loose; (entspannt) relaxed ⟨*position, muscles*⟩; slack ⟨*rope, rein*⟩; (fig.) relax ⟨*regulation, law, etc.*⟩ [2] *adv.* **~ sitzen** ⟨*tooth, screw, nail*⟩ be loose; (entspannt, ungezwungen) loosely

locker|lassen *unr. itr. V.* (ugs.) **nicht ~:** not give up

lockern [1] *tr. V.* loosen; slacken [off] ⟨*rope etc.*⟩; relax ⟨*muscles, limbs*⟩ [2] *refl. V.* ⟨*brick, tooth, etc.*⟩ work itself loose; ⟨*person*⟩ loosen up

Lockerung *die;* ~, ~en (a) loosening; (fig.: von Bestimmung, Gesetz usw.) relaxation (b) (Entspannung) loosening up; relaxation

lǫckig *Adj.* curly

Lǫck·vogel *der* decoy

Loden·mantel *der* loden coat

Löffel *der;* ~s, ~: spoon; (als Maßangabe) spoonful; (Jägerspr.) ear

löffeln *tr. V.* spoon [up]

log *1. u. 3. Pers. Sg. Prät. v.* LÜGEN

Logarịthmus *der;* ~, Logarịthmen (Math.) logarithm; log

Loge /'lo:ʒə/ *die;* ~, ~n box

logieren *itr. V.* (veralt.) stay

Logik *die;* ~: logic

Log-in /lɔk'ɪn/*das;* ~s, ~s (DV) login

logisch ☐1 *Adj.* logical
☐2 *adv.* logically

logischer·weise *Adv.* logically; (selbstverständlich) naturally

logo *Adj.* (salopp) **[ist doch]** ~! you bet! (coll.); of course!

Lohn *der;* ~[e]s, Löhne (a) wage[s *pl.*]; pay *no indef. art., no pl.*
(b) (Belohnung) reward

Lohn·büro *das* payroll office

lohnen ☐1 *refl., itr. V.* be worth it
☐2 *tr. V.* be worth

lohnend *Adj.* rewarding

Lohn·steuer *die* income tax

Lohn-: ~**steuer·karte** *die* income-tax card; ~**streifen** *der* payslip; ~**tüte** *die* pay packet (Brit.); wage packet

lokal *Adj.* local

Lokal *das;* ~s, ~e pub (Brit. coll.); bar (Amer.); (Speise~) restaurant

Lokalität *die;* ~, ~en locality

Lokal-: ~**blatt** *das* local paper; ~**patriotismus** *der* local patriotism; ~**teil** *der* (Zeitungsw.) local section; ~**termin** *der* (Rechtsspr.) visit to the scene [of the crime]

Lǫk·führer *der,* **Lǫk·führerin** *die:* ▶ LOKOMOTIVFÜHRER

Lokomotive /lokomo'ti:və/ *die;* ~, ~n locomotive

Lokomotịv·führer *der,* **Lokomotịv·führerin** *die* engine driver (Brit.); engineer (Amer.)

Lokus *der;* ~ *od.* ~ses, ~ *od.* ~se (salopp) loo (Brit. coll.); john (Amer. coll.)

London (*das*); ~s London

Londoner ☐1 *indekl. Adj.* London
☐2 *der;* ~s, ~: Londoner

Londonerin *die;* ~, ~nen Londoner

Lǫrbeer *der;* ~s, ~en (a) laurel
(b) (Gewürz) bayleaf

Lore *die;* ~, ~n car; (kleiner) tub

los ☐1 *Adj.* (a) (gelöst, ab) off
(b) **es ist etwas** ~: there is something going on
(c) **jmdn./etw.** ~ **sein** be rid of sb./sth.

☐2 *Adv.* (als Aufforderung) come on!

Los *das;* ~es, ~e (a) lot
(b) (Lotterie~) ticket

Lösch·blatt *das* piece of blotting paper

löschen *tr. V.* (a) put out; extinguish; **seinen Durst** ~ (fig.) quench one's thirst
(b) (tilgen) delete ⟨*entry*⟩; erase ⟨*recording, memory, etc.*⟩

Lösch-: ~**fahrzeug** *das* fire engine; ~**papier** *das* blotting paper

lose ☐1 *Adj.* loose
☐2 *adv.* loosely

Löse·geld *das* ransom

losen *itr. V.* draw lots (**um** for)

lösen ☐1 *tr. V.* (a) remove ⟨*stamp, wallpaper*⟩; **etw. von etw.** ~: remove sth. from sth.
(b) (lockern) undo ⟨*screw, belt, tie*⟩
(c) (klären) solve; resolve ⟨*contradiction, conflict*⟩
(d) (annullieren) break off ⟨*engagement*⟩; cancel ⟨*contract*⟩; sever ⟨*relationship*⟩
(e) (kaufen) buy, obtain ⟨*ticket*⟩
☐2 *refl. V.* (a) (lose werden) come off; (sich lockern) ⟨*wallpaper, plaster*⟩ come off; ⟨*packing, screw*⟩ come loose
(b) (sich klären) ⟨*puzzle, problem*⟩ be solved
(c) (sich auflösen) dissolve

los-: ~**fahren** *unr. itr. V.; mit sein* set off; (wegfahren) move off; ~**gehen** *unr. itr. V.; mit sein* (a) (aufbrechen) set off; (b) (ugs.: beginnen) start; (c) (ugs.: abgehen) ⟨*button, handle, etc.*⟩ come off; ~**kommen** *unr. itr. V.; mit sein* (ugs.) (a) get away; (b) (freikommen) get free; ~**lassen** *unr. tr. V.* (a) (nicht festhalten) let go of; (b) (freilassen) let ⟨*person, animal*⟩ go; ~**legen** *unr. itr. V.* (ugs.) get going

löslich *Adj.* soluble

Löslichkeit *die;* ~: solubility

los|machen *tr. V.* (ugs.) let ⟨*animal*⟩ loose; untie ⟨*string, line, rope*⟩; unhitch ⟨*trailer*⟩

Los-nummer *die* [lottery-]ticket number

los-: ~|**reißen** *unr. refl. V.* break free or loose; ~|**sagen** *refl. V.* **sich von jmdm./ etw.** ~sagen break with sb./sth.

Löss, *Löß *der;* Lösses, Lösse (Geol.) loess

los|schlagen *unr. itr. V.* (bes. Milit.) attack; launch one's attack

Losung *die;* ~, ~en slogan; (Milit.: Kennwort) password

Lösung *die;* ~, ~en (a) solution (Gen., für to)
(b) ▶ LÖSEN 1D: breaking off; cancellation; severing

los|werden *unr. tr. V.; mit sein* get rid of

Lot *das;* ~[e]s, ~e plumb [bob]; **[nicht] im** ~ **sein** be [out of] plumb

löten *tr. V.* solder

Lotion *die;* ~, ~en lotion

Löt·kolben *der* soldering iron

lot·recht ☐1 *Adj.* perpendicular; vertical

---

*alte Schreibung – vgl. Hinweis auf S. x

2 *adv.* perpendicularly; vertically

Lotse *der;* ~n, ~n (Seew.) pilot

lotsen *tr. V.* guide

Lotsin *die* ▶ LOTSE

Lotterie *die;* ~, ~n lottery

Lotto *das;* ~s, ~s national lottery

Lotto-: ~**schein** *der* national-lottery coupon; ~**zahlen** *Pl.* winning national-lottery numbers

Löt·zinn *das* [tin-lead] solder

Löwe *der;* ~n, ~n (a) lion (b) (Astrol.) Leo; the Lion

Löwen-: ~**anteil** *der* lion's share; ~**mäulchen** *das;* ~~s, ~~: snapdragon; ~**zahn** *der* dandelion

Löwin *die;* ~, ~nen lioness

loyal /loa'ja:l/ 1 *Adj.* loyal 2 *adv.* loyally

Loyalität *die;* ~: loyalty

LP /ɛl'pe:/ *die;* ~, ~[s] *Abk.* = **Langspielplatte** LP

LSD /ɛl|ɛs'de:/ *das;* ~[s] LSD

Luchs *der;* ~es, ~e lynx

Lücke *die;* ~, ~n gap

lücken-, Lücken-: ~**büßer** *der,* ~~s, ~~, ~**büßerin** *die;* ~~, ~~~nen (ugs.) stopgap; ~**haft** *Adj.* sketchy; ~**los** *Adj.* complete

lud 1. u. 3. Pers. Sg. Prät. v. LADEN

Luder *das;* ~s, ~ (salopp) so-and-so (coll.)

Luft *die;* ~, Lüfte air; **an die frische ~ gehen** get out in[to] the fresh air; **die ~ anhalten** hold one's breath; **tief ~ holen** take a deep breath; **in die ~ gehen** (fig. ugs.) blow one's top (coll.)

luft-, Luft-: ~**angriff** *der* (Milit.) air raid; ~**ballon** *der* balloon; ~**brücke** *die* airlift; ~**dicht** *Adj.* airtight; ~**druck** *der* (a) (Physik) air pressure; (b) (Druckwelle) blast

lüften 1 *tr. V.* (a) air ⟨room, clothes, etc.⟩ (b) raise ⟨hat⟩ (c) disclose ⟨secret⟩ 2 *itr. V.* air the room/house etc.

luft-, Luft-: ~**fahrt** *die* aviation *no art.;* ~**feuchtigkeit** *die* [atmospheric] humidity; ~**gekühlt** *Adj.* air-cooled; ~**getrocknet** *Adj.* air-dried; ~**gewehr** *das* air rifle; airgun

luftig *Adj.* airy ⟨room, building, etc.⟩; light ⟨clothes⟩

Luft·kissen·boot *das* hovercraft

luft-, Luft-: ~**leer** *Adj.* ein ~leerer Raum a vacuum; ~**linie** *die* 1000 km ~linie 1,000 km. as the crow flies; ~**loch** *das* air hole; ~**matratze** *die* airbed; air mattress; Lilo®; ~**pirat** *der,* ~**piratin** *die* [aircraft] hijacker; ~**post** *die* airmail; etw. per od. mit ~**post** schicken send sth. [by] airmail; ~**pumpe** *die* air pump; (für Fahrrad) [bicycle] pump; ~**qualität** *die* air quality; ~**röhre** *die* (Anat.) windpipe; ~**schiff** *das* airship; ~**schloss,** ***~**schloß** *das*

castle in the air; ~**schutz** *der* air-raid protection *no art.;* ~**schutz·bunker,** ~**schutz·keller,** ~**schutz·raum** *der* air-raid shelter; ~**verschmutzung** *die* air pollution; ~**waffe** *die* air force; ~**zug** *der* [gentle] breeze; (in Zimmern, Gebäuden) draught

Lüge *die;* ~, ~n lie

lügen *itr., tr. V.* lie; **das ist gelogen!** that's a lie!

Lügner *der;* ~s, ~, **Lügnerin** *die;* ~, ~nen liar

Luke *die;* ~, ~n (Dach~) skylight; (bei Schiffen) hatch; (Keller~) trapdoor

lukrativ 1 *Adj.* lucrative 2 *adv.* lucratively

Lümmel *der;* ~s, ~: lout; (ugs., fam.: Bengel) rascal

Lump *der;* ~en, ~en scoundrel

lumpen (ugs.) *tr. V.* sich nicht ~ lassen splash out (coll.)

Lumpen *der;* ~s, ~ rag

Lumpen-: ~**sammler** *die* rag-and-bone man; ~**sammlerin** *die* rag-and-bone woman

Lunge *die;* ~, ~n lungs *pl.*

Lungen-: ~**entzündung** *die* pneumonia *no indef. art.;* ~**krebs** *der* lung cancer; ~**zug** *der* inhalation

Lunte *die;* ~, ~n fuse; match

Lupe *die;* ~, ~n magnifying glass

Lurch *der;* ~[e]s, ~e amphibian

Lust *die;* ~ (a) ~ haben, etw. zu tun feel like doing sth. (b) (Vergnügen) pleasure; joy

lustig 1 *Adj.* (a) merry; jolly; enjoyable ⟨time⟩ (b) (komisch) funny 2 *adv.* (a) merrily (b) (komisch) funnily

lust-, Lust-: ~**los** 1 *Adj.* listless; 2 *adv.* listlessly; ~**spiel** *das* comedy

lutherisch *Adj.* Lutheran

lutschen 1 *tr. V.* suck 2 *itr. V.* suck; **an etw.** (*Dat.*) ~: suck sth.

Luxemburg (*das*); ~s Luxembourg

luxuriös 1 *Adj.* luxurious 2 *adv.* luxuriously

Luxus *der;* ~: luxury

Lymphe *die;* ~, ~n lymph

Lymph·knoten *der* lymph node

lynchen *tr. V.* lynch

Lyrik *die;* ~: lyric poetry

Lyriker *der;* ~s, ~, **Lyrikerin** *die;* ~, ~nen lyric poet; lyricist

lyrisch *Adj.* lyrical; lyric ⟨poetry⟩

Lyzeum *das;* ~s, Lyzeen girls' high school

Mm

m, M /ɛm/ *das;* ~, ~ m/M
m *Abk.* = **Meter** m
Mach·art *die* style; (Schnitt) cut
machbar *Adj.* feasible
machen ① *tr. V.* **(a)** make; **aus Plastik/
Holz** *usw.* **gemacht** made of plastic/wood
etc.; **sich** (*Dat.*) **etw.** ~ **lassen** have sth.
made; **etw. aus jmdm.** ~: make sb. into sth.;
jmdn. zum Präsidenten *usw.* ~: make sb.
president *etc.;* **jmdm./sich [einen] Kaffee**
~: make [some] coffee for sb./oneself
(b) (verursachen) **jmdm. Arbeit** ~: make
[extra] work for sb.; **das macht das Wetter**
that's [because of] the weather
(c) (ausführen) do 〈*job, repair, etc.*〉; **einen
Spaziergang** ~: go for a walk; **eine Reise**
~: go on a journey; **einen Besuch [bei
jmdm.]** ~: pay [sb.] a visit
(d) (tun) do; **was machst du da?** what are
you doing?; **so etwas macht man nicht** that
[just] isn't done
(e) was macht ...? (wie ist es um ... bestellt?)
how is ...?; **was macht die Gesundheit/
Arbeit?** how are you keeping/how is the job
[getting on]?
(f) (ergeben) (beim Rechnen) be; (bei
Geldbeträgen) come to; **zwei mal zwei macht
vier** two times two is four; **das macht
12 Euro** that is 12 euros; (Endsumme) that
comes to 12 euros
(g) (schaden) **was macht das schon?** what
does it matter?; **macht nichts!** (ugs.) it
doesn't matter
(h) (teilnehmen an) **einen Kursus** *od.* **Lehrgang**
~: take a course
(i) mach's gut! (ugs.) look after yourself!; (auf
Wiedersehen) so long!
② *refl. V.* **(a) sich an etw.** (*Akk.*) ~: get
down to sth.
(b) (ugs.: sich entwickeln) do well
(c) mach dir nichts daraus! (ugs.) don't let it
bother you
③ *itr. V.* **(a) mach schon!** (ugs.) get a move
on! (coll.)
(b) das macht hungrig/durstig it makes
you hungry/thirsty; **das macht dick** it's
fattening
Machenschaften *Pl.* (abwertend)
wheeling and dealing *sing.*
Macher *der;* ~s, ~, **Macherin** *die;* ~,
~nen (ugs.) doer; **der Typ des Machers** the
dynamic type who just gets on with things
Macho /ˈmatʃo/ *der;* ~s, ~s (abwertend)
macho
Macht *die;* ~, **Mächte** power; **an die**

~ kommen come to power
Macht-: ~**bereich** *der* sphere of
influence; ~**haber** *der;* ~~s, ~~,
~**haberin** *die;* ~~, ~~**nen** ruler
mächtig ① *Adj.* **(a)** powerful
(b) (beeindruckend groß) mighty
② *adv.* (ugs.) terribly (coll.)
macht-, Macht-: ~**kampf** *der* power
struggle; ~**los** *Adj.* powerless; **gegen etw.**
~**los sein** be powerless in the face of sth.;
~**probe** *die* trial of strength
Mach·werk *das* (abwertend) shoddy effort
Macke *die;* ~, ~**n (a)** (salopp: Tick) fad
(b) (ugs.: Defekt) defect
Mädchen *das;* ~s, ~ **(a)** girl
(b) (Haus~) maid
mädchenhaft *Adj.* girlish
Mädchen·name *der* **(a)** girl's name
(b) (Name vor der Ehe) maiden name
Made *die;* ~, ~**n** maggot
madig *Adj.* maggoty; **jmdn./etw.** ~ **machen**
(ugs.) run sb./sth. down
Madonna *die;* ~, **Madonnen** madonna
mag *1. u. 3. Pers. Sg. Präsens v.* MÖGEN
Magazin *das;* ~s, ~**e (a)** (Lager) store; (für
Waren) stockroom
(b) (für Patronen, Dias, Film usw.; Zeitschrift)
magazine
Magazin·sendung *die* magazine
programme
Magen *der;* ~s, **Mägen** *od.* ~: stomach
magen-, Magen-: ~**bitter** *der;* ~~s,
~~, bitters *pl.;* ~**geschwür** *das* stomach
ulcer; ~**krebs** *der* cancer of the stomach;
~**schmerzen** *Pl.* stomach ache *sing.*
mager *Adj.* **(a)** thin
(b) (fettarm) low-fat; low in fat *pred.;* lean 〈*meat*〉
(c) (fig.) poor 〈*soil, harvest*〉; meagre
〈*profit, increase, success, report, etc.*〉; thin
〈*programme*〉
Mager-: ~**milch** *die* skim[med] milk;
~**quark** *der* low-fat curd cheese; ~**sucht**
die (Med.) wasting disease; (Anorexie)
anorexia
Magie *die;* ~: magic
Magier /ˈmaːgiɐ/ *der;* ~s, ~, **Magierin**
die; ~, ~**nen** (auch fig.) magician
magisch *Adj.* magic 〈*powers*〉;
(geheimnisvoll) magical
Magistrat *der;* ~[e]s, ~**e** City Council
Magnat *der;* ~**en**, ~**en** magnate
Magnet *der;* ~**en** *od.* ~[e]s, ~**e** magnet
Magnet·band *das; Pl.* **Magnet·bänder**
magnetic tape
magnetisch ① *Adj.* magnetic

---

*old spelling – see note on page x

2 *adv.* magnetically

magnetisieren *tr. V.* magnetize

Magnetismus *der;* ~: magnetism

Magnet-: ~**nadel** *die* [compass] needle; ~**schwebebahn** *die* maglev [system]

Mahagoni *das;* ~s mahogany

Mäh·drescher *der* combine harvester

mähen 1 *tr. V.* mow; cut ⟨corn⟩
2 *itr. V.* mow; (Getreide ~) reap

Mahl *das;* ~[e]s, **Mähler** (geh.) meal; repast (formal)

mahlen *unr. tr., itr. V.* grind

Mahl·zeit meal

Mähne *die;* ~, ~n mane

mahnen *tr. V.* urge; remind ⟨debtor⟩

Mahn-: ~**mal** *das; Pl.* ~~e od. ~mäler memorial (erected as a warning to future generations); ~**schreiben** *das* reminder

Mahnung *die;* ~, ~en (a) exhortation; (Warnung) admonition
(b) ▸ MAHNSCHREIBEN

Mai *der;* ~[e]s od. ~: May

Mai-: ~**baum** *der* maypole; ~**feiertag** *der* May Day *no def. art.;* ~**glöckchen** *das* lily of the valley; ~**käfer** *der* May bug

Mais *der;* ~es maize; corn (esp. Amer.); (als Gericht) sweet corn

Mais·kolben *der* corn cob; (als Gericht) corn on the cob

Majestät *die;* ~, ~en (a) (Titel) Majesty; **Eure** ~: Your Majesty
(b) (geh.) majesty

majestätisch 1 *Adj.* majestic
2 *adv.* majestically

Majonäse *die;* ~, ~n mayonnaise

Major *der;* ~s, ~e (Milit.) major

Majoran *der;* ~s, ~e marjoram

makaber *Adj.* macabre

Makedonien /make'do:niən/ (*das*); ~s Macedonia

Makel *der;* ~s, ~ (geh.) (a) (Schmach) stigma
(b) (Fehler) blemish

makel·los 1 *Adj.* flawless; spotless ⟨white, cleanness⟩
2 *adv.* immaculately; spotlessly ⟨clean⟩

Make-up /me:k'|ap/ *das;* ~s, ~s make-up

Makkaroni *Pl.* macaroni *sing.*

Makler *der;* ~s, ~, **Maklerin** *die;* ~, ~nen (a) (Häusermakler) estate agent (Brit.); realtor (Amer.)
(b) (Börsenmakler) broker

Makrele *die;* ~, ~n mackerel

Makro *der od. das;* ~s, ~s (DV) macro

Makrone *die;* ~, ~n macaroon

mal 1 *Adv.* times; (bei Flächen) by
2 *Partikel* **komm** ~ **her!** come here!

Mal[1] *das;* ~[e]s, ~e **das erste/zweite** ~, **zum ersten/zweiten** ~: for the first/second time; **beim ersten/zweiten** ~: the first/second time; **das letzte, zum letzten**

~: for the last time; **letztes, beim letzten** ~: last time; **jedes** ~: every time; **mit einem** ~[e] all at once

Mal[2] *das;* ~[e]s, ~e od. **Mäler** mark; (Muttermal) birthmark; (braun) mole

Malaie *der;* ~n, ~n, **Malaiin** *die;* ~, ~nen Malay

Malaria *die;* ~: malaria

Malaysia (*das*); ~s Malaysia

Mal·buch *das* colouring book

malen *tr., itr. V.* paint; decorate ⟨flat, room, walls⟩

Maler *der;* ~s, ~: painter

Malerei *die;* ~, ~en painting

Malerin *der;* ~, ~nen painter

malerisch 1 *Adj.* picturesque
2 *adv.* picturesquely

mal|nehmen *unr. tr., itr. V.* multiply (mit by)

malträtieren *tr. V.* maltreat; ill-treat

Malz·bier *das* malt beer

Mama *die;* ~, ~s (fam.) mamma

Mami *die;* ~, ~s (fam.) mummy (Brit. coll.); mommy (Amer. coll.)

Mammut *das;* ~s, ~e od. ~s mammoth

mampfen *tr., itr. V.* (salopp) munch; nosh (coll.)

man *Indefinitpron. im Nom.* one; you *2nd person;* (irgendjemand) somebody; (die Behörden, die Leute dort) they *pl.;* (die Menschen im Allgemeinen) people *pl;* ~ **hat mir gesagt** …: I was told …

Management /'mɛnɪdʒmənt/ *das;* ~s, ~s management

managen /'mɛnɪdʒn̩/ *tr. V.* (a) (ugs.) fix; organize
(b) (betreuen) manage ⟨singer, artist, player⟩

Manager /'mɛnɪdʒɐ/ *der;* ~s, ~, **Managerin** *die;* ~, ~nen manager; (eines Fußballvereins) club secretary

manch *Indefinitpron.* (a) *attr.* many a; in [so] ~**er Beziehung** in many respects
(b) *allein stehend* ~**er** many a person/man; ~**e** *Pl.* some; (viele) many; [so] ~**es** a number of things; (allerhand Verschiedenes) all kinds of things

mancherlei *indekl. Adj.* (a) *attr.* various; a number of
(b) *allein stehend* various things

manch·mal *Adv.* sometimes

Mandant *der;* ~en, ~en, **Mandantin** *die;* ~, ~nen client

Mandarine *die;* ~, ~n mandarin [orange]

Mandel *die;* ~, ~n (a) almond
(b) (Anat.) tonsil

Mandel·entzündung *die* tonsillitis *no indef. art.*

Manege /ma'ne:ʒə/ *die;* ~, ~n (im Zirkus) ring; (in der Reitschule) arena

Mangel[1] *der;* ~s, **Mängel** (a) (Fehlen) lack (an + *Dat.* of); (Knappheit) shortage, ⋯⋗

lack (**an** + *Dat.* of)
(b) (Fehler) defect
Mangel² *die;* ~, ~n [large] mangle
mangelhaft ① *Adj.* faulty ⟨*goods,
German, English, etc.*⟩; (unzulänglich)
inadequate ⟨*knowledge, lighting*⟩; (Schulw.)
die Note „~**"** the mark 'unsatisfactory'; (bei
Prüfungen) the fail mark
② *adv.* faultily; (unzulänglich) inadequately
mangeln¹ *itr. V.; unpers.* **es mangelt an
etw.** (*Dat.*) (etw. fehlt) there is a lack of sth.;
(etw. ist unzureichend vorhanden) there is a
shortage of sth.; **jmdm./einer Sache mangelt
es an etw.** (*Dat.*) sb./sth. lacks sth.
mangeln² *tr. V.* mangle
mangels *Präp. mit Gen.* in the absence of
Mango *die;* ~, ~s mango
Mangold *der;* ~[e]s [Swiss] chard
Manie *die;* ~, ~n mania
Manier *die;* ~, ~en **(a)** manner
(b) *Pl.* (Umgangsformen) manners
manierlich ① *Adj.* **(a)** (fam.) well-
mannered; well-behaved ⟨*child*⟩
(b) (ugs.: einigermaßen gut) decent
② *adv.* **(a)** (fam.) nicely
(b) (ugs.: einigermaßen gut) **ganz/recht**
~: quite/really nicely
Manifest *das;* ~[e]s, ~e manifesto
Maniküre *die;* ~: manicure
maniküren *tr. V.* manicure
Manipulation *die;* ~, ~en (geh.)
manipulation
manipulieren *tr. V.* manipulate; rig
⟨*election result etc.*⟩
Manko *das;* ~s, ~s shortcoming;
deficiency
Mann *der;* ~[e]s, **Männer (a)** man
(b) (Ehemann) husband
Männchen *das;* ~s, ~ **(a)** little man
(b) (Tier~) male; ~ **machen** ⟨*animal*⟩ sit up
and beg
Mannequin /ˈmanəkɛ̃/ *das;* ~s, ~s
mannequin; [fashion] model
männer-, Männer-: ~**beruf** *der*
all-male profession; (überwiegend von Männern
ausgeübt) male-dominated profession;
~**mordend** *Adj.* (ugs. scherzh.) man-
eating (fig.); ~**sache** *die:* **das ist** ~**sache**
that's men's business; ~**überschuss,**
*~**überschuß** *der* surplus of men
mannig·fach *Adj.* multifarious
männlich ① *Adj.* **(a)** male
(b) ▶ MASKULIN 1
② *adv.* in a masculine way
Mannschaft *die;* ~, ~en (Sport, auch fig.)
team; (Schiffs-, Flugzeugbesatzung) crew; (Milit.)
unit
Mannschafts-: ~**führer** *der,*
~**führerin** *die* (Sport) team captain;
~**kapitän** *der,* ~**kapitänin** *die* (Sport)

team captain; ~**spiel** *das* (Sport) team game
Manöver *das;* ~s, ~ **(a)** (Milit.) exercise; ~
Pl. manœuvres
(b) (Bewegung; fig. abwertend: Trick) manœuvre
manövrieren *itr., tr. V.* manœuvre
Mansarde *die;* ~, ~n attic; (Zimmer) attic
room
Manschette *die;* ~, ~n cuff
Manschetten·knopf *der* cuff link
Mantel *der;* ~s, **Mäntel** coat
Manteltarif·vertrag *der* (Wirtsch.)
framework collective agreement [on
working conditions]
Manuskript *das;* ~[e]s, ~e
(a) manuscript; (Typoskript) typescript
(b) (Notizen) notes *pl.*
Mappe *die;* ~, ~n **(a)** folder
(b) (Aktentasche) briefcase; (Schul~)
schoolbag
Marathon·lauf /...tɔn.../ *der* marathon
Märchen *das;* ~s, ~: fairy story; fairy
tale; (ugs.: Lüge) [tall] story (coll.)
Märchen·buch *das* book of fairy stories
märchenhaft ① *Adj.* magical
② *adv.* magically; (ugs.) fantastically (coll.)
Margarine *die;* ~: margarine
Margerite *die;* ~, ~n ox-eye daisy
Maria (*die*); ~s *od.* (Rel.) **Mariä** Mary
Marien·käfer *der* ladybird
Marihuana *das;* ~s marijuana
Marinade *die;* ~, ~n (Kochk.) marinade;
(Salatsoße) [marinade] dressing
Marine *die;* ~, ~n fleet; (Kriegs~) navy
marinieren *tr. V.* marinade; **marinierte
Heringe** soused herrings
Marionette *die;* ~, ~n puppet;
marionette
Marionetten·theater *das* puppet
theatre
Mark¹ *die;* ~, ~: mark; **Deutsche
~: Deutschmark
Mark² *das;* ~[e]s **(a)** (Knochen~) marrow
(b) (Frucht~) pulp
markant *Adj.* striking; prominent ⟨*figure,
nose, chin*⟩; clear-cut ⟨*features, profile*⟩
Marke *die;* ~, ~n **(a)** (Waren~) brand;
(Fabrikat) make
(b) (Brief~, Rabatt~, Beitrags~) stamp
(c) (Essen~) meal ticket
(d) (Erkennungs~) [identification] disc;
(Dienst~) [police] identification badge;
≈ warrant card (Brit.) *or* (Amer.) ID card
Marken-: ~**artikel** *der* proprietary *or*
(Brit.) branded article; ~**zeichen** *das* trade
mark
Marketing *das;* ~s (Wirtsch.) marketing
markieren ① *tr. V.* **(a)** mark
(b) (ugs.: vortäuschen) sham ⟨*illness,
breakdown, etc.*⟩
② *itr. V.* (ugs.: simulieren) put it on (coll.)
Markierung *die;* ~, ~en marking

---

*alte Schreibung – vgl. Hinweis auf S. x

Markt der; ~[e]s, Märkte market; (~platz) market place or square; **freitags ist ~**: Friday is market day

markt-, Markt-: ~**anteil** der share of the market; ~**beherrschend** Adj. market-dominating attrib.; ~**einführung** die launch; ~**forschung** die market research no def. art.; ~**frau** die market woman; ~**führer** der, ~**führerin** die market leader; ~**halle** die covered market; ~**lücke** die gap in the market; ~**platz** der market place; ~**stand** der market stall; ~**wirtschaft** die market economy

Marmelade die; ~, ~n jam; (Orangen~) marmalade

Marmor der; ~s marble

Marokkaner der; ~s, ~, **Marokkanerin** die; ~, ~nen Moroccan

marokkanisch Adj. Moroccan

Marokko (das); ~s Morocco

Marone die; ~, ~n [sweet] chestnut

Mars der; ~: Mars no def. art.

Marsch[1] der; ~[e]s, Märsche march; (Wanderung) [long] walk

Marsch[2] die; ~, ~en fertile marshland

Marsch·flug·körper der cruise missile

marschieren itr. V.; mit sein march; (wandern) walk

Marsch-: ~**musik** die march music; ~**verpflegung** die (Milit.) marching rations pl.;

Mars-: ~**mensch** der Martian; ~**sonde** die (Raumfahrt) Mars probe

Marter die; ~, ~n (geh.) torture; (seelisch) torment

martern tr. V. (geh.) torture

Märtyrer der; ~s, ~, **Märtyrerin** die; ~, ~nen martyr

Martyrium das; ~s, Martyrien martyrdom

Marxismus der; ~: Marxism no art.

Marxist der; ~en, ~en, **Marxistin** die; ~, ~nen Marxist

marxistisch Adj. Marxist

März der; ~[es] March

Marzipan das; ~s marzipan

Masche die; ~, ~n stitch; (Lauf~) run; ladder (Brit.); (beim Netz) mesh

Maschen·draht der wire netting

Maschine die; ~, ~n (a) (auch ugs.: Motorrad) machine
(b) (ugs.: Automotor) engine
(c) (Flugzeug) [aero]plane
(d) (Schreib~) typewriter; ~ **schreiben** type

maschine·geschrieben Adj. typewritten

maschinell [1] Adj. machine attrib.; by machine postpos.
[2] adv. by machine; ~ **hergestellt** machine-made

Maschinen-: ~**gewehr** das machine gun; ~**pistole** die sub-machine gun;

~**schlosser** der, ~**schlosserin** die fitter

*****maschine|schreiben** ▶ MASCHINE D

Masern Pl. measles sing. or pl.

Maserung die; ~, ~en [wavy] grain

Maske die; ~, ~n mask

Masken-: ~**ball** der masked ball; ~**bildner** der; ~~s, ~~, ~**bildnerin** die; ~~, ~~nen make-up artist

Maskerade die; ~, ~n [fancy-dress] costume

maskieren [1] tr. V. mask
[2] refl. V. put on a mask/masks

Maskottchen das; ~s, ~: [lucky] mascot

maskulin /auch: '---/ [1] Adj. (auch Sprachw.) masculine
[2] adv. in a masculine way

Masochismus der; ~ (Psych.) masochism no art.

Masochist der; ~en, ~en, **Masochistin** die; ~, ~nen (Psych.) masochist

masochistisch (Psych.) [1] Adj. masochistic
[2] adv. masochistically; ~ **veranlagt sein** have masochistic tendencies

maß 1. u. 3. Pers. Sg. Prät. v. MESSEN

Maß[1] das; ~es, ~e (a) measure (**für** of); (fig.) **das ~ ist voll** enough is enough
(b) (Größe) measurement
(c) (Grad) degree (**an** + Dat. of); **in großem/gewissem ~e** to a great/certain extent
(d) ~ **halten** exercise moderation

Maß[2] die; ~, ~[e] (bayr., österr.) litre [of beer]

Massage /ma'sa:ʒə/ die; ~, ~n massage

Massaker das; ~s, ~: massacre

Maß-: ~**anzug** der made-to-measure suit; ~**arbeit** die (a) custom-made item; (Kleidungsstück) made-to-measure item; (b) (genaue Arbeit) neat work

Masse die; ~, ~n (a) mass
(b) (Gemisch) mixture

Maß·einheit die unit of measurement

Massen-: ~**arbeitslosigkeit** die mass unemployment; ~**entlassungen** Pl. mass redundancies pl.; ~**grab** das mass grave

massenhaft [1] Adj. in huge numbers postpos.
[2] adv. on a huge scale

massen-, Massen-: ~**karambolage** die multiple crash; ~**kommunikations·mittel** das medium of mass communication; mass medium; ~**medium** das mass medium; ~**mörder** der, ~**mörderin** die mass murderer; ~**produktion** die mass production; ~**vernichtung** die mass extermination; ~**vernichtungs·waffen** Pl. weapons of mass destruction; ~**weise** Adv. in huge numbers

Masseur /ma'søːɐ̯/ *der;* ~s, ~e masseur
Masseurin *die;* ~, ~nen, **Masseuse**
/ma'søːzə/ *die;* ~, ~n masseuse
maß-gebend, maß-geblich [1] *Adj.*
authoritative ⟨*book, expert, opinion*⟩;
definitive ⟨*text*⟩; influential ⟨*person, circles, etc.*⟩; decisive ⟨*factor, influence, etc.*⟩
[2] *adv.* ⟨*influence*⟩ to a considerable extent;
(entscheidend) decisively
*****maß|halten** ▸ Mass¹ D
massieren *tr. V.* massage
mäßig [1] *Adj.* moderate; (mittel~) mediocre
[2] *adv.* in moderation; moderately ⟨*gifted, talented*⟩; (mittel~) indifferently
mäßigen *refl. V.* (geh.) **(a)** practise *or*
exercise moderation
(b) (sich beherrschen) control *or* restrain
oneself
Mäßigkeit *die;* ~: moderation
Mäßigung *die;* ~: moderation
massiv [1] *Adj.* **(a)** solid
(b) (heftig) massive ⟨*demand*⟩; crude
⟨*accusation, threat*⟩; strong ⟨*attack, criticism, pressure*⟩
[2] *adv.* ⟨*attack*⟩ strongly; ⟨*accuse, threaten*⟩
crudely
maß-, Maß-: ~**krug** *der* (südd., österr.)
litre beer mug; (aus Steingut) stein; ~**los**
[1] *Adj.* extreme; gross ⟨*exaggeration, insult*⟩; excessive ⟨*demand, claim*⟩;
boundless ⟨*ambition, greed, sorrow, joy*⟩;
[2] *adv.* extremely; ⟨*exaggerate*⟩ grossly;
~**nahme** *die;* ~~, ~~n measure;
~**regel** *die* regulation; (Maßnahme)
measure; ~**regeln** *tr. V.* (zurechtweisen)
reprimand; (bestrafen) discipline; ~**stab** *der*
(a) standard; **(b)** (einer Karte, eines Modells usw.)
scale; ~**voll** [1] *Adj.* moderate; [2] *adv.* in
moderation
Mast *der;* ~[e]s, ~en, *auch:* ~e (Schiffs~,
Antennen~) mast; (Stange, Fahnen~) pole;
(Hochspannungs~) pylon
mästen *tr. V.* fatten
Masturbation *die;* ~, ~en masturbation
masturbieren *itr., tr. V.* masturbate
Match /mɛtʃ/ *das od. der;* ~[e]s, ~s *od.*
~e match
Material *das;* ~s, ~ien material; (Bau~;
Hilfsmittel) materials *pl.*
Materialismus *der;* ~: materialism
Materialist *der;* ~en, ~en,
Materialistin *die;* ~, ~nen materialist
materialistisch [1] *Adj.* materialistic
[2] *adv.* materialistically
Materie *die;* ~, ~n **(a)** matter
(b) (geh.: Thema, Gegenstand) subject matter
materiell [1] *Adj.* (finanziell) financial
[2] *adv.* materially; (finanziell) financially
Mathe *die;* ~ (ugs.) maths *sing.* (Brit. coll.);
math (Amer. coll.)

Mathematik *die;* ~: mathematics *sing.,
no art.*
mathematisch [1] *Adj.* mathematical
[2] *adv.* mathematically
Matjes *der;* ~, ~: matie [herring]
Matratze *die;* ~, ~n mattress
Matrose *der;* ~n, ~n sailor; seaman
Matsch *der;* ~[e]s (ugs.) mud; (breiiger
Schmutz) sludge; (Schnee~) slush
matschig *Adj.* (ugs.) **(a)** muddy; slushy
⟨*snow*⟩
(b) (weich) mushy; squashy ⟨*fruit*⟩
matt [1] *Adj.* **(a)** weak; feeble ⟨*applause, reaction*⟩
(b) (glanzlos) matt; dull ⟨*metal, mirror, etc.*⟩
(c) (undurchsichtig) frosted ⟨*glass*⟩; pearl
⟨*lightbulb*⟩
(d) subdued; (Schach) checkmated; ~!
checkmate!
[2] *adv.* **(a)** (kraftlos) weakly
(b) (mäßig) ⟨*protest, contradict*⟩ feebly
Matte *die;* ~, ~n mat
Matt-scheibe *die* (ugs.) telly (Brit. coll.);
box (coll.)
Matur *die;* ~ (schweiz.), **Matura** *die;* ~a
(österr., schweiz.) ▸ Abitur
Mätzchen *das;* ~s, ~: ~ machen (ugs.)
fool about *or* around
Mauer *die;* ~, ~n wall
mauern [1] *tr. V.* build
[2] *itr. V.* lay bricks
Mauer-: ~**segler** *der* swift; ~**werk**
das **(a)** masonry; (aus Ziegeln) brickwork;
(b) (Mauern) walls *pl.*
Maul *das;* ~[e]s, Mäuler (von Tieren) mouth;
(derb: Mund) gob (sl.)
Maul-: ~**esel** *der* mule; ~**korb** *der* (auch
fig.) muzzle; ~**tier** *das* mule
Maul-wurf *der* mole
Maulwurfs-: ~**haufen** *der,* ~**hügel**
der molehill
Maurer *der;* ~s, ~, **Maurerin** *die;* ~,
~nen bricklayer
Maus *die;* ~, Mäuse mouse
Mauschelei *die;* ~, ~en (ugs. abwertend)
shady wheeling and dealing *no indef. art.*
mauscheln *itr. V.* (ugs. abwertend) engage
in shady wheeling and dealing
Mäuschen *das;* ~s, ~: little mouse
mäuschen-still *Adj.* ~ sein be as quiet
as a mouse
Mause-falle *die* mousetrap
mausern *refl. V.* moult
Maus-: ~**klick** *der;* ~~s, ~~s (DV)
mouse click; ~**pad** /-pɛt/ *das;* ~~s, ~~s
(DV) mouse mat; ~**taste** *die* (DV) mouse
button; ~**zeiger** *der* (DV) mouse pointer
Maut *die;* ~, ~en toll
maximal [1] *Adj.* maximum
[2] *adv.* ~ zulässige Geschwindigkeit
maximum permitted speed

*****old spelling – see note on page x

Maxime *die;* ~, ~n maxim
maximieren *tr. V.* maximize
Maximum *das;* ~s, Maxima maximum (an + *Dat.* of)
Maxi·single *die* maxi-single
Mayonnaise /majɔ'nɛːzə/ *die;* ~, ~n mayonnaise
Mäzen *der;* ~s, ~e (geh.) patron
Mäzenin *die;* ~, ~nen patroness
MdB, M.d.B. *Abk.* = **Mitglied des Bundestages** Member of the Bundestag
m. E. *Abk.* = **meines Erachtens** in my opinion *or* view
Mechanik *die;* ~: mechanics *sing., no art.*
Mechaniker *der;* ~s, ~,
Mechanikerin *die;* ~, ~nen mechanic
mechanisch [1] *Adj.* mechanical; power attrib. ‹loom, press›
[2] *adv.* mechanically
Mechanismus *der;* ~, Mechanismen mechanism
meckern *itr. V.* (a) (auch fig.) bleat
(b) (ugs.: nörgeln) grumble; moan
Mecklenburg-Vorpommern *(das);* ~s Mecklenburg-Western Pomerania
Medaille /me'daljə/ *die;* ~, ~n medal
Medaillen·gewinner *der,*
Medaillen·gewinnerin *die* medallist; medal winner
Medaillon /medal'jõː/ *das;* ~s, ~s
(a) locket
(b) (Kochk., bild. Kunst) medallion
medial *Adj.* (in den Medien) in the media *postpos.;* (von den Medien) by the media *postpos.;* eine ~e Präsenz a media presence; ein ~es Spektakel a media spectacle
Medien-: ~**angebot** *das* range of media; ~**konzern** *der* media concern; ~**landschaft** *die* media scene; ~**politik** *die* media policy; ~**präsenz** *die* media presence
Medikament *das;* ~[e]s, ~e medicine; (Droge) drug
Meditation *die;* ~, ~en meditation
meditieren *itr. V.* meditate (**über** + *Akk.* [up]on)
Medium *das;* ~s, Medien medium
Medizin *die;* ~, ~en medicine
Mediziner *der;* ~s, ~, **Medizinerin** *die;* ~, ~nen doctor; (Student[in]) medical student
medizinisch [1] *Adj.* medical; medicinal ‹bath etc.›; medicated ‹toothpaste, soap, etc.›
[2] *adv.* medically
Meer *das;* ~[e]s, ~e (auch fig.) sea; **am** ~: by the sea
Meer·enge *die* straits *pl.;* strait
Meeres-: ~**boden** *der* sea bed *or* bottom *or* floor; ~**bucht** *die* bay; ~**früchte** *Pl.* (Kochk.) seafood *sing.;* ~**kunde** *die* oceanography *no art.;* ~**spiegel** *der* sea level

Meer-: ~**jungfrau** *die* mermaid; ~**katze** *die* guenon; ~**rettich** *der* horseradish; ~**schweinchen** *das;* ~~s, ~~: guinea pig; ~**wasser** *das* sea water
Meeting /'miːtɪŋ/ *das;* ~s, ~s meeting
mega-, Mega- mega-
Mega·byte *das* (DV) megabyte
Megaphon *das;* ~s, ~e megaphone; loud hailer
Mehl *das;* ~[e]s flour
mehlig *Adj.* (a) floury
(b) mealy ‹potato, apple, etc.›
Mehl-: ~**sack** *der* flour sack; (Sack voll Mehl) sack of flour; ~**tau** *der* mildew; ~**wurm** *der* mealworm
mehr [1] *Indefinitpron.* more
[2] *Adv.* (a) more
(b) **nicht** ~: not ... any more; no longer; **es war niemand** ~ **da** there was no one left; **das wird nie** ~ **vorkommen** it will never happen again; **da ist nichts** ~ **zu machen** there is nothing more to be done
mehr-, Mehr-: ~**bändig** *Adj.* in several volumes *postpos.;* ~**bereichs·öl** *das* (Technik) multi-purpose oil; ~**deutig** [1] *Adj.* ambiguous; [2] *adv.* ambiguously
mehren (geh.) *refl. V.* increase
mehrer... *Indefinitpron. u. unbest. Zahlwort* (a) attr. several
(b) *allein stehend* ~e several people; ~es several things *pl.*
mehr·fach [1] *Adj.* multiple; (wiederholt) repeated
[2] *adv.* several times; (wiederholt) repeatedly
Mehrheit *die;* ~, ~en majority
Mehrheits-: ~**beschluss,** ***beschluß** *der,* ~**entscheidung** *die* majority decision
mehr-, Mehr-: ~**jährig** *Adj.* lasting several years *postpos.;* ~**malig** *Adj.;* nicht präd. repeated; ~**mals** *Adv.* several times; (wiederholt) repeatedly; ~**parteien·system** *das* multi-party system; ~**sprachig** *Adj.* multilingual; ~**spurig** *Adj.* multi-lane ‹highway, motorway›; ~**stimmig** (Musik) [1] *Adj.* for several voices *postpos.;* **ein** ~stimmiges Lied a part-song; [2] *adv.* ~stimmig singen sing in harmony; ~**teilig** *Adj.* in several parts *postpos.*
Mehrweg-: ~**flasche** *die* returnable *or* reusable bottle; ~**verpackung** *die* reusable packaging
Mehr-: ~**wert** *der* (Wirtsch.) surplus value; ~**wert·steuer** *die* (Wirtsch.) value added tax (Brit.); VAT (Brit.); sales tax (Amer.); ~**zahl** *die* (a) (Sprachw.) plural; (b) (Mehrheit) majority
meiden unr. *tr. V.* (geh.) avoid
Meile *die;* ~, ~n mile
mein *Possessivpron.* my; ~e Damen und Herren ladies and gentlemen; **das Buch dort, ist das** ~[e]s? that book over there, is it mine?

Mein·eid *der* perjury *no indef. art.;* **einen ~ schwören** commit perjury

meinen 1 *itr. V.* think
2 *tr. V.* **(a)** think
(b) (sagen wollen, im Sinn haben) mean
(c) (beabsichtigen) mean; intend; **es gut mit jmdm. ~:** mean well by sb.
(d) (sagen) say

meiner *Gen. von* ICH (geh.) **gedenkt ~:** remember me; **erbarme dich ~:** have mercy upon me

meinerseits *Adv.* for my part; **ganz ~:** the pleasure is [all] mine

meinetwegen *Adv.* **(a)** because of me; (mir zuliebe) for my sake; (um mich) about me
(b) /auch: --'--/ (von mir aus) as far as I'm concerned; **~!** if you like

Meinung *die; ~, ~en* opinion (**zu** on, **über** + *Akk.* about); **er ist der ~, dass ...** he is of the opinion *or* takes the view that ...; **meiner ~ nach** in my opinion; **ganz meine ~:** I agree entirely; **einer ~ sein** be of the same opinion

Meinungs-: ~forschung *die* opinion research; **~freiheit** *die* freedom to form and express one's own opinions; (Redefreiheit) freedom of speech; **~umfrage** *die* [public] opinion poll; **~verschiedenheit** *die* difference of opinion

Meise *die; ~, ~n* tit[mouse]

Meißel *der; ~s, ~:* chisel

meißeln *tr. V.* chisel; carve ⟨*statue, sculpture*⟩ with a chisel

meist *Adv.* mostly

meist... *Indefinitpron. u. unbest. Zahlw.* most; **die ~en Leute ...:** most people ...; **am ~en** most

meistens *Adv.* ▸ MEIST

Meister *der; ~s, ~* **(a)** master
(b) (Werk~, Polier~) foreman
(c) (Sport) champion

Meister·brief *der* master craftsman's diploma *or* certificate

meisterhaft 1 *Adj.* masterly
2 *adv.* in a masterly manner

Meisterin *die; ~, ~nen* ▸ MEISTER A, C

meistern *tr. V.* master

Meister·prüfung *die* examination for the/one's master craftsman's diploma *or* certificate

Meisterschaft *die; ~, ~en* **(a)** mastery
(b) (Sport) championship

Meister-: ~stück *das* masterpiece (**an** + *Dat.* of); **~titel** *der* (Sport) championship [title]; **~werk** *das* masterpiece (**an** + *Dat.* of)

Melancholie /melaŋko:'li:/ *die; ~* (Gemütszustand) melancholy; (Psych.) melancholia

melancholisch 1 *Adj.* melancholy; melancholy, melancholic ⟨*person,*

---

temperament⟩
2 *adv.* melancholically

melden 1 *tr. V.* report; (registrieren lassen) register ⟨*birth, death, etc.*⟩ (*Dat.* with)
2 *refl. V.* **(a)** report
(b) (am Telefon) answer
(c) (ums Wort bitten) put one's hand up
(d) (von sich hören lassen) get in touch (**bei** with)

Meldung *die; ~, ~en* **(a)** report; (Nachricht) piece of news
(b) (Wort~) request to speak

meliert *Adj.* mottled; **[grau] ~es Haar** hair streaked with grey

melken *regelm.* (*auch unr.*) *tr. V.* milk

Melodie *die; ~, ~n* melody; (Weise) tune

melodisch 1 *Adj.* melodic
2 *adv.* melodically

Melone *die; ~, ~n* **(a)** melon
(b) (ugs.: Hut) bowler [hat]

Membran *die; ~, ~en* **(a)** (Technik) diaphragm
(b) (Biol., Chemie) membrane

Memoiren /me'mǫa:rǝn/ *Pl.* memoirs

Menge *die; ~, ~n* **(a)** quantity; amount
(b) (große) lot (coll.); **eine ~** (ugs.) lots [of it/them] (coll.)
(c) (Menschen~) crowd
(d) (Math.) set

Mengen-: ~lehre *die* set theory *no art.;* **~rabatt** *der* bulk discount

Meniskus *der; ~,* Menisken (Anat., Optik) meniscus

Menopause *die; ~, ~n* (Physiol.) menopause

Mensa *die; ~, ~s od.* Mensen refectory, canteen (*of university, college*)

Mensch *der; ~en, ~en* **(a)** (Gattung) **der ~:** man; **die ~en** man *sing.;* human beings; mankind *sing.*
(b) (Person) person; man/woman; **~en** people

menschen-, Menschen-: ~affe *der* anthropoid [ape]; **~auflauf** *der* crowd [of people]; **~feind** *der,* **~feindin** *die* misanthropist; **~fresser** *der* (ugs.) cannibal; **~freund** *der,* **~freundin** *die* philanthropist; **~handel** *der* trade *or* traffic in human beings; **~kenner** *der,* **~kennerin** *die* judge of human nature; **~kenntnis** *die;* ability to judge human nature; **~leben** *das* life; **~leer** *Adj.* deserted; **~menge** *die* crowd [of people]; **~recht** *das* human right; **~rechtler** *der;* **~~s, ~~,** **~rechtlerin** *die;* **~~, ~~nen** human rights campaigner; **~schlag** *der* breed [of people]; **~seele** *die:* **keine ~seele** not a [living] soul

Menschens·kind: ~! (salopp) (erstaunt) good heavens; good grief; (vorwurfsvoll) for heaven's sake

menschen-, Menschen-: ~unwürdig 1 *Adj.* ⟨*accommodation*⟩

---

*alte Schreibung – vgl. Hinweis auf S. x

unfit for human habitation; ⟨*conditions*⟩
unfit for human beings; ⟨*behaviour*⟩
unworthy of a human being; **2** *adv.* ⟨*treat*⟩
in a degrading and inhumane way; ⟨*live,
be housed*⟩ in conditions unfit for human
beings; **~verstand** *der* human intellect;
~würde *die* human dignity *no art.*
Menschheit *die;* ~: mankind *no art.;*
humanity *no art.;* human race
menschlich **1** *Adj.* (a) human
(b) (annehmbar) civilized
(c) (human) humane ⟨*person, treatment, etc.*⟩
2 *adv.* (a) er ist mir ~ sympathisch I like
him as a person
(b) (human) humanely
Menschlichkeit *die;* ~: humanity *no
art.*
Mensen ▸ Mensa
Menstruation *die;* ~, ~en (Physiol.)
menstruation; (Periode) [menstrual] period
Mentalität *die;* ~, ~en mentality
Menü *das;* ~s, ~s (auch DV) menu
Menü·leiste *die* (DV) menu bar
merkbar **1** *Adj.* noticeable
2 *adv.* noticeably
Merk·blatt leaflet
merken **1** *tr. V.* notice
2 *refl. V.* sich (*Dat.*) etw. ~: remember sth.
merklich ▸ MERKBAR
Merkmal *das;* ~s, ~e feature
Merkur *der;* ~s Mercury
merkwürdig **1** *Adj.* strange; odd
2 *adv.* strangely; oddly
messbar, *meßbar *Adj.* measurable
Messe¹ *die;* ~, ~n (Gottesdienst, Musik) mass
Messe² *die;* ~, ~n (Ausstellung) [trade] fair
messen **1** *unr. tr. V.* (a) *auch itr.*
measure
(b) (beurteilen) judge (**nach** by)
2 *unr. refl. V.* (geh.) compete (**mit** with)
Messer *das;* ~s, ~: knife
messer-, Messer-: ~**scharf** **1** *Adj.*
razor-sharp; (fig.) incisive ⟨*logic*⟩; razor-
sharp ⟨*wit, intellect*⟩; **2** *adv.* (fig. ugs.)
⟨*argue*⟩ incisively; **~stecherei** *die;*
~~, ~~en knife fight; fight with knives;
~stich *der* knife thrust; (Wunde) knife
wound
Mess·gerät, *Meß·gerät *das*
measuring device; (Zähler) meter
Messias *der;* ~, ~se Messiah
Messing *das;* ~s brass
**Mess·instrument,
*Meß·instrument** *das* measuring
instrument
Messung *die;* ~, ~en measurement
Metall *das;* ~s, ~e metal
metallic *indekl. Adj.* metallic [grey/blue/
etc.]
Metall·industrie *die* metal-processing
and metal-working industries *pl.*

metallisch *Adj.* metallic; metal *attrib.,*
metallic ⟨*conductor*⟩
Metapher *die;* ~, ~n metaphor
metaphorisch (Stilk.) **1** *Adj.*
metaphorical
2 *adv.* metaphorically
Meta·physik *die;* ~: metaphysics *sing.,
no art.*
Metastase *die;* ~, ~n (Med.) metastasis
Meteor *der;* ~s, ~e meteor
Meteorit *der;* ~en *od.* ~s, ~e[n] meteorite
Meteorologe *der;* ~n, ~n meteorologist
Meteorologie *die;* ~: meteorology *no art.*
Meteorologin *die;* ~, ~nen
meteorologist
meteorologisch **1** *Adj.* meteorological
2 *adv.* meteorologically
Meter *der od. das;* ~s, ~: metre
meter-, Meter-: ~**dick** *Adj.* (sehr dick)
metres thick *postpos.;* ~**hoch** *Adj.* metres
high *postpos.;* ⟨*snow*⟩ metres deep; ~**maß**
das tape measure; (Stab) [metre] rule
Methan *das;* ~s methane
Methode *die;* ~, ~n method
methodisch **1** *Adj.* methodological;
(nach einer Methode vorgehend) methodical
2 *adv.* methodologically; (nach einer Methode)
methodically
Metier /me'tie:/ *das;* ~s, ~s profession
Metrik *die;* ~, ~en metrics
metrisch **1** *Adj.*(a) (Verslehre, Musik)
metrical
(b) (auf den Meter bezogen) metric
2 *adv.* metrically
Metropole *die;* ~, ~n metropolis
Mett·wurst *die: soft smoked sausage made
of minced pork and beef*
Metzger *der;* ~s, ~ (bes. westmd., südd.,
schweiz.) butcher
Metzgerei *die;* ~, ~en (bes. westmd., südd.,
schweiz.) butcher's [shop]
Meute *die;* ~, ~n (a) (Jägerspr.) pack
(b) (ugs. abwertend) mob
Meuterei *die;* ~, ~en mutiny
meutern *itr. V.* (a) mutiny; ⟨*prisoners*⟩ riot
(b) (ugs.: Unwillen äußern) moan
Mexikaner *der;* ~s, ~, **Mexikanerin**
die; ~, ~ Mexican
mexikanisch *Adj.* Mexican
Mexiko (*das*) ~s, ~s Mexico
MEZ *Abk.* = **mitteleuropäische Zeit**
CET
mg *Abk.* = **Milligramm** mg
MG /ɛm'ge:/ *das;* ~s, ~s *Abk.* =
Maschinengewehr
Mi. *Abk.* = **Mittwoch** Wed.
miau *Interj.* miaow
miauen *itr. V.* miaow
mich **1** *Akk. von* ICH me
2 *Akk. des Reflexivpron. der 1. Pers. Sg.*
myself

mick[e]rig *Adj.* (ugs.) miserable; measly (coll.); puny ⟨person⟩

mied *1. u. 3. Pers. Sg. Prät. v.* MEIDEN

Mieder·waren *Pl.* corsetry *sing.*

Miene *die;* ~, ~n expression

mies (ugs.) [1] *Adj.* lousy (coll.) [2] *adv.* lousily (coll.)

Mies-: ~**macher** *der,* ~**macherin** *die* (ugs. abwertend) carping critic; (Spielverderber) killjoy; ~**muschel** *die* [common] mussel

Miete *die;* ~, ~n rent; (für ein Auto, Boot) hire charge; zur ~ wohnen live in rented accommodation

mieten *tr. V.* rent; (für kürzere Zeit) hire

Mieter *der;* ~s, ~, **Mieterin** *die;* ~, ~nen tenant

Miet-: ~**erhöhung** *die* rent increase

Miets·haus *das* block of rented flats (Brit.) or (Amer.) apartments

Miet-: ~**vertrag** *der* tenancy agreement; ~**wagen** *der* hire car

Migräne *die;* ~, ~n migraine

Migrant *der;* ~en, ~en, **Migrantin** *die;* ~, ~nen migrant

mikro-, Mikro- micro-

Mikrobe *die;* ~, ~n microbe

mikro-, Mikro-: ~**film** *der* microfilm; ~**phon** /--'-/ *das;* ~~s, ~~e microphone; ~**skop** /--'-/ *das;* ~~s, ~~e microscope; ~**skopisch** /--'--'-/ [1] *Adj.* microscopic; [2] *adv.* microscopically; ~**welle** *die* (ugs.) microwave [oven]

Milbe *die;* ~, ~n mite

Milch *die;* ~: milk

Milch·flasche *die* milk bottle

milchig [1] *Adj.* milky [2] *adv.* ~ weiß milky-white

Milch-: ~**kaffee** *der* coffee with plenty of milk; ~**kännchen** *das;* ~~s, ~~: milk jug; ~**reis** *der* rice pudding; ~**straße** *die* Milky Way; Galaxy; ~**zahn** *der* milk tooth

mild, milde [1] *Adj.* mild; lenient ⟨judge, judgement⟩; soft ⟨light⟩; smooth ⟨brandy⟩ [2] *adv.* (gütig) leniently; (gelinde) mildly

Milde *die;* ~: mildness; (Güte) leniency

mildern *tr. V.* moderate; mitigate ⟨punishment⟩

Milderung *die;* ~: ▸ MILDERN: moderation; mitigation

Milieu /mi'ljø:/ *das;* ~~s, ~~s environment

militant *Adj.* militant

Militär¹ *das;* ~~s armed forces *pl.;* military; (Soldaten) soldiers *pl.*

Militär² *der;* ~~s, ~~s [high-ranking military] officer

Militär-: ~**dienst** *der* military service; ~**diktatur** *die* military dictatorship

militärisch *Adj.* military

militarisieren *tr. V.* militarize

Militarismus *der;* ~ (abwertend) militarism

Militarist *der;* ~en, ~en (abwertend) militarist

Militär-: ~**macht** *die* military power; ~**putsch** *der* military putsch

Military /'mɪlɪtərɪ/ *die;* ~, ~s (Reiten) three-day event

Miliz *die;* ~, ~en militia; (Polizei) police

Mill. *Abk.* = **Million** m.

milli-, Milli- milli-

Milliarde *die;* ~, ~n billion

Milli-: ~**gramm** *das* milligram; ~**meter** *der od. das* millimetre; ~**meter·papier** *das* [graph] paper ruled in millimetre squares

Million *die;* ~, ~en million

Millionär *der;* ~s, ~e millionaire

Millionen-: ~**schaden** *der* damage no *pl.,* no indef. *art.* running into millions; ~**stadt** *die* town with over a million inhabitants

millionst... *Ordinalz.* millionth

Milz *die;* ~: spleen

Mimik *die;* ~: gestures and facial expressions *pl.*

Mimose *die;* ~, ~n (a) mimosa (b) (fig.) oversensitive person

mimosenhaft [1] *Adj.* oversensitive [2] *adv.* oversensitively

minder *Adv.* (geh.) less

minder... *Adj.* inferior ⟨goods, brand⟩

minder·bemittelt *Adj.* without much money *postpos., not pred.;* ~ sein not have much money; geistig ~ (fig. salopp abwertend) not all that bright (coll.)

Minderheit *die;* ~, ~en minority

minder·jährig *Adj.* ⟨child etc.⟩ who is/was a minor

Minder·jährige *der/die; adj. Dekl.* minor

mindern *tr. V.* (geh.) reduce

Minderung *die;* ~, ~en reduction (Gen. in)

minder·wertig *Adj.* inferior

mindest... *Adj.* least; (geringst...) slightest; das ist das Mindeste *od.* ~e, was du tun kannst it is the least you can do

mindestens *Adv.* at least

Mindest·haltbarkeits·datum *das* best-before date

Mine *die;* ~, ~n (a) (Bergwerk, Sprengkörper) mine (b) (Bleistift~) lead; (Kugelschreiber~, Filzschreiber~) refill

Mineral *das;* ~~s, ~~e od. Mineralien mineral

Mineralogie *die;* ~: mineralogy no art.

Mineral-: ~**öl** *das* mineral oil; ~**wasser** *das* mineral water

Mini *das;* ~~s, ~~s (Mode) mini

Mini- mini-

---

*old spelling – see note on page x

Miniatur *die;* ∼, ∼**en** miniature

minimal ① *Adj.* minimal; marginal ⟨*advantage, lead*⟩; very slight ⟨*benefit, profit*⟩
② *adv.* minimally

minimieren *tr. V.* (bes. Math.) minimize

Minimum *das;* ∼s, Minima minimum (**an** + *Dat.* of)

Minister *der;* ∼s, ∼, **Ministerin** *die;* ∼, ∼**nen** minister (**für** for); (eines britischen Hauptministeriums) Secretary of State (**für** for); (eines amerikanischen Hauptministeriums) Secretary (**für** of)

Ministerium *das;* ∼s, Ministerien Ministry; Department (Amer.)

Minister-präsident *der*, **Minister-präsidentin** *die* (a) (eines deutschen Bundeslandes) minister-president (b) (Premierminister[in]) Prime Minister

Minister-rat *der* Council of Ministers

Ministrant *der;* ∼en, ∼en, **Ministrantin** *die;* ∼, ∼nen (kath. Kirche) server

Minorität *die;* ∼, ∼en ▶ MINDERHEIT

minus *Konj., Adv.* (bes. Math.) minus

Minus *das;* ∼: deficit

Minus-zeichen *das* minus sign

Minute *die;* ∼, ∼n minute

minuten-lang ① *Adj.* lasting [for] several minutes *postpos.*
② *adv.* for several minutes

Minuten-zeiger *der* minute hand

Mio. *Abk.* = **Million[en]** m.

mir ① *Dat. von* ICH to me; (nach Präpositionen) me; **Freunde von** ∼: friends of mine; **gehen wir zu** ∼: let's got to my place; **von** ∼ **aus** as far as I'm concerned
② *Dat. des Reflexivpron. der 1. Pers. Sg.* myself

Mirabelle *die;* ∼, ∼n mirabelle

Misch-: ∼**brot** *das* bread made from wheat and rye flour; ∼**ehe** *die* mixed marriage

mischen ① *tr. V.* mix
② *refl. V.* (a) (sich ver∼) mix (**mit** with); ⟨*smell, scent*⟩ blend (**mit** with) (b) (sich ein∼) **sich in etw.** (*Akk.*) ∼: interfere in sth.

Misch-farbe *die* non-primary colour

Mischling *der;* ∼s, ∼e half-caste

Mischmasch *der;* ∼[e]s, ∼e (ugs., meist abwertend) hotchpotch; mishmash

Misch-pult *das* (Film, Rundf., Ferns.) mixing desk *or* console

Mischung *die;* ∼, ∼en mixture; (Tee∼, Kaffee∼, Tabak∼) blend; (Pralinen∼) assortment

Misch-wald *der* mixed [deciduous and coniferous] forest

miserabel (ugs.) ① *Adj.* dreadful (coll.)
② *adv.* dreadfully (coll.); **ihm geht es gesundheitlich** ∼: he's in a bad way

Misere *die;* ∼, ∼n (geh.) wretched *or* dreadful state; (Elend) misery; (Not) distress

miss, *miß *Imperativ Sg. v.* MESSEN

miss-achten, *miß-achten *tr. V.*
(a) (ignorieren) disregard; ignore
(b) (geringschätzen) be contemptuous of

miss-billigen, *miß-billigen *tr. V.* disapprove of

Miss-billigung, *Miß-billigung *die* disapproval

Miss-brauch, *Miß-brauch *der:*
▶ MISSBRAUCHEN: abuse; misuse

miss-brauchen, *miß-brauchen *tr. V.* abuse; misuse; abuse ⟨*trust*⟩

missen *tr. V.* (geh.) jmdn./etw. nicht ∼ mögen not want to be without sb./sth.

Miss-erfolg, *Miß-erfolg *der* failure

Misse-tat *die* (geh. veralt.) misdeed

miss-fallen, *miß-fallen *unr. itr. V.* etw. missfällt jmdm. sb. dislikes sth.

Missfallen, *Mißfallen *das;* ∼s displeasure; (Missbilligung) disapproval

Miss-geschick, *Miß-geschick *das* mishap

miss-glücken, *miß-glücken *itr. V.; mit sein* fail

miss-gönnen, *miß-gönnen *tr. V.* jmdm. etw. ∼: begrudge sb. sth.

Miss-griff, *Miß-griff *der* error of judgement

miss-handeln, *miß-handeln *tr. V.* maltreat

Miss-handlung, *Miß-handlung *die* maltreatment

Mission *die;* ∼, ∼en mission

Missionar *der;* ∼s, ∼e, **Missionarin** *die;* ∼, ∼nen missionary

Miss-kredit, *Miß-kredit *der:* jmdn./etw. in ∼ bringen bring sb./sth. into discredit

misslang, *mißlang *1. u. 3. Pers. Sg. Prät. v.* MISSLINGEN

missliebig, *mißliebig *Adj.* unpopular

misslingen, *mißlingen *unr. itr. V.; mit sein* fail

Misslingen, *Mißlingen *das;* ∼s failure

misslungen, *mißlungen *2. Part. v.* MISSLINGEN

Miss-mut, *Miß-mut *der* ill humour *no indef. art.*

miß-mutig, *miss-mutig ① *Adj.* bad-tempered; sullen ⟨*face*⟩
② *adv.* bad-temperedly

Miss-stand, *Miß-stand *der* deplorable state of affairs *no pl.*

misst, *mißt *2. u. 3. Pers. Sg. Präsens v.* MESSEN

miss-trauen, *miß-trauen *itr. V.* jmdm./einer Sache ∼: mistrust *or* distrust sb./sth.

Misstrauen, *Miß·trauen *das;* ~s
mistrust, distrust (**gegen** of)

misstrauisch, *miß·trauisch 1 *Adj.*
mistrustful; distrustful
2 *adv.* mistrustfully; distrustfully

**miss·verständlich,
*miß·verständlich** 1 *Adj.* unclear;
⟨*formulation, concept, etc.*⟩ that could be
misunderstood
2 *adv.* ⟨*express oneself, describe*⟩ in a way
that could be misunderstood

**Miss·verständnis,
*Miß·verständnis** *das*
misunderstanding

mi ss·verstehen, *mi ß·verstehen
unr. tr. V. ich missverstehe,
missverstanden, misszuverstehen
misunderstand

Miss·wirtschaft, *Miß·wirtschaft
die mismanagement

Mist *der;* ~[e]s **(a)** dung; (Dünger) manure;
(mit Stroh usw. gemischt) muck
(b) (Misthaufen) dung/manure/muck heap
(c) (ugs. abwertend) (Unsinn) rubbish *no indef.
art.;* (Minderwertiges) junk *no indef. art.*

Mistel *die;* ~, ~n mistletoe

Mist·haufen *der* dung/manure/muck
heap

mit 1 *Präp. mit Dat.* with; **ein Zimmer**
~ **Frühstück** a room with breakfast
included; ~ **50 [km/h] fahren** drive at
50 [k.p.h]; ~ **der Bahn/dem Auto fahren** go
by train/car; ~ **20 [Jahren]** at [the age of]
twenty
2 *adv.* **(a)** too; as well
(b) **seine Arbeit war** ~ **am besten** (ugs.) his
work was among the best

Mit·arbeit *die* collaboration (**bei/an** + *Dat.*
on); (Mithilfe) assistance (**bei, in** + *Dat.* in);
(Beteiligung) participation (**in** + *Dat.* in)

mit|arbeiten *itr. V.* collaborate (**bei/an**
+ *Dat.* on) (sich beteiligen) participate (**in**
+ *Dat.* in)

Mit·arbeiter *der,* **Mit·arbeiterin** *die*
(a) collaborator; **freier** ~: freelance worker
(b) (Angestellter) employee

mit|bekommen *unr. tr. V.* **(a)** etw. ~: be
given sth. to take with one
(b) (wahrnehmen) be aware of; (durch Hören,
Sehen) hear/see

mit|bestimmen 1 *itr. V.* have a say
2 *tr. V.* have an influence on

Mit·bestimmung *die* participation (**bei**
in); (der Arbeitnehmer) co-determination

mit|bringen *unr. tr. V.* **(a)** etw. ~: bring
sth. with one; jmdm./sich etw. ~: bring sth.
with one for sb./bring sth. back for oneself
(b) (haben) have ⟨*ability, gift, etc.*⟩

Mitbringsel *das;* ~s, ~: [small] present;
(Andenken) [small] souvenir

Mit·bürger *der,* **Mit·bürgerin** *die* fellow

citizen; **ältere Mitbürger** (Amtsspr.) senior
citizens

mit·einander *Adv.* **(a)** with each other or
one another; ~ **sprechen** talk to each other
or one another
(b) (gemeinsam) together

mit|erleben *tr. V.* **(a)** witness ⟨*events etc.*⟩
(b) (mitmachen) be alive during

mit|fahren *unr. itr. V.; mit sein* **bei jmdm.**
[im Auto] ~: go/travel with sb. [in his/her
car]; (mitgenommen werden) get a lift with sb.
[in his/her car]

Mitfahr·zentrale *die: office for putting
those wanting lifts in touch with those who
can offer them*

mit·fühlend 1 *Adj.* sympathetic
2 *adv.* sympathetically

mit|führen *tr. V.* **(a)** (Amtsspr.: bei sich tragen)
etw. ~: carry sth. [with one]
(b) (transportieren) ⟨*river, stream*⟩ carry along

mit|geben *unr. tr. V.* jmdm. etw. ~: give
sb. sth. to take with him/her; (fig.) provide
sb. with sth.

Mit·gefühl *das* sympathy

mit|gehen *unr. itr. V.; mit sein* **(a)** go too;
mit jmdm. ~: go with sb.
(b) (sich mitreißen lassen) **begeistert**
~: respond enthusiastically

Mit·gift *die;* ~, ~en (veralt.) dowry

Mit·glied *das* member (*Gen.,* **in** + *Dat.* of)

Mitglieder·versammlung *die* general
meeting

Mitglieds-: ~**ausweis** *der* membership
card; ~**beitrag** *der* membership
subscription

Mitgliedschaft *die;* ~: membership
(+ *Gen.,* **in** + *Dat.*) of

Mitglied[s]·staat *der* member state or
country

mit|halten *unr. itr. V.* keep up (**bei** in, **mit**
with)

mit|helfen *unr. itr. V.* help (**bei, in** + *Dat.*
with)

mit·hilfe 1 *Präp. mit Gen.* with the help
or aid of
2 *Adv.* ~ **von** with the help or aid of

Mit·hilfe *die* help; assistance

mit|hören 1 *tr. V.* listen to; (zufällig)
overhear ⟨*conversation, argument, etc.*⟩;
(abhören) listen in on
2 *itr. V.* listen; (zufällig) overhear

mit|kommen *unr. itr. V.; mit sein*
(a) come too; **kommst du mit?** are you
coming [with me/us]?
(b) (Schritt halten) keep up

Mit·läufer *der,* **Mit·läuferin** *die*
(abwertend) [mere] supporter

Mit·laut *der* consonant

Mit·leid *das* pity, compassion (**mit** for);
(Mitgefühl) sympathy (**mit** for)

Mit·leidenschaft *die:* jmdn./etw. in
~ **ziehen** affect sb./sth.

mit·leidig ① *Adj.* compassionate; (mitfühlend) sympathetic ② *adv.* compassionately; (mitfühlend) sympathetically

mit|machen ① *tr. V.* **(a)** (teilnehmen an) go on ‹*trip*›; join in ‹*joke*›; follow ‹*fashion*›; fight in ‹*war*›; do ‹*course, seminar*›; **das mache ich nicht mit** (ugs.) I can't go along with it **(b)** (ugs.: erleiden) **zwei Weltkriege/viele Bombenangriffe mitgemacht haben** have been through two world wars/many bomb attacks ② *itr. V.* **(a)** (sich beteiligen) join in **(b)** (ugs.: funktionieren) **mein Herz/Kreislauf macht nicht mit** my heart/circulation can't take it

Mit·mensch *der* fellow human being

mit|nehmen *unr. tr. V.* **(a)** jmdn. ~: take sb. with one; etw. ~: take sth. with one; (verhüll.: stehlen) walk off with sth. (coll.); (kaufen) take sth.; **Essen/Getränke zum Mitnehmen** food/drinks to take away *or* (Amer.) to go **(b)** (in Mitleidenschaft ziehen) jmdn. ~: take it out of sb.

mit|reden *itr. V.* **(a)** join in the conversation **(b)** (mitbestimmen) have a say

Mit·reisende *der/die* fellow passenger

mit|reißen *unr. tr. V.* **die Begeisterung/ seine Rede hat alle Zuhörer mitgerissen** the audience was carried away with enthusiasm/by his speech

mit·samt *Präp. mit Dat.* together with

mit|schneiden *unr. tr. V.* (Rundf., Ferns.) record [live]

Mit·schuld *die* share of the blame *or* responsibility (**an** + *Dat.* for)

Mit·schüler *der*, **Mit·schülerin** *die* schoolfellow

mit|spielen *itr. V.* **(a)** join in the game **(b)** (in einem Film ~: be in a film; **in einem Orchester/in** *od.* **bei einem Fußballverein** ~: play in an orchestra/for a football club

Mit·spieler *der*, **Mit·spielerin** *die* player; (in derselben Mannschaft) teammate

*****mittag** ▸ Mittag

Mittag *der;* ~s, ~e **(a)** midday *no art.;* **gegen** ~: around midday; **zu** ~ **essen** have lunch; **heute/Montag** ~: at midday today/on Monday **(b)** (ugs.: Mittagspause) lunch hour

Mittag·essen *das* lunch

mittags *Adv.* at midday; **12 Uhr** ~: 12 noon

Mittags-: ~**pause** *die* lunch hour; ~**ruhe** *die* period of quiet after lunch; ~**zeit** *die* **(a)** (Zeit gegen 12 Uhr) lunchtime *no art.;* **(b)** (Mittagspause) lunch hour

Mitte *die;* ~, ~n middle; (eines Kreises, einer Kugel, Stadt) centre; ~ **des Monats/Jahres** in the middle of the month/year

mit|teilen *tr. V.* jmdm. etw. ~: tell sb. sth.;

(informieren) inform sb. of sth.

mitteilsam *Adj.* communicative; (gesprächig) talkative

Mit·teilung *die* communication; (Bekanntgabe) announcement

Mittel *das;* ~s, ~ **(a)** means; (Methode) way; method; (Werbe~, Propaganda~ usw.) device (*Gen.* for); **mit allen** ~**n versuchen, etw. zu tun** try by every means to do sth. **(b)** (Arznei) **ein** ~ **gegen Husten** *usw.* a cure for coughs *etc.* **(c)** *Pl.* (Geldmittel) funds; [financial] resources; (Privatmittel) means

Mittel·alter *das* Middle Ages *pl.*

mittel·alterlich *Adj.* medieval

mittelbar ① *Adj.* indirect ② *adv.* indirectly

mittel-, Mittel-: ~**ding** *das* ein ~ding sein be something in between; ~**europa** *(das)* Central Europe; ~**finger** *der* middle finger; ~**gebirge** *das* low mountains *pl.;* ~**groß** *Adj.* medium-sized; ‹*person*› of medium height; ~**klasse·wagen** *der* medium-sized car; ~**linie** *die* centre line; (Fußball) half-way line; ~**los** *Adj.* without means *postpos.;* ~**mäßig** *Adj.* mediocre; ~**meer** *das* Mediterranean [Sea]; ~**punkt** *der* **(a)** (Geom.) centre; (einer Strecke) midpoint; **(b)** (Mensch/Sache im Zentrum) centre of attention; ~**scheitel** *der* centre parting; ~**schule** *die* ▸ Realschule; ~**stand** *der* middle class; ~**strecken·rakete** *die* medium-range missile; ~**streifen** *der* central reservation; median strip (Amer.); ~**weg** *der* middle course; ~**welle** *die* (Physik, Rundf.) medium wave

mitten *Adv.* ~ **an/auf etw.** (*Akk./Dat.*) in the middle of sth.; ~ **durch die Stadt** right through the town

mitten-: ~**drin** *Adv.* [right] in the middle; ~**durch** *Adv.* [right] through the middle

Mitter·nacht *die* midnight *no art.*

Mitternachts·sonne *die* midnight sun

Mittler *der;* ~s, ~ mediator

mittler... *Adj.* middle; moderate ‹*speed*›; medium-sized ‹*company, town*›; medium ‹*quality, size*›; (durchschnittlich) average; **die** ~**e Reife** (Schulw.) standard of achievement for school-leaving certificate at a Realschule or for entry to the sixth form in a Gymnasium

Mittlerin *die;* ~, ~nen mediator

Mittler·rolle *die* mediating role

mittler·weile *Adv.* since then; (bis jetzt) by now; (unterdessen) in the meantime

Mittwoch *der;* ~[e]s, ~e Wednesday; *s. auch* Dienstag

mittwochs *Adv.* on Wednesday[s]

mit·unter *Adv.* from time to time

mit·wirken *itr. V.* **an etw.** (*Dat.*)/**bei etw.** ~: collaborate on/be involved in sth.; **in einem Orchester/**

Theaterstück ∼: play in an orchestra/act *or* appear in a play

Mitwirkende *der/die adj. Dekl.* (an einer Sendung) participant; (in einer Show) performer; (in einem Theaterstück) actor

Mit·wisser *der;* ∼s ∼, **Mit·wisserin** *die;* ∼, ∼nen: ∼ einer Sache (*Gen.*) sein be an accessory to sth.

mixen *tr. V.* mix; **sich** (*Dat.*) **einen Drink** ∼: fix oneself a drink

Mixer *der;* ∼s, ∼, (a) (Bar∼) barman; bartender (Amer.)
(b) (Gerät) blender and liquidizer

Mixerin *die;* ∼, ∼nen barmaid

mm *Abk.* = **Millimeter** mm.

Mo. *Abk.* = **Montag** Mon.

Mob *der;* ∼s (abwertend) mob

Möbel *das;* ∼s, ∼ (a) *Pl.* furniture *sing.*, *no indef. art.*
(b) piece of furniture

Möbel·wagen *der* furniture van; removal van

mobil *Adj.* (a) mobile; *s. auch* MOBILMACHEN;
(b) (ugs.) (lebendig) lively

Mobiliar *das;* ∼s furnishings *pl.*

mobilisieren *tr. V.* (a) (Milit., fig.) mobilize
(b) (aktivieren) activate

mobil|machen *itr. V.* mobilize

Mobilmachung *die;* ∼, ∼en mobilization

Mobil·telefon *das* cellular phone

möblieren *tr. V.* furnish

mochte *1. u. 3. Pers. Sg. Prät. v.* MÖGEN

möchte *1. u. 3. Pers. Sg. Konjunktiv II v.* MÖGEN

Mode *die;* ∼, ∼n fashion

Mode·farbe *die* fashionable colour

Modell *das;* ∼s, ∼e (auch fig.) model; **jmdm.** ∼ **sitzen** *od.* **stehen** sit for sb.

modellieren *tr. V.* model, mould ⟨*figures, objects*⟩; mould ⟨*clay, wax*⟩

Modell·kleid *das* model dress

Modem *der od. das;* ∼s, ∼s (DV) modem

Moden·schau *die* fashion show

Moder *der;* ∼s mould; (∼geruch) mustiness

Moderation *die;* ∼, ∼en (Rundf., Fems.) presentation

Moderator *der;* ∼s, ∼en, **Moderatorin** *die;* ∼, ∼nen (Rundf., Fems.) presenter

moderieren *tr. V.* (Rundf., Fems.) present ⟨*programme*⟩

modern[1] *itr. V.; auch mit sein* go mouldy

modern[2] ① *Adj.* modern; (modisch) fashionable
② *adv.* in a modern manner; (modisch) fashionably

modernisieren *tr. V.* modernize

Mode-: ∼**schöpfer** *der* couturier;

∼**schöpferin** *die* couturière;
∼**wort** *das; Pl.* ∼wörter vogue word;
∼**zeitschrift** *die* fashion magazine

modifizieren *tr. V.* (geh.) modify

modisch ① *Adj.* fashionable
② *adv.* fashionably

Mofa *das;* ∼s, ∼s [low-powered] moped

Mogelei *die;* ∼, ∼en (ugs.) cheating *no pl.*

mogeln *itr. V.* cheat

Mogel·packung *die* (abwertend) deceptive packaging

mögen ① *unr. Modalverb; 2.Part.* mögen:
(a) (wollen) want to; **das hätte ich sehen** ∼: I would have liked to see that
(b) (geh.: sollen) **das mag genügen** that should be enough
(c) (Vermutung, Möglichkeit) **sie mag/mochte vierzig sein** she must be/must have been [about] forty; **[das] mag sein** maybe
(d) *Konjunktiv II* (den Wunsch haben) **ich/sie möchte gern wissen ...:** I would/she would like to know ...
② *unr. tr. V.* like; **sie mag keine Rosen** she does not like roses; **sie** ∼ **sich** they're fond of one another; **möchten Sie ein Glas Wein?** would you like a glass of wine?; **ich möchte lieber Tee** I would prefer tea
③ *unr. itr. V.* (a) (es wollen) like to
(b) **ich möchte nach Hause** I want to go home; **er möchte zu Herrn A** he would like to see Mr A

möglich *Adj.* possible; **es war ihm nicht** ∼ **[zu kommen]** he was unable [to come]; **alles Mögliche** (ugs.) all sorts of things; **[das ist doch] nicht** ∼**!** impossible!; **sein Möglichstes tun** do one's utmost

möglicher·weise *Adv.* possibly

Möglichkeit *die;* ∼, ∼en (a) possibility; (Methode) way; **es besteht die** ∼, **dass ...:** there is a possibility that ...
(b) (Gelegenheit) opportunity; chance

möglichst *Adv.* (a) if [at all] possible
(b) ∼ **schnell** as fast as possible

Mohammed (*der*) Muhammad

Mohammedaner *der;* ∼s, ∼, **Mohammedanerin** *die;* ∼, ∼nen Muslim; Muhammadan

mohammedanisch *Adj.* Muslim; Muhammadan

Mohn *der;* ∼s poppy; (Samen) poppy seed; (auf Brot, Kuchen) poppy seeds *pl.*

Mohn-: ∼**blume** *die* poppy;
∼**brötchen** *das* poppy-seed roll;
∼**kuchen** *der* poppy-seed cake

Möhre *die;* ∼, ∼n carrot

Mohren·kopf *der* chocolate marshmallow

Mohr·rübe *die* carrot

mokieren *refl. V.* (geh.) **sich über etw.** (*Akk.*) ∼: scoff at sth.; **sich über jmdn.** ∼: mock sb.

Mokka *der;* ∼s strong black coffee

Molch *der;* ∼[e]s, ∼e newt

Mole *die;* ~, ~n [harbour] mole
Molekül *das;* ~s, ~e molecule
molekular *Adj.* molecular
molk *1. u. 3. Pers. Sg. Prät. v.* MELKEN
Molkerei *die;* ~, ~en dairy
Moll *das;* ~ (Musik) minor [key]
mollig ① *Adj.* (a) (rundlich) plump
(b) (warm) snug
② *adv.* snugly; ~ **warm** warm and snug
Moment[1] *der;* ~[e]s, ~e moment; **jeden** ~
(ugs.) [at] any moment; **im** ~: at the moment
Moment[2] *das;* ~[e]s, ~e factor, element
(**für** in)
momentan ① *Adj.* (a) present
(b) (vorübergehend) temporary; (flüchtig)
momentary
② *adv.* (a) at present
(b) (vorübergehend) temporarily
Monaco *(das)*; ~s Monaco
Monarch *der;* ~en, ~en monarch
Monarchie *die;* ~, ~n monarchy
Monarchin *die;* ~, ~nen monarch
Monat *der;* ~s, ~e month; **im** ~ **April** in
the month of April
monatelang ① *Adj.* lasting for months
postpos., not pred.
② *adv.* for months [on end]
monatlich ① *Adj.* monthly
② *adv.* every month; (pro Monat) per month
Monats-: ~**ende** *das* end of the month;
~**erste** *der; adj. Dekl.* first [day] of the
month; ~**hälfte** *die* half of the month;
~**karte** *die* monthly season ticket;
~**letzte** *der; adj. Dekl.* last day of the
month
Mönch *der;* ~[e]s, ~e monk
Mond *der;* ~[e]s, ~e moon; **auf** *od.* **hinter**
dem ~ **leben** (fig. ugs.) be a bit behind the
times; **nach dem** ~ **gehen** (ugs.) ⟨clock,
watch⟩ be hopelessly wrong
Mond-: ~**fähre** *die* (Raumf.) lunar module;
~**finsternis** *die* eclipse of the moon;
~**landung** *die* moon landing; ~**licht** *das*
moonlight; ~**phase** *die* moon's phase
Mongole *der;* ~n, ~n (a) Mongol
(b) (Bewohner der Mongolei) Mongolian
Mongolei *die;* ~: Mongolia
Mongolin *die;* ~, ~nen ▶ MONGOLE
Monitor *der;* ~s, ~en monitor
mono-, Mono-: mono-
Mono·gramm *das;* ~s, ~e monogram
Monographie *die;* ~, ~n monograph
Monolog *der;* ~s, ~e monologue
Monopol *das;* ~s, ~e monopoly (**auf**
+ *Akk.*, **für** in, of)
monoton ① *Adj.* monotonous
② *adv.* monotonously
Monotonie *die;* ~, ~n monotony
Monster *das;* ~s, ~: monster; (hässlich)
[hideous] brute
Monstren ▶ MONSTRUM

monströs *Adj.* monstrous
Monstrum *das;* ~s, Monstren (a) monster
(b) (Sache) hulking great thing (coll.)
Monsun *der;* ~s, ~e (Geogr.) monsoon
Mon·tag *der* Monday; *s. auch* DIENSTAG
Montage /mɔn'taːʒə/ *die;* ~, ~n
(a) (Zusammenbau) assembly; (Einbau)
installation; (Aufstellen) erection; (Anbringen)
fitting (**an** + *Akk. od. Dat.* to); mounting (**auf**
+ *Akk. od. Dat.* to)
(b) (Film, bild. Kunst, Literaturw.) montage
montags *Adv.* on Monday[s]
montieren *tr. V.* (a) (zusammenbauen)
assemble (**aus** from); erect ⟨building⟩
(b) (anbringen) fit (**an** + *Akk. od. Dat.* to; **auf**
+ *Akk. od. Dat.* on); (einbauen) install (**in**
+ *Akk.* in); (befestigen) fix (**an** + *Akk. od. Dat.*
to)
Monument *das;* ~[e]s, ~e monument
monumental *Adj.* monumental
Moor *das;* ~[e]s, ~e bog; (Bruch) marsh
Moos *das;* ~es, ~e moss
Moped /'moːpɛt/ *das;* ~s, ~s moped
Mops *der;* ~es, Möpse pug [dog]; (salopp:
dicke Person) podge (coll.)
Moral *die;* ~ (a) (Norm) morality
(b) (Sittlichkeit) morals *pl.*
(c) (Selbstvertrauen) morale
(d) (Lehre) moral
moralisch ① *Adj.* (a) moral
(b) (tugendhaft) virtuous
② *adv.* (a) morally
(b) (tugendhaft) virtuously
moralisieren *itr. V.* (geh.) moralize
Moralist *der;* ~en, ~en, **Moralistin** *die;*
~, ~nen moralist
Moral·predigt *die* (abwertend) [moralizing]
lecture; homily
Morast *der;* ~[e]s, ~e *od.* Moräste (a) bog;
swamp
(b) (Schlamm) mud
Mord *der;* ~[e]s, ~e murder (**an** + *Dat.*
of); (durch ein Attentat) assassination; **einen**
~ **begehen** commit murder
Mord-: ~**anschlag** *der* attempted
murder (**auf** + *Akk.* of); (Attentat)
assassination attempt (**auf** + *Akk.* on);
~**drohung** *die* murder threat
morden *tr., itr. V.* murder
Mörder *der;* ~s, ~: murderer (esp. Law);
killer; (politischer) assassin
Mörderin *die;* ~, ~nen murderer;
murderess; (politische) assassin
mörderisch ① *Adj.* murderous
② *adv.* (ugs.) dreadfully (coll.)
Mord·fall *der* murder case
mords-,
Mords- (ugs.) terrific (coll.)
mords·mäßig *Adj.* terrific (coll.);
tremendous (coll.); (entsetzlich) terrible
(coll.)   ····⦂

Mord-: ~**verdacht** der suspicion of murder; ~**versuch** der attempted murder; (Attentat) assassination attempt; ~**waffe** die murder weapon

morgen Adv. tomorrow; ~ **in einer Woche** tomorrow week; **a week tomorrow**; ~ **um diese Zeit** this time tomorrow; **bis** ~**!** until tomorrow!; see you tomorrow!

Morgen der; ~**s,** ~**:** morning; **am** ~**:** in the morning; **am folgenden** od. **nächsten** ~**:** next morning; **früh am** ~, **am frühen** ~**:** early in the morning; **heute** ~**:** this morning; **guten** ~**!** good morning!

morgendlich Adj. morning

Morgen-: ~**grauen** das daybreak; ~**mantel** der dressing gown; ~**rot** das (geh.) rosy dawn

morgens Adv. in the morning; (jeden Morgen) every morning; **Dienstag** od. **dienstags** ~**:** on Tuesday morning[s]; **von** ~ **bis abends** from morning to evening

morgig Adj. tomorrow's

Morphium das; ~**s** morphine

morphium·süchtig Adj. addicted to morphine pred.

morsch Adj. (auch fig.) rotten

Mörser der; ~**s,** ~ (Gefäß, Geschütz) mortar

Mörtel der; ~**s** mortar

Mosaik das; ~**s,** ~**en** od. ~**e** mosaic

Mosambik (das); ~**s** Mozambique

Moschee die; ~, ~**n** mosque

Moschus der; ~**:** musk

Mosel die; ~**:** Moselle

Mosel·wein der Moselle [wine]

mosern itr. V. (ugs.) gripe (coll.) (**über** + Akk.)

Moskau (das); ~**s** Moscow

Moskauer 1 indekl. Adj. Moscow attrib. 2 der; ~**s,** ~**:** Muscovite

Moskauerin die; ~, ~**nen** Muscovite

Moskito der; ~**s,** ~**s** mosquito

Moslem der; ~**s,** ~**s** ▶ MUSLIM

Moslemin die; ~, ~**nen** ▶ MUSLIMIN

moslemisch ▶ MUSLIMISCH

Most der; ~**[e]s,** ~**e** (a) [cloudy fermented] fruit juice (b) (landsch.: neuer Wein) new wine

Mostrich der; ~**s** (nordostd.) mustard

Motel das; ~**s,** ~**s** motel

Motherboard /'maðɐbɔːd/ das; ~**s,** ~**s** (DV) motherboard

Motiv das; ~**s,** ~**e** (a) motive (b) (fachspr.: Thema) motif; theme; (Kunst) subject

Motor der; ~**s,** ~**en** engine; (Elektro~) motor

Motor·haube die (Kfz-W.) bonnet (Brit.); hood (Amer.)

motorisieren tr. V. motorize

Motor-: ~**rad** das motor cycle; ~**rad·fahrer** der, ~**rad·fahrerin** die motorcyclist; ~**roller** der motor scooter; ~**schaden** der engine trouble no indef. art.

Motte die; ~, ~**n** moth

Motten·kugel die mothball

Motto das; ~**s,** ~**s** motto; (Schlagwort) slogan

Möwe die; ~, ~**n** gull

Mrd. Abk. = **Milliarde** bn.

Mücke die; ~, ~**n** midge; (größer) mosquito

Mücken·stich der midge/mosquito bite

Mucks der; ~**es,** ~**e** (ugs.) murmur [of protest]; **keinen** ~ **sagen** not utter a [single] word

müde 1 Adj. tired; (ermattet) weary; (schläfrig) sleepy; **jmdn./etw.** od. **jmds./einer Sache** ~ **sein** (geh.) be tired of sb./sth. 2 adv. wearily; (schläfrig) sleepily

Müdigkeit die; ~**:** tiredness

muffelig (ugs.) 1 Adj. grumpy 2 adv. grumpily

muffig Adj. musty

Mühe die; ~, ~**n** trouble; **sich** (Dat.) **mit jmdm./etw.** ~ **geben** take [great] pains over sb./sth.; **mit Müh und Not** with great difficulty

mühelos 1 Adj. effortless 2 adv. effortlessly

mühe·voll Adj. laborious; painstaking ‹work›

Mühle die; ~, ~**n** (a) mill; (Kaffee~) [coffee] grinder (b) (Spiel) nine men's morris

Mühsal die; ~, ~**e** (geh.) tribulation; (Strapaze) hardship

mühsam 1 Adj. laborious 2 adv. laboriously

müh·selig (geh.) 1 Adj. laborious; arduous ‹journey, life› 2 adv. with [great] difficulty

Mulde die; ~, ~**n** hollow

Mull der; ~**[e]s** (Stoff) mull; (Verband~) gauze

Müll der; ~**s** refuse; rubbish; garbage (Amer.); trash (Amer.); (Industrie~) [industrial] waste

Müll-: ~**abfuhr** die refuse or (Amer.) garbage collection; ~**ablade·platz** der [refuse] dump or (Brit.) tip

Müll·binde die gauze bandage

Müll·deponie die (Amtsspr.) refuse disposal site

Müller der; ~**s,** ~**:** miller

Müll-: ~**halde** die refuse dump; ~**kippe** die ▶ MÜLLABLADEPLATZ; ~**mann** der (ugs.) dustman (Brit.); garbage man (Amer.); ~**sack** der refuse bag; ~**schlucker** der rubbish (Brit.) or (Amer.) garbage chute; ~**tonne** die dustbin (Brit.); garbage or trash can (Amer.); ~**tüte** die bin bag; ~**wagen** der dustcart (Brit.); garbage truck (Amer.)

---

*alte Schreibung – vgl. Hinweis auf S. x

mulmig *Adj.* (ugs.) uneasy
Multimedia·technik *die* (DV) multimedia technology
Multiplex *das;* ~es, ~e multiplex
Multiplikation *die;* ~, ~en (Math.) multiplication
multiplizieren *tr. V.* multiply (**mit** by)
Mumie /'mu:miə/ *die;* ~, ~n mummy
Mumm *der;* ~s (ugs.) (Mut) guts *pl.* (coll.); (Tatkraft) drive; zap (coll.); (Kraft) muscle power
Mumps *der od. die;* ~: mumps *sing.*
München (*das*); ~s Munich
Münch[e]ner ① *indekl. Adj.* Munich *attrib*
② *der;* ~s, ~: inhabitant/native of Munich
Münch[e]nerin *die;* ~, ~nen
▶ Münch[e]ner 2
Mund *der;* ~[e]s, Münder mouth; **er küsste sie auf den** ~: he kissed her on the lips; **mit vollem** ~ **sprechen** speak with one's mouth full; **den** ~ **nicht aufmachen** (fig. ugs.) not say anything; **den** *od.* **seinen** ~ **halten** (ugs.) (zu sprechen aufhören) shut up (coll.); (nichts sagen) not say anything; (nichts verraten) keep quiet (**über** + *Akk.* about); **sie ist nicht auf den** ~ **gefallen** (fig. ugs.) she's never at a loss for words
Mund·art *die* dialect
münden *itr. V.; mit sein* **in etw.** (*Akk.*) ~: ⟨*river*⟩ flow into sth.; ⟨*corridor, street*⟩ lead into sth.
mund-, Mund-: ~**faul** *Adj.* (ugs.) uncommunicative; ~**gerecht** *Adj.* bite-sized; ~**geruch** *der* bad breath *no indef. art.;* ~**harmonika** *die* mouth organ
mündig *Adj.* of age *pred.;* ~ **werden** come of age
mündlich ① *Adj.* oral
② *adv.* orally
Mund·stück *das* mouthpiece; (bei Zigaretten) tip
mund·tot *Adj.* jmdn. ~ **machen** silence sb.
Mündung *die;* ~, ~en (a) mouth; (größere Trichter~) estuary
(b) (bei Feuerwaffen) muzzle
Mund·wasser *das; Pl.* ~wässer mouthwash
Mund-zu-Mund-Beatmung *die* mouth-to-mouth resuscitation
Munition *die;* ~: ammunition
munkeln *tr., itr. V.* (ugs.) **man munkelt, dass ...:** there is a rumour that ...
Münster *das;* ~s, ~: minster; (Dom) cathedral
munter ① *Adj.* (a) cheerful; (lebhaft) lively ⟨*eyes, game*⟩
(b) (wach) awake
② *adv.* cheerfully
Munterkeit *die;* ~: cheerfulness
Münz·automat *der* slot machine
Münze *die;* ~, ~n coin

Münz-: ~**fernsprecher** *der* payphone; pay station (Amer.); ~**tankstelle** *die* coin-in-the-slot petrol (Brit.) *or* (Amer.) gas station; ~**wechsler** *der* change machine
mürbe *Adj.* crumbly ⟨*biscuit, cake, etc.*⟩; tender ⟨*meat*⟩; soft ⟨*fruit*⟩; jmdn. ~ **machen** (fig.) wear sb. down
Murmel *die;* ~, ~n marble
murmeln *tr., itr. V.* mumble; mutter; (sehr leise) murmur
Murmel·tier *das* marmot
murren *itr. V.* grumble
mürrisch ① *Adj.* grumpy
② *adv.* grumpily
Mus *das od. der;* ~es, ~e purée
Muschel *die;* ~, ~n (a) mussel; (Schale) [mussel] shell
(b) (am Telefon) (Hör~) earpiece; (Sprech~) mouthpiece
Muse *die;* ~, ~n muse
Museum *das;* ~s, Museen museum
Musik *die;* ~, ~en music
musikalisch ① *Adj.* musical
② *adv.* musically
Musikant *der;* ~en, ~en, **Musikantin** *die;* ~, ~nen musician
Musik·box *die* jukebox
Musiker *der;* ~s, ~, **Musikerin** *die;* ~, ~nen musician
Musik-: ~**hochschule** *die* college of music; ~**instrument** *das* musical instrument; ~**saal** *der* (in der Schule) music room; ~**sender** *der* music station; ~**stück** *das* piece of music; **ein** ~**stück Chopins/von Chopin** a piece by Chopin; ~**stunde** *die* music lesson; ~**szene** *die* music scene
musisch ① *Adj.* artistic; ⟨*education*⟩ in the arts
② *adv.* artistically
musizieren *itr. V.* play music; (bes. unter Laien) make music
Muskat *der;* ~[e]s, ~e nutmeg
Muskat·nuss, *Muskat·nuß *die* nutmeg
Muskel *der;* ~s, ~n muscle
Muskel-: ~**kater** *der* stiff muscles *pl.;* ~**kraft** *die* muscle power; ~**krampf** *der* cramp; ~**pille** *die* (scherz.) muscle-building pill; muscle builder ~**protz** *der* (ugs.) muscleman; ~**zerrung** *die* (Med.) pulled muscle; **sich** (*Dat.*) **eine** ~**zerrung zuziehen** pull a muscle
Muskulatur *die;* ~, ~en musculature; muscular system
muskulös *Adj.* muscular
Müsli *das;* ~s, ~s muesli
Muslim *der;* ~s, ~e *od.* ~s Muslim
Muslimin *die;* ~, ~nen Muslim [woman]
muslimisch ① *Adj.* Muslim
② *adv.* on Muslim principles; ~ **erzogen werden** be brought up in the Muslim faith

muss, *muß 1. u. 3.Pers. Sg. Präsens v.
MÜSSEN

Muss, *Muß das; ~: necessity; must (coll.)

Muße die; ~: leisure

müssen ① unr. Modalverb; 2. Part.
müssen: **(a)** have to; **er muss es tun** he must
do it; he has to or (coll.) has got to do it; **das
muss 1968 gewesen sein** it must have been
in 1968; **er muss gleich hier sein** he will be
here at any moment
(b) Konjunktiv II **es müsste doch möglich
sein** it ought to be possible; **reich müsste
man sein!** how nice it would be to be rich!
② unr. itr. V. **ich muss nach Hause** I have
to or must go home; **ich muss mal** (fam.) I
need to spend a penny (Brit. coll.) or (Amer.
coll.) go to the john

müßig ① Adj. idle ⟨person⟩; ⟨hours, weeks,
life⟩ of leisure
② adv. idly

Müßig-: ~**gang** der leisure; (Untätigkeit)
idleness ~**gänger** der; ~~s, ~~,
~**gängerin** die; ~~, ~~nen idler;
~**gänger** Pl. people with time on their hands

musste, *mußte 1. u. 3. Pers. Sg. Prät.
v. MÜSSEN

Muster das; ~s, ~ **(a)** (Vorlage) pattern
(b) (Vorbild) model (**an** + Dat. of)
(c) (Verzierung) pattern
(d) (Warenprobe) sample

muster-, Muster-: ~**beispiel**
das perfect example; ~**gültig** ① Adj.
exemplary; impeccable ⟨order⟩; ② adv. in
an exemplary fashion

mustern tr. V. **(a)** eye
(b) (Milit.: ärztlich untersuchen) **jmdn.** ~: give sb.
his medical

Muster-prozess, *Muster-prozeß
der test case

Musterung die; ~, ~en **(a)** scrutiny
(b) (Milit.: von Wehrpflichtigen) medical
examination; medical

Mut der; ~[e]s courage

mutig ① Adj. brave
② adv. bravely

mut·los Adj. dejected; (entmutigt)
disheartened

Mut·losigkeit die; ~: dejection

mutmaßen tr., itr. V. conjecture

mutmaßlich Adj. supposed; suspected
⟨murderer etc.⟩

Mutmaßung die; ~, ~en conjecture

Mut·probe die test of courage

Mutter¹ die; ~, Mütter mother

Mutter² die; ~, ~n nut

mütterlich ① Adj. **(a)** maternal ⟨line,
love, instincts, etc.⟩
(b) (fürsorglich) motherly ⟨woman, care⟩
② adv. in a motherly way

mütterlicher·seits Adv. on the/his/her
etc. mother's side

Mütterlichkeit die; ~: motherliness;
(mütterliche Gefühle) motherly feeling

Mutter-: ~**liebe** die motherly love no
art.; ~**mal** das; ~~e birthmark

Mutterschaft die; ~: motherhood

Mutterschafts·urlaub der maternity
leave

mutter-, Mutter-: ~**seelen·allein**
Adj. all alone; ~**söhnchen** das mummy's
or (Amer.) mama's boy; ~**sprache** die
mother tongue; ~**tag** der Mother's Day no
def. art.

Mutti die; ~, ~s mummy (Brit. coll.); mum
(Brit. coll.); mommy (Amer. coll.); mom (Amer. coll.)

mut·willig ① Adj. wilful; wanton
⟨destruction⟩
② adv. wilfully

Mütze die; ~, ~n cap

MW Abk. (Rundf.) = **Mittelwelle** MW

Mw.-St., MwSt. Abk. =
Mehrwertsteuer VAT

mysteriös ① Adj. mysterious
② adv. mysteriously

Mystery- /ˈmɪstəri/ mystery attrib.

Mystik die; ~: mysticism

Mythologie die; ~, ~n mythology

mythologisch Adj. mythology

Mythos der; ~, Mythen myth

Nn

n, N /ɛn/ das; ~, ~: n/N

N Abk. = **Nord[en]** N

na Interj. (ugs.) well; **na so [et]was!** well
I never!; **na und?** (wennschon) so what?;
(beschwichtigend) **na, na, na!** now, now, come
along; (triumphierend) **na also!** there you are!;

(unsicher) **na, ich weiß nicht** hmm, I'm not
sure; (ärgerlich) **na, was soll das denn?** now
what's all this about?; (drohend) **na warte!**
just [you] wait!

Nabe die; ~, ~n hub

Nabel der; ~s, ~: navel

Nabel-: ~**bruch** der (Med.) umbilical
hernia; ~**frei** Adj. **ein** ~**freies Top** a

---

crop top; ~**frei gehen** wear a crop top;
~**schnur** die umbilical cord
Naben·schaltung die hub gear
nach 1 *Präp. mit Dat.* (a) (räumlich) to; der
Zug ~ **München** the train for Munich *or*
the Munich train; ~ **Hause gehen** go home;
~ **Osten [zu]** eastwards; [towards the] east
(b) (zeitlich) after; **zehn [Minuten]** ~ **zwei** ten
[minutes] past two
(c) (mit bestimmten Verben, bezeichnet das Ziel der
Handlung) for
(d) (bezeichnet [räumliche und zeitliche]
Reihenfolge) after; ~ **Ihnen/dir!** after you
(e) (gemäß) according to; ~ **meiner Ansicht**
od. Meinung, meiner Ansicht *od.* Meinung
~: in my view *or* opinion; ~ **der neusten**
Mode gekleidet dressed in [accordance
with] the latest fashion; **dem Gesetz** ~: in
accordance with the law; by law; ~ **etw.**
schmecken/riechen taste/smell of sth.
2 *Adv.* (a) (räumlich) **[alle] mir** ~!
[everybody] follow me!
(b) (zeitlich) ~ **und** ~: little by little;
gradually; ~ **wie vor** still
nach|ahmen tr. V. imitate
Nachahmung die; ~, ~en imitation
Nachbar der; ~n, ~n neighbour
Nachbar·haus das house next door
Nachbarin die; ~, ~nen neighbour
Nachbar·land das neighbouring country
Nachbarschaft die; ~, ~en (a) the
whole neighbourhood
(b) (Beziehungen) **gute** ~: good
neighbourliness
(c) (Gegend) neighbourhood; (Nähe) vicinity
Nach·beben das aftershock
nach|bestellen tr. V. **[noch] etw.**
~: order more of sth.; ⟨shop⟩ reorder sth.
Nach·bildung die (a) copying
(b) (Gegenstand) copy
nach|blicken tr. V. (geh.) **jmdm./einer**
Sache ~: gaze after sb./sth.
nach|datieren tr. V. backdate
nach·dem Konj. (a) after
(b) ▶ JE¹ 3
nach|denken unr. itr. V. think; **denk mal**
[gut *od.* **scharf] nach** have a [good] think
Nach·denken das thought
nachdenklich 1 Adj. thoughtful
2 adv. thoughtfully
Nach·druck der; Pl. ~e (a) mit
~: emphatically
(b) (Druckw.) reprint
nachdrücklich 1 Adj. emphatic
2 adv. emphatically
Nachdrücklichkeit die; ~: emphatic
nature
nach|dunkeln itr. V.; mit sein get darker
Nach·durst der morning-after thirst
nach|eifern itr. V. **jmdm.** ~: emulate sb.
nach·einander Adv. one after the other
nach|empfinden unr. tr. V. empathize

with ⟨feeling⟩; share ⟨delight, sorrow⟩
Nach·erzählung die retelling [of a story];
(Schulw.) reproduction
Nachfahr der; ~en, ~en, **Nachfahrin**
die; ~, ~nen (geh.) descendant
nach|fahren unr. itr. V.; mit sein follow
[on]; **jmdm.** ~: follow sb.
Nach·folge die succession
Nachfolger der; ~s, ~, **Nachfolgerin**
die; ~, ~nen successor
Nach·forschung die investigation
Nach·frage die demand (**nach** for)
nach|fragen itr. V. ask; inquire; **bei**
jmdm. ~: ask sb.; **ob ich mal** ~ **soll?** should
I ask about it *or* make inquiries?
nach|fühlen tr. V. empathize with; **das**
kann ich dir ~! I know how you feel!
nach|füllen tr. V. top up; **Salz/Wein**
~: put [some] more salt/wine in
nach|geben unr. itr. V. give way
Nach·gebühr die excess postage
nach|gehen unr. itr. V.; mit sein
(a) **jmdm./einer Sache** ~: follow sb./sth.;
einer Sache ~ (fig.) look into a matter; **einem**
Beruf ~: practise a profession
(b) (nicht aus dem Kopf gehen) **jmdm.** ~: remain
on sb.'s mind
(c) ⟨clock, watch⟩ be slow; **[um] eine Stunde**
~: be an hour slow
Nach·geschmack der aftertaste
nach·giebig Adj. indulgent
Nachgiebigkeit die; ~: indulgence
nach·haltig 1 Adj. (a) lasting
(b) (Ökologie) sustainable
2 adv. (a) (auf längere Zeit) for a long time
(b) (Ökologie) sustainably
Nach·hause·weg der way home
nach|helfen unr. itr. V. help
nach·her /auch: '--/ Adv. afterwards;
(später) later [on]; **bis** ~! see you later!
Nach·hilfe die coaching
Nachhilfe·unterricht der coaching
***nach·hinein, Nachhinein:** im ~
(nachträglich) afterwards; later; (zurückblickend)
with hindsight
nach|holen tr. V. (nachträglich erledigen)
catch up on ⟨work, sleep⟩; make up for
⟨working hours missed⟩
nach|jagen itr. V.; mit sein **jmdm./einer**
Sache ~: chase after sb./sth.
Nachkomme der; ~n, ~n descendant
nach|kommen unr. itr. V.; mit sein
follow [later]; come [on] later
Nachkommenschaft die; ~:
descendants pl.
Nachkömmling der; ~s, ~e much
younger child (than the rest)
Nach·kriegs- post-war ⟨generation,
period, etc.⟩
Nach·lass, *Nach·laß der; Nachlasses,
Nachlasse *od.* Nachlässe (a) estate

(b) (Kaufmannsspr.: Rabatt) discount
nach|lassen ① *unr. itr. V.* let up;
⟨*pain, stress, pressure*⟩ ease; ⟨*effect*⟩
wear off; ⟨*interest, enthusiasm, strength,
courage*⟩ wane; ⟨*health, hearing, memory*⟩
deteriorate; ⟨*business*⟩ drop off
② *unr. tr. V.* (Kaufmannsspr.) give a discount
of
nach·lässig ① *Adj.* careless
② *adv.* carelessly
Nach·lässigkeit *die;* ~, ~en
carelessness
Nachlass·verwalter *der,*
Nachlass·verwalterin, *die* (Rechtsw.)
executor
nach|laufen *unr. itr. V.; mit sein* jmdm./
einer Sache ~: run after sb./sth.
nach|lesen *unr. tr. V.* look up
nach|lösen ① *tr. V.* eine Fahrkarte
~: buy a ticket [on the train, bus, etc.]
② *itr. V.* pay the excess [fare]
nach|machen *tr. V.* (auch tun) copy;
(imitieren) imitate; (genauso herstellen)
reproduce ⟨*period furniture etc.*⟩; forge
⟨*signature*⟩
*****nach·mittag** ▸ NACHMITTAG
Nach·mittag *der* afternoon; am ~: in
the afternoon; am späten ~: late in the
afternoon; heute ~: this afternoon
nach·mittags *Adv.* in the afternoon;
dienstags *od.* Dienstag ~: on Tuesday
afternoons; um vier Uhr ~: at four in the
afternoon; at 4 p.m.
Nachnahme *die;* ~, ~n: per ~: cash on
delivery; COD
Nach·name *der* surname
Nach·porto *das* excess postage
nachprüfbar *Adj.* verifiable
nach|prüfen *tr., itr. V.* check
nach|rechnen *tr. V.* check ⟨*figures*⟩
Nach·rede *die:* üble ~: malicious gossip;
(Rechtsw.) defamation [of character]
nach|rennen *unr. itr. V.:* ▸ NACHLAUFEN
Nachricht *die;* ~, ~en **(a)** news *no pl.;*
das ist eine gute ~: that is [a piece of] good
news; eine ~ hinterlassen leave a message
(b) *Pl.* (Ferns., Rundf.) news *sing.;* ~en hören
listen to the news
Nachrichten-: ~**sprecher** *der,*
~**sprecherin** *die* newsreader
nach|rücken *itr. V.; mit sein* move up
Nach·ruf *der* obituary (auf + *Akk.* of)
nach|rufen *unr. tr., itr. V.* jmdm. [etw.]
~: call [sth.] after sb.
nach|rüsten ① *itr. V.* counter-arm
② *tr. V.* (Technik: zusätzlich ausstatten) mit etw.
~ (+ *Akk.*) equip additionally with sth.;
upgrade ⟨*television, hi-fi, etc.*⟩ with sth.
nach|sagen *tr. V.* **(a)** (wiederholen) repeat
(b) man sagt ihm nach, er sei ...: he is said

to be ...; jmdm. **Schlechtes** ~: speak ill of sb.
Nach·saison *die* late season
nach|schicken *tr. V.* **(a)** (durch die Post o.
Ä.) forward
(b) jmdm. jmdn. ~: send sb. after sb.
Nach·schlag *der* (ugs.: zusätzliche Portion)
second helping; seconds *pl.*
nach|schlagen ① *unr. tr. V.* look up
② *unr. itr. V.* im Lexikon/Wörterbuch
~: consult the encyclopaedia/dictionary
Nachschlage·werk *das* work of
reference
Nach·schlüssel *der* duplicate key
nach|schmeißen *unr. tr. V.* (ugs.) man
kriegt sie nachgeschmissen you get them
for next to nothing
Nach·schub *der* (Milit.) **(a)** supply (an
+ *Dat.* of)
(b) (~material) supplies *pl.* (an + *Dat.* of)
nach|sehen ① *unr. itr. V.* **(a)** jmdm./
einer Sache ~: gaze after sb./sth.
(b) (kontrollieren) check
(c) (nachschlagen) have a look
② *unr. tr. V.* **(a)** (nachlesen) look up
(b) (überprüfen) check [over]
Nach·sehen *das:* das ~ haben not get
a look-in; (nichts abbekommen) be left with
nothing
nach|senden *unr. od. regelm. tr. V.*
forward
Nach·sicht *die* leniency
nachsichtig ① *Adj.* lenient (gegen, mit
towards)
② *adv.* leniently
Nachsichtigkeit *die;* ~: leniency
Nach·silbe *die* (Sprachw.) suffix
nach|sitzen *unr. itr. V.* be in detention;
[eine Stunde] ~ müssen have [an hour's]
detention
Nach·spann *der;* ~[e]s, ~e (Film, Ferns.)
[final] credits *pl.*
Nach·speise *die* dessert; sweet
Nach·spiel *das:* die Sache wird noch ein
~ haben this affair will have repercussions;
ein gerichtliches ~ haben result in court
proceedings
nach|spionieren *itr. V.* jmdm. ~: spy
on sb.
nach|sprechen *unr. tr. V.* [jmdm.] etw.
~: repeat sth. [after sb.]
nächst... *Sup. zu* NAH: *Adj.* next; (kürzest)
shortest ⟨*way*⟩; am ~en Tag the next day;
beim ~en Mal, das ~e Mal the next time;
der ~e bitte! next [one], please; wer kommt
als ~er dran? whose turn is it next?
Nächste *der; adj. Dekl.* (geh.) neighbour
nach|stehen *unr. itr. V.* jmdm. an etw.
(*Dat.*) nicht ~: be sb.'s match in sth.;
jmdm./einer Sache in nichts ~: be in no way
inferior to sb./sth.
nach·stehend ① *Adj.* following
② *adv.* below

---

*alte Schreibung – vgl. Hinweis auf S. x

Nächsten·liebe *die* charity [to one's neighbour]

nächstens *Adv.* (a) shortly
(b) (ugs.: wenn es so weitergeht) if it goes on like this

nächst-: ∼**liegend** *Adj.* first, immediate ⟨*problem*⟩; [most] obvious ⟨*explanation etc.*⟩; ∼**möglich** *Adj.* earliest possible

nach|suchen *itr. V.* (geh.) **um etw.** ∼: request sth.; (bes. schriftlich) apply for sth.

*****nacht** ▸ NACHT

Nacht *die;* ∼, Nächte night; gestern/ morgen/Dienstag ∼: last night/tomorrow night/on Tuesday night; **heute** ∼: tonight; **bei** ∼, **in der** ∼: at night[-time]; **über** ∼ **bleiben** stay overnight; **gute** ∼! good night!

nacht-, Nacht-: ∼**arbeit** *die* night work *no art.;* ∼**blind** *Adj.* night-blind; ∼**blindheit** *die* night blindness; ∼**creme** *die* night cream; ∼**dienst** *der* night duty; ∼**dienst haben** be on night duty; ⟨*chemist's shop*⟩ be open late

Nach·teil *der* disadvantage

nachteilig ① *Adj.* detrimental; harmful ② *adv.* detrimentally; harmfully

Nacht-: ∼**essen** *das* (bes. südd., schweiz.) ▸ ABENDESSEN; ∼**hemd** *das* nightshirt

Nachtigall *die;* ∼, ∼**en** nightingale

nächtigen *itr. V.* (österr., sonst geh.) spend the night

Nach·tisch *der* dessert; sweet

nächtlich *Adj.* nocturnal; night ⟨*sky*⟩; ⟨*darkness, stillness*⟩ of the night

Nacht·lokal *das* night spot (coll.)

nach|tragen *unr. tr. V.* (schriftlich ergänzen) insert; add

nach·tragend *Adj.* unforgiving; (rachsüchtig) vindictive

nachträglich ① *Adj.* later; subsequent ⟨*apology*⟩; (verspätet) belated ⟨*greetings, apology*⟩
② *adv.* afterwards; subsequently; (verspätet) belatedly

nach|trauern *itr. V.* jmdm./einer Sache ∼: bemoan the passing of sb./sth.

Nacht·ruhe *die* night's sleep

nachts *Adv.* at night; Montag *od.* montags ∼: on Monday nights; um 3 Uhr ∼: at 3 o'clock in the morning

Nacht-: ∼**schicht** *die* night shift; ∼**schwester** *die* night nurse; ∼**tisch** *der* bedside table; ∼**tisch·lampe** *die* bedside light; ∼**topf** *der* chamber pot; ∼**wächter, ∼wächterin** *die* nightwatchman

Nach·untersuchung *die* follow-up examination; check-up

nach|vollziehen *unr. tr. V.* reconstruct; (begreifen) comprehend

nach|wachsen *unr. itr. V.; mit sein* [wieder] ∼: grow again

Nach·wehen *Pl.* (Med.) afterpains; (fig. geh.) unpleasant after-effects

Nachweis *der;* ∼es, ∼e proof *no indef. art.* (Gen., über + Akk. of); (Zeugnis) certificate (über + Akk. of)

nachweisbar ① *Adj.* demonstrable ⟨*fact, truth, error, defect, guilt*⟩; detectable ⟨*substance, chemical*⟩
② *adv.* demonstrably

nach|weisen *unr. tr. V.* prove

nachweislich *Adv.* as can be proved

Nach·welt *die* posterity *no art.;* future generations *pl., no art.*

nach|winken *itr. V.* jmdm./einer Sache ∼: wave after sb./sth.

Nach·wirkung *die* after-effect

Nach·wort *das; Pl.* ∼**e** afterword

Nach·wuchs *der* (a) (fam.: Kind[er]) offspring
(b) (junge Kräfte) new blood; (für eine Branche usw.) new recruits *pl.;* (in der Ausbildung) trainees *pl.*

nach|zahlen *tr., itr. V.* (a) pay later
(b) (zusätzlich zahlen) 25 Euro ∼: pay another 25 euros

nach|zählen *tr., itr. V.* [re]count

Nach·zahlung *die* additional payment

nach|ziehen *unr. itr. V.*(a) (ugs.: ebenso handeln) do likewise; follow suit
(b) *mit sein* (nachträglich übersiedeln) jmdm. ∼: [go to] join sb.

Nachzügler *der;* ∼**s**, ∼, **Nachzüglerin** *die;* ∼, ∼**nen** straggler; (spät Ankommende[r]) latecomer

Nackedei *der;* ∼**s**, ∼**s** (fam. scherzh.) [kleiner] ∼: naked little thing

Nacken *der;* ∼**s**, ∼: back *or* nape of the neck; (Hals) neck

nackt *Adj.* naked; bare ⟨*feet, legs, arms, skin, fists*⟩; (fig.) plain ⟨*truth, fact*⟩; bare ⟨*existence*⟩

Nackt·bade·strand *der* nudist beach

Nackte *der/die; adj. Dekl.* naked man/woman

Nackt·foto *das* nude photo

Nadel *die;* ∼, ∼**n** needle; (Steck∼, Hut∼, Haar∼) pin; **an der** ∼ **hängen** (fig. ugs.) be on the needle (sl.)

Nadel·baum *der* conifer

Nadeldrucker *der* (DV) dot-matrix printer

nadeln *itr. V.* ⟨*tree*⟩ shed its needles

Nadel·wald *der* coniferous forest

Nagel *der;* ∼**s**, Nägel nail; **den** ∼ **auf den Kopf treffen** (fig. ugs.) hit the nail on the head

Nagel-: ∼**bürste** *die* nailbrush; ∼**feile** *die* nail file; ∼**lack** *der* nail varnish (Brit.); nail polish

nageln *tr. V.* nail (an + Akk. to, auf + Akk. on); (Med.) pin

nagel·neu *Adj.* (ugs.) brand-new

n

Nagel·schere die nail scissors pl.
nagen ① itr. V. gnaw; **an etw.** (Dat.)
~: gnaw [at] sth.
② tr. V. gnaw off; **ein Loch ins Holz**
~: gnaw a hole in the wood
Nage·tier das rodent
nah ▶ NAHE
Nah·aufnahme die (Fot.) close-up
[photograph]
nahe /'naːə,/ **näher** /'nɛːɐ,/ **nächst...** ① Adj.
(a) (räumlich) near pred.; close pred.; nearby
attrib.
(b) (zeitlich) imminent; near pred.
(c) (eng) close ⟨relationship etc.⟩
② adv. (a) (räumlich) ~ **an** (+ Dat./Akk.),
~ **bei** close to; ~ **gelegen** nearby; **von**
~**m** od. **Nahem** from close up; **jmdm.**
~ **gehen** affect sb. deeply; **eine Sache**
(Dat.) ~ **kommen** come close to sth.;
⟨amount⟩ approximate to sth.; **jmdm/sich**
[menschlich] ~ **kommen** get to know sb./one
another well; **jmdm/sich [menschlich]**
näher kommen get on closer terms with sb.;
jmdm. ~ **stehen** be on intimate terms with
sb.; **jmdm. etw.** ~ **legen** (fig.) suggest sth. to
sb.; **einen Verdacht/einen Gedanken** usw.
~ **legen** give rise to a suspicion/thought
etc.; ~ **liegen** (fig.) ⟨thought⟩ suggest itself;
⟨suspicion, question⟩ arise
(b) (zeitlich) ~ **an die achtzig** (ugs.) pushing
eighty (coll.)
(c) (eng) closely
③ Präp. mit Dat. (geh.) near; close to
Nähe die; ~: closeness
nahe-: ~**bei** Adv. nearby; close by;
~|**gehen** usw. ▶ NAHE 2A; ~**liegend**
Adj. obvious ⟨reason, solution⟩
nahen itr. V.; mit sein (geh.) draw near;
sein/ihr usw. ▶ NAHE 2A; ~**zu** Adv.
nähen ① itr. V. sew; (Kleider machen) make
clothes
② tr. V. (a) sew ⟨seam, hem⟩; make ⟨dress
etc.⟩
(b) (Med.) stitch
näher ① Komp. zu nahe;
② Adj. (a) (kürzer) shorter ⟨way, road⟩
(b) (genauer) more precise ⟨information⟩;
closer ⟨investigation, inspection⟩
③ adv. (a) **bitte treten Sie** ~! please come
in/nearer/this way
(b) (genauer) more closely; (im Einzelnen) in
[more] detail
***näher|kommen** ▶ NAHE 2A
nähern refl. V. approach; **sich jmdm./einer**
Sache ~: approach sb./sth.
nahe-: *~|**stehen** ▶ NAHE 2A; ~**zu** Adv.
almost; nearly; (mit Zahlenangabe) close on
Näh-: ~**garn** das [sewing] cotton;
~**kasten** der sewing box
nahm 1. u. 3. Pers. Sg. Prät. v. NEHMEN
Näh-: ~**maschine** die sewing machine;

~**nadel** die sewing needle
nah·östlich Adj. Middle Eastern
Nähr·boden der culture medium; (fig.)
breeding ground
nähren ① tr. V. feed (mit on)
② refl. V. (geh.) **sich von etw.** ~: live on sth.;
⟨animal⟩ feed on sth.
nahrhaft Adj. nourishing
Nahrung die; ~: food
Nahrungs·mittel das food [item]; ~ Pl.
foodstuffs
Nähr·wert der nutritional value
Näh·seide die sewing silk
Naht die; ~, **Nähte** seam
naht·los ① Adj. seamless; (fig.) perfectly
smooth ⟨transition⟩
② adv. **Studium und Beruf gehen nicht**
~ **ineinander über** there is not a perfectly
smooth transition from study to work
Nah-: ~**verkehr** der local traffic;
~**verkehrs·zug** der local train
Näh·zeug das sewing things pl.
naiv ① Adj. naive
② adv. naively
Naivität die; ~: naivety
Name der; ~ns, ~n name
namens Adv. by the name of
Namens-: ~**schild** das (a) (an Türen usw.)
nameplate; (b) (zum Anstecken) name badge;
~**tag** der name day
namentlich ① Adj. by name postpos.
② adv. by name
③ adv. (besonders) particularly
namhaft Adj. (a) (berühmt) noted
(b) (ansehnlich) noteworthy ⟨sum, difference⟩;
notable ⟨contribution, opportunity⟩
nämlich Adv. (a) **er kann nicht kommen, er**
ist ~ **krank** he cannot come, as he is ill
(b) (und zwar) namely
nannte 1. u. 3. Pers. Sg. Prät. v. NENNEN
nanu Interj. ~, **was machst du denn hier?**
hello, what are you doing here?; ~, **Sie**
gehen schon? what, you're going already?
Napf der; ~[e]s, **Näpfe** bowl (esp. for animal's
food)
Narbe die; ~, ~n scar
narbig Adj. scarred
Narkose die; ~, ~n (Med.) narcosis
narkotisieren tr. V. (Med.) anaesthetize
⟨patient⟩; put ⟨patient⟩ under a general
anaesthetic
Narr der; ~en, ~en fool
Narren·freiheit die freedom to do as one
pleases
Närrin die; ~, ~nen fool
närrisch ① Adj. crazy; carnival-crazy
⟨season⟩
② adv. crazily
Narzisse die; ~, ~n narcissus
naschen ① itr. V. (Süßes essen) eat sweet
things; (heimlich essen) have a nibble

---

[2] *tr. V.* eat ⟨*sweets, chocolate, etc.*⟩; **er hat Milch genascht** he has been at the milk
Nascherei *die;* ~, ~**en (a)** [continually] eating sweet things; **hör auf mit der** ~! don't keep eating sweet things all the time! **(b)** (Süßigkeit) ~**en** sweets
naschhaft *Adj.* sweet-toothed; ~ **sein** have a sweet tooth
Nase *die;* ~, ~**n** nose; **die** ~ **voll haben** (ugs.) have had enough
Nasen-: ~**bluten** *das;* ~~**s** bleeding from the nose; ~**loch** *das* nostril; ~**spitze** *die* tip of the/one's nose; **jmdm. etw. an der** ~**spitze ansehen** (fig. ugs.) tell sth. by sb.'s face; ~**tropfen** *Pl.* nose drops; ~**wurzel** *die* root of the nose
nase-: ~**rümpfend** [1] *Adj.* disapproving; [2] *adv.* disdainfully; ~**weis** [1] *Adj.* precocious; pert ⟨*remark, reply*⟩; [2] *adv.* precociously
Nas·horn *das* rhinoceros
nass, *naß; nasser *od.* nässer, nassest... *od.* nässest...: *Adj.* wet; **sich/das Bett** ~ **machen** wet oneself/one's bed
Nässe *die;* ~: wetness
nass-kalt, *naß-kalt *Adj.* cold and wet
Nass·rasur, *Naß·rasur *die* wet shaving *no art.*
Nation *die;* ~, ~**en** nation
national [1] *Adj.* national [2] *adv.* nationally
National-: ~**elf** *die* (Fußball) national side; ~**hymne** *die* national anthem
Nationalisierung *die;* ~, ~**en** nationalization
Nationalismus *der;* ~: nationalism *usu. no art.*
nationalistisch [1] *Adj.* nationalist; nationalistic [2] *adv.* nationalistically
Nationalität *die;* ~, ~**en** nationality
national-, National-: ~**mannschaft** *die* national team; ~**sozialismus** *der* National Socialism; ~**sozialist** *der,* ~**sozialistin** *die* National Socialist; ~**sozialistisch** *Adj.* National Socialist; ~**spieler** *der,* ~**spielerin** *die* (Sport) national player; international; ~**staat** *der* nation state; ~**stolz** *der* national pride; ~**versammlung** *die* National Assembly
NATO, Nato *die;* ~: NATO, Nato *no art.*
Natron *das;* ~**s [doppeltkohlensaures]** ~: sodium bicarbonate; **[kohlensaures]** ~: sodium carbonate
Natter *die;* ~, ~**n** colubrid
Natur *die;* ~, ~**en** nature; **die freie** ~: [the] open countryside
Naturalien /natu'ra:li̯ən/ *Pl.* natural produce *sing.* (used as payment); **in** ~ (*Dat.*) **bezahlen** pay in kind
Naturalismus *der;* ~: naturalism

naturalistisch [1] *Adj.* naturalistic [2] *adv.* naturalistically
Naturell *das;* ~**s,** ~**e** temperament
natur-, Natur-: ~**erscheinung** *die* natural phenomenon; ~**farben** *Adj.* natural-coloured; ~**freund** *der,* ~**freundin** *die* nature lover; ~**gemäß** *Adv.* naturally; ~**geschichte** *die* natural history; ~**gesetz** *das* law of nature; ~**getreu** [1] *Adj.* lifelike ⟨*portrait, imitation*⟩; faithful ⟨*reproduction*⟩; [2] *adv.* ⟨*draw*⟩ true to life; ⟨*reproduce*⟩ faithfully; ~**heilkunde** *die* naturopathy *no art.;* ~**katastrophe** *die* natural disaster
natürlich [1] *Adj.* natural [2] *adv.* ⟨*laugh, behave*⟩ naturally [3] *Adv.* **(a)** (selbstverständlich, wie erwartet) naturally; of course **(b)** (zwar) of course
Natürlichkeit *die;* ~: naturalness
Natur-, Natur-: ~**park** *der* ≈ national park; ~**produkt** *das* natural product; ~**schutz** *der* [nature] conservation; **unter** ~**schutz** (*Dat.*) **stehen** be protected by law; be a protected species/variety/area *etc.*; ~**schutz·gebiet** *das* nature reserve; ~**talent** *das* [great] natural talent *or* gift; (begabter Mensch) naturally talented *or* gifted person; ~**verbunden** *Adj.* ⟨*person*⟩ in tune with nature; ~**volk** *das* primitive people; ~**wissenschaft** *die* natural science *no art.;* ~**wissenschaftler** *der,* ~**wissenschaftlerin** *die* [natural] scientist; ~**wissenschaftlich** [1] *Adj.* scientific; [2] *adv.* scientifically; ~**wunder** *das* miracle *or* wonder of nature
Navigation *die;* ~: navigation *no art.*
navigieren *tr., itr. V.* navigate
n. Chr. *Abk.* = **nach Christus** AD
Neandertaler *der;* ~**s,** ~: Neanderthal man
Nebel *der;* ~**s,** ~: fog; (weniger dicht) mist
nebelig ▸ NEBLIG
Nebel-: ~**scheinwerfer** *der* fog lamp; ~**schluss·leuchte,** ***~schluß·leuchte** *die* rear fog lamp; ~**schwaden** *Pl.* swathes of mist; ~**wand** *die* wall of fog
neben [1] *Präp. mit Dat.* **(a)** (Lage) next to; beside **(b)** (außer) apart from; aside from (Amer.) **(c)** (verglichen mit) beside [2] *Präp. mit Akk.* (Richtung) next to; beside
neben-, Neben-: ~**an** *Adv.* next door; ~**bei** *Adv.* **(a)** ⟨*work*⟩ on the side; (zusätzlich) as well; **(b)** (beiläufig) ⟨*remark, ask*⟩ by the way; ⟨*mention*⟩ in passing; ~**beruf** *der* second job; sideline; ~**beruflich** [1] *Adj.* **eine** ~**berufliche Tätigkeit** a second job; [2] *adv.* on the side; **er arbeitet** ~**beruflich als Übersetzer** he translates as a sideline; ~**beschäftigung** *die* second job; sideline; ~**buhler** *der,* ~**buhlerin** *die* rival

neben·einander *Adv.* **(a)** next to each other; ⟨*be sitting, standing*⟩ next to one another, side by side; (fig.: zusammen) ⟨*live, exist*⟩ side by side; ~ **wohnen** live next door to each other; ~ **legen** (+ *Akk.*) lay or place ⟨*objects*⟩ next to each other *or* side by side **(b)** (gleichzeitig) together

***nebeneinander|legen** *usw.*

▶ NEBENEINANDER A

Neben-: ~**erwerb** *der* secondary occupation; ~**fach** *das* subsidiary subject; minor (Amer.); ~**fluss,** *~***fluß** *der* tributary; ~**gebäude** *das* **(a)** annexe; outbuilding; **(b)** (Nachbargebäude) neighbouring building; ~**geräusch** *das* background noise; ~**haus** *das* house next door

neben·her *Adv.* ▶ NEBENBEI

nebenher-: ~|**fahren** *unr. itr. V.; mit sein* drive/ride alongside; ~|**gehen** *unr. itr. V.; mit sein* walk alongside

neben-, Neben-: ~**höhle** *die* (Anat.) paranasal sinus; ~**kläger** *der,* ~**klägerin** *die* (Rechtsw.) accessory prosecutor; ~**kosten** *Pl.* **(a)** additional costs; **(b)** (bei Mieten) heating, lighting, and services; ~**produkt** *das* by-product; ~**rolle** *die* supporting role; ~**sache** *die* minor matter; ~**sachen** inessentials; ~**sächlich** *Adj.* of minor importance *postpos.;* unimportant; minor ⟨*detail*⟩; ~**sächlichkeit** *die;* ~~, ~~**en** (Unwichtiges) matter of minor importance; unimportant matter; ~**satz** *der* (Sprachw.) subordinate clause; ~**stelle** *die* extension; ~**straße** *die* side street; ~**tätigkeit** *die* second job; sideline; ~**tisch** *der* next table; ~**verdienst** *der* additional income; ~**wirkung** *die* side effect; ~**zimmer** *das* next room

neblig *Adj.* foggy; (weniger dicht) misty

Necessaire /nesɛˈsɛːɐ̯/ *das;* ~**s,** ~**s** sponge bag (Brit.); toilet bag (Amer.)

necken *tr. V.* tease

Neckerei *die;* ~: teasing

nee (ugs.) no; nope (Amer. coll.)

Neffe *der;* ~**n,** ~**n** nephew

negativ ① *Adj.* negative ② *adv.* ⟨*answer*⟩ in the negative

Negativ *das;* ~**s,** ~**e** (Fot.) negative

Neger *der;* ~**s,** ~: Negro

Negerin *die;* ~, ~**nen** Negress

nehmen *unr. tr. V.* take; **sich** (*Dat.*) **etw.** ~: take sth.; (sich bedienen) help oneself to sth.; **auf sich** (*Akk.*) ~: take on ⟨*responsibility, burden*⟩; **jmdm./einer Sache etw.** ~: deprive sb./sth. of sth.; **was nehmen Sie dafür?** how much do you charge for it?

Neid *der;* ~**[e]s** envy; jealousy

neiden *tr. V.* (geh.) **jmdm. etw.** ~: envy sb. [for] sth.

---

*alte Schreibung – vgl. Hinweis auf S. x

Neid·hammel *der* (salopp abwertend) envious sod (sl.)

neidisch ① *Adj.* envious ② *adv.* enviously

neigen ① *tr. V.* tip; tilt; incline ⟨*head, upper part of body*⟩ ② *refl. V.:* ⟨*person*⟩ lean; ⟨*ship*⟩ heel over, list; ⟨*scales*⟩ tip ③ *itr. V.* **(a) zu Erkältungen/Krankheiten** ~: be prone to colds/illnesses **(b)** (tendieren) tend

Neigung *die;* ~, ~**en (a)** (Vorliebe) inclination **(b)** (Tendenz) tendency

nein *Interj.* no

Nein *das;* ~**[s],** ~**[s]** no

Nein·stimme *die* no-vote

Nektar *der;* ~**s,** ~**e** (Bot.) nectar

Nektarine *die;* ~, ~**n** nectarine

Nelke *die;* ~, ~**n (a)** pink; (Dianthus caryophyllus) carnation **(b)** (Gewürz) clove

nennen ① *unr. tr. V.* **(a)** call **(b)** (angeben) give ⟨*name, date of birth, address, reason, price, etc.*⟩ **(c)** (anführen) give ⟨*example*⟩; (erwähnen) mention ⟨*person, name*⟩ ② *unr. refl. V.* ⟨*person, thing*⟩ be called

nennens·wert *Adj.* considerable ⟨*influence, changes, delays, damage*⟩; **kaum** ~**e Veränderungen** changes scarcely worth mentioning

Nenner *der;* ~**s,** ~ (Math.) denominator

neo-, Neo- neo-

neo-: ~**konservativ** *Adj.* neo-conservative; neo-con (coll.); ~**liberal** *Adj.* neo-liberal

Neon *das;* ~**s** neon

Neo·nazi *der* neo-Nazi

Neon-: ~**licht** *das* neon light; ~**röhre** *die* neon tube

Nepal (*das*); ~**s** Nepal

Nepp *der;* ~**s** (ugs. abwertend) daylight robbery *no art.;* rip-off (coll.)

neppen *tr. V.* (ugs. abwertend) rook; rip ⟨*tourist, customer, etc.*⟩ off (sl.)

Nepper *der;* ~**s,** ~, **Nepperin** *die;* ~, ~**nen** (ugs. abwertend) shark; rip-off merchant (coll.)

Nepp·lokal *das* (ugs. abwertend) clip joint (coll.)

Nerv *der;* ~**s,** ~**en** nerve; **die** ~**en verlieren** lose control [of oneself]; **jmdm. auf die** ~**en gehen** od. **fallen** get on sb.'s nerves

nerven (salopp) ① *tr. V.* **jmdn.** ~: get on sb.'s nerves ② *itr. V.* be wearing on the nerves

nerven-, Nerven-: ~**aufreibend** *Adj.* nerve-racking; ~**bündel** *das* (ugs.) bundle of nerves (coll.); ~**gift** *das* neurotoxin; ~**heil·anstalt** *die* (veralt.) psychiatric hospital; ~**krank** *Adj.* ⟨*person*⟩ suffering from a nervous disease; ~**probe** *die* mental trial; ~**säge** *die* (salopp) pain in the neck (coll.); ~**zusammen·bruch** *der* nervous breakdown

nęrvig *Adj.* (auch fig.) sinewy

nęrvlich *Adj.* nervous ⟨*strain*⟩

nervös 1 *Adj.* (auch Med.) nervous; jittery ⟨*person*⟩
2 *adv.* nervously

Nervosität *die;* ~ nervousness

nęrv·tötend *Adj.* nerve-racking ⟨*wait*⟩; soul-destroying ⟨*activity, work*⟩

Nęrz *der;* ~**es,** ~**e** mink

Nęrz·mantel *der* mink coat

Nęssel *die;* ~**,** ~**n** nettle

Nęst *das;* ~**[e]s,** ~**er (a)** nest
(b) (fam.: Bett) bed
(c) (ugs. abwertend: kleiner Ort) little place

nętt 1 *Adj.* nice; (freundlich) kind
2 *adv.* nicely; (freundlich) nicely; kindly

netter·wẹise *Adv.* kindly

nętto *Adv.* ⟨*weigh, earn, etc.*⟩ net

Nętto-: ~**einkommen** *das* net income; ~**gehalt** *das* net salary; ~**preis** *der* net price

Nętz *das;* ~**es,** ~**e (a)** net; (Einkaufs~) string bag; (Gepäck~) [luggage] rack
(b) (Spinnen~) web
(c) (Netzwerk) network; (für Strom, Wasser, Gas) mains *pl.*

Nętz-: ~**haut** *die* (Anat.) retina; ~**werk** *das* (auch Elektrot.) network; **soziales** ~**werk** social networking site

neu 1 *Adj.* new; **die** ~**este Mode** the latest fashion; **das ist mir** ~: that is news to me; **der/die Neue** the new man/woman/boy/girl
2 *adv.* **(a)** ~ **tapeziert/gestrichen** repapered/repainted; **sich** ~ **einrichten** refurnish one's home
(b) (gerade erst) **diese Ware ist** ~ **eingetroffen** this item has just come in; ~ **eröffnet** newly-opened; (wieder eröffnet) reopened

neu·artig *Adj.* new; ~**e Lebensmittel** novel foods

Neu·artigkeit *die;* ~~: novelty

neu-, Neu-: ~**bau** *der; Pl.* ~~**ten** new house/building/build; ~**bau·wohnung** *die* flat (Brit.) *or* (Amer.) apartment in a new block/house/build; ~**beginn** *der* new beginning

neuerdings *Adv.* **er trägt** ~ **eine Brille** he has recently started wearing glasses

*****neu·eröffnet** ▶ NEU 2B

Neu·eröffnung *die* **(a)** opening
(b) (Wiedereröffnung) reopening

Neuerung *die;* ~**,** ~**en** innovation

neu·geboren *Adj.* newborn

Neu·gier,

Neugierde *die;* ~: curiosity; (Wissbegierde) inquisitiveness

neu·gierig 1 *Adj.* curious; inquisitive; inquisitive ⟨*person*⟩; **ich bin** ~**, was er dazu**

sagt I'm curious to know what he'll say about it
2 *adv.* ⟨*ask*⟩ inquisitively; ⟨*peer*⟩ nosily (coll. derog.)

Neuheit *die;* ~**,** ~**en (a)** novelty
(b) (Neues) new product/gadget/article *etc.*

Neuigkeit *die;* ~**,** ~**en** piece of news; ~**en** news *sing.*

Neu: ~**jahr** *das* New Year's Day; ~**land** *das* (fig.) new ground

neulich *Adv.* recently; ~ **morgens** the other morning

Neuling *der;* ~**s,** ~**e** newcomer; (auf einem Gebiet) novice

Neu·mond *der* new moon

neun *Kardinalz.* nine

Neun *die;* ~**,** ~**en** nine

neun-: ~**hundert** *Kardinalz.* nine hundred; ~**jährig** *Adj.* (9 Jahre alt) nine-year-old ⟨*attrib.*⟩; (9 Jahre dauernd) nine-year ⟨*attrib.*⟩; ~**mal** *Adv.* nine times

neunt... *Ordinalz.* ninth

neun·tausend *Kardinalz.* nine thousand

Neuntel *das* (schweiz. meist *der*); ~**s,** ~: ninth

neuntens *Adv.* ninthly

neun·zehn *Kardinalz.* nineteen

neunzig *Kardinalz.* ninety

neunziger *indekl. Adj.* **die** ~ **Jahre** the nineties

neunzigst... *Ordinalz.* ninetieth

neuralgisch *Adj.* **(a)** (Med.) neuralgic
(b) (empfindlich) **das ist mein** ~**er Punkt** it's a sore *or* touchy point with me

neu·reich *Adj.* nouveau riche

Neurodermitis *die;* ~**,** **Neurodermitiden** (Med.) neurodermatitis

Neurologe *der;* ~**n,** ~**n** neurologist

Neurologie *die;* ~: neurology

Neurologin *die;* ~**,** ~**nen** neurologist

neurologisch *Adj.* neurological

Neurose *die;* ~**,** ~**n** (Med., Psych.) neurosis

Neurotiker *der;* ~**s,** ~**, Neurotikerin** *die;* ~**,** ~**nen** (Med., Psych., auch ugs.) neurotic

neurotisch *Adj.* (Med., Psych., auch ugs.) neurotic

Neu·see·land (*das*); ~**s** New Zealand

Neuseeländer *der;* ~**s,** ~**,** **Neuseeländerin** *die;* ~**,** ~**nen** New Zealander

neutral 1 *Adj.* neutral
2 *adv.* **sich** ~ **verhalten** remain neutral

Neutralität *die;* ~**,** ~**en** neutrality

Neutron *das;* ~**s,** ~**en** neutron

Neutrum *das;* ~**s, Neutra** (österr. nur so) *od.* **Neutren** (Sprachw.) neuter

neu-, Neu-: ~**wert** *der* value when new; ~**wertig** *Adj.* as new; ~**zeit** *die* modern age; ~**zeitlich** *Adj.* modern

nicht *Adv.* not; ~**!** [no,] don't!; ~ **rostend** non-rusting ⟨*blade*⟩; stainless ⟨*steel*⟩; ⋯⋗

~ **[wahr]?** isn't it/he/she *etc.;* don't you/we/they *etc.;* **du magst das,** ~ **[wahr]?** you like that, don't you?; **was du** ~ **sagst!** you don't say!

nicht-, Nicht- non-

Nicht·angriffs·pakt *der* nonaggression pact

Nichte *die;* ~, ~n niece

nichtig *Adj.* **(a)** (geh.) vain ⟨*things, pleasures, etc.*⟩; trivial ⟨*reason*⟩ **(b)** (Rechtsspr.) void

Nicht·raucher *der* non-smoker; „~raucher" 'no smoking'

*nicht·rostend ▶ NICHT

nichts *Indefinitpron.* nothing; **ich möchte** ~: I don't want anything; ~ **sagend** (fig.) empty; (ausdruckslos) expressionless ⟨*face*⟩

nichts·desto·weniger *Adv.* nevertheless; none the less

nichts-, Nichts-: ~**nutz** *der;* ~~es, ~~e (veralt.) good-for-nothing; ~**nutzig** *Adj.* (veralt.) good-for-nothing *attrib.;* worthless ⟨*existence*⟩; *~**sagend** ▶ NICHTS; ~**tun** *das* idleness *no art.*

Nicht·wähler *der,* **Nicht·wählerin,** *die* non-voter; abstainer

Nickel *das;* ~s nickel

nicken *itr. V.* nod

nie *Adv.* never

nieder ① *Adj.; nicht präd.* lower ⟨*class, intelligence*⟩; minor ⟨*official*⟩; lowly ⟨*family, origins, birth*⟩; menial ⟨*task*⟩ ② *Adv.* down

nieder-, Nieder-: ~**gang** *der* fall; decline; ~**gehen** *unr. itr. V.; mit sein* ⟨*plane etc., rain, avalanche*⟩ come down; ~**geschlagen** *Adj.* dejected; ~**geschlagenheit** *die;* ~: dejection; ~**lage** *die* defeat

Nieder·lande *Pl.:* **die** ~: the Netherlands

Niederländer *der;* ~s, ~: Dutchman

Niederländerin *die;* ~, ~nen Dutchwoman

niederländisch *Adj.* Dutch; Netherlands *attrib.* ⟨*government, embassy, etc.*⟩

nieder-, Nieder-: ~**lassen** *unr. refl. V.* **(a)** set up in business; ⟨*doctor, lawyer*⟩ set up in practice; **(b)** (seinen Wohnsitz nehmen) settle; ~**lassung** *die;* ~~, ~~en (Wirtsch.) branch; ~**legen** *tr. V.* **(a)** (geh.: hinlegen) lay *or* put down; lay ⟨*wreath*⟩; **(b)** (fig.) resign [from] ⟨*office*⟩; relinquish ⟨*command*⟩

Nieder·sachsen *(das)* Lower Saxony

nieder-, Nieder-: ~**schlag** *der* precipitation; ~**schlagen** *unr. tr. V.* **(a)** jmdn. ~schlagen knock sb. down; **(b)** (beenden) suppress, put down ⟨*revolt, uprising, etc.*⟩; **(c)** (senken) lower ⟨*eyes, eyelids*⟩; ~**schmetternd** *Adj.* shattering ⟨*experience, news*⟩; devastating ⟨*result, review*⟩; ~**trächtig** ① *Adj.*

malicious ⟨*person, slander, lie, etc.*⟩; (verachtenswert) despicable ⟨*person*⟩; base ⟨*misrepresentation, slander, lie*⟩; ② *adv.* ⟨*betray, lie, treat*⟩ in a despicable way; ~**trächtigkeit** *die;* ~~, ~~en **(a)** ▶ ~TRÄCHTIG 1: maliciousness; despicableness; baseness; **(b)** (gemeine Handlung) despicable act

Niederung *die;* ~, ~en low-lying area; (an Flussläufen, Küsten) flats *pl.;* (Tal) valley

niedlich ① *Adj.* sweet; cute (Amer. coll.) ② *adv.* sweetly

niedrig ① *Adj.* low; lowly ⟨*origins, birth*⟩; base ⟨*instinct, desire, emotion*⟩; vile ⟨*motive*⟩ ② *adv.* ⟨*hang, fly*⟩ low

Niedrig-: ~**lohn·land** *das* country with a low-wage country; ~**wasser** *das* **(a)** (von Seen/Flüssen) **bei** ~**wasser** when the [level of the] lake/river is low; **(b)** (bei Ebbe) low tide; low water; **bei** ~**wasser** at low tide *or* low water

niemals *Adv.* never

niemand *Indefinitpron.* nobody; no one

Niemands·land *das* (auch fig.) no man's land

Niere *die;* ~, ~n kidney

Nieren-: ~**entzündung** *die* nephritis; ~**stein** *der* kidney stone

nieseln *unpers. itr. V.* drizzle

Niesel·regen *der* drizzle

niesen *itr. V.* sneeze

Niete¹ *die;* ~, ~n **(a)** (Los) blank **(b)** (ugs.: Mensch) dead loss (coll.) **(in** + *Dat.* at)

Niete² *die;* ~, ~n rivet

nieten *tr. V.* rivet

niet- und nagelfest: [alles] was nicht ~ **ist** (ugs.) [everything] that's not nailed *or* screwed down

Nikolaus /'nɪkolaʊs/ *der;* ~, ~e (ugs.) Nikoläuse **(a)** St Nicholas **(b)** (Tag) St Nicholas' Day

Nikotin *das;* ~s nicotine

nikotin·arm *Adj.* low-nicotine *attrib.;* low in nicotine *pred.*

Nikotin·sucht *die* nicotine addiction

Nil *der;* ~[s] Nile

Nil·pferd *das* hippopotamus

nimm *Imperativ Sg. v.* NEHMEN

nippen *itr. V.* sip

nirgends, nirgend·wo *Adv.* nowhere

Nische *die;* ~, ~n niche; (Erweiterung eines Raumes) recess

nisten *itr. V.* nest

Nitrat *das;* ~[e]s, ~e nitrate

Niveau /ni'vo:/ *das;* ~s, ~s level; (Qualitäts~) standard

Nixe *die;* ~, ~n nixie; (mit Fischschwanz) mermaid

nobel *Adj.* **(a)** (geh.) noble; noble[-minded] ⟨*person*⟩ **(b)** (oft spött.: luxuriös) elegant; posh (coll.)

Nobel·preis *der* Nobel prize

noch [1] *Adv.* **(a)** ([wie] bisher) still; ~ **nicht** not yet; **sie sind immer** ~ **nicht da** they're still not here; **ich habe Großvater** ~ **gekannt** I'm old enough to have known grandfather; **er hat** ~ **Glück gehabt** he was lucky; **das geht** ~: that's [still] all right
(b) (als Rest einer Menge) **ich habe [nur]** ~ **zehn Euro** I've [only] ten euros left; **es sind** ~ **10 km bis zur Grenze** it's another 10 km. to the border
(c) (bevor etw. anderes geschieht) just; **ich will** ~ **[schnell] duschen** I just want to have a [quick] shower
(d) (irgendwann einmal) some time; one day; **er wird** ~ **anrufen/kommen** he will still call/come
(e) (womöglich) if you're/he's *etc.* not careful; **du kommst** ~ **zu spät!** you'll be late if you're not careful
(f) (drückt eine geringe zeitliche Distanz aus) only; **gestern habe ich ihn** ~ **gesehen** I saw him only yesterday
(g) (nicht später als) ~ **am selben Abend** the [very] same evening
(h) (außerdem, zusätzlich) **wer war** ~ **da?** who else was there?; ~ **etwas Kaffee?** [would you like] some more coffee?; **Geld/Kleider** *usw.* ~ **und** ~ heaps and heaps of money/clothes *etc.* (coll.)
(i) er ist ~ **größer [als Karl]** he is even taller [than Karl]; **er will** ~ **mehr haben** he wants even more; **jeder** ~ **so dumme Mensch versteht das** anyone, however stupid, can understand that
(j) wie heißt sie [doch] ~? [now] what's her name again?
[2] *Partikel* **das ist** ~ **Qualität!** that's what I call quality; **der wird sich** ~ **wundern** (ugs.) he's in for a surprise; **er kann** ~ **nicht einmal lesen** he can't even read
[3] *Konj.* (und auch nicht) nor; **weder ... noch** neither ... nor
noch·mals *Adv.* again
Nominativ *der;* ~**s,** ~**e** (Sprachw.) nominative [case]
nominieren *tr. V.* nominate
Nominierung *die;* ~, ~**en** nomination
Nonne *die;* ~, ~**n** nun
Nord (bes. Seemannsspr., Met.) ▶ NORDEN
nord-, Nord-: ~**afrika** (*das*) North Africa; ~**amerika** (*das*) North America; ~**deutsch** *Adj.* North German
Norden *der;* ~**s** north; **der** ~: the North; **nach** ~: northwards
Nord·irland (*das*) Northern Ireland
nordisch *Adj.* Nordic
Nord·kap *das* North Cape
nördlich [1] *Adj.* **(a)** (im Norden gelegen) northern
(b) (nach, aus dem Norden) northerly
(c) (aus dem Norden kommend, für den Norden typisch) Northern
[2] *adv.* northwards; ~ **von ...:** [to the]

north of ...
[3] *Präp. mit Gen.* [to the] north of
Nord-: ~**licht** *das* northern lights *pl.;* aurora borealis; **ein** ~**licht/**~**lichter** the northern lights; ~**pol** *der* North Pole
Nordrhein-Westfalen (*das*); ~**s** North Rhine-Westphalia
Nord·see *die;* ~: North Sea
nord·wärts *Adv.* northwards
Nord·wind *der* northerly wind
Nörgelei *die;* ~ (abwertend) grumbling
nörgeln *itr. V.* (abwertend) moan, grumble (**an** + *Dat.* about)
Norm *die;* ~, ~**en (a)** norm
(b) (geforderte Arbeitsleistung) quota
(c) (Sport) qualifying standard
(d) (technische, industrielle ~) standard
normal [1] *Adj.* normal
[2] *adv.* normally
Normal-benzin *das* ≈ two-star petrol (Brit.); regular (Amer.)
normalerweise *Adv.* normally
normalisieren [1] *tr. V.* normalize
[2] *refl. V.* return to normal
Normalität *die;* ~: normality *no def. art.*
Normal-zustand *der* normal state
Normandie *die;* ~: Normandy
normen *tr. V.,* **normieren** *tr. V.* standardize
Norwegen (*das*); ~**s** Norway
Norweger *der;* ~**s,** ~, **Norwegerin** *die;* ~, ~**nen** Norwegian
norwegisch *Adj.* Norwegian
Nostalgie *die;* ~: nostalgia
Not *die;* ~, **Nöte (a)** (Gefahr) **in** ~ **sein** be in desperate straits
(b) (Mangel, Armut) need; poverty [and hardship]; ~ **leiden** suffer poverty [and hardship]; **in** ~ **geraten/sein** encounter hard times/be suffering want [and deprivation]
(c) (Verzweiflung) distress
(d) (Sorge, Mühe) trouble; **mit knapper** ~: by the skin of one's teeth
(e) (veralt.: Notwendigkeit) necessity; **zur** ~: if need be
Notar *der;* ~**s,** ~**e** notary
Notariat *das;* ~**[e]s,** ~**e (a)** (Amt) notaryship
(b) (Kanzlei) notary's office
not-, Not-: ~**arzt** *der* doctor on [emergency] call; ~**aufnahme** *die* casualty department; casualty *no art.;* ~**ausgang** *der* emergency exit; ~**bremse** *die* emergency brake; ~**dienst** *der* ▶ BEREITSCHAFTSDIENST; ~**durft** *die;* ~ (geh.) **seine [große/kleine]** ~**durft verrichten** relieve oneself; ~**dürftig** [1] *Adj.* makeshift ‹shelter, repair›; scanty ‹cover, clothing›; [2] *adv.* scantily ‹clothed›
Note *die;* ~, ~**n (a)** (Zeichen) note
(b) *Pl.* (Text) music *sing.* ⋯⋗

(c) (Schul∼) mark

(d) (Eislauf, Turnen) score

Notebook /'nǝʊtbʊk; *das;* ∼s, ∼s (DV) notebook [computer]

not-, Not-: ∼**fall** *der* (a) emergency; (b) im ∼fall (nötigenfalls) if need be; ∼**falls** *Adv.* if need be; ∼**gedrungen** *Adv.* of necessity

notieren [1] *tr. V.* [sich (*Dat.*)] etw. ∼: make a note of sth.
[2] *itr. V.* (Börsenw., Wirtsch.) be quoted (mit at)

Notierung *die;* ∼, ∼en (Börsenw., Wirtsch.) quotation; (Preis) quoted [price] (für of); (von Devisen) rate (für for)

nötig [1] *Adj.* necessary; etw./jmdn. ∼ haben need sth./sb.
[2] *adv.* er braucht ∼ Hilfe he is in urgent need of help

nötigen *tr. V.* compel; force; (Rechtsspr.) coerce

Nötigung *die;* ∼, ∼en (bes. Rechtsspr.) intimidation; coercion

Notiz *die;* ∼, ∼en note; (Zeitungs∼) brief report; von jmdm./etw. [keine] ∼ nehmen take [no] notice of sth./sb.

Notiz-: ∼**block** *der; Pl.* ∼blocks, *schweiz.:* ∼blöcke notepad; ∼**buch** *das* notebook

not-, Not-: ∼**lage** *die* serious difficulties *pl.;* ∼**landen** *itr. V.; mit sein;* ich notlande, notgelandet, notzulanden do an emergency landing; ∼**landung** *die* emergency landing; ∼**leidend** *Adj.* needy; ∼**lösung** *die* stopgap; ∼**lüge** *die* evasive lie; (aus Rücksichtnahme) white lie

notorisch [1] *Adj.* notorious
[2] *adv.* notoriously

Not-: ∼**ruf** *der* (a) (Hilferuf) emergency call; (eines Schiffes) Mayday call; (b) (Nummer) emergency number; ∼**ruf·nummer** *die* emergency number; ∼**ruf·säule** *die* emergency telephone (mounted in a pillar); ∼**stand** *der* crisis; (Staatsrecht) state of emergency; ∼**unterkunft** *die* emergency accommodation *no pl., no indef. art.;* ∼**wehr** *die* self-defence

not·wendig *Adj.* necessary

Notwendigkeit *die;* ∼, ∼en necessity

Not·zucht *die* (Rechtsw. veralt.) rape; ∼ [an jmdm.] begehen *od.* verüben commit rape [on sb.]

Novelle *die;* ∼, ∼n (Literaturw.) novella

November *der;* ∼[s], ∼: November

Novität *die;* ∼, ∼en novelty; (neue Erfindung) innovation; (neue Schallplatte) new release; (neues Buch) new publication

Nr. *Abk.* = **Nummer** No

Nu *der:* im Nu in no time

Nuance /'nyãːsǝ/ *die;* ∼, ∼n nuance; (Grad) shade

nüchtern [1] *Adj.* (nicht betrunken; realistisch)

sober; (ungeschminkt) bare, plain ⟨*fact*⟩; der Patient muss ∼ sein the patient's stomach must be empty
[2] *adv.* soberly

Nüchternheit *die;* ∼: sobriety

nuckeln (ugs.) *itr. V.* suck (an + *Dat.* at)

Nudel *die;* ∼, ∼n piece of spaghetti/vermicelli/tortellini *etc.;* (als Suppeneinlage) noodle; ∼n (Teigwaren) pasta *sing.;* (als Suppeneinlage) noodles

Nugat /'nuːgat/ *der; auch das;* ∼s nougat

nuklear [1] *Adj.* nuclear
[2] *adv.* ∼ angetrieben nuclear-powered

Nuklear-: ∼**medizin** *die* nuclear medicine *no art.;* ∼**waffe** *die* nuclear weapon

null *Kardinalz.* nought; ∼ Komma sechs [nought] point six; gegen ∼ Uhr around twelve midnight

Null *die;* ∼, ∼en (a) nought; zero; in ∼ Komma nichts (ugs.) in less than no time; gleich ∼ sein (fig.) be practically zero; auf ∼ stehen ⟨*indicator, needle, etc.*⟩ be at zero (b) (ugs.: Versager) failure; dead loss (coll.)

Null-: ∼**punkt** *der* zero; ∼**summen·spiel** *das* zero-sum game

*****numerieren** ▶ NUMMERIEREN

*****Numerierung** ▶ NUMMERIERUNG

Numerus clausus *der;* ∼: *fixed number of students admissible to a university to study a particular subject;* numerus clausus

Nummer *die;* ∼, ∼n (a) number; ein Wagen mit [einer] Münchner ∼: a car with a Munich registration; ich bin unter der ∼ 242679 zu erreichen I can be reached on 242679
(b) (Ausgabe) issue
(c) (Größe) size

nummerieren *tr. V.* number

Nummerierung *die;* ∼, ∼en numbering

Nummern·schild *das* number plate; license plate (Amer.)

nun [1] *Adv.* now
[2] *Partikel* now; das hast du ∼ davon! it serves you right!; kommst du ∼ mit oder nicht? now are you coming or not?; ∼ gut [well], all right; ∼, ∼! now, come on; ∼ ja ...: well, yes ...

nur [1] *adv.* (a) (nicht mehr als) only; just (b) (ausschließlich) only; nicht ∼ ..., sondern auch ...: not only ..., but also ...; ∼ so zum Spaß just for fun
[2] *Konj.* but; ich kann dir das Buch leihen, ∼ nicht heute I can lend you the book, only not today
[3] *Partikel* wenn er ∼ hier wäre if only he were here; ∼ zu! go ahead; lass dich ∼ nicht erwischen just don't let me/them *etc.* catch you; was sollen wir ∼ tun? what on earth are we going to do?; so schnell er ∼ konnte just as fast as he could

Nürnberg (*das*); ∼s Nuremberg

nuscheln *tr., itr. V.* (ugs.) mumble

---

n

Nuss, *Nuß *die;* ~, **Nüsse** nut

Nuss-, *Nuß-: ~**baum** *der* walnut
tree; ~**knacker** *der* nutcrackers *pl.;*
~**schale** *die* nutshell

Nüster *die;* ~, ~**n** nostril

Nut *die;* ~, ~**en** (Technik) groove

Nutte *die;* ~, ~**n** (derb) tart (sl.); hooker
(Amer. sl.)

nutz-: ~**bar** *Adj.* usable; exploitable,
utilizable ⟨*mineral resources, invention*⟩;
cultivatable ⟨*land, soil*⟩; ~**bringend**
[1] *Adj.* useful; (gewinnbringend) profitable;
[2] *adv.* profitably

nutzen [1] *tr. V.* **(a)** use; exploit, utilize
⟨*natural resources*⟩; cultivate ⟨*land, soil*⟩;
harness ⟨*energy source*⟩; exploit ⟨*advantage*⟩
(b) (be-, ausnutzen) use; make use of
[2] *itr. V.* ▶ NÜTZEN 1

Nutzen *der;* ~**s** **(a)** benefit; **[jmdm.] von**
~ **sein** be of use [to sb.]
(b) (Profit) profit

nützen [1] *itr. V.* be of use (*Dat.* to); **nichts**
~: be no use
[2] *tr. V.* ▶ NUTZEN 1

nützlich *Adj.* useful

Nützlichkeit *die;* ~: usefulness

nutzlos [1] *Adj.* useless; (vergeblich) vain
attrib.; in vain *pred.*
[2] *adv.* uselessly; (vergeblich) in vain

Nutz·losigkeit *die;* ~: uselessness;
(Vergeblichkeit) futility

Nutznießer *der;* ~**s**, ~, **Nutznießerin**
die; ~, ~**nen** beneficiary

Nutzung *die;* ~, ~**en** use; (des Landes,
des Bodens) cultivation; (von Bodenschätzen)
exploitation; utilization; (einer Energiequelle)
harnessing

Nylon Ⓦ /'nailɔn/ *das;* ~**s** nylon

Nymphe *die;* ~, ~**n** (Myth., Zool.) nymph

Nymphomanin *die;* ~, ~**nen** (Psych.)
nymphomaniac

Oo

---

o, O *das;* ~, ~: o/O

ö, Ö *das;* ~, ~: o/O umlaut

O *Abk.* = **Ost[en]** E

Oase *die;* ~, ~**n** (auch fig.) oasis

ob *Konj.* **(a)** whether
(b) und ob! of course!

OB *Abk.* = **Oberbürgermeister[in]**

Obacht *die;* ~ (bes. südd.) caution; ~ **auf**
jmdn./etw. geben take care of sb./sth.;
(aufmerksam sein) pay attention to sb./sth.

Obdach *das;* ~**[e]s** (geh.) shelter

obdach·los *Adj.* homeless

Obdachlose *der/die; adj. Dekl.* homeless
person/man/woman; **die** ~**n** the homeless

Obdachlosen-: ~**heim** *das* hostel for
the homeless; ~**siedlung** *die* estate of
houses for the homeless

Obdachlosigkeit *die;* ~: homelessness

Obduktion *die;* ~, ~**en** (Med., Rechtsw.)
post mortem [examination]; autopsy

obduzieren *tr. V.* carry out *or* perform
a/the postmortem [examination] *or* autopsy
on

O-Beine *Pl.* bandy legs; bow legs

oben *Adv.* **(a)** hier/dort ~: up here/there;
weiter ~: further up; **nach** ~: upwards;
von ~: from above; **von** ~ **herab** (fig.)
condescendingly
(b) (im Gebäude) upstairs; **nach** ~: upstairs
(c) (am oberen Ende, zum oberen Ende hin) at
the top; **nach** ~ **[hin]** towards the top; **von**

~: from the top; ~ **ohne** topless
(d) (an der Oberseite) on top
(e) (in einer Hierarchie, Rangfolge) at the top
(f) ([weiter] vorn im Text) above; ~ **genannt**
above-mentioned

*oben·genannt ▶ OBEN F

Ober *der;* ~**s**, ~: waiter; **Herr** ~**!** waiter!

ober... *Adj.* upper *attrib.;* top *attrib.*

Ober-: ~**arm** *der* upper arm;
~**bekleidung** *die* outer clothing;
~**bürgermeister** *der* mayor;
~**cool** *Adj.* (ugs.) **(a)** (sehr gelassen)
ultra-cool; **(b)** (fabelhaft) really cool (coll.);
~**fläche** *die* surface; (Flächeninhalt) surface
area

oberflächlich [1] *Adj.* superficial
[2] *adv.* superficially

Ober·geschoss, *Ober·geschoß *das*
upper storey; **im fünften** ~: on the fifth floor
(Brit.) *or* (Amer.) the sixth floor

ober·halb [1] *Adv.* above; ~ **von** above
[2] *Präp. mit Gen.* above

Ober-: ~**hand** *die* **die** ~**hand [über**
jmdn./etw.] haben have the upper hand
[over sb./sth.]; **die** ~**hand [über jmdn./etw.]**
gewinnen/bekommen gain *or* get the upper
hand [over sb./sth.]; ~**haupt** *das* head;
(einer Verschwörung) leader; ~**hemd** *das*
shirt; ~**kiefer** *der* upper jaw; ~**körper**
der upper part of the body; ~**lippen·bart**
der moustache; ~**schenkel** *der* thigh;
~**schicht** *die* (Soziol.) upper class; ⋯⋮

∼schule *die* secondary school; **∼seite** *die* top

oberst... ▷ OBER...

Ober-: **∼stufe** *die* (Schulw.) upper school; **∼teil** *das od. der* top [part]; (eines Bikinis, Anzugs, Kleids usw.) top [half]; **∼wasser** *das* headwater; (fig.) **∼wasser haben** feel in a strong position; **∼wasser bekommen/kriegen** have one's hand strengthened

ob·gleich *Konj.* ▷ OBWOHL

obig *Adj.* above

Objekt *das;* ∼s, ∼e object; (Kaufmannsspr.: Immobilie) property

objektiv 1 *Adj.* objective
2 *adv.* objectively

Objektiv *das;* ∼s, ∼e lens

Objektivität *die;* ∼: objectivity

Obrigkeit *die;* ∼, ∼en authorities *pl.*

ob·schon *Konj.* (geh.) although

Obst *das;* ∼[e]s fruit

Obst-: **∼baum** *der* fruit tree; **∼garten** *der* orchard; **∼kuchen** *der* fruit flan

Obstler *der;* ∼s, ∼ (bes. südd.) fruit brandy

Obst-: **∼saft** *der* fruit juice; **∼salat** *der* fruit salad; **∼wein** *der* fruit wine

obszön 1 *Adj.* obscene
2 *adv.* obscenely

Obszönität *die;* ∼, ∼en obscenity

ob·wohl *Konj.* although; though

Ochse /ˈɔksə/ *der;* ∼n, ∼n (a) ox; bullock
(b) (salopp) numskull (coll.)

Ochsen·schwanz·suppe *die* oxtail soup

od. *Abk.* = **oder**

öde *Adj.* (a) deserted; desolate ⟨*area, landscape*⟩
(b) (unfruchtbar) barren
(c) (langweilig) tedious; dreary ⟨*life, time, existence*⟩

Öde *die;* ∼ ▷ ÖDE: desertedness; desolateness; barrenness; tediousness; dreariness

oder *Konj.* or; (in Fragen) **er ist doch hier, ∼?** he is here, isn't he? (zweifelnd) he is here – or isn't he?

Öd·land *das* uncultivated land

Œuvre /ˈøːvrə/ *das;* ∼, ∼s (geh.) œuvre

OEZ *Abk.* = **osteuropäische Zeit** EET

Ofen *der;* ∼s, Öfen heater; (Kohle∼) stove; (Back∼) oven; (Brenn∼, Trocken∼) kiln

Ofen·rohr *das* [stove] flue

offen 1 *Adj.* (a) open; **∼ bleiben** stay open; **etw. ∼ lassen** leave sth. open; **∼ stehen** be open; **ein ∼es Hemd** a shirt with the collar unfastened; **∼ haben** *od.* **sein** be open; **∼es Licht** a naked light
(b) (frei) vacant ⟨*job, post*⟩
(c) (ungewiss, ungeklärt) open ⟨*question*⟩; uncertain ⟨*result*⟩; **∼ bleiben** remain open;

⟨*decision*⟩ be left open
(d) (noch nicht bezahlt) outstanding ⟨*bill*⟩
(e) (freimütig, aufrichtig) frank [and open] ⟨*person*⟩; frank, candid ⟨*look, opinion, reply*⟩
2 *adv.* openly; **∼ gesagt** frankly; **to be frank**

offen·bar 1 *Adj.* obvious
2 *adv.* obviously

Offenbarung *die;* ∼, ∼en revelation

*****offen|bleiben** ▷ OFFEN 1A, C

Offen·heit *die;* ∼ ▷ OFFEN E: frankness [and openness]; candour

offen-: **∼kundig** 1 *Adj.* obvious;
2 *adv.* obviously; *****∼|lassen** ▷ OFFEN 1A;
∼sichtlich 1 *Adj.* obvious; 2 *adv.* obviously

offensiv 1 *Adj.* (a) offensive
(b) (Sport) attacking
2 *adv.* (a) offensively
(b) (Sport) **∼ spielen** play an attacking game

Offensive *die;* ∼, ∼n (auch Sport) offensive

*****offen|stehen** ▷ OFFEN 1A

öffentlich 1 *Adj.* public; state *attrib.*, [state-]maintained ⟨*school*⟩; **der ∼e Dienst** the civil service
2 *adv.* publicly; ⟨*perform, appear*⟩ in public

Öffentlichkeit *die;* ∼: public

offiziell 1 *Adj.* official
2 *adv.* officially

Offizier *der;* ∼s, ∼e, **Offizierin** *die;* ∼, ∼nen officer

öffnen 1 *tr. V.* open; turn on ⟨*tap*⟩; undo ⟨*coat, blouse, button, zip*⟩
2 *itr. V.* (a) [jmdm.] ∼: open the door [to sb.]
(b) (geöffnet werden) ⟨*shop, bank, etc.*⟩ open
3 *refl. V.* open

Öffner *der;* ∼s, ∼: opener

Öffnung *die;* ∼, ∼en opening

Öffnungs·zeiten *Pl.* opening times

Offroader /ɔfˈrəʊdɐ/ *der;* ∼s, ∼: offroader

oft *Adv.* **öfter, am öftesten** often; **wie oft soll ich dir noch sagen, dass ...?** how many [more] times do I have to tell you that ...?

öfter *Adv.* now and then

oftmals *Adv.* often; frequently

OG *Abk.* = **Obergeschoss**

ohne 1 *Präp. mit Akk.* without; **∼ mich!** [you can] count me out!; **∼ weiteres** *od.* **Weiteres** (leicht, einfach) easily; (ohne Einwand) readily
2 *Konj.* **∼ zu zögern** without hesitation

ohne·hin *Adv.* anyway

Ohnmacht *die;* ∼, ∼en (a) faint; **in ∼ fallen** faint
(b) (Machtlosigkeit) powerlessness; impotence

ohnmächtig 1 *Adj.* (a) unconscious; **∼ werden** faint; **∼ sein** have fainted
(b) (machtlos) powerless; impotent
2 *adv.* impotently; **∼ zusehen** watch helplessly

Ohr *das;* ∼[e]s, ∼en ear; **gute/schlechte ∼en haben** have good/poor hearing *sing.;*

jmdn. übers ∼ hauen (fig. ugs.) put one over on sb. (coll.)

Öhr *das,* ∼[e]s, ∼e eye

ohren-, Ohren-: ∼**arzt,** *der,* ∼**ärztin,** *die* otologist; ear specialist; ∼**betäubend** [1] *Adj.* ear-splitting; deafening; deafening ⟨applause⟩; [2] *adv.* deafeningly; ∼**sausen** *das;* ∼∼s ringing in the *or* one's ears; tinnitus (Med.); ∼**schmerz** *der* earache; ∼**schmerzen haben** have [an] earache *sing.*

ohr-, Ohr-: ∼**feige** *die* box on the ears; ∼**feigen** *tr. V.* jmdn. ∼feigen box sb.'s ears; **ich könnte mich** ∼**feigen!** (ugs.) I could kick myself!; ∼**läppchen** *das* ear lobe; ∼**ring** *der* earring; ∼**wurm** *der* **(a)** earwig; **(b)** (ugs.: Melodie) catchy tune; **ein** ∼**wurm sein** be really catchy

okay /o'ke/ (ugs.) *Interj., Adj., adv.* OK (coll.); okay (coll.)

öko-, Öko- eco-

Ökologie *die;* ∼: ecology

ökologisch [1] *Adj.* ecological [2] *adv.* ecologically

ökonomisch [1] *Adj.* **(a)** economic **(b)** (sparsam) economical [2] *adv.* economically

Öko-: ∼**produkt** *das* ecoproduct; environmentally friendly *or* safe product; ∼**steuer** *die* eco-tax; ∼**system** *das* ecosystem; ∼**tourismus** *der* ecotourism

Oktober *der;* ∼[s], ∼: October

ökumenisch *Adj.* (christl. Rel.) ecumenical

Öl *das;* ∼[e]s, ∼e oil; **in Öl malen** paint in oils

Öl-embargo *das* oil embargo

ölen *tr. V.* oil

Öl-: ∼**farbe** *die* **(a)** oil-based paint; **(b)** (zum Malen) oil paint; ∼**gemälde** *das* oil painting

ölig *Adj.* oily

Olive *die;* ∼, ∼n olive

Oliven-: ∼**baum** *der* olive tree; ∼**öl** *das* olive oil

Öl-: ∼**ofen** *der* oil heater; ∼**pest** *die* oil pollution *no indef. art.;* ∼**quelle** *die* oil well; ∼**sardine** *die* sardine in oil; **eine Dose** ∼**sardinen** a tin of sardines; ∼**teppich** *der* oil slick; ∼**wechsel** *der* (bes. Kfz-W.) oil change

Olympiade *die;* ∼, ∼n Olympic Games *pl.;* Olympics *pl.*

Olympia-: ∼**sieger** *der,* ∼**siegerin** *die* Olympic champion; ∼**stadion** *das* Olympic stadium

olympisch *Adj.* Olympic; **die Olympischen Spiele** the Olympic Games; the Olympics

Oma *die;* ∼, ∼s (fam.) granny (coll./child lang.)

Omelett /ɔm(ə)'lɛt/ *das;* ∼[e]s, ∼e *od.* ∼s omelette

Omi *die;* ∼, ∼s ▶ OMA

Omnibus *der;* ∼ses, ∼se omnibus (formal); (Privat- und Reisebus auch) coach

Onanie *die;* ∼: onanism *no art.;* masturbation *no art.*

onanieren *itr. V.* masturbate

Onkel *der;* ∼s, *od.* (ugs.) ∼s uncle

online /'ɔnlaɪn/ [1] *Adj.* online; ∼ **gehen** go online [2] *Adv.* online

Online-: ∼**banking** /-bɛŋkɪŋ/ *das;* ∼∼s (DV) online banking; ∼**shopping** *das* online shopping;

OP /o:'pe:/ *der;* ∼[s], ∼[s] *Abk.* = **Operationssaal**

Opa *der;* ∼s, ∼s (fam.) grandad (coll./child lang.)

Opal *der;* ∼s, ∼e opal

OPEC /'o:pɛk/ *die;* ∼: *Abk.* OPEC

Oper *die;* ∼, ∼n opera; (Opernhaus) Opera; opera house

Operation *die;* ∼, ∼en operation

Operations·saal *der* operating theatre (Brit.) *or* room

operativ [1] *Adj.*(Med.) operative [2] *adv.* (Med.) by operative surgery; **etw.** ∼ **entfernen** operate to remove sth.

Operette *die;* ∼, ∼n operetta

operieren [1] *tr. V.* operate on ⟨patient⟩ [2] *itr. V.* operate

Opern·glas *das* opera glass[es *pl.*]

Opfer *das;* ∼s, ∼ **(a)** sacrifice **(b)** (Geschädigter) victim

opfern *tr. V.* (auch fig.) sacrifice; offer up ⟨fruit, produce, etc.⟩

Opi *der* ∼s, ∼s ▶ OPA

Opium *das;* ∼s opium

opponieren *itr. V.* gegen jmdn./etw. ∼: oppose sb./sth.

Opposition *die;* ∼, ∼en opposition

oppositionell *Adj.* opposition *attrib.* ⟨group, movement, etc.⟩; ⟨newspaper, writer, artist, etc.⟩ opposed to the government

Optik *die;* ∼: optics *sing., no art.*

Optiker *der;* ∼s, ∼, **Optikerin** *die;* ∼, ∼nen optician

optimal [1] *Adj.* optimal; optimum *attrib.* [2] *adv.* jmdn. ∼ **beraten** give sb. the best possible advice

optimieren *tr. V.* optimize

Optimierung *die;* ∼, ∼en optimization

Optimismus *der;* ∼: optimism

Optimist *der;* ∼en, ∼en, **Optimistin** *die;* ∼, ∼nen optimist

optimistisch [1] *Adj.* optimistic [2] *adv.* optimistically

optisch [1] *Adj.* optical; visual ⟨impression⟩; **eine** ∼**e Täuschung** an optical illusion [2] *adv.* optically; visually ⟨impressive, effective⟩

orange /o'rãːʒ(ə)/ *indekl. Adj.* orange

Orange *die;* ∼, ∼n orange ⋯❖

Orangen-: ∼**marmelade** *die* orange marmalade; ∼**saft** *der* orange juice

Orchester /ɔr'kɛstɐ/ *das;* ∼s, ∼: orchestra

Orden *der;* ∼s, ∼ **(a)** order **(b)** (Ehrenzeichen) decoration

ordentlich ① *Adj.* **(a)** [neat and] tidy; neat ⟨*handwriting, clothes*⟩ **(b)** (anständig) respectable; proper ⟨*manners*⟩ **(c)** (planmäßig) ordinary ⟨*meeting*⟩; ∼**es Mitglied** full member **(d)** (ugs.: richtig) proper; real; **ein** ∼**es Stück Kuchen** a nice big piece of cake **(e)** (ugs.: recht gut) decent ⟨*wine, flat, marks, etc.*⟩; **ganz** ∼: pretty good ② *adv.* **(a)** tidily; neatly; ⟨*write*⟩ neatly **(b)** (anständig) properly **(c)** (ugs.: gehörig) ∼ **feiern** have a real good celebration (coll.) **(d)** (ugs.: recht gut) ⟨*ski, speak, etc.*⟩ really well

ordern *tr., itr. V.* (Kaufmannsspr.) order

Ordinal·zahl *die* ordinal [number]

ordinär ① *Adj.* vulgar ② *adv.* vulgarly

Ordinate *die;* ∼, ∼**n** (Math.) ordinate

ordnen *tr. V.* arrange; **sein Leben/seine Finanzen** ∼: straighten out one's life/put one's finances in order

Ordner *der;* ∼s, ∼ (Hefter) file

Ordnung *die;* ∼, ∼**en** order; (geregelter Ablauf) routine; ∼ **halten** keep things tidy; **in** ∼ **sein** (ugs.) be OK (coll.) *or* all right; **hier ist etw. nicht in** ∼: there's something wrong here; **sie ist in** ∼ (ugs.) she's OK (coll.); **in** ∼**!** (ugs.) OK! (coll.); all right!

ordnungs-, Ordnungs-: ∼**gemäß** ① *Adj.* ⟨*conduct etc.*⟩ in accordance with the regulations; ② *adv.* in accordance with the regulations; ∼**halber** *Adv.* as a matter of form; ∼**widrig** (Rechtsw.) ① *Adj.* ⟨*actions, behaviour, etc.*⟩ contravening the regulations; illegal ⟨*parking*⟩; ② *adv.* ∼**widrig parken** park illegally; ∼**widrigkeit** *die* (Rechtsw.) infringement of the regulations; ∼**zahl** *die* ordinal [number]

Organ *das;* ∼s, ∼**e** organ; (ugs.: Stimme) voice

Organisation *die;* ∼, ∼**en** organization

Organisator *der;* ∼s, ∼**en**, **Organisatorin** *die;* ∼, ∼**nen** organizer

organisatorisch *Adj.* organizational

organisch ① *Adj.* organic ② *adv.* organically

organisieren ① *tr. V.* organize ② *itr. V.* **gut** ∼ **können** be a good organizer ③ *refl. V.* organize

Organismus *der;* ∼, Organismen organism

Organist *der;* ∼en, ∼en, **Organistin** *die;* ∼, ∼**nen** organist

Organ·spender *der,* **Organ·spenderin** *die* organ donor

Orgasmus *der;* ∼, Orgasmen orgasm

Orgel *die;* ∼, ∼**n** organ

Orgie /'ɔrgiə/ *die;* ∼, ∼**n** (auch fig.) orgy

Orient /'oːriɛnt/ *der;* ∼s Middle East and south-western Asia (*including Afghanistan and Nepal*); **der Vordere** ∼: the Middle East

orientalisch *Adj.* oriental

orientieren ① *refl. V.* **(a)** get one's bearings **(b)** **sich über etw.** (*Akk.*) ∼ (fig.) inform oneself about sth. **(c)** **sich an etw.** (*Dat.*) ∼ (fig.) be oriented towards sth.; ⟨*policy, advertising*⟩ be geared towards sth ② *tr. V.* (unterrichten) inform (**über** + *Akk.* about)

Orientierung *die;* ∼ **(a)** **die** ∼ **verlieren** lose one's bearings **(b)** (Unterrichtung) **zu Ihrer** ∼: for your information

Orientierungs·sinn *der* sense of direction

original ① *Adj.* original ② *adv.* ∼ **italienischer Espresso** genuine Italian espresso coffee; **etw.** ∼ **übertragen** broadcast sth. live

Original *das;* ∼s, ∼**e** original

Original-: ∼**fassung** *die* original version; ∼**gemälde** *das* original painting

Originalität *die;* ∼: originality

Original·ton *der; Pl.* Original·töne (Film, Ferns.) direct sound; original sound

originell ① *Adj.* original ② *adv.* with originality

Orkan *der;* ∼[e]s, ∼**e** hurricane

Ornament *das;* ∼[e]s, ∼**e** ornament

Ort¹ /ɔrt/ *der;* ∼[e]s, ∼**e** place; (Dorf) village; (Stadt) town; **an** ∼ **und Stelle** there and then

Ort²: **vor** ∼ (fig.) on the spot

orthodox *Adj.* orthodox

Orthographie *die;* ∼, ∼**n** orthography

orthographisch ① *Adj.* orthographic; ∼**e Fehler** spelling mistakes ② *adv.* orthographically

Orthopäde *der;* ∼**n**, ∼**n** orthopaedic specialist

orthopädisch ① *Adj.* orthopaedic ② *adv.* orthopaedically

örtlich ① *Adj.* (auch Med.) local ② *adv.* (auch Med.) locally; ∼ **betäubt werden** be given a local anaesthetic

Ortschaft *die;* ∼, ∼**en** (Dorf) village; (Stadt) town

Orts-: ∼**gespräch** *das* (Fernspr.) local call; ∼**name** *der* place name; ∼**netz·kennzahl** *die* (Fernspr.) dialling code; area code (Amer.)

Öse *die;* ∼, ∼**n** eye

Ossi *der;* ∼s, ∼s (salopp) East German

Ost (bes. Seemannsspr., Met.) ▶ OSTEN

ost-, Ost-: ~**block** der Eastern bloc; ~**deutsch** Adj. Eastern German; (hist.: auf die DDR bezogen) East German; ~**deutschland** (das) Eastern Germany; (hist.: DDR) East Germany

Osten der; ~s east; der ~: the East; der **Ferne** ~: the Far East; der **Nahe** ~: the Middle East

Oster-: ~**ei** das Easter egg; ~**glocke** die daffodil; ~**hase** der Easter hare (said to bring children their Easter Eggs); ~**montag** der Easter Monday no def. art.

Ostern das; ~, ~: Easter; **Frohe** od. **Fröhliche** ~: Happy Easter!; **zu** ~: at Easter

Österreich (das); ~s Austria

Österreicher der; ~s, **Österreicherin** die ~, ~nen Austrian

österreichisch Adj. Austrian

Oster-sonntag der Easter Sunday no def. art.

Ost-europa (das) Eastern Europe

Ostler der; ~s, ~, **Ostlerin** die; ~, ~nen (ugs.) East German

östlich [1] Adj. (a) (im Osten gelegen) eastern (b) (nach, aus dem Osten) easterly

(c) (aus dem Osten kommend, für den Osten typisch; Politik) Eastern; ⟨influence, policies⟩ of the East
[2] adv. eastwards; ~ **von** …: [to the] east of …
[3] Präp. mit Gen. [to the] east of

Ost-see die; ~: Baltic [Sea]

ost-wärts Adv. eastwards

Ost-wind der easterly wind

Otter[1] der; ~s, ~ (Fisch~) otter

Otter[2] die; ~, ~n (Viper) adder; viper

Otto-motor der Otto engine

out /aut/ Adj. ~ **sein** (ugs.) be out

Outfit /'autfit/ das; ~[s], ~s outfit

Ouvertüre /uvɛr'tyːrə/ die; ~, ~n (auch fig.) overture (Gen. to)

oval Adj. oval

Ovation die; ~, ~en ovation; jmdm. ~**en darbringen** give sb. an ovation

Ozean der; ~s, ~e ocean

Ozean-dampfer der ocean liner

Ozon der od. das; ~s ozone

Ozon-: ~**alarm** der ozone alert; ~**loch** das hole in the ozone layer; ~**schicht** die ozone layer; ~**zerstörung** die ozone destruction

Pp

p, P /peː/ das; ~, ~: p/P

paar indekl. Indefinitpron. **ein** ~ …: a few …; (zwei od. drei) a couple of …

Paar das; ~[e]s, ~e pair; (Mann und Frau) couple; **ein** ~ **Würstchen** two sausages

paaren refl. V. ⟨animals⟩ mate; ⟨people⟩ copulate

Paar-lauf der pairs pl.

paar-mal Adv. **ein** ~ a few times; (zwei- oder dreimal) a couple of times

Paarung die; ~, ~en (Zool.) mating

paar-weise Adv. in pairs

Pacht die; ~, ~en lease; **etw. in** ~ **nehmen** lease sth.; **etw. in** ~ **haben** have sth. on lease; **etw. in** ~ **geben** lease sth.

pachten tr. V. lease

Pächter der; ~s, ~, **Pächterin** die; ~, ~nen leaseholder; (eines Hofes) tenant

Pacht-: ~**vertrag** der lease; ~**zins** der; Pl. ~~e rent

Pack[1] der; ~[e]s, ~e od. **Päcke (a)** pack (b) ▶ PACKEN

Pack[2] das; ~[e]s (ugs. abwertend) rabble

Päckchen das; ~s, ~ (a) package; (auch Postw.) small parcel; (Bündel) packet

(b) ▶ PACKUNG A

packen [1] tr. V. (a) pack (b) (fassen) grab [hold of]; (fig.) **Furcht packte ihn/er wurde von Furcht gepackt** he was seized with fear
[2] itr. V. (Koffer usw. ~) pack

Packen der; ~s, ~: pile; (zusammengeschnürt) bundle; (von Geldscheinen) wad

packend [1] Adj. gripping
[2] adv. grippingly

Pack-papier das [stout] wrapping paper

Packung die; ~, ~en (a) packet; pack (esp. Amer.) (b) (Med., Kosmetik) pack

Pädagoge der; ~n, ~n (Erzieher, Lehrer) teacher; (Wissenschaftler) educationalist

Pädagogik die; ~: [theory and methodology of] education

Pädagogin die; ~, ~nen ▶ PÄDAGOGE

pädagogisch [1] Adj. educational; **seine** ~**en Fähigkeiten** his teaching ability sing.
[2] adv. educationally ⟨sound, wrong⟩

Paddel das; ~s, ~: paddle

Paddel-boot das canoe

paddeln itr. V.; mit sein paddle; (als Sport) canoe

Päderast *der;* ∼en, ∼en pederast
pädophil *Adj.* paedophile
Pädophile *der; adj. Dekl.* paedophile
paffen ① *tr. V.* puff at ⟨*pipe etc.*⟩
② *itr. V.* puff away
Page /'pa:ʒə/ *der;* ∼n, ∼n bellboy
Paket *das;* ∼[e]s, ∼e pile;
(zusammengeschnürt) bundle; (Eingepacktes,
Post∼) parcel; (Packung) packet; pack (esp.
Amer.)
Paket-: ∼**karte** *die* parcel dispatch form;
∼**schalter** *der* parcels counter
Pakistan (*das*); ∼s Pakistan
Pakistaner *der;* ∼s, ∼, **Pakistanerin**
die; ∼, ∼nen, **Pakistani** *der;* ∼[s], ∼[s]
Pakistani
pakistanisch *Adj.* Pakistani
Pakt *der;* ∼[e]s, ∼e pact
paktieren *itr. V.* make *or* do a deal/deals
Palast *der;* ∼[e]s, **Paläste** palace
Palästina (*das*); ∼s Palestine
Palästinenser *der;* ∼s, ∼,
Palästinenserin *die;* ∼, ∼nen
Palestinian
palästinensisch *Adj.* Palestinian
Palaver /pa'la:vɐ/ *das;* ∼s, ∼ (ugs.
abwertend) palaver
palavern *itr. V.* (ugs. abwertend) palaver
Palette *die;* ∼, ∼n (a) palette
(b) (bes. Werbespr.: Vielfalt) diverse range; **die
ganze** ∼: the whole range
(c) (Technik, Wirtsch.: Untersatz) pallet
paletti *Adj.* **alles** ∼ (ugs.) everything's OK
(coll.) *or* all right
Palme *die;* ∼, ∼n palm [tree]
Palmtop ⓌZ /'pa:mtɔp/ *der;* ∼s, ∼s
palmtop
Pampelmuse *die;* ∼, ∼n grapefruit
Panade *die;* ∼, ∼n (Kochk.) breadcrumb
coating
Panama (*das*); ∼s Panama
Panama-kanal *der;* ∼s Panama Canal
Panel /'pɛnl̩/ *das;* ∼s, ∼s panel
Pan·flöte *die* pan pipes *pl.*
panieren *tr. V.* bread; coat ⟨*sth.*⟩ with
breadcrumbs
Panier·mehl *das* breadcrumbs *pl.*
Panik *die;* ∼, ∼en panic
Panik-: ∼**mache** *die;* ∼ (abwertend)
panicmongering; ∼**macher** *der,*
∼**macherin** *die* (abwertend) panicmonger
Panne *die;* ∼, ∼n (a) breakdown; (Reifen∼)
puncture; flat [tyre]
(b) (Missgeschick) mishap
Pannen-dienst *der* breakdown service
Panorama *das;* ∼s, **Panoramen** panorama
Panter, *Panther *der;* ∼s, ∼: panther
Pantoffel *der;* ∼s, ∼n backless slipper

Pantomime *die;* ∼, ∼n mime
Panzer *der;* ∼s, ∼ (a) (Milit.) tank
(b) (Zool.) armour *no indef. art.;* (von
Schildkröten, Krebsen) shell
Panzer·glas *das* bulletproof glass
panzern *tr. V.* armour[-plate]
Panzer·schrank *der* safe
Papa *der;* ∼s, ∼s (ugs.) daddy (coll.)
Papagei *der;* ∼en *od.* ∼s, ∼e[n] parrot
Paparazzo *der;* ∼s, **Paparazzi** paparazzo
Paperback /'peɪpəbæk/ *das;* ∼s, ∼s
paperback
Papi *der;* ∼s, ∼s (ugs.) daddy (coll.)
Papier *das;* ∼s, ∼e (a) paper
(b) *Pl.* (Ausweis[e]) [identity] papers
(c) (Finanzw.: Wert∼) security
Papier-: ∼**geld** *das* paper money;
∼**korb** *der* waste-paper basket
Pappe *die;* ∼, ∼n cardboard
Pappel *die;* ∼, ∼n poplar
päppeln *tr. V.* feed up
Papp·karton *der* cardboard box
Paprika *der;* ∼s, ∼[s] (a) pepper
(b) (Gewürz) paprika
Papst *der;* ∼[e]s, **Päpste**, **Päpstin** *die;* ∼,
∼nen pope
päpstlich *Adj.* papal
Para *der;* ∼s, ∼s para (coll.)
Parabel *die;* ∼, ∼n (a) (bes. Literaturw.)
parable
(b) (Math.) parabola
Parade *die;* ∼, ∼n parade
Parade-beispiel *das* perfect example
Paradeiser *der;* ∼s, ∼ (österr.) tomato
Paradies *das;* ∼es, ∼e paradise
paradiesisch *Adj.* paradisical; (herrlich)
heavenly
Paradigma *das;* ∼s, **Paradigmen**
paradigm
paradox *Adj.* paradoxical
Para·gleiten *das;* ∼s, **Para·gliding**
/'paraglaɪdɪŋ/ *das;* ∼s paragliding
Paragraph *der;* ∼en, ∼en section; (in
Vertrag) clause
parallel ① *Adj.* parallel
② *adv.* ∼ **verlaufen** run parallel (**mit, zu** to)
Parallele *die;* ∼, ∼n parallel
Parallelogramm *das;* ∼s, ∼e
parallelogram
Parallel·straße *die* street running
parallel (*Gen.* to)
Paralympiker *der;* ∼s, ∼,
Paralympikerin *die;* ∼, ∼nen
Paralympian
paralympisch *Adj.* Paralympic; **die
Paralympischen Spiele** the Paralympic
Games; the Paralympics
Para·nuss, *Para·nuß *die* Brazil nut
Parasit *der;* ∼en, ∼en (auch fig.) parasite
parat *Adj.* ready

Pardon /par'dõ/ *der od. das;* ~s pardon; ~!
I beg your pardon
Parfum /par'fõ:/, **Parfüm** *das;* ~s, ~s
perfume
Parfümerie *die;* ~, ~en perfumery
parfümieren *tr. V.* perfume
Pariser [1] *indekl. Adj.* Parisian; Paris
attrib.
  [2] *der;* ~s, ~ (a) (Einwohner) Parisian
  (b) (ugs.: Kondom) French letter (coll.)
Pariserin *die;* ~, ~nen Parisian
Parität *die;* ~, ~en parity
Park /park/ *der;* ~s, ~s park;
  (Schloss~ usw.) grounds *pl.*
Parka *der;* ~s, ~s parka
parken *tr., itr. V.* park; „Parken verboten!"
'No Parking'
Parkett *das;* ~[e]s, ~e (a) parquet floor
  (b) (Theater) [front] stalls *pl.;* parquet (Amer.)
Parkett-: ~**[fuß]boden** *der* parquet
floor; ~**handel** *der* (Börsenw.) floor trading
Park-: ~**gebühr** *die* parking fee; ~**haus**
das multi-storey car park
parkieren *tr., itr. V.* (schweiz.) ▶ PARKEN
Park-: ~**lücke** *die* parking space;
~**platz** *der* car park; parking lot (Amer.);
  (für ein einzelnes Fahrzeug) parking space;
~**scheibe** *die* parking disc; ~**schein**
der car park ticket; ~**uhr** *die* parking
meter; ~**verbot** *das* ban on parking;
im ~verbot stehen be parked illegally;
~**verbots·schild** *das* no-parking sign
Parlament *das;* ~[e]s, ~e parliament
Parlamentarier *der;* ~s, ~,
  Parlamentarierin *die;* ~, ~nen
member of parliament
parlamentarisch *Adj.* parliamentary
Parodie *die;* ~, ~n parody (auf + *Akk.* of)
Parole *die;* ~, ~n (a) (Wahlspruch) motto;
  (Schlagwort) slogan
  (b) (bes. Milit.: Kennwort) password
Partei *die;* ~, ~en (a) (Politik, Rechtsw.) party
  (b) (Gruppe, Mannschaft) side; **für jmdn.**
~ **ergreifen** *od.* **nehmen** side with sb.
Partei·gänger *der;* ~~s, ~~,
  Partei·gängerin *die;* ~, ~~nen (oft
abwertend) [loyal] party supporter
parteiisch [1] *Adj.* biased
  [2] *adv.* in a biased manner
parteilich [1] *adj.* (parteiisch) biased
  [2] *Adv.* in a biased manner
Parteilichkeit *die;* ~ (einseitige
Parteinahme) bias; partiality
partei-, Partei-: ~**los** *Adj.* (Politik)
independent ‹MP›; ~**lose** *der/die;*
adj. Dekl. (Politik) independent; person
not attached to a party; ~**nahme** *die;*
~~, ~~n partisanship; taking sides *no
art.;* ~**politik** *die* party politics *sing.;*
~**politisch** [1] *Adj.* party political;
  [2] *adv.* from a party political point of
view; ~**tag** *der* party conference *or* (Amer.)

convention
Parterre *das;* ~s, ~s ground floor; first
floor (Amer.)
Partie *die;* ~, ~n (a) part
  (b) (Spiel, Sport: Runde) game; (Golf) round
  (c) eine gute ~ **[für jmdn.] sein** be a good
match [for sb.]
Partisan *der;* ~s *od.* ~en, ~en,
  Partisanin *die;* ~, ~nen guerrilla; (gegen
Besatzungstruppen im Krieg) partisan
Partitur *die;* ~, ~en (Musik) score
Partizip *das;* ~s, ~ien /-'tsi:piən/
  (Sprachw.) participle
Partner *der;* ~s, ~, **Partnerin** *die;* ~,
~nen partner
Partnerschaft *die;* ~, ~en partnership
partnerschaftlich [1] *Adj.* ‹cooperation
etc.› on a partnership basis
  [2] *adv.* in a spirit of partnership
Partner-: ~**schule** *die* partner school;
~**stadt** *die* twin town (Brit.); sister
city *or* town (Amer.); ~**vermittlung**
die (a) matchmaking; (b) (Agentur)
[introduction and] matchmaking
agency; ~**vermittlungs·büro** *das:*
  ▶ PARTNER·VERMITTLUNG B
Party /'pa:ɐti/ *die;* ~, ~s party
Parzelle *die;* ~, ~n [small] plot [of land]
Pass, *Paß *der;* Passes, Pässe
  (a) (Reisepass) passport
  (b) (Gebirgspass; Ballspiele) pass
passabel [1] *Adj.* reasonable; presentable
  ‹appearance›
  [2] *adv.* reasonably well
Passage /pa'sa:ʒə/ *die;* ~, ~n
  (a) [shopping] arcade
  (b) (Abschnitt) passage
Passagier /pasa'ʒi:ɐ/ *der;* ~s, ~e
passenger; **blinder** ~: stowaway
Passagier-: ~**dampfer** *der* passenger
steamer; ~**flugzeug** *das* passenger
aircraft
Passagierin *die;* ~, ~nen passenger
Passagier·liste *die* passenger list
Pass·amt, *Paß·amt *das* passport office
Passant *der;* ~en, ~en, **Passantin** *die;*
~, ~nen passer-by
Pass·bild, *Paß·bild *das* passport
photograph
Pässe ▶ PASS
passen *itr. V.* (a) (die richtige Größe/Form
haben) fit
  (b) (geeignet sein) be suitable (auf + *Akk.*, zu
for); (harmonieren) ‹colour etc.› match; **zu etw./**
jmdm. ~: go well with sth./be well suited to
sb.; **zueinander** ~ ‹things› go well together;
  ‹two people› be suited to each other
  (c) (genehm sein) **jmdm.** ~ ‹time› suit sb.
  (d) (Kartenspiel) pass
passend *Adj.* (a) (geeignet) suitable ‹dress,
present, etc.›; right ‹words, expression,
moment› ⋯⋗

(b) (harmonierend) matching ⟨*shoes etc.*⟩
Pạss·foto, *Pạß·foto *das* ▸ PASSBILD
passierbar *Adj.* passable ⟨*road*⟩;
navigable ⟨*river*⟩; negotiable ⟨*path*⟩
passieren 1 *tr. V.* pass; **die Grenze**
∼: cross the border
2 *itr. V.; mit sein* happen
Passion *die;* ∼, ∼en **(a)** passion
(b) (christl. Rel.) Passion
passioniert *Adj.* passionate ⟨*collector,
card player, huntsman*⟩
passiv 1 *Adj.* passive
2 *adv.* passively
Passiv *das;* ∼s, ∼e (Sprachw.) passive
Passivität *die;* ∼: passivity
Pạssivraucher *der,*
Pạssivraucherin *die* passive smoker
pass-, *paß-, Pass-, *Paß-:
∼**kontrolle** *die* passport check;
∼**straße** *die* [mountain] pass road;
∼**wort** *das; Pl.* ∼wörter (DV) password;
∼**wort·geschützt** (DV) 1 *Adj.*
password-protected; 2 *adv.* with password
protection; ∼**zwang** *der* obligation to
carry a passport
Pạste *die;* ∼, ∼n paste
Pastẹll *das;* ∼[e]s, ∼e **(a)** (Farbton) pastel
shade
(b) (Maltechnik) pastel *no art.*
Pastẹll-: ∼**farbe** *die* pastel colour;
∼**ton** *der* pastel shade
Pastẹte *die;* ∼, ∼n **(a)** (gefüllte) vol-au-vent
(b) (in einer Schüssel o. Ä. gegart) pâté; (in einer
Hülle aus Teig gebacken) pie
pasteurisieren *tr. V.* pasteurize
Pastịlle *die;* ∼, ∼n pastille
Pạstor *der;* ∼s, ∼en, **Pastọrin** *die;* ∼,
∼nen pastor
Pate *der;* ∼n, ∼n godfather; (männlich od.
weiblich) godparent
Paten-: ∼**kind** *das* godchild; ∼**onkel**
der godfather; ∼**stadt** *die* ▸ PARTNERSTADT
patent (ugs.) 1 *Adj.* **(a)** (tüchtig) capable
(b) (zweckmäßig) ingenious
2 *adv.* ingeniously; neatly ⟨*solved*⟩
Patẹnt *das;* ∼[e]s, ∼e **(a)** (Schutz) patent;
etw. zum *od.* **als** ∼ **anmelden** apply for a
patent for sth.
(b) (Erfindung) [patented] invention
Patẹnt·amt *das* Patent Office
Paten·tante *die* godmother
patentieren *tr. V.* patent
Patẹnt-: ∼**lösung** *die* patent remedy
(für, zu for); ∼**rezept** *das* patent remedy
(gegen, für for)
Pater *der;* ∼s, ∼ *od.* **Pạtres** (kath. Kirche)
Father
Paternọster *der;* ∼s, ∼ (Aufzug)
paternoster [lift]
pathẹtisch 1 *Adj.* emotional ⟨*speech,*

manner⟩; melodramatic ⟨*gesture*⟩; pompous
⟨*voice*⟩
2 *adv.* emotionally; (dramatisch)
[melo]dramatically
Pathos *das;* ∼: emotionalism
Patience /pa'si̯ā:s/ *die;* ∼, ∼n [game of]
patience; ∼n/eine ∼ legen play patience/a
game of patience
Patient /pa'tsi̯ɛnt/ *der;* ∼en, ∼en,
Patiẹntin *die;* ∼, ∼nen patient
Patin *die;* ∼, ∼nen godmother
Patres ▸ PATER
Patriọt *der;* ∼en, ∼en, **Patriọtin** *die;* ∼,
∼nen patriot
patriọtisch 1 *Adj.* patriotic
2 *adv.* patriotically
Patriotịsmus *der;* ∼: patriotism
Patrọne *die;* ∼, ∼n cartridge
Patrouille /pa'trʊljə/ *die;* ∼, ∼n patrol
patrouillieren /patrʊl'ji:rən/ *itr. V.; auch
mit sein* be on patrol
Pạtsche *die;* ∼, ∼n (ugs.) ▸ KLEMME
pạtschen *itr. V., mit sein* (ugs.) splash
patsch·nạss, *pạtsch·naß *Adj.* (ugs.)
sopping wet
patt *Adj.* (Schach) stalemated
Pạtt *das;* ∼s, ∼s (Schach; auch fig.) stalemate
Pạtt·situation *die* [position of] stalemate
Pạtzer *der;* ∼s, ∼ (ugs.) slip (coll.); boob (coll.)
pạtzig (ugs.) 1 *Adj.* snotty (coll.); (frech)
cheeky
2 *adv.* snottily (coll.); (frech) cheekily
Pauke *die;* ∼, ∼n kettledrum; **auf die**
∼ **hauen** (ugs.) (feiern) paint the town red
(coll.); (sich lautstark äußern) come right out
with it
pauken (ugs.) 1 *tr. V.* swot up (Brit. sl.),
bone up on (Amer. coll.) ⟨*facts, figures, etc.*⟩;
Latein/Mathe ∼: swot up one's Latin/maths
2 *itr. V.* swot (Brit. sl.); (fürs Examen) cram
(coll.)
pausbäckig *Adj.* chubby-faced; chubby
⟨*face*⟩
pauschal 1 *Adj.* **(a)** all-inclusive ⟨*price,
settlement*⟩
(b) (verallgemeinernd) sweeping ⟨*judgement,
criticism, statement*⟩; indiscriminate
⟨*prejudice*⟩; wholesale ⟨*discrimination*⟩
2 *adv.* **(a)** ⟨*cost*⟩ all in all; ⟨*pay*⟩ in a lump
sum
(b) (ohne zu differenzieren) wholesale
Pauschale *die;* ∼, ∼n flat-rate payment
Pauschal-: ∼**preis** *der* flat rate;
(Inklusivpreis) all-in price; ∼**reise** *die*
package holiday; (mit mehreren Reisezielen)
package tour
Pause *die;* ∼, ∼n break; (Ruhe∼) rest;
(Theater) interval (Brit.); intermission (Amer.)
pausen *tr. V.* trace; (eine Lichtpause machen)
Photostat (*Brit.* ®)
pausen-, Pausen-: ∼**brot** *das*
sandwich (*eaten during break*); ∼**hof** *der*

---
*alte Schreibung – vgl. Hinweis auf S. x

school yard; **~los** 1 *Adj.* incessant ⟨*noise, moaning, questioning*⟩; continous ⟨*work, operation*⟩; 2 *adv.* incessantly; ⟨*work*⟩ non-stop

Pavian /'paːvi̯aːn/ *der;* ~s, ~e baboon

Pavillon /'pavɪljɔn/ *der;* ~s, ~s pavilion

Pazifik *der;* ~s Pacific

pazifisch *Adj.* Pacific ⟨*area*⟩; **der Pazifische Ozean** the Pacific Ocean

Pazifismus *der;* ~: pacifism *no art.*

Pazifist *der;* ~en, ~en, **Pazifistin** *die;* ~, ~nen pacifist

pazifistisch 1 *Adj.* pacifist 2 *adv.* in a pacifist way

PC *der;* ~[s], ~[s] (DV) PC

PDS *Abk.* = **Partei des Demokratischen Sozialismus** Party of Democratic Socialism

Peanuts /'piːnʌts/ *Pl.* peanuts (coll.)

Pech *das;* ~[e]s, ~e (a) pitch (b) (Missgeschick) bad luck

pech·schwarz *Adj.* (ugs.) jet-black

Pedal *das;* ~s, ~e pedal

Pedant *der;* ~en, ~en, **Pedantin** *die;* ~, ~nen pedant

pedantisch 1 *Adj.* pedantic 2 *adv.* pedantically

Pediküre *die;* ~, ~n pedicure

pediküren *tr. V.* pedicure

Pegel *der;* ~s, ~ (a) water level indicator; (Tide~) tide gauge (b) (Wasserstand) water level

peilen *tr. V.* take a bearing on ⟨*transmitter, fixed point*⟩

Pein *die;* ~ (geh.) torment

peinigen *tr. V.* (geh.) torment; (foltern) torture

peinlich 1 *Adj.* (a) embarrassing; awkward ⟨*question, position, pause*⟩; **es ist mir sehr ~:** I feel very bad (coll.) *or* embarrassed about it (b) (äußerst genau) meticulous 2 *adv.* (a) unpleasantly ⟨*surprised*⟩ (b) (überaus [genau]) meticulously

Peinlichkeit *die;* ~, ~en (a) embarrassment; **die ~ der Situation** the awkwardness of the situation (b) (Genauigkeit) meticulousness (c) (peinliche Situation) embarrassing situation

Peitsche *die;* ~, ~n whip

peitschen *tr. V.* whip; (fig.) ⟨*storm, waves, rain*⟩ lash

Pelikan *der;* ~s, ~e pelican

Pelle *die;* ~, ~n (bes. nordd.) skin; (abgeschält) peel

pellen (bes. nordd.) *tr., refl. V.* peel

Pell·kartoffel *die* potato boiled in its skin

Pelz *der;* ~es, ~e (a) fur; coat; (des toten Tieres) skin; pelt (b) (Material) fur; (~mantel) fur coat

Pelz·mantel *der* fur coat

Pendel *das;* ~s, ~: pendulum

pendeln *itr. V.* (a) swing [to and fro]; (mit weniger Bewegung) dangle (b) *mit sein* ⟨*bus, ferry, etc.*⟩ operate a shuttle service; ⟨*person*⟩ commute

Pendler *der;* ~s, ~, **Pendlerin** *die;* ~, ~nen commuter

penetrant 1 *Adj.* (a) penetrating ⟨*smell, taste*⟩; overpowering ⟨*stink, perfume*⟩ (b) (aufdringlich) pushing, (coll.) pushy ⟨*person*⟩; overbearing ⟨*tone, manner*⟩; aggressive ⟨*question*⟩ 2 *adv.* (a) overpoweringly (b) (aufdringlich) overbearingly

penibel 1 *Adj.* over-meticulous ⟨*person*⟩; (pedantisch) pedantic 2 *adv.* painstakingly; over-meticulously ⟨*dressed*⟩

Penis *der;* ~, ~se penis

pennen *itr. V.* (salopp) (a) (schlafen) kip (coll.) (b) (fig.: nicht aufpassen) be half asleep (c) (koitieren) **mit jmdm. ~:** sleep with sb.

Penner *der;* ~s, ~, **Pennerin** *die;* ~, ~nen (salopp) tramp (Brit.); hobo (Amer.)

Pensen ▸ PENSUM

Pension /pãˈzi̯oːn/ *die;* ~, ~en (a) (Ruhestand) **in ~ gehen** retire; **in ~ sein** be retired (b) (Ruhegehalt) [retirement] pension (c) (Haus für [Ferien]gäste) guest house (d) (Unterkunft u. Verpflegung) board

Pensionär /pãzi̯oˈnɛːɐ̯/ *der;* ~s, ~e, **Pensionärin** *die;* ~, ~nen retired civil servant

pensionieren *tr. V.* pension off; retire; **sich [vorzeitig] ~ lassen** take [early] retirement; **ein pensionierter Schulmeister/ Politiker** a retired schoolmaster/politician

Pensionierung *die;* ~, ~en retirement

Pensions-: **~alter** *das* retirement age; **~anspruch** *der* pension entitlement

Pensum *das;* ~s, **Pensen** work quota

per *Präp. mit Akk.* (a) (mittels) by; **~ Adresse X** care of X; c/o X (b) (Kaufmannsspr.: [bis] zum) by; (am) on (c) (Kaufmannsspr.: pro) per

perfekt 1 *Adj.* (a) perfect ⟨*crime, host*⟩; faultless ⟨*English, French, etc.*⟩ (b) **~ sein** (ugs.: abgeschlossen, fertig sein) be finalized 2 *adv.* perfectly

Perfekt *das;* ~s (Sprachw.) perfect

Perfektion *die;* ~: perfection

perfektionieren *tr. V.* perfect

Perfektionismus *der;* ~: perfectionism

Perfektionist *der;* ~en, ~en, **Perfektionistin** *die;* ~, ~nen perfectionist

perfektionistisch 1 *Adj.* perfectionist ⟨*standards etc.*⟩ 2 *adv.* in a perfectionist manner

Pergament·papier *das* greaseproof paper

Periode *die;* ~, ~n period

Perle *die;* ~, ~n **(a)** (auch fig.) pearl **(b)** (aus Holz, Glas o. Ä.) bead

Perlmutt *das;* ~s mother-of-pearl

Perlon ⓦ *das;* ~s ≈ nylon

Perser *der;* ~s, ~ **(a)** Persian **(b)** ▶ PERSERTEPPICH

Perserin *die;* ~, ~nen Persian

Perser·teppich *der* Persian carpet

Persianer *der;* ~s, ~ (Mantel) Persian lamb coat

Persien (*das*); ~s Persia

persisch *Adj.* Persian

Person *die;* ~, ~en person; (in der Dichtung, im Film) character

Personal *das;* ~s (in einem Betrieb o. Ä.) staff; (im Haushalt) domestic staff *pl.*

Personal-: ~**abbau** *der* reduction in staff; (in mehreren Abteilungen/Betrieben) staff cuts *pl.;* ~**abteilung** *die* personnel department; ~**ausweis** *der* identity card; ~**büro** *das* personnel office; ~**chef** *der,* ~**chefin** *die* personnel manager

Personalien *Pl.* personal particulars

Personal-: ~**kosten** *Pl.* (Wirtsch., Verwaltung) staff costs; ~**mangel** *der* staff shortage; ~**pronomen** *das* (Sprachw.) personal pronoun; ~**rat** *der* **(a)** (Ausschuss) staff council (*for civil servants*); **(b)** (Mitglied) staff council representative; ~**rätin** *die:* ▶ ~RAT B

Personen-: ~**kraftwagen** *der* (bes. Amtsspr.) private car *or* (Amer.) automobile; ~**nahverkehr** *der* local public transport; ~**name** *der* personal name; ~**wagen** *der* (Auto) [private] car; automobile (Amer.); (im Unterschied zum Lastwagen) passenger car *or* (Amer.) automobile; ~**zug** *der* stopping train

Personifikation *die;* ~, ~en personification

personifizieren *tr. V.* personify

Personifizierung *die;* ~, ~en personification

persönlich ① *Adj.* personal; ~ werden get personal ② *adv.* personally; (auf Briefen) 'private [and confidential]'

Persönlichkeit *die;* ~, ~en **(a)** personality **(b)** (Mensch) person of character; eine ~ sein have a strong personality; ~en des öffentlichen Lebens public figures

Perspektive *die;* ~, ~n perspective; (Blickwinkel) angle; (Zukunftsaussicht) prospect

Peru (*das*); ~s Peru

Peruaner *der;* ~s, ~, **Peruanerin** *die;* ~, ~nen Peruvian

peruanisch *Adj.* Peruvian

Perücke *die;* ~, ~n wig

pervers *Adj.* perverted

Perversion *die;* ~, ~en perversion

Pessimismus *der;* ~: pessimism

Pessimist *der;* ~en, ~en, **Pessimistin** *die;* ~, ~nen pessimist

pessimistisch ① *Adj.* pessimistic ② *adv.* pessimistically

Pest *die;* ~: plague

Pestizid *das;* ~s, ~e pesticide

Petersilie /petɐ'zi:liə/ *die;* ~: parsley

Petition *die;* ~, ~en (Amtsspr.) petition

Petroleum /pe'tro:leʊm/ *das;* ~s paraffin (Brit.); kerosene (Amer.)

Petrus (*der*); **Petri** (christl. Rel.: Apostel) St Peter

petzen (Schülerspr.) ① *itr. V.* tell tales; sneak (Brit. school coll.). ② *tr. V.* ~, **dass** ...: tell teacher/sb.'s parents that ...

Pf *Abk.* = **Pfennig**

Pfad *der;* ~[e]s, ~e path

Pfad-: ~**finder** *der* Scout; ~**finderin** *die;* ~, ~nen Guide (Brit.); girl scout (Amer.)

Pfaffe *der;* ~n, ~n (abwertend) cleric; Holy Joe (derog.)

Pfahl *der;* ~[e]s, Pfähle post; stake

Pfand *das;* ~[e]s, Pfänder **(a)** security; pledge (esp. fig.) **(b)** (für Flaschen usw.) deposit (**auf** + *Dat.* on)

pfänden *tr. V.* seize [under distress] (Law) ⟨*goods, chattels*⟩; attach ⟨*wages etc.*⟩ (Law)

pfand-, Pfand-: ~**flasche** *die* returnable bottle (*on which a deposit is payable*); ~**pflichtig** *Adj.* ⟨*container*⟩ on which a deposit is payable

Pfändung *die;* ~, ~en seizure; distraint (Law); (von Geldsummen, Vermögensrechten) attachment (Law)

Pfanne *die;* ~, ~n [frying] pan

Pfann·kuchen *der* **(a)** pancake **(b)** (Berliner) doughnut

Pfarrei *die;* ~, ~en **(a)** (Bezirk) parish **(b)** (Dienststelle) parish office **(c)** ▶ PFARRHAUS

Pfarrer *der;* ~s, ~ pastor; (anglikanisch) vicar; (von Freikirchen) minister

Pfarrerin *die;* ~, ~nen [woman] pastor; (in Freikirchen) [woman] minister

Pfarr·haus *das* vicarage; (katholisch) presbytery; (in Schottland) manse

Pfau *der;* ~[e]s, ~en peacock

Pfauen·auge *das* peacock butterfly

Pfd. *Abk.* = **Pfund** lb.

Pfeffer *der;* ~s, ~: pepper

Pfeffer-: ~**kuchen** *der* ≈ gingerbread; ~**minze** *die* peppermint [plant]; ~**minz·tee** *der* peppermint tea; ~**mühle** *die* pepper mill

pfeffern *tr. V.* season with pepper

Pfeffer·streuer *der;* ~s, ~: pepper pot

Pfeife *die;* ~, ~n pipe; (Triller~) whistle

pfeifen ···⟩ Pharmakologie ····

pfeifen ① *unr. itr. V.* whistle; ⟨*bird*⟩ sing; (auf einer Trillerpfeife o. Ä.) ⟨*policeman, referee, etc.*⟩ blow one's whistle; **auf jmdn./etw.** ~ (ugs.) not give a damn about sb./sth. ② *unr. tr. V.* whistle ⟨*tune etc.*⟩; ⟨*bird*⟩ sing ⟨*song*⟩; (auf einer Pfeife) pipe, play ⟨*tune etc.*⟩

Pfeil *der;* ~[e]s, ~e arrow

Pfeiler *der;* ~s, ~: pillar; (Brücken~) pier

Pfennig *der;* ~s, ~e pfennig; **es kostete damals 20** ~: it cost 20 pfennig[s] at that time

pferchen *tr. V.* cram; pack

Pferd *das;* ~[e]s, ~e horse; (Schachfigur) knight; **mit ihr kann man** ~**e stehlen** (ugs.) she's game for anything

Pferde-: ~**rennen** *das* horse race; (Sportart) horseracing; ~**schwanz** *der* (Frisur) ponytail; ~**stall** *der* stable

pfiff *1. u. 3. Pers. Sg. Prät. v.* PFEIFEN

Pfiff *der;* ~[e]s, ~e **(a)** whistle **(b)** (ugs.: besonderer Reiz) style

Pfifferling *der;* ~s, ~e chanterelle; **keinen** *od.* **nicht einen** ~ **wert sein** (ugs.) be not worth a bean (coll.)

pfiffig ① *Adj.* smart; bright ⟨*idea*⟩; artful ⟨*smile, expression*⟩ ② *adv.* artfully

Pfingsten *das;* ~, ~: Whitsun

Pfingst-: ~**montag** *der* Whit Monday *no def. art.;* ~**sonntag** *der* Whit Sunday *no def. art.*

Pfirsich *der;* ~s, ~e peach

Pflanze *die;* ~, ~n plant

pflanzen *tr. V.* plant

Pflanzen-öl *das* vegetable oil

pflanzlich *Adj.* plant *attrib.* ⟨*life, motif*⟩; vegetable ⟨*dye, fat*⟩

Pflaster *das;* ~s, ~ **(a)** (Straßen~) road surface; (auf dem Gehsteig) pavement; **ein teures/gefährliches** ~ (ugs.) an expensive/ dangerous place *or* spot to be **(b)** (Wund~) sticking plaster

pflastern *tr. (auch itr.) V.* surface; (mit Kopfsteinpflaster, Steinplatten) pave

Pflaster·stein *der* paving stone; (Kopfstein) cobblestone

Pflaume *die;* ~, ~n plum; **getrocknete** ~n [dried] prunes

Pflege *die;* ~: care; (Maschinen~, Fahrzeug~) maintenance; (fig.: von Beziehungen, Kunst, Sprache) cultivation; **jmdn./etw. in** ~ (*Akk.*) **nehmen** look after sb./sth.

pflege-, Pflege-: ~**bedürftig** *Adj.* needing care *or* attention *postpos.;* ⟨*person*⟩ in need of care; ~**bedürftig sein** need looking after; need attention; ~**eltern** *Pl.* foster-parents; ~**fall** *der;* **ein** ~**fall sein** be in [permanent] need of nursing; ~**heim** *das* nursing home (esp. Brit.); ~**kind** *das* foster-child; ~**leicht** *Adj.* easy-care *attrib.* ⟨*textiles, flooring*⟩

pflegen ① *tr. V.* look after; care for; take care of ⟨*skin, teeth, floor*⟩; look after ⟨*bicycle,*

car, machine⟩; look after, tend ⟨*garden, plants*⟩; cultivate ⟨*relations, arts, interests*⟩; foster ⟨*contacts, cooperation*⟩; pursue ⟨*hobby*⟩ ② *mod. V.* **etw. zu tun** ~: usually do sth.

Pflege·personal *das* nursing staff

Pfleger *der;* ~s, ~ **(a)** (Krankenpfleger) [male] nurse **(b)** (Tierpfleger) keeper

Pflegerin *die;* ~, ~nen **(a)** (Krankenpflegerin) nurse **(b)** (Tierpflegerin) keeper

Pflege·versicherung *die* (long-term) [nursing-]care insurance

Pflicht *die;* ~, ~en duty

pflicht-, Pflicht-: ~**bewusst,** ***~**bewußt** ① *Adj.* conscientious; ② *adv.* with a sense of duty; ~**bewusstsein,** ***~**bewußtsein** *das,* sense of duty; ~**fach** *das* compulsory subject; ~**gefühl** *das* sense of duty; ~**übung** *die* (fig.) ritual exercise; ~**verteidiger** *der,* ~**verteidigerin** *die* (Rechtsw.) defense counsel appointed by the court; assigned counsel

Pflock *der;* ~[e]s, Pflöcke peg

pflücken *tr. V.* pick

Pflug *der;* ~[e]s, Pflüge plough

pflügen *tr., itr. V.* plough

Pforte *die;* ~, ~n (Tor) gate; (Tür) door; (Eingang) entrance

Pförtner *der;* ~s, ~, **Pförtnerin** *die;* ~, ~nen porter; (eines Wohnblocks, Büros) doorkeeper; (am Tor) gatekeeper

Pförtner·loge *die* porter's lodge

Pfosten *der;* ~s, ~: post

Pfote *die;* ~, ~n paw

Pfropf *der;* ~[e]s, ~e blockage

pfropfen *tr. V.* (ugs.) cram; stuff; **gepfropft voll** crammed [full]; packed

Pfropfen *der;* ~s, ~: stopper; (Korken) cork; (für Fässer) bung

pfui *Interj.* ugh; ~ **rufen** boo

Pfund *das;* ~[e]s, ~e pound

Pfusch *der;* ~[e]s **(a)** (ugs. abwertend) **das ist** ~: it's a botch-up **(b)** (österr.: Schwarzarbeit) work done on the side (*and not declared for tax*); (nach Feierabend) moonlighting (coll.)

pfuschen *itr. V.* **(a)** (ugs. abwertend) botch it; do a botched-up job **(b)** (österr.: schwarzarbeiten) do work on the side (*not declared for tax*); (nach Feierabend) moonlight (coll.)

Pfütze *die;* ~, ~n puddle

Phänomen *das;* ~s, ~e phenomenon

Phantasie *usw.:* ▶ FANTASIE *usw.*

Pharma-: ~**berater** *der,* ~**beraterin** *die:* ▶ ~REFERENT; ~**industrie** *die* pharmaceutical industry

Pharmakologie *die;* ~: pharmacology *no art.*

Pharma·referent der,
Pharma·referentin die pharmaceutical
representative
pharmazeutisch Adj. pharmaceutical
Phase die; ~, ~n phase
Philosoph der; ~en, ~en philosopher
Philosophie die; ~, ~n philosophy
philosophieren itr. (auch tr.) V.
philosophize
Philosophin die; ~, ~nen philosopher
philosophisch ① Adj. philosophical;
⟨dictionary, principles⟩ of philosophy
② adv. philosophically
Phosphat das; ~[e]s, ~e (Chemie)
phosphate
Photo das; ~s, ~s ▸ Foto
photo-, Photo-: ~voltaik·anlage
/-vɔl'taɪk-/ die photovoltaic array;
~voltaisch /-vɔl'taɪʃ/ ① Adj.
photovoltaic; ② adv. photovoltaically
Phrase die; ~, ~n (abwertend) [empty]
phrase; cliché
Physik die; ~: physics sing., no art.
physikalisch Adj. physics attrib.
⟨experiment, formula, research, institute⟩;
physical ⟨map, process⟩
Physiker der; ~s, ~, **Physikerin** die;
~, ~nen physicist
physisch ① Adj. physical
② adv. physically
Pianist der; ~en, ~en, **Pianistin** die; ~,
~nen pianist
Pickel der; ~s, ~: pimple
picken ① itr. V. peck (nach at; an + Akk.,
gegen on, against)
② tr. V. ⟨bird⟩ peck; (ugs.) ⟨person⟩ pick
Picknick das; ~s, ~e od. ~s picnic
piek·fein (ugs.) ① Adj. posh (coll.)
② adv. poshly (coll.)
piepe, piep·egal Adj. [jmdm.] ~ sein
(ugs.) not matter at all [to sb.]; es ist mir ~
(ugs.) I don't give a damn
Piepen Pl. (salopp: Geld) dough sing. (coll.)
piep[s]en itr. V. (ugs.) squeak; ⟨small bird⟩
cheep; bei dir piept's wohl! (salopp) you must
be off your rocker (coll.); zum Piepen sein
(ugs.) be a hoot or a scream (coll.)
Pietät /piˈtɛːt/ die; ~: respect; (Ehrfurcht)
reverence
Pik das; ~[s], ~[s] (Kartenspiel) (a) (Farbe)
spades pl.
(b) (Karte) spade
pikant ① Adj. (a) piquant
(b) (fig.: witzig) ironical
(c) (verhüll.: schlüpfrig) racy ⟨joke, story⟩
② adv. piquantly ⟨seasoned⟩
pikiert ① Adj. piqued
② adv. ⟨reply, say⟩ in an aggrieved tone
Pilger der; ~s, ~, **Pilgerin** die; ~, ~nen
pilgrim

pilgern itr. V.; mit sein go on a pilgrimage
Pille die; ~, ~n pill
Pilot der; ~en, ~en, **Pilotin** die; ~, ~nen
pilot
Pils das; ~, ~: Pils
Pilz der; ~es, ~e fungus; (Speise~, auch fig.)
mushroom
PIN /pɪn/ die; ~, ~s PIN
Pinguin der; ~s, ~e penguin
Pinie /ˈpiːni̯ə/ die; ~, ~n [stone or
umbrella] pine
pinkeln itr. V. (salopp) pee (coll.)
Pinsel der; ~s, ~: brush; (Mal~)
paintbrush
Pinzette die; ~, ~n tweezers pl.
Pionier der; ~s, ~e (Milit.) sapper; (fig.:
Wegbereiter) pioneer
Pionier·arbeit die pioneering work
Pionierin die; ~, ~nen pioneer
Pipi das; ~s (Kinderspr.) ~ machen do wee-
wees (sl.); ~ müssen have to do wee-wees or
have a wee (sl.)
Pirat der; ~en, ~en, **Piratin** die; ~, ~nen
pirate
pissen itr. V. (derb) piss (coarse)
Pistazie /pɪsˈtaːtsi̯ə/ die; ~, ~n pistachio
Piste die; ~, ~n (Ski~) piste; (Renn~)
course; (Flugw.) runway
Pistole die; ~, ~n pistol
Pizza die; ~, ~s od. Pizzen pizza
Pkw, PKW /ˈpeːkaːveː/ der; ~[s], ~[s]
[private] car; automobile (Amer.)
plädieren itr. V. (Rechtsw.) plead (auf
+ Akk. for); (fig.) argue
Plädoyer /plɛdo̯aˈjeː/ das; ~s, ~s
(Rechtsw.) summing up (for the defence/
prosecution); (fig.) plea
Plage die; ~, ~n (a) nuisance
(b) (ugs.: Mühe) bother; trouble
plagen ① tr. V. (a) torment
(b) (ugs.: bedrängen) harass; (mit Bitten, Fragen)
pester
② refl. V. (a) (sich abmühen) slave away
(b) (leiden) sich mit etw. ~: be bothered by
sth.
Plagiat das; ~[e]s, ~e plagiarism no art.
Plakat das; ~[e]s, ~e poster
Plakette die; ~, ~n badge
Plan der; ~[e]s, Pläne (a) plan
(b) (Karte) map; plan
Plane die; ~, ~n tarpaulin
planen tr., itr. V. plan
Planet der; ~en, ~en planet
planieren tr. V. level; grade
Planier·raupe die bulldozer
Planke die; ~, ~n plank
plan-: ~los ① Adj. aimless; (ohne System)
unsystematic; ② adv. ▸ 1: aimlessly;
unsystematically; ~mäßig ① Adj.
(a) scheduled ⟨service, steamer⟩; ~mäßige
Ankunft/Abfahrt scheduled time of arrival/

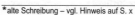

departure; **(b)** (systematisch) systematic;
2 *adv.* **(a)** (wie geplant) according to plan;
(pünktlich) on schedule; **(b)** (systematisch)
systematically

Plansch·becken *das* paddling pool

planschen *itr. V.* splash [about]

Plantage /plan'ta:ʒə/ *die;* ~, ~n
plantation

Planung *die;* ~, ~en planning

Plan·wirtschaft *die* planned economy

Plastik¹ *die;* ~, ~en sculpture

Plastik² *das;* ~s (ugs.) plastic

Plastik·beutel *der,* **Plastik·tüte** *die*
plastic bag

Platane *die;* ~, ~n plane tree

Platin *das;* ~s platinum

platschen *itr. V.* **(a)** splash
(b) *mit sein* (~d auftreffen) splash (**an** + *Akk.,*
gegen against)

plätschern *itr. V.* **(a)** splash; ⟨*rain*⟩
patter; ⟨*stream*⟩ burble
(b) *mit sein* ⟨*stream*⟩ burble along

platt *Adj.* flat; **ein Platter** (ugs.) a flat (coll.);
etw. ~ **machen** (salopp abwertend) close sth.
down

Platt *das;* ~[s] [local] Low German dialect

Plättchen *das;* ~s, ~: small plate *or* disc

platt·deutsch *Adj.* Low German

Platte *die;* ~, ~n (a) (Stein~) slab; (Metall~)
plate; sheet; (Span~, Hartfaser~ usw.) board;
(Tisch~) [table] top; (Grab~) [memorial] slab
(b) (Koch~) hotplate
(c) (Schall~) [gramophone] record
(d) (Teller) plate; (zum Servieren, aus Metall)
dish; **kalte** ~: selection of cold meats [and
cheese]

Platten·spieler *der* record player

Platt·fuß *der* **(a)** flat foot
(b) (ugs.: Reifenpanne) flat (coll.)

Platz *der;* ~es, Plätze **(a)** square
(b) (Sport~) ground; (Spielfeld) field; (Tennis~,
Volleyball~ usw.) court; (Golf~) course
(c) (Stelle, wo jmd., etw. hingehört) place; **nicht**
od. **fehl am** ~[e] **sein** (fig.) be out of place
(d) (Sitz~) seat; (am Tisch, Steh~ usw.) place;
~ **nehmen** sit down
(e) (bes. Sport: Platzierung) place
(f) (Ort) place; **am** ~: in the town/village
(g) (Raum) space; room; ~ **machen** make
room (*Dat.* for)

Platz·angst *die* (volkst.: Klaustrophobie)
claustrophobia

Plätzchen *das;* ~s, ~ **(a)** little place
(b) (Keks) biscuit (Brit.); cookie (Amer.)

platzen *itr. V.; mit sein* **(a)** burst;
(explodieren) explode
(b) (ugs.: scheitern) fall through; **der Wechsel/
das Treffen ist geplatzt** the bill has bounced
(coll.)/the meeting is off
(c) **in eine Versammlung** ~ (ugs.) burst into
a meeting

Platz-: ~**karte** *die* reserved-seat ticket;

~**konzert** *das* open-air concert (*by a
military or brass band*); ~**mangel** *der*
lack of space; ~**not** *die* [acute] lack of
space; ~**regen** *der* cloudburst; ~**wunde**
die lacerated wound

Plauderei *die;* ~, ~en chat

plaudern *itr. V.* chat

plausibel *Adj.* plausible

Play·boy /'pleɪbɔɪ/ *der* playboy

Player /'pleɪɐ/ *der;* ~, ~: player

pleite (ugs.) ~ **sein** ⟨*person*⟩ be broke (coll.);
⟨*company*⟩ have gone bust (coll.); *s. auch*
PLEITE A

Pleite *die;* ~, ~n (ugs.) **(a)** (Bankrott)
bankruptcy *no def. art.;* ~ **gehen/machen**
go bust (coll.)
(b) (Misserfolg) washout (coll.)

Pleite-: ~**geier** *der* (ugs.) spectre of
bankruptcy; ~**wirtschaft** *die* (ugs.)
bankrupt economy

Plissee *das;* ~s, ~s accordion pleats *pl.*

Plombe *die;* ~, ~n (a) (Siegel) [lead] seal
(b) (veralt.: Zahnfüllung) filling

plombieren *tr. V.* **(a)** (versiegeln) seal
(b) (veralt.) fill ⟨*tooth*⟩

plötzlich **1** *Adj.* sudden
2 *adv.* suddenly

Plötzlichkeit *die;* ~: suddenness

plump **1** *Adj.* **(a)** (dick) plump; (unförmig)
ungainly ⟨*shape*⟩; (rundlich) bulbous
(b) (schwerfällig) clumsy ⟨*movements, style*⟩
(c) (fig.) (dreist) crude ⟨*lie, deception, trick*⟩;
(leicht durchschaubar) blatantly obvious;
(unbeholfen) clumsy ⟨*excuse, advances*⟩; crude
⟨*joke, forgery*⟩
2 *adv.* **(a)** (schwerfällig) clumsily
(b) (fig.) in a blatantly obvious manner

Plumpheit *die;* ~ **(a)** (Dicke) plumpness;
(Unförmigkeit) ungainliness; (Rundlichkeit)
bulbousness
(b) (Schwerfälligkeit) clumsiness
(c) (abwertend: Dreistigkeit) blatant nature

plumps *Interj.* bump; thud; (ins Wasser)
splash; ~ **machen** go bump

Plumps *der;* ~es, ~e (ugs.) bump; thud; (ins
Wasser) splash

plumpsen *itr. V.* fall with a bump; thud;
(ins Wasser) splash

Plünderer *der;* ~s, ~, **Plünderin** *die;*
~, ~nen looter

plündern *itr., tr. V.* **(a)** loot; plunder
⟨*town*⟩
(b) (scherzh.) raid ⟨*larder, fridge, account*⟩

Plünderung *die;* ~, ~en looting; (einer
Stadt) plundering; ~en cases of looting/
plundering

Plural *der;* ~s, ~e plural

Pluralismus *der;* ~: pluralism

pluralistisch **1** *Adj.* pluralistic
2 *adv.* pluralistically; along pluralistic
lines

plus *Konj., Adv.* plus

Plus *das;* ∼: surplus; (Vorteil) advantage

Plüsch *der;* ∼[e]s, ∼e plush

Plusquam·perfekt *das* pluperfect [tense]

PLZ *Abk.* = **Postleitzahl**

Po *der;* ∼s, ∼s (ugs.) bottom

Pöbel *der;* ∼s rabble

pöbeln *itr. V.* make rude *or* coarse remarks

pochen *itr. V.* (klopfen) knock (**gegen/an** + *Akk.* at, on); (geh.: pulsieren) ⟨*heart*⟩ pound

Pocken *Pl.* smallpox *sing.*

Podest *das od. der;* ∼[e]s, ∼e rostrum

Podium *das;* ∼s, **Podien** (Plattform) platform; (Bühne) stage; (trittartige Erhöhung) rostrum

Poesie *die;* ∼: poetry

Poet *der;* ∼en, ∼en (veralt.) poet; bard (literary)

poetisch ⓵ *Adj.* poetic[al] ⓶ *adv.* poetically

Pogrom *das od. der;* ∼s, ∼e pogrom

Pointe /'poɛ̃:tə/ *die;* ∼, ∼n (eines Witzes) punch line; (einer Geschichte) point; (eines Sketches) curtain line

pointiert /poɛ̃'ti:ɐt/ ⓵ *Adj.* pointed ⟨*remark*⟩ ⓶ *adv.* pointedly

Pokal *der;* ∼s, ∼e (a) (Trinkgefäß) goblet (b) (Siegestrophäe, ∼wettbewerb) cup

Pökel·fleisch *das* salt meat

pökeln *tr. V.* salt

Poker *das od. der;* ∼s poker

Poker·gesicht *das* poker face

pokern *itr. V.* play poker

Pol *der;* ∼s, ∼e pole

Polar·licht *das* aurora; polar lights *pl.*

Polaroid·kamera Ⓦ *die* Polaroid camera ®

Pole *der;* ∼n, ∼n Pole

polemisch ⓵ *Adj.* polemic[al] ⓶ *adv.* polemically

Polen *das;* ∼s Poland

Polente *die;* ∼ (salopp) cops *pl.* (coll.)

Police /po'li:sə/ *die;* ∼, ∼n (Versicherungsw.) policy

polieren *tr. V.* polish

Poli·klinik *die* outpatients' clinic

Polin *die;* ∼n, ∼nen Pole

Polit·büro *das* politburo

Politik *die;* ∼, ∼en (a) politics *sing., no art.* (b) (eine spezielle ∼) policy

Politiker *der;* ∼s, ∼, **Politikerin** *die;* ∼, ∼nen politician

politisch ⓵ *Adj.* political ⓶ *adv.* politically

politisieren ⓵ *itr. V.* talk politics ⓶ *tr. V.* make politically active

Politur *die;* ∼, ∼en polish

Polizei *die;* ∼, ∼en police *pl.*

Polizei-: ∼**auto** *das* police car; ∼**beamte** *der* police officer; ∼**kontrolle** *die* police check

polizeilich ⓵ *Adj.* police; ∼e **Meldepflicht** obligation to register with the police ⓶ *adv.* by the police

Polizei-: ∼**präsidium** *das* police headquarters *sing. or pl.;* ∼**revier** *das* police station; ∼**streife** *die* police patrol; ∼**stunde** *die* closing time; ∼**wache** *die* police station

Polizist *der;* ∼en, ∼en policeman

Polizistin *die;* ∼, ∼nen policewoman

Pollen *der;* ∼s, ∼ (Bot.) pollen

Poller *der;* ∼s, ∼: bollard

polnisch *Adj.* Polish

Polster *das;* ∼s, ∼: upholstery *no pl., no indef. art.*

Polster·möbel *Pl.* upholstered furniture *sing.*

polstern *tr. V.* upholster ⟨*furniture*⟩

poltern *itr. V.* (a) crash about (b) *mit sein* **der Karren polterte über das Pflaster** the cart clattered over the cobblestones

Polyp *der;* ∼en, ∼en (Zool., Med.) polyp

Pommern (*das*) ∼s Pomerania

Pommes frites /pɔm'frit/ *Pl.* chips (Brit.); French fries (Amer.)

pompös ⓵ *Adj.* grandiose ⓶ *adv.* grandiosely

Pony¹ /'poni/ *das;* ∼s, ∼s pony

Pony² *der;* ∼s, ∼s (Frisur) fringe

Popel *der;* ∼s, ∼ (ugs.) bogy (sl.)

popelig (ugs. abwertend) ⓵ *Adj.* crummy (coll.); lousy (coll.); (durchschnittlich) second-rate ⓶ *adv.* crummily (sl.)

Popeline·mantel *der* poplin coat

popeln *itr. V.* (ugs.) [**in der Nase**] ∼: pick one's nose

Pop-: ∼**musik** *die* pop music; ∼**star** *der* pop star

populär ⓵ *Adj.* popular (**bei** with) ⓶ *adv.* popularly

popularisieren *tr. V.* popularize

Popularität *die;* ∼: popularity

Pore *die;* ∼, ∼n pore

Porno *der;* ∼s, ∼s (ugs.) porn[o] film/ magazine *etc.*

Pornographie *die;* ∼: pornography

pornographisch ⓵ *Adj.* pornographic ⓶ *adv.* pornographically

Porree *der;* ∼s leek

Portal *das;* ∼s, ∼e portal

Portemonnaie /pɔrtmɔ'ne:/ *das;* ∼s, ∼s purse

Porti *Pl.* ▶ PORTO

Portier /pɔr'tie:/ *der;* ∼s, ∼s, österr.: /pɔr'ti:ɐ/ *der;* ∼s, ∼e porter

Portion /pɔr'tsi̯o:n/ *die;* ∼, ∼en (a) (beim Essen) portion; helping

(b) (ugs.: Anteil) amount

Porto *das;* ~s, ~s *od.* **Porti** postage (**für** on, for)

Portugal (*das*); ~s Portugal

Portugiese *der;* ~n, ~n, **Portugiesin** *die;* ~, ~nen Portuguese

portugiesisch *Adj.* Portuguese

Portwein *der* port

Porzellan *das;* ~s porcelain; china

Posaune *die;* ~, ~n trombone

Position /pozi'tsio:n/ *die;* ~, ~en position

positiv ☐ *Adj.* positive
☐ *adv.* positively

Positiv *das;* ~s, ~e (Fot.) positive

Possessiv·pronomen *das* (Sprachw.) possessive pronoun

Post *die;* ~, ~en (a) post (Brit.); mail; **etw. mit der** *od.* **per** ~ **schicken** send sth. by post *or* mail; **die** ~ **geht ab** (fig. ugs.) it's all happening; **ab 20 Uhr geht die** ~ **ab** (fig. ugs.)it'll all be happening from 8 o'clock; **auch beim Publikum geht die** ~ **ab** (fig. ugs.) the audience is having a ball too (coll.)
(b) (Postamt) post office

Post-: ~**amt** *das* post office; ~**anweisung** *die* postal remittance form; ~**auto** *das* mail van; ~**bote** *der* (ugs.) postman (Brit.); mailman (Amer.); ~**botin** *die* (ugs.) postwoman (Brit.); mailwoman (Amer.)

Posten *der;* ~s, ~ (a) post
(b) (bes. Milit.: Wachmann) sentry

post-, Post-: ~**fach** *das* post office *or* PO box; (im Büro, Hotel usw.) pigeonhole; ~**karte** *die* postcard; ~**lagernd** *Adj., adv.* poste restante; general delivery (Amer.); ~**leit·zahl** *die* postcode; Zip code (Amer.); ~**stempel** *der* (Abdruck) postmark; ~**wendend** *Adv.* by return [of post]

potent *Adj.* potent

Potenz *die;* ~, ~en (a) potency
(b) (Math.) power

potenzieren *tr. V.* (Math.) **mit 5** ~: raise to the power [of] 5

Pracht *die;* ~: splendour

prächtig,

pracht·voll ☐ *Adj.* splendid
☐ *adv.* splendidly

prädestiniert *Adj.* predestined

Prädikat *das;* ~[e]s, ~e (a) (Auszeichnung) rating
(b) (Sprachw.) predicate

Prag (*das*); ~s Prague

prägen *tr. V.* (a) emboss
(b) mint ⟨coin⟩
(c) (fig.: beeinflussen) shape

prägnant ☐ *Adj.* concise; succinct
☐ *adv.* concisely; succinctly

Prägung *die;* ~, ~en embossing; (von Münzen) minting

prahlen *itr. V.* boast, brag (**mit** about)

Prahler *der;* ~s, ~: boaster; braggart

Prahlerei *die;* ~, ~en (abwertend) boasting; bragging; ~en boasts

Prahlerin *die;* ~, ~nen boaster; braggart

Praktik *die;* ~, ~en practice

Praktika ▸ PRAKTIKUM

praktikabel *Adj.* practicable; practical

Praktikant *der;* ~en, ~en, **Praktikantin** *die;* ~, ~nen (a) (in einem Betrieb) student trainee
(b) (an der Hochschule) physics/chemistry student (*doing a period of practical training*)

Praktikum *das;* ~s, **Praktika** period of practical training

praktisch ☐ *Adj.* practical; ~**er Arzt** general practitioner
☐ *adv.* practically; (auf die Praxis bezogen; wirklich) in practice

praktizieren *tr. V.* practise

Praline *die;* ~, ~n [filled] chocolate

prall *Adj.* (a) hard ⟨ball⟩; bulging ⟨sack, wallet, bag⟩; big strong *attrib.* ⟨thighs, muscles, calves⟩; well-rounded ⟨breasts⟩
(b) (intensiv) blazing ⟨sun⟩

prallen *itr. V.; mit sein* crash (**gegen/auf/an** + *Akk.* into); collide (**gegen/auf/an** + *Akk.* with)

Prämie /'prɛ:miə/ *die;* ~, ~n
(a) (Leistungs~; Wirtschaft) bonus; (Belohnung) reward; (Spar~, Versicherungs~) premium
(b) (einer Lotterie) [extra] prize

prämieren *tr. V.* award a prize to ⟨person, film⟩; give an award for ⟨best essay etc.⟩

Pranger *der;* ~s, ~ (hist.) pillory

Pranke *die;* ~, ~n paw

Präparat *das;* ~[e]s, ~e preparation

präparieren ☐ *tr. V.* prepare
☐ *refl. V.* (geh.: sich vorbereiten) prepare oneself

Präposition *die;* ~, ~en (Sprachw.) preposition

Prärie *die;* ~, ~n prairie

Präsens /'prɛ:zɛns/ *das;* ~ (Sprachw.) present [tense]

präsentieren *tr. V.* present

Präservativ *das;* ~s, ~e condom

Präsident *der;* ~en, ~en, **Präsidentin** *die;* ~, ~nen president

Präsidium *das;* ~s, **Präsidien**
(a) committee
(b) (Vorsitz) chairmanship
(c) (Polizei~) police headquarters *sing. or pl.*

prasseln *itr. V.* pelt down; ⟨shots⟩ clatter; ⟨fire⟩ crackle

prassen *itr. V.* live extravagantly; (schlemmen) feast

Präteritum *das;* ~s (Sprachw.) preterite [tense]

Prävention *die;* ~, ~en prevention

Praxis *die;* ~, **Praxen (a)** (im Unterschied zur Theorie) practice *no art.;* (Erfahrung) [practical] experience ····⟫

p

(b) (eines Arztes, Anwalts usw.) practice; (Räume) (eines Arztes) surgery (Brit.); office (Amer.); (eines Anwalts usw.) office

präzise ⊡ *Adj.* precise
⊡ *adv.* precisely

Präzision *die;* ~: precision

predigen ⊡ *itr. V.* deliver a/the sermon
⊡ *tr. V.* preach

Prediger *der;* ~s, ~, **Predigerin** *die;* ~, ~nen preacher

Predigt *die;* ~, ~en sermon

Preis *der;* ~es, ~e **(a)** (Kaufpreis) price (**für** of)
(b) (Belohnung) prize

Preis-: ~**anstieg** *der* rise *or* increase in prices; ~**aus·schreiben** *das* [prize] competition; ~**bindung** *die* (Wirtsch.) price-fixing

Preisel·beere *die* cranberry

preisen *unr. tr. V.* (geh.) praise

preis-, Preis-: ~**erhöhung** *die* price increase *or* rise; ~**geld** *das* prize money; ~**günstig** ⊡ *Adj.* ⟨goods⟩ available at unusually low prices; ⟨purchases⟩ at favourable prices; inexpensive ⟨holiday⟩; **das** ~**günstigste Angebot** the best bargain *or* value; **das ist [sehr] ~günstig** that is [very] good value; ⊡ *adv.* at a low price; **etw. ~günstig herstellen/verkaufen/ bekommen** produce/sell/get sth. at a low price; ~**kampf** *der* price war; ~**liste** *die* price list; ~**nachlass**, ***~**nachlaß** *der* price reduction; ~**richter** *der*, ~**richterin** *die* judge; ~**schild** *das* price tag; ~**senkung** *die* price reduction *or* cut; ~**steigerung** *die* rise *or* increase in prices; ~**tafel** *die* price list; ~**träger** *der*, ~**trägerin** *die* prizewinner; ~**verleihung** *die* presentation [of prizes/awards]; ~**wert** ⊡ *Adj.* good value *pred.*; ⊡ *adv.* ⟨eat⟩ at a reasonable price; **dort kann man ~wert einkaufen** you get good value for money there

prellen *tr. V.* **(a)** (betrügen) cheat (**um** out of); **die Zeche** ~: avoid paying the bill
(b) (verletzen) bash; bruise

Prellung *die;* ~, ~en bruise

Premiere /prə'mi̯e:rə/ *die;* ~, ~n opening night

Presse *die;* ~, ~n **(a)** press; (Zitronen~) squeezer
(b) (Zeitungen) press

Presse-: ~**erklärung** *die* press statement; ~**freiheit** *die* freedom of the press; ~**information** *die* press release; ~**konferenz** *die* press conference; ~**meldung** *die* press report

pressen *tr. V.* press

Presse·sprecher *der*, ~**sprecherin** *die* spokesman; press officer

Press·luft-, *Preß·luft-: ~**bohrer**

der pneumatic drill; ~**hammer** *der* pneumatic hammer

Prestige /prɛs'ti:ʒə/ *das;* ~s prestige

prickeln *itr. V.* tingle

pries *1. u. 3. Pers. Sg. Prät. v.* PREISEN

Priester *der;* ~s, ~: priest

Priesterin *die;* ~, ~nen priestess

prima (ugs.) ⊡ *indekl. Adj.* great (coll.)
⊡ *adv.* ⟨taste⟩ great (coll.); ⟨sleep⟩ fantastically well (coll.)

primär ⊡ *Adj.* primary
⊡ *adv.* primarily

Primel *die;* ~, ~n primula; (Schlüsselblume) cowslip

primitiv ⊡ *Adj.* primitive; (einfach, schlicht) simple
⊡ *adv.* primitively; (einfach, schlicht) in a simple manner

Prim·zahl *die* (Math.) prime [number]

Prinz *der;* ~en, ~en prince

Prinzessin *die;* ~, ~nen princess

Prinzip *das;* ~s, ~ien /-'tsi:pi̯ən/ principle; **aus** ~: on principle; **im** ~: in principle

prinzipiell ⊡ *Adj.* in principle *postpos., not pred.*; ⟨rejection⟩ on principle
⊡ *adv.* (im Prinzip) in principle; (aus Prinzip) on principle

Prion *das;* ~s, ~en (Biol.) prion

Prise *die;* ~, ~n pinch

privat ⊡ *Adj.* private; (persönlich) personal
⊡ *adv.* privately

Privat-: ~**adresse** *die* private *or* home address; ~**angelegenheit** *die* private matter; ~**besitz** *der* private property; ~**eigentum** *das* private property

privatisieren *tr. V.* (Wirtsch.) privatize; transfer into private ownership

Privatisierung *die;* ~, ~en (Wirtsch.) privatization; transfer into private ownership

Privat-: ~**leben** *das* private life; ~**lehrer** *der*, ~**lehrerin** *die* private tutor; ~**patient** *der*, ~**patientin** *die* private patient; ~**schule** *die* private school; (Eliteschule in Großbritannien) public school; ~**unterricht** *der* private tuition; ~**vermögen** *das* private fortune; ~**versicherung** *die* private insurance; ~**weg** *der* private way; ~**wirtschaftlich** *Adj.* private-sector *attrib.*

privilegiert *Adj.* privileged

pro *Präp. mit Akk.* per; ~ **Stück** each; a piece

pro- pro-; ~**westlich**/~**kommunistisch** pro-western/pro-communist

Probe *die;* ~, ~n **(a)** test
(b) (Muster, Teststück) sample
(c) (Theater~, Orchester~) rehearsal

Probe-: ~**fahrt** *die* trial run; (vor dem Kauf, nach einer Reparatur) test drive; ~**jahr** *das* probationary year

---

proben *tr., itr. V.* rehearse

probe-weise *Adv.* ⟨*employ*⟩ on a trial basis

Probe-zeit *die* probationary period

probieren ① *tr. V.* (a) try; have a go at (b) (kosten) taste; try (c) (aus~) try out; (an~) try on ⟨*clothes, shoes*⟩ ② *itr. V.* (a) (versuchen) try (b) (kosten) have a taste

Problem *das;* ~s, ~e problem

problematisch *Adj.* problematic[al]

problematisieren *tr. V. etw.* ~: expound the problems of sth.

problem-los ① *Adj.* problem-free ② *adv.* without any problems

Product placement /'prɔdaktpleɪsmənt/ *das;* ~s, ~s product placement

Produkt *das;* ~[e]s, ~e (auch Math., fig.) product

Produktion *die;* ~, ~en production

produktiv ① productive; prolific ⟨*writer, artist, etc.*⟩ ② *adv.* ⟨*work, cooperate*⟩ productively

Produktivität *die;* ~: productivity

Produzent *der;* ~en, ~en, **Produzentin** *die;* ~, ~nen producer

produzieren *tr. V.* produce

Prof. *Abk.* = **Professor** Prof.

professionell ① *Adj.* professional ② *adv.* professionally

Professor *der;* ~s, ~en, **Professorin** *die;* ~, ~nen professor

Professur *die;* ~, ~en professorship, chair (**für** in)

Profi *der;* ~s, ~s (ugs.) pro (coll.)

Profil *das;* ~s, ~e (a) (Seitenansicht) profile; **im** ~: in profile (b) (von Reifen, Schuhsohlen) tread

Profit *der;* ~[e]s, ~e profit

profitieren *itr. V.* profit (**von, bei** by)

profund *Adj.* (geh.) profound; deep

Prognose *die;* ~, ~n prognosis; (Wetter~, Wirtschafts~) forecast

prognostizieren *tr. V.* (geh.) forecast; predict

Programm *das;* ~s, ~e programme; program (Amer., Comp.); (Ferns.: Sender) channel

Programm-: ~**fehler** *der* (DV) program error; error in the/a program; ~**heft** *das* programme; ~**hinweis** *der* programme announcement

programmieren *tr. V.* (a) (DV) program (b) (auf etw. festlegen) programme

Programmierer *der;* ~s, ~, **Programmiererin** *die;* ~, ~nen (DV) programmer

Programm-: ~**vorschau** *die* (im Fernsehen) preview [of the week's/evening's *etc.* viewing]; (im Kino) trailers *pl.;*

~**zeitschrift** *die* radio and television magazine

progressiv ① *Adj.* progressive ② *adv.* progressively

Projekt *das;* ~[e]s, ~e project

Projekt-management *das* project management

Projektor /pro'jɛktɔr/ *der;* ~s, ~en / -'toːrən/ projector

Projekt-tage *Pl.* (Schulw.) project[-work] days

projizieren /proji'tsiːrən/ *tr. V.* (Optik) project

proklamieren *tr. V.* proclaim

Prolet *der;* ~en, ~en (abwertend) peasant

Proletariat *das;* ~[e]s proletariat

Proletarier /prole'taːriɐ/ *der;* ~s, ~: proletarian

proletarisch *Adj.* proletarian

prollig *Adj.* (salopp) boorish

Promenade *die;* ~, ~n promenade

Promille *das;* ~s, ~: [part] per thousand; **er fährt nur ohne** ~ (ugs.) he never drinks and drives; **er hatte 1,8** ~: he had a blood alcohol level of 1.8 per thousand

Promille-grenze *die* (ugs.) legal [alcohol] limit

prominent *Adj.* prominent

Prominente *der/die; adj. Dekl.* prominent figure

Prominenz *die;* ~: prominent figures *pl.*

Promotion /promo'tsioːn/ *die;* ~ (Wirtsch.) promotion; **für etw.** ~ **machen** promote sth.

promovieren ① *itr. V.* (a) (die Doktorwürde erlangen) gain *or* obtain a/one's doctorate (b) (eine Dissertation schreiben) do a doctorate (**über** + *Akk.* on) ② *tr. V.* confer a doctorate *or* the degree of doctor on

prompt ① *Adj.* prompt ② *adv.* (a) promptly (b) (ugs., meist iron.: wie erwartet) [and] sure enough

Promptheit *die;* ~: promptness

Pronomen *das;* ~s, ~ *od.* **Pronomina** (Sprachw.) pronoun

Propaganda *die;* ~: propaganda

propagieren *tr. V.* propagate

Propan-gas *das* propane

Propeller *der;* ~s, ~ propeller

Prophet *der;* ~en, ~en, **Prophetin** *die;* ~, ~nen prophet

prophezeien *tr. V.* prophesy (*Dat.* for); predict ⟨*result, weather*⟩

Proportion *die;* ~, ~en proportion

Prosa *die;* ~: prose

Prosa-literatur *die* prose writing

prosit *Interj.* your [very good] health; ~ **Neujahr!** happy New Year!

Prospekt *der od.* (bes. österr.) *das;* ~[e]s, ~e (Werbeschrift) brochure; (Werbezettel) leaflet

prost *Interj.* (ugs.) cheers (Brit. coll.)
Prostituierte *die/der; adj. Dekl.*
prostitute
Prostitution *die;* ~: prostitution *no art.*
Protagonist *der;* ~en, ~en,
Protagonistin *die;* ~, ~nen (geh.)
protagonist
Protest *der;* ~[e]s, ~e protest
Protestant *der;* ~en, ~en,
Protestantin *die;* ~, ~nen Protestant
protestantisch *Adj.* Protestant
Protestantismus *der;* ~: Protestantism
no art.
protestieren *itr. V.* protest, make a
protest (**gegen** against, about)
Protest·kundgebung *die* protest rally
Prothese *die;* ~, ~n artificial limb;
prosthesis (Med.); (Zahn~) set of dentures;
dentures *pl.*
Protokoll *das;* ~s, ~e (a) (wörtlich
mitgeschrieben) transcript; (Ergebnis~)
minutes *pl.;* (bei Gericht) record; **etw. zu**
~ **geben** make a statement about sth.
(b) (diplomatisches Zeremoniell) protocol
protokollieren 1 *tr. V.* take down; take
the minutes of ⟨*meeting*⟩; minute ⟨*remark*⟩
2 *itr. V.* take the minutes; (bei Gericht) keep
the record
protzen *itr. V.* (ugs.) swank (coll.); show off;
mit etw. ~: show sth. off
protzig (ugs. abwertend) 1 *Adj.* swanky
(coll.); showy
2 *adv.* swankily (coll.)
Proviant *der;* ~s, ~e provisions *pl.*
Provinz *die;* ~, ~en province
provinziell 1 *Adj.* provincial
2 *adv.* provincially
Provision *die;* ~, ~en (Kaufmannsspr.)
commission
provisorisch 1 *Adj.* provisional;
temporary
2 *adv.* temporarily
Pro·vitamin *das* provitamin
Provokation *die;* ~, ~en provocation
provozieren *tr. V.* provoke
Prozedur *die;* ~, ~en procedure
Prozent *das;* ~[e]s, ~e (a) *nach*
Zahlenangaben Pl. ungebeugt per cent *sing.;*
fünf ~: five per cent
(b) *Pl.* (ugs.) (Gewinnanteil) share *sing.* of
the profits; (Rabatt) discount *sing.;* **auf etw.**
(*Akk.*) ~**e bekommen** get a discount on sth.
-prozentig *adj.* -per-cent
Prozent-: ~**punkt** *der* percentage point;
~**rechnung** *die* percentage calculation;
~**satz** *der* percentage
prozentual 1 *Adj.* percentage
2 *adv.* ~ **am Gewinn beteiligt sein** have a
percentage share in the profits

Prozess, *Prozeß *der;* Prozesses,
Prozesse (a) trial; (Fall) [court] case; **einen**
~ **gewinnen/verlieren** win/lose a case
(b) (Vorgang) process
prozessieren *itr. V.* go to court; **gegen**
jmdn. ~: bring an action against sb.
Prozess·kosten, *Prozeß·kosten
Pl. legal costs
Prozessor *der;* ~s, ~en (DV) [central]
processor
prüde (abwertend) 1 *Adj.* prudish
2 prudishly
Prüderie *die;* ~ (abwertend) prudery;
prudishness
prüfen *tr. V.* (a) *auch itr.* examine ⟨*pupil,*
student, etc.⟩; **mündlich/schriftlich geprüft**
werden have an oral/a written examination
(b) (untersuchen) examine (**auf** + *Akk.* for);
check ⟨*device, machine, calculation*⟩ (**auf**
+ *Akk.* for); investigate ⟨*complaint*⟩; (testen)
test (**auf** + *Akk.* for)
(c) (kontrollieren) check; examine ⟨*accounts,*
books⟩
(d) (vor einer Entscheidung) check ⟨*price*⟩;
examine ⟨*offer*⟩; consider ⟨*application*⟩
Prüfer *der;* ~s, ~, **Prüferin** *die;* ~, ~nen
(a) inspector; (Buch~) auditor
(b) (im Examen) examiner
Prüfling *der;* ~s, ~e examinee;
[examination] candidate
Prüfung *die;* ~, ~en (a) examination;
exam (coll.); **eine** ~ **machen** *od.* **ablegen** take
an examination
(b) ▶ PRÜFEN B–D: examination; check;
investigation; test; consideration
Prügel *Pl.* (Schläge) beating *sing.;* (als Strafe
für Kinder) hiding (coll.)
Prügelei *die;* ~, ~en (ugs.) punch-up (coll.);
fight
Prügel·knabe *der* whipping boy
prügeln 1 *tr.* (*auch itr.*) *V.* beat
2 *refl. V.* **sich** ~: fight; **sich mit jmdm. [um**
etw.] ~: fight sb. [over *or* for sth.]
Prunk *der;* ~[e]s splendour; magnificence
Prunk-: ~**bau** *der; Pl.* ~~ten magnificent
building; ~**stück** *das* showpiece
PS /pe:'|ɛs/ *das;* ~, ~: *Abk.*
= **Pferdestärke** h.p.
Psalm *der;* ~s, ~en psalm
Psychiater *der;* ~s, ~, **Psychiaterin**
die; ~, ~nen psychiatrist
Psychiatrie *die;* ~: psychiatry *no art.*
psychisch 1 *Adj.* psychological; mental
⟨*process, illness*⟩
2 *adv.* psychologically; ~ **gesund/krank**
sein be mentally fit/ill
psycho-, Psycho- /psyço-/: ~**loge**
der; ~~n, ~~n psychologist; ~**logie**
die; ~~: psychology; ~**login** *die;* ~~,
~~nen psychologist; ~**logisch** 1 *Adj.*
psychological; 2 *adv.* psychologically;
~**path** *der;* ~~en, ~~en, ~**pathin** *die;*
~~, ~~nen psychopath

Psychose *die;* ~, ~n psychosis
psychotisch *Adj.* psychotic
pubertär *Adj.* pubertal
Pubertät *die;* ~: puberty
pubertieren *itr. V.* reach puberty; ~d
pubescent
publik *Adj.* ~ **sein/werden** be/become
public knowledge
Publikum *das;* ~s (a) (Zuschauer, Zuhörer)
audience; (bei Sportveranstaltungen) crowd
(b) (Kreis von Interessierten) public; (eines
Schriftstellers) readership
(c) (Besucher) clientele
Publikums-: ~**erfolg** *der* success
with the public; ~**liebling** *der* idol of the
public; ~**sport** *der* spectator sport
publizieren *tr. (auch itr.) V.* publish
Publizität *die;* ~: publicity
Pudding *der;* ~s, ~e *od.* ~s thick, *usually
flavoured, milk-based dessert;* ≈ blancmange
Pudel *der;* ~s, ~: poodle
Puder *der;* ~s, ~: powder
Puder-dose *die* powder compact
pudern *tr. V.* powder
Puder-zucker *der* icing sugar (Brit.);
confectioners' sugar (Amer.)
Puff¹ *der;* ~[e]s, Püffe (ugs.) (a) (Stoß)
thump; (leichter/kräftiger Stoß mit dem Ellenbogen)
nudge/dig
(b) (Knall) bang
Puff² *der od. das;* ~s, ~s (salopp: Bordell)
knocking shop (Brit. sl.); brothel
puffen (ugs.) *tr. V.:* ▶ Puff¹ A: thump;
nudge; dig
Puff-reis *der* puffed rice
Pulli *der;* ~s, ~s (ugs.), **Pullover** *der;* ~s,
~: pullover; sweater
Pullunder *der;* ~s, ~: slipover
Puls *der;* ~es, ~e pulse
Puls-ader *die* artery
Pult *das;* ~[e]s, ~e desk; (Lese~) lectern
Pulver *das;* ~s, ~: powder
pulverisieren *tr. V.* pulverize; powder
Pulver-kaffee *der* instant coffee
pumm[e]lig *Adj.* (ugs.) chubby
Pumpe *die;* ~, ~n pump
pumpen *tr., itr. V.* **(a)** (auch fig.) pump
(b) (salopp) ▶ LEIHEN A, B
Pump-: ~**spray** *das* pump spray;
~**zerstäuber** *der* pump-action atomizer
Punkt *der;* ~[e]s, ~e **(a)** (Tupfen) dot;
(größer) spot
(b) (Satzzeichen) full stop
(c) (I-Punkt) dot
(d) (Stelle) point; **ein schwacher/wunder** ~
(fig.) a weak/sore point
(e) (Gegenstand, Thema, Abschnitt) point; (einer
Tagesordnung) item
(f) (Bewertungs~) point; (bei einer Prüfung)
mark
(g) ~ **12 Uhr** at 12 o'clock on the dot

pünktlich ①*Adj.* punctual
②*adv.* punctually; on time
Pünktlichkeit *die;* ~: punctuality
Punsch *der;* ~[e]s, ~e *od.* Pünsche punch
Pupille *die;* ~, ~n pupil
Puppe *die;* ~, ~n (a) doll[y]
(b) (Marionette) puppet; marionette
Puppen-: ~**stube** *die* doll's house;
dollhouse (Amer.); ~**wagen** *der* doll's pram
pur *Adj.* **(a)** (rein) pure
(b) (unvermischt) neat ⟨whisky etc.⟩; straight
Püree *das;* ~s, ~s (a) purée
(b) ▶ KARTOFFELBREI
pürieren *tr. V.* (Kochk.) purée ⟨potatoes,
apples, etc.⟩; (zerstampfen) mash
Purpur *der;* ~s crimson
purzeln *itr. V.; mit sein* (fam.) tumble
pushen *tr. V.* **(a)** (Drogenjargon) push
(b) (Journalistenjargon) push
Puste *die;* ~ (salopp) puff; breath
Pustel *die;* ~, ~n pimple; pustule (Med.)
pusten (ugs.) *tr., itr. V.* blow
Pute *die;* ~, ~n turkey hen; (als Braten)
turkey
Puter *der;* ~s, ~: turkeycock; (als Braten)
turkey
Putsch *der;* ~[e]s, ~e putsch; coup [d'état]
putschen *itr. V.* organize a putsch *or* coup
Putsch-versuch *der* attempted putsch
or coup
Putz *der;* ~es plaster; (für Außenmauern)
rendering
putzen *tr. V.* **(a)** (blank reiben) polish
(b) (säubern) clean; groom ⟨horse⟩; [sich
(*Dat.*)] **die Zähne/die Nase** ~: clean *or* brush
one's teeth/blow one's nose
(c) *auch itr.* (sauber machen) clean ⟨room,
shop, etc.⟩; ~ **gehen** work as a cleaner
(d) (vorbereiten) wash and prepare
⟨vegetables⟩
Putz-: ~**fimmel** *der* (ugs. abwertend) mania
for cleaning; ~**frau** *die* cleaner
putzig *Adj.* (ugs.) (entzückend) sweet; cute
(Amer.); (possierlich) funny; comical
Putz-: ~**lappen** *der* [cleaning] rag; cloth;
~**leute** *Pl.* cleaners; ~**mann** *der* cleaner;
~**mittel** *das* cleaning agent; ~**tuch** *das;*
Pl. ~**tücher** cloth; (Lappen) [cleaning] rag
puzzeln /'pʊzl̩n/ *itr. V.* do jigsaw puzzles/a
jigsaw [puzzle]
Puzzle /'pʊzl/ *das;* ~s, ~s, **Puzzlespiel**
das jigsaw [puzzle]
Pyjama /pɪ'dʒaːma/ *der* (österr., schweiz.
auch: das); ~s, ~s pyjamas *pl.*
Pyramide *die;* ~, ~n pyramid
pyramiden-förmig *Adj.* pyramidal;
pyramid-shaped
Python *der;* ~s, ~s *od.* ~en,
Python-schlange *die* python

p

Qq

q, Q /kuː/ *das;* ~, ~: q, Q
Quacksalber *der;* ~s, ~,
 Quacksalberin *die;* ~, ~nen (abwertend)
 quack [doctor]
Quader *der;* ~s, ~ *od.* (österr.:) ~n
 (a) (Steinblock) ashlar block; [rectangular]
 block of stone
 (b) (Geom.) rectangular parallelepiped;
 cuboid
Quadrat *das;* ~[e]s, ~e square
quadratisch *Adj.* square
Quadrat-: ~**meter** *der od. das* square
 metre; ~**wurzel** *die* (Math.) square root
 (aus of); ~**zahl** *die* square number
quaken *itr. V.* ⟨*duck*⟩ quack; ⟨*frog*⟩ croak
Qual *die;* ~, ~en **(a)** torment
 (b) (Schmerzen) agony; ~en pain *sing.;* agony
 sing.; (seelisch) torment *sing.*
quälen *tr. V.* **(a)** torment ⟨*person, animal*⟩;
 be cruel to ⟨*animal*⟩; (foltern) torture
 (b) (plagen) ⟨*cough etc.*⟩ plague; (belästigen)
 pester
Quälerei *die;* ~, ~en **(a)** torment; (Folter)
 torture; (Grausamkeit) cruelty
 (b) (das Belästigen) pestering
Qualifikation *die;* ~, ~en **(a)** (Ausbildung)
 qualifications *pl.*
 (b) (Sport) qualification
qualifizieren *refl. V.* **(a)** gain
 qualifications
 (b) (Sport) qualify
qualifiziert *Adj.* **(a)** ⟨*work, post*⟩ requiring
 particular qualifications
 (b) (sachkundig) competent; skilled ⟨*work*⟩
Qualität *die;* ~, ~en quality
qualitativ ① *Adj.* qualitative; ⟨*difference,
 change*⟩ in quality
 ② *adv.* with regard to quality
Qualitäts-erzeugnis *das* quality
 product
Qualle *die;* ~, ~n jellyfish
Qualm *der;* ~[e]s [thick] smoke
qualmen *itr. V.* **(a)** give off clouds of
 [thick] smoke
 (b) (ugs.: rauchen) puff away
qualmig *Adj.* (ugs.) thick with smoke
 postpos.; smoke-filled
qual·voll ① *Adj.* agonizing
 ② *adv.* agonizingly
Quantität *die;* ~, ~en quantity
quantitativ ① *Adj.* quantitative
 ② *adv.* quantitatively
Quantum *das;* ~s, Quanten quota (an

+ *Dat.* of); (Dosis) dose
Quarantäne /karanˈtɛːnə/ *die;* ~, ~n
 quarantine
Quark *der;* ~s quark
Quark·speise *die* quark dish
Quartal *das;* ~s, ~e quarter [of the year]
Quartett *das;* ~[e]s, ~e **(a)** quartet
 (b) (Spiel) ≈ Happy Families; (Satz von vier
 Karten) set [of four]
Quartier *das;* ~s, ~e accommodation *no
 indef. art.;* accommodations *pl.* (Amer.); place
 to stay; (Mil.) quarters *pl.*
Quarz *der;* ~es, ~e quartz
Quarz·uhr *die* quartz clock; (Armbanduhr)
 quartz watch
quasi *Adv.* [so] ~: more or less; (so gut wie)
 as good as
quasseln (ugs.) ① *itr. V.* chatter; rabbit on
 (Brit. coll.) (von about)
 ② *tr. V.* spout, babble ⟨*nonsense*⟩
Quaste *die;* ~, ~n tassel
Quatsch *der;* ~[e]s (ugs.) **(a)** (Äußerung)
 rubbish
 (b) (Handlung) nonsense; (Unfug) messing
 about; **lass den** ~: stop that nonsense
quatschen (ugs.) ① *itr. V.* **(a)** (dumm reden)
 rabbit on (Brit. coll.)
 (b) (klatschen) gossip; **es wird so viel
 gequatscht** there is so much gossip
 (c) (sich unterhalten) [have a] chat *or* (coll.)
 natter
 ② *tr. V.* (äußern) spout ⟨*nonsense, rubbish*⟩
Quatsch·kopf *der* (salopp) stupid
 chatterbox; (Schwätzer, Schwafler) windbag
Queck·silber *das* mercury
Quell·bewölkung *die* (Met.) cumulus
 clouds *pl.*
Quelle *die;* ~, ~n spring; (eines Flusses; fig.)
 source
quellen *unr. itr. V.; mit sein* **(a)** ⟨*liquid*⟩
 gush, stream; (aus der Erde) well up; ⟨*smoke*⟩
 billow
 (b) (sich ausdehnen) swell [up]
Quell·wasser *das; Pl.* ~ *od.* Quell·wässer
 spring water
quengeln *itr. V. (auch tr.) V.* (ugs.) **(a)** (weinen)
 ⟨*baby*⟩ whimper, (coll.) grizzle
 (b) (drängen) nag
 (c) (nörgeln) carp
quer *Adv.* sideways; (schräg) diagonally;
 (rechtwinklig) at right angles; ~ **durch/über**
 (+ *Akk.*) straight through/across
Quer-: ~**achse** *die* transverse axis;
 ~**denker** *der,* ~**denkerin** *die* lateral
 thinker

---

*alte Schreibung – vgl. Hinweis auf S. x

Quere *die* jmdm. in die ~ **kommen** bump into sb. (coll.); (fig.: jmdn. behindern) get in sb.'s way (coll.)

quer-, Quer-: ~**flöte** *die* transverse flute; ~**format** *das* landscape format; ~**kopf** *der* (ugs.) awkward cuss (coll.); (komischer Kauz) oddball (coll.); ~**köpfig** *Adj.* awkward; perverse; ~**schläger** *der* deflected shot; ricochet; ~**schnitt** *der* (*auch fig.*) cross section; ~**schnitt[s]·gelähmt** *Adj.* (Med.) paraplegic; ~**straße** *die* intersecting road; ~**treiber** *der;* ~~s, ~~, ~**treiberin** *die;* ~~, ~~**nen** (ugs. abwertend) troublemaker

Querulant *der;* ~en, ~en, **Querulantin** *die;* ~, ~**nen** (abwertend) malcontent

quetschen *tr. V.* crush; sich (*Dat.*) die **Hand** ~: get one's hand caught

Quetschung *die;* ~, ~en bruise; contusion (Med.)

quietschen *itr. V.* squeak; ⟨brakes, tyres⟩

squeal, screech; (ugs.) ⟨person⟩ squeal, shriek

Quirl *der;* ~[e]s, ~e *long-handled blender with a star-shaped head*

quirlig *Adj.* lively; (flink) nimble

quitt *Adj.* (ugs.) quits

Quitte *die;* ~, ~n quince

quittieren *tr. V.* (a) *auch itr.* acknowledge, confirm ⟨receipt, condition⟩; give a receipt for ⟨sum, invoice⟩
(b) etw. mit etw. ~: react *or* respond to sth. with sth.

Quittung *die;* ~, ~en (a) receipt
(b) (fig.) come-uppance (coll.)

Quiz /kvɪs/ *das;* ~, ~: quiz

Quiz-: ~**sendung** *die* quiz programme; ~**show** *die* quiz show

quoll *1. u. 3. Pers. Sg. Prät. v.* QUELLEN

Quote *die;* ~, ~n proportion

Quoten·regelung *die: requirement that women should be adequately represented*

Quotient *der;* ~en, ~en (Math.) quotient (aus of)

Rr

r, R /ɛr/ *das;* ~, ~: r, R

Rabatt *der;* ~[e]s, ~e discount

Rabatte *die;* ~, ~n border

Rabbi *der;* ~[s], ~nen *od.* ~s (a) (Titel) Rabbi
(b) (Person) rabbi

Rabbiner *der;* ~s, ~: rabbi

Rabe *der;* ~n, ~n raven

Rabenmutter *die; Pl.* Rabenmütter (abwertend) uncaring [brute of a] mother

rabiat ⟨1⟩ *Adj.* violent; brutal; ruthless ⟨methods⟩
⟨2⟩ *adv.* (gewalttätig) violently; brutally

Rache *die;* ~: revenge; [an jmdm.] ~ nehmen take revenge [on sb.]

Rache·akt *der* (geh.) act of revenge, reprisal (*Gen.* by, on the part of)

rächen ⟨1⟩ *tr. V.* avenge ⟨person, crime⟩; take revenge for ⟨insult, crime⟩
⟨2⟩ *refl. V.* (a) take one's revenge
(b) ⟨mistake etc.⟩ take its/their toll

Rachen *der;* ~s, ~ (a) (Schlund) pharynx (Anat.)
(b) (Maul) mouth; maw (literary); (fig.) jaws *pl.*

Rachitis *die;* ~ (Med.) rickets *sing.*

Rach·sucht *die* (geh.) lust for revenge

rach·süchtig (geh.) ⟨1⟩ *Adj.* vengeful
⟨2⟩ *adv.* vengefully

Rad *das;* ~es, Räder (a) wheel; das fünfte ~ am Wagen sein (fig. ugs.) be superfluous;

ein ~ abhaben (fig. ugs.) have a screw loose (coll.)
(b) (Fahrrad) bicycle; bike (coll.); ~ fahren cycle; ride a bicycle *or* (coll.) bike

Radar *der od. das;* ~s radar

Radar-: ~**falle** *die* (ugs.) [radar] speed trap; ~**kontrolle** *die* [radar] speed check; ~**schirm** *der* radar screen

Rad·dampfer *der* paddle steamer

radeln *itr. V.;* mit sein (ugs., bes. südd.) cycle

Rädels·führer *der,* **Rädels·führerin** *die* (abwertend) ringleader

rad-, Rad-: **~***fahren** ▸ RAD B; ~**fahrer** *der,* ~**fahrerin** *die* cyclist; ~**fahr·streifen** *der* bicycle lane; ~**fahr·weg** *der* cycle path; cycle track

Radien ▸ RADIUS

radieren *tr.* (*auch itr.*) *V.* erase

Radier·gummi *der* rubber [eraser]

Radierung *die;* ~, ~en (Grafik) etching

Radieschen *das;* ~s, ~: radish

radikal ⟨1⟩ *Adj.* radical; drastic ⟨measure, method, cure⟩
⟨2⟩ *adv.* radically; (vollständig) totally

Radikalismus *der;* ~: radicalism

Radikalität *die;* ~: radicalness; radical nature

Radio *das* (südd., schweiz. auch: *der*); ~s, ~s radio; ~ hören listen to the radio ⋯‣

radio-, Radio-: ~**aktiv** /----'-/ ⑴ *Adj.*
radioactive; ⑵ *adv.* radioactively;
~**aktivität** /-----'-/ *die* radioactivity;
~**sender** *der* radio station; ~**wecker**
der radio alarm clock

Radius *der;* ~, **Radien** radius

Rad-: ~**kappe** *die* hubcap; ~**lager** *das*
wheel bearing

Radler *der;* ~**s,** ~: (a) cyclist
(b) (bes. südd.: Getränk) shandy

Radlerin *die;* ~, ~**nen** cyclist

Rad-: ~**rennbahn** *die* cycle racing track;
~**rennen** *das* cycle race; (Sport) cycle
racing; ~**sport** *der* cycling *no def. art.;*
~**tour** *die* cycling tour; ~**weg** *der* cycle
path *or* track

raffen *tr. V.* (a) snatch; rake in (coll.)
⟨money⟩; **etw. [an sich]** ~: seize sth.; (eilig)
snatch sth.
(b) gather ⟨*material, curtain*⟩

Raffinerie *die;* ~, ~**n** refinery

Raffinesse *die;* ~, ~**n** (a) (Schlauheit)
guile; ingenuity
(b) (Finesse) refinement

raffiniert ⑴ *Adj.* (a) ingenious ⟨*plan,
design*⟩; (verfeinert) refined, subtle ⟨*colour;
scheme, effect*⟩; sophisticated ⟨*dish, cut (of
clothes)*⟩
(b) (gerissen) cunning ⟨*person, trick*⟩
⑵ *adv.* (a) ingeniously; (verfeinert) with great
refinement/sophistication
(b) (gerissen) cunningly

Raffiniertheit *die;* ~(a) (Klugheit)
ingenuity; (Verfeinerung) refinement;
sophistication
(b) (Gerissenheit) cunning

Raft *das;* ~**s,** ~**s** raft

raften *itr. V.* raft

Rafting *das;* ~**s** rafting

Rage /'ra:ʒə/ *die;* ~ (ugs.) fury

ragen *itr. V.* (a) (vertikal) rise [up];
⟨*mountains*⟩ tower up
(b) (horizontal) project, stick out (**in** + *Akk.*
into; **über** + *Akk.* over)

Ragout /ra'guː/ *das;* ~**s,** ~**s** ragout

Rahm *der;* ~**[e]s** cream

rahmen *tr. V.* frame

Rahmen *der;* ~**s,** ~ (a) frame; (Fahrgestell)
chassis
(b) (fig.) framework

Rakete *die;* ~, ~**n** rocket; (Lenkflugkörper)
missile

rammen *tr. V.* ram

Rampe *die;* ~, ~**n** (a) (Lade~) [loading]
platform
(b) (schiefe Fläche) ramp

Rampen·licht *das:* im ~ [der
Öffentlichkeit] stehen be in the limelight

Ramsch *der;* ~**[e]s,** ~**e** (ugs.) (a) (Ware)
trashy goods *pl.*

(b) (Kram) junk

ran *Adv.* (ugs.) (a) ▶ HERAN
(b) (fang[t] an) off you go; (fangen wir an) let's
go
(c) (greif[t] an) go at him/them!

Rand *der;* ~**[e]s, Ränder** (a) edge;
(Einfassung) border; (Hut~) brim; (Brillen~,
Gefäß~, Krater~) rim; (eines Abgrunds) brink;
(auf einem Schriftstück) margin; (Weg~) verge;
(Stadt~) outskirts *pl.*
(b) (Schmutz~) mark; (rund) ring

randalieren *itr. V.* riot

Randalierer *der;* ~**s,** ~,
Randaliererin *die;* ~, ~**nen** hooligan

rand-, Rand-: ~**bemerkung** *die*
marginal note *or* comment; ~**gruppe** *die*
(Soziol.) fringe *or* marginal group; ~**stein**
der kerb; ~**voll** *Adj.* ⟨*glass etc.*⟩ full to the
brim

rang *1. u. 3. Pers. Sg. Prät. v.* RINGEN

Rang *der;* ~**[e]s, Ränge** (a) rank; (in der
Gesellschaft) status
(b) (im Theater) circle; **erster** ~: dress circle;
zweiter ~: upper circle; **dritter** ~: gallery

rangieren /raŋ'ʒiːrən/ *tr. V.* shunt ⟨*trucks
etc.*⟩; switch ⟨*cars*⟩ (Amer.)

Rang-: ~**liste** *die* ranking list; **Nummer
eins der internationalen** ~**liste** number one
in the world rankings; ~**ordnung** *die*
order of precedence; (Verhaltensf.) pecking
order

Ranke *die;* ~, ~**n** (Bot.) tendril

ranken *refl. V.* climb, grow (**an** + *Dat.* up,
über + *Akk.* over)

Ranking /'rænkɪŋ/ *das;* ~**s** ranking

rann *1. u. 3. Pers. Sg. Prät. v.* RINNEN

rannte *1. u. 3. Pers. Sg. Prät. v.* RENNEN

Ranzen *der;* ~**s,** ~: satchel

ranzig *Adj.* rancid

Rap /ræp/ *der;* ~**[s],** ~**s** rap

Rappe *der;* ~**n,** ~**n** black horse

rappen /'ræpn̩/ *itr. V.* rap

Rappen *der;* ~**s,** ~: [Swiss] centime

Rapper/'ræpɐ/ *der;* ~**s,** ~, **Rapperin**
die; ~, ~**nen** rapper

Raps *der;* ~**es** (Bot.) rape

rar *Adj.* scarce; (selten) rare

Rarität *die;* ~, ~**en** rarity

rasant (ugs.) ⑴ *Adj.* tremendously fast
(coll.) ⟨*car, horse, etc.*⟩
⑵ *adv.* at terrific speed (coll.)

rasch ⑴ *Adj.* quick; speedy, swift ⟨*end,
action, decision, progress*⟩
⑵ *adv.* quickly; ⟨*decide, end, proceed*⟩
swiftly, rapidly

rascheln *itr. V.* rustle; ⟨*mouse etc.*⟩ make a
rustling noise

rasen *itr. V.* (a) *mit sein* (ugs.: eilen) dash *or*
rush [along]; (fahren) tear *or* race along; (fig.)
⟨*pulse*⟩ race
(b) (toben) ⟨*person*⟩ rage

---
*old spelling – see note on page x

Rasen *der;* ~s, ~: grass *no indef. art.;* (gepflegte Rasenfläche) lawn

rasend ⓵ *Adj.* **(a)** (sehr schnell) breakneck *attrib.* ⟨speed⟩
(b) (tobend) raging
(c) (heftig) violent
⓶ *adv.* (ugs.) incredibly (coll.)

Rasen·mäher *der;* ~s, ~: lawn-mower

Raser *der;* ~s, ~ (ugs. abwertend) speed merchant (coll.); (rücksichtslos) road hog

Raserei *die;* ~, ~en (ugs.) tearing along *no art.*

Raserin *die;* ~, ~nen ▶ RASER

Rasier·apparat *der* [safety] razor; (elektrisch) electric shaver

rasieren *tr. V.* shave; **sich** ~: shave; **sich nass/trocken/elektrisch** ~: have a wet shave/have a dry shave/use an electric shaver

Rasierer *der;* ~s, ~ (ugs.) [electric] shaver

Rasier-: ~**klinge** *die* razor blade; ~**messer** *das* cutthroat razor; ~**pinsel** *der* shaving brush; ~**schaum** *der* shaving foam; ~**seife** *die* shaving soap; ~**wasser** *das* aftershave; (vor der Rasur) pre-shave lotion

Räson /rɛˈzɔŋ/ *die* zur ~ kommen come to one's senses; jmdn. zur ~ bringen make sb. see reason

Rasse *die;* ~, ~n **(a)** breed
(b) (Menschen~) race

Rassel *die;* ~, ~n rattle

rasseln *itr. V.* rattle

Rassen-: ~**hass,** **~**haß** *der* racial hatred *no art.;* ~**krawall** *der* race riot; ~**trennung** *die* racial segregation *no art.*

Rassismus *der;* ~: racism; racialism

Rassist *der;* ~en, ~en, **Rassistin** *die;* ~, ~nen racist; racialist

rassistisch *Adj.* racist; racialist

Rast *die;* ~, ~en rest; ~ **machen** stop for a break

rasten *itr. V.* rest; take a rest *or* break

Raster *der;* ~s, ~ **(a)** (Druckw.) screen
(b) (fig.) [conceptual] framework; set pattern

Rast-: ~**haus** *das* roadside café; (an der Autobahn) motorway restaurant; ~**hof** *der* [motorway] motel [and service area]; ~**platz** *der* **(a)** place to rest; **(b)** (an Autobahnen) parking place (*with benches and WCs*); picnic area; ~**stätte** *die* service area

Rasur *die;* ~, ~en shave

rät *3. Pers. Sg. Präsens v.* RATEN

Rat *der;* ~[e]s, Räte **(a)** advice; ein ~: a word of advice
(b) (Gremium) council

Rate *die,* ~, ~n **(a)** (Teilbetrag) instalment; etw. auf ~n kaufen buy sth. by instalments *or* (Brit.) on hire purchase *or* (Amer.) on the installment plan
(b) (Statistik) rate

raten ⓵ *unr. itr. V.* **(a)** jmdm. ~: advise sb.
(b) (schätzen) guess
⓶ *tr. V.* **(a)** jmdm. ~, etw. zu tun advise sb. to do sth.
(b) (erraten) guess

Raten·zahlung *die* payment by instalments

Rat·haus *das* town hall

Ratifizierung *die;* ~, ~en ratification

Rätin *die;* ~, ~nen councillor

Ration *die;* ~, ~en ration

rational *Adj.* rational

rationalisieren *tr., itr. V.* rationalize

rationell ⓵ *Adj.* efficient; (wirtschaftlich) economic
⓶ *adv.* efficiently; (wirtschaftlich) economically

rationieren *tr. V.* ration

rat·los ⓵ *Adj.* baffled; helpless ⟨look⟩
⓶ *adv.* helplessly

Rat·losigkeit *die;* ~: helplessness

ratsam *Adj.* advisable

Rat·schlag *der* [piece of] advice

Rätsel *das;* ~s, ~ **(a)** riddle; (Bilder~, Kreuzwort~ usw.) puzzle
(b) (Geheimnis) mystery

rätselhaft ⓵ *Adj.* mysterious; (unergründlich) enigmatic
⓶ *adv.* mysteriously; (unergründlich) enigmatically

rätseln *itr. V.* puzzle, rack one's brains (über + *Akk.* over); ~, wer …/ob …: try to work out who …/whether …

Ratte *die;* ~, ~n (auch fig.) rat

rau ⓵ *Adj.* **(a)** (nicht glatt) rough
(b) (nicht mild) harsh, raw ⟨climate, winter⟩; raw ⟨wind⟩
(c) (kratzig) husky, hoarse ⟨voice⟩
(d) (entzündet) sore ⟨throat⟩
(e) (grob, nicht feinfühlig) rough; harsh ⟨words, tone⟩
⓶ *adv.* **(a)** (kratzig) ⟨speak etc.⟩ huskily, hoarsely
(b) (grob, nicht feinfühlig) roughly

Raub *der;* ~[e]s **(a)** robbery
(b) (Beute) stolen goods *pl.*

Raub·bau *der* overexploitation (an + *Dat.* of); ~ an etw. (*Dat.*) treiben over-exploit sth.

rauben *tr. V.* steal; kidnap ⟨person⟩; jmdm. etw. ~: rob sb. of sth.; (geh.: wegnehmen) deprive sb. of sth.

Räuber *der;* ~s, ~, **Räuberin** *die;* ~, ~nen robber

Raub-: ~**fisch** *der* predatory fish; ~**kopie** *die* pirated copy; ~**mord** *der* (Rechtsw.) murder (an + *Dat.* of) in the course of a robbery *or* with robbery as motive; ~**tier** *das* predator; ~**überfall** *der* robbery (auf + *Akk.* of); ~**vogel** *der* bird of prey

Rauch *der;* ~[e]s smoke ⋯⟫

rauchen ① *itr. V.* smoke
  ② *tr. (auch itr.) V.* smoke ⟨*cigarette, pipe, etc.*⟩; „Rauchen verboten" 'No smoking'
Raucher *der;* ~s, ~: smoker
Raucher-: ~**abteil** *das* smoking compartment; smoker; ~**husten** *der* smoker's cough
Raucherin *die;* ~, ~nen smoker
räuchern *tr. V.* smoke ⟨*meat, fish*⟩
rauch·frei *Adj.* smoke-free
rauchig *Adj.* smoky; husky ⟨*voice*⟩
Rauch-: ~**melder** *der* smoke detector; ~**schwaden** *der* cloud of smoke; ~**verbot** *das* ban on smoking; ~**wolke** *die* cloud of smoke
räudig *Adj.* mangy
rauf *Adv.* (ugs.) up; ~ mit euch! up you go!; *s. auch* HERAUF; HINAUF
Rau·faser·tapete *die* woodchip wallpaper
raufen ① *itr., refl. V.* fight
  ② *tr. V.* sich (*Dat.*) die Haare/den Bart ~: tear one's hair/at one's beard
Rauferei *die;* ~, ~en fight
*****rauh** *usw.* ▶ RAU *usw.*
Raum *der;* ~[e]s, Räume (a) (Wohn~, Nutz~) room
  (b) (Gebiet) area; region
  (c) (Platz) room; space
räumen *tr. V.* (a) clear [away]; clear ⟨*snow*⟩
  (b) (an einen Ort) clear; move
  (c) (frei machen) clear ⟨*street, building, warehouse, stocks, etc.*⟩
  (d) (verlassen) vacate
Raum·fahrt *die;* ~: space travel
räumlich ① *Adj.* (a) spatial; aus ~en Gründen for reasons of space
  (b) (dreidimensional) three-dimensional; stereoscopic ⟨*vision*⟩
  ② *adv.* (a) spatially
  (b) (dreidimensional) three-dimensionally
Räumlichkeit *die;* ~, ~en(a) *Pl.* rooms
  (b) (räumliche Wirkung) three-dimensionality
Raum-: ~**schiff** *das* spaceship; ~**sonde** *die* space probe
Räumung *die;* ~, ~en (a) clearing
  (b) (das Verlassen) vacation; vacating
  (c) (wegen Gefahr) evacuation
  (d) (eines Lagers) clearance
Räumungs·verkauf *der* (Kaufmannsspr.) clearance sale
raunen *tr., itr. V.* (geh.) whisper
Raupe *die;* ~, ~n caterpillar
Rau·reif *der* hoar frost
raus *Adv.* (ugs.) out; ~ mit euch! out you go!; *s. auch* HERAUS; HINAUS
Rausch *der;* ~[e]s, Räusche (a) state of drunkenness
  (b) (starkes Gefühl) transport; **der** ~ **der**

Geschwindigkeit the exhilaration *or* thrill of speed
rauschen *itr. V.* ⟨*water, wind, torrent*⟩ rush; ⟨*trees, leaves*⟩ rustle; ⟨*skirt, curtains, silk*⟩ swish; ⟨*waterfall, strong wind*⟩ roar; ⟨*rain*⟩ pour down
Rausch·gift *das* drug; narcotic; ~ **nehmen** take drugs; be on drugs
Rauschgift-: ~**händler** *der,* ~**händlerin** *die* drug trafficker; ~**sucht** *die* drug addiction
raus|fliegen *unr. itr. V.; mit sein* (ugs.) be fired (coll.)
räuspern *refl. V.* clear one's throat
raus|schmeißen *unr. tr. V.* (ugs.) chuck (coll.) ⟨*objects*⟩ out *or* away; give ⟨*employee*⟩ the push (coll.) *or* sack (coll.); chuck (coll.) *or* throw ⟨*customer, drunk, tenant*⟩ out (**aus** of)
Raute *die;* ~, ~n (Geom.) rhombus
Rave /reɪv/ *der;* ~s, ~s rave
Raver /'reɪvɐ/ *der;* ~s, ~, **Raverin** *die;* ~, ~nen raver
Razzia *die;* ~, Razzien raid
reagieren *itr. V.* react (**auf** + *Akk.* to)
Reaktion *die;* ~, ~en reaction (**auf** + *Akk.* to)
reaktionär *Adj.* reactionary
Reaktionär *der;* ~s, ~e reactionary
Reaktor *der;* ~s, ~en /-'to:rən/ reactor
real ① *Adj.* real
  ② *adv.* actually
realisieren *tr. V.* (geh.) realize
Realismus *der;* ~: realism
Realist *der;* ~en, ~en, **Realistin** *die;* ~, ~nen realist
realistisch ① *Adj.* realistic
  ② *adv.* realistically
Realität *die;* ~, ~en reality
Real·schule *die* ≈ secondary modern school (Brit. Hist.)
Rebe *die;* ~, ~n (a) vine shoot
  (b) (Weinstock) [grape] vine
Rebell *der;* ~en, ~en, **Rebellin** *die;* ~, ~nen rebel
rebellieren *itr. V.* rebel (**gegen** against)
Rebellion *die;* ~, ~en rebellion
rebellisch *Adj.* rebellious
Reb-: ~**huhn** *das* partridge; ~**stock** *der* vine
rechen *tr. V.* (bes. südd.) rake
Rechen *der;* ~s, ~ (bes. südd.) rake
Rechen-: ~**fehler** *der* arithmetical error; ~**maschine** *die* calculator
Rechenschaft *die;* ~: account; **jmdn. für etw. zur** ~ **ziehen** call *or* bring sb. to account for sth.
Rechenschafts·bericht *der* report
Recherche /re'ʃɛrʃə/ *die;* ~, ~n (a) (geh.) investigation; enquiry
  (b) (DV) search
recherchieren *itr., tr. V.* (geh.) investigate

---

rẹchnen ☐ *tr. V.* **(a) eine Aufgabe** ∼: work out a problem
(b) (veranschlagen) reckon; estimate; **gut/rund gerechnet** at a generous/rough estimate
(c) (berücksichtigen) take into account
(d) (einbeziehen) count
②itr. *V.* **(a)** do *or* make a calculation/calculations; **gut/schlecht** ∼ **können** be good/bad at figures
(b) (zählen) reckon
(c) (ugs.: berechnen) calculate; estimate
(d) (wirtschaften) budget carefully
(e) auf jmdn./etw. *od.* **mit jmdm./etw.** ∼: count on sb./sth.
(f) mit etw. ∼ (etw. einkalkulieren) reckon with sth.; (etw. erwarten) expect sth.

Rẹchnen *das;* ∼s arithmetic

Rẹchner *der;* ∼s, ∼: calculator; (Computer) computer

rẹchnerisch *Adj.* arithmetical

Rẹchnung *die;* ∼, ∼en **(a)** calculation
(b) (schriftliche Kosten∼) bill; invoice (Commerc.); **[jmdm.] etw. in** ∼ **stellen** charge [sb.] for sth.

rẹcht ☐ *Adj.* **(a)** (geeignet, richtig) right
(b) (gesetzmäßig, anständig) right; proper;
∼ **und billig** right and proper
(c) (wunschgemäß) **jmdm.** ∼ **sein** be all right with sb.
(d) (wirklich, echt) real
②*adv.* **(a)** (geeignet) **du kommst gerade** ∼: you are just in time
(b) (richtig) correctly
(c) (gesetzmäßig, anständig) properly
(d) (wunschgemäß) **es jmdm.** ∼ **machen** please sb.
(e) (wirklich, echt) really
(f) (ziemlich) quite; rather; *s. auch* RECHT D

Rẹcht *das;* ∼[e]s, ∼e **(a)** (Rechtsordnung) law
(b) (Rechtsanspruch) right; **sein** ∼ **fordern** *od.* **verlangen** demand one's rights
(c) (Berechtigung) right (**auf** + *Akk.* to);
gleiches ∼ **für alle!** equal rights for all!; **im** ∼ **sein** be in the right; **zu** ∼: rightly
(d) ∼ **haben** be right; **jmdm.** ∼ **geben** admit that sb. is right

rẹcht... *Adj.* **(a)** right; right[-hand] ⟨*edge*⟩
(b) (außen, sichtbar) right ⟨*side*⟩
(c) (in der Politik) right-wing

rẹcht·fertigen *tr. V.* justify (**vor** + *Dat.* to)
Rẹcht·fertigung *die* justification
rẹchtlich ☐ *Adj.* legal
②*adv.* legally
Rẹchtlichkeit *die;* ∼ *s.:* RECHTMÄSSIGKEIT
rẹcht·los *Adj.* without rights *postpos.*
Rẹchtlosigkeit *die;* ∼: lack of rights
rẹchtmäßig ☐ *Adj.* lawful; rightful; legitimate ⟨*claim*⟩
②*adv.* lawfully; rightfully
Rẹchtmäßigkeit *die;* ∼: legality; (eines Anspruchs) legitimacy
rẹchts *Adv.* **(a)** on the right; **von** ∼: from the right

(b) (Politik) on the right wing
Rẹchts-: ∼**abbieger** *der,*
∼**abbiegerin** *die* (Verkehrsw.) motorist/cyclist/car *etc.* turning right; ∼**anwalt** *der,* ∼**anwältin** *die* lawyer; solicitor (Brit.); attorney (Amer.); (vor Gericht) barrister (Brit.); attorney[-at-law] (Amer.); advocate (Scot.);
∼**außen** /-'--/ *der;* ∼, ∼ (Ballspiele) right wing; outside right
rẹcht-, Rẹcht-: ∼**schaffen** ☐ *Adj.* honest; ②*adv.* honestly;
∼**schreib·fehler** *der* spelling mistake;
∼**schreibung** *die* orthography
rẹchts-, Rẹchts-: ∼**empfinden** *das* sense of [what is] right and wrong;
∼**extremist** *der,* ∼**extremistin** *die* (Politik) right-wing extremist; ∼**händer** *der;* ∼∼s, ∼∼, ∼**händerin** *die;* ∼∼, ∼∼**nen** right-hander; ∼**kräftig** (Rechtsw.) ☐ *Adj.* final [and absolute] ⟨*decision, verdict, etc.*⟩; ②*adv.* **jmdn.** ∼**kräftig verurteilen** pass a final sentence on sb.;
∼**kurve** *die* right-hand bend
Rẹcht·sprechung *die;* ∼, ∼en administration of justice; (eines Gerichts) jurisdiction
rẹchts-, Rẹchts-: ∼**radikal** (Politik) ☐ *Adj.* radical right-wing; ②*adv.* **eine** ∼**radikal orientierte Gruppe** a group with a radical right-wing orientation;
∼**radikale** *der/die* right-wing radical;
∼**radikalismus** *der* right-wing radicalism; ∼**staat** *der* [constitutional] state founded on the rule of law;
∼**staatlich** *Adj.* founded on the rule of law *postpos.;* ∼**verkehr** *der* driving *no art.* on the right; ∼**verletzung** *die* (Rechtsw.) infringement *or* violation of the law; ∼**widrig** ☐ *Adj.* unlawful;
②*adv.* unlawfully; ∼**widrigkeit** *die* **(a)** unlawfulness; **(b)** (Handlung) unlawful act
rẹcht-: ∼**wink[e]lig** *Adj.* right-angled;
∼**zeitig** ☐ *Adj.* timely; (pünktlich) punctual;
②*adv.* in time; (pünktlich) on time
Rẹck *das;* ∼[e]s, ∼e *od.* ∼s horizontal bar
rẹcken ☐ *tr. V.* stretch
②*refl. V.* stretch oneself
recycelbar /ri'saikl]ba:ɐ̯/ *Adj.* recyclable
recyceln /ri'saikln/ *tr. V.; 2. Part.* **recycelt** recycle
Recycling /ri'saiklɪŋ/ *das;* ∼s recycling
recycling-, Recycling-: ∼**fähig** *Adj.* recyclable; ∼**papier** *das* recycled paper
Redakteur /redak'tø:ɐ̯/ *der;* ∼s, ∼e, **Redakteurin** *die;* ∼, ∼nen editor
Redaktion *die;* ∼, ∼en **(a)** (Redakteure) editorial staff
(b) (Büro) editorial department *or* office/offices *pl.*
redaktionẹll ☐ *Adj.* editorial
②*adv.* editorially

r

Rede *die;* ~, ~n **(a)** (Ansprache) address; speech; **eine** ~ **halten** give *or* make a speech **(b)** (Vortrag) rhetoric **(c)** (Äußerung, Ansicht) **nicht der** ~ **wert sein** be not worth mentioning; **jmdn. zur** ~ **stellen** make someone explain himself/herself; **von jmdm./etw. ist die** ~: there is some talk about sb./sth.; **es ist die** ~ **davon, dass …:** it is being said *or* people are saying that …; **davon kann keine** ~ **sein** it's out of the question

reden ① *tr. V.* talk; **Unsinn** ~: talk nonsense; **kein Wort** ~: not say *or* speak a word ② *itr. V.* **(a)** (sprechen) talk; speak; **viel/wenig** ~: talk a lot (coll.)/not talk much **(b)** (sich äußern, eine Rede halten) speak; **gut** ~ **können** be a good speaker **(c)** (sich unterhalten) talk; **mit jmdm./über jmdn.** ~: talk to/about sb.

Redens·art *die* **(a)** expression; (Sprichwort) saying **(b)** *Pl.* (Phrase) empty *or* meaningless words

Rede·wendung *die* (Sprachw.) idiom

redlich ① *Adj.* honest ② *adv.* honestly

Redlichkeit *die;* ~: honesty

Redner *der;* ~s, ~, **Rednerin** *die* ~, ~nen **(a)** speaker **(b)** (Rhetoriker) orator

red·selig *Adj.* talkative

reduzieren ① *tr. V.* reduce (**auf** + *Akk.* to) ② *refl. V.* decrease; diminish

Reeder *der;* ~s, ~: shipowner

Reederei *die;* ~, ~en shipping firm

Reederin *die;* ~, ~nen shipowner

reell ① *Adj.* honest, straight ⟨*person, deal, etc.*⟩; sound, solid ⟨*business, firm, etc.*⟩; straight ⟨*offer*⟩ ② *adv.* honestly

Reet *das;* ~s (nordd.) reeds *pl.*

Referat *das;* ~[e]s, ~e **(a)** paper **(b)** (kurzer schriftlicher Bericht) report

Referendar *der;* ~s, ~e, **Referendarin** *die;* ~, ~nen *candidate for a higher civil-service post who has passed the first state examination and is undergoing in-service training*

Referenz *die;* ~, ~en (Person, Stelle) referee; **jmdn. als** ~ **angeben** give sb.'s name *or* give sb. as a reference

referieren *itr. V.* **über etw.** (*Akk.*) ~: present a paper on sth.; (zusammenfassend) give a report on sth.

reflektieren *tr. V.* reflect

Reflex *der;* ~es, ~e reflex

Reflexion *die;* ~, ~en reflection

Reflexiv·pronomen *das* (Sprachw.) reflexive pronoun

Reform *die;* ~, ~en reform

Reformation *die;* ~ (hist.) Reformation

Reformations·fest *das* Reformation Day

Reform·haus *das* health food shop

reformieren *tr. V.* reform

Refrain /rə'frɛ̃ː/ *der;* ~s, ~s chorus

Regal *das;* ~s, ~e [set *sing.* of] shelves *pl.*

rege ① *Adj.* **(a)** (betriebsam) busy ⟨*traffic*⟩; brisk ⟨*demand, trade, business, etc.*⟩ **(b)** (lebhaft) lively; keen ⟨*interest*⟩ ② *adv.* **(a)** (betriebsam) actively **(b)** (lebhaft) actively

Regel *die;* ~, ~n (a) rule; **nach allen** ~n **der Kunst** (fig.) well and truly **(b)** rule; custom; **die** ~ **sein** be the rule; **in der** *od.* **aller** ~: as a rule **(c)** (Menstruation) period

regel·mäßig ① *Adj.* regular ② *adv.* regularly

Regel·mäßigkeit *die* regularity

regeln ① *tr. V.* **(a)** settle ⟨*matter, question, etc.*⟩; put ⟨*finances, affairs, etc.*⟩ in order **(b)** (einstellen, regulieren) regulate; (steuern) control ② *refl. V.* take care of itself

regelrecht ① *Adj.* (ugs.: richtiggehend) proper (coll.); real; real ⟨*shock*⟩; real, absolute ⟨*scandal*⟩; complete, utter ⟨*flop, disaster*⟩; **ich hatte** ~e **Angst** I was really afraid ② *adv.* (ugs.: richtiggehend) really

Regelung *die;* ~, ~en **(a)** ▸ REGELN 1A, B: settlement; putting in order; regulation; control **(b)** (Vorschrift) regulation

regen ① *tr. V.* (geh.) move ② *refl. V.* **(a)** (sich bewegen) move **(b)** (geh.) ⟨*hope, doubt, desire, conscience*⟩ stir

Regen *der;* ~s, ~ **(a)** rain; **vom** *od.* **aus dem** ~ **in die Traufe kommen** (fig.) jump out of the frying pan into the fire **(b)** (fig.) shower

Regen-: ~**bogen** *der* rainbow; ~**mantel** *der* raincoat; mackintosh; ~**schirm** *der* umbrella; ~**tag** *der* rainy day; ~**wald** *der* (Geogr.) rainforest; ~**wasser** *das* rainwater; ~**wetter** *das* wet weather; ~**wolke** *die* rain cloud; ~**wurm** *der* earthworm; ~**zeit** *die* rainy season

Regie /re'ʒiː/ *die;* ~ **(a)** (Theater, Film, Ferns., Rundf.) direction; **die** ~ **bei etw. haben** *od.* **führen** direct sth. **(b)** (Leitung, Verwaltung) management

regieren ① *itr. V.* rule (**über** + *Akk.* over); ⟨*party, administration*⟩ govern ② *tr. V.* rule; govern; ⟨*monarch*⟩ reign over

Regierung *die;* ~, ~en **(a)** (Herrschaft) rule; (eines Monarchen) reign **(b)** (Kabinett) government

Regierungs·sitz *der* seat of government

Regime /re'ʒiːm/ *das;* ~s, ~ /re'ʒiːmə/ (abwertend) regime

Regiment *das;* ~[e]s, ~e *od.* ~er **(a)** *Pl.* ~e (Herrschaft) rule **(b)** *Pl.* ~er (Milit.) regiment

---

*old spelling – see note on page x

Regime·wechsel *der* regime change
Region *die;* ~, ~en region
regional ⓵ *Adj.* regional
  ⓶ *adv.* regionally
Regisseur /reʒɪ'søːɐ̯/ *der;* ~s, ~e,
  Regisseurin *die;* ~, ~nen director
Register *das;* ~s, ~ (a) index
  (b) (amtliche Liste) register
  (c) (Musik) (bei Instrumenten) register; (Orgel~)
  stop
registrieren *tr. V.* (a) register
  (b) (bewusst wahrnehmen) note; register
Regler *der;* ~s, ~ (Technik) regulator;
  (Kybernetik) control
reg·los *Adj.* motionless
regnen ⓵ *itr., tr. V.* (unpers.) rain; **es
  regnet** it is raining
  ⓶ *itr. V.; mit sein* (fig.) rain down
regnerisch *Adj.* rainy
regulär *Adj.* (a) proper; normal *⟨working
  hours⟩*
  (b) (normal, üblich) normal
regulieren *tr. V.* regulate
Regulierung *die;* ~, ~en regulation
Regung *die;* ~, ~en (geh.: Gefühl) stirring
regungs·los *Adj.* motionless
Reh *das;* ~[e]s, ~e roe deer
Reha /'reːha/ *die;* ~, ~s rehab; **in** ~ **sein/
  gehen** be in/go into rehab
Rehabilitation *die;* ~, ~en
  rehabilitation
rehabilitieren *tr. V.* rehabilitate
Reh-: ~**bock** *der* roebuck; ~**kitz** *das*
  fawn [of a/the roe deer]
Reibach *der;* ~s (ugs.) profits *pl.;* **einen
  [kräftigen]** ~ **machen** make a killing (coll.)
Reibe *die;* ~, ~n, **Reib·eisen** *das* grater
reiben ⓵ *unr. tr. V.* (a) rub
  (b) (zerkleinern) grate
  ⓶ *unr. itr. V.* rub **(an** + *Dat.* on)
Reib·fläche *die* striking surface *(of
  matchbox)*
Reibung *die;* ~, ~en (Physik, fig.) friction
reibungs·los ⓵ *Adj.* smooth
  ⓶ *adv.* smoothly
reich ⓵ *Adj.* **(a)** (vermögend) rich
  (b) (prächtig) costly *⟨goods, gifts⟩;* rich *⟨décor,
  finery⟩*
  (c) (üppig) rich; abundant *⟨harvest⟩;*
  abundant *⟨mineral resources⟩;* ~ **an etw.**
  (Dat.) **sein** be rich in sth.
  (d) (vielfältig) rich *⟨collection, possibilities⟩;*
  wide, large *⟨selection, choice⟩;* wide
  ⟨knowledge, experience⟩
  ⓶ *adv.* richly
Reich *das;* ~[e]s, ~e **(a)** empire; (König~)
  kingdom; realm; **das [Deutsche]** ~ (hist.) the
  German Reich *or* Empire; **das Dritte** ~ (hist.)
  the Third Reich
  (b) (fig.) realm
reichen ⓵ *itr. V.* **(a)** (ausreichen) be enough;
  das Geld reicht nicht I/we *etc.* haven't got

enough money; **jetzt reichts mir aber!** now
I've had enough!; **danke, es reicht** that's
enough, thank you
  (b) (sich erstrecken) reach; *⟨forest, fields, etc.⟩*
  extend
  ⓶ *tr. V.* **(a)** pass; hand; **jmdm. die Hand**
  ~: hold out one's hand to sb.; **sich** *(Dat.)* **die
  Hand** ~: shake hands
  (b) (servieren) serve *⟨food, drink⟩*
reich·haltig *Adj.* extensive; varied
  ⟨programme⟩; substantial *⟨meal⟩*
Reich·haltigkeit *die;* ~~: extensiveness;
  (eines Programms) varied content; (einer
  Mahlzeit) substantialness
reichlich ⓵ *Adj.* large; ample *⟨space,
  time⟩;* good *⟨hour, year⟩*
  ⓶ *adv.* **(a)** amply
  (b) (mehr als) over; more than
  (c) (ugs.: ziemlich, sehr) a bit too *⟨cheeky, dear,
  late⟩*
Reichtum *der;* ~s, **Reichtümer (a)** wealth
  (an + *Dat.* of)
  (b) *Pl.* (Vermögenswerte) riches
Reich·weite *die* reach; (eines Geschützes,
  Senders, Flugzeugs) range
reif *Adj.* **(a)** ripe *⟨fruit, grain, cheese⟩;*
  mature *⟨brandy, cheese⟩;* ~ **für etw. sein**
  (ugs.) be ready for sth.
  (b) (erwachsen, ausgewogen) mature
Reif¹ *der;* ~[e]s hoar frost
Reif² *der;* ~[e]s, ~e (geh.) ring; (Arm~)
  bracelet; (Diadem) circlet
Reife *die;* ~ **(a)** ripeness; (von Menschen,
  Gedanken, Produkten) maturity
  (b) (Reifung) ripening
  (c) mittlere ~ (Schulw.) school-leaving
  *certificate usually taken after the fifth year of
  secondary school*
reifen ⓵ *itr. V.; mit sein* **(a)** *⟨fruit, cereal,
  cheese⟩* ripen
  (b) (geh.: älter, reifer werden) mature **(zu** into)
  (c) *⟨idea, plan, decision⟩* mature
  ⓶ *tr. V.* ripen *⟨fruit, cereal⟩*
Reifen *der;* ~s, ~ **(a)** hoop
  (b) (Gummi~) tyre
  (c) ▶ REIF²
Reifen-: ~**druck** *der; Pl.* ~drücke
  tyre pressure; ~**panne** *die* puncture;
  ~**wechsel** *der* tyre change
Reif·glätte *die* ice on the roads
reiflich ⓵ *Adj.* [very] careful
  ⓶ *adv.* [very] carefully
Reifung *die;* ~: ▶ REIFEN 1: ripening;
  maturing; maturation
Reigen *der;* ~s, ~ **(a)** round dance
  (b) (fig.) **den** ~ **eröffnen** start off
Reihe *die;* ~, ~n **(a)** row; **in Reih und Glied**
  (Milit.) in rank and file; **aus der** ~ **tanzen** (fig.
  ugs.) be different
  (b) (Reihenfolge) series; **er/sie** *usw.* **ist an der**
  ~: it's his/her *etc.* turn; **der** ~ **nach, nach
  der** ~: in turn
  (c) (größere Anzahl) number

⋯⟩

~**leiterin** die courier

reihen (geh.) tr. V. string; thread

reisen itr. V.; mit sein **(a)** travel
(b) (abreisen) leave; set off

Reihen-: ~**folge** die order; ~**haus** das terraced house

Reisende der/die; adj. Dekl. traveller; (Fahrgast) passenger

Reiher der; ~s, ~: heron

Reim der; ~[e]s, ~e rhyme

reimen ①ⅠⅠ itr. V. make up rhymes ②ⅠⅠ tr., refl. V. rhyme (**auf** + Akk. with)

Reise-: ~**pass**, *~**paß** der passport; ~**planung** die travel planning; die ~**planung umstellen** change one's travel plans; ~**prospekt** der travel brochure; ~**route** die route; ~**scheck** der traveller's cheque; ~**tasche** die holdall; ~**verkehr** der holiday traffic; ~**wetterbericht** der holiday weather forecast; ~**ziel** das destination

rein¹ Adv. (ugs.) ~ **mit dir!** in you go/come!

rein² ① Adj. **(a)** (unvermischt) pure **(b)** (nichts anderes als) pure; sheer; plain, unvarnished ⟨truth⟩ **(c)** (frisch, sauber) clean; fresh ⟨clothes, sheet of paper, etc.⟩; pure, clean ⟨water, air⟩; clear ⟨complexion⟩; **etw. ins Reine schreiben** make a fair copy of sth.; **etw. ins Reine bringen** clear sth. up ② Adv. purely; ~ **gar nichts** (ugs.) absolutely nothing

Reisig das; ~s brushwood

Reiß·brett das drawing board

reißen ① unr. tr. V. **(a)** tear; (in Stücke) tear up **(b)** (ziehen an) pull; (heftig) yank (coll.) **(c)** (werfen, ziehen) **jmdn. zu Boden/in die Tiefe** ~: knock sb. to the ground/drag sb. down into the depths **(d)** (töten) ⟨wolf, lion, etc.⟩ kill ⟨prey⟩ **(e) etw. an sich** ~ (fig.) seize sth. ② unr. itr. V. **(a)** mit sein ⟨paper, fabric⟩ tear, rip; ⟨rope, thread⟩ break, snap; ⟨film⟩ break; ⟨muscle⟩ tear **(b)** (ziehen) **an etw.** (Dat.) ~: pull at sth. ③ unr. refl. V. (ugs.: sich bemühen um) **sie** ~ **sich um die Eintrittskarten** they are fighting each other to get tickets

Rein·fall der (ugs.) let-down

rein|fallen unr. itr. V.; mit sein (ugs.) ▶ HEREINFALLEN

Rein·gewinn der net profit

Reinheit die; ~ **(a)** purity **(b)** (Sauberkeit) cleanness; (des Wassers, der Luft) purity; (der Haut) clearness

reinigen tr. V. clean; purify ⟨effluents, air, water, etc.⟩; **Kleider [chemisch]** ~ **lassen** have clothes [dry-]cleaned

reißend Adj. rapacious ⟨animal⟩; raging ⟨torrent⟩; ~**en Absatz finden** sell like hot cakes

reißerisch (abwertend) ① Adj. sensational; lurid ⟨headline⟩; garish, lurid ⟨colour⟩ ② adv. sensationally

Reinigung die; ~, ~**en (a)** ▶ REINIGEN: cleaning; purification; dry-cleaning **(b)** (Betrieb) [dry-]cleaner's

Reiß-: ~**leine** die (Flugw.) ripcord; ~**nagel** der: ▶ ~ZWECKE; ~**verschluss**, *~**verschluß** der zip [fastener]; ~**zwecke** die drawing pin (Brit.); thumbtack (Amer.)

reinlich Adj. cleanly

Reinlichkeit die; ~: cleanliness

rein, Rein-: ~**rassig** Adj. thoroughbred ⟨animal⟩; ~|**reiten** tr. V. (ugs.) **jmdn.** ~**reiten** drag sb. in (fig.); ~**schrift** die fair copy

reiten ① unr. itr. V.; meist mit sein ride ② unr. tr. V.; auch mit sein ride; **Schritt/Trab/ Galopp** ~: ride at a walk/trot/gallop

Reiten das; ~s riding no art.

rein|ziehen unr. tr. V. **(a)** ▶ HINEINZIEHEN **(b) sich** (Dat.) **etw.** ~**ziehen** (salopp) take ⟨drug⟩; watch ⟨film, show, video⟩

Reiter der; ~s, ~, **Reiterin** die; ~, ~**nen** rider

Reis der; ~es rice

Reit-: ~**hose** die riding breeches pl.; ~**pferd** das saddle horse; ~**stiefel** der riding boot

Reis·brei der rice pudding

Reise die; ~, ~**n** journey; (kürzere Fahrt, Geschäfts~) trip; (Ausflug) outing; trip; (Schiffs~) voyage; **eine** ~ **machen** go on a trip/an outing; **auf** ~**n sein** travel; (nicht zu Hause sein) be away; **glückliche** od. **gute** ~! have a good journey

Reiz der; ~**es**, ~**e (a)** (Physiol.) stimulus **(b)** (Anziehungskraft) attraction; appeal no pl.; (des Verbotenen, der Ferne usw.) lure **(c)** (Zauber) charm

reizbar Adj. irritable

Reizbarkeit die; ~: irritability

reise-, Reise-: ~**andenken** das souvenir; ~**boom** das tourist boom; ~**büro** das travel agent's; travel agency; ~**bus** das coach; ~**freiheit** die freedom of travel; ~**führer** der **(a)** (Reiseleiter) courier; **(b)** (Buch) guidebook; ~**führerin** die courier; ~**gepäck** das luggage (Brit.); baggage (Amer.); (am Flughafen) baggage; ~**gesellschaft** die **(a)** (Reisegruppe) party of tourists; **(b)** (ugs.: Reiseveranstalter) tour operator; ~**kosten** Pl. travel expenses; ~**krank** Adj. travel-sick; ~**krankheit** die travel sickness no pl.; ~**leiter** der;

reizen ① tr. V. **(a)** annoy; tease ⟨animal⟩; (herausfordern, provozieren) provoke; s. auch GEREIZT **(b)** (Physiol.) irritate **(c)** (Interesse erregen bei) **jmdn.** ~: attract sb.; appeal to sb.

(d) (Kartenspiele) bid
[2] *itr. V.* (Kartenspiele) bid
reizend [1] *Adj.* charming; delightful;
lovely ⟨*child*⟩
[2] *adv.* charmingly
reizlos *Adj.* unattractive; ⟨*landscape,
scenery*⟩ lacking in charm
reizvoll *Adj.* **(a)** (hübsch) charming
(b) (interessant) attractive
rekeln *refl. V.* (ugs.) stretch
Reklamation /reklama'tsịo:n/ *die;* ∼,
∼en complaint (**wegen** about)
Reklame *die;* ∼, ∼n **(a)** advertising *no
indef. art.;* ∼ **für jmdn./etw. machen** promote
sb./advertise *or* promote sth.
(b) (ugs.: Werbemittel) advert (Brit. coll.); ad
(coll.); (im Fernsehen, Radio auch) commercial
Reklame-: ∼**schild** *das* advertising
sign; ∼**tafel** *die* advertising hoarding;
(klein) advertising board
reklamieren [1] *itr. V.* complain
[2] *tr. V.* **(a)** complain about (**bei** to, **wegen** on
account of)
(b) (beanspruchen) claim
rekonstruieren *tr. V.* reconstruct
Rekọrd *der;* ∼[e]s, ∼e record
Rekọrd·halter *der,* **Rekọrd·halterin**
die, **Rekọrd·inhaber** *der,*
Rekọrd·inhaberin *die* record holder
Rekrụt *der;* ∼en, ∼en (Milit.) recruit
Rektor *der;* ∼s, ∼en **(a)** (einer Schule)
head[master]
(b) (Universitäts∼) Rector; ≈ Vice-Chancellor
(Brit.); (einer Fachhochschule) principal
Rektorin *die;* ∼, ∼nen **(a)** (einer Schule)
head[mistress]
(b) ▶ REKTOR B
Relation *die;* ∼, ∼en relation
relativ [1] *Adj.* relative
[2] *adv.* relatively
relativieren *tr. V.* relativize
Relativierung *die;* ∼, ∼en relativization
Relativ-: ∼**pronomen** *das* (Sprachw.)
relative pronoun; ∼**satz** *der* (Sprachw.)
relative clause
relaxed /ri'lɛkst/ *Adj.* (salopp) laid-back
(coll.)
relevant /rele'vant/ *Adj.* relevant (**für** to)
Relevạnz *die;* ∼: relevance (**für** to)
Relief *das;* ∼s, ∼s *od.* ∼e relief
Religion *die;* ∼, ∼en religion
religiös [1] *Adj.* religious
[2] *adv.* in a religious manner
Religiosität *die;* ∼: religiousness
Relịkt *das;* ∼[e], ∼e relic
Reling *die;* ∼, ∼s *od.* ∼e [deck] rail
Reliquie /re'li:kvịə/ *die;* ∼, ∼n relic
Remis *das;* ∼ /rə'mi:(s)/, ∼ /rə'mi:s/ (bes.
Schach) draw
Ren *das;* ∼s, ∼s *od.* ∼e reindeer
Renaissance /rənɛ'sãːs/ *die;* ∼, ∼n

(a) Renaissance
(b) (Wiederaufleben) revival
Rendezvous /rãde'vu:/ *das;* ∼ /...'vu:(s)/,
∼ /'rãde'vu:s/ rendezvous
Rẹnn·bahn *die* (Sport) racetrack; (für Pferde)
racecourse
rẹnnen *unr. itr. V.; mit sein* run; **an/gegen
jmdn./etw.** ∼: run *or* bang into sb./sth.
Rẹnnen *das;* ∼s, ∼: running; (Pferde∼,
Auto∼) racing; (Wettbewerb) race
Rẹnner *der;* ∼s, ∼ (ugs.: Verkaufserfolg) big
seller
Rẹnn-: ∼**fahrer** *der,* ∼**fahrerin** *die*
racing driver; ∼**pferd** *das* racehorse;
∼**rad** *das* racing cycle; ∼**wagen** *der*
racing car
renommiert *Adj.* renowned
renovieren *tr. V.* renovate; redecorate
⟨*room, flat*⟩
Renovierung *die;* ∼, ∼en renovation;
(eines Zimmers, einer Wohnung) redecoration
rentabel [1] *Adj.* profitable
[2] *adv.* profitably
Rentabilität *die;* ∼ (bes. Wirtsch.)
profitability
Rẹnte *die;* ∼, ∼n **(a)** pension
(b) (Kapitalertrag) annuity
Rẹnten-: ∼**alter** *das* pensionable
age *no art.;* ∼**empfänger** *der,*
∼**empfängerin** *die* pensioner;
∼**versicherung** *die* pension scheme
Rẹn·tier *das* reindeer
rentieren *refl. V.* be profitable; ⟨*equipment,
machinery*⟩ pay its way
Rẹntner *der;* ∼s, ∼, **Rẹntnerin** *die;* ∼,
∼nen pensioner
Reparatur *die;* ∼, ∼en repair (**an** + *Dat.*
to)
Reparatur·werkstatt *die* repair
[work]shop; (für Autos) garage
reparieren *tr. V.* repair; mend
Repertoire /repɛ'toaːɐ̯/ *das;* ∼s, ∼s
repertoire
Repọrt *der;* ∼[e]s, ∼e, **Reportage**
/repɔr'taːʒə/ *die;* ∼, ∼n report
Repọrter *der;* ∼s, ∼, **Repọrterin** *die;*
∼, ∼nen reporter
Repräsentạnt *der;* ∼en, ∼en,
Repräsentạntin *die;* ∼, ∼nen
representative
repräsentativ *Adj.* representative
repräsentieren *tr. V.* represent
Repressalie /reprɛ'saːlịə/ *die;* ∼, ∼n
repressive measure
Reproduktion *die* reproduction
reproduzieren *tr. V.* reproduce
Reptịl *das;* ∼s, ∼ien reptile
Republịk *die;* ∼, ∼en republic
republikạnisch *Adj.* republican
Reservạt *das;* ∼[e]s, ∼e **(a)** reservation
(b) (Naturschutzgebiet) reserve   ····⋗

Reserve *die;* ~, ~n reserve
Reserve-: ~**rad** *das* spare wheel;
~**reifen** *der* spare tyre
reservieren *tr. V.* reserve
reserviert [1] *Adj.* reserved
  [2] *adv.* in a reserved way
Reserviertheit *die;* ~: reserve
Reservierung *die;* ~, ~en reservation
Reservoir /rɛzɛr'voaːɐ̯/ *das;* ~s, ~e (auch
  fig.) reservoir (**an** + *Dat.* of)
Residenz *die;* ~, ~en (a) residence
  (b) (Hauptstadt) [royal] capital
Resignation *die;* ~, ~en resignation
resignieren *itr. V.* give up
resigniert [1] *Adj.* resigned
  [2] *adv.* resignedly
resolut [1] *Adj.* resolute
  [2] *adv.* resolutely
Resolution *die;* ~, ~en resolution
Resonanz *die;* ~, ~en resonance
resozialisieren *tr. V.* (bes. Rechtsspr.)
  reintegrate into society
Resozialisierung *die;* ~, ~en (bes.
  Rechtsspr.) reintegration into society
Respekt *der;* ~[e]s (a) (Achtung) respect
  (**vor** + *Dat.* for)
  (b) (Furcht) jmdm. ~ **einflößen** intimidate sb.
respektabel [1] *Adj.* respectable
  [2] *adv.* respectably
respektieren *tr. V.* respect
respekt·los [1] *Adj.* disrespectful
  [2] *adv.* disrespectfully
Respekt·losigkeit *die;*
  ~: disrespectfulness
respekt·voll [1] *Adj.* respectful
  [2] *adv.* respectfully
Ressort /rɛ'soːɐ̯/ *das;* ~s, ~s area of
  responsibility; (Abteilung) department
Ressource /rɛ'sʊrsə/ *die;* ~, ~n resource
Rest *der;* ~[e]s, ~e (a) rest; **ein** ~ **von** a
  little bit of
  (b) (Endstück) remnant
  (c) (Math.) remainder
Rest·alkohol *der* residual alcohol
Restaurant /rɛsto'rãː/ *das;* ~s, ~s
  restaurant
restaurieren *tr. V.* restore
restlich *Adj.* remaining
rest·los [1] *Adj.* complete
  [2] *adv.* completely
Rest·müll *der* general waste; non-
  recyclable waste
Resultat *das;* ~[e]s, ~e result
resultieren *itr. V.* result
Retorte *die;* ~, ~n retort
Retorten·baby *das* (ugs.) test tube baby
Retrospektive *die;* ~, ~n (a) (Rückblick)
  retrospective view; **in der** ~: in retrospect
  (b) (Ausstellung) retrospective

retten [1] *tr. V.* save; (vor Gefahr) save; rescue;
  (befreien) rescue; jmdm. **das Leben** ~: save
  sb.'s life
  [2] *refl. V.* (fliehen) escape (**aus** from)
Retter *der;* ~s, ~, **Retterin** *die;* ~, ~nen
  rescuer
Rettich *der;* ~s, ~e radish
Rettung *die* rescue; (vor Zerstörung) saving
rettungs-, Rettungs-: ~**aktion** *die*
  rescue operation; ~**boot** *das* lifeboat;
  ~**hubschrauber** *der* rescue helicopter;
  ~**los** [1] *Adj.* hopeless; inevitable
  ⟨*disaster*⟩; [2] *adv.* hopelessly; ~**ring** *der*
  lifebelt
Return·taste /ri'tɝ:n-/ *die* (DV) return key
Reue *die;* ~: remorse (**über** + *Akk.* for);
  (Rel.) repentance
reuen *tr. V.* etw. reut jmdn. sb. regrets sth.
reu·mütig *Adj.* remorseful; repentant
  ⟨*sinner*⟩
Reuse *die;* ~, ~n fish trap
Revanche /re'vãː.ʃ(ə)/ *die;* ~, ~n revenge;
  (Sport) return match/fight/game
revanchieren *refl. V.* (a) get one's
  revenge, (coll.) get one's own back (**bei** on)
  (b) sich bei jmdm. für eine Einladung ~
  (ugs.) return sb.'s invitation
Revers /rə've:ɐ̯/ *das od.* (österr.) *der;* ~
  /rə'vɛːɐ̯(s)/, ~ /rə'vɛːɐ̯s/ lapel
reversibel /revɛr'ziːbl̩/ *Adj.* (Technik, Med.)
  reversible
revidieren /revi'diːrən/ *tr. V.* (abändern)
  revise; amend ⟨*law, contract*⟩
Revier /re'viːɐ̯/ *das;* ~s, ~e
  (a) (Aufgabenbereich) province
  (b) (Zool.) territory
  (c) (Polizei~) (Dienststelle) [police] station;
  (Bereich) district; (des einzelnen Polizisten) beat
Revision /revi'zjoːn/ *die;* ~, ~en
  (a) revision; (Änderung) amendment
  (b) (Rechtsw.) appeal [on a point/points of
  law]; ~ **einlegen, in die** ~ **gehen** lodge an
  appeal [on a point/points of law]
Revolte /re'vɔltə/ *die;* ~, ~n revolt
revoltieren /revɔl'tiːrən/ *itr. V.* revolt,
  rebel (**gegen** against); (fig.) ⟨*stomach*⟩ rebel
Revolution /revolu'tsjoːn/ *die;* ~, ~en
  (auch fig.) revolution
revolutionär [1] *Adj.* revolutionary
  [2] *adv.* in a revolutionary way
Revolutionär *der;* ~s, ~e,
Revolutionärin *die;* ~, ~nen
  revolutionary
Revolver /re'vɔlvɐ/ *der;* ~s, ~: revolver
Rezept *das;* ~[e]s, ~e (a) (Med.)
  prescription
  (b) (Anleitung) recipe
rezept·frei [1] *Adj.* ~e Mittel medicines
  obtainable without a prescription
  [2] *adv.* etw. ~ verkaufen/erhalten
  sell/obtain sth. without a prescription *or*
  over the counter

Rezeption *die;* ~, ~en reception *no art.*
rezept·pflichtig *Adj.* ⟨*drug etc.*⟩ obtainable only on prescription
Rezession *die;* ~, ~en (Wirtsch.) recession
R-Gespräch /'ɛr-/ *das* (Fernspr.) reverse-charge call (Brit.); collect call (Amer.)
Rhabarber *der;* ~s rhubarb
Rhein *der;* ~[e]s Rhine
rheinisch *Adj.* Rhenish; ⟨*speciality etc.*⟩ of the Rhine region
Rhein·land *das;* ~[e]s Rhineland
Rheinland-Pfalz *(das);* ~: the Rhineland-Palatinate
Rhetorik *die;* ~, ~en rhetoric
Rheuma *das;* ~s (ugs.) rheumatism
rheumatisch (Med.) **1** *Adj.* rheumatic **2** *adv.* rheumatically
Rheumatismus *der;* ~, Rheumatismen (Med.) rheumatism
Rhinozeros *das;* ~[ses], ~se rhinoceros; rhino (coll.)
Rhododendron *der od. das;* ~s, Rhododendren rhododendron
rhythmisch **1** *Adj.* rhythmical; rhythmic **2** *adv.* rhythmically
Rhythmus *der;* ~, Rhythmen (auch fig.) rhythm
richten **1** *tr. V.* **(a)** direct ⟨*gaze*⟩ **(auf + *Akk.* at, towards); turn ⟨*eyes, gaze*⟩ (auf + *Akk.* towards); point ⟨*torch, telescope, gun*⟩ (auf + *Akk.* at); aim ⟨*gun, missile, telescope, searchlight*⟩ (auf + *Akk.* on); (fig.) direct ⟨*activity, attention*⟩ (auf + *Akk.* towards); address ⟨*letter, remarks, words*⟩ (an + *Akk.* to); level ⟨*criticism*⟩ (an + *Akk.* at) **(b)** (gerade richten) straighten **(c)** (aburteilen) judge; (verurteilen) condemn; *s. auch* ZUGRUNDE A **2** *refl. V.* **(a)** (sich hinwenden) **sich auf jmdn./etw.** ~ (auch fig.) be directed towards sb./sth. **(b) sich an jmdn./etw.** ~ ⟨*person*⟩ turn on sb./sth.; ⟨*appeal, explanation*⟩ be directed at sb./sth.; **sich gegen jmdn./etw.** ~ ⟨*person*⟩ criticize sb./sth.; ⟨*criticism, accusations, etc.*⟩ be aimed *or* levelled at sb./sth. **(c)** (sich orientieren) **sich nach jmdm./jmds. Wünschen** ~: fit in with sb./sb.'s wishes **(d)** (abhängen) **sich nach jmdm./etw.** ~: depend on sb./sth. **3** *itr. V.* (urteilen) judge
Richter *der;* ~s, ~, **Richterin** *die;* ~, ~nen judge
Richt·geschwindigkeit *die* recommended maximum speed
richtig **1** *Adj.* **(a)** right; (zutreffend) right; correct; accurate ⟨*prophecy, premonition*⟩; **etw.** ~ **stellen** correct sth. **(b)** (ordentlich) proper **(c)** (wirklich, echt) real **2** *adv.* **(a)** right; correctly **(b)** (ordentlich) properly **(c)** (richtiggehend) really

richtig·gehend **1** *Adj.* real; proper (coll.) **2** *adv.* really
Richtigkeit *die;* ~: correctness; **etw. hat seine** ~, **mit etw. hat es seine** ~: sth. is right; **das wird schon seine** ~ **haben** I'm sure it's all right *or* (coll.) OK
***richtig|stellen** ▸ RICHTIG 1A
Richt-: ~**linie** *die* guideline; ~**schnur** *die; Pl.* ~~en (fig.) guiding principle
Richtung *die;* ~, ~en **(a)** direction; **in** ~ **Ulm** in the direction of Ulm **(b)** (fig.: Tendenz) movement; trend
richtung·weisend *Adj.* ⟨*idea, resolution, paper, speech*⟩ that points the way ahead
rieb *1. u. 3. Pers. Sg. Prät. v.* REIBEN
riechen **1** *unr. tr. V.* **(a)** smell **(b)** (wittern) ⟨*dog etc.*⟩ pick up the scent of **2** *unr. itr. V.* **(a)** smell; **an jmdm./etw.** ~: smell sb./sth. **(b)** (einen Geruch haben) smell (nach of)
rief *1. u. 3. Pers. Sg. Prät. v.* RUFEN
Riegel *der;* ~s, ~ **(a)** bolt **(b) ein** ~ **Schokolade** a bar of chocolate
Riemen *der;* ~s, ~ **(a)** strap; (Treib~, Gürtel) belt; **sich am** ~ **reißen** (ugs.) pull oneself together; get a grip on oneself **(b)** (Ruder) [long] oar
Riese *der;* ~n, ~n giant
rieseln *itr. V.; mit Richtungsangabe mit sein* trickle [down]; ⟨*snow*⟩ fall gently
Riesen- giant; enormous ⟨*selection, profit, portion*⟩; tremendous (coll.) ⟨*effort, rejoicing, success*⟩; terrific (coll.), terrible (coll.) ⟨*stupidity, scandal, fuss*⟩
riesen-, Riesen-: ~**groß** *Adj.* enormous; huge; terrific (coll.) ⟨*surprise*⟩; ~**schritt** *der* giant stride; ~**welle** *die* giant wave
riesig **1** *Adj.* enormous; huge; vast ⟨*country*⟩; tremendous ⟨*effort, progress*⟩ **2** *adv.* (ugs.) tremendously (coll.); terribly (coll.)
Riesin *die;* ~, ~nen giantess
Riesling *der;* ~s, ~e Riesling
Riester-Rente *die: state-supported private pension*
riet *1. u. 3. Pers. Sg. Prät. v.* RATEN
Riff *das;* ~[e]s, ~e reef
rigoros **1** *Adj.* rigorous **2** *adv.* rigorously
Rille *die;* ~, ~n groove
Rind *das;* ~[e]s, ~er **(a)** cow; (Stier) bull; ~er cattle *pl.* **(b)** (~fleisch) beef
Rinde *die;* ~, ~n **(a)** (Baum~) bark **(b)** (Brot~) crust; (Käse~) rind
Rinder·braten *der* roast beef *no indef. art.*; (roh) roasting beef *no indef. art.*
Rinder·wahnsinn *der* mad cow disease
Rind-: ~**fleisch** *das* beef; ~**vieh** *das* **(a)** cattle *pl.;* **(b)** (ugs. abwertend) ass; [stupid] fool

Ring *der;* ~[e]s, ~e ring
Ringel·natter *die* ring snake
ringen ① *unr. tr. V.* (Sport, fig.) wrestle; (fig.: kämpfen) struggle, fight (**um** for; **gegen, mit** with); **nach Luft** ~: struggle for breath
② *unr. tr. V.* **die Hände** ~: wring one's hands
Ringen *das;* ~s (Sport) wrestling *no art.*
Ring-: ~**finger** *der* ring finger; ~**kampf** *der* **(a)** [stand-up] fight; **(b)** (Sport) wrestling bout
rings *Adv.* all around
rings·herum *Adv.* all around [it/them *etc.*]
Ring·straße *die* ring road
rings-: ~**um**, ~**umher** *Adv.* all around
Rinne *die;* ~, ~n channel; (Dach~, Rinnstein) gutter; (Abfluss) drainpipe
rinnen *unr. itr. V.; mit sein* run
Rinn·stein *der* gutter
Rippchen *das;* ~s, ~ (Kochk. südd.) rib [of pork]
Rippe *die;* ~, ~n rib
Rippen·bruch *der* (Med.) rib fracture
Risiko *das;* ~s, Risiken risk
Risiko-: ~**faktor** *der* risk factor; ~**gruppe** *die* risk group
riskant ① *Adj.* risky
② *adv.* riskily
riskieren *tr. V.* risk
riss, *riß 1. u. 3. Pers. Sg. Prät. v. REISSEN
Riss, *Riß *der;* Risses, Risse tear; (Spalt, Sprung) crack
rissig *Adj.* cracked; chapped ⟨lips⟩
ritt 1. u. 3. Pers. Sg. Prät. v. REITEN
Ritt *der;* ~[e]s, ~e ride
Ritter *der;* ~s, ~: knight
Ritter·sporn *der* delphinium
rittlings *Adv.* astride
Ritze *die;* ~, ~n crack; [narrow] gap
ritzen *tr. V.* scratch
Rivale *der;* ~n, ~n, **Rivalin** *die;* ~, ~nen rival
Rivalität *die;* ~, ~en rivalry *no indef. art.*
Roastbeef /'ro:stbi:f/ *das;* ~s, ~s roast [sirloin (Brit.) of] beef
Robbe *die;* ~, ~n seal
Robe *die;* ~, ~n robe; (schwarz) gown
Roboter *der;* ~s, ~: robot
robust *Adj.* robust
roch 1. u. 3. Pers. Sg. Prät. v. RIECHEN
Rochade *die;* ~, ~n (Schach) castling
röcheln *itr. V.* ⟨dying person⟩ give the death rattle
Rock¹ *der;* ~[e]s, Röcke skirt
Rock² *der;* ~[s] (Musik) rock [music]
Rock and Roll /'rɔk ɛnt 'rɔl/ *der;* ~[s], ~[s] rock and roll *no pl.*
Rock·band *die* rock band
rocken *itr. V.* rock

Rocker *der;* ~s, ~: rocker
rockig *Adj.* rock ⟨music⟩; rock-like ⟨jazz etc.⟩
Rock·musik *die* rock music
Rodel·bahn *die* toboggan run; (Sport) luge run
rodeln *itr. V.; mit sein* sledge; toboggan
roden *tr. V.* clear ⟨wood, land⟩; (ausgraben) grub up ⟨tree⟩
Rogen *der;* ~s, ~: roe
Roggen *der;* ~s rye
Roggen-: ~**brot** *das* rye bread; **ein** ~**brot** a loaf of rye bread; ~**brötchen** *das* rye-bread roll
roh ① *Adj.* **(a)** raw ⟨food⟩; unboiled ⟨milk⟩; unfinished ⟨wood⟩
(b) (ungenau) rough
(c) (brutal) brutish; brute *attrib.* ⟨force⟩
② *adv.* **(a)** (ungenau) roughly
(b) (brutal) brutishly; (grausam) callously; (grob) coarsely
Roh-: ~**bau** *der* shell [of a/the building]; ~**kost** *die* raw fruit and vegetables *pl.;* ~**material** *das* raw material; ~**öl** *das* crude oil
Rohr *das;* ~[e]s, ~e **(a)** (Leitungs~) pipe; (als Bauteil) tube
(b) *o. Pl.* (Röhricht) reeds *pl.*
(c) *o. Pl.* (Werkstoff) reed
Röhre *die;* ~, ~n tube; (Elektronen~) valve (Brit.); tube (Amer.)
Roh·stoff *der* raw material
Rokoko *das;* ~[s] rococo
*Rolladen ▶ ROLLLADEN
Roll·bahn *die* (Flugw.) taxiway
Rolle *die;* ~, ~n **(a)** (Spule) reel
(b) (zylindrischer [Hohl]körper; Zusammengerolltes) roll
(c) (Walze) roller
(d) (Rad) [small] wheel; (an Möbeln usw.) castor; (für Gardine, Schiebetür usw.) runner
(e) (Turnen, Kunstflug) roll
(f) (Theater, Film usw., fig.) role; part; (Soziol.) role; **es spielt keine** ~: it is of no importance; (es macht nichts aus) it doesn't matter
rollen ① *tr. V.* roll
② *itr. V. mit sein* ⟨ball, wheel, etc.⟩ roll; ⟨vehicle⟩ move; ⟨aircraft⟩ taxi
Roller *der;* ~s, ~: scooter
Roll-: ~**feld** *das* runway[s] and taxiway[s]; ~**kragen** *der* polo neck; ~**laden** *der* [roller] shutter; ~**mops** *der* rollmops; ~**schuh** *der* roller skate; ~**schuh laufen** roller-skate; ~**splitt** *der* loose chippings *pl.;* ~**stuhl** *der* wheelchair; ~**treppe** *die* escalator
Rom (*das*); ~s Rome
Roman *der;* ~s, ~e novel
Romantik *die;* ~: romanticism; **die** ~: Romanticism

romạntisch [1] *Adj.* romantic
[2] *adv.* romantically

Romạnze *die;* ∼, ∼n romance

Römer *der;* ∼s, ∼, **Römerin** *die;* ∼,
∼nen Roman

römisch-katholisch *Adj.* Roman
Catholic

röntgen *tr. V.* X-ray

Röntgen-: ∼**aufnahme** *die,* ∼**bild**
das X-ray [image/photograph *or* picture];
∼**strahlen** *Pl.* X-rays

rosa [1] *indekl. Adj.* pink
[2] *adv.* pink

Rosa *das;* ∼s, ∼ *od.* ∼s pink

Rose *die;* ∼, ∼n rose

rosé *indekl. Adj.* pale pink

Rosé *der;* ∼s, ∼s rosé [wine]

Rosen-: ∼**kohl** *der* [Brussels] sprouts
pl.; ∼**kranz** *der* (kath. Kirche) rosary; **einen**
∼**kranz beten** say a rosary; ∼**montag** *der*
the day before Shrove Tuesday

rosig *Adj.* (a) rosy; pink ⟨*piglet etc.*⟩
(b) (fig.) rosy; optimistic ⟨*mood*⟩

Rosine *die;* ∼, ∼n raisin

Rosmarin *der;* ∼s rosemary

Ross, *Roß *das;* Rosses, Rosse *od.*
Rösser horse; steed (poet./joc.); **hoch zu**
∼: on horseback; **auf dem** *od.* **seinem hohen**
∼ **sitzen** (fig.) be on one's high horse

Ross-, *Roß-: ∼**haar** *das* horsehair;
∼**kastanie** *die* horse chestnut

Rost¹ *der;* ∼[e]s, ∼e (a) (Gitter) grating;
(eines Ofens, einer Feuerstelle) grate; (Brat∼)
grill
(b) (Bett∼) base

Rost² *der;* ∼[e]s rust

Rost-: ∼**braten** *der* grilled steak;
∼**bratwurst** *die* grilled sausage

rosten *itr. V.; auch mit sein* rust

rösten /'rœstn̩, 'rø:stn̩/ *tr. V.* roast; toast
⟨*bread*⟩

rost·frei *Adj.* stainless ⟨*steel*⟩

Rösti *die;* ∼ (schweiz. Kochk.) thinly sliced
fried potatoes *pl.*

rostig *Adj.* rusty

rot [1] *Adj.* red; ∼ **werden** turn red; ⟨*person*⟩
blush; ⟨*traffic light*⟩ change to red
[2] *adv.* red

Rot *das;* ∼s, ∼ *od.* ∼s red

Rot·barsch *der* rosefish

Röte *die;* ∼: red[ness]

röten [1] *tr. V.* redden
[2] *refl. V.* go or turn red

rot-, Rot-: ∼**haarig** *Adj.* red-haired;
∼**hirsch** *der* red deer; ∼**grün** *Adj.* (Politik)
⟨*coalition*⟩ of Greens and Socialists; red-
green ⟨*coalition*⟩

rotieren *itr. V.* (a) rotate
(b) (ugs.: hektisch sein) get into a flap (coll.)

Rot-: ∼**käppchen** *das;* ∼∼s Little Red
Riding Hood; ∼**kehlchen** *das;* ∼∼s,

∼∼: robin [redbreast]; ∼**kohl** *der,* (bes.
südd., österr.) ∼**kraut** *das* red cabbage

rötlich *Adj.* reddish

Rot-: ∼**licht** *das* red light; **bei** ∼**licht**
under a red light; ∼**stift** *der* red pencil

Rötung *die;* ∼, ∼en reddening

Rot·wein *der* red wine

Rotz *der;* ∼es (salopp) snot (sl.)

rotzen (derb) [1] *itr. V.* (a) blow one's nose
loudly
(b) (Schleim in den Mund ziehen) sniff back
one's snot (sl.)
(c) (ausspucken) gob (sl.)
[2] *tr. V.* spit

rotz·frech (salopp) [1] *Adj.* insolent; snotty
(sl.)
[2] *adv.* insolently; snottily (sl.)

Rouge /ru:ʒ/ *das;* ∼s, ∼s rouge

Roulade /ru:la:də/ *die;* ∼, ∼n (Kochk.)
[beef/veal/pork] olive

Route /'ru:tə/ *die;* ∼, ∼n route

Router /'ru:tɐ/ *der;* ∼s, ∼ (DV) router

Routine /ru'ti:nə/ *die;* ∼ (a) (Erfahrung)
experience; (Übung) practice
(b) (Gewohnheit) routine *no def. art.*

routiniert /ruti'ni:ɐt/ [1] *Adj.* (gewandt)
expert; skilled; (erfahren) experienced
[2] *adv.* expertly; skilfully

Rowdy /'raudi/ *der;* ∼s, ∼s (abwertend)
hooligan

Rübe *die;* ∼, ∼n turnip; **Rote** ∼: beetroot;
Gelbe ∼ (südd.) carrot

rüber *Adv.* (ugs.) over

Rubin *der;* ∼s, ∼e ruby

Rubrik *die;* ∼, ∼en column; (fig.: Kategorie)
category

Ruck *der;* ∼[e]s, ∼e jerk

Rück·blick *der* look back (**auf** + *Akk.* at);
retrospective view (**auf** + *Akk.* of)

rücken *itr., tr. V.* move

Rücken *der;* ∼s, ∼: back; (Buch∼) spine

Rücken-: ∼**deckung** *die* (a) (bes. Milit.)
rear cover; (b) (fig.) backing; ∼**lehne** *die*
[chair/seat] back; ∼**mark** *das* (Anat.) spinal
cord; ∼**schmerzen** *Pl.* backache *sing.;*
∼**schwimmen** *das* backstroke; ∼**wind**
der tail wind

rück-, Rück-: ∼|**erstatten** *tr. V.; nur
im Inf. u. 2. Part.* repay; ∼**erstattung**
die repayment; ∼**fahr·karte** *die,*
∼**fahr·schein** *der* return [ticket];
∼**fahrt** *die* return journey; ∼**fall** *der*
(Med., auch fig.) relapse; ∼**fällig** *Adj.* (Med.,
auch fig.) relapsed ⟨*patient, alcoholic, etc.*⟩;
∼**fällig werden** have a relapse; ⟨*alcoholic
etc.*⟩ go back to one's old ways; ⟨*criminal*⟩
commit a second offence; ∼**flug** *der*
return flight; ∼**frage** *die* query; ∼**gabe**
die return; ∼**gang** *der* drop, fall (*Gen.*
in); ∼**gängig** *Adj.* ∼**gängig machen**
cancel ⟨*agreement, decision, etc.*⟩; ∼**grat**
das; ∼∼[e]s, ∼∼e spine; (bes. fig.) ····⟩

backbone; ∼**halt** *der* support; backing;
∼**halt·los** [1] *Adj.* unreserved, unqualified
⟨*support*⟩; [2] *adv.* unreservedly; ∼**kehr**
die; ∼∼: return; ∼**kopp[e]lung** *die*
(Elektrot.) feedback; ∼**lage** *die* savings
pl.; ∼**läufig** *Adj.* decreasing ⟨*number*⟩;
declining ⟨*economic growth etc.*⟩; falling
⟨*rate, production, etc.*⟩; ∼**licht** *das* rear *or*
tail light
rücklings *Adv.* on one's back
Rück-: ∼**nahme** *die;* ∼∼: taking back;
∼**reise** *die* return journey; ∼**ruf** *der*
(Fernspr.) return call
Ruck·sack *der* rucksack; (Touren∼)
backpack
Rucksack·urlaub *der* backpacking
holiday
rück-, Rück-: ∼**schlag** *der* setback;
∼**schritt** *der* retrograde step; ∼**seite**
die back; (einer Münze usw.) reverse; far
side; ∼**sicht** *die* consideration; ∼**sicht**
auf jmdn. nehmen show consideration
for *or* towards sb.; ∼**sicht·nahme** *die;*
∼∼: consideration; ∼**sichts·los** [1] *Adj.*
inconsiderate; thoughtless; (verantwortungslos)
reckless ⟨*driver*⟩; (schonungslos) ruthless;
[2] *adv. s. Adj:* inconsiderately; recklessly;
ruthlessly; ∼**sichtslosigkeit** *die;*
∼∼, ∼∼**en** ▸ RÜCKSICHTSLOS: lack of
consideration; recklessness; ruthlessness;
∼**sichts·voll** [1] *Adj.* considerate,
[2] *adv.* considerately; ∼**sitz** *der* back
seat; ∼**spiegel** *der* rear-view mirror;
∼**sprache** *die* consultation; ∼**stand**
der **(a)** (Rest) residue; **(b)** (ausstehende
Zahlung) arrears *pl.;* **(c)** (Zurückbleiben hinter
dem gesetzten Ziel) backlog; (bes. Sport: hinter
dem Gegner) deficit; **[mit etw.] im** ∼**stand**
sein/in ∼**stand** (*Akk.*) **geraten** be/get behind
[with sth.]; ∼**ständig** *Adj.* **(a)** backward;
(b) (schon länger fällig) outstanding ⟨*payment,*
amount⟩; ⟨*wages*⟩ still owing; ∼**strahler**
der reflector; ∼**tritt** *der* resignation (**von**
from); (von einer Kandidatur, einem Vertrag usw.)
withdrawal (**von** from)
rückwärts *Adv.* backwards
Rückwärts·gang *der* (Kfz-W.) reverse
[gear]
rück-, Rück-: ∼**weg** *der* return
journey; ∼**wirkend** [1] *Adj.* retrospective;
backdated ⟨*pay increase*⟩; [2] *adv.* retrospectively;
∼**zahlung** *die* repayment; ∼**zug** *der*
retreat
Rüde *der;* ∼**n,** ∼**n** [male] dog
Rudel *das;* ∼**s,** ∼: herd; (von Wölfen, Hunden)
pack
Ruder *das;* ∼**s,** ∼ **(a)** (Riemen) oar
(b) (Steuer∼) rudder
Ruder·boot *das* rowboat; rowing boat
(Brit.)
Rudergänger *der;* ∼∼**s,** ∼∼, ∼**gast**
der (Seemannsspr.) helmsman

---

rudern [1] *itr. V.; mit sein* row
[2] *tr. V.* row
Ruder·regatta *die* rowing regatta
Ruf *der;* ∼**[e]s,** ∼**e (a)** call; (Schrei) shout;
cry; (Tierlaut) call
(b) (fig.: Forderung) call (**nach** for)
(c) (Telefonnummer) telephone [number]
(d) (Leumund) reputation
rufen [1] *unr. itr. V.* call (**nach** for); (schreien)
shout (**nach** for); ⟨*animal*⟩ call
[2] *unr. tr. V.* **(a)** (ausrufen) call; (schreien) shout
(b) (herbeirufen, anrufen) **jmdn.** ∼: call sb.;
jmdn. zu Hilfe ∼: call to sb. to help
Ruf-: ∼**mord** *der* character assassination;
∼**mord·kampagne** *die* smear
campaign; ∼**name** *der* first name (*by*
which one is generally known); ∼**nummer**
die telephone number
Rüge *die;* ∼, ∼**n** reprimand
rügen *tr. V.* reprimand ⟨*person*⟩ (**wegen** for);
censure ⟨*carelessness etc.*⟩
Ruhe *die;* ∼ **(a)** (Stille) silence; ∼ **[bitte]!**
quiet *or* silence [please]!
(b) (Ungestörtheit) peace; **jmdn. mit etw.**
∼ **lassen** stop bothering sb. with sth.
(c) (Unbewegtheit) rest
(d) (Erholung) rest *no def. art.*
(e) (Gelassenheit) calm[ness]; composure;
[die] ∼ **bewahren/die** ∼ **verlieren** keep calm/
lose one's composure; **in [aller]** ∼: [really]
calmly
ruhe·los [1] *Adj.* restless
[2] *adv.* restlessly
ruhen *itr. V.* **(a)** (ausruhen) rest
(b) (geh.: schlafen) sleep
(c) (stillstehen) ⟨*work, business*⟩ have stopped;
⟨*production, firm*⟩ be at a standstill
Ruhe-: ∼**pause** *die* break; ∼**stand** *der*
retirement; **in den** ∼**stand gehen/versetzt**
werden go into retirement/be retired;
∼**störung** *die* disturbance; (Rechtsw.)
disturbance of the peace; ∼**tag** *der* closing
day; „Dienstag ∼**tag**" 'closed on Tuesdays'
ruhig [1] *Adj.* **(a)** (still, leise) quiet
(b) (friedlich, ungestört) peaceful ⟨*times, life,*
valley, etc.⟩; quiet ⟨*talk, reflection, life*⟩
(c) (unbewegt) calm ⟨*sea, weather*⟩; still ⟨*air*⟩;
(fig.) peaceful ⟨*melody*⟩; (gleichmäßig) steady
⟨*breathing, hand, steps*⟩; smooth ⟨*flight,*
crossing⟩
(d) (gelassen) calm ⟨*voice etc.*⟩; quiet, calm
⟨*person*⟩
[2] *adv.* **(a)** (still, leise) quietly; **sich**
∼ **verhalten** keep quiet
(b) (friedlich, ohne Störungen) peacefully; (ohne
Zwischenfälle) uneventfully; ⟨*work, think*⟩ in
peace
(c) (unbewegt) ⟨*sit, lie, stand*⟩ still;
(gleichmäßig) ⟨*burn, breathe*⟩ steadily; ⟨*run,*
fly⟩ smoothly
(d) (gelassen) ⟨*speak, watch, sit*⟩ calmly
[3] *Adv.* by all means
Ruhm *der;* ∼**[e]s** fame

rühmen 1 *tr. V.* praise
  2 *refl. V.* boast (+ *Gen.* about)
ruhm·reich *Adj.* glorious ⟨*victory, history*⟩; celebrated ⟨*general, army, victory*⟩
Ruhr *die;* ∼, ∼**en** dysentery *no art.*
Rühr·ei *das* scrambled egg[s *pl.*]
rühren 1 *tr. V.* (a) (umrühren) stir; (einrühren) stir ⟨*egg, powder, etc.*⟩ (an, in + *Akk.* into)
  (b) (bewegen) move ⟨*limb, fingers, etc.*⟩
  (c) (fig.) move; touch
  2 *itr. V.* (a) (umrühren) stir
  (b) (geh.: herrühren) **das rührt daher, dass ...:** that stems from the fact that ...
  3 *refl. V.* (a) (sich bewegen) move
  (b) (Milit.) **rührt euch!** at ease!
rührend 1 *Adj.* touching
  2 *adv.* touchingly
rühr·selig 1 *Adj.* (a) emotional ⟨*person*⟩
  (b) (allzu gefühlvoll) over-sentimental; ⟨*manner, mood, etc.*⟩; maudlin, (coll.) tear-jerking ⟨*play, song, etc.*⟩
  2 *adv.* (allzu gefühlvoll) in an over-sentimental manner
Rühr·seligkeit *die* sentimentality
Rührung *die;* ∼: emotion
Ruine *die;* ∼, ∼**n** ruin
ruinieren *tr. V.* ruin
rülpsen *itr. V.* (ugs.) burp
rum *Adv.* (ugs.) ▶ HERUM
Rum *der;* ∼**s**, ∼**s** rum
Rumäne *der;* ∼**n**, ∼**n** Romanian
Rumänien *(das);* ∼**s** Romania
Rumänin *die;* ∼, ∼**nen** Romanian
rumänisch *Adj.* Romanian
Rummel *der;* ∼**s** (ugs.) (a) commotion; (Aufhebens) fuss (**um** about)
  (b) (Jahrmarkt) fair
Rummel·platz *der* (bes. nordd.) fairground
Rumpel·kammer *die* (ugs.) boxroom (Brit.); junk room
rumpeln *itr. V.* (ugs.) bump and bang about
Rumpf *der;* ∼**[e]s**, Rümpfe (a) trunk [of the body]
  (b) (beim Schiff) hull
  (c) (beim Flugzeug) fuselage
rümpfen *tr. V.* **die Nase [bei etw.]** ∼: wrinkle one's nose [at sth.]; **über jmdn./ etw. die Nase rümpfen** (fig.) look down one's nose at sb./turn up one's nose at sth.
Rumpsteak /'rʊmpsteːk/ *das;* ∼**s**, ∼**s** rump steak
rum|treiben *unr. refl. V.* (ugs.)
  ▶ HERUMTREIBEN
rund 1 *Adj.* (a) round
  (b) (dicklich) plump ⟨*arms etc.*⟩; chubby ⟨*cheeks*⟩; fat ⟨*stomach*⟩
  (c) (ugs.: ganz) round ⟨*dozen, number, etc.*⟩
  2 *Adv.* (a) (ugs.: etwa) about
  (b) ∼ **um jmdn./etw.** [all] around sb./sth
Rund-: ∼**blick** *der* panorama; view in all directions; ∼**brief** *der* circular [letter]
Runde *die;* ∼, ∼**n** (a) (Sport: Strecke) lap

  (b) (Sport: Durchgang usw.) round; **über die** ∼**n kommen** (fig. ugs.) get by; manage
  (c) (Personenkreis) circle; (Gesellschaft) company
  (d) (Rundgang) round
  (e) (Lage) round
rund-, Rund-: ∼**erneuern** *tr. V.;* ich runderneuere, runderneuert, rundzuerneuern (Kfz-W.) remould; ∼**fahrt** *die* tour (**durch** of); ∼**funk** *der* (a) radio;
  (b) (Einrichtung, Gebäude) radio station
Rundfunk-: ∼**anstalt** *die* broadcasting corporation; ∼**gebühren** *Pl.* radio licence fees; ∼**gerät** *das* radio set; ∼**sendung** *die* radio programme; ∼**sprecher** *der,* ∼**sprecherin** *die* radio announcer
rund-, Rund-: ∼**gang** *der* round (**durch** of); ∼**herum** *Adv.* (a) (ringsum) all around;
  (b) (völlig) completely
rundlich *Adj.* (a) roundish
  (b) (mollig) plump
Rund-: ∼**reise** *die* [circular] tour (**durch** of); ∼**schreiben** *das;* ▶ ∼BRIEF; ∼**weg** *der* circular path *or* walk
runter *Adv.* (ugs.) ∼ **[da]!** get off [there]; *s. auch* HERUNTER; HINUNTER
runter|scrollen *tr. auch itr. V* (DV) scroll down
Runzel *die;* ∼, ∼**n** wrinkle
runz[e]lig *Adj.* wrinkled
runzeln *tr. V.* **die Stirn/die Brauen** ∼: wrinkle one's brow/knit one's brows; (ärgerlich) frown
rupfen *tr. V.* (a) pluck ⟨*goose, hen, etc.*⟩
  (b) (abreißen) pull up ⟨*weeds, grass*⟩; pull off ⟨*leaves etc.*⟩
ruppig *Adj.* (abwertend) gruff ⟨*person, behaviour*⟩; sharp ⟨*tone*⟩; **er war** ∼ **zu ihr** he was short with her; he snapped at her
Rüsche *die;* ∼, ∼**n** ruche; frill
Ruß *der;* ∼**es** soot
Russe *der;* ∼**n**, ∼**n** Russian
Rüssel *der;* ∼**s**, ∼ (des Elefanten) trunk; (des Schweins) snout; (bei Insekten u. Ä.) proboscis
rußen *itr. V.* give off sooty smoke
Russin *die;* ∼, ∼**nen** Russian
russisch 1 *Adj.* Russian
  2 *adv.* (auf ∼) in Russian
Russisch *das;* ∼**[s]** Russian
Russ-land, *Ruß-land *(das);* ∼**s** Russia
rüsten *itr. V.* arm
rüstig *Adj.* sprightly; active
rustikal 1 *Adj.* country-style ⟨*food, inn, clothes, etc.*⟩; rustic ⟨*furniture*⟩
  2 *adv.* in [a] country style
Rüstung *die;* ∼, ∼**en** (a) armament *no art.;* (Waffen) arms *pl.;* weapons *pl.*
  (b) (hist.) suit of armour
Rüstungs-: ∼**industrie** *die* armaments *or* arms industry; ····❯

∼kontrolle *die* arms control; **∼stopp** *der* arms freeze; **∼wettlauf** *der* arms race
Rute *die;* ∼, ∼n switch; (Birken∼, Angel∼, Wünschel∼) rod
Rutsch *der* **guten** ∼ **[ins neue Jahr]!** (ugs.) happy New Year!

Rutsch·bahn *die* slide
Rutsche *die;* ∼, ∼n chute
rutschen *itr. V.; mit sein* slide; ⟨*clutch, carpet*⟩ slip
rutschig *Adj.* slippery
rütteln *tr., itr. V.* shake

Ss

s, S /ɛs/ *das;* ∼, ∼ s, S
s *Abk.* = **Sekunde** sec.; s.
s. *Abk.* = **siehe**
S *Abk.* **(a)** = **Süden** S.
  (b) (österr.) = **Schilling** Sch
S. *Abk.* = **Seite** p.
Sa. *Abk.* = **Samstag** Sat.
Saal *der;* ∼[e]s, **Säle (a)** hall; (Ballsaal) ballroom
  (b) (Publikum) audience
Saar·land *das;* ∼[e]s Saarland; Saar (esp. Hist.)
Saat *die;* ∼, ∼en **(a)** (das Gesäte) [young] crops *pl.*
  (b) (das Säen) sowing
  (c) (Samenkörner) seed[s *pl.*]
Säbel *der;* ∼s, ∼: sabre
Sabotage /zabo'ta:ʒə/ *die;* ∼, ∼n sabotage *no art.*
Sabotage·akt *der* act of sabotage
sabotieren *tr. V.* sabotage
Sach-: ∼**bearbeiter** *der;* ∼**bearbeiterin** *die* person responsible (für for); (Experte) specialist, expert (für on); ∼**beschädigung** *die* (Rechtsw.) wilful damage to property; ∼**buch** *das* [popular] non-fiction book; ∼**bücher lesen** read non-fiction *sing.*
sach·dienlich *Adj.* useful
Sache *die;* ∼, ∼n **(a)** things
  (b) (Angelegenheit) matter; business (esp. derog.); **zur** ∼ **kommen** come to the point
  (c) (Rechtssache) case
  (d) (Anliegen) cause
sach-, Sach-: ∼**gebiet** *das* subject [area]; field; ∼**gemäß,** ∼**gerecht** ① *Adj.* proper; correct; ② *adv.* properly; correctly; ∼**kenntnis** *die* expertise; knowledge of the subject; ∼**kundig** ① *Adj.* with a knowledge of the subject *postpos., not pred.;* ② *adv.* expertly
sachlich ① *Adj.* **(a)** (objektiv) objective; (nüchtern) functional ⟨*building, style, etc.*⟩; matter-of-fact ⟨*letter etc.*⟩
  (b) (sachbezogen) factual ⟨*error*⟩

② *adv.* **(a)** (objektiv) objectively; ⟨*state*⟩ as a matter of fact; (nüchtern) ⟨*furnished*⟩ in a functional style; ⟨*written*⟩ in a matter-of-fact way
  (b) (sachbezogen) factually ⟨*wrong*⟩
sächlich *Adj.* (Sprachw.) neuter
Sachlichkeit *die;* ∼: objectivity; (Nüchternheit) functionalism
Sach-: ∼**register** *das* [subject] index; ∼**schaden** *der* damage [to property] *no indef. art.*
Sachse *der;* ∼n, ∼n Saxon
Sachsen (*das*)*;* ∼s Saxony
Sachsen-Anhalt (*das*)*;* ∼s Saxony-Anhalt
Sächsin *die;* ∼, ∼nen Saxon
sacht, sachte ① *Adj.* **(a)** (behutsam) gentle
  (b) (leise) quiet
  ② *adv.* **(a)** gently
  (b) (leise) quietly
Sach-: ∼**verhalt** *der;* ∼∼[e]s, ∼∼e facts *pl.* [of the matter]; ∼**verstand** *der* expertise; grasp of the subject; ∼**verständige** *der/die; adj. Dekl.* expert
Sack *der;* ∼[e]s, **Säcke** sack; (aus Papier, Kunststoff) bag
Sack-: ∼**gasse** *die* cul-de-sac; ∼**hüpfen** *das;* ∼∼s sack race
Sadismus *der;* ∼: sadism *no art.*
Sadist *der;* ∼en, ∼en, **Sadistin** *die;* ∼, ∼nen sadist
sadistisch ① *Adj.* sadistic
  ② *adv.* sadistically
säen *tr.* (auch itr.) *V.* sow
Saft *der;* ∼[e]s, **Säfte (a)** juice
  (b) (in Pflanzen) sap
saftig *Adj.* **(a)** juicy; sappy ⟨*stem*⟩; lush ⟨*meadow, green*⟩
  (b) (ugs.) hefty ⟨*slap, blow*⟩; steep (coll.) ⟨*prices, bill*⟩; crude ⟨*joke, song, etc.*⟩; strongly-worded ⟨*letter etc.*⟩
saft-, Saft-: ∼**laden** *der* (salopp abwertend) lousy outfit (coll.); ∼**los** *Adj.* **(a)** juiceless; **(b)** (fig.) feeble, anodyne ⟨*language*⟩; ∼**- und kraftlos** feeble; wishy-washy; ⟨*adv.*⟩ without any zest; ∼**sack** *der* (derb abwertend) bastard (coll.)

*alte Schreibung – vgl. Hinweis auf S. x

Sage *die;* ∼, ∼n legend; (bes. nordische) saga
Säge *die;* ∼, ∼n saw
Säge-: ∼**blatt** *das* saw blade; ∼**mehl** sawdust
sagen [1] *tr. V.* (a) say; **was ich noch** ∼ **wollte** [oh] by the way; **unter uns gesagt** between you and me
(b) (mitteilen) jmdm. etw. ∼: say sth. to sb.; (zur Information) tell sb. sth.
(c) (nennen) **zu jmdm./etw. X** ∼: call sb./sth. X
(d) (anordnen, befehlen) tell
[2] *refl. V.* **sich** (*Dat.*) **etw.** ∼: say sth. to oneself
sägen *tr., itr. V.* saw
Säge-: ∼**späne** *Pl.* wood shavings; ∼**werk** *das* sawmill
sah *1. u. 3. Pers. Sg. Prät. v.* SEHEN
Sahne *die;* ∼: cream
Saison /zɛˈzõ:/ *die;* ∼, ∼s season
saisonal /zɛzoˈnaːl/ [1] *Adj.* seasonal
[2] *adv.* ⟨fluctuate⟩ according to the season
Saite *die;* ∼, ∼n string
Saiten·instrument *das* stringed instrument
Sakko *der od. das;* ∼s, ∼s jacket
Sakrament *das;* ∼[e]s, ∼e sacrament
Sakristei *die;* ∼, ∼en sacristy
säkularisieren *tr. V.* secularize ⟨property, art, etc.⟩; deconsecrate ⟨church⟩
Salami *die;* ∼, ∼[s] salami
Salami·taktik *die* step-by-step policy
Salat *der;* ∼[e]s, ∼e (a) salad
(b) [grüner] ∼: lettuce; **ein Kopf** ∼: a [head of] lettuce
Salat-: ∼**besteck** *das* salad servers *pl.;* ∼**soße** *die* salad dressing
Salbe *die;* ∼, ∼n ointment
Salbei *der od. die;* ∼: sage
Saldo *der;* ∼s, ∼s *od.* **Saldi** (Buchf., Finanzw.) balance
Säle ▶ SAAL
Salmiak *der od. das;* ∼: sal ammoniac
Salmonelle *die;* ∼, ∼n salmonella
Salon /zaˈlõ:/ *der;* ∼s, ∼s (a) (Raum) drawing room
(b) (Geschäft) [hair *etc.*] salon
salopp [1] *Adj.* casual ⟨clothes⟩; informal ⟨behaviour⟩; slangy ⟨expression⟩
[2] *adv.* ⟨dress⟩ casually
Salto *der;* ∼s, ∼s *od.* **Salti** somersault; (beim Turnen auch) salto
Salut *der;* ∼[e]s, ∼e (Milit.) salute; ∼ **schießen** fire a salute
salutieren *itr. V.* (bes. Milit.) salute
Salut·schuss, *Salut·schuß *der* (Milit.) gun salute
Salve *die;* ∼, ∼n (Milit.) salvo; (aus Gewehren) volley
Salz *das;* ∼es, ∼e salt
salzen *tr. V.* salt

salzig *Adj.* salty
Salz-: ∼**kartoffel** *die* boiled potato; ∼**säure** *die* (Chemie) hydrochloric acid; ∼**stange** *die* salt stick; ∼**streuer** *der;* ∼∼s, ∼∼: salt sprinkler; salt shaker (Amer.); ∼**wasser** *das* (a) (zum Kochen) salted water; (b) (Meerwasser) salt water
Sambia (*das*); ∼s Zambia
Samen *der;* ∼s, ∼ (a) (Samenkorn) seed
(b) (Samenkörner) seed[s *pl.*]
(c) (Sperma) sperm; semen
Samen-: ∼**bank** *die; Pl.* ∼∼en (Med., Tiermed.) sperm bank; ∼**erguss,** *∼**erguß** *der* ejaculation; ∼**korn** *das* seed; ∼**spender** *der* (Med.) sperm donor
Sammel-: ∼**büchse** *die* collecting box; ∼**mappe** *die* folder; file
sammeln [1] *tr. (auch itr.) V.* (a) collect; gather ⟨honey, firewood, fig.: experiences, impressions, etc.⟩; gather, pick ⟨berries etc.⟩
(b) (zusammenkommen lassen) gather ⟨people⟩ [together]; assemble ⟨people⟩; cause ⟨light rays⟩ to converge
[2] *refl. V.* gather [together]
Sammler *der;* ∼s, ∼: collector
Sammlung *die;* ∼, ∼en (a) collection
(b) [innere] ∼: composure
Samstag *der;* ∼[e]s, ∼e Saturday; *s. auch* DIENSTAG
samstags *Adv.* on Saturdays
samt [1] *Präp. mit Dat.* together with
[2] *Adv.* ∼ **und sonders** one and all
Samt *der;* ∼[e]s, ∼e velvet
samten *Adj.* velvet
Samt·handschuh *der* velvet glove; **jmdn. mit** ∼**en anfassen** (fig.) handle sb. with kid gloves
samtig *Adj.* velvety
sämtlich *Indefinitpron. u. unbest. Zahlwort* all the
Sand *der;* ∼[e]s sand
Sandale *die;* ∼, ∼n sandal
Sand-: ∼**bank** *die; Pl.* ∼bänke sandbank; ∼**dorn** *der; Pl.* ∼∼e (Bot.) hippophaë; [Echter] ∼**dorn** sea buckthorn ∼**düne** *die* sand dune
sandig *Adj.* sandy
sand-, Sand-: ∼**kasten** *der* [child's] sandpit; sandbox (Amer.); ∼**kuchen** *der* Madeira cake; ∼**mann** *der;* ∼**männchen** *das* sandman; ∼**stein** *der* sandstone; ∼**strahlen** *tr. V.* (Technik) sandblast; ∼**strand** *der* sandy beach
sandte *1. u. 3. Pers. Sg. Prät. v.* SENDEN
sanft [1] *Adj.* gentle; (leise) soft; (friedlich) peaceful
[2] *adv.* gently; (leise) softly; (friedlich) peacefully
Sänfte *die;* ∼, ∼n litter; (geschlossen) sedan chair
Sanftheit *die;* ∼: gentleness; (von Klängen, Licht, Farben) softness

S

Sanftmut *die;* ∼: gentleness; **mit**
∼: gently; (nachsichtig) leniently

sanftmütig ①*Adj.* gentle; docile ⟨*horse*⟩
②*adv.* gently

Sanftmütigkeit *die;* ∼: gentleness;
(Fügsamkeit) docility

sang *1. u. 3. Pers. Sg. Prät. v.* SINGEN

Sänger *der;* ∼s, ∼, **Sängerin** *die;* ∼,
∼nen singer

sanieren ①*tr. V.* (a) redevelop ⟨*area*⟩;
rehabilitate ⟨*building*⟩; (renovieren) renovate
[and improve] ⟨*flat etc.*⟩
(b) (Wirtsch.) restore ⟨*firm*⟩ to profitability
②*refl. V.* ⟨*company etc.*⟩ restore itself to
profitability; ⟨*person*⟩ get oneself out of the
red

Sanierung *die;* ∼, ∼en (a) ▶ SANIEREN A:
redevelopment; rehabilitation; renovation
(b) ▶ SANIEREN B: restoration to profitability

sanitär *Adj.* sanitary

Sanitäter *der;* ∼s, ∼, **Sanitäterin** *die;*
∼, ∼nen first-aid worker; (im Krankenwagen)
ambulance worker

sank *1. u. 3. Pers. Sg. Prät. v.* SINKEN

Sanktion *die;* ∼, ∼en sanction

sanktionieren *tr. V.* sanction

Sanktionierung *die;* ∼, ∼en sanctioning
no indef. art.

sann *1. u. 3. Pers. Sg. Prät. v.* SINNEN

Saphir *der;* ∼s, ∼e sapphire

Sardelle *die;* ∼, ∼n anchovy

Sardine *die;* ∼, ∼n sardine

Sarg *der;* ∼[e]s, Särge coffin

Sarkasmus *der;* ∼: sarcasm

sarkastisch ①*Adj.* sarcastic
②*adv.* sarcastically

SARS, Sars /zars/ *das;* ∼: SARS

saß *1. u. 3. Pers. Sg. Prät. v.* SITZEN

Satan *der* (bibl.) Satan *no def. art.*

Satellit *der;* ∼en, ∼en satellite

Satelliten-: ∼**aufnahme** *die* satellite
photograph; ∼**fernsehen** *das* satellite
television; ∼**navigation** *die* satellite
navigation; ∼**schüssel** *die* (ugs.) satellite
dish; ∼**technologie** *die* satellite
technology

Satire *die;* ∼, ∼n satire

satirisch ①*Adj.* satirical
②*adv.* satirically; with a satirical touch

satt *Adj.* (a) full [up] *pred.;* well-fed; **sich**
∼ **essen/trinken** eat/drink as much as one
wants; eat/drink one's fill
(b) **jmdn./etw.** ∼ **haben** (ugs.) be fed up with
sb./sth. (coll.)

Sattel *der;* ∼s, Sättel saddle

satteln ①*tr. V.* saddle
②*itr. V.* saddle the/one's horse

sättigen *itr. V.* be filling

---
*old spelling – see note on page x

Sattler *der;* ∼s, ∼, **Sattlerin** *die;* ∼,
∼nen saddler; (allgemein) leather worker

Satz *der;* ∼es, Sätze (a) (sprachliche Einheit)
sentence
(b) (Musik) movement
(c) (Tennis, Volleyball) set; (Tischtennis, Badminton)
game
(d) (Sprung) leap; jump
(e) (Amtsspr.: Tarif) rate
(f) (Set) set
(g) (Bodensatz) sediment; (von Kaffee) grounds
pl.

Satz·glied *das,* **Satz·teil** *der* (Sprachw.)
component part [of a/the sentence]

Satzung *die;* ∼, ∼en articles of
association *pl.;* statutes *pl.*

Satz·zeichen *das* punctuation mark

sau-, Sau- (salopp) bloody ... (Brit. sl.);
damn ... (coll.)

Sau *die;* ∼, Säue (a) (weibliches Schwein) sow
(b) (bes. südd.: Schwein) pig
(c) **die** ∼ **rauslassen** (fig. ugs.) let one's hair
down

sauber ①*Adj.* (a) clean; **etw.** ∼ **machen**
clean sth.; ∼ **machen** (putzen) clean; do the
cleaning
(b) (sorgfältig) neat
②*adv.* (a) (sorgfältig) neatly
(b) (fehlerlos) **[sehr]** ∼: [quite] perfectly

Sauberkeit *die;* ∼: cleanness

säuberlich ①*Adj.* neat
②*adv.* neatly; **fein** ∼ **geordnet/verpackt**
usw. neatly arranged/packed *etc.*

*****sauber|machen** ▶ SAUBER 1A

säubern *tr. V.* (a) clean
(b) (befreien) clear, rid (**von** of); purge ⟨*party,
government, etc.*⟩ (**von** of)

Säuberung *die;* ∼, ∼en (a) cleaning
(b) (Entfernung) purging
(c) (Politik) purge; **ethnische** ∼ (verhüll.)
ethnic cleansing

Säuberungs·aktion *die* (Politik) purge;
clean-up operation

Sauce ▶ SOSSE

Saudi *der;* ∼s, ∼s Saudi

Saudi-Arabien *(das)* Saudi Arabia

sauer ①*Adj.* (a) sour; pickled ⟨*herring,
gherkin, etc.*⟩; acid[ic] ⟨*wine, vinegar*⟩; **saurer
Regen** acid rain
(b) (ugs.: verärgert) cross, annoyed (**auf** + *Akk.*
with)
②*adv.* in vinegar

Sauer·braten *der: braised beef marinated
in vinegar and herbs;* sauerbraten (Amer.)

Sauerei *die;* ∼, ∼en (salopp abwertend)
(a) (Unflätigkeit) obscenity
(b) (Gemeinheit) bloody scandal (coll.)

Sauer-: ∼**kirsche** *die* sour cherry;
∼**kraut** *das* sauerkraut

säuerlich *Adj.* **[leicht]** ∼: slightly sour;
slightly sharp ⟨*sauce*⟩

Sauer-: ~**stoff** *der* oxygen;
~**stoff·gerät** *das* oxygen apparatus;
~**stoff·mangel** *der* lack of oxygen;
~**teig** *der* leaven

saufen [1] *unr. itr. V.* (salopp: trinken) drink; swig (coll.); (Alkohol trinken) drink; booze (coll.)
[2] *unr. tr. V.* (salopp: trinken) drink

Säufer *der;* ~**s,** ~ (salopp) boozer (coll.)

säuft *3. Pers. Sg. Präsens v.* SAUFEN

saugen [1] *tr. V.* (a) *auch unr.* suck
(b) *auch itr.* (staubsaugen) vacuum; hoover (coll.)
[2] *regelm. (auch unr.) itr. V.* an etw. (*Dat.*)
~: suck [at] sth.
[3] *unr. (auch regelm.) refl. V.* sich voll etw.
~: become soaked with sth.

säugen *tr. V.* suckle

Säuge·tier *das* (Zool.) mammal

Säugling *der;* ~**s,** ~**e** baby

Säuglings-: ~**alter** *das* infancy; babyhood; ~**pflege** *die* baby care

Säule *die;* ~**,** ~**n** column; (nur als Stütze, auch fig.) pillar

Saum *der;* ~**[e]s,** Säume hem

säumen *tr. V.* hem; (fig. geh.) line

säumig (geh.) *Adj.* tardy

Sauna *die;* ~**,** ~**s** *od.* Saunen sauna

Säure *die;* ~**,** ~**n** (a) (von Früchten) sourness; (von Wein, Essig) acidity; (von Soßen) sharpness
(b) (Chemie) acid

säure-: ~**beständig** *Adj.* acid-resistant;
~**frei** *Adj.* acid-free

Saure·gurken·zeit, Saure-Gurken-Zeit *die* (ugs.) silly season (Brit.)

Saurier /'zauriɐ/ *der;* ~**s,** ~: large prehistoric reptile

Saus: in ~ und Braus leben live the high life

säuseln [1] *itr. V.* ⟨*leaves, branches, etc.*⟩ rustle; ⟨*wind*⟩ murmur
[2] *tr. V.* (iron.: sagen) whisper

sausen *itr. V.* (a) ⟨*wind*⟩ whistle; ⟨*storm*⟩ roar; ⟨*head, ears*⟩ buzz
(b) *mit sein* ⟨*person*⟩ rush; ⟨*vehicle*⟩ roar
(c) *mit sein* ⟨*whip, bullet, etc.*⟩ whistle

sau-, Sau-: ~**stall** *der* (fig. salopp abwertend) hole (coll.); dump (coll.); ~**stark** *Adj.* (salopp) bloody brilliant (sl.); ~**wetter** *das* (salopp abwertend) lousy weather (coll.);
~**wohl** *Adj.* sich ~wohl fühlen (salopp) feel bloody (Brit. sl.) *or* (coll.) damn good *or* great

Savanne /za'vanə/ *die;* ~**,** ~**n** savannah

Saxophon *das;* ~**s,** ~**e** saxophone

SB- /ɛs'be:-/ self-service *attrib.*

S-Bahn /'ɛs-/ *die* city and suburban railway

Scanner /'skænɐ/ *der;* ~**s,** ~ (DV, Med., graf. Technik) scanner

Schabe *die;* ~**,** ~**n** cockroach

schaben *tr., itr. V.* scrape

Schaber *der;* ~**s,** ~: scraper

schäbig [1] *Adj.* (a) (abgenutzt) shabby
(b) (jämmerlich, gering) pathetic

(c) (gemein) shabby
[2] *adv.* (a) (abgenutzt) shabbily
(b) (jämmerlich) miserably
(c) (gemein) meanly

Schablone *die;* ~**,** ~**n** pattern

Schach *das;* ~**s,** ~**s** (a) (Spiel) chess
(b) (Stellung) check; jmdn./etw. in ~ halten (ugs. fig.) keep sb./sth. in check

Schach-: ~**brett** *das* chessboard;
~**figur** *die* chess piece; ~**spiel** *das*
(a) (Spiel) chess; (das Spielen) chess-playing;
(b) (Brett und Figuren) chess set

Schacht *der;* ~**[e]s,** Schächte shaft

Schachtel *die;* ~**,** ~**n** (a) box; eine
~ Zigaretten a packet *or* (Amer.) pack of cigarettes
(b) alte ~ (salopp abwertend) old bag (sl.)

schade *Adj.* [ach, wie] ~! [what a] pity *or* shame; [es ist] ~ um jmdn./etw. it's a pity *or* shame about sb./sth.; für jmdn./für *od.* zu etw. zu ~ sein be too good for sb./sth.

Schädel *der;* ~**s,** ~: skull; (Kopf) head

Schädel·basis·bruch *der* (Med.) basal skull fracture

Schädel·bruch *der* (Med.) skull fracture

schaden *itr. V.* jmdm./einer Sache
~: damage *or* harm sb./sth.

Schaden *der;* ~**s,** Schäden (a) damage *no pl., no indef. art.;* ein kleiner/großer
~: little/major damage
(b) (Nachteil) disadvantage

schaden-, Schaden-: ~**ersatz**
der (Rechtsw.) damages *pl.;* ~**freude**
die malicious pleasure; ~**froh** [1] *Adj.* gloating; ~froh sein gloat; [2] *adv.* with malicious pleasure

schadhaft *Adj.* defective

Schadhaftigkeit *die;* ~: defectiveness

schädigen *tr. V.* damage ⟨health, reputation, interests⟩; harm, hurt ⟨person⟩; cause losses to ⟨firm, industry, etc.⟩

Schädigung *die;* ~**,** ~**en** damage *no pl., no indef. art.* (Gen. to)

schädlich *Adj.* harmful

Schädling *der;* ~**s,** ~**e** pest

Schad·stoff *der* harmful chemical

schadstoff·arm *Adj.* (bes. Kfz-W.) low in harmful substances *postpos.;* clean-exhaust *attrib.* ⟨vehicle⟩

Schaf *das;* ~**[e]s,** ~**e** (a) sheep
(b) (ugs.: Dummkopf) twit (Brit. coll.)

Schaf·bock *der* ram

Schäfchen *das;* ~**s,** ~: [little] sheep; (Lamm) lamb

Schäfchen·wolke *die* fleecy cloud

Schäfer *der;* ~**s,** ~: shepherd

Schäfer·hund *der* sheepdog; [deutscher]
~: Alsatian

Schäferin *die;* ~**,** ~**nen** shepherdess

Schaf·fell *das* sheepskin

schaffen [1] *unr. tr. V.* (a) create
(b) *auch regelm.* (herstellen) create ⋯⋗

S

⟨*conditions, jobs, situation, etc.*⟩; make ⟨*room, space, fortune*⟩
2 *tr. V.* **(a)** (bewältigen) manage; **es ~, etw. zu tun** manage to do sth.
(b) (ugs.: erschöpfen) wear out
(c) etw. aus etw./in etw. (*Akk.*) **~**: get sth. out of/into sth.
3 *itr. V.* **(a)** (südd.: arbeiten) work
(b) sich (*Dat.*) **zu ~ machen** busy oneself; **jmdm. zu ~ machen** cause sb. trouble
Schaffner *der; ~s ~* (im Bus) conductor; (im Zug) guard (Brit.); conductor (Amer.)
Schaffnerin *die; ~, ~nen* (im Bus) conductress (Brit.); (im Zug) guard (Brit.); conductress (Amer.)
Schaffung *die; ~*: creation
Schafott *das; ~[e]s, ~e* scaffold
Schafs·käse *der* sheep's milk cheese
Schaf·wolle *die* sheep's wool
Schakal *der; ~s, ~e* jackal
schal *Adj.* stale ⟨*drink, taste, smell, joke*⟩; empty ⟨*words, feeling*⟩
Schal *der; ~s, ~s od. ~e* scarf
Schale *die; ~, ~n* **(a)** (Obstschale) skin; (abgeschälte ~) peel *no pl.*
(b) (Nussschale, Eierschale) shell
(c) (Schüssel) bowl; (flacher) dish
(d) sich in ~ werfen *od.* **schmeißen** (ugs.) get dressed [up] to the nines
schälen **1** *tr. V.* peel ⟨*fruit, vegetable*⟩; shell ⟨*egg, nut, pea*⟩
2 *refl. V.* peel
Schall *der; ~[e]s, ~e od.* **Schälle** sound
Schall·dämpfer *der* **(a)** silencer
(b) (Musik) mute
schall·dicht *Adj.* soundproof
schallen *regelm. (auch unr.) itr. V.* ring out; **~des Gelächter** ringing laughter
Schall-: ~**geschwindigkeit** *die* speed *or* velocity of sound; ~**mauer** *die* sound *or* sonic barrier; ~**platte** *die* record
Schalotte *die; ~, ~n* shallot
schalt *1. u. 3. Pers. Sg. Prät. v.* SCHELTEN
schalten **1** *tr. V.* switch
2 *itr. V.* **(a)** (Schalter betätigen) switch, turn (**auf** + *Akk.* to)
(b) ⟨*machine*⟩ switch (**auf** + *Akk.* to)
(c) (im Auto) change [gear]
(d) ~ und walten manage one's affairs
(e) (ugs.: begreifen) twig (coll.); catch on (coll.)
Schalter *der; ~s, ~* **(a)** switch
(b) (Post-, Bankschalter usw.) counter
Schalter-: ~**beamte** *der,* ~**beamtin** *die* counter clerk; (im Bahnhof) ticket clerk; ~**halle** *die* hall; (im Bahnhof) booking hall (Brit.); ticket office
Schalt·jahr *das* leap year
Schaltung *die; ~, ~en* (Elektrot.) circuit; wiring system
Scham *die; ~*: shame

schämen *refl. V.* be ashamed (*Gen.*, **für, wegen** of)
Scham·gefühl *das* sense of shame
schamhaft **1** *Adj.* bashful
2 *adv.* bashfully
scham·los **1** *Adj.* **(a)** (skrupellos, dreist) shameless
(b) (unanständig) indecent; shameless ⟨*person*⟩
2 *adv.* **(a)** (skrupellos, dreist) shamelessly
(b) (unanständig) indecently
Schampon *das; ~s, ~s* ▸ SHAMPOO
schamponieren *tr. V.* shampoo
Schande *die; ~*: disgrace
schändlich **1** *Adj.* disgraceful
2 *adv.* disgracefully
Schändlichkeit *die; ~*: disgracefulness
Schar *die; ~, ~en* crowd; horde
scharen·weise *Adv.* in swarms *or* hordes
scharf; schärfer, schärfst... **1** *Adj.*
(a) sharp
(b) (stark gewürzt, brennend, stechend) hot; strong ⟨*drink, vinegar, etc.*⟩; caustic ⟨*chemical*⟩; pungent ⟨*smell*⟩
(c) (durchdringend) shrill; (hell) harsh; (kalt) biting ⟨*cold, wind, etc.*⟩; sharp ⟨*frost*⟩
(d) (deutlich wahrnehmend) keen
(e) (schnell) fast; hard ⟨*ride, gallop, etc.*⟩
(f) (explosiv) live; (Ballspiele) powerful ⟨*shot*⟩
(g) das ~e S (bes. österr.) the letter 'ß'
(h) ~ auf jmdn./etw. sein (ugs.) really fancy sb. (coll.)/be really keen on sth.
2 *adv.* **(a) ~ würzen/abschmecken** season/flavour highly; **~ riechen** smell pungent
(b) (durchdringend) shrilly; (hell) harshly; (kalt) bitingly
(c) (deutlich wahrnehmend) ⟨*listen, watch, etc.*⟩ closely, intently; ⟨*think, consider, etc.*⟩ hard
(d) (deutlich hervortretend) sharply
(e) (schonungslos) ⟨*attack, criticize, etc.*⟩ sharply, strongly; ⟨*watch, observe, etc.*⟩ closely
(f) (schnell) fast; **~ bremsen** brake hard *or* sharply
Schärfe *die; ~* **(a)** sharpness
(b) (von Geschmack) hotness; (von Chemikalien) causticity; (von Geruch) pungency
(c) (Intensität) shrillness; (des Frostes) sharpness
schärfen **1** *tr. V.* (auch fig.) sharpen
2 *refl. V.* become sharper *or* keener
scharf-, Scharf-: ~**kantig** *Adj.* sharp-edged; ~**macher** *der* (ugs.) rabble-rouser; ~**macherei** *die; ~~, ~~en** (ugs.) rabble-rousing; ~**macherin** *die:* ▸~MACHER; ~**sichtig** *Adj.* sharp-sighted; perspicacious; ~**sinn** *der* astuteness; ~**sinnig** **1** *Adj.* astute; **2** *adv.* astutely
Scharlach *der; ~s* (Med.) scarlet fever
Scharlatan *der; ~s, ~e* (abwertend) charlatan
Scharnier *das; ~s, ~e* hinge

scharren ⬚1 *itr. V.* **(a)** scrape
(b) (wühlen) scratch
⬚2 *tr. V.* scrape, scratch out ‹*hole, hollow, etc.*›
Schaschlik *der od. das;* ~s, ~s (Kochk.) shashlik
Schatten *der;* ~s, ~ **(a)** shadow
(b) (schattiger Bereich) shade
Schatten-: ~**kabinett** *das* (Politik) shadow cabinet; ~**riss,** **~**riß** *der* silhouette; ~**seite** *die* shady side; **die** ~**seiten des Lebens kennen lernen** (fig.) get to know the dark side of life
schattig *Adj.* shady
Schatz *der;* ~es, **Schätze** treasure *no indef. art.*
schätzen ⬚1 *tr. V.* **(a)** estimate; **sich glücklich** ~: deem oneself lucky
(b) (ugs.: annehmen) reckon
(c) (würdigen, hoch achten) **jmdn.** ~: hold sb. in high esteem
⬚2 *itr. V.* guess
Schätzung *die;* ~, ~en estimate
Schätz·wert *der* estimated value
Schau *die;* ~, ~en **(a)** (Ausstellung) exhibition
(b) (Vorführung) show
(c) zur ~ **stellen** (ausstellen) exhibit; display; (offen zeigen) display
Schauder *der;* ~s, ~: shiver
schauderhaft ⬚1 *Adj.* terrible
⬚2 *adv.* terribly
schaudern *itr. V.* **(a)** (vor Kälte) shiver
(b) (vor Angst) shudder
schauen (bes. südd., österr., schweiz.) ⬚1 *itr. V.*
(a) look
(b) (sich kümmern um) **nach jmdm./etw.** ~: take *or* have a look at sb./sth.
(c) (achten) **auf etw.** (*Akk.*) ~: set store by sth.
(d) (ugs.: sich bemühen) **schau, dass du ...:** see *or* mind that you ...
(e) (nachsehen) have a look
⬚2 *tr. V.* **Fernsehen** ~: watch television
Schauer *der;* ~s, ~: shower
Schauer·geschichte *die* horror story
schauerlich ⬚1 *Adj.* **(a)** horrifying
(b) (ugs.: fürchterlich) terrible (coll.)
⬚2 *adv.* (ugs.: fürchterlich) terribly (coll.)
Schaufel *die;* ~, ~n shovel; (Kehr~) dustpan
schaufeln *tr. V.* shovel; (graben) dig
Schau·fenster *das* shop window
Schaufenster-: ~**bummel** *der:* **einen** ~**bummel machen** go window shopping; ~**einbruch** *der* raid on a shop window
Schaukel *die;* ~, ~n **(a)** swing
(b) (Wippe) see-saw
schaukeln ⬚1 *itr. V.* **(a)** swing; (im Schaukelstuhl) rock
(b) (sich hin und her bewegen) sway [to and fro]; (sich auf und ab bewegen) ‹*ship, boat*› pitch and

toss; ‹*vehicle*› bump [up and down]
⬚2 *tr. V.* rock
Schaukel-: ~**pferd** *das* rocking horse; ~**stuhl** *der* rocking chair
Schau·lustige *der/die; adj. Dekl.* curious onlooker
Schaum *der;* ~s, **Schäume (a)** foam; (von Seife usw.) lather; (von Getränken, Suppen usw.) froth
(b) (Geifer) foam; froth
schäumen *itr. V.* foam; froth; ‹*soap etc.*› lather; ‹*beer, fizzy drink, etc.*› froth [up]
Schaum·gummi *der* foam rubber
schaumig *Adj.* frothy; **Butter und Zucker** ~ **rühren** beat butter and sugar until fluffy
Schaum-: ~**schläger** *der* (abwertend) boaster; ~**schlägerei** *die* (abwertend) boasting; ~**schlägerin** *die:* ▶~SCHLÄGER; ~**stoff** *der* [plastic] foam; ~**wein** *der* sparkling wine
Schau·platz *der* scene
schaurig *Adj.* (furchtbar) dreadful; frightful; (unheimlich) eerie
Schau-: ~**spiel** *das* **(a)** (Drama) drama *no art.;* **(b)** (ernstes Stück) play; **(c)** (geh.: Anblick) spectacle; ~**spieler** *der* actor; ~**spielerin** *die* actress; ~**steller** *der;* ~~s, ~~: showman; ~**stellerin** *die;* ~~, ~~**nen** showwoman
Scheck *der;* ~s, ~s cheque
Scheck-: ~**heft** *das* chequebook; ~**karte** *die* cheque card
scheel (ugs.) ⬚1 *Adj.* disapproving; (neidisch) envious; jealous
⬚2 *adv.* disapprovingly; (neidisch) enviously; jealously
scheffeln *tr. V.* (ugs.) rake in (coll.)
Scheibe *die;* ~, ~n **(a)** disc
(b) (abgeschnittene ~) slice
(c) (Glasscheibe) pane [of glass]; (Fensterscheibe) [window] pane
Scheiben-: ~**bremse** *die* disc brake; ~**wasch·anlage** *die* (Kfz-W.) windscreen washer system *or* unit; ~**wischer** *der* windscreen wiper
Scheide *die;* ~, ~n **(a)** sheath
(b) (Anat.) vagina
scheiden *unr. tr. V.* dissolve ‹*marriage*›; divorce ‹*married couple*›; **sich** ~ **lassen** get divorced *or* get a divorce
Scheidung *die;* ~, ~en divorce
Schein *der;* ~[e]s, ~e **(a)** (Lichtschein) light
(b) (Anschein) appearances *pl., no art.;* (Täuschung) pretence; **etw. nur zum** ~ **tun** [only] pretend to do sth.; make a show of doing sth.
(c) (Geldschein) note
scheinbar ⬚1 *Adj.* apparent; seeming
⬚2 *adv.* seemingly
scheinen *unr. itr. V.* **(a)** shine
(b) (den Eindruck erwecken) seem; appear; **mir scheint, [dass] ...:** it seems *or* appears to me that ...   ⋯⊱

schein-, Schein-: ~**heilig** [1] *Adj.*
hypocritical; [2] *adv.* hypocritical;
~**heiligkeit** *die* hypocrisy; ~**tot** *Adj.*
(a) (Med.) apparently *or* seemingly dead;
(b) (salopp: sehr alt) with one foot in the grave
postpos.; ~**werfer** *der* floodlight; (am Auto)
headlight; ~**werfer·licht** *das* floodlight;
(des Autos) headlights *pl.;* (im Theater, Museum
usw.) spotlight [beam]

Scheiße *die;* ~ (derb) shit (coarse); crap
(coarse)

scheiß·egal *Adj.* (derb) ~ **sein** not matter
a damn (sl.); **das ist mir** ~: I don't give a
damn (sl.) *or* (coarse) shit

scheißen *unr. itr. V.* (derb) [have *or* (Amer.)
take a] shit (coarse); crap (coarse); have a crap
(coarse)

Scheiß·kerl *der* (derb) bastard (coll.)

Scheitel *der;* ~s, ~: parting

scheiteln *tr. V.* part ⟨hair⟩

scheitern *itr. V.; mit sein* fail; ⟨talks,
marriage⟩ break down; ⟨plan, project⟩ fail,
fall through

Schelle *die;* ~, ~n bell

schellen *itr. V.* (westd.) ▶ KLINGELN

Schell·fisch *der* haddock

Schelm *der;* ~[e]s, ~e rascal; rogue

schelmisch [1] *Adj.* roguish
[2] *adv.* roguishly

Schelte *die;* ~, ~n (geh.) scolding

schelten (südd., geh.) [1] *unr. itr. V.* **auf** od.
über jmdn./etw. ~: moan about sb./sth.
[2] *unr. tr. V.* scold

Schema *das;* ~s, ~s od. ~ta od. **Schemen**
pattern

schematisch [1] *Adj.* (a) diagrammatic
(b) (mechanisch) mechanical
[2] *adv.* (a) in diagram form
(b) (mechanisch) mechanically

Schemel *der;* ~s, ~ (a) stool
(b) (südd.: Fußbank) footstool

Schenkel *der;* ~s, ~: thigh

schenken *tr. V.* (a) give; **jmdm. etw. [zum
Geburtstag]** ~: give sb. sth. *or* sth. to sb. [as
a birthday present *or* for his/her birthday]
(b) (ugs.: erlassen) **jmdm./sich etw.** ~: spare
sb./oneself sth.

scheppern *itr. V.* (ugs.) clank

Scherbe *die;* ~, ~n fragment

Schere *die;* ~, ~n (a) scissors *pl.;* **eine**
~: a pair of scissors
(b) (Zool.) claw

scheren[1] *unr. tr. V.* crop; (von Haar befreien)
shear, clip ⟨sheep⟩

scheren[2] *tr., refl. V.* **sich um jmdn./etw.
nicht** ~: not care about sb./sth.

Schererei en *Pl.* (ugs.) trouble *no pl.*

Scherz *der;* ~es, ~e joke

scherzen *itr. V.* joke

scherzhaft [1] *Adj.* jocular
[2] *adv.* jocularly

scheu [1] *Adj.* shy; timid ⟨animal⟩;
(ehrfürchtig) awed
[2] *adv.* shyly; (von Tieren) timidly

Scheu *die;* ~ (a) shyness; (Ehrfurcht) awe
(b) (von Tieren) timidity

scheuchen *tr. V.* shoo; drive

scheuen [1] *tr. V.* shrink from; shun
⟨people, light, company, etc.⟩
[2] *refl. V.* **sich vor etw.** (*Dat.*) ~: be afraid of
or shrink from sth.
[3] *itr. V.* ⟨horse⟩ shy (**vor** + *Dat.* at)

scheuern [1] *tr., itr. V.* (a) (reinigen) scour;
scrub
(b) (reiben) rub; chafe
[2] *tr. V.* (reiben an) rub

Scheuer-: ~**pulver** *das* scouring
powder; ~**tuch** *das; Pl.* ~**tücher** scouring
cloth

Scheune *die;* ~, ~n barn

Scheusal *das;* ~s, ~e monster

scheußlich [1] *Adj.* (a) dreadful
(b) (ugs.: äußerst unangenehm) dreadful (coll.);
ghastly (coll.) ⟨weather, taste, smell⟩
[2] *adv.* (a) dreadfully
(b) (ugs.: sehr) dreadfully (coll.)

Scheußlichkeit *die;* ~, ~en
(a) dreadfulness
(b) (etw. Scheußliches) dreadful thing

Schi *usw.* ▶ SKI *usw.*

Schicht *die;* ~, ~en (a) (Lage) layer; (Geol.)
stratum; (von Farbe) coat; (sehr dünn) film
(b) (Gesellschaftsschicht) stratum
(c) (Arbeitsschicht) shift; ~ **arbeiten** work
shifts; be on shift work

Schicht·arbeit *die* shift work

schichten *tr. V.* stack

schick [1] *Adj.* (a) stylish; chic ⟨clothes,
fashions⟩; smart ⟨woman, girl, man⟩
(b) (ugs.: großartig, toll) great (coll.); fantastic
(coll.)
[2] *adv.* stylishly; smartly ⟨furnished,
decorated⟩

schicken [1] *tr. V.* send; **jmdm. etw.** ~, **etw.
an jmdn.** ~: send sth. to sb.; send sb. sth.
[2] *itr. V.* **nach jmdm.** ~: send for sb.
[3] *refl. V.* (veralt.: sich ziemen) be proper *or*
fitting

Schickeria *die;* ~ (ugs.) smart set

Schicksal *das;* ~s, ~e: [**das**] ~: fate;
destiny; (schweres Los) fate

Schicksals·schlag *der* stroke of fate

Schiebe·dach *das* sunroof

schieben [1] *unr. tr. V.* (a) push
(b) (stecken) put
(c) **etw. auf jmdn./etw.** ~: blame sb./sth. for
sth.
[2] *unr. refl. V.* **sich durch die Menge** ~: push
one's way through the crowd
[3] *unr. itr. V.* push; (heftig) shove

Schiebe·tür *die* sliding door

Schiebung ⋯⟶ Schirmständer ⋯⋯

Schiebung *die;* ~, ~en (ugs.) **(a)** shady deal
(b) (Begünstigung) pulling strings
schied *1. u. 3. Pers. Sg. Prät. v.* SCHEIDEN
Schieds·richter *der;*
Schieds·richterin *die* referee; (Tennis, Hockey, Kricket) umpire
schief 1 *Adj.* **(a)** (schräg) leaning ⟨*wall, fence, post*⟩; (nicht parallel) crooked; sloping ⟨*surface*⟩; worn[-down] ⟨*heels*⟩
(b) (fig.: verzerrt) distorted ⟨*picture, presentation, view, impression*⟩; false ⟨*comparison*⟩
2 *adv.* **(a)** (schräg) **das Bild hängt/der Teppich liegt** ~: the picture/carpet is crooked; **der Tisch steht** ~: the table isn't level
(b) (fig.: verzerrt) **etw.** ~ **darstellen** give a distorted account of sth.
(c) ~ **gehen** *od.* **laufen** (ugs.) go wrong
Schiefer *der;* ~s (Gestein) slate
***schief-:** ~|**gehen,** ~|**laufen**
▶ SCHIEF 2c
schielen *itr. V.* **(a)** squint; **auf dem rechten Auge** ~: have a squint in one's right eye
(b) (ugs.: blicken) look out of the corner of one's eye
schien *1. u. 3. Pers. Sg. Prät. v.* SCHEINEN
Schien·bein *das* shinbone
Schiene *die;* ~, ~n **(a)** rail
(b) (Gleitschiene) runner
(c) (Med.: Stütze) splint
schienen *tr. V.* **jmds. Arm/Bein** ~: put sb.'s arm/leg in a splint/splints
schießen 1 *unr. itr. V.* **(a)** shoot; **auf jmdn./etw.** ~: shoot/fire at sb./sth.
(b) *mit sein* (strömen) gush; (spritzen) spurt
(c) *mit sein* (schnell wachsen) shoot up
2 *unr. tr. V.* **(a)** shoot; fire ⟨*bullet, missile, rocket*⟩
(b) (Fußball) score ⟨*goal*⟩
(c) (ugs.: fotografieren) **einige Aufnahmen** ~: take a few snaps
Schießerei *die;* ~, ~en **(a)** shooting *no indef. art., no pl.*
(b) (Schusswechsel) gun battle
Schiff *das;* ~[e]s, ~e **(a)** ship; **mit dem** ~: by ship *or* sea
(b) (Archit.) (Mittelschiff) nave; (Querschiff) transept; (Seitenschiff) aisle
***Schiffahrt** ▶ SCHIFFFAHRT
schiffbar *Adj.* navigable
Schiff-: ~**bau** *der* shipbuilding *no art.;* ~**bruch** *der* (veralt.) shipwreck; **[mit etw.]** ~**bruch erleiden** (fig.) fail [in sth.]; ~**brüchige** *der/die; adj. Dekl.* shipwrecked man/woman
Schiffer *der;* ~s, ~, **Schifferin** *die;* ~, ~**nen** boatman/boatwoman; (eines Lastkahns) bargee; (Kapitän[in]) skipper
Schiff·fahrt *die* shipping *no indef. art.;* (Schifffahrtskunde) navigation
Schiffs-: ~**arzt** *der* ship's doctor;

~**brücke** *die* pontoon bridge; ~**junge** *der* ship's boy; ~**reise** *die* voyage; (Vergnügungsreise) cruise; ~**verkehr** *der* shipping traffic
Schikane *die;* ~, ~n **(a)** harassment *no indef. art.*
(b) **mit allen** ~**n** (ugs.) ⟨*kitchen, house*⟩ with all mod cons (Brit. coll.); ⟨*car, bicycle, stereo*⟩ with all the extras
schikanieren *tr. V.* harass
Schild[1] *der;* ~[e]s, ~e shield
Schild[2] *das;* ~[e]s, ~er sign; (Nummernschild) number plate; (Namensschild) nameplate; (auf Denkmälern, Gebäuden usw.) plaque; (Etikett) label
Schild·drüse *die* (Med.) thyroid [gland]
schildern *tr. V.* describe
Schild·kröte *die* tortoise; (Meeresschildkröte) turtle
Schilf *das;* ~[e]s **(a)** reed
(b) (Röhricht) reeds *pl.*
schillern *itr. V.* shimmer
Schilling *der;* ~s, ~e schilling
schilt *3. Pers. Sg. Präsens v.* SCHELTEN
Schimmel *der;* ~s, ~ **(a)** mould; (auf Leder, Papier) mildew
(b) (Pferd) white horse
schimmelig *Adj.* mouldy; mildewy ⟨*paper, leather*⟩
schimmeln *itr. V.; auch mit sein* go mouldy; ⟨*leather, paper*⟩ get covered with mildew
Schimmel·pilz *der* mould
Schimmer *der;* ~s (Schein) gleam; (von Seide) shimmer; sheen; **keinen** ~ **[von etw.] haben** (ugs.) not have the faintest idea [about sth.] (coll.)
schimmern *itr. V.* gleam; ⟨*water, sea*⟩ glisten, shimmer; ⟨*metal*⟩ glint, gleam; ⟨*silk etc.*⟩ shimmer
schimmlig ▶ SCHIMMELIG
Schimpanse *der;* ~n, ~n chimpanzee
schimpfen 1 *itr. V.* **(a)** carry on (coll.) **(auf, über** + *Akk.* about); (meckern) grumble, moan **(auf, über** + *Akk.* at)
(b) **mit jmdm.** ~: tell sb. off; scold sb.
2 *tr. V.* **jmdn.** ~: tell sb. off
Schimpf·wort *das; Pl.* **Schimpf·wörter** (Beleidigung) insult; (derbes Wort) swear word
schinden *unr. tr. V.* maltreat; ill-treat; **Zeit** ~ (ugs.) play for time
Schinderei *die;* ~, ~en (Strapaze, Qual) struggle; (Arbeit) toil
Schinken *der;* ~s, ~: ham
Schinken·speck *der* bacon
Schippe *die;* ~, ~n (Schaufel) shovel
Schirm *der;* ~[e]s, ~e umbrella; brolly (Brit. coll.); (Sonnenschirm) sunshade
Schirm-: ~**herr** *der* patron; ~**herrin** *die* patroness; ~**herrschaft** *die* patronage; ~**ständer** *der* umbrella stand

S

schiss, **schiß 1. u. 3. Pers. Sg. Prät. v.*
SCHEISSEN
Schlacht *die;* ~, ~en battle
schlachten *tr. (auch itr.) V.* slaughter; kill
⟨*rabbit, chicken, etc.*⟩
Schlachter *der;* ~s, ~ (nordd.) butcher
Schlachterei *die;* ~, ~en (nordd.)
butcher's [shop]
Schlacht-: ~**feld** *das* battlefield; ~**hof**
der abattoir; ~**tier** *das* animal kept for
meat; (kurz vor der Schlachtung) animal for
slaughter
Schlachtung *die;* ~, ~en slaughter[ing]
Schlacht·vieh *das* animals *pl.* kept for
meat; (kurz vor der Schlachtung) animals *pl.* for
slaughter
Schlacke *die;* ~, ~n cinders *pl.;*
(Hochofen~) slag
Schlaf *der;* ~[e]s sleep; **einen leichten/
festen/gesunden** ~ **haben** be a light/heavy/
good sleeper
Schlaf·anzug *der* pyjamas *pl.*
Schläfchen *das;* ~s, ~: nap; snooze (coll.)
Schläfe *die;* ~, ~n temple
schlafen *unr. itr. V.* **(a)** (auch fig.) sleep;
tief *od.* **fest** ~: be sound asleep; **lange**
~: sleep for a long time; (am Morgen) sleep in;
~ **gehen** go to bed
(b) (ugs.: nicht aufpassen) be asleep
Schläfer *der;* ~s, ~, **Schläferin** *die;* ~,
~nen sleeper
schlaff ① *Adj.* **(a)** slack; flabby ⟨*stomach,
muscles*⟩
(b) (schlapp, matt) limp ⟨*body, hand,
handshake*⟩; shaky ⟨*knees*⟩
② *adv.* **(a)** slackly
(b) (schlapp, matt) limply
Schlaf-: ~**gelegenheit** *die* place to
sleep; ~**mittel** *das* sleep-inducing drug
schläfrig ① *Adj.* sleepy
② *adv.* sleepily
Schläfrigkeit *die;* ~: sleepiness
Schlaf-: ~**saal** *der* dormitory; ~**sack**
sleeping bag
schläft *3. Pers. Sg. Präsens v.* SCHLAFEN
Schlaf-: ~**tablette** *die* sleeping pill;
~**wagen** *der* sleeping car; sleeper;
~**zimmer** *das* bedroom
Schlag *der;* ~[e]s, **Schläge (a)** blow;
(Faust~) punch; (Klaps) slap; (Tennis, Golf)
stroke; shot; ~ **auf** ~ (fig.) in quick
succession
(b) (Aufprall) bang; (dumpf) thud; (Klopfen)
knock
(c) (des Herzens, Pulses) beating; (eines Pendels)
swinging
(d) (einzelne rhythmische Bewegung) beat; (eines
Pendels) swing
(e) (Töne) (einer Uhr) striking; (einer Glocke)
ringing

(f) (einzelner Ton) (Stundenschlag) stroke;
(Glockenschlag) ring; ~ **acht Uhr** on the stroke
of eight
schlag-, Schlag-: ~**ader** *die* artery;
~**anfall** *der* stroke; ~**artig** ① *Adj.*
very sudden; ② *adv.* quite suddenly;
~**baum** *der* barrier; ~**bohrer** *der,*
~**bohr·maschine** *die* percussion drill;
hammer drill
schlagen ① *unr. tr. V.* **(a)** hit; beat; strike;
(mit der Faust) punch; hit; (mit der flachen Hand)
slap
(b) (mit Richtungsangabe) hit ⟨*ball*⟩; **einen
Nagel in etw.** (*Akk.*) ~: knock a nail into sth.
(c) (rühren) beat ⟨*mixture*⟩; whip ⟨*cream*⟩; (mit
einem Schneebesen) whisk
(d) (läuten) ⟨*clock*⟩ strike; ⟨*bell*⟩ ring
(e) (legen) throw
(f) (einwickeln) wrap (**in** + *Akk.* in)
(g) (besiegen, übertreffen) beat
② *unr. itr. V.* **(a)** er schlug mit der Faust auf
den Tisch he beat the table with his fist
(b) mit den Flügeln ~ ⟨*bird*⟩ beat or flap its
wings
(c) *mit sein* (prallen) bang; **mit dem Kopf auf
etw.** (*Akk.*)/**gegen etw.** ~: bang one's head
on/against sth.
(d) *mit sein* **jmdm. auf den Magen** ~: affect
sb.'s stomach
(e) (pulsieren) ⟨*heart, pulse*⟩ beat; (heftig)
⟨*heart*⟩ pound; ⟨*pulse*⟩ throb
(f) (läuten) ⟨*clock*⟩ strike; ⟨*bell*⟩ ring
③ *unr. refl. V.* fight; **sich mit jmdm.** ~: fight
with sb.
Schlager *der;* ~s, ~ **(a)** pop song
(b) (Erfolg) (Buch) best seller; (Ware) best-
selling line; (Film, Stück, Lied) hit
Schläger *der;* ~s, ~ **(a)** (Raufbold) tough;
thug
(b) (Tennis, Federball, Squash) racket;
(Tischtennis, Kricket) bat; ([Eis]hockey, Polo) stick;
(Golf) club
Schlägerei *die;* ~, ~en brawl; fight
Schlägerin *die;* ~, ~nen ▸ SCHLÄGER A
Schlager·sänger *der,*
Schlager·sängerin *die* pop singer
schlag-, Schlag-: ~**fertig** *Adj.*
quick-witted ⟨*reply*⟩; ⟨*person*⟩ who is quick
at repartee; ~**fertigkeit** *die* quickness at
repartee; ~**licht** *das* (Kunst, Fot.) shaft of
light; **ein** ~**licht auf etw. werfen** highlight
sth.; ~**loch** *das* pothole; ~**obers** *das;*
~~ (österr.), ~**rahm** *der* (bes. südd., österr.,
schweiz.), ~**sahne** *die* whipping cream;
(geschlagen) whipped cream; ~**seite**
die list; [**starke** *od.* **schwere**] ~**seite
haben/bekommen** be listing [heavily] *or*
have a [heavy] list/develop a [heavy] list;
~**stock** *der* cudgel; (für Polizei) truncheon;
~**wort** *das* **(a)** *Pl. meist* ~~e (Parole)
slogan; catchphrase; **(b)** *Pl.* ~**wörter** (Buchw.:
Stichwort) headword; ~**zeile** *die* headline;
~**zeug** *das* drums *pl.*
schlaksig (ugs.) *Adj.* gangling; lanky

Schlamassel *der od. das;* ~s (ugs.) mess
Schlamm *der;* ~[e]s, ~e *od.* **Schlämme**
(a) mud
(b) (Schlick) sludge
schlammig *Adj.* (a) muddy
(b) (schlickig) sludgy; muddy
Schlamperei *die;* ~, ~en (ugs. abwertend) sloppiness
schlampig (ugs. abwertend) ①*Adj.*
(a) (liederlich) slovenly
(b) (nachlässig) sloppy, slipshod *‹work›*
②*adv.* (a) (liederlich) in a slovenly way
(b) (nachlässig) sloppily
schlang *1. u. 3. Pers. Sg. Prät. v.* SCHLINGEN
Schlange *die;* ~, ~n (a) snake
(b) (Warteschlange) queue; line (Amer.);
~ **stehen** queue; stand in line (Amer.)
(c) (Autoschlange) tailback (Brit.); backup (Amer.)
schlängeln *refl. V.* *‹snake›* wind [its way]; *‹road›* wind, snake [its way]
Schlangen·linie *die* wavy line
schlank *Adj.* slim *‹person›*; slim, slender *‹build, figure›*
Schlankheit *die;* ~ ▶ SCHLANK: slimness; slenderness
Schlankheits·kur *die* slimming diet
schlapp *Adj.* (a) worn out; tired out; (wegen Schwüle) listless; (wegen Krankheit) run-down
(b) (ugs.: ohne Schwung) wet (coll.); feeble
(c) slack *‹rope, cable›*; loose *‹skin›*; flabby *‹stomach, muscles›*
Schlappe *die;* ~, ~n setback
schlapp|machen *itr. V.* (ugs.) flag; (zusammenbrechen) flake out (coll.); (aufgeben) give up
Schlaraffen·land *das;* ~[e]s Cockaigne
schlau ①*Adj.* (a) shrewd; astute; (gerissen) wily; crafty; cunning
(b) (ugs.: gescheit) clever; bright; smart; **aus jmdm. nicht** ~ **werden** (ugs.) not be able to make sb. out
②*adv.* shrewdly; astutely; (gerissen) craftily; cunningly
Schlauch *der;* ~[e]s, Schläuche (a) hose
(b) (im Reifen) tube
Schlauch·boot *das* rubber dinghy; inflatable [dinghy]
schlauchen (ugs.) *tr., auch itr. V.* **jmdn.** ~: take it out of sb.
schlauch·los *Adj.* tubeless *‹tyre›*
Schläue *die;* ~: shrewdness; astuteness; (Gerissenheit) wiliness; craftiness; cunning
Schlaufe *die;* ~, ~n loop
schlecht ①*Adj.* (a) bad; poor, bad *‹food, quality, style, harvest, health, circulation›*; poor *‹salary, eater, appetite›*; poor-quality *‹goods›*; bad, weak *‹eyes›*; **um jmdn./mit etw. steht es** ~: sb./sth. is in a bad way; **jmdn.** ~ **machen** run sb. down; disparage sb.
(b) (böse) bad; wicked
(c) (ungenießbar) off; **das Fleisch ist**

~ **geworden** the meat has gone off
②*adv.* (a) badly; **er sieht/hört** ~: his sight is poor/he has poor hearing; **über jmdn.** *od.* **von jmdm.** ~ **sprechen** speak ill of sb.; ~ **bezahlt** badly *or* poorly paid
(b) (schwer) **heute geht es** ~: today is difficult
(c) ~ **und recht, mehr** ~ **als recht** after a fashion
schlecht-: ***~**bezahlt** ▶ SCHLECHT 2A; ***~**|gehen** ▶ GEHEN I; ***~**gelaunt** ▶ GELAUNT
Schlechtigkeit *die;* ~: badness; wickedness
*****schlecht|machen** ▶ SCHLECHT 1A
schlecken (bes. südd., österr.) *tr. V.* lap up
schleichen ①*unr. itr. V.; mit sein* creep; (heimlich) creep; sneak; *‹cat›* slink, creep; (langsam fahren) crawl along
②*unr. refl. V.* creep; sneak; *‹cat›* slink, creep
schleichend *Adj.* insidious *‹disease›*; slow[-acting] *‹poison›*; creeping *‹inflation›*; gradual *‹crisis›*
Schleich·werbung *die* surreptitious advertising
Schleier *der;* ~s, ~: veil
schleier·haft *Adj.* **jmdm.** ~ **sein/bleiben** be/remain a mystery to sb.
Schleife *die;* ~, ~n (a) bow; (Fliege) bow tie
(b) (starke Biegung) loop
schleifen¹ *unr. tr. V.* grind; cut *‹diamond, glass›*; (mit Schleifpapier usw.) sand; (schärfen) sharpen
schleifen² ①*tr. V.* (a) (auch fig.) drag
(b) (niederreißen) raze *‹sth.›* [to the ground]
②*itr. V.; auch mit sein* drag; **die Kupplung** ~ **lassen** (Kfz-W.) slip the clutch
Schleim *der;* ~[e]s, ~e mucus; (im Hals) phlegm; (von Schnecken) slime
schleimig *Adj.* (auch fig.) slimy; (Physiol., Zool.) mucous
schlemmen *itr. V.* have a feast
Schlemmer *der;* ~s, ~: gourmet
schlendern *itr. V.; mit sein* stroll
Schlenker *der;* ~s, ~ (ugs.) swerve; **einen** ~ **machen** swerve
schlenkern *tr., itr. V.* swing; **mit den Armen** ~: swing one's arms
Schleppe *die;* ~, ~n train
schleppen ①*tr. V.* (a) (ziehen) tow *‹vehicle, ship›*
(b) (tragen) carry; lug
(c) (ugs.: mitnehmen) drag
②*refl. V.* drag *or* haul oneself
schleppend *Adj.* (nicht zügig) slow
Schlepper *der;* ~s, ~ (a) (Schiff) tug
(b) (Traktor) tractor
Schlepper·organisation *die:* organization smuggling illegal immigrants and emigrants ⋯⟫

S

Schlepp-: ~**lift** der T-bar [lift]; ~**tau** das
towline; **in jmds.** ~**tau** (fig.) in sb.'s wake
Schleswig-Holstein (das); ~**s**
Schleswig-Holstein
Schleuder die; ~, ~n sling; (mit
Gummiband) catapult (Brit.); slingshot (Amer.)
schleudern ① tr. V. hurl
② itr. V.; mit sein ⟨vehicle⟩ skid
schleunigst Adv. (a) (auf der Stelle) at once;
immediately; straight away
(b) (eilends) hastily; with all haste
Schleuse die; ~, ~n lock
schlich 1. u. 3. Pers. Sg. Prät. v. SCHLEICHEN
schlicht ① Adj. (a) simple; plain ⟨pattern,
furniture⟩
(b) (unkompliziert) simple, unsophisticated
⟨person, view, etc.⟩
② adv. simply; simply, plainly ⟨dressed,
furnished⟩
schlichten ① tr. V. settle ⟨argument etc.⟩;
settle ⟨industrial dispute etc.⟩ by mediation
② itr. V. mediate
Schlichtheit die; ~ ▸ SCHLICHT A, B:
simplicity; plainness; unsophisticatedness
Schlick der; ~[e]s, ~e silt
schlief 1. u. 3. Pers. Sg. Prät. v. SCHLAFEN
Schließe die; ~, ~n clasp; (Schnalle) buckle
schließen ① unr. tr. V. (a) close; shut;
turn off ⟨tap⟩; fasten ⟨belt, bracelet⟩; do
up ⟨button, zip⟩; close ⟨street, route, border,
electrical circuit⟩; fill, close ⟨gap⟩
(b) (außer Betrieb setzen) close [down] ⟨shop,
school⟩
(c) etw./jmdn./sich in etw. (Akk.) ~: lock
sth./sb./oneself in sth.
(d) (beenden) close ⟨meeting, proceedings,
debate⟩; end, conclude ⟨letter, speech, lecture⟩
(e) (eingehen, vereinbaren) conclude ⟨treaty,
pact, ceasefire, agreement⟩; reach ⟨settlement,
compromise⟩; enter into ⟨contract⟩
(f) (folgern) infer (aus from)
② unr. itr. V. (a) close, shut
(b) (enden) end; conclude
(c) [aus etw.] auf etw. (Akk.) ~: infer sth.
[from sth.]
③ unr. refl. V. ⟨door, window⟩ close, shut;
⟨wound, circle⟩ close
Schließ·fach das locker; (bei der Post) PO
box; (bei der Bank) safe-deposit box
schließlich Adv. (a) finally; in the end
(b) (immerhin, doch) after all
schliff 1. u. 3. Pers. Sg. Prät. v. SCHLEIFEN
Schliff der; ~[e]s, ~e (a) cutting; (von
Messern, Sensen usw.) sharpening
(b) (Art, wie etw. geschliffen wird) cut; (von
Messern, Scheren usw.) edge
(c) einem Brief/Text usw. den letzten
~ geben put the finishing touches pl. to a
letter/text etc.
schlimm ① Adj. (a) grave, serious ⟨error,
mistake, accusation, offence⟩; bad, serious

⟨error, mistake⟩
(b) (übel) bad; nasty, bad ⟨experience⟩; **[das
ist alles] halb so** ~: it's not as bad as all
that; **ist nicht** ~! [it] doesn't matter
② adv. ~ **dran sein** be in a bad way; (in einer
Notlage) be in dire straits
schlimmsten·falls Adv. if the worst
comes to the worst
Schlinge die; ~, ~n (a) loop; (für den Arm)
sling; (zum Erhängen) noose
(b) (Fanggerät) snare
Schlingel der; ~s, ~: rascal; rogue
schlingen ① unr. tr. V. etw. um etw.
~: loop sth. round sth.
② unr. refl. V. sich um etw. ~: wind itself
round sth.
③ unr. itr. V. bolt one's food
schlingern itr. V.; mit sein ⟨ship, boat⟩ roll;
⟨train, vehicle⟩ lurch from side to side
Schlips der; ~es, ~e tie
Schlitten der; ~s, ~: sledge; sled;
(Pferdeschlitten) sleigh; (Rodelschlitten)
toboggan; ~ **fahren** go tobogganing
schlittern itr. V. slide
Schlitt-: ~**schuh** der [ice] skate;
~**schuh laufen** od. **fahren** [ice-]skate;
~**schuh-laufen** das [ice] skating no art.;
~**schuh-läufer** der, ~**schuh-läuferin**
die [ice] skater
Schlitz der; ~es, ~e (a) slit; (am Briefkasten,
Automaten) slot
(b) (Hosenschlitz) flies pl.; fly
schlitz-, Schlitz-: ~**auge** das slit eye;
~**äugig** Adj. slit-eyed; ~**ohr** das (ugs.)
wily or crafty devil; ~**ohrig** (ugs.) ① Adj.
wily; crafty; ② adv. craftily
schloss, *schloß 1. u. 3. Pers. Sg. Prät.
v. SCHLIESSEN
Schloss, *Schloß das; Schlosses,
Schlösser (a) lock; (Vorhänge~) padlock;
hinter ~ und Riegel (ugs.) behind bars
(b) (Verschluss) clasp
(c) (Wohngebäude) castle; (Palast) palace;
(Herrschaftshaus) mansion
Schlosser der; ~s, ~, **Schlosserin**
die; ~, ~nen metalworker;
(Maschinenschlosser) fitter; (für Schlösser)
locksmith
Schlot der; ~[e]s, ~e od. **Schlöte** chimney
[stack]; (eines Schiffes) funnel
schlottern itr. V. (a) shake
(b) ⟨clothes⟩ hang loose
Schlucht die; ~, ~en ravine
schluchzen itr. V. sob
Schluck der; ~[e]s, ~e od. **Schlücke**
swallow; mouthful; (großer ~) gulp;
(kleiner ~) sip
Schluck·auf der; ~s hiccups pl.
Schlückchen das; ~s, ~: sip
schlucken ① tr. V. swallow; **etw. hastig**
~: gulp sth. down
② itr. V. swallow

---

*old spelling – see note on page x

Schlucker *der;* ~s, ~: armer ~ (ugs.) poor devil *or* (Brit. coll.) blighter

schluderig ▸ SCHLUDRIG

schludern *itr. V.* (ugs.) work sloppily

schludrig (ugs.) [1] *Adj.* **(a)** slipshod ⟨*work, examination*⟩; botched ⟨*job*⟩; slapdash ⟨*person, work*⟩

(b) (schlampig [aussehend]) scruffy

[2] *adv.* **(a)** in a slipshod *or* slapdash way

(b) (schlampig) scruffily

schlug *1. u. 3. Pers. Sg. Prät. v.* SCHLAGEN

Schlummer *der;* ~s (geh.) slumber (poet./rhet.)

schlummern *itr. V.* (geh.) slumber (poet./rhet.)

Schlund *der;* ~[e]s, Schlünde [back of the] throat; pharynx (Anat.)

schlüpfen *itr. V.; mit sein* slip; [aus dem Ei] ~ ⟨*chick*⟩ hatch out

Schlüpfer *der;* ~s, ~ (für Damen) knickers *pl.* (Brit.); panties *pl.;* (für Herren) [under]pants *pl. or* trunks *pl.*

schlüpfrig *Adj.* **(a)** slippery

(b) (anstößig) lewd

Schlüpfrigkeit *die;* ~, ~en **(a)** (feuchte Glätte) slipperiness

(b) (Anstößigkeit) lewdness

schlurfen *itr. V.; mit sein* shuffle

schlürfen [1] *tr. V.* slurp [up] (coll.)

[2] *itr. V.* slurp (coll.)

Schluss, *Schluß *der;* Schlusses, Schlüsse **(a)** end; (eines Vortrags o. Ä.) conclusion; (eines Buchs, Schauspiels usw.) ending; **am** *od.* **zum** ~: at the end; (schließlich) in the end

(b) (Folgerung) conclusion

Schlüssel *der;* ~s, ~: key

Schlüssel-: ~**bein** *das* collarbone; clavicle (Anat.); ~**blume** *die* cowslip; (Primel) primula; ~**bund** *der od. das* bunch of keys; ~**figur** *die* key figure; ~**loch** *das* keyhole; ~**stellung** *die* key position

schluss·folgern, *schlußfolgern *tr. V.* conclude (**aus** from)

Schluss·folgerung, *Schluß·folgerung *die* conclusion, inference (**aus** from); ~**en ziehen** draw conclusions

schlüssig [1] *Adj.* **(a)** conclusive ⟨*proof, evidence*⟩; convincing, logical ⟨*argument, conclusion*⟩

(b) sich (*Dat.*) ~ **werden** make up one's mind

[2] *adv.* conclusively

Schlüssigkeit *die;* ~: conclusiveness

Schluss-, *Schluß-: ~**licht** *das* tail *or* rear light; ~**strich** *der* [bottom] line; ~**verkauf** *der* [end-of-season] sale[s *pl.*]

schmächtig *Adj.* slight

schmackhaft *Adj.* tasty

Schmähung *die;* ~, ~en diatribe; ~en abuse *sing.;* invective *sing.*

schmal; ~er *od.* schmäler, ~st... *od.* schmälst... *Adj.* narrow; slim, slender ⟨*hips, hands, figure, etc.*⟩; thin ⟨*lips, face, nose, etc.*⟩

schmälern *tr. V.* diminish; restrict ⟨*rights*⟩

Schmalz¹ *das;* ~es dripping; (Schweineschmalz) lard

Schmalz² *der;* ~es (abwertend) schmaltz (coll.)

Schmalz·brot *das* slice of bread and dripping

schmalzig (abwertend) [1] *Adj.* schmaltzy (coll.)

[2] *adv.* with slushy sentimentality

schmarotzen *itr. V.* (fig.) sponge; freeload (coll.)

Schmarren *der;* ~s, ~ (österr., auch südd.) *pancake broken up with a fork after frying*

schmatzen *itr. V.* smack one's lips; (geräuschvoll essen) eat noisily

Schmaus *der;* ~es, Schmäuse (veralt., scherzh.) [good] spread (coll.)

schmecken [1] *itr. V.* taste (**nach** of); [gut] ~: taste good; **schmeckt es [dir]?** are you enjoying it *or* your meal?

[2] *tr. V.* taste; (kosten) sample

schmeicheln *itr. V.* jmdm. ~: flatter sb.

Schmeichler *der;* ~s, ~, **Schmeichlerin** *die;* ~, ~nen flatterer

schmeißen (ugs.) [1] *unr. tr. V.* chuck (coll.); sling (coll.); (schleudern) fling; hurl

[2] *unr. refl. V.* throw oneself; (mit Wucht) hurl oneself

[3] *unr. itr. V.* **mit etw. [nach jmdm.]** ~: chuck sth. [at sb.] (coll.)

Schmeiß·fliege *die* blowfly; (blaue) bluebottle

schmelzen [1] *unr. itr. V.; mit sein* melt; (fig.) ⟨*doubts, apprehension, etc.*⟩ dissolve, fade away

[2] *unr. tr. V.* melt; smelt ⟨*ore*⟩; render ⟨*fat*⟩

Schmelz-: ~**käse** *der* processed cheese; ~**wasser** *das* melted snow and ice; meltwater (Geol.)

Schmerz *der;* ~es, ~en **(a)** (physisch) pain; (dumpf u. anhaltend) ache; **wo haben Sie** ~en? where does it hurt?; ~en haben be in pain

(b) (psychisch) pain; (Kummer) grief

schmerz·empfindlich *Adj.* sensitive to pain *pred.*

Schmerz·empfindlichkeit *die;* ~: sensitivity to pain

schmerzen [1] *tr. V.* jmdn. ~: hurt sb.; (jmdm. Kummer bereiten) grieve sb.; cause sb. sorrow

[2] *itr. V.* hurt

schmerz·frei *Adj.* free of pain *pred.;* painless ⟨*operation*⟩

Schmerz·grenze *die* (fig.) **jetzt/dann ist die** ~ **erreicht** this/that is the absolute limit

schmerzhaft *Adj.* painful ⋯⟶

schmerzlich ① *Adj.* painful; distressing ② *adv.* painfully

schmerz-, Schmerz-: ~**lindernd** *Adj.* pain-relieving; ~**los** ① *Adj.* painless; ② *adv.* painlessly; ~**stillend** *Adj.* pain-killing; ~**tablette** *die* pain-killing tablet

Schmetterling *der;* ~**s,** ~**e** butterfly

schmettern ① *tr. V.* (a) hurl (**an** + *Akk.* at, **gegen** against)
(b) (laut spielen, singen usw.) blare out ⟨*march, music*⟩; ⟨*person*⟩ sing lustily ⟨*song*⟩
(c) (Tennis usw.) smash ⟨*ball*⟩
② *itr. V.* ⟨*trumpet, music, etc.*⟩ blare out

Schmied *der;* ~**[e]s,** ~**e** blacksmith

Schmiede *die;* ~, ~**n** smithy; forge

schmieden *tr. V.* (auch fig.) forge

Schmiedin *die;* ~, ~**nen** ▶ SCHMIED

schmiegen ① *refl. V.* snuggle, nestle (**in** + *Akk.* in); **sich an jmdn.** ~: snuggle [close] up to sb.
② *tr. V.* press (**an** + *Akk.* against)

schmieren ① *tr. V.* (a) lubricate
(b) (streichen) spread ⟨*butter, jam, etc.*⟩ (**auf** + *Akk.* on); **Brote** ~: spread slices of bread
② *itr. V.* (a) ⟨*oil, grease*⟩ lubricate
(b) (ugs.: unsauber schreiben) ⟨*person*⟩ scrawl, scribble; ⟨*pen, ink*⟩ smudge, make smudges

schmierig *Adj.* greasy

Schmier-: ~**mittel** *das* lubricant; ~**seife** *die* soft soap

schmilzt 2. u. 3. Pers. Sg. Präsens v. SCHMELZEN

Schminke *die;* ~, ~**n** make-up

schminken ① *tr. V.* make up ⟨*face, eyes*⟩ ② *refl. V.* make oneself up

schmirgeln *tr. V.* rub down; (bes. mit Sandpapier) sand

Schmirgel·papier *das* emery paper; (Sandpapier) sandpaper

schmiss, *schmiß 1. u. 3. Pers. Sg. Prät. v. SCHMEISSEN

Schmöker *der;* ~**s,** ~ (ugs.) lightweight adventure story/romance

schmökern (ugs.) ① *itr. V.* bury oneself in a book
② *tr. V.* bury oneself in ⟨*book*⟩

schmollen *itr. V.* sulk

Schmoll·mund *der* pouting mouth

schmolz 1. u. 3. Pers. Sg. Prät. v. SCHMELZEN

Schmor·braten *der* braised beef

schmoren ① *tr. V.* braise
② *itr. V.* (a) braise
(b) (ugs.: schwitzen) swelter

schmuck *Adj.* attractive

Schmuck *der;* ~**[e]s (a)** jewelry; jewellery (esp. Brit.)
(b) ▶ SCHMUCKSTÜCK
(c) (Zierde) decoration

schmücken *tr. V.* decorate; embellish

⟨*writings, speech*⟩

schmuck-, Schmuck-: ~**kästchen** *das,* ~**kasten** *der* jewelry or (esp. Brit.) jewellery box; ~**los** *Adj.* plain; bare ⟨*room*⟩; ~**losigkeit** *die;* ~: plainness; (eines Zimmers) bareness; ~**stück** *das* piece of jewelry or (esp. Brit.) jewellery

schmuddelig *Adj.* (ugs.) grubby; mucky (coll.); (schmutzig u. unordentlich) messy; grotty (Brit. coll.)

Schmuggel *der;* ~**s** smuggling *no art.*

schmuggeln *tr., itr. V.* smuggle (**in** + *Akk.* into; **aus** out of)

Schmuggler *der;* ~**s,** ~, **Schmugglerin** *die;* ~, ~**nen** smuggler

schmunzeln *itr. V.* smile to oneself

schmusen *itr. V.* (ugs.) cuddle; ⟨*couple*⟩ kiss and cuddle

Schmutz *der;* ~**es** dirt; (Schlamm) mud

schmutzen *itr. V.* get dirty

schmutzig *Adj.* dirty

Schmutz·wasser *das* dirty water; (Abwasser) sewage

Schnabel *der;* ~**s, Schnäbel (a)** beak
(b) (ugs.: Mund) gob (sl.)

Schnake *die;* ~, ~**n (a)** daddy-long-legs
(b) (bes. südd.: Stechmücke) mosquito

Schnalle *die;* ~, ~**n** buckle

schnallen *tr. V.* (a) (mit einer Schnalle festziehen) buckle ⟨*shoe, belt*⟩; fasten ⟨*strap*⟩
(b) (mit Riemen/Gurten befestigen) strap (**auf** + *Akk.* on to)

schnalzen *itr. V.* [**mit der Zunge/den Fingern**] ~: click one's tongue/snap one's fingers

Schnäppchen *das;* ~**s,** ~ (ugs.) snip (Brit. coll.); [real] bargain; **ein** ~ **machen** get a [real] bargain

schnappen ① *itr. V.* **nach jmdm./etw.** ~ ⟨*animal*⟩ snap at sb./sth.; **nach Luft** ~: gasp for breath
② *tr. V.* ⟨*dog, bird, etc.*⟩ snatch; [**sich** (*Dat.*)] **jmdn./etw.** ~ (ugs.) ⟨*person*⟩ grab sb./sth.; (mit raschem Zugriff) snatch sb./sth

Schnapp·schuss, *Schnapp·schuß *der* snapshot

Schnaps *der;* ~**es, Schnäpse (a)** spirit; (Klarer) schnapps
(b) (Spirituosen) spirits *pl.*

schnarchen *itr. V.* snore

schnattern *itr. V.* (a) ⟨*goose etc.*⟩ cackle, gaggle
(b) (ugs.: eifrig schwatzen) jabber [away]; chatter

schnauben *itr. V.* snort (**vor** with)

schnaufen *itr. V.* puff (**vor** with)

Schnauze *die;* ~, ~**n (a)** (von Tieren) muzzle; (der Maus usw.) snout; (Maul) mouth
(b) (derb: Mund) gob (sl.); [**halt die**] ~! shut your trap! (sl.)

schnauzen *tr., itr. V.* (ugs.) bark; (ärgerlich) snap; snarl

---

*alte Schreibung – vgl. Hinweis auf S. x

Schnecke *die* snail; (Nacktschnecke) slug
Schnecken·haus *das* snail shell
Schnee *der;* ∼s snow
schnee-, Schnee-: ∼**ball** *der* snowball; ∼**besen** *der* whisk; ∼**flocke** *die* snowflake; ∼**gestöber** *das* snow flurry; ∼**glöckchen** *das* snowdrop; ∼**kette** *die* snow chain; ∼**matsch** *der* slush; ∼**pflug** *der* snowplough; ∼**schmelze** *die;* ∼∼, ∼∼n melting of the snow; thaw; ∼**sturm** *der* snowstorm; ∼**treiben** *das* driving snow; ∼**wehe** *die* snowdrift; ∼**weiß** *Adj.* snow-white; as white as snow *postpos.*
Schneewittchen *das;* ∼s Snow White
Schneid·brenner *der* (Technik) cutting torch; oxyacetylene cutter
Schneide *die;* ∼, ∼n [cutting] edge
schneiden 1 *unr. itr. V.* cut (in + *Akk.* into) 2 *unr. tr. V.* (a) cut; (in Scheiben) slice ⟨*bread, sausage, etc.*⟩; (klein ∼) cut up, chop ⟨*wood, vegetables*⟩; (stutzen) prune ⟨*tree, bush*⟩; trim ⟨*beard*⟩; cut, mow ⟨*grass*⟩; **sich** (*Dat.*) **die Haare** ∼ **lassen** have one's hair cut (b) **eine Kurve** ∼: cut a corner
Schneider *der;* ∼s, ∼: tailor; (Damenschneider) dressmaker
Schneiderei *die;* ∼, ∼en tailor's shop; (Damenschneider) dressmaker's shop
Schneiderin *die;* ∼, ∼nen ▶ SCHNEIDER
schneidern *tr. V.* make; make, tailor ⟨*suit*⟩
Schneide·zahn *der* incisor
schneien 1 *itr., tr. V.* (*unpers.*) snow; **es schneit** it is snowing 2 *itr. V.; mit sein* (fig.) rain down; fall like snow
Schneise *die;* ∼, ∼n (Wald∼) aisle; (als Feuerschutz) firebreak
schnell 1 *Adj.* quick ⟨*journey, decision, service, etc.*⟩; fast ⟨*car, skis, road, track, etc.*⟩; quick, swift ⟨*progress, movement, blow, action*⟩ 2 *adv.* quickly; ⟨*drive, move, etc.*⟩ fast, quickly; ⟨*spread*⟩ quickly, rapidly; (bald) soon ⟨*sold, past, etc.*⟩; **mach** ∼**!** (ugs.) move it! (coll.)
schnellen *itr. V.; mit sein* shoot (**aus** + *Dat.* out of; **in** + *Akk.* into)
Schnelligkeit *die;* ∼, ∼en speed
Schnell-: ∼**imbiss,** ***∼**imbiß** *der* snackbar; ∼**koch·topf** *der* pressure cooker
schnellstens *Adv.* as quickly as possible
Schnell-: ∼**straße** *die* expressway; ∼**zug** *der* express [train]
Schnepfe *die;* ∼, ∼n snipe
schneuzen 1 *tr. V.* **sich/einem Kind die Nase** ∼: blow one's/a child's nose 2 *refl. V.* blow one's nose
schnippeln (ugs.) 1 *itr. V.* snip [away] (**an** + *Dat.* at) 2 *tr. V.* shred ⟨*vegetables*⟩; chop ⟨*beans etc.*⟩ [finely]

schnippen 1 *itr. V.* snap one's fingers (nach at) 2 *tr. V.* flick (**von** off, from)
schnippisch 1 *Adj.* pert ⟨*reply, tone, etc.*⟩ 2 *adv.* pertly
Schnipsel *der od. das;* ∼s, ∼: scrap; (aus Papier, Stoff) snippet; shred
schnipseln ▶ SCHNIPPELN
schnitt *1. u. 3. Pers. Sg. Prät. v.* SCHNEIDEN
Schnitt *der;* ∼[e]s, ∼e (a) cut (b) (das Mähen) (von Gras) mowing; (von Getreide) harvest
Schnitt-: ∼**blume** *die* cut flower; ∼**bohne** *die* French bean
Schnittchen *das;* ∼s, ∼: canapé; [small] open sandwich
Schnitte *die;* ∼, ∼n slice; **eine** ∼ [Brot] a slice of bread
Schnitt·fläche *die* cut surface
schnittig 1 *Adj.* stylish, smart ⟨*suit, appearance, etc.*⟩; (sportlich) racy ⟨*car, yacht, etc.*⟩ 2 *adv.* stylishly; (sportlich) racily
Schnitt-: ∼**lauch** *der* chives *pl.;* ∼**menge** *die* (Math.) intersection; ∼**punkt** *der* intersection; (Geom.) point of intersection; ∼**stelle** *die* (DV) interface; ∼**wunde** *die* cut; (lang u. tief) gash
Schnitzel *das;* ∼s, ∼ (a) (Fleisch) [veal/pork] escalope (b) (von Papier) scrap; (von Holz) shaving
schnitzeln *tr. V.* chop up ⟨*vegetables*⟩ [into small pieces]; shred ⟨*cabbage*⟩
schnitzen *tr., itr. V.* carve
schnodderig (ugs.) 1 *Adj.* brash 2 *adv.* brashly
schnöde (geh.) 1 *Adj.* (a) (verachtenswert) contemptible (b) (gemein) contemptuous, scornful ⟨*glance, reply, etc.*⟩ 2 *adv.* (gemein) contemptuously; ⟨*exploit, misuse*⟩ flagrantly
Schnorchel *der;* ∼s, ∼: snorkel
Schnörkel *der;* ∼s, ∼: scroll; (der Handschrift, in der Rede) flourish
schnorren *tr., itr. V.* (ugs.) scrounge (coll.) (**bei, von** + *Dat.* off)
Schnorrer *der;* ∼s, ∼, **Schnorrerin** *die;* ∼, ∼nen (ugs.) scrounger (coll.)
Schnösel *der;* ∼s, ∼ (ugs. abwertend) young whippersnapper
schnüffeln *itr. V.* (a) sniff (b) (ugs.: spionieren) snoop [about] (coll.) (c) (Drogenjargon: Dämpfe ∼) sniff [glue/paint etc.]
Schnüffler *der;* ∼s, ∼, **Schnüfflerin** *die;* ∼, ∼nen (a) (ugs.) Nosey Parker; (Spion) snooper (coll.) (b) (Drogenjargon) [glue-, paint-, *etc.*]sniffer
Schnulze *die;* ∼, ∼n (ugs. abwertend) (Lied/Melodie) slushy song/tune; (Theaterstück, Film, Fernsehspiel) tear jerker (coll.); slushy play

schnupfen ① *tr. V.* sniff; **Tabak** ~: take
snuff
② *itr. V.* take snuff
Schnupfen *der;* ~s, ~: [head] cold; [den
od. einen] ~ **haben** have a [head] cold
Schnupf·tabak *der* snuff
schnuppe: das/er ist mir ~/mir völlig ~
(ugs.) I don't care/I couldn't care less about
it/him (coll.)
schnuppern *itr. V.* sniff; **an etw.** *(Dat.)*
~: sniff sth.
Schnur *die;* ~, **Schnüre (a)** (Bindfaden) piece
of string; (Kordel) piece of cord
(b) (ugs.: Kabel) flex (Brit.); lead; cord (Amer.)
schnüren *tr. V.* tie ⟨*bundle, string, etc.*⟩; tie,
lace up ⟨*shoe, corset, etc.*⟩
schnur·los *Adj.* cordless
Schnurr·bart *der* moustache
schnurren *itr. V.* ⟨*cat*⟩ purr; ⟨*machine*⟩ hum
Schnür-: ~**schuh** *der* lace-up shoe;
~**senkel** *der;* ~~s, ~~ (bes. nordd.)
[shoe]lace; (für Stiefel) bootlace
schnur·stracks *Adv.* (ugs.) straight
schob *1. u. 3. Pers. Prät. v.* SCHIESSEN
Schock *der;* ~[e]s, ~s shock
schockieren *tr. V.* shock; **über etw.** *(Akk.)*
schockiert sein be shocked at sth.
Schöffe *der;* ~n, ~n lay judge ⟨*acting
together with another lay judge and a
professional judge*⟩
Schöffen·gericht *das: court presided
over by a professional judge and two lay
judges*
Schöffin *die;* ~, ~**nen** ▶ SCHÖFFE
Schoko /'ʃoːko/ *die;* ~, ~[s] (ugs.) choccy
(coll.)
Schokolade *die;* ~, ~n **(a)** chocolate
(b) (Getränk) [drinking] chocolate
Schokolade[n]-: ~**eis** *das* chocolate
ice cream; ~**guss**, *~**guß** *der* chocolate
icing; ~**pudding** *der* chocolate
blancmange; ~**torte** *die* chocolate cake
or gateau
scholl *1. u. 3. Pers. Sg. Prät. v.* SCHALLEN
Scholle *die;* ~, ~n **(a)** (Erdscholle) clod [of
earth]
(b) (Eisscholle) [ice] floe
(c) (Fisch) plaice
schon ① *Adv.* **(a)** (bereits) (oft nicht übersetzt)
already; (in Fragen) yet; **wie lange bist du
~ hier?** how long have you been here?
(b) (fast gleichzeitig) there and then
(c) (jetzt) ~ **[mal]** now; (inzwischen)
meanwhile
(d) (selbst, sogar) even; (nur) only
(e) (ohne Ergänzung, ohne weiteren Zusatz) on its
own; **[allein]** ~ **der Gedanke daran** the mere
thought of it; ~ **deshalb** for this reason
alone
(f) (wohl) really; **Lust hätte ich ~, aber ...:** I'd

certainly like to, but ...
② *Partikel* **(a)** (ugs.: ungeduldig: endlich) **nun
komm ~!** come on!; hurry up!
(b) (beruhigend: bestimmt) all right
(c) (durchaus) **das ist ~ möglich** that is quite
possible
schön ① *Adj.* **(a)** beautiful; handsome
⟨*youth, man*⟩
(b) (angenehm) pleasant, nice ⟨*day, holiday,
dream, relaxation, etc.*⟩; fine ⟨*weather*⟩;
(nett) nice; **das war eine ~e Zeit** those were
wonderful days
(c) (gut) good
(d) (in Höflichkeitsformeln) ~**e Grüße** best
wishes; ~**en Dank für ...:** thank you
very much for ...
(e) ~**!** (ugs.: einverstanden) OK (coll.); all right
(f) (iron.: leer) ~**e Worte** fine[-sounding]
words; (schmeichlerisch) honeyed words
(g) (ugs.: beträchtlich) handsome, (coll.)
tidy ⟨*sum, fortune, profit*⟩; considerable
⟨*quantity, distance*⟩; pretty good ⟨*pension*⟩
(h) (iron.: unerfreulich) nice (coll. iron.); **das sind
ja ~e Aussichten!** this is a fine lookout *sing.*
(iron.)
(i) sich ~ machen smarten oneself up
② *adv.* **(a)** beautifully
(b) (angenehm, erfreulich) nicely; ~ **warm/
weich/langsam** nice and warm/soft/slow
(c) (gut) well
(d) (in Höflichkeitsformeln) **bitte ~, können Sie
mir sagen, ...:** excuse me, could you tell
me ...
(e) (iron.) **wie es so ~ heißt, wie man so
~ sagt** as they say
(f) (ugs.: beträchtlich) really; (vor einem Adjektiv)
pretty; **ganz ~ arbeiten müssen** have to
work jolly hard (Brit. coll.)
③ *Partikel* (ugs.) **bleib ~ liegen!** lie there
and be good
schonen ① *tr. V.* treat ⟨*clothes, books,
furniture, etc.*⟩ with care; (schützen) protect
⟨*hands, furniture*⟩; (nicht strapazieren) spare
⟨*voice, eyes, etc.*⟩; conserve ⟨*strength*⟩
② *refl. V.* take things easy
Schönheit *die;* ~, ~en beauty
Schönheits-: ~**chirurgie** *die* cosmetic
surgery *no art.;* ~**pflege** *die* beauty care
no art.
Schon·kost *die* light food
***schön|machen** (ugs.) ▶ SCHÖN 1i
Schonung *die;* ~, ~en **(a)** (Nachsicht)
consideration; (nachsichtige Behandlung)
considerate treatment; (nach Krankheit/
Operation) [period of] rest; (von Gegenständen)
careful treatment
(b) (Jungwald) [young] plantation
schonungs·los ① *Adj.* unsparing,
ruthless ⟨*criticism etc.*⟩; blunt ⟨*frankness*⟩
② *adv.* unsparingly; ⟨*say*⟩ without mincing
one's words
Schonungslosigkeit *die;*
~: ruthlessness; (Strenge) rigour
Schopf *der;* ~[e]s, **Schöpfe** shock of hair

schöpfen *tr. V.* (a) scoop [up] ⟨*water, liquid*⟩; (mit einer Kelle) ladle ⟨*soup*⟩ (b) (geh.: einatmen) draw, take ⟨*breath*⟩

Schöpfer *der;* ~s, ~: creator; (Gott) Creator

Schöpferin *die;* ~, ~nen creator

schöpferisch ☐1 *Adj.* creative ☐2 *adv.* creatively

Schöpf-: ~kelle *die,* ~löffel *der* ladle

Schöpfung *die;* ~, ~en (geh.) creation; die ~ (die Welt) Creation

Schoppen *der;* ~s, ~: [quarter-litre/half-litre] glass of wine/beer

schor *1. u. 3. Pers. Sg. Prät. v.* SCHEREN

Schorf *der;* ~[e]s, ~e scab

Schorle *die;* ~, ~n wine with mineral water; ≈ spritzer

Schorn·stein *der* chimney; (Lokomotive, Schiff usw.) funnel

Schornstein·feger *der;* ~s, ~, **Schornstein·fegerin** *die;* ~, ~nen chimney sweep

schoss, *schoß *1. u. 3. Pers. Sg. Prät. v.* SCHIESSEN

Schoß *der;* ~es, Schöße lap

Schote *die;* ~, ~n pod

Schotte *der;* ~n, ~n Scot; Scotsman; die ~n the Scots; the Scottish

Schotten·rock *der* tartan skirt; (Kilt) kilt

Schottin *die;* ~, ~nen Scot; Scotswoman

schottisch *Adj.* Scottish; ~er Whisky Scotch whisky

Schottland *(das);* ~s Scotland

schräg ☐1 *Adj.* diagonal ⟨*line, beam, cut, etc.*⟩; sloping ⟨*surface, roof, wall, side, etc.*⟩; slanting, slanted ⟨*writing, eyes, etc.*⟩; tilted ⟨*position of the head etc., axis*⟩ ☐2 *adv.* at an angle; (diagonal) diagonally

Schräge *die;* ~, ~n (a) (schräge Fläche) sloping surface (b) (Neigung) slope

Schräg·strich *der* oblique stroke

schrak *1 u. 3. Pers. Sg. Prät. v.* SCHRECKEN

Schramme *die;* ~, ~n scratch

schrammen *tr. V.* scratch

Schrank *der;* ~[e]s, Schränke cupboard; closet (Amer.); (Glas~; kleiner Wand~) cabinet; (Kleiderschrank) wardrobe; (Bücher~) bookcase

Schränkchen *das;* ~s, ~: cabinet

Schranke *die;* ~, ~n (a) (auch fig.) barrier (b) (fig.: Grenze) limit

Schraube *die;* ~, ~n bolt; (Holz-, Blechschraube) screw

schrauben *tr. V.* (a) ▶ SCHRAUBE: bolt/screw (**an, auf** + *Akk.* on to) (b) (drehen) screw ⟨*nut, hook, lightbulb, etc.*⟩ (**auf** + *Akk.* on to; **in** + *Akk.* into)

Schrauben-: ~schlüssel *der* spanner; ~zieher *der;* ~s, ~: screwdriver

Schraub·verschluss, *Schraub·verschluß *der* screw top

Schreber·garten *der* ≈ allotment

(cultivated primarily as a garden)

Schreck *der;* ~[e]s, ~e fright; scare; (Schock) shock; jmdm. einen ~ einjagen give sb. a fright

schrecken *regelm. (auch unr.) itr. V.* start [up]; **aus dem Schlaf** ~: awake with a start; start from one's sleep

Schrecken *der;* ~s, ~: fright; scare; (Entsetzen) horror; (große Angst) terror; jmdm. einen ~ einjagen give sb. a fright

schreckhaft *Adj.* easily scared

Schreckhaftigkeit *die;* ~: easily scared nature; tendency to take fright

schrecklich ☐1 *Adj.* terrible ☐2 *adv.* terribly

Schredder *der;* ~s, ~: shredder

schreddern *tr. V.* shred

Schrei *der;* ~[e]s, ~e cry; (lauter Ruf) shout; (durchdringend) yell; (gellend) scream; (kreischend) shriek

Schreib·block *der; Pl.* ~s od. **Schreib·blöcke** writing pad

schreiben ☐1 *unr. itr. V.* write; (mit der Schreibmaschine) type; **an einem Roman** *usw.* ~: be writing a novel *etc.;* jmdm. od. an jmdn. ~: write to sb. ☐2 *unr. tr. V.* write; (mit der Schreibmaschine) type; **wie schreibt man dieses Wort?** how is this word spelt? ☐3 *unr. refl. V.* be spelt

Schreiben *das;* ~s, ~ (a) writing *no def. art.* (b) (Brief) letter

Schreiber *der;* ~s, ~: writer; (Verfasser) author

Schreiberin *die;* ~, ~en writer; (Verfasserin) authoress

Schreib-: ~marke *die* (DV) cursor; ~maschine *die* typewriter; ~maschinen·papier *das* typing paper; ~papier *das* writing paper; ~schutz *der* (DV) write protection; ~tisch *der* desk

Schreibung *die;* ~, ~en spelling

Schreib-: ~waren *Pl.* stationery *sing.;* ~waren·geschäft *das* stationer's

schreien *unr. itr. V.* ⟨person⟩ cry [out]; (laut rufen/sprechen) shout; (durchdringend) yell; (gellend) scream; ⟨baby⟩ yell, bawl; **zum Schreien sein** (ugs.) be a scream (coll.)

Schrei·hals *der* (ugs.) (a) (Kind) bawler (b) (abwertend: Randalierer) rowdy

Schreiner *der;* ~s, ~, (bes. südd.) ▶ TISCHLER

Schreinerei *die;* ~, ~en (bes. südd.) ▶ TISCHLEREI

Schreinerin *die;* ~, ~nen (bes. südd.) ▶ TISCHLERIN

schreiten *unr. itr. V.; mit sein* (geh.) walk; (mit großen Schritten) stride

schrickst *2. Pers. Sg. Präsens v.* SCHRECKEN

schrickt *3. Pers. Sg. Präsens v.* SCHRECKEN

schrie *1. u. 3. Pers. Sg. Prät. v.* SCHREIEN

schrieb *1. u. 3. Pers. Sg. Prät. v.* SCHREIBEN
Schrieb *der;* ~**[e]s,** ~**e** (ugs.) missive (coll.)
Schrift *die;* ~**,** ~**en (a)** (System) script; (Alphabet) alphabet
(b) (Handschrift) [hand]writing
(c) (Werk) work
Schrift-art *die* (Druckw.) [type]face
schriftlich ① *Adj.* written
② *adv.* in writing
Schrift-: ~**steller** *der;* ~~**s,** ~~**,** ~**stellerin** *die;* ~~**,** ~~**nen** writer; ~**stück** *das* [official] document; ~**wechsel** *der* correspondence; ~**zeichen** *das* character; ~**zug** *der* (Namenszug) lettering; (als Firmenzeichen) logo
schrill ① *Adj.* shrill
② *adv.* shrilly
schrillen *itr. V.* shrill; sound shrilly
schritt *1. u. 3. Pers. Sg. Prät. v.* SCHREITEN
Schritt *der;* ~**[e]s,** ~**e (a)** step; **einen** ~ **machen** *od.* **tun** take a step
(b) *Pl.* (Geräusch) footsteps
(c) (Entfernung) pace
(d) (Gleich~) **aus dem** ~ **kommen** get out of step
(e) (Gangart) walk; **seinen** ~ **verlangsamen/ beschleunigen** slow/quicken one's pace; **[mit jmdm./etw.]** ~ **halten** (auch fig.) keep up *or* keep pace with sb./sth.]
(f) (Schrittgeschwindigkeit) walking pace; „~ **fahren**' 'dead slow'
(g) (fig.: Maßnahme) step; measure
Schritt-: ~**geschwindigkeit** *die* walking pace; ~**macher** *der;* ~**macherin** *die* pacemaker
schroff ① *Adj.* **(a)** precipitous ‹rock etc.›
(b) (plötzlich) sudden ‹transition, change›; (krass) stark ‹contrast›
(c) (barsch) curt ‹refusal, manner›; brusque ‹manner, behaviour, tone›
② *adv.* **(a)** ‹rise, drop› sheer; ‹fall away› precipitously
(b) (plötzlich, unvermittelt) suddenly
(c) (barsch) curtly; ‹interrupt› abruptly; ‹treat› brusquely
schröpfen *tr. V.* (ugs.) fleece
Schrot *der od. das;* ~**[e]s,** ~**e (a)** coarse meal; (aus Getreide) whole meal (Brit.); whole grain
(b) (Munition) shot
schroten *tr. V.* grind ‹grain etc.› [coarsely]; crush ‹malt› [coarsely]
Schrot-: ~**flinte** *die* shotgun; ~**kugel** *die* pellet
Schrott *der;* ~**[e]s,** ~**e (a)** scrap [metal]; **ein Auto zu** ~ **fahren** (ugs.) write a car off
(b) (salopp fig.) rubbish
schrott-reif *Adj.* ready for the scrap heap *postpos.*
schrubben *tr. (auch itr.) V.* scrub
Schrubber *der;* ~**s,** ~**:** [long-handled]

scrubbing brush
Schrulle *die;* ~**,** ~**n** cranky idea; (Marotte) quirk
schrumpelig *Adj.* (ugs.) wrinkly
schrumpeln *itr. V.; mit sein* (ugs.) ‹skin› go wrinkled; ‹apple etc.› shrivel
schrumpfen *itr. V.; mit sein* shrink; ‹metal, rock› contract; ‹apple etc.› shrivel; ‹skin› go wrinkled; (abnehmen) decrease; ‹supplies, capital, hopes› dwindle
Schrumpf-: ~**leber** *die* cirrhotic liver; ~**niere** *die* cirrhotic kidney
Schub *der;* ~**[e]s, Schübe (a)** (Physik) thrust
(b) (Med.: Phase) phase; stage
(c) (Gruppe, Anzahl) batch
Schuber *der;* ~**s,** ~**:** slip case
Schub-: ~**fach** *das* drawer; ~**karre** *die,* ~**karren** *der* wheelbarrow; ~**lade** *die* drawer
Schubs *der;* ~**es,** ~**e** (ugs.) shove
schubsen *tr. (auch itr.) V.* (ugs.) push; shove
schub-weise *Adv.* (Med.) in phases *or* stages
schüchtern ① *Adj.* **(a)** shy ‹person, smile, etc.›; shy, timid ‹voice, knock, etc.›
(b) (fig.: zaghaft) tentative, cautious ‹attempt, beginnings, etc.›
② *adv.* shyly; ‹knock, ask, etc.› timidly
Schüchternheit *die;* ~**:** shyness
Schuft *der;* ~**[e]s,** ~**e** scoundrel
schuften (ugs.) *itr. V.* slave away
Schufterei *die;* ~ (ugs.) slaving away *no indef. art.;* slog
Schuh *der;* ~**[e]s,** ~**e** shoe; (hoher ~, Stiefel) boot; **jmdm. etw. in die** ~**e schieben** (fig. ugs.) pin the blame for sth. on sb.
Schuh-: ~**anzieher** *der;* ~~**s,** ~~**:** shoehorn; ~**band** *das; Pl.* ~**bänder** (bes. südd.) shoelace; ~**creme** *die* shoe polish; ~**größe** *die* shoe size; **welche** ~**größe hast du?** what size shoe[s] do you take?; ~**löffel** *der* shoehorn; ~**macher** *der,* ~**macherin** *die* shoemaker; ~**sohle** *die* sole [of a/one's shoe]
Schul-: ~**abschluss,** ***~**abschluß** *der* school-leaving qualification; ~**arbeit** *die* **(a)** ► ▶AUFGABE; **(b)** (österr.: Klassenarbeit) [written] class test; ~**aufgabe** *die* item of homework; ~**aufgaben** homework *sing.;* ~**beirat** *der* school advisory board; ~**buch** *das* school book; ~**bus** *der* school bus
schuld ▶ SCHULD B
Schuld *die;* ~**,** ~**en (a)** guilt; **er ist sich** *(Dat.)* **keiner** ~ **bewusst** he is not conscious of having done any wrong
(b) (Verantwortlichkeit) blame; **es ist [nicht] seine** ~**:** it is [not] his fault; **[an etw.** *(Dat.)***]** ~ **haben** *od.* **schuld sein** be to blame [for sth.]
(c) (Verpflichtung zur Rückzahlung) debt; **5000 Euro** ~**en haben** have debts of 5,000 euros; owe 5,000 marks

---

**alte Schreibung – vgl. Hinweis auf S. x

schuld·bewusst, *schuld·bewußt
[1] *Adj.* guilty ‹*look, face, etc.*›
[2] *adv.* guiltily

schulden *tr. V.* owe; **was schulde ich Ihnen?** how much do I owe you?

Schuld·gefühl *das* feeling of guilt

schuldig *Adj.* **(a)** guilty; **der [an dem Unfall] ~e Autofahrer** the driver to blame [for the accident]
(b) jmdm. etw. ~ sein/bleiben owe sb. sth.
(c) (gebührend) due; proper

Schuldige *der/die; adj. Dekl.* guilty person; (im Strafprozess) guilty party

Schuldigkeit *die;* ~, ~en duty; **meine [verdammte] Pflicht und ~:** my bounden duty; **seine ~ getan haben** (fig.) have served its/his purpose

Schul·direktor *der,* **Schul·direktorin** *die* head teacher; headmaster/headmistress

schuld-, Schuld-: ~**los** *Adj.* innocent (an + *Dat.* of); ~**spruch** *der* verdict of guilty

Schule *die;* ~, ~n school; **zur** *od.* **in die ~ gehen, die ~ besuchen** go to school; **auf** *od.* **in der ~:** at school

schulen *tr. V.* train

Schüler *der;* ~s, ~: pupil; (Schuljunge) schoolboy

Schüler·austausch *der* school exchange

Schülerin *die;* ~, ~nen pupil; (Schulmädchen) schoolgirl

Schüler·mit·verwaltung *die* pupil participation *no art.* in school administration

schul-, Schul-: ~**ferien** *Pl.* school holidays *or* (Amer.) vacation *sing.;* ~**fernsehen** *das* educational television; television for schools; ~**fest** *das* school open day; ~**frei** *Adj.* ‹*day*› off school; **morgen ist/haben wir ~frei** there is/we have no school tomorrow; ~**frei bekommen** be let off school; ~**hof** *der* school yard; ~**jahr** *das* **(a)** school year; **(b)** (Klasse) year; ~**junge** *der* schoolboy; ~**kind** *das* schoolchild; ~**klasse** *die* [school] class; ~**land·heim** *das* [school's] country hostel (*visited by school classes*); ~**mädchen** *das* schoolgirl; ~**ordnung** *die* school rules *pl.;* ~**pflicht** *die* obligation to attend school; **die Einführung der [allgemeinen] ~pflicht** the introduction of compulsory school attendance [for all children]; ~**pflichtig** *Adj.* required to attend school *postpos.;* ~**pflichtig sein** have to attend school; **im ~pflichtigen Alter** of school age; ~**ranzen** *der* [school] satchel; ~**sportfest** *das* inter-school sports day; ~**sprecher** *der* pupils' representative; ≈ head boy; ~**sprecherin** *die* pupils' representative; ≈ head girl; ~**tag** *der* school day; ~**tasche** *die* schoolbag; (Ranzen) [school] satchel

Schulter *die;* ~, ~n shoulder; **jmdm. auf die ~ klopfen** pat sb. on the shoulder *or* (fig.) back

Schulter·blatt *das* (Anat.) shoulder blade

schultern *tr. V.* shoulder; **das Gewehr ~:** shoulder arms

Schul-: ~**uniform** *die* school uniform; ~**weg** *der* way to school; ~**zeit** *die* schooldays *pl.*

Schummelei *die;* ~, ~en (ugs.)
▶ MOGELEI

schummeln *itr., tr., refl. V.* (ugs.) ▶ MOGELN

schummerig *Adj.* dim ‹*light etc.*›; dimly lit ‹*room etc.*›

Schummler *der;* ~s, ~, **Schummlerin** *die;* ~, ~nen (ugs.) cheat

Schund *der;* ~[e]s trash

Schuppe *die;* ~, ~n **(a)** scale
(b) *Pl.* (auf dem Kopf) dandruff *sing.;* (auf der Haut) flaking skin *sing.*

schuppen [1] *tr. V.* scale ‹*fish*›
[2] *refl. V.* ‹*skin*› flake; ‹*person*› have flaking skin

Schuppen *der;* ~s, ~ **(a)** shed
(b) (ugs.: Lokal) joint (coll.)

schüren *tr. V.* **(a)** poke ‹*fire*›
(b) (fig.) stir up ‹*hatred, envy, etc.*›

schürfen [1] *itr. V.* scrape
[2] *tr. V.* **(a) sich** (*Dat.*) **das Knie** *usw.* **~:** graze one's knee *etc.*
(b) (Bergbau) mine ‹*ore etc.*› open-cast *or* (Amer.) opencut

Schürf·wunde *die* graze; abrasion

Schurke *der;* ~n, ~n rogue

Schurken·staat *der* (abwertend) rogue state

Schurkin *die;* ~, ~nen rogue

Schur·wolle *die* new wool

Schürze *die;* ~, ~n apron; (Latzschürze) pinafore

Schuss, *Schuß *der;* **Schusses, Schüsse**
(a) shot (auf + *Akk.* at); **weit** *od.* **weitab vom ~** (fig. ugs.) well away from the action
(b) (Menge Munition/Schießpulver) round; **drei ~ Munition** three rounds of ammunition
(c) (Schusswunde) gunshot wound
(d) (kleine Menge) dash
(e) (Drogenjargon) shot; fix (sl.)
(f) (Skisport) schuss; **~ fahren** schuss
(g) (ugs.) **etw. in ~ bringen/halten** get sth. into/keep sth. in [good] shape

Schüssel *die;* ~, ~n bowl; (flacher) dish

schusselig (ugs.) [1] *Adj.* scatterbrained
[2] *adv.* in a scatterbrained way

Schusseligkeit *die;* ~ (ugs.) scatterbrained way

Schuss-, *Schuß-: ~**linie** *die* line of fire; **in die/jmds. ~linie geraten** *od.* **kommen** (auch fig.) come under fire/come under fire from sb.; ~**verletzung** *die* gunshot wound; ~**waffe** *die* weapon (*firing a projectile*); (Gewehr usw.) firearm; ~**wechsel** *der* exchange of shots

Schuster *der;* ~s, ~, **Schusterin** *die;* ~, ~**nen** (ugs.) shoemaker; (jmd., der schuhe repariert) shoe repairer

Schutt *der;* ~[e]s rubble; „~ **abladen verboten**" 'no tipping'; 'no dumping'

Schüttel·frost *der* [violent] shivering fit

schütteln ① *tr. V.* **(a)** shake; **den Kopf [über etw.** *(Akk.)]* ~: shake one's head [over sth.]; **jmdm. die Hand** ~: shake sb.'s hand; shake sb. by the hand
(b) *(unpers.)* **es schüttelte ihn [vor Kälte]** he was shaking [with *or* from cold]
② *refl. V.* shake oneself/itself
③ *itr. V.* **mit dem Kopf** ~: shake one's head

schütten ① *tr. V.* pour ⟨*liquid, flour, etc.*⟩; (unabsichtlich) spill ⟨*liquid, flour, etc.*⟩; tip ⟨*rubbish, coal, etc.*⟩
② *itr. V.* *(unpers.)* (ugs.: regnen) pour [down]

schütter *Adj.* sparse; thin

Schutt-: ~**halde** *die* pile *or* heap of rubble; ~**haufen** *der* pile of rubble; (Abfallhaufen) rubbish heap

Schutz *der;* ~es protection (**vor** + *Dat.,* **gegen** against); (Zuflucht) refuge; ~ **suchend** seeking protection *postpos.*

schutz-, Schutz-: ~**bedürftig** *Adj.* in need of protection *postpos.;* ~**behauptung** *die* (bes. Rechtsw.) attempt to justify one's behaviour; ~**blech** *das* mudguard; ~**brief** *der* (Kfz-W.) travel insurance; (Dokument) travel insurance certificate

Schütze *der;* ~n, ~n **(a)** marksman
(b) (Fußball usw.) scorer
(c) (Milit.: einfacher Soldat) private
(d) (Astrol.) Sagittarius

schützen ① *tr. V.* protect (**vor** + *Dat.* from, **gegen** against); safeguard ⟨*interest, property, etc.*⟩ (**vor** + *Dat.* from); **gesetzlich geschützt** registered [as a trade mark]
② *itr. V.* provide *or* give protection (**vor** + *Dat.* from, **gegen** against); (vor Wind, Regen) give shelter (**vor** + *Dat.* from)

Schützen·fest *das;* shooting competition with fair

Schutz·engel *der* guardian angel

Schützen-: ~**graben** *der* trench; ~**panzer** *der* armoured personnel carrier; ~**verein** *der* rifle club

Schutz-: ~**helm** *der* helmet; (bei Motorradfahrern usw.) crash helmet; (bei Bauarbeitern usw.) safety helmet; ~**hütte** *die* **(a)** (Unterstand) shelter; **(b)** (Berghütte) mountain hut; ~**impfung** *die* vaccination

Schützin *die;* ~, ~**nen (a)** markswoman
(b) (Fußball usw.) scorer

Schützling *der;* ~s, ~e protégé; (Anvertrauter) charge

schutz-, Schutz-: ~**los** *Adj.* defenceless; ~**mann** *der;* *Pl.* ~**männer** *od.* ~**leute** (ugs. veralt.) [police] constable; copper

(Brit. coll.); ~**patron** *der,* ~**patronin** *die* patron saint; ~**schicht** *die* protective layer (**aus** of); (flüssig aufgetragen) protective coating; *~**suchend** ▶ SCHUTZ; ~**umschlag** *der* dust jacket

schwabbelig *Adj.* flabby ⟨*stomach, person, etc.*⟩; wobbly ⟨*jelly etc.*⟩

schwabbeln *itr. V.* (ugs.) wobble

Schwabe *der;* ~n, ~n Swabian

Schwaben *(das);* ~s Swabia

Schwäbin *die;* ~, ~**nen** Swabian

schwäbisch *Adj.* Swabian

schwach; schwächer, schwächst...
① *Adj.* **(a)** weak; weak, delicate ⟨*child, woman*⟩; frail ⟨*invalid, old person*⟩; low-powered ⟨*engine, bulb, amplifier, etc.*⟩; weak, poor ⟨*eyesight, memory, etc.*⟩; poor ⟨*hearing*⟩; delicate ⟨*health, constitution*⟩; ~ **werden** grow weak; (fig.: schwanken) weaken; (fig.: nachgeben) give in
(b) (nicht gut) poor ⟨*pupil, player, performance, result, etc.*⟩; weak ⟨*argument, opponent, play, film, etc.*⟩
(c) (gering, niedrig) poor, low ⟨*attendance etc.*⟩; slight ⟨*effect, resistance, gradient, etc.*⟩; light ⟨*wind, rain, current*⟩; faint ⟨*voice, pressure, hope, smile, smell*⟩; weak, faint ⟨*pulse*⟩; faint, dim ⟨*light*⟩; pale ⟨*colour*⟩
(d) (wenig konzentriert) weak ⟨*solution, coffee, poison, etc.*⟩
(e) (Sprachw.) weak
② *adv.* **(a)** weakly
(b) (nicht gut) poorly
(c) (in geringem Maße) poorly ⟨*attended, developed*⟩; slightly ⟨*poisonous, sweetened, inclined*⟩; ⟨*rain*⟩ slightly; ⟨*remember, glow, smile*⟩ faintly
(d) (Sprachw.) ~ **gebeugt** weak

Schwäche *die;* ~, ~n weakness; **eine ~ für jmdn./etw. haben** have a soft spot for sb./a weakness for sth.

Schwäche·anfall *der* sudden feeling of faintness

schwächen *tr. V.* weaken

schwächlich *Adj.* weakly ⟨*person*⟩; frail ⟨*old person, constitution*⟩

Schwächling *der;* ~s, ~e weakling

schwach-, Schwach-: ~**punkt** *der* weak point; ~**sinn** *der* **(a)** (Med.) mental deficiency; **(b)** (ugs.) [idiotic (coll.)] rubbish; ~**sinnig** ① *Adj.* **(a)** (Med.) mentally deficient; **(b)** (ugs.) idiotic (coll.), nonsensical ⟨*measure, policy, etc.*⟩; rubbishy ⟨*film etc.*⟩; ② *adv.* (ugs.) idiotically (coll.); stupidly

Schwächung *die;* ~, ~en weakening

Schwaden *der;* ~s, ~: [thick] cloud

schwafeln (ugs.) ① *itr. V.* rabbit on (Brit. coll.), waffle (**von** about)
② *tr. V.* blether ⟨*nonsense*⟩

Schwager *der;* ~s, **Schwäger** brother-in-law

Schwägerin *die;* ~, ~**nen** sister-in-law

Schwalbe *die;* ~, ~n swallow

---

*old spelling – see note on page x

Schwall *der;* ~[e]s, ~e torrent

schwamm *1. u. 3. Pers. Sg. Prät. v.*
SCHWIMMEN

Schwamm *der;* ~[e]s, Schwämme
(a) sponge; ~ **drüber!** (ugs.) [let's] forget it
(b) (südd., österr.: Pilz) mushroom

Schwammerl *das;* ~s, ~[n] (bayr., österr.)
mushroom

schwammig 1 *Adj.* (a) spongy
(b) (aufgedunsen) flabby, bloated *(face, body, etc.)*
(c) (abwertend: unpräzise) woolly *(concept, manner of expression, etc.)*
2 *adv.* (unpräzise) vaguely

Schwammigkeit *die;* ~ (a) sponginess
(b) (abwertend: Aufgedunsenheit) flabbiness; bloated appearence
(c) (abwertend: Vagheit) woolliness

Schwan *der;* ~[e]s, Schwäne swan

schwand *1. u. 3. Pers. Sg. Prät. v.*
SCHWINDEN

schwang *1. u. 3. Pers. Sg. Prät. v.*
SCHWINGEN

schwanger *Adj.* pregnant (**von** by)

Schwangere *die; adj. Dekl.* expectant
mother; pregnant woman

schwängern *tr. V.* make *(woman)*
pregnant

Schwangerschaft *die;* ~, ~en
pregnancy

Schwangerschafts-: ~**abbruch**
der termination of pregnancy; abortion;
~**verhütung** *die* contraception;
~**vertretung** *die* (a) maternity[-leave]
cover; **die** ~**vertretung für jmdn. machen**
cover for sb. while she is on maternity leave;
(b) (Person) person covering [a period of]
maternity leave

Schwank *der;* ~[e]s, Schwänke comic
tale; (auf der Bühne) farce

schwanken *itr. V.; mit Richtungsangabe
mit sein* (a) sway; *(boat)* rock; (heftiger) roll;
(ground, floor) shake
(b) (fig.: unbeständig sein) *(prices, temperature, etc.)* fluctuate; *(number, usage, etc.)* vary
(c) (fig.: unentschieden sein) waver; (zögern)
hesitate

Schwankung *die;* ~, ~en variation; (der
Kurse usw.) fluctuation

Schwanz *der;* ~es, Schwänze (a) tail
(b) (salopp: Penis) prick (coarse); cock (coarse)

Schwänzchen *das;* ~s, ~(a) [little] tail
(b) (fam.: Penis) willy (coll.)

schwänzeln *itr. V.* wag its tail/their tails

schwänzen *tr., itr. V.* (ugs.) skip, cut
(lesson etc.); [**die Schule**] ~: play truant *or*
(Amer.) hookey

schwappen *itr. V.* slosh

Schwarm *der;* ~[e]s, Schwärme
(a) swarm
(b) (fam.: Angebetete[r]) idol; heart-throb

schwärmen *itr. V.* (a) *mit
Richtungsangabe mit sein* swarm
(b) (begeistert sein) **für jmdn./etw.** ~: be mad
about *or* really keen on sb./sth.; **von etw.**
~: go into raptures about sth.

schwärmerisch 1 *Adj.* rapturous
2 *adv.* rapturously

Schwarte *die;* ~, ~n (a) rind
(b) (ugs.: dickes Buch) tome

schwarz; schwärzer, schwärzest... 1 *Adj.*
(a) black; Black *(person)*; filthy[-black]
(hands, fingernails, etc.); **mir wurde** ~ **vor
den Augen** everything went black **der
Schwarze Erdteil** *od.* **Kontinent** the Dark
Continent; **das Schwarze Meer** the Black
Sea; **ins Schwarze treffen** (fig.) hit the nail
on the head
(b) (illegal) illicit *(deal, exchange, etc.)*; **der**
~**e Markt** the black market
(c) ~ **sehen** look on the black side; be
pessimistic (**für** about)
2 *adv.* (illegal) illegally

Schwarz *das;* ~[es], ~: black

Schwarz·brot *das* black bread

Schwarze *der/die; adj. Dekl.* Black

schwärzen *tr. V.* blacken

schwarz-, Schwarz-: ~|**fahren**
unr. itr. V.; mit sein dodge paying the fare;
~**fahrer** *der,* ~**fahrerin** *die* fare dodger;
~**haarig** *Adj.* black-haired; ~**handel**
der black market (**mit** in); (Tätigkeit) black
marketeering (**mit** in); ~**markt** *der*
black market; ~|**sehen** *unr. itr. V.* watch
television without a licence; *s. auch*
SCHWARZ 1c; ~**seher** *der,* ~**seherin**
die (a) (ugs.) pessimist; (b) (jmd, der schwarz
fernsieht) [television] licence dodger

Schwärzung *die;* ~, ~en blackening

schwarz-, Schwarz-: ~**wald** *der;*
~[e]s Black Forest; ~**weiß** *Adj.* black and
white; ~**weiß·film** *der* black and white
film; ~**weiß·foto** *das* black and white
photo; ~**wurzel** *die* black salsify

schwatzen, (bes. südd.) **schwätzen**
1 *itr. V.* chat; (über belanglose Dinge) chatter;
natter (coll.)
2 *tr. V.* say; talk *(nonsense, rubbish)*

Schwätzer *der;* ~s, ~, **Schwätzerin**
die; ~, ~nen chatterbox; (klatschhafter Mensch)
gossip

schwatzhaft *Adj.* talkative; (klatschhaft)
gossipy

Schwatzhaftigkeit *die;*
~: talkativeness; (Klatschsucht) gossipiness

Schwebe *die;* **in der** ~ **sein/bleiben** (fig.)
be/remain in the balance

Schwebe-: ~**bahn** *die* cableway;
~**balken** *der* (Turnen) [balance] beam

schweben *itr. V.* (a) *(bird, balloon, etc.)*
hover; *(cloud, balloon, mist)* hang; **in
Gefahr** ~ (fig.) be in danger
(b) *mit sein* (durch die Luft) float

Schwede *der;* ~n, ~n Swede ⋯⟩

Schweden *(das);* ~s Sweden
Schwedin *die;* ~, ~nen Swede
schwedisch *Adj.* Swedish
Schwefel *der;* ~s sulphur
Schwefel-: ~**dioxid, ~dioxyd** *das*
(Chemie) sulphur dioxide; ~**säure** *die*
(Chemie) sulphuric acid; ~**wasserstoff**
der (Chemie) hydrogen sulphide
Schweif *der;* ~[e]s, ~e tail
schweifen *itr. V.; mit sein* (geh.; auch fig.)
wander
Schweige·geld *das* hush money
schweigen *unr. itr. V.* remain *or* stay
silent; say nothing; **ganz zu** ~ **von** ...: not to
mention ...
Schweigen *das;* ~s silence
schweigsam *Adj.* silent; quiet
Schweigsamkeit *die;* ~: silence;
quietness
Schwein *das;* ~[e]s, ~e **(a)** pig
(b) (Fleisch) pork
(c) (salopp: gemeiner Mensch) swine; (Schmutzfink)
mucky devil (coll.); mucky pig (coll.)
(d) (salopp: Mensch) **ein armes** ~: a poor
devil; **kein** ~ **war da** there wasn't a bloody
(Brit. sl.) *or* (coll.) damn soul there
(e) (ugs.: Glück) **[großes]** ~ **haben** have a [big]
stroke of luck; (davonkommen) get away with
it (coll.)
Schweine-: ~**braten** *der* roast
pork *no indef. art.;* ~**fleisch** *das* pork;
~**kotelett** *das* (Kochk.) pork chop
Schweinerei *die;* ~, ~en (ugs.)
(a) (Schmutz) mess
(b) (Gemeinheit) mean *or* dirty trick
Schweine-: ~**schnitzel** *das* escalope
of pork; ~**stall** *der* (auch fig.) pigsty; pigpen
(Amer.); ~**steak** *das* pork steak
schweinisch (ugs.) *Adj.* **(a)** (schmutzig) filthy
(b) (unanständig) dirty; smutty
Schweins·leder *das* pigskin
Schweiß *der;* ~es sweat; **mir brach der**
~ **aus** I broke out in a sweat
Schweiß-: ~**ausbruch** *der* sweat;
~**brenner** *der* welding torch; ~**drüse**
die (Anat.) sweat gland
schweißen *tr., itr. V.* weld
Schweißer *der;* ~s, ~, **Schweißerin**
die; ~, ~nen welder
schweiß-, Schweiß-: ~**fuß** sweaty
foot; ~**gebadet** *Adj.* bathed in sweat
postpos.; ~**nass,** ***~**naß** *Adj.* sweaty;
damp with sweat *pred.;* ~**perle** *die* bead
of sweat
Schweiz *die;* ~: Switzerland *no art.*
Schweizer *der;* ~s, ~: Swiss
schweizer·deutsch *Adj.* Swiss German
Schweizerin *die;* ~, ~nen Swiss
schweizerisch *Adj.* Swiss
schwelen (auch fig.) smoulder

---

*alte Schreibung – vgl. Hinweis auf S. x

schwelgen *itr. V.* feast
Schwelle *die;* ~, ~n **(a)** threshold
(b) (Eisenbahnschwelle) sleeper (Brit.); [cross]
tie (Amer.)
schwellen *unr. itr. V.; mit sein* swell; ‹*limb,
face, cheek, etc.*› swell [up]
Schwellen·land *das:* country at the stage
of economic take-off
Schwellung *die;* ~, ~en (Med.) swelling
Schwemme *die;* ~, ~n glut (**an** + *Dat.* of)
Schwemm·land *das* alluvial land
Schwengel *der;* ~s, ~ **(a)** (der Glocke)
clapper
(b) (der Pumpe) handle
Schwenk *der;* ~s, ~s **(a)** (Drehung) swing
(b) (Film, Ferns.) pan
schwenken ① *tr. V.* **(a)** swing; wave ‹*flag,
handkerchief*›
(b) (spülen) rinse
② *itr. V.; mit sein* ‹*marching column*› swing,
wheel; ‹*camera*› pan; ‹*path, road, car*› swing
schwer ① *Adj.* **(a)** heavy; **2 Kilo** ~ **sein**
weigh two kilos
(b) (mühevoll) heavy ‹*work*›; hard, tough
‹*job*›; hard ‹*day*›; difficult ‹*birth*›; **es**
~**/nicht** ~ **haben** have it hard/easy; **sich**
mit *od.* **bei etw.** ~ **tun** (ugs.) have trouble
with sth.; **jmdm. fällt etw.** ~: sb. finds sth.
difficult; **jmdm./sich etw.** ~ **machen** make
sth. difficult for sb./oneself
(c) (schlimm) severe ‹*shock, disappointment,
strain, storm*›; serious, grave ‹*wrong,
injustice, error, illness, blow, reservation*›;
serious ‹*accident, injury*›; heavy
‹*punishment, strain, loss, blow*›; **etw.**
~ **nehmen** take sth. seriously
② *adv.* **(a)** heavily ‹*built, laden, armed*›;
~ **tragen** be carrying sth. heavy [with
difficulty]
(b) ‹*work*› hard; ‹*breathe*› heavily; ~ **hören**
be hard of hearing
(c) (schwierig) with difficulty; ~ **verdaulich**
(auch fig.) hard to digest *pred.*
(d) (sehr) seriously ‹*injured, ill*›; greatly,
deeply ‹*disappointed*›; ‹*punish*› severely,
heavily; ~ **verunglücken** have a serious
accident
Schwer-: ~**arbeiter** *der* worker
engaged in heavy physical work;
~**behinderte** *der/die* severely
handicapped person; (körperlich auch)
severely disabled person; **die** ~**behinderten**
the severely handicapped/disabled;
~**beschädigte** *der/die; adj. Dekl.*
severely disabled person
Schwere *die;* ~ **(a)** weight
(b) (Schwerkraft) gravity
(c) ▶ SCHWER 1c: severity; seriousness;
gravity; heaviness
schwere·los *Adj.* weightless
Schwerelosigkeit *die;*
~: weightlessness

schwer-, Schwer-: *~|**fallen**
▸ SCHWER 1B; ~**fällig** 〔1〕 *Adj.* (auch fig.)
ponderous; cumbersome ⟨*bureaucracy,
procedure*⟩; 〔2〕 *adv.* ponderously;
~**fälligkeit** *die;* ▸~FÄLLIG:
ponderousness; cumbersomeness;
~**gewicht** *das* **(a)** (Sport) heavyweight;
(b) (Schwerpunkt) main focus; ~**hörig** *Adj.*
hard of hearing *pred.;* ~**hörigkeit** *die;*
~~: hardness of hearing; ~**industrie**
die heavy industry; ~**kraft** *die* gravity;
*~**krank** ▸ SCHWER 2D
schwerlich *Adv.* hardly
schwer-, Schwer-: *~|**machen**
▸ SCHWER 1B; ~**metall** *das* heavy
metal; ~**mütig** 〔1〕 *Adj.* melancholic;
〔2〕 *adv.* melancholically; *~|**nehmen**
▸ SCHWER 1C; ~**punkt** *der* centre of
gravity; (fig.) main focus; (Hauptgewicht) main
stress
Schwert *das;* ~[e]s, ~er sword
Schwert-: ~**fisch** *der* swordfish; ~**lilie**
die iris
schwer|tun ▸ SCHWER 1B
Schwert·wal *der* (Orka) killer whale
schwer-, Schwer-: ~**verbrecher**
der, ~**verbrecherin** *die* serious
offender; *~**verdaulich** ▸ SCHWER 2C;
*~**verletzt** ▸ SCHWER 2D; ~**wiegend**
Adj. serious; momentous ⟨*decision*⟩
Schwester *die;* ~, ~n **(a)** sister
(b) (Krankenschwester) nurse
schwesterlich 〔1〕 *Adj.* sisterly
〔2〕 *adv.* ~ **handeln** act in a sisterly way
schwieg *1. u. 3. Pers. Prät. v.* SCHWEIGEN
Schwieger-: ~**eltern** *Pl.* parents-in-
law; ~**mutter** *die; Pl.* ~**mütter** mother-in-
law; ~**sohn** *der* son-in-law; ~**tochter** *die*
daughter-in-law; ~**vater** *der* father-in-law
Schwiele *die;* ~, ~n callus; ~n **an den
Händen** horny hands
schwielig *Adj.* callused; ~e Hände horny
hands
schwierig *Adj.* difficult
Schwierigkeit *die;* ~, ~en difficulty
Schwierigkeits·grad *der* degree of
difficulty; (von Lehrmaterial usw.) level of
difficulty
Schwimm-: ~**bad** *das* swimming baths
pl. (Brit.); swimming pool; ~**becken** *das*
swimming pool
schwimmen 〔1〕 *unr. itr. V.* **(a)** *meist mit
sein* swim
(b) *meist mit sein* (treiben, nicht untergehen)
float
(c) (ugs.: unsicher sein) be all at sea; **ins
Schwimmen geraten** start to flounder
〔2〕 *unr. tr. V.; auch mit sein* swim
Schwimmen *das;* ~s: swimming *no art.*
Schwimmer *der;* ~s, ~ **(a)** swimmer
(b) (Technik) float
Schwimmerin *die;* ~, ~nen swimmer

Schwimm-: ~**flosse** *die* flipper;
~**lehrer** *der,* ~**lehrerin** *die* swimming
instructor; ~**weste** *die* life jacket
Schwindel *der;* ~s **(a)** dizziness; giddiness
(b) (Betrug) swindle; (Lüge) lie
schwindel·frei *Adj.* ~ **sein** have a head
for heights
schwindelig ▸ SCHWINDLIG
schwindeln *itr. V.* **(a)** (unpers.) **mich** *od.*
mir schwindelt I feel dizzy *or* giddy
(b) (lügen) tell fibs
schwinden *unr. itr. V.; mit sein* fade;
⟨*supplies, money*⟩ run out; ⟨*effect*⟩ wear off;
⟨*fear, mistrust*⟩ lessen; ⟨*powers, influence*⟩
wane
Schwindler *der;* ~s, ~, **Schwindlerin**
die; ~, ~nen (Lügner[in]) liar; (Betrüger[in])
swindler; (Hochstapler[in]) confidence trickster
schwindlig *Adj.* dizzy; giddy; **jmdm. wird
es** ~: sb. gets dizzy *or* giddy
schwingen 〔1〕 *unr. itr. V.* **(a)** *mit sein* swing
(b) (vibrieren) vibrate
〔2〕 *unr. tr. V.* swing; wave ⟨*flag, wand*⟩;
brandish ⟨*sword, axe, etc.*⟩
〔3〕 *unr. refl. V.* **sich aufs Pferd/Fahrrad**
~: leap on to one's horse/bicycle
Schwingung *die;* ~, ~en **(a)** swinging;
(Vibration) vibration
(b) (Physik) oscillation
Schwips *der;* ~es, ~e (ugs.) **einen**
~ **haben** be tipsy
schwirren *itr. V. mit sein* ⟨*arrow, bullet,
etc.*⟩ whiz; ⟨*bird*⟩ whirl; ⟨*insect*⟩ buzz
schwitzen *itr. V.* (auch fig.) sweat
schwor *1. u. 3. Pers. Sg. Prät. v.* SCHWÖREN
schwören 〔1〕 *unr. tr., itr. V.* swear ⟨*fidelity,
friendship*⟩; swear, take ⟨*oath*⟩
〔2〕 *unr. itr. V.* swear an/the oath
Schwuchtel *die;* ~, ~n (salopp) queen (sl.)
schwul *Adj.* (ugs.) gay (coll.)
schwül *Adj.* sultry; close
Schwule *der; adj. Dekl.* (ugs.) gay (coll.);
(abwertend) queer (sl.)
Schwüle *die;* ~: sultriness
schwülstig 〔1〕 *Adj.* bombastic; pompous;
over-ornate ⟨*art, architecture*⟩
〔2〕 *adv.* bombastically; pompously
Schwund *der;* ~[e]s decrease, drop (Gen.
in); (an Interesse) waning; falling off
Schwung *der;* ~[e]s, **Schwünge**
(a) (Bewegung) swing
(b) (Linie) sweep
(c) (Geschwindigkeit) momentum; ~ **holen**
build *or* get up momentum
(d) (Antrieb) drive; energy
(e) (mitreißende Wirkung) sparkle
schwung·haft *Adj.* thriving; brisk,
flourishing ⟨*trade, business*⟩
schwung·voll 〔1〕 *Adj.* **(a)** lively
(b) (kraftvoll) vigorous; sweeping ⟨*movement,
gesture*⟩; bold ⟨*handwriting, line, stroke*⟩
〔2〕 *adv.* spiritedly; (kraftvoll) with great vigour

S

Schwur *der;* ∼[e]s, Schwüre (a) (Gelöbnis) vow
(b) (Eid) oath

Schwur·gericht *das: court with a jury*

scrollen /'skrolən/ *itr., tr. V.* (DV) scroll

sechs *Kardinalz.* six

Sechs *die;* ∼, ∼en six

sechs-, Sechs-: ∼**eck** *das* hexagon; ∼**eckig** *Adj.* hexagonal; ∼**fach** *Vervielfältigungsz.* sixfold; ∼**hundert** *Kardinalz.* six hundred; ∼**mal** *Adv.* six times

sechst... *Ordinalz.* sixth

sechs·tausend *Kardinalz.* six thousand

sechstel *Bruchz.* sixth

Sechstel *das,* (*schweiz. meist der*); ∼s, ∼: sixth

sechstens *Adv.* sixthly

sechzehn *Kardinalz.* sixteen

sechzig *Kardinalz.* sixty

sechzigst... *Ordinalz.* sixtieth

SED *Abk.* (DDR) = **Sozialistische Einheitspartei Deutschlands** Socialist Unity Party of Germany (*state party of the former DDR*)

See[1] *der;* ∼s, ∼n lake

See[2] *die;* ∼: **die** ∼: the sea; **an die** ∼ **fahren** go to the seaside; **auf hoher** ∼: on the high seas

see-, See-: ∼**bad** *das* seaside health resort; ∼**fahrt** *die* seafaring *no art.;* sea travel *no art.;* ∼**gang** *der* **leichter/starker** *od.* **hoher** *od.* **schwerer** ∼**gang** light/heavy *or* rough sea; ∼**hund** *der* [common] seal; (Pelz) seal[skin]; ∼**igel** *der* sea urchin; ∼**krank** *Adj.* seasick; ∼**krankheit** *die* seasickness; ∼**lachs** *der* pollack

Seele *die;* ∼, ∼n soul; (Psyche) mind

Seelen·leben *das* (geh.) inner life

seelen·ruhig [1] *Adj.* calm; unruffled [2] *adv.* calmly

seelisch [1] *Adj.* psychological ⟨*cause, damage, tension*⟩; mental ⟨*equilibrium, breakdown, illness, health*⟩ [2] *adv.* ∼ **bedingt sein** have psychological causes; ∼ **krank** mentally ill

Seel·sorge *die* pastoral care

Seelsorger *der;* ∼s, ∼, **Seelsorgerin** *die;* ∼, ∼nen pastoral worker; (Geistliche[r]) pastor

see-, See-: ∼**macht** *die* sea power; ∼**mann** *der; Pl.* ∼**leute** seaman; sailor; ∼**meile** *die* nautical mile; ∼**not** *die* distress [at sea]; **in** ∼**not geraten** get into difficulties *pl.;* ∼**pferd[chen]** *das* sea horse; ∼**räuber** *der,* ∼**räuberin** *die* pirate; ∼**reise** *die* voyage; (Kreuzfahrt) cruise; ∼**rose** *die* waterlily; ∼**stern** *der* starfish; ∼**tüchtig** *Adj.* seaworthy; ∼**zunge** *die* sole

---

*old spelling – see note on page x

Segel *das;* ∼s, ∼: sail

Segel-: ∼**boot** *das* sailing boat; ∼**flieger** *der,* ∼**fliegerin** *die* glider pilot; ∼**flugzeug** *das* glider

segeln *itr. V.; mit sein* sail

Segel-: ∼**schiff** *das* sailing ship; ∼**tuch** *das; Pl.* ∼∼e sailcloth

Segen *der;* ∼s, ∼: blessing; (Gebet in der Messe) benediction

Segler *der;* ∼s, ∼: yachtsman

Seglerin *die;* ∼, ∼nen yachtswoman

segnen *tr. V.* bless

seh·behindert *Adj.* partially sighted; visually handicapped

sehen [1] *unr. itr. V.* (a) see; **schlecht/gut** ∼: have bad/good eyesight; **mal** ∼, **wir wollen** *od.* **werden** ∼ (ugs.) we'll see; **siehste!** (ugs.) there, you see!
(b) (hinsehen) look (**auf** + *Akk.* at); **sieh mal** *od.* **doch!** look!; **siehe da!** lo and behold!
[2] *unr. tr. V.* (a) (auch fig.) see; **jmdn./etw. [nicht] zu** ∼ **bekommen** [not] get to see sb./sth.; **ich habe ihn kommen [ge]**∼: I saw him coming
(b) (ansehen) watch ⟨*television programme*⟩

sehens·wert *Adj.* worth seeing *postpos.*

Sehens·würdigkeit *die;* ∼, ∼en sight

Seher *der;* ∼s, ∼, **Seherin** *die;* ∼, ∼nen seer; prophet/prophetess

Seh-: ∼**fehler** *der* sight defect; defect of vision; ∼**kraft** *die* sight

Sehne *die;* ∼, ∼n (a) tendon
(b) (Bogen∼) string

sehnen *refl. V.* **sich nach jmdm./etw.** ∼: long *or* yearn for sb./sth.

sehnig *Adj.* (a) stringy ⟨*meat*⟩
(b) (kräftig) sinewy ⟨*figure, legs, etc.*⟩

sehnlichst [1] *Adj.* **das ist mein** ∼**es Verlangen/mein** ∼**er Wunsch** that's what I long for most/that's my dearest wish
[2] *adv.* **etw.** ∼ **herbeiwünschen** look forward longingly to sth.

Sehn·sucht *die* longing; ∼ **nach jmdm. haben** long to see sb.

sehn·süchtig *Adj.* longing *attrib.,* yearning *attrib.* ⟨*desire, look, gaze, etc.*⟩

sehr *Adv.* (a) *mit Adj. u. Adv.* very; ∼ **viel** a great deal; **jmdn.** ∼ **gern haben** like sb. a lot (coll.) *or* a great deal
(b) *mit Verben* very much; greatly; **danke** ∼! thank you *or* thanks [very much]; **bitte** ∼, **Ihr Steak!** here's your steak, sir/madam

Seh-: ∼**schärfe** *die* visual acuity; ∼**test** *der* eye test; ∼**vermögen** *das* sight

sei *1. u. 3. Pers. Sg. Präsens Konjunktiv u. Imperativ Sg. v.* SEIN

seicht [1] *Adj.* (auch fig.) shallow
[2] *adv.* (fig.) shallowly

Seichtheit *die;* ∼ (auch fig.) shallowness

seid *2. Pers. Pl. Präsens u. Imperativ Pl. v.* SEIN

Seide *die;* ∼, ∼n silk

Seidel *das;* ~s, ~: beer mug
seiden *Adj.* silk
Seiden·papier *das* tissue paper
seidig [1] *Adj.* silky
[2] *adv.* silkily
Seife *die;* ~, ~n soap
Seifen-: ~**blase** *die* soap bubble;
~**oper** *die* (ugs.) soap opera; ~**schale** *die*
soap dish; ~**schaum** *der* lather
Seil *das;* ~s, ~e rope; (Drahtseil) cable
Seil·bahn *die* cableway
seil|hüpfen *itr. V.; nur im Inf. u. 2. Part.;*
mit sein ▶ SEILSPRINGEN
Seilschaft *die;* ~, ~en (Bergsteigen) rope;
(fig.) followers *pl.*
seil-, Seil-: ~|**springen** *unr. itr. V.; nur*
im Inf. u. 2. Part.; mit sein skip; **wie dem auch sei**
der, ~**tänzerin** *die* tightrope walker;
~**winde** *die* cable winch
sein[1] [1] *unr. itr. V.* be; (existieren) be; exist;
(sich ereignen) be; happen; **wie dem auch sei**
be that as it may; **er ist Schwede/Lehrer** he
is Swedish *or* a Swede/a teacher; **bist du es?**
is that you?; **mir ist kalt/besser** I am *or* feel
cold/better; **mir ist schlecht** I feel sick; **drei**
und vier ist *od.* (ugs.) **sind sieben** three and
four is *or* makes seven; **es ist drei Uhr/Mai/**
Winter it is three o'clock/May/winter; **er ist**
aus Berlin he is *or* comes from Berlin; **was**
darf es ~**?** (im Geschäft) what can I get you?;
es war einmal ein Prinz once upon a time
there was a prince
[2] *mod. V. (in der Funktion von* können/
müssen + *Passiv)* **es ist niemand zu**
sehen there's no one to be seen; **das war**
zu erwarten that was to be expected; **die**
Schmerzen sind kaum zu ertragen the pain
is hardly bearable; **die Richtlinien sind**
strengstens zu beachten the guidelines are
to be strictly followed
[3] *Hilfsverb* **(a)** (zur Perfektumschreibung) have;
er ist gestorben he has died
(b) (zur Bildung des Zustandspassivs) be; **wir sind**
gerettet worden/wir waren gerettet we were
saved
sein[2] *Possessivpron.* (einer männlichen Person)
his; (einer weiblichen Person) her; (einer Sache,
eines Tiers) its; (nach man) one's; his (Amer.)
Sein *das;* ~s (Philos.) being; (Dasein)
existence; ~ **und Schein** appearance and
reality
seiner (geh.) *Gen. von* ER: **sich** ~ **erbarmen**
have pity on him; ~ **gedenken** remember
him
seiner-: ~**seits** *Adv.* for his part; (von ihm)
on his part; ~**zeit** *Adv.* at that time
seines·gleichen *indekl. Pron.* his own
kind
seinet·wegen *Adv.* ▶ MEINETWEGEN:
because of him; for his sake; about him; as
far as he is concerned
seismo-, Seismo-: ~**graph** *der;*
~~en, ~~en seismograph; ~**loge** *der;*

~~**n**, ~~**n** seismologist; ~**logie** *die;*
~~: seismology *no art.;* ~**login** *die;* ~~,
~~**nen** seismologist; ~**logisch** [1] *Adj.*
seismological; [2] *adv.* seismologically
seit [1] *Präp. mit Dat.* (Zeitpunkt) since;
(Zeitspanne) for; **ich bin** ~ **zwei Wochen hier**
I've been here [for] two weeks
[2] *Konj.* since; ~ **du hier wohnst** since you
have been living here
seit·dem [1] *Adv.* since then
[2] *Konj.* ▶ SEIT 2
Seite *die;* ~, ~n **(a)** side; **zur** *od.* **auf die**
~ **gehen** move aside *or* to one side; ~ **an**
~: side by side; **jmdm. zur** ~ **stehen** stand
by sb.; **von allen** ~**n** (auch fig.) from all sides;
nach allen ~**n** in all directions; (fig.) on all
sides
(b) (Buch-, Zeitungsseite) page
Seiten-: ~**airbag** *der* (Kfz.-W.) side
airbag; ~**ansicht** *die* side view;
~**aufprall·schutz** *der* side impact
protection; ~**hieb** *der* (fig.) sideswipe (**auf**
+ *Akk.* at); ~**ruder** *das* (Flugw.) rudder
seitens *Präp. mit Gen.* (Papierdt.) on the
part of
Seiten-: ~**sprung** *der* infidelity;
~**straße** *die* side street; ~**wind** *der*
side wind; crosswind; ~**zahl** *die* **(a)** page
number; **(b)** (Anzahl der Seiten) number of
pages
seit·her *Adv.* since then
seitlich [1] *Adj.* at the side (postpos.)
[2] *adv.* (an der Seite) at the side; (von der Seite)
from the side; (nach der Seite) to the side
seit·wärts *Adv.* sideways
Sekretär *der;* ~s, ~e **(a)** secretary
(b) (Schreibschrank) bureau (Brit.)
Sekretariat *das;* ~[e]s, ~e [secretary's/
secretaries'] office
Sekretärin *die;* ~, ~nen secretary
Sekt *der;* ~[e]s, ~e high-quality sparkling
wine; ≈champagne
Sekte *die;* ~, ~n sect
Sektor *der;* ~s, ~en **(a)** (Fachgebiet)
field; sphere; **industrieller/wirtschaftlicher**
~: industrial/economic sector
(b) (Geom.; Besatzungszone) sector
sekundär [1] *Adj.* secondary
[2] *adv.* secondarily
Sekundar-: ~**schule** *die* (schweiz.)
secondary school; ~**stufe** *die* secondary
stage *(of education)*
Sekunde *die;* ~, ~n **(a)** (auch Math., Musik)
second
(b) (ugs.: Augenblick) second; moment
Sekunden·zeiger *der* second hand
selb... *Demonstrativpron.* same;
selber *indekl. Demonstrativpron.*
▶ SELBST 1
selbst [1] *indekl. Demonstrativpron.*
myself/yourself/himself/herself/itself/
ourselves/yourselves/themselves; **von** ⋯⋗

~: automatically; ~ **gemacht** home-made
2 *Adv.* even
Selbst·achtung *die* self-respect; self-
esteem
selb·ständig 1 *Adj.* independent; self-
employed ⟨*business man, tradesman, etc.*⟩;
sich ~ **machen** set up on one's own
2 *adv.* independently; ~ **denken** think for
oneself
Selbständigkeit *die;* ~: independence
selbst-, Selbst-: ~**auslöser** *der*
(Fot.) delayed-action shutter release;
~**bedienung** *die* self-service *no art.;*
~**befriedigung** *die* masturbation *no
art.;* ~**beherrschung** *die* self-control
no art.; ~**bestätigung** *die* (Psych.)
self-affirmation *no art.;* ~**bewusst,**
*~**bewußt** 1 *Adj.* self-confident; 2 *adv.*
self-confidently; ~**bewusstsein,**
*~**bewußtsein** *das* self-confidence *no
art.;* ~**erkenntnis** *die* self-knowledge
no art.; ~**gefällig** 1 *Adj.* self-satisfied;
smug; 2 *adv.* smugly; ~**gefälligkeit**
die self-satisfaction; smugness;
*~**gemacht** ▸ SELBST 1; ~**gespräch**
das conversation with oneself; ~**hilfe**
die self-help *no art.;* Hilfe zur ~**hilfe**
leisten help people to help themselves;
~**hilfe·gruppe** *die* self-help group;
~**los** 1 *Adj.* selfless; 2 *adv.* selflessly;
unselfishly; ~**mord** *der* suicide *no art.;*
~**mord·anschlag** *der* suicide attack;
~**mörder** *der,* ~**mörderin** *die* suicide;
~**sicher** 1 *Adj.* self-confident; 2 *adv.*
in a self-confident manner; ~**ständig**
usw.: ▸ SELBSTÄNDIG *usw.;* ~**süchtig**
1 *Adj.* selfish; 2 *adv.* selfishly; ~**tätig**
1 *Adj.* automatic; 2 *adv.* automatically;
~**verständlich** 1 *Adj.* natural; etw.
für ~verständlich halten regard sth. as a
matter of course; (für gegeben hinnehmen)
take sth. for granted; 2 *adv.* naturally;
of course; ~**verständlichkeit** *die*
matter of course; etw. mit der größten
~verständlichkeit tun do sth. as if it
were the most natural thing in the world;
~**vertrauen** *das* self-confidence;
~**verwaltung** *die* self-government *no
art.;* ~**zweck** *der* end in itself
selektieren *tr. V.* select; pick out
Selektion *die;* ~, ~en selection
selektiv 1 *Adj.* selective
2 *adv.* selectively
selig 1 *Adj.* (a) (Rel.) blessed
(b) (tot) late [lamented]
(c) (glücklich) blissful ⟨*idleness, slumber, etc.*⟩;
blissfully happy ⟨*person*⟩
2 *adv.* blissfully
Seligkeit *die;* ~, ~en bliss *no pl.;* [blissful]
happiness *no pl.*
Sellerie *der;* ~s, ~[s] *od.* die; ~,
~: celeriac; (Stangen~) celery

---

selten 1 *Adj.* rare; infrequent ⟨*visit,
visitor*⟩
2 *adv.* (a) rarely
(b) (sehr) exceptionally; uncommonly
Seltenheit *die;* ~, ~en rarity
Seltenheits·wert *der;* ~[es] rarity value
Selters·wasser *das* seltzer [water]
seltsam 1 *Adj.* strange; odd
2 *adv.* strangely
Semester *das;* ~s, ~: semester
Semester·ferien *Pl.* [university]
vacation *sing.*
Semi·finale *das* (Sport) semi-final
Semi·kolon *das;* ~s, ~s semicolon
Seminar *das;* ~s, ~e (a) seminar (über
+ *Akk.* on)
(b) (Institut) department
Semit *der;* ~en, ~en, **Semitin** *die;* ~,
~nen Semite
semitisch *Adj.* Semitic
Semmel *die;* ~, ~n (bes. österr., bayr., ostmd.)
[bread] roll
Semmel·knödel *der* (bayr., österr.) bread
dumpling
Senat *der;* ~[e]s, ~e senate
Senator *der;* ~s, ~en, **Senatorin** *die;*
~, ~nen senator
senden[1] *unr.* (*auch regelm.*) *tr. V.* (geh.) send
senden[2] *regelm.* (*schweiz. unr.*) *tr., itr. V.*
broadcast ⟨*programme, play, etc.*⟩; transmit
⟨*signals, Morse, etc.*⟩
Sender *der;* ~s, ~: [broadcasting] station;
(Anlage) transmitter
Sende·reihe *die* series [of programmes]
Sender·such·lauf *der* (Rundf., Ferns.)
[automatic] station search
Sende·schluss, *Sende·schluß *der*
close down
Sende·zeit *die* (Rundf., Ferns.) broadcasting
time; die ~ um zehn Minuten überschreiten
overrun by ten minutes
Sendung *die;* ~, ~en (a) consignment
(b) (Rundf., Ferns.) programme
Senf *der;* ~[e]s, ~e mustard
senil 1 *Adj.* (Med., auch abwertend) senile
2 *adv.* in a senile manner
senior *nach Personennamen* senior
Senior *der;* ~s, ~en (a) (Kaufmannsspr.)
senior partner
(b) (Sport) senior [player]
(c) (Rentner) senior citizen
Senioren·heim *das* home for the elderly
Seniorin *die;* ~, ~nen ▸ SENIOR
Senke *die;* ~, ~n hollow
senken 1 *tr. V.* lower
2 *refl. V.* ⟨*curtain, barrier, etc.*⟩ fall, come
down; ⟨*ground, building, road*⟩ subside,
sink; ⟨*water level*⟩ fall, sink
senk-, Senk-: ~**fuß** *der* flat foot;
~**recht** 1 *Adj.* vertical; ~recht zu etw.
perpendicular to sth.; 2 *adv.* vertically;

~rechte *die;* ~~, ~~n; *auch adj. Dekl.*
vertical; (Geom.: Gerade) perpendicular
Sensation *die;* ~, ~en sensation
sensationell [1] *Adj.* sensational
[2] *adv.* sensationally
Sense *die;* ~, ~n scythe
sensibel [1] *Adj.* sensitive
[2] *adv.* sensitively
sensibilisieren *tr. V.* (geh.) make ⟨person⟩
more sensitive (**für** to)
Sensibilität *die;* ~: sensitivity
sentimental [1] *Adj.* sentimental
[2] *adv.* sentimentally
Sentimentalität *die;* ~, ~en
sentimentality
separat [1] *Adj.* separate; self-contained
⟨flat etc.⟩
[2] *adv.* separately
September *der;* ~[s], ~: September
Serbe *der;* ~n, ~n Serb; Serbian
Serbien (das); ~s Serbia
Serbin *die;* ~, ~nen ▶ SERBE
serbisch *Adj.* Serbian
Serenade *die;* ~, ~n serenade
Serie /'ze:ri̯ə/ *die;* ~, ~n series
serien·mäßig [1] *Adj.* standard ⟨product,
model, etc.⟩
[2] *adv.* (a) ~ **gefertigt** *od.* **gebaut** produced
in series
(b) (nicht als Sonderausstattung) ⟨fitted, supplied,
etc.⟩ as standard
seriös respectable ⟨person, hotel, etc.⟩;
trustworthy ⟨firm, partner, etc.⟩; serious
⟨offer, applicant, artist, etc.⟩
Seriosität *die;* ~ (geh.) (a) (Solidität)
respectability; (Vertrauenswürdigkeit)
trustworthiness
(b) (Ernsthaftigkeit) seriousness
Serotonin /zeroto'ni:n/ *das;* ~s, ~e (Biol.)
serotonin
Serpentine *die;* ~, ~n hairpin bend
Serum *das;* ~s, Seren serum
Server /'sə:vɐ/ *der;* ~s, ~ (DV) server
Service[1] /zɐ'vi:s/ *das;* ~, ~: [dinner etc.]
service
Service[2] /'zø:ɐ̯vɪs/ *der;* ~, ~s /'zø:ɐ̯vɪsɪs/
(Bedienung, Kundendienst) service
servieren *tr. V.* serve
Serviererin *die;* ~, ~nen waitress
Serviette /zɐ'vi̯ɛtə/ *die;* ~, ~n napkin;
serviette (Brit.)
Servo-: ~**bremse** *die* servo[-assisted]
brake; ~**lenkung** *die* power[-assisted]
steering *no indef. art.*
Servus /'zɛrvʊs/ *Interj.* (bes. südd., österr.)
(beim Abschied) goodbye; so long (coll.); (zur
Begrüßung) hello
Sesam *der;* ~s sesame seeds *pl.*
Sessel *der;* ~s, ~ (a) armchair
(b) (österr.: Stuhl) chair
Sessel·lift *der* chairlift

sesshaft, *seßhaft *Adj.* settled;
~ **werden** settle down
Sesshaftigkeit, *Seßhaftigkeit *die;*
~: settled way of life
Set *das od. der;* ~[s], ~s (a) set,
combination (**aus** of)
(b) (Deckchen) table- *or* place mat
setzen [1] *refl. V.* (a) sit [down]; setzen Sie
sich sit down; take a seat; sich aufs Sofa
usw. ~: sit on the sofa etc.
(b) ⟨coffee, froth, etc.⟩ settle; ⟨sediment⟩ sink
to the bottom
[2] *tr. V.* (a) put
(b) (einpflanzen) plant ⟨tomatoes, potatoes,
etc.⟩
(c) (aufziehen) hoist ⟨flag etc.⟩; set ⟨sails,
navigation lights⟩
(d) (Druckw.) set ⟨manuscript etc.⟩
[3] *itr. V.* (a) *meist mit sein* (springen) leap;
jump
(b) **über einen Fluss** ~ (mit einer Fähre o. Ä.)
cross a river
(c) (beim Wetten) bet; **auf ein Pferd/auf Rot**
~: back a horse/put one's money on red
Setzer *der;* ~s, ~, **Setzerin** *die;* ~,
~nen (Druckw.) [type]setter
Setzling *der;* ~s, ~e seedling
Seuche *die;* ~, ~n epidemic
Seuchen·gefahr *die* danger of an
epidemic
seufzen *itr., tr. V.* sigh
Seufzer *der;* ~s, ~: sigh
Sex *der;* ~[es] sex *no art.*
Sexismus *der;* ~: sexism *no art.*
sexistisch [1] *Adj.* sexist
[2] *adv.* ⟨behave, think, etc.⟩ in a sexist
manner
Sexualität *die;* ~: sexuality *no art.*
Sexual-: ~**kunde** *die* (Schulw.) sex
education *no art.;* ~**leben** *das* sex life;
~**partner** *der,* ~**partnerin** *die* sexual
partner; ~**trieb** *der* sex[ual] drive *or*
urge; ~**verbrechen** *das* sex crime;
~**verbrecher** *der* sex offender
sexuell [1] *Adj.* sexual
[2] *adv.* sexually
sezieren *tr. V.* dissect ⟨corpse⟩
sfr., sFr. *Abk.* = **Schweizer Franken**
Shampoo /ʃam'pu:/, **Shampoon**
/ʃam'po:n/ *das;* ~s, ~s shampoo
Shareholdervalue /'ʃeəhoʊldəvælju:/
der; ~s, ~s shareholder value
Sherry /'ʃɛrɪ/ *der;* ~s, ~s sherry
Show /ʃoʊ/ *die;* ~, ~s show
siamesisch *Adj.* Siamese
Siam·katze *die* Siamese cat
Sibirien (das); ~s Siberia
sich *Reflexivpron. der 3. Pers. Sg. und Pl.*
Akk. und Dat. (a) himself/herself/itself/
themselves; (auf man *bezogen*) oneself;
(auf das Anredepronomen Sie *bezogen*)
yourself/yourselves; ~ **freuen/wundern/** ⋯⃗

schämen/täuschen be pleased/surprised/ ashamed/mistaken; ~ **sorgen** worry

(b) (reziprok) one another, each other

Sichel *die;* ~, ~n sickle

sicher [1] *Adj.* **(a)** safe ⟨*road, procedure, etc.*⟩; secure ⟨*job, investment, etc.*⟩

(b) reliable ⟨*evidence, source*⟩; certain ⟨*proof*⟩; reliable, sure ⟨*judgment, taste, etc.*⟩

(c) (selbstbewusst) [self-]assured ⟨*person, manner*⟩

(d) (gewiss) certain; sure

[2] *adv.* **(a)** safely

(b) (zuverlässig) reliably; ~ **[Auto] fahren** be a safe driver

(c) (selbstbewusst) [self-]confidently

[3] *Adv.* certainly

sicher|gehen *unr. itr. V.; mit sein* play safe

Sicherheit *die;* ~, ~en **(a)** safety; (der Öffentlichkeit) security; **jmdn./etw. in ~ [vor etw. (***Dat.***)] bringen** save *or* rescue sb./sth. [from sth.]

(b) (Gewissheit) certainty

(c) (Wirtsch.: Bürgschaft) security

sicherheits-, Sicherheits-: ~**abstand** *der* (Verkehrsw.) safe distance between vehicles; ~**gurt** *der* seat belt; ~**halber** *Adv.* to be on the safe side; ~**nadel** *die* safety pin; ~**schloss,** *****~**schloß** *das* safety lock

sicherlich *Adv.* certainly

sichern *tr. V.* **(a)** make ⟨*door etc.*⟩ secure; (garantieren) safeguard ⟨*rights, peace*⟩; (schützen) protect ⟨*rights etc.*⟩; **sich (***Dat.***) etw. ~:** secure sth.

(b) (DV) back up

sicher|stellen *tr. V.* **(a)** impound ⟨*goods, vehicle*⟩

(b) guarantee ⟨*supply, freedom, etc.*⟩

Sicher·stellung *die*

(a) ▸ SICHERSTELLEN A: impounding

(b) (Gewährleistung) guarantee

Sicherung *die;* ~, ~en **(a)** safeguarding; (das Schützen) protection

(b) (Elektrot.) fuse

(c) (techn. Vorrichtung) safety catch

Sicherungs·kopie *die* (DV) back-up [copy]

Sicht *die;* ~: view (**auf** + *Akk.,* **in** + *Akk.* of); **gute** *od.* **klare/schlechte ~:** good/poor visibility; **in ~ kommen** come into sight; **außer ~ sein** be out of sight

sichtbar [1] *Adj.* visible; (fig.) apparent ⟨*reason*⟩

[2] *adv.* visibly

sichten *tr. V.* sight

sichtlich [1] *Adj.* obvious; evident

[2] *adv.* obviously; evidently; visibly ⟨*impressed*⟩

Sichtung *die;* ~, ~en sighting

Sicht-: ~**verhältnisse** *Pl.* visibility *sing.;* ~**vermerk** *der* visa; ~**weite** *die*

visibility *no art.;* **außer/in ~weite sein** be out of/in sight

sickern *itr. V.; mit sein* seep; (spärlich fließen) trickle

sie [1] *Personalpron.; 3. Pers. Sg. Nom. Fem.* she; (betont) her; (bei Dingen, Tieren) it; *s. auch* IHR[1], IHRER A

[2] *Personalpron.; 3. Pers. Pl. Nom.* they; (betont) them; *s. auch* IHNEN; IHRER B

[3] *Akk. von* SIE 1: her; (bei Dingen, Tieren) it

[4] *Akk. von* SIE 2A: them

Sie *Personalpron.; 3. Pers. Pl. Nom. u. Akk; Anrede an eine od. mehrere Personen* you; *s. auch* IHNEN; IHRER

Sieb *das;* ~[e]s, ~e sieve; (für Tee) strainer

sieben[1] *tr. V.* **(a)** sieve ⟨*flour etc.*⟩; riddle ⟨*sand, gravel, etc.*⟩

(b) (auswählen) screen ⟨*candidates*⟩

sieben[2] *Kardinalz.* seven

Sieben *die;* ~, ~en seven

sieben-, Sieben-: ~**fach** *Vervielfältigungsz.* sevenfold; ~**mal** *Adj.* seven times; ~**sachen** *Pl.* (ugs.) meine/ deine *usw.* ~**sachen** my/your *etc.* belongings *or* (coll.) bits and pieces

siebt... *Ordinalz.* seventh

siebtel *Bruchz.* seventh

Siebtel *das,* (schweiz. meist der); ~s, ~: seventh

siebtens *Adv.* seventhly

sieb·zehn *Kardinalz.* seventeen

siebzig *Kardinalz.* seventy

siebzigst... *Ordinalz.* seventieth

siedeln *itr. V.* settle

sieden *unr. od. regelm. itr. V.* boil

Siede·punkt *der* (auch fig.) boiling point

Siedler *der;* ~s, ~: settler

Siedlung *die;* ~, ~en **(a)** (Wohngebiet) [housing] estate

(b) (Niederlassung) settlement

Sieg *der;* ~[e]s, ~e victory, (bes. Sport) win (**über** + *Akk.* over)

Siegel *das;* ~s, ~: seal; (von Behörden) stamp

siegen *itr. V.* win; **über jmdn. ~:** gain *or* win a victory over sb.; (bes. Sport) win against sb.; beat sb.

Sieger *der;* ~s, ~: winner; (Mannschaft) winners *pl.;* (einer Schlacht) victor

Sieger·ehrung *die* presentation ceremony; awards ceremony

Siegerin *die;* ~, ~nen winner

sieges·sicher *Adj., adv.* confident of victory

sieg·gewohnt *Adj.* ⟨*army*⟩ accustomed to victory; ⟨*team*⟩ used to winning

sieh, siehe *Imperativ Sg. v.* SEHEN

siehst *2. Pers. Sg. Präsens v.* SEHEN

sieht *3. Pers. Sg. Präsens v.* SEHEN

siezen *tr. V.* call ⟨*sb.*⟩ 'Sie' (*the polite form of address*)

Signal *das;* ~s, ~e signal
signalisieren *tr. V.* indicate ⟨*danger, change, etc.*⟩
Signatur *die;* ~, ~en **(a)** initials *pl.;* (Kürzel) abbreviated signature; (des Künstlers) autograph
(b) (Unterschrift) signature
(c) (in einer Bibliothek) shelf mark
signieren *tr. V.* sign; autograph ⟨*one's own work*⟩
Silbe *die;* ~, ~n syllable
Silber *das;* ~s **(b)** (silbernes Gerät) silver[ware]
(b) (silbernes Gerät) silver[ware]
Silber·medaille *die* silver medal
silbern ①*Adj.* silver; silvery ⟨*moonlight, shade, gleam, etc.*⟩
②*adv.* ⟨*shine, shimmer, etc.*⟩ with a silvery lustre
Silber·papier *das* silver paper
Silhouette /zi'luɛtə/ *die;* ~, ~n silhouette
Silicium *das;* ~s silicon
Silikon *das;* ~s, ~e (Chemie) silicone
Silo *der od. das;* ~s, ~s silo
Silvester *der od. das;* ~s, ~: New Year's Eve
Silvester·nacht *die* night of New Year's Eve
Simbabwe *(das);* ~s Zimbabwe
Sim-Karte, SIM-Karte /'zɪm-/ *die* SIM card
simpel ①*Adj.* **(a)** simple ⟨*question, task*⟩
(b) (beschränkt) simple-minded ⟨*person*⟩; simple ⟨*mind*⟩
②*adv.* **(a)** simply
(b) (beschränkt) in a simple-minded manner
Simpel *der;* ~s, ~ (bes. südd. ugs.) simpleton; fool
Sims *der od. das;* ~es, ~e ledge; sill; (Kamin~) mantelpiece
simsen /'zɪmzn̩/ *itr. V.* (ugs.) send a text message/text messages
Simulant *der;* ~en, ~en **Simulantin** *die;* ~, ~nen malingerer
Simulation *die;* ~, ~en simulation
simulieren ①*tr. V.* feign, sham ⟨*illness, emotion, etc.*⟩; simulate ⟨*situation, condition, etc.*⟩
②*itr. V.* feign illness
simultan ①*Adj.* simultaneous
②*adv.* simultaneously
sind *1. u. 3. Pers. Pl. Präsens v.* SEIN¹
Sinfonie *die;* ~, ~n symphony
Sinfonie·orchester *das* symphony orchestra
singen *unr. tr., itr. V.* sing
Single¹ /'zɪŋl/ *die;* ~, ~s (Schallplatte) single
Single² *der;* ~s, ~s single person; ~s single people *no art.*
Single³ *das;* ~s, ~s (Badminton, Tennis) singles *sing. or pl.*
Singular *der;* ~s singular

Sing·vogel *der* songbird
sinken *unr. itr. V.; mit sein* **(a)** ⟨*ship, sun*⟩ sink, go down; ⟨*plane, balloon*⟩ descend, go down
(b) (niedersinken) fall
(c) (niedriger werden) ⟨*temperature, level*⟩ fall, drop
(d) (an Wert verlieren; nachlassen; abnehmen) fall, go down
Sinn *der;* ~[e]s, ~e **(a)** sense
(b) *Pl.* (geh.: Bewusstsein) senses; mind *sing.;* nicht bei ~en sein be out of one's senses *or* mind
(c) (Gefühl, Verständnis) feeling
(d) (Bedeutung) meaning
(e) (Ziel u. Zweck) point
Sinn·bild *das* symbol
Sinnes-: ~organ *das* sense organ; sensory organ; ~täuschung *die* trick of the senses
sinn·gemäß ①*Adj.* eine ~e Übersetzung a translation which conveys the general sense
②*adv.* etw. ~ übersetzen/wiedergeben translate the general sense of sth./give the gist of sth.
sinnlich *Adj.* sensory ⟨*impression, perception, stimulus*⟩; sensual ⟨*love, mouth*⟩; sensuous ⟨*pleasure, passion*⟩
Sinnlichkeit *die;* ~: sensuality
sinn·los ①*Adj.* **(a)** senseless
(b) (zwecklos) pointless
②*adv.* **(a)** senselessly
(b) (zwecklos) pointlessly
Sinnlosigkeit *die;* ~ **(a)** senselessness
(b) (Zwecklosigkeit) pointlessness
sinn·voll ①*Adj.* **(a)** (vernünftig) sensible
(b) (einen Sinn ergebend) meaningful
②*adv.* **(a)** (vernünftig) sensibly
(b) (einen Sinn ergebend) meaningfully
Sint·flut *die* Flood; Deluge
sintflut·artig ①*Adj.* torrential
②*adv.* in torrents
Sinto *der;* ~, Sinti Sinte
Sippe *die;* ~, ~n **(a)** (Völkerk.) sib
(b) (ugs.: Verwandtschaft) clan
Sippschaft *die;* ~, ~en (ugs.) ▶ SIPPE B
Sirene *die;* ~, ~n siren
Sirup *der;* ~s, ~e syrup
Sitte *die;* ~, ~n **(a)** (Brauch) custom; tradition
(b) (moralische Norm) common decency
(c) *Pl.* (Benehmen) manners
sitten·widrig *Adj.* **(a)** (Rechtsw.) illegal ⟨*methods, advertising, etc.*⟩
(b) (unmoralisch) immoral ⟨*behaviour*⟩
sittlich ①*Adj.* moral
②*adv.* morally
Sittlichkeit *die;* ~: morality
Sittlichkeits-: ~verbrechen *das* sexual crime; ~verbrecher *der,* ~verbrecherin *die* sex offender

S

Situation die; ~, ~en situation

situiert Adj. gut/schlechter (usw.) ~ well off/worse off etc.

Sitz der; ~es, ~e (a) seat
(b) (Verwaltungssitz) headquarters sing. or pl.
(c) (von Kleidungsstücken) fit

Sitz·bank die; Pl. Sitzbänke bench

sitzen unr. itr. V.; südd., österr., schweiz. mit sein (a) sit
(b) (sein) be
(c) ([gut] passen) fit
(d) ~ bleiben (nicht versetzt werden) stay down [a year]; (unverheiratet bleiben) be left on the shelf; auf etw. (Dat.) ~ bleiben (für etw. keinen Käufer finden) be left or (coll.) stuck with sth.; jmdn. ~ lassen (ugs.) (nicht heiraten) jilt sb.; (im Stich lassen) leave sb. in the lurch; etw. nicht auf sich (Dat.) ~lassen not take sth.

sitzen-: *~\|**bleiben** ▶ SITZEN D;
*~\|**lassen** ▶ SITZEN D

Sitz·platz der seat

Sitzplatz·stadion das all-seater stadium

Sitzung die; ~, ~en meeting; (eines Parlaments) sitting; session

Sitzungs·saal der conference hall

Skala die; ~, Skalen scale

Skalp der; ~s, ~e scalp

Skalpell das; ~s, ~e scalpel

skalpieren tr. V. scalp

Skandal der; ~s, ~e scandal

skandalös Adj. scandalous

Skandinavien (das); ~s Scandinavia

Skandinavier der; ~s, ~: Scandinavian

skandinavisch Adj. Scandinavian

Skat der; ~[e]s, ~e od. ~s skat

Skateboard /'skeɪtbɔːd/ das; ~s, ~s skateboard

Skateboarder /'skeɪtbɔːdɐ/ der; ~s, ~, **Skateboarderin** die; ~, ~nen skateboarder

Skelett das; ~[e]s, ~e skeleton

Skepsis die; ~: scepticism

skeptisch [1] Adj. sceptical
[2] adv. sceptically

Ski /ʃiː/ der; ~s, ~er od. ~: ski; ~ laufen od. fahren ski

Ski-: ~läufer der, ~läuferin die skier; ~lehrer der, ~lehrerin die ski instructor; ~lift der ski lift

Skinhead /'skɪnhɛd/ der; ~s, ~s skinhead

Ski·springen das; ski jumping no art.

Skizze die; ~, ~n sketch

Skizzen·block der sketch pad

skizzieren tr. V. sketch

Sklave der; ~n, ~n slave

Sklaven·händler der, **Sklaven·händlerin** die slave trader

Sklaverei die; ~: slavery no art.

Sklavin die; ~, ~nen slave

sklavisch [1] Adj. slavish
[2] adv. slavishly

Skonto der od. das; ~s, ~s (Kaufmannsspr.) [cash] discount

Skorbut der; ~[e]s scurvy no art.

Skorpion der; ~s, ~e scorpion; (Astrol.) Scorpio

Skrupel der; ~s, ~: scruple

skrupel·los [1] Adj. unscrupulous
[2] adv. unscrupulously

Skrupellosigkeit die;
~: unscrupulousness

Skulptur die; ~, ~en sculpture

skurril [1] Adj. absurd; droll ⟨person⟩
[2] adv. absurdly

Skurrilität die; ~, ~en absurdity

Slalom der; ~s, ~s slalom

Slash /slɛʃ/ der; ~s, ~s [forward] slash

Slawe der; ~n, ~n, **Slawin** die; ~, ~nen Slav

slawisch Adj. Slav[ic]; Slavonic

Slip der; ~s, ~s briefs pl.

Slogan /'sloːgn̩/ der; ~s, ~s slogan

Slowake der; ~n, ~n Slovak

Slowakei die; ~: Slovakia no art.

Slowakin die; ~, ~nen Slovak

Slowene der; ~n, ~n Slovene; Slovenian

Slowenien /sloˈveːni̯ən/ (das); ~s Slovenia

Slowenin die; ~, ~nen Slovene; Slovenian

Slum /slam/ der; ~s, ~s slum

Smaragd der; ~[e]s, ~e emerald

Smog der; ~[s], ~s smog

Smoking der; ~s, ~s dinner jacket or (Amer.) tuxedo and dark trousers

SMS die; ~, ~: SMS (message)

Snowboard /'snoʊbɔːd/ das; ~s, ~s snowboard

Snowboarder /'snoʊbɔːdɐ/ der; ~s, ~, **Snowboarderin** die; ~, ~nen snowboarder

so [1] Adv. (a) (auf diese Weise; in, von dieser Art) like this/that; this/that way; **weiter so!** carry on in the same way!; **so genannt** so-called
(b) (dermaßen, überaus) so
(c) (genauso) as; **so wenig/viel wie** od. **als** as little/much as; **halb/doppelt so viel** half/twice as much; **so weit wie möglich** as far as possible; **so weit** (im großen Ganzen) by and large; (bis jetzt) up to now; **so weit sein** (ugs.) be ready; **so gut ich konnte** as best I could
(d) (ugs.: solch) such; **so ein Idiot!** what an idiot!; **so einer/eine/eins** one like that
(e) betont (eine Zäsur ausdrückend) right; OK (coll.)
(f) (ugs.: schätzungsweise) about
[2] Partikel (a) just; **ach, das hab' ich nur so gesagt** oh, I didn't mean anything by that

s

(b) (in Aufforderungssätzen verstärkend) **so komm doch** come on now

s. o. *Abk.* = **siehe oben**

So. *Abk.* = **Sonntag** Sun.

Soap /soʊp/ *die;* ~, ~s soap [opera]

sobald *Konj.* as soon as

Socke *die;* ~, ~n sock

Sockel *der;* ~s, ~ **(a)** (einer Säule, Statue) plinth

(b) (unterer Teil eines Hauses, Schrankes) base

so·dass, *sodaß *Konj.* **(a)** (damit) so that

(b) (und deshalb) and so

Soda·wasser *das* soda; soda water

Sod·brennen *das;* ~s heartburn

so·eben *Adv.* just

Sofa *das;* ~s, ~s sofa; settee

so·fern *Konj.* provided [that]

soff *1. u. 3. Pers. Sg. Prät. v.* SAUFEN

so·fort *Adv.* immediately; at once

sofortig *Adj.* (unmittelbar) immediate

Sofort·maßnahme *die* immediate measure

Software /'sɔftvɛːɐ̯/ *die;* ~, ~s (DV) software

sog *1. u. 3. Pers. Sg. Prät. v.* SAUGEN

Sog *der;* ~[e]s, ~e suction; (bei Schiffen) wake; (bei Fahr-, Flugzeugen) slipstream; (von Wasser, auch fig.) current

so·gar *Adv.* even

***so·genannt** ▶ so 1A

so·gleich *Adv.* immediately; at once

Sohle *die;* ~, ~n **(a)** (Schuh~) sole; (Einlege~) insole

(b) (Fuß~) sole [of the foot]

Sohn *der;* ~es, Söhne son

Soja-: ~**bohne** *die* soy[a] bean; ~**soße** *die* soy[a] sauce

so·lang[e] *Konj.* so *or* as long as

solar *Adj.* solar

Solar·energie *die* (Physik.) solar energy

Solarium *das;* ~s, Solarien solarium

Solar-: ~**kraftwerk** *das:* ▶ SONNENKRAFTWERK; ~**technik** *die* (Energietechnik) solar technology *no art.;* ~**zelle** *die* (Physik, Elektrot.) solar cell

solch *Demonstrativpron.* **(a)** *attr.* such; **das macht** ~**en Spaß!** it's so much fun!

(b) *allein stehend* ~**e wie die** people like that

Sold *der;* ~[e]s, ~e [military] pay

Soldat *der;* ~en, ~en soldier

Soldaten·friedhof *der* military *or* war cemetery

Soldatin *die;* ~, ~nen [female *or* woman] soldier

soldatisch ① *Adj.* military ⟨discipline, expression, etc.⟩; soldierly ⟨figure, virtue⟩ ② *adv.* in a military manner

Söldner *der;* ~s, ~, **Söldnerin** *die;* ~, ~nen mercenary

solidarisch ① *Adj.* ~**es Verhalten zeigen** show one's solidarity ② *adv.* ~ **handeln/sich** ~ **verhalten** act in/show solidarity

solidarisieren *refl.* V. show [one's] solidarity

Solidarität *die;* ~: solidarity

solide ① *Adj.* **(a)** solid; sturdy ⟨shoes, material⟩; [good-]quality ⟨goods⟩

(b) (gut fundiert) sound ⟨work, education, knowledge⟩; solid ⟨firm⟩

(c) (anständig) respectable ⟨person, life, profession⟩ ② *adv.* **(a)** solidly ⟨built⟩; sturdily ⟨made⟩

(b) (gut fundiert) soundly ⟨educated, constructed⟩

(c) (anständig) ⟨live⟩ respectably, steadily

Solidität *die;* ~: ▶ SOLIDE 1 A-C: solidness; sturdiness; soundness; respectability

Solist *der;* ~en, ~en, **Solistin** *die;* ~, ~nen soloist

Soll *das;* ~[s], ~[s] **(a)** (Bankw.) debit

(b) (Arbeits~) quota; **sein** ~ **erfüllen** *od.* **erreichen** achieve one's target

sollen ① *unr. Modalverb; 2. Part.* **sollen:** **(a)** (bei Aufforderung, Anweisung, Auftrag) **was soll ich als Nächstes tun?** what should I do next?; **[sagen Sie ihm,] er soll hereinkommen** tell him to come in

(b) (bei Wunsch, Absicht, Vorhaben) **das sollte ein Witz sein** that was meant to be a joke; **was soll denn das heißen?** what is that supposed to mean?

(c) (bei Ratlosigkeit) **was soll ich nur machen?** what am I to do?

(d) (Notwendigkeit ausdrückend) **man soll so etwas nicht unterschätzen** it shouldn't be taken so lightly

(e) *häufig im Konjunktiv II* (Erwartung, Wünschenswertes ausdrückend) **du solltest dich schämen** you ought to be ashamed of yourself; **das hättest du besser nicht tun** ~: it would have been better if you hadn't done it

(f) (jmdm. beschieden sein) **er sollte seine Heimat nicht wieder sehen** he was never to see his homeland again

(g) *im Konjunktiv II* (eine Möglichkeit ausdrückend) **wenn du ihn sehen solltest, sage ihm bitte …:** if you should see him, please tell him …

(h) *im Präsens* (sich für die Wahrheit nicht verbürgend) **das Restaurant soll sehr teuer sein** the restaurant is supposed *or* said to be very expensive

(i) *im Konjunktiv II* (Zweifel ausdrückend) **sollte das sein Ernst sein?** is he really being serious?

(j) (können) **mir soll es gleich sein** it's all the same to me ② *tr., itr. V.* **was soll das?** what's the idea?; **was soll ich dort?** what would I do there?

Solo *das;* ~s, ~s *od.* **Soli** solo

so·mit /*auch:* '--/ *Adv.* consequently; therefore

Sommer *der;* ∼s, ∼: summer
Sommer·ferien *Pl.* summer holidays
sommerlich ⟨1⟩ *Adj.* summer; summery ⟨*warmth, weather*⟩; summer's *attrib.* ⟨*day, evening*⟩
⟨2⟩ *adv.* **es war** ∼ **warm** it was as warm as summer
sommer-, Sommer-: ∼**reifen** *der* standard tyre; ∼**schluss·verkauf,** **∼**schluß·verkauf** *der* summer sale/ sales; ∼**sprosse** *die* freckle; ∼**sprossig** *Adj.* freckled; ∼**zeit** *die* (Uhrzeit) summer time
Sonate *die;* ∼, ∼n (Musik) sonata
Sonde *die;* ∼, ∼n probe; (zur Ernährung) tube
Sonder-: ∼**angebot** *das* special offer; ∼**ausgabe** *die* **(a)** special edition; **(b)** (Steuerw.: private Aufwendungen) tax-deductible expenditure; **(c)** (Extraausgabe) extra expense
sonderbar ⟨1⟩ *Adj.* strange; odd
⟨2⟩ *adv.* strangely; oddly
sonderbarer·weise *Adv.* strangely *or* oddly enough
Sonder-: ∼**fall** *der* special case; ∼**genehmigung** *die* special permit
sonder·gleichen *Adv., nachgestellt* **eine Frechheit/Unverschämtheit** ∼: the height of cheek/impudence
sonderlich *Adv.* particularly
Sonderling *der;* ∼s, ∼e strange *or* odd person
Sonder-: ∼**marke** *die* special issue [stamp]; ∼**müll** *der* hazardous waste
sondern¹ *tr. V.* (geh.) separate (**von** from)
sondern² *Konj.* but; **nicht nur ...,** ∼ **[auch] ...:** not only ... but also ...
Sonder-: ∼**nummer** *die* special edition *or* issue; ∼**preis** *der* special *or* reduced price; ∼**schule** *die* special school; ∼**schul·lehrer** *der,* ∼**schul·lehrerin** *die* teacher at a special school; ∼**wunsch** *der* special request *or* wish; ∼**zug** *der* special train
sondieren *tr. V.* sound out
Sonett *das;* ∼[e]s, ∼e sonnet
Sonn·abend *der* (bes. nordd.) Saturday; *s. auch* DIENSTAG
sonn·abends *Adv.* on Saturday[s]
Sonne *die;* ∼, ∼n sun; (Licht der ∼) sun[light]
sonnen *refl. V.* sun oneself
sonnen-, Sonnen-: ∼**aufgang** *der* sunrise; ∼**baden** *itr. V.* sunbathe; ∼**blume** *die* sunflower; ∼**brand** *der* sunburn *no indef. art.;* ∼**brille** *die* sunglasses *pl.;* ∼**energie** *die* solar energy; ∼**finsternis** *die* solar eclipse; ∼**hut** *der* sun hat; ∼**kollektor** *der* (Energietechnik) solar collector; ∼**kraftwerk** *das* solar power station; ∼**licht** *das* sunlight;

∼**milch** *die* suntan lotion; ∼**öl** *das* sun oil; ∼**schein** *der* sunshine; ∼**schirm** *der* sunshade; ∼**schutz·creme** *die* suntan lotion; ∼**stich** *der* sunstroke *no indef. art.;* ∼**strahl** *der* ray of sun[shine]; ∼**uhr** *die* sundial; ∼**untergang** *der* sunset
sonnig *Adj.* sunny
Sonn·tag *der* Sunday; *s. auch* DIENSTAG
sonn·täglich ⟨1⟩ *Adj.* Sunday *attrib.*
⟨2⟩ *adv.* ∼ **gekleidet** dressed in one's Sunday best
sonntags *Adv.* on Sunday[s]
sonst *Adv.* **(a) der** ∼ **so freundliche Mann ...:** the man, who is/was usually so friendly, ...; **alles war wie** ∼: everything was [the same] as usual; ∼ **was** (ugs.) something else; (fragend, verneint) anything else; ∼ **wer** (ugs.) somebody else; (fragend, verneint) anybody else; ∼ **wo** (ugs.) somewhere else; (fragend, verneint) anywhere else; ∼ **noch was?** (ugs., auch iron.) anything else?; **wer/was/wie/wo [denn]** ∼**?** who/what/how/ where else?
(b) (andernfalls) otherwise; or
sonstig... *Adj.* other; further
****sonst·was** *usw.* ► SONST A
so·oft *Konj.* whenever
sophistisch ⟨1⟩ *Adj.* sophistic[al]
⟨2⟩ *adv.* sophistically
Sopran *der;* ∼s, ∼e (Musik) soprano; (im Chor) sopranos *pl.*
Sopranistin *die;* ∼, ∼nen soprano
Sorge *die;* ∼, ∼n worry; **keine** ∼**!** don't [you] worry!
sorgen ⟨1⟩ *refl. V.* worry (**um** about)
⟨2⟩ *itr. V.* **für jmdn./etw.** ∼: take care of sb./sth
sorgen-, Sorgen-: ∼**frei** ⟨1⟩ *Adj.* carefree; ⟨2⟩ *adv.* ∼ **frei leben** live in a carefree manner; ∼**kind** *das* (auch fig.) problem child; ∼**voll** ⟨1⟩ *Adj.* worried; ⟨2⟩ *adv.* worriedly
Sorg·falt *die;* ∼: care
sorg·fältig ⟨1⟩ *Adj.* careful
⟨2⟩ *adv.* carefully
sorg·los ⟨1⟩ *Adj.* **(a)** (ohne Sorgfalt) careless
(b) (unbekümmert) carefree
⟨2⟩ *adv.* ∼ **mit etw. umgehen** treat sth. carelessly
Sorglosigkeit *die;* ∼ **(a)** (Mangel an Sorgfalt) carelessness
(b) (Unbekümmertheit) carefreeness
sorgsam ⟨1⟩ *Adj.* careful
⟨2⟩ *adv.* carefully
Sorte *die;* ∼, ∼n **(a)** sort; type; kind
(b) *Pl.* (Devisen) foreign currency *sing.*
Sorten·kurs *der* (Bankw.) exchange rate
sortieren *tr. V.* sort [out] ⟨*pictures, letters, washing, etc.*⟩; grade ⟨*goods etc.*⟩
Sortiment *das;* ∼[e]s, ∼e range (**an** + *Dat.* of)
so·sehr *Konj.* however much

**old spelling – see note on page x

Soße *die;* ~, ~n sauce; (Bratensoße) gravy; sauce; (Salatsoße) dressing
sott *1. u. 3. Pers. Sg. Prät. v.* SIEDEN
Souffleur /zu'flø:ɐ̯/ *der;* ~s, ~e,
Souffleuse /zu'flø:zə/ *die;* ~, ~n prompter
soufflieren /zu'fli:rən/ *tr. V.* prompt
Sound-: ~**check** /'saʊndtʃɛk/ *der;* ~~s, ~~s sound check; ~**karte** *die* (DV) sound card
Souvenir /suvə'ni:ɐ̯/ *das;* ~s, ~s souvenir
souverän /zuvə'rɛːn/ *Adj.* sovereign
Souveränität *die;* ~: sovereignty
so·viel *Konj.* as *or* so far as; *s. auch* SO 1B
so·weit *Konj.* (a) as *or* so far as; *s. auch* SO 1B
(b) (in dem Maße, wie) [in] so far as; *s. auch* SO 1B
***so·wenig** ▶ SO 1B
so·wie *Konj.* (a) (und) as well as
(b) (sobald) as soon as
so·wie·so *Adv.* anyway
sowjetisch *Adj.* Soviet
Sowjet·union *die* (1922–1991) Soviet Union
so·wohl *Konj.* ~ ... als *od.* wie [auch] ...: both ... and ...; ... as well as ...
sozial ⬚1 *Adj.* social
⬚2 *adv.* socially
sozial-, Sozial-: ~**abgaben** *Pl.* social welfare contributions; ~**arbeiter** *der,* ~**arbeiterin** *die* social worker; ~**demokrat** *der,* ~**demokratin** *die* Social Democrat; ~**demokratisch** *Adj.* social democratic; ~**dienst** *der* community services department; ~**hilfe** *die* social welfare; ~**hilfe·empfänger** *der,* ~**hilfe·empfängerin** *die* welfare recipient
Sozialismus *der;* ~: socialism *no art.;*
Sozialist *der;* ~en, ~en, **Sozialistin** *die;* ~, ~nen socialist
sozialistisch ⬚1 *Adj.* socialist
⬚2 ~ regierte Länder countries with socialist governments
Sozial-: ~**kunde** *die* social studies *sing., no art.;* ~**politik** *die* social policy; ~**produkt** *das* (Wirtsch.) national product; ~**staat** *der* welfare state
Soziologe *der;* ~n, ~n sociologist
Soziologie *die;* ~: sociology
Soziologin *die;* ~, ~nen sociologist
soziologisch ⬚1 *Adj.* sociological
⬚2 *adv.* sociologically
Sozius *der;* ~, ~se (a) *Pl. auch:* Sozii (Wirtsch.: Teilhaber) partner
(b) (beim Motorrad) pillion
so·zu·sagen *Adv.* as it were
Spachtel *der;* ~s, ~ *od. die;* ~, ~n putty knife; (zum Malen) palette knife
Spachtel·masse *die* filler

spachteln *tr. V.* (a) stop, fill ⟨*hole, crack, etc.*⟩; smooth over ⟨*wall, panel, surface, etc.*⟩
(b) (ugs.: essen) put away (coll.) ⟨*food, meal*⟩
Spagat *der od. das;* ~[e]s, ~e splits *pl.;* [einen] ~ machen do the splits
Spaghetti *Pl.* spaghetti *sing.*
spähen *itr. V.* peer; (durch ein Loch, eine Ritze usw.) peep
Späher *der;* ~s, ~, **Späherin** *die;* ~, ~nen (Milit.) scout; (Posten) lookout; (Spitzel) informer
Spalier *das;* ~s, ~e (a) trellis
(b) (Ehren~) guard of honour; ~ stehen line the route; ⟨*soldiers*⟩ form a guard of honour
Spalt *der;* ~[e]s, ~e opening; (im Fels) fissure; crevice; (zwischen Vorhängen) chink; gap; (langer Riss) crack
Spalte *die;* ~, ~n (a) crack; (Felsspalte) crevice
(b) (Druckw.) column
spalten *unr. (auch regelm.) tr., refl. V.* split
Spaltung *die;* ~, ~en (auch fig.) splitting; (fig.: das Gespaltensein) split
Spam /spɛm/ *das;* ~s, ~s (DV) spam
Span *der;* ~[e]s, Späne (Hobelspan) shaving
Span·ferkel *das* suckling pig
Spange *die;* ~, ~n clasp; (Haarspange) hairslide (Brit.); barrette (Amer.); (Armspange) bracelet; bangle
Spaniel /'ʃpa:niəl/ *der;* ~s, ~s spaniel
Spanien /'ʃpa:niən/ *(das);* ~s Spain
Spanier /'ʃpa:niɐ̯/ *der;* ~s, ~, **Spanierin** *die;* ~, ~nen Spaniard
spanisch *Adj.* Spanish
Span·korb *der* chip basket; chip
spann *1. u. 3. P. Sing. Prät. v.* SPINNEN
spannen ⬚1 *tr. V.* (a) tighten ⟨*violin string, violin bow, etc.*⟩; draw ⟨*bow*⟩; tension ⟨*spring, tennis net, drumhead, saw blade*⟩; stretch ⟨*fabric, shoe, etc.*⟩; draw *or* pull ⟨*line*⟩ tight *or* taut; flex ⟨*muscle*⟩; cock ⟨*gun, camera shutter*⟩
(b) (befestigen) put up ⟨*washing line*⟩; stretch ⟨*net, wire, tarpaulin, etc.*⟩ (über + *Akk.* over)
(c) (schirren) harness (vor, an + *Akk.* to)
⬚2 *refl. V.* (a) become *or* go taut; ⟨*muscles*⟩ tense
(b) (geh.: sich wölben) **sich über etw.** (*Akk.*) ~: span sth.
⬚3 *itr. V.* ⟨*clothing*⟩ be [too] tight; ⟨*skin*⟩ be taut
spannend ⬚1 *Adj.* exciting; (stärker) thrilling
⬚2 *adv.* excitingly; (stärker) thrillingly
Spannung *die;* ~, ~en (a) excitement; (Neugier) suspense
(b) (eines Romans, Films usw.) suspense
(c) (Zwistigkeit, Nervosität) tension
(d) (Elektrot.) voltage
Spannungs·gebiet *das* (Politik.) area of tension
Spann·weite *die* [wing]span

S

Span·platte die chipboard

Spar-: ~**buch** das savings book; ~**büchse** die money box

sparen ① tr. V. save
② itr. V. (a) save; **für** od. **auf etw.** (Akk.) ~: save up for sth.
(b) (sparsam wirtschaften) economize (**mit** on); **an etw.** (Dat.) ~: be sparing with sth.; (beim Einkauf) economize on sth.

Sparer der; ~s, ~, **Sparerin** die; ~, ~nen saver

Spargel der; ~s, ~, (schweiz. auch) die; ~, ~n asparagus no pl., no indef. art.

Spar-: ~**groschen** der (ugs.) nest egg; savings pl.; ~**kasse** die savings bank; ~**konto** das savings or deposit account

spärlich ① Adj. sparse ⟨vegetation, beard, growth⟩; thin ⟨hair, applause⟩; scanty ⟨leftovers, knowledge, news, evidence, clothing⟩; poor ⟨lighting⟩
② adv. sparsely, thinly ⟨populated, covered⟩; poorly ⟨lit, attended⟩; scantily ⟨dressed⟩

sparsam ① Adj. thrifty ⟨person⟩; (wirtschaftlich) economical; **mit etw.** ~ **sein** be economical with sth.
② adv. ~ **mit der Butter/dem Papier umgehen** use butter/paper sparingly; economize on butter/paper

Sparsamkeit die; ~: thrift[iness]; (Wirtschaftlichkeit) economicalness

Sparte die; ~, ~n (a) (Teilbereich) area; (eines Geschäfts) line [of business]
(b) (Rubrik) section

Sparten·kanal der special-interest channel

Spar-: ~**vertrag** der savings agreement; ~**zins** der; Pl. ~~**en** interest no pl. on a savings account

Spaß der; ~es, Späße (a) (Vergnügen) fun; ~ **an etw.** (Dat.) **haben** enjoy sth.; **[jmdm.]** ~ **machen** be fun [for sb.]; **viel** ~! have a good time!
(b) (Scherz) joke; (Streich) prank; **er macht nur** ~: he's only joking; ~ **beiseite!** joking aside; ~ **muss sein!** there's no harm in a joke; ~ **verstehen** be able to take a joke; **im** od. **zum** od. **aus** ~: as a joke; for fun

spaßen itr. V. (a) (Spaß machen) joke
(b) **er lässt nicht mit sich** ~: he won't stand for any nonsense; **mit ihm/damit ist nicht zu** ~: he/it is not to be trifled with

spaßes·halber Adv. for the fun of it; for fun

spaßig Adj. funny; comical; amusing

Spaß·macher der, **Spaß·macherin** die joker

spät ① Adj. late; **wie** ~ **ist es?** what time is it?
② adv. late; ~ **am Abend** late in the evening

Spaten der; ~s, ~: spade

---

*alte Schreibung – vgl. Hinweis auf S. x

später ① Adj. (a) later ⟨years, generations, etc.⟩
(b) (zukünftig) future ⟨owner, wife, etc.⟩
② Adv. later; **bis** ~! see you later!

spätestens Adv. at the latest

Spatz der; ~en, ~en (a) sparrow
(b) (fam.: Liebling) pet

Spätzle Pl. spaetzle; kind of noodles

spazieren itr. V.; mit sein stroll; ~ **gehen** go for a walk; ~ **fahren** go for a ride; **ein Kind [im Kinderwagen]** ~ **fahren** take a baby for a walk [in a pram]

***spazieren|fahren** usw. ▶ SPAZIEREN

Spazier-: ~**gang** der walk; ~**gänger** der; ~~s, ~~, ~**gängerin** die; ~~, ~~nen person out for a walk

SPD ~ Abk. = **Sozialdemokratische Partei Deutschlands** SPD

Specht der; ~[e]s, ~e woodpecker

Speck der; ~[e]s, ~e (a) bacon fat; (Schinkenspeck) bacon
(b) (ugs. scherzh.: Fettpolster) fat; flab (coll.)

speckig Adj. greasy

Spediteur /ʃpedi'tøːɐ̯/ der; ~s, ~e, **Spediteurin** die; ~, ~nen carrier; haulage contractor; (Möbelspediteur) furniture remover

Spedition die; ~, ~en ▶ SPEDITIONSFIRMA

Speditions·firma die forwarding agency; (per Schiff) shipping agency; (Transportunternehmen) haulage firm; firm of hauliers; (per Schiff) firm of carriers; (Möbelspedition) removal firm

Speer der; ~[e]s, ~e (a) spear
(b) (Sportgerät) javelin

Speichel der; ~s saliva

Speicher der; ~s, ~ (a) storehouse; (Lagerhaus) warehouse
(b) (südd.: Dachboden) loft
(c) (Elektronik) memory

Speicher·kapazität die storage capacity; (DV) memory or storage capacity

speichern tr. V. store

speien (geh.) unr. tr., itr. V. spit

Speise die; ~, ~n (a) (Gericht) dish
(b) (geh.: Nahrung) food

Speise-: ~**eis** das ice cream; ~**fisch** der food fish; ~**gaststätte** die restaurant; ~**kammer** die larder; ~**karte** die menu; ~**lokal** das restaurant

speisen (geh.) ① itr. V. eat; (dinieren) dine
② tr. V. eat; (dinieren) dine on

Speise-: ~**saal** der dining hall; (im Hotel, in einer Villa usw.) dining room; ~**wagen** der restaurant car (Brit.); ~**zettel** der menu

Spektakel der; ~s, ~ (ugs.) (Lärm) row (coll.); rumpus (coll.)

spektakulär ① Adj. spectacular
② adv. spectacularly

Spekulation die; ~, ~en speculation

spekulieren itr. V. (a) (ugs.) **darauf** ~, **etw. tun zu können** count on being able to do sth.

(b) (Wirtsch.) speculate (**mit** in)
Spelunke *die;* ∼, ∼n (ugs. abwertend) dive (coll.)
Spelze *die;* ∼, ∼n husk
Spende *die;* ∼, ∼n donation; contribution
spenden *tr., itr. V.* **(a)** donate; give
  (b) (fig. geh.) give ⟨*light*⟩; afford, give ⟨*shade*⟩; give off ⟨*heat*⟩
Spenden·aktion *die* campaign for donations
Spender *der;* ∼s, ∼, **Spenderin** *die;* ∼, ∼nen donor; donator; (Organspender, Blutspender) donor
Spender·organ *das* donor organ
spendieren *tr. V.* (ugs.) get, buy ⟨*drink, meal, etc.*⟩; stand ⟨*round*⟩
Spengler *der;* ∼s, ∼, **Spenglerin** *die;* ∼, ∼nen (südd., österr., schweiz.) ▶ KLEMPNER
Sperling *der;* ∼s, ∼e sparrow
Sperma *das;* ∼s, Spermen sperm; semen
Sperma·bank *die; Pl.* ∼en sperm bank
sperr-, Sperr-: ∼**angel·weit** *Adv.* (ugs.) ∼angel·weit offen *od.* geöffnet wide open; ∼**bezirk** *der* (a) restricted *or* prohibited area; **(b)** (für Prostituierte) *area in which prostitution is prohibited;* **(c)** (Gesundheitswesen) infected area
Sperre *die;* ∼, ∼n **(a)** barrier; (Straßensperre) roadblock; (Milit.) obstacle
  (b) (fig.) ban; (Handelssperre) embargo; (Import-, Exportsperre) blockade; (Nachrichten∼) [news] blackout
sperren ① *tr. V.* **(a)** close; close off ⟨*area*⟩; block ⟨*entrance, access, etc.*⟩; lock ⟨*mechanism etc.*⟩
  (b) cut off ⟨*water, gas, electricity, etc.*⟩
  (c) (Bankw.) stop ⟨*cheque, overdraft facility*⟩; freeze ⟨*bank account*⟩
  (d) (einsperren) **ein Tier/jmdn. in etw.** (*Akk.*) ∼: shut an animal/sb. in sth.
  (e) (Sport: von der Teilnahme ausschließen) ban
  (f) (Druckw.: spationieren) print ⟨*word, text*⟩ with the letters spaced
  ② *refl. V.* **sich [gegen etw.]** ∼: balk [at sth.]
Sperr·holz *das* plywood
sperrig *Adj.* unwieldy
Sperr-: ∼**müll** *der* bulky refuse (*for which there is a separate collection service*); ∼**sitz** *der* (im Kino) seat in the back stalls; (im Zirkus) front seat; (im Theater) seat in the front stalls; ∼**stunde** *die* closing time
Sperrung *die;* ∼, ∼en ▶ SPERREN A-C, E: closing; closing off; cutting off; stopping; freezing; banning
Spesen *Pl.* expenses; **auf** ∼: on expenses
Spezi *der;* ∼s, ∼[s] (südd., österr., schweiz. ugs.) [bosom] pal (coll.); chum (coll.)
spezialisieren *refl. V.* specialize (**auf** + *Akk.* in)
Spezialist *der;* ∼en, ∼en, **Spezialistin** *die;* ∼, ∼nen specialist
Spezialität *die;* ∼, ∼en speciality

speziell ① *Adj.* special; specific ⟨*question, problem, etc.*⟩
  ② *Adv.* especially; (eigens) specially
spezifisch ① *Adj.* specific; characteristic ⟨*smell, style*⟩
  ② *adv.* specifically
Sphäre *die;* ∼, ∼n (auch fig.) sphere
spicken *tr. V.* lard
spie *1. u. 3. Pers. Sg. Prät. v.* SPEIEN
Spiegel *der;* ∼s, ∼ **(a)** mirror
  (b) (Wasserspiegel, fig.: Konzentration) level
spiegel-, Spiegel-: ∼**bild** *das* reflection; ∼**blank** *Adj.* shining; ∼**ei** *das* fried egg; ∼**glatt** *Adj.* like glass *postpos.;* as smooth as glass *postpos.*
spiegeln ① *itr. V.* **(a)** (glänzen) shine; gleam
  (b) (als Spiegel wirken) reflect the light
  ② *tr. V.* reflect; mirror
  ③ *refl. V.* be mirrored *or* reflected
Spiegel·reflex·kamera *die* reflex camera
Spiegelung *die;* ∼, ∼en **(a)** (auch fig., Math.) reflection
  (b) (Med.) speculum examination
spiegel·verkehrt ① *Adj.* back-to-front ⟨*lettering*⟩; **eine** ∼**e Abbildung** a mirror image
  ② *adv.* **etw.** ∼ **abbilden** reproduce sth. as a *or* in mirror image
Spiel *das;* ∼[e]s, ∼e **(a)** play
  (b) (Glücks, Gesellschaftsspiel) game; (Wettspiel) game; match; **auf dem** ∼ **stehen** be at stake; **etw. aufs** ∼ **setzen** put sth. at stake; risk sth.
Spiel·bank *die; Pl.* ∼en casino
spielen ① *itr. V.* **(a)** play; **auf der Gitarre** ∼: play the guitar; **um Geld** ∼: play for money
  (b) (als Schauspieler) act; perform
  (c) **der Roman/Film spielt im 17. Jahrhundert/in Berlin** the novel/film is set in the 17th century/in Berlin
  (d) (fig.) **das Blau spielt ins Violette** the blue is tinged with purple
  ② *tr. V.* **(a)** play; **Cowboy** ∼: play at being a cowboy; **Geige** *usw.* ∼: play the violin *etc.*
  (b) (aufführen, vorführen) put on ⟨*play*⟩; show ⟨*film*⟩; perform ⟨*piece of music*⟩; play ⟨*record*⟩; **den Beleidigten/Unschuldigen** ∼ (fig.) act offended/play the innocent
spielend *Adv.* easily
Spieler *der;* ∼s, ∼: player; (Glücksspieler) gambler
Spielerei *die;* ∼, ∼en **(a)** playing *no art.;* (im Glücksspiel) gambling *no art.*
  (b) **eine** ∼ **mit Worten/Zahlen** playing [around] with words/numbers
Spiel·ergebnis *das* match result
Spielerin *die;* ∼, ∼nen ▶ SPIELER
spielerisch *Adj.* playful
Spiel-: ∼**feld** *das* field; pitch (Brit.); (Tennis, Squash, Volleyball usw.) court; ∼**film** *der* feature film; ∼**kamerad** *der* playmate; ∼**karte** *die* playing card; ⋯⬥

S

∼leitung *die* **(a)** (Sport) control of the match; **(b)** ▶ REGIE; **∼plan** *der* programme; **∼platz** *der* playground; **∼raum** *der* room to move (fig.); scope; latitude; **∼regel** *die* (auch fig.) rule of the game; **gegen die ∼regeln verstoßen** (auch fig.) break the rules; **∼sachen** *Pl.* toys; **∼verderber** *der;* **∼∼s,** **∼∼,** **∼verderberin** *die;* **∼∼,** **∼∼nen** spoilsport; **∼waren** *Pl.* toys; **∼zeit** *die* **(a)** (Theater: Saison) season; **(b)** (Sport) playing time; **die normale ∼zeit** normal time; **∼zeug** *das* **(a)** toy; (fig.) toy; plaything; **(b)** (Gesamtheit) toys *pl.*

Spieß *der;* **∼es,** **∼e (a)** (Waffe) spear; **den ∼ umdrehen** *od.* **umkehren** (ugs.) turn the tables
(b) (Bratspieß) spit
(c) (Fleischspieß) kebab
(d) (Soldatenspr.) [company] sergeant major
Spieß·bürger *der,* **Spießbürgerin** *die* (abwertend) [petit] bourgeois
Spießer *der;* **∼s,** **∼,** **Spießerin** *die;* **∼,** **∼nen** (abwertend) [petit] bourgeois
spießig (abwertend) **①** *Adj.* [petit] bourgeois **②** *adv.* ⟨*think, behave, etc.*⟩ in a [petit] bourgeois way
Spinat *der;* **∼[e]s,** **∼e** spinach
Spind *der od. das;* **∼[e]s,** **∼e** locker
Spindel *die;* **∼,** **∼n** spindle
Spinne *die;* **∼,** **∼n** spider
spinnen **①** *unr. tr. V.* spin (fig.); plot ⟨*intrigue*⟩; think up ⟨*idea*⟩; hatch ⟨*plot*⟩ **②** *unr. itr. V.* **(a)** spin
(b) (ugs.: verrückt sein) be crazy *or* (coll.) nuts
Spinnen·netz *das* spider's web
Spinner *der;* **∼s,** **∼ (a)** (Beruf) spinner
(b) (ugs. abwertend) nutcase (coll.); idiot
Spinnerei *die;* **∼,** **∼en** spinning mill
Spinnerin *die;* **∼,** **∼nen** ▶ SPINNER
Spinn-: **∼rad** *das* spinning wheel; **∼webe** *die;* **∼∼,** **∼∼n** cobweb
Spion *der;* **∼s,** **∼e (a)** spy
(b) (Guckloch) spyhole
Spionage /ʃpioˈnaːʒə/ *die;* **∼:** spying; espionage
spionieren *itr. V.* spy
Spionin *die;* **∼,** **∼nen** spy
Spirale *die;* **∼,** **∼n** spiral
Spiral·feder *die* coil spring
Spirituose *die;* **∼,** **∼n** spirit *usu. in pl.*
Spiritus *der;* **∼,** **∼se** spirit; ethyl alcohol
Spiritus·kocher *der* spirit stove
Spital *das;* **∼s,** **Spitäler** (bes. österr., schweiz.) hospital
spitz **①** *Adj.* **(a)** pointed; sharp ⟨*pencil, needle, stone, etc.*⟩; fine ⟨*pen nib*⟩; (Geom.) acute ⟨*angle*⟩
(b) (schrill) shrill ⟨*cry etc.*⟩
(c) (boshaft) cutting ⟨*remark etc.*⟩
② *adv.* **(a)** **∼ zulaufen** taper to a point;

∼ zulaufend pointed
(b) (boshaft) cuttingly
Spitz *der;* **∼es,** **∼e** spitz
spitz-, Spitz-: **∼bart** *der* goatee; **∼bube** *der* (scherzh.: Schlingel) rascal; **∼bübisch** **①** *Adj.* mischievous; **②** *adv.* mischievously
spitze *indekl. Adj.* (ugs.) ▶ KLASSE
Spitze *die;* **∼,** **∼n (a)** point; (Pfeil∼, Horn∼ usw.) tip
(b) (oberes Ende) top; (eines Berges) summit
(c) (Zigarren-, Haar-, Zweigspitze) end; (Schuhspitze) toe; (Finger-, Nasenspitze) tip
(d) (vorderes Ende) front; **an der ∼ liegen** (Sport) be in the lead *or* in front
(e) (führende Position) top
(f) (einer Firma, Organisation usw.) head; (einer Hierarchie) top; (leitende Gruppe) management
(g) (Höchstwert) maximum; peak
(h) [absolute/einsame] **∼ sein** (ugs.) be [absolutely] great (coll.)
(i) (fig.: Angriff) dig (**gegen** at)
(j) (Textilwesen) lace
Spitzel *der;* **∼s,** **∼:** informer
spitzen *tr. V.* sharpen ⟨*pencil*⟩; purse ⟨*lips, mouth*⟩; prick up ⟨*ears*⟩
Spitzen-: **∼erzeugnis** *das* top-quality product; **∼kandidat** *der,* **∼kandidatin** *die* leading *or* top candidate; **∼klasse** *die* top class; **∼qualität** *die* top quality; **∼reiter** *der* **(a)** top rider; (fig.) leader; **(b)** (Mannschaft) top team; **(c)** (Ware) top *or* best seller; **∼reiterin** *die;* ▶ **∼**REITER A; **∼sportler** *der* top sportsman; **∼sportlerin** *die* top sportswoman
Spitzer *der;* **∼s,** **∼:** [pencil] sharpener
spitz-, Spitz-: **∼findig** *Adj.* hair-splitting; **∼findigkeit** *die;* **∼∼,** **∼∼en** **(a)** hair-splitting; **(b)** (etwas Spitzfindiges) nicety; **∼hacke** *die* pick; **∼kriegen** *tr. V.* (ugs.) tumble to (coll.); **∼maus** *die* shrew; **∼name** *der* nickname
Spleen /ʃpliːn/ *der;* **∼s,** **∼e** *od.* **∼s** strange habit; eccentricity
Splitt *der;* **∼[e]s,** **∼e** [stone] chippings *pl.;* (zum Streuen) grit
Splitter *der;* **∼s,** **∼:** splinter; (Granat-, Bombensplitter) splinter
splitter·faser·nackt *Adj.* (ugs.) absolutely stark naked; completely starkers *pred.* (Brit. coll.)
splittern *itr. V.* **(a)** (Splitter bilden) splinter
(b) *mit sein* (in Splitter zerbrechen) ⟨*glass, windscreen, etc.*⟩ shatter
splitter·nackt *Adj.* (ugs.) stark naked; starkers *pred.* (Brit. coll.)
Splitter·partei *die* splinter party
SPÖ *Abk.* = **Sozialistische Partei Österreichs** Austrian Socialist Party
sponsern *tr. V.* sponsor
Sponsor *der;* **∼s,** **∼en** sponsor
spontan **①** *Adj.* spontaneous **②** *adv.* spontaneously

Spontaneität /ʃpɔntanei'tɛːt/ *die;*
~: spontaneity
sporadisch ⓵ *Adj.* sporadic
⓶ *adv.* sporadically
Spore *die;* ~, ~n spore
Sporn *der;* ~[e]s, Sporen (des Reiters) spur;
einem Pferd die Sporen geben spur a horse
Sport *der;* ~[e]s (a) sport; (als Unterrichtsfach)
sport; PE; ~ **treiben** do sport
(b) (Hobby, Zeitvertreib) hobby; pastime
Sport-: ~**art** *die* [form of] sport; ~**fest**
das sports festival; (einer Schule) sports day;
~**flugzeug** *das* sports plane; ~**geist**
der sportsmanship; ~**halle** *die* sports
hall; ~**journalist** *der,* ~**journalistin**
die sports journalist; ~**kleidung** *die*
sportswear
Sportler *der;* ~s, ~: sportsman
Sportlerin *die;* ~, ~nen sportswoman
sportlich ⓵ *Adj.* (a) sporting *attrib.*
(b) (fair) sportsmanlike; sporting
(c) (fig.: flott, rasant) sporty ⟨car, driving, etc.⟩
(d) (zu sportlicher Leistung fähig) sporty, athletic
⟨person⟩
(e) (jugendlich wirkend) sporty, smart but
casual ⟨clothes⟩; smart but practical
⟨hairstyle⟩
⓶ *adv.* (a) as far as sport is concerned
(b) (fair) sportingly
(c) (fig.: flott, rasant) in a sporty manner
Sport-: ~**platz** *der* sports field; (einer
Schule) playing field/fields *pl.;* ~**schuh**
der sports shoe; ~**stadion** *das* [sports]
stadium; ~**teil** *der* sport[s] section;
~**verein** *der* sports club; ~**wagen**
der (a) (Auto) sports car; (b) (Kinderwagen)
pushchair (Brit.); stroller (Amer.);
~**zentrum** *das* sports centre
Spot /spɔt/ *der;* ~s, ~s (a) (Werbespot)
commercial; advertisement; ad (coll.)
(b) (Leuchte) spotlight; spotlamp
Spott *der;* ~[e]s mockery; (höhnischer)
ridicule; derision
spott·billig *Adj., adv.* (ugs.) dirt cheap
spötteln *itr. V.* mock [gently]; poke *or* make
[gentle] fun
spotten *itr. V.* (a) mock; poke *or* make fun;
(höhnischer) ridicule; be derisive
(b) einer Sache (Gen.) ~: be contemptuous
of *or* scorn sth.
Spötter *der;* ~s, ~, **Spötterin** *die;* ~,
~nen mocker
spöttisch ⓵ *Adj.* mocking; (höhnischer)
derisive
⓶ *adv.* mockingly
Spott·preis *der* (ugs.) ridiculously low
price
sprach *1. u. 3. Pers. Sg. Prät. v.* SPRECHEN
Sprache *die;* ~, ~n (a) language; **in
englischer** ~: in English
(b) (Sprechweise) way of speaking; speech;
(Stil) style
(c) etw. zur ~ **bringen** bring sth. up; raise

sth.; **heraus mit der** ~! come on, out with it!
Sprachen·schule *die* language school
Sprach-: ~**fehler** *der* speech
impediment *or* defect; ~**führer** *der* phrase
book; ~**grenze** *die* language boundary;
~**kenntnisse** *Pl.* knowledge *sing.* of a
language/languages; ~**kurs** *der* language
course; ~**labor** *das* language laboratory
or (coll.) lab
sprachlich ⓵ *Adj.* linguistic
⓶ *adv.* linguistically
sprach-, Sprach-: ~**los** *Adj.*
(überrascht) speechless; ~**problem** *das*
language problem; ~**rohr** *das* (Repräsentant)
spokesman; (Propagandist) mouthpiece;
~**schule** *die* language school;
~**unterricht** *der* language teaching
sprang *1. u. 3. Pers. Sg. Prät. v.* SPRINGEN
Spray /ʃpreː/ *das od. der;* ~s, ~s spray
Spray·dose *die* aerosol [can]
sprayen *tr., itr. V.* spray
Sprech-: ~**anlage** *die* intercom (coll.);
~**chor** *der* chorus
sprechen ⓵ *unr. itr. V.* speak (über
+ *Akk.* about; von about, of); (sich unterhalten,
sich besprechen auch) talk (über + *Akk.,* von
about); ⟨parrot etc.⟩ talk; **deutsch/flüsternd**
~: speak German/in a whisper; **für/gegen**
etw. ~: speak in favour of/against sth.; **mit**
jmdm. ~: speak *or* talk with *or* to sb.; **mit
wem spreche ich?** who is speaking please?
⓶ *unr. tr. V.* (a) speak ⟨language, dialect⟩;
say ⟨word, sentence⟩; „**Hier spricht man
Deutsch**" 'German spoken'
(b) (rezitieren) say, recite ⟨poem, text⟩; say
⟨prayer⟩
(c) jmdn. ~: speak to sb.
(d) (aussprechen) pronounce ⟨name, word, etc.⟩
Sprecher *der;* ~s, ~, **Sprecherin** *die;*
~, ~nen (a) spokesman/spokeswoman
(b) (Ansager[in]) announcer; (Nachrichtensprecher[in]) newscaster; newsreader
(c) (Kommentator[in], Erzähler[in]) narrator
Sprech-: ~**funk·gerät** *das* radio-
telephone; (Walkie-talkie) walkie-talkie;
~**stunde** *die* consultation hours *pl.;* (eines
Arztes) surgery; ~**stunden·hilfe** *die*
(eines Arztes) receptionist; (eines Zahnarztes)
assistant; ~**zimmer** *das* consulting room
spreizen *tr. V.* spread ⟨fingers, toes, etc.⟩;
die Beine ~: spread one's legs apart; open
one's legs
Spreiz·fuß *der* (Med.) spread foot
sprengen *tr. V.* (a) blow up; blast ⟨rock⟩;
etw. in die Luft ~: blow sth. up
(b) (gewaltsam öffnen, aufbrechen) force
[open] ⟨door⟩; force ⟨lock⟩; burst, break
⟨bonds, chains⟩; (fig.) break up ⟨meeting,
demonstration⟩
(c) (besprengen) water ⟨flower bed, lawn⟩;
sprinkle ⟨street, washing⟩ with water;
(verspritzen) sprinkle; (mit dem Schlauch)
spray ⋯⫶›

S

Spreng-: ~**stoff** der explosive; ~**stoff·anschlag** der bomb attack

Sprenkel der; ~s, ~: spot; dot; speckle

sprenkeln tr. V. sprinkle spots of ‹colour›; sprinkle ‹water›

Spreu die; ~: chaff

sprich Imperativ Sg. v. SPRECHEN

sprichst 2. Pers. Sg. Präsens v. SPRECHEN

spricht 3. Pers. Sg. Präsens v. SPRECHEN

Sprich·wort das; Pl. Sprichwörter proverb

sprießen unr. itr. V.; mit sein ‹leaf, bud› shoot, sprout; ‹seedlings› come or spring up; ‹beard› sprout

Spring·brunnen der fountain

springen 1 unr. itr. V. (a) mit sein (auch Sport) jump; (mit Schwung) leap; spring; jump; ‹frog, flea› hop, jump; (sich in Sprüngen fortbewegen) bound

(b) mit sein (fig.) ‹pointer, milometer, etc.› jump (auf + Akk. to); ‹traffic lights› change (auf + Akk. to); ‹spark› leap; ‹ball› bounce

(c) mit sein ‹string, glass, porcelain, etc.› break; (Risse, Sprünge bekommen) crack

2 unr. tr. V.; auch mit sein (Sport) perform ‹somersault, twist dive, etc.›

Springer der; ~s, ~ (a) (Sport) jumper

(b) (Schachfigur) knight

Springerin die; ~, ~nen (Sport) jumper

spring·lebendig Adj. extremely lively; full of beans pred. (coll.)

Spring·reiten das showjumping no art.

Sprinkler der; ~s, ~: sprinkler

sprinten itr. (auch tr.) V.; mit sein sprint

Sprinter der; ~s, ~, **Sprinterin** die; ~, ~nen (Sport) sprinter

Sprit der; ~[e]s, ~e (a) (ugs.: Treibstoff) gas (Amer. coll.); juice (sl.); petrol (Brit.)

(b) (ugs.: Schnaps) shorts pl.

Spritze die; ~, ~n (a) syringe

(b) (Injektion) injection

(c) (der Feuerwehr) hose; (Löschfahrzeug) fire engine

spritzen 1 tr. V. (a) (versprühen) spray; (verspritzen) splash; (in Form eines Strahls) spray, squirt ‹water, foam, etc.›; pipe ‹cream etc.›

(b) (bespritzen, besprühen) water ‹lawn, tennis court›; water, spray ‹street, yard›; spray ‹plants, crops, etc.›; (mit Lack) spray ‹car etc.›; jmdn. nass ~: splash sb.; (mit Wasserpistole, Schlauch) spray sb.

(c) (injizieren) inject ‹drug etc.›; (ugs.: einer Injektion unterziehen) jmdn./sich ~: give sb. an injection/inject oneself

2 itr. V.; mit Richtungsangabe mit sein ‹hot fat› spit; ‹mud etc.› spatter, splash; ‹blood, water› spurt

Spritzer der; ~s, ~ (kleiner Tropfen) splash; (von Farbe) splash; spot

spritzig 1 Adj. (a) sparkling ‹wine›; tangy ‹fragrance, perfume›

---

*alte Schreibung – vgl. Hinweis auf S. x

(b) lively ‹show, music, article›; sparkling ‹performance›; racy ‹style›; nippy (coll.); zippy ‹car, engine›; agile ‹person›

2 adv. sparklingly ‹produced, performed, etc.›; racily ‹written›

Spritz·tour die (ugs.) spin

spröd, spröde Adj. (a) brittle ‹glass, plastic, etc.›; dry ‹hair, lips, etc.›; (rissig) chapped ‹lips, skin›; (rauh) rough ‹skin›

(b) (fig.: abweisend) aloof ‹person, manner, nature›

Sprödheit, Sprödigkeit die; ~

(a) ▶ SPRÖDE A: brittleness; dryness; roughness

(b) (fig.: abweisendes Wesen) aloofness

spross, *sproß 1. u. 3. Pers. Sg. Prät. v. SPRIESSEN

Spross, *Sproß der; Sprosses, Sprosse (Bot.) shoot

Sprosse die; ~, ~n (a) (auch fig.) rung

(b) (eines Fensters) glazing bar

Sprössling, *Sprößling der; ~s, ~e (ugs. scherzh.) offspring; **seine** ~e his offspring pl.

Sprotte die; ~, ~n sprat

Spruch der; ~[e]s, Sprüche (Wahlspruch) motto; (Sinnspruch) maxim; (Ausspruch) saying; aphorism; (Zitat) quotation

spruch·reif Adj. das ist noch nicht ~: that's not definite, so people mustn't start talking about it yet

Sprudel der; ~s, ~ (a) sparkling mineral water

(b) (österr.) fizzy drink

sprudeln itr. V.; mit sein bubble; ‹lemonade, champagne, etc.› fizz, effervesce

Sprudel·wasser das sparkling mineral water

Sprüh·dose die aerosol [can]

sprühen 1 tr. V. spray

2 itr. V.; mit Richtungsangabe mit sein ‹sparks, spray› fly; (fig.) ‹eyes› sparkle (**vor** + Dat. with); ‹intellect, wit› sparkle

Sprüh·regen der drizzle; fine rain

Sprung der; ~[e]s, Sprünge (a) (auch Sport) jump; (schwungvoll) leap; (Satz) bound; (fig.) leap; **keine großen Sprünge machen können** (fig. ugs.) not be able to afford many luxuries; **auf dem** ~[e] **sein** (fig. ugs.) be in a rush

(b) (ugs.: kurze Entfernung) stone's throw

(c) (Riss) crack

Sprung·brett das (auch fig.) springboard

sprunghaft 1 Adj. (a) erratic ‹person, character, manner›; disjointed ‹conversation, thoughts›

(b) (unvermittelt) sudden

(c) (ruckartig) rapid ‹change›; sharp ‹increase›

2 adv. ▶ 1B–C: disjointedly; suddenly; rapidly; sharply

Sprunghaftigkeit die; ~: SPRUNGHAFT 1 A: erraticness; disjointedness

Sprung·tuch das; Pl. Sprungtücher safety blanket

Spucke *die;* ~: spit

spucken ⟨1⟩ *itr. V.* spit; **in die Hände** ~ (fig.: an die Arbeit gehen) go to work with a will
⟨2⟩ *tr. V.* spit; cough up ⟨*blood, phlegm*⟩

Spuk *der;* ~[e]s, ~e [ghostly *or* supernatural] manifestation

spuken *itr. V.; unpers.* hier/in dem Haus spukt es this place/the house is haunted

Spül·bürste *die* washing-up brush

Spule *die;* ~, ~n spool; (für Tonband, Film) spool; reel

Spüle *die;* ~, ~n sink unit; (Becken) sink

spulen *tr., itr. V.* spool; (am Tonbandgerät) wind

spülen ⟨1⟩ *tr. V.* (a) rinse; bathe ⟨*wound*⟩
(b) (landsch.: abwaschen) wash up ⟨*dishes, glasses, etc.*⟩; **Geschirr** ~: wash up
⟨2⟩ *itr. V.* (a) (beim WC) flush [the toilet]
(b) (den Mund ausspülen) rinse out [one's mouth]
(c) (landsch.) ▸ ABWASCHEN 2

Spül-: ~**maschine** *die* dishwasher; ~**mittel** *das* washing-up liquid; ~**tuch** *das; Pl.* ~tücher dish cloth; ~**wasser** *das* (a) rinse water; (b) (Abwaschwasser) dishwater

Spund *der;* ~[e]s, ~e/Spünde (a) *Pl.* Spünde (Zapfen) bung
(b) *Pl.* ~e (ugs.) [**junger** *od.* **grüner**] ~ young greenhorn *or* tiro

Spur *die;* ~, ~en (a) (Abdruck im Boden) track; (Folge von Abdrücken) tracks *pl.;* **eine heiße** ~ (fig.) a hot trail; **jmdm./einer Sache auf der** ~ **sein** be on to the track *or* trail of sb./sth.
(b) (Anzeichen) trace; (eines Verbrechens) clue (*Gen.* to)
(c) (sehr kleine Menge; auch fig.) trace
(d) (Verkehrsw.: Fahrspur) lane; **die** ~ **wechseln** change lanes

spürbar ⟨1⟩ *Adj.* noticeable; distinct, perceptible ⟨*improvement*⟩; evident ⟨*relief, embarrassment*⟩
⟨2⟩ *adv.* noticeably; perceptibly; (sichtlich) clearly ⟨*relieved, on edge*⟩

spüren *tr. V.* feel; (instinktiv) sense

spur·los ⟨1⟩ *Adj.* total, complete ⟨*disappearance*⟩
⟨2⟩ *adv.* ⟨*disappear*⟩ completely *or* without trace

Spür·sinn *der* (feiner Instinkt) intuition

Spurt *der;* ~[e]s, ~s *od.* ~e spurt

spurten *itr. V.* (a) mit Richtungsangabe mit *sein* spurt
(b) *mit sein* (ugs.: schnell laufen) sprint

sputen *refl. V.* (veralt.) make haste

St. *Abk.* (a) = **Sankt** St.
(b) = **Stück**

Staat *der;* ~[e]s, ~en state

staatlich ⟨1⟩ *Adj.* state *attrib.;* ⟨*power, unity, etc.*⟩ of the state; state-owned ⟨*factory etc.*⟩

⟨2⟩ *adv.* by the state; ~ anerkannt/geprüft state-approved/-certified

staats-, Staats-: ~**angehörige** *der/die* national; ~**angehörigkeit** *die* nationality; ~**anwalt** *der,* ~**anwältin** *die* public prosecutor; ~**bürger** *der,* ~**bürgerin** *die* citizen; **er ist deutscher** ~**bürger** he is a German citizen *or* national; ~**bürgerlich** *Adj.* civil ⟨*rights*⟩; civic ⟨*duties, loyalty*⟩; ⟨*education, attitude*⟩ as a citizen; ~**bürgerschaft** *die* ▸ ~ANGEHÖRIGKEIT; ~**gewalt** *die* authority of the state; (Exekutive) executive power; ~**grenze** *die* state frontier *or* border; ~**mann** *der; Pl.* -**männer** statesman; ~**oberhaupt** *das* head of state; ~**präsident** *der,* ~**präsidentin** *die* [state] president; ~**sicherheit** *die* (a) state security; (b) (DDR ugs.) ▸ ~SICHERHEITSDIENST; ~**sicherheits·dienst** *der* (DDR) State Security Service

Stab *der;* ~[e]s, Stäbe (a) rod; (länger) pole; (eines Käfigs, Gitters, Geländers) bar
(b) (Milit.) staff
(c) (Team) team

Stäbchen *das;* ~s, ~ (a) (kleiner Stab) little rod; [small] stick
(b) (Essstäbchen) chopstick

stabil ⟨1⟩ *Adj.* sturdy ⟨*chair, cupboard*⟩; robust, sound ⟨*health*⟩; stable ⟨*prices, government, economy, etc.*⟩
⟨2⟩ *adv.* ~ **gebaut** solidly built

stabilisieren ⟨1⟩ *tr. V.* stabilize
⟨2⟩ *refl. V.* (a) stabilize
(b) ⟨*health, circulation, etc.*⟩ become stronger

Stabilität *die;* ~ (a) (einer Konstruktion) sturdiness; (von Gesundheit, Konstitution usw.) robustness; (von Preisen, Regierung usw.) soundness
(b) (das Beständigsein) stability

Stab·lampe *die* torch (Brit.); flashlight (Amer.)

Stabs·arzt *der,* **Stabs·ärztin** *die* (Milit.) medical officer, MO (*with the rank of captain*)

stach *1. u. 3. Pers. Sg. Prät. v.* STECHEN

Stachel *der;* ~s, ~n (a) spine; (Dorn) thorn
(b) (Giftstachel) sting
(c) (Spitze) spike; (an Stacheldraht) barb

Stachel-: ~**beere** *die* gooseberry; ~**draht** *der* barbed wire

stachelig *Adj.* prickly

Stadion *das;* ~s, Stadien stadium

Stadium *das;* ~s, Stadien stage

Stadt *die;* ~, Städte (a) town; (Großstadt) city; **die** ~ **Basel** the city of Basel; **in die** ~ **gehen** go into town; go downtown (Amer.)
(b) (Verwaltung) town council; (in der Großstadt) city council; city hall *no art.* (Amer.)

Stadt-: ~**bahn** *die* urban railway; ~**bummel** *der* (ugs.) **einen** ~**bummel machen** take a stroll through the town/city centre

Städter der; ~s, ~, **Städterin** die; ~,
~nen (a) town-dweller; (Großstädter, -städterin)
city-dweller
(b) (Stadtmensch) townie (coll.)

Städte·tour die city tour

Stadt-: ~**führer** der town/city
guidebook; ~**führung** die guided tour
of the town/city; ~**gespräch** das:
~gespräch sein be the talk of the town

städtisch ① Adj. (a) (kommunal) municipal
(b) (urban) urban ‹life, way of life, etc.›
② adv. (kommunal) municipally

Stadt-: ~**mauer** die town/city wall;
~**mitte** die town centre; (einer Großstadt)
city centre; downtown area (Amer.); ~**park**
der municipal park; ~**plan** der [town/city]
street plan or map; ~**rand** der outskirts
pl. of the town/city; **am** ~**rand** on the
outskirts of the town/city; ~**rundfahrt**
die sightseeing tour round a/the town/city;
~**teil** der district; part [of a/the town];
~**tor** das town/city gate; ~**viertel** das
district

Staffel die; ~, ~n (a) (Sport: Mannschaft)
relay team
(b) (Sport: Staffellauf) relay race
(c) (Luftwaffe: Einheit) flight
(d) (Eskorte) escort formation

Staffelei die; ~, ~en easel

staffeln tr. V. (a) (aufstellen, formieren)
arrange in a stagger or in an echelon
(b) (einteilen, abstufen) grade ‹salaries, fees,
prices›; stagger ‹times, arrivals, starting
places›

stahl *1. u. 3. Pers. Sg. Prät. v.* STEHLEN

Stahl der; ~[e]s, Stähle od. ~e steel

Stahl-: ~**beton** der reinforced concrete;
~**blech** das sheet steel

stählern Adj. steel

stak *1. u. 3. Pers. Sg. Prät. v.* STECKEN

Stall der; ~[e]s, Ställe (Pferde-, Rennstall)
stable; (Kuhstall) cowshed; (Hühnerstall)
[chicken] coop; (Schweinestall) [pig]sty; (für
Kaninchen, Kleintiere) hutch; (für Schafe) pen

Stallung die; ~, ~en (Pferdestall) stable;
(Kuhstall) cowshed; (Schweinestall) [pig]sty

Stamm der; ~[e]s, Stämme (a) (Baumstamm)
trunk
(b) (Volksstamm) tribe

Stamm-: ~**aktie** die (Wirtsch.) ordinary
share; ~**baum** der family tree; (eines Tieres)
pedigree

stammeln tr., itr. V. stammer

stammen itr. V. come (aus, von from);
(datieren) date (aus, von from)

Stamm-: ~**gast** der (im Lokal/Hotel)
regular customer/visitor; regular (coll.);
~**tisch** der (a) (Tisch) regulars' table
(coll.); (b) (Runde) group of regulars (coll.);
(c) (Treffen) get-together with the regulars
(coll.); ~**zelle** die (Biol.) stem cell

---

*old spelling – see note on page x

stampfen ① itr. V. (a) (laut auftreten) stamp
(b) mit sein (sich fortbewegen) tramp; (mit
schweren Schritten) trudge
② tr. V. (a) mit den Füßen den Rhythmus
~: tap the rhythm with one's feet
(b) (feststampfen) compress
(c) (zerkleinern) mash ‹potatoes›

stand *1. u. 3. Pers. Sg. Prät. v.* STEHEN

Stand der; ~[e]s, Stände (a) (das Stehen)
standing position; [bei jmdm. od. gegen
jmdn.] einen schweren ~ haben (fig.) have a
tough time [of it] [with sb.]
(b) (Standort) position
(c) (Verkaufsstand; Box für ein Pferd) stall;
(Messestand, Informationsstand) stand;
(Zeitungsstand) [newspaper] kiosk
(d) (erreichte Stufe; Zustand) state; etw. auf
den neu[e]sten ~ bringen bring sth. up to
date; außer ~[e] ► AUSSERSTANDE; im ~[e]
► IMSTANDE
(e) (des Wassers, Flusses) level; (des
Thermometers, Zählers, Barometers) reading; (der
Kasse, Finanzen) state; (eines Himmelskörpers)
position
(f) (Familienstand) status
(g) (Gesellschaftsschicht) class; (Berufsstand)
trade; (Ärzte, Rechtsanwälte) [professional]
group

Standard der; ~s, ~s standard

standardisieren tr. V. standardize

Standardisierung die; ~, ~en
standardization

Ständchen das; ~s, ~: serenade; jmdm.
ein ~ bringen serenade sb.

Ständer der; ~s, ~: stand; (Kleider~) coat
stand; (Wäsche~) clothes horse

standes-, Standes-: ~**amt** das
registry office; ~**amtlich** ① Adj.
registry office ‹wedding, document›; ② adv.
~amtlich heiraten get married in a registry
office; ~**beamte** der, ~**beamtin** die
registrar

stand-, Stand-: ~**fest** Adj. steady;
stable; strong ‹stalk, stem›; ~**haft**
① Adj. steadfast; ② adv. steadfastly;
~**haftigkeit** die; ~~: steadfastness;
~**|halten** unr. itr. V. stand firm; einer
Sache (Dat.) ~halten withstand sth.

ständig ① Adj. constant ‹noise, worry,
pressure, etc.›; permanent ‹residence,
correspondent, staff, member, etc.›; standing
‹committee›; regular ‹income›
② adv. constantly

Stand-: ~**licht** das (Kfz-W.) sidelights pl.;
~**ort** der (a) position; (eines Betriebes usw.)
location; site; (b) (Milit.: Garnison) garrison;
base; ~**punkt** der (fig.) point of view;
viewpoint; auf dem ~punkt stehen, dass ...:
take the view that ...; ~**spur** die (Verkehrsw.)
hard shoulder; ~**uhr** die grandfather clock

Stange die; ~, ~n pole; (aus Metall) bar;
(dünner) rod; (Kleiderstange) rail; (Vogelstange)
perch; ein Anzug von der ~ (ugs.) an off-the-
peg-suit

Stängel *der;* ~s, ~: stem; stalk
Stangen-: ~**brot** *das* French bread;
~**spargel** *der* asparagus spears *pl.*
stank *1. u. 3. Pers. Sg. Prät. v.* STINKEN
Stapel *der;* ~s, ~: pile; **ein** ~ **Holz** a pile *or*
stack of wood
stapeln 1 *tr. V.* pile up; stack
2 *refl. V.* pile up
stapfen *itr. V.; mit sein* tramp
Star¹ *der;* ~[e]s, ~e *od.* (schweiz.) ~**en**
(Vogel) starling
Star² *der;* ~s, ~s (berühmte Persönlichkeit) star
Star³ *der;* ~[e]s (Med.) **grauer** ~: cataract;
grüner ~: glaucoma
starb *1. u. 3. Pers. Sg. Prät. v.* STERBEN
stark; stärker, stärkst… 1 *Adj.* (a) strong;
potent ⟨drink, medicine, etc.⟩; powerful
⟨engine, lens, voice, etc.⟩; (ausgezeichnet)
excellent; *s. auch* STÜCK c
(b) (dick) thick; stout ⟨rope, string⟩; (verhüll.:
korpulent) well-built (euphem.)
(c) (zahlenmäßig groß, umfangreich) sizeable,
large; big ⟨demand⟩; **eine 100 Mann** ~**e**
Truppe a 100-strong unit
(d) (heftig, intensiv) heavy; severe ⟨frost, pain⟩;
strong ⟨impression, current, resistance,
dislike⟩; grave ⟨doubt, reservations⟩; great
⟨exaggeration, interest⟩; loud ⟨applause⟩
(e) (Jugendspr.: großartig) great (coll.); fantastic
(coll.)
2 *adv.* (a) (sehr, überaus, intensiv) (mit Adj.)
very; heavily ⟨indebted, stressed⟩; greatly
⟨increased, reduced, enlarged⟩; strongly
⟨emphasized, characterized⟩; badly
⟨damaged, worn, affected⟩; (mit Verb) heavily;
⟨exaggerate, impress⟩ greatly; ⟨enlarge,
reduce, increase⟩ considerably; ⟨support,
oppose, suspect⟩ strongly; ⟨remind⟩ very
much; ~ **erkältet sein** have a heavy *or* bad
cold
(b) (Jugendspr.: großartig) fantastically (coll.)
Stark·bier *das* strong beer
Stärke *die;* ~, ~n (a) strength; (eines
Motors) power; (einer Glühbirne) wattage
(b) (Dicke) thickness; (Technik) gauge
(c) (zahlenmäßige Größe) strength
(d) (besondere Fähigkeit, Vorteil) strength; **jmds.**
~/**nicht jmds.** ~ **sein** be sb.'s forte/not be
sb.'s strong point
(e) (Intensität) strength; (von Sturm, Schmerzen,
Abneigung) intensity; (von Frost) severity; (von
Lärm, Verkehr) volume
(f) (organischer Stoff) starch
stärken 1 *tr. V.* (a) strengthen; boost
⟨power, prestige⟩; ⟨drink, food, etc.⟩ fortify
⟨person⟩
(b) (steif machen) starch ⟨washing etc.⟩
2 *refl. V.* refresh oneself
Stärkung *die;* ~, ~en (a) strengthening
(b) (Erfrischung) refreshment
starr 1 *Adj.* (a) rigid; (steif) stiff (**vor**
+ *Dat.* with); fixed ⟨expression, smile, stare⟩
(b) (nicht abwandelbar) inflexible, rigid ⟨law,

rule, principle⟩
(c) (unnachgiebig) inflexible ⟨person, attitude,
etc.⟩
2 *adv.* rigidly; (steif) stiffly
starren *itr. V.* (a) stare (**in** + *Akk.* into, **auf,**
an, gegen + *Akk.* at); **jmdm. ins Gesicht**
~: stare sb. in the face
(b) **vor/von Schmutz** ~: be filthy
starr-, Starr-: ~**sinn** *der*
pigheadedness; ~**sinnig** *Adj.* pigheaded;
~**sinnigkeit** *die* pigheadedness
Start *der;* ~[e]s, ~e start; (eines Flugzeugs)
take-off; (einer Rakete) launch
Start·bahn *die* [take-off] runway
start·bereit *Adj.* ready to start *postpos.;*
⟨aircraft⟩ ready for take-off
starten 1 *itr. V.; mit sein* (a) start;
⟨aircraft⟩ take off; ⟨rocket⟩ blast off, be
launched
(b) (den Motor anlassen) start the engine
2 *tr. V.* start; launch ⟨rocket, satellite,
attack⟩; start [up] ⟨engine, machine, car⟩
Stasi *die;* ~: *Abk.* (DDR ugs.)
= **Staatssicherheit**
Stasi·akte *die* Stasi file
Station *die;* ~, ~en (a) station
(b) (Haltestelle) stop
(c) (Zwischenhalt, Aufenthalt) stopover;
~ **machen** stop over *or* off
(d) (im Krankenhaus) ward
stationär 1 *Adj.* (Med.) ⟨treatment⟩ in
hospital, as an inpatient
2 *adv.* (Med.) in hospital; **jmdn.**
~ **behandeln** treat sb. as an inpatient
stationieren *tr. V.* station ⟨troops⟩; deploy
⟨weapons, bombers, etc.⟩
Stationierung *die;* ~, ~en stationing;
(von Waffen, Raketen usw.) deployment
Stations-: ~**arzt** *der,* ~**ärztin** *die* ward
doctor; ~**schwester** *die* ward sister;
~**taste** *die* (Rundf.) preset [tuning] button;
preset
statisch *Adj.* static
Statistik *die;* ~: statistics *sing., no art.*
statistisch 1 *Adj.* statistical
2 *adv.* statistically
statt 1 *Präp. mit Gen.* instead of; *s. auch*
STATTDESSEN
2 *Konj.* ▶ ANSTATT
statt·dessen *Adv.* instead [of this]
statt|finden *unr. V.* take place;
⟨process, development⟩ occur
statthaft *Adj.* permissible
stattlich 1 *Adj.* (a) well-built; imposing
⟨figure, stature, building, etc.⟩; fine ⟨farm,
estate⟩; impressive ⟨trousseau, collection⟩
(b) (beträchtlich) considerable
2 *adv.* impressively
Statue *die;* ~, ~n statue
Statur *die;* ~, ~en build
Status *der;* ~, ~ /'ʃta:tu:s/ status
Status quo *der;* ~ (geh.) status quo

Statut *das;* ∼[e]s, ∼en statute

Stau *der;* ∼[e]s, ∼s *od.* ∼e (a) build-up
(b) (von Fahrzeugen) tailback (Brit.); backup
(Amer.)

Staub *der;* ∼[e]s dust; ∼ **wischen** dust;
∼ **saugen** vacuum *or* (Brit. coll.) hoover; **sich
aus dem** ∼[e] **machen** (fig. ugs.) make oneself
scarce (coll.)

stauben *itr. V.* cause dust

staubig *Adj.* dusty

staub-, Staub-: ∼**saugen** *itr., tr. V.* ich
staubsauge, staubgesaugt, staubzusaugen
vacuum; (Brit. coll.) hoover; ∼**sauger** *der*
vacuum cleaner; Hoover (*Brit. ®*); ∼**tuch**
das; Pl. ∼**tücher** duster

Stau·damm *der* dam

Staude *die;* ∼, ∼n (Bot.) herbaceous
perennial

stauen 1 *tr. V.* dam [up] ⟨*stream, river*⟩;
staunch ⟨*blood*⟩
2 *refl. V.* ⟨*water, blood, etc.*⟩ accumulate,
build up; ⟨*people*⟩ form a crowd; ⟨*traffic*⟩
form a tailback/tailbacks (Brit.) *or* (Amer.)
backup/backups

staunen *itr. V.* be amazed *or* astonished
(**über** + *Akk.* at); (beeindruckt sein) marvel
(**über** + *Akk.* at); ∼**d** with *or* in amazement

Staunen *das;* ∼s amazement (**über** + *Akk.*
at); (Bewunderung) wonderment

Stau-: ∼**see** *der* reservoir; ∼**stufe** *die*
barrage

Stauung *die;* ∼, ∼en (a) (eines Bachs,
Flusses) damming; (des Blutes, Wassers)
stemming the flow; (das Sichstauen) build-up
(b) (Verkehrsstau) tailback (Brit.); backup
(Amer.); jam

Std. *Abk.* = **Stunde** hr.

Steak /steːk/ *das;* ∼s, ∼s steak

stechen 1 *unr. itr. V.* (a) prick; ⟨*wasp, bee*⟩
sting; ⟨*mosquito*⟩ bite
(b) (hineinstechen) **mit etw. in etw.** (*Akk.*)
∼: stick *or* jab sth. into sth.
2 *unr. tr. V.* (mit dem Messer, Schwert) stab;
(mit der Nadel, mit einem Dorn usw.) prick; ⟨*bee,
wasp*⟩ sting; ⟨*mosquito*⟩ bite; **sich in den
Finger** ∼: prick one's finger

stechend *Adj.* penetrating, pungent
⟨*smell*⟩; penetrating ⟨*glance, eyes*⟩

Stech-: ∼**mücke** *die* mosquito; gnat;
∼**uhr** *die* time clock

Steck-: ∼**brief** *der* description [of a/the
wanted person]; (Plakat) 'wanted' poster;
∼**dose** *die* socket; power point

stecken 1 *tr. V.* (a) put
(b) (mit Nadeln) pin ⟨*hem, lining, etc.*⟩; pin [on]
⟨*badge*⟩; pin up ⟨*hair*⟩
2 *itr. V.* be; ∼ **bleiben** get stuck; **den
Schlüssel [im Schloss]** ∼ **lassen** leave the
key in the lock; **wo steckt meine Brille?**
(ugs.) where have my glasses got to *or* gone?;
hinter etw. (*Dat.*) ∼ (fig. ugs.) be behind sth.

stecken-, Stecken-: *∼|bleiben
▶ STECKEN 2; *∼|lassen ▶ STECKEN 2;
∼**pferd** *das* (a) (Spielzeug) hobby horse;
(b) (Liebhaberei) hobby

Stecker *der;* ∼s, ∼: plug

Steck·nadel *die* pin

Steg *der;* ∼[e]s, ∼e (Brücke) [narrow]
bridge; (Laufbrett) gangplank; (Boots∼)
landing stage

Steg·reif *der:* aus dem ∼: impromptu

Steh·auf·männchen *das* tumbling
figure; tumbler

stehen *unr. itr. V.;* **südd., österr., schweiz.
mit sein** (a) stand
(b) (sich befinden) be; ⟨*upright object,
building*⟩ stand
(c) (einen bestimmten Stand haben) **auf etw.**
(*Dat.*) ∼ ⟨*needle, hand*⟩ point to sth.;
das Barometer steht tief/auf Regen the
barometer is reading low/indicating rain;
das Spiel/es steht 1: 1 (Sport) the score is one
all; **die Sache steht gut/schlecht** things are
going well/badly
(d) (einen bestimmten Kurs, Wert haben)
⟨*currency*⟩ stand (**bei** at); **wie steht das
Pfund?** what is the rate for the pound?
(e) (nicht in Bewegung sein) be stationary;
⟨*machine etc.*⟩ be at a standstill; **meine
Uhr steht** my watch has stopped;
∼ **bleiben** (anhalten) stop; ⟨*traffic*⟩ come to
a standstill; (stehen gelassen werden) stay; be
left; (zurückgelassen werden) be left behind;
(der Zerstörung entgehen) ⟨*building*⟩ be left
standing; **etw.** ∼ **lassen** (nicht entfernen) leave
sth.; (vergessen) leave sth. [behind]
(f) (geschrieben, gedruckt sein) be; **in der Zeitung
steht, dass …** it says in the paper that …
(g) (Sprachw.: gebraucht werden) ⟨*subjunctive
etc.*⟩ occur; be found
(h) **jmdm. [gut]** ∼ ⟨*dress etc.*⟩ suit sb. [well]
(i) **auf etw.** (*Akk.*) ∼ (ugs., bes. Jugendspr.:
mögen) be into sth. (coll.); **sie steht total auf
ihn** she's nuts about him

***stehen|bleiben, *stehen|lassen
▶ STEHEN E

Steh·lampe *die* standard lamp (Brit.); floor
lamp (Amer.)

stehlen *unr. tr., itr. V.* steal; *s. auch*
GESTOHLEN 2

Steh·platz *der* (im Theater usw.) standing
place; (im Bus) space to stand

Steiermark *die;* ∼: Styria *no art.*

steif 1 *Adj.* (a) stiff; (ugs.: erigiert) erect
⟨*penis*⟩
(b) (Seemannsspr.: stark) stiff ⟨*wind, breeze*⟩
(c) (förmlich) stiff; formal
2 *adv.* stiffly

Steifheit *die;* (a) ∼ stiffness
(b) (Förmlichkeit) formality; stiffness

steigen 1 *unr. itr. V.; mit sein* (a) climb;
⟨*mist, smoke, sun*⟩ rise; ⟨*balloon*⟩ climb,
rise; **auf die Leiter** ∼: get on to the ladder;
in den/aus dem Bus/Zug ∼: board *or* get
on/get off *or* out of the bus/train

S

(b) (ansteigen, zunehmen) rise; ⟨price, cost, salary, output⟩ increase, rise; ⟨debts, tension⟩ increase, mount; ⟨chances⟩ improve [2] unr. tr. V.; mit sein climb ⟨stairs, steps⟩

Steiger der; ~s, ~ (Bergbau) overman

steigern [1] tr. V. **(a)** increase ⟨speed, value, sales, consumption, etc.⟩ **(auf** + Akk. to); step up ⟨demands, production, etc.⟩; raise ⟨standards, requirements⟩; (verstärken) intensify ⟨fear, tension⟩; heighten ⟨effect⟩ **(b)** (Sprachw.) compare ⟨adjective⟩ [2] refl. V. ⟨confusion, speed, profit, etc.⟩ increase; ⟨pain, excitement, tension, etc.⟩ become more intense; ⟨costs⟩ escalate; ⟨effect⟩ be heightened

Steigerung die; ~, ~en **(a)** increase (Gen. in); (Verstärkung) intensification; (einer Wirkung) heightening; (Verbesserung) improvement (Gen. in); (bes. Sport: Leistungssteigerung) improvement [in performance] **(b)** (Sprachw.) comparison

Steigung die; ~, ~en gradient

steil [1] Adj. steep; meteoric ⟨career⟩; rapid ⟨rise⟩ [2] adv. steeply

Steil-: ~**hang** der steep escarpment; ~**küste** die (Geogr.) cliffs pl.

Stein der; ~[e]s, ~e stone; (Fels) rock; (Baustein) [stone]block; **mir fällt ein ~ vom Herzen** that's a weight off my mind

Stein-: ~**bock** der **(a)** ibex; **(b)** (Astrol.) Capricorn; the Goat; ~**bruch** der quarry

steinern Adj. stone

Stein·gut das earthenware

stein·hart Adj. rock-hard

steinig Adj. stony

steinigen tr. V. stone ⟨person⟩

Stein-: ~**kohle** die [hard] coal; ~**metz** der; ~~en, ~~en, ~**metzin** die; ~~, ~~nen stonemason; ~**obst** das stone fruit; ~**pilz** der cep; ~**schlag** der rock fall; „**Achtung** ~**schlag**" 'beware falling rocks'; ~**zeit** die Stone Age; (fig.) stone age

Steiß·bein das (Anat.) coccyx

Stelle die; ~, ~n **(a)** place; an jmds. ~ **treten** take sb.'s place; **ich an deiner ~ ...:** ... if I were you; **an achter ~ liegen** be in eighth place; **die erste ~ hinter** od. **nach dem Komma** (Math.) the first decimal place; **an ~** (+ Gen.) instead of; **auf der ~:** immediately **(b)** (begrenzter Bereich) patch; (am Körper) spot **(c)** (Passage) passage; (Punkt im Ablauf einer Rede usw.) point **(d)** (Arbeitsstelle) job; post; **eine freie ~:** a vacancy **(e)** (Dienststelle) office; (Behörde) authority

stellen [1] tr. V. **(a)** put; (mit Sorgfalt) place; (aufrecht hin~) stand **(b)** (ein~) set ⟨points, clock, scales⟩; **den Wecker auf 6 Uhr ~:** set the alarm for 6 o'clock; **die Heizung höher/niedriger ~:** turn the heating up/down

(c) (bereitstellen) provide **(d)** jmdn. besser ~: ⟨firm⟩ improve sb.'s pay; **gut/schlecht/besser gestellt** comfortably/badly/better off **(e)** (verblasst) put ⟨question⟩; set ⟨task, topic, condition⟩; make ⟨application, demand, request⟩; **jmdm. eine Frage ~:** ask sb. a question [2] refl. V. **(a)** place oneself; **sich auf die Zehenspitzen ~:** stand on tiptoe **(b)** **sich schlafend/taub/tot usw. ~:** feign sleep/deafness/death etc.; pretend to be asleep/deaf/dead etc.

stell-, Stell-: ~**angebot** das offer of a job; (Inserat) job advertisement; „~**angebote**" 'situations vacant'; ~**anzeige** die job advertisement; ~**gesuch** das 'situation wanted' advertisement; ~**markt** der job market; ~**profil** das job profile; ~**suche** die job-hunting no art.; search for a job; ~**weise** Adv. in places; ~**wert** der **(a)** (Math.) place value; **(b)** (fig.: Bedeutung) standing; status

Stellung die; ~, ~en position; **zu etw. ~ nehmen** express one's opinion on sth.

Stellungnahme die; ~, ~n opinion; (kurze Äußerung) statement

stell-, Stell-: ~**vertretend** [1] Adj. acting; (von Amts wegen) deputy ⟨minister, director, etc.⟩; [2] adv. as a deputy; ~**vertreter** der, ~**vertreterin** die deputy

Stelze die; ~, ~n stilt

stelzen itr. V.; mit sein strut; stalk

stemmen [1] tr. V. **(a)** (hochstemmen) lift [above one's head] **(b)** (drücken) brace ⟨feet, knees⟩ (**gegen** against) [2] refl. V. **sich gegen etw. ~:** brace oneself against sth.

Stempel der; ~s, ~: stamp; (Poststempel) postmark

stempeln tr. V. stamp ⟨passport, form⟩; postmark ⟨letter⟩; cancel ⟨postage stamp⟩

***Stengel** ▸ STÄNGEL

steno-, Steno-: ~**gramm** das shorthand text; ~**graph** der; ~~en, ~~en stenographer; ~**graphie** die; ~~, ~~en stenography no art.; shorthand no art.; ~**graphieren** itr. V. do shorthand; ~**graphin** die; ~~, ~~nen stenographer; ~**typistin** die; ~~, ~~nen shorthand typist

Stepp·decke die quilt

Steppe die; ~, ~n steppe

steppen[1] tr. (auch itr.) V. backstitch

steppen[2] itr. V. (tanzen) tap dance

Steppke der; ~s, ~s (ugs., bes. berlin.) lad; nipper (coll.)

sterben unr. itr. V.; mit sein die; **im Sterben liegen** lie dying

sterbens·krank Adj. mortally ill

sterblich Adj. mortal

S

Sterbliche *der/die; adj. Dekl.* mortal; **ein gewöhnlicher ~r** an ordinary mortal *or* person

Sterblichkeit *die; ~:* mortality

stereo *Adv.* in stereo

Stereo *das; ~s* stereo

Stereo-: **~anlage** *die* stereo [system]; **~aufnahme** *die* stereo recording

steril *Adj.* sterile

Sterling /'stɛːlɪŋ/: **Pfund ~:** pound/pounds sterling

Stern *der; ~[e]s, ~e* star

Sternchen *das; ~s, ~* (Druckw.) asterisk

Stern·schnuppe *die; ~, ~n* shooting star

Stethoskop *das; ~s, ~e* (Med.) stethoscope

Steuer¹ *das; ~s, ~:* [steering] wheel; (von Schiffen) helm

Steuer² *die; ~, ~n* tax

steuer-, Steuer-: **~belastung** *die* tax burden; **~berater** *der,* **~beraterin** *die* tax consultant *or* adviser; **~bord** *das od.* (österr.) *der* (Seew., Flugw.) starboard; **~erhöhung** *die* tax increase; **~erklärung** *die* tax return; **~ermäßigung** *die* tax relief; **~frau** *die* (Rudersport) cox; **~frei** *Adj.* tax-free

steuerlich ① *Adj.* tax ⟨*advantages, benefits, etc.*⟩ ② *adv.* **~ absetzbar** tax-deductible

Steuer·mann *der; Pl.* **~leute** *od.* **~männer** (Rudersport) cox

steuern ① *tr. V.* (fahren) steer; (fliegen) pilot, fly ⟨*aircraft*⟩; fly ⟨*course*⟩ ② *itr. V.* **(a)** be at the wheel; (auf dem Schiff) be at the helm **(b)** *mit sein* (Kurs nehmen, ugs.: sich hinbewegen; auch fig.) head

Steuer-: **~oase** *die* (ugs.) tax haven; **~senkung** *die* (Steuerw.) tax cut; reduction in taxation

Steuerung *die; ~, ~en* **(a)** (System) controls *pl.* **(b)** ▶ STEUERN 1: steering; piloting; flying

Steward /'stjuːɐt/ *der; ~s, ~s* steward

Stewardess, *Stewardeß /'stjuːɐdɛs/ *die; ~, Stewardessen* stewardess

stich *Imper. Sg. v.* STECHEN

Stich *der; ~[e]s, ~e* **(a)** (mit einer Waffe) stab **(b)** (mit einem Dorn, einer Nadel) prick; (von Wespe, Biene usw.) sting; (Mückenstich usw.) bite **(c)** (Stichwunde) stab wound **(d)** (beim Nähen) stitch **(e)** (Schmerz) stabbing *or* shooting pain **(f)** (Kartenspiel) trick **(g)** **jmdn./etw. im ~ lassen** leave sb. in the lurch/abandon sth.

Stichelei *die; ~, ~en* (ugs. abwertend) **(a)** (Bemerkung) dig; gibe

(b) **hör auf mit deiner ~:** stop getting at me/him *etc.* (coll.)

sticheln *itr. V.* make snide remarks (coll.) **(gegen** about)

stich-, Stich-: **~flamme** *die* tongue of flame; **~haltig** *Adj.* sound ⟨*argument, reason*⟩; valid ⟨*assertion, reply*⟩; conclusive ⟨*evidence*⟩; **~haltigkeit** *die;* **~~:** ▶ **~HALTIG:** soundness; validity; conclusiveness

Stichling *der; ~s, ~e* stickleback

Stich·probe *die* [random] sample; (bei Kontrollen) spot check

stichst *2. Pers. Sg. Präsens v.* STECHEN

sticht *3. Pers. Sg. Präsens v.* STECHEN

Stich-: **~tag** *der* set date; deadline; **~wunde** *die* stab wound

sticken ① *itr. V.* do embroidery ② *tr. V.* embroider

Stickerei *die; ~, ~en* embroidery *no pl.;* (gestickte Arbeit) piece of embroidery

Stick·garn *das* embroidery thread

stickig *Adj.* stuffy; stale ⟨*air*⟩

Stick-: **~oxid, ~oxyd** *das* nitrogen oxide; **~oxid·emission, ~oxyd·emission** *die* nitrogen oxide emission; **~stoff** *der* nitrogen; **~stoff·oxid, ~stoff·oxyd** *das* nitrogen oxide

Stief- step ⟨*brother, child, mother, etc.*⟩

Stiefel *der; ~s, ~* boot

stief-, Stief-: **~mutter** *die; Pl.* **~mütter** stepmother; **~mütterchen** *das; ~s, ~~* (Bot.) pansy; **~mütterlich** ① *Adj.* poor, shabby ⟨*treatment*⟩; ② *adv.* **~mütterlich behandeln** treat ⟨*person*⟩ poorly *or* shabbily; neglect ⟨*pet, flowers, doll, problem*⟩; **~vater** *der* stepfather

stieg *1. u. 3. Pers. Sg. Prät. v.* STEIGEN

Stieglitz *der; ~es, ~e* goldfinch

stiehl *Imp. Sg. v.* STEHLEN

stiehlst *2. Pers. Sg. Präsens v.* STEHLEN

stiehlt *3. Pers. Sg. Präsens v.* STEHLEN

Stiel *der; ~[e]s, ~e* (Griff) handle; (Besenstiel) [broom]stick; (für Süßigkeiten) stick; (bei Gläsern) stem; (bei Blumen) stem; (an Obst usw.) stalk

Stier *der; ~[e]s, ~e* bull; (Astrol.) Taurus; the Bull

stieren *itr. V.* stare [vacantly] **(auf** + *Akk.* at)

Stier·kampf *der* bullfight

stieß *1. u. 3. Pers. Sg. Prät. v.* STOSSEN

Stift *der; ~[e]s, ~e* **(a)** (aus Metall) pin; (aus Holz) peg **(b)** (Bleistift) pencil; (Malstift) crayon; (Schreibstift) pen

stiften *tr. V.* **(a)** found, establish ⟨*monastery, hospital, etc.*⟩; endow ⟨*prize, scholarship*⟩; (als Spende) donate, give **(für** to) **(b)** (herbeiführen) cause ⟨*unrest, confusion, strife, etc.*⟩; bring about ⟨*peace, order, etc.*⟩; arrange ⟨*marriage*⟩

---

*old spelling – see note on page x

Stifter der; ~s, ~, **Stifterin** die; ~, ~nen founder; (Spender) donor

Stiftung die; ~, ~en (Rechtsspr.) foundation; endowment

Stift·zahn der (Zahnmed.) post crown

stigmatisieren tr. V. stigmatize

Stil der; ~[e]s, ~e style

Stil·bruch der inconsistency of style

stilistisch [1] Adj. stylistic
[2] adv. stylistically

still [1] Adj. quiet; (ohne Geräusche) silent; still; (reglos) still; (wortlos) silent; (heimlich) secret; **der Stille Ozean** the Pacific [Ocean]
[2] adv. quietly; (geräuschlos) silently; (wortlos) in silence

Stille die; ~: quiet; (Geräuschlosigkeit) silence; stillness

***stilllegen** ▶ STILLLEGEN

stillen [1] tr. V. (a) **ein Kind** ~: breastfeed a baby
(b) (befriedigen) satisfy; quench ⟨thirst⟩
(c) (eindämmen) stop ⟨bleeding, tears, pain⟩
[2] itr. V. breastfeed

still-, Still-: ~|**halten** unr. itr. V. keep or stay still; ~|**legen** tr. V. close or shut down; close ⟨railway line⟩; ~**schweigen** das silence; ~**schweigen bewahren** maintain silence; keep silent; ~**schweigend**
[1] Adj. silent; (ohne Abmachung) tacit ⟨assumption, agreement⟩; [2] adv. in silence; (ohne Abmachung) tacitly; ~|**sitzen** unr. itr. V. sit still; ~**stand** der standstill; ~|**stehen** unr. itr. V. (a) ⟨factory, machine⟩ stand idle; ⟨traffic⟩ be at a standstill; ⟨heart etc.⟩ stop; (b) (Milit.) stand to attention

Stimm·bruch der: **er ist im** ~: his voice is breaking

Stimme die; ~, ~n (a) voice
(b) (bei Wahlen) vote

stimmen [1] itr. V. (a) be right or correct; **stimmt es, dass ...?** is it true that ...?
(b) (seine Stimme geben) vote; **mit Ja** ~: vote yes or in favour
[2] tr. V. (a) (in eine Stimmung versetzen) make
(b) (Musik) tune ⟨instrument⟩

Stimm-: ~**enthaltung** die abstention; ~**gabel** die (Musik) tuning fork

stimmig Adj. harmonious; **die Argumentation ist [in sich** (Dat.)] ~: the argument is consistent

Stimm-: ~**lage** die (a) voice; (b) (Musik) voice; register; ~**recht** das right to vote

Stimmung die; ~, ~en (a) mood
(b) (Atmosphäre) atmosphere

stimmungs·voll [1] Adj. atmospheric
[2] adv. ⟨describe, light⟩ atmospherically; ⟨sing, recite⟩ with great feeling

Stimm·zettel der ballot paper

stimulieren tr. V. stimulate

Stink·bombe die stink bomb

stinken unr. itr. V. stink (nach of)

stink·faul Adj. (salopp abwertend) bone idle (coll.)

stinkig Adj. (salopp abwertend) stinking; smelly

stink-: ~**normal** (salopp) [1] Adj. dead (coll.) or boringly ordinary; [2] adv. in a dead ordinary way (coll.); ~**reich** Adj. (salopp) stinking rich (coll.)

Stipendium das; ~s, Stipendien (als Auszeichnung) scholarship; (als finanzielle Unterstützung) grant

stirb Imp. Sg. v. STERBEN

stirbst 2. Pers. Sg. Präsens v. STERBEN

stirbt 3. Pers. Sg. Präsens v. STERBEN

Stirn die; ~, ~en forehead; brow

Stirn-: ~**höhle** die (Anat.) frontal sinus; ~**runzeln** das; ~~s frown; ~**seite** die front [side]

stöbern itr. V. (ugs.) rummage

stochern itr. V. poke

Stock¹ der; ~[e]s, Stöcke (a) stick; (Zeigestock) pointer; stick; (Taktstock) baton; (Skistock) pole; stick
(b) (Pflanze) (Rosenstock) [rose] bush; (Rebstock) vine

Stock² der; ~[e]s, ~ (Etage) floor; storey; **in welchem** ~? on which floor?

stock·dunkel Adj. (ugs.) pitch-dark

stocken itr. V. (a) ⟨traffic⟩ be held up; ⟨conversation, production⟩ stop; ⟨business⟩ slacken; ⟨journey⟩ be interrupted
(b) (innehalten) falter

Stöckel·schuhe Pl. high heels

stock·finster Adj. (ugs.) pitch-dark

-stöckig -storey attr.; -storeyed

stock·nüchtern Adj. (ugs.) stone-cold sober

Stockung die; ~, ~en hold-up (Gen. in)

Stockwerk das floor; storey

Stoff der; ~[e]s, ~e (a) material; fabric
(b) (Materie) substance
(c) (Philos.) matter
(d) (Thema) subject [matter]; (Gesprächsthema) topic
(e) (salopp: Rauschgift) stuff (sl.); dope (sl.)

stofflich Adj. material

Stofflichkeit die; ~: materiality

Stoff·wechsel der metabolism

stöhnen itr. V. moan; (vor Schmerz) groan

Stola die; ~, Stolen shawl; (Pelzstola) stole

Stollen der; ~s, ~ (a) (Kuchen) Stollen
(b) (Bergbau) gallery
(c) (bei Sportschuhen) stud

stolpern itr. V.; mit sein stumble; trip

stolz [1] Adj. proud (auf + Akk. of); **eine** ~**e Summe** (ugs.) a tidy sum
[2] adv. proudly

Stolz der; ~es pride (auf + Akk. in)

stolzieren itr. V.; mit sein strut

stop /stɔp/ Interj. stop; (Verkehrsw.) halt

S

stopfen *tr. V.* (a) darn
(b) (hineintun) stuff
(c) (füllen) stuff ⟨*cushion, quilt, etc.*⟩; fill ⟨*pipe*⟩; plug, stop [up] ⟨*hole, leak*⟩
Stopf-: ∼**garn** *das* darning cotton; ∼**nadel** *die* darning needle
Stopp *der;* ∼**s,** ∼**s** stop; (Einstellung) freeze (*Gen.* on)
Stoppel *die;* ∼, ∼**n** stubble *no pl.*
stoppelig *Adj.* stubbly
stoppen *tr., itr. V.* stop
Stopp-: ∼**licht** *das* stop light; ∼**schild** *das* stop sign; ∼**uhr** *die* stopwatch
Stöpsel *der;* ∼**s,** ∼: plug
Stör *der;* ∼**s,** ∼**e** sturgeon
Storch *der;* ∼**[e]s,** Störche stork
stören ① *tr. V.* (a) disturb; disrupt ⟨*court proceedings, lecture, church service, etc.*⟩; interfere with ⟨*transmitter, reception*⟩
(b) (missfallen) bother
② *itr. V.* (a) disturb
(b) (Unruhe stiften) make *or* cause trouble
③ *refl. V.* **sich an jmdm./etw.** ∼: take exception to sb./sth
Störenfried *der;* ∼**[e]s,** ∼**e** troublemaker
Stör·fall *der* (Technik) fault
störrisch ① *Adj.* stubborn
② *adv.* stubbornly
Störung *die;* ∼, ∼**en** (a) disturbance; (einer Gerichtsverhandlung, Vorlesung, eines Gottesdienstes usw.) disruption; **bitte entschuldigen Sie die** ∼**, aber ...:** I'm sorry to bother you, but ...
(b) **eine technische** ∼: a technical fault
Stoß *der;* ∼**es,** Stöße (a) (mit der Faust) punch; (mit dem Fuß) kick; (mit dem Kopf, den Hörnern) butt; (mit dem Ellbogen) dig
(b) (mit einer Waffe) (Stich) thrust; (Schlag) blow
(c) (beim Schwimmen, Rudern) stroke
(d) (Stapel) pile; stack
stoßen ① *unr. tr. V.* (a) *auch itr.:* (mit der Faust) punch; (mit dem Fuß) kick; (mit dem Kopf, den Hörnern) butt; (mit dem Ellbogen) dig
(b) (hineintreiben) plunge, thrust ⟨*dagger, knife*⟩; push ⟨*stick, pole*⟩
(c) (schleudern) push; **die Kugel** ∼: put the shot
② *unr. itr. V.* (a) *mit sein* (auftreffen) bump ⟨**gegen** into⟩; **mit dem Kopf gegen etw.** ∼: bump one's head on sth.
(b) *mit sein* (fig.) **auf etw.** (*Akk.*) ∼ ⟨etw. entdecken⟩ come upon sth.; **auf Ablehnung** ∼ (abgelehnt werden) meet with disapproval
(c) (grenzen) **an etw.** (*Akk.*) ∼ ⟨*room, property, etc.*⟩ be [right] next to sth.
③ *unr. refl. V.* bump *or* knock oneself; **sich an etw.** (*Dat.*) ∼ (fig.) object to sth.
Stoß-: ∼**seufzer** *der* heartfelt groan; ∼**stange** *die* bumper
stößt 3. *Pers. Sg. Präsens v.* STOSSEN
stoß-, Stoß-: ∼**weise** *Adv.*
(a) spasmodically; (b) (in Stapeln) by the pile;

in piles; ∼**zahn** *der* tusk; ∼**zeit** *die* peak time; (Hauptverkehrszeit) rush hour
Stotterer *der;* ∼**s,** ∼, **Stotterin** *die;* ∼, ∼**nen** stutterer
stottern ① *itr. V.* stutter
② *tr. V.* stutter [out]
Str. *Abk.* = **Straße** St./Rd.
stracks *Adv.* (a) (direkt) straight
(b) (sofort) straight away
straf·bar *Adj.* punishable
Strafe *die;* ∼, ∼**n** punishment; (Rechtsspr.) penalty; (Freiheitsstrafe) sentence; (Geldstrafe) fine
strafen *tr. V.* punish
straff ① *Adj.* (a) tight, taut ⟨*rope, lines, etc.*⟩; firm ⟨*breasts, skin*⟩
(b) (energisch) tight ⟨*organization, planning, etc.*⟩; strict ⟨*discipline, leadership, etc.*⟩
② *adv.* (a) [zu] ∼ **sitzen** ⟨*clothes*⟩ be [too] tight
(b) (energisch) tightly, strictly
straf·fällig *Adj.* ∼ **werden** commit a criminal offence
straffen *tr. V.* (a) tighten; firm ⟨*skin*⟩
(b) (fig.) tighten up ⟨*text, procedure, organization, etc.*⟩
straf-, Straf-: ∼**frei** *Adj.* ∼**frei ausgehen** go unpunished; ∼**freiheit** *die* exemption from punishment; ∼**gefangene** *der/die* prisoner; ∼**gericht** *das* (fig.) judgement; **ein** ∼**gericht des Himmels** divine judgement; ∼**gesetz·buch** *das* penal code
sträflich ① *Adj.* criminal
② *adv.* criminally
Sträfling *der;* ∼**s,** ∼**e** prisoner
straf-, Straf-: ∼**los** *Adj.* unpunished; ∼**rechtlich** ① *Adj.* criminal *attrib.* ⟨*case, investigation, responsibility*⟩; ② *adv.* under criminal law; **etw.** ∼**rechtlich verfolgen** prosecute sth.; ∼**tat** *die* criminal offence; ∼**täter** *der,* ∼**täterin** *die* offender; ∼**verfahren** *das* criminal proceedings *pl.;* ∼**vollzug** *der* (System) penal system; ∼**zettel** *der* (ugs.) [parking, speeding, *etc.*] ticket
Strahl *der;* ∼**[e]s,** ∼**en** (auch Phys., Math., fig.) ray; (von Scheinwerfern, Taschenlampen) beam; (von Flüssigkeit) jet
Strahle·mann *der* (ugs.) man/boy with the smiling face
strahlen *itr. V.* (a) shine; **bei** ∼**dem Wetter/Sonnenschein** in glorious sunny weather/in glorious sunshine; ∼**d weiß** sparkling white
(b) (glänzen) sparkle
(c) (lächeln) beam ⟨**vor** + *Dat.* with⟩
Strahler *der;* ∼**s,** ∼ (a) radiator
(b) (Heizstrahler) radiant heater
Strahlung *die;* ∼, ∼**en** radiation
Strähne *die;* ∼, ∼**n** strand; **eine graue** ∼: a grey streak
strähnig ① *Adj.* straggly ⟨*hair*⟩
② *adv.* in strands

---

stramm 1 *Adj.* **(a)** (straff) tight, taut ‹*rope, line, etc.*›; tight ‹*clothes*›
(b) (kräftig) strapping ‹*girl, boy*›; sturdy ‹*legs, body*›
(c) (gerade) upright, erect ‹*posture, etc.*›
2 *adv.* **(a)** (straff) tightly
(b) (kräftig) sturdily ‹*built*›

strampeln *itr. V.* ‹*baby*› kick [his/her feet]

Strand *der;* **~[e]s, Strände** beach; **am ~:** on the beach

Strand-: ~bad *das* bathing beach (*on river, lake*); **~burg** *die* sand den (*built as a windbreak*)

stranden *itr. V.; mit sein* ‹*ship*› run aground

Strand-: ~korb *der* basket chair; **~urlaub** *der* beach holiday; beach vacation (Amer.)

Strang *der;* **~[e]s, Stränge** rope

Strapaze *die;* **~, ~n** strain *no pl.*

strapazieren *tr. V.* be a strain on ‹*person, nerves*›

strapazier·fähig *Adj.* hard-wearing ‹*clothes, shoes*›; durable ‹*material*›

Straße *die;* **~, ~n** (in Ortschaften) street; road; (außerhalb) road

Straßen-: ~bahn *die* tram (Brit.); streetcar (Amer.); **~bahn·haltestelle** *die* tram stop (Brit.); **~bau·arbeiten** *Pl.* roadworks; **~café** *das* pavement café; street café; **~ecke** *die* street corner; **~feger** *der,* **~fegerin** *die;* **~~, ~~nen** (bes. nordd.) road sweeper; **~graben** *der* ditch [at the side of the road]; **~karte** *die* road map; **~kehrer** *der;* **~~s, ~~, ~kehrerin** *die;* **~~, ~~nen** (bes. südd.) road sweeper; **~kriminalität** *die* street crime; **~musikant** *der,* **~musikantin** *die* street musician; busker; **~raub** *der* street robbery; (gewalttätig) mugging; **~räuber** *der,* **~räuberin** *die* street robber; (gewalttätig) mugger; **~schild** *das* street name sign; **~sperre** *die* roadblock; **~verkehr** *der* traffic

Strategie *die;* **~, ~n** strategy

strategisch 1 *Adj.* strategic
2 *adv.* strategically

Strato·sphäre *die* stratosphere

sträuben 1 *tr. V.* ruffle [up] ‹*feathers*›; bristle ‹*fur, hair*›
2 *refl. V.* **(a)** ‹*hair, fur*› bristle, stand on end; ‹*feathers*› become ruffled
(b) (sich widersetzen) resist

Strauch *der;* **~[e]s, Sträucher** shrub

straucheln *itr. V.; mit sein* (geh.) stumble

Strauß[1] *der;* **~es, Sträuße** bunch of flowers; bouquet [of flowers]

Strauß[2] *der;* **~es, ~e** (Vogel) ostrich

Sträußchen *das;* **~s, ~:** posy

streben *itr. V.* **(a)** *mit sein* make one's way briskly
(b) (trachten) strive (**nach** for)

Streber *der;* **~s; ~** (abwertend) pushy person (coll.); (in der Schule) swot (Brit. coll.); grind (Amer. coll.)

strebsam *Adj.* ambitious and industrious

Strecke *die;* **~, ~n** distance; (Abschnitt, Route) route; (Eisenbahn~) line

strecken 1 *tr. V.* (gerade machen) stretch ‹*arms, legs*›; (dehnen) stretch [out] ‹*arms, legs, etc.*›; **den Kopf aus dem Fenster ~:** stick one's head out of the window (coll.)
2 *refl. V.* stretch out

strecken·weise *Adv.* in places; (fig.: zeitweise) at times

Streich *der;* **~[e]s, ~e** trick; prank; **jmdm. einen ~ spielen** play a trick on sb.

streicheln *tr. V.* stroke

streichen 1 *unr. tr. V.* **(a)** stroke
(b) (anstreichen) paint; **„frisch gestrichen"** 'wet paint'
(c) (auftragen) spread ‹*butter, jam, ointment, etc.*›; (bestreichen) **ein Brötchen mit Butter/mit Honig ~:** butter a roll/spread honey on a roll
(d) (tilgen) delete; cancel ‹*train, flight*›
2 *unr. itr. V.* **(a)** stroke; **jmdm. über den Kopf ~:** stroke sb.'s head
(b) (anstreichen) paint

Streicher *der;* **~s, ~, Streicherin** *die;* **~, ~nen** (Musik) string player; **die Streicher:** the strings

Streich-: ~holz *das* match; **~instrument** *das* string[ed] instrument; **~käse** *der* cheese spread; **~wurst** *die* [soft] sausage for spreading; ≈ meat spread

Streife *die;* **~, ~n (a)** (Personen) patrol
(b) (Streifengang) patrol

streifen 1 *tr. V.* **(a)** (leicht berühren) touch; ‹*shot*› graze
(b) (kurz behandeln) touch [up]on ‹*problem, subject, etc.*›
(c) den Ring vom Finger ~: slip the ring off one's finger; **die Ärmel nach oben ~:** pull/push up one's sleeves
2 *itr. V. mit sein* roam

Streifen *der;* **~s, ~ (a)** stripe
(b) (Stück, Abschnitt) strip

Streifen·wagen *der* patrol car

streifig *Adj.* streaky

Streif·licht *das* streak of light; **ein ~licht auf etw.** (*Akk.*) **werfen** (fig.) highlight sth.

Streik *der;* **~[e]s, ~s** strike; **in den ~ treten** come out *or* go on strike

Streik·brecher *der,* **Streik·brecherin** *die;* **~, ~nen** strikebreaker; blackleg (derog.)

streiken *itr. V.* **(a)** strike; be on strike; (in den Streik treten) come out *or* go on strike; strike
(b) (ugs.: nicht mitmachen) go on strike
(c) (ugs.: nicht funktionieren) pack up (coll.)

Streikende *der/die; adj. Dekl.* striker

Streik·posten *der* picket

Streit *der;* **~[e]s, ~e** (Zank) quarrel; (Auseinandersetzung) dispute; argument ⇢

streiten *unr. itr., refl. V.* quarrel; argue; (sich zanken) quarrel

Streiterei *die; ~, ~en* arguing *no pl., no indef. art.;* (Gezänk) quarrelling *no pl.*

Streitigkeit *die; ~, ~en meist Pl.*
(a) quarrel; argument
(b) (Streitfall) dispute

Streit·kräfte *Pl.* armed forces

streng ☐1 *Adj.* (a) strict; severe ⟨*punishment*⟩; stringent, strict ⟨*rule, regulation, etc.*⟩; stringent ⟨*measure*⟩; rigorous ⟨*examination, check, test, etc.*⟩; stern ⟨*reprimand, look*⟩; absolute ⟨*discretion*⟩; complete ⟨*rest*⟩
(b) (schmucklos, herb) austere, severe ⟨*cut, collar, style, etc.*⟩; severe ⟨*face, features, hairstyle, etc.*⟩
(c) (durchdringend) pungent, sharp ⟨*taste, smell*⟩
(d) (rau) severe ⟨*winter*⟩; sharp, severe ⟨*frost*⟩
☐2 *adv.* ⟨*mark, judge, etc.*⟩ strictly, severely; ⟨*punish*⟩ severely; ⟨*look, reprimand*⟩ sternly; ⟨*smell*⟩ strongly

Strenge *die; ~* (a) ▶ STRENG A: strictness; severity; stringency; rigour; sternness
(b) (von [Gesichts]zügen) severity
(c) (von Geruch, Geschmack) pungency; sharpness
(d) ▶ STRENG D: severity; sharpness

strengstens *Adv.* [most] strictly

Stress, *Streß *der;* Stresses stress

stressen (ugs.) ☐1 *tr. V.* **jmdn. ~:** put sb. under stress; **vollkommen gestresst sein** be under an enormous amount of stress; **die gestressten Großstädter** the stressed city-dwellers
☐2 *itr. V.* be stressful

Streu *die; ~, ~en* straw

Streubombe *die* cluster bomb

streuen *tr. V.* (a) spread ⟨*manure, sand, grit*⟩; sprinkle ⟨*salt, herbs, etc.*⟩; strew, scatter ⟨*flowers*⟩
(b) *auch itr.* **die Straßen [mit Sand/Salz] ~:** grit/salt the roads

streunen *itr. V.; meist mit sein* wander or roam about or around; **~de Katzen/Hunde** stray cats/dogs

Streusel·kuchen *der* streusel cake

strich *1. u. 3. Pers. Sg. Prät. v.* STREICHEN

Strich *der; ~[e]s, ~e* (Linie) line; (Gedankenstrich) dash; (Schrägstrich) diagonal; (Binde-, Trennungsstrich) hyphen; **auf den ~ gehen** (salopp) walk the streets

stricheln *tr. V.* (a) sketch in [with short lines]
(b) (schraffieren) hatch

Strich-: **~junge** *der* (salopp) [young] male prostitute; **~mädchen** *das* (salopp) streetwalker; hooker (Amer. sl.); **~punkt** *der* semicolon

Strick *der; ~[e]s, ~e* cord; (Seil) rope;

jmdm. aus etw. einen **~ drehen** (fig.) use sth. against sb.

stricken *tr., itr. V.* knit

Strick-: **~jacke** *die* cardigan; **~nadel** *die* knitting needle; **~zeug** *das* knitting

striegeln *tr. V.* groom ⟨*horse*⟩

strikt ☐1 *Adj.* strict
☐2 *adv.* strictly

Strip *der; ~s, ~s* strip[tease]

Strippe *die; ~, ~n* (ugs.) string; **an der ~ hängen** (fig.) be on the phone (coll.); (dauernd) hog the phone (coll.)

Stripper *der; ~s, ~,* **Stripperin** *die; ~, ~nen* (ugs.) stripper

Striptease /'ʃtrɪptiːs/ *der od. das; ~:* striptease

stritt *1. u. 3. Pers. Sg. Prät. v.* STREITEN

strittig *Adj.* contentious ⟨*point, problem*⟩; disputed ⟨*territory*⟩; ⟨*question*⟩ in dispute, at issue

Stroh *das; ~[e]s* straw

Stroh-: **~blume** *die* (a) (Immortelle) immortelle; (b) (Korbblütler) strawflower; **~halm** *der* straw; **~witwe** *die* (ugs. scherzh.) grass widow; **~witwer** *der* (ugs. scherzh.) grass widower

Strolch *der; ~[e]s, ~e* (fam. scherzh.: Junge) rascal

Strom *der; ~[e]s, Ströme* river; (fig.) stream; (Strömung; Elektrizität) current; (~versorgung) electricity; **unter ~ stehen** be live

strom-: **~abwärts** *Adv.* downstream; **~auf[wärts]** *Adv.* upstream

strömen *itr. V.; mit sein* stream

Strömung *die; ~, ~en* current; (Met.) airstream; (fig.) trend

Strophe *die; ~, ~n* verse; (einer Ode) strophe

strotzen *itr. V.* **von** *od.* **vor etw.** (*Dat.*) **~:** be full of sth.; **von** *od.* **vor Gesundheit ~:** be bursting with health

strubbelig *Adj.* tousled

Strudel *der; ~s, ~* (a) whirlpool
(b) (bes. südd., österr.: Gebäck) strudel

Struktur *die; ~, ~en* structure

strukturieren *tr. V.* structure; **neu ~:** restructure

Strumpf *der; ~[e]s, Strümpfe* stocking; (Socke, Knie~) sock

Strumpf-: **~band** *das* garter; (Straps) suspender (Brit.); garter (Amer.); **~hose** *die* tights *pl.* (Brit.); pantyhose (esp. Amer.)

Strunk *der; ~[e]s, Strünke* stem; stalk; (Baumstrunk) stump

struppig *Adj.* shaggy; tangled, tousled ⟨*hair*⟩

Stube *die; ~, ~n* (a) (veralt.: Wohnraum) [living] room; parlour (dated)
(b) (Milit.) [barrack] room

Stuben·fliege *die* [common] housefly

Stück *das;* ~**[e]s,** ~**e (a)** piece; (kleines) bit; (Teil, Abschnitt) part; **ein** ~ **Kuchen** a piece *or* slice of cake; **ein** ~ **Zucker/Seife** a lump of sugar/a piece *or* bar of soap; **im** *od.* **am** ~: unsliced ⟨*sausage, cheese, etc.*⟩
(b) (Einzelstück) item; (Exemplar) specimen; **ich nehme 5** ~: I'll take five [of them]; **30 Cent das** ~: thirty cents each; ~ **für** ~: piece by piece; (eins nach dem andern) one by one; **das ist [ja] ein starkes** ~ (ugs.) that's a bit much; **ein faules/freches** ~ (salopp) a lazy/cheeky thing *or* devil
(c) (Bühnenstück) play; (Musikstück) piece
Stückchen *das;* ~**s,** ~: [little] piece; bit
stückeln *tr. V.* put together ⟨*sleeve, curtain*⟩ with patches
Student *der;* ~**en,** ~**en (a)** student
(b) (österr.: Schüler) [secondary-school] pupil
Studenten·wohnheim *das* student hostel; hall of residence
Studentin *die;* ~**,** ~**nen** ▶ STUDENT
Studie /ˈʃtuːdiə/ *die;* ~**,** ~**n** study
Studien-: ~**aufenthalt** *der* study visit (**in** + *Dat.* to); ~**dauer** *die* length of study; **eine neunsemestrige** ~**dauer** nine semesters of study; ~**freund** *der,* ~**freundin** *die* university/college friend; ~**gebühr** *die* tuition fee; ~**platz** *der* university/college place; ~**reise** *die* study trip
studieren *tr., itr. V.* study
Studierende *der/die; adj. Dekl.* student
Studio *das;* ~**s,** ~**s** studio
Studium *das;* ~**s, Studien** study; (Studiengang) course of study
Stufe *die;* ~**,** ~**n (a)** step; (einer Treppe) stair; „**Vorsicht,** ~!" 'mind the step'
(b) (Raketenstufe, Geol., fig.: Stadium) stage; (Niveau) level; (Grad) degree; (Rang) grade
Stuhl *der;* ~**[e]s, Stühle** chair
Stuhl-: ~**gang** *der* bowel movement[s]; (Kot) stool; ~**lehne** *die* (Rückenlehne) chair back; (Armlehne) chair arm
stülpen *tr. V.* etw. auf *od.* über etw. (*Akk.*) ~: pull/put sth. on to *or* over sth.
stumm *Adj.* dumb ⟨*person*⟩; (schweigsam) silent; (wortlos) wordless; mute ⟨*glance, gesture*⟩
Stumme *der/die; adj. Dekl.* mute; **die** ~**n** the dumb
Stummel *der;* ~**s,** ~: stump; (Bleistiftstummel) stub; (Zigaretten-/Zigarrenstummel) [cigarette/cigar] butt
Stumm·film *der* silent film
Stümper *der;* ~**s,** ~: botcher; bungler
stümperhaft [1] *Adj.* incompetent; botched ⟨*job*⟩; (laienhaft) amateurish ⟨*attempt, drawing*⟩
[2] *adv.* incompetently; (laienhaft) amateurishly
Stümperin *die;* ~**,** ~**nen** botcher; bungler
stümpern *itr. V.* work incompetently; (pfuschen) bungle

stumpf *Adj.* **(a)** blunt ⟨*pin, needle, knife, etc.*⟩
(b) (glanzlos, matt) dull ⟨*paint, hair, metal, colour, etc.*⟩
Stumpf *der;* ~**[e]s, Stümpfe** stump
Stumpf·sinn *der* **(a)** apathy
(b) (Monotonie) monotony; tedium
stumpf·sinnig [1] *Adj.* **(a)** apathetic; vacant ⟨*look*⟩
(b) (monoton) tedious; soul-destroying ⟨*job, work*⟩
[2] *adv.* **(a)** apathetically; ⟨*stare*⟩ vacantly
(b) (monoton) tediously
stünde *1. u. 3. Pers. Sg. Konjunktiv II v.* STEHEN
Stunde *die;* ~**,** ~**n** hour; (Unterrichts~) lesson; **eine** ~ **Aufenthalt/Pause** an hour's stop/break; **a stop/break of an hour**
stunden *tr. V.* jmdm. einen Betrag *usw.* ~: allow sb. to defer payment of a sum *etc.*
stunden-, Stunden-: ~**kilometer** *der* kilometre per hour; k.p.h.; ~**lang** [1] *Adj.* lasting hours *postpos.;* [2] *adv.* for hours; ~**lohn** *der* hourly wage; ~**plan** *der* timetable; ~**zeiger** *der* hour hand
-stündig *adj.* -hour
stündlich *Adj., adv.* hourly
-stündlich *adj.* -hourly; **zwei**~**/ halb**~: two-hourly/half-hourly; *adv.* every two hours/half an hour
Stundung *die;* ~**,** ~**en** deferment of payment
Stups *der;* ~**es,** ~**e** (ugs.) push; shove; (leicht) nudge
stupsen *tr. V.* (ugs.) push; shove; (leicht) nudge
Stups·nase *die* snub nose
stur (ugs.) [1] *Adj.* **(a)** obstinate; dogged ⟨*insistence*⟩; (phlegmatisch) dour
(b) (unbeirrbar) dogged; persistent
(c) (stumpfsinnig) tedious
[2] *adv.* **(a)** obstinately
(b) (unbeirrbar) doggedly
(c) (stumpfsinnig) tediously; ⟨*learn, copy*⟩ mechanically
stürbe *1. u. 3. Pers. Sg. Konjunktiv II v.* STERBEN
Sturheit *die;* ~ (ugs.) **(a)** obstinacy; pigheadedness; (phlegmatisches Wesen) dourness
(b) (Stumpfsinnigkeit) deadly monotony
Sturm *der;* ~**[e]s, Stürme (a)** storm; (heftiger Wind) gale
(b) (Milit.) assault (**auf** + *Akk.* on); ~ **klingeln** ring the [door]bell like mad
stürmen [1] *itr. V.* **(a)** unpers. es stürmt [heftig] it's blowing a gale
(b) mit sein (rennen) rush; (verärgert) storm
[2] *tr. V.* (Milit.) storm ⟨*town, position, etc.*⟩; (fig.) besiege ⟨*booking office, shop, etc.*⟩
Stürmer *der;* ~**s,** ~ (Sport) striker; forward
stürmisch [1] *Adj.* **(a)** stormy; (fig.) tempestuous, turbulent   ⋯⟩

(b) (ungestüm) tumultuous ⟨applause, welcome, reception⟩; wild ⟨enthusiasm⟩; passionate ⟨lover, embrace, temperament⟩; vehement ⟨protest⟩

2 adv. ⟨protest⟩ vehemently; ⟨embrace⟩ impetuously, passionately; ⟨demand⟩ clamorously; ⟨applaud⟩ wildly

Sturz der; -es, Stürze **(a)** fall; (Unfall) accident

(b) (fig.: von Preis, Temperatur usw.) [sharp] fall, drop (Gen. in)

(c) (Verlust des Amtes, der Macht) fall; (Absetzung) overthrow; (Amtsenthebung) removal from office

Sturz·bach der [mountain] torrent; (fig.: von Fragen usw.) torrent

sturz·besoffen Adj (ugs.) paralytic [drunk] (coll.)

stürzen 1 itr. V.; mit sein **(a)** fall; (fig.) ⟨temperature, exchange rate, etc.⟩ drop [sharply]; ⟨prices⟩ tumble; ⟨government⟩ fall, collapse

(b) (laufen) rush; dash

(c) (fließen) stream; pour

2 refl. V. sich auf jmdn./etw. ~ (auch fig.) pounce on sb./sth.; sich in etw. (Akk.) ~: throw oneself into sth.

3 tr. V. **(a)** throw; (mit Wucht) hurl

(b) (umdrehen) upturn ⟨mould⟩; turn out ⟨pudding, cake, etc.⟩

(c) (des Amtes entheben) oust ⟨person⟩ [from office]; (gewaltsam) overthrow ⟨leader, government⟩

Sturz-: ~flug der (Flugw.) [nose]dive; im ~flug in a [nose]dive; ~helm der crash helmet

Stuss, *Stuß der; Stusses (ugs. abwertend) rubbish; twaddle (coll.)

Stute die; ~, ~n mare

Stütze die; ~, ~n (auch fig.) support

stutzen¹ itr. V. stop short

stutzen² tr. V. trim; dock ⟨tail⟩; clip ⟨ear, hedge, wing⟩; prune ⟨tree, bush⟩

stützen 1 tr. V. support; (mit Pfosten o. Ä.) prop up; (aufstützen) rest ⟨head, hands, arms, etc.⟩

2 refl. V. sich auf jmdn./etw. ~: lean or support oneself on sb./sth

stutzig Adj. ~ werden begin to wonder; jmdn. ~ machen make sb. wonder

Styropor ⓦ das; ~s polystyrene [foam]

s. u. Abk. = **siehe unten** see below

Subjekt das; ~[e]s, ~e **(a)** subject

(b) (abwertend: Mensch) creature

subjektiv 1 Adj. subjective

2 adv. subjectively

Subjektivität die; ~: subjectivity

***substantiell** ▶ SUBSTANZIELL

Substantiv das; ~s, ~e (Sprachw.) noun

Substanz die; ~, ~en **(a)** (auch fig.) substance

(b) (Grundbestand) die ~: the reserves pl.

substanziell 1 Adj. substantial

2 adv. substantially

subtil 1 Adj. subtle

2 adv. subtly

Subtilität die; ~, ~en subtlety

sub·tropisch Adj. subtropical

Subvention die; ~, ~en (Wirtsch.) subsidy

Suche die; ~, ~n search (nach for); auf der ~ [nach jmdm./etw.] sein be looking/ (intensiver) searching [for sb./sth.]

suchen 1 tr. V. **(a)** look for; (intensiver) search for; „Leerzimmer gesucht" 'unfurnished room wanted'

(b) (bedacht sein auf, sich wünschen) seek ⟨protection, advice, company, warmth, etc.⟩; look for ⟨adventure⟩

2 itr. V. search; nach jmdm./etw. ~: look/ search for sb./sth

Sucherei die; ~, ~en (ugs., oft abwertend) [endless] searching no pl.

Such·maschine die (DV) search engine

Sucht die; ~, Süchte od. ~en **(a)** addiction (nach to); [bei jmdm.] zur ~ werden (auch fig.) become addictive [in sb.'s case]

(b) Pl. Süchte (übermäßiges Verlangen) craving (nach for)

süchtig Adj. **(a)** addicted

(b) (fig.) nach etw. ~ sein be obsessed with sth.

Sucht·kranke die/der addict

Süd (bes. Seemannsspr., Met.) ▶ SÜDEN

Süd-: ~afrika (das) South Africa; ~amerika (das) South America

Sudan (das); ~s od. der; ~s Sudan

Süden der; ~s south; der ~: the South;

Süd·frucht die tropical [or sub-tropical] fruit

Südländer der; ~s, ~, **Südländerin** die; ~, ~nen Southern European

südländisch Adj. Southern [European]; Latin ⟨temperament⟩; ~ aussehen have Latin looks

südlich 1 Adj. **(a)** southern

(b) (nach, von Süden) southerly

(c) (aus dem Süden) Southern

2 adv. southwards

3 Präp. mit Gen. [to the] south of

süd-, Süd-: ~licht das southern lights pl.; (einzelne Erscheinung) display of the southern lights; ~pol der South Pole; ~see die; ~~: die ~see: the South Seas pl.; ~see-insel die South Sea island; ~tirol (das) South Tyrol; ~wärts Adv. southwards; ~wind der south or southerly wind

Sues·kanal der; ~s Suez Canal

Sühne die; ~, ~n (geh.) atonement; expiation

sühnen tr., itr. V. [für] etw. ~: atone for or pay the penalty for sth.

Sultanine die; ~, ~n sultana

---

*alte Schreibung – vgl. Hinweis auf S. x

Sülze ⋯⋮⋗ Szenenwechsel ⋯⋯

Sülze *die;* ~, ~n **(a)** diced meat/fish in aspic; (vom Schweinskopf) brawn **(b)** (Aspik) aspic

sülzen *tr., itr. V.* (salopp) ▶ QUATSCHEN 1 A, 2

Summe *die;* ~, ~n sum

summen 1 *itr. V.* hum; (lauter, heller) buzz 2 *tr. V.* hum ⟨*tune, song, etc.*⟩

summieren *refl. V.* add up (**auf** + *Akk.* to)

Sumpf *der;* ~[e]s, Sümpfe marsh; (bes. in den Tropen) swamp

sumpfig *Adj.* marshy

Sund *der;* ~[e]s, ~e (Geogr.) sound

Sünde *die;* ~, ~n sin; (fig.) misdeed; transgression

Sünden·bock *der* (ugs.) scapegoat

Sünder *der;* ~s, ~, **Sünderin** *die;* ~, ~nen sinner

sündigen *itr. V.* sin

Super *das;* ~s, ~: four star (Brit.); premium (Amer.)

super- ultra-⟨*long, high, fast, modern, masculine, etc.*⟩

Super- super⟨*hero, car, group, etc.*⟩; terrific (coll.), tremendous (coll.) ⟨*success, offer, chance, idea, etc.*⟩

Super·benzin *das* four-star petrol (Brit.); premium (Amer.)

Superlativ *der;* ~s, ~e (Sprachw.) superlative

Super-: ~**macht** *die* super power; ~**markt** *der* supermarket

Suppe *die;* ~; ~n soup

Suppen·löffel *der* soup spoon

Surf·brett /'sə:f-/ *das* surfboard

surfen /'sə:fn̩/ *itr. V.* surf

Surfer /'sə:fe/ *der;* ~s, ~, **Surferin** *die;* ~, ~nen surfer

surren *itr. V.* **(a)** (summen) hum; ⟨*camera, fan*⟩ whirr **(b)** *mit sein* (schwirren) whirr

suspekt 1 *Adj.* suspicious; **jmdm.** ~ **sein** arouse sb.'s suspicions 2 *adv.* suspiciously

süß 1 *Adj.* sweet 2 *adv.* sweetly

süßen *tr. V.* sweeten

Süßigkeit *die;* ~, ~en sweet (Brit.); candy (Amer.); ~**en** sweets (Brit.); candy *sing.* (Amer.); (als Ware) confectionery *sing.*

süßlich 1 *Adj.* **(a)** [slightly] sweet; on the sweet side *pred.* **(b)** (sentimental) mawkish 2 *adv.* ⟨*write, paint*⟩ mawkishly

süß-, Süß-: ~**most** *der* unfermented fruit juice; ~**-sauer** 1 *Adj.* sweet-and-sour; (fig.) wry ⟨*smile, face*⟩; 2 *adv.* **(a)** etw. ~**-sauer zubereiten** give sth. a sweet-and-sour flavour; **(b)** (fig.) ⟨*smile*⟩ wryly; ~**speise** *die* sweet; dessert; ~**stoff** *der* sweetener; ~**wasser** *das* fresh water

Symbol *das;* ~s, ~e symbol

symbolisch 1 *Adj.* symbolic 2 *adv.* symbolically

Sympathie *die;* ~, ~n sympathy (**für** with)

sympathisch 1 *Adj.* congenial, likeable ⟨*person, manner*⟩; appealing ⟨*voice, appearance, material*⟩ 2 *adv.* in an appealing way; (angenehm) agreeably

Symphonie *usw.* ▶ SINFONIE *usw.*

Symptom *das;* ~s, ~e (Med., geh.) symptom (*Gen.*, **für**, **von** of)

symptomatisch (Med., geh.) *Adj.* symptomatic (**für** of)

Synagoge *die;* ~, ~n synagogue

synchron 1 *Adj.* **(a)** synchronous **(b)** (Sprachw.) synchronic 2 *adv.* **(a)** synchronously **(b)** (Sprachw.) synchronically

Synchronisation *die;* ~, ~en ▶ SYNCHRONISIERUNG

synchronisieren *tr. V.* **(a)** (Film) dub ⟨*film*⟩ **(b)** (Technik, fig.) synchronize ⟨*watches, operations, etc.*⟩; **synchronisiertes Getriebe** synchromesh [gearbox]

Synchronisierung *die;* ~, ~en **(a)** (Film) dubbing **(b)** (Technik, fig.) synchronization

Synthese *die;* ~, ~n synthesis (*Gen.*, **von**, **aus** of)

Synthesizer /'sɪntəsaɪze/ *der;* ~s, ~ (Musik) synthesizer

synthetisch 1 *Adj.* synthetic 2 *adv.* synthetically

Syrer *der;* ~s, ~, **Syrerin** *die;* ~, ~nen Syrian

Syrien /'zy:riən/ *(das);* ~s Syria

syrisch *Adj.* Syrian

System *das;* ~s, ~e system

systematisch 1 *Adj.* systematic 2 *adv.* systematically

System·fehler *der* fault in the system

Szenario *das;* ~s, ~s scenario

Szene /'stse:nə/ *die;* ~, ~n (auch fig.) scene

Szenen·wechsel *der* (Theater) scene change

S

Tt

t, T /te:/*das;* ~, ~: t/T
t *Abk.* = **Tonne** t
Tab. *Abk.* = **Tabelle**
Tabak *der;* ~s, ~e tobacco
Tabaks·pfeife *die* [tobacco] pipe
tabellarisch *Adj.* tabular; **ein** ~**er Lebenslauf** a curriculum vitae in tabular form
Tabelle *die;* ~, ~n table
Tabellen·kalkulation *die* (DV) performing calculations using a spreadsheet; (Program) spreadsheet program
Tabernakel *das od. der;* ~s, ~: tabernacle
Tablett *das;* ~[e]s, ~s *od.* ~e tray
Tablette *die;* ~, ~n tablet
tabletten·süchtig *Adj.* addicted to pills *postpos.*
tabu *Adj.* taboo
Tabu *das;* ~s, ~s taboo
tabuisieren *tr. V.* etw. ~: taboo sth.; make sth. taboo
Ta·cheles [mit jmdm.] ~ reden (ugs.) do some straight talking [to sb.]
Tacho *der;* ~s, ~s (ugs.) speedo (coll.)
Tacho-: ~**meter** *der od. das* speedometer; ~**stand** *der* (ugs.: Kilometerstand) mileometer *or* odometer reading
Tadel *der;* ~s, ~ (a) censure (b) (im Klassenbuch) black mark
tadel·los ① *Adj.* impeccable; immaculate ⟨hair, clothing, suit, etc.⟩; perfect ⟨condition, teeth, pronunciation, German, etc.⟩ ② *adv.* ⟨dress⟩ impeccably; ⟨fit, speak, etc.⟩ perfectly; ⟨live, behave, etc.⟩ irreproachably
tadeln *tr. V.* jmdn. [für *od.* wegen etw.] ~: rebuke sb. [for sth.]
Tafel *die;* ~, ~n (a) (Schiefertafel) slate; (Wandtafel) blackboard (b) (plattenförmiges Stück) slab; **eine** ~ **Schokolade** a bar of chocolate (c) (Gedenktafel) plaque (d) (geh.: festlicher Tisch) table
Täfelchen *das;* ~s, ~: ▶ TAFEL B: [small] slab; [small] bar
tafeln *itr. V.* (geh.) feast
täfeln *tr. V.* panel
Tafel-: ~**spitz** *der* (österr.) boiled fillet of beef; ~**wasser** *das* [bottled] mineral water; ~**wein** *der* table wine
taff *Adj.* (ugs.) tough
Taft *der;* ~[e]s, ~e taffeta

Tag *der;* ~[e]s, ~e day; **am** ~[e] during the day[time]; **guten** ~! hello; (bei Vorstellung) how do you do?; **an diesem** ~: on this day; **dreimal am** ~: three times a day; **am folgenden** ~: the next day; **eines** ~**es** one day; some day
tag·aus *Adv.* ~, **tagein** day in, day out; day after day
Tage·buch *das* diary
tag·ein *Adv.* ▶ TAGAUS
tage·lang ① *Adj.* lasting for days *postpos.;* **nach** ~**em Regen** after days of rain ② *adv.* for days [on end]
tagen *itr. V.* meet; **das Gericht/Parlament tagt** the court/parliament is in session
tages-, Tages-: ~**aktuell** *Adj.* **die** ~**aktuellen Nachrichten** the [current] news of the day; **die** ~**aktuellen Kurse** the rates of exchange current on the day; ~**anbruch** *der* daybreak; dawn; ~**ausflug** *der* day's outing; ~**geld·konto** *das* (Bankw.) no-notice account; ~**karte** *die* (a) (Gastron.) menu of the day; (b) (Fahr-, Eintrittskarte) day ticket; ~**kasse** *die* (a) box office (open during the day); (b) (Tageseinnahme) day's takings *pl.;* ~**licht** *das* daylight; ~**licht·projektor** *der* overhead projector; ~**zeit** *die* time of day; ~**zeitung** *die* daily newspaper; daily
-tägig (a) (… Tage alt) **ein sechstägiges Küken** a six-day-old chick (b) (… Tage dauernd) **nach dreitägiger Vorbereitung** after three days' preparation
täglich ① *Adj.* daily ② *adv.* every day; **zweimal** ~: twice a day; ~ **drei Tabletten einnehmen** take three tablets daily
tags *Adv.* (a) by day; in the daytime (b) ~ **zuvor/davor** the day before; ~ **darauf** the next *or* following day; the day after
tags·über *Adv.* during the day
tag·täglich (intensivierend) ① *Adj.* day-to-day; daily ② *adv.* every single day
Tagung *die;* ~, ~en conference
Taifun *der;* ~s, ~e typhoon
Taille /'taljə/ *die;* ~, ~n waist
Taiwan *(das)* ~s Taiwan
Takt *der;* ~[e]s, ~e (a) (Musik) time; (Einheit) bar; measure (Amer.); **aus dem** ~ **kommen** lose the beat (b) (rhythmischer Bewegungsablauf) rhythm (c) (Feingefühl) tact
Takt·gefühl *das* sense of tact
taktieren *itr. V.* proceed tactically; **vorsichtig/klug** ~: use caution/clever tactics

Taktik *die;* ∼, ∼en: [eine] ∼: tactics *pl.*

taktisch ① *Adj.* tactical
② *adv.* tactically

taktlos ① *Adj.* tactless
② *adv.* tactlessly

Taktlosigkeit *die;* ∼, ∼en (a) (taktlose Art) tactlessness
(b) (taktlose Handlung) piece of tactlessness

Takt·verkehr *der* regular service; **im** ∼ **at** regular intervals

taktvoll ① *Adj.* tactful
② *adv.* tactfully

Tal *das;* ∼[e]s, **Täler** valley

Talent *das;* ∼[e]s, ∼e talent (**zu, für** for); (Mensch) talented person

talentiert *Adj.* talented

Talg *der;* ∼[e]s, ∼e suet; (zur Herstellung von Seife, Kerzen usw.) tallow

Talisman *der;* ∼s, ∼e talisman

Tampon *der;* ∼s, ∼s tampon

Tamtam *das;* ∼s (ugs. abwertend) **[großes]** ∼: [a big] fuss

Tang *der;* ∼[e]s, ∼e seaweed

Tangente *die;* ∼, ∼n (Math.) tangent

Tank *der;* ∼s, ∼s tank

tanken *tr., itr. V.* fill up; **Öl** ∼: fill up with oil

Tanker *der;* ∼s, ∼: tanker

Tank-: ∼**säule** *die* petrol pump (Brit.); gasoline pump (Amer.); ∼**stelle** *die* petrol station (Brit.); gas station (Amer.); ∼**wagen** *der* tanker; ∼**wart** *der;* ∼∼s, ∼∼e, ∼**wartin** *die;* ∼∼, ∼∼nen petrol pump attendant (Brit.); gas station attendant (Amer.)

Tanne *die;* ∼, ∼n fir [tree]

Tannen-: ∼**baum** *der* (ugs.) fir tree; (Weihnachtsbaum) Christmas tree; ∼**grün** *das* fir sprigs *pl.;* ∼**zapfen** *der* fir cone; ∼**zweig** *der* fir branch

Tansania *(das);* ∼s Tanzania

Tante *die;* ∼, ∼n (a) aunt
(b) (Kinderspr.: Frau) lady
(c) (ugs.: Frau) woman

Tanz *der;* ∼es, **Tänze** dance

Tanz-: ∼**abend** *der* evening dance; ∼**bar** *die* night spot (coll.) with dancing; ∼**café** *das* coffee house with dancing

tanzen *itr., tr. V.* dance

Tänzer *der;* ∼s, ∼, **Tänzerin** *die;* ∼, ∼nen dancer; (Balletttänzer[in]) ballet dancer

Tanz-: ∼**fläche** *die* dance floor; ∼**lokal** *das* café/restaurant with dancing; ∼**orchester** *das* dance band; ∼**stunde** *die* (a) (∼kurs) dancing class; (b) (einzelne Stunde) dancing lesson

Tapete *die;* ∼, ∼n wallpaper

Tapeten·wechsel *der* (ugs.) change of scene

tapezieren *tr. V.* [wall]paper

tapfer ① *Adj.* brave
② *adv.* bravely

Tapferkeit *die;* ∼: courage; bravery

tappen *itr. V.* (a) *mit sein* patter
(b) (tastend greifen) grope (**nach** for)

Taps *der;* ∼es, ∼e (ugs. abwertend) clumsy oaf

Tarif *der;* ∼s, ∼e charge; (Post-, Wassertarif) rate; (Verkehrstarif) fares *pl.;* (Zolltarif) tariff; (Lohntarif) [wage] rate; (Gehaltstarif) [salary] scale

tarnen ① *tr., itr. V.* camouflage
② *refl. V.* camouflage oneself

Tasche *die;* ∼, ∼n bag; (in Kleidung, Rucksack usw.) pocket; **jmdm. auf der** ∼ **liegen** (fig. ugs.) live off sb.

Taschen-: ∼**buch** *das* paperback; ∼**dieb** *der,* ∼**diebin** *die* pickpocket; ∼**geld** *das* pocket money; ∼**lampe** *die* [pocket] torch (Brit.) *or* (Amer.) flashlight; ∼**messer** *das* penknife; ∼**rechner** *der* pocket calculator; ∼**tuch** *das; Pl.* ∼**tücher** handkerchief; ∼**uhr** *die* pocket watch

Tasse *die;* ∼, ∼n cup

Tastatur *die;* ∼, ∼en keyboard

Taste *die;* ∼, ∼n (a) (eines Musikinstruments, einer Schreibmaschine) key
(b) (Pedal) pedal [key]
(c) (am Telefon, Radio, Fernsehgerät, Taschenrechner usw.) button

tasten ① *itr. V.* (fühlend suchen) grope, feel (**nach** for)
② *refl. V.* (sich tastend bewegen) grope *or* feel one's way

Tasten-: ∼**feld** *das* (Elektrot.) keypad; ∼**telefon** *das* push-button telephone

tat 1. u. 3. Pers. Sg. Prät. v. TUN

Tat *die;* ∼, ∼en act; (das Tun) action; **eine gute** ∼: a good deed; **in der** ∼ (verstärkend) actually; (zustimmend) indeed

Tatar *das;* ∼[s] steak tartare

Tat·bestand *der* (a) facts *pl.* [of the matter *or* case]
(b) (Rechtsw.) elements *pl.* of an offence

Täter *der;* ∼s, ∼, **Täterin** *die;* ∼, ∼nen culprit

tätig *Adj.* (a) ∼ **sein** work
(b) (rührig, aktiv) active

tätigen *tr. V.* (Kaufmannsspr., Papierdt.) transact ‹*business, deal, etc.*›

Tätigkeit *die;* ∼, ∼en activity; (Arbeit) job

tat-, Tat-: ∼**kraft** *die* energy; drive; ∼**kräftig** ① *Adj.* energetic ‹*person*›; ② *adv.* energetically

tätlich ① *Adj.* physical ‹*clash, attack, resistance, etc.*›; **gegen jmdn.** ∼ **werden** become violent towards sb.
② *adv.* physically; **jmdn.** ∼ **angreifen** attack sb. physically; assault sb.

Tat·ort *der* scene of a/the crime

tätowieren *tr. V.* tattoo

Tätowierung *die;* ∼, ∼en tattoo

Tat·sache *die* fact

tatsächlich ① *Adj.* actual; real ···⊱

2 *adv.* actually; really

tätscheln *tr. V.* pat

Tattoo /tɛˈtuː/ *das;* ~s, ~s tattoo

tat·verdächtig *Adj.* suspected

Tat·waffe *die* weapon [used in the crime]

Tatze *die;* ~, ~n paw

Tat·zeit *die* time of the crime

Tau[1] *der;* ~[e]s dew

Tau[2] *das;* ~[e]s, ~e (Seil) rope

taub *Adj.* **(a)** deaf
(b) (wie abgestorben) numb
(c) empty ⟨*nut*⟩

Taube[1] *die;* ~, ~n pigeon; (Turteltaube; auch Politik fig.) dove

Taube[2] *der/die; adj. Dekl.* deaf person; deaf man/woman; **die** ~n the deaf

Taubheit *die;* ~: deafness

taub·stumm *Adj.* deaf and dumb

Taub·stumme *der/die; adj. Dekl.* deaf mute

tauchen [1] *itr. V.* **(a)** *auch mit* **sein** dive (**nach** for)
(b) *mit* **sein** (eintauchen) dive; (auftauchen) rise; emerge
2 *tr. V.* **(a)** (eintauchen) dip
(b) (untertauchen) duck

Taucher *der;* ~s, ~: diver; (mit Flossen und Atemgerät) skin diver

Taucher-: ~**anzug** *der* diving suit; ~**brille** *die* diving goggles *pl.*

Taucherin *die;* ~, ~nen ▶ TAUCHER

Tauch·sieder *der;* ~s, ~: portable immersion heater

tauen [1] *itr. V.* **(a)** *unpers.* **es taut** it's thawing
(b) *mit* **sein** (schmelzen) melt
2 *tr. V.* melt; thaw

Taufe *die;* ~, ~n (christl. Rel.) **(a)** (Sakrament) baptism
(b) (Zeremonie) christening; baptism

taufen *tr. V.* **(a)** baptize
(b) (einen Namen geben) christen

taugen *itr. V.* **nichts/nicht viel/etwas** ~: be no/not much/some good *or* use

tauglich *Adj.* **[nicht]** ~: [un]suitable; (für Militärdienst) fit [for service]

Taumel *der;* ~s **(a)** [feeling of] dizziness
(b) (Rausch) frenzy; fever

taumelig *Adj.* dizzy; giddy

taumeln *itr. V.* **(a)** *auch mit* **sein** (wanken) reel, sway (**vor** + *Dat.* with)
(b) *mit* **sein** (taumelnd gehen) stagger

Tausch *der;* ~[e]s, ~e exchange; **ein guter/schlechter** ~: a good/bad deal

tauschen [1] *tr. V.* exchange (**gegen** for); **sie tauschten die Plätze** they changed places
2 *itr. V.* **mit jmdm.** ~ (fig.) change places with sb.

täuschen [1] *tr. V.* deceive; **wenn mich nicht alles täuscht** unless I'm completely mistaken
2 *itr. V.* be deceptive
3 *refl. V.* be wrong *or* mistaken (**in** + *Dat.* about)

täuschend [1] *Adj.* remarkable, striking ⟨*similarity, imitation*⟩
2 *adv.* remarkably

Täuschung *die;* ~, ~en deception; (Selbst~) delusion

tausend *Kardinalz.* **(a)** a *or* one thousand
(b) (ugs.: sehr viele) thousands of; ~ **Dank/ Küsse** a thousand thanks/kisses

Tausend *das;* ~s, ~e thousand

tausend·ein[s] *Kardinalz.* a *or* one thousand and one

Tausender *der;* ~s, ~ (ugs.) (Tausendmarkschein usw.) thousand-mark/-dollar *etc.* note; (Betrag) thousand marks/dollars *etc.*

tausenderlei *indekl. Adj.* (ugs.) a thousand and one different ⟨*answers, kinds, etc.*⟩

tausend·mal *Adv.* a thousand times

Tausend·mark·schein *der* thousand-mark note

tausendst... *Ordinalz.* thousandth; *s. auch* ACHT...

tausendstel *Bruchz.* thousandth

Tausendstel *das* (schweiz. meist der); ~s, ~: thousandth

Tau-: ~**wasser** *das* meltwater; ~**wetter** *das* thaw; ~**ziehen** *das;* ~~s (auch fig.) tug-of-war

Taxe *die;* ~, ~n **(a)** (Taxi) taxi
(b) (Gebühr) charge

Taxi *das;* ~s, ~s taxi

taxieren *tr. V.* estimate

Taxi-: ~**fahrer** *der,* ~**fahrerin** *die* taxi driver; ~**stand** *der* taxi rank (Brit.); taxi stand

Tb /teˈbeː/, **Tbc** /teːbeːˈtseː/ *die;* ~: *Abk.* = **Tuberkulose** TB

Team /tiːm/ *das;* ~s, ~s team

Team·arbeit *die* teamwork

Technik *die;* ~, ~en **(a)** technology; (Studienfach) engineering *no art.*
(b) (technische Ausrüstung) equipment
(c) (Arbeitsweise, Verfahren) technique

Techniker *der;* ~s, ~, **Technikerin** *die;* ~, ~nen technical expert

technisch [1] *Adj.* technical; technological ⟨*progress, age*⟩
2 *adv.* technically; technologically ⟨*advanced*⟩

Techno /ˈtɛkno/ *das od. der;* ~s techno

Technologie *die;* ~, ~n technology

technologisch [1] *Adj.* technological
2 *adv.* technologically

Techno·party *die* techno party

Tee *der;* ~s, ~s tea

TEE /teːeːˈʔeː/ *der;* ~[s], ~[s] *Abk.* = **Trans-Europ-Express** TEE

Tee-: ~**beutel** *der* tea bag; ~**kanne** *die* teapot; ~**löffel** *der* teaspoon

Teenie /'tiːni/ *der;* ~s, ~s (ugs.) young teenager

Tee-: ~**sieb** *das* tea strainer; ~**tasse** *die* teacup

Teich *der;* ~[e]s, ~e pond

Teig *der;* ~[e]s, ~e dough; (Kuchen-, Biskuitteig) pastry; (Pfannkuchen-, Waffelteig) batter

Teig·waren *Pl.* pasta *sing.*

Teil (a) *der;* ~[e]s, ~e part; **fünfter** ~: fifth
(b) *der od. das;* ~[e]s, ~e (Anteil; Beitrag) share
(c) *der;* ~[e]s, ~e (beteiligte Person[en]; Rechtsw.: Partei) party
(d) *das;* ~[e]s, ~e (Einzelteil) part

teil·bar *Adj.* divisible (**durch** by)

Teilbarkeit *die;* ~: divisibility

Teilchen *das;* ~s, ~ (a) (kleines Stück) [small] part
(b) (Partikel) particle

teilen [1] *tr. V.* (a) divide (**durch** by)
(b) (aufteilen) share (**unter** + *Dat.* among)
[2] *refl. V.* **sich** (*Dat.*) **etw.** [mit jmdm.] ~: share sth. [with sb.]

Teiler *der;* ~s, ~ (Math.) factor

teil|haben *unr. itr. V.* share (**an** + *Dat.* in)

Teilhaber *der;* ~s, ~, **Teilhaberin** *die;* ~, ~nen partner

Teil·kasko·versicherung *die: insurance giving limited cover*

Teilnahme *die;* ~, ~n (a) participation (**an** + *Dat.* in); ~ **an einem Kurs** attendance at a course
(b) (Interesse) interest (**an** + *Dat.* in)
(c) (geh.: Mitgefühl) sympathy

teilnahms·los *Adj.* indifferent

Teilnahmslosigkeit *die;* ~: indifference

teilnahms·voll [1] *Adj.* compassionate [2] *adv.* compassionately

teil|nehmen *unr. itr. V.* [an etw. (*Dat.*)] ~: take part [in sth.]; [an einem Lehrgang] ~: attend [a course]

Teilnehmer *der;* ~s, ~, **Teilnehmerin** *die;* ~, ~nen
(a) participant (*Gen.,* **an** + *Dat.* in); (bei Wettbewerb auch) competitor, contestant (**an** + *Dat.* in)
(b) (Fernspr.) subscriber

teils *Adv.* partly

Teilung *die;* ~, ~en division

teil·weise [1] *Adv.* partly [2] *adj.* partial

Teilzeit-: ~**arbeit** *die* part-time work *no indef. art.;* ~**beschäftigt** *Adj.* ⟨person⟩ in part-time work; ~**beschäftigt sein** work part-time; ~**beschäftigte** *der/die; adj. Dekl.* part-time employee; ~**job** *der* part-time job

Teint /tɛ̃ː/ *der;* ~s, ~s complexion

Tektonik /tɛk'toːnɪk/ *die;* ~ (Geol.) tectonics *sing., no art.*

tektonisch *Adj.* tectonic

Telefon /'teːlefoːn, *auch* teleˈfoːn/ *das;* ~s, ~e telephone; phone; **ans** ~ **gehen** answer the [tele]phone

Telefon-: ~**anruf** *der* [tele]phone call; ~**anschluss**, *⋆*~**anschluß** *der* telephone; line; ~**apparat** *der* telephone

Telefonat *das;* ~[e]s, ~e telephone call

Telefon-: ~**buch** *das* [tele]phone book *or* directory; ~**gespräch** *das* telephone conversation

telefonieren *itr. V.* make a [tele]phone call; **mit jmdm.** ~: talk to sb. [on the telephone]

telefonisch [1] *Adj.* telephone *attrib.* [2] *adv.* by telephone

Telefonist *der;* ~en, ~en, **Telefonistin** *die;* ~, ~nen telephonist; (in einer Firma) switchboard operator

Telefon-: ~**karte** *die* phonecard; ~**nummer** *die* [tele]phone number; ~**rechnung** *die* [tele]phone bill; ~**verzeichnis** *das* [tele]phone list; ~**zelle** *die* [tele]phone booth *or* (Brit.) box; call box (Brit.); ~**zentrale** *die* telephone exchange

Telegraf *der;* ~en, ~en telegraph

Telegrafie *die;* S : telegraphy *no art.*

telegrafieren *itr., tr. V.* telegraph

telegrafisch [1] *Adj.* telegraphic [2] *adv.* by telegraph *or* telegram

Telegramm *das* telegram

Tele·objektiv *das* (Fot.) telephoto lens

Tele·text *der* teletext *no art.*

Teller *der;* ~s, ~: plate

Tempel *der;* ~s, ~: temple

Temperament *das;* ~[e]s, ~e
(a) (Wesensart) temperament
(b) (Schwung) **eine Frau mit** ~: a woman with spirit; **das** ~ **geht oft mit mir durch** I often lose my temper

temperament·voll *Adj.* spirited ⟨person, speech, dance, etc.⟩

Temperatur *die;* ~, ~en temperature

Temperatur-: ~**anstieg** *der* rise in temperature; ~**rückgang** *der* drop *or* fall in temperature

Tempo *das;* ~s, ~s *od.* **Tempi** (a) *Pl.* ~s speed
(b) (Musik) tempo; time

Tempo·limit *das* (Verkehrsw.) speed limit

Tempus *das;* ~, **Tempora** (Sprachw.) tense

Tendenz *die;* ~, ~en trend

tendieren *itr. V.* tend (**zu** towards)

Teneriffa *(das);* ~s Tenerife

Tennis *das;* ~: tennis *no art.*

Tennis-: ~**ball** *der* tennis ball; ~**platz** *der* tennis court; ~**schläger** *der* tennis racket; ~**schuh** *der* tennis shoe; ⋯⟶

∼**schule** die tennis school; ∼**spieler**
der, ∼**spielerin** die tennis player
Tenor der; ∼s, Tenöre, (österr. auch:) ∼e
(Musik) tenor; (im Chor) tenors pl.; tenor
voices pl.
Teppich der; ∼s, ∼e carpet; (kleiner) rug
Teppich·boden der fitted carpet
Termin der; ∼s, ∼e date; (Anmeldung)
appointment; (Verabredung) engagement;
(Rechtsw.) hearing
Terminal /'tø:ɐ̯minəl/ das; ∼s, ∼s
terminal
Termin-: ∼**geschäft** das (Börsenw.)
forward transaction or operation;
∼**kalender** der appointments book
Terminus der; ∼, Termini term
Terpentin das, (österr. meist:) der; ∼s
(a) (Harz) turpentine
(b) (ugs.: Terpentinöl) turps sing. (coll.)
Terpentin·öl das oil of turpentine
Terrain /tɛ'rɛ̃:/ das; ∼s, ∼s terrain
Terrasse die; ∼, ∼n terrace
Terrier /'tɛriɐ̯/ der; ∼s, ∼: terrier
Terrine die; ∼, ∼n tureen
Territorium das; ∼s, Territorien territory
Terror der; ∼s terrorism no art.
Terror-: ∼**angriff** der terrorist attack;
∼**anschlag** der terrorist attack;
∼**gruppe** die terrorist group
terrorisieren tr. V. (a) terrorize
(b) (ugs.: belästigen) pester
Terrorismus der; ∼: terrorism no art.
Terrorist der; ∼en, ∼en, **Terroristin**
die; ∼, ∼nen terrorist
Terror-: ∼**netz** das terrorist network;
∼**verdächtige** der/die terrorist suspect;
∼**zelle** die terrorist cell
Terz die; ∼, ∼en (Musik) third
Test der; ∼[e]s, ∼s od. ∼e test
Testament das; ∼[e]s, ∼e (a) will
(b) (christl. Rel.) Testament
Test·bogen der test paper
testen tr. V. test (auf + Akk. for)
teuer ① Adj. expensive; dear usu. pred.;
wie ∼ war das? how much did that cost?
② adv. expensively; dearly; etw. ∼ kaufen/
verkaufen pay a great deal for sth./sell sth.
at a high price
Teuerung die; ∼, ∼en rise in prices
Teuerungs·rate die rate of price
increases
Teufel der; ∼s, ∼: devil
Teufels·zeug das (ugs.) terrible stuff (coll.)
teuflisch ① Adj. (a) devilish, fiendish
⟨plan, trick, etc.⟩; diabolical ⟨laughter,
pleasure, etc.⟩
(b) (ugs.: groß, intensiv) terrible (coll.); dreadful
(coll.)
② adv. (a) diabolically

(b) (ugs.) terribly (coll.)
Text der; ∼[e]s, ∼e text; (Wortlaut) wording;
(eines Theaterstücks) script; (einer Oper) libretto;
(eines Liedes, Chansons usw.) words pl.; (eines
Schlagers) words pl.; lyrics pl.; (zu einer
Abbildung) caption
texten tr. V. write ⟨song, advertisement,
etc.⟩
Textilien Pl. (a) textiles
(b) (Fertigwaren) textile goods
Textil·industrie die textile industry
Text·verarbeitung die text processing;
word processing
Thailand (das); ∼s Thailand
Theater das; ∼s, ∼ (a) theatre; ins
∼ gehen go to the theatre; im ∼: at the
theatre; ∼ spielen act; (fig.) play-act; pretend
(b) (fig. ugs.) fuss
Theater-: ∼**abonnement** das theatre
subscription [ticket]; ∼**stück** das [stage]
play
Theke die; ∼, ∼n (a) (Schanktisch) bar
(b) (Ladentisch) counter
Thema das; ∼s, Themen subject; topic;
(einer Abhandlung) subject; theme; (Leitgedanke)
theme
Themse die; ∼: Thames
Theologe der; ∼n, ∼n theologian
Theologie die; ∼, ∼n theology no art.
Theologin die; ∼, ∼: theologian
theologisch ① Adj. theological
② adv. theologically
theoretisch ① Adj. theoretical
② adv. theoretically
Theorie die; ∼, ∼n theory
Therapeut der; ∼en, ∼en,
Therapeutin die; ∼, ∼nen therapist;
therapeutist
therapeutisch ① Adj. therapeutic
② adv. therapeutically
Therapie die; ∼, ∼n therapy (gegen for)
therapieren tr. V. treat
Thermo·meter das (österr. u. schweiz.
der od. das) thermometer
Thermos·flasche Ⓦⓩ die Thermos flask
® vacuum flask
Thermostat der; ∼[e]s od. ∼en, ∼e od.
∼en thermostat
These die; ∼, ∼n thesis
Thron der; ∼[e]s, ∼e throne
Thun·fisch der tuna
Thüringen (das); ∼s Thuringia
Thüringer Wald der; ∼ ∼[e]s
Thuringian Forest
Thymian der; ∼s, ∼e thyme
Tick der; ∼[e]s, ∼s (a) (ugs.: Schrulle) quirk;
thing (coll.)
(b) (ugs.: Nuance) tiny bit; shade
ticken itr. V. tick; du tickst wohl nicht
richtig (salopp) you must be off your rocker
(coll.)

Ticket *das;* ~s, ~s ticket

tief 1 *Adj.* (auch fig.) deep; (niedrig) low; low ⟨*neckline, bow*⟩; deep; intense ⟨*pain, suffering*⟩
2 *adv.* deep; (niedrig) low; (intensiv) deeply; ⟨*stoop, bow*⟩ low; ⟨*breathe, inhale*⟩ deeply

Tief *das;* ~s, ~s (Met.) low

tief·blau *Adj.* deep blue

Tief·druck *der* (Met.) low pressure

Tiefe *die;* ~, ~n depth; **in die** ~ **stürzen** plunge into the depths

tief-, Tief-: ~**garage** *die* underground car park; ~**greifend** 1 *Adj.* profound; profound, deep ⟨*crisis*⟩; far-reaching ⟨*improvement*⟩; 2 *adv.* profoundly; ~**gründig** *Adj.* profound; ~|**kühlen** *tr. V.* [deep-]freeze

Tief·kühl-: ~**fach** *das* freezer [compartment]; ~**kost** *die* frozen food

tief-, Tief-: ~**punkt** *der* low [point]; ~**schlag** *der* (Boxen) low punch; punch below the belt (lit. or fig.); ~**see** *die* (Geogr.) deep sea; ~**sinnig** 1 *Adj.* profound; 2 *adv.* profoundly

Tiefst·temperatur *die* minimum or lowest temperature

Tiegel *der;* ~s, ~ (zum Kochen) pan; (Schmelztiegel) crucible; (Behälter) pot

Tier *das;* ~[e]s, ~e animal

Tier-: ~**arzt** *der,* ~**ärztin** *die* veterinary surgeon; vet; ~**garten** *der* zoo; zoological garden; ~**heim** *das* animal home

tierisch 1 *Adj.* (a) animal *attrib.;* savage ⟨*cruelty, crime*⟩
(b) (ugs.: unerträglich groß) terrible (coll.); ~**er Ernst** deadly seriousness
2 *adv.* (a) ⟨*roar*⟩ like an animal; savagely ⟨*cruel*⟩
(b) (ugs.: unerträglich) terribly (coll.)

tier-, Tier-: ~**kreis** *der* (Astron., Astrol.) zodiac; ~**kreis·zeichen** *das* (Astron., Astrol.) sign of the zodiac; ~**lieb** *Adj.* animal-loving *attrib.;* fond of animals *postpos.;* ~**park** *der* zoo; ~**pfleger** *der,* ~**pflegerin** *die* animal keeper; ~**quälerei** /---'-/ *die* cruelty to animals; ~**rechtler** *der;* ~~s, ~~, ~**rechtlerin** *die;* ~~, ~~nen animal rights campaigner; ~**reich** *das* animal kingdom;

Tiger *der;* ~s, ~: tiger

tilgen *tr. V.* (a) (geh.) delete ⟨*word, letter, error*⟩; erase ⟨*record, endorsement*⟩; (fig.) wipe out ⟨*shame, guilt, traces*⟩
(b) (Wirtsch., Bankw.) repay; pay off

Tilgung *die;* ~, ~en (a) (geh.) ▶ TILGEN A: deletion; erasure; wiping out
(b) (Wirtsch., Bankw.) repayment

Tilsiter *der;* ~s, ~: Tilsit [cheese]

Tinte *die;* ~, ~n ink; **in der** ~ **sitzen** (ugs.) be in the soup (coll.)

Tinten-: ~**fisch** *der* cuttlefish; (Krake) octopus; ~**strahl·drucker** *der* (DV) ink-jet printer

*****Tip, Tipp** *der;* ~s, ~s (a) (ugs.) tip
(b) (bei Toto, Lotto usw.) [row of] numbers

tippen 1 *itr. V.* (a) **an/gegen etw.** (*Akk.*) ~: tap sth.
(b) (ugs.: Maschine schreiben) type
(c) (wetten) do the pools/lottery *etc.;* **im Lotto** ~: do the lottery
2 *tr. V.* (a) tap
(b) (ugs.: mit der Maschine schreiben) type
(c) (setzen auf) choose; **sechs Richtige** ~: make six correct selections

Tipp-: ~**fehler** *der* typing error or mistake; ~**gemeinschaft** *die* pools/lottery *etc.* syndicate

tipp·topp (ugs.) 1 *Adj.* (tadellos) immaculate; (erstklassig) tip-top
2 *adv.* immaculately

Tirol *(das);* ~s [the] Tyrol

Tiroler *der;* ~s, ~, **Tirolerin** *die;* ~, ~nen Tyrolese; Tyrolean

Tisch *der;* ~[e]s, ~e table; **reinen** ~ **machen** (ugs.) sort things out

Tisch-: ~**dame** *die* dinner partner; ~**decke** *die* tablecloth; ~**gebet** *das* grace *no pl.;* ~**herr** *der* dinner partner; ~**lampe** *die* table lamp

Tischler *der;* ~s, ~: joiner; (bes. Kunst~) cabinetmaker

Tischlerei *die;* ~, ~en ▶ TISCHLER:
(a) (Werkstatt) joiner's/cabinetmaker's [workshop]
(b) (Handwerk) joinery/cabinetmaking

Tischlerin *die;* ~, ~nen ▶ TISCHLER

Tisch-: ~**nachbar** *der* person next to one [at table]; ~**platte** *die* table top; ~**tennis** *das* table tennis; ~**tuch** *das; Pl.* ~tücher tablecloth; ~**wäsche** *die* table linen; ~**wein** *der* table wine; ~**zeit** *die* lunchtime

Titel *der;* ~s, ~ (a) title
(b) (ugs.: Musikstück, Song usw.) number

Titel-: ~**bild** *das* cover picture; ~**blatt** *das* title page; ~**rolle** *die* title role; ~**seite** *die* (a) (einer Zeitung, Zeitschrift) [front] cover; (b) (eines Buchs) title page

Titte *die;* ~, ~n (derb) tit (coarse)

titulieren *tr. V.* call

tja /tja(:)/ *Interj.* [yes] well; (Resignation ausdrückend) oh, well

Toast /to:st/ *der;* ~[e]s, ~e *od.* ~s toast

Toast·brot *das* [sliced white] bread for toasting

toasten *tr. V.* toast

Toaster *der;* ~s, ~: toaster

toben *itr. V.* (a) go wild (**vor** + *Dat.* with); (fig.) ⟨*storm, sea, battle*⟩ rage
(b) (tollen) romp or charge about
(c) *mit sein* (laufen) charge

Tochter *die;* ~, Töchter (a) daughter
(b) (Wirtsch.) subsidiary

Tochter·gesellschaft *die* (Wirtsch.) subsidiary [company]

Tod *der;* ~[e]s, ~e death; **eines natürlichen/ gewaltsamen** ~**es sterben** die a natural/ violent death; **jmdn. zum** ~**e verurteilen** sentence sb. to death

tod·ernst ① *Adj.* deadly serious
② *adv.* deadly seriously

Todes-: ~**anzeige** *die* (a) (in einer Zeitung) death notice; **(b)** (Karte) *card announcing a person's death;* ~**fall** *der* death; (in der Familie) bereavement; ~**nachricht** *die* news of his/her/their *etc.* death; ~**opfer** *das* death; fatality; ~**strafe** *die* death penalty; ~**ursache** *die* cause of death; ~**urteil** *das* death sentence; ~**verachtung** *die* [utter] fearlessness in the face of death; **etw. mit** ~**verachtung essen/trinken** (ugs.) force sth. down [without showing one's distaste]

Tod·feind *der,* **Tod·feindin** *die* deadly enemy

tod·krank *Adj.* critically ill

tödlich ① *Adj.* (a) fatal ⟨*accident, illness, outcome, etc.*⟩; lethal, deadly ⟨*poison, bite, shot, trap, etc.*⟩; lethal ⟨*dose*⟩
(b) (sehr groß, ausgeprägt) deadly ⟨*hatred, seriousness, certainty, boredom*⟩
② *adv.* (a) fatally
(b) (sehr) terribly (coll.)

tod-, Tod-: ~**müde** *Adj.* dead tired; ~**schick** (ugs.) ① *Adj.* dead smart (coll.); ② *adv.* dead smartly (coll.); ~**sicher** (ugs.) ① *Adj.* sure-fire (coll.); ② *adv.* for certain *or* sure; ~**sünde** *die* (auch fig.) deadly *or* mortal sin; ~**unglücklich** *Adj.* (ugs.) extremely *or* desperately unhappy

Toilette /tɔaˈlɛtə/ *die;* ~, ~n toilet

Toiletten·papier *das* toilet paper

toi, toi, toi /ˈtɔy ˈtɔy ˈtɔy/ *Interj.* good luck!; (unberufen!) touch wood!

Tokio *(das);* ~s Tokyo

tolerant ① *Adj.* tolerant **(gegen)** ② *adv.* tolerantly

Toleranz *die;* ~: tolerance

tolerierbar *Adj.* tolerable

tolerieren *tr. V.* tolerate

toll ① *Adj.* (a) (ugs.) (großartig) great (coll.); fantastic (coll.); (erstaunlich) amazing; (heftig, groß) enormous ⟨*respect*⟩; terrific (coll.) ⟨*noise, storm*⟩
(b) (wild) wild
② *adv.* (a) (ugs.: großartig) terrifically well (coll.)
(b) (ugs.: heftig) ⟨*rain, snow*⟩ like billy-o (coll.)
(c) (wild) **bei dem Fest ging es** ~ **zu** it was a wild party

Tolle *die;* ~, ~n quiff

tollen *itr. V.* (a) romp about
(b) *mit sein* romp

tollkühn ① *Adj.* daredevil *attrib.;* daring; ② *adv.* daringly

Tollpatsch *der;* ~[e]s, ~e (ugs.) clumsy *or* awkward creature

tollpatschig (ugs.) ① *Adj.* clumsy; awkward
② *adv.* clumsily; awkwardly

toll-, Toll-: ~**wut** *die* rabies *sing.;* ~**wütig** *Adj.* rabid

*****Tolpatsch** *usw.* ▶ TOLLPATSCH *usw.*

Tölpel *der;* ~s, ~: fool

tölpelhaft ① *Adj.* foolish
② *adv.* foolishly

Tomate *die;* ~, ~n tomato

Tomaten·mark *das* tomato purée

Tombola *die;* ~, ~s raffle

Ton¹ *der;* ~[e]s, ~e clay

Ton² *der;* ~[e]s, **Töne** (a) (auch Physik, Musik; beim Telefon) tone; (Klang) note
(b) (Film, Ferns. usw., Tonwiedergabe) sound
(c) (ugs.: Äußerung) word
(d) (Farb~) shade
(e) (Akzent) stress

ton-, Ton-: ~**angebend** *Adj.* predominant; ~**art** *die* (a) (Musik) key;
(b) (fig.) tone; ~**band** *das; Pl.* ~bänder tape; ~**band·gerät** *das* tape recorder; ~**effekt** *der* sound effect

tönen ① *itr. V.* (geh.) sound; ⟨*bell*⟩ sound, ring; (schallen, widerhallen) resound
② *tr. V.* (färben) tint

Ton-: ~**fall** *der* tone; (Intonation) intonation; ~**höhe** *die* pitch; ~**leiter** *die* (Musik) scale

Tonne *die;* ~, ~n (a) (Behälter) drum; (Mülltonne) bin; (Regentonne) water butt
(b) (Gewicht) tonne

tonnen·weise *Adv., adj.* by the ton

Ton·qualität *die* sound quality

Tönung *die;* ~, ~en tint; shade

Tool /tuːl/ *das;* ~s, ~s (DV) tool

Topf *der;* ~es, **Töpfe** (a) pot; (Braten~, Schmor~) casserole; (Stielkasserolle) saucepan
(b) (zur Aufbewahrung) pot
(c) (Krug) jug
(d) (Nachttopf) chamber pot; (für Kinder) potty (Brit. coll.)
(e) (Blumentopf) [flower]pot

Topf·blume *die* [flowering] pot plant

Töpfchen *das;* ~s, ~: potty (Brit. coll.)

Töpfer *der;* ~s, ~ potter

Töpferei *die;* ~, ~en (a) (Handwerk) pottery *no art.*
(b) (Werkstatt) pottery; potter's workshop
(c) (Erzeugnis) piece of pottery; ~en pottery *sing.*

Töpferin *die;* ~, ~nen ▶ TÖPFER

Topf-: ~**lappen** *der* oven cloth; ~**pflanze** *die* pot plant

Tor¹ *das;* ~[e]s, ~e (a) gate; (einer Garage, Scheune) door; (fig.) gateway
(b) (Ballspiele) goal
(c) (Ski) gate

Tor² *der;* ~en, ~en (geh.: Narr) fool

Torf *der;* ~[e]s, ~e peat

Torheit *die;* ~, ~en (geh.) (a) foolishness

(b) (Handlung) foolish act

Tor·hüter *der,* **Tor·hüterin** *die* (Ballspiele) goalkeeper

töricht (geh.) ⟨1⟩ *Adj.* foolish
⟨2⟩ *adv.* foolishly

torkeln *itr. V.; mit sein* stagger

Tor·mann *der; Pl.* Tormänner *od.* Torleute (Ballspiele) goalkeeper

Tornister /tɔr'nɪstɐ/ *der;* ∼s, ∼: knapsack; (Schulranzen) satchel

torpedieren *tr. V.* (Milit., fig.) torpedo

Torpedo *der;* ∼s, ∼s torpedo

Törtchen *das;* ∼s, ∼: tartlet

Torte *die;* ∼, ∼n (Creme-, Sahnetorte) gateau; (Obsttorte) [fruit] flan

Torten-: ∼**boden** *der* flan case; (ohne Rand) flan base; ∼**guss,** **∼***guß** *der* glaze; ∼**heber** *der;* ∼∼s, ∼∼: cake slice

Tortur *die;* ∼, ∼en **(a)** ordeal
(b) (veralt.: Folter) torture

Tor-: ∼**wart** *der;* ∼∼[e]s, ∼∼e, ∼**wartin** *die;* ∼∼, ∼∼nen (Ballspiele) goalkeeper; ∼**weg** *der* gateway

tosen *itr. V.* roar; ⟨storm⟩ rage

tot *Adj.* dead; ∼ umfallen drop dead; **sich** ∼ **stellen** pretend to be dead; play dead; ∼ **geboren** stillborn

total ⟨1⟩ *Adj.* total
⟨2⟩ *adv.* totally

Total·ausverkauf *der* clearance sale

totalitär (Politik) ⟨1⟩ *Adj.* totalitarian
⟨2⟩ *adv.* in a totalitarian way; ⟨organized, run⟩ along totalitarian lines

Total·schaden *der* (Versicherungsw.) an beiden Fahrzeugen entstand ∼: both vehicles were a write-off

tot|ärgern *refl. V.* (ugs.) get livid (coll.)

Tote *der/die; adj. Dekl.* dead person; **die** ∼**n** the dead

töten *tr., itr. V.* kill; deaden ⟨nerve etc.⟩

toten-, Toten-: ∼**blass,** **∼***blaß,** ∼**bleich** *Adj.* deathly pale; ∼**gräber** *der;* ∼∼s, ∼∼, ∼**gräberin** *die;* ∼∼, ∼∼nen gravedigger; ∼**kopf** *der* **(a)** skull; **(b)** (als Symbol) death's head; (mit gekreuzten Knochen) skull and crossbones; ∼**schädel** *der* skull; ∼**sonntag** *der* (ev. Kirche) *Sunday before Advent on which the dead are commemorated;* ∼**still** *Adj.* deathly quiet; ∼**stille** *die* deathly silence; ∼**wache** *die* vigil by the body

tot-, Tot-: ∼|**fahren** *unr. tr. V.* [run over and] kill; **∼***geboren** ▶ TOT; ∼**geburt** *die* still birth; ∼|**lachen** *refl. V.* (ugs.) kill oneself laughing; **zum Totlachen sein** be killing (coll.)

Toto *das od. der;* ∼s, ∼s **(a)** (Pferdetoto) tote (coll.); **im** ∼: on the tote
(b) (Fußballtoto) [football] pools *pl.;* **[im]** ∼ **spielen** do the pools

Toto·schein *der:* ▶ TOTO: pools coupon/ (coll.) tote ticket

tot-, Tot-: ∼|**schießen** *unr. tr. V.* (ugs.) jmdn. ∼schießen shoot sb. dead; ∼**schlag** *der* (Rechtsspr.) manslaughter *no indef. art.;* ∼|**schlagen** *unr. tr. V.* beat to death; **∼*|**stellen** ▶ TOT; ∼|**treten** *unr. tr. V.* trample ⟨person⟩ to death; step on and kill ⟨insect⟩

Tötung *die;* ∼, ∼en killing; **fahrlässige** ∼ (Rechtsspr.) manslaughter by culpable negligence

Touch /tatʃ/ *der;* ∼s, ∼s (ugs.) touch

tough /taf/ *Adj.* (ugs.) tough

Toupet /tu'peː/ *das;* ∼s, ∼s toupee

toupieren /tu'piːrən/ *tr. V.* backcomb

Tour /tuːɐ̯/ *die;* ∼, ∼en tour **(durch** of); (kürzere Fahrt, Ausflug) trip; (mit dem Auto) drive; (mit dem Fahrrad) ride; (feste Strecke) route; **in einer** ∼ (ugs.) the whole time

touren /'tuːrən/ *itr. V.; mit sein* tour

Tourismus /tu'rɪsmʊs/ *der;* ∼: tourism *no art.*

Tourismus·branche *die* tourism industry; tourist industry;

Tourist *der;* ∼en, ∼en tourist

Touristen-: ∼**klasse** *die* tourist class; ∼**paradies** *das* tourist paradise; ∼**zentrum** *das* tourist centre

Touristin *die;* ∼, ∼nen tourist

Tournee /tʊr'neː/ *die;* ∼, ∼s *od.* ∼n tour; **auf** ∼ **sein/gehen** be/go on tour

Trab *der;* ∼[e]s trot; **im** ∼: at a trot; **im** ∼ **reiten** trot

traben *itr. V.; mit sein* (auch ugs.: laufen) trot

Tracht *die;* ∼, ∼en **(a)** (Volkstracht) national costume; (Berufstracht) uniform
(b) eine ∼ **Prügel** a thrashing; (als Strafe) a hiding

trachten *itr. V.* (geh.) strive **(nach** for, after)

Tradition *die;* ∼, ∼en tradition

traditionell ⟨1⟩ *Adj.* traditional
⟨2⟩ *adv.* traditionally

traf *1. u. 3. Pers. Sg. Prät. v.* TREFFEN

träfe *1. u. 3. Pers. Sg. Konjunktiv II v.* TREFFEN

Trafik *die;* ∼, ∼en (österr.) tobacconist's [shop]

Trag·bahre *die* stretcher

tragbar *Adj.* **(a)** portable
(b) wearable ⟨clothes⟩
(c) (finanziell) supportable ⟨cost, debt, etc.⟩
(d) (erträglich) bearable; tolerable

träge ⟨1⟩ *Adj.* sluggish
⟨2⟩ *adv.* sluggishly

Trage *die;* ∼, ∼n **(a)** (Bahre) stretcher
(b) (Traggestell) pannier

tragen ⟨1⟩ *unr. tr. V.* **(a)** carry
(b) (bringen) take
(c) (ertragen) bear ⟨fate, destiny⟩; bear, endure ⟨suffering⟩
(d) (halten) hold; **einen/den linken Arm in der Schlinge** ∼: have one's arm/ one's left arm in a sling ⋯⋗

(e) (von unten stützen) support
(f) (belastbar sein durch) be able to carry *or* take ⟨*weight*⟩
(g) (übernehmen, aufkommen für) bear, carry ⟨*costs etc.*⟩; take ⟨*blame, responsibility, consequences*⟩
(h) (am Körper) wear ⟨*clothes, wig, glasses, jewellery, etc.*⟩
(i) have ⟨*false teeth, beard, etc.*⟩
(j) (hervorbringen) ⟨*tree*⟩ bear ⟨*fruit*⟩; ⟨*field*⟩ produce ⟨*crops*⟩
2 *unr. itr. V.* **(a)** carry
(b) (am Körper) **man trägt [wieder] kurz/lang** short/long skirts are in fashion [again]
(c) der Baum trägt gut the tree produces a good crop

tragend *Adj.* (Stabilität gebend) load-bearing; supporting ⟨*wall, column, function, etc.*⟩
Träger *der;* ~s, ~ **(a)** porter
(b) (Austräger) paper boy/girl; delivery boy/girl
(c) (Bauw.) girder; [supporting] beam
(d) (an Kleidung) strap; (Hosenträger) braces *pl.*
(e) (Inhaber) (eines Amts) holder; (eines Namens, Titels) bearer; (eines Preises) winner
Trägerin *die;* ~, ~nen ▶ TRÄGER A, B, E
Trage·tasche *die* carrier bag
Trag-: ~**fähigkeit** *die* load-bearing capacity; ~**fläche** *die* wing; ~**flügel·boot** *das* hydrofoil
Trägheit *die;* ~, ~en sluggishness
Tragik *die;* ~: tragedy
tragi·komisch 1 *Adj.* tragicomic
2 *adv.* tragicomically
tragisch 1 *Adj.* tragic; **das ist nicht [so]** ~ (ugs.) it's not the end of the world (coll.)
2 *adv.* tragically
Tragödie /tra'gøː.diə/ *die;* ~, ~n tragedy
Trag·weite *die* consequences *pl.*
Trainer /'trɛːnɐ/ *der;* ~s, ~, **Trainerin** *die;* ~, ~nen coach; trainer; (einer Fußballmannschaft) manager
trainieren 1 *tr. V.* **(a)** train; coach ⟨*swimmer, tennis player*⟩; manage ⟨*football team*⟩; exercise ⟨*muscles etc.*⟩
(b) (üben, einüben) practise ⟨*exercise, jump, etc.*⟩; **Fußball** ~: do football training
2 *itr. V.* train
Training /'trɛːnɪŋ/ *das;* ~s, ~s training *no indef. art.*
Trainings-: ~**anzug** *der* track suit; ~**hose** *die* track-suit bottoms *pl.* ~**lager** *das* training camp
Trakt *der;* ~[e]s, ~e section; (Flügel) wing
Traktor *der;* ~s, ~en tractor
trällern *itr., tr. V.* warble
trampeln 1 *itr. V.* **(a)** [mit den Füßen] ~: stamp one's feet
(b) *mit sein* (treten) trample (**auf** + *Akk.* on)
2 *tr. V.* trample
Trampel·pfad *der* [beaten] path

---

trampen /'trɛmpn̩/ *itr. V. mit sein* hitch-hike
Tramper *der;* ~s, ~, **Tramperin** *die;* ~, ~nen hitch-hiker
Trampolin *das;* ~s, ~e trampoline
Tramway /'tramveː/ *die;* ~, ~s (österr.) tram (Brit.); streetcar (Amer.)
Tran *der;* ~[e]s train-oil
Trance /'trãːs(ə)/ *die;* ~, ~n trance; **in** ~: in a trance
tranchieren /trãˈʃiːrən/ *tr. V.* carve
Träne *die;* ~, ~n tear; ~**n lachen** laugh till one cries
tränen *itr. V.* ⟨*eyes*⟩ water
tranig *Adj.* (ugs. abwertend: langsam) sluggish; slow
trank *1. u. 3. Pers. Sg. Prät. v.* TRINKEN
Tränke *die;* ~, ~n watering place
tränken *tr. V.* **(a)** water
(b) (sich voll saugen lassen) soak
Transfer *der;* ~s, ~s (bes. Wirtsch., Sport) transfer
Transfer·summe *die* transfer fee
Trans·formator *der;* ~s, ~en transformer
Transistor *der;* ~s, ~en transistor
Transit /tranˈziːt, *auch:* ˈtranzɪt/ *das;* ~s, ~s transit visa
transitiv (Sprachw.) 1 *Adj.* transitive
2 *adv.* transitively
Transit·verkehr *der* transit traffic
transparent *Adj.* transparent; (Licht durchlassend) translucent
Transparent *das;* ~[e]s, ~e (Spruchband) banner; (Bild) transparency
Transparenz *die;* ~ transparency
Transport *der;* ~[e]s, ~e
(a) transportation
(b) (beförderte Lebewesen od. Sachen) (mit dem Zug) trainload; (mit mehreren Fahrzeugen) convoy; (Fracht) consignment
transportabel *Adj.* transportable; (tragbar) portable
Transporteur /…ˈtøːɐ̯/ *der;* ~s, ~e, **Transporteurin** *die;* ~, ~nen carrier
transport·fähig *Adj.* moveable
transportieren *tr. V.* transport ⟨*goods, people*⟩; move ⟨*patient*⟩
Transport·kosten *Pl.* carriage *sing.*; transport costs
Transvestit *der;* ~en, ~en transvestite
Trapez *das;* ~es, ~e **(a)** (Geom.) trapezium (Brit.); trapezoid (Amer.)
(b) (im Zirkus) trapeze
trappeln *itr. V.; mit sein* patter [along]; ⟨*feet*⟩ patter; ⟨*hoofs*⟩ go clip-clop
Trara *das;* ~s (ugs.) razzmatazz (coll.)
Trasse *die;* ~, ~n (Verkehrsweg) [marked-out] route *or* line
trat *1. u. 3. Pers. Sg. Prät. v.* TRETEN
Tratsch *der;* ~[e]s (ugs.) gossip; tittle-tattle

tratschen itr. V. (ugs.) gossip; (schwatzen) chatter

Traube die; ~, ~n (a) bunch; (von Johannisbeeren usw.) cluster
(b) (Weinbeere~) grape
(c) (Menschenmenge) bunch; cluster

trauen 1 itr. V. jmdm./einer Sache ~: trust sb./sth.
2 refl. V. dare
3 tr. V. (verheiraten) ⟨vicar, registrar, etc.⟩ marry

Trauer die; ~ (a) grief (über + Akk. over); (um einen Toten) mourning (um + Akk. for)
(b) (Trauerzeit) [period of] mourning
(c) ~ tragen be in mourning

Trauer-: ~fall der bereavement; ~feier die memorial ceremony; (beim Begräbnis) funeral ceremony; ~karte die [pre-printed] card of condolence; ~kleidung die mourning clothes pl.

trauern itr. V. mourn; um jmdn. ~: mourn for sb.

Trauer-: ~spiel das tragedy; (fig. ugs.) deplorable business; ~weide die weeping willow

träufeln tr. V. [let] trickle (in + Akk. into); drip ⟨ear drops etc.⟩

Traum der; ~[e]s, Träume /'trɔymə/ dream

Trauma das; ~s, Traumen od. ~ta (Psych., Med.) trauma

traumatisch (Psych., Med.) 1 Adj. traumatic
2 adv. traumatically

traumatisieren (Psych., Med.) 1 tr. V. traumatize.
2 itr. V. have a traumatizing effect

träumen 1 itr. V. dream (von of, about); (unaufmerksam sein) [day]dream
2 tr. V. dream

Träumer der; ~s, ~, **Träumerin** die; ~, ~nen dreamer

träumerisch 1 Adj. dreamy
2 adv. dreamily

traumhaft (ugs.) 1 Adj. marvellous; fabulous (coll.)
2 adv. fabulously (coll.)

Traum-urlaub der dream holiday

traurig 1 Adj. (a) sad; unhappy ⟨childhood, youth⟩; painful ⟨duty⟩
(b) (kümmerlich) sorry ⟨state etc.⟩; miserable ⟨result⟩
2 adv. sadly

Traurigkeit die; ~: sadness; sorrow

Trau-: ~ring der wedding ring; ~schein der marriage certificate

Trauung die; ~, ~en wedding [ceremony]

Trau-zeuge der, **Trau-zeugin** die witness (at wedding ceremony)

Trecker der; ~s, ~: tractor

Treff der; ~s, ~s (ugs.) rendezvous; (Ort) meeting place

treffen 1 unr. tr. V. (a) hit; ⟨punch, blow, object⟩ strike; **ihn trifft keine Schuld** he is in no way to blame
(b) (erschüttern) affect [deeply]; (verletzen) hurt
(c) (begegnen) meet
(d) (vorfinden) come upon, find ⟨anomalies etc.⟩; **es gut/schlecht ~:** be or strike lucky/be unlucky
(e) (als Funktionsverb) make ⟨arrangements, choice, preparations, decision, etc.⟩
2 unr. itr. V. (a) ⟨person, shot, etc.⟩ hit the target; **nicht ~:** miss [the target]
(b) **mit sein auf etw.** (Akk.) ~: come upon sth.; **auf Widerstand/Ablehnung/Schwierigkeiten ~:** meet with resistance/rejection/difficulties
3 unr. refl. V. (a) sich mit jmdm. ~: meet sb.
(b) unpers. **es trifft sich gut/schlecht** it is convenient/inconvenient

Treffen das; ~s, ~: meeting

treffend 1 Adj. apt
2 adv. aptly

Treffer der; ~s, ~ (a) (Milit., Boxen, Fechten usw.) hit; (Schlag) blow; (Ballspiele) goal
(b) (Gewinn) win; (Los) winner

trefflich (geh.) 1 Adj. excellent; splendid ⟨person⟩
2 adv. excellently; splendidly

treff-, Treff-: ~punkt der meeting place; ~sicher 1 Adj. accurate ⟨language, mode of expression⟩; unerring ⟨judgement⟩; 2 adv. accurately; ~sicherheit die accuracy

Treib-eis das drift-ice

treiben 1 unr. tr. V. (a) drive
(b) (sich beschäftigen mit) go in for ⟨farming, cattle breeding, etc.⟩; study ⟨French etc.⟩; carry on, pursue ⟨studies, trade, craft⟩; **viel Sport ~:** do a lot of sport; **es wüst/übel/toll ~** (ugs.) lead a dissolute/bad life/live it up
2 unr. itr. V. meist. mit Richtungsangabe nur, mit sein drift

Treiben das; ~s (a) (Durcheinander) bustle
(b) (Tun) activities pl.; doings pl.

Treiber der; ~s, ~ (DV) driver

Treib-: ~gas das propellant; ~haus das hothouse; ~haus-effekt der greenhouse effect; ~haus-gas das greenhouse gas; ~stoff der fuel

trekken /'trɛkṇ/ itr. V.; mit sein trek

Trekking das; ~s trekking

Trenchcoat /'trɛntʃkoʊt/ der; ~s, ~s trench coat

Trend der; ~s, ~s trend (zu + Dat. towards); (Mode) vogue

trendig Adj. (ugs.) modern and fashionable

trennen 1 tr. V. (a) separate (von from); sever ⟨head, arm⟩
(b) (auftrennen) unpick ⟨dress, seam⟩
(c) (teilen) divide ⟨word, parts of a room etc., fig.: people⟩
2 refl. V. (a) (voneinander weggehen) part [company]

····⟶

(b) (eine Partnerschaft auflösen) ⟨*couple, partners*⟩ split up
(c) sich von etw. ~: part with sth.
Trennung *die;* ~, ~en (von Menschen) separation (von from); (von Gegenständen) parting; (von Wörtern) division
trepp-: ~**ab** *Adv.* down the stairs; ~**auf** *Adv.* up the stairs
Treppe *die;* ~, ~n staircase; [flight *sing.* of] stairs *pl.;* (im Freien, auf der Bühne) [flight *sing.* of] steps *pl.*
Treppen-: ~**absatz** *der* half-landing; ~**geländer** *das* banisters *pl.;* ~**haus** *das* stairwell; ~**stufe** *die* stair; (im Freien) step
Tresen *der;* ~s, ~ (bes. nordd.) bar; (Ladentisch) counter
Tresor *der;* ~s, ~e safe
Tret·boot *das* pedalo
treten 1 *unr. itr. V.* **(a)** *mit sein* step (in + *Akk.* into, auf + *Akk.* on to)
(b) (seinen Fuß setzen) auf etw. (*Akk.*) ~ tread on sth.
(c) (ausschlagen) kick
2 *unr. tr. V.* **(a)** (Tritt versetzen) kick ⟨*person, ball, etc.*⟩
(b) (trampeln) trample ⟨*path*⟩
(c) (mit dem Fuß niederdrücken) step on ⟨*brake, pedal*⟩; operate ⟨*bellows, clutch*⟩
treu 1 *Adj.* faithful; loyal; faithful ⟨*husband, wife*⟩; loyal ⟨*ally, subject*⟩; jmdm. ~ sein be true to sb.; sich selbst (*Dat.*)/seinem Glauben ~ bleiben be true to oneself/one's faith
2 *adv.* faithfully; loyally
Treue *die;* ~ **(a)** loyalty; (von [Ehe]partnern) fidelity
(b) (*Genauigkeit*) accuracy
treu-, Treu-: ~**hand[anstalt]** *die* (Wirtschaft) German privatization agency; ~**herzig** 1 *Adj.* ingenuous; (naiv) naive; (unschuldig) innocent; 2 *adv.* ingenuously; (naiv) naively; (unschuldig) innocently; ~**herzigkeit** *die;* ~~: ingenuousness; (Naivität) naivety; (Unschuld) innocence; ~**los** 1 *Adj.* disloyal, faithless ⟨*friend, person*⟩; unfaithful ⟨*husband, wife, lover*⟩; 2 *adv.* faithlessly
Tribunal *das;* ~s, ~e tribunal
Tribüne *die;* ~, ~n [grand]stand
Tribut *der;* ~[e]s, ~e (fig.) due; einer Sache (*Dat.*) ~ zollen pay the price for sth.
Trichter *der;* ~s, ~ funnel
Trick *der;* ~s, ~s trick; (fig.: List) ploy
Trick·film *der* animated cartoon [film]
trieb 1. u. 3. Pers. Sg. Prät. v. TREIBEN
Trieb *der;* ~[e]s, ~e **(a)** (innerer Antrieb) impulse; (Drang) urge; (Verlangen) [compulsive] desire
(b) (Spross) shoot
trieb-, Trieb-: ~**feder** *die* mainspring;

(fig.) driving *or* motivating force; ~**haft** 1 *Adj.* compulsive; carnal ⟨*sensuality*⟩; 2 *adv.* compulsively; ~**täter** *der,* ~**täterin** *die,* ~**verbrecher** *der,* ~**verbrecherin** *die: offender committing a crime in gratifying a compulsive desire;* (Sexualtäter) sexual offender; ~**wagen** *der* (Eisenb.) railcar; ~**werk** *das* engine
triefen *unr. od. regelm. itr. V.* **(a)** *mit sein* (fließen) (in Tropfen) drip; (in kleinen Rinnsalen) trickle
(b) (nass sein) be dripping wet; ⟨*nose*⟩ run
triff *Imperativ Sg. v.* TREFFEN
trifft 3. *Pers. Sg. Präsens v.* TREFFEN
triftig *Adj.* good ⟨*reason, excuse*⟩; valid, convincing ⟨*motive, argument*⟩
Trikot[1] /tri'ko:/ *der od. das;* ~s, ~s (Stoff) cotton jersey
Trikot[2] /tri'ko:/ *das;* ~s, ~ (ärmellos) singlet; (eines Tänzers) leotard; (eines Fußballspielers) shirt
Triller *der;* ~s, ~: trill
trillern 1 *itr. V.* trill
2 *tr. V.* warble ⟨*song*⟩
Triller·pfeife *die* police/referee's whistle
Trillion *die;* ~, ~en quintillion
Trimm-dich-Pfad *der* keep-fit trail
trimmen *tr. V.* (durch Sport) get ⟨*person*⟩ into shape
trinken 1 *unr. itr. V.* drink; auf jmdn./etw. ~: drink to sb./sth.
2 *unr. tr. V.* drink; einen Kaffee/ein Bier ~: have a coffee/beer
Trinker *der;* ~s, ~: alcoholic
Trinkerei *die;* ~, ~en drinking *no art.*
Trinkerin *die;* ~, ~nen alcoholic
Trink-: ~**geld** *das* tip; ~**halle** *die* **(a)** (in einem Heilbad) pump room; **(b)** (Kiosk) refreshment kiosk; (größer) refreshment stall; ~**wasser** *das* drinking water; „kein ~wasser" 'not for drinking'
Trio *das;* ~s, ~s (Musik, fig.) trio
Trip *der;* ~s, ~s **(a)** (ugs.: Ausflug) trip; jaunt
(b) (Drogenjargon: Rausch) trip (coll.)
(c) (Drogenjargon: Dosis) fix (sl.)
trippeln *itr. V.; mit sein* trip; ⟨*child*⟩ patter
trist *Adj.* dreary; dismal
tritt *Imperativ Sg. u. 3. Pers. Sg. Präsens v.* TRETEN
Tritt *der;* ~[e]s, ~e (Schritt; Trittbrett) step; (Fußtritt) kick
Tritt-: ~**brett** *das* step; ~**brett·fahrer** *der,* ~**brett·fahrerin** *die* (fig. abwertend) ≈ free rider (Amer.); *person who profits from another's work*
Triumph *der;* ~[e]s, ~e triumph
triumphieren *itr. V.* **(a)** exult
(b) (siegen) be triumphant; triumph (lit. or fig.) (über + *Akk.* over)
trivial 1 *Adj.* **(a)** (platt) banal; trite; (unbedeutend) trivial
(b) (alltäglich) humdrum ⟨*life, career*⟩

---

*alte Schreibung – vgl. Hinweis auf S. x

2 *adv.* (platt) banally; ⟨*say etc.*⟩ tritely

trocken 1 *Adj.* (auch fig.) dry

2 *adv.* drily

Trocken·haube *die* [hood-type] hairdrier

Trockenheit *die;* ~, ~en **(a)** dryness

(b) (Dürreperiode) drought

trocken-, Trocken-: ~|**legen**

tr. V. **(a)** ein Baby ~legen change a baby's nappies (Brit.) *or* (Amer.) diapers;

(b) (entwässern) drain ⟨*marsh, pond, etc.*⟩;

~**milch** *die* dried milk; ~|**reiben** *unr. tr. V.* rub ⟨*hair, child, etc.*⟩ dry; wipe ⟨*crockery, window, etc.*⟩ dry

trocknen 1 *itr. V.; meist mit* sein dry

2 *tr. V.* dry

Troddel *die;* ~, ~n tassel

Trödel *der;* ~s (ugs.) junk; (für den Flohmarkt) jumble

trödeln *itr. V.* **(a)** (ugs.) dawdle (**mit** over)

(b) *mit sein* (ugs.: schlendern) saunter

Trödler *der;* ~s, ~, **Trödlerin** *die;* ~, ~nen (ugs.) junk dealer

troff *1. u. 3. Pers. Sg. Prät. v.* TRIEFEN

trog *1. u. 3. Pers. Sg. Prät. v.* TRÜGEN

Trog *der;* ~[e]s, Tröge trough

trollen (ugs.) *refl. V.* push off (coll.)

Trommel *die;* ~, ~n drum

Trommel·bremse *die* drum brake

trommeln *itr. V.* **(a)** beat the drum; (als Beruf, Hobby usw.) play the drums

(b) [auf etw.] schlagen, auftreffen) drum (**auf** + *Akk.* on, **an** + *Akk.* against)

Trommel·wirbel *der* drum roll

Trommler *der;* ~s, ~ drummer

Trompete *die;* ~, ~n trumpet

trompeten 1 *itr. V.* play the trumpet; (fig.) ⟨*elephant*⟩ trumpet

2 *tr. V.* play ⟨*piece*⟩ on the trumpet

Trompeter *der;* ~s, ~, **Trompeterin** *die;* ~, ~nen trumpeter

Tropen *Pl.* tropics

Tropen- tropical

Tropen·helm *der* sun helmet

Tropf *der;* ~[e]s, ~e (Med.) drip

Tröpfchen *das;* ~s, ~: droplet; (kleine Menge) drop

tröpfeln 1 *itr. V.* **(a)** *mit sein* drip (**auf** + *Akk.* on to, **aus, von** from)

(b) *unpers.* (ugs.: leicht regnen) es tröpfelt it's spitting [with rain]

2 *tr. V.* let ⟨*sth.*⟩ drip (**in** + *Akk.* into, **auf** + *Akk.* on to)

tropfen 1 *itr. V.; mit Richtungsangabe mit sein* drip; ⟨*tears*⟩ fall; *unpers.* **es tropft [vom Dach usw.]** water is dripping from the roof *etc.*

2 *tr. V.* let ⟨*sth.*⟩ drip (**in** + *Akk.* into, **auf** + *Akk.* on to)

Tropfen *der;* ~s, ~ drop; **ein guter/edler** ~: a good/fine vintage

Tropf·stein·höhle *die* limestone cave

with stalactites and/or stalagmites

Trophäe *die;* ~, ~n (hist., Jagd, Sport) trophy

tropisch *Adj.* tropical

Tross, *Troß *der;* Trosses, Trosse

(a) (Milit.) baggage train

(b) (Gefolge) retinue; (fig.: Zug) procession [of hangers-on]

Trost *der;* ~[e]s consolation; (bes. geistlich) comfort; **nicht [ganz** *od.* **recht] bei** ~ **sein** (ugs.) be out of one's mind

trösten 1 *tr. V.* comfort, console (**mit** with)

2 *refl. V.* console oneself

tröstlich *Adj.* comforting

trost·los *Adj.* **(a)** hopeless; (verzweifelt) in despair *postpos.*

(b) (deprimierend, öde) miserable; dreary; hopeless ⟨*situation*⟩

Trostlosigkeit *die;* ~ **(a)** (einer Person, der Lage usw.) hopelessness; (Verzweiflung) despair

(b) (Öde) dreariness

Trost·preis *der* consolation prize

Tröstung *die;* ~, ~en comfort *no indef. art.*

Trott *der;* ~[e]s, ~e trot; (fig.) routine

Trottel *der;* ~s, ~ (ugs.) fool

trottelig (ugs.) 1 *Adj.* doddery

2 *adv.* in a feeble-minded way

trotten *itr. V.; mit sein* trot [along]

trotz *Präp. mit Gen., seltener mit Dat.* in spite of; despite

Trotz *der;* ~es defiance

trotz·dem /*auch:* '-'-/ *Adv.* nevertheless

trotzen *itr. V.* **(a)** (geh.: widerstehen) jmdm./ einer Sache ~ (auch fig.) defy sb./sth.

(b) (trotzig sein) be contrary

trotzig 1 *Adj.* defiant; (widerspenstig) contrary; difficult ⟨*child*⟩

2 *adv.* defiantly

trüb[e] 1 *Adj.* **(a)** (nicht klar) murky ⟨*stream, water*⟩; cloudy ⟨*liquid, wine, juice*⟩; (schlammig) muddy ⟨*puddle*⟩; (schmutzig) dirty ⟨*glass, window pane*⟩; dull ⟨*eyes*⟩

(b) (nicht hell) dim ⟨*light*⟩; dull, dismal ⟨*day, weather*⟩; grey, overcast ⟨*sky*⟩

2 *adv.* ⟨*shine, light*⟩ dimly

Trubel *der;* ~s [hustle and] bustle; **sie stürzten sich in den dicksten** ~: they plunged into the thick of the hurly-burly

trüben 1 *tr. V.* **(a)** make ⟨*liquid*⟩ cloudy; cloud ⟨*liquid*⟩

(b) (beeinträchtigen) dampen ⟨*mood*⟩; mar ⟨*relationship*⟩; cloud ⟨*judgement*⟩

2 *refl. V.* ⟨*liquid*⟩ become cloudy; ⟨*eyes*⟩ become dull; ⟨*sky*⟩ darken

Trübsal *die;* ~, ~e (geh.) **(a)** (Leiden) affliction

(b) (Kummer) grief; ~ **blasen** (ugs.) mope (**wegen** over, about)

trüb-, Trüb-: ~**selig** 1 *Adj.* **(a)** (öde) dreary, depressing ⟨*place, area, colour*⟩;

(b) (traurig) gloomy; 2 *adv.* (traurig) ···⟩

gloomily; ~**seligkeit** *die:* **(a)** (Ödheit) dreariness; **(b)** (Traurigkeit) gloom; ~**sinn** *der* melancholy; ~**sinnig** ① *Adj.* melancholy; ② *adv.* gloomily

Trübung *die;* ~, ~en **(a)** clouding; (des Auges) dimming **(b)** (Beeinträchtigung) deterioration; (der Stimmung) dampening

trudeln *itr. V. mit sein* roll

Trüffel *die;* ~, ~n truffle

trug *1. u. 3. Pers. Prät. v.* TRAGEN

trüge *1. u. 3. Pers. Sg. Konjunktiv II v.* TRAGEN

trügen ① *unr. tr. V.* deceive ② *unr. itr. V.* be deceptive; ⟨*feeling, deception*⟩ be a delusion

trügerisch ① *Adj.* deceptive; false ⟨*hope, sign, etc.*⟩; treacherous ⟨*ice*⟩ ② *adv.* deceptively

Truhe *die;* ~, ~n chest

Trümmer *Pl.* (eines Gebäudes) rubble *sing.;* (Ruinen) ruins; (eines Flugzeugs usw.) wreckage *sing.;* (kleinere Teile) debris *sing.*

Trümmer·haufen *der* pile *or* heap of rubble

Trumpf *der;* ~[e]s, Trümpfe (auch fig.) trump [card]; (Farbe) trumps *pl.;* ~ **sein** (fig.: Mode sein) be the in thing

trumpfen *itr. V.* play a trump

Trunk *der;* ~[e]s, Trünke (geh.) (Getränk) drink; beverage (formal)

Trunkenheit *die;* ~: drunkenness; ~ **am Steuer** drink-driving

Trunk·sucht *die* alcoholism *no art.*

trunk·süchtig *Adj.* alcoholic; ~ **sein** be an alcoholic

Trupp *der;* ~s, ~s troop; (von Arbeitern, Gefangenen) gang; (von Soldaten, Polizisten) squad

Truppe *die;* ~, ~n **(a)** (Einheit der Streitkräfte) unit **(b)** *Pl.* (Soldaten) troops **(c)** (Streitkräfte) [armed] forces *pl.;* (Heer) army **(d)** (Gruppe von Schauspielern, Artisten) troupe; (von Sportlern) squad

Trut·hahn *der* turkey [cock]

tschau *Interj.* (ugs.) ciao (coll.)

Tscheche *der;* ~n, ~n Czech

Tschechien *(das);* ~s Czech Republic

Tschechin *die;* ~, ~nen Czech

tschechisch *Adj.* Czech

Tschechoslowakei *die;* ~ (hist.) Czechoslovakia *no art.*

tschechoslowakisch *Adj.* (hist.) Czechoslovak[ian]

Tschetschene /tʃeˈtʃeːnə/ *der;* ~n, ~n Chechen; **die** ~**n** the Chechen[s]

Tschetschenien /tʃeˈtʃeːniən/ *das;* ~s Chechenia; Chechnya

Tschetschenin /tʃeˈtʃeːnɪn/ *die;* ~, ~nen Chechen

---

tschetschenisch *Adj.* Chechen

tschüs *Interj.* (ugs.) bye (coll.)

Tsd. *Abk.* = **Tausend**

T-Shirt /ˈtiːʃəːt/ *das;* ~s, ~s T-shirt

Tsunami /tsuˈnaːmi/ *der;* ~[s], ~s tsunami

Tube *die;* ~, ~n tube

Tuberkulose *die;* ~, ~n (Med.) tuberculosis *no art.*

Tuch *das;* ~[e]s, Tücher *od.* ~e **(a)** *Pl.* Tücher cloth; (Kopf-, Halstuch) scarf **(b)** *Pl.* ~e (Gewebe) cloth

Tuch·fühlung *die* (scherzh.) physical contact

tüchtig ① *Adj.* **(a)** efficient; (fähig) capable, competent (**in** + *Dat.* at) **(b)** (ugs.: beträchtlich) sizeable ⟨*piece, portion*⟩; big ⟨*gulp*⟩; hearty ⟨*eater, appetite*⟩ ② *adv.* **(a)** efficiently; (fähig) competently **(b)** (ugs.: sehr) really ⟨*cold, warm*⟩; ⟨*snow, rain*⟩ good and proper (coll.); ⟨*eat*⟩ heartily

Tüchtigkeit *die;* ~: efficiency; (Fähigkeit) ability; competence; (Fleiß) industry

Tücke *die;* ~, ~n **(a)** (Hinterhältigkeit) deceit[fulness]; (List) guile **(b)** ([verborgene] Gefahr/Schwierigkeit) [hidden] danger/difficulty

tuckern *itr. V.; mit Richtungsangabe mit sein* chug

tückisch ① *Adj.* **(a)** (hinterhältig) wily; (betrügerisch) deceitful **(b)** (gefährlich) treacherous ⟨*bend, slope, spot, etc.*⟩ ② *adv.* craftily

tüfteln *itr. V.* (ugs.) fiddle (**an** + *Dat.* with); do finicky work (**an** + *Dat.* on); (geistig) rack one's brains (**an** + *Dat.* over)

Tugend *die;* ~, ~en virtue

tugendhaft ① *Adj.* virtuous ② *adv.* virtuously

Tüll *der;* ~s, ~e tulle

Tülle *die;* ~, ~n (bes. nordd.) spout

Tulpe *die;* ~, ~n tulip

tummeln *refl. V.* romp [about]

Tummel·platz *der* (auch fig.) playground

Tumor *der;* ~s, ~en (Med.) tumour

Tümpel *der;* ~s, ~: pond

Tumult *der;* ~[e]s, ~e tumult; commotion; (Protest) uproar

tun ① *unr. tr. V.* **(a)** do; **so etwas tut man nicht** that is just not done; **[etwas] mit etw./jmdm. zu** ~ **haben** be concerned with sth./have dealings with sb. **(b)** *als Funktionsverb* make ⟨*remark, catch, etc.*⟩; take ⟨*step, jump*⟩; do ⟨*deed*⟩ **(c)** (bewirken) work, perform ⟨*miracle*⟩ **(d)** (antun) jmdm. etw. ~: do sth. to sb. **(e)** es ~ (ugs.: genügen) be good enough **(f)** (ugs.: irgendwohin bringen) put ② *unr. itr. V.* **(a)** (ugs.: funktionieren) work **(b)** freundlich/geheimnisvoll ~: pretend to be *or* (coll.) act friendly/act mysteriously

---

3 *unr. refl. V.; unpers.* **es hat sich einiges getan** quite a bit has happened

Tünche *die;* ~, ~n distemper; wash; **[weiße]** ~: whitewash

tünchen *tr. (auch itr.) V.* distemper; **weiß** ~: whitewash

Tunell *das;* ~s, ~s (südd., österr., schweiz.) ▶ Tunnel

tunen /'tjuːnən/ *tr. V.* (Kfz-W.) tune

Tuner /'tjuːnɐ/ *der;* ~s, ~(a) (Elektronik) tuner
(b) (Kfz-W.) tuner; tuning expert

Tunesien /tuˈneːzi̯ən/ *(das);* ~s Tunisia

tunesisch *Adj.* Tunisian

Tunke *die;* ~, ~n (bes. ostmd.) sauce; (Bratensoße) gravy

tunken *tr. V.* (bes. ostmd.) dip

tunlichst *Adv.* (geh.) **(a)** (möglichst) as far as possible
(b) (unbedingt) at all costs

Tunnel *der;* ~s, od. ~s tunnel

tupfen *tr. V.* **(a)** dab
(b) (mit Tupfen versehen) dot

Tupfen *der;* ~s, ~: dot; (größer) spot

Tupfer *der;* ~s, ~ (Med.) swab

Tür *die;* ~, ~en door; (Garten~) gate; **an die** ~ **gehen** (öffnen) [go and] answer the door; **vor die** ~ **gehen** go outside

Turban *der;* ~s, ~e turban

Turbine *die;* ~, ~n turbine

turbulent **1** *Adj.* (auch fachspr.) turbulent
2 *adv.* (auch fachspr.) turbulently

Turbulenz *die;* ~, ~en (auch Physik, Astron., Met.) turbulence *no pl.*

Tür·griff *der* door handle

Türke *der;* ~n, ~n Turk

Türkei *die;* ~: Turkey *no art.*

türken *tr. V.* (ugs.) fake ⟨scene, letter, document, etc.⟩; make up ⟨story, report⟩

Türkin *die;* ~, ~nen Turk

türkis *indekl. Adj.* turquoise

Türkis *der;* ~es, ~e turquoise

türkisch *Adj.* Turkish

Tür·klinke *die* door handle

Turm *der;* ~[e]s, Türme **(a)** tower; (spitzer Kirchturm) spire; steeple
(b) (Schach) rook
(c) (Sprungturm) diving platform

Türmchen *das;* ~s, ~: turret

türmen¹ **1** *tr. V.* (stapeln) stack up; (häufen) pile up
2 *refl. V.* be piled up; ⟨clouds⟩ gather

türmen² *itr. V.; mit sein* (salopp) scarper

(Brit. coll.)

Turm·falke *der* kestrel

turnen **1** *itr. V.* do gymnastics; (Schulw.) do gym
2 *tr. V.* do, perform ⟨exercise, routine⟩

Turnen *das;* ~s gymnastics *sing., no art.;* (Schulw.) gym *no art.;* PE *no art.*

Turner *der;* ~s, ~, **Turnerin** *die;* ~, ~nen gymnast

Turn-: ~**halle** *die* gymnasium; ~**hemd** *das* [gym] singlet; ~**hose** *die* gym shorts *pl.*

Turnier *das;* ~s, ~e (auch hist.) tournament; (Reitturnier) show; (Tanzturnier) competition

Turn·schuh *der* gym shoe

Turnus *der;* ~, ~se regular cycle

Turn·verein *der* gymnastics club

Tür-: ~**öffner** *der* door-opener; ~**rahmen** *der* doorframe

turteln *itr. V.* (scherzh.: zärtlich sein) bill and coo

Tusch *der;* ~[e]s, ~e fanfare

Tusche *die;* ~, ~n Indian (Brit.) *or* (Amer.) India ink

Tuschelei *die;* ~, ~en **(a)** (das Tuscheln) whispering
(b) (Äußerung) whisper

tuscheln *itr., tr. V.* whisper

Tussi *die;* ~, ~s (salopp) female (derog.)

Tüte *die;* ~, ~n bag

tuten *itr. V.* hoot; ⟨siren, [fog]horn⟩ sound

Tutor *der;* ~s, ~en, **Tutorin** *die;* ~, ~nen (Päd.) tutor

Tycoon /taiˈkuːn/ *der;* ~s, ~s tycoon

Typ *der;* ~s, ~en **(a)** type
(b) *Gen. auch* ~en (ugs.: Mann) bloke (Brit. coll.)

Type *die;* ~, ~n (Druck-, Schreibmaschinentype) type

Typhus *der;* ~: typhoid [fever]

typisch **1** *Adj.* typical (**für** of)
2 *adv.* typically

Typographie *die;* ~, ~n (Druckw.) typography

typographisch (Druckw.) **1** *Adj.* typographical
2 *adv.* typographically

Tyrann *der;* ~en, ~en (auch fig.) tyrant

Tyrannei *die;* ~, ~en (auch fig.) tyranny

Tyrannin *die;* ~, ~nen ▶ Tyrann

tyrannisch **1** *Adj.* tyrannical
2 *adv.* tyrannically

tyrannisieren *tr. V.* tyrannize

Uu

u, U /uː/ *das;* ∼, ∼: u, U
u. *Abk.* = **und**
ü, Ü /yː/ *das;* ∼, ∼: u umlaut
U-Bahn *die* underground (Brit.); subway (Amer.); (bes. in London) tube
U-Bahnhof *der;* **U-Bahn-Station** *die* underground station (Brit.); subway station (Amer.); (bes. in London) tube station
übel *Adj.* **(a)** foul, nasty ⟨*smell, weather*⟩; bad, nasty ⟨*headache, cold, taste*⟩; nasty ⟨*consequences, situation*⟩; sorry ⟨*state, affair*⟩; foul, (coll.) filthy ⟨*mood*⟩; **nicht** ∼ (ugs.) not bad at all
(b) (unwohl) **jmdm. ist/wird** ∼: sb. feels sick
(c) (verwerflich) bad; wicked; nasty, dirty ⟨*trick*⟩
(d) **jmdm. etw.** ∼ **nehmen** hold sth. against sb.; **etw.** ∼ **nehmen** take offence at sth.
Übel *das;* ∼s, ∼: evil
Übelkeit *die;* ∼, ∼en nausea
*übel|nehmen ▶ ÜBEL D
Übel·täter *der,* **Übel·täterin** *die* wrongdoer
üben *tr. V.* **(a)** (*auch itr.*) practise; rehearse ⟨*scene, play*⟩; practise on ⟨*musical instrument*⟩
(b) (trainieren, schulen) exercise ⟨*fingers*⟩; train ⟨*memory*⟩
über ① *Präp. mit Dat.* **(a)** (Lage, Standort) over; above; (in einer Rangfolge) above; ∼ **jmdm. wohnen** live above sb.; **zehn Grad** ∼ **Null** ten degrees above zero; **sie trug eine Jacke** ∼ **dem Kleid** she wore a jacket over her dress
(b) (während) during; ∼ **dem Lesen/der Arbeit einschlafen** fall asleep over one's book/magazine *etc.*/over one's work
② *Präp. mit Akk.* **(a)** (Richtung) over; (quer hinüber) across; ∼ **Ulm nach Stuttgart** via Ulm to Stuttgart
(b) (während) over; (für die Dauer von) for
(c) (betreffend) about; ∼ **etw. reden/schreiben** talk/write about sth.; **ein Scheck/eine Rechnung** ∼ **100 Euro** a cheque/bill for 100 euros
(d) Kinder ∼ **10 Jahre** children over ten [years of age]
③ *Adv.* **(a)** (mehr als) over
(b) ∼ **und** ∼: all over
über·all /od. --'-/ *Adv.* **(a)** everywhere
(b) (bei jeder Gelegenheit) always
überall-: ∼**her** *Adv.* from all over the place; ∼**hin** *Adv.* everywhere
Über·angebot *das* surplus (**an** + *Dat.* of);

(Schwemme) glut (**an** + *Dat.* of)
über·anstrengen *tr. V.; ich überanstrenge, überanstrengt, zu überanstrengen* overtax ⟨*person, energy*⟩; strain ⟨*eyes, nerves, heart*⟩; **sich** ∼: overexert oneself
über·arbeiten ① *tr. V.* rework; revise ⟨*text, edition*⟩
② *refl. V.* overwork
über·aus *Adv.* (geh.) extremely
über·backen *unr. tr. V.* **etw. mit Käse** *usw.* ∼: top sth. with cheese *etc.* and brown it lightly [under the grill/in a hot oven]
Über·bein *das* (Med.) ganglion
überbelichten *tr. V.; ich überbelichte, überbelichtet, überzubelichten* (Fot.) overexpose
über·bieten *unr. tr. V.* **(a)** outbid (**um** by)
(b) (übertreffen) surpass; outdo ⟨*rival*⟩; break ⟨*record*⟩ (**um** by); exceed ⟨*target*⟩ (**um** by)
Über·blick *der* **(a)** view; **einen guten** ∼ **über etw.** (*Akk.*) **haben** have a good view over sth.
(b) (Abriss) survey
(c) (Einblick) overall view
über·blicken *tr. V.* ▶ ÜBERSEHEN A, B
über·bringen *unr. tr. V.* deliver; convey ⟨*greetings, congratulations*⟩
über·brücken *tr. V.* bridge ⟨*gap, gulf*⟩; reconcile ⟨*difference*⟩
Überbrückung *die;* ∼, ∼en (fig.) bridging; (von Gegensätzen) reconciliation
über·buchen *tr. V.* overbook
überdacht *Adj.* covered ⟨*terrace, station platform, etc.*⟩
über·dauern *tr. V.* survive ⟨*war, separation, hardship*⟩
über·dehnen *tr. V.* overstretch; strain ⟨*muscle*⟩
über·dies *Adv.* moreover
Über·dosis *die* overdose
Über·druck *der; Pl.* Überdrücke excess pressure
Überdruss, *Überdruß *der;* Überdrusses surfeit (**an** + *Dat.* of)
überdrüssig *Adj.* **jmds./einer Sache** ∼ **sein/werden** be/grow tired of sb./sth.
über·eignen *tr. V.* **jmdm. etw.** ∼: transfer sth. *or* make sth. over to sb.
Über·eignung *die* transfer (**an** + *Akk.* to)
über·eilen *tr. V.* rush; **übereilt** overhasty
über·einander *Adv.* **(a)** one on top of the other; **Holzscheite** *usw.:* ∼ **legen** lay pieces of wood *etc.* one on top of the other; **Arme/Beine** ∼ **schlagen** fold one's

---

*alte Schreibung – vgl. Hinweis auf S. x

arms/cross one's legs
(b) ⟨*talk etc.*⟩ about each other
*übereinạnder|legen *usw.*
▸ ÜBEREINANDER A

überein|kommen *unr. itr. V.; mit sein*
agree; come to an agreement
Überein·kommen *das;* ~s, ~,
Überẹinkunft *die;* ~, Überẹinkünfte
agreement

überein|stimmen *itr. V.* **(a)** (einer Meinung
sein) agree (**in** + *Dat.* on)
(b) (sich gleichen) ⟨*colours, styles*⟩ match;
⟨*figures, statements, reports, results*⟩ tally,
agree; ⟨*views, opinions*⟩ coincide

Überein·stimmung *die* agreement (**in**
+ *Dat.* on; *Gen.* between)

über·empfindlich ☐1 *Adj.* oversensitive
(**gegen** to); (Med.) hypersensitive (**gegen** to).
☐2 *adv.* oversensitively; (Med.)
hypersensitively

Über·empfindlichkeit *die*
oversensitivity (**gegen** to); (Med.)
hypersensitivity (**gegen** to)

über|fahren[1] ☐1 *unr. tr. V.* jmdn. ~: ferry
or take sb. over
☐2 *unr. itr. V.; mit sein* cross over

über·fahren[2] *unr. tr. V.* **(a)** run over
(b) (hinwegfahren über) cross; go over
⟨*crossroads*⟩

Über·fahrt *die* crossing (**über** + *Akk.* of)

Über·fall *der* attack (**auf** + *Akk.* on); (aus
dem Hinterhalt) ambush (**auf** + *Akk.* on); (mit
vorgehaltener Waffe) hold-up; (auf eine Bank o. Ä.)
raid (**auf** + *Akk.* on)

über·fallen *unr. tr. V.* **(a)** attack; raid
⟨*bank, enemy position, village, etc.*⟩;
(hinterrücks) ambush; (mit vorgehaltener Waffe)
hold up
(b) (überkommen) ⟨*tiredness, homesickness,
fear*⟩ come over

über·fällig *Adj.* overdue
über·fischen *tr. V.* overfish
über·fliegen *unr. tr. V.* **(a)** fly over;
overfly
(b) (flüchtig lesen) skim [through]

über·flügeln *tr. V.* outshine; outstrip

Über·fluss, *Über·fluß *der* abundance
(**an** + *Dat.* of); (Wohlstand) affluence

über·flüssig *Adj.* superfluous;
unnecessary ⟨*purchase, words, work*⟩

über·fluten *tr. V.* (auch fig.) flood

Über|flutung *die;* ~, ~en (auch fig.)
flooding

über·fordern *tr. V.* jmdn. [mit etw.]
~: overtax sb. [with sth.]; ask *or* demand
too much of sb. [with sth.]

über·fragen *tr. V.* da bin ich überfragt I
don't know the answer to that

über·fremden *tr. V.* überfremdet
werden/sein ⟨*country*⟩ be dominated [by
foreign influences]

Über·fremdung *die;* ~, ~en domination

[by foreign influences]

über·frieren *unr. itr. V.; mit sein* freeze
over; ~de Nässe black ice

über|führen[1] *tr. V.* transfer

über·führen[2] *tr. V.* **(a)** ▸ ÜBERFÜHREN[1]
(b) jmdn. [eines Verbrechens] ~: find sb.
guilty [of a crime]; convict sb. [of a crime]

Über·führung *die* **(a)** transfer
(b) (eines Verdächtigen) conviction
(c) (Brücke) bridge; (Hochstraße) overpass; (für
Fußgänger) [foot]bridge

über·füllt *Adj.* crammed full (**von** with);
(mit Menschen) overcrowded (**von** with);
oversubscribed ⟨*course*⟩

Über·gabe *die* **(a)** handing over (**an** + *Akk.*
to); (von Macht) handing over
(b) (Auslieferung an den Gegner) surrender (**an**
+ *Akk.* to)

Über·gang *der* **(a)** crossing
(b) (Stelle zum Überqueren) crossing;
(Bahnübergang) level crossing (Brit.); grade
crossing (Amer.); (Grenzübergang) crossing
point
(c) (Wechsel, Überleitung) transition (**zu, auf**
+ *Akk.* to)

über·geben ☐1 *unr. tr. V.* **(a)** hand over;
pass ⟨*baton*⟩
(b) (übereignen) transfer, make over (*Dat.* to)
(c) (ausliefern) surrender (*Dat.,* **an** + *Akk.* to)
(d) eine Straße dem Verkehr ~: open a road
to traffic
☐2 *unr. refl. V.* (sich erbrechen) vomit

über|gehen[1] *unr. itr. V.; mit sein* **(a)** pass
(b) zu etw. ~: go over to sth.
(c) in etw. (*Akk.*) ~ (zu etw. werden) turn into
sth.

über·gehen[2] *unr. tr. V.* **(a)** (nicht beachten)
ignore
(b) (auslassen, überspringen) skip [over]
(c) (nicht berücksichtigen) pass over

über·geordnet *Adj.* higher ⟨*court,
authority, position*⟩; greater ⟨*significance*⟩;
superordinate ⟨*concept*⟩

Über·gewicht *das* **(a)** excess weight
(b) (fig.) predominance

über·gewichtig *Adj.* overweight

über·glücklich *Adj.* blissfully happy;
(hocherfreut) overjoyed

über|greifen *unr. itr. V.* auf etw. (*Akk.*)
~: spread to sth.

Über·griff *der* (unrechtmäßiger Eingriff)
encroachment (**auf** + *Akk.* on); infringement
(**auf** + *Akk.* of); (Angriff) attack (**auf** + *Akk.* on)

Über·größe *die* outsize

überhand: ~ nehmen get out of
hand; ⟨*attacks, muggings, etc.*⟩ increase
alarmingly; ⟨*weeds*⟩ run riot

über|hängen *tr. V.* sich (*Dat.*) eine Jacke
~: put a jacket round one's shoulders; sich
(*Dat.*) das Gewehr/die Tasche ~: hang the
rifle/bag over one's shoulder

über·häufen *tr. V.* jmdn. mit etw. ~: heap
or shower sth. on sb.

überhaupt *Adv.* (a) in general
(b) ~ **nicht** not at all; ~ **keine Zeit haben** have no time at all; ~ **nichts** nothing at all

überheblich ⓵ *Adj.* arrogant; supercilious ⟨*grin*⟩
⓶ *adv.* arrogantly; ⟨*grin*⟩ superciliously

Überheblichkeit *die;* ~: arrogance

über·holen ⓵ *tr. V.* (a) overtake (esp. Brit.); pass (esp. Amer.)
(b) (übertreffen) outstrip
(c) (wieder instand setzen) overhaul
⓶ *itr. V.* overtake (esp. Brit.); pass (esp. Amer.)

Überholspur *die* overtaking lane (esp. Brit.); pass lane (esp. Amer.)

überholt *Adj.* (veraltet) outdated

Überholung *die;* ~, ~en overhaul

Überhol·verbot *das* ban on overtaking

über·hören *tr. V.* not hear

über·irdisch ⓵ *Adj.* celestial; heavenly; (übernatürlich) supernatural
⓶ *adv.* celestially; (übernatürlich) supernaturally

über|kochen *itr. V.; mit sein* (auch fig. ugs.) boil over

über·kommen *unr. tr. V.* Mitleid/Ekel/ Furcht überkam mich I was overcome by pity/revulsion/fear

über·laden *unr. tr. V.* (auch fig.) overload

über·lassen *unr. tr. V.* (a) jmdm. etw. ~: let sb. have sth.
(b) sich (*Dat.*) selbst ~ sein be left to one's own devices
(c) etw. jmdm. ~ (etw. jmdn. entscheiden/tun lassen) leave sth. to sb.

über·lasten *tr. V.* overload; overtax ⟨*person*⟩; (mit Arbeit) overwork ⟨*person*⟩

Über·lauf *der* overflow

über|laufen[1] *unr. itr. V.; mit sein*
(a) overflow
(b) (auf die gegnerische Seite überwechseln) defect; ⟨*partisan*⟩ go over to the other side

über·laufen[2] *unr. tr. V.* seize; **ein Frösteln/Schauer überlief mich, es überlief mich [eis]kalt** a cold shiver ran down my spine

überlaufen[3] *Adj.* overcrowded

Über·läufer *der,* **Über·läuferin** *die* (auch fig.) defector

über·leben *tr. V.* survive

Über·lebende *der/die; adj. Dekl.* survivor

über|legen[1] *tr. V.* jmdm. etw. ~: put sth. over sb.

über·legen[2] ⓵ *tr. V.* consider; think about; **es sich anders** ~: change one's mind
⓶ *itr. V.* think

überlegen[3] ⓵ *Adj.* (a) superior; clear, convincing ⟨*win, victory*⟩; **jmdm.** ~ **sein** be superior to sb. (**an** + *Dat.* in)
(b) (herablassend) supercilious

⓶ *adv.* (a) in a superior manner; ⟨*play*⟩ much the better: ⟨*win, argue*⟩ convincingly
(b) (herablassend) superciliously

Überlegenheit *die;* ~: superiority

überlegt ⓵ *Adj.* carefully considered
⓶ *adv.* in a carefully considered way

Überlegung *die;* ~, ~en (a) thought
(b) (Gedanke) idea; ~en (Gedankengang) thoughts

über·liefern *tr. V.* hand down

Über·lieferung *die* tradition

überlisten *tr. V.* outwit

überm *Präp.* + *Art.* = über dem

Über·macht *die* superior strength; (zahlenmäßig) superior numbers *pl.*

über·mannen *tr. V.* overcome

Über·maß *das* excessive amount, excess (**an** + *Dat.* of)

über·mäßig ⓵ *Adj.* excessive
⓶ *adv.* excessively

über·menschlich *Adj.* superhuman

über·mitteln *tr. V.* send; (als Mittler weitergeben) pass on, convey ⟨*greetings, regards, etc.*⟩

über·morgen *Adv.* the day after tomorrow

über·müden *tr. V.* overtire; **übermüdet** overtired; exhausted

Übermüdung *die;* ~: overtiredness; exhaustion

Über·mut *der* high spirits *pl.*

übermütig ⓵ *Adj.* high-spirited
⓶ *adv.* high-spiritedly

über·nächst... *Adj.* **im** ~**en Jahr,** ~**es Jahr** the year after next; **am** ~**en Tag** two days later

über·nachten *itr. V.* stay overnight

übernächtigt *Adj.* ⟨*person*⟩ tired *or* worn out [through lack of sleep]; tired ⟨*face, look, etc.*⟩

Übernachtung *die;* ~, ~en overnight stay; ~ **und Frühstück** bed and breakfast

Übernahme *die;* ~ (von Waren, einer Sendung) taking delivery *no art.;* (einer Idee usw.) adoption, taking over *no indef. art.;* (der Macht, einer Praxis usw.) take over

über·natürlich *Adj.* supernatural

über·nehmen ⓵ *unr. tr. V.* (a) take delivery of ⟨*goods, consignment*⟩; take over ⟨*power, practice, business, etc.*⟩; take on ⟨*job, position, etc.*⟩; undertake to pay ⟨*costs*⟩
(b) (sich zu Eigen machen) adopt ⟨*ideas, methods, subject, etc.*⟩ (**von** from); borrow ⟨*word, phrase*⟩ (**von** from)
⓶ *unr. refl. V.* overdo things *or* it; **sich mit etw.** ~: take on too much with sth.

Über·produktion *die* (Wirtsch., Med.) overproduction

über·prüfen *tr. V.* check (**auf** + *Akk.* for); review ⟨*issue, situation, results*⟩

Über·prüfung *die* (a) checking *no indef. art.* (**auf** + *Akk.* for)

(b) (Kontrolle) check; (einer Lage, Frage usw.) review

über·queren tr. V. cross

über·ragen tr. V. **(a)** jmdn./etw. ∼: tower above sb./sth

(b) (übertreffen) jmdn. an etw. (Dat.) ∼: be head and shoulders above sb. in sth.

überragend ⑴ Adj. outstanding

⑵ adv. outstandingly

über·raschen tr. V. surprise

Überraschung die; ∼, ∼en surprise

über·reden tr. V. persuade

Überredung die; ∼: persuasion

über·regional ⑴ Adj. national ⟨newspaper, radio station⟩

⑵ adv. nationally

über·reichen tr. V. [jmdm.] etw. ∼: present sth. [to sb.]

Überreichung die; ∼: presentation

über·reif Adj. over-ripe

über·rumpeln tr. V. jmdn. ∼: take sb. by surprise

über·runden tr. V. **(a)** (Sport) lap

(b) (übertreffen) outstrip

übers Präp. + Art. = über das

über·sättigen tr. V. supersaturate ⟨solution⟩; glut ⟨market⟩; satiate ⟨public⟩

Überschall-: ∼flugzeug das supersonic aircraft;

∼geschwindigkeit die supersonic speed

über·schatten tr. V. overshadow; cast its/their shadow over; (fig.) cast a shadow over

über·schätzen tr. V. overestimate; overrate ⟨artist, talent, etc.⟩

Über·schätzung die ▸ ÜBERSCHÄTZEN: overestimation; overrating

überschaubar Adj. eine ∼e Menge/Zahl a manageable quantity/number

über·schauen tr. V. ▸ ÜBERSEHEN A, B

Über·schlag der **(a)** rough calculation or estimate

(b) (Turnen) handspring

(c) ▸ LOOPING

über|schlagen¹ ⑴ unr. tr. V. die Beine ∼: cross one's legs

⑵ unr. itr. V.; mit sein ⟨wave⟩ break

über·schlagen² ⑴ unr. tr. V. **(a)** skip ⟨chapter, page, etc.⟩

(b) (ungefähr berechnen) calculate or estimate roughly

⑵ unr. refl. V. go head over heels; ⟨car⟩ turn over

über|schnappen itr. V.; mit sein (ugs.) go crazy

über·schneiden unr. refl. V. cross, intersect; (fig.) overlap

über·schreiben unr. tr. V. **(a)** entitle; head ⟨chapter, section⟩

(b) etw. jmdm. od. auf jmdn. ∼: transfer sth. to sb.

(c) (DV) overwrite

über·schreiten unr. itr. V. cross; (fig.) exceed

Über·schrift die heading; (in einer Zeitung) headline; (Titel) title

Über·schuss, *Über·schuß der surplus (an + Dat. of)

überschüssig Adj. surplus

über·schütten tr. V. cover

Überschwang der; ∼[e]s exuberance

über·schwänglich ⑴ Adj. effusive ⟨words etc.⟩; wild ⟨joy, enthusiasm⟩

⑵ adv. effusively

über·schwemmen tr. V. (auch fig.) flood

Überschwemmung die; ∼, ∼en flood; (das Überschwemmen) flooding no pl.

***über·schwenglich**

▸ ÜBERSCHWÄNGLICH

Über·see: aus od. von ∼: from overseas; in/nach ∼: overseas

über·sehen unr. tr. V. **(a)** look out over

(b) (abschätzen) assess ⟨damage, situation, consequences, etc.⟩

(c) (nicht sehen) overlook; miss; miss ⟨turning, signpost⟩

(d) (ignorieren) ignore

über·senden unr. (auch regelm.) tr. V. send

über|setzen¹ ⑴ tr. V. ferry over

⑵ itr. V.; auch mit sein cross [over]

über·setzen² tr., itr. V. (auch fig.) translate

Über·setzer der, **Übersetzerin** die; ∼, ∼nen translator

Übersetzung die; ∼, ∼en translation

Über·sicht die **(a)** overall view, overview (über + Akk. of)

(b) (Darstellung) survey; (Tabelle) summary

über·sichtlich ⑴ Adj. clear; ⟨crossroads⟩ which allows a clear view

⑵ adv. clearly

Übersichtlichkeit die; ∼: clarity; (einer Kreuzung) clear layout

über|siedeln¹, über·siedeln² itr. V.; mit sein move (nach to)

Über·siedler der, **Über·siedlerin** die migrant

überspannt Adj. exaggerated ⟨ideas, behaviour, gestures⟩; extreme ⟨views⟩; inflated ⟨demands, expectations⟩

über·spielen tr. V. **(a)** (hinweggehen über) cover up; smooth over ⟨difficult situation⟩

(b) (aufnehmen) [auf ein Tonband] ∼: transfer ⟨record⟩ to tape; put ⟨record⟩ on tape

über·spitzen tr. V. etw. ∼: push or carry sth. too far

über·springen unr. tr. V. **(a)** jump ⟨obstacle⟩

(b) (auslassen) miss out

über|stehen¹ unr. itr. V.; südd., österr., schweiz. mit sein jut out

über·stehen² unr. tr. V. come through ⟨danger, war, operation⟩; get over ⟨illness⟩

über·steigen *unr. tr. V.* **(a)** climb over
(b) (fig.) exceed

über·stimmen *tr. V.* outvote

über|streifen *tr. V.* **[sich** (*Dat.*)**]** etw.
~: slip sth. on

über|stülpen *tr. V.* pull on ⟨*hat etc.*⟩

Über·stunde *die:* ~n machen do overtime

über·stürzen ① *tr. V.* rush
② *refl. V.* rush; (rasch aufeinander folgen)
⟨*events, news, etc.*⟩ come thick and fast

überstürzt ① *Adj.* hurried ⟨*escape,
departure*⟩; overhasty ⟨*decision*⟩
② *adv.* ⟨*decide, act*⟩ overhastily; ⟨*depart*⟩
hurriedly

über·tölpeln *tr. V.* dupe; con (coll.)

über·tönen *tr. V.* drown out

Übertrag *der;* ~[e]s, **Überträge** (bes. Buchf.)
carry-over

über·tragbar *Adj.* transferable (**auf**
+ *Akk.* to); (auf etw. anderes anwendbar)
applicable (**auf** + *Akk.* to); (übersetzbar)
translatable; (ansteckend) infectious ⟨*disease*⟩

über·tragen *unr. tr. V.* **(a)** transfer (**auf**
+ *Akk.* to); transmit ⟨*power, torque, etc.*⟩ (**auf**
+ *Akk.* to); communicate ⟨*disease, illness*⟩
(**auf** + *Akk.* to); carry over ⟨*subtotal*⟩; (auf
etw. anderes anwenden) apply (**auf** + *Akk.* to);
(übersetzen) translate
(b) (senden) broadcast ⟨*concert, event, match,
etc.*⟩; (im Fernsehen) televise
(c) (geben) **jmdm. Aufgaben/Pflichten**
usw. ~: hand over tasks/duties *etc.* to sb.;
(anvertrauen) entrust sb. with tasks/duties *etc.*

Übertragung *die;* ~, ~en
(a) ▶ ÜBERTRAGEN A: transference;
transmission; communication; carrying
over; application; translation
(b) (das Senden) broadcasting; (Sendung)
broadcast; (im Fernsehen) televising/
television broadcast

über·treffen *unr. tr. V.* **(a)** surpass, outdo
(**an** + *Dat.* in); break ⟨*record*⟩
(b) (übersteigen) exceed

über·treiben *unr. tr. V.* **(a)** auch itr.
exaggerate
(b) (zu weit treiben) overdo

Übertreibung *die;* ~, ~en exaggeration

über|treten[1] *unr. itr. V.; mit sein* change
sides; **zum Katholizismus/Islam** ~: convert
to Catholicism/Islam

über·treten[2] *unr. tr. V.* contravene ⟨*law*⟩;
violate ⟨*regulation, prohibition*⟩

Übertretung *die;* ~, ~en
(a) ▶ ÜBERTRETEN[2]: contravention; violation
(b) (Vergehen) misdemeanour

übertrieben *Adj.* ① exaggerated;
(übermäßig) excessive ⟨*care, thrift, etc.*⟩
② *adv.* excessively

Über·tritt *der* change of allegiance, switch
(**zu** to); (Rel.) conversion (**zu** to)

über·trumpfen *tr. V.* outdo

über·tünchen *tr. V.* cover with
whitewash; (fig.) cover up

über·vorteilen *tr. V.* cheat

über·wachen *tr. V.* keep under
surveillance ⟨*suspect, agent, area, etc.*⟩;
supervise ⟨*factory, workers, process*⟩; control
⟨*traffic*⟩; monitor ⟨*progress, production
process, experiment, patient*⟩

Überwachung *die;* ~, ~en
▶ ÜBERWACHEN: surveillance; supervision;
controlling; monitoring

über·wältigen *tr. V.* **(a)** overpower
(b) (fig.) ⟨*sleep, emotion, fear, etc.*⟩ overcome;
⟨*sight, impressions, beauty, etc.*⟩ overwhelm

überwältigend ① *Adj.* overwhelming
⟨*sight, impression, victory, majority, etc.*⟩;
overpowering ⟨*smell*⟩; stunning ⟨*beauty*⟩
② *adv.* stunningly ⟨*beautiful*⟩

über·weisen *unr. tr. V.* **(a)** transfer
⟨*money*⟩ (**an, auf** + *Akk.* to)
(b) refer ⟨*patient*⟩ (**an** + *Akk.* to)

Über·weisung *die* **(a)** transfer (**an, auf**
+ *Akk.* to)
(b) (Summe) remittance
(c) (eines Patienten) referral (**an** + *Akk.* to)

überwiegend ① /*auch* --'--/ *Adj.*
overwhelming
② *adv.* mainly

über·winden ① *unr. tr. V.* overcome; get
past ⟨*stage*⟩
② *unr. refl. V.* overcome one's reluctance;
sich [dazu] ~, **etw. zu tun** bring oneself to do
sth.

Über·windung *die* **(a)** ▶ ÜBERWINDEN 1:
overcoming; getting past
(b) (das Sichüberwinden) **es war eine große**
~ **für ihn** it cost him a great effort

über·wuchern *tr. V.* overgrow

Über·zahl *die* majority

überzählig *Adj.* surplus

über·zeugen ① *tr. V.* convince
② *itr. V.* be convincing

überzeugend ① *Adj.* convincing
② *adv.* convincingly

überzeugt *Adj.* convinced

Über·zeugung *die* (feste Meinung)
conviction

über|ziehen[1] *unr. tr. V.* pull on

über·ziehen[2] *unr. tr. V.* **(a)** etw. mit etw.
~: cover sth. with sth.
(b) overdraw ⟨*account*⟩ (**um** by)

Überziehungs·kredit *der* (Finanzw.)
overdraft facility

überzüchtet *Adj.* overbred; over-
sophisticated ⟨*engines, systems*⟩

Überzug *der* **(a)** (Beschichtung) coating
(b) (Bezug) cover

üblich *Adj.* usual; (normal) normal;
(gebräuchlich) customary

üblicher·weise *Adv.* usually

U-Boot *das* submarine; sub (coll.)

übrig *Adj.* remaining *attrib.;* (ander...) other;

alle ∼en Gäste ...: all the other guests ...;
im Übrigen besides; **es ist etwas ∼**: there
is some left; **∼ bleiben** be left; ⟨food, drink⟩
be left over; **∼ lassen** (+ Akk.) leave; leave
⟨food, drink⟩ over

***übrig|bleiben** ▸ ÜBRIG

übrigens Adv. by the way

***übrig|lassen** ▸ ÜBRIG

Übung die; ∼, ∼en **(a)** exercise
(b) (das Üben, Geübtsein) practice

UdSSR Abk. die; ∼ (1922–1991) =
**Union der Sozialistischen
Sowjetrepubliken** USSR

Ufer das; ∼s, ∼: bank; (des Meers) shore

UG Abk. = **Untergeschoss**

Uganda (das); ∼s Uganda

Uhr die; ∼, ∼en **(a)** clock; (Armband-,
Taschenuhr) watch; (Wasser-, Gasuhr) meter; (an
Messinstrumenten) dial; gauge; **auf die** od. **nach
der ∼ sehen** look at the time; **rund um die ∼**
(ugs.) round the clock
(b) acht ∼: eight o'clock; **wie viel ∼ ist es?**
what's the time?; what time is it?

Uhr-: ∼**armband** das watch strap;
∼**kette** die watch chain; ∼**macher**
der, ∼**macherin** die watchmaker/
clockmaker; ∼**werk** das clock/watch
mechanism; ∼**zeiger** der clock/watch
hand; ∼**zeiger·sinn** der: im/entgegen
dem ∼zeigersinn clockwise/anticlockwise;
∼**zeit** die time; jmdn. nach der ∼zeit fragen
ask sb. the time

Uhu der; ∼s, ∼s eagle owl

Ukraine die; ∼: Ukraine

Ukrainer der; ∼s, ∼, **Ukrainerin** die;
∼, ∼nen Ukrainian

UKW Abk. = **Ultrakurzwelle** VHF

UKW-Sender der VHF station; ≈ FM
station

Ulk der; ∼s, ∼e lark (coll.); (Streich) trick;
[practical] joke

ulkig (ugs.) **⒈** Adj. funny
⒉ adv. in a funny way

Ulme die; ∼, ∼n elm

Ultimatum das; ∼s, Ultimaten ultimatum

Ultra·kurz·welle die ultra-short wave;
(Rundf.: Wellenbereich) very high frequency;
VHF

Ultra·schall der (Physik, Med.) ultrasound

Ultraschall·untersuchung die (Med.)
ultrasound examination

ultra·violett Adj. ultraviolet

um ⒈ Präp. mit Akk. **(a)** (räumlich) [a]round;
um die Ecke round the corner
(b) (zeitlich) (genau) at; (etwa) around [about]
(c) (zeitlich) **um Tag/Stunde um Stunde** day after
day/hour after hour
(d) (bei Maß- u. Mengenangaben) by
⒉ Adv. around; about; **um [die] 10 Euro/50
Personen [herum]** around or about ten
euros/50 people
⒊ Konj. **(a)** (final) **um ... zu** [in order] to

(b) (konsekutiv) **er ist groß genug/ist noch zu
klein, um ... zu ...:** he is big enough/is still
too young to ...

um|ändern tr. V. change; revise ⟨text,
novel⟩; alter ⟨garment⟩

um·armen tr. V. embrace; (an sich drücken)
hug

Umarmung die; ∼, ∼en embrace; hug

Um·bau der; ∼[e]s, ∼ten ▸ UMBAUEN:
rebuilding; alteration; conversion; (fig.)
reorganization

um|bauen tr., auch itr. V. rebuild; (leicht
ändern) alter; (zu etw. anderem) convert
(**zu** into); (fig.) reorganize ⟨system,
administration, etc.⟩

um|benennen unr. tr. V. change the
name of; rename

um|biegen ⒈ unr. tr. V. bend
⒉ unr. itr. V.; mit sein turn

um|binden unr. tr. V. put on

um|blättern ⒈ tr. V. turn [over]
⒉ itr. V. turn the page/pages

um|blicken refl. V. **(a)** look around
(b) (zurückblicken) [turn to] look back (**nach**
at)

um|bringen unr. tr. V. kill

Um·bruch der **(a)** radical change;
(Umwälzung) upheaval
(b) (Druckw.) make-up; (Ergebnis) page proofs
pl.

um|buchen ⒈ tr. V. change (**auf** + Akk.
to)
⒉ itr. V. change one's booking (**auf** + Akk.
to)

Um·buchung die change of booking

um|datieren tr. V. change the date of;
redate ⟨contract, letter, etc.⟩

um|denken unr. itr. V. revise one's
thinking; rethink; **ein Prozess des
Umdenkens** a process of rethinking

um|drehen ⒈ tr. V. turn round; turn over
⟨coin, hand, etc.⟩; turn ⟨key⟩
⒉ refl. V. turn round; (den Kopf wenden) turn
one's head
⒊ itr. V.; auch mit sein (ugs.: umkehren) turn
back; (ugs.: wenden) turn round

Um·drehung die turn; (eines Motors usw.)
revolution; rev (coll.)

um·einander Adv. **sich ∼ kümmern/
sorgen** take care of/worry about each other
or one another

um|fahren[1] unr. tr. V. knock down

um·fahren[2] unr. tr. V. go round; make
a detour round ⟨obstruction etc.⟩; (im Auto)
drive round; (im Schiff) sail round; (auf einer
Umgehungsstraße) bypass ⟨town, village, etc.⟩

um|fallen unr. itr. V.; mit sein **(a)** fall over
(b) (zusammenbrechen) collapse; **tot ∼**: fall
down dead

Um·fang der **(a)** circumference; (eines
Quadrats usw.) perimeter; (eines Baums,
Menschen usw.) girth
⋯⋗

(b) (Größe) size
(c) (Ausmaß) extent
um·fang·reich *Adj.* extensive; substantial
⟨*book*⟩
um·fassen *tr. V.* **(a)** grasp; (umarmen)
embrace
(b) (enthalten) contain; (einschließen) include;
span, cover ⟨*period*⟩
umfassend ⟨1⟩ *Adj.* full ⟨*reply,*
information, survey, confession⟩; extensive,
wide ⟨*knowledge, powers*⟩
⟨2⟩ *adv.* ⟨*inform*⟩ fully
Um·feld *das* (Psych., Soziol.) milieu
um|formen *tr. V.* reshape; revise ⟨*poem,*
novel⟩; transform ⟨*person*⟩
Um·frage *die* survey; (Politik) opinion poll
um|füllen *tr. V.* etw. in etw. (*Akk.*)
∼: transfer sth. into sth.
um|funktionieren *tr. V.* change the
function of; **etw. zu etw.** ∼: turn sth. into
sth.
Um·gang *der* **(a)** (gesellschaftlicher Verkehr)
contact
(b) (das Umgehen) **den** ∼ **mit Pferden lernen**
learn how to handle horses
umgänglich *Adj.* affable; (gesellig) sociable
Umgangs-: ∼**form** *die* **gute/schlechte/**
keine ∼**formen haben** have good/bad/no
manners; ∼**sprache** *die* colloquial
language
um·garnen *tr. V.* beguile
um·geben *unr. tr. V.* **(a)** surround; ⟨*hedge,*
fence, wall, etc.⟩ enclose
(b) etw. mit etw. ∼: surround sth. with sth.;
(einfrieden) enclose sth. with sth.
Umgebung *die;* ∼, ∼**en** surroundings *pl.;*
(Nachbarschaft) neighbourhood; (eines Ortes)
surrounding area
um|gehen¹ *unr. itr. V.; mit sein* **(a)** (im
Umlauf sein) ⟨*list, rumour, etc.*⟩ go round,
circulate; ⟨*illness, infection*⟩ go round
(b) (spuken) **hier geht ein Gespenst um** this
place is haunted
(c) (behandeln) **mit jmdm. freundlich/liebevoll**
usw. ∼: treat sb. kindly/lovingly *etc.;* **er**
kann mit Geld nicht ∼: he can't handle
money
um·gehen² *unr. tr. V.* **(a)** go round; make
a detour round; (auf einer Umgehungsstraße)
bypass ⟨*town etc.*⟩
(b) (vermeiden) avoid; evade ⟨*question, issue*⟩
(c) (nicht befolgen) circumvent ⟨*law,*
restriction, etc.⟩; evade ⟨*obligation, duty*⟩
umgehend ⟨1⟩ *Adj.* immediate
⟨2⟩ *adv.* immediately
Umgehung *die;* ∼, ∼**en (a) durch** ∼ **der**
Innenstadt by bypassing *or* avoiding the
town centre
(b) ▶ UMGEHEN² C: circumvention; evasion
Umgehungs·straße *die* bypass
umgekehrt ⟨1⟩ *Adj.* inverse ⟨*ratio,*

proportion⟩; reverse ⟨*order*⟩; opposite ⟨*sign*⟩
⟨2⟩ *adv.* inversely ⟨*proportional*⟩; **vom**
Englischen ins Deutsche und ∼ **übersetzen**
translate from English into German and
vice versa
um|gestalten *tr. V.* reshape; remodel;
redesign ⟨*square, park, room, etc.*⟩
um|graben *unr. tr. V.* dig over
Um·hang *der* cape
um|hängen *tr. V.* **(a)** etw. ∼: hang sth.
somewhere else
(b) jmdm./sich einen Mantel/eine Decke
∼: drape a coat/blanket round sb.'s/one's
shoulders
um|hauen *unr. tr. V.* fell; (fig.) knock down
um·her *Adv.* around
umher- ▸ HERUM-
um|hören *refl. V.* keep one's ears open;
(direkt fragen) ask around
um|jubeln *tr. V.* cheer
um|kehren ⟨1⟩ *itr. V.; mit sein* turn back
⟨2⟩ *tr. V.* turn upside down; turn over ⟨*sheet*
of paper⟩; (nach links drehen) turn ⟨*garment*
etc.⟩ inside out; (nach rechts drehen) turn
⟨*garment etc.*⟩ right side out
um|kippen ⟨1⟩ *itr. V.; mit sein* **(a)** fall over;
⟨*boat*⟩ capsize, turn over; ⟨*vehicle*⟩ overturn
(b) (ugs.: ohnmächtig werden) keel over
(c) (Ökologie) ⟨*river, lake*⟩ reach the stage of
biological collapse
⟨2⟩ *tr. V.* tip over; knock over ⟨*lamp, vase,*
glass, cup⟩; capsize ⟨*boat*⟩; turn ⟨*boat*⟩ over;
overturn ⟨*vehicle*⟩
um|klappen *tr. V.* fold down
Umkleide·kabine *die* changing cubicle
um|knicken *itr. V.; mit sein* **(a)** [mit dem
Fuß] ∼: go over on one's ankle
(b) bend; ⟨*branch*⟩ bend and snap
um|kommen *unr. itr. V.; mit sein* die;
(bei einem Unglück, durch Gewalt) get killed; die;
⟨*food*⟩ go off
Um·kreis *der* surrounding area; **im** ∼ **von**
5 km within a radius of 5 km.
um·kreisen *tr. V.* circle; ⟨*spacecraft,*
satellite⟩ orbit; ⟨*planet*⟩ revolve [a]round
Um·lauf *der* **(a)** (von Planeten) revolution
(b) (Zirkulation) circulation; **in** *od.* **im** ∼ **sein**
be circulating; ⟨*coin, banknote*⟩ be in
circulation; **in** ∼ **bringen** circulate; bring
⟨*coin, banknote*⟩ into circulation
Umlauf·bahn *die* (Astron., Raumf.) orbit
Um·laut *der* (Sprachw.) umlaut
um|legen *tr. V.* **(a)** (um einen Körperteil) put
on
(b) (verlegen) transfer ⟨*patient, telephone*
call⟩
(c) (salopp: ermorden) **jmdn.** ∼: bump sb. off
(coll.)
um|leiten divert
Um·leitung *die* diversion
umliegend *Adj.* surrounding ⟨*area*⟩;
(nahe) nearby ⟨*building*⟩

---

*old spelling – see note on page x

um|modeln *tr. V.* (ugs.) change ⟨*house, flat*⟩ round; refashion, alter ⟨*jacket etc.*⟩

um·nạchtet *Adj.* (geh.) deranged

Umnạchtung *die;* ~, ~en (geh.) derangement

um|pflanzen *tr. V.* transplant

um|pflügen *tr. V.* plough up

um|räumen ⟨1⟩ *tr. V.* rearrange
⟨2⟩ *itr. V.* rearrange things

um|rechnen *tr. V.* convert (**in** + *Akk.* into)

Ụm·rechnung *die* conversion (**in** + *Akk.* into)

Ụmrechnungs·kurs *der* exchange rate

um|reißen[1] *unr. tr. V.* pull ⟨*mast, tree*⟩ down; knock ⟨*person*⟩ down; ⟨*wind*⟩ tear ⟨*tent etc.*⟩ down

um·reißen[2] *unr. tr. V.* outline; summarize ⟨*subject, problem, situation*⟩

u̱m|rennen *unr. tr. V.* [run into and] knock down

um·rịngen *tr. V.* surround

Ụm·riss, *Ụm·riß *der* (auch fig.) outline

um|rühren *tr. (auch itr.) V.* stir

um|rüsten *tr. V.* (Technik) convert (**auf** + *Akk.* to, **zu** into)

ums /ʊms/ *Präp.* + *Art.* (**a**) = um das;
(**b**) ~ Leben kommen lose one's life

um|satteln *itr. V.* (ugs.) change jobs; ⟨*student*⟩ change courses

Ụm·satz *der* turnover; (Verkauf) sales *pl.* (**an** + *Dat.* of); ~ machen (ugs.) make money

um|säumen *tr. V.* hem

um|schalten ⟨1⟩ *tr. V.* (auch fig.) switch [over] (**auf** + *Akk.* to); move ⟨*lever*⟩
⟨2⟩ *itr. V.* switch *or* change over (**auf** + *Akk.* to)

Ụmschalt·taste *die* shift key

Ụm·schlag *der* (**a**) cover
(**b**) (Briefumschlag) envelope
(**c**) (Schutzumschlag) jacket; (einer Broschüre, eines Heftes) cover
(**d**) (Med.: Wickel) compress; (warm) poultice

um|schlagen ⟨1⟩ *unr. tr. V.* (**a**) turn up ⟨*sleeve, collar, trousers*⟩; turn over ⟨*page*⟩
(**b**) (umladen, verladen) turn round, trans-ship ⟨*goods*⟩
⟨2⟩ *unr. itr. V.; mit sein* change (**in** + *Akk.* into); ⟨*wind*⟩ veer [round]

um|schreiben[1] *unr. tr. V.* rewrite

um·schreiben[2] *unr. tr. V.* (**a**) (in Worte fassen) describe; (definieren) define ⟨*meaning, sb.'s task, etc.*⟩; (paraphrasieren) paraphrase ⟨*word, expression*⟩
(**b**) (Sprachw.) construct (**mit** with)

Ụm·schreibung *die* description; (Definition) definition; (Verhüllung) circumlocution (*Gen.* for)

Ụm·schrift *die* (Sprachw.) transcription

um|schulen ⟨1⟩ *tr. V.* (beruflich) retrain
⟨2⟩ *itr. V.* retrain (**auf** + *Akk.* as)

Ụmschulung *die;* ~: retraining (**auf**

+ *Akk.* as)

um|schütten *tr. V.* (**a**) pour [into another container]; decant ⟨*liquid*⟩
(**b**) (verschütten) spill

Ụm·schweif *der* circumlocution; ohne ~e without beating about the bush

Ụm·schwung *der* complete change; (in der Politik usw.) U-turn

um|sehen *unr. refl. V.* (**a**) look; sich im Zimmer ~: look [a]round the room
(**b**) (zurücksehen) look round *or* back

umseitig *Adj., adv.* overleaf

um|setzen *tr. V.* (**a**) move; (auf anderen Posten usw.) move, transfer (**in** + *Akk.* to); (umpflanzen) transplant; (in anderen Topf) repot
(**b**) (verwirklichen) implement ⟨*plan*⟩; translate ⟨*plan, intention, etc.*⟩ into action *or* reality; realize ⟨*ideas*⟩
(**c**) (Wirtsch.) turn over, have a turnover of ⟨*x euros etc.*⟩; sell ⟨*shares, goods*⟩

Ụm·sicht *die* circumspection

um·sichtig ⟨1⟩ *Adj.* circumspect
⟨2⟩ *adv.* circumspectly

um|siedeln ⟨1⟩ *tr. V.* resettle
⟨2⟩ *itr. V.; mit sein* move (**in** + *Akk., nach* to)

um·so *Konj.* je ... ~: the ..., the; ~ besser/ schlimmer! all the better/worse!

um·sọnst *Adv.* (**a**) (unentgeltlich) free; for nothing
(**b**) (vergebens) in vain

Ụm·stand *der* (**a**) (Gegebenheit) circumstance; (Tatsache) fact; unter Umständen possibly
(**b**) (Aufwand) business; macht keine [großen] Umstände please don't go to any bother

umstände·halber *Adv.* owing to circumstances; „~ zu verkaufen" 'forced to sell'

umständlich ⟨1⟩ *Adj.* involved, elaborate ⟨*procedure, method, description, explanation, etc.*⟩; elaborate, laborious ⟨*preparation, check, etc.*⟩; awkward, difficult ⟨*journey, job*⟩; (weitschweifig) long-winded; (Umstände machend) awkward ⟨*person*⟩
⟨2⟩ *adv.* in an involved *or* roundabout way; (weitschweifig) at great length

Ụmstands·kleid *das* maternity dress

umstehend *Adj.* standing round *postpos.*

um|steigen *unr. itr. V.* change (**in** + *Akk.* [on] to)

um|stellen[1] ⟨1⟩ *tr. V.* (**a**) rearrange, change round ⟨*furniture, books, etc.*⟩; reorder ⟨*words etc.*⟩; transpose ⟨*two words*⟩
(**b**) (anders einstellen) reset ⟨*lever, switch, points, clock*⟩
(**c**) (ändern) change *or* switch over (**auf** + *Akk.* to)
⟨2⟩ *refl. V.* adjust (**auf** + *Akk.* to)

um·stellen[2] *tr. V.* surround

um|stimmen *tr. V.* win ⟨*person*⟩ round

um|stoßen *unr. tr. V.* (**a**) knock over
(**b**) (rückgängig machen) change ⟨*plan, decision*⟩; (zunichte machen) upset, wreck ⟨*plan, theory*⟩

u

umstritten *Adj.* disputed; controversial ‹*book, author, policy, etc.*›

Ụm·sturz *der* coup

ụm|stürzen ① *tr. V.* overturn; (fig.) topple, overthrow ‹*political system, government*› ② *itr. V.* overturn; ‹*wall, building, chimney*› fall down

ụmstürzlerisch *Adj.* subversive

Ụmsturz·versuch *der* attempted coup

Ụm·tausch *der* exchange

ụm|tauschen *tr. V.* exchange ‹*goods, article*› (**gegen** for); change ‹*dollars, pounds, etc.*› (**in** + *Akk.* into)

ụm|topfen *tr. V.* repot ‹*plant*›

Ụm·trunk *der* communal drink

ụm|tun *unr. refl. V.* (ugs.) look [a]round; **sich nach etw. ~:** be on the lookout for sth.

Ụmwälzung *die;* ~, ~**en** (fig.) revolution

ụm|wandeln *tr. V.* convert ‹*substance, building, etc.*› (**in** + *Akk.* into); (ändern) change; alter

Ụm·weg *der* detour

Ụm·welt *die* **(a)** environment **(b)** (Menschen) people *pl.* around sb.

umwelt-, Umwelt-: ~**bedingt** *Adj.* caused by the *or* one's environment *postpos.;* ~**belastung** *die* environmental pollution *no indef. art.;* ~**bewusst, *~bewußt** *Adj.* environmentally conscious *or* aware; ~**feindlich** ① *Adj.* inimical to the environment *postpos.;* ecologically undesirable; ② *adv.* in an ecologically undesirable way; ‹*drive, behave*› without regard for the environment; ~**freundlich** ① *Adj.* environmentally-friendly; ② *adv.* in an environmentally friendly way; ~**katastrophe** *die* environmental disaster; ~**schädlich** ① *Adj.* harmful to the environment *postpos.;* ecologically harmful; ② *adv.* in an ecologically harmful way; ~**schutz** *der* environmental protection *no art.;* ~**schützer** *der;* ~~**s,** ~~, ~**schützerin** *die;* ~~, ~, ~**nen** environmentalist; conservationist; ~**verschmutzung** *die* pollution [of the environment]

ụm|wenden *regelm. (auch unr.) tr. V.* **(a)** turn over ‹*page, joint, etc.*› **(b)** turn round ‹*vehicle, horse*›

um·wẹrben *unr. tr. V.* court; woo; **viel umworben** much-courted

ụm|wẹrfen *unr. tr. V.* **(a)** knock over; knock ‹*person*› down *or* over; (fig. ugs.: aus der Fassung bringen) bowl ‹*person*› over; stun ‹*person*› **(b)** (fig. ugs.: umstoßen) knock ‹*plan*› on the head (coll.)

ụmwerfend (ugs.) ① *Adj.* fantastic (coll.); stunning (coll.); ② *adv.* fantastically [well] (coll.); brilliantly

um·wị̈ckeln *tr. V.* wrap; bind; (mit einem Verband) bandage

Umzäunung *die;* ~, ~**en** fence, fencing (Gen. round)

ụm|ziehen ① *unr. itr. V.; mit sein* move (**an** + *Akk.,* **in** + *Akk.,* **nach** to) ② *unr. tr. V.* **jmdn. ~:** change sb. *or* get sb. changed; **sich ~:** change *or* get changed

um·zịngeln *tr. V.* surround; encircle

Umzịngelung *die;* ~: encirclement

Ụm·zug *der* **(a)** move; (von Möbeln) removal **(b)** (Festzug) procession

UN *Pl.* UN *sing.*

unabạ̈nderlich ① *Adj.* unalterable; irrevocable ‹*decision*› ② *adv.* irrevocably

unabhạ̈ngig ① *Adj.* independent (**von** of); (unbeeinflusst) unaffected (**von** by) ② *adv.* independently (**von** of); ~ **davon, ob …/was …/wo …** *usw.* irrespective *or* regardless of whether …/what …/where … *etc.*

Ụnabhängigkeit *die;* ~: independence

unabkọ̈mmlich *Adj.* indispensable; **sie ist im Moment ~:** she is otherwise engaged

unablạ̈ssig ① *Adj.* incessant ② *adv.* incessantly

unabsịchtlich ① *Adj.* unintentional ② *adv.* unintentionally

unabwẹndbar *Adj.* inevitable

unạchtsam ① *Adj.* **(a)** inattentive **(b)** (nicht sorgfältig) careless ② *adv.* (ohne Sorgfalt) carelessly

Ụnachtsamkeit *die;* ~ **(a)** inattentiveness **(b)** (mangelnde Sorgfalt) carelessness

unạngebracht *Adj.* inappropriate

unạngefochten *Adj.* unchallenged; (Rechtsw.) uncontested ‹*verdict, will, etc.*›

unạngenehm ① *Adj.* unpleasant (*Dat.* for); (peinlich) embarrassing ‹*question, situation*› ② *adv.* unpleasantly

unannẹhmbar *Adj.* unacceptable

Ụnannehmlichkeit *die;* ~, ~**en** trouble

unạnsehnlich *Adj.* unprepossessing; plain ‹*girl*›

unạnständig ① *Adj.* improper; (anstößig) indecent; dirty ‹*joke*›; rude ‹*word, song*› ② *adv.* improperly

Ụnanständigkeit *die;* ~, ~**en** impropriety; indecency; (Obszönität) obscenity

unạppetitlich ① *Adj.* unappetizing; (fig.) unsavoury ‹*joke*›; disgusting ‹*washbasin, nails, etc.*› ② *adv.* unappetizingly

Ụnart *die;* ~, ~**en** bad habit

unạrtig *Adj.* naughty

unạ̈sthetisch *Adj.* unpleasant ‹*sight etc.*›; ugly ‹*building etc.*›

unạuffällig ① *Adj.* inconspicuous; unobtrusive ‹*scar, defect, skill, behaviour,*

surveillance, etc.⟩; discreet ⟨*signal, elegance*⟩
   2 *adv.* inconspicuously; unobtrusively
unauffindbar *Adj.* untraceable; ∼ **sein**
  od. bleiben be nowhere to be found
unaufgefordert *Adv.* without being
  asked
unaufhaltsam 1 *Adj.* inexorable
  2 *adv.* inexorably
unaufmerksam *Adj.* inattentive
  (**gegenüber** to); careless ⟨*driver*⟩
unaufrichtig *Adj.* insincere
Unaufrichtigkeit *die;* ∼, ∼**en**
  insincerity
unausbleiblich *Adj.* inevitable
unausgegoren *Adj.* (abwertend) immature
unausstehlich *Adj.* unbearable ⟨*person,
  noise, smell, etc.*⟩; insufferable ⟨*person*⟩;
  intolerable ⟨*noise, smell*⟩.
unausweichlich *Adj.* unavoidable;
  inevitable
unbändig 1 *Adj.* (a) boisterous
  (b) (überaus groß/stark) unbridled
  2 *adv.* (a) wildly
  (b) (sehr, äußerst) unrestrainedly;
  tremendously (coll.)
unbarmherzig *Adj.* merciless
unbeabsichtigt 1 *Adj.* unintentional
  2 *adv.* unintentionally
unbeachtet *Adj.* unnoticed
unbedacht 1 *Adj.* rash; thoughtless
  2 *adv.* rashly; thoughtlessly
unbedenklich *adv.* without second
  thoughts
unbedeutend 1 *Adj.* insignificant;
  minor ⟨*artist, poet*⟩; slight, minor
  ⟨*improvement, change, error*⟩
  2 *adv.* slightly
unbedingt 1 *Adj.* absolute
  2 *adv.* absolutely
  3 *Adv.* (auf jeden Fall) whatever happens
unbefangen *Adj.* (a) (ungehemmt)
  uninhibited
  (b) (unvoreingenommen) impartial
Unbefangenheit *die;* ▸ UNBEFANGEN A,
  B: uninhibitedness; impartiality
unbefriedigend *Adj.* unsatisfactory
unbefristet 1 *Adj.* for an indefinite
  period *postpos.;* indefinite ⟨*strike*⟩;
  unlimited ⟨*visa*⟩
  2 *adv.* for an indefinite period
unbefugt 1 *Adj.* unauthorized
  2 *adv.* without authorization
unbegreiflich *Adj.* incomprehensible
  (*Dat.,* **für** to); incredible ⟨*love, goodness,
  stupidity, carelessness, etc.*⟩
unbegrenzt 1 *Adj.* unlimited
  2 *adv.* ⟨*stay, keep, etc.*⟩ indefinitely
Unbehagen *das;* ∼**s** uneasiness, disquiet;
  (Sorge) concern (**an** + *Dat.* about)
unbehaglich 1 *Adj.* uneasy ⟨*feeling,
  atmosphere*⟩; uncomfortable ⟨*thought, room*⟩
  2 *adv.* uneasily

unbeherrscht *Adj.* uncontrolled; **er ist**
  ∼: he has no self-control
Unbeherrschtheit *die;* ∼: lack of self-
  control
unbeholfen 1 *Adj.* clumsy
  2 *adv.* clumsily
unbekannt *Adj.* (a) unknown; (nicht
  vertraut) unfamiliar; unidentified ⟨*caller,
  donor*⟩; „**Empfänger** ∼" 'not known at this
  address'
  (b) (nicht vielen bekannt) little known; obscure
  ⟨*poet, painter, etc.*⟩
Unbekannte[1] *der/die; adj. Dekl.*
  unknown *or* unidentified man/woman;
  (Fremde[r]) stranger
Unbekannte[2] *die; adj. Dekl.* (Math.; auch
  fig.) unknown
unbekleidet *Adj.* without any clothes on
  postpos.; bare ⟨*torso etc.*⟩; naked ⟨*corpse*⟩
unbekümmert 1 *Adj.* carefree; (ohne
  Bedenken, lässig) casual
  2 *adv.* (a) in a carefree way
  (b) (ohne Bedenken) without caring *or*
  worrying
unbeleuchtet *Adj.* unlit ⟨*street, corridor,
  etc.*⟩; ⟨*vehicle*⟩ without [any] lights
unbeliebt *Adj.* unpopular (**bei** with)
unbemannt *Adj.* unmanned
unbemerkt *Adj., adv.* unnoticed
unbenutzt *Adj.* unused
unbequem 1 *Adj.* (a) uncomfortable
  (b) (lästig) awkward, embarrassing
  ⟨*question, opinion*⟩; troublesome ⟨*politician
  etc.*⟩; unpleasant ⟨*criticism, truth, etc.*⟩
  2 *adv.* uncomfortably
unberechenbar 1 *Adj.* unpredictable
  2 *adv.* unpredictably
unberechtigt *Adj.* (a) (ungerechtfertigt)
  unjustified
  (b) (unbefugt) unauthorized
unberührt *Adj.* untouched; **sie ist noch**
  ∼: she is still a virgin
unbescheiden *Adj.* presumptuous
unbeschrankt *Adj.* ⟨*crossing*⟩ without
  gates, with no gates
unbeschreiblich 1 *Adj.* indescribable;
  unimaginable ⟨*fear, beauty*⟩; ⟨*fear, beauty*⟩
  beyond description
  2 *adv.* indescribably ⟨*beautiful*⟩;
  unbelievably ⟨*busy*⟩
unbesorgt *Adj.* unconcerned; **seien Sie**
  ∼: don't [you] worry
unbeständig *Adj.* changeable ⟨*weather*⟩;
  fickle ⟨*lover etc.*⟩
unbestimmt 1 *Adj.* (a) indefinite;
  indeterminate ⟨*age, number*⟩; (ungewiss)
  uncertain
  (b) (ungenau) vague
  (c) (Sprachw.) indefinite ⟨*article, pronoun*⟩
  2 *adv.* (ungenau) vaguely
unbestreitbar *Adj.* indisputable;
  unquestionable

unbestritten ① *Adj.* undisputed; ∼ **ist, dass** ... it is undisputed that ...; there is no disputing that ...
② *adv.* indisputably

unbewacht *Adj.* unsupervised; unattended ⟨*car park*⟩

unbewaffnet *Adj.* unarmed

unbeweglich *Adj.* motionless; still ⟨*air, water*⟩; fixed ⟨*gaze, expression*⟩

unbewegt *Adj.* motionless; fixed ⟨*expression*⟩

unbewohnbar *Adj.* uninhabitable

unbewohnt *Adj.* uninhabited ⟨*area*⟩; unoccupied ⟨*house, flat*⟩

unbewusst, *unbewußt *Adj.* unconscious

unbrauchbar *Adj.* unusable; (untauglich) useless ⟨*method, person*⟩

und *Konj.* and; (folglich) [and] so; **ich ∼ tanzen?** what, me dance?; **sei so gut ∼ mach das Fenster zu** be so good as to shut the window

Undank *der;* ∼**[e]s:** ingratitude

undankbar *Adj.* ungrateful ⟨*person, behaviour*⟩

undenkbar *Adj.* unthinkable; inconceivable

undeutlich ① *Adj.* unclear; indistinct; (ungenau) vague ⟨*idea, memory, etc.*⟩
② *adv.* indistinctly; (ungenau) vaguely

undicht *Adj.* leaky; leaking; ∼**e Fenster** windows which do not fit tightly

Unding *das* **ein ∼ sein** be preposterous *or* ridiculous

undurchführbar *Adj.* impracticable

undurchlässig *Adj.* impermeable; (wasserdicht) watertight; waterproof; (luftdicht) airtight

uneben *Adj.* uneven

Unebenheit *die;* ∼*,* ∼**en (a)** unevenness **(b)** (unebene Stelle) lumpy *or* uneven patch

unehelich *Adj.* illegitimate ⟨*child*⟩; unmarried ⟨*mother*⟩

unehrlich ① *Adj.* dishonest
② *adv.* dishonestly; by dishonest means

uneigennützig *Adj.* unselfish

Uneigennützigkeit *die;* ∼**:** unselfishness

uneinig *Adj.* ⟨*party*⟩ divided by disagreement; [**sich** (*Dat.*)] ∼ **sein** disagree

Uneinigkeit *die;* ∼**:** disagreement (**in** + *Dat.* on)

uneins *Adj.* ∼ **sein** be divided (**in** + *Dat.* on); ⟨*persons*⟩ be at variance *or* at cross purposes (**in** + *Dat.* over)

unempfindlich *Adj.* **(a)** insensitive (**gegen** to)
(b) (immun) immune (**gegen** to, against)
(c) (strapazierfähig) hard-wearing

unendlich ① *Adj.* infinite; boundless; (zeitlich) endless; (Math.) infinite
② *adv.* infinitely ⟨*lovable, sad*⟩; immeasurably ⟨*happy*⟩; ⟨*happy*⟩ beyond measure

unentbehrlich *Adj.* indispensable (*Dat.,* **für** to)

unentgeltlich /*od.* '----/ ① *Adj.* free
② *adv.* free of charge; ⟨*work*⟩ for nothing, without pay

unentschieden ① *Adj.* unsettled; undecided ⟨*question*⟩; (Sport, Schach) drawn
② *adv.* ∼ **spielen** draw

Unentschieden *das;* ∼**s,** ∼ (Sport, Schach) draw

unentwegt /*od.* --'-/ ① *Adj.* **(a)** (beharrlich) persistent ⟨*fighter, champion, efforts*⟩
(b) (unaufhörlich) constant; incessant
② *adv.* **(a)** (beharrlich) persistently
(b) (unaufhörlich) constantly; incessantly

unerbittlich ① *Adj.* (auch fig.) inexorable; unsparing ⟨*critic*⟩; relentless ⟨*battle, struggle*⟩; implacable ⟨*hate, enemy*⟩
② *adv.* (auch fig.) inexorably

unerfahren *Adj.* inexperienced

unerfreulich ① *Adj.* unpleasant; bad ⟨*news*⟩
② *adv.* unpleasantly

unerheblich *Adj.* insignificant

unerhört ① *Adj.* (empörend) outrageous
② *adv.* outrageously

unerlaubt ① *Adj.* unauthorized
② *adv.* without authorization

unerledigt *Adj.* not dealt with *postpos.*

unermüdlich ① *Adj.* tireless, untiring (**bei, in** + *Dat.* in)
② *adv.* tirelessly

unerreichbar *Adj.* inaccessible; (fig.) unattainable

unerreicht *Adj.* unequalled

unersättlich *Adj.* insatiable

unerschöpflich *Adj.* inexhaustible

unersetzlich *Adj.* irreplaceable

unerträglich /*od.* '----/ *Adj.* unbearable; intolerable ⟨*situation, conditions, etc.*⟩

unerwartet ① *Adj.* unexpected; **es kam für alle** ∼**:** it came as a surprise to everybody
② *adv.* unexpectedly

unerwünscht *Adj.* unwanted; unwelcome ⟨*interruption, visit, visitor*⟩; undesirable ⟨*side effects*⟩

unethisch ① *Adj.* unethical
② *adv.* unethically

unfähig *Adj.* **(a)** ∼ **sein, etw. zu tun** (ständig) be incapable of doing sth.; (momentan) be unable to do sth.
(b) (inkompetent) incompetent

Unfähigkeit *die* **(a)** inability
(b) (Inkompetenz) incompetence

unfair ① *Adj.* unfair (**gegen** to)
② *adv.* unfairly

Un·fall *der;* ∼**[e]s, Unfälle** accident

---

u

Unfall-: ~**arzt** der, ~**ärztin** die casualty doctor; ~**flucht** die (Rechtsspr.) ~**flucht begehen** fail to stop after [being involved in] an accident; ~**opfer** das accident victim; ~**stelle** die scene of an/the accident; ~**versicherung** die accident insurance

unfehlbar Adj. infallible

Unfehlbarkeit die; ~: infallibility

unförmig Adj. shapeless; huge ⟨legs, hands, body⟩; bulky, ungainly ⟨shape, shoes, etc.⟩

unfrei Adj. not free pred.; subject, dependent ⟨people⟩; ⟨life⟩ of bondage

unfreiwillig ⟦1⟧ Adj. involuntary; (erzwungen) enforced ⟨stay⟩; (nicht beabsichtigt) unintended ⟨publicity, joke, humour⟩ ⟦2⟧ adv. involuntarily; without wanting to; (unbeabsichtigt) unintentionally

unfreundlich ⟦1⟧ Adj. unfriendly (zu, gegen to); unkind ⟨words, remark⟩ ⟦2⟧ adv. in an unfriendly way

Unfreundlichkeit die; ~: unfriendliness

unfrisiert Adj. ungroomed ⟨hair⟩

unfruchtbar Adj. infertile; (fig.) unproductive

Unfruchtbarkeit die; ~: infertility; (fig.) unproductiveness

Unfug der; ~[e]s **(a)** [piece of] mischief; **grober** ~: public nuisance **(b)** (Unsinn) nonsense

Ungar der; ~n, ~n, **Ungarin** die; ~, ~nen Hungarian

ungarisch Adj. Hungarian

Ungarn (das); ~s Hungary

ungeachtet Präp. mit Gen. (geh.) notwithstanding; despite

ungebildet Adj. uneducated

ungeboren Adj. unborn

ungebräuchlich Adj. uncommon; rare; rarely used ⟨method, process⟩

ungebrochen Adj. (fig.) unbroken ⟨will, person⟩; undiminished ⟨strength, courage⟩

ungedeckt Adj. uncovered ⟨cheque⟩

Ungeduld die; ~: impatience

ungeduldig ⟦1⟧ Adj. impatient ⟦2⟧ adv. impatiently

ungeeignet Adj. unsuitable; (für eine Aufgabe) unsuited (für, zu to, for)

ungefähr ⟦1⟧ Adj. approximate; rough ⟨idea, outline⟩ ⟦2⟧ adv. approximately; roughly

ungefährlich Adj. safe; harmless ⟨animal, person, illness, etc.⟩

ungeheizt Adj. unheated

ungeheuer ⟦1⟧ Adj. enormous; tremendous ⟨strength, energy, effort, enthusiasm, fear, success, pressure, etc.⟩; vast, immense ⟨fortune, knowledge⟩; (schrecklich) terrible (coll.), terrific (coll.) ⟨pain, rage⟩ ⟦2⟧ adv. tremendously; terribly (coll.) ⟨difficult, clever⟩

Ungeheuer das; ~s, ~ (auch fig.) monster

ungeheuerlich Adj. monstrous; outrageous

Ungeheuerlichkeit die; ~, ~en **(a)** monstrous nature; outrageousness **(b)** (Vorgang) monstrous or outrageous thing

ungehindert Adj. unimpeded

ungehörig ⟦1⟧ Adj. improper; (frech) impertinent ⟦2⟧ adv. improperly; (frech) impertinently

ungehorsam Adj. disobedient (gegenüber to)

Ungehorsam der; ~s disobedience (gegenüber to)

ungekürzt Adj. unabridged ⟨edition, book⟩; uncut ⟨film, speech⟩

ungelegen ⟦1⟧ Adj. **das kommt mir sehr** ~/nicht ~: that is very inconvenient or awkward/quite convenient for me ⟦2⟧ adv. inconveniently

ungelernt Adj. unskilled

ungemütlich ⟦1⟧ Adj. uninviting, cheerless ⟨room, flat⟩; uncomfortable, unfriendly ⟨atmosphere⟩ ⟦2⟧ adv. uncomfortably ⟨furnished⟩

ungenau ⟦1⟧ Adj. inaccurate; imprecise, inexact ⟨definition, formulation, etc.⟩; (undeutlich) vague ⟨memory, idea, impression⟩ ⟦2⟧ adv. inaccurately; ⟨define⟩ imprecisely, inexactly; ⟨remember⟩ vaguely

ungeniert /'ʊnʒeniːɐt/ ⟦1⟧ Adj. free and easy; uninhibited ⟦2⟧ adv. openly; ⟨yawn⟩ unconcernedly; ⟨undress etc.⟩ without any embarrassment

ungenießbar Adj. (nicht essbar) inedible; (nicht trinkbar) undrinkable; (fig. ugs.) unbearable

ungenügend ⟦1⟧ Adj. inadequate; **die Note „**~**"/ein Ungenügend** (Schulw.) the/an 'unsatisfactory' [mark] ⟦2⟧ adv. inadequately

ungepflegt Adj. neglected ⟨garden, park, car, etc.⟩; unkempt ⟨person, appearance, hair⟩; uncared-for ⟨hands⟩

ungerade Adj. odd ⟨number⟩

ungerecht ⟦1⟧ Adj. unjust, unfair (gegen, zu, gegenüber to) ⟦2⟧ adv. unjustly; unfairly

Ungerechtigkeit die; ~, ~en injustice

ungern Adv. reluctantly; **etw.** ~ **tun** not like or dislike doing sth.

ungerührt Adj. unmoved

ungeschält Adj. unpeeled ⟨fruit⟩

ungeschehen Adj. **etw.** ~ **machen** undo sth.

Ungeschicklichkeit die; ~, ~en **(a)** clumsiness **(b)** (etwas Ungeschicktes) piece of clumsiness

ungeschickt ⟦1⟧ Adj. clumsy; awkward ⟦2⟧ adv. clumsily; awkwardly

ungesetzlich ⟦1⟧ Adj. unlawful; illegal ⟦2⟧ adv. unlawfully; illegally

u

ungestempelt *Adj.* uncancelled ⟨*stamp*⟩
ungestört *Adj.* undisturbed; uninterrupted ⟨*development*⟩
ungesund *Adj.* (auch fig.) unhealthy
Ungetüm *das;* ~s, ~e monster
ungewiss, *ungewiß *Adj.* uncertain; über etw. (*Akk.*) **im Ungewissen sein** be uncertain *or* unsure about sth.
Ungewissheit, *Ungewißheit *die;* ~, ~en uncertainty
ungewöhnlich ① *Adj.* (a) unusual (b) (sehr groß) exceptional ⟨*strength, beauty, ability, etc.*⟩; outstanding ⟨*achievement, success*⟩
② *adv.* (a) ⟨*behave*⟩ abnormally, strangely (b) (enorm) exceptionally
ungewohnt ① *Adj.* unaccustomed; (nicht vertraut) unfamiliar ⟨*method, work, surroundings, etc.*⟩
② *adv.* unusually
ungewollt ① *Adj.* unwanted; (unbeabsichtigt) unintentional; inadvertent
② *adv.* unintentionally; inadvertently
Ungeziefer *das;* ~s vermin *pl.*
ungezogen ① *Adj.* naughty; badly behaved; bad ⟨*behaviour*⟩; (frech) cheeky
② *adv.* naughtily; ⟨*behave*⟩ badly
ungezwungen *Adj.* natural, unaffected ⟨*person, behaviour, cheerfulness*⟩; (nicht förmlich) informal, free and easy ⟨*tone, conversation, etc.*⟩
ungläubig ① *Adj.* (a) disbelieving (b) (Rel.) unbelieving
② *adv.* in disbelief
unglaublich ① *Adj.* incredible
② *adv.* (ugs.: äußerst) incredibly (coll.)
unglaubwürdig *Adj.* implausible; untrustworthy, unreliable ⟨*witness etc.*⟩
ungleich ① *Adj.* unequal; odd, unmatching ⟨*socks, gloves, etc.*⟩; (unähnlich) dissimilar
② *adv.* (a) unequally (b) (ungleichmäßig) unevenly
ungleichmäßig ① *Adj.* uneven
② *adv.* unevenly
Unglück *das;* ~[e]s, ~e (a) (Unfall) accident; (Flugzeugunglück, Zugunglück) crash; accident
(b) (Not) misfortune; (Leid) suffering
(c) (Pech) bad luck; ~ **haben** be unlucky; **das bringt** ~: that's unlucky
(d) (Schicksalsschlag) misfortune
unglücklich ① *Adj.* (a) unhappy (b) (nicht vom Glück begünstigt) unfortunate ⟨*person*⟩; (bedauernswert, arm) hapless ⟨*person, animal*⟩
(c) (ungünstig, ungeschickt) unfortunate ⟨*moment, combination, meeting, etc.*⟩; unhappy ⟨*end, choice, solution*⟩
② *adv.* (a) unhappily (b) (ungünstig) unfortunately; (ungeschickt)

unhappily, clumsily ⟨*translated, expressed*⟩
unglücklicher·weise *Adv.* unfortunately
Unglücks·fall *der* accident
Ungnade *die* [bei jmdm.] **in** ~ (*Akk.*) **fallen/in** ~ (*Dat.*) **sein** fall/be out of favour [with sb.]
ungnädig *Adj.* bad-tempered; grumpy
ungültig *Adj.* invalid; void (esp. Law); spoilt ⟨*vote, ballot paper*⟩; disallowed ⟨*goal*⟩
Ungunst *die* **zu jmds.** ~en to sb.'s disadvantage
ungünstig ① *Adj.* (a) unfavourable; unfortunate, bad ⟨*shape, layout*⟩
(b) (unpassend) inconvenient ⟨*time*⟩; (ungeeignet) inappropriate, inconvenient ⟨*time, place*⟩
② *adv.* (a) unfavourably; badly ⟨*designed, laid out*⟩
(b) (unpassend) inconveniently
ungut *Adj.* **nichts für** ~! no offence [meant]! (coll.)
unhandlich *Adj.* unwieldy
Unheil *das;* ~s disaster
unheilbar ① *Adj.* incurable
② *adv.* incurably
unheil·voll *Adj.* disastrous; (verhängnisvoll) fateful
unheimlich ① *Adj.* (a) eerie (b) (ugs.) (schrecklich) terrible (coll.) ⟨*hunger, headache, etc.*⟩ terrific (coll.) ⟨*fun etc.*⟩
② *adv.* (a) eerily (b) (ugs.: äußerst) terribly (coll.); incredibly (coll.) ⟨*quick, long*⟩
unhöflich ① *Adj.* impolite
② *adv.* impolitely
Unhöflichkeit *die;* ~, ~en impoliteness
unhygienisch ① *Adj.* unhygienic
② *adv.* unhygienically
Uni *die;* ~, ~s (ugs.) university
Uniform *die;* ~, ~en uniform
uninteressant *Adj.* uninteresting; (nicht von Belang) of no interest *postpos.;* unimportant
Union *die;* ~, ~en union
Universität *die;* ~, ~en university
Universum *das;* ~s universe
unkenntlich *Adj.* unrecognizable ⟨*person, face*⟩; indecipherable ⟨*writing, stamp*⟩
Unkenntnis *die;* ~: ignorance
unklar *Adj.* unclear; **sich** (*Dat.*) **über etw.** (*Akk.*) **im Unklaren sein** be unclear *or* unsure about sth.
unkonventionell ① *Adj.* unconventional
② *adv.* unconventionally
Unkosten *Pl.* (a) [extra] expense *sing.;* expenses
(b) (ugs.: Ausgaben) costs; expenditure *sing.*
Unkosten·beitrag *der* contribution towards expenses
Unkraut *das;* ~[e]s, **Unkräuter** weeds *pl.*

unkultiviert *Adj.* uncultivated

unlauter *Adj.* (geh.) dishonest; ~er Wettbewerb (Rechtsspr.) unfair competition

unleserlich [1] *Adj.* illegible
[2] *adv.* illegibly

unmäßig [1] *Adj.* immoderate; excessive
[2] *adv.* excessively; ⟨*eat, drink*⟩ to excess

Unmenge *die* mass; enormous number/ amount

Unmensch *der;* ~en, ~en brute

unmenschlich [1] *Adj.* (a) inhuman; brutal; appalling ⟨*conditions*⟩
(b) (entsetzlich) appalling
[2] *adv.* (a) in an inhuman way
(b) (entsetzlich) appallingly (coll.)

unmissverständlich, **unmißverständlich* [1] *Adj.*
(a) (eindeutig) unambiguous
(b) (offen, direkt) blunt ⟨*answer, refusal*⟩; unequivocal ⟨*language*⟩
[2] *adv.* (a) (eindeutig) unambiguously
(b) (offen, direkt) bluntly; unequivocally

unmittelbar [1] *Adj.* immediate; direct ⟨*contact, connection, influence, etc.*⟩
[2] *adv.* immediately; directly

unmöbliert *Adj.* unfurnished

unmodern [1] *Adj.* old-fashioned; (nicht modisch) unfashionable
[2] *adv.* in an old-fashioned way; (nicht modisch) unfashionably

unmöglich [1] *Adj.* impossible; (ugs.: seltsam) incredible
[2] *adv.* (ugs.) ⟨*behave*⟩ impossibly; ⟨*dress*⟩ ridiculously
[3] *Adv.* (ugs.) ich/es *usw.* kann ~ ...: I/it *etc.* can't possibly ...

unmoralisch [1] *Adj.* immoral
[2] *adv.* immorally

unmündig *Adj.* under-age

Unmut *der;* ~[e]s (geh.) displeasure; annoyance

unnachsichtig [1] *Adj.* merciless; unmerciful
[2] *adv.* mercilessly; ⟨*punish*⟩ unmercifully

unnahbar *Adj.* unapproachable

unnatürlich [1] *Adj.* unnatural; forced ⟨*laugh*⟩
[2] *adv.* unnaturally; ⟨*laugh*⟩ in a forced way; ⟨*speak*⟩ affectedly

unnötig [1] *Adj.* unnecessary
[2] *adv.* unnecessarily

unnütz *Adj.* useless

UNO *die;* ~: UN

unordentlich [1] *Adj.* (a) untidy
(b) (ungeregelt) disorderly ⟨*life*⟩
[2] *adv.* untidily; ⟨*tie, treat, etc.*⟩ carelessly

Unordnung *die;* ~: disorder; mess

unparteiisch [1] *Adj.* impartial
[2] *adv.* impartially

unpassend [1] *Adj.* inappropriate; unsuitable ⟨*dress etc.*⟩
[2] *adv.* inappropriately; unsuitably

⟨*dressed etc.*⟩

unpersönlich [1] *Adj.* impersonal; distant, aloof ⟨*person*⟩
[2] *adv.* impersonally; ⟨*answer, write*⟩ in impersonal terms

unpraktisch [1] *Adj.* unpractical
[2] *adv.* in an unpractical way

unproblematisch *Adj.* unproblematic

unproduktiv *Adj.* unproductive

unpünktlich [1] *Adj.* unpunctual ⟨*person*⟩; late, unpunctual ⟨*payment*⟩
[2] *adv.* late

Unpünktlichkeit *die;* ~: lack of punctuality

Unrecht *das;* ~[e]s wrong; zu ~: wrongly; ~ haben be wrong; jmdm. ~ tun do sb. an injustice

unrechtmäßig [1] *Adj.* unlawful
[2] *adv.* unlawfully

unredlich (geh.) [1] *Adj.* dishonest
[2] *adv.* dishonestly

Unredlichkeit *die;* ~, ~en
(a) dishonesty
(b) (Handlung) dishonest act

unregelmäßig [1] *Adj.* irregular
[2] *adv.* irregularly

Unregelmäßigkeit *die;* ~, ~en irregularity

unreif *Adj.* (a) unripe
(b) (nicht erwachsen) immature

unrentabel *Adj.* unprofitable

Unruhe *die;* ~, ~n (auch fig.) unrest; (Lärm) noise; (Unrast) restlessness; (Besorgnis) anxiety

unruhig [1] *Adj.* (a) restless; (besorgt) anxious; unsettled, troubled ⟨*time*⟩
(b) (laut) noisy
(c) (ungleichmäßig) uneven ⟨*breathing, pulse, etc.*⟩; fitful ⟨*sleep*⟩; disturbed ⟨*night*⟩
[2] *adv.* (a) restlessly; (besorgt) anxiously
(b) (ungleichmäßig) unevenly; ⟨*sleep*⟩ fitfully

uns [1] (a) *Akk. von* WIR us
(b) *Dat. von* WIR; gib es ~: give it to us; bei ~: at our home *or* (coll.) place
[2] *Reflexivpron. der 1. Pers. Pl.* (a) refl. ourselves
(b) *reziprok* one another

unsachlich [1] *Adj.* unobjective
[2] *adv.* without objectivity

unsauber [1] *Adj.* (a) dirty
(b) (nachlässig) untidy; sloppy
[2] *adv.* (nachlässig) untidily

unschädlich *Adj.* harmless

unscharf *Adj.* blurred ⟨*photo, picture*⟩

unscheinbar *Adj.* inconspicuous

unschlagbar *Adj.* unbeatable

Unschuld *die;* ~: innocence; (Jungfräulichkeit) virginity

unschuldig [1] *Adj.* innocent
[2] *adv.* innocently

unselbständig, unselbstständig *Adj.* dependent [on other people]

unser¹ *Possessivpron. der 1. Pers. Pl.* our; **das ist ∼s** that is ours

unser² *Gen. von* WIR (geh.) of us; **in ∼ aller/beider Interesse** in the interest of all/both of us

unser·einer,

unsereins *Indefinitpron.* (ugs.) the likes of us *pl.;* our sort (coll.)

unserer·seits *Adv.* for our part; (von uns) on our part

unser[e]s·gleichen *indekl. Indefinitpron.* people *pl.* like us

unsert·wegen *Adv.:* ▸ MEINETWEGEN: because of us; for our sake; about us; as far as we are concerned

unsicher ⓵ *Adj.* uncertain; (nicht selbstsicher) insecure
⓶ *adv.* ⟨walk, stand, etc.⟩ unsteadily; (nicht selbstsicher) ⟨smile, look⟩ diffidently

Unsicherheit *die; ∼:* uncertainty; (fehlende Selbstsicherheit) insecurity

unsichtbar *Adj.* invisible (**für** to)

Unsinn *der; ∼[e]s* nonsense; **∼ machen** mess *or* fool about

unsinnig *Adj.* nonsensical ⟨statement, talk, etc.⟩; absurd, ridiculous ⟨demand etc.⟩

Unsitte *die; ∼, ∼n* bad habit

unsittlich ⓵ *Adj.* indecent
⓶ *adv.* indecently

unsr... ▸ UNSER¹

unsterblich *Adj.* immortal

Unsterblichkeit *die; ∼:* immortality

unstreitig ⓵ *Adj.* indisputable
⓶ *adv.* indisputably

unsympathisch *Adj.* uncongenial, disagreeable ⟨person⟩; unpleasant ⟨characteristic, nature, voice⟩

Untat *die; ∼, ∼en* misdeed; evil deed

untätig *Adj.* idle; **∼ herumsitzen/zusehen** sit around doing nothing/stand idly by

untauglich *Adj.* unsuitable; (für Militärdienst) unfit [for service] *postpos.*

unten *Adv.* (a) down; **hier/da ∼:** down here/there; **von ∼:** from below
(b) (in Gebäuden) downstairs; **nach ∼:** downstairs
(c) (am unteren Ende, zum unteren Ende hin) at the bottom; **∼ [links] auf der Seite/im Schrank** at the bottom [left] of the page/cupboard
(d) (an der Unterseite) underneath
(e) (im Text) below; **∼ genannt** undermentioned (Brit.); mentioned below *postpos.*

*unten·genannt ▸ UNTEN E

unter ⓵ *Präp. mit Dat.* (Lage, Standort) under; (zwischen) among[st]; **Mengen ∼ 100 Stück** quantities of less than 100; **∼ Angst/ Tränen** in *or* out of fear/in tears
⓶ *Präp. mit Akk.* under; (zwischen) among[st]; **∼ Null sinken** drop below zero

⓷ *Adv.* less than; **∼ 30 [Jahre alt] sein** be under 30 [years of age]

unter... *Adj.* lower; bottom; (ganz unten) bottom; (in der Rangfolge o. Ä.) lower

Unter·arm *der* forearm

unterbelichten *tr. V.;* **ich unterbelichte, unterbelichtet, unterzubelichten** (Fot.) underexpose

Unter·bewusstsein,
*Unter·bewußtsein *das* subconscious

unter·bleiben *unr. itr. V.; mit* sein **etw.** unterbleibt sth. does not occur *or* happen

unter·brechen *unr. tr. V.* interrupt; break ⟨journey, silence⟩

Unter·brechung *die* ▸ UNTERBRECHEN: interruption; break (*Gen.* in)

unter|bringen *unr. tr. V.* **(a)** put **(b)** (beherbergen) put up

Unterbringung *die; ∼, ∼en* accommodation *no indef. art.*

unter|buttern *tr. V.* (ugs.) push aside (fig.)

*unter-der-hand ▸ HAND

unter·dessen ▸ INZWISCHEN

unter·drücken *tr. V.* suppress; hold back ⟨comment, question, answer, criticism, etc.⟩; oppress ⟨minority etc.⟩

Unterdrückung *die; ∼, ∼en* **(a)** (das Unterdrücken) suppression **(b)** (das Unterdrücktwerden, -sein) oppression

unter·einander *Adv.* **(a)** (räumlich) one below the other **(b)** (miteinander) among[st] ourselves/themselves *etc.*

unter·ernährt *Adj.* undernourished

Unter·ernährung *die* malnutrition

Unter·finanzierung *die* underfunding (no art.)

Unter·führung *die* underpass; (für Fußgänger) subway (Brit.); [pedestrian] underpass (Amer.)

unter-, Unter-: **∼gang** *der* **(a)** (Sonnenuntergang, Monduntergang usw.) setting; **(b)** (von Schiffen) sinking; **(c)** (das Zugrundegehen) decline; **∼|gehen** *unr. itr. V.; mit* sein **(a)** ⟨sun, star, etc.⟩ set; ⟨ship⟩ sink, go down; ⟨person⟩ drown, go under; **(b)** (zugrunde gehen) come to an end; **∼geordnet** *Adj.* secondary ⟨role, importance, etc.⟩; subordinate ⟨position, post, etc.⟩; **∼geschoss,** ***∼geschoß** *das* basement; **∼gewicht** *das* underweight; **∼grund** *der* (bes. Politik) underground; **∼grund·bahn** *die* underground [railway] (Brit.); subway (Amer.); **∼|haken** *tr. V.* (ugs.) jmdn. **∼haken** take sb.'s arm; **∼halb** ⓵ *Adv.* below; **∼halb von** below; **∼halb** ⓶ *Präp. mit Gen.* below; **∼halt** *der* **(a)** living; **(b)** (Zahlung) maintenance; **(c)** (Instandhaltung[skosten]) upkeep

unter-, Unter-: **∼halten** ⓵ *unr. tr. V.* **(a)** support; **(b)** (instand halten) maintain ⟨building⟩; **(c)** (betreiben) run, keep ⟨car,

---
*old spelling – see note on page x

hotel); **(d)** (pflegen) maintain, keep up ⟨*contact, correspondence*⟩; ⟨*guest, audience*⟩; ② *unr. refl. V.* **(a)** talk; converse; **(b)** (sich vergnügen) enjoy oneself; **∼haltsam** *Adj.* entertaining; **∼haltung** *die* **(a)** (Versorgung) support; **(b)** (Instandhaltung) maintenance; **(c)** (Gespräch) conversation; **(d)** (Zeitvertreib) entertainment

unter-, Unter-: **∼händler** *der*, **∼händlerin** *die* (bes. Politik) negotiator; **∼hemd** *das* vest (Brit.); undershirt (Amer.); **∼holz** *das* underwood; undergrowth; **∼hose** *die* (für Männer) briefs *pl.*; [under]pants *pl.*; (für Frauen) panties *pl.*; knickers *pl.* (Brit.); **∼irdisch** ① *Adj.* underground; ② *adv.* underground; **∼|jubeln** *tr. V.* (ugs.) jmdm. etw. **∼jubeln** palm sth. off on sb.; **∼kiefer** *der* lower jaw; **∼|kommen** *unr. itr. V.; mit sein* find accommodation; **∼kühlt** *Adj.* **∼kühlt sein** be suffering from hypothermia *or* exposure

Unterkunft *die;* **∼**, Unterkünfte accommodation *no indef. art.;* lodging *no indef. art.;* **∼ und Frühstück** bed and breakfast; **∼ und Verpflegung** board and lodging

Unter·lage *die* **(a)** (Schreibunterlage) pad; (für eine Schreibmaschine usw.) mat **(b)** *Pl.* documents; papers

unter-, Unter-: **∼lassen** *unr. tr. V.* refrain from [doing]; **∼lassung** *die;* **∼∼**, **∼∼en** omission; failure; **∼lassungs·sünde** *die* (ugs.) sin of omission; **∼laufen** *unr. itr. V.; mit sein* occur; jmdm. ist ein Fehler/Irrtum **∼laufen** sb. made a mistake; **∼legen** *Adj.* inferior; jmdm. **∼legen sein** be inferior to sb. (**an** + *Dat.* in); **∼leib** *der* lower abdomen

unter·liegen *unr. itr. V.* **(a)** *mit sein* (besiegt werden) lose; be beaten *or* defeated **(b)** (unterworfen sein) be subject to

Unter·lippe *die* lower lip

unterm *Präp.* + *Art.* = unter dem

unter·malen *tr. V.* accompany

Unter·malung *die;* **∼**, **∼en** accompaniment (*Gen.* to)

unter·mauern *tr. V.* (mit Argumenten, Fakten absichern) back up

Unter-: **∼miete** *die* subtenancy; sublease; **∼mieter** *der*, **∼mieterin** *die* subtenant; lodger

untern (ugs.) *Präp.* + *Art.* = unter den

unter-, Unter-: **∼nehmen** *unr. tr. V.* **(a)** (durchführen) undertake; make; take ⟨*steps*⟩; **(b)** etwas **∼nehmen** do something; **∼nehmen** *das;* **∼∼s**, **∼∼** **(a)** (Vorhaben) enterprise; **(b)** (Firma) concern; **∼nehmer** *der;* **∼∼s**, **∼∼**, **∼nehmerin** *die;* **∼∼**, **∼∼nen** employer

unternehmerisch ① *Adj.* entrepreneurial ② *adv.* ⟨*think*⟩ in an entrepreneurial *or* businesslike way

unter·nehmungs·lustig *Adj.* active; **sie ist sehr ∼** she is always out doing things

Unter·offizier *der* **(a)** non-commissioned officer **(b)** (Dienstgrad) corporal

unter|ordnen ① *tr. V.* subordinate ② *refl. V.* accept a subordinate role

Unterredung *die;* **∼**, **∼en** discussion

Unterricht *der;* **∼[e]s**, **∼e** instruction; (Schulunterricht) teaching; (Schulstunden) classes *pl.*

unterrichten ① *tr. V.* **(a)** teach **(b)** (informieren) inform (**über** + *Akk.* of, about) ② *itr. V.* (Unterricht geben) teach ③ *refl. V.* (sich informieren) inform oneself (**über** + *Akk.* about)

Unterrichts·stunde *die* lesson; period

Unter·rock *der* [half] slip

unter|rühren *tr. V.* stir in

unters *Präp.* + *Art.* = unter das

unter·sagen *tr. V.* forbid; prohibit

Unter·satz *der* ▸ UNTERSETZER

unter-, Unter-: **∼schätzen** *tr. V.* underestimate ⟨*amount, effect, etc.*⟩; underrate ⟨*talent, ability, etc.*⟩; **∼scheiden** ① *unr. tr. V.* distinguish; ② *unr. refl. V.* differ (**durch** in, **von** from); **∼scheidung** *die* (Vorgang) differentiation; (Resultat) distinction

Unter-: **∼schenkel** *der* shank; lower leg; **∼schicht** *die* (Soziol.) lower class

Unter·schied *der;* **∼[e]s**, **∼e** difference

unterschiedlich ① *Adj.* different; (uneinheitlich) variable; varying ② *adv.* [sehr/ganz] **∼:** in [very/quite] different ways

unterschieds·los ① *Adj.* uniform; equal ⟨*treatment*⟩ ② *adv.* ⟨*treat*⟩ equally; (ohne Benachteiligung) without discrimination

unter·schlagen *unr. tr. V.* embezzle ⟨*money, funds, etc.*⟩; (unterdrücken) intercept ⟨*letter*⟩; withhold ⟨*fact, news, information, etc.*⟩

Unter·schlupf *der;* **∼[e]s**, **∼e** shelter; (Versteck) hiding place; hideout

unter|schlüpfen *itr. V.; mit sein* (ugs.) hide out

unter·schreiben *unr. itr., tr. V.* sign

Unter-: **∼schrift** *die* signature; (Bild**∼**) caption; **∼see-boot** *das* submarine; **∼setzer** *der* mat; (für Gläser) coaster

untersetzt *Adj.* stocky

Unter·stand *der* (Schutzbunker) dugout; (Unterschlupf) shelter

unter|stehen ① *unr. itr. V.* jmdm. **∼:** be subordinate *or* answerable to sb. ② *unr. refl. V.* dare

unter|stellen¹ ① *tr. V.* (zur Aufbewahrung) keep; store ⟨*furniture*⟩ ② *refl. V.* take shelter

unter·stellen[2] tr. V. (a) jmdm.
eine Abteilung ∼: put sb. in charge
of a department; **die Behörde ist dem
Ministerium unterstellt** the office is under
the ministry
(b) (unterschieben) jmdm. **böse Absichten**
usw. ∼: insinuate that sb.'s intentions *etc.*
are bad
Unter·stellung *die* (falsche Behauptung)
insinuation
unter·streichen *unr. tr. V.* (a) underline
(b) (hervorheben) emphasize
Unter·streichung *die;* ∼, ∼en
(a) underlining
(b) (das Betonen) emphasizing
unter·stützen *tr. V.* support
Unter·stützung *die;* ∼, ∼en (a) support
(b) (finanzielle Hilfe) allowance; (für Arbeitslose)
[unemployment] benefit *no art.*
unter·suchen *tr. V.* examine; (überprüfen)
test (**auf** + *Akk.* for); (aufzuklären suchen)
investigate; (durchsuchen) search (**auf** + *Akk.*,
nach for)
Untersuchung *die;* ∼, ∼en
(a) ▸ UNTERSUCHEN: examination; test;
investigation; search
(b) (wissenschaftliche Arbeit) study
Untersuchungs·haft *die* imprisonment
or detention while awaiting trial
Unter·tasse *die* saucer
unter|tauchen [1] *itr. V.; mit sein* (a) (im
Wasser) dive [under]
(b) (verschwinden) disappear
[2] *tr. V.* duck
Unter·teil *das od. der* bottom part
unter·teilen *tr. V.* divide; (gliedern)
subdivide
Unter·titel *der* subtitle
unter·treiben *unr. itr. V.* play things
down
Untertreibung *die;* ∼, ∼en
understatement
unter·vermieten *tr., itr. V.* sublet
unter·wandern *tr. V.* infiltrate
Unter·wanderung *die* infiltration *no
indef. art.*
Unter·wäsche *die* underwear
unterwegs *Adv.* on the way; (nicht zu
Hause) out [and about]
unter·weisen *unr. tr. V.* (geh.) instruct
Unter·welt *die;* ∼: underworld
unter·werfen [1] *unr. tr. V.* (a) subjugate
⟨people, country⟩
(b) (unterziehen) subject (*Dat.* to)
[2] *unr. refl. V.* **sich [jmdm./einer Sache]**
∼: submit [to sb./sth.]
Unterwerfung *die;* ∼, ∼en (a) (das
Unterwerfen) subjugation (**unter** + *Akk.* to)
(b) (das Sichunterwerfen) submission (**unter**
+ *Akk.* to)

unterwürfig [1] *Adj.* obsequious
[2] *adv.* obsequiously
unter·zeichnen *tr. V.* sign
unter·ziehen [1] *unr. tr. V.* **etw. einer
Untersuchung/Überprüfung** (*Dat.*)
∼: examine/check sth.
[2] *unr. refl. V.* **sich einer Operation** (*Dat.*)
∼: undergo *or* have an operation
untragbar *Adj.* unbearable
untreu *Adj.* disloyal; (in der Ehe, Liebe)
unfaithful
Untreue *die;* ∼: disloyalty; (in der Ehe, Liebe)
unfaithfulness
untröstlich *Adj.* inconsolable
Untugend *die;* ∼, ∼en bad habit
unüberlegt [1] *Adj.* rash
[2] *adv.* rashly
unübersehbar [1] *Adj.* (a) (offenkundig)
conspicuous
(b) (sehr groß) enormous
[2] *adv.* (sehr) extremely
unübersichtlich [1] *Adj.* unclear;
confusing ⟨arrangement⟩; blind ⟨bend⟩;
broken ⟨country etc.⟩
[2] *adv.* unclearly; confusingly ⟨arranged⟩
unübertrefflich [1] *Adj.* superb
[2] *adv.* superbly
unübertroffen *Adj.* unsurpassed
unumgänglich *Adj.* [absolutely]
necessary
Unumgänglichkeit *die;* ∼: absolute
necessity
unumwunden [1] *Adj.* frank
[2] *adv.* frankly; openly
ununterbrochen [1] *Adj.* incessant
[2] *adv.* incessantly
unveränderlich *Adj.* unchangeable
unverantwortlich [1] *Adj.* irresponsible
[2] *adv.* irresponsibly
unverbesserlich *Adj.* incorrigible
unverbindlich [1] *Adj.* (a) not binding
pred.; without obligation *postpos*
(b) (reserviert) non-committal ⟨answer,
words⟩; impersonal ⟨attitude, person⟩
[2] *adv.* ⟨send, reserve⟩ without obligation
unverbleit *Adj.* unleaded
unverblümt [1] *Adj.* blunt
[2] *adv.* bluntly
unverbraucht *Adj.* untouched; unspent
⟨energy⟩; fresh ⟨air⟩
unverdaut *Adj.* undigested
unverdorben *Adj.* unspoilt
unverdrossen *Adj.* undeterred;
(unverzagt) undaunted
unvereinbar *Adj.* incompatible (**mit** with)
Unvereinbarkeit *die;* ∼: incompatibility
(**mit** with)
unverfänglich *Adj.* harmless
unverfroren *Adj.* insolent; impudent
unvergänglich *Adj.* immortal ⟨fame⟩;
unchanging ⟨beauty⟩; abiding ⟨recollection⟩

unvergẹsslich, *unvergẹßlich *Adj.* unforgettable

unverglẹichlich ⒈ *Adj.* incomparable ⒉ *adv.* incomparably

unverheiratet *Adj.* unmarried

unverhọfft ⒈ *Adj.* unexpected ⒉ *adv.* unexpectedly

unverhọhlen ⒈ *Adj.* unconcealed ⒉ *adv.* openly

unverkäuflich *Adj.* **diese Vase ist ∼:** this vase is not for sale/ (nicht absetzbar) unsaleable

unvermẹidlich *Adj.* unavoidable; (sich als Folge ergebend) inevitable

Ụnvermögen *das;* ∼s lack of ability

unvermutet ⒈ *Adj.* unexpected ⒉ *adv.* unexpectedly

unvernụ̈nftig *Adj.* stupid; foolish

unverrịchtet *Adj.* ∼er Dinge without having achieved anything

unverschämt ⒈ *Adj.* (a) impertinent ⟨*person, manner, words, etc.*⟩; barefaced ⟨*lie*⟩ (b) (ugs.: sehr groß) outrageous ⟨*price, luck, etc.*⟩ ⒉ *adv.* impertinently; ⟨*lie*⟩ barefacedly; blatantly

Ụnverschämtheit *die;* ∼, ∼en impertinence

unversẹhens *Adv.* suddenly

unversẹhrt *Adj.* unscathed; (unbeschädigt) undamaged

unverstạ̈ndlich *Adj.* incomprehensible

Ụnverständnis *das;* ∼ses lack of understanding

unverträglich *Adj.* (a) quarrelsome (b) incompatible ⟨*blood groups, medicines, transplant tissue*⟩

unverwẹchselbar *Adj.* unmistakable; distinctive

unverwụ̈stlich *Adj.* indestructible

unverzẹihlich *Adj.* unforgivable

unverzụ̈glich ⒈ *Adj.* prompt ⒉ *adv.* promptly

unvọllkommen ⒈ *Adj.* (a) imperfect (b) (unvollständig) incomplete ⒉ *adv.* (a) imperfectly (b) (unvollständig) incompletely

Ụnvollkommenheit *die;* ∼: (a) imperfectness (b) (Unvollständigkeit) incompleteness

unvọllständig *Adj.* incomplete

Ụnvollständigkeit *die;* ∼: incompleteness

unvorhergesehen *Adj.* unforeseen; unexpected ⟨*visit*⟩

unvorhersehbar *Adj.* unforeseeable

unvorsichtig ⒈ *Adj.* careless; (unüberlegt) rash ⒉ *adv.* carelessly; (unüberlegt) rashly

Ụnvorsichtigkeit *die;* ∼ ▶ UNVORSICHTIG 1: carelessness; rashness

unvorstẹllbar ⒈ *Adj.* inconceivable ⒉ *adv.* unimaginably

unvorteilhaft *Adj.* (a) unattractive ⟨*figure, appearance*⟩ (b) (ohne Vorteil) unfavourable, poor ⟨*purchase, exchange*⟩; unprofitable ⟨*business*⟩

unwahr *Adj.* untrue

Ụnwahrheit *die;* ∼, ∼en (a) untruthfulness (b) (Äußerung) untruth

unwahrschẹinlich ⒈ *Adj.* (a) improbable; unlikely (b) (ugs.: sehr viel) incredible (coll.) ⒉ *adv.* (ugs.: sehr) incredibly (coll.)

Ụnwahrscheinlichkeit *die;* ∼: improbability

unwẹgsam *Adj.* [almost] impassable

unwẹiblich *Adj.* unfeminine

unwẹigerlich ⒈ *Adj.* inevitable ⒉ *adv.* inevitably

Ụnwesen *das;* sein ∼ treiben (abwertend) be up to one's mischief *or* one's tricks

Ụnwetter *das;* ∼s, ∼: [thunder]storm

unwịchtig *Adj.* unimportant

Ụnwichtigkeit *die;* ∼, ∼en (a) unimportance (b) (etw. Unwichtiges) unimportant thing

unwiderrụflich ⒈ *Adj.* irrevocable ⒉ *adv.* irrevocably

unwiderstẹhlich *Adj.* irresistible

unwiederbrịnglich (geh.) ⒈ *Adj.* irretrievable ⒉ *adv.* irretrievably

Ụnwille[n] *der;* Ụnwillens displeasure

unwịllig ⒈ *Adj.* indignant; (widerwillig) unwilling ⒉ *adv.* indignantly; (widerwillig) unwillingly

unwịllkürlich ⒈ *Adj.* (a) spontaneous ⟨*cry, sigh*⟩; instinctive ⟨*reaction, movement, etc.*⟩ (b) (Physiol.) involuntary ⟨*movement etc.*⟩ ⒉ *adv.* (a) ⟨*shout etc.*⟩ spontaneously; ⟨*react, move, etc.*⟩ instinctively (b) (Physiol.) ⟨*move etc.*⟩ involuntarily

unwịrklich (geh.) *Adj.* unreal

Ụnwirklichkeit *die;* ∼, ∼en unreality

unwịrksam *Adj.* ineffective

Ụnwirksamkeit *die;* ∼: ineffectiveness

unwịrsch ⒈ *Adj.* surly; ill-natured ⒉ *adv.* ill-naturedly

unwịrtschaftlich ⒈ *Adj.* uneconomic ⟨*procedure etc.*⟩; (nicht sparsam) uneconomical ⟨*driving etc.*⟩ ⒉ *adv.* ⟨*work, drive, etc.*⟩ uneconomically

Ụnwissenheit *die;* ∼: ignorance

unwịssentlich ⒈ *Adj.* unconscious ⒉ *adv.* unknowingly; unwittingly

unwọhl *Adv.* unwell; **mir ist ∼:** I don't feel well

Ụnwohlsein *das;* ∼s indisposition

u

unwürdig *Adj.* **(a)** undignified ‹*person, behaviour*›; degrading ‹*treatment*› **(b)** (unangemessen) unworthy

unzählig *Adj.* innumerable; countless

Unze *die;* ∼, ∼n ounce

unzeitgemäß *Adj.* anachronistic

unzerbrechlich *Adj.* unbreakable

unzertrennlich *Adj.* inseparable

Unzucht *die:* ∼ **treiben** fornicate; **gewerbsmäßige** ∼: prostitution

unzüchtig **1** *Adj.* obscene ‹*letter, gesture*› **2** *adv.* ‹*touch, approach, etc.*› indecently; ‹*speak*› obscenely

unzufrieden *Adj.* dissatisfied; (stärker) unhappy

Unzufriedenheit *die;* ∼: dissatisfaction; (stärker) unhappiness

unzugänglich *Adj.* inaccessible ‹*area, building, etc.*›; unapproachable ‹*character, person, etc.*›

unzulänglich (geh.) **1** *Adj.* insufficient **2** *adv.* insufficiently

unzumutbar *Adj.* unreasonable

unzurechnungsfähig *Adj.* not responsible for one's actions *pred.;* (geistesgestört) of unsound mind *postpos.*

unzustellbar *Adj.* (Postw.) „∼": 'not known [at this address]'

unzutreffend *Adj.* inappropriate; (falsch) incorrect

unzuverlässig *Adj.* unreliable

Unzuverlässigkeit *die;* ∼: unreliability

unzweckmäßig **1** *Adj.* unsuitable; (unpraktisch) impractical **2** *adv.* unsuitably; (unpraktisch) impractically

Update /'apdeit/ *das;* ∼s, ∼s (DV) update

üppig **1** *Adj.* lush ‹*vegetation*›; thick ‹*hair, beard*›; full ‹*bosom, lips*›; voluptuous ‹*figure, woman*›; (fig.) sumptuous, opulent ‹*meal*› **2** *adv.* luxuriantly; (fig.) sumptuously

Ur·abstimmung *die* [esp. strike] ballot

Ural *der;* ∼[s] Urals *pl.;* Ural Mountains *pl.*

ur·alt *Adj.* very old; ancient

Uran *das;* ∼s uranium

Ur·aufführung *die* première; first night *or* performance; (eines Films) première; first showing

urbar *Adj.* **ein Stück Land** ∼ **machen** cultivate a piece of land

Ur·einwohner *der,* **Ur·einwohnerin** *die* native inhabitant

Ur·enkel *der* great-grandson

Urgroß-: ∼**eltern** *Pl.* great-grandparents; ∼**mutter** *die; Pl.* ∼mütter great-grandmother; ∼**vater** *der* great-grandfather

Ur·heber *der;* ∼s, ∼: originator; initiator; (bes. Rechtsspr.: Verfasser, Autor) author

Urheber·recht *das* copyright

urig *Adj.* natural ‹*person*›; real ‹*beer*›; cosy ‹*pub*›

Urin *der;* ∼s, ∼e (Med.) urine

urinieren *itr. V.* urinate

Ur·knall *der* big bang

Ur·kunde *die;* ∼, ∼n document; (Bescheinigung, Siegerurkunde, Diplom usw.) certificate

Urlaub *der;* ∼[e]s, ∼e holiday[s] (Brit.); vacation; (esp. Amer.); (bes. Milit.) leave

urlaubs-, Urlaubs-: ∼**geld** *das* holiday pay *or* money; (gespartes Geld) holiday money; ∼**ort** *der* holiday resort; ∼**reif** *Adj.* ∼reif sein (ugs.) be ready for a holiday; ∼**reise** *die* holiday [trip]; ∼**zeit** *die* holiday period *or* season

Urne *die;* ∼, ∼n urn; (Wahlurne) [ballot] box

Ur·oma *die* (fam.) great-granny (coll./child lang.)

Ur·opa *der* (fam.) great-grandpa (coll./child lang.)

Ur·sache *die* cause

Ur·sprung *der* origin

ur·sprünglich **1** *Adj.* **(a)** original ‹*plan, price, form, material, etc.*› **(b)** (natürlich) natural **2** *adv.* **(a)** originally **(b)** (natürlich) naturally

Urteil *das;* ∼s, ∼e judgement; (Strafe) sentence; (Gerichtsurteil) verdict

urteilen *itr. V.* form an opinion; judge; **über etw./jmdn.** ∼: judge sth./sb.

urteils-, Urteils-: ∼**fähig** *Adj.* competent *or* able to judge *postpos.;* ∼**fähigkeit** *die* competence *or* ability to judge; ∼**vermögen** *das* competence to judge

Ur·wald *der* primeval forest; (tropisch) jungle

ur·wüchsig *Adj.* natural ‹*landscape, power*›; earthy ‹*language, humour*›

Urwüchsigkeit *die;* ∼ ▶ URWÜCHSIG: naturalness; earthiness

USA *Pl.* USA

User /'ju:zɐ/ *der;* ∼s, ∼, **Userin** *die;* ∼, ∼nen (bes. DV, Drogenjargon) user

usw. *Abk.* = **und so weiter** etc.

Utensil *das;* ∼s, ∼ien /...iən/ piece of equipment; ∼ien equipment *sing.*

Utopie *die;* ∼, ∼n utopian dream

utopisch *Adj.* utopian

UV *Abk.* = **Ultraviolett** UV

---

*old spelling – see note on page x

Vv

v, V /vaʊ/ *das;* ~, ~: v, V

v. *Abk.* = **von**

vage /'va:gə/ [1] *Adj.* vague
[2] *adv.* vaguely

Vagina /va'gi:na/ *die;* ~, **Vaginen** (Anat.) vagina

vaginal *Adj.* (Anat.) vaginal

vakant /va'kant/ *Adj.* vacant

Vakuum *das;* ~s, **Vakuen** vacuum

vakuum·verpackt *Adj.* vacuum-packed

Valentins·tag /'va:lɛnti:ns-/ *der* [St] Valentine's Day

Van /væn/ *der;* ~s, ~s (Kfz.-W.) multi-purpose vehicle; MPV

Vandale /van'da:la/ *usw.:* ▶ Wandale

Vanille /va'nɪljə/ *die;* ~: vanilla

Vanille-: ~**eis** *das* vanilla ice cream;
~**pudding** *der* vanilla pudding;
~**zucker** *der* vanilla sugar

variabel /va'ria:bl̩/ [1] *Adj.* variable
[2] *adv.* variably

Variante /va'rianta/ *die;* ~, ~n (geh.) variant; variation

variieren *tr., itr. V.* vary

Vase /'va:zə/ *die;* ~, ~n vase

Vaseline /vaze'li:nə/ *die;* ~: Vaseline ®

Vater *der;* ~s, **Väter** father; **Gott** ~: God the Father

Vater·land *das* fatherland

väterlich [1] *Adj.* (a) paternal ⟨line, love, instincts, etc.⟩
(b) (fürsorglich) fatherly
[2] *adv.* in a fatherly way

väterlicherseits *Adv.* on the/his/her *etc.* father's side

Vaterschaft *die;* ~, ~en fatherhood

Vater-: ~**tag** *der* Father's Day *no def. art.;*
~**unser** *das;* ~~s, ~~: Lord's Prayer

Vati *der;* ~s, ~s (fam.) dad[dy] (coll.)

Vatikan /vati'ka:n/ *der;* ~s Vatican

v. Chr. *Abk.* = **vor Christus** BC

Vegetarier /vege'ta:riɐ/ *der;* ~s, ~,
Vegetarierin *die;* ~, ~nen vegetarian

vegetarisch [1] *Adj.* vegetarian
[2] *adv.* **er isst** *od.* **lebt** ~: he is a vegetarian

Vegetation *die;* ~, ~en vegetation *no indef. art.*

vegetieren *itr. V.* vegetate

Veilchen *das;* ~s, ~: violet

Vene /'ve:nə/ *die;* ~, ~n vein

Venedig /ve'ne:dɪç/ *(das)* ~s Venice

Venezolaner /venetso'la:nɐ/ *der;* ~s,
~, **Venezolanerin** *die;* ~, ~nen
Venezuelan

venezolanisch *Adj.* Venezuelan

Venezuela *(das);* ~s Venezuela

Ventil /vɛn'ti:l/ *das;* ~s, ~e valve

Ventilator /vɛnti'la:tɔr/ *der;* ~s, ~en ventilator

Venus /'ve:nʊs/ *die;* ~: Venus *no def. art.*

verabreden [1] *tr. V.* arrange
[2] *refl. V.* **sich im Park/zum Tennis/für den folgenden Abend** ~: arrange to meet in the park/for tennis/next evening

Verabredung *die;* ~, ~en
(a) arrangement
(b) (verabredete Zusammenkunft) appointment;
eine ~ **absagen** call off a meeting

verabscheuen *tr. V.* detest; loathe

verabschieden [1] *tr. V.* (a) say goodbye to
(b) (aus dem Dienst) retire ⟨general, civil servant, etc.⟩
[2] *refl. V.* **sich [von jmdm.]** ~: say goodbye [to sb.]

Verabschiedung *die;* ~, ~en (a) leave-taking
(b) (aus dem Dienst) retirement

verachten *tr. V.* despise

verächtlich [1] *Adj.* (a) contemptuous
(b) (verachtenswürdig) contemptible
[2] *adv.* contemptuously

Verächtlichkeit *die;* ~: contempt; contemptuousness

Verachtung *die;* ~: contempt

verallgemeinern *tr., itr. V.* generalize

Verallgemeinerung *die;* ~, ~en generalization

veralten *itr. V.; mit sein* become obsolete

Veranda /ve'randa/ *die;* ~, **Veranden** veranda; porch

veränderlich *Adj.* changeable

verändern *tr., refl. V.* change

Veränderung *die;* ~, ~en change (*Gen.* in)

verängstigen *tr. V.* frighten; scare

verankern *tr. V.* fix ⟨tent, mast, pole, etc.⟩; (mit einem Anker) anchor

veranlagen *tr. V.* (Steuerw.) assess (**mit** at)

veranlagt *Adj.* **künstlerisch/praktisch** ~ **sein** have an artistic bent/be practically minded

Veranlagung *die;* ~, ~en [pre]disposition

veranlassen *tr. V.* cause; induce; ~, **dass ...** see to it that ...

Veranlassung *die;* ~, ~en reason

veranschaulichen *tr. V.* illustrate

veranschlagen *tr. V.* estimate (**mit** at)

veranstalten *tr. V.* organize; hold, give ⟨*party*⟩; hold ⟨*auction*⟩; do ⟨*survey*⟩

Veranstalter *der;* ~s, ~,

Veranstalterin *die;* ~, ~nen organizer

Veranstaltung *die;* ~, ~en (a) (das Veranstalten) organizing; organization
(b) (etw., was veranstaltet wird) event

verantworten ① *tr. V.* etw. ~: take responsibility for sth.
② *refl. V.* **sich für etw.** ~: answer for sth.; **sich vor jmdm.** ~: answer to sb.

verantwortlich *Adj.* responsible

Verantwortung *die;* ~, ~en responsibility (**für** for)

verantwortungs-: ~**bewusst,** *****~**bewußt** *Adj.* responsible; ~**los** *Adj.* irresponsible; ~**voll** *Adj.* responsible

verarbeiten *tr. V.* use; **etw. zu etw.** ~: make sth. into sth.; (geistig bewältigen) assimilate ⟨*film, experience, impressions*⟩

Verarbeitung *die;* ~, ~en (a) (das Verarbeiten) use
(b) (Art der Fertigung) finish; **Schuhe in erstklassiger** ~: shoes with a first-class finish

verärgern *tr. V.* annoy

verarzten *tr. V.* (ugs.) patch up (coll.) ⟨*person*⟩; fix (coll.) ⟨*wound etc.*⟩

verausgaben *refl. V.* wear oneself out; **sie hat sich total verausgabt** (finanziell) she has completely spent out

veräußern *tr. V.* dispose of ⟨*property*⟩

Verb /vɛrp/ *das;* ~s, ~en verb

verbal /vɛr'ba:l/ *Adj.* ① (auch Sprachw.) verbal
② *adv.* verbally

Verband *der* (a) (Binde) bandage; dressing
(b) (Vereinigung) association

verbandeln *tr. V.* link closely

Verband[s]-: ~**kasten** *der* first-aid box; ~**material** *das* dressing materials *pl.*

Verband-zeug *das* first-aid things *pl.*

Verbannung *die;* ~, ~en banishment

verbeamten *tr. V.* make ⟨*person*⟩ a civil servant

verbergen *unr. tr. V.* hide; conceal

verbessern ① *tr. V.* (a) improve
(b) (korrigieren) correct
② *refl. V.* (a) improve
(b) ([beruflich] aufsteigen) better oneself

Verbesserung *die* (a) improvement
(b) (Korrektur) correction

Verbesserungs-vorschlag *der* suggestion for improvement

verbeugen *refl. V.* bow (**vor** + *Dat.* to)

Verbeugung *die;* ~, ~en bow

verbeulen *tr. V.* dent

verbieten *unr. tr. V.* (a) forbid; jmdm. etw. ~: forbid sb. sth.; „**Betreten des Rasens/ Rauchen verboten**" 'keep off the grass'/'no smoking'
(b) (für unzulässig erklären) ban

verbinden ① *unr. tr. V.* (a) (bandagieren) bandage; dress
(b) (zubinden) bind; **jmdm. die Augen** ~: blindfold sb.
(c) (zusammenfügen) join
(d) (in Beziehung bringen) connect (**durch** by); link ⟨*towns, lakes, etc.*⟩ (**durch** by)
(e) (verknüpfen) combine ⟨*abilities, qualities, etc.*⟩
(f) *auch itr.* (telefonisch) jmdn. [mit jmdm.] ~: put sb. through [to sb.]
② *unr. refl. V.* (a) (auch Chemie) combine (**mit** with)
(b) (sich zusammentun) join [together]; join forces

verbindlich ① *Adj.* (a) friendly
(b) (bindend) obligatory; compulsory; binding ⟨*agreement, decision, etc.*⟩
② *adv.* (a) (freundlich) in a friendly manner
(b) ~ **zusagen** definitely agree; **jmdm. etw.** ~ **zusagen** make sb. a firm offer of sth.

Verbindung *die;* ~, ~en (a) (das Verknüpfen) linking
(b) (Zusammenhalt) join; connection
(c) (verknüpfende Strecke) link
(d) (durch Telefon, Funk, Verkehrsmittel) connection (**nach** to)
(e) (Kombination) combination; **in** ~ **mit etw.** in conjunction with sth.
(f) (Kontakt) contact; **sich mit jmdm. in** ~ **setzen** *or* get in touch *or* contact with sb.
(g) (Zusammenhang) connection

verbissen ① *Adj.* dogged; doggedly determined
② *adv.* doggedly

verbitten *unr. refl. V.* sich (*Dat.*) etw. ~: refuse to tolerate sth.

verbittern *tr. V.* embitter

Verbitterung *die;* ~, ~en bitterness; embitterment

verblassen *itr. V.; mit sein* (auch fig. geh.) fade

Verbleib *der;* ~[e]s (geh.) whereabouts *pl.*

verbleiben *unr. itr. V.; mit sein* remain; **wie seid ihr verblieben?** what did you arrange?

verbleien *tr. V.* (Technik) lead ⟨*petrol*⟩

Verblendung *die;* ~, ~en blindness

verblüffen *tr.* (*auch itr.*) *V.* amaze

verblüffend ① *Adj.* amazing
② *adv.* amazingly

Verblüffung *die;* ~, ~en amazement

verblühen *itr. V.; mit sein* (auch fig.) fade

verbluten *itr.* (*auch refl.*) *V.; mit sein* bleed to death

verbohrt *Adj.* pigheaded

verborgen *Adj.* (abgelegen) secluded; (nicht sichtbar) hidden

Verbot *das;* ∼[e]s, ∼e ban (*Gen.,* **von** on)
Verbots-schild *das; Pl.* ∼er sign (prohibiting sth.); (Verkehrsw.) prohibitive sign
Verbrauch *der;* ∼[e]s consumption (**von, an** + *Dat.* of)
verbrauchen *tr. V.* use; consume ⟨*food, drink*⟩; use up ⟨*provisions*⟩; spend ⟨*money*⟩; consume, use ⟨*fuel*⟩; (fig.) use up ⟨*strength, energy*⟩
Verbraucher *der;* ∼s, ∼ consumer
verbraucher-: ∼**feindlich** 1 *Adj.* not in the interests of consumers *postpos.;* 2 *adv.* against the interests of consumers; ∼**freundlich** 1 *Adj.* consumer-friendly; 2 *adv.* in a consumer-friendly way
Verbraucherin *die;* ∼, ∼nen consumer
Verbraucher-schutz *der* consumer protection
Verbrechen *das;* ∼s, ∼: crime (**an** + *Dat.,* **gegen** against)
Verbrechens-: ∼**rate** *die* crime rate; ∼**verhütung** *die* crime prevention
Verbrecher *der;* ∼s, ∼, **Verbrecherin** *die;* ∼, ∼nen criminal
verbrecherisch *Adj.* criminal
verbreiten 1 *tr. V.* spread; radiate ⟨*optimism, calm, etc.*⟩ 2 *refl. V.* spread
Verbreitung *die;* ∼, ∼en (a) ▸ VERBREITEN 1: spreading; radiation (b) (Ausbreitung) spread
verbrennen 1 *unr. itr. V.; mit sein* burn 2 *tr. V.* burn; cremate ⟨*dead person*⟩; sich (*Dat.*) den Mund ∼ (fig.) say too much
Verbrennung *die;* ∼, ∼en (a) ▸ VERBRENNEN 2: burning; cremation (b) (Wunde) burn
Verbrennungs-anlage *die* incineration plant; incinerator
verbringen *unr. tr. V.* spend
verbummeln *tr. V.* (ugs.) (a) waste ⟨*time*⟩ (b) (vergessen) forget [all] about; clean forget; (verlieren) lose
verbünden *refl. V.* form an alliance
Verbündete *der/die; adj. Dekl.* ally
verbüßen *tr. V.* serve ⟨*sentence*⟩
Verdacht *der;* ∼[e]s, ∼e *od.* Verdächte suspicion; wen hast du in ∼? who do you suspect?
verdächtig 1 *Adj.* suspicious 2 *adv.* suspiciously
Verdächtige *der/die; adj. Dekl.* suspect
verdächtigen *tr. V.* suspect
Verdächtigung *die;* ∼, ∼en suspicion
verdammen *tr. V.* condemn; (Rel.) damn ⟨*sinner*⟩
verdampfen 1 *itr. V.; mit sein* evaporate 2 *tr. V.* evaporate
verdanken *tr. V.* jmdm./einer Sache etw. ∼: owe sth. to sb./sth.

verdarb *1. u. 3. Pers. Sg. Prät. v.* VERDERBEN
verdattert (ugs.) *Adj.* flabbergasted; (verwirrt) dazed; stunned
verdauen 1 *tr. V.* (auch fig.) digest 2 *itr. V.* digest [one's food]
verdaulich *Adj.* digestible
Verdauung *die;* ∼: digestion
Verdeck *das;* ∼[e]s, ∼e top; hood (Brit.); (bei Kinderwagen) hood
verdecken *tr. V.* hide; cover
verderben 1 *unr. itr. V.; mit sein* go bad *or* off; spoil 2 *unr. tr. V.* spoil; (stärker) ruin; spoil ⟨*appetite, enjoyment, fun, etc.*⟩ 3 *unr. refl. V.* sich (*Dat.*) den Magen/die Augen ∼: give oneself an upset stomach/ ruin one's eyesight
Verderben *das;* ∼s ruin
verderblich *Adj.* perishable ⟨*food*⟩; pernicious ⟨*influence, effect, etc.*⟩
verdeutlichen *tr. V.* etw. ∼: make sth. clear; (erklären) explain sth.
verdichten *refl. V.* ⟨*fog, smoke*⟩ thicken, become thicker; (fig.) ⟨*suspicion, rumour*⟩ grow; ⟨*feeling*⟩ intensify
verdienen 1 *tr. V.* (a) earn (b) (wert sein) deserve 2 *itr. V.* beide Eheleute ∼: husband and wife are both earning
Verdiener *der;* ∼s, ∼, **Verdienerin** *die;* ∼, ∼nen wage earner
Verdienst¹ *der;* ∼[e]s, ∼e income; earnings *pl.*
Verdienst² *das;* ∼[e]s, ∼e merit
verdienst-voll 1 *Adj.* commendable; ⟨*person*⟩ of outstanding merit 2 *adv.* commendably
verdient 1 *Adj.* (a) ⟨*person*⟩ of outstanding merit; sich um etw. ∼ machen render outstanding services to sth. (b) (gerecht, zustehend) well-deserved 2 *adv.* deservedly
verdientermaßen *Adv.* deservedly
verdoppeln 1 *tr. V.* double; (fig.) double, redouble ⟨*efforts etc.*⟩ 2 *refl. V.* double
verdorben *2. Part. v.* VERDERBEN
verdorren *itr. V.; mit sein* wither [and die]; ⟨*meadow*⟩ scorch
verdrängen *tr. V.* (a) drive out ⟨*inhabitants*⟩; (fig.: ersetzen) displace (b) (Psych.) repress; (bewusst) suppress
verdrehen *tr. V.* (a) twist ⟨*joint*⟩; roll ⟨*eyes*⟩ (b) (ugs. abwertend: entstellen) twist ⟨*words, facts, etc.*⟩
verdrießen *unr. tr. V.* (geh.) irritate; annoy
verdrießlich 1 *Adj.* morose 2 *adv.* morosely

verdross, *verdroß *1. u. 3. Pers. Sg.*
Prät. v. VERDRIESSEN
verdrossen [1] *Adj.* (missmutig) morose;
(missmutig und lustlos) sullen
　[2] *adv.* (missmutig) morosely; (missmutig und
lustlos) sullenly
Verdruss, *Verdruß *der;* Verdrusses,
Verdrusse annoyance
verdunkeln *tr. V.* darken; (vollständig)
black out ⟨*room, house, etc.*⟩
Verdunk[e]lung *die;* ∼, ∼en darkening;
(vollständig) blackout
verdünnen *tr. V.* dilute
verdunsten *itr. V.; mit sein* evaporate
Verdunstung *die;* ∼: evaporation
verdursten *itr. V.; mit sein* die of thirst
verdutzt *Adj.* taken aback *pred.;*
nonplussed; (verwirrt) baffled
Verdutztheit *die;* ∼: bafflement
verehren *tr. V.* (a) venerate
　(b) (geh.: bewundern) admire; (ehrerbietig lieben)
worship
Verehrer *der;* ∼s, ∼, **Verehrerin** *die;*
∼, ∼en admirer
Verehrung *die;* ∼ (a) veneration
　(b) (Bewunderung) admiration
vereidigen *tr. V.* swear in
Vereidigung *die;* ∼, ∼en swearing in
Verein *der;* ∼s, ∼e organization; (der
Kunstfreunde usw.) association; society;
(Sportverein) club
vereinbar *Adj.* compatible
vereinbaren *tr. V.* agree; arrange
⟨*meeting etc.*⟩
Vereinbarung *die;* ∼, ∼en (a) agreeing;
(eines Termins usw.) arranging
　(b) (Abmachung) agreement
vereinfachen *tr. V.* simplify
Vereinfachung *die;* ∼, ∼en
simplification
vereinheitlichen *tr. V.* standardize
Vereinheitlichung *die;* ∼, ∼en
standardization
vereinigen *tr., refl. V.* unite; (in der
Wirtschaft) merge
vereinigt *Adj.* united
Vereinigung *die;* ∼, ∼en (a) organization
　(b) (das Vereinigen) uniting; (von Unternehmen)
merging
vereinsamen *itr. V.; mit sein* become
[increasingly] lonely *or* isolated
Vereinsamung *die;* ∼: loneliness;
isolation
vereinzelt [1] *Adj.* occasional
　[2] *adv.* (zeitlich) occasionally; (örtlich) here
and there
Vereinzelung *die;* ∼, ∼en isolation
vereisen *itr. V.; mit sein* freeze *or* ice over;
⟨*wing*⟩ ice up; ⟨*lock*⟩ freeze up

vereiteln *tr. V.* thwart
Vereitelung *die;* ∼: thwarting
vereitern *itr. V.; mit sein* go septic
verenden *itr. V.; mit sein* perish; die
verengen *refl. V.* narrow; ⟨*pupils*⟩
contract
vererben *tr. V.* leave, bequeath ⟨*property*⟩
(*Dat.,* an + *Akk.* to)
Vererbung *die;* ∼, ∼en heredity *no art.*
verewigen [1] *tr. V.* immortalize
　[2] *refl. V.* (ugs.: Spuren hinterlassen) leave one's
mark
verfahren [1] *unr. refl. V.* lose one's way
　[2] *unr. itr. V.; mit sein* proceed
Verfahren *das;* ∼s, ∼ (a) procedure;
(Technik) process; (Methode) method
　(b) (Rechtsw.) proceedings *pl.*
Verfall *der;* ∼[e]s (a) decay; (fig.: der Preise,
einer Währung) collapse
　(b) (Auflösung) decline
verfallen *unr. itr. V.; mit sein* (a) (baufällig
werden) fall into disrepair
　(b) (körperlich) ⟨*strength*⟩ decline
　(c) (untergehen) ⟨*empire*⟩ decline; ⟨*morals,
morale*⟩ deteriorate
　(d) (ungültig werden) expire
Verfalls·datum *das* use-by date;
(ugs.: Mindesthaltbarkeitsdatum) best-before date
verfälschen *tr. V.* distort, misrepresent
⟨*statement, message*⟩; falsify, misrepresent
⟨*facts, history, truth*⟩; falsify ⟨*painting,
banknote*⟩; adulterate ⟨*wine, milk, etc.*⟩
Verfälschung *die* ▶ VERFÄLSCHEN:
distortion; misrepresentation; falsification;
adulteration
verfassen *tr. V.* write; draw up
⟨*resolution*⟩
Verfasser *der;* ∼s, ∼, **Verfasserin**
die; ∼, ∼nen writer; (eines Buchs, Artikels usw.)
author; writer
Verfassung *die;* ∼, ∼en (a) (Politik)
constitution
　(b) (Zustand) state [of health/mind]; **in
guter/schlechter ∼ sein** be in good/poor
shape
verfassungs·gemäß [1] *Adj.*
constitutional; in accordance with the
constitution *postpos.*
　[2] *adv.* constitutionally; in accordance with
the constitution
verfaulen *itr. V.; mit sein* rot
verfehlen *tr. V.* miss
Verfehlung *die;* ∼, ∼en misdemeanour;
(Rel.: Sünde) transgression
verfeinden *refl. V.* sich ∼ mit make an
enemy of
verfeinern *tr. V.* improve; refine ⟨*method,
procedure*⟩
Verfeinerung *die;* ∼, ∼en
▶ VERFEINERN: improvement; refinement
verfertigen *tr. V.* produce
verfilmen *tr. V.* film; make a film of

Verfilmung *die;* ~, ~en (a) (das Verfilmen) filming
(b) (Film) film [version]
verfinstern [1] *tr. V.* obscure ⟨sun etc.⟩
[2] *refl. V.* (auch fig.) darken
Verfinsterung *die;* ~, ~en darkening
verflixt (ugs.) [1] *Adj.* **(a)** (ärgerlich) awkward, unpleasant ⟨situation, business, etc.⟩
(b) (verdammt) blasted (Brit.); blessed; confounded; ~ **[noch mal]!** [damn and] blast! (Brit. coll.)
(c) (sehr groß) **er hat ~es Glück gehabt** he was damned lucky (coll.)
[2] *adv.* (sehr) damned (coll.)
verflossen *Adj.* (ugs.) former
verfluchen *tr. V.* curse
verflucht [1] *Adj.* (salopp) damned (coll.); bloody (Brit. sl.); ~ **[noch mal]!** damn [it]! (coll.)
[2] *adv.* (sehr) damned (coll.)
verfolgen *tr. V.* pursue; hunt, track ⟨animal⟩; **etw. [strafrechtlich]** ~: prosecute sth.
Verfolgte *der/die; adj. Dekl.* victim of persecution
Verfolgung *die;* ~, ~en (a) pursuit; (eines Ziels, Plans usw.) pursuance
(b) [strafrechtliche] ~: prosecution
Verfolgungs-: ~**jagd** *die* pursuit; chase; ~**wahn** *der* (Psych.) persecution mania
verfressen *Adj.* (salopp) greedy
verfügen [1] *tr. V.* (anordnen) order; (dekretieren) decree
[2] *itr. V.* **über etw.** (*Akk.*) **[frei]** ~ **können** be free to decide what to do with sth.; **über etw.** (*Akk.*) ~ (etw. haben) have sth. at one's disposal
Verfügung *die;* ~, ~en (a) (Anordnung) order; (Dekret) decree
(b) (Disposition) **etw. zur** ~ **haben** have sth. at one's disposal; **jmdm. etw. zur** ~ **stellen** put sth. at sb.'s disposal
verführen *tr. V.* **(a)** (verleiten) tempt
(b) (sexuell) seduce
Verführer *der;* ~s, ~: seducer
Verführerin *die;* ~, ~nen seductress
verführerisch [1] *Adj.* **(a)** (verlockend) tempting
(b) (aufreizend) seductive
[2] *adv.* **(a)** (verlockend) temptingly
(b) (aufreizend) seductively
Verführung *die;* ~, ~en (a) temptation
(b) (sexuell) seduction
vergangen *Adj.* **(a)** (vorüber, vorbei) bygone, former ⟨times, years, etc.⟩
(b) (letzt...) last ⟨year, week, etc.⟩
Vergangenheit *die;* ~ (a) past
(b) (Grammatik: Präteritum) past tense
vergänglich *Adj.* transient; transitory; ephemeral

Vergänglichkeit *die;* ~: transience
Vergaser *der;* ~s, ~: carburettor
vergaß *1. u. 3. Pers. Sg. Prät. v.* VERGESSEN
Vergasung *die;* ~, ~en (a) (von Kohle) gasification
(b) (Tötung) gassing
(c) bis zur ~ (ugs.) ad nauseam
vergeben *unr. tr. V.* **(a)** *auch itr.* (geh.: verzeihen) forgive; **jmdm. etw.** ~: forgive sb. [for] sth.
(b) throw away ⟨chance, goal, etc.⟩
(c) (geben) place ⟨order⟩ **(an** + *Akk.* with); award ⟨grant, prize⟩ **(an** + *Akk.* to)
vergebens [1] *Adv.* in vain; vainly
[2] *adj.* **es war** ~: it was of *or* to no avail
vergeblich [1] *Adj.* futile; vain, futile ⟨attempt, efforts⟩
[2] *adv.* in vain
Vergebung *die;* ~: (geh.) forgiveness
vergegenwärtigen /od. ---'---/ *refl. V.* **sich** (*Dat.*) **etw.** ~: imagine sth.; (erinnern) recall sth.
vergehen *unr. itr. V.; mit sein* ⟨time⟩ pass [by], go by; ⟨pain⟩ wear off, pass; ⟨pleasure⟩ fade
Vergehen *das;* ~s, ~: crime; (Rechtsspr.) offence
vergeigen *tr. V.* (ugs.) botch up ⟨test, performance, etc.⟩; lose ⟨game, match⟩
vergelten *unr. tr. V.* repay
Vergeltung *die* **(a)** repayment
(b) (Rache) revenge; ~ **an jmdm./etw. üben** take revenge on sb./sth.
vergessen *unr. tr. V.* (*auch itr.*) *V.* forget
Vergessenheit *die;* ~: oblivion
vergesslich, *vergeßlich *Adj.* forgetful
vergeuden *tr. V.* waste
Vergeudung *die;* ~, ~en waste
vergewaltigen *tr. V.* rape
Vergewaltigung *die;* ~, ~en rape
vergewissern *refl. V.* make sure (*Gen.* of)
vergießen *unr. tr. V.* spill; **Tränen** ~: shed tears
vergiften *tr. V.* (auch fig.) poison
Vergiftung *die;* ~, ~en poisoning
vergiss, *vergiß *Imper. Sg. v.* VERGESSEN
Vergiss·mein·nicht, *Vergiß·mein·nicht *das;* ~[e]s, ~[e] forget-me-not
vergisst, *vergißt *2. u. 3. Pers. Sg. Präs. v.* VERGESSEN
Vergleich *der;* ~[e]s, ~e (a) comparison; **im** ~ **zu** *od.* **mit etw.** in comparison with sth.; compared with *or* to sth.
(b) (Rechtsw.) settlement
vergleichbar *Adj.* comparable
vergleichen *unr. tr. V.* compare
Vergleichs·form *die* (Sprachw.) comparative/superlative form

verglühen itr. V.; mit sein ⟨log, wick, fire, etc.⟩ smoulder and go out; ⟨satellite, rocket, wire, etc.⟩ burn out

vergnügen refl. V. enjoy oneself; have a good time

Vergnügen das; ~s, ~: pleasure; (Spaß) fun; **viel** ~! (auch iron.) have fun!

vergnüglich Adj. amusing; entertaining

vergnügt ① Adj. cheerful ② adv. cheerfully

Vergnügungs-viertel das pleasure district

vergolden tr. V. gold-plate ⟨jewellery etc.⟩; (mit Blattgold) gild

vergraben unr. tr. V. bury

vergrämt Adj. careworn

vergraulen tr. V. (ugs.) put off

vergreifen unr. refl. V. **sich an jmdm.** ~: assault sb.

vergriffen Adj. out of print pred.

vergrößern ① tr. V. (a) (erweitern) extend ⟨room, area, building, etc.⟩
(b) (vermehren) increase
(c) (größer reproduzieren) enlarge ⟨photograph etc.⟩
② refl. V. (a) (größer werden) ⟨firm, business, etc.⟩ expand
(b) (zunehmen) increase
③ itr. V. ⟨lens etc.⟩ magnify

Vergrößerung die; ~, ~en
(a) ▶ VERGRÖSSERN 1, 2: extension; increase; enlargement; expansion
(b) (Foto) enlargement

Vergrößerungs-glas das magnifying glass

Vergünstigung die; ~, ~en privilege

vergüten tr. V. (a) (erstatten) jmdm. etw. ~: reimburse sb. for sth.
(b) (bes. Papierdt.: bezahlen) remunerate, pay for ⟨work, services⟩

Vergütung die; ~, ~en (a) (Rückerstattung) reimbursement
(b) (Geldsumme) remuneration

verhaften tr. V. arrest; **Sie sind verhaftet** you are under arrest

Verhaftung die; ~, ~en arrest

verhalten unr. refl. V. (a) behave; (reagieren) react
(b) (beschaffen sein) be

Verhalten das; ~s behaviour

Verhaltens-weise die behaviour

Verhältnis das; ~ses, ~se (a) ein ~ von drei zu eins a ratio of three to one
(b) (persönliche Beziehung) relationship (zu with); **mit jmdm. ein** ~ **haben** (ugs.) have an affair with sb.
(c) Pl. (Umstände) conditions

verhältnis-mäßig Adv. relatively; comparatively

Verhältnis-wort das; Pl. ~wörter

(Sprachw.) preposition

verhandeln ① itr. V. (a) negotiate (**über** + Akk. about)
(b) (strafrechtlich) try a case; (zivilrechtlich) hear a case
② tr. V. (a) etw. ~: negotiate over sth.
(b) (strafrechtlich) try ⟨case⟩; (zivilrechtlich) hear ⟨case⟩

Verhandlung die; ~, ~en (a) ~en negotiations
(b) (strafrechtlich) trial; (zivilrechtlich) hearing; **die** ~ **gegen X** the trial of X

verhängen tr. V. impose ⟨fine, punishment⟩ (**über** + Akk. on); declare ⟨state of emergency, state of siege⟩; (Sport) award, give ⟨penalty etc.⟩

Verhängnis das; ~ses, ~se undoing

verhängnis-voll Adj. disastrous

verharmlosen tr. V. play down

Verharmlosung die; ~, ~en playing down

verhärmt Adj. careworn

verharren itr. V. (geh.) remain

verhärten ① tr. V. harden; make ⟨person⟩ hard
② refl. V. ⟨tissue⟩ become hardened

verhasst, *verhaßt Adj. hated; detested

verhätscheln tr. V. (ugs.) pamper

verhauen (ugs.) unr. tr. V. beat up; (als Strafe) beat

verheben unr. refl. V. do oneself an injury [while lifting sth.]

verheeren tr. V. devastate; lay waste [to]

verheerend Adj. (a) devastating
(b) (ugs.: scheußlich) ghastly (coll.)

verhehlen tr. V. (geh.) conceal (Dat. from)

verheilen itr. V.; mit sein ⟨wound⟩ heal [up]

verheimlichen tr. V. [jmdm.] etw. ~: keep sth. secret [from sb.]

Verheimlichung die; ~, ~en concealment

verheiraten refl. V. get married; **sich mit jmdm.** ~: marry sb.; get married to sb.

Verheiratete der/die; adj. Dekl. married person; married man/woman

Verheiratung die; ~, ~en marriage

verheizen tr. V. (a) burn; use as fuel
(b) (abwertend: rücksichtslos einsetzen) burn out ⟨athlete, skier, etc.⟩; use ⟨troops⟩ as cannon fodder

verhelfen unr. itr. V. jmdm./einer Sache zu etw. ~: help sb./sth. to get/achieve sth.

verherrlichen tr. V. glorify

Verherrlichung die; ~, ~en glorification

verheult Adj. (ugs.) ⟨eyes⟩ red from crying; ⟨face⟩ puffy or swollen from crying

verhexen tr. V. (auch fig.) bewitch

verhindern tr. V. prevent

Verhinderung die; ~, ~en prevention

verhöhnen tr. V. mock

Verhöhnung *die;* ~, ~en mockery
Verhör *das;* ~[e]s, ~e interrogation; questioning; (bei Gericht) examination
verhören ① *tr. V.* interrogate; question; (bei Gericht) examine
② *refl. V.* mishear
verhüllen *tr. V.* cover; (fig.) disguise
verhüllend *Adj.* (Literaturw.) euphemistic
Verhüllung *die;* ~, ~en covering; (fig.) disguising
verhungern *itr. V.; mit sein* die of starvation; starve [to death]
verhunzen *tr. V.* (ugs. abwertend) ruin; mess up; ruin ⟨landscape, townscape, etc.⟩
verhüten *tr. V.* prevent
Verhütung *die;* ~, ~en prevention; (Empfängnisverhütung) contraception
Verhütungs·mittel *das* contraceptive
verirren *refl. V.* (a) get lost; lose one's way; ⟨animal⟩ stray
(b) (irgendwohin gelangen) stray (**in, an** + *Akk.* into)
verjagen *tr. V.* chase away
verjüngen ① *tr. V.* rejuvenate
② *refl. V.* (schmaler werden) taper; become narrower; narrow
verkalken *itr. V.; mit sein* (a) ⟨tissue⟩ calcify; ⟨arteries⟩ become hardened
(b) (ugs.: senil werden) become senile
Verkauf *der;* ~[e]s, Verkäufe sale
verkaufen *tr. V.* (auch fig.) sell (*Dat.,* **an** + *Akk.* to); „zu ~" 'for sale'
Verkäufer *der;* ~s, ~ **Verkäuferin** *die;* ~, ~nen (a) seller; vendor (formal)
(b) (Berufsbez.) sales *or* shop assistant; (im Außendienst) salesman/saleswoman
verkäuflich *Adj.* (zum Verkauf geeignet) saleable; (zum Verkauf bestimmt) for sale postpos.
verkaufs·offen *Adj.* **der** ~**e** Samstag Saturday on which the shops are open all day
Verkaufs·preis *der* retail price
Verkehr *der;* ~s (a) traffic
(b) (Kontakt) contact; communication
(c) (Geschlechtsverkehr) intercourse
verkehren *itr. V.* (a) *auch mit sein* (fahren) run; ⟨aircraft⟩ fly
(b) (in Kontakt stehen) **mit jmdm.** ~: associate with sb.
(c) (zu Gast sein) **bei jmdm.** ~: visit sb. regularly
verkehrs-, Verkehrs-: ~**ampel** *die* traffic lights *pl.;* ~**amt** *das* tourist information office; ~**aufkommen** *das* volume of traffic; ~**hindernis** *das* obstruction to traffic; ~**knotenpunkt** *der* [traffic] junction; ~**kontrolle** *die* traffic check; ~**meldung** *die* traffic announcement *or* flash; ~**mittel** *das* means of transport; **die öffentlichen** ~**mittel** public transport *sing.;* ~**polizist**

der traffic policeman; ~**polizistin** *die* traffic policewoman; ~**schild** *das; Pl.* ~~**er** traffic sign; road sign; ~**sicher** *Adj.* roadworthy; ~**teilnehmer** *der,* ~**teilnehmerin** *die* road user; ~**unfall** *der* road accident; ~**weg** *der* traffic route; ~**zeichen** *das* traffic sign; road sign
verkehrt ① *Adj.* wrong
② *adv.* wrongly; **alles** ~ **machen** do everything wrong
verkennen *unr. tr. V.* fail to recognize; misjudge ⟨situation⟩
verklagen *tr. V.* sue; take to court; **eine Firma auf Schadenersatz** ~: sue a company for damages
verkleben ① *itr. V.; mit sein* stick together
② *tr. V.* (zukleben) seal up ⟨hole⟩; (festkleben) stick [down] ⟨floor covering etc.⟩
verkleiden *tr. V.* disguise; (kostümieren) dress up; **sich** ~: disguise oneself/dress [oneself] up
Verkleidung *die;* ~, ~en (a) disguising; (das Kostümieren) dressing up
(b) (Kleidung) disguise; (bei einer Party) fancy dress
verkleinern ① *tr. V.* (a) make smaller
(b) (verringern) reduce ⟨size, number, etc.⟩
(c) (kleiner reproduzieren) reduce ⟨photograph etc.⟩
② *refl. V.* become smaller; ⟨number⟩ decrease
Verkleinerungs·form *die* (Sprachw.) diminutive form
verknallen *refl. V.* (ugs.: sich verlieben) fall head over heels in love (**in** + *Akk.* with); **in jmdn. verknallt sein** be crazy about sb. (coll.)
verknittern *tr. V.* crumple
verknoten *tr. V.* tie; knot
verknüpfen *tr. V.* (a) (knoten) tie; knot
(b) (in Beziehung setzen) link
verkochen *itr. V.; mit sein* (a) boil away
(b) (breiig werden, zerfallen) boil down to a pulp
verkohlen *itr. V.* char
verkommen¹ *unr. itr. V.; mit sein* go to the dogs; (moralisch, sittlich) go to the bad
verkommen² *Adj.* depraved
verköstigen *tr. V.* feed; provide with meals
verkraften *tr. V.* cope with
verkrampfen *refl. V.* ⟨muscle⟩ become cramped; ⟨person⟩ tense up
Verkrampfung *die;* ~, ~en tenseness; tension
verkriechen *unr. refl. V.* ⟨animal⟩ creep [away]; ⟨person⟩ hide [oneself away]
verkrümeln *refl. V.* (ugs.: sich entfernen) slip off *or* away
verkrümmt *Adj.* bent ⟨person⟩; crooked ⟨finger⟩; curved ⟨spine⟩
Verkrümmung *die;* ~, ~en crookedness
verkrüppeln *tr. V.* cripple

verkümmern itr. V.; mit sein ⟨person, animal⟩ go into a decline; ⟨plant etc.⟩ become stunted; ⟨talent, emotional life, etc.⟩ wither away

verkünden tr. V. announce; pronounce ⟨judgement⟩; promulgate ⟨law, decree⟩

verkündigen tr. V. (geh.) announce; proclaim

Verkündigung die; ~, ~en announcement; proclamation

Verkündung die; ~, ~en announcement; (von Urteilen) pronouncement; (von Gesetzen, Verordnungen) promulgation

verkürzen tr. V. (a) (verringern) reduce; (abkürzen) shorten
(b) (abbrechen) cut short ⟨stay, life⟩; put an end to, end ⟨suffering⟩

verladen unr. tr. V. load

Verlag der; ~[e]s, ~e publishing house or firm; publisher's

verlagern tr. V. shift; (an einen anderen Ort) move; (fig.) transfer; shift ⟨emphasis⟩

Verlagerung die moving; eine ~ des Schwergewichts (fig.) a shift in emphasis

verlanden itr. V.; mit sein silt up

Verlandung die; ~, ~en silting up

verlangen tr. V. demand; (nötig haben) require, call for ⟨patience, knowledge, experience, skill, etc.⟩; (berechnen) charge; (sehen/sprechen wollen) ask for; **du wirst am Telefon verlangt** you're wanted on the phone (coll.)

Verlangen das; ~s, ~ (a) desire (**nach** for)
(b) **auf ~**: on request

verlängern tr. V. extend; lengthen, make longer ⟨skirt, sleeve, etc.⟩; renew ⟨passport, driving licence, etc.⟩

Verlängerung die; ~, ~en
▶ VERLÄNGERN: extension; lengthening; renewal

Verlängerungs-schnur die extension lead or (Amer.) cord

verlangsamen tr. V. das Tempo/seine Schritte ~: reduce speed/slacken one's pace; slow down

verlassen¹ ① unr. refl. V. rely, depend (**auf** + Akk. on)
② unr. tr. V. (a) leave
(b) (sich trennen von) desert; abandon; forsake; leave, desert ⟨wife, family, etc.⟩

verlassen² Adj. deserted ⟨street etc.⟩; empty ⟨house⟩; (öd) desolate ⟨region etc.⟩

verlässlich, *verläßlich ① Adj. reliable
② adv. reliably

Verlauf der; ~[e]s, Verläufe course

verlaufen ① unr. itr. V.; mit sein (a) (sich erstrecken) run
(b) (ablaufen) ⟨test, rehearsal, etc.⟩ go; ⟨party

etc.⟩ go off
② unr. refl. V. get lost; lose one's way

Verlaufs-form die (Sprachw.) progressive or continuous form

verlautbaren tr. V. announce [officially]

Verlautbarung die; ~, ~en announcement

verlauten itr. V.; mit sein be reported; **wie verlautet** according to reports

verleben tr. V. spend

verlebt Adj. dissipated

verlegen¹ tr. V. (a) mislay
(b) (verschieben) postpone (**auf** + Akk. until); (vor~) bring forward (**auf** + Akk. to); **einen Termin ~**: alter an appointment
(c) (verlagern) move; transfer ⟨patient⟩
(d) (legen) lay ⟨cable, pipe, carpet, etc.⟩

verlegen² ① Adj. embarrassed
② adv. in embarrassment

Verlegenheit die; ~, ~en
(a) (Befangenheit) embarrassment; **jmdn. in ~ bringen** embarrass sb.
(b) (Unannehmlichkeit) embarrassing situation

Verleger der; ~s, ~, **Verlegerin** die; ~, ~nen publisher

Verleih der; ~[e]s, ~e (a) hiring out; (von Autos) renting or hiring out
(b) (Unternehmen) hire firm; (Filmverleih) distribution company; (Videoverleih) video library; (Autoverleih) rental or hire firm

verleihen unr. tr. V. (a) hire out; rent or hire out ⟨car⟩; (umsonst) lend [out]
(b) (überreichen) award; confer ⟨award, honour⟩

Verleihung die; ~, ~en
(a) ▶ VERLEIHEN A: hiring out; renting out; lending [out]
(b) ▶ VERLEIHEN B: awarding; conferring; (Zeremonie) award; conferment

verleiten tr. V. jmdn. dazu ~, etw. zu tun lead or induce sb. to do sth.

verlernen tr. V. forget

verlesen ① unr. tr. V. read out
② unr. refl. V. (falsch lesen) make a mistake/ mistakes in reading

verletzen tr. V. (a) injure; (durch Schuss, Stich) wound
(b) (kränken) hurt ⟨person, feelings⟩
(c) (verstoßen gegen) violate; infringe ⟨regulation⟩; break ⟨agreement, law⟩

verletzlich Adj. vulnerable

Verletzlichkeit die; ~: vulnerability

Verletzte der/die; adj. Dekl. casualty; (durch Schuss, Stich) wounded person

Verletzung die; ~, ~en (a) (Wunde) injury
(b) (Kränkung) hurting
(c) ▶ VERLETZEN C: violation; infringement; breaking

verleugnen tr. V. deny; disown ⟨friend, relation⟩

Verleugnung die; ~, ~en denial; (eines Freundes, Verwandten) disownment

verleumden *tr. V.* slander; (schriftlich) libel
verleumderisch *Adj.* slanderous; (in Schriftform) libellous
Verleumdung *die;* ∼, ∼en slander; (in Schriftform) libel
verlieben *refl. V.* fall in love (**in** + *Akk.* with)
Verliebte *der/die; adj. Dekl.* lover
verlieren *unr. tr., itr. V.* lose
Verlierer *der;* ∼s, ∼, **Verliererin** *die;* ∼, ∼nen loser
verloben *refl. V.* get engaged; **verlobt sein** be engaged
Verlobte *der/die; adj. Dekl.* fiancé/fiancée
verlockend *Adj.* tempting
Verlockung *die;* ∼, ∼en temptation
verlogen *Adj.* lying, mendacious 〈*person*〉; false 〈*morality etc.*〉
verlor *1. u. 3. Pers. Sg. Prät. v.* VERLIEREN
verloren ① *2. Part. v.* VERLIEREN
　② *Adj.* lost; wasted 〈*effort*〉; ∼ **gehen** get lost
***verloren|gehen** ▶ VERLOREN 2
verlosen *tr. V.* raffle
Verlosung *die;* ∼, ∼en raffle; draw
verlottern *itr. V.; mit sein* 〈*person*〉 go to seed
Verlust *der;* ∼[e]s, ∼e loss (**an** + *Dat.* of)
vermachen *tr. V.* **jmdm. etw.** ∼: leave *or* bequeath sth. to sb.; (fig.: schenken, überlassen) give sth. to sb.
vermählen *refl. V.* (geh.) **sich [jmdm.** *od.* **mit jmdm.]** ∼: marry *or* wed [sb.]
Vermählung *die;* ∼, ∼en (geh.)
(a) marriage
(b) (Fest) wedding ceremony
vermarkten *tr. V.* market 〈*goods etc.*〉
Vermarktung *die;* ∼, ∼en marketing
vermehren ① *tr. V.* increase (**um** by)
　② *refl. V.* (a) increase
(b) (sich fortpflanzen) reproduce
Vermehrung *die;* ∼, ∼en (a) increase (*Gen.* in)
(b) (Fortpflanzung) reproduction
vermeiden *unr. tr. V.* avoid
Vermeidung *die;* ∼, ∼en avoidance
vermeintlich *Adj.* supposed
vermengen *tr. V.* mix (**miteinander** together)
Vermerk *der;* ∼[e]s, ∼e note; (amtlich) remark
vermerken *tr. V.* make a note of; note [down]; (in Akten, Wachbuch usw.) record
vermessen[1] *unr. tr. V.* measure; survey 〈*land, site*〉
vermessen[2] *Adj.* (geh.) presumptuous
vermieten *tr. (auch itr.) V.* rent [out], let [out] (**an** + *Akk.* to); hire [out] 〈*boat, car, etc.*〉; „**Zimmer zu** ∼‟ 'room to let'
Vermieter *der;* ∼s, ∼: landlord
Vermieterin *die;* ∼, ∼nen landlady

Vermietung *die;* ∼, ∼en
　▶ VERMIETEN: renting [out]; letting [out]; hiring [out]
vermindern ① *tr. V.* reduce; decrease; reduce, lessen 〈*danger, stress*〉; lower 〈*resistance*〉; reduce 〈*debt*〉
　② *refl. V.* decrease; 〈*resistance*〉 diminish
Verminderung *die*
　▶ VERMINDERN 1: reduction; decreasing; lessening; lowering; **eine** ∼ **der Einnahmen** a decrease in revenues
verminen *tr. V.* mine
vermischen ① *tr. V.* mix (**miteinander** together); blend 〈*teas, tobaccos, etc.*〉
　② *refl. V.* mix; (fig.) mingle; 〈*races, animals*〉 interbreed
Vermischung *die;* ∼
　▶ VERMISCHEN: mixing; blending; (fig.) mingling
vermissen *tr. V.* (a) miss
(b) (nicht haben) **ich vermisse meinen Ausweis** my identity card is missing
Vermißte, ***Vermißte** *der/die; adj. Dekl.* missing person
vermitteln ① *itr. V.* mediate, act as [a] mediator (**in** + *Dat.* in)
　② *tr. V.* (a) (herbeiführen) arrange; negotiate 〈*transaction, ceasefire, compromise*〉
(b) (besorgen) **jmdm. eine Stelle** ∼: find sb. a job
(c) (weitergeben) impart 〈*knowledge, insight, values, etc.*〉; communicate 〈*message, information, etc.*〉; convey 〈*feeling*〉; pass on 〈*experience*〉
Vermittler *der;* ∼s, ∼, **Vermittlerin** *die;* ∼, ∼nen (a) (Mittler) mediator
(b) ▶ VERMITTELN 2C: imparter; communicator; conveyer
(c) (von Berufs wegen) agent
Vermittlung *die;* ∼, ∼en (a) (Schlichtung) mediation
(b) ▶ VERMITTELN 2A: arrangement; negotiation
(c) ▶ VERMITTELN 2C: imparting; communicating; conveying
(d) (Telefonzentrale) exchange; (in einer Firma) switchboard
vermöbeln *tr. V.* (ugs.) beat up; (als Strafe) thrash
vermögen (geh.) *unr. tr. V.* **etw. zu tun** ∼: be able to do sth.; be capable of doing sth.
Vermögen *das;* ∼s, ∼ (a) (geh.: Fähigkeit) ability
(b) (Besitz) fortune; **er hat** ∼: he has money
vermögend *Adj.* wealthy; well-off
Vermögen[s]-steuer *die* wealth tax
vermummen *tr. V.* wrap up [warmly]; (verbergen) disguise
vermurksen *tr. V.* (ugs.) mess up; muck up (Brit. sl.)
vermuten *tr. V.* suspect; **das ist zu** ∼: that is what one would suppose *or* expect; we may assume that;

vermutlich [1] *Adj.* probable
[2] *Adv.* presumably; (wahrscheinlich) probably
Vermutung *die;* ~, ~**en** supposition
vernachlässigen *tr. V.* neglect;
(unberücksichtigt lassen) ignore; disregard
Vernachlässigung *die;* ~, ~**en** neglect
vernarben *itr. V.; mit sein* [form a] scar;
heal (lit. or fig.)
vernehmbar *Adj.* (geh.) audible
vernehmen *unr. tr. V.* (a) (geh.: hören,
erfahren) hear
(b) (verhören) question
vernehmlich [1] *Adj.* [clearly] audible
[2] *adv.* audibly
Vernehmung *die;* ~, ~**en** questioning
verneigen *refl. V.* (geh.) bow (**vor** + *Dat.* to,
(literary) before)
verneinen *tr. (auch itr.) V.* (a) say 'no' to
(question); answer (question) in the negative
(b) (Sprachw.) negate
Verneinung *die;* ~, ~**en** (Sprachw.)
negation
vernetzen *tr. V.* (Chemie, Technik) interlink
vernichten *tr. V.* destroy; exterminate
(pests, vermin)
vernichtend [1] *Adj.* crushing (defeat);
shattering (blow); (fig.) devastating
(criticism); devastating, withering (glance)
[2] *adv.* **den Feind** ~ **schlagen** inflict a
crushing defeat on the enemy
Vernichtung *die;* ~, ~**en** destruction;
(von Schädlingen) extermination
Vernichtungs-: ~**lager** *das*
extermination camp; ~**waffe** *die* weapon
of annihilation
Vernunft *die;* ~: reason
vernünftig [1] *Adj.* (a) sensible
(b) (ugs.: ordentlich, richtig) decent
[2] *adv.* (a) sensibly
(b) (ugs.: ordentlich, richtig) (talk, eat) properly;
(dress) sensibly
veröffentlichen *tr. V.* publish
Veröffentlichung *die;* ~, ~**en**
publication
verordnen *tr. V.* [jmdm. etw.] ~: prescribe
[sth. for sb.]
Verordnung *die;* ~, ~**en** prescribing
verpachten *tr. V.* lease
verpacken *tr. V.* pack; wrap up (present,
parcel)
Verpackung *die* (a) packing
(b) (Umhüllung) packaging *no pl.;* wrapping
verpassen *tr. V.* miss
verpennen (salopp) [1] *itr. V.* oversleep
[2] *tr. V.* (a) (vergessen) forget
(b) (verschlafen) sleep through (morning etc.)
verpesten *tr. V.* (abwertend) pollute
Verpestung (abwertend) *die;* ~, ~**en**
pollution

verpflanzen *tr. V.* (auch Med.) transplant;
graft (skin)
Verpflanzung *die;* ~, ~**en** (Med.)
transplant[ing]; (von Haut) graft
verpflegen *tr. V.* cater for; feed
Verpflegung *die;* ~, ~**en** (a) catering *no
indef. art.* (Gen. for)
(b) (Nahrung) food; **Unterkunft und** ~: board
and lodging
verpflichten [1] *tr. V.* (a) oblige; commit;
(festlegen, binden) bind
(b) (einstellen, engagieren) engage (manager,
actor, etc.)
[2] *refl. V.* undertake; promise; **sich
vertraglich** ~: sign a contract
Verpflichtung *die;* ~, ~**en** (a) obligation;
commitment
(b) (Engagement) engaging; engagement
verpfuschen *tr. V.* (ugs.) make a mess of;
muck up (Brit. sl.)
verpissen *refl. V.* (salopp) piss off (Brit. sl.);
beat it (coll.)
verpönt *Adj.* scorned; (tabu) taboo
verprügeln *tr. V.* beat up; (zur Strafe)
thrash
Verputz *der;* ~**es** plaster; (auf Außenwänden)
rendering
verputzen *tr. V.* plaster; render (outside
wall)
verquer *Adj.* (absonderlich) weird,
outlandish (idea)
verquirlen *tr. V.* mix [with a whisk];
whisk
verquollen *Adj.* swollen
verrammeln *tr. V.* barricade
Verrat *der;* ~**[e]s** betrayal (**an** + *Dat.* of)
verraten *unr. tr. V.* (a) betray (**an** + *Akk.*
to)
(b) (ugs.: mitteilen) **jmdm. den Grund** *usw.*
~: tell sb. the reason *etc.*
(c) (erkennen lassen) show, betray (feelings,
surprise, fear, etc.); show (influence, talent)
Verräter *der;* ~**s**, ~: traitor
Verräterin *die;* ~, ~**nen** traitress
verräterisch *Adj.* treacherous (plan,
purpose, act, etc.)
verraucht *Adj.* smoke-filled; smoky
verrechnen [1] *tr. V.* include (amount
etc.); (gutschreiben) credit (cheque etc.) to
another account
[2] *refl. V.* miscalculate
Verrechnungs-scheck *der* crossed
cheque
verregnen *itr. V.; mit sein* be spoilt *or*
ruined by rain
verreiben *unr. tr. V.* rub in
verreisen *itr. V.; mit sein* go away
verrenken *tr. V.* dislocate
Verrenkung *die;* ~, ~**en** dislocation
verrichten *tr. V.* perform
verriegeln *tr. V.* bolt

---

verringern ① *tr. V.* reduce
② *refl. V.* decrease
Verringerung *die;* ~: reduction; decrease
(*Gen.,* **von** in)
Verriss, *Verriß *der* (ugs.) damning
review *or* criticism (**über** + *Akk.* of)
verrosten *itr. V.; mit sein* rust; **verrostet**
rusty
verrückt (ugs.) ① *Adj.* (a) mad; ~ **werden**
go mad *or* insane
(b) (überspannt, ausgefallen) crazy ⟨*idea,
fashion, prank, day, etc.*⟩
② *adv.* crazily; ⟨*behave*⟩ crazily *or* like a
madman; ⟨*dress etc.*⟩ in a mad *or* crazy way
Verrückte *der/die; adj. Dekl.* (ugs.)
madman/madwoman; lunatic
verrufen *Adj.* disreputable
verrühren *tr. V.* stir together; mix
verrutschen *itr. V.* slip
Vers *der;* ~**es,** ~**e** verse
versagen *itr. V.* fail; ⟨*machine, engine*⟩
stop [working]; **menschliches Versagen**
human error
Versager *der;* ~**s,** ~, **Versagerin** *die;*
~, ~**nen** failure
versalzen *unr. tr. V.* put too much salt
in/on; (fig. ugs.) spoil
versammeln *tr., refl. V.* assemble
Versammlung *die;* ~, ~**en** (a) meeting
(b) (Gremium) assembly
Versand *der;* ~**[e]s** (a) dispatch
(b) (ugs.: Versandhaus) mail order firm
Versand-: ~**handel** *der* mail order
business; ~**haus** *das* mail order firm
versauen *tr. V.* (salopp) (a) (verschmutzen)
mess up; make mucky (coll.)
(b) (verderben) foul up (coll.)
versäumen *tr. V.* (a) (verpassen) miss; lose
⟨*time, sleep*⟩
(b) (vernachlässigen, unterlassen) neglect ⟨*duty,
task*⟩
verschaffen *tr. V.* jmdm. etw. ~: provide
sb. with sth.; get sb. sth.; **sich** (*Dat.*) **etw.**
~: get hold of sth.; obtain sth.
verschämt ① *Adj.* bashful
② *adv.* bashfully
verschandeln *tr. V.* (ugs.) spoil; ruin
verschenken *tr. V.* give away
verscheuchen *tr. V.* chase away
verscheuern *tr. V.* (ugs.) flog (Brit. sl.)
(*Dat.,* **an** + *Akk.* to)
verschicken *tr. V.* ▶ VERSENDEN
verschieben ① *unr. tr. V.* (a) shift; move
(b) (aufschieben) put off, postpone (**auf** + *Akk.*
till)
② *unr. refl. V.* be postponed (**um** for); ⟨*start*⟩
be put back *or* delayed (**um** by)
Verschiebung *die;* ~, ~**en**
postponement
verschieden ① *Adj.* (a) different (**von**
from)
(b) (vielfältig) various; **die** ~**sten** ...: all sorts

of ...; **die** ~**en** ...: the various ...
(c) **Verschiedenes** various things *pl.*
② *adv.* differently
verschieden·artig ① *Adj.* different in
kind *pred.;* (mehr als zwei) diverse
② *adv.* diversely
Verschiedenheit *die;* ~, ~**en**
difference; (unter mehreren) diversity
verschiedentlich *Adv.* on various
occasions
verschimmeln *itr. V.; mit sein* go
mouldy; **verschimmelt** mouldy
verschlafen¹ ① *unr. itr. (auch refl.) V.*
oversleep
② *unr. tr. V.* (a) (schlafend verbringen) sleep
through ⟨*morning, journey, etc.*⟩
(b) (versäumen) not wake up in time for
⟨*appointment*⟩; not wake up in time to catch
⟨*train, bus*⟩
(c) (ugs.: vergessen) forget about ⟨*appointment
etc.*⟩
verschlafen² *Adj.* half asleep; (fig.) sleepy
⟨*town*⟩
Verschlag *der;* ~**[e]s, Verschläge** shed
verschlagen¹ *unr. tr. V.* **die Seite** ~: lose
one's place *or* page; **jmdm. die Sprache**
~: leave sb. speechless
verschlagen² ① *Adj.* sly; shifty
② *adv.* slyly; shiftily
verschlechtern ① *tr. V.* make worse
② *refl. V.* get worse; deteriorate
Verschlechterung *die;* ~, ~**en**
worsening, deterioration (*Gen.* in)
Verschleiß *der;* ~**es,** ~**e** (a) wear *no
indef. art.*
(b) (Verbrauch) consumption (**an** + *Dat.* of)
verschleißen ① *unr. itr. V.; mit sein*
wear out
② *unr. tr. V.* wear out; (fig.) run down, ruin
⟨*one's nerves, one's health*⟩; use up ⟨*energy,
ability, etc.*⟩
verschleppen *tr. V.* (a) carry off; take
away ⟨*person*⟩
(b) (weiterverbreiten) carry, spread ⟨*disease,
bacteria, mud, etc.*⟩
(c) (verzögern) delay; (in die Länge ziehen) draw
out; let ⟨*illness*⟩ drag on [and get worse]
verschleudern *tr. V.* (a) sell dirt cheap
(coll.); (mit Verlust) sell at a loss
(b) (verschwenden) squander
verschließbar *Adj.* closable; lockable
⟨*suitcase, drawer, etc.*⟩; **[luftdicht]**
~: sealable ⟨*container etc.*⟩
verschließen *unr. tr. V.* (a) close; stop
(mit einem Korken) cork ⟨*bottle*⟩
(b) (abschließen) lock; lock up ⟨*house etc.*⟩
(c) (wegschließen) lock away (**in** + *Dat. od.
Akk.* in)
verschlimmern ① *tr. V.* make worse
② *refl. V.* get worse; ⟨*position, conditions*⟩
deteriorate, worsen
Verschlimmerung *die;* ~, ~**en**
worsening

V

verschlingen *unr. tr. V.* **(a)** [inter]twine ⟨*threads etc.*⟩ (**zu** into)
(b) (essen, fressen) devour ⟨*food*⟩; (fig.) devour ⟨*novel, money, etc.*⟩

verschlissen 2. *Part. v.* VERSCHLEISSEN 2

verschlossen *Adj.* (wortkarg) taciturn; (zurückhaltend) reserved

Verschlossenheit *die;* ~: taciturnity; (Zurückhaltung) reserve

verschlucken ⓵ *tr. V.* swallow
⓶ *refl. V.* choke

Verschluss, *Verschluß *der* (am BH, an Schmuck usw.) fastener; fastening; (an Taschen, Schmuck) clasp; (an Schuhen, Gürteln) buckle; (am Schrank, Fenster, Koffer usw.) catch; (an Flaschen) top; (Stöpsel) stopper

verschmähen *tr. V.* (geh.) spurn

verschmerzen *tr. V.* get over

verschmieren *tr. V.* smear ⟨*window etc.*⟩; (beim Schreiben) mess up ⟨*paper*⟩; scrawl all over ⟨*page*⟩; smudge ⟨*ink*⟩

verschmitzt ⓵ *Adj.* mischievous
⓶ *adv.* mischievously

verschmutzen ⓵ *itr. V.; mit sein* get dirty; ⟨*river etc.*⟩ become polluted
⓶ *tr. V.* dirty; soil; pollute ⟨*air, water, etc.*⟩

Verschmutzung *die;* ~, ~en (der Umwelt) pollution; (von Stoffen, Teppichen usw.) soiling

verschnaufen *itr.* (*auch refl.*) *V.* have *or* take a breather

verschneit *Adj.* snow-covered *attrib.;* covered with snow *postpos.*

verschnörkelt *Adj.* ornate

verschnüren *tr. V.* tie up

verschollen *Adj.* missing

verschonen *tr. V.* spare; **jmdn. mit etw.** ~: spare sb. sth.

verschönern *tr. V.* brighten up

verschränken *tr. V.* fold ⟨*arms*⟩; cross ⟨*legs*⟩; clasp ⟨*hands*⟩

verschrecken *tr. V.* frighten *or* scare [off *or* away]

verschreiben ⓵ *unr. tr. V.*
(Med.: verordnen) prescribe
⓶ *unr. refl. V.* **(a)** make a slip of the pen
(b) sich einer Sache (*Dat.*) ~: devote oneself to sth.

verschreibungs·pflichtig *Adj.* available only on prescription *postpos.*

verschrie[e]n *Adj.* notorious (**wegen** for)

verschroben *Adj.* eccentric, cranky ⟨*person*⟩; cranky, weird ⟨*ideas*⟩

verschrotten *tr. V.* scrap

Verschrottung *die;* ~, ~en scrapping

verschulden ⓵ *tr. V.* be to blame for ⟨*accident, death, etc.*⟩
⓶ *refl. V.* get into debt

Verschulden *das;* ~s guilt; **durch eigenes** ~: through one's own fault

verschuldet *Adj.* in debt *postpos.* (**bei** to);

hoch ~: deeply in debt

verschütt: ~ **gehen** (ugs.) do a vanishing trick *or* disappearing act (coll.)

verschütten *tr. V.* **(a)** spill
(b) (begraben) bury ⟨*person*⟩ [alive]

*verschütt|gehen ▸ VERSCHÜTT

verschwägert *Adj.* related by marriage *postpos.*

verschweigen *unr. tr. V.* conceal (*Dat.* from)

verschwenden *tr. V.* waste (**an** + *Akk.* on)

Verschwender *der;* ~s, ~,
Verschwenderin *die;* ~, ~nen (von Geld) spendthrift; (von Dingen) wasteful person

verschwenderisch ⓵ *Adj.* wasteful ⟨*person*⟩; ⟨*life*⟩ of extravagance
⓶ *adv.* wastefully

Verschwendung *die;* ~, ~en wastefulness; extravagance

verschwiegen *Adj.* discreet; (still, einsam) secluded

Verschwiegenheit *die;* ~: secrecy; (Diskretion) discretion

verschwimmen *unr. itr. V.; mit sein* blur

verschwinden *unr. itr. V.; mit sein* disappear; vanish; **verschwinde [hier]!** off with you!; go away!; hop it! (coll.); **ich muss mal** ~ (ugs. verhüll.) I have to pay a visit (coll.) *or* (Brit. coll.) spend a penny

verschwindend ⓵ *Adj.* tiny
⓶ *adv.* ~ **klein** tiny; minute; ~ **wenig** a tiny amount

verschwommen ⓵ *Adj.* blurred ⟨*photograph, vision*⟩; blurred, hazy ⟨*outline*⟩; vague, woolly ⟨*idea, concept, formulation, etc.*⟩
⓶ *adv.* vaguely; ⟨*remember*⟩ hazily

versehen ⓵ *unr. tr. V.* **(a)** (ausstatten) provide; equip ⟨*car, factory, machine, etc.*⟩
(b) (ausüben, besorgen) perform ⟨*duty etc.*⟩
⓶ *unr. refl. V.* make a slip; slip up

Versehen *das;* ~s, ~: oversight; slip; **aus** ~: by mistake; inadvertently

versehentlich ⓵ *Adv.* by mistake; inadvertently
⓶ *adj.* inadvertent

Versehrte *der/die; adj. Dekl.* disabled person; **die** ~n the disabled

versenden *unr.* (*auch regelm.*) *tr. V.* send ⟨*letter, parcel*⟩; send out ⟨*invitations*⟩; dispatch ⟨*goods*⟩

versetzen ⓵ *tr. V.* **(a)** move; transfer; move ⟨*employee*⟩; (in die nächsthöhere Klasse) move ⟨*pupil*⟩ up, (Amer.) promote ⟨*pupil*⟩ (**in** + *Akk.* to); (umpflanzen) transplant, move ⟨*plant*⟩; (fig.) transport (**in** + *Akk.* to)
(b) (nicht geradlinig anordnen) stagger
(c) (verpfänden) pawn
(d) (verkaufen) sell
(e) (ugs.: vergeblich warten lassen) stand ⟨*person*⟩ up (coll.)

(f) (vermischen) mix
(g) (erwidern) retort
(h) etw. in Bewegung/Tätigkeit ∼: set sth. in motion/operation; **jmdn. in die Lage** ∼, **etw. zu tun** put sb. in a position to do sth.; **jmdn. einen Stoß/Fußtritt/Schlag** *usw.* ∼: give sb. a push/kick/deal sb. a blow *etc.*
2 *refl. V.* **sich in jmds. Lage** (*Akk.*) ∼: put oneself in sb.'s position *or* place
Versetzung *die;* ∼, ∼en (eines Schülers) moving up, (Amer.) promotion (**in** + *Akk.* to); (eines Angestellten) transfer
verseuchen *tr. V.* (auch fig.) contaminate; **radioaktiv** ∼: contaminate with radioactivity
Verseuchung (auch fig.) *die;* ∼, ∼en contamination
Versicherer *der;* ∼s, ∼, **Versicherin** *die;* ∼, ∼nen insurer
versichern *tr. V.* **(a)** assert ⟨*sth.*⟩ **(b)** (vertraglich schützen) insure (**bei** with)
Versicherte *der/die; adj. Dekl.* insured [person]
Versicherung *die* **(a)** (Beteuerung) assurance
(b) (Schutz durch Vertrag) insurance; (Vertrag) insurance [policy] (**über** + *Akk.* for); (Gesellschaft) insurance [company]
Versicherungs-: ∼**beitrag** *der* insurance premium; ∼**betrug** *der* insurance fraud; ∼**gesellschaft** *die* insurance company; ∼**nehmer** *der;* ∼∼s, ∼∼, ∼**nehmerin** *die;* ∼∼, ∼∼nen policy holder; ∼**police** *die* insurance policy
versickern *itr. V.; mit sein* ⟨*river etc.*⟩ drain *or* seep away
versiegeln *tr. V.* seal
versiegen *itr. V.; mit sein* (geh.) dry up; run dry
versinken *unr. itr. V.; mit sein* sink; **im Schlamm** ∼: sink into the mud
verslumen /'slamən/ *itr. V.; mit sein* turn into a slum; **ein verslumter Stadtteil** a slum district
versoffen *Adj.* (salopp abwertend) boozy (coll.)
versöhnen **1** *refl. V.* **sich [miteinander]** ∼: become reconciled; **sich mit jmdm.** ∼: make it up with sb.
2 *tr. V.* reconcile
Versöhnung *die;* ∼, ∼en reconciliation
versonnen **1** *Adj.* dreamy
2 *adv.* dreamily
versorgen *tr. V.* **(a)** supply
(b) (unterhalten, ernähren) provide for ⟨*children, family*⟩
(c) (sorgen für) look after; **jmdn. ärztlich** ∼: give sb. medical care; (kurzzeitig) give sb. medical attention
Versorger *der;* ∼s, ∼, **Versorgerin** *die;* ∼, ∼nen breadwinner
Versorgung *die;* ∼, ∼en **(a)** supply[ing]
(b) (Unterhaltung, Ernährung) support[ing]

(c) (Bedienung, Pflege) care; **ärztliche** ∼: medical care *or* treatment; (kurzzeitig) medical attention
Verspannung *die* (Med.: der Muskulatur) tension
verspäten *refl. V.* be late
verspätet *Adj.* late ⟨*arrival etc.*⟩; belated ⟨*greetings, thanks*⟩; ∼ **eintreffen** arrive late
Verspätung *die;* ∼, ∼en lateness; (verspätetes Eintreffen) late arrival; **[fünf Minuten]** ∼ **haben** be [five minutes] late
versperren *tr. V.* block; obstruct ⟨*view*⟩
verspielen *tr. V.* gamble away; (fig.) squander, throw away ⟨*opportunity, chance*⟩; forfeit ⟨*right, credibility, etc*⟩
verspielt **1** *Adj.* (auch fig.) playful; fanciful, fantastic ⟨*form, design, etc.*⟩
2 *adv.* playfully (lit. or fig.); ⟨*dress, designed*⟩ fancifully, fantastically
verspotten *tr. V.* mock; ridicule
Verspottung *die;* ∼, ∼en mocking; ridiculing
versprechen **1** *unr. tr. V.* promise; **sich** (*Dat.*) **etw. von etw./jmdm.** ∼: hope for sth. *or* to get sth. from sth./sb.
2 *unr. refl. V.* make a slip/slips of the tongue
Versprechen *das;* ∼s, ∼, **Versprechung** *die;* ∼, ∼en promise
versprühen *tr. V.* spray
verspüren *tr. V.* feel
verstaatlichen *tr. V.* nationalize
Verstaatlichung *die;* ∼, ∼en nationalization
Verstand *der;* ∼[e]s (Fähigkeit zu denken) reason *no art.;* (Fähigkeit, Begriffe zu bilden) mind; (Vernunft) [common] sense *no art.;* **hast du denn den** ∼ **verloren?** (ugs.) have you taken leave of your senses?
verständig **1** *Adj.* sensible
2 *adv.* sensibly
verständigen **1** *tr. V.* notify, inform (**von, über** + *Akk.* of)
2 *refl. V.* **(a)** make oneself understood; **sich mit jmdm.** ∼: communicate with sb.
(b) (sich einigen) **sich [mit jmdm.] über/auf etw.** (*Akk.*) ∼: come to an understanding [with sb.] about *or.* on sth.
Verständigkeit *die;* ∼: understanding; intelligence
Verständigung *die;* ∼, ∼en
(a) notification
(b) (das Sichverständlichmachen) communication *no art.*
(c) (Einigung) understanding
Verständigungs-schwierigkeit *die* difficulty of communication
verständlich **1** *Adj.* **(a)** comprehensible; (deutlich) clear ⟨*pronunciation, presentation, etc.*⟩; **sich** ∼ **machen** make oneself understood; **jmdm. etw.** ∼ **machen** make sth. clear to sb.
(b) (begreiflich, verzeihlich) understandable ⋯❖

2 adv. comprehensibly; (deutlich) ⟨speak, express oneself, present⟩ clearly

verständlicher·weise Adv. understandably

Verständlichkeit die;
~: comprehensibility; clarity

Verständnis das; ~ses, ~se understanding; **ich habe volles ~ dafür, dass …**: I fully understand that …; **für die Unannehmlichkeiten bitten wir um [Ihr] ~**: we apologize for the inconvenience caused

verständnis-: ~**los** **1** Adj. uncomprehending; **2** adv. uncomprehendingly; ~**voll** **1** Adj. understanding; **2** adv. understandingly

verstärken **1** tr. V. **(a)** strengthen **(b)** (zahlenmäßig) reinforce ⟨troops etc.⟩ (um by); enlarge ⟨orchestra, choir⟩ (um by) **(c)** (intensiver machen) intensify, increase ⟨effort, contrast⟩; strengthen, increase ⟨impression, suspicion⟩; (größer machen) increase ⟨pressure, voltage, effect, etc.⟩; (lauter machen) amplify ⟨signal, sound, guitar, etc.⟩ **2** refl. V. increase

Verstärker der; ~s, ~: amplifier

Verstärkung die; ~, ~en **(a)** strengthening **(b)** (zahlenmäßig) reinforcement (esp. Mil.) **(c)** (Zunahme) increase (Gen. in); (der Lautstärke) amplification **(d)** (zusätzliche Person[en]) reinforcements pl.

verstauben itr. V.; mit sein get dusty; gather dust (lit. or fig.)

verstaubt Adj. (fig. abwertend) old-fashioned; outmoded

verstauchen tr. V. sprain; **sich** (Dat.) **den Fuß/die Hand ~**: sprain one's ankle/wrist

Verstauchung die; ~, ~en sprain

verstauen tr. V. pack (in + Dat. od. Akk. in[to]); (bes. im Boot/Auto) stow (in + Dat. od. Akk. in)

Versteck das; ~[e]s, ~e hiding place: ~ **spielen** play hide-and-seek

verstecken **1** tr. V. hide (vor + Dat. from) **2** refl. V. sich [vor jmdm./etw.] ~: hide [from sb./sth.]

versteckt Adj. hidden; (heimlich) secret ⟨malice, activity, etc.⟩; disguised ⟨foul⟩

verstehen **1** unr. tr. V. understand; **wie soll ich das ~?** how am I to interpret that?; **jmdn./etw. falsch ~**: misunderstand sb./sth. **2** unr. refl. V. **sich mit jmdm. ~**: get on with sb.; **das versteht sich [von selbst]** that goes without saying

versteigern tr. V. auction; **etw. ~ lassen** put sth. up for auction

Versteigerung die; ~, ~en auction

versteinern itr. V.; mit sein ⟨plant, animal⟩ fossilize, become fossilized; ⟨wood

etc.⟩ petrify, become petrified

Versteinerung die; ~, ~en **(a)** (das Versteinern) fossilization; (von Holz) petrification **(b)** (Fossil) fossil

verstellbar Adj. adjustable

verstellen **1** tr. V. **(a)** (falsch platzieren) misplace **(b)** (anders einstellen) adjust ⟨seat etc.⟩; alter [the adjustment of] ⟨mirror etc.⟩; reset ⟨alarm clock, points, etc.⟩ **(c)** (versperren) block, obstruct **(d)** (zur Täuschung verändern) disguise ⟨voice, handwriting⟩ **2** refl. V. pretend

Verstellung die; ~, ~en pretence; (der Stimme, Schrift) disguising

versteuern tr. V. pay tax on

verstimmen tr. V. put ⟨person⟩ in a bad mood; (verärgern) annoy

verstimmt Adj. **(a)** (Musik) out of tune pred. **(b)** (verärgert) put out, peeved, disgruntled (über + Akk. by, about); **ein ~er Magen** an upset stomach

Verstimmung die; ~, ~en bad mood

verstockt Adj. obdurate; stubborn

Verstocktheit die; ~: obduracy; stubbornness

verstohlen **1** Adj. furtive **2** adv. furtively

verstopfen **1** tr. V. block; **verstopft sein** ⟨pipe, drain, jet, nose, etc.⟩ be blocked [up] (durch, von with) **2** itr. V.; mit sein become blocked

Verstopfung die; ~, ~en (Med.) constipation

verstorben Adj. late (deceased)

Verstorbene der/die; adj. Dekl. (geh.) deceased

verstören tr. V. distress

verstört Adj. distraught

Verstoß der; ~es, Verstöße violation (gegen of)

verstoßen **1** unr. tr. V. disown **2** unr. itr. V. gegen etw. ~: infringe sth.

verstreichen **1** unr. tr. V. apply, put on ⟨paint⟩; spread ⟨butter etc.⟩ **2** unr. itr. V.; mit sein (geh.) ⟨time⟩ pass [by]

verstreuen tr. V. scatter; put down ⟨bird food, salt⟩; (versehentlich) spill

verstricken **1** tr. V. jmdn. in etw. (Akk.) ~: involve sb. in sth.; draw sb. into sth. **2** refl. V. sich in etw. (Akk.) ~: become entangled or caught up in sth.

verstümmeln tr. V. mutilate; (fig.) garble ⟨report⟩; chop, mutilate ⟨text⟩

verstummen itr. V.; mit sein (geh.) fall silent; ⟨music, noise, conversation⟩ cease

Versuch der; ~[e]s, ~e attempt; (Experiment) experiment (an + Dat. on); (Probe) test

---

v

versuchen *tr. V.* (a) try; attempt
(b) (probieren) try ⟨*cake etc.*⟩
versündigen *refl. V.* **sich an jmdm./etw.**
~: sin against sb./sth.
versüßen *tr. V.* **jmdm./sich etw. ~** (fig.)
make sth. more pleasant for sb./oneself
vertauschen *tr. V.* exchange; switch;
reverse ⟨*roles, poles*⟩; **etw. mit** *od.* **gegen etw.**
~: exchange sth. for sth.
verteidigen *tr. V.* defend
Verteidiger *der;* **~s, ~, Verteidigerin**
die; **~, ~nen** (auch Sport) defender; (Rechtsw.)
defence counsel
Verteidigung *die,* **~, ~en** defence
Verteidigungs‑minister *der,*
Verteidigungs‑ministerin *die*
minister of defence
verteilen *tr. V.* distribute, hand out
⟨*leaflets, prizes, etc.*⟩ (**an** + *Akk.* to, **unter**
+ *Akk.* among); share [out], distribute
⟨*money, food*⟩ (**an** + *Akk.* to, **unter** + *Akk.*
among); allocate ⟨*work*⟩; distribute ⟨*weight
etc.*⟩ (**auf** + *Akk.* over); spread ⟨*cost*⟩ (**auf**
+ *Akk.* among); distribute, spread ⟨*butter,
seed, dirt, etc.*⟩
Verteilung *die;* **~, ~en** distribution; (der
Rollen, der Arbeit) allocation
verteuern 1 *tr. V.* make ⟨*goods*⟩ more
expensive
2 *refl. V.* become more expensive
verteufeln *tr. V.* condemn; denigrate
Verteufelung *die;* **~, ~en** condemnation;
denigration
vertiefen 1 *tr. V.* (auch fig.) deepen (**um**
by)
2 *refl. V.* **sich ~ in** (+ *Akk.*) bury oneself in
⟨*book, work, etc.*⟩; **in etw.** (*Akk.*) **vertieft sein**
be engrossed in sth.
Vertiefung *die;* **~, ~en** (Mulde)
depression; hollow
vertikal 1 *Adj.* vertical
2 *adv.* vertically
Vertikale *die;* **~, ~n ▶** SENKRECHTE
vertilgen *tr. V.* (a) (vernichten) exterminate
⟨*vermin*⟩; kill off ⟨*weeds*⟩
(b) (ugs.: verzehren) devour, (joc.) demolish
⟨*food*⟩
vertonen *tr. V.* set ⟨*text, poem*⟩ to music
Vertonung *die;* **~, ~en** setting
Vertrag *der;* **~[e]s, Verträge** contract;
(zwischen Staaten) treaty
vertragen 1 *unr. tr. V.* endure; tolerate
(esp. Med.); (aushalten, leiden können) stand;
bear; **ich vertrage keinen Kaffee** coffee
disagrees with me
2 *unr. refl. V.* **sich mit jmdm. ~:** get on *or*
along with sb.; (passen) **sich mit etw. ~:** go
with sth.
vertraglich 1 *Adj.* contractual
2 *adv.* contractually; by contract
verträglich *Adj.* (a) digestible ⟨*food*⟩
(b) (umgänglich) goodnatured; easy to get on

with *pred.*
vertrauen *itr. V.* **jmdm./einer Sache**
~: trust sb./sth.; **auf etw.** (*Akk.*) **~:** [put
one's] trust in sth.
Vertrauen *das;* **~s** trust; confidence;
jmdn. ins ~ ziehen take sb. into one's
confidence
vertrauen‑erweckend *Adj.* inspiring
vertrauens‑, Vertrauens‑: **~bruch**
der breach of trust; **~lehrer** *der,*
~lehrerin *die* (Schulw.) liaison teacher
(liaising between staff and pupils); **~person** *die*
person in a position of trust; **~sache** *die*
matter *or* question of trust; **~selig** *Adj.*
all too trusting; **~voll** 1 *Adj.* trusting
⟨*relationship*⟩; ⟨*collaboration, cooperation*⟩
based on trust; (zuversichtlich) confident;
2 *adv.* trustingly; (zuversichtlich) confidently;
~würdig *Adj.* trustworthy
vertraulich 1 *Adj.* (a) confidential
(b) (freundschaftlich, intim) familiar ⟨*manner,
tone, etc.*⟩; intimate ⟨*conversation*⟩
2 *adv.* (a) confidentially
(b) (freundschaftlich, intim) in a familiar way
Vertraulichkeit *die;* **~, ~en**
(a) confidentiality
(b) (vertrauliche Information) confidence
(c) (distanzloses Verhalten) familiarity; (Intimität)
intimacy
vertraut *Adj.* (a) close ⟨*friend etc.*⟩;
intimate ⟨*circle, conversation, etc.*⟩
(b) (bekannt) familiar; **jmdn./sich mit etw.**
~ machen familiarize sb./oneself with sth.
Vertraute *der/die; adj. Dekl.* close friend
vertreiben *unr. tr. V.* (a) drive out (**aus**
of); drive away ⟨*animal, smoke, clouds*⟩ (**aus**
from); fight off ⟨*tiredness, troubles*⟩
(b) (verkaufen) sell
vertreten 1 *unr. tr. V.* (a) stand in *or*
deputize for ⟨*colleague etc.*⟩; ⟨*teacher*⟩ cover
for ⟨*colleague*⟩
(b) (eintreten für, repräsentieren) represent
⟨*person, firm, interests, constituency, country,
etc.*⟩; (Rechtsw.) act for ⟨*person, prosecution,
etc.*⟩; **~ sein** be represented
(c) (einstehen für, verfechten) support ⟨*point of
view, principle*⟩; hold ⟨*opinion*⟩; advocate
⟨*thesis etc.*⟩
2 *unr. refl. V.* **sich** (*Dat.*) **die Füße** *od.* **Beine**
~ (ugs.) stretch one's legs
Vertreter *der;* **~s, ~, Vertreterin** *die;*
~, ~nen (a) (Stellvertreter[in]) deputy; stand‑in
(b) (Repräsentant[in]) representative;
(Handelsvertreter[in]) sales representative;
commercial traveller
(c) (Verfechter[in], Anhänger[in]) supporter;
advocate
Vertretung *die;* **~, ~en** deputy;
(Delegierte[r]) representative; (Delegation)
delegation (Handelsvertretung) [sales] agency;
eine diplomatische ~: a diplomatic mission
Vertriebene *der/die; adj. Dekl.* expellee
[from his/her homeland]
vertrocknen *itr. V.; mit sein* dry up

vertrödeln tr. V. (ugs. abwertend) dawdle away, waste ⟨time⟩

vertrösten tr. V. put ⟨person⟩ off (auf + Akk. until)

vertun [1] unr. tr. V. waste
[2] unr. refl. V. (ugs.) make a slip

vertuschen tr. V. hush up ⟨scandal etc.⟩; keep ⟨truth etc.⟩ secret

Vertuschung die; ~, ~en hushing up; eine ~: a hush-up or cover-up

verübeln tr. V. jmdm. eine Äußerung usw. ~: take sb.'s remark etc. amiss

verüben tr. V. commit ⟨crime etc.⟩

verunglücken itr. V.; mit sein have an accident; ⟨car etc.⟩ be involved in an accident; mit dem Auto/Flugzeug ~: be in a car/an air accident or crash

Verunglückte der/die; adj. Dekl. accident victim; casualty

verunreinigen tr. V. pollute; contaminate ⟨water, milk, flour, oil⟩

verunsichern tr. V. jmdn. ~: make sb. feel unsure or uncertain

verunstalten tr. V. disfigure

Verunstaltung die; ~, ~en disfigurement

veruntreuen tr. V. embezzle

Veruntreuung die; ~, ~en embezzlement

verunzieren tr. V. spoil the look of

verursachen tr. V. cause

verurteilen tr. V. pass sentence on; sentence; (fig.) condemn ⟨behaviour, action⟩; jmdn. zum Tode ~: sentence or condemn sb. to death

Verurteilte der/die; adj. Dekl. convicted man/woman

Verurteilung die; ~, ~en sentencing; (fig.) condemnation

vervollkommnen tr. V. perfect

vervollständigen tr. V. complete

verwachsen Adj. deformed

verwählen refl. V. misdial

verwahren [1] tr. V. keep [safe]
[2] refl. V. protest

verwahrlosen itr. V.; mit sein get in a bad state; ⟨house, building⟩ fall into disrepair; ⟨garden, hedge⟩ become overgrown; ⟨person⟩ let oneself go; verwahrlost neglected; overgrown ⟨hedge, garden⟩; dilapidated ⟨house, building⟩; unkempt ⟨person, appearance, etc.⟩; (in der Kleidung) ragged ⟨person⟩

Verwahrlosung die; ~: (eines Gebäudes) dilapidation; (einer Person) advancing decrepitude

verwaisen itr. V. be orphaned

verwalten tr. V. (a) administer ⟨estate, property⟩; run ⟨house⟩; hold ⟨money⟩ in trust
(b) (leiten) run, manage ⟨hostel, kindergarten,

etc.⟩; (regieren) administer ⟨area, colony, etc.⟩; govern ⟨country⟩

Verwalter der; ~s, ~, **Verwalterin** die; ~, ~nen administrator; (eines Amts usw.) manager; (eines Nachlasses) trustee

Verwaltung die; ~, ~en
(a) administration; (eines Landes) government; (eines Amtes) tenure; (einer Aufgabe) performance
(b) (Organ) administration

verwandeln [1] tr. V. convert (in + Akk., zu into); (völlig verändern) transform (in + Akk., zu into)
[2] refl. V. sich in etw. (Akk.) od. zu etw. ~: turn or change into sth.; (bei chemischen Vorgängen usw.) be converted into sth.

Verwandlung die; ~, ~en conversion (in + Akk., zu into); (völlige Veränderung, das Sichverwandeln) transformation (in + Akk., zu into)

verwandt[1] 2. Part. v. VERWENDEN

verwandt[2] Adj. related (mit to); (fig.) similar ⟨views, ideas, forms⟩

Verwandte der/die; adj. Dekl. relative; relation

Verwandtschaft die; ~, ~en
(a) relationship (mit to); (fig.) affinity
(b) (Verwandte) relatives pl.; relations pl.; die ganze ~: all one's relatives

verwandtschaftlich Adj. family ⟨ties, relationships, etc.⟩

verwarnen tr. V. warn, caution (wegen for)

Verwarnung die; ~, ~en warning; caution

verwechseln tr. V. (a) [miteinander] ~: confuse ⟨two things/people⟩; etw. mit etw./jmdn. mit jmdm. ~: mistake sth. for sth./sb. for sb.; confuse sth. with sth./sb. with sb.
(b) (vertauschen) mix up

Verwechslung die; ~, ~en (a) [case of] confusion
(b) (Vertauschung) mixing up; eine ~: a mix-up

verwegen [1] Adj. daring; (auch fig.) audacious
[2] adv. (auch fig.) audaciously

Verwegenheit die; ~: daring; (auch fig.) audacity

verwehren tr. V. jmdm. etw. ~: refuse or deny sb. sth.

Verwehung die; ~, ~en [snow]drift

verweigern tr. V. refuse

Verweigerung die; ~, ~en refusal

Verweis der; ~es, ~e (a) reference (auf + Akk. to); (Querverweis) cross reference
(b) (Tadel) reprimand

verweisen unr. tr. V. (a) jmdn./einen Fall usw. an jmdn./etw. ~ (auch Rechtsspr.) refer sb./a case etc. to sb./sth.
(b) (wegschicken) jmdn. von der Schule/aus dem Saal ~: expel sb. from the school/send

---

sb. out of the room; **einen Spieler vom Platz**
~: send a player off [the field]
(c) *auch itr.* (hinweisen) **[jmdn.] auf etw.**
(*Akk.*) **~**: refer [sb.] to sth.
verwelken *itr. V.; mit sein* wilt
verwendbar *Adj.* usable
Verwendbarkeit *die;* **~**: usability
verwenden *unr. od. regelm. tr. V.* **(a)** use
(**zu, für** for)
(b) (aufwenden) spend ⟨*time*⟩ (**auf** + *Akk.* on)
Verwendung *die;* **~, ~en** use
verwerfen *unr. tr. V.* reject; dismiss
⟨*thought*⟩
verwerflich (geh.) ☐1 *Adj.* reprehensible
☐2 *adv.* reprehensibly
verwertbar *Adj.* utilizable; usable
verwerten *tr. V.* utilize, use (**zu** for); make
use of ⟨*suggestion, experience, knowledge,*
etc.⟩
verwesen *itr. V.; mit sein* decompose
verwestlichen *itr. V.; mit sein* become
westernized
Verwesung *die;* **~**: decomposition
verwickeln ☐1 *refl. V.* get tangled up *or*
entangled; **sich in etw.** (*Akk. od. Dat.*) **~**: get
caught [up] in sth.
☐2 *tr. V.* involve
Verwicklung *die;* **~, ~en** complication
verwildern *itr. V.* ⟨*garden*⟩ become
overgrown; ⟨*domestic animal*⟩ return to
the wild
verwirklichen ☐1 *tr. V.* realize ⟨*dream*⟩;
realize, put into practice ⟨*plan, proposal,*
idea, etc.⟩; carry out ⟨*project, intention*⟩
☐2 **(a)** *refl. V.* ⟨*hope, dream*⟩ be realized
(b) (sich voll entfalten) **sich [selbst]** **~**: realize
one's [full] potential; fulfil oneself
Verwirklichung *die;* **~, ~en** realization;
(eines Wunsches, einer Hoffnung) fulfilment
verwirren *tr. V.* (*auch itr.*) *V.* confuse;
verwirrt ⟨*cloud, sb.*⟩; **~d** bewildering
Verwirrung *die;* **~, ~en** confusion
verwischen *tr. V.* smudge ⟨*signature,*
writing, etc.⟩; smear ⟨*paint*⟩; (fig.) cover up
⟨*tracks*⟩
verwittern *itr. V.; mit sein* weather
Verwitterung *die;* **~, ~en** weathering
verwitwet *Adj.* widowed
verwöhnen *tr. V.* spoil
verwöhnt *Adj.* spoilt; (anspruchsvoll)
discriminating; ⟨*taste, palate*⟩ of a gourmet
verworren *Adj.* confused, muddled ⟨*ideas,*
situation, etc.⟩
verwunden *tr. V.* wound; injure
Verwundete *der/die; adj. Dekl.* casualty;
die ~n the wounded
Verwundung *die;* **~, ~en** wound
verwünschen *tr. V.* curse
verwüsten *tr. V.* devastate
Verwüstung *die;* **~, ~en** devastation
verzagen *itr. V.; mit sein od. haben*

despair; lose heart; **verzagt sein** be
despondent
Verzagtheit *die;* **~**: despondency; despair
verzählen *refl. V.* miscount
verzanken *refl. V.* (ugs.) **sich [mit jmdm.**
wegen etw.] ~: fall out [with sb. over sth.]
verzaubern *tr. V.* cast a spell on;
bewitch; (fig.) enchant; **jmdn. in etw.** (*Akk.*)
~: transform sb. into sth.
Verzehr *der;* **~[e]s** consumption
verzehren *tr. V.* consume
Verzeichnis *das;* **~ses, ~se** list; (Register)
index
verzeihen *unr. tr., itr. V.* forgive;
(entschuldigen) excuse ⟨*behaviour, remark,*
etc.⟩; **~ Sie [bitte], können Sie mir sagen ...?**
excuse me, could you tell me ...?
Verzeihung *die;* **~**: forgiveness; **~!**
sorry!; **jmdn. um ~ bitten** apologize to sb.
verzerren *tr. V.* **(a)** contort ⟨*face etc.*⟩ (**zu**
into)
(b) (akustisch, optisch) distort ⟨*sound, image*⟩;
etw. verzerrt darstellen (fig.) present a
distorted account *or* picture of sth.
Verzicht *der;* **~[e]s, ~e (a)** renunciation
(**auf** + *Akk.* of)
(b) (auf Reichtum, ein Amt usw.) relinquishment
(**auf** + *Akk.* of)
verzichten *itr. V.* do without; **~ auf**
(+ *Akk.*) do without; (sich enthalten) refrain
from; (aufgeben) give up ⟨*share, smoking,*
job, etc.⟩; renounce ⟨*inheritance*⟩; relinquish
⟨*right, privilege*⟩; (opfern) sacrifice ⟨*holiday,*
salary⟩
verziehen[1] *2. Part. v.* VERZEIHEN
verziehen[2] ☐1 *unr. tr. V.* **(a)** screw up
⟨*face, mouth, etc.*⟩
(b) (schlecht erziehen) spoil
☐2 *unr. refl. V.* **(a)** (aus der Form geraten) go out
of shape; ⟨*wood*⟩ warp
(b) (wegziehen) ⟨*clouds, storm*⟩ move away,
pass over; ⟨*fog, mist*⟩ disperse
(c) (ugs.: weggehen) take oneself off
☐3 *unr. itr. V.; mit sein* move [away];
„Empfänger [unbekannt] verzogen" 'no
longer at this address'
verzieren *tr. V.* decorate
Verzierung *die;* **~, ~en** decoration
verzögern ☐1 *tr. V.* **(a)** delay (**um** by)
(b) (verlangsamen) slow down
☐2 *refl. V.* be delayed (**um** by)
Verzögerung *die;* **~, ~en** delay (*Gen.* in);
(Verlangsamung) slowing down
verzollen *tr. V.* pay duty on
Verzug *der;* **~[e]s** delay; **im ~ sein/in**
~ kommen be/fall behind
verzweifeln *itr. V.; mit sein* despair; **über**
etw./jmdn. ~: despair at sth./of sb.
verzweifelt ☐1 *Adj.* despairing ⟨*person*⟩;
desperate ⟨*situation, attempt, effort,*
struggle, etc⟩; **~ sein** be in despair
☐2 *adv.* desperately   ⋯⋗

Verzweiflung *die;* ~: despair
verzweigen *refl. V.* branch [out]
Veteran /vete'raːn/ *der;* ~en, ~en,
  Veteranin *die;* ~, ~nen (auch fig.) veteran
Vetter *der;* ~s, ~n cousin
vgl. *Abk.* = **vergleiche** cf.
v. H. *Abk.* = **vom Hundert** per cent
via /'viːa/ *Präp.* via
Viadukt /via'dʊkt/ *das od.* **der;** ~[e]s, ~e
  viaduct
Viagra ⓦⓩ/'viagra/ *das;* ~s Viagra ®
vibrieren /vi'briːrən/ *itr. V.* vibrate
video-, Video- /'viːdeo-/: video
Video *das;* ~s, ~s (ugs.) video
Video-: ~**clip** *der;* ~~s, ~~s video;
  ~**gerät** *das* video machine; ~**kassette**
  die video cassette; ~**konferenz**
  die videoconference; ~**recorder,**
  ~**rekorder** *der* video recorder; ~**text**
  der videotex[t]
Videothek *die;* ~, ~en video library
Vieh *das;* ~[e]s (a) (Nutztiere) livestock *sing.*
  or pl.
  (b) (Rinder) cattle *pl.*
Vieh·zucht *die* [live]stock/cattle breeding
  no art.
viel ① *Indefinitpron. u. unbest. Zahlw.*
  (a) *Sg.* a great deal of; a lot of (coll.);
  wie/nicht/zu ~: how/not/too much; ~**[es]**
  (vielerlei) much; **der** ~**e Regen** all the rain;
  um ~**es jünger** a great deal younger
  (b) *Pl.* many; **gleich** ~**[e]** the same number
  of; **die** ~**en Menschen** all the people
  ② *Adv.* (a) (oft, lange) a great deal; a lot (coll.)
  (b) (wesentlich) much; a great deal; a lot (coll.);
  ~ **zu klein** much too small
vielerlei *indekl. Adj.* (a) *attr.* many
  different; all kinds *or* sorts of
  (b) *allein stehend* all kinds of things
viel-, Viel-: ~**fach** ① *Adj.* (a) multiple;
  die ~**fache Menge** many times the amount;
  (b) (vielfältig) many kinds of; ② *adv.* many
  times; ~**falt** *die;* ~~: diversity; ~**fältig**
  ① *Adj.* many and diverse; ② *adv.* in many
  different ways
vielleicht *Adv.* perhaps; maybe
viel-: ~**mals** *Adv.* **ich bitte** ~**mals um**
  Entschuldigung I'm very sorry; **danke**
  ~**mals** thank you very much; ~**mehr**
  /od. '·'-/ Konj. u. Adv. rather; ~**sagend**
  ① *Adj.* meaningful; ② *adv.* meaningfully;
  ~**seitig** *Adj.* versatile ⟨*person*⟩;
  ~**versprechend** ① *Adj.* [very]
  promising; ② *adv.* [very] promisingly
vier *Kardinalz.* four
Vier *die;* ~, ~en four; **eine** ~ **schreiben/**
  bekommen (Schulw.) ≈ get a D
vier-, Vier-: (*s. auch* ACHT-, ACHT-);
  ~**beiner** *der;* ~~s, ~~ (ugs.) four-
  legged friend; ~**beinig** *Adj.* four-legged;

 V

~**eck** *das* quadrilateral; (Rechteck)
  rectangle; (Quadrat) square; ~**eckig** *Adj.*
  quadrilateral; (rechteckig) rectangular;
  ~**fach** *Vervielfältigungsz.* fourfold;
  quadruple; ~**fache** *das; adj. Dekl.* **um das**
  ~**fache:** fourfold; by four times the amount;
  ~**hundert** *Kardinalz.* four hundred
Vierling *der;* ~s, ~e quadruplet
vier-, Vier-: ~**mal** *Adv.* four times;
  ~**spurig** *Adj.* four-lane ⟨*road, motorway*⟩;
  ~**spurig sein** have four lanes; ~**stellig**
  Adj. four-figure *attrib.;* ~**sterne·hotel**
  /-'----/ *das* four-star hotel
viert... *Ordinalz.* fourth
viert·tausend *Kardinalz.* four thousand;
viertel /'fɪrtl/ *Bruchz.* quarter; **ein** ~ **Pfund**
  a quarter of a pound; **drei** ~ **Liter** three
  quarters of a litre
Viertel /'fɪrtl/ *das* ((schweiz. meist) *der*); ~s,
  ~ (a) quarter; ~ **vor/nach eins** [a] quarter
  to/past one; **drei** ~: three-quarters
  (b) (Stadtteil) quarter; district
viertel-, Viertel-: ~**finale** *das* (Sport)
  quarter-final; ~**jahr** *das* three months
  pl.; ~**jährlich** ① *Adj.* quarterly; ② *adv.*
  quarterly; ~**liter** *der* quarter of a litre;
  ~**note** *die* (Musik) crotchet (Brit.); quarter
  note (Amer.); ~**pfund** *das* quarter [of a]
  pound; ~**stunde** *die* quarter of an hour;
  ~**stündig** *Adj.* quarter-of-an-hour;
  ~**stündlich** *Adj., adv.* every quarter of
  an hour
viertens *Adv.* fourthly
viertürig *Adj.* four-door *attrib.;* ~ **sein**
  have four doors
Vierwaldstätter See, (schweiz.:)
Vierwaldstättersee *der* Lake Lucerne
vier- /'fɪr-:/ ~**zehn** *Kardinalz.*
  fourteen; **für vierzehn Tage** for a
  fortnight; ~**zehn·tägig** *Adj.* two-week;
  ~**zehn·täglich** ① *Adj.* fortnightly;
  ② *adv.* fortnightly
vierzig /'fɪrtsɪç/ *Kardinalz.* forty; *s. auch*
  ACHTZIG
vierzigst... *Ordinalz.* fortieth; *s. auch*
  ACHT...
Vikar /vi'kaːɐ̯/ *der;* ~s, ~e, **Vikarin** *die;*
  ~, ~nen (a) (kath. Kirche) locum tenens
  (b) (ev. Kirche) ≈ [trainee] curate
Villa /'vɪla/ *die;* ~, **Villen** villa
Villen·viertel *das* exclusive residential
  district
violett /vio'lɛt/ purple; violet
Violett *das;* ~s, ~e *od.* ugs. ~s purple;
  violet; (im Spektrum) violet
Violine /vio'liːnə/ *die;* ~, ~n (Musik) violin
Viper /'viːpɐ/ *die;* ~, ~n viper; adder
Viren ▶ VIRUS
Viren·schutz *der* (DV, Med.) virus
  protection
virtuell /vɪr'tu̯ɛl/ ① *Adj.* (a) potential
  (b) (DV, Optik) virtual ⟨*memory, image;*⟩ ~**e**

---

*alte Schreibung – vgl. Hinweis auf S. x

Wirklichkeit virtual reality
2 *adv.* virtually
virtuos /vɪrˈtuoːs/ 1 *Adj.* virtuoso
⟨*performance etc.*⟩
2 *adv.* in a virtuoso manner
Virtuose *der;* ~n, ~n, **Virtuosin** *die;* ~,
~nen virtuoso
Virtuosität *die;* ~: virtuosity
Virus /ˈviːrʊs/ *das;* ~, Viren virus
Visa ▶ VISUM
Visage /viˈzaːʒə/ *die;* ~, ~n (salopp
abwertend) mug (coll.); (Miene) expression
Visen ▶ VISUM
Visier /viˈziːɐ̯/ *das;* ~s, ~e (am Helm) visor;
(an der Waffe) backsight
Vision /viˈzioːn/ *die;* ~, ~en vision
Visite /viˈziːtə/ *die;* ~, ~n round;
~ **machen** do one's round
Visiten·karte *die* visiting card
Visum /ˈviːzʊm/ *das;* ~s, Visa *od.* Visen
visa
vital *Adj.* vital
Vitalität *die;* ~: vitality
Vitamin /vitaˈmiːn/ *das;* ~s, ~e vitamin
vitamin-, Vitamin-: ~**arm** *Adj.* low in
vitamins *postpos.;* ~**mangel** *der* vitamin
deficiency; ~**reich** *Adj.* rich in vitamins
postpos.
Vitrine /viˈtriːnə/ *die;* ~, ~n display case;
(Möbel) display cabinet
Vize- vice-
Vogel *der;* ~s, Vögel bird; einen ~ haben
(salopp) be off one's rocker (coll.)
Vogel-: ~**grippe** *die* bird flu; ~**käfig**
der birdcage; ~**nest** *das* bird's nest;
~**perspektive** *die* bird's-eye view;
~**scheuche** *die;* ~~, ~~n scarecrow
Voicemail /ˈvɔysmeɪl/ *die;* ~, ~s
voicemail
Vokabel /voˈkaːbḷ/ *die;* ~, ~n word; ~n
vocabulary *sing.*
Vokal /voˈkaːl/ *der;* ~s, ~e (Sprachw.) vowel
Volk *das;* ~[e]s, Völker people
volks-, Volks-: ~**abstimmung** *die*
plebiscite; ~**eigen** *Adj.* (DDR) publicly
or nationally owned; ~**entscheid** *der*
(Politik) referendum; ~**fest** *das* public
festival; (Jahrmarkt) fair; ~**hochschule**
die adult education centre; ~**kammer**
die (DDR) Volkskammer; People's Chamber;
~**kunde** *die* folklore; ~**lied** *das* folk
song; ~**musik** *die* folk music; ~**polizei**
die (DDR) People's Police; ~**republik** *die*
People's Republic; ~**stamm** *der* tribe;
~**tanz** *der* folk dance; ~**tracht** *die*
traditional costume; (eines Landes) national
costume; ~**trauer·tag** *der* (Bundesrepublik
Deutschland) national remembrance day
volkstümlich 1 *Adj.* popular
2 *adv.* ~ schreiben write in terms readily
comprehensible to the layman
volks-, Volks-: ~**verhetzung**

die; ~~: incitement of the people;
~**vertreter** *der,* ~**vertreterin** *die*
representative of the people; ~**wirt** *der,*
~**wirtin** *die* economist; ~**wirtschaft**
die national economy; (Fach) economics
sing., no art.; ~**wirtschaftlich**
1 *Adj.* economic; 2 *adv.* economically;
~**zählung** *die* [national] census; ~**zorn**
der public anger
voll 1 *Adj.* full; ample ⟨*bosom*⟩;
(salopp: betrunken) plastered (sl.); ~ **von** *od.* **mit**
etw. sein be full of sth.; ~ **laufen** fill up; etw.
~ **laufen lassen** fill sth. [up]; etw. ~ **füllen**
fill sth. up; etw. ~ **gießen** fill sth. [up]; etw.
~ **tanken** fill sth. up; **bitte** ~ **tanken** fill it
up, please; etw. ~ **machen** fill sth. up; [sich]
(*Dat.*)] die Hosen/Windeln ~ **machen** (ugs.)
mess one's pants/nappy; **jmdn. nicht für**
~ **nehmen** not take sb. seriously
2 *adv.* fully; ~ **und ganz** completely
*****vollabern** ▶ VOLLLABERN
voll·auf /*od.* '--/ *Adv.* completely
*****vollaufen** ▶ VOLL 1
voll-, Voll-: ~**automatisch** 1 *Adj.*
fully automatic; 2 *adv.* fully automatically;
~**bad** *das* bath; ~**bart** *der* full beard;
~**bringen** /-'--/ *unr. tr. V.* (geh.)
accomplish; achieve
Völle·gefühl *das* feeling of fullness
voll·enden *tr. V.* complete
vollendet 1 *Adj.* accomplished
⟨*performance*⟩; perfect ⟨*gentleman, host,*
manners, reproduction⟩
2 *adv.* ⟨*play*⟩ in an accomplished manner
vollends *Adv.* completely
Voll·endung *die* completion
voller *indekl. Adj.* full of; ~ **Flecken**
covered with stains
Volley·ball /ˈvɔlibal/ *der* volleyball
voll-, Voll-: ~**führen** /-'--/ *tr. V.* perform;
*****~|füllen** ▶ VOLL 1; ~**gas** *das* ~**gas**
geben put one's foot down; mit ~**gas** at full
throttle; *****~|gießen** ▶ VOLL 1
völlig 1 *Adj.* complete; total
2 *adv.* completely; totally; du hast ~ Recht
you are absolutely right
voll-, Voll-: ~**jährig** *Adj.* of age
pred.; ~**jährig werden** come of age;
~**jährigkeit** *die;* ~: majority *no art.;*
~**kasko·versicherung** *die* fully
comprehensive insurance
voll·kommen 1 *Adj.* (a) /-'-- *od.* '---/
(vollendet) perfect
(b) /'---/ (vollständig) complete; total
2 /'---/ *adv.* completely; totally
voll-, Voll-: ~**korn·brot** *das* wholemeal
(Brit.) *or* (Amer.) wholewheat bread;
~**labern** *tr. V.* (ugs.) jmdn. ~**labern** rabbit
on at sb. (Brit. coll.); *****~|laufen** ▶ VOLL 1;
*****~|machen** ▶ VOLL 1; ~**macht** *die;* ~~,
~~en (a) authority; (b) (Urkunde) power of
attorney; ~**milch** *die* full-cream milk;
~**milch·schokolade** *die* full-cream ···⟶

milk chocolate; ~**mond** *der* full moon;
~**pension** *die* full board *no art.;*
~**ständig** ① *Adj.* complete; full ⟨*text, address, etc.*⟩; ② *adv.* completely; ⟨*list*⟩ in full; ~**ständigkeit** *die;* ~: completeness; ~**strecken** /-'--/ *tr. V.* enforce ⟨*penalty, fine, law*⟩; carry out ⟨*sentence*⟩ (**an** + *Dat.* on); **~|**tanken** ▶ VOLL 1; ~**treffer** *der* direct hit; **ein** ~**treffer sein** (fig.) hit the bull's eye; ~**versammlung** *die* general meeting; (der UNO) General Assembly; ~**zählig** *Adj.* complete; ~**zeit·beschäftigt** *Adj.* employed full-time *postpos.;* ~**zeit·beschäftigte** *der/die* full-time employee

voll·ziehen *unr. tr. V.* carry out (**an** + *Dat.* on); execute, carry out ⟨*order*⟩; perform ⟨*sacrifice, ceremony, sexual intercourse*⟩

Voll·zug *der:* ▶ VOLLZIEHEN: carrying out; execution; performance

Volt /vɔlt/ *das;* ~ *od.* ~**[e]s,** ~: (Physik, Elektrot.) volt

Volumen /vo'lu:mən/ *das;* ~**s,** ~: volume

vom *Präp.* + *Art.* **(a)** = **von dem;** **(b)** (räumlich) from the; **links/rechts** ~ **Eingang** to the left/right of the entrance; ~ **Stuhl aufspringen** jump up out of one's chair **(c)** (zeitlich) ~ **Morgen bis zum Abend** from morning till night; ~ **ersten Januar an** [as] from the first of January **(d)** (zur Angabe der Ursache) **das kommt** ~ **Rauchen/Alkohol** that comes from smoking/drinking alcohol; **jmdn.** ~ **Sehen kennen** know sb. by sight

von *Präp. mit Dat.* **(a)** (räumlich) from; **nördlich/südlich** ~ **Mannheim** to the north/south of Mannheim; **rechts/links** ~ **mir** on my right/left; ~ **hier an** *od.* (ugs.) **ab** from here on[ward]; ~ **Mannheim aus** from Mannheim **(b)** (zeitlich) from; ~ **jetzt an** *od.* (ugs.) **ab** from now on; ~ **heute/morgen an** [as] from today/tomorrow; starting today/tomorrow; **in der Nacht** ~ **Freitag auf** *od.* **zu Samstag** during Friday night; **das Brot ist** ~ **gestern** it's yesterday's bread **(c)** (anstelle eines Genitivs) of; **acht** ~ **hundert/zehn** eight out of a hundred/ten **(d)** (zur Angabe des Urhebers, der Ursache, beim Passiv) by; **der Roman ist** ~ **Fontane** the novel is by Fontane; **müde** ~ **der Arbeit sein** be tired from work[ing]; **sie hat ein Kind** ~ **ihm** she has a child by him **(e)** (zur Angabe von Eigenschaften) of; **eine Fahrt** ~ **drei Stunden** a three-hour drive

von·einander *Adv.* from each other *or* one another

vonstatten *Adv.* ~ **gehen** proceed

vor ① *Präp. mit Dat.* **(a)** (räumlich) in front of; (weiter vorn) ahead of; in front of; (nicht ganz so weit wie) before; (außerhalb) outside; **kurz**

~ **der Abzweigung** just before the turn-off; ~ **der Stadt** outside the town; **etw.** ~ **sich haben** (fig.) have sth. before one; **das liegt noch** ~ **mir** (fig.) I still have that to come *or* have that ahead of me **(b)** (zeitlich) before; **es ist fünf [Minuten]** ~ **sieben** it is five [minutes] to seven **(c)** (bei Reihenfolge, Rangordnung) before; **knapp** ~ **jmdm. siegen** win just ahead *or* in front of sb. **(d)** (aufgrund von) with; ~ **Freude strahlen** beam with joy; ~ **Hunger/Durst umkommen** (ugs.) die of hunger/thirst **(e)** ~ **fünf Minuten/10 Jahren/Wochen** *usw.* five minutes/ten years/weeks ago; **heute** ~ **einer Woche** a week ago today ② *Präp. mit Akk.* in front of; ~ **sich hin** to oneself

Vor·abend *der* **(a)** evening before; (fig.) eve **(b)** (Ferns.) early evening

Vor·ahnung *die* premonition; presentiment; **dunkle/schlimme** ~**en** dark forebodings

vor·an *Adv.* forward[s] ahead; first

voran-: ~|**gehen** *unr. itr. V.; mit sein* **(a)** go first; **(b)** (Fortschritte machen) make progress; ~|**kommen** *unr. itr. V.; mit sein* **(a)** make headway; **(b)** (Fortschritte machen) make progress; ~|**treiben** *unr. tr. V.* push ahead

Vor·arbeiter *der* foreman

Vor·arbeiterin *die* forewoman

vor·aus ① /-'-/ *Präp. mit Dat., nachgestellt* in front; **jmdm./seiner Zeit** ~ **sein** (fig.) be ahead of sb./one's time ② *Adv.* **im Voraus** /'--/ in advance

voraus-, Voraus-: ~|**gehen** *unr. itr. V.; mit sein* **(a)** go [on] ahead; **(b)** (zeitlich) **einem Ereignis** ~**gehen** precede an event; ~**sage** *die* ▶ VORHERSAGE; ~|**sagen** *tr. V.* predict; ~|**sehen** *unr. tr. V.* foresee; ~|**setzen** *tr. V.* **(a)** (als gegeben ansehen) assume; ~**gesetzt, [dass]** …: provided [that] …; **(b)** (erfordern) require ⟨*skill, experience, etc.*⟩; presuppose ⟨*good organization, planning, etc.*⟩; ~**setzung** *die;* ~~, ~**en (a)** (Annahme) assumption; (Prämisse) premiss; **(b)** (Vorbedingung) prerequisite; **unter der** ~**setzung, dass** …: on condition *or* on the precondition that …; ~**sichtlich** ① *Adj.* anticipated; ② *adv.* probably

Vor·bau *der; Pl.* ~**ten** porch

Vorbehalt *der;* ~**[e]s,** ~**e** reservation; **unter dem** ~, **dass** …: with the reservation that …

vor|behalten *unr. tr. V.* **sich** (*Dat.*) **etw.** ~: reserve oneself sth.; „**Änderungen** ~" 'subject to alterations'

vorbehalt·los ① *Adj.* unreserved; unconditional ② *adv.* unreservedly; without reservation[s]

**old spelling – see note on page x

vor·bei *Adv.* **(a)** (räumlich) past; by; **an etw.** (*Dat.*) ~: past sth.
(b) (zeitlich) past; over; (beendet) finished; over; **es ist acht Uhr** ~ (ugs.) it is past *or* gone eight o'clock

vorbei-: ~|**fahren** *unr. itr. V.; mit sein* **(a)** drive/ride past; pass; **an jmdm.** ~**fahren** drive/ride past *or* pass sb.; **(b)** (ugs.: einen kurzen Besuch machen) **[bei jmdm./der Post]** ~**fahren** drop in (coll.) [at sb.'s/at the post office]; ~|**gehen** *unr. itr. V.; mit sein* **(a)** pass; go past; **an jmdm./etw.** ~**gehen** pass *or* go past sb./sth.; **der Schuss ist** ~**gegangen** the shot missed; **(b)** (ugs.: einen kurzen Besuch machen) **[bei jmdm./der Post]** ~**gehen** drop in (coll.) [at sb.'s/at the post office]; **(c)** (vergehen) pass; ~|**kommen** *unr. itr. V.; mit sein* pass sth.; ~|**reden** *itr. V.* **an etw.** (*Dat.*) ~**reden** talk round sth. without getting to the point; **aneinander** ~**reden** talk at cross purposes; ~|**schießen** *unr. itr. V.* miss

vor·belastet *Adj.* handicapped (**durch** by); **erblich** ~ **sein** have an inherited defect

vor|bereiten *tr. V.* prepare; **jmdn./sich auf** *od.* **für etw.** ~: prepare sb./oneself for sth.

Vor·bereitung *die;* ~, ~**en** preparation; ~**en [für etw.] treffen** make preparations for sth.

vor|bestellen *tr. V.* order in advance
Vor·bestellung *die* advance order

vor·bestraft *Adj.* with a previous conviction/previous convictions *postpos., not pred.*

vor|beugen **1** *tr. V.* bend ⟨head, upper body⟩ forward; **sich** ~: lean forward
2 *itr. V.* **einer Sache** (*Dat.*) *od.* **gegen etw.** ~: prevent sth.

Vor·beugung *die* prevention (**gegen** of); **zur** ~: as a preventive

Vor·bild *das* model; **jmdm. ein gutes** ~ **sein** be a good example to sb.

vor·bildlich **1** *Adj.* exemplary
2 *adv.* in an exemplary way

vor|bringen *unr. itr. V.* say; **eine Forderung/ein Anliegen** ~: make a demand/express a desire; **Argumente** ~: present arguments

vor·christlich *Adj.* pre-Christian
vor|datieren *tr. V.* postdate
vorder... *Adj.* front; **der Vordere Orient** the Middle East

Vorder-: ~**grund** *der* foreground; **im** ~**grund stehen** (fig.) be prominent *or* to the fore; ~**mann** *der; Pl.* ~**männer** person in front; **jmdn. auf** ~**mann bringen** (ugs.) lick sb. into shape

vor|drängen *refl. V.* push [one's way] forward *or* to the front; (fig.) push oneself forward

vor|dringen *unr. itr. V.; mit sein* push forward; advance

vor·dringlich **1** *Adj.* **(a)** priority *attrib.* ⟨treatment⟩
(b) (dringlich) urgent
2 *adv.* **(a)** as a matter of priority
(b) (dringlich) as a matter of urgency

Vor·druck *der; Pl.* ~**e** form

vor·eilig **1** *Adj.* rash
2 *adv.* rashly

vor·einander *Adv.* **(a)** one in front of the other
(b) (einer dem anderen gegenüber) opposite each other; face to face
(c) Angst ~ **haben** be afraid of each other

vor·eingenommen *Adj.* prejudiced; biased; **für/gegen jmdn.** ~ **sein** be prejudiced in sb.'s favour/against sb.

Vor·eingenommenheit *die;* ~, ~**en** prejudice; bias

vorenthalten *unr. tr. V.; ich enthalte vor* (*od. seltener:* vorenthalte), vorenthalten, vorzuenthalten: **jmdm. etw.** ~: withhold sth. from sb.

vor·erst /*od.* '-'-/ *Adv.* for the present
Vorfahr *der;* ~**en**, ~**en** forefather
vor|fahren *unr. itr. V.; mit sein*
(a) (ankommen) drive/ride up
(b) (weiter nach vorn fahren) ⟨person⟩ drive *or* move forward; ⟨car⟩ move forward
(c) (vorausfahren) drive *or* go on ahead

Vor·fahrt *die* right of way; „~ **beachten/ gewähren"** 'give way'

Vorfahrt[s]-: ~**schild** *das; Pl.* ~~**er** right-of-way sign; ~**straße** *die* main road

Vor·fall *der* incident; occurrence

vor|fallen *unr. itr. V.; mit sein* **(a)** (sich ereignen) happen; occur
(b) (nach vorn fallen) fall forward

Vor·film *der* supporting film

vor|finden *unr. tr. V.* find

Vor·freude *die* anticipation

vor|führen *tr. V.* show ⟨film, slides, etc.⟩; present ⟨circus act, programme⟩; perform ⟨play, trick, routine⟩; (demonstrieren) demonstrate; **jmdn. dem Richter** ~: bring sb. before the judge

Vor·führung *die* show; (eines Theaterstücks) performance

Vor·gang *der* occurrence; (Amtsspr.) file

Vorgänger *der;* ~**s**, ~, **Vorgängerin** *die;* ~, ~**nen** predecessor

Vor·garten *der* front garden

vor|geben *unr. tr. V.* pretend

Vor·gebirge *das* promontory

vor·gefasst, *vor·gefaßt *Adj.* preconceived

vor|gehen *unr. itr. V.; mit sein*
(a) (ugs.: nach vorn gehen) go forward
(b) (vorausgehen) go on ahead; **jmdn.** ~ **lassen** let sb. go first
(c) ⟨clock⟩ be fast
(d) (einschreiten) **gegen jmdn./etw.** ~: take action against sb./sth.   ⋯⋮⟶

(e) (verfahren) proceed

(f) (sich abspielen) happen; go on

(g) (Vorrang haben) have priority; come first

Vor·geschmack *der* foretaste

Vor·gesetzte *der/die; adj. Dekl.* superior

vor·gestern *Adv.* the day before yesterday

vor|greifen *unr. itr. V.* jmdm.
~: anticipate sb.; jump in ahead of sb.

vor|haben *unr. tr. V.* intend; (geplant haben) plan

Vor·haben *das;* ~**s,** ~: plan; (Projekt) project

Vor·halle *die* entrance hall; (eines Theaters, Hotels) foyer

vor|halten *unr. tr. V.* **(a)** hold up; **mit vorgehaltener Schusswaffe** at gunpoint **(b)** (zum Vorwurf machen) **jmdm. etw.**
~: reproach sb. for sth.

Vor·haltungen *Pl.* jmdm. [wegen etw.]
~ machen reproach sb. [for sth.]

vorhanden *Adj.* existing; (verfügbar) available; ~ **sein** exist *or* be in existence/be available

Vor·hang *der* (auch Theater) curtain

Vorhänge·schloss,
***Vorhänge·schloß** *das* padlock

Vor·haut *die* foreskin

vor·her /*od.* -'-/ beforehand; (davor) before

vorher|gehen *unr. itr. V.; mit sein* **in den** ~**den Wochen** in the preceding weeks

Vor·herrschaft *die* supremacy

vor|herrschen *itr. V.* predominate

vorher-, Vorher-: ~**sage** *die* prediction; (des Wetters) forecast; ~|**sagen** *tr. V.* predict; forecast *‹weather›*; ~|**sehen** *unr. tr. V.* ▶ VORAUSSEHEN

vor·hin /*od.* -'-/ *Adv.* a short time *or* while ago

vorig... *Adj.* last

Vor·jahr *das* previous year

vor·jährig *Adj.* of the previous year

Vor·kämpfer *der,* **Vor·kämpferin** *die* pioneer

Vorkehrungen *Pl.* precautions

Vor·kenntnis *die* background knowledge

vor|kommen *unr. itr. V.; mit sein* **(a)** (sich ereignen) happen **(b)** (vorhanden sein) occur **(c)** (erscheinen) seem; **das Lied kommt mir bekannt vor** I seem to know the song

Vorkommnis *das;* ~**ses,** ~**se** incident; occurrence

vor|laden *unr. tr. V.* summon

Vor·ladung *die* summons

Vor·lage *die* **(a)** ▶ VORLEGEN: presentation; showing; production; submission; tabling **(b)** (Entwurf) draft **(c)** (Muster) pattern; (Modell) model

Vor·lauf *der* (eines Bandgeräts) fast forward

Vor·läufer *der,* **Vor·läuferin** *die* precursor; forerunner

vor·läufig **1** *Adj.* temporary; provisional; interim *‹order, agreement›* **2** *adv.* for the time being

vor·laut **1** *Adj.* forward **2** *adv.* forwardly

vor|legen *tr. V.* present; show, produce *‹certificate, identity card, etc.›*; show *‹sample›*; submit *‹evidence›*; table *‹parliamentary bill›*

vor|lesen *unr. tr., itr. V.* read aloud *or* out; read *‹story, poem, etc.›* aloud; **jmdm. [etw.]**
~: read [sth.] to sb.

Vor·lesung *die* lecture; (Vorlesungsreihe) series *or* course of lectures

vor·letzt... *Adj.* last but one; penultimate *‹page, episode, etc.›*

vorlieb: **mit jmdm./etw.** ~ **nehmen** put up with sb./sth.; (sich begnügen) make do with sb./sth.

Vor·liebe *die* preference

***vorlieb|nehmen** ▶ VORLIEB

vor|liegen *unr. itr. V.* jmdm. ~: be with sb.; **die Ergebnisse liegen uns noch nicht vor** we do not have the results yet; **im** ~**den Fall** in the present case

vor|lügen *unr. tr. V.* (ugs.) **jmdm. etwas**
~: lie to sb.

vorm *Präp. + Art.* **(a)** = vor dem; **(b)** (räumlich) in front of the **(c)** (zeitlich, bei Reihenfolge) before the

vor|machen *tr. V.* (ugs.) **jmdm. etw.**
~: show sb. sth.; (vortäuschen) kid (coll.) *or* fool sb.

vormalig *Adj.* former

vormals *Adv.* formerly

Vor·marsch *der* (auch fig.) advance

vor|merken *tr. V.* make a note of; **ich habe Sie für den Kurs vorgemerkt** I've put you down for the course

***vor·mittag** ▶ VORMITTAG

Vor·mittag *der* morning; **heute/morgen/ gestern** ~: this/tomorrow/yesterday morning

vor·mittags *Adv.* in the morning

Vor·mund *der; Pl.* ~**e** *od.* **Vormünder** guardian

Vor·name *der* first *or* Christian name

vorn[e] *Adv.* at the front; **nach** ~: to the front; **von** ~: from the front; **noch einmal von** ~ **anfangen** start afresh; **von** ~ **bis hinten** (ugs.) from beginning to end

vornehm **1** *Adj.* (nobel; adelig) noble; (kultiviert) distinguished; (elegant) exclusive *‹district, hotel, restaurant, resort›*; elegant *‹villa, clothes›* **2** *adv.* nobly; (elegant) elegantly

vor|nehmen *unr. refl. V.* **sich** *(Dat.)*
etw. ~: plan sth.; **sich** *(Dat.)* ~**, mit dem Rauchen aufzuhören** resolve to give up smoking

---

*alte Schreibung – vgl. Hinweis auf S. x

vorn-: **∼her|ein:** von ∼herein from the outset; **∼über** *Adv.* forwards

Vor·ort *der* suburb

vor|programmieren *tr. V.* (auch fig.) pre-programme

Vor·rang *der* **(a)** priority (**vor** + *Dat.* over); **(b)** (bes. österr.: Vorfahrt) right of way

Vor·rat *der* supply, stock (**an** + *Dat.* of)

vorrätig *Adj.* in stock *postpos.*

Vor·raum *der* anteroom

vor|rechnen *tr. V.* **jmdm. etw. ∼:** work sth. out *or* calculate sth. for sb.; **jmdm. seine Fehler ∼** (fig.) enumerate sb.'s mistakes

Vor·recht *das* privilege

Vor·redner *der,* **Vor·rednerin** *die* previous speaker; **mein Vorredner:** the previous speaker

Vor·richtung *die* device

vor|rücken **1** *tr. V.* move forward; advance ‹chess piece› **2** *itr. V.; mit sein* move forward; **auf den 5. Platz ∼:** move up to fifth place

Vor·ruhestand *der* early retirement

vors *Präp.* + *Art.* = **vor das**

vor|sagen *tr. V.* **(a)** *auch itr.* jmdm. [die Antwort] ∼: tell sb. the answer; (flüsternd) whisper the answer to sb. **(b)** (aufsagen) recite

Vor·saison *die* start of the season; early [part of the] season

Vor·satz *der* intention

vorsätzlich **1** *Adj.* intentional; wilful ‹murder, arson, etc.› **2** *adv.* intentionally

Vor·schau *die* preview

Vor·schein *der:* **zum ∼ kommen** appear; (entdeckt werden) come to light

vor|schieben *unr. tr. V.* **(a)** push ‹bolt› across **(b)** (nach vorn schieben) push forward

vor|schießen *unr. tr. V.* jmdm. Geld ∼: advance sb. money

Vorschlag *der* suggestion; proposal

vor|schlagen *unr. tr. V.* **[jmdm.] etw. ∼:** suggest *or* propose sth. [to sb.]

vor|schreiben *unr. tr. V.* stipulate, set ‹conditions›; lay down ‹rules›; prescribe ‹dose›

Vor·schrift *die* instruction; order; (gesetzliche od. amtliche Bestimmung) regulation

vorschrifts·mäßig **1** *Adj.* correct; proper **2** *adv.* correctly; properly

Vor·schub *der* **jmdm./einer Sache ∼ leisten** encourage sb./encourage *or* promote *or* foster sth.

Vorschul·alter *das* preschool age

Vor·schuss, *Vor·schuß *der* advance

vor|schwärmen *itr. V.* jmdm. von jmdm./etw. ∼: rave about sb./sth. to sb. (coll.)

vor|schweben *itr. V.* jmdm. schwebt etw. vor sb. has sth. in mind

vor|sehen **1** *unr. tr. V.* **(a)** plan; **etw. für/als etw. ∼:** intend sth. for/as sth. **(b)** ‹law, plan, contract, etc.› provide for **2** *unr. refl. V.* **sich [vor jmdm./etw.] ∼:** be careful [of sb./sth.]

vor|setzen *tr. V.* jmdm. etw. ∼: serve sb. sth.; (fig.) serve *or* dish sb. up sth.

Vor·sicht *die* care; (bei Risiko, Gefahr) caution; care; **zur ∼:** as a precaution; **∼! be careful!;** „∼, Stufe!" 'mind the step!'

vorsichtig **1** *Adj.* careful; (bei Risiko, Gefahr) cautious; **sei ∼! be careful!;** take care!

2 *adv.* carefully; with care

vorsichts·halber *Adv.* as a precaution; to be on the safe side

Vorsichts·maßnahme *die* precautionary measure; precaution

Vor·silbe *die* [monosyllabic] prefix

vor|singen *unr. tr. V.* **[jmdm.] etw. ∼:** sing sth. [to sb.]

Vor·sitz *der* chairmanship

Vorsitzende *der/die; adj. Dekl.* chair[person]; (bes. Mann) chairman; (Frau auch) chairwoman

Vor·sorge *die* precautions *pl.;* (für den Todesfall, Krankheit, Alter) provisions *pl.*

vor|sorgen *itr. V.* **für etw. ∼:** make provisions for sth.; provide for sth.

Vorsorge-untersuchung *die* (Med.) medical check-up

vorsorglich *adv.* as a precaution

Vor·spann *der* (Film, Ferns.) opening credits *pl.*

Vor·speise *die* starter; hors d'œuvre

Vor·spiel *das* (Theater) prologue; (Musik) prelude

vor|spielen *tr. V.* **(a)** play ‹piece of music› (*Dat.* to, for); act out, perform ‹scene› (*Dat.* for, in front of) **(b)** (vorspiegeln) jmdm. etw. ∼: feign sth. to sb.

vor|sprechen **1** *unr. tr. V.* **(a)** (zum Nachsprechen) jmdm. etw. ∼: pronounce *or* say sth. first for sb. **(b)** (zur Prüfung) recite **2** *unr. itr. V.* audition

Vor·sprung *der* lead (**vor** + *Dat.* over)

Vor·stadt *die* suburb

Vor·stand *der* (einer Firma) board [of directors]; (eines Vereins, einer Gesellschaft) executive committee; (einer Partei) executive

vor|stehen *unr. itr. V.* **(a)** project; jut out; ‹teeth, chin› stick out; **∼de Zähne** buck teeth; projecting teeth **(b)** (geh.: leiten) **einer Institution ∼:** be the head of an institution

vorstell·bar *Adj.* conceivable; imaginable; **es ist durchaus/[nur] schwer ∼, dass …:** it is quite/scarcely conceivable that … ⋯⋗

vor|stellen ① *tr. V.* jmdn./sich jmdm. ∼: introduce sb./oneself to sb.; (bei Bewerbung) **sich** ∼: come/go for [an] interview; **die Uhr [um eine Stunde]** ∼: put the clock forward [one hour] ② *refl. V.* **sich** (*Dat.*) **etw.** ∼: imagine sth.

Vor·stellung *die* (a) (Begriff) idea (b) (Fantasie) imagination (c) (Aufführung) performance; (im Kino) showing

Vorstellungs·gespräch *das* interview

Vor·stoß *der* advance

vor|stoßen *unr. itr. V.; mit sein* advance; push forward

Vor·strafe *die* previous conviction

vor|strecken *tr. V.* stretch ⟨arm, hand⟩ out; advance ⟨money, sum⟩

Vor·tag *der* day before

vor|täuschen *tr. V.* feign; simulate ⟨reality etc.⟩; fake ⟨crime⟩

Vor·teil /*od.* 'fɔrtail/ *der* advantage

vorteilhaft ① *Adj.* advantageous ② *adv.* advantageously

Vortrag *der;* ∼**[e]s, Vorträge** talk; (wissenschaftlich) lecture; **einen** ∼ **halten** give a talk/lecture

vor|tragen *unr. tr. V.* (a) sing ⟨song⟩; perform, play ⟨piece of music⟩; recite ⟨poem⟩ (b) (darlegen) present ⟨case, matter, request, demands⟩; lodge, make ⟨complaint⟩; express ⟨wish, desire⟩

vor·trefflich ① *Adj.* excellent ② *adv.* excellently

Vortrefflichkeit *die;* ∼: excellence

vorüber *Adv.* over; (räumlich) past

vorüber|gehen *unr. itr. V.; mit sein* (a) go *or* walk past; pass by; **an jmdm./etw.** ∼: go past sb./sth.; pass sb./sth.; (achtlos) pass sb./sth. by (b) (vergehen) pass; ⟨pain⟩ go

vorübergehend ① *Adj.* temporary; passing ⟨interest, infatuation⟩; brief ⟨illness, stay⟩ ② *adv.* temporarily; (für kurze Zeit) for a short time; briefly

Vor·urteil *das* bias; (voreilige Schlussfolgerung) prejudice

Vor·vergangenheit *die* (Sprachw.) pluperfect

Vor·verkauf *der* advance sale of tickets

vor|verlegen *tr. V.* (zeitlich) bring forward

(auf + *Akk.* to; um by)

Vor·wahl *die,* **Vorwähl·nummer** *die* (Fernspr.) dialling code

Vorwand *der;* ∼**[e]s, Vorwände** pretext; (Ausrede) excuse

vor|warnen *tr. V.* jmdn. ∼: give sb. advance warning; warn sb. [in advance]; **vorgewarnt sein** be forewarned

Vor·warnung *die* [advance] warning

vor·wärts *Adv.* forwards; (weiter) onwards; ∼ **kommen** make progress; (im Beruf, Leben) get on; get ahead

*****vorwärts|kommen** ▸ VORWÄRTS

vor·weg *Adv.* beforehand

vorweg|nehmen *unr. tr. V.* anticipate

vor|weisen *unr. tr. V.* produce

vor|werfen *unr. tr. V.* jmdm. etw. ∼: reproach sb. with sth.; (beschuldigen) accuse sb. of sth.

vor·wiegend *Adv.* mainly

vor·witzig *Adj.* bumptious; pert ⟨child⟩

Vor·wort *das; Pl.* ∼**e** foreword

Vor·wurf *der* reproach; (Beschuldigung) accusation

vorwurfs·voll ① *Adj.* reproachful ② *adv.* reproachfully

Vor·zeichen *das* (a) (Omen) omen (b) (Math.) [algebraic] sign

vor|zeigen *tr. V.* produce; show

Vor·zeit *die* prehistory

vorzeitig ① *Adj.* premature; early ⟨retirement⟩ ② *adv.* prematurely

vor|ziehen *unr. tr. V.* prefer

Vor·zimmer *das* outer office

Vor·zug *der* (a) preference (**gegenüber** over) (b) (gute Eigenschaft) good quality; merit

vorzüglich ① *Adj.* excellent; first-rate ② *adv.* excellently

vulgär /vʊl'gɛːɐ̯/ ① *Adj.* vulgar ② *adv.* in a vulgar way

Vulgarität /vʊlgari'tɛːt/ *die;* ∼, ∼**en** vulgarity

Vulkan /vʊl'kaːn/ *der;* ∼**s,** ∼**e** volcano

vulkanisch *Adj.* volcanic

vulkanisieren *tr. V.* vulcanize

v. u. Z. *Abk.* = **vor unserer Zeit[rechnung]** BC

Ww

w, W /veː/ *das;* ~s, ~: w, W

W *Abk.* **(a)** = **West, Westen** W.
(b) = **Watt** W

Waage *die;* ~, ~n **(a)** [pair *sing.* of] scales *pl.*
(b) (Astrol.) **[die]** ~: Libra; **er ist [eine]** ~: he is a Libra *or* Libran

waage·recht ⨂ *Adj.* horizontal
⨂ *adv.* horizontally

Waage·rechte *die;* ~, ~n; *also adj. Dekl.* horizontal

Waag·schale *die* scale pan

Wabe *die;* ~, ~n honeycomb

wach ⨂ *Adj.* awake
⨂ *adv.* alertly; attentively

Wache *die;* ~, ~n **(a)** (Milit.) guard *or* sentry duty; (Seew.) watch [duty]
(b) (Wächter, Milit.) guard; (Seew.) watch
(c) (Polizei~) police station

wachen *itr. V.* (geh.) be awake; **bei jmdm.** ~: stay up at sb.'s bedside; sit up with sb.

Wachheit *die;* ~: alertness

Wach·hund *der* guard dog

Wacholder *der;* ~s, ~: juniper

Wach·posten *der* (Milit.) guard

Wachs *das;* ~es, ~e wax

wachsam *Adj.* watchful; vigilant

Wachsamkeit *die;* ~: vigilance

wachsen¹ *unr. itr. V.; mit sein* grow

wachsen² *tr. V.* wax

Wachs-: ~**figur** *die* waxwork; ~**figuren·kabinett** *das* waxworks *sing. or pl.;* waxworks museum

wächst 2. *u.* 3. *Pers. Sg. Präsens v.* WACHSEN

Wachs·tuch *das Pl.* Wachstücher (Tischtuch) oilcloth tablecloth

Wachstum *das;* ~s growth

Wachtel *die;* ~, ~n quail

Wächter *der;* ~s, ~: guard; (Nacht-, Turmwächter) watchman; (Parkwächter) [park-]keeper

Wächterin *die;* ~, ~nen ▶ WÄCHTER

Wach[t]·turm *der* watchtower

wackelig *Adj.* **(a)** wobbly ⟨chair, table, etc.⟩; loose ⟨tooth⟩
(b) (ugs.: kraftlos, schwach) frail

Wackel·kontakt *der* (Elektrot.) loose connection

wackeln *itr. V.* wobble; ⟨tooth etc.⟩ be loose; ⟨house, window, etc.⟩ shake; **mit dem Kopf/den Ohren** ~: waggle one's head/ears

wacker (veralt.) ⨂ *Adj.* upright
⨂ *adv.* valiantly; **sich** ~ **halten** put up a good show

Wade *die;* ~, ~n (Anat.) calf

Waden·krampf *der* cramp in one's calf

Waffe *die;* ~, ~n weapon

Waffel *die;* ~, ~n waffle; (dünne Waffel, Eiswaffel) wafer; (Eistüte) cone

Waffen-: ~**gewalt** *die* mit ~**gewalt** by force of arms; ~**handel** *der* arms trade; ~**händler** *der*, ~**händlerin** *die* arms dealer; ~**schein** *der* firearms licence; ~**stillstand** *der* armistice

Wage·mut *der* daring

wage·mutig *Adj.* daring

wagen ⨂ *tr. V.* risk; **[es]** ~, **etw. zu tun** dare to do sth.
⨂ *refl. V.* **sich irgendwohin/nicht irgendwohin** ~: venture somewhere/not dare to go somewhere

Wagen *der;* ~s, ~: (PKW) car; (Pferdewagen) cart; (Eisenb.: Personenwagen) coach; (Eisenb.: Güterwagen) truck; (Straßenbahnwagen) car; (Kinder-, Puppenwagen) pram (Brit.); baby carriage (Amer.); (Sportwagen) pushchair (Brit.); stroller (Amer.)

Wagen·heber *der* jack

Waggon /vaˈɡɔŋ, *südd., österr.:* vaˈɡoːn/ *der;* ~s, ~s, *südd., österr.:* ~s, ~e wagon; truck (Brit.); car (Amer.)

waghalsig ⨂ *Adj.* daring; (leichtsinnig) reckless
⨂ *adv.* daringly; ⟨speculate⟩ riskily; (leichtsinnig) recklessly

Wagnis *das;* ~ses, ~se daring exploit *or* feat; (Risiko) risk

Wahl *die;* ~, ~en **(a)** choice; **eine/seine** ~ **treffen** make a/one's choice
(b) (in ein Gremium, Amt usw.) election; **geheime** ~: secret ballot

wahl·berechtigt *Adj.* eligible *or* entitled to vote *postpos.*

Wahl·beteiligung *die* turn-out

wählen ⨂ *tr. V.* **(a)** choose; (aus~) select
(b) (Fernspr.) dial ⟨number⟩
(c) (durch Stimmabgabe) elect
(d) (stimmen für) vote for ⟨party, candidate⟩
⨂ *itr. V.* **(a)** choose
(b) (Fernspr.) dial
(c) (stimmen) vote

Wähler *der;* ~s, ~: voter

Wahl·ergebnis *das* election result

Wählerin *die;* ~, ~nen voter

wählerisch *Adj.* choosy; particular (**in** + *Dat.* about)

Wählerschaft *die;* ~, ~en electorate; **die** ~ **der SPD** the SPD's voters *pl.;* those who vote for the SPD ⋯▸

wahl-, Wahl-: ~**fach** das (Schulw.) optional subject; ~**gang** der ballot; ~**geheimnis** das secrecy of the ballot; ~**geschenk** das pre-election bonus; ~**kabine** die polling booth; ~**kampf** der election campaign; ~**kreis** der constituency; ~**lokal** das polling station; ~**los** ⓵ Adj. indiscriminate; ⓶ adv. indiscriminately; ~**niederlage** die election defeat; ~**recht** das right to vote

Wähl·scheibe die (Fernspr.) dial

Wahl-: ~**sieg** der election victory; ~**spruch** der motto; ~**system** das electoral system; ~**urne** die ballot box

Wahn der; ~[e]s mania; delusion

Wahn·sinn der (a) insanity; madness (b) (ugs.: Unvernunft) madness; lunacy

wahnsinnig ⓵ Adj. (a) (geistesgestört) insane; mad (b) (ugs.: ganz unvernünftig) mad; crazy (c) (ugs.: groß, heftig, intensiv) terrific (coll.) ⟨effort, speed, etc.⟩; terrible (coll.) ⟨fright, job, pain⟩ ⓶ adv. (ugs.) incredibly (coll.); terribly (coll.)

wahr Adj. (a) true; nicht ~? translation depends on preceding verb form: du hast Hunger, nicht ~? you're hungry, aren't you?; nicht ~, er weiß es doch? he does know, doesn't he? (b) (wirklich) real ⟨reason, motive, feelings, joy, etc.⟩; actual ⟨culprit⟩; (echt) true, real ⟨friend, friendship, love, art⟩

wahren tr. V. (geh.) preserve ⟨balance, equality, neutrality, etc.⟩; maintain ⟨authority, right⟩; (verteidigen) defend

währen itr. V. (geh.) last

während ⓵ Konj. (a) (zeitlich) while (b) (adversativ) whereas ⓶ Präp. mit Gen. during; (über einen Zeitraum von) for

wahr|haben unr. tr. V. etw. nicht ~ wollen not want to admit sth.

wahrhaft (geh.) ⓵ Adj. true ⓶ adv. truly

wahrhaftig ⓵ Adj. (geh.) truthful ⟨person⟩ ⓶ adv. really; genuinely

Wahrheit die; ~, ~en truth

wahrheits·getreu ⓵ Adj. truthful; faithful ⟨account⟩ ⓶ adv. truthfully; ⟨portray⟩ faithfully

wahr|nehmen unr. tr. V. (a) (mit den Sinnen erfassen) perceive; (spüren) feel; detect ⟨sound, smell⟩; (bemerken) notice; (erkennen, ausmachen) make out (b) (nutzen) take advantage of ⟨opportunity⟩; exploit ⟨advantage⟩; exercise ⟨right⟩ (c) (vertreten) look after ⟨sb.'s interests, affairs⟩ (d) (erfüllen, ausführen) carry out, perform ⟨function, task, duty⟩; fulfil ⟨responsibility⟩

Wahrnehmung die; ~, ~en (a) perception; (eines Sachverhalts) awareness; (eines Geruchs, eines Tons) detection (b) (Nutzung) (eines Rechts) exercise; (einer Gelegenheit, eines Vorteils) exploitation (c) (Vertretung) representation (d) (einer Funktion, Aufgabe, Pflicht) performance; execution; (einer Verantwortung) fulfilment

wahr·sagen 2. Part. gewahrsagt ⓵ itr. V. tell fortunes ⓶ tr. V. predict, foretell ⟨future⟩

Wahrsager der; ~s, ~, **Wahrsagerin** die; ~, ~nen fortune-teller

wahrscheinlich ⓵ Adj. probable; likely ⓶ adv. probably

Wahrscheinlichkeit die; ~, ~en probability; likelihood

Währung die; ~, ~en currency

Währungs-: ~**reform** die currency reform; ~**union** die currency union; ~**-, Wirtschafts- und Sozialunion** social, economic, and currency union

Wahr·zeichen das symbol; (einer Stadt, einer Landschaft) [most famous] landmark

Waise die; ~, ~n orphan

Waisen·haus das orphanage

Wal der; ~[e]s, ~e whale

Wald der; ~[e]s, Wälder wood; (größer) forest

Wald·brand der forest fire

Wäldchen das; ~s, ~: copse

Wald-: ~**meister** der (Bot.) woodruff; ~**sterben** das; ~~s death of the forest [as a result of pollution]

Wal·fang der whaling no def. art.; auf ~ gehen/sein go/be whaling

Waliser der; ~s, ~: Welshman

Waliserin die; ~, ~nen Welshwoman

walisisch Adj. Welsh

Walkman Ⓦ /ˈwɔkmən/ der; ~s, Walkmen /ˈwɔkmən/ Walkman ®; personal stereo

Wall der; ~[e]s, Wälle earthwork; embankment; rampart (esp. Mil.)

Wall-: ~**fahrer** der pilgrim; ~**fahrt** die pilgrimage; ~**fahrts·ort** der place of pilgrimage

Wal·nuss, *Wal·nuß die walnut

Wal·ross, *Wal·roß das; Pl. -rosse walrus

walten itr. V. (geh.) ⟨good sense, good spirit⟩ prevail; ⟨peace, silence, harmony, etc.⟩ reign

Walze die; ~, ~n roller; (Straßen~) [road] roller; (Schreib~) platen

walzen tr. V. roll ⟨field, road, steel, etc.⟩

wälzen ⓵ tr. V. roll; heave ⟨heavy object⟩; (fig.) shove ⟨blame, responsibility⟩ (auf + Akk. on); etw. in Mehl usw. ~ (Kochk.) toss sth. in flour etc.; Probleme ~ (fig. ugs.) mull over problems ⓶ refl. V. roll; (auf der Stelle) roll about or around; (im Krampf, vor Schmerzen) writhe around

Walzer der; ~s, ~: waltz

w

wand *1. u. 3. Pers. Sg. Prät. v.* WINDEN

Wand *die;* ~, **Wände** wall; (Trennwand) partition; (bewegliche Trennwand) screen; (eines Behälters, Schiffs) side

Wandale *der;* ~n, ~n, **Wandalin** *die;* ~, ~nen vandal

Wandalismus *der;* ~: vandalism

Wandel *der;* ~s change

wandeln *refl., tr. V.* change (**in** + *Akk.* into)

Wanderer *der;* ~s, ~, **Wanderin** *die;* ~, ~nen rambler; hiker

Wander·karte *die* rambler's [path] map

wandern *itr. V.; mit sein* **(a)** hike; ramble **(b)** (ugs.: gehen; fig.) wander (lit. or fig.) **(c)** (ziehen, reisen) travel; (ziellos) roam; ‹exhibition, circus, theatre› tour, travel; ‹animal, people, tribe› migrate

Wander·tag *der* day's hike (*for a class or school*)

Wanderung *die;* ~, ~en **(a)** hike; walking tour; **eine** ~ **machen** go on a hike/tour/trek **(b)** (Zool., Soziol.) migration

Wander-: ~**urlaub** *der* walking holiday; ~**weg** *der* footpath (*constructed for ramblers*)

Wand-: ~**gemälde** *das* mural; ~**lampe** *die* wall light

Wandlung *die;* ~, ~en change; (grundlegend) transformation

Wand-: ~**malerei** *die* (Bild) mural; ~**schrank** *der* wall cupboard *or* (Amer.) closet

wandte *1. u. 3. Pers. Prät. v.* WENDEN

Wange *die;* ~, ~n (geh.) cheek

wankel-, Wankel-: ~**mut** *der* (geh.) vacillation; ~**mutig** *Adj.* (geh.) vacillating

wanken *itr. V.* **(a)** sway; ‹person› totter; (unter einer Last) stagger **(b)** *mit sein* (unsicher gehen) stagger; totter

wann *Adv.* when; **seit** ~ **wohnst du dort?** how long have you been living there?

Wanne *die;* ~, ~n bath[tub]

Wanze *die;* ~, ~n bug (coll.)

Wappen *das;* ~s, ~: coat of arms

wappnen *refl. V.* (geh.) forearm oneself

war *1. u. 3. Pers. Sg. Prät. v.* SEIN

warb *1. u. 3. Pers. Sg. Prät. v.* WERBEN

ward (geh.) *1. u. 3. Pers. Sg. Prät. v.* WERDEN

Ware *die;* ~, ~n **(a)** ~[n] goods *pl.* **(b)** (Artikel) article; commodity (Econ., fig.); (Erzeugnis) product

Waren-: ~**angebot** *das* supply [of goods]; (Sortiment) range of goods; ~**haus** *das* department store; ~**korb** *der* (Statistik) basket of goods; ~**lager** *das* (einer Fabrik o. Ä.) stores *pl.;* (eines Geschäftes) stockroom; (größer) warehouse; ~**muster** *das,* ~**probe** *die* sample; ~**zeichen** *das* trade mark

warf *1. u. 3. Pers. Sg. Prät. v.* WERFEN

warm; wärmer, wärmst … ① *Adj.* (auch fig.) warm; hot ‹meal, food, bath, spring›; keen, lively ‹interest›; **das Essen** ~ **machen** heat up the food; „~" (auf Wasserhahn) 'hot' ② *adv.* warmly; ~ **essen/duschen** have a hot meal/shower

Wärme *die;* ~: warmth; (Hitze; auch Physik) heat

wärmen ① *tr. V.* warm; (aufwärmen) warm up ‹food, drink› ② *itr. V.* be warm; (warm halten) keep one warm

Wärme·pumpe *die* (Technik) heat pump

Warm·front *die* (Met.) warm front

warm|halten *unr. tr. V.* (ugs.) **sich** (*Dat.*) **jmdn.** ~: keep on the right side of sb.

Warm·wasser-: ~**bereiter** *der;* ~s, ~: water heater; ~**heizung** *die* hot-water heating

Warn-: ~**blinkanlage** *die* (Kfz-W.) hazard warning lights *pl.;* ~**dreieck** *das* (Kfz-W.) hazard warning triangle

warnen *tr. (auch itr.) V.* warn (**vor** + *Dat.* of, about); **jmdn. [davor]** ~, **etw. zu tun** warn sb. against doing sth.

Warn-: ~**schild** *das; Pl.* ~**er** warning sign; ~**schuss,** **~**schuß*** *der* warning shot; ~**signal** *das* warning signal; ~**streik** *der* token strike

Warnung *die;* ~, ~en warning (**vor** + *Dat.* of, about)

Warschau (*das*) ~s Warsaw

Warte-: ~**halle** *die* waiting room; (Flugw.) departure lounge; ~**liste** *die* waiting list

warten ① *itr. V.* wait (**auf** + *Akk.* for) ② *tr. V.* service ‹car etc.›

Wärter *der;* ~s, ~, **Wärterin** *die;* ~, ~nen attendant; (Tier-, Zoo-, Leuchtturmwärter[in]) keeper; (Krankenwärter[in]) orderly; (Gefängniswärter[in]) warder

Warte-: ~**saal** *der* waiting room; ~**zimmer** *das* waiting room

Wartung *die;* ~, ~en service; (das Warten) servicing; (Instandhaltung) maintenance

warum *Adv.* why

Warze *die;* ~, ~n wart; (Brust~) nipple

was ① *Interrogativpron. Nom. u. Akk. u. (nach Präp.) Dat. Neutr.;* ~ **kostet das?** what *or* how much does that cost?; **ach** ~**!** (ugs.) oh, come on!; ~ **für ein …/**~ **für …:** what sort *or* kind of … ② *Relativpron. Nom. u. Akk. u. (nach Präp.) Dat. Neutr.;* **[das,]** ~: what; **alles,** ~ **…:** everything *or* all that …; **vieles/nichts/ etwas,** ~ **…:** much/nothing/something that …; ~ **mich betrifft, [so]** …: as far as I'm concerned, … ③ *Indefinitpron. Nom. u. Akk. u. (nach Präp.) Dat. Neutr.* (ugs.) ▶ ETWAS ④ *Adv.* (ugs.) (warum, wozu) why; what … for

Wasch-: ~**anlage** *die* car wash; ~**automat** *der* washing machine; ~**becken** *das* washbasin

Wäsche *die;* ∼, ∼n (a) (zu waschende
Textilien) washing; (für die Wäscherei) laundry
(b) (Unterwäsche) underwear
(c) (das Waschen) washing *no pl.;* (einmalig)
wash; **in der** ∼ **sein** be in the wash
wasch·echt *Adj.* (a) colour-fast ⟨*textile,
clothes*⟩; fast ⟨*colour*⟩
(b) (fig.) genuine
Wäsche-: ∼**klammer** *die* clothes
peg (Brit.); clothespin (Amer.); ∼**korb** *der*
laundry basket; ∼**leine** *die* clothes line
waschen ① *unr. tr. V.* wash; **sich**
∼: wash [oneself]; have a wash; **Wäsche**
∼: do the/some washing
② *unr. itr. V.* do the washing
Wäscherei *die;* ∼, ∼en laundry
Wäsche-: ∼**schleuder** *die* spin drier;
∼**trockner** *der* (a) (Maschine) tumble
drier; (b) (Gestell) clothes airer
wasch-, Wasch-: ∼**gelegenheit**
die washing facilities *pl.;* ∼**küche** *die*
laundry room; ∼**lappen** *der* [face] flannel;
washcloth (Amer.); ∼**maschine** *die*
washing machine; ∼**maschinen·fest**
Adj. machine washable; ∼**mittel** *das*
detergent; ∼**pulver** *das* washing powder;
∼**raum** *der* washing room; ∼**schüssel**
die washing bowl; ∼**straße** *die*
[automatic] car wash
wäscht *3. Pers. Sg. Präsens v.* WASCHEN
Wasch·wasser *das* washing water
Wasser *das;* ∼s, ∼/Wässer (a) water
(b) *Pl.* Wässer (Mineral-, Tafelwasser) mineral
water; (Heilwasser) water
(c) (Gewässer) **ein fließendes/stehendes** ∼:
a moving/stagnant stretch of water
(d) ∼ **lassen** pass water
wasser-, Wasser-: ∼**bad** *das* (Kochk.)
bain-marie; ∼**ball** *der* (a) beachball;
(b) (Spiel) water polo; ∼**dampf** *der* steam;
∼**dicht** *Adj.* waterproof ⟨*clothing, watch,
etc.*⟩; watertight ⟨*container, seal, etc.*⟩; ∼**fall**
der waterfall; ∼**farbe** *die* watercolour;
∼**hahn** *der* water tap; faucet (Amer.)
wässerig ▶ WÄSSRIG
Wasser-: ∼**kessel** *der* kettle;
∼**leitung** *die* water pipe; (Hauptleitung)
water main; ∼**mann** *der* (Astrol.) [*der*]
∼**mann** Aquarius; **er/sie ist [ein]** ∼∼: he/
she is an Aquarian
wassern *itr. V.; mit sein* land [on the
water]
wässern *tr. V.* soak; (Fot.) wash ⟨*negative,
print*⟩
wasser-, Wasser-: ∼**pflanze** *die*
aquatic plant; ∼**qualität** *die* water
quality; ∼**rohr** *das* water pipe; ∼**scheu**
Adj. scared of water; ∼**schlauch** *der*
[water] hose; ∼**schutz·polizei** *die*
river/lake police; ∼**ski**[1] *der* waterski;
∼**ski fahren** waterski; ∼**ski**[2] *das;* ∼∼s

waterskiing *no art.;* ∼**spiegel** *der*
(a) (Oberfläche) surface [of the water];
(b) (Niveau) water level; ∼**sport** *der* water
sport *no art.;* ∼**spülung** *die* flush
Wasser·stoff *der* hydrogen
Wasser·stoff-: ∼**bombe** *die* hydrogen
bomb; ∼**per·oxid**, ∼**per·oxyd**,
∼**super·oxid**, ∼**super·oxyd** *das*
(Chemie) hydrogen peroxide
Wasser-: ∼**strahl** *der* jet of water;
∼**straße** *die* waterway; ∼**temperatur**
die water temperature; ∼**tiefe** *die* depth
of the water; ∼**tropfen** *der* drop of water;
∼**turm** *der* water tower; ∼**werfer** *der*
water cannon; ∼**werk** *das* waterworks
sing.; ∼**zeichen** *das* watermark
wässrig, *wäßrig *Adj.* watery
waten *itr. V.; mit sein* wade
Waterloo *das;* ∼s, ∼s Waterloo *no art.;*
sein ∼ **erleben** meet one's Waterloo
watscheln *itr. V.; mit sein* waddle
Watt[1] *das;* ∼[e]s, ∼en mudflats *pl.*
Watt[2] *das;* ∼s, ∼ (Technik, Physik) watt
Watte *die;* ∼, ∼n cotton wool
Watte·bausch *der* wad of cotton wool
Watten·meer *das* tidal shallows *pl.*
wattiert *Adj.* quilted; padded ⟨*shoulder
etc., envelope*⟩
WC *das;* ∼[s], ∼[s] toilet; WC
Web /wɛp/ *das;* ∼s (DV) web; **im** ∼ **surfen**
surf the web
Web·cam /'wɛpkæm/ *die;* ∼∼, ∼∼s (DV)
webcam
weben *tr., itr. V.* weave
Weber *der;* ∼s, ∼, **Weberin** *die;* ∼,
∼nen weaver
Web-/'wɛp-/**:** ∼**seite** *die* (DV) web page;
∼**site** /-sa͜it/ *die;* ∼, ∼s (DV) website
Web·stuhl *der* loom
Wechsel *der;* ∼s, ∼ (a) (das Auswechseln)
change; (Geldwechsel) exchange
(b) (Aufeinanderfolge) alternation; **im**
∼: alternately; (bei mehr als zwei) in rotation
(c) (das Überwechseln) move; (Sport) transfer
(d) (Bankw.) bill of exchange (**über** + *Akk.*
for)
wechsel-, Wechsel-: ∼**geld** *das*
change; ∼**haft** *Adj.* changeable; ∼**jahre**
Pl. change of life *sing.;* menopause *sing.;*
∼**kurs** *der* exchange rate
wechseln ① *tr. V.* (a) change; **das
Hemd** ∼: change one's shirt; **die Wohnung**
∼: move home
(b) ([aus]tauschen) exchange ⟨*letters, glances,
etc.*⟩
(c) (umwechseln) change ⟨*money, note, etc.*⟩ (**in**
+ *Akk.* into)
② *itr. V.* change
wechsel-, Wechsel-: ∼**seitig**
① *Adj.* mutual; ② *adv.* mutually; ∼**strom**
der (Elektrot.) alternating current; ∼**stube**
die bureau de change; ∼**wähler** *der,*

---

*old spelling – see note on page x

∼wählerin *die* (Politik) floating voter;
∼wirkung *die* interaction

wecken *tr. V.* jmdn. [aus dem Schlaf]
∼: wake sb. [up]; (fig.: hervorrufen) arouse
⟨*interest, curiosity, anger*⟩

Wecker *der;* ∼s, ∼: alarm clock

wedeln *itr. V.* ⟨*tail*⟩ wag; [mit dem
Schwanz] ∼ ⟨*dog*⟩ wag its tail

weder *Konj.* ∼ A noch B neither A nor B

weg *Adv.* away; (verschwunden, weggegangen)
gone; **er ist schon seit einer Stunde** ∼: he
left an hour ago; **weit** ∼: far away; a long
way away

Weg *der;* ∼[e]s,∼e (a) (Fußweg) path;
(Feldweg) track
(b) (Zugang) way; (Passage, Durchgang)
passage; **sich** (*Dat.*) **einen** ∼ **durch etw.
bahnen** clear a path *or* way through sth.
(c) (Route, Verbindung) way; route
(d) (Strecke, Entfernung) distance; (Gang) walk;
(Reise) journey; **auf dem kürzesten** ∼: by
the shortest route; **auf halbem** ∼[e] (auch
fig.) half-way; **sich auf den** ∼ **machen** set off;
etw. in die ∼**e leiten** get sth. under way
(e) (ugs.: Besorgung) errand
(f) (Methode) way; (Mittel) means

weg-: ∼|**bleiben** *unr. itr. V.; mit sein*
(nicht kommen) stay away; (nicht nach Hause
kommen) stay out; ∼|**bringen** *unr. tr. V.*
take away; (zur Reparatur, Wartung usw.) take in

Wegelagerei *die;* ∼: highway robbery

Wegelagerer *der;* ∼s, ∼: highwayman

Wegelagerin *die;* ∼, ∼nen
highwaywoman

wegen *Präp. mit Gen.* (a) because of;
∼ **Umbau[s] geschlossen** closed for
alterations
(b) (um ... willen) for the sake of; ∼ **der
Kinder**/(ugs.) **dir** for the children's/your sake
(c) (bezüglich) about; regarding

weg-: ∼|**fahren** ① *unr. itr. V.; mit sein*
(a) leave; (im Auto) drive off; (losfahren) set
off; **(b)** (irgendwohin fahren) go away; ② *unr.
tr. V.* drive away; (mit dem Handwagen usw.)
take away; ∼|**fallen** *unr. itr. V.; mit sein* be
discontinued; (nicht mehr zutreffen) no longer
apply; ∼|**fliegen** *unr. itr. V.; mit sein* fly
away; (weggeblasen werden) fly off; ∼|**gehen**
unr. itr. V. **(a)** leave; (ugs.: ausgehen) go out;
(ugs.: wegziehen) move away; **(b)** (verschwinden)
⟨*spot, fog, etc.*⟩ go away; **(c)** (sich entfernen
lassen) ⟨*stain*⟩ come out; ∼|**jagen** *tr. V.*
chase away; ∼|**kommen** *unr. itr. V.; mit
sein* **(a)** get away; **(b)** (abhanden kommen)
go missing; **(c)** **gut**/**schlecht** *usw.* [bei
etw.] ∼**kommen** (ugs.) come off well/badly
etc. [in sth.]; ∼|**kriegen** *tr. V.* get rid of
⟨*cold, pain, etc.*⟩; get out, get rid of ⟨*stain*⟩;
∼|**lassen** *unr. tr. V.* **(a)** jmdn. ∼**lassen**
let sb. go; (ausgehen lassen) let sb. go out;
(b) (auslassen) leave out; omit; ∼|**laufen**
unr. itr. V.; mit sein run away (**von, vor**

+ *Dat.* from); ∼|**legen** *tr. V.* put aside; (an
seinen Platz legen) put away; ∼|**nehmen**
unr. tr. V. **(a)** take away; move ⟨*head, arm*⟩;
(b) jmdm. etw. ∼nehmen take sth. away
from sb.; ∼|**schicken** *tr. V.* **(a)** send off
⟨*letter, parcel*⟩; **(b)** send ⟨*person*⟩ away;
∼|**schmeißen** *unr. tr. V.* (ugs.) chuck
away (coll.); ∼|**schnappen** *tr. V.* (ugs.)
jmdm. etw. ∼schnappen/vor der Nase
∼schnappen snatch sth. away from
sb./from under sb.'s nose; ∼|**schütten**
tr. V. pour away; ∼|**sehen** *unr. itr. V.* look
away; ∼|**stellen** *tr. V.* put away; (beiseite
stellen) put aside; ∼|**stoßen** *unr. tr. V.*
push *or* shove away; ∼|**tragen** *unr. tr. V.*
carry away

Weg·weiser *der;* ∼s, ∼: signpost

weg-: ∼|**werfen** *unr. tr. V.* (auch fig.)
throw away; ∼**werfend** *Adj.* dismissive
⟨*gesture, remark*⟩; ∼|**wischen** *tr. V.*
wipe away; ∼|**zappen** (ugs.) ① *tr. V.*
etw. ∼zappen: switch sth. off [by
changing channels]; ② *itr. V.* switch to
another channel; ∼|**ziehen** ① *unr.
tr. V.* pull away; draw back ⟨*curtain*⟩;
pull off ⟨*blanket*⟩; ② *unr. itr. V.; mit sein*
(a) (umziehen) move away; **(b)** (wandern)
⟨*animals, nomads, etc.*⟩ leave [on their
migration]

weh (ugs.) *Adj.* sore; *s. auch* WEHTUN

Wehe *die;* ∼, ∼n: ∼n haben have
contractions; **in den** ∼**n liegen** be in labour

wehen *itr. V.* **(a)** (blasen) blow
(b) (flattern) flutter

weh-, Weh-: ∼**leidig** (abwertend) ① *Adj.*
(überempfindlich) soft; (weinerlich) whining
attrib.; ② *adv.* self-pityingly; (weinerlich)
whiningly; ∼**mut** *die;* ∼ (geh.) wistful
nostalgia; ∼**mütig** *Adj.* wistfully nostalgic

Wehr¹ *die;* ∼, ∼en: **sich [gegen jmdn./etw.]
zur** ∼ **setzen** make a stand [against sb./sth.];
resist [sb./sth.]

Wehr² *das;* ∼[e]s, ∼e weir

Wehrdienst *der* military service *no art.;*
seinen ∼ **ableisten** do one's military service

Wehr·dienst-: ∼**verweigerer**
der; ∼s, ∼: conscientious objector;
∼**verweigerung** *die* conscientious
objection

wehren *refl. V.* defend oneself

wehr-, Wehr-: ∼**los** *Adj.* defenceless;
∼**losigkeit** *die;* ∼∼: defencelessness;
∼**pflicht** *die* military service; **die
allgemeine** ∼**pflicht** compulsory military
service; ∼**pflichtig** *Adj.* liable for
military service *postpos.;* ∼**sold** *der*
military pay; ∼**übung** *die* reserve duty
[re]training exercise

weh|tun *unr. itr. V.* (ugs.) hurt; **mir tut der
Magen/Kopf/Rücken weh** my stomach/head/
back is aching *or* hurts; **jmdm./sich** ∼: hurt
sb./oneself

Weib *das;* ~[e]s, ~er (veralt., ugs.) woman; female (derog.)

Weibchen *das;* ~s, ~: female

Weiber·held *der* (ugs.) ladykiller

weiblich 1 *Adj.* (a) female
(b) (für die Frau typisch; Sprachw.) feminine
2 *adv.* femininely

Weiblichkeit *die;* ~: femininity

Weibs·bild *das* (a) (ugs.) woman
(b) (salopp abwertend) female

weich 1 *Adj.* (auch fig.) soft; **ein** ~es *od.*
~ **gekochtes Ei** a soft-boiled egg
2 *adv.* softly

Weiche¹ *die;* ~, ~n (Flanke) flank

Weiche² *die;* ~, ~n points *pl.* (Brit.); switch (Amer.)

weichen *unr. itr. V.; mit sein* move; **vor jmdm./einer Sache** ~: give way to sb./sth.

*weich-gekocht ▶ WEICH 1

weichlich 1 *Adj.* soft; (ohne innere Festigkeit) weak
2 *adv.* softly

Weich·macher *der* (Chemie, Technik) plasticizer

Weide¹ *die;* ~, ~n willow

Weide² *die;* ~, ~n pasture

weiden *itr., tr. V.* graze

Weiden·kätzchen *das* willow catkin

weigern *refl. V.* refuse

Weigerung *die;* ~, ~en refusal

Weih·bischof *der* (kath. Kirche) suffragan bishop

Weihe *die;* ~, ~n (Rel.) consecration; (kath. Kirche: Priester-, Bischofsweihe) ordination

weihen *tr. V.* (a) (Rel.) consecrate; (zueignen) dedicate (*Dat.* to)
(b) (kath. Kirche: ordinieren) ordain

Weiher *der;* ~s, ~: [small] pond

Weihnachten *das;* ~, ~: Christmas; **frohe** *od.* **fröhliche** *od.* **gesegnete** ~! Merry *or* Happy Christmas!

weihnachtlich *Adj.* Christmassy

Weihnachts-: ~**baum** *der* Christmas tree; ~**feiertag** *der:* **der erste/zweite** ~**feiertag** Christmas Day/Boxing Day; ~**fest** *das* Christmas; ~**geld** *das* Christmas bonus; ~**geschenk** *das* Christmas present *or* gift; ~**lied** *das* Christmas carol; ~**mann** *der; Pl.* ~**männer** Father Christmas; Santa Claus; ~**markt** *der* Christmas fair; ~**tag** *der:* ▶ ~FEIERTAG; ~**zeit** *die* Christmas time

Weih-: ~**rauch** *der* incense; ~**wasser** *das* (kath. Kirche) holy water

weil *Konj.* because

Weile *die;* ~: while

weilen *itr. V.* (geh.) stay; (sein) be

Wein *der;* ~[e]s, ~e wine

Wein-: ~**berg** *der* vineyard;

~**berg·schnecke** *die* [edible] snail; ~**brand** *der* brandy

weinen *itr. V.* cry (**über** + *Akk.* over, about); (aus Trauer, Kummer) cry, weep (**um** for)

weinerlich 1 *Adj.* tearful; weepy
2 *adv.* tearfully

wein-, Wein-: ~**essig** *der* wine vinegar; ~**flasche** *die* wine bottle; ~**glas** *das* wineglass; ~**handlung** *die* wine merchant's; ~**karte** *die* wine list; ~**krampf** *der* crying fit; fit of crying; ~**lokal** *das* wine bar; ~**probe** *die* wine-tasting [session]; ~**rebe** *die* grapevine; ~**rot** *Adj.* wine-red; ~**schaum·creme** *die* (Kochk.) zabaglione; ~**stock** *der; Pl.* ~**stöcke** [grape]vine; ~**stube** *die* wine bar; ~**traube** *die* grape

weise 1 *Adj.* wise
2 *adv.* wisely

Weise *die;* ~, ~n (a) (Art, Verfahren) way
(b) (Melodie) tune; melody

weisen 1 *unr. tr. V.* (geh.: zeigen) show; **jmdn. aus dem Zimmer** ~: send sb. out of the room
2 *unr. itr. V.* (irgendwohin zeigen) point

Weisheit *die;* ~, ~en (a) wisdom
(b) (Erkenntnis) wise insight; (Spruch) wise saying

Weisheits·zahn *der* wisdom tooth

weis|machen *tr. V.* (ugs.) **das kannst du mir nicht** ~! you can't expect me to swallow that!

weiß¹ *1. u. 3. Pers. Sg. Präsens v.* WISSEN

weiß² *Adj.* white

Weiß *das;* ~[e]s, ~: white

weis·sagen *tr. V.* prophesy

Weissagung *die;* ~, ~en prophecy

Weiß-: ~**bier** *das* wheat beer; white beer; ~**brot** *das* white bread; ~**dorn** *der;* ~~s, ~~e hawthorn

Weiße *der/die; adj. Dekl.* white; white man/woman

weißen *tr. V.* paint white; (tünchen) whitewash

weiß-, Weiß-: ~**gold** *das* white gold; ~**haarig** *Adj.* white-haired; ~**haarig sein** have white hair; ~**herbst** *der* ≈ rosé wine; ~**kohl** *der,* (bes. südd., österr.) ~**kraut** *das* white cabbage

weißlich *Adj.* whitish

Weiß·macher *der* whitener

weißt *2. Pers. Sg. Präsens v.* WISSEN

Weiß-: ~**wein** *der* white wine; ~**wurst** *die* veal sausage

Weisung *die;* ~, ~en (geh., sonst Amtsspr.) instruction; (Direktive) directive

Weisungs·befugnis *die* authority to issue instructions/directives

weit 1 *Adj.* wide; long ⟨*way*⟩; **jmdm. zu** ~ **sein** ⟨*clothes*⟩ be too loose on sb.
2 *adv.* (a) (räumlich ausgedehnt) ~ **geöffnet**

---
*alte Schreibung – vgl. Hinweis auf S. x

wide open; ∼ **und breit war niemand zu sehen** there was no one to be seen anywhere; ∼ **verbreitet** widespread; common; common ⟨*plant, animal*⟩; ∼ **gereist** widely travelled
(b) (lang) far; ∼**er** further; farther; **am** ∼**esten** [the] furthest *or* farthest; ∼ **[entfernt** *od.* **weg] wohnen** live a long way away *or* off; live far away; ∼ **reichend** long-range; (fig.) far-reaching ⟨*importance, consequences*⟩; sweeping ⟨*changes, powers*⟩; extensive ⟨*relations, influence*⟩; **von** ∼**em** *od.* **Weitem** from a distance; **das geht zu** ∼ (fig.) that is going too far
(c) (zeitlich entfernt) ∼ **nach Mitternacht** well past midnight
(d) (in der Entwicklung) far
Weit·blick *der* far-sightedness
Weite *die;* ∼, ∼n **(a)** (räumliche Ausdehnung) expanse
(b) (bes. Sport: Entfernung) distance
(c) (eines Kleidungsstückes) width
weiten [1] *tr. V.* widen
[2] *refl. V.* widen; ⟨*pupil*⟩ dilate
weiter *Adv.* **(a)** ▸ WEIT 2
(b) und so ∼: and so on
(c) (weithin, anschließend) then
(d) (außerdem, sonst) ∼ **nichts** nothing more *or* else
weiter... *Adj.* further; **bis auf** ∼**es** *od.* **Weiteres** for the time being; *s. auch* OHNE
weiter-, Weiter-: ∼**|bilden** *tr. V.:* ▸ FORTBILDEN; ∼**bildung** *die:* ▸ FORTBILDUNG; ∼**|bringen** *unr. tr. V.* **die Diskussion brachte uns nicht** ∼: the discussion did not get us any further [forward]; ∼**|erzählen** *tr. V.* **(a)** continue telling; *itr.* **erzähl weiter!** do carry *or* go on; **(b)** (∼sagen) pass on; ∼**|fahren** *unr. itr. V.; mit sein* continue [on one's way]; (weiterreisen) travel on; ∼**|führen** *tr., itr. V.* continue; ∼**|geben** *unr. tr. V.* pass on; ∼**|gehen** *unr. itr. V.; mit sein* go on; **bitte** ∼**gehen!** please move along *or* keep moving!; ∼**hin** *Adv.* **(a)** (immer noch) still; **(b)** (künftig) in future; **(c)** (außerdem) in addition; ∼**|kommen** *unr. itr. V.; mit sein* **(a)** get further; **(b)** (Fortschritte machen) make progress; **im Beruf** ∼**kommen** get on in one's career; ∼**|machen** (ugs.) *itr. V.* carry on; go on; ∼**|reichen** *tr. V.* pass on; ∼**|sagen** *tr. V.* pass on; ∼**|sehen** *unr. itr. V.* see
Weiterungen *Pl.* complications; difficulties
weiter-, Weiter-: ∼**verarbeiten** *tr. V.* process; ∼**verarbeitung** *die* processing
weit-, Weit-: ∼**gehend** [1] *Adj.* extensive, wide, sweeping ⟨*powers*⟩; far-reaching ⟨*support, concessions, etc.*⟩; wide ⟨*support, agreement, etc.*⟩; general ⟨*renunciation*⟩; [2] *adv.* to a large *or* great extent; *∗*∼**gereist** ▸ WEIT 2A; ∼**hin**

Adv. for miles around; ∼**läufig** [1] *Adj.* **(a)** (ausgedehnt) extensive; (geräumig) spacious; **(b)** (entfernt) distant; [2] *adv.* **(a)** (ausgedehnt) spaciously; **(b)** (entfernt) distantly; ∼**räumig** [1] *Adj.* spacious ⟨*room, area, etc.*⟩; wide ⟨*gap, space*⟩; [2] *adv.* spaciously; *∗*∼**reichend** ▸ WEIT 2B; ∼**sichtig** *Adj.* long-sighted; ∼**sichtigkeit** *die;* ∼∼: long-sightedness; ∼**sprung** *der* (Sport) long jump (Brit.); broad jump (Amer.); *∗*∼**verbreitet** ▸ WEIT 2A; ∼**winkel·objektiv** *das* wide-angle lens
Weizen *der;* ∼s wheat
Weizen·bier *das:* ▸ WEISSBIER
welch [1] *Interrogativpron.* (bei Wahl aus einer unbegrenzten Menge) what; (bei Wahl aus einer begrenzten Menge) (*adj.*) which; (*subst.*) which one
[2] *Relativpron.* (bei Menschen) who; (bei Sachen) which
[3] *Indefinitpron.* some; (in Fragen) any
welk *Adj.* withered ⟨*skin, hands, etc.*⟩; wilted ⟨*leaves, flower*⟩; limp ⟨*lettuce*⟩
welken *itr. V.; mit sein* ⟨*plant, flower*⟩ wilt
Well·blech *das* corrugated iron
Welle *die;* ∼, ∼n **(a)** (auch fig.) wave; (Rundf.: Wellenlänge) wavelength
(b) (Technik) shaft
wellen-, Wellen-: ∼**bad** *das* artificial wave pool; ∼**bereich** *der* (Rundf.) waveband; ∼**brecher** *der* breakwater; ∼**gang** *der* swell; **bei starkem** ∼**gang** in heavy seas; ∼**kraftwerk** *das* wave farm; ∼**länge** *die* wavelength; ∼**sittich** *der* budgerigar
Well·fleisch *das* boiled belly pork
wellig *Adj.* wavy ⟨*hair*⟩; undulating ⟨*scenery, hills, etc.*⟩; uneven ⟨*surface, track, etc.*⟩
Well·pappe *die* corrugated cardboard
Wels *der;* ∼es, ∼e catfish
Welt *die;* ∼, ∼en **(a)** world; **auf der** ∼: in the world; **die Alte/Neue** ∼: the Old/New World; **die Dritte/Vierte** ∼ the Third/Fourth World; **auf die** *od.* **zur** ∼ **kommen** be born; **alle** ∼ (fig. ugs.) the whole world; everybody
(b) (Weltall) universe
welt-, Welt-: ∼**all** *das* universe; ∼**anschauung** *die* world view; ∼**ausstellung** *die* world fair; ∼**berühmt** *Adj.* world-famous; ∼**bevölkerung** *die* world population; population of the world
Welten·bummler *der;* ∼s, ∼, **Welten·bummlerin** *die;* ∼, ∼nen globetrotter
welt-, Welt-: ∼**erfolg** *der* worldwide success; ∼**fremd** [1] *Adj.* unworldly; [2] *adv.* unrealistically; ∼**frieden** *der* world peace; ∼**karte** *die* map of the world; ∼**klima** *das* world climate; ∼**krieg** *der* world war; **der Erste/Zweite** ∼**krieg** the First/Second World War

weltlich *Adj.* (a) worldly
(b) (nicht geistlich) secular

welt-, Welt-: ~**literatur** *die* world
literature *no art.;* ~**macht** *die* world
power; ~**markt** *der* (Wirtsch.) world
market; ~**meister** *der,* ~**meisterin**
die world champion; ~**meisterschaft**
die world championship; ~**musik** *die*
world music; ~**politik** *die* world politics
pl.; ~**rangliste** *die* world ranking list;
world rankings *pl.;* ~**raum** *der* space *no
art.;* ~**reise** *die* world tour; ~**rekord**
der world record; ~**religion** *die* world
religion; ~**sicherheits·rat** *der* (Pol.)
[United Nations] Security Council;
~**sprache** *die* world language; ~**stadt**
die cosmopolitan city; ~**weit** ① *Adj.*
worldwide; ② *adv.* throughout the world;
~**wirtschaft** *die* world economy;
~**wunder** *das:* **die sieben** ~**wunder** the
Seven Wonders of the World

wem *Dat. von* WER ① *Interrogativpron.* to
whom; who ... to; **mit/von/zu** ~: with/from/
to whom; who ... with/from/to
② *Relativpron.* the person to whom ...; the
person who ... to
③ *Indefinitpron.* (ugs.: jemandem) to
somebody *or* someone; (fragend od. verneint) to
anybody *or* anyone

wen *Akk. von* WER ① *Interrogativpron.*
whom; who (coll.); **an/für** ~: to/for whom ...;
who ... to/for
② *Relativpron.* the person whom
③ *Indefinitpron.* (ugs.: jemanden) somebody;
someone; (fragend od. verneint) anybody;
anyone

Wende *die;* ~, ~**n** change (**zu** for)

Wende-kreis *der* (a) (Geogr.) tropic
(b) (Kfz-W.) turning circle

Wendel·treppe *die* spiral staircase

wenden¹ ① *tr., auch itr. V.* (auf die andere
Seite) turn [over]; (in die entgegengesetzte
Richtung) turn [round]; **bitte** ~**!** please turn
over
② *itr. V.* turn [round]
③ *refl. V.* **sich zum Besseren/Schlechteren**
~: take a turn for the better/worse

wenden² ① *unr. (auch regelm.) tr. V.* turn
② *unr. (auch regelm.) refl. V.* (a) ⟨person⟩
turn
(b) (sich richten) **sich an jmdn. [um Rat]**
~: turn to sb. [for advice]

Wende-: ~**platz** *der* turning area;
~**punkt** *der* turning point

wendig ① *Adj.* (a) agile; manœuvrable
⟨vehicle, boat, etc.⟩
(b) (gewandt) astute
② *adv.* (a) (beweglich) agilely
(b) (gewandt) astutely

Wendigkeit *die;* ~ (a) agility; (eines
Flugzeugs) manœuvrability
(b) (Gewandtheit) astuteness

---
*old spelling – see note on page x

Wendung *die;* ~, ~**en** (a) (Änderung der
Richtung) turn
(b) (Veränderung) change

wenig ① *Indefinitpron. u. unbest. Zahlw.*
(a) *Sing.* little; **das ist** ~: that isn't much;
zu ~ **Zeit/Geld haben** not have enough
time/money; **ein Exemplar/50 Euro zu**
~: one copy too few/50 euros too little
(b) *Pl.* a few; **mit** ~**en Worten** in a few words
② *Adv.* little; ~ **mehr** not much more

weniger ① *Komp. von* WENIG;
Indefinitpron. u. unbest. Zahlw. (+ *Sg.*) less;
(+ *Pl.*) fewer; **immer** ~: less and less
② *Komp. von* WENIG; *Adv.* less; **das ist**
~ **angenehm/erfreulich/schön** that is not
very pleasant/pleasing/nice; *s. auch* MEHR 1
③ *Konj.* less; **fünf** ~ **drei** five, take away
three

wenigst... ① *Sup. von* WENIG 1; least; **am**
~**en** least
② *Sup. von* WENIG 2: **am** ~**en** the least

wenigstens *Adv.* at least

wenn *Konj.* (a) (konditional) if; **außer**
~: unless; ~ **es nicht anders geht** if there's
no other way
(b) (temporal) when; **jedes Mal** *od.* **immer,**
~: whenever
(c) (konzessiv) **wenn ... auch** even though
(d) (in Wunschsätzen) if only

wenn·gleich *Konj.* (geh.) even though;
although

wer *Nom. Mask. u. Fem.; s. auch*
(*Gen.*) WESSEN; (*Dat.*) WEM; (*Akk.*) WEN
① *Interrogativpron.* who; ~ **von ...:** which
of ...
② *Relativpron.* the person who; (jeder, der)
anyone *or* anybody who
③ *Indefinitpron.* (ugs.: jemand) someone; (in
Fragen, Konditionalsätzen) anyone; anybody

Werbe-: ~**abteilung** *die* advertising
or publicity department; ~**agentur**
die advertising agency; ~**aktion** *die*
advertising campaign; ~**block** *der; pl.*
~**blöcke** commercial break; ~**fernsehen**
das television commercials *pl.;* ~**funk** *der*
radio commercials *pl.;* ~**geschenk** *das*
[promotional] free gift

werben ① *unr. itr. V.* advertise; **für etw.**
~: advertise sth.
② *unr. tr. V.* attract ⟨readers, customers,
etc.⟩; recruit ⟨soldiers, members, etc.⟩

Werbe-: ~**pause** *die* commercial break;
~**spot** *der* commercial; advertisement; ad
(coll.); ~**spruch** *der* advertising slogan

Werbung *die;* ~: advertising; **für etw.**
~ **machen** advertise sth.

Werde·gang *der* career

werden ① *unr. itr. V.; mit sein* become;
get; **älter** ~: get or grow old[er]; **wahnsinnig**
od. **verrückt** ~: go mad; **das muss anders**
~: things have to change; **wach** ~: wake
up; **rot** ~: go or turn red; **Arzt/Professor**
~: become a doctor/professor; **zu etw.**
~: become sth.; **es wird [höchste] Zeit** it is

[high] time; **es wird 10 Uhr** it is nearly 10 o'clock; **es wird Herbst** autumn is coming; **sind die Fotos [etwas] geworden?** (ugs.) have the photos turned out [well]?

☐2 *Hilfsverb; 2. Part.* **worden (a)** (zur Bildung des Futurs) **wir ∼ uns um ihn kümmern** we will take care of him; **es wird gleich regnen** it is going to rain any minute; **es wird um die 80 Euro kosten** (ich vermute, es kostet um die 80 Euro) it will cost around 80 euros **(b)** (zur Bildung des Passivs) **du wirst gerufen** you are being called; **er wurde gebeten** he was asked

werfen ☐1 *unr. tr. V.* throw; drop ‹*bombs*› ☐2 *unr. itr. V.* **(a)** throw; **mit etw. ∼:** throw sth. **(b)** (Junge kriegen) give birth; ‹*dog, cat*› litter ☐3 *unr. refl. V.* throw oneself; **sich vor einen Zug ∼:** throw oneself under a train

Werft *die; ∼, ∼en* shipyard

Werk *das; ∼[e]s, ∼e* **(a)** work **(b)** (Betrieb, Fabrik) factory; works *sing. or pl.;* **ab ∼:** ex works

Werk·bank *die; Pl.* **Werkbänke** workbench

werken *itr. V.* work

Werken *das; ∼s* (Schulw.) handicraft

Werk[s]-: **∼angehörige** *der/die* factory *or* works employee; **∼arzt** *der,* **∼ärztin** *die* factory *or* works doctor

werk-, Werk-: **∼statt** *die; ∼statt,* **∼stätten** workshop; (Kfz-W.) garage; **∼stoff** *der* material; **∼tag** *der* working day; workday; **∼tags** *Adv.* on weekdays; **∼tätig** *Adj.* working; **∼tätige** *der/die; adj. Dekl.* worker; **∼zeug** *das* (auch fig.) tool; (Gesamtheit von Werkzeugen) tools *pl.*

Werkzeug-: **∼kasten** *der* toolbox; **∼macher** *der,* **∼macherin** *die* tool maker

Wermut *der; ∼[e]s, ∼s* **(a)** (Pflanze) wormwood **(b)** (Wein) vermouth

wert *Adj.* (geh.) esteemed; (als Anrede) my dear ...; **etw./nichts ∼ sein** be worth sth./be worthless

Wert *der; ∼[e]s, ∼e* value; **im ∼[e] von ...:** worth ...; **∼ auf etw.** (*Akk.*) **legen** set great store by *or* on sth.

wert·beständig *Adj.* of lasting value *postpos.*

werten *tr., itr. V.* judge; assess

wert-, Wert-: **∼gegenstand** *der* valuable object; **∼gegenstände** valuables; **∼los** *Adj.* worthless; valueless; **∼papier** *das* (Wirtsch.) security; **∼sache** *die* valuable item; **∼sachen** valuables; **∼sendung** *die* (Postw.) registered item; **∼stoff** *der* recyclable material

Wertung *die; ∼, ∼en* judgement

Wert·urteil *das* value judgement

wert·voll *Adj.* valuable; (moralisch) estimable

Wesen *das; ∼s* nature

wesentlich ☐1 *Adj.* fundamental (**für** to); **im W∼en** essentially ☐2 *adv.* (erheblich) considerably; much

wes·halb *Adv.* ▶ WARUM

Wespe *die; ∼, ∼n* wasp

Wespen·nest *das* wasp's nest; **in ein ∼ stechen** (fig. ugs.) stir up a hornets' nest

wessen *Interrogativpron.* **(a)** *Gen. von* WER whose **(b)** *Gen. von* WAS: **∼ wird er beschuldigt?** what is he accused of?

Wessi *der; ∼s, ∼s* (salopp) West German

West (bes. Seemannsspr., Met.) ▶ WESTEN

west·deutsch *Adj.* Western German; (hist.: auf die alte BRD bezogen) West German

West·deutschland *(das)* Western Germany; (hist.: alte BRD) West Germany

Weste *die; ∼, ∼n* waistcoat (Brit.); vest (Amer.)

Westen *der; ∼s* west; **der ∼:** the West

Western *der; ∼[s], ∼:* western

West·europa *(das)* Western Europe

Westfalen *(das); ∼s* Westphalia

westfälisch *Adj.* Westphalian

West·indien *(das)* the West Indies *pl.*

westlich ☐1 *Adj.* **(a)** western **(b)** (nach Westen) westerly **(c)** (aus dem Westen) Western ☐2 *adv.* westwards ☐3 *Präp. mit Gen.* [to the] west of

west·wärts *Adv.* [to the] west

West·wind *der* west[erly] wind

wes·wegen *Adv.* ▶ WARUM

Wett·bewerb *der; ∼[e]s, ∼e* **(a)** competition **(b)** (Wirtsch.) competition *no indef. art.*

Wette *die; ∼, ∼n* bet; **eine ∼ [mit jmdm.] abschließen** make a bet [with sb.]; **mit jmdm. um die ∼ laufen** race sb.

wett·eifern *itr. V.; 2. Part.* **gewetteifert: mit jmdm. [um etw.] ∼:** compete with sb. [for sth.]

wetten *itr. V.* bet; **mit jmdm. ∼:** have a bet with sb.; **mit jmdm. um etw. ∼:** bet sb. sth.

Wetter *das; ∼s* weather

wetter-, Wetter-: **∼aussichten** *Pl.* weather outlook *sing.;* **∼bedingungen** *die Pl.* weather conditions; **∼bericht** *der* weather report; (Vorhersage) weather forecast; **∼dienst** *der* weather *or* meteorological service; **∼fühlig** *Adj.* sensitive to [changes in] the weather *postpos.;* **∼fühligkeit** *die; ∼, ∼:* sensitivity to [changes in] the weather; **∼karte** *die* weather chart; weather map; **∼lage** *die* weather situation; **∼satellit** *der* weather satellite; **∼vorhersage** *die* weather forecast; **∼warte** *die* weather station

wett-, Wett-: **∼kampf** *der* competition; **∼lauf** *der* race; **∼|machen** *tr. V.* make up for (durch with); **∼rennen** *das* race; **∼rüsten** *das; ∼∼s* arms race; **∼streit** *der* contest

W

wẹtzen *tr. V.* sharpen; whet

WEZ *Abk.* = **Westeuropäische Zeit** GMT

Whirlpool /'wə:lpu:l/ *der;* ~s, ~s whirlpool [bath]

Whiskey /'vɪskɪ/ *der;* ~s ~s whiskey

Whisky /'vɪskɪ/ *der;* ~s, ~s whisky

wịch *1. u. 3. Pers. Sg. Prät. v.* WEICHEN

wịchtig *Adj.* important

Wịchtigkeit *die;* ~: importance

Wịcke *die;* ~, ~n vetch; (im Garten) sweet pea

Wịckel *der;* ~s, ~: compress

wịckeln *tr. V.* wind; (einwickeln) wrap (in + *Akk.* in); (auswickeln) unwrap (aus + *Dat.* from); (abwickeln) unwind (von from); ein Kind ~: change a baby's nappy

Wịdder *der;* ~s, ~: (a) ram (b) (Astrol.) Aries

wịder *Präp. mit Akk.* (geh.) against

wider-: ~**fahren** *unr. itr. V.; mit sein* (geh.) etw. ~fährt jmdm. sth. happens to sb.; ~**legen** *tr. V.* etw. ~legen refute sth.; jmdn. ~legen prove sb. wrong

wịderlich ① *Adj.* revolting; repulsive ⟨person, behaviour, etc.⟩; awful ⟨headache etc.⟩ ② *adv.* revoltingly; ⟨behave⟩ in a repugnant or repulsive manner; awfully ⟨cold, sweet, etc.⟩

Wịderlichkeit *die;* ~, ~en (abwertend) (a) repulsiveness (b) (Äußerung/Handlung) revolting remark/ action

wịder-, Wịder-: ~**rede** *die:* keine ~rede! don't argue!; ~**ruf** *der* retraction; [bis] auf ~ruf until revoked; ~**rufen** /--'--/ *unr. tr., auch itr. V.* retract ⟨statement, claim, confession, etc.⟩; ~**setzen** /--'--/ *refl. V.* sich jmdm./einer Sache ~setzen oppose sb./sth.; ~**spenstig** ① *Adj.* unruly; stubborn ⟨horse, mule, etc.⟩; ② *adv.* wilfully; ~**|spiegeln**, ~**spiegeln** /--'--/ ① *tr. V.* mirror; (fig.) reflect; ② *refl. V.* be mirrored; (fig.) be reflected; ~**sprechen** /--'--/ *unr. itr. V.* contradict; ~**spruch** *der* (a) (Widerrede, Protest) opposition; protest; (b) (etw. Unvereinbares) contradiction; in ~spruch zu *od.* mit etw. stehen contradict sth.; be contradictory to sth.; ~**sprüchlich** *Adj.* contradictory ⟨news, statements, etc.⟩; inconsistent ⟨behaviour, attitude, etc.⟩

Wịder·stand *der* (a) resistance (gegen to) (b) (Hindernis) opposition

wịderstands-, Wịderstands-: ~**fähig** *Adj.* robust; resistant ⟨material etc.⟩; hardy ⟨animal, plant⟩; ~**fähigkeit** *die* robustness; (von Material usw.) resistance; (von Tier, Pflanze) hardiness; ~**los** *Adj., adv.* without resistance *postpos.*

---

*alte Schreibung – vgl. Hinweis auf S. x

wịder-, Wịder-: ~**stehen** /--'--/ *unr. itr. V.* (a) (nicht nachgeben) [jmdm./ einer Sache] ~stehen resist [sb./sth.]; (b) (standhalten) jmdm./einer Sache ~stehen withstand sb./sth.; ~**streben** /--'--/ *itr. V.* etw. ~strebt jmdm. sb. dislikes or detests sth.; ~**wärtig** ① *Adj.* revolting, repugnant ⟨smell, taste, etc.⟩; offensive ⟨person, behaviour, etc.⟩; ② *adv.* ⟨behave etc.⟩ in an offensive manner; ~**wille** *der* aversion (gegen to); ~**willig** ① *Adj.* reluctant; unwilling; ② *adv.* reluctantly; unwillingly

wịdmen ① *tr. V.* (a) dedicate (b) (verwenden für/auf) devote ② *refl. V.* sich jmdm./einer Sache ~: attend to sb./sth.; (ausschließlich) devote oneself to sb./sth

Wịdmung *die;* ~, ~en dedication (an + *Akk.* to)

wịdrig *Adj.* unfavourable; adverse

Wịdrigkeit *die;* ~, ~en adversity

wie ① *Interrogativadv.* how; ~ viel/viele how much/many; ~ [bitte]? [I beg your] pardon?; ~ spät ist es? what time is it? ② *Relativadv.* ~ er es tut the way or manner in which he does it ③ *Konj.* (a) *Vergleichspartikel* as; [so] ... ~ ...: as ... as ...; ich fühlte mich ~ ...: I felt as if I were ...; „N ~ Nordpol" N for November (b) (zum Beispiel) like; such as (c) (und, sowie) as well as; both

wieder *Adv.* again; alles ist ~ beim Alten everything is back as it was before; ich bin gleich ~ da I'll be right back (coll.); etw. ~ finden find sth. again; etw. ~ gutmachen make sth. good; put sth. right; den Schaden ~ gutmachen pay for the damage; jmdn. ~ wählen re-elect sb.; jmdn. ~ beleben revive or resuscitate sb.; jmdn./etw. ~ erkennen recognize sb./sth.

wieder-, Wieder-: ~**aufbau** /--'--/ *der* reconstruction; rebuilding; der wirtschaftliche ~aufbau economic recovery; ~**|bekommen** *unr. tr. V.* get back; *~**|beleben** ▶ WIEDER; ~**belebungs·versuch** *der* attempt at resuscitation; ~**eingliederung** *die* reintegration (in + *Akk.* in); *~**|erkennen** ▶ WIEDER; *~**|finden** ▶ WIEDER; ~**gabe** *die* (Bericht) report; (Übersetzung) rendering; (Reproduktion) reproduction; ~**|geben** *unr. tr. V.* (a) (zurückgeben) give back; (b) (berichten) report; (wiederholen) repeat; ~**geburt** *die* (christl. Rel., fig. geh.) rebirth

***wieder·gut|machen** ▶ WIEDER

wieder|haben *unr. tr. V.* (auch fig.) have back

wieder-: ~**her|stellen** *tr. V.* (a) re-establish ⟨contact, peace⟩; (b) (reparieren) restore ⟨building⟩; ~**holen**¹ ① *tr. V.* repeat; (repetieren) revise ⟨lesson, vocabulary,

etc.›; ② *refl. V.* **(a)** (wieder dasselbe sagen) repeat oneself; **(b)** (erneut geschehen) happen again; **(c)** (wiederkehren) be repeated; recur
wieder|holen² *tr. V.* fetch *or* get back
wiederholt ① *Adj.* repeated
② *adv.* repeatedly
Wiederholung *die;* ~, ~en repetition; (eines Fußballspiels usw.) replay; (einer Sendung) repeat; (einer Aufführung) repeat performance; (von Lernstoff) revision
Wiederholungs·täter *der,* **Wiederholungs·täterin** *die* habitual offender
Wieder·hören *das;* [auf *od.* Auf] ~! goodbye! (*at end of telephone call*)
wieder-, Wieder-: ~**kehr** *die;* ~~ (geh.) return; ~|**kehren** *itr. V.; mit sein* (geh.) return; ~|**kommen** *unr. itr. V.; mit sein* **(a)** (zurückkommen) return; come back; **(b)** (noch einmal kommen) come back *or* again; **(c)** (sich noch einmal ereignen) ‹*opportunity, past*› come again; ~|**kriegen** *tr. V.* (ugs.) get back; ~**schauen** *das;* [auf] ~schauen! (südd., österr.) goodbye!; ~|**sehen** *unr. tr. V.* see again; ~**sehen** *das;* ~s, ~: reunion; [auf] ~sehen! goodbye!; ~**um** *Adv.* **(a)** (erneut) again; **(b)** (andererseits) on the other hand; ~**verwendung** *die* reuse; ~**verwertung** *die* recycling; ~**wahl** *die* re-election; ***~|**wählen** *tr. V.* ▶ WIEDER
Wiege *die;* ~, ~n (auch fig.) cradle
wiegen¹ *unr. itr., tr. V.* weigh
wiegen² *tr. V.* rock; shake ‹*head*›
Wiegen·lied *das* lullaby; cradle song
wiehern *itr. V.* whinny; (lauter) neigh
Wien *(das);* ~s Vienna
Wiener¹ *der;* ~s, ~: Viennese
Wiener² *Adj.* Viennese; *s. auch* WÜRSTCHEN
Wienerin *die;* ~, ~nen Viennese
wienerisch *Adj.* Viennese
wies *1. u. 3. Pers. Sg. Prät. v.* WEISEN
Wiese *die;* ~, ~n meadow; (Rasen) lawn
wie·so *Interrogativadv.* why
***wie·viel */od. '--/* ▶ VIEL, WIE, UHR B
wie·viel·mal */od. -'--/ Interrogativadv.* how many times
wievielt... */od. '--/ Interrogativadj.* der ~e Band? which number volume?; der Wievielte ist heute? what is the date today?
wie·weit *Interrogativadv.* to what extent; how far
wild ① *Adj.* (auch fig.) wild; (wütend) furious ‹*cursing, shouting, etc.*›; ~es Parken illegal parking; ~er Streik wildcat strike; ~ auf etw./jmdn. sein (ugs.) be mad *or* crazy about sth./sb. (coll.); ~ werden get furious; jmdn. ~ machen infuriate sb.
② *adv.* **(a)** wildly; wie ~ (ugs.) like mad (coll.)
(b) (ordnungswidrig) illegally
Wild *das;* ~[e]s **(a)** (Tiere, Fleisch) game
(b) (einzelnes Tier) [wild] animal

Wild·bret */-brɛt/ das;* ~s (geh.) game
Wilde *der/die; adj. Dekl.* savage
Wilderei *die;* ~, ~en poaching *no pl., no art.*
Wilderer *der;* ~s, ~, **Wilderin** *die;* ~, ~nen poacher
wild·fremd *Adj.* completely strange
Wild·gans *die* wild goose
Wildheit *die;* ~: wildness
Wild-: ~**katze** *die* wild cat; ~**leder** *das* suede
Wildnis *die;* ~, ~se wilderness
Wild-: ~**pferd** *das* wild horse; ~**schwein** *das* wild boar; ~**wasser** *das Pl.* ~~: mountain torrent; ~**wechsel** *der* game crossing; ~**west·film** *der* western
will *1. u. 3. Pers. Sg. Präsens v.* WOLLEN
Wille *der;* ~ns will; (Wunsch) wish
willen *Präp. mit Gen.* um jmds./einer Sache ~: for sb.'s/sth.'s sake
Willen *der;* ~s ▶ WILLE
willen·los ① *Adj.* will-less
② *adv.* will-lessly
willens *Adj.* ~ sein, etw. zu tun (geh.) be willing to do sth.
willens-, Willens-: ~**schwach** *Adj.* weak-willed; ~**schwäche** *die* weakness of will; ~**stark** *Adj.* strong-willed; ~**stärke** *die* strength of will
willentlich ① *Adj.* deliberate
② *adv.* deliberately; on purpose
willig ① *Adj.* willing
② *adv.* willingly
will·kommen *Adj.* welcome; jmdn. ~ heißen welcome sb.
Will·kür *die;* ~: arbitrary use of power; (Handlung o. Ä.) arbitrariness
willkürlich ① *Adj.* arbitrary; (vom Willen gesteuert) voluntary ‹*muscle, movement, etc.*›
② *adv.* arbitrarily; (vom Willen gesteuert) voluntarily
wimmeln *itr. V.* von Fischen/Fehlern ~: be teeming with fish/mistakes
wimmern *itr. V.* whimper
Wimpel *der;* ~s, ~: pennant
Wimper *die;* ~, ~n [eye]lash
Wimpern·tusche *die* mascara
Wind *der;* ~[e]s, ~e wind
Wind·beutel *der* cream puff
Winde *die;* ~, ~n winch
Windel *die;* ~, ~n nappy (Brit.); diaper (Amer.)
Windel·höschen *das* nappy pants *pl.*
winden ① *unr. tr. V.* (geh.) make ‹*wreath, garland*›; etw. um etw. ~: wind sth. around sth.
② *unr. refl. V.* ‹*plant, tendrils*› wind (um around); ‹*snake*› coil [itself], wind itself (um around); sich vor Schmerzen ~: writhe in pain
Windes·eile *die;* in ~: in next to no time
Wind-: ~**hose** *die* (Met.) whirlwind; ~**hund** *der* greyhound

W

windig *Adj.* windy

Wind-: ~**kanal** *der* (Technik) wind tunnel; ~**mühle** *die* windmill; ~**park** *der* wind farm; ~**pocken** *Pl.* chickenpox *sing.;* ~**schatten** *der* lee; ~**schutz·scheibe** *die* windscreen (Brit.); windshield (Amer.); ~**stärke** *die;* ~stärke 7/9 *usw.* wind force 7/9 *etc.;* ~**still** *Adj.* windless; still; ~**stoß** *der* gust of wind; ~**surfer** *der,* ~**surferin** *die* windsurfer; ~**surfing** *das;* ~~s windsurfing *no art.*

Windung *die;* ~, ~en **(a)** bend **(b)** (spiralförmiger Verlauf) spiral; (einer Spule usw.) winding

Wink *der;* ~[e]s, ~e sign; (Hinweis) hint; (Ratschlag) tipp; hint

Winkel *der;* ~s, ~ **(a)** (Math.) angle; **toter** ~: blind spot **(b)** (Ecke; auch fig.) corner

winkelig *Adj.* twisty ⟨streets⟩

winken ① *itr. V.* **(a)** wave; **mit etw.** ~: wave sth. **(b)** (auffordern heranzukommen) **jmdm.** ~: beckon sb. over; **einem Taxi** ~: hail a taxi ② *tr. V.* beckon; **jmdn. zu sich** ~: beckon sb. over [to one]

winklig *Adj.* ▶ WINKELIG

winseln *itr. V.* ⟨dog⟩ whimper

Winter *der;* ~s, ~ winter

Winter-: ~**anfang** *der* beginning of winter; ~**garten** *der* conservatory

winterlich ① *Adj.* wintry; winter *attrib.* ⟨clothing, break⟩ ② *adv.* ~ **kalt** cold and wintry

Winter-: ~**reifen** *der* winter tyre; ~**schlussverkauf,** ***~**schlußverkauf** *der* winter sale[s *pl.*]; ~**sport** *der* winter sports *pl.;* ~**urlaub** *der* winter holiday; ~**zeit** *die* wintertime

Winzer *der;* ~s, ~, **Winzerin** *die;* ~, ~nen winegrower

winzig ① *Adj.* tiny ② *adv.* ~ **klein** tiny; minute

Winzigkeit *die;* ~, ~en **(a)** tininess; minuteness **(b)** (Kleinigkeit) tiny thing; triviality

Wipfel *der;* ~s, ~: treetop

Wippe *die;* ~, ~n see-saw

wippen *itr. V.* bob up and down; (hin und her) bob about; (auf einer Wippe) see-saw

wir *Personalpron.;* 1. *Pers. Pl. Nom.* we; *s. auch* ⟨Gen.⟩ UNSER; ⟨Dat.⟩ UNS; ⟨Akk.⟩ UNS

wirb *Imperativ Sg. v.* WERBEN

Wirbel *der;* ~s, ~ **(a)** (kreisende Bewegung) (im Wasser) whirlpool; (in der Luft) whirlwind; (kleiner) eddy; (von Rauch, beim Tanz) whirl **(b)** (Trubel) hurly-burly **(c)** (Aufsehen) fuss **(d)** (Anat.) vertebra

wirbeln ① *itr. V. mit sein* whirl; ⟨water, snowflakes⟩ swirl ② *tr. V.* swirl ⟨leaves, dust⟩; whirl ⟨dancer⟩

Wirbel-: ~**säule** *die* spinal column; ~**sturm** *der* cyclone

wirbt 3. *Pers. Sg. Präsens v.* WERBEN

wird 3. *Pers. Sg. Präsens v.* WERDEN

wirf *Imperativ Sg. v.* WERFEN

wirft 3. *Pers. Sg. Präsens v.* WERFEN

wirken *itr. V.* **(a)** (eine Wirkung haben) have an effect; **gegen etw.** ~: be effective against sth. **(b)** (erscheinen) seem; appear

wirklich ① *Adj.* real ② *Adv.* really

Wirklichkeit *die;* ~, ~en reality; **in** ~: in reality

wirksam ① *Adj.* effective ② *adv.* effectively

Wirksamkeit *die;* ~: effectiveness

Wirk·stoff *der* active agent

Wirkung *die;* ~, ~en effect (auf + *Akk.* on); **mit** ~ **vom 1. Juli** (Amtsspr.) with effect from 1 July

wirkungs-, Wirkungs-: ~**grad** *der* (Technik) efficiency; ~**los** ① *Adj.* ineffective; ② *adv.* ineffectively; ~**losigkeit** *die;* ~~: ineffectiveness; ~**voll** ① *Adj.* effective; ② *adv.* effectively

wirr *Adj.* (unordentlich) tousled ⟨hair, beard⟩; tangled ⟨ropes, roots⟩; (unklar, verwirrt) confused

Wirren *Pl.* turmoil *sing.*

Wirrwarr *der;* ~s chaos; (von Stimmen) clamour

Wirsing *der;* ~s, **Wirsing·kohl** *der* savoy [cabbage]

Wirt *der;* ~[e]s, ~e landlord

Wirtin *die;* ~, ~nen landlady

Wirtschaft *die;* ~, ~en **(a)** economy; (Geschäftsleben) commerce and industry **(b)** (Gaststätte) public house; pub (Brit. coll.); bar (Amer.) **(c)** (Haushalt) household **(d)** (ugs. abwertend: Unordnung) mess; shambles *sing.*

wirtschaften *itr. V.* **mit dem Geld gut** ~: manage one's money well; **mit Verlust/ Gewinn** ~: run at a loss/profit

wirtschaftlich ① *Adj.* **(a)** economic **(b)** (finanziell) financial **(c)** (sparsam, rentabel) economical ② *adv.;* *s. Adj.:* economically; financially

Wirtschaftlichkeit *die;* ~: economic viability

Wirtschafts-: ~**hilfe** *die* economic aid *no indef. art.;* ~**krieg** *der* economic war; (Kriegsführung) economic warfare; ~**kriminalität** *die* economic crime *no art.;* ~**krise** *die* economic crisis; ~**lehre** *die* economics *sing.;* ~**minister** *der,* ~**ministerin** *die* minister for economic affairs; **~politik** *die* economic policy; **~union** *die* economic union; *s. auch* Währungsunion; **~wunder** *das* (ugs.) economic miracle

Wirts-: **~haus** *das* pub (Brit. coll.); **~leute** *Pl.* landlord and landlady

Wisch *der;* ~[e]s, ~e (salopp) piece *or* bit of paper

wischen *itr., tr. V.* wipe; **Staub ~:** do the dusting; dust

wispern *itr., tr. V.* whisper

wiss-, *wiß-, Wiss-, *Wiß-: **~begier, ~begierde** *die* thirst for knowledge; **~begierig** *Adj.* eager for knowledge; ⟨*child*⟩ eager to learn

wissen [1] *unr. tr. V.* know; **von jmdm./ etw. nichts [mehr] ~ wollen** want to have nothing [more] to do with sb./sth [2] *unr. itr. V.* **von etw./um etw. ~:** know about sth.

Wissen *das;* ~s knowledge; **meines/ unseres ~s** to my/our knowledge

Wissenschaft *die;* ~, ~en science

Wissenschaftler *der;* ~s ~, **Wissenschaftlerin** *die;* ~, ~nen academic; (Naturwissenschaft) scientist

wissenschaftlich [1] *Adj.* scholarly; (naturwissenschaftlich) scientific [2] *adv.* in a scholarly manner; (naturwissenschaftlich) scientifically

wissens-wert *Adj.* ~ **sein** be worth knowing

wissentlich [1] *Adj.* deliberate [2] *adv.* knowingly; deliberately

wittern [1] *itr. V.* sniff the air [2] *tr. V.* get wind of; (fig.: ahnen) sense

Witterung *die;* ~, ~en (a) (Wetter) weather *no indef. art* (b) (Jägerspr.) (Geruchssinn) sense of smell; (Geruch) scent

Witwe *die;* ~, ~n widow; ~ **werden** be widowed

Witwen-rente *die* widow's pension

Witwer *der;* ~s, ~: widower; ~ **werden** be widowed

Witz *der;* ~es, ~e joke

Witz-: **~blatt** *das* humorous magazine; **~bold** *der;* ~es, ~e joker

Witzelei *die;* ~, ~en (a) teasing (b) (witzelnde Bemerkung) joke

witzeln *itr. V.* joke (**über** + *Akk.* about)

Witz-figur *die* (a) (in Witzen) joke character (b) (ugs. abwertend) figure of fun

witzig [1] *Adj.* funny [2] *adv.* amusingly

witz-los *Adj.* (a) dull (b) (ugs.: sinnlos) pointless

wo [1] *Adv.* where [2] *Konj.* (a) (da, weil) seeing that (b) (obwohl) although; when

wo-anders *Adv.* somewhere else

wo-bei *Adv.* (a) (interrogativ) ~ **hast du sie**

ertappt? what did you catch her doing? (b) (relativisch) **er gab sechs Schüsse ab,** ~ **einer der Täter getötet wurde** he fired six shots – one of the criminals was killed

Woche *die;* ~, ~n week; **in dieser/der nächsten/der letzten ~:** this/next/last week; **heute in/vor einer ~:** a week today/a week ago today

wochen-, Wochen-: **~bett** *das:* **im ~bett liegen** be lying in; **~ende** *das* weekend; **~lang** [1] *Adj.* lasting weeks *postpos;* [2] *adv.* for weeks [on end]; **~stunde** *die* (Schulw.) period per week; **~tag** *der* weekday (*including Saturday*); **~tags** *Adv.* on weekdays [and Saturdays]

wöchentlich *Adj., adv.* weekly

Wochen-zeitung *die* weekly newspaper

-wöchig (a) (... Wochen alt) ... -week-old (b) (... Wochen dauernd) ... week's/weeks'; ...-week

Wöchnerin *die;* ~, ~nen woman who has just given birth

Wodka *der;* ~s, ~s vodka

wo-durch *Adv.* (a) (interrogativ) how (b) (relativisch) as a result of which

wo-für *Adv.* (a) (interrogativ) for what (b) (relativisch) for which

wog *1. u. 3. Pers. Sg. Prät. v.* wiegen

Woge *die;* ~, ~n wave

wo-gegen [1] *Adv.* (a) (interrogativ) against what; what ... against (b) (relativisch) against which; which ... against [2] *Konj.* whereas

wogen *itr. V.* (geh.) ⟨*sea*⟩ surge; (fig.) ⟨*corn*⟩ wave

wo-her *Adv.* (a) (interrogativ) where ... from; ~ **weißt du das?** how do you know that? (b) (relativisch) where ... from

wo-hin *Adv.* (a) (interrogativ) where [... to] (b) (relativisch) where

wo-hingegen *Konj.* whereas

wohl [1] *Adv.* (a) well; **jmdm. ist nicht ~, jmd. fühlt sich nicht ~:** sb. does not feel well (b) (behaglich) at ease; happy; **leb ~!/leben Sie ~!** farewell! (c) (durchaus) well (d) (ungefähr) about (e) **etw. tut jmdm. ~:** sth. does sb. good [2] *Partikel* probably; ~ **kaum** hardly

Wohl *das;* ~[e]s welfare; **auf jmds. ~ trinken** drink sb.'s health; **zum ~!** cheers!

wohl-, Wohl-: **~auf** /-'-/ *Adj.* (geh.) **~auf sein** be well; **~befinden** *das* well-being; **~behagen** *das* sense of well-being; **~behalten** *Adj.* safe and well ⟨*person*⟩; undamaged ⟨*thing*⟩; **~fahrts-staat** *der* welfare state; **~gefallen** *das;* ~~s pleasure; **~gemerkt** *Adv.* please note; **~habend** *Adj.* prosperous; **~habenheit** *die;* ~~: prosperity

wohlig [1] *Adj.* pleasant; agreeable [2] *adv.* ⟨*sigh, purr, etc.*⟩ with pleasure ····⟶

wohl-, Wohl-: ∼**klang** der (geh.)
melodious sound; ∼**schmeckend**
Adj. (geh.) delicious; ∼**stand** der
prosperity; ∼**stands·gesellschaft**
die affluent society; ∼**tat** die (a) (gute Tat)
good deed; (Gefallen) favour; (b) (Genuss)
blissful relief; ∼**tätig** Adj. charitable;
∼**tuend** Adj. agreeable; *∼|**tun**
▶ WOHL 1 E; ∼**verdient** Adj. well-earned;
∼**weislich** Adv. deliberately; ∼**wollen**
das; ∼∼s goodwill; ∼**wollend** 1 Adj.
benevolent; favourable ⟨judgement,
opinion⟩; 2 adv. benevolently; ⟨judge,
consider⟩ favourably

Wohn-: ∼**anhänger** der caravan; trailer
(Amer.); ∼**block** der; Pl. ∼∼s, od. ∼**blöcke**
residential block

wohnen itr. V. live; (kurzfristig) stay

wohn-, Wohn-: ∼**gemeinschaft**
die group sharing a flat (Brit.) or (Amer.)
apartment/house; ∼**haft** Adj. resident (**in**
+ Dat. in); ∼**heim** das (für Alte, Behinderte)
home; (für Obdachlose, Lehrlinge) hostel; (für
Studenten) hall of residence

wohnlich Adj. homely

Wohn-: ∼**mobil** das; ∼∼s, ∼∼e
motor home; ∼**ort** der place of residence;
∼**siedlung** die residential estate; (mit
gleichartigen Häusern) housing estate; ∼**sitz**
der place of residence; **ohne festen** ∼**sitz** of
no fixed abode

Wohnung die; ∼, ∼en (a) flat (Brit.);
apartment (Amer.)
(b) (Unterkunft) lodging

Wohnungs-: ∼**not** die housing crisis;
serious housing shortage; ∼**schlüssel**
der key to the flat (Brit.) or (Amer.) apartment;
∼**suche** die search for a flat (Brit.) or
(Amer.) apartment; **auf** ∼**suche sein** be
flat-hunting; ∼**tür** die door of the flat (Brit.)
or (Amer.) apartment; ∼**verlust** der loss of
one's home

Wohn-: ∼**verhältnisse** Pl. living
conditions; ∼**wagen** der caravan; trailer
(Amer.); ∼**zimmer** das living room

wölben 1 tr. V. curve; vault, arch ⟨roof,
ceiling⟩
2 refl. V. curve; ⟨bridge, ceiling⟩ arch

Wölbung die; ∼, ∼en curve; (einer Decke)
arch; vault

Wolf der; ∼[e]s, **Wölfe** wolf

Wolke die; ∼, ∼n cloud

wolken-, Wolken-: ∼**bruch** der
cloudburst; ∼**bruch·artig** Adj. torrential;
∼**decke** die [unbroken] cloud no indef.
art.; **die** ∼**decke riss auf** the clouds broke;
∼**kratzer** der skyscraper; ∼**los** Adj.
cloudless

wolkig Adj. cloudy

Wolle die; ∼, ∼n wool

wollen¹ Adj. woollen

wollen² 1 unr. Modalverb; 2. Part. wollen:
etw. tun ∼ (den Wunsch haben, etw. zu tun) want
to do sth.; (die Absicht haben, etw. zu tun) be
going to do sth.; **die Wunde will nicht heilen**
the wound [just] won't heal
2 unr. itr. V. **du musst nur** ∼, **dann** … you
only have to want to enough, then … **ganz
wie du willst** just as you like; **ich will nach
Hause** (ugs.) I want to go home; **zu wem**
∼ **Sie?** whom do you want to see?
3 unr. tr. V. want; **das habe ich nicht
gewollt** I never meant that to happen

wo·mit Adv. (a) (interrogativ) ∼ **schreibst
du?** what do you write with?
(b) (relativisch) ∼ **du schreibst** which or that
you write with; (more formal) with which you
write

wo·möglich Adv. possibly

wo·nach Adv. (a) (interrogativ) after what;
what … after; ∼ **suchst du?** what are you
looking for?
(b) (relativisch) after which; which … after

Wonne die; ∼, ∼n (geh.) bliss no pl.;
ecstasy; (etw., was Freude macht) joy

wonnig Adj. sweet

woran Adv. (a) (interrogativ) ∼ **denkst du?**
what are you thinking of?
(b) (relativisch) **nichts,** ∼ **man sich anlehnen
könnte** nothing one could lean against

worauf (a) (interrogativ) ∼ **wartest du?** what
are you waiting for?
(b) (relativisch) **etwas,** ∼ **man sich verlassen
kann** something one can rely on
(c) (relativisch: woraufhin) whereupon

woraus Adv. (a) (interrogativ) ∼ **schließt du
das?** what do you infer that from?
(b) (relativisch) **es gab nichts,** ∼ **wir den Wein
hätten trinken können** there was nothing for
us to drink the wine out of

worden 2. Part. v. WERDEN 2

worin Adv. (a) (interrogativ) in what; what … in
(b) (relativisch) in which; which … in

Workaholic /wɔːkəˈhɒlɪk/ der; ∼s, ∼s:
workaholic

Wort das; ∼[e]s, **Wörter**/∼e (a) Pl. **Wörter,**
(auch:) ∼e word; ∼ **für** ∼: word for word;
ˋ**1000 (in** ∼**en: tausend)** €1,000 (in words:
one thousand)
(b) Pl. ∼e (Äußerung) word; **mir fehlen die** ∼e
I'm lost for words; **Dr. Meyer hat das** ∼: it's
Dr Meyer's turn to speak
(c) Pl. ∼e (Spruch) saying; (Zitat) quotation
(d) Pl. ∼e (geh.: Text) words pl.; **in** ∼ **und Bild**
in words and pictures
(e) Pl. ∼e (Versprechen) word; **[sein]** ∼ **halten**
keep one's word

Wort·bruch der breaking one's word no
art.

wort·brüchig Adj. ∼ **werden** break one's
word

Wörter·buch das dictionary

wort-, Wort-: ∼**getreu** Adj. word-for-
word; ∼**karg** 1 Adj. taciturn ⟨person⟩;

---

w

2 *adv.* taciturnly; ~**kargheit** *die* taciturnity; ~**laut** *der* wording; **im [vollen]** ~**laut** verbatim

wörtlich 1 *Adj.* (a) word-for-word (b) (der eigentlichen Bedeutung entsprechend) literal
2 *adv.: s. Adj.:* word for word; literally

wort-, Wort-: ~**los** 1 *Adj.* silent; wordless; 2 *adv.* without saying a word; ~**meldung** *die:* **gibt es noch** ~**meldungen?** does anyone else wish to speak?; ~**spiel** *das* play on words; pun; ~**wechsel** *der* exchange of words; ~**wörtlich** *Adj.* word-for-word

worüber *Adv.* (a) (interrogativ) over what ...; what ... over (b) (relativisch) over which; which ... over

worum *Adv.* (a) (interrogativ) around what; what ... around (b) (relativisch) around which; which ... around

worunter *Adv.* (a) (interrogativ) under what; what ... under (b) (relativisch) under which; which ... under

wo·von *Adv.* (a) (interrogativ) from where; where ... from (b) (relativisch) from which; which ... from

wo·vor *Adv.* (a) (interrogativ) in front of what; what ... in front of (b) (relativisch) in front of which; which ... in front of

wo·zu *Adv.* (a) (interrogativ) to what; what ... to; (wofür) what ... for (b) (relativisch) ~ **du dich auch entschließt** whatever you decide on

Wrack *das;* ~**[e]s,** ~**s** *od.* ~**e** wreck

wrang *1. und 3. Pers. Sg. Prät. v.* WRINGEN

wringen *unr. tr. V.* (bes. nordd.) wring

Wucher *der;* ~**s** profiteering; (beim Verleihen von Geld) usury

wuchern *itr. V.* (a) *auch mit sein ⟨plants, weeds, etc.⟩* proliferate, run wild (b) (Wucher treiben) **[mit etw.]** ~: profiteer [on sth.]; (beim Verleihen von Geld) lend [sth.] at extortionate interest rates

Wucherung *die;* ~, ~**en** growth

wuchs *1. u. 3. Pers. Sg. Prät. v.* WACHSEN

Wuchs *der;* ~**es** (Gestalt) stature

Wucht *die;* ~: force; (von Schlägen) power; weight

wuchtig 1 *Adj.* (a) (voller Wucht) powerful; mighty (b) (schwer, massig) massive
2 *adv.* powerfully

wühlen 1 *itr. V.* (a) dig; (mit der Schnauze, dem Schnabel) root (**nach** for); ⟨*mole*⟩ tunnel, burrow (b) (ugs.: suchen) rummage [around] (**nach** for) 2 *tr. V.* burrow; tunnel out ⟨*burrow*⟩

wulstig *Adj.* bulging

wund *Adj.* sore; **sich** ~ **liegen** get bed sores

Wunde *die;* ~, ~**n** wound

wunder, Wunder¹ (ugs.): **er denkt, er sei** ~ **wer** he thinks he's really something; **sie bildet sich** ~ **was darauf ein** she's terribly pleased with herself about it (coll.)

Wunder² *das;* ~**s,** ~ (a) miracle; ~ **wirken** (fig. ugs.) work wonders; **ein/kein** ~ **sein** (ugs.) be a/no wonder (b) (etw. Erstaunliches) wonder

wunderbar 1 *Adj.* (a) miraculous (b) (sehr schön, herrlich) wonderful; marvellous
2 *adv.* (a) (sehr schön, herrlich) wonderfully; marvellously (b) (ugs.: sehr) wonderfully

Wunder-: ~**kerze** *die* sparkler; ~**kind** *das* child prodigy

wunderlich 1 *Adj.* strange; odd 2 *adv.* strangely; oddly

wundern 1 *tr. V.* surprise; **mich wundert** *od.* **es wundert mich, dass** ...: I'm surprised that ... 2 *refl. V.* **sich über jmdn./etw.** ~: be surprised at sb./sth

wunder-: ~**schön** 1 *Adj.* simply beautiful; (herrlich) simply wonderful; 2 *adv.* quite beautifully; ~**voll** 1 *Adj.* wonderful; 2 *adv.* wonderfully

***wund|liegen** ▶ WUND

Wund·starr·krampf *der* (Med.) tetanus

Wunsch *der;* ~**[e]s, Wünsche** wish (**nach** to have); (Sehnen) desire (**nach** for); **haben Sie [sonst] noch einen** ~? will there be anything else?; **auf jmds.** ~: at sb.'s wish; **mit den besten/herzlichsten Wünschen** with best/warmest wishes

wünschbar *Adj.* (bes. schweiz.) desirable

Wünschel-: ~**rute** *die* divining rod; ~**ruten·gänger** *der;* ~~**s,** ~~, ~**ruten·gängerin** *die;* ~~, ~~**nen** diviner

wünschen *tr. V.* (a) **sich** (*Dat.*) **etw.** ~: want sth.; (im Stillen) wish for sth. (b) (in formelhaften Wünschen) wish; **jmdm. alles Gute/frohe Ostern** ~: wish sb. all the best/a happy Easter (c) *auch itr. V.* (begehren) want; **was** ~ **Sie?, Sie** ~? (im Lokal) what would you like?; (in einem Geschäft) can I help you?

Wunsch-: ~**kind** *das* wanted child; ~**konzert** *das* request concert; (im Rundfunk) request programme; ~**zettel** *der* (zum Geburtstag usw.) list of presents one would like

wurde *1. u. 3. Pers. Sg. Prät. v.* WERDEN

würde *1. u. 3. Pers. Sg. Konjunktiv II v.* WERDEN

Würde *die;* ~: dignity

würde·los 1 *Adj.* undignified; (schimpflich) disgraceful 2 *adv.* in an undignified way; (schimpflich) disgracefully

Würdelosigkeit *die;* ~ ▶ WÜRDELOS: lack of dignity; disgracefulness

Würden·träger *der,*
Würden·trägerin *die* dignitary
würde·voll ① *Adj.* dignified
  ② *adv.* with dignity
würdig ① *Adj.* (a) dignified
  (b) (wert) worthy
  ② *adv.* (a) with dignity
  (b) (angemessen) worthily
würdigen *tr. V.* (a) (anerkennen, beachten)
recognize; (schätzen) appreciate; (lobend
hervorheben) acknowledge
  (b) (für wert halten) **jmdn. keines Blickes/**
keiner Antwort ∼: not deign to look
at/answer sb.
Wurf *der;* ∼[e]s, Würfe (a) throw; (beim
Kegeln) bowl
  (b) *o. Pl.* (das Werfen) throwing/pitching/
bowling
  (c) (Zool.) litter
Würfel *der;* ∼s, ∼: cube; (Spielwürfel) dice;
die (formal)
Würfel·becher *der* dice cup
würfeln ① *itr. V.* throw the dice; **um etw.**
∼: play dice for sth.
  ② *tr. V.* (a) throw
  (b) (in Würfel schneiden) dice
Würfel-: ∼**spiel** *das* dice; (Brettspiel) dice
game; ∼**zucker** *der* cube sugar
Wurf·geschoss, *Wurf·geschoß *das*
missile
würgen ① *tr. V.* strangle; throttle
  ② *itr. V.* (Brechreiz haben) retch
Wurm *der;* ∼[e]s, Würmer worm; (Made)
maggot
wurmig *Adj.,* **wurm·stichig** *Adj.* worm-
eaten; (madig) maggoty
Wurst *die;* ∼, Würste sausage; **es geht um**
die ∼ (fig. ugs.) the crunch has come; **jmdm.**
ist jmd./etw. ∼ (ugs.) sb. doesn't care about
sb./sth.
Wurst·bude *die* ▶ WÜRSTCHENBUDE

Würstchen *das;* ∼s, ∼ (a) [small]
sausage; **Frankfurter/Wiener** ∼: frankfurter/
wienerwurst
  (b) (fig. ugs.) nobody; (hilfloser Mensch) poor
soul
Würstchen·bude *die* sausage stand
Wurstelei *die;* ∼, ∼en (ugs. abwertend)
pottering about *no pl.*
wursteln *itr. V.* (ugs.) potter
Wurst·salat *der: piquant salad with pieces*
of sausage, onion rings, boiled eggs and/or
cheese
Würze *die;* ∼, ∼n spice; seasoning
Wurzel *die;* ∼, ∼n (auch fig.) root
wurzeln *itr. V.* take root
würzen *tr. V.* season
würzig *Adj.* tasty; full-flavoured ⟨beer,
wine⟩; aromatic ⟨fragrance⟩; tangy ⟨air⟩
Würzigkeit *die;* ∼ ▶ WÜRZIG 1: tastiness;
full flavour; aromatic fragrance; tanginess
wusch *1. u. 3. Pers. Sg. Prät. v.* WASCHEN
wusste, *wußte *1. und 3. Pers. Sg. Prät.*
v. WISSEN
wüsste, *wüßte *1. und 3. Pers. Sg.*
Konjunktiv II v. WISSEN
wüst ① *Adj.* (a) (öde) desolate
  (b) (unordentlich) chaotic
  (c) (ungezügelt) wild; (unanständig) rude
  ② *adv.* (a) (unordentlich) chaotically
  (b) (ungezügelt) wildly
Wust *der;* ∼[e]s (abwertend) jumble; (fig.)
welter; **ein** ∼ **von Daten/Vorschriften** a mass
of data/regulations
Wüste *die;* ∼, ∼n desert
Wüsten·bildung *die* desertification
Wut *die;* ∼: rage; fury
wüten *itr. V.* (auch fig.) rage; (zerstören)
wreak havoc
wütend ① *Adj.* furious; angry ⟨voice, mob⟩
  ② *adv.* furiously; in a fury

Xx

x¹, X /ɪks/ *das;* ∼, ∼: x, X
x² *unbest. Zahlwort* (ugs.) umpteen (coll.)
x-Achse *die* (Math.) x-axis
X-Beine *Pl.* knock knees
x-beinig *Adj.* knock-kneed
x-beliebig *Adj.* (ugs.) **[irgend]ein** ∼**er/**
[irgend]eine ∼**e/[irgend]ein** ∼**es** any old
(coll. attrib.); **jeder** ∼**e Ort** any old place (coll.)

X-Chromosom *das* (Biol.) X-chromosome
x-fach ① *Vervielfältigungsz.* **die** ∼**e Menge**
(Math.) x times the amount; (ugs.) umpteen
times the amount (coll.)
  ② *adv.* (ugs.) ∼ **erprobt sein** ⟨tested etc.⟩
umpteen times (coll.)
x-mal *Adv.* (ugs.) umpteen times (coll.)
x-t... *Ordinalz.* (ugs.) umpteenth (coll.)
Xylophon *das;* ∼s, ∼e xylophone

---

*old spelling – see note on page x

Yy

y, Y /'ʏpsilɔn/ *das;* ~, ~: y, Y
y-Achse *die* (Math.) y-axis
Yacht ▸ JACHT

Y-Chromosom *das* (Biol.) Y-chromosome
Yoga ▸ JOGA
Ypsilon *das;* ~[s], ~s y, Y; (im griechischen Alphabet) upsilon

Zz

z, Z /tsɛt/ *das;* ~, ~: z, Z
Zack: auf ~ sein (ugs.: tüchtig sein) be on the ball (coll.) *or* one's toes; **jmdn. auf** ~ **bringen** (ugs.) knock sb. into shape (coll.)
Zacke *die;* ~, ~n point; peak; (einer Säge, eines Kamms) tooth; (einer Gabel, Harke) prong
Zacken *der;* ~s: ▸ ZACKE
zackig ① *Adj.* **(a)** (gezackt) jagged; (mit kleinen, regelmäßigen Zacken) serrated **(b)** (schneidig) dashing; smart; rousing ⟨*music*⟩; brisk ⟨*orders, tempo*⟩; lively ⟨*organization*⟩
② *adv.* **(a)** (gezackt) jaggedly **(b)** (schneidig) smartly; ⟨*play music*⟩ rousingly
zaghaft ① *Adj.* timid; (zögernd) hesitant ② *adv.* timidly; (zögernd) hesitantly
Zaghaftigkeit *die;* ~: timidity; (Zögern) hesitancy
zäh ① *Adj.* **(a)** tough; heavy ⟨*dough, soil*⟩; (dickflüssig) glutinous; viscous ⟨*oil*⟩ **(b)** (widerstandsfähig) tough ⟨*person*⟩ **(c)** (beharrlich) tenacious; tough ⟨*negotiations*⟩; dogged ⟨*resistance*⟩ ② *adv.* **(b)** (beharrlich) tenaciously; ⟨*resist*⟩ doggedly
Zähheit *die;* ~: **(a)** (Festigkeit) toughness; (des Teigs, Bodens) heaviness; (Dickflüssigkeit) glutinousness; (von Öl) viscosity **(b)** (Widerstandsfähigkeit) toughness **(c)** (Beharrlichkeit) tenacity; (des Widerstands) doggedness
Zähigkeit *die;* ~ **(a)** (Widerstandsfähigkeit) toughness **(b)** (Beharrlichkeit) tenacity; **mit** ~: tenaciously
Zahl *die;* ~, ~en number; (Ziffer) numeral; (Zahlenangabe, Geldmenge) figure; **in den roten/schwarzen** ~en in the red/black
zahlbar *Adj.* (Kaufmannsspr.) payable
zahlen ① *tr. V.* pay (an + *Akk.* to) ② *itr. V.* pay; **[ich möchte]** bitte ~ (im Lokal) [can I have] the bill, please!
zählen ① *itr. V.* **(a)** count; **zu einer Gruppe** *usw.* ~: be one of *or* belong to a group *etc.* **(b)** auf jmdn./etw. ~: count on sb./sth ② *tr. V.* count; **jmdn. zu seinen Freunden** ~: count sb. among one's friends
zahl-, Zahl-: ~**karte** *die* (Postw.) paying-in slip; ~**los** *Adj.* countless; ~**reich** *Adj.* numerous
Zahlung *die;* ~, ~en payment
Zählung *die;* ~, ~en counting; **eine** ~: a count
zahlungs-, Zahlungs-: ~**bilanz** *die* (Wirtsch.) balance of payments; ~**fähig** *Adj.* solvent; ~**fähigkeit** *die* solvency; ~**mittel** *das* means of payment; ~**unfähig** *Adj.* insolvent; ~**unfähigkeit** *die* insolvency
Zahl·wort *das; Pl.* **Zahl·wörter** (Sprachw.) numeral
zahm ① *Adj.* tame ② *adv.* tamely
zähmen *tr. V.* (auch fig.) tame
Zahn *der;* ~[e]s, **Zähne** tooth; (Reißzahn) fang; (an einer Briefmarke usw.) serration
Zahn-: ~**arzt** *der,* ~**ärztin** *die* dentist; (mit chirurgischer Ausbildung) dental surgeon; ~**bürste** *die* toothbrush
zahnen *itr. V.* ⟨*baby*⟩ be teething
zahn-, Zahn-: ~**ersatz** *der* denture; ~**fleisch** *das* gum; (als Ganzes) gums *pl.;* ~**fleisch·bluten** *das;* ~~s bleeding gums *pl.;* ~**los** *Adj.* toothless; ~**lücke** *die* gap in one's teeth; ~**pasta** *die;* ~~, ~**pasten** toothpaste; ~**pflege** *die* dental care; ~**prothese** *die* dentures *pl.;* [set *sing.* of] false teeth *pl.;* ~**rad** *das* gearwheel; (für Ketten) sprocket; ~**schmerzen** *Pl.* toothache *sing.;* ~**seide** *die* dental floss; ~**spange** *die* [tooth] brace; ~**stein** *der* tartar; ~**stocher** *der;* ~~s, ~~: toothpick; ~**weh** *das* (ugs.) toothache
Zange *die;* ~, ~n **(a)** (Werkzeug) pliers *pl.;* (Eiswürfel-, Zuckerzange) tongs *pl.;* ⋯⋗

(Geburtszange) forceps *pl.;* (Kneifzange) pincers *pl.;* **eine** ∼: a pair of pliers/tongs/forceps/pincers
(b) (bei Tieren) pincer

Zank *der;* ∼[e]s squabble; row

zanken *refl. (auch itr.) V.* squabble, bicker (**um** *od.* **über** + *Akk.* over)

zänkisch *Adj.* quarrelsome

Zäpfchen *das;* ∼s, ∼: suppository

zapfen *tr. V.* tap, draw ⟨*beer, wine*⟩

Zapfen *der;* ∼s, ∼ **(a)** (Bot.) cone
(b) (Stöpsel) bung

Zapf·säule *die* petrol pump (Brit.); gasoline pump (Amer.)

zappeln *itr. V.* wriggle; ⟨*child*⟩ fidget

zappen /'zɛpn̩/ *itr. V.* (ugs.) zap (coll.)

Zar *der;* ∼en, ∼en (hist.) Tsar

Zarin *die;* ∼, ∼nen (hist.) Tsarina

zart ⌐1⌐ *Adj.* (auch fig.) delicate; soft ⟨*skin*⟩; tender ⟨*bud, shoot; meat, vegetables*⟩; fine ⟨*biscuits*⟩; gentle ⟨*kiss, touch*⟩; soft ⟨*pastel colours*⟩
⌐2⌐ *adv.* (empfindlich) delicately; ⟨*kiss, touch*⟩ gently

Zartheit *die;* ∼: delicacy; (der Haut) softness; (von Fleisch, Gemüse) tenderness; (eines Kusses, einer Berührung) gentleness

zärtlich ⌐1⌐ *Adj.* tender
⌐2⌐ *adv.* tenderly

Zärtlichkeit *die;* ∼, ∼en **(a)** (Zuneigung) tenderness; affection
(b) (Liebkosung) caress

Zauber *der;* ∼s, ∼ **(a)** (auch fig.) magic; (Bann) [magic] spell
(b) (ugs. abwertend: Aufheben) fuss

Zauberei *die;* ∼, ∼en **(a)** (das Zaubern) magic
(b) (Zaubertrick) magic trick

Zauberer *der;* ∼s, ∼: magician

zauber·haft ⌐1⌐ *Adj.* enchanting
⌐2⌐ *adv.* enchantingly

Zauberin *die;* ∼, ∼nen **(a)** sorceress
(b) (Zauberkünstlerin) conjurer

Zauber·künstler *der,*
Zauberkünstlerin *die* conjurer; magician

zaubern ⌐1⌐ *itr. V.* **(a)** do magic
(b) (Zaubertricks ausführen) do conjuring tricks
⌐2⌐ *tr. V.* (auch fig.) conjure

zaudern *itr. V.* (geh.) delay

Zaum *der;* ∼[e]s, Zäume bridle

zäumen *tr. V.* bridle

Zaum·zeug *das* bridle

Zaun *der;* ∼[e]s, Zäune fence

Zaun·könig *der* wren

z. B. *Abk.* = **zum Beispiel** e.g.

ZDF *das;* ∼: *Abk.* = **Zweites Deutsches Fernsehen** Second

German Television Channel

Zebra *das;* ∼s, ∼s zebra

Zebra·streifen *der* zebra crossing (Brit.); pedestrian crossing

Zeche *die;* ∼, ∼n **(a)** (Rechnung) bill (Brit.); check (Amer.)
(b) (Bergwerk) pit; mine

zechen *itr. V.* (veralt., scherzh.) tipple

Zecke *die;* ∼, ∼n (Zool.) tick

Zeder *die;* ∼, ∼n cedar

Zedern·holz *das* cedarwood

Zeh *der;* ∼s, ∼en, **Zehe** *die;* ∼, ∼n **(a)** toe
(b) (Knoblauchzehe) clove

Zehen·spitze *die:* auf ∼n on tiptoe

zehn *Kardinalz.* ten

Zehn *die;* ∼, ∼en ten

Zehn·cent·stück *das* ten-cent piece

Zehner *der;* ∼s, ∼ **(a)** (ugs.: Geldschein, Münze) ten
(b) (ugs.: Autobus) number ten
(c) (Math.) ten

Zehn·euro·schein *der* ten-euro note

zehn·fach *Vervielfältigungsz.* tenfold

Zehnfache *das; adj. Dekl.* **das** ∼: ten times as much

zehn-, Zehn-: ∼**kampf** *der* (Sport) decathlon; ∼**mal** *Adv.* ten times

zehnt... *Ordinalz.* tenth;

zehn·tausend *Kardinalz.* ten thousand

zehntel *Bruchz.* tenth

Zehntel *das* (schweiz. meist *der*); ∼s, ∼: tenth

zehntens *Adv.* tenthly

zehren *itr. V.* von etw. ∼: live on *or* off sth.

Zeichen *das;* ∼s, ∼: sign; (Markierung) mark; (Chemie, Math., auf Landkarten usw.) symbol; (Schrift∼) character; **jmdm. ein** ∼ **geben** signal to sb.

Zeichen-: ∼**setzung** *die;*
∼∼: punctuation; ∼**sprache** *die* sign language

zeichnen ⌐1⌐ *tr. V.* draw; (fig.) portray ⟨*character*⟩
⌐2⌐ *itr. V.* draw

Zeichner *der;* ∼s, ∼, **Zeichnerin** *die;* ∼, ∼nen graphic artist; (Technik) draughtsman/-woman

Zeichnung *die;* ∼, ∼en drawing

zeichnungs·berechtigt *Adj.* with signatory powers *postpos.;* ∼ **sein** have signatory powers

Zeige·finger *der* index finger; forefinger

zeigen ⌐1⌐ *itr. V.* point
⌐2⌐ *tr. V.* show
⌐3⌐ *refl. V.* **(a)** (sich sehen lassen) appear
(b) (sich erweisen) prove to be; **es wird sich** ∼, ...: time will tell ...

Zeiger *der;* ∼s, ∼: pointer; (Uhrzeiger) hand

Zeile *die;* ∼, ∼n line; (Reihe) row

zeit *Präp. mit Gen.* ∼ **meines** *usw.*/**unseres** *usw.* **Lebens** all my *etc.* life/our *etc.* lives

---

*alte Schreibung – vgl. Hinweis auf S. x

Zeit *die;* ~, ~en **(a)** time *no art.;* **mit der** ~: with *or* in time; (allmählich) gradually; **eine** ~ **lang** for a while **(b)** (Zeitpunkt) time; **alles zu seiner** ~: all in good time; ***zur** ~: at the moment **(c)** (Zeit-, Lebensabschnitt) time; period; (Geschichtsabschnitt) age; period **(d)** (Sprachw.) tense

zeit-, Zeit-: ~**alter** *das* age; era; ~**arbeit** *die* (Wirtsch.) temporary work; work as a temp (coll.); ~**druck** *der* pressure of time; **unter** ~**druck** under pressure; **unter** ~**druck stehen** be pressed for time; ~**geist** *der* spirit of the age; ~**gemäß** *Adj.* (modern) up-to-date; (aktuell) topical ⟨*theme*⟩; contemporary ⟨*views*⟩; ~**genosse** *der,* ~**genossin** *die* contemporary; ~**genössisch** *Adj.* contemporary; ~**geschehen** *das:* **das [aktuelle]** ~**geschehen** current events *pl.;* ~**geschichte** *die* contemporary history *no art.*

zeitig *Adj., adv.* early

zeit-, Zeit-: ~**karte** *die* (Verkehrsw.) season ticket; *~**lang** ▸ ZEIT A; ~**lebens** *Adv.* all my/his/her *etc.* life

zeitlich ① *Adj.* ⟨*length, interval*⟩ in time; chronological ⟨*order, sequence*⟩ ② *adv.* with regard to time

zeit-, Zeit-: ~**los** ① *Adj.* timeless; classic ⟨*fashion, shape*⟩; ② *adv.* timelessly; ~**lupe** *die* slow motion; ~**mangel** *der* lack of time; ~**punkt** *der* moment; ~**raubend** *Adj.* time-consuming; ~**raum** *der* period; ~**schrift** *die* magazine; (bes. wissenschaftlich) journal; periodical; ~**spanne** *die* period

Zeitung *die;* ~, ~en [news]paper

Zeitungs-: ~**ausschnitt** *der* newspaper cutting; ~**bericht** *der* newspaper report; ~**notiz** *die* newspaper item

zeit-, Zeit-: ~**unterschied** *der* time difference; ~**verschwendung** *die* waste of time; ~**vertreib** *der;* ~~**[e]s,** ~~**e** pastime; **zum** ~**vertreib** to pass the time; ~**weilig** ① *Adj.* temporary; ② *adv.* temporarily; ~**weise** *Adv.* (gelegentlich) occasionally; (von Zeit zu Zeit) from time to time; ~**wort** *das; Pl.* ~**wörter** (Sprachw.) verb; ~**zünder** *der* time fuse

Zelle *die;* ~, ~n cell

Zelluloid /tsɛlu'lɔyt/ *das;* ~**[e]s** celluloid

Zelt *das;* ~**[e]s,** ~**e** tent; (Festzelt) marquee; (Zirkuszelt) big top

zelten *itr. V.* camp

Zelt-: ~**lager** *das* camp; ~**plane** *die* tarpaulin

Zement *der;* ~**[e]s,** ~**e** cement

Zensur *die;* ~, ~en **(a)** (Schulw.: Note) mark; grade (Amer.) **(b)** (Kontrolle) censorship **(c)** (Behörde) censors *pl.*

Zenti-: ~**meter** *der, auch: das* centimetre; ~**meter·maß** *das* [centimetre] measuring tape

Zentner *der;* ~**s,** ~ **(a)** metric hundredweight **(b)** (österr., schweiz.) ▸ DOPPELZENTNER

zentral ① *Adj.* central ② *adv.* centrally

Zentral·bank *die; Pl.* ~**en** (Finanzw.) central bank

Zentrale *die;* ~, ~**n (a)** (zentrale Stelle) head *or* central office; (der Polizei, einer Partei) headquarters *sing. or pl.;* (Funkzentrale) control centre **(b)** (Telefonzentrale) [telephone] exchange; (eines Hotels, einer Firma o. Ä.) switchboard

Zentral-: ~**figur** *die* central figure; ~**heizung** *die* central heating; ~**speicher** *der* (DV) main memory

Zentren ▸ ZENTRUM

Zentrifugal·kraft *die* (Physik) centrifugal force

Zentrifuge *die;* ~, ~**n** centrifuge

Zentrum *das;* ~**s,** Zentren centre; **im** ~: at the centre; (im Stadtzentrum) in the town/city centre

Zeppelin *der;* ~**s,** ~**e** Zeppelin

Zepter *das, auch: der;* ~**s,** ~: sceptre

zerbeißen *unr. tr. V.* bite in two

zerbersten *unr. itr. V.; mit sein* burst apart

zerbrechen ① *unr. itr. V.; mit sein* break [into pieces]; smash [to pieces]; ⟨*glass*⟩ shatter; (fig.) ⟨*marriage, relationship*⟩ break up ② *unr. tr. V.* break; smash, shatter ⟨*dishes, glass*⟩

zerbrechlich *Adj.* fragile; (fig.) frail

Zerbrechlichkeit *die;* ~: fragility; (fig.) frailty

zerbröckeln ① *itr. V.; mit sein* crumble away ② *tr. V.* break into small pieces

zerdrücken *tr. V.* mash

Zeremonie *die;* ~, ~**n** ceremony; (fig.) ritual

Zeremoniell *das;* ~**s,** ~**e** ceremonial

zerfallen *unr. itr. V.; mit sein* (auch fig.) disintegrate (in + *Akk.,* **zu** into); ⟨*building*⟩ fall into ruin, decay; ⟨*corpse*⟩ decompose, decay

zerfetzen *tr. V.* rip *or* tear to pieces; (fig.) tear apart ⟨*body, limb*⟩

zerfleischen *tr. V.* tear ⟨*person, animal*⟩ limb from limb

zerfressen *unr. tr. V.* **(a)** eat away; ⟨*moth etc.*⟩ eat holes in **(b)** (zersetzen) corrode ⟨*metal*⟩; eat away ⟨*bone*⟩

zergehen *unr. itr. V.; mit sein* melt; (in Wasser, im Mund) ⟨*tablet etc.*⟩ dissolve

zerhacken *tr. V.* chop up (**zu** into)

Z

zerhauen *unr. tr. V.* chop up
zerkleinern *tr. V.* chop up; (zermahlen) crush ⟨*rock etc.*⟩
zerknautschen *tr. V.* (ugs.) crumple
zerknirscht ① *Adj.* remorseful
② *adv.* remorsefully
zerknittern *tr. V.* crease; crumple
zerknüllen *tr. V.* crumple up [into a ball]
zerkratzen *tr. V.* scratch
zerkrümeln *tr. V.* crumble up
zerlegen *tr. V.* (a) dismantle; take to pieces (b) (zerschneiden) cut up ⟨*animal, meat*⟩; carve ⟨*joint*⟩
zerlumpt *Adj.* ragged ⟨*clothes, person*⟩
zerplatzen *itr. V.; mit sein* burst
Zerr·bild *das* distorted image
zerreiben *unr. tr. V.* crush
zerreißen ① *unr. tr. V.* (a) tear up; (in kleine Stücke) tear to pieces; break ⟨*thread*⟩ (b) (beschädigen) tear ⟨*stocking, trousers, etc.*⟩ (an + *Dat.* on)
② *unr. itr. V.; mit sein* ⟨*thread, string, rope*⟩ break; ⟨*paper, cloth, etc.*⟩ tear
Zerreiß·probe *die* acid test
zerren ① *tr. V.* (a) drag (b) sich ⟨*Dat.*⟩ einen Muskel/eine Sehne ∼: pull a muscle/tendon
② *itr. V.* an etw. ⟨*Dat.*⟩ ∼: tug *or* pull at sth.
Zerrung *die; ∼, ∼en* pulled muscle/tendon
zerrütten *tr. V.* ruin; shatter ⟨*nerves*⟩
zerschellen *itr. V.; mit sein* be dashed *or* smashed to pieces
zerschlagen ① *unr. tr. V.* smash ⟨*plate, windscreen, etc.*⟩; smash up ⟨*furniture*⟩; (fig.) smash ⟨*spy ring etc.*⟩
② *unr. refl. V.* ⟨*plan, deal*⟩ fall through
zerschmettern *tr. V.* smash; shatter ⟨*glass, leg, bone*⟩
zerschneiden *unr. tr. V.* cut; (in Stücke) cut up; (in zwei Teile) cut in two
zersetzen *tr. V.* corrode ⟨*metal*⟩; decompose ⟨*organism*⟩
zersplittern *itr. V.; mit sein* ⟨*wood, bone*⟩ splinter; ⟨*glass*⟩ shatter
zerspringen *unr. itr. V.; mit sein* shatter; (Sprünge bekommen) crack
zerstäuben *tr. V.* spray
zerstören *tr. V.* destroy; ⟨*hooligan*⟩ smash up, vandalize; (fig.) ruin ⟨*health, life*⟩
Zerstörung *die; ∼, ∼en* ▶ ZERSTÖREN: destruction; smashing up; vandalization; (fig.) ruin[ation]
Zerstörungs·wut *die* destructive frenzy
zerstreuen ① *tr. V.* scatter; disperse ⟨*crowd*⟩; jmdn./sich ∼ (ablenken) take sb.'s/one's mind off things
② *refl. V.* disperse; (schneller) scatter
zerstreut ① *Adj.* distracted; (vergesslich) absent-minded

② *adv.* absentmindedly
Zerstreuung *die; ∼, ∼en* (Ablenkung) diversion
zerstückeln *tr. V.* break ⟨*sth.*⟩ up into small pieces; (zerschneiden) cut *or* chop ⟨*sth.*⟩ up into small pieces; dismember ⟨*corpse*⟩
zerteilen *tr. V.* divide into pieces; (zerschneiden) cut into pieces; cut up
Zertifikat *das; ∼[e]s, ∼e* certificate
zertrampeln *tr. V.* trample all over ⟨*flower bed etc.*⟩; trample ⟨*child etc.*⟩ underfoot
zertreten *unr. tr. V.* stamp on; stamp out ⟨*cigarette, match*⟩
zertrümmern *tr. V.* smash; smash, shatter ⟨*glass*⟩; smash up ⟨*furniture*⟩; wreck ⟨*car, boat*⟩; reduce ⟨*building*⟩ to ruins
Zerwürfnis *das; ∼ses, ∼se* (geh.) quarrel; dispute; (Bruch) rift
zerzausen *tr. V.* ruffle; zerzaust aussehen look dishevelled
zetern *itr. V.* scold [shrilly]; (sich beklagen) moan (über + *Akk.* about)
Zettel *der; ∼s, ∼:* slip *or* piece of paper; (mit einigen Zeilen) note; (Bekanntmachung) notice; (Formular) form; (Kassenzettel) receipt; (Handzettel) leaflet
Zeug *das; ∼[e]s, ∼e* (a) (ugs.) stuff; dummes ∼: nonsense; rubbish (b) (Kleidung) things *pl.*
Zeuge *der; ∼n, ∼n* witness
zeugen *tr. V.* procreate; ⟨*man*⟩ father ⟨*child*⟩
Zeugen·aussage *die* testimony
Zeugin *die; ∼, ∼nen* witness
Zeugnis *das; ∼ses, ∼se* (a) (Schulw.) report (b) (Arbeitszeugnis) reference; testimonial (c) (Gutachten) certificate
Zeugung *die; ∼, ∼en* procreation; (eines Kindes) fathering
zeugungs·fähig *Adj.* fertile
z.Hd. *Abk.* = **zu Händen** attn.
Zicke *die; ∼, ∼n* (a) ▶ ZIEGE (b) *Pl.* (ugs.: Dummheiten) stupid tricks; monkey business *sing.* (coll.); ∼n machen mess about; (Schwierigkeiten machen) make trouble
Zickzack *der; ∼[e]s, ∼e* zigzag
Ziege *die; ∼, ∼n* goat; (Schimpfwort: Frau) cow (sl. derog.)
Ziegel *der; ∼s, ∼* brick; (Dachziegel) tile
Ziegelei *die; ∼, ∼en* brickworks *sing.*
Ziegel·stein *der* brick
Ziegen-: ∼**bock** *der* he- *or* billy goat; ∼**käse** *der* goat's cheese
ziehen ① *unr. tr. V.* (a) pull; (sanfter) draw; (zerren) tug; (schleppen) drag; etw. nach sich ∼ (fig.) result in sth.; entail sth. (b) (herausziehen) extract ⟨*tooth*⟩; take out, remove ⟨*stitches*⟩; draw ⟨*cord, sword, pistol*⟩; den Hut ∼: raise one's hat; die

[Quadrat]wurzel ~ (Math.) extract the square root

(c) (dehnen) stretch ⟨*elastic etc.*⟩; stretch out ⟨*sheets etc.*⟩

(d) (Gesichtspartien bewegen) make ⟨*face, grimace*⟩

(e) (bei Brettspielen) move ⟨*chessman etc.*⟩

(f) (zeichnen) draw ⟨*line etc.*⟩

(g) (anlegen) dig ⟨*trench*⟩; build ⟨*wall*⟩; erect ⟨*fence*⟩; put up ⟨*washing line*⟩; run, lay ⟨*cable, wires*⟩; draw ⟨*frontier*⟩

(h) (aufziehen) grow ⟨*plants, flowers*⟩; breed ⟨*animals*⟩

2 *unr. itr. V.* **(a)** (reißen) pull; **an etw.** (*Dat.*) ~: pull on sth.

(b) (funktionieren) ⟨*stove, pipe, chimney*⟩ draw

(c) *mit sein* (umziehen) move (**nach, in** + *Akk.* to)

(d) *mit sein* (gehen) go; (marschieren) march; (umherstreifen) roam; (weggehen) go away; leave; ⟨*fog, clouds*⟩ drift

(e) (saugen) draw; **an einer Zigarette/Pfeife** ~: draw on a cigarette/pipe

(f) ⟨*tea, coffee*⟩ draw

(g) (Kochk.) simmer

(h) *unpers.* **es zieht** there's a draught

3 *unr. refl. V.* ⟨*road*⟩ run, stretch; ⟨*frontier*⟩ run

Zieh·harmonika *die* piano accordion

Ziehung *die;* ~, ~en draw

Ziel *das;* ~[e]s, ~e **(a)** destination

(b) (Sport) finish; (Ziellinie) finishing line; (Pferderennen) finishing post

(c) (Zielscheibe; auch Milit.) target

(d) (Zweck) aim; goal; **sein** ~ **erreichen** achieve one's objective *or* aim

ziel·bewusst, *ziel·bewußt 1 *Adj.* determined

2 *adv.* determinedly

zielen *itr. V.* aim (**auf** + *Akk.*, at); (fig.) **auf jmdn./etw.** ~ ⟨*reproach, efforts, etc.*⟩ be aimed at sb./sth.

ziel-, Ziel-: ~**gruppe** *die* target group; ~**los** 1 *Adj.* aimless; 2 *adv.* aimlessly; ~**losigkeit** *die;* ~~: aimlessness; ~**scheibe** *die* (auch fig.) target (*Gen.* for); ~**strebig** 1 *Adj.* **(a)** purposeful; **(b)** (energisch) single-minded ⟨*person*⟩; 2 *adv.* **(a)** purposefully; **(b)** (energisch) single-mindedly; ~**strebigkeit** *die;* ~~ ▸ ~STREBIG: **(a)** purposefulness; **(b)** single-mindedness; ~**wahl** *die* (Fernspr.) one-touch dialling

ziemlich 1 *Adj.* (ugs.) fair, sizeable ⟨*quantity, number*⟩

2 *adv.* **(a)** quite; fairly

(b) (ugs.: fast) pretty well

Zierde *die;* ~, ~n (auch fig.) ornament

zieren *refl. V.* be coy

zierlich 1 *Adj.* dainty; petite, dainty ⟨*woman, figure*⟩

2 *adv.* daintily

Zierlichkeit *die;* ~: daintiness; (einer Frau, Gestalt) petiteness; daintiness

Zier·pflanze *die* ornamental plant

Ziffer *die;* ~, ~n numeral; (in einer mehrstelligen Zahl) digit; figure

Ziffer·blatt *das* dial; face

zig *unbest. Zahlwort* (ugs.) umpteen (coll.)

Zigarette *die;* ~, ~n cigarette

Zigaretten·werbung *die* cigarette advertising

Zigarillo *der od. das;* ~s, ~s cigarillo; small cigar

Zigarre *die;* ~, ~n cigar

Zigeuner *der;* ~s, ~, **Zigeunerin** *die;* ~, ~nen gypsy

zig·mal *Adv.* (ugs.) umpteen times (coll.)

zig·tausend *unbest. Zahlwort* (ugs.) umpteen thousand (coll.)

Zimmer *das;* ~s, ~: room

Zimmer·mädchen *das* chambermaid

zimmern *tr. V.* make ⟨*shelves etc.*⟩

Zimmer-: ~**suche** *die* room-hunt; ~**vermittlung** *die* accommodation office

zimperlich 1 *Adj.* timid; (leicht angeekelt) squeamish; (prüde) prissy

2 *adv.: s. Adj.:* timidly; squeamishly; prissily

Zimperlichkeit *die;* ~, ~en (abwertend) timidity; (Neigung zum Ekel) squeamishness; (Prüderie) prissiness

Zimt *der;* ~[e]s, ~e cinnamon

Zink *das;* ~[e]s zinc

Zinke *die;* ~, ~n prong; (eines Kamms) tooth

Zinn *das;* ~[e]s tin; (Gegenstände) pewter[ware]

Zins *der;* ~es, ~en interest

Zinses·zins *der* compound interest

zins·los 1 *Adj.* interest-free

2 *adv.* free of interest

Zins·satz *der* interest rate

Zipfel *der;* ~s, ~ (einer Decke, eines Tisch-, Handtuchs usw.) corner; (Wurstzipfel, eines Halstuchs) [tail] end

Zipfel·mütze *die* [long-]pointed cap

zirka *Adv.* about; approximately

Zirkulation *die,* ~, ~en circulation

zirkulieren *itr. V.; auch mit sein* circulate

Zirkus *der;* ~, ~se **(a)** circus

(b) (ugs.) (Trubel) hustle and bustle; (Krach) to-do

zirpen *itr. V.* chirp

zischeln *tr. V.* whisper angrily

zischen *itr. V.* **(a)** hiss; ⟨*hot fat*⟩ sizzle

(b) *mit sein* hiss

Zitat *das;* ~[e]s, ~e quotation (**aus** from)

zitieren *tr., itr. V.* **(a)** quote; (Rechtsspr.) cite

(b) (rufen) summon

Zitronat *das;* ~[e]s candied lemon peel

Zitrone *die;* ~, ~n lemon

Zitronen-: ~**limonade** *die* lemonade; ~**presse** *die* lemon squeezer; ~**saft** *der* lemon juice

Z

Zitrus·frucht die citrus fruit
zittern itr. V. tremble (**vor** + Dat. with); (vor Kälte) shiver; (beben) ⟨walls, windows⟩ shake; **vor jmdm./etw. ~:** be terrified of sb./sth.
Zitter·partie die nail-biting affair
zittrig Adj. shaky; doddery ⟨old man⟩
Zitze die; ~, ~n teat
zivil 1 Adj. (a) civilian; non-military ⟨purposes⟩; civil ⟨aviation, marriage, law, defence⟩
(b) (annehmbar) decent
2 adv. (annehmbar) decently
Zivil das; ~s civilian clothes pl.
Zivil·bevölkerung die civilian population
Zivilisation /tsiviliza'tsi̯o:n/ die; ~, ~en civilization
zivilisieren tr. V. civilize
zivilisiert 1 Adj. civilized
2 adv. in a civilized way
Zivilist der; ~en, ~en, **Zivilistin** die; ~, ~nen civilian
Zivil·kleidung die civilian clothes pl.
Zofe die; ~, ~n (hist.) lady's maid
zoffen refl. V. (ugs.) quarrel (**mit** with)
zog 1. u. 3. Pers. Sg. Prät. v. ZIEHEN
zögerlich 1 Adj. hesitant; tentative
2 adv. hesitantly; tentatively
zögern itr. V. hesitate; **ohne zu ~:** without hesitation
Zoll der; ~[e]s, Zölle (a) [customs] duty
(b) (Behörde) customs pl.
zoll-, Zoll-: ~**amt** das customs house or office; ~**beamte** der, ~**beamtin** die customs officer; ~**erklärung** die customs declaration; ~**frei** 1 Adj. duty-free; free of duty pred.; 2 adv. free of duty; ~**kontrolle** die customs examination or check; ~**stock** der folding rule
Zone die; ~, ~n zone
Zoo der; ~s, ~s zoo
Zoologe der; ~n, ~n zoologist
Zoologie die; ~: zoology no art.
Zoologin die; ~, ~nen zoologist
zoologisch Adj. zoological; ~**er Garten** zoological gardens pl.
Zoom das; ~s, ~s (Film, Fot.) zoom
Zoom-objektiv das (Film, Fot.) zoom lens
Zopf der; ~[e]s, Zöpfe plait; (am Hinterkopf) pigtail
Zorn der; ~[e]s anger; (stärker) wrath; fury
zornig 1 Adj. furious
2 adv. furiously
Zote die; ~, ~n dirty joke
zotig 1 Adj. smutty; dirty ⟨joke⟩
2 adv. smuttily
zottig Adj. shaggy
zu 1 Präp. mit Dat. (a) (Richtung) to; **zu ... hin** towards ...

(b) (zusammen mit) with; **zu dem Käse gab es Wein** there was wine with the cheese
(c) (Lage) at; **zu beiden Seiten** on both sides
(d) (zeitlich) at; **zu Weihnachten** at Christmas
(e) (Art u. Weise) **zu meiner Zufriedenheit/ Überraschung** to my satisfaction/surprise; (bei Mengenangaben) **zu Dutzenden/zweien** by the dozen/in twos
(f) (ein Zahlenverhältnis ausdrückend) **ein Verhältnis von 3 zu 1** a ratio of 3 to 1
(g) (einen Preis zuordnend) at; for
(h) (Zweck) for
(i) (Ziel, Ergebnis) into; **zu etw. werden** turn into sth.
(j) (über) about; on; **sich zu etw. äußern** comment on sth.
(k) (gegenüber) **freundlich/hässlich zu jmdm. sein** be friendly/nasty to sb.; s. auch ZUM; ZUR
2 Adv. (a) (allzu) too; **zu sehr/viel** too much; **zu wenig** too little
(b) nachgestellt (Richtung) towards
3 Konj. (a) mit Infinitiv to; **was gibts da zu lachen?** what is there to laugh about?
(b) mit 1. Part. **die zu erledigende Post** the letters pl. to be dealt with
Zubehör das; ~[e]s, ~e od. schweiz. ~den accessories pl.; (eines Staubsaugers, Mixers usw.) attachments pl.; (Ausstattung) equipment
zu|bereiten tr. V. prepare ⟨meal etc.⟩; make up ⟨medicine, ointment⟩; (kochen) cook ⟨fish, meat, etc.⟩
zu|billigen tr. V. jmdm. etw. ~: grant or allow sb. sth.
zu|binden unr. tr. V. tie [up]
zu|blinzeln itr. V. jmdm. ~: wink at sb.
zu|bringen unr. tr. V. spend
Zu·bringer der; ~s, ~ (a) (Straße) access road
(b) (Verkehrsmittel) shuttle
Zucht die; ~, ~en (a) breeding; (von Pflanzen) cultivation; **ein Pferd aus deutscher ~:** a German-bred horse
(b) (geh.: Disziplin) discipline
züchten tr. V. (auch fig.) breed; cultivate ⟨plants⟩; culture ⟨bacteria, pearls⟩
Züchter der; ~s, ~, **Züchterin** die; ~, ~nen breeder; (von Pflanzen) grower [of new varieties]
züchtigen tr. V. (geh.) beat; thrash; (fig.: bestrafen) castigate
Züchtigung die; ~, ~en (geh.) beating; thrashing; (fig.: Bestrafung) castigation
Züchtung die; ~, ~en (a) breeding; (von Pflanzen) cultivation
(b) (Zuchtergebnis) strain
zucken itr. V.; mit Richtungsangabe mit sein twitch; ⟨body, arm, leg, etc.⟩ jerk; (vor Schreck) start; ⟨flames⟩ flicker; **mit den Achseln/Schultern ~:** shrug one's shoulders
zücken tr. V. draw ⟨sword, dagger, knife⟩
Zucker der; ~s, ~ (a) sugar
(b) (ugs.: Diabetes) diabetes; **~ haben** be a diabetic

---
*alte Schreibung – vgl. Hinweis auf S. x

Z

zucker-, Zucker-: ∼**dose** *die* sugar bowl; ∼**hut** *der* sugar loaf; ∼**krank** *Adj.* diabetic

zuckern *tr. V.* sugar

Zucker·wasser *das* sugar water

Zuckung *die;* ∼, ∼**en** twitch

zu|decken *tr. V.* cover up; cover [over] ⟨*well, ditch*⟩; **jmdn./sich** ∼: tuck sb./oneself up

zu|drehen *tr. V.* **(a)** (abdrehen) turn off **(b)** (zuwenden) **jmdm. den Rücken** ∼: turn one's back on sb.

zu·dringlich ⟨1⟩ *Adj.* pushy (coll.), pushing ⟨*person, manner*⟩; (sexuell) importunate ⟨*person, manner*⟩; prying ⟨*glance*⟩ ⟨2⟩ *adv.* importunately

Zu·dringlichkeit *die;* ∼, ∼**en** **(a)** pushiness (coll.); (in sexueller Hinsicht) importunate manner **(b)** (Handlung) ∼**en** insistent advances *or* attentions

zu|drücken *tr. V.* press shut; push ⟨*door*⟩ shut; **jmdm. die Kehle** ∼: choke *or* throttle sb.

zu·einander *Adv.* to one another

zu·erst *Adv.* **(a)** first **(b)** (anfangs) at first; to start with **(c)** (erstmals) first

Zu·fahrt *die* **(a)** access [for vehicles] **(b)** (Straße, Weg) access road; (zum Haus) driveway

Zufahrts·straße *die* access road

Zu·fall *der* chance; (zufälliges Zusammentreffen von Ereignissen) coincidence; **durch** ∼: by chance

zu|fallen *unr. itr. V.; mit sein* **(a)** ⟨*door etc.*⟩ slam shut; ⟨*eyes*⟩ close **(b)** (zukommen) **jmdm.** ∼ ⟨*task*⟩ fall to sb.; ⟨*prize, inheritance*⟩ go to sb.

zu·fällig ⟨1⟩ *Adj.* accidental; chance *attrib.* ⟨*meeting, acquaintance*⟩; random ⟨*selection*⟩ ⟨2⟩ *adv.* by chance; **wissen Sie** ∼, **wie spät es ist?** (ugs.) do you by any chance know the time?

Zufalls·treffer *der* fluke

zu|fassen *itr. V.* make a snatch *or* grab

zu|faxen *tr. V.* **jmdm. etw.** ∼: fax sth. to sb.; fax sb. sth.

zu|fliegen *unr. itr. V.; mit sein* (ugs.) ⟨*door, window, etc.*⟩ slam shut

Zu·flucht *die* refuge (**vor** + *Dat.* from); (vor Unwetter o. Ä.) shelter (**vor** + *Dat.* from)

Zufluchts·ort *der* place of refuge; sanctuary

Zu·fluss, *Zu·fluß *der* **(a)** (das Zufließen) inflow; supply; (fig.) influx **(b)** (Gewässer) feeder stream/river

zu|flüstern *tr. V.* **jmdm. etw.** ∼: whisper sth. to sb.

zu·folge *Präp. mit Dat.; nachgestellt* according to

zu·frieden ⟨1⟩ *Adj.* contented; (befriedigt)

satisfied; **mit etw.** ∼ **sein** be satisfied with sth.; **sich** ∼ **geben** be satisfied; **jmdn.** ∼ **stellen** satisfy sb. ⟨2⟩ *adv.* contentedly

*zufrieden|geben ▶ ZUFRIEDEN 1

Zufriedenheit *die;* ∼: contentment; (Befriedigung) satisfaction

*zufrieden|stellen ▶ ZUFRIEDEN 1

zufriedenstellend ⟨1⟩ *Adj.* satisfactory ⟨2⟩ *adv.* satisfactorily

zu|frieren *unr. itr. V.; mit sein* freeze over

zu|fügen *tr. V.* **jmdm. etw.** ∼: inflict sth. on sb.; **jmdm. Schaden/[ein] Unrecht** ∼: do sb. harm/an injustice

Zufuhr *die;* ∼: supply; (Material) supplies *pl.*

zu|führen ⟨1⟩ *itr. V.* **auf etw.** (*Akk.*) ∼: lead towards sth. ⟨2⟩ *tr. V.* **(a)** (zuleiten) **einer Sache** (*Dat.*) **etw.** ∼: supply sth. to sth. **(b)** (bringen) **einer Partei Mitglieder** ∼: bring new members to a party

Zug *der;* ∼**[e]s, Züge** **(a)** (Bahn) train **(b)** (Kolonne) column; (Umzug) procession; (Demonstrationszug) march **(c)** (das Ziehen) pull; traction (Phys.) **(d)** (Vorrichtung) pull **(e)** (Wanderung) migration **(f)** (beim Brettspiel) move **(g)** (Schluck) swig (coll.); mouthful; (großer Schluck) gulp; **das Glas auf einen** *od.* **in einem** ∼ **leeren** empty the glass at one go **(h)** (beim Rauchen) pull; drag (coll.) **(i)** (Atemzug) breath **(j)** (Zugluft; beim Ofen) draught **(k)** (Gesichtszug) feature; (Wesenszug) characteristic; trait

Zu·gabe *die* **(a)** (Geschenk) [free] gift **(b)** (im Konzert, Theater) encore

Zu·gang *der* **(a)** (Weg, auch fig.) access; (Eingang) entrance **(b)** (das Hinzukommen) (von Personen) intake; (von Patienten) admission **(c)** (Zuwachs) increase (**von** in)

zu·gange: ∼ **sein** (ugs.) be busy *or* occupied

zugänglich *Adj.* **(a)** accessible; (geöffnet) open **(b)** (zur Verfügung stehend) available (*Dat.,* **für** to); (verständlich) accessible (*Dat.,* **für** to) **(c)** (aufgeschlossen) approachable ⟨*person*⟩

zu|geben *unr. tr. V.* admit; admit to ⟨*deed, crime*⟩

zu·gegen *Adj.* ∼ **sein** be present

zu|gehen *unr. itr. V.; mit sein* **(a)** **auf jmdn./etw.** ∼: approach sb./sth. **(b)** **jmdm.** ∼ (zugeschickt werden) be sent to sb. **(c)** (ugs.: sich schließen) close; shut; **die Tür geht nicht zu** the door will not shut

zu·gehörig *Adj.* belonging to it/them *postpos., not pred.*

Zugehörigkeit *die;* ∼: belonging (**zu** to)

Zügel *der;* ~s, ~: rein
zügel·los (fig.) ① *Adj.* unrestrained;
unbridled ⟨*rage, passion*⟩
② *adv.* without restraint
Zügellosigkeit *die;* ~, ~en lack of
restraint; (Unzüchtigkeit) licentiousness
zügeln *tr. V.* rein [in] ⟨*horse*⟩; (fig.) curb,
restrain ⟨*desire etc.*⟩
zu|gesellen *refl. V.* sich jmdm./einer
Sache ~: join sb./sth.
Zu·geständnis *das* concession
zu|gestehen *unr. tr. V.* admit; concede
zu·getan *Adj.* jmdm. [herzlich] ~ sein
(geh.) be [very] attached to sb.
zugig *Adj.* draughty, (im Freien) windy
⟨*corner etc.*⟩
zügig ① *Adj.* speedy; rapid
② *adv.* speedily; rapidly
Zügigkeit *die;* ~: speediness; rapidity
zu·gleich *Adv.* at the same time
Zug-: ~**luft** *die* draught; ~**maschine**
die tractor; (von Sattelzug) tractor [unit]
zu|greifen *unr. itr. V.* (a) take hold
(b) (sich bedienen) help oneself
(c) (fleißig arbeiten) [hart *od.* kräftig]
~: [really] knuckle down to it
Zu·griff *der* (Zugang) access (auf + *Akk.* to)
zu·grunde *Adv.* (a) ~ gehen (sterben) die
(an + *Dat.* of); (zerstört werden) be destroyed
(an + *Dat.* by); ~ richten destroy; (finanziell)
ruin ⟨*company, person*⟩
(b) etw. einer Sache (*Dat.*) ~ legen base
sth. on sth.; etw. liegt einer Sache ~: sth. is
based on sth.
zu|gucken *itr. V.* (ugs.) ▶ ZUSEHEN
zu·gunsten ① *Präp. mit Gen.* in favour of
② *Adv.* ~ von in favour of
zu·gute *Adv.* jmdm. seine Unerfahrenheit
usw. ~ halten (geh.) make allowances for
sb.'s inexperience *etc.*; sich (*Dat.*) etwas/viel
auf etw. (*Akk.*) ~ tun *od.* halten (geh.) be
proud/very proud of sth.; jmdm./einer Sache
~ kommen stand sb./sth. in good stead
zu|haben *unr. itr. V.* (ugs.) ⟨*shop, office*⟩ be
shut *or* closed
zu|halten *unr. tr. V.* hold closed; (nicht
öffnen) keep closed
zu|hängen *tr. V.* cover ⟨*window, cage*⟩
zu|hauen (ugs.) ① *unr. itr. V.* bang *or* slam
⟨*door, window*⟩ shut
② *unr. itr. V.* hit *or* strike out
Zu·hause *das;* ~s home
Zuhilfenahme *die;* ~: utilization;
ohne/unter ~ einer Sache (*Gen.*)/von etw.
without/with the aid of sth.
zu|hören *itr. V.* jmdm./einer Sache
~: listen to sb./sth.
Zu·hörer *der,* **Zu·hörerin** *die* listener
zu|kleben *tr. V.* seal ⟨*letter, envelope*⟩
zu|knallen (ugs.) ① *tr. V.* slam

② *itr. V.; mit sein* slam
zu|knöpfen *tr. V.* button up
zu|kommen *itr. V.; mit sein* auf jmdn.
~: approach sb.
Zukunft *die;* ~: future
Zukunfts·technologie *die* technology
of the future
Zu·lage *die* extra pay *no indef. art.;*
additional allowance *no indef. art.*
zu|lassen *unr. tr. V.* (a) allow; permit
(b) (teilnehmen lassen) admit
(c) (mit einer Lizenz usw. versehen) jmdn. als
Arzt ~: register sb. as a doctor
(d) (Kfz-W.) register ⟨*vehicle*⟩
(e) (geschlossen lassen) leave closed *or* shut
⟨*door, window, etc.*⟩
zu·lässig *Adj.* permissible; admissible
⟨*appeal*⟩
Zulassung *die;* ~, ~en registration
Zu·lauf *der* ⟨viel⟩ ~ haben ⟨*shop,
restaurant, etc.*⟩ enjoy a large clientele;
⟨*doctor, lawyer*⟩ have a large practice
zu|laufen *unr. itr. V.; mit sein* (a) auf
jmdn./etw. ~ (auch fig.) run towards sb./sth.
(b) jmdm. ~ ⟨*cat, dog, etc.*⟩ adopt sb. as a
new owner
zu|legen *refl. V.* sich (*Dat.*) etw. ~: get
oneself sth.
zu·letzt *Adv.* (a) last [of all]
(b) (als letzter/letzte/letztes) last
(c) (fig.: am wenigsten) least of all
(d) (schließlich, am Ende) in the end; bis
~: [right up] to *or* until the end
zu·liebe *Adv.* jmdm./einer Sache ~: for
sb.'s sake/for the sake of sth.
Zulieferer *der;* ~s, ~, **Zulieferin** *die;*
~, ~nen supplier
zum *Präp.* + *Art.* (a) = zu dem;
(b) (räumlich: Richtung) to the
(c) (räumlich: Lage) etw. ~ Fenster
hinauswerfen throw sth. out of the window
(d) (Hinzufügung) Milch ~ Tee nehmen take
milk with [one's] tea
(e) (zeitlich) ~ 15. April; ~ spätestens ~ 15. April by
15 April at the latest
(f) (Zweck) ~ Spaß/Vergnügen for
fun/pleasure
(g) (Folge) ~ Ärger seines Vaters to the
annoyance of his father
zu|machen *tr. V.* close; fasten, do up
⟨*dress*⟩; seal ⟨*envelope, letter*⟩; turn off ⟨*tap*⟩;
put the top on ⟨*bottle*⟩; (stilllegen) close *or*
shut down ⟨*factory, mine, etc.*⟩
zu·mal ① *Adv.* especially; particularly
② *Konj.* especially *or* particularly since
zumindest *Adv.* at least
zu|müllen *tr. V.* (ugs.) etw. ~: bury sth.
under rubbish; mit etw. zugemüllt werden
be buried under sth.; von etw. zugemüllt
werden (fig.) be buried under sth.
zu·mute *Adj.* jmdm. ist unbehaglich *usw.*
~: sb. feels uncomfortable *etc.;* mir war nicht
danach ~: I didn't feel like it *or* in the mood

zu|muten *tr. V.* **jmdm. etw.** ~ (abverlangen) expect *or* ask sth. of sb.; (antun) expect sb. to put up with sth.

Zumutung *die;* ~, ~en unreasonable demand; **eine** ~ **sein** be unreasonable

zu·nächst *Adv.* **(a)** (als erstes) first; (anfangs) at first

(b) (im Moment, vorläufig) for the moment

Zunahme *die;* ~, ~n increase (*Gen.,* an + *Dat.* in)

Zu·name *der* surname; last name

zünden ① *tr. V.* ignite ⟨*gas, fuel, etc.*⟩; detonate ⟨*bomb, explosive device, etc.*⟩; let off ⟨*fireworks*⟩; fire ⟨*rocket*⟩

② *itr. V.* ⟨*rocket, engine*⟩ fire; ⟨*lighter, match*⟩ light; ⟨*gas, fuel, explosive*⟩ ignite

Zünd-: ~**holz** *das* (bes. südd., österr.) match; ~**schlüssel** *der* (Kfz-W.) ignition key

Zündung *die;* ~, ~en **(a)** ▶ ZÜNDEN 1: ignition; detonation; letting off; firing

(b) (Kfz-W.: Anlage) ignition

zu|nehmen *unr. itr. V.* **(a)** increase (an + *Dat.* in); ⟨*moon*⟩ wax

(b) (schwerer werden) put on *or* gain weight

Zu·neigung *die* affection

Zunge *die;* ~, ~n tongue; **[jmdm.] die** ~ **herausstrecken** put one's tongue out [at sb.]

Zungen·piercing *das* **(a)** tongue-piercing;

(b) (Schmuck) tongue stud

zu·nichte *Adj.* **etw.** ~ **machen** ruin sth.

zu·oberst *Adv.* [right] on [the] top

zu·pass, *zu·paß: **jmdm.** ~ **kommen** come [to sb.] at just the right time *or* moment

zupfen ① *itr. V.* **an etw.** (*Dat.*) ~: pluck *or* pull at sth.

② *tr. V.* **(a)** etw. aus/von *usw.* etw. ~: pull sth. out of/from *etc.* sth.

(b) (auszupfen) pull out; pluck ⟨*eyebrows*⟩

(c) pluck ⟨*string, guitar, tune*⟩

(d) jmdn. am Ärmel ~: pull *or* tug [at] sb.'s sleeve

zur *Präp.* + *Art.* **(a)** = zu der;

(b) (räumlich, fig.: Richtung) to the; ~ **Schule/ Arbeit gehen** go to school/work

(c) (räumlich: Lage) ~ **Tür hereinkommen** come [in] through the door

(d) (Zusammengehörigkeit, Hinzufügung) with the

(e) (zeitlich) at the; ~ **Stunde** at the moment; at present; ~ **Zeit** ▶ ZURZEIT

(f) (Zweck) ~ **Entschuldigung** by way of [an] excuse

(g) (Folge) ~ **vollen Zufriedenheit ihres Chefs** to the complete satisfaction of her boss

zurechnungs·fähig *Adj.* sound of mind *pred.*

zurecht-: ~|**finden** *unr. refl. V.* find one's way [around]; ~|**kommen** *unr. itr. V.; mit sein* get on (mit with); ~|**legen** *tr. V.* lay out [ready]; **jmdm. etw.** ~**legen** lay

sth. out ready for sb.; ~|**machen** *tr. V.* (ugs.) **(a)** (vorbereiten) get ready; **(b)** (herrichten) do up; **(c)** jmdn./sich ~**machen** get sb. ready/get [oneself] ready; (schminken) make sb. up/put on one's make-up; ~|**weisen** *unr. tr. V.* rebuke; reprimand ⟨*pupil, subordinate, etc.*⟩

zu|reden *itr. V.* **jmdm.** ~: persuade sb.; (ermutigen) encourage sb.

Zürich *(das);* ~s Zurich

zu·rück *Adv.* back; (weiter hinten) behind; **einen Schritt** ~: a step backwards; ~! get *or* go back!

zurück-, Zurück-: ~|**behalten** *unr. tr. V.* **(a)** keep [back]; retain; **(b)** be left with ⟨*scar, heart defect, etc.*⟩; ~|**bekommen** *unr. tr. V.* get back; **Sie bekommen 10 Euro** ~: you get 10 euros change; ~|**bleiben** *unr. itr. V.; mit sein* **(a)** remain; **(b)** (nicht mithalten) lag behind; (fig.) fall behind; **(c)** (bleiben) remain; ~|**blicken** *itr. V.* look back; ~|**erstatten** *tr. V.* refund; **jmdm. etw.** ~**erstatten** refund sth. to sb.; ~|**fahren** *unr. itr. V.; mit sein* **(a)** go back; return; **(b)** (nach hinten fahren) go back[wards]; ~|**fallen** *unr. itr. V.; mit sein* **(a)** (in Rückstand geraten) fall behind; **(b)** (auf einen niedrigeren Rang) drop (auf + *Akk.* to); **(c)** an jmdn. ~**fallen** ⟨*property*⟩ revert to sb.; **(d)** auf jmdn. ~**fallen** ⟨*actions, behaviour*⟩ reflect [up]on sb.; ~|**fliegen** *unr. itr. V.; mit sein* fly back; ~|**führen** *tr. V.* etw. auf etw. (*Akk.*) ~**führen** attribute sth. to sth.; ~|**geben** *unr. tr. V.* give back; return; take back ⟨*defective goods*⟩; ~|**gehen** *unr. itr. V.; mit sein* **(a)** go back; return; **(b)** (nach hinten) go back; **(c)** (verschwinden) disappear; ⟨*swelling, inflammation*⟩ go down; ⟨*pain*⟩ subside; **(d)** (sich verringern) decrease; ⟨*fever*⟩ abate; ⟨*flood*⟩ subside; ⟨*business*⟩ fall off; **(e)** (zurückgeschickt werden) be returned *or* sent back; ~|**greifen** *unr. itr. V.* auf jmdn./etw. ~**greifen** fall back on sb./sth.; ~|**halten** ① *unr. tr. V.* **(a)** jmdn. ~**halten** hold sb. back; (von etw. abhalten) stop sb.; **(b)** (am Vordringen hindern) keep back ⟨*crowd, mob, etc.*⟩; **(c)** (behalten) withhold ⟨*news, letter, etc.*⟩; **(d)** (nicht austreten lassen) hold back ⟨*tears etc.*⟩; ② *unr. refl. V.* restrain *or* control oneself; **sich in einer Diskussion** ~**halten** keep in the background in a discussion; ~|**haltend** ① *Adj.* **(a)** reserved; **(b)** (kühl, reserviert) cool, restrained ⟨*reception, response*⟩; **(c)** (Wirtsch.: schwach) slack ⟨*demand*⟩; ② *adv.* ⟨*behave*⟩ with reserve *or* restraint; (kühl, reserviert) coolly; ~|**haltung** *die* reserve; (Kühle, Reserviertheit) coolness; (Wirtsch.) caution; ~|**kehren** *itr. V.; mit sein* return; come back; ~|**kommen** *unr. itr. V.; mit sein* come back; return; (zurückgelangt) get back; ~**kommen auf** (+ *Akk.*) come back to ⟨*subject, question, point*⟩; **kriegen** *tr. V.* (ugs.) ▶ ~BEKOMMEN; ~|**lassen** *unr. tr. V.* leave; ~|**legen** *tr. V.* **(a)** put

Z

back; **(b)** (reservieren) put aside, keep ⟨*Dat.,*
für for⟩; **(c)** (sparen) put away; **(d)** (hinter sich
bringen) cover ⟨*distance*⟩; ~|**lehnen** *refl.*
V. lean back; ~|**nehmen** *unr. tr. V.* (auch
fig. widerrufen) take back; ~|**rufen** *unr.*
tr. V. **(a)** call back; recall ⟨*ambassador*⟩;
(b) *auch itr.* (telefonisch) call *or* (Brit.) ring
back; ~|**schauen** *itr. V.* (bes. südd., österr.,
schweiz.) ▶ ~BLICKEN; ~|**schicken** *tr. V.*
send back; ~|**schlagen** ① *unr. tr. V.*
(a) (nach hinten schlagen) fold back ⟨*cover,*
hood, etc.⟩; turn down ⟨*collar*⟩; **(b)** (durch
einen Schlag zurückbefördern) hit back; (mit dem
Fuß) kick back; **(c)** (zum Rückzug zwingen,
abwehren) beat off, repulse ⟨*enemy, attack*⟩;
② *unr. itr. V.* **(a)** hit back; ⟨*enemy*⟩ strike
back, retaliate; **(b)** *mit sein* ⟨*pendulum*⟩
swing back; ~|**schrecken** *regelm.,*
(veralt.) *unr. itr. V., mit sein vor etw.* (*Dat.*)
~**schrecken** (fig.) shrink from sth.; **er**
schreckt vor nichts ~: he will stop at
nothing; ~|**senden** *unr. od. regelm. tr. V.*
(geh.) ▶ ~SCHICKEN; ~|**treten** *unr. itr. V.;*
mit sein step back; (von einem Amt) resign;
step down; ⟨*government*⟩ resign; (von einem
Vertrag usw.) withdraw (**von** from); back out
(**von** of); (fig.: in den Hintergrund treten) become
less important; ~|**weisen** *unr. tr. V.* reject
⟨*proposal, question, demand, application,*
etc.⟩; turn down, refuse ⟨*offer, request, help,*
etc.⟩; turn away ⟨*petitioner, unwelcome*
guest⟩; repudiate ⟨*accusation, claim, etc.*⟩;
~|**werfen** *unr. tr. V.* throw back; reflect
⟨*light, sound*⟩; repulse ⟨*enemy*⟩; (fig.: in einer
Entwicklung) set back; ~|**zahlen** *tr. V.* pay
back; ~|**ziehen** ① *unr. tr. V.* **(a)** pull
back; draw back ⟨*bolt, curtains, one's hand,*
etc.⟩; **(b)** (abziehen, zurückbeordern) withdraw
⟨*troops*⟩; recall ⟨*ambassador*⟩; **(c)** (rückgängig
machen) withdraw; cancel ⟨*order,*
instruction⟩; ② *unr. refl. V.* withdraw
Zu·ruf *der* shout
zu|rufen *unr. tr. V.* **jmdm. etw. ~:** shout
sth. to sb.
zur·zeit *Adv.* at the moment
Zu·sage *die* **(a)** (auf eine Einladung hin)
acceptance; (auf eine Stellenbewerbung hin) offer
(b) (Versprechen) promise; undertaking
zu|sagen ① *itr. V.* **(a)** accept
(b) jmdm. ~ (gefallen) appeal to sb.
② *tr. V.* promise
zusammen *Adv.* together; **~ sein**
(zusammenleben) be *or* live together
zusammen-, Zusammen-: ~**arbeit**
die cooperation *no indef. art.*; ~|**arbeiten**
itr. V. cooperate; ~|**binden** *unr. tr. V.*
tie together; ~|**brechen** *unr. itr. V.; mit*
sein collapse; (fig.) ⟨*order, communications,*
system, telephone network⟩ break down;
⟨*traffic*⟩ come to a standstill; ~**bruch**
der collapse; (fig., auch psychisch, nervlich)
breakdown; ~|**drücken** *tr. V.* press
together; ~|**fahren** *unr. itr. V.; mit sein*

(zusammenzucken) start; jump; ~|**fallen** *unr.*
itr. V.; mit sein **(a)** collapse; **(b)** [zeitlich]
~**fallen** coincide; ~|**fassen** *tr. V.*
summarize; ~**fassung** *die* summary;
~|**fegen** *tr. V.* (bes. nordd.) sweep together;
~|**fließen** *unr. itr. V.; mit sein* ⟨*rivers,*
streams⟩ flow into each other; ~**fluss,**
~*fluß** *der* confluence; ~|**fügen** *tr. V.*
fit together; ~|**führen** *tr. V.* bring
together; ~|**gehören** *itr. V.* belong
together; ~**gehörig** *Adj.* [closely] related
or connected ⟨*subjects, problems, etc.*⟩;
matching *attrib.* ⟨*pieces of tea service,*
cutlery, etc.⟩; ~**gehörigkeit** *die;*
~~: ein starkes Gefühl der ~gehörigkeit
a strong sense of belonging together;
~**gehörigkeits-gefühl** *das* sense *or*
feeling of belonging together; ~**hang**
der connection; (einer Geschichte, Rede)
coherence; (Kontext) context; ~|**hängen**
unr. itr. V. **(a)** be joined [together]; **(b)** mit
etw. ~**hängen** (fig.) be related to sth.; (durch
etw. [mit] verursacht sein) be the result of
sth.; ~|**kehren** *tr. V.* (bes. südd.) sweep
together; ~**klappbar** *Adj.* folding;
~|**klappen** *tr. V.* fold up; ~|**kommen**
unr. itr. V.; mit sein **(a)** meet; **mit jmdm.**
~**kommen** meet sb.; **(b)** (zueinanderkommen;
auch fig.) get together; (gleichzeitig auftreten)
occur *or* happen together; ~**kunft** *die;*
~~, ~künfte meeting; ~|**laufen** *unr.*
itr. V.; mit sein **(a)** ⟨*people, crowd*⟩ gather,
congregate; **(b)** ⟨*rivers, streams*⟩ flow into
each other, join up; ~|**leben** *itr. V.* live
together; ~**leben** *das* living together
no art.; ~|**legen** ① *tr. V.* **(a)** put *or*
gather together; (zusammenfalten) fold
[up]; **(c)** (miteinander verbinden) amalgamate,
merge ⟨*classes, departments, etc.*⟩; combine
⟨*events*⟩; **(d)** put ⟨*patients, guests, etc.*⟩
together [in the same room]; ② *itr. V.*
club together; ~|**nehmen** ① *unr.*
tr. V. summon up ⟨*courage, strength,*
understanding⟩; ② *unr. refl. V.* get *or*
take a grip on oneself; **nimm dich ~!** pull
yourself together!; ~|**passen** *itr. V.* go
together; ⟨*persons*⟩ be suited to each other;
~**prall** *der;* **~~[e]s, ~~e** collision;
~|**prallen** *itr. V.; mit sein* collide (**mit**
with); ~|**schlagen** *unr. tr. V.* (verprügeln)
beat up; **~*|**sein** ▶ ZUSAMMEN; ~|**setzen**
① *tr. V.* put together; ② *refl. V.* **(a) sich aus**
etw. ~setzen be made up *or* composed of
sth.; **(b)** (sich zueinander setzen) sit together;
(zu einem Gespräch) get together; ~**setzung**
die; **~~, ~~en** **(a)** putting together;
(b) (Aufbau) composition; „**~setzung: …**" (als
Aufschrift auf Medikamentenpackung) 'ingredients:
…'; **(c)** (Sprachw.) compound; ~**spiel** *das*
(a) (von Musikern) ensemble playing; (von
Darstellern) ensemble acting; (einer Mannschaft)
teamwork; **(b)** (fig.) interplay; ~|**stehen**
unr. itr. V. stand together; ~|**stellen** *tr. V.*
put together; draw up ⟨*list*⟩; ~**stoß** *der*
collision; (fig.) clash (**mit** with); ~|**stoßen**

---

unr. itr. V.; mit sein collide (**mit** with);
∼**treffen** *unr. itr. V.; mit sein* (**a**) meet;
mit jmdm. ∼**treffen** meet sb.; (**b**) (zeitlich)
coincide; ∼**wachsen** *unr. itr. V.; mit
sein* grow together; join [up]; ⟨*bones*⟩ knit
together; (fig.) ⟨*towns*⟩ merge into one;
∼**zählen** *tr. V.* add up; ∼**ziehen** *unr.
itr. V.; mit sein* move in together; **mit jmdm.**
∼**ziehen** move in with sb.; ∼**zucken**
itr. V.; mit sein start; jump
Zu·satz *der* addition; (Zugesetztes, Additiv)
additive
zusätzlich 1 *Adj.* additional
2 *adv.* in addition
zu|**schauen** *itr. V.* (südd., österr., schweiz.)
▶ ZUSEHEN
Zu·schauer *der,* **Zu·schauerin** *die;* ∼,
∼**nen** spectator; (im Theater, Kino) member of
the audience; (an einer Unfallstelle) onlooker;
(Fernsehzuschauer) viewer; **die Zuschauer** (im
Theater, Kino) the audience *sing.*
Zuschauerzahl *die* (bes. Ferns.) audience
[numbers]; (Sport) attendance
zu|**schicken** *tr. V.* send; **jmdm. etw.**
∼: send sth. to sb.
zu|**schieben** *unr. tr. V.* (**a**) push ⟨*drawer,
door*⟩ shut
(**b**) (fig.) **jmdm. die Schuld** ∼: lay the blame
on sb.
Zu·schlag *der* (**a**) additional *or* extra
charge; (für Nacht-, Feiertagsarbeit usw.)
additional *or* extra payment
(**b**) (Eisenb.) supplement
zu|**schlagen** 1 *unr. tr. V.* bang *or* slam
⟨*door, window, etc.*⟩ shut; close ⟨*book*⟩;
(heftig) slam ⟨*book*⟩ shut
2 *unr. itr. V.* (**a**) *mit sein* ⟨*door, trap*⟩ slam
or bang shut
(**b**) (einen Schlag/Schläge führen) throw a
blow/blows; (losschlagen) hit *or* strike out;
(fig.) ⟨*army, police, murderer*⟩ strike
zu|**schließen** 1 *unr. tr. V.* lock
2 *unr. itr. V.* lock up
zu|**schnüren** *tr. V.* tie up
zu|**schrauben** *tr. V.* screw the lid *or* top
on ⟨*jar, flask*⟩; screw ⟨*lid, top*⟩ on
Zu·schrift *die* letter; (auf eine Anzeige) reply
Zu·schuss, ***Zu·schuß** *der* contribution
(**zu** towards)
zu|**sehen** *unr. itr. V.* (**a**) watch; **jmdm.
[beim Arbeiten** *usw.*] ∼: watch sb. [working
etc.]
(**b**) (dafür sorgen) make sure; see to it
zu|**senden** *unr. od. regelm. tr. V.*
▶ ZUSCHICKEN
Zu·sendung *die* sending
zu|**spitzen** *refl. V.* become aggravated
zu|**sprechen** 1 *unr. tr. V.* (**a**) **er sprach
ihr Trost/Mut zu** his words gave her
comfort/courage
(**b**) **jmdm. ein Erbe** *usw.* ∼: award sb. an
inheritance *etc.*
2 *unr. itr. V.* **jmdm. ermutigend/tröstend**

usw. ∼: speak encouragingly/comfortingly
to sb.
Zu·stand *der* (**a**) condition; (bes. abwertend)
state
(**b**) (Stand der Dinge) state of affairs
zu·stande *Adv. etw.* ∼ **bringen** [manage
to] bring about sth.; ∼ **kommen** come into
being; (geschehen) take place
zu·ständig *Adj.* appropriate relevant
⟨*authority, office, etc.*⟩; **[für etw.]** ∼ **sein**
(verantwortlich) be responsible [for sth.]
Zuständigkeit *die;* ∼, ∼**en**
(Verantwortlichkeit) responsibility; (Kompetenz)
competence
zu|**stehen** *unr. itr. V.* **etw. steht jmdm. zu**
sb. is entitled to sth.
zu|**steigen** *unr. itr. V.; mit sein* get on; **ist
noch jemand zugestiegen?** (im Bus) ≈ any
more fares, please?; (im Zug) ≈ tickets, please!
zu|**stellen** *tr. V.* deliver ⟨*letter, parcel, etc.*⟩
zu|**stimmen** *itr. V.* agree; **jmdm. [in einem
Punkt]** ∼: agree with sb. [on a point]; **einer
Sache** (*Dat.*) ∼: agree to sth.
Zu·stimmung *die* (Billigung) approval (**zu**
of); (Einverständnis) agreement (**zu** to, with)
zu|**stoßen** *unr. itr. V.; mit sein* **jmdm.**
∼: happen to sb.
Zu·tat *die* ingredient
zu·teil *Adv.* **jmdm./einer Sache** ∼ **werden**
(geh.) be granted to sb./sth.
zu|**teilen** *tr. V.* **jmdm. jmdn./etw.** ∼: allot
or assign sb./sth. to sb.; **jmdm. seine Portion**
∼: mete out his/her share to sb.
zu|**tragen** *unr. refl. V.* (geh.) occur
zuträglich *Adj.* healthy ⟨*climate*⟩; **jmdm./
einer Sache** ∼ **sein** be good for sb./sth.; be
beneficial to sb./sth.
zu|**trauen** *tr. V.* **jmdm. etw.** ∼: believe sb.
[is] capable of [doing] sth.; **sich** (*Dat.*) **etw.**
∼: think one can do *or* is capable of doing
sth.
Zutrauen *das;* ∼**s** confidence, trust (**zu** in)
zutraulich 1 *Adj.* trusting
2 *adv.* trustingly
Zutraulichkeit *die;* ∼: trust[fulness]
zu|**treffen** *unr. itr. V.* (**a**) be correct
(**b**) **auf** *od.* **für jmdn./etw.** ∼: apply to sb./sth
zutreffend 1 *Adj.* (**a**) correct; (treffend)
accurate
(**b**) (geltend) applicable; relevant
2 *adv.* correctly
zu|**trinken** *unr. itr. V.* **jmdm.** ∼: raise
one's glass and drink to sb.
Zu·tritt *der* entry; admittance; „**kein** ∼",
„∼ **verboten**" 'no entry'; 'no admittance';
∼ **[zu etw.] haben** have access [to sth.]
Zu·tun *das;* ∼**s: ohne jmds.** ∼: without
sb.'s being involved
zu·unterst *Adv.* right at the bottom
zuverlässig 1 *Adj.* reliable; (verlässlich)
dependable ⟨*person*⟩
2 *adv.* reliably

Z

Zuverlässigkeit *die;* ∼: reliability; (Verlässlichkeit) dependability

Zuversicht *die;* ∼: confidence

zuversichtlich ⒈ *Adj.* confident ⒉ *adv.* confidently

*zuviel ▸ ZU 2A

zu-vor *Adv.* before

zuvor|kommen *unr. itr. V.; mit sein* (a) jmdm. ∼: beat sb. to it (b) einer Sache (*Dat.*) ∼: anticipate sth.

zuvorkommend ⒈ *Adj.* obliging; (höflich) courteous ⒉ *adv.* obligingly; (höflich) courteously

Zuvorkommenheit *die;* ∼: courteousness; courtesy

Zuwachs *der;* ∼es, Zuwächse increase (*Gen.,* an + *Dat.* in)

Zuwachs-rate *die* (bes. Wirtsch.) growth rate

Zu-wanderer *der,* **Zu-wanderin** *die* immigrant

Zu-wanderung *die* immigration

zu-weilen *Adv.* (geh.) now and again

zu|weisen *unr. tr. V.* jmdm. etw. ∼: allocate *or* allot sb. sth.

zu|wenden *unr. od. regelm. refl. V.* sich jmdm./einer Sache ∼ (auch fig.) turn to sb./sth.

*zu·wenig ▸ ZU 2A

zuwider *Adj.* jmdm. ∼ sein be repugnant to sb.

zu|winken *itr. V.* jmdm./einander ∼: wave to sb./one another

zu|zahlen *tr. V.* pay ⟨*five euros etc.*⟩ extra

zu|ziehen ⒈ *unr. tr. V.* pull ⟨*door*⟩ shut; draw ⟨*curtain*⟩; do up ⟨*zip*⟩ ⒉ *unr. refl. V.* sich (*Dat.*) eine Krankheit ∼: catch an illness ⒊ *unr. itr. V.; mit sein* move into the area

Zu-zug *der* influx

zuzüglich *Präp. mit Gen.* plus

zwang *1. u. 3. Pers. Sg. Prät. v.* ZWINGEN

Zwang *der;* ∼[e]s, Zwänge (a) compulsion (b) (unwiderstehlicher Drang) irresistible urge

zwängen ⒈ *tr. V.* squeeze ⒉ *refl. V.* squeeze [oneself]

zwanghaft *Adj.* obsessive

zwanglos ⒈ *Adj.* (a) informal; casual ⟨*behaviour*⟩ (b) (unregelmäßig) haphazard ⟨*arrangement*⟩ ⒉ *adv.* (a) informally (b) (unregelmäßig) haphazardly ⟨*arranged*⟩

Zwanglosigkeit *die;* ∼: (a) informality (b) (Unregelmäßigkeit) haphazard *or* casual manner

Zwangs-lage *die* predicament

zwangs-läufig ⒈ *Adj.* inevitable ⒉ *adv.* inevitably

zwanzig *Kardinalz.* twenty; *s. auch* ACHTZIG

zwanziger *indekl. Adj.* die ∼ Jahre the twenties

Zwanzig-euro-schein *der* twenty-euro note

zwanzigst... *Ordinalz.* twentieth

zwar *Adv.* (a) admittedly (b) und ∼: to be precise

Zweck *der;* ∼[e]s, ∼e purpose; (Sinn) point; es hat keinen ∼: it's pointless; es hat keinen ∼, das zu tun there is no point in doing that

zweck-, Zweck-: ∼**entfremden** *tr. V.* use for another purpose; ∼**los** *Adj.* pointless; ∼**losigkeit** *die;* ∼∼: pointlessness; ∼**mäßig** ⒈ *Adj.* appropriate; expedient ⟨*behaviour, action*⟩; functional ⟨*building, fittings, furniture*⟩; ⒉ *adv.* appropriately ⟨*arranged, clothed*⟩; ⟨*act*⟩ expediently; ⟨*equip, furnish*⟩ functionally; ∼**mäßigkeit** *die* appropriateness; (einer Handlung) expediency; (eines Gebäudes) functionalism

zwecks *Präp. mit Gen.* (Papierdt.) for the purpose of

zwei *Kardinalz.* two; *s. auch* ACHT[1]

Zwei *die;* ∼, ∼en (a) (Zahl) two (b) (Schulnote) B

zwei-, Zwei-: ∼**bettzimmer** *das* twin-bedded room; ∼**deutig** ⒈ *Adj.* ambiguous; (fig.: schlüpfrig) suggestive ⟨*remark, joke*⟩; ⒉ *adv.* ambiguously; (fig.) suggestively; ∼**deutigkeit** *die;* ∼∼, ∼∼en ambiguity; (fig.) suggestiveness; ∼**dimensional** ⒈ *Adj.* two-dimensional; ⒉ *adv.* two-dimensionally; ∼**ein-halb** *Bruchz.* two and a half

zweierlei *indekl. Adj.* (a) *attr.* two sorts *or* kinds of; two different ⟨*sizes, kinds, etc.*⟩; odd ⟨*socks, gloves*⟩ (b) *allein stehend* two [different] things

zwei-fach *Vervielfältigungsz.* double; (zweimal) twice

Zwei-fache *das; adj. Dekl.* das ∼: twice as much

Zweifel *der;* ∼s, ∼: doubt (an + *Dat.* about); etw. in ∼ ziehen question sth.

zweifelhaft *Adj.* (a) doubtful (b) (fragwürdig) dubious; (suspekt) suspicious

zweifel-los *Adv.* undoubtedly

zweifeln *itr. V.* doubt; an jmdm./etw. ∼: have doubts about sb./sth.

zweifels-, Zweifels-: ∼**fall** *der* case of doubt; doubtful *or* problematic case; im ∼fall[e] in case of doubt; if in doubt; ∼**ohne** *Adv.* undoubtedly; without doubt

Zweig *der;* ∼[e]s, ∼e [small] branch; (meist ohne Blätter) twig

zwei-, Zwei-: ∼**hundert** *Kardinalz.* two hundred; ∼**mal** *Adv.* twice; ∼**mark-stück** *das* two-mark piece; ∼**pfennig-stück** *das* two-pfennig piece; ∼**reiher** *der* double-breasted suit/coat/ jacket; ∼**schneidig** *Adj.* double-edged; ∼**sprachig** ⒈ *Adj.* bilingual; ⟨*sign*⟩ in

---

*old spelling – see note on page x

two languages; ⟨2⟩ *adv.* bilingually; ⟨*written*⟩ in two languages; ⟨*published*⟩ in a bilingual edition; ∼**spurig** *Adj.* (a) two-lane ⟨*road*⟩; (b) two-track ⟨*vehicle*⟩; (c) two- *or* twin-track ⟨*recording*⟩; ∼**stellig** *Adj.* two-figure *attrib.* ⟨*number, sum*⟩; ∼**stöckig** *Adj.* two-storey *attrib.;* ∼**stöckig sein** have two storeys

zweit... *Ordinalz.* second; **jeder Zweite** every other one; *s. auch* ERST...

zwei·tägig *Adj.* (2 Tage alt) two-day-old *attrib.;* (2 Tage dauernd) two-day *attrib.*

zwei·ältest... *Adj.* second oldest

zwei·tausend *Kardinalz.* two thousand

zwei·best... *Adj.* second best

***zweite·mal** ▶ MAL¹

***zweiten·mal** ▶ MAL¹

zweitens *Adv.* secondly; in the second place

Zweite[r]-Klasse-Abteil *das* second-class compartment

zweit·rangig *Adj.* of secondary importance *postpos.;* (zweitklassig) second-rate

Zweit·stimme *die* second vote

zwei·türig *Adj.* two-door ⟨*car*⟩

Zweit-: ∼**wagen** *der* second car; ∼**wohnung** *die* second home

Zwei·zimmer·wohnung *die* two-room flat (Brit.) *or* (Amer.) apartment

Zwerch·fell *das* (Anat.) diaphragm

Zwerg *der;* ∼[e]s, ∼e dwarf; (Gartenzwerg) gnome

Zwetsche *die;* ∼, ∼n damson plum

Zwieback *der;* ∼[e]s, ∼e *od.* **Zwiebäcke** rusk; (unzählbar) rusks *pl.*

Zwiebel *die;* ∼, ∼n onion; (Blumenzwiebel) bulb

zwie-, Zwie-: ∼**gespräch** *das* (geh.) dialogue; ∼**spalt** *der;* ∼∼[e]s, ∼∼e *od.* ∼spälte [inner] conflict; ∼**spältig** *Adj.* conflicting ⟨*mood, feelings*⟩; discordant ⟨*impression*⟩; (widersprüchlich) contradictory ⟨*nature, attitude, person, etc.*⟩

Zwilling *der;* ∼s, ∼e (a) twin (b) *Pl.* (Astrol.) Gemini; the Twins; **er/sie ist [ein]** ∼: he/she is a Gemini

Zwillings-: ∼**bruder** *der* twin brother; ∼**paar** *das* pair of twins; ∼**schwester** *die* twin sister

zwingen *unr. tr. V.* force; **jmdn. [dazu]** ∼, **etw. zu tun** force *or* compel sb. to do sth.

zwingend *Adj.* compelling ⟨*reason, logic*⟩; conclusive ⟨*proof, argument*⟩; imperative ⟨*necessity*⟩

zwinkern *itr. V.* [mit den Augen] ∼: blink; (als Zeichen) wink

Zwirn *der;* ∼[e]s, ∼e [strong] thread *or* yarn

zwischen *Präp. mit Dat./Akk.* between; (mitten unter) among[st]

zwischen-, Zwischen-: ∼**durch** /-'-'-/ *Adv.* (zeitlich) between times; (zwischen zwei Zeitpunkten) in between; (von Zeit zu Zeit) from time to time; ∼**fall** *der* incident; ∼**kriegszeit** *die* period between the wars; inter-war years *pl.;* ∼|**landen** *itr. V.; mit sein* **in X** ∼**landen** land in X on the way; ∼**mahlzeit** *die* snack [between meals]; ∼**menschlich** ⟨1⟩ *Adj.* interpersonal ⟨*relations*⟩; ⟨*contacts*⟩ between people; ⟨2⟩ *adv.* on a personal level; ∼**raum** *der* space; gap; (Lücke) gap; ∼**ruf** *der* interruption; **viele** ∼**rufe** a great deal of heckling *sing.;* ∼**wand** *die* dividing wall; partition; ∼**zeit** *die* interim

Zwist *der;* ∼[e]s, ∼e (geh.) strife *no indef. art.;* (Fehde) feud; dispute

Zwistigkeit *die;* ∼, ∼en (geh.) dispute

zwitschern *itr. (auch tr.) V.* chirp

Zwitter *der;* ∼s, ∼ (Biol.) hermaphrodite

zwo *Kardinalz.* (ugs.; bes. zur Verdeutlichung) two

zwölf *Kardinalz.* twelve; ∼ **Uhr mittags/ nachts** [twelve o'clock] midday/midnight; *s. auch* ACHT¹

zwölft... *Ordinalz.* twelfth; *s. auch* ACHT...

zwölftel *Bruchz.* twelfth; *s. auch* ACHTEL...

Zwölftel *das* (schweiz. meist *der*); ∼s, ∼: twelfth

zwot... *Ordinalz.* (ugs.; bes. zur Verdeutlichung) second

zwotens *Adv.* (ugs.; bes. zur Verdeutlichung) secondly

Zylinder /tsi'lɪndɐ/ *der;* ∼s, ∼ (a) cylinder (b) (Hut) top hat

zylindrisch ⟨1⟩ *Adj.* cylindrical ⟨2⟩ *adv.* cylindrically

Zyniker *der;* ∼s, ∼, **Zynikerin** *die;* ∼, ∼nen cynic

zynisch ⟨1⟩ *Adj.* cynical ⟨2⟩ *adv.* cynically

Zynismus *der;* ∼: cynicism

Zypern *(das);* ∼s Cyprus

Zyprer *der;* ∼s, ∼, **Zyprerin** *die;* ∼, ∼nen Cypriot

Zypresse *die;* ∼, ∼n cypress

Zypriot *der;* ∼en, ∼en, **Zypriotin** *die;* ∼, ∼nen Cypriot

zypriotisch,

zyprisch *Adj.* Cypriot

Zyste *die;* ∼, ∼n (Med.) cyst

Z

Calendar

Traditions, festivals, and holidays in German-speaking countries

1 January Neujahr (New Year's Day) is always a public holiday and tends to be a quiet day when people are recovering from the *Silvester* celebrations.

6 January Heilige Drei Könige Epiphany or Twelfth Night is a public holiday in Austria and some parts of southern Germany. In some areas, children dress up as the Three Kings and go from house to house to bless homes for the coming year and collect money for charity.

2 February Mariä Lichtmess Candlemas is celebrated in the Catholic Church but is not a public holiday.

1 April Erster April April Fool's Day is the time to make an April fool of your family and friends (*jmdn. in den April schicken*) or to play an April fool trick (*Aprilscherz*).

1 May Erster Mai May Day is a public holiday in Germany, Austria, and Switzerland. It is celebrated by trade unions as Labour Day, often with rallies and demonstrations. Many people go on a family outing; in rural areas maypoles are put up in the villages.

3 October Tag der deutschen Einheit Germany's national holiday, the Day of German Unity, commemorates German reunification on 3 October 1990.

26 October Nationalfeiertag Austria's national holiday.

31 October Reformationstag Reformation Day is a public holiday in some mainly Protestant parts of Germany and commemorates the Reformation.

1 November Allerheiligen All Saints' Day is a public holiday in Catholic parts of Germany and Austria.

2 November Allerseelen All Souls' Day is the day when Catholics remember their dead by visiting the cemeteries to pray and place wreaths, flowers, and candles on the graves. This is often done on 1 November as *Allerseelen* is not a public holiday.

11 November Martinstag (St Martin's Day) is not a public holiday, but in Catholic areas the charitable saint is commemorated with processions where children carry lanterns and sing songs. Traditional food includes the *Martinsgans* (roast goose) and *Martinsbrezel* (a soft pretzel).

6 December Nikolaustag On the eve of St Nicholas' Day, children put out their boots in the hope of finding presents and fruit, nuts, and sweets in the morning. St Nicholas is always depicted as looking much like Santa Claus or Father Christmas.

25 December Weihnachten (Christmas) is a family event in Germany, and preparations begin with the *Adventskranz*, an Advent wreath with four candles. On each Sunday of Advent one more candle is lit. Christmas decorations are generally very traditional, with fir branches, candles and wooden Christmas figurines, which can be bought at the *Weihnachtsmarkt* (Christmas market). Typical Christmas baking includes *Stollen* or *Christstollen* (a rich fruit bread), *Lebkuchen* (spicy honey biscuits), and lots of biscuits in the shape of stars, bells, etc. The decorated Christmas tree should only be seen by the children on *Heiligabend* (Christmas Eve), when presents are given out. The *erster Weihnachtstag* (Christmas Day) is a public holiday in Germany, Austria, and Switzerland. It tends to be a quiet day for family gatherings, often with a traditional lunch of goose or carp. The *zweiter Weihnachtstag* (Boxing Day) is also a public holiday; in Austria and Switzerland it is called *Stephanstag* (St Stephen's Day).

31 December **Silvester** New Year's Eve is not a bank holiday, but firms and shops tend to close early. Many people celebrate with a party, or a meal with friends, toasting in the new year at midnight with *Sekt* (German sparkling wine), and watching fireworks.

Movable feasts

Rosenmontag The day before Shrove Tuesday is not an official holiday but many people, especially in the Rhineland, get the day off to take part in the *Karneval* celebrations, including masked balls, fancy-dress parties, and parades. Almost every town has its own carnival prince and princess. The street parades in Düsseldorf, Cologne, Mainz, and other cities are attended by thousands of revellers wearing fancy dress and shown live on television.

Faschingsdienstag Shrove Tuesday is the final day of *Fasching* (Carnival) in southern Germany, with processions and fancy-dress parties similar to *Rosenmontag* in the northwest. In the far south, ancient customs to drive out the winter with bells and drums survive.

Aschermittwoch Ash Wednesday marks the end of the carnival season and the beginning of Lent. It is celebrated in the Catholic Church but it is not a pubic holiday.

Karfreitag Good Friday is a public holiday and generally quiet. Catholics and many Protestants traditionally eat fish on this day.

Ostern Easter traditions include hiding Easter eggs (often dyed hardboiled eggs, or the chocolate variety) in the garden for the children, supposedly left by the *Osterhase* (Easter bunny). *Ostermontag* (Easter Monday) is also a public holiday.

Weißer Sonntag (Sunday after Easter) In the Catholic Church, first communion is traditionally taken on this Sunday.

Muttertag (second Sunday in May). On Mother's Day, children of all ages give their mothers small gifts, cards, or flowers.

Christi Himmelfahrt (40 days after Easter). Ascension Day is a public holiday in Germany, Austria, and Switzerland. This is also Father's Day, when fathers traditionally go out on day trips or pub crawls.

Pfingsten (Whitsun – seventh Sunday after Easter). As *Pfingstmontag* (Whit Monday) is a public holiday in Germany, Austria, and Switzerland, Whitsun is a popular time to have a long weekend away.

Fronleichnam (second Thursday after Whitsun). Corpus Christi is a public holiday in Austria and in parts of Germany and Switzerland. In Catholic areas, processions and open-air masses are held.

Erntedankfest Harvest festival is not a legal holiday in Germany, but is celebrated with church services on the first Sunday in October in many rural areas. In Switzerland there is a harvest thanksgiving holiday in mid-September.

Buß- und Bettag (third Wednesday in November). This day of 'repentance and prayer' is a public holiday only in the German Land of Sachsen.

Volkstrauertag (second Sunday before the beginning of Advent). In Germany, this is a national day of mourning to commemorate the dead of both world wars, and the victims of the Nazis.

Totensonntag (last Sunday before the beginning of Advent). Protestants remember their dead on this day.

Advent The four weeks leading up to Christmas, beginning with the *1. Adventssonntag* (first Sunday in Advent), still have a special significance in Germany, even for people who are not religious.

A–Z of life and culture in German-speaking countries

Abendbrot, Abendessen For most Germans, MITTAGESSEN is still the main meal of the day. *Abendbrot* or *Abendessen* normally consists of bread, cheese, meats, perhaps a salad, and a hot drink. It is eaten by the whole family at about 6 or 7 p.m. *Abendessen* can also refer to a cooked meal, especially for people who are out at work all day.

Abitur The *Abitur*, or *Matura* in Austria, is the final exam taken by pupils at a GYMNASIUM, usually when they are aged about 18. The result is based on continuous assessment during the last two years before the *Abitur*, plus examinations in four subjects. On passing the *Abitur*, a *Zeugnis der allgemeinen Hochschulreife* is issued. This certificate is the obligatory qualification for university entrance.

Adventskranz A garland made of fir springs, traditionally decorated with ribbons and four candles. The wreath is either suspended from the ceiling or put on a table. One candle is lit on the first Sunday in Advent, two on the next, and so on until the fourth Sunday.

Allerheiligen see the Calendar section.

Allerseelen see the Calendar section.

Amerikahaus In Germany and Austria, *Amerikahäuser* are US information centres. They have reference libraries and offer language courses and lectures.

Ampelkoalition A term describing any coalition between the SPD (the party colour is red), the FDP (yellow), and the Green Party (*see* BÜNDNIS 90). This type of coalition has become increasingly common in local government over the last ten years, with some LÄNDER ruled in this way.

Amtsgericht *Amtsgerichte* (local or district courts) are the lowest level of ordinary courts in Germany. They work in a two-tier system with the *Landgerichte* (regional courts) and deal with minor cases. There are four levels of ordinary courts hearing both civil and criminal cases: beside the *Amtsgericht* and *Landgericht* there are the *Oberlandesgericht* (higher regional court) and the *Bundesgerichtshof* (federal supreme court). Most legal proceedings at the local court are handled by magistrates. The regional courts, which handle more serious cases and deal with local court appeals, are presided over by a panel of lay judges and a professional judge.

Arbeitsagentur The local employment office to be found in every German town (formerly called *Arbeitsamt*). It provides career guidance, helps the unemployed find new jobs, and processes all claims for ARBEITSLOSENGELD I and related benefits. Unemployed people have to report to the *Arbeitsagentur* once every three months to prove that they are still looking for work.

Arbeitsgericht Industrial tribunals are held at administrative courts (local, higher, and federal), which handle all proceedings under administrative law. They deal with disputes between employers and employees or between employers and trade unions, and matters connected with the *Betriebsverfassungsgesetz* (industrial relations law).

Arbeitslosengeld I, or earnings-related unemployment benefit, is paid to all unemployed people who are looking for a new job and have already made a minimum contribution to the ARBEITSLOSENVERSICHERUNG. The benefit is a proportion of the person's previous pay, and is higher for people supporting children. It is generally paid for up to one year. People unemployed for longer than twelve months, or those who are not entitled to *Arbeitslosengeld I*, can apply for the so-called *Arbeitslosengeld II* (unemployment benefit II), which has replaced *Arbeitslosenhilfe* and is a reduced-rate benefit.

Arbeitsamt ▶ ARBEITSAGENTUR

Arbeitslosenversicherung This is the compulsory state-run insurance against unemployment. All employees have to pay into this scheme and in return are entitled to ARBEITSLOSENGELD I and related benefits. Employees and employers each pay half of the contributions. This area has been subject to wide-ranging reforms in recent years.

Archiv der Jugendkulturen Since 1998 the Archive of Youth Culture in Berlin has been collecting and cataloguing books, magazines, CDs, and other materials of special interest to young people. The Archive is open to the public and publishes a magazine called *Journal der Jugendkulturen* (Journal of Youth Culture).

ARD – Arbeitsgemeinschaft der öffentlich-rechtlichen Rundfunkanstalten der Bundesrepublik Deutschland An umbrella organization for the regional broadcasting stations of the various German LÄNDER, financed by licence fees plus a certain amount of advertising. The ARD broadcasts das ERSTE.

Aschermittwoch see the Calendar section.

AStA — Allgemeiner Studentenausschuss A students' union which consists of twelve student boards elected by a student parliament that is voted in annually. AStA deals with all student issues, including financial, cultural, and social concerns, offering advice and support.

Ausbildungsplatz Over 500,000 firms in all sectors of the economy, including the independent professions and the public sector, provide trainee posts for AZUBIS. Young people can only apply for these in state-recognized occupations for which vocational training is required. Large firms have their own training workshops, but smaller firms train their apprentices on the job.

Autobahn Germany's motorway network is very extensive and not subject to a general speed limit, other than a recommended limit of about 80 mph (130 km/h). But increasingly speed limits are in force on long stretches of the *Autobahn*. Many motorways have only two lanes. To ease congestion, lorries are not allowed to use the *Autobahn* on Sundays. German motorways are free for passenger traffic. Lorries over twelve tonnes pay a toll known as *Autobahngebühren*. On Austrian and Swiss motorways, all vehicles must display a VIGNETTE.

Azubi Trainees and apprentices are known as *Azubis* or *Auszubildende*. They are trained within the German dual system (*das duale Ausbildungssystem*), which combines practical on-the-job training in recognized occupations with theoretical instruction at a BERUFSSCHULE.

During the training period, *Azubis* receive a small wage from their employer. In order to gain professional qualifications, *Azubis* take an examination at the end of their two- or three-year apprenticeship; this is conducted by a board of examiners such as the chamber of industry and commerce, the chamber of crafts, or representatives of employers and vocational schoolteachers.

Bachfest This ten-day music festival is held annually in honour of the great German composer Johann Sebastian Bach (1685–1750), and takes place in Leipzig, where Bach spent many years of his life. The *Bachfest* is one of more than a hundred important music festivals in Germany.

BAföG – Bundesausbildungsförderungsgesetz Federal education and training assistance, which about a quarter of German students receive from the state. Whether they are entitled to a *BAföG* grant or loan, and how much they get, depends on the students' and their parents' financial circumstances. Half of this assistance is awarded in the form of a grant, and the rest as an interest-free loan which usually has to be repaid within five years of the end of the maximum entitlement period. The payments are made by the STUDENTENWERKE (student welfare services).

BahnCard A rail pass for frequent rail travellers within Germany. *BahnCard 25/BahnCard 50/BahnCard 100* entitle the holder to 25 per cent, 50 per cent, or 100 per cent discount respectively. There are a number of other passes and saver tickets offering reductions throughout Germany, Austria, Switzerland, and neighbouring countries.

Bauhaus A school of architecture and the applied arts founded in 1919 in Weimar and later housed at Dessau. Under the leadership of Walter Gropius (1883–1969) and Ludwig Mies van der Rohe (1886–1969), it became the centre of modern design in the 1920s and played a key role in establishing a relationship between architecture, technology, and functionality. The *Bauhaus* was closed down by the Nazis in 1933.

Bausparen German building societies expect people to have saved up a sizeable sum towards the purchase of a house before they will give them a mortgage. For this reason, many Germans have a *Bausparvertrag* (a tax-efficient savings contract for an agreed sum) with a building society, even if they are not planning to buy their EIGENHEIM for some time.

Bayern Bayern, or Bavaria, the largest and most southerly of Germany's LÄNDER, is known for its beautiful scenery (the Alps and their foothills, as well as forests, rivers, and lakes, picturesque towns and villages), its excellent BIER (beer) and food, and its lively cosmopolitan capital, München (Munich). The Bavarians are said to be warm and hospitable, but also fiercely independent and very conservative.

Bayreuth The Franconian city of Bayreuth in Bavaria is a magnet for opera fans. The German composer Richard Wagner (1813–83) lived there from 1872. In most years since 1876 the Richard Wagner Festival has been staged in the Festspielhaus, the festival theatre built between 1872 and 1876 with funding from the Bavarian King Ludwig II, one of Wagner's greatest admirers.

Beamte This term, meaning 'official', covers civil servants and other local government officers, but also teachers and lecturers. *Beamte* are legally obliged to support the democratic system in Germany and are not allowed to go on strike. In return, they enjoy many privileges, such as total job security, private health insurance, and exemption from social security contributions.

Berlin After WIEDERVEREINIGUNG, Berlin took over from Bonn as the capital of Germany, though the German government did not start moving there until 1998. This vibrant city lies on the River Spree. It has about 3.5 million inhabitants and is a major cultural and commercial centre.

Berlinale This is the short name for the Internationale Filmfestspiele Berlin, an annual film festival that was first held in 1951. A *Goldener Bär* (Golden Bear) statuette is awarded for the best film, and a *Gläserner Bär* (Glass Bear) for the best children's film. The bear is Berlin's symbol.

Berliner Theatertreffen Founded in 1964, the Berlin Theatre Encounter presents the best German-language plays. Some dramatic productions are broadcast on 3SAT, which also presents one of the *Theatertreffen* prizes, awarded for innovative drama.

Berufsfachschule A full-time vocational college that offers preparation courses for a period of one to three years. Only pupils with a *Haupt-* or

Realschulabschluss (school-leaving certificates) can attend a *Berufsfachschule*. The courses count as part of an apprenticeship, or can even replace it. *See also* SCHULE.

Berufsschule A college for young people who are doing a LEHRE. They attend *Berufsschule* one or two days a week (or sometimes in blocks of several weeks) to continue their general education and receive formal training in their chosen type of job.

Besenwirtschaft An inn set up temporarily by a local winegrower for a few weeks after the new wine has been made. A blown-up pig's bladder hung outside the door indicates that the new vintage may be sampled here. This is mainly found in southern Germany and is similar to the Austrian HEURIGER. *See also* STRAUSSWIRTSCHAFT.

Betriebsrat The staff in any German company with at least five employees are entitled to have a *Betriebsrat*. This is a committee elected by the workers to represent their interests, as opposed to those of management. It allows workers to participate in decisions on pay and other benefits, redundancies, and even some business matters.

Bier Germany and Austria rank among the world's top beer producers and consumers, with a vast range of beer varieties (*Bock, Alt, Dunkel, Export, Hell, Kölsch, Lager, Malzbier, Pils, Märzen, Weizenbier* or *Weißbier*, and *Berliner Weiße*) to choose from. The standard everyday pale beer most people order is a *Helles*. Germans brew more than 5,000 varieties, and each beer tastes different depending on the ratio of ingredients, brewing temperature and technique, alcoholic content, ageing time, and colour. Although there are now some big brewing conglomerates, the local brews from small independent breweries (there are about 1,300 in Germany) are still the best and most popular. German beer is brewed according to the *Reinheitsgebot* (beer purity regulation) of 1516, which stipulates that no ingredients other than hops, malted barley, yeast, and water can be used. Dortmund and Munich are among the top beer-producing cities in the world. Drinking beer is a vital part of everyday life for many people; they regularly meet up at their STAMMTISCH in a *Kneipe* (pub) or BIERGARTEN.

Biergarten A rustic open-air pub, or beer garden, which is traditional in Bavaria and Austria but can now also be found throughout Germany. It is usually set up for the summer in the yard of a pub or restaurant and serves beer and simple meals. In Munich beer gardens, the drink comes in a litre-sized glass, called a *Maß*.

Bild Zeitung Germany's largest-selling daily newspaper, *Bild* is a typical tabloid with huge headlines, lots of photos, scandal stories, gossip, and nude models. It is known for its right-wing views. *Bild* sells about 4.5

Culture

million copies every day, almost eight times more than any other newspaper in Germany. Its Sunday edition is called *Bild am Sonntag*.

Bioladen A health-food shop which sells only organically grown products.

Biotonne ▶ RECYCLING

BKJ ▶ DBJR

Blauer Brief A letter sent by a school to inform parents that their son or daughter is in danger of having to repeat the year, a concept colloquially known as SITZEN BLEIBEN.

Blauer Engel The Blue Angel label on goods for sale shows consumers that the product is environmentally friendly.

Bodensee This is the German name for Lake Constance, Germany's biggest lake, bordered by Germany, Switzerland, and Austria. The River Rhine flows through it. This popular recreation area enjoys a particularly mild climate, especially on the three islands, Lindau, Mainau, and Reichenau.

Bonn Bonn was the capital of the Federal Republic of Germany (*see* BUNDESREPUBLIK DEUTSCHLAND) from 1949 until Berlin was made the capital of reunified Germany in 1991. It is still home to a number of government institutions. This relatively small city of about 300,000 inhabitants enjoys a picturesque location on the River Rhine.

Brandenburger Tor Once a symbol of divided Berlin, the Brandenburg Gate triumphal arch has become a symbol of reunited Germany. It was designed in the neoclassical style by Karl Gotthard Langhans (1732–1808) and opened in 1791 as an entrance to the boulevard Unter den Linden. Topped by the goddess of peace, the monument was part of the closed border between East and West Berlin from 1961 to 1989.

Brothers Grimm ▶ KINDER- UND HAUSMÄRCHEN

Bund This term refers to the federal state as the top level of government, as opposed to the individual LÄNDER which make up the BUNDESREPUBLIK. *Bund* and *Länder* have different responsibilities, with the *Bund* in charge of foreign policy, defence, transport, health, employment, etc.

Bundesbank Properly called the *Deutsche Bundesbank*, Germany's central bank is an autonomous non-governmental institution located in Frankfurt am Main. With the introduction of the EURO in 1999, some of the bank's functions passed to the European Central Bank (also in Frankfurt).

Bundesheer The *Bundesheer* is the Austrian federal army, which ensures the country's neutrality. All 18-year-old Austrian males must serve for a compulsory six months, plus two further months reserve duty at later dates. Conscientious objectors do public service. No foreign military bases are allowed on Austrian territory. *See also* WEHRDIENST, ZIVILDIENST.

Bundeskanzler The chancellor is the head of government in Germany and Austria. The German chancellor is normally elected for four years by the members of the BUNDESTAG after being proposed by the BUNDESPRÄSIDENT. The *Bundeskanzler* chooses the ministers and decides on government policies.

Bundesländer ▶ LÄNDER

Bundesliga The German national soccer league is split into two divisions of eighteen teams: the *Bundesliga* and the *2.* (or *Zweite*) *Bundesliga*. League games attract hundreds of thousands of spectators every week during the regular season.

Bundesminister The Federal Government consists of the BUNDESKANZLER and the *Bundesminister* (federal ministers). The chancellor appoints ministers and determines their number and responsibilities in the Cabinet. Ministers run their ministries independently but within the framework of the guidelines of the chancellor's policy.

Bundespräsident The president is the head of state in Germany and Austria. The German president is elected for five years by the members of the BUNDESTAG and delegates from the LÄNDER. The *Bundespräsident* acts mainly as a figurehead, representing Germany abroad, and does not get involved in party politics, although he often takes a moral lead in major issues and can exercise personal authority through his neutral mediating function. The *Bundespräsident* can only be re-elected once.

Bundesrat This is the upper house of the German parliamentary system. The *Bundesrat* members are appointed by the LÄNDER governments and represent them. The *Bundesrat* has to approve laws affecting the *Länder*, and also any changes to the GRUNDGESETZ. The opposition parties can sometimes hold a majority in the *Bundesrat*, which allows them to influence German legislation.

Bundesrepublik Deutschland, or Bundesrepublik for short, is the official name of the German state (the Federal Republic of Germany, or FRG). During the period when Germany was divided, it was the official name of West Germany. The short form was then used particularly to distinguish West Germany from East Germany (see GDR). Established on 23 May 1949, the republic became fully independent from British, French, and US control in May 1955. In October 1990 the Federal Republic merged with the GDR to form a single, unified Germany. *See also* WIEDERVEREINIGUNG.

Bundestag The lower house of the German parliament, which is elected every four years by the German people. The Bundestag is responsible for federal legislation, the federal budget, and electing the BUNDESKANZLER. Half of the members are elected directly and half by proportional representation, in a system in which each voter has two votes. *See also* NATIONALRAT.

Bundesverfassungsgericht As the supreme court in Germany, the federal constitutional court in Karlsruhe is the guardian of the GRUNDGESETZ and the final arbiter in any German legal appeal. It passes judgement on constitutional complaints and has the power to order a party's dissolution if it is unconstitutional and may pose a threat to democracy. The Federal Government has to accept the judges' ruling, however controversial the case may be. The *Bundesverfassungsgericht* consists of two panels, each with eight judges, who are elected for a single twelve-year term. Half of the panel is elected by the BUNDESTAG and half by the BUNDESRAT.

Bundeswappen The German coat of arms is the eagle. This heraldic bird – emblem of the Roman emperors – was adopted by Charlemagne and became the coat of arms of the German Empire when it was founded in 1871. The Weimar Republic adopted it in its present form in 1919, and since 1950 it has been used by the BUNDESREPUBLIK DEUTSCHLAND.

Bundeswehr This is the name for the German armed forces, which come under the control of the defence minister. The *Bundeswehr* consists of professional soldiers and conscripts serving their WEHRDIENST. Until 1994, the GRUNDGESETZ did not allow German forces to be deployed abroad, but they now take part in certain operations, notably UN peacekeeping missions.

Bündnis 90/Die Grünen This party came into being in 1993 as a result of the merger of the West German Green party and civil-rights movements of the former East Germany (GDR). It is an important force in the German parliament, committed to environmental and social issues.

Burschenschaft A students' duelling society, like a fraternity, which was founded in Jena in 1815 to strengthen patriotic feeling. The tradition was abolished in 1935, but a decade later male students formed a new fraternity, the *Deutsche Burschenschaft*. Most of these generally right-wing social organizations for students are now called *studentische Verbindungen* (*Verbindung* means 'link' or 'connection'). There are now also Verbindungen for women.

CDU – Christlich-Demokratische Union One of the main German political parties, it was founded in 1945 and is committed to Christian and conservative values. Led by Angela Merkel, the CDU and its sister party, the CSU, were well ahead in opinion polls at the start of the 2005 election campaign. However, results announced after the 18 September ballot showed the CDU/CSU had gained only four more seats than its rivals, the

SPD, headed by former chancellor Gerhard Schröder. Extended negotiations between the SPD and CDU/CSU resulted in an agreement to form a Grand Coalition between the parties, with Merkel as BUNDESKANZLER.

Christkind Traditionally, it is *das Christkind* (the Christ child) who brings Christmas presents to children on Christmas Eve. The concept of *der Weihnachtsmann* (Father Christmas or Santa Claus) is relatively new in Germany and confined mainly to the protestant North.

Christopher Street Day Gay Pride festivals and parades in Germany and Switzerland are called Christopher Street Days (or CSDs), after the New York street in which the gay protests known as the Stonewall Rebellion took place in 1969. Pride parades are held in most German cities, and the most famous are in Berlin and Cologne. In Austria, the parade is called the *Regenbogenparade* (Rainbow Parade).

CSU – Christlich-Soziale Union The Bavarian sister party of the CDU was founded in 1946 and has enjoyed an absolute majority in Bavaria for over 30 years. It now forms part of the governing Grand Coalition in Germany.

DAAD – Deutscher Akademischer Austauschdienst The German Academic Exchange Service is a joint organization of universities and other institutions of higher education for the promotion of academic exchange. The DAAD is the central source of information on study and research opportunities in Germany and abroad. It awards scholarships to students and academics and acts as a national agency for grants from the European Union.

DBJR – Deutscher Bundesjugendring The German Federal Youth Association, based in Berlin, is made up of twenty-four national youth organizations and sixteen regional youth councils. The *Bundesjugendring* aims to represent young people in their everyday lives. The *Bundesvereinigung Kulturelle Jugendbildung* (BKJ), a separate Federation of Youth Cultural Associations based in Remscheid, specializes in cultural activities that are followed by more than 12 million young people.

Deutsche Bibliothek The German Library in Frankfurt am Main is the central archive of all German-language writing, and the national bibliographical information centre of the BUNDESREPUBLIK. The first national library bringing together all German-language literature under one roof was set up in Leipzig in 1912. The division of Germany after the Second World War resulted in a new national library, established in 1947 in Frankfurt. After reunification in 1990, the German library in Leipzig was merged with the Frankfurt library.

Deutsche Post The previously state-run German postal system has undergone wide-ranging reforms in recent years, which has effectively removed the Deutsche Post monopoly. The number of post offices has been reduced, but small post-office agencies can now be found in shops, newsagents, and petrol stations. German letter boxes are yellow. Postal charges are relatively high, but the service is very reliable.

Deutsche Telekom The previously state-run German telecommunications service has undergone extensive reforms and gradual privatization and is now a public limited company. Since 1998, when the market was opened up to competition, Deutsche Telekom has ceased to have a monopoly.

Deutsche Welle Aimed at listeners abroad, this radio station is financed and controlled by the German government and broadcasts programmes on German politics, business, arts, and culture.

Deutscher Kulturrat The German Arts Council was founded in 1981 as a non-governmental commission representing cultural associations and institutions. The Arts Council comprises eight independent organizations, among them the Sociocultural Council (SOZIOKULTUR). The function of the *Kulturrat* is to coordinate, advise, and inform on matters concerning cultural affairs, make recommendations on cultural policy, and further international cultural relations.

Deutscher Sportbund – DSB Around 27 million people are members of a sports club in Germany, while another 12 million take part in sport. The German Sports Federation (DSB) has 16 regional sports federations and many individual sports associations. There are more than 2.5 million volunteer coaches and officials working for the Sports Federation. The DSB also promotes programmes such as *Trimm dich* (Get fit), a programme aimed at physical fitness, and *Sport für alle* (Sport for all), a programme encouraging people to run, swim, cycle, ski, and hike. About 750,000 people a year pass DSB tests and qualify for a gold, silver, or bronze sports medal.

Deutschlandlied This has been the German national anthem since 1922, when it was chosen by the first president of the Weimar Republic. The song entitled *Lied der Deutschen* (Song of the Germans) was written by Hoffmann von Fallersleben in 1841 and set to a melody composed by Joseph Haydn (1732–1809). Only the third stanza of the song is now used as the national anthem.

Diplomprüfung Final (degree) examination at a university or equivalent higher education institution in a technical or scientific subject, especially in engineering, business administration, design, agriculture, and social work. Those passing the exam are awarded a degree or diploma.

Duales System This waste-disposal and recycling system was introduced in Germany in 1993 and is operated by the private company DSD. All packaging materials marked with the GRÜNER PUNKT symbol are collected separately, and sorted into plastics, glass, paper, and metal for recycling. All other waste is still collected by the local refuse collection service. *See also* RECYCLING.

Eigenheim Germany and Switzerland have the lowest levels of home ownership in Europe, while Austria has among the highest. In Germany, many people happily live in rented flats or houses, but most dream of buying or building their *Eigenheim* (own home) one day, and save up towards it through the system of BAUSPAREN. First-time buyers are usually middle-aged and expect to stay in their home for the rest of their lives.

Einwohnermeldeamt (residents' registration office) Anybody who moves to Germany or relocates within Germany is legally obliged to register their address with the *Einwohnermeldeamt* within a week.

Eisschießen, Eisstockschießen Ice-stick shooting or Bavarian curling is a popular sport in Bavaria and Austria. There are two kinds of *Eisschießen*: in one, the aim is to slide the ice stick, a heavy metal plate with a handle, as far as possible across the ice; in the other, players slide a metal-plated wooden ice stick as close as possible to the *Daube*, a wooden tee.

Elternzeit A German mother or father who looks after a child at home is entitled to up to three years' extended maternity or paternity leave. At the end of this *Elternzeit* – formerly called *Erziehungsurlaub* ('child-raising leave') – they are entitled to return to their old job. Around 95 per cent of German mothers take time out of work for at least one year after the birth.

Entwerter In many German cities, *Entwerter* (ticket-cancelling machines) are located on U-Bahn and S-Bahn platforms, or on trains, trams, or buses. When travelling on public transport in Germany, it is important to remember to cancel (*entwerten*) the ticket in one of the machines. Even if just bought from the driver, your ticket may not be valid without this stamp.

Erntedankfest see the Calendar section.

Erste, Das Also called *Erstes Programm*, this is the first German public TV channel, broadcast by ARD. Programming includes news, information, films, and entertainment. There is a limited amount of advertising, which is concentrated in blocks at certain times of day and not after 8 p.m.

Erziehungsgeld A state benefit paid for up to two years to any mother or father who stays at home after the birth of a child to look after it. In 98 per cent of cases, it is still the mother who claims *Erziehungsgeld*. In addition to this, parents receive *Kindergeld* (child benefit) for each child.

Erziehungsurlaub ▶ ELTERNZEIT

Euro The *Euro* was introduced as a *gemeinsame Währung* (common currency) in twelve states of the European Union in 2002. It replaced the *Mark* in Germany and the *Schilling* in Austria. Switzerland is not a member of the EU and retained the *Franken*.

Eurocheque The *Eurocheque* is the standard cheque issued by banks in Germany. It is backed up by the *Eurochequekarte*, which can also be used at cash machines and for payments in shops. Plastic cards are still not quite as widely accepted in Germany as in many other countries.

Fachhochschule This type of college provides shorter, more vocational and practical courses than those available at a HOCHSCHULE. A third of new students now enrol at a *Fachhochschule* to take the DIPLOMPRÜFUNG.

Fachhochschulreife ▶ FACHOBERSCHULE

Fachoberschule This vocationally orientated college takes students with an intermediate school certificate and leads to the *Fachhochschulreife*, a certificate qualifying students for the FACHHOCHSCHULE. Courses last for two to three years and cover theoretical instruction as well as on-the-job training.

Fasching, Fastnachtszeit This is the carnival season, which begins in November and ends on Aschermittwoch for Lent. Depending on the region it is called *Karneval*, *Fastnacht*, *Fasnet*, or *Fasching*, and is celebrated in Germany, Austria, and Switzerland. Every town and village has its own carnival customs. Whether it is the Kölner Karneval or the Münchner Fasching, celebrations reach a climax in the last week, especially on Rosenmontag and Faschingsdienstag. On Ash Wednesday everything returns to normal. *See also* ASCHERMITTWOCH, FASCHINGSDIENSTAG, ROSENMONTAG in the Calendar section.

Faschingsdienstag see the Calendar section.

FDP – Freie Demokratische Partei The German Liberal party, founded in 1948. This relatively small party has held the balance of power in coalitions in the past, even though it tends to gain only 5 to 10 per cent of the vote at general elections (9.9 per cent in 2005). It supports a free-market economy and the freedom of the individual.

Flohmarkt There is a *Flohmarkt* (flea market) on Sundays in most big cities. Stalls are set up in a main street, park, or central square to sell knick-knacks, second-hand clothes, furniture, and other bargains.

Focus A relatively new weekly news and current affairs magazine published in Munich. It was set up in 1993 and is aimed at a centre-right, professional readership. *Focus* has become a serious competitor of DER SPIEGEL, with shorter, easier-to-read articles, and a more modern presentation.

Formel 1 Formula 1 motor racing enjoys a large following in Germany, particularly since local hero Michael Schumacher won the drivers' world championship a record seven times between 1994 and 2004. The German Grand Prix, which was won three times by Michael and once by his brother Ralf, takes place each year at Hockenheim near Mannheim. The European Grand Prix was held at the Nürburgring in Rheinland-Pfalz from 1999 to 2007.

FPÖ – Freiheitliche Partei Österreichs The Austrian Freedom Party, also known as *Die Freiheitlichen*, was founded in 1955. It is right-wing and is the third largest party. It advocates a minimum monthly wage and stricter asylum policies.

Frankfurter Allgemeine Zeitung (FAZ) One of Germany's most serious and widely respected daily newspapers. It tends to have a centre-left to liberal outlook.

Frankfurter Buchmesse The annual Book Fair was first held in Frankfurt in 1964. Since then it has become the most important publishing trade fair in the world. Held every October, it includes the award of the *Friedenspreis des deutschen Buchhandels* (Peace Prize of the German Book Trade). Leipzig also stages an important annual book fair.

Die Freiheitlichen ▶ FPÖ

FRG – Federal Republic of Germany ▶ BUNDESREPUBLIK DEUTSCHLAND

Frühstück Breakfast in Germany typically consists of strong coffee, slices of bread or fresh rolls with butter, jam, honey, sliced cheese and meat, and maybe a boiled egg. For working people and schoolchildren, who have little time for breakfast first thing in the morning, a *zweites Frühstück* is common at around 10 a.m.

Fünfprozentklausel The 5 per cent clause, introduced in 1953, stipulates that only parties gaining at least 5 per cent of the valid second votes, or at least three constituency seats, can be represented in parliament.

Fußballweltmeisterschaft The Football World Cup took place in Germany in 2006, with matches spread across twelve cities, including the opening match in Munich and the final in Berlin. The German team won in 1954, 1974, and 1990 and has been runner-up four times. Women's football is also strong in Germany; the German team won the Women's World Cup in 2003 and 2007.

Gastarbeiter The term used for workers from foreign countries, mainly Turkey, former Yugoslavia, and Italy, many of whom came to Germany in the 1960s and 1970s. Despite the time that they have lived in Germany, and the fact that their children have grown up there, the issue of integration is still widely discussed.

Culture

GDR – German Democratic Republic The communist state, established in the Soviet-occupied zone of Germany after the Second World War. Also known as East Germany, or the *Deutsche Demokratische Republik* (*DDR*), it lasted from 1949 to 1990. *See also* BUNDESREPUBLIK DEUTSCHLAND, MAUER, WIEDERVEREINIGUNG.

Gemeinde The lowest level of local government, run by a local council chaired by the *Bürgermeister* (mayor). *Gemeinden* have their own budget, with income from local taxes. They pass local legislation and administer local affairs.

Gesamthochschule A type of higher-education institution that existed in some LÄNDER from the 1960s until 2003, combining HOCHSCHULE and FACHHOCHSCHULE under one roof. Most have since become universities.

Gesamtschule A comprehensive secondary school introduced in the 1970s and designed to replace the traditional division into GYMNASIUM, REALSCHULE, and HAUPTSCHULE. Pupils are taught different subjects at their own level and may take any of the school-leaving exams, including the ABITUR.

Glascontainer ▶ RECYCLING

Goethe-Institut An organization promoting German language and culture abroad. It is based in Munich and runs about 140 institutes in over seventy countries, offering German language classes, cultural events such as exhibitions, films, and seminars, and a library, which is open to the public, of German books and magazines and other documentation.

Goldener Bär ▶ BERLINALE

Grundgesetz The written German constitution which came into force in May 1949. It lays down the basic rights of German citizens, the relationship between BUND and LÄNDER, and the legal framework of the German state.

Grundschule The primary school which all German children attend for four years from the age of six (some children do not start until they are seven). Lessons are intense but pupils only attend school for about four hours a day. At the end of the *Grundschule*, teachers and parents decide together which type of secondary school – HAUPTSCHULE, REALSCHULE, GESAMTSCHULE, or GYMNASIUM – the child should attend. Parents usually accept the *Lehrerempfehlung* (teacher's recommendation), which is binding in some Länder.

Grünen, Die ▶ BÜNDNIS 90

Grüner Punkt A symbol used to mark packaging materials that can be recycled. Any packaging carrying this logo is collected separately under the DUALES SYSTEM recycling scheme. Manufacturers have to buy a licence from the recycling company DSD (Duales System Deutschland) to entitle them to use this symbol.

Culture

Gruppe 47 This German literary group was founded (in 1947, hence its name) by the writer Hans Werner Richter (1908–93), who organized regular meetings to encourage young German-language authors in the postwar era. The group's two most famous representatives both won Nobel Prizes in Literature: Heinrich Böll in 1972, for his 'renewal of German literature', and Günter Grass, in 1999, for portraying 'the forgotten face of history'.

Gymnasium The secondary school which prepares pupils for the ABITUR. The GYMNASIUM is attended after the GRUNDSCHULE by the most academically inclined pupils. They spend nine years at this school (to be reduced to eight by 2012), and during the last three years they have some choice as to which subjects they study. *See also* SCHULE.

Hansestadt *Hansestädte* (Hanseatic cities), such as Bremen and Hamburg, were once part of an association of trading cities along the North Sea and Baltic coasts. The *Hanse* (Hanseatic League or Hansa) was formed in the 13th century to protect the economic interests of its

members. Meetings were held at Lübeck, where members developed a system of commercial laws. The *Hanse* remained a powerful force until the late sixteenth century, after which it declined.

Hauptschule The secondary school which prepares pupils for the *Hauptschulabschluss* (school-leaving certificate). The *Hauptschule* aims to give less academically inclined pupils a sound educational grounding. Pupils stay at the *Hauptschule* for five or six years after the GRUNDSCHULE. *See also* LEHRE, SCHULE.

Hausordnung These 'house rules' are what a tenant has to adhere to in order to maintain a harmonious relationship with neighbours. They might cover the maintenance of common areas and the appearance of the house or apartment block; for example, forbidding a tenant from hanging washing from a front window. But usually the *Hausordnung*, whether written or unwritten, includes restrictions on noise, possibly even from running a late-night bath. *See also* RUHEZEIT.

Heiligabend see the Calendar section.

Heilige Drei Könige see the Calendar section.

Heuriger This is an Austrian term for both a new wine and an inn with new wine on tap, especially an inn with its own vineyard in the environs of Vienna. On warm, late summer evenings Viennese wine devotees sit on wooden benches and sample the new wine of the year. A garland of pine twigs outside the gates of the *Heuriger* shows that the barrel has been breached. *See also* BESENWIRTSCHAFT and STRAUSSWIRTSCHAFT.

Hochdeutsch There are many regional variations and dialects in Germany, Austria, and Switzerland (64 per cent of Swiss people speak

Schwyzerdütsch). *Hochdeutsch* is the standard German that can be understood by all German speakers. It is probably the only way for a Bavarian, Austrian, or Swiss to communicate with a North German. Newspapers and other publications are generally printed in *Hochdeutsch*, which is regarded as 'proper' German.

Hochschule German *Hochschulen* (universities and colleges) have generally not charged fees, but some LÄNDER recently introduced fees of 500 euros per semester. Anybody who has passed the ABITUR is entitled to go to university (except for some subjects which have a restriction on numbers, or NUMERUS CLAUSUS). They tend to be very large and impersonal institutions. Students may receive a BAFÖG grant and often take more than the minimum eight semesters (four years) to complete their course.

Hochzeit Church weddings are not legally recognized in Germany, Austria, or Switzerland, and all couples must be married in a civil ceremony. The civil ceremony is held in a *Standesamt* (registry office, called a *Zivilstandsamt* in Switzerland). The civil marriage tends to be a private family affair; if the couple also has a church ceremony afterwards, that is usually a more public event. Various traditions are associated with weddings: often a car procession takes place (where the wedding party and guests drive around honking their horns, and well-wishers honk back), or children strew flowers in front of the couple for good luck. The bachelor party or stag night is known as *Junggesellenabschied*, and there is often also an informal party held before the wedding known as POLTERABEND. Since 2001, same-sex couples have been able to register a civil union called a *Lebenspartnerschaft*.

ICE – Intercityexpresszug This high-speed train runs at one- or two-hour intervals on a number of main routes in Germany, offering shorter journey times and better facilities than ordinary trains.

IM – inoffizieller Mitarbeiter This term refers to 'unofficial collaborators' of the STASI. These informers were often ordinary people in the former GDR who had been recruited or pressurized by the *Stasi* to spy on neighbours, family, and friends. However, some were prominent figures in the West.

Jüdisches Museum The new Jewish Museum in Berlin opened in 1999, a stunning, angular silver building designed by the American architect Daniel Libeskind. It stands in dramatic contrast to its Baroque neighbour, a former appeal court built in 1734–35. The collection covers two millennia of German Jewish history, and includes a Holocaust Tower memorial.

Kaffee This refers not only to coffee as a drink but also to the small meal taken at about four in the afternoon, consisting of coffee and cakes or biscuits. It is often a social occasion, as it is common to invite family or

Culture

friends for *Kaffee und Kuchen* (rather than for tea or dinner), especially on birthdays and other family occasions.

Kanton The name for the individual autonomous states that make up Switzerland. There are 26 *Kantone*, each with its own government and constitution.

Karneval ▶ FASCHING, FASTNACHTSZEIT

Kfz-Kennzeichen This is the number plate on German motor vehicles, which have to be licensed by the *Zulassungsstelle* (vehicle registration office) for the owner's registered place of residence. The first letter or group of letters indicate the town or district that the vehicle comes from.

KI.KA – Kinderkanal This publicly funded children's TV channel was set up in 1997 by ARD and ZDF. Based in Erfurt, the channel broadcasts German children's favourites, as well as classic programmes from around the world.

Kindergarten Every German pre-school child has the right to attend *Kindergarten* (nursery or play school) between the ages of three and six. *Kindergarten* concentrates on play, crafts, singing, etc., and aims to foster the child's social and emotional development. There is no formal teaching at all, this being reserved for the GRUNDSCHULE.

Kindertagesstätte Often called *Kita* for short, these day nurseries are intended for the children of working parents and usually cater for babies to 6-year-olds, though some *Kitas* also offer after-school care for older children.

Kinder- und Hausmärchen Jakob Grimm (1785–1863) and his brother Wilhelm (1786–1859) collected fairy tales for their book of *Kinder- und Hausmärchen* (Household and Nursery Tales). In 1852 they started compiling a comprehensive German dictionary, but the work was so vast that it was only completed in 1961, a century after their deaths.

Kirchensteuer Any taxpayer who is a member of one of the established churches in Germany (mainly Catholic and Protestant) has to pay *Kirchensteuer* (church tax). It is calculated as a proportion of income tax and is collected at source by the tax office, which then passes on the money to the relevant church.

Kita ▶ KINDERTAGESSTÄTTE

Knecht Ruprecht ▶ KRAMPUS

Krampus – Knecht Ruprecht The legendary figure known as Krampus in Austria and Bavaria, and Knecht Ruprecht in other regions, is St Nicholas's helper. While St Nicholas carries presents, Krampus is a scary – sometimes horned – figure, who carries a sack in which he is supposed to place disobedient children. Other traditions have him carrying a birch and a sack full of coal for the naughty ones. He visits on St Nicholas' Day (6 December). He is also believed to help the CHRISTKIND carry Christmas presents. See also the Calendar section.

Krankenkasse There are many different health insurance organizations in Germany. Contributions are high, due to the high standard (and cost) of health care in Germany. Members of the *Krankenkassen* are given plastic cards entitling them to treatment by the doctor of their choice.

Kriminalpolizei – Kripo The criminal investigation department deals with serious offences, including murder, terrorism, and organized crime.

Kulturstadt Weimar This thousand-year-old city has played an important role in Germany's cultural history. The composer Johann Sebastian Bach (1685–1750) and the artist Lucas Cranach (1472–1553) lived and worked here. Other important writers and poets such as Johann Wolfgang von Goethe (1749–1832), Johann Gottfried von Herder (1744–1803) and Christoph Martin Wieland (1733–1813) – who translated Shakespeare's plays – made the city their home. Friedrich von Schiller (1759–1805) wrote many of his plays in Weimar, while the composer Franz Liszt (1811–86) composed and gave concerts here. In 1919 the Bauhaus was founded in Weimar; in the same year, the constitution of the first German republic – the Weimar Republic – was drafted in the city.

Kur A health cure in a spa town lasting about three to six weeks and usually involving a special diet, exercise programmes, physiotherapy, massage, etc. These are intended for people with minor complaints or recovering from illness. *Kuren* are paid for by the KRANKENKASSEN, with the patient making a contribution. The *Kur* is not taken as frequently as it once was.

Kuratorium Junger Deutscher Film Young creative directors are given financial support by the LÄNDER. The Young German Film Board awards prizes for first films (sometimes also second films) of artistic value. The *Filmförderungsanstalt* – FFA (German Film Board) – provides financial assistance for film productions and cinemas.

Ladenschlusszeit Strict regulations governing *Ladenschlusszeit* (shop closing time) in Germany were relaxed in 1996. Shops are allowed to stay open until 8 p.m. on weekdays and Saturdays, and bakeries may open for three hours on Sundays. However, actual opening times vary, depending on the location and size of the shop.

Länder Germany is a federal republic consisting of sixteen member states called *Länder* or *Bundesländer*. Five so-called *neue Bundesländer* were added after reunification in 1990. Each *Land* has a degree of autonomy and is responsible for educational and cultural affairs, the police, the environment, and local government. Austria is a federal state consisting of

Culture

nine *Länder*. The Swiss equivalent of a German or Austrian *Land* is a KANTON.

Landtag The parliament of a *Land*. It is elected every four to five years using a similar mixed system of voting as for the BUNDESTAG elections.

Lebenspartnerschaft ▶ HOCHZEIT

Lehre This type of apprenticeship is still the normal way to learn a trade or train for a practical career in Germany. A *Hauptschulabschluss* is the minimum requirement, although many young people with a *Realschulabschluss* or ABITUR opt to train in this way. A *Lehre* takes about two to three years and involves practical training by a MEISTER(IN) backed up by lessons at a BERUFSSCHULE, with an exam at the end.

Linkspartei, Die (Left Party) Formerly known as the PDS, this ultra-left-wing party was formed in 1990 from the old East German SED, the Communist party which ruled in the former GDR. In the 2005 federal elections, the Left Party joined forces with the newly formed *Arbeit & soziale Gerechtigkeit – Die Wahlalternative*, or WASG (the Labour and Social Justice Party) and won an 8.7 per cent share of the vote.

Loveparade A techno music and dance festival which takes place in Berlin every summer, with hundreds of thousands of mainly young people attending. Originally a celebration of youth culture, it has become a major tourist attraction.

Markt Weekly markets are still held in most German cities and towns, usually laid out very attractively in the picturesque market squares. Fresh fruit and vegetables, flowers, eggs, cheese and other dairy products, bread, meat, and fish are available directly from the producer. Many Germans still buy most of their provisions '*auf dem Markt*'.

Matura ▶ ABITUR

Mauer *Die Mauer*, or the Berlin Wall, a 42-km (26-mile) structure of concrete blocks, was put up almost overnight in 1961. It was designed to halt the exodus of inhabitants from the Communist-controlled East of the city to the West. Over the following twenty-eight years, numerous people were killed trying to escape East Berlin. On 9 November 1989, an announcement by the East German Government that border checkpoints in the city had been abandoned resulted in a flood of people crossing to the West, the gradual dismantling of the wall, and eventually the WIEDERVEREINIGUNG. Parts of the Berlin Wall were sold to museums and private collectors. A few small sections remain as a memorial and tourist attraction.

Meister(in) A master craftsman or craftswoman who has completed rigorous training in his/her trade or vocation and has passed a final exam after several years' experience in a job. A *Meister(in)* is allowed to set up in business and train young people who are doing their LEHRE.

Meldepflicht An 'obligation to register' that applies to all German residents, regardless of nationality. Residents must inform the EINWOHNERMELDEAMT every time they change their address. The applicant is issued with an *Abmeldebestätigung* (notification of intention to leave) and must then register the new address. The system means that every resident can quickly be traced.

Mitfahrzentrale An agency that puts drivers and passengers in contact with each other (including via the Internet) to save petrol costs and reduce pollution. The Mitfahrzentrale charges a small fee, complies with particular requests (non-smoking, female drivers, etc.), and is popular throughout Germany for long-distance travel.

Mittagessen This is a cooked meal eaten in the middle of the day and is the main meal of the day for most Germans. Schoolchildren come home from school in time for *Mittagessen*, and most large companies have canteens where hot meals are served at lunchtime. On a Sunday, *Mittagessen* might consist of a starter such as clear broth, followed by a roast with gravy, boiled potatoes and vegetables, and a dessert.

Museumsinsel The Museum Island on the River Spree in Berlin is home to the renowned Pergamon Museum of Antiquities, attracting more than 850,000 visitors a year, as well as to the *Altes Museum* and *Neues Museum*. The island was designated a World Heritage Site by UNESCO in 1999.

Namenstag This day is celebrated by many Germans, especially Catholics, in the same way as a birthday. It is the day dedicated to the saint whose name the person carries, so someone called Martin, for example, would celebrate their *Namenstag* on *Martinstag* (11 November). See also the Calendar section.

Nationalrat In Austria the *Nationalrat* is the Federal Assembly's lower house, whose 183 members are elected for four years under a system of proportional representation. The BUNDESKANZLER commands the majority in the *Nationalrat*. The BUNDESRAT, the 64-member upper house, is elected by provincial assemblies. In Switzerland, the National Council is made up of 200 representatives, and together with the STÄNDERAT forms the Federal Assembly.

Neue Kronen Zeitung An Austrian tabloid that is published in Vienna and is read by around half the population. It is regarded as right-wing, as is the *Kurier*, Austria's other tabloid.

Neue Zürcher Zeitung A Swiss quality daily which is held in high esteem at home and abroad.

Culture

Numerus clausus The *Numerus clausus* system is used to limit the number of students studying certain oversubscribed subjects such as medicine at German universities. It means that only those students who have achieved a minimum average mark in their ABITUR are admitted.

Oktoberfest Germany's most famous beer festival (the Munich October Festival) actually starts each year in September. Over 5 million litres of beer are drunk over a period of sixteen days. The *Oktoberfest* goes back to the year 1810, when the Bavarian crown prince (later King Ludwig I) married Therese of Saxony-Hildburghausen. A horse race was organized in honour of the couple on the *Theresienwiese* (Therese's Meadow, named after the bride), and almost the entire population of Munich joined in the celebrations. The party was such a success that it became an annual event. Today the *Wies'n* (meadow), as the locals call the *Oktoberfest*, looks more like a giant fairground, with huge marquees in which the big breweries set up beer halls for visitors to drink many a *Maß* (a litre of beer) and eat *Weißwurst*

(veal sausage), *Schweinshaxe* (pork knuckles), and giant *Brezen* (pretzels) while listening and singing along to Bavarian music.

Orientierungsstufe A two-year orientation stage following GRUNDSCHULE, during which pupils can find out if they are more suited to a HAUPTSCHULE, GESAMTSCHULE, GYMNASIUM, or REALSCHULE. Students can transfer to a different school during this phase.

Ossi A colloquial and sometimes derogatory term for someone from the former East Germany (GDR), as opposed to a WESSI (someone from the former West Germany).

Ostern see the Calendar section.

ÖVP – Österreichische Volkspartei The conservative People's Party is Austria's centrist party. It was founded in 1945 and is the second largest party.

Papiertonne ▶ RECYCLING

Parkscheibe In Germany, some areas only allow limited parking time; here you have to display a *Parkscheibe* (parking disc) on your windscreen, with the hands of its clock set to your arrival time. These blue cardboard or plastic discs are available at newsagents and department stores.

Passionsspiel The famous Passion Play is held every ten years in the small Bavarian mountain village of Oberammergau. It has its origin in a vow sworn by the villagers in 1633 that they would perform the passion of Jesus if God delivered them from the plague.

PDS – Partei des Demokratischen Sozialismus ▶ LINKSPARTEI

Personalausweis The standard German identity card, with the holder's photograph and particulars, should in theory be carried at all times. If you are stopped by the police without any ID, you might be taken to a police station and kept there for up to six hours. The *Personalausweis* acts as a passport for Germans and Austrians travelling within the EU.

Pflegeversicherung Compulsory nursing-care insurance which all employees have to pay into as part of their SOZIALABGABEN. It was introduced in Germany in 1995 and pays for the long-term nursing care of the elderly and the severely disabled. Employers and employees make equal contributions to the scheme.

Pinakothek der Moderne This gallery of modern art, design, graphics, and architecture opened in Munich in 2002. Its collections concentrate on 20th- and 21st-century art, complementing the nearby Neue Pinakothek (exhibiting 19th-century art) and Alte Pinakothek (14th–18th century art).

Polterabend In Germany the *Polterabend* usually takes place a few days before the wedding and takes the form of a large party for the family and friends of both bride and groom. Traditionally, the guests smash some crockery, as this is supposed to bring good luck to the couple. *See also* HOCHZEIT.

Popmusik At the beginning of the 1980s, the *Neue Deutsche Welle* (New German Wave) of popular music brought German pop groups to the fore. Today all the different pop genres are represented by German groups, and in 2005 the German hip-hop band *Die Fantastischen Vier* won an ECHO music award. Some chart-topping German pop groups such as No Angels and Bro'Sis were discovered via the 'Popstars' REALITY-TV show.

Post ▶ DEUTSCHE POST

Prater Vienna's largest and most popular amusement park. In 1766 Joseph II, the son of Empress Maria Theresa, decreed that *Der Prater* should be open to everyone. Earlier it had been forbidden to enter forests and meadows reserved for imperial hunts. Now the Prater has old-fashioned swings, skittle alleys, and merry-go-rounds, including the oldest carousel in Europe. A *Riesenrad* (big wheel) with a diameter of 67 m (200 ft) was put up for the World Exhibition of 1897 and is a famous Viennese landmark.

Premiere Germany's main pay-TV channel, introduced in 1991, can be received via satellite or cable. Premiere subscribers can watch feature films, sports events, documentaries, and so on, uninterrupted by advertising.

Pro 7 Germany's third largest private television channel, Pro 7 is financed entirely by advertising. It offers documentaries, films, and news programmes.

profil An Austrian news and current affairs magazine, with a circulation of over 100,000. It has a reputation for hard-hitting journalism.

Culture

Reality-TV *Reality-Shows* are as popular in the German-speaking world as elsewhere. They include *Big Brother* (shown on RTL II in Germany and TV3 in Switzerland) and a mobile version called *Taxi Orange*, shown on ORF, the public broadcaster in Austria, in which contestants have to run a taxi company in Vienna and live off the profits. So-called *Casting-Shows* such as Popstars have produced chart-topping pop groups. *See also* POPMUSIK.

Realschule The secondary school that prepares pupils for the *Realschulabschluss* (school-leaving certificate). It is in between HAUPTSCHULE and GYMNASIUM, catering for less academic students who will probably train for a practical career. Pupils stay at the *Realschule* for six years after the GRUNDSCHULE. *See also* LEHRE, SCHULE.

Rechtschreibreform After much controversy, a reform aiming to simplify the rules governing German spelling was implemented in 1998. The old spellings were officially acceptable for a transitional period until 2005, and further modifications to the reform were agreed during that period. The new spellings are still controversial and are only binding for schools and public authorities. Some newspapers have retained or returned to the old spellings, so it remains to be seen whether the changes will gain general acceptance.

Recycling All *Hausmüll* (domestic waste) in Germany is collected in at least three bins, and waste materials are recycled and reused. The *Biotonne* is for biodegradable kitchen waste (vegetable and fruit peel, meat, cheese, nutshells, tea leaves, and coffee filters, etc.). The *Wertstofftonne* can be used for plastic containers, metal objects, cans, aluminium, textiles, etc., and anything with a GRÜNER PUNKT. A separate *Papiertonne* is used for paper and cardboard, although most wrapping is discarded at source or reused – German supermarkets don't hand out a free supply of plastic bags. The *Restmüll* is for sweepings and general household rubbish. Bottles and glass are taken to the *Glascontainer* (bottle bank). A deposit on drinks bottles encourages returning empties to the shop. There are also collection points for fridges, freezers, and bulky items. *See also* DUALES SYSTEM.

Regenbogenparade ▶ CHRISTOPHER STREET DAY

Reichstagsgebäude This historic building in the centre of Berlin became the seat of the BUNDESTAG in 1999. Its refurbishment, designed by the British architect Norman Foster, included the addition of a glass cupola, with a walkway open to visitors, which provides a spectacular viewing platform and further enhances the Berlin skyline.

Religion In Germany, the Christian community is divided almost equally between Roman Catholics (26.6 million people) and Protestants (26.3 million), who are mostly Lutheran. In April 2005, a German, Cardinal Joseph Ratzinger, was appointed head of the Roman Catholic Church as

Papst Benedikt XVI (Pope Benedict XVI). There are also more than 3 million Muslims, mostly from Turkey and former Yugoslavia, living in Germany. Eighty-eight per cent of Austrians are Catholic, while in Switzerland there are slightly more Catholics than Protestants, with Muslims – again mainly from Turkey and former Yugoslavia – making up just over 4 per cent of the population. *See also* KIRCHENSTEUER.

Rentenversicherung This is the compulsory state pension insurance in Germany. All employees have to pay into it as part of their SOZIALABGABEN, with employers and the state also making a contribution. The amount of the German state pension depends on the contributions made by the individual, with allowances for years spent as a student or carer.

Restmüll ▶ RECYCLING

Rosenmontag see the Calendar section.

RTL – Radio Télévision Luxembourg Germany's largest privately owned television channel is the market leader in commercial television. It broadcasts films, sport, news, and entertainment, and regularly achieves top viewing figures.

Ruhezeit This is the accepted 'quiet time', usually between one and three o'clock in the afternoon, late evening, and on Sundays. *Ruhezeit* prohibits loud music and any noisy work, including drilling and vacuuming. But many young Germans no longer adhere to the letter of the *Ruhezeit*. *See also* HAUSORDNUNG.

Salzburger Festspiele Since 1920, this annual festival has been held in Salzburg, the home of Wolfgang Amadeus Mozart (1756–91), as a tribute to the great composer.

SAT 1 Germany's second largest privately owned television channel broadcasts films, news, sport, and entertainment. It was the first commercial channel in the country.

3SAT This satellite TV channel is run jointly by ARD, ZDF, and Swiss and Austrian TV. It offers programmes that are not broadcast by other TV stations, and almost half of 3SAT's output is devoted to cultural reports.

S-Bahn ▶ U-BAHN

Schnellimbiss Usually a *Schnellimbiss* is just a stand, selling different kinds of *Würstchen* (sausages), rissoles, *Döner* (doner kebab) or *Leberkäse* (meat loaf), depending on which region you are in. You can eat there or take the snack away. *Currywurst* – sausages served with ketchup (or a tomato-based sauce) mixed with curry powder – is a *Schnellimbiss* favourite.

Schrebergarten A *Schrebergarten* is an enclosed mini-garden in a large common garden, usually just outside an urban area. As most German city-dwellers live in blocks of flats, many rent a *Schrebergarten* to provide them with a place where they can grow fruit and flowers and relax. The gardens are named after the Leipzig physician D. G. M. Schreber (1808–61), who had the idea of creating playgrounds for children and small gardens for adults, set within a common plot. By law, the size of each mini-garden is limited to no more than 400 sq. m (4,306 sq. ft). Most *Schrebergärten* have a shed or summer house at one end that often looks like a fairy-tale cottage, and tidy flower beds. The gardeners are members of an association (*Schrebergartenverein*) which represents their interests.

Schule German children have to attend school from the ages of 6 to 18. Full-time schooling is compulsory for nine or ten years, until pupils are at least 15. All children go to a GRUNDSCHULE for four years (six in Berlin) and move on to a HAUPTSCHULE, REALSCHULE, GYMNASIUM, or GESAMTSCHULE, depending on their ability. From the age of 15, some pupils attend a BERUFSSCHULE, a part-time vocational school. Some students stay at school until they are over 20, due to the system of SITZEN BLEIBEN.

Schultüte The first day at school (*der 1. Schultag*) is a big event for a German child, involving a ceremony at school and sometimes at church. The child is given a *Schultüte*, a large cardboard cone containing pens, small gifts, and sweets, to mark this special occasion.

Schützenfest An annual festival celebrated in most towns, involving a shooting competition, parade, and fair. The winners of the shooting competition are crowned *Schützenkönig* and *Schützenkönigin* (shooting king and queen) for the year.

Schutzpolizei (Schupo) Colloquially referred to as the Schupo, the Schutzpolizei is the general police force dealing with public security, order, and traffic offences. Most people know the Schupo only as traffic police.

Schwarzwald The Black Forest, a mountainous area in Baden-Württemberg in southwestern Germany, is a popular holiday destination for Germans and foreign tourists alike. The name refers to the large coniferous forests in the region. *See also* WALDSTERBEN.

Schweizerische Eidgenossenschaft The Swiss Confederation is the official name for Switzerland. The confederation was established in 1291 when farmers from the mountain cantons of Uri, Schwyz, and Unterwalden swore that they would jointly defend their traditional rights against the House of Habsburg. The unified federal state as it is today, with twenty-six self-governing cantons, was formed in 1848. *See also* KANTON.

Seniorenbüro There are 170 *Seniorenbüros* (senior citizens' offices) spread throughout Germany. They were set up in the early 1990s to organize events, publicize sources of help and advice, and help older people take part in volunteer work. They are government funded.

Culture (margin text)

siezen/duzen German has two forms for 'you', the formal *Sie* and the familiar *du*. *Du* is used when speaking to a friend, a child, or a family member. Young people always address each other as *du*. If someone says, *wir duzen uns* (we call each other *du*), it means that they are friends. When speaking to a person you do not know very well, the polite form *Sie* is used. Even though there has been a tendency for less formality in recent years, it is still best to say *Sie*, especially in work situations and when you would normally address someone in English as Mrs or Mr.

sitzen bleiben If German pupils fail more than one subject in their end-of-year school report, they have to repeat the year. This is colloquially referred to as *sitzen bleiben*. Some students might even have to repeat two years, not sitting their ABITUR until they are 20.

Skat A popular card game for three players playing with thirty-two German cards. Keen players even join a *Skat* club.

Solidaritätszuschlag A tax surcharge introduced to help pay for the cost of German reunification and rebuilding the economy in former East Germany (GDR). It is payable by every German taxpayer and firm.

Sozialabgaben This term refers to the contributions every German taxpayer has to make towards the four main state insurance schemes: pension, health, nursing care, and unemployment. This amounts to over 40 per cent of gross income, with employee and employer paying half each.

Soziokultur The sociocultural movement has its origins in the alternative cultural scene which developed in the 1970s in Germany. Groups of artists and performers developed new, independent centres such as theatres, art schools, and women's cultural groups.

SPD — Sozialdemokratische Partei Deutschlands One of the main German political parties. Reformed after the war in 1945, it is a workers' party supporting social-democratic values. In the 2005 federal elections, the SPD gained only 1 per cent fewer votes than the CDU/CSU; after protracted negotiations, the three parties agreed to form a Grand Coalition, headed by the CDU leader, Angela Merkel.

Der Spiegel One of Germany's best-selling weekly news and current affairs magazines, *Der Spiegel* was founded in 1947 and is published in Hamburg. It has a liberal outlook and has become synonymous with investigative journalism in Germany, as it has brought to light a number of major scandals in German business and politics over the years.

SPÖ — Sozialistische Partei Österreichs The Austrian Social-Democratic Party was founded in 1888 as the Sozialdemokratische

Arbeiterpartei Österreichs (Social Democratic Workers' Party of Austria). It was reformed in 1945 and is the largest political party in Austria.

Stadtumbau Ost This government programme was set up to regenerate inner-city housing and improve the urban environment between the years 2002 and 2009 in the eastern part of Germany (the former GDR).

Stammtisch A large table reserved for regulars in most German pubs. The word is also used to refer to the group of people who meet around the table for a drink and lively discussion.

Der Standard An Austrian daily printed on pink paper and considered to be liberal in its views.

Ständerat The Ständerat (Council of States) is the upper chamber in Switzerland. It is composed of forty-six representatives from the various cantons. *See also* KANTON.

Stasi, Staatssicherheitsdienst *Stasi* is the shortened nickname of the State Security Service, the much-despised secret police and their agents in the former GDR. With the help of an extensive network of informers, the *Stasi* built up personal files on a third of the East German population. It was disbanded a year before the WIEDERVEREINIGUNG. Since then there have been many charges relating to political crimes committed by *Stasi* agents, as well as enquiries into the number of former GDR citizens who cooperated with the *Stasi*. *See also* IM.

Straußwirtschaft An inn set up temporarily by a local winegrower for a few weeks after the new wine has been made. A bunch of flowers and vine leaves above the door shows that the new vintage is ready for tasting. *See also* BESENWIRTSCHAFT and HEURIGER.

Studentenwerke The *Studentenwerke* (student welfare services) are responsible for the economic, social, cultural, and health care of students at higher educational institutions.

Süddeutsche Zeitung This respected daily national newspaper was founded in 1945 and is published in Munich. It has a liberal outlook and is read mainly in southern Germany.

Tempolimit Speed limits are either compulsory – 50 km/h (30 mph) in towns, 100 km/h (60 mph) on other roads – or recommended when driving in bad weather conditions, on dangerous stretches, and in urban areas. On the *Autobahn* the *Richtgeschwindigkeit* (recommended maximum speed) is 130 km/h (80 mph). In residential areas the limit can be as low as 30 km/h (20 mph); the 30-Zone was introduced to protect children and pedestrians.

Trabant A make of car produced in the former GDR. A Trabant, or Trabi, with its two-stroke engine and plastic body, was a prized possession, and

Culture

people had to wait for years to get one. After reunification, the Trabant came to symbolize the GDR era and has achieved cult status in Germany.

U-Bahn Most large cities have a *U-Bahn* (*Untergrundbahn*) (underground railway network) that connects with an *S-Bahn* (*Schnellbahn* or *Stadtbahn*) (city and suburban railway). The same ticket can normally be used for both services.

Umweltschutz (Environmental protection) Most Germans feel a strong sense of responsibility for the environment, especially after seeing so many forests dying (WALDSTERBEN). The *Bundesumweltministerium* is the government ministry responsible for all environmental matters. Its policy is based on the 'polluter must pay' principle, by which manufacturers are obliged to collect, sort, and recycle their waste; on the cooperation principle, by which every individual is responsible for the environment; and on the prevention principle, which encourages manufacturers to develop environmentally friendly products. Other focal points are a more efficient use of energy, a clean air and water programme, less road traffic, and cleaner fuels, nature conservation, and soil protection. *See also* DUALES SYSTEM, GRÜNER PUNKT, RECYCLING.

Verein There are over 300,000 officially registered *Vereine* (clubs or associations) with their own constitution and by-laws. Millions of Germans belong to a club; nearly one in four is a member of a sports club, and there are around 15 million hiking-club members. Stamp collectors, marksmen, dog breeders, music fans – in fact those who follow any kind of activity or hobby – are soon organized into a *Verein*. Membership fees are usually low, and everybody is encouraged to socialize at club level.

Vignette In order to be able to use Austrian or Swiss motorways, all vehicles must display a sticker on the windscreen called a *Vignette*. These stickers are usually valid for one year, but foreign tourists in Austria can buy stickers for a period of ten days or two months. Each sticker can be bought at border crossings and petrol stations.

Volkshochschule (VHS) A local adult education centre that can be found in every German town. The *VHS* offers low-cost day and evening classes in a wide range of subjects, including crafts, languages, music, and exercise.

Waldsterben *Waldsterben* (the death of forests) is due mainly to pollution from factories and cars. By 1996 over half of Germany's trees were damaged. The threat to forests has strengthened support for Germany's ecological political movement, BÜNDNIS 90/DIE GRÜNEN.

WASG ▶ LINKSPARTEI

Wehrdienst Compulsory military service for young men in Germany (nine months), Switzerland (three months), and Austria (six months). Young Germans are generally called up when they are 18 or 19, although there are certain exemptions. Conscientious objectors may apply to do ZIVILDIENST instead.

Weihnachten see the Calendar section.

Weihnachtsmarkt During the weeks of Advent, Christmas markets take place in most German towns, selling Christmas decorations, handmade toys and crib figures, traditional Christmas biscuits, and mulled wine to sustain the shoppers.

Wein Germany, Switzerland, and Austria are wine-producing countries, best known for their white wines. Germany's main wine regions are Franconia, the Rhineland-Palatinate, the Moselle area, and Baden-Württemberg. Rhine wine is traditionally sold in tall brown bottles and

wine from the Moselle in green bottles; Franconian *Bocksbeutel* comes in wide, bulbous bottles. There are two categories of German wine, the cheap *Tafelwein* (table wine) and the superior *Qualitätswein* (quality wine). The best wines are designated *Qualitätswein mit Prädikat*. *Sekt* is a champagne-like sparkling wine. In August and September there are festivals in German wine towns and villages. Austria grows red and white wines, mainly in the Burgenland, in Styria, and around the Neusiedler See where the HEURIGER is celebrated. More than a third of the total area of grape cultivation in Austria is devoted to *Grüner Veltliner*, a full-bodied, fruity white wine. Wines from Switzerland are mostly drunk locally and are produced in the Thurgau region. The Swiss reputation rests with their spirits, such as *Kirsch*, *Pflümli*, *Mirabelle*, and *Enzian*. *See also* BESENWIRTSCHAFT and STRAUSSWIRTSCHAFT.

Weinstube A cosy wine bar which offers a wide choice of wines and usually also serves a few dishes that are considered to go well with wine. A *Weinstube* can be more upmarket than an ordinary pub, or else fairly rustic, especially in wine-growing areas.

Die Welt A national daily newspaper published in Hamburg. It has a large business section and is considered right-wing in its views.

Wende This word can refer to any major political or social change or turning point, but it is used especially to refer to the collapse of Communism in 1989, symbolized by the fall of die MAUER (the Berlin Wall), which eventually led to the WIEDERVEREINIGUNG in 1990.

Wertstofftonne ▶ RECYCLING

Wessi A colloquial and sometimes derogatory term for someone from West Germany, as opposed to an OSSI. The expression *Besserwessi*, a pun on

Besserwisser (know-all), is sometimes used to describe overly confident West Germans.

Westdeutsche Allgemeine Zeitung (WAZ) Germany's highest-circulation serious national paper. It is published in Essen, and caters mainly for the densely populated Ruhr area.

Wiedervereinigung The reunification of Germany, which officially took place on 3 October 1990, when the former GDR was incorporated into the BUNDESREPUBLIK. The huge financial and social costs of reunification are still being felt throughout Germany. *See also* SOLIDARITÄTSZUSCHLAG.

Wirtschaftswunder, The German 'economic miracle', which resulted from the country's rapid reconstruction after the Second World War. The economy boomed in the decades after 1950.

Die Woche A relatively new weekly newspaper, which was founded in 1993 and is published in Hamburg. It is less comprehensive and easier to read than DIE ZEIT, but is also an important opinion leader with a liberal outlook offering background information, analyses, and reports.

ZDF – Zweites Deutsches Fernsehen The second German public TV channel, founded in 1961. It broadcasts the *Zweites Programm* with entertainment, news, information, and a limited amount of advertising.

Die Zeit Germany's 'heaviest' weekly newspaper, published in Hamburg, is considered essential reading for academics and intellectuals. Former BUNDESKANZLER Helmut Schmidt is a joint editor. The paper offers in-depth analysis of current issues in politics, society, culture, and the arts.

Zeugnis der allgemeinen Hochschulreife ▶ ABITUR

Zivildienst Community service, which recognized conscientious objectors in Germany, Austria, and Switzerland can choose to carry out instead of WEHRDIENST. It lasts longer than WEHRDIENST and usually involves caring for children or elderly, disabled, or sick people.

Culture

Letter-writing / Briefeschreiben

Holiday postcard

- Beginnings (informal): 'Lieber' here because it's a man; if it's a woman, use e.g. Liebe Elke.

  To two people, repeat 'Liebe(r)': Lieber Hans, liebe Elke.

  To a family: Liebe Schmidts, Liebe Familie Schmidt, or just Liebe Leute.

- Address: Note that the title (Herrn, Frau, Fräulein) stands on the line above the name. Herr always has an n on the end in addresses.

  The house number comes after the street name.

  The postcode comes before the place, and if you're writing from outside the country put a D- for Germany, A- for Austria or CH- for Switzerland in front of it.

Heidelberg, den 6.8. 2008

Lieber Hans!

Einen schönen Gruß aus Alt-Heidelberg! Wir sind erst zwei Tage hier, aber schon sehr angetan von der Stadt und Umgebung, trotz der vielen Touristen. Allerdings ist es ziemlich schwül. Wir waren gestern abend in einem Konzert im Schlosshof, eine wunderbare Stimmung! Und dann die herrliche Aussicht auf Altstadt und Neckar von der Terrasse. Morgen machen wir eine Bootsfahrt, dann geht's am Donnerstag wieder nach Hause. Hoffentlich ist deine Mutter inzwischen wieder gesund.

Bis bald

Max und Sophie

Herrn

Hans Matthäus

Brucknerstr. 26

91052 Erlangen

- Endings (informal): Herzlich or Herzlichst, Herzliche Grüße; more affectionately: Alles Liebe; Bis bald = See you soon .

Letters

. . . .

Postkarte aus dem Urlaub

■ *Anrede: sehr einfach auf Postkarten, immer 'Dear' und der Vorname, der im englischen Sprachraum viel häufiger verwendet wird. Die Anrede kann auch entfallen.*

■ *Meist keine Ortsangabe, wenn der Ort aus dem Inhalt oder dem Bild auf der Postkarte klar hervorgeht.*
Datum – in den USA verwendet man die Reihenfolge Monat, Tag, Jahr, wenn ein Datum mit Ziffern angegeben ist – 8.6.2008

■ *Adresse: Der Titel (Mr, Mrs, Miss, Ms) steht direkt vor dem Namen auf der gleichen Zeile.*

Das Haus hat oft einen Namen anstelle einer (oder zusätzlich zur) Hausnummer, die übrigens vor dem Straßennamen steht.

Es folgen (in GB) Ortschaft, meist auch Grafschaft, dann Postleitzahl (postcode), alles jeweils auf einer eigenen Zeile; in den USA Ortschaft und Postleitzahl (zipcode), mit dem auf zwei Buchstaben abgekürzten Namen des Staates davor:

John Splaine Jr.
1067 Blackwall Avenue
Studio City
CA 91604
USA

Letters

6.8.2008

Dear John,

Greetings from old Heidelberg! Got here ① a couple of days ago, but already in love with the place (in spite of all the tourists). It's pretty sultry though. Last night we went to a concert in the castle courtyard, very atmospheric. And a terrific view of the river and the old town from the terrace. Tomorrow we're taking a boat trip, and then on Thursday we head for home. Hope ① your mother's fully recovered by now.

See you soon,

   Mark and Juliet

Mr J. Roberts
The Willows
49 North Terrace
Kings Barton
Nottinghamshire
NG8 4LQ
England

■ *Schlussformel:*
All the best, Best wishes, *oder einfach* Yours; *auch* Love (from), *wenn man den Addressaten näher steht.*

① *Telegrammstil: die Angabe der Person entfällt auf Postkarten oft.*

. . . .

Christmas and New Year wishes

On a card:

Frohe Weihnachten und viel Glück im neuen Jahr

A bit more formal: Ein gesegnetes Weihnachtsfest und die besten Wünsche zum neuen Jahr

A bit less formal: Fröhliche Weihnachten und einen guten Rutsch ins neue Jahr

In a letter:

- *On most personal letters German speakers don't put their address at the top, but just the name of the place and the date*

Würzburg, den 20.12.2008

Liebe Karin, lieber Ferdinand,

euch und euren Kindern wünschen wir von Herzen frohe Weihnachten und ein glückliches neues Jahr. Wir hoffen, es geht euch allen gut, und dass wir uns bald mal wieder sehen werden. Es kommt uns so vor, als hätten wir uns eine Ewigkeit nicht gesehen.

Das vergangene Jahr war für uns sehr ereignisreich. Thomas hatte im Sommer einen Unfall mit dem Fahrrad, und brach sich den Arm und das Schlüsselbein. Sabine hat das Abitur gerade noch bestanden und ist jetzt an der Uni in Erlangen, studiert Sport. Der arme Michael ist im Oktober arbeitslos geworden und sucht immer noch nach einer Stelle.

Ihr müsst unbedingt vorbeikommen, wenn ihr das nächste Mal in der Gegend seid. Ruft doch einfach ein paar Tage vorher an, damit wir etwas ausmachen können.

Mit herzlichen Grüßen

Eure Gabi und Michael

Letter-writing / Briefeschreiben

. . . .

Weihnachts- und Neujahrsgrüße

Auf einer Karte:

[Best wishes for a] Happy ① Christmas and a Prosperous New Year

All best wishes for Christmas and the New Year

Wishing you every happiness this Christmas[tide] and in the New Year

① *Oder etwas altmodisch:* Merry

In einem Brief:

> 44 Louis Gardens
> London NW6 4GM
>
> December 20th 2008

Dear Peter and Claire,

First of all, a very happy Christmas and all the best for the New Year
to you and the children.① We hope you're all well② and that we'll
see you again soon. It seems ages since we last met up.

We've had a very eventful year. Last summer Gavin came off his
bike and broke his arm and collarbone. Kathy scraped through her
A levels and is now at Sussex doing European Studies. Poor Tony was
made redundant in October and is still looking for a job.

Do come and see us next time you are over this way. Just give us a
ring a couple of days before so we can fix something.

All best wishes

Tony and Ann

Letters

① *Oder (vor allem, wenn die Kinder älter sind):* to you and the family.
② *Informeller:* flourishing.

Letters

Invitation (informal)

> Hamm, den 22.4.2009
>
> Liebe Jennie,
>
> wäre es möglich, dass du ① in den Sommerferien zu uns kommst? Katrin und Gottfried würden sich riesig freuen (ich und mein Mann natürlich auch). Wir planen eine Reise zum Bodensee Ende Juli/Anfang August, du ① könntest gerne mitfahren. Es ist wirklich sehr schön dort unten. Wir werden wahrscheinlich zelten – hoffentlich hast du ① nichts dagegen!
>
> Schreib bald, ob das für dich ① in Frage kommt.
>
> Herzliche Grüße
>
> Monika Pfortner

- *Beginning: if you put a comma after the name on the first line (which is usual), the letter proper should start with a small letter.*

① du, dich, dein etc.: although many people still write these with a capital in letters, this is not necessary. But the formal Sie, Ihnen, Ihr must always have a capital.

Invitation (formal)

Invitations to parties are usually by word of mouth, while for weddings, announcements rather than invitations are usually sent out:

> Irene Brinkmann   Stefan Hopf
>
> Wir heiraten am Samstag, den 25. April 2009,
> um 14 Uhr in der Pfarrkirche Landsberg.
>
> Goethestraße 12   Ulrichsweg 4
>
> Landsberg   Altötting

Einladung (informell)

- *Die Absenderadresse befindet sich oben auf dem Brief selbst, entweder rechts oder in der Mitte, darunter das Datum.*

- *Das Datum im Englischen hat viele Formen:* May 10, 10 May, May 10th, 10th May *sind alle möglich und gleichermaßen richtig. In den USA verwendet man die Reihenfolge Monat, Tag, Jahr, wenn das Datum in Ziffern angegeben wird:* 05/10/2009

35 Winchester Drive
Stoke Gifford
Bristol
BS34 8PD

April 22nd 2009

Dear Klaus,

Is there any chance of your coming to stay with us in the summer holidays? Roy and Debbie would be delighted if you could (as well as David and me, of course). We hope to go to North Wales at the end of July/beginning of August, and you'd be very welcome to come too. It's really beautiful up there. We'll probably take tents – I hope that's OK by you.

Let me know as soon as possible if you can manage it.

All best wishes

Rachel Hemmings

Letters

Einladung (förmlich)
Zu einer Hochzeit mit anschließendem Empfang

Mr and Mrs Peter Thompson

request the pleasure of your company
at the marriage of their daughter

Hannah Louise
to
Steven David Warner

at St. Mary's Church, Little Bourton
on Saturday 25th July 2009 at 2 p.m.
and afterwards at the
Golden Cross Hotel, Billing

R.S.V.P.   23 Santers Lane
Little Bourton
Northampton
NN6 1AZ

Accepting an invitation

Edinburgh, den 2.5.2009

Liebe Frau Pfortner,

recht herzlichen Dank für Ihre liebe Einladung. Da ich noch keine festen Pläne für die Sommerferien habe, möchte ich sie sehr gerne annehmen. Allerdings darf ich nicht mehr als vier bis fünf Tage weg sein, da es meiner Mutter nicht sehr gut geht. Sie ① müssen mir sagen, was ich mitbringen soll (außer Edinburgh Rock!). Ist es sehr warm am Bodensee? Kann man im See schwimmen?

Natürlich habe ich nichts gegen Zelten. Auch hier in Schottland bei Wind und Regen macht es mir Spaß!

Ich freue mich auf ein baldiges Wiedersehen.

Herzliche Grüße

Jennie Stewart

① *Since this is a letter from a younger person writing to the mother of a friend, she uses the formal Sie form and possessive Ihr (always with capitals), and writes to her as* "Frau Pfortner". *On the other hand it was quite natural for* Frau Pfortner *to use the* du *form to her.*

Antwort auf eine Einladung (informell)

Mozartstraße 5
32756 Detmold
Germany

2 May 2009

Dear Mrs Hemmings,

Many thanks for your letter and kind invitation. Since I don't have anything fixed yet for the summer holidays, I'd be delighted to come. However I mustn't be away for more than four or five days since my mother hasn't been very well.

You must let me know what I should bring. How warm is it in North Wales? Can one swim in the sea? Camping is fine as far as I'm concerned, we take our tent everywhere.

Looking forward to seeing you again soon,

Yours

Klaus

Antwort auf eine Einladung (förmlich)

Greenacres
Westway
Balsall Common
West Midlands
CV7 8RR

■ Man wiederholt die Details von der Einladung, etwas vereinfacht.

Annahme:
Richard Willis has great pleasure in accepting Mr and Mrs Peter Thompson's kind invitation to the marriage of their daughter Hannah Louise to Steven Warner at St. Mary's Church, Little Bourton, on Saturday 25th July.

■ Im Falle einer Absage ist es oft höflicher, einen Brief zu schreiben, vor allem wenn man die Brauteltern gut kennt.

Absage:
Richard Willis regrets that he is unable to accept Mr and Mrs Peter Thompson's kind invitation ... , due to a prior engagement.

Letters

Replying to a job advertisement

David Baker
67 Whiteley Avenue
St George
Bristol
BS5 6TW

Softwarehaus WSO GmbH
Personalabteilung
Kanalstr. 75
D-75757 Pforzheim   Bristol, den 26.2.2009

Ihre Stellenanzeige im Tagblatt vom 23.2.2009

Sehr geehrte Damen und Herren, ①

ich interessiere mich für die von Ihnen im Tagblatt vom 23. Februar
ausgeschriebene Stelle eines Computergrafikers und würde mich freuen, wenn
Sie mir nähere Informationen zuschicken könnten. ②

Derzeit bin ich bei der Firma Wondersoft Ltd in Bristol tätig, aber mein Vertrag
läuft schon Ende des Monats aus, ③ und ich möchte gerne in Deutschland
arbeiten. Wie Sie meinem Lebenslauf entnehmen können, verfüge ich über
ausgezeichnete Sprachkenntnisse sowie die geforderten Qualifikationen und
einschlägige Berufserfahrung.

Zu einem Vorstellungsgespräch stehe ich jederzeit ab dem 6. März zur Verfügung.
Sie können mich ab diesem Datum unter der folgenden Adresse in Deutschland
erreichen:

bei Gerber
Rudolfstr. 22
81925 München
Tel. (089) 460 99 507

Ich freue mich darauf, von Ihnen zu hören. ④

Mit freundlichen Grüßen

David Baker

Anlage: Lebenslauf

---

① *Correct if the letter is addressed to the personnel department, but if it is addressed to the personnel manager* (An den Personalleiter, ...) *the letter begins:* Sehr geehrter Herr XY *or* Sehr geehrte Frau XY.

② *Or if you have enough details and want to apply for the job right away:* und möchte mich um diese Stellung bewerben.

③ *Or if you are unemployed:* Derzeit bin ich arbeitslos, ...

④ *Or:* Ihre Antwort erwarte ich mit Interesse.

. . . .

Bewerbung auf eine Stellenanzeige hin

Humboldtweg 16
60247 Frankfurt a. M.
Germany
Tel. (069) 724 689

13th February 2009

The Personnel Manager ①
Patterson Software plc
Milton Estate
Bath BA6 8YZ

Dear Sir or Madam, ②

I am interested in the post of programmer advertised in the Guardian of 12th February and would be grateful if you could send me further particulars. ③

I am currently working for the Sempo Corporation in Frankfurt, but my contract finishes at the end of the month, and I would like ④ to come and work in the UK. As you can see from my CV (enclosed), I have an excellent command of English and also the required qualifications and experience.

I will be available for interview any time after 6th March, from which date I can be contacted at the following address in the UK:

c/o Lewis
51 Dexter Road
London N7 6BW
Tel. 0207 607 5512

I look forward to hearing from you. ⑤

Yours sincerely

Rita Steinmüller

Encl.

Letters

① *Den Brief so addressieren, wenn in der Anzeige kein Name vorkommt; aber wenn es z.B. heißt* "Reply to Angela Summers", *dann* "Ms Angela Summers, …"

② *Wenn der Name bekannt ist, dann* "Dear Ms Summers", "Dear Mr Wright" *etc.*

③ *Oder falls Sie schon genügend Informationen haben und sich bewerben wollen:* "and would like to apply for this position".

④ *Oder falls Sie arbeitslos sind:* "I am currently unemployed and would like …"

⑤ *Oder:* "Thanking you in anticipation".

Curriculum Vitae (CV) or (*Amer.*) Résumé

Lebenslauf

David Baker
67 Whiteley Avenue
St George
Bristol
BS5 6TW
Großbritannien

Tel. +43 (0)117 945 3421

geboren am 30.06.1980 in London, ledig①

<u>Ausbildung</u>

1996 GCSEs in 9 Fächern (ungefähr = mittlere Reife), John Radcliffe School, Croydon

1998 A Levels in Mathematik, Höherer Mathematik, Informatik, Deutsch (ungefähr = Abitur), Croydon Sixth Form College

1999 Teilzeitarbeit in München, Abendkurse an der VHS

2000-04 University of Aston, Birmingham, B.Sc in Informatik

<u>Berufstätigkeit</u>

08/04 - 08/07 Traineeausbildung, anschließend Sotwareentwickler bei IBM

seit 09/07 Programmierer bei Wondersoft plc, Bristol

Entwicklung von Programmen für die Industrie; Schwerpunkt: Grafiksoftware

<u>Besondere Kenntnisse</u>

Fremdsprachen: Deutsch (fließend), Französisch (gut)

① *Or:* Verheiratet (mit einem Kind/zwei Kindern etc.); Geschieden (mit einem Kind/zwei Kindern etc.)

Lebenslauf

CURRICULUM VITAE ①

Name:	Rita Steinmüller
Address:	Humboldtweg 16 60247 Frankfurt a. M. Germany
Telephone:	+44 (0)69 724 689
Nationality:	German
Date of Birth:	11/3/1983
Marital status:	Single ②

Education:

2001-2005	Degree Course in Information Technology at Stuttgart University
1994-2001	Theodor-Heuss-Gymnasium, Eichborn Abitur examination (approx. A Level) in Mathematics, Physics, Economics and English

Employment:

2006-present	Program development engineer with Sempo-Informatik, Frankfurt, specializing in computer graphics
2005-2006	Trainee programmer with Oregon Germany, Rüsselsheim

Further skills:

Languages:	German (mother tongue), English (fluent spoken and written), French (good)
Interests:	Travel (many trips to the UK), chess, tennis

---

① Oder (Amer.): RÉSUMÉ
② Oder: Married (with one/two/three etc. children), Divorced (with one/two/three etc. children)

Letters

Letter-writing / Briefeschreiben

. . . .

Booking a hotel room

Hotel Goldener Pflug
Ortsstraße 7
69235 Steinbach

Tobias Schwarz
Gartenstr. 19
76530 Baden-Baden

16. Juli 2009

Sehr geehrte Damen und Herren,

Ich wurde durch die Broschüre "Hotels und Pensionen im Naturpark Odenwald
(Ausgabe 2008)" auf ihr Hotel aufmerksam.

Ich möchte für mich und meine Frau für die Zeit vom 2. bis 11. August (neun Nächte)
ein ruhiges Doppelzimmer mit Dusche reservieren, sowie ein Einzelzimmer für unseren
Sohn.

Falls Sie für diese Zeit etwas Passendes haben, informieren Sie mich doch bitte über
den Preis und darüber, ob Sie eine Anzahlung wünschen.

Mit freundlichen Grüßen

Tobias Schwarz

Booking a campsite

Camilla Stumpf
Saalgasse 10
60311 Frankfurt

Camping am See
Frau Bettina Sattler
Auweg 6-10
87654 Waldenkirchen

■ *For a business letter to a particular person, use "Sehr geehrte(r)"
and the name. (If this letter were to a man, it would start "Sehr geehrter
Herr Sattler").*

Frankfurt, den 16.04.2009

Sehr geehrte Frau Sattler,

Ihr Campingplatz wurde mir von Herrn Stephan Seidel empfohlen, der schon mehrmals
bei Ihnen war. ① Ich würde nun gerne vom 18. bis 25. Juli mit zwei Freunden eine
Woche bei Ihnen verbringen. Könnten Sie uns bitte einen Zeltplatz ② möglichst in
unmittelbarer Nähe des Sees ③ reservieren?

Würden Sie mir freundlicherweise mitteilen, ob Sie meine Reservierung annehemen
können und ob Sie eine Anzahlung wünschen?

Außerdem wäre ich Ihnen dankbar für eine kurze Wegbeschreibung von der Autobahn.

Mit vielem Dank im Voraus und freundlichen Grüßen

Camilla Stumpf

① *Or if you have found the campsite in a guide, say e.g.:* "Ich habe Ihre Anschrift dem ACDA-
Campingführer 2008 entnommen".
② *Or if you have a caravan:* "einen Stellplatz für einen Wohnwagen".
③ *Alternatives:* "in schattiger/geschützter Lage".

Letters

Letter-writing / Briefeschreiben

Hotelzimmerreservierung

The Manager	35 Prince Edward Road
Torbay Hotel	Oxford OX7 3AA
Dawlish	
Devon	Tel. 01865 322435
EX37 2LR	23rd April 2009

Dear Sir or Madam,

I saw your hotel listed in the Inns of Devon guide for last year, and wish to reserve a double (or twin-bedded) room with shower ① in a quiet position from August 2nd – 11th (nine nights), also a single room for our son.

If you have anything suitable for this period please let me know the price and whether you require a deposit.

Yours sincerely

Charles Fairhurst

① *Alternativen:* "with bath", "with ensuite".

Campingplatzreservierung

22 Daniel Avenue
Caldwood
Leeds LS8 7RR
Tel. 01132 998767

25th April 2009

Mr Joseph Vale
Lakeside Park
Rydal
Cumbria
LA22 9RZ

Dear Mr Vale

Your campsite was recommended to me by James Dallas, who knows it from several visits. ① I and two friends would like to come for a week from July 18th to 25th. Could you please reserve us a site for one tent, ② preferably close to the shore. ③

Please confirm the booking and let me know if you require a deposit. Would you also be good enough to send me instructions on how to reach you from the motorway.

Yours sincerely

Frances Good

① *Oder falls Sie den Campingplatz einem Führer entnommen haben, etwa:* "I found your site in the Tourist Board's list/ the Good Camper's Guide" *etc.*
② *Oder falls Sie einen Wohnwagen haben:* "a caravan site".
③ *Andere Möglichkeiten:* "in a shady/sheltered spot".

Letter-writing / Briefeschreiben

Sending an e-mail

The illustration shows a typical interface for sending e-mail.

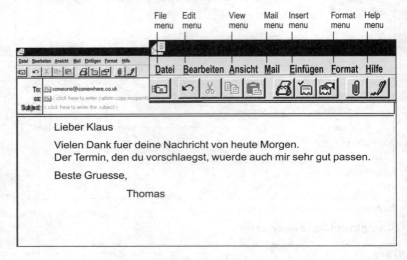

Das Verschicken von E-Mails

Die Abbildung zeigt eine typische Oberfläche zum Verschicken von E-Mails.

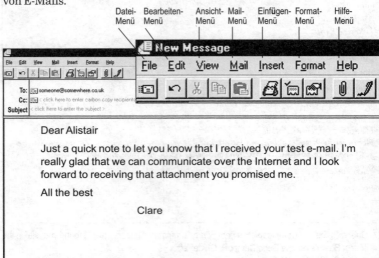

SMS (electronic text-messaging)

The basic principles governing German SMS abbreviations are similar to those governing English SMS. Certain words or syllables are represented by letters or numbers that sound the same. Most punctuation is usually omitted, umlauts are rarely used, and there are no strict rules about upper and lower case. For example 'viele Grüße' can be 'vlg'. Sentences are shortened by leaving out certain letters – 'bist du noch wach?' might read 'bidunowa'. Often just the initial letter of a word is used, as in 'ff' for 'Fortsetzung folgt'. Many English abbreviations have made it into German text messages. For example '4u' (for you) is often used for 'für dich'.

Glossary of German SMS abbreviations

Abbreviation	Meaning		Abbreviation	Meaning
8ung	Achtung		sms	schreib mir schnell
ads	alles deine Schuld		sz	schreib zurück
akla?	alles klar?		tabu	tausend Bussis
aws	auf Wiedersehen		vegimini	vergiss mich nicht
bb	bis bald		vlg	viele Grüße
bda	bis dann		vv	viel Vergnügen
bidunowa?	bist du noch wach?		wamaduheu?	was machst du heute?
braduhi?	brauchst du Hilfe?		waudi	warte auf dich
bs	bis später		we	Wochenende
dad	denke an dich		zdom?	zu dir oder zu mir?
d	der			
div	danke im Voraus		*Emoticons*	
dubido	du bist doof			
ff	Fortsetzung folgt		:-)	lächeln, glücklich
g	grinsen		:-))	sehr glücklich
g&k	Gruß und Kuss		:-|	Stirnrunzeln
gn8	gute Nacht		:-e	enttäuscht
gngn	geht nicht, gibts nicht		:-(	unglücklich, traurig
hahu	habe Hunger		:-((	sehr unglücklich
hdl	habe dich lieb		:->	sarkastisch
hdos	halt die Ohren steif		%-)	verwirrt
hegl	herzlichen Glückwunsch		:~(or :'-(	weinen
ild	ich liebe dich		;-)	zwinkern
jon	jetzt oder nie		|-o	müde
katze?	kannst du tanzen?		:-\	skeptisch
ko5mispä	komme 5 Minuten später		:-D	lachen
l8er	later = später		:-<>	erstaunt
lg	liebe Grüße		:-p	rausgestreckte Zunge
lidumino	liebst du mich noch?		:-O	schreien
mamima	mail mir mal		O:-)	Engel
mumidire	muss mit dir reden		:-* or :-x	Kuss
n8	Nacht		:-o	Schock
nfd	nur für dich		@}-,-'—	Rose
pg	Pech gehabt			
rumian	ruf mich an			
sfh	Schluss für heute			
siw	soweit ich weiß			

SMS

SMS (elektronische Textmitteilungen über das Handy)

SMS ist die englische Abkürzung für "Short Message Service", was sich als "Kurznachrichtendienst" übersetzen lässt. Im Englischen gibt es zahllose Abkürzungen, die es erlauben, viele Informationen mit wenigen Zeichen und Zahlen zu übermitteln. Zum Beispiel: 2L8 = 'too late'. Für die meisten Nachrichten tippt man nur die Anfangsbuchstaben jedes Wortes ein, zum Beispiel: ttyl = 'talk to you later' oder fyi = 'for your information'.

Verzeichnis von englischen SMS-Abkürzungen

Abkürzung	Bedeutung	Abkürzung	Bedeutung	Abkürzung	Bedeutung
adn	any day now	lol	lots of luck/ laughing out loud	yr	your
afaik	as far as I know			2	to, too
atb	all the best	mob	mobile	2day	today
b	be	msg	message	2l8	too late
b4	before	myob	mind your own business	2moro	tomorrow
b4n	bye for now	ne	any	2nite	tonight
bbl	be back late(r)	ne1	anyone	3sum	threesome
bcnu	be seeing you	no1	no one	4	for
bfn	bye for now	oic	oh, I see		
brb	be right back	otoh	on the other hand	*Emoticons*	
btw	by the way	pcm	please call me	:-)	smiling, happy face
bwd	backward	pls	please	:-))	very happy face
c	see	ppl	people	:-|	frowning
cu	see you	r	are		
cul8r	see you later	rofl	rolling on the floor, laughing	:-e	disappointed
f2f	face to face			:-(	unhappy, sad face
f2t	free to talk	ru	are you	:-((	very unhappy face
fwd	forward	ruok	are you OK?	:->	sarcastic
fwiw	for what it's worth	sit	stay in touch	%-)	confused
fyi	for your information	som1	someone	:-(or :'-(	crying
gal	get a life	spk	speak	;-)	winking happy face
gr8	great	thkq	thank you	|-o	tired, asleep
h8	hate	ttyl	talk to you later	:-\	sceptical
hand	have a nice day	tx	thanks	:-D	big smile, laughing face
hak	hugs and kisses	u	you		
hth	hope this helps	ur	you are	:-<>	amazed
ic	I see	w/	with	X=	fingers crossed
iluvu	I love you	wan2	want to	:-p	tongue sticking out
imho	in my humble opinion	wan2 tlk	want to talk?	:-O	shouting
imo	in my opinion	werv u bin	where have you been?	O:-)	angel
iow	in other words	wknd	weekend	:-* or :-x	big kiss!
jic	just in case	wot	what	:-o	shocked face
jk	just kidding	wu	what's up?	@}-,-'—	a rose
kit	keep in touch	x	kiss		
kwim	know what I mean?	xlnt	excellent		
l8	late	xoxoxo	hugs and kisses		
l8r	later				

SMS

A, a¹ /eɪ/ *n.* A, a, *das;* **A road** Straße 1. Ordnung; ≈ Bundesstraße, *die*

a² /ə, *stressed* eɪ/ *indef. art.* ein/eine/ein; **he is a gardener/a Frenchman** er ist Gärtner/Franzose; **she did not say a word** sie sagte kein Wort

AA *abbr.* (Brit.) = **Automobile Association** *britischer Automobilklub*

A & E *abbr.* accident and emergency

aback /ə'bæk/ *adv.* **be taken ~:** erstaunt sein

abacus /'æbəkəs/ *n., pl.* **~es** *or* **abaci** /'æbəsaɪ/ Abakus, *der*

abandon /ə'bændən/ *v.t.* verlassen ⟨*Ort, Person*⟩; aufgeben ⟨*Prinzip*⟩; **~ed** verlassen, ausgesetzt ⟨*Kind, Tier*⟩

abase /ə'beɪs/ *v.t.* erniedrigen

abashed /ə'bæʃt/ *adj.* beschämt

abate /ə'beɪt/ *v.i.* nachlassen

abattoir /'æbətwɑː(r)/ *n.* Schlachthof, *der*

abbey /'æbɪ/ *n.* Abtei, *die*

abbot /'æbət/ *n.* Abt, *der*

abbreviate /ə'briːvɪeɪt/ *v.t.* abkürzen

ab'breviated dialling *n.* (Teleph.) Kurzwahl, *die*

abbreviation /əbriːvɪ'eɪʃn/ *n.* Abkürzung, *die*

abdicate /'æbdɪkeɪt/ *v.t.* abdanken

abdication /æbdɪ'keɪʃn/ *n.* Abdankung, *die*

abdomen /'æbdəmən/ *n.* Bauch, *der*

abdominal /æb'dɒmɪnl/ *adj.* Bauch-

abduct /əb'dʌkt/ *v.t.* entführen

abduction /əb'dʌkʃn/ *n.* Entführung, *die*

aberration /æbə'reɪʃn/ *n.* Abweichung, *die*

abet /ə'bet/ *v.t.,* **-tt-** helfen (+ *Dat.*); **aid and ~:** Beihilfe leisten (+ *Dat.*)

abhor /əb'hɔː(r)/ *v.t.,* **-rr-** verabscheuen

abhorrent /əb'hɒrənt/ *adj.* abscheulich

abide /ə'baɪd/ ① *v.i.* **~ by** befolgen ⟨*Gesetz, Vorschrift*⟩; [ein]halten ⟨*Versprechen*⟩ ② *v.t.* ertragen; **I can't ~ dogs** ich kann Hunde nicht ausstehen

ability /ə'bɪlɪtɪ/ *n.* (a) (capacity) Fähigkeit, *die;* **have the ~ to do sth.** etw. können (b) (cleverness) Intelligenz, *die* (c) (talent) Begabung, *die*

abject /'æbdʒekt/ *adj.* elend; bitter ⟨*Armut*⟩; demütig ⟨*Entschuldigung*⟩

ablaze /ə'bleɪz/ *adj.* **be ~:** in Flammen stehen

able /'eɪbl/ *adj.* (a) **be ~ to do sth.** etw. tun können

(b) (competent) fähig

able-bodied /'eɪblbɒdɪd/ *adj.* kräftig; tauglich ⟨*Soldat, Matrose*⟩

ably /'eɪblɪ/ *adv.* geschickt; gekonnt

abnormal /æb'nɔːml/ *adj.* abnorm; a[b]normal ⟨*Interesse, Verhalten*⟩

abnormality /æbnɔ'mælɪtɪ/ *n.* Abnormität, *die*

aboard /ə'bɔːd/ ① *adv.* an Bord ② *prep.* an Bord (+ *Gen.*); **~ the bus** im Bus; **~ ship** an Bord

abode /ə'bəʊd/ *n.* **of no fixed ~:** ohne festen Wohnsitz

abolish /ə'bɒlɪʃ/ *v.t.* abschaffen

abolition /æbə'lɪʃn/ *n.* Abschaffung, *die*

abominable /ə'bɒmɪnəbl/ *adj.* abscheulich; scheußlich

aborigine /æbə'rɪdʒɪnɪ/ *n.* Ureinwohner, *der*

abort /ə'bɔːt/ *v.t.* abtreiben ⟨*Baby*⟩

abortion /ə'bɔːʃn/ *n.* Abtreibung, *die;* **back-street ~:** illegale Abtreibung (durch Engelmacherin)

a'bortion pill *n.* Abtreibungspille, *die*

abortive /ə'bɔːtɪv/ *adj.* misslungen ⟨*Plan*⟩; fehlgeschlagen ⟨*Versuch*⟩

abound /ə'baʊnd/ *v.i.* **~ in sth.** an etw. (*Dat.*) reich sein

about /ə'baʊt/ ① *adv.* (a) (all around) rings[her]um; (here and there) überall; **all ~:** ringsumher (b) (near) **be ~:** da sein; hier sein (c) **be ~ to do sth.** gerade etw. tun wollen (d) **be out and ~:** aktiv sein (e) (approximately) ungefähr ② *prep.* (a) (all round) um [… herum] (b) (concerning) über (+ *Akk.*); **know ~ sth.** von etw. wissen; **a question ~ sth.** eine Frage zu etw.; **what was it ~?** worum ging es?

above /ə'bʌv/ ① *adv.* (a) (position) oben; (higher up) darüber (b) (direction) nach oben ② *prep.* (position) über (+ *Dat.*); (direction, more than) über (+ *Akk.*); **~ all** vor allem

above 'board *pred. adj.* einwandfrei; korrekt

a'bove-mentioned *adj.* oben erwähnt *od.* genannt

abrasion /ə'breɪʒn/ *n.* (graze) Hautabschürfung, *die*

abrasive /ə'breɪsɪv/ ① *adj.* (a) scheuernd; Scheuer- (b) (fig.: harsh) aggressiv ② *n.* Scheuermittel, *das* ⋯⟫

abreast /ə'brest/ adv. (a) nebeneinander (b) (fig.) keep ∼ of sth. sich über etw. (Akk.) auf dem Laufenden halten

abroad /ə'brɔːd/ adv. im Ausland; (direction) ins Ausland

abrupt /ə'brʌpt/ adj., **a'bruptly** adv. (a) (sudden[ly]) abrupt; plötzlich (b) (brusque[ly]) schroff

ABS abbr. = **anti-lock brake** or **braking system** ABS

abscess /'æbsɪs/ n. Abszess, der

abscond /əb'skɒnd/ v.t. sich entfernen

absence /'æbsəns/ n. Abwesenheit, die; the ∼ of sth. der Mangel an etw. (Dat.)

absent /'æbsənt/ adj. abwesend; **be** ∼ **from school/work** in der Schule/am Arbeitsplatz fehlen

absentee /æbsən'tiː/ n Fehlende, der/die; Abwesende, der/die; ∼ **ballot** (Amer.) Briefwahl, die; ∼ **landlord** nicht auf seinem Gut lebender Gutsherr

absenteeism /æbsən'tiːɪzm/ n. [häufiges] Fernbleiben; (without good reason) Krankfeiern, das (ugs.)

absent-minded /æbsənt'maɪndɪd/ adj. geistesabwesend; (habitually) zerstreut

absolute /'æbsəluːt/ adj. absolut; ausgemacht ⟨Lüge, Skandal⟩; ∼ **majority** absolute Mehrheit

abso'lutely adv. absolut; völlig ⟨verrückt⟩; **you're** ∼ **right!** du hast völlig Recht; ∼ **not!** auf keinen Fall!

absolve /əb'zɒlv/ v.t. ∼ **from** entbinden von ⟨Pflichten⟩; lossprechen von ⟨Schuld⟩

absorb /əb'sɔːb/ v.t. (a) aufsaugen ⟨Flüssigkeit⟩ (b) abfangen ⟨Schlag, Stoß⟩ (c) (fig.: engross) ausfüllen

absorbency /əb'sɔːbənsɪ/ n. Saugfähigkeit, die

absorbent /əb'sɔːbənt/ adj. saugfähig

ab'sorbing adj. faszinierend

abstain /əb'steɪn/ v.i. ∼ **from** sth. sich einer Sache (Gen.) enthalten; ∼ **[from voting]** sich der Stimme enthalten

abstemious /əb'stiːmɪəs/ adj. enthaltsam

abstention /əb'stenʃn/ n. (from voting) Stimmenthaltung, die

abstinence /'æbstɪnəns/ n. Abstinenz, die

abstinent /'æbstɪnənt/ adj. abstinent

abstract /'æbstrækt/ 1 adj. abstrakt 2 n. Zusammenfassung, die

absurd /əb'sɜːd/ adj. absurd; (ridiculous) lächerlich

absurdity /əb'sɜːdɪtɪ/ n. Absurdität, die

ab'surdly adv. lächerlich

abundance /ə'bʌndəns/ n. [an] ∼ **of** sth. eine Fülle von etw.

abundant /ə'bʌndənt/ adj. reich (**in** an + Dat.)

abuse 1 /ə'bjuːz/ v.t. beschimpfen 2 /ə'bjuːs/ n. Beschimpfungen Pl.

abusive /ə'bjuːsɪv/ adj. beleidigend; **become** ∼: ausfallend werden

abysmal /ə'bɪzml/ adj. (coll.: bad) katastrophal (ugs.)

abyss /ə'bɪs/ n. Abgrund, der

AC abbr. = **alternating current** Ws

academic /ækə'demɪk/ adj. akademisch

academy /ə'kædəmɪ/ n. Akademie, die

accede /æk'siːd/ v.i. (a) zustimmen (**to** Dat.) (b) ∼ **[to the throne]** den Thron besteigen

accelerate /ək'seləreɪt/ 1 v.t. beschleunigen 2 v.i. sich beschleunigen; ⟨Auto, Fahrer:⟩ beschleunigen

acceleration /əkselə'reɪʃn/ n. Beschleunigung, die

accelerator /ək'seləreɪtə(r)/ n. ∼ **[pedal]** Gas[pedal], das

accent /'æksənt/ n. Akzent, der

accentuate /ək'sentjʊeɪt/ v.t. betonen

accept /ək'sept/ v.t. (a) annehmen; entgegennehmen ⟨Dank, Spende⟩; übernehmen ⟨Verantwortung⟩ (b) (acknowledge) akzeptieren

acceptable /ək'septəbl/ adj. akzeptabel; annehmbar ⟨Preis, Gehalt⟩

acceptance /ək'septəns/ n. (a) Annahme, die (b) (acknowledgement) Anerkennung, die

access /'ækses/ n. (a) (admission) **gain** ∼: Einlass finden (b) (opportunity to use or approach) Zugang, der (**to** zu)

accessible /ək'sesɪbl/ adj. (a) (reachable) erreichbar (b) (available, understandable) zugänglich (**to** für)

accession /ək'seʃn/ n. Amtsantritt, der; ∼ **[to the throne]** Thronbesteigung, die

accessory /ək'sesərɪ/ n. (a) **accessories** pl. Zubehör, das (b) (dress article) Accessoire, das

'access road n. Zufahrtsstraße, die

accident /'æksɪdənt/ n. (a) Unfall, der (b) (chance) Zufall, der; **by** ∼: zufällig (c) (mistake) Versehen, das; **by** ∼: versehentlich

accidental /æksɪ'dentl/ adj. (chance) zufällig; (unintended) unbeabsichtigt

acci'dentally adv. (by chance) zufällig; (by mistake) versehentlich

accident and e'mergency department n. Unfallstation, die; Notaufnahme[station], die

'accident-prone adj. ∼ **person** Unfäller, der (Psych.); **he's such an** ∼ **boy** mit dem Jungen ist aber auch immer irgendwas (ugs.)

acclaim /ə'kleɪm/ v.t. feiern

acclimatisation, acclimatise
▸ ACCLIMATIZ-
acclimatization /əklaɪmətaɪ'zeɪʃn/ *n.*
(lit. or fig.) Akklimatisation, *die*
acclimatize /ə'klaɪmətaɪz/ *v.t.* get *or*
become ∼d sich akklimatisieren
accolade /'ækəleɪd/ *n.* ∼**[s]** (praise) Lob,
das
accommodate /ə'kɒmədeɪt/ *v.t.*
(a) unterbringen; (hold) Platz bieten (+ *Dat.*)
(b) (oblige) gefällig sein (+ *Dat.*)
accommodating /ə'kɒmədeɪtɪŋ/ *adj.*
zuvorkommend
accommodation /əkɒmə'deɪʃn/ *n.*
Unterkunft, *die*
accommo'dation address *n.*
Gefälligkeitsadresse, *die*
accompaniment /ə'kʌmpənɪmənt/ *n.*
Begleitung, *die*
accompanist /ə'kʌmpənɪst/ *n.* Begleiter,
der/Begleiterin, *die*
accompany /ə'kʌmpəni/ *v.t.* begleiten
accomplice /ə'kʌmplɪs/ *n.* Komplize,
der/Komplizin, *die*
accomplish /ə'kʌmplɪʃ/ *v.t.* vollbringen
⟨*Tat*⟩; erfüllen ⟨*Aufgabe*⟩
accomplished /ə'kʌmplɪʃt/ *adj.* fähig;
he is an ∼ speaker/dancer er ist ein
erfahrener Redner/vollendeter Tänzer
ac'complishment *n.* (a) (completion)
Vollendung, *die*
(b) (achievement) Leistung, *die;* (skill)
Fähigkeit, *die*
accord /ə'kɔːd/ **1** *n.* Übereinstimmung,
die; of one's own ∼: aus eigenem Antrieb;
with one ∼: geschlossen
2 *v.t.* ∼ sb. sth. jmdm. etw. gewähren
accordance /ə'kɔːdəns/ *n.* in ∼ with in
Übereinstimmung mit
ac'cording *adv.* ∼ to nach; ∼ to him nach
seiner Aussage
ac'cordingly *adv.* (as appropriate)
entsprechend; (therefore) folglich
accordion /ə'kɔːdɪən/ *n.* Akkordeon, *das*
accost /ə'kɒst/ *v.t.* ansprechen
account /ə'kaʊnt/ *n.* (a) (Finance)
Rechnung, *die;* (at bank, shop) Konto, *das*
(b) (consideration) take ∼ of sth., take sth.
into ∼: etw. berücksichtigen; take no ∼ of
sth./sb. etw./jmdn. unberücksichtigt lassen;
don't change your plans on my ∼: ändert
nicht meinetwegen eure Pläne; on ∼ of
wegen; on no ∼: auf [gar] keinen Fall
(c) (report) Bericht, *der*
(d) call sb. to ∼: jmdn. zur Rechenschaft
ziehen
■ **ac'count for** *v.t.* Rechenschaft ablegen
über; (explain) erklären
accountable /ə'kaʊntəbl/ *adj.*
verantwortlich
accountancy /ə'kaʊntənsi/ *n.*
Buchhaltung, *die*

accountant /ə'kaʊntənt/ *n.*
[Bilanz]buchhalter, *der*/-halterin, *die*
account: ∼ **holder** *n.* Kontoinhaber,
der/-inhaberin, *die;* ∼ **number** *n.*
Kontonummer, *die*
accredited /ə'kredɪtɪd/ *adj.* anerkannt
⟨*Schule, Anstalt, Buch, Regierung*⟩;
akkreditiert ⟨*Botschafter, Diplomat*⟩;
zugelassen ⟨*Journalist*⟩
accrue /ə'kruː/ *v.i.* ⟨*Zinsen:*⟩ auflaufen;
∼ to sb. ⟨*Reichtümer, Einnahmen:*⟩ jmdm.
zufließen
accumulate /ə'kjuːmjʊleɪt/ **1** *v.t.*
sammeln
2 *v.i.* ⟨*Menge, Staub:*⟩ sich ansammeln;
⟨*Geld:*⟩ sich anhäufen
accumulation /əkjuːmjʊ'leɪʃn/ *n.*
[An]sammeln, *das;* (being accumulated)
Anhäufung, *die*
accuracy /'ækjʊrəsi/ *n.* Genauigkeit, *die*
accurate /'ækjʊrət/ *adj.,* **'accurately**
adv. genau; (correct[ly]) richtig
accusation /ækju:'zeɪʃn/ *n.*
Anschuldigung, *die;* (Law) Anklage, *die*
accusative /ə'kjuːzətɪv/ *adj. & n.*
∼ **[case]** Akkusativ, *der*
accuse /ə'kjuːz/ *v.t.* beschuldigen; (Law)
anklagen (of wegen + *Gen.*)
accustom /ə'kʌstəm/ *v.t.* gewöhnen (to
an + *Akk.*); grow/be ∼ed to sth. sich an etw.
(*Akk.*) gewöhnen/an etw. (*Akk.*) gewöhnt
sein
accustomed /ə'kʌstəmd/ *attrib. adj.*
gewohnt; üblich
ace /eɪs/ **1** *n.* As, *das*
2 *adj.* (coll.) klasse (ugs.); spitze (ugs.)
ache /eɪk/ **1** *v.i.* schmerzen; wehtun
2 *n.* Schmerz, *der*
achieve /ə'tʃiːv/ *v.t.* zustande bringen;
erreichen ⟨*Ziel, Standard*⟩
a'chievement *n.* (a) ▸ ACHIEVE:
Zustandebringen, *das;* Erreichen, *das*
(b) (thing accomplished) Leistung, *die*
acid /'æsɪd/ **1** *adj.* sauer
2 *n.* Säure, *die*
'acid house *n.* Acidhouse, *das;* ∼ **music/
party** Acidhousemusik, *die*/Acidhouseparty,
die
acidic /ə'sɪdɪk/ *adj.* säuerlich
acidity /ə'sɪdɪti/ *n.* Säure, *die*
acid: ∼ **'rain** *n.* saurer Regen; ∼ **test** *n.*
(fig.) Feuerprobe, *die*
acknowledge /ək'nɒlɪdʒ/ *v.t.*
(a) zugeben ⟨*Tatsache, Fehler, Schuld*⟩
(b) sich erkenntlich zeigen für ⟨*Dienste,
Bemühungen*⟩; erwidern ⟨*Gruß*⟩
(c) bestätigen ⟨*Empfang, Bewerbung*⟩;
∼ a letter den Empfang eines Briefes
bestätigen
acknowledg[e]ment /ək'nɒlɪdʒmənt/
n. (a) (admission) Eingeständnis, *das*
(b) (thanks) Dank, *der* (of für) ⋯⋮

a

(c) (of letter) Bestätigung [des Empfangs]

acne /'æknɪ/ n. Akne, die

acorn /'eɪkɔːn/ n. Eichel, die

acoustic /ə'kuːstɪk/ adj. akustisch

a'coustics n. pl. Akustik, die

acquaint /ə'kweɪnt/ v.t. be ~ed with sb. mit jmdm. bekannt sein

acquaintance /ə'kweɪntəns/ n.
(a) ~ with sb. Bekanntschaft mit jmdm.; make sb.'s ~: jmds. Bekanntschaft machen
(b) (person) Bekannte, der/die

acquiesce /ækwɪ'es/ v.i. einwilligen (in in + Akk.)

acquire /ə'kwaɪə(r)/ v.t. sich (Dat.) anschaffen ‹Gegenstände›; erwerben ‹Besitz, Kenntnisse›

acquisition /ækwɪ'zɪʃn/ n. Erwerb, der; (thing) Anschaffung, die

acquisitive /ə'kwɪzɪtɪv/ adj. raffsüchtig

acquit /ə'kwɪt/ v.t., -tt- freisprechen

acquittal /ə'kwɪtl/ n. Freispruch, der

acre /'eɪkə(r)/ n. Acre, der

acrid /'ækrɪd/ adj. beißend ‹Geruch, Rauch›; bitter ‹Geschmack›

acrimonious /ækrɪ'məʊnɪəs/ adj. bitter; erbittert ‹Streit›

acrobat /'ækrəbæt/ n. Akrobat, der/Akrobatin, die

acrobatic /ækrə'bætɪk/ adj. akrobatisch

acrobatics /ækrə'bætɪks/ n. Akrobatik, die

acronym /'ækrənɪm/ n. Akronym, das

across /ə'krɒs/ ① adv. (from one side to the other) darüber; (from here to there) hinüber; be 9 miles ~: 9 Meilen breit sein ② prep. über (+ Akk.); (on the other side of) auf der anderen Seite (+ Gen.)

a'cross-the-board adj. pauschal; an ~ pay rise eine pauschale od. generelle Lohnerhöhung

acrylic /ə'krɪlɪk/ ① adj. aus Acryl nachgestellt; Acryl-; ~ paint/fibre Acrylfarbe, die/-faser, die ② n. Acryl, das

act /ækt/ ① n. (a) (deed) Tat, die
(b) (Theatre) Akt, der
(c) (pretence) Theater, das; put on an ~: Theater spielen
(d) (Law) Gesetz, das
② v.t. spielen ‹Stück›
③ v.i. (a) (perform actions) handeln
(b) (behave) sich verhalten; ~ as fungieren als
(c) (perform play) spielen
(d) (have effect) ~ on sth. auf etw. (Akk.) wirken

'acting ① n. (Theatre etc.) die Schauspielerei ② adj. (temporary) stellvertretend

action /'ækʃn/ n. (a) (doing sth.) Handeln, das; take ~: Schritte od. etwas unternehmen; put a plan into ~: einen Plan in die Tat umsetzen; put sth. out of ~: etw.

außer Betrieb setzen
(b) (act) Tat, die
(c) (legal process) [Gerichts]verfahren, das
(d) die in ~: im Kampf fallen

action: ~ **committee,** ~ **group** ns. [Eltern-/Bürger- usw.]initiative, die; ~-**packed** adj. spannend ‹Buch, Roman›; an ~-packed film ein Film mit viel Aktion; ~ **'replay** n. Wiederholung [in Zeitlupe]

activate /'æktɪveɪt/ v.t. (a) in Gang setzen
(b) (Chem., Phys.) aktivieren

active /'æktɪv/ adj., **'actively** adv. aktiv

activist /'æktɪvɪst/ n. Aktivist, der/Aktivistin, die

activity /æk'tɪvɪtɪ/ n. Aktivität, die; outdoor activities Betätigung an der frischen Luft; ~ **holiday** Aktivurlaub, der

actor /'æktə(r)/ n. Schauspieler, der

actress /'æktrɪs/ n. Schauspielerin, die

actual /'æktʃʊəl/ adj. eigentlich; wirklich ‹Name›

'actually adv. (in fact) eigentlich; (by the way) übrigens; (believe it or not) sogar

acumen /'ækjʊmen/ Scharfsinn, der; business ~: Geschäftssinn, der

acupressure /'ækjuːpreʃə(r)/ n. (Med.) Akupressur, die

acupuncture /'ækjʊpʌnktʃə(r)/ n. Akupunktur, die

acute /ə'kjuːt/ adj. (a) spitz ‹Winkel›
(b) (critical; Med.) akut

ad /æd/ n. (coll.) Annonce, die

AD abbr. = **Anno Domini** n.Chr.

adamant /'ædəmənt/ adj. unnachgiebig; be ~ that ...: darauf bestehen, dass ...

adapt /ə'dæpt/ v.t. (a) anpassen (to Dat.); ~ oneself to sth. sich an etw. (Akk.) gewöhnen
(b) bearbeiten ‹Text, Theaterstück›

adaptable /ə'dæptəbl/ adj. anpassungsfähig

adaptation /ædəp'teɪʃn/ n.
(a) Anpassung, die
(b) (version) Adap[ta]tion, die; (of story, text) Bearbeitung, die

adapter, adaptor /ə'dæptə(r)/ n. Adapter, der

add /æd/ ① v.t. hinzufügen (to Dat.); ~ two and two zwei und zwei zusammenzählen ② v.i. ~ to vergrößern ‹Schwierigkeiten, Einkommen›

■ **add 'up** ① v.i. ~ up to sth. (fig.) auf etw. (Akk.) hinauslaufen ② v.t. zusammenzählen

adder /'ædə(r)/ n. Viper, die

addict ① /ə'dɪkt/ v.t. be ~ed süchtig sein (to nach); be ~ed to alcohol/smoking/drugs alkohol-/nikotin-/drogensüchtig sein ② /'ædɪkt/ n. Süchtige, der/die

addiction /ə'dɪkʃn/ n. Sucht, die (to nach)

addictive /ə'dɪktɪv/ adj. be ~: süchtig machen

addition /əˈdɪʃn/ n. (a) Hinzufügen, *das;* (adding up) Addieren, *das;* (process) Addition, *die;* in ∼: außerdem; in ∼ to zusätzlich zu
(b) (thing added) Ergänzung, *die* (to zu)
additional /əˈdɪʃənl/ adj. zusätzlich
additionally /əˈdɪʃənəlɪ/ adv. außerdem
additive /ˈædɪtɪv/ n. Zusatz, *der*
'**add-on** ☐ n. (accessory) Zubehörteil, *das;* (for electrical appliance) Zusatzgerät, *das;* (addition) Zusatz, *der*
② adj. ∼ **accessory** Zubehörteil, *das;* (for electrical appliance) Zusatzgerät, *das*
address /əˈdres/ ☐ v.t. (a) (mark with address) adressieren (to an + *Akk.*)
(b) (speak to) anreden; sprechen zu ⟨*Zuhörern*⟩
② n. (a) (on letter) Adresse, *die*
(b) (speech) Ansprache, *die*
ad'dress book n. Adressenbüchlein, *das*
addressee /ædreˈsiː/ n. Adressat, *der*/Adressatin, *die*
ad'dress label n. Adressenaufkleber, *der*
adept /ˈædept, əˈdept/ adj. geschickt (in, at in + *Dat.*)
adequate /ˈædɪkwət/ adj. (a) angemessen (to *Dat.*); (suitable) passend
(b) (sufficient) ausreichend
'**adequately** adv. (a) (sufficiently) ausreichend
(b) (suitably) angemessen ⟨*gekleidet, qualifiziert usw.*⟩
adhere /ədˈhɪə(r)/ v.i. haften, (by glue) kleben (to an + *Dat.*)
adhesion /ədˈhiːʒn/ n. Haften, *das*
adhesive /ədˈhiːsɪv/ ☐ adj. gummiert ⟨*Briefmarke*⟩; Klebe⟨*band*⟩; ∼ **plaster** Heftpflaster, *das*
② n. Klebstoff, *der*
adjacent /əˈdʒeɪsənt/ adj. angrenzend; ∼ **to** neben (position: + *Dat.;* direction: + *Akk.*)
adjective /ˈædʒɪktɪv/ n. Adjektiv, *das*
adjoin /əˈdʒɔɪn/ v.t. grenzen an (+ *Akk.*)
adjourn /əˈdʒɜːn/ ☐ v.t. (break off) unterbrechen; (put off) aufschieben
② v.i. sich vertagen; ∼ **for lunch/half an hour** eine Mittagspause/halbstündige Pause einlegen
a'djournment n. (of court) Vertagung, *die;* (of meeting) Unterbrechung, *die*
adjudicate /əˈdʒuːdɪkeɪt/ v.i. (in court, tribunal) das Urteil fällen; (in contest) entscheiden
adjust /əˈdʒʌst/ ☐ v.t. einstellen; ∼ **sth.** [**to sth.**] etw. [an etw. (*Akk.*)] anpassen
② v.i. ⟨*Person:*⟩ sich anpassen (to an + *Akk.*)
adjustable /əˈdʒʌstəbl/ adj. einstellbar; verstellbar ⟨*Gerät*⟩
a'djustment n. Einstellung, *die;* (to situation etc.) Anpassung, *die*
ad-lib /ædˈlɪb/ ☐ adj. improvisiert
② v.i., -bb- improvisieren

adman/ˈædmæn/ n. Werbe-, Reklamefachmann, *der*
admin /ˈædmɪn/ n. (coll.) Verwaltung, *die;* an ∼ **problem** ein Verwaltungsproblem
administer /ædˈmɪnɪstə(r)/ (a) (manage) verwalten
(b) leisten ⟨*Hilfe*⟩; verabreichen ⟨*Medikamente*⟩
administration /ədmɪnɪˈstreɪʃn/ n. Verwaltung, *die*
administrative /ədˈmɪnɪstrətɪv/ adj. Verwaltungs-; an ∼ **job** ein Verwaltungsposten
administrator /ədˈmɪnɪstreɪtə(r)/ n. Administrator, *der;* Verwalter, *der*
admirable /ˈædmərəbl/ adj. bewundernswert
admiral /ˈædmərəl/ n. Admiral, *der*
admiration /ædməˈreɪʃn/ n. Bewunderung, *die* (of, for für)
admire /ədˈmaɪə(r)/ v.t. bewundern
admirer /ədˈmaɪərə(r)/ n. Bewunderer, *der*/Bewunderin, *die*
admiring /ədˈmaɪərɪŋ/ adj. bewundernd
admission /ədˈmɪʃn/ n. (a) (entry) Zutritt, *der*
(b) (charge) Eintritt, *der*
(c) (confession) Eingeständnis, *das*
admission: ∼ **charge,** ∼ **fee** ns. Eintrittspreis, *der;* ∼ **money** n. Eintrittsgeld, *das;* ∼ **price** n. Eintrittspreis, *der;* ∼ **ticket** n. Eintrittskarte, *die*
admit /ədˈmɪt/ v.t., **-tt-**: (a) (let in) hinein-/hereinlassen
(b) (acknowledge) zugeben
admittance /ədˈmɪtəns/ n. Zutritt, *der*
admittedly /ədˈmɪtɪdlɪ/ adv. zugegeben[ermaßen]
admonish /ədˈmɒnɪʃ/ v.t. ermahnen
ado /əˈduː/ n. **without more** ∼: ohne weiteres Aufheben
adolescence /ædəˈlesns/ n. die Zeit des Erwachsenenwerdens
adolescent /ædəˈlesnt/ ☐ n. Heranwachsende, *der/die*
② adj. heranwachsend
adopt /əˈdɒpt/ v.t. (a) adoptieren
(b) (take over) annehmen ⟨*Glaube, Kultur*⟩
(c) (take up) übernehmen ⟨*Methode*⟩; einnehmen ⟨*Standpunkt, Haltung*⟩
adoption /əˈdɒpʃn/ n. (a) Adoption, *die*
(b) (taking over) Annahme, *die*
(c) (taking up) Übernahme, *die;* (of point of view) Einnahme, *die*
a'doption agency n. Adoptionsagentur, *die*
adorable /əˈdɔːrəbl/ adj. bezaubernd
adoration /ædəˈreɪʃn/ n. Verehrung, *die*
adore /əˈdɔː(r)/ v.t. verehren
adorn /əˈdɔːn/ v.t. schmücken
a'dornment n. Verzierung, *die;* ∼**s** Schmuck, *der*

adrenalin /ə'drenəlɪn/ n. Adrenalin, *das*

Adriatic /eɪdrɪ'ætɪk/ pr. n. ~ [Sea] Adriatisches Meer

adrift /ə'drɪft/ adj. be ~: treiben

adroit /ə'drɔɪt/ adj. geschickt

ADSL abbr. (Teleph.) = **asymmetric digital subscriber line** ADSL

adulation /ædjʊ'leɪʃn/ n. Vergötterung, *die*

adult /'ædʌlt, ə'dʌlt/ [1] adj. erwachsen; **an ~ film/book** etc. ein Film/Buch *usw.* [nur] für Erwachsene
[2] n. Erwachsene, *der/die;* **~ education** Erwachsenenbildung, *die*

adulterate /ə'dʌltəreɪt/ v.t. verunreinigen

adultery /ə'dʌltərɪ/ n. Ehebruch, *der*

advance /əd'vɑːns/ [1] v.t. (a) (also Mil.) vorrücken lassen
(b) (put forward) vorbringen ⟨Plan, Meinung⟩
(c) (further) fördern
(d) (pay before due date) vorschießen; ⟨Bank:⟩ leihen
[2] v.i. (a) (also Mil.) vorrücken; ⟨Prozession:⟩ sich vorwärts bewegen
(b) (fig.: make progress) vorankommen
[3] n. (a) Vorrücken, *das;* (fig.: progress) Fortschritt, *der*
(b) usu. in pl. Annäherungsversuch, *der*
(c) (on salary) Vorschuss, *der*
(d) **in ~:** im Voraus

ad'vance booking n. (for a film, play) [vorherige] Kartenreservierung; (of a table in a restaurant) [vorherige] Tischreservierung

advanced /əd'vɑːnst/ adj. fortgeschritten

advance: ~ **'notice** n. **a week's ~ notice** Benachrichtigung eine Woche [im] Voraus; **give sb. ~ notice of sth.** jmdn. im Voraus von etw. in Kenntnis setzen; ~ **'payment** n. Vorauszahlung, *die*

advantage /əd'vɑːntɪdʒ/ n. Vorteil, *der;* **take ~ of sb.** jmdn. ausnutzen; **be to one's ~:** für jmdn. von Vorteil sein; **turn sth. to [one's] ~:** etw. ausnutzen

advantageous /ædvən'teɪdʒəs/ adj. vorteilhaft

advent /'ædvent/ n. Beginn, *der;* **A~:** Advent, *der*

adventure /əd'ventʃə(r)/ n. Abenteuer, *das*

adventure: ~ **holiday** n Abenteuerurlaub, *der;* ~ **playground** n. (Brit.) Abenteuerspielplatz, *der*

adventurous /əd'ventʃərəs/ adj. abenteuerlustig

adverb /'ædvɜːb/ n. Adverb, *das*

adversary /'ædvəsərɪ/ n. (enemy) Widersacher, *der/*Widersacherin, *die;* (opponent) Kontrahent, *der/*Kontrahentin, *die*

adverse /'ædvɜːs/ adj. (a) (unfavourable) ungünstig
(b) (contrary) widrig ⟨Wind, Umstände⟩

adversity /əd'vɜːsɪtɪ/ n. (a) no pl. Not, *die*
(b) usu. in pl. Widrigkeit, *die*

advert /'ædvɜːt/ (Brit. coll.) ▶ ADVERTISEMENT

advertise /'ædvətaɪz/ [1] v.t. werben für; (by small ad) inserieren; ausschreiben ⟨Stelle⟩
[2] v.i. werben; (in newspaper) inserieren; annoncieren

advertisement /əd'vɜːtɪsmənt/ n. Anzeige, *die;* **TV ~:** Fernsehspot, *der;* **classified ~:** Kleinanzeige, *die*

advertiser /'ædvətaɪzə(r)/ n. (in newspaper) Inserent, *der/*Inserentin, *die;* (on radio, TV) Auftraggeber/Auftraggeberin [der Werbesendung]

advertising /'ædvətaɪzɪŋ/ n. Werbung, *die; attrib.* Werbe-; ~ **agency/campaign/ industry** Werbeagentur, *die/*-kampagne, *die/*-branche, *die*

advice /əd'vaɪs/ n. Rat, *der;* **take sb.'s ~:** jmds. Rat (Dat.) folgen

advisable /əd'vaɪzəbl/ adj. ratsam

advise /əd'vaɪz/ v.t. beraten; ~ **sth.** zu etw. raten; (inform) unterrichten (**of** über + Akk.); ~ **sb. to do sth.** jmdm. raten, etw. zu tun

adviser, advisor /əd'vaɪzə(r)/ n. Berater, *der/*Beraterin, *die*

advisory /əd'vaɪzərɪ/ adj. beratend

advocate [1] /'ædvəkət/ n. (of a cause) Befürworter, *der/*Befürworterin, *die;* (Law) [Rechts]anwalt, *der/*-anwältin, *die*
[2] /'ædvəkeɪt/ v.t. befürworten

advt. abbr. = **advertisement**

aerial /'eərɪəl/ [1] adj. Luft-; ~ **bombardment** Bombardierung [aus der Luft]; ~ **photograph/photography** Luftaufnahme, *die/*Luftaufnahmen Pl.
[2] n. Antenne, *die*

aero- /eərəʊ/ in comb. Aero-

aerobic /eə'rəʊbɪk/ adj. (Biol.) aerob

ae'robics n. Aerobic, *das*

aerody'namic adj. aerodynamisch

aerogenerator /'eərəʊdʒenəreɪtə(r)/ n. Windgenerator, *der*

aeronautics /eərə'nɔːtɪks/ n. Aeronautik, *die*

aeroplane /'eərəpleɪn/ n. (Brit.) Flugzeug, *das*

aerosol /'eərəsɒl/ n. (spray) Spray, *der od. das;* (container) ~ **[spray]** Spraydose, *die*

'aerospace n., no art. Erdatmosphäre und Weltraum; (technology) Luft- und Raumfahrt, *die*

aesthetic /iːs'θetɪk/ adj. ästhetisch

afar /ə'fɑː/ adv. **from ~:** aus der Ferne

affable /'æfəbl/ adj. freundlich

affair /ə'feə(r)/ n. (a) (concern) Angelegenheit, *die*
(b) in pl. (business) Geschäfte Pl.
(c) (love affair) Affäre, *die;* **have an ~ with sb.** eine Affäre od. ein Verhältnis mit jmdm. haben

affect /əˈfekt/ v.t. (a) sich auswirken auf (+ Akk.)
(b) (emotionally) betroffen machen
affectation /æfekˈteɪʃn/ n. (studied display) Verstellung, die; (artificiality) Affektiertheit, die
affected /əˈfektɪd/ adj. affektiert; gekünstelt ⟨Sprache, Stil⟩
affection /əˈfekʃn/ n. Zuneigung, die
affectionate /əˈfekʃənət/ adj. anhänglich; liebevoll ⟨Umarmung⟩
afˈfectionately adv. liebevoll
affiliate /əˈfɪlɪeɪt/ v.t. be ⁓d to sth. an etw. (Akk.) angegliedert sein
affinity /əˈfɪnɪtɪ/ n. (a) (relationship) Verwandtschaft, die (to mit)
(b) (liking) Neigung, die (for zu); feel an ⁓ to or for sb./sth. sich zu jmdm./etw. hingezogen fühlen
affirm /əˈfɜːm/ v.t. (assert) bekräftigen ⟨Absicht⟩; beteuern ⟨Unschuld⟩; (state as a fact) bestätigen
affirmation /æfəˈmeɪʃn/ n. (of intention) Bekräftigung, die; (of fact) Bestätigung, die
affirmative /əˈfɜːmətɪv/ ①adj. affirmativ; bejahend ⟨Antwort⟩
②n. answer in the ⁓: bejahend antworten
affirmative ˈaction n. (Amer.) positive Diskriminierung (fachspr.); Bevorzugung, die
afflict /əˈflɪkt/ v.t. (physically) plagen; (mentally) quälen; peinigen; be ⁓ed with sth. von etw. befallen sein
affliction /əˈflɪkʃn/ n. Leiden, das
affluence /ˈæflʊəns/ n. Reichtum, der
affluent /ˈæflʊənt/ adj. reich; the ⁓ society die Überflussgesellschaft
afford /əˈfɔːd/ v.t. (a) sich (Dat.) leisten
(b) (provide) bieten; gewähren ⟨Schutz⟩
affordable /əˈfɔːdəbl/ adj. erschwinglich
affray /əˈfreɪ/ n. Schlägerei, die
affront /əˈfrʌnt/ ①v.t. beleidigen
②n. Beleidigung, die
afield /əˈfiːld/ adv. far ⁓ (direction) weit hinaus; (place) weit draußen
afloat /əˈfləʊt/ pred. adj. (a) (floating) über Wasser; flott ⟨Schiff⟩
(b) (at sea) auf See; be ⁓: auf dem Meer treiben
afoot /əˈfʊt/ pred. adj. im Gange
aforementioned /əˈfɔːmenʃnd/, **aforesaid** /əˈfɔːsed/ adjs. oben erwähnt od. genannt
afraid /əˈfreɪd/ adj. be ⁓ [of sb./sth.] [vor jmdm./etw.] Angst haben; be ⁓ to do sth. Angst davor haben, etw. zu tun; I'm ⁓ so/not ich fürchte ja/nein
afresh /əˈfreʃ/ adv. von neuem
Africa /ˈæfrɪkə/ pr. n. Afrika (das)
African /ˈæfrɪkən/ ①adj. afrikanisch; sb. is ⁓: jmd. ist Afrikaner/Afrikanerin
②n. Afrikaner, der/Afrikanerin, die
Afro-Caribˈbean ①adj. afrokaribisch
②n. Mensch afrokaribischer Herkunft od.

Abstammung
after /ˈɑːftə(r)/ ①adv. (a) (later) danach
(b) (behind) hinterher
②prep. (a) (in time) nach; two days ⁓: zwei Tage danach
(b) (behind) hinter (+ Dat.)
(c) ask ⁓ sb./sth. nach jmdm./etw. fragen
(d) ⁓ all schließlich
③conj. nachdem
after: ⁓**care** n. (Med.) Nachbehandlung, die; ⁓**-effect** n. Nachwirkung, die
aftermath /ˈɑːftəmæθ, ˈɑːftəmɑːθ/ n. Nachwirkungen Pl.
after: ⁓**ˈnoon** n. Nachmittag, der; this/ tomorrow ⁓noon: heute/morgen Nachmittag; in the ⁓noon: am Nachmittag; (regularly) nachmittags; ⁓**-sales service** n. Kundendienst, der; ⁓**shave** n. Aftershave, das; ⁓**taste** n. Nachgeschmack, der; ⁓**thought** n. nachträglicher Einfall
afterwards /ˈɑːftəwədz/ adv. danach
again /əˈgen, əˈgeɪn/ adv. wieder; (one more time) noch einmal; ⁓ and ⁓, time and [time] ⁓: immer wieder; back ⁓: wieder zurück
against /əˈgenst, əˈgeɪnst/ prep. gegen
age /eɪdʒ/ ①n. (a) Alter, das; what ⁓ are you? wie alt bist du?; at the ⁓ of im Alter von; come of ⁓: volljährig werden; be under ⁓: zu jung sein
(b) (great period) Zeitalter, das; ⁓s (coll.: a long time) eine Ewigkeit
②v.t. altern lassen
③v.i. altern
ˈage bracket n. Altersstufe, die
aged adj. (a) /eɪdʒd/ be ⁓ five fünf Jahre alt sein; a boy ⁓ five ein fünfjähriger Junge
(b) /ˈeɪdʒɪd/ (elderly) bejahrt
ˈage group n. Altersgruppe, die
ageism /ˈeɪdʒɪzm/ n. Diskriminierung aufgrund des Alters
ageist /ˈeɪdʒɪst/ adj. das Alter diskriminierend
ageless /ˈeɪdʒlɪs/ adj. nicht alternd ⟨Person⟩; (eternal) zeitlos
ˈage limit n. Altersgrenze, die
agency /ˈeɪdʒənsɪ/ n. (business establishment) Geschäftsstelle, die; (news/advertising ⁓) Agentur, die
agenda /əˈdʒendə/ n. Tagesordnung, die
agent /ˈeɪdʒənt/ n. Vertreter, der/ Vertreterin, die; (spy) Agent, der/Agentin, die
age: ⁓**-old** adj. uralt; ⁓ **range** n. Altersstufe, die
aggravate /ˈægrəveɪt/ v.t. (a) (make worse) verschlimmern
(b) (annoy) aufregen; ärgern
aggravating /ˈægrəveɪtɪŋ/ adj. ärgerlich
aggravation /ægrəˈveɪʃn/ n.
(a) Verschlimmerung, die
(b) (annoyance) Ärger, der

aggregate /'ægrɪɡət/ ☐ *n.* Gesamtmenge, *die*
☐ *adj.* gesamt

aggression /ə'greʃn/ *n.* Aggression, *die*

aggressive /ə'gresɪv/ *adj.*,
ag'gressively *adv.* aggressiv

ag'gressiveness *n.* Aggressivität, *die*

aggressor /ə'gresə(r)/ *n.* Aggressor, *der*

aggrieved /ə'gri:vd/ *v.t.* (resentful)
verärgert; (offended) gekränkt

aggro /'ægrəʊ/ *n.* (Brit. sl.) Zoff, *der* (ugs.);
Krawall, *der;* **they are looking for ~:** sie
suchen Streit

aghast /ə'gɑ:st/ *pred. adj.* bestürzt (**über**
+ *Akk.*)

agile /'ædʒaɪl/ *adj.* beweglich; flink
⟨*Bewegung*⟩

agility /ə'dʒɪlɪtɪ/ *n.* Beweglichkeit, *die;* (of
movement) Flinkheit, *die*

agitate /'ædʒɪteɪt/ ☐ *v.t.* (a) (shake)
schütteln
(b) (disturb) erregen
☐ *v.i.* agitieren

agitation /ædʒɪ'teɪʃn/ *n.* (a) (shaking)
Schütteln, *das*
(b) (emotional) Erregung, *die*

agitator /'ædʒɪteɪtə(r)/ *n.* Agitator, *der*

AGM *abbr.* = **Annual General
Meeting** JHV

agnostic /æg'nɒstɪk/ *n.* Agnostiker,
der/Agnostikerin, *die*

ago /ə'gəʊ/ *adv.* **ten years ~:** vor zehn
Jahren; **[not] long ~:** vor [nicht] langer Zeit

agog /ə'gɒg/ *pred. adj.* gespannt

agonize /'ægənaɪz/ *v.i.* **~ over sth.** sich
(*Dat.*) den Kopf über etw. (*Akk.*) zermartern

agony /'ægənɪ/ *n.* Todesqualen *Pl.*

'agony aunt *n.* (coll.) Briefkastentante, *die*
(ugs. scherzh.)

agoraphobia /ægərə'fəʊbɪə/ *n.* (Psych.)
Agoraphobie, *die;* Platzangst, *die*

agoraphobic /ægərə'fəʊbɪk/ *adj.* (Psych.)
an Agoraphobie *od.* Platzangst leidend; **be
~:** an Agoraphobie *od.* Platzangst leiden

agree /ə'gri:/ ☐ *v.i.* (a) (consent)
einverstanden sein (**to, with** mit)
(b) (hold similar opinion) einer Meinung sein;
they ~d [with me] sie waren derselben
Meinung [wie ich]
(c) (reach similar opinion) **~ on sth.** sich über
etw. (*Akk.*) einigen
(d) (harmonize) übereinstimmen
(e) **~ with sb.** (suit) jmdn. bekommen
☐ *v.t.* vereinbaren

agreeable /ə'gri:əbl/ *adj.* (a) (pleasing)
angenehm
(b) **be ~ [to sth.]** [mit etw.] einverstanden
sein

agreeably /ə'gri:əblɪ/ *adv.* angenehm

agreed /ə'gri:d/ *adj.* einig; vereinbart
⟨*Summe, Zeit*⟩

a'greement *n.* Übereinstimmung, *die;*
be in ~ [about sth.] sich (*Dat.*) [über etw.
(*Akk.*)] einig sein

agricultural /ægrɪ'kʌltʃərl/ *adj.*
landwirtschaftlich

agriculture /'ægrɪkʌltʃə(r)/ *n.*
Landwirtschaft, *die*

aground /ə'graʊnd/ *adj.* **go** *or* **run ~:** auf
Grund laufen

aha /ɑ:'hɑ:/ *int.* aha

ahead /ə'hed/ *adv.* voraus; **~ of** vor
(+ *Dat.*); **be ~ of the others** (fig.) den anderen
voraus sein

AI *abbr.* = **artificial intelligence** KI

aid /eɪd/ ☐ *v.t.* (a) **~ sb. [to do sth.]** jmdm.
helfen[, etw. zu tun]; **~ed by** unterstützt von
(b) (promote) fördern
☐ *n.* (a) (help) Hilfe, *die;* **with the ~ of
sth./sb.** mit Hilfe einer Sache (*Gen.*)/mit
jmds. Hilfe; **in ~ of sb./sth.** zugunsten von
jmdm./etw.
(b) (source of help) Hilfsmittel, *das* (**to** für)

'aid agency *n.* Hilfsorganisation, *die;*
Hilfswerk, *das*

aide /eɪd/ *n.* Berater, *der*/Beraterin, *die*

Aids /eɪdz/ *n.* Aids (*das*); **~ test** Aidstest, *der*

'Aids-related *adj.* **~ disease/illness**
durch Aids hervorgerufene Krankheit

'aid worker *n.* Helfer, *der*/Helferin, *die;*
~s Hilfskräfte *Pl.;* Hilfspersonal, *das*

ailment /'eɪlmənt/ *n.* Gebrechen, *das*

aim /eɪm/ ☐ *v.t.* ausrichten ⟨*Schusswaffe,
Rakete*⟩; **~ sth. at sb./sth.** etw. auf
jmdn./etw. richten
☐ *v.i.* (a) zielen (**at** auf + *Akk.*)
(b) **~ to do sth.** beabsichtigen, etw. zu tun;
~ at *or* **for sth.** (fig.) etwas anstreben
☐ *n.* Ziel, *das;* **take ~ [at sth./sb.]** [auf
etw./jmdn.] zielen

'aimless *adj.,* **'aimlessly** *adv.* ziellos

air /eə(r)/ ☐ *n.* (a) Luft, *die;* **be/go on the
~:** senden; ⟨*Programm:*⟩ gesendet werden;
by ~: mit dem Flugzeug; (by ~ mail) mit
Luftpost
(b) (facial expression) Miene, *die*
(c) **put on ~s** sich aufspielen
☐ *v.t.* (ventilate) lüften; (make public)
[öffentlich] darlegen

air: **~ bag** *n.* (Motor Veh.) Airbag *der;*
side ~ bag Seitenairbag, *der;* **~base**
n. Luftwaffenstützpunkt, *der;* **~bed** *n.*
Luftmatratze, *die;* **~borne** *adj.* **be ~borne**
sich in der Luft befinden; **~ brake** *n.*
Druckluftbremse, *die;* (flap) Luftbremse, *die;*
~brush *n.* Spritzpistole, *die;* **~ bubble**
n. Luftblase, *die;* **~ bus** *n.* Airbus, *der;*
~-conditioned *adj.* klimatisiert;
~ conditioner *n.* Klimaanlage, *die;*
~ conditioning *n.* Klimaanlage, *die;*
~-cooled *adj.* luftgekühlt; **~craft** *n.,*
pl. same Flugzeug, *das;* **~craft carrier** *n.*
Flugzeugträger, *der;* **~ crew** *n.* Besatzung,
die; Flugpersonal, *das;* **~ cushion** *n.*

Luftkissen, *das;* ~ **fare** *n.* Flugpreis, *der;* ~**field** *n.* Flugplatz, *der;* ~ **force** *n.* Luftwaffe, *die;* ~ **freshener** *n.* Lufterfrischer, *der;* Luftverbesserer, *der;* ~**gun** *n.* Luftgewehr, *das;* ~ **hostess** *n.* Stewardess, *die*

airing /'eərɪŋ/ *n.* Auslüften, *das;* **these clothes need a good** ~: diese Kleider müssen gründlich gelüftet werden

airless /'eəlɪs/ *adj.* stickig ⟨*Zimmer, Büro*⟩; windstill ⟨*Nacht*⟩

air: ~ **letter** *n.* Aerogramm, *das;* ~**lift** *n.* Luftbrücke, *die* (**of für**); ~**line** *n.* Fluggesellschaft, *die;* Fluglinie, *die;* ~**line pilot** [für eine Fluggesellschaft fliegender] Pilot; ~ **liner** *n.* Verkehrsflugzeug, *das;* ~ **mail** *n.* Luftpost, *die;* **by** ~ **mail** mit Luftpost; ~**man** /'eəmən/ *n., pl.* ~**men** /-mən/ Flieger, *der;* ~ **mile** *n.* Flugmeile, *die;* ~**plane** *n.* (Amer.) Flugzeug, *das;* ~**play** *n.* (Radio) das Spielen einer Platte im *Radio;* **the record receives** *or* **gets no/a great deal of** ~**play** die Platte wird [überhaupt] nicht/wird sehr häufig im Radio gespielt; ~ **pocket** *n.* (Aeronaut.) Luftloch, *das;* ~ **pollution** *n.* Luftverschmutzung, *die;* ~**port** *n.* Flughafen, *der;* ~**port tax** Flughafengebühr, *die;* ~ **pressure** *n.* Luftdruck, *der;* ~ **raid** *n.* Luftangriff, *der;* ~**-raid shelter** *n.* Luftschutzraum, *der;* ~ **rifle** *n.* Luftgewehr, *das;* ~**-sea** '**rescue** *n.* Seenotrettungseinsatz aus der Luft; ~**ship** *n.* Luftschiff, *das;* ~ **show** *n.* Flugschau, *die;* ~**sick** *adj.* luftkrank; ~**stream** *n.* (Meteorol.) Luftströmung, *die;* ~ **strike** *n.* Luftanschlag, *der;* ~ **terminal** *n.* [Air-]Terminal, *der od. das;* ~**tight** *adj.* luftdicht; ~**time** *n.* Sendezeit, *die;* ~ **traffic** *n.* Flugverkehr, *der;* ~**-traffic control** *n.* Flugsicherung, *die;* ~**-traffic controller** *n.* Fluglotse, *der;* ~ **travel** *n.* Fliegen, *das;* ~**waves** *n. pl.* Äther, *das*

'**airy** *adj.* luftig ⟨*Büro, Zimmer*⟩

aisle /aɪl/ *n.* Gang, *der;* (of church) Seitenschiff, *das*

ajar /ə'dʒɑː(r)/ *adj.* **be** ~: einen Spaltbreit offen stehen

a.k.a. *abbr.* = **also known as** al.

akin /ə'kɪn/ *adj.* **be** ~ **to sth.** einer Sache (*Dat.*) ähnlich sein

alarm /ə'lɑːm/ [1] *n.* (a) Alarm, *der;* **give** *or* **raise the** ~: Alarm schlagen
(b) (fear) Angst, *die*
[2] *v.t.* aufschrecken

alarm: ~ **call** *n.* Weck[an]ruf, *der;* ~ **clock** *n.* Wecker, *der*

alas /ə'læs/ *int.* ach

Albania /æl'beɪnɪə/ *pr. n.* Albanien (*das*)

Albanian /æl'beɪnɪən/ [1] *adj.* albanisch; **sb. is** ~: jmd. ist Albaner/Albanerin
[2] *n.* (a) (person) Albaner, *der*/Albanerin, *die*
(b) (language) Albanisch, *das; see also*

albatross /'ælbətrɒs/ *n.* Albatros, *der*

album /'ælbəm/ *n.* Album, *das*

alcohol /'ælkəhɒl/ *n.* Alkohol, *der*

'**alcohol-free** *adj.* alkoholfrei

alcoholic /ælkə'hɒlɪk/ [1] *adj.* alkoholisch
[2] *n.* Alkoholiker, *der*/Alkoholikerin, *die*

Alcoholics A'nonymous *n.* die Anonymen Alkoholiker

alcoholism /'ælkəhɒlɪzm/ *n.* Alkoholismus, *der*

alcopop /'ælkəʊpɒp/ *n.* Alcopop, *der od. das*

alcove /'ælkəʊv/ *n.* Alkoven, *der*

ale /eɪl/ *n.* Ale, *das*

alert /ə'lɜːt/ [1] *adj.* wachsam
[2] *n.* Alarmbereitschaft, *die;* **on the** ~: auf der Hut
[3] *v.t.* alarmieren; ~ **sb.** [**to sth.**] jmdn. [vor etw. (*Dat.*)] warnen

'**A level** *n.* (Brit. Sch.) ≈ Abitur, *das*

algebra /'ældʒɪbrə/ *n.* Algebra, *die*

Algeria /æl'dʒɪərɪə/ *pr. n.* Algerien (*das*)

Algerian /æl'dʒɪərɪən/ [1] *adj.* algerisch; **sb. is** ~: jmd. ist Algerier/Algerierin
[2] *n.* Algerier, *der*/Algerierin, *die*

alias /'eɪlɪəs/ [1] *adv.* alias
[2] *n.*(a) angenommener Name
(b) (Comp.) Alias, *das*

alibi /'ælɪbaɪ/ *n.* Alibi, *das*

alien /'eɪlɪən/ [1] *adj.* (a) (strange) fremd
(b) (foreign) ausländisch
[2] *n.* (a) (from another world) Außerirdische, *der/die*
(b) (Admin.: foreigner) Ausländer, *der*/Ausländerin, *die*

alienate /'eɪlɪəneɪt/ *v.t.* befremden

alienation /eɪlɪə'neɪʃn/ *n.* Entfremdung, *die*

alight¹ /ə'laɪt/ *v.i.* (a) aussteigen (**from** aus)
(b) ⟨*Vogel:*⟩ sich niedersetzen

alight² *adj.* **be/catch** ~: brennen; **set sth.** ~: etw. in Brand setzen

align /ə'laɪn/ *v.t.* (a) (place in a line) ausrichten
(b) (bring into line) in eine Linie bringen

a'lignment *n.* Ausrichtung, *die;* **out of** ~: nicht richtig ausgerichtet

alike /ə'laɪk/ *pred. adj.* ähnlich; (indistinguishable) gleich

alimony /'ælɪmənɪ/ *n.* Unterhaltszahlung, *die*

alive /ə'laɪv/ *pred. adj.* (a) lebendig
(b) (aware) **be** ~ **to sth.** sich (*Dat.*) einer Sache (*Gen.*) bewusst sein
(c) (swarming) **be** ~ **with** wimmeln von

alkali /'ælkəlaɪ/ *n., pl.* ~**s** *or* ~**es** Alkali, *das*

alkaline /'ælkəlaɪn/ *adj.* alkalisch

all /ɔːl/ [1] *attrib. adj.* (a) (entire extent or quantity of) ganz; ~ **day** den ganzen Tag; ~ **my money** all mein Geld; mein ganzes Geld
⋯⟩

(b) (entire number of) alle; ~ **the books** alle Bücher; ~ **my books** all[e] meine Bücher; ~ **the others** alle anderen
(c) (any whatever) jeglicher/jegliche/jegliches
(d) (greatest possible) in ~ **innocence** in aller Unschuld
2 *n.* **(a)** (~ persons) alle; ~ **of us** wir alle; **the happiest of** ~: der/die Glücklichste unter *od.* von allen
(b) (every bit) ~ **of it** alles; ~ **of the money** das ganze Geld
(c) ~ **of** (coll.: as much as) **be** ~ **of seven feet tall** gut sieben Fuß groß sein
(d) (~ things) alles; ~ **I need is the money** ich brauche nur das Geld; **that is** ~: das ist alles; **the most beautiful of** ~: der/die/das Schönste von allen; **most of** ~: am meisten; **it was** ~ **but impossible** es war fast unmöglich; **it's** ~ **the same to me** es ist mir ganz egal; **can I help you at** ~? kann ich Ihnen irgendwie behilflich sein?; **she has no talent at** ~: sie hat überhaupt kein Talent; **nothing at** ~: gar nichts; **not at** ~ **happy/ well** überhaupt nicht glücklich/gesund; **not at** ~! überhaupt nicht!; (acknowledging thanks) gern geschehen!; **if at** ~: wenn überhaupt; **in** ~: insgesamt; ~ **in** ~: alles in allem
(e) (Sport) **two [goals]** ~: zwei zu zwei; (Tennis) **thirty** ~: dreißig beide
3 *adv.* ganz; ~ **but** fast; ~ **the better/worse [for that]** um so besser/schlimmer; ~ **at once** (suddenly) plötzlich; **be** ~ **'in** (exhausted) total erledigt sein (ugs.); **sth. is** ~ **right** etw. ist in Ordnung; (tolerable) etw. ist ganz gut; **I'm** ~ **right** mir geht es ganz gut; **yes,** ~ **right** ja, gut; **it's** ~ **right by me** das ist mir recht

allay /ə'leɪ/ *v.t.* zerstreuen ⟨*Besorgnis, Befürchtungen*⟩

all: ~**-'clear** *n.* Entwarnung, *die;* ~**-day** *adj.* ganztägig ⟨*Ausflug, Versammlung*⟩

allegation /ælɪ'geɪʃn/ *n.* Behauptung, *die;* **make** ~**s against sb.** Beschuldigungen gegen jmdn. erheben

allege /ə'ledʒ/ *v.t.* behaupten

alleged /ə'ledʒd/ *adj.,* **allegedly** /ə'ledʒɪdlɪ/ *adv.* angeblich

allegiance /ə'li:dʒəns/ *n.* Loyalität, *die* (**to** gegenüber)

allegorical /ælɪ'gɒrɪkl/ *adj.* allegorisch

allegory /'ælɪgərɪ/ *n.* Allegorie, *die*

allergic /ə'lɜ:dʒɪk/ *adj.* allergisch (**to** gegen)

allergy /'ælədʒɪ/ *n.* Allergie, *die*

alleviate /ə'li:vɪeɪt/ *v.t.* abschwächen

alley /'ælɪ/ *n.* [schmale] Gasse

alliance /ə'laɪəns/ *n.* Bündnis, *das;* (league) Allianz, *die*

allied /'ælaɪd/ *adj.* **be** ~ **to** *or* **with sb./sth.** mit jmdm./etw. verbündet sein

alligator /'ælɪgeɪtə(r)/ *n.* Alligator, *der*

all: ~**-in** *adj.* Pauschal-; ~**-night** *adj.* die ganze Nacht dauernd ⟨*Sitzung*⟩; nachts durchgehend geöffnet ⟨*Gaststätte*⟩

allocate /'æləkeɪt/ *v.t.* zuweisen, zuteilen (**to** *Dat.*)

allocation /ælə'keɪʃn/ *n.* Zuweisung, *die;* (ration) Zuteilung, *die*

allot /ə'lɒt/ *v.t.,* -tt-: ~ **sth. to sb.** jmdm. etw. zuteilen

al'lotment *n.* (Brit.: plot of land) ≈ Schrebergarten, *der*

all: ~**-out** *attrib. adj.* mit allen [verfügbaren] Mitteln *nachgestellt;* ~**-over** *attrib. adj.* ~**-over tan** nahtlose Bräune

allow /ə'laʊ/ **1** *v.t.* erlauben; zulassen; ~ **sb. to do sth.** jmdm. erlauben, etw. zu tun; **be** ~**ed to do sth.** etw. tun dürfen **2** *v.i.* ~ **for sth.** etw. berücksichtigen

allowance /ə'laʊəns/ *n.* **(a)** Zuteilung, *die;* (for special expenses) Zuschuss, *der* **(b) make** ~**s for sth./sb.** etw./jmdn. berücksichtigen

alloy /'ælɔɪ/ *n.* Legierung, *die*

all: ~**-purpose** *adj.* Universal-; Allzweck-; ~**-risks** *attrib. adj.* **an** ~**-risks insurance** eine alle gängigen Risiken abdeckende Versicherung; ~**-round** *adj.* Allround-; ~**-'rounder** *n.* Allroundtalent, *das;* ~**-seater** *adj.* voll bestuhlt ⟨*Stadion*⟩; ~**-time** *adj.* ~**-time record** absoluter Rekord

allude /ə'lu:d/ *v.i.* ~ **to** sich beziehen auf (+ *Akk.*); (indirectly) anspielen auf (+ *Akk.*)

allusion /ə'lu:ʒn/ *n.* Hinweis, *der;* (indirect) Anspielung, *die*

ally /'ælaɪ/ *n.* Verbündete, *der/die;* **the Allies** die Alliierten

almighty /ɔ:l'maɪtɪ/ *adj.* allmächtig; **the A**~: der Allmächtige

almond /'ɑ:mənd/ *n.* Mandel, *die*

almost /'ɔ:lməʊst/ *adv.* fast; beinahe

alms /ɑ:mz/ *n.* Almosen, *das*

alone /ə'ləʊn/ **1** *pred. adj.* allein; alleine (ugs.) **2** *adv.* allein

along /ə'lɒŋ/ **1** *prep.* entlang (*position: + Dat.; direction: + Akk.*) **2** *adv.* weiter; **I'll be** ~ **shortly** ich komme gleich; **all** ~: die ganze Zeit [über]

along'side 1 *adv.* daneben **2** *prep.* neben (*position: + Dat.; direction: + Akk.*)

aloof /ə'lu:f/ **1** *adv.* abseits; **hold** ~ **from sb.** sich von jmdm. fern halten **2** *adj.* distanziert

aloud /ə'laʊd/ *adv.* laut; **read [sth.]** ~: [etw.] vorlesen

alphabet /'ælfəbet/ *n.* Alphabet, *das*

alphabetical /ælfə'betɪkl/ *adj.,* **alpha'betically** *adv.* alphabetisch

alpine /'ælpaɪn/ *adj.* alpin

Alps /ælps/ *pr. n. pl.* **the** ~: die Alpen

already /ɔ:l'redɪ/ *adv.* schon

Alsatian /æl'seɪʃn/ *n.* [deutscher] Schäferhund

also /'ɔːlsəʊ/ *adv.* auch; (moreover) außerdem

altar /'ɔːltə(r), 'ɒltə(r)/ *n.* Altar, *der*

alter /'ɔːltə(r), 'ɒltə(r)/ **1** *v.t.* ändern
2 *v.i.* sich verändern

alteration /ɔːltə'reɪʃn, ɒltə'reɪʃn/ *n.*
Änderung, *die*

alternate **1** /ɔːl'tɜːnət/ *adj.* sich
abwechselnd
2 /'ɔːltəneɪt/ *v.t.* abwechseln lassen
3 /'ɔːltəneɪt/ *v.i.* sich abwechseln

al'ternately *adv.* abwechselnd

'alternating current *n.* (Electr.)
Wechselstrom, *der*

alternative /ɔːl'tɜːnətɪv/ **1** *adj.*
alternativ; Alternativ-
2 *n.* (a) (choice) Alternative, *die;*
~ **energy** alternative Energie;
~ **fuel** Alternativkraftstoff, *der* (*für
Verbrennungsmotoren*); ~ **medicine**
Alternativmedizin, *die*
(b) (possibility) Möglichkeit, *die*

al'ternatively *adv.* oder aber; **or** ~: oder
aber auch

although /ɔːl'ðəʊ/ *conj.* obwohl

altimeter /'æltɪmiːtə(r)/ *n.* Höhenmesser,
der

altitude /'æltɪtjuːd/ *n.* Höhe, *die*

altogether /ɔːltə'geðə(r)/ *adv.* völlig; (on
the whole) im Großen und Ganzen; (in total)
insgesamt; **not** ~ **[true/convincing]** nicht
ganz [wahr/überzeugend]

altruist /'æltrʊɪst/ *n.* Altruist, *der*/
Altruistin, *die* (geh.)

altruistic /æltrʊ'ɪstɪk/ *adj.* altruistisch

aluminium /æljʊ'mɪnɪəm/ (Brit.),
aluminum /ə'luːmɪnəm/ (Amer.) *ns.*
Aluminium, *das*

always /'ɔːlweɪz/ *adv.* immer; (repeatedly)
ständig

Alzheimer's disease /'æltshaɪməz
dɪziːz/ *n.* Alzheimerkrankheit, *die*

am ▶ BE

a.m. /eɪ'em/ *adv.* vormittags; **[at] one/four**
~: [um] ein/vier Uhr früh

AM *abbr.* = **amplitude modulation**
AM

amalgamate /ə'mælɡəmeɪt/ **1** *v.t.*
vereinigen
2 *v.i.* sich vereinigen; ⟨*Firmen:*⟩
fusionieren

amalgamation /əmælɡə'meɪʃn/ *n.*
Vereinigung, *die;* (of firms) Fusion, *die*

amass /ə'mæs/ *v.t.* anhäufen

amateur /'æmətə(r)/ *n.* Amateur, *der;*
attrib. Amateur-; Laien-

'amateurish *adj.* laienhaft; amateurhaft

amaze /ə'meɪz/ *v.t.* verblüffen;
verwundern

a'mazement *n.* Verblüffung, *die;*
Verwunderung, *die*

amazing /ə'meɪzɪŋ/ *adj.* (remarkable)
erstaunlich; (astonishing) verblüffend

Amazon /'æməzən/ *pr. n.* **the** ~: der
Amazonas

ambassador /æm'bæsədə(r)/ *n.*
Botschafter, *der*/Botschafterin, *die*

amber /'æmbə(r)/ **1** *n.* **(a)** Bernstein, *der*
(b) (traffic light) Gelb, *das*
2 *adj.* Bernstein-; (colour) bernsteinfarben;
gelb ⟨*Verkehrslicht*⟩

ambiguity /æmbɪ'ɡjuːɪtɪ/ *n.*
Zweideutigkeit, *die*

ambiguous /æm'bɪɡjʊəs/ *adj.* zweideutig

ambition /æm'bɪʃn/ *n.* Ehrgeiz, *der;*
(aspiration) Ambition, *die*

ambitious /æm'bɪʃəs/ *adj.* ehrgeizig

ambivalent /æm'bɪvələnt/ *adj.* ambivalent

amble /'æmbl/ *v.i.* schlendern

ambulance /'æmbjʊləns/ *n.*
Krankenwagen, *der;* Ambulanz, *die*

ambulance: ~ **chaser** *n.* (Amer.)
*Anwalt oder sein Agent, der Unfallopfer dazu
überredet, auf Schadenersatz zu klagen;*
~ **driver** *n.* Fahrer/Fahrerin eines/des
Krankenwagens; ~ **man** *n.* Sanitäter, *der;*
~ **service** *n.* Rettungsdienst, *der*

ambush /'æmbʊʃ/ **1** *n.* Hinterhalt, *der;* **lie
in** ~: im Hinterhalt liegen
2 *v.t.* [aus dem Hinterhalt] überfallen

amen /ɑː'men, eɪ'men/ **1** *int.* amen
2 *n.* Amen, *das*

amenable /ə'miːnəbl/ *adj.* zugänglich,
aufgeschlossen (**to** *Dat.*)

amend /ə'mend/ *v.t.* berichtigen; abändern
⟨*Gesetzentwurf, Antrag*⟩

a'mendment *n.* (to motion)
Abänderungsantrag, *der;* (to bill)
Änderungsantrag, *der*

amends /ə'mendz/ *n. pl.* **make** ~ **[to sb.]** es
[bei jmdm.] wieder gutmachen; **make** ~ **for**
sth. etw. wieder gutmachen

amenity /ə'miːnɪtɪ/ *n., usu. in pl.*
amenities (of town) kulturelle und
Freizeiteinrichtungen

America /ə'merɪkə/ *pr. n.* Amerika (*das*)

American /ə'merɪkən/ **1** *adj.*
amerikanisch; **sb. is** ~: jmd. ist
Amerikaner/Amerikanerin; ~ **English**
amerikanisches Englisch
2 *n.* (person) Amerikaner, *der*/
Amerikanerin, *die*

American: ~ **'football** *n.* Football, *der;*
~ **'Indian** *n.* Indianer, *der*/Indianerin, *die*

Americanism /ə'merɪkənɪzm/ *n.* (Ling.)
Amerikanismus, *der*

Americanization /əmerɪkənaɪ'zeɪʃn/ *n.*
Amerikanisierung, *die*

Americanize /ə'merɪkənaɪz/ *v.t.*
amerikanisieren

amiable /'eɪmɪəbl/ *adj.* umgänglich

amicable /'æmɪkəbl/ *adj.*
freundschaftlich; gütlich ⟨*Einigung*⟩

amicably /'æmɪkəblɪ/ *adv.* in [aller]
Freundschaft

a

amid[st] /ə'mɪd(st)/ *prep.* inmitten; (fig.: during) bei

amiss /ə'mɪs/ ① *pred. adj.* verkehrt; **is anything ~?** stimmt irgendetwas nicht? ② *adv.* **take sth. ~:** etw. übel nehmen

ammonia /ə'məʊnɪə/ *n.* Ammoniak, *das*

ammunition /æmjʊ'nɪʃn/ *n.* Munition, *die*

amnesia /æm'ni:zɪə/ Amnesie, *die*

amnesty /'æmnɪstɪ/ *n.* Amnestie, *die*

amniocentesis /æmnɪəʊsen'ti:sɪs/ *n.* (Med.) Fruchtwasserentnahme, *die*

amok /ə'mɒk/ *adv.* **run ~:** Amok laufen

among[st] /ə'mʌŋ(st)/ *prep.* unter (+ *Dat.*); **~ other things** unter anderem; **they often quarrel ~ themselves** sie streiten oft miteinander

amoral /eɪ'mɒrl/ *adj.* amoralisch

amorous /'æmərəs/ *adj.* verliebt; amourös ⟨*Abenteuer, Beziehung*⟩

amorphous /ə'mɔ:fəs/ *adj.* formlos; amorph ⟨*Masse*⟩

amount /ə'maʊnt/ ① *v.i.* **~ to sth.** sich auf etw. (*Akk.*) belaufen; (fig.) etw. bedeuten ② *n.* **(a)** (total) Betrag, *der;* Summe, *die* **(b)** (quantity) Menge, *die*

amp /æmp/ *n.* Ampere, *das*

amphetamine /æm'fetəmɪn/ *n.* (Med.) Amphetamin, *das*

amphibian /æm'fɪbɪən/ ① *adj.* amphibisch ② *n.* Amphibie, *die*

amphibious /æm'fɪbɪəs/ *adj.* amphibisch

amphitheatre /'æmfɪθɪətə(r)/ *n.* Amphitheater, *das*

ample /'æmpl/ *adj.* **(a)** (spacious) weitläufig ⟨*Garten, Räume*⟩; reichhaltig ⟨*Mahl*⟩ **(b)** (enough) **~ room/food** reichlich Platz/zu essen

amplifier /'æmplɪfaɪə(r)/ *n.* Verstärker, *der*

amplify /'æmplɪfaɪ/ *v.t.* verstärken; (enlarge on) weiter ausführen

amputate /'æmpjʊteɪt/ *v.t.* amputieren

amputation /æmpjʊ'teɪʃn/ *n.* Amputation, *die*

amuse /ə'mju:z/ *v.t.* **(a)** (interest) unterhalten; **~ oneself by doing sth.** sich (*Dat.*) die Zeit damit vertreiben, etw. zu tun **(b)** (make laugh or smile) amüsieren

a'musement *n.* Belustigung, *die;* **~ arcade** Spielhalle, *die*

amusing /ə'mju:zɪŋ/ *adj.* amüsant

an /ən, *stressed* æn/ *indef. art. see also* A²: ein/eine/ein

anaemia /ə'ni:mɪə/ *n.* Blutarmut, *die;* Anämie, *die*

anaemic /ə'ni:mɪk/ *adj.* blutarm; anämisch

anaesthetic /ænɪs'θetɪk/ *n.* Anästhetikum, *das;* general

~: Narkosemittel, *das;* **local ~:** Lokalanästhetikum, *das*

anaesthetist /ə'ni:sθətɪst/ *n.* Anästhesist, *der*/Anästhesistin, *die;* Narkose[fach]arzt, *der*/-ärztin, *die*

anagram /'ænəgræm/ *n.* Anagramm, *das*

analgesia /ænæl'dʒi:zɪə/ *n.* (Med.) Analgesie, *die*

analgesic /ænæl'dʒi:sɪk/ (Med.) ① *adj.* analgetisch ② *n.* Analgetikum, *das*

analog (Amer.) ▸ ANALOGUE

analogue /'ænəlɒg/ *n.* Entsprechung, *die;* Analogon, *das* (geh.); **~ computer** Analogrechner, *der;* **~ watch** Analoguhr, *die*

analogy /ə'nælədʒɪ/ *n.* Analogie, *die*

analyse /'ænəlaɪz/ *v.t.* analysieren

analysis /ə'nælɪsɪs/ *n., pl.* **analyses** /ə'nælɪsi:z/ Analyse, *die*

analyst /'ænəlɪst/ *n.* **(a)** (Psych.) Analytiker, *der*/Analytikerin, *die* **(b)** (Econ., Polit., etc.) Experte, *der*/Expertin, *die*

analytic /ænə'lɪtɪk/, **analytical** /ænə'lɪtɪkl/ *adj.* analytisch

analyze (Amer.) ▸ ANALYSE

anarchic /ə'nɑ:kɪk/, **anarchical** /ə'nɑ:kɪkl/ *adj.* anarchisch; (anarchistic) anarchistisch

anarchist /'ænəkɪst/ *n.* Anarchist, *der*/Anarchistin, *die*

anarchy /'ænəkɪ/ *n.* Anarchie, *die*

anatomical /ænə'tɒmɪkl/ *adj.* anatomisch

anatomy /ə'nætəmɪ/ *n.* Anatomie, *die*

ANC *abbr.* = **African National Congress** ANK

ancestor /'ænsestə(r)/ *n.* Vorfahr, *der*

ancestry /'ænsestrɪ/ *n.* Abstammung, *die*

anchor /'æŋkə(r)/ ① *n.* Anker, *der* ② *v.t.* verankern ③ *v.i.* ankern

anchorage /'æŋkərɪdʒ/ *n.* Ankerplatz, *der*

anchorman /'æŋkəmæn/ *n.* (Telev., Radio) Moderator, *der*

anchovy /'æntʃəvɪ/ *n.* Sardelle, *die*

ancient /'eɪnʃənt/ *adj.* alt; historisch ⟨*Gebäude usw.*⟩; (of antiquity) antik

and /ənd, *stressed* ænd/ *conj.* und; **for weeks ~ weeks** wochenlang; **better ~ better** immer besser

androgynous /æn'drɒdʒɪnəs/ *adj.* (Biol.) zwittrig

anecdote /'ænɪkdəʊt/ *n.* Anekdote, *die*

anemia, anemic (Amer.) ▸ ANAEM-

angel /'eɪndʒl/ *n.* Engel, *der*

angelic /æn'dʒelɪk/ *adj.* engelhaft

anger /'æŋgə(r)/ ① *n.* Zorn, *der* (at über + *Akk.*); (fury) Wut, *die* (at über + *Akk.*) ② *v.t.* verärgern; (infuriate) wütend machen

angina [pectoris] /æn'dʒaɪnə ('pektərɪs)/ *n.* (Med.) Angina pectoris, *die*

angle¹ /'æŋgl/ *n.* **(a)** (Geom.) Winkel, *der;*
at an ~ of 60° im Winkel von 60°; **at an**
~: schief
(b) (fig.) Gesichtspunkt, *der*
angle² *v.i.* angeln; (fig.) ~ **for sth.** sich um
etw. bemühen
angle: ~ **brackets** *n. pl.* spitze
Klammern; ~ **grinder** *n.* Winkelschleifer,
der; (with cutting disc) Flex, *die;* **~-parking** *n.*
Schrägparken, *das*
angler /'æŋglə(r)/ *n.* Angler, *der*/Anglerin,
die
Anglican /'æŋglɪkən/ ☐1 *adj.* anglikanisch
☐2 *n.* Anglikaner, *der*/Anglikanerin, *die*
Anglo- /æŋgləʊ/ *in comb.* anglo-/Anglo-
Anglo-Saxon /-'sæksn/ ☐1 *n.*
Angelsachse, *der*/Angelsächsin, *die;*
(language) Angelsächsisch, *das*
☐2 *adj.* angelsächsisch
angora [wool] /æŋ'gɔːrə/ *n.*
Angorawolle, *die;* Mohair, *der*
angrily /'æŋgrɪlɪ/ *adv.* verärgert; (stronger)
zornig
angry /'æŋgrɪ/ *adj.* böse; verärgert ‹*Person,*
Stimme, Geste›; (stronger) zornig; wütend;
be ~ at or about sth. wegen etw. böse sein;
be ~ with or at sb. mit jmdm. *od.* auf jmdn.
böse sein; **get ~:** böse werden
anguish /'æŋgwɪʃ/ *n.* Qualen *Pl.*
angular /'æŋgjʊlə(r)/ *adj.* eckig ‹*Gebäude,*
Struktur›; kantig ‹*Gesicht*›
animal /'ænɪməl/ ☐1 *n.* Tier, *das*
☐2 *adj.* tierisch
animal: A~ Libe'ration Front
n. Tierbefreiungsfront, *die;* ~ **lover**
n. Tierfreund, *der*/-freundin, *die;*
~ **pro'tectionist** *n.* Tierschützer, *der*/
-schützerin, *die;* ~ **'rights** *n. pl.* Tierrechte
Pl.; ~ rights supporter Tierrechtler,
der/Tierrechtlerin, *die*
animate ☐1 /'ænɪmeɪt/ *v.t.* beleben
☐2 /'ænɪmət/ *adj.* beseelt ‹*Leben, Körper*›;
belebt ‹*Objekt, Welt*›
animated /'ænɪmeɪtɪd/ *adj.* lebhaft
‹*Diskussion, Gebärde*›; ~ **cartoon**
Zeichentrickfilm, *der*
animation /ænɪ'meɪʃn/ *n.*
(a) Lebhaftigkeit, *die*
(b) (Cinemat.) Animation, *die*
animosity /ænɪ'mɒsɪtɪ/ *n.* Feindseligkeit,
die
aniseed /'ænɪsiːd/ *n.* Anis[samen], *der*
ankle /'æŋkl/ *n.* Fußgelenk, *das*
ankle: **~-deep** *adj.* knöcheltief; ~ **sock**
n. Socke, *die;* (esp. for children) Söckchen, *das*
annex ☐1 /ə'neks/ *v.t.* annektieren ‹*Land,*
Territorium›
☐2 /'æneks/ *n.* Anbau, *der*
annexation /ænɪk'seɪʃn/ *n.* Annexion,
die; Annektierung, *die*
annexe ▶ ANNEX 2
annihilate /ə'naɪɪleɪt/ *v.t.* vernichten

annihilation /ənaɪɪ'leɪʃn/ *n.* Vernichtung,
die
anniversary /ænɪ'vɜːsərɪ/ *n.* Jahrestag,
der; wedding ~: Hochzeitstag, *der*
annotate /'ænəteɪt/ *v.t.* kommentieren
announce /ə'naʊns/ *v.t.* bekannt geben;
ansagen ‹*Programm*›; (over Tannoy etc.)
durchsagen; (in newspaper) anzeigen ‹*Heirat*
usw.›
an'nouncement *n.* Bekanntgabe, *die;*
(over Tannoy etc.) Durchsage, *die;* (in newspaper)
Anzeige, *die*
an'nouncer *n.* Ansager, *der*/Ansagerin, *die*
annoy /ə'nɔɪ/ *v.t.* **(a)** ärgern
(b) (harass) schikanieren
annoyance /ə'nɔɪəns/ *n.* Verärgerung,
die; (nuisance) Plage, *die*
annoyed /ə'nɔɪd/ *adj.* be ~ [at or with
sb./sth.] ärgerlich [auf *od.* über jmdn./über
etw.] sein; **he got very ~:** er hat sich
darüber sehr geärgert
an'noying *adj.* ärgerlich; lästig
‹*Gewohnheit, Person*›
annual /'ænjʊəl/ ☐1 *adj.* **(a)** (reckoned by
the year) Jahres-; ~ **income/subscription/**
rent/turnover/production/leave/salary
Jahreseinkommen, *das*/-abonnement, *das*/
-miete, *die*/-umsatz, *der*/-produktion, *die*/
-urlaub, *der*/-gehalt, *das;* ~ **rainfall** jährliche
Regenmenge
(b) (recurring yearly) [alljährlich ‹*Ereignis,*
Feier›; Jahres ‹*bericht, -hauptversammlung*›
☐2 *n.* **(a)** Jahrbuch, *das;* (of comic etc.)
Jahresalbum, *das*
(b) (plant) einjährige Pflanze
'annually *adv.* jährlich
annul /ə'nʌl/ *v.t.,* -ll- annullieren; auflösen
‹*Vertrag*›
anodyne/'ænədaɪn/ *adj.* (fig.) wohltuend;
(soothing) einlullend
anon. /ə'nɒn/ *abbr.* = **anonymous**
[author] anon.
anonymity /ænə'nɪmɪtɪ/ *n.* Anonymität, *die*
anonymous /ə'nɒnɪməs/ *adj.* anonym
anorak /'ænəræk/ *n.* Anorak, *der*
anorexia /ænə'reksɪə/ *n.* Anorexie, *die*
(Med.); Magersucht, *die*
anorexic /ænə'reksɪk/ *adj.* anorektisch
(fachspr.); magersüchtig; **be ~:** an Anorexie
(Med.) *od.* Magersucht leiden
another /ə'nʌðə(r)/ ☐1 *pron.* **(a)** (an
additional one) noch einer/eine/eins; ein
weiterer/eine weitere/ein weiteres
(b) (counterpart) wieder einer/eine/eins
(c) (a different one) ein anderer/eine andere/
ein anderes
☐2 *adj.* **(a)** (additional) noch eine/eine;
weiterer/eine weitere/ein weiteres; **after**
~ **six weeks** nach weiteren sechs Wochen
(b) (different) ein anderer/eine andere/ein
anderes
answer /'ɑːnsə(r)/ ☐1 *n.* **(a)** (reply)   ┈┈┊>
Antwort, *die* (to auf + *Akk.*)

(b) (to problem) Lösung, *die* **(to** *Gen.*); (to calculation) Ergebnis, *das*
2 *v.t.* **(a)** beantworten ⟨*Brief, Frage*⟩; antworten auf (+ *Akk.*) ⟨*Frage, Hilferuf, Einladung, Inserat*⟩; eingehen auf (+ *Akk.*) ⟨*Angebot, Vorschlag*⟩; sich stellen zu ⟨*Beschuldigung*⟩; erhören ⟨*Gebet*⟩; erfüllen ⟨*Bitte, Wunsch*⟩; **~ sb.** jmdm. antworten **(b) ~ the door/bell** an die Tür gehen
3 *v.i.* **(a)** (reply) antworten; **~ to sth.** sich zu etw. äußern
(b) (be responsible) **~ for sth.** für etw. die Verantwortung übernehmen
(c) ~ to a description einer Beschreibung (*Dat.*) entsprechen

answerable /'ɑːnsərəbl/ *adj.* verantwortlich **(for** für; **to** *Dat.*)

answering: ~ machine *n.* Anrufbeantworter, *der;* **~ service** *n.* Fernsprechauftragsdienst, *der*

'answerphone (Brit.) ▶ ANSWERING MACHINE

ant /ænt/ *n.* Ameise, *die*

antagonism /æn'tægənɪzm/ *n.* Feindseligkeit, *die* **(towards, against** gegenüber)

antagonist /æn'tægənɪst/ *n.* Gegner, *der*/Gegnerin, *die*

antagonistic /æntægə'nɪstɪk/ *adj.* feindlich

antagonize /æn'tægənaɪz/ *v.t.* **~ sb.** sich (*Dat.*) jmdn. zum Feind machen

antarctic /ænt'ɑːktɪk/ 1 *adj.* antarktisch
2 *n.* **the A~:** die Antarktis

antelope /'æntɪləʊp/ *n.* Antilope, *die*

antenatal /æntɪ'neɪtl/ *adj.* (concerning pregnancy) Schwangerschafts-; Schwangeren-; **~ care** Schwangerenfürsorge, *die;* **~ clinic** Klinik für werdende Mütter

antenna /æn'tenə/ *n.* **(a)** *pl.* **~e** /æn'teniː/ (Zool.) Fühler, *der*
(b) *pl.* **~s** (tech., Amer.: aerial) Antenne, *die*

anthem /'ænθəm/ *n.* Chorgesang, *der*

anthology /æn'θɒlədʒɪ/ *n.* Anthologie, *die*

anthropologist /ænθrə'pɒlədʒɪst/ *n.* Anthropologe, *der*/Anthropologin, *die*

anthropology /ænθrə'pɒlədʒɪ/ *n.* Anthropologie, *die*

anthropomorphism /ænθrəpə'mɔːfɪzm/ *n., no pl.* Anthropomorphismus, *der*

anti /'æntɪ/ 1 *prep.* gegen
2 *adj.* ablehnend

anti- /æntɪ/ *pref.* anti-/Anti-

anti: ~a'bortion *attrib. adj.* **~-abortion protester** Abtreibungsgegner, *der*/-gegnerin, *die;* **~-abortion protest/law** Protest/Gesetz gegen Abtreibung; **~-abortion demonstration/ movement** Antiabtreibungsdemonstration, *die*/-bewegung, *die;* **~-abortionist** /æntɪə'bɔːʃənɪst/ *n.* Abtreibungsgegner, *der*/-gegnerin, *die;* **~-'aircraft** *adj.* (Mil.) Flugabwehr-; **~-aircraft gun** Flak, *die*

antibiotic /æntɪbaɪ'ɒtɪk/ *n.* Antibiotikum, *das*

'antibody *n.* Antikörper, *der*

antic /'æntɪk/ *n.* (trick) Mätzchen, *das* (ugs.); (of clown) Possen, *der*

anticipate /æn'tɪsɪpeɪt/ *v.t.* **(a)** (expect) erwarten; (foresee) voraussehen; **~ trouble** mit Ärger rechnen
(b) (consider before due time) vorwegnehmen

anticipation /æntɪsɪ'peɪʃn/ *n.* Erwartung, *die*

anti'climax *n.* Abstieg, *der*

anti'clockwise *adv., adj.* gegen den Uhrzeigersinn

anti'cyclone *n.* Hochdruckgebiet, *das*

antidepressant /æntɪdɪ'presənt/ *n.* Antidepressivum, *das*

antidote /'æntɪdəʊt/ *n.* Gegenmittel, *das* **(for, against, to** gegen)

'antifreeze *n.* Frostschutzmittel, *das*

antiglobalization /æntɪgləʊbəlaɪ'zeɪʃn/ *n.* Antiglobalisierung, *die*

'anti-hero *n.* Antiheld, *der*

antihistamine /æntɪ'hɪstəmɪn/ *n.* (Med.) Antihistamin[ikum], *das*

'anti-lock *adj.* Antiblockier-; **~ brake** *or* **braking system** Antiblockiersystem, *das*

anti'nuclear *adj.* Anti-Atom[kraft]-

antipathy /æn'tɪpəθɪ/ *n.* Antipathie, *die;* Abneigung, *die*

anti-person'nel *adj.* gegen Menschen gerichtet; **~ mine** Schützenmine, *die*

antiperspirant /æntɪ'pɜːspɪrənt/
1 *adj.* schweißhemmend; **~ spray** Deodorantspray, *der od. das*
2 *n.* Antitranspirant, *das*

antiquated /'æntɪkweɪtɪd/ *adj.* antiquiert; veraltet

antique /æn'tiːk/ 1 *adj.* antik ⟨*Möbel, Schmuck usw.*⟩
2 *n.* Antiquität, *die;* **~ shop** Antiquitätenladen, *der*

antiquity /æn'tɪkwɪtɪ/ *n.* Altertum, *das;* Antike, *die*

anti-Semitic /æntɪsɪ'mɪtɪk/ *adj.* antisemitisch; judenfeindlich

anti-Semitism /æntɪ'semɪtɪzm/ *n.* Antisemitismus, *der;* Judenhass, *der*

anti'septic 1 *adj.* antiseptisch
2 *n.* Antiseptikum, *das*

anti'social *adj.* asozial

anti-'theft *attrib. adj.* Antidiebstahl-

antithesis /æn'tɪθəsɪs/ *n., pl.* **antitheses** /æn'tɪθəsiːz/ Gegenstück, *das* **(of, to** zu)

anti: ~'toxin *n.* (Med.) Antitoxin, *das;* **~'virus** *attrib. adj.* (Comp.) Antivirus-; **~virus software** Antivirensoftware, *die*

antivivisectionist /æntɪvɪvɪ'sekʃənɪst/ *n.* Vivisektionsgegner, *der*/-gegnerin, *die*

antler /'æntlə(r)/ *n.* Geweihsprosse, *die;* **[pair of] ~s** Geweih, *das*

anvil /'ænvɪl/ n. Amboss, der
anxiety /æŋ'zaɪətɪ/ n. Angst, die; (concern about future) Sorge, die (about wegen)
anxious /'æŋkʃəs/ adj. (a) (troubled) besorgt (about um)
(b) (eager) sehnlich; be ∼ for sth. sich nach etw. sehnen
'**anxiously** adv. (a) besorgt
(b) (eagerly) sehnsüchtig
any /'enɪ/ ① adj. (a) (some) [irgend]ein/ [irgend]eine; not ∼: kein/keine; have you ∼ wool/wine? haben Sie Wolle/Wein?
(b) (one) ein/eine
(c) (all, every) jeder/jede/jedes; [at] ∼ time jederzeit
(d) (whichever) jeder/jede/jedes [beliebige]; choose ∼ [one] book/∼ books you like suchen Sie sich (Dat.) irgendein Buch/ irgendwelche Bücher aus
② pron. (a) (some) in condit., interrog., or neg. sentence (replacing sing. n.) einer/ eine/ein[e]s; (replacing collect. n.) welcher/ welche/welches; (replacing pl. n.) welche; not ∼: keiner/keine/kein[e]s/Pl. keine; without ∼: ohne
(b) (no matter which) irgendeiner/irgendeine/ irgendein[e]s/irgendwelche Pl.
③ adv. do you feel ∼ better today? fühlen Sie sich heute [etwas] besser?; if it gets ∼ colder wenn es noch kälter wird; I can't wait ∼ longer ich kann nicht [mehr] länger warten
'**anybody** n. & pron. (a) (whoever) jeder
(b) (somebody) [irgend]jemand; after neg. niemand
'**anyhow** adv. (a) ▶ ANYWAY
(b) (haphazardly) irgendwie
'**anyone** ▶ ANYBODY
'**anything** ① n. & pron. (a) (whatever thing) was [immer]; alles, was
(b) (something) irgendetwas; after neg. nichts
(c) (a thing of any kind) alles
② adv. not ∼ like as ... as keineswegs so ... wie
'**anyway** adv. (a) (in any case, besides) sowieso
(b) (at any rate) jedenfalls
'**anywhere** adv. (a) (in any place) (wherever) überall, wo; wo [immer]; (somewhere) irgendwo; not ∼ near as ... as (coll.) nicht annähernd so ... wie
(b) (to any place) (wherever) wohin [auch immer]; (somewhere) irgendwohin
aorta /eɪ'ɔːtə/ n. (Anat.) Aorta, die
apart /ə'pɑːt/ adv. (a) (separately) getrennt; ∼ from ...: außer ...
(b) (into pieces) auseinander
apartheid /ə'pɑːteɪt/ n. Apartheid, die
apartment /ə'pɑːtmənt/ n. (a) (room) Apartment, das
(b) (Amer.: flat) Wohnung, die
apathetic /æpə'θetɪk/ adj. apathisch (about gegenüber)

apathy /'æpəθɪ/ n. Apathie, die (about gegenüber)
ape /eɪp/ ① n. [Menschen]affe, der
② v.t. nachahmen
aperitif /əperɪ'tiːf/ n. Aperitif, der
aperture /'æpətʃə(r)/ n. Öffnung, die
apex /'eɪpeks/ n. Spitze, die
aphid /'eɪfɪd/ n. Blattlaus, die
aphrodisiac /æfrə'dɪzɪæk/ n. Aphrodisiakum, das
apiece /ə'piːs/ adv. je; they cost a penny ∼: sie kosten einen Penny das Stück
apolitical /eɪpə'lɪtɪkl/ adj. apolitisch; unpolitisch
apologetic /əpɒlə'dʒetɪk/ adj. entschuldigend; be ∼: sich entschuldigen
apologize /ə'pɒlədʒaɪz/ v.i. sich entschuldigen (to bei)
apology /ə'pɒlədʒɪ/ n. Entschuldigung, die; make an ∼: sich entschuldigen (to bei)
apoplectic /æpə'plektɪk/ adj. apoplektisch; ∼ fit Schlaganfall, der
apoplexy /'æpəpleksɪ/ n. Apoplexie, die (fachspr.); Schlaganfall, der
apostle /ə'pɒsl/ n. Apostel, der
apostrophe /ə'pɒstrəfɪ/ n. Apostroph, der; Auslassungszeichen, das
appal (Amer.: **appall**) /ə'pɔːl/ v.t., -ll- entsetzen
ap'palling adj. entsetzlich
apparatus /æpə'reɪtəs/ n. (equipment) Gerät, das; (gymnastic apparatus) Geräte Pl.; (machinery, lit. or fig.) Apparat, der; a piece of ∼: ein Gerät
apparel /ə'pærəl/ n. Kleidung, die; Gewänder Pl. (geh.)
apparent /ə'pærənt/ adj. (a) (clear) offensichtlich; offenbar ⟨Bedeutung, Wahrheit⟩
(b) (seeming) scheinbar
ap'parently adv. (a) (clearly) offensichtlich
(b) (seemingly) scheinbar
apparition /æpə'rɪʃn/ n. [Geister]erscheinung, die
appeal /ə'piːl/ ① v.i. (a) (Law etc.) Einspruch einlegen
(b) (make earnest request) ∼ to sb. for sth./to do sth. jmdn. um etw. ersuchen/jmdn. ersuchen, etw. zu tun
(c) (address oneself) ∼ to sb./sth. an jmdn./ etw. appellieren
(d) (be attractive) ∼ to sb. jmdm. zusagen
② n. (a) (Law etc.) Einspruch, der (to bei); (to higher court) Berufung, die (to bei)
(b) (request) Appell, der; an ∼ to sb. for sth. eine Bitte an jmdn. um etw.
(c) (attraction) Reiz, der
ap'pealing adj. (a) (imploring) flehend
(b) (attractive) ansprechend; verlockend ⟨Idee⟩
appear /ə'pɪə(r)/ v.i. (a) (become visible, arrive) erscheinen; ⟨Licht, Mond:⟩ ⋯⋗

auftauchen; (present oneself) auftreten
(b) (occur) vorkommen
(c) (seem) ~ **[to be]** …: scheinen … [zu sein]
appearance /əˈpɪərəns/ n. **(a)** (becoming visible) Auftauchen, das; (arrival) Erscheinen, das; (of performer etc.) Auftritt, der
(b) (look) Äußere, das; **to all ~s** allem Anschein nach
(c) (semblance) Anschein, der
(d) (occurrence) Vorkommen, das
appease /əˈpiːz/ v.t. besänftigen; (Polit.) beschwichtigen
append /əˈpend/ v.t. anhängen (**to** an + Akk.); (add) anfügen (+ Dat.)
appendage /əˈpendɪdʒ/ n. Anhängsel, das; (addition) Anhang, der
appendicitis /əpendɪˈsaɪtɪs/ n. Blinddarmentzündung, die
appendix /əˈpendɪks/ n., pl. **appendices** /əˈpendɪsiːz/ or ~**es** **(a)** Anhang, der (**to** zu)
(b) (Anat.) Blinddarm, der
appetite /ˈæpɪtaɪt/ n. **(a)** Appetit, der (**for** auf + Akk.)
(b) (fig.) Verlangen, das (**for** nach)
appetizer /ˈæpɪtaɪzə(r)/ n. Appetitanreger, der
appetizing /ˈæpɪtaɪzɪŋ/ adj. appetitlich
applaud /əˈplɔːd/ 1 v.i. applaudieren; [Beifall] klatschen
2 v.t. applaudieren (+ Dat.)
applause /əˈplɔːz/ n. Beifall, der; Applaus, der
apple /ˈæpl/ n. Apfel, der
apple: ~ **'pie** gedeckte Apfeltorte; ~ **'sauce** n. Apfelmus, das
applet /ˈæplɪt/ n. (Comp.) Applet, das
'apple tree n. Apfelbaum, der
appliance /əˈplaɪəns/ n. Gerät, das
applicable /əˈplɪkəbl/ adj. **(a)** anwendbar (**to** auf + Akk.)
(b) (appropriate) geeignet; zutreffend ⟨Fragebogenteil⟩
applicant /ˈæplɪkənt/ n. Bewerber, der/Bewerberin, die (**for** um); (claimant) Antragsteller, der/-stellerin, die
application /æplɪˈkeɪʃn/ n. **(a)** (request) Bewerbung, die (**for** um); (for passport, licence, etc.) Antrag, der (**for** auf + Akk.); ~ **form** Antragsformular, das
(b) (putting) Auftragen, das (**to** auf + Akk.)
(c) (use) Anwendung, die
(d) (Comp.) Applikation, die
applicator /ˈæplɪkeɪtə(r)/ n. Applikator, der
apply /əˈplaɪ/ 1 v.t. **(a)** auftragen ⟨Creme, Farbe⟩ (**to** auf + Akk.)
(b) (make use of) anwenden
2 v.i. **(a)** (have relevance) zutreffen (**to** auf + Akk.)
(b) ~ **[to sb.] for sth.** [jmdn.] um etw. bitten; (for passport etc.) [bei jmdm.] etw. beantragen; (for job) sich [bei jmdm.] um etw. bewerben
appoint /əˈpɔɪnt/ v.t. **(a)** (fix) bestimmen; festlegen ⟨Zeitpunkt, Ort⟩

(b) (to job) einstellen; (to office) ernennen
appointee /əpɔɪnˈtiː/ n. Ernannte, der/die; Berufene, der/die
ap'pointment n. **(a)** (to job) Einstellung, die; (to office) Ernennung, die (**as** zum/zur)
(b) (job) Stelle, die
(c) (arrangement) Termin, der; **make an ~ with sb.** sich (Dat.) von jmdm. einen Termin geben lassen; **by ~:** nach Anmeldung
appraisal /əˈpreɪzl/ n. (evaluation) Bewertung, die
appraise /əˈpreɪz/ v.t. (evaluate) bewerten
appreciable /əˈpriːʃəbl/ adj.
(a) (perceptible) nennenswert ⟨Unterschied, Einfluss⟩; spürbar ⟨Veränderung, Wirkung⟩; merklich ⟨Verringerung, Anstieg⟩
(b) (considerable) beträchtlich
appreciably /əˈpriːʃəblɪ/ adv.
(a) (perceptibly) spürbar ⟨verändern⟩; merklich ⟨sich unterscheiden⟩
(b) (considerably) beträchtlich
appreciate /əˈpriːʃɪeɪt/ 1 v.t.
(a) ([correctly] estimate) [richtig] einschätzen; (understand) verstehen; (be aware of) sich (Dat.) bewusst sein (+ Gen.)
(b) (be grateful for) schätzen; (enjoy) genießen
2 v.i. im Wert steigen
appreciation /əpriːʃɪˈeɪʃn/ n. **(a)** ([correct] estimation) [richtige] Einschätzung; (understanding) Verständnis, das (**of** für); (awareness) Bewusstsein, das
(b) (gratefulness) Dankbarkeit, die; (enjoyment) Gefallen, das (**of** an + Dat.)
appreciative /əˈpriːʃətɪv/ adj. (grateful) dankbar (**of** für); (approving) anerkennend
apprehend /æprɪˈhend/ v.t. **(a)** (arrest) festnehmen
(b) (understand) erfassen
apprehension /æprɪˈhenʃn/ n. Besorgnis, die
apprehensive /æprɪˈhensɪv/ adj. besorgt
apprentice /əˈprentɪs/ n. Lehrling, der (**to** bei)
ap'prenticeship n. (training) Lehre, die; (learning period) Lehrzeit, die
approach /əˈprəʊtʃ/ 1 v.i. sich nähern; (in time) nahen
2 v.t. **(a)** (come near to) sich nähern (+ Dat.)
(b) (approximate to) nahe kommen (+ Dat.)
(c) (appeal to) sich wenden an (+ Akk.)
3 n. **(a)** [Heran]nahen, das
(b) (approximation) Annäherung, die (**to** an + Akk.)
(c) (appeal) Herantreten, das (**to** an + Akk.)
(d) (access) Zugang, der; (road) Zufahrtsstraße, die
approachable /əˈprəʊtʃəbl/ adj.
(a) (friendly) umgänglich
(b) (accessible) zugänglich
ap'proach road n. Zufahrtsstraße, die
appropriate 1 /əˈprəʊprɪət/ adj. geeignet (**to, for** für)

2 /əˈprəʊprɪeɪt/ *v.t.* sich (*Dat.*) aneignen
appropriately /əˈprəʊprɪətlɪ/ *adv.*
gebührend; passend ⟨*gekleidet, genannt*⟩
approval /əˈpruːvl/ *n.* **(a)** (sanctioning)
Genehmigung, *die;* (of proposal) Billigung, *die;*
(agreement) Zustimmung, *die*
(b) on ∼ (Commerc.) zur Probe
approve /əˈpruːv/ 1 *v.t.* **(a)** (sanction)
genehmigen ⟨*Plan, Projekt*⟩; billigen
⟨*Vorschlag*⟩
(b) (find good) gutheißen
2 *v.i.* ∼ of billigen; zustimmen (+ *Dat.*)
⟨*Plan*⟩
approving /əˈpruːvɪŋ/ *adj.* zustimmend
⟨*Worte*⟩; anerkennend ⟨*Blicke*⟩
approx. /əˈprɒks/ *abbr.*
= **approximately** ca.
approximate /əˈprɒksɪmət/ *adj.*
ungefähr *attr.*
apˈproximately *adv.* ungefähr
approximation /əprɒksɪˈmeɪʃn/ *n.*
(a) Annäherung, *die* (**to** an + *Dat.*)
(b) (estimate) Annäherungswert, *der*
Apr. *abbr.* = **April** Apr.
APR *abbr.* = **annualized percentage
rate** Jahreszinssatz, *der*
après-ski /æpreɪˈskiː/ *n.* Après-Ski, *der;*
attrib. Après-Ski-
apricot /ˈeɪprɪkɒt/ *n.* Aprikose, *die*
April /ˈeɪprəl/ *n.* April, *der;* ∼ **fool**
April[s]narr, *der; see also* AUGUST
apron /ˈeɪprən/ *n.* Schürze, *die*
apt /æpt/ *adj.* **(a)** (suitable) passend; treffend
⟨*Bemerkung*⟩
(b) be ∼ to do sth. dazu neigen, etw. zu tun
aptitude /ˈæptɪtjuːd/ *n.* Begabung, *die*
ˈaptly *adv.* passend
aqualung /ˈækwəlʌŋ/ *n.* Tauchgerät, *das*
aquaplane /ˈækwəpleɪn/ *v.i.* ⟨*Reifen:*⟩
aufschwimmen; ⟨*Fahrzeug:*⟩ [durch
Aquaplaning] ins Rutschen geraten
aquarium /əˈkweərɪəm/ *n., pl.* ∼s *or*
aquaria /əˈkweərɪə/ Aquarium, *das*
Aquarius /əˈkweərɪəs/ *n.* (Astrol., Astron.)
der Wassermann
aquatic /əˈkwætɪk/ *adj.* aquatisch;
Wasser-; ∼ **plant** Wasserpflanze, *die*
aqueduct /ˈækwɪdʌkt/ *n.* Aquädukt, *der*
od. das
aqueous /ˈeɪkwɪəs, ˈækwɪəs/ *adj.*
wässerig; wässrig
Arab /ˈærəb/ 1 *adj.* arabisch
2 *n.* Araber, *der*/Araberin, *die*
Arabian /əˈreɪbɪən/ 1 *adj.* arabisch
2 *n.* Araber, *der*/Araberin, *die*
Arabic /ˈærəbɪk/ 1 *adj.* arabisch
2 *n.* Arabisch, *das; see also* ENGLISH 2A
arable /ˈærəbl/ *adj.* bebaubar,
landwirtschaftlich nutzbar ⟨*Land*⟩; ∼ **land**
(cultivated) Ackerland, *das*
arbitrary /ˈɑːbɪtrərɪ/ *adj.* willkürlich

arbitrate /ˈɑːbɪtreɪt/ 1 *v.t.* schlichten
⟨*Streit*⟩
2 *v.i.* ∼ [**upon sth.**] [in einer Sache]
vermitteln
arbitration /ɑːbɪˈtreɪʃn/ *n.* Vermittlung,
die; (in industry) Schlichtung, *die*
arbitrator /ˈɑːbɪtreɪtə(r)/ *n.* Vermittler,
der; (in industry) Schlichter, *der*
arboretum /ɑːbəˈriːtəm/ *n., pl.* arboreta
/ɑːbəˈriːtə/ *or* (Amer.) ∼s Arboretum, *das;*
Baumgarten, *der*
arbour /ˈɑːbə(r)/ *n.* (Brit.) Laube, *die*
arc /ɑːk/ *n.* [Kreis]bogen, *der;* ∼ **lamp,**
∼ **light** Lichtbogenlampe, *die;* ∼ **welding**
Lichtbogen-, Elektroschweißung, *die*
arcade /ɑːˈkeɪd/ *n.* Arkade, *die*
arch /ɑːtʃ/ 1 *n.* Bogen, *der;* (of foot)
Wölbung, *die*
2 *v.t.* beugen ⟨*Rücken*⟩; ∼ **its back** ⟨*Katze:*⟩
einen Buckel machen
arch- *pref.* Erz-
archaeological /ɑːkɪəˈlɒdʒɪkl/ *adj.*
archäologisch
archaeologist /ɑːkɪˈɒlədʒɪst/ *n.*
Archäologe, *der*/Archäologin, *die*
archaeology /ɑːkɪˈɒlədʒɪ/ *n.* Archäologie,
die
archaic /ɑːˈkeɪɪk/ *adj.* veraltet
archˈbishop *n.* Erzbischof, *der*
arch-ˈenemy *n.* Erzfeind, *der*/Erzfeindin,
die
archeology etc. (Amer.) ▶ ARCHAEOLOGY
etc.
archer /ˈɑːtʃə(r)/ *n.* Bogenschütze, *der*
archery /ˈɑːtʃərɪ/ *n.* Bogenschießen, *das*
archetype /ˈɑːkɪtaɪp/ *n.* (original)
Urfassung, *die;* (typical specimen) Prototyp, *der*
architect /ˈɑːkɪtekt/ *n.* Architekt, *der*/
Architektin, *die*
architectural /ɑːkɪˈtektʃərl/ *adj.*
architektonisch
architecture /ˈɑːkɪtektʃə(r)/ *n.*
Architektur, *die*
archive /ˈɑːkaɪv/ 1 *n.* Archiv, *das;* ∼s
Archiv, *das*
2 *v.t.* archivieren
arctic /ˈɑːktɪk/ 1 *adj.* arktisch; A∼ **Circle**
nördlicher Polarkreis; A∼ **Ocean**
Nordpolarmeer, *das*
2 *n.* the A∼: die Arktis
ardent /ˈɑːdənt/ *adj.* leidenschaftlich;
brennend ⟨*Wunsch*⟩; (eager) begeistert
ardor (Amer.), **ardour** (Brit.) /ˈɑːdə(r)/ *n.*
Leidenschaft, *die*
arduous /ˈɑːdjʊəs/ *adj.* anstrengend
are ▶ BE
area /ˈeərɪə/ *n.* **(a)** (surface measure) Fläche,
die; Flächeninhalt, *der*
(b) (region) Gelände, *das;* (of wood, marsh,
desert) Gebiet, *das;* (of city, country) Gegend, *die;*
parking/picnic ∼: Park-/Picknickplatz, *der*
(c) (subject field) Gebiet, *das*

'area code *n.* (Amer. Teleph.)
Gebietsvorwahl[nummer], *die*
arena /ə'riːnə/ *n.* Arena, *die;* **the political**
~: die politische Arena
aren't /ɑːnt/ (coll.) = **are not;** ▶ BE
Argentina /ɑːdʒən'tiːnə/ *pr. n.*
Argentinien (*das*)
Argentinian /ɑːdʒən'tɪnɪən/ ⚊ *adj.*
argentinisch; **sb. is** ~: jmd. ist Argentinier/
Argentinierin
② *n.* Argentinier, *der*/Argentinierin, *die*
arguable /'ɑːgjʊəbl/ *adj.* (questionable)
fragwürdig
arguably /'ɑːgjʊəblɪ/ *adv.* möglicherweise
argue /'ɑːgjuː/ ⚊ *v.t.* (a) (maintain)
~ **that ...:** die Ansicht vertreten, dass ...
(b) (with reasoning) darlegen ⟨*Grund,
Standpunkt*⟩
② *v.i.* ~ **with sb.** sich mit jmdm. streiten;
~ **for/against sth.** für/gegen etw. eintreten;
~ **about sth.** sich über/um etw. (*Akk.*)
streiten
argument /'ɑːgjʊmənt/ *n.* (a) (reason)
Begründung, *die;* ~**s for/against sth.**
Argumente für/gegen etw.
(b) (reasoning process) Argumentieren, *das*
(c) (disagreement, quarrel)
Auseinandersetzung, *die*
argumentative /ɑːgjʊ'mentətɪv/ *adj.*
widerspruchsfreudig
arid /'ærɪd/ *adj.* trocken
Aries /'eəriːz/ *n.* (Astrol., Astron.) der Widder
arise /ə'raɪz/ *v.i.,* **arose** /ə'rəʊz/, **arisen**
/ə'rɪzn/ (a) (originate) entstehen
(b) (present itself) auftreten; ⟨*Gelegenheit:*⟩
sich bieten
(c) (result) ~ **from** *or* **out of sth.** von etw.
herrühren
aristocracy /ærɪ'stɒkrəsɪ/ *n.*
Aristokratie, *die*
aristocrat /'ærɪstəkræt/ *n.* Aristokrat,
der/Aristokratin, *die*
aristocratic /ærɪstə'krætɪk/ *adj.*
aristokratisch
arithmetic /ə'rɪθmətɪk/ *n.* Arithmetik, *die*
arm[1] /ɑːm/ *n.* Arm, *der*
arm[2] ⚊ *n.* (a) *usu. in pl.* (weapon) Waffe, *die;*
up in ~**s** (fig.) in Harnisch (**about** wegen)
(b) *in pl.* (heraldic device) Wappen, *das*
② *v.t.* bewaffnen
armada /ɑː'mɑːdə/ *n.* Armada, *die*
arm: ~**band** *n.* Armbinde, *die;* ~**chair**
n. Sessel, *der;* ~**chair politician/strategist**
politischer Amateur/Amateurstratege, *der;*
~**chair critic** Hobby- *od.* Amateurkritiker,
der; ~**chair travel** Reisen *Pl.* in der Fantasie
armed /ɑːmd/ *adj.* bewaffnet; ~ **forces**
Streitkräfte *Pl.*
armistice /'ɑːmɪstɪs/ *n.* Waffenstillstand,
der
armor (Amer.), **armour** (Brit.) /'ɑːmə(r)/ *n.*
(a) (Hist.) Rüstung, *die*

(b) (steel plates) Panzerung, *die*
arm: ~**pit** *n.* Achselhöhle, *die;* ~**rest** *n.*
Armlehne, *die*
arms: ~ **control** *n.* Rüstungskontrolle,
die; attrib. Rüstungskontroll-; ~ **race**
n. Rüstungswettlauf, *der;* ~ **trade** *n.*
Waffenhandel, *der*
army /'ɑːmɪ/ *n.* Heer, *das;* **join the** ~: zum
Militär gehen
aroma /ə'rəʊmə/ *n.* Duft, *der*
aromatherapy /ərəʊmə'θerəpɪ/ *n.*
Aromatherapie, *die*
aromatic /ærə'mætɪk/ *adj.* aromatisch
arose ▶ ARISE
around /ə'raʊnd/ ⚊ *adv.* (a) (on every side)
[all] ~: überall
(b) (round) herum
(c) (in various places) **ask/look**
~: herumfragen/sich umsehen
② *prep.* (a) um [... herum]
(b) (approximately) ~ **3 o'clock** gegen 3 Uhr;
sth. [costing] ~ **£2** etw. für ungefähr 2
Pfund
arouse /ə'raʊz/ *v.t.* (a) (awake) [auf]wecken
(b) (excite) erregen; erwecken ⟨*Interesse,
Begeisterung*⟩; ~ **suspicion** Verdacht
erregen
arrange /ə'reɪndʒ/ ⚊ *v.t.* (a) (order)
anordnen
(b) (settle, agree) ausmachen, vereinbaren
⟨*Termin*⟩; planen ⟨*Urlaub*⟩; **they** ~**d to meet
the following day** sie verabredeten sich für
den nächsten Tag
② *v.i.* (plan) sorgen (**for** für)
ar'rangement *n.* (a) (ordering, order)
Anordnung, *die*
(b) (settling, agreement) Vereinbarung, *die*
(c) *in pl.* (plans) Vorkehrungen *Pl.;* **make** ~**s**
Vorkehrungen treffen
arrears /ə'rɪəz/ *n. pl.* Schulden *Pl.;* **be in**
~ **with sth.** mit etw. im Rückstand sein; **be
paid in** ~: rückwirkend bezahlt werden
arrest /ə'rest/ ⚊ *v.t.* (a) verhaften,
(temporarily) festnehmen ⟨*Person*⟩
(b) (stop) aufhalten
② *n.* Verhaftung, *die;* **under**
~: festgenommen
arrival /ə'raɪvl/ *n.* Ankunft, *die;* **new** ~**s**
Neuankömmlinge
arrive /ə'raɪv/ *v.i.* (a) ankommen; ~ **at**
a conclusion/an agreement zu einem
Schluss/einer Einigung kommen
(b) ⟨*Stunde, Tag, Augenblick:*⟩ kommen
arrogance /'ærəgəns/ *n.* Arroganz, *die*
arrogant /'ærəgənt/ *adj.* arrogant
arrow /'ærəʊ/ *n.* Pfeil, *der*
arse /ɑːs/ *n.* (coarse) Arsch, *der* (derb)
■ **arse a'bout, arse a'round** *v. i.* (Brit.
coarse) herumalbern (ugs.); herumblödeln (ugs.)
'arsehole *n.* (coarse) Arschloch, *das* (derb)
arsenal /'ɑːsənl/ *n.* Waffenlager, *das*
arsenic /'ɑːsənɪk/ *n.* (a) Arsenik, *das*
(b) (element) Arsen, *das*

arson /'ɑːsn/ *n*. Brandstiftung, *die;* ∼ **attack** Brandanschlag, *der*

arsonist /'ɑːsənɪst/ *n*. Brandstifter, *der*/Brandstifterin, *die*

art /ɑːt/ *n*. **(a)** Kunst, *die;* works of ∼: Kunstwerke *Pl.;* ∼ **college** *or* **school** Kunsthochschule, *die;* ∼**s and crafts** Kunsthandwerk, *das*
(b) *in pl.* (branch of study) Geisteswissenschaften *Pl.*

artery /'ɑːtərɪ/ *n*. (Anat.) Schlagader, *die;* Arterie, *die* (bes. fachspr.)

artful /'ɑːtfl/ *adj*. schlau

'art gallery *n*. Kunstgalerie, *die*

arthritic /ɑː'θrɪtɪk/ *adj*. arthritisch

arthritis /ɑː'θraɪtɪs/ *n*. Arthritis, *die* (fachspr.); Gelenkentzündung, *die*

artichoke /'ɑːtɪtʃəʊk/ *n*. [globe] ∼: Artischocke, *die*

article /'ɑːtɪkl/ *n*. **(a)** (in magazine, newspaper; Ling.) Artikel, *der*
(b) an ∼ **of furniture/clothing** ein Möbel-/ Kleidungsstück; **an** ∼ **of value** ein Wertgegenstand

articulate /ɑː'tɪkjʊlət/ *adj*. redegewandt; **be** ∼**/not very** ∼: sich gut/nicht sehr gut ausdrücken [können]

articulated /ɑː'tɪkjʊleɪtɪd/ *adj*. ∼ **'lorry** Sattelzug, *der*

artificial /ɑːtɪ'fɪʃl/ *adj*. **(a)** künstlich; Kunst-; (not real) unecht; ∼ **limb** Prothese, *die*
(b) (affected) gekünstelt

artificial: ∼ **insemi'nation** *n*. künstliche Befruchtung; (of animal) künstliche Besamung; ∼ **in'telligence** *n*. künstliche Intelligenz; ∼ **'language** *n*. Kunstsprache, *die;* ∼ **respi'ration** *n*. künstliche Beatmung

artillery /ɑː'tɪlərɪ/ *n*. Artillerie, *die*

artisan /'ɑːtɪzn, ɑːtɪ'zæn/ *n*. [Kunst]handwerker, *der*

artist /'ɑːtɪst/ *n*. Künstler, *der*/Künstlerin, *die*

artiste /ɑː'tiːst/ *n*. Artist, *der*/Artistin, *die*

artistic /ɑː'tɪstɪk/ *adj*. **(a)** (of art) Kunst-; künstlerisch
(b) (naturally skilled in art) künstlerisch veranlagt

'artless *adj*. arglos

art nouveau /ɑː nuː'vəʊ/ *n*. Jugendstil, *der*

'art room *n*. Zeichensaal, *der*

'arts centre *n*. Kunstzentrum, *das*

'art work *n*. Bildmaterial, *das*

as /əz, *stressed* æz/ **1** *adv.*, *conj.* **(a)** **he is as tall as I am** er ist so groß wie ich; **as quickly as you can/as possible** so schnell du kannst/wie möglich
(b) (though) **small as he was** obwohl er klein war
(c) (however much) **try as he might/would, he could not concentrate** sosehr er sich

auch bemühte, er konnte sich nicht konzentrieren
(d) *expr. manner* wie; **as you may already have heard, …:** wie Sie vielleicht schon gehört haben, …; **as it were** sozusagen
(e) *expr. time* als; während; **as we climbed the stairs** als wir die Treppe hinaufgingen; **as we were talking** während wir uns unterhielten
(f) *expr. reason* da
2 *prep.* **(a)** (in the function of) als; **as an artist** als Künstler; **speaking as a mother …:** als Mutter …
(b) (like) wie
(c) the same as …: der-/die-/dasselbe wie …; **such as** wie zum Beispiel
3 as for …: was … angeht *od.* betrifft; **as [it] is** wie die Dinge liegen; **the place is untidy enough as it is** es ist hier [so] schon unordentlich genug; **as of …:** (Amer.) von … an; **as to** hinsichtlich (+ *Gen.*); **as yet** bis jetzt; noch

a.s.a.p. *abbr.* = **as soon as possible**

asbestos /æz'bestɒs/ *n*. Asbest, *der*

asbestosis /æzbes'təʊsɪs/ *n*. (Med.) Asbestose, *die*

ASBO /'æzbəʊ/ *abbr.* (Brit.) = **antisocial behaviour order** Verfügung gegen antisoziales Verhalten

ascend /ə'send/ **1** *v.i.* **(a)** (go up) hinaufsteigen; (climb up) hinaufklettern; (by vehicle) hinauffahren
(b) (rise) aufsteigen; ⟨Hubschrauber:⟩ höhersteigen
(c) (slope upwards) ⟨Hügel, Straße:⟩ ansteigen
2 *v.t.* **(a)** (go up) hinaufsteigen ⟨Treppe, Leiter, Berg⟩
(b) ∼ **the throne** den Thron besteigen

Ascension Day /ə'senʃn/ *n*. Himmelfahrtstag, *der*

ascent /ə'sent/ *n*. Aufstieg, *der*

ascertain /æsə'teɪn/ *v.t.* feststellen; ermitteln ⟨Fakten, Daten⟩

ascribe /ə'skraɪb/ *v.t.* zuschreiben (**to** Dat.)

asexual /eɪ'sekʃʊəl/ *adj*. (without sexuality) asexuell

ash¹ /æʃ/ *n*. (tree) Esche, *die*

ash² *n*. (from fire etc.) Asche, *die*

ashamed /ə'ʃeɪmd/ *adj*. beschämt; **be** ∼: sich schämen (**of** wegen)

ash: ∼ **bin** *n*. Mülleimer, *der;* ∼ **blonde** **1** *adj*. aschblond; **2** *n*. Aschblonde, *der*/*die;* ∼**can** (Amer.) ▸ ∼ BIN

ashen /'æʃn/ *adj*. aschfahl ⟨Gesicht⟩

ashore /ə'ʃɔː(r)/ *adv.* an Land

'ashtray *n*. Aschenbecher, *der*

Ash 'Wednesday *n*. Aschermittwoch, *der*

Asia /'eɪʃə/ *pr. n.* Asien (*das*)

Asian /'eɪʃən/ **1** *adj*. asiatisch
2 *n*. Asiat, *der*/Asiatin, *die*

aside /ə'saɪd/ *adv.* beiseite; zur Seite

ask /ɑːsk/ ① *v.t.* (a) fragen; ∼ sb. [sth.]
jmdn. [nach etw.] fragen
(b) (seek to obtain) ∼ sth. um etw. bitten; **how
much are you ∼ing for that car?** wie viel
verlangen Sie für das Auto?; ∼ **sb. to do sth.**
jmdn. [darum] bitten, etw. zu tun
(c) (invite) einladen
② *v.i.* ∼ **after sb./sth.** nach jmdm./etw.
fragen; ∼ **for sth./sb.** etw./jmdn. verlangen
askance /əˈskæns, əˈskɑːns/ *adv.* **look
∼ at sb.** jmdn. befremdet ansehen
askew /əˈskjuː/ *adv., pred. adj.* schief
asleep /əˈsliːp/ *pred. adj.* schlafend; **be/lie
∼:** schlafen; **fall ∼:** einschlafen
asparagus /əˈspærəgəs/ *n.* Spargel, *der*
aspect /ˈæspekt/ *n.* Aspekt, *der*
aspersion /əˈspɜːʃn/ *n.* **cast ∼s on
sb./sth.** jmdn./etw in den Schmutz ziehen
asphalt /ˈæsfælt/ *n.* Asphalt, *der*
asphyxiate /æsˈfɪksɪeɪt/ *v.t. & i.* ersticken
aspiration /æspəˈreɪʃn/ *n.* Streben, *das*
aspire /əˈspaɪə(r)/ *v.i.* ∼ **to** *or* **after sth.**
nach etw. streben
aspirin /ˈæspərɪn/ *n.* Aspirin ⓦⓏ, *das;*
Kopfschmerztablette, *die*
ass¹ /æs/ *n.* Esel, *der*
ass² (Amer.) ▸ ARSE
assailant /əˈseɪlənt/ *n.* Angreifer, *der/*
Angreiferin, *die*
assassin /əˈsæsɪn/ *n.* Mörder, *der/*
Mörderin, *die*
assassinate /əˈsæsɪneɪt/ *v.t.* ermorden;
be ∼d einem Attentat zum Opfer fallen
assassination /əsæsɪˈneɪʃn/ *n.* Mord,
der (**of** an + *Dat.*); ∼ **attempt** Attentat, *das*
(**on** auf + *Akk.*)
assault /əˈsɔːlt/ ① *n.* Angriff, *der;* (fig.)
Anschlag, *der*
② *v.t.* angreifen
assemble /əˈsembl/ ① *v.t.*
(a) zusammentragen; zusammenrufen
⟨*Menschen*⟩
(b) (fit together) zusammenbauen
② *v.i.* sich versammeln
assembly /əˈsemblɪ/ *n.* (a) (meeting)
Versammlung, *die;* (in school)
Morgenandacht, *die*
(b) (fitting together) Zusammenbau, *der*
as'sembly line *n.* Fließband, *das*
assent /əˈsent/ ① *v.i.* zustimmen (**to** *Dat.*)
② *n.* Zustimmung, *die*
assert /əˈsɜːt/ *v.t.* (a) geltend machen;
∼ **oneself** sich durchsetzen
(b) (declare) behaupten; beteuern ⟨*Unschuld*⟩
assertion /əˈsɜːʃn/ *n.* (a) Geltendmachen,
das
(b) (declaration) Behauptung, *die*
assertive /əˈsɜːtɪv/ *adj.* energisch
⟨*Person*⟩; bestimmt ⟨*Ton, Verhalten*⟩
assertiveness /əˈsɜːtɪvnɪs/ *n.*
Bestimmtheit, *die*

assess /əˈses/ *v.t.* einschätzen; festsetzen
⟨*Steuer*⟩ (**at** auf + *Akk.*)
as'sessment *n.* (a) Einschätzung, *die*
(b) (tax to be paid) Steuerbescheid, *der*
asset /ˈæset/ *n.* (a) Vermögenswert, *der*
(b) (useful quality) Vorzug, *der* (**to** für); (person)
Stütze, *die;* (thing) Hilfe, *die*
'asset-stripping *n.: Ankauf unrentabler
Unternehmen, von denen einzelne Teile
Gewinn bringend weiterverkauft werden*
assiduous /əˈsɪdjʊəs/ *adj.* (a) (diligent)
eifrig
(b) (conscientious) gewissenhaft
assign /əˈsaɪn/ *v.t.* (a) (allot) zuweisen (**to**
Dat.)
(b) (appoint) zuteilen; ∼ **sb. to do sth.** jmdn.
damit betrauen, etw. zu tun
as'signment *n.* (a) (allotment) Zuweisung,
die; (appointment) Zuteilung, *die*
(b) (task) Aufgabe, *die*
assimilate /əˈsɪmɪleɪt/ *v.t.* angleichen (**to,
with** an + *Akk.*)
assimilation /əsɪmɪˈleɪʃn/ *n.*
Angleichung, *die* (**to, with** an + *Akk.*)
assist /əˈsɪst/ ① *v.t.* helfen (+ *Dat.*)
② *v.i.* helfen; ∼ **with sth./in doing sth.** bei
etw. helfen/helfen, etw. zu tun
assistance /əˈsɪstəns/ *n.* Hilfe, *die*
assistant /əˈsɪstənt/ *n.* (helper) Helfer,
*der/*Helferin, *die;* (subordinate) Mitarbeiter,
*der/*Mitarbeiterin, *die;* (of professor, artist)
Assistent, *der/*Assistentin, *die;* (in shop)
Verkäufer, *der/*Verkäuferin, *die;* ∼ **manager**
stellvertretender Geschäftsführer
assisted 'suicide *n.* Beihilfe zur
Selbsttötung; assistierter Suizid
associate ① /əˈsəʊʃɪət, əˈsəʊsɪət/
n. (partner) Partner, *der/*Partnerin, *die;*
(colleague) Kollege, *der/*Kollegin, *die*
② /əˈsəʊʃɪeɪt, əˈsəʊsɪeɪt/ *v.t.* in Verbindung
bringen; **be ∼d** in Verbindung stehen
③ /əˈsəʊʃɪeɪt, əˈsəʊsɪeɪt/ *v.i.* ∼ **with sb.** mit
jmdm. Umgang haben
association /əsəʊsɪˈeɪʃn/ *n.*
(a) (organization) Vereinigung, *die*
(b) (mental connection) Assoziation, *die*
(c) (connection) Verbindung, *die*
assorted /əˈsɔːtɪd/ *adj.* gemischt
assortment /əˈsɔːtmənt/ *n.* Sortiment,
das; **a good ∼ of hats [to choose from]** eine
gute Auswahl an Hüten
Asst. *abbr.* = **Assistant** Ass.
assume /əˈsjuːm/ *v.t.* (a) voraussetzen;
assuming that …: vorausgesetzt, dass …
(b) (undertake) übernehmen ⟨*Amt, Pflichten*⟩
(c) (take on) annehmen ⟨*Namen, Rolle*⟩
assumption /əˈsʌmpʃn/ *n.* Annahme,
die; **going on the ∼ that …:** vorausgesetzt,
dass …; **the A∼** (Relig.) Mariä Himmelfahrt
assurance /əˈʃʊərəns/ *n.*
(a) Zusicherung, *die*
(b) (self-confidence) Selbstsicherheit, *die*
assure /əˈʃʊə(r)/ *v.t.* (a) versichern (+ *Dat.*)

(b) (convince) ~ **sb./oneself** jmdn./sich überzeugen
(c) (make certain or safe) gewährleisten
assured /ə'ʃʊəd/ *adj.* gewährleistet 〈*Erfolg*〉; **be** ~ **of sth.** sich (*Dat.*) einer Sache (*Gen.*) sicher sein
asterisk /'æstərɪsk/ *n.* Sternchen, *das*
astern /ə'stɜ:n/ *adv.* (Naut., Aeronaut.) achtern; (towards the rear) achteraus
asteroid /'æstərɔɪd/ *n.* Asteroid, *der*
asthma /'æsmə/ *n.* Asthma, *das*
asthmatic /æs'mætɪk/ ⓵ *adj.* asthmatisch
⓶ *n.* Asthmatiker, *der*/Asthmatikerin, *die*
astonish /ə'stɒnɪʃ/ *v.t.* erstaunen
a'stonishing *adj.* erstaunlich
a'stonishment *n.* Erstaunen, *das*
astound /ə'staʊnd/ *v.t.* verblüffen
a'stounding *adj.* erstaunlich
astray /ə'streɪ/ *adv.* **sth. goes** ~ (is mislaid) etw. wird verlegt; (is lost) etw. geht verloren; **go/lead** ~ (fig.) in die Irre gehen/führen
astride /ə'straɪd/ ⓵ *adv.* rittlings 〈*sitzen*〉
⓶ *prep.* rittlings auf (+ *Dat.*)
astringent /ə'strɪndʒənt/ ⓵ *adj.* scharf
⓶ *n.* Adstringens, *das*
astrologer /ə'strɒlədʒə(r)/ *n.* Astrologe, *der*/Astrologin, *die*
astrological /æstrə'lɒdʒɪkl/ *adj.* astrologisch
astrology /ə'strɒlədʒɪ/ *n.* Astrologie, *die*
astronaut /'æstrənɔ:t/ *n.* Astronaut, *der*/Astronautin, *die*
astronautics /æstrə'nɔ:tɪks/ *n.* Astronautik, *die;* Raumfahrt, *die*
astronomer /ə'strɒnəmə(r)/ *n.* Astronom, *der*/Astronomin, *die*
astronomical /æstrə'nɒmɪkl/ *adj.* astronomisch
astronomy /ə'strɒnəmɪ/ *n.* Astronomie, *die*
astrophysics /æstrəʊ'fɪzɪks/ *n.* Astrophysik, *die*
astute /ə'stju:t/ *adj.* scharfsinnig
asylee /æsaɪ'li:/ *n* Asylant, *der*/Asylantin, *die*
asylum /ə'saɪləm/ *n.* (a) (Polit.) Asyl, *das;* **grant sb.** ~: jmdm. Asyl gewähren; ~ **seeker** Asylsuchende, *der*/*die*
(b) ▸ LUNATIC ASYLUM
asymmetric /æsɪ'metrɪk, eɪsɪ'metrɪk/ *adj.* asymmetrisch; unsymmetrisch
at /ət, *stressed* æt/ *prep.* **(a)** *expr. place* an (+ *Dat.*); **at the station** am Bahnhof; **at the baker's/butcher's/grocer's** beim Bäcker/ Fleischer/Kaufmann; **at the chemist's** in der Apotheke/Drogerie; **at the supermarket** im Supermarkt; **at the party** auf der Party; **at the office/hotel** im Büro/Hotel; **at Dover** in Dover
(b) *expr. time* **at Christmas** [zu *od.* an] Weihnachten; **at six o'clock** um sechs Uhr; **at midnight** um Mitternacht; **at midday** am

Mittag; **at [the age of] 40** mit 40; im Alter von 40; **at this/the moment** in diesem/im Augenblick *od.* Moment
(c) *expr. price* **at £2.50 [each]** zu *od.* für [je] 2,50 Pfund
(d) *expr. speed* **at 30 m.p.h.** *etc.* mit dreißig Meilen pro Stunde *usw.*
(e) at that (at that point) dabei; (at that provocation) daraufhin; (moreover) noch dazu
ate ▸ EAT
atheism /'eɪθɪɪzm/ *n.* Atheismus, *der*
atheist /'eɪθɪɪst/ *n.* Atheist, *der*/Atheistin, *die*
Athens /'æθɪnz/ *pr. n.* Athen (*das*)
athlete /'æθli:t/ *n.* Athlet, *der*/Athletin, *die;* (runner, jumper) Leichtathlet, *der*/ -athletin, *die*
athletic /æθ'letɪk/ *adj.* sportlich
ath'letics *n.* Leichtathletik, *die*
Atlantic /ət'læntɪk/ ⓵ *adj.* atlantisch; ~ **Ocean** Atlantischer Ozean
⓶ *pr. n.* Atlantik, *der*
atlas /'ætləs/ *n.* Atlas, *der*
ATM *abbr.* = **automated teller machine**
atmosphere /'ætməsfɪə(r)/ *n.* Atmosphäre, *die*
atmospheric /ætməs'ferɪk/ *adj.*
(a) atmosphärisch
(b) (fig.: evocative) stimmungsvoll
atom /'ætəm/ *n.* Atom, *das*
'atom bomb *n.* Atombombe, *die*
atomic /ə'tɒmɪk/ *adj.* Atom-
atomizer /'ætəmaɪzə(r)/ *n.* Zerstäuber, *der*
atone /ə'təʊn/ *v.i.* es wieder gutmachen; ~ **for sth.** etw. wieder gutmachen
a'tonement *n.* Buße, *die*
atrocious /ə'trəʊʃəs/ *adj.* grauenhaft; scheußlich 〈*Wetter, Benehmen*〉
a'trociously *adv.* grauenhaft; scheußlich 〈*sich benehmen*〉
atrocity /ə'trɒsɪtɪ/ *n.* **(a)** (wickedness) Grauenhaftigkeit, *die*
(b) (deed) Gräueltat, *die*
'at sign *n.* At-Zeichen, *das;* Klammeraffe, *der* (ugs.)
attach /ə'tætʃ/ *v.t.* **(a)** (fasten) befestigen (to an + *Dat.*); **please find** ~**ed a copy of the letter** beigeheftet ist eine Kopie des Briefes
(b) (fig.) ~ **importance to sth.** einer Sache (*Dat.*) Gewicht beimessen
attaché /ə'tæʃeɪ/ *n.* Attaché, *der*
at'taché case *n.* Diplomatenkoffer, *der*
attached /ə'tætʃt/ *adj.* (emotionally) **be** ~ **to sb./sth.** an jmdn./etw. hängen
at'tachment *n.* **(a)** (act or means of fastening) Befestigung, *die*
(b) (affection) Anhänglichkeit, *die* (**to** an + *Akk.*)
(c) (accessory) Zusatzgerät, *das*
(d) (Comp.) Attachment, *das;* Anlage, *die*

attack /əˈtæk/ 1 v.t. (a) angreifen; (ambush, raid) überfallen; (fig.: criticize) attackieren
(b) (affect) ⟨Krankheit:⟩ befallen
2 v.i. angreifen
3 n. Angriff, der; (ambush) Überfall, der; (fig.: criticism) Attacke, die; (of illness) Anfall, der
at'tacker n. Angreifer, der/Angreiferin, die
at'tack helicopter n. Kampfhubschrauber, der
attacking /əˈtækɪŋ/ adj. offensiv ⟨Spielweise, Spieler⟩; angreifend ⟨Truppen⟩
attain /əˈteɪn/ v.t. erreichen
attainable /əˈteɪnəbl/ adj. erreichbar ⟨Ziel⟩; realisierbar ⟨Hoffnung, Ziel⟩
at'tainment n. Verwirklichung, die
attempt /əˈtempt/ 1 v.t. versuchen
2 n. Versuch, der
attend /əˈtend/ 1 v.i. (a) (give care and thought) aufpassen; (apply oneself) ~ to sth. (deal with sth.) sich um etw. kümmern
(b) (be present) anwesend sein (at bei)
2 v.t. (a) (be present at) teilnehmen an (+ Dat.); (go regularly to) besuchen
(b) (wait on) bedienen (+ Dat.)
(c) ⟨Arzt:⟩ behandeln
attendance /əˈtendəns/ n. Anwesenheit, die; (number of people) Teilnehmerzahl, die
attendant /əˈtendənt/ n. (a) [lavatory] ~: Toilettenmann, der/-frau, die; [cloakroom] ~: Garderobenmann, der/-frau, die; museum ~: Museumswärter, der/-wärterin, die
(b) (member of entourage) Begleiter, der/Begleiterin, die
attention /əˈtenʃn/ 1 n.
(a) Aufmerksamkeit, die; attract [sb.'s] ~: [jmdn.] auf sich (Akk.) aufmerksam machen; pay ~ to sb./sth. jmdn./etw. beachten; pay ~! gib Acht!; pass auf!; hold sb.'s ~: jmds. Interesse wach halten; ~ Miss Jones (on letter) zu Händen [von] Miss Jones
(b) (Mil.) stand to ~: stillstehen
2 int. (a) Achtung
(b) (Mil.) stillgestanden
attentive /əˈtentɪv/ adj. aufmerksam
attic /ˈætɪk/ n. (room) Dachboden, der; (habitable) Dachkammer, die
attire /əˈtaɪə(r)/ n. Kleidung, die
attitude /ˈætɪtjuːd/ n. (a) Haltung, die
(b) (mental ~) Einstellung, die
attn. abbr. = **for the attention of** z. H[d].
attorney /əˈtɜːnɪ/ n. (a) Bevollmächtigte, der/die; power of ~: Vollmacht, die
(b) (Amer.: lawyer) [Rechts]anwalt, der/-anwältin, die
attract /əˈtrækt/ v.t. (a) (draw) anziehen; auf sich (Akk.) ziehen ⟨Interesse, Blick, Kritik⟩
(b) (arouse pleasure in) anziehend wirken auf (+ Akk.)

(c) (arouse interest in) reizen (about an + Dat.)
attraction /əˈtrækʃn/ n. (a) Anziehung, die; (force, lit. or fig.) Anziehung[skraft], die
(b) (fig.: thing that attracts) Attraktion, die; (charm) Verlockung, die; Reiz, der
attractive /əˈtræktɪv/ adj. (a) anziehend
(b) (fig.) attraktiv; reizvoll ⟨Vorschlag, Möglichkeit, Idee⟩
attribute 1 /ˈætrɪbjuːt/ n. Eigenschaft, die
2 /əˈtrɪbjuːt/ v.t. zuschreiben (to Dat.)
attributive /əˈtrɪbjʊtɪv/ adj. (Ling.) attributiv
atypical /eɪˈtɪpɪkl/ adj. atypisch; untypisch
aubergine /ˈəʊbəʒiːn/ n. Aubergine, die
auburn /ˈɔːbən/ adj. rötlich braun
auction /ˈɔːkʃn/ 1 n. Versteigerung, die
2 v.t. versteigern
auctioneer /ɔːkʃəˈnɪə(r)/ n. Auktionator, der/Auktionatorin, die
audacious /ɔːˈdeɪʃəs/ adj. (a) (daring) kühn; verwegen
(b) (impudent) dreist
audacity /ɔːˈdæsɪtɪ/ n. (a) (daringness) Kühnheit, die; Verwegenheit, die
(b) (impudence) Dreistigkeit, die
audible /ˈɔːdɪbl/ adj. hörbar
audience /ˈɔːdɪəns/ n. (a) Publikum, das
(b) (formal interview) Audienz, die (with bei)
audio /ˈɔːdɪəʊ/ adj. Ton-; ~ frequency Tonfrequenz, die; ~ equipment Audioanlage, die
audio- : ~book n. Hörbuch, das; ~ cassette n. Audiokassette, die; Tonkassette, die; ~ typist n. Phonotypist, der/-typistin, die; ~visual adj. audiovisuell
audit /ˈɔːdɪt/ 1 n. ~ [of the accounts] Rechnungsprüfung, die
2 v.t. prüfen
audition /ɔːˈdɪʃn/ 1 n. (singing) Vorsingen, das; (dancing) Vortanzen, das; (acting) Vorsprechen, das
2 v.i. (sing) vorsingen; (dance) vortanzen; (act) vorsprechen
3 v.t. vorsingen/vortanzen/vorsprechen lassen
auditor /ˈɔːdɪtə(r)/ n. Buchprüfer, der/-prüferin, die
auditorium /ɔːdɪˈtɔːrɪəm/ n. Zuschauerraum, der
Aug. abbr. = **August** Aug.
augment /ɔːgˈment/ v.t. verbessern ⟨Einkommen⟩; aufstocken ⟨Fonds⟩
augur /ˈɔːgə(r)/ 1 v.t. bedeuten; versprechen ⟨Erfolg⟩
2 v.i. ~ well/ill for sth./sb. ein gutes/schlechtes Zeichen für etw./jmdn. sein
August /ˈɔːgəst/ n. August, der; in ~: im August; last/next ~: letzten/nächsten August; the first of/on the first of ~: der

erste/am ersten August

aunt /ɑːnt/ n. Tante, die

auntie, aunty /'ɑːntɪ/ n. (coll.) Täntchen, das; (with name) Tante, die

au pair /əʊ 'peə(r)/ n. Aupairmädchen, das

aura /'ɔːrə/ n. Aura, die

auspices /'ɔːspɪsɪs/ n. pl. under the ~ of sb./sth. unter jmds./einer Sache Schirmherrschaft

auspicious /ɔː'spɪʃəs/ adj. günstig; viel versprechend ⟨Anfang⟩

Aussie /'ɒzɪ/ (coll.) **1** adj. australisch **2** n. Australier, der/Australierin, die

austere /ɒ'stɪə(r)/ adj. **(a)** (strict, stern) streng
(b) (severely simple) karg

austerity /ɒ'sterɪtɪ/ n. **(a)** (strictness) Strenge, die
(b) (severe simplicity) Kargheit, die
(c) (lack of luxuries) wirtschaftliche Einschränkung

Australia /ɒ'streɪlɪə/ pr. n. Australien (das)

Australian /ɒ'streɪlɪən/ **1** adj. australisch; sb. is ~: jmd. ist Australier/Australierin
2 n. Australier, der/Australierin, die

Austria /'ɒstrɪə/ pr. n. Österreich (das)

Austrian /'ɒstrɪən/ **1** adj. österreichisch sb. is ~: jmd. ist Österreicher/Österreicherin
2 n. Österreicher, der/Österreicherin, die

authentic /ɔː'θentɪk/ adj. authentisch

authenticate /ɔː'θentɪkeɪt/ v.t. authentifizieren; ~ sth. die Echtheit einer Sache (Gen.) bestätigen

authentication /ɔːˌθentɪ'keɪʃn/ n. Bestätigung der Echtheit; (of information, report) Bestätigung, die

authenticity /ɔːθen'tɪsɪtɪ/ n. Authentizität, die

author /'ɔːθə(r)/ n. Autor, der/Autorin, die; (profession) Schriftsteller, der/Schriftstellerin, die

authoritarian /ɔːˌθɒrɪ'teərɪən/ **1** adj. autoritär
2 n. autoritäre Person

authoritative /ɔː'θɒrɪtətɪv/ adj. maßgebend; zuverlässig ⟨Bericht, Information⟩

authority /ɔː'θɒrɪtɪ/ n. **(a)** Autorität, die; in ~: verantwortlich
(b) the authorities die Behörde[n]

authorization /ɔːθəraɪ'zeɪʃn/ n. Genehmigung, die

authorize /'ɔːθəraɪz/ v.t. **(a)** ermächtigen; bevollmächtigen
(b) (sanction) genehmigen

autism /'ɔːtɪzm/ n., no pl. (Psych., Med.) Autismus, der

autistic /ɔː'tɪstɪk/ adj. (Psych., Med.) autistisch

auto /'ɔːtəʊ/ n., pl. ~s (Amer. coll.) Auto, das

auto- /ɔːtəʊ/ in comb. auto-/Auto-

autobio'graphical adj. autobiographisch

autobi'ography n. Autobiographie, die

autocrat /'ɔːtəkræt/ n. Autokrat, der/Autokratin, die

autocratic /ɔːtə'krætɪk/ adj. autokratisch

'autocross n. Autocross, das

Autocue ® /'ɔːtəʊkjuː/ n. Teleprompter ⒲, der

'autofocus n. (Photog.) Autofokus, der

autograph /'ɔːtəgrɑːf/ **1** n. Autogramm, das
2 v.t. signieren

auto-im'mune adj. (Med.) autoimmun; ~ response Autoimmunantwort, die

automat /'ɔːtəmæt/ n. (Amer.) **(a)** (slot machine) [Münz]automat, der
(b) (cafeteria) Automatenrestaurant, das

automate /'ɔːtəmeɪt/ v.t. automatisieren

automated 'teller machine n. Geldautomat, der

automatic /ɔːtə'mætɪk/ **1** adj. automatisch; ~ gear system, ~ transmission Automatikgetriebe, das
2 n. (weapon) automatische Waffe; (vehicle) Fahrzeug mit Automatikgetriebe

automatically /ɔːtə'mætɪkəlɪ/ adv. automatisch

automation /ɔːtə'meɪʃn/ n. Automation, die

automaton /ɔː'tɒmətən/ n., pl. ~s or automata /ɔː'tɒmətə/ Automat, der

automobile /'ɔːtəməbiːl/ n. (Amer.) Auto, das

autonomous /ɔː'tɒnəməs/ adj. autonom

autonomy /ɔː'tɒnəmɪ/ n. Autonomie, die

'autopilot n. Autopilot, der; [fly] on ~: mit Autopilot [fliegen]

autopsy /'ɔːtɒpsɪ/ n. Autopsie, die

auto: ~**save** (Comp.) **1** n. automatisches Speichern; **2** v.t. automatisch speichern; ~-**suggestion** n. Autosuggestion, die; ~**timer** n. [automatische] Schaltuhr

autumn /'ɔːtəm/ n. Herbst, der; in [the] ~: im Herbst

autumnal /ɔː'tʌmnl/ adj. herbstlich

auxiliary /ɔːg'zɪljərɪ/ **1** adj. Hilfs-
2 n. **(a)** Hilfskraft, die
(b) (Ling.) Hilfsverb, das

avail /ə'veɪl/ **1** n. be of no ~: nichts nützen; to no ~: vergebens
2 v. refl. ~ oneself of sth. von etw. Gebrauch machen

available /ə'veɪləbl/ adj. **(a)** (at one's disposal) verfügbar
(b) (obtainable) erhältlich; lieferbar ⟨Waren⟩

avalanche /'ævəlɑːnʃ/ n. Lawine, die

avarice /'ævərɪs/ n. Geldgier, die; Habsucht, die

avaricious /ævə'rɪʃəs/ adj. geldgierig; habsüchtig

avenge /ə'vendʒ/ *v.t.* rächen

avenue /'ævənjuː/ *n.* Allee, *die;* (fig.) Weg, *der* (**to** zu)

average /'ævərɪdʒ/ **1** *n.* Durchschnitt, *der;* **on** ~: im Durchschnitt; durchschnittlich
2 *adj.* durchschnittlich
3 *v.t.* **(a)** (find the ~ of) den Durchschnitt ermitteln von
(b) (amount on ~ to) durchschnittlich betragen
4 *v.i.* ~ **out at** im Durchschnitt betragen

averse /ə'vɜːs/ *adj.* **be** ~ **to sth.** einer Sache (*Dat.*) abgeneigt sein

aversion /ə'vɜːʃn/ *n.* Abneigung, *die* (**to** gegen)

avert /ə'vɜːt/ *v.t.* abwenden; verhüten ⟨*Unfall*⟩

aviary /'eɪvɪərɪ/ *n.* Vogelhaus, *das*

aviation /eɪvɪ'eɪʃn/ *n.* Luftfahrt, *die*

avid /'ævɪd/ *adj.* (enthusiastic) begeistert; **be** ~ **for sth.** (eager, greedy) begierig auf etw. (*Akk.*) sein

avocado /ævə'kɑːdəʊ/ *n., pl.* ~**s:** ~ **[pear]** Avocado[birne], *die*

avoid /ə'vɔɪd/ *v.t.* **(a)** meiden ⟨*Ort*⟩; ~ **a cyclist** einem Radfahrer ausweichen; ~ **the boss when he's in a temper** geh dem Chef aus dem Weg, wenn er schlechte Laune hat
(b) (refrain from, escape) vermeiden

avoidable /ə'vɔɪdəbl/ *adj.* vermeidbar

avoidance /ə'vɔɪdəns/ *n.* Vermeidung, *die*

await /ə'weɪt/ *v.t.* erwarten

awake /ə'weɪk/ **1** *v.i.,* awoke /ə'wəʊk/, awoken /ə'wəʊkn/ erwachen
2 *v.t.,* awoke, awoken wecken
3 *pred. adj.* wach; **wide** ~: hellwach

awaken /ə'weɪkn/ *v.t. & i.* (esp. fig.)
▶ AWAKE 1, 2

award /ə'wɔːd/ **1** *v.t.* verleihen ⟨*Preis, Auszeichnung*⟩; zusprechen ⟨*Sorgerecht, Entschädigung*⟩; gewähren ⟨*Zahlung, Gehaltserhöhung*⟩
2 *n.* (prize) Auszeichnung, *die*

a'ward-winning *adj.* preisgekrönt

aware /ə'weə(r)/ *adj.* **be** ~ **of sth.** sich (*Dat.*) einer Sache (*Gen.*) bewusst sein; **be** ~ **that** ...: sich (*Dat.*) [dessen] bewusst sein, dass ...

a'wareness *n.* Bewusstsein, *das*

awash /ə'wɒʃ/ *adj.* **be** ~ (flooded) unter Wasser stehen

away /ə'weɪ/ **1** *adv.* **(a)** (at a distance) entfernt; **play** ~ (Sport) auswärts spielen
(b) (to a distance) weg; fort
(c) (absent) nicht da
2 *adj.* (Sport) auswärts *präd.;* Auswärts-; ~ **match** Auswärtsspiel, *das;* ~ **team** Gastmannschaft, *die*

awe /ɔː/ *n.* Ehrfurcht, *die* (**of** vor + *Dat.*)

'awe-inspiring *adj.* Ehrfurcht gebietend; beeindruckend

awesome /'ɔːsəm/ *adj.* **(a)** überwältigend; eindrucksvoll ⟨*Schweigen*⟩; übergroß ⟨*Verantwortung*⟩
(b) (coll.: wonderful, excellent) geil (ugs.)

awe: ~**stricken,** ~**struck** *adj.* [von Ehrfurcht] ergriffen; ehrfurchtsvoll ⟨*Ausdruck, Staunen*⟩

awful /'ɔːfl/ *adj.,* **'awfully** *adv.* furchtbar

awkward /'ɔːkwəd/ *adj.* **(a)** (difficult to use) ungünstig; **be** ~ **to use** unhandlich sein
(b) (clumsy) unbeholfen
(c) (embarrassing) peinlich
(d) (difficult) schwierig; ungünstig ⟨*Zeitpunkt*⟩

awning /'ɔːnɪŋ/ *n.* (on house) Markise, *die;* (of tent) Vordach, *das*

awoke, awoken ▶ AWAKE

awry /ə'raɪ/ *adv.* schief; **go** ~ (fig.) schief gehen (ugs.); ⟨*Plan:*⟩ fehlschlagen

axe (*Amer.:* **ax**) /æks/ *n.* Axt, *die;* Beil, *das*

axis /'æksɪs/ *n., pl.* **axes** /'æksiːz/ Achse, *die*

axle /'æksl/ *n.* Achse, *die*

Bb

B, b /biː/ *n.* B, b, *das;* **B road** Straße 2. Ordnung; ≈ Landstraße, *die*

BA *abbr.* = **Bachelor of Arts**

babble /'bæbl/ *v.i.* **(a)** (talk incoherently) stammeln
(b) (talk foolishly) [dumm] schwatzen
(c) ⟨*Bach:*⟩ plätschern

baboon /bə'buːn/ *n.* Pavian, *der*

baby /'beɪbɪ/ *n.* **(a)** Baby, *das;* **have a** ~**/be going to have a** ~: ein Kind bekommen; throw out *or* away the ~ **with the bathwater** (fig.) das Kind mit dem Bade ausschütten
(b) (childish person) **be a** ~: sich wie ein kleines Kind benehmen

baby: ~ **boom** *n.* Babyboom, *der;*
~**-bouncer** *n.: federnd aufgehängter Sitz für Kleinkinder, in dem sie durch Wippen ihre Beine kräftigen sollen;* ~ **buggy,**
~ **carriage** *ns.* (Amer.) Kinderwagen, *der;* ~ **clothes** *n. pl.* Babykleidung, *die;*
~ **food** *n.* Babynahrung, *die*

'**babyish** *adj.* kindlich ⟨*Aussehen*⟩; kindisch ⟨*Benehmen, Person*⟩

baby: ⁓**minder** *n.* Tagesmutter, *die;* ⁓**sit** *v.i., forms as* sɪᴛ 1: babysitten (ugs.); auf das Kind/die Kinder aufpassen; ⁓**sitter** *n.* Babysitter, *der*/Babysitterin, *die;* ⁓**sitting** *n.* Babysitting, *das;* ⁓**snatcher** *n.* Kindesentführer, *der*/-entführerin, *die;* ⁓**talk** *n.* Babysprache, *die;* ⁓ **walker** *n.* Laufstuhl, *der;* ⁓ **wipe** *n.* feuchtes Baby[pflege]tuch

bachelor /'bætʃələ(r)/ *n.* **(a)** Junggeselle, *der*
(b) (Univ.) B⁓ **of Arts/Science** Bakkalaureus der philosophischen Fakultät/der Naturwissenschaften

back /bæk/ **1** *n.* **(a)** (of person, animal) Rücken, *der;* (of house, cheque) Rückseite, *die;* (of vehicle) Heck, *das;* (inside car) Rücksitz, *der;* **stand ⁓ to ⁓**: Rücken an Rücken stehen; **⁓ to front** verkehrt rum; **turn one's ⁓ on sb.** jmdm. den Rücken zuwenden; (fig.) jmdn. im Stich lassen; **turn one's ⁓ on sth.** (fig.) sich um etw. nicht kümmern; **get** *or* **put sb.'s ⁓ up** (fig.) jmdn. wütend machen; **be glad to see the ⁓ of sb./sth.** (fig.) froh sein, jmdn./etw. nicht mehr sehen zu müssen; **have one's ⁓ to the wall** (fig.) mit dem Rücken zur Wand stehen; **put one's ⁓ into sth.** (fig.) sich für etw. mit allen Kräften einsetzen; **with the ⁓ of one's hand** mit dem Handrücken; **at the ⁓ [of the book]** hinten [im Buch]
(b) (Sport: player) Verteidiger, *der*
2 *adj.* hinter...
3 *adv.* zurück; **two miles ⁓**: vor zwei Meilen; **⁓ and forth** hin und her; **there and ⁓**: hin und zurück; **a week/month ⁓**: vor einer Woche/vor einem Monat
4 *v.t.* **(a)** (assist) unterstützen
(b) (bet on) wetten *od.* setzen auf (+ *Akk.*)
(c) zurücksetzen [mit] ⟨*Fahrzeug*⟩
5 *v.i.* zurücksetzen; **⁓ into/out of sth.** rückwärts in etw. (*Akk.*)/aus etw. fahren; **⁓ on to sth.** hinten an etw. (*Akk.*) grenzen
■ **back 'down** *v.i.* nachgeben
■ **back 'out** *v.i.* rückwärts herausfahren; **⁓ out of sth.** (fig.) von etw. zurücktreten
■ **back 'up** *v.t.* **(a)** unterstützen; untermauern ⟨*Anspruch, These*⟩
(b) (Comp.) sichern ⟨*Daten, Dokumente*⟩; **⁓ up a file on to a floppy disk** von einer Datei eine Sicherungskopie auf Diskette machen

back: ⁓**ache** *n.* Rückenschmerzen *Pl.;* ⁓**-bencher** /bæk'bentʃə(r)/ *n.* (Brit. Parl.) [einfacher] Abgeordneter/[einfache] Abgeordnete; ⁓**bone** *n.* Rückgrat, *das;* ⁓**chat** *n.* (coll.) [freche] Widerrede; ⁓**date** *v.t.* zurückdatieren (**to** auf + *Akk.*); ⁓ '**door** *n.* Hintertür, *die*
'**backer** *n.* Geldgeber, *der*
back: ⁓'**fire** *v.i.* knallen; (fig.) fehlschlagen; **it ⁓fired on me/him** *etc.*

der Schuss ging nach hinten los (ugs.); ⁓**gammon** /'bækgæmən/ *n.* (game) Backgammon, *das;* ≈ Tricktrack, *das;* ≈ Puff, *das;* ⁓**ground** *n.* Hintergrund, *der;* (social status) Herkunft, *die;* ⁓**hand** (Tennis etc.) **1** *adj.* Rückhand-; **2** *n.* Rückhand, *die;* ⁓'**handed** *adj.* **(a)** (Tennis etc.) Rückhand-; **(b)** (fig.) indirekt; zweifelhaft ⟨*Kompliment*⟩; ⁓'**hander** *n.* (coll.: bribe) Schmiergeld, *das*

'**backing** *n.* (support) Unterstützung, *die*

back: ⁓ **issue** ▶⁓ NUMBER; ⁓**lash** *n.* (fig.) Gegenreaktion, *die;* ⁓**log** *n.* Rückstand, *der;* ⁓ **number** *n.* (of periodical, magazine) alte Nummer; ⁓**pack** **1** *n.* Rucksack, *der;* **2** *v.i.* mit dem Rucksack [ver]reisen; ⁓**packer** *n.* Rucksackreisende, *der/die;* Rucksacktourist, *der*/-touristin, *die;* (hiker) Wanderer, *der*/Wanderin, *die* mit Rucksack; ⁓**packing** *n.* das [Ver]reisen mit dem Rucksack; (hiking) das Wandern mit dem Rucksack; *attrib.* ⟨*Reise usw.*⟩ mit dem Rucksack; ⁓ **pay** *n.* ausstehender Lohn/ ausstehendes Gehalt; **he was reinstated with ⁓ pay** er wurde wieder eingestellt und erhielt eine Lohn-/Gehaltsnachzahlung; **she was awarded £7,850 in ⁓ pay** sie erhielt eine Nachzahlung von 7 850 Pfund; ⁓-**pedal** *v.i.* **(a)** die Pedale rückwärts treten; **(b)** (fig.) einen Rückzieher machen (ugs.); ⁓**scratching** *n.* (fig. coll.) [mutual] ⁓scratching Klüngelei, *die* (abwertend); ⁓ '**seat** *n.* Rücksitz, *der;* ⁓**side** *n.* Hinterteil, *das* (ugs.); ⁓**space** *v.i.* die Rücktaste betätigen; ⁓'**stage** *adv.* **go ⁓stage** hinter die Bühne gehen; ⁓ **street** *n.* kleine Seitenstraße; ⁓**stroke** *n.* Rückenschwimmen, *das;* ⁓**track** *v.i.* wieder zurückgehen; (fig.) eine Kehrtwendung machen; ⁓-**up** *n.* (support) Unterstützung, *die;* ⁓-up [copy] (Comp.) Sicherungskopie, *die*

backward /'bækwəd/ **1** *adj.*
(a) rückwärts gerichtet; Rückwärts-
(b) (reluctant, shy) zurückhaltend
(c) (underdeveloped) rückständig ⟨*Land, Region*⟩
2 *adv.* ▶ BACKWARDS

backwards /'bækwədz/ *adv.* **(a)** nach hinten; **the child fell [over] ⁓ into the water** das Kind fiel rückwärts ins Wasser; **bend** *or* **lean over ⁓ to do sth.** (fig. coll.) sich zerreißen, um etw. zu tun (ugs.)
(b) (oppositely to normal direction) rückwärts; **⁓ and forwards** hin und her

back: ⁓**water** *n.* (fig.) Kaff, *das* (ugs.); ⁓ '**yard** *n.* Hinterhof, *der*

bacon /'beɪkn/ *n.* [Frühstücks]speck, *der*

bacterial /bæk'tɪərɪəl/ *adj.* bakteriell

bacterium /bæk'tɪərɪəm/ *n., pl.* **bacteria** /bæk'tɪərɪə/ Bakterie, *die*

bad /bæd/ *adj., worse* /wɜːs/, *worst* / wɜːst/ **(a)** schlecht; (rotten) schlecht, ⋯⋯

verdorben ⟨*Fleisch, Fisch, Essen*⟩; faul ⟨*Ei, Apfel*⟩; **not** ~ (coll.) nicht schlecht; nicht übel
(b) (naughty) ungezogen, böse ⟨*Kind, Hund*⟩
(c) (offensive) **[use]** ~ **language** Kraftausdrücke [benutzen]
(d) (regretful) **feel** ~ **about sth.** etw. bedauern; **I feel** ~ **about him** ich habe seinetwegen ein schlechtes Gewissen
(e) (serious) schlimm ⟨*Sturz, Krise*⟩; schwer ⟨*Fehler, Krankheit, Unfall*⟩
(f) (Commerc.) **a** ~ **debt** eine uneinbringliche Schuld
bade ▸ BID 1B
badge /bædʒ/ *n.* Abzeichen, *das*
badger /'bædʒə(r)/ *n.* Dachs, *der*
'badly *adv.*, **worse** /wɜːs/, **worst** /wɜːst/
(a) schlecht
(b) schwer ⟨*verletzt, beschädigt*⟩
(c) (urgently) dringend
bad-mannered /bæd'mænəd/ *adj.* **be** ~: schlechte Manieren haben
badminton /'bædmɪntən/ *n.* Federball, *der;* (als Sport) Badminton, *das*
bad-tempered /bæd'tempəd/ *adj.* griesgrämig
baffle /'bæfl/ *v.t.* ~ **sb.** jmdm. unverständlich sein
baffling /'bæflɪŋ/ *adj.* rätselhaft
bag /bæg/ ① *n.* Tasche, *die;* (sack) Sack, *der;* (hand~) Handtasche, *die;* (plastic ~) Beutel, *der;* (small paper ~) Tüte, *die;* ~**s of** (coll.: large amount) jede Menge
② *v.t.*, **-gg-: (a)** in Säcke/Beutel/Tüten füllen
(b) (claim possession of) sich (*Dat.*) schnappen (ugs.)
baggage /'bægɪdʒ/ *n.* Gepäck, *das*
baggage: ~ **allowance** *n.* Freigepäck, *das;* **be over/within one's** ~ **allowance** Übergepäck/kein Übergepäck haben; ~ **handler** *n.* Gepäckverlader, *der/*-verladerin, *die;* ~ **handling** *n.* Gepäckverladung, *die;* ~ **reclaim** *n.* Gepäckausgabe, *die*
baggy /'bægɪ/ *adj.* weit [geschnitten] ⟨*Kleid, Hose*⟩; (through long use) ausgebeult ⟨*Hose*⟩
'bagpipe[s] *n.* [*pl.*] Dudelsack, *der*
baguette /bæ'get/ *n.* Baguette, *die;* [französisches] Stangenweißbrot
Bahamas /bə'hɑːməz/ *pr. n. pl.* **the** ~: die Bahamas *Pl.*
bail¹ /beɪl/ ① *n.* Kaution, *die;* **be [out] on** ~: gegen Kaution auf freiem Fuß sein
② *v.t.* ~ **sb. out** jmdn. gegen Kaution freibekommen; (fig.) jmdm. aus der Klemme helfen (ugs.)
bail² *v.t.* (scoop) ~ **[out]** ausschöpfen
▪ **'bail out** *v.i.* ⟨*Pilot:*⟩ abspringen
bailiff /'beɪlɪf/ *n.* ≈ Gerichtsvollzieher, *der*
bait /beɪt/ ① *v.t.* mit einem Köder versehen
② *n.* Köder, *der*
bake /beɪk/ *v.t. & i.* backen; ~**d beans**

gebackene Bohnen [in Tomatensoße]; ~**d potato** [in der Schale] gebackene Kartoffel
'baker *n.* Bäcker, *der*
bakery /'beɪkərɪ/ *n.* Bäckerei, *die*
baking: ~ **powder** *n.* Backpulver, *das;* ~ **sheet** *n.* Backblech, *das;* ~ **soda** *n.* Natron, *das;* ~ **tin** *n.* Backform, *die;* ~ **tray** *n.* Kuchenblech, *das*
balance /'bæləns/ ① *n.* **(a)** (instrument) Waage, *die*
(b) (fig.) **be** *or* **hang in the** ~: in der Schwebe sein
(c) (steady position) Gleichgewicht, *das;* **keep/lose one's** ~: das Gleichgewicht halten/verlieren; (fig.) sein Gleichgewicht bewahren/verlieren; **strike a** ~ between (fig.) den Mittelweg finden zwischen (+ *Dat.*)
(d) (Bookk.: difference) Bilanz, *die;* (state of bank account) Kontostand, *der;* **on** ~ (fig.) alles in allem; ~ **sheet** Bilanz, *die*
(e) (Econ.) ~ **of payments** Zahlungsbilanz, *die;* ~ **of trade** Handelsbilanz, *die*
(f) (remainder) Rest, *der*
② *v.t.* **(a)** (weigh up) abwägen
(b) (bring into or keep in ~) balancieren; auswuchten ⟨*Rad*⟩
(c) (equal, neutralize) ausgleichen; ~ **each other,** be ~**d** sich (*Dat.*) die Waage halten
'balanced *adj.* ausgewogen; ausgeglichen ⟨*Person, Team, Gemüt*⟩
balcony /'bælkənɪ/ *n.* Balkon, *der*
bald /bɔːld/ *adj.* kahl ⟨*Kopf*⟩; kahlköpfig, glatzköpfig ⟨*Person*⟩; **be/go** ~: eine Glatze haben/bekommen
bald: ~**head** *n.* kahlköpfiger *od.* glatzköpfiger Mensch; Kahlkopf, *der* (ugs.); Glatzkopf, *der* (ugs.); ~-**'headed** *adj.* glatzköpfig; kahlköpfig
'balding *adj.* mit beginnender Glatze *nachgestellt;* **be** ~: kahl werden
'baldness *n.* Kahlheit, *die*
bale /beɪl/ *n.* Ballen, *der*
balk /bɔːlk/ ① *v.t.* **they were** ~**ed in their plan** ihr Plan wurde blockiert
② *v.i.* sich sträuben (at gegen)
Balkan /'bɔːlkən/ ① *adj.* Balkan-
② *n. pl.* **the** ~**s** der Balkan
ball¹ /bɔːl/ *n.* **(a)** Ball, *der;* (Billiards etc., Croquet) Kugel, *die;* **be on the** ~ (coll.: be alert) auf Zack sein (ugs.)
(b) (of wool, string, fluff, etc.) Knäuel, *das*
ball² *n.* (dance) Ball, *der*
ballad /'bæləd/ *n.* Ballade, *die*
ballast /'bæləst/ *n.* Ballast, *der*
ball: ~ **'bearing** *n.* Kugellager, *das;* ~**boy** *n.* Balljunge, *der;* ~**cock** *n.* Schwimmer[regel]ventil, *das*
ballerina /bælə'riːnə/ *n.* Ballerina, *die*
ballet /'bæleɪ/ *n.* Ballett, *das;* ~ **dancer** *n.* Balletttänzer, *der/*-tänzerin, *die*
'ball game *n.* **(a)** Ballspiel, *das*
(b) (Amer.) Baseballspiel, *das;* **a whole new** ~

(fig. coll.) eine ganz neue Geschichte (ugs.); **a different** ~ (fig. coll.) eine andere Sache

ballistic /bə'lɪstɪk/ *adj.* ballistisch; **go** ~ (fig. coll.) ausrasten (salopp)

balloon /bə'lu:n/ *n.* **(a)** Ballon, *der;* **hot-air** ~: Heißluftballon, *der* **(b)** (toy) Luftballon, *der*

ballot /'bælət/ *n.* Abstimmung, *die;* **[secret]** ~: geheime Wahl

ballot: ~ **box** *n.* Wahlurne, *die;* ~ **paper** *n.* Stimmzettel, *der*

ball: ~**park** *n.* (Amer.) Baseballfeld, *das;* **your estimate is not in the right** ~**park** (fig.) mit deiner Schätzung liegst du völlig falsch (ugs.); ~ **pen,** ~**point 'pen** *ns.* Kugelschreiber, *der;* ~**room** *n.* Tanzsaal, *der*

balls-up /'bɔ:lzʌp/ *n.* (coarse) Scheiß, *der* (salopp abwertend); **make a** ~ **of sth.** bei etw. Scheiße bauen (derb)

balm /bɑ:m/ *n.* Balsam, *der*

balmy /'bɑ:mɪ/ *adj.* (mild) mild

balsa /'bɔ:lsə, 'bɒlsə/ *n.* ~ **[wood]** Balsaholz, *das*

balsamic vinegar /bælsæmɪk 'vɪnɪgə(r)/ *n.* Balsamessig, *der*

Baltic /'bɔ:ltɪk/ ① *pr.* n. Ostsee, *die* ② *adj.* ~ **Sea** Ostsee, *die*

balustrade /bælə'streɪd/ *n.* Balustrade, *die*

bamboo /bæm'bu:/ *n.* Bambus, *der*

ban /bæn/ ① *v.t.*, **-nn-** verbieten; ~ **sb. from doing sth.** jmdm. verbieten, etw. zu tun ② *n.* Verbot, *das*

banal /bə'nɑ:l/ *adj.* banal

banality /bə'nælɪtɪ/ *n.* Banalität, *die*

banana /bə'nɑ:nə/ *n.* Banane, *die*

ba'nana skin *n.* Bananenschale, *die*

band /bænd/ ① *n.* **(a)** Band, *das;* **a** ~ **of light/colour** ein Streifen Licht/Farbe **(b)** (range of values) Bandbreite, *die* **(c)** (organized group) Gruppe, *die;* (of robbers, outlaws, etc.) Bande, *die* **(d)** (Mus.) [Musik]kapelle, *die;* (pop group, jazz ~) Band, *die* ② *v.i.* ~ **together [with sb.]** sich [mit jmdm.] zusammenschließen

bandage /'bændɪdʒ/ ① *n.* Verband, *der;* (as support) Bandage, *die* ② *v.t.* verbinden; bandagieren ⟨*verstauchtes] Gelenk usw.*⟩

b. & b. /bi: ən 'bi:/ *abbr.* = **bed & breakfast**

bandit /'bændɪt/ *n.* Bandit, *der*

band: ~**stand** *n.* Musiktribüne, *die;* ~**wagon** *n.* **climb** *or* **jump on [to] the** ~**wagon** (fig.) auf den fahrenden Zug aufspringen (fig.)

bandy[1] /'bændɪ/ *v.t.* **they were** ~**ing words/insults** sie stritten sich/beschimpften sich gegenseitig

bandy[2] *adj.* krumm; **he is** ~**-legged** er hat O-Beine (ugs.)

bang /bæŋ/ ① *v.t.* knallen (ugs.); schlagen; zuknallen (ugs.) ⟨*Tür, Fenster, Deckel*⟩; ~ **one's head on sth.** mit dem Kopf an etw. (*Akk.*) knallen (ugs.) ② *v.i.* (strike) ~ **[against sth.]** [gegen etw.] knallen (ugs.); ~ **shut** ⟨*Tür:*⟩ zuknallen (ugs.) ③ *n.* **(a)** (blow) Schlag, *der* **(b)** (noise) Knall, *der* ④ *adv.* **go** ~ ⟨*Gewehr, Feuerwerkskörper:*⟩ krachen

'banger *n.* (coll.) **(a)** (sausage) Würstchen, *das* **(b)** (firework) Kracher, *der* (ugs.) **(c)** (car) Klapperkiste, *die* (ugs.)

bangle /'bæŋgl/ *n.* Armreif, *der*

banish /'bænɪʃ/ *v.t.* verbannen (**from** aus)

banister /'bænɪstə(r)/ *n.* [Treppen]geländer, *das*

banjo /'bændʒəʊ/ *n., pl.* ~**s** *or* ~**es** Banjo, *das*

bank[1] /bæŋk/ *n.* **(a)** (slope) Böschung, *die* **(b)** (of river) Ufer, *das*

bank[2] ① *n.* (Finance) Bank, *die* ② *v.i.* ~ **at/with …**: ein Konto haben bei …; ~ **on sth.** (fig.) auf etw. (*Akk.*) zählen ③ *v.t.* zur Bank bringen

bank: ~ **account** *n.* Bankkonto, *das;* ~ **balance** *n.* Kontostand, *der;* ~ **book** *n.* Sparbuch, *das;* ~ **card** *n.* Scheckkarte, *die;* ~ **charges** *n. pl.* Kontoführungskosten *Pl.;* ~ **clerk** *n.* Bankangestellte, *der/die;* ~ **draft** *n.* Bankakzept, *das*

'banker *n.* Bankier, *der*

banker's: ~ **card** ▸ BANK CARD; ~ **draft** ▸ BANK DRAFT; ~ **'order** *n.* Bankanweisung, *die*

bank 'holiday *n.* (Brit.) Feiertag, *der*

'banking *n.* Bankwesen, *das*

bank: ~ **loan** *n.* Bankdarlehen, *das;* **take out a** ~ **loan** bei einer Bank einen Kredit *od.* ein Darlehen aufnehmen; ~ **manager** *n.* Zweigstellenleiter/-leiterin [einer/der Bank]; ~**note** *n.* Banknote, *die*

bankrupt /'bæŋkrʌpt/ ① *n.* Bankrotteur, *der* ② *adj.* **go** ~: Bankrott machen ③ *v.t.* Bankrott machen

bankruptcy /'bæŋkrʌptsɪ/ *n.* Konkurs, *der;* Bankrott, *der*

bank statement *n.* Kontoauszug, *der*

banner /'bænə(r)/ *n.* Banner, *das;* (on two poles) Spruchband, *das*

banns /bænz/ *n. pl.* Aufgebot, *das*

banquet /'bæŋkwɪt/ *n.* Bankett, *das*

bap /bæp/ *n.* ≈ Brötchen, *das*

baptism /'bæptɪzm/ *n.* Taufe, *die*

Baptist /'bæptɪst/ *n.* Baptist, *der/* Baptistin, *die*

baptize /bæp'taɪz/ *v.t.* taufen

bar /bɑ:(r)/ ① *n.* **(a)** Stange, *die;* (shorter, thinner also) Stab, *der;* (of cage, prison) ⋯

Gitterstab, *der;* a ~ of soap ein Stück Seife;
a ~ of chocolate eine Tafel Schokolade
(b) (for refreshment) Bar, *die;* (counter) Theke, *die*
[2] *v.t.,* -rr-: **(a)** (fasten) verriegeln
(b) ~ sb.'s way jmdm. den Weg versperren
(c) (prohibit, hinder) verbieten; ~ sb. from
doing sth. jmdn. daran hindern, etw. zu tun
[3] *prep.* abgesehen von; ~ none ohne
Einschränkung
barb /bɑːb/ *n.* Widerhaken, *der*
barbarian /bɑːˈbeərɪən/ *n.* Barbar, *der*
barbaric /bɑːˈbærɪk/ *adj.* barbarisch
barbarity /bɑːˈbærɪtɪ/ *n.* Grausamkeit, *die*
barbecue /ˈbɑːbɪkjuː/ [1] *n.* **(a)** (party)
Grillparty, *die*
(b) (food) Grillgericht, *das;* ~ sauce
Grillsoße, *die;* Barbecuesoße, *die*
[2] *v.t.* grillen
barbed wire /bɑːbd ˈwaɪə(r)/ *n.*
Stacheldraht, *der*
barber /ˈbɑːbə(r)/ *n.* [Herren]friseur, *der;*
~'s shop (Brit.) Friseursalon, *der*
barbiturate /bɑːˈbɪtjʊrət/ *n.* (Chem.)
Barbiturat, *das*
bar: ~ **chart** *n.* Stabdiagramm, *das;*
~ **code** *n.* Strichcode, *der*
bare /beə(r)/ [1] *adj.* nackt; (leafless,
unfurnished) kahl; (empty) leer; äußerst
⟨*Notwendige*⟩; do sth. with one's ~ hands
etw. mit den bloßen Händen tun
[2] *v.t.* entblößen ⟨*Kopf, Arm, Bein*⟩; blecken
⟨*Zähne*⟩
bare: ~**faced** /ˈbeəfeɪst/ *adj.* (fig.)
unverhüllt; ~**foot** [1] *adj.* barfüßig;
[2] *adv.* barfuß
barely /ˈbeəlɪ/ *adv.* kaum; knapp
⟨*vermeiden, entkommen*⟩
bargain /ˈbɑːgɪn/ [1] *n.* **(a)** (agreement)
Abmachung, *die;* into the ~: darüber hinaus
(b) (thing offered cheap) günstiges Angebot;
(thing acquired cheaply) guter Kauf
[2] *v.i.* **(a)** (discuss) handeln
(b) ~ for or on sth. (expect sth.) mit etw.
rechnen
bargain: ~ '**basement** *n.*
Untergeschoss mit Sonderangeboten;
~ **hunter** *n.* Schnäppchenjäger, *der*/
-jägerin, *die;* ~ **price** *n.* Sonderpreis, *der*
barge /bɑːdʒ/ [1] *n.* Kahn, *der*
[2] *v.i.* ~ into sb. jmdn. anrempeln; ~ in
(intrude) hineinplatzen/hereinplatzen (ugs.)
baritone /ˈbærɪtəʊn/ [1] *n.* Bariton, *der*
[2] *adj.* Bariton-
bark¹ /bɑːk/ *n.* (of tree) Rinde, *die*
bark² [1] *n.* (of dog) Bellen, *das*
[2] *v.i.* bellen; be ~ing up the wrong tree auf
dem Holzweg sein
barley /ˈbɑːlɪ/ *n.* Gerste, *die*
bar: ~**maid** *n.* (Brit.) Bardame, *die;*
~**man** /ˈbɑːmən/ *n., pl.* ~**men** /ˈbɑːmən/
Barmann, *der*
barmy /ˈbɑːmɪ/ *adj.* (coll.: crazy) bescheuert
(salopp)

barn /bɑːn/ *n.* (Brit.: for grain etc.) Scheune, *die;*
(Amer.: for animals) Stall, *der*
barnacle /ˈbɑːnəkl/ *n.* Rankenfüßer, *der*
barn: ~ **dance** *n.* ≈ Schottische,
der; ~**storming** /ˈbɑːnstɔːmɪŋ/ *adj.*
mitreißend
barometer /bəˈrɒmɪtə(r)/ *n.* Barometer,
das
baron /ˈbærn/ *n.* Baron, *der;* Freiherr, *der*
baroness /ˈbærənɪs/ *n.* Baronin, *die;*
Freifrau, *die*
baroque /bəˈrɒk/ [1] *n.* Barock, *das*
[2] *adj.* barock
barracks /ˈbærəks/ *n. pl.* Kaserne, *die*
barrage /ˈbærɑːʒ/ *n.* (Mil.) Sperrfeuer, *das;*
a ~ of questions ein Bombardement von
Fragen
barrel /ˈbærl/ *n.* **(a)** Fass, *das*
(b) (of gun) Lauf, *der*
barren /ˈbærn/ *adj.* unfruchtbar
barricade /bærɪˈkeɪd/ [1] *n.* Barrikade,
die
[2] *v.t.* verbarrikadieren
barrier /ˈbærɪə(r)/ *n.* Barriere, *die;* (at level
crossing etc.) Schranke, *die*
barring /ˈbɑːrɪŋ/ *prep.* außer im Falle
(+ *Gen.*)
barrister /ˈbærɪstə(r)/ *n.* (Brit.) ~[-at-law]
Barrister, *der;* ≈ [Rechts]anwalt/-anwältin
vor höheren Gerichten
barrow /ˈbærəʊ/ *n.* **(a)** Karre, *die;* Karren,
der
(b) ▶ WHEELBARROW
barter /ˈbɑːtə(r)/ [1] *v.t.* [ein]tauschen;
~ sth. for sth. [else] etw. für *od.* gegen etw.
[anderes] [ein]tauschen
[2] *v.i.* Tauschhandel treiben
[3] *n.* Tauschhandel, *der*
base /beɪs/ [1] *n.* **(a)** (of lamp, mountain) Fuß,
der; (of cupboard, statue) Sockel, *der;* (fig.:
support) Basis, *die*
(b) (Mil.) Basis, *die;* Stützpunkt, *der*
[2] *v.t.* **(a)** be ~d on sth. sich auf etw. (*Akk.*)
gründen; ~ sth. on sth. etw. auf etw. (*Dat.*)
aufbauen
(b) *in pass.* be ~d in Paris (permanently) in
Paris sitzen; (temporarily) in Paris sein
base: ~**ball** *n.* Baseball, *der;* ~**line** *n.*
Grundlinie, *die*
basement /ˈbeɪsmənt/ *n.* Untergeschoss,
das; a ~ flat eine Kellerwohnung
'**base rate** *n.* (Finance) Eckzins, *der*
bash /bæʃ/ *v.t.* [heftig] schlagen
bashful /ˈbæʃfl/ *adj.* schüchtern
basic /ˈbeɪsɪk/ *adj.* grundlegend;
Grund⟨*prinzip, -bestandteil, -lohn, -gehalt
usw.*⟩; Haupt⟨*problem, -grund, -sache*⟩; be
~ to sth. wesentlich für etw. sein
basically /ˈbeɪsɪkəlɪ/ *adv.* im Grunde;
grundsätzlich ⟨*übereinstimmen*⟩; (mainly)
hauptsächlich
basil /ˈbæzɪl/ *n.* Basilikum, *das*

basin /'beɪsn/ n. (a) Becken, das; (wash∼) Waschbecken, das; (bowl) Schüssel, die (b) (of river) Becken, das

basis /'beɪsɪs/ n., pl. **bases** /'beɪsiːz/ Basis, die; Grundlage, die

bask /bɑːsk/ v.i. sich [wohlig] wärmen

basket /'bɑːskɪt/ n. Korb, der

'basketball n. Basketball, der

Basle /bɑːl/ pr. n. Basel (das)

bass /beɪs/ ① n. (a) Bass, der (b) (coll.) (double ∼) [Kontra]bass, der; (∼ guitar) Bass, der ② adj. Bass-

bass gui'tar n. Bassgitarre, die

bassoon /bə'suːn/ n. Fagott, das

'bass player n. Bassist, der/Bassistin, die

bastard /'bɑːstəd/ ① adj. unehelich ② n. (a) uneheliches Kind (b) (sl.: disliked person) Schweinehund, der (derb)

baste /beɪst/ v.t. [mit Fett] begießen

bastion /'bæstɪən/ n. Bastei, die

bat¹ /bæt/ n. (Zool.) Fledermaus, die

bat² ① n. (Sport) Schlagholz, das; (for table tennis) Schläger, der; **do sth. off one's own ∼** (fig.) etw. auf eigene Faust tun ② v.t., **-tt-** schlagen

bat³ v.t. **not ∼ an eyelid** nicht mit der Wimper zucken

batch /bætʃ/ n. (a) (of loaves) Schub, der (b) (of people) Gruppe, die; (of books, papers) Stapel, der

batch: ∼ file n. (Comp.) Stapeldatei, die; **∼ 'processing** n. (Comp.) Schub-, Stapelverarbeitung, die

bated /'beɪtɪd/ v.t. **with ∼ breath** mit angehaltenem Atem

bath /bɑːθ/ ① n., pl. **∼s** /bɑːðz/ (a) Bad, das; **have or take a ∼:** ein Bad nehmen (b) (tub) Badewanne, die; **room with ∼:** Zimmer mit Bad (c) usu. in pl. (building) Bad, das ② v.t. & i. baden

'bath cubes n. pl. Badesalz, das

bathe /beɪð/ v.t. & i. baden

bather /'beɪðə(r)/ n. Badende, der/die

bathing /'beɪðɪŋ/ n. Baden, das

bathing: ∼ beach n. Badestrand, der; **∼ costume, ∼ suit** ns. Badeanzug, der; **∼ trunks** n. pl. Badehose, die

bath: ∼ mat n. Badematte, die; **∼robe** n. Bademantel, der; **∼room** n. Badezimmer, das; **∼ salts** n. pl. Badesalz, das; **∼ towel** n. Badetuch, das; **∼tub** ▸ BATH 1B; **∼water** n. Badewasser, das

baton /'bætn/ n. (a) (truncheon) Schlagstock, der (b) (Mus.) Taktstock, der

batsman /'bætsmən/ n., pl. **batsmen** /'bætsmən/ Schlagmann, der

battalion /bə'tælJən/ n. Bataillon, das

batter¹ /'bætə(r)/ v.t. (strike) einschlagen auf (+ Akk.)

batter² n. (Cookery) [Back]teig, der

battery /'bætərɪ/ n. Batterie, die

battery: ∼ charger n. Batterieladegerät, das; **∼ 'chicken** n. Batteriehuhn, das; **∼ 'farming** n. Batteriehaltung, die; **∼ 'hen** n. Batteriehuhn, das; **∼-operated** adj. batteriebetrieben

battle /'bætl/ ① n. Schlacht, die; (fig.) Kampf, der ② v.i. kämpfen

battle: ∼axe n. (coll.: woman) Schreckschraube, die (ugs.); **∼field, ∼ground** ns. Schlachtfeld, das

battlements /'bætlmənts/ n. pl. Zinnen Pl.

'battleship n. Schlachtschiff, das

batty /'bætɪ/ adj. (coll.) bekloppt (salopp)

bauble /'bɔːbl/ n. Flitter, der

baulk ▸ BALK

Bavaria /bə'veərɪə/ pr. n. Bayern (das)

Bavarian /bə'veərɪən/ ① adj. bay[e]risch; **sb. is ∼:** jmd. ist Bayer/Bayerin ② n. Bayer, der/Bayerin, die

bawdy /'bɔːdɪ/ adj. zweideutig; (stronger) obszön

bay¹ /beɪ/ n. (of sea) Bucht, die

bay² n. (a) (space in room) Erker, der (b) (parking) ∼: Stellplatz, der

bay³ n. **hold or keep sb./sth. at ∼:** sich (Dat.) jmdn./etw. vom Leib halten

'bayleaf n. Lorbeerblatt, das

bayonet /'beɪənɪt/ n. Bajonett, das

bayonet: ∼ fitting n. Bajonettfassung, die; **∼ plug** n. Stecker mit Bajonettverschluss od. -fassung; **∼ socket** n. Steckdose mit Bajonettfassung

bay 'window n. Erkerfenster, das

bazaar /bə'zɑː(r)/ n. Basar, der

BBC abbr. = **British Broadcasting Corporation** BBC, die

BBQ abbr. = **barbecue**

BC abbr. = **before Christ** v.Chr.

be /biː/ v., pres. t. **I am** /əm, stressed æm/, **he is** /ɪz/, **we are** /ə(r), stressed ɑː(r)/; p.t. **I was** /wəz, stressed wɒz/, **we were** /wə(r), stressed wɜː(r)/; pres.p. **being** /'biːɪŋ/; p.p. **been** /bɪn, stressed biːn/ ① copula (a) sein; **she is a mother/an Italian/a teacher** sie ist Mutter/Italienerin/Lehrerin; **be sensible!** sei vernünftig!; **be ill/unwell** krank sein/sich nicht wohl fühlen; **I am well** es geht mir gut; **I am hot** mir ist heiß; **I am freezing** mich friert es; **how are you/is she?** wie gehts (ugs.)/geht es ihr?; **it is the 5th today** heute haben wir den Fünften; **who's that?** wer ist das?; **if I were you** an deiner Stelle; **it's hers** es ist ihrs (b) (cost) kosten; **how much are the**

····⟶

eggs? was kosten die Eier?; **two times three
is six, two threes are six** zweimal drei ist *od.*
sind sechs
(c) (constitute) bilden
2 *v.i.* **(a)** (exist) [vorhanden] sein; **there
is/are …:** es gibt …; **for the time being**
vorläufig; **be that as it may** wie dem auch sei
(b) (remain) bleiben; **I shan't be a moment**
ich komme sofort; **let it be** lass es sein; **let
him/her be** lass ihn/sie in Ruhe
(c) (happen) stattfinden; sein
(d) (go, come) **be off with you!** geh/geht!;
I'm off home ich gehe jetzt nach Hause;
she's from Australia sie stammt *od.* ist aus
Australien
(e) (go or come on visit) sein; **have you [ever]
been to London?** bist du schon einmal in
London gewesen?; **has anyone been?** ist
jemand da gewesen?
3 *v. aux.* **(a)** *forming passive* werden; **the
child was found** das Kind wurde gefunden;
German is spoken here hier wird Deutsch
gesprochen
(b) *forming continuous tenses, active* **he
is reading** er liest [gerade]; **I am leaving
tomorrow** ich reise morgen [ab]; **the train
was departing when I got there** der Zug fuhr
gerade ab, als ich ankam
(c) *forming continuous tenses, passive*
the house is/was being built das Haus
wird/wurde [gerade] gebaut
(d) *expr. arrangement, obligation* **be to**
sollen; **I am to go/to inform you** ich soll
gehen/Sie unterrichten
(e) *expr. destiny* **they were never to meet
again** sie sollten sich nie wieder treffen
(f) *expr. condition* **if I were to tell you that …:**
wenn ich dir sagen würde, dass …
4 **bride-/husband-to-be** zukünftige
Braut/zukünftiger Ehemann

beach /biːtʃ/ *n.* Strand, *der;* **on the ~:** am
Strand; **~ hat/holiday/shoe** Strandhut/
-urlaub/-schuh, *der*

beach: ~ball *n.* Wasserball, *der;* **~wear**
n. Strandkleidung, *die*

beacon /'biːkn/ *n.* Leuchtfeuer, *das;* (Naut.)
Leuchtbake, *die*

bead /biːd/ *n.* Perle, *die;* **~s** Perlen *Pl.;*
Perlenkette, *die;* **~s of dew/sweat** Tau-/
Schweißtropfen

beady /'biːdɪ/ *adj.* **~ eyes** Knopfaugen *Pl.*

beak /biːk/ *n.* Schnabel, *der*

beaker /'biːkə(r)/ *n.* Becher, *der*

beam /biːm/ **1** *n.* **(a)** (timber etc.) Balken, *der*
(b) (ray etc.) [Licht]strahl, *der*
2 *v.i.* **(a)** (shine) strahlen; glänzen
(b) (smile) strahlen; **~ at sb.** jmdn. anstrahlen

bean /biːn/ *n.* Bohne, *die;* **full of ~s** (fig. coll.)
putzmunter (ugs.)

bean: ~bag *n.* **(a)** *mit Bohnen gefülltes
Säckchen zum Spielen;* **(b)** (cushion)
Knautschsessel, *der;* **~ curd** *n.*
Soja[bohnen]quark, *der;* **~pole** *n.* (lit.
or fig.) Bohnenstange, *die;* **~sprout** *n.*

Sojabohnenkeim, *der*

bear¹ /beə(r)/ *n.* Bär, *der*

bear² **1** *v.t.,* **bore** /bɔː(r)/, **borne** /bɔːn/
(a) tragen; aufweisen ⟨*Spuren, Ähnlichkeit*⟩;
tragen, führen ⟨*Namen, Titel*⟩; **~ some/little
relation to sth.** einen gewissen/wenig Bezug
zu etw. haben
(b) (endure, tolerate) ertragen ⟨*Schmerz,
Kummer*⟩; *with neg.* ertragen, aushalten
⟨*Schmerz*⟩; ausstehen ⟨*Geruch, Lärm*⟩
(c) (be fit for) vertragen; **it will not ~ scrutiny**
es hält einer Überprüfung nicht stand; **it
does not ~ thinking about** daran darf man
gar nicht denken
(d) (give birth to) gebären ⟨*Kind, Junges*⟩
2 *v.i.,* **bore, borne:** **~ left** ⟨*Person:*⟩ sich
links halten; **the path ~s to the left** der Weg
führt nach links
■ **bear 'out** *v.t.* (fig.) bestätigen ⟨*Bericht,
Erklärung*⟩; **~ sb. out** jmdm. Recht geben
■ **'bear with** *v.t.* Nachsicht haben mit

bearable /'beərəbl/ *adj.* erträglich

beard /bɪəd/ *n.* Bart, *der*

'bearded *adj.* bärtig. **be ~:** einen Bart
haben

'bearer *n.* (carrier) Träger, *der/*Trägerin,
die; (of message, cheque) Überbringer,
*der/*Überbringerin, *die*

'bear hug *n.* kräftige Umarmung

'bearing *n.* **(a)** (behaviour) Verhalten, *das*
(b) (relation) Bezug, *der;* **have some/no ~ on
sth.** relevant/irrelevant für etw. sein
(c) (Mech. Engin.) Lager, *das*
(d) (compass **~**) Position, *die;* **take a compass
~:** den Kompasskurs feststellen; **get one's
~s** sich orientieren; (fig.) sich zurechtfinden

beast /biːst/ *n.* Tier, *das;* (fig.: brutal person)
Bestie, *die*

'beastly *adj., adv.* (coll.) scheußlich

beat /biːt/ **1** *v.t.,* **beat, beaten** /'biːtn/
schlagen; klopfen ⟨*Teppich*⟩; (surpass)
brechen ⟨*Rekord*⟩; **hard to ~:** schwer zu
schlagen; **it ~s me how/why …:** es ist mir
ein Rätsel wie/warum …; **~ time** den Takt
schlagen; **~ it!** (coll.) hau ab! (ugs.); *see also*
BEATEN 2
2 *v.i.,* **beat, beaten** schlagen (**on** auf
+ *Akk.*); ⟨*Regen, Hagel:*⟩ prasseln (**against**
gegen)
3 *n.* **(a)** (stroke, throbbing) Schlagen, *das;*
(*Mus.*) (rhythm) Takt, *der;* (single **~**) Schlag,
der
(b) (of policeman) Runde, *die*
■ **beat 'off** *v.t.* abwehren ⟨*Angriff*⟩
■ **beat 'up** *v.t.* zusammenschlagen
⟨*Person*⟩

beaten /'biːtn/ **1** ▶ BEAT 1, 2
2 *adj.* **(a)** **off the ~ track** weit abgelegen
(b) gehämmert ⟨*Silber, Gold*⟩

'beating *n.* **(a)** (punishment) **a ~:** Schläge
Pl.; Prügel *Pl.*
(b) (defeat) Niederlage, *die*
(c) **take some/a lot of ~:** nicht leicht zu
übertreffen sein

'beat-up *adj.* (coll.) ramponiert (ugs.)

beautician /bjuː'tɪʃn/ *n.* Kosmetiker, *der*/Kosmetikerin, *die*

beautiful /'bjuːtɪfl/ *adj.* schön; wunderschön ⟨*Augen, Aussicht, Morgen*⟩

beautify /'bjuːtɪfaɪ/ *v.t.* verschönern

beauty /'bjuːtɪ/ *n.* Schönheit, *die;* (beautiful feature) Schöne, *das;* **the ~ of it** das Schöne daran

beauty: ~ competition, ~ contest *ns.* Schönheitswettbewerb, *der;* **~ parlour** ▸**~ SALON; ~ queen** *n.* Schönheitskönigin, *die;* **~ salon** *n.* Kosmetiksalon, *der;* **~ spot** *n.* Schönheitsfleck, *der;* (place) schönes Fleckchen [Erde]; **~ treatment** *n.* Schönheitsbehandlung, *die*

beaver /'biːvə(r)/ *n.* Biber, *der*

became ▸ BECOME

because /bɪ'kɒz/ [1] *conj.* weil
[2] *adv.* **~ of** wegen (+ *Gen.*)

beckon /'bekn/ *v.t. & i.* winken (**to sb.** jmdm.); (fig.) locken

become /bɪ'kʌm/ [1] *copula*, **became** /bɪ'keɪm/, **become** werden; **~ a politician** Politiker werden; **~ a nuisance/rule** zu einer Plage/zur Regel werden
[2] *v.i.*, **became, become** werden; **what has ~ of him?** was ist aus ihm geworden?
[3] *v.t.*, **became, become** (suit) **~ sb.** jmdm. stehen

becoming /bɪ'kʌmɪŋ/ *adj.* (a) (fitting) schicklich (geh.)
(b) (flattering) vorteilhaft ⟨*Hut, Kleid, Frisur*⟩

bed /bed/ *n.* (a) Bett, *das;* (without bedstead) Lager, *das;* **in ~:** im Bett; **~ and breakfast** Zimmer mit Frühstück; **get out of/into ~:** aufstehen/ins Bett gehen; **go to ~:** ins Bett gehen; **put sb. to ~:** jmdn. ins Bett bringen; **make the ~:** das Bett machen
(b) (flat base) Unterlage, *die;* (of machine) Bett, *das*
(c) (in garden) Beet, *das*
(d) (of sea, lake) Grund, *der;* (of river) Bett, *das*

'bedclothes *n. pl.* Bettzeug, *das*

bedding /'bedɪŋ/ *n.* Matratze und Bettzeug

'bedding plant *n.* Freilandpflanze, *die*

bedlam /'bedləm/ *n., no indef. art.* Tumult, *der*

bed: ~linen *n.* Bettwäsche, *die;* **~pan** *n.* Bettpfanne, *die*

bedraggled /bɪ'drægld/ *adj.* (soaked) durchnässt; (with mud) verdreckt

bed: ~ridden *adj.* bettlägerig; **~room** *n.* Schlafzimmer, *das;* **~ set'tee** *n.* Bettcouch, *die;* **~side** *n.* Seite des Bettes, *die;* **~side table/lamp** Nachttisch, *der/* Nachttischlampe, *die;* **~sit, ~'sitter** *ns.* (coll.) Wohnschlafzimmer, *das;* **~spread** *n.* Tagesdecke, *die;* **~stead** *n.* Bettgestell, *das;* **~time** *n.* Schlafenszeit, *die;* **at ~time** vor dem Zubettgehen; **a ~time story** eine Gutenachtgeschichte; **~-wetting** *n.*

Bettnässen, *das*

bee /biː/ *n.* Biene, *die*

beech /biːtʃ/ *n.* Buche, *die*

beef /biːf/ [1] *n.* (a) Rindfleisch, *das*
(b) (coll.: muscles) Muskeln *Pl.*
[2] *v.t.* **~ up** stärken

beef: ~burger *n.* Beefburger, *der;* **~cake** *n.* (Amer. coll.) Muskeln *Pl.;* Bizeps, *der* (ugs.)

bee: ~hive *n.* Bienenstock, *der;* **~-keeper** *n.* Imker, *der*/Imkerin, *die;* **~-keeping** *n.* Imkerei, *die;* **~line** *n.* **make a ~line for sth./sb.** schnurstracks auf etw./jmdn. zustürzen

been ▸ BE

beep /biːp/ [1] *n.* Piepton, *der;* (of car horn) Tuten, *das*
[2] *v.i.* piepen; ⟨*Signalhorn:*⟩ hupen
[3] *v.t.* (esp. Amer.) ▸ BLEEP 3

beeper /'biːpə(r)/ *n.* Piepser, *der*

beer /bɪə(r)/ *n.* Bier, *das*

beer: ~ barrel *n.* Bierfass, *das;* **~ belly** *n.* (coll.) Bierbauch, *der* (ugs.); **~ bottle** *n.* Bierflasche, *die;* **~ can** *n.* Bierdose, *die;* **~ cellar** *n.* Bierkeller, *der;* **~ drinker** *n.* Biertrinker, *der;* **~ garden** *n.* Biergarten, *der;* **~ glass** *n.* Bierglas, *das;* **~ mat** *n.* Bierdeckel, *der;* Bieruntersetzer, *der;* **~ mug** *n.* Bierkrug, *der*

beet /biːt/ *n.* Rübe, *die*

beetle /'biːtl/ *n.* Käfer, *der*

'beetroot *n.* rote Beete *od.* Rübe

before /bɪ'fɔː(r)/ [1] *adv.* (a) (of time) vorher; (already) schon; **the day ~:** am Tag zuvor; **never ~:** noch nie
(b) (ahead in position) vor[aus]
[2] *prep.* (of time; position) vor (+ *Dat.*); (direction) vor (+ *Akk.*); **the day ~ yesterday** vorgestern; **~ now/then** früher/vorher; **~ Christ** vor Christus; **~ leaving, he phoned** bevor er wegging, rief er an
[3] *conj.* bevor

be'forehand *adv.* vorher; (in anticipation) im Voraus

befriend /bɪ'frend/ *v.t.* (a) (act as a friend to) sich anfreunden mit
(b) (help) sich annehmen (+ *Gen.*)

beg /beg/ [1] *v.t.*, **-gg-:** (a) betteln um
(b) (ask earnestly for) **~ sth.** um etw. bitten
[2] *v.i.*, **-gg-** betteln (**for** um)

began ▸ BEGIN

beggar /'begə(r)/ *n.* (a) Bettler, *der*/Bettlerin, *die*
(b) (coll.) **poor ~:** armer Teufel

begin /bɪ'gɪn/ [1] *v.t.*, **-nn-**, **began** /bɪ'gæn/, **begun** /bɪ'gʌn/ **~ sth.** [mit] etw. beginnen; **~ doing** *or* **to do sth.** anfangen *od.* beginnen, etw. zu tun
[2] *v.i.*, **-nn-**, **began, begun** anfangen; **~ [up]on sth.** etw. anfangen

be'ginner *n.* Anfänger, *der*/Anfängerin, *die*

be'ginning *n.* Anfang, *der;* **at** *or* **in the** ~: am Anfang; **at the** ~ **of** February/the month Anfang Februar/des Monats; **from the** ~: von Anfang an

begrudge /bɪˈɡrʌdʒ/ *v.t.* ~ **sb. sth.** jmdm. etw. missgönnen; ~ **doing sth.** etw. ungern tun

begun ▸ BEGIN

behalf /bɪˈhɑːf/ *n.* **on** *or* (Amer.) **in** ~ **of sb./sth.** für jmdn./etw.; (more formally) im Namen von jmdm./etw.

behave /bɪˈheɪv/ ① *v.i.* sich verhalten; sich benehmen; **well-/ill-** *or* **badly** ~d brav/ungezogen
② *v. refl.* ~ **oneself** sich benehmen

behaviour /bɪˈheɪvjə(r)/ *n.* Verhalten, *das*

behead /bɪˈhed/ *v.t.* enthaupten

behind /bɪˈhaɪnd/ ① *adv.* hinten; (further back) **be miles** ~: kilometerweit zurückliegen; **stay** ~: dableiben; **leave sb./sth.** ~: jmdn./etw. zurücklassen; **fall** ~: zurückbleiben; (fig.) in Rückstand geraten; **be/get** ~ **with one's payments/rent** mit seinen Zahlungen/der Miete im Rückstand sein/in Rückstand geraten
② *prep.* (a) hinter (+ *Dat.*); **one** ~ **the other** hintereinander
(b) (towards rear of) hinter (+ *Akk.*)

beige /beɪʒ/ ① *n.* Beige, *das*
② *adj.* beige

being /ˈbiːɪŋ/ *n.* (a) (existence) Dasein, *das;* **in** ~: bestehend; **come into** ~: entstehen
(b) (person etc.) Wesen, *das*

belated /bɪˈleɪtɪd/ *adj.,* **be'latedly** *adv.* verspätet

belch /beltʃ/ ① *v.i.* heftig aufstoßen; rülpsen (ugs.)
② *n.* Rülpser, *der* (ugs.)

beleaguer /bɪˈliːɡə(r)/ *v.t.* (lit. or fig.) belagern

belfry /ˈbelfrɪ/ *n.* Glockenturm, *der*

Belgian /ˈbeldʒən/ ① *adj.* belgisch; **sb. is** ~: jmd. ist Belgier/Belgierin
② *n.* Belgier, *der*/Belgierin, *die*

Belgium /ˈbeldʒəm/ *pr. n.* Belgien (*das*)

belie /bɪˈlaɪ/ *v.t.,* **belying** /bɪˈlaɪɪŋ/ hinwegtäuschen über ⟨Tatsachen, wahren Zustand⟩; nicht erfüllen ⟨Versprechen⟩; nicht entsprechen ⟨Vorstellung (Dat.)⟩

belief /bɪˈliːf/ *n.* (a) Glaube, *der* (**in** an + *Akk.*); **in the** ~ **that** ...: in der Überzeugung, dass ...
(b) (Relig.) Glaube[n], *der*

believable /bɪˈliːvəbl/ *adj.* glaubhaft

believe /bɪˈliːv/ ① *v.i.* glauben (**in** an + *Dat.*); (have faith) glauben (**in** an + *Akk.*) ⟨Gott, Himmel usw.⟩; **I** ~ **so/not** ich glaube schon/nicht
② *v.t.* glauben; ~ **sb.** jmdm. glauben; **I don't** ~ **you** das glaube ich dir nicht; **make** ~ **that** ...: so tun, als ob ...

believer /bɪˈliːvə(r)/ *n.* (a) Gläubige, *der/die*

(b) **be a great** *or* **firm** ~ **in sth.** viel von etw. halten

Belisha beacon /bəliːʃə ˈbiːkn/ *n.* (Brit.) *gelbes Blinklicht an Zebrastreifen*

belittle /bɪˈlɪtl/ *v.t.* herabsetzen

bell /bel/ *n.* Glocke, *die;* (door~) Klingel, *die*

belligerent /bɪˈlɪdʒərənt/ *adj.* Krieg führend ⟨Nation⟩; streitlustig ⟨Person⟩

bellow /ˈbeləʊ/ ① *v.i.* brüllen
② *v.t.* ~ [**out**] brüllen ⟨Befehl⟩

bellows /ˈbeləʊz/ *n. pl.* Blasebalg, *der*

bell: ~**ringer** *n.* Glöckner, *der;* ~**ringing** *n.* Glockenläuten, *das*

belly /ˈbelɪ/ *n.* Bauch, *der*

belly: ~**ache** *n.* Bauchschmerzen *Pl.;* ~ **button** *n.* (coll.) Bauchnabel, *der;* ~ **dance** *n.* Bauchtanz, *der*

belong /bɪˈlɒŋ/ *v.i.* ~ **to sb./sth.** jmdm./zu etw. gehören; ~ **to a club** einem Verein angehören; **where does this** ~? wo gehört das hin?

be'longings *n. pl.* Habe, *die;* Sachen *Pl.;* **personal** ~: persönlicher Besitz; persönliches Eigentum

beloved /bɪˈlʌvɪd/ ① *adj.* geliebt
② *n.* Geliebte, *der/die*

below /bɪˈləʊ/ ① *adv.* (a) (position) unten; (lower down) darunter; **from** ~: von unten [herauf]
(b) (direction) nach unten; hinunter
② *prep.* unter (*position: + Dat.; direction: + Akk.*)

belt /belt/ *n.* Gürtel, *der;* (for tools, weapons, ammunition) Gurt, *der;* (of trees) Streifen, *der*
■ **belt along** *v.i.* (coll.) rasen (ugs.)
■ **belt 'up** *v.i.* (Brit. coll.) die Klappe halten (salopp)

bemused /bɪˈmjuːzd/ *adj.* verwirrt

bench /bentʃ/ *n.* Bank, *die;* (work table) Werkbank, *die*

bench: ~**mark** *n.* Höhenmarke, *die;* (fig.) Maßstab, *der;* Fixpunkt, *der;* ~**marking** *n.* Benchmarking, *das* (fachspr.); Leistungsvergleich, *der*

bend /bend/ ① *n.* Beuge, *die;* (in road) Kurve, *die*
② *v.t.,* **bent** /bent/ biegen; beugen ⟨Arm, Knie⟩; anwinkeln ⟨Bein⟩
③ *v.i.,* **bent** sich biegen; (bow) sich bücken
■ **bend 'down** *v.i.* sich bücken
■ **bend 'over** *v.i.* sich nach vorn beugen

beneath /bɪˈniːθ/ *prep.* (a) (unworthy of) ~ **sb.,** ~ **sb.'s dignity** unter jmds. Würde (*Dat.*)
(b) (arch./literary: under) unter (+ *Dat.*)

benefactor /ˈbenɪfæktə(r)/ *n.* Wohltäter, *der;* (patron) Gönner, *der*

beneficial /benɪˈfɪʃl/ *adj.* nützlich; vorteilhaft ⟨Einfluss⟩

benefit /ˈbenɪfɪt/ ① *n.* (a) Vorteil, *der;* **be of** ~ **to sb./sth.** jmdm./einer Sache von Nutzen sein; **have the** ~ **of** den Vorteil (+ *Gen.*) haben; **with the** ~ **of** mit Hilfe

(+ *Gen.*); **for sb.'s** ∼: in jmds. Interesse
(*Dat.*)
(b) (allowance) Beihilfe, *die;* **unemployment**
∼: Arbeitslosenunterstützung, *die*
② *v.t.* nützen (+ *Dat.*)
③ *v.i.* ∼ **by/from sth.** von etw. profitieren
benevolent /bɪ'nevələnt/ *adj.* **(a)** gütig
(b) wohltätig ⟨*Institution, Verein*⟩
benign /bɪ'naɪn/ *adj.* gütig; (Med.) gutartig
bent /bent/ ① ▶ BEND 2, 3
② *n.* (liking) Neigung, *die* (**for** zu)
③ **(a)** *adj.* krumm
(b) (Brit. sl.: corrupt) link (salopp)
bequeath /bɪ'kwiːð/ *v.t.* ∼ **sth. to sb.**
jmdm. etw. hinterlassen
bequest /bɪ'kwest/ *n.* Legat, *das* (**to** an
+ *Akk.*)
bereaved /bɪ'riːvd/ *n.* **the** ∼: der/die
Hinterbliebene/die Hinterbliebenen
bereavement /bɪ'riːvmənt/ *n.*
Trauerfall, *der*
beret /'bereɪ/ *n.* Baskenmütze, *die*
Berlin /bɜːˈlɪn/ *pr. n.* Berlin (*das*)
Berne /bɜːn/ *pr. n.* Bern (*das*)
berry /'berɪ/ *n.* Beere, *die*
berserk /bə'sɜːk/ *adj.* rasend; **go**
∼: durchdrehen (ugs.)
berth /bɜːθ/ *n.* (for ship) Liegeplatz, *der;*
(sleeping place) (in ship) Koje, *die;* (in train)
Schlafwagenbett, *das*
beside /bɪ'saɪd/ *prep.* **(a)** neben (+ *Dat.*);
∼ **the sea/lake** am Meer/See
(b) be ∼ **the point** nichts damit zu tun
haben
(c) ∼ **oneself** außer sich
besides /bɪ'saɪdz/ ① *adv.* außerdem
② *prep.* außer
besiege /bɪ'siːdʒ/ *v.t.* belagern
besotted /bɪ'sɒtɪd/ *adj.* **be** ∼ **by** *or* **with**
sb. in jmdn. vernarrt sein
bespectacled /bɪ'spektəkld/ *adj.*
bebrillt
best /best/ ① *adj.* best…; **the** ∼ **part of an**
hour fast eine ganze Stunde
② *adv.* am besten
③ *n.* **the** ∼: der/die/das Beste; **do one's**
∼: sein Bestes tun; **make the** ∼ **of it** das
Beste daraus machen; **at** ∼: bestenfalls
best: ∼**-before date** *n.*
Mindesthaltbarkeitsdatum, *das;* ∼ **'friend**
n. bester Freund/beste Freundin; **be**
∼ **friends with sb.** sehr gut mit jmdm.
befreundet sein; ∼ **'man** *n.* Trauzeuge, *der*
(*des Bräutigams*); ∼ **'seller** *n.* Bestseller,
der; (author) Bestsellerautor, *der;* ∼**-selling**
attrib. adj. meistverkauft ⟨*Schallplatte*⟩;
∼**-selling book/novel** Bestseller, *der;* **a**
∼**-selling author/novelist** ein
Bestsellerautor
bet /bet/ ① *v.t. & i.,* **-tt-,** ∼ *or* ∼**ted** wetten;
I ∼ **him £10** ich habe mit ihm um 10 Pfund
gewettet; ∼ **on sth.** auf etw. (*Akk.*) setzen
② *n.* Wette, *die;* (fig. coll.) Tipp, *der*

beta-blocker /'biːtəblɒkə(r)/ *n.* (Med.)
Beta[rezeptoren]blocker, *der*
betray /bɪ'treɪ/ *v.t.* verraten (**to** an + *Akk.*)
betrayal /bɪ'treɪəl/ *n.* Verrat, *der*
better /'betə(r)/ ① *adj.* besser; ∼ **and**
∼: immer besser; **be much** ∼ (recovered) sich
viel besser fühlen; **get** ∼ (recover) besser
werden; **the** ∼ **part of sth.** der größte Teil
einer Sache (*Gen.*)
② *adv.* besser; ∼ **'off** (financially) [finanziell]
besser gestellt; **be** ∼ **off than sb.** besser
als jmd. dran sein (ugs.); **be** ∼ **off without**
sb./sth. ohne jmdn./etw. besser dran sein;
I'd ∼ **be off now** ich gehe jetzt besser
③ *n.* **get the** ∼ **of sb./sth.** jmdn./etw.
unterkriegen (ugs.); **a change for the** ∼: eine
vorteilhafte Veränderung
④ *v.t.* übertreffen
better-'quality *attrib. adj.* qualitativ
besser
'betting shop *n.* Wettbüro, *das*
between /bɪ'twiːn/ ① *prep.* **(a) [in]**
∼: zwischen (*position:* + *Dat.; direction:*
+ *Akk.*)
(b) (amongst) unter (+ *Dat.*); ∼ **ourselves,**
∼ **you and me** unter uns (*Dat.*) gesagt
(c) ∼ **them/us** (by joint action of) gemeinsam;
∼ **us we had 40p** wir hatten zusammen
40 Pence
② *adv.* **[in]** ∼: dazwischen; (in time)
zwischendurch
beverage /'bevərɪdʒ/ *n.* Getränk, *das*
beware /bɪ'weə(r)/ *v.t. & i.; only in imper.*
and inf. ∼ **[of] sb./sth.** sich vor jmdm./etw.
in Acht nehmen; ∼ **of doing sth.** sich davor
hüten, etw. zu tun; '∼ **of the dog'** „Vorsicht,
bissiger Hund!"
bewilder /bɪ'wɪldə(r)/ *v.t.* verwirren
be'wildering *adj.* verwirrend
be'wilderment *n.* Verwirrung, *die*
bewitch /bɪ'wɪtʃ/ *v.t.* verzaubern; (fig.)
bezaubern
beyond /bɪ'jɒnd/ ① *adv.* **(a)** (in space)
jenseits; (on other side of wall, mountain range,
etc.) dahinter
(b) (in time) darüber hinaus
(c) (in addition) außerdem
② *prep.* **(a)** (at far side of) jenseits (+ *Gen.*)
(b) (later than) nach
(c) (out of reach or comprehension or range)
über … (+ *Akk.*) hinaus
bias /'baɪəs/ ① *n.* Voreingenommenheit,
die
② *v.t.,* **-s-** *or* **-ss-** beeinflussen; **be** ∼**ed in**
favour of/against sth./sb. für etw./jmdn.
eingestellt sein/gegen etw./jmdn.
voreingenommen sein
biathlon /baɪ'æθlən/ *n.* (Sport) Biathlon, *das*
bib /bɪb/ *n.* Lätzchen, *das*
Bible /'baɪbl/ *n.* Bibel, *die*
biblical /'bɪblɪkl/ *adj.* biblisch
bibliography /bɪblɪ'ɒɡrəfɪ/ *n.*
Bibliographie, *die*

biceps /'baɪseps/ n. Bizeps, der
bicker /'bɪkə(r)/ v.i. sich zanken
bicycle /'baɪsɪkl/ ① n. Fahrrad, das; attrib. Fahrrad-
② v.i. Radfahren
bicycle: ~ **clip** n. Hosenklammer, die; ~ **courier** n. Fahrradkurier, der/-kurierin, die; ~ **lane** n. (reserved for cyclists) Radfahrstreifen, der; (with priority for cyclists) Schutzstreifen, der [für Radfahrer]; ~ **path** n. [Fahr]radweg, der
bid /bɪd/ ① v.t. (a) -dd-, bid (at auction) bieten (b) -dd-, bade /bæd, beɪd/ or bid, bidden /'bɪdn/ or bid: ~ sb. welcome/goodbye jmdn. willkommen heißen/sich von jmdm. verabschieden
② v.i., -dd-, bid (a) werben (for um) (b) (at auction) bieten
③ n. (a) (at auction) Gebot, das (b) (attempt) Versuch, der
bidden ▶ BID 1B
'bidder n. Bieter, der/Bieterin, die
bide /'baɪd/ v.t. ~ one's time den richtigen Augenblick abwarten
biennial /baɪ'enɪəl/ n. (Bot.) zweijährige Pflanze; Bienne, die (fachspr.)
bifocal /baɪ'fəʊkl/ ① adj. Bifokal-
② n. in pl. Bifokalgläser Pl.
big /bɪg/ adj. groß
bigamist /'bɪgəmɪst/ n. Bigamist, der/Bigamistin, die
bigamy /'bɪgəmɪ/ n. Bigamie, die
big: ~**head** n. (coll.) Fatzke, der (ugs. abwertend); ~-'**headed** adj. (coll.) eingebildet
bigot /'bɪgət/ n. borniter Mensch; (Relig.) bigotter Mensch
bigoted /'bɪgətɪd/ adj. borniert
big: ~ 'toe n. große Zehe; ~ 'top n. Zirkuszelt, das; ~ 'wheel n. (at fair) Riesenrad, das
bike /baɪk/ (coll.) ① n. (bicycle) Rad, das; (motor cycle) Maschine, die
② v.i. Radfahren/[mit dem] Motorrad fahren
bike: ~ **courier,** ~ **messenger** ns. (on motorbike) Motorradkurier, der/-kurierin, die; (on bicycle) Fahrradkurier, der/-kurierin, die; ~ **path** (esp. Amer.) ▶ BICYCLE PATH
bikini /bɪ'ki:nɪ/ n. Bikini, der
bilingual /baɪ'lɪŋgwəl/ adj. zweisprachig
bilious /'bɪljəs/ adj. (Med.) Gallen-; ~ **attack** Gallenanfall, der
bill¹ /bɪl/ n. (of bird) Schnabel, der
bill² n. (a) (Parl.) Gesetzentwurf, der (b) (note of charges) Rechnung, die; could we have the ~ please? wir möchten zahlen (c) (poster) '[stick] no ~s" „[Plakate] ankleben verboten"
'billboard n. Reklametafel, die
billet /'bɪlɪt/ ① n. Quartier, das
② v.t. einquartieren (with, on bei)

'billfold n. (Amer.) Brieftasche, die
'billiard ball n. Billardkugel, die
billiards /'bɪljədz/ n. Billard[spiel], das
billion /'bɪljən/ n. (a) (thousand million) Milliarde, die (b) (esp. Brit. dated: million million) Billion, die
billionaire /bɪljə'neə(r)/ n. (Amer.) Milliardär, der
billy goat /'bɪlɪgəʊt/ n. Ziegenbock, der
bimbo /'bɪmbəʊ/ n. (coll. derog.) Puppe, die (salopp)
bin /bɪn/ n. Behälter, der; (for bread) Brotkasten, der; (for rubbish) Mülleimer, der
binary /'baɪnərɪ/ adj. binär
'bin bag n. Müllbeutel, der
bind /baɪnd/ v.t., **bound** /baʊnd/ (a) fesseln ‹Person, Tier›; (bandage) wickeln ‹Glied, Baum›; verbinden ‹Wunde› (with mit) (b) (fasten together) zusammenbinden (c) binden ‹Buch› (d) be bound up with sth. (fig.) eng mit etw. verbunden sein (e) be bound to do sth. (required) verpflichtet sein, etw. zu tun; (certain) etw. ganz bestimmt tun; it is bound to rain es wird bestimmt regnen
'binder n. (for papers) Hefter, der; (for magazines) Mappe, die
'binding ① adj. bindend ‹Vertrag, Abkommen› (on für)
② n. (of book) Einband, der
binge-drinking /'bɪndʒ-/ Komasaufen, das
bingo /'bɪŋgəʊ/ n. Bingo, das
'bin liner n. Müllbeutel, der
binoculars /bɪ'nɒkjʊləz/ n. pl. [pair of] ~: Fernglas, das
bio'chemistry n. Biochemie, die
biodegradable /baɪəʊdɪ'greɪdəbl/ adj. biologisch abbaubar
biode'grade v.i. sich biologisch abbauen
biodi'versity n., no pl. biologische Vielfalt
bio'ethics n. Bioethik, die
'biofuel n. Biobrennstoff, der; (for vehicle) Biokraftstoff, der
biographer /baɪ'ɒgrəfə(r)/ n. Biograph, der/Biographin, die
biographical /baɪə'græfɪkl/ adj. biographisch
biography /baɪ'ɒgrəfɪ/ n. Biographie, die
'biohazard n. Biogefahr, die
biological /baɪə'lɒdʒɪkl/ adj. biologisch
biological: ~ 'clock n. biologische Uhr; ~ 'warfare n. biologische Kriegführung; Bakterienkrieg, der; ~ 'waste n. Bio-Abfall, der; Biomüll, der
biologist /baɪ'ɒlədʒɪst/ n. Biologe, der/Biologin, die
biology /baɪ'ɒlədʒɪ/ n. Biologie, die
biopsy /'baɪɒpsɪ/ n. Biopsie, die

'biorhythm *n.* Biorhythmus, *der*

biose'curity *n., no pl.* Biosicherheit, *die;* biologische Sicherheit

'biosphere *n.* Biosphäre, *die*

biotech /'baɪəʊtek/ *n., no pl.* Biotechnologie, *die*

biotech'nology *n.* Biotechnologie, *die*

bio'terrorism *n.* Bioterrorismus, *der*

bipolar disorder /baɪˈpəʊlə/ (Psych. Med.) bipolare Störung

birch /bɜːtʃ/ *n.* Birke, *die*

bird /bɜːd/ *n.* Vogel, *der*

bird: ∼ **bath** *n.* Vogelbad, *das;* ∼ **cage** *n.* Vogelkäfig, *der;* ∼ **flu** *n.* Vogelgrippe, *die;* ∼**'s-eye 'view** *n.* Vogelperspektive, *die;* ∼**'s nest** *n.* Vogelnest, *das;* ∼ **table** *n.* Futterstelle für Vögel; ∼**watcher** *n.* Vogelbeobachter, *der*/-beobachterin, *die;* ∼**-watching** *n.* das Beobachten von Vögeln

Biro ® /'baɪrəʊ/ *n., pl.* ∼**s** Kugelschreiber, *der;* Kuli, *der* (ugs.)

birth /bɜːθ/ *n.* (a) Geburt, *die;* give ∼ ⟨*Frau:*⟩ entbinden; ⟨*Tier:*⟩ jungen; werfen; **give ∼ to a child** ein Kind zur Welt bringen (b) (of movement, fashion, etc.) Aufkommen, *das*

birth: ∼ **certificate** *n.* Geburtsurkunde, *die;* ∼ **control** *n.* Geburtenkontrolle, *die;* ∼**day** *n.* Geburtstag, *der; attrib.* Geburtstags-

'birthing pool *n.* Gebärwanne, *die*

birth: ∼**mark** *n.* Muttermal, *das;* ∼**place** *n.* Geburtsort, *der;* ∼ **rate** *n.* Geburtenrate, *die*

biscuit /'bɪskɪt/ *n.* (Brit.) Keks, *der*

bisect /baɪˈsekt/ *v.t.* halbieren

bisexual /baɪˈseksjʊəl/ ① *adj.* bisexuell ② *n.* Bisexuelle, *der*/*die*

bishop /'bɪʃəp/ *n.* (a) (Eccl.) Bischof, *der* (b) (Chess) Läufer, *der*

bit¹ /bɪt/ *n.* (a) (for horse) Gebiss, *das* (b) (of drill) [Bohr]einsatz, *der*

bit² *n.* (piece) Stück, *das;* **not a** *or* **one** ∼ (not at all) überhaupt nicht; **a** ∼ **tired/too early** ein bisschen müde/zu früh; **be a** ∼ **of a coward/bully** ein ziemlicher Feigling sein/den starken Mann markieren (ugs.)

bit³ *n.* (Comp.) Bit, *das*

bit⁴ ▸ BITE 1, 2

bitch /bɪtʃ/ *n.* (a) (dog) Hündin, *die* (b) (sl. derog.: woman) Miststück, *das* (derb)

bitchy /'bɪtʃɪ/ *adj.* (coll.) gemein; gehässig

bite /baɪt/ ① *v.t.,* **bit** /bɪt/, **bitten** /'bɪtn/ beißen; ⟨*Moskito usw.:*⟩ stechen ② *v.i.,* bit, bitten beißen/stechen; (take bait) anbeißen ③ *n.* Biss, *der;* (piece) Bissen, *der;* (wound) Bisswunde, *die;* (by mosquito etc.) Stich, *der* ■ **bite 'off** *v.t.* abbeißen

'bite-size *adj.* mundgerecht

biting /'baɪtɪŋ/ *adj.* beißend

bitten ▸ BITE 1, 2

bitter /'bɪtə(r)/ *adj.* bitter

'bitterly *adv.* bitterlich ⟨*weinen, sich beschweren*⟩; ∼ **cold** bitterkalt

'bitterness *n.* Bitterkeit, *die*

bizarre /bɪ'zɑː(r)/ *adj.* bizarr

black /blæk/ ① *adj.* (a) schwarz; ∼ **and blue** (fig.) grün und blau; **in** ∼ **and white** (fig.) schwarz auf weiß; ∼ **and white film** Schwarzweißfilm, *der;* **in the** ∼ (in credit) in den schwarzen Zahlen (b) B∼ (dark-skinned) schwarz ② *n.* (a) Schwarz, *das* (b) B∼ (person) Schwarze, *der*/*die* ③ *v.t.* bestreiken ⟨*Betrieb*⟩; boykottieren ⟨*Arbeit*⟩ ■ **black 'out** ① *v.t.* verdunkeln ② *v.i.* das Bewusstsein verlieren

black: ∼**berry** /'blækbərɪ/ *n.* Brombeere, *die;* ∼**bird** *n.* Amsel, *die;* ∼**board** *n.* [Wand]tafel, *die;* '**box** *n.* (flight recorder) Flugschreiber, *der;* ∼**'currant** *n.* schwarze Johannisbeere

blacken /'blækn/ *v.t.* schwärzen; verfinstern ⟨*Himmel*⟩

black: ∼ **'eye** *n.* blaues Auge; B∼ '**Forest** *pr. n.* Schwarzwald, *der;* ∼ '**hole** *n.* (Astron.) schwarzes Loch; ∼ '**ice** *n.* Glatteis, *das;* ∼**leg** *n.* (Brit.) Streikbrecher, *der*/-brecherin, *die;* ∼ **list** *n.* schwarze Liste; ∼**list** *v.t.* auf die schwarze Liste setzen; ∼**mail** ① *v.t.* erpressen; ② *n.* Erpressung, *die;* ∼ **market** *n.* schwarzer Markt

'blackness *n.* Schwärze, *die;* (darkness) Finsternis, *die*

black: ∼**out** *n.* (a) Verdunkelung, *die;* (Theatre, Radio) Blackout, *der;* (b) (Med.) **have a** ∼**out** das Bewusstsein verlieren; ∼ '**pudding** *n.* Blutwurst, *die;* B∼ '**Sea** *pr. n.* Schwarze Meer, *das;* ∼**smith** *n.* Schmied, *der;* ∼ **spot** *n.* Gefahrenstelle, *die*

bladder /'blædə(r)/ *n.* Blase, *die*

blade /bleɪd/ *n.* (a) (of sword, knife, razor, etc.) Klinge, *die;* (of saw, oar, propeller) Blatt, *das* (b) (of grass) Spreite, *die*

blame /bleɪm/ ① *v.t.* ∼ sb. [for sth.] jmdm. die Schuld [an etw. (*Dat.*)] geben; **be to** ∼ **[for sth.]** an etw. (*Dat.*) schuld sein; ∼ **sth. [for sth.]** etw. [für etw.] verantwortlich machen ② *n.* Schuld, *die*

'blameless *adj.* untadelig

blancmange /blə'mɒnʒ/ *n.* Flammeri, *der*

bland /blænd/ *adj.* mild; (suave) verbindlich

blank /blæŋk/ ① *adj.* (a) leer; kahl ⟨*Wand, Fläche*⟩ (b) (empty) frei ② *n.* (a) (space) Lücke, *die* (b) (cartridge) Platzpatrone, *die* (c) **draw a** ∼: kein Glück haben

blank 'cheque *n.* Blankoscheck, *der;* (fig.) Blankovollmacht, *die*

blanket /'blæŋkɪt/ n. Decke, die; **wet '~** (fig.) Trauerkloß, der (ugs.)

blare /'bleə(r)/ [1] v.i. ⟨Lautsprecher:⟩ plärren; ⟨Trompete:⟩ schmettern
[2] v.t. **~ [out]** [hinaus]plärren ⟨Worte⟩; [hinaus]schmettern ⟨Melodie⟩

blasé /'blɑːzeɪ/ adj. blasiert

blasphemous /'blæsfəməs/ adj. lästerlich

blasphemy /'blæsfəmɪ/ n. Blasphemie, die

blast /blɑːst/ [1] n. **(a) a ~ [of wind]** ein Windstoß
(b) (of horn) Tuten, das
[2] v.t. (blow up) sprengen
■ **blast 'off** v.i. abheben
[3] int. verdammt

blasted /'blɑːstɪd/ adj. (damned) verdammt (salopp)

'blast-off n. Abheben, das

blatant /'bleɪtənt/ adj. **(a)** (flagrant) eklatant;
(b) (unashamed) unverhohlen; unverfroren ⟨Lüge⟩

'blatantly adv. ▶ BLATANT: eklatant; unverhohlen

blaze /bleɪz/ [1] n. Feuer, das
[2] v.i. brennen; lodern (geh.)

blazer /'bleɪzə(r)/ n. Blazer, der

bleach /bliːtʃ/ [1] v.t. bleichen
[2] n. Bleichmittel, das

bleak /bliːk/ adj. **(a)** öde ⟨Landschaft usw.⟩
(b) (unpromising) düster

bleat /bliːt/ v.i. ⟨Schaf:⟩ blöken; ⟨Ziege:⟩ meckern

bled ▶ BLEED

bleed /bliːd/ v.i., bled /bled/ bluten

bleep /bliːp/ [1] n. Piepen, das
[2] v.i. ⟨Geigerzähler, Funksignal:⟩ piepen
[3] v.t. **~ sb.** jmdn. über seinen Kleinempfänger od. (ugs.) Piepser rufen

bleeper /'bliːpə(r)/ n. Kleinempfänger, der; Piepser, der (ugs.)

blemish /'blemɪʃ/ n. Fleck, der

blend /blend/ [1] v.t. mischen
[2] v.i. sich mischen lassen
[3] n. Mischung, die

'blender n. Mixer, der

bless /bles/ v.t. segnen; **~ you!** (after sb. sneezes) Gesundheit!

blessed /'blesɪd/ adj. **(a)** (revered) heilig
(b) (cursed) verdammt (salopp)

'blessing n. Segen, der

blew ▶ BLOW¹

blight /blaɪt/ n. (fig.) Fluch, der

blind /blaɪnd/ [1] adj. blind; **~ in one eye** auf einem Auge blind
[2] adv. blindlings
[3] n. **(a)** Jalousie, die; (made of cloth) Rouleau, das; (of shop) Markise, die
(b) pl. **the ~:** die Blinden Pl.
[4] v.t. blenden

blind: ~ 'alley n. (lit. or fig.) Sackgasse, die; **~ 'corner** n. unübersichtliche Ecke;

~ 'date n. Verabredung mit einem/einer Unbekannten; **~fold** [1] v.t. die Augen verbinden (+ Dat.); [2] adj. mit verbundenen Augen nachgestellt.

'blinding adj. blendend; **a ~ headache** rasende Kopfschmerzen Pl.

'blindly adv. [wie] blind; (fig.) blindlings

'blindness n. Blindheit, die

'blind spot n. (Motor Veh.) toter Winkel; (fig.: weak spot) schwacher Punkt;

blink /blɪŋk/ v.i. **(a)** blinzeln
(b) (shine intermittently) blinken

'blinkers n. pl. Scheuklappen Pl.

blip /blɪp/ n. **(a)** (minor deviation from trend) Delle, die
(b) (Radar: image) Echozeichen, das

bliss /blɪs/ n. [Glück]seligkeit, die

blissful /'blɪsfl/ adj. [glück]selig

blister /'blɪstə(r)/ [1] n. Blase, die
[2] v.i. ⟨Haut:⟩ Blasen bekommen; ⟨Anstrich:⟩ Blasen werfen

'blister pack n. Klarsichtpackung, die

blizzard /'blɪzəd/ n. Schneesturm, der

bloated /'bləʊtɪd/ adj. (having overeaten) aufgedunsen; **I feel ~:** ich bin voll (ugs.)

blob /blɒb/ n. (drop) Tropfen, der; (small mass) Klacks, der (ugs.)

block /blɒk/ [1] n. **(a)** Klotz, der; (for chopping on) Hackklotz, der; (of concrete or stone, building stone) Block, der
(b) (building) [Häuser]block, der; **~ of flats/offices** Wohnblock, der/Bürohaus, das
[2] v.t. versperren ⟨Tür, Straße, Durchgang, Sicht⟩; verstopfen ⟨Pfeife, Abfluss⟩; verhindern ⟨Fortschritt⟩
■ **block 'out** v.t. ausschließen ⟨Licht, Lärm⟩
■ **block 'up** v.t. verstopfen; versperren ⟨Eingang⟩

blockade /blɒ'keɪd/ [1] n. Blockade, die
[2] v.t. blockieren

blockage /'blɒkɪdʒ/ n. Block, der; (of pipe, gutter) Verstopfung, die

block: ~ 'booking n. Gruppenbuchung, die; **~buster** n. **(a)** (bomb) [große] Fliegerbombe; **(b)** (fig.) Knüller, der (ugs.); **~ 'capital** n. Blockbuchstabe, der; **~head** n. Dummkopf, der; **~ 'letters** n. pl. Blockschrift, die

blog /blɒg/ (Comp.) [1] n. Blog, das (Jargon)
[2] v.i. ein Weblog unterhalten

blogger /'blɒgə(r)/ n. (author of a weblog) Weblogautor, der/-autorin, die

bloke /bləʊk/ n. (Brit. coll.) Typ, der (ugs.)

blonde /blɒnd/ [1] adj. blond
[2] n. Blondine, die

blood /blʌd/ n. Blut, das

blood: ~ bank n. Blutbank, die; **~bath** n. Blutbad, das; **~ cell** n. Blutkörperchen, das; **~ clot** n. Blutgerinnsel, das; **~ donor** n. Blutspender, der/-spenderin, die; **~ group** n. Blutgruppe, die;

~**hound** n. Bluthund, der; ~ **plasma** n. Blutplasma, das; ~ **poisoning** n. Blutvergiftung, die; ~ **pressure** n. Blutdruck, der; ~ **sample** n. Blutprobe, die; ~**shed** n. Blutvergießen, das; ~**shot** adj. blutunterlaufen; ~ **sports** n. pl. Hetzjagd, die; ~**stain** n. Blutfleck, der; ~**stained** adj. blutbefleckt; ~**stream** n. Blutstrom, der; ~ **sugar** n. Blutzucker, der; ~ **test** n. Blutprobe, die; ~**thirsty** adj. blutrünstig; ~ **transfusion** n. Bluttransfusion, die; ~ **vessel** n. Blutgefäß, das

'**bloody** ①① adj. (a) blutig; (running with blood) blutend
(b) (sl.: damned) verdammt (salopp)
②② adv. (sl.: damned) verdammt (salopp)

bloom /blu:m/ ①① n. Blüte, die; be in ~: in Blüte stehen
②② v.i. blühen

blossom /'blɒsəm/ ①① n. (flower) Blüte, die; (mass) Blütenmeer, das (geh.)
②② v.i. blühen; ⟨Mensch:⟩ aufblühen

blot /blɒt/ ①① n. (of ink) Tintenklecks, der; (stain) Fleck, der
②② v.t., -tt- ablöschen ⟨Tinte, Papier⟩
■ **blot** '**out** v.t. (fig.) auslöschen

blotchy /'blɒtʃɪ/ adj. fleckig

'**blotting paper** n. Löschpapier, das

blouse /blaʊz/ n. Bluse, die

blow¹ /bləʊ/ ①① v.i., blew /blu:/, blown /bləʊn/ ⟨Wind:⟩ wehen; ⟨Sturm:⟩ blasen
②② v.t., blew, blown: (a) blasen; ⟨Wind:⟩ wehen; machen ⟨Seifenblase⟩; ~ sb. a kiss jmdm. eine Kusshand zuwerfen
(b) ~ one's nose sich (Dat.) die Nase putzen
(c) ~ sth. to pieces etw. in die Luft sprengen
■ **blow** '**out** ①① v.t. ausblasen
②② v.i. ausgeblasen werden
■ **blow** '**over** ①① v.i. umgeblasen werden; ⟨Streit, Sturm:⟩ sich legen
②② v.t. umblasen
■ **blow** '**up** ①① v.t. (a) (shatter) [in die Luft] sprengen
(b) aufblasen ⟨Ballon⟩; aufpumpen ⟨Reifen⟩
(c) (coll.: exaggerate) hochspielen
②② v.i. (explode) explodieren

blow² n. (a) Schlag, der; (with axe) Hieb, der; come to ~s handgreiflich werden
(b) (disaster) [schwerer] Schlag

blow: ~**-dry** v.t. fönen; ~**lamp**, ~ **torch** n. Lötlampe, die

blown ▸ BLOW¹

blubber /'blʌbə(r)/ n. Walspeck, der

blue /blu:/ ①① adj. blau
②② n. (a) Blau, das
(b) have the ~s deprimiert sein
(c) (Mus.) the ~s der Blues
(d) out of the ~: aus heiterem Himmel

blue: ~**bell** n. Glockenblume, die; ~ '**blood** n. blaues Blut; ~**bottle** n. Schmeißfliege, die; ~ '**cheese** n. Blauschimmelkäse, der; Edelpilzkäse, der; ~**-collar** adj. ~**-collar worker**

Arbeiter, der/Arbeiterin, die; ~**-eyed** adj. blauäugig; be ~**-eyed** blaue Augen haben; ~ '**jeans** n. pl. Blue jeans Pl.; ~ '**moon** n. once in a ~ moon alle Jubeljahre (ugs.); ~**print** n. (fig.) Entwurf, der; ~ **tit** n. (Ornith.) Blaumeise, die; ~ '**whale** n. Blauwal, der

bluff /blʌf/ ①① n. Bluff, der (ugs.); call sb.'s ~: es darauf ankommen lassen (ugs.)
②② v.i. & t. bluffen (ugs.)

blunder /'blʌndə(r)/ ①① n. [schwerer] Fehler
②② v.i. (a) (make mistake) einen [schweren] Fehler machen
(b) (move blindly) tappen

blunt /blʌnt/ ①① adj. (a) stumpf
(b) (outspoken) direkt; glatt (ugs.) ⟨Ablehnung⟩
②② v.t. ~ [the edge of] stumpf machen

'**bluntly** adv. direkt; glatt ⟨ablehnen⟩

blur /blɜ:(r)/ ①① v.t., -rr-: (a) verwischen
(b) (become indistinct) verschwimmen; his vision was ~red er sah alles verschwommen
②② n. (smear) Fleck, der; (dim image) verschwommener Fleck

blurt /blɜ:t/ v.t. ~ out herausplatzen mit (ugs.)

blush /blʌʃ/ ①① v.i. rot werden
②② n. Rotwerden, das

bluster /'blʌstə(r)/ v.i. sich aufplustern (ugs.)

'**blustery** /'blʌstərɪ/ adj. stürmisch

BO abbr. (coll.) = **body odour** Körpergeruch, der

boar /bɔ:(r)/ n. [wild] ~: Keiler, der

board /bɔ:d/ ①① n. (a) Brett, das; (black~) Tafel, die; (notice~) schwarzes Brett; above ~ (fig.) einwandfrei; korrekt
(b) (Commerc.) ~ [of directors] Vorstand, der; (supervisory ~) Aufsichtsrat, der
(c) (Naut., Aeronaut.) on ~: an Bord
(d) ~ and lodging Unterkunft und Verpflegung; full ~: Vollpension, die
②② v.t. ~ the ship/plane an Bord des Schiffes/Flugzeuges gehen; ~ the train/bus in den Zug/Bus einsteigen
■ **board** '**up** v.t. mit Brettern vernageln

'**boarder** n. (Sch.) Internatsschüler, der/ -schülerin, die

'**board game** n. Brettspiel, das

boarding: ~ **house** n. Pension, die; ~ **pass** n. Bordkarte, die; ~ **school** n. Internat, das

board: ~ **meeting** n. Vorstandssitzung, die; ~**room** n. Sitzungssaal, der

boast /bəʊst/ v.i. prahlen

boastful /'bəʊstfl/ adj. prahlerisch

boat /bəʊt/ n. Boot, das

boat: ~**house** n. Bootshaus, das; ~ **trip** n. Bootsfahrt, die

bob¹ /bɒb/ v.i., -bb-: ~ [up and down] sich auf und nieder bewegen

bob² n. (~sled) Bob, der

bobbin /'bɒbɪn/ n. Spule, die

bob: ~**sled,** ~**sleigh** ns. Bobschlitten, der

bodice /'bɒdɪs/ n. Mieder, das; (part of dress) Oberteil, das

bodily /'bɒdɪlɪ/ adj. körperlich; ~ **needs** leibliche Bedürfnisse

body /'bɒdɪ/ n. (a) Körper, der
(b) (corpse) Leiche, die
(c) (group) Gruppe, die; (with particular function) Organ, das

body: ~ **bag** n. Leichensack, der;
~**building** ① n. Bodybuilding, das;
② adj. ~building **food** Aufbaukost, die;
~ **clock** ▸ BIOLOGICAL CLOCK; ~**guard** n. (single) Leibwächter, der; (group) Leibwache, die; ~ **language** n. Körpersprache, die;
~ **odour** n. Körpergeruch, der; ~ **part** n. Körperteil, der; ~ **piercing** n. Piercing, das; ~ **weight** n. Körpergewicht, das;
~**work** n. Karosserie, die

bog /bɒg/ ① n. Moor, das; (marsh, swamp) Sumpf, der
② v.t., **-gg-:** be/get ~ged down (fig.) sich verzettelt haben/sich verzetteln

boggle /'bɒgl/ v.i. (coll.) the mind ~s da kann man nur [noch] staunen

bogus /'bəʊgəs/ adj. falsch

boil¹ /bɔɪl/ ① v.i. & t. kochen
② n. come to/go off the ~: zu kochen anfangen/aufhören; bring to the ~: zum Kochen bringen
■ **boil 'down** v.i. ~ down to sth. (fig.) auf etw. hinauslaufen
■ **boil 'over** v.i. überkochen

boil² n. (Med.) Furunkel, der

'boiler n. Kessel, der

boiler: ~**room** n. Kesselraum, der;
~ **suit** n. Overall, der

'boiling point n. Siedepunkt, der

boisterous /'bɔɪstərəs/ adj. ausgelassen

bold /bəʊld/ adj. (a) (courageous) mutig; (daring) kühn
(b) auffallend ⟨Farbe, Muster⟩

'boldly adv. (courageously) mutig; (daringly) kühn

Bolivia /bə'lɪvɪə/ pr. n. Bolivien (das)

bollard /'bɒlɑːd/ n. (Brit.) Poller, der

bollocks /'bɒləks/ (coarse) ① n. pl. Eier (derb)
② int. Scheiße

bolster /'bəʊlstə(r)/ ① n. (pillow) Nackenrolle, die
② v.t. (fig.) stärken

bolt /bəʊlt/ ① n. (a) (on door or window) Riegel, der; (on gun) Kammerverschluss, der
(b) (metal pin) Schraube, die; (without thread) Bolzen, der
② v.i. davonlaufen; ⟨Pferd:⟩ durchgehen; ⟨Fuchs, Kaninchen:⟩ flüchten
③ v.t. (a) verriegeln ⟨Tür, Fenster⟩

(b) (fasten with ~s) verschrauben/mit Bolzen verbinden
(c) ~ [down] hinunterschlingen ⟨Essen⟩
④ adv. ~ upright kerzengerade

bomb /bɒm/ ① n. Bombe, die; ~ **attack** Bombenanschlag, der
② v.t. bombardieren

bombard /bɒm'bɑːd/ v.t. beschießen

bom'bardment n. Beschuss, der

bombastic /bɒm'bæstɪk/ adj. bombastisch

bomb: ~ **blast** n. (blast wave) Druckwelle, die; (explosion) Bombenexplosion, die;
~ **disposal** n. Räumung von Bomben;
~ **disposal squad** Bombenräumkommando, das

bomber /'bɒmə(r)/ n. (Air Force) Bomber, der (ugs.)

bombing /'bɒmɪŋ/ n. Bombardierung, die

bomb: ~ **scare** n. Bombendrohung, die;
~**shell** n. Bombe, die; (fig.) Sensation, die

bond /bɒnd/ n. (a) Band, das; in pl. (shackles) Fesseln Pl.
(b) (adhesion) Verbindung, die
(c) (Commerc.) Anleihe, die

bone /bəʊn/ ① n. Knochen, der; (of fish) Gräte, die
② v.t. den/die Knochen herauslösen aus; entgräten ⟨Fisch⟩

bone: ~ **'china** n. Knochenporzellan, das; ~ **'dry** adj. knochentrocken (ugs.);
~ **'idle** adj. stinkfaul (salopp); ~ **marrow** n. (Anat.) Knochenmark, das; ~**meal** n. Knochenmehl, das

bonfire /'bɒnfaɪə(r)/ n. Freudenfeuer, das; (for rubbish) Feuer, das; B~ **Night** (Brit.) [Abend des] Guy Fawkes Day (mit Feuerwerk)

bonnet /'bɒnɪt/ n. (a) (woman's) Haube, die; (child's) Häubchen, das
(b) (Brit. Motor Veh.) Motorhaube, die

bonus /'bəʊnəs/ n. zusätzliche Leistung; (to shareholders) Bonus, der; **Christmas** ~: Weihnachtsgratifikation, die

bony /'bəʊnɪ/ adj. (a) Knochen-; (like bone) knochenartig
(b) (skinny) knochendürr (ugs.); spindeldürr

boo /buː/ ① int. (to surprise sb.) huh; (expr. disapproval, contempt) buh
② n. Buh, das (ugs.)
③ v.t. ausbuhen (ugs.)
④ v.i. buhen (ugs.)

boob /buːb/ (Brit. coll.) n. (a) (mistake) Fehler, der; Schnitzer, der (ugs.)
(b) (breast) Titte, die (derb)

booby /'buːbɪ/ n. Trottel, der (ugs.)

booby: ~ **prize** n. Preis für den schlechtesten Teilnehmer an einem Wettbewerb; ~ **trap** n. (a) Falle, mit der man jmdm. einen Streich spielen will;
(b) (Mil.) versteckte Sprengladung

book /bʊk/ ① n. Buch, das; (for accounts) Rechnungsbuch, das; (for exercises)

[Schreib]heft, *das*
2 *v.t.* buchen ⟨*Reise, Flug, Platz* [*im Flugzeug*]⟩; [vor]bestellen ⟨*Eintrittskarte, Tisch, Zimmer, Platz* [*im Theater*]⟩
3 *v.i.* buchen
■ **book 'in** **1** *v.i.* sich eintragen
2 *v.t.* eintragen
■ **book 'up** *v.i. & t.* buchen; **be** ~**ed up** ⟨*Hotel usw.:*⟩ ausgebucht sein
book: ~**case** *n.* Bücherschrank, *der;* ~ **club** *n.* Buchklub, *der;* Buchgemeinschaft, *die;* ~**ends** *n. pl.* Buchstützen *Pl.*
bookie /'bʊkɪ/ *n.* (coll.) Buchmacher, *der*
'**booking office** *n.* [Fahrkarten]schalter, *der*
book: ~**keeper** *n.* Buchhalter, *der/* -halterin, *die;* ~**keeping** *n.* Buchführung, *die;* Buchhaltung, *die*
booklet /'bʊklɪt/ *n.* Broschüre, *die*
book: ~**maker** *n.* (in betting) Buchmacher, *der;* ~**mark** *n.* **1** (also Comp.) Lesezeichen, *das;* **2** *v.t.* (Comp.) mit einem Lesezeichen versehen; ~**seller** *n.* Buchhändler, *der/* -händlerin, *die;* ~**shelf** *n.* Bücherbord, *das;* ~**shop** *n.* Buchhandlung, *die;* ~**stall** *n.* Bücherstand, *der;* ~**store** *n.* (Amer.) Buchhandlung, *die;* ~ **token** *n.* Büchergutschein, *der;* ~**worm** *n.* Bücherwurm, *der*
boom¹ /buːm/ *n.* (a) (for camera or microphone) Ausleger, *der*
(b) (Naut.) Baum, *der*
boom² **1** *v.i.* (a) dröhnen
(b) ⟨*Geschäft, Verkauf, Gebiet:*⟩ sich sprunghaft entwickeln
2 *n.* (a) Dröhnen, *das*
(b) (in business or economy) Boom, *der*
boomerang /'buːməræŋ/ *n.* Bumerang, *der*
boon /buːn/ *n.* Segen, *der* (**to** für)
boor /bʊər/ *n.* Rüpel, *der*
boorish /'bʊərɪʃ/ *adj.* rüpelhaft
boost /buːst/ **1** *v.t.* ankurbeln ⟨*Wirtschaft*⟩; in die Höhe treiben ⟨*Preis, Wert*⟩; stärken ⟨*Selbstvertrauen, Moral*⟩
2 *n.* Auftrieb, *der*
boot /buːt/ **1** *n.* (a) Stiefel, *der;* **give sb. the** ~ (fig. coll.) jmdn. rausschmeißen (ugs.)
(b) (Brit.: of car) Kofferraum, *der*
2 *v.t.* (a) (coll.: kick) kicken (ugs.)
(b) (Comp.) ~ [**up**] booten
bootable /'buːtəbl/ *adj.* (Comp.) bootbar ⟨*System*⟩; ~ **disk** Bootdiskette, *die*
'**boot disk** *n.* (Comp.) Bootdiskette, *die*
booth /buːð/ *n.* (a) Bude, *die*
(b) (telephone ~) Zelle, *die*
'**bootleg** *adj.* (illegally sold/distilled) schwarz verkauft/gebrannt
booze /buːz/ (coll.) **1** *v.i.* saufen (derb)
2 *n.* Alkohol, *der*
'**booze-up** *n.* (coll.) Besäufnis, *das* (salopp); **have a** ~: saufen gehen (salopp)/(ugs.)

border /'bɔːdə(r)/ **1** *n.* (a) Rand, *der;* (of tablecloth, handkerchief) Bordüre, *die*
(b) (of country) Grenze, *die*
(c) (flower bed) Rabatte, *die*
2 *attrib. adj.* Grenz⟨*stadt, -streit*⟩
3 *v.t.* (a) (adjoin) [an]grenzen an (+ *Akk.*)
(b) (put a ~ to, act as a ~ to) umranden; einfassen
4 *v.i.* ~ **on (a)** ▶ 3A
(b) (resemble) grenzen an (+ *Akk.*)
border: ~ **crossing** *n.* Grenzübergang, *der;* ~**line** **1** *n.* Grenzlinie, *die;* **2** *adj.* **be** ~**line** auf der Grenze liegen; **a** ~**line case/candidate** ein Grenzfall
bore¹ /bɔː(r)/ **1** *v.t.* bohren
2 *n.* (of firearm) Kaliber, *das*
bore² **1** *n.* (a) **it's a real** ~: es ist wirklich ärgerlich; **what a** ~! wie ärgerlich!
(b) (person) Langweiler, *der* (ugs.)
2 *v.t.* langweilen; **be** ~**d** sich langweilen
bore³ ▶ BEAR²
boredom /'bɔːdəm/ *n.* Langeweile, *die*
'**borehole** *n.* Bohrloch, *das*
boring /'bɔːrɪŋ/ *adj.* langweilig
born /bɔːn/ **1** **be** ~: geboren werden
2 *adj.* geboren; **be a** ~ **orator** der geborene Redner sein
borne ▶ BEAR²
borough /'bʌrə/ *n.* (town) Stadt, *die;* (village) Gemeinde, *die*
borrow /'bɒrəʊ/ *v.t.* leihen (**from** von, bei); (from library) entleihen
'**borrower** *n.* (from bank) Kreditnehmer, *der;* (from library) Entleiher, *der*
Bosnia /'bɒznɪə/ *n.* Bosnien (*das*)
Bosnian /'bɒznɪən/ **1** *adj.* bosnisch; **sb. is** ~: jmd. ist Bosnier/Bosnierin
2 *n.* Bosnier, *der/*Bosnierin, *die*
bosom /'bʊzəm/ *n.* Brust, *die*
boss /bɒs/ (coll.) **1** *n.* Boss, *der* (ugs.); Chef, *der*
2 *v.t.* ~ [**about** *or* **around**] herumkommandieren (ugs.)
'**bossy** *adj.* (coll.) herrisch
botanical /bə'tænɪkl/ *adj.* botanisch
botanist /'bɒtənɪst/ *n.* Botaniker, *der/*Botanikerin, *die*
botany /'bɒtənɪ/ *n.* Botanik, *die*
botch /bɒtʃ/ **1** *v.t.* pfuschen bei (ugs.)
2 *v.i.* pfuschen (ugs.)
■ **botch 'up** *v.t.* (bungle) verpfuschen (ugs.)
both /bəʊθ/ **1** *adj.* beide; ~ [**the**] **brothers** beide Brüder
2 *pron.* beide; ~ [**of them**] **are dead** beide sind tot; ~ **of you/them are …**: ihr seid/sie sind beide …
3 *adv.* ~ **A and B** sowohl A als [auch] B; **he and I were** ~ **there** er und ich waren beide da
bother /'bɒðə(r)/ **1** *v.t.* (a) **I can't be** ~**ed** ich habe keine Lust
(b) (annoy) lästig sein (+ *Dat.*); ⟨*Lärm,* ···⟶

Licht:) stören; ⟨*Schmerz, Zahn:*⟩ zu
schaffen machen (+ *Dat.*); **I'm sorry to
~ you, but ...**: es tut mir Leid, wenn ich
Sie störe, aber ...
(c) (worry) Sorgen machen (+ *Dat.*);
⟨*Problem, Frage:*⟩ beschäftigen
2 *v.i.* **don't ~ to do it** Sie brauchen es nicht
zu tun; **you needn't/shouldn't have ~ed** das
wäre nicht nötig gewesen; **don't ~!** nicht
nötig!
3 *n.* **(a)** (trouble) Ärger, *der*
(b) (effort) Mühe, *die*
4 *int.* (coll.) wie ärgerlich!
bottle /'bɒtl/ **1** *n.* Flasche, *die;* **a ~ of beer**
eine Flasche Bier
2 *v.t.* **(a)** (put into ~s) in Flaschen [ab]füllen
(b) **~d beer** Flaschenbier, *das*
(c) (preserve in jars) einmachen
■ **bottle 'up** *v.t.* **(a)** (conceal) in sich (*Dat.*)
aufstauen
(b) (trap) einschließen
bottle: ~ bank *n.* Altglasbehälter, *der;*
~neck *n.* (fig.) Flaschenhals, *der* (ugs.);
~-opener *n.* Flaschenöffner, *der;* **~ top**
n. Flaschenverschluss, *der*
bottom /'bɒtəm/ **1** *n.* **(a)** unteres Ende; (of
cup, glass, box) Boden, *der;* (of valley, well, shaft)
Sohle, *die;* (of hill, cliff, stairs) Fuß, *der*
(b) (buttocks) Hinterteil, *das* (ugs.)
(c) (of sea, lake) Grund, *der*
(d) (farthest point) **at the ~ of the garden/
street** hinten im Garten/am Ende der Straße
(e) (underside) Unterseite, *die*
(f) (fig.) **start at the ~:** ganz unten anfangen;
be ~ of the class der/die Letzte in der
Klasse sein
2 *adj.* **(a)** (lowest) unterst...; (lower) unter...
(b) (fig.: last) letzt...
'bottomless *adj.* bodenlos; unendlich tief
⟨*Meer, Ozean*⟩
'botulism /'bɒtjuːlɪzm/ *n.* (Med.)
Botulismus, *der*
bough /baʊ/ *n.* Ast, *der*
bought ▸ BUY 1
boulder /'bəʊldə(r)/ *n.* Felsbrocken, *der*
boulevard /'buːləvɑːd/ *n.* Boulevard, *der*
bounce /baʊns/ **1** *v.i.* **(a)** springen
(b) (coll.) ⟨*Scheck:*⟩ platzen (ugs.)
2 *v.t.* aufspringen lassen ⟨*Ball*⟩
3 *n.* Aufprall, *der*
'bouncer *n.* (coll.) Rausschmeißer, *der* (ugs.)
bouncing /'baʊnsɪŋ/ *adj.* stramm ⟨*Baby*⟩
bouncy /'baʊnsɪ/ *adj.* gut springend ⟨*Ball*⟩;
(fig.: lively) munter
bouncy 'castle *n.* Hüpfburg, *die*
bound¹ /baʊnd/ **1** *n., usu. in pl.* (limit)
Grenze, *die;* **within the ~s of possibility** im
Bereich des Möglichen; **sth. is out of ~s [to
sb.]** der Zutritt zu etw. ist [für jmdn.] verboten
2 *v.t.* **be ~ed by sth.** durch etw. begrenzt
werden
bound² **1** *v.i.* hüpfen
2 *n.* Satz, *der*

bound³ *pred. adj.* **be ~ for home/Frankfurt**
auf dem Heimweg/nach Frankfurt
unterwegs sein; **homeward ~:** auf dem Weg
nach Hause
bound⁴ ▸ BIND
boundary /'baʊndərɪ/ *n.* Grenze, *die*
'boundless *adj.* grenzenlos
bounty /'baʊntɪ/ *n.* Kopfgeld, *das*
bouquet /bʊ'keɪ/ *n.* [Blumen]strauß, *der*
bourgeois /'bʊəʒwɑː/ **1** *n., pl. same*
Bürger, *der*/Bürgerin, *die*
2 *adj.* bürgerlich
bout /baʊt/ *n.* **(a)** (contest) Wettkampf, *der*
(b) (fit) Anfall, *der*
boutique /buː'tiːk/ *n.* Boutique, *die*
bow¹ /bəʊ/ **(a)** (curve, weapon, Mus.) Bogen,
der
(b) (knot, ribbon) Schleife, *die*
bow² /baʊ/ **1** *v.i.* **(a)** **~ [to sb.]** sich [vor
jmdm.] verbeugen
(b) (submit) sich beugen (**to** *Dat.*)
2 *n.* Verbeugung, *die*
bow³ /baʊ/ *n.* (Naut.) Bug, *der*
bowel /'baʊəl/ *n.* (Anat.) **~s** *pl.*, (Med.)
~: Darm, *der*
bowl¹ /bəʊl/ *n.* (basin) Schüssel, *die;*
(shallower) Schale, *die;* (of spoon) Schöpfteil,
der; (of pipe) Kopf, *der*
bowl² **1** *n.* **(a)** (ball) Kugel, *die*
(b) *in pl.* (game) Bowls, *das*
2 *v.i.* **(a)** (play ~s) Bowls spielen
(b) (Cricket) werfen
bow-legged /'bəʊlegɪd/ o-beinig (ugs.)
bowler¹ /'bəʊlə(r)/ *n.* (Cricket) Werfer, *der*
bowler² *n.* **~ [hat]** Bowler, *der*
'bowling *n.* **[tenpin] ~:** Bowling, *das;* **go
~:** bowlen gehen
bowling: ~ alley *n.* Bowlingbahn, *die;*
~ green *n.:* Rasenfläche für Bowls
bow /bəʊ/ **~string** *n.* Bogensehne,
die; **~ 'tie** *n.* Fliege, *die;* **~ window** *n.*
Erkerfenster, *das*
box¹ /bɒks/ *n.* **(a)** Kasten, *der;* (bigger) Kiste,
die; (of cardboard) Schachtel, *die*
(b) **the ~** (coll.: television) der Kasten (ugs.
abwertend); die Flimmerkiste (scherzh.)
box² **1** *n.* **he gave him a ~ on the ear[s]** er
gab ihm eine Ohrfeige
2 *v.t.* **(a)** **he ~ed his ears** *or* **~ed him
round the ears** er ohrfeigte ihn
(b) (Sport) **~ sb.** gegen jmdn. boxen
3 *v.i.* (Sport) boxen
■ **box 'in** *v.t.* (enclose tightly) einklemmen
'boxer *n.* Boxer, *der*
'boxer shorts *n. pl.* Boxershorts *Pl.*
'boxing *n.* Boxen, *das*
boxing: B~ Day *n.* zweiter
Weihnachtsfeiertag; **~ glove** *n.*
Boxhandschuh, *der;* **~ match** *n.*
Boxkampf, *der;* **~ ring** *n.* Boxring, *der*
box: ~ junction *n.* (Brit.) *gelb markierter
Kreuzungsbereich, in den man bei Stau nicht*

einfahren darf; ~ **number** *n.* (at newspaper office) Chiffre, *die;* (at post office) Postfach, *das;* ~ **office** *n.* Kasse, *die;* **be a** ~ **office success** ein Kassenerfolg sein; ~**room** *n.* (Brit.) Abstellraum, *der*

boy /bɔɪ/ *n.* Junge, *der*

'boy band *n.* Boyband, *die*

boycott /'bɔɪkɒt/ **1** *v.t.* boykottieren **2** *n.* Boykott, *der*

'boyfriend *n.* Freund, *der*

'boyish *adj.* jungenhaft

boy 'scout ▶ SCOUT 1A

bra /brɑː/ *n.* BH, *der* (ugs.); *attrib.* ~ **strap** BH-Träger, *der*

brace /breɪs/ **1** *n.* **(a)** (connecting piece) Klammer, *die;* (strut) Strebe, *die;* (Dent.) [Zahn]spange, *die*
(b) *in pl.* (trouser straps) Hosenträger. *Pl.*
2 *v. refl.* ~ **oneself for sth.** sich auf etw. (*Akk.*) vorbereiten

bracelet /'breɪslɪt/ *n.* Armband, *das*

bracing /'breɪsɪŋ/ *adj.* belebend

bracken /'brækn/ *n.* [Adler]farn, *der*

bracket /'brækɪt/ **1** *n.* **(a)** (support) Konsole, *die*
(b) (mark) Klammer, *die*
2 *v.t.* einklammern

brag /bræg/ *v.i. & t.,* **-gg-** prahlen (**about** mit)

braid /breɪd/ **1** *n.* **(a)** (plait) Flechte, *die* (geh.); Zopf, *der*
(b) (woven band) Borte, *die;* (on uniform) Litze, *die*
2 *v.t.* flechten

Braille /breɪl/ *n.* Blindenschrift, *die*

brain /breɪn/ *n.* Gehirn, *das*

brain: ~**child** *n.* (coll.) Geistesprodukt, *das;* ~**dead** *adj.* **(a)** (Med.) hirntot;
(b) (coll. derog.) hirnlos ⟨*Person*⟩; ~**less** *adj.* hirnlos; ~**storm** *n.* **(a)** Anfall geistiger Umnachtung; **(b)** (Amer. coll.) ▶ ~WAVE;
~**storming** *n.* Brainstorming, *das;*
~ **tumour** *n.* Gehirntumor, *der;* ~**wash** *v.t.* einer Gehirnwäsche unterziehen;
~**wave** *n.* (coll.: inspiration) genialer Einfall

'brainy *adj.* intelligent

brake /breɪk/ **1** *n.* Bremse, *die*
2 *v.t. & i.* bremsen

brake: ~ **block** *n.* Bremsklotz, *der;*
~ **cable** *n.* Bremszug, *der;* Bremsseil, *das;*
~ **fluid** *n.* Bremsflüssigkeit, *die;* ~ **light** *n.* Bremslicht, *das;* ~ **pad** *n.* Bremsbelag, *der;* ~ **shoe** *n.* Bremsbacke, *die*

'braking distance *n.* Bremsweg, *der*

bramble /'bræmbl/ *n.* Dornenstrauch, *der*

bran /bræn/ *n.* Kleie, *die*

branch /brɑːntʃ/ **1** *n.* **(a)** (bough) Ast, *der;* (twig) Zweig, *der*
(b) (of artery, antlers) Ast, *der*
(c) (office) Zweigstelle, *die;* (shop) Filiale, *die*
2 *v.i.* sich verzweigen

■ **branch 'off** *v.i.* abzweigen

■ **branch 'out** *v.i.* (fig.) ~ **out into sth.** sich auch mit etw. befassen

branch: ~ **line** *n.* (Railw.) Nebenstrecke, *die;* ~ **manager** *n.* Filialleiter, *der/* -leiterin, *die;* ~ **office** *n.* Zweigstelle, *die*

brand /brænd/ *n.* **(a)** (trade mark) Markenzeichen, *das;* (goods of particular make) Marke, *die*
(b) (mark) Brandmal, *das*

'brand image *n.* Markenimage, *das*

brandish /'brændɪʃ/ *v.t.* schwenken; schwingen ⟨*Waffe*⟩

brand: ~ **leader** *n.* (product) marktführendes Produkt; (brand) führende Marke; ~ **name** *n.* Markenname, *der;*
~-'**new** *adj.* nagelneu (ugs.)

brandy /'brændɪ/ *n.* Weinbrand, *der;* Kognak, *der*

brash /bræʃ/ *adj.* dreist

brass /brɑːs/ *n.* Messing, *das; attrib.* Messing-; **the** ~ (Mus.) das Blech; ~ **player** (Mus.) Blechbläser, *der;* **get down to** ~ **tacks** zur Sache kommen

brass 'band *n.* Blaskapelle, *die*

brassière /'bræzjə(r)/ *n.* Büstenhalter, *der*

brat /bræt/ *n.* Balg, *das od. der* (ugs.)

bravado /brə'vɑːdəʊ/ *n.* **do sth. out of** ~: so waghalsig sein, etw. zu tun

brave /breɪv/ **1** *adj.* tapfer
2 *n.* [indianischer] Krieger
3 *v.t.* trotzen (+ *Dat.*)

'bravely *adv.* tapfer

bravery /'breɪvərɪ/ *n.* Tapferkeit, *die*

bravo /brɑː'vəʊ/ *int.* bravo

brawl /brɔːl/ **1** *v.i.* sich schlagen
2 *n.* Schlägerei, *die*

brawny /'brɔːnɪ/ *adj.* muskulös

bray /breɪ/ **1** *n.* Iah, *das*
2 *v.i.* ⟨*Esel*⟩ iahen

brazen /'breɪzn/ **1** *adj.* dreist; (shameless) schamlos
2 *v.t.* ~ **[out]** trotzen (+ *Dat.*); ~ **it out** (deny guilt) es abstreiten; (not admit guilt) es nicht zugeben

brazier /'breɪzɪə(r)/ *n.* Kohlenbecken, *das*

Brazil /brə'zɪl/ *pr. n.* Brasilien (*das*)

Bra'zil nut *n.* Paranuss, *die*

breach /briːtʃ/ **1** *n.* **(a)** (violation) Verstoß, *der* (of gegen); ~ **of faith/duty** Vertrauensbruch, *der*/Pflichtverletzung, *die*
(b) (of relations) Bruch, *der*
(c) (gap) Bresche, *die;* (fig.) Riss, *der*
2 *v.t.* durchbrechen

bread /bred/ *n.* Brot, *das;* **a piece of** ~ **and butter** ein Butterbrot

bread: ~ **bin** *n.* Brotkasten, *der;*
~**board** *n.* [Brot]brett, *das;* ~**crumb** *n.* Brotkrume, *die;* ~**crumbs** (coating) Paniermehl, *das;* ~ **knife** *n.* Brotmesser, *das;* ~**line** *n.* **be** *or* **live on/below the** ~**line** gerade noch/nicht einmal mehr ⸱⸱⸱⸱>

das Notwendigste zum Leben haben;
~ **'roll** n. Brötchen, das
breadth /bredθ/ n. Breite, die
'breadwinner n. Ernährer, der/
Ernährerin, die
break /breɪk/ **1** v.t., **broke** /brəʊk/, **broken**
/'brəʊkn/ **(a)** brechen; (so as to damage)
zerbrechen; kaputtmachen (ugs.); zerreißen
⟨Seil⟩; (fig.: interrupt) unterbrechen; brechen
⟨Bann, Zauber, Schweigen⟩; **the TV/my
watch is broken** der Fernseher/meine Uhr
ist kaputt (ugs.); ~ **the habit** es sich (Dat.)
abgewöhnen
(b) (fracture) sich (Dat.) brechen ⟨Arm, Bein
usw.⟩
(c) brechen ⟨Vertrag, Versprechen⟩;
verstoßen gegen ⟨Regel, Gesetz⟩
(d) (surpass) brechen ⟨Rekord⟩
(e) (cushion) auffangen ⟨Schlag, jmds. Fall⟩
2 v.i., **broke, broken (a)** kaputtgehen (ugs.);
⟨Faden, Seil:⟩ [zer]reißen; ⟨Glas, Tasse,
Teller:⟩ zerbrechen; ⟨Eis:⟩ brechen; ~ **in
two/in pieces** durchbrechen/zerbrechen
(b) ~ **into** einbrechen in (+ Akk.) ⟨Haus⟩;
aufbrechen ⟨Auto, Safe⟩; ~ **into laughter/
tears** in Gelächter/Tränen ausbrechen;
~ **into a trot/run** zu traben/laufen anfangen
(c) (escape) ~ **out of prison** aus dem
Gefängnis ausbrechen; ~ **free** or **loose** sich
losreißen
(d) ⟨Welle:⟩ sich brechen **(on/against** an
+ Dat.)
(e) ⟨Tag:⟩ anbrechen; ⟨Sturm:⟩ losbrechen
(f) sb's **voice is** ~**ing** jmd. kommt in den
Stimmbruch
3 n. **(a)** Bruch, der; (of rope) Reißen, das; **a**
~ **with sb./sth.** ein Bruch mit jmdm./etw.
(b) (gap) Lücke, die; (broken place) Sprung, der
(c) (dash) **they made a sudden** ~: sie
stürmten plötzlich davon
(d) (interruption) Unterbrechung, die; (pause,
holiday) Pause, die; **take** or **have a** ~: Pause
machen
(e) (coll.: chance) Chance, die
▪ **break 'down** **1** v.i. zusammenbrechen;
⟨Verhandlungen:⟩ scheitern; ⟨Auto:⟩ eine
Panne haben
2 v.t. **(a)** aufbrechen ⟨Tür⟩; brechen
⟨Widerstand⟩; niederreißen ⟨Barriere,
Schranke⟩
(b) (analyse) aufgliedern
▪ **break 'in** **1** v.i. (into building etc.)
einbrechen
2 v.t. **(a)** zureiten ⟨Pferd⟩
(b) einlaufen ⟨Schuhe⟩
(c) ~ **the door** in die Tür aufbrechen
▪ **'break into** ▶ ~ 2.
▪ **break 'off** **1** v.t. abbrechen; abreißen
⟨Faden⟩; auflösen ⟨Verlobung⟩
2 v.i. **(a)** abbrechen
(b) (cease) aufhören
▪ **break 'out** v.i. ausbrechen; ~ **out
in spots/a rash** Pickel/einen Ausschlag
bekommen
▪ **break 'up** **1** v.t. **(a)** (~ into pieces)

zerkleinern; ausschlachten ⟨Auto⟩;
aufbrechen ⟨Erde⟩
(b) (disband) auflösen
2 v.i. **(a)** (~ **into pieces,** lit. or fig.) zerbrechen
(b) (disband) sich auflösen; ⟨Schule:⟩
schließen; ⟨Schüler, Lehrer:⟩ in die Ferien
gehen
(c) ~ **up [with sb.]** sich [von jmdm.] trennen
breakable /'breɪkəbl/ **1** adj.
zerbrechlich
2 n. ~**s** zerbrechliche Dinge
breakage /'breɪkɪdʒ/ n. Zerbrechen, das;
~**s must be paid for** zerbrochene Ware
muss bezahlt werden
'breakdown n. **(a)** (of vehicle) Panne,
die; (in machine) Störung, die; ~ **truck/van**
Abschleppwagen, der
(b) (Med.) Zusammenbruch, der
(c) (analysis) Aufschlüsselung, die
'breaker n. **(a)** (wave) Brecher, der
(b) ~**'s [yard]** Autoverwertung, die
breakfast /'brekfəst/ **1** n. Frühstück,
das; **for** ~: zum Frühstück
2 v.i. frühstücken
breakfast: ~ **cereal** n. ≈
Frühstücksflocken Pl.; ~ **'television** n.
Frühstücksfernsehen, das
'break-in n. Einbruch, der
'breaking n. ~ **and entering** (Law)
Einbruch, der; **be at** ~ **point** (mentally) die
Grenze der Belastbarkeit erreicht haben
break: ~**neck** adj. halsbrecherisch;
~**through** n. Durchbruch, der; ~**-up** n.
Auflösung, die; (of relationship) Bruch, der;
~**water** n. Wellenbrecher, der
breast /brest/ n. Brust, die
breast: ~**bone** n. Brustbein, das;
~ **cancer** n. Brustkrebs, der; ~**feed**
v.t. & i. stillen; ~**stroke** n.
Brustschwimmen, das
breath /breθ/ n. **(a)** Atem, der; **get one's**
~ **back** wieder zu Atem kommen; **hold one's**
~: den Atem anhalten; **be out of** ~: außer
Atem sein; **say sth. under one's** ~: etw. vor
sich (Akk.) hin murmeln
(b) (one respiration) Atemzug, der
Breathalyser (Brit.), **Breathalyzer**®
/'breθəlaɪzə(r)/ n. Alcotest-Röhrchen ⓌⓏ,
das; ~ **test** Alcotest ⓌⓏ, der
breathe /briːð/ **1** v.i. atmen; ~ **in**
einatmen; ~ **out** ausatmen
2 v.t. **(a)** ~ **[in/out]** ein-/ausatmen
(b) (utter) hauchen
'breather /'briːðə(r)/ n. Verschnaufpause,
die
'breathing space n. Zeit zum Luftholen;
(fig.) Atempause, die
'breathless adj. atemlos (**with** vor + Dat.)
breath: ~**taking** adj. atemberaubend;
~ **test** n. Alcotest ⓌⓏ, der
bred ▶ BREED 1, 2
breeches /'brɪtʃɪz/ n. pl. **[pair
of]** ~: [Knie]bundhose, die;

[riding]~: Reithose, *die*

breed /briːd/ ① *v.t.*, **bred** /bred/ **(a)** (cause) erzeugen
(b) züchten ‹*Tiere, Pflanzen*›
② *v.i.*, **bred** sich vermehren
③ *n.* (of animals) Rasse, *die*

'**breeding** *n.* [good] ~: gute Erziehung

'**breeding ground** *n.* (lit. or fig.) Brutstätte, *die*

breeze /briːz/ *n.* Brise, *die*

'**breeze block** *n.* (Building) ≈ Leichtstein, *der*

breezy /'briːzɪ/ *adj.* windig

brevity /'brevɪtɪ/ *n.* Kürze, *die*

brew /bruː/ ① *v.t.* brauen ‹*Bier*›; ~ [up] kochen ‹*Kaffee, Tee usw.*›
② *v.i.* **(a)** ‹*Bier:*› gären; ‹*Kaffee, Tee:*› ziehen
(b) ‹*Unwetter:*› sich zusammenbrauen
③ *n.* (brewed beer/tea) Bier, *das*/Tee, *der*

'**brewer** *n.* Brauer, *der;* (firm) Brauerei, *die*

brewery /'bruːərɪ/ *n.* Brauerei, *die*

bribe /braɪb/ ① *n.* Bestechung, *die*
② *v.t.* bestechen; ~ **sb. to do/into doing sth.** jmdn. bestechen, damit er etw. tut

bribery /'braɪbərɪ/ *n.* Bestechung, *die*

brick /brɪk/ ① *n.* Ziegelstein, *der;* (toy) Bauklötzchen, *das*
② *adj.* Ziegelstein-

brick: ~**layer** *n.* Maurer, *der;*
~**laying** *n.* Mauern, *das;* ~ '**wall** *n.* Backsteinmauer, *die;* **bang one's head against a** ~ **wall** (fig.) mit dem Kopf gegen die Wand rennen (fig.)

bridal /'braɪdl/ *adj.* Braut-

bride /braɪd/ *n.* Braut, *die*

'**bridegroom** *n.* Bräutigam, *der*

bridesmaid /'braɪdzmeɪd/ *n.* Brautjungfer, *die*

bridge¹ /brɪdʒ/ ① *n.* **(a)** Brücke, *die*
(b) (Naut.) [Kommando]brücke, *die*
(c) (of nose) Nasenbein, *das*
(d) (of spectacles) Steg, *der*
② *v.t.* eine Brücke bauen über (+ *Akk.*)

bridge² *n.* (Cards) Bridge, *das*

'**bridging loan** *n.* (Commerc.) Überbrückungskredit, *der*

bridle /'braɪdl/ *n.* Zaum, *der*

'**bridle path** *n.* Reitweg, *der*

brief¹ /briːf/ *adj.* **(a)** kurz; gering ‹*Verspätung*›
(b) (concise) knapp; **in** ~, **to be** ~: kurz gesagt

brief² ① *n.* (instructions) Instruktionen *Pl.;* (Law: case) Mandat, *das*
② *v.t.* Instruktionen geben (+ *Dat.*); (inform) unterrichten

'**briefcase** *n.* Aktentasche, *die*

'**briefing** *n.* Briefing, *das;* (of reporters) Unterrichtung, *die*

'**briefly** *adv.* **(a)** kurz
(b) (concisely) knapp; kurz

briefs /briːfs/ *n. pl.* [pair of] ~: Slip, *der*

brigade /brɪ'ɡeɪd/ *n.* (Mil.) Brigade, *die*

brigadier /brɪɡə'dɪə(r)/ *n.* Brigadegeneral, *der*

bright /braɪt/ *adj.* **(a)** hell; grell ‹*Scheinwerfer[licht], Sonnenlicht*›; strahlend ‹*Sonnenschein, Augen, Tag*›; leuchtend ‹*Farbe, Blume*›; ~ **intervals/periods** Aufheiterungen *Pl.*
(b) (cheerful) fröhlich
(c) (clever) intelligent

brighten /'braɪtn/ ① *v.t.* ~ [up] aufhellen
② *v.i.* **the weather** *or* **it is** ~**ing [up]** es klärt sich auf

'**brightly** *adv.* **(a)** hell
(b) (cheerfully) fröhlich

'**brightness** *n.* ▸ BRIGHT: **(a)** Helligkeit, *die;* Grelle, *die;* Strahlen, *das;* Leuchtkraft, *die*
(b) Fröhlichkeit, *die*
(c) Intelligenz, *die*

brilliance /'brɪljəns/ *n.* ▸ BRILLIANT:
(a) Helligkeit, *die;* Leuchten, *das*
(b) Genialität, *die;* Glanz, *der*

brilliant /'brɪljənt/ *adj.* **(a)** hell ‹*Licht*›; leuchtend ‹*Farbe*›
(b) genial ‹*Mensch, Gedanke, Leistung*›; glänzend ‹*Verstand, Aufführung, Idee*›

brim /brɪm/ ① *n.* Rand, *der;* (of hat) [Hut]krempe, *die*
② *v.i.*, **-mm-:** **be** ~**ming with sth.** randvoll mit etw. sein

brim-'full *pred. adj.* randvoll (**with** mit)

brine /braɪn/ *n.* Salzwasser, *das*

bring /brɪŋ/ *v.t.*, **brought** /brɔːt/ **(a)** bringen; (as a present or favour) mitbringen; ~ **sth. with one** etw. mitbringen
(b) ~ **sb. to do sth.** jmdn. dazu bringen, etw. zu tun; **I could not** ~ **myself to do it** ich konnte es nicht über mich bringen, es zu tun

■ **bring a'bout** *v.t.* verursachen

■ **bring 'back** *v.t.* **(a)** (return) zurückbringen; (from a journey) mitbringen
(b) (recall) in Erinnerung bringen
(c) (restore, reintroduce) wieder einführen

■ **bring 'down** *v.t.* **(a)** herunterbringen
(b) (kill, wound) zur Strecke bringen
(c) senken ‹*Preise, Inflationsrate, Fieber*›

■ **bring 'forward** *v.t.* **(a)** nach vorne bringen
(b) vorbringen ‹*Argument*›; zur Sprache bringen ‹*Fall, Angelegenheit*›
(c) vorverlegen ‹*Termin*› (**to** auf + *Akk.*)

■ **bring 'in** *v.t.* hereinbringen; einbringen ‹*Gesetzesvorlage, Verdienst, Summe*›

■ **bring 'off** *v.t.* (conduct successfully) zustande bringen

■ **bring 'on** *v.t.* **(a)** (cause) verursachen
(b) (Sport) einsetzen

■ **bring 'out** *v.t.* **(a)** herausbringen
(b) hervorheben ‹*Unterschied*›
(c) einführen ‹*Produkt*›; herausbringen ‹*Buch, Zeitschrift*› ····⊹

b

■ **bring** 'up *v.t.* (a) heraufbringen
(b) (educate) erziehen; (rear) aufziehen
(c) zur Sprache bringen ⟨*Angelegenheit, Thema, Problem*⟩

brink /'brɪŋk/ *n.* Rand, *der;* be on the ∼ of doing sth. nahe daran sein, etw. zu tun

brisk /brɪsk/ *adj.* flott ⟨*Gang*⟩; forsch ⟨*Person, Art*⟩; frisch ⟨*Wind*⟩; (fig.) rege ⟨*Handel, Nachfrage*⟩; lebhaft ⟨*Geschäft*⟩

'**briskly** *adv.* flott

bristle /'brɪsl/ ⟨1⟩ *n.* Borste, *die*
⟨2⟩ *v.i.* (a) ∼ [up] ⟨*Haare:*⟩ sich sträuben
(b) ∼ with (fig.) starren vor (+ *Dat.*)

'**bristly** /'brɪslɪ/ *adj.* borstig

Brit /brit/ *n.* (coll.) Brite, *der*/Britin, *die;* Engländer, *der*/Engländerin, *die* (ugs.)

Britain /'brɪtn/ *pr. n.* Großbritannien ⟨*das*⟩

British /'brɪtɪʃ/ ⟨1⟩ *adj.* britisch; he/she is ∼: er ist Brite/sie ist Britin
⟨2⟩ *n. pl.* the ∼: die Briten

British '**Isles** *pr. n. pl.* Britische Inseln

Briton /'brɪtn/ *n.* Brite, *der*/Britin, *die*

Brittany /'brɪtənɪ/ *pr. n.* Bretagne, *die*

brittle /'brɪtl/ *adj.* spröde ⟨*Material*⟩

broach /brəʊtʃ/ *v.t.* anschneiden ⟨*Thema*⟩

broad /brɔːd/ *adj.* (a) breit; (extensive) weit ⟨*Ebene, Land*⟩; ausgedehnt ⟨*Fläche*⟩
(b) (explicit) klar ⟨*Hinweis*⟩; breit ⟨*Lächeln*⟩
(c) (main) grob; (generalized) allgemein
(d) stark ⟨*Akzent*⟩

broadband *n.* (Comp.) Breitband, *das;* attrib. Breitband-

broad '**bean** *n.* Saubohne, *die*

broadcast /'brɔːdkɑːst/ ⟨1⟩ *n.* Sendung, *die;* (live) Übertragung, *die*
⟨2⟩ *v.t.,* broadcast senden; übertragen ⟨*Livesendung*⟩
⟨3⟩ *v.i.,* broadcast senden

'**broadcaster** *n.* (Radio, Telev.) jmd., *der* durch häufige Auftritte im Rundfunk und Fernsehen, besonders als Interviewpartner, Diskussionsteilnehmer od. Kommentator, bekannt ist

'**broadcasting** *n.* Senden, *das;* (live) Übertragen, *das;* work in ∼: beim Funk arbeiten

broaden /'brɔːdn/ ⟨1⟩ *v.t.* (a) verbreitern
(b) ausweiten ⟨*Diskussion*⟩
⟨2⟩ *v.i.* sich verbreitern; (fig.) sich erweitern

'**broadly** *adv.* (a) deutlich ⟨*hinweisen*⟩; breit ⟨*grinsen, lächeln*⟩
(b) (in general) allgemein ⟨*beschreiben*⟩; ∼ speaking allgemein gesagt

broad: ∼-'**minded** *adj.* tolerant;
∼**sheet** *n.* (a) (Printing) Einblattdruck, *der;* (b) (pamphlet) Flugblatt, *das;*
∼-'**shouldered** *adj.* breitschultrig;
∼**side** *n.* Breitseite, *die*

brocade /brə'keɪd/ *n.* Brokat, *der*

broccoli /'brɒkəlɪ/ *n.* Brokkoli, *der*

brochure /'brəʊʃə(r)/ *n.* Broschüre, *die;* Prospekt, *der*

broil /'brɔɪl/ *v.t.* (esp. Amer.) grillen

broke /brəʊk/ ⟨1⟩ ▶ BREAK 1, 2
⟨2⟩ *pred. adj.* (coll.) pleite (ugs.)

broken /'brəʊkn/ ⟨1⟩ ▶ BREAK 1, 2
⟨2⟩ *adj.* (a) zerbrochen; gebrochen ⟨*Bein, Hals*⟩; verletzt ⟨*Haut*⟩; abgebrochen ⟨*Zahn*⟩; gerissen ⟨*Seil*⟩; kaputt (ugs.) ⟨*Uhr, Fernsehen, Fenster*⟩; ∼ glass Glasscherben *Pl.*
(b) (imperfect) gebrochen; in ∼ English in gebrochenem Englisch
(c) (fig.) ruiniert ⟨*Ehe*⟩; gebrochen ⟨*Mensch, Herz*⟩

broken: ∼-**down** *adj.* baufällig ⟨*Gebäude*⟩; kaputt (ugs.) ⟨*Wagen*⟩;
∼-'**hearted** *adj.* untröstlich

broker /'brəʊkə(r)/ *n.* Makler, *der*

brolly /'brɒlɪ/ *n.* (Brit. coll.) [Regen]schirm, *der*

bronchitis /brɒŋ'kaɪtɪs/ *n.* Bronchitis, *die*

bronze /brɒnz/ ⟨1⟩ *n.* Bronze, *die*
⟨2⟩ *attrib. adj.* Bronze-; (coloured like ∼) bronzefarben

brooch /brəʊtʃ/ *n.* Brosche, *die*

brood /bruːd/ ⟨1⟩ *n.* Brut, *die*
⟨2⟩ *v.i.* [vor sich (*Akk.*) hin] brüten

brook /brʊk/ *n.* Bach, *der*

broom /bruːm/ *n.* (a) Besen, *der*
(b) (Bot.) Ginster, *der*

broom: ∼ **cupboard** *n.* Besenschrank, *der;* ∼**stick** *n.* Besenstiel, *der*

broth /brɒθ/ *n.* Brühe, *die*

brothel /'brɒθl/ *n.* Bordell, *das*

brother /'brʌðə(r)/ *n.* Bruder, *der;* my ∼s and sisters meine Geschwister

'**brotherhood** *n.* (organization) Bruderschaft, *die*

'**brother-in-law** *n., pl.* brothers-in-law Schwager, *der*

brought ▶ BRING

brow /braʊ/ *n.* (a) (eye∼) Braue, *die*
(b) (forehead) Stirn, *die*
(c) (of hill) Kuppe, *die*

'**browbeat** *v.t., forms as* BEAT 1 einschüchtern

brown /braʊn/ ⟨1⟩ *adj.* braun
⟨2⟩ *n.* Braun, *das*

brown: ∼ '**bread** *n.* ≈ Mischbrot, *das;*
∼-**eyed** *adj.* braunäugig; be ∼-eyed braune Augen haben

'**brownfield site** *n.* Industriebrache, *die*

Brownie /'braʊnɪ/ *n.* Wichtel, *die*

brown: ∼ '**paper** *n.* Packpapier, *das;*
∼ **rice** *n.* Naturreis, *der*

browse /braʊz/ *v.i.* ⟨1⟩ (a) weiden
(b) (in shop) sich umsehen; (read) blättern (through in + *Dat.*)
(c) (Comp.) suchen; ∼ through sth. etw. durchsuchen
⟨2⟩ (a) abgrasen ⟨*Weide*⟩; abfressen ⟨*Blätter*⟩
(b) (Comp.) ∼ sth in etw. (*Dat.*) suchen

browser /'braʊzə(r)/ *n.* (Comp.) Browser, *der*

bruise /bruːz/ 1 n. **(a)** (Med.) blauer Fleck
(b) (on fruit) Druckstelle, *die*
2 v.t. quetschen ⟨*Obst, Pflanzen*⟩;
~ **oneself/one's leg** sich stoßen/sich am
Bein stoßen

brunch /brʌntʃ/ n. (coll.) Brunch, *der;*
ausgedehntes, spätes Frühstück

brunette /bruːˈnet/ 1 n. Brünette, *die*
2 adj. brünett

brunt /brʌnt/ n. **bear the** ~ **of the attack/**
financial cuts von dem Angriff/von den
Einsparungen am meisten betroffen sein

brush /brʌʃ/ 1 n. **(a)** Bürste, *die;* (for
sweeping) Besen, *der;* (with short handle)
Handfeger, *der;* (for painting or writing) Pinsel, *der*
(b) (skirmish) Zusammenstoß, *der*
(c) (light touch) flüchtige Berührung
2 v.t. **(a)** kehren; fegen; abbürsten
⟨*Kleidung*⟩; ~ **one's teeth/hair** sich (*Dat.*)
die Zähne putzen/die Haare bürsten
(b) (touch in passing) streifen
3 v.i. ~ **past sb./sth.** jmdn./etw. streifen
■ **brush 'up** v.t. & i. ~ **up [on]** auffrischen
⟨*Kenntnisse usw.*⟩

brusque /brʌsk/ adj., **'brusquely** adv.
schroff

Brussels /ˈbrʌslz/ pr. n. Brüssel (*das*)

Brussels 'sprouts n. pl. Rosenkohl, *der*

brutal /ˈbruːtl/ adj. brutal

brutality /bruːˈtælɪtɪ/ n. Brutalität, *die*

brutally /ˈbruːtəlɪ/ adv. brutal

brute /bruːt/ 1 n. **(a)** (animal) Bestie, *die*
(b) (person) Rohling, *der*
2 attrib. adj. **by** ~ **force** mit roher Gewalt

B.Sc. abbr. = **Bachelor of Science**

BSE abbr. = **bovine spongiform**
encephalopathy BSE

BST abbr. = **British Summer Time**
Britische Sommerzeit

bubble /ˈbʌbl/ 1 n. Blase, *die;* (small)
Perle, *die*
2 v.i. ⟨*Wasser, Schlamm, Lava:*⟩ Blasen
bilden

bubble: ~ **bath** n. Schaumbad, *das;*
~ **pack** n. Klarsichtpackung, *die;*
~**-wrapped** adj. in Luftpolsterfolie
verpackt

buck[1] /bʌk/ n. (deer, chamois) Bock, *der;*
(rabbit, hare) Rammler, *der*

buck[2] n. **pass the** ~ **to sb.** jmdm. die
Verantwortung aufhalsen

buck[3] (coll.) 1 v.i. ~ **'up (a)** (make haste)
sich ranhalten (ugs.)
(b) (cheer up) ~ **up!** Kopf hoch!
2 v.t. ~ **one's ideas up** (coll.) sich
zusammenreißen

buck[4] n. (Amer. coll.) Dollar, *der*

bucket /ˈbʌkɪt/ n. Eimer, *der*

bucketful /ˈbʌkɪtfʊl/ n. Eimer [voll]

bucket: ~ **seat** n. Schalensitz,
der; ~ **shop** n. [nicht ganz seriöses]
Maklerbüro; (for air tickets) Reisebüro (*das vor*

allem Billigflüge vermittelt)

buckle /ˈbʌkl/ 1 n. Schnalle, *die*
2 v.t. **(a)** zuschnallen; ~ **sth. on/up** etw.
anschnallen/festschnallen
(b) verbiegen ⟨*Stoßstange, Rad*⟩
3 v.i. ⟨*Rad, Metallplatte:*⟩ [sich] verbiegen

bud /bʌd/ 1 n. Knospe, *die;* **come into** ~/**be**
in ~: Knospen treiben
2 v.i., -dd- Knospen treiben

Buddha /ˈbʊdə/ n. Buddha, *der*

Buddhism /ˈbʊdɪzm/ n. Buddhismus, *der*

Buddhist /ˈbʊdɪst/ 1 n. Buddhist,
der/Buddhistin, *die*
2 adj. buddhistisch

budge /bʌdʒ/ 1 v.i. sich rühren;
⟨*Gegenstand:*⟩ sich bewegen
2 v.t. bewegen

budgerigar /ˈbʌdʒərɪɡɑː(r)/ n.
Wellensittich, *der*

budget /ˈbʌdʒɪt/ 1 n. Etat, *der;*
Haushalt[splan], *der*
2 v.i. ~ **for sth.** etw. [im Etat] einplanen

budget: ~ **account** n. Konto für
laufende Zahlungen; ~ **'airline** n.
Billigfluglinie, *die*

budgie /ˈbʌdʒɪ/ n. (coll.) Wellensittich, *der*

buff /bʌf/ 1 adj. gelbbraun
2 n. (coll.: enthusiast) Fan, *der* (ugs.)

buffalo /ˈbʌfələʊ/ n., pl. ~**es** or same
Büffel, *der*

buffer /ˈbʌfə(r)/ n. Prellbock, *der;* (on vehicle;
also fig.) Puffer, *der*

buffet /ˈbʊfeɪ/ n. Büfett, *das*

'buffet car n. Büfettwagen, *der*

bug /bʌɡ/ n. (also coll.: microphone) Wanze, *die*

bugger /ˈbʌɡə(r)/ (coarse) 1 n. (as insult)
Scheißkerl, *der* (derb)
2 v.t. (damn) ~ **you/him** du kannst/der kann
mich mal (derb); ~ **it!** ach du Scheiße! (derb)
■ ~ **'off** v.i. abhauen (ugs.)

buggy /ˈbʌɡɪ/ n. (pushchair) Sportwagen, *der*

bugle /ˈbjuːɡl/ n. Bügelhorn, *das*

build /bɪld/ 1 v.t., **built** /bɪlt/ bauen; (fig.)
aufbauen ⟨*System, Gesellschaft, Zukunft*⟩
2 v.i., **built** bauen
3 n. Körperbau, *der*
■ **build 'in** v.t. einbauen
■ **build 'on** v.t. aufbauen auf (+ *Dat.*);
bebauen ⟨*Gebiet*⟩
■ **build 'up** 1 v.t. aufhäufen ⟨*Reserven,*
Mittel⟩; kräftigen ⟨*Personen, Körper*⟩;
steigern ⟨*Produktion, Kapazität*⟩; stärken
⟨*[Selbst]vertrauen*⟩; aufbauen ⟨*Firma,*
Geschäft⟩
2 v.i. ⟨*Spannung, Druck:*⟩ zunehmen;
⟨*Schlange, Rückstau:*⟩ sich bilden;
⟨*Verkehr:*⟩ sich verdichten

'builder n. Bauunternehmer, *der*

'building n. **(a)** Bau, *der*
(b) (structure) Gebäude, *das*

building: ~ **site** n. Baustelle, *die;*
~ **society** n. (Brit.) Bausparkasse, *die*

built ▶ BUILD 1, 2
built: ~**-in** *adj.* **(a)** eingebaut;
Einbau‹*schrank, -küche usw.*›; **(b)** (fig.:
instinctive) angeboren; ~**-up** *adj.* bebaut;
~**-up area** Wohngebiet, *das;* (Motor Veh.)
geschlossene Ortschaft
bulb /bʌlb/ *n.* **(a)** (Bot., Hort.) Zwiebel, *die*
(b) (of lamp) [Glüh]birne, *die*
Bulgaria /bʌl'geərɪə/ *pr. n.* Bulgarien
(*das*)
Bulgarian /bʌl'geərɪən/ ⟦1⟧ *adj.*
bulgarisch; **sb. is** ~: jmd. ist Bulgare/
Bulgarin
⟦2⟧ *n.* **(a)** (person) Bulgare, *der*/Bulgarin, *die*
(b) (language) Bulgarisch, *das; see also*
ENGLISH 2A
bulge /bʌldʒ/ ⟦1⟧ *n.* Ausbeulung, *die;*
ausgebeulte Stelle
⟦2⟧ *v.i.* sich wölben
bulimia (nervosa) /bʊ'liːmɪə
(nɜː'vəʊsə)/ *n.* Bulimie, *die;* Bulimia
nervosa, *die* (fachspr.)
bulimic /bʊ'lɪmɪk/ ⟦1⟧ *n.* Bulimiker,
der/Bulimikerin, *die*
⟦2⟧ *adj.* bulimisch
bulk /bʌlk/ *n.* **(a)** (large quantity) **in** ~: in
großen Mengen
(b) (large shape) massige Gestalt
(c) (size) Größe, *die*
(d) (greater part) der größte Teil; (of population,
votes) Mehrheit, *die*
bulk 'buying *n.* Großeinkauf, *der*
'**bulky** *adj.* sperrig ‹*Gegenstand*›; massig
‹*Gestalt, Körper*›
bull /bʊl/ *n.* Bulle, *der;* (esp. for bullfight) Stier,
der
bull: ~ **bar** *n.* Rammschutz, *der;*
Rammbügel, *der;* ~**dog** *n.* Bulldogge, *die*
bulldozer /'bʊldəʊzə(r)/ *n.* Planierraupe,
die
bullet /'bʊlɪt/ *n.* Kugel, *die*
'**bullet hole** *n.* Einschuss, *der;*
Einschussloch, *das*
bulletin /'bʊlɪtɪn/ *n.* Bulletin, *das*
'**bulletin board** *n.* (Comp.) schwarzes
Brett
'**bulletproof** *adj.* kugelsicher
bull: ~**fight** *n.* Stierkampf, *der;*
~**fighter** *n.* Stierkämpfer, *der;*
~**fighting** *n.* Stierkämpfe *Pl.*
bullion /'bʊljən/ *n.* **gold** ~: Goldbarren *Pl.*
'**bull neck** *n.* Stiernacken, *der*
bullock /'bʊlək/ *n.* Ochse, *der*
bull: ~**ring** *n.* Stierkampfarena, *die;*
~**seye** *n.* (of target) Schwarze, *das;* ~**shit**
(coarse) *n.* Scheiße, *die* (salopp abwertend)
bully /'bʊlɪ/ ⟦1⟧ *n.* (schoolboy etc.) ≈ Rabauke,
der; (boss) Tyrann, *der*
⟦2⟧ *v.t.* schikanieren; (frighten) einschüchtern
bullying /'bʊlɪŋ/ *n.* Schikanieren, *das*
bum¹ /bʌm/ *n.* (Brit. coll.) Hintern, *der* (ugs.)
bum² *n.* (Amer. coll.: tramp) Penner, *der* (salopp)

bumble-bee /'bʌmblbiː/ *n.* Hummel, *die*
bumf /bʌmf/ *n.* (Brit. coll. derog.: papers)
Papierkram, *der* (ugs.)
bump /bʌmp/ ⟦1⟧ *n.* **(a)** (sound) Bums, *der;*
(impact) Stoß, *der*
(b) (swelling) Beule, *die*
(c) (hump) Buckel, *der* (ugs.)
⟦2⟧ *adv.* bums
⟦3⟧ *v.t.* anstoßen
■ '**bump into** *v.t.* **(a)** stoßen an (+ *Akk.*)
(b) (meet by chance) zufällig [wieder]treffen
'**bumper** ⟦1⟧ *n.* Stoßstange, *die;* ~**-to-**~
Stoßstange an Stoßstange
⟦2⟧ *attrib. adj.* Rekord‹*ernte, -jahr*›
'**bumpy** *adj.* holp[e]rig ‹*Straße, Fahrt,*
Fahrzeug›; uneben ‹*Fläche*›; unruhig ‹*Flug*›
bun /bʌn/ *n.* süßes Brötchen; (currant ~)
Korinthenbrötchen, *das*
bunch /bʌntʃ/ *n.* **(a)** (of flowers) Strauß, *der;*
(of grapes, bananas) Traube, *die;* (of parsley,
radishes) Bund, *das;* ~ **of flowers**/**grapes**
Blumenstrauß, *der*/Traube, *die;* **a** ~ **of keys**
ein Schlüsselbund
(b) (lot) Anzahl, *die;* **the best** *or* **pick of the**
~: der/die/das Beste [von allen]
(c) (of people) Haufen, *der* (ugs.)
bundle /'bʌndl/ *n.* Bündel, *das;* (of papers)
Packen, *der*
bung /bʌŋ/ ⟦1⟧ *n.* Spund, *der*
⟦2⟧ *v.t.* (coll.) schmeißen (ugs.)
■ **bung 'up** *v.i.* be/get ~ed up verstopft
sein/verstopfen
bungalow /'bʌŋgələʊ/ *n.* Bungalow, *der*
'**bungee jumping** /'bʌndʒɪ/ *n.*
Bungeespringen, *das*
bungle /'bʌŋgl/ *v.t.* stümpern bei
bunk /bʌŋk/ *n.* (in ship, lorry) Koje, *die;* (in
sleeping car) Bett, *das;* (~ bed) Etagenbett, *das*
bunker /'bʌŋkə(r)/ *n.* Bunker, *der*
bunny /'bʌnɪ/ *n.* Häschen, *das*
buoy /bɔɪ/ *n.* Boje, *die*
buoyancy /'bɔɪənsɪ/ *n.* Auftrieb, *der*
buoyant /'bɔɪənt/ *adj.* **(a)** schwimmend;
be ~: schwimmen
(b) (fig.) rege, lebhaft ‹*Markt*›; heiter,
munter ‹*Person*›; **in** ~ **spirits** in
Hochstimmung
burden /'bɜːdn/ ⟦1⟧ *n.* Last, *die;* **become a**
~ (fig.) zur Last werden
⟦2⟧ *v.t.* belasten (**with** mit)
bureau /'bjʊərəʊ, bjʊə'rəʊ/ *n.* **(a)** (Brit.:
writing desk) Sekretär, *der*
(b) (office) Büro, *das*
bureaucracy /bjʊə'rɒkrəsɪ/ *n.*
Bürokratie, *die*
bureaucrat /'bjʊərəkræt/ *n.* Bürokrat,
der/Bürokratin, *die*
bureaucratic /bjʊərə'krætɪk/ *adj.*
bürokratisch
burger /'bɜːgə(r)/ *n.* (coll.) Hamburger, *der*
'**burger bar** *n.* (coll.) Hamburgerlokal, *das*
burglar /'bɜːglə(r)/ *n.* Einbrecher, *der*

burglar: ∼ **alarm** *n.* Alarmanlage, *die;*
∼**-proof** *adj.* einbruch[s]sicher
burglary /'bɜːglərɪ/ *n.* Einbruch, *der*
burgle /'bɜːgl/ *v.t.* einbrechen in (+ *Akk.*);
the shop/he was ∼d in dem Laden/bei ihm
wurde eingebrochen
burial /'berɪəl/ *n.* Begräbnis, *das*
burka /'bɜːkə/ *n.* Burka, *die*
burly /'bɜːlɪ/ *adj.* stämmig
Burma /'bɜːmə/ *pr. n.* Birma (*das*)
Burmese /bɜː'miːz/ ⟨1⟩ *adj.* birmanisch;
sb. is ∼: jmd. ist Birmane/Birmanin
⟨2⟩ *n., pl. same* **(a)** (person) Birmane,
der/Birmanin, *die*
(b) (language) Birmanisch, *das; see also*
ENGLISH 2A
burn /bɜːn/ ⟨1⟩ *n.* (on the skin) Verbrennung,
die; (on material) Brandfleck, *der*
⟨2⟩ *v.t.,* ∼t /bɜːnt/ *or* ∼ed **(a)** verbrennen;
∼ oneself/one's hand sich verbrennen/sich
(*Dat.*) die Hand verbrennen; ∼ a hole in sth.
ein Loch in etw. (*Akk.*) brennen
(b) als Brennstoff verwenden ⟨*Gas, Öl
usw.*⟩; heizen mit ⟨*Kohle, Holz, Torf*⟩
(c) (spoil) anbrennen lassen ⟨*Fleisch,
Kuchen*⟩; be ∼t angebrannt sein
(d) (Comp.) brennen ⟨*CD, CD-ROM*⟩
⟨3⟩ *v.i.,* ∼t *or* ∼ed brennen; ∼ to death
verbrennen; she ∼s easily sie bekommt
leicht einen Sonnenbrand
■ **burn** '**down** *v.t. & i.* niederbrennen
'**burned-out** *adj.* (lit. or fig.) ausgebrannt
'**burner** *n.* Brenner, *der*
'**burning** *adj.* glühend ⟨*Leidenschaft,
Hass, Wunsch*⟩; brennend ⟨*Wunsch, Frage,
Problem*⟩
'**burn-out** *n.* Burn-out, *das* (Med.);
totale Erschöpfung *od.* Entkräftung; risk
∼: Gefahr laufen, sich zu übernehmen
burnt ▸ BURN 2, 3
'**burnt-out** ▸ BURNED-OUT
burp /bɜːp/ (coll.) ⟨1⟩ *n.* Rülpser, *der* (ugs.)
⟨2⟩ *v.i.* rülpsen (ugs.)
burrow /'bʌrəʊ/ ⟨1⟩ *n.* Bau, *der*
⟨2⟩ *v.i.* [sich (*Dat.*)] einen Gang graben
burst /bɜːst/ ⟨1⟩ *n.* **(a)** (split) Bruch, *der*
(b) (of firing) Salve, *die*
(c) (fig.) a ∼ of applause/cheering ein
Beifallsausbruch/Beifallsrufe *Pl.*
⟨2⟩ *v.t.,* burst zum Platzen bringen; platzen
lassen ⟨*Luftballon*⟩; ∼ pipe Rohrbruch, *der*
⟨3⟩ *v.i.,* burst **(a)** platzen; ⟨*Bombe:*⟩
explodieren; ⟨*Damm:*⟩ brechen; ⟨*Flussufer:*⟩
überschwemmt werden; ⟨*Furunkel,
Geschwür:*⟩ aufgehen
(b) be ∼ing with sth. zum Bersten voll sein
mit etw.; be ∼ing with pride/impatience/
excitement vor Stolz/Ungeduld platzen/vor
Aufregung außer sich sein
■ '**burst into** *v.t.* **(a)** eindringen in
(b) ∼ into tears/laughter in Tränen/
Gelächter ausbrechen; ∼ into flames in
Brand geraten

■ **burst** '**out** *v.i.* **(a)** herausstürzen
(b) (exclaim) losplatzen
(c) ∼ out laughing/crying in Lachen/Tränen
ausbrechen
bury /'berɪ/ *v.t.* **(a)** begraben
(b) (hide) vergraben; ∼ one's face in one's
hands das Gesicht in den Händen vergraben
(c) ∼ one's teeth in sth. seine Zähne in etw.
(*Akk.*) graben
bus /bʌs/ *n.* Bus, *der*
bus: ∼ **company** *n.* ≈ Verkehrsbetrieb,
der; ∼ **conductor** *n.* Busschaffner, *der/*
-schaffnerin, *die;* ∼ **depot** ▸ ∼ GARAGE;
∼ **driver** *n.* Busfahrer, *der/*-fahrerin, *die;*
∼ **fare** *n.* [Bus]fahrpreis, *der;* ∼ **garage**
n. Busdepot, *das*
bush /bʊʃ/ *n.* **(a)** Busch, *der*
(b) (shrubs) Gebüsch, *das*
'**bushy** *adj.* buschig
busily /'bɪzɪlɪ/ *adj.* eifrig
business /'bɪznɪs/ *n.* **(a)** (trading operation)
Geschäft, *das;* (company, firm) Betrieb, *der;*
(large) Unternehmen, *das;* how's ∼ with
you? (lit. or fig.) was machen die Geschäfte
[bei Ihnen]?; ∼ is ∼ (fig.) Geschäft ist
Geschäft; go out of ∼: Pleite gehen (ugs.); go
into ∼: Geschäftsmann/-frau werden
(b) (buying and selling) Geschäfte *Pl.*
(c) (task, province) Aufgabe, *die;* mind your
own ∼! kümmere dich um deine [eigenen]
Angelegenheiten!
(d) (difficult matter) Problem, *das*
business: ∼ **address** *n.*
Geschäftsadresse, *die;* ∼ **card** *n.*
Geschäftskarte, *die;* ∼ **class** ⟨1⟩ *n.,*
no pl. Businessklasse, *die; attrib.*
Businessklasse-; ⟨2⟩ *adv.* fly/travel
∼ class in der Businessklasse fliegen/
reisen; ∼ **correspondence**
n. Geschäftskorrespondenz, *die;*
∼ **hours** *n. pl.* Geschäftszeit, *die;*
(in office) Dienstzeit, *die;* ∼ **letter**
n. Geschäftsbrief, *der;* ∼**-like** *adj.*
geschäftsmäßig ⟨*Art*⟩; geschäftstüchtig
⟨*Person*⟩; ∼ **lunch** *n.* Arbeitsessen,
das; ∼**man** *n.* Geschäftsmann, *der;*
∼ **park** *n.* Gewerbepark, *der;* ∼ **plan**
n. Geschäftsplan, *der;* ∼ **premises**
n. pl. Geschäftsräume *Pl.;* ∼ **school**
n. kaufmännische Fachschule;
∼ **studies** *n. pl.* Wirtschaftslehre,
die; ∼ **trip** *n.* Geschäftsreise, *die;* on a
∼ trip auf Geschäftsreise; ∼**woman** *n.*
Geschäftsfrau, *die*
busk /bʌsk/ *v.i.* Straßenmusik machen
busker /'bʌskə(r)/ *n.* Straßenmusikant,
der
bus: ∼ **lane** *n.* (Brit.) Busspur, *die;*
∼ **ride** *n.* Busfahrt, *die;* B. is only
an hour's ∼ ride away B. ist nur eine
Busstunde entfernt; ∼ **route** *n.* Buslinie,
die; ∼ **service** *n.* Omnibusverkehr,
der; (specific service) Busverbindung, *die;*
∼ **shelter** *n.* Wartehäuschen, *das;* ····⟩

∼ **station** n. Omnibusbahnhof, der;
∼ **stop** n. Bushaltestelle, die
bust[1] /bʌst/ n. (a) (sculpture) Büste, die
(b) ∼ [measurement] Oberweite, die
bust[2] (coll.) [1] adj. kaputt (ugs.)
[2] v.t., ∼ed or **bust** (break) kaputtmachen
(ugs.); ∼ **sth. open** etw. aufbrechen
[3] v.i., ∼ed or **bust** kaputtgehen (ugs.)
bus: ∼ **terminal** n. Busbahnhof,
der; ∼ **ticket** n. Busfahrkarte, die;
Busfahrschein, der
bustle /'bʌsl/ [1] v.i. ∼ **about** geschäftig
hin und her eilen
[2] n. Betrieb, der
bustling /'bʌslɪŋ/ adj. belebt ⟨Straße,
Stadt, Markt usw.⟩; rege ⟨Tätigkeit⟩
busy /'bɪzɪ/ [1] adj. (a) beschäftigt (at,
with mit); arbeitsreich ⟨Leben⟩; ziemlich
hektisch ⟨Zeit⟩; **I'm** ∼ **now** ich habe jetzt zu
tun; **he was** ∼ **packing** er war mit Packen
beschäftigt
(b) (Amer. Teleph.) besetzt
[2] v. refl. ∼ **oneself** sich beschäftigen (with
mit)
busybody n. G[e]schaftlhuber, der
but [1] /bət, stressed bʌt/ conj. aber; correcting
after a negative sondern; **not that book** ∼ **this**
one nicht das Buch, sondern dieses
[2] /bət/ prep. außer (+ Dat.); **the next/last**
∼ **one** der/die/das übernächste/vorletzte
butcher /'bʊtʃə(r)/ [1] n. Fleischer,
der/Fleischerin, die
[2] v.t. (murder) niedermetzeln
butler /'bʌtlə(r)/ n. Butler, der
butt[1] /bʌt/ n. (a) (of rifle) Kolben, der
(b) (of cigarette, cigar) Stummel, der
butt[2] n. (object of teasing or ridicule) Zielscheibe,
die
butt[3] [1] n. (push) (by person) [Kopf]stoß, der;
(by animal) Stoß [mit den Hörnern]
[2] v.t. & i. mit dem Kopf/den Hörnern
stoßen
■ **butt 'in** v.i. dazwischenreden
butter /'bʌtə(r)/ [1] n. Butter, die
[2] v.t. buttern
butter: ∼ **bean** n. Mondbohne, die;
∼**cup** n. Butterblume, die; ∼ **dish**
n. Butterdose, die; ∼**fingers** n. sing.
Tollpatsch, der ⟨beim Fangen usw.⟩;
∼**fly** n. (a) Schmetterling, der; (b) ∼**fly**
[stroke] Delphinstil, der; ∼ **mountain** n.
Butterberg, der
buttock /'bʌtək/ n. Hinterbacke, die;
Gesäßhälfte, die; ∼s Gesäß, das
button /'bʌtn/ [1] n. Knopf, der
[2] v.t. ∼ [up] zuknöpfen
buttonhole [1] n. (a) Knopfloch, das
(b) (flower) Knopflochblume, die
[2] v.t. zu fassen kriegen (ugs.)
buttress /'bʌtrɪs/ n. (Archit.) Mauerstütze,
die
buxom /'bʌksəm/ adj. drall
buy /baɪ/ [1] v.t., bought /bɔːt/ kaufen;

∼ **sb./oneself sth.** jmdm./sich etw. kaufen
[2] n. [Ein]kauf, der; **be a good** ∼: preiswert
sein
■ **buy 'up** v.t. aufkaufen
'buyer n. (a) Käufer, der/Käuferin, die
(b) (Commerc.) Einkäufer, der/Einkäuferin,
die
'buying power /'baɪɪŋ/ n. Kaufkraft, die
'buyout n. Aufkauf, der; Management-Buy-
Out, das (Wirtsch.)
buzz /bʌz/ [1] n. Summen, das
[2] v.i. summen
■ **buzz 'off** v.i. (coll.) abhauen (salopp)
'buzzer n. Summer, der
by /baɪ/ [1] prep. (a) (near, beside) an (+ Dat.);
bei; (next to) neben; ∼ **the window/river** am
Fenster/Fluss
(b) (to position beside) zu
(c) (about, in the possession of) bei
(d) [all] **by herself/himself** etc. [ganz]
allein[e]
(e) (along) entlang; (via) über (+ Akk.)
(f) (passing) vorbei an (+ Dat.)
(g) (during) bei; **by day/night** bei Tag/Nacht
(h) (through the agency of) von; **written by** ...:
geschrieben von ...
(i) (through the means of) durch; **by bus/ship**
etc. mit dem Bus/Schiff usw.; **by air/sea** mit
dem Flugzeug/Schiff
(j) (not later than) bis; **by now/this time**
inzwischen
(k) (indicating unit) pro; **by the minute/hour** pro
Minute/Stunde; **day by day/month by month**
Tag für Tag/Monat für Monat; **10 ft. by 20 ft.**
10 [Fuß] mal 20 Fuß
(l) (indicating amount) **one by one** einzeln; **two**
by two/three by three zu zweit/dritt
(m) (indicating factor) durch; **8 divided by 2 is 4**
8 geteilt durch 2 ist 4
(n) (indicating extent) um; **wider by a foot** um
einen Fuß breiter
(o) (according to) nach
[2] adv. (a) (past) vorbei
(b) (near) **close/near by** in der Nähe
(c) **by and large** im Großen und Ganzen
bye[-bye] /'baɪ(baɪ)/ int. (coll.) tschüs (ugs.)
bye-law ▶ BY-LAW
'by-election n. Nachwahl, die
bygone /'baɪgɒn/ adj. vergangen
'by-law n. (esp. Brit.) Verordnung, die
'bypass [1] n. (a) Umgehungsstraße, die
(b) (Med.) Bypass, der; ∼ **surgery** (Med.) eine
Bypassoperation/Bypassoperationen Pl.
[2] v.t. (a) **the road** ∼**es the town** die Straße
führt um die Stadt herum
(b) (fig.) übergehen
'by-product n. Nebenprodukt, das
'byroad n. Nebenstraße, die
bystander /'baɪstændə(r)/ n. Zuschauer,
der/Zuschauerin, die
byte /baɪt/ n. (Comp.) Byte, das
'byway n. Seitenweg, der
'byword n. Inbegriff, der (for Gen.)

Cc

C, c /siː/ *n.* C, c, *das*

C. *abbr.* (a) = **Celsius** C
(b) = **Centigrade** C

cab /kæb/ *n.* (a) (taxi) Taxi, *das*
(b) (of lorry, truck) Fahrerhaus, *das;* (of train) Führerstand, *der*

cabaret /'kæbəreɪ/ *n.* Varietee, *das;*
(satirical) Kabarett, *das*

cabbage /'kæbɪdʒ/ *n.* Kohl, *der;* red/white ∼: Rot-/Weißkohl, *der*

'cab driver *n.* Taxifahrer, *der*/-fahrerin, *die*

cabin /'kæbɪn/ *n.* (in ship) (for passengers) Kabine, *die;* (for crew) Kajüte, *die;* (in aircraft) Kabine, *die*

cabinet /'kæbɪnɪt/ *n.* (a) Schrank, *der;*
(in bathroom, for medicines) Schränkchen, *das;*
[display] ∼: Vitrine, *die*
(b) the C∼ (Polit.) das Kabinett; C∼ Minister Minister, *der*

cable /'keɪbl/ ① *n.* (a) (rope) Kabel, *das;* (of ∼ car etc.) Seil, *das*
(b) (Electr., Teleph.) Kabel, *das*
(c) (message) Kabel, *das*
② *v.t.* kabeln ⟨Mitteilung, Nachricht⟩

cable: ∼ **car** *n.* Drahtseilbahn, *die;* ∼ **'television,** ∼ **T'V** *ns.* Kabelfernsehen, *das*

'cab rank *n.* (Brit.) Taxistand, *der;* Droschken[halte]platz, *der* (Amtsspr.)

cache /kæʃ/ *n.* (a) (hiding place) geheimes [Waffen-/Proviant-]lager
(b) (Comp.) Cache, *der*

cackle /'kækl/ ① *n.* (a) (of hen) Gackern, *das*
(b) (laughter) [meckerndes] Gelächter
② *v.i.* (a) ⟨Henne:⟩ gackern
(b) (laugh) meckernd lachen

cactus /'kæktəs/ *n., pl.* **cacti** /'kæktaɪ/ *or* ∼es Kaktus, *der*

CAD *abbr.* = **computer-aided design** CAD

caddie /'kædɪ/ *n.* (Golf) Caddie, *der*

caddy /'kædɪ/ *n.* Dose, *die*

cadet /kə'det/ *n.* Offiziersschüler, *der;* naval/police ∼: Marinekadett/Anwärter für den Polizeidienst

cadge /kædʒ/ *v.t.* [sich ⟨Dat.⟩] erbetteln

café, cafe /'kæfeɪ/ *n.* Lokal, *das;* (tea room) Café, *das*

cafeteria /kæfɪ'tɪərɪə/ *n.* Cafeteria, *die*

cafetière /kæfə'tjeə/ *n.* Kaffeebereiter, *der*

caffeinated /'kæfɪneɪtɪd/ *adj.* koffeinhaltig

caffeine /'kæfiːn/ *n.* Koffein, *das*

cage /keɪdʒ/ ① *n.* (a) Käfig, *der*
(b) (of lift) Fahrkabine, *die*
② *v.t.* einsperren

cagey /'keɪdʒɪ/ *adj.* (coll.) zugeknöpft (ugs.); be ∼ about sth. mit etw. hinterm Berg halten (ugs.)

Cairo /'kaɪərəʊ/ *pr. n.* Kairo (*das*)

cajole /kə'dʒəʊl/ *v.t.* ∼ sb. into sth./doing sth. jmdm. etw. einreden/jmdm. einreden, etw. zu tun

cake /keɪk/ ① *n.* Kuchen, *der;* a ∼ of soap ein Riegel *od.* Stück Seife
② *v.t.* verkrusten; ∼d with dirt/blood schmutz-/blutverkrustet

cal. *abbr.* = **calorie[s]** cal.

calamity /kə'læmɪtɪ/ *n.* Unheil, *das*

calcium /'kælsɪəm/ *n.* Kalzium, *das*

calculate /'kælkjʊleɪt/ ① *v.t.*
(a) berechnen; (by estimating) ausrechnen
(b) be ∼d to do sth. darauf abzielen, etw. zu tun
② *v.i.* ∼ on doing sth. damit rechnen, etw. zu tun

'calculated *adj.* kalkuliert ⟨Risiko⟩; vorsätzlich ⟨Handlung⟩

calculation /kælkjʊ'leɪʃn/ *n.* (a) (result) Rechnung, *die;* he is out in his ∼s er hat sich verrechnet
(b) (calculating) Berechnung, *die*

calculator /'kælkjʊleɪtə(r)/ *n.* Rechner, *der*

calculus /'kælkjuːləs/ *n.* differential/ integral ∼: Differenzial-/Integralrechnung, *die*

calendar /'kælɪndə(r)/ *n.* Kalender, *der;* *attrib.* Kalender-

calf[1] /kɑːf/ *n., pl.* **calves** Kalb, *das*

calf[2] *n., pl.* **calves** (Anat.) Wade, *die*

calibre (Brit.; Amer.: **caliber**) /'kælɪbə(r)/ *n.* Kaliber, *das*

calico /'kælɪkəʊ/ *n.* Kattun, *der*

California /kælɪ'fɔːnɪə/ *pr. n.* Kalifornien (*das*)

caliper ▶ CALLIPER

call /kɔːl/ ① *v.i.* (a) rufen; ∼ to sb. jmdm. etwas zurufen; ∼ [out] for help um Hilfe rufen
(b) (pay brief visit) [kurz] besuchen (at *Akk.*); ∼ on sb. jmdn. besuchen; ∼ round vorbeikommen (ugs.); ∼ at a port/station einen Hafen anlaufen/an einem Bahnhof halten
(c) (Teleph.) who is ∼ing, please? wer spricht da, bitte?; thank you for ∼ing vielen Dank für Ihren Anruf! ⋯▶

2 *v.t.* **(a)** rufen; aufrufen ⟨Namen, Nummer⟩
(b) (cry to, summon) rufen; (to a duty, to do sth.) aufrufen
(c) (by radio/telephone) rufen/anrufen; (initially) Kontakt aufnehmen mit
(d) (rouse) wecken
(e) einberufen ⟨Konferenz⟩; ausrufen ⟨Streik⟩
(f) (name) nennen; **he is ~ed Bob** er heißt Bob; **what is it ~ed in English?** wie heißt das auf Englisch?
3 *n.* **(a)** Ruf, *der;* **a ~ for help** ein Hilferuf; **be on ~:** Bereitschaftsdienst haben
(b) (visit) Besuch, *der;* **make** *or* **pay a ~ on sb., make** *or* **pay sb. a ~:** jmdn. besuchen
(c) (telephone ~) Anruf, *der;* **give sb. a ~:** jmdn. anrufen; **make a ~:** telefonieren
(d) (invitation, summons) Aufruf, *der*
(e) (need, occasion) Anlass, *der*
■ **call 'back** **1** *v.t.* zurückrufen
2 *v.i.* zurückrufen; (come back) zurückkommen
■ **'call for** *v.t.* **(a)** (send for, order) bestellen
(b) (collect) abholen
(c) (require, demand) erfordern; **this ~s for a celebration** das muss gefeiert werden
■ **call 'in** **1** *v.i.* vorbeikommen (ugs.) (on bei)
2 *v.t.* zu Rate ziehen ⟨Fachmann usw.⟩
■ **call 'off** *v.t.* absagen ⟨Treffen, Verabredung⟩; rückgängig machen ⟨Geschäft⟩; lösen ⟨Verlobung⟩; (end) abbrechen ⟨Streik⟩
■ **'call on** *v.t.* **(a)** ▶ ~ 1B
(b) ▶ ~ [UP]ON
■ **call 'out** **1** *v.t.* alarmieren ⟨Truppen⟩; zum Streik aufrufen ⟨Arbeitnehmer⟩
2 *v.i.* ▶ ~ 1A
■ **call 'up** *v.t.* **(a)** (by telephone) anrufen
(b) (Mil.) einberufen
■ **'call [up]on** *v.t.* **~ upon sb.'s generosity** an jmds. Großzügigkeit (*Akk.*) appellieren; **~ [up]on sb. to do sth.** jmdn. auffordern, etw. zu tun
'call box *n.* Telefonzelle, *die*
'caller *n.* (visitor) Besucher, *der*/Besucherin, *die;* (on telephone) Anrufer, *der*/Anruferin, *die*
'call girl *n.* Callgirl, *das*
'calling *n.* Beruf, *der*
calliper /'kælɪpə(r)/ *n.* **(a)** **[a pair of] ~s** Tasterzirkel, *der*
(b) (Med.) Beinschiene, *die*
callous /'kæləs/ *adj.* gefühllos; herzlos ⟨Handlung, Verhalten⟩
'call-up *n.* (Mil.) Einberufung, *die*
calm /kɑːm/ **1** *n.* (stillness) Stille, *die;* (serenity) Ruhe, *die*
2 *adj.* ruhig
3 *v.t.* **~ sb. [down]** jmdn. beruhigen
4 *v.i.* **~ [down]** sich beruhigen
'calmly *adv.* ruhig; gelassen
'calmness *n.* Ruhe, *die;* (of water) Stille, *die*
Calor gas ® /'kælə gæs/ *n.* Butangas, *das*

calorie /'kælərɪ/ *n.* Kalorie, *die*
calorific /kælə'rɪfɪk/ *adj.* **~ value** Heizwert, *der*
calves *pl.* of CALF[1, 2]
CAM *abbr.* = **computer-aided manufacturing** CAM
camber /'kæmbə(r)/ *n.* Wölbung, *die*
camcorder /'kæmkɔːdə(r)/ *n.* Camcorder, *der;* Kamerarecorder, *der*
came ▶ COME
camel /'kæml/ *n.* Kamel, *das*
camera /'kæmərə/ *n.* Kamera, *die*
camera: ~ case *n.* Kameratasche, *die;* **~ crew** *n.* Kamerateam, *das;* **~man** *n.* Kameramann, *der;* **~work** *n., no indef. art.* Kameraführung, *die*
camomile /'kæməmaɪl/ *n.* Kamille, *die;* **~ tea** Kamillentee, *der*
camouflage /'kæməflɑːʒ/ **1** *n.* Tarnung, *die*
2 *v.t.* tarnen
camp /kæmp/ **1** *n.* Lager, *das*
2 *v.i.* **~ [out]** campen; (in tent) zelten; **go ~ing** Campen/Zelten fahren/gehen
campaign /kæm'peɪn/ **1** *n.* **(a)** (Mil.) Feldzug, *der*
(b) (organized action) Kampagne, *die;* **publicity ~:** Werbekampagne, *die*
2 *v.i.* **~ for/against sth.** sich für etw. einsetzen/gegen etw. etwas unternehmen; **be ~ing** ⟨Politiker:⟩ im Wahlkampf stehen
'camp bed *n.* Campingliege, *die*
'camper *n.* **(a)** (person) Camper, *der*/Camperin, *die*
(b) (vehicle) **~ [van]** Wohnmobil, *das*
'campfire *n.* Lagerfeuer, *das*
'camping *n.* Camping, *das;* (in tent) Zelten, *das*
camping: ~ ground ▶ ~ SITE; **~ holiday** *n.* Campingurlaub, *der;* **~ site** *n.* Campingplatz, *der;* **~ stove** *n.* Campingkocher, *der*
'campsite *n.* Campingplatz, *der*
campus /'kæmpəs/ *n.* Campus, *der*
can[1] /kæn/ **1** *n.* **(a)** (milk ~, watering ~) Kanne, *die;* (for oil, petrol) Kanister, *der;* (Amer.: for refuse) Eimer, *der*
(b) (for preserving) [Konserven]dose, *die;* **a ~ of tomatoes/beer** eine Dose Tomaten/Bier
2 *v.t.,* **-nn-** konservieren
can[2] /kən, *stressed* kæn/ *v. aux., only in pres.* **can**, *neg.* **cannot** /'kænɒt/, (coll.) **can't** /kɑːnt/, *past* **could** /kʊd/, *neg.* (coll.) **couldn't** /'kʊdnt/ können; (have right, be permitted) dürfen; können; **I can't do that** das kann ich nicht; (it would be wrong) das kann ich nicht tun; **you can't smoke here** hier dürfen Sie nicht rauchen; **could you ring me tomorrow?** könnten Sie mich morgen anrufen?; **I could have killed him** ich hätte ihn umbringen können; **[that] could be [so]** das könnte *od.* kann sein

Canada /'kænədə/ *pr. n.* Kanada (*das*)
Canadian /kə'neɪdɪən/ ⓵ *adj.* kanadisch;
sb. is ~: jmd. ist Kanadier/Kanadierin
⓶ *n.* Kanadier, *der*/Kanadierin, *die*
canal /kə'næl/ *n.* Kanal, *der*
canary /kə'neərɪ/ *n.* Kanarienvogel, *der*
Ca'nary Islands *pr. n. pl.* Kanarische
Inseln *Pl.*
cancel /'kænsl/ ⓵ *v.t.,* (Brit.) -ll-
(a) absagen ⟨*Besuch, Urlaub, Reise,
Sportveranstaltung*⟩; ausfallen lassen
⟨*Veranstaltung, Vorlesung, Zug, Bus*⟩;
fallen lassen ⟨*Pläne*⟩; rückgängig machen
⟨*Einladung, Vertrag*⟩; zurücknehmen
⟨*Befehl*⟩; stornieren ⟨*Bestellung, Auftrag*⟩;
kündigen ⟨*Abonnement*⟩; abbestellen
⟨*Zeitung*⟩
(b) (Comp.) abbrechen
⓶ *v.i.,* (Brit.) -ll-: (a) ~ [out] sich
[gegenseitig] aufheben
(b) (Comp.) abbrechen
cancellation /kænsə'leɪʃn/ *n.*
▶ CANCEL 1 A: Absage, *die;* Ausfall, *der;*
Fallenlassen, *das;* Rückgängigmachen,
das; Zurücknahme, *die;* Stornierung, *die;*
Kündigung, *die;* Abbestellung, *die*
cancer /'kænsə(r)/ *n.* (a) (Med.) Krebs, *der;*
~ **of the liver** Leberkrebs, *der*
(b) **C**~ (Astrol., Astron.) der Krebs
candelabra /kændɪ'lɑːbrə/ *n.* Leuchter,
der
candid /'kændɪd/ *adj.* offen; ehrlich
⟨*Ansicht, Bericht*⟩
candidate /'kændɪdət, 'kændɪdeɪt/ *n.*
Kandidat, *der*/Kandidatin, *die*
candle /'kændl/ *n.* Kerze, *die*
candle: ~**light** *n.* Kerzenlicht, *das;*
~**stick** *n.* Kerzenhalter, *der;* (elaborate)
Leuchter, *der;* ~**wick** *n.* (material)
Frottierplüsch, *der*
candour (*Brit., Amer.:* **candor**)
/'kændə(r)/ *n.* ▶ CANDID: Offenheit, *die;*
Ehrlichkeit, *die*
candy /'kændɪ/ *n.* (Amer.) (sweets)
Süßigkeiten *Pl.;* (sweet) Bonbon, *das od. der*
'candyfloss /'kændɪflɒs/ *n.* Zuckerwatte,
die
cane /keɪn/ ⓵ *n.* (a) (stem) Rohr, *das;* (of
raspberry, blackberry) Spross, *der*
(b) (material) Rohr, *das*
(c) (stick) [Rohr]stock, *der*
⓶ *v.t.* [mit dem Stock] schlagen
'cane sugar *n.* Rohrzucker, *der*
canine /'keɪnaɪn/ *adj.* (a) (of dog[s]) Hunde-
(b) ~ **tooth** Eckzahn, *der*
canister /'kænɪstə(r)/ *n.* Büchse, *die;* (for
petrol, oil, etc.) Kanister, *der*
cannabis /'kænəbɪs/ *n.* (hashish)
Haschisch, *das;* (marijuana) Marihuana, *das*
canned /kænd/ *adj.* Dosen-; in Dosen
nachgestellt; ~ **meat/fruit** Fleisch-/
Obstkonserven *Pl.;* ~ **beer** Dosenbier;
~ **food** [Lebensmittel]konserven *Pl.;*

~ **music** Musikkonserve, *die*
cannibal /'kænɪbl/ *n.* Kannibale,
der/Kannibalin, *die*
cannibalism /'kænɪbəlɪzm/ *n.*
Kannibalismus, *der*
cannon /'kænən/ ⓵ *n.* Kanone, *die*
⓶ *v.i.* (Brit.) ~ **into sb./sth.** mit etw./jmdm.
zusammenprallen
'cannon ball *n.* Kanonenkugel, *die*
cannot ▶ CAN²
canny /'kænɪ/ *adj.* (shrewd) schlau
canoe /kə'nuː/ *n.* Paddelboot, *das;* (Indian
~, Sport) Kanu, *das*
canoeing /kə'nuːɪŋ/ *n.* Paddeln, *das;*
(Sport) Kanufahren, *das;* Kanusport, *der*
canoeist /kə'nuːɪst/ *n.* Paddelbootfahrer,
der/-fahrerin, *die*
canon /'kænən/ *n.* (a) (general law, criterion)
Grundregel, *die*
(b) (Eccl.: person) Kanoniker, *der*
canonize /'kænənaɪz/ *v.t.* kanonisieren
⟨*Heiligen*⟩; heilig sprechen ⟨*Märtyrer*⟩
'can-opener *n.* Dosenöffner, *der*
canopy /'kænəpɪ/ *n.* Baldachin, *der;* (over
entrance) Vordach, *das*
can't /kɑːnt/ (coll.) = CANNOT; ▶ CAN²
cantankerous /kæn'tæŋkərəs/ *adj.*
streitsüchtig
canteen /kæn'tiːn/ *n.* Kantine, *die*
canter /'kæntə(r)/ ⓵ *n.* Handgalopp, *der*
⓶ *v.i.* leicht galoppieren
canvas /'kænvəs/ *n.* Leinwand, *die*
canvass /'kænvəs/ ⓵ *v.t.* Wahlwerbung
treiben in ⟨*einem Wahlkreis, Gebiet*⟩;
Wahlwerbung treiben bei ⟨*Wählern,
Bürgern*⟩
⓶ *v.i.* werben (**on behalf of** für); ~ **for votes**
um Stimmen werben
'canvasser *n.* (for votes) Wahlhelfer, *der*/
-helferin, *die*
canyon /'kænjən/ *n.* Cañon, *der*
cap /kæp/ ⓵ *n.* (a) Mütze, *die;* (nurse's,
servant's) Haube, *die;* (with peak) Schirmmütze,
die; (skull~) Kappe, *die*
(b) (of bottle, jar) [Verschluss]kappe, *die;* (petrol
~, radiator ~) Deckel, *der*
⓶ *v.t.,* -pp-: (a) verschließen ⟨*Flasche*⟩;
zudecken ⟨*Bohrloch*⟩; mit einer Schutzkappe
versehen ⟨*Zahn*⟩
(b) (fig.) überbieten; **to** ~ **it all** obendrein
CAP *abbr.* = **Common Agricultural
Policy** gemeinsame Agrarpolitik
capability /keɪpə'bɪlɪtɪ/ *n.* Fähigkeit, *die*
capable /'keɪpəbl/ *adj.* (a) **be** ~ **of sth.**
⟨*Person:*⟩ zu etw. imstande sein
(b) (gifted, able) fähig
capacity /kə'pæsɪtɪ/ *n.*
(a) Fassungsvermögen, *das;* **the machine
is working to** ~: die Maschine ist voll
ausgelastet; **a seating** ~ **of 300** 300 Sitzplätze
(b) (measure) Rauminhalt, *der;* Volumen,
das; **measure of** ~: Hohlmaß, *das* ⋯⟫

(c) (position) Eigenschaft, *die;* **in his ~ as ...:** in seiner Eigenschaft als ...

cape¹ /keɪp/ *n.* (garment) Umhang, *der;* Cape, *das*

cape² *n.* (Geog.) Kap, *das;* **the C~** [of Good Hope] das Kap der Guten Hoffnung; **C~ Town** Kapstadt (*das*)

caper /'keɪpə(r)/ *v.i.* **~ [about]** [herum]tollen

capful /'kæpfʊl/ *n.* **one ~:** der Inhalt einer Verschlusskappe

capillary /kə'pɪlərɪ/ *n.* Kapillare, *die* (fachspr.)

capital /'kæpɪtl/ ① *attrib. adj.* **(a)** Todes⟨strafe, -urteil⟩; Kapital⟨verbrechen⟩ **(b)** groß, Groß⟨buchstabe⟩ **(c)** (principal) Haupt⟨stadt⟩ ② *n.* **(a)** (letter) Großbuchstabe, *der* **(b)** (city, town) Hauptstadt, *die* **(c)** (stock, wealth) Kapital, *das*

capitalism /'kæpɪtəlɪzm/ *n.* Kapitalismus, *der*

capitalist /'kæpɪtəlɪst/ ① *n.* Kapitalist, *der*/Kapitalistin, *die* ② *adj.* kapitalistisch

capitalize /'kæpɪtəlaɪz/ ① *v.t.* großschreiben ⟨Buchstaben, Wort⟩ ② *v.i.* **~ on sth.** aus etw. Kapital schlagen (ugs.)

capital 'punishment *n.* Todesstrafe, *die*

capitulate /kə'pɪtjʊleɪt/ *v.i.* kapitulieren

capitulation /kəpɪtjʊ'leɪʃn/ *n.* Kapitulation, *die*

cappuccino /kɑːpʊ'tʃiːnəʊ/ *n., pl.* **~s** Cappuccino, *der*

capricious /kə'prɪʃəs/ *adj.* launisch

Capricorn /'kæprɪkɔːn/ *n.* (Astrol., Astron.) der Steinbock

capsize /kæp'saɪz/ ① *v.t.* zum Kentern bringen ② *v.i.* kentern

'caps lock *n.* Feststelltaste, *die*

capsule /'kæpsjuːl/ *n.* Kapsel, *die*

Capt. *abbr.* = **Captain** Kapt.; Hptm.

captain /'kæptɪn/ ① *n.* Kapitän, *der;* (Army) Hauptmann, *der* ② *v.t.* **~ a team** Kapitän einer Mannschaft sein

caption /'kæpʃn/ *n.* (heading) Überschrift, *die;* (under photograph, drawing) Bildunterschrift, *die;* (Cinemat., Telev.) Untertitel, *der*

captivate /'kæptɪveɪt/ *v.t.* fesseln

captivating /'kæptɪveɪtɪŋ/ *adj.* bezaubernd; einnehmend ⟨Lächeln⟩

captive /'kæptɪv/ ① *adj.* gefangen; **be taken ~:** gefangen genommen werden; **~ audience** unfreiwilliges Publikum ② *n.* Gefangener, *der*/Gefangene, *die*

captivity /kæp'tɪvɪtɪ/ *n.* Gefangenschaft, *die;* **be held in ~:** gefangen gehalten werden

captor /'kæptə(r)/ *n.* **his ~:** der, der/die, die ihn gefangen nahm

capture /'kæptʃə(r)/ ① *n.* **(a)** (of thief etc.) Festnahme, *die;* (of town) Einnahme, *die* **(b)** (thing, person) Fang, *der* ② *v.t.* festnehmen ⟨Person⟩; [ein]fangen ⟨Tier⟩; einnehmen ⟨Stadt⟩; gefangen nehmen ⟨Fantasie⟩

car /kɑː(r)/ *n.* Auto, *das;* Wagen, *der;* **by ~:** mit dem Auto

carafe /kə'ræf/ *n.* Karaffe, *die*

caramel /'kærəmel/ *n.* Karamell, *der;* (toffee) Karamellbonbon, *das*

carat /'kærət/ *n.* Karat, *das;* **a 22-~ gold ring** ein 22-karätiger Goldring

caravan /'kærəvæn/ *n.* (Brit.) Wohnwagen, *der*

'caravan site *n.* Campingplatz für Wohnwagen

carbohydrate /kɑːbəʊ'haɪdreɪt/ *n.* Kohlenhydrat, *das*

'car bomb *n.* Autobombe, *die*

carbon /'kɑːbən/ *n.* Kohlenstoff, *der*

carbon: ~ 'copy *n.* Durchschlag, *der;* **~ 'cycle** *n.* Kohlenstoffkreislauf, *der;* **~ dioxide** /- daɪ'ɒksaɪd/ *n.* Kohlendioxid, *das;* **~ 'footprint** *n.* CO_2-Bilanz, *die;* **~ monoxide** /- mə'nɒksaɪd/ *n.* (Chem.) Kohlenmonoxid *das;* **~-'neutral** *adj.* CO_2-neutral; **~ 'offsetting** *n.* CO_2-Ausgleich, *der;* **~ paper** *n.* Kohlepapier, *das;* **~ tax** *n.* CO_2-Steuer, *die;* **~ 'trading** *n.* CO_2-Handel, *der*

car 'boot sale *n.:* Trödelmarkt, bei dem die Händler ihre Waren aus dem Kofferraum ihrer Autos heraus verkaufen

carburettor (*Amer.:* **carburetor**) /kɑːbə'retə(r)/ *n.* Vergaser, *der*

carcass (*Brit. also:* **carcase**) /'kɑːkəs/ *n.* Kadaver, *der*

'car crash *n.* Autounfall, *der*

card /kɑːd/ *n.* Karte, *die;* **play ~s** Karten spielen

card: ~board *n.* Pappe, *die;* **~board 'box** *n.* [Papp]karton, *der;* (smaller) [Papp]schachtel, *die;* **~ game** *n.* Kartenspiel, *das;* **~holder** *n.* Karteninhaber, *der/*-inhaberin, *die*

cardiac /'kɑːdɪæk/ *adj.* (of heart) Herz-

cardiac ar'rest *n.* Herzstillstand, *der*

cardigan /'kɑːdɪɡən/ *n.* Strickjacke, *die*

cardinal /'kɑːdɪnl/ ① *adj.* grundlegend ⟨Frage, Doktrin, Pflicht⟩; Kardinal⟨fehler, -problem⟩; Haupt⟨punkt, -merkmal⟩ ② *n.* (Eccl.) Kardinal, *der*

cardinal: ~ 'number *n.* Kardinalzahl, *die;* **~ 'sin** *n.* Todsünde, *die*

'cardphone *n.* Kartentelefon, *das*

care /keə(r)/ ① *n.* **(a)** (anxiety) Sorge, *die* **(b)** (pains) Sorgfalt, *die* **(c)** (caution) Vorsicht, *die;* **take ~:** aufpassen **(d)** **medical ~:** ärztliche Betreuung

(e) (charge) Obhut, *die* (geh.); **put sb. in ~/take sb. into ~:** jmdn. in Pflege geben/nehmen; **~ of** (on letter) bei; **take ~ of sb./sth.** (ensure safety of) auf jmdn./etw. aufpassen; (attend to) sich um jmdn./etw. kümmern
⎾2⏋ *v.i.* **~ for sb./sth.** (look after) sich um jmdn./etw. kümmern; (like) jmdn./etw. mögen; **~ to do sth.** etw. tun mögen; **I don't ~ [whether/how/what** *etc.*] es ist mir gleich[, ob/wie/was *usw.*]
career /kə'rɪə(r)/ ⎾1⏋ *n.* Beruf, *der*
⎾2⏋ *v.i.* rasen; ⟨*Pferd, Reiter:*⟩ galoppieren
career: ~ break *n.* Karriereknick, *der;* **~s adviser** *n.* Berufsberater, *der*/ -beraterin, *die;* **~s [advisory] service** *n.* Berufsberatung, *die;* **~ woman** *n.* Karrierefrau, *die*
'carefree *adj.* sorgenfrei
careful /'keəfl/ *adj.* (thorough) sorgfältig; (cautious) vorsichtig; **[be] ~!** Vorsicht!; **be ~ of sb./sth.** (be cautious of) sich vor jmdn./ etw. in Acht nehmen; **be ~ with sb./sth.** vorsichtig mit jmdn./etw. umgehen
'carefully *adv.* (thoroughly) sorgfältig; (attentively) aufmerksam; (cautiously) vorsichtig
careless /'keəlɪs/ *adj.* **(a)** (inattentive) unaufmerksam; (thoughtless) gedankenlos; leichtsinnig ⟨*Fahrer*⟩; nachlässig ⟨*Arbeiter, Arbeit*⟩; gedankenlos ⟨*Bemerkung, Handlung*⟩; unachtsam ⟨*Fahren*⟩ **(b)** (nonchalant) ungezwungen
'carelessly *adv.* (without care) nachlässig; (thoughtlessly) gedankenlos
'carelessness *n.* (lack of care) Nachlässigkeit, *die;* (thoughtlessness) Gedankenlosigkeit, *die*
carer /'keərə(r)/ *n.* (for sick person) Pfleger, *der*/Pflegerin, *die*
caress /kə'res/ ⎾1⏋ *n.* Liebkosung, *die*
⎾2⏋ *v.t.* liebkosen
'caretaker *n.* Hausmeister, *der*/ -meisterin, *die*
'car ferry *n.* Autofähre, *die*
cargo /'kɑːgəʊ/ *n.* Fracht, *die*
'cargo boat, 'cargo ship *ns.* Frachter, *der*
'car hire *n.* Autovermietung, *die*
Caribbean /kærɪ'biːən/ ⎾1⏋ *n.* **the ~:** die Karibik
⎾2⏋ *adj.* karibisch
caricature /'kærɪkətjʊə(r)/ ⎾1⏋ *n.* Karikatur, *die*
⎾2⏋ *v.t.* karikieren
caring /'keərɪŋ/ *adj.* sozial ⟨*Gesellschaft*⟩; fürsorglich ⟨*Person*⟩
carnage /'kɑːnɪdʒ/ *n.* Gemetzel, *das*
carnal /'kɑːnl/ *adj.* sinnlich
carnation /kɑː'neɪʃn/ *n.* [Garten]nelke, *die*
carnet /'kɑːneɪ/ *n.* (of motorist) Triptyk, *das;* **[camping] ~:** Ausweis für Camper

carnival /'kɑːnɪvl/ *n.* Volksfest, *das*
carnivorous /kɑː'nɪvərəs/ *adj.* Fleisch fressend
carol /'kærl/ *n.* **[Christmas] ~:** Weihnachtslied, *das*
'car owner *n.* Autobesitzer, *der*/ -besitzerin, *die*
carp /kɑːp/ *n., pl. same* Karpfen, *der*
car: ~ park *n.* Parkplatz, *der;* (building) Parkhaus, *das;* **~ parking** *n.* Parken, *das;* **~ parking facilities are available** Parkplätze [sind] vorhanden
carpenter /'kɑːpɪntə(r)/ *n.* Zimmermann, *der;* (for furniture) Tischler, *der*/Tischlerin, *die*
carpentry /'kɑːpɪntrɪ/ *n.* Zimmerhandwerk, *das;* (in furniture) Tischlerhandwerk, *das*
carpet /'kɑːpɪt/ *n.* Teppich, *der*
carpet: ~ slipper *n.* Hausschuh, *der;* **~ sweeper** *n.* Teppichkehrer, *der*
car: ~ phone *n.* Autotelefon, *das;* **~port** *n.* Einstellplatz, *der;* **~ radio** *n.* Autoradio, *das;* **~ rental** ▶ CAR HIRE
carriage /'kærɪdʒ/ *n.* **(a)** (horse-drawn) Kutsche, *die* **(b)** (Railw.) Wagen, *der*
'carriageway *n.* Fahrbahn, *die*
'car ride *n.* Autofahrt, *die*
carrier /'kærɪə(r)/ *n.* **(a)** (bearer) Träger, *der* **(b)** (firm) Transportunternehmen, *das*
carrier: ~ bag *n.* Tragetasche, *die;* **~ pigeon** *n.* Brieftaube, *die*
carrot /'kærət/ *n.* Möhre, *die*
carry /'kærɪ/ *v.t.* **(a)** tragen; (emphasizing destination) bringen **(b)** (possess) besitzen ⟨*Autorität, Gewicht*⟩
■ **carry a'way** *v.t.* forttragen; **be** *or* **get carried away** sich hinreißen lassen
■ **carry 'on** ⎾1⏋ *v.t.* fortführen; **~ on [doing sth.]** weiterhin etw. tun
⎾2⏋ *v.i.* weitermachen
■ **carry 'out** *v.t.* durchführen; ausführen ⟨*Anweisung, Auftrag*⟩; vornehmen ⟨*Verbesserungen*⟩
carry: ~cot *n.* Babytragetasche, *die;* **~-out** *n.* **~-out [meal]** Essen *od.* Mahlzeit zum Mitnehmen; **get a ~-out** sich (*Dat.*) in einem Restaurant was zu essen holen
'carsick *adj.* **children are often ~:** Kindern wird beim Autofahren oft schlecht
cart /kɑːt/ ⎾1⏋ *n.* Wagen, *der*
⎾2⏋ *v.t.* (coll.) schleppen
'car thief *n.* Autodieb, *der*/-diebin, *die*
cartilage /'kɑːtɪlɪdʒ/ *n.* Knorpel, *der*
carton /'kɑːtn/ *n.* **[Papp]karton, *der;* (of drink) Tüte, *die;* (of cream, yoghurt) Becher, *der*
cartoon /kɑː'tuːn/ *n.* humoristische Zeichnung; (satirical) Karikatur, *die;* (film) Zeichentrickfilm, *der*
cartridge /'kɑːtrɪdʒ/ *n.* **(a)** (for gun) Patrone, *die* **(b)** (of film; cassette) Kassette, *die*

'cartwheel *n.* (Gymnastics) Rad, *das;* **turn** *or* do **∼s** Radschlagen

carve /kɑːv/ ① *v.t.* **(a)** tranchieren ⟨*Fleisch, Braten, Hähnchen*⟩ **(b)** (from wood) schnitzen; (from stone) meißeln ② *v.i.* **∼ in** wood/stone in Holz schnitzen/in Stein meißeln

carving /'kɑːvɪŋ/ *n.* (in or from wood) Schnitzerei, *die;* (in or from stone) Skulptur, *die*

'carving knife *n.* Tranchiermesser, *das*

'car wash *n.* Waschanlage, *die*

cascade /kæs'keɪd/ *n.* Kaskade, *die*

case[1] /keɪs/ *n.* **(a)** (instance, matter, set of arguments) Fall, *der;* **it is [not] the ∼ that …:** es trifft [nicht] zu, dass …; **in ∼ …:** falls …; **[just] in ∼:** für alle Fälle; **in ∼ of emergency** im Notfall; **in any ∼:** jedenfalls; **in that ∼:** in diesem Fall; **in any ∼** (regardless of anything else) jedenfalls; **I don't need it in any ∼:** ich brauche es sowieso nicht **(b)** (Med., Police, Soc. Serv., etc.) Fall, *der* **(c)** (Law) Fall, *der;* (action) Verfahren, *das* **(d)** (Ling.) Fall, *der;* Kasus, *der* (fachspr.)

case[2] *n.* **(a)** Koffer, *der;* (brief∼) [Akten]tasche, *die* **(b)** (for spectacles, cigarettes) Etui, *das* **(c)** (crate) Kiste, *die* **(d)** [display] ∼: Schaukasten, *der*

cash /kæʃ/ ① *n.* Bargeld, *das;* **pay [in] ∼, pay ∼ down** bar zahlen ② *v.t.* einlösen ⟨*Scheck*⟩

cash: ∼ account *n.* Kassekonto, *das;* **∼ and 'carry** *n.* cash and carry; (store) Cash-and-carry-Laden, *der;* **∼back** *n.,* no *art.: Barauszahlung eines Differenzbetrages bei Kauf mit Geldkarte;* **∼card** *n.* Geldautomatenkarte, *die;* **∼ desk** *n.* (Brit.) Kasse, *die;* **∼ discount** *n.* Skonto, *der od. das;* Barzahlungsrabatt, *der;* **∼ dispenser** *n.* Geldautomat, *der*

cashew nut /'kæʃuː/ *n.* Cashewnuss, *die*

'cash flow *n.* Cashflow, *der*

cashier /kæ'ʃɪə(r)/ *n.* Kassierer, *der*/Kassiererin, *die*

'cashless *adj.* bargeldlos; **the ∼ society** die bargeldlose Gesellschaft

'cash machine *n.* Geldautomat, *der*

cashmere /'kæʃmɪə(r)/ *n.* Kaschmir, *der;* **∼ wool/sweater** Kaschmirwolle, *die*/Kaschmirpullover, *der*

cash: ∼ payment *n.* Barzahlung, *die;* **make ∼ payment** bar bezahlen; **∼point** *n.* Geldautomat, *der;* **∼ register** *n.* [Registrier]kasse, *die*

casino /kə'siːnəʊ/ *n.* Kasino, *das*

cask /kɑːsk/ *n.* Fass, *das*

casket /'kɑːskɪt/ *n.* **(a)** Kästchen, *das* **(b)** (Amer.: coffin) Sarg, *der*

casserole /'kæsərəʊl/ *n.* Schmortopf, *der*

cassette /kə'set, kæ'set/ *n.* Kassette, *die*

cassette: ∼ deck *n.* Kassettendeck, *das;* **∼ player** *n.* Kassettengerät, *das;*

∼ recorder *n.* Kassettenrekorder, *der*

cast /kɑːst/ ① *v.t.,* **cast (a)** werfen **(b)** (shape, form) gießen **(c)** abgeben ⟨*Stimme*⟩ ② *n.* **(a)** (Med.) Gipsverband, *der* **(b)** (actors) Besetzung, *die* ▪ **cast a'side** *v.t.* beiseite schieben ⟨*Vorschlag*⟩; vergessen ⟨*Sorgen*⟩; fallen lassen ⟨*Hemmungen*⟩ ▪ **cast 'off** *v.i. & t.* (Naut.) losmachen

castanets /kæstə'nets/ *n. pl.* Kastagnetten *Pl.*

'castaway *n.* Schiffbrüchige, *der*/*die*

caste /kɑːst/ *n.* Kaste, *die*

cast 'iron *n.* Gusseisen, *das*

castle /'kɑːsl/ *n.* Burg, *die;* (mansion) Schloss, *das*

'cast-offs *n. pl.* abgelegte Sachen *Pl.*

castor /'kɑːstə(r)/ *n.* (wheel) Rolle, *die*

castor: ∼ 'oil *n.* Rizinusöl, *das;* **∼ sugar** *n.* Raffinade, *die*

castrate /kæ'streɪt/ *v.t.* kastrieren

castration /kæ'streɪʃn/ *n.* Kastration, *die*

casual /'kæʒjʊəl/ *adj.* ungezwungen; leger ⟨*Kleidung*⟩; beiläufig ⟨*Bemerkung*⟩; flüchtig ⟨*Bekannter, Bekanntschaft, Blick*⟩; unbekümmert ⟨*Haltung, Einstellung*⟩

casual 'labour *n.* Gelegenheitsarbeit, *die*

'casually *adv.* ungezwungen; beiläufig ⟨*bemerken*⟩; flüchtig ⟨*anschauen*⟩; leger ⟨*sich kleiden*⟩

casualty /'kæʒjʊəltɪ/ *n.* **(a)** (injured person) Verletzte, *der*/*die;* (in battle) Verwundete, *der*/*die;* (dead person) Tote, *der*/*die* **(b)** (hospital department) Unfallstation, *die*

'casualty ward *n.* Unfallstation, *die*

cat /kæt/ *n.* Katze, *die*

catalogue (*Amer.:* **catalog**) /'kætəlɒg/ ① *n.* Katalog, *der* ② *v.t.* katalogisieren

catalyst /'kætəlɪst/ *n.* Katalysator, *der*

catalytic /kætə'lɪtɪk/ *adj.* **∼ converter** Katalysator, *der*

catamaran /kætəmə'ræn/ *n.* Katamaran, *der*

catapult /'kætəpʌlt/ ① *n.* Katapult, *das* ② *v.t.* katapultieren

cataract /'kætərækt/ *n.* **(a)** Katarakt, *der* **(b)** (Med.) grauer Star

catarrh /kə'tɑː(r)/ *n.* Katarrh, *der*

catastrophe /kə'tæstrəfɪ/ *n.* Katastrophe, *die*

catastrophic /kætə'strɒfɪk/ *adj.* katastrophal

catch /kætʃ/ ① *v.t.,* **caught** /kɔːt/ **(a)** fangen; **∼ hold of sb./sth.** jmdn./etw. festhalten; (to stop oneself falling) sich an jmdm./etw. festhalten; **get sth. caught** *or* **∼ sth. on/in sth.** mit etw. an/in etw. (*Dat.*) hängen bleiben; **∼ one's finger in the door** sich (*Dat.*) den Finger in der Tür einklemmen

(b) (travel by) nehmen; (be in time for) [noch] erreichen
(c) (surprise) ~ **sb. doing sth.** jmdn. [dabei] erwischen, wie er etw. tut (ugs.)
(d) (become infected with) sich (*Dat.*) zuziehen; ~ **sth. from sb.** sich bei jmdm. mit etw. anstecken; ~ **a cold** sich erkälten; ~ **it** (fig. coll.) etwas kriegen (ugs.)
(e) ~ **sb.'s attention/interest** jmds. Aufmerksamkeit erregen/jmds. Interesse wecken
② *v.i.,* **caught (a)** (begin to burn) [anfangen zu] brennen
(b) (become hooked up) hängenbleiben; ⟨*Haar, Faden:*⟩ sich verfangen
③ *n.* **(a)** (of ball) **make a ~:** fangen
(b) (amount caught, lit. or fig.) Fang, *der*
(c) (difficulty) Haken, *der* (in an + *Dat.*)
(d) (of door) Schnapper, *der*
■ **catch 'on** *v.i.* (coll.) **(a)** (become popular) [gut] ankommen (ugs.)
(b) (understand) kapieren (ugs.)
■ **catch 'up** ① *v.t.* ~ **sb. up,** ~ **up with sb.** jmdn. einholen
② *v.i.* ~ **up** gleichziehen; ~ **up on sth.** etw. nachholen
'**catching** *adj.* ansteckend
'**catchphrase** *n.* Slogan, *der*
'**catchy** *adj.* eingängig
'**cat door** *n.* Katzentür, *die*
categorical /kætɪ'gɒrɪkl/ *adj.* kategorisch
categorize (categorise) /'kætɪgəraɪz/ *v.t.* kategorisieren
category /'kætɪgərɪ/ *n.* Kategorie, *die*
cater /'keɪtə(r)/ *v.i.* ~ **for sb./sth.** für jmdn./etw. [die] Speisen und Getränke liefern; (fig.) auf jmdn./etw. eingestellt sein
'**caterer** *n.* Lieferant von Speisen und Getränken
'**catering** *n.* **(a)** (trade) Gastronomie, *die*
(b) (service) Lieferung von Speisen und Getränken
caterpillar /'kætəpɪlə(r)/ *n.* Raupe, *die*
'**cat flap** ▶ CAT DOOR
cathedral /kə'θi:drl/ *n.* Dom, *der*
Catherine wheel /'kæθrɪn wi:l/ *n.* Feuerrad, *das*
Catholic /'kæθəlɪk/ ① *adj.* katholisch
② *n.* Katholik, *der*/Katholikin, *die*
Catholicism /kə'θɒlɪsɪzm/ *n.* Katholizismus, *der*
catkin /'kætkɪn/ *n.* (Bot.) Kätzchen, *das*
'**Cat's-eye** ® *n.* (Brit.: on road) Bodenrückstrahler, *der*
cattle /'kætl/ *n. pl.* Rinder *Pl.*
'**cattle market** *n.* Viehmarkt, *der;* (fig.) Fleischbeschau, *die* (ugs. scherzh.)
'**catwalk** *n.* Laufsteg, *der*
caught ▶ CATCH 1, 2
cauldron /'kɔ:ldrən/ *n.* Kessel, *der*
cauliflower /'kɒlɪflaʊə(r)/ *n.* Blumenkohl, *der*

cause /kɔ:z/ ① *n.* **(a)** Ursache, *die* (of für *od. Gen.*); (person) Verursacher, *der*/Verursacherin, *die;* **be the ~ of sth.** etw. verursachen
(b) (reason) Grund, *der;* ~ **for sth.** Grund zu etw.
(c) (object of support) Sache, *die;* [in] **a good ~:** [für] eine gute Sache
② *v.t.* verursachen; erregen ⟨*Aufsehen, Ärgernis*⟩; hervorrufen ⟨*Unruhe, Verwirrung*⟩; ~ **sb. worry/pain** jmdm. Sorge/Schmerzen bereiten; ~ **sb. to do sth.** jmdn. veranlassen, etw. zu tun
causeway /'kɔ:zweɪ/ *n.* Damm, *der*
caustic /'kɔ:stɪk/ *adj.* ätzend; (fig.) bissig; beißend ⟨*Spott*⟩
caution /'kɔ:ʃn/ ① *n.* **(a)** Vorsicht, *die*
(b) (warning) Warnung, *die*
② *v.t.* (warn) warnen; (warn and reprove) verwarnen (**for** wegen)
cautious /'kɔ:ʃəs/ *adj.,* '**cautiously** *adv.* vorsichtig
cavalry /'kævəlrɪ/ *n.* Kavallerie, *die*
cave /keɪv/ *n.* Höhle, *die*
■ **cave 'in** *v.i.* einbrechen
'**caveman** *n.* Höhlenbewohner, *der*
cavern /'kævən/ *n.* Höhle, *die*
cavernous /'kævənəs/ *adj.* höhlenartig
caviar[e] /'kævɪɑ:(r)/ *n.* Kaviar, *der*
cavity /'kævɪtɪ/ *n.* Hohlraum, *der;* (in tooth) Loch, *das*
'**cavity wall** *n.* Hohlmauer, *die*
CB *abbr.* = **citizen's band** CB
cc /si:'si:/ *abbr.* = **cubic centimetre(s)** cm³
CCTV *abbr.* = **closed-circuit television** CCTV
CD *abbr.* = **compact disc** CD, *die;* CD burner CD-Brenner, *der;* CD player CD-Spieler, *der*
CD-ROM /si:di:'rɒm/ *n.* CD-ROM, *die;* ~ **drive** CD-ROM-Laufwerk, *das*
cease /si:s/ ① *v.i.* aufhören
② *v.t.* **(a)** (stop) aufhören
(b) (end) aufhören mit; einstellen ⟨*Bemühungen*⟩
'**ceasefire** *n.* Waffenruhe, *die*
cedar /'si:də(r)/ *n.* Zeder, *die*
Ceefax ® /'si:fæks/ *n.* Bildschirmtextdienst der BBC
ceiling /'si:lɪŋ/ *n.* **(a)** Decke, *die*
(b) (upper limit) Maximum, *das*
celebrate /'selɪbreɪt/ *v.t. & i.* feiern
'**celebrated** *adj.* berühmt
celebration /selɪ'breɪʃn/ *n.* Feier, *die*
celebrity /sɪ'lebrɪtɪ/ *n.* Berühmtheit, *die*
celery /'selərɪ/ *n.* Sellerie, *der od. die*
celibate /'selɪbət/ *adj.* zölibatär (Rel.); ehelos
cell /sel/ *n.* Zelle, *die*
cellar /'selə(r)/ *n.* Keller, *der*

cellist /'tʃelɪst/ n. Cellist, der/Cellistin, die

cello /'tʃeləʊ/ n., pl. ∼s Cello, das

Cellophane ® /'seləfeɪn/ n. Cellophan Ⓦ, das

'cellphone n., **cellular 'phone** /'seljʊlə(r)/ Mobiltelefon, das

cellulite /'seljʊlaɪt/ n., no indef. art.: überschüssige Fettdepots an Oberschenkeln und Hüften

Celsius /'selsɪəs/ adj. Celsius

cement /sɪ'ment/ ① n. Zement, der ② v.t. zementieren; (stick together) zusammenkleben

ce'ment mixer n. Betonmischmaschine, die

cemetery /'semɪtərɪ/ n. Friedhof, der

censor /'sensə(r)/ ① n. Zensor, der ② v.t. zensieren

'censorship n. Zensur, die

censure /'senʃə(r)/ v.t. tadeln

census /'sensəs/ n. Volkszählung, die

cent /sent/ n. Cent, der

centenary /sen'ti:nərɪ/ adj. & n. ∼ **[celebrations]** Hundertjahrfeier, die

center (Amer.) ▸ CENTRE

centigrade /'sentɪgreɪd/ ▸ CELSIUS

centimetre (Brit.; Amer.: **centimeter**) /'sentɪmi:tə(r)/ n. Zentimeter, der

centipede /'sentɪpi:d/ n. Tausendfüßler, der

central /'sentrl/ adj. zentral

Central: ∼ **A'merica** pr. n. Mittelamerika (das); ∼ **'Europe** pr. n. Mitteleuropa (das); ∼ **Euro'pean** adj. mitteleuropäisch; **c**∼ **'heating** n. Zentralheizung, die

centralize /'sentrəlaɪz/ v.t. zentralisieren

central: ∼ **'locking** n. (Motor Veh.) Zentralverriegelung, die; ∼ **'nervous system** n. Zentralnervensystem, das; ∼ **'processing unit** n. (Comp.) Zentraleinheit, die; ∼ **reservation** n. (Brit.) Mittelstreifen, der

centre /'sentə(r)/ (Brit.) ① n. (a) Mitte, die; (of circle) Mittelpunkt, der (b) (of area, city) Zentrum, das ② adj. mittler... ③ v.i. ∼ **on sth.** sich auf etw. (Akk.) konzentrieren; ∼ **[a]round sth.** sich um etw. drehen ④ v.t. (a) in der Mitte anbringen (b) (concentrate) **be** ∼**d [a]round sth.** etw. zum Mittelpunkt haben; ∼ **sth. on sth.** etw. auf etw. (Akk.) konzentrieren

centre 'forward n. Mittelstürmer, der

centrifugal /sentrɪ'fju:gl/ adj. ∼ **force** Zentrifugalkraft, die; Fliehkraft, die

century /'sentʃərɪ/ n. (hundred-year period from a year ..00) Jahrhundert, das; (hundred years) hundert Jahre

ceramic /sɪ'ræmɪk/ adj. keramisch

ceramic 'hob n. [Glas]keramikkochfeld, das

cereal /'sɪərɪəl/ n. Getreide, das; (breakfast dish) Getreideflocken Pl.

cerebral /'serɪbrl/ adj. (intellectual) intellektuell

ceremonial /serɪ'məʊnɪəl/ ① adj. feierlich; (prescribed for ceremony) zeremoniell ② n. Zeremoniell, das

ceremony /'serɪmənɪ/ n. Feier, die; (formal act) Zeremonie, die

certain /'sɜ:tn, 'sɜ:tɪn/ adj. (a) (settled, definite) bestimmt (b) **be** ∼ **to do sth.** etw. bestimmt tun (c) (confident, sure to happen) sicher (d) (indisputable) unbestreitbar (e) **a** ∼ **Mr Smith** ein gewisser Herr Smith; **to a** ∼ **extent** in gewisser Weise

'certainly adv. (a) (admittedly) sicher[lich]; (definitely) bestimmt (b) (in answer) [aber] sicher; **[most]** ∼ **'not!** auf [gar] keinen Fall!

certainty /'sɜ:tntɪ, 'sɜ:tɪntɪ/ n. (a) **be a** ∼: sicher sein (b) (absolute conviction) Gewissheit, die

certificate /sə'tɪfɪkət/ n. Urkunde, die; (of action performed) Schein, der

certify /'sɜ:tɪfaɪ/ v.t. bescheinigen; bestätigen; **this is to** ∼ **that ...:** hiermit wird bescheinigt od. bestätigt, dass ...

cf. abbr. = **compare** vgl.

CFC abbr. = **chlorofluorocarbon** FCKW, das; ∼**-free** FCKW-frei

chafe /tʃeɪf/ v.t. wund scheuern

chaff /tʃɑ:f/ n. Spreu, die

chaffinch /'tʃæfɪntʃ/ n. Buchfink, der

chagrin /'ʃægrɪn/ n. Kummer, der

chain /tʃeɪn/ ① n. Kette, die; ∼ **of shops/ hotels** Laden-/Hotelkette, die ② v.t. [an]ketten (**to an** + Akk.)

chain: ∼ **re'action** n. Kettenreaktion, die; ∼**saw** n. Kettensäge, die; ∼**-smoke** v.t. & i. Kette rauchen (ugs.); ∼**-smoker** n. Kettenraucher, der/-raucherin, die; ∼ **store** n. Kettenladen, der

chair /tʃeə(r)/ ① n. (a) Stuhl, der; (arm∼, easy ∼) Sessel, der (b) (professorship) Lehrstuhl, der (c) (at meeting) Vorsitz, der; (∼person) Vorsitzende, der/die ② v.t. den Vorsitz haben bei

chair: ∼ **back** n. Rückenlehne, die; ∼**lift** n. Sessellift, der; ∼**man** /'tʃeəmən/ n., pl. ∼**men** /'tʃeəmən/ Vorsitzende, der/die; ∼**person** n. Vorsitzende, der/die; ∼**woman** n. Vorsitzende, die

chalet /'ʃæleɪ/ n. Chalet, das

chalk /tʃɔ:k/ ① n. Kreide, die ② v.t. mit Kreide schreiben/malen usw.

challenge /'tʃælɪndʒ/ ① n. Herausforderung, die ② v.t. (a) (to contest etc.) herausfordern (b) (fig.) auffordern; (question) infrage stellen

challenged /'tʃælɪndʒd/ *adj.* (euphem. or joc.) behindert; **mentally ~:** geistig behindert

'**challenger** *n.* Herausforderer, *der*/Herausforderin, *die*

challenging /'tʃælɪndʒɪŋ/ *adj.* herausfordernd; fesselnd ⟨*Problem*⟩; anspruchsvoll ⟨*Arbeit*⟩

chamber /'tʃeɪmbə(r)/ *n.* Kammer, *die*

chamber: ~**maid** *n.* Zimmermädchen, *das;* ~ **music** *n.* Kammermusik, *die;* **C~ of 'Commerce** *n.* Industrie- und Handelskammer, *die;* ~ **pot** *n.* Nachttopf, *der*

chameleon /kə'miːljən/ *n.* Chamäleon, *das*

chamois /'ʃæmwɑː/ *n.* (a) Gämse, *die* (b) /'ʃæmɪ/ ~ **[leather]** Chamois[leder], *das*

champagne /ʃæm'peɪn/ *n.* Sekt, *der;* (from Champagne) Champagner, *der*

cham'pagne glass *n.* Sektglas, *das*

champion /'tʃæmpɪən/ ⏹1 *n.* (a) (defender) Verfechter, *der*/Verfechterin, *die* (b) (Sport) Meister, *der*/Meisterin, *die* ⏹2 *v.t.* verfechten ⟨*Sache*⟩; sich einsetzen für ⟨*Person*⟩

'**championship** *n.* Meisterschaft, *die*

chance /tʃɑːns/ ⏹1 *n.* (a) (fortune, trick of fate) Zufall, *der; attrib.* zufällig; ~ **encounter** Zufallsbegegnung, *die;* **game of ~:** Glücksspiel, *das;* **by ~:** zufällig; **take a ~:** es riskieren; **the ~s are that …:** es ist wahrscheinlich, dass …; **by [any] ~, by some ~ or other** zufällig (b) (opportunity, possibility) Chance, *die;* **get a/the ~ to do sth.** eine/die Gelegenheit haben, etw. zu tun ⏹2 *v.t.* riskieren

chancellor /'tʃɑːnsələ(r)/ *n.* Kanzler, *der;* **C~ of the Exchequer** (Brit.) Schatzkanzler, *der*

chandelier /ʃændə'lɪə(r)/ *n.* Kronleuchter, *der*

change /tʃeɪndʒ/ ⏹1 *n.* (a) Veränderung, *die;* Änderung, *die;* (of job, surroundings, government, etc.) Wechsel, *der* (b) (for the sake of variety) Abwechslung, *die;* **for a ~:** zur Abwechslung (c) (money) Wechselgeld, *das;* **[loose or small]** ~: Kleingeld, *das;* **[here is] £5 ~:** 5 Pfund zurück; **keep the ~:** [es] stimmt so ⏹2 *v.t.* (a) (switch) wechseln; auswechseln ⟨*Glühbirne, Batterie*⟩; ~ **one's clothes** sich umziehen; ~ **one's address/name** seine Anschrift/seinen Namen ändern; ~ **trains/buses** umsteigen (b) (transform) verwandeln (**into** in + *Akk.*); (alter) ändern (c) (exchange) eintauschen (**for** für); wechseln ⟨*Geld*⟩ ⏹3 *v.i.* (a) (alter) sich ändern; ⟨*Person, Land:*⟩ sich verändern (b) (into something else) sich verwandeln (c) (put on other clothes) sich umziehen (d) (~ trains, buses, etc.) umsteigen

■ **change 'over** *v.i.* ~ **over from sth. to sth.** von etw. zu etw. übergehen

changeable /'tʃeɪndʒəbl/ *adj.* veränderlich

'**change[-giving] machine** *n.* Geldwechsler, *der*

'**changeover** *n.* Wechsel, *der;* ~ **from sth. to sth.** Umstellung von etw. auf etw. (*Akk.*)

'**changing room** *n.* (Brit.) Umkleideraum, *der*

channel /'tʃænl/ ⏹1 *n.* (also Telev., Radio) Kanal, *der;* **the C~** (Brit.) der [Ärmel]kanal ⏹2 *v.t.* (fig.) lenken

Channel: c~-hop *v.i.* (coll.) (a) (Telev.) zappen (ugs.); (b) (cross the English Channel) kurz mal über den Kanal fahren; ~ **Islands** *pr. n. pl.* Kanalinseln *Pl.;* ~ '**Tunnel** *n.* [Ärmel]kanaltunnel, *der*

chant /tʃɑːnt/ ⏹1 *v.t.* skandieren; (Eccl.) singen ⏹2 *v.i.* Sprechchöre anstimmen; (Eccl.) singen ⏹3 *n.* Sprechchor, *der;* (Eccl.) Gesang, *der*

chaos /'keɪɒs/ *n.* Chaos, *das*

chaotic /keɪ'ɒtɪk/ *adj.* chaotisch

chap[1] /tʃæp/ *n.* (Brit. coll.) Bursche, *der;* Kerl, *der*

chap[2] *v.t.,* **-pp-** aufplatzen lassen

chapel /'tʃæpl/ *n.* Kapelle, *die*

chaperon /'ʃæpərəʊn/ ⏹1 *n.* Anstandsdame, *die* ⏹2 *v.t.* beaufsichtigen

chaplain /'tʃæplɪn/ *n.* Kaplan, *der*

chapter /'tʃæptə(r)/ *n.* Kapitel, *das*

char /tʃɑː(r)/ *v.t. & i.,* **-rr-** verkohlen

character /'kærɪktə(r)/ *n.* (a) Charakter, *der* (b) (in novel etc.) Figur, *die* (c) (coll.: extraordinary person) Original, *das* (d) (symbol) Zeichen, *das*

characteristic /kærɪktə'rɪstɪk/ ⏹1 *adj.* charakteristisch (**of** für) ⏹2 *n.* charakteristisches Merkmal

characterize /'kærɪktəraɪz/ *v.t.* charakterisieren

'**characterless** *adj.* nichts sagend

charade /ʃə'rɑːd/ *n.* Scharade, *die;* (fig.) Farce, *die*

charcoal /'tʃɑːkəʊl/ *n.* Holzkohle, *die*

charge /tʃɑːdʒ/ ⏹1 *n.* (a) (price) Preis, *der;* (for services) Gebühr, *die* (b) **be in ~ of sth.** für etw. die Verantwortung haben; **take ~:** die Verantwortung übernehmen (c) (Law: accusation) Anklage, *die* (d) (attack) Angriff, *der* (e) (of explosives, electricity) Ladung, *die* ⏹2 *v.t.* (a) ~ **sb. sth.,** ~ **sth. to sb.** jmdm. etw. berechnen (b) (Law: accuse) anklagen (**with** wegen) (c) (Electr.) [auf]laden ⟨*Batterie*⟩ (d) (rush at) angreifen ⋯>

3 *v.i.* **(a)** (attack) angreifen
(b) (coll.: hurry) sausen
charge: ~ **account** *n.* (Amer.)
Kreditkonto, *das;* ~ **card** *n.* Kreditkarte,
die
charisma /kə'rızmə/ *n.* Charisma, *das*
charitable /'tʃærɪtəbl/ *adj.* **(a)** wohltätig
(b) (lenient) großzügig
charity /'tʃærɪtɪ/ *n.* **(a)** Wohltätigkeit, *die*
(b) (organization) wohltätige Organisation
charity: ~ **concert** *n.* Benefizkonzert,
das; ~ **match** *n.* Benefizspiel, *das;*
~ **performance** *n.* Benefizvorstellung,
die; Wohltätigkeitsvorstellung, *die;*
~ **shop** *n.:* Secondhandladen, dessen
Erlöse einem wohltätigen Zweck dienen
charlady /'tʃɑːleɪdɪ/ *n.* (Brit.) Putzfrau, *die*
charlatan /'ʃɑːlətən/ *n.* Scharlatan, *der*
charm /tʃɑːm/ **1** *n.* **(a)** (act) Zauber, *der*
(b) (talisman) Talisman, *der*
(c) (attractiveness) Reiz, *der;* (of person)
Charme, *der*
2 *v.t.* bezaubern
'**charming** *adj.* bezaubernd
chart /tʃɑːt/ **1** *n.* **(a)** (map) Karte, *die*
(b) (graph etc.) Schaubild, *das*
(c) the ~s die Hitliste
2 *v.t.* (fig.: describe) schildern
charter /'tʃɑːtə(r)/ **1** *n.* **(a)** Charta, *die*
(b) on ~ gechartert
2 *v.t.* chartern ⟨*Schiff, Flugzeug*⟩
chartered: ~ **ac'countant** *n.* (Brit.)
Wirtschaftsprüfer, *der*/-prüferin, *die;*
~ '**aircraft** *n.* Charterflugzeug, *das;*
Chartermaschine, *die*
charter: ~ **flight** *n.* Charterflug, *der;*
~ **plane** ▶ CHARTERED AIRCRAFT
charwoman /'tʃɑːwʊmən/ *n.* Putzfrau,
die
chase /tʃeɪs/ **1** *n.* Verfolgungsjagd, *die*
2 *v.t.* (pursue) jagen; ~ **sth.** (fig.) einer Sache
(*Dat.*) nachjagen
3 *v.i.* ~ **after sb./sth.** hinter jmdm./etw.
herjagen
■ **chase 'up** *v.t.* (coll.) ausfindig machen
chasm /'kæzm/ *n.* Kluft, *die*
chassis /'ʃæsɪ/ *n., pl. same* /'ʃæsɪz/
Chassis, *das;* Fahrgestell, *das*
chaste /tʃeɪst/ *adj.* keusch
chastening /'tʃeɪsənɪŋ/ *adj.* ernüchternd
chastise /tʃæ'staɪz/ *v.t.* züchtigen
chastity /'tʃæstɪtɪ/ *n.* Keuschheit, *die*
chat /tʃæt/ **1** *n.* Schwätzchen, *das*
2 *v.i.,* **-tt-:** **(a)** plaudern; ~ **with** *or* **to sb.**
about sth. mit jmdm. von etw. plaudern
(b) (Comp.) chatten
■ **chat 'up** *v.t.* (Brit. coll.) anmachen (ugs.)
chat: ~ **line** *n.* Chatline, *die;* ~ **room**
n. (Comp.) Chat-Room, *der;* ~ **show** *n.*
Talkshow, *die*
chattels /'tʃætəlz/ *n. pl.* bewegliche Habe
(geh.)

chatter /'tʃætə(r)/ **1** *v.i.* **(a)** schwatzen
(b) ⟨*Zähne:*⟩ klappern
2 *n.* Schwatzen, *das*
'**chatterbox** *n.* Quasselstrippe, *die* (ugs.)
chatty /'tʃætɪ/ *adj.* gesprächig
chauffeur /'ʃəʊfə(r)/ **1** *n.* Fahrer, *der;*
Chauffeur, *der*
2 *v.t.* fahren
chauvinist /'ʃəʊvɪnɪst/ *n.* Chauvinist,
der/Chauvinistin, *die*
chauvinistic /ʃəʊvɪ'nɪstɪk/ *adj.*
chauvinistisch
cheap /tʃiːp/ *adj., adv.* billig
cheapen /'tʃiːpn/ *v.t.* (fig.) herabsetzen
'**cheaply** *adv.* billig
cheat /tʃiːt/ **1** *n.* Schwindler, *der*/
Schwindlerin, *die*
2 *v.t. & i.* betrügen
Chechen /'tʃetʃn/ **1** *adj.* tschetschenisch;
he/she is ~: er ist Tschetschene/sie ist
Tschetschenin
2 *n.* **(a)** (Person) Tschetschene, *der*/
Tschetschenin, *die*
(b) (language) Tschetschenisch, *das*
Chechenia, Chechnya /tʃeʃ'nɪɑː/ *pr.*
ns. Tschetschenien (*das*)
Chechen Re'public /tʃetʃn rɪ'pʌblɪk/
n. Tschetschenische Republik
check¹ /tʃek/ **1** *n.* **(a)** Kontrolle, *die;*
make/keep a ~ on kontrollieren
(b) (Amer.: bill) Rechnung, *die*
2 *v.t.* **(a)** (restrain) unter Kontrolle halten
(b) (examine) nachprüfen; kontrollieren
⟨*Fahrkarte*⟩
(c) (stop) aufhalten
3 *v.i.* ~ **on sth.** etw. überprüfen; ~ **with sb.**
bei jmdm. nachfragen
■ **check 'in** *v.t. & i.* (at airport) einchecken
■ **check 'out** **1** *v.t.* überprüfen
2 *v.i.* abreisen
■ **check 'up** *v.i.* ~ **up [on]** überprüfen
check² *n.* (pattern) Karo, *das*
checkers /'tʃekəz/ (Amer.) ▶ DRAUGHTS
check: ~**in** *n.* Abfertigung, *die;*
~**list** *n.* Checkliste, *die;* ~**mate** **1** *n.*
[Schach]matt, *das;* **2** *int.* [schach]matt;
~**out [desk]** *n.* Kasse, *die;* ~**point**
n. Kontrollpunkt, *der;* ~**-up** *n.* (Med.)
Untersuchung, *die*
cheek /tʃiːk/ *n.* **(a)** Backe, *die;* Wange, *die*
(geh.)
(b) (impertinence) Frechheit, *die*
'**cheekbone** *n.* Backenknochen, *der*
'**cheekily** *adv.,* '**cheeky** *adj.* frech
cheep /tʃiːp/ **1** *v.i.* piep[s]en
2 *n.* Piep[s]en, *das*
cheer /tʃɪə(r)/ **1** *n.* **(a)** (applause)
Beifallsruf, *der*
(b) *in pl.* (Brit. coll.: as a toast) prost!
(c) (Brit. coll.: thank you) danke
2 *v.t.* **(a)** (applaud) ~ **sth./sb.** etw. bejubeln/
jmdm. zujubeln
(b) (gladden) aufmuntern

③ *v.i.* jubeln

■ **cheer 'on** *v.t.* anfeuern ‹*Sportler*›

■ **cheer 'up** ① *v.t.* aufheitern

② *v.i.* bessere Laune bekommen; ∼ **up!** Kopf hoch!

cheerful /'tʃɪəfl/ *adj.* (in good spirits) fröhlich; (bright, pleasant) heiter

'**cheerfully** *adv.* vergnügt

'**cheering** ① *adj.* fröhlich stimmend

② *n.* Jubeln, *das*

cheerio /tʃɪərɪ'əʊ/ *int.* (Brit. coll.) tschüs (ugs.)

'**cheery** *adj.* fröhlich

cheese /tʃiːz/ *n.* Käse, *der*

cheese: ∼**board** *n.* Käseplatte, *die;* ∼**cake** *n.* Käsetorte, *die*

cheetah /'tʃiːtə/ *n.* Gepard, *der*

chef /ʃef/ *n.* Küchenchef, *der;* (as profession) Koch, *der*

chemical /'kemɪkl/ ① *adj.* chemisch

② *n.* Chemikalie, *die*

chemical 'warfare *n.* chemische Krieg[s]führung

chemist /'kemɪst/ *n.* (a) (scientist) Chemiker, *der*/Chemikerin, *die*

(b) (Brit.: pharmacist) Drogist, *der*/Drogistin, *die;* ∼'**s [shop]** Drogerie, *die*

chemistry /'kemɪstrɪ/ *n.* Chemie, *die*

chemotherapy /kiːmə'θerəpɪ/ *n.* Chemotherapie, *die*

cheque /tʃek/ *n.* Scheck, *der;* **pay by** ∼: mit [einem] Scheck bezahlen

cheque: ∼**book** *n.* Scheckbuch, *das;* ∼**book 'journalism** *n.* Scheckbuchjournalismus, *der;* ∼ **card** *n.* Scheckkarte, *die*

cherish /'tʃerɪʃ/ *v.t.* hegen ‹*Hoffnung, Gefühl*›; in Ehren halten ‹*[Erinnerungs]ge genstand*›

cherry /'tʃerɪ/ *n.* Kirsche, *die*

chess /tʃes/ *n., no art.* das Schach[spiel]

chess: ∼**board** *n.* Schachbrett, *das;* ∼**man** *n.* Schachfigur, *die;* ∼ **player** *n.* Schachspieler, *der*/-spielerin, *die*

chest /tʃest/ *n.* (a) Kiste, *die*

(b) (Anat.) Brust, *die;* **get sth. off one's** ∼ (fig. coll.) sich (*Dat.*) etw. von der Seele reden

(c) ∼ **[measurement]** Brustumfang, *der*

chestnut /'tʃesnʌt/ ① *n.* (a) Kastanie, *die*

(b) (colour) Kastanienbraun, *das*

② *adj.* (colour) ∼**[-brown]** kastanienbraun

'**chestnut tree** *n.* Kastanie, *die*

chest of 'drawers *n.* Kommode, *die*

chew /tʃuː/ *v.t. & i.* kauen

'**chewing gum** *n.* Kaugummi, *der od. das*

chic /ʃiːk/ *adj.* schick; elegant

chick /tʃɪk/ *n.* (a) Küken, *das*

(b) (sl.: young woman) Biene, *die* (ugs.)

chicken /'tʃɪkɪn/ ① *n.* (a) Huhn, *das;* (grilled, roasted) Hähnchen, *das*

(b) (coll.: coward) Angsthase, *der*

② *adj.* (coll.) feig[e]

③ *v.i.* ∼ **out** (coll.) kneifen

chicken: ∼**pox** /-pɒks/ *n.* Windpocken *Pl.;* ∼ '**soup** *n.* Hühnersuppe, *die;* ∼ **wire** *n.* Maschendraht, *der*

'**chick flick** *n.: unterhaltsamer, emotionaler Film für Frauen*

'**chickpea** *n.* Kichererbse, *die*

chicory /'tʃɪkərɪ/ *n.* (plant) Chicorée, *der od. die;* (for coffee) Zichorie, *die*

chief /tʃiːf/ ① *n.* (a) Oberhaupt, *das;* (of tribe) Häuptling, *der*

(b) (of department) Leiter, *der;* ∼ **of police** Polizeipräsident, *der*

② *adj., usu. attrib.* (a) Haupt-

(b) (leading) führend

chief ex'ecutive [officer] *n.* Hauptgeschäftsführer, *der*/-führerin, *die*

'**chiefly** *adv.* hauptsächlich

chieftain /'tʃiːftən/ *n.* Stammesführer, *der*

chilblain /'tʃɪlbleɪn/ *n.* Frostbeule, *die*

child /tʃaɪld/ *n., pl.* ∼**ren** /'tʃɪldrən/ Kind, *das*

child: ∼ **abuse** *n.* (sexual) sexueller Missbrauch von Kindern; (physical) Kindesmisshandlung, *die;* ∼ **allowance** *n.* (tax allowance) Kinderfreibetrag, *der;* ∼**bearing** ① *n.* Schwangerschaften *Pl.;* ② *adj.* ∼**bearing age** Gebäralter, *das;* **of** ∼**bearing age** im gebärfähigen Alter; ∼**birth** *n.* Geburt, *die;* ∼**care** *n.* Kinderbetreuung *die*

'**childhood** *n.* Kindheit, *die*

'**childish** /'tʃaɪldɪʃ/ *adj.,* '**childishly** *adv.* kindisch

'**childishness** *n.* (behaviour) kindisches Benehmen

child: ∼**less** *adj.* kinderlos; ∼**like** *adj.* kindlich; ∼**minder** /-maɪndə(r)/ *n.* (Brit.) Tagesmutter, *die;* ∼**proof** *adj.* kindersicher; ∼**proof door lock** (in car) Kindersicherung, *die*

children *pl. of* CHILD

'**child's play** *n.* (fig.) ein Kinderspiel

Chile /'tʃɪlɪ/ *pr. n.* Chile (*das*)

chill /tʃɪl/ ① *n.* Kühle, *die;* (illness) Erkältung, *die*

② *v.t.* kühlen

■ **chill out** *v.i.* (Amer. coll.) (relax) sich entspannen; (calm down) sich abregen (ugs.)

chilli /'tʃɪlɪ/ *n., pl.* ∼**es** Chili, *der*

chilling /'tʃɪlɪŋ/ *adj.* (fig.) ernüchternd

'**chilly** *adj.* kühl; **I am rather** ∼: mir ist ziemlich kühl

chime /tʃaɪm/ ① *n.* Geläute, *das*

② *v.i.* läuten; ‹*Turmuhr:*› schlagen

chimney /'tʃɪmnɪ/ *n.* Schornstein, *der*

chimney: ∼ **breast** *n.* Kaminmantel, *der;* ∼ **pot** *n.* ≈ Schornsteinkopf, *der;* ∼ **sweep** *n.* Schornsteinfeger, *der*

chimpanzee /tʃɪmpən'ziː/ *n.* Schimpanse, *der*

chin /tʃɪn/ *n.* Kinn, *das*

china *n.* Porzellan, *das;* (crockery) Geschirr, *das*

China /'tʃaɪnə/ pr. n. China (das)

Chinese /tʃaɪ'niːz/ **1** adj. chinesisch; **sb. is ∼:** jmd. ist Chinese/Chinesin **2** n. **(a)** pl. same (person) Chinese, der/Chinesin, die **(b)** (language) Chinesisch, das; see also ENGLISH 2A

chink n. (gap) Spalt, der

chip /tʃɪp/ **1** n. **(a)** Splitter, der **(b)** in pl. (Brit.: potato ∼s) Pommes frites Pl. **(c)** (Gambling, Comp.) Chip, der **2** v.t., -pp- anschlagen

■ **chip 'in** (coll.) **1** v.i. **(a)** (interrupt) sich einmischen **(b)** (contribute money) etwas beisteuern **2** v.t. (contribute) beisteuern

'**chipboard** n. Spanplatte, die

chipmunk /'tʃɪpmʌŋk/ n. Chipmunk, das

chippy /'tʃɪpɪ/ n. (Brit. coll.) Pommes-frites-Bude, die; Frittenbude, die (ugs.)

'**chip shop** (Brit.) ▶ CHIPPY

chiropodist /kɪ'rɒpədɪst/ n. Fußpfleger, der/-pflegerin, die

chiropody /kɪ'rɒpədɪ/ n. Fußpflege, die

chirp /tʃɜːp/ **1** v.i. zwitschern; ⟨Grille:⟩ zirpen **2** n. Zwitschern, das; Zirpen, das

chisel /'tʃɪzl/ **1** n. Meißel, der; (for wood) Stemmeisen, das **2** v.t., (Brit.) -ll- meißeln; (in wood) hauen

chit /tʃɪt/ n. Notiz, die

chit-chat /'tʃɪttʃæt/ n. Plauderei, die

chivalrous /'ʃɪvlrəs/ adj. ritterlich

chivalry /'ʃɪvlrɪ/ n. Ritterlichkeit, die

chives /tʃaɪvz/ n. Schnittlauch, der

chloride /'klɔːraɪd/ n. Chlorid, das

chlorine /'klɔːriːn/ n. Chlor, das

chlorofluorocarbon /klɔːrəʊflʊərəʊ'kɑːbən/ n. Chlorfluorkohlenstoff, der

chock /tʃɒk/ n. Bremsklotz, der

'**chock-a-block** pred adj. voll gepfropft

chocoholic /tʃɒkə'hɒlɪk/ n. (coll.) [absoluter] Schokofan (ugs.); (addict) Schokoladensüchtige, der/die

chocolate /'tʃɒklət/ n. Schokolade, die

chocolate 'biscuit n. Schokoladenkeks, der

choice /tʃɔɪs/ **1** n. **(a)** Wahl, die; from ∼: freiwillig **(b)** (variety) Auswahl, die **2** adj. ausgewählt

choir /kwaɪə(r)/ n. Chor, der

'**choirboy** n. Chorknabe, der

choke /tʃəʊk/ **1** v.t. **(a)** ersticken **(b)** (block up) verstopfen **2** v.i. (temporarily) keine Luft [mehr] bekommen; (permanently) ersticken (on an + Dat.) **3** n. (Motor Veh.) Choke, der

cholera /'kɒlərə/ n. Cholera, die

cholesterol /kə'lestərɒl/ n. Cholesterin, das

choose /tʃuːz/ **1** v.t., chose /tʃəʊz/, chosen /'tʃəʊzn/ **(a)** wählen **(b)** (decide) ∼/∼ not to do sth. sich dafür/ dagegen entscheiden, etw. zu tun **2** v.i., chose, chosen wählen (between zwischen); ∼ from sth. aus etw./(from several) unter etw. (Dat.) [aus]wählen

choos[e]y /'tʃuːzɪ/ adj. wählerisch

chop /tʃɒp/ **1** n. **(a)** Hieb, der **(b)** (of meat) Kotelett, das **(c) get the ∼** (coll.: be dismissed) rausgeworfen werden (ugs.) **2** v.t., -pp- hacken ⟨Holz⟩; klein schneiden ⟨Fleisch, Gemüse⟩

'**chopper** n. (axe) Beil, das; (cleaver) Hackbeil, das

'**chopping board** n. Hackbrett, das

'**choppy** adj. bewegt

'**chopstick** n. [Ess]stäbchen, das

choral /'kɔːrl/ adj. Chor-

chord /kɔːd/ n. (Mus.) Akkord, der

chore /tʃɔː(r)/ n. [lästige] Routinearbeit

choreographer /kɒrɪ'ɒgrəfə(r)/ n. Choreograph, der/Choreographin, die

choreography /kɒrɪ'ɒgrəfɪ/ n. Choreographie, die

chortle /'tʃɔːtl/ **1** v.i. vor Lachen glucksen **2** n. Glucksen, das

chorus /'kɔːrəs/ n. **(a)** Chor, der **(b)** (of song) Refrain, der; (in jazz) Chorus, der

chose, chosen ▶ CHOOSE

chow /tʃaʊ/ n. (Amer. sl.: food) Futter, das (salopp)

Christ /kraɪst/ n. Christus (der)

christen /'krɪsn/ v.t. taufen

'**christening** n. Taufe, die

Christian /'krɪstjən/ **1** adj. christlich **2** n. Christ, der/Christin, die

Christianity /krɪstɪ'ænɪtɪ/ n. das Christentum

'**Christian name** n. Vorname, der

Christmas /'krɪsməs/ n. Weihnachten, das od. Pl.; **merry** or **happy ∼:** frohe od. fröhliche Weihnachten; **at ∼:** [zu] Weihnachten

Christmas: ∼ cake n. Weihnachtskuchen, der; **∼ card** n. Weihnachtskarte, die; **∼ 'carol** n. Weihnachtslied, das; **∼ 'Day** n. erster Weihnachtsfeiertag; **∼ 'Eve** n. Heiligabend, der; **∼ present** n. Weihnachtsgeschenk, das; **∼ tree** n. Weihnachtsbaum, der

chrome /krəʊm/, **chromium** /'krəʊmɪəm/ ns. Chrom, das

'**chromium-plated** adj. verchromt

chromosome /'krəʊməsəʊm/ n. Chromosom, das

chronic /'krɒnɪk/ adj. chronisch; **∼ fatigue syndrome** chronisches Müdigkeitssyndrom

chronically /'krɒnɪkəlɪ/ adv. chronisch

chronicle /'krɒnɪkl/ n. Chronik, die

chronological /krɒnə'lɒdʒɪkl/ adj. chronologisch

chrysalis /'krɪsəlɪs/ n., pl. ~es Puppe, die

chrysanthemum /krɪ'sænθɪməm/ n. Chrysantheme, die

chubby /'tʃʌbɪ/ adj. pummelig

chuck /tʃʌk/ v.t. (coll.) schmeißen (ugs.).
■ **chuck 'away, chuck 'out** v.t. (coll.) wegschmeißen (ugs)

chuckle /'tʃʌkl/ [1] v.i. leise [vor sich hin] lachen (**at** über + Akk.)
[2] n. leises, glucksendes Lachen

chug /tʃʌg/ v.i., **-gg-** tuckern

chum /tʃʌm/ n. (coll.) Kumpel, der (salopp)

chunk /tʃʌŋk/ n. dickes Stück

'**chunky** adj. (a) (small and sturdy) stämmig
(b) dick ⟨Pullover⟩

Chunnel /'tʃʌnl/ n. (Brit. coll.) [Ärmel]kanaltunnel, der

church /tʃɜːtʃ/ n. Kirche, die; **go to** ~: in die Kirche gehen; **the C~ of England** die Kirche von England

'**churchyard** n. Friedhof, der (bei einer Kirche); Kirchhof, der (veralt.)

churlish /'tʃɜːlɪʃ/ adj. (ill-bred) ungehobelt; (surly) griesgrämig

churn /tʃɜːn/ n. (Brit.) Butterfass, das

churn out v.t. massenweise produzieren (ugs.)

chute /ʃuːt/ n. Schütte, die; (for persons) Rutsche, die

chutney /'tʃʌtnɪ/ n. Chutney, das

CIA abbr. (Amer.) = **Central Intelligence Agency** CIA, der od. die

cicada /sɪ'kɑːdə/ n. Zikade, die

CID abbr. (Brit.) = **Criminal Investigation Department** C.I.D.; **the** ~: die Kripo

cider /'saɪdə(r)/ n. ≈ Apfelwein, der

cigar /sɪ'gɑː(r)/ n. Zigarre, die

cigarette /sɪgə'ret/ n. Zigarette, die

cigarette: ~ **end** n. Zigarettenstummel, der; ~ **lighter** n. Feuerzeug, das; ~ **packet** n. Zigarettenschachtel, die; ~ **paper** n. Zigarettenpapier, das

cinders /'sɪndəz/ n. pl. Asche, die

cine /'sɪnɪ/: ~ **camera** n. Filmkamera, die; ~ **film** n. Schmalfilm, der

cinema /'sɪnɪmə/ n. Kino, das; **go to the** ~: ins Kino gehen

cinema: ~ **complex** n. Kinocenter, das; ~**-goer** n. (Brit.) Kinogänger, der/ -gängerin, die

cinematography /sɪnɪmə'tɒgrəfɪ/ n. Kinematographie, die

cinnamon /'sɪnəmən/ n. Zimt, der

cipher /'saɪfə(r)/ n. Geheimschrift, die; **in** ~: chiffriert

circle /'sɜːkl/ [1] n. Kreis, der

[2] v.i. kreisen
[3] v.t. umkreisen

circuit /'sɜːkɪt/ n. **(a)** (Electr.) Schaltung, die
(b) (Motor racing) Rundkurs, der

circular /'sɜːkjʊlə(r)/ [1] adj. (round) kreisförmig
[2] n. (letter, notice) Rundbrief, der; Rundschreiben, das; (advertisement) Werbeprospekt, der

circular: ~ **'letter** ▶ CIRCULAR 2; ~ '**saw** n. Kreissäge, die

circulate /'sɜːkjʊleɪt/ [1] v.i. zirkulieren; ⟨Personen, Wein usw.:⟩ herumgehen (ugs.)
[2] v.t. in Umlauf setzen; herumgehen lassen ⟨Buch, Bericht⟩ (**around** in + Dat.)

circulation /sɜːkjʊ'leɪʃn/ n. **(a)** (Physiol.) Kreislauf, der; **poor** ~: Kreislaufstörungen Pl.
(b) (copies sold) verkaufte Auflage

circulatory /sɜːkjʊ'leɪtərɪ, 'sɜːkjʊleɪtərɪ/ adj. (Physiol., Bot.) Kreislauf-; ~ **system** Kreislauf, der

circumcise /'sɜːkəmsaɪz/ v.t. beschneiden

circumcision /sɜːkəm'sɪʒn/ n. Beschneidung, die

circumference /sə'kʌmfərəns/ n. Umfang, der

circumstances /'sɜːkəmstənsɪz/ n. pl. Umstände Pl.; **in** or **under the** ~: unter diesen Umständen; **under no** ~: unter keinen Umständen

circus /'sɜːkəs/ n. Zirkus, der

CIS abbr. = **Commonwealth of Independent States** GUS

cissy /'sɪsɪ/ ▶ SISSY

cistern /'sɪstən/ n. Wasserkasten, der; (in roof) Wasserbehälter, der

citation /saɪ'teɪʃn/ n. Zitat, das

cite /saɪt/ v.t. (quote) zitieren; anführen ⟨Beispiel⟩

citizen /'sɪtɪzən/ n. **(a)** (of town, city) Bürger, der/Bürgerin, die
(b) (of state) [Staats]bürger, der/-bürgerin, die

'**citizenship** n. Staatsbürgerschaft, die

citrus /'sɪtrəs/ n. ~ **[fruit]** Zitrusfrucht, die

city /'sɪtɪ/ n. [Groß]stadt, die

city 'centre n. Stadtzentrum, das

civic /'sɪvɪk/ adj. [staats]bürgerlich; ~ **centre** Verwaltungszentrum der Stadt

civil /'sɪvl/ adj. **(a)** (not military) zivil
(b) (polite, obliging) höflich
(c) (Law) Zivil-

civil: ~ **engi'neer** n. Bauingenieur, der/-ingenieurin, die; ~ **engi'neering** n. Hoch- und Tiefbau, der

civilian /sɪ'vɪljən/ [1] n. Zivilist, der
[2] adj. Zivil-

civility /sɪ'vɪlɪtɪ/ n. Höflichkeit, die

civilization /sɪvɪlaɪ'zeɪʃn/ n. Zivilisation, die

civilized /'sɪvɪlaɪzd/ adj. zivilisiert

civil: ~ **'law** n. Zivilrecht, das; ~ **'rights** n. pl. Bürgerrechte Pl.; ~ **'servant** n. ≈ Staatsbeamte, der/ -beamtin, die; **C~** '**Service** n. öffentlicher Dienst; ~ **'war** n. Bürgerkrieg, der

CJD abbr. = **Creutzfeldt-Jakob disease**

clad /klæd/ adj. (arch./literary) gekleidet (**in** in + Akk.)

claim /kleɪm/ **1** v.t. (a) beanspruchen ⟨Thron, Gebiete⟩; fordern ⟨Lohnerhöhung, Schadensersatz⟩; beantragen ⟨Sozialhilfe usw.⟩
(b) (assert) behaupten
2 v.i. (Insurance) Ansprüche geltend machen
3 n. Anspruch, der (**to** auf + Akk.); **lay** ~ **to sth.** auf etw. (Akk.) Anspruch erheben

claimant /'kleɪmənt/ n. Antragsteller, der/-stellerin, die

'claim form n. (a) (Insurance) Antragsformular, das
(b) (for expenses) Spesenabrechnungsformular, das

clairvoyant /kleə'vɔɪənt/ **1** n. Hellseher, der/Hellseherin, die
2 adj. hellseherisch

clam /klæm/ **1** n. Klaffmuschel, die
2 v.i., **-mm-:** ~ **up** (coll.) den Mund nicht [mehr] aufmachen

clamber /'klæmbə(r)/ v.i. klettern

clammy /'klæmɪ/ adj. feucht; kalt und schweißig ⟨Haut⟩; klamm ⟨Kleidung⟩

clamour (Brit.; Amer.: **clamor**) /'klæmə(r)/ **1** n. (noise, shouting) Lärm, der; lautes Geschrei
2 v.i. ~ **for sth.** nach etw. schreien

clamp /klæmp/ **1** n. Klammer, die; (for holding) Schraubzwinge, die
2 v.t. klemmen; einspannen ⟨Werkstück⟩
3 v.i. (fig.) ~ **down on sb./sth.** gegen jmdn./etw. rigoros vorgehen

clan /klæn/ n. Sippe, die; (of Scottish Highlanders) Clan, der

clandestine /klæn'destɪn/ adj. heimlich

clang /klæŋ/ **1** n. (of bell) Läuten, das; (of hammer) Klingen, das
2 v.i. ⟨Glocke:⟩ läuten; ⟨Hammer:⟩ klingen

clap /klæp/ **1** n. (a) Klatschen, das
(b) ~ **of thunder** Donnerschlag, der
2 v.i., **-pp-** klatschen
3 v.t., **-pp-:** ~ **one's hands** in die Hände klatschen; ~ **sth.** etw. beklatschen; ~ **sb.** jmdm. Beifall klatschen

'clapping n. Applaus, der

claret /'klærət/ **1** n. roter Bordeauxwein
2 adj. weinrot

clarification /klærɪfɪ'keɪʃn/ n. Klarstellung, die

clarify /'klærɪfaɪ/ v.t. klären ⟨Situation usw.⟩; (by explanation) klarstellen; erläutern ⟨Bedeutung, Aussage⟩

clarinet /klærɪ'net/ n. Klarinette, die

clarity /'klærɪtɪ/ n. Klarheit, die

clash /klæʃ/ **1** v.i. (a) scheppern (ugs.)
(b) (meet in conflict) zusammenstoßen
(c) (disagree) sich streiten
(d) ⟨Interesse, Ereignis:⟩ kollidieren; ⟨Farbe:⟩ sich beißen (ugs.) (**with** mit)
2 v.t. gegeneinander schlagen
3 n. (a) (of cymbals) Dröhnen, das
(b) (meeting in conflict) Zusammenstoß, der
(c) (disagreement) Auseinandersetzung, die
(d) (of personalities, colours) Unverträglichkeit, die; (of events) Überschneiden, das

clasp /klɑːsp/ **1** n. Verschluss, der
2 v.t. umklammern

class /klɑːs/ **1** n. Klasse, die; (in society) Gesellschaftsschicht, die; (Sch.: lesson) Stunde, die
2 v.t. einstufen (**as** als)

'class-conscious adj. klassenbewusst

classic /'klæsɪk/ **1** adj. klassisch
2 n. Klassiker, der; ~**s** Altphilologie, die

classical /'klæsɪkl/ adj. klassisch

classifiable /'klæsɪfaɪəbl/ adj. klassifizierbar

classification /klæsɪfɪ'keɪʃn/ n. Klassifikation, die

classified /'klæsɪfaɪd/ adj. (a) (secret) geheim
(b) ~ **advertisement** Kleinanzeige, die

classify /'klæsɪfaɪ/ v.t. klassifizieren

'classless adj. klassenlos ⟨Gesellschaft⟩

class: ~**mate** n. Klassenkamerad, der/-kameradin, die; ~**room** n. Klassenzimmer, das; ~**room assistant** n. Unterrichtsassistent, der/-assistentin, die; ~ **trip** n. Klassenfahrt, die; Klassenausflug, der

'classy adj. (coll.) klasse

clatter /'klætə(r)/ **1** n. Klappern, das
2 v.i. (a) klappern
(b) (move or fall with a ~) poltern

clause /klɔːz/ n. (a) Klausel, die
(b) (Ling.) Teilsatz, der; **[subordinate]** ~: Nebensatz, der

claustrophobia /klɒstrə'fəʊbɪə/ n. Klaustrophobie, die

claustrophobic /klɒstrə'fəʊbɪk/ adj. beengend ⟨Ort⟩

claw /klɔː/ **1** n. Kralle, die; (of crab etc.) Schere, die
2 v.t. kratzen

clay /kleɪ/ n. Lehm, der; (for pottery) Ton, der

clean /kliːn/ **1** adj. sauber; frisch ⟨Wäsche, Hemd⟩
2 adv. glatt
3 v.t. sauber machen; putzen ⟨Zimmer, Schuh⟩; reinigen ⟨Teppich, Kleidung, Wunde⟩; ~ **one's teeth** sich (Dat.) die Zähne putzen
4 n. **give sth. a** ~: etw. putzen
■ **clean 'out** v.t. (a) sauber machen
(b) (coll.) ~ **sb. out** (take all sb.'s money) jmdn. [total] schröpfen (ugs.)

■ **clean 'up** 1 *v.t.* (a) aufräumen
(b) (fig.) säubern
2 *v.i.* aufräumen

'**clean-cut** *adj.* klar [umrissen]; **his**
∼ **features** seine klar geschnittenen
Gesichtszüge

'**cleaner** *n.* (a) Raumpfleger, *der/*
-pflegerin, *die;* (woman also) Putzfrau, *die*
(b) *usu. in pl.* (dry-∼) Reinigung, *die;* **take**
sth. to the ∼'**s** etw. in die Reinigung bringen

cleanliness /'klɛnlɪnɪs/ *n.* Reinlichkeit,
die

'**clean-living** *adj.* von untadeligem
Lebenswandel *nachgestellt*

cleanly /'kli:nlɪ/ *adv.* sauber

cleanse /klɛnz/ *v.t.* [gründlich] reinigen

'**cleanser** *n.* Reinigungsmittel, *das*

'**clean-shaven** *adj.* glatt rasiert

'**cleansing cream** *n.* Reinigungscreme,
die

clear /klɪə(r)/ 1 *adj.* (a) klar; scharf
⟨*Bild*⟩; **make oneself** ∼: sich deutlich
[genug] ausdrücken; **make it** ∼ [**to sb.**]
that ...: [jmdm.] klar und deutlich sagen,
dass ...
(b) (complete) **three** ∼ **days** volle drei Tage
(c) (unobstructed) frei; **keep sth.** ∼ (not block)
etw. freihalten
2 *adv.* **keep** ∼ **of sth./sb.** etw./jmdn.
meiden; **please stand** *or* **keep** ∼ **of the door**
bitte von der Tür zurücktreten
3 *v.t.* (a) räumen ⟨*Straße*⟩; abräumen
⟨*Schreibtisch*⟩; freimachen ⟨*Abfluss, Kanal*⟩;
∼ **a space for sb./sth.** für jmdn./etw. Platz
machen
(b) (empty) räumen; leeren ⟨*Briefkasten*⟩
(c) (remove) wegräumen; beheben
⟨*Verstopfung*⟩
(d) (show to be innocent) freisprechen
(e) (get permission for) ∼ **sth. with sb.** etw. von
jmdm. genehmigen lassen
4 *v.i.* (a) ⟨*Wetter, Himmel:*⟩ sich aufheitern
(b) (disperse) sich verziehen
5 *n.* **we're in the** ∼ (free of suspicion) auf uns
fällt kein Verdacht; (free of trouble) wir haben
es geschafft

■ **clear 'off** *v.i.* abhauen (salopp)

■ **clear 'out** 1 *v.t.* ausräumen
2 *v.i.* (coll.) verschwinden

■ **clear 'up** 1 *v.t.* (a) wegräumen
⟨*Abfall*⟩; aufräumen ⟨*Platz, Sachen*⟩
(b) (explain) klären
2 *v.i.* (a) aufräumen
(b) ⟨*Wetter:*⟩ sich aufhellen

clearance /'klɪərəns/ *n.* (a) (of obstruction)
Beseitigung, *die*
(b) (clear space) Spielraum, *der*

'**clearance sale** *n.* Räumungsverkauf,
der

'**clear cut** *adj.* klar umrissen; klar
⟨*Abgrenzung, Ergebnis*⟩

'**clearing** *n.* Lichtung, *die*

'**clearing bank** *n.* Clearingbank, *die*

'**clearly** *adv.* (a) (distinctly) klar; deutlich
⟨*sprechen*⟩
(b) (manifestly, unambiguously) eindeutig; klar
⟨*denken*⟩

'**clearway** *n.* (Brit.) Straße mit Halteverbot

cleavage /'kli:vɪdʒ/ *n.* (between breasts)
Dekolleté, *das*

cleaver /'kli:və(r)/ *n.* Hackbeil, *das*

clef /klɛf/ *n.* Notenschlüssel, *der*

cleft /klɛft/ *n.* Spalte, *die*

clematis /'klɛmətɪs, klə'meɪtɪs/ *n.*
Klematis, *die*

clementine /'klɛmənti:n, 'klɛməntaɪn/ *n.*
Klementine, *die*

clench /klɛntʃ/ *v.t.* zusammenpressen;
∼ **one's fist** *or* **fingers** die Faust ballen;
∼ **one's teeth** die Zähne zusammenbeißen

clergy /'klɜ:dʒɪ/ *n. pl.* Geistlichkeit, *die;*
Klerus, *der*

clergyman /'klɜ:dʒɪmən/ *n., pl.* ∼**men**
/'klɜ:dʒɪmən/ Geistliche, *der*

clerical /'klɛrɪkl/ *adj.* Büro⟨*arbeit,*
-personal⟩; ∼ **error** Schreibfehler, *der*

clerk /klɑ:k/ *n.* (in bank) Bankangestellte,
der/die; (in office) Büroangestellte, *der/die*

clever /'klɛvə(r)/ *adj.* (a) klug
(b) (skilful) geschickt
(c) (ingenious) geistreich ⟨*Idee, Argument*⟩
(d) (smart, cunning) clever

'**cleverly** *adv.* (a) klug
(b) (skilfully) geschickt

cliché /'kli:ʃeɪ/ *n.* Klischee, *das*

click /klɪk/ 1 *n.* Klicken, *das*
2 *v.i.* klicken
3 *v.t.* (Comp.) drücken ⟨*Maustaste*⟩

■ **click on** *v.t.* (Comp.) anklicken

client /'klaɪənt/ *n.* (a) Klient, *der/*Klientin,
die
(b) (customer) Kunde, *der/*Kundin, *die*

clientele /kli:ɒn'tel/ *n.* (of shop)
Kundschaft, *die*

cliff /klɪf/ *n.* Kliff, *das*

'**cliffhanger** *n.* Thriller, *der*

climate /'klaɪmət/ *n.* Klima, *das*

'**climate change** *n.* Klimawechsel, *der*

climatic /klaɪ'mætɪk/ *adj.* klimatisch

climax /'klaɪmæks/ *n.* Höhepunkt, *der*

climb /klaɪm/ 1 *v.t.* hinaufsteigen;
klettern auf ⟨*Baum*⟩; ⟨*Auto:*⟩ hinaufkommen
⟨*Hügel*⟩
2 *v.i.* (a) klettern (**up** auf + *Akk.*)
(b) ⟨*Flugzeug, Sonne:*⟩ aufsteigen
3 *n.* Aufstieg, *der*

■ **climb 'down** *v.i.* (a) hinunterklettern
(b) (fig.) nachgeben

'**climbdown** *n.* Rückzieher, *der* (ugs.)

climber /'klaɪmə(r)/ *n.* Bergsteiger, *der*

'**climbing frame** *n.* Klettergerüst, *das*

clinch /klɪntʃ/ 1 *v.t.* zum Abschluss
bringen; perfekt machen (ugs.) ⟨*Geschäft*⟩
2 *n.* (Boxing) Clinch, *der*

cling /klɪŋ/ v.i., **clung** /klʌŋ/ sich
klammern (**to** an + Akk.)
'cling film n. Klarsichtfolie, die
clinic /'klɪnɪk/ n. Klinik, die
clinical /'klɪnɪkl/ adj. (a) (Med.) klinisch
(b) (dispassionate) nüchtern
clink /klɪŋk/ ① n. (of glasses) Klirren, das;
(of coins) Klimpern, das
② v.i. ⟨Flaschen:⟩ klirren; ⟨Münzen:⟩
klimpern
③ v.t. klirren mit ⟨Glas⟩; klimpern mit
⟨Kleingeld⟩
clip¹ /klɪp/ ① n. Klammer, die; (for paper)
Büroklammer, die
② v.t., **-pp-** klammern (**[on] to** an + Akk.)
clip² v.t., **-pp-** (cut) schneiden ⟨Fingernägel,
Haar, Hecke⟩; stutzen ⟨Flügel⟩
clip: ~board n. (a) Klemmbrett, das;
(b) (Comp.) Zwischenablage, die; **~ frame**
n. [rahmenloser] Bilderhalter
clipping /'klɪpɪŋ/ n. (a) (piece clipped off)
Schnipsel, der od. das
(b) (newspaper cutting) Ausschnitt, der
clique /kliːk/ n. Clique, die
clitoris /'klɪtərɪs/ n. Kitzler, der; Klitoris,
die (fachspr.)
cloak /kləʊk/ ① n. Umhang, der
② v.t. [ein]hüllen
'cloakroom n. Garderobe, die; (Brit.
euphem.: lavatory) Toilette, die
clock /klɒk/ ① n. (a) Uhr, die; [work]
against the ~: gegen die Zeit [arbeiten];
round the ~ rund um die Uhr
(b) (coll.) (speedometer) Tacho, der (ugs.);
(milometer) ≈ Kilometerzähler, der
② v.t. **~ [up]** zu verzeichnen haben
⟨Erfolg⟩; erreichen ⟨Geschwindigkeit⟩
▪ **clock 'in, clock 'on** v.i. [bei
Arbeitsantritt] stechen
▪ **clock 'off, clock 'out** v.i. [bei
Arbeitsschluss] stechen
clock 'radio n. Radiowecker, das
'clockwise adv., adj. im Uhrzeigersinn
'clockwork n. Uhrwerk, das; **a ~ car** ein
Aufziehauto; **as regular as ~** (fig.) absolut
regelmäßig
clod /klɒd/ n. (of earth) Scholle, die
clog /klɒg/ ① n. Clog, der; (traditional)
Holzschuh, der
② v.t., **-gg-: ~ [up]** verstopfen
cloister /'klɔɪstə(r)/ n. Kreuzgang, der
clone /kləʊn/ ① n. Klon, der
② v.t. klonen
close ① /kləʊs/ adj. (a) (in space) dicht;
nahe; **be ~ to sth.** nahe bei od. an etw. (Dat.)
sein; **at ~ quarters** aus der Nähe betrachtet
(b) (in time) nahe (**to** an + Dat.)
(c) eng ⟨Freund, Zusammenarbeit⟩; nahe
⟨Verwandte, Bekanntschaft⟩
(d) eingehend ⟨Untersuchung, Prüfung
usw.⟩
(e) hart ⟨Wett[kampf], Spiel⟩; knapp
⟨Ergebnis⟩; **that was a ~ call** or **shave!** (coll.)

das war knapp!
② /kləʊs/ adv. nah[e]; **~ by** in der Nähe;
~ to sb./sth. nahe bei jmdm./etw
③ /kləʊz/ v.t. (a) (shut) schließen; zuziehen
⟨Vorhang⟩; schließen ⟨Laden, Fabrik⟩;
sperren ⟨Straße⟩
(b) (conclude) schließen ⟨Diskussion,
Versammlung⟩
④ /kləʊz/ v.i. (a) (shut) sich schließen
(b) ⟨Laden, Fabrik:⟩ schließen, (ugs.)
zumachen
⑤ /kləʊz/ n. Ende, das; Schluss, der; **come**
or **draw to a ~:** zu Ende gehen; **bring** or
draw sth. to a ~: etw. zu Ende bringen
▪ **close 'down** /kləʊz/ ① v.t. schließen;
stilllegen ⟨Werk⟩
② v.i. geschlossen werden; ⟨Werk:⟩
stillgelegt werden
▪ **close 'in** v.i. ⟨Nacht, Dunkelheit:⟩
hereinbrechen; ⟨Tage:⟩ kürzer werden; **~ in**
on umzingeln
▪ **close 'off** v.t. [ab]sperren
close-cropped /'kləʊskrɒpt/ adj. kurz
geschoren
closed /kləʊzd/ adj. geschlossen; **we're**
~: wir haben geschlossen
'closed-circuit adj. **~ television**
interne Fernsehanlage; (for supervision)
Videoüberwachungsanlage, die
close-down /'kləʊzdaʊn/ n. (Radio, Telev.)
Sendeschluss, der
closed 'shop n. Closed Shop, der
close-knit /kləʊs'nɪt/ adj. fest
zusammengewachsen
closely /'kləʊslɪ/ adv. (a) dicht
(b) (intimately) eng
(c) genau ⟨befragen, prüfen⟩; streng
⟨bewachen⟩
'close-range /'kləʊsreɪndʒ/ adj. ⟨Sicht,
Betrachtung⟩ aus nächster Nähe
closet /'klɒzɪt/ n. (Amer.: cupboard) Schrank,
der
close-up /'kləʊsʌp/ n. **~ [picture/shot]**
Nahaufnahme, die
closing /'kləʊzɪŋ/: **~ date** n. (for
competition) Einsendeschluss, der; (to take
part) Meldefrist, die; **~ time** n. (of pub)
Polizeistunde, die
closure /'kləʊʒə(r)/ n. Schließung, die; (of
road) Sperrung, die
clot /klɒt/ ① n. (a) (blood) Gerinnsel, das
(b) (Brit. coll.: stupid person) Trottel, der
② v.i., **-tt-** ⟨Blut:⟩ gerinnen
cloth /klɒθ/ n., pl. **~s** /klɒθs/ (a) Stoff, der;
Tuch, das
(b) (dish~) Spültuch, das; (table~)
[Tisch]decke, die
clothe /kləʊð/ v.t. kleiden
clothes /kləʊðz/ n. pl. Kleider Pl.; **put**
one's ~ on sich anziehen; **take one's ~ off**
sich ausziehen
clothes: ~ brush n. Kleiderbürste,
die; **~ hanger** n. Kleiderbügel, der;

~ **horse** n. Wäscheständer, der; ~ **line** n. Wäscheleine, die; ~ **peg** (Brit.), **~pin** (Amer.) ns. Wäscheklammer, die

clothing /'kləʊðɪŋ/ n. Kleidung, die

clotted cream /klɒtɪd 'kriːm/ n. sehr fetter Rahm

cloud /klaʊd/ n. (a) Wolke, die; **every ~ has a silver lining** (prov.) es hat alles sein Gutes

(b) ~ **of dust/smoke** Staub-/Rauchwolke, die

■ **cloud 'over** v.i. sich bewölken

'**cloudburst** n. Wolkenbruch, der

'**cloudless** adj. wolkenlos

'**cloudy** adj. bewölkt ⟨Himmel⟩; trübe ⟨Wetter, Flüssigkeit, Glas⟩

clout /klaʊt/ (coll.) ① n. Schlag, der ② v.t. hauen (ugs.)

clove¹ /kləʊv/ n. ~ **[of garlic]** [Knoblauch]zehe, die

clove² n. (spice) [Gewürz]nelke, die

clover /'kləʊvə(r)/ n. Klee, der

'**cloverleaf** n. Kleeblatt, das

clown /klaʊn/ ① n. Clown, der ② v.i. ~ **[about** or **around]** den Clown spielen

cloying /'klɔɪɪŋ/ adj. süßlich

club /klʌb/ ① n. (a) (weapon) Keule, die; (golf ~) Schläger, der

(b) (association) Klub, der; Verein, der

(c) (disco) Club, der; Disco, die

(d) (Cards) Kreuz, das; ~**s are trumps** Kreuz ist Trumpf; **the ace/seven of ~s** das Kreuzas/die Kreuzsieben

② v.t., -bb- (beat) prügeln; (with ~) knüppeln ③ v.i., -bb-: ~ **together** (to buy something) zusammenlegen

clubber /'klʌbə(r)/ n. Nachtklubgänger, der/-gängerin, die; (disco-goer) Clubber, der; Discogänger, der/-gängerin, die

clubbing /'klʌbɪŋ/ n., no pl. Clubbing, das; Besuch von Nachtlokalen/Discos; **go ~**: clubbing gehen; Nachtlokale/Discos aufsuchen

club 'sandwich n. (Amer.) Club-Sandwich, das; Doppeldecker, der (ugs.)

cluck /klʌk/ ① n. Gackern, das ② v.i. gackern

clue /kluː/ n. Anhaltspunkt, der; (in criminal investigation) Spur, die; **not have a ~:** keine Ahnung haben

'**clueless** adj. (coll.) unbedarft (ugs.)

clump /klʌmp/ n. Gruppe, die; (of grass) Büschel, das

clumsily /'klʌmzɪlɪ/ adv. ▶ CLUMSY: schwerfällig; unbeholfen; plump

clumsiness /'klʌmzɪnɪs/ n. ▶ CLUMSY: Schwerfälligkeit, die; Plumpheit, die

clumsy /'klʌmzɪ/ adj. schwerfällig, unbeholfen ⟨Person, Bewegung⟩; plump ⟨Form, Figur, Nachahmung⟩

clung ▶ CLING

cluster /'klʌstə(r)/ ① n. (of grapes, berries) Traube, die; (of fruit, flowers) Büschel, das; (of stars, huts) Haufen, der

② v.i. ~ **[a]round sb./sth.** sich um jmdn./ etw. scharen od. drängen

'**cluster bomb** n. Streubombe, die

clutch /klʌtʃ/ ① v.t. umklammern ② v.i. ~ **at sth.** nach etw. greifen; (fig.) sich an etw. (Akk.) klammern

③ n. (a) in pl. (fig.: control) Klauen

(b) (Motor Veh.) Kupplung, die

clutter /'klʌtə(r)/ ① n. Durcheinander, das

② v.t. ~ **[up] the table/room** überall auf dem Tisch/im Zimmer herumliegen

cm. abbr. = **centimetre[s]** cm

c/o abbr. = **care of** bei; c/o

Co. abbr. (a) = **company** Co.

(b) = **county**

coach /kəʊtʃ/ ① n. (a) (horse-drawn) Kutsche, die

(b) (Railw.) Wagen, der

(c) (bus) [Reise]bus, der; **by ~:** mit dem Bus

(d) (Sport) Trainer, der/Trainerin, die

② v.t. trainieren

coaching /'kəʊtʃɪŋ/ n. (a) (teaching) Privatunterricht, der

(b) (Sport) Training, das

coach: ~ **party** n. Reisegesellschaft, die; ~ **station** n. Busbahnhof, der; ~ **tour** n. Rundreise [im Omnibus]

coagulate /kəʊ'ægjʊleɪt/ ① v.t. gerinnen lassen

② v.i. gerinnen

coal /kəʊl/ n. Kohle, die

coal: ~**field** n. Kohlenrevier, das; ~ **fire** n. Kohlenfeuer, das; ~**-fired** adj. mit Kohle beheizt; kohlebeheizt

coalition /kəʊə'lɪʃn/ n. (Polit.) Koalition, die

coal: ~ **mine** n. [Kohlen]bergwerk, das; ~ **miner** n. [im Kohlenbergbau tätiger] Grubenarbeiter; ~ **mining** n. Kohlenbergbau, der

coarse /kɔːs/ adj. (a) (in texture) grob

(b) (unrefined, obscene) derb

coast /kəʊst/ ① n. Küste, die ② v.i. im Freilauf fahren

coastal /'kəʊstl/ adj. Küsten-

'**coaster** n. (a) (mat) Untersetzer, der

(b) (ship) Küstenmotorschiff, das

coast: ~**guard** n. Küstenwache, -wacht, die; ~**line** n. Küste, die

coat /kəʊt/ ① n. (a) Mantel, der

(b) (layer) Schicht, die; (of paint) Anstrich, der

(c) (animal's hair, fur, etc.) Fell, das

② v.t. überziehen; (with paint) streichen

'**coat hanger** n. Kleiderbügel, der

'**coating** n. Schicht, die

coat of 'arms n. Wappen, das

coax /kəʊks/ v.t. überreden

cobble /'kɒbl/ n. Kopfstein, der

cobbler /'kɒblə(r)/ n. Schuster, der

'**cobblestone** ▸ COBBLE

cobra /'kɒbrə/ n. Kobra, die

cobweb /'kɒbweb/ n. Spinnengewebe, das; Spinnennetz, das

cocaine /kə'keɪn/ n. Kokain, das

cock /kɒk/ 1 n. Hahn, der
2 v.t. spitzen ⟨Ohren⟩; ∼ a/the gun den Hahn spannen

cock-a-hoop /kɒkə'huːp/ adj. überschwänglich

cockatoo /kɒkə'tuː/ n. Kakadu, der

'**cockcrow** n. at ∼: beim ersten Hahnenschrei

cockerel /'kɒkərəl/ n. junger Hahn

cock-eyed /'kɒkaɪd/ adj. (a) (crooked) schief
(b) (absurd) verrückt

cockle /'kɒkl/ n. Herzmuschel, die

cockney /'kɒknɪ/ 1 adj. Cockney-
2 n. Cockney, der

'**cockpit** n. Cockpit, das

cockroach /'kɒkrəʊtʃ/ n. [Küchen-, Haus-] schabe, die

cocktail /'kɒkteɪl/ n. Cocktail, der

cocktail: ∼ **cabinet** n. Hausbar, die; ∼ **party** n. Cocktailparty, die

cocoa /'kəʊkəʊ/ n. Kakao, der

coconut /'kəʊkənʌt/ n. Kokosnuss, die

cocoon /kə'kuːn/ n. (Zool.) Kokon, der

cod /kɒd/ n., pl. same Kabeljau, der

COD abbr. = **cash on delivery,** (Amer.) = **collect on delivery** p. Nachn.

code /kəʊd/ 1 n. (a) (statutes etc.) Gesetzbuch, das; ∼s of behaviour Verhaltensnormen
(b) (system of signals) Code, der; be in ∼: verschlüsselt sein
2 v.t. chiffrieren; verschlüsseln

code: ∼ **name** n. Deckname, der; ∼ **word** n. Kennwort, das

cod-liver '**oil** n. Lebertran, der

co-driver /'kəʊdraɪvə(r)/ n. Beifahrer, der/-fahrerin, die

coed /'kəʊed/ (esp. Amer. coll.) 1 n. Studentin, die
2 adj. ∼ school gemischte Schule

coeducational /kəʊedjʊ'keɪʃnl/ adj. koedukativ; Koedukations-

coerce /kəʊ'ɜːs/ v.t. zwingen; ∼ sb. into sth. jmdn. zu etw. zwingen

coercion /kəʊ'ɜːʃn/ n. Zwang, der

coexist /kəʊɪg'zɪst/ v.i. koexistieren

coexistence /kəʊɪg'zɪstəns/ n. Koexistenz, die

C. of E. /siːəv'iː/ abbr. = **Church of England**

coffee /'kɒfɪ/ n. Kaffee, der; three black/ white ∼s drei [Tassen] Kaffee ohne/mit Milch

coffee: ∼ **bar** n. Café, das; ∼ **bean** n. Kaffeebohne, die; ∼ **break** n. Kaffeepause, die; ∼ **cup** n. Kaffeetasse, die; ∼ **machine**, ∼ **maker** ns. Kaffeeautomat, der; ∼ **pot** n. Kaffeekanne, die; ∼ **shop** n. Kaffeestube, die; ∼ **table** n. Couchtisch, der

coffin /'kɒfɪn/ n. Sarg, der

cog /kɒg/ n. (Mech.) Zahn, der

cogent /'kəʊdʒənt/ adj. überzeugend ⟨Argument⟩; zwingend ⟨Grund⟩

cognac /'kɒnjæk/ n. Cognac, der ⓦ

cog: ∼ **railway** n. Zahnradbahn, die; ∼**wheel** n. Zahnrad, das

cohabit /kəʊ'hæbɪt/ v.i. zusammenleben; in eheähnlicher Gemeinschaft leben (Rechtsspr.)

cohere /kəʊ'hɪə(r)/ v.i. zusammenhalten

coherent /kəʊ'hɪərənt/ adj. zusammenhängend

coherently /kəʊ'hɪərəntlɪ/ adv. zusammenhängend; im Zusammenhang

coil /kɔɪl/ 1 v.t. aufwickeln; (twist) aufdrehen
2 v.i. ∼ round sth. etw. umschlingen
3 n. (a) ∼s of rope/wire aufgerollte Seile Pl./aufgerollter Draht
(b) (single turn) Windung, die
(c) (Electr.) Spule, die

'**coil spring** n. Spiralfeder, die

coin /kɔɪn/ 1 n. Münze, die
2 v.t. prägen ⟨Wort, Redewendung⟩

coincide /kəʊɪn'saɪd/ v.i. (a) (in time) zusammenfallen
(b) (agree) übereinstimmen (with mit)

coincidence /kəʊ'ɪnsɪdəns/ n. Zufall, der

coincidental /kəʊɪnsɪ'dentl/ adj. zufällig

coincidentally /kəʊɪnsɪ'dentəlɪ/ adv. gleichzeitig; (by coincidence) zufälligerweise

'**coin-operated** adj. Münz-

coke /kəʊk/ n. Koks, der

Col. abbr. = **Colonel** Obst.

colander /'kʌləndə(r)/ n. Sieb, das

cold /kəʊld/ 1 adj. (a) kalt; I am/feel ∼: mir ist kalt
(b) (fig.) [betont] kühl ⟨Person, Aufnahme, Begrüßung⟩
2 adv. kalt
3 n. (a) Kälte, die
(b) (illness) Erkältung, die; ∼ [in the head] Schnupfen, der; have a ∼: eine Erkältung/ [einen] Schnupfen haben

cold-blooded /'kəʊldblʌdɪd/ adj. (a) wechselwarm ⟨Tier⟩
(b) kaltblütig ⟨Person, Mord⟩

'**coldly** adv. [betont] kühl

cold: ∼-'**shoulder** v.t. schneiden (fig.); ∼ '**storage** n. Kühllagerung, die; ∼ '**war** n. kalter Krieg

coleslaw /'kəʊlslɔː/ n. Krautsalat, der

collaborate /kə'læbəreɪt/ v.i. (a) zusammenarbeiten; ∼ [with sb.] on

sth. zusammen [mit jmdm.] an etw. (*Dat.*)
arbeiten
(b) (with enemy) kollaborieren
collaboration /kəlæbə'reɪʃn/ *n.*
Zusammenarbeit, *die;* (with enemy)
Kollaboration, *die*
collaborator /kə'læbəreɪtə(r)/ *n.*
Mitarbeiter, *der*/-arbeiterin, *die;* (with enemy)
Kollaborateur, *der*/Kollaborateurin, *die*
collage /'kɒlɑːʒ/ *n.* Collage, *die*
collapse /kə'læps/ ① *n.* **(a)** (of person)
Zusammenbruch, *der*
(b) (of structure) Einsturz, *der*
(c) (of negotiations) Scheitern, *das;* (of company)
Zusammenbruch, *der*
② *v.i.* **(a)** 〈*Person:*〉 zusammenbrechen
(b) 〈*Stuhl:*〉 zusammenbrechen; 〈*Gebäude:*〉
einstürzen
(c) 〈*Verhandlungen:*〉 scheitern;
〈*Unternehmen:*〉 zusammenbrechen
(d) (fold down) 〈*Regenschirm, Fahrrad,
Tisch:*〉 sich zusammenklappen lassen
collapsible /kə'læpsɪbl/ *adj.* Klapp〈*stuhl,
-tisch, -fahrrad*〉
collar /'kɒlə(r)/ ① *n.* **(a)** Kragen, *der*
(b) (for dog) [Hunde]halsband, *das*
② *v.t.* schnappen (ugs.)
'collarbone *n.* Schlüsselbein, *das*
col'lateral damage *n.*, *no pl.*
Kollateralschäden *Pl.*
colleague /'kɒliːg/ *n.* Kollege, *der*/
Kollegin, *die*
collect /kə'lekt/ ① *v.i.* sich versammeln;
〈*Staub, Müll usw.:*〉 sich ansammeln
② *v.t.* sammeln; aufsammeln 〈*Müll, leere
Flaschen usw.*〉; (fetch) abholen 〈*Menschen,
Dinge*〉; ～ one's wits/thoughts seine
Gedanken sammeln
col'lected *adj.* **(a)** (gathered) gesammelt
(b) (calm) gesammelt; gelassen
collection /kə'lekʃn/ *n.* **(a)** (collecting)
Sammeln, *das;* (of goods, persons) Abholen, *das*
(b) (amount of money collected) Sammlung, *die;*
(in church) Kollekte, *die*
(c) (from postbox) Leerung, *die*
(d) (of stamps etc.) Sammlung, *die*
collective /kə'lektɪv/ *adj.* kollektiv *nicht
präd*
collective 'bargaining *n.*
Tarifverhandlungen *Pl.*
collector /kə'lektə(r)/ *n.* **(a)** (of stamps etc.)
Sammler, *der*/Sammlerin, *die*
(b) (of taxes) Einnehmer, *der*/Einnehmerin,
die
**col'lector's item, col'lector's
piece** *ns.* Sammlerstück, *das*
college /'kɒlɪdʒ/ *n.* **(a)** (esp. Brit. Univ.)
College, *das*
(b) (place of further education)
Fach[hoch]schule, *die;* go to ～ (esp. Amer.)
studieren
collide /kə'laɪd/ *v.i.* zusammenstoßen
(with mit)

collie /'kɒlɪ/ *n.* Collie, *der*
colliery /'kɒljərɪ/ *n.* Kohlengrube, *die*
collision /kə'lɪʒn/ *n.* Zusammenstoß, *der;*
on a ～ course (lit. or fig.) auf Kollisionskurs
colloquial /kə'ləʊkwɪəl/ *adj.*
umgangssprachlich
collusion /kə'luːʒn/ *n.* geheime Absprache
cologne ▶ EAU-DE-COLOGNE
Cologne /kə'ləʊn/ ① *pr. n.* Köln (*das*)
② *attrib. adj.* Kölner
Colombia /kə'lɒmbɪə/ *pr. n.* Kolumbien
(*das*)
colon¹ /'kəʊlən/ *n.* Doppelpunkt, *der*
colon² /'kəʊlən, 'kəʊlɒn/ *n.* (Anat.)
Grimmdarm, *der*
colonel /kɜːnl/ *n.* Oberst, *der*
colonial /kə'ləʊnɪəl/ *adj.* Kolonial-;
kolonial
colonize /'kɒlənaɪz/ *v.t.* kolonisieren
colony /'kɒlənɪ/ *n.* Kolonie, *die*
color *etc.* (*Amer.*) ▶ COLOUR *etc.*
colossal /kə'lɒsl/ *adj.* ungeheuer;
gewaltig 〈*Bauwerk*〉
colour /'kʌlə(r)/ (Brit.) ① *n.* Farbe, *die;*
what ～ is it? welche Farbe hat es?; change
～: die Farbe ändern; he is off ～: ihm ist
nicht gut
② *v.t.* **(a)** (give ～ to) Farbe geben (+ *Dat.*)
(b) (paint) malen
(c) (stain, dye) färben
③ *v.i.* **[up]** erröten
'colour-blind *adj.* farbenblind
coloured /'kʌləd/ (Brit.) ① *adj.* **(a)** farbig
(b) (of non-white descent) farbig; ～ people
Farbige *Pl.*
② *n.* Farbige, *der*/*die*
colour: ～-fast *adj.* farbecht; ～ film *n.*
Farbfilm, *der*
colourful /'kʌləfl/ *adj.* (Brit.) bunt;
anschaulich 〈*Sprache, Stil, Bericht*〉
'colouring *n.* (Brit.) **(a)** (colours) Farben *Pl.*
(b) ～ **[matter]** (in food etc.) Farbstoff, *der*
'colourless *adj.* (Brit.) farblos
colour: ～ photograph *n.*
Farbaufnahme, *die;* ～ **printer** *n.*
Farbdrucker, *der;* ～ **scheme** *n.* Farb[en]
zusammenstellung, *die;* ～ **supplement**
n. Farbbeilage, *die;* ～ **television** *n.*
Farbfernsehen, *das;* (set) Farbfernsehgerät,
das; ～ **transparency** *n.* Farbdia, *das*
colt /kəʊlt/ *n.* [Hengst]fohlen, *das*
column /'kɒləm/ *n.* **(a)** Säule, *die*
(b) (of page) Spalte, *die;* sports ～: Sportteil,
der
columnist /'kɒləmɪst/ *n.* Kolumnist,
der/Kolumnistin, *die*
coma /'kəʊmə/ *n.* Koma, *das;* in a ～: im
Koma
comb /kəʊm/ ① *n.* Kamm, *der*
② *v.t.* **(a)** kämmen; ～ sb.'s/one's hair
jmdm./sich die Haare kämmen
(b) (search) durchkämmen

c

combat /'kɒmbæt/ ①　*n.* Kampf, *der*
② *v.t.* bekämpfen
combatant /'kɒmbətənt/ *n.* Kombattant, *der*
combination /kɒmbɪ'neɪʃn/ *n.* Kombination, *die;* in ∼: zusammen
combi'nation lock *n.* Kombinationsschloss, *das*
combine ① /kəm'baɪn/ *v.t.* zusammenfügen (**into** zu); verbinden ⟨*Substanzen*⟩
② *v.i.* (join together) ⟨*Stoffe:*⟩ sich verbinden
③ /'kɒmbaɪn/ *n.* ∼ **[harvester]** Mähdrescher, *der*
combustible /kəm'bʌstɪbl/ *adj.* brennbar
combustion /kəm'bʌstʃn/ *n.* Verbrennung, *die*
come /kʌm/ *v.i.,* came /keɪm/, come /kʌm/ kommen; ∼ **here!** komm [mal] her!; **[I'm] coming!** [ich] komme schon!; **the train came into the station** der Zug fuhr in den Bahnhof ein; **Christmas is coming** bald ist Weihnachten; **the handle has** ∼ **loose** der Griff ist lose; **nothing came of it** es ist nichts daraus geworden
■ **come a'bout** *v.i.* passieren
■ **come across** ① /--'-'-/ *v.i.* (be understood) verstanden werden
② /'---/ *v.t.* begegnen (+ *Dat.*)
■ **come a'long** *v.i.* (coll.) **(a)** (hurry up) ∼ **along!** komm/kommt!
(b) (make progress) ∼ **along nicely** gute Fortschritte machen
(c) (to place) mitkommen (**with** mit)
■ **come 'back** *v.i.* zurückkommen
■ **come by** ① /--'-/ *v.t.* (obtain) bekommen
② /-'-/ *v.i.* vorbeikommen
■ **come 'down** *v.i.* **(a)** (fall) ⟨*Schnee, Regen, Preis:*⟩ fallen
(b) (∼ lower) herunterkommen
(c) (land) [not]landen; (crash) abstürzen
■ **come 'in** *v.i.* (enter) hereinkommen; ∼ **in!** herein!
■ **'come into** *v.t.* **(a)** (enter) hereinkommen in (+ *Akk.*)
(b) (inherit) erben
■ **come off** ① /-'-/ *v.i.* **(a)** ⟨*Griff, Knopf:*⟩ abgehen; (be removable) sich abnehmen lassen
(b) (succeed) ⟨*Pläne, Versuche:*⟩ Erfolg haben
(c) (take place) stattfinden
② /'--/ *v.t.* ∼ **off a horse/bike** vom Pferd/ Fahrrad fallen; ∼ **'off it!** (coll.) nun mach mal halblang! (ugs.)
■ **come on** ① /-'-/ *v.i.* **(a)** (continue coming, follow) kommen; ∼ **on!** komm, komm/ kommt, kommt!; (encouraging) na, komm!
(b) (make progress) ∼ **on very well** gute Fortschritte machen
② /'--/ *v.t.* ∼ UPON
■ **come 'out** *v.i.* **(a)** herauskommen
(b) (fig.) ⟨*Sonne, Wahrheit, Buch:*⟩ herauskommen

(c) ∼ **out with** herausrücken mit (ugs.)
■ **come 'over** ① *v.i.* herüberkommen
② *v.t.* kommen über (+ *Akk.*)
■ **come 'round** *v.i.* **(a)** (visit) vorbeischauen
(b) (recover) wieder zu sich kommen
■ **come 'through** ① *v.i.* durchkommen
② *v.t.* (survive) überleben
■ **come to** ① /'--/ *v.t.* (amount to) ⟨*Rechnung, Kosten:*⟩ sich belaufen auf (+ *Akk.*)
② /-'-/ *v.i.* wieder zu sich kommen
■ **'come under** *v.t.* **(a)** (be classed as or among) kommen unter (+ *Akk.*)
(b) (be subject to) kommen unter (+ *Akk.*)
■ **come 'up** *v.i.* **(a)** (∼ higher) hochkommen
(b) ∼ **up to sb.** (approach for talk) auf jmdn. zukommen
(c) (present itself) sich ergeben
(d) ∼ **up to** (reach) reichen bis an (+ *Akk.*); entsprechen (+ *Dat.*) ⟨*Erwartungen*⟩
(e) ∼ **up against sth.** (fig.) auf etw. (*Akk.*) stoßen
(f) ∼ **up with** vorbringen ⟨*Vorschlag*⟩; wissen ⟨*Lösung, Antwort*⟩
■ **'come upon** *v.t.* (meet by chance) begegnen (+ *Dat.*)
'comeback *n.* (to profession etc.) Comeback, *das*
comedian /kə'miːdɪən/ *n.* Komiker, *der*
comedienne /kəmiːdɪ'en/ *n.* Komikerin, *die*
'comedown *n.* Abstieg, *der*
comedy /'kɒmɪdɪ/ **(a)** *n.* Lustspiel, *das;* Komödie, *die*
(b) (humour) Witz, *der;* Witzigkeit, *die*
comer /'kʌmə(r)/ *n.* **the competition is open to all** ∼**s** an dem Wettbewerb kann sich jeder beteiligen; **the first** ∼: derjenige, der zuerst kommt
comet /'kɒmɪt/ *n.* Komet, *der*
comeuppance /kʌm'ʌpəns/ *n.* **get one's** ∼: die Quittung kriegen (fig.)
comfort /'kʌmfət/ ①　*n.* **(a)** (consolation) Trost, *der*
(b) (physical well-being) Behaglichkeit, *die*
(c) in *pl.* Komfort, *der*
② *v.t.* trösten
comfortable /'kʌmfətəbl/ *adj.*
(a) bequem ⟨*Bett, Schuhe*⟩; komfortabel ⟨*Haus, Zimmer*⟩; **a** ∼ **victory** ein leichter Sieg
(b) (at ease) **be/feel** ∼: sich wohl fühlen
comfortably /'kʌmfətəblɪ/ *adv.* bequem; leicht ⟨*gewinnen*⟩
comforting /'kʌmfətɪŋ/ *adj.* beruhigend ⟨*Gedanke*⟩; tröstend ⟨*Worte*⟩; wohlig ⟨*Wärme*⟩
'comfort station *n.* (Amer.) öffentliche Toilette
comfy /'kʌmfɪ/ *adj.* (coll.) bequem; gemütlich ⟨*Haus, Zimmer*⟩
comic /'kɒmɪk/ ①　*adj.* komisch
② *n.* **(a)** (comedian) Komiker, *der*/

Komikerin, *die*
(b) (periodical) Comicheft, *das*
comical /'kɒmɪkl/ *adj*. komisch
coming /'kʌmɪŋ/ ① *adj*. in the ～ **week** kommende Woche
② *n*. ～s **and goings** das Kommen und Gehen
comma /'kɒmə/ *n*. Komma, *das*
command /kə'mɑːnd/ ① *v.t.* **(a)** (order) befehlen **(sb.** jmdm.)
(b) (be in ～ of) befehligen ⟨*Schiff, Armee*⟩
(c) verfügen über (+ *Akk.*) ⟨*Gelder, Wortschatz*⟩
② *n*. **(a)** Kommando, *das;* (in writing) Befehl, *der;* **have/take** ～ **of** das Kommando über (+ *Akk.*) … haben/übernehmen
(b) (mastery, possession) Beherrschung, *die*
commandeer /kɒmən'dɪə(r)/ *v.t.* requirieren
com'mander *n*. Führer, *der*
com'manding *adj.* **(a)** gebieterisch ⟨*Erscheinung, Stimme*⟩; imposant ⟨*Gestalt*⟩
(b) beherrschend ⟨*Ausblick, Lage*⟩
commanding 'officer *n*. Befehlshaber, *der*/Befehlshaberin, *die*
com'mandment *n*. Gebot, *das*
commemorate /kə'meməreɪt/ *v.t.* gedenken (+ *Gen.*)
commemoration /kəmemə'reɪʃn/ *n*. Gedenken, *das;* **in** ～ **of** zum Gedenken an (+ *Akk.*)
commemorative /kə'memərətɪv/ *adj.* Gedenk-; ～ **of** zum Gedenken an (+ *Akk.*)
commence /kə'mens/ *v.t. & i.* beginnen
com'mencement *n*. Beginn, *der*
commend /kə'mend/ *v.t.* (praise) loben
commendable /kə'mendəbl/ *adj.* lobenswert; löblich
commendation /kɒmen'deɪʃn/ *n*. (praise) Lob, *das;* (official) Belobigung, *die;* (award) Auszeichnung, *die*
comment /'kɒment/ ① *n*. Bemerkung, *die* (on über + *Akk.*); (note) Anmerkung, *die* (on über + *Akk.*); **no** ～! (coll.) kein Kommentar!
② *v.i.* ～ **on sth.** über etw. (*Akk.*) Bemerkungen machen; **he** ～ed **that** …: er bemerkte, dass …
commentary /'kɒməntərɪ/ *n*.
(a) Kommentar, *der* (on zu)
(b) (Radio, Telev.) **[live** *or* **running]** ～: Livereportage, *die*
commentate /'kɒmənteɪt/ *v.i.* ～ **on sth.** etw. kommentieren
commentator /'kɒmənteɪtə(r)/ *n*. Kommentator, *der*/Kommentatorin, *die;* (Sport) Reporter, *der*/Reporterin, *die*
commerce /'kɒmɜːs/ *n*. Handel, *der*
commercial /kə'mɜːʃl/ ① *adj.* Handels-; kaufmännisch ⟨*Ausbildung*⟩
② *n*. Werbespot, *der*
commercial: ～ **'bank** *n*. private Geschäftsbank; ～ **'break** *n*. Werbepause, *die*

commercialism /kə'mɜːʃəlɪzm/ *n*. Kommerzialismus, *der*
commercialize /kə'mɜːʃəlaɪz/ *v.t.* kommerzialisieren
commercial: ～ **'radio** *n*. Werbefunk, *der;* ～ **'television** *n*. Werbefernsehen, *das;* ～ **'traveller** *n*. Handelsvertreter, *der*/-vertreterin, *die;* ～ **'vehicle** *n*. Nutzfahrzeug, *das*
commiserate /kə'mɪzəreɪt/ *v.i.* ～ **with sb.** jmdm. sein Mitgefühl aussprechen (on zu)
commission /kə'mɪʃn/ ① *n*. **(a)** (official body) Kommission, *die*
(b) (instruction, piece of work) Auftrag, *der*
(c) (Mil.) Ernennungsurkunde, *die*
(d) (pay of agent) Provision, *die*
(e) in/out of ～ ⟨*Auto, Maschine*⟩ in/außer Betrieb
② *v.t.* beauftragen ⟨*Künstler*⟩; in Auftrag geben ⟨*Gemälde usw.*⟩
commissionaire /kəmɪʃə'neə(r)/ *n*. (esp. Brit.) Portier, *der*
commissioner /kə'mɪʃənə(r)/ *n*. (of police) Präsident, *der*
commit /kə'mɪt/ *v.t.,* -tt-: **(a)** begehen ⟨*Verbrechen, Fehler, Ehebruch*⟩
(b) (pledge, bind) ～ **oneself/sb. to doing sth.** sich/jmdn. verpflichten, etw. zu tun
(c) (entrust) anvertrauen (to *Dat.*)
(d) ～ **sb. for trial** jmdm. dem Gericht überstellen
com'mitment *n*. Verpflichtung (to gegenüber)
com'mitted *adj.* engagiert
committee /kə'mɪtɪ/ *n*. Ausschuss, *der*
commodity /kə'mɒdɪtɪ/ *n*. **(a)** household ～: Haushaltsartikel, *der*
(b) (St. Exch.) [vertretbare] Ware; (raw material) Rohstoff, *der*
common /'kɒmən/ ① *adj.* **(a)** (belonging to all) gemeinsam
(b) (public) öffentlich
(c) (usual) gewöhnlich; (frequent) häufig; allgemein verbreitet ⟨*Sitte, Redensart*⟩
(d) (vulgar) ordinär
② *n*. **(a)** (land) Gemeindeland, *das*
(b) **have sth./nothing/a lot in** ～ **[with sb.]** etw./nichts/viel [mit jmdm.] gemein[sam] haben
common 'cold *n*. Erkältung, *die*
'commoner *n*. Bürgerliche *der/die*
common: ～ **'ground** *n*. gemeinsame Basis; ～ **'knowledge** *n*. it's [a matter of] ～ **knowledge that** … es ist allgemein bekannt, dass …; ～**-law** *adj.* she's his ～-law wife sie lebt mit ihm in eheähnlicher Gemeinschaft
'commonly *adv.* im Allgemeinen
common: C～ **'Market** *n*. gemeinsamer Markt; ～**place** ① *n*. Gemeinplatz, *der;* ② *adj.* alltäglich; ～ **room** *n*. (Brit.) Gemeinschaftsraum, *der;* (for lecturers) Dozentenzimmer, *das*

Commons /'kɒmənz/ n. pl. the [House of] ~: das Unterhaus

common: ~ **'sense** n. gesunder Menschenverstand; ~**-sense** adj. vernünftig; gesund ‹Ansicht, Standpunkt›; ~**wealth** n. the [British] C~**wealth** das Commonwealth

commotion /kə'məʊʃn/ n. Tumult, der

communal /'kɒmjʊnl/ adj. (a) (of or for the community) gemeindlich (b) (for common use) gemeinsam

commune /'kɒmjuːn/ n. Kommune, die

communicate /kə'mjuːnɪkeɪt/ 1 v. t. übertragen ‹Krankheit›; übermitteln ‹Informationen›; vermitteln ‹Gefühle, Ideen› 2 v.i. ~ with sb. mit jmdm. kommunizieren

communication /kəmjuːnɪ'keɪʃn/ n. (a) (of information) Übermittlung, die (b) (message) Mitteilung, die (to an + Akk.)

communication: ~ **cord** n. Notbremse, die; ~**s satellite** n. Nachrichtensatellit, der

communicative /kə'mjuːnɪkətɪv/ adj. gesprächig

Communion /kə'mjuːnɪən/ n. [Holy] ~ (Protestant Ch.) das [heilige] Abendmahl; (RC Ch.) die [heilige] Kommunion

communiqué /kə'mjuːnɪkeɪ/ n. Kommuniqué, das

communism /'kɒmjʊnɪzm/ n. Kommunismus, der; C~: der Kommunismus

Communist, communist /'kɒmjʊnɪst/ 1 n. Kommunist, der/ Kommunistin, die 2 adj. kommunistisch

community /kə'mjuːnɪtɪ/ n. (a) (organized body) Gemeinwesen, das; the Jewish ~: die jüdische Gemeinde (b) no pl. (public) Öffentlichkeit, die

community: ~ **'care** n. ≈ ambulante Betreuung; ~ **centre** n. Gemeindezentrum, das; ~ **'charge** n. (Brit.) Gemeindesteuer, die; ~ **'service** n.: [freiwilliger od. als Strafe auferlegter] sozialer Dienst; ~ **spirit** n. Gemeinschaftsgeist, der

commute /kə'mjuːt/ 1 v.t. umwandeln ‹Strafe› (to in + Akk.) 2 v.i. pendeln

commuter /kə'mjuːtə(r)/ n. Pendler, der/Pendlerin, die

com'muter: ~ **belt** n. großstädtischer Einzugsbereich; ~ **train** n. Pendlerzug, der

compact[1] /kəm'pækt/ adj. kompakt

compact[2] /'kɒmpækt/ n. Puderdose [mit Puder(stein)]

compact 'disc n. Compactdisc, die; ~ **player** CD-Spieler, der

companion /kəm'pænjən/ n. Begleiter, der/Begleiterin, die

com'panionship n. Gesellschaft, die

company /'kʌmpənɪ/ n. (a) (persons assembled, companionship) Gesellschaft, die; expect ~: Besuch od. Gäste erwarten; keep sb. ~: jmdm. Gesellschaft leisten (b) (firm) Gesellschaft, die; ~ car Firmenwagen, der; ~ policy Unternehmenspolitik, die; Firmenpolitik, die (c) (of actors) Truppe, die; Ensemble, das (d) (Mil.) Kompanie, die

comparable /'kɒmpərəbl/ adj. vergleichbar (to, with mit)

comparably /'kɒmpərəblɪ/ adv. in vergleichbarer Weise; vergleichbar

comparative /kəm'pærətɪv/ 1 adj. (a) (relative) relativ; in ~ comfort relativ komfortabel (b) (Ling.) komparativ (fachspr.); a ~ adjective/adverb ein Adjektiv/Adverb im Komparativ 2 n. (Ling.) Komparativ, der

com'paratively adv. verhältnismäßig

compare /kəm'peə(r)/ 1 v.t. vergleichen (to, with mit); ~d with or to sb./sth. verglichen mit od. im Vergleich zu jmdm./etw 2 v.i. sich vergleichen lassen

comparison /kəm'pærɪsn/ n. Vergleich, der; in or by ~ [with sb./sth.] im Vergleich [zu jmdm./etw.]

compartment /kəm'pɑːtmənt/ n. (in drawer, desk, etc.) Fach, das; (of railway carriage) Abteil, das

compass /'kʌmpəs/ n. (a) in pl. [a pair of] ~es ein Zirkel (b) (for navigating) Kompass, der

compassion /kəm'pæʃn/ n. Mitgefühl, das (for mit)

compassionate /kəm'pæʃənət/ adj. mitfühlend; on ~ grounds aus persönlichen Gründen; (for family reasons) aus familiären Gründen

compatibility /kəmpætɪ'bɪlɪtɪ/ n. Vereinbarkeit, die; (of people) Zueinanderpassen, das; (Comp.) Kompatibilität, die

compatible /kəm'pætɪbl/ adj. vereinbar; zueinander passend ‹Personen›; (Comp.) kompatibel

compel /kəm'pel/ v.t., -ll- zwingen

compelling /kəm'pelɪŋ/ adj. bezwingend

compendium /kəm'pendɪəm/ n. Kompendium, das

compensate /'kɒmpenseɪt/ 1 v.i. ~ for sth. etw. ersetzen 2 v.t. ~ sb. for sth. jmdn. für etw. entschädigen

compensation /kɒmpen'seɪʃn/ n. Ersatz, der; (for damages, injuries, etc.) Schaden[s]ersatz, der

compère /'kɒmpeə(r)/ n. (Brit.) Conférencier, der

compete /kəm'piːt/ *v.i.* konkurrieren **(for** um); (Sport) kämpfen

competence /'kɒmpɪtəns/ *n.* Fähigkeiten *Pl.*

competent /'kɒmpɪtənt/ *adj.* fähig; **not ~ to do sth.** nicht kompetent, etw. zu tun

'competently *adv.* kompetent

competition /kɒmpɪ'tɪʃn/ *n.* **(a)** (contest) Wettbewerb, *der;* (in magazine etc.) Preisausschreiben, *das* **(b)** (those competing) Konkurrenz, *die*

competitive /kəm'petɪtɪv/ *adj.* wettbewerbsfähig 〈*Preis, Unternehmen*〉; **~ sports** Leistungssport, *der*

competitor /kəm'petɪtə(r)/ *n.* Konkurrent, *der*/Konkurrentin, *die;* (in contest, race) Teilnehmer, *der*/-nehmerin, *die*

compile /kəm'paɪl/ *v.t.* zusammenstellen

complacency /kəm'pleɪsənsɪ/ *n.* Selbstzufriedenheit, *die*

complacent /kəm'pleɪsənt/ *adj.* selbstzufrieden

complain /kəm'pleɪn/ *v.i.* sich beklagen **(about, at** über + *Akk.;* **to** bei); **~ of sth.** über etw. (*Akk.*) klagen

complaint /kəm'pleɪnt/ *n.* **(a)** Beschwerde, *die* **(b)** (ailment) Leiden, *das*

complement ⓵ /'kɒmplɪmənt/ *n.* **(a)** (what completes) Vervollständigung, *die* **(b)** (full number) **a [full] ~:** die volle Zahl; (of people) die volle Stärke ⓶ /'kɒmplɪment/ *v.t.* ergänzen

complementary /kɒmplɪ'mentərɪ/ *adj.* **(a)** (completing) ergänzend **(b)** (completing each other) einander ergänzend

complementary 'medicine *n.* Komplementärmedizin, *die*

complete /kəm'pliːt/ ⓵ *adj.* **(a)** vollständig; (in number) vollzählig **(b)** (finished) fertig **(c)** (absolute) völlig 〈*Idiot*〉; absolut 〈*Katastrophe*〉; total, (ugs.) blutig 〈*Anfänger*〉 ⓶ *v.t.* **(a)** (finish) beenden; fertig stellen 〈*Gebäude, Arbeit*〉 **(b)** ausfüllen 〈*Formular*〉

com'pletely *adv.* völlig; absolut 〈*erfolgreich*〉

completion /kəm'pliːʃn/ *n.* Beendigung, *die;* (of building, work) Fertigstellung, *die*

complex /'kɒmpleks/ ⓵ *adj.* kompliziert ⓶ *n.* Komplex, *der*

complexion /kəm'plekʃn/ *n.* Gesichtsfarbe, *die;* (fig.) Gesicht, *das*

-complexioned /kəm'plekʃnd/ *adj.* in comb. **sallow-/fair-~:** mit gelblichem Teint/mit hellem Teint

complexity /kəm'pleksɪtɪ/ *n.* Kompliziertheit, *die*

complicate /'kɒmplɪkeɪt/ *v.t.* komplizieren.

'complicated *adj.* kompliziert

complication /kɒmplɪ'keɪʃn/ *n.* Komplikation, *die*

complicity /kəm'plɪsɪtɪ/ *n.* Mittäterschaft, *die* **(in bei)**

compliment ⓵ /'kɒmplɪmənt/ *n.* Kompliment, *das; in pl.* (formal greetings) Grüße *Pl.;* **pay sb. a ~:** jmdn. ein Kompliment machen ⓶ /'kɒmplɪment/ *v.t.* **~ sb. on sth.** jmdm. Komplimente wegen etw. machen

complimentary /kɒmplɪ'mentərɪ/ *adj.* **(a)** schmeichelhaft **(b)** (free) Frei-

comply /kəm'plaɪ/ *v.i.* **~ with sth.** sich nach etw. richten; **he refused to ~:** er wollte sich nicht danach richten

component /kəm'pəʊnənt/ ⓵ *n.* Bestandteil, *der* ⓶ *adj.* **a ~ part** ein Bestandteil

compose /kəm'pəʊz/ *v.t.* **(a)** bilden; **be ~d of** sich zusammensetzen aus **(b)** verfassen 〈*Rede, Gedicht*〉; abfassen 〈*Brief*〉 **(c)** (Mus.) komponieren

com'posed *adj.* (calm) gefasst

com'poser *n.* Komponist, *der*/ Komponistin, *die*

composition /kɒmpə'zɪʃn/ *n.* **(a)** (constitution) (of soil etc.) Zusammensetzung, *die;* (of picture) Aufbau, *der* **(b)** (essay) Aufsatz, *der;* (Mus.) Komposition, *die*

compost /'kɒmpɒst/ *n.* Kompost, *der*

compostable /'kɒmpɒstəbl/ *adj.* kompostierbar

'compost heap *n.* Komposthaufen, *der*

composure /kəm'pəʊʒə(r)/ *n.* Gleichmut, *der*

compound¹ ⓵ /'kɒmpaʊnd/ *adj.* **(a)** zusammengesetzt **(b)** (Med.) **~ fracture** komplizierter Bruch ⓶ /'kɒmpaʊnd/ *n.* **(a)** (mixture) Mischung, *die* **(b)** (Ling.) Kompositum, *das* **(c)** (Chem.) Verbindung, *die* ⓷ /'kəm'paʊnd/ *v.t.* verschlimmern 〈*Schwierigkeiten, Verletzung usw.*〉

compound² /'kɒmpaʊnd/ *n.* umzäuntes Gelände

compound 'interest *n.* Zinseszinsen *Pl.*

comprehend /kɒmprɪ'hend/ *v.t.* verstehen

comprehensible /kɒmprɪ'hensɪbl/ *adj.* verständlich

comprehension /kɒmprɪ'henʃn/ *n.* Verständnis, *das*

comprehensive /kɒmprɪ'hensɪv/ ⓵ *adj.* **(a)** umfassend **(b)** **~ school** Gesamtschule, *die* **(c)** (insurance) Vollkasko- ⓶ *n.* Gesamtschule, *die*

compress ⓵ /kəm'pres/ *v.t.* **(a)** (squeeze) zusammenpressen **(into** zu)   ····>

(b) komprimieren ⟨*Luft, Gas, Bericht*⟩
(c) (Comp.) komprimieren
2 /'kɒmpres/ *n.* Kompresse, *die*
compression /kəm'preʃn/ *n.*
Kompression, *die*
compressor /kəm'presə(r)/ *n.*
Kompressor, *der*
comprise /kəm'praɪz/ *v.t.* (include)
umfassen; (consist of) bestehen aus
compromise /'kɒmprəmaɪz/ **1** *n.*
Kompromiss, *der*
2 *v.i.* Kompromisse/einen Kompromiss
schließen
3 *v.t.* kompromittieren
compromising /'kɒmprəmaɪzɪŋ/ *adj.*
kompromittierend
compulsion /kəm'pʌlʃn/ *n.* Zwang, *der;*
be under no ～ to do sth. keineswegs etw.
tun müssen
compulsive /kəm'pʌlsɪv/ *adj.*
(a) zwanghaft; he is a ～ gambler er ist dem
Spiel verfallen
(b) this book is ～ reading von diesem Buch
kann man sich nicht losreißen
compulsory /kəm'pʌlsəri/ *adj.*
obligatorisch
compunction /kəm'pʌŋkʃn/ *n.*
Schuldgefühle
computer /kəm'pjuːtə(r)/ *n.* Computer,
der
computer: ～-**aided** *adj.*
computergestützt; ～ **ani'mation** *n.*
Computeranimation, *die;* ～-**assisted**
adj. computergestützt; ～ '**dating**
n. Partnervermittlung per Computer;
～ **dating agency/service** Computer-Partn
ervermittlung[sagentur], *die;* ～ **game** *n.*
Computerspiel, *das;* ～ '**graphics** *n. pl.*
Computergraphik, *die*
computerisation, computerise
▶ COMPUTERIZ-
computerization /kəmpjuːtəraɪ'zeɪʃn/
n. Computerisierung, *die*
computerize /kəm'pjuːtəraɪz/ *v.t.*
computerisieren
computer: ～-'**literate** *adj.* mit
Computern vertraut; ～-'**operated** *adj.*
computergesteuert; rechnergesteuert;
～ **program** *n.* Programm, *das;*
～ **programmer** *n.* Programmierer, *der/*
Programmiererin, *die;* ～ **programming**
n. Programmieren, *das;* ～ **room** *n.*
Computerraum, *der;* ～ '**science** *n.*
Computerwissenschaft, *die;* ～ **terminal**
n. Terminal, *das;* ～ '**typesetting**
n. Computersatz, *der;* ～ **virus** *n.*
[Computer]virus, *das od. der*
computing /kəm'pjuːtɪŋ/ *n.* EDV, *die;*
elektronische Datenverarbeitung; ～ **skills**
Computerkenntnisse *Pl.*
comrade /'kɒmreɪd, 'kɒmrɪd/ *n.*
Kamerad, *der/*Kameradin, *die*
'**comradeship** *n.* Kameradschaft, *die*

con /kɒn/ (coll.) **1** *n.* Schwindel, *der*
2 *v.t.,* -**nn**- reinlegen (ugs.); ～ **sb. into sth.**
jmdm. etw. aufschwatzen (ugs.)
concave /'kɒnkeɪv/ *adj.* konkav
conceal /kən'siːl/ *v.t.* verbergen (**from** vor
+ *Dat.*)
con'cealment *n.* Verbergen, *das*
concede /kən'siːd/ *v.t.* zugeben
conceit /kən'siːt/ *n.* Einbildung, *die*
con'ceited *adj.* eingebildet
conceivable /kən'siːvəbl/ *adj.*
vorstellbar; it is scarcely ～ that …: man
kann sich (*Dat.*) kaum vorstellen, dass …
conceivably /kən'sɪːvəblɪ/ *adj.*
möglicherweise; he cannot ～ have done it
er kann es unmöglich getan haben
conceive /kən'siːv/ **1** *v.t.* **(a)** empfangen
⟨*Kind*⟩
(b) (form in mind) sich (*Dat.*) vorstellen; haben
⟨*Idee, Plan*⟩
2 *v.i.* **(a)** (become pregnant) empfangen
(b) ～ **of sth.** sich (*Dat.*) etw. vorstellen
concentrate /'kɒnsəntreɪt/ **1** *v.t.*
konzentrieren
2 *v.i.* sich konzentrieren (**on** auf + *Akk.*)
'**concentrated** *adj.* konzentriert
concentration /kɒnsən'treɪʃn/ *n.*
Konzentration, *die*
concen'tration camp *n.*
Konzentrationslager, *das;* KZ, *das*
concentric /kən'sentrɪk/ *adj.*
konzentrisch
concept /'kɒnsept/ *n.* Begriff, *der;* (idea)
Vorstellung, *die*
conception /kən'sepʃn/ **(a)** Vorstellung,
die (**of** von)
(b) (of child) Empfängnis, *die*
conceptual /kən'septjʊəl/ *adj.* begrifflich
conceptualize /kən'septjʊəlaɪz/ *v.t.*
begrifflich fassen
concern /kən'sɜːn/ **1** *v.t.* **(a)** (affect)
betreffen; so far as … is ～ed was … betrifft;
'to whom it may ～' ≈ „Bestätigung"; (on
certificate, testimonial) ≈ „Zeugnis"
(b) (interest) ～ **oneself with** *or* **about sth.** sich
mit etw. befassen
(c) (trouble) beunruhigen
2 *n.* **(a)** (anxiety) Besorgnis, *die;* (interest)
Interesse, *das*
(b) (matter) Angelegenheit, *die*
(c) (firm) Unternehmen, *das*
con'cerned /kən'sɜːnd/ *adj.* **(a)** (involved)
betroffen; (interested) interessiert; as *or* so far
as I'm ～: was mich betrifft
(b) (troubled) besorgt
con'cerning *prep.* bezüglich
concert /'kɒnsət/ *n.* Konzert, *das*
concerted /kən'sɜːtɪd/ *adj.* vereint
concert: ～-**goer** *n.* Konzertbesucher,
der/-besucherin, *die;* ～ **hall** *n.* Konzertsaal,
der
concertina /kɒnsə'tiːnə/ *n.* Konzertina, *die*

concerto /kən'tʃeətəʊ/ *n.* Konzert, *das*
concession /kən'seʃn/ *n.* Konzession, *die*
concessionary /kən'seʃənərɪ/ *adj.*
Konzessions-; ~ **rate/fare** ermäßigter Tarif
conciliatory /kən'sɪljətərɪ/ *adj.*
versöhnlich
concise /kən'saɪs/ *adj.* kurz und
prägnant; knapp, konzis ‹*Stil*›
conclude /kən'kluːd/ ① *v.t.* (a) (end)
beschließen
(b) (infer) schließen (**from** aus)
(c) (reach decision) beschließen
② *v.i.* (end) schließen
concluding /kən'kluːdɪŋ/ *adj.*
abschließend
conclusion /kən'kluːʒn/ *n.* (a) (end)
Abschluss, *der;* **in** ~: zum Abschluss
(b) (result) Ausgang, *der*
(c) (inference) Schluss, *der;* **draw** *or* **reach a**
~: zu einem Schluss kommen
conclusive /kən'kluːsɪv/ *adj.*,
con'clusively *adv.* schlüssig
concoct /kən'kɒkt/ *v.t.* zubereiten;
zusammenbrauen ‹*Trank*›
concoction /kən'kɒkʃn/ *n.* Gebräu, *das*
concourse /'kɒnkɔːs/ *n.* Halle, *die;* **station**
~: Bahnhofshalle, *die*
concrete /'kɒnkriːt/ ① *adj.* konkret
② *n.* Beton, *der; attrib.* Beton-; aus Beton
präd
concrete/'kɒnkriːt/**:** ~ **mixer** *n.*
Betonmischer, *der;* Betonmischmaschine,
die; ~ **'poetry** *n.* konkrete Poesie
concur /kən'kɜː(r)/ *v.i.*, **-rr-:** ~ [**with sb.**] [**in**
sth.] [jmdm.] [in etw. (*Dat.*)] zustimmen
concurrent /kən'kʌrənt/ *adj.*,
con'currently *adv.* gleichzeitig
concussion /kən'kʌʃn/ *n.*
Gehirnerschütterung, *die*
condemn /kən'dem/ *v.t.* (a) (censure)
verdammen
(b) (Law: sentence) verurteilen (**to** zu)
(c) für unbewohnbar erklären ‹*Gebäude*›
condemnation /kɒndem'neɪʃn/ *n.*
Verdammung, *die*
condensation /kɒnden'seɪʃn/ *n.*
(a) (condensing) Kondensation, *die*
(b) (water) Kondenswasser, *das*
condense /kən'dens/ ① *v.t.*
(a) komprimieren; ~**d milk** Kondensmilch,
die
(b) (Phys., Chem.) kondensieren
② *v.i.* kondensieren
condescend /kɒndɪ'send/ *v.i.* ~ **to do**
sth. sich dazu herablassen, etw. zu tun
conde'scending *adj.* herablassend
condescension /kɒndɪ'senʃn/ *n.* (derog.:
patronizing manner) Herablassung, *die*
condiment /'kɒndɪmənt/ *n.* Gewürz, *das*
condition /kən'dɪʃn/ *n.* (a) (stipulation)
[Vor]bedingung, *die;* **on** [**the**] ~ **that** ...:
unter der Voraussetzung, dass ...

(b) *in pl.* (circumstances) Umstände *Pl.;*
weather/living ~**s** Witterungs-/
Wohnverhältnisse; **working** ~**s**
Arbeitsbedingungen
(c) (of athlete etc.) Form, *die;* (of thing) Zustand,
der; (of patient) Verfassung, *die*
(d) (Med.) Leiden, *das*
conditional /kən'dɪʃənl/ *adj.* (a) bedingt;
be ~ [**up**]**on sth.** von etw. abhängen
(b) (Ling.) Konditional-
con'ditioner *n.* Frisiermittel, *das*
condolence /kən'dəʊləns/ *n.*
Anteilnahme, die; **letter of** ~: Beileidsbrief,
der
condom /'kɒndɒm/ *n.* Kondom, *das od. der*
condominium /'kɒndə'mɪnɪəm/
n. (Amer.) Appartementhaus [mit
Eigentumswohnungen]
condone /kən'dəʊn/ *v.t.* hinwegsehen
über (+ *Akk.*); (approve) billigen
conducive /kən'djuːsɪv/ *adj.* **be** ~ **to sth.**
einer Sache (*Dat.*) förderlich sein
conduct ① /'kɒndʌkt/ *n.* (a) (behaviour)
Verhalten, *das*
(b) (way of ~ing) Führung, *die*
② /kən'dʌkt/ *v.t.* (a) führen
(b) (Mus.) dirigieren
(c) (Phys.) leiten
(d) ~**ed tour** Führung, *die*
conduction /kən'dʌkʃn/ *n.* (Phys.)
Leitung, *die*
conductor /kən'dʌktə(r)/ *n.* (a) (Mus.)
Dirigent, *der*/Dirigentin, *die*
(b) (of bus, tram) Schaffner, *der*
conductress /kən'dʌktrɪs/ *n.*
Schaffnerin, *die*
conduit /'kɒndjʊɪt/ *n.* (a) Leitung, *die;*
Kanal, *der* (auch fig.)
(b) (Electr.) Isolierrohr, *das*
cone /kəʊn/ *n.* (a) Kegel, *der;* (traffic ~)
Leitkegel, *der*
(b) (Bot.) Zapfen, *der*
(c) ice-cream ~: Eistüte, *die*
confectioner /kən'fekʃənə(r)/ *n.* ~**'s**
[shop] Süßwarengeschäft, *das*
con'fectionery *n.* Süßwaren *Pl.*
confederate /kən'fedərət/ *adj.* verbündet
confederation /kən'fedə'reɪʃn/ *n.*
[Staaten]bund, *der*
confer /kən'fɜː(r)/ ① *v.t.*, **-rr-:** ~ **sth.**
[**up**]**on sb.** jmdm. etw. verleihen
② *v.i.*, **-rr-:** ~ **with sb.** sich mit jmdm.
beraten
conference /'kɒnfərəns/ *n.*
(a) Konferenz, *die*
(b) **be in** ~: in einer Besprechung sein
conference: ~ **room** *n.*
Konferenzraum, *der;* ~ **table** *n.*
Konferenztisch, *der*
confess /kən'fes/ ① *v.t.* (a) gestehen
(b) (Eccl.) beichten
② *v.i.* (a) ~ **to sth.** etw. gestehen
(b) (Eccl.) beichten (**to sb.** jmdm.)

confession /kən'feʃn/ n. (a) Geständnis, das
(b) (Eccl.: of sins etc.) Beichte, die
confetti /kən'fetɪ/ n. Konfetti, das
confidant /'kɒnfɪdænt, kɒnfɪ'dænt/ n. Vertraute, der
confidante /'kɒnfɪdænt, kɒnfɪ'dænt/ n. Vertraute, die
confide /kən'faɪd/ ☐1 v.i. ~ in sb. sich jmdm. anvertrauen
☐2 v.t. ~ sth. to sb. jmdm. etw. anvertrauen
confidence /'kɒnfɪdəns/ n. (a) (firm trust) Vertrauen, das; **have ~ in sb./sth.** Vertrauen zu jmdm./etw. haben; **have [absolute] ~ that ...:** [absolut] sicher sein, dass ...
(b) (assured expectation) Gewissheit, die
(c) (self-reliance) Selbstvertrauen, das
(d) **in ~:** im Vertrauen; **this is in [strict] ~:** das ist [streng] vertraulich
'**confidence trick** n. (Brit.) Trickbetrug, der
confident /'kɒnfɪdənt/ adj. zuversichtlich (**about** in Bezug auf + Akk.)
confidential /kɒnfɪ'denʃl/ adj. vertraulich
confidentiality /kɒnfɪdenʃɪ'ælɪtɪ/ n. Vertraulichkeit, die
confi'dentially adv. vertraulich
'**confidently** adv. zuversichtlich
confiding /kən'faɪdɪŋ/ adj.,
con'fidingly adv. vertrauensvoll
configure /kən'fɪgə(r)/ v.t. (esp. Comp.) konfigurieren
confine /kən'faɪn/ v.t. (a) einsperren; **be ~d to bed/the house** ans Bett/Haus gefesselt sein
(b) (fig.) ~ **oneself to doing sth.** sich darauf beschränken, etw. zu tun
con'fined adj. begrenzt
con'finement n. (imprisonment) Einsperrung, die
confines /'kɒnfaɪnz/ n. pl. Grenzen
confirm /kən'fɜːm/ v.t. bestätigen
confirmation /kɒnfə'meɪʃn/ n.
(a) Bestätigung, die
(b) (Protestant Ch.) Konfirmation, die; (RC Ch.) Firmung, die
con'firmed adj. eingefleischt ⟨Junggeselle⟩; überzeugt ⟨Vegetarier⟩
confiscate /'kɒnfɪskeɪt/ v.t. beschlagnahmen
confiscation /kɒnfɪs'keɪʃn/ n. Beschlagnahme, die
conflict ☐1 /'kɒnflɪkt/ n. (a) (fight) Kampf, der
(b) (clashing) Konflikt, der
☐2 /kən'flɪkt/ v.i. (be incompatible) sich (Dat.) widersprechen; ~ **with sth.** einer Sache (Dat.) widersprechen
con'flicting adj. widersprüchlich
conform /kən'fɔːm/ v.i. (a) entsprechen (**to** Dat.)

(b) (comply) sich einfügen; ~ **to** or **with sth./with sb.** sich nach etw./jmdm. richten
conformist /kən'fɔːmɪst/ n. Konformist, der/Konformistin, die
conformity /kən'fɔːmɪtɪ/ n. Übereinstimmung, die (**with, to** mit)
confound /kən'faʊnd/ v.t. (a) (defeat) vereiteln
(b) (confuse) verwirren
con'founded adj. (coll. derog.) verdammt
confront /kən'frʌnt/ v.t.
(a) gegenüberstellen; ~ **sb. with sth./sb.** jmdn. mit etw./[mit] jmdm. konfrontieren
(b) (stand facing) gegenüberstehen (+ Dat.)
confrontation /kɒnfrən'teɪʃn/ n. Konfrontation, die
confuse /kən'fjuːz/ v.t. (a) (disorder) durcheinander bringen
(b) (mix up mentally) verwechseln
(c) (perplex) verwirren
con'fused adj. konfus; wirr ⟨Gedanken, Gerüchte⟩; verworren ⟨Lage, Situation⟩
confusing /kən'fjuːzɪŋ/ adj. verwirrend
confusion /kən'fjuːʒn/ n. (a) Verwirrung, die; (mixing up) Verwechslung, die
(b) (embarrassment) Verlegenheit, die
congeal /kən'dʒiːl/ v.i. gerinnen
congenial /kən'dʒiːnɪəl/ adj. (agreeable) angenehm
congenital /kən'dʒenɪtl/ adj. angeboren; kongenital (fachspr.)
conger /'kɒŋgə(r)/ n. ~ [eel] Seeaal, der
congested /kən'dʒestɪd/ adj. verstopft ⟨Straße, Nase⟩
congestion /kən'dʒestʃn/ n. (of traffic) Stauung, die; **nasal ~:** verstopfte Nase
con'gestion charge n. Staugebühr, die
conglomerate /kən'glɒmərət/ n. (Commerc.) Großkonzern, der
conglomeration /kənglɒmə'reɪʃn/ n. Anhäufung, die
congratulate /kən'grætjʊleɪt/ v.t. gratulieren (+ Dat.); ~ **sb./oneself on sth.** jmdm./sich zu etw. gratulieren
congratulations /kəngrætjʊ'leɪʃnz/ ☐1 int. ~! herzlichen Glückwunsch! (**on** zu); (on passing exam etc.) ich gratuliere!
☐2 n. pl. Glückwünsche Pl.
congregate /'kɒŋgrɪgeɪt/ v.i. sich versammeln
congregation /kɒŋgrɪ'geɪʃn/ n. (Eccl.) Gemeinde, die
congress /'kɒŋgres/ n. Kongress, der; **C~** (Amer.) der Kongress
congressional /kən'greʃənl/ adj. Kongress-
conical /'kɒnɪkl/ adj. kegelförmig
conifer /'kɒnɪfə(r)/ n. Nadelbaum, der
coniferous /kə'nɪfərəs/ adj. Nadel-; ~ **tree** Nadelbaum, der; Konifere, die
conjecture /kən'dʒektʃə(r)/ ☐1 n. Vermutung, die

☑ *v.t.* vermuten
☒ *v.i.* Vermutungen anstellen
conjugate /'kɒndʒʊɡeɪt/ *v.t.* (Ling.)
konjugieren
conjugation /kɒndʒʊ'ɡeɪʃn/ *n.* (Ling.)
Konjugation, *die*
conjunction /kən'dʒʌŋkʃn/ *n.*
(a) Verbindung, *die;* in ∼ with in
Verbindung mit
(b) (Ling.) Konjunktion, *die*
conjure /'kʌndʒə(r)/ *v.i.* zaubern;
conjuring trick Zaubertrick, *der*
■ **conjure 'up** *v.t.* heraufbeschwören
conjurer, conjuror /'kʌndʒərə(r)/ *n.*
Zauberkünstler, *der*/-künstlerin, *die*
connect /kə'nekt/ ☐ *v.t.* verbinden **(to,**
with mit)
☒ *v.i.* ∼ with sth. mit etw.
zusammenhängen
con'nected *adj.* zusammenhängend
connection, (Brit. also) **connexion**
/kə'nekʃn/ *n.* **(a)** (act, state) Verbindung, *die*
(b) (fig.: of ideas) Zusammenhang, *der;* in
∼ with im Zusammenhang mit
(c) (train, bus, etc.) Anschluss, *der*
connoisseur /kɒnə'sɜ:(r)/ *n.* Kenner, *der*
connotation /kɒnə'teɪʃn/ *n.* Assoziation,
die
conquer /'kɒŋkə(r)/ *v.t.* besiegen; erobern
⟨Land⟩
conqueror /'kɒŋkərə(r)/ *n.* (of a country)
Eroberer, *der*
conquest /'kɒŋkwest/ *n.* Eroberung, *die*
conscience /'kɒnʃəns/ *n.* Gewissen, *das;*
have a clear/guilty ∼: ein gutes/schlechtes
Gewissen haben
'conscience-stricken,
'conscience-struck *adjs.*
schuldbewusst
conscientious /kɒnʃɪ'enʃəs/ *adj.*
pflichtbewusst; (meticulous) gewissenhaft;
∼ objector Wehrdienstverweigerer [aus
Gewissensgründen]
consci'entiously *adv.* pflichtbewusst;
(meticulously) gewissenhaft
conscious /'kɒnʃəs/ *adj.* **(a)** he is not
∼ of it es ist ihm nicht bewusst
(b) *pred.* (awake) bei Bewusstsein *präd.*
(c) (realized by doer) bewusst ⟨Versuch,
Bemühung⟩
'consciously *adv.* bewusst
'consciousness *n.* Bewusstsein, *das*
conscript ☐ /kən'skrɪpt/ *v.t.* einberufen
☒ /'kɒnskrɪpt/ *n.* Einberufene, *der*/*die*
conscription /kən'skrɪpʃn/ *n.*
Wehrpflicht, *die*
consecrate /'kɒnsɪkreɪt/ *v.t.* weihen
consecutive /kən'sekjʊtɪv/ *adj.*
aufeinander folgend ⟨Monate, Jahre⟩;
fortlaufend ⟨Zahlen⟩
con'secutively *adj.* hintereinander
consensus /kən'sensəs/ *n.* Einigkeit, *die*

consent /kən'sent/ ☐ *v.i.* zustimmen
☒ *n.* (agreement) Zustimmung, *die* **(to**
zu); by common *or* general ∼: nach
allgemeiner Auffassung; age of ∼: ≈
Ehemündigkeitsalter, *das*
consequence /'kɒnsɪkwəns/ *n.*
(a) (result) Folge, *die;* in ∼: folglich; as a
∼: infolgedessen
(b) (importance) Bedeutung, *die*
consequent /'kɒnsɪkwənt/ *adj.* daraus
folgend
'consequently *adv.* infolgedessen
conservation /kɒnsə'veɪʃn/ *n.*
Erhaltung, *die;* wildlife ∼: Schutz wild
lebender Tierarten
conser'vation area *n.* (Brit.) (rural)
Landschaftsschutzgebiet, *das;* (urban) unter
Denkmalschutz stehendes Gebiet
conservationist /kɒnsə'veɪʃənɪst/ *n.*
Naturschützer, *der*/-schützerin, *die*
conservative /kən'sɜ:vətɪv/ ☐ *adj.*
(a) konservativ
(b) vorsichtig ⟨Schätzung⟩
(c) C∼ (Brit. Polit.) konservativ; the C∼ Party
die Konservative Partei
☒ *n.* C∼ (Brit. Polit.) Konservative, *der*/*die*
con'servatively *adv.* vorsichtig
⟨geschätzt⟩
conservatory /kən'sɜ:vətəri/ *n.*
Wintergarten, *der*
conserve /kən'sɜ:v/ *v.t.* erhalten; schonen
⟨Kräfte⟩
consider /kən'sɪdə(r)/ *v.t.* **(a)** (think about)
∼ sth. an etw. (Akk.) denken; he's ∼ing
emigrating er denkt daran, auszuwandern
(b) (reflect on) sich (Dat.) überlegen
(c) (regard as) halten für; all things ∼ed alles
in allem
considerable /kən'sɪdərəbl/ *adj.,*
con'siderably *adv.* erheblich
considerate /kən'sɪdərət/ *adj.*
rücksichtsvoll; (thoughtfully kind)
entgegenkommend
considerately /kən'sɪdərətlɪ/ *adv.*
rücksichtsvoll; (obligingly) entgegenkommend
consideration /kənsɪdə'reɪʃn/ *n.*
(a) Überlegung, *die;* take sth. into ∼: etw.
berücksichtigen; the matter is under ∼: die
Angelegenheit wird geprüft
(b) (thoughtfulness) Rücksichtnahme, *die*
considered /kən'sɪdəd/ *adj.*
(a) ∼ opinion feste *od.* ernsthafte
Überzeugung
(b) be highly ∼ [by others] [bei anderen] in
hohem Ansehen stehen
con'sidering *prep.* ∼ sth. wenn man etw.
bedenkt; ∼ [that] ...: wenn man bedenkt,
dass ...
consign /kən'saɪn/ *v.t.* anvertrauen **(to**
Dat.)
con'signment *n.* (Commerc.) Sendung, *die;*
(large) Ladung, *die*
consist /kən'sɪst/ *v.i.* ∼ of bestehen aus

consistency /kən'sɪstənsɪ/ n. (a) (density) Konsistenz, die
(b) (being consistent) Konsequenz, die
consistent /kən'sɪstənt/ adj.
(a) (compatible) [miteinander] vereinbar
(b) (uniform) gleich bleibend ⟨Qualität⟩
(c) (unchanging) konsequent
consolation /kɒnsə'leɪʃn/ n. Trost, der
conso'lation prize n. Trostpreis, der
console /kən'səʊl/ v.t. trösten
consolidate /kən'sɒlɪdeɪt/ v.t. festigen
consolidation /kənsɒlɪ'deɪʃn/ n. Festigung, die
consoling /kən'səʊlɪŋ/ adj. tröstlich
consonant /'kɒnsənənt/ n. Konsonant, der
consort /kən'sɔːt/ v.i. verkehren (with mit)
consortium /kən'sɔːtɪəm/ n., pl. consortia /kən'sɔːtɪə/ Konsortium, das
conspicuous /kən'spɪkjʊəs/ adj.
(a) (visible) unübersehbar
(b) (obvious) auffallend
con'spicuously adv. (a) (visibly) unübersehbar
(b) (obviously) auffallend
conspiracy /kən'spɪrəsɪ/ n. (conspiring) Verschwörung, die; (plot) Komplott, das
conspire /kən'spaɪə(r)/ v.i. sich verschwören
constable /'kʌnstəbl, 'kɒnstəbl/ n. (Brit.) Polizist, der/Polizistin, die
constabulary /kən'stæbjʊlərɪ/ n. Polizei, die
constant /'kɒnstənt/ adj. (a) (unceasing) ständig
(b) (unchanging) gleich bleibend
'constantly adv. (a) (unceasingly) ständig
(b) (unchangingly) konstant
constellation /kɒnstə'leɪʃn/ n. Sternbild, das
consternation /kɒnstə'neɪʃn/ n. Bestürzung, die
constipated /'kɒnstɪpeɪtɪd/ adj. be ~: an Verstopfung leiden
constipation /kɒnstɪ'peɪʃn/ n. Verstopfung, die
constituency /kən'stɪtjʊənsɪ/ n. Wahlkreis, der
constituent /kən'stɪtjʊənt/ n. (a) (part) Bestandteil, der
(b) (Polit.) Wähler, der/Wählerin, die
constitute /'kɒnstɪtjuːt/ v.t. (a) (form, be) sein; ~ a threat to eine Gefahr sein für
(b) (make up) bilden
constitution /kɒnstɪ'tjuːʃn/ n. (a) (of person) Konstitution, die
(b) (of state) Verfassung, die
constitutional /kɒnstɪ'tjuːʃənl/ adj. (of constitution) der Verfassung nachgestellt; (in harmony with constitution) verfassungsmäßig
constrain /kən'streɪn/ v.t. zwingen

constraint /kən'streɪnt/ n. (limitation) Einschränkung, die
constrict /kən'strɪkt/ v.t. verengen
constriction /kən'strɪkʃn/ n. Verengung, die
construct /kən'strʌkt/ v.t. bauen; (fig.) erstellen ⟨Plan⟩
construction /kən'strʌkʃn/ n.
(a) (constructing) Bau, der; be under ~: im Bau sein
(b) (thing constructed) Bauwerk, das
constructive /kən'strʌktɪv/ adj. konstruktiv
consul /'kɒnsl/ n. Konsul, der
consulate /'kɒnsjʊlət/ n. Konsulat, das
consult /kən'sʌlt/ v.t. konsultieren ⟨Arzt, Fachmann⟩; ~ a book in einem Buch nachsehen
consultant /kən'sʌltənt/ n. Berater, der/ Beraterin, die; (Med.) Chefarzt, der/-ärztin, die
consultation /kɒnsəl'teɪʃn/ n. Beratung, die
con'sulting room n. Sprechzimmer, das
consume /kən'sjuːm/ v.t. verbrauchen; (eat, drink) konsumieren
con'sumer n. Verbraucher, der/ Verbraucherin, die
con'sumer goods n. pl. Konsumgüter Pl.
consumerism /kən'sjuːmərɪzm/ n., no art. Konsumerismus, der
consumer: ~ **pro'tection** n. Verbraucherschutz, der; ~ **research** n. Verbrauchsforschung, die; Konsumforschung, die
consumption /kən'sʌmpʃn/ n. Verbrauch, der (of an + Dat.); (eating or drinking) Verzehr, der (of von)
cont. abbr. = **continued** Forts.
contact ① /'kɒntækt/ n. Berührung, die; (fig.) Kontakt, der; be in ~ with sth. etw. berühren; be in ~ with sb. (fig.) mit jmdm. Kontakt haben
② /'kɒntækt, kən'tækt/ v.t. sich in Verbindung setzen mit
'contact lens n. Kontaktlinse, die
'contactless adj. kontaktlos; berührungslos
contagious /kən'teɪdʒəs/ adj. ansteckend
contain /kən'teɪn/ v.t. (a) (hold, include) enthalten
(b) (prevent from spreading) aufhalten
con'tainer n. Behälter, der; (cargo ~) Container, der; cardboard/wooden ~: Pappkarton, der/Holzkiste, die
contaminate /kən'tæmmeɪt/ v.t. verunreinigen; (with radioactivity) verseuchen
contamination /kəntæmɪ'neɪʃn/ n. Verunreinigung, die; (with radioactivity) Verseuchung, die
contemplate /'kɒntəmpleɪt/ v.t.
(a) betrachten; (mentally) nachdenken über (+ Akk.)

contemplation ⋯⫶ contrary ⋯⫶

(b) (expect) rechnen mit; (consider) ~ sth./ doing sth. an etw. (*Akk.*) denken/daran denken, etw. zu tun

contemplation /kɒntəmˈpleɪʃn/ n. Betrachtung, *die;* (mental) Nachdenken, *das* (of über + *Akk.*)

contemporary /kənˈtempərərɪ/ **1** *adj.* zeitgenössisch

2 *n.* Zeitgenosse, *der/*-genossin, *die*

contempt /kənˈtempt/ n. Verachtung, *die* (of, for für)

contemptible /kənˈtemptɪbl/ *adj.* verachtenswert

contemptuous /kənˈtemptjʊəs/ *adj.* verächtlich

contend /kənˈtend/ *v.i.* be able to/have to ~ with fertig werden können/müssen mit

conˈtender n. Bewerber, *der/*Bewerberin, *die*

content¹ /ˈkɒntent/ n. **(a)** *in pl.* Inhalt, *der;* [table of] ~s Inhaltsverzeichnis, *das* **(b)** (amount contained) Gehalt, *der* (of an + *Dat.*)

content² /kənˈtent/ **1** *pred. adj.* zufrieden **2** *v.t.* zufrieden stellen; ~ oneself with sth./sb. sich mit etw./jmdm. zufrieden geben

conˈtented *adj.,* **conˈtentedly** *adv.* zufrieden

contention /kənˈtenʃn/ n. **(a)** Streit, *der* **(b)** (point asserted) Behauptung, *die*

contentious /kənˈtenʃəs/ *adj.* strittig ‹Punkt, Thema›

conˈtentment n. Zufriedenheit, *die*

contest **1** /ˈkɒntest/ n. Wettbewerb, *der* **2** /kənˈtest/ *v.t.* **(a)** bestreiten; infrage stellen ‹Behauptung› **(b)** (Brit.: compete for) kandidieren für

contestant /kənˈtestənt/ n. (competitor) Teilnehmer, *der/*Teilnehmerin, *die*

context /ˈkɒntekst/ n. Kontext, *der;* in/out of ~: im/ohne Kontext; in this ~: in diesem Zusammenhang

contextual /kənˈtekstjʊəl/ *adj.* kontextuell

contextualize /kənˈtekstjʊəlaɪz/ *v.t.* (place in context) in einen Kontext einordnen

continent /ˈkɒntɪnənt/ n. Kontinent, *der;* the C~: das europäische Festland

continental /kɒntɪˈnentl/ *adj.* **(a)** kontinental **(b)** C~ (mainland European) kontinental[europäisch]

continental: ~ ˈbreakfast n. kontinentales Frühstück; ~ ˈquilt n. (Brit.) [Stepp]federbett, *das*

conˈtingency plan /kənˈtɪndʒənsɪ/ n. Alternativplan, *der*

contingent /kənˈtɪndʒənt/ n. Kontingent, *das*

continual /kənˈtɪnjʊəl/ *adj.,* **conˈtinually** *adv.* (frequent[ly]) ständig;

(without stopping) unaufhörlich

continuation /kəntɪnjʊˈeɪʃn/ n. Fortsetzung, *die*

continue /kənˈtɪnjuː/ **1** *v.t.* fortsetzen; '~d on page 2' „Fortsetzung auf Seite 2"; ~ doing *or* to do sth. etw. weiter tun; it ~d to rain es regnete weiter **2** *v.i.* (persist) ‹Wetter, Zustand, Krise usw.›: andauern; (persist in doing sth.) nicht aufhören; ~ with sth. mit etw. fortfahren

continuity /kɒntɪˈnjuːɪtɪ/ n. Kontinuität, *die*

continuous /kənˈtɪnjʊəs/ *adj.* **(a)** ununterbrochen; anhaltend ‹Regen, Sonnenschein›; ständig ‹Kritik, Streit›; durchgezogen ‹Linie› **(b)** (Ling.) ~ [form] Verlaufsform, *die*

conˈtinuously *adv.* ununterbrochen; ständig ‹sich ändern›

contort /kənˈtɔːt/ *v.t.* verdrehen

contortion /kənˈtɔːʃn/ n. Verdrehung, *die*

contour /ˈkɒntʊə(r)/ n. Kontur, *die;* ~ map Höhenlinienkarte, *die*

contraband /ˈkɒntrəbænd/ n. Schmuggelware, *die*

contraception /kɒntrəˈsepʃn/ n. Empfängnisverhütung, *die*

contraceptive /kɒntrəˈseptɪv/ **1** *adj.* empfängnisverhütend **2** *n.* Verhütungsmittel, *das*

contract **1** /ˈkɒntrækt/ n. Vertrag, *der;* ~ of employment Arbeitsvertrag, *der;* be under ~ to do sth. vertraglich verpflichtet sein, etw. zu tun **2** /kənˈtrækt/ *v.t.* (Med.) sich (*Dat.*) zuziehen **3** /kənˈtrækt/ *v.i.* **(a)** ~ to do sth. sich vertraglich verpflichten, etw. zu tun **(b)** (become smaller, be drawn together) sich zusammenziehen

contraction /kənˈtrækʃn/ n. Kontraktion, *die*

ˈcontract killer n. Auftragskiller, *der/* -killerin, *die*

contractor /kənˈtræktə(r)/ n. Auftragnehmer, *der/*-nehmerin, *die*

contradict /kɒntrəˈdɪkt/ *v.t.* widersprechen (+ *Dat.*)

contradiction /kɒntrəˈdɪkʃn/ n. Widerspruch, *der;* in ~ to sb./sth. im Widerspruch zu jmdm./etw.

contradictory /kɒntrəˈdɪktərɪ/ *adj.* widersprüchlich

contraflow /ˈkɒntrəfləʊ/ n. ~ system Gegenverkehr auf einem Fahrstreifen

contralto /kənˈtræltəʊ/ n., *pl.* ~s Alt, *der*

contraption /kənˈtræpʃn/ n. (coll.) [komisches] Gerät

contrary /ˈkɒntrərɪ/ **1** *adj.* **(a)** entgegengesetzt; be ~ to sth. im Gegensatz zu etw. stehen **(b)** /kənˈtreərɪ/ (perverse) widerspenstig **2** *n.* the ~: das Gegenteil; on the ~: im Gegenteil ⋯⫶

3 *adv.* ~ **to sth.** entgegen einer Sache

contrast 1 /kən'trɑːst/ *v.t.*
gegenüberstellen
2 /'kɒntrɑːst/ *n.* Kontrast, *der* (**with** zu); **in**
~, …: im Gegensatz dazu, …; [**be**] **in** ~ **with**
sth. im Gegensatz zu etw. [stehen]
con'trasting *adj.* gegensätzlich

contravene /kɒntrə'viːn/ *v.t.* verstoßen
gegen

contravention /kɒntrə'venʃn/ *n.*
Verstoß, *der* (**of** gegen)

contribute /kən'trɪbjuːt/ 1 *v.t.* ~ **sth.** [to
or **towards sth.**] etw. [zu etw.] beitragen
2 *v.i.* ~ **to charity** für karitative Zwecke
spenden; ~ **to the success of sth.** zum
Erfolg einer Sache (*Gen.*) beitragen

contribution /kɒntrɪ'bjuːʃn/ *n.* Beitrag,
der; (for charity) Spende, *die* (**to** für); **make a**
~: einen Beitrag leisten; (to charity) etwas
spenden

contributor /kən'trɪbjʊtə(r)/ *n.*
(to encyclopaedia etc.) Mitarbeiter, *der*/
Mitarbeiterin, *die*

'con trick (Brit. coll.) ▶ CONFIDENCE TRICK

contrite /'kɒntraɪt/ *adj.* zerknirscht

contrive /kən'traɪv/ *v.t.* ~ **to do sth.** es
fertig bringen, etw. zu tun

contrived /kən'traɪvd/ *adj.* künstlich

control /kən'trəʊl/ 1 *n.* (a) Kontrolle,
die (**of** über + *Akk.*); **keep** ~ **of sth.** etw.
unter Kontrolle halten; **be in** ~ [**of sth.**] die
Kontrolle [über etw. (*Akk.*)] haben; [**go** *or*
get] **out of** ~: außer Kontrolle [geraten];
[**get sth.**] **under** ~: [etw.] unter Kontrolle
[bringen]
(b) (device) Regler, *der;* ~**s** Schalttafel, *die*
2 *v.t.*, **-ll-** kontrollieren; lenken ⟨*Auto*⟩;
zügeln ⟨*Zorn*⟩; regeln ⟨*Verkehr*⟩

control: ~ **centre** *n.* Kontrollzentrum,
das; ~ **desk** *n.* Schaltpult, *das*

con'troller *n.* (director) Leiter, *der*/Leiterin,
die

control: ~ **panel** *n.* Schalttafel, *die;*
~ **room** *n.* Kontrollraum, *der;* ~ **tower**
n. Kontrollturm, *der*

controversial /kɒntrə'vɜːʃl/ *adj.*
umstritten

controversy /'kɒntrəvɜːsɪ, kən'trɒvəsɪ/
n. Auseinandersetzung, *die*

conurbation /kɒnɜː'beɪʃn/ *n.*
Konurbation, *die* (Soziol.); ≈ Stadtregion, *die*

convalesce /kɒnvə'les/ *v.i.* genesen

convalescence /kɒnvə'lesəns/ *n.*
Genesung, *die*

convection /kən'vekʃn/ *n.* (Phys.,
Meteorol.) Konvektion, *die*

convector /kən'vektə(r)/ *n.* Konvektor,
der

convene /kən'viːn/ 1 *v.t.* einberufen
2 *v.i.* zusammenkommen

convenience /kən'viːnɪəns/ *n.* (a) **for**
sb.'s ~ zu jmds. Bequemlichkeit; **at your**

~: wann es Ihnen passt
(b) (toilet) [**public**] ~: [öffentliche] Toilette

con'venience food *n.* Fertignahrung,
die

convenient /kən'viːnɪənt/ *adj.* günstig;
(useful) praktisch; **would it be** ~ **to** *or* **for**
you? würde es Ihnen passen?

con'veniently *adv.* (a) günstig ⟨*gelegen,
angebracht*⟩
(b) (opportunely) angenehmerweise

convent /'kɒnvənt/ *n.* Kloster, *das*

convention /kən'venʃn/ *n.* (a) Brauch,
der
(b) (assembly) Konferenz, *die*
(c) (agreement) Konvention, *die*

conventional /kən'venʃənl/ *adj.*
konventionell

converge /kən'vɜːdʒ/ *v.i.* ~ [**on each**
other] aufeinander zulaufen

conversant /kən'vɜːsənt/ *pred. adj.*
vertraut (**with** mit)

conversation /kɒnvə'seɪʃn/ *n.*
Unterhaltung, *die;* **have a** ~: ein Gespräch
führen

conversational /kɒnvə'seɪʃənl/ *adj.*
~ **English** gesprochenes Englisch

converse[1] /kən'vɜːs/ *v.i.* (formal) ~ [**with**
sb.] [**about** *or* **on sth.**] sich [mit jmdm.] [über
etw. (*Akk.*)] unterhalten

converse[2] /'kɒnvɜːs/ 1 *adj.*
entgegengesetzt; umgekehrt ⟨*Fall, Situation*⟩
2 *n.* Gegenteil, *das*

conversely /kən'vɜːslɪ/ *adj.* umgekehrt

conversion /kən'vɜːʃn/ *n.*
(a) Umwandlung, *die* (**into** in + *Akk.*)
(b) (adaptation) Umbau, *der*
(c) (of person) Bekehrung, *die* (**to** zu)

con'version table *n.*
Umrechnungstabelle, *die*

convert 1 /kən'vɜːt/*v.t.* umwandeln (**into**
in + *Akk.*); (Comp.) konvertieren ⟨*Daten*⟩;
~ **sb.** [**to sth.**] jmdn. [zu etw.] bekehren
2 /kən'vɜːt/ *v.i.* ~ **into sth.** sich in etw.
(*Akk.*) umwandeln lassen
3 /'kɒnvɜːt/ *n.* Konvertit, *der*/Konvertitin,
die

convertible /kən'vɜːtɪbl/ 1 *adj.* **be**
~ **into sth.** sich in etw. (*Akk.*) umwandeln
lassen
2 *n.* Kabrio[lett], *das*

convex /'kɒnveks/ *adj.* konvex

convey /kən'veɪ/ *v.t.* (a) befördern
(b) (impart) vermitteln

conveyance /kən'veɪəns/ *n.*
(a) (transportation) Beförderung, *die*
(b) (formal: vehicle) Beförderungsmittel, *das*

con'veyancing *n.* (Law) ~ [**of property**]
[Eigentums]übertragung, *die*

conveyor /kən'veɪə(r)/ *n.* ~ [**belt**]
Förderband, *das*

convict 1 /'kɒnvɪkt/ *n.* Strafgefangene,
der/*die*

2 /kən'vɪkt/ v.t. verurteilen

conviction /kən'vɪkʃn/ n. (a) (Law) Verurteilung, die (for wegen) (b) (belief) Überzeugung, die

convince /kən'vɪns/ v.t. überzeugen; ~ sb. that …: jmdn. davon überzeugen, dass …; be ~d that …: davon überzeugt sein, dass …

convincing /kən'vɪnsɪŋ/ adj., **con'vincingly** adv. überzeugend

convivial /kən'vɪvɪəl/ adj. fröhlich

convoluted /'kɒnvəluːtɪd/ adj. (complex) kompliziert

convoy /'kɒnvɔɪ/ n. Konvoi, der; in ~: im Konvoi

convulse /kən'vʌls/ v.t. be ~d with sich krümmen vor (+ Dat.)

convulsions /kən'vʌlʃnz/ n. pl. Krämpfe Pl.

convulsive /kən'vʌlsɪv/ adj., **con'vulsively** adv. konvulsivisch

coo /kuː/ v.i. gurren

cook /kʊk/ 1 n. Koch, der/Köchin, die 2 v.t. kochen ‹Mahlzeit›; (fry, roast) braten; (boil) kochen 3 v.i. kochen

■ **cook 'up** v.t. erfinden ‹Geschichte›

'**cookbook** n. (Amer.) Kochbuch, das

'**cooker** n. (Brit.) Herd, der

cookery /'kʊkərɪ/ n. Kochen, das

'**cookery book** n. (Brit.) Kochbuch, das

cookie /'kʊkɪ/ n. (a) (Amer.) Keks, der (b) (Comp.) Cookie, der

'**cooking** n. Kochen, das

cooking: ~ **apple** n. Kochapfel, der; ~ **utensil** n. Küchengerät, das

cool /kuːl/ 1 adj. (a) kühl; store in a ~ place kühl aufbewahren (b) (unemotional, unfriendly) kühl; (calm) ruhig 2 n. Kühle, die 3 v.i. abkühlen 4 v.t. kühlen; (from high temperature) abkühlen

■ **cool 'down, cool 'off** v.i. & t. abkühlen

cool: ~ **box** n. Kühlbox, die; ~**-headed** adj. kühl; nüchtern

coolly /'kuːllɪ/ adv. (calmly) ruhig; (unemotionally) kühl

coop /kuːp/ 1 n. (for poultry) Hühnerstall, der 2 v.t. ~ up einpferchen

cooperate /kəʊ'ɒpəreɪt/ v.i. mitarbeiten (in bei); (with each other) zusammenarbeiten (in bei)

cooperation /kəʊɒpə'reɪʃn/ n. Zusammenarbeit, die

cooperative /kəʊ'ɒpərətɪv/ 1 adj. kooperativ; (helpful) hilfsbereit 2 n. Genossenschaft, die

coordinate /kəʊ'ɔːdɪneɪt/ v.t. koordinieren

coordination /kəʊɔːdɪ'neɪʃn/ n. Koordination, die

co-owner /kəʊ'əʊnə(r)/ n. Miteigentümer, der/-eigentümerin, die; (of business) Mitinhaber, der/-inhaberin, die

cop /kɒp/ n. (coll.: police officer) Bulle, der (salopp)

cope /kəʊp/ v.i. ~ with sb./sth. mit jmdm./etw. fertig werden

Copenhagen /kəʊpn'heɪgn/ pr. n. Kopenhagen (das)

copier /'kɒpɪə(r)/ n. (machine) Kopiergerät, das

co-pilot /'kəʊpaɪlət/ n. Kopilot, der/Kopilotin, die

copious /'kəʊpɪəs/ adj. reichhaltig

'**cop-out** n. (coll.) Drückebergerei, die (ugs. abwertend); that's a ~: das ist Drückebergerei (ugs. abwertend)

copper¹ /'kɒpə(r)/ n. Kupfer, das

copper² (Brit. coll.) ▸ COP

coppice /'kɒpɪs/, **copse** /kɒps/ ns. Wäldchen, das

'**cop shop** n. (Brit. coll.) Wache, die; Revier, das

copula /'kɒpjʊlə/ n. (Ling.) Kopula, die

copulate /'kɒpjʊleɪt/ v.i. kopulieren

copy /'kɒpɪ/ 1 n. (a) (reproduction) Kopie, die (b) (specimen) Exemplar, das 2 v.t. & i. kopieren; (transcribe) abschreiben

copy: ~**cat** n. (coll.) you're such a ~cat! du musst immer alles nachmachen!; ~ **editor** n. Redakteur, der/Redakteurin, die (der/die nur nach schriftlichen Vorlagen arbeitet); ~ **protection** n. (Comp.) Kopierschutz, der; ~**right** n. Urheberrecht, das; ~**writer** n. [Werbe]texter, der/-texterin, die

coral /'kɒrl/ n. Koralle, die

cord /kɔːd/ n. (a) (Kordel, die; (strong string) Schnur, die (b) (cloth) Cord, der (c) in pl. (trousers) [pair of] ~s Cordhose, die

cordial /'kɔːdɪəl/ 1 adj. herzlich 2 n. (drink) Sirup, der

cordiality /kɔːdɪ'ælɪtɪ/ n. Herzlichkeit, die

'**cordially** adv. herzlich

cordless /'kɔːdlɪs/ adj. (without flex) ohne Kabel nachgestellt

cordless 'phone n. Schnurlostelefon, das

cordon /'kɔːdn/ 1 n. Kordon, der 2 v.t. ~ [off] absperren

corduroy /'kɔːdərɔɪ, 'kɔːdjʊrɔɪ/ n. Cordsamt, der

core /kɔː(r)/ 1 n. (of fruit) Kerngehäuse, das 2 v.t. entkernen

co-respondent /kəʊrɪ'spɒndənt/ n. Mitbeklagte, der/die (im Scheidungsprozess)

cork /kɔːk/ 1 n. (a) (bark) Kork, der (b) (bottle stopper) Korken, der 2 v.t. zukorken

cork: ~screw n. Korkenzieher, der;
~ **'tile** n. Korkplatte, die
cormorant /'kɔːmərənt/ n. Kormoran, der
corn¹ /kɔːn/ n. Getreide, das
corn² n. (on foot) Hühnerauge, das
cornea /'kɔːnɪə/ n. (Anat.) Hornhaut, die;
Cornea, die (fachspr.)
corned beef /kɔːnd 'biːf/ n. Cornedbeef,
das
corner /'kɔːnə(r)/ [1] n. (a) Ecke, die;
(curve) Kurve, die; **on the ~:** an der Ecke/in
der Kurve
(b) (of mouth, eye) Winkel, der
[2] v.t. (fig.) in die Enge treiben
[3] v.i. die Kurve nehmen
corner: ~ kick n. (Footb.) Eckball, der;
~ **shop** n. Tante-Emma-Laden, der (ugs.);
~stone n. (fig.) Eckpfeiler, der
cornet /'kɔːnɪt/ n. (a) (Brit.: for ice cream)
[Eis]tüte, die
(b) (Mus.) Kornett, das
corn: ~flakes n. pl. Cornflakes Pl.;
~flour (Brit.) n. Maismehl, das; **~flower**
n. Kornblume, die; **~starch** (Amer.) n.
Maismehl, das
'corny adj. (coll.: trite) abgedroschen
coronary /'kɒrənərɪ/ [1] adj. (Anat.)
koronar
[2] n. (Med.) ▶ CORONARY THROMBOSIS
coronary: ~ 'artery n.
Herzkranzarterie, die; Koronararterie,
die (fachspr.); ~ **throm'bosis** n.
Koronarthrombose, die
coronation /kɒrə'neɪʃn/ n. Krönung, die
coroner /'kɒrənə(r)/ n. Coroner, der;
Beamter, der gewaltsame od. unnatürliche
Todesfälle untersucht
coronet /'kɒrənet/ n. Krone, die
corporal¹ /'kɔːpərl/ adj. körperlich
corporal² n. ≈ Hauptgefreite, der
corporate /'kɔːpərət/ adj.
körperschaftlich
corporation /kɔːpə'reɪʃn/ n.
Stadtverwaltung, die
corpo'ration tax n.
Körperschaftssteuer, die
corps /kɔː(r)/ n., pl. same /kɔːz/ Korps, das
corpse /kɔːps/ n. Leiche, die
corpulent /'kɔːpjʊlənt/ adj. korpulent
Corpus Christi /kɔːpəs 'krɪstɪ/ n. (Eccl.)
Fronleichnam (der)
corpuscle /'kɔːpəsl/ n. **[blood]** ~
Blutkörperchen, das
corral /kə'rɑːl/ (Amer.) [1] n. Pferch, der
[2] v.t., -ll- einpferchen
correct /kə'rekt/ [1] v.t. korrigieren
[2] adj. korrekt; **that is** ~: das stimmt
correction /kə'rekʃn/ n. Korrektur, die
cor'rectly adv. korrekt
correspond /kɒrɪ'spɒnd/ v.i. (a) ~ **[to**
each other] einander entsprechen; ~ **to sth.**

einer Sache (Dat.) entsprechen
(b) (communicate) ~ **with sb.** mit jmdm.
korrespondieren
correspondence /kɒrɪ'spɒndəns/ n.
(a) (Übereinstimmung, die (**with, to** mit)
(b) (communication) Briefwechsel, der
corre'spondence course n.
Fernkurs, der
correspondent /kɒrɪ'spɒndənt/
n. (reporter) Korrespondent, der/
Korrespondentin, die
corre'sponding adj. entsprechend (**to**
Dat.)
corre'spondingly adv. entsprechend
corridor /'kɒrɪdɔː(r)/ n. (a) Flur, der
(b) (Railw.) [Seiten]gang, der
corroborate /kə'rɒbəreɪt/ v.t. bestätigen
corroboration /kərɒbə'reɪʃn/ n.
Bestätigung, die
corrode /kə'rəʊd/ [1] v.t. zerfressen
[2] v.i. zerfressen werden
corrosion /kə'rəʊʒn/ n. Korrosion, die
corrugated /'kɒrəgeɪtɪd/ adj.
~ **cardboard** Wellpappe, die; ~ **iron**
Wellblech, das
corrupt /kə'rʌpt/ [1] adj. (depraved)
verdorben (geh.); (influenced by bribery) korrupt
[2] v.t. (deprave) korrumpieren; (bribe)
bestechen
corruption /kə'rʌpʃn/ n. (moral deterioration)
Verdorbenheit, die (geh.); (corrupt practices)
Korruption, die
corset /'kɔːsɪt/ n. Korsett, das
Corsica /'kɔːsɪkə/ pr. n. Korsika (das)
cortège /kɔː'teɪʒ/ n. Trauerzug, der
cortisone /'kɔːtɪzəʊn/ n. Kortison, das;
Cortison, das (fachspr.)
cosh /kɒʃ/ (Brit. coll.) [1] n. Totschläger, der
[2] v.t. niederknüppeln
cosmetic /kɒz'metɪk/ [1] adj. kosmetisch
[2] n. Kosmetikum, das
cosmic /'kɒzmɪk/ adj. kosmisch
cosmonaut /'kɒzmənɔːt/ n. Kosmonaut,
der/Kosmonautin, die
cosmopolitan /kɒzmə'pɒlɪtən/ adj.
kosmopolitisch
cosmos /'kɒzmɒs/ n. Kosmos, der
cosset /'kɒsɪt/ v.t. [ver]hätscheln
cost /kɒst/ [1] n. (a) Kosten Pl.
(b) (fig.) Preis, der; **at all ~s, at any** ~: um
jeden Preis
[2] v.t. (a) p.t., p.p. **cost** (lit. or fig.) kosten; **how**
much does it ~? was kostet es?
(b) p.t., p.p. **costed** (Commerc.: fix price of)
~ **sth.** den Preis für etw. kalkulieren
co-star /'kəʊstɑː(r)/ (Cinemat., Theatre) [1] n.
be a/the ~: eine der Hauptrollen/die zweite
Hauptrolle spielen
[2] v.i., **-rr-** eine der Hauptrollen spielen
[3] v.t., **-rr-: the film ~red Robert Redford**
der Film zeigte Robert Redford in einer der
Hauptrollen

cost: ~ **cutting** *n.* Kostensenkung, *die;* ~**-cutting** *adj.* Spar-; ~**-effective** *adj.* rentabel

'**costly** *adj.* teuer

cost: ~ **of** '**living** *n.* Lebenshaltungskosten *Pl.;* ~-of-living index Lebenshaltungsindex, *der;* ~ **price** *n.* Selbstkostenpreis, *der*

costume /'kɒstju:m/ *n.* Kleidermode, *die;* (theatrical ~) Kostüm, *das*

costume '**jewellery** *n.* Modeschmuck, *der*

cosy /'kəʊzı/ *adj.* gemütlich

cot /kɒt/ *n.* Kinderbett, *das*

'**cot death** *n.* (Brit.) plötzlicher Kindstod; Cot-death, *der* (Med.)

cottage /'kɒtɪdʒ/ *n.* Cottage, *das*

cottage: ~ '**cheese** *n.* Hüttenkäse, *der;* ~ '**hospital** *n.: kleines [Land]krankenhaus ohne ständige ärztliche Betreuung;* ~ **industry** *n.* Heimarbeit, *die;* ~ '**pie** *n.: mit Kartoffelbrei überbackenes Hackfleisch*

cotton /'kɒtən/ ① *n.* Baumwolle, *die;* (thread) Baumwollgarn, *das* ② *attrib. adj.* Baumwoll- ③ *v.i.* ~ '**on** (coll.) kapieren (ugs.)

cotton: ~ **reel** *n.* [Näh]garnrolle, *die;* ~ '**wool** *n.* Watte, *die*

couch /kaʊtʃ/ *n.* Couch, *die*

couchette /ku:'ʃet/ *n.* (Railw.) Liegewagenplatz, *der*

couch po'tato *n.* (coll.) Couchpotato[e], *der*

cough /kɒf/ ① *n.* Husten, *der* ② *v.i.* husten

cough: ~ **medicine** *n.* Hustenmittel, *das;* ~ **mixture** *n.* Hustensaft, *der*

could ▶ CAN²

couldn't /'kʊdnt/ (coll.) = could not; ▶ CAN²

council /'kaʊnsl/ *n.* Rat, *der;* **local** ~: Gemeinderat, *der;* **city/town** ~: Stadtrat, *der;* **C**~ **of Ministers** Ministerrat, *der*

council: ~ **estate** *n.* Wohnviertel mit Sozialwohnungen; ~ **flat** *n.* Sozialwohnung, *die;* ~ **house** *n.* Haus des sozialen Wohnungsbaus; ~ **housing** *n.* sozialer Wohnungsbau

councillor /'kaʊnsələ(r)/ *n.* Ratsmitglied, *das*

'**council tax** *n.* (Brit.) Gemeindesteuer, *die*

counsel /'kaʊnsl/ ① *n.* (a) Rat[schlag], *der* (b) *pl. same* (Law) Rechtsanwalt, *der/* -anwältin, *die* ② *v.t.,* (Brit.) -**ll**- beraten

counselling (*Amer.:* **counseling**) /'kaʊnsəlɪŋ/ *n.* Beratung, *die;* **marriage** ~: Eheberatung, *die*

counsellor, (*Amer.* **counselor**) /'kaʊnsələ(r)/ *n.* Berater, *der/*Beraterin, *die*

count¹ /kaʊnt/ ① *n.* Zählen, *das;* **keep** ~ [**of sth.**] [etw.] zählen; **lose** ~: sich verzählen ② *v.t.* (a) zählen (b) (include) mitzählen; **not** ~**ing** abgesehen von (c) (consider) halten für; ~ **oneself lucky** sich glücklich schätzen können ③ *v.i.* (a) zählen; ~ [**up**] **to ten** bis zehn zählen (b) (be included) zählen ∎ '**count on** *v.t.* ~ **on sb./sth.** sich auf jmdn./etw. verlassen ∎ **count** '**up** *v.t.* zusammenzählen

count² *n.* (nobleman) Graf, *der*

'**countdown** *n.* Count-down, *der od. das*

countenance /'kaʊntɪnəns/ ① *n.* (literary: face) Antlitz, *das* ② *v.t.* (formal: approve) gutheißen

counter¹ /'kaʊntə(r)/ *n.* (a) (in shop) Ladentisch, *der;* (in cafeteria) Büfett, *das;* (in bank) Schalter, *der* (b) (for games) Spielmarke, *die*

counter² ① *adj.* Gegen- ② *v.t.* (a) (oppose) begegnen (+ *Dat.*) (b) (act against) kontern ③ *adv.* **go** ~ **to** zuwiderlaufen (+ *Dat.*)

counter: ~'**act** *v.t.* entgegenwirken (+ *Dat.*); ~**attack** *n.* Gegenangriff, *der;* ~**balance** *v.t.* (fig.) ausgleichen; ~-'**espionage** *n.* Spionageabwehr, *die*

counterfeit /'kaʊntəfɪt/ ① *adj.* gefälscht; ~ **money** Falschgeld, *das* ② *v.t.* fälschen

'**counterfeiter** *n.* Fälscher, *der/* Fälscherin, *die*

counterfoil /'kaʊntəfɔɪl/ *n.* Kontrollabschnitt, *der*

counter: ~**part** *n.* Gegenstück, *das* (of zu); ~**pro'ductive** *adj.* **sth. is** ~**productive** etw. bewirkt das Gegenteil des Gewünschten; ~**sign** *v.t.* gegenzeichnen; ~**weight** *n.* Gegengewicht, *das*

countess /'kaʊntɪs/ *n.* Gräfin, *die*

'**countless** *adj.* zahllos

countrified /'kʌntrɪfaɪd/ *adj.* ländlich

country /'kʌntrɪ/ *n.* (a) Land, *das;* **sb's** [**home**] ~: jmds. Heimat (b) (~side) Landschaft, *die;* **in the** ~: auf dem Land; ~ **road/air** Landstraße, *die*/Landluft, *die*

country '**dancing** *n.* Kontertanz, *der*

countryfied ▶ COUNTRIFIED

country: ~**man** /'kʌntrɪmən/, *n. pl.* ~**men** /'kʌntrɪmən/ Landsmann, *der;* ~**side** *n.* (a) (rural areas) Land, *das;* (b) (rural scenery) Landschaft, *die*

county /'kaʊntɪ/ *n.* (Brit.) Grafschaft, *die*

coup /ku:/ *n.* (a) Coup, *der* (b) ▶ COUP D'ÉTAT

coup d'état /ku: deɪ'ta:/ *n.* Staatsstreich, *der*

coupé /'ku:peɪ/ *n.* Coupé, *das*

couple /kʌpl/ ① **(a)** n. (pair) Paar, *das;*
(married) [Ehe]paar, *das*
(b) a ~ **[of]** (a few) ein paar; (two) zwei
② *v.t.* koppeln
coupon /'ku:pɒn/ n. **(a)** (for rations) Marke,
die
(b) (in advertisement) Coupon, *der*
courage /'kʌrɪdʒ/ n. Mut, *der*
courageous /kə'reɪdʒəs/ *adj.,*
cou'rageously *adv.* mutig
courgette /kʊə'ʒet/ n. (Brit.) Zucchino, *der*
courier /'kʊrɪə(r)/ n. **(a)** (Tourism)
Reiseleiter, *der*/-leiterin, *die*
(b) (messenger) Kurier, *der*
'courier company n. Kurierdienst, *der*
course /kɔːs/ n. **(a)** (of ship, plane) Kurs, *der;*
~ **[of action]** Vorgehensweise, *die*
(b) of ~: natürlich
(c) in due ~: zu gegebener Zeit; in the ~ of
the day/his life im Lauf[e] des Tages/seines
Lebens
(d) (of meal) Gang, *der*
(e) (Sport) Kurs, *der;* **[golf]**~: [Golf]platz, *der*
(f) (Educ.) Kurs[us], *der;* go to *or* attend/do
a ~ in sth. einen Kurs in etw. (*Dat.*)
besuchen/machen
(g) (Med.) a ~ of treatment eine Kur
court /kɔːt/ ① n. **(a)** Hof, *der*
(b) (Tennis, Squash) Platz, *der*
(c) (Law) Gericht, *das*
② *v.t.* ~ sb. jmdn. umwerben
courteous /'kɜːtɪəs/ *adj.* höflich
courtesy /'kɜːtəsɪ/ n. Höflichkeit, *die*
'courtesy light n. (Motor Veh.)
Innenbeleuchtung, *die*
court: ~ **house** n. (Law)
Gerichtsgebäude, *das;* ~ **'martial** n., pl.
~s martial (Mil.) Kriegsgericht, *das;* ~**room**
n. (Law) Gerichtssaal, *der*
courtship /'kɔːtʃɪp/ n. Werben, *das*
court: ~ **shoe** n. Pumps, *der;* ~**yard** n.
Hof, *der*
cousin /'kʌzn/ n. **[first]** ~: Cousin,
der/Cousine, *die*
couturier /ku:'tjʊərjeɪ/ n. Couturier, *der;*
Modeschöpfer, *der*
cove /kəʊv/ n. (Geog.) [kleine] Bucht
covenant /'kʌvənənt/ n. formelle
Übereinkunft
cover /'kʌvə(r)/ ① n. **(a)** (piece of cloth)
Decke, *die;* (of cushion, bed) Bezug, *der;* (lid)
Deckel, *der;* (of hole, engine, typewriter, etc.)
Abdeckung, *die*
(b) (of book) Einband, *der;* (of magazine)
Umschlag, *der*
(c) [send sth.] under separate ~: [etw.] mit
getrennter Post [schicken]
(d) take ~ [from sth.] Schutz [vor etw.
(*Dat.*)] suchen; under ~ (from rain) überdacht
② *v.t.* **(a)** bedecken; beziehen ⟨Sessel,
Kissen⟩; zudecken ⟨Pfanne⟩; the roses are
~ed with greenfly die Rosen sind voller
Blattläuse

(b) (include) abdecken
(c) (Journ.) berichten über (+ *Akk.*)
(d) decken ⟨Kosten⟩
■ **cover 'up** ① *v.t.* zudecken; (fig.)
vertuschen
② *v.i.* ~ up for sb. jmdn. decken
coverage /'kʌvərɪdʒ/ n. (Journ.)
Berichterstattung, *die*
'cover charge n. [Preis für das] Gedeck
'covering n. Decke, *die;* (of chair, bed)
Bezug, *der*
'covering letter n. Begleitbrief, *der*
'cover story n. (Journ.) Titelgeschichte,
die
covert /'kʌvət/ *adj.* versteckt
cover: ~-**up** n. Verschleierung, *die;*
~ **version** n. Coverversion, *die*
covet /'kʌvɪt/ *v.t.* begehren (geh.)
covetous /'kʌvɪtəs/ *adj.* begehrlich (geh.)
cow /kaʊ/ n. Kuh, *die*
coward /'kaʊəd/ n. Feigling, *der*
cowardice /'kaʊədɪs/ n. Feigheit, *die*
'cowardly *adj.* feig[e]
'cowboy n. Cowboy, *der*
cower /'kaʊə(r)/ *v.i.* sich ducken
cowherd n. Kuhhirte, *der*
'co-worker n. Kollege, *der*/Kollegin, *die*
cow: ~ **parsley** n. (Bot.) Wiesenkerbel,
der; ~**pat** n. Kuhfladen, *der;* ~**shed** n.
Kuhstall, *der;* ~**slip** n. Schlüsselblume, *die*
coy /kɔɪ/ *adj.* gespielt schüchtern
cozy (Amer.) ▶ COSY
CPU *abbr.* (Comp.) = **central
processing unit** ZE
crab /kræb/ n. Krabbe, *die*
'crab apple n. Holzapfel, *der*
crack /kræk/ ① n. **(a)** (noise) Krachen, *das*
(b) (in china etc.) Sprung, *der;* (in rock) Spalte,
die; (chink) Spalt, *der*
(c) (coll.: try) have a ~ at sth./doing sth.
versuchen, etw. zu tun
(d) (sl.: drug) ~ **[cocaine]** Crack, *das*
② *attrib. adj.* (coll.) erstklassig
③ *v.t.* **(a)** knacken ⟨Nuss, Problem, Kode⟩
(b) (make a ~ in) anschlagen ⟨Porzellan usw.⟩
(c) ~ a joke einen Witz machen
(d) ~ a whip mit einer Peitsche knallen
④ *v.i.* ⟨Porzellan usw.:⟩ einen Sprung/
Sprünge bekommen
■ **crack 'down** *v.i.* (coll.) ~ down [on
sb./sth.] [gegen jmdn./etw.] [hart] vorgehen
■ **crack 'up** *v.i.* (coll.) ⟨Person:⟩
zusammenbrechen
'crack-down n. (coll.) there will be a
~: man wird hart durchgreifen; have/order
a ~ on sb./sth. drastische Maßnahmen
gegen jmdn./etw. ergreifen/anordnen
cracked /krækt/ *adj.* gesprungen
⟨Porzellan usw.⟩; rissig ⟨Verputz⟩
cracker /'krækə(r)/ n. **(a)** **[Christmas]** ~
≈ Knallbonbon, *der od. das*
(b) (biscuit) Cracker, *der*

'**crackers** *pred. adj.* (Brit. coll.) übergeschnappt (ugs.)

crackle /'kræk̩l/ ① *v.i.* knistern; ⟨*Feuer:*⟩ prasseln
② *n.* Knistern, *das*

cradle /'kreɪd̩l/ ① *n.* Wiege, *die*
② *v.t.* wiegen

cradle: ~-**snatch** *v.i.* (coll.) **Your boyfriend/girlfriend is much younger than you You're** ~-**snatching** Dein Freund/deine Freundin ist viel jünger als du. Du vergreifst dich ja an kleinen Kindern (ugs. scherzh.); ~-**snatcher** *n.* (fig. coll.) *jmd., der mit einer sehr viel jüngeren Person eine Liebesbeziehung eingeht*

craft /krɑːft/ *n.* **(a)** (trade) Handwerk, *das;* (art) Kunsthandwerk, *das*
(b) *pl. same* (boat) Boot, *das*

craftily /'krɑːftɪlɪ/ *adv.* listig

craftsman /'krɑːftsmən/ *n., pl.* **craftsmen** /'krɑːftsmən/ Handwerker, *der*

craftsmanship /'krɑːftsmənʃɪp/ *n.* (skilled workmanship) handwerkliches Können

crafty /'krɑːftɪ/ *adj.* listig

crag /kræg/ *n.* Felsspitze, *die*

'**craggy** *adj.* **(a)** felsig
(b) zerfurcht ⟨*Gesicht*⟩

cram /kræm/ ① *v.t.,* **-mm-** (overfill) voll stopfen (ugs.); (force) stopfen
② *v.i.,* **-mm-** (for exam) büffeln (ugs.)

cramp /kræmp/ ① *n.* (Med.) Krampf, *der*
② *v.t.* einengen

cramped /kræmpt/ *adj.* eng ⟨*Raum*⟩; gedrängt ⟨*Handschrift*⟩

cranberry /'krænbərɪ/ *n.* Preiselbeere, *die*

crane /kreɪn/ ① *n.* Kran, *der*
② *v.t.* ~ **one's neck** den Hals recken

crane: ~ **driver** *n.* Kranführer, *der/* -führerin, *die;* ~ **fly** *n.* Schnake, *die*

crank[1] /kræŋk/ *n.* (Mech. Engin.) [Hand]kurbel, *die*

crank[2] *n.* Irre, *der/die* (salopp)

crank: ~ **arm** *n.* (of bicycle) Tretkurbel, *die;* ~**shaft** *n.* (Mech. Engin.) Kurbelwelle, *die*

'**cranky** *adj.* (eccentric) schrullig

cranny /'krænɪ/ *n.* Ritze, *die*

crap /kræp/ *n.* (coarse) **(a)** (faeces) Scheiße, *die* (derb); **have a** ~: scheißen (derb)
(b) (nonsense) Scheiß, *der* (salopp)

crash /kræʃ/ ① *n.* **(a)** (noise) Krachen, *das*
(b) (collision) Zusammenstoß, *der;* **have a** ~: einen Unfall haben
② *v.i.* **(a)** (make a noise, go noisily) krachen
(b) (have a collision) einen Unfall haben; ⟨*Flugzeug, Flieger:*⟩ abstürzen; ~ **into sth.** gegen etw. krachen
(c) (Finance etc., Computing) zusammenbrechen
③ *v.t.* **(a)** (smash) schmettern
(b) (cause to have collision) einen Unfall haben mit

crash: ~ **barrier** *n.* Leitplanke, *die;* ~ **course** *n.* Intensivkurs, *der;* ~ **diet** *n.*

radikale Diät; ≈ Nulldiät, *die;* ~ **helmet** *n.* Sturzhelm, *der;* ~-**land** ① *v.t.* ~-**land a plane** mit einem Flugzeug bruchlanden; ② *v.i.* bruchlanden; ~-**landing** *n.* Bruchlandung, *die*

crass /kræs/ *adj.* haarsträubend ⟨*Dummheit, Unwissenheit*⟩; (grossly stupid) strohdumm

crate /kreɪt/ *n.* Kiste, *die*

crater /'kreɪtə(r)/ *n.* Krater, *der*

cravat /krə'væt/ *n.* Krawatte, *die*

crave /kreɪv/ *v.t.* **(a)** (beg) erbitten
(b) (long for) sich sehnen nach

'**craving** *n.* Verlangen, *das* (**for** nach)

crawl /krɔːl/ ① *v.i.* **(a)** kriechen; ⟨*Baby, Insekt:*⟩ krabbeln
(b) (coll.) ~ **to sb.** vor jmdm. kriechen
② *n.* **(a) go at a** ~: im Schneckentempo fahren
(b) (swimming stroke) Kraulen, *das*

'**crawler lane** *n.* Kriechspur, *die*

crayfish /'kreɪfɪʃ/ *n., pl. same* Flusskrebs, *der*

crayon /'kreɪən/ *n.* **[coloured]** ~: Buntstift, *der;* (wax) Wachsmalstift, *der*

craze /kreɪz/ *n.* Begeisterung, *die*

crazy /'kreɪzɪ/ *adj.* verrückt; **be** ~ **about sb./sth.** (coll.) nach jmdm./etw. verrückt sein (ugs.)

creak /kriːk/ ① *n.* Knarren, *das*
② *v.i.* knarren

cream /kriːm/ ① *n.* **(a)** Sahne, *die*
(b) (dessert, cosmetic) Creme, *die*
② *adj.* ~-**[-coloured]** creme[farben]

cream: ~ **cake** *n.* Cremetorte, *die;* (small) Cremetörtchen, *das;* (with whipped ~) Sahnetorte, *die/*Sahnetörtchen, *das;* ~ '**cheese** *n.* ≈ Frischkäse, *der;* ~ '**cracker** *n.* ≈ Cracker, *der;* ~ '**tea** *n.* Tee mit Marmeladetörtchen und Sahne

'**creamy** *adj.* (with cream) sahnig; (like cream) cremig

crease /kriːs/ ① *n.* (pressed) Bügelfalte, *die;* (accidental) Falte, *der*
② *v.t.* (press) eine Falte bügeln in (+ *Akk.*); (accidentally) zerknittern
③ *v.i.* Falten bekommen; knittern

'**crease-resistant** *adj.* knitterfrei

create /kriː'eɪt/ *v.t.* schaffen; verursachen ⟨*Verwirrung*⟩; machen ⟨*Eindruck*⟩

creation /kriː'eɪʃn/ *n.* Schaffung, *die;* (of the world) Schöpfung, *die* (geh.)

creative /kriː'eɪtɪv/ *adj.* kreativ

creator /kriː'eɪtə(r)/ *n.* Schöpfer, *der/*Schöpferin, *die*

creature /'kriːtʃə(r)/ *n.* Geschöpf, *das*

crèche /kreʃ/ *n.* [Kinder]krippe, *die*

credentials /krɪ'denʃlz/ *n. pl.* Zeugnis, *das*

credibility /kredɪ'bɪlɪtɪ/ *n.* Glaubwürdigkeit, *die*

credible /'kredɪbl/ *adj.* glaubwürdig

credit /'kredɪt/ 1 n. (a) (honour) Ehre, *die;* take the ~ for sth. die Anerkennung für etw. einstecken
(b) (Commerc.) Kredit, *der*
(c) ~s, ~ titles (at beginning of film) Vorspann, *der;* (at end) Nachspann, *der*
2 *v.t.* (a) glauben
(b) (Finance) gutschreiben

creditable /'kredɪtəbl/ *adj.* anerkennenswert

creditably /'kredɪtəblɪ/ *adv.* achtbar

credit: ~ account *n.* Kreditkonto, *das;* ~ **card** *n.* Kreditkarte, *die;* ~ **crunch** *n.* Kreditklemme, *die;* ~ **facilities** *n. pl.* [Kredit]fazilität, *die* (fachspr.); ~ **limit** *n.* Kreditlinie, *die*

creditor /'kredɪtə(r)/ *n.* Gläubiger, *der*/Gläubigerin, *die*

credit: ~ rating *n.* [Einschätzung *der*] Kreditwürdigkeit; **have a good/bad** ~ **rating** als kreditwürdig/kreditunwürdig eingeschätzt werden; ~**worthy** *adj.* kreditwürdig

creed /kri:d/ *n.* Glaubensbekenntnis, *das*

creek /kri:k/ *n.* (a) (Brit.: of coast) [kleine] Bucht
(b) (of river) [kurzer] Flussarm

creep /kri:p/ 1 *v.i.,* crept [krept] kriechen; (move timidly, slowly, stealthily) schleichen
2 *n.* (a) (coll.: person) Fiesling, *der* (salopp)
(b) (coll.) **give sb. the** ~**s** jmdn. nicht [ganz] geheuer sein

'creeper *n.* Kletterpflanze, *die*

'creepy *adj.* unheimlich

cremate /krɪ'meɪt/ *v.t.* einäschern

cremation /krɪ'meɪʃn/ *n.* Einäscherung, *die*

crematorium /kremə'tɔ:rɪəm/ *n.* Krematorium, *das*

creosote /'kri:əsəʊt/ *n.* Kreosot, *das*

crept ▶ CREEP 1

crescendo /krɪ'ʃendəʊ/ *n., pl.* ~s (Mus.) Crescendo, *das;* (fig.) Zunahme, *die*

crescent /'kresənt/ *n.* Mondsichel, *die*

cress /kres/ *n.* Kresse, *die*

crest /krest/ *n.* Kamm, *der*

'crestfallen *adj.* niedergeschlagen

Crete /kri:t/ *pr. n.* Kreta (*das*)

cretin /'kretɪn/ *n.* (coll.) Trottel, *der*

Creutzfeldt-Jakob disease /'krɔɪtsfelt'jækɒb/ *n.* Creutzfeldt-Jakob-Krankheit, *die*

crevasse /krɪ'væs/ *n.* Gletscherspalte, *die*

crevice /'krevɪs/ *n.* Spalt, *der*

crew /kru:/ *n.* Besatzung, *die*

crew: ~cut *n.* Bürstenschnitt, *der;* ~ **neck** *n.* enger, runder Halsausschnitt; **a** ~**-neck pullover** ein Pullover mit engem, rundem Halsausschnitt

crib /krɪb/ 1 *n.* Krippe, *die*
2 *v.t.,* -bb- (coll.) abkupfern (salopp)

crick /krɪk/ *n.* **a** ~ [in one's neck/back] ein steifer Hals/Rücken

cricket¹ /'krɪkɪt/ *n.* Kricket, *das*

cricket² *n.* (Zool.) Grille, *die*

cricket: ~ ball *n.* Kricketball, *der;* ~ **bat** Schlagholz, *das*

'cricketer *n.* Kricketspieler, *der*/-spielerin, *die*

'cricket match *n.* Kricketspiel, *das*

cried ▶ CRY

crime /kraɪm/ *n.* (a) Verbrechen, *das*
(b) collect. **a wave of** ~: eine Welle von Straftaten; ~ **doesn't pay** Verbrechen lohnen sich nicht

crime: ~ prevention *n.* Verbrechensverhütung, *die;* C~ **Prevention Officer** *Polizeibeamter, dessen/-beamtin, deren Aufgabe aktive, vorbeugende Verbrechensbekämpfung ist;* ~ **rate** *n.* Kriminalitätsrate, *die;* ~ **wave** *n.* Welle von Straftaten; ~ **writer** *n.* Kriminalschriftsteller, *der*/-schriftstellerin, *die*

criminal /'krɪmɪnl/ 1 *adj.* kriminell; strafbar; ~ **act** *or* deed/offence Straftat, *die*
2 *n.* Kriminelle, *der*/*die*

criminal: ~ charge *n.* Anklage, *die;* **face** ~ **charges [for sth.]** sich [wegen etw.] vor Gericht zu verantworten haben; **there are** ~ **charges against him** er steht unter Anklage; ~ **court** *n.* Strafgericht, *das;* ~ **'law** *n.* Strafrecht, *das;* ~ **'lawyer** *n.* Anwalt/Anwältin für Strafsachen; ~ **'record** *n.* Strafregister, *das;* **have a** ~ **record** vorbestraft sein

crimson /'krɪmzn/ 1 *adj.* purpurrot
2 *n.* Purpurrot, *das*

cringe /krɪndʒ/ *v.i.* zusammenzucken

crinkle /'krɪŋkl/ 1 *n.* Knitterfalte, *die*
2 *v.t.* zerknittern
3 *v.i.* knittern

cripple /'krɪpl/ 1 *n.* Krüppel, *der*
2 *v.t.* zum Krüppel machen; (fig.) lähmen

crippled /'krɪpld/ *adj.* verkrüppelt

crippling /'krɪplɪŋ/ *adj.* zur Verkrüppelung führend ‹*Krankheit, Verletzung*›; (fig.) erdrückend ‹*Preise, Inflationsrate, Steuern, Mieten*›; lähmend ‹*Streik, Schmerzen*›

crisis /'kraɪsɪs/ *n., pl.* crises /'kraɪsi:z/ Krise, *die*

crisis: ~ area *n.* Krisengebiet, *das;* ~ **'management** *n.* Krisenmanagement, *das*

crisp /krɪsp/ 1 *adj.* knusprig
2 *n.*(a) *usu. in pl.* (Brit.: potato ~) [Kartoffel]chip, *der*
(b) **be burned to a** ~: verbrannt sein

'crispbread *n.* Knäckebrot, *das*

'crispy *adj.* knusprig

criss-cross /'krɪskrɒs/ 1 *adj.* ~ **pattern** Muster aus gekreuzten Linien

2 *adv.* kreuz und quer

3 *v.t.* wiederholt schneiden

criterion /kraɪ'tɪərɪən/ *n., pl.* **criteria** /kraɪ'tɪərɪə/ Kriterium, *das*

critic /'krɪtɪk/ *n.* Kritiker, *der*/Kritikerin, *die*

critical /'krɪtɪkl/ *adj.* kritisch; **be ∼ of sb./sth.** jmdn./etw. kritisieren

critically /'krɪtɪkəlɪ/ *adv.* kritisch; **∼ ill** ernstlich krank

critical 'mass *n.* (Phys.) kritische Masse

criticism /'krɪtɪsɪzm/ *n.* Kritik, *die* (**of** an + *Dat.*)

criticize /'krɪtɪsaɪz/ *v.t.* kritisieren (**for** wegen)

critique /krɪ'tiːk/ *n.* Kritik, *die*

croak /krəʊk/ **1** *n.* (of frog) Quaken, *das;* (of person) Krächzen, *das*
   2 *v.i.* ⟨*Frosch:*⟩ quaken; ⟨*Person:*⟩ krächzen
   3 *v.t.* krächzen

Croat /'krəʊæt/ *n.* (a) (person) Kroate, *der*/Kroatin, *die*
   (b) (language) Kroatisch, *das*

Croatia /krəʊ'eɪʃə/ *pr. n.* Kroatien (*das*)

Croatian /krəʊ'eɪʃən/ **1** *adj.* kroatisch; **sb. is ∼:** jmd. ist Kroate/Kroatin
   2 *n.* ▶ CROAT

crochet /'krəʊʃeɪ/ **1** *n.* Häkelarbeit, *die;* **∼ hook** Häkelhaken, *der*
   2 *v.t.* häkeln

crock /krɒk/ *n.* (coll.) **[old]** ∼ (person) altes Wrack, *das* (fig.); (vehicle) [alte] Klapperkiste (ugs.)

crockery /'krɒkərɪ/ *n.* Geschirr, *das*

crocodile /'krɒkədaɪl/ *n.* Krokodil, *das*

crocus /'krəʊkəs/ *n.* Krokus, *der*

croft /krɒft/ *n.* (a) [kleines] Stück Acker-/Weideland
   (b) (smallholding) [kleines] Pachtgut

'crofter *n.* (Brit.) Pächter, *der*/Pächterin, *die*

croissant /'krwɑːsɑː/ *n.* Hörnchen, *das*

crony /'krəʊnɪ/ *n.* Kumpel, *der* (ugs.)

crook /krʊk/ *n.* (a) (coll.: rogue) Gauner, *der*
   (b) (shepherd's) Hirtenstab, *der*

crooked /'krʊkɪd/ *adj.* krumm; (fig.: dishonest) betrügerisch

crop /krɒp/ **1** *n.* [Feld]frucht, *die;* (season's yield) Ernte, *die*
   2 *v.t.* stutzen ⟨*Haare usw.*⟩
  ■ **crop 'up** *v.i.* auftauchen

'crop dusting *n.* Schädlingsbekämpfung aus der Luft

'cropper *n.* (coll.) **come a ∼:** einen Sturz bauen (ugs.)

crop: ∼-spraying *n.* Schädlingsbekämpfung (*mit Sprühmitteln*); **∼ top** *n.* bauch- *od.* nabelfreies Top

croquet /'krəʊkeɪ/ *n.* Krocket[spiel], *das*

croquette /krə'ket/ *n.* Krokette, *die*

cross /krɒs/ **1** *n.* (a) Kreuz, *das*

(b) (mixture) Mischung, *die* (**between** aus)
   2 *v.t.* (a) [über]kreuzen; **∼ one's arms/legs** die Arme verschränken/die Beine übereinander schlagen; **keep one's fingers ∼ed [for sb.]** (fig.) [jmdm.] die od. den Daumen drücken
   (b) (go across) kreuzen; überqueren ⟨*Straße, Gebirge*⟩; durchqueren ⟨*Land, Zimmer*⟩; **∼ sb.'s mind** (fig.) jmdm. einfallen; **'∼ now'** „Gehen"
   (c) (Brit.) **a ∼ed cheque** ein Verrechnungsscheck
   (d) **∼ oneself** sich bekreuzigen
   3 *v.i.* aneinander vorbeigehen; **∼ [in the post]** ⟨*Briefe:*⟩ sich kreuzen
   4 *adj.* verärgert; **sb. will be ∼:** jmd. wird ärgerlich *od.* böse werden; **be ∼ with sb.** böse auf jmdn. sein
  ■ **cross 'out** *v.t.* ausstreichen
  ■ **cross 'over** *v.t.* überqueren; *abs.* hinübergehen

cross: ∼bar *n.* (a) [Fahrrad]stange, *die;* (b) (Sport) Querlatte, *die;* **∼bones** *n. pl.* gekreuzte Knochen *Pl.* (*unter Totenkopf*); **∼bow** /'krɒsbəʊ/ *n.* Armbrust, *die;* **∼-breed** **1** *n.* Hybride, *die;* (animal) Bastard, *der;* **2** *v.t.* kreuzen; **∼-Channel** *adj.* **∼-Channel traffic/ferry** Verkehr/Fähre über den Kanal; **∼-check** **1** *n.* Gegenprobe, *die;* **2** *v.t.* [nochmals] nachprüfen; nachkontrollieren; **∼-country** **1** *adj.* Querfeldein-; **2** *adv.* querfeldein; **∼-cultural** *adj.* interkulturell; **∼-dressing** *n.* Crossdressing, *das;* **∼-examination** *n.* Kreuzverhör, *das;* **∼-examine** *v.t.* ins Kreuzverhör nehmen; **∼-eyed** /'krɒsaɪd/ *adj.* [nach innen] schielend; **be ∼-eyed** schielen; **∼-'fertilize** *v.t.* fremdbestäuben; kreuzbefruchten; (fig.) sich gegenseitig befruchten; **∼fire** *n.* Kreuzfeuer, *das;* **get caught in the ∼fire** (fig.) ins Kreuzfeuer geraten

'crossing *n.* (a) (act) Überquerung, *die* (b) (pedestrian ∼) Überweg, *der*

cross-legged /'krɒslegd/ *adv.* mit gekreuzten Beinen; (with feet across thighs) im Schneidersitz

'crossly *adv.* verärgert

cross: ∼ 'purposes *n. pl.* **talk at ∼ purposes** aneinander vorbeireden; **∼-'question** *v.t.* ins Kreuzverhör nehmen; **∼-refer** *v.i.* einen Querverweis machen (**to** auf + *Akk.*); **∼ reference** *n.* Querverweis, *der;* **∼roads** *n. sing.* Kreuzung, *die;* (fig.) Wendepunkt, *der;* **∼ section** *n.* Querschnitt, *der;* **∼word** *n.* **∼word [puzzle]** Kreuzworträtsel, *das*

crotch /krɒtʃ/ *n.* (of trousers, body) Schritt, *der*

crotchet /'krɒtʃɪt/ *n.* (Brit. Mus.) Viertelnote, *die*

crouch /kraʊtʃ/ *v.i.* [sich zusammen]kauern

croupier /ˈkruːpɪə(r), ˈkruːpɪeɪ/ n.
Croupier, *der*

crow /krəʊ/ n. Krähe, *die; as the* ~ flies
Luftlinie

'**crowbar** n. Brechstange, *die*

crowd /kraʊd/ ① n. [Menschen]menge, *die*
② v.t. füllen
③ v.i. sich sammeln

'**crowded** adj. überfüllt

'**crowd-puller** n. (coll.) Publikumsmagnet,
der

crown /kraʊn/ ① n. Krone, *die*
② v.t. (a) krönen
(b) überkronen ⟨*Zahn*⟩

crown 'jewels n. pl. Kronjuwelen Pl.

'**crow's-foot** n., usu. in pl. Krähenfuß, *der*

crucial /ˈkruːʃl/ adj. entscheidend (**to** für)

crucially /ˈkruːʃəlɪ/ adv. entscheidend;
be ~ **important** von entscheidender
Wichtigkeit sein

crucifix /ˈkruːsɪfɪks/ n. Kruzifix, *das*

crucifixion /kruːsɪˈfɪkʃn/ n. Kreuzigung,
die

crucify /ˈkruːsɪfaɪ/ v.t. kreuzigen

crude /kruːd/ adj. (a) roh; ~ **oil** Rohöl, *das*
(b) (fig.) grob ⟨*Entwurf, Worte*⟩

cruel /ˈkruːəl/ adj. grausam

cruelty /ˈkruːəltɪ/ n. Grausamkeit, *die*

cruet /ˈkruːɪt/ n. (a) Essig-/Ölfläschchen,
das
(b) ▶ CRUET STAND

'**cruet stand** n. Menage, *die*

cruise /kruːz/ ① v.i. (at random) ⟨*Fahrzeug,
Fahrer:*⟩ herumfahren
② n. Kreuzfahrt, *die*

'**cruise missile** n. Marschflugkörper, *der*

'**cruiser** n. Kreuzer, *der*

crumb /krʌm/ n. Krümel, *der*

crumble /ˈkrʌmbl/ ① v.t. zerkrümeln
⟨*Keks, Kuchen*⟩
② v.i. ⟨*Mauer:*⟩ zusammenfallen

crumbly /ˈkrʌmblɪ/ adj. krümelig ⟨*Keks,
Kuchen*⟩; bröckelig ⟨*Gestein*⟩

crumpet /ˈkrʌmpɪt/ n.: *weiches
Hefeküchlein zum Toasten*

crumple /ˈkrʌmpl/ ① v.t. (a) (crush)
zerdrücken
(b) (wrinkle) zerknittern
② v.i. knittern

'**crumple zone** n. (Motor Veh.)
Knautschzone, *die*

crunch /krʌntʃ/ ① v.t. [geräuschvoll]
knabbern ⟨*Keks*⟩
② v.i. ⟨*Schnee, Kies:*⟩ knirschen
③ n. Knirschen, *das; when it comes to the*
~: wenn es hart auf hart geht

'**crunchy** adj. knusprig

crusade /kruːˈseɪd/ ① n. (Hist.; also fig.)
Kreuzzug, *der*
② v.i. (fig.) zu Felde gehen

cru'sader n. (Hist.) Kreuzfahrer, *der*

crush /krʌʃ/ ① v.t. (a) quetschen
(b) (powder) zerstampfen
(c) (fig.) niederschlagen
② n. (a) (crowd) Gedränge, *das*
(b) (coll.) **have/get a** ~ **on sb.** in jmdn.
verknallt sein/sich in jmdn. verknallen
(ugs.)

crush: ~ **bar** n. Bar, *die (im Foyer eines
Theaters)*; ~-**barrier** n. Absperrgitter, *das*

crushing /ˈkrʌʃɪŋ/ adj. niederschmetternd
⟨*Antwort*⟩; vernichtend ⟨*Niederlage, Schlag*⟩

crust /krʌst/ n. Kruste, *die*

'**crusty** adj. knusprig

crutch /krʌtʃ/ n. Krücke, *die; go about on*
~es an Krücken gehen

crux /krʌks/ n. **the** ~ **of the matter** der
springende Punkt bei der Sache

cry /kraɪ/ ① n. (of grief) Schrei, *der;* (of words)
Schreien, *das; a far* ~ **from** … (fig.) etwas
ganz anderes als …
② v.i. (a) rufen; (loudly) schreien
(b) (weep) weinen (**over** wegen)
■ **cry 'off** v.i. absagen
■ **cry 'out** v.i. aufschreien

'**crying** adj. **it's a** ~ **shame** es ist eine
wahre Schande

crypt /krɪpt/ n. Krypta, *die*

cryptic /ˈkrɪptɪk/ adj. geheimnisvoll

crystal /ˈkrɪstl/ ① n. (a) Kristall, *der*
(b) (glass) Bleikristall, *das*
② adj. (made of ~ glass) kristallen;
Kristall⟨*schale, -vase*⟩

crystal: ~ '**clear** adj. kristallklar; (fig.)
glasklar; ~ '**glass** n. Bleikristall, *das;*
Kristallglas, *das*

crystallize /ˈkrɪstəlaɪz/ v.i.
kristallisieren; (fig.) feste Form annehmen

cub /kʌb/ n. (a) Junge, *das;* (of wolf, fox, dog)
Welpe, *der*
(b) Cub ▶ CUB SCOUT

Cuba /ˈkjuːbə/ pr. n. Kuba (*das*)

cubby[hole] /ˈkʌbɪ(həʊl)/ n.
Kämmerchen, *das*

cube /kjuːb/ n. Würfel, *der*

'**cube sugar** n. Würfelzucker, *der*

cubic /ˈkjuːbɪk/ adj. (a) würfelförmig
(b) Kubik⟨*meter usw.*⟩

cubicle /ˈkjuːbɪkl/ n. Kabine, *die*

cubism /ˈkjuːbɪzm/ n. (Art) Kubismus, *der*

cubist /ˈkjuːbɪst/ n. (Art) Kubist,
der/Kubistin, *die*

'**Cub Scout** n. Wölfling, *der*

cuckoo /ˈkʊkuː/ n. Kuckuck, *der*

'**cuckoo clock** n. Kuckucksuhr, *die*

cucumber /ˈkjuːkʌmbə(r)/ n.
[Salat]gurke, *die*

cuddle /ˈkʌdl/ ① n. enge Umarmung
② v.t. schmusen mit; hätscheln ⟨*kleines
Kind*⟩
③ v.i. schmusen

cuddly /ˈkʌdlɪ/ adj. zum Schmusen
nachgestellt

cuddly 'toy n. Plüschtier, das

cudgel /'kʌdʒl/ n. Knüppel, der

cue¹ /kju:/ n. (Billiards etc.) Queue, das

cue² n. (Theatre) Stichwort, das

cuff¹ /kʌf/ n. (a) Manschette, die; **off the** ~ (fig.) aus dem Stegreif
(b) (Amer.: trouser turn-up) [Hosen]aufschlag, der

cuff² [1] v.t. ~ **sb.** jmdm. einen Klaps geben [2] n. Klaps, der

'cuff link n. Manschettenknopf, der

cuisine /kwɪ'zi:n/ n. Küche, die

cul-de-sac /'kʌldəsæk/ n. Sackgasse, die

culinary /'kʌlɪnərɪ/ adj. kulinarisch

culminate /'kʌlmɪneɪt/ v.i. gipfeln; ~ **in sth.** in etw. (Dat.) seinen Höchststand erreichen

culmination /kʌlmɪ'neɪʃn/ n. Höhepunkt, der

culottes /kju:'lɒts/ n. pl. Hosenrock, der

culpable /'kʌlpəbl/ adj. schuldig ⟨Person⟩; strafbar ⟨Handlung⟩

culprit /'kʌlprɪt/ n. Täter, der/Täterin, die

cult /kʌlt/ n. Kult, der

cultivate /'kʌltɪveɪt/ v.t. kultivieren (auch fig.); bestellen ⟨Acker, Land⟩; anbauen ⟨Pflanzen⟩

cultivated /'kʌltɪveɪtɪd/ adj. kultiviert ⟨Manieren, Sprache, Geschmack⟩; kultiviert, gebildet ⟨Person⟩

cultivation /kʌltɪ'veɪʃn/ n. ▶ CULTIVATE: Kultivierung, die; Bestellen das; Anbau, der

culture /'kʌltʃə(r)/ n. Kultur, die

'cultured adj. kultiviert

'culture shock n. Kulturschock, der

cumbersome /'kʌmbəsəm/ adj. hinderlich ⟨Kleider⟩; sperrig ⟨Pakete⟩; schwerfällig ⟨Arbeitsweise⟩

cunning /'kʌnɪŋ/ [1] n. Schläue, die [2] adj. schlau

cup /kʌp/ n. (a) Tasse, die
(b) (prize, competition) Pokal, der
(c) (~ful) Tasse, die; **a** ~ **of coffee/tea** eine Tasse Kaffee/Tee

cupboard /'kʌbəd/ n. Schrank, der

'Cup Final n. Pokalendspiel, das

cupful /'kʌpfl/ n. Tasse, die; **a** ~ **of water** eine Tasse Wasser

'cup tie n. Pokalspiel, das

curable /'kjʊərəbl/ adj. heilbar

curate /'kjʊərət/ n. Kurat, der

curator /kjʊə'reɪtə(r)/ n. (of museum) Direktor, der/Direktorin, die

curb /kɜ:b/ v.t. zügeln

'curd cheese n. ≈ Quark, der

curdle /'kɜ:dl/ v.i. gerinnen

cure /kjʊə(r)/ [1] n. [Heil]mittel, das (**for** gegen); (fig.) Mittel, das [2] v.t. (a) heilen
(b) [ein]pökeln ⟨Fleisch⟩

'cure-all n. Allheilmittel, das

curfew /'kɜ:fju:/ n. Ausgangssperre, die

curiosity /kjʊərɪ'ɒsɪtɪ/ n. (a) Neugier[de], die
(b) (object) Wunderding, das

curious /'kjʊərɪəs/ adj. (a) (inquisitive) neugierig
(b) (strange, odd) seltsam

curl /kɜ:l/ [1] n. Locke, die [2] v.t. locken [3] v.i. (a) sich locken
(b) ⟨Straße, Fluss:⟩ sich winden

'curler n. Lockenwickler, der

'curly adj. lockig

'curly-haired adj. lockenköpfig; mit lockigem Haar

currant /'kʌrənt/ n. Korinthe, die

currency /'kʌrənsɪ/ n. (money) Währung, die; **foreign currencies** Devisen Pl.

current /'kʌrənt/ [1] adj. (a) verbreitet ⟨Meinung⟩; gebräuchlich ⟨Wort⟩
(b) laufend ⟨Jahr, Monat⟩
(c) (the present) aktuell ⟨Ereignis, Mode⟩; Tages⟨politik, -preis⟩; ~ **affairs** Tagespolitik, die
[2] n. (a) (of water, air) Strömung, die
(b) (Electr.) Strom, der

'current account n. Girokonto, das

'currently adv. zur Zeit

curriculum /kə'rɪkjʊləm/ n. Lehrplan, der

curriculum vitae /- 'vi:taɪ/ n. Lebenslauf, der

curry¹ /'kʌrɪ/ n. Curry[gericht], das

curry² v.t. ~ **favour [with sb.]** sich [bei jmdm.] einschmeicheln

curse /kɜ:s/ [1] n. Fluch, der [2] v.t. verfluchen [3] v.i. fluchen

cursor /'kɜ:sə(r)/ n. Läufer, der; (on screen) Cursor, der; Schreibmarke, die

cursory /'kɜ:sərɪ/ adj. flüchtig

curt /kɜ:t/ adj. kurz angebunden; kurz und schroff ⟨Brief⟩

curtail /kɜ:'teɪl/ v.t. kürzen; abkürzen ⟨Urlaub⟩; beschneiden ⟨Macht⟩

curtain /'kɜ:tən/ n. Vorhang, der; **draw or pull the** ~**s** (open) die Vorhänge aufziehen; (close) die Vorhänge zuziehen

curtain: ~ **call** n. Vorhang, der; ~ **hook** n. Gardinenhaken, der; ~ **rod** n. Gardinenstange, die

curtsy /'kɜ:tsɪ/ [1] n. Knicks, der [2] v.i. einen Knicks machen (**to** vor + Dat.)

curvaceous /kɜ:'veɪʃəs/ adj. kurvenreich (ugs.); **a** ~ **figure** eine üppige Figur

curve /kɜ:v/ [1] v.t. krümmen [2] v.i. ⟨Straße, Fluss:⟩ eine Biegung machen [3] n. Kurve, die

cushion /'kʊʃn/ [1] n. Kissen, das [2] v.t. dämpfen ⟨Aufprall, Stoß⟩

cushy /'kʊʃɪ/ adj. (coll.) bequem

custard /'kʌstəd/ n. ≈ Vanillesoße, *die*

'**custard powder** n. Vanillesoßenpulver, *das*

custodian /kʌs'təʊdɪən/ n. (of museum) Wächter, *der*/Wächterin, *die;* (of valuables) Hüter, *der*/Hüterin, *die*

custody /'kʌstədɪ/ n. (a) (care) Obhut, *die* (b) (imprisonment) [be] in ∼: in Haft [sein]; take sb. into ∼: jmdn. verhaften *od.* festnehmen

custom /'kʌstəm/ n. (a) Brauch, *der* (b) *in pl.* (duty on imports) Zoll, *der*

customary /'kʌstəmərɪ/ adj. üblich

'**custom-built** adj. spezial[an]gefertigt

customer /'kʌstəmə(r)/ n. Kunde, *der*/Kundin, *die*

customize (customise) /'kʌstəmaɪz/ v.t. speziell anfertigen; (alter) umbauen

'**custom-made** adj. spezial[an]gefertigt; maßgeschneidert ‹Kleidung›

customs: ∼ **duty** n. Zoll, *der;* ∼ **inspection** n. Zollkontrolle, *die;* ∼ **officer** n. Zollbeamter, *der*/-beamtin, *die*

cut /kʌt/ ①v.t., **-tt-, cut (a)** schneiden; durchschneiden ‹Seil›; ∼ one's leg sich (*Dat. od. Akk.*) ins Bein schneiden (b) abschneiden ‹Scheibe›; schneiden ‹Hecke›; mähen ‹Getreide, Gras›; ∼ one's nails sich (*Dat.*) die Nägel schneiden (c) (reduce) senken ‹Preise›; kürzen ‹Lohn›; abbauen ‹Arbeitsplätze› (d) ∼ sth. short (interrupt) etw. abbrechen (e) (Comp.) ∼ and paste ausschneiden und einfügen ②v.i., **-tt-, cut (a)** ‹Messer:› schneiden (b) ∼ through *or* across the field/park [quer] über das Feld/durch den Park gehen ③n. (a) (act of cutting) Schnitt, *der* (b) (stroke, blow) (with knife) Schnitt, *der;* (with sword, whip) Hieb, *der* (c) (reduction) Kürzung, *die;* (in prices) Senkung, *die;* (in services) Verringerung, *die* (d) (of meat) Stück, *das*

■ **cut a'way** v.t. abschneiden

■ **cut 'back** v.t. (a) (reduce) einschränken (b) (prune) stutzen

■ **cut 'down** ①v.t. (a) fällen ‹Baum› (b) (reduce) einschränken ②v.i. ∼ down on sth. etw. einschränken

■ **cut 'off** v.t. abschneiden; unterbrechen ‹Telefongespräch, Sprecher›

■ **cut 'out** ①v.t. (a) ausschneiden (of aus) (b) be ∼ out for geeignet sein zu ②v.i. ‹Motor:› aussetzen

■ **cut 'up** v.t. zerschneiden

cut: ∼**back** n. (reduction) Kürzung, *die;* ∼ '**glass** n. Kristall[glas], *das;* ∼**-glass**

adj. Kristall-

cutlery /'kʌtlərɪ/ n. Besteck, *das*

cutlet /'kʌtlɪt/ n. Kotelett, *das*

cut: ∼**-off** n. ∼**-off** point Trennungslinie, *die;* ∼**-out** n. (figure) Ausschneidefigur, *die;* ∼**-price** adj. herabgesetzt; ∼**-price offer** Billigangebot, *das*

'**cutting** ① adj. beißend ‹Bemerkung, Antwort› ② n. (from newspaper) Ausschnitt, *der*

'**cutting edge** n. be at the ∼ of technology auf dem Gebiet der Technologie führend sein; die Speerspitze der Technologie sein; be at the ∼ of fashion auf dem Gebiet der Mode führend sein

c. v. abbr. = **curriculum vitae**

cyber: ∼**cafe** /'saɪbəkæfeɪ/ n. Internet-Café *das;* ∼**sex** /'saɪbəseks/ n., *no art.* Cybersex, *der;* ∼**space** /'saɪbəspeɪs/ n., *no art.* Cyberspace, *der*

cycle /'saɪkl/ ① n. (a) (recurrent period) Zyklus, *der* (b) (bicycle) Rad, *das* ② v.i. Rad fahren

cycle: ∼ **lane** n. Fahrradspur, *die;* ∼ **race** n. Radrennen, *das;* ∼ **track** n. Rad[fahr]weg, *der;* (for racing) Radrennbahn, *die*

cycling /'saɪklɪŋ/ n. (activity) Radfahren, *das;* (sport) Radsport, *der;* ∼ **shorts** Radlerhose, *die*

cyclist /'saɪklɪst/ n. Radfahrer, *der*/-fahrerin, *die*

cyclone /'saɪkləʊn/ n. (violent hurricane) Zyklon, *der*

cylinder /'sɪlɪndə(r)/ n. Zylinder, *der*

cylindrical /sɪ'lɪndrɪkl/ adj. zylindrisch

cymbal /'sɪmbl/ n. Beckenteller, *der;* ∼s Becken *Pl.*

cynic /'sɪnɪk/ n. Zyniker, *der*

cynical /'sɪnɪkl/ adj. zynisch; bissig ‹Bemerkung, Worte›

cynicism /'sɪnɪsɪzm/ n. Zynismus, *der*

Cyprus /'saɪprəs/ pr. n. Zypern (*das*)

czar ▶ TSAR

Czech /tʃek/ ① adj. tschechisch; sb. is ∼: jmd. ist Tscheche/Tschechin ② n. (a) (language) Tschechisch, *das* (b) (person) Tscheche, *der*/Tschechin, *die*

Czechoslovakia /tʃekəʊslə'vækɪə/ pr. n. (Hist.) die Tschechoslowakei

Czechoslovakian /tʃekəʊslə'vækɪən/ (Hist.) ① adj. tschechoslowakisch ② n. Tschechoslowake, *der*/Tschechoslowakin, *die*

Czech Re'public pr. n. Tschechische Republik; Tschechien (*das*)

Dd

D, d /diː/ *n.* D, d, *das*

dab /dæb/ ① *n.* Tupfer, *der*
② *v.t.*, **-bb-** abtupfen; ~ **sth. on** *or* **against sth.** etw. auf etw. (*Akk.*) tupfen

dabble /'dæbl/ *v.i.* ~ **in sth.** sich in etw. (*Dat.*) versuchen

dachshund /'dækshʊnd/ *n.* Dackel, *der*

dad /dæd/ *n.* (coll.) Vater, *der*

daddy /'dædɪ/ *n.* (coll.) Vati, *der* (fam.)

daddy-'long-legs *n.* Schnake, *die*

daffodil /'dæfədɪl/ *n.* Osterglocke, *die*

daft /dɑːft/ *adj.* doof (ugs.)

dagger /'dægə(r)/ *n.* Dolch, *der*

daily /'deɪlɪ/ ① *adj.* täglich; ~ **[news]paper** Tageszeitung, *die*
② *adv.* täglich
③ *n.* Tageszeitung, *die*

dainty /'deɪntɪ/ *adj.* zierlich; anmutig ⟨*Bewegung, Person*⟩; zart ⟨*Gesichtszüge*⟩

dairy /'deərɪ/ *n.* (a) Molkerei, *die*
(b) (shop) Milchladen, *der*

dairy: ~ **cattle** *n.* Milchvieh, *das;*
~ **farm** *n.* Milchbetrieb, *der;* ~ **farmer** *n.* Milchbauer, *der;* ~ **produce** *n.*,
~ **products** *n. pl.* Molkereiprodukte

dais /'deɪɪs/ *n.* Podium, *das*

daisy /'deɪzɪ/ *n.* Gänseblümchen, *das*

'daisy chain *n.* Kranz aus Gänseblümchen

dam /dæm/ ① *n.* [Stau]damm, *der*
② *v.t.*, **-mm-**: (a) ~ **[up] sth.** etw. abblocken
(b) aufstauen ⟨*Fluss*⟩

damage /'dæmɪdʒ/ ① *n.* Schaden, *der*
② *v.t.* beschädigen

damaging /'dæmɪdʒɪŋ/ *adj.* schädlich (**to** für)

damn /dæm/ ① *v.t.* verdammen
② *adj., adv., int.* (coll.) verdammt (ugs.)
③ *n.* **he doesn't give** *or* **care a** ~: ihm ist es völlig wurscht (ugs.)

damp /dæmp/ ① *adj.* feucht
② *v.t.* ▸ DAMPEN
③ *n.* Feuchtigkeit, *die*

dampen /'dæmpn/ *v.t.* befeuchten; (fig.) dämpfen ⟨*Begeisterung, Eifer*⟩

'dampness *n.* Feuchtigkeit, *die*

'damp-proof *adj.* feuchtigkeitsbeständig;
~ **course** Sperrschicht, *die* ⟨*gegen aufsteigende Bodenfeuchtigkeit*⟩

dance /dɑːns/ ① *v.i. & t.* tanzen
② *n.* (a) Tanz, *der*
(b) (party) Tanzveranstaltung, *die;* (private) Tanzparty, *die*

dance: ~ **floor** *n.* Tanzfläche, *die;*
~ **hall** *n.* Tanzsaal, *der*

'dancer *n.* Tänzer, *der*/Tänzerin, *die*

'dance step *n.* Tanzschritt, *der*

dandelion /'dændɪlaɪən/ *n.* Löwenzahn, *der*

dandruff /'dændrʌf/ *n.* [Kopf]schuppen *Pl.*

Dane /deɪn/ *n.* Däne, *der*/Dänin, *die*

danger /'deɪndʒə(r)/ *n.* Gefahr, *die;* **in/out of** ~: in/außer Gefahr; **be in** ~ **of doing sth.** ⟨*Person:*⟩ Gefahr laufen, etw. zu tun

danger: ~ **area** *n.* Gefahrenzone, *die;*
~ **list** *n.* **be on/off the** ~ **list** in/außer Lebensgefahr sein

dangerous /'deɪndʒərəs/ *adj.*,
'dangerously *adv.* gefährlich

danger: ~ **signal** *n.* Warnzeichen, *das;*
~ **zone** *n.* Gefahrenzone, *die*

dangle /'dæŋgl/ ① *v.i.* baumeln (**from** an + *Dat.*)
② *v.t.* baumeln lassen

Danish /'deɪnɪʃ/ ① *adj.* dänisch; **sb. is** ~: jmd. ist Däne/Dänin
② *n.* Dänisch, *das; see also* ENGLISH 2A

dank /dæŋk/ *adj.* feucht

Danube /'dænjuːb/ *pr. n.* Donau, *die*

dare /deə(r)/ ① *v.t.* (a) [es] wagen; ~ **to do sth.** [es] wagen, etw. zu tun
(b) (challenge) ~ **sb. to do sth.** jmdn. aufstacheln, etw. zu tun; **I** ~ **you!** trau dich!
② *n.* Mutprobe, *die*

daring /'deərɪŋ/ *adj.* (bold) kühn; waghalsig ⟨*Kunststück, Tat*⟩; (fearless) wagemutig

dark /dɑːk/ ① *adj.* dunkel; (dark-haired) dunkelhaarig; ~**-blue/-brown** dunkelblau/ -braun; ~ **glasses** dunkle Brille
② *n.* (a) Dunkel, *das;* **in the** ~: im Dunkeln; **keep sb. in the** ~ (fig.) jmdn. im Dunkeln lassen
(b) *no art.* (nightfall) Einbruch der Dunkelheit

darken /'dɑːkn/ *v.t.* verdunkeln

dark: ~**-haired** *adj.* dunkelhaarig;
~ **'horse** *n.* **be a** ~ **horse** ein stilles Wasser sein; ~ **matter** *n.*, *no pl.* (Astron.) Dunkelmaterie, *die*

'darkness *n.* Dunkelheit, *die*

'darkroom *n.* Dunkelkammer, *die*

darling /'dɑːlɪŋ/ *n.* Liebling, *der*

darn /dɑːn/ *v.t.* stopfen

dart /dɑːt/ ① *n.* (a) (missile) Pfeil, *der*
(b) (Sport) Wurfpfeil, *der;* ~**s** *sing.* (game) Darts, *das*
② *v.i.* sausen

'dartboard n. Dartsscheibe, die
dash /dæʃ/ **1** v.i. sausen
2 v.t. (fling) schleudern
3 n. (a) make a ∼: rasen (ugs.) (for zu)
(b) (horizontal stroke) Gedankenstrich, der
(c) (small amount) Schuss, der
'dashboard n. Armaturenbrett, das
data /'deɪtə, 'dɑːtə/ n. Daten Pl.
data: ∼**base** n. Datenbank, die;
∼ **capture** n. (Comp.) Datenerfassung,
die; ∼ **file** n. (Comp.) Datei, die;
∼ **highway** n. (Comp.) Datenautobahn,
die; ∼ **processing** n. (Comp.)
Datenverarbeitung, die; ∼ **pro'tection**
n. (Comp.) Datenschutz, der; ∼ **retrieval**
n. (Comp.) Retrieval, das; Datenabruf,
der; ∼ **security** n. (Comp.)
Datensicherung, die; ∼ **storage** n.
(Comp.) Datenspeicherung, die; (capacity)
Speicherkapazität, die
date¹ /deɪt/ n. (Bot.) Dattel, die
date² **1** n. (a) Datum, das; (on coin etc.)
Jahreszahl, die; ∼ **of birth** Geburtsdatum,
das; **be out of** ∼: altmodisch sein; **to** ∼: bis
heute
(b) (coll.: appointment) Verabredung, die; **have/
make a** ∼ **with sb.** mit jmdm. verabredet
sein/sich mit jmdm. verabreden
2 v.t. **(a)** datieren
(b) (coll.: make seem old) alt machen
3 v.i. ∼ **back to/**∼ **from** stammen aus
dated /'deɪtɪd/ adj. altmodisch
date: ∼ **line** n. Datumsgrenze, die;
∼ **rape** n.: Vergewaltigung der eigenen
Freundin oder Vergewaltigung einer
Frau während einer Verabredung mit
ihr; ∼ **stamp** n. Datumsstempel, der;
∼**-stamp** v.t. abstempeln; mit einem
Datumsstempel versehen
'dating agency /'deɪtɪŋ/ n.
Partnervermittlung, die
dative /'deɪtɪv/ adj. & n. ∼ **[case]** Dativ,
der
daub /dɔːb/ v.t. (smear) beschmieren; (put
crudely) schmieren
daughter /'dɔːtə(r)/ n. Tochter, die
'daughter-in-law n., pl. **daughters-in-law**
Schwiegertochter, die
daunt /dɔːnt/ v.t. entmutigen
dawdle /'dɔːdl/ v.i. bummeln (ugs.)
dawn /dɔːn/ **1** v.i. dämmern; sth. ∼**s
[up]on sb.** etw. dämmert jmdm
2 n. [Morgen]dämmerung, die; **at** ∼: im
Morgengrauen
dawn 'chorus n. morgendlicher Gesang
der Vögel
day /deɪ/ n. Tag, der; **all** ∼ **[long]** den ganzen
Tag [lang]; **for two** ∼**s** zwei Tage [lang];
the ∼ **before yesterday/after tomorrow**
vorgestern/übermorgen; ∼ **after** ∼: Tag
für Tag; ∼ **in** ∼ **out** tagaus, tagein; **in the**
∼**s when** ...: zu der Zeit, als ...; **these** ∼**s**
heutzutage; **in those** ∼**s** damals

day: ∼**bed** n. Liegesofa, das; ∼**break**
n. Tagesanbruch, der; ∼ **care** n.
Ganztagsbetreuung, die; ∼**dream**
1 n. Tagtraum, der; **2** v.i. träumen;
∼**dreamer** n. Tagträumer, der/
-träumerin, die; ∼**light** n. Tageslicht,
das; **in broad** ∼**light** am helllichten
Tag[e]; ∼ **release** n. (Brit.) [tageweise]
Freistellung zur Fortbildung; ∼ **re'turn**
n. Tagesrückfahrkarte, die; ∼**time** n.
Tag, der; ∼**-to-**∼ adj. [tag]täglich; ∼ **trip**
n. Tagesausflug, der; ∼ **tripper** n.
Tagesausflügler, der/-ausflüglerin, die
daze /'deɪz/ v.t. benommen machen
dazed /'deɪzd/ adj. benommen
dazzle /'dæzl/ v.t. blenden
DC abbr. = **direct current** GS
dead /ded/ **1** adj. (a) tot
(b) plötzlich ⟨Halt⟩; genau ⟨Mitte⟩
(c) (numb) taub
2 adv. völlig; ∼ **straight** schnurgerade;
∼ **easy/slow** kinderleicht/ganz langsam;
∼ **on time** auf die Minute; ∼ **tired** todmüde
3 n. pl. **the** ∼: die Toten Pl.
deaden /'dedn/ v.t. dämpfen; betäuben
⟨Schmerz⟩
dead: ∼ **'end** n. Sackgasse, die; ∼ **'heat**
n. totes Rennen; ∼**line** n. [letzter] Termin;
∼**lock** n. völliger Stillstand; ∼ **'loss** n.
(coll.) (worthless thing) totaler Reinfall (ugs.);
(person) hoffnungsloser Fall (ugs.)
deadly /'dedlɪ/ adj. tödlich; (fig. coll.: boring)
todlangweilig
dead: ∼**pan** adj. unbewegt; **he looked**
∼**pan** or **had a** ∼**pan expression** er verzog
keine Miene; **D**∼ **'Sea** pr. n. Totes Meer;
∼ **'wood** n. (fig.) **be just** ∼ **wood** völlig
überflüssig sein
deaf /def/ adj. **1** taub; ∼ **and dumb**
taubstumm
2 n. pl. **the** ∼: die Gehörlosen Pl.
'deaf aid n. Hörgerät, das
deafen /'defn/ v.t. ∼ **sb.** bei jmdm. zur
Taubheit führen; **I was** ∼**ed by the noise**
(fig.) ich war von dem Lärm wie betäubt
'deafening adj. ohrenbetäubend
'deafness n. Taubheit, die
deal¹ /diːl/ **1** v.t., **dealt** /delt/ (a) (Cards)
austeilen
(b) ∼ **sb. a blow** jmdm. einen Schlag
versetzen
2 v.i., **dealt** (a) (do business) ∼ **in sth.** mit
etw. handeln
(b) ∼ **with sth.** (occupy oneself) sich mit etw.
befassen; (manage) mit etw. fertig werden;
(be about) von etw. handeln; ∼ **with sb.** mit
jmdm. fertig werden
3 n. (coll.: arrangement) Geschäft, das; **it's a**
∼! abgemacht!; **big** ∼! (iron.) na, und?
■ **deal 'out** v.t. verteilen
deal² n. **a great** or **good** ∼: viel; (often)
ziemlich viel; **a great** or **good** ∼ **of** viel
'dealer n. (a) Händler, der

(b) (Cards) Geber, *der;* he's the ∼: er gibt

'dealings *n. pl.* have ∼ with sb. mit jmdm. zu tun haben

dealt ▶ DEAL¹ 1, 2

dean /diːn/ *n.* (Eccl.) Dechant, *der*

dear /dɪə(r)/ [1] *adj.* **(a)** lieb; sb./sth. is ∼ to sb.['s heart] jmd. liebt jmdn./etw.; (beginning letter) D∼ Sir/Madam Sehr geehrter Herr/Sehr geehrte Dame; D∼ Mr Jones/Mrs Jones Sehr geehrter Herr Jones/Sehr geehrte Frau Jones; D∼ Malcolm/Emily Lieber Malcolm/Liebe Emily

(b) (expensive) teuer

[2] *int.* ∼, ∼!, ∼ me!, oh ∼! [ach] du liebe *od.* meine Güte!

'dearly *adv.* **(a)** von ganzem Herzen

(b) (at high price) teuer

dearth /dɜːθ/ *n.* Mangel, *der* (of an + *Dat.*)

death /deθ/ *n.* **(a)** Tod, *der;* ... to ∼: zu Tode ...; **bleed to** ∼: verbluten

(b) (instance) Todesfall, *der*

death: ∼**bed** *n.* Totenbett, *das;* on one's ∼bed auf dem Sterbebett; ∼ **certificate** *n.* (from doctor) Totenschein, *der*

deathly /'deθlɪ/ [1] *adj.* tödlich

[2] *adv.* tödlich; ∼ **still/quiet** totenstill

death: ∼ **penalty** *n.* Todesstrafe, *die;* ∼ **sentence** *n.* Todesurteil, *das;* ∼ **threat** *n.* Morddrohung, *die;* ∼ **trap** *n.* lebensgefährliche Sache

debatable /dɪ'beɪtəbl/ *adj.* (questionable) fraglich

debate /dɪ'beɪt/ *n.* Debatte, *die*

debilitating /dɪ'bɪlɪteɪtɪŋ/ *adj.* anstrengend ⟨*Klima*⟩; schwächend ⟨*Krankheit*⟩

debit /'debɪt/ [1] *n.* Soll, *das*

[2] *v.t.* belasten ⟨*Konto*⟩

'debit card Debitkarte, *die*

debris /'debriː/ *n.* Trümmer *Pl.*

debt /det/ *n.* Schuld, *die;* be in ∼: Schulden haben; **get into** ∼: in Schulden geraten

debtor /'detə(r)/ *n.* Schuldner, *der/* Schuldnerin, *die*

debug /diː'bʌg/ *v.t.*, **-gg-** (coll.: remove defects from) von Fehlern befreien

début (*Amer.:* **debut**) /'deɪbuː, 'deɪbjuː/ *n.* Debüt, *das*

Dec. *abbr.* = **December** Dez.

decade /'dekeɪd/ *n.* Jahrzehnt, *das*

decadent /'dekədənt/ *adj.* dekadent

decaf, decaff /'diːkæf/ *n.* (coll.) *or* ℗ koffeinfreier Kaffee

decaffeinated /diː'kæfɪneɪtɪd/ *adj.* entkoffeiniert

decanter /dɪ'kæntə(r)/ *n.* Karaffe, *die*

decay /dɪ'keɪ/ [1] *v.i.* verrotten; ⟨*Gebäude:*⟩ zerfallen; ⟨*Zahn:*⟩ faul werden

[2] *n.* Verrotten, *das;* (of building) Zerfall, *der;* (of tooth) Fäule, *die*

deceased /dɪ'siːst/ [1] *adj.* verstorben

[2] *n.* Verstorbene, *der/die*

deceit /dɪ'siːt/ *n.* Täuschung, *die*

deceitful /dɪ'siːtfl/ *adj.* falsch ⟨*Person, Art*⟩; hinterlistig ⟨*Trick*⟩

deceive /dɪ'siːv/ *v.t.* täuschen; (be unfaithful to) betrügen

December /dɪ'sembə(r)/ *n.* Dezember, *der; see also* AUGUST

decency /'diːsənsɪ/ *n.* Anstand, *der*

decent /'diːsənt/ *adj.* anständig

decentralization /diːsentrəlaɪ'zeɪʃn/ *n.* Dezentralisierung, *die*

decentralize /diː'sentrəlaɪz/ *v.t.* dezentralisieren

deception /dɪ'sepʃn/ *n.* Betrug, *der;* (being deceived) Täuschung, *die*

deceptive /dɪ'septɪv/ *adj.* trügerisch

decibel /'desɪbel/ *n.* Dezibel, *das*

decide /dɪ'saɪd/ [1] *v.t.* **(a)** (settle, judge) entscheiden über (+ *Akk.*)

(b) (resolve) ∼ that ...: beschließen, dass ...; ∼ to do sth. sich entschließen, etw. zu tun

[2] *v.i.* sich entscheiden (in favour of zugunsten von, against gegen)

de'cided *adj.,* **de'cidedly** *adv.* entschieden

deciduous /dɪ'sɪdjʊəs/ *adj.* ∼ tree ≈ Laubbaum, *der*

decimal /'desɪml/ [1] *n.* Dezimalbruch, *der*

[2] *adj.* Dezimal-

decimal: ∼ **'currency** *n.* Dezimalwährung, *die;* ∼ **'fraction** *n.* Dezimalbruch, *der;* ∼ **'point** *n.* Komma, *das*

decimate /'desɪmeɪt/ *v.t.* dezimieren

decipher /dɪ'saɪfə(r)/ *v.t.* entziffern

decision /dɪ'sɪʒn/ *n.* Entscheidung, *die*

decisive /dɪ'saɪsɪv/ *adj.* entscheidend

deck /dek/ *n.* **(a)** Deck, *das;* on ∼: an Deck; **below** ∼[s] unter Deck

(b) (Amer.: pack) **a** ∼ **of cards** ein Spiel Karten

'deckchair *n.* Liegestuhl, *der*

declaration /deklə'reɪʃn/ *n.* Erklärung, *die*

declare /dɪ'kleə(r)/ *v.t.* erklären; kundtun (geh.) ⟨*Wunsch, Absicht*⟩; ∼ sth./sb. [to be] sth. etw./jmdn. für etw. erklären

declension /dɪ'klenʃn/ *n.* Deklination, *die*

decline /dɪ'klaɪn/ [1] *v.i.* nachlassen; ⟨*Anzahl:*⟩ sinken

[2] *v.t.* **(a)** ablehnen

(b) (Ling.) deklinieren

[3] *n.* ▶ 1: Nachlassen, *das*/Sinken, *das* (in *Gen.*); be on the ∼: nachlassen/sinken

declutter /diː'klʌtə(r)/ *v.t.* entrümpeln

decode /diː'kəʊd/ *v.t.* entziffern

decommission /diːkə'mɪʃən/ *v.t.* stilllegen; außer Dienst stellen ⟨*Schiff*⟩

decompose /diːkəm'pəʊz/ *v.i.* sich zersetzen

décor /'deɪkɔː(r)/ *n.* Ausstattung, *die*

decorate /'dekəreɪt/ *v.t.* **(a)** schmücken
⟨*Raum, Straße, Baum*⟩; verzieren ⟨*Kuchen,
Kleid*⟩; (paint) streichen; (wallpaper) tapezieren
(b) (award medal etc. to) auszeichnen

decoration /dekə'reɪʃn/ *n.*
(a) Schmücken, *das;* (with paint) Streichen,
das; (with wallpaper) Tapezieren, *das;* (of cake,
dress) Verzieren, *das*
(b) (adornment) Schmuck, *der*
(c) (medal etc.) Auszeichnung, *die*

decorative /'dekərətɪv/ *adj.* dekorativ

decorator /'dekəreɪtə(r)/ *n.* Maler, *der;*
(paperhanger) Tapezierer, *der*

decorous /'dekərəs/ *adj.,* '**decorously**
adv. schicklich (geh.)

decorum /dɪ'kɔːrəm/ *n.* Schicklichkeit,
die (geh.)

decoy /'diːkɔɪ/ *n.* Lockvogel, *der*

decrease ① /dɪ'kriːs/ *v.i.* abnehmen;
⟨*Stärke:*⟩ nachlassen
② /dɪ'kriːs/ *v.t.* [ver]mindern ⟨*Wert, Lärm*⟩;
schmälern ⟨*Popularität, Macht*⟩
③ /'diːkriːs/ *n.* Rückgang, *der;* (in weight)
Abnahme, *die;* (in strength) Nachlassen, *das;*
(in value, noise) Minderung, *die*

decree /dɪ'kriː/ ① *n.* Dekret, *das;* Erlass,
der
② *v.t.* verfügen

decrepit /dɪ'krepɪt/ *adj.* altersschwach;
(dilapidated) heruntergekommen

decriminalize /diː'krɪmɪnəlaɪz/ *v.t.*
entkriminalisieren

dedicate /'dedɪkeɪt/ *v.t.* ∼ sth. to sb.
jmdm. etw. widmen

'**dedicated** *adj.* **(a)** (devoted) be ∼ to
sth./sb. nur für etw./jmdn. leben
(b) (to vocation) hingebungsvoll; a ∼ **teacher**
ein Lehrer mit Leib und Seele

dedication /dedɪ'keɪʃn/ *n.* **(a)** Widmung,
die (to *Dat.*)
(b) (devotion) Hingabe, *die*

deduce /dɪ'djuːs/ *v.t.* ∼ sth. [from sth.]
etw. [aus etw.] schließen

deduct /dɪ'dʌkt/ *v.t.* ∼ sth. [from sth.] etw.
[von etw.] abziehen

deduction /dɪ'dʌkʃn/ *n.* **(a)** (deducting)
Abzug, *der*
(b) (deducing, thing deduced) Ableitung, *die*
(c) (amount) Abzüge *Pl.*

deed /diːd/ *n.* **(a)** Tat, *die*
(b) (Law) Urkunde, *die*

deejay /'diːdʒeɪ/ *n.* (coll.) Diskjockey, *der*

deem /diːm/ *v.t.* erachten für

deep /diːp/ ① *adj.* (lit. or fig.) tief; tiefgründig
⟨*Bemerkung*⟩; **water ten feet** ∼: drei Meter
tiefes Wasser; **take a** ∼ **breath** tief Atem
holen; **be** ∼ **in thought** in Gedanken
versunken sein
② *adv.* tief

'**deepen** ① *v.t.* vertiefen
② *v.i.* sich vertiefen

deep: ∼-'**freeze** *v.t.* tiefgefrieren;
∼-**fried** *adj.* frittiert

'**deeply** *adv.* (lit. or fig.) tief; äußerst
⟨*interessiert, dankbar*⟩

deep-'rooted *adj.* tief ⟨*Abneigung*⟩; tief
verwurzelt ⟨*Tradition*⟩

deer /dɪə(r)/ *n., pl. same* Hirsch, *der;* (roe
∼) Reh, *das*

de-escalate /diː'eskəleɪt/ *v.t.*
deeskalieren

deface /dɪ'feɪs/ *v.t.* verunstalten

defamation /defə'meɪʃn/ *n.*
Diffamierung, *die*

defamatory /dɪ'fæmətərɪ/ *adj.*
diffamierend

default /dɪ'fɔːlt, dɪ'fɒlt/ ① *n.* **(a)** lose/go
by ∼: durch Abwesenheit verlieren/nicht
zur Geltung kommen; **win by** ∼: durch
Nichterscheinen des Gegners gewinnen
(b) (Comp.) Voreinstellung, *die*
② *v.i.* ∼ **on one's payments/debts**
seinen Zahlungsverpflichtungen nicht
nachkommen

defeat /dɪ'fiːt/ ① *v.t.* besiegen
② *n.* (being ∼ed) Niederlage, *die;* (∼ing) Sieg,
der (of über + *Akk.*)

de'featist *adj.* defätistisch

defect ① /'diːfekt/ *n.* **(a)** (lack) Mangel, *der*
(b) (shortcoming) Fehler, *der*
② /dɪ'fekt/ *v.i.* überlaufen (**to** zu)

defection /dɪ'fekʃn/ *n.* Flucht, *die*

defective /dɪ'fektɪv/ *adj.* defekt
⟨*Maschine*⟩; fehlerhaft ⟨*Material, Arbeiten,
Methode*⟩

defector /dɪ'fektə(r)/ *n.* Überläufer, *der/*
-läuferin, *die*

defence /dɪ'fens/ *n.* (Brit.) Verteidigung,
die; (means of ∼) Schutz, *der*

de'fenceless *adj.* wehrlos

de'fence mechanism *n.* (Physiol.,
Psych.) Abwehrmechanismus, *der*

defend /dɪ'fend/ *v.t.* verteidigen

defendant /dɪ'fendənt/ *n.* (Law) (accused)
Angeklagte, *der/die;* (sued) Beklagte, *der/die*

de'fender *n.* Verteidiger, *der*

defense etc. (*Amer.*) ▶ DEFENCE etc.

defensive /dɪ'fensɪv/ ① *adj.* defensiv
② *n.* be on the ∼: in der Defensive sein

defer¹ /dɪ'fɜː(r)/ *v.t.,* -rr- aufschieben

defer² *v.i.,* -rr-: ∼ [to sb.] sich [jmdm.]
beugen

deference /'defərəns/ *n.* Respekt, *der;* in
∼ to sb./sth. aus Achtung vor jmdm./etw.

deferential /defə'renʃl/ *adj.* respektvoll

defiance /dɪ'faɪəns/ *n.* Trotz, *der;* in ∼ of
sb./sth. jmdm./einer Sache zum Trotz

defiant /dɪ'faɪənt/ *adj.,* **de'fiantly** *adv.*
trotzig

deficiency /dɪ'fɪʃənsɪ/ *n.* Mangel, *der*

deficient /dɪ'fɪʃənt/ *adj.* unzulänglich;
sb./sth. is ∼ in sth. jmdm./einer Sache

mangelt es an etw. (*Dat.*)

deficit /'defɪsɪt/ *n.* Defizit, *das* (of an + *Dat.*)

defile /dɪ'faɪl/ *v.t.* verpesten ⟨*Luft*⟩; beflecken ⟨*Reinheit, Unschuld*⟩

define /dɪ'faɪn/ *v.t.* definieren

definite /'defɪnɪt/ *adj.* bestimmt; eindeutig ⟨*Antwort, Entscheidung, Beschluss, Verbesserung*⟩; klar umrissen ⟨*Ziel, Plan*⟩; klar ⟨*Vorstellung*⟩; genau ⟨*Zeitpunkt*⟩

'definitely ① *adv.* bestimmt; eindeutig ⟨*festlegen, größer sein, verbessert*⟩; endgültig ⟨*entscheiden*⟩
② *int.* (coll.) na, klar (ugs.)

definition /defɪ'nɪʃn/ *n.* Definition, *die;* (Telev., Phot.) Schärfe, *die*

definitive /dɪ'fɪnɪtɪv/ *adj.* endgültig ⟨*Beschluss, Antwort, Urteil*⟩; (authoritative) maßgeblich

deflate /dɪ'fleɪt/ *v.t.* die Luft ablassen aus; (fig.) ernüchtern

deflation /dɪ'fleɪʃn/ *n.* (Econ.) Deflation, *die*

deflect /dɪ'flekt/ *v.t.* brechen ⟨*Licht*⟩; ~ sb./sth. [from sb./sth.] jmdn./etw. [von jmdm./einer Sache] ablenken

deforestation /diːfɒrɪ'steɪʃn/ *n.* Entwaldung, *die;* Abholzung, *die*

deform /dɪ'fɔːm/ *v.t.* deformieren

deformed /dɪ'fɔːmd/ *adj.* entstellt ⟨*Gesicht*⟩; verunstaltet ⟨*Person, Körperteil*⟩

deformity /dɪ'fɔːmɪtɪ/ *n.* (malformation) Verunstaltung, *die*

defraud /dɪ'frɔːd/ *v.t.* ~ sb. [of sth.] jmdn. [um etw.] betrügen

defray /dɪ'freɪ/ *v.t.* bestreiten

defrost /diː'frɒst/ *v.t.* auftauen ⟨*Speisen*⟩; abtauen ⟨*Kühlschrank*⟩

deft /deft/ *adj.,* **'deftly** *adv.* sicher und geschickt

defunct /dɪ'fʌŋkt/ *adj.* defekt ⟨*Maschine*⟩; veraltet ⟨*Gesetz*⟩

defuse /diː'fjuːz/ *v.t.* entschärfen

defy /dɪ'faɪ/ *v.t.* (a) (resist openly) ~ sb. jmdm. trotzen
(b) (refuse to obey) ~ sb./sth. sich jmdm./ einer Sache widersetzen

degenerate /dɪ'dʒenəreɪt/ *v.i.* ~ [into sth.] [zu etw.] verkommen

degradation /degrə'deɪʃn/ *n.* Erniedrigung, *die*

degrade /dɪ'greɪd/ *v.t.* erniedrigen

degrading /dɪ'greɪdɪŋ/ *adj.* entwürdigend; erniedrigend

degree /dɪ'griː/ *n.* (a) Grad, *der;* **20 ~s** 20 Grad
(b) (academic rank) [akademischer] Grad

de'gree course *n.* Studium, *das*

dehydrate /diː'haɪdreɪt/ *v.t.* austrocknen ⟨*Körper*⟩; ~d dehydratisiert (fachspr.)

dehydration /diːhaɪ'dreɪʃn/ *n.* Dehydration, *die* (fachspr.); Austrocknung, *die*

de-ice /diː'aɪs/ *v.t.* enteisen

deign /deɪn/ *v.t.* ~ to do sth. sich [dazu] herablassen, etw. zu tun

deity /'diːɪtɪ/ *n.* Gottheit, *die*

dejected /dɪ'dʒektɪd/ *adj.* niedergeschlagen

dejection /dɪ'dʒekʃn/ *n.* Niedergeschlagenheit, *die*

delay /dɪ'leɪ/ ① *v.t.* (make late) aufhalten; verzögern ⟨*Ankunft, Abfahrt*⟩; **the train has been ~ed** der Zug hat Verspätung
② *v.i.* warten
③ *n.* (a) Verzögerung, *die* (to bei)
(b) (Transport) Verspätung, *die*

delectable /dɪ'lektəbl/ *adj.* köstlich

delegate ① /'delɪgət/ *n.* Delegierte, *der/die*
② /'delɪgeɪt/ *v.t.* delegieren (to an + *Akk.*)

delegation /delɪ'geɪʃn/ *n.* Delegation, *die*

delete /dɪ'liːt/ *v.t.* streichen (from in + *Dat.*); (Comp.) löschen

de'lete key *n.* (Comp.) Löschtaste, *die*

deletion /dɪ'liːʃn/ *n.* Streichung, *die;* (Comp.) Löschung, *die*

deli /'delɪ/ (coll.) ▶ DELICATESSEN

deliberate /dɪ'lɪbərət/ *adj.* (a) (intentional) absichtlich; bewusst ⟨*Lüge, Irreführung*⟩
(b) (fully considered) wohl überlegt

de'liberately *adv.* absichtlich

deliberation /dɪlɪbə'reɪʃn/ *n.* Überlegung, *die;* (discussion) Beratung, *die*

delicacy /'delɪkəsɪ/ *n.* (a) (tactfulness and care) Feingefühl, *das*
(b) (food) Delikatesse, *die*

delicate /'delɪkət/ *adj.* zart; (requiring careful handling) empfindlich; delikat ⟨*Frage, Angelegenheit*⟩

delicatessen /delɪkə'tesən/ *n.* Feinkostgeschäft, *das*

delicious /dɪ'lɪʃəs/ *adj.* köstlich

delight /dɪ'laɪt/ ① *v.t.* erfreuen
② *v.i.* ~s in doing sth. es macht jmdm. Freude, etw. zu tun
③ *n.* Freude, *die* (at über + *Akk.;* in an + *Dat.*)

de'lighted *adj.* be ~ ⟨*Person:*⟩ hocherfreut sein; be ~ by *or* with sth. sich über etw. (*Akk.*) freuen

delightful /dɪ'laɪtfl/ *adj.* wunderbar; köstlich ⟨*Geschmack*⟩; reizend ⟨*Person, Landschaft*⟩

de'lightfully *adv.* wunderbar

delinquent /dɪ'lɪŋkwənt/ ① *n.* Randalierer, *der*
② *adj.* kriminell

delirious /dɪ'lɪrɪəs/ *adj.* be ~: im Delirium sein; be ~ [with sth.] (fig.) außer sich [vor etw. (*Dat.*)] sein

delirium /dɪ'lɪrɪəm/ *n.* Delirium, *das*

deliver /dɪ'lɪvə(r)/ *v.t.* (a) bringen; liefern ⟨*Ware*⟩; zustellen ⟨*Post, Telegramm*⟩; überbringen ⟨*Botschaft*⟩
(b) halten ⟨*Rede*⟩

delivery /dɪˈlɪvərɪ/ n. Lieferung, die; (of letters, parcels) Zustellung, die

delivery: ~ **date** n. Liefertermin, der; ~ **note** n. Lieferschein, der; ~ **service** n. Zustelldienst, der; ~ **van** n. Lieferwagen, der

delta /ˈdeltə/ n. Delta, das

delude /dɪˈljuːd/ v.t. täuschen

deluge /ˈdeljuːdʒ/ ① n. sintflutartiger Regen
② v.t. überschwemmen

delusion /dɪˈljuːʒn/ n. Illusion, die

de luxe /dəˈlʌks/ adj. Luxus-

demand /dɪˈmɑːnd/ ① n. Forderung, die (for nach); (for commodity) Nachfrage, die; sth./sb. is in ~: etw. ist gefragt/jmd. ist begehrt
② v.t. verlangen (of, from von); fordern ⟨Recht⟩

deˈmanding adj. anspruchsvoll

demean /dɪˈmiːn/ v. refl. (lower one's dignity) ~ **oneself [to do sth.]** sich [dazu] erniedrigen[, etw. zu tun]; ~ **oneself by sth./doing sth.** sich durch etw. erniedrigen/ sich dadurch erniedrigen, dass man etw. tut

demeaning /dɪˈmiːnɪŋ/ adj. erniedrigend

demeanour (Brit.; Amer.: **demeanor**) /dɪˈmiːnə(r)/ n. Benehmen, das

demented /dɪˈmentɪd/ adj. wahnsinnig

dementia /dɪˈmenʃə/ n. (Med.) Demenz, die

demerara /deməˈreərə/ n. ~ [**sugar**] brauner Zucker; Farin, der

demise /dɪˈmaɪz/ n. (death) Ableben, das (geh.); (of firm, party, etc.) Untergang, der

demo /ˈdeməʊ/ n., pl. ~**s** (coll.) Demo, die (ugs.)

deˈmobilize v.t. demobilisieren ⟨Armee, Kriegsschiff⟩; aus dem Kriegsdienst entlassen ⟨Soldat⟩

democracy /dɪˈmɒkrəsɪ/ n. Demokratie, die

Democrat /ˈdeməkræt/ n. (Amer. Polit.) Demokrat, der/Demokratin, die

democratic /deməˈkrætɪk/ adj., **democratically** /deməˈkrætɪkəlɪ/ adv. demokratisch

demolish /dɪˈmɒlɪʃ/ v.t. abreißen

demolition /deməˈlɪʃn/ n. Abriss, der; ~ **work** Abbrucharbeit, die

demon /ˈdiːmən/ n. Dämon, der

demonstrably /ˈdemənstrəblɪ, dɪˈmɒnstrəblɪ/ adv. nachweislich

demonstrate /ˈdemənstreɪt/ ① v.t. zeigen; (be proof of) zeigen; beweisen
② v.i. demonstrieren

demonstration /demənˈstreɪʃn/ n. (also Pol. etc.) Demonstration, die; (proof) Beweis, der

demonstrative /dəˈmɒnstrətɪv/ adj.
(a) offen ⟨Person⟩
(b) (Ling.) Demonstrativ-

demonstrator /ˈdemənstreɪtə(r)/ n. (Pol. etc.) Demonstrant, der/Demonstrantin, die

demoralize /dɪˈmɒrəlaɪz/ v.t. demoralisieren

demote /diːˈməʊt/ v.t. degradieren (**to** zu)

demotion /diːˈməʊʃn/ n. Degradierung, die (**to** zu)

demur /dɪˈmɜː(r)/ v.i., -**rr**- Einwände erheben

demure /dɪˈmjʊə(r)/ adj. betont zurückhaltend

den /den/ n. Höhle, die

denial /dɪˈnaɪəl/ n. (refusal) Verweigerung, die; (of request) Ablehnung, die; **be in** ~: die Augen vor der Wahrheit schließen

denier /ˈdenjə(r)/ n. Denier, das; 20 ~ **stockings** 20-den-Strümpfe

denim /ˈdenɪm/ n. Denim Ⓦⓩ, der; Jeansstoff, der; ~ **jacket** Jeansjacke, die; ~**s** Bluejeans Pl.

Denmark /ˈdenmɑːk/ pr. n. Dänemark (das)

denomination /dɪnɒmɪˈneɪʃn/ n. (Relig.) Konfession, die

denote /dɪˈnəʊt/ v.t. bezeichnen

dénouement, denouement /deɪˈnuːmɑ̃/ n. Ausgang, der

denounce /dɪˈnaʊns/ v.t. denunzieren; (accuse publicly) beschuldigen

dense /dens/ adj. (a) dicht; massiv ⟨Körper⟩
(b) (stupid) dumm

ˈdensely adv. dicht; ~ **packed** dicht gedrängt

density /ˈdensɪtɪ/ n. Dichte, die

dent /dent/ ① n. Beule, die
② v.t. einbeulen

dental /ˈdentl/ adj. Zahn-; ~ **care** Zahnpflege, die; ~ **treatment** zahnärztliche Behandlung

dental: ~ **floss** /ˈdentl flɒs/ n. Zahnseide, die; ~ **practitioner,** ~ **surgeon** ns. Zahnarzt, der/-ärztin, die

dentist /ˈdentɪst/ n. Zahnarzt, der/-ärztin, die

dentistry /ˈdentɪstrɪ/ n. Zahnheilkunde, die

denture /ˈdentʃə(r)/ n. ~**[s]** Zahnprothese, die

denunciation /dɪnʌnsɪˈeɪʃn/ n. Denunziation, die; (public accusation) Beschuldigung, die

deny /dɪˈnaɪ/ v.t. (declare untrue) bestreiten; (refuse) ~ **sb. sth.** jmdm. etw. verweigern; ~ **sb.'s request** jmdm. seine Bitte abschlagen

deodorant /diːˈəʊdərənt/ ① adj. deodorierend
② n. Deodorant, das

depart /dɪˈpɑːt/ v.i. (a) (go away) weggehen (b) (set out, leave) abfahren; (on one's journey) abreisen
(c) (fig.: deviate) abweichen (**from** von)

department /dɪ'pɑ:tmənt/ n. Abteilung, *die;* (government ⁓) Ministerium, *das;* (of university) Seminar, *das*

de'partment store n. Kaufhaus, *das*

departure /dɪ'pɑ:tʃə(r)/ n. **(a)** Abreise, *die;* (of train, bus, ship) Abfahrt, *die;* (of aircraft) Abflug, *der*
(b) (deviation) ⁓ **from sth.** Abweichen von etw.

departure: ⁓ **gate** n. Flugsteig, *der;* ⁓ **lounge** n. Abflughalle, *die;* ⁓ **time** n. (of train, bus) Abfahrtzeit, *die;* (of aircraft) Abflugzeit, *die*

depend /dɪ'pend/ v.i. **(a)** ⁓ [up]on abhängen von; it/that ⁓s es kommt drauf an
(b) (rely, trust) ⁓ [up]on sich verlassen auf (+ *Akk.*); (have to rely on) angewiesen sein auf (+ *Akk.*)

dependable /dɪ'pendəbl/ adj. zuverlässig

dependant /dɪ'pendənt/ n. Abhängige, *der/die*

dependence /dɪ'pendəns/ n. Abhängigkeit, *die*

dependent /dɪ'pendənt/ adj. ▢1 n.
▸ DEPENDANT
▢2 adj. abhängig

depict /dɪ'pɪkt/ v.t. darstellen

deplete /dɪ'pli:t/ v.t. erheblich verringern

deplorable /dɪ'plɔ:rəbl/ adj. beklagenswert

deplore /dɪ'plɔ:(r)/ v.t. **(a)** (disapprove of) verurteilen
(b) (regret) beklagen

deploy /dɪ'plɔɪ/ v.t. einsetzen

deport /dɪ'pɔ:t/ v.t. ausweisen

deportation /di:pɔ:'teɪʃn/ n. Ausweisung, *die*

depose /dɪ'pəʊz/ v.t. absetzen

deposit /dɪ'pɒzɪt/ ▢1 n. **(a)** (in bank) Depot, *das;* (credit) Guthaben, *das;* (Brit.: at interest) Sparguthaben, *das*
(b) (first instalment) Anzahlung, *die;* put down a ⁓ on sth. eine Anzahlung für etw. leisten
(c) (on bottle) Pfand, *das*
▢2 v.t. **(a)** (lay down) ablegen; abstellen ‹*etw. Senkrechtes*›
(b) (in bank) deponieren

de'posit account n. (Brit.) Sparkonto, *das*

depot /'depəʊ/ n. Depot, *das*

depraved /dɪ'preɪvd/ adj. verdorben

depravity /dɪ'prævɪtɪ/ n. Verdorbenheit, *die*

depreciate /dɪ'pri:ʃɪeɪt/ v.i. an Wert verlieren

depreciation /dɪpri:ʃɪ'eɪʃn/ n. Wertverlust, *der*

depress /dɪ'pres/ v.t. **(a)** (deject) deprimieren
(b) (push down) herunterdrücken

depressed /dɪ'prest/ adj. deprimiert

de'pressing adj., **de'pressingly** adv. deprimierend

depression /dɪ'preʃn/ n. **(a)** Depression, *die*
(b) (sunk place) Vertiefung, *die*
(c) (Meteorol.) Tief[druckgebiet], *das*
(d) (Econ.) Wirtschaftskrise, *die*

deprivation /deprɪ'veɪʃn/ n. Entbehrung, *die*

deprive /dɪ'praɪv/ v.t. ⁓ **sb. of sth.** jmdm. etw. nehmen; (prevent from having) jmdm. etw. vorenthalten

deprived /dɪ'praɪvd/ adj. benachteiligt ‹*Kind, Familie usw.*›

depth /depθ/ n. Tiefe, *die;* in ⁓: gründlich; in the ⁓s of winter im tiefsten Winter

'depth charge n. Wasserbombe, *die*

deputation /depjʊ'teɪʃn/ n. Abordnung, *die*

deputize /'depjʊtaɪz/ v.i. ⁓ **for sb.** jmdn. vertreten

deputy /'depjʊtɪ/ n. [Stell]vertreter, *der/* -vertreterin, *die; attrib.* stellvertretend

derail /dɪ'reɪl/ v.t. be ⁓ed entgleisen

de'railment n. Entgleisung, *die*

deranged /dɪ'reɪndʒd/ adj. **[mentally]** ⁓: geistesgestört

deregulate /di:'regjʊleɪt/ v.t. deregulieren (fachspr.); dem freien Wettbewerb überlassen

deregulation /di:regjʊ'leɪʃn/ n. Deregulation, *die* (fachspr.); Deregulierung, *die* (fachspr.)

derelict /'derɪlɪkt/ ▢1 adj. verlassen und verfallen
▢2 n. Ausgestoßene, *der/die*

deride /dɪ'raɪd/ v.t. sich lustig machen über (+ *Akk.*)

derision /dɪ'rɪʒn/ n. Spott, *der*

derisive /dɪ'raɪsɪv/ adj. (ironical) spöttisch; (scoffing) verächtlich

derisory /dɪ'raɪzərɪ/ adj. (ridiculously inadequate) lächerlich

derivation /derɪ'veɪʃn/ n. Ableitung, *die*

derivative /dɪ'rɪvətɪv/ ▢1 adj. abgeleitet; (lacking originality) nachahmend
▢2 n. Ableitung, *die*

derive /dɪ'raɪv/ ▢1 v.t. ⁓ **sth. from sth.** etw. aus etw. gewinnen; ⁓ **pleasure from sth.** Freude an etw. (*Dat.*) haben
▢2 v.i. ⁓ **from** beruhen auf (+ *Dat.*)

derogatory /dɪ'rɒgətərɪ/ adj. abfällig

derrick /'derɪk/ n. [Derrick]kran, *der*

derv /dɜ:v/ n. Diesel[kraftstoff], *der*

descale /di:'skeɪl/ v.t. entkalken

descend /dɪ'send/ ▢1 v.i. **(a)** (go down) hinuntergehen/-steigen/-klettern/-fahren; (come down) herunterkommen; ‹*Fallschirm, Flugzeug:*› niedergehen
(b) (slope downwards) abfallen
(c) ⁓ **on sb.** jmdn. überfallen
▢2 v.t. (go/come down) hinunter- /heruntergehen/-steigen/-klettern/-fahren

descendant /dɪˈsendənt/ n. Nachkomme, der

de'scended adj. be ⁓ from sb. von jmdm. abstammen

descent /dɪˈsent/ n. **(a)** Abstieg, der; (of parachute, plane) Niedergehen, das **(b)** (lineage) Herkunft, die; be of Russian ⁓: russischer Abstammung sein

describe /dɪˈskraɪb/ v.t. beschreiben

description /dɪˈskrɪpʃn/ n. **(a)** Beschreibung, die **(b)** (sort, class) Art, die

descriptive /dɪˈskrɪptɪv/ adj. beschreibend; (vivid) anschaulich; **a purely ⁓ report** ein reiner Tatsachenbericht

desecrate /ˈdesɪkreɪt/ v.t. entweihen

desert[1] /ˈdezət/ n. Wüste, die

desert[2] /dɪˈzɜːt/ ◾1 v.t. verlassen ◾2 v.i. ⟨Soldat:⟩ desertieren

de'serted adj. verlassen

de'serter n. Deserteur, der

desertification /dezɜːtɪfɪˈkeɪʃn/ n., no pl. Verwüstung, die; Desertifikation, die

desertion /dɪˈzɜːʃn/ n. Desertion, die

desert 'island /dezət ˈaɪlənd/ n. einsame Insel

deserts /dɪˈzɜːts/ n. pl. **get one's [just] ⁓:** das bekommen, was man verdient hat

deserve /dɪˈzɜːv/ v.t. verdienen

deserving /dɪˈzɜːvɪŋ/ adj. verdienstvoll; **a ⁓ cause** ein guter Zweck

design /dɪˈzaɪn/ ◾1 n. Entwurf, der; (pattern) Muster, das; (established form of machine, engine, etc.) Bauweise, die; (general idea, construction) Konstruktion, die ◾2 v.t. entwerfen; **be ⁓ed to do sth.** etw. tun sollen

designate /ˈdezɪgneɪt/ v.t. **(a)** bezeichnen **(b)** (appoint) designieren (geh.)

designation /dezɪgˈneɪʃn/ n. Bezeichnung, die

'designer n. Designer, der/Designerin, die; (of machines) Konstrukteur, der/ Konstrukteurin, die; attrib. Modell ⟨-kleidung, -jeans⟩

desirability /dɪzaɪərəˈbɪlɪtɪ/ n. Wunschbarkeit, die

desirable /dɪˈzaɪərəbl/ adj. wünschenswert

desire /dɪˈzaɪə(r)/ ◾1 n. Wunsch, der (for nach); (longing) Sehnsucht, die (for nach) ◾2 v.t. sich (Dat.) wünschen; (long for) sich sehnen nach

desist /dɪˈzɪst/ v.i. (literary) einhalten (geh.); **⁓ from sth.** von etw. ablassen (geh.)

desk /desk/ n. **(a)** Schreibtisch, der; (in school) Tisch, der **(b)** (cash ⁓) Kasse, die; (reception ⁓) Rezeption, die

desk: ⁓-bound adj. an den Schreibtisch gefesselt (fig.); **⁓ calendar, ⁓ diary** ns. Tischkalender, der; **⁓ editor** n.

Manuskriptbearbeiter, der/-bearbeiterin, die; Lektor, der/Lektorin, die; **⁓ lamp** n. Schreibtischlampe, die; **⁓top** adj. **⁓top publishing** Desktoppublishing, das; **⁓top computer** Tischcomputer, der

desolate /ˈdesələt/ adj. trostlos

desolation /desəˈleɪʃn/ n. Trostlosigkeit, die

despair /dɪˈspeə(r)/ ◾1 n. Verzweiflung, die; **be the ⁓ of sb.** jmdn. zur Verzweiflung bringen ◾2 v.i. verzweifeln

desperate /ˈdespərət/ adj. verzweifelt; extrem ⟨Maßnahmen⟩; **be ⁓ for sth.** etw. dringend brauchen

desperation /despəˈreɪʃn/ n. Verzweiflung, die

despicable /dɪˈspɪkəbl/ adj. verabscheuungswürdig

despise /dɪˈspaɪz/ v.t. verachten

despite /dɪˈspaɪt/ prep. trotz

despondent /dɪˈspɒndənt/ adj. bedrückt

despot /ˈdespɒt/ n. Despot, der

dessert /dɪˈzɜːt/ n. Nachtisch, der

dessert: ⁓spoon n. Esslöffel, der; **⁓spoonful** n. Esslöffel, der; **⁓ wine** n. Dessertwein, der

destabilize /diːˈsteɪbɪlaɪz/ v.t. (Polit.) destabilisieren

destination /destɪˈneɪʃn/ n. Reiseziel, das; (of goods) Bestimmungsort, der; (of train, bus) Zielort, der

destine /ˈdestɪn/ v.t. bestimmen; **be ⁓d to do sth.** dazu bestimmt sein, etw. zu tun

destiny /ˈdestɪnɪ/ n. Schicksal, das

destitute /ˈdestɪtjuːt/ adj. mittellos

destroy /dɪˈstrɔɪ/ v.t. zerstören

de'stroyer n. (also Naut.) Zerstörer, der

destruction /dɪˈstrʌkʃn/ n. Zerstörung, die

destructive /dɪˈstrʌktɪv/ adj. zerstörerisch; verheerend ⟨Sturm, Feuer⟩

desultory /ˈdesəltərɪ/ adj. sprunghaft; zwanglos, ungezwungen ⟨Gespräch⟩

detach /dɪˈtætʃ/ v.t. entfernen; abnehmen ⟨wieder zu Befestigendes⟩; herausnehmen ⟨innen Befindliches⟩

detachable /dɪˈtætʃəbl/ adj. abnehmbar

detached /dɪˈtætʃt/ adj. **(a)** (impartial) unvoreingenommen; (unemotional) unbeteiligt **(b)** **a ⁓ house** ein Einzelhaus

de'tachment n. **(a)** ▸ DETACH: Entfernen, das; Abnehmen, das; Herausnehmen, das **(b)** (Mil.) Abteilung, die

detail /ˈdiːteɪl/ ◾1 n. Einzelheit, die; Detail, das; **in ⁓:** Punkt für Punkt; **go into ⁓[s] ins** Detail gehen ◾2 v.t. **(a)** einzeln ausführen **(b)** (Mil.) abkommandieren

detailed /ˈdiːteɪld/ adj. detailliert; eingehend ⟨Studie⟩

detain /dɪ'teɪn/ v.t. **(a)** festhalten; (take into confinement) verhaften **(b)** (delay) aufhalten

detainee /di:teɪ'ni:/ n. Verhaftete, der/die

detect /dɪ'tekt/ v.t. entdecken; wahrnehmen ⟨Bewegung⟩; aufdecken ⟨Irrtum, Verbrechen⟩

detection /dɪ'tekʃn/ n. Entdeckung, die; (of error, crime) Aufdeckung, die

detective /dɪ'tektɪv/ n. Detektiv, der; **private ~**: Privatdetektiv, der; **~ work** Ermittlungsarbeit, die; **~ story** Detektivgeschichte, die

detector /dɪ'tektə(r)/ n. Detektor, der

detention /dɪ'tenʃn/ n. **(a)** Festnahme, die; (confinement) Haft, die **(b)** (Sch.) Nachsitzen, das

de'tention centre n. (Brit.) Jugendstrafanstalt, die

deter /dɪ'tɜ:(r)/ v.t., **-rr-** abschrecken

detergent /dɪ'tɜ:dʒənt/ n. Waschmittel, das

deteriorate /dɪ'tɪərɪəreɪt/ v.i. sich verschlechtern; ⟨Haus:⟩ verfallen

deterioration /dɪtɪərɪə'reɪʃn/ n. ▶ DETERIORATE: Verschlechterung, die; Verfall, der

determination /dɪtɜ:mɪ'neɪʃn/ n. Entschlossenheit, die

determine /dɪ'tɜ:mɪn/ v.t. **(a)** (decide) beschließen **(b)** (be a decisive factor for) bestimmen **(c)** (ascertain) feststellen

determined /dɪ'tɜ:mɪnd/ adj. **(a) be ~ to do sth.** etw. unbedingt tun wollen **(b)** (resolute) entschlossen

deterrent /dɪ'terənt/ n. Abschreckungsmittel, das **(to** für)

detest /dɪ'test/ v.t. verabscheuen

detestable /dɪ'testəbl/ adj. verabscheuenswert

detonate /'detəneɪt/ **1** v.t. zünden **2** v.i. detonieren

detonation /detə'neɪʃn/ n. Detonation, die

detonator /'detəneɪtə(r)/ n. Sprengkapsel, die

detour /'di:tʊə(r)/ n. Umweg, der; (diversion) Umleitung, die

detoxify /di:'tɒksɪfaɪ/ v.t. entgiften; unschädlich machen ⟨Gift usw.⟩

detract /dɪ'trækt/ v.i. **~ from sth.** etw. beeinträchtigen

detriment /'detrɪmənt/ n. **to the ~ of sth.** zum Nachteil einer Sache (Gen.)

detrimental /detrɪ'mentl/ adj. schädlich; **be ~ to sth.** einer Sache (Dat.) schaden

deuce /dju:s/ n. (Tennis) Einstand, der

devaluation /di:vælju:'eɪʃn/ n. Abwertung, die

devalue /di:'vælju:/ v.t. abwerten

devastate /'devəsteɪt/ v.t. verwüsten; (fig.) niederschmettern

devastating /'devəsteɪtɪŋ/ adj. verheerend; (fig.) niederschmetternd

devastation /devə'steɪʃn/ n. Verwüstung, die

develop /dɪ'veləp/ **1** v.t. entwickeln; erschließen ⟨natürliche Ressourcen⟩; bekommen ⟨Krankheit, Fieber, Lust⟩; **~ a taste for sth.** Geschmack an etw. (Akk.) finden **2** v.i. sich entwickeln (**from** aus; **into** zu)

de'veloper n. **(a)** (Photog.) Entwickler, der **(b)** (of land) Bauunternehmer, der

developing: ~ country n. Entwicklungsland, das; **~ world** n. Entwicklungsländer Pl.

de'velopment n. Entwicklung, die (**from** aus; **into** zu); (of natural resources etc.) Erschließung, die

de'velopment area n. (Brit.) Entwicklungsgebiet, das

deviant /'di:vɪənt/ adj. abweichend

deviate /'di:vɪeɪt/ v.i. abweichen

deviation /di:vɪ'eɪʃn/ n. Abweichung, die

device /dɪ'vaɪs/ n. Gerät, das; (as part of sth.) Vorrichtung, die; **leave sb. to his own ~s** jmdn. sich (Dat.) selbst überlassen

devil /'devl/ n. Teufel, der; **the D~:** der Teufel

'devilish adj. teuflisch

devious /'di:vɪəs/ adj. **(a)** (winding) verschlungen; **~ route** Umweg, der **(b)** (unscrupulous, insincere) hinterhältig

devise /dɪ'vaɪz/ v.t. entwerfen; schmieden ⟨Pläne⟩

devoid /dɪ'vɔɪd/ adj. **~ of sth.** (lacking) ohne etw.; (free from) frei von etw.

devolution /di:və'lu:ʃn/ n. (Polit.) Dezentralisierung, die

devote /dɪ'vəʊt/ v.t. widmen (**to** Dat.)

de'voted adj. treu; aufrichtig ⟨Freundschaft, Liebe, Verehrung⟩; **be ~ to sb.** jmdn. innig lieben

devotion /dɪ'vəʊʃn/ n. **~ to sb./sth.** Hingabe an jmdn./etw.

devour /dɪ'vaʊə(r)/ v.t. verschlingen

devout /dɪ'vaʊt/ adj. fromm

dew /dju:/ n. Tau, der

'dewdrop n. Tautropfen, der

dexterity /dek'sterɪtɪ/ n. Geschicklichkeit, die

dextrous /'dekstrəs/ adj. geschickt

diabetes /daɪə'bi:ti:z/ n. Zuckerkrankheit, die

diabetic /daɪə'betɪk/ **1** adj. zuckerkrank ⟨Person⟩ **2** n. Diabetiker, der/Diabetikerin, die

diabolical /daɪə'bɒlɪkl/ adj. teuflisch

diagnose /daɪəg'nəʊz/ v.t. diagnostizieren; feststellen ⟨Fehler⟩

diagnosis /daɪəg'nəʊsɪs/ *n., pl.* **diagnoses** /daɪəg'nəʊsiːz/ Diagnose, *die;* **make a ∼:** eine Diagnose stellen

diagonal /daɪ'ægənl/ ① *adj.* diagonal ② *n.* Diagonale, *die*

di'agonally *adv.* diagonal

diagram /'daɪəgræm/ *n.* Diagramm, *das*

dial /'daɪəl/ ① *n.* (of clock or watch) Zifferblatt, *das;* (of gauge, meter, etc.) Skala, *die;* (Teleph.) Wählscheibe, *die* ② *v.t. & i.,* (Brit.) **-ll-** (Teleph.) wählen; ∼ **direct** selbst wählen; (dial extension) durchwählen

dialect /'daɪəlekt/ *n.* Dialekt, *der*

dialling, (Amer.) **dialing:** ∼ **code** *n.* Vorwahl, *die;* ∼ **tone** Wählton, *der*

dialogue /'daɪəlɒg/ *n.* Dialog, *der*

'dialogue box *n.* (Comp.) Dialogbox, *die;* Dialogfenster, *das*

'dial tone *n.* (Amer.) Wählton, *der*

dialysis /daɪ'ælɪsɪs/ *n.* [Hämo]dialyse, *die* (fachspr.); Blutwäsche, *die;* ∼ **machine** Dialyseapparat, *der*

diameter /daɪ'æmɪtə(r)/ *n.* Durchmesser, *der*

diametrical /daɪə'metrɪkl/ *adj.,* **dia'metrically** *adv.* diametral

diamond /'daɪəmənd/ *n.* (a) Diamant, *der* (b) (figure) Raute, *die* (c) (Cards) Karo, *das; see also* CLUB 1C

diaper /'daɪəpə(r)/ *n.* (Amer.) Windel, *die*

diaphragm /'daɪəfræm/ *n.* Diaphragma, *das* (fachspr.); (Anat. also) Zwerchfell, *das;* (Photog. also) Blende, *die*

diarrhoea (*Amer.:* **diarrhea** /daɪə'riːə/ *n.* Durchfall, *der*

diary /'daɪərɪ/ *n.* (a) Tagebuch, *das* (b) (for appointments) Terminkalender, *der*

dice /daɪs/ ① *n.* Würfel, *der* ② *v.t.* (Cooking) würfeln

dicey /'daɪsɪ/ *adj.* (coll.) riskant

Dictaphone ® /'dɪktəfəʊn/ *n.* Diktaphon, *das* (fachspr.); Diktiergerät, *das*

dictate /dɪk'teɪt/ *v.t. & i.* diktieren; (prescribe) vorschreiben; ∼ **to** Vorschriften machen (+ *Dat.*)

dic'tating machine *n.* Diktiergerät, *das*

dictation /dɪk'teɪʃn/ *n.* Diktat, *das*

dictator /dɪk'teɪtə(r)/ *n.* Diktator, *der*

dictatorial /dɪktə'tɔːrɪəl/ *adj.* diktatorisch

dic'tatorship *n.* Diktatur, *die*

dictionary /'dɪkʃənərɪ/ *n.* Wörterbuch, *das*

did ▶ DO

diddle /'dɪdl/ *v.t.* (coll.) übers Ohr hauen (ugs.)

didn't /'dɪdnt/ (coll.) = **did not;** ▶ DO

die /daɪ/ *v.i.,* **dying** /'daɪɪŋ/ sterben (**of, from** an + *Dat.*); (*Tier, Pflanze:*) eingehen; **be dying to do sth.** darauf brennen, etw. zu tun; **be dying for sth.** etw. unbedingt brauchen

■ **die 'down** *v.i.* ⟨*Sturm, Wind, Protest:*⟩ sich legen; ⟨*Flammen:*⟩ kleiner werden; ⟨*Feuer:*⟩ herunterbrennen; ⟨*Lärm:*⟩ leiser werden

■ **die 'out** *v.i.* aussterben

'diehard *n.* Ewiggestrige, *der/die*

diesel /'diːzl/ *n.* ∼ **[engine]** Diesel[motor], *der;* ∼ **[fuel]** Diesel[kraftstoff], *der*

diet /'daɪət/ ① *n.* Diät, *die;* **be/go on a** ∼: eine Schlankheitskur machen ② *v.i.* eine Schlankheitskur machen

'diet sheet *n.* Diätplan, *der*

differ /'dɪfə(r)/ *v.i.* (be different) sich unterscheiden

difference /'dɪfərəns/ *n.* (a) Unterschied, *der;* **make no** ∼ **[to sb.]** [jmdm.] nichts ausmachen; **it makes a** ∼**:** es ist ein *od.* (ugs.) macht einen Unterschied (b) (disagreement) Meinungsverschiedenheit, *die*

different /'dɪfərənt/ *adj.* verschieden; (*pred. also*) anders; (*attrib. also*) ander...; **be** ∼ **from** *or* (esp. Brit.) **to** *or* (Amer.) **than** ...: anders sein als ...

differentiate /dɪfə'renʃɪeɪt/ *v.t. & i.* unterscheiden (**between** zwischen + *Dat.*)

differently *adv.* anders (**from,** *esp. Brit.* **to** als)

difficult /'dɪfɪkəlt/ *adj.* schwierig

'difficulty *n.* Schwierigkeit, *die;* **with [great]** ∼**:** [sehr] mühsam; **get into difficulties** in Schwierigkeiten kommen

diffident /'dɪfɪdənt/ *adj.* zaghaft; (modest) zurückhaltend

diffuse ① /dɪ'fjuːz/ *v.t.* verbreiten ② *v.i.* sich ausbreiten (**through** in + *Dat.*) ③ /dɪ'fjuːs/ *adj.* diffus

dig /dɪg/ ① *v.i.,* **-gg-,** dug /dʌg/ graben (**for** nach) ② *v.t.,* **-gg-,** dug graben; umgraben ⟨*Erde, Garten*⟩

■ **dig 'out** *v.t.* ausgraben

■ **dig 'up** *v.t.* ausgraben; umgraben ⟨*Garten*⟩; aufreißen ⟨*Straße*⟩

digest /dɪ'dʒest, daɪ'dʒest/ *v.t.* verdauen

digestion /dɪ'dʒestʃn, daɪ'dʒestʃn/ *n.* Verdauung, *die*

'digger *n.* Bagger, *der*

digit /'dɪdʒɪt/ *n.* Ziffer, *die*

digital /'dɪdʒɪtl/ *adj.* Digital-; ∼ **audio tape** Digitaltonband, *das;* ∼ **camera** Digitalkamera, *die;* ∼ **radio** Digitalradio, *das;* ∼ **television** Digitalfernsehen, *das;* ∼ **video disc** DVD, *die;* Digital Video Disc, *die*

dignified /'dɪgnɪfaɪd/ *adj.* würdig; (stately) würdevoll

dignify /'dɪgnɪfaɪ/ *v.t.* Würde verleihen (+ *Dat.*)

dignitary /'dɪgnɪtərɪ/ *n.* Würdenträger, *der;* **dignitaries** (prominent people) Honoratioren *Pl.*

dignity /'dɪgnɪtɪ/ n. Würde, die
digress /daɪ'gres/ v.i. abschweifen
digression /daɪ'greʃn/ n. Abschweifung, die
dike /daɪk/ n. Deich, der
dilapidated /dɪ'læpɪdeɪtɪd/ adj. verfallen ⟨Gebäude⟩; verwahrlost ⟨Erscheinung⟩
dilate /daɪ'leɪt/ ① v.i. sich weiten ② v.t. ausdehnen
dilemma /dɪ'lemə, daɪ'lemə/ n. Dilemma, das
diligence /'dɪlɪdʒəns/ n. Fleiß, der
diligent /'dɪlɪdʒənt/ adj., **'diligently** adv. fleißig
dilute ① /daɪ'lju:t, 'daɪlju:t/ adj. verdünnt ② /daɪ'lju:t/ v.t. verdünnen
dim /dɪm/ ① adj. (a) schwach ⟨Licht, Flackern⟩; dunkel ⟨Zimmer⟩; verschwommen ⟨Gestalt⟩
(b) (vague) verschwommen
(c) (coll.: stupid) beschränkt
② v.i. schwächer werden
dime /daɪm/ n. (Amer. coll.) Zehncentstück, das
dimension /dɪ'menʃn, daɪ'menʃn/ n. Dimension, die; ~s (measurements) Abmessungen; Maße
diminish /dɪ'mɪnɪʃ/ ① v.i. nachlassen; ⟨Vorräte, Einfluss:⟩ abnehmen; ⟨Wert, Ansehen:⟩ geringer werden
② v.t. verringern; schmälern ⟨Ansehen, Ruf⟩
dimple /'dɪmpl/ n. Grübchen, das
dim: ~wit n. (coll.) Dummkopf, der (ugs.); **~-witted** /'dɪmwɪtɪd/ adj. (coll.) dusselig (salopp)
din /dɪn/ n. Lärm, der
dine /daɪn/ v.i. [zu Mittag/zu Abend] essen **'diner** n. Gast, der
dinghy /'dɪŋgɪ, 'dɪŋɪ/ n. Ding[h]i, das; (inflatable) Schlauchboot, das
dingy /'dɪndʒɪ/ adj. schmuddelig
dining /'daɪnɪŋ/: ~ **area** n. ≈ Essecke, die; ~ **car** n. Speisewagen, der; ~ **room** n. Esszimmer, das; (in hotel etc.) Speisesaal, der; ~ **table** n. Esstisch, der
dinner /'dɪnə(r)/ n. (at midday) Mittagessen, das; (in the evening) Abendessen, das; (formal) Diner, das
dinner: ~ jacket n. (Brit.) Dinnerjacket, das; ~ **party** n. Abendeinladung, das (mit Essen); (more formal) Abendgesellschaft, die; ~ **plate** n. flacher Teller; Essteller, der; ~ **table** n. Esstisch, der; ~ **time** n. Essenszeit, die; at ~ time zur Essenszeit; (12-2 p.m.) mittags
dinosaur /'daɪnəsɔ:(r)/ n. Dinosaurier, der
dint /dɪnt/ n. by ~ of durch; by ~ of doing sth. indem jmd. etw. tut
dip /dɪp/ ① v.t., -pp-: (a) [ein]tauchen (in in + Akk.)
(b) ~ one's headlights abblenden

② v.i. sinken; (incline) abfallen
③ n. (a) (in road) Senke, die
(b) (bathe) [kurzes] Bad
diphtheria /dɪf'θɪərɪə/ n. Diphtherie, die
diphthong /'dɪfθɒŋ/ n. Diphthong, der
diploma /dɪ'pləumə/ n. Diplom, das
diplomacy /dɪ'pləuməsɪ/ n. Diplomatie, die
diplomat /'dɪpləmæt/ n. Diplomat, der/Diplomatin, die
diplomatic /dɪplə'mætɪk/ adj., **diplo'matically** adv. diplomatisch
diplo'matic service n. diplomatischer Dienst
'dipstick n. [Öl-/Benzin]messstab, der
dire /'daɪə(r)/ adj. furchtbar
direct /dɪ'rekt, daɪ'rekt/ ① v.t. (a) (turn) richten (to[wards] auf + Akk.); ~ sb. to a place jmdn. den Weg zu einem Ort weisen
(b) (control) leiten; regeln ⟨Verkehr⟩
(c) (order) anweisen
(d) (Theatre, Cinemat., etc.) Regie führen bei
② adj. direkt; durchgehend ⟨Zug⟩; unmittelbar ⟨Ursache, Auswirkung, Erfahrung, Verantwortung⟩; genau ⟨Gegenteil⟩; direkt ⟨Widerspruch⟩; diametral ⟨Gegensatz⟩; ~ **speech** direkte Rede
③ adv. direkt
direct: ~ 'current n. (Electr.) Gleichstrom, der; ~ **'debit** n. (Brit.) Lastschriftverfahren, das; ~ **'dialling** n. Durchwahl, die; we will soon have ~ dialling wir werden bald ein Durchwahlsystem haben; ~ **'flight** n. Direktflug, der; ~ **'hit** n. Volltreffer, der
direction /dɪ'rekʃn, daɪ'rekʃn/ n.
(a) Richtung, die; in the ~ of London in Richtung London
(b) (guidance) Führung, die; (Theatre, Cinemat., etc.) Regie, die; Spielleitung, die
(c) usu. in pl. (order) Anordnung, die; ~s [for use] Gebrauchsanweisung, die
di'rectly adv. (a) direkt; unmittelbar ⟨folgen, verantwortlich sein⟩
(b) (exactly) genau
(c) (at once) umgehend
(d) (shortly) gleich
di'rect object n. direktes Objekt
director /daɪ'rektə(r), dɪ'rektə(r)/ n.
(a) (Commerc.) Direktor, der/Direktorin, die; board of ~s Aufsichtsrat, der
(b) (Theatre, Cinemat., etc.) Regisseur, der/Regisseurin, die
directory /daɪ'rektərɪ, dɪ'rektərɪ/ n. (telephone ~) Telefonbuch, das; (of tradesmen etc.) Branchenverzeichnis, das; (Comp.) Verzeichnis, das; ~ **enquiries** (Brit.), ~ **information** (Amer.) [Fernsprech]auskunft, die
dirt /dɜ:t/ n. Schmutz, der; ~ **cheap** (coll.) spottbillig
'dirty ① adj. schmutzig; get sth. ~: etw. schmutzig machen ⋯⊹

2 *v.t.* schmutzig machen

disa'bility *n.* Behinderung, *die*

disa'bility allowance *n.* Erwerbsunfähigkeitsentschädigung, *die*

disabled /dɪs'eɪbld/ *adj.* behindert

disad'vantage *n.* Nachteil, *der;* **at a** ~: im Nachteil

disad'vantaged *adj.* benachteiligt

disa'gree *v.i.* anderer Meinung sein; ~ **with sb./sth.** mit jmdm./etw. nicht übereinstimmen; ~ **[with sb.] about** *or* **over sth.** sich [mit jmdm.] über etw. (*Akk.*) nicht einig sein

disa'greeable *adj.* unangenehm

disa'greement *n.* **(a)** (difference of opinion) Uneinigkeit, *die;* **be in** ~ **with sb./sth.** mit jmdm./etw. nicht übereinstimmen **(b)** (quarrel) Meinungsverschiedenheit, *die* **(c)** (discrepancy) Diskrepanz, *die*

disal'low *v.t.* verbieten; (Sport) nicht geben ⟨*Tor*⟩

disap'pear *v.i.* verschwinden; ⟨*Brauch, Tierart:*⟩ aussterben

disap'pearance *n.* Verschwinden, *das*

disap'point *v.t.* enttäuschen

disap'pointed *adj.* enttäuscht

disap'pointing *adj.* enttäuschend

disap'pointment *n.* Enttäuschung, *die*

disap'proval *n.* Missbilligung, *die*

disap'prove *v.i.* dagegen sein; ~ **of sb./sth.** jmdn. ablehnen/etw. missbilligen

dis'arm *v.t.* entwaffnen

disarmament /dɪs'ɑːməmənt/ *n.* Abrüstung, *die*

disarray /dɪsə'reɪ/ *n.* Unordnung, *die;* **in** ~: in Unordnung

disaster /dɪ'zɑːstə(r)/ *n.* Katastrophe, *die;* ~ **area** Katastrophengebiet, *das;* ~ **fund** Nothilfefonds, *der*

disastrous /dɪ'zɑːstrəs/ *adj.* katastrophal; verhängnisvoll ⟨*Irrtum, Entscheidung, Politik*⟩

dis'band 1 *v.t.* auflösen 2 *v.i.* sich auflösen

disbe'lief *n.* Unglaube, *der;* **in** ~: ungläubig

disbe'lieve *v.t.* ~ **sb./sth.** jmdm./etw. nicht glauben

disc /dɪsk/ *n.* **(a)** Scheibe, *die;* (record) Platte, *die* **(b)** (Comp.) ▶ DISK A

discard /dɪs'kɑːd/ *v.t.* wegwerfen; fallenlassen ⟨*Vorschlag, Idee*⟩

'disc brake *n.* Scheibenbremse, *die*

discern /dɪ'sɜːn/ *v.t.* wahrnehmen

discernible /dɪ'sɜːnɪbl/ *adj.* erkennbar

di'scerning *adj.* kritisch

discharge 1 /dɪs'tʃɑːdʒ/ *v.t.* **(a)** entlassen (from aus); freisprechen ⟨*Angeklagte*⟩ **(b)** ablassen ⟨*Flüssigkeit, Gas*⟩ 2 /'dɪstʃɑːdʒ/ *n.* **(a)** Entlassung, *die* (from

aus); (of defendant) Freispruch, *der* **(b)** (emission) Ausfluss, *der*

disciple /dɪ'saɪpl/ *n.* **(a)** (Relig.) Jünger, *der* **(b)** (follower) Anhänger, *der*/Anhängerin, *die*

disciplinary /dɪsɪ'plɪnərɪ/ *adj.* disziplinarisch; ~ **action** Disziplinarmaßnahmen *Pl.*

discipline /'dɪsɪplɪn/ 1 *n.* Disziplin, *die* 2 *v.t.* disziplinieren; (punish) bestrafen

disciplined /'dɪsɪplɪnd/ *adj.* diszipliniert

'disc jockey *n.* Diskjockey, *der*

dis'claim *v.t.* abstreiten

dis'claimer *n.* Gegenerklärung, *die;* (Law) Verzichterklärung, *die*

disclose /dɪs'kləʊz/ *v.t.* enthüllen; bekannt geben ⟨*Information, Nachricht*⟩

dis'closure *n.* Enthüllung, *die;* (of information, news) Bekanntgabe, *die*

disco /'dɪskəʊ/ *n., pl.* ~**s** (coll.) Disko, *die*

'disco dancing *n.* Diskotanz, *der*

dis'colour (*Brit.; Amer.:* **discolor**) *v.t.* verfärben

dis'comfort *n.* **(a)** *no pl.* (slight pain) Beschwerden *Pl.* **(b)** (hardship) Unannehmlichkeit, *die*

'disco music *n.* Diskomusik, *die*

disconcert /dɪskən'sɜːt/ *v.t.* irritieren

discon'nect *v.t.* abtrennen; abstellen ⟨*Telefon*⟩

disconsolate /dɪs'kɒnsələt/ *adj.* **(a)** (unhappy) unglücklich **(b)** (inconsolable) untröstlich

discon'tent *n.* Unzufriedenheit, *die*

discon'tented *adj.* unzufrieden

discon'tinue *v.t.* einstellen

discord /'dɪskɔːd/ *n.* **(a)** Zwietracht, *die* **(b)** (Mus.) Dissonanz, *die*

discordant /dɪs'kɔːdənt/ *adj.* **(a)** (conflicting) gegensätzlich **(b)** **a** ~ **note** ein Misston

discothèque /'dɪskətek/ *n.* Diskothek, *die*

discount 1 /'dɪskaʊnt/ *n.* (Commerc.) Rabatt, *der* (**on** auf + *Akk.*) 2 /dɪ'skaʊnt/ *v.t.* (disbelieve) unberücksichtigt lassen

discourage /dɪ'skʌrɪdʒ/ *v.t.* **(a)** entmutigen **(b)** (advise against) abraten

di'scouragement *n.* **(a)** Entmutigung, *die* **(b)** (depression) Mutlosigkeit, *die*

discouraging /dɪ'skʌrɪdʒɪŋ/ *adj.* entmutigend

dis'courteous *adj.* unhöflich

dis'courtesy *n.* Unhöflichkeit, *die*

discover /dɪ'skʌvə(r)/ *v.t.* entdecken; (by search) herausfinden

di'scovery *n.* Entdeckung, *die*

dis'credit 1 *n.* Misskredit, *der;* **bring** ~ **on sb./sth., bring sb./sth. into** ~: jmdn./

etw. in Misskredit bringen
2 *v.t.* in Misskredit bringen
discreet /dɪ'skriːt/ *adj.*, **di'screetly**
adv. diskret
discrepancy /dɪ'skrepənsɪ/ *n.*
Diskrepanz, *die*
discrepant /dɪ'skrepənt/ *adj.*
[voneinander] abweichend
discretion /dɪ'skreʃn/ *n.* (prudence)
Umsicht, *die*
discriminate /dɪ'skrɪmɪneɪt/ *v.i.*
(a) unterscheiden
(b) ~ against/in favour of sb. jmdn.
diskriminieren/bevorzugen
discrimination /dɪskrɪmɪ'neɪʃn/ *n.*
(a) Unterscheidung, *die*
(b) Diskriminierung, *die* (against *Gen.*);
~ in favour of Bevorzugung (+ *Gen.*)
discus /'dɪskəs/ *n.* Diskus, *der*
discuss /dɪ'skʌs/ *v.t.* besprechen; (debate)
diskutieren über (+ *Akk.*)
discussion /dɪ'skʌʃn/ *n.* Gespräch, *das;*
(debate) Diskussion, *die*
disdain /dɪs'deɪn/ **1** *n.* Verachtung, *die*
2 *v.t.* verachten; ~ to do sth. zu stolz sein,
etw. zu tun
disdainful /dɪs'deɪnfl/ *adj.* verächtlich
disease /dɪ'ziːz/ *n.* Krankheit, *die*
diseased /dɪ'ziːzd/ *adj.* krank
disem'bark *v.i.* von Bord gehen
disen'chant *v.t.* ernüchtern; he became
~ed with her/it sie/es hat ihn desillusioniert
disen'gage *v.t.* lösen (from aus, von);
~ the clutch auskuppeln
disen'tangle *v.t.* entwirren; (extricate)
befreien (from aus)
dis'figure *v.t.* entstellen
disgrace /dɪs'greɪs/ **1** *n.* Schande, *die*
(to für)
2 *v.t.* Schande machen (+ *Dat.*); ~ oneself
sich blamieren
di'sgraceful /dɪs'greɪsfl/ *adj.* skandalös;
it's a ~: es ist ein Skandal
disgruntled /dɪs'grʌntld/ *adj.* verstimmt
disguise /dɪs'gaɪz/ **1** *v.t.* verkleiden
‹*Person*›; verstellen ‹*Stimme*›; tarnen
‹*Gegenstand*›
2 *n.* Verkleidung, *die*
disgust /dɪs'gʌst/ **1** *n.* (nausea) Ekel, *der*
(at vor + *Dat.*); (revulsion) Abscheu, *der* (at
vor + *Dat.*); (indignation) Empörung, *die* (at
über + *Akk.*)
2 *v.t.* anwidern; (fill with nausea) ekeln; (fill
with indignation) empören
dis'gusted *adj.* angewidert; (nauseated)
angeekelt; (indignant) empört
dis'gusting *adj.* widerlich
dish /dɪʃ/ *n.* **(a)** Schale, *die;* (deeper)
Schüssel, *die;* ~es (crockery) Geschirr, *das;*
wash *or* (coll.) do the ~es Geschirr spülen
(b) (type of food) Gericht, *das*

■ **dish 'out** *v.t.* **(a)** austeilen ‹*Essen*›.
(b) (coll.: distribute) verteilen.
■ **dish 'up** *v.t.* auftragen
'dishcloth *n.* Spültuch, *das*
dis'hearten *v.t.* entmutigen
dishevelled (*Amer.:* **disheveled**)
/dɪ'ʃevld/ *adj.* zerzaust ‹*Haar*›; ungepflegt
‹*Erscheinung*›
dis'honest *adj.*, **dis'honestly** *adv.*
unehrlich
dis'honesty *n.* Unehrlichkeit, *die*
dis'honour **1** *n.* Unehre, *die*
2 *v.t.* beleidigen
dishonourable /dɪs'ɒnərəbl/ *adj.*
unehrenhaft
dish: ~ **rack** *n.* Abtropfgestell, *das;* (in
dishwasher) Geschirrwagen, *der;* ~**washer**
n. Geschirrspülmaschine, *die*
disil'lusion **1** *v.t.* ernüchtern
2 *n.* Desillusion, *die* (with über + *Akk.*)
disil'lusionment *n.* Desillusionierung,
die
disincentive /dɪsɪn'sentɪv/ *n.* Hemmnis,
das; act as *or* be a ~ to sth. jmdn.
davon abhalten, etw. zu tun
disin'fect *v.t.* desinfizieren
disinfectant /dɪsɪn'fektənt/ **1** *adj.*
desinfizierend
2 *n.* Desinfektionsmittel, *das*
disinformation /dɪsɪnfə'meɪʃn/ *n.*
Desinformation, *die*
disingenuous /dɪsɪn'dʒenjʊəs/ *adj.*
unaufrichtig
dis'integrate *v.i.* zerfallen
disinte'gration *n.* Zerfall, *der*
dis'interested *adj.* **(a)** (impartial)
unvoreingenommen
(b) (coll.: uninterested) desinteressiert
disjointed /dɪs'dʒɔɪntɪd/ *adj.*
unzusammenhängend
disk *n.* **(a)** (Comp.) **[floppy]** ~: Floppydisk,
die; Diskette, *die;* **[hard]** ~ (exchangeable)
[harte] Magnetplatte; (fixed) Festplatte, *die*
(b) ▶ DISC A
'disk drive *n.* (Comp.) Diskettenlaufwerk,
das
diskette /dɪ'sket/ *n.* Diskette, *die*
dis'like **1** *v.t.* nicht mögen; ~ doing sth.
etw. ungern tun
2 *n.* Abneigung, *die* (of, for gegen); take
a ~ to sb./sth. eine Abneigung gegen
jmdn./etw. empfinden
dislocate /'dɪsləkeɪt/ *v.t.* ausrenken;
auskugeln ‹*Schulter, Hüfte*›
dis'lodge *v.t.* entfernen (from aus)
dis'loyal *adj.* illoyal (to gegenüber)
dis'loyalty *n.* Illoyalität, *die* (to
gegenüber)
dismal /'dɪzməl/ *adj.* trist
dismantle /dɪs'mæntl/ *v.t.* demontieren;
abbauen ‹*Schuppen, Gerüst*›

dismay /dɪsˈmeɪ/ ① *v.t.* bestürzen
② *n.* Bestürzung, *die* (**at** über + *Akk.*)
dismiss /dɪsˈmɪs/ *v.t.* entlassen; (reject) ablehnen
dismissal /dɪsˈmɪsl/ *n.* Entlassung, *die*
dismissive /dɪsˈmɪsɪv/ *adj.* abweisend; (disdainful) abschätzig
dis'mount *v.i.* absteigen
diso'bedience *n.* Ungehorsam, *der*
diso'bedient *adj.* ungehorsam
diso'bey *v.t.* nicht gehorchen (+ *Dat.*); nicht befolgen ‹*Befehl*›
dis'order *n.* (a) Durcheinander, *das* (b) (Med.) Störung, *die*
dis'orderly *adj.* (untidy) unordentlich; ~ **conduct** ungebührliches Benehmen
dis'organized *adj.* chaotisch
dis'orientated, dis'oriented *adjs.* desorientiert
dis'own *v.t.* verleugnen
disparage /dɪˈspærɪdʒ/ *v.t.* herabsetzen
disparaging /dɪˈspærɪdʒɪŋ/ *adj.* abschätzig
disparity /dɪˈspærɪtɪ/ *n.* Ungleichheit, *die*
dispatch /dɪˈspætʃ/ ① *v.t.* (a) schicken (b) (kill) töten
② *n.* Bericht, *der*
di'spatch note *n.* Versandanzeige, *die*
dispel /dɪˈspel/ *v.t.,* -**ll**- vertreiben; zerstreuen ‹*Besorgnis, Befürchtung*›
dispensable /dɪˈspensəbl/ *adj.* entbehrlich
dispensary /dɪˈspensərɪ/ *n.* Apotheke, *die*
dispense /dɪˈspens/ *v.i.* ~ **with** verzichten auf (+ *Akk.*)
dispensing 'chemist *n.* Apotheker, *der*/Apothekerin, *die*
dispersal /dɪˈspɜːsl/ *n.* Zerstreuung, *die*
disperse /dɪˈspɜːs/ ① *v.t.* zerstreuen
② *v.i.* sich zerstreuen
dispirited /dɪˈspɪrɪtɪd/ *adj.* entmutigt
dis'place *v.t.* verschieben; (supplant) ersetzen
displaced 'person *n.* Vertriebene, *der*/*die*
display /dɪˈspleɪ/ ① *v.t.* (a) zeigen; ausstellen ‹*Waren*›
(b) (Comp.) anzeigen
② *n.* (a) Ausstellung, *die;* (of goods) Auslage, *die;* (ostentatious show) Zurschaustellung, *die* (b) (Comp. etc.) Display, *das;* Anzeige, *die*
dis'please *v.t.* ~ **sb.** jmds. Missfallen erregen
dis'pleasure *n.* Missfallen, *das*
disposable /dɪˈspəʊzəbl/ *adj.* Wegwerf-
disposal /dɪˈspəʊzl/ *n.* Beseitigung, *die;* **have sth./sb. at one's** ~: etw./jmdn. zur Verfügung haben; **be at sb.'s** ~: jmdm. zur Verfügung stehen
dispose /dɪˈspəʊz/ *v.t.* ~ **sb. to sth.** jmdn. zu etw. veranlassen; ~ **sb. to do sth.** jmdn.

dazu veranlassen, etw. zu tun
■ **di'spose of** *v.t.* beseitigen; (settle) erledigen
disposed /dɪˈspəʊzd/ *adj.* **be** ~ **to do sth.** dazu neigen, etw. zu tun; **be well** ~ **towards sb./sth.** jmdm. wohl gesinnt sein/einer Sache (*Dat.*) positiv gegenüberstehen
disposition /dɪspəˈzɪʃn/ *n.* Veranlagung, *die;* (nature) Art, *die*
dis'prove *v.t.* widerlegen
disputable /dɪˈspjuːtəbl, ˈdɪspjʊtəbl/ *adj.* strittig
dispute /dɪˈspjuːt/ ① *n.* Streit, *der* (**over** um)
② *v.t.* (a) (discuss) sich streiten über (+ *Akk.*)
(b) (oppose) bestreiten
disqualifi'cation *n.* Ausschluss, *der;* (Sport) Disqualifikation, *die*
dis'qualify *v.t.* ausschließen (**from** von); (Sport) disqualifizieren
disre'gard ① *v.t.* ignorieren
② *n.* Missachtung, *die* (**of, for** *Gen.*); (of wishes, feelings) Gleichgültigkeit, *die* (**for, of** gegenüber)
dis'reputable *adj.* verrufen
disrepute /dɪsrɪˈpjuːt/ *n.* Verruf, *der;* **bring sb./sth. into** ~: jmdn./etw. in Verruf bringen
disre'spect *n.* Missachtung, *die;* **show** ~ **for sb./sth.** keine Achtung vor jmdm./etw. haben
disre'spectful *adj.* respektlos
disrupt /dɪsˈrʌpt/ *v.t.* stören
disruption /dɪsˈrʌpʃn/ *n.* Störung, *die*
disruptive /dɪsˈrʌptɪv/ *adj.* störend
dissatis'faction *n.* Unzufriedenheit, *die*
dis'satisfied *adj.* unzufrieden
dissect /dɪˈsekt/ *v.t.* sezieren
disseminate /dɪˈsemɪneɪt/ *v.t.* verbreiten
dissent /dɪˈsent/ ① *v.i.* (a) (refuse to assent) nicht zustimmen; ~ **from sth.** mit etw. nicht übereinstimmen
(b) (disagree) ~ **from sth.** von etw. abweichen
② *n.* Ablehnung, *die;* (from majority) Abweichung, *die*
dissertation /dɪsəˈteɪʃn/ *n.* Dissertation, *die*
dis'service *n.* **do sb. a** ~: jmdm. einen schlechten Dienst erweisen
dissident /ˈdɪsɪdənt/ *n.* Dissident, *der*/Dissidentin, *die*
dis'similar *adj.* unähnlich (**to** *Dat.*)
dissociate /dɪˈsəʊʃɪeɪt/ *v.t.* trennen; ~ **oneself** sich distanzieren (**from** von)
dissolve /dɪˈzɒlv/ ① *v.t.* auflösen
② *v.i.* sich auflösen
dissuade /dɪˈsweɪd/ *v.t.* abbringen (**from** von)
distance /ˈdɪstəns/ *n.* (a) Entfernung, *die* (**from** zu)
(b) (way to cover) Strecke, *die;* **from a** ~: von

weitem; **in/into the** ~: in der/die Ferne

'distance learning n. Fernstudium, *das*

distant /'dɪstənt/ *adj.* **(a)** fern; entfernt 〈*Ähnlichkeit, Verwandtschaft, Verwandte*〉 **(b)** (reserved) distanziert

dis'taste n. Abneigung, *die* **(for** gegen)

dis'tasteful *adj.* unangenehm

distend /dɪ'stend/ *v.t.* erweitern

distil, (Amer.) **distill** /dɪ'stɪl/ *v.t.* destillieren; brennen 〈*Branntwein*〉

distillation /dɪstɪ'leɪʃn/ *n.* Destillation, *die*

distillery /dɪ'stɪlərɪ/ *n.* Brennerei, *die*

distinct /dɪ'stɪŋkt/ *adj.* deutlich; (different) verschieden

distinction /dɪ'stɪŋkʃn/ *n.* Unterschied, *der*

distinctive /dɪ'stɪŋktɪv/ *adj.* unverwechselbar

dis'tinctly *adv.* deutlich

distinguish /dɪ'stɪŋgwɪʃ/ ① *v.t.* **(a)** (make out) erkennen **(b)** (differentiate) unterscheiden **(c)** (characterize) kennzeichnen **(d)** ~ **oneself [by sth.]** sich [durch etw.] hervortun ② *v.i.* unterscheiden; ~ **between** auseinander halten

distinguished /dɪ'stɪŋgwɪʃt/ *adj.* angesehen; glänzend 〈*Laufbahn*〉; vornehm 〈*Aussehen*〉

distort /dɪ'stɔːt/ *v.t.* verzerren; (fig.) verdrehen

distortion /dɪ'stɔːʃn/ *n.* Verzerrung, *die;* (fig.) Verdrehung, *die*

distract /dɪ'strækt/ *v.t.* ablenken; ~ **sb.['s attention from sth.]** jmdn. [von etw.] ablenken

di'stracted *adj.* von Sinnen *nachgestellt;* (mentally far away) abwesend

distraction /dɪ'strækʃn/ *n.* **(a)** (diversion) Ablenkung, *die;* (interruption) Störung, *die* **(b) drive sb. to** ~: jmdn. zum Wahnsinn treiben

distraught /dɪ'strɔːt/ *adj.* aufgelöst **(with** vor + *Dat.*); verstört 〈*Blick*〉

distress /dɪ'stres/ ① *n.* **(a)** Kummer, *der* **(at** über + *Akk.*) **(b)** (pain) Qualen *Pl.* **(c) an aircraft/ship in** ~: ein Flugzeug in Not/ein Schiff in Seenot ② *v.t.* nahe gehen (+ *Dat.*)

di'stressing *adj.* erschütternd

di'stress signal n. Notsignal, *das*

distribute /dɪ'strɪbjuːt/ *v.t.* verteilen **(to** an + *Akk.;* **among** unter + *Akk.*); (Commerc.) vertreiben

distribution /dɪstrɪ'bjuːʃn/ *n.* Verteilung, *die;* (Commerc.) Vertrieb, *der*

distributor /dɪ'strɪbjʊtə(r)/ *n.* Verteiler, *der*/Verteilerin, *die;* (Commerc.) Vertreiber, *der*

district /'dɪstrɪkt/ *n.* Gegend, *die;* (Admin.) Bezirk, *der*

district: ~ **at'torney** n. (Amer. Law) [Bezirks]staatsanwalt, *der*/-anwältin, *die;* ~ **'nurse** n. (Brit.) Gemeindeschwester, *die*

dis'trust /dɪs'trʌst/ ① *n.* Misstrauen, *das* (of gegen) ② *v.t.* misstrauen (+ *Dat.*)

dis'trustful *adj.* misstrauisch

disturb /dɪ'stɜːb/ *v.t.* **(a)** stören; **'do not** ~!' „bitte nicht stören!" **(b)** (worry) beunruhigen

disturbance /dɪ'stɜːbəns/ *n.* Störung, *die;* **political** ~s politische Unruhen

disturbed /dɪ'stɜːbd/ *adj.* besorgt; **[mentally]** ~: geistig gestört

disturbing /dɪs'tɜːbɪŋ/ *adj.* bestürzend

disuse /dɪs'juːs/ *n.* **fall into** ~: außer Gebrauch kommen

disused /dɪs'juːzd/ *adj.* stillgelegt; leer stehend 〈*Gebäude*〉

ditch /dɪtʃ/ ① *n.* Graben, *der* ② *v.t.* (coll.) sausen lassen 〈*Plan*〉; sitzen lassen 〈*Familie, Freund*〉

dither /'dɪðə(r)/ *v.i.* schwanken

ditto /'dɪtəʊ/ *n., pl.* ~**s** ebenso; ditto; ~ **marks** Unterführungszeichen, *das*

divan /dɪ'væn/ *n.* [Polster]liege, *die*

dive /daɪv/ ① *v.i.,* **dived** or (Amer.) **dove** /dəʊv/ **(a)** einen Kopfsprung machen; (when already in water) tauchen **(b)** 〈*Vogel, Flugzeug usw.:*〉 einen Sturzflug machen ② *n.* **(a)** Kopfsprung, *der;* (of bird, aircraft, etc.) Sturzflug, *der* **(b)** (coll.: place) Spelunke, *die*

'diver n. **(a)** (Sport) Kunstspringer, *der*/-springerin, *die* **(b)** (as profession) Taucher, *der*/Taucherin, *die*

diverge /daɪ'vɜːdʒ/ *v.i.* auseinander gehen

divergent /daɪ'vɜːdʒənt/ *adj.* auseinander gehend

diverse /daɪ'vɜːs/ *adj.* verschieden

diversify /daɪ'vɜːsɪfaɪ, dɪ'vɜːsɪfaɪ/ *v.i.* 〈*Firma:*〉 sich auf neue Produktions-/Produktbereiche umstellen

diversion /daɪ'vɜːʃn/ *n.* **(a)** Ablenkung, *die;* **create a** ~: ein Ablenkungsmanöver durchführen **(b)** (Brit.: alternative route) Umleitung, *die*

diversity /daɪ'vɜːsɪtɪ/ *n.* Vielfalt, *die*

divert /daɪ'vɜːt/ *v.t.* umleiten 〈*Verkehr, Fluss*〉; ablenken 〈*Aufmerksamkeit*〉

divide /dɪ'vaɪd/ ① *v.t.* **(a)** teilen; ~ **sth. in two etc.** [in zwei Teile] zerteilen **(b)** (distribute) aufteilen **(among/between** unter + *Akk. od. Dat.*) **(c)** (Math.) dividieren (fachspr.), teilen **(by** durch) ② *v.i.* sich teilen; ~ **[from sth.]** von etw. abzweigen ⋯⟫

■ **divide 'out** *v.t.* aufteilen (among/between unter + *Akk. od. Dat.*); (distribute) verteilen an (+ *Akk.*)

■ **divide 'up** *v.t.* aufteilen

dividend /'dɪvɪdend/ *n.* Dividende, *die*

dividers /dɪ'vaɪdəz/ *n. pl.* Stechzirkel, *der*

divine /dɪ'vaɪn/ *adj.* göttlich

diving /'daɪvɪŋ/ *n.* Kunstspringen, *das*

diving: ~ **board** *n.* Sprungbrett, *das;* ~ **suit** *n.* Taucheranzug, *der*

divinity /dɪ'vɪnɪtɪ/ *n.* (a) Göttlichkeit, *die* (b) (god) Gottheit, *die*

divisible /dɪ'vɪzɪbl/ *adj.* teilbar (by durch)

division /dɪ'vɪʒn/ *n.* (a) Teilung, *die* (b) (Math.) Dividieren, *das;* do ~: dividieren; long ~: ausführliche Division (*mit Aufschreiben der Zwischenprodukte*); short ~: verkürzte Division (*ohne Aufschreiben der Zwischenprodukte*) (c) (section, part) Abteilung, *die* (d) (group) Gruppe, *die* (e) (Mil. etc.) Division, *die* (f) (Footb. etc.) Liga, *die;* Spielklasse, *die;* (in British football) Division, *die*

divorce /dɪ'vɔːs/ ⎡1⎤ *n.* [Ehe]scheidung, *die* ⎡2⎤ *v.t.* ~ one's husband/wife sich von seinem Mann/seiner Frau scheiden lassen

divorced /dɪ'vɔːst/ *adj.* geschieden; get ~: sich scheiden lassen

divorcee /dɪvɔː'siː/ *n.* Geschiedene, *der/die;* be a ~: geschieden sein

divulge /daɪ'vʌldʒ/ *v.t.* preisgeben

DIY *abbr.* = **do-it-yourself**

dizzy /'dɪzɪ/ *adj.* schwind[e]lig; I feel ~: mir ist schwindlig

DJ /diː'dʒeɪ/ *abbr.* = **disc jockey** Diskjockey, *der*

DNA *abbr.* = **deoxyribonucleic acid** DNS

do /də, *stressed* duː/ ⎡1⎤ *v.t.*, neg. (coll.) **don't** /dəʊnt/, pres.t. **he does** /dʌz/, neg. (coll.) **doesn't** /'dʌznt/, p.t. **did** /dɪd/, neg. (coll.) **didn't** /'dɪdnt/, pres.p. **doing** /'duːɪŋ/, p. p. **done** /dʌn/ (a) machen ⟨Hausaufgaben, Hausarbeit, Examen, Übersetzung, Kopie, Bett, Handstand⟩; erfüllen ⟨Pflicht⟩; verrichten ⟨Arbeit⟩; vorführen ⟨Trick, Nummer, Tanz⟩; durchführen ⟨Test⟩; schaffen ⟨Pensum⟩; (clean) putzen; (arrange) [zurecht]machen ⟨Haare⟩; schminken ⟨Lippen, Augen, Gesicht⟩; machen (ugs.) ⟨Nägel⟩; (cut) schneiden ⟨Nägel⟩; (paint) machen (ugs.) ⟨Zimmer⟩; streichen ⟨Haus, Möbel⟩; (repair) in Ordnung bringen; do the **shopping/washing-up/cleaning** einkaufen [gehen]/abwaschen/sauber machen; **what can I do for you?** (in shop) was darfs sein?; **do sth. about sth./sb.** etw. gegen etw./jmdn. unternehmen (b) (cook) braten; **well done** durch[gebraten] (c) (solve) lösen ⟨Problem, Rätsel⟩; machen ⟨Puzzle, Kreuzworträtsel⟩ (d) (coll.: swindle) reinlegen (ugs.); **do sb. out**

of sth. jmdn. um etw. bringen (e) (satisfy) zusagen (+ *Dat.*) ⎡2⎤ *v.i., forms as* 1: (a) (act) tun; **do as they do** mach es wie sie (b) (fare) **how are you doing?** wie gehts dir? (c) (get on) vorankommen; (in exams) abschneiden; **do well/badly at school** gut/schlecht in der Schule sein (d) **how do you do?** (formal) guten Tag/Morgen/Abend! (e) (serve purpose) es tun; (suffice) [aus]reichen; (be suitable) gehen; **that won't do** das geht nicht; **that will do!** jetzt aber genug! ⎡3⎤ *v. substitute, forms as* 1: **you mustn't act as he does** du darfst nicht so wie er handeln; **You went to Paris, didn't you?** – **Yes, I did** Du warst doch in Paris, nicht wahr? – Ja[, stimmt]; **come in, do!** komm doch herein! ⎡4⎤ *v. aux. forms as* 1: **I do love Greece** Griechenland gefällt mir wirklich gut; **little did he know that ...:** er hatte keine Ahnung, dass ...; **do you know him?** kennst du ihn?; **what does he want?** was will er?; **I don't** *or* **do not wish to take part** ich möchte nicht teilnehmen; **don't be so noisy!** seid [doch] nicht so laut! ⎡5⎤ *n.* /duː/, *pl.* **do's** *or* **dos** /duːz/ (Brit. coll.) Feier, *die;* Fete, *die* (ugs.)

■ **do a'way with** *v.t.* abschaffen

■ **'do for** *v.t.* (coll.) do for sb. jmdn. fertig machen (ugs.); **be done for** erledigt sein

■ **do 'in** *v.t.* (sl.) kaltmachen (salopp)

■ **do 'up** *v.t.* (a) (fasten) zumachen; binden ⟨Schnürsenkel, Fliege⟩ (b) (wrap) einpacken

■ **'do with** *v.t.* I could do with ...: ich brauche ...

■ **'do without** *v.t.* do without sth. auf etw. (*Akk.*) verzichten

docile /'dəʊsaɪl/ *adj.* sanft; (submissive) unterwürfig

dock[1] /dɒk/ ⎡1⎤ *n.* (a) Dock, *das* (b) *usu. in pl.* (area) Hafen, *der* ⎡2⎤ *v.t.* [ein]docken ⎡3⎤ *v.i.* anlegen

dock[2] *n.* (in lawcourt) Anklagebank, *die;* **stand/be in the ~:** ≈ auf der Anklagebank sitzen

'docker *n.* Hafenarbeiter, *der*

dock: ~**land** *n.* das Hafenviertel; ~**yard** *n.* Schiffswerft, *die*

doctor /'dɒktə(r)/ ⎡1⎤ *n.* (a) Arzt, *der/*Ärztin, *die; as address* Herr/Frau Doktor (b) (holder of degree) Doktor, *der* ⎡2⎤ *v.t.* (coll.) verfälschen

doctorate /'dɒktərət/ *n.* Doktorwürde, *die*

doctrine /'dɒktrɪn/ *n.* Lehre, *die*

docudrama /'dɒkjuːdrɑːmə/ *n.* Dokudrama, *das*

document /'dɒkjʊmənt/ *n.* (a) Dokument, *das;* Urkunde, *die* (b) (Comp.) Dokument, *das*

documentary /dɒkjʊ'mentərɪ/ **1** *adj.*
dokumentarisch
2 *n.* (film) Dokumentarfilm, *der*
documentation /dɒkjʊmen'teɪʃn/ *n.*
(material) beweiskräftige Dokumente *Pl.*
dodge /dɒdʒ/ **1** *v.i.* ausweichen
2 *v.t.* ausweichen (+ *Dat.*) ⟨*Schlag,
Hindernis usw.*⟩; entkommen (+ *Dat.*)
⟨*Polizei, Verfolger*⟩
3 *n.* (trick) Trick, *der*
dodgems /'dɒdʒəmz/ *n. pl.*
[Auto]skooterbahn, *die;* **have a ride/go on
the ~:** Autoskooter fahren
dodgy /'dɒdʒɪ/ *adj.* (Brit. coll.) (unreliable)
unsicher; (risky) gewagt
doe /dəʊ/ *n.* (deer) Damtier, *das;* (rabbit)
[Kaninchen]weibchen, *das*
does /dʌz/ ▸ DO
doesn't /'dʌznt/ (coll.) = does not; ▸ DO
dog /dɒg/ **1** *n.* Hund, *der*
2 *v.t.,* -gg- verfolgen; (fig.) heimsuchen
dog: ~ biscuit *n.* Hundekuchen, *der;*
~ collar *n.* [Hunde]halsband, *das;* (joc.:
clerical collar) Kollar, *das;* **~-eared** *adj.* **a
~-eared book** ein Buch mit Eselsohren;
~-end *n.* (coll.) Kippe, *die* (ugs.)
dogged /'dɒgɪd/ *adj.* hartnäckig
⟨*Weigerung, Verurteilung*⟩; zäh
⟨*Durchhaltevermögen, Ausdauer*⟩
'dog licence *n.*
Hundesteuerbescheinigung, *die*
dogma /'dɒgmə/ *n.* Dogma, *das*
dogmatic /dɒg'mætɪk/ *adj.* dogmatisch
do-gooder /du:'gʊdə(r)/ *n.* Wohltäter,
der (iron.)
dog: ~sbody *n.* (Brit. coll.) Mädchen für
alles; **~'s life** *n.* **a ~'s life** ein Hundeleben;
give *or* **lead sb. a ~'s life** jmdn. schäbig
behandeln; **~-'tired** *adj.* hundemüde
doing /'du:ɪŋ/ *n.* Tun, *das*
do-it-yourself /du:ɪtjə'self/ **1** *adj.*
Do-it-yourself-
2 *n.* Heimwerken, *das*
doldrums /'dɒldrəmz/ *n. pl.* **in the ~** (in
low spirits) niedergeschlagen; (Econ.) in einer
Flaute
dole /dəʊl/ **1** *n.* (coll.) **the ~:** Stempelgeld,
das (ugs.); **be/go on the ~:** stempeln gehen
(ugs.)
2 *v.t.* **~ out** [in kleinen Mengen] verteilen
doll /dɒl/ *n.* Puppe, *die*
dollar /'dɒlə(r)/ *n.* Dollar, *der*
dollar: ~ 'bill *n.* Dollarnote, *die;*
Dollarschein, *der;* **~ sign** *n.* Dollarzeichen,
das
dollop /'dɒləp/ *n.* (coll.) Klacks, *der* (ugs.)
'doll's house *n.* Puppenhaus, *das*
dolphin /'dɒlfɪn/ *n.* Delphin, *der*
domain /də'meɪn/ *n.* (a) Gebiet, *das*
(b) (Comp.) Domäne, *die;* Domain, *die;*
~ name Domänenname, *der*
dome /dəʊm/ *n.* Kuppel, *die*

domestic /də'mestɪk/ *adj.* (a) (household)
häuslich; (family) familiär ⟨*Angelegenheit,
Reibereien*⟩
(b) (Econ.) inländisch; Binnen-
(c) **~ animal/cat** Haustier, *das/*-katze, *die*
domesticated /də'mestɪkeɪtɪd/ *adj.*
gezähmt ⟨*Tier*⟩; (fig.) häuslich
domesticity /dəʊmes'tɪsɪtɪ, dɒmes'tɪsɪtɪ/
n. (being domestic) Häuslichkeit, *die*
domestic 'science *n.*
Hauswirtschaftslehre, *die*
dominant /'dɒmɪnənt/ *adj.* vorherrschend
dominate /'dɒmɪneɪt/ *v.t.* beherrschen
domination /dɒmɪ'neɪʃn/ *n.*
[Vor]herrschaft, *die* (**over** über + *Akk.*)
domineering /dɒmɪ'nɪərɪŋ/ *adj.* herrisch
domino /'dɒmɪnəʊ/ *n.* Domino[stein], *der;*
~es *sing.* (game) Domino[spiel], *das;* **play
~es** Domino spielen
'domino effect *n.* Dominoeffekt, *der*
don¹ /dɒn/ *v.t.* (Liter.) anlegen (geh.)
don² *n.* (Univ.) Dozent, *der*
donate /dəʊ'neɪt/ *v.t.* spenden; (on large
scale) stiften
donation /də'neɪʃn/ *n.* Spende, *die* (**to** für);
(large-scale) Stiftung, *die*
done /dʌn/ ▸ DO
donkey /'dɒŋkɪ/ *n.* Esel, *der*
donor /'dəʊnə(r)/ *n.* Spender, *der/*
Spenderin, *die*
don't /dəʊnt/ (coll.) = do not; ▸ DO
doodle /'du:dl/ *v.i.* [herum]kritzeln
doom /du:m/ **1** *n.* Verhängnis, *das*
2 *v.t.* verurteilen; **be ~ed** verloren sein;
be ~ed to fail *or* **failure** zum Scheitern
verurteilt sein
door /dɔ:(r)/ *n.* Tür, *die;* (of castle, barn) Tor,
das; **out of ~s** im Freien; **go out of ~s** nach
draußen gehen
door: ~bell *n.* Türklingel, *die;* **~frame**
n. Türrahmen, *der;* **~ handle** *n.*
Türklinke, *die;* **~keeper** *n.* Pförtner, *der;*
Portier, *der;* **~knob** *n.* Türknopf, -knauf,
der; **~man** *n.* Portier, *der;* **~mat** *n.*
Fußmatte, *die;* **~step** *n.* Türstufe, *die;* **on
one's/the ~step** (fig.) vor jmds. Tür; **~way**
n. Eingang, *der*
dope /dəʊp/ **1** *n.* (a) (sl.: narcotic) Stoff, *der*
(salopp)
(b) (coll.: fool) Dussel, *der*
2 *v.t.* dopen ⟨*Pferd, Athleten*⟩
dormant /'dɔ:mənt/ *adj.* ruhend ⟨*Tier,
Pflanze*⟩; untätig ⟨*Vulkan*⟩
dormitory /'dɔ:mɪtərɪ/ *n.* Schlafsaal, *der*
dormouse /'dɔ:maʊs/ *n., pl.* dormice
/'dɔ:maɪs/ Haselmaus, *die*
DOS /dɒs/ *abbr.* (Comp.) = **disk
operating system** DOS
dosage /'dəʊsɪdʒ/ *n.* (size of dose) Dosis, *die*
dose /dəʊs/ **1** *n.* Dosis, *die*
2 *v.t.* **~ sb. with sth.** jmdm. etw. geben

dot /dɒt/ *n.* Punkt, *der;* **on the ∼:** auf den Punkt genau

dot.com /'dɒtkɒm/ ⟦1⟧ *adj.* Dot-com- ⟦2⟧ *n.* Dot-com-Firma, *die*

dote /dəʊt/ *v.i.* **∼ on sb./sth.** jmdn./etw. abgöttisch lieben

'**dot matrix** *n.* (Comp.) Punktmatrix, *die;* **∼ printer** Nadeldrucker, *der*

dotted /'dɒtɪd/ *adj.* gepunktet

dotty /'dɒtɪ/ *adj.* (coll.) (silly) dümmlich; (feeble-minded) vertrottelt (ugs.); (absurd) blödsinnig (ugs.)

double /'dʌbl/ ⟦1⟧ *adj.* doppelt; **∼ bed/room** Doppelbett, *das/*-zimmer, *das;* **be ∼ the height/width/length** doppelt so hoch/breit/lang sein ⟦2⟧ *adv.* doppelt ⟦3⟧ *n.* (a) Doppelte, *das* (b) (twice as much) doppelt so viel; (twice as many) doppelt so viele (c) (person) Doppelgänger, *der/*-gängerin, *die* (d) *in pl.* (Tennis etc.) Doppel, *das* (e) **at the ∼** (Mil.) im Laufschritt; (fig.) ganz schnell ⟦4⟧ *v.t.* verdoppeln ⟦5⟧ *v.i.* sich verdoppeln

■ **double 'back** *v.i.* kehrtmachen (ugs.).

■ **double 'up** *v.i.* sich krümmen (**with** vor + *Dat.*)

double: **∼ 'agent** *n.* Doppelagent, *der/* -agentin, *die;* **∼-barrelled** (*Amer.:* **∼-barreled**) /'dʌblbærəld/ *adj.* doppelläufig; **∼-barrelled surname** (Brit.) Doppelname, *der;* **∼ 'bass** *n.* Kontrabass, *der;* **∼ 'bill** *n.* Doppelprogramm, *das;* **∼-breasted** /dʌbl'brestɪd/ *adj.* zwei- *od.* doppelreihig; **∼-breasted jacket** Zweireiher, *der;* **∼-'check** *v.t.* (verify twice) zweimal kontrollieren; (verify in two ways) zweifach überprüfen; **∼ 'chin** *n.* Doppelkinn, *das;* **∼-click** (Comp.) ⟦1⟧ *v.i.* doppelklicken; ⟦2⟧ *v.t.* **∼-click sth.** auf etw. (*Dat.*) doppelklicken; **∼ 'cream** *n.* Sahne mit hohem Fettgehalt; **∼-'cross** *v.t.* ein Doppelspiel treiben mit; **∼-decker** /dʌbl'dekə(r)/ *n.* Doppeldeckerbus, *der*

double entendre /duːbl ɑː'tɑ̃dr/ *n.* Zweideutigkeit, *die*

double: **∼-'glazed** *adj.* Doppel⟨fenster⟩; **∼ 'glazing** *n.* Doppelverglasung, *die;* **∼-'jointed** *adj.* sehr gelenkig; **∼ lesson** *n.* Doppelstunde, *die;* **∼-'lock** *v.t.* zweimal abschließen; **∼ 'meaning** ▶ DOUBLE ENTENDRE; **∼-page 'spread** *n.* **the advertisement was a ∼-page spread** die Anzeige war doppelseitig; **∼-'parking** *n.* Parken in der zweiten Reihe; **∼ 'room** *n.* Doppelzimmer, *das;* **∼ 'standard** *n.* (rule) Doppelmoral, *die;* **apply** *or* **operate a ∼ standard** *or* **∼ standards** mit zweierlei Maß messen; **∼ 'vision** *n.* Doppeltsehen, *die;* **∼ yellow 'lines** *n. pl.:* **am Fahrbahnrand verlaufende gelbe Doppellinie, die ein Halteverbot signalisiert**

doubly /'dʌblɪ/ *adv.* doppelt

doubt /daʊt/ ⟦1⟧ *n.* Zweifel, *der* (**about, as to, of** an + *Dat.*); **∼[s]** [**about** *or* **as to sth./as to whether …**] (as to future) Ungewissheit, (as to fact) Unsicherheit [über etw. (*Akk.*)/ darüber, ob …]; **there's no ∼ that …:** es besteht kein Zweifel daran, dass …; **∼[s]** (hesitations) Bedenken *Pl.* (**about** gegen); **no ∼** (certainly) gewiss; (probably) sicherlich ⟦2⟧ *v.i.* zweifeln ⟦3⟧ *v.t.* zweifeln an (+ *Dat.*); **I don't ∼ that** *or* **it ich bezweifle das nicht; I ∼ whether** *or* **if** *or* **that …:** ich bezweifle, dass …

doubtful /'daʊtfl/ *adj.* skeptisch ⟨Wesen⟩; ungläubig ⟨Blick⟩

doubtless /'daʊtlɪs/ *adv.* (a) (certainly) gewiss (b) (probably) sicherlich

dough /dəʊ/ *n.* (a) Teig, *der* (b) (coll.: money) Knete, *die* (salopp)

'**doughnut** *n.* [Berliner] Pfannkuchen, *der*

douse /daʊs/ *v.t.* übergießen; (extinguish) ausmachen

dove[1] /dʌv/ *n.* Taube, *die*

dove[2] /dəʊv/ ▶ DIVE 1

dovecot, dovecote /'dʌvkɒt/ *n.* Taubenschlag, *der;* **flutter the ∼cots** (fig.) für einige Aufregung sorgen

dowdy /'daʊdɪ/ *adj.* unansehnlich; (shabby) schäbig

down[1] /daʊn/ *n.* (feathers) Daunen *Pl.*

down[2] ⟦1⟧ *adv.* (a) (to lower place) herunter/ hinunter; (in lift) abwärts (b) (in lower place, downstairs) unten; **∼ there/ here** da/hier unten; **the next floor ∼:** ein Stockwerk tiefer; **be ∼ with an illness** eine Krankheit haben; **be three points/games ∼:** mit drei Punkten/Spielen zurückliegen ⟦2⟧ *prep.* herunter/hinunter; **lower ∼ the river** weiter unten am Fluss; **walk ∼ the hill/ road** den Berg/die Straße heruntergehen; **fall ∼ the stairs/steps** die Treppe/Stufen herunterstürzen; **fall ∼ a hole/ditch** in ein Loch/ einen Graben fallen; **go ∼ the pub** in die Kneipe gehen; **live just ∼ the road** ein Stück weiter unten in der Straße wohnen; **be ∼ the pub/town** in der Kneipe/Stadt sein; **I've got coffee [all] ∼ my skirt** mein ganzer Rock ist voll Kaffee ⟦3⟧ *v.t.* (coll.) schlucken (ugs.) ⟨Getränk⟩; **∼ tools** die Arbeit niederlegen

down: **∼-and-'out** *n.* Stadtstreicher, *der/*-streicherin, *die;* **∼-cast** *adj.* niedergeschlagen; **∼-fall** *n.* Untergang, *der;* **∼-'hearted** *adj.* niedergeschlagen; **∼-'hill** *adv.* bergab; **∼-load** *v.t.* (Comp.) herunterladen; **∼-market** *adj.* weniger anspruchsvoll; **∼ payment** *n.* Anzahlung, *die;* **∼-pour** *n.* Regenguss, *der;* **∼-right** *adj.* ausgemacht; glatt ⟨Lüge⟩; **∼-size** ⟦1⟧ *v.t.* verschlanken; ⟦2⟧ *v.i.* abspecken; **∼-stairs** ⟦1⟧ /-'-/ *adv.* die Treppe hinunter⟨gehen, -fallen, -kommen⟩; unten ⟨wohnen, sein⟩; ⟦2⟧ /'--/ *adj.* im Erdgeschoss

nachgestellt; ~**'stream** *adv.* flussabwärts;
~**-to-'earth** *adj.* sachlich; ~**town** *adv.*
im/(direction) ins Stadtzentrum; ~**trodden**
adj. unterdrückt; ~**turn** *n.* (Econ., Commerc.)
Abschwung, *der;* ~ **'under** *adv.* (coll.)
in/(to) nach Australien/Neuseeland
downward /'daʊnwəd/ ⓵ *adj.* nach
unten gerichtet
⓶ *adv.* abwärts ⟨*sich bewegen*⟩; nach unten
⟨*sehen, gehen*⟩
downwards /'daʊnwədz/ ▶ DOWNWARD 2
dowry /'daʊrɪ/ *n.* Aussteuer, *die*
doz. *abbr.* = **dozen** Dtzd.
doze /dəʊz/ ⓵ *v.i.* dösen (ugs.)
⓶ *n.* Nickerchen, *das* (ugs.)
■ **doze 'off** *v.i.* eindösen (ugs.)
dozen /'dʌzn/ *n.* (a) Dutzend, *das;* half a
~: sechs
(b) *in pl.* (coll.: many) Dutzende *Pl.*
Dr *abbr.* = **doctor** Dr.
drab /dræb/ *adj.* langweilig; trostlos
⟨*Landschaft*⟩; eintönig ⟨*Leben*⟩
draft /drɑːft/ ⓵ *n.* (a) (of speech) Konzept,
das; (of treaty, bill) Entwurf, *der*
(b) (Amer.) ▶ DRAUGHT
⓶ *v.t.* entwerfen
drafty (Amer.) ▶ DRAUGHTY
drag /dræg/ ⓵ *v.t.,* -gg- schleppen; (Comp.)
ziehen; ~ **and drop** ziehen und ablegen
⓶ *v.i.,* -gg- schleifen; (fig.: pass slowly) sich
[hin]schleppen
⓷ *n.* (a) (coll.) **in** ~: in Frauenkleidung
(b) (coll.: at cigarette) Zug, *der*
■ **drag 'down** *v.t.* nach unten ziehen;
~ **sb. down to one's own level** (fig.) jmdn.
auf sein Niveau herabziehen
■ **drag 'on** *v.i.* sich [da]hinschleppen
dragon /'drægn/ *n.* Drache, *der*
'dragonfly *n.* Libelle, *die*
drain /dreɪn/ ⓵ *n.* Abflussrohr, *das;*
(underground) Kanalisationsrohr, *das;* (grating
at roadside) Gully, *der;* **go down the** ~ (fig.
coll.) für die Katz sein (ugs.)
⓶ *v.t.* (a) trockenlegen ⟨*Teich*⟩; entwässern
⟨*Land*⟩; ableiten ⟨*Wasser*⟩
(b) (Cookery) abgießen ⟨*Wasser, Gemüse*⟩
(c) austrinken ⟨*Glas*⟩
⓷ *v.i.* ⟨*Flüssigkeit:*⟩ ablaufen; ⟨*Geschirr,
Gemüse:*⟩ abtropfen
drainage /'dreɪnɪdʒ/ *n.* Kanalisation, *die*
'draining board (Brit.; Amer.:
'drainboard) *n.* Abtropfbrett, *das*
'drainpipe *n.* Regen[abfall]rohr, *das*
drake /dreɪk/ *n.* Enterich, *der*
drama /'drɑːmə/ *n.* Drama, *das*
dramatic /drə'mætɪk/ *adj.* dramatisch
dramatist /'dræmətɪst/ *n.* Dramatiker,
der/Dramatikerin, *die*
dramatize /'dræmətaɪz/ *v.t.*
dramatisieren
drank ▶ DRINK 2

drape /dreɪp/ ⓵ *v.t.* drapieren
⓶ *n.* (Amer.: curtain) Vorhang, *der*
'draper *n.* (Brit.) Textilkaufmann, *der;* ~**'s**
[shop] Textilgeschäft, *das*
drastic /'dræstɪk/ *adj.* drastisch
draught /drɑːft/ *n.* [Luft]zug, *der;* **there's a**
~: es zieht
draught: ~ **'beer** *n.* Fassbier, *das;*
~ **board** *n.* (Brit.) Damebrett, *das;*
~ **excluder** *n.* Abdichtvorrichtung, *die;*
Zugluft-Verhinderer, *der;* ~**proof** *adj.*
winddicht
draughts /drɑːfts/ *n.* (Brit.) Damespiel, *das*
'draughtsman /-mən/ *n., pl.*
draughtsmen /-mən/ Zeichner,
der/Zeichnerin, *die*
'draughty *adj.* zugig
draw /drɔː/ ⓵ *v.t.,* drew /druː/, drawn
/drɔːn/ (a) (pull) ziehen; ~ **the curtains/
blinds** (close) die Vorhänge zuziehen/die
Jalousien herunterlassen; ~ **sth. towards
one** etw. zu sich heranziehen
(b) (attract) anlocken; **be** ~**n to sb.** von
jmdm. angezogen werden
(c) (take out) herausziehen; schöpfen
⟨*Wasser*⟩; ~ **money from the bank** Geld bei
der Bank holen/abheben
(d) beziehen ⟨*Gehalt, Rente,
Arbeitslosenunterstützung*⟩
(e) ziehen ⟨*Strich*⟩; zeichnen ⟨*geometrische
Figur, Bild*⟩
(f) ziehen ⟨*Parallele, Vergleich*⟩;
herausstellen ⟨*Unterschied*⟩
⓶ *v.i.* (a) drew, drawn: ~ **to an end** zu Ende
gehen
(b) (Sport) **they drew [three-all]** sie spielten
[3 : 3] unentschieden
⓷ *n.* (a) (raffle) Tombola, *die*
(b) (of lottery) Ziehung, *die*
(c) ([result of] drawn game) Unentschieden, *das;*
end in a ~: mit einem Unentschieden enden
■ **draw 'back** ⓵ *v.t.* zurückziehen
⓶ *v.i.* zurückweichen
■ **draw 'in** *v.i.* einfahren; ⟨*Tage:*⟩ kürzer
werden
■ **draw 'out** *v.i.* abfahren; ⟨*Tage:*⟩ länger
werden
■ **draw 'up** ⓵ *v.t.* (a) aufsetzen ⟨*Vertrag*⟩;
aufstellen ⟨*Liste*⟩
(b) (pull closer) heranziehen
⓶ *v.i.* [an]halten
draw: ~**back** *n.* Nachteil, *der;* ~**bridge**
n. Zugbrücke, *die*
drawer /drɔː(r), 'drɔːə(r)/ *n.* Schublade, *die*
'drawing *n.* (sketch) Zeichnung, *die*
drawing: ~ **board** *n.* Zeichenbrett, *das;*
~ **pin** *n.* (Brit.) Reißzwecke, *die;* ~ **room**
n. Salon, *der*
drawl /drɔːl/ ⓵ *v.i.* gedehnt sprechen
⓶ *n.* gedehntes Sprechen
drawn ▶ DRAW 1, 2
dread /dred/ ⓵ *v.t.* sich sehr fürchten
vor (+ *Dat.*); **the** ~**ed day/moment** der ⋯⟶

gefürchtete Tag/Augenblick
[2] *n.* Angst, *die*
dreadful /'dredfl/ *adj.* schrecklich; (coll.:
very bad) fürchterlich; **I feel** ~ (unwell) ich
fühle mich scheußlich (ugs.)
'**dreadfully** *adv.* schrecklich; (coll.: very
badly) fürchterlich
dream /driːm/ [1] *n.* Traum, *der; attrib.*
traumhaft; Traum‹haus, -auto, -urlaub›;
have a ~ **about sb./sth.** von jmdm./etw.
träumen
[2] *v.i. & t.* dreamt /dremt/ *or* dreamed
träumen
'**dreamer** *n.* (in sleep) Träumende, *der/die;*
(day~) Träumer, *der/*Träumerin, *die*
dreary /'drɪərɪ/ *adj.* trostlos
dredge /dredʒ/ *v.t.* ausbaggern
'**dredger** *n.* Bagger, *der*
dregs /dregz/ *n. pl.* [Boden]satz, *der*
drench /drentʃ/ *v.t.* durchnässen
dress /dres/ [1] *n.* Kleid, *das;* (clothing)
Kleidung, *die*
[2] *v.t.* (a) anziehen; **be well** ~ed gut
gekleidet sein; **get** ~ed sich anziehen
(b) verbinden ‹*Wunde*›
[3] *v.i.* sich anziehen
▪ **dress 'up** *v.i.* sich fein machen
dress: ~ **circle** *n.* (Theatre) erster Rang;
~ **designer** *n.* Modeschöpfer, *der/*
-schöpferin, *die*
'**dresser** *n.* (a) Anrichte, *die*
(b) (Amer.) ▸ DRESSING TABLE
'**dressing** *n.* (a) *no pl.* Anziehen, *das*
(b) (Cookery) Dressing, *das*
(c) (Med.) Verband, *der*
dressing: ~ **gown** *n.* Bademantel,
der; ~ **room** *n.* (Sport) Umkleideraum,
der; (for actor) Garderobe, *die;* ~ **table** *n.*
Frisierkommode, *die*
dress: ~**maker** *n.* Damenschneider,
der/-schneiderin, *die;* ~**making** *n.*
Damenschneiderei, *die;* ~ **rehearsal** *n.*
Generalprobe, *die*
drew ▸ DRAW 1, 2
dribble /'drɪbl/ *v.i.* (a) (slobber) sabbern
(b) (Sport) dribbeln
dried /draɪd/ *adj.* getrocknet; ~ **fruit[s]**
Dörrobst, *das;* ~ **milk** Trockenmilch, *die*
drier /'draɪə(r)/ *n.* (for hair) Trockenhaube,
die; (hand-held) Föhn, *der;* (for laundry)
[Wäsche]trockner, *der*
drift /drɪft/ [1] *n.* (a) (of snow or sand)
Verwehung, *die*
(b) (gist) **get** *or* **catch the** ~ **of sth.** etw im
Wesentlichen verstehen
[2] *v.i.* (a) treiben; ‹*Wolke:*› ziehen
(b) ‹*Sand, Schnee:*› zusammengeweht
werden
'**driftwood** *n.* Treibholz, *das*
drill /drɪl/ [1] *n.* (a) (tool) Bohrer, *der*
(b) (Mil.: training) Drill, *der*
[2] *v.t. & i.* bohren (**for** nach)

'**drill bit** *n.* Bohrer, *der*
drink /drɪŋk/ [1] *n.* Getränk, *das;* (alcoholic)
Glas, *das;* (not with food) Drink, *der;* **have a** ~:
[etwas] trinken; (alcoholic) ein Glas trinken
[2] *v.t. & i.* drank /dræŋk/, drunk /drʌŋk/
trinken
drinkable /'drɪŋkəbl/ *adj.* trinkbar
'**drink-driving** *n.* Fahren unter
Alkoholeinfluss; Alkohol am Steuer;
~ **offence** Alkoholdelikt, *das*
drinker /'drɪŋkə(r)/ *n.* Trinker,
*der/*Trinkerin, *die*
drinking /'drɪŋkɪŋ/: ~ **fountain**
n. Trinkbrunnen, *der;* ~ **water** *n.*
Trinkwasser, *das*
drip /drɪp/ [1] *n.* (a) Tropfen, *das*
(b) (coll.: feeble person) Schlappschwanz, *der*
(salopp)
[2] *v.i.,* **-pp-** tropfen; **be** ~**ping with water/**
moisture triefend nass sein
'**drip-dry** *adj.* bügelfrei
'**dripping** *n.* (Cookery) Schmalz, *das*
drive /draɪv/ [1] *n.* (a) Fahrt, *die*
(b) (private road) Zufahrt, *die;* (entrance) (to
small building) Einfahrt, *die;* (to large building)
Auffahrt, *die*
(c) (energy) Tatkraft, *die*
(d) (Psych.) Trieb, *der*
(e) (Motor Veh.) **left-hand/right-hand** ~:
Links-/Rechtssteuerung, *die*
[2] *v.t.,* **drove** /drəʊv/, **driven** /'drɪvn/
(a) fahren
(b) treiben ‹*Tier*›
(c) (compel to move) vertreiben (**out of, from**
aus)
(d) (fig.) ~ **sb. to sth.** jmdn. zu etw. treiben;
~ **sb. to do sth.** *or* **into doing sth.** jmdn.
dazu treiben, etw. zu tun
(e) (power) antreiben
[3] *v.i.,* **drove, driven** (a) fahren; **can you** ~?
kannst du Auto fahren?
(b) (go by car) mit dem [eigenen] Auto fahren
▪ '**drive at** *v.t.* (fig.) hinauswollen auf
(+ *Akk.*); **what are you driving at?** worauf
wollen Sie hinaus?
▪ **drive a'way** [1] *v.i.* wegfahren
[2] *v.t.* (a) wegfahren
(b) (chase away) vertreiben
▪ **drive 'off** ▸ DRIVE AWAY
▪ **drive 'on** *v.i.* weiterfahren
▪ **drive 'up** *v.i.* vorfahren (**to** vor + *Dat.*)
'**drive-in** *adj.* Drive-in-; ~ **cinema** *or* (Amer.)
movie [theater] *n.* Autokino, *das*
drivel /'drɪvl/ *n.* Gefasel, *das* (ugs.); **talk**
~: faseln (ugs.)
driven ▸ DRIVE 2, 3
driver /'draɪvə(r)/ *n.* (a) Fahrer,
*der/*Fahrerin, *die;* (of locomotive) Führer,
*der/*Führerin, *die;* ~'**s license** (Amer.)
Führerschein, *der*
(b) (Comp.) Treiber, *der*
driving /'draɪvɪŋ/ [1] *n.* Fahren, *das*
[2] *adj.* peitschend ‹*Regen*›

driving: ∼ **force** n. treibende Kraft; Triebfeder, die; the ∼ **force behind sth.** die treibende Kraft hinter etw.; ∼ **gloves** n. pl. Autohandschuhe Pl.; ∼ **instructor** n. Fahrlehrer, der/-lehrerin, die; ∼ **lesson** n. Fahrstunde, die; ∼ **licence** n. Führerschein, der; ∼ **mirror** n. Rückspiegel, der; ∼ **school** n. Fahrschule, die; ∼ **test** n. Fahrprüfung, die

drizzle /'drɪzl/ ① n. Nieseln, das ② v.i. it's drizzling es nieselt

drone /drəʊn/ ① v.i. (a) ⟨Biene:⟩ summen; ⟨Maschine:⟩ brummen (b) ⟨Rezitator:⟩ leiern ② n. ▶ 1: Summen, das; Brummen, das; Geleier, das

drool /dru:l/ v.i. ∼ over eine kindische Freude haben an (+ Dat.)

droop /dru:p/ v.i. herunterhängen; ⟨Blume:⟩ den Kopf hängen lassen

drop /drɒp/ ① n. (a) Tropfen, der; in ∼s tropfenweise (b) (decrease) Rückgang, der ② v.i., -pp-: (a) (fall) (accidentally) [herunter]fallen; (deliberately) sich [hinunter]fallen lassen (b) (in amount etc.) sinken; ⟨Preis, Wert:⟩ sinken, fallen; ⟨Wind:⟩ sich legen; ⟨Stimme:⟩ sich senken ③ v.t., -pp-: (a) fallen lassen; abwerfen ⟨Bomben, Nachschub⟩ (b) (discontinue, abandon) fallen lassen; ∼ out of university/the course das Studium abbrechen od. aufgeben (c) (omit) auslassen
■ **drop 'by, drop 'in** v.i. vorbeikommen
■ **drop 'off** ① v.i. (a) (fall off) abfallen (b) (fall asleep) einnicken ② v.t. absetzen ⟨Fahrgast⟩
■ **drop 'out** v.i. (a) herausfallen (of aus) (b) (withdraw) aussteigen (ugs.) (of aus); (beforehand) seine Teilnahme absagen

drop: ∼-**down menu** n. (Comp.) Dropdownmenü, das; ∼ **handlebars** n. pl. Rennlenker, der; ∼ **kick** n. (Football) Dropkick, der

droplet /'drɒplɪt/ n. Tröpfchen, das

dropout /'drɒpaʊt/ n. Aussteiger, der/Aussteigerin, die

dropper /'drɒpə(r)/ n. (esp. Med.) Tropfer, der

drop shot n. (Tennis etc.) Stoppball, der

drought /draʊt/ n. Dürre, die

drove ▶ DRIVE 2, 3

drown /draʊn/ ① v.i. ertrinken ② v.t. ertränken; be ∼ed ertrinken

drowse /draʊz/ v.i. [vor sich hin]dösen

drowsy /'draʊzɪ/ adj. schläfrig; (on just waking) verschlafen

drudgery /'drʌdʒərɪ/ n. Schufterei, die

drug /drʌg/ ① n. (a) (Med.) [Arznei]mittel, das (b) (narcotic) Droge, die; be on ∼s Rauschgift

nehmen ② v.t., -gg- betäuben ⟨Person⟩; ∼ sb.'s food/drink jmds. Essen/Getränk (Dat.) ein Betäubungsmittel beimischen

drug: ∼ **abuse** n. Drogenmissbrauch, der; ∼ **abuser** n. Drogenmissbrauch Treibender/Treibende; ∼ **addict** n. Drogensüchtige, der/die; ∼ **addiction** n. Drogensucht, die; ∼ **dealer** n. Drogenhändler, der/-händlerin, die; Dealer, der/Dealerin, die (Drogenjargon); ∼ **peddler** ▶ DRUG DEALER; ∼-**related** adj. Drogen⟨tote, -kriminalität, -delikt, -probleme⟩; ∼ **scene** n. Drogenszene, die; ∼**store** n. (Amer.) Drugstore, der; ∼-**taking** n. Drogeneinnahme, die; ∼ **test** n. Dopingkontrolle, die/ Dopingtest, der; ∼ **trafficking** n. Drogenhandel, der; ∼ **user** n. Drogenkonsument, der/ -konsumentin, die

drum /drʌm/ ① n. (a) Trommel, die (b) in pl. (in jazz or pop) Schlagzeug, das (c) (container) Fass, das ② v.i. trommeln
■ **drum 'up** v.i. auftreiben

'drum beat n. Trommelschlag, der

'drummer n. Schlagzeuger, der

'drumstick n. (a) Trommelschlägel, der (b) (Cookery) Keule, die

drunk /drʌŋk/ ① adj. be ∼: betrunken sein; get ∼: betrunken werden (on von); (intentionally) sich betrinken (on mit) ② n. Betrunkene, der/die

drunkard /'drʌŋkəd/ n. Trinker, der/Trinkerin, die

drunken /'drʌŋkn/ attrib. adj. betrunken; (habitually) ständig betrunken; ∼ **driving** Trunkenheit am Steuer

'drunkenness n. Betrunkenheit, die; (habitual) Trunksucht, die

dry /draɪ/ ① adj. trocken; (very ∼) herb ⟨Wein⟩; ausgetrocknet ⟨Flussbett⟩; get or become ∼: trocknen ② v.t. (a) trocknen ⟨Haare, Wäsche⟩; abtrocknen ⟨Geschirr, Baby⟩; ∼ oneself sich abtrocknen; ∼ one's eyes or tears/hands sich (Dat.) die Tränen abwischen/die Hände abtrocknen (b) (preserve) trocknen; dörren ⟨Obst, Fleisch⟩ ③ v.i. trocknen
■ **dry 'out** v.t. & i. trocknen
■ **dry 'up** ① v.t. abtrocknen ② v.i. (a) (∼ the dishes) abtrocknen (b) ⟨Brunnen, Quelle:⟩ versiegen; ⟨Fluss, Teich:⟩ austrocknen

dry: ∼-'**clean** v.t. chemisch reinigen; ∼-'**cleaner's** n. chemische Reinigung; ∼-'**cleaning** n. chemische Reinigung

'dryer ▶ DRIER

dry: ∼-**eyed** adj. ohne Rührung; ∼ '**ice** n. Trockeneis, das

drying-'up n. Abtrocknen, das; do the ∼ abtrocknen; attrib. ∼ **cloth** Geschirrtuch, das

'dryness n. Trockenheit, die

dry 'rot n. Trockenfäule, die

dual /'dju:əl/ adj. doppelt

dual: ~ **'carriageway** n. (Brit.)
Straße mit Mittelstreifen; ~ **con'trol** n.
(Aeronaut.) Doppelsteuerung, die; (Motor Veh.)
doppelte Bedienungselemente Pl.;
~-'**purpose** adj. zweifach verwendbar

dub /dʌb/ v.t., -bb- (Cinemat.)
synchronisieren

dubious /'dju:bɪəs/ adj. (doubting)
unschlüssig; (suspicious) zweifelhaft

duchess /'dʌtʃɪs/ n. Herzogin, die

duck /dʌk/ [1] n. Ente, die
[2] v.i. sich [schnell] ducken
[3] v.t. ~ one's head den Kopf einziehen

duckling /'dʌklɪŋ/ n. Entenküken, das

'duck pond n. Ententeich, der

duct /dʌkt/ n. Rohr, das; (for air) Ventil, das

dud /dʌd/ [1] n. (useless thing) Niete, die
(ugs.); (counterfeit) Fälschung, die
[2] adj. mies (ugs.); schlecht; (fake) gefälscht;
geplatzt ⟨Scheck⟩

dude /dju:d, du:d/ n. (esp. Amer. coll.) Typ,
der (ugs.)

due /dju:/ [1] adj. (a) (owed) geschuldet;
zustehend ⟨Eigentum, Recht usw.⟩; there's
sth. ~ to me, I've got sth. ~: mir steht etw.
zu
(b) (immediately payable) fällig
(c) (that it is proper to give or use) gebührend;
angemessen ⟨Belohnung⟩; be ~ to sb. jmdm.
gebühren; with all ~ respect bei allem
gebotenen Respekt
(d) (attributable) the mistake was ~ to
negligence der Fehler war durch
Nachlässigkeit verursacht; it's ~ to her that
we missed the train ihretwegen verpassten
wir den Zug
(e) (scheduled, expected); be ~ to do sth. etw.
tun sollen; be ~ [to arrive] ankommen
sollen
(f) (likely to get, deserving) be ~ for sth. etw.
verdienen
[2] adv. (a) ~ north genau nach Norden
(b) ~ to aufgrund (+ Gen.); auf Grund
(+ Gen.)
[3] n. (a) give sb. his ~: jmdm.
Gerechtigkeit widerfahren lassen
(b) ~s (fees) Gebühren usw.

duel /'dju:əl/ n. Duell, das

duet /dju:'et/ n. (for voices) Duett, das;
(instrumental) Duo, das

duffle /'dʌfl/: ~ **bag** n. Matchbeutel, der;
~ **coat** n. Dufflecoat, der

dug ▶ DIG

duke /dju:k/ n. Herzog, der

dull /dʌl/ [1] adj. (a) (stupid) beschränkt;
(slow to understand) begriffsstutzig
(b) (boring) langweilig
(c) (gloomy) trübe ⟨Wetter, Tag⟩
[2] v.t. abstumpfen ⟨Geist, Sinne, Verstand⟩

duly /'dju:lɪ/ adv. ordnungsgemäß

dumb /dʌm/ adj. (a) stumm
(b) (coll.: stupid) doof (ugs.)

■ **dumb down** v.t. & i. (coll.) verflachen

dumbfounded /dʌm'faʊndɪd/ adj.
sprachlos

dummy /'dʌmɪ/ n. (a) (of tailor)
Schneiderpuppe, die; (in shop)
Schaufensterpuppe, die; (of ventriloquist)
Puppe, die; (stupid person) Dummkopf, der
(ugs.); like a stuffed ~: wie ein Ölgötze (ugs.)
(b) (imitation) Attrappe, die
(c) (esp. Brit.: for baby) Schnuller, der

dump /dʌmp/ [1] n. (a) (place) Müllkippe,
die; (heap) Müllhaufen, der; (permanent)
Müllhalde, die
(b) (Mil.) Depot, das
(c) (coll.: town) Kaff, das (ugs.)
[2] v.t. (dispose of) werfen; (deposit) abladen
⟨Sand, Müll usw.⟩; (leave) lassen; (place)
abstellen

'dumping ground n. Müllkippe, die; (fig.)
Abstellplatz, der

dumpling /'dʌmplɪŋ/ n. Kloß, der

dumps /dʌmps/ n. pl. be or feel down in the
~: ganz down sein (ugs.)

'dump truck n. Kipper, der

dunce /dʌns/ n. Null, die (ugs.)

dune /dju:n/ n. Düne, die

dung /dʌŋ/ n. Dung, der

dungarees /dʌŋgə'ri:z/ n. pl. Latzhose,
die

dungeon /'dʌndʒən/ n. Kerker, der

dunk /dʌŋk/ v.t. tunken

dupe /dju:p/ [1] v.t. übertölpeln
[2] n. Dumme, der/die

duplex /'dju:pleks/ adj. (esp. Amer.) (two-
storey) zweistöckig ⟨Wohnung⟩; (two-family)
Zweifamilien⟨haus⟩

duplicate [1] /'dju:plɪkət/ adj. (a) (identical)
Zweit-
(b) (twofold) doppelt
[2] n. Kopie, die; (second copy of letter/document/
key) Duplikat, das; in ~: in doppelter
Ausfertigung
[3] /'dju:plɪkeɪt/ v.t. (a) (make a copy of, make in
~) ~ sth. eine zweite Anfertigung von etw.
machen
(b) (on machine) vervielfältigen
(c) (do twice) noch einmal tun

duplicity /dju:'plɪsɪtɪ/ n. Falschheit, die

durability /djʊərə'bɪlɪtɪ/ n. (of friendship,
peace, etc.) Dauerhaftigkeit, die; (of garment,
material) Haltbarkeit, die

durable /'djʊərəbl/ adj. haltbar; dauerhaft
⟨Friede, Freundschaft usw.⟩

duration /djʊə'reɪʃn/ n. Dauer, die

duress /djʊə'res/ n. Zwang, der

during /'djʊərɪŋ/ prep. während; (at a point
in) in (+ Dat.)

dusk /dʌsk/ n. Einbruch der Dunkelheit

dust /dʌst/ [1] n. Staub, der
[2] v.t. abstauben ⟨Möbel⟩; ~ a room/ house

in einem Zimmer/Haus Staub wischen
3 *v.i.* Staub wischen
dust: ~bin *n.* (Brit.) Mülltonne, *die;* **~cart**
n. (Brit.) Müllwagen, *der;* **~ cloth** *n.*
Schonbezug, *der;* (duster) Staubtuch, *das*
'duster *n.* Staubtuch, *das*
dust: ~ jacket *n.* Schutzumschlag, *der;*
~man /-mən/ *n., pl.* **~men** /-mən/ (Brit.)
Müllmann, *der;* **~pan** *n.* Kehrschaufel, *die*
'dusty *adj.* staubig; verstaubt ⟨*Bücher,
Möbel*⟩
Dutch /dʌtʃ/ **1** *adj.* holländisch; *sb.* is ~:
jmd. ist Holländer/Holländerin
2 *n.* (a) (language) Holländisch, *das; see also*
ENGLISH 2A
(b) the ~ *pl.* die Holländer *usw.*
Dutch: ~ 'courage *n.* angetrunkener
Mut; ~ **'elm disease** *n.* Ulmensterben,
das; **~man** /-mən/ *n., pl.* **~men** /-mən/
Holländer, *der;* **~woman** *n.* Holländerin,
die
dutiful /'djuːtɪfl/ *adj.,* **'dutifully** *adv.*
pflichtbewusst
duty /'djuːtɪ/ *n.* (a) Pflicht, *die;* (task)
Aufgabe, *die;* **be on** ~: Dienst haben; **off**
~: nicht im Dienst; **be off** ~: keinen Dienst
haben; ⟨*ab … Uhr*⟩ dienstfrei sein
(b) (tax) Zoll, *der;* **pay** ~ **on sth.** Zoll für etw.
bezahlen
'duty-free *adj., adv.* zollfrei

duvet /'duːveɪ/ *n.* Federbett, *das;* ~ **cover**
Bettbezug, *der*
DVD *abbr.* = **digital video disc** DVD;
~ **drive** DVD-Laufwerk, *das;* ~ **player** DVD-
Spieler, *der;* DVD-Player, *der;* ~ **burner,**
~ **writer** DVD-Brenner, *der*
dwarf /dwɔːf/ *n., pl.* ~s *or* dwarves
/'dwɔːvz/ Zwerg, *der*/Zwergin, *die*
dwell /dwel/ *v.i.,* dwelt /dwelt/ (literary)
wohnen
■ **'dwell [up]on** *v.t.* (in discussion) sich
ausführlich befassen mit; (in thought) in
Gedanken verweilen bei
'dwelling *n.* Wohnung, *die*
dwelt ▶ DWELL
dwindle /'dwɪndl/ *v.i.* ~ **[away]** abnehmen;
⟨*Unterstützung, Interesse:*⟩ nachlassen;
⟨*Vorräte:*⟩ schrumpfen
dye /daɪ/ **1** *n.* Färbemittel, *das*
2 *v.t.,* ~**ing** /'daɪɪŋ/ färben
dying /'daɪɪŋ/ *adj.* sterbend; absterbend
⟨*Baum*⟩
dyke ▶ DIKE
dynamic /daɪ'næmɪk/ *adj.* dynamisch
dynamism /'daɪnəmɪzm/ *n.* Dynamik, *die*
dynamite /'daɪnəmaɪt/ *n.* Dynamit, *das*
dynamo /'daɪnəməʊ/ *n.* Dynamo, *der;* (in
car) Lichtmaschine, *die*
dynasty /'dɪnəstɪ/ *n.* Dynastie, *die*
dysentery /'dɪsəntrɪ/ *n.* Ruhr, *die*

Ee

E, e /iː/ *n.* E, e, *das*
E. *abbr.* (a) = **east** O
(b) = **eastern** ö
each /iːtʃ/ **1** *adj.* jeder/jede/jedes; **they
cost** *or* **are a pound** ~: sie kosten ein Pfund
pro Stück
2 *pron.* (a) jeder/jede/jedes
(b) ~ **other** sich
eager /'iːɡə(r)/ *adj.* eifrig; **be** ~ **to do sth.**
etw. unbedingt tun wollen
'eagerly *adv.* eifrig; gespannt ⟨*warten*⟩
eagle /'iːɡl/ *n.* Adler, *der*
eagle-'eyed *adj.* adleräugig
ear¹ /ɪə(r)/ *n.* Ohr, *das;* **up to one's** ~**s in
work/debt** bis zum Hals in Arbeit/Schulden;
be[come] all ~**s** [plötzlich] ganz Ohr sein;
play by ~ (Mus.) nach dem Gehör spielen
ear² *n.* (Bot.) Ähre, *die*
ear: ~ache *n.* Ohrenschmerzen *Pl.;*
~ **clip** *n.* Ohr[en]klipp, *der;* ~ **drops**
n. pl. (a) (Med.) Ohrentropfen *Pl.;*

(b) (earrings) Ohrgehänge, *das;* ~**drum** *n.*
Trommelfell, *das*
earl /ɜːl/ *n.* Graf, *der*
'ear lobe *n.* Ohrläppchen, *das*
early /'ɜːlɪ/ **1** *adj.* früh
2 *adv.* früh; **I am a bit** ~: ich bin etwas zu
früh gekommen; ~ **next week** Anfang der
nächsten Woche; ~ **in June** Anfang Juni; **from**
~ **in the morning till late at night** von früh
[morgens] bis spät [nachts]; ~ **on** schon früh
early: ~ 'closing *n.* **it is** ~ **closing** die
Geschäfte haben nachmittags geschlossen;
~**-'closing day** *n.:* Tag, an dem die
Geschäfte nachmittags geschlossen haben
ear: ~mark *v.t.* vorsehen; ~**muffs** *n. pl.*
Ohrenschützer, *Pl.*
earn /ɜːn/ *v.t.* verdienen; (bring in as income or
interest) einbringen
earnest /'ɜːnɪst/ **1** *adj.* ernsthaft
2 *n.* **in** ~: mit vollem Ernst
earnings /'ɜːnɪŋz/ *n. pl.* Verdienst,
der; (of business etc.) Ertrag, *der*

ear: ~phones *n. pl.* Kopfhörer, *der;*
~piece *n.* Hörmuschel, *die;* **~-piercing**
1 *adj.* durch Mark und Bein gehend ‹*Lärm*›;
2 *n.* Durchstechen der Ohrläppchen;
~plug *n.* Ohropax, *das* ⓌⓏ*;* **~ring** *n.*
Ohrring, *der;* **~shot** *n.* out of/within **~**shot
außer/in Hörweite; **~-splitting** *adj.*
ohrenbetäubend

earth /ɜ:θ/ **1** *n.* (also Brit. Electr.) Erde, *die;*
how/what *etc.* on **~** …? wie/was *usw.* in
aller Welt …?
2 *v.t.* (Brit. Electr.) erden

earthenware /'ɜ:θnweə(r)/ **1** *n.*
Tonwaren *usw.*
2 *adj.* Ton-

earthly /'ɜ:θlɪ/ *adj.* irdisch; **no ~** use *etc.*
(coll.) nicht der geringste Nutzen *usw.*

earth: ~quake *n.* Erdbeben, *das;*
~ sciences *n. pl.* Geowissenschaften *Pl.;*
~worm *n.* Regenwurm, *der*

'earthy *adj.* (a) erdig
(b) (coarse) derb

'earwax *n.* Ohrenschmalz, *das*

earwig /'ɪəwɪɡ/ *n.* Ohrwurm, *der*

ease /i:z/ **1** *n.* (a) set sb. at **~:** jmdn.
beruhigen; **at [one's] ~:** entspannt; **be** *or*
feel **at [one's] ~:** sich wohl fühlen; **[stand] at**
~! (Mil.) rührt euch!
(b) **with ~** (without difficulty) mit Leichtigkeit
2 *v.t.* lindern ‹*Schmerz, Kummer*›;
entspannen ‹*Lage*›; verringern ‹*Belastung,*
Druck, Spannung›
3 *v.i.* nachlassen

easel /'i:zl/ *n.* Staffelei, *die*

easily /'i:zɪlɪ/ *adv.* leicht

easiness /'i:zɪnɪs/ *n.* Leichtigkeit, *die*

east /i:st/ **1** *n.* (a) Osten, *der;* **in/to[wards]/**
from the ~: im/nach/von Osten; **to the ~ of**
östlich von
(b) *usu.* **E~** (Geog., Polit.) Osten, *der*
2 *adj.* östlich; Ost‹*küste, -wind, -grenze*›
3 *adv.* nach Osten; **~ of** östlich von

'East Ber'lin *pr. n.* (Hist.) Ostberlin, *das*

'eastbound *adj.* ‹*Zug, Verkehr usw.*› in
Richtung Osten

Easter /'i:stə(r)/ *n.* Ostern, *das od. Pl.*

'Easter egg *n.* Osterei, *das*

easterly /'i:stəlɪ/ *adj.* östlich; ‹*Wind*› aus
östlichen Richtungen

Easter 'Monday *n.* Ostermontag, *der*

eastern /'i:stən/ *adj.* östlich; Ost‹*grenze,*
-hälfte, -seite›; **~ Germany** Ostdeutschland
(das)

Eastern: ~ 'Europe *pr. n.*
Osteuropa, *(das);* **~ Euro'pean**
1 *adj.* osteuropäisch; **2** *n.* Osteuropäer,
der/Osteuropäerin, *die*

Easter 'Sunday *n.* Ostersonntag, *der*

East: ~ 'German (Hist.) **1** *adj.*
ostdeutsch; **he/she is ~ German** er ist
Ostdeutscher/sie ist Ostdeutsche; **2** *n.*
Ostdeutsche, *der/die;* **~ 'Germany** *pr. n.*

(Hist.) Ostdeutschland *(das);* **~ 'Timor**
/'ti:mɔ:(r)/ *pr. n.* Osttimor *(das)*

eastward(s) /i:stwəd(z)/ *adv.* ostwärts

easy /'i:zɪ/ **1** *adj.* (a) leicht; **on ~ terms**
auf Raten ‹*kaufen*›
(b) sorglos ‹*Leben, Zeit*›
(c) (free from constraint) ungezwungen
2 *adv.* leicht; **easier said than done** leichter
gesagt als getan; **take it ~!** (calm down!)
beruhige dich!

easy: ~-care *attrib. adj.* pflegeleicht;
~ chair *n.* Sessel, *der;* **~-'going** *adj.*
gelassen; (lax) nachlässig; **~ 'money** *n.*
leicht verdientes Geld

eat /i:t/ *v.t. & i.,* ate /et, eɪt/, eaten /'i:tn/
essen; ‹*Tier:*› fressen

■ **eat a'way** *v.t.* ‹*Rost, Säure:*› zerfressen

■ **eat 'out** *v.i.* essen gehen

■ **eat 'up** *v.t.* aufessen; ‹*Tier:*› auffressen

'eat-by date *n.* Verfallsdatum, *das*

eaten ▸ EAT

eating: ~ apple *n.* Essapfel, *der;*
~ disorder *n.* Essstörung, *die (meist Pl.);*
~ place *n.* Essgelegenheit, *die*

eau-de-Cologne /əʊdəkə'ləʊn/ *n.*
Kölnischwasser, *das*

eaves /i:vz/ *n. pl.* Dachgesims, *das*

'eavesdrop *v.i.* lauschen; **~ on**
belauschen

'eavesdropper *n.* Lauscher, *der*/
Lauscherin, *die*

'e-banking *n.* E-banking, *das*

ebb /eb/ **1** *n.* Ebbe, *die;* **be at a low ~**
(fig.) ‹*Person, Stimmung, Moral:*› auf dem
Nullpunkt sein
2 *v.i.* zurückgehen; **~ away** (fig.)
dahinschwinden

'ebb tide *n.* Ebbe, *die*

ebony /'ebənɪ/ *n.* Ebenholz, *das*

EC *abbr.* = **European Community** EG

eccentric /ɪk'sentrɪk/ **1** *adj.* exzentrisch
2 *n.* Exzentriker, *der*/Exzentrikerin, *die*

eccentricity /eksen'trɪsɪtɪ/ *n.*
Exzentrizität, *die*

ecclesiastical /ɪkli:zɪ'æstɪkl/ *adj.*
kirchlich; geistlich ‹*Musik*›

ECG *abbr.* = **electrocardiogram** EKG

echo /'ekəʊ/ **1** *n.* Echo, *das*
2 *v.t.* zurückwerfen; (fig.: repeat)
wiederholen

éclair /eɪ'kleə(r)/ *n.* Eclair, *das*

eclipse /ɪ'klɪps/ *n.* (Astron.) Finsternis, *die;*
~ of the sun Sonnenfinsternis, *die*

eco-friendly /'i:kəʊ-/ *adj.*
umweltfreundlich

ecological /i:kə'lɒdʒɪkl/ *adj.* ökologisch

eco'logically *adv.* ökologisch; **~ aware/**
sound/harmful umweltbewusst/-gerecht/
-schädlich

ecologist /i:'kɒlədʒɪst/ *n.* Ökologe,
der/Ökologin, *die*

ecology /i:'kɒlədʒɪ/ *n.* Ökologie, *die*

e-commerce /iː'kɒmɜːs/ *n.* (Comp.)
elektronischer Handel; E-Commerce, *der*

economic /iːkə'nɒmɪk/ *adj.*
(a) Wirtschafts⟨*politik, -abkommen,
-system, -krise, -wunder*⟩; wirtschaftlich
⟨*Entwicklung, Zusammenbruch*⟩; ~ **refugee**
Wirtschaftsflüchtling, *der*
(b) (giving adequate return) wirtschaftlich

economical /iːkə'nɒmɪkl/ *adj.*
wirtschaftlich; sparsam ⟨*Person*⟩; **be** ~ **with
sth.** mit etw. haushalten

eco'nomically *adv.* wirtschaftlich; (not
wastefully) sparsam

economics /iːkə'nɒmɪks/ *n.*
Wirtschaftswissenschaft, *die (meist Pl.)*

economist /ɪ'kɒnəmɪst/ *n.*
Wirtschaftswissenschaftler, *der*/
-wissenschaftlerin, *die*

economize /ɪ'kɒnəmaɪz/ *v.i.* sparen; ~ **on
sth.** etw. sparen

economy /ɪ'kɒnəmɪ/ *n.* **(a)** (frugality)
Sparsamkeit, *die*
(b) (instance) Einsparung, *die;* **make
economies** zu Sparmaßnahmen greifen
(c) (of country etc.) Wirtschaft, *die*

economy: ~ **class** *n.* Touristenklasse,
die; Economyklasse, *die;* ~-**class syndrome**
Economyclasssyndrom, *das;* ~ **size** *n.*
Haushaltspackung, *die*

eco /'iːkəʊ/: ~**sphere** *n.* Ökosphäre,
die; ~**system** *n.* Ökosystem, *das;*
~**terrorism** *n., no pl.* **(a)** (terrorism carried
out by environmentalist groups) Ökoterrorismus,
der; **(b)** (damage to the environment) Ökoterror,
der; ~**tourism** *n.* Ökotourismus, *der;*
~**tourist** *n.* Ökotourist, *der*/-touristin, *die;*
~-**warrior** *n.* Ökokrieger, *der*/-kriegerin,
die

ecstasy /'ekstəsɪ/ *n.* **(a)** Ekstase, *die*
(b) E~ (drug) Ecstasy, *das*

ecstatic /ɪk'stætɪk/ *adj.* ekstatisch

ecu, ECU /'eɪkjuː/ *abbr.* = **European
currency unit** Ecu, *der od. die*

eddy /'edɪ/ *n.* Strudel, *der*

edge /edʒ/ **1** *n.* **(a)** (of knife, razor, weapon)
Schneide, *die;* **on** ~ (fig.) nervös *od.* gereizt
(about wegen)
(b) (of solid, bed, table) Kante, *die;* (of sheet of
paper, road, forest, cliff) Rand, *der*
2 *v.i.* sich schieben

edgy /'edʒɪ/ *adj.* nervös

edible /'edɪbl/ *adj.* essbar

edict /'iːdɪkt/ *n.* Erlass, *der*

edit /'edɪt/ *v.t.* herausgeben ⟨*Zeitung*⟩;
redigieren ⟨*Buch, Artikel, Manuskript*⟩

edition /ɪ'dɪʃn/ *n.* Ausgabe, *die*

editor /'edɪtə(r)/ *n.* Redakteur,
der/Redakteurin, *die;* (of particular work)
Bearbeiter, *der*/Bearbeiterin, *die;* (of
newspaper) Herausgeber, *der*/Herausgeberin,
die

editorial /edɪ'tɔːrɪəl/ **1** *n.* Leitartikel, *der*
2 *adj.* redaktionell

EDP *abbr.* = **electronic data
processing** EDV

educate /'edjʊkeɪt/ *v.t.* **(a)** (bring up)
erziehen; (train mind and character of) bilden
(b) (provide schooling for) **he was** ~**d at ...:** er
hat seine Ausbildung in ... erhalten

educated /'edjʊkeɪtɪd/ *adj.* gebildet

education /edjʊ'keɪʃn/ *n.* Erziehung, *die;*
(system) Erziehungswesen, *das*

educational /edjʊ'keɪʃənl/ *adj.*
pädagogisch; Lehr⟨*film, -spiele, -anstalt*⟩;
Erziehungs⟨*methoden, -arbeit*⟩

edu'cation system *n.* Bildungssystem,
das

EEC *abbr.* = **European Economic
Community** EWG

eel /iːl/ *n.* Aal, *der*

eerie /'iːrɪ/ *adj.* unheimlich

eff /ef/ *v.i.* (sl.) ~ **and blind** fluchen

effect /ɪ'fekt/ *n.* **(a)** Wirkung, *die* (**on**
auf + *Akk.*); **the** ~**s of sth. on sth.** die
Auswirkungen einer Sache (*Gen.*) auf etw.
(*Akk.*); **take** ~: die erwünschte Wirkung
erzielen; **in** ~: in Wirklichkeit
(b) **come into** ~: gültig werden; ⟨*Gesetz:*⟩
in Kraft treten; **put into** ~: in Kraft setzen
⟨*Gesetz*⟩; verwirklichen ⟨*Plan*⟩; **with** ~ **from
2 November/Monday** mit Wirkung vom 2.
November/von Montag
(c) **personal** ~**s** persönliches Eigentum;
Privateigentum, *das;* **household** ~**s**
Hausrat, *der*

effective /ɪ'fektɪv/ *adj.* **(a)** wirksam
⟨*Mittel, Maßnahmen*⟩; **be** ~ ⟨*Arzneimittel:*⟩
wirken
(b) (in operation) gültig; ~ **from/as of** mit
Wirkung vom

ef'fectively *adv.* (in fact) effektiv; (with
effect) wirkungsvoll

effectual /ɪ'fektjʊəl/ *adj.* wirksam

effeminate /ɪ'femɪnət/ *adj.* unmännlich

effervescent /efə'vesənt/ *adj.* sprudelnd;
(fig.) übersprudelnd

effete /e'fiːt/ *adj.* verweichlicht

efficiency /ɪ'fɪʃənsɪ/ *n.* (of person)
Fähigkeit, *die;* Tüchtigkeit, *die;* (of machine,
factory, engine) Leistungsfähigkeit, *die;* (of
organization, method) gutes Funktionieren

efficient /ɪ'fɪʃənt/ *adj.* fähig ⟨*Person*⟩;
tüchtig ⟨*Arbeiter, Sekretärin*⟩;
leistungsfähig ⟨*Maschine, Motor, Fabrik*⟩;
gut funktionierend ⟨*Methode, Organisation*⟩

ef'ficiently *adv.* gut

effigy /'efɪdʒɪ/ *n.* Bildnis, *das*

effing /'efɪŋ/ *adj.* (sl.) Scheiß- (salopp)

effluent /'efluənt/ Abwässer *Pl.*

effort /'efət/ *n.* **(a)** Anstrengung, *die;*
Mühe, *die;* **make an/every** ~ (physically) sich
anstrengen; (mentally) sich bemühen
(b) (attempt) Versuch, *der*

'effortless *adj.* mühelos

effrontery /ɪ'frʌntərɪ/ n. Dreistigkeit, die; **have the ~ to do sth.** die Stirn besitzen, etw. zu tun

effusive /ɪ'fjuːsɪv/ adj. überschwänglich; exaltiert (geh.) ⟨Person⟩

EFL abbr. = **English as a foreign language**

e.g. /iː'dʒiː/ abbr. = **for example** z.B.

egg /eg/ n. Ei, das
■ **egg 'on** v.t. anstacheln

egg: ~cup n. Eierbecher, der; **~plant** n. Aubergine, die; (fruit also) Eierfrucht, die; (plant also) Eierpflanze, die; **~shell** n. Eierschale, die; **~ timer** n. Eieruhr, die; **~ white** n. Eiweiß, das; **~ yolk** n. Eigelb, das

ego /'egəʊ, 'iːgəʊ/ n., pl. **~s (a)** (Psych.) Ego, das
(b) (self-esteem) Selbstbewusstsein, das

egotism /'egətɪzm/ n. **(a)** Egotismus, der (fachspr.); Ichbezogenheit, die
(b) (self-conceit) Egotismus, der; Selbstgefälligkeit, die

egotist /'egətɪst/ n. Egotist, der/Egotistin, die (fachspr.); (self-centred person) Egozentriker, der/Egozentrikerin, die

egotistic /egə'tɪstɪk/, **egotistical** /egə'tɪstɪkl/ adj. **(a)** ichbezogen ⟨Rede, Gespräch⟩
(b) selbstsüchtig, selbstgefällig ⟨Person⟩

Egypt /'iːdʒɪpt/ pr. n. Ägypten (das)

Egyptian /ɪ'dʒɪpʃn/ **1** adj. ägyptisch; **sb. is ~:** jmd. ist Ägypter/Ägypterin
2 n. (person) Ägypter, der/Ägypterin, die

eiderdown /'aɪdədaʊn/ n. Federbett, das

eight /eɪt/ **1** adj. acht; **at ~:** um acht; **half past ~:** halb neun; **~ thirty** acht Uhr dreißig; **~ ten/fifty** zehn nach acht/vor neun; (esp. in timetable) acht Uhr zehn/fünfzig; **~-year-old boy** achtjähriger Junge; **an ~-year-old** ein Achtjähriger/eine Achtjährige; **at [the age of] ~, aged ~:** mit acht Jahren; **~ times** achtmal
2 n. Acht, die; **the first/last ~:** die ersten/letzten acht; **there were ~ of us present** wir waren [zu] acht

eighteen /eɪ'tiːn/ **1** adj. achtzehn
2 n. Achtzehn, die. See also EIGHT

eighteenth /eɪ'tiːnθ/ **1** adj. achtzehnt...
2 n. (fraction) Achtzehntel, das. See also EIGHTH

eighth /eɪtθ/ **1** adj. acht...; **be/come ~:** Achter sein/als Achter ankommen; **~-largest** achtgrößt...
2 n. (in sequence, rank) Achte, der/die/das; (fraction) Achtel, das; **the ~ of May** der achte Mai

eightieth /'eɪtɪɪθ/ adj. achtzigst...

eighty /'eɪtɪ/ **1** adj. achtzig
2 n. Achtzig, die; **the eighties** (years) die Achtzigerjahre; **be in one's eighties** in den Achtzigern sein. See also EIGHT

Eire /'eərə/ pr. n. Irland, das; Eire, das

either /'aɪeə(r), 'iːeə(r)/ **1** adj. **(a)** (each) **at ~ end of the table** an beiden Enden des Tisches
(b) (one or other) [irgend]ein ... [von beiden]; **take ~ one** nimm einen/eine/eins von [den] beiden
2 pron. **(a)** (each) beide Pl.; **I can't cope with ~:** ich kann mit keinem von beiden fertig werden
(b) (one or other) einer/eine/ein[e]s [von beiden]
3 adv. auch [nicht]; **'I don't like that ~:** ich mag es auch nicht
4 conj. **~ ... or ...:** entweder ... oder ...; (after negation) weder ... noch ...

ejaculate /ɪ'dʒækjʊleɪt/ **1** v.t. (utter suddenly) ausstoßen
2 v.i. (eject semen) ejakulieren

eject /ɪ'dʒekt/ **1** v.t. **(a)** (from hall, meeting) hinauswerfen (**from** aus)
(b) ⟨Gerät:⟩ auswerfen, ⟨Person:⟩ herausholen ⟨Kassette⟩
2 v.i. sich hinauskatapultieren

ejector seat /ɪ'dʒektə siːt/ n. Schleudersitz, der

eke out /iːk 'aʊt/ v.t. strecken; **~ out a living** sich (Dat.) seinen Lebensunterhalt notdürftig verdienen

elaborate **1** /ɪ'læbərət/ adj. kompliziert; kunstvoll [gearbeitet] ⟨Arrangement, Verzierung⟩
2 /ɪ'læbəreɪt/ v.i. mehr ins Detail gehen; **~ on** näher ausführen

elapse /ɪ'læps/ v.i. ⟨Zeit:⟩ vergehen

elastic /ɪ'læstɪk/ **1** adj. elastisch
2 n. (~ band) Gummiband, das

elastic 'band n. Gummiband, das

elated /ɪ'leɪtɪd/ adj. freudig erregt; **be or feel ~:** in Hochstimmung sein

elation /ɪ'leɪʃn/ n. freudige Erregung

elbow /'elbəʊ/ **1** n. Ell[en]bogen, der
2 v.t. **~ sb. aside** jmdn. mit dem Ellenbogen zur Seite stoßen

elbow: ~ grease n. (joc.) Muskelkraft, die; **~ room** n. Ell[en]bogenfreiheit, die

elder¹ /'eldə(r)/ **1** attrib. adj. älter...
2 n. **(a)** (senior) Ältere, der/die
(b) (village ~, church ~) Älteste, der/die

elder² n. (Bot.) Holunder, der

'elderberry n. Holunderbeere, die

elderly /'eldəlɪ/ **1** adj. älter
2 n. pl. **the ~:** ältere Menschen

eldest /'eldɪst/ adj. ältest...

elect /ɪ'lekt/ **1** adj. postpos. gewählt; **the President ~:** der designierte Präsident
2 v.t. wählen; **~ sb. chairman** jmdn. zum Vorsitzenden wählen

election /ɪ'lekʃn/ n. Wahl, die; **general ~:** allgemeine Wahlen Pl.; **~ results** Wahlergebnisse Pl.

e'lection campaign n. Wahlkampagne, die

electioneer /ɪlekʃə'nɪə(r)/ *v.i.* be/go ~ing Wahlkampf machen
elector /ɪ'lektə(r)/ *n.* Wähler, *der*/ Wählerin, *die*
electoral /ɪ'lektərl/ *adj.* Wahl-
electoral 'college *n.* Wahlmännergremium, *das;* Wahlausschuss, *der*
electorate /ɪ'lektərət/ *n.* Wähler *Pl.*
electric /ɪ'lektrɪk/ *adj.* elektrisch; Elektro⟨kabel, -motor, -herd, -kessel⟩; Strom⟨versorgung⟩; (fig.) spannungsgeladen ⟨Atmosphäre⟩
electrical /ɪ'lektrɪkl/ *adj.* elektrisch; Elektro⟨abteilung, -handel, -geräte⟩
electric: ~ **'blanket** *n.* Heizdecke, *die;* ~ **'chair** *n.* elektrischer Stuhl; ~ **cooker** *n.* Elektroherd, *der;* ~ **'fire** *n.* [elektrischer] Heizofen; ~ **gui'tar** *n.* elektrische Gitarre; E-Gitarre, *die*
electrician /ɪlek'trɪʃn/ *n.* Elektriker, *der*/Elektrikerin, *die*
electricity /ɪlek'trɪsɪtɪ/ *n.* Elektrizität, *die*
electricity: ~ **bill** *n.* Stromrechnung, *die;* ~ **man** *n.* (fitter) Elektroinstallateur, *der;* (meter reader, collector) Stromableser, *der;* ~ **meter** *n.* Stromzähler, *der*
electric 'shock *n.* Stromschlag, *der*
electrify /ɪ'lektrɪfaɪ/ *v.t.* elektrifizieren; (fig.) elektrisieren
electro'cardiogram *n.* Elektrokardiogramm, *das*
electrocute /ɪ'lektrəkjuːt/ *v.t.* durch Stromschlag töten
electrode /ɪ'lektrəʊd/ *n.* Elektrode, *die*
electro'magnet *n.* Elektromagnet, *der*
electromag'netic *adj.* elektromagnetisch
electron /ɪ'lektrɒn/ *n.* Elektron, *das*
electronic /ɪlek'trɒnɪk/ *adj.* elektronisch
electronic: ~ **'cash** *n.* elektronisches Geld; ~ **'mail** *n.* elektronische Post; ~ **'publishing** *n.* elektronisches Publizieren
electronics /ɪlek'trɒnɪks/ *n.* Elektronik, *die*
electronic: ~ **'shopping basket** *n.* elektronischer Warenkorb; ~ **'storefront** *n.* elektronisches Schaufenster
electron 'microscope *n.* Elektronenmikroskop, *das*
elegance /'elɪgəns/ *n.* Eleganz, *die*
elegant /'elɪgənt/ *adj.* elegant
elegy /'elɪdʒɪ/ *n.* Elegie, *die*
element /'elɪmənt/ *n.* **(a)** Element, *das* **(b)** (Electr.) Heizelement, *das* **(c)** ~s (rudiments) Grundlagen *Pl.*
elementary /elɪ'mentərɪ/ *adj.* elementar; grundlegend ⟨Fakten, Wissen⟩; Grundschul⟨bildung⟩; Grund⟨kurs, -ausbildung, -kenntnisse⟩

elementary: ~ **'particle** *n.* (Phys.) Elementarteilchen, *das;* ~ **school** *n.* Grundschule, *die*
elephant /'elɪfənt/ *n.* Elefant, *der;* white ~ (fig.) nutzloser Besitz; be a white ~ ⟨Gebäude, Einkaufszentrum usw.:⟩ reine Geldverschwendung sein
elevate /'elɪveɪt/ *v.t.* [empor]heben
elevation /elɪ'veɪʃn/ *n.* **(a)** (height) Höhe, *die* **(b)** (Archit.) Aufriss, *der*
elevator /'elɪveɪtə(r)/ *n.* (Amer.) Aufzug, *der;* Fahrstuhl, *der*
eleven /ɪ'levn/ [1] *adj.* elf [2] *n.* (also Sport) Elf, *die. See also* EIGHT
elevenses /ɪ'levnzɪz/ *n. sing. or pl.* (Brit. coll.) ≈ zweites Frühstück [gegen elf Uhr]
eleventh /ɪ'levnθ/ [1] *adj.* elft...; at the ~ hour in letzter Minute [2] *n.* (fraction) Elftel, *das. See also* EIGHTH
elf /elf/ *n., pl.* **elves** /elvz/ Elf, *der*/ Elfe, *die*
elicit /ɪ'lɪsɪt/ *v.t.* entlocken (from *Dat.*); gewinnen ⟨Unterstützung⟩
eligible /'elɪdʒɪbl/ *adj.* be ~ for sth. (fit) für etw. geeignet sein; (entitled) zu etw. berechtigt sein
eliminate /ɪ'lɪmɪneɪt/ *v.t.* **(a)** (remove) beseitigen; ausschließen ⟨Möglichkeit⟩ **(b)** (exclude) ausschließen; be ~d (Sport) ausscheiden
elimination /ɪlɪmɪ'neɪʃn/ *n.* **(a)** (removal) Beseitigung, *die;* process of ~: Ausleseverfahren, *das* **(b)** (exclusion) Ausschluss, *der;* (Sport) Ausscheiden, *das*
élite /eɪ'liːt/ *n.* Elite, *die*
élitist /eɪ'liːtɪst/ *adj.* elitär; Elite⟨denken⟩
elk /elk/ *n., pl.* ~s *or same* **(a)** (deer) Elch, *der* **(b)** (moose) Riesenelch, *der*
ellipse /ɪ'lɪps/ *n.* Ellipse, *die*
elliptical /ɪ'lɪptɪkl/ *adj.* elliptisch
elm /elm/ *n.* Ulme, *die*
elocution /elə'kjuːʃn/ *n.* (art) Sprechkunst, *die*
elongated /'iːlɒŋgeɪtɪd/ *adj.* lang gestreckt
elope /ɪ'ləʊp/ *v.i.* durchbrennen (ugs.)
eloquence /'eləkwəns/ *n.* Beredtheit, *die*
eloquent /'eləkwənt/ *adj.* beredt ⟨Person⟩; gewandt ⟨Stil, Redner⟩
else /els/ *adv.* **(a)** (besides) sonst [noch]; somebody/something ~: [noch] jemand anders/noch etwas; everybody/everything ~: alle anderen/alles andere; who/what/when/how ~? wer/was/wann/wie sonst noch?; why ~? warum sonst? **(b)** (instead) ander...; sb. ~'s hat der Hut von jmd. anders; anybody/anything ~? [irgend]jemand anders/[irgend]etwas anderes?; somebody/something ~: ⋯⁍

jemand anders/etwas anderes; **everybody/ everything** ∼: alle anderen/alles andere **(c)** (otherwise) sonst; **or** ∼: oder aber; **do it or** ∼ ...! tun Sie es, sonst ...!

'elsewhere *adv.* woanders

elude /ɪ'lju:d/ *v.t.* (avoid) ausweichen (+ *Dat.*); (escape from) entkommen (+ *Dat.*)

elusive /ɪ'lju:sɪv/ *adj.* schwer zu erreichen ⟨*Person*⟩; schwer zu fassen ⟨*Straftäter*⟩; schwer definierbar ⟨*Begriff, Sinn*⟩

elves *pl. of* ELF

emaciated /ɪ'meɪsɪeɪtɪd/ *adj.* abgezehrt

email /'i:meɪl/ **1** *n.* E-Mail, *die;* ∼ **address** E-Mail-Adresse, *die;* ∼ **message** E-Mail, *die* **2** *v.t.* per E-Mail übermitteln ⟨*Ergebnisse, Datei usw.*⟩; ∼ **sb.** jmdm. eine E-Mail schicken

emancipated /ɪ'mænsɪpeɪtɪd/ *adj.* emanzipiert: **become** ∼: sich emanzipieren

emancipation /ɪmænsɪ'peɪʃn/ *n.* Emanzipation, *die*

embalm /ɪm'bɑ:m/ *v.t.* einbalsamieren

embankment /ɪm'bæŋkmənt/ *n.* Damm, *der*

embargo /em'bɑ:gəʊ/ *n., pl.* ∼**es** Embargo, *das;* **put** *or* **lay an** ∼ **on sth.** etw. mit einem Embargo belegen

embark /ɪm'bɑ:k/ *v.i.* **(a)** sich einschiffen (for nach) **(b)** ∼ **[up]on sth.** etw. in Angriff nehmen

embarkation /embɑ:'keɪʃn/ *n.* Einschiffung, *die*

embarrass /ɪm'bærəs/ *v.t.* in Verlegenheit bringen

embarrassed /ɪm'bærəst/ *adj.* verlegen; **feel** ∼: verlegen sein

em'barrassing *adj.* peinlich

em'barrassment *n.* Verlegenheit, *die*

embassy /'embəsɪ/ *n.* Botschaft, *die*

embed /ɪm'bed/ *v.t.*, **-dd-**: (fix) einlassen; ∼ **sth. in cement/concrete** etw. einzementieren/einbetonieren; ∼**ded in the mud** im Schlamm versunken; ∼**ded journalist** eingebetteter Journalist; ∼**ded sentence** (Ling.) eingeschobener Satz

embellish /em'belɪʃ/ *v.t.* beschönigen ⟨*Wahrheit*⟩; ausschmücken ⟨*Geschichte, Bericht*⟩

embers /'embəz/ *n. pl.* Glut, *die*

embezzle /ɪm'bezl/ *v.t.* unterschlagen

embitter /ɪm'bɪtə(r)/ *v.t.* verbittern

emblem /'embləm/ *n.* Emblem, *das*

embody /ɪm'bɒdɪ/ *v.t.* verkörpern

embrace /ɪm'breɪs/ **1** *v.t.* umarmen; (fig.: accept, adopt) annehmen **2** *v.i.* sich umarmen **3** *n.* Umarmung, *die*

embroider /ɪm'brɔɪdə(r)/ *v.t.* sticken ⟨*Muster*⟩; besticken ⟨*Tuch, Kleid*⟩; (fig.) ausschmücken

embroidery /ɪm'brɔɪdərɪ/ *n.* Stickerei, *die*

embroil /ɪm'brɔɪl/ *v.t.* **become/be** ∼**ed in sth. in etw.** (*Akk.*) verwickelt werden/sein

embryo /'embrɪəʊ/ *n.* Embryo, *der;* ∼ **research** Embryonenforschung, *die*

embryonic /embrɪ'ɒnɪk/ *adj.* (Biol., fig.) Embryonal⟨*entwicklung, -struktur, -zustand, -stadium*⟩; unausgereift ⟨*Vorstellung*⟩

emerald /'emərəld/ **1** *n.* Smaragd, *der* **2** *adj.* smaragdgrün; **the E**∼ **Isle** die Grüne Insel

emerald 'green *n.* Smaragdgrün, *das*

emerge /ɪ'mɜ:dʒ/ *v.i.* auftauchen (**from** aus, **from behind** hinter + *Dat.*); ⟨*Wahrheit:*⟩ an den Tag kommen; **it** ∼**s that** ...: es stellt sich heraus, dass ...

emergency /ɪ'mɜ:dʒənsɪ/ **1** *n.* Notfall, *der;* **in an** *or* **in case of** ∼: im Notfall; **declare a state of** ∼: den Ausnahmezustand ausrufen **2** *adj.* Not-

emergency: ∼ **exit** *n.* Notausgang, *der;* ∼ **services** *n. pl.* Hilfsdienste *Pl.*

'emery paper *n.* Schmirgelpapier, *das*

emetic /ɪ'metɪk/ (Med.) *n.* Emetikum, *das* (fachspr.); Brechmittel, *das*

emigrant /'emɪgrənt/ *n.* Auswanderer, *der*/Auswanderin, *die*

emigrate /'emɪgreɪt/ *v.i.* auswandern (**to** nach, **from** aus)

emigration /emɪ'greɪʃn/ *n.* Auswanderung, *die* (**to** nach, **from** aus)

eminence /'emɪnəns/ *n.* hohes Ansehen

eminent /'emɪnənt/ *adj.* bedeutend; herausragend

emission /ɪ'mɪʃn/ *n.* Emission, *die* (fachspr.); (process also) Abgabe, *die*

emit /ɪ'mɪt/ *v.t.*, **-tt-** abgeben, emittieren (fachspr.) ⟨*Wärme, Strahlung usw.*⟩; ausstoßen ⟨*Rauch*⟩

emoticon /ɪ'mɒtɪkɒn/ *n.* (Comp.) Emoticon, *das*

emotion /ɪ'məʊʃn/ *n.* Gefühl, *das*

emotional /ɪ'məʊʃənl/ *adj.* emotional; Gemüts⟨*zustand, -störung*⟩; gefühlvoll ⟨*Stimme*⟩

e'motionally *adv.* emotional; gefühlvoll ⟨*sprechen*⟩; ∼ **disturbed** seelisch gestört

emotive /ɪ'məʊtɪv/ *adj.* emotional

empathize /'empəθaɪz/ *v.i.* ∼ **with sb.** sich in jmdn. hineinversetzen; ∼ **with sth.** etw. nachempfinden

empathy /'empəθɪ/ *n.* Empathie, *die* (Psych.); Einfühlung, *die*

emperor /'empərə(r)/ *n.* Kaiser, *der*

emphasis /'emfəsɪs/ *n., pl.* **emphases** /'emfəsi:z/ Betonung, *die;* **lay** *or* **place** *or* **put** ∼ **on sth.** etw. betonen

emphasize /'emfəsaɪz/ *v.t.* betonen

emphatic /ɪm'fætɪk/ *adj.* nachdrücklich; demonstrativ ⟨*Ablehnung*⟩; **be** ∼ **that** ...: darauf bestehen, dass ...

em'phatically *adv.* nachdrücklich

empire /'empaɪə(r)/ *n.* Reich, *das*

empirical /ɪm'pɪrɪkl/ *adj.* empirisch

employ /ɪm'plɔɪ/ *v.t.* **(a)** (take on) einstellen; (have working for one) beschäftigen; **be ∼ed by a company** bei einer Firma arbeiten **(b)** (use) einsetzen **(for, in, on** für); anwenden ⟨*Methode, List*⟩ **(for, in, on** bei)

employee (*Amer.:* **employe**) /emplɔɪˈiː, emˈplɔɪiː/ *n.* Angestellte, *der/die*

employer /ɪm'plɔɪə(r)/ *n.* Arbeitgeber, *der*/-geberin, *die*

employment /ɪm'plɔɪmənt/ *n.* **(a)** (work) Arbeit, *die* **(b)** (regular trade or profession) Beschäftigung, *die*

employment: ∼ agency *n.* Stellenvermittlung, *die;* **∼ office** *n.* (Brit.) Arbeitsamt, *das*

empower /ɪm'paʊə(r)/ *v.t.* (authorize) ermächtigen; (enable) befähigen

empress /'emprɪs/ *n.* Kaiserin, *die*

emptiness /'emptɪnɪs/ *n.* Leere, *die*

empty /'emptɪ/ ⓵ *adj.* leer; frei ⟨*Sitz, Parkplatz*⟩ ⓶ *v.t.* leeren; (pour) schütten (**over** über + *Akk.*) ⓷ *v.i.* sich leeren

'empty-handed *adj.* mit leeren Händen

EMS *abbr.* = **European Monetary System** EWS

emu /'iːmjuː/ *n.* (Ornith.) Emu, *der*

EMU *abbr.* = **Economic and Monetary Union** WWU

emulate /'emjʊleɪt/ *v.t.* nacheifern (+ *Dat.*)

emulsion /ɪ'mʌlʃn/ *n.* **(a)** Emulsion, *die* **(b)** ▶ EMULSION PAINT

e'mulsion paint *n.* Dispersionsfarbe, *die*

enable /ɪ'neɪbl/ *v.t.* **∼ sb. to do sth.** es jmdm. ermöglichen, etw. zu tun

enamel /ɪ'næml/ ⓵ *n.* Email, *das* ⓶ *v.t.,* (Brit.) **-ll-** emaillieren

enchant /ɪn'tʃɑːnt/ *v.t.* verzaubern; (delight) entzücken

en'chanted *adj.* verzaubert

en'chanting *adj.* entzückend

en'chantment *n.* Verzauberung, *die;* (fig.) Zauber, *der*

encircle /ɪn'sɜːkl/ *v.t.* umgeben

encl. *abbr.* = **enclosed, enclosure[s]** Anl.

enclave /'enkleɪv/ *n.* Enklave, *die*

enclose /ɪn'kləʊz/ *v.t.* **(a)** (surround) umgeben; (shut up or in) einschließen **(b)** (with letter) beilegen (**with, in** *Dat.*); **please find ∼d** anbei erhalten Sie

enclosure /ɪn'kləʊʒə(r)/ *n.* **(a)** (in zoo) Gehege, *das* **(b)** (with letter) Anlage, *die*

encode /ɪn'kəʊd/ *v.t.* verschlüsseln; chiffrieren

encore /'ɒŋkɔː(r)/ ⓵ *int.* Zugabe! ⓶ *n.* Zugabe, *die*

encounter /ɪn'kaʊntə(r)/ ⓵ *v.t.* (as adversary) treffen auf (+ *Akk.*); (by chance) begegnen (+ *Dat.*); stoßen auf (+ *Akk.*) ⟨*Problem, Widerstand usw.*⟩ ⓶ *n.* (chance meeting) Begegnung, *die*

encourage /ɪn'kʌrɪdʒ/ *v.t.* ermutigen; (promote) fördern

encouragement *n.* Ermutigung, *die* (**from** durch)

encroach /ɪn'krəʊtʃ/ *v.i.* **∼ on** eindringen in (+ *Akk.*); in Anspruch nehmen ⟨*Zeit*⟩

encrypt /en'krɪpt/ *v.t.* (Comp.) verschlüsseln ⟨*Daten etc.*⟩

encryption /en'krɪpʃn/ *n.* Verschlüsselung, *die*

encumber /ɪn'kʌmbə(r)/ *v.t.* belasten

encumbrance /ɪn'kʌmbrəns/ *n.* Belastung, *die*

encyclopaedia /ɪnsaɪklə'piːdɪə/ *n.* Lexikon, *das;* Enzyklopädie, *die*

encyclopaedic /ɪnsaɪklə'piːdɪk/ *adj.* enzyklopädisch

end /end/ ⓵ *n.* **(a)** Ende, *das;* (of nose, hair, finger) Spitze, *die;* **from ∼ to ∼:** von einem Ende zum anderen; **at the ∼ of 1987/March** Ende 1987/März; **in the ∼:** schließlich; **come to an ∼:** ein Ende nehmen; **be at an ∼:** zu Ende sein **(b)** (of box, packet, etc.) Schmalseite, *die;* (top/bottom surface) Ober-/Unterseite, *die;* **on ∼:** hochkant; **make ∼s meet** (fig.) zurechtkommen; **no ∼ of** (coll.) unendlich viel/viele **(c)** (remnant) Rest, *der;* (of cigarette) Stummel, *der* **(d)** (purpose, object) Ziel, *das;* **∼ in itself** Selbstzweck, *der* ⓶ *v.t.* beenden ⓷ *v.i.* enden ∎ **end 'up** *v.i.* enden; **∼ up in** (coll.) landen in (+ *Dat.*); **∼ up [as] a teacher** (coll.) schließlich Lehrer werden

endanger /ɪn'deɪndʒə(r)/ *v.t.* gefährden

endear /ɪn'dɪə(r)/ *v.t.* **∼ sb./sth./oneself to sb.** jmdn./etw./sich bei jmdm. beliebt machen

en'dearing *adj.* reizend; gewinnend ⟨*Lächeln, Art*⟩

endeavour (*Brit.;* *Amer.:* **endeavor**) /ɪn'devə(r)/ ⓵ *v.i.* **∼ to do sth.** sich bemühen, etw. zu tun ⓶ *n.* Bemühung, *die;* (attempt) Versuch, *der*

'ending *n.* Schluss, *der;* (of word) Endung, *die*

endive /'endaɪv/ *n.* Endivie, *die*

'endless *adj.* endlos

'endlessly *adv.* unaufhörlich ⟨*streiten, schwatzen*⟩

endorse /ɪn'dɔːs/ *v.t.* **(a)** indossieren ⟨*Scheck*⟩ **(b)** beipflichten (+ *Dat.*) ⟨*Meinung*⟩; ····⟶

billigen ⟨*Entscheidung, Handlung*⟩;
unterstützen ⟨*Vorschlag*⟩
(c) (Brit. Law) einen Strafvermerk machen
auf (+ *Akk. od. Dat.*)
en'dorsement *n.* **(a)** (of cheque)
Indossament, *das*
(b) (support) Billigung, *die;* (of proposal)
Unterstützung, *die*
(c) (Brit. Law) Strafvermerk, *der*
endow /ɪn'daʊ/ *v.t.* [über Stiftungen/
eine Stiftung] finanzieren; stiften ⟨*Preis,
Lehrstuhl*⟩; **be ~ed with charm/a talent
for music** Charme/musikalisches Talent
besitzen
en'dowment mortgage *n.* ≈
Tilgungslebensversicherung, *die;*
end: ~ 'product *n.* Endprodukt, *das;*
~ re'sult *n.* Ergebnis, *das;* (consequence)
Folge, *die*
endurable /ɪn'djʊərəbl/ *adj.* erträglich
endurance /ɪn'djʊərəns/ *n.* Ausdauer, *die*
en'durance test *n.* Belastungsprobe,
die
endure /ɪn'djʊə(r)/ *v.t.* ertragen
enema /'enəmə/ *n.* Einlauf, *der*
enemy /'enəmɪ/ ⑴ *n.* Feind, *der* (of, to
Gen.)
⑵ *adj.* feindlich
energetic /enə'dʒetɪk/ *adj.*
energiegeladen; (active) tatkräftig
energy /'enədʒɪ/ *n.* Energie, *die*
energy: ~ consumption *n.*
Energieverbrauch, *der;* **~ crisis** *n.*
Energiekrise, *die;* **~ resources** *n. pl.*
Energieressourcen *Pl.;* **~-saving**
adj. Energie sparend; **~-saving lamp**
Energiesparlampe, *die*
enforce /ɪn'fɔːs/ *v.t.* durchsetzen; sorgen
für ⟨*Disziplin*⟩; **~d** erzwungen ⟨*Schweigen*⟩;
unfreiwillig ⟨*Untätigkeit*⟩
ENG *abbr.* = **electronic news-
gathering** elektronische
Berichterstattung; EB
engage /ɪn'geɪdʒ/ ⑴ *v.t.* **(a)** (hire)
einstellen ⟨*Arbeiter*⟩; engagieren ⟨*Sänger*⟩
(b) wecken ⟨*Interesse*⟩; auf sich (*Akk.*)
ziehen ⟨*Aufmerksamkeit*⟩
(c) ~ the clutch/first gear einkuppeln/den
ersten Gang einlegen
⑵ *v.i.* **~ in sth.** sich an etw. (*Dat.*)
beteiligen; **~ in politics** sich politisch
engagieren
engaged /ɪn'geɪdʒd/ *adj.* **(a) be ~ [to be
married] [to sb.]** [mit jmdm.] verlobt sein;
get ~ [to be married] [to sb.] sich [mit
jmdm.] verloben
(b) be ~ in sth./in doing sth. mit etw.
beschäftigt sein/damit beschäftigt sein,
etw. zu tun; **be otherwise ~:** etwas anderes
vorhaben
(c) besetzt ⟨*Toilette, [Telefon]anschluss,
Nummer*⟩; **~ signal** *or* **tone** (Brit.)
Besetztzeichen, *das*

en'gagement *n.* **(a)** (to be married)
Verlobung, *die* (**to** mit)
(b) (appointment) Verabredung, *die*
en'gagement ring *n.* Verlobungsring,
der
engaging /ɪn'geɪdʒɪŋ/ *adj.* bezaubernd;
einnehmend ⟨*Persönlichkeit, Art*⟩
engine /'endʒɪn/ *n.* **(a)** Motor, *der;* (rocket/jet
~) Triebwerk, *das*
(b) (locomotive) Lok[omotive], *die*
'engine driver *n.* Lok[omotiv]führer, *der*
engineer /endʒɪ'nɪə(r)/ ⑴ *n.*
(a) Ingenieur, *der*/Ingenieurin, *die;* (service
~, installation **~**) Techniker, *der*/Technikerin,
die
(b) (Amer.: engine driver) Lok[omotiv]führer,
der
⑵ *v.t.* arrangieren
engi'neering *n.* Technik, *die*
England /'ɪŋglənd/ *pr. n.* England (*das*)
English /'ɪŋglɪʃ/ ⑴ *adj.* englisch; **he/she is
~:** er ist Engländer/sie ist Engländerin
⑵ *n.* **(a)** Englisch, *das;* **say sth. in ~:** etw.
auf Englisch sagen; **I cannot** *or* **do not speak
~:** ich spreche kein Englisch; **translate
into/from [the] ~:** ins Englische/aus dem
Englischen übersetzen
(b) *pl.* **the ~:** die Engländer *usw.*
English: ~ 'breakfast *n.* englisches
Frühstück; **~ 'Channel** *pr. n.* the
~ Channel der [Ärmel]kanal; **~man**
/-mən/ *n., pl.* **~men** /-mən/ Engländer, *der;*
~woman *n.* Engländerin, *die*
engrave /ɪn'greɪv/ *v.t.* gravieren;
eingravieren ⟨*Namen, Figur usw.*⟩
engraving /ɪn'greɪvɪŋ/ *n.* Stich, *der;* (from
wood) Holzschnitt, *der*
engross /ɪn'grəʊs/ *v.t.* fesseln; **be ~ed in
sth.** in etw. (*Akk.*) vertieft sein; **become** *or*
get ~ed in sth. sich in etw. (*Akk.*) vertiefen
engrossing /ɪn'grəʊsɪŋ/ *adj.* fesselnd
engulf /ɪn'gʌlf/ *v.t.* verschlingen
enhance /ɪn'hɑːns/ *v.t.* erhöhen ⟨*Wert,
Aussichten, Schönheit*⟩; verstärken
⟨*Wirkung*⟩; heben ⟨*Aussehen*⟩
enigma /ɪ'nɪgmə/ *n.* Rätsel, *das*
enigmatic /enɪg'mætɪk/ *adj.* rätselhaft
enjoy /ɪn'dʒɔɪ/ ⑴ *v.t.* **(a) I ~ed the book/
work** das Buch/die Arbeit hat mir gefallen;
he ~s reading/travelling er liest/reist gern
(b) genießen ⟨*Rechte, Privilegien, Vorteile*⟩
⑵ *v. refl.* sich amüsieren
enjoyable /ɪn'dʒɔɪəbl/ *adj.* schön;
angenehm ⟨*Empfindung, Arbeit*⟩;
unterhaltsam ⟨*Buch, Film, Stück*⟩
en'joyment *n.* Vergnügen, *das* (of an
+ *Dat.*)
enlarge /ɪn'lɑːdʒ/ ⑴ *v.t.* vergrößern;
verbreitern ⟨*Straße, Durchgang*⟩
⑵ *v.i.* **~ [up]on sth.** etw. weiter ausführen
en'largement *n.* Vergrößerung, *die;*
(making wider) Verbreiterung, *die*

enlighten /ɪnˈlaɪtn/ *v.t.* aufklären (**on, as to** über + *Akk.*).

en'lightenment *n.* Aufklärung, *die*

enlist /ɪnˈlɪst/ 1 *v.t.* (obtain) gewinnen
2 *v.i.* ~ **[for the army/navy]** in die Armee/Marine eintreten; ~ **[as a soldier]** Soldat werden

enliven /ɪnˈlaɪvn/ *v.t.* beleben

enmity /ˈenmɪtɪ/ *n.* Feindschaft, *die*

enormous /ɪˈnɔːməs/ *adj.* enorm; riesig, gewaltig ‹*Figur, Tier, Menge*›

e'normously *adv.* enorm

enough /ɪˈnʌf/ 1 *adj.* genug; **there's ~ room** es ist Platz genug
2 *n.* genug; **be ~ to do sth.** genügen, etw. zu tun; **have had ~ [of sb./sth.]** genug [von jmdm./etw.] haben; **I've had ~!** jetzt reicht's mir aber!
3 *adv.* genug; **oddly/funnily ~:** merkwürdigerweise/(ugs.) komischerweise

enquire /ɪnˈkwaɪə(r)/ 1 *v.i.* sich erkundigen (**about, after** nach, **of** bei); ~ **into** untersuchen
2 *v.t.* sich erkundigen nach ‹*Weg, Namen*›

enquiring /ɪnˈkwaɪərɪŋ, ɪŋˈkwaɪərɪŋ/ *adj.* fragend; forschend ‹*Geist*›

enquiry /ɪnˈkwaɪərɪ/ *n.* **(a)** (question) Erkundigung, *die* (**into** über + *Akk.*); **make enquiries** Erkundigungen einziehen
(b) (investigation) Untersuchung, *die*

enquiry desk, enquiry office *n.* Auskunft, *die*

enrage /ɪnˈreɪdʒ/ *v.t.* wütend machen; **be ~d by sth.** über etw. (*Akk.*) wütend werden

enrich /ɪnˈrɪtʃ/ *v.t.* reich machen; (fig.) bereichern

enrol (*Amer.:* **enroll**) /ɪnˈrəʊl/ 1 *v.i.,* -ll- sich einschreiben; ~ **for a course** sich zu einem Kurs anmelden
2 *v.t.* einschreiben

en'rolment (*Amer.:* **en'rollment**) *n.* Einschreibung, *die*

en route /ɑ̃ ˈruːt/ *adv.* unterwegs; ~ **to Scotland/for Edinburgh** auf dem Weg nach Schottland/Edinburgh

ensign /ˈensaɪn, ˈensn/ *n.* Hoheitszeichen, *das*

enslave /ɪnˈsleɪv/ *v.t.* versklaven

ensue /ɪnˈsjuː/ *v.i.* folgen (**from** aus); **the discussion which ~d** die anschließende Diskussion

ensure /ɪnˈʃʊə(r)/ *v.t.* ~ **that ...** (see to it that) gewährleisten, dass ...; ~ **sth.** etw. gewährleisten

entail /ɪnˈteɪl/ *v.t.* mit sich bringen; **sth. ~s doing sth.** etw. bedeutet, dass man etw. tun muss

entangle /ɪnˈtæŋgl/ *v.t.* sich verfangen lassen; **get** *or* **become ~d in** *or* **with sth.** sich in etw. (*Dat.*) verfangen

enter /ˈentə(r)/ 1 *v.i.* **(a)** hineingehen; ‹*Fahrzeug:*› hineinfahren; (come in) hereinkommen; (into room) eintreten
(b) (register as competitor) sich zur Teilnahme anmelden (**for** an + *Dat.*)
2 *v.t.* **(a)** [hinein]gehen in (+ *Akk.*); ‹*Fahrzeug:*› [hinein]fahren in (+ *Akk.*); betreten ‹*Gebäude, Zimmer*›; einlaufen in (+ *Akk.*) ‹*Hafen*›; einreisen in (+ *Akk.*) ‹*Land*›; (come into) [herein]kommen in (+ *Akk.*)
(b) teilnehmen an (+ *Dat.*) ‹*Rennen, Wettbewerb*›
(c) (in book etc.) eintragen (**in** in + *Akk.*)
(d) (Comp.) eingeben ‹*Daten usw.*›; **press ~:** 'Enter' drücken

■ **'enter into** *v.t.* aufnehmen ‹*Verhandlungen*›; eingehen ‹*Verpflichtung*›; schließen ‹*Vertrag*›

■ **'enter [up]on** *v.t.* beginnen

'enter key *n.* (Comp.) Entertaste, *die;* Eingabetaste, *die*

enterprise /ˈentəpraɪz/ *n.* **(a)** (undertaking) Unternehmen, *das;* **free/private ~:** freies/privates Unternehmertum
(b) (enterprising spirit) Unternehmungsgeist, *der*

enterprising /ˈentəpraɪzɪŋ/ *adj.* unternehmungslustig

entertain /entəˈteɪn/ *v.t.* **(a)** (amuse) unterhalten
(b) (receive as guest) bewirten
(c) haben ‹*Vorstellung*›; hegen (geh.) ‹*Gefühl, Verdacht, Zweifel*›; (consider) in Erwägung ziehen

enter'tainer *n.* Unterhalter, *der*/Unterhalterin, *die*

enter'taining *adj.* unterhaltsam

enter'tainment *n.* **(a)** (amusement) Unterhaltung, *die*
(b) (performance, show) Veranstaltung, *die*

enthral (*Amer.:* **enthrall**) /ɪnˈθrɔːl/ *v.t.,* -ll- gefangen nehmen (fig.)

enthuse /ɪnˈθjuːz/ 1 *v.i.* in Begeisterung ausbrechen (**about** über + *Akk.*)
2 *v.t.* begeistern

enthusiasm /ɪnˈθjuːzɪæzm/ *n.* Begeisterung, *die*

enthusiast /ɪnˈθjuːzɪæst/ *n.* Enthusiast, *der;* (for sports) Fan, *der;* **a great DIY ~:** ein begeisterter Heimwerker

enthusiastic /ɪnθjuːzɪˈæstɪk/ *adj.* begeistert; **not be very ~ about doing sth.** keine große Lust haben, etw. zu tun

entice /ɪnˈtaɪs/ *v.t.* locken (**into** in + *Akk.*); ~ **sb. into doing** *or* **to do sth.** jmdn. dazu verleiten, etw. zu tun

entire /ɪnˈtaɪə(r)/ *adj.* **(a)** (whole) ganz
(b) (intact) vollständig

en'tirely *adv.* **(a)** (wholly) völlig
(b) (solely) ganz ‹*für sich behalten*›; voll ‹*verantwortlich sein*›; **it's up to you ~:** es liegt ganz bei dir

entirety /ɪn'taɪərətɪ/ n. in its ∼: in seiner/ihrer Gesamtheit

entitle /ɪn'taɪtl/ v.t. berechtigen (to zu); ∼ sb. to do sth. jmdm. das Recht geben, etw. zu tun; be ∼d to [claim] sth. Anspruch auf etw. (Akk.) haben; be ∼d to do sth. das Recht haben, etw. zu tun

entomologist /entə'mɒlədʒɪst/ n. Entomologe, der/Entomologin, die

entomology /entə'mɒlədʒɪ/ n. Entomologie, die; Insektenkunde, die

entourage /ɒntʊ'rɑːʒ/ n. Gefolge, das

entrails /'entreɪlz/ n. pl. Eingeweide Pl.

entrance¹ /ɪn'trɑːns/ v.t. hinreißen

entrance² /'entrəns/ n. (way in) Eingang, der (to Gen. od. zu); (for vehicles) Einfahrt, die

entrance /'entrəns/: ∼ **examination** n. Aufnahmeprüfung, die; ∼ **fee** n. Eintrittsgeld, das; ∼ **hall** n. Eingangshalle, die; ∼ **ticket** n. Eintrittskarte, die

entrant /'entrənt/ n. (for competition, race, etc.) Teilnehmer, der/Teilnehmerin, die (for Gen., an + Dat.)

entreat /ɪn'triːt/ v.t. anflehen

en'treaty n. flehentliche Bitte

entrepreneur /ɒntrəprə'nɜː(r)/ n. Unternehmer, der/Unternehmerin, die

entrepreneurial /ɒntrəprə'nɜːrɪəl/ adj. unternehmerisch

entrust /ɪn'trʌst/ v.t. ∼ sb. with sth. jmdm. etw. anvertrauen; ∼ sb./sth. to sb. jmdm. jmdn./etw. jmdm./einer Sache anvertrauen; ∼ a task to sb. jmdn. mit einer Aufgabe betrauen

entry /'entrɪ/ n. (a) Eintritt, der (into in + Akk.); (into country) Einreise, die; 'no ∼' (for people) „Zutritt verboten"; (for vehicles) „Einfahrt verboten" (b) (way in) Eingang, der; (for vehicle) Einfahrt, die (c) (registration, item) Eintragung, die (in, into in + Akk. od. Dat.); (in dictionary, encyclopaedia) Eintrag, der

entry: ∼ **fee** n. Eintrittsgeld, das; ∼ **form** n. Anmeldeformular, das; ∼ **visa** n. Einreisevisum, das

envelop /ɪn'veləp/ v.t. (ein)hüllen (in in + Akk.); be ∼ed in flames ganz von Flammen umgeben sein

envelope /'envələʊp, 'ɒnvələʊp/ n. [Brief]umschlag, der

enviable /'envɪəbl/ adj. beneidenswert

envious /'envɪəs/ adj. neidisch (of auf + Akk.)

environment /ɪn'vaɪərənmənt/ n. Umwelt, die; (surrounding objects, region) Umgebung, die

environmental /ɪnvaɪərən'mentl/ adj. Umwelt(verschmutzung, -schutz, -katastrophe); for ∼ reasons aus Gründen des Umweltschutzes; ∼ **group** Umweltschutzorganisation, die;

∼ protection Umweltschutz, der

environmental 'health n. Umwelthygiene, die; ∼ **health officer** Umwelthygienebeauftragte, der/die; ∼ **health department** Umwelthygieneamt, das

environ'mentalist n. Umweltschützer, der/-schützerin, die

environ'mentally adv. ∼ **friendly** umweltfreundlich; ∼ **sensitive** ökologisch sensibel; ∼ **sound** umweltverträglich; umweltgerecht

envisage /ɪn'vɪzɪdʒ/, **envision** /ɪn'vɪʒn/ v.t. sich (Dat.) vorstellen

envoy /'envɔɪ/ n. Gesandte, der/Gesandtin, die

envy /'envɪ/ ① n. Neid, der; you'll be the ∼ of all your friends alle deine Freunde werden dich beneiden ② v.t. beneiden; ∼ sb. sth. jmdn. um etw. beneiden

enzyme /'enzaɪm/ n. Enzym, das

ephemeral /ɪ'femərl/ adj. kurzlebig

epic /'epɪk/ ① adj. episch ② n. Epos, das

epidemic /epɪ'demɪk/ ① adj. epidemisch ② n. Epidemie, die

epilepsy /'epɪlepsɪ/ n. Epilepsie, die

epileptic /epɪ'leptɪk/ ① adj. epileptisch; ∼ **fit** epileptischer Anfall ② n. Epileptiker, der/Epileptikerin, die

Epiphany /ɪ'pɪfənɪ/ n. [Feast of the] ∼: Epiphanias, das; Dreikönigsfest, das; at ∼: am Dreikönigstag

episode /'epɪsəʊd/ n. (a) Episode, die (b) (of serial) Folge, die

epistle /ɪ'pɪsl/ n. Epistel, die

epitaph /'epɪtɑːf/ n. Grab[in]schrift, die

epithet /'epɪθet/ n. Beiname, der; (as term of abuse) Schimpfname, der

epitome /ɪ'pɪtəmɪ/ n. Inbegriff, der

epitomize /ɪ'pɪtəmaɪz/ v.t. ∼ sth. der Inbegriff einer Sache (Gen.) sein

epoch /'iːpɒk/ n. Epoche, die

'epoch-making adj. Epoche machend

equal /'iːkwl/ ① adj. (a) gleich; ∼ in or of ∼ **height/size/importance** etc. gleich hoch/groß/wichtig usw. (b) be ∼ to sth./sb. (strong, clever, etc. enough) einer Sache/jmdm. gewachsen sein ② n. Gleichgestellte, der/die; have no ∼: nicht seines-/ihresgleichen haben ③ v.t., (Brit.) -ll-: ∼ sb. es jmdm. gleichtun; three times four ∼s twelve drei mal vier ist [gleich] zwölf

equality /ɪ'kwɒlɪtɪ/ n. Gleichheit, die; (equal rights) Gleichberechtigung, die; ∼ **between the sexes** Gleichheit von Mann und Frau

equalize /'iːkwəlaɪz/ v.i. (Sport) den Ausgleich[streffer] erzielen

'equalizer n. (Sport) Ausgleich[streffer], der

'equally *adv.* gleich; (just as) ebenso; in gleiche Teile ⟨*aufteilen*⟩; gleichmäßig ⟨*verteilen*⟩

Equal Oppor'tunities Commission *n.* (Brit.) *Ausschuss für Chancengleichheit;* ≈ Gleichstellungsausschuss, *der*

equal oppor'tunity *n.* Chancengleichheit, *die*

'equals sign *n.* (Math.) Gleichheitszeichen, *das*

equanimity /ekwə'nɪmɪtɪ/ *n.* Gelassenheit, *die*

equate /ɪ'kweɪt/ *v.t.* gleichsetzen (**with** mit)

equation /ɪ'kweɪʒn/ *n.* (Math.) Gleichung, *die*

equator /ɪ'kweɪtə(r)/ *n.* Äquator, *der*

equilibrium /iːkwɪ'lɪbrɪəm/ *n.*, *pl.* **equilibria** /iːkwɪ'lɪbrɪə/ *or* ∼s Gleichgewicht, *das*

equinox /'ekwɪnɒks/ *n.* Tagundnachtgleiche, *die*

equip /ɪ'kwɪp/ *v.t.*, **-pp-** ausrüsten ⟨*Fahrzeug, Armee*⟩; ausstatten ⟨*Küche*⟩; **fully** ∼**ped** komplett ausgerüstet/ausgestattet; ∼ **sb./oneself [with sth.]** jmdn./sich [mit etw.] ausrüsten

e'quipment *n.* Ausrüstung, *die;* (of kitchen, laboratory) Ausstattung, *die;* (needed for activity) Geräte *Pl.*

equity /'ekwɪtɪ/ *n.*(a) (fairness) Gerechtigkeit, *die;* **with** ∼: gerecht
(b) *in pl.* (stocks and shares without fixed interest) [Stamm]aktien *Pl.*
(c) (value of shares) Eigenkapital, *das*
(d) (net value of mortgaged property) *Wert eines Besitzes nach Abzug der Belastungen*

'equity market *n.* (Commerc.) Aktienmarkt, *der*

equivalent /ɪ'kwɪvələnt/ ① *adj.* gleichwertig; **be** ∼ **to sth.** einer Sache (*Dat.*) entsprechen
② *n.* (a) (thing, person) Pendant, *das;* Gegenstück, *das* (**of** zu)
(b) **be the** ∼ **of sth.** (have same result) einer Sache (*Dat.*) entsprechen

equivocal /ɪ'kwɪvəkl/ *adj.* zweideutig

er /ɜː(r)/ *int.* äh

era /'ɪərə/ *n.* Ära, *die*

eradicate /ɪ'rædɪkeɪt/ *v.t.* ausrotten

erase /ɪ'reɪz/ *v.t.* auslöschen; (with rubber, knife) ausradieren; (from tape, also Comp.) löschen

e'raser *n.* [pencil] ∼: Radiergummi, *der*

erect /ɪ'rekt/ ① *adj.* aufrecht
② *v.t.* errichten; aufstellen ⟨*Standbild, Mast, Verkehrsschild, Gerüst, Zelt*⟩

erection /ɪ'rekʃn/ *n.* (a) ▶ ERECT 2: Errichtung, *die;* Aufstellen, *das*
(b) (Physiol.) Erektion, *die*

ergonomic /ɜːɡə'nɒmɪk/ *adj.*, **ergo'nomically** *adv.* ergonomisch

ermine /'ɜːmɪn/ *n.* Hermelin, *der*

erode /ɪ'rəʊd/ *v.t.* (a) ⟨*Säure, Rost:*⟩ angreifen; ⟨*Wasser:*⟩ auswaschen; ⟨*Wind:*⟩ verwittern lassen
(b) (fig.) unterminieren

erosion /ɪ'rəʊʒn/ *n.* (a) ▶ ERODE A: Angreifen, *das;* Auswaschung, *die;* Verwitterung, *die*
(b) (fig.) Unterminierung, *die*

erotic /ɪ'rɒtɪk/ *adj.* erotisch

err /ɜː(r)/ *v.i.* sich irren

errand /'erənd/ *n.* Botengang, *der;* (shopping) Besorgung, *die;* **go on** *or* **run an** ∼: einen Botengang/eine Besorgung machen

'errand boy *n.* Laufbursche, *der*

erratic /ɪ'rætɪk/ *adj.* unregelmäßig; sprunghaft ⟨*Wesen, Person, Art*⟩; launenhaft ⟨*Verhalten*⟩

erroneous /ɪ'rəʊnɪəs/ *adj.* falsch; irrig ⟨*Schlussfolgerung, Annahme*⟩

error /'erə(r)/ *n.* (mistake) Fehler, *der;* (wrong opinion) Irrtum, *der;* **in** ∼: irrtümlich[erweise]

'error message *n.* (Comp.) Fehlermeldung, *die*

erudite /'eruːdaɪt/ *adj.* gelehrt

erupt /ɪ'rʌpt/ *v.i.* ausbrechen

eruption /ɪ'rʌpʃn/ *n.* Ausbruch, *der*

escalate /'eskəleɪt/ *v.i.* ① sich ausweiten (**into** zu); ⟨*Preise, Kosten:*⟩ [ständig] steigen
② *v.t.* ausweiten (**into** zu)

escalator /'eskəleɪtə(r)/ *n.* Rolltreppe, *die*

escapade /eskə'peɪd/ *n.* Eskapade, *die* (geh.)

escape /ɪ'skeɪp/ ① *n.* Flucht, *die* (**from** aus); **have a narrow** ∼: gerade noch einmal davonkommen
② *v.i.* (a) fliehen (**from** aus); (successfully) entkommen (**from** *Dat.*)
(b) ⟨*Gas:*⟩ ausströmen; ⟨*Flüssigkeit:*⟩ auslaufen
③ *v.t.* (a) entkommen (+ *Dat.*) ⟨*Verfolger, Feind*⟩; entgehen (+ *Dat.*) ⟨*Bestrafung, Gefangennahme, Tod*⟩; verschont bleiben von ⟨*Zerstörung, Auswirkungen*⟩
(b) (not be remembered by) entfallen sein (+ *Dat.*)

escape: ∼ **artist** ▶ ESCAPOLOGIST; ∼ **attempt,** ∼ **bid** *ns.* Fluchtversuch, *der;* (from prison) Ausbruchsversuch, *der;* ∼ **hatch** *n.* Notausstieg, *der;* (fig.) Rettungsanker, *der;* ∼ **key** *n.* (Comp.) Escapetaste, *die;* ∼ **road** *n.* Auslaufstrecke, *die;* ∼ **route** *n.* Fluchtweg, *der*

escapism /ɪ'skeɪpɪzm/ *n.* Realitätsflucht, *die*

escapologist /eskə'pɒlədʒɪst/ *n.* (Brit.) Entfesselungskünstler, *der*/-künstlerin, *die*

escarpment /ɪ'skɑːpmənt/ *n.* (Geog.) Steilhang, *der*

escort ① /'eskɔːt/ *n.* (a) Begleitung, *die;* (Mil.) Eskorte, *die* ⋯◈

(b) (hired companion) Begleiter, *der*/ Begleiterin, *die* 2 /ɪˈskɔːt/ *v.t.* begleiten; (lead) führen; (Mil.) eskortieren

Eskimo /ˈeskɪməʊ/ 1 *adj.* Eskimo- 2 *n.*, *pl.* ~s *or same* Eskimo, *der*/ Eskimofrau, *die;* the ~s die Eskimos

esoteric /esəʊˈterɪk/ *adj.* esoterisch

especial /ɪˈspeʃl/ *attrib. adj.* [ganz] besonder...

especially /ɪˈspeʃəlɪ/ *adv.* besonders

espionage /ˈespɪənɑːʒ/ *n.* Spionage, *die*

esplanade /espləˈneɪd, espləˈnɑːd/ *n.* Esplanade, *die* (geh.)

espouse /ɪˈspaʊz/ *v.t.* eintreten für

espresso /eˈspresəʊ/ *n.*, *pl.* ~s (coffee) Espresso, *der*

eˈspresso bar *n.* Espressobar, *die*

Esq. /ɪˈskwaɪə(r)/ *abbr.* = **Esquire** ≈ Hr.; (on letter) ≈ Hrn.; **Jim Smith,** ~: Hr./Hrn. Jim Smith

essay /ˈeseɪ/ *n.* Essay, *der;* Aufsatz, *der* (bes. Schulw.)

essence /ˈesəns/ *n.* **(a)** Wesen, *das;* (gist) Wesentliche, *das;* in ~: im Wesentlichen **(b)** (Cookery) Essenz, *die*

essential /ɪˈsenʃl/ 1 *adj.* **(a)** (fundamental) wesentlich **(b)** (indispensable) unentbehrlich; lebensnotwendig ⟨*Versorgungseinrichtungen, Güter*⟩; unabdingbar ⟨*Qualifikation, Voraussetzung*⟩; **it is ~ that ...:** es ist unbedingt notwendig, dass ... 2 *n. pl.* **the ~s** (fundamentals) das Wesentliche; (items) das Notwendigste

esˈsentially *adv.* im Grunde

establish /ɪˈstæblɪʃ/ *v.t.* **(a)** schaffen ⟨*Einrichtung, Präzedenzfall*⟩; gründen ⟨*Organisation, Institut*⟩; errichten ⟨*Geschäft, System*⟩ **(b)** (secure acceptance for) etablieren; **become ~ed** sich einbürgern **(c)** (prove) beweisen **(d)** (discover) feststellen

established /ɪˈstæblɪʃt/ *adj.* bestehend ⟨*Ordnung*⟩; etabliert ⟨*Schriftsteller*⟩; (accepted) üblich; fest ⟨*Brauch*⟩; feststehend ⟨*Tatsache*⟩; **become ~:** sich durchsetzen

eˈstablishment *n.* **(a)** (setting up, foundation) Gründung, *die* **(b)** [business] ~: Unternehmen, *das*

estate /ɪˈsteɪt/ *n.* **(a)** (landed property) Gut, *das* **(b)** (Brit.: housing ~) [Wohn]siedlung, *die* **(c)** (of deceased person) Erbmasse, *die*

estate: ~ **agent** *n.* (Brit.) Grundstücksmakler, *der*/-maklerin, *die;* ~ **car** *n.* (Brit.) Kombiwagen, *der;* ~ **duty** (Brit.), ~ **tax** (Amer.) *ns.* Erbschaftssteuer, *die*

esteem /ɪˈstiːm/ 1 *n.* Wertschätzung, *die* (geh.) (for *Gen.*, für)

2 *v.t.* schätzen; **highly ~ed** hoch geschätzt

estimate 1 /ˈestɪmət/ *n.* **(a)** Schätzung, *die;* **at a rough ~:** grob geschätzt **(b)** (Commerc.) Kostenvoranschlag, *der* 2 /ˈestɪmeɪt/ *v.t.* schätzen (at auf + *Akk.*)

estimation /estɪˈmeɪʃn/ *n.* Schätzung, *die;* **in sb.'s ~:** nach jmds. Schätzung

Estonia /eˈstəʊnɪə/ *pr. n.* Estland (*das*)

Estonian /eˈstəʊnɪən/ 1 *adj.* estländisch; estnisch; **sb. is ~:** jmd. ist Este/Estin 2 *n.* **(a)** (language) Estnisch, *das;* Estländisch, *das; see also* ENGLISH 2A **(b)** (person) Este, *der*/Estin, *die;* Estländer, *der*/Estländerin, *die*

estuary /ˈestjʊərɪ/ *n.* [Trichter]mündung, *die*

ETA *abbr.* = **estimated time of arrival** voraussichtliche Ankunftszeit

etc. *abbr.* = **et cetera** usw.

etch /etʃ/ *v.t.* ätzen (on auf + *Akk.*); (on metal also) ⟨*bes. Künstler:*⟩ radieren; (fig.) einprägen (in, on *Dat.*)

ˈetching *n.* (Art) Radierung, *die*

eternal /ɪˈtɜːnl/ *adj.*, **eˈternally** *adv.* ewig

eternity /ɪˈtɜːnɪtɪ/ *n.* Ewigkeit, *die*

ether /ˈiːθə(r)/ *n.* Äther, *der*

ethereal /ɪˈθɪərɪəl/ *adj.* ätherisch

ethical /ˈeθɪkl/ *adj.* ethisch

ethics /ˈeθɪks/ *n.* **(a)** Moral, *die;* (moral philosophy) Ethik, *die* **(b)** *usu. constr. as pl.* (moral code) Ethik, *die* (geh.)

Ethiopia /iːθɪˈəʊpɪə/ *pr. n.* Äthiopien (*das*)

Ethiopian /iːθɪˈəʊpɪən/ 1 *adj.* äthiopisch; **sb. is ~:** jmd. ist Äthiopier/Äthiopierin 2 *n.* Äthiopier, *der*/Äthiopierin, *die*

ethnic /ˈeθnɪk/ *adj.* ethnisch; ~ **minority** ethnische Minderheit

ethnic ˈcleansing *n.* ethnische Säuberung

ethnology /eθˈnɒlədʒɪ/ *n.* Ethnologie, *die*

ethos /ˈiːθɒs/ *n.* (guiding beliefs) Gesinnung, *die;* (fundamental values) Ethos, *das* (geh.); (characteristic spirit) Geist, *der*

etiquette /ˈetɪket/ *n.* Etikette, *die*

etymology /etɪˈmɒlədʒɪ/ *n.* Etymologie, *die*

EU *abbr.* = **European Union** EU

eulogy /ˈjuːlədʒɪ/ *n.* Lobrede, *die*

euphemism /ˈjuːfəmɪzm/ *n.* Euphemismus, *der*

euphemistic /juːfəˈmɪstɪk/ *adj.* verhüllend

euphoria /juːˈfɔːrɪə/ *n.* Euphorie, *die* (geh.)

euro /ˈjʊərəʊ/ *n* Euro, *der*

Euro: ~**cheque** *n.* Euroscheck, *der;* ~**land** *n.* Euroland, *das;* ~**-MP** *n.* Europaabgeordnete, *der*/*die*

Europe /ˈjʊərəp/ *pr. n.* Europa (*das*)

European /jʊərə'pi:ən/ ① *adj.*
europäisch; **sb. is** ~: jmd. ist Europäer/
Europäerin; ~ **[Economic] Community**
Europäische [Wirtschafts]gemeinschaft
② *n.* Europäer, *der*/Europäerin, *die*
European: ~ **Central 'Bank**
n. Europäische Zentralbank;
~ **Com'mission** *n.* Europäische
Kommission; ~ **'Council** *n.*
Europäischer Rat; ~ **Court of**
'Justice *n.* Europäischer Gerichtshof;
~ **'Cup** *n.* (Footb.) Europacup, *der;*
Europapokal, *der;* ~ **'currency unit**
n. Europäische Währungseinheit;
~ **'Monetary System** *n.* Europäisches
Währungssystem; ~ **Monetary**
'Union *n.* Europäische Währungsunion;
~ **'Parliament** *n.* Europäisches
Parlament; ~ **'Union** *n.* Europäische
Union
Euro-: ~**rebel** *n.* (esp. Brit.)
[innerparteilicher] Europagegner/
[innerparteiliche] Europagegnerin;
~**sceptic** *n.* Euroskeptiker, *der*/
-skeptikerin, *die;* ~**star** ® *n.* Eurostar,
der; **go by** ~**star** mit dem Eurostar fahren;
e~**zone** *n.* Eurozone, *die*
euthanasia /ju:θə'neɪzɪə/ *n.* Euthanasie,
die
evacuate /ɪ'vækjʊeɪt/ *v.t.* evakuieren
(from aus)
evacuation /ɪvækjʊ'eɪʃn/ *n.*
Evakuierung, *die* **(from** aus)
evade /ɪ'veɪd/ *v.t.* ausweichen (+ *Dat.*)
⟨*Angriff, Angreifer, Schlag, Problem,*
Frage⟩; sich entziehen (+ *Dat.*) ⟨*Verhaftung,*
Verantwortung⟩; entkommen (+ *Dat.*)
⟨*Verfolger, Verfolgung*⟩; hinterziehen
⟨*Steuern*⟩; ~ **doing sth.** vermeiden, etw.
zu tun
evaluate /ɪ'væljʊeɪt/ *v.t.* einschätzen;
bewerten ⟨*Daten*⟩
evangelical /i:væn'dʒelɪkl/ *adj.*
missionarisch (fig.); (Protestant) evangelikal
evangelist /ɪ'vændʒəlɪst/ *n.* Evangelist,
der
evaporate /ɪ'væpəreɪt/ ① *v.i.* verdunsten
② *v.t.* verdunsten lassen
evaporated 'milk *n.* Kondensmilch, *die*
evaporation /ɪvæpə'reɪʃn/ *n.*
Verdunstung, *die*
evasion /ɪ'veɪʒn/ *n.* Umgehung, *die;* (of
responsibility, question) Ausweichen, *das* **(of** vor
+ *Dat.*); **tax** ~: Steuerhinterziehung, *die*
evasive /ɪ'veɪsɪv/ *adj.* **(a)** be/become
~: ausweichen
(b) ausweichend ⟨*Antwort*⟩
eve /i:v/ *n.* Vorabend, *der* **(of** *Gen.*); (day)
Vortag, *der* **(of** *Gen.*)
even /'i:vn/ ① *adj.* **(a)** eben ⟨*Boden,*
Fläche⟩; gleich hoch ⟨*Stapel, Stuhl-,*
Tischbein⟩; **be of** ~ **height/length** gleich
hoch/lang sein

(b) gerade ⟨*Zahl, Seite, Hausnummer*⟩
(c) be *or* get ~ **with sb.** (quits) es jmdm.
heimzahlen; **break** ~: die Kosten decken
② *adv.* sogar; selbst; sogar noch ⟨*weniger,*
schlimmer usw.⟩; ~ **if** selbst wenn; ~ **so**
[aber] trotzdem; **not** *or* **never** ~ ...: [noch]
nicht einmal ...
■ **even 'up** *v.t.* ausgleichen
evening /'i:vnɪŋ/ *n.* Abend, *der;*
this/tomorrow ~: heute/morgen Abend; **in**
the ~: am Abend; (regularly) abends
evening: ~ **class** *n.* Abendkurs,
der; ~ **dress** *n.* Abendkleidung, *die;*
~ **'meal** *n.* Abendessen, *das;* ~ **'paper**
n. Abendzeitung, *die*
'evenly *adv.* gleichmäßig
'even-numbered *adj.* gerade
event /ɪ'vent/ *n.* **(a) in the** ~ **of his**
dying *or* **death im Falle seines Todes; in**
the ~: letzten Endes; **in the** ~ **of rain** bei
Regenwetter
(b) (occurrence) Ereignis, *das*
(c) (planned public or social occasion)
Veranstaltung *die*
e'ventful *adj.* ereignisreich
eventual /ɪ'ventjʊəl/ *adj.* **predict sb.'s**
~ **downfall** vorhersagen, dass jmd.
schließlich zu Fall kommen wird; **the career**
of Napoleon and his ~ **defeat** der Aufstieg
Napoleons und schließlich seine Niederlage
eventuality /ɪventjʊ'ælɪtɪ/ *n.*
Eventualität, *die*
e'ventually *adv.* schließlich
ever /'evə(r)/ *adv.* **(a)** (always) immer; **for**
~: für immer; ewig ⟨*lieben, da sein, leben*⟩;
~ **since [then]** seit [dieser Zeit]
(b) (at any time) je[mals]; **hardly** ~: so gut wie
nie; **as** ~: wie gewöhnlich
(c) *in comb. with compar. adj. or adv.* noch;
~**-increasing** ständig zunehmend
(d) what ~ **does he want?** was will er nur?;
why ~ **not?** warum denn nicht?
'ever: ~**green** ① *adj.* immergrün; ② *n.*
immergrüne Pflanze; ~**lasting** *adj.*
(a) (eternal) immer während; ewig ⟨*Leben*⟩;
unvergänglich ⟨*Ruhm, Ehre*⟩; **(b)** (incessant)
endlos
every /'evrɪ/ *adj.* **(a)** jeder/jede/jedes;
~ **one** jeder/jede [einzelne]; **your**
~ **wish** all[e] deine Wünsche; **she comes**
~ **day** sie kommt jeden Tag; ~ **three/few**
days alle drei/paar Tage; ~ **other** (~ second,
almost ~) jeder/jede/jedes zweite
(b) (the greatest possible) all ⟨*Respekt, Aussicht*⟩
every: ~**body** *n. & pron.* jeder; ~**body**
else alle anderen; ~**day** *attrib. adj.*
alltäglich; Alltags⟨*kleidung, -sprache*⟩;
in ~**day life** im Alltag; ~**one** ▸ ~BODY;
~**place** (Amer.) ▸ ~WHERE; ~**thing** *n. &*
pron. alles; ~**where** *adv.* überall; ~**where**
you go/look wohin man auch geht/sieht
evict /ɪ'vɪkt/ *v.t.* ~ **sb. [from his home]**
jmdn. zur Räumung [seiner Wohnung]
zwingen

eviction /ɪ'vɪkʃn/ n. Zwangsräumung,
die; the ∼ of the tenant die zwangsweise
Vertreibung des Mieters

evidence /'evɪdəns/ n. (a) Beweis, *der;*
(indication) Anzeichen, *das;* be ∼ of sth. etw.
beweisen
(b) (Law) Beweismaterial, *das;* give
∼: aussagen

evident /'evɪdənt/ adj. offensichtlich; be
∼ to sb. jmdm. klar sein; it soon became
∼ that …: es stellte sich bald heraus, dass …

'evidently adv. offensichtlich

evil /'iːvl, 'iːvɪl/ ① adj. böse; schlecht
⟨*Charakter, Einfluss, System*⟩
② n. (a) Böse, *das*
(b) (bad thing) Übel, *das*

evocative /ɪ'vɒkətɪv/ adj. be ∼ of sth.
etw. heraufbeschwören

evoke /ɪ'vəʊk/ v.t. heraufbeschwören;
hervorrufen ⟨*Bewunderung, Überraschung*⟩;
erregen ⟨*Interesse*⟩

evolution /iːvə'luːʃn/ n. Entwicklung, *die;*
(Biol.) Evolution, *die*

evolve /ɪ'vɒlv/ ① v.i. sich entwickeln
(from aus, into zu)
② v.t. entwickeln

ewe /juː/ n. Mutterschaf, *das*

ex¹ /eks/ n. (coll.) Verflossene, *der/die* (ugs.)

ex² prep. (Commerc.) ex works/store ⟨*Güter*⟩
ab Werk/Lager

ex- pref. Ex-⟨*Freundin, Präsident,
Champion*⟩; Alt-⟨*[bundes]kanzler*⟩

exacerbate /ek'sæsəbeɪt/ v.t.
verschärfen ⟨*Lage*⟩; verschlechtern
⟨*Zustand*⟩

exact /ɪg'zækt/ ① adj. genau
② v.t. fordern; erheben ⟨*Gebühr*⟩

exacting /ɪg'zæktɪŋ/ n. anspruchsvoll;
hoch ⟨*Anforderung*⟩

exactitude /ɪg'zæktɪtjuːd/ Genauigkeit,
die

exactly /ɪg'zæktlɪ/ adv. genau; not ∼ (coll.
iron.) nicht gerade

exactness /ɪg'zæktnɪs/ n. Genauigkeit,
die

exaggerate /ɪg'zædʒəreɪt/ v.t.
übertreiben

exaggeration /ɪgzædʒə'reɪʃn/ n.
Übertreibung, *die*

exam /ɪg'zæm/ (coll.) ▶ EXAMINATION B

examination /ɪgzæmɪ'neɪʃn/ n.
(a) (inspection; Med.) Untersuchung, *die*
(b) (Sch. etc.) Prüfung, *die;* (final ∼ at university)
Examen, *das*

exami'nation paper n. (a) ∼[s]
schriftliche Prüfungsaufgaben *Pl.*
(b) (with candidate's answers) ≈ Klausurarbeit,
die

examine /ɪg'zæmɪn/ v.t. (a) (inspect;
Med.) untersuchen (for auf + *Akk.*); prüfen
⟨*Dokument, Gewissen*⟩; kontrollieren
⟨*Ausweis, Gepäck*⟩

(b) (Sch. etc.) prüfen (in in + *Dat.*)
(c) (Law) verhören

examiner /ɪg'zæmɪnə(r)/ n. Prüfer,
*der/*Prüferin, *die*

example /ɪg'zɑːmpl/ n. Beispiel, *das;*
for ∼: zum Beispiel; make an ∼ of sb. ein
Exempel an jmdm. statuieren

exasperate /ɪg'zæspəreɪt/ v.t. (irritate)
verärgern; (infuriate) zur Verzweiflung
bringen

exasperation /ɪg'zæspəreɪʃn/ n.
▶ EXASPERATE: Ärger, *der/*Verzweiflung,
die (with über + *Akk.*); in ∼: verärgert/
verzweifelt

excavate /'ekskəveɪt/ v.t.
(a) ausschachten; (with machine) ausbaggern
(b) (Archaeol.) ausgraben

excavation /ekskə'veɪʃn/ n.
(a) Ausschachtung, *die;* (with machine)
Ausbaggerung, *die*
(b) (Archaeol.) Ausgrabung, *die*

excavator /'ekskəveɪtə(r)/ n. Bagger, *der*

exceed /ɪk'siːd/ v.t. (a) (be greater than)
übertreffen (in an + *Dat.*); ⟨*Kosten, Summe,
Anzahl:*⟩ übersteigen (by um)
(b) (go beyond) überschreiten; hinausgehen
über (+ *Akk.*) ⟨*Auftrag, Befehl*⟩

ex'ceedingly adv. äußerst;
ausgesprochen ⟨*hässlich, dumm*⟩

excel /ɪk'sel/ ① v.t., -ll- übertreffen;
∼ oneself (lit. or iron.) sich selbst übertreffen
② v.i., -ll- sich hervortun (at, in in + *Dat.*)

excellence /'eksələns/ n. hervorragende
Qualität

excellent /'eksələnt/ adj. hervorragend

except /ɪk'sept/ ① prep. ∼ [for] außer
(+ *Dat.*); ∼ for (in all respects other than)
abgesehen von
② v.t. ausnehmen (from bei); ∼ed
ausgenommen

ex'cepting prep. außer (+ *Dat.*)

exception /ɪk'sepʃn/ n. Ausnahme, *die;*
take ∼ to Anstoß nehmen an (+ *Dat.*)

exceptional /ɪk'sepʃənl/ adj.
außergewöhnlich

ex'ceptionally adv. (a) (as an exception)
ausnahmsweise
(b) (remarkably) ungewöhnlich

excerpt /'eksɜːpt/ n. Auszug, *der* (from aus)

excess /ɪk'ses/ n. (a) Übermaß, *das* (of
an + *Dat.*); eat/drink to ∼: übermäßig
essen/trinken
(b) esp. in pl. (over-indulgence) Exzess, *der*
(c) be in ∼ of sth. etw. übersteigen
(d) (surplus) Überschuss, *der*

excess /'ekses/: ∼ **'baggage** n.
Mehrgepäck, *das;* ∼ **'fare** n. Mehrpreis,
der; pay the ∼ **fare** nachlösen

excessive /ɪk'sesɪv/ adj. übermäßig;
übertrieben ⟨*Forderung, Lob, Ansprüche*⟩;
unmäßig ⟨*Esser, Trinker*⟩

ex'cessively adv. übertrieben; unmäßig
⟨*essen, trinken*⟩

excess ~ **'luggage** ▶ ~ BAGGAGE; ~ **'postage** *n.* Nachgebühr, *die*

exchange /ɪks'tʃeɪndʒ/ **1** *v.t.*
(a) tauschen ⟨*Plätze, Ringe, Küsse*⟩; umtauschen ⟨*Geld*⟩; wechseln ⟨*Blicke, Worte*⟩; ~ **insults** sich beleidigen
(b) (give in place of another) eintauschen (**for** für, gegen); umtauschen ⟨*[gekaufte] Ware*⟩ (**for** gegen)
2 *n.* (a) Tausch, *der;* **in** ~: dafür; **in** ~ **for** sth. für etw.
(b) (Educ.) Austausch, *der;* **an** ~ **student** ein Austauschstudent/eine Austauschstudentin
(c) (of money) Umtausch, *der;* ~ **rate, rate of** ~: Wechselkurs, *der*
(d) (Teleph.) Fernmeldeamt, *das*

exchequer /ɪks'tʃekə(r)/ *n.* (Brit.) Schatzamt, *das*

excise /'eksaɪz/ *n.* Verbrauchsteuer, *die;* **Customs and E**~ (Brit.) *Amt für Zölle und Verbrauchsteuer*

excitable /ek'saɪtəbl/ *adj.* leicht erregbar

excite /ɪk'saɪt/ *v.t.* (a) (thrill) begeistern
(b) (agitate) aufregen

ex'cited *adj.* aufgeregt (**at** über + *Akk.*); **get** ~: sich aufregen

ex'citement *n.* Aufregung, *die;* (enthusiasm) Begeisterung, *die*

exciting /ɪk'saɪtɪŋ/ *adj.* aufregend; (full of suspense) spannend

exclaim /ɪk'skleɪm/ **1** *v.t.* ausrufen
2 *v.i.* aufschreien

exclamation /eksklə'meɪʃn/ *n.* Ausruf, *der*

excla'mation mark, (Amer.) **excla'mation point** *ns.*
Ausrufezeichen, *das*

exclude /ɪk'sklu:d/ *v.t.* ausschließen

excluding /ɪk'sklu:dɪŋ/ *prep.* ~ **drinks/ VAT** Getränke ausgenommen/ohne Mehrwertsteuer

exclusion /ɪk'sklu:ʒn/ *n.* Ausschluss, *der*

exclusive /ɪk'sklu:sɪv/ *adj.* (a) alleinig ⟨*Besitzer, Kontrolle*⟩; Allein⟨*eigentum*⟩; (Journ.) Exklusiv⟨*bericht, -interview*⟩
(b) (select) exklusiv
(c) ~ **of** ohne

ex'clusively *adv.* ausschließlich

excommunicate /ekskə'mju:nɪkeɪt/ *v.t.* exkommunizieren

excrement /'ekskrɪmənt/ *n.* Kot, *der* (geh.)

excrete /ɪk'skri:t/ *v.t.* ausscheiden

excruciating /ɪk'skru:'ʃeɪtɪŋ/ *adj.* unerträglich

excursion /ɪk'skɜ:ʃn/ *n.* Ausflug, *der*

excusable /ɪk'skju:zəbl/ *adj.* entschuldbar; verzeihlich

excuse **1** /ɪk'skju:z/ *v.t.*
(a) entschuldigen; ~ **oneself** sich entschuldigen; ~ **me** Entschuldigung
(b) (release, exempt) befreien (**from** von)

2 /ɪk'skju:s/ *n.* Entschuldigung, *die*

ex-di'rectory *adj.* (Brit. Teleph.) Geheim⟨*nummer, -anschluss*⟩; **be** ~: nicht im Telefonbuch stehen

execute /'eksɪkju:t/ *v.t.* (a) hinrichten
(b) (put into effect) ausführen

execution /eksɪ'kju:ʃn/ *n.*
(a) Hinrichtung, *die*
(b) (putting into effect) Ausführung, *die*

exe'cutioner *n.* Scharfrichter, *der*

executive /ɪg'zekjʊtɪv/ **1** *n.* leitender Angestellter/leitende Angestellte
2 *adj.* leitend ⟨*Stellung, Funktion*⟩

executive: ~ **'stress** *n.* Managerstress, *der;* ~ **'toy** *n.* Managerspielzeug, *das*

executor /ɪg'zekjʊtə(r)/ *n.* (Law) Testamentsvollstrecker, *der*

exemplary /ɪg'zemplərɪ/ *adj.* (a) (model) vorbildlich
(b) (deterrent) exemplarisch

exemplify /ɪg'zemplɪfaɪ/ *v.t.* veranschaulichen

exempt /ɪg'zempt/ **1** *adj.* [**be**] ~ [**from** sth.] [von etw.] befreit [sein]
2 *v.t.* befreien

exemption /ɪg'zempʃn/ *n.* Befreiung, *die*

exercise /'eksəsaɪz/ **1** *n.* (a) Übung, *die*
(b) *no pl.* (physical exertion) Bewegung, *die;* **take** ~: sich (*Dat.*) Bewegung schaffen
2 *v.t.* ausüben ⟨*Recht, Macht, Einfluss*⟩; walten lassen ⟨*Vorsicht*⟩
3 *v.i.* sich (*Dat.*) Bewegung schaffen

exercise: ~ **bicycle,** (coll.) ~ **bike** *ns.* Heimtrainer, *der;* ~ **book** *n.* [Schul]heft, *das*

exert /ɪg'zɜ:t/ **1** *v.t.* aufbieten ⟨*Kraft*⟩; ausüben ⟨*Einfluss, Druck*⟩
2 *v. refl.* sich anstrengen

exertion /ɪg'zɜ:ʃn/ *n.* (a) (of strength, force) Aufwendung, *die;* (of influence, pressure) Ausübung, *die*
(b) (effort) Anstrengung, *die*

exhale /eks'heɪl/ *v.t. & i.* ausatmen

exhaust /ɪg'zɔ:st/ **1** *v.t.* erschöpfen; erschöpfend behandeln ⟨*Thema*⟩
2 *n.* (Motor Veh.) Auspuff, *der;* (gases) Auspuffgase *Pl.;* ~ **emissions** Auspuffabgase *Pl.;* ~ **emissions test** Abgasuntersuchung, *die*

ex'hausted *adj.* erschöpft

ex'hausting *adj.* anstrengend

exhaustion /ɪg'zɔ:stʃn/ *n.* Erschöpfung, *die*

exhaustive /ɪg'zɔ:stɪv/ *adj.* umfassend

ex'haust pipe *n.* Auspuffrohr, *das*

exhibit /ɪg'zɪbɪt/ **1** *v.t.* ausstellen; zeigen ⟨*Mut, Symptome, Angst usw.*⟩
2 *n.* Ausstellungsstück, *die*

exhibition /eksɪ'bɪʃn/ *n.* Ausstellung, *die;* **make an** ~ **of oneself** sich unmöglich aufführen

e

exhibitionism /eksɪˈbɪʃənɪzm/ n. Exhibitionismus, der

exhibitionist /eksɪˈbɪʃənɪst/ n. Exhibitionist, der/Exhibitionistin, die

exhibitor /ɪgˈzɪbɪtə(r)/ n. Aussteller, der/Ausstellerin, die

exhilarated /ɪgˈzɪləreɪtɪd/ adj. belebt

exhilarating /ɪgˈzɪləreɪtɪŋ/ adj. belebend

exhilaration /ɪgzɪləˈreɪʃn/ n. [feeling of] ∼: Hochgefühl, das

exhort /ɪgˈzɔːt/ v.t. ermahnen

exile /ˈeksaɪl/ ① n. (a) Exil, das; in/into ∼: im/ins Exil
(b) (person) Verbannte, der/die
② v.t. verbannen

exist /ɪgˈzɪst/ v.i. existieren; ⟨Zweifel, Gefahr, Problem, Einrichtung:⟩ bestehen; ∼ on sth. von etw. leben

existence /ɪgˈzɪstəns/ n. Existenz, die; (mode of living) Dasein, das; be in/come into ∼: existieren/entstehen

exit /ˈeksɪt/ n. (way out) Ausgang, der (from aus); (for vehicle) Ausfahrt, die

exit: ∼ permit n. Ausreiseerlaubnis, die; **∼ poll** n.: Befragung der ein Wahllokal verlassenden Wähler; **∼ visa** n. Ausreisevisum, das

exonerate /ɪgˈzɒnəreɪt/ v.t. entlasten

exorbitant /ɪgˈzɔːbɪtənt/ adj. [maßlos] überhöht

exorcize /ˈeksɔːsaɪz/ v.t. austreiben

exotic /ɪgˈzɒtɪk/ adj. exotisch

expand /ɪkˈspænd/ ① v.i. (a) sich ausdehnen; (Commerc.) expandieren
(b) ∼ on weiter ausführen
② v.t. ausdehnen; (Commerc.) erweitern

expanse /ɪkˈspæns/ n. [weite] Fläche

expansion /ɪkˈspænʃn/ n. Ausdehnung, die; (Commerc.) Expansion, die

expect /ɪkˈspekt/ v.t. (a) erwarten; ∼ to do sth. damit rechnen, etw. zu tun; ∼ sb. to do sth. damit rechnen, dass jmd. etw. tut; (require) von jmdm. erwarten, dass er etw. tut
(b) (coll.: think, suppose) glauben; I ∼ so ich glaube schon

expectancy /ɪkˈspektənsɪ/ n. Erwartung, die

expectant /ɪkˈspektənt/ adj. erwartungsvoll; ∼ mother werdende Mutter

ex'pectantly adv. erwartungsvoll; gespannt ⟨warten⟩

expectation /ekspekˈteɪʃn/ n. Erwartung, die

expedient /ɪkˈspiːdɪənt/ ① adj. angebracht
② n. Mittel, das

expedition /ekspɪˈdɪʃn/ n. Expedition, die

expel /ɪkˈspel/ v.t., -ll- ausweisen (from aus); ∼ sb. from school jmdn. von der Schule verweisen

expend /ɪkˈspend/ v.t. (a) aufwenden ([up]on für)

(b) (use up) aufbrauchen ([up]on für)

expendable /ɪkˈspendəbl/ adj. entbehrlich; be ∼: geopfert werden können

expenditure /ɪkˈspendɪtʃə(r)/ n.
(a) (amount spent) Ausgaben Pl. (on für)
(b) (spending) Ausgabe, die

expense /ɪkˈspens/ n. (a) Kosten Pl.; at sb.'s ∼: auf jmds. Kosten (Akk.); at one's own ∼: auf eigene Kosten
(b) usu. in pl. (Commerc. etc.: amount spent [and repaid]) Spesen Pl.
(c) (fig.) [be] at the ∼ of sth. auf Kosten von etw. [gehen]

ex'pense account n. Spesenabrechnung, die; put sth. on one's ∼: etw. als Spesen abrechnen

expensive /ɪkˈspensɪv/ adj., **ex'pensively** adv. teuer

experience /ɪkˈspɪərɪəns/ ① n. Erfahrung, die; (incident) Erlebnis, das
② v.t. erleben; haben ⟨Schwierigkeiten⟩; verspüren ⟨Kälte, Schmerz, Gefühl⟩

ex'perienced adj. erfahren

experiment ① /ɪkˈsperɪmənt/ n.
(a) Experiment, das, Versuch, der (on an + Dat.)
(b) (fig.) Experiment, das
② /ɪkˈsperɪment/ v.i. Versuche anstellen (on an + Dat.)

experimental /ɪksperɪˈmentl/ adj. experimentell; Experimentier⟨theater, -kino⟩

expert /ˈekspɜːt/ ① adj. ausgezeichnet; be ∼ in or at sth. Fachmann od. Experte für etw. sein; be ∼ in or at doing sth. etw. ausgezeichnet können
② n. Fachmann, der; Experte, der/Expertin, die; be an ∼ in or at/on sth. Fachmann od. Experte in etw. (Dat.)/für etw. sein

expertise /ekspɜːˈtiːz/ n. Fachkenntnisse Pl.; (skill) Können, das

expert: ∼ system n. (Comp.) Expertensystem, das; **∼ 'witness** n. sachverständiger Zeuge

expire /ɪkˈspaɪə(r)/ v.i. ablaufen

expiry /ɪkˈspaɪərɪ/ n. Ablauf, der

explain /ɪkˈspleɪn/ ① v.t., also abs. erklären
② v. refl., often abs. please ∼ [yourself] bitte erklären Sie mir das
■ **explain a'way** v.t. eine [plausible] Erklärung finden für

explanation /ekspləˈneɪʃn/ n. Erklärung, die; need ∼: einer Erklärung bedürfen

explanatory /ɪkˈsplænətərɪ/ adj. erklärend; erläuternd ⟨Bemerkung⟩

explicable /ɪkˈsplɪkəbl/ adj. erklärbar

explicit /ɪkˈsplɪsɪt/ adj. klar; ausdrücklich ⟨Zustimmung, Erwähnung⟩

ex'plicitly adv. ausdrücklich; deutlich ⟨beschreiben, ausdrücken⟩

explode /ɪkˈspləʊd/ ① v.i. explodieren
② v.t. zur Explosion bringen

exploit ⚊ /'eksplɔɪt/ n. Heldentat, *die* ⚋ /ɪk'splɔɪt/ v.t. ausbeuten ⟨*Arbeiter usw.*⟩; ausnutzen ⟨*Gutmütigkeit, Freund, Unwissenheit*⟩

exploitation /eksplɔɪ'teɪʃn/ n.
► EXPLOIT 2: Ausbeutung, *die;* Ausnutzung, *die*

exploration /eksplə'reɪʃn/ n. Erforschung, *die;* (fig.) Untersuchung, *die*

exploratory /ɪk'splɒrətərɪ/ adj. Forschungs-

explore /ɪk'splɔː(r)/ v.t. erforschen; (fig.) untersuchen

ex'plorer n. Entdeckungsreisende, *der/die*

explosion /ɪk'spləʊʒn/ n. Explosion, *die*

explosive /ɪk'spləʊzɪv/ ⚊ adj. explosiv ⚋ n. Sprengstoff, *der*

export ⚊ /ɪk'spɔːt, 'ekspɔːt/ v.t. exportieren; ausführen ⚋ /'ekspɔːt/ n. Export, *der*

export /'ekspɔːt/: ~ **drive** n. Exportkampagne, *die;* ~ **duty** n. Exportzoll, *der*

ex'porter n. Exporteur, *der*

export /'ekspɔːt/: ~ **licence** n. Ausfuhrlizenz, *die;* ~ **market** n. Exportmarkt, *der;* ~ **permit** n. Exporterlaubnis, *die;* Ausfuhrerlaubnis, *die*

expose /ɪk'spəʊz/ v.t. (a) (uncover) freilegen; entblößen ⟨*Haut, Körper*⟩ (b) offenbaren ⟨*Schwäche*⟩; aufdecken ⟨*Missstände, Verbrechen*⟩; entlarven ⟨*Täter, Spion*⟩ (c) (subject) ~ **to sth.** einer Sache (*Dat.*) aussetzen (d) (Photog.) belichten

exposed /ɪk'spəʊzd/ adj. (unprotected) ungeschützt; ~ **position** exponierte Stellung

exposure /ɪk'spəʊʒə(r)/ n. (a) (to cold etc.) die of/suffer from ~: an Unterkühlung (*Dat.*) sterben/leiden (b) (Photog.) (exposing time) Belichtung, *die;* (picture) Aufnahme, *die*

ex'posure meter n. Belichtungsmesser, *der*

expound /ɪk'spaʊnd/ v.t. darlegen

express /ɪk'spres/ ⚊ v.t. ausdrücken; äußern ⟨*Meinung, Wunsch, Dank, Bedauern*⟩; ~ **oneself** sich ausdrücken ⚋ *attrib. adj.* (a) Eil⟨*brief, -bote usw.*⟩; Schnell⟨*paket, -sendung*⟩ (b) ausdrücklich ⟨*Wunsch, Absicht*⟩ ⚌ *adv.* als Eilsache ⟨*senden*⟩ ⚍ n. (train) Schnellzug, *der*

express de'livery n. Eilzustellung, *die*

expression /ɪk'spreʃn/ n. Ausdruck, *der*

expressive /ɪk'spresɪv/ adj. ausdrucksvoll

express: ~ **'letter** n. Eilbrief, *der;* ~ **'lift** n. Schnellaufzug, *der*

ex'pressly adv. ausdrücklich

express: ~ **'train** n. D-Zug, *der;* ~**way** n. (Amer.) Schnellstraße, *die*

expulsion /ɪk'spʌlʃn/ n. Ausweisung, *die* (from aus); (from school) Verweisung, *die* (from von)

exquisite /'ekskwɪzɪt, ɪk'skwɪzɪt/ adj. erlesen

ex'quisitely adv. vorzüglich; kunstvoll ⟨*verziert, geschnitzt*⟩

extend /ɪk'stend/ ⚊ v.t. verlängern; ausstrecken ⟨*Arm, Bein, Hand*⟩; ausziehen ⟨*Leiter, Teleskop*⟩; verlängern lassen ⟨*Leihbuch, Visum*⟩; ausdehnen ⟨*Einfluss, Macht*⟩; vergrößern ⟨*Haus, Geschäft, Fabrik*⟩; gewähren ⟨*[Gast]freundschaft, Hilfe, Kredit*⟩ (to *Dat.*); ~ **the time limit** den Termin hinausschieben ⚋ v.i. sich erstrecken; **the season ~s from November to March** die Saison geht von November bis März

extended 'family n. Großfamilie, *die*

extension /ɪk'stenʃn/ n. (a) Verlängerung, *die* (b) (part of house) Anbau, *der* (c) (telephone) Nebenanschluss, *der;* (number) Apparat, *der*

extension: ~ **cord** (Amer.) ► ~ LEAD; ~ **ladder** n. Ausziehleiter, *die;* ~ **lead** n. (Brit.) Verlängerungsschnur, *die*

extensive /ɪk'stensɪv/ adj. ausgedehnt; umfangreich ⟨*Reparatur, Wissen, Nachforschungen*⟩; beträchtlich ⟨*Schäden*⟩; weit reichend ⟨*Änderungen*⟩

ex'tensively adv. beträchtlich ⟨*ändern, beschädigen*⟩; ausführlich ⟨*berichten, schreiben*⟩

extent /ɪk'stent/ n. Ausdehnung, *die;* (scope) Umfang, *der;* (of damage) Ausmaß, *das;* **to what ~?** inwieweit?

exterior /ɪk'stɪərɪə(r)/ ⚊ adj. äußer...; Außen⟨*fläche, -wand*⟩ ⚋ n. Äußere, *das;* (of house) Außenwände *usw.*

exterminate /ɪk'stɜːmɪneɪt/ v.t. ausrotten ⟨*Nation, Volk*⟩; vertilgen ⟨*Ungeziefer*⟩; liquidieren ⟨*Person*⟩

extermination /ɪkstɜːmɪ'neɪʃn/ n. Ausrottung, *die;* (of pests) Vertilgung, *die*

extermi'nation camp n. Vernichtungslager, *das*

external /ɪk'stɜːnl/ adj. äußer...; Außen⟨*fläche, -abmessungen*⟩; **purely ~:** rein äußerlich; **for ~ use only** nur äußerlich anzuwenden

extinct /ɪk'stɪŋkt/ adj. erloschen ⟨*Vulkan*⟩; ausgestorben ⟨*Art, Rasse, Gattung*⟩

extinction /ɪk'stɪŋkʃn/ n. Aussterben, *das*

extinguish /ɪk'stɪŋgwɪʃ/ v.t. löschen

ex'tinguisher n. Feuerlöscher, *der*

extol /ɪk'stɒl/ v.t., **-ll-** rühmen; preisen

extort /ɪk'stɔːt/ v.t. erpressen (out of von)

extortion /ɪk'stɔːʃn/ n. Erpressung, *die*

extortionate /ɪk'stɔːʃənət/ adj. ⸱⸱⸱⸱⟩

Wucher⟨*preis, -zinsen usw.*⟩; maßlos
überzogen ⟨*Forderung*⟩
extra /'ekstrə/ **1** *adj.* zusätzlich;
Mehr⟨*arbeit, -kosten, -ausgaben*⟩;
Sonder⟨*bus, -zug*⟩
2 *adv.* **(a)** (more than usually) besonders;
extra ⟨*lang, stark, fein*⟩
(b) (additionally) extra; **packing and postage
~:** zuzüglich Verpackung und Porto
3 *n.* **(a)** (added to services, salary, etc.)
zusätzliche Leistung; (on car etc.) Extra, *das*
(b) (in play, film, etc.) Statist, *der*/Statistin, *die*
extract 1 /'ekstrækt/ *n.* **(a)** Extrakt, *der*
(fachspr. auch: *das*)
(b) (from book, music, etc.) Auszug, *der*
2 /ık'strækt/ *v.t.* ziehen ⟨*Zahn*⟩;
herausziehen ⟨*Dorn, Splitter usw.*⟩
extraction /ık'strækʃn/ *n.* (of tooth)
Extraktion, *die;* (of thorn, splinter, etc.)
Herausziehen, *das*
ex'tractor fan *n.* Entlüfter, *der*
extra-curricular /ekstrəkə'rıkjʊlə(r)/
adj. extracurricular (fachspr.); ⟨*Aktivität*⟩
außerhalb des Lehrplans
extradite /'ekstrədaıt/ *v.t.* ausliefern
extradition /ekstrə'dıʃn/ *n.* Auslieferung,
die
extra'marital *adj.* außerehelich
extraordinary /ık'strɔːdınərı/ *adj.*
außergewöhnlich; merkwürdig ⟨*Benehmen*⟩;
how ~! wie seltsam!
extraordinary rendition /ren'dıʃn/
außerordentliche Auslieferung
extravagance /ık'strævəgəns/ *n.*
(a) Extravaganz, *die*
(b) (extravagant thing) Luxus, *der*
extravagant /ık'strævəgənt/ *adj.*
verschwenderisch; aufwendig ⟨*Lebensstil*⟩;
teuer ⟨*Geschmack*⟩
extreme /ık'striːm/ **1** *adj.* **(a)** äußerst…
⟨*Spitze, Rand, Ende*⟩; extrem ⟨*Gegensätze,
Hitze, Kälte*⟩; höchst… ⟨*Gefahr*⟩; äußerst…
⟨*Notfall, Höflichkeit, Bescheidenheit*⟩
stärkst… ⟨*Schmerzen*⟩; größt…
⟨*Wichtigkeit*⟩; **at the ~ edge/left** ganz am
Rand/ganz links
(b) (not moderate) extrem; drastisch
⟨*Maßnahme*⟩
2 *n.* Extrem, *das;* **go to ~s** vor nichts

zurückschrecken; **go from one ~ to the
other** von einem Extrem ins andere fallen
ex'tremely *adv.* äußerst
extreme 'sport *n.* Extremsportart, *die*
extremist /ık'striːmıst/ *n.* Extremist,
der/Extremistin, *die; attrib.* extremistisch
extremity /ık'stremıtı/ *n.* äußerstes Ende
extricate /'ekstrıkeıt/ *v.t.* **~ sth. from sth.**
etw. aus etw. herausziehen; **~ oneself/sb.
from sth.** sich/jmdn. aus etw. befreien
extrovert /'ekstrəvɜːt/ **1** *n.*
extravertierter Mensch; **be an
~:** extravertiert sein
2 *adj.* extravertiert
exuberant /ıg'zjuːbərənt/ *adj.* **be ~:** sich
überschwänglich freuen
exude /ıg'zjuːd/ *v.t.* absondern; (fig.)
ausstrahlen
exult /ıg'zʌlt/ *v.i.* jubeln (**in, at, over** über
+ *Akk.*)
eye /aı/ **1** *n.* **(a)** Auge, *das;* **keep an ~ on
sb./sth.** auf jmdn./etw. aufpassen; **see ~ to
~:** einer Meinung sein; **with one's ~s shut**
(fig.) blind; (easily) im Schlaf; **be up to one's
~s in work/debt** bis über beide Ohren in
Arbeit/Schulden stecken (ugs.)
(b) (of needle) Öhr, *das;* (metal loop) Öse, *die*
2 *v.t.,* beäugen; **~ sb. up and down** jmdn.
von oben bis unten mustern
eye: ~ball *n.* Augapfel, *der;* **~brow**
n. Augenbraue, *die;* **~-catching** *adj.*
ins Auge springend *od.* fallend ⟨*Inserat,
Plakat, Buchhülle usw.*⟩; **be [very]
~-catching** ein [wirkungsvoller] Blickfang
sein; **~ drops** *n. pl.* (Med.) Augentropfen
Pl.; **~ hospital** *n.* Augenklinik, *die;*
~lash *n.* Augenwimper, *die;* **~ level** *n.*
Augenhöhe, *die;* **at ~ level** in Augenhöhe;
~-level *attrib.* in Augenhöhe *nachgestellt;*
~lid *n.* Augenlid, *das;* **~ make-up**
n. Augen-Make-up, *das;* **~shadow** *n.*
Lidschatten, *der;* **~sight** *n.* Sehkraft,
die; **have good ~sight** gute Augen haben;
his ~sight is poor er hat schlechte Augen;
~sore *n.* Schandfleck, *der;* **~wash**
n. **(a)** (Med.: lotion) Augenwasser, *das;*
(b) (coll.) (nonsense) Gewäsch, *das* (ugs.);
(concealment) Augen[aus]wischerei, *die* (ugs.);
~witness *n.* Augenzeuge, *der*/-zeugin, *die*

Ff

F, f /ef/ n. F, f, das
fable /'feɪbl/ n. Fabel, die; (myth, lie) Märchen, das
fabric /'fæbrɪk/ n. Gewebe, das
fabricate /'fæbrɪkeɪt/ v.t. (invent) erfinden
fabrication /fæbrɪkeɪʃn/ n. Erfindung, die
'fabric softener /'sɒfənə(r)/ n. Weichspülmittel, das; Weichspüler, der
fabulous /'fæbjʊləs/ adj. (a) sagenhaft (b) (coll.: marvellous) fabelhaft (ugs.)
façade /fə'sɑːd/ n. (lit. or fig.) Fassade, die; that's just a ∼ (fig.) das ist alles nur Fassade
face /feɪs/ ① n. (a) Gesicht, das; lie ∼ down[ward] ⟨Person/Buch:⟩ auf dem Bauch/Gesicht liegen; make or pull a ∼/∼s Grimassen schneiden; on the ∼ of it dem Anschein nach; in the ∼ of sth. trotz etw. (Gen.)
(b) (of mountain, cliff) Wand, die; (of clock, watch) Zifferblatt, das; (of dice) Seite, die; (of coin, playing card) Vorderseite, die
② v.t. (a) sich wenden zu; [stand] facing one another sich (Dat.) gegenüber[stehen]
(b) (fig.) ins Auge sehen (+ Dat.) ⟨Tod, Vorstellung⟩; stehen vor (+ Dat.) ⟨Ruin, Entscheidung⟩; ∼ the facts den Tatsachen ins Gesicht sehen; be ∼d with sth. sich einer Sache (Dat.) gegenübersehen
(c) (coll.: bear) verkraften
③ v.i. (in train etc.) ∼ backwards/forwards ⟨Person:⟩ entgegen der/in Fahrtrichtung sitzen
■ **face 'up to** v.t. ins Auge sehen (+ Dat.); sich abfinden mit ⟨Möglichkeit⟩
face: ∼ **cream** n. Gesichtscreme, die; ∼ **flannel** n. (Brit.) Waschlappen, der; ∼**less** /'feɪslɪs/ adj. (anonymous) anonym (fig.); ∼**lift** n. (a) Facelifting, das; have or get a ∼lift sich liften lassen; (b) (fig.) Verschönerung, die; ∼ **pack** n. [Gesichts]maske, die; ∼**-saving** adj. zur Wahrung des Gesichts nachgestellt
facet /'fæsɪt/ n. Facette, die; (fig.) Aspekt, der
facetious /fə'siːʃəs/ adj. [gewollt] witzig
face: ∼**-to-**∼ adj. persönlich ⟨Gespräch, Treffen⟩; ∼ **value** n. Nennwert, der; accept sth. at [its] ∼ value (fig.) etw. für bare Münze nehmen
facial /'feɪʃl/ adj. Gesichts-
facile /'fæsaɪl/ adj. nichts sagend
facilities /fə'sɪlɪtɪz/ n. pl. Einrichtungen Pl.; cooking/washing ∼: Koch-/Waschgelegenheit, die; sports ∼: Sportanlagen Pl.; shopping ∼: Einkaufsmöglichkeiten Pl.

facsimile /fæk'sɪmɪlɪ/ n. (a) Faksimile, das
(b) ▶ FAX 1
fact /fækt/ n. Tatsache, die; ∼s and figures Fakten und Zahlen; the ∼ remains that …: Tatsache bleibt: …; the true ∼s of the case or matter der wahre Sachverhalt; know for a ∼ that …: genau wissen, dass …; in ∼: tatsächlich
faction /'fækʃn/ n. Splittergruppe, die
factor /'fæktə(r)/ n. Faktor, der
factory /'fæktərɪ/ n. Fabrik, die
factory: ∼ '**farm** n. [voll]automatisierter landwirtschaftlicher Betrieb; ∼ '**farming** n. [fabrikmäßige] Massentierhaltung; the ∼ farming of salmon die massenweise Lachsproduktion; ∼ **worker** n. Fabrikarbeiter, der/-arbeiterin, die
'**fact sheet** n. Infoblatt, das
factual /'fæktjʊəl/ adj. sachlich
faculty /'fækəltɪ/ n. (a) Fähigkeit, die; mental ∼: geistige Kraft
(b) (Univ.) Fakultät, die
fad /fæd/ n. Marotte, die
fade /feɪd/ v.i. (a) ⟨Blätter, Blumen:⟩ [ver]welken
(b) ∼ [in colour] [ver]bleichen; the light ∼d es dunkelte
(c) ⟨Laut:⟩ verklingen
(d) (fig.) verblassen; ⟨Schönheit:⟩ verblühen; ⟨Hoffnung:⟩ schwinden
(e) (blend) übergehen (into in + Akk.)
■ **fade a'way** v.i. schwinden; ⟨Laut:⟩ verklingen (into in + Dat.)
faded /'feɪdɪd/ adj. welk ⟨Blume, Blatt, Laub⟩; verblichen ⟨Stoff, Farbe⟩
faeces /'fiːsiːz/ n. pl. Fäkalien Pl.
fag /fæg/ n. (a) (Brit. coll.) Schinderei, die (ugs.)
(b) (coll.: cigarette) Stäbchen, das (ugs.)
fail /feɪl/ ① v.i. (a) scheitern; (in examination) nicht bestehen, (ugs.) durchfallen (in in + Dat.)
(b) (become weaker) ⟨Augenlicht, Gehör, Stärke:⟩ nachlassen
(c) (break down, stop) ⟨Versorgung:⟩ zusammenbrechen; ⟨Motor:⟩ aussetzen; ⟨Batterie, Pumpe:⟩ ausfallen; ⟨Bremse:⟩ versagen
② v.t. (a) ∼ to do sth. (not succeed in doing) etw. nicht tun [können]; ∼ to achieve one's purpose/aim seine Absicht/sein Ziel verfehlen
(b) (be unsuccessful in) nicht bestehen, (ugs.) durchfallen in (+ Dat.) ⟨Prüfung⟩
(c) (reject) durchfallen lassen (ugs.) ⟨Prüfling⟩ ⋯⃗

(d) ~ **to do sth.** (not do) etw. nicht tun;
(neglect to do) [es] versäumen, etw. zu tun; **not**
~ **to do sth.** etw. tun
(e) words ~ me mir fehlen die Worte; **his
courage** ~ed him ihn verließ der Mut
3 *n.* without ~: auf jeden Fall
'**failing** **1** *n.* Schwäche, *die*
2 *prep.* ~ that andernfalls
failure /ˈfeɪljə(r)/ *n.* **(a)** (omission, neglect)
Versäumnis, *das*
(b) (lack of success) Scheitern, *das;* **end in**
~: scheitern
(c) (person or thing) Versager, *der;* **our
plan/attempt was a** ~: unser Plan/Versuch
war fehlgeschlagen
faint /feɪnt/ **1** *adj.* **(a)** matt ⟨*Licht, Farbe,
Stimme, Lächeln*⟩; schwach ⟨*Geruch, Duft*⟩;
leise ⟨*Flüstern, Geräusch, Stimme*⟩; entfernt
⟨*Ähnlichkeit*⟩; undeutlich ⟨*Umriss, Linie,
Spur, Fotokopie*⟩
(b) (giddy, weak) matt; **she felt** ~: ihr war
schwindelig
2 *v.i.* ohnmächtig werden (**from** vor + *Dat.*)
3 *n.* Ohnmacht, *die*
faint-'hearted *adj.* hasenherzig; zaghaft
⟨*Versuch*⟩
'**faintly** *adv.* schwach; entfernt ⟨*sich
ähneln*⟩
fair¹ /feə(r)/ *n.* (fun~) Jahrmarkt, *der;*
(exhibition) Messe, *die;* **book-/trade** ~: Buch-/
Handelsmesse, *die*
fair² *adj.* **(a)** (just) gerecht; begründet
⟨*Beschwerde, Annahme*⟩; fair ⟨*Spiel, Kampf,
Prozess, Preis, Beurteilung, Handel*⟩; ~ **play**
Fairness, *die*
(b) (not bad, pretty good) ganz gut ⟨*Bilanz,
Anzahl, Chance*⟩; ziemlich ⟨*Maß,
Geschwindigkeit*⟩
(c) (blond) blond ⟨*Haar, Person*⟩; (light) hell
⟨*Haut*⟩; (~-skinned) hellhäutig ⟨*Person*⟩
(d) schön ⟨*Wetter, Tag*⟩
fair: ~**ground** *n.* Festplatz, *der;*
~**-haired** *adj.* blond; ~**-haired boy** (Amer.
fig.) Liebling, *der;* Favorit, *der*
'**fairly** *adv.* **(a)** fair ⟨*kämpfen, spielen*⟩;
gerecht ⟨*bestrafen, beurteilen, behandeln*⟩
(b) (rather) ziemlich
'**fair-minded** *adj.* unvoreingenommen
'**fairness** *n.* Gerechtigkeit, *die;* **in all** ~ [**to
sb.**] um fair [gegen jmdn.] zu sein
fairy /ˈfeərɪ/ *n.* Fee, *die*
fairy: ~ '**godmother** *n.* gute Fee;
~ **story,** ~ **tale** *ns.* Märchen, *das*
faith /feɪθ/ *n.* **(a)** (reliance, trust)
Vertrauen, *die* (**in** zu); have ~ **in oneself**
Selbstvertrauen haben; **in good** ~: in gutem
Glauben
(b) (religious belief) Glaube, *der*
faithful /ˈfeɪθfl/ *adj.* **(a)** treu (**to** *Dat.*)
(b) (conscientious) pflichtbewusst; [ge]treu
⟨*Diener*⟩
(c) (accurate) [wahrheits]getreu;
originalgetreu ⟨*Wiedergabe, Kopie*⟩

'**faithfully** *adv.* **(a)** treu ⟨*dienen*⟩;
pflichtbewusst ⟨*überbringen, zustellen*⟩;
hoch und heilig ⟨*versprechen*⟩
(b) (accurately) wahrheitsgetreu ⟨*erzählen*⟩;
originalgetreu ⟨*wiedergeben*⟩; genau
⟨*befolgen*⟩
(c) yours ~: hochachtungsvoll
faith: ~ **group** *n.* Glaubensgemeinschaft,
die; ~ **healer** *n.* Gesundbeter, *der/*
-beterin, *die;* ~ **healing** *n.* Gesundbeten,
das; ~ **school** *n.* religiöse Schule
fake /feɪk/ **1** *adj.* unecht; gefälscht
⟨*Dokument, Banknote, Münze*⟩
2 *n.* **(a)** Imitation, *die;* (painting) Fälschung,
die
(b) (person) Schwindler, *der/*Schwindlerin,
die
3 *v.t.* fälschen ⟨*Unterschrift*⟩; vortäuschen
⟨*Krankheit, Unfall*⟩
falcon /ˈfɔːlkn/ *n.* Falke, *der*
fall /fɔːl/ **1** *n.* **(a)** Fallen, *das;* (of person)
Sturz, *der;* ~ **of snow/rain** Schnee-/
Regenfall, *der;* **have a** ~: stürzen
(b) (collapse, defeat) Fall, *der;* (of dynasty,
empire) Untergang, *der*
(c) (decrease) Rückgang, *der*
(d) (Amer.: autumn) Herbst, *der*
2 *v.i.,* **fell** /fel/, **fallen** /ˈfɔːln/ **(a)** fallen;
⟨*Baum:*⟩ umstürzen; ⟨*Pferd:*⟩ stürzen;
~ **off sth.,** ~ **down from sth.** von etw.
[herunter]fallen; ~ **down [into] sth.**
in etw. (*Akk.*) [hinein]fallen; ~ **to the
ground** auf den Boden fallen; ~ **down the
stairs** *or* **downstairs** die Treppe herunter-/
hinunterfallen
(b) ⟨*Nacht, Dunkelheit:*⟩ hereinbrechen;
⟨*Abend:*⟩ anbrechen
(c) ⟨*Blätter:*⟩ [ab]fallen
(d) (sink) sinken; ⟨*Barometer:*⟩ fallen;
⟨*Absatz, Verkauf:*⟩ zurückgehen; ~ **by 10
per cent/from 10[°C] to 0[°C]** um 10%/von
10[°C] auf 0[°C] sinken
(e) (be killed) ⟨*Soldat:*⟩ fallen
(f) (collapse) einstürzen; ~ **to pieces,** ~ **apart**
auseinander fallen
(g) (occur) fallen (**on** auf + *Akk.*)
■ **fall 'back** *v.i.* zurückweichen
■ **fall 'back on** *v.t.* zurückgreifen auf
(+ *Akk.*)
■ **fall 'down** *v.i.* **(a)** ▸ FALL 2A
(b) ⟨*Brücke, Gebäude:*⟩ einstürzen
■ '**fall for** *v.t.* (coll.) ~ **for sb.** sich in jmdn.
verknallen (ugs.); ~ **for sth.** auf etw. (*Akk.*)
hereinfallen (ugs.)
■ **fall 'in** *v.i.* **(a)** hineinfallen
(b) (Mil.) antreten; ~ **in!** angetreten!
(c) ⟨*Gebäude, Wand usw.:*⟩ einstürzen
■ **fall 'off** *v.i.* **(a)** herunterfallen
(b) (diminish) nachlassen
■ **fall 'out** *v.i.* **(a)** herausfallen; ⟨*Haare,
Federn:*⟩ ausfallen
(b) (quarrel) ~ **out [with sb.]** sich [mit jmdm.]
streiten
■ **fall 'over** *v.i.* umfallen; ⟨*Person:*⟩
[hin]fallen

■ **fall 'through** *v.i.* (fig.) ins Wasser fallen (ugs)

fallacy /'fæləsɪ/ *n.* Irrtum, *der*

fallen ▸ FALL 2

fallible /'fælɪbl/ *adj.* nicht unfehlbar; fehlbar ⟨*Person*⟩

'**fallout** *n.* radioaktiver Niederschlag

fallow /'fæləʊ/ *adj.* brachliegend; ~ **ground/land** Brache, *die*/Brachland, *das;* **lie** ~: brachliegen

false /fɔːls, fɒls/ *adj.* falsch; gefälscht ⟨*Urkunde, Dokument*⟩; künstlich ⟨*Wimpern*⟩; **under a** ~ **name** unter falschem Namen

false a'larm *n.* blinder Alarm

'**falsely** *adv.* falsch; fälschlich[erweise] ⟨*annehmen, glauben, behaupten, beschuldigen*⟩

false: ~ '**move** ▸ FALSE STEP; ~ **pre'tences** *n. pl.* Vorspiegelung falscher Tatsachen; ~ '**start** *n.* Fehlstart, *der;* ~ '**step** *n.* (lit. or fig.) falscher Schritt; **make a** ~ **step** einen falschen Schritt tun; ~ '**teeth** *n. pl.* [künstliches] Gebiss

falsify /'fɔːlsɪfaɪ/ *v.t.* (alter) fälschen; (misrepresent) verfälschen ⟨*Tatsachen, Wahrheit*⟩

falter /'fɔːltə(r)/ *v.i.* stocken

fame /feɪm/ *n.* Ruhm, *der*

familiar /fə'mɪljə(r)/ *adj.* (a) vertraut; bekannt ⟨*Gesicht, Name, Lied*⟩; **he looks** ~: er kommt mir bekannt vor

(b) (informal) ungezwungen ⟨*Sprache, Art*⟩

familiarity /fəmɪlɪ'ærɪtɪ/ *n.* Vertrautheit, *die*

familiarize /fə'mɪljəraɪz/ *v.t.* vertraut machen (**with** mit)

family /'fæməlɪ/ *n.* Familie, *die*

family: ~ '**doctor** *n.* Hausarzt, *der;* ~ '**name** *n.* Familienname, *der;* ~ '**planning** *n.* Familienplanung, *die;* ~ '**tree** *n.* Stammbaum, *der*

famine /'fæmɪn/ *n.* Hungersnot, *die*

famished /'fæmɪʃt/ *adj.* ausgehungert; **I'm absolutely** ~ (coll.) ich sterbe vor Hunger (ugs.)

famous /'feɪməs/ *adj.* berühmt

fan[1] /fæn/ ① *n.* Fächer, *der;* (apparatus) Ventilator, *der*

② *v.t.*, -**nn**- fächeln ⟨*Gesicht*⟩; anfachen ⟨*Feuer*⟩; ~ **oneself/sb.** sich/jmdm. Luft zufächeln

■ **fan 'out** *v.i.* fächern; ⟨*Soldaten:*⟩ ausfächern

fan[2] *n.* (devotee) Fan, *der*

fanatic /fə'nætɪk/ *n.* Fanatiker, *der*/Fanatikerin, *die*

fanatical /fə'nætɪkl/ *adj.* fanatisch

fanaticism /fə'nætɪsɪzm/ *n.* Fanatismus, *der*

'**fan belt** *n.* Keilriemen, *der*

fanciful /'fænsɪfl/ *adj.* überspannt ⟨*Vorstellung, Gedanke*⟩; fantastisch

⟨*Gemälde, Design*⟩

'**fan club** *n.* Fanklub, *der*

fancy /'fænsɪ/ ① *n.* (a) (taste, inclination) **he has taken a** ~ **to a new car/her** ein neues Auto/sie hat es ihm angetan; **take** *or* **catch sb.'s** ~: jmdm. gefallen

(b) (whim) Laune, *die;* **tickle sb.'s** ~: jmdn. reizen

② *attrib. adj.* kunstvoll ⟨*Arbeit, Muster*⟩; fein[st...] ⟨*Kuchen, Spitzen*⟩

③ *v.t.* (a) (imagine) sich ⟨*Dat.*⟩ einbilden; ~ **that!** (coll.) sieh mal einer an!

(b) (suppose) glauben

(c) (wish to have) mögen; **what do you** ~ **for dinner?** was hättest du gern zum Abendessen?; **do you think he fancies him?** glaubst du, sie mag ihn?

fancy 'dress *n.* [Masken]kostüm, *das;* **in** ~: kostümiert; **fancy-dress party** Kostümfest, *das;* **fancy-dress ball** Maskenball, *der*

fanfare /'fænfeə(r)/ *n.* Fanfare, *die*

fang /fæŋ/ *n.* Reißzahn, *der;* (of snake) Giftzahn, *der*

fan: ~ **heater** *n.* Heizlüfter, *der;* ~**light** *n.* Oberlicht, *das;* ~ **mail** *n.* Fanpost, *die;* ~ **oven** *n.* Heißluftofen, *der*

fantastic /fæn'tæstɪk/ *adj.* (a) (grotesque, quaint) bizarr

(b) (coll.: excellent) fantastisch (ugs.)

fantasy /'fæntəzɪ/ *n.* Fantasie, *die;* (mental image) Fantasiegebilde, *das*

FAQ /fæk/ *abbr.* (Comp.) FAQ

far /fɑː(r)/ ① *adv.* weit; ~ **above/below** hoch über/tief unter (+ *Dat.*); hoch oben/tief unten; **as** ~ **as Munich/the church** bis [nach] München/bis zur Kirche; ~ **and wide** weit und breit; **from** ~ **and wide** von fern und nah; ~ **too viel zu;** ~ **longer/better** weit[aus] länger/besser; **as** ~ **as I remember/know** soweit ich mich erinnere/weiß; **go so** ~ **as to do sth.** so weit gehen und etw. tun; **so** ~ (until now) bisher; **so** ~ **so good** so weit, so gut; **by** ~: bei weitem; ~ **from easy/good** alles andere als leicht/gut

② *adj.* (a) (remote) weit entfernt; (in time) fern; **in the** ~ **distance** in weiter Ferne

(b) (more remote) weiter entfernt; **the** ~ **bank of the river/side of the road** das andere Flussufer/die andere Straßenseite; **the** ~ **door/wall** etc. die hintere Tür/Wand *usw.*

farce /fɑːs/ *n.* Farce, *die*

farcical /'fɑːsɪkl/ *adj.* (absurd) farcenhaft

fare /feə(r)/ *n.* (a) (price) Fahrpreis, *der;* (money) Fahrgeld, *das;* **what** *or* **how much is the** ~? was kostet die Fahrt?

(b) (food) Kost, *die*

Far: ~ '**East** *n.* **the** ~ **East** der Ferne Osten; ~ '**Eastern** *adj.* fernöstlich; des Fernen Ostens *nachgestellt*

farewell /feə'wel/ ① *int.* leb[e] wohl (veralt.)

② *n. attrib.* ~ **speech/gift** Abschiedsrede, *die*/-geschenk, *das*

far-'fetched *adj.* weit hergeholt

farm /fɑːm/ **1** *n.* [Bauern]hof, *der;* (larger) Gut, *das;* ~ **animals** Nutzvieh, *das*
2 *v.t.* bebauen ⟨*Land*⟩
3 *v.i.* Landwirtschaft treiben

'farmer *n.* Landwirt, *der*/-wirtin, *die;* ~**'s market** Bauernmarkt, *der*

farm: ~**hand** *n.* Landarbeiter, *der*/-arbeiterin, *die;* ~**house** *n.* Bauernhaus, *das;* (larger) Gutshaus, *das*

'farming *n.* Landwirtschaft, *die*

farm: ~**land** *n.* Acker- und Weideland, *das;* ~**worker** *n.* Landarbeiter, *der*/-arbeiterin, *die;* ~**yard** *n.* Hof, *der*

far: ~**'reaching** *adj.* weit reichend; ~**sighted** *adj.* **(a)** (fig.) weit blickend; **(b)** (Amer.: long-sighted) weitsichtig

fart /fɑːt/ (coarse) **1** *v.i.* furzen (derb)
2 *n.* Furz, *der* (derb)

farther /'fɑːðə(r)/ ▸ FURTHER 1A, 2

farthest /'fɑːðɪst/ ▸ FURTHEST

fascinate /'fæsɪneɪt/ *v.t.* fesseln; bezaubern

fascinated /'fæsɪneɪtɪd/ *adj.* fasziniert

fascinating /'fæsɪneɪtɪŋ/ *adj.* faszinierend (geh.); bezaubernd; hochinteressant ⟨*Thema, Faktum, Meinung*⟩; spannend, fesselnd ⟨*Buch*⟩

fascination /fæsɪ'neɪʃn/ *n.* Zauber, *der;* **have a ~ for sb.** einen besonderen Reiz auf jmdn. ausüben

fascism /'fæʃɪzm/ *n.* Faschismus, *der*

fascist /'fæʃɪst/ **1** *n.* Faschist, *der*/Faschistin, *die*
2 *adj.* faschistisch

fashion /'fæʃn/ **1** *n.* **(a)** Mode, *die*
(b) (manner) Art [und Weise]; **talk/behave in a peculiar ~:** merkwürdig sprechen/sich merkwürdig verhalten
2 *v.t.* formen (**out of, from** aus; [in]to zu)

fashionable /'fæʃənəbl/ *adj.* modisch; vornehm ⟨*Hotel, Restaurant*⟩; Mode⟨*farbe, -autor*⟩

fashionably /'fæʃənəblɪ/ *adv.* modisch

fashion: ~**-conscious** *adj.* modebewusst; ~ **designer** *n.* Modeschöpfer, *der*/-schöpferin, *die;* ~ **parade,** ~ **show** *ns.* Mode[n]schau, *die*

fast¹ /fɑːst/ **1** *v.i.* fasten
2 *n.* Fasten, *das*

fast² **1** *adj.* **(a)** (fixed, attached) fest; **make [the boat] ~:** das Boot festmachen; **hard and ~:** fest; bindend ⟨*Regel*⟩; klar ⟨*Entscheidung*⟩
(b) (rapid) schnell; ~ **train** Schnellzug, *der;* D-Zug, *der*
(c) be [ten minutes] ~ ⟨*Uhr:*⟩ [zehn Minuten] vorgehen
2 *adv.* **(a) be ~ asleep** fest schlafen; (when one should be awake) fest eingeschlafen sein
(b) (quickly) schnell

'fastback *n.* (back of car) Fließheck, *das;* Fastback, *das;* (car) Wagen mit Fließheck; Fastback, *das*

fasten /'fɑːsn/ *v.t.* befestigen (**on, to** an + *Dat.*); zumachen ⟨*Kleid, Spange, Jacke*⟩; [ab]schließen ⟨*Tür*⟩; anstecken ⟨*Brosche*⟩ (**to** an + *Akk.*); ~ **one's seat belt** sich anschnallen

'fastener, 'fastening *ns.* Verschluss, *der*

fast: ~ **'food** *n.: im Schnellrestaurant angebotenes Essen;* Fastfood, *das; attrib.* ~**-food restaurant** Schnellrestaurant, *das;* ~ **'forward** *n.* schneller Vorlauf; (playback) Zeitrafferwiedergabe, *die;* ~**-forward** **1** *attrib. adj.* Vorspul⟨*taste, -funktion*⟩; **2** *v.t. & i.* vorspulen

fastidious /fæ'stɪdɪəs/ *adj.* wählerisch; (hard to please) heikel

fast: ~ **lane** *n.* Überholspur, *die;* **life in the ~ lane** (fig.) Leben auf vollen Touren (ugs.); ~ **track** *n.* Überholspur, *die;* **a career on the ~ track** eine Blitzkarriere; **be on the ~ track** eine Blitzkarriere machen; ~**-track** **1** *v.t.* beschleunigen ⟨*Projekt*⟩; **2** *attrib. adj.* Schnell-

fat /fæt/ **1** *adj.* dick; rund ⟨*Wangen, Gesicht*⟩
2 *n.* Fett, *das;* **animal/vegetable ~:** tierisches/pflanzliches Fett

fatal /'feɪtl/ *adj.* **(a)** (disastrous) verheerend (**to** für); **it would be ~:** das wäre das Ende **(b)** (deadly) tödlich ⟨*Unfall, Verletzung*⟩

fatality /fə'tælɪtɪ/ *n.* Todesopfer, *das*

'fatally *adv.* tödlich; **be ~ ill** todkrank sein

fate /feɪt/ *n.* Schicksal, *das*

fat-free *adj.* fettfrei

'fathead *n.* Dummkopf, *der* (ugs.)

father /'fɑːðə(r)/ *n.* Vater, *der*

father: **F~ 'Christmas** *n.* der Weihnachtsmann; ~ **figure** *n.* Vaterfigur, *die*

fatherhood /'fɑːðəhʊd/ *n.* Vaterschaft, *die*

'father-in-law *n., pl.* ~**s-in-law** Schwiegervater, *der*

'fatherly *adj.* väterlich

'Father's Day *n.* Vatertag, *der*

fathom /'fæðəm/ **1** *n.* (Naut.) Faden, *der*
2 *v.t.* (comprehend) verstehen; ~ **sb./sth. out** jmdn./etw. ergründen

fatigue /fə'tiːg/ **1** *n.* Ermüdung, *die*
2 *v.t.* ermüden

'fatness *n.* Dicke, *die*

fatten /'fætn/ *v.t.* herausfüttern ⟨*Person*⟩; mästen ⟨*Tier*⟩

'fattening *adj.* **be ~:** dick machen

fatty /'fætɪ/ *adj.* fett ⟨*Fleisch, Soße*⟩; fetthaltig ⟨*Speise, Nahrungsmittel*⟩

faucet /'fɔːsɪt/ *n.* (Amer.) Wasserhahn, *der*

fault /fɔːlt, fɒlt/ *n.* **(a)** Fehler, *der* **(b)** (responsibility) Schuld, *die;* **it's your ~:** du bist schuld; **it isn't my ~:** ich habe keine

Schuld; **be at ~:** im Unrecht sein
(c) (in machinery; also Electr.) Defekt, *der*
'faultless *adj.* einwandfrei
'faulty *adj.* fehlerhaft; defekt ⟨*Gerät, usw.*⟩
fauna /'fɔːnə/ *n., pl.* ~e /'fɔːniː/ *or* ~s
Fauna, *die*
favor *etc.* (*Amer.*) ▶ FAVOUR *etc.*
favour /'feɪvə(r)/ **1** *n.* **(a)** Gunst, *die*
(b) (kindness) Gefallen, *der;* **ask sb. a ~, ask
a ~ of sb.** jmdn. um einen Gefallen bitten;
do sb. a ~, do a ~ for sb. jmdm. einen
Gefallen tun; **as a ~:** aus Gefälligkeit
(c) be in ~ of sth. für etw. sein
2 *v.t.* bevorzugen
favourable /'feɪvərəbl/ *adj.* (Brit.)
(a) günstig ⟨*Eindruck, Licht*⟩; gewogen
⟨*Haltung, Einstellung*⟩; freundlich
⟨*Erwähnung*⟩; positiv ⟨*Bericht[erstattung],
Bemerkung*⟩
(b) (helpful) günstig (**to** für) ⟨*Wetter, Wind,
Umstand*⟩
favourably /'feɪvərəblɪ/ *adv.* (Brit.)
wohlwollend; **be ~ disposed towards
sb./sth.** jmdm./einer Sache positiv
gegenüberstehen
favourite /'feɪvərɪt/ (Brit.) **1** *adj.*
Lieblings-
2 *n.* **(a)** Liebling, *der;* (food/country etc.)
Lieblingsessen, *das*/-land, *das usw.;* **this/he
is my ~:** das/ihn mag ich am liebsten
(b) (Sport) Favorit, *der*/Favoritin, *die*
favouritism /'feɪvərɪtɪzm/ *n.* (Brit.)
Begünstigung, *die;* (when selecting sb. for a post
etc.) Günstlingswirtschaft, *die*
fawn /fɔːn/ **1** *n.* **(a)** (colour) Rehbraun, *das*
(b) (young deer) [Dam]kitz, *das*
2 *adj.* rehfarben
fax /fæks/ **1** *n.* [Tele]fax, *das*
2 *v.t.* faxen
fax: ~ machine *n.* Faxgerät, *das;*
~ modem *n.* (Comp.) Faxmodem, *das;*
~ number *n.* Faxnummer, *die*
FBI *abbr.* (Amer.) **= Federal Bureau of
Investigation** FBI, *das*
fear /fɪə(r)/ **1** *n.* Angst, *die* (**of** vor + *Dat.*);
(instance) Befürchtung, *die;* **~ of death** *or*
dying/heights Todes-/Höhenangst, *die;*
~ of doing sth. Angst davor, etw. zu tun; **in
~:** angstvoll; **no ~!** (coll.) keine Bange! (ugs.)
2 *v.t.* **(a) ~ sb./sth.** vor jmdn./etw. Angst
haben; **~ to do** *or* **doing sth.** Angst haben,
etw. zu tun
(b) (be worried about) befürchten; **~ [that …]**
fürchten[, dass …]
fearful /'fɪəfl/ *adj.* **(a)** (terrible) furchtbar
(b) (frightened) ängstlich; **be ~ of sth./sb.** vor
etw./jmdm. Angst haben
'fearless *adj.,* **'fearlessly** *adv.* furchtlos
feasibility /fiːzɪ'bɪlɪtɪ/ *n.*
Durchführbarkeit, *die*
feasible /'fiːzɪbl/ *adj.* durchführbar
feast /fiːst/ **1** *n.* **(a)** (Relig.) Fest, *das*
(b) (banquet) Festessen, *das*

2 *v.i.* schlemmen; **~ on sth.** sich an etw.
(*Dat.*) gütlich tun
feat /fiːt/ *n.* Meisterleistung, *die*
feather /'feðə(r)/ *n.* Feder, *die*
feather: ~ 'bed *n.* mit Federn gefüllte
Matratze; **~ 'duster** *n.* Flederwisch, *der;*
~weight *n.* (Boxing) Federgewicht, *das*
feature /'fiːtʃə(r)/ **1** *n.* **(a)** *usu. in pl.* (of
face) Gesichtszug, *der*
(b) (characteristic) [charakteristisches]
Merkmal; **be a ~ of sth.** charakteristisch
für etw. sein
(c) (Journ.) Feature, *das*
(d) (Cinemat.) **~ [film]** Hauptfilm, *der*
2 *v.t.* vorrangig vorstellen; (in film) in der
Hauptrolle zeigen
3 *v.i.* vorkommen; **~ in** (be important) eine
bedeutende Rolle haben bei
Feb. *abbr.* **= February** Febr.
February /'febrʊərɪ/ *n.* Februar, *der*
feces (Amer.) ▶ FAECES
fed /fed/ **1** ▶ FEED 1, 2
2 *pred. adj.* (coll.) **be/get ~ up with sb./sth.**
jmdn./etw. satt haben/kriegen (ugs.); **I'm
~ up** ich hab die Nase voll (ugs.)
federal /'fedərl/ *adj.* Bundes-; föderativ
⟨*System*⟩
federation /fedə'reɪʃn/ *n.* Föderation, *die*
fee /fiː/ *n.* Gebühr, *die;* (of doctor, lawyer, etc.)
Honorar, *das*
feeble /'fiːbl/ *adj.* schwach; wenig
überzeugend ⟨*Entschuldigung*⟩; zaghaft
⟨*Versuch*⟩; lahm (ugs.) ⟨*Witz*⟩
feed /fiːd/ **1** *v.t.,* fed /fed/ **(a)** füttern;
~ sb./an animal with sth. jmdm. etw. zu
essen/einem Tier [etw.] zu fressen geben
(b) (provide food for) ernähren (**on,** mit mit)
2 *v.i.,* fed ⟨*Tier:*⟩ fressen (**from** aus);
⟨*Person:*⟩ essen (**off** von); **~ on sth.** ⟨*Tier:*⟩
etw. fressen
3 *n.* **(a)** (for baby) Mahlzeit, *die*
(b) (fodder) Futter, *das*
'feedback *n.* Reaktion, *die*
feel /fiːl/ **1** *v.t.,* felt /felt/ **(a)** (explore by
touch) befühlen
(b) (perceive by touch) fühlen; (become aware of)
bemerken; (have sensation of) spüren
(c) (experience) empfinden; verspüren
⟨*Drang*⟩; **~ the cold/heat** unter der
Kälte/Hitze leiden; **~ [that] …:** das Gefühl
haben, dass …; (think) glauben, dass …
2 *v.i.,* felt: **(a) ~ [about] in sth. [for sth.]** in
etw. (*Dat.*) [nach etw.] [herum]suchen
(b) (be conscious that one is) sich … fühlen;
~ angry/sure/disappointed böse/sicher/
enttäuscht sein; **~ like sth./doing sth.** auf
etw. (*Akk.*) Lust haben/Lust haben, etw. zu
tun
(c) (be consciously perceived as) sich …
anfühlen
■ **'feel for** *v.t.* **~ for sb.** mit jmdm. Mitleid
haben
'feeler *n.* Fühler, *der*

'**feeling** *n.* **(a)** Gefühl, *das;* (sense of touch)
[sense of] ∼: Tastsinn, *der;* **hurt sb.'s** ∼**s**
jmdn. verletzen
(b) (opinion) Ansicht, *die*

feet *pl. of* FOOT

feign /feɪn/ *v.t.* vortäuschen; ∼ **to do sth.**
vorgeben, etw. zu tun

feline /'fiːlaɪn/ *adj.* (of cat[s]) Katzen-; (catlike)
katzenartig; katzenhaft

fell¹ ▶ FALL 2

fell² /fel/ *v.t.* fällen ⟨*Baum*⟩

fell³ *adj.* **in one** ∼ **swoop** auf einen Schlag

fellow /'feləʊ/ ① *n.* **(a)** (comrade) Kamerad,
der
(b) (Brit. Univ.) Fellow, *der*
(c) (of academy or society) Mitglied, *das*
(d) (coll.: man, boy) Kerl, *der* (ugs.)
② *attrib. adj.* Mit-; ∼ **man** *or* **human being**
Mitmensch, *der*

fellowship /'feləʊʃɪp/ *n.* (companionship)
Gesellschaft, *die*

felt¹ /felt/ *n.* Filz, *der*

felt² ▶ FEEL

felt[-tipped] 'pen *n.* Filzstift, *der*

female /'fiːmeɪl/ ① *adj.* weiblich;
Frauen⟨*stimme, -chor, -verein*⟩
② *n.* Frau, *die;* (foetus, child) Mädchen, *das;*
(animal) Weibchen, *das*

feminine /'femɪnɪn/ *adj.* weiblich;
Frauen⟨*angelegenheit, -leiden*⟩; (womanly)
feminin

femininity /femɪ'nɪnɪtɪ/ *n.* Weiblichkeit,
die

feminism /'femɪnɪzm/ *n.* Feminismus, *der*

feminist /'femɪnɪst/ ① *adj.* feministisch;
Feministen⟨*bewegung, -gruppe*⟩
② *n.* Feministin, *die*/Feminist, *der*

fence /fens/ ① *n.* Zaun, *der*
② *v.i.* (Sport) fechten
③ *v.t.* ∼ **[in]** einzäunen

'**fencer** *n.* Fechter, *der*/Fechterin, *die*

fencing /'fensɪŋ/ *n.* (Sport) Fechten, *das*

fend /fend/ *v.i.* ∼ **for oneself** für sich selbst
sorgen; (in hostile surroundings) sich allein
durchschlagen
∎ **fend 'off** *v.t.* abwehren

fender /'fendə(r)/ *n.* **(a)** (for fire)
Kaminschutz, *der*
(b) (Amer.) (car bumper) Stoßstange, *die;* (car
mudguard) Kotflügel, *der*

ferment /fə'ment/ ① *v.i.* gären
② *v.t.* zur Gärung bringen

fermentation /fɜːmen'teɪʃn/ *n.* Gärung,
die

fern /fɜːn/ *n.* Farnkraut, *das*

ferocious /fə'rəʊʃəs/ *adj.* wild

ferocity /fə'rɒsɪtɪ/ *n.* Wildheit, *die*

ferret /'ferɪt/ *n.* Frettchen, *das*

ferrous /'ferəs/ *adj.* (containing iron)
eisenhaltig; Eisen-

ferry /'ferɪ/ ① *n.* Fähre, *die;* (service)

Fährverbindung, *die*
② *v.t.* (in boat) ∼ **[across** *or* **over]** übersetzen

'**ferry service** *n.* **(a)** Fährverbindung, *die*
(b) (business) Fährbetrieb, *der*

fertile /'fɜːtaɪl/ *adj.* (fruitful) fruchtbar;
(capable of developing) befruchtet

fertility /fɜː'tɪlɪtɪ/ *n.* Fruchtbarkeit, *die*

fer'tility drug *n.* Hormonpräparat, *das*
(*zur Steigerung der Fruchtbarkeit*)

fertilization /fɜːtɪlaɪ'zeɪʃn/ *n.* **(a)** (Biol.)
Befruchtung, *die*
(b) (Agric.) Düngung, *die*

fertilize /'fɜːtɪlaɪz/ *v.t.* befruchten

'**fertilizer** *n.* Dünger, *der*

fervent /'fɜːvənt/ *adj.* leidenschaftlich;
inbrünstig ⟨*Gebet, Wunsch, Hoffnung*⟩

fervour (*Brit.; Amer.:* **fervor**) /'fɜːvə(r)/ *n.*
Leidenschaftlichkeit, *die*

fester /'festə(r)/ *v.i.* eitern

festival /'festɪvl/ *n.* **(a)** (feast day) Fest, *das*
(b) (of music etc.) Festival, *das*

festive /'festɪv/ *adj.* festlich; fröhlich; **the**
∼ **season** die Weihnachtszeit

festivity /fe'stɪvɪtɪ/ *n.* **(a)** (gaiety)
Feststimmung, *die*
(b) (celebration) Feier, *die;* **festivities**
Feierlichkeiten *Pl.*

festoon /fe'stuːn/ ① *n.* Girlande, *die*
② *v.t.* schmücken (**with** mit)

fetch /fetʃ/ *v.t.* **(a)** holen; (collect) abholen
(from von); ∼ **sb. sth.,** ∼ **sth. for sb.** jmdm.
etw. holen
(b) (be sold for) erzielen ⟨*Preis*⟩

'**fetching** *adj.* einnehmend

fête /feɪt/ *n.* [Wohltätigkeits]basar, *der*

fetish /'fetɪʃ/ *n.* Fetisch, *der*

fetishism /'fetɪʃɪzm/ *n.* Fetischismus, *der*

fetishist /'fetɪʃɪst/ *n.* Fetischist,
der/Fetischistin, *die*

fetter /'fetə(r)/ *v.t.* fesseln

fetus (Amer.) ▶ FOETUS

feud /fjuːd/ *n.* Fehde, *die*

feudal /'fjuːdl/ *adj.* Feudal-; feudalistisch;
∼ **system** Feudalsystem, *das*

fever /'fiːvə(r)/ *n.* **(a)** (high temperature)
Fieber, *das;* **have a [high]** ∼: [hohes] Fieber
haben
(b) (disease) Fieberkrankheit, *die*

'**feverish** *adj.* **(a)** (Med.) fiebrig; **be**
∼: Fieber haben
(b) (excited) fiebrig

'**fever pitch** *n.* Siedepunkt, *der* (fig.); **reach**
∼: auf dem Siedepunkt angelangt sein; **at**
∼: auf dem Siedepunkt

few /fjuː/ ① *adj.* **(a)** (not many) wenige;
abs. nur wenige; **with very** ∼ **exceptions**
mit ganz wenigen Ausnahmen; **his**
∼ **belongings** seine paar Habseligkeiten; **a**
∼ ...: wenige ...
(b) (some) wenige; **a** ∼ ...: ein paar ...; **a**
∼ **more** ...: noch ein paar ...
② *n.* **(a)** (not many) wenige; **a** ∼: wenige;

just a ~ of you/her friends nur ein paar von euch/ihrer Freunde
(b) (some) with a ~ of our friends mit einigen unserer Freunde; quite a ~: ziemlich viele

fiancé /fɪˈɑ̃seɪ/ n. Verlobte, der

fiancée /fɪˈɑ̃seɪ/ n. Verlobte, die

fiasco /fɪˈæskəʊ/ n., pl. ~s Fiasko, das

fib /fɪb/ [1] n. Flunkerei, die (ugs.); tell ~s flunkern (ugs.)
[2] v.i., -bb- flunkern (ugs.)

fibre (Brit.; Amer.: **fiber**) /ˈfaɪbə(r)/ n.
(a) Faser, die
(b) (material) [Faser]gewebe, das

fibre: ~glass n. (plastic) glasfaserverstärkter Kunststoff; ~ **optic 'cable** n. Glasfaserkabel, das; ~ **'optics** n. Faseroptik, die

fibrous /ˈfaɪbrəs/ adj. faserig ⟨Aufbau, Beschaffenheit, Eigenschaft⟩; Faser⟨gewebe, -holz, -stoff⟩

fiche /fiːʃ/ n., pl. same or ~s Mikrofiche, das od. der

fickle /ˈfɪkl/ adj. unberechenbar

fiction /ˈfɪkʃn/ n. erzählende Literatur; a ~/~s eine Erfindung

fictional /ˈfɪkʃənl/ adj. erfunden ⟨Geschichte⟩; fiktiv ⟨Figur⟩

'fiction writer n. Belletrist, der/ Belletristin, die

fictitious /fɪkˈtɪʃəs/ adj. fingiert; falsch ⟨Name, Identität⟩

fiddle /ˈfɪdl/ [1] n. **(a)** (Mus.) (coll./derog.) Fiedel, die; (violin for traditional music) Geige, die; [as] fit as a ~: kerngesund
(b) (coll.: swindle) Gaunerei, die
[2] v.t. (coll.) frisieren (ugs.) ⟨Bücher, Rechnungen⟩
[3] v.i. herumspielen (with mit)

fiddler /ˈfɪdlə(r)/ n. Geiger, der/Geigerin, die

fiddly /ˈfɪdlɪ/ adj. (coll.) knifflig

fidelity /fɪˈdelɪtɪ/ n. Treue, die (to zu)

fidget /ˈfɪdʒɪt/ [1] v.i. ~ [about] herumrutschen
[2] n. (person) Zappelphilipp, der (ugs.)

'fidgety adj. unruhig; zappelig ⟨Kind⟩

field /fiːld/ n. **(a)** Feld, das
(b) (for game) Platz, der; [Spiel]feld, das
(c) (subject area) [Fach]gebiet, das; in the ~ of medicine auf dem Gebiet der Medizin; that is outside my ~: das fällt nicht in mein Fach

field: ~ day n. have a ~ day seinen großen Tag haben; ~ **events** n. pl. technische Disziplinen Pl.; ~ **glasses** n. pl. Feldstecher, der; F~ **'Marshal** n. (Brit. Mil.) Feldmarschall, der; ~ **mouse** n. Brandmaus, die; ~ **trip** n. Exkursion, die

fiend /fiːnd/ n. **(a)** (wicked person) Scheusal, das
(b) (evil spirit) böser Geist

'fiendish adj. **(a)** teuflisch
(b) (very awkward) höllisch

fierce /ˈfɪəs/ adj. wild; erbittert ⟨Widerstand, Kampf⟩; scharf ⟨Kritik⟩

'fiercely adv. heftig ⟨angreifen, Widerstand leisten⟩; wütend ⟨brüllen⟩; aufs heftigste ⟨kritisieren, bekämpfen⟩

fiery /ˈfaɪərɪ/ adj. glühend; (looking like fire) feurig; (blazing red) feuerrot

fifteen /fɪfˈtiːn/ [1] adj. fünfzehn
[2] n. Fünfzehn, die. See also EIGHT

fifteenth /fɪfˈtiːnθ/ [1] adj. fünfzehnt...
[2] n. (fraction) Fünfzehntel, das. See also EIGHTH

fifth /fɪfθ/ [1] adj. fünft...
[2] n. (in sequence, rank) Fünfte, der/die/das; (fraction) Fünftel, das. See also EIGHTH

fiftieth /ˈfɪftɪɪθ/ adj. fünfzigst...

fifty /ˈfɪftɪ/ [1] adj. fünfzig
[2] n. Fünfzig, die. See also EIGHT; EIGHTY 2

fig /fɪg/ n. Feige, die

fig. abbr. = **figure** Abb.

fight /faɪt/ [1] v.i., fought /fɔːt/ **(a)** kämpfen; (with fists) sich schlagen
(b) (squabble) [sich] streiten (about wegen)
[2] v.t., fought: **(a)** ~ sb./sth. gegen jmdn./etw. kämpfen; (using fists) ~ sb. sich mit jmdm. schlagen
(b) (seek to overcome) bekämpfen; (resist) ~ sb./sth. gegen jmdn./etw. ankämpfen
(c) ~ a battle einen Kampf austragen
(d) kandidieren bei ⟨Wahl⟩
[3] n. Kampf, der (for um)

■ **'fight against** v.t. kämpfen gegen; ankämpfen gegen ⟨Wellen, Wind⟩

■ **fight 'back** [1] v.i. zurückschlagen
[2] v.t. (suppress) zurückhalten

■ **fight 'off** v.t. abwehren

■ **fight 'with** v.t. **(a)** kämpfen mit
(b) (squabble with) [sich] streiten mit

'fighter n. Kämpfer, der/Kämpferin, die; (aircraft) Kampfflugzeug, das

'fighting n. Kämpfe Pl.

fighting 'chance n. have a ~ of succeeding/of doing sth. Aussicht auf Erfolg haben/gute Chancen haben, etw. zu tun

'fig leaf n. (lit. or fig.) Feigenblatt, das

figment /ˈfɪgmənt/ n. a ~ of one's or the imagination pure Einbildung

'fig tree n. Feigenbaum, der

figurative /ˈfɪgərətɪv/ adj. übertragen

figure /ˈfɪgə(r)/ [1] n. **(a)** (shape) Form, die
(b) (carving, sculpture, one's bodily shape) Figur, die
(c) (illustration) Abbildung, die
(d) (person as seen) Gestalt, die; (literary ~) Figur, die
(e) (numerical symbol) Ziffer, die; (number) Zahl, die; (amount of money) Betrag, der
(f) ~ of speech Redewendung, die
[2] v.i. **(a)** vorkommen
(b) that ~s (coll.) das kann gut sein   ⋯⫶

■ **figure** '**out** *v.t.* (a) (by arithmetic)
ausrechnen
(b) (understand) verstehen
figure: ~**head** *n.* (lit. or fig.) Galionsfigur,
die; ~ **skating** *n.* Eiskunstlauf, *der*
filament /'fɪləmənt/ *n.* (a) Faden, *der*
(b) (Electr.) Glühfaden, *der*
filch /'fɪltʃ/ *v.t.* stibitzen (ugs.)
file[1] /faɪl/ ① *n.* Feile, *die*
② *v.t.* feilen ⟨*Fingernägel*⟩; mit der Feile
bearbeiten ⟨*Holz, Eisen*⟩
file[2] ① *n.* (a) (holder) Ordner, *der;* (box)
Kassette, *die*
(b) (papers) Ablage, *die;* (cards) Kartei, *die*
② *v.t.* (a) [in die Kartei] einordnen/[in die
Akten] aufnehmen
(b) einreichen ⟨*Antrag*⟩
file[3] ① *n.* (Mil. etc.) Reihe, *die;* [in] single *or*
Indian ~: [im] Gänsemarsch
② *v.i.* ~ [in/out] in einer Reihe [hinein-/
hinaus]gehen
file: ~ **copy** *n.* Belegexemplar, *das;* (of
letter) Kopie für die Akten; ~ **extension**
n. (Comp.) Dateierweiterung, *die;* ~ **name**
n. (Comp.) Dateiname
filigree /'fɪlɪgriː/ *n.* Filigran, *das*
'**filing cabinet** *n.* Aktenschrank, *der*
filings /'faɪlɪŋz/ *n. pl.* Späne *Pl.*
fill /fɪl/ ① *v.t.* (a) füllen; besetzen
⟨*Sitzplätze*⟩; (fig.) ausfüllen ⟨*Gedanken, Zeit*⟩;
(pervade) erfüllen; ~**ed with** voller ⟨*Reue,
Bewunderung, Neid usw.*⟩
(b) (appoint sb. to) besetzen ⟨*Posten*⟩
② *v.i.* ~ [with sth.] sich [mit etw.] füllen
③ *n.* eat/drink one's ~: sich satt essen/
trinken
■ **fill** '**in** ① *v.t.* (a) füllen; zuschütten
⟨*Erdloch*⟩
(b) (complete) ausfüllen
(c) ~ sb. in [on sth.] (coll.) jmdn. [über etw.
(*Akk.*)] ins Bild setzen
② *v.i.* ~ in for sb. für jmdn. einspringen
■ **fill** '**out** *v.t.* ausfüllen
■ **fill** '**up** *v.t.* (a) füllen (with mit)
(b) (put petrol into) ~ up the tank tanken;
~ her up! (coll.) voll [tanken]!
fillet /'fɪlɪt/ ① *n.* Filet, *das*
② *v.t.* entgräten ⟨*Fisch*⟩
'**filling** *n.* (a) (for teeth) Füllung, *die*
(b) (for pancakes etc.) Füllung, *die;* (for
sandwiches etc.) Belag, *der;* (for spreading)
Aufstrich, *der*
'**filling station** *n.* Tankstelle, *die*
'**filly** /'fɪlɪ/ *n.* junge Stute
film /fɪlm/ ① *n.* (a) Film, *der*
(b) (thin layer) Schicht, *die*
② *v.t.* filmen; drehen ⟨*Kinofilm, Szene*⟩
film: ~ **crew** *n.* Kamerateam,
das; ~ **director** *n.* Filmregisseur,
der/-regisseurin, *die;* ~ **industry**
n. Filmindustrie, *die;* ~ **music** *n.*
Filmmusik, *die;* ~ **poster** *n.* Filmplakat,
das; ~ **projector** *n.* Projektor, *der;*

~ **script** *n.* Drehbuch, *das;* ~ **set** *n.*
Dekoration, *die;* ~ **star** *n.* Filmstar, *der;*
~**strip** *n.* Filmstreifen, *der;* ~ **studio** *n.*
Filmstudio, *das*
Filofax ® /'faɪləʊfæks/ *n.* ≈ Terminplaner,
der
filter /'fɪltə(r)/ ① *n.* Filter, *der*
② *v.t.* filtern
■ **filter** '**through** *v.t.* durchsickern
filter: ~ **ciga'rette** *n.* Filterzigarette,
die; ~ **coffee** *n.* Filterkaffee, *der;* ~ **lane**
n. Abbiegespur, *die;* ~**-tip** *n.* (a) Filter, *der;*
(b) ~**-tip [cigarette]** Filterzigarette, *die*
filth /fɪlθ/ *n.* Dreck, *der*
'**filthy** *adj.* dreckig (ugs.); schmutzig
fin /fɪn/ *n.* Flosse, *die*
final /'faɪnl/ ① *adj.* letzt...; End⟨*spiel,
-stadium, -stufe, -ergebnis*⟩; endgültig
⟨*Entscheidung*⟩
② *n.* (a) (Sport etc.) Finale, *das*
(b) ~**s** *pl.* (university examination) Examen, *das*
finale /fɪ'nɑːlɪ/ *n.* Finale, *das*
finalist /'faɪnəlɪst/ *n.* Teilnehmer/
Teilnehmerin in der Endausscheidung;
(Sport) Finalist, *der/*Finalistin, *die*
finality /faɪ'nælɪtɪ/ *n.* Endgültigkeit, *die;* (of
tone of voice) Entschiedenheit, *die*
finalize /'faɪnəlaɪz/ *v.t.* [endgültig]
beschließen; (complete) zum Abschluss
bringen
'**finally** /'faɪnəlɪ/ *adv.* (a) (in the end)
schließlich; (expressing impatience etc.) endlich
(b) (in conclusion) abschließend
(c) (conclusively) entschieden ⟨*sagen*⟩
finance /faɪ'næns, 'faɪnæns/ ① *n.* (a) *in
pl.* (resources) Finanzen *Pl.*
(b) (management of money) Geldwesen, *das*
(c) (support) Geldmittel *usw.*
② *v.t.* finanzieren
'**finance company** *n.*
Finanzierungsgesellschaft, *die*
financial /faɪ'nænʃl/ *adj.* finanziell;
Finanz⟨*mittel, -experte, -lage*⟩; ~ **year**
Geschäftsjahr, *das*
fi'nancially *adv.* finanziell
financier /faɪ'nænsɪə(r)/ *n.*
Finanzexperte, *der/*-expertin, *die*
finch /fɪntʃ/ *n.* Fink[envogel], *der*
find /faɪnd/ ① *v.t.,* **found** /faʊnd/ finden;
(come across unexpectedly) entdecken;
auftreiben ⟨*Geld, Gegenstand*⟩; aufbringen
⟨*Kraft, Energie*⟩; **want to** ~: suchen;
~ **that** ...: herausfinden, dass ...; ~ **sth.
necessary** etw. für nötig erachten; ~ **sth./
sb. to be** ...: herausfinden, dass etw./jmd. ...
ist/war; **you will** ~ **[that]** ...: Sie werden
sehen, dass ...
② *n.* Fund, *der*
■ **find** '**out** *v.t.* herausfinden
'**finder** *n.* Finder, *der/*Finderin, *die*
'**findings** *n. pl.* Ergebnisse *Pl.*
fine[1] /faɪn/ ① *n.* Geldstrafe, *die*

2 *v.t.* mit einer Geldstrafe belegen

fine² *adj.* **(a)** hochwertig ⟨*Qualität, Lebensmittel*⟩; fein ⟨*Gewebe, Spitze*⟩; edel ⟨*Holz, Wein*⟩
(b) (delicate) fein; zart ⟨*Porzellan*⟩; (thin) hauchdünn; **cut** *or* **run it** ∼: knapp kalkulieren
(c) (in small particles) [hauch]fein ⟨*Sand, Staub*⟩; ∼ **rain** Nieselregen, *der*
(d) (sharp) scharf ⟨*Spitze, Klinge*⟩; spitz ⟨*Nadel, Schreibfeder*⟩
(e) (excellent) ausgezeichnet ⟨*Sänger, Schauspieler*⟩
(f) (satisfactory) schön; **that's** ∼ **by** *or* **with me** ja, ist mir recht
(g) (in good health or state) gut; **feel** ∼: sich wohl fühlen
(h) schön ⟨*Wetter*⟩

fine 'arts *n. pl.* schöne Künste *Pl.*

finery /'faɪnərɪ/ *n.* Pracht, *die;* (garments etc.) Staat, *der*

finger /'fɪŋɡə(r)/ 1 *n.* Finger, *der*
2 *v.t.* berühren; (meddle with) befingern

finger: ∼**mark** *n.* Fingerabdruck, *der;* ∼**nail** *n.* Fingernagel, *der;* ∼**print** *n.* Fingerabdruck, *der;* ∼**tip** *n.* Fingerspitze, *die;* **have sth. at one's** ∼**tips** (fig.) etw. im kleinen Finger haben (ugs.)

finish /'fɪnɪʃ/ 1 *v.t.* **(a)** beenden ⟨*Unterhaltung*⟩; erledigen ⟨*Arbeit*⟩; abschließen ⟨*Kurs, Ausbildung*⟩; **have** ∼**ed sth.** etw. fertig haben; ∼ **writing/reading sth.** etw. zu Ende schreiben/lesen
(b) aufessen ⟨*Mahlzeit*⟩; auslesen ⟨*Buch, Zeitung*⟩; austrinken ⟨*Flasche, Glas*⟩
2 *v.i.* **(a)** aufhören; **have you** ∼**ed?** sind Sie fertig?; **when does the concert** ∼? wann ist das Konzert aus?; **have you** ∼**ed with the sugar?** brauchen Sie der Zucher noch?; ∼ **with one's boyfriend/girlfriend** Schluss mit seinem Freund/seiner Freundin machen
(b) (in race) das Ziel erreichen
3 *n.* **(a)** Ende, *das*
(b) (∼ing line) Ziel, *das*
■ **finish 'off** *v.t.* abschließen

finishing: ∼ **post** *n.* Zielpfosten, *der;* ∼ '**touch** *n.* **as a** ∼ **touch to sth.** zur Vollendung *od.* Vervollkommnung einer Sache; **put the** ∼ **touches to sth.** einer Sache (*Dat.*) den letzten Schliff geben

finite /'faɪnaɪt/ *adj.* begrenzt

Finland /'fɪnlənd/ *pr. n.* Finnland (*das*)

Finn /fɪn/ *n.* Finne, *der*/Finnin, *die*

Finnish /'fɪnɪʃ/ 1 *adj.* finnisch; **sb. is** ∼: jmd. ist Finne/Finnin
2 *n.* Finnisch, *das; see also* ENGLISH 2A

fiord /fɪ'ɔːd/ *n.* Fjord, *der*

fir /fɜː(r)/ *n.* Tanne, *die*

fire /'faɪə(r)/ 1 *n.* **(a)** Feuer, *das;* **be on** ∼: brennen; **catch** ∼: Feuer fangen; ⟨*Wald, Gebäude:*⟩ in Brand geraten; **set** ∼ **to sth.** etw. anzünden
(b) (in grate) [offenes] Feuer; (electric or gas ∼) Heizofen, *der;* **light the** ∼: den Ofen

anstecken; (in grate) das [Kamin]feuer anmachen
(c) (destructive burning) Brand, *der*
(d) (of guns) **come/be under** ∼: unter Beschuss geraten/beschossen werden
2 *v.t.* **(a)** abschießen ⟨*Gewehr*⟩; abfeuern ⟨*Kanone*⟩; abgeben ⟨*Schuss*⟩; ∼ **one's gun/pistol/rifle at sb.** auf jmdn. schießen; **two shots were** ∼**d** es fielen zwei Schüsse; ∼ **questions at sb.** jmdn. mit Fragen bombardieren
(b) (coll.: dismiss) feuern (ugs.)
3 *v.i.* feuern; ∼ **at/on** schießen auf (+ *Akk.*); ∼! Feuer!

fire: ∼ **alarm** *n.* Feuermelder, *der;* ∼**arm** *n.* Schusswaffe, *die;* ∼**bomb** *n.* Brandsatz, *der;* (aerial bomb) Brandbombe, *die;* ∼ **brigade** (Brit.). ∼ **department** (Amer.) *ns.* Feuerwehr, *die;* ∼ **drill** *n.* Probe[feuer]alarm, *der;* ∼ **engine** *n.* Löschfahrzeug, *das;* ∼ **escape** *n.* (staircase) Feuertreppe, *die;* ∼ **exit** *n.* Notausgang, *der;* ∼ **extinguisher** *n.* Feuerlöscher, *der;* ∼**fighter** *n.* Feuerwehrmann, *der/*-frau, *die;* ∼**fighting** *n.* Feuerbekämpfung, *die;* Brandbekämpfung, *die;* ∼ **hazard** *n.* Brandrisiko, *das;* ∼**lighter** *n.* (Brit.) Feueranzünder, *der;* ∼**man** /'faɪəmən/ *n., pl.* ∼**men** /-mən/ Feuerwehrmann, *der;* ∼**place** *n.* Kamin, *der;* ∼ **precautions** *n. pl.* Feuerschutz, *der;* ∼**proof** 1 *adj.* feuerfest; 2 *v.t.* feuerfest machen; ∼**-resistant** *adj.* feuerbeständig; ∼ **risk** ▶ ∼ HAZARD; ∼**side** *n.* **at** *or* **by the** ∼**side** am Kamin; ∼ **station** *n.* Feuerwache, *die;* ∼ **tongs** *n. pl.* Feuerzange; **a pair of** ∼ **tongs** eine Feuerzange; ∼**wood** *n.* Brennholz, *das;* ∼**work** *n.* Feuerwerkskörper, *der;* ∼**works** (display) Feuerwerk, *das*

firm¹ /fɜːm/ *n.* Firma, *die*

firm² *adj.* **(a)** fest; stabil ⟨*Konstruktion, Stuhl*⟩
(b) (resolute, strict) bestimmt

'**firmly** *adv.* **(a)** fest
(b) (resolutely, strictly) bestimmt

first /fɜːst/ 1 *adj.* erst...; **he was** ∼ **to arrive** er kam als Erster an
2 *adv.* **(a)** (before anyone else) zuerst; als Erster/Erste ⟨*sprechen, ankommen*⟩; (before anything else) an erster Stelle ⟨*stehen, kommen*⟩; ∼ **come** ∼ **served** wer zuerst kommt, mahlt zuerst (Spr.)
(b) (beforehand) vorher
(c) (for the ∼ time) zum ersten Mal
(d) ∼ **of all** zuerst; (in importance) vor allem
3 *n.* **(a)** the ∼ (in sequence, rank) der/die/das Erste; *pl.* die Ersten
(b) **at** ∼: zuerst; **from the** ∼: von Anfang an

first: ∼ '**aid** *n.* erste Hilfe; ∼**-aid box/kit** Verbandkasten, *der/*Erste-Hilfe-Ausrüstung, *die;* ∼**-class** 1 /'--/ *adj.*
(a) erster Klasse *nachgestellt;* Erste[r]-Klasse-⟨*Fahrkarte, Abteil, Post,* ⸽⸽⸽⸽

Brief usw.⟩; **(b)** (excellent) erstklassig; ② /-'-/ *adv.* erster Klasse ⟨*reisen*⟩

'**firstly** *adv.* zunächst [einmal]; (followed by 'secondly') erstens

first: ∼ **name** *n.* Vorname, *der;* ∼ '**night** *n.* (Theatre) Premiere, *die;* ∼ **of'fender** *n.* Ersttäter, *der*/-täterin, *die;* ∼-**rate** *adj.* erstklassig; ∼ **school** *n.* (Brit.) ≈ Grundschule, *die*

'**fir tree** *n.* Tanne, *die*

fish /fɪʃ/ ① *n.* Fisch, *der* ② *v.i.* fischen; (with rod) angeln; **go** ∼**ing** fischen/angeln gehen
∎ **fish 'out** *v.t.* (coll.) herausfischen (ugs.)

fish: ∼ **bone** *n.* [Fisch]gräte, *die;* ∼ **cake** *n.* Fischfrikadelle, *die*

fisherman /'fɪʃəmən/ *n., pl.* **fishermen** /'fɪʃəmən/ Fischer, *der;* (angler) Angler, *der*

fish: ∼**eye lens** *n.* Fischaugenobjektiv, *das;* ∼ **farm** *n.* Fischzucht[anlage], *die;* ∼ **farming** *n.* Fischzucht, *die;* ∼ '**finger** *n.* Fischstäbchen, *das;* ∼ **hook** *n.* Angelhaken, *der*

'**fishing** *n.* Fischen, *das;* (with rod) Angeln, *das*

fishing: ∼ **boat** *n.* Fischerboot, *das;* ∼ **industry** *n.* Fischerei[industrie], *die;* ∼ **net** *n.* Fischernetz, *das;* ∼ **rod** *n.* Angelrute, *die* ∼ **tackle** *n.* Angelgeräte *Pl.;* ∼ **vessel** *n.* Fischereifahrzeug, *das;* ∼ **village** *n.* Fischerdorf, *das*

fish: ∼ **kettle** *n.* Fischkessel, *der;* ∼**monger** /'fɪʃmʌŋgə(r)/ *n.* (Brit.) Fischhändler, *der*/-händlerin, *die;* ∼ **pond** *n.* Fischteich, *der;* ∼ **shop** *n.* Fischgeschäft, *das;* ∼ **slice** *n.* Wender, *der;* ∼ **tank** *n.* Fischkasten, *der;* Fischbehälter, *der*

'**fishy** *adj.* **(a)** fischartig; Fisch⟨*geschmack, -geruch*⟩ **(b)** (coll.: suspicious) verdächtig

fist /fɪst/ *n.* Faust, *die*

fit[1] /fɪt/ *n.* Anfall, *der;* (fig.) [plötzliche] Anwandlung; **be in** ∼**s of laughter** sich vor Lachen biegen; **in a** ∼ **of** …: in einem Anfall von …

fit[2] ① *adj.* **(a)** (suitable) geeignet; ∼ **to eat** essbar **(b)** (worthy) würdig; wert **(c)** (proper) richtig; **see** *or* **think** ∼ **[to do sth.]** es für richtig halten[, etw. zu tun] **(d)** (healthy) fit (ugs.); **keep** ∼: sich fit halten ② *n.* Passform, *die;* **it is a good/bad** ∼: es sitzt *od.* passt gut/nicht gut ③ *v.t.,* **-tt-: (a)** ⟨*Kleider:*⟩ passen (+ *Dat.*); ⟨*Deckel, Bezug:*⟩ passen auf (+ *Akk.*) **(b)** (put into place) anbringen (**to** an + *Dat. od. Akk.*); einbauen ⟨*Motor, Ersatzteil*⟩ ④ *v.i.,* **-tt-** passen
∎ **fit 'in** ① *v.t.* unterbringen ② *v.i.* **(a)** ⟨*Person:*⟩ sich anpassen (**with** an + *Akk.*) **(b)** (be in accordance with) ∼ **in with sth.** mit etw. übereinstimmen

fitful /'fɪtfl/ *adj.* unbeständig; unruhig ⟨*Schlaf*⟩; launisch ⟨*Brise*⟩

'**fitment** *n.* Einrichtung, *die*

'**fitness** *n.* **(a)** (physical) Fitness, *die* **(b)** (suitability) Eignung, *die*

'**fitness studio** *n.* Fitnessstudio, *das*

'**fitted** *adj.* **(a)** (suited) geeignet (**for** für, zu) **(b)** (shaped) tailliert ⟨*Kleider*⟩; Einbau⟨*küche, schrank*⟩; ∼ **carpet** Teppichboden, *der*

'**fitter** *n.* Monteur, *der;* (of pipes) Installateur, *der;* (of machines) Maschinenschlosser, *der*

'**fitting** ① *adj.* (appropriate) passend; (becoming) schicklich (geh.) ⟨*Benehmen*⟩ ② *n.* **(a)** (usu. in pl. (fixture) Anschluss, *der;* ∼s (furniture) Ausstattung, *die* **(b)** (Brit.: size) Größe, *die*

'**fitting-room** *n.* Anprobe, *die*

five /faɪv/ ① *adj.* fünf ② *n.* Fünf, *die.* See also EIGHT

fiver /'faɪvə(r)/ *n.* (Brit. coll.) Fünfpfundschein, *der*

five: ∼-**star** *adj.* Fünf-Sterne-⟨*Hotel, General*⟩; (fig.) ausgezeichnet; ∼-'**year plan** *n.* Fünfjahresplan, *der*

fix /fɪks/ ① *v.t.* **(a)** befestigen **(b)** festsetzen ⟨*Termin, Preis, Grenze*⟩; (agree on) ausmachen **(c)** (repair) reparieren **(d)** (arrange) arrangieren ② *n.* (coll.: predicament) Klemme, *die* (ugs.); **be in a** ∼: in der Klemme sitzen
∎ **fix 'up** *v.t.* **(a)** (arrange) arrangieren; festsetzen ⟨*Termin, Treffpunkt*⟩ **(b)** (provide) versorgen; ∼ **sb. up with sth.** jmdm. etw. verschaffen

fixed: ∼ **price** Festpreis, *der;* ∼-**rate** *attrib. adj.* Festzins-; mit festem Zins *nachgestellt*

fixture /'fɪkstʃə(r)/ *n.* **(a)** (furnishing) eingebautes Teil **(b)** (Sport) Veranstaltung, *die*

fizz /fɪz/ *v.i.* [zischend] sprudeln

fizzle /'fɪzl/ *v.i.* zischen
∎ **fizzle 'out** *v.i.* ⟨*Kampagne:*⟩ im Sande verlaufen

fizzy /'fɪzɪ/ *adj.* sprudelnd; ∼ **lemonade** Brause[limonade], *die*

flabbergast /'flæbəgɑːst/ *v.t.* umhauen (ugs.)

flabby /'flæbɪ/ *adj.* schlaff

flag[1] /flæg/ *n.* Fahne, *die;* (national ∼, on ship) Flagge, *die*

flag[2] *v.i.,* **-gg-** ⟨*Person:*⟩ abbauen; ⟨*Kraft, Begeisterung usw..:*⟩ nachlassen

flagon /'flægn/ *n.* Kanne, *die*

'**flagpole** *n.* Flaggenmast, *der*

flagrant /'fleɪgrənt/ *adj.* eklatant; flagrant ⟨*Verstoß*⟩

'**flagstone** *n.* Steinplatte, *die*

flair /fleə(r)/ *n.* Gespür, *das;* (special ability) Talent, *das*

flak /flæk/ *n.* Flakfeuer, *das* (Milit.); (gun)

0629

flake ···⟫ flesh wound ····

Flak, *die* (Milit.); **get a lot of** ∼ **for sth.** (fig.) wegen etw. [schwer] unter Beschuss geraten

flake /fleɪk/ ① *n.* Flocke, *die;* (of dry skin) Schuppe, *die*
② *v.i.* abblättern

'**flak jacket** *n.* kugelsichere Weste

flaky /'fleɪkɪ/ *adj.* blättrig ⟨Kruste⟩; ∼ **pastry** Blätterteig, *der*

flamboyant /flæm'bɔɪənt/ *adj.* extravagant

flame /fleɪm/ *n.* Flamme, *die;* **be in** ∼**s** in Flammen stehen

'**flameproof** nicht entflammbar; flammfest

flan /flæn/ *n.* [fruit] ∼: [Obst]torte, *die*

flank /flæŋk/ *n.* Seite, *die;* (of animal; also Mil.) Flanke, *die*

flannel /'flænl/ *n.* **(a)** (fabric) Flanell, *der* **(b)** (Brit.: for washing) Waschlappen, *der*

flap /flæp/ ① *v.t.,* **-pp-:** ∼ **its wings** mit den Flügeln schlagen
② *v.i.,* **-pp-** ⟨Flügel:⟩ schlagen; ⟨Segel, Fahne, Vorhang:⟩ flattern
③ *n.* **(a)** Klappe, *die;* (envelope seal, of shoe) Lasche, *die*
(b) (fig. coll.) **in a** ∼**:** furchtbar aufgeregt

flare /fleə(r)/ ① *v.i.* flackern; (fig.) ausbrechen; **tempers** ∼**d** die Gemüter erhitzten sich
② *n.* Leuchtsignal, *das*
■ **flare 'up** *v.i.* **(a)** aufflackern **(b)** (break out) [wieder] ausbrechen

flash /flæʃ/ ① *n.* Aufleuchten, *das;* (as signal) Lichtsignal, *das;* ∼ **of lightning** Blitz, *der;* **in a** ∼**:** (quickly) im Nu
② *v.t.* **(a)** aufleuchten lassen; ∼ **one's headlights** die Lichthupe betätigen; ∼ **sb. a smile/glance** jmdm. ein Lächeln/einen Blick zuwerfen
(b) (display briefly) kurz zeigen
③ *v.i.* aufleuchten; ∼ **by** *or* **past** ⟨Zeit, Ferien:⟩ wie im Fluge vergehen

flash: ∼**back** *n.* Rückblende, *die* (**to** auf + *Akk.*); ∼ **bulb** *n.* Blitzbirnchen, *das;* ∼ **cube** *n.* Blitzwürfel, *der;* ∼ **flood** *n.* Überschwemmung, *die* (durch heftige Regenfälle); ∼**gun** *n.* Blitzgerät, *das;* ∼**light** *n.* **(a)** (for signals) Blinklicht, *das;* **(b)** (Amer.: torch) Taschenlampe, *die;* ∼**point** *n.* Flammpunkt, *der;* (fig.) Siedepunkt, *der*

'**flashy** *adj.* auffällig

flask /flɑ:sk/ *n.* **(a)** ▶ THERMOS **(b)** (for wine, oil) [bauchige] Flasche **(c)** (Chem.) Kolben, *der*

flat¹ /flæt/ *n.* (Brit.) Wohnung, *die*

flat² ① *adj.* **(a)** flach; eben ⟨Fläche⟩; platt ⟨Nase, Reifen⟩
(b) (downright) glatt (ugs.) ⟨Absage, Weigerung, Widerspruch⟩
(c) (Mus.) [um einen Halbton] erniedrigt ⟨Note⟩
(d) schal, abgestanden ⟨Bier, Sekt⟩
(e) leer ⟨Batterie⟩

② *adv.* (Mus.) zu tief

'**flatbed scanner** *n.* (Comp.) Flachbettscanner, *der*

flat: ∼**-chested** /flæt'tʃestɪd/ *adj.* flachbrüstig; flachbusig; ∼ '**feet** *n. pl.* Plattfüße *Pl.;* ∼'**fish** *n.* Plattfisch, *der;* ∼-'**footed** *adj.* plattfüßig; ∼**-heeled** *adj.* ⟨Schuh⟩ mit flachem Absatz; flach ⟨Schuh⟩

flatlet /'flætlɪt/ *n.* (Brit.) Appartement, *das*

'**flatly** *adv.* rundweg

flat: ∼ **mate** *n.* (Brit.) Mitbewohner, *der*/Mitbewohnerin, *die;* **they were** ∼ **mates** sie haben zusammen gewohnt; ∼ '**out** *adv.* (at top speed) **he ran/worked** ∼ **out** er rannte/arbeitete, so schnell er konnte; ∼**pack** *adj.* ⟨Möbel⟩ zum Selbstbauen; ∼ **rate** *n.* Einheitstarif, *der;* ∼ **screen** *n.* (Comp.) Flachbildschirm, *der;* ∼ '**spin** *n.* (Aeronaut.) Flachtrudeln, *das;* **go into a** ∼ **spin** (fig. coll.) durchdrehen (ugs.)

flatten /'flætn/ ① *v.t.* flach drücken ⟨Schachtel⟩; dem Erdboden gleichmachen ⟨Stadt, Gebäude⟩
② *v. refl.* ∼ **oneself against sth.** sich flach gegen etw. drücken

flatter /'flætə(r)/ *v.t.* schmeicheln (+ *Dat.*)

'**flattering** *adj.* schmeichelhaft

'**flattery** *n.* Schmeichelei, *die*

flat 'tyre *n.* Reifenpanne, *die*

flatulence /'flætjʊləns/ *n.* Blähungen *Pl.;* Flatulenz, *die* (Med.)

flaunt /flɔ:nt/ *v.t.* zur Schau stellen

flavor etc. (Amer.) ▶ FLAVOUR etc.

flavour /'fleɪvə(r)/ (Brit.) ① *n.* **(a)** Geschmack, *der* **(b)** (fig.) Anflug, *der*
② *v.t.* abschmecken

'**flavouring** *n.* (Brit.) Aroma, *das*

'**flavourless** *adj.* (Brit.) fade

flavoursome /'fleɪvəsəm/ *adj.* (Brit.) schmackhaft

flaw /flɔ:/ *n.* Fehler, *der;* (imperfection) Makel, *der;* (in workmanship or goods) Mangel, *der*

flax /flæks/ *n.* Flachs, *der*

flea /fli:/ *n.* Floh, *der*

flea: ∼ **bite** *n.* Flohbiss, *der;* ∼ **market** *n.* (coll.) Flohmarkt, *der*

fled ▶ FLEE

flee /fli:/ ① *v.i.,* **fled** /fled/ fliehen; ∼ **from sth./sb.** aus etw./vor jmdm. flüchten
② *v.t.,* **fled** fliehen aus

fleece /fli:s/ ① *n.* **(a)** [Schaf]fell, *das* **(b)** (garment) Fleece, *das*
② *v.t.* (fig.) ausplündern

fleecy /'fli:sɪ/ *adj.* flauschig

fleet /fli:t/ *n.* Flotte, *die*

fleeting /'fli:tɪŋ/ *adj.* flüchtig

flesh /fleʃ/ *n.* Fleisch, *das;* (of fruit, plant) [Frucht]fleisch, *das*

flesh: ∼**-coloured** *adj.* fleischfarben; ∼ **wound** *n.* Fleischwunde, *die*

'fleshy adj. fett; fleischig ⟨Hände⟩

flew ▶ FLY² 1, 2

flex¹ /fleks/ n. (Brit. Electr.) Kabel, das

flex² v.t. beugen ⟨Arm, Knie⟩; ~ one's muscles seine Muskeln spielen lassen

flexible /'fleksɪbl/ adj. (a) biegsam; elastisch
(b) (fig.) flexibel; ~ working hours or time gleitende Arbeitszeit

flexitime /'fleksɪtaɪm/ (Brit.), **flextime** /'flekstaɪm/ (Amer.) ns. Gleitzeit, die; be on or work ~: gleitende Arbeitszeit haben

flick /flɪk/ v.t. schnippen; anknipsen ⟨Schalter⟩; verspritzen ⟨Tinte⟩
■ **'flick through** v.t. durchblättern

flicker /'flɪkə(r)/ ① v.i. flackern; ⟨Fernsehapparat:⟩ flimmern
② n. Flackern, das; (of TV) Flimmern, das

'flick knife n. (Brit.) Schnappmesser, das

flight¹ /flaɪt/ n. (a) Flug, der
(b) ~ [of stairs or steps] Treppe, die

flight² n. (fleeing) Flucht, die; take ~: die Flucht ergreifen; put to ~: in die Flucht schlagen

flight: ~ **attendant** n. Flugbegleiter, der/-begleiterin, die; ~ **control** n. ≈ Flugsicherung, die; ~ **controller** n. (Aeronaut.) Fluglotse, der; ~ **deck** n. (a) (of aircraft carrier) Flugdeck, das; (b) (of aircraft) Cockpit, das; ~ **number** n. Flugnummer, die; ~ **path** n. (Aeronaut.) Flugweg, der; (Astronaut.) Flugbahn, die; ~ **recorder** n. Flugschreiber, der

flimsy /'flɪmzɪ/ adj. (a) dünn; nicht sehr haltbar ⟨Verpackung⟩
(b) (fig.) fadenscheinig ⟨Entschuldigung, Argument⟩

flinch /flɪntʃ/ v.i. zurückschrecken (from vor + Dat.); (wince) zusammenzucken

fling /flɪŋ/ ① n. have a or one's ~: sich ausleben
② v.t., flung /flʌŋ/ werfen; ~ oneself into sth. (fig.) sich in etw. (Akk.) stürzen

flint /flɪnt/ n. Feuerstein, der

flip /flɪp/ v.t., -pp- schnipsen; ~ [over] (turn over) umdrehen
■ **'flip through** v.t. durchblättern

flippant /'flɪpənt/ adj. leichtfertig

flipper /'flɪpə(r)/ n. Flosse, die

'flip side n. B-Seite, die

flirt /flɜːt/ v.i. flirten

flirtation /flɜː'teɪʃn/ n. Flirt, der

flirtatious /flɜː'teɪʃəs/ adj. kokett ⟨Blick, Art⟩

flit /flɪt/ v.i. huschen

float /fləʊt/ ① v.i. treiben; (in air) schweben
② n. (for carnival) Festwagen, der
③ v.t. (set afloat) flottmachen; (fig.) lancieren ⟨Plan, Idee⟩

floating: ~ **'dock** n. Schwimmdock, das; ~ **'voter** n. Wechselwähler, der/-wählerin, die

flock /flɒk/ ① n. (a) Herde, die; (of birds) Schwarm, der
(b) (of people) Schar, die
② v.i. strömen; ~ round sb. sich um jmdn. scharen

flog /flɒg/ v.t., -gg-: (a) auspeitschen
(b) (Brit. coll.: sell) verscheuern (salopp)

flood /flʌd/ ① n. Überschwemmung, die; the F~ (Bibl.) die Sintflut
② v.i. ⟨Fluss:⟩ über die Ufer treten; (fig.) strömen
③ v.t. überschwemmen

flood: ~ **damage** n. Hochwasserschaden, der; the area suffered extensive ~ damage in dem Gebiet gab es beträchtliche Hochwasserschäden; ~**gate** n. (Hydraulic Engin.) Schütze, die; open the ~**gates to sth.** (fig.) einer Sache (Dat.) Tür und Tor öffnen; ~**light** ① n. Scheinwerfer, der. ② v.t., floodlit /'flʌdlɪt/ anstrahlen; ~ **tide** n. Flut, die; ~ **warning** n. Hochwasserwarnung, die; ~ **water** n. Hochwasser, das

floor /flɔː(r)/ ① n. (a) Boden, der
(b) (storey) Stockwerk, das; first ~ (Amer.) Erdgeschoss, das; first ~ (Brit.), second ~ (Amer.) erster Stock; ground ~: Erdgeschoss, das; Parterre, das
② v.t. (a) (confound) überfordern
(b) (knock down) zu Boden schlagen

floor: ~**board** n. Dielenbrett, das; ~**cloth** n. (Brit.) Scheuertuch, das; ~ **polish** n. Bohnerwachs, das; ~ **show** n. ≈ Unterhaltungsprogramm, das

flop /flɒp/ ① v.i., -pp-: (a) plumpsen
(b) (coll.: fail) fehlschlagen; ⟨Theaterstück, Show:⟩ durchfallen
② n. (coll.: failure) Reinfall, der (ugs.)

floppy /'flɒpɪ/ adj. weich und biegsam

floppy disk n. (Comp.) Floppy Disk, die; Diskette, die

flora /'flɔːrə/ n. Flora, die

floral /'flɔːrl, 'flɒrl/ adj. geblümt ⟨Kleid, Stoff⟩; Blumen⟨muster⟩

Florence /'flɒrəns/ pr. n. Florenz (das)

florid /'flɒrɪd/ adj. blumig ⟨Stil, Redeweise⟩; gerötet ⟨Teint⟩

florist /'flɒrɪst/ n. Florist, der/Floristin, die

flotsam /'flɒtsəm/ n. ~ [and jetsam] Treibgut, das

flounder /'flaʊndə(r)/ v.i. taumeln

flour /'flaʊə(r)/ n. Mehl, das

flourish /'flʌrɪʃ/ ① v.i. gedeihen; ⟨Geschäft:⟩ florieren, gut gehen
② v.t. schwingen
③ n. do sth. with a ~: etw. schwungvoll tun

flout /flaʊt/ v.t. missachten

flow /fləʊ/ ① v.i. fließen; ⟨Körner, Sand:⟩ rinnen, rieseln; ⟨Gas:⟩ strömen
② n. (a) Fließen, das; ~ of water/people Wasser-/Menschenstrom, der; ~ of information Informationsfluss, der
(b) (of tide, river) Flut, die

'flow chart n. Flussdiagramm, *das*

flower /'flaʊə(r)/ ☐1 n. (blossom) Blüte, *die;* (plant) Blume, *die;* **come into** ∼: zu blühen beginnen
☐2 v.i. blühen

'flower bed n. Blumenbeet, *das*

flowering /'flaʊərɪŋ/ adj. ∼ **cherry/shrub** Zierkirsche, *die*/Blütenstrauch, *der*

'flowerpot n. Blumentopf, *der*

'flowery adj. geblümt ⟨*Stoff, Muster*⟩; (fig.) blumig ⟨*Sprache*⟩

'flowing adj. fließend; wallend ⟨*Haar*⟩

flown ▶ FLY² 1, 2

flu /fluː/ n. (coll.) Grippe, *die*

fluctuate /'flʌktjʊeɪt/ v.i. schwanken

fluctuation /flʌktjʊ'eɪʃn/ n. Schwankung, *die*

fluency /'fluːənsɪ/ n. Gewandtheit, *die;* (spoken) Redegewandtheit, *die*

fluent /'fluːənt/ adj. gewandt ⟨*Stil, Redeweise, Redner, Schreiber*⟩; **be** ∼ **in Russian, speak** ∼ **Russian** fließend Russisch sprechen

fluff /flʌf/ n. Flusen Pl.; Fusseln Pl.

fluffy /'flʌfɪ/ adj. [flaum]weich ⟨*Kissen, Küken*⟩; flauschig ⟨*Spielzeug, Decke*⟩

fluid /'fluːɪd/ ☐1 n. Flüssigkeit, *die*
☐2 adj. flüssig

fluke /fluːk/ n. (piece of luck) Glücksfall, *der*

flung ▶ FLING 2

fluorescent /flʊə'resənt/ adj. fluoreszierend

fluorescent 'light n. Leuchtstofflampe, *die*

fluoride /'flʊəraɪd/ n. Fluorid, *das;* ∼ **toothpaste** fluorhaltige Zahnpasta

flurry /'flʌrɪ/ n. **(a)** Aufregung, *die* **(b)** (of rain/snow) [Regen-/Schnee]schauer, *der*

flush¹ /flʌʃ/ ☐1 v.i. rot werden
☐2 v.t. ausspülen ⟨*Becken*⟩; ∼ **the toilet** or **lavatory** spülen
☐3 n. Rotwerden, *das*

flush² adj. (level) bündig; **be** ∼ **with sth.** mit etw. bündig abschließen

flush 'toilet n. Toilette mit Wasserspülung

fluster /'flʌstə(r)/ v.t. aus der Fassung bringen

flustered /'flʌstəd/ adj. nervös

flute /fluːt/ n. Flöte, *die*

flutter /'flʌtə(r)/ ☐1 v.i. flattern
☐2 v.t. flattern mit ⟨*Flügel*⟩

flux /flʌks/ n. **in a state of** ∼: im Fluss

fly¹ /flaɪ/ n. Fliege, *die*

fly² ☐1 v.i., **flew** /fluː/, **flown** /fləʊn/ **(a)** fliegen; ∼ **away** or **off** wegfliegen
(b) (fig.) ∼ **[by** or **past]** wie im Fluge vergehen
(c) ⟨*Fahne:*⟩ gehisst sein
☐2 v.t., **flew, flown** fliegen ⟨*Flugzeug, Fracht, Einsatz usw.*⟩; fliegen über (+ Akk.) ⟨*Strecke*⟩

☐3 n. in sing. or pl. (on trousers) Hosenschlitz, *der*

■ **fly 'in** v.i. [mit dem Flugzeug] eintreffen (from aus)

■ **fly 'out** v.i. abfliegen (of von)

'fly-fishing n. Fliegenfischerei, *die*

flying /'flaɪɪŋ/: ∼ **'doctor** n.: Arzt, der seine Krankenbesuche mit dem Flugzeug macht; ∼ **'saucer** n. fliegende Untertasse; ∼ **'start** n. (Sport) fliegender Start; ∼ **'visit** n. Stippvisite, *die* (ugs.)

fly: ∼**leaf** n. Vorsatzblatt, *das;* ∼**over** n. (Brit.) [Straßen]überführung, *die;* ∼ **spray** n. Insektenspray, *der od. das;* ∼ **swatter** n. Fliegenklappe, *die;* Fliegenklatsche, *die*

foal /fəʊl/ n. Fohlen, *das*

foam /fəʊm/ ☐1 n. Schaum, *der*
☐2 v.i. schäumen

foam: ∼**-backed** adj. schaumstoffverstärkt; ∼ **'mattress** n. Schaumgummimatratze, *die;* ∼ **'rubber** n. Schaumgummi, *der*

fob /fɒb/ v.t., **-bb-:** ∼ **sb. off with sth.** jmdn. mit etw. abspeisen (ugs.)

'focal point n. Brennpunkt, *der* (auch fig.)

focus /'fəʊkəs/ ☐1 n., pl. ∼**es** or **foci** /'fəʊsaɪ/ Brennpunkt, *der;* **out of/in** ∼: unscharf/ scharf eingestellt; unscharf/scharf ⟨*Foto, Film usw.*⟩; (fig.) **be the** ∼ **of attention** im Brennpunkt des Interesses stehen
☐2 v.t., **-s-** or **-ss-** einstellen (on auf + Akk.); bündeln ⟨*Licht, Strahlen*⟩
☐3 v.i., **-s-** or **-ss-** (fig.) sich konzentrieren (on auf + Akk.)

'focus group n. Fokusgruppe, *die*

fodder /'fɒdə(r)/ n. [Vieh]futter, *das*

foe /fəʊ/ n. (poet./rhet.) Feind, *der*

foetus /'fiːtəs/ n. Fötus, *der*

fog /fɒg/ n. Nebel, *der*

foggy /'fɒgɪ/ adj. neblig

'foglight n. Nebelscheinwerfer, *der*

fogy /'fəʊgɪ/ n. [old] ∼: [alter] Opa (salopp)/[alte] Oma (salopp)

foible /'fɔɪbl/ n. Eigenheit, *die*

foil¹ /fɔɪl/ n. Folie, *die*

foil² v.t. vereiteln

foist /fɔɪst/ v.t. ∼ **[off] on to sb.** jmdm. andrehen (ugs.); auf jmdn. abwälzen ⟨*Probleme, Verantwortung*⟩

fold /fəʊld/ ☐1 v.t. [zusammen]falten; ∼ **one's arms** die Arme verschränken
☐2 v.i. **(a)** (become ∼ed) sich zusammenfalten
(b) (be able to be ∼ed) sich falten lassen
(c) (go bankrupt) Konkurs machen
☐3 n. Falte, *die;* (line made by ∼ing) Kniff, *der*

■ **fold 'up** v.t. zusammenfalten ⟨*Laken*⟩; zusammenklappen ⟨*Stuhl*⟩

'folder n. **(a)** Mappe, *die* **(b)** (Comp.) Ordner, *der*

foliage /'fəʊlɪɪdʒ/ n. Blätter Pl.; (of tree also) Laub, *das*

folk /fəʊk/ n. **(a)** Volk, das
(b) in pl. ~[s] (people) Leute Pl.

folk: ~ **dance** n. Volkstanz, der;
~ **hero** n. Volksheld, der; ~**lore** /-lɔː(r)/
n. Folklore, die; ~ **music** n. Volksmusik,
die; ~ **singer** n. Sänger/Sängerin von
Volksliedern; (modern) Folksänger, der/
-sängerin, die; ~ **song** Volkslied, das;
(modern) Folksong, der

follow /'fɒləʊ/ ① v.t. **(a)** folgen (+ Dat.)
(b) entlanggehen/-fahren ‹Straße usw.›
(c) (come after) folgen auf (+ Akk.)
(d) (result from) die Folge sein von
(e) (treat or take as guide) sich orientieren an
(+ Dat.)
(f) folgen (+ Dat.) ‹Prinzip, Instinkt,
Trend›; verfolgen ‹Politik›; befolgen ‹Regel,
Vorschrift, Rat, Warnung›; sich halten an
(+ Akk.) ‹Konventionen, Diät›
(g) (grasp meaning of) folgen (+ Dat.); **do you
~ me?** verstehst du, was ich meine?
② v.i. **(a)** (go, come) ~ **after sb./sth.**
jmdm./einer Sache folgen
(b) (come next in order or time) folgen; **as ~s**
wie folgt
(c) ~ **from sth.** (result) die Folge von etw.
sein; (be deducible) aus etw. folgen
■ **follow 'on** v.i. (continue) ~ **on from sth.**
die Fortsetzung von etw. sein
■ **follow 'up** v.t. **(a)** ausbauen ‹Erfolg,
Sieg›
(b) nachgehen (+ Dat.) ‹Hinweis›

'follower n. Anhänger, der/Anhängerin,
die

'following ① adj. folgend; **the
~:** Folgendes
② prep. nach
③ n. Anhängerschaft, die

folly /'fɒlɪ/ n. Torheit, die (geh.)

fond /fɒnd/ adj. liebevoll; lieb
‹Erinnerung›; **be ~ of sb.** jmdn. mögen; **be
~ of doing sth.** etw. gern tun

fondle /'fɒndl/ v.t. streicheln

'fondness n. Liebe, die; ~ **for sth.**
Vorliebe für etw.

font¹ /fɒnt/ n. Taufstein, der

font² n. (Comp., Printing) Schrift, die; Font,
der (fachspr.); ~ **size** Schriftgröße, die;
Fontgröße, die

food /fuːd/ n. **(a)** Nahrung, die; (for animals)
Futter, das
(b) (as commodity) Lebensmittel Pl.
(c) (in solid form) Essen, das
(d) (particular kind) Nahrungsmittel, das; Kost,
die

food: ~ **chain** n. Nahrungskette, die;
~ **mile** ≈ Lebensmittelkilometer, das
~ **poisoning** n. Lebensmittelvergiftung,
die; ~ **processor** n. Küchenmaschine,
die; ~ **shop,** ~ **store** ns.
Lebensmittelgeschäft, das; ~**stuff** n.
Nahrungsmittel, das; perishable ~stuffs
leicht verderbliche Lebensmittel

fool /fuːl/ ① n. Dummkopf, der (ugs.)

② v.t. ~ **sb. into doing sth.** jmdn. [durch
Tricks] dazu bringen, etw. zu tun
■ **fool a'bout, fool a'round** v.i.
Unsinn machen

foolhardy /'fuːlhɑːdɪ/ adj. tollkühn

'foolish adj. töricht; verrückt (ugs.) ‹Idee,
Vorschlag›

'foolproof adj. (infallible) absolut sicher

foot /fʊt/ ① n., pl. **feet** /fiːt/ **(a)** Fuß, der;
on ~: zu Fuß; **put one's ~ in it** (fig. coll.) ins
Fettnäpfchen treten (ugs.)
(b) (far end) unteres Ende; (of bed) Fußende,
das
(c) (measure) Fuß, der (30,48 cm)
② v.t. ~ **the bill** die Rechnung bezahlen

football /'fʊtbɔːl/ n. (game, ball) Fußball, der

'football boot n. Fußballschuh, der

'footballer n. Fußballspieler, der/
-spielerin, die

football: ~ **pitch** n. Fußballplatz, der;
~ **pools** n. pl. **the ~ pools** das Fußballtoto

foot: ~ **brake** n. Fußbremse, die;
~ **bridge** n. Fußgängerbrücke, die;
~**hold** n. Halt, der

'footing n. **(a)** (fig.) be on an equal ~ [with
sb.] [jmdm.] gleichgestellt sein
(b) (foothold) Halt, der

foot: ~**note** n. Fußnote, die;
~ **passenger** n. Fußpassagier, der;
~**path** n. Fußweg, der; ~**print** n.
Fußabdruck, der; ~**rest** n. Fußstütze, die;
(on bicycle or motorcycle) Fußraste, die; ~**step**
n. Schritt, der; **follow in sb.'s ~steps** (fig.)
in jmds. Fußstapfen (Akk.) treten; ~**stool**
n. Fußbank, die; Fußschemel, der; ~**wear**
n. Schuhe Pl.; ~**work** n. (Sport, Dancing)
Beinarbeit, die

for /fə(r), stressed fɔː(r)/ ① prep. **(a)** für;
what is it ~? wofür ist das?; **reason
~ living** Grund zu leben; **a request ~ help**
eine Bitte um Hilfe; **study ~ a university
degree** auf einen Hochschulabschluss hin
studieren; **take sb. ~ a walk** mit jmdm.
einen Spaziergang machen; **be '~ doing sth.**
(in favour) dafür sein, etw. zu tun; **cheque/bill
~ £5** Scheck/Rechnung über 5 Pfund; **what
have you got ~ a cold?** was haben Sie gegen
Erkältungen da?
(b) (on account of, as penalty of) wegen; **were it
not ~ you/ your help** ohne dich/deine Hilfe;
~ **fear of** aus Angst vor (+ Dat.)
(c) (in spite of) ~ **all …:** trotz …; ~ **all that, …:**
trotzdem …
(d) ~ **all I know/care …:** möglicherweise/
was mich betrifft, …; ~ **one thing, …:**
zunächst einmal …
(e) (during) **stay ~ a week** eine Woche
bleiben; **we've/we haven't been here ~ three
years** wir sind seit drei Jahren hier/nicht
mehr hier gewesen
(f) **walk ~ 20 miles** 20 Meilen gehen
② conj. denn

forage /'fɒrɪdʒ/ ① n. Futter, das
② v.i. ~ **for sth.** auf der Suche nach etw. sein

forbad, forbade ▸ FORBID

forbid /fə'bɪd/ *v.t.*, **-dd-, forbad** /fə'bæd/ *or* **forbade** /fə'bæd, fə'beɪd/, **forbidden** /fə'bɪdn/ ~ sb. to do sth. jmdm. verbieten, etw. zu tun; ~ [sb.] sth. [jmdm.] etw. verbieten; **it is ~den [to do sth.]** es ist verboten[, etw. zu tun]

forbidden ▸ FORBID

for'bidding *adj.* Furcht einflößend

force /fɔːs/ **1** *n.* (a) (strength, power) Stärke, *die;* (of explosion, storm) Wucht, *die;* (Phys.; physical strength) Kraft, *die;* **in ~:** mit einem großen Aufgebot

(b) (validity) Kraft, *die;* **in ~:** in Kraft; **come into ~** ‹*Gesetz usw.:*› in Kraft treten

(c) (violence) Gewalt, *die;* **by ~:** gewaltsam

(d) (group) (of workers) Kolonne, *die;* Trupp, *der;* (Mil.) Armee, *die;* **the ~** (Police) die Polizei; **the ~s** die Armee; **be in the ~s** beim Militär sein

2 *v.t.* (a) zwingen; **~ sth. [up]on sb.** jmdm. etw. aufzwingen

(b) **~ [open]** aufbrechen; **~ one's way in** sich (*Dat.*) mit Gewalt Zutritt verschaffen

forced /fɔːst/ *adj.* (a) (contrived, unnatural) gezwungen

(b) (compelled by force) erzwungen; Zwangs‹*arbeit*›

forced 'landing *n.* Notlandung, *die*

'force-feed *v.t.* zwangsernähren

forceful /'fɔːsfl/ *adj.* stark ‹*Persönlichkeit, Charakter*›; energisch ‹*Person, Art*›; eindrucksvoll ‹*Sprache*›

forceps /'fɔːseps/ *n., pl. same* [**pair of**] ~: Zange, *die*

forcible /'fɔːsɪbl/ *adj.,* **forcibly** /'fɔːsɪblɪ/ *adv.* gewaltsam

ford /fɔːd/ **1** *n.* Furt, *die* **2** *v.t.* durchqueren; (wade through) durchwaten

fore /fɔː(r)/ **1** *adj., esp. in comb.* vorder…; Vorder‹*teil, -front usw.*›

2 *n.* **to the ~:** im Vordergrund

'forearm *n.* Unterarm, *der*

foreboding /fɔː'bəʊdɪŋ/ *n.* Vorahnung, *die*

'forecast **1** *v.t.,* **forecast** *or* **forecasted** vorhersagen

2 *n.* Voraussage, *die*

'forecaster *n.* Meteorologe, *der/* Meteorologin, *die*

'forecourt *n.* Vorhof, *der*

'forefather *n., usu. in pl.* Vorfahr, *der*

'forefinger *n.* Zeigefinger, *der*

'forefront *n.* **[be] in the ~ of** in vorderster Linie (+ *Gen.*) [stehen]

'foregone *adj.* **be a ~ conclusion** von vornherein feststehen; (be certain) so gut wie sicher sein

'foreground *n.* Vordergrund, *der*

forehead /'fɒrɪd, 'fɔːhed/ *n.* Stirn, *die*

foreign /'fɒrɪn/ *adj.* (a) (from abroad) ausländisch; Fremd‹*kapital, -sprache*›; **he is**

~: er ist Ausländer

(b) (abroad) fremd; Außen‹*politik, -handel*›; **from a ~ country** aus einem anderen Land; aus dem Ausland; **~ countries** Ausland, *das*

(c) (from outside) fremd; **~ body/substance** Fremdkörper, *der*

foreign corre'spondent *n.* (Journ.) Auslandskorrespondent, *der/* -korrespondentin, *die*

'foreigner *n.* Ausländer, *der/*Ausländerin, *die*

foreign: **~ ex'change** *n.* Devisen *Pl.;* **~ 'language** *n.* Fremdsprache, *die;* **~-language assistant** Fremdsprachenassistent, *der/* -assistentin, *die;* **~-language newspaper/broadcast** fremdsprachige Zeitung/Rundfunksendung; **~-language teaching** Fremdsprachenunterricht, *der;* **F~ 'Minister** *n.* Außenminister, *der/*-ministerin, *die;* **F~ 'Ministry** *n.* Außenministerium, *das;* **F~ Office** *n.* (Brit. Hist./coll.) Außenministerium, *das;* **~ policy** *n.* Außenpolitik, *die;* **F~ 'Secretary** *n.* (Brit.) Außenminister, *der/*-ministerin, *die;* **~ trade** *n.* Außenhandel, *der*

foreman /'fɔːmən/ *n., pl.* **foremen** /'fɔːmən/ Vorarbeiter, *der*

foremost /'fɔːməʊst, 'fɔːməst/ **1** *adj.* (a) vorderst…

(b) (fig.) führend

2 *adv.* **first and ~:** zunächst einmal

'forename *n.* Vorname, *der*

forensic /fə'rensɪk/ *adj.* **~ medicine** Gerichtsmedizin, *die;* **~ science** Kriminaltechnik, *die*

'foreplay *n.* Vorspiel, *das*

'forerunner *n.* Vorläufer, *der/*Vorläuferin, *die*

foresaw ▸ FORESEE

foresee /fɔː'siː/ *v.t., forms as* SEE voraussehen

foreseeable /fɔː'siːəbl/ *adj.* vorhersehbar; **in the ~ future** in nächster Zukunft

foreseen ▸ FORESEE

'foresight *n.* Weitblick, *der*

foreskin *n.* (Anat.) Vorhaut, *die*

forest /'fɒrɪst/ *n.* Wald, *der;* (commercially exploited) Forst, *der*

fore'stall *v.t.* zuvorkommen (+ *Dat.*)

forested /'fɒrɪstɪd/ *adj.* bewaldet

forestry /'fɒrɪstrɪ/ *n.* Forstwirtschaft, *die*

foretaste *n.* Vorgeschmack, *der*

fore'tell *v.t.,* **fore'told** voraussagen

'forethought *n.* (prior deliberation) [vorherige] Überlegung; (care for the future) Vorausdenken, *das*

forever /fə'revə(r)/ *adv.* (constantly) ständig

fore'warn *v.t.* vorwarnen

fore'warning *n.* Vorwarnung, *die*

'foreword n. Vorwort, das

forfeit /'fɔːfɪt/ ☐ v.t. verlieren; verwirken (geh.) ⟨Recht, jmds. Gunst⟩

☐ n. Strafe, die; (games) Pfand, das

forgave ▶ FORGIVE

forge¹ /fɔːdʒ/ ☐ n. (a) (workshop) Schmiede, die

(b) (blacksmith's hearth) Esse, die

☐ v.t. (a) schmieden (into zu)

(b) (fig.) schmieden ⟨Plan⟩; schließen ⟨Vereinbarung, Freundschaft⟩

(c) (counterfeit) fälschen

forge² v.i. ~ ahead [das Tempo] beschleunigen; (fig.) Fortschritte machen

'forger n. Fälscher, der/Fälscherin, die

forgery /'fɔːdʒərɪ/ n. Fälschung, die

forget /fə'get/ v.t., -tt-, forgot /fə'gɒt/, forgotten /fə'gɒtn/ vergessen; (~ learned ability) verlernen

☐ v.i., -tt-, forgot, forgotten es vergessen; ~ about sth. etw. vergessen; ~ about it! (coll.) schon gut!

forgetful /fə'getfl/ adj. vergesslich

for'getfulness n. Vergesslichkeit, die

for'get-me-not n. (Bot.) Vergissmeinnicht, das

forgettable /fə'getəbl/ adj. easily ~: leicht zu vergessen

forgive /fə'gɪv/ v.t., forgave /fə'geɪv/, forgiven /fə'gɪvn/ verzeihen; vergeben ⟨Sünden⟩; ~ sb. [sth. or for sth.] jmdm. [etw.] verzeihen

for'giveness n. Verzeihung, die; (of sins) Vergebung, die

for'giving /fə'gɪvɪŋ/ adj. versöhnlich

forgo /fɔː'gəʊ/ v.t., forms as GO: verzichten auf (+ Akk.)

forgone ▶ FORGO

forgot, forgotten ▶ FORGET

fork /fɔːk/ ☐ n. (a) Gabel, die; knives and ~s Besteck, das

(b) (in road) Gabelung, die; (one branch) Abzweigung, die

☐ v.i. (divide) sich gabeln; (turn) abbiegen; ~ left links abbiegen

■ **fork 'out** v.i. (coll.) blechen (ugs.)

forked 'lightning n., no indef. art. Linienblitz, der

'forklift truck n. Gabelstapler, der

forlorn /fə'lɔːn/ adj. (a) (desperate) verzweifelt

(b) (forsaken) verlassen

form /fɔːm/ ☐ n. (a) (shape, type, style) Form, die; take ~: Gestalt annehmen

(b) (printed sheet) Formular, das

(c) (Brit. Sch.) Klasse, die

(d) (bench) Bank, die

(e) (Sport: physical condition) Form, die; (fig.) true to ~: wie üblich

☐ v.t. (a) bilden

(b) (shape) formen, gestalten (into zu)

(c) sich (Dat.) bilden ⟨Meinung, Urteil⟩;

gewinnen ⟨Eindruck⟩; fassen ⟨Plan⟩; entwickeln ⟨Vorliebe, Gewohnheit⟩; schließen ⟨Freundschaft⟩

(d) (set up) bilden ⟨Regierung⟩; gründen ⟨Bund, Firma, Partei⟩

☐ v.i. sich bilden; ⟨Idee:⟩ Gestalt annehmen

formal /'fɔːml/ adj. formell; förmlich ⟨Person, Art, Einladung, Begrüßung⟩; (official) offiziell; a ~ 'yes'/'no' eine bindende Zusage/endgültige Absage

formality /fɔː'mælɪtɪ/ n. (a) (requirement) Formalität, die

(b) (being formal) Förmlichkeit, die

formalize /'fɔːməlaɪz/ v.t. (a) (specify and systematize) formalisieren

(b) (make official) formell bekräftigen

format /'fɔːmæt/ n. ☐ (also Comp.) Format, das

☐ v.t., -tt- (Comp.) formatieren

formation /fɔː'meɪʃn/ n. (a) ▶ FORM 2A, D: Bildung, die; Gründung, die

(b) (Mil., Aeronaut.) Formation, die

formative /'fɔːmətɪv/ adj. formend, prägend ⟨Einfluss⟩; the ~ years of life die entscheidenden Lebensjahre

former /'fɔːmə(r)/ attrib. adj. ehemalig; in ~ times früher; the ~ (as noun) der/die/das Erstere; pl. die Ersteren

'formerly adv. früher

formidable /'fɔːmɪdəbl/ adj. gewaltig; gefährlich ⟨Herausforderung, Gegner⟩

formula /'fɔːmjʊlə/ n. Formel, die

formulate /'fɔːmjʊleɪt/ v.t. formulieren; (devise) entwickeln

formulation /fɔːmjʊ'leɪʃn/ n. Formulierung, die

forsake /fə'seɪk/ v.t., forsook /fə'sʊk/, ~n /fə'seɪkn/ (a) (give up) verzichten auf (+ Akk.)

(b) (desert) verlassen

for'saken adj. verlassen

forsook ▶ FORSAKE

fort /fɔːt/ n. (Mil.) Fort, das

forte /'fɔːteɪ/ n. Stärke, die

forth /fɔːθ/ adv. and so ~: und so weiter; see also BACK 3

forthcoming /'---, -'--/ adj. (a) (approaching) bevorstehend; in Kürze erscheinend ⟨Buch usw.⟩

(b) pred. be ~ ⟨Geld, Antwort:⟩ kommen; ⟨Hilfe:⟩ geleistet werden; not be ~: ausbleiben

(c) (responsive) mitteilsam ⟨Person⟩

'forthright adj. direkt

forth'with adv. unverzüglich

fortieth /'fɔːtɪɪθ/ adj. vierzigst...

fortify /'fɔːtɪfaɪ/ v.t. (a) (Mil.) befestigen

(b) (strengthen) stärken

fortitude /'fɔːtɪtjuːd/ n. innere Stärke

fortnight /'fɔːtnaɪt/ n. vierzehn Tage Pl.

fortnightly /'fɔːtnaɪtlɪ/ ☐ adj. vierzehntäglich; zweiwöchentlich

2 *adv.* alle vierzehn Tage; alle zwei Wochen

fortress /'fɔːtrɪs/ *n.* Festung, *die*

fortuitous /fɔː'tjuːɪtəs/ *adj.*, **for'tuitously** *adv.* zufällig

fortunate /'fɔːtʃənət/ *adj.* glücklich **'fortunately** *adv.* glücklicherweise

fortune /'fɔːtʃən, 'fɔːtʃuːn/ *n.* **(a)** (wealth) Vermögen, *das* **(b)** (luck) Schicksal, *das;* **bad/good** ∼**:** Pech/ Glück, *das*

'fortune teller *n.* Wahrsager, *der/* Wahrsagerin, *die*

forty /'fɔːtɪ/ **1** *adj.* vierzig; **have** ∼ **'winks** ein Nickerchen machen (ugs.) **2** *n.* Vierzig, *die.* See also EIGHT; EIGHTY 2

forum /'fɔːrəm/ *n.* Forum, *das*

forward /'fɔːwəd/ **1** *adv.* **(a)** (in direction faced) vorwärts **(b)** (to the front) nach vorn; vor⟨*laufen, -rücken, -schieben*⟩ **(c)** (closer) heran; **he came** ∼ **to greet me** er kam auf mich zu, um mich zu begrüßen **(d) come** ∼ ⟨*Zeuge, Helfer:*⟩ sich melden **2** *adj.* **(a)** (directed ahead) vorwärts gerichtet **(b)** (at or to the front) Vorder-; vorder… **3** *n.* (Sport) Stürmer, *der/*Stürmerin, *die* **4** *v.t.* (send on) nachschicken ⟨*Post*⟩ **(to an + *Akk.*)**

forwarding ad'dress /'fɔːwədɪŋ/ *n.* Nachsendeanschrift, *die*

forward: ∼**-looking** *adj.* vorausschauend; ∼ **'planning** *n.* Vorausplanung, *die*

forwards /'fɔːwədz/ ▶ FORWARD 1A, B

'forward slash *n.* Schrägstrich, *der*

forwent ▶ FORGO

fossil /'fɒsɪl/ *n.* Fossil, *das;* ∼ **fuel** fossiler Brennstoff

foster /'fɒstə(r)/ **1** *v.t.* **(a)** fördern; pflegen ⟨*Freundschaft*⟩ **(b)** in Pflege haben ⟨*Kind*⟩ **2** *adj.* ∼**:** Pflege⟨*kind, -eltern, -sohn usw.*⟩

fought ▶ FIGHT 1, 2

foul /faʊl/ **1** *adj.* **(a)** abscheulich ⟨*Geruch, Geschmack*⟩ **(b)** (polluted) verschmutzt ⟨*Wasser, Luft*⟩; (putrid) faulig ⟨*Wasser*⟩; stickig ⟨*Luft*⟩ **(c)** (coll.: awful) scheußlich (ugs.); anstößig ⟨*Sprache*⟩ **2** *n.* (Sport) Foul, *das* **3** *v.t.* **(a)** beschmutzen; verpesten ⟨*Luft*⟩ **(b)** (Sport) foulen

foul: ∼**-mouthed** /'faʊlmaʊðd/ *adj.* unanständig; unflätig; ∼**-smelling** *adj.* übel riechend

found¹ /faʊnd/ *v.t.* **(a)** (establish) gründen; stiften ⟨*Krankenhaus, Kloster*⟩; begründen ⟨*Wissenschaft, Religion*⟩ **(b)** (fig.: base) begründen; **be** ∼**ed [up]on sth.** [sich] auf etw. (*Akk.*) gründen

found² ▶ FIND 1

foundation /faʊn'deɪʃn/ *n.* **(a)** Gründung, *die;* (of hospital, monastery) Stiftung, *die* **(b)** *usu. in pl.* ∼**[s]** (lit. or fig.) Fundament, *das;* **be without** ∼ (fig.) unbegründet sein

foundation: ∼ **course** *n.* (Univ. etc.) Grundkurs, *der;* ∼ **cream** *n.* Grundierungscreme, *die;* ∼ **stone** *n.* (lit. or fig.) Grundstein, *der*

'founder¹ *n.* Gründer, *der/*Gründerin, *die;* (of hospital) Stifter, *der/*Stifterin, *die*

founder² *v.i.* **(a)** ⟨*Schiff:*⟩ sinken **(b)** (fig.: fail) sich zerschlagen

foundry /'faʊndrɪ/ *n.* Gießerei, *die*

fountain /'faʊntɪn/ *n.* Fontäne, *die;* (structure) Springbrunnen, *der;* (fig.) Quelle, *die*

'fountain pen *n.* Füllfederhalter, *der*

four /fɔː(r)/ **1** *adj.* vier **2** *n.* Vier, *die;* **on all** ∼**s** auf allen vieren (ugs.). See also EIGHT

four: ∼**-by-**∼ **1** *adj.* Allrad-; **2** *n.* Allradler, *der;* Allradfahrzeug, *das;* ∼**-door** *attrib. adj.* viertürig ⟨*Auto*⟩; ∼**fold** /'fɔːfəʊld/ *adj., adv.* vierfach; **a** ∼**fold increase** ein Anstieg auf das Vierfache; ∼**-legged** /'fɔːlegɪd, 'fɔːlegd/ *adj.* vierbeinig; ∼**-letter 'word** *n.* vulgärer Ausdruck; (expressing anger) ≈ Kraftausdruck, *der;* ∼**-poster** *n.* Himmelbett, *das;* ∼**some** /'fɔːsəm/ *n.* Quartett, *das;* **go in** *or* **as a** ∼**some** zu viert gehen; ∼**-star** *n.* ∼-star [petrol] Super[benzin], *das*

fourteen /fɔː'tiːn/ **1** *adj.* vierzehn **2** *n.* Vierzehn, *die.* See also EIGHT

fourteenth /fɔː'tiːnθ/ **1** *adj.* vierzehnt… **2** *n.* (fraction) Vierzehntel, *das.* See also EIGHTH

fourth /fɔːθ/ **1** *adj.* viert… **2** *n.* (in sequence, rank) Vierte, *der/die/das;* (fraction) Viertel, *das.* See also EIGHTH

'fourthly *adv.* viertens

four-wheel 'drive *n.* (Motor Veh.) Vier- *od.* Allradantrieb, *der*

fowl /faʊl/ *n.* Haushuhn, *das;* (collectively) Geflügel, *das*

fox /fɒks/ **1** *n.* Fuchs, *der* **2** *v.t.* verwirren

'fox-hunting *n.* Fuchsjagd, *die*

foyer /'fɔɪeɪ/ *n.* Foyer, *das*

fraction /'frækʃn/ *n.* **(a)** (Math.) Bruch, *der* **(b)** (small part) Bruchteil, *der*

fracture /'fræktʃə(r)/ **1** *n.* Bruch, *der* **2** *v.t.* brechen

fragile /'frædʒaɪl/ *adj.* zerbrechlich

fragility /frə'dʒɪlɪtɪ/ *n.* Zerbrechlichkeit, *die*

fragment /'frægmənt/ *n.* Bruchstück, *das*

fragmentary /'frægməntərɪ/ *adj.* bruchstückhaft

fragrance /'freɪgrəns/ *n.* Duft, *der*

fragrant /'freɪgrənt/ *adj.* duftend

frail /freɪl/ *adj.* zerbrechlich; gebrechlich ⟨*Greis, Greisin*⟩

frame /freɪm/ [1] *n.* **(a)** (of vehicle) Rahmen, *der;* (of bed) Gestell, *das*
(b) (border) Rahmen, *der;* [spectacle] ~s [Brillen]gestell, *das*
[2] *v.t.* **(a)** rahmen
(b) formulieren ⟨*Frage, Antwort*⟩
(c) (coll.: incriminate) ~ sb. jmdm. etwas anhängen (ugs.)

frame: ~-**up** *n.* (coll.) abgekartetes Spiel (ugs.); ~**work** *n.* Gerüst, *das*

franc /fræŋk/ *n.* Franc, *der;* (Swiss) Franken, *der*

France /frɑːns/ *pr. n.* Frankreich (*das*)

franchise /'fræntʃaɪz/ *n.* **(a)** Stimmrecht, *das*
(b) (Commerc.) Lizenz, *die*

frank[1] *adj.* offen; freimütig ⟨*Geständnis, Äußerung*⟩; be ~ with sb. zu jmdm. offen sein

frank[2] *v.t.* (Post) frankieren

frankfurter /'fræŋkfɜːtə(r)/ ⟨*Amer.:* **frankfurt** /'fræŋkfɜːt/⟩ *n.* Frankfurter [Würstchen]

frankly *adv.* offen; (honestly) offen gesagt

frantic /'fræntɪk/ *adj.* **(a)** verzweifelt ⟨*Hilferufe, Gestikulieren*⟩; be ~ with fear/rage *etc.* außer sich (*Dat.*) sein vor Angst/Wut *usw.*
(b) hektisch ⟨*Aktivität, Suche*⟩

frantically /'fræntɪkəlɪ/, **franticly** *adv.* verzweifelt

fraternal /frə'tɜːnl/ *adj.* brüderlich

fraternize /'frætənaɪz/ *v.i.* ~ [with sb.] sich verbrüdern [mit jmdm.]

fraud /frɔːd/ *n.* **(a)** *no pl.* Betrug, *der*
(b) (trick) Schwindel, *der*
(c) (person) Betrüger, *der*/Betrügerin, *die*

fraudulent /'frɔːdjʊlənt/ *adj.* betrügerisch

fraught /frɔːt/ *adj.* be ~ with danger voller Gefahren sein

fray[1] /freɪ/ *n.* [Kampf]getümmel, *das;* enter *or* join the ~: sich in den Kampf stürzen

fray[2] *v.i.* [sich] durchscheuern; ⟨*Hosenbein, Teppich, Seilende:*⟩ ausfransen; our nerves/ tempers began to ~ (fig.) wir verloren langsam die Nerven/unsere Gemüter erhitzten sich

freak /friːk/ *n.* **(a)** Missgeburt, *die; attrib.* ungewöhnlich ⟨*Wetter, Ereignis*⟩
(b) (coll.: fanatic) Freak, *der*

freakish /'friːkɪʃ/ *adj.* (capricious) launisch; verrückt (ugs.); (abnormal) absonderlich

freaky /'friːkɪ/ *adj.* **(a)** ▶ FREAKISH
(b) (coll.: bizarre) irre (salopp); verrückt (ugs.)

freckle /'frekl/ *n.* Sommersprosse, *die*

freckled *adj.* sommersprossig

free /friː/ [1] *adj.,* **freer** /'friːə(r)/, **freest** /'friːɪst/ **(a)** frei; get ~: freikommen; set ~: freilassen; ~ of charge/cost gebührenfrei/ kostenlos; sb. is ~ to do sth. es steht jmdm. frei, etw. zu tun; ~ time Freizeit, *die;* he's ~ in the mornings er hat morgens Zeit

(b) (without payment) kostenlos; frei ⟨*Unterkunft, Verpflegung*⟩; Frei⟨*karte, -exemplar*⟩; Gratis⟨*probe*⟩; 'admission ~' „Eintritt frei"; for ~ (coll.) umsonst
[2] *adv.* gratis; umsonst
[3] *v.t.* (set at liberty) freilassen; (disentangle) befreien (of, from von); ~ sb./oneself from jmdn./sich befreien aus ⟨*Gefängnis, Sklaverei*⟩

free 'agent *n.* be a ~: sein eigener Herr sein

freedom /'friːdəm/ *n.* Freiheit, *die;* ~ of the press Pressefreiheit, *die;* ~ of action/ speech/movement Handlungs-/Rede-/ Bewegungsfreiheit, *die;* ~ of information Auskunftsrecht, *das*

'freedom fighter *n.* Freiheitskämpfer, *der*/-kämpferin, *die*

free: ~ 'enterprise *n.* freies Unternehmertum; ~ 'fall *n.* freier Fall; ~-fall parachuting Fallschirmspringen mit freiem Fall; F~fone ® /'friːfəʊn/ *n.* ≈ Service 130; phone us on F~fone 0800 343 027 rufen Sie uns unter 0800 343 027 zum Nulltarif an; ~ 'gift *n.* Gratisgabe, *die;* ~hold [1] *n.* Besitzrecht, *das;* [2] *adj.* Eigentums-; ~holder *n.* Grundeigentümer, *der;* ~ house *n.* (Brit.) *brauereiunabhängiges Wirtshaus;* ~ 'kick *n.* (Footb.) Freistoß, *der;* ~lance [1] *n.* freier Mitarbeiter/freie Mitarbeiterin; [2] *adj.* freiberuflich; ~lancer /'friːlɑːnsə(r)/ ▶ ~LANCE 1

'freely *adv.* (willingly) großzügig; freimütig ⟨*eingestehen*⟩; (without restriction) frei; (frankly) offen

free: ~ 'market *n.* (Econ.) freier Markt; F~mason *n.* Freimaurer, *der;* F~phone ▶ FREEFONE; ~-range *adj.* frei laufend ⟨*Huhn*⟩; ~-range eggs Eier von frei laufenden Hühnern; ~ speech *n.* Redefreiheit; ~standing *adj.* frei stehend; ~ware /'friːweə(r)/ *n., no indef. art.* (Comp.) Freeware, *die;* kostenlose Software; ~way *n.* (Amer.) Autobahn, *die;* ~-wheel *v.i.* im Freilauf fahren; ~ 'world *n.* freie Welt

freeze /friːz/ [1] *v.i.,* **froze** /frəʊz/, **frozen** /'frəʊzn/ **(a)** frieren; (become covered with ice) zufrieren; ⟨*Straße:*⟩ vereisen; ⟨*Flüssigkeit:*⟩ gefrieren; ⟨*Rohr, Schloss:*⟩ einfrieren
(b) (become rigid) steif frieren
[2] *v.t.,* **froze, frozen (a)** (preserve) tiefkühlen
(b) einfrieren ⟨*Kredit, Löhne, Preise usw.*⟩

'freeze-dry *v.t.* gefriertrocknen

'freezer *n.* Tiefkühltruhe, *die;* [upright] ~: Tiefkühlschrank, *der;* ~ compartment Tiefkühlfach, *das*

freezing /'friːzɪŋ/ [1] *adj.* (lit. or fig.) frostig; it's ~: es ist eiskalt
[2] *n.* above/below ~: über/unter dem/den Gefrierpunkt

freezing: ~ 'fog *n.* gefrierender Nebel; ~ point *n.* Gefrierpunkt, *der*

freight /freɪt/ *n.* Fracht, *die*
'freighter *n.* Frachter, *der*
'freight train *n.* Güterzug, *der*
French /frentʃ/ ① *adj.* französisch; **he/she is** ∼: er ist Franzose/sie ist Französin ② *n.* (a) (language) Französisch, *das; see also* ENGLISH 2A (b) **the** ∼ *pl.* die Franzosen *usw.*
French: ∼ **'bean** *n.* (Brit.) Gartenbohne, *die;* ∼ **'bread** *n.* französisches [Stangen]weißbrot; ∼ **'dressing** *n.* Vinaigrette, *die;* ∼ **'fries** *n. pl.* Pommes frites *Pl.;* ∼ **'kiss** *n.* französischer Kuss (ugs.); Zungenkuss, *der;* ∼**man** /'frentʃmən/ *n., pl.* ∼**men** /'frentʃmən/ Franzose, *der;* ∼ **'polish** *n.* Schellackpolitur, *die;* ∼ **'window** *n.* französisches Fenster; ∼**woman** *n.* Französin, *die*
frenzied /'frenzɪd/ *adj.* rasend
frenzy /'frenzɪ/ *n.* Wahnsinn, *der;* (fury) Raserei, *die*
frequency /'fri:kwənsɪ/ *n.* (a) Häufigkeit, *die* (b) (Phys.) Frequenz, *die*
frequent ① /'fri:kwənt/ *adj.* (a) häufig; **become less** ∼: seltener werden (b) (habitual) eifrig ② /fri:'kwent/ *v.t.* häufig besuchen ‹Café, Klub, usw.›
frequently /'fri:kwəntlɪ/ *adv.* häufig
fresco /'freskəʊ/ *n. pl.* ∼**es** *or* ∼**s** Fresko, *das*
fresh /freʃ/ *adj.* frisch; neu ‹Beweise, Anstrich, Mut, Energie›; ∼ **supplies** Nachschub, *der* (**of** an + *Dat.*); **make a** ∼ **start** noch einmal von vorne anfangen; (fig.) neu beginnen
freshen /'freʃn/ *v.i.* auffrischen
■ **freshen 'up** *v.i.* sich auffrischen
'freshly *adv.* frisch
'freshness *n.* Frische, *die*
fresh 'water *n.* Süßwasser, *das*
fret /fret/ *v.i.,* **-tt-** sich (*Dat.*) Sorgen machen
fretful /'fretfl/ *adj.* verdrießlich; quengelig (ugs.)
'fretsaw *n.* Laubsäge, *die*
Fri. *abbr.* = **Friday** Fr.
friar /'fraɪə(r)/ *n.* Ordensbruder, *der*
friction /'frɪkʃn/ *n.* Reibung, *die*
Friday /'fraɪdeɪ, 'fraɪdɪ/ *n.* Freitag, *der;* **on** ∼: [am] Freitag; **on a** ∼, **on** ∼**s** freitags; ∼ **13 August** Freitag, der 13. August; (at top of letter etc.) Freitag, den 13. August; **next/last** ∼: [am] nächsten/letzten Freitag; **Good** ∼: Karfreitag, *der*
fridge /frɪdʒ/ *n.* (Brit. coll.) Kühlschrank, *der*
fried ▶ FRY¹
friend /frend/ *n.* Freund, *der*/Freundin, *die;* **be** ∼**s with sb.** mit jmdm. befreundet sein; **make** ∼**s [with sb.]** [mit jmdm.] Freundschaft schließen

friendliness /'frendlɪnɪs/ *n.* Freundlichkeit, *die*
'friendly ① *adj.* freundlich (**to** zu); freundschaftlich ‹Rat, Beziehungen, Wettkampf› ② *n.* (Sport) Freundschaftsspiel, *das*
'friendship *n.* Freundschaft, *die*
fries /fraɪz/ *n. pl.* (Amer.) Pommes frites *Pl.*
frigate /'frɪgət/ *n.* (Naut.) Fregatte, *die*
fright /fraɪt/ *n.* Schreck, *der;* **take** ∼: erschrecken
frighten /'fraɪtn/ *v.t.* ‹Explosion, Schuss:› erschrecken; ‹Gedanke, Drohung:› Angst machen (+ *Dat.*); **be** ∼**ed at** *or* **by sth.** vor etw. (*Dat.*) erschrecken
'frightful *adj.,* **'frightfully** *adv.* furchtbar
frigid /'frɪdʒɪd/ *adj.* frostig; (sexually) frigid[e]
frill /frɪl/ *n.* (a) Rüsche, *die* (b) *in pl.* (embellishments) Beiwerk, *das*
'frilly *adj.* mit Rüschen besetzt; Rüschen‹kleid, -bluse›
fringe /frɪndʒ/ *n.* (a) Fransenkante, *die* (**on** an + *Dat.*) (b) (hair) [Pony]fransen *Pl.* (ugs.) (c) (edge) Rand, *der*
frisk /frɪsk/ ① *v.i.* ∼ **[about]** [herum]springen ② *v.t.* (coll.) filzen (ugs.)
'frisky *adj.* munter
fritter¹ /'frɪtə(r)/ *n.* apple *etc.* ∼**s** Apfelstücke *usw.* in Pfannkuchenteig
fritter² *v.t.* ∼ **away** vergeuden
frivolity /frɪ'vɒlɪtɪ/ *n.* Oberflächlichkeit, *die*
frivolous /'frɪvələs/ *adj.* (a) frivol (b) (trifling) belanglos
frizzy /'frɪzɪ/ *adj.* kraus
fro /frəʊ/ *adv.* ▶ TO 2
frock /frɒk/ *n.* Kleid, *das*
frog /frɒg/ *n.* Frosch, *der*
frog: ∼**man** /'frɒgmən/ *n., pl.* ∼**men** /'frɒgmən/ Froschmann, *der;* ∼**spawn** *n.* Froschlaich, *der*
frolic /'frɒlɪk/ *v.i.,* **-ck-:** ∼ **[about** *or* **around]** [herum]springen
from /frəm, *stressed* frɒm/ *prep.* von; (∼ within; expr. origin) aus; ∼ **Paris** aus Paris; ∼ **Paris to Munich** von Paris nach München; **be a mile** ∼ **sth.** eine Meile von etw. entfernt sein; **where do you come** ∼?, **where are you** ∼? woher kommen Sie?; **painted** ∼ **life** nach dem Leben gemalt; **weak** ∼ **hunger** schwach vor Hunger; ∼ **the year 1972** seit 1972; ∼ **[the age of] 18** ab 18 Jahre; ∼ **4 to 6 eggs** 4 bis 6 Eier
front /frʌnt/ ① *n.* (a) Vorderseite, *die;* (of house) Vorderfront, *die;* **in** *or* **at the** ∼ **[of sth.]** vorn [in etw. *position: Dat., movement: Akk.*]; **to the** ∼: nach vorn; **in** ∼: vorn[e]; **be in** ∼ **of sth./sb.** vor etw./jmdm. sein ┄┄⟩

(b) (Mil.) Front, *die*
(c) (at seaside) Strandpromenade, *die*
(d) (Metereol.) Front, *die*
(e) (bluff) Fassade, *die*
2 *adj.* vorder…; Vorder⟨*rad, -zimmer, -zahn*⟩; ∼ **garden** Vorgarten, *der;* ∼ **row** erste Reihe

frontal /'frʌntl/ *adj.* Frontal-

front 'door *n.* (of flat) Wohnungstür, *die;* (of house) Haustür, *die*

frontier /'frʌntɪə(r)/ *n.* Grenze, *die*

front: ∼ **'page** *n.* Titelseite, *die;* ∼**-wheel drive** 1 *n.* Vorderradantrieb, *der;* Frontantrieb, *der;* 2 *adj.* a ∼**-wheel drive vehicle** ein Fahrzeug mit Vorderradod. Frontantrieb

frost /frɒst/ 1 *n.* Frost, *der;* **ten degrees of** ∼ (Brit.) zehn Grad minus
2 *v.t.* ∼**ed glass** Mattglas, *das*

'frostbite *n.* Erfrierung, *die*

'frosting *n.* (esp. Amer.) Glasur, *die*

'frosty *adj.* frostig

froth /frɒθ/ 1 *n.* Schaum, *der*
2 *v.i.* schäumen

'frothy *adj.* schaumig

frown /fraʊn/ 1 *v.i.* die Stirn runzeln ([up]on über + *Akk.*)
2 *n.* Stirnrunzeln, *das*

froze ▸ FREEZE

frozen /'frəʊzn/ 1 ▸ FREEZE
2 *adj.* (a) zugefroren ⟨*Fluss, See*⟩; eingefroren ⟨*Wasserleitung*⟩; **I'm** ∼ (fig.) mir ist eiskalt
(b) (to preserve) tiefgekühlt; ∼ **food** Tiefkühlkost, *die*

frugal /'fru:gl/ *adj.* genügsam ⟨*Lebensweise, Mensch*⟩; frugal ⟨*Mahl*⟩

fruit /fru:t/ *n.* Frucht, *die; collect.* Obst, *das*

'fruit cake *n.* englischer Teekuchen

fruitful /'fru:tfl/ *adj.* fruchtbar

'fruit juice *n.* Obstsaft, *der*

'fruitless *adj.* nutzlos ⟨*Versuch, Gespräch*⟩; fruchtlos ⟨*Verhandlung, Suche*⟩

fruit: ∼ **machine** *n.* (Brit.) Spielautomat, *der;* ∼ **'salad** *n.* Obstsalat, *der*

'fruity *adj.* fruchtig ⟨*Geschmack, Wein*⟩

frustrate /frʌ'streɪt/ *v.t.* vereiteln ⟨*Plan, Versuch*⟩; zunichte machen ⟨*Hoffnung, Bemühungen*⟩

'frustrated *adj.* frustriert

frustration /frʌ'streɪʃn/ *n.* Frustration, *die*

fry[1] /fraɪ/ *v.t. & i.,* fried /fraɪd/ braten; **fried egg** Spiegelei, *das*

fry[2] *n.* (fishes) Brut, *die;* **small** ∼ (fig.) unbedeutende Leute

'frying pan *n.* Bratpfanne, *die*

ft. *abbr.* = **feet, foot** ft.

fuchsia /'fju:ʃə/ *n.* (Bot.) Fuchsie, *die*

fuck /fʌk/ (coarse) 1 *v.t. & i.* ficken (vulg.); [oh,] ∼!, [oh,] ∼ **it!** [au,] Scheiße! (derb.)
2 *n.* Fick, *der* (vulg.)

fuddy-duddy /'fʌdɪdʌdɪ/ (coll.) 1 *adj.* verkalkt (ugs.)
2 *n.* Fossil, *das* (fig.)

fudge /fʌdʒ/ *n.* Karamellbonbon, *der od. das*

fuel /'fju:əl/ *n.* Brennstoff, *der;* (for vehicle) Kraftstoff, *der;* (for ship, aircraft) Treibstoff, *der*

fuel: ∼ **consumption** *n.* (of vehicle) Kraftstoffverbrauch, *der;* ∼ **gauge** *n.* Kraftstoffanzeiger *der;* ∼ **injection** *n.* Benzineinspritzung, *die*

fugitive /'fju:dʒɪtɪv/ *n.* Flüchtige, *der/die*

fugue /fju:g/ *n.* (Mus.) Fuge, *die*

fulfil (Amer.: **fulfill**) /fʊl'fɪl/ *v.t.,* -ll- erfüllen; halten ⟨*Versprechen;*⟩ ∼ **oneself** sich selbst verwirklichen

ful'filment (Amer.: **ful'fillment**) *n.* Erfüllung, *die*

full /fʊl/ 1 *adj.* (a) voll; satt ⟨*Person*⟩; ∼ **of** voller; **be** ∼ **up** voll [besetzt] sein; ⟨*Behälter:*⟩ randvoll sein; ⟨*Flug:*⟩ völlig ausgebucht sein; **I'm** ∼ **[up]** (coll.) ich bin voll [bis obenhin] (ugs.); **be** ∼ **of oneself** sehr von sich eingenommen sein
(b) ausführlich ⟨*Bericht, Beschreibung*⟩; erfüllt ⟨*Leben*⟩; ganz ⟨*Stunde, Jahr, Monat, Seite*⟩; voll ⟨*Name, Bezahlung, Verständnis*⟩; ∼ **details** alle Einzelheiten; **at** ∼ **speed** mit Höchstgeschwindigkeit
(c) voll ⟨*Gesicht*⟩; füllig ⟨*Figur*⟩; weit ⟨*Rock*⟩
2 *n.* **in** ∼: vollständig
3 *adv.* (exactly) genau

full: ∼**-blown** *adj.* ausgewachsen ⟨*Skandal*⟩; ausgereift ⟨*Theorie, Plan, Gedanke*⟩; ∼**-blown AIDS** Vollbild-Aids, *das;* ∼**-bodied** *adj.* vollmundig, (fachspr.) körperreich ⟨*Wein*⟩; ∼**-cream** *adj.* ∼**-cream milk/cheese** Vollmilch, *die/*Vollfettkäse, *der;* ∼**-length** *adj.* lang ⟨*Kleid*⟩; ∼ **'moon** *n.* Vollmond, *der;* ∼**-scale** *adj.* (a) in Originalgröße;
(b) groß angelegt ⟨*Untersuchung, Suchaktion*⟩; ∼ **'stop** *n.* Punkt, *der;* ∼**-time** *adj.* ganztägig; Ganztags⟨*arbeit*⟩; ∼**-'timer** *n.* Ganztagsbeschäftigte, *der/die*

fully /'fʊlɪ/ *adv.* voll [und ganz]; reich ⟨*belohnt*⟩; ausführlich ⟨*erklären*⟩

fulsome /'fʊlsəm/ *adj.* übertrieben

fumble /'fʌmbl/ *v.i.* ∼ **at** *or* **with** [herum]fingern an (+ *Dat.*); ∼ **in one's pockets for sth.** in seinen Taschen nach etw. kramen (ugs.)

fume /fju:m/ 1 *n. in pl.* ∼**s** Dämpfe *Pl.* (from car exhaust) Abgase *usw.*
2 *v.i.* vor Wut schäumen

fumigate /'fju:mɪgeɪt/ *v.t.* ausräuchern

fun /fʌn/ *n.* Spaß, *der;* **have** ∼**!** viel Spaß!; **make** ∼ **of sb.** sich über jmdn. lustig machen; **for** ∼, **for the** ∼ **of it** zum Spaß

function /'fʌŋkʃn/ 1 *n.* Aufgabe, *die;* Funktion, *die;* (formal event) Veranstaltung, *die*

2 *v.i.* ⟨*Maschine, System:*⟩ funktionieren; ∼ **as** fungieren als; ⟨serve as⟩ dienen als

functional /ˈfʌŋkʃənl/ *adj.* **(a)** (useful) funktionell
(b) (working) funktionsfähig

'**function key** *n.* (Comp.) Funktionstaste, *die*

fund /fʌnd/ **1** *n.* **(a)** (money) Fonds, *der*
(b) (fig.: stock) Fundus, *der* (**of** von, an + *Dat.*)
2 *v.t.* finanzieren

fundamental /fʌndəˈmentl/ *adj.* grundlegend (**to** für); elementar ⟨*Bedürfnisse*⟩

fundamentalism /fʌndəˈmentəlɪzm/ *n.* Fundamentalismus, *der*

fundamentalist /fʌndəˈmentəlɪst/ *n.* Fundamentalist, *der*/Fundamentalistin, *die*

funda'mentally *adv.* grundlegend; von Grund auf ⟨*verschieden, ehrlich*⟩

fund: ∼-**raiser** /ˈfʌndreɪzə(r)/ *n.* **(a)** (person) Geldbeschaffer, *der*/-beschafferin, *die;* **(b)** (event) Benefizveranstaltung, *die;* ∼-**raising** /ˈfʌndreɪzɪŋ/ *n.* Geldbeschaffung, *die; attrib.* zur Geldbeschaffung *nachgestellt*

funeral /ˈfjuːnərl/ *n.* Beerdigung, *die.* ∼ **director** Bestattungsunternehmer, *der;* ∼ **service** Trauerfeier, *die*

'**funfair** *n.* (Brit.) Jahrmarkt, *der*

fungus /ˈfʌŋgəs/ *n., pl.* **fungi** /ˈfʌŋgaɪ, ˈfʌndʒaɪ/ *or* ∼**es** Pilz, *der*

funicular /fjuːˈnɪkjʊlə(r)/ *adj. & n.* ∼ [**railway**] [Stand]seilbahn, *die*

'**fun-loving** *adj.* lebenslustig

funnel /ˈfʌnl/ *n.* Trichter, *der;* (of ship etc.) Schornstein, *der*

funnily /ˈfʌnɪlɪ/ *adv.* komisch; ∼ **enough** komischerweise

funny /ˈfʌnɪ/ *adj.* **(a)** komisch; lustig; witzig ⟨*Mensch, Einfall*⟩
(b) (strange) komisch

'**funny bone** *n.* Musikantenknochen, *der*

fur /fɜː(r)/ *n.* **(a)** Fell, *das;* (garment) Pelz, *der;* ∼ **coat** Pelzmantel, *der*
(b) (in kettle) Kesselstein, *der*

furious /ˈfjʊərɪəs/ *adj.* wütend; heftig ⟨*Streit*⟩; wild ⟨*Tanz, Tempo, Kampf*⟩; **be** ∼ **with sb.** wütend auf jmdn. sein

'**furiously** *adv.* wütend; wild ⟨*kämpfen*⟩; wie wild (ugs.) ⟨*arbeiten*⟩

furl /fɜːl/ *v.t.* einrollen ⟨*Segel, Flagge*⟩

furnace /ˈfɜːnɪs/ *n.* Ofen, *der*

furnish /ˈfɜːnɪʃ/ *v.t.* **(a)** möblieren
(b) (supply) liefern; ∼ **sb. with sth.** jmdm. etw. liefern

'**furnishings** *n. pl.* Einrichtungsgegenstände *Pl.*

furniture /ˈfɜːnɪtʃə(r)/ *n.* Möbel *Pl.;* **piece of** ∼: Möbel[stück], *das*

furniture: ∼ **polish** *n.* Möbelpolitur, *die;*

∼ **van** *n.* Möbelwagen, *der*

furrow /ˈfʌrəʊ/ *n.* Furche, *die*

furry /ˈfɜːrɪ/ *adj.* haarig; ∼ **animal** (toy) Plüschtier, *das*

further /ˈfɜːðə(r)/ **1** *adj.* **(a)** (in space) weiter entfernt
(b) (additional) weiter…
2 *adv.* weiter
3 *v.t.* fördern

further edu'cation *n.* Weiterbildung, *die;* (for adults also) Erwachsenenbildung, *die*

further'more *adv.* außerdem

'**furthermost** *adj.* äußerst…

furthest /ˈfɜːðɪst/ **1** *adj.* am weitesten entfernt
2 *adv.* am weitesten ⟨*springen, laufen*⟩; am weitesten entfernt ⟨*sein, wohnen*⟩

furtive /ˈfɜːtɪv/ *adj.*, **furtively** *adv.* verstohlen

fury /ˈfjʊərɪ/ *n.* Wut, *die;* (of sea, battle) Wüten, *das*

fuse[1] /fjuːz/ **1** *v.t.* (blend) verschmelzen (**into** zu)
2 *v.i.* ∼ **together** miteinander verschmelzen

fuse[2] *n.* **[time]** ∼: [Zeit]zünder, *der;* (cord) Zündschnur, *die*

fuse[3] (Electr.) **1** *n.* Sicherung, *die*
2 *v.i.* **the lights have** ∼**d** die Sicherung ist durchgebrannt

'**fuse box** *n.* Sicherungskasten, *der*

fuselage /ˈfjuːzəlɑːʒ/ *n.* [Flugzeug]rumpf, *der*

fusion /ˈfjuːʒn/ *n.* **(a)** Verschmelzung, *die*
(b) (Phys.) Fusion, *die*

fuss /fʌs/ **1** *n.* Theater, *das* (ugs.); **make a** ∼ **[about sth.]** einen Wirbel [um etw.] machen
2 *v.i.* Wirbel machen; (get agitated) sich [unnötig] aufregen

'**fussy** *adj.* (fastidious) eigen; penibel; **I'm not** ∼ (I don't mind) ich bin nicht wählerisch

futile /ˈfjuːtaɪl/ *adj.* vergeblich ⟨*Versuch, Bemühung*⟩; zum Scheitern verurteilt ⟨*Plan*⟩

futility /fjuːˈtɪlɪtɪ/ *n.* (of attempt, effort) Vergeblichkeit, *die;* (of plan) Zwecklosigkeit, *die*

futon /ˈfuːtɒn/ *n.* Futon, *der*

future /ˈfjuːtʃə(r)/ **1** *adj.* [zu]künftig; **at some** ∼ **date** zu einem späteren Zeitpunkt
2 *n.* **(a)** Zukunft, *die;* **in** ∼: in Zukunft; künftig
(b) (Ling.) Futur, *das;* Zukunft, *die*
(c) *in pl.* (Commerc.) Terminware, *die;* (contracts) Lieferungsverträge *usw.*

futuristic /fjuːtʃəˈrɪstɪk/ *adj.* futuristisch

fuze /fjuːz/ ▶ **FUSE**[2]

fuzzy /ˈfʌzɪ/ *adj.* **(a)** (frizzy) kraus
(b) (blurred) verschwommen

Gg

G, g /dʒiː/ n. G, g, das

gab /gæb/ n. (coll.) **have the gift of the**
∼: reden können

gabble /'gæbl/ v.i. brabbeln (ugs.)

gable /'geɪbl/ n. Giebel, der

gad /gæd/ v.i., **-dd-** (coll.) ∼ **about**
herumziehen (ugs.)

gadget /'gædʒɪt/ n. Gerät, das

gadgetry /'gædʒɪtrɪ/ n. [hoch technisierte]
Ausstattung

Gaelic /'geɪlɪk, 'gælɪk/ 1 adj. gälisch
2 n. Gälisch, das

gaffe /gæf/ n. Fauxpas, der

'gaffer tape n., no pl. Lassoband, das

gag /gæg/ 1 n. (a) Knebel, der
(b) (joke) Gag, der
2 v.t., **-gg-** knebeln

gaiety /'geɪətɪ/ n. Fröhlichkeit, die

gaily /'geɪlɪ/ adv. fröhlich; in leuchtenden
Farben ⟨bemalt, geschmückt⟩

gain /geɪn/ 1 n. (a) Gewinn, der
(b) (increase) Zunahme, die (in an + Dat.)
2 v.t. (a) gewinnen; finden ⟨Zugang,
Zutritt⟩; erwerben ⟨Wissen, Ruf⟩; erlangen
⟨Freiheit⟩; erzielen ⟨Vorteil, Punkte⟩;
verdienen ⟨Lebensunterhalt, Geldsumme⟩;
∼ **weight/five pounds [in weight]** zunehmen/
fünf Pfund zunehmen; ∼ **speed** schneller
werden
(b) ⟨Uhr:⟩ vorgehen um
3 v.i. (a) ∼ **by sth.** von etw. profitieren
(b) ⟨Uhr:⟩ vorgehen

gainful /'geɪnfl/ adj. ∼ **employment**
Erwerbstätigkeit, die

gainfully /'geɪnfəlɪ/ adv. ∼ **employed**
erwerbstätig

gait /geɪt/ n. Gang, der

gala /'gɑːlə, 'geɪlə/ n. Festveranstaltung,
die; attrib. Gala⟨abend, -vorstellung⟩;
swimming ∼: Schwimmfest, das

galaxy /'gæləksɪ/ n. Galaxie, die

gale /geɪl/ n. Sturm, der

gall /gɔːl/ n. Unverschämtheit, die

gallant /'gælənt/ adj. (brave) tapfer;
(chivalrous) ritterlich

gallantry /'gæləntrɪ/ n. (bravery)
Tapferkeit, die

'gall bladder n. Gallenblase, die

gallery /'gælərɪ/ n. (a) Galerie, die
(b) (Theatre) dritter Rang

galley /'gælɪ/ n. (a) (ship's kitchen) Kombüse,
die
(b) (Hist.) Galeere, die

gallivant /'gælɪvænt/ v.i. (coll.)
herumziehen (ugs.)

gallon /'gælən/ n. Gallone, die

gallop /'gæləp/ 1 n. Galopp, der
2 v.i. ⟨Pferd, Reiter:⟩ galoppieren

gallows /'gæləʊz/ n. sing. Galgen, der

Gallup poll ® /'gæləp pəʊl/ n.
Meinungsumfrage, die

galore /gə'lɔː(r)/ adv. im Überfluss; in
Hülle und Fülle

galvanize /'gælvənaɪz/ v.t. wachrütteln;
∼ **sb. into action** jmdn. veranlassen, sofort
aktiv zu werden

gambit /'gæmbɪt/ n. Gambit, das

gamble /'gæmbl/ v.i. (a) [um Geld] spielen;
∼ **at cards/on horses** um Geld Karten
spielen/auf Pferde wetten
(b) (fig.) spekulieren; ∼ **on sth.** sich auf etw.
(Akk.) verlassen

gambler /'gæmblə(r)/ n. Glücksspieler,
der

gambling /'gæmblɪŋ/ n. Spiel[en], das;
Glücksspiel, das; (on horses, dogs) Wetten, das

game¹ /geɪm/ n. (a) Spiel, das; (of [table]
tennis, chess, cards, cricket) Partie, die
(b) (fig.: scheme) Vorhaben, das
(c) in pl. (athletic contests) Spiele Pl.; (in school)
(sports) Sport, der; (athletics) Leichtathletik,
die
(d) (Hunting, Cookery) Wild, das

game² adj. mutig; **be** ∼ **to do sth.** bereit
sein, etw. zu tun

'gamekeeper n. Wildheger, der

'games console n. Spielkonsole, die

'game show n. Gameshow, die;
Spielshow, die

gamma rays /'gæmə/ n. pl. (Phys.)
Gammastrahlen Pl.

gammon /'gæmən/ n. Räucherschinken,
der

gamut /'gæmət/ n. Skala, die

gander /'gændə(r)/ n. Gänserich, der

gang /gæŋ/ 1 n. Bande, die; (of workmen,
prisoners) Trupp, der
2 v.i. ∼ **up against** or **on** (coll.) sich
verbünden gegen

gangling /'gæŋglɪŋ/ schlaksig (ugs.)

gangster /'gæŋstə(r)/ n. Gangster, der

gang warfare n. Bandenkrieg, der

'gangway n. Gangway, die; (Brit.: between
seats) Gang, der

gaol /dʒeɪl/ n. ▶ JAIL

gap /gæp/ n. (a) Lücke, die
(b) (in time) Pause, die

(c) (divergence) Kluft, *die*

gape /geɪp/ *v.i.* **(a)** den Mund aufsperren; ⟨*Loch, Abgrund, Wunde:*⟩ klaffen
(b) (stare) Mund und Nase aufsperren (ugs.); ∼ **at sb./sth.** jmdn./etw. mit offenem Mund anstarren

'gap year *n.* (Brit.) Zwischenjahr, *das*

garage /'gærɪdʒ/ *n.* Garage, *die;* (selling petrol) Tankstelle, *die;* (for repairing cars) [Kfz-]Werkstatt, *die*

garb /gɑːb/ *n.* Tracht, *die*

garbage /'gɑːbɪdʒ/ *n.* **(a)** Abfall, *der;* Müll, *der*
(b) (coll.: nonsense) Quatsch, *der* (salopp)

garbage: ∼ **can** *n.* (Amer.) Mülltonne, *die;* ∼ **dis'posal unit,** ∼ **disposer** *ns.* Abfallvernichter, *der;* Müllwolf, *der*

garble /'gɑːbl/ *v.t.* verstümmeln

garden /'gɑːdn/ *n.* Garten, *der*

garden: ∼ **centre** *n.* Gartencenter, *das;* ∼ **'city** *n.* Gartenstadt, *die*

gardener /'gɑːdnə(r)/ *n.* Gärtner, *der*/Gärtnerin, *die*

gardening /'gɑːdnɪŋ/ *n.* Gartenarbeit, *die*

garden: ∼ **'shed** *n.* Geräteschuppen, *der* ∼ **'waste** *n.* Gartenabfälle *Pl.;* Gartenabfall, *der*

gargle /'gɑːgl/ *v.i.* gurgeln

gargoyle /'gɑːgɔɪl/ *n.* (Archit.) Wasserspeier, *der*

garish /'geərɪʃ/ *adj.* grell ⟨*Farbe, Licht*⟩; knallbunt ⟨*Kleidung*⟩

garland /'gɑːlənd/ *n.* Girlande, *die*

garlic /'gɑːlɪk/ *n.* Knoblauch, *der*

garment /'gɑːmənt/ *n.* Kleidungsstück, *das;* ∼**s** *pl.* (clothes) Kleidung, *die;* Kleider *Pl.*

garnish /'gɑːnɪʃ/ 1 *v.t.* garnieren
2 *n.* Garnierung, *die*

garret /'gærət/ *n.* Dachkammer, *die*

garrison /'gærɪsn/ *n.* Garnison, *die*

garter /'gɑːtə(r)/ *n.* Strumpfband, *das*

gas /gæs/ 1 *n.* **(a)** *pl.* ∼**es** /'gæsɪz/ Gas, *das*
(b) (Amer. coll.: petrol) Benzin, *das*
2 *v.t.,* **-ss-** mit Gas vergiften

gas: ∼ **chamber** *n.* Gaskammer, *die;* ∼ **'cooker** *n.* (Brit.) Gasherd, *der;* ∼ **cylinder** *n.* Gasflasche, *die;* ∼ **'fire** *n.* Gasofen, *der*

gash /gæʃ/ 1 *n.* Schnittwunde, *die*
2 *v.t.* aufritzen ⟨*Haut*⟩; ∼ **one's finger** sich (*Dat. od. Akk.*) in den Finger schneiden

gas: ∼ **heater** *n.* Gasofen, *der;* ∼ **mask** *n.* Gasmaske, *die;* ∼ **meter** *n.* Gaszähler, *der*

gasoline (gasolene) /'gæsəliːn/ *n.* (Amer.) Benzin, *das*

gasometer /gæ'sɒmɪtə(r)/ *n.* Gasometer, *der*

gasp /gɑːsp/ 1 *v.i.* nach Luft schnappen (**with** vor); **he was** ∼**ing for air** er rang nach Luft

2 *v.t.* ∼ **out** hervorstoßen
3 *n.* Keuchen, *das*

'gas station *n.* (Amer.) Tankstelle, *die*

gastric: ∼ **'flu** (coll.), ∼ **influ'enza** *ns.* Darmgrippe, *die;* ∼ **'ulcer** *n.* Magengeschwür, *das*

gastro-enteritis /gæstrəʊentə'raɪtɪs/ *n.* Gastroenteritis, *die* (fachspr.); Magen-Darm-Katarrh, *der*

gastronomy /gæ'strɒnəmɪ/ *n.* Gastronomie, *die*

'gasworks *n. sing.* Gaswerk, *das*

gate /geɪt/ *n.* Tor, *das;* (barrier) Sperre, *die;* (to field etc.) Gatter, *das;* (of level crossing) [Bahn]schranke, *die;* (in airport) Flugsteig, *der*

gateau /'gætəʊ/ *n., pl.* ∼**s** or ∼**x** /'gætəʊz/ Torte, *die*

gate: ∼**crasher** /'geɪtkræʃə(r)/ *n.* ungeladener Gast; ∼**way** *n.* Tor, *das*

gather /'gæðə(r)/ 1 *v.t.* **(a)** sammeln; zusammentragen ⟨*Informationen*⟩; pflücken ⟨*Obst, Blumen*⟩
(b) (infer, deduce) schließen (**from** aus)
(c) ∼ **speed/force** schneller/stärker werden
2 *v.i.* sich versammeln; ⟨*Wolken:*⟩ sich zusammenziehen

'gathering *n.* Versammlung, *die*

GATT /gæt/ *abbr.* = **General Agreement on Tariffs and Trade** GATT, *das*

gauche /ɡəʊʃ/ *adj.* linkisch

gaudy /'ɡɔːdɪ/ *adj.* protzig; grell ⟨*Farben*⟩

gauge /geɪdʒ/ *n.* 1 **(a)** (measure) Maß, *das*
(b) (instrument) Messgerät, *das*
2 *v.t.* messen; (fig.) beurteilen

gaunt /ɡɔːnt/ *adj.* hager

gauntlet /'ɡɔːntlɪt/ *n.* Stulpenhandschuh, *der*

gauze /ɡɔːz/ *n.* Gaze, *die*

gave ▸ GIVE 1, 2

gay /geɪ/ 1 *adj.* **(a)** fröhlich; (brightly coloured) farbenfroh
(b) (coll.: homosexual) schwul (ugs.); Schwulen⟨*lokal*⟩
2 *n.* (coll.) Schwule, *der* (ugs.)

gay 'rights *n. pl.* Schwulenrechte *Pl.*

gaze /geɪz/ *v.i.* blicken; (fixedly) starren; ∼ **at sb./sth.** jmdn./etw. anstarren

gazebo /ɡə'ziːbəʊ/ *n.* (building) Aussichtspavillon, *der;* (tent-like) Zeltling, *der*

GB *abbr.* = **Great Britain** GB

GCSE *abbr.* (Brit.) = **General Certificate of Secondary Education**

gear /ɡɪə(r)/ 1 *n.* **(a)** (Motor Veh.) Gang, *der;* **top/bottom** ∼ (Brit.) der höchste/erste Gang; **change** *or* **shift** ∼: schalten; **put the car into** ∼: einen Gang einlegen; **out of** ∼: im Leerlauf
(b) (coll.: clothes) Aufmachung, *die*
(c) (equipment) Gerät, *das;* Ausrüstung, *die*
2 *v.t.* ausrichten (**to** auf + *Akk.*)

gear: ∼**box** n. Getriebekasten, der; ∼ **lever,** (Amer.) ∼ **shift** ns. Schalthebel, der

geese pl. of GOOSE

geezer /'giːzə(r)/ (coll.: old man) Opa, der (ugs.)

gel /dʒel/ n. Gel, das

gelatin /'dʒelətɪn/, (Brit.) **gelatine** /'dʒelətiːn/ n. Gelatine, die

gelignite /'dʒelɪɡnaɪt/ n. Gelatinedynamit, das

gem /dʒem/ n. Edelstein, der

Gemini /'dʒemɪnaɪ, 'dʒemɪnɪ/ n. (Astrol., Astron.) Zwillinge Pl.

'**gemstone** n. Edelstein, der

gender /'dʒendə(r)/ n. (Ling.) [grammatisches] Geschlecht

gene /dʒiːn/ n. (Biol.) Gen, das

general /'dʒenrl/ [1] adj. allgemein; weit verbreitet ⟨Ansicht⟩; (true of [nearly] all cases) allgemein gültig; ungefähr ⟨Vorstellung, Beschreibung usw.⟩; **the** ∼ **public** weite Kreise der Bevölkerung; **in** ∼ **use** allgemein verbreitet; **as a** ∼ **rule, in** ∼: im Allgemeinen
[2] n. (Mil.) General, der

general: ∼ **e'lection** ▶ ELECTION; ∼ '**hospital** n. Allgemeinkrankenhaus, das

generalization /dʒenrəlaɪ'zeɪʃn/ n. Verallgemeinerung, die

generalize /'dʒenrəlaɪz/ [1] v.t. verallgemeinern
[2] v.i. ∼ **about sth.** etw. verallgemeinern

general 'knowledge n. Allgemeinwissen, das

generally /'dʒenrəlɪ/ adv. (a) allgemein; ∼ **available** überall erhältlich; ∼ **speaking** im Allgemeinen
(b) (usually) im Allgemeinen

general: ∼ '**manager** n. [leitender] Direktor/[leitende] Direktorin; ∼ '**meeting** n. Generalversammlung, die; Hauptversammlung, die; ∼ **National Vo'cational Qualification** n. (Brit.) staatliches Berufsausbildungsprogramm; ∼ **prac'titioner** n. (Med.) Arzt/Ärztin für Allgemeinmedizin

generate /'dʒenəreɪt/ v.t. erzeugen (**from** aus); (result in) führen zu

generation /dʒenə'reɪʃn/ n.
(a) Generation, die
(b) (production) Erzeugung, die

generator /'dʒenəreɪtə(r)/ n. Generator, der

generosity /dʒenə'rɒsɪtɪ/ n. Großzügigkeit, die

generous /'dʒenərəs/ adj. großzügig; reichlich ⟨Vorrat, Portion⟩

'**generously** adv. großzügig

genetic /dʒɪ'netɪk/ adj. genetisch

genetically /dʒɪ'netɪkəlɪ/ adv. genetisch; ∼ **modified** gentechnisch verändert; ∼ **engineered** gentechnisch verändert ⟨Organismen, Pflanzen, Tiere, Nahrungsmittel⟩; genetisch hergestellt ⟨Medikament, Enzym⟩

genetic engi'neering n. Gentechnologie, die

genetics /dʒɪ'netɪks/ n. Genetik, die

genetic 'test n. Gentest, der

Geneva /dʒɪ'niːvə/ [1] pr. n. Genf (das) [2] attrib. adj. Genfer

genial /'dʒiːnɪəl/ adj. freundlich

genitals /'dʒenɪtlz/ n. pl. Geschlechtsorgane Pl.

genitive /'dʒenɪtɪv/ adj. & n. ∼ **[case]** Genitiv, der

genius /'dʒiːnɪəs/ n. **(a)** (person) Genie, das **(b)** (ability) Talent, das

genome /'dʒiːnəʊm/ n. (Biol.) Genom, das

genre /'ʒɑ̃rə/ n. Genre, das

gent /dʒent/ n. **(a)** (coll./joc.) Gent, der (iron.) **(b)** the G∼s (Brit. coll.) die Herrentoilette

genteel /dʒen'tiːl/ adj. vornehm

gentle /'dʒentl/ adj., ∼**r** /'dʒentlə(r)/, ∼**st** /'dʒentlɪst/ sanft; liebenswürdig ⟨Person, Verhalten⟩; leicht, schwach ⟨Brise⟩; leise ⟨Geräusch⟩; gemächlich ⟨Spaziergang, Tempo⟩; mäßig ⟨Hitze⟩

gentleman /'dʒentlmən/ n., pl. **gentlemen** /'dʒentlmən/ Herr, der; (well-mannered) Gentleman, der; **Ladies and Gentlemen!** meine Damen und Herren!; '**Gentlemen'** (sign) „Herren"

'**gentleness** n. Sanftheit, die; (of nature) Sanftmütigkeit, die

gently /'dʒentlɪ/ adv. (tenderly) zart; zärtlich; (mildly) sanft; (carefully) behutsam; (quietly, softly) leise

genuine /'dʒenjʊɪn/ adj. **(a)** (real) echt **(b)** (true) aufrichtig; wahr ⟨Grund, Not⟩

'**genuinely** adv. wirklich

genus /'dʒiːnəs, 'dʒenəs/ n., pl. **genera** /'dʒenərə/ (Biol.) Gattung, die

geographical /dʒiːə'ɡræfɪkl/ adj. geographisch

geography /dʒɪ'ɒɡrəfɪ/ n. Geographie, die; Erdkunde, die (Schulw.)

geological /dʒiːə'lɒdʒɪkl/ adj. geologisch

geologist /dʒɪ'ɒlədʒɪst/ n. Geologe, der/Geologin, die

geology /dʒɪ'ɒlədʒɪ/ n. Geologie, die

geometric /dʒiːə'metrɪk/, **geometrical** /dʒiːə'metrɪkl/ adj. geometrisch

geometry /dʒɪ'ɒmɪtrɪ/ n. Geometrie, die

geranium /dʒə'reɪnɪəm/ n. Geranie, die; Pelargonie, die

geriatric /dʒerɪ'ætrɪk/ adj. geriatrisch

germ /dʒɜːm/ n. Keim, der

German /'dʒɜːmən/ **1** *adj.* deutsch; **he/ she is** ~: er ist Deutscher/sie ist Deutsche **2** *n.* **(a)** (person) Deutsche, *der/die* **(b)** (language) Deutsch, *das; see also* ENGLISH 2A

German Democratic Re'public *pr. n.* (Hist.) Deutsche Demokratische Republik

Germanic /dʒɜːˈmænɪk/ *adj.* germanisch **German 'measles** *n.* Röteln *Pl.*

Germany /'dʒɜːmənɪ/ *pr. n.* Deutschland (*das*); **Federal Republic of** ~: Bundesrepublik Deutschland, *die*

germinate /'dʒɜːmɪneɪt/ *v.i.* keimen

germ 'warfare *n.* Bakterienkrieg, *der*

gesticulate /dʒeˈstɪkjʊleɪt/ *v.i.* gestikulieren

gesticulation /dʒestɪkjʊˈleɪʃn/ *n.* Gesten *Pl.*

gesture /'dʒestʃə(r)/ *n.* Geste, *die*

get /get/ **1** *v.t.,* **-tt-,** got /gɒt/, **got** *or* (Amer.) **gotten** /'gɒtn/ **(a)** (obtain, receive) bekommen; kriegen (ugs.); sich (*Dat.*) besorgen ⟨*Visum, Genehmigung*⟩; sich (*Dat.*) beschaffen ⟨*Geld*⟩; (find) finden ⟨*Zeit*⟩; (fetch) holen; (buy) kaufen; **where did you** ~ **that?** wo hast du das her?; ~ **sb. a job/taxi,** ~ **a job/taxi for sb.** jmdm. einen Job verschaffen/ein Taxi besorgen; ~ **oneself sth.** sich (*Dat.*) etw. zulegen

(b) ~ **the bus** *etc.* (be in time for, catch) den Bus *usw.* erreichen *od.* (ugs.) kriegen; (travel by) den Bus *usw.* nehmen

(c) (prepare) machen (ugs.), zubereiten ⟨*Essen*⟩

(d) (win) bekommen; finden ⟨*Anerkennung*⟩; erzielen ⟨*Tor, Punkt, Treffer*⟩; gewinnen ⟨*Spiel, Preis, Belohnung*⟩; ~ **permission** die Erlaubnis erhalten

(e) finden ⟨*Schlaf, Ruhe*⟩; bekommen ⟨*Einfall, Vorstellung, Gefühl, Kopfschmerzen, Grippe*⟩; gewinnen ⟨*Eindruck*⟩

(f) have got (coll.: have) haben; **have got a cold** eine Erkältung haben; **have got to do sth.** etw. tun müssen

(g) (succeed in placing, bringing, etc.) bringen; kriegen (ugs.); ~ **a message to sb.** jmdm. eine Nachricht zukommen lassen; ~ **things going** *or* **started** die Dinge in Gang bringen

(h) ~ **everything packed/prepared** alles [ein]packen/vorbereiten; ~ **sth. ready/done** etw. fertig machen; ~ **one's feet wet** nasse Füße kriegen; ~ **one's hands dirty** sich (*Dat.*) die Hände schmutzig machen; ~ **one's hair cut** sich *Dat.* die Haare schneiden lassen; ~ **sb. to do sth.** (induce) jmdn. dazu bringen, etw. zu tun

(i) ~ **sb. [on the telephone]** jmdn. [telefonisch] erreichen

(j) (coll.) (understand) kapieren (ugs.); (hear) mitkriegen (ugs.)

2 *v.i.,* **-tt-,** got, **got** *or* (Amer.) **gotten (a)** (succeed in coming or going) kommen; ~ **to London before dark** London vor Einbruch

der Dunkelheit erreichen

(b) (come to be) ~ **working** sich an die Arbeit machen; ~ **going** *or* **started** (leave) losgehen; (become lively or operative) in Schwung kommen; ~ **going on** *or* **with sth.** mit etw. anfangen

(c) ~ **to know sb.** jmdn. kennen lernen

(d) (become) werden; ~ **ready/washed** sich fertig machen/waschen; ~ **frightened/ hungry** Angst/Hunger kriegen

■ **get a'bout** *v.i.* **(a)** (travel) herumkommen **(b)** ⟨*Gerücht:*⟩ sich verbreiten

■ **'get at** *v.t.* **(a)** herankommen an (+ *Akk.*) **(b)** (find out) [he]rausfinden ⟨*Wahrheit usw.*⟩; **what are you** ~**ting at?** worauf wollen Sie hinaus?

(c) (coll.: attack, taunt) anmachen (salopp)

■ **get a'way** *v.i.* **(a)** (leave) wegkommen **(b)** (escape) entkommen

■ **get 'back** **1** *v.i.* zurückkommen; ~ **back home** nach Hause kommen

2 *v.t.* (recover) zurückbekommen; ~ **one's own back** (coll.) sich rächen

■ **get 'by** *v.i.* **(a)** vorbeikommen **(b)** (coll.: manage) über die Runden kommen (ugs.)

■ **get 'down** **1** *v.i.* hinunter-/ heruntersteigen; ~ **down to sth.** (start) sich an etw. (*Akk.*) machen

2 *v.t.* **(a)** ~ **sb./sth. down** jmdn./etw. hinunter-/herunterbringen

(b) (coll.: depress) fertig machen (ugs.)

■ **get 'in** **1** *v.i.* (into bus etc.) einsteigen; (arrive) ankommen

2 *v.t.* (fetch) reinholen

■ **get 'off** **1** *v.i.* **(a)** (alight) aussteigen; (dismount) absteigen

(b) (leave) [weg]gehen

(c) (escape punishment) davonkommen

2 *v.t.* **(a)** (remove) ausziehen ⟨*Kleidung usw.*⟩; entfernen ⟨*Fleck usw.*⟩; abbekommen ⟨*Deckel usw.*⟩

(b) (alight from) aussteigen aus; absteigen von ⟨*Fahrrad*⟩

(c) ~ **off the subject** vom Thema abkommen

■ **get 'on** *v.i.* **(a)** (mount) aufsteigen; (enter vehicle) einsteigen

(b) (make progress) vorankommen; **he's** ~**ting on well** es geht ihm gut

(c) (manage) zurechtkommen

■ **get 'on with** *v.t.* **(a)** weitermachen mit **(b)** ~ **on [well] with sb.** mit jmdm. [gut] auskommen

■ **get 'out** **1** *v.i.* **(a)** rausgehen/ rausfahren (**of** aus)

(b) (alight) aussteigen

(c) (escape) ausbrechen (**of** aus); (fig.) herauskommen; ~ **out of** (avoid) herumkommen um (ugs.)

2 *v.t.* **(a)** (cause to leave) rausbringen

(b) (withdraw) abheben ⟨*Geld*⟩ (**of** von)

■ **get 'over** *v.t.* **(a)** (cross) gehen über (+ *Akk.*); (climb) klettern über (+ *Akk.*)

(b) (recover from) überwinden; hinwegkommen über (+ *Akk.*) ···**>**

■ **get 'round** *v.i.* ~ round to doing sth. dazu kommen, etw. zu tun

■ **get 'through** *v.i.* durchkommen

■ **get 'up** *v.i.* aufstehen

■ **get 'up to** *v.t.* ~ up to mischief etwas anstellen

get: ~**away** *n.* Flucht, *die; attrib.* Flucht⟨*plan, -wagen*⟩; **make one's** ~**away** entkommen; ~**-together** *n.* (coll.) gemütliches Beisammensein; ~**-up** *n.* (coll.) Aufmachung, *die*

geyser /'giːzə(r)/ *n.* **(a)** (spring) Geysir, *der* **(b)** (Brit.) Durchlauferhitzer, *der*

ghastly /'gɑːstlɪ/ *adj.* grauenvoll; entsetzlich ⟨*Verletzungen*⟩; schrecklich ⟨*Fehler*⟩

gherkin /'gɜːkɪn/ *n.* Essiggurke, *die*

ghetto /'getəʊ/ *n., pl.* ~**s** Getto, *das*

ghetto blaster /'getəʊblɑːstə(r)/ *n.* (coll.) [großer, tragbarer] Radiorekorder

ghost /gəʊst/ *n.* Geist, *der;* Gespenst, *das*

'ghostly *adj.* gespenstisch

ghost: ~ **story** *n.* Gespenstergeschichte, *die;* ~ **writer** *n.* Ghostwriter, *der*

giant /'dʒaɪənt/ 1 *n.* Riese, *der* 2 *attrib. adj.* riesig

gibberish /'dʒɪbərɪʃ/ *n.* Kauderwelsch, *das*

gibe /dʒaɪb/ *n.* Stichelei, *die*

giblets /'dʒɪblɪts/ *n. pl.* [Geflügel]klein, *das*

giddiness /'gɪdɪnɪs/ *n.* Schwindel, *der*

giddy /'gɪdɪ/ *adj.* schwind[e]lig

gift /gɪft/ *n.* **(a)** Geschenk, *das;* **make sb. a** ~ **of sth., make a** ~ **of sth. to sb.** jmdm. etw. schenken; **a** ~ **box/pack** eine Geschenkpackung **(b)** (talent) Begabung, *die;* **have a** ~ **for languages / mathematics** sprachbegabt/ mathematisch begabt sein

'gifted *adj.* begabt (**in, at** für)

gift: ~ **shop** *n.* Geschenkboutique, *die;* Geschenkladen, *der;* ~ **token**, ~ **voucher** *ns.* Geschenkgutschein, *der;* ~**-wrap** *v.t.* als Geschenk einpacken; in Geschenkpapier einpacken

'gigabyte *n.* (Comp.) Gigabyte, *das*

gigantic /dʒaɪ'gæntɪk/ *adj.* gigantisch; riesig; enorm ⟨*Verbesserung, Appetit*⟩

giggle /'gɪgl/ 1 *n.* Kichern, *das* 2 *v.i.* kichern

gild /gɪld/ *v.t.* vergolden

gill /gɪl/ *n.* Kieme, *die*

gilt /gɪlt/ 1 *n.* Goldauflage, *die;* (paint) Goldfarbe, *die* 2 *adj.* vergoldet

gimmick /'gɪmɪk/ *n.* (coll.) Gag, *der*

gin /dʒɪn/ *n.* Gin, *der*

ginger /'dʒɪndʒə(r)/ *n.* **(a)** Ingwer, *der* **(b)** (colour) Rötlichgelb, *das*

ginger: ~ **'beer** *n.* Ingwerbier, *das;* ~**bread** *n.* Pfefferkuchen, *der*

gingerly /'dʒɪndʒəlɪ/ *adv.* vorsichtig

gipsy ▶ GYPSY

giraffe /dʒɪ'rɑːf/ *n.* Giraffe, *die*

girder /'gɜːdə(r)/ *n.* Träger, *der*

girdle /'gɜːdl/ *n.* Hüfthalter, *der*

girl /gɜːl/ *n.* Mädchen, *das;* (teenager) junges Mädchen

girl: ~**band** *n.* Girlgroup, *die;* ~**friend** *n.* Freundin, *die*

'girlish *adj.* mädchenhaft

'girl power *n.* (coll.) Girlpower, *die*

giro /'dʒaɪərəʊ/ *n.* **(a)** Giro, *das; attrib.* Giro-; **bank** ~: Giroverkehr, *der* **(b)** (cheque) Scheck, *der*

girth /gɜːθ/ *n.* **(a)** Umfang, *der* **(b)** (for horse) Bauchgurt, *der*

gismo /'gɪzməʊ/ *n.* (coll.) Ding, *das* (ugs.)

gist /dʒɪst/ *n.* Wesentliche, *das;* (of tale, question, etc.) Kern, *der*

give /gɪv/ 1 *v.t.,* gave /geɪv/, given /'gɪvn/ **(a)** geben (**to** *Dat.*) **(b)** (as gift) schenken; ~ sb. sth., ~ sth. to sb. jmdm. etw. schenken; ~ and take (fig.) Kompromisse eingehen **(c)** (assign) aufgeben ⟨*Hausaufgaben usw.*⟩; (grant, award, offer, allow to have) geben; verleihen ⟨*Preis, Titel usw.*⟩; lassen ⟨*Wahl, Zeit*⟩; verleihen ⟨*Gewicht, Nachdruck*⟩; bereiten, machen ⟨*Freude, Mühe, Kummer*⟩; bieten ⟨*Schutz*⟩; leisten ⟨*Hilfe*⟩; gewähren ⟨*Unterstützung*⟩; be ~n sth. etw. bekommen; ~n that (because) da; (if) wenn; ~ sb. hope jmdm. Hoffnung machen **(d)** (tell) angeben ⟨*Namen, Anschrift, Alter, Grund*⟩; nennen ⟨*Einzelheiten*⟩; geben ⟨*Rat, Befehl, Anweisung, Antwort*⟩; fällen ⟨*Urteil, Entscheidung*⟩; sagen ⟨*Meinung*⟩; bekannt geben ⟨*Nachricht*⟩; ~ him my best wishes richte ihm meine besten Wünsche aus **(e)** (perform, sing, etc.) geben ⟨*Vorstellung, Konzert*⟩; halten ⟨*Vortrag, Seminar*⟩ **(f)** (produce) geben ⟨*Licht, Milch*⟩; ergeben ⟨*Zahlen, Resultat*⟩ **(g)** (make, show) geben ⟨*Zeichen, Stoß, Tritt*⟩; machen ⟨*Satz, Ruck*⟩; ausstoßen ⟨*Schrei, Seufzer, Pfiff*⟩; ~ sb. a [friendly] look jmdm. einen [freundlichen] Blick zuwerfen **(h)** (inflict) versetzen ⟨*Schlag, Stoß*⟩; sth. ~s me a headache von etw. bekomme ich Kopfschmerzen **(i)** geben ⟨*Party, Essen usw.*⟩ 2 *v.i.,* gave, given (yield) nachgeben; ⟨*Knie:*⟩ weich werden; ⟨*Bett:*⟩ federn 3 *n.* Nachgiebigkeit, *die;* (elasticity) Elastizität, *die*

■ **give a'way** *v.t.* **(a)** verschenken **(b)** (in marriage) dem Bräutigam zuführen **(c)** (betray) verraten

■ **give 'back** *v.t.* zurückgeben

■ **give in** 1 /'--/ *v.t.* abgeben 2 /-'-/ *v.i.* nachgeben (**to** *Dat.*)

■ **give 'off** *v.t.* ausströmen ⟨*Geruch*⟩; aussenden ⟨*Strahlen*⟩

■ **give 'up** 1 *v.i.* aufgeben

2 *v.t.* aufgeben; widmen ⟨*Zeit*⟩; ∼ sth. up (abandon habit) sich (*Dat.*) etw. abgewöhnen; ∼ **oneself up** sich stellen

■ **give 'way** *v.i.* (a) (yield) nachgeben (b) (in traffic) ∼ **way [to traffic from the right]** [dem Rechtsverkehr] die Vorfahrt lassen; '**G∼ Way**' „Vorfahrt beachten" (c) (collapse) einstürzen

given ▶ GIVE 1, 2

'**given name** *n.* (Amer.) Vorname, *der*

give-'way sign *n.* (Brit.) Vorfahrtsschild, *das*

gizmo ▶ GISMO

glacier /'glæsɪə(r)/ *n.* Gletscher, *der*

glad /glæd/ *adj.* froh; **be** ∼ **of sth.** über etw. (*Akk.*) froh sein; **für etw. dankbar sein**

gladden /'glædn/ *v.t.* erfreuen

glade /gleɪd/ *n.* Lichtung, *die*

'**gladly** *adv.* gern

glamor (Amer.) ▶ GLAMOUR

glamorous /'glæmərəs/ *adj.* glanzvoll; glamourös ⟨*Filmstar*⟩

glamour /'glæmə(r)/ *n.* Glanz, *der;* (of person) Ausstrahlung, *die*

glance /glɑːns/ 1 *n.* Blick, *der* 2 *v.i.* blicken; ∼ **at sb./sth.** jmdn./etw. anblicken; ∼ **at one's watch** auf seine Uhr blicken; ∼ **at the newspaper** *etc.* einen Blick in die Zeitung *usw.* werfen; ∼ **round [the room]** sich [im Zimmer] umsehen

gland /glænd/ *n.* Drüse, *die*

glandular /'glændjʊlə(r)/ *adj.* Drüsen-

glare /gleə(r)/ 1 *n.* (a) grelles Licht (b) (hostile look) feindseliger Blick; **with a** ∼: feindselig 2 *v.i.* (glower) [finster] starren; ∼ **at sb./sth.** jmdn./etw. anstarren

glaring /'gleərɪŋ/ *adj.* grell; (fig.: conspicuous) schreiend; grob ⟨*Fehler*⟩; krass ⟨*Gegensatz*⟩

glass /glɑːs/ *n.* (a) (substance) Glas, *das;* **pieces of/broken** ∼: Glasscherben *Pl.;* (smaller) Glassplitter *Pl.* (b) (drinking ∼) Glas, *das;* **a** ∼ **of milk** ein Glas Milch (c) (pane) [Glas]scheibe, *die* (d) *in pl.* (spectacles) **[a pair of]** ∼**es** eine Brille

glass 'ceiling *n.* (fig.) unsichtbare Barriere

'**glassy** *adj.* gläsern

glaze /gleɪz/ 1 *n.* Glasur, *die* 2 *v.t.* (a) glasieren (b) (fit with glass) verglasen

glazed /gleɪzd/ *adj.* glasig ⟨*Blick*⟩

glazier /'gleɪzɪə(r)/ *n.* Glaser, *der*

gleam /gliːm/ 1 *n.* Schein, *der;* (fainter) Schimmer, *der;* ∼ **of hope** Hoffnungsschimmer, *der* 2 *n.* ⟨*Licht:*⟩ scheinen; ⟨*Fußboden, Stiefel:*⟩ glänzen; ⟨*Zähne:*⟩ blitzen; ⟨*Augen:*⟩ leuchten

'**gleaming** *adj.* glänzend

glean /gliːn/ *v.t.* zusammentragen ⟨*Informationen usw.*⟩; ∼ **sth. from sth.** einer Sache (*Dat.*) etw. entnehmen

glee /gliː/ *n.* Freude, *die;* (gloating joy) Schadenfreude, *die*

gleeful /'gliːfl/ *adj.* freudig; (gloating) schadenfroh

glen /glen/ *n.* [schmales] Tal

glib /glɪb/ *adj.* aalglatt ⟨*Person*⟩; leicht dahingesagt ⟨*Antwort*⟩

glide /glaɪd/ *v.i.* gleiten; (through the air) schweben

'**glider** *n.* Segelflugzeug, *das*

glimmer /'glɪmə(r)/ 1 *n.* Schimmer, *der* (of von); (of fire) Glimmen, *das* 2 *v.i.* glimmen

glimpse /glɪmps/ 1 *n.* [kurzer] Blick; **catch** *or* **have** *or* **get a** ∼ **of sb./sth.** jmdn./ etw. [kurz] zu sehen bekommen 2 *v.t.* flüchtig sehen

glint /glɪnt/ 1 *n.* Schimmer, *der* 2 *v.i.* blinken; glitzern

glisten /'glɪsn/ *v.i.* glitzern

glitter /'glɪtə(r)/ 1 *v.i.* glitzern; ⟨*Juwelen, Sterne:*⟩ funkeln 2 *n.* Glitzern, *das;* (of diamonds) Funkeln, *das*

glitz /glɪts/ *n.* Glanz, *der*

glitzy /'glɪtsɪ/ *adj.* glanzvoll

gloat /gləʊt/ *v.i.* ∼ **over sth.** sich hämisch über etw. (*Akk.*) freuen

global /'gləʊbl/ *adj.* weltweit; **G∼ Positioning System** GPS [-Navigationssystem], *das;* ∼ **warming** globaler Temperaturanstieg; **the** ∼ **village** das Weltdorf

globalization /gləʊbəlaɪ'zeɪʃn/ *n.* Globalisierung, *die*

globalize /'gləʊbəlaɪz/ *v.t.* globalisieren

globe /gləʊb/ *n.* (a) (sphere) Kugel, *die* (b) (with map) Globus, *der* (c) (world) **the** ∼: der Globus; der Erdball

'**globetrotter** *n.* Globetrotter, *der;* Weltenbummler, *der*

gloom /gluːm/ *n.* (a) (darkness) Dunkel, *das* (geh.) (b) (despondency) düstere Stimmung

'**gloomy** *adj.* (a) (dark) düster; finster (b) (depressing) düster; (depressed) trübsinnig ⟨*Person*⟩

glorify /'glɔːrɪfaɪ/ *v.t.* verherrlichen; **a glorified messenger boy** ein besserer Botenjunge

glorious /'glɔːrɪəs/ *adj.* (a) (illustrious) ruhmreich ⟨*Held, Sieg*⟩ (b) (delightful) wunderschön; herrlich

glory /'glɔːrɪ/ 1 *n.* (a) (splendour) Schönheit, *die;* (majesty) Herrlichkeit, *die* (b) (fame) Ruhm, *der* 2 *v.i.* ∼ **in sth.** (be proud of) sich einer Sache (*Gen.*) rühmen

gloss /glɒs/ *n.* Glanz, *der;* ∼ **paint** Lackfarbe, *die* ⋯⋯

■ **'gloss over** *v.t.* bemänteln; beschönigen ⟨*Fehler*⟩

glossary /'glɒsərɪ/ *n.* Glossar, *das*

'glossy **1** *adj.* glänzend; (fig.) glanzvoll **2** *n.* (coll.) (magazine) auf [Hoch]glanzpapier gedruckte Zeitschrift

glove /glʌv/ *n.* Handschuh, *der*

glove: ~ **box** *n.* (a) ▶ ~ COMPARTMENT; **(b)** (for toxic material etc.) Handschuhkasten, *der;* ~ **compartment** *n.* Handschuhfach, *das;* ~ **puppet** *n.* Handpuppe, *die*

glow /gləʊ/ *v.i.* **(a)** glühen; ⟨*Lampe, Leuchtfarbe:*⟩ schimmern, leuchten **(b)** (fig.) (with warmth or pride) ⟨*Gesicht, Wangen:*⟩ glühen (**with** vor + *Dat.*); (with health or vigour) strotzen (**with** vor + *Dat.*)

glower /'glaʊə(r)/ *v.i.* finster dreinblicken; ~ **at sb.** jmdn. finster anstarren

'glowing *adj.* glühend; begeistert ⟨*Bericht*⟩

'glow-worm *n.* Glühwürmchen, *das*

glucose /'glu:kəʊz/ *n.* Glucose, *die*

glue /glu:/ **1** *n.* Klebstoff, *der* **2** *v.t.* kleben; ~ **sth. to sth.** etw. an etw. (*Dat.*) an- *od.* festkleben

'glue-sniffing *n.* Schnüffeln, *das* (ugs.); Sniefen, *das* (ugs.)

glum /glʌm/ *adj.* verdrießlich

glut /glʌt/ *n.* Überangebot, *das* (**of** an, von + *Dat.*)

glutton /'glʌtən/ *n.* Vielfraß, *der* (ugs.); a ~ **for punishment** (iron.) ein Masochist (fig.)

gluttony /'glʌtənɪ/ *n.* Gefräßigkeit, *die*

glycerine /'glɪsəri:n/ (*Amer.:* **glycerin** /'glɪsərɪn/) *n.* Glyzerin, *das*

gm. *abbr.* = **gram[s]** g

GM *abbr.* = **genetically modified**; GM **crops/food** gentechnisch veränderte Feldfrüchte *Pl.*/Nahrungsmittel *Pl.*

GMO *abbr.* = **genetically modified organism** GVO

GMT *abbr.* = **Greenwich Mean Time** GMT; WEZ

gnarled /nɑ:ld/ *adj.* knorrig; knotig ⟨*Hand*⟩

gnash /næʃ/ *v.t.* ~ **one's teeth** mit den Zähnen knirschen

gnat /næt/ *n.* [Stech]mücke, *die*

gnaw /nɔ:/ **1** *v.i.* ~ **[away] at sth.** an etw. (*Dat.*) nagen **2** *v.t.* nagen an (+ *Dat.*); abnagen ⟨*Knochen*⟩

gnome /nəʊm/ *n.* Gnom, *der*

GNVQ *abbr.* = **General National Vocational Qualification**

go /gəʊ/ **1** *v.i., pres.* **he goes** /gəʊz/, *p.t.* **went** /went/, *pres. p.* **going** /'gəʊɪŋ/, *p.p.* **gone** /gɒn/ **(a)** gehen; ⟨*Fahrzeug:*⟩ fahren; ⟨*Flugzeug:*⟩ fliegen; ⟨*Vierfüßer:*⟩ laufen; (on horseback etc.) reiten; (in lift) fahren; (on outward journey) weg-, abfahren; (travel regularly) ⟨*Verkehrsmittel:*⟩ verkehren (**from ... to** zwischen + *Dat.* ... und); **go by bicycle/car/** bus/train *or* rail/boat *or* sea *or* ship mit dem [Fahr]rad/Auto/Bus/Zug/Schiff fahren; **go by plane** *or* **air** fliegen; **go on foot** zu Fuß gehen; laufen (ugs.); **go on a journey** verreisen; **have far to go** es weit haben; **go to the toilet/cinema/a museum** auf die Toilette/ins Kino/ins Museum gehen; **go to the doctor['s]** *etc.* zum Arzt *usw.* gehen; **go bathing** baden gehen; **go cycling** Rad fahren; **go to see sb.** jmdn. aufsuchen; **go and see whether ...:** nachsehen [gehen], ob ...; **I'll go!** ich geh schon!; (answer phone) ich geh ran *od.* nehme ab; (answer door) ich mache auf **(b)** (start) losgehen; (in vehicle) losfahren **(c)** (pass, circulate) gehen; **a shiver went up** *or* **down my spine** ein Schauer lief mir über den Rücken; **go to** (be given to) ⟨*Preis, Gelder, Job:*⟩ gehen an (+ *Akk.*); ⟨*Titel, Besitz:*⟩ übergehen auf (+ *Akk.*); **go towards** (be of benefit to) zugute kommen (+ *Dat.*) **(d)** (act, function effectively) gehen; ⟨*Mechanismus, Maschine:*⟩ laufen; **keep going** (in movement) weitergehen/-fahren; (in activity) weitermachen; (not fail) sich aufrecht halten; **keep sth. going** etw. in Gang halten; **make sth. go, get/set sth. going** etw. in Gang bringen **(e)** **go to work** zur Arbeit gehen; **go to school** in die Schule gehen; **go to a comprehensive school** auf eine Gesamtschule gehen **(f)** (depart) ⟨*Bus, Zug:*⟩ [ab]fahren; ⟨*Post:*⟩ rausgehen (ugs.) **(g)** (cease to function) kaputtgehen; ⟨*Sicherung:*⟩ durchbrennen; (break) brechen; ⟨*Seil usw.:*⟩ reißen **(h)** (disappear) weggehen; ⟨*Mantel, Hut, Fleck:*⟩ verschwinden; ⟨*Geruch, Rauch:*⟩ sich verziehen; ⟨*Geld, Zeit:*⟩ draufgehen (ugs.) (**in, on** für) **(i)** **to go** (still remaining) **have sth. [still] to go** [noch] etw. übrig haben; **one week** *etc.* **to go to ...:** noch eine Woche *usw.* bis ...; **there's hours to go** es dauert noch Stunden **(j)** (be sold) weggehen (ugs.); verkauft werden; **going! going! gone!** zum Ersten! zum Zweiten! zum Dritten!; **go to sb.** an jmdn. gehen **(k)** (run) ⟨*Grenze, Straße usw.:*⟩ verlaufen; (lead) gehen; führen; (extend) reichen; **as** *or* **so far as he/it goes** so weit **(l)** (turn out, progress) ⟨*Projekt, Interview, Abend:*⟩ verlaufen; **how did your holiday go?** wie war Ihr Urlaub?; **things have been going well/badly** in der letzten Zeit läuft alles gut/schief **(m)** (be, have form or nature) sein; ⟨*Sprichwort, Gedicht, Titel:*⟩ lauten; **that's the way it goes** so ist es nun mal; **go hungry** hungern; **go without food/water** es ohne Essen/Wasser aushalten **(n)** (become) werden; **the tyre has gone flat** der Reifen ist platt **(o)** (have usual place) kommen; (belong) gehören; **where does the box go?** wo kommt *od.* gehört die Kiste hin?

(p) (fit) passen; **go in[to]** sth. in etw. (*Akk.*) gehen *od.* [hinein]passen; **go through** sth. durch etw. [hindurch]gehen

(q) (match) passen (**with** zu)

(r) ⟨*Turmuhr, Gong:*⟩ schlagen; ⟨*Glocke:*⟩ läuten

(s) (coll.: be acceptable or permitted) erlaubt sein; **it/that goes without saying** es/das ist doch selbstverständlich. *See also* GOING 2

2 *n., pl.* **goes** /gəʊz/ (coll.) **(a)** (attempt, try) Versuch, *der;* (chance) Gelegenheit, *die;* **have a go** es versuchen; **let me have a go/can I have a go?** lass mich [auch ein]mal/kann ich [auch ein]mal? (ugs.); **it's 'my go** ich bin an der Reihe *od.* dran; **at one go** auf einmal; **at the first go** auf Anhieb

(b) (vigorous activity) **it's all go** es ist alles eine einzige Hetzerei (ugs.); **be on the go** auf Trab sein (ugs.)

(c) (success) **make a go of** sth. mit etw. Erfolg haben

▪ **go a'head** *v.i.* **(a)** (in advance) vorausgehen (**of** *Dat.*)

(b) (proceed) weitermachen; (make progress) ⟨*Arbeit:*⟩ fortschreiten, vorangehen

▪ **go a'long with** *v.t.* **go along with** sth. (agree to) sich einer Sache (*Dat.*) anschließen

▪ **go a'way** *v.i.* weggehen; (on holiday or business) verreisen

▪ **go 'back** *v.i.* zurückgehen/-fahren; (restart) ⟨*Schule, Fabrik:*⟩ wieder anfangen; (fig.) zurückgehen; **go back to the beginning** noch mal von vorne anfangen

▪ **go by** **1** /'--/ *v.t.* **go by** sth. sich nach etw. richten; (adhere to) sich an etw. (*Akk.*) halten **2** /-'-/ *v.i.* ⟨*Zeit:*⟩ vergehen

▪ **go 'down** *v.i.* hinuntergehen/-fahren; ⟨*Sonne:*⟩ untergehen; ⟨*Schiff:*⟩ untergehen; (fall to ground) ⟨*Flugzeug usw.:*⟩ abstürzen

▪ **'go for** *v.t.* **go for** sb./sth. (go to fetch) jmdn./etw. holen; (apply to) für jmdn./etw. gelten; (like) jmdn./etw. gut finden

▪ **go 'in** *v.i.* hineingehen; reingehen (ugs.)

▪ **go 'off** **1** *v.i.* **(a)** go off **with** sb./sth. sich mit jmdm./etw. auf- und davonmachen (ugs.)

(b) ⟨*Alarm, Schusswaffe:*⟩ losgehen; ⟨*Wecker:*⟩ klingeln; ⟨*Bombe:*⟩ hochgehen

(c) (turn bad) schlecht werden

(d) ⟨*Strom:*⟩ ausfallen

2 *v.t.* (begin to dislike) **go off** sth. von etw. abkommen

▪ **go 'on** *v.i.* **(a)** weitergehen/-fahren

(b) (continue) weitermachen

(c) (happen) passieren

▪ **go 'out** *v.i.* ausgehen; **go out to work/for a meal** arbeiten/essen gehen; **go out with** sb. (date sb.) mit jmdm. gehen (ugs.)

▪ **go over** **1** /-'--/ *v.i.* hinübergehen **2** /'---, -'--/ *v.t.* (re-examine) durchgehen

▪ **go 'round** *v.i.* **(a)** (call) **go round** and *or* **to see** sb. bei jmdm. vorbeigehen (ugs.)

(b) (look round) sich umschauen

(c) (suffice) reichen; langen (ugs.)

(d) (spin) sich drehen

▪ **go through** **1** /-'-/ *v.i.* ⟨*Ernennung:*⟩ durchkommen; ⟨*Antrag:*⟩ durchgehen

2 /'--/ **(a)** (rehearse) durchgehen

(b) (examine) durchsehen

(c) (endure) durchmachen

▪ **go 'through with** *v.t.* zu Ende führen

▪ **go 'under** *v.i.* untergehen; (fig.: fail) eingehen

▪ **go 'up** *v.i.* **(a)** hinaufgehen/-fahren; ⟨*Ballon:*⟩ aufsteigen; (Theatre) ⟨*Vorhang:*⟩ aufgehen; ⟨*Lichter:*⟩ angehen

(b) (increase) ⟨*Zahl:*⟩ wachsen; ⟨*Preis, Wert, Niveau:*⟩ steigen; (in price) ⟨*Ware:*⟩ teurer werden

▪ **go without** **1** /'---/ *v.t.* verzichten auf (+ *Akk.*)

2 /-'-/ *v.i.* verzichten

goad /gəʊd/ *v.t.* ~ **sb. into** sth./**doing** sth. jmdn. zu etw. anstacheln/dazu anstacheln, etw. zu tun

'go-ahead **1** *adj.* unternehmungslustig; (progressive) fortschrittlich

2 *n.* **give sb./sth. the** ~: jmdm./einer Sache grünes Licht geben

goal /gəʊl/ *n.* **(a)** (aim) Ziel, *das*

(b) (Footb., Hockey) Tor, *das;* **score/kick a** ~: einen Treffer erzielen

goalie /'gəʊlɪ/ *n.* (coll.) Tormann, *der*

goal: ~**keeper** *n.* Torwart, *der;* ~**post** *n.* Torpfosten, *der;* **move the** ~**posts** (fig. coll.) sich nicht an die Spielregeln halten

goat /gəʊt/ *n.* Ziege, *die*

gobble /'gɒbl/ **1** *v.t.* ~ [**down** *or* **up**] hinunterschlingen

2 *v.i.* schlingen

'go-between *n.* Vermittler, *der/* Vermittlerin, *die*

goblet /'gɒblɪt/ *n.* Kelchglas, *das*

goblin /'gɒblɪn/ *n.* Kobold, *der*

god /gɒd/ *n.* **(a)** Gott, *der*

(b) **God** (Theol.) Gott

god: ~**child** *n.* Patenkind, *das;* ~**daughter** *n.* Patentochter, *die*

goddess /'gɒdɪs/ *n.* Göttin, *die*

god: ~**father** *n.* Pate, *der;* **G**~**forsaken** *adj.* gottverlassen; ~**mother** *n.* Patentante, *die;* ~**send** *n.* Gottesgabe, *die;* **be a** ~**send to** sb. für jmdn. ein Geschenk des Himmels sein; ~**son** *n.* Patensohn, *der*

'go-getter *n.* Draufgänger, *der*

'goggle-box *n.* (Brit. coll.) Glotze, *die* (salopp); Glotzkiste, *die* (salopp)

goggles /'gɒglz/ *n. pl.* Schutzbrille, *die*

going /'gəʊɪŋ/ **1** *n.* (progress) Vorankommen, *das;* **while the** ~ **is good** solange es noch geht

2 *adj.* **(a)** (available) erhältlich; **there is sth.** ~: es gibt etw.

(b) **be** ~ **to do** sth. etw. tun [werden/ wollen]; **I was** ~ **to say** ich wollte sagen; **it's** ~ **to snow** es wird schneien; **a** ~ **concern** eine gesunde Firma

(c) (current) [derzeit/damals/dann] geltend; **the** ~ **rate of exchange** der augenblickliche Wechselkurs

⋯⟶

(d) a ~ **concern** eine gesunde Firma
goings-'on *n. pl.* Ereignisse *Pl.*
gold /gəʊld/ [1] *n.* Gold, *das*
[2] *attrib. adj.* golden; Gold‹münze, -kette
usw.›
'gold-digger *n.* Goldgräber, *der;* **she's a**
~**-digger** (fig. coll.) sie ist nur auf das Geld
der Männer aus
golden /'gəʊldn/ *adj.* golden
golden 'wedding *n.* goldene Hochzeit
gold: ~**fish** *n.* Goldfisch, *der;* ~**fish
bowl** *n.* Goldfischglas, *das;* **like being in a**
~**fish bowl** (fig.) wie auf dem Präsentierteller;
~ **'medal** *n.* Goldmedaille, *die;*
~ **'medallist** *n.* Goldmedaillengewinner,
der/-gewinnerin, *die;* ~ **mine** *n.* Goldmine.
die; (fig.) Goldgrube, *die;* ~**-'plated** *adj.*
vergoldet; ~**smith** *n.* Goldschmied, *der/*
-schmiedin, *die*
golf /gɒlf/ *n.* Golf, das
golf: ~ **ball** *n.* Golfball, *der;* ~ **club**
n. **(a)** (implement) Golfschläger, *der;* **(b)**
(association) Golfklub, *der;* ~**course** *n.*
Golfplatz, *der*
'golfer *n.* Golfer, *der/*Golferin, *die*
golf links *n.* Golfplatz, *der*
gondola /'gɒndələ/ *n.* Gondel, *die*
gondolier /gɒndə'lɪə(r)/ *n.* Gondoliere, *der*
gone /gɒn/ [1] ▸ GO 1
[2] *pred. adj.* **(a)** (away) weg; **it's time you
were** ~: es ist *od.* wird Zeit, dass du gehst
(b) (of time: after) nach; **it's** ~ **ten o'clock** es
ist zehn Uhr vorbei
gong /gɒŋ/ *n.* Gong, *der*
good /gʊd/ [1] *adj.,* **better** /'betə(r)/,
best /best/ **(a)** gut; günstig ‹Gelegenheit,
Angebot›; ausreichend ‹Vorrat›; ausgiebig
‹Mahl›; **as** ~ **as** so gut wie; **his** ~ **eye/leg**
sein gesundes Auge/Bein; **in** ~ **time**
frühzeitig; **all in** ~ **time** alles zu seiner Zeit;
be ~ **at sth.** in etw. (*Dat.*) gut sein; **too** ~ **to
be true** zu schön, um wahr zu sein; **apples
are** ~ **for you** Äpfel sind gesund; **be too
much of a** ~ **thing** zu viel des Guten sein;
~ **times** eine schöne Zeit; **feel** ~: sich wohl
fühlen; **take a** ~ **look round** sich gründlich
umsehen; **give sb. a** ~ **beating/scolding**
jmdn. tüchtig verprügeln/ausschimpfen;
~ **afternoon/day** guten Tag!; ~ **evening/
morning** guten Abend/Morgen!; ~ **night**
gute Nacht!
(b) (enjoyable) schön ‹Leben, Urlaub,
Wochenende›; **the** ~ **life** das angenehme[,
sorglose] Leben; **have a** ~ **time!** viel Spaß!;
have a ~ **journey!** gute Reise!
(c) (well-behaved) gut; brav; **be** ~**!, be a**
~ **girl/boy!** sei brav *od.* lieb!; **[as]** ~ **as gold**
ganz artig *od.* brav
(d) (virtuous) rechtschaffen; (kind) nett; gut
‹Absicht, Wünsche, Benehmen, Tat›; **be** ~ **to
sb.** gut zu jmdm. sein; **would you be so**
~ **as to** *or* ~ **enough to do that?** wären Sie
so freundlich *od.* nett, das zu tun?; **that/it is**
~ **of you** das/es ist nett *od.* lieb von dir

(e) (commendable) gut; ~ **for 'you** *etc.* (coll.)
bravo!
(f) (attractive) schön; gut ‹Figur›; **look** ~: gut
aussehen
(g) (considerable) [recht] ansehnlich
‹Menschenmenge›; ganz schön, ziemlich
(ugs.) ‹Entfernung, Strecke›; gut ‹Preis,
Erlös›
(h) make ~ (succeed) erfolgreich sein;
(compensate for) wieder gutmachen; (indemnify)
ersetzen
[2] *n.* **(a)** (use) Nutzen, *der;* **be some** ~ **to
sb./sth.** jmdm./einer Sache nützen; **be
no** ~ **to sb./sth.** für jmdn./etw. nicht zu
gebrauchen sein; **it is no/not much** ~ **doing
sth.** es hat keinen/kaum einen Sinn, etw. zu
tun; **what's the** ~ **of …?, what** ~ **is …?** was
nützt …?
(b) (benefit) **for your/his** *etc.* **own** ~: zu
deinem/seinem *usw.* Besten; **do no/little**
~: nichts/wenig helfen *od.* nützen; **do
sb./sth.** ~: jmdm./einer Sache nützen;
‹Ruhe, Erholung:› jmdm./einer Sache gut
tun; ‹Arznei:› jmdm./einer Sache helfen
(c) (goodness) Gute, *das;* **be up to no**
~: nichts Gutes im Sinn haben
(d) for ~ (finally) ein für alle Mal; (permanently)
für immer
(e) *in pl.* (wares etc.) Waren *Pl.;* (belongings)
Habe, *die;* (Brit. Railw.) Fracht, *die; attrib.*
Güter‹wagen, -zug›
good: ~**'bye** (*Amer.:* ~**'by**) *int.*
auf Wiedersehen!; (on telephone) auf
Wiederhören!; ~**-for-nothing** [1] *adj.*
nichtsnutzig; [2] *n.* Taugenichts, *der;*
~**-'looking** *adj.* gut aussehend
'goodness [1] *n.* Güte, *die*
[2] *int.* **[my]** ~**!** meine Güte! (ugs.)
good: ~**s train** *n.* (Brit.) Güterzug, *der;*
~**-'tempered** *adj.* ausgeglichen;
verträglich ‹Person›; ~**'will** *n.* guter Wille;
attrib. Goodwill‹botschaft, -reise usw.›
'goody *n.* (coll.: hero) Gute, *der/die*
gooey /'guːɪ/ *adj.,* **gooier** /'guːɪə(r)/,
gooiest /'guːɪɪst/ (coll.) klebrig
goose /guːs/ *n., pl.* **geese** /giːs/ Gans, *die*
gooseberry /'gʊzbərɪ/ *n.* Stachelbeere,
die
goose bumps (Amer.), **goose
pimples** *ns. pl.* **have** ~: eine Gänsehaut
haben
gore¹ /gɔː(r)/ *v.t.* [mit den Hörnern]
aufspießen *od.* durchbohren
gore² *n.* Blut, *das*
gorge /gɔːdʒ/ [1] *n.* Schlucht, *die*
[2] *v.i. & refl.* ~ **[oneself]** sich voll stopfen
(ugs.) (on mit)
gorgeous /'gɔːdʒəs/ *adj.* prächtig;
hinreißend ‹Frau, Mann, Lächeln›
gorilla /gə'rɪlə/ *n.* Gorilla, *der*
gormless /'gɔːmlɪs/ *adj.* (Brit. coll.) dämlich
(ugs.)
gorse /gɔːs/ *n.* Stechginster, *der*

gory /'gɔːrɪ/ *adj.* (fig.) blutrünstig
gosh /gɒʃ/ *int.* (coll.) Gott!
'go-slow *n.* (Brit.) Bummelstreik, *der*
gospel /'gɒspl/ *n.* Evangelium, *das*
'gospel singer *n.* Gospelsänger, *der*/ -sängerin, *die*
gossamer /'gɒsəmə(r)/ *n.* Altweibersommer, *der; attrib.* hauchdünn
gossip /'gɒsɪp/ ① *n.* (a) (talk) Klatsch, *der* (ugs.)
  (b) (person) Klatschbase, *die* (ugs.)
  ② *v.i.* klatschen (ugs.)
gossip: ∼ column *n.* Klatschspalte, *die* (ugs.); **∼ columnist** *n.* Klatschspaltenkolumnist, *der*/-kolumnistin, *die*
got ▸ GET
Gothic /'gɒθɪk/ *adj.* gotisch
gotten ▸ GET
gouge /gaʊdʒ/ *v.t.* aushöhlen
goulash /'guːlæʃ/ *n.* Gulasch, *das od. der*
gourmet /'gʊəmeɪ/ *n.* Gourmet, *der*
gout /gaʊt/ *n.* Gicht, *die*
govern /'gʌvn/ ① *v.t.* (a) regieren ⟨Land, Volk⟩; verwalten ⟨Provinz⟩
  (b) (dictate) bestimmen
  ② *v.i.* regieren
governess /'gʌvənɪs/ *n.* Gouvernante, *die* (veraltet); Hauslehrerin, *die*
government /'gʌvnmənt/ *n.* Regierung, *die; attrib.* Regierungs-
government: ∼ department *n.* Regierungsstelle, *die;* **∼-funded** *adj.* staatlich finanziert; **∼ official** *n.* Regierungsbeamte, *der*/-beamtin, *die*
governor /'gʌvənə(r)/ *n.* (a) (of province etc.) Gouverneur, *der*
  (b) (of institution) Direktor, *der*/Direktorin, *die;* **[board of] ∼s** Vorstand, *der*
  (c) (coll.: employer) Boss, *der* (ugs.)
gown /gaʊn/ *n.* (a) [elegantes] Kleid
  (b) (official or uniform robe) Talar, *der*
GP *abbr.* = **general practitioner**
GPS *abbr.* = **Global Positioning System**
grab /græb/ ① *v.t.,* -bb- greifen nach; (seize) packen; **∼ the chance** die Gelegenheit ergreifen; **∼ hold of sb./sth.** sich ⟨Dat.⟩ jmdn./etw. schnappen (ugs.)
  ② *v.i.,* -bb-: **∼ at sth.** nach etw. greifen
  ③ *n.* **make a ∼ at *or* for sb./sth.** nach jmdm./etw. greifen
grace /greɪs/ *n.* (a) (charm) Anmut, *die* (geh.)
  (b) (decency) **have the ∼ to do sth.** so anständig sein und etw. tun
  (c) (delay) Frist, *die;* **give sb. a day's ∼:** jmdm. einen Tag Aufschub gewähren
  (d) (prayers) **say ∼:** das Tischgebet sprechen
graceful /'greɪsfl/ *adj.* elegant; graziös ⟨Bewegung, Eleganz⟩
gracious /'greɪʃəs/ ① *adj.*
  (a) liebenswürdig

  (b) (merciful) gnädig
  ② *int.* **good ∼!** [ach] du meine Güte!
grade /greɪd/ ① *n.* (a) Rang, *der;* (Mil.) Dienstgrad, *der*
  (b) (position) Stufe, *die*
  (c) (Amer. Sch.: class) Klasse, *die*
  (d) (Sch., Univ.: mark) Note, *die;* Zensur, *die*
  ② *int.* einstufen ⟨Schüler⟩; [nach Größe/Qualität] sortieren ⟨Eier, Kartoffeln⟩
  (b) (mark) benoten
gradient /'greɪdɪənt/ *n.* (ascent) Steigung, *die;* (descent) Gefälle, *das*
gradual /'grædʒʊəl/ *adj.,* **gradually** *adv.* allmählich
graduate ① /'grædʒʊət/ *n.* Graduierte, *der*/*die;* (who has left university) Akademiker, *der*/Akademikerin, *die;* **university ∼:** Hochschulabsolvent, *der*/-absolventin, *die*
  ② /'grædʒʊeɪt/ *v.i.* einen akademischen Grad/Titel erwerben; (Amer. Sch.) die [Schul]abschlussprüfung bestehen (**from** an + *Dat.*)
graduation /grædʒʊ'eɪʃn/ *n.* (a) (Univ.) Graduierung, *die*
  (b) (Amer. Sch.) Entlassung, *die*
graffiti /grə'fiːtiː/ *n. sing. or pl.* Graffiti *Pl.;* **∼ artist** Graffitikünstler, *der*/-künstlerin, *die*
graft /grɑːft/ ① *n.* (a) (Bot.) Edelreis, *das*
  (b) (Med.) (operation) Transplantation, *die;* (thing ∼ed) Transplantat, *das*
  (c) (Brit. coll.: work) Plackerei, *die* (ugs.)
  ② *v.t.* (a) (Bot.) pfropfen
  (b) (Med.) transplantieren
  ③ *v.i.* (Brit. coll.) schuften (ugs.)
grain /greɪn/ *n.* (a) Korn, *das; collect.* Getreide, *das*
  (b) (particle) Korn, *das*
  (c) (in wood) Maserung, *die;* (in paper) Faser, *die;* (in leather) Narbung, *die;* **go against the ∼ [for sb.]** (fig.) jmdm. gegen den Strich gehen (ugs.)
'grainy *adj.* körnig; gemasert ⟨Holz⟩; genarbt ⟨Leder⟩
gram /græm/ *n.* Gramm, *das*
grammar /'græmə(r)/ *n.* Grammatik, *die*
grammar: ∼ book *n.* Grammatik, *die;* **∼ school** *n.* (Brit.) ≈ Gymnasium, *das*
grammatical /grə'mætɪkl/ *adj.*
  (a) grammat[ikal]isch richtig *od.* korrekt
  (b) (of grammar) grammatisch
grammatically /grə'mætɪkəlɪ/ *adv.* grammati[kal]isch ⟨richtig, falsch⟩
gramme ▸ GRAM
gramophone /'græməfəʊn/ *n.* Plattenspieler, *der* (dated)
gran /græn/ *n.* (coll./child lang.) Oma, *die* (Kinderspr./ugs.)
granary /'grænərɪ/ *n.* Getreidesilo, *der od. das;* Kornspeicher, *der*
'granary bread *n.* Ganzkornbrot, *das*
grand /grænd/ *adj.* (a) (most or very important) groß; **∼ finale** großes Finale ┄┄⟶

(b) (splendid) grandios
(c) (coll.: excellent) großartig
grandad /'grændæd/ *n.* (coll./child lang.);
Opa, *der* (Kinderspr./ugs.)
grand: ~child *n.* Enkel, *der*/Enkelin, *die*;
Enkelkind, *das;* **~dad[dy]** /'grændæd(i)/
▶ GRANDAD; **~daughter** *n.* Enkelin, *die*
grandeur /'grændʒə(r), 'grændjə(r)/ *n.*
Erhabenheit, *die*
'**grandfather** *n.* Großvater, *der;* ~ **clock**
Standuhr, *die*
grandiose /'grændɪəʊs/ *adj.* grandios;
(pompous) bombastisch
grand: ~ma *n.* (coll./child lang.) Oma,
die (Kinderspr./ugs.); **~mother** *n.*
Großmutter, *die;* **~pa** *n.* (coll./child lang.)
Opa, *der* (Kinderspr./ugs.); **~parent** *n.* (male)
Großvater, *der;* (female) Großmutter, *die;*
~parents Großeltern *Pl.;* ~ **pi'ano** *n.*
[Konzert]flügel, *der;* **~son** *n.* Enkel, *der;*
~stand *n.* [Haupt]tribüne, *die*
granite /'grænɪt/ *n.* Granit, *der*
granny /'grænɪ/ *n.* (coll./child lang.) Oma, *die*
(Kinderspr./ugs.)
'**granny flat** *n.* Einliegerwohnung, *die*
grant /grɑːnt/ 1 *v.t.* **(a)** erfüllen ⟨Wunsch⟩;
stattgeben (+ *Dat.*) ⟨Gesuch⟩
(b) (concede, give) gewähren; geben ⟨Zeit⟩;
bewilligen ⟨Geldmittel⟩; zugestehen ⟨Recht⟩;
erteilen ⟨Erlaubnis⟩
(c) (in argument) zugeben; **take sb./sth. for
~ed** sich (*Dat.*) jmds. sicher sein/etw. für
selbstverständlich halten
2 *n.* Zuschuss, *der;* (financial aid [to
student]) [Studien]beihilfe, *die;* (scholarship)
Stipendium, *das*
granulated sugar /grænjʊleɪtɪd
'ʃʊgə(r)/ *n.* Kristallzucker, *der*
granule /'grænjuːl/ *n.* Körnchen, *das*
grape /greɪp/ *n.* Weintraube, *die;* **a bunch
of ~s** eine Traube
grape: ~fruit *n., pl. same* Grapefruit,
die; ~ **juice** *n.* Traubensaft, *der;* **~vine**
n. (fig.) **the ~vine** die Flüsterpropaganda;
I heard on the ~vine that ...: es wird
geflüstert, dass ...
graph /grɑːf/ *n.* grafische Darstellung;
~ **paper** Diagrammpapier, *das*
graphic /'græfɪk/ *adj.* **(a)** grafisch
(b) (vivid) plastisch; anschaulich
graphically /'græfɪkəlɪ/ *adv.* **(a)** (vividly)
plastisch
(b) (using graphics) grafisch
graphic 'arts *n. pl.* Grafik, *die*
graphics /'græfɪks/ *n.* (use of diagrams)
grafische Darstellung; **computer ~:**
Computergraphik, *die*
grapple /'græpl/ *v.i.* handgemein werden;
~ **with** (fig.) sich auseinander setzen mit
grasp /grɑːsp/ 1 *v.i.* **~ at** ergreifen; sich
stürzen auf (+ *Akk.*) ⟨Angebot⟩
2 *v.t.* **(a)** (seize) ergreifen
(b) (hold firmly) festhalten

(c) (understand) verstehen; erfassen
⟨Bedeutung⟩
3 *n.* **(a)** (firm hold) Griff, *der*
(b) (mental ~) **have a good ~ of sth.** etw. gut
beherrschen
'**grasping** *adj.* habgierig
grass /grɑːs/ *n.* **(a)** Gras, *das*
(b) (lawn) Rasen, *der*
(c) (Brit. sl.: police informer) Spitzel, *der*
grass: ~hopper *n.* Grashüpfer, *der;*
~-root[s] *attrib. adj.* (Polit.) Basis-;
~ **seed** *n.* Grassamen, *der;* (collect.)
Grassamen *Pl.*
grassy /'grɑːsɪ/ *adj.* mit Gras bewachsen
grate[1] /greɪt/ *n.* Rost, *der;* (recess) Kamin,
der
grate[2] *v.t.* **(a)** reiben; (less finely) raspeln
(b) (grind) ~ **one's teeth** mit den Zähnen
knirschen
grateful /'greɪtfl/ *adj.* dankbar (**to** *Dat.*)
'**gratefully** *adv.* dankbar
'**grater** *n.* Reibe, *die;* Raspel, *die*
gratify /'grætɪfaɪ/ *v.t.* freuen; **be gratified
by** *or* **with** *or* **at sth.** über etw. (*Akk.*) erfreut
sein
'**gratifying** *adj.* erfreulich
grating /'greɪtɪŋ/ *n.* Gitter, *das*
gratitude /'grætɪtjuːd/ *n.* Dankbarkeit, *die*
(**to** gegenüber)
gratuitous /grə'tjuːɪtəs/ *adj.* (motiveless)
grundlos
gratuity /grə'tjuːɪtɪ/ *n.* Trinkgeld, *das*
grave[1] /greɪv/ *n.* Grab, *das*
grave[2] *adj.* **(a)** (important, solemn) ernst
(b) (serious) schwer ⟨Fehler, Irrtum⟩; ernst
⟨Situation, Lage⟩; groß ⟨Gefahr⟩; schlimm
⟨Nachricht⟩
'**gravedigger** *n.* Totengräber, *der*
gravel /'grævl/ *n.* Kies, *der*
grave: ~stone *n.* Grabstein, *der;* **~yard**
n. Friedhof, *der*
gravity /'grævɪtɪ/ *n.* **(a)** (of mistake, offence)
Schwere, *die;* (of situation) Ernst, *der*
(b) (Phys., Astron.) Gravitation, *die;*
Schwerkraft, *die*
gravy /'greɪvɪ/ *n.* **(a)** (juices) Bratensaft, *der*
(b) (dressing) [Braten]soße, *die*
gravy: ~ boat *n.* Sauciere, *die;*
Soßenschüssel, *die;* ~ **train** *n.* **ride/board
the ~ train** (coll.) leichtes Geld machen (ugs.)
gray etc. (Amer.) ▶ GREY etc.
graze[1] /greɪz/ *v.i.* grasen; weiden
graze[2] 1 *n.* Schürfwunde, *die*
2 *v.t.* **(a)** (touch lightly) streifen
(b) (scrape) abschürfen ⟨Haut⟩; zerkratzen
⟨Oberfläche⟩
grease /griːs/ 1 *n.* Fett, *das;* (lubricant)
Schmierfett, *das*
2 *v.t.* einfetten; (lubricate) schmieren
'**greaseproof** *adj.* fettdicht; ~ **paper**
Pergament- *od.* Butterbrotpapier, *das*

greasy /'griːsɪ/ *adj.* fettig; fett ⟨*Essen*⟩; (lubricated) geschmiert; (dirty with lubricant) schmierig

great /greɪt/ *adj.* **(a)** groß; **a ~ many** sehr viele; sehr gut ⟨*Freund*⟩; (impressive; coll.: splendid) großartig; **be a ~ one for sth.** etw. sehr gern tun
(b) Groß⟨*onkel, -tante, -neffe, -nichte*⟩; Ur⟨*großmutter, -großvater, -enkel, -enkelin*⟩

great: G~ 'Bear *n.* (Astron.) Großer Bär; **G~ 'Britain** *pr. n.* Großbritannien (*das*)

'greatly *adv.* sehr; höchst ⟨*verärgert*⟩; stark ⟨*beeinflusst*⟩; bedeutend ⟨*verbessert*⟩

'greatness *n.* Größe, *die*

Great 'War *n.* Erster Weltkrieg

Greece /griːs/ *pr. n.* Griechenland (*das*)

greed /griːd/ *n.* Gier, *die* (**for** nach); (gluttony) Gefräßigkeit, *die*

'greedy *adj.* gierig; (gluttonous) gefräßig

Greek /griːk/ ① *adj.* griechisch; **sb. is ~:** jmd. ist Grieche/Griechin
② *n.* **(a)** (person) Grieche, *der*/Griechin, *die* **(b)** (language) Griechisch, *das; see also* ENGLISH 2A

green /griːn/ ① *adj.* **(a)** grün **(b)** (environmentally safe) ökologisch; **~ electricity** Ökostrom, *der* **(c)** (gullible) naiv; (inexperienced) grün **(d)** (Polit.) **G~:** grün; **the G~s** die Grünen ② *n.* **(a)** (colour) Grün, *das* **(b)** (piece of land) Grünfläche, *die;* **village ~:** Dorfanger, *der* **(c)** *in pl.* (~ vegetables) Grüngemüse, *das*

green: ~ belt *n.* Grüngürtel, *der;* **~ 'card** *n.* (Motor Veh.) grüne Karte

greenery /'griːnərɪ/ *n.* Grün, *das*

green: ~fly *n.* (Brit.) grüne Blattlaus; **~gage** /'griːngeɪdʒ/ *n.* Reineclaude, *die;* **~grocer** *n.* (Brit.) Obst- und Gemüsehändler, *der/*-händlerin, *die*

'greenhouse *n.* Gewächshaus, *das*

greenhouse: ~ effect *n.* Treibhauseffekt, *der;* **~ gas** *n.* Treibhausgas, *das*

green: ~ light *n.* **(a)** grünes Licht; (as signal) Grün, *das;* **(b)** (fig.) **give sb./get the ~:** jmdm. grünes Licht geben/grünes Licht erhalten; **G~ Party** *n.* (Polit.) die Grünen *Pl.*

greet /griːt/ *v.t.* begrüßen; (in passing) grüßen; (receive) empfangen

'greeting *n.* Begrüßung, *die;* (in passing) Gruß, *der;* (words) Grußformel, *die*

'greetings card *n.* Grußkarte, *die;* (for birthday) Glückwunschkarte, *die*

gregarious /grɪ'geərɪəs/ *adj.* gesellig

grenade /grɪ'neɪd/ *n.* Granate, *die*

grew ▶ GROW

grey /greɪ/ ① *adj.* grau ② *n.* Grau, *das*

grey: ~-haired *adj.* grauhaarig; **~hound** *n.* Windhund, *der;* **~hound**

racing *n.* Windhundrennen, *das*

greyish /'greɪɪʃ/ *adj.* gräulich

grid /grɪd/ *n.* **(a)** (grating) Rost, *der* **(b)** (of lines) Gitter[netz], *das* **(c)** (for supply) Versorgungsnetz, *das*

grid: ~lock *n.* Verkehrsinfarkt, *der;* (fig.) völliger Stillstand; **~locked** /'grɪdlɒkt/ *adj.* total verstopft ⟨*Straße, Stadt*⟩; (fig.) festgefahren

grief /griːf/ *n.* Kummer, *der* (**over, at** über + *Akk.,* um); (at loss of sb.) Trauer, *die* (**for** um); **come to ~** (fail) scheitern

'grief-stricken *adj.* untröstlich (**at** über + *Akk.*)

grievance /'griːvəns/ *n.* (complaint) Beschwerde, *die;* (grudge) Groll, *der*

grieve /griːv/ ① *v.t.* betrüben; bekümmern ② *v.i.* trauern (**for** um)

grievous /'griːvəs/ *adj.* schwer ⟨*Verwundung, Krankheit;*⟩ **~ bodily harm** (Law) schwere Körperverletzung

grill¹ /grɪl/ ① *v.t.* (cook) grillen; (fig.: question) in die Mangel nehmen (ugs.) ② *n.* **(a)** **mixed ~:** gemischte Grillplatte **(b)** (on cooker) Grill, *der*

grille (grill²) *n.* **(a)** Gitter, *das* **(b)** (Motor Veh.) [Kühler]grill, *der*

grim /grɪm/ *adj.* (stern) streng; grimmig ⟨*Lächeln, Schweigen*⟩; (unrelenting) erbittert ⟨*Widerstand, Kampf*⟩; (ghastly) grauenvoll ⟨*Aufgabe, Nachricht*⟩; trostlos ⟨*Aussichten*⟩

grimace /grɪ'meɪs/ ① *n.* Grimasse, *die* ② *v.i.* Grimassen schneiden; **~ with pain** vor Schmerz das Gesicht verziehen

grime /graɪm/ *n.* Schmutz, *der*

grimy /'graɪmɪ/ *adj.* schmutzig

grin /grɪn/ ① *n.* Grinsen, *das* ② *v.i.,* **-nn-** grinsen; **~ at sb.** jmdn. angrinsen

grind /graɪnd/ ① *v.t.,* **ground** /graʊnd/ **(a)** **~ [up]** zermahlen; mahlen ⟨*Kaffee, Pfeffer, Getreide*⟩ **(b)** (sharpen) schleifen ⟨*Schere, Messer*⟩; schärfen ⟨*Klinge*⟩ **(c)** (rub harshly) zerquetschen; **~ one's teeth** mit den Zähnen knirschen ② *v.i.,* **ground:** **~ to a halt** ⟨*Fahrzeug:*⟩ quietschend zum Stehen kommen; (fig.) ⟨*Verkehr:*⟩ zum Erliegen kommen ③ *n.* (coll.) Plackerei, *die* (ugs.)

'grinder *n.* Schleifmaschine, *die;* (coffee ~ etc.) Mühle, *die*

'grindstone *n.* Schleifstein, *der*

grip /grɪp/ ① *n.* **(a)** (firm hold) Halt, *der;* (fig.: power) Umklammerung, *die;* **have a ~ on sth.** etw. festhalten; (fig.) etwas im Griff haben; **loosen one's ~:** loslassen; **lose one's ~** (fig.) nachlassen **(b)** (strength or way of ~ping) Griff, *der* ② *v.t.,* **-pp-** [fest] halten; ⟨*Reifen:*⟩ greifen; (fig.) fesseln ⟨*Publikum, Aufmerksamkeit*⟩ ③ *v.i.,* **-pp-** ⟨*Räder, Bremsen usw.:*⟩ greifen

gripe /graɪp/ *v.i.* (coll.) meckern (ugs.) (**about** über + *Akk.*)

gripping /ˈgrɪpɪŋ/ *adj.* (fig.) packend

grisly /ˈgrɪzlɪ/ *adj.* grausig

gristle /ˈgrɪsl/ *n.* Knorpel, *der*

grit /grɪt/ ① *n.* (a) Sand, *der*
(b) (coll.: courage) Schneid, *der* (ugs.)
② *v.t.*, **-tt-:** (a) streuen ⟨*Straßen*⟩
(b) ~ one's teeth die Zähne zusammenbeißen (ugs.)

grizzly /ˈgrɪzlɪ/ *n.* ~ [**bear**] Grislybär, *der*

groan /grəʊn/ ① *n.* Stöhnen, *das;* (of thing) Ächzen, *das*
② *v.i.* [auf]stöhnen (**at** bei); ⟨*Tisch, Planken:*⟩ ächzen
③ *v.t.* stöhnen

grocer /ˈgrəʊsə(r)/ *n.* Lebensmittelhändler, *der*/-händlerin, *die*

grocery /ˈgrəʊsərɪ/ *n.* (a) *in pl.* (goods) Lebensmittel *Pl.*
(b) ~ [**store**] Lebensmittelgeschäft, *das*

groggy /ˈgrɒgɪ/ *adj.* groggy *präd.* (ugs.)

groin /grɔɪn/ *n.* Leistengegend, *die*

groom /gruːm, grʊm/ ① *n.* (a) (stable boy) Stallbursche, *der*
(b) (bride~) Bräutigam, *der*
② *v.t.* striegeln ⟨*Pferd*⟩; (fig.) vorbereiten (**for** auf + *Akk.*)

groove /gruːv/ *n.* Rille, *die*

grope /grəʊp/ *v.i.* tasten (**for** nach)

gross¹ /grəʊs/ *adj.* (a) (flagrant) grob ⟨*Fahrlässigkeit, Fehler*⟩
(b) (obese) fett
(c) (total) Brutto-

gross² *n., pl. same* Gros, *das*

'grossly *adj.* (flagrantly) äußerst; grob ⟨*übertreiben*⟩

grotesque /grəʊˈtesk/ *adj.* grotesk

grotto /ˈgrɒtəʊ/ *n., pl.* ~es *or* ~s Grotte, *die*

grotty /ˈgrɒtɪ/ *adj.* (Brit. coll.) mies (ugs.)

ground¹ /graʊnd/ ① *n.* (a) Boden, *der;* **get off the** ~ (coll.) konkrete Gestalt annehmen
(b) [**sports**] ~: Sportplatz, *der*
(c) *in pl.* (attached to house) Anlage, *die*
(d) (reason) Grund, *der;* **on the** ~[**s**] **of** auf Grund (+ *Gen.*); **on the** ~[**s**] **that** …: unter Berufung auf die Tatsache, dass …
(e) *in pl.* (sediment) Satz, *der*
② *v.t.* (Aeronaut.) am Boden festhalten

ground² ① ▸ GRIND 1, 2
② *adj.* gemahlen ⟨*Kaffee, Getreide*⟩

ground: ~ **control** *n.* (Aeronaut.: personnel, equipment, etc.;) Flugsicherungskontrolldienst, *der;*
~ **'floor** ▸ FLOOR 1B; ~ **forces** *n. pl.* Bodentruppen *Pl.;* ~ **frost** *n.* Bodenfrost, *der*

'grounding *n.* Grundkenntnisse *Pl.*

'groundless *adj.* unbegründet

ground: ~**sheet** *n.* Bodenplane, *die;*
~**sman** /ˈgraʊndzmən/ *n., pl.* **-smen**

/ˈgraʊndzmən/ (Sport) Platzwart, *der;*
~**work** *n.* Vorarbeiten *Pl.;* ~ **'zero** *n.* [Boden]nullpunkt, *der*

group /gruːp/ ① *n.* Gruppe, *die*
② *v.t.* gruppieren

group: ~ **practice** *n.* Gemeinschaftspraxis, *die;* ~ **therapy** *n.* Gruppentherapie, *die*

grouse¹ /graʊs/ *n., pl. same* Raufußhuhn, *das;* [**red**] ~ (Brit.) Schottisches Moorschneehuhn

grouse² *v.i.* (coll.) meckern (ugs.)

grove /grəʊv/ *n.* Wäldchen, *das*

grovel /ˈgrɒvl/ *v.i.*, (Brit.) **-ll-** (fig.) katzbuckeln

grow /grəʊ/ ① *v.i.*, grew /gruː/, grown /grəʊn/ (a) wachsen; ~ **out of** *or* **from** sth. sich aus etw. entwickeln; (from sth. abstract) von etw. herrühren; ~ **in** gewinnen an (+ *Dat.*) ⟨*Größe, Bedeutung*⟩
(b) (become) werden; ~ **apart** (fig.) sich auseinander leben; ~ **to love/hate** sb./sth. jmdn. lieben lernen/hassen lernen; ~ **to like** sb./sth. nach und nach Gefallen an jmdm./etw. finden
② *v.t.*, grew, grown ziehen; (on a large scale) anpflanzen; züchten ⟨*Blumen*⟩
■ **grow 'up** *v.i.* (a) aufwachsen; (become adult) erwachsen werden
(b) ⟨*Legende:*⟩ entstehen

growl /graʊl/ ① *n.* Knurren, *das;* (of bear) Brummen, *das*
② *v.i.* knurren; ⟨*Bär:*⟩ [böse] brummen

grown /grəʊn/ ① ▸ GROW
② *adj.* erwachsen

'grown-up ① *n.* Erwachsene, *der/die*
② *adj.* erwachsen

growth /grəʊθ/ *n.* (a) Wachstum, *das* (**of, in** *Gen.*); (increase) Zunahme, *die* (**of, in** *Gen.*)
(b) (Med.) Gewächs, *das*

growth: ~ **area** *n.* Wachstumsbereich, *der;* ~ **industry** *n.* Wachstumsindustrie, *die;* ~ **rate** *n.* Wachstumsrate, *die*

grub /grʌb/ *n.* (a) Larve, *die;* (maggot) Made, *die*
(b) (coll.: food) Fressen, *das* (salopp)

grubby /ˈgrʌbɪ/ *adj.* schmudd[e]lig (ugs.)

grudge /grʌdʒ/ ① *v.t.* ~ sb. sth. jmdm. etw. missgönnen; ~ **doing** sth. etw. ungern tun
② *n.* Groll, *der;* **bear** sb. a. ~ *or* a ~ **against** sb. jmdm. gegenüber nachtragend sein

grudging /ˈgrʌdʒɪŋ/ *adj.* widerwillig; widerwillig gewährt ⟨*Zuschuss*⟩

'grudgingly *adv.* widerwillig

gruelling (*Amer.:* **grueling**) /ˈgruːəlɪŋ/ *adj.* aufreibend; strapaziös ⟨*Reise*⟩

gruesome /ˈgruːsəm/ *adj.* grausig

gruff /grʌf/ *adj.* barsch; rau ⟨*Stimme*⟩

grumble /ˈgrʌmbl/ *v.i.* murren; ~ **about** *or* **over** sth. sich über etw. (*Akk.*) beklagen

grumpily /ˈgrʌmpɪlɪ/ *adv.* unleidlich

grumpy /'grʌmpɪ/ *adj.* unleidlich

grunge /grʌndʒ/ *n.* Grunge, *der*

grunt /grʌnt/ ⟦1⟧ *n.* Grunzen, *das*
⟦2⟧ *v.i.* grunzen

guarantee /gærən'tiː/ ⟦1⟧ *v.t.*
(a) garantieren für; [eine] Garantie geben
auf (+ *Akk.*); **the clock is ~d for a year** die
Uhr hat ein Jahr Garantie
(b) (promise) garantieren (ugs.); (ensure)
bürgen für ⟨*Qualität*⟩
⟦2⟧ *n.* (a) (Commerc. etc.) Garantie, *die;*
(document) Garantieschein, *der*
(b) (promise) Garantie, *die* (ugs.); **give sb. a
~ that …:** jmdm. garantieren, dass …

guarantor /'gærəntə(r), gærən'tɔː(r)/ *n.*
Bürge, *der*/Bürgin, *die*

guaranty /'gærəntɪ/ *n.* (basis of security)
Garantie, *die;* Gewähr, *die*

guard /gɑːd/ ⟦1⟧ *n.* (a) (guardsman)
Wachtposten, *der;* (group of soldiers) Wache,
die; **be on ~:** Wache haben; **be on [one's] ~**
(lit. or fig.) sich hüten
(b) (Brit. Railw.) [Zug]schaffner, *der*/
-schaffnerin, *die*
(c) (Amer.: prison warder) [Gefängnis]wärter,
der/-wärterin, *die*
(d) (safety device) Schutz, *der*
⟦2⟧ *v.t.* bewachen; hüten ⟨*Geheimnis*⟩;
schützen ⟨*Leben*⟩; beschützen ⟨*Prominenten*⟩
■ **'guard against** *v.t.* sich hüten vor
(+ *Dat.*); vorbeugen (+ *Dat.*) ⟨*Krankheit,
Irrtum*⟩

guard: ~ **dog** *n.* Wachhund, *der;*
~ **duty** *n.* Wachdienst, *der*

'guarded *adj.* zurückhaltend

guardian /'gɑːdɪən/ *n.* (a) Hüter, *der;*
Wächter, *der*
(b) (Law) Vormund, *der*

guardian 'angel *n.* Schutzengel, *der*

guerrilla /gə'rɪlə/ *n.* Guerillakämpfer,
der/-kämpferin, *die; attrib.* Guerilla-

guess /ges/ ⟦1⟧ *v.t.* (a) (estimate) schätzen;
(surmise) raten; (surmise correctly) erraten;
raten ⟨*Rätsel*⟩; ~ **what!** (coll.) stell dir vor!
(b) (esp. Amer.: suppose) **I ~:** ich glaube
⟦2⟧ *v.i.* (estimate) schätzen; (make assumption)
vermuten; (surmise correctly) es erraten; ~ **at**
sth. etw. schätzen; **keep sb. ~ing** (coll.) jmdn.
im Unklaren lassen
⟦3⟧ *n.* Schätzung, *die;* **make** *or* **have a**
~: schätzen

guesstimate /'gestɪmət/ *n.* (coll.) grobe
Schätzung

'guesswork *n.* **be ~:** eine Vermutung
sein

guest /gest/ *n.* Gast, *der*

guest: ~ **house** *n.* Pension, *die;* ~ **list**
n. Gästeliste, *die;* ~ **room** *n.* Gästezimmer,
das; ~ **worker** *n.* Gastarbeiter, *der*/
-arbeiterin, *die*

guffaw /gʌ'fɔː/ ⟦1⟧ *n.* brüllendes Gelächter
⟦2⟧ *v.i.* brüllend lachen

guidance /'gaɪdəns/ *n.* (a) (leadership)

Führung, *die;* (by teacher etc.) [An]leitung, *die*
(b) (advice) Rat, *der*

guide /gaɪd/ ⟦1⟧ *n.* (a) Führer, *der*/
Führerin, *die;* (Tourism) [Fremden]führer,
der/-führerin, *die*
(b) (indicator) **be a [good]** ~ **to sth.** ein [guter]
Anhaltspunkt für etw. sein; **be no** ~ **to sth.**
keine Rückschlüsse auf etw. (*Akk.*) zulassen
(c) (Brit.) **[Girl] G~:** Pfadfinderin, *die*
(d) (handbook) Handbuch, *das*
(e) (for tourists) [Reise]führer, *der*
⟦2⟧ *v.t.* führen; (fig.) bestimmen ⟨*Handeln,
Urteil*⟩; **be ~d by sth./sb.** sich von
etw./jmdm. leiten lassen

'guidebook *n.* [Reise]führer, *der*

guided 'missile *n.* Lenkflugkörper, *der*

'guide dog *n.* Blinden[führ]hund, *der*

guided 'tour *n.* Führung, *die* (**of** durch)

'guideline *n.* Richtlinie, *die*

guild /gɪld/ *n.* (a) Verein, *der*
(b) (Hist.) Gilde, *die;* Zunft, *die*

guile /gaɪl/ *n.* Hinterlist, *die*

guillotine /'gɪlətiːn/ *n.* Guillotine, *die*

guilt /gɪlt/ *n.* (a) Schuld, *die* (**of, for** an + *Dat.*)
(b) (guilty feeling) Schuldgefühle *Pl.*

'guiltless *adj.* unschuldig (**of** an + *Dat.*)

'guilty *adj.* (a) schuldig; **be** ~ **of murder**
des Mordes schuldig sein; **find sb.** ~**/not**
~ **[of sth.]** jmdn. [an etw. (*Dat.*)] schuldig
sprechen/[von etw.] freisprechen; **feel** ~ ein
schlechtes Gewissen haben
(b) schuldbewusst ⟨*Miene, Blick, Verhalten*⟩;
schlecht ⟨*Gewissen*⟩

guinea: ~**fowl,** ~ **hen** *ns.* Perlhuhn,
das; ~ **pig** *n.* (a) (animal) Meerschweinchen,
das; (b) (fig.: subject of experiment) (person)
Versuchsperson, *die;* Versuchskaninchen,
das (ugs. abwertend); (thing) Versuchsobjekt,
das; **act as** ~ **pig:** Versuchskaninchen
spielen

guise /gaɪz/ *n.* Gestalt, *die;* **in the** ~ **of** in
Gestalt (+ *Gen.*)

guitar /gɪ'tɑː(r)/ *n.* Gitarre, *die*

guitarist /gɪ'tɑːrɪst/ *n.* Gitarrist,
der/Gitarristin, *die*

gulf /gʌlf/ *n.* (a) (Geog.) Golf, *der*
(b) (wide gap) Kluft, *die*

gull /gʌl/ *n.* Möwe, *die*

gullet /'gʌlɪt/ *n.* (a) Speiseröhre, *die*
(b) (throat) Kehle, *die*

gullible /'gʌlɪbl/ *adj.* leichtgläubig

gully /'gʌlɪ/ *n.* (artificial channel) Abzugsrinne,
die; (drain) Gully, *der*

gulp /gʌlp/ ⟦1⟧ *v.t.* hinunterschlingen;
hinuntergießen ⟨*Getränk*⟩
⟦2⟧ *n.* (a) Schlucken, *das*
(b) (large mouthful of drink) kräftiger Schluck
■ **gulp 'down** *v.t.* hinunterschlingen;
hinuntergießen ⟨*Getränk*⟩

gum¹ /gʌm/ *n.* (Anat.) ~[s] Zahnfleisch, *das*

gum² ⟦1⟧ *n.* (a) Gummi, *das;* (glue)
Klebstoff, *der* ⋯▷

(b) (Amer.) ▶ CHEWING GUM
2 *v.t.*, **-mm-: (a)** (smear with ∼) mit Klebstoff bestreichen; gummieren ⟨*Briefmarken, Etiketten usw.*⟩
(b) (fasten with ∼) kleben

'**gumboot** *n.* Gummistiefel, *der*

gumption /'gʌmpʃn/ *n.* (coll.) Grips, *der*

gun /gʌn/ *n.* Schusswaffe, *die;* (rifle) Gewehr, *das;* (pistol) Pistole, *die;* (revolver) Revolver, *der*

■ **gun** '**down** *v.t.* niederschießen

gun: ∼**fight** *n.* (Amer. coll.) Schießerei, *die;* ∼**fire** *n.* Geschützfeuer, *das;* ∼ **laws** *pl.* Waffengesetze *Pl.;* ∼**man** /'gʌnmən/ *n., pl.* ∼**men** /'gʌnmən/ bewaffneter Mann; ∼**powder** *n.* Schießpulver, *das;* ∼**shot** *n.* Schuss, *der;* ∼**shot wound** Schusswunde, *die;* ∼**smith** *n.* Büchsenmacher, *der*

gurgle /'gɜːgl/ 1 *n.* Gluckern, *das;* (of brook) Plätschern, *das*
2 *v.i.* gluckern; ⟨*Bach:*⟩ plätschern; ⟨*Baby:*⟩ lallen; (with delight) glucksen

guru /'gʊruː/ *n.* Guru, *der*

gush /gʌʃ/ 1 *n.* Schwall, *der*
2 *v.i.* **(a)** strömen; ∼ **out** herausströmen
(b) (fig.: enthuse) schwärmen

'**gushing** *adj.* **(a)** reißend ⟨*Strom*⟩
(b) (effusive) exaltiert

gust /gʌst/ *n.* ∼ **[of wind]** Bö[e], *die*

gusto /'gʌstəʊ/ *n.* Genuss, *der;* (vitality) Schwung, *der*

'**gusty** *adj.* böig

gut /gʌt/ 1 *n.* **(a)** (material) Darm, *der*
(b) *in pl.* (bowels) Eingeweide *Pl.;* Gedärme *Pl.*
(c) *in pl.* (coll.: courage) Schneid, *der* (ugs.)
2 *v.t.*, **-tt-: (a)** (remove ∼s of) ausnehmen
(b) (remove fittings from) ausräumen; **the house**

was ∼**ted [by fire]** das Haus brannte aus
3 *attrib. adj.* ∼ **feeling** instinktives Gefühl; **have a** ∼ **feeling that** ... es im Gefühl *od.* (salopp) Urin haben, dass ...

gutter /'gʌtə(r)/ *n.* (below edge of roof) Dachrinne, *die;* (at side of street) Rinnstein, *der;* Gosse, *die*

'**guttering** *n.* (on roof) Dachrinnen *Pl.*

gutter '**press** *n.* Sensationspresse, *die*

guttural /'gʌtərl/ *adj.* guttural; kehlig

guy /gaɪ/ *n.* **(a)** (coll.: man) Typ, *der* (ugs.)
(b) *in pl.* (Amer.: everyone) **[listen,] you** ∼**s!** [hört mal,] Kinder! (ugs.)

'**guy rope** *n.* Zelt[spann]leine, *die*

guzzle /'gʌzl/ 1 *v.t.* (eat) hinunterschlingen; (drink) hinuntergießen
2 *v.i.* schlingen

gym /dʒɪm/ *n.* (coll.) **(a)** (gymnasium) Turnhalle, *die*
(b) (gymnastics) Turnen, *das*

gymnasium *n.* /dʒɪm'neɪzɪəm/ *n., pl.* ∼**s** *or* **gymnasia** /dʒɪm'neɪzɪə/ Turnhalle, *die*

gymnast /'dʒɪmnæst/ *n.* Turner, *der*/Turnerin, *die*

gymnastic /dʒɪm'næstɪk/ *adj.* turnerisch ⟨*Können*⟩; ∼ **equipment** Turngeräte *Pl.*

gymnastics /dʒɪm'næstɪks/ *n.* Gymnastik, *die;* (esp. with apparatus) Turnen, *das*

'**gymslip** *n.* Trägerrock, *der*

gynaecologist /gaɪnɪ'kɒlədʒɪst/ *n.* Frauenarzt, *der*/-ärztin, *die*

gynaecology /gaɪnɪ'kɒlədʒɪ/ *n.* Gynäkologie, *die*

gypsy, Gypsy /'dʒɪpsɪ/ *n.* Zigeuner, *der*/Zigeunerin, *die*

gyrate /dʒaɪə'reɪt/ *v.i.* sich drehen

Hh

H¹, h /eɪtʃ/ *n.* H, h, *das*

haberdashery /'hæbədæʃərɪ/ *n.* (goods) Kurzwaren *Pl.;* (Amer.: menswear) Herrenmoden *Pl.*

habit /'hæbɪt/ *n.* **(a)** Gewohnheit, *die;* **good/bad** ∼: gute/schlechte [An]gewohnheit; **get** *or* **fall into a** *or* **the** ∼ **of doing sth.** [es] sich (*Dat.*) angewöhnen, etw. zu tun
(b) (coll.: addiction) Süchtigkeit, *die*

habitable /'hæbɪtəbl/ *adj.* bewohnbar

habitat /'hæbɪtæt/ *n.* Habitat, *das*

habitation /hæbɪ'teɪʃn/ *n.* **fit/unfit for human** ∼: bewohnbar/unbewohnbar

habitual /hə'bɪtjʊəl/ *adj.* **(a)** gewohnt
(b) (given to habit) gewohnheitsmäßig;

Gewohnheits⟨*trinker*⟩

ha·bitually *adv.* (regularly) regelmäßig

hack¹ /hæk/ *v.t.* **(a)** hacken ⟨*Holz*⟩; ∼ **sth. to bits** *or* **pieces** etw. in Stücke hacken
(b) (Comp.) eindringen in (+ *Akk.*) ⟨*Computersystem*⟩; ∼ **into sth.** in etw. (*Akk.*) eindringen

■ **hack** '**off** *v.t.* abhacken

■ **hack** '**out** *v.t.* heraushauen (**from** aus)

hack² *n.* (derog.: writer) Schreiberling, *der*

hacker /'hækə(r)/ *n.* (Comp.) Hacker, *der*

hackneyed /'hæknɪd/ *adj.* abgegriffen; abgedroschen (ugs.)

'**hacksaw** *n.* [Metall]bügelsäge, *die*

had ▶ HAVE

haddock /'hædək/ *n., pl. same* Schellfisch, *der*

hadn't /'hædnt/ (coll.) = had not; ▶ HAVE

haemoglobin /hiːmə'gləʊbɪn/ *n.* Hämoglobin, *das*

haemophilia /hiːmə'fɪlɪə/ *n.* Hämophilie, *die* (fachspr.); Bluterkrankheit, *die*

haemophiliac /hiːmə'fɪlɪæk/ *n.* Bluter, *der*/Bluterin, *die*

haemorrhage /'hemərɪdʒ/ *n.* Blutung, *die*

haemorrhoid /'hemərɔɪd/ *n.* Hämorrhoide, *die*

hag /hæg/ *n.* [alte] Hexe

haggard /'hægəd/ *adj.* ausgezehrt; (with worry) abgehärmt

haggle /'hægl/ *v.i.* sich zanken (**over, about** wegen); (over price) feilschen (**over, about** um)

Hague /heɪg/ *pr. n.* **The** ∼: Den Haag (*das*)

hail¹ /heɪl/ **1** *n.* Hagel, *der* **2** *v.i.* it ∼s or is hageIt; ∼ **down** (fig.) niederprasseln (**on** auf + *Akk.*)

hail² *v.t.* **(a)** (call out to) anrufen; (signal to) anhalten ⟨*Taxi*⟩ **(b)** (acclaim) zujubeln (+ *Dat.*); bejubeln (**as** als)

'hailstone *n.* Hagelkorn, *das*

hair /heə(r)/ *n.* **(a)** (one strand) Haar, *das* **(b)** collect. Haar, *das;* Haare *Pl.; attrib.* Haar-; **have** *or* **get one's** ∼ **done** sich (*Dat.*) das Haar *od.* die Haare machen lassen (ugs.)

hair: ∼**brush** *n.* Haarbürste, *die;* ∼ **conditioner** *n.* Pflegespülung, *die;* ∼ **cream** *n.* Haarcreme, *die;* Pomade, *die;* ∼ **curler** *n.* Lockenwickler, *der;* ∼**cut** *n.* **(a)** (act) Haareschneiden, *das;* **go for/need a** ∼**cut** zum Friseur gehen/müssen; **get/have a** ∼**cut** sich (*Dat.*) die Haare schneiden lassen; **(b)** (style) Haarschnitt, *der;* ∼**do** *n.* (style) Frisur, *die;* ∼**dresser** *n.* Friseur, *der*/Friseurin, *die;* **go to the** ∼**dresser's** zum Friseur gehen; ∼ **dye** *n.* Haarfärbemittel, *das;* ∼**grip** *n.* (Brit.) Haarklammer, *die;* ∼**line** *n.* **(a)** (edge of hair) Haaransatz, *der;* **his** ∼**line is receding, he has a receding** ∼**line** er bekommt eine Stirnglatze; **(b)** (crack) Haarriss ∼**line fracture** (Med.) Fissur, *die;* ∼**pin** *n.* Haarnadel, *die;* ∼**pin 'bend** *n.* Haarnadelkurve, *die;* ∼**-raising** /'heəreɪzɪŋ/ *adj.* haarsträubend; ∼**spray** *n.* Haarspray, *das;* ∼**style** *n.* Frisur, *die*

'hairy *adj.* **(a)** behaart; flauschig ⟨*Pullover, Teppich*⟩ **(b)** (coll.: difficult) haarig

hale /heɪl/ *adj.* ∼ **and hearty** gesund und munter

half /hɑːf/ **1** *n., pl.* **halves** /hɑːvz/ **(a)** Hälfte, *die;* ∼ **[of sth.]** die Hälfte [von etw.]; ∼ **of Europe** halb Europa; **one and a** ∼ **hours, one hour and a** ∼: anderthalb *od.* eineinhalb Stunden; **divide sth. in** ∼ *or* **into halves** etw. halbieren; **she is three and a** ∼:

sie ist dreieinhalb **(b)** (Footb. etc.: period) Halbzeit, *die* **2** *adj.* halb; ∼ **the house/books/time** die Hälfte des Hauses/der Bücher/der Zeit; ∼ **an hour** eine halbe Stunde **3** *adv.* **(a)** zur Hälfte; halb ⟨*schließen, aufessen, fertig, voll, geöffnet*⟩; (almost) fast ⟨*ersticken, tot sein*⟩; ∼ **as much/many** halb so viel/viele; **only** ∼ **hear what** ...: nur zum Teil hören, was ... **(b)** ∼ **past** *or* (coll.) ∼ **one/two/three** *etc.* halb zwei/drei/vier *usw.;* ∼ **past twelve** halb eins

half: ∼**'board** *n.* Halbpension, *die;* ∼**-caste** *n.* Mischling, *der;* ∼**-'hearted** *adj.* halbherzig; ∼**-'hour** *n.* halbe Stunde; ∼ **'mast** *n.* **be [flown] at** ∼ **mast** auf Halbmast stehen; ∼ **'moon** *n.* Halbmond, *der;* ∼ **note** *n.* (Amer. Mus.) halbe Note; ∼**-'price** **1** *n.* halber Preis; **2** *adj.* zum halben Preis *nachgestellt;* **3** *adv.* zum halben Preis; ∼**-'term** *n.* (Brit.) (holiday) ∼**-term [holiday/break]** Ferien in der Mitte des Trimesters; ∼**-'time** *n.* (Sport) Halbzeit, *die;* ∼**-'way** **1** *adj.* ∼**-way point** Mitte, *die;* **2** *adv.* die Hälfte des Weges ⟨*begleiten, fahren*⟩; ∼**wit** *n.* Schwachkopf, *der;* (scatterbrain) Schussel, *der*

halibut /'hælɪbət/ *n., pl. same* Heilbutt, *der*

hall /hɔːl/ *n.* **(a)** Saal, *der;* (building) Halle, *die;* **school/church** ∼: Aula, *die*/Gemeindehaus, *das* **(b)** (entrance ∼) Flur, *der* **(c)** (Univ.) ∼ **[of residence]** Studentenwohnheim, *das*

'hallmark *n.* [Feingehalts]stempel, *der;* (fig.) Kennzeichen, *das*

hallo /hə'ləʊ/ *int.* **(a)** (to call attention) hallo **(b)** (Brit.) ▶ HELLO

Hallowe'en /hæləʊ'iːn/ *n.* Halloween, *das; Abend vor Allerheiligen*

hallucination /həluːsɪ'neɪʃn/ *n.* Halluzination, *die*

hallucinogen /hə'luːsɪnədʒen/ *n.* (Med.) Halluzinogen, *das*

hallucinogenic /həluːsɪnə'dʒenɪk/ *adj.* (Med.) halluzinogen

'hallway *n.* Flur, *der*

halo /'heɪləʊ/ *n., pl.* ∼**es** Heiligenschein, *der*

halt /hɒlt, hɔːlt/ **1** *n.* **(a)** Pause, *die;* (interruption) Unterbrechung, *die;* **call a** ∼ **to sth.** mit etw. Schluss machen **(b)** (Brit. Railw.) Haltepunkt, *der* **2** *v.i.* **(a)** stehen bleiben; ⟨*Fahrer:*⟩ anhalten; (for a rest) eine Pause machen; (esp. Mil.) Halt machen; ∼, **who goes there?** (Mil.) halt, wer da? **(b)** (end) eingestellt werden **3** *v.t.* anhalten; einstellen ⟨*Projekt*⟩

'halting *adj.* schleppend; zögernd ⟨*Antwort*⟩

halve /hɑːv/ *v.t.* halbieren

halves *pl. of* HALF

ham /hæm/ *n.* Schinken, *der*
hamburger /'hæmbɜːɡə(r)/ *n.* Hacksteak, *das;* (in roll) Hamburger, *der*
hamlet /'hæmlɪt/ *n.* Weiler, *der*
hammer /'hæmə(r)/ [1] *n.* Hammer, *der*
[2] *v.t.* hämmern
[3] *v.i.* hämmern (**at** an + *Dat.*)
■ **hammer 'out** *v.t.* ausklopfen ⟨Delle, Beule⟩; (fig.: devise) ausarbeiten
hammock /'hæmək/ *n.* Hängematte, *die*
hamper[1] /'hæmpə(r)/ *n.* [Deckel]korb, *der*
hamper[2] *v.t.* behindern
hamster /'hæmstə(r)/ *n.* Hamster, *der*
'hamstring [1] *n.* (Anat.) Kniesehne, *die*
[2] *vt.* (fig.) lähmen
hand /hænd/ [1] *n.* (a) Hand, *die;* **by** ∼ (manually) mit der *od.* von Hand; **give** *or* **lend [sb.] a** ∼ **[with** *or* **in sth.]** [jmdm.] [bei etw.] helfen
(b) (share) **have a** ∼ **in sth.** bei etw. seine Hände im Spiel haben
(c) (worker) Arbeiter, *der;* (Naut.: seaman) Matrose, *der*
(d) (of clock or watch) Zeiger, *der*
(e) **at** ∼: in der Nähe; **on the one** ∼ ..., **[but] on the other [∼]** ...: einerseits ..., andererseits ...
(f) (Cards) Karte, *die*
[2] *v.t.* geben; ⟨Überbringer:⟩ übergeben ⟨Sendung, Lieferung⟩
■ **hand 'in** *v.t.* abgeben (**to, at** bei); einreichen ⟨Petition⟩
■ **hand 'out** *v.t.* austeilen
■ **hand 'over** *v.t.* übergeben (**to** *Dat.*)
hand: ∼**bag** *n.* Handtasche, *die;* ∼ **baggage** *n.* Handgepäck, *das;* ∼**book** *n.* Handbuch, *das;* ∼**brake** *n.* Handbremse, *die;* ∼**cuff** [1] *n., usu. in pl.* Handschelle, *die;* [2] *v.t.* ∼**cuff sb.** jmdm. Handschellen anlegen
handful /'hændfʊl/ *n.* Handvoll, *die;* **be a** ∼: (fig. coll.) einen ständig auf Trab halten (ugs.)
hand: ∼ **grenade** *n.* Handgranate, *die;* ∼**gun** *n.* Faustfeuerwaffe, *die;* ∼**-held** *adj.* ∼**-held camera** Handkamera, *die*
handicap /'hændɪkæp/ [1] *n.* (a) (Sport, also fig.) Handikap, *das*
(b) (physical) Behinderung, *die*
[2] *v.t., -pp-* benachteiligen
handicapped /'hændɪkæpt/ *adj.* **[mentally/physically]** ∼: [geistig/körperlich] behindert
handicraft /'hændɪkrɑːft/ *n.* [Kunst]handwerk, *das;* (needlework, knitting, etc.) Handarbeit, *die*
handiwork /'hændɪwɜːk/ *n.* handwerkliche Arbeit; **it's all his own** ∼: das hat er selbst gemacht
handkerchief /'hæŋkətʃɪf/ *n., pl.* ∼**s** *or* **handkerchieves** /'hæŋkətʃiːvz/ Taschentuch, *das*
handle /'hændl/ [1] *n.* Griff, *der;* (of

door) Klinke, *die;* (of axe, brush, comb, broom, saucepan) Stiel, *der;* (of cup, jug) Henkel, *der*
[2] *v.t.* (a) (touch, feel) anfassen
(b) (control) handhaben ⟨Fahrzeug, Flugzeug⟩
(c) (deal/cope with) umgehen/fertig werden mit
'handlebars *n. pl.* Lenkstange, *die*
'handling charge /'hændlɪŋ/ *n.* (Commerc.) Bearbeitungsgebühr, *die*
hand: ∼ **lotion** *n.* Handlotion, *die;* ∼ **luggage** *n.* Handgepäck, *das;* ∼**made** *adj.* handgearbeitet; ∼**over** *n.* Übergabe, *die;* ∼**-painted** *adj.* handbemalt; ∼**-picked** *adj.* sorgfältig ausgewählt; ∼**s-free** *adj.* Freisprech⟨einrichtung, -betrieb⟩; ∼**s-free kit** Freisprechanlage, *die;* Freisprecheinrichtung, *die;* ∼**shake** *n.* Händedruck, *der*
handsome /'hænsəm/ *adj.* gut aussehend
hand: ∼**s-'on** *adj.* praktisch; ∼**stand** *n.* Handstand, *der;* ∼ **towel** *n.* [Hände]handtuch, *das;* ∼**writing** *n.* [Hand]schrift, *die;* ∼**written** *adj.* handgeschrieben; handschriftlich
handy /'hændɪ/ *adj.* greifbar; **keep/have sth.** ∼: etw. greifbar haben
'handyman *n.* Handwerker, *der;* **[home]** ∼: Heimwerker, *der*
hang /hæŋ/ [1] *v.t.* (a) *p.t., p.p.* hung /hʌŋ/ hängen; aufhängen ⟨Bild, Gardinen⟩; ankleben ⟨Tapete⟩
(b) *p.t., p.p.* hanged (execute) hängen (**for** wegen); ∼ **oneself** sich erhängen
[2] *v.i.*, hung (a) hängen; ⟨Kleid usw.:⟩ fallen
(b) (be executed) hängen
[3] *n.* **get the** ∼ **of sth.** (coll.) mit etw. klarkommen (ugs.)
■ **hang a'bout, hang a'round** *v.i.*
(a) (loiter) herumlungern (salopp)
(b) (coll.: wait) warten
■ **hang 'on** *v.i.* (a) sich festhalten (**to** an + *Dat.*)
(b) (coll.: wait) warten
(c) ∼ **on to** (coll.: keep) behalten
■ **hang 'out** [1] *v.t.* aufhängen ⟨Wäsche⟩
[2] *v.i.* (a) heraushängen
(b) (coll.) (live) wohnen; (be often present) sich herumtreiben (ugs.)
■ **hang 'up** *v.t.* [1] aufhängen
[2] *v.i.* (Teleph.) auflegen
hangar /'hæŋə(r)/ *n.* Hangar, *der*
'hanger *n.* Bügel, *der*
hang: ∼**-glider** *n.* Hängegleiter, *der;* Drachen, *der;* ∼**-glider pilot** Drachenflieger, *der/*-fliegerin, *die;* ∼**-gliding** *n.* Drachenfliegen, *das*
'hanging [1] *n.* (execution) Hinrichtung, *die* [durch den Strang]
[2] *adj.* ∼ **basket** Hängekorb, *der*
hang: ∼**man** /hæŋmən/ *n., pl.* ∼**men** /hæŋmən/ Henker, *der;* ∼**over** *n.* Kater, *der* (ugs.); ∼**-up** *n.* (coll.) Macke, *die* (ugs.)
hanker /'hæŋkə(r)/ *v.i.* ∼ **after** ein heftiges

Verlangen haben nach

hanky /'hæŋkɪ/ *n.* (coll.) Taschentuch, *das*

Hanover /'hænəʊvə(r)/ *pr. n.* Hannover (*das*)

haphazard /hæp'hæzəd/ *adj.,* **hap'hazardly** *adv.* willkürlich

happen /'hæpn/ *v.i.* geschehen; ‹*Vorhergesagtes:*› eintreffen; ~ **to sb.** jmdm. passieren; ~ **to do sth./be sb.** zufällig etw. tun/jmd. sein; **as it** ~**s** *or* **it so** ~**s I have …:** zufällig habe ich …

'**happening** *n.* Ereignis, *das*

happily /'hæpɪlɪ/ *adv.* (a) glücklich ‹*lächeln*›; vergnügt ‹*spielen, lachen*› (b) (gladly) mit Vergnügen

happiness /'hæpɪnɪs/ *n.* ▶ HAPPY A: Glück, *das;* Heiterkeit, *die;* Zufriedenheit, *die*

happy /'hæpɪ/ *adj.* (a) (joyful) glücklich; heiter ‹*Bild, Veranlagung*›; erfreulich ‹*Erinnerung, Szene*›; froh ‹*Ereignis*›; (contented) zufrieden (b) be ~ to do sth. (glad) etw. gern tun

happy: ~ '**ending** *n.* Happyend, *das;* ~-**go**-'**lucky** *adj.* sorglos

harass /'hærəs/ *v.t.* schikanieren

harassed /'hærəst/ *adj.* geplagt (**with** von); gequält ‹*Blick, Ausdruck*›

'**harassment** *n.* Schikanierung, *die;* **sexual** ~: [sexuelle] Belästigung

harbour (*Brit.; Amer.:* **harbor**) /'hɑːbə(r)/ ① *n.* Hafen, *der;* **in** ~: im Hafen ② *v.t.* Unterschlupf gewähren (+ *Dat.*) ‹*Verbrecher, Flüchtling*›; hegen (geh.) ‹*Groll, Verdacht*›

hard /hɑːd/ ① *adj.* (a) hart; fest ‹*Gelee*›; stark ‹*Regen*›; streng ‹*Frost, Winter*›; gesichert ‹*Beweis, Daten*› (b) (difficult) schwer; **this is** ~ **to believe** das ist kaum zu glauben; **do sth. the** ~ **way** es sich (*Dat.*) bei etw. unnötig schwer machen (c) (strenuous) hart (d) (vigorous) kräftig ‹*Schlag, Stoß, Tritt*› (e) (harsh) hart ② *adv.* (a) (strenuously) hart ‹*arbeiten, trainieren*›; fleißig ‹*studieren, üben*›; genau ‹*überlegen*›; gut ‹*aufpassen, zuhören*›; **try** ~: sich sehr bemühen (b) (vigorously) heftig; fest ‹*schlagen, drücken, klopfen*› (c) (severely) hart; **be** ~ **up** knapp bei Kasse sein (ugs.); **feel** ~ **done by** sich schlecht behandelt fühlen

hard: ~**back** *n.* gebundene Ausgabe; ~**board** *n.* Hartfaserplatte, *die;* ~-**boiled** *adj.* (a) hart gekocht ‹*Ei*›; (b) (tough) hartgesotten; ~ '**cash** *n.* in ~ **cash** in bar ‹*bezahlen*›; ~ **copy** *n.* (Comp.) Hardcopy, *die;* ~-**core** *attrib. adj.* hart ‹*Pornographie*›; ~ **court** *n.* (Tennis) Hartplatz, *der;* ~ '**currency** *n.* harte Währung; ~ '**disk** ▶ DISK A; ~ **drug** *n.* harte Droge; ~-**earned** *adj.* schwer verdient

harden /'hɑːdn/ ① *v.t.* härten; (fig.) abhärten (**to** gegen) ② *v.i.* hart werden; (become confirmed) sich verhärten

hardened /'hɑːdnd/ *adj.* abgehärtet (**to** gegen); hartgesotten ‹*Verbrecher*›

hard: ~ '**hat** *n.* Schutzhelm, *der;* ~-**headed** *adj.* nüchtern; ~-**hearted** *adj.* hartherzig (**towards** gegenüber); ~-'**hitting** *adj.* (fig.) aggressiv ‹*Rede, Politik, Kritik*›; ~ '**labour** *n.* Zwangsarbeit, *die*

hardly /'hɑːdlɪ/ *adv.* kaum; ~ **anyone** *or* **anybody/anything** fast niemand/nichts; ~ **ever** so gut wie nie; ~ **at all** fast überhaupt nicht

'**hardness** *n.* Härte, *die*

hard: ~ **porn** (coll.), ~ **pornography** *ns.* harte Pornographie; harte Pornos *Pl.* (ugs.); ~ '**pressed** *adj.* hart bedrängt; **be** ~ **pressed** große Schwierigkeiten haben; ~ **sell** *n.* aggressive Verkaufsmethoden *Pl.*

'**hardship** *n.* (a) Not, *die;* Elend, *das* (b) (instance) Notlage, *die*

hard: ~ '**shoulder** *n.* (Brit.) Standspur, *die;* ~**ware** *n.* (a) (goods) Eisenwaren *Pl.; attrib.* Eisenwaren‹*geschäft*›; (b) (Comp.) Hardware, *die;* ~-**wearing** *adj.* strapazierfähig; ~**wood** *n.* Hartholz, *das;* ~-**working** *adj.* fleißig

hardy /'hɑːdɪ/ *adj.* abgehärtet; zäh ‹*Rasse*›; winterhart ‹*Pflanze*›

hare /heə(r)/ *n.* Hase, *der*

harem /'hɑːriːm, hɑː'riːm/ *n.* Harem, *der*

hark /hɑːk/ *v.i.* [**just**] ~ **at him** hör ihn dir/hört ihn euch nur an!; ~ **back to** zurückkommen auf (+ *Akk.*)

harm /hɑːm/ ① *n.* Schaden, *der;* **do sb.** ~, **do** ~ **to sb.** jmdm. schaden ② *v.t.* etwas [zuleide] tun (+ *Dat.*); schaden (+ *Dat.*) ‹*Beziehungen, Land, Ruf*›

harmful /'hɑːmfl/ *adj.* schädlich (**to** für)

'**harmless** *adj.* harmlos

harmonica /hɑː'mɒnɪkə/ *n.* Mundharmonika, *die*

harmonious /hɑː'məʊnɪəs/ *adj.* harmonisch

harmonize /'hɑːmənaɪz/ ① *v.t.* aufeinander abstimmen ② *v.i.* harmonieren (**with** mit)

harmony /'hɑːmənɪ/ *n.* Harmonie, *die;* **be in** ~: harmonieren

harness /'hɑːnɪs/ ① *n.* Geschirr, *das* ② *v.t.* anschirren; (fig.) nutzen

harp /hɑːp/ ① *n.* Harfe, *die* ② *v.i.* ~ **on** [**about**] sth. immer wieder von etw. reden; (critically) auf etw. (*Dat.*) herumreiten (salopp)

harpoon /hɑː'puːn/ *n.* Harpune, *die*

harpsichord /'hɑːpsɪkɔːd/ *n.* Cembalo, *das*

harrowing /'hærəʊɪŋ/ *adj.* entsetzlich; grauenhaft ‹*Anblick, Geschichte*›

harsh /hɑ:ʃ/ adj. (a) rau ‹Gewebe, Klima›; schrill ‹Ton, Stimme›; grell ‹Licht›; hart ‹Bedingungen, Leben›
(b) (excessively severe) [sehr] hart; [äußerst] streng ‹Disziplin›; rücksichtslos ‹Tyrann, Herrscher, Politik›

'**harshly** adv. [sehr] hart

harvest /'hɑ:vɪst/ ① n. Ernte, die
② v.t. ernten

harvest 'festival n. Erntedankfest, das

has ▸ HAVE

has-been /'hæzbiːn/ n. (coll.) be a ∼: seine besten Jahre hinter sich haben

hash /hæʃ/ n. (a) (Cookery) Haschee, das
(b) make a ∼ of sth. (coll.) etw. verpfuschen (ugs.)

'**hash browns** n. pl.: Bratkartoffeln mit Zwiebeln; ≈ Rösti mit Zwiebeln

hashish /'hæʃɪʃ/ n. Haschisch, das

hasn't /'hæznt/ = has not; ▸ HAVE

hassle /'hæsl/ (coll.) ① n. Ärger, der
② v.t. schikanieren

haste /heɪst/ n. Eile, die; (rush) Hast, die; make ∼: sich beeilen

hasten /'heɪsn/ ① v.t. beschleunigen
② v.i. eilen

hastily /'heɪstɪlɪ/ adv. (hurriedly) eilig; (rashly) übereilt

hasty /'heɪstɪ/ adj. eilig; flüchtig ‹Skizze, Blick›; (rash) übereilt

hat /hæt/ n. Hut, der

hatch¹ /hætʃ/ n. Luke, die; (serving ∼) Durchreiche, die

hatch² ① v.t. ausbrüten
② v.i. [aus]schlüpfen

■ **hatch 'out** ① v.i. ausschlüpfen
② v.t. ausbrüten

'**hatchback** n. (car) Schräghecklimousine, die

hatchet /'hætʃɪt/ n. Beil, das; bury the ∼ (fig.) das Kriegsbeil begraben

hate /heɪt/ ① n. Hass, der
② v.t. hassen; I ∼ to say this (coll.) ich sage das nicht gern

hateful /'heɪtfl/ adj. abscheulich

'**hate mail** n. hasserfüllte Briefe Pl.

'**hatpin** n. Hutnadel, die

hatred /'heɪtrɪd/ n. Hass, der

hat: ∼**stand** n. Hutständer, der; ∼ **trick** n. Hattrick, der

haughty /'hɔ:tɪ/ adj. hochmütig

haul /hɔ:l/ ① v.i. & t. ziehen
② n. (a) Ziehen, das
(b) (catch) Fang, der; (fig.) Beute, die

haulage /'hɔ:lɪdʒ/ n. Transport, der

haunch /hɔ:ntʃ/ n. sit on one's/its ∼es auf seinem Hinterteil sitzen

haunt /hɔ:nt/ v.t. ∼ a house/castle in einem Haus/Schloss spuken; a ∼ed house ein Haus, in dem es spukt

'**haunting** adj. sehnsüchtig

have ① /hæv/ v.t., pres. he has /hæz,/ p.t. & p.p. had /hæd/ haben; (obtain) bekommen; (take) nehmen; bekommen ‹Kind›;
∼ breakfast/dinner/lunch frühstücken/zu Abend/zu Mittag essen; ∼ a cup of tea eine Tasse Tee trinken; ∼ sb. to stay jmdn. zu Besuch haben; you've had it now (coll.) jetzt ist es aus (ugs.); ∼ a game of football Fußball spielen
② /həv, əv, stressed hæv/ v. aux., he has /həz, əz, stressed hæz/, had /həd, əd, stressed hæd/ I ∼/I had read ich habe/hatte gelesen; I ∼/I had gone ich bin/war gegangen; if I had known …: wenn ich gewusst hätte …; ∼ sth. made etw. machen lassen; ∼ to müssen

■ **have 'on** v.t. (a) (wear) tragen
(b) (Brit. coll.: deceive) ∼ sb. on jmdn. auf den Arm nehmen (ugs.)

■ **have 'out** v.t. (a) ∼ a tooth/one's tonsils out sich (Dat.) einen Zahn ziehen lassen/ sich (Dat.) die Mandeln herausnehmen lassen
(b) ∼ it out with sb. mit jmdm. offen sprechen

haven /'heɪvn/ n. geschützte Anlegestelle, die; (fig.) Zufluchtsort, der

haven't /'hævnt/ = have not; ▸ HAVE

haversack /'hævəsæk/ n. Brotbeutel, der

havoc /'hævək/ n. (a) (devastation) Verwüstungen Pl.; cause or wreak ∼: Verwüstungen anrichten
(b) (confusion) Chaos; play ∼ with sth. etw. völlig durcheinander bringen

hawk¹ /hɔ:k/ n. Falke, der

hawk² v.t. hausieren mit

'**hawker** n. Hausierer, der/Hausiererin, die

hawthorn /'hɔ:θɔ:n/ n. (Bot.) (white) Weißdorn, der; (red) Rotdorn, der

hay /heɪ/ n. Heu, das

hay: ∼ **fever** n. Heuschnupfen, der; ∼**making** n. Heuernte, die; ∼**stack** n. Heuschober, der (südd.); Heudieme, die (nordd.); ∼**wire** adj. (coll.) go ∼wire ‹Instrument:› verrückt spielen (ugs.)

hazard /'hæzəd/ ① n. Gefahr, die
② v.t. ∼ a guess es mit Raten probieren

'**hazard lights** n. pl. Warnblinkanlage, die

hazardous /'hæzədəs/ adj. gefährlich; ∼ waste Sondermüll, der

hazard 'warning lights ▸ HAZARD LIGHTS

haze /heɪz/ n. Dunst[schleier], der

hazel /'heɪzl/ adj. haselnussbraun

hazelnut /'heɪzlnʌt/ n. Haselnuss, die

hazy /'heɪzɪ/ adj. dunstig; (fig.) vage

HDTV abbr. = **high-definition television** HDTV

he /hɪ, stressed hiː/ pron. er

head /hed/ ① n. (a) Kopf, der; ∼ first mit dem Kopf voran; ∼ over heels kopfüber; keep/lose one's ∼: einen klaren Kopf behalten/den Kopf verlieren; in one's ∼: im Kopf; enter sb.'s ∼: jmdm. in den Sinn

kommen; **use your** ∼: gebrauch deinen Verstand; **a** *or* **per** ∼: pro Kopf
(b) *in pl.* (on coin) ∼s Kopf; ∼s **or tails?** Kopf oder Zahl?
(c) (leader) Leiter, *der*/Leiterin, *die*
(d) (on beer) Blume, *die*
2 *attrib. adj.* ∼ **waiter** Oberkellner, *der;* ∼ **office** Hauptverwaltung, *die;* ∼ **boy/girl** ≈ Schulsprecher, *der*/-sprecherin, *die* (*vom Lehrkörper eingesetzt*)
3 *v.t.* **(a)** (stand at top of) anführen ⟨*Liste*⟩; (lead) leiten; führen ⟨*Bewegung*⟩
(b) (Football) köpfen
4 *v.i.* steuern; ∼ **for London** ⟨*Flugzeug, Schiff:*⟩ Kurs auf London nehmen; ⟨*Auto:*⟩ in Richtung London fahren; **you're** ∼**ing for trouble** du wirst Ärger bekommen

head: ∼**ache** n. Kopfschmerzen *Pl.;*
∼**band** n. Stirnband, *das;* ∼**board** n. Kopfende, *das;* ∼ **count** n. Kopfzahl, *die*
'**header** n. (Footb.) Kopfball, *der*
'**headgear** n. Kopfbedeckung, *die*
'**heading** n. Überschrift, *die*
head: ∼**lamp** n. Scheinwerfer, *der;*
∼**land** n. Landspitze, *die;* ∼**light** n. Scheinwerfer, *der;* ∼**line** n. Schlagzeile, *die;* **be** ∼**line news, make [the]** ∼**lines, hit the** ∼**lines** Schlagzeilen machen; ∼**long** *adv.* kopfüber; ∼'**master** n. Schulleiter, *der;* ∼'**mistress** n. Schulleiterin, *die;*
∼ '**office** n. Hauptsitz, *der;* ∼**-on** **1** /'⋯/ *adj.* frontal; Frontal⟨*zusammenstoß*⟩;
2 /-'⋯/ *adv.* frontal; ∼**phones** n. pl. Kopfhörer, *der;* ∼'**quarters** n. sing. *or pl.* Hauptquartier, *das;* ∼**rest** n. Kopfstütze, *die;* ∼**room** n. [lichte] Höhe, *die;* ∼**scarf** n. Kopftuch, *das;*
∼**set** n. Kopfhörer, *der;* ∼**stone** n. **(a)** (gravestone) Grabstein, *der;* **(b)** (of building) Grundstein, *der;* (fig.) Grundpfeiler, *der;*
∼**strong** *adj.* eigensinnig; ∼ '**teacher** ▸ ∼MASTER; ∼MISTRESS; ∼**way** n. **make** ∼**way** Fortschritte machen; ∼ **wind** n. Gegenwind, *der*
heady /'hedɪ/ *adj.* berauschend
heal /hiːl/ **1** *v.t.* heilen
2 *v.i.* ∼ **[up]** [ver]heilen
healer /'hiːlə(r)/ n. (person) Heilkundige, *der*/*die*
health /helθ/ n. Gesundheit, *die;* **in good/ very good** ∼: bei guter/bester Gesundheit; **good** *or* **your** ∼**!** auf deine Gesundheit!
health: ∼ **care** n. Gesundheitsfürsorge, *die;* ∼ **care worker** im Gesundheitswesen Beschäftigte, *der*/*die;* **inadequate** ∼ **care** unzureichende medizinische Versorgung; ∼ **centre** n. Poliklinik, *die;* ∼ **certificate** n. Gesundheitszeugnis, *das;* ∼ **check** n. Gesundheitsuntersuchung, *die;*
∼ **farm** n. Gesundheitsfarm, *die* (ugs.); ∼ **food** n. Reformkost, *die;* ∼ **food shop** Reformhaus, *das;* ∼ **hazard** n. Gesundheitsrisiko, *das*

healthily /'helθɪlɪ/ *adv.* gesund
health: ∼ **insurance** n. Krankenversicherung, *die;* ∼ **resort** n. Kurort, *der;* ∼ **service** n. Gesundheitsdienst, *der;* ∼ **visitor** n. Krankenschwester/-pfleger im Sozialdienst; ∼ **warning** n. Warnhinweis, *der; Hinweis auf die Gesundheitsgefährdung*
healthy /'helθɪ/ *adj.* gesund
heap /hiːp/ **1** n. Haufen, *der;* ∼**s of** (coll.) jede Menge (ugs.)
2 *v.t.* aufhäufen
hear /hɪə(r)/ **1** *v.t.,* **heard** /hɜːd/ **(a)** hören
(b) (understand) verstehen
2 *v.i.,* **heard:** ∼ **about sb./sth.** von jmdm./etw. [etwas] hören; **he wouldn't** ∼ **of it** er wollte nichts davon hören
3 *int.* H∼! H∼! bravo!; richtig!
▪ **hear 'out** *v.t.* ausreden lassen
heard ▸ HEAR 1, 2
'**hearing** n. Gehör, *das;* **be hard of** ∼: schwerhörig sein
'**hearing aid** n. Hörgerät, *das*
hearsay /'hɪəseɪ/ n. Gerücht, *das;* **it's only** ∼: es ist nur ein Gerücht
hearse /hɜːs/ n. Leichenwagen, *der*
heart /hɑːt/ n. (also Cards) Herz, *das;* **by** ∼: auswendig; **at** ∼: im Grunde seines/ ihres Herzens; **take/lose** ∼: Mut schöpfen/ verlieren; **my** ∼ **sank** mein Mut sank; **the** ∼ **of the matter** der wahre Kern der Sache; *see also* CLUB 1C
heart: ∼**ache** n. [seelische] Qual; ∼ **attack** n. Herzanfall, *der;* (fatal) Herzschlag, *der;* ∼**beat** n. Herzschlag, *der;* ∼**breaking** *adj.* herzzerreißend; ∼**broken** *adj.* **she was** ∼**broken** ihr Herz war gebrochen; ∼**burn** n. Sodbrennen, *das;*
∼ **disease** n. Herzkrankheiten *Pl.*
hearten /'hɑːtn/ *v.t.* ermutigen
'**heartening** *adj.* ermutigend
heart: ∼ **failure** n. Herzversagen, *das;* ∼**felt** *adj.* tief empfunden ⟨*Beileid*⟩; aufrichtig ⟨*Dankbarkeit*⟩
hearth /hɑːθ/ n.: Platz vor dem Kamin
'**hearthrug** n. Kaminvorleger, *der*
heartily /'hɑːtɪlɪ/ *adv.* von Herzen; **eat** ∼: tüchtig essen
'**heartless** *adj.* herzlos
heart: ∼ **rate** n. Herzfrequenz, *die;*
∼**-shaped** *adj.* herzförmig;
∼**-throb** n. Idol, *das;* ∼ **transplant** n. Herztransplantation, *die* (fachspr.);
∼**-warming** *adj.* herzerfreuend
hearty /'hɑːtɪ/ *adj.* herzlich; ungeteilt ⟨*Zustimmung*⟩; herzhaft ⟨*Mahlzeit*⟩
heat /hiːt/ **1** n. **(a)** (hotness) Hitze, *die*
(b) (Phys.) Wärme, *die*
(c) (Sport) Vorlauf, *der*
2 *v.t.* heizen
▪ **heat 'up** *v.t.* heiß machen
'**heated** *adj.* (angry) hitzig

'**heater** n. Ofen, der; (for water) Boiler, der
heath /hi:θ/ n. Heide, die
heathen /'hi:ðn/ [1] adj. heidnisch
[2] n. Heide, der/Heidin, die
heather /'heðə(r)/ n. Heidekraut, das
'**heating** n. Heizung, die
heat: ~**proof** adj. feuerfest; ~ **rash**
n. Hitzebläschen Pl.; ~**-resistant**
adj. hitzebeständig; ~**stroke** n.
Hitzschlag, der; ~ **treatment** n. (Med.)
Wärmebehandlung, die; ~**wave** n.
Hitzewelle, die
heave /hi:v/ [1] v.t. (a) heben
(b) (coll.: throw) schmeißen (ugs.)
(c) ~ a sigh aufseufzen
[2] v.i. (pull) ziehen
[3] n. Zug, der
heaven /'hevn/ n. Himmel, der; in ~: im
Himmel; for H~'s sake! um Gottes willen!
'**heavenly** adj. himmlisch
heavily /'hevɪlɪ/ adj. schwer; (to a great
extent) stark; schwer ⟨bewaffnet⟩; tief
⟨schlafen⟩; dicht ⟨bevölkert⟩; smoke/drink
~: ein starker Raucher/Trinker sein; it
rained/snowed ~: es regnete/schneite stark
heavy /'hevɪ/ adj. schwer; unmäßig
⟨Trinken, Rauchen⟩; a ~ smoker/drinker ein
starker Raucher/Trinker; be a ~ sleeper
sehr fest schlafen
heavy: ~**-duty** adj. strapazierfähig
⟨Kleidung, Material⟩; schwer ⟨Werkzeug,
Maschine⟩; ~ '**goods vehicle** n. (Brit.)
Schwerlastwagen, der; ~**-'handed**
adj. (clumsy) ungeschickt ⟨Person⟩;
~ '**industry** n. Schwerindustrie, die;
~ '**metal** n. (a) Schwermetall, das;
(b) (Mus.) Heavy metal, das; ~**weight** n.
Schwergewicht, das
Hebrew /'hi:bru:/ [1] adj. hebräisch
[2] n. (language) Hebräisch, das
heckle /'hekl/ v.t. durch Zwischenrufe
unterbrechen
heckler /'heklə(r)/ n. Zwischenrufer,
der/Zwischenruferin, die
hectic /'hektɪk/ adj. hektisch
he'd /hɪd, stressed hi:d/ (a) = he had;
(b) = he would
hedge /hedʒ/ [1] n. Hecke, die
[2] v.t. ~ one's bets (fig.) nicht alles auf eine
Karte setzen
[3] v.i. sich nicht festlegen
'**hedge clippers** n. pl. Heckenschere, die
hedgehog /'hedʒhɒg/ n. Igel, der
'**hedgerow** n. Hecke, die [als
Feldbegrenzung]
hedonism /'hi:dənɪzm/ n. Hedonismus,
der
hedonist /'hi:dənɪst/ n. Hedonist,
der/Hedonistin, die
heed /hi:d/ [1] v.t. beachten; beherzigen
⟨Rat, Lektion⟩; ~ the danger/risk sich (Dat.)
der Gefahr/des Risikos bewusst sein

[2] n. give or pay ~ to, take ~ of Beachtung
schenken (+ Dat.)
'**heedless** adj. unachtsam; be ~ of sth.
auf etw. (Akk.) nicht achten
heel /hi:l/ n. Ferse, die; (of shoe) Absatz, der;
Achilles' ~ (fig.) Achillesferse, die; down at
~ (fig.) heruntergekommen; take to one's
~s Fersengeld geben (ugs.)
hefty /'heftɪ/ adj. kräftig; (heavy) schwer
height /haɪt/ n. (a) Höhe, die; (of person,
animal, building) Größe, die
(b) (fig.: highest point) Höhepunkt, der
heighten /'haɪtn/ v.t. aufstocken; (fig.)
verstärken
heir /eə(r)/ n. Erbe, der/Erbin, die
heiress /'eərɪs/ n. Erbin, die
heirloom /'eəlu:m/ n. Erbstück, das
held ▸ HOLD² 1, 2
helicopter /'helɪkɒptə(r)/ n.
Hubschrauber, der
helicopter 'gunship n.
Kampfhubschrauber, der
heliport /'helɪpɔ:t/ n. Heliport, der
helium /'hi:lɪəm/ n. Helium, das
hell /hel/ n. (a) Hölle, die
(b) (coll.) [oh] ~! verdammter Mist! (ugs.);
what the ~! ach, zum Teufel! (ugs.); run like
~: wie der Teufel rennen (ugs.)
he'll /hɪl, stressed hi:l/ = he will
hello /hə'ləʊ, he'ləʊ/ int. (greeting) hallo;
(surprise) holla
hell's 'angel n. Rocker, der
helm /helm/ n. (Naut.) Ruder, das
helmet /'helmɪt/ n. Helm, der
help /help/ [1] v.t. (a) ~ sb. [to do sth.]
jmdm. helfen[, etw. zu tun]; can I ~ you? (in
shop) was möchten Sie bitte?
(b) (serve) ~ oneself sich bedienen;
~ oneself to sth. (Dat.) etw. nehmen;
(coll.: steal) etw. mitgehen lassen (ugs.)
(c) (avoid) if I/you can ~ it wenn es irgend zu
vermeiden ist; (remedy) I can't ~ it ich kann
nichts dafür (ugs.); it can't be ~ed es lässt
sich nicht ändern
(d) (refrain from) I can't ~ thinking or can't
~ but think that ...: ich kann mir nicht
helfen, ich glaube, ...; I can't ~ laughing ich
muss einfach lachen
[2] n. Hilfe, die; with the ~ of ...: mit Hilfe ...
(+ Gen.); be of [some]/no/much ~ to sb.
jmdm. eine gewisse/keine/eine große Hilfe
sein
■ **help 'out** [1] v.i. aushelfen
[2] v.t. ~ sb. out jmdm. helfen
'**help desk** n. Help Desk, das (fachspr.);
Auskunftsstelle für Computerbenutzer
'**helper** n. Helfer, der/Helferin, die
helpful /'helpfl/ adj. (willing) hilfsbereit;
(useful) hilfreich; nützlich
'**helping** [1] adj. lend [sb.] a ~ hand [with
sth.] (fig.) [jmdm.] [bei etw.] helfen
[2] n. Portion, die

'helpless *adj.*, **'helplessly** *adv.* hilflos

'helpline *n.* Hotline, *die*

helter-skelter /heltə'skeltə(r)/ *n.* [spiralförmige] Rutschbahn

hem /hem/ **1** *n.* Saum, *der*
2 *v.t.*, -mm- säumen
■ **hem 'in** *v.t.* einschließen; **feel ∼med in** sich eingeengt fühlen

hemisphere /'hemɪsfɪə(r)/ *n.* Halbkugel, *die*

'hemline *n.* Saum, *der*

hemo- (Amer.) ▶ HAEMO-

hemp /hemp/ *n.* Hanf, *der*

hen /hen/ *n.* Huhn, *das;* Henne, *die*

hence /hens/ *adv.* (therefore) daher

hence'forth *adv.* von nun an

henchman /'hentʃmən/ *n., pl.* **henchmen** /'hentʃmən/ Handlanger, *der*

hen: ∼ **party** *n.* (coll.) [Damen]kränzchen, *das;* ∼**pecked** /'henpekt/ *adj.* a ∼ **husband** ein Pantoffelheld, *der* (ugs.)

hepatitis /hepə'taɪtɪs/ *n.* (Med.) Leberentzündung, *die*

her¹ /hə(r), *stressed* hɜː(r)/ *pron.* sie; *as indirect object* ihr; **it was ∼:** sie wars

her² *poss. pron. attr.* ihr

herald /'herəld/ **1** *n.* Herold, *der*
2 *v.t.* ankündigen

heraldic /he'rældɪk/ *adj.* heraldisch

heraldry /'herəldrɪ/ *n.* Heraldik, *die*

herb /hɜːb/ *n.* Kraut, *das*

herbaceous /hɜː'beɪʃəs/ *adj.* krautartig; ∼ **border** Staudenrabatte, *die*

herbal /'hɜːbl/ *attrib. adj.* Kräuter-

herbivore /'hɜːbɪvɔː(r)/ *n.* Pflanzenfresser, *der*

'herb tea *n.* Kräuteraufguss, *der*

herd /hɜːd/ **1** *n.* Herde, *die;* (of wild animals) Rudel, *das*
2 *v.t.* **(a)** treiben; ∼ **people together** Menschen zusammenpferchen
(b) (tend) hüten

here /hɪə(r)/ **1** *adv.* **(a)** (in or at this place) hier; **down/in/up ∼:** hier unten/drin/oben; ∼ **you are** (coll.: giving sth.) hier
(b) (to this place) hierher; **in[to]** ∼: hierherein; **come/bring ∼:** hierher kommen/bringen
2 *int.* (attracting attention) he

here'by *adv.* (formal) hiermit

hereditary /hɪ'redɪtərɪ/ *adj.* **(a)** erblich ⟨Titel, Amt⟩
(b) (Biol.) angeboren

heresy /'herɪsɪ/ *n.* Ketzerei, *die*

heretic /'herɪtɪk/ *n.* Ketzer, *der*/Ketzerin, *die*

heretical /hɪ'retɪkl/ *adj.* ketzerisch

here'with *adv.* in der Anlage

heritage /'herɪtɪdʒ/ *n.* Erbe, *das*

hermetic /hɜː'metɪk/ *adj.* luftdicht

hermetically /hɜː'metɪkəlɪ/ *adv.* hermetisch

hermit /'hɜːmɪt/ *n.* Einsiedler, *der*/ Einsiedlerin, *die*

hernia /'hɜːnɪə/ *n.* Bruch, *der*

hero /'hɪərəʊ/ *n., pl.* ∼**es** Held, *der*

heroic /hɪ'rəʊɪk/ *adj.* heldenhaft

heroin /'herəʊɪn/ *n.* Heroin, *das*

heroine /'herəʊɪn/ *n.* Heldin, *die*

heroism /'herəʊɪzm/ *n.* Heldentum, *das*

heron /'hern/ *n.* Reiher, *der*

herpes /'hɜːpiːz/ *n.* (Med.) Herpes, *der*

herring /'herɪŋ/ *n.* Hering, *der*

hers /hɜːz/ *poss. pron. pred.* ihrer/ihre/ ihres; **the book is ∼:** das Buch gehört ihr

her'self *pron.* **(a)** *emphat.* selbst; **[all] by ∼:** [ganz] allein[e]
(b) *refl.* sich; allein[e] ⟨tun, wählen⟩; **younger than/as heavy as ∼:** jünger als/so schwer wie sie selbst

he's /hɪz, *stressed* hiːz/ **(a)** = he is;
(b) = he has

hesitant /'hezɪtənt/ *adj.* zögernd ⟨Reaktion⟩; stockend ⟨Rede⟩

hesitate /'hezɪteɪt/ *v.i.* zögern; (falter) ins Stocken geraten; ∼ **to do sth.** Bedenken haben, etw. zu tun

hesitation /hezɪ'teɪʃn/ *n.* **(a)** (indecision) Unentschlossenheit, *die;* **without ∼:** ohne zu zögern
(b) (instance of faltering) Unsicherheit, *die*
(c) (reluctance) Bedenken *Pl.*

hetero /'hetərəʊ/ *n.* (coll.) *n.* Hetero *der*/die

heterosexual /hetərəʊ'seksjʊəl/ **1** *adj.* heterosexuell
2 *n.* Heterosexuelle, *der*/die

het up /het 'ʌp/ *adj.* aufgeregt

hew /hjuː/ *v.t., p.p.* **hewn** /hjuːn/ *or* **hewed** /hjuːd/ hacken ⟨Holz⟩; losschlagen ⟨Kohle, Gestein⟩

hewn ▶ HEW

hexagon /'heksəgən/ *n.* Sechseck, *das*

hey /heɪ/ *int.* he; ∼ **presto!** simsalabim!

heyday /'heɪdeɪ/ *n.* Blütezeit, *die*

HGV *abbr.* (Brit.) = **heavy goods vehicle**

hi /haɪ/ *int.* hallo (ugs.)

hiatus /haɪ'eɪtəs/ *n.* Unterbrechung, *die*

hibernate /'haɪbəneɪt/ *v.i.* Winterschlaf halten

hibernation /haɪbə'neɪʃn/ *n.* Winterschlaf, *der*

hiccup /'hɪkʌp/ **1** *n.* **(a)** Schluckauf, *der;* **have/get [the] ∼s** den Schluckauf haben/bekommen
(b) (fig.: stoppage) Störung, *die*
2 *v.i.* schlucksen (ugs.)

hid ▶ HIDE¹

hidden ▶ HIDE¹

hide¹ /haɪd/ **1** *v.t.*, **hid** /hɪd/, **hidden** /'hɪdn/ **(a)** verstecken ⟨Gegenstand, ⋯⟶

Person usw.⟩ (**from** vor + *Dat.*); verbergen
⟨*Gefühle, Sinn usw.*⟩ (**from** vor + *Dat.*);
verheimlichen ⟨*Tatsache, Absicht usw.*⟩
(**from** *Dat.*)
(**b**) (obscure) verdecken
☐2 *v.i.,* **hid, hidden** sich verstecken (**from** vor
+ *Dat.*)
hide² *n.* Haut, *die;* (of furry animal) Fell, *das;*
(dressed) Leder, *das*
hide-and-'seek *n.* Versteckspiel, *das;*
play ∼: Verstecken spielen
hideous /'hɪdɪəs/ *adj.* scheußlich
'**hideout** *n.* Versteck, *das*
hiding¹ /'haɪdɪŋ/ *n.* **go into** ∼: sich
verstecken; (to avoid police, public attention)
untertauchen; **be in** ∼: sich versteckt
halten; (to avoid police, public attention)
untergetaucht sein
hiding² *n.* (coll.: beating) Tracht Prügel; **give
sb. a [good]** ∼: jmdm. eine [ordentliche]
Tracht Prügel verpassen (ugs.)
'**hiding place** *n.* Versteck, *das*
hierarchic /haɪə'rɑːkɪk/, **hierarchical**
/haɪə'rɑːkɪkl/ *adj.* hierarchisch
hierarchy /'haɪərɑːkɪ/ *n.* Hierarchie, *die*
hi-fi /'haɪfaɪ/ (coll.) ☐1 *adj.* Hi-Fi-
☐2 *n.* Hi-Fi-Anlage, *die*
high /haɪ/ ☐1 *adj.* (**a**) hoch; groß ⟨*Höhe*⟩;
stark ⟨*Wind*⟩
(**b**) (coll.: on a drug) high (ugs.)
(**c**) it's ∼ **time you left** es ist höchste Zeit,
dass du gehst
☐2 *adv.* hoch; **search** *or* **look** ∼ **and low**
überall suchen
☐3 *n.* (**a**) (∼est level/figure) Höchststand, *der*
(**b**) (Meteorol.) Hoch, *das*
(**c**) (coll.: drug-induced euphoria)
Rausch[zustand], *der;* **give sb. a** ∼ ⟨*Droge:*⟩
jmdn. high machen (ugs.)
high: ∼**brow** ☐1 *n.* Intellektuelle, *der/die;*
☐2 *adj.* intellektuell ⟨*Person, Gerede usw.*⟩;
hochgestochen (abwertend) ⟨*Person, Musik,
Literatur usw.*⟩; ∼ **chair** *n.* Hochstuhl,
der; ∼**-definition** '**television** *n.* hoch
auflösendes Fernsehen
higher edu'cation *n.* Hochschulbildung,
die
high: ∼ **fi'nance** *n.* Hochfinanz,
die; ∼'**flier,** ∼'**flyer** *n.* (successful
person) Senkrechtstarter, *der;* (person
with great potential) Hochbegabte, *der/die;*
∼ '**frequency** *n.* Hochfrequenz,
die; ∼'**handed** *adj.* selbstherrlich;
∼**-heeled** /haɪ'hiːld/ *adj.* ⟨*Schuhe*⟩
mit hohen Absätzen; ∼**-income**
adj. einkommensstark; ∼ **jump** *n.*
Hochsprung, *der;* ∼**land** /'haɪlənd/
n. Hochland, *das;* ∼**light** ☐1 *n.*
(**a**) Höhepunkt, *der;* (**b**) (bright area) Licht,
das; ☐2 *v.t.,* ∼**lighted** ein Schlaglicht werfen
auf (+ *Akk.*) ⟨*Probleme usw.*⟩
'**highly** *adv.* sehr; hoch ⟨*angesehen,
bezahlt*⟩; hoch⟨*interessant, -gebildet*⟩; leicht
⟨*entzündlich*⟩; stark ⟨*gewürzt*⟩; **think** ∼ **of**

sb./sth. eine hohe Meinung von jmdm./etw.
haben; **speak** ∼ **of sb./sth.** jmdn./etw. sehr
loben
highly-strung /'haɪlɪstrʌŋ/ *adj.*
übererregbar
Highness /'haɪnɪs/ *n.* **His/her** *etc.*
∼: Seine/Ihre *usw.* Hoheit
high: ∼**-pitched** /'haɪpɪtʃt/ *adj.* hoch
⟨*Ton, Stimme*⟩; ∼**-powered** /'haɪpaʊəd/
adj. (forceful) dynamisch ⟨*Geschäftsmann*⟩;
∼ '**pressure** *n.* (**a**) (Meteorol.) Hochdruck,
der; (**b**) (Mech. Engin.) Überdruck, *der;*
∼**-rise** *adj.* ∼**-rise building** Hochhaus,
das; ∼**-rise block of flats/office block**
Wohn-/ Bürohochhaus, *das;* ∼**-risk**
attrib. adj. risikoreich; Risiko⟨*gruppe,
-sportart*⟩; **a** ∼**-risk investment** eine
Geldanlage mit hohem Risiko; ∼ **school**
n. ≈ Oberschule, *die;* ∼ '**seas** *n. pl.*
the ∼ **seas** die hohe See; ∼ **season** *n.*
Hochsaison, *die;* ∼**-speed** *adj.* ∼**-speed
train** Hochgeschwindigkeitszug, *der;*
∼ **street** *n.* Hauptstraße, *die;* ∼ '**tech**
(coll.) ▶ ∼ TECHNOLOGY; ∼**-tech** *adj.*
(coll.) Hightech-; ∼ **tech'nology** *n.*
Spitzentechnologie, *die;* Hochtechnologie,
die; ∼'**voltage** *adj.* Hochspannungs-;
∼**way** *n.* öffentliche Straße
hijab /hɪ'dʒɑːb/ *n.* Hijab, *der*
hijack /'haɪdʒæk/ *v.t.* entführen
'**hijacker** *n.* Entführer, *der;* (of aircraft)
Hijacker, *der*
hike /haɪk/ *n.* Wanderung, *die*
'**hiker** *n.* Wanderer, *der*/Wanderin, *die*
hilarious /hɪ'leərɪəs/ *adj.* urkomisch
hill /hɪl/ *n.* Hügel, *der;* (higher) Berg, *der;*
(slope) Hang, *der*
hill: ∼**billy** /'hɪlbɪlɪ/ *n.* (Amer.)
Hinterwäldler, *der*/Hinterwäldlerin, *die;*
∼**side** *n.* Hang, *der;* ∼**top** *n.* [Berg]gipfel,
der
'**hilly** *adj.* hüg[e]lig
hilt /hɪlt/ *n.* Griff, *der;* [**up] to the** ∼ (fig.) voll
und ganz
him /ɪm, stressed hɪm/ *pron.* ihn; *as indirect
object* ihm; **it was** ∼: er war's
Himalayas /hɪmə'leɪəz/ *pr. n. pl.*
Himalaya, *der*
him'self *pron.* (**a**) *emphat.* selbst
(**b**) *refl.* sich. *See also* HERSELF
hind /haɪnd/ *adj.* hinter...; ∼ **legs**
Hinterbeine *Pl.*
hinder /'hɪndə(r)/ *v.t.* (impede) behindern;
(delay) verzögern ⟨*Vollendung einer Arbeit,
Vorgang*⟩; aufhalten ⟨*Person*⟩; ∼ **sb. from
doing sth.** jmdn. daran hindern, etw. zu tun
'**hindquarters** *n. pl.* Hinterteil, *das*
hindrance /'hɪndrəns/ *n.* Hindernis, *das*
(**to** für)
'**hindsight** *n.* **with [the benefit of]** ∼: im
Nachhinein
Hindu /'hɪnduː, hɪn'duː/ ☐1 *n.* Hindu, *der*
☐2 *adj.* hinduistisch; Hindu⟨*gott, -tempel*⟩

Hinduism /'hɪnduːɪzm/ n. Hinduismus, der

hinge /hɪndʒ/ [1] n. Scharnier, das
[2] v.t. mit Scharnieren versehen
[3] v.i. (depend) abhängen ([up]on von)

hint /hɪnt/ [1] n. (a) (suggestion) Wink, der
(b) (slight trace) Spur, die (of von); the ∼/no
∼ of a smile der Anflug/nicht die Spur eines
Lächelns
(c) (information) Tipp, der (on für)
[2] v.i. ∼ at andeuten

hip /hɪp/ n. Hüfte, die

hip: ∼ **bone** n. Hüftbein, das; ∼ **flask** n.
Taschenflasche, die; ∼ **joint** n. Hüftgelenk,
das

hippie /'hɪpɪ/ n. (coll.) Hippie, der

hippopotamus /hɪpə'pɒtəməs/ n.
Nilpferd, das

hippy ▶ HIPPIE

hire /haɪə(r)/ [1] n. Mieten, das; be on ∼ [to
sb.] [an jmdm.] vermietet sein; for ∼: zu
vermieten
[2] v.t. (a) (employ) anwerben; engagieren
⟨Anwalt, Berater usw.⟩
(b) (obtain use of) mieten; ∼ sth. from sb. etw.
bei jmdm. mieten
(c) (grant use of) ∼ [out] vermieten; ∼ sth.
[out] to sb. etw. jmdm. od. an jmdn.
vermieten

hire: ∼ **car** n. Mietwagen, der;
∼ **purchase** n. (Brit.) Ratenkauf, der;
attrib. Raten-; pay for/buy sth. on ∼: etw. in
Raten bezahlen/auf Raten kaufen

his /ɪz, stressed hɪz/ poss. pron. (a) attrib.
sein
(b) pred. seiner/seine/sein[e]s; see also HERS

hiss /hɪs/ [1] n. Zischen, das
[2] v.i. zischen

historian /hɪ'stɔːrɪən/ n. Historiker,
der/Historikerin, die

historic /hɪ'stɒrɪk/ adj. historisch

historical /hɪ'stɒrɪkl/ adj. historisch;
geschichtlich ⟨Belege, Hintergrund⟩

history /'hɪstərɪ/ n. Geschichte, die

hit /hɪt/ [1] v.t., -tt-, hit schlagen; (with missile)
treffen; ⟨Geschoss, Ball usw.:⟩ treffen;
⟨Fahrzeug:⟩ prallen gegen; ⟨Schiff:⟩ laufen
gegen; ∼ one's head on sth. mit dem Kopf
gegen etw. stoßen; ∼ it off with sb. gut mit
jmdm. auskommen
[2] v.i., -tt-, hit schlagen
[3] n. (a) (blow) Schlag, der; (shot or bomb
striking target) Treffer, der
(b) (success) Erfolg, der; (in entertainment)
Schlager, der; Hit, der (ugs.)
■ **hit 'back** v.t. & i. zurückschlagen
■ **'hit [up]on** v.t. kommen auf (+ Akk.)
⟨Idee⟩; finden ⟨richtige Antwort, Methode⟩

hit-and-'run adj. unfallflüchtig ⟨Fahrer⟩;
∼ accident Unfall mit Fahrerflucht

hitch /hɪtʃ/ [1] v.t. (a) binden ⟨Seil⟩ (round
um + Akk.); [an]koppeln ⟨Anhänger usw.⟩
(to an + Akk.); spannen ⟨Zugtier usw.⟩ (to

vor + Akk.)
(b) ∼ a lift or ride (coll.) per Anhalter fahren
[2] n. (problem) Problem, das
■ **hitch 'up** v.t. hochheben ⟨Rock⟩

'hitch-hike v.i. per Anhalter fahren

'hitch-hiker n. Anhalter, der/Anhalterin,
die

hit: ∼ **man** n. (Amer.) Killer, der (salopp);
∼-**or**-'**miss** adj. (coll.: random) unsicher,
unzuverlässig ⟨Methode⟩; ∼ **parade** n.
Hitparade, die; ∼ '**record** n. Hit, der (ugs.)

HIV abbr. = **human
immunodeficiency virus** HIV;
∼-**positive**/-**negative** HIV-positiv/-negativ

hive /haɪv/ n. [Bienen]stock, der

HMS abbr. (Brit.) = **Her/His Majesty's
Ship** H.M.S.

hoard /hɔːd/ [1] n. Vorrat, der
[2] v.t. ∼ [up] horten; hamstern
⟨Lebensmittel⟩

hoarding /'hɔːdɪŋ/ n. (fence) Bauzaun, der;
(Brit.: for advertisements) Reklamewand, die

hoar frost /'hɔːfrɒst/ n. [Rau]reif, der

hoarse /hɔːs/ adj. heiser

hoax /həʊks/ [1] v.t. anführen (ugs.); foppen
[2] n. (deception) Schwindel, der; (practical joke)
Streich, der; (false alarm) blinder Alarm

hob /hɒb/ n. [Koch]platte, die

hobble /'hɒbl/ v.i. ∼ [about]
[herum]humpeln

hobby /'hɒbɪ/ n. Hobby, das

'hobby horse n. Steckenpferd, das

hobnailed /'hɒbneɪld/ adj. Nagel⟨schuh,
-stiefel⟩

hobo /'həʊbəʊ/ n., pl. -es (Amer.)
Landstreicher, der/-streicherin, die

hockey /'hɒkɪ/ n. Hockey, das

'hockey stick n. Hockeyschläger, der

hoe /həʊ/ [1] n. Hacke, die
[2] v.t. & i. hacken

hog /hɒg/ [1] n. [Mast]schwein
[2] v.t., -gg- (coll.) mit Beschlag belegen

hoist /hɔɪst/ [1] v.t. hochziehen, hissen
⟨Flagge usw.⟩; hieven ⟨Last⟩; setzen ⟨Segel⟩
[2] n. [Lasten]aufzug, der

hold¹ /həʊld/ n. (of ship) Laderaum, der; (of
aircraft) Frachtraum, der

hold² [1] v.t., held /held/ (a) halten; (carry)
tragen; (keep fast) festhalten; ∼ the door
open for sb. jmdm. die Tür aufhalten; ∼ sth.
in place etw. halten
(b) (contain) enthalten; (be able to contain)
fassen ⟨Liter, Personen usw.⟩
(c) (possess) besitzen; haben
(d) (keep possession of) halten ⟨Stützpunkt,
Stadt, Stellung⟩; ∼ the line (Teleph.) am
Apparat bleiben; ∼ one's own sich
behaupten
(e) (cause to take place) stattfinden lassen;
abhalten ⟨Veranstaltung, Konferenz,
Gottesdienst, Sitzung⟩; veranstalten
⟨Festival, Auktion⟩; austragen ⋯❖

⟨*Meisterschaften*⟩; führen ⟨*Unterhaltung,
Gespräch*⟩; durchführen ⟨*Untersuchung*⟩;
halten ⟨*Vortrag, Rede*⟩
(f) (think, believe) ~ a view *or* an opinion
eine Ansicht haben (**on** über + *Akk.*);
~ **that** …: der Ansicht sein, dass …;
~ **oneself responsible for sth.** sich für etw.
verantwortlich fühlen; ~ **sth. against sb.**
jmdm. etw. vorwerfen
2 *v.i.*, **held** halten; ⟨*Wetter:*⟩ sich halten
3 *n.* **(a)** (grasp) Griff, *der;* **grab** *or* **seize**
~ **of sth.** etw. ergreifen; **get** *or* **lay** *or* **take**
~ **of sth.** etw. fassen *od.* packen; **keep**
~ **of sth.** etw. festhalten; **get** ~ **of sth.** (fig.)
etw. auftreiben; **get** ~ **of sb.** (fig.) jmdn.
erreichen
(b) (influence) Einfluss, *der* (**on, over** auf
+ *Akk.*)
(c) (Sport) Griff, *der*
■ **hold 'back** 1 *v.t.* zurückhalten
2 *v.i.* zögern
■ **hold 'on** 1 *v.t.* [fest]halten
2 *v.i.* **(a)** sich festhalten; ~ **on to** sich
festhalten an (+ *Dat.*); (keep) behalten
(b) (coll.: wait) warten
■ **hold 'out** 1 *v.t.* ausstrecken ⟨*Hand,
Arm usw.*⟩; hinhalten ⟨*Tasse, Teller*⟩
2 *v.i.* (resist) sich halten
■ **hold 'up** *v.t.* **(a)** (raise) hochhalten; heben
⟨*Hand, Kopf*⟩
(b) (delay) aufhalten
(c) (rob) überfallen
■ **'hold with** *v.t.* **not** ~ **with sth.** etw.
ablehnen
'holdall *n.* Reisetasche, *die*
'holder *n.* **(a)** (of post, title) Inhaber,
der/Inhaberin, *die*
(b) ⟨*Zigaretten*⟩spitze, *die;* ⟨*Papier-,
Zahnputzglas*⟩halter, *der*
'hold-up *n.* **(a)** (robbery) [Raub]überfall, *der*
(b) (delay) Verzögerung, *die*
hole /həʊl/ *n.* Loch, *das;* (of fox, badger, rabbit)
Bau, *der;* **pick** ~**s in** (fig.) zerpflücken (ugs.)
holiday /'hɒlɪdeɪ/ *n.* **(a)** [arbeits]freier Tag;
(public ~) Feiertag, *der*
(b) *in sing. or pl.* (Brit.: vacation) Urlaub, *der;*
(Sch.) [Schul]ferien *Pl.*
holiday: ~ **home** *n.* Feriendomizil,
das; ~ **job** *n.* Ferienjob, *der;* ~**maker** *n.*
Urlauber, *der*/Urlauberin, *die;* ~ **resort** *n.*
Ferienort, *der;* ~ **season** *n.* Urlaubszeit,
die
Holland /'hɒlənd/ *pr. n.* Holland (*das*)
hollow /'hɒləʊ/ 1 *adj.* hohl; eingefallen
⟨*Wangen, Schläfen*⟩; (fig.) leer ⟨*Versprechen*⟩
2 *n.* [Boden]senke, *die*
3 *v.t.* ~ **out** aushöhlen
holly /'hɒlɪ/ *n.* Stechpalme, *die*
holocaust /'hɒləkɔːst/ *n.* (destruction)
Massenvernichtung, *die;* **the H**~: der
Holocaust
hologram /'hɒləgræm/ *n.* Hologramm, *der*
holster /'həʊlstə(r)/ *n.* [Pistolen]halfter,
die od. das

holy /'həʊlɪ/ *adj.* heilig
Holy: H~ **'Bible** *n.* Heilige Schrift;
~ **'Ghost** ▶ ~ SPIRIT; ~ **Land** *n.* the
~ **Land** das Heilige Land; ~ **'Spirit** *n.*
Heiliger Geist
homage /'hɒmɪdʒ/ *n.* Huldigung, *die* (**to an**
+ *Akk.*); **pay** *or* **do** ~ **to** sb./sth. jmdm./einer
Sache huldigen
home /həʊm/ 1 *n.* **(a)** Heim, *das;* (flat)
Wohnung, *die;* (house) Haus, *das;* (household)
[Eltern]haus, *das;* (native country) Heimat, *die;*
at ~: zu Hause; **be/feel at** ~ (fig.) sich wohl
fühlen; **make yourself at** ~: fühl dich wie
zu Hause
(b) (institution) Heim, *das*
2 *adj.* **(a)** Haus-
(b) (Sport) Heim-; ~ **match** Heimspiel, *das*
3 *adv.* nach Hause
home: ~ **address** *n.* Privatanschrift,
die; ~ **'banking** *n.* Homebanking,
das; ~**-based** /'həʊmbeɪst/ *adj.* zu
Hause arbeitend; **be** ~**-based** zu Hause
arbeiten; seinen Arbeitsplatz zu Hause
haben; ~**coming** *n.* Heimkehr, *die;*
~ **com'puter** *n.* Heimcomputer,
der; ~ **'ground** *n.* **on** ~ **ground** auf
heimischem Boden; (fig.) zu Hause (ugs.);
~**-grown** *adj.* selbst gezogen; ~**land**
n. Heimat, *die;* ~**land security** (esp. Amer.)
Heimatschutz
'homeless 1 *adj.* obdachlos
2 *n. pl.* **the** ~: die Obdachlosen *Pl.*
'homelessness *n.* Obdachlosigkeit, *die*
homely /'həʊmlɪ/ *adj.* wohnlich ⟨*Zimmer
usw.*⟩; behaglich ⟨*Atmosphäre*⟩
home: ~**-made** *adj.* selbst gemacht;
selbst gebacken ⟨*Brot*⟩; hausgemacht
⟨*Lebensmittel*⟩; **H**~ **Office** *n.* (Brit.)
Innenministerium, *das*
homeopathic *etc.* (Amer.) ▶ HOMOEO-
home: ~**owner** *n.* Eigenheimbesitzer,
der/-besitzerin, *die;* ~ **page** *n.* (Comp.)
Homepage, *die;* **H**~ **'Secretary** *n.*
(Brit.) Innenminister, *der;* ~ **'shopping**
n. Teleshopping, *das;* ~**sick** *adj.*
heimwehkrank; **become/be** ~**sick** Heimweh
bekommen/haben; ~**sickness** *n.*
Heimweh, *das;* ~ **'town** *n.* Heimatstadt,
die; ~**work** *n.* Hausaufgaben *Pl.;* **piece of**
~**work** Hausaufgabe, *die*
homicide /'hɒmɪsaɪd/ *n.* Tötung, *die;*
(manslaughter) Totschlag, *der*
homoeopathic /həʊmɪə'pæθɪk,
hɒmɪə'pæθɪk/ *adj.* homöopathisch
homoeopathy /həʊmɪ'ɒpəθɪ,
hɒmɪ'ɒpəθɪ/ *n.* Homöopathie, *die*
homoe'rotic *adj.* homoerotisch
homophobia /hɒmə'fəʊbɪə/ *n., no pl.*
Homophobie, *die*
homophobic /hɒmə'fəʊbɪk/ *adj.*
homophob
homosexual /həʊməʊ'seksjʊəl/ 1 *adj.*
homosexuell

2 *n.* Homosexuelle, *der/die*
homosexu'ality *n.* Homosexualität, *die*
hone /həʊn/ *v.t.* wetzen
honest /'ɒnɪst/ *adj.* ehrlich
'**honestly** *adv.* ehrlich; redlich ⟨*handeln*⟩;
∼! ehrlich!; (annoyed) also wirklich!
honesty /'ɒnɪstɪ/ *n.* Ehrlichkeit, *die*
honey /'hʌnɪ/ *n.* Honig, *der*
honey: ∼ **bee** *n.* Honigbiene, *die;*
∼**comb** *n.* Honigwabe, *die;* ∼**moon** *n.*
Flitterwochen *Pl.;* (journey) Hochzeitsreise,
die; ∼**suckle** *n.* Geißblatt, *das*
honk /hɒŋk/ 1 *v.i.* ⟨*Fahrzeug, Fahrer:*⟩
hupen
2 *n.* Hupen, *das*
honor, honorable (Amer.) ▶ HONOUR,
HONOURABLE
honorary /'ɒnərərɪ/ *adj.* Ehren⟨*mitglied,*
-präsident, -doktor, -bürger⟩
honour /'ɒnə(r)/ (Brit.) 1 *n.* (a) Ehre, *die*
(b) (distinction) Auszeichnung, *die*
2 *v.t.* ehren; (Commerc.) honorieren
honourable /'ɒnərəbl/ *adj.* (Brit.)
ehrenwert (geh.)
'**honours degree** *n.* Examen mit
Auszeichnung
hood /hʊd/ *n.* (a) Kapuze, *die*
(b) (Amer. Motor Veh.) Motorhaube, *die*
(c) (of pram) Verdeck, *das*
hoodlum /'huːdləm/ *n.* Rowdy, *der*
hoodwink /'hʊdwɪŋk/ *v.t.* hinters Licht
führen
hoof /huːf/ *n., pl.* ∼s *or* **hooves** /huːvz/
Huf, *der*
hook /hʊk/ 1 *n.* Haken, *der;* **by** ∼ **or by**
crook mit allen Mitteln
2 *v.t.* (a) (grasp) mit Haken/mit einem
Haken greifen
(b) (fasten) mit Haken/mit einem Haken
befestigen (**to** an + *Dat.*)
(c) **be** ∼**ed [on sth.]** (addicted) [von etw.]
abhängig sein; (harmlessly) auf etw. (*Akk.*)
stehen (ugs.)
■ **hook** '**up** *v.t.* festhaken (**to** an + *Akk.*)
hooligan /'huːlɪgən/ *n.* Rowdy, *der*
hooliganism /'huːlɪgənɪzm/ *n.*
Rowdytum, *das*
hoop /huːp/ *n.* Reifen, *der*
hooray /hʊ'reɪ/ *int.* hurra
hoot /huːt/ 1 *v.i.* (a) (call out) johlen
(b) ⟨*Eule:*⟩ schreien
(c) ⟨*Fahrzeug, Fahrer:*⟩ hupen
2 *n.* (a) (shout) ∼s **of derision** verächtliches
Gejohle
(b) (of owl) Schrei, *der*
(c) (of vehicle) Hupen, *das*
'**hooter** *n.* (Brit.: siren) Sirene, *die*
hoover /'huːvə(r)/ (Brit.) 1 *n.* (a) H∼ ®
[Hoover]staubsauger, *der*
(b) (made by any company) Staubsauger, *der*
2 *v.t.* staubsaugen
hooves *pl. of* HOOF

hop¹ /hɒp/ *n.* (a) (plant) Hopfen, *der*
(b) *in pl.* (Brewing) Hopfen, *der*
hop² 1 *v.i.,* -pp-: (a) hüpfen; ⟨*Hase:*⟩
hoppeln
(b) (fig. coll.) ∼ **out of bed** aus dem Bett
springen; ∼ **into the car/on [to] the bus/train**
sich ins Auto/in den Bus/Zug schwingen
(ugs.)
2 *v.t.,* -pp- (Brit. coll.) ∼ **it** sich verziehen
(ugs.)
3 *n.* (a) Hüpfer, *der*
(b) (Brit. coll.) **catch sb. on the** ∼: jmdn.
überraschen
hope /həʊp/ 1 *n.* Hoffnung, *die;* **sb.'s** ∼[s]
of sth. jmds. Hoffnung auf etw. (*Akk.*); **raise**
sb.'s ∼**s** jmdm. Hoffnung machen
2 *v.i. & t.* hoffen (**for** auf + *Akk.*); **I** ∼ **so/not**
hoffentlich/hoffentlich nicht; ∼ **for the best**
das Beste hoffen
hopeful /'həʊpfl/ *adj.* (a) zuversichtlich;
be ∼ **of sth./of doing sth.** auf etw. (*Akk.*)
hoffen/voller Hoffnung sein, etw. zu tun
(b) (promising) viel versprechend
'**hopefully** *adv.* (a) (expectantly) voller
Hoffnung
(b) (coll.: it is hoped that) hoffentlich
'**hopeless** *adj.,* '**hopelessly**
adv.(a) hoffnungslos
(b) (inadequate) miserabel
'**hopelessness** *n.* Hoffnungslosigkeit, *die*
hopscotch /'hɒpskɒtʃ/ *n.* Himmel-und-
Hölle-Spiel, *das*
horde /hɔːd/ *n.* Horde, *die*
horizon /hə'raɪzn/ *n.* Horizont, *der;* **on the**
∼: am Horizont; (fig.) **broaden one's/sb.'s**
∼**s** seinen/jmds. Horizont erweitern
horizontal /hɒrɪ'zɒntl/ *adj.* horizontal;
waagerecht
hori'zontally *adv.* horizontal; (flat)
waagerecht
hormone /'hɔːməʊn/ *n.* Hormon, *das*
hormone re'placement therapy *n.*
Hormonsubstitutionstherapie, *die*
horn /hɔːn/ *n.* Horn, *das;* (of vehicle) Hupe, *die*
hornet /'hɔːnɪt/ *n.* Hornisse, *die*
'**horny** *adj.* (hard) hornig
horoscope /'hɒrəskəʊp/ *n.* Horoskop, *das*
horrendous /hə'rendəs/ *adj.* (coll.)
schrecklich (ugs.)
horrible /'hɒrɪbl/ *adj.* grauenhaft;
grausig ⟨*Monster*⟩; grauenvoll ⟨*Verbrechen,*
Albtraum⟩
horrid /'hɒrɪd/ *adj.* scheußlich
horrific /hə'rɪfɪk/ *adj.* schrecklich
horrify /'hɒrɪfaɪ/ *v.t.* mit Schrecken
erfüllen; **be horrified** (shocked, scandalized)
entsetzt sein (**at, by** über + *Akk.*)
'**horrifying** *adj.* grauenhaft
horror /'hɒrə(r)/ 1 *n.* Entsetzen, *das* (**at**
über + *Akk.*); (repugnance) Grausen, *das;*
(horrifying thing) Gräuel, *der*
2 *attrib. adj.* Horror-; ∼ **film/story** ⋯⋗

h

Horrorfilm, *der/*-geschichte, *die*

'horror-stricken, 'horror-struck
adjs. von Entsetzen gepackt

hors d'œuvre /ɔː'dɜːvr/ *n.* Horsd'œuvre,
das; ≈ Vorspeise, *die*

horse /hɔːs/ *n.* Pferd, *das*

horse: ~**back** *n.* on ~back zu Pferd;
~ '**chestnut** *n.* Rosskastanie, *die;* ~**fly**
n. Pferdebremse, *die;* ~**man** /'hɔːsmən/
n., pl. ~**men** /'hɔːsmən/ ([skilled] rider)
[guter] Reiter; ~**play** *n.* Balgerei, *die;*
~**power** *n., pl. same* (Mech.) Pferdestärke,
die; ~**racing** *n.* Pferderennsport, *der;*
~**radish** *n.* Meerrettich, *der;* ~**shoe** *n.*
Hufeisen, *das*

horticulture /'hɔːtɪkʌltʃə(r)/ *n.*
Gartenbau, *der*

hose /həʊz/, **'hosepipe** *ns.* Schlauch, *der*

hospice /'hɒspɪs/ *n.* (Brit.: for the terminally ill)
Sterbehospiz, *das*

hospitable /hɒ'spɪtəbl/ *adj.*
gastfreundlich ‹*Person, Wesensart*›; be ~ to
sb. jmdn. gastfreundlich aufnehmen

hospital /'hɒspɪtl/ *n.* Krankenhaus, *das;* in
~ (Brit.), in the ~ (Amer.) im Krankenhaus

'hospital bed *n.* Krankenhausbett, *das*

hospitality /hɒspɪ'tælɪtɪ/ *n.*
Gastfreundschaft, *die*

'hospital nurse *n.* ≈ Krankenschwester,
die

host[1] /həʊst/ *n.* (large number) Menge, *die;* a
~ of people/children eine Menge Leute/eine
Schar von Kindern

host[2] *n.* Gastgeber, *der/*-geberin, *die*

hostage /'hɒstɪdʒ/ *n.* Geisel, *die*

'host country *n.* Gastland, *das*

hostel /'hɒstl/ *n.* (Brit.) Wohnheim, *das*

hostess /'həʊstɪs/ *n.* Gastgeberin, *die;* (in
nightclub) Animierdame, *die*

hostile /'hɒstaɪl/ *adj.* **(a)** feindlich
(b) (unfriendly) feindselig (to[wards]
gegenüber); be ~ to sth. etw. ablehnen

hostility /hɒ'stɪlɪtɪ/ *n.* Feindseligkeit, *die*

hot /hɒt/ *adj.* **(a)** heiß; warm ‹*Mahlzeit,
Essen*›; I am/feel ~ mir ist heiß
(b) (pungent) scharf ‹*Gewürz, Senf usw.*›;
scharf gewürzt ‹*Essen*›
(c) (recent) noch warm ‹*Nachrichten*›
(d) (coll.: illegally obtained) heiß ‹*Ware, Geld*›

hot: ~ '**air** *n.* (coll.) leeres Gerede (ugs.);
~**bed** *n.* (Hort.) Mistbeet, *das;* (fig.: of vice,
corruption) Brutstätte, *die* (of für)

hotchpotch /'hɒtʃpɒtʃ/ *n.* Mischmasch,
der (ugs.) (of aus)

hot: ~**-desking** *n.*: Mehrfachnutzung
von Arbeitsplätzen; ~ **dog** *n.* (coll.) Hotdog,
der od. das

hotel /həʊ'tel/ *n.* Hotel, *das*

hotelier /hə'telɪə(r)/ *n.* Hotelier, *der*

ho'tel room *n.* Hotelzimmer, *das*

hot: ~**head** *n.* Hitzkopf, *der;* ~**house**
n. Treibhaus, *das;* ~ **line** *n.* Hotline, *die;*

(Polit.) heißer Draht

'hotly *adv.* heftig

hot: ~**plate** *n.* Kochplatte, *die;* (to keep food
~) Warmhalteplatte, *die;* ~ **seat** *n.* (coll.)
be in the ~ seat den Kopf hinhalten müssen
(ugs.); ~**-tempered** *adj.* heißblütig;
~-'**water bottle** *n.* Wärmflasche, *die*

hound /haʊnd/ [1] *n.* Jagdhund, *der*
[2] *v.t.* verfolgen

hour /'aʊə(r)/ *n.* **(a)** Stunde, *die;* half
an ~: eine halbe Stunde; an ~ and a
half anderthalb Stunden; be paid by the
~: stundenweise bezahlt werden; the
24-~ clock die Vierundzwanzigstundenuhr
(b) (time o'clock) Zeit, *die;* the small ~s [of
the morning] die frühen Morgenstunden;
0100/0200/1700/1800 ~s (on 24-~ clock)
1.00/2.00/17.00/18.00 Uhr

'hourly *adj., adv.* stündlich; be paid ~:
stundenweise bezahlt werden

house [1] /haʊs/ *n., pl.* ~s /'haʊzɪz/ Haus,
das; to/at my ~: zu mir [nach Hause]/bei
mir [zu Hause]
[2] /haʊz/ *v.t.* **(a)** ein Heim geben (+ *Dat.*)
(b) (keep, store) unterbringen

house/haʊs/**:** ~ **arrest** *n.* Hausarrest,
der; ~**boat** *n.* Hausboot, *das;* ~**-bound**
adj. ans Haus gefesselt

household /'haʊshəʊld/ *n.* Haushalt, *der;*
attrib. Haushalts-

'householder *n.* Wohnungsinhaber, *der/*
-inhaberin, *die*

household 'name *n.* geläufiger Name;
be a ~: ein Begriff sein

house /haʊs/**:** ~ **husband** *n.* Hausmann,
der; ~**keeper** *n.* Haushälterin, *die;*
~**keeping** *n.* Hauswirtschaft, *die;*
~ **plant** *n.* Zimmerpflanze, *die;*
~**-proud** *adj.* he/she is ~-proud Ordnung
und Sauberkeit [im Haushalt] gehen
ihm/ihr über alles; ~**-sit** *v.i.* das Haus
hüten; ~**-sitter** *n.* Housesitter, *der* (ugs.);
Person, die für jemanden das Haus hütet;
~**-trained** *adj.* (Brit.) stubenrein ‹*Hund,
Katze*›; ~**-warming** *n.* ~-warming [party]
Einzugsfeier, *die;* ~**wife** *n.* Hausfrau, *die;*
~**work** *n.* Hausarbeit, *die*

housing /'haʊzɪŋ/ *n.* (dwellings)
Wohnungen *Pl.;* (provision of dwellings)
Wohnungsbeschaffung, *die*

housing: ~ **association** *n.* (Brit.)
Gesellschaft für sozialen Wohnungsbau;
~ **benefit** *n.* (Brit.) Wohngeld, *das;*
~ **estate** *n.* (Brit.) Wohnsiedlung, *die;*
~ **shortage** *n.* Wohnraummangel, *der*

hovel /'hɒvl/ *n.* [armselige] Hütte

hover /'hɒvə(r)/ *v.i.* **(a)** schweben
(b) (linger) sich herumdrücken (ugs.)

'hovercraft *n., pl. same* Hovercraft, *das;*
Luftkissenfahrzeug, *das*

'hover mower *n.* Luftkissenmäher, *der*

how /haʊ/ *adv.* wie; learn ~ to ride a
bike/swim Rad fahren/schwimmen lernen;

∼ **'are you?** wie geht es dir?; (greeting) guten Morgen/Tag/Abend!; ∼ **do you 'do?** (formal) guten Morgen/Tag/Abend!; ∼ **much?** wieviel?; ∼ **many?** wie viel?; wie viele?

however /haʊ'evə(r)/ *adv.* **(a)** wie ... auch **(b)** (nevertheless) jedoch; aber

howl /haʊl/ ☐ *n.* (of animal) Heulen, *das;* (of distress) Schrei, *der;* ∼s **of laughter** brüllendes Gelächter

② *v.i.* ⟨*Tier, Wind:*⟩ heulen; (with distress) schreien

③ *v.t.* [hinaus]schreien

howler /'haʊlə(r)/ *n.* (coll.: blunder) Schnitzer, *der* (ugs.)

HP *abbr.* (Brit.) = **hire purchase**

HQ *abbr.* = **headquarters** HQ

HTML *abbr.* (Comp.) = **hypertext markup language** HTML

hub /hʌb/ *n.* [Rad]nabe, *die;* (fig.) Mittelpunkt, *der;* (Aeronaut.) Drehkreuz, *das*

hubbub /'hʌbʌb/ *n.* Lärm, *der;* **a** ∼ **of voices** ein Stimmengewirr

hub: ∼**cap** *n.* Radkappe, *die;* ∼ **dynamo** *n.* Nabendynamo, *der;* ∼ **gear** *n.* Nabenschaltung, *die*

huddle /'hʌdl/ *v.i.* sich drängen; ∼ **together** sich zusammendrängen

∎ **huddle 'up** *v.i.* (nestle up) sich zusammenkauern; (crowd together) sich [zusammen]drängen

hue¹ /hju:/ *n.* Farbton, *der*

hue² *n.* ∼ **and cry** lautes Geschrei; (protest) Gezeter, *das*

huff /hʌf/ ☐ *v.i.* ∼ **and puff** schnaufen und keuchen

② *n.* **in a** ∼: beleidigt

hug /hʌg/ ☐ *n.* Umarmung, *die;* **give sb. a** ∼: jmdn. umarmen

② *v.t.,* **-gg-** umarmen

huge /hju:dʒ/ *adj.* riesig; gewaltig ⟨*Unterschied, Verbesserung, Interesse*⟩

hulking /'hʌlkɪŋ/ *adj.* (coll.) ∼ **great** klobig

hull /hʌl/ *n.* (Naut.) Schiffskörper, *der*

hum /hʌm/ ☐ *v.i.,* **-mm-:** **(a)** summen; ⟨*Maschine:*⟩ brummen

(b) ∼ **and haw** (coll.) herumdrucksen (ugs.)

② *v.t.,* **-mm-** summen

③ *n.* **(a)** Summen, *das;* (of machinery) Brummen, *das*

(b) (of voices, conversation) Gemurmel, *das;* (of traffic) Brausen, *das*

human /'hju:mən/ ☐ *adj.* menschlich; **the** ∼ **race** die menschliche Rasse

② *n.* Mensch, *der*

human 'being *n.* Mensch, *der*

humane /hju:'meɪn/ *adj.* human

humanitarian /hju:mænɪ'teərɪən/ *adj.* humanitär

humanity /hju:'mænɪtɪ/ *n.* **(a)** (mankind) Menschheit, *die;* (people collectively) Menschen *Pl.*

(b) (being humane) Humanität, *die*

human 'rights *n. pl.* Menschenrechte *Pl.;* ∼ **rights activist** Menschenrechtsaktivist, *der/*-aktivistin, *die;* ∼ **rights group** Menschenrechtsorganisation, *die*

humble /'hʌmbl/ ☐ *adj.* **(a)** demütig **(b)** (modest) bescheiden

(c) (low-ranking) einfach; niedrig ⟨*Status, Rang usw.*⟩

② *v.t.* **(a)** demütigen; ∼ **oneself** sich demütigen *od.* erniedrigen

(b) (defeat decisively) [vernichtend] schlagen

humbly /'hʌmblɪ/ *adv.* demütig

humdrum /'hʌmdrʌm/ *adj.* alltäglich; eintönig ⟨*Leben*⟩

humid /'hju:mɪd/ *adj.* feucht

humidifier /hju:'mɪdɪfaɪə(r)/ *n.* Luftbefeuchter, *der*

humidify /hju:'mɪdɪfaɪ/ *v.t.* befeuchten

humidity /hju:'mɪdɪtɪ/ *n.* Feuchtigkeit, *die*

humiliate /hju:'mɪlɪeɪt/ *v.t.* demütigen

humiliation /hju:mɪlɪ'eɪʃn/ *n.* Demütigung, *die*

humility /hju:'mɪlɪtɪ/ *n.* Demut, *die*

humor (Amer.) ▶ HUMOUR

humorous /'hju:mərəs/ *adj.* lustig, komisch ⟨*Geschichte, Name, Situation*⟩; witzig ⟨*Bemerkung*⟩

humour /'hju:mə(r)/ (Brit.) ☐ *n.* **(a)** Humor, *der;* **sense of** ∼: Sinn für Humor; **have no sense of** ∼: keinen Humor haben

(b) (mood) Laune, *die*

② *v.t.* ∼ **sb.** jmdm. seinen Willen lassen

hump /hʌmp/ ☐ *n.* **(a)** (of person) Buckel, *der;* (of animal) Höcker, *der*

(b) (mound) Hügel, *der*

② *v.t.* (Brit. coll.: carry) schleppen

humpback 'bridge *n.* gewölbte Brücke

hunch¹ /hʌntʃ/ *v.t.* ∼ **[up]** hochziehen

hunch² *n.* (feeling) Gefühl, *das*

'hunchback *n.* (back) Buckel, *der;* (person) Bucklige, *der/die;* **be a** ∼: einen Buckel haben

hundred /'hʌndrəd/ ☐ *adj.* hundert; **a** *or* **one** ∼: [ein]hundert; **two/several** ∼: zweihundert/mehrere hundert; **a** *or* **one** ∼ **and one** [ein]hundert[und]eins

② *n.* **(a)** (number) hundert; **a** *or* **one/two** ∼: [ein]hundert/zweihundert

(b) (written figure; group) Hundert, *das*

(c) (indefinite amount) ∼**s** Hunderte. *See also* EIGHT

hundredth /'hʌndrədθ/ ☐ *adj.* hundertst...; **a** ∼ **part** ein Hundertstel

② *n.* (fraction) Hundertstel, *das;* (in sequence, rank) Hundertste, *der/die/das*

'hundredweight *n., pl.* **same** (Brit.) 50,8 kg; ≈ Zentner, *der*

hung ▶ HANG 1, 2

Hungarian /hʌŋ'geərɪən/ ☐ *adj.* ungarisch; **sb. is** ∼: jmd. ist Ungar/Ungarin

② *n.* **(a)** (person) Ungar, *der/*Ungarin, *die*

(b) (language) Ungarisch, *das; see also* ENGLISH 2A

Hungary /'hʌŋgərɪ/ *pr. n.* Ungarn (*das*)
hunger /'hʌŋgə(r)/ 1 *n.* Hunger, *der*
 2 *v.i.* ~ **after** *or* **for sb./sth.** [heftiges]
 Verlangen nach jmdm./etw. haben
'**hunger strike** *n.* Hungerstreik, *der;* **go**
 on ~: in den Hungerstreik treten
hung '**over** *adj.* (coll.) verkatert (ugs.)
hungry /'hʌŋgrɪ/ *adj.* hungrig; **be**
 ~: Hunger haben; **go** ~: hungern
hunk /hʌŋk/ *n.* [großes] Stück
hunt /hʌnt/ 1 *n.* Jagd, *die;* (search) Suche,
 die
 2 *v.t.* jagen; (search for) Jagd machen auf
 (+ *Akk.*) ⟨*Mörder usw.*⟩
 3 *v.i.* jagen; **go** ~**ing** auf die Jagd gehen;
 ~ **after** *or* **for** Jagd machen auf (+ *Akk.*);
 (seek) suchen
'**hunter** *n.* Jäger, *der*
'**hunting** *n.* die Jagd (of auf + *Akk.*);
 (searching) Suche, *die* (**for** nach)
hurdle /'hɜ:dl/ *n.* Hürde, *die*
hurl /hɜ:l/ *v.t.* werfen; (violently) schleudern;
 ~ **insults at sb.** jmdm. Beleidigungen ins
 Gesicht schleudern
hurly-burly /'hɜ:lɪbɜ:lɪ/ *n.* Tumult, *der;* **the**
 ~ **of city life** der Großstadttrummel (ugs.)
hurrah /hʊ'rɑ:/, **hurray** /hʊ'reɪ/ *int.*
 hurra
hurricane /'hʌrɪkən/ *n.* (tropical cyclone)
 Hurrikan, *der;* (storm, lit. or fig.) Orkan, *der*
hurried /'hʌrɪd/ *adj.* eilig; überstürzt
 ⟨*Abreise*⟩; in Eile ausgeführt ⟨*Arbeit*⟩
hurry /'hʌrɪ/ 1 *n.* Eile, *die;* **in a** ~: eilig;
 be in a ~: es eilig haben; **there's no** ~: es
 eilt nicht
 2 *v.t.* antreiben ⟨*Person*⟩;
 hinunterschlingen ⟨*Essen*⟩; ~ **one's work**
 seine Arbeit in zu großer Eile erledigen
 3 *v.i.* sich beeilen; (to or from place) eilen
■ **hurry** '**up** 1 *v.i.* sich beeilen
 2 *v.t.* antreiben
hurt /hɜ:t/ 1 *v.t.,* **hurt (a)** wehtun (+ *Dat.*);
 (injure) verletzen; ~ **oneself** sich (*Dat.*) weh
 tun; (injure oneself) sich verletzen; ~ **one's**
 arm/back sich (*Dat.*) am Arm/Rücken
 wehtun; (injure) sich (*Dat.*) den Arm/am
 Rücken verletzen
 (b) (damage, be detrimental to) schaden (+ *Dat.*)
 (c) (upset) verletzen ⟨*Person, Stolz*⟩
 2 *v.i.,* **hurt (a)** wehtun
 (b) (cause damage, be detrimental) schaden
 3 *adj.* gekränkt ⟨*Tonfall, Miene*⟩
 4 *n.* (emotional pain) Schmerz, *der*
hurtful /'hɜ:tfl/ *adj.* verletzend
hurtle /'hɜ:tl/ *v.i.* rasen (ugs.)
husband /'hʌzbənd/ *n.* Ehemann, *der;*
 my/your/her ~: mein/dein/ihr Mann; ~ **and**
 wife Mann und Frau
hush /hʌʃ/ 1 *n.* (silence) Schweigen, *das;*
 (stillness) Stille, *die*
 2 *v.t.* (silence) zum Schweigen bringen; (still)
 beruhigen
 3 *v.i.* still sein; ~! still!

■ **hush** '**up** *v.t.* vertuschen
husk /hʌsk/ *n.* Spelze, *die*
husky[1] /'hʌskɪ/ *adj.* heiser
husky[2] *n.* Eskimohund, *der*
hustle /'hʌsl/ 1 *v.t.* drängen (**into** zu)
 2 *n.* ~ **and bustle** geschäftiges Treiben
hut /hʌt/ *n.* Hütte, *die*
hutch /hʌtʃ/ *n.* Stall, *der*
hyacinth /'haɪəsɪnθ/ *n.* Hyazinthe, *die*
hybrid /'haɪbrɪd/ 1 *n.* Hybride, *die od. der*
 (between aus); (fig.: mixture) Mischung, *die*
 2 *adj.* hybrid ⟨*Züchtung*⟩
'**hybrid bike** *n.* Crossrad, *das*
hydrangea /haɪ'dreɪndʒə/ *n.* Hortensie,
 die
hydrant /'haɪdrənt/ *n.* Hydrant, *der*
hydraulic /haɪ'drɔ:lɪk/ *adj.* hydraulisch
hydrochloric acid /haɪdrəklɔ:rɪk
 'æsɪd/ *n.* Salzsäure, *die*
hydroelectric /haɪdrəʊɪ'lektrɪk/
 adj. hydroelektrisch; ~ **power station**
 Wasserkraftwerk, *das*
hydrofoil /'haɪdrəfɔɪl/ *n.* Tragflächenboot,
 das
hydrogen /'haɪdrədʒən/ *n.* Wasserstoff,
 der; ~ **bomb** *n.* Wasserstoffbombe, *die*
hyena /haɪ'i:nə/ *n.* Hyäne, *die*
hygiene /'haɪdʒi:n/ *n.* Hygiene, *die*
hygienic /haɪ'dʒi:nɪk/ *adj.* hygienisch
hymn /hɪm/ *n.* Hymne, *die;* (sung in service)
 Kirchenlied, *das*
'**hymn book** *n.* Gesangbuch, *das*
hyper /'haɪpə(r)/ *adj.* (coll.) aufgedreht (ugs.)
hyperactive /haɪpə'ræktɪv/ *adj.*
 überaktiv
hyperbole /haɪ'pɜ:bəlɪ/ *n.* (Rhet.)
 Hyperbel, *die*
hyper: ~**link** *n.* (Comp.) Hyperlink, *der;*
 ~**market** *n.* (Brit.) Verbrauchermarkt,
 der; ~**text** *n.* (Comp.) Hypertext, *der;*
 ~'**ventilate** *v.i.* hyperventilieren
hyphen /'haɪfn/ 1 *n.* Bindestrich, *der*
 2 *v.t.* mit Bindestrich schreiben
hyphenate /'haɪfəneɪt/ ▶ HYPHEN 2
hyphenation /haɪfə'neɪʃn/ *n.* Kopplung,
 die
hypnosis /hɪp'nəʊsɪs/ *n., pl.* **hypnoses**
 /hɪp'nəʊsi:z/ Hypnose, *die;* (act, process)
 Hypnotisierung, *die;* **under** ~: in Hypnose
 (*Dat.*)
hypnotic /hɪp'nɒtɪk/ *adj.* hypnotisch
hypnotism /'hɪpnətɪzm/ *n.* Hypnotik, *die;*
 (act) Hypnotisieren, *das*
hypnotist /'hɪpnətɪst/ *n.* Hypnotiseur,
 der/Hypnotiseurin, *die*
hypnotize /'hɪpnətaɪz/ *v.t.* hypnotisieren
hypochondria /haɪpə'kɒndrɪə/ *n.*
 Hypochondrie, *die*
hypochondriac /haɪpə'kɒndrɪæk/ *n.*
 Hypochonder, *der*

hypocrisy /hɪˈpɒkrɪsɪ/ n. Heuchelei, *die*
hypocrite /ˈhɪpəkrɪt/ n. Heuchler, *der*/Heuchlerin, *die*
hypocritical /hɪpəˈkrɪtɪkl/ *adj.* heuchlerisch
hypodermic /haɪpəˈdɜːmɪk/ *adj. & n.* ~ **[syringe]** Injektionsspritze, *die*
hypotenuse /haɪˈpɒtənjuːz/ n. Hypotenuse, *die*
hypothermia /haɪpəˈθɜːmɪə/ n. (Med.) Hypothermie, *die* (fachspr.); Unterkühlung, *die*

hypothesis /haɪˈpɒθɪsɪs/ n., pl. **hypotheses** /haɪˈpɒθɪsiːz/ Hypothese, *die*
hypothetical /haɪpəˈθetɪkl/ *adj.* hypothetisch
hysterectomy /hɪstəˈrektəmɪ/ n. (Med.) Hysterektomie, *die* (fachspr.)
hysteria /hɪˈstɪərɪə/ n. Hysterie, *die*
hysterical /hɪˈsterɪkl/ *adj.* hysterisch
hysterics /hɪˈsterɪks/ n. pl. (laughter) hysterischer Lachanfall; (crying) hysterischer Weinkrampf; **have** ~: hysterisch lachen/weinen

• •

• •

I¹, i /aɪ/ n. I, i, *das*
I² *pron.* ich
ice /aɪs/ ☐**1** n. (a) Eis, *das;* **feel/be like** ~ (be very cold) eiskalt sein
(b) (~ **cream**) [Speise]eis, *das;* **an** ~/**two** ~**s** ein/zwei Eis
☐**2** *v.t.* glasieren ⟨Kuchen⟩
■ **ice 'over, ice 'up** *v.i.* ⟨Gewässer:⟩ zufrieren
'ice age n. Eiszeit, *die*
iceberg /ˈaɪsbɜːg/ n. Eisberg, *der*
ice: ~**box** n. (Amer.) Kühlschrank, *der;* ~ **bucket** n. Eisbehälter, *der;* ~**-cold** *adj.* eiskalt; ~ **'cream** n. Eis, *das;* Eiscreme, *die;* **one** ~ **cream**/**two**/**too many** ~ **creams** ein/zwei/zu viel Eis; ~ **'cream parlour** n. Eisdiele, *die;* ~ **cube** n. Eiswürfel, *die*
iced /aɪst/ *adj.* (a) (cooled) eisgekühlt; ~ **coffee/tea** Eiskaffee, *der*/Eistee, *der*
(b) (with icing) glasiert
ice hockey n. Eishockey, *das*
Iceland /ˈaɪslənd/ *pr. n.* Island (*das*)
Icelandic /aɪsˈlændɪk/ ☐**1** *adj.* isländisch
☐**2** n. Isländisch, *das; see also* ENGLISH 2A
ice: ~ **'lolly** n. Eis am Stiel; ~ **rink** n. Eisbahn, *die;* ~ **skate** n. Schlittschuh, *der;* ~**-skate** *v.i.* Schlittschuh laufen; ~ **skating** n. Schlittschuhlaufen, *das*
icicle /ˈaɪsɪkl/ n. Eiszapfen, *der*
icing /ˈaɪsɪŋ/ n. Zuckerguss, *der*
'icing sugar n. (Brit.) Puderzucker, *der*
icon /ˈaɪkɒn/ n. (a) Ikone, *die*
(b) (Comp.) Icon, *das*
icy /ˈaɪsɪ/ *adj.* (a) vereist ⟨Berge, Landschaft, Straße⟩; eisreich ⟨Region, Land⟩; **in** ~ **conditions** bei Eis
(b) (very cold) eiskalt; eisig; (fig.) frostig
I'd /aɪd/ (a) = **I had**;
(b) = **I would**

idea /aɪˈdɪə/ n. Idee, *die;* Gedanke, *der;* (mental picture) Vorstellung, *die;* (vague notion) Ahnung, *die;* **have you any** ~ **[of] how ...?** weißt du ungefähr, wie ...?; **have no** ~ **[of] where ...:** keine Ahnung haben, wo ...; **not have the slightest** *or* **faintest** ~: nicht die leiseste Ahnung haben
ideal /aɪˈdɪəl/ ☐**1** *adj.* ideal; vollendet ⟨Ehemann, Gastgeber⟩; vollkommen ⟨Welt⟩
☐**2** n. Ideal, *das*
idealism /aɪˈdɪəlɪzm/ n. Idealismus, *der*
idealist /aɪˈdɪəlɪst/ n. Idealist, *der*/Idealistin, *die*
idealistic /aɪdɪəˈlɪstɪk/ *adj.* idealistisch
idealize /aɪˈdɪəlaɪz/ *v.t.* idealisieren
ideally /aɪˈdɪəlɪ/ *adv.* ideal; ~, ...: idealerweise *od.* im Idealfall ...
identical /aɪˈdentɪkl/ *adj.* identisch; **be** ~: sich (*Dat.*) völlig gleichen; ~ **twins** eineiige Zwillinge
identification /aɪdentɪfɪˈkeɪʃn/ n. Identifizierung, *die;* (of plants, animals) Bestimmung, *die*
identifi'cation parade n. (Brit.) Gegenüberstellung [zur Identifizierung], *die*
identify /aɪˈdentɪfaɪ/ ☐**1** *v.t.* identifizieren; bestimmen ⟨Pflanze, Tier⟩
☐**2** *v.i.* ~ **with sb.** sich mit jmdm. identifizieren
Identikit ® /aɪˈdentɪkɪt/ n. Phantombild, *das*
identity /aɪˈdentɪtɪ/ n. Identität, *die;* **proof of** ~: Identitätsnachweis, *der;* **[case of] mistaken** ~: [Personen]verwechslung, *die*
identity: ~ **card** n. [Personal]ausweis, *der;* ~ **crisis** n. Identitätskrise, *die;* ~ **parade** ▸ IDENTIFICATION PARADE; ~ **theft** n. Identitätsdiebstahl. *der*
ideological /aɪdɪəˈlɒdʒɪkl/ *adj.* ideologisch
ideology /aɪdɪˈɒlədʒɪ/ n. Ideologie, *die*

idiocy /'ɪdɪəsɪ/ *n.* Idiotie, *die*

idiom /'ɪdɪəm/ *n.* [Rede]wendung, *die*

idiomatic /ɪdɪə'mætɪk/ *adj.* idiomatisch

idiosyncrasy /ɪdɪə'sɪŋkrəsɪ/ *n.* Eigentümlichkeit, *die*

idiosyncratic /ɪdɪəsɪŋ'krætɪk/ *adj.* eigenwillig

idiot /'ɪdɪət/ *n.* Idiot, *der* (ugs.)

idiotic /ɪdɪ'ɒtɪk/ *adj.* idiotisch (ugs.)

idle /'aɪdl/ 1 *adj.* (a) (lazy) faul
(b) (not in use) außer Betrieb *nachgestellt;* be ∼ ⟨*Maschinen, Fabrik:* ⟩ stillstehen
(c) bloß ⟨*Neugier, Spekulation*⟩; leer ⟨*Geschwätz*⟩
2 *v.i.* ⟨*Motor:* ⟩ leer laufen
▪ **idle a'way** *v.t.* vertun

'idleness *n.* Faulheit, *die*

idol /'aɪdl/ *n.* Idol, *das*

idolize /'aɪdəlaɪz/ *v.t.* vergöttern

idyllic /ɪ'dɪlɪk/ *adj.* idyllisch

i.e. /aɪ'iː/ *abbr.* = **that is** d.h.; i.e.

if /ɪf/ *conj.* (a) wenn; if anyone should ask ...: falls jemand fragt, ...; if I knew what to do ...: wenn ich wüsste, was ich tun soll ...; if I were you an deiner Stelle; if so/not wenn ja/nein *od.* nicht; if then/that/at all wenn überhaupt; **as if** als ob; if I only knew, if only I knew! wenn ich das nur wüsste!; if it isn't Ronnie! das ist doch Ronnie!
(b) (whenever) [immer] wenn
(c) (whether) ob
(d) (though) auch *od.* selbst wenn
(e) (despite being) wenn auch

iffish /'ɪfɪʃ/, **iffy** /'ɪfɪ/ *adjs.* (coll.) ungewiss; zweifelhaft

igloo /'ɪgluː/ *n.* Iglu, *der od. das*

ignite /ɪg'naɪt/ 1 *v.t.* anzünden
2 *v.i.* sich entzünden

ignition /ɪg'nɪʃn/ *n.* (a) (igniting) Zünden, *das*
(b) (Motor Veh.) Zündung, *die;* ∼ key Zündschlüssel, *der*

ignorance /'ɪgnərəns/ *n.* Unwissenheit, *die;* keep sb. in ∼ of sth. jmdn. in Unkenntnis über etw. (*Akk.*) lassen

ignorant /'ɪgnərənt/ *adj.* unwissend; be ∼ of sth. (uninformed) über etw. (*Akk.*) nicht informiert sein

ignore /ɪg'nɔː(r)/ *v.t.* ignorieren; nicht befolgen ⟨*Befehl, Rat*⟩; übergehen ⟨*Frage, Bemerkung*⟩

ill /ɪl/ 1 *adj.,* worse /wɜːs/, worst /wɜːst/ krank; fall ∼: krank werden
2 *adv.* be ∼ at ease sich nicht wohl fühlen
3 *n.* Übel, *das*

I'll /aɪl/ (a) = I shall
(b) = I will

'ill-advised *adj.* unklug

illegal /ɪ'liːgl/ *adj.,* **il'legally** *adv.* illegal

il'legal immigrant *n.* illegaler Einwanderer/illegale Einwanderin

illegality /ɪlɪ'gælɪtɪ/ *n.* Ungesetzlichkeit, *die*

illegible /ɪ'ledʒɪbl/ *adj.* unleserlich

illegitimate /ɪlɪ'dʒɪtɪmət/ *adj.* unehelich ⟨*Kind*⟩

ill 'health *n.* schwache Gesundheit

illicit /ɪ'lɪsɪt/ *adj.* unerlaubt ⟨*Beziehung, [Geschlechts]verkehr*⟩; Schwarz⟨*handel, -verkauf, -arbeit*⟩

'ill-informed *adj.* schlecht informiert

illiteracy /ɪ'lɪtərəsɪ/ *n.* Analphabetentum, *das;* Analphabetismus, *der*

illiterate /ɪ'lɪtərət/ *adj.* des Lesens und Schreibens unkundig; analphabetisch ⟨*Bevölkerung*⟩

illness /'ɪlnɪs/ *n.* Krankheit, *die*

illogical /ɪ'lɒdʒɪkl/ *adj.* unlogisch

ill-'treat *v.t.* misshandeln

ill-'treatment *n.* Misshandlung, *die*

illuminate /ɪ'luːmɪneɪt/ *v.t.* beleuchten

illuminating /ɪ'luːmɪneɪtɪŋ/ *adj.* aufschlussreich

illumination /ɪluːmɪ'neɪʃn/ *n.* Beleuchtung, *die*

illusion /ɪ'luːʒn/ *n.* Illusion, *die;* be under the ∼ that ...: sich (*Dat.*) einbilden, dass ...

illusory /ɪ'luːsərɪ/ *adj.* illusorisch

illustrate /'ɪləstreɪt/ *v.t.* (a) (serve as example of) veranschaulichen
(b) illustrieren ⟨*Buch, Erklärung*⟩

illustration /ɪlə'streɪʃn/ *n.* (a) (example) Beispiel, *das* (of für)
(b) (picture) Abbildung, *die*

illustrious /ɪ'lʌstrɪəs/ *adj.* berühmt ⟨*Person*⟩

ill 'will *n.* Böswilligkeit, *die*

I'm /aɪm/ = I am

image /'ɪmɪdʒ/ *n.* (a) Bildnis, *das* (geh.)
(b) (Optics) Bild, *das*
(c) [public] ∼: Image, *das*

'image-conscious *adj.* imagebewusst

imaginable /ɪ'mædʒɪnəbl/ *adj.* the best solution ∼: die denkbar beste Lösung

imaginary /ɪ'mædʒɪnərɪ/ *adj.* imaginär (geh.); eingebildet ⟨*Krankheit*⟩

imagination /ɪmædʒɪ'neɪʃn/ *n.*
(a) Fantasie, *die*
(b) (fancy) Einbildung, *die*

imaginative /ɪ'mædʒɪnətɪv/ *adj.* fantasievoll; (showing imagination) einfallsreich

imagine /ɪ'mædʒɪn/ *v.t.* (a) sich (*Dat.*) vorstellen
(b) (suppose) glauben
(c) (get the impression) ∼ that ...: sich (*Dat.*) einbilden[, dass ...]

imbalance /ɪm'bæləns/ *n.* Unausgeglichenheit, *die*

imbecile /'ɪmbɪsiːl/ *n.* Idiot, *der* (ugs.)

IMF *abbr.* = **International Monetary Fund** IWF, *der*

imitate /'ɪmɪteɪt/ *v.t.* nachahmen

imitation /ɪmɪ'teɪʃn/ *n.* (a) Nachahmung, *die*

(b) (counterfeit) Imitation, *die*

immaculate /ɪˈmækjʊlət/ *adj.* (spotless)
makellos; (faultless) tadellos

immaterial /ɪməˈtɪərɪəl/ *adj.* unerheblich

immature /ɪməˈtjʊə(r)/ *adj.* unreif; noch
nicht voll entwickelt ⟨*Lebewesen*⟩

immaturity /ɪməˈtjʊərɪtɪ/ *n.* Unreife, *die*

immediate /ɪˈmiːdjət/ *adj.*
(a) unmittelbar; (nearest) nächst...
⟨*Nachbar*[*schaft*], *Umgebung, Zukunft*⟩;
engst... ⟨*Familie*⟩
(b) (occurring at once) prompt; unverzüglich
⟨*Handeln, Maßnahmen*⟩; umgehend
⟨*Antwort*⟩

imˈmediately ⎡1⎤ *adv.* **(a)** unmittelbar
(b) (without delay) sofort
⎡2⎤ *conj.* sobald

immemorial /ɪmɪˈmɔːrɪəl/ *adj.* **from time
~:** seit undenklichen Zeiten

immense /ɪˈmens/ *adj.* **(a)** ungeheuer
(b) (coll.: great) enorm

imˈmensely *adv.* **(a)** ungeheuer
(b) (coll.: very much) unheimlich (ugs.)

immerse /ɪˈmɜːs/ *v.t.* [ein]tauchen; **be
~d in thought/one's work** in Gedanken
versunken/in seine Arbeit vertieft sein

immersion /ɪˈmɜːʃn/ *n.* Eintauchen, *das*

imˈmersion heater *n.*
Heißwasserbereiter, *der*

immigrant /ˈɪmɪɡrənt/ ⎡1⎤ *n.*
Einwanderer, *der*/Einwanderin, *die*
⎡2⎤ *adj.* Einwanderer-; **~ workers**
ausländische Arbeitnehmer *Pl.*

immigration /ɪmɪˈɡreɪʃn/ *n.*
Einwanderung *die* (**into** nach, **from**
aus); *attrib.* Einwanderungs⟨*kontrolle,
-gesetz*⟩; **~ officer** Beamter/Beamtin der
Einwanderungsbehörde; **~ authorities**
Einwanderungsbehörden *Pl.;* **go through
~:** durch die Passkontrolle gehen

imminent /ˈɪmɪnənt/ *adj.* unmittelbar
bevorstehend; drohend ⟨*Gefahr*⟩; **be
~:** unmittelbar bevorstehen/drohen

immobile /ɪˈməʊbaɪl/ *adj.* (immovable)
unbeweglich

immobilize /ɪˈməʊbɪlaɪz/ *v.t.* verankern;
(fig.) lähmen

immobilizer /ɪˈməʊbɪlaɪzə(r)/ *n.* (Motor
Veh.) Wegfahrsperre, *die*

immodest /ɪˈmɒdɪst/ *adj.* unbescheiden;
(improper) unanständig

immoral /ɪˈmɒrəl/ *adj.* unmoralisch; (in
sexual matters) sittenlos

immorality /ɪməˈrælɪtɪ/ *n.* Unmoral, *die;*
(in sexual matters) Sittenlosigkeit, *die*

immortal /ɪˈmɔːtl/ *adj.* unsterblich

immortality /ɪmɔːˈtælɪtɪ/ *n.*
Unsterblichkeit, *die*

immortalize /ɪˈmɔːtəlaɪz/ *v.t.* unsterblich
machen

immovable /ɪˈmuːvəbl/ *adj.* unbeweglich;
be ~: sich nicht bewegen lassen

immune /ɪˈmjuːn/ *adj.* **(a)** (exempt) sicher
(**from** vor + *Dat.*)
(b) (not susceptible) unempfindlich (**to** gegen)
(c) (Med.) immun (**to** gegen); **~ therapy**
Immuntherapie, *die;* **~ system**
Immunsystem, *das*

immunity /ɪˈmjuːnɪtɪ/ *n.* **(a)** diplomatic
~: diplomatische Immunität
(b) (Med.) Immunität, *die*

immunization /ɪmjʊnaɪˈzeɪʃn/ *n.*
Immunisierung, *die*

immunize /ˈɪmjʊnaɪz/ *v.t.* immunisieren

immunodeficiency
/ɪˈmjuːnəʊdɪfɪʃənsɪ/ *n.* Immunschwäche, *die*

immunology /ɪmjʊˈnɒlədʒɪ/ *n.*
Immunologie, *die*

immunotherapy /ɪmjuːnəʊˈθerəpɪ/ *n.*
Immuntherapie, *die*

immutable /ɪˈmjuːtəbl/ *adj.*
unveränderlich

imp /ɪmp/ *n.* **(a)** Kobold, *der*
(b) (fig.: child) Racker, *der* (fam.)

impact /ˈɪmpækt/ *n.* **(a)** Aufprall,
der (**on, against** auf + *Akk.*); (collision)
Zusammenprall, *der*
(b) (fig.) Wirkung, *die*

impair /ɪmˈpeə(r)/ *v.t.* beeinträchtigen;
schaden (+ *Dat.*) ⟨*Gesundheit*⟩

impale /ɪmˈpeɪl/ *v.t.* aufspießen

impart /ɪmˈpɑːt/ *v.t.* **(a)** (give) [ab]geben (**to**
an + *Akk.*)
(b) (communicate) kundtun (geh.) (**to** *Dat.*);
vermitteln ⟨*Kenntnisse*⟩ (**to** *Dat.*)

impartial /ɪmˈpɑːʃl/ *adj.* unparteiisch;
gerecht ⟨*Entscheidung, Urteil*⟩

impassable /ɪmˈpɑːsəbl/ *adj.*
unpassierbar (**to** für); (to vehicles)
unbefahrbar (**to** für)

impasse /ˈæmpɑːs/ *n.* Sackgasse, *die*

impassive /ɪmˈpæsɪv/ *adj.* ausdruckslos

impatience /ɪmˈpeɪʃəns/ *n.* Ungeduld, *die*
(**at** über + *Akk.*)

impatient /ɪmˈpeɪʃənt/ *adj.* ungeduldig;
~ at sth./with sb. ungeduldig über etw.
(*Akk.*)/mit jmdm.

imˈpatiently *adv.* ungeduldig

impeccable /ɪmˈpekəbl/ *adj.* makellos;
tadellos ⟨*Manieren*⟩

impeccably /ɪmˈpekəblɪ/ *adv.* tadellos;
makellos ⟨*rein*⟩

impede /ɪmˈpiːd/ *v.t.* behindern

impediment /ɪmˈpedɪmənt/ *n.*
(a) Hindernis, *das* (**to** für)
(b) (speech defect) Sprachfehler, *der*

impel /ɪmˈpel/ *v.t.,* **-ll-** treiben; **feel ~led to
do sth.** sich genötigt *od.* gezwungen fühlen,
etw. zu tun

impending /ɪmˈpendɪŋ/ *adj.* bevorstehend

impenetrable /ɪmˈpenɪtrəbl/ *adj.*
undurchdringlich (**by, to** für)

imperative /ɪmˈperətɪv/ ⎡1⎤ *adj.*
dringend erforderlich ⋯⋗

$\boxed{2}$ *n.* (Ling.) Imperativ, *der*

imperceptible /ɪmpə'septɪbl/ *adj.*
nicht wahrnehmbar; (very slight or gradual)
unmerklich

imperfect /ɪm'pɜːfɪkt/ $\boxed{1}$ *adj.*
(a) (incomplete) unvollständig
(b) (faulty) mangelhaft
$\boxed{2}$ *n.* (Ling.) Imperfekt, *das*

imperfection /ɪmpə'fekʃn/ *n.*
(a) (incompleteness) Unvollständigkeit, *die*
(b) (fault) Mangel, *der*

im'perfectly *adv.* **(a)** (incompletely)
unvollständig
(b) (faultily) fehlerhaft

imperial /ɪm'pɪərɪəl/ *adj.* kaiserlich

imperialism /ɪm'pɪərɪəlɪzm/ *n.*
Imperialismus, *der*

imperil /ɪm'perəl/ *v.t.,* (Brit.) -**ll**- gefährden

imperious /ɪm'pɪərɪəs/ *adj.* herrisch

impermeable /ɪm'pɜːmɪəbl/ *adj.*
undurchlässig

impersonal /ɪm'pɜːsənl/ *adj.* unpersönlich

impersonate /ɪm'pɜːsəneɪt/ *v.t.* sich
ausgeben als; (to entertain) imitieren;
nachmachen

impersonator /ɪm'pɜːsəneɪtə(r)/ *n.*
(entertainer) Imitator, *der*/Imitatorin, *die*

impertinence /ɪm'pɜːtɪnəns/ *n.*
Unverschämtheit, *die*

impertinent /ɪm'pɜːtɪnənt/ *adj.*
unverschämt

imperturbable /ɪmpə'tɜːbəbl/ *adj.*
gelassen; **be completely** ~: durch nichts zu
erschüttern sein

impervious /ɪm'pɜːvɪəs/ *adj.*
undurchlässig; **be** ~ **to sth.** (fig.)
unempfänglich für etw. sein

impetuous /ɪm'petjʊəs/ *adj.* unüberlegt;
impulsiv ⟨*Person*⟩

impetus /'ɪmpɪtəs/ *n.* **(a)** Kraft, *die*
(b) (fig.) Motivation, *die*

impinge /ɪm'pɪndʒ/ *v.i.* ~ **on sth.** auf etw.
(*Akk.*) Einfluss nehmen

'impish *adj.* lausbübisch

implacable /ɪm'plækəbl/ *adj.*
unversöhnlich; erbittert ⟨*Gegner*⟩

implausible /ɪm'plɔːzɪbl/ *adj.*
unglaubwürdig

implement $\boxed{1}$ /'ɪmplɪmənt/ *n.* Gerät, *das*
$\boxed{2}$ /'ɪmplɪment/ *v.t.* [in die Tat] umsetzen
⟨*Politik, Plan usw.*⟩

implicate /'ɪmplɪkeɪt/ *v.t.* belasten; **be** ~**d**
in a scandal in einen Skandal verwickelt
sein

implication /ɪmplɪ'keɪʃn/ *n.* Implikation,
die; **by** ~: implizit

implicit /ɪm'plɪsɪt/ *adj.* **(a)** (implied) implizit
(geh.); unausgesprochen ⟨*Drohung, Zweifel*⟩
(b) (resting on authority) unbedingt; blind
⟨*Vertrauen*⟩

implicitly /ɪm'plɪsɪtlɪ/ *adv.* **(a)** (by
implication) implizit (geh.)

(b) (unquestioningly) blind ⟨*vertrauen,
gehorchen usw.*⟩

implode /ɪm'pləʊd/ *v.i.* implodieren

implore /ɪm'plɔː(r)/ *v.t.* anflehen (**for** um)

imply /ɪm'plaɪ/ *v.t.* **(a)** implizieren (geh.);
(say indirectly) hindeuten auf (+ *Akk.*)
(b) (insinuate) unterstellen

impolite /ɪmpə'laɪt/ *adj.* unhöflich

import $\boxed{1}$ /ɪm'pɔːt/ *v.t.* importieren,
einführen ⟨*Waren*⟩ (**from** aus, **into** nach)
$\boxed{2}$ /'ɪmpɔːt/ *n.* **(a)** (process) Import, *der*
(b) (article) Importgut, *das*

importance /ɪm'pɔːtəns/ *n.* Wichtigkeit,
die (**to** für); (significance) Bedeutung, *die;* **be**
of ~: wichtig sein; **full of one's own** ~: von
seiner eigenen Wichtigkeit überzeugt

important /ɪm'pɔːtənt/ *adj.* wichtig (**to**
für); (significant) bedeutend

'import duty *n.* Einfuhrzoll, *der*

im'porter *n.* Importeur, *der*

impose /ɪm'pəʊz/ *v.t.* auferlegen (geh.)
⟨*Bürde, Verpflichtung*⟩ (**[up]on** *Dat.*);
erheben ⟨*Steuer*⟩ (**on** auf + *Akk.*); verhängen
⟨*Kriegsrecht*⟩; anordnen ⟨*Rationierung*⟩
■ **im'pose on** *v.t.* ausnutzen
⟨*Gutmütigkeit, Toleranz usw.*⟩; ~ **on sb.**
sich jmdm. aufdrängen

imposing /ɪm'pəʊzɪŋ/ *adj.* imposant

imposition /ɪmpə'zɪʃn/ *n.*
(a) Auferlegung, *die;* (of tax) Erhebung, *die*
(b) (unreasonable demand) Zumutung, *die*

impossibility /ɪmpɒsɪ'bɪlɪtɪ/ *n.*
Unmöglichkeit, *die*

impossible /ɪm'pɒsɪbl/ *adj.,*
impossibly /ɪm'pɒsɪblɪ/ *adv.* unmöglich

impostor /ɪm'pɒstə(r)/ *n.* Hochstapler,
der/-staplerin, *die;* (swindler) Betrüger,
der/Betrügerin, *die*

impotence /'ɪmpətəns/ *n.*
(a) (powerlessness) Machtlosigkeit, *die*
(b) (lack of sexual power) Impotenz, *die*

impotent /'ɪmpətənt/ *adj.* **(a)** (powerless)
machtlos
(b) (lacking in sexual power; in popular use: sterile)
impotent

impound /ɪm'paʊnd/ *v.t.* beschlagnahmen

impoverished /ɪm'pɒvərɪʃt/ *adj.*
be/become ~: verarmt sein/verarmen

impracticable /ɪm'præktɪkəbl/ *adj.*
undurchführbar

impractical /ɪm'præktɪkl/ *adj.*
(a) (unpractical) unpraktisch
(b) ▶ IMPRACTICABLE

imprecise /ɪmprɪ'saɪs/ *adj.* ungenau

impregnable /ɪm'pregnəbl/ *adj.*
uneinnehmbar ⟨*Festung, Bollwerk*⟩; (fig.)
unanfechtbar ⟨*Ruf, Stellung*⟩

impregnate /'ɪmpregneɪt/ *v.t.*
imprägnieren

impress /ɪm'pres/ *v.t.* beeindrucken; *abs.*
Eindruck machen; **be** ~**ed by** *or* **with sth.**
von etw. beeindruckt sein

■ **im'press [up]on** *v.t.* einschärfen (+ *Dat.*); ∼ **sth. [up]on sb.'s memory** jmdm. etw. einschärfen

impression /ɪm'preʃn/ *n.* **(a)** Eindruck, *der;* **form an** ∼ **of sb.** sich (*Dat.*) ein Bild von jmdm. machen **(b)** (impersonation) **do an** ∼ **of sb.** jmdn. imitieren; **do** ∼**s** andere Leute imitieren

impressionable *adj.* beeinflussbar

impressionist /ɪm'preʃənɪst/ *n.* Impressionist, *der*/Impressionistin, *die*

impressive /ɪm'presɪv/ *adj.* beeindruckend; imponierend

imprint ⊡ /'ɪmprɪnt/ *n.* Abdruck, *der;* (fig.) Stempel, *der*
⊡ /ɪm'prɪnt/ *v.t.* aufdrucken; (fig.) einprägen (**on** *Dat.*)

imprison /ɪm'prɪzn/ *v.t.* in Haft nehmen; **be** ∼**ed** sich in Haft befinden

im'prisonment *n.* Haft, *die;* **a long term of** ∼: eine lange Haftstrafe

improbable /ɪm'prɒbəbl/ *adj.* unwahrscheinlich

impromptu /ɪm'prɒmptju:/ ⊡ *adj.* improvisiert; **an** ∼ **speech** eine Stegreifrede ⊡ *adv.* aus dem Stegreif

improper /ɪm'prɒpə(r)/ *adj.* **(a)** (wrong) unrichtig **(b)** (unseemly) unpassend; (indecent) unanständig

im'properly *adv.* ▶ IMPROPER: unrichtig; unpassend; unanständig

improvable /ɪm'pru:vəbl/ *adj.* verbesserungsfähig

improve /ɪm'pru:v/ ⊡ *v.i.* besser werden; ⟨*Person, Wetter:*⟩ sich bessern ⊡ *v.t.* verbessern ⊡ *v. refl.* ∼ **oneself** sich weiterbilden

■ **im'prove [up]on** *v.t.* überbieten ⟨*Rekord, Angebot*⟩; verbessern ⟨*Leistung*⟩

improvement /ɪm'pru:vmənt/ *n.* Verbesserung, *die* (**on, over** gegenüber); **make** ∼**s to sth.** Verbesserungen an etw. (*Dat.*) vornehmen

improvisation /ɪmprəvaɪ'zeɪʃn/ *n.* Improvisieren, *das*

improvise /'ɪmprəvaɪz/ *v.t.* improvisieren

imprudent /ɪm'pru:dənt/ *adj.* unklug; (showing rashness) unbesonnen

impudence /'ɪmpjʊdəns/ *n.* Unverschämtheit, *die;* (brazenness) Dreistigkeit, *die*

impudent /'ɪmpjʊdənt/ *adj.*, **'impudently** *adv.* unverschämt; (brazen[ly]) dreist

impulse /'ɪmpʌls/ *n.* Impuls, *der;* **on [an]** ∼: impulsiv

'impulse buying *n.* Spontankäufe *Pl.*

impulsive /ɪm'pʌlsɪv/ *adj.* impulsiv

impunity /ɪm'pju:nɪtɪ/ *v.t.* **with** ∼: ungestraft

impure /ɪm'pjʊə(r)/ *adj.* unrein

impurity /ɪm'pjʊərɪtɪ/ *n.* Unreinheit, *die;* (foreign body) Fremdstoff, *der*

impute /ɪm'pju:t/ *v.t.* zuschreiben (**to** *Dat.*)

in /ɪn/ ⊡ *prep.* (position; also fig.) in (+ *Dat.*); (into) in (+ *Akk.*); **in this heat** bei dieser Hitze; **two feet in diameter** mit einem Durchmesser von zwei Fuß; **there are three feet in a yard** ein Yard hat drei Fuß; **draw in crayon/ink** mit Kreide/Tinte zeichnen; **pay in pounds/dollars** in Pfund/Dollars bezahlen; **in fog/rain** *etc.* bei Nebel/Regen *usw.;* **in the 20th century** im 20. Jahrhundert; **4 o'clock in the morning/afternoon** 4 Uhr morgens/abends; **in 1990** [im Jahre] 1990; **in three minutes/years** in drei Minuten/Jahren; **in doing this, he** ...: indem er das tut/tat, ... er ...: **in that** ...; insofern als ...
⊡ *adv.* **(a)** (inside) hinein⟨*gehen usw.*⟩; herein⟨*kommen usw.*⟩ **(b)** (at home, work, etc.) **be in** da sein **(c)** **have it in for sb.** es auf jmdn. abgesehen haben (ugs.); **sb. is in for sth.** (about to undergo) jmdm. steht etw. bevor
⊡ *adj.* (coll.: in fashion) in (ugs.)
⊡ *n.* **know the ins and outs of sth.** sich in einer Sache genau auskennen

in. *abbr.* = **inch[es]**

ina'bility *n.* Unfähigkeit, *die*

inaccessible /ɪnək'sesɪbl/ *adj.* unzugänglich

in'accuracy *n.* **(a)** (incorrectness) Unrichtigkeit, *die* **(b)** (imprecision) Ungenauigkeit, *die*

in'accurate *adj.* **(a)** (incorrect) unrichtig **(b)** (imprecise) ungenau

in'active *adj.* untätig

inac'tivity *n.* Untätigkeit, *die*

inadequacy /ɪn'ædɪkwəsɪ/ *n.* **(a)** (insufficiency) Unzulänglichkeit, *die* **(b)** (incompetence) mangelnde Eignung

in'adequate *adj.* unzulänglich; (incompetent) ungeeignet; **feel** ∼: sich überfordert fühlen

inadvertent /ɪnəd'vɜːtənt/ *adj.*, **inad'vertently** *adv.* versehentlich

inad'visable *adj.* nicht ratsam

inane /ɪn'eɪn/ *adj.* dümmlich

in'animate *adj.* unbelebt

inap'plicable *adj.* nicht zutreffend

inap'propriate *adj.* unpassend

in'apt *adj.* unpassend

inar'ticulate *adj.* **(a)** **she's rather/very** ∼: sie kann sich ziemlich schlecht/sehr schlecht ausdrücken **(b)** (indistinct) unverständlich

inat'tentive *adj.* unaufmerksam (**to** gegenüber)

in'audible *adj.* unhörbar

inau'spicious *adj.* (ominous) unheilvoll; (unlucky) unglücklich

'inborn *adj.* angeboren (in *Dat.*)

'in-box *n.* (Comp.) Inbox, *die;* Posteingang, *der*

in'bred *adj.* they are/have become ∼: bei ihnen herrscht Inzucht

in'breeding *n.* Inzucht, *die*

'inbuilt *adj.* jmdm./einer Sache eigen

Inc. *abbr.* (Amer.) = **Incorporated** e. G.

incalculable /ɪnˈkælkjʊləbl/ *adj.* (very great) unermesslich

in'capable *adj.* (a) be ∼ of doing sth. außerstande sein, etw. zu tun; be ∼ of sth. zu etw. unfähig sein
(b) be ∼ of nicht zulassen ⟨Beweis, Messung usw.⟩

incapacitate /ɪnkəˈpæsɪteɪt/ *v.t.* unfähig machen

incarcerate /ɪnˈkɑːsəreɪt/ *v.t.* einkerkern (geh.)

incarceration /ɪnkɑːsəˈreɪʃn/ *n.* Einkerkerung, *die* (geh.)

incendiary /ɪnˈsendɪərɪ/ *adj. & n.*
∼ device Brandsatz, *der;* ∼ [bomb] Brandbombe, *die*

incense¹ /ˈɪnsens/ *n.* Weihrauch, *der*

incense² /ɪnˈsens/ *v.t.* erzürnen

incentive /ɪnˈsentɪv/ *n.* Anreiz, *der*

incessant /ɪnˈsesənt/ *adj.*,
in'cessantly *adv.* unablässig

incest /ˈɪnsest/ *n.* Inzest, *der*

incestuous /ɪnˈsestjʊəs/ *adj.* inzestuös

inch /ɪntʃ/ ⏍1⏍ *n.* Inch, *der;* Zoll, *der* (veralt.)
⏍2⏍ *v.t. & i.* ∼ [one's way] forward sich Zoll für Zoll vorwärts bewegen

incident /ˈɪnsɪdənt/ *n.* (a) (notable event) Vorfall, *der*
(b) (clash) Zwischenfall, *der*

incidental /ɪnsɪˈdentl/ *adj.* beiläufig ⟨Bemerkung⟩; Neben⟨ausgaben, -einnahmen⟩

incidentally /ɪnsɪˈdentəlɪ/ *adv.* nebenbei [bemerkt]

inci'dental music *n.* Begleitmusik, *die*

incinerate /ɪnˈsɪnəreɪt/ *v.t.* verbrennen

incineration /ɪnsɪnəˈreɪʃn/ *n.*, no pl. Verbrennung, *die*

incinerator /ɪnˈsɪnəreɪtə(r)/ *n.* Verbrennungsofen, *der*

incision /ɪnˈsɪʒn/ *n.* Einschnitt, *der*

incisive /ɪnˈsaɪsɪv/ *adj.* schneidend ⟨Ton⟩; scharf ⟨Verstand⟩; scharfsinnig ⟨Kritik, Frage, Bemerkung, Argument⟩

incite /ɪnˈsaɪt/ *v.t.* anstiften; aufstacheln ⟨Massen, Volk⟩

in'citement *n.* Anstiftung, *die*/ Aufstachelung, *die*

incl. *abbr.* = **including** inkl.

inclination /ɪnklɪˈneɪʃn/ *n.* Neigung, *die*

incline ⏍1⏍ /ɪnˈklaɪn/ *v.t.* (a) (bend) neigen
(b) (dispose) veranlassen
⏍2⏍ *v.i.* (be disposed) neigen (to[wards] zu)
⏍3⏍ /ˈɪnklaɪn/ *n.* Steigung, *die*

inclined /ɪnˈklaɪnd/ *adj.* geneigt; they are ∼ to be slow sie neigen zur Langsamkeit; if

you feel [so] ∼: wenn Sie Lust [dazu] haben

include /ɪnˈkluːd/ *v.t.* einschließen; (contain) enthalten; ∼d in the price im Preis inbegriffen

including /ɪnˈkluːdɪŋ/ *prep.* einschließlich (+ Gen.); ∼ VAT inklusive Mehrwertsteuer

inclusion /ɪnˈkluːʒn/ *n.* Aufnahme, *die*

inclusive /ɪnˈkluːsɪv/ *adj.* einschließlich; be ∼ of sth. etw. einschließen; from 2 to 6 January ∼: vom 2. bis einschließlich 6. Januar; cost £50 ∼: 50 Pfund kosten, alles inbegriffen

incognito /ɪnkɒgˈniːtəʊ/ *adj., adv.* inkognito

inco'herent *adj.* zusammenhanglos

income /ˈɪnkʌm/ *n.* Einkommen, *das*

income: ∼ **bracket,** ∼ **group** *ns.* Einkommensklasse, *die;* ∼ **sup'port** *n.* (Brit.) zusätzliche Hilfe zum Lebensunterhalt; ∼ **tax** *n.* Einkommensteuer, *die;* (on wages, salary) Lohnsteuer, *die*

'incoming *adj.* ankommend; landend ⟨Flugzeug⟩; einfahrend ⟨Zug⟩; eingehend ⟨Telefongespräch, Auftrag⟩

incomings /ˈɪnkʌmɪŋz/ *n. pl.* (revenue, income) Einnahmen *Pl.*

in'comparable *adj.* unvergleichlich

incom'patible *adj.* unvereinbar; be ∼ ⟨Menschen:⟩ nicht zueinander passen

in'competence /ɪnˈkɒmpɪtəns/ *n.* Unfähigkeit, *die;* Unvermögen, *das*

in'competent *adj.* unfähig

incom'plete *adj.* unvollständig

incompre'hensible *adj.* unbegreiflich; unverständlich ⟨Rede, Argument⟩

incon'ceivable *adj.* unvorstellbar

incon'clusive *adj.* ergebnislos; nicht schlüssig ⟨Beweis, Argument⟩

incongruous /ɪnˈkɒŋgrʊəs/ *adj.* unpassend

inconsequential /ɪnkɒnsɪˈkwenʃl/ *adj.* belanglos

incon'siderate *adj.* rücksichtslos

incon'sistency *n.* ▸ INCONSISTENT: Widersprüchlichkeit, *die;* Inkonsequenz, *die;* Unbeständigkeit, *die*

incon'sistent *adj.* widersprüchlich; (illogical) inkonsequent; (irregular) unbeständig

inconsolable /ɪnkənˈsəʊləbl/ *adj.* untröstlich

incon'spicuous *adj.* unauffällig

incontinence /ɪnˈkɒntɪnəns/ *n.* (Med.) Inkontinenz, *die*

incontinent /ɪnˈkɒntɪnənt/ *adj.* (Med.) inkontinent; be ∼: an Inkontinenz leiden

incontrovertible /ɪnkɒntrəˈvɜːtəbl/ *adj.* unbestreitbar; unwiderlegbar ⟨Beweis⟩

incon'venience ⏍1⏍ *n.* Unannehmlichkeiten *Pl.* (to für); put sb. to a lot of ∼: jmdm. große Unannehmlichkeiten bereiten
⏍2⏍ *v.t.* Unannehmlichkeiten bereiten

(+ *Dat.*); (disturb) stören

incon'venient *adj.* unbequem; ungünstig ⟨*Lage, Standort*⟩; **come at an ~ time** zu ungelegener Zeit kommen; **be ~ for sb.** jmdm. nicht passen

incorporate /ɪn'kɔːpəreɪt/ *v.t.* aufnehmen (**in**[**to**], **with** in + *Akk.*)

incorporated /ɪn'kɔːpəreɪtɪd/ *adj.* eingetragen ⟨[*Handels*]*gesellschaft*⟩

incor'rect *adj.* (a) unrichtig; **be ~:** nicht stimmen; **it is ~ to say that ...:** es stimmt nicht, dass ...
(b) (improper) inkorrekt

incor'rectly *adv.* (a) unrichtigerweise; falsch ⟨*beantworten, aussprechen*⟩
(b) (improperly) inkorrekt

incorrigible /ɪn'kɒrɪdʒɪbl/ *adj.* unverbesserlich

increase ①/ɪn'kriːs/ *v.i.* zunehmen; ⟨*Lärm:* ⟩ größer werden; ⟨*Preise, Nachfrage:*⟩ steigen; **~ in weight/size/price** schwerer/größer/teurer werden
② *v.t.* (a) (make greater) erhöhen
(b) (intensify) verstärken
③ /'ɪnkriːs/ *n.* Zunahme, *die* (in *Gen.*); **be on the ~:** ständig zunehmen

increasing /ɪn'kriːsɪŋ/ *adj.* steigend; **an ~ number of people** mehr und mehr Menschen

in'creasingly *adv.* in zunehmendem Maße; **become ~ apparent** immer deutlicher werden

in'credible *adj.* (also coll.: remarkable) unglaublich

in'credibly *adv.* (also coll.: remarkably) unglaublich

incredulity /ɪnkrɪ'djuːlɪtɪ/ *n.* Ungläubigkeit, *die*

incredulous /ɪn'kredjʊləs/ *adj.* ungläubig

increment /'ɪnkrɪmənt/ *n.* Erhöhung, *die;* (amount of growth) Zuwachs, *der*

incriminate /ɪn'krɪmɪneɪt/ *v.t.* belasten

incubate /'ɪŋkjʊbeɪt/ *v.t.* bebrüten; (to hatching) ausbrüten

incubation /ɪŋkjʊ'beɪʃn/ *n.* Bebrütung, *die*

incubator /ɪŋkjʊ'beɪtə(r)/ *n.* Inkubator, *der;* (for babies also) Brutkasten, *der*

incur /ɪn'kɜː(r)/ *v.t.* **-rr-** sich (*Dat.*) zuziehen ⟨*Unwillen, Ärger*⟩; **~ debts/expenses/risks** Schulden machen/Ausgaben haben/Risiken eingehen

in'curable *adj.* unheilbar

incurably /ɪn'kjʊərəblɪ/ *adv.* unheilbar ⟨*krank*⟩

incursion /ɪn'kɜːʃn/ *n.* Eindringen, *das;* (by sudden attack) Einfall, *der*

indebted /ɪn'detɪd/ *pred. adj.* **be** [**much**] **~ to sb. for sth.** jmdm. für etw. [sehr] zu Dank verpflichtet sein

in'decency *n.* Unanständigkeit, *die*

in'decent *adj.,* **in'decently** *adv.* unanständig

indecipherable /ɪndɪ'saɪfərəbl/ *adj.* unentzifferbar

inde'cision *n.* Unentschlossenheit, *die*

inde'cisive *adj.* (a) ergebnislos ⟨*Streit, Diskussion*⟩; nichtssagend ⟨*Ergebnis*⟩
(b) (hesitating) unentschlossen

indeed /ɪn'diːd/ *adv.* (a) in der Tat; **thank you very much ~:** haben Sie vielen herzlichen Dank; **~ it is** in der Tat
(b) (in fact) ja sogar; **~, he can ...:** ja, er kann sogar ...
(c) (admittedly) zugegebenermaßen

indefatigable /ɪndɪ'fætɪɡəbl/ *adj.* unermüdlich

indefensible /ɪndɪ'fensɪbl/ *adj.* (intolerable) unverzeihlich

in'definite *adj.* (a) (vague) unbestimmt
(b) (unlimited) unbegrenzt

in'definitely *adv.* (a) (vaguely) unbestimmt
(b) (unlimitedly) unbegrenzt; auf unbestimmte Zeit ⟨*verschieben*⟩

indelible /ɪn'delɪbl/ *adj.* unauslöschlich; **~ ink** Wäschetinte, *die*

indelibly /ɪn'delɪblɪ/ *adv.* unauslöschlich

indemnify /ɪn'demnɪfaɪ/ *v.t.* absichern (**against** gegen); (compensate) entschädigen

indemnity /ɪn'demnɪtɪ/ *n.* Absicherung, *die;* (compensation) Entschädigung, *die*

indentation /ɪnden'teɪʃn/ *n.* (a) (indenting, notch) Einkerbung, *die*
(b) (recess) Einschnitt, *der*

inde'pendence *n.* Unabhängigkeit, *die*

inde'pendent *adj.,* **inde'pendently** *adv.* unabhängig (**of** von)

indescribable /ɪndɪ'skraɪbəbl/ *adj.* unbeschreiblich

indestructible /ɪndɪ'strʌktɪbl/ *adj.* unzerstörbar

indeterminable /ɪndɪ'tɜːmɪnəbl/ *adj.* unbestimmbar

indeterminate /ɪndɪ'tɜːmɪnət/ *adj.* unbestimmt; unklar ⟨*Konzept*⟩

index /'ɪndeks/ ① *n.* Register, *das*
② *v.t.* mit einem Register versehen

index: ~ card *n.* Karteikarte, *die;* **~ finger** *n.* Zeigefinger, *der;* **~ gears** *pl.* Indexschaltung, *die;* **~-linked** *adj.* (Econ.) indexiert; dynamisch ⟨*Rente*⟩; **~ number** *n.* Indexzahl, *die*

India /'ɪndɪə/ *n.* Indien (*das*)

Indian /'ɪndɪən/ ① *adj.* (a) indisch; **sb. is ~:** jmd. ist Inder/Inderin
(b) [American] **~:** indianisch
② *n.* (a) Inder/Inderin, *die*
(b) [American] **~:** Indianer, *der*/Indianerin, *die*

Indian: ~ 'Ocean *pr. n.* Indischer Ozean; **~ 'summer** *n.* Altweibersommer, *der*

indicate /'ɪndɪkeɪt/ ① *v.t.* (a) (be a sign of) erkennen lassen ⋯⇢

(b) (state briefly) andeuten
(c) (mark, point out) anzeigen
(d) (suggest, make evident) zum Ausdruck
bringen (**to** gegenüber)
2 *v.i.* (Motor Veh.) blinken
indication /ɪndɪˈkeɪʃn/ *n.* [An]zeichen,
das (**of** Gen., für)
indicative /ɪnˈdɪkətɪv/ 1 *adj.* **(a)** be ~ **of**
sth. auf etw. (*Akk.*) schließen lassen
(b) (Ling.) indikativisch
2 *n.* (Ling.) Indikativ, *der*
indicator /ˈɪndɪkeɪtə(r)/ *n.* (on vehicle)
Blinker, *der*
indict /ɪnˈdaɪt/ *v.t.* anklagen (**for, on a
charge of** Gen.)
indie /ˈɪndɪ/ (coll.) 1 *adj.* Indie-⟨*Gruppe,
Szene, Charts etc.*⟩
2 *n.* (record company) Indie-Label, *das;* (band)
Indie-Band, *die*
in'difference *n.* Gleichgültigkeit, *die*
(**to[wards]** gegenüber)
in'different *adj.* **(a)** gleichgültig
(b) (not good) mittelmäßig
indigenous /ɪnˈdɪdʒɪnəs/ *adj.*
einheimisch; eingeboren ⟨*Bevölkerung*⟩
indigestible /ɪndɪˈdʒestɪbl/ *adj.* (lit. or fig.)
unverdaulich
indi'gestion *n.* Magenverstimmung, *die;*
(chronic) Verdauungsstörungen *Pl.*
indignant /ɪnˈdɪgnənt/ *adj.* entrüstet (**at,
over, about** über + *Akk.*); indigniert ⟨*Blick,
Geste*⟩
in'dignantly *adv.* entrüstet; indigniert
indignation /ɪndɪgˈneɪʃn/ *n.* Entrüstung,
die (**about, at, against, over** über + *Akk.*)
in'dignity *n.* Demütigung, *die*
indigo /ˈɪndɪgəʊ/ 1 *adj.* ~ **[blue]**
indigoblau
2 *n.* ~ **[blue]** Indigoblau, *das*
indi'rect *adj.* indirekt; ~ **speech** indirekte
Rede
indi'rectly *adv.* indirekt
indirect 'object *n.* indirektes Objekt; (in
German) Dativobjekt, *das*
indiscipline /ɪnˈdɪsɪplɪn/ *n.*, no indef. art.
Disziplinlosigkeit, *die*
indi'screet *adj.* indiskret
indi'scretion *n.* Indiskretion, *die*
indiscriminate /ɪndɪˈskrɪmɪnət/ *adj.*
(lacking judgement) unkritisch; (random,
unrestrained) wahllos
indi'spensable *adj.* unentbehrlich (**to**
für); unabdingbar ⟨*Voraussetzung*⟩
indisposed /ɪndɪˈspəʊzd/ *adj.* (unwell)
unpässlich; indisponiert ⟨*Sänger,
Schauspieler*⟩
indisputable /ɪndɪˈspjuːtəbl/ *adj.*,
indisputably /ɪndɪˈspjuːtəblɪ/ *adv.*
unbestreitbar
indi'stinct *adj.,* **indi'stinctly** *adv.*
undeutlich

indi'stinguishable *adj.* nicht
unterscheidbar
individual /ɪndɪˈvɪdjʊəl/ 1 *adj.*
(a) einzeln
(b) (distinctive, characteristic) individuell
2 *n.* Einzelne, *der/die*
individualist /ɪndɪˈvɪdjʊəlɪst/ *n.*
Individualist, *der/*Individualistin, *die*
individualistic /ɪndɪvɪdjʊəˈlɪstɪk/ *adj.*
individualistisch
individuality /ɪndɪvɪdjʊˈælɪtɪ/ *n.*
(character) eigene Persönlichkeit
indi'vidually *adv.* einzeln
indi'visible *adj.* unteilbar
indoctrinate /ɪnˈdɒktrɪneɪt/ *v.t.*
indoktrinieren
indoctrination /ɪndɒktrɪˈneɪʃn/ *n.*
Indoktrination, *die*
indolence /ˈɪndələns/ *n.* Trägheit, *die*
indolent /ˈɪndələnt/ *adj.* träge
indomitable /ɪnˈdɒmɪtəbl/ *adj.*
unbeugsam
Indonesia /ɪndəˈniːzɪə/ *pr. n.* Indonesien
(*das*)
'indoor *adj.* ~ **swimming pool/sports**
Hallenbad, *das/*-sport, *der;* ~ **plants**
Zimmerpflanzen; ~ **games** Spiele im Haus;
(Sport) Hallenspiele
indoors /ɪnˈdɔːz/ *adv.* drinnen; im Haus;
go/come ~: nach drinnen gehen/kommen
indubitable /ɪnˈdjuːbɪtəbl/ *adj.*
unzweifelhaft
indubitably /ɪnˈdjuːbɪtəblɪ/ *adv.*
zweifellos; zweifelsohne
induce /ɪnˈdjuːs/ *v.t.* ~ **sb. to do sth.** jmdn.
dazu bringen, etw. zu tun
in'ducement *n.* (incentive) Anreiz, *der*
induction /ɪnˈdʌkʃn/ *n.* Amtseinführung,
die; ~ **course** Einführungskurs[us], *der*
indulge /ɪnˈdʌldʒ/ 1 *v.t.* **(a)** nachgeben
(+ *Dat.*) ⟨*Wunsch, Verlangen, Verlockung*⟩;
frönen (geh.) (+ *Dat.*) ⟨*Leidenschaft*⟩
(b) (please) verwöhnen
2 *v.i.* ~ **in** frönen (geh.) (+ *Dat.*)
⟨*Leidenschaft*⟩
indulgence /ɪnˈdʌldʒəns/ *n.*
(a) Nachsicht, *die;* (humouring)
Nachgiebigkeit, *die* (**with** gegenüber)
(b) (thing indulged in) Luxus, *der*
indulgent /ɪnˈdʌldʒənt/ *adj.* nachsichtig
(**with, to[wards]** gegenüber)
industrial /ɪnˈdʌstrɪəl/ *adj.* industriell;
Arbeits⟨*unfall, -medizin, -psychologie*⟩
industrial: ~ **'action** *n.*
Arbeitskampfmaßnahmen *Pl.;* **take**
~ **action** in den Ausstand treten; ~ **area**
n. Industriegebiet, *das;* ~ **di'sease**
n. Berufskrankheit, *die;* ~ **dispute** *n.*
Arbeitskonflikt, *der;* ~ **espionage**
n. Industriespionage, *die;* ~ **estate**
n. Industriegebiet, *das* ~ **'injury** *n.*
Arbeitsverletzung, *die*

industrialist /ɪn'dʌstrɪəlɪst/ n.
Industrielle, der/die
industrialization /ɪndʌstrɪəlaɪ'zeɪʃn/ n.
Industrialisierung, die
industrialize /ɪn'dʌstrɪəlaɪz/ v.t.
industrialisieren
industrial: ~ **park** n. Industriegebiet,
das; ~ **plant** n. Industrieanlage, die;
~ **re'lations** n. pl. Industrialrelations
Pl.; ~ **town** n. Industriestadt, die;
~ **tribunal** n. Arbeitsgericht, das;
~ **waste** n. Industriemüll, der
industrious /ɪn'dʌstrɪəs/ adj. fleißig;
(busy) emsig
industry /'ɪndəstrɪ/ n. (a) Industrie, die
(b) ▶ INDUSTRIOUS: Fleiß, der; Emsigkeit, die
inebriated /ɪ'niːbrɪeɪtɪd/ adj. betrunken
inebriation /ɪniːbrɪ'eɪʃn/ n.
Betrunkenheit, die; betrunkener Zustand
in'edible adj. ungenießbar
inef'fective adj. unwirksam; fruchtlos
〈Anstrengung, Versuch〉
ineffectual /ɪnɪ'fektjʊəl/ adj. unwirksam;
fruchtlos 〈Versuch, Bemühung〉; ineffizient
〈Methode, Person〉
inef'ficiency n. Leistungsschwäche,
die; (of organization, method) schlechtes
Funktionieren
inef'ficient adj. leistungsschwach;
schlecht funktionierend 〈Organisation,
Methode〉
in'elegant adj. unelegant
in'eligible adj. ungeeignet; be ~ for
nicht infrage kommen für 〈Beförderung,
Position〉; nicht berechtigt sein zu
〈Leistungen des Staats usw.〉
inept /ɪ'nept/ adj. unbeholfen
ineptitude /ɪ'neptɪtjuːd/ n.
Unbeholfenheit, die
ine'quality n. Ungleichheit, die
inert /ɪ'nɜːt/ adj. (a) reglos; (sluggish) träge
(b) (Chem.) inert; ~ **gas** Edelgas, das
inertia /ɪ'nɜːʃə/ n. Trägheit, die
inertia reel 'seat belt n.
Automatikgurt, der
inescapable /ɪnɪ'skeɪpəbl/ adj.
unausweichlich
ines'sential adj. unwesentlich;
(dispensable) entbehrlich
inestimable /ɪn'estɪməbl/ adj.
unschätzbar
inevitable /ɪn'evɪtəbl/ adj.
unvermeidbar; unabwendbar 〈Ereignis,
Krieg, Schicksal〉; zwangsläufig 〈Ergebnis,
Folge〉
inevitably /ɪn'evɪtəblɪ/ adv. zwangsläufig
ine'xact adj. ungenau
inex'cusable adj. unverzeihlich
inexhaustible /ɪnɪg'zɔːstɪbl/ adj.
unerschöpflich; unverwüstlich 〈Person〉
inexorable /ɪn'eksərəbl/ adj. unerbittlich

inex'pensive adj. preisgünstig
inex'perience n. Unerfahrenheit, die
inex'perienced adj. unerfahren; ~ in
sth. wenig vertraut mit etw.
inexpert /ɪn'ekspɜːt/ adj. unerfahren
inex'plicable adj. unerklärlich
inexpressive /ɪnɪk'spresɪv/ adj.
ausdruckslos 〈Gesicht, Augen〉; trocken
〈Ausdrucksweise, Sprache〉
inextricably /ɪn'ekstrɪkəblɪ/ adv.
become ~ entangled sich vollkommen
verheddern (ugs.); [be] ~ linked untrennbar
verbunden [sein]
infallibility /ɪnfælɪ'bɪlɪtɪ/ n.
Unfehlbarkeit, die
in'fallible adj. unfehlbar
infamous /'ɪnfəməs/ adj. berüchtigt
infancy /'ɪnfənsɪ/ n. frühe Kindheit; be in
its ~ (fig.) noch in den Anfängen stecken
infant /'ɪnfənt/ n. kleines Kind
infantile /'ɪnfəntaɪl/ adj. kindlich; (childish)
kindisch
infant mor'tality n.
Säuglingssterblichkeit, die
infantry /'ɪnfəntrɪ/ n. Infanterie, die
'infant school n. (Brit.) ≈ Vorschule, die
infatuated /ɪn'fætjʊeɪtɪd/ adj. be ~ with
sb. in jmdn. vernarrt sein
infect /ɪn'fekt/ v.t. anstecken; infizieren;
the wound became ~ed die Wunde
entzündete sich
infection /ɪn'fekʃn/ n. Infektion, die;
throat/ear/eye ~: Hals-/Ohren-/
Augenentzündung, die
infectious /ɪn'fekʃəs/ adj. ansteckend; be ~
〈Person〉 eine ansteckende Krankheit haben
infer /ɪn'fɜː(r)/ v.t. ⁑rr- schließen (from aus);
ziehen 〈Schlussfolgerung〉
inference /'ɪnfərəns/ n.
[Schluss]folgerung, die
inferior /ɪn'fɪərɪə(r)/ ⌈1⌉ adj. (of lower quality)
minderwertig 〈Ware〉; minder… 〈Qualität〉;
unterlegen 〈Gegner〉; ~ **to sth.** schlechter
als etw.; feel ~: Minderwertigkeitsgefühle
haben
⌈2⌉ n. Untergebene, der/die
inferiority /ɪnfɪərɪ'ɒrɪtɪ/ n.
Minderwertigkeit, die; (of opponent)
Unterlegenheit, die
inferi'ority complex n.
Minderwertigkeitskomplex, der
infernal /ɪn'fɜːnl/ adj. (a) (of hell) höllisch
(b) (coll.) verdammt (salopp)
inferno /ɪn'fɜːnəʊ/ n. Inferno, das
in'fertile adj. unfruchtbar
infer'tility n. Unfruchtbarkeit, die
infest /ɪn'fest/ v.t. 〈Ungeziefer:〉 befallen;
〈Unkraut:〉 überwuchern; ~ed with
befallen/überwuchert von
infestation /ɪnfes'teɪʃn/ n. ~ of rats/
insects Ratten-/Insektenplage, die

infidelity /ɪnfɪˈdelɪtɪ/ n. Untreue, die (**to** gegenüber)

'**infighting** n. (in organization) interne Machtkämpfe Pl.

infiltrate /ˈɪnfɪltreɪt/ v.t. (a) infiltrieren; unterwandern ‹Partei, Organisation› (b) einschleusen ‹Agenten›

infinite /ˈɪnfɪnɪt/ adj. (a) (endless) unendlich (b) (very great) ungeheuer

infinitesimal /ɪnfɪnɪˈtesɪml/ adj. (a) (Math.) infinitesimal (b) (very small) äußerst gering; winzig ‹Menge›

infinitive /ɪnˈfɪnɪtɪv/ n. Infinitiv, der

infinity /ɪnˈfɪnɪtɪ/ n. Unendlichkeit, die

infirm /ɪnˈfɜːm/ adj. gebrechlich

infirmary /ɪnˈfɜːmərɪ/ n. (hospital) Krankenhaus, das

infirmity /ɪnˈfɜːmɪtɪ/ n. Gebrechlichkeit, die; (malady) Gebrechen, das

inflamed /ɪnˈfleɪmd/ adj. (Med.) be/become ~: entzündet sein/sich entzünden

inflammable /ɪnˈflæməbl/ adj. feuergefährlich

inflammation /ɪnfləˈmeɪʃn/ n. (Med.) Entzündung, die

inflammatory /ɪnˈflæmətərɪ/ adj. aufrührerisch; **an** ~ **speech** eine Hetzrede

inflatable /ɪnˈfleɪtəbl/ adj. aufblasbar; ~ **dinghy** Schlauchboot, das

inflate /ɪnˈfleɪt/ v.t. aufblasen; (with pump) aufpumpen

inflated /ɪnˈfleɪtɪd/ adj. (lit or fig.) aufgeblasen

inflation /ɪnˈfleɪʃn/ n. (Econ.) Inflation, die

in'flexible adj. (a) (stiff) unbiegsam (b) (obstinate) [geistig] unbeweglich

inflict /ɪnˈflɪkt/ v.t. zufügen ‹Leid, Schmerzen›, beibringen ‹Wunde›, versetzen ‹Schlag› (**on** Dat.)

infliction /ɪnˈflɪkʃn/ n. ▶ INFLICT: Zufügen, das; Beibringen, das; Versetzen, das

'**in-flight** adj. Bord‹verpflegung, -programm›

influence /ˈɪnfluəns/ ① n. Einfluss, der; **be a good/bad** ~ [**on sb.**] einen guten/ schlechten Einfluss [auf jmdn.] ausüben ② v.t. beeinflussen

influential /ɪnfluˈenʃl/ adj. einflussreich

influenza /ɪnfluˈenzə/ n. Grippe, die

influx /ˈɪnflʌks/ n. Zustrom, der

info /ˈɪnfəʊ/ n. (coll.) Infos Pl. (ugs.)

inform /ɪnˈfɔːm/ ① v.t. informieren (**of, about** über + Akk.); **keep sb.** ~**ed** jmdn. auf dem Laufenden halten ② v.i. ~ **against** or **on sb.** jmdn. denunzieren (**to** bei)

in'formal adj. (a) zwanglos (b) (unofficial) informell

infor'mality n. Zwanglosigkeit, die

informant /ɪnˈfɔːmənt/ n. Informant, der/Informantin, die

information /ɪnfəˈmeɪʃn/ n. Informationen Pl.; **give** ~ **on sth.** Auskunft über etw. (Akk.) erteilen; **piece** or **bit of** ~: Information, die

information: ~ **bureau,** ~ **centre** ns. Auskunftsbüro, das; ~ **desk** n. Informationsschalter, der; ~ **explosion** n. Informationsflut, die; ~ **highway** n. (Comp.) Datenautobahn, die; ~ **office** ▶ ~ BUREAU; ~ **pack** n. Informationspaket, das; (folder etc.) Informationsmappe, die; ~ **retrieval** n. (Comp.) Retrieval, das; ~ **science** n. Informatik, die; ~ **superhighway** n. (Comp.) Datenautobahn, die; Datensuperhighway, der; ~ **system** n. Informationssystem, das; ~ **technology** n. Informationstechnologie, die

informative /ɪnˈfɔːmətɪv/ adj. informativ; **not very** ~: nicht sehr aufschlussreich ‹Dokument, Schriftstück›

informed /ɪnˈfɔːmd/ adj. informiert

in'former n. Denunziant, der/ Denunziantin, die

infra-red /ɪnfrəˈred/ adj. infrarot

infrastructure /ˈɪnfrəstrʌktʃə(r)/ n. Infrastruktur, die

infrequency /ɪnˈfriːkwənsɪ/ n. Seltenheit, die

in'frequent adj., **in'frequently** adv. selten

infringe /ɪnˈfrɪndʒ/ v.t. & i. ~ [**on**] verstoßen gegen

in'fringement n. Verstoß, der (**of** gegen)

infuriate /ɪnˈfjʊərɪeɪt/ v.t. wütend machen; **be** ~**d** wütend sein (**by** über + Akk.)

infuriating /ɪnˈfjʊərɪeɪtɪŋ/ adj. ärgerlich

ingenious /ɪnˈdʒiːnɪəs/ adj. einfallsreich; genial ‹Methode, Idee›; raffiniert ‹Spielzeug, Maschine›

ingenuity /ɪndʒɪˈnjuːɪtɪ/ n. Genialität, die

ingot /ˈɪŋgət/ n. Ingot, der

ingratiate /ɪnˈgreɪʃɪeɪt/ v. refl. ~ **oneself with sb.** sich bei jmdm. einschmeicheln

in'gratitude n. Undankbarkeit, die (**to[wards]** gegenüber)

ingredient /ɪnˈgriːdɪənt/ n. Zutat, die

ingrowing /ˈɪŋgrəʊɪŋ/ adj. eingewachsen ‹Zehennagel usw.›

inhabit /ɪnˈhæbɪt/ v.t. bewohnen

inhabitable /ɪnˈhæbɪtəbl/ adj. bewohnbar

inhabitant /ɪnˈhæbɪtənt/ n. Bewohner, der/Bewohnerin, die

inhale /ɪnˈheɪl/ v.t. & i. einatmen; inhalieren (ugs.) ‹Zigarettenrauch usw.›

inherent /ɪnˈhɪərənt, ɪnˈherənt/ adj. adj. (belonging by nature) innewohnend (geh.); natürlich ‹Anmut, Eleganz›

inherit /ɪnˈherɪt/ v.t. erben

inheritance /ɪn'herɪtəns/ n. Erbe, das; (inheriting) Erbschaft, die

in'heritance tax n. Erbschaftssteuer, die

inhibit /ɪn'hɪbɪt/ v.t. hemmen

in'hibited adj. gehemmt

inhibition /ɪnhɪ'bɪʃn/ n. Hemmung, die

inho'spitable adj. ungastlich ‹Person, Verhalten›; unwirtlich ‹Gegend, Klima›

'in-house adj. hausintern

in'human adj. unmenschlich

inhumane /ɪnhju:'meɪn/ adj. unmenschlich

initial /ɪ'nɪʃl/ **1** adj. anfänglich; Anfangs‹stadium, -schwierigkeiten› **2** n. esp. in pl. Initiale, die **3** v.t. (Brit.) -ll- abzeichnen ‹Scheck, Quittung›; paraphieren ‹Vertrag, Abkommen usw.›

initial 'letter n. Anfangsbuchstabe, der

i'nitially adv. anfangs; am Anfang

initiate /ɪ'nɪʃɪeɪt/ v.t. (a) (introduce) einführen (**into** in + Akk.); (into knowledge, mystery) einweihen (**into** in + Akk.) (b) (begin) einleiten

initiation /ɪnɪʃɪ'eɪʃn/ n. (a) (introduction) Einführung, die (b) (into knowledge, mystery) Einweihung, die

initiative /ɪ'nɪʃətɪv/ n. Initiative, die; **lack** ∼: keine Initiative haben

inject /ɪn'dʒekt/ v.t. [ein]spritzen; injizieren (Med.)

injection /ɪn'dʒekʃn/ n. Spritze, die; Injektion, die

injure /'ɪndʒə(r)/ v.t. (a) verletzen; **his leg was** ∼**d** er wurde/(state) war am Bein verletzt (b) (impair) schaden (+ Dat.)

injured /'ɪndʒəd/ adj. verletzt; verwundet ‹Soldat›

injury /'ɪndʒərɪ/ n. Verletzung, die (**to** Gen.)

'injury time n. (Brit. Footb.) Nachspielzeit, die; **be into/play** ∼: nachspielen

in'justice n. Ungerechtigkeit, die

ink /ɪŋk/ n. Tinte, die

'ink-jet printer n. Tintenstrahldrucker, der

inkling /'ɪŋklɪŋ/ n. Ahnung, die; **have an** ∼ **of sth.** etw. ahnen

'ink pad n. Stempelkissen, das

inland /'ɪnlənd, 'ɪnlænd/ adj. Binnen-; binnenländisch

Inland 'Revenue n. (Brit.) ≈ Finanzamt, das

'in-laws n. pl. (coll.) Schwiegereltern Pl.

inlet /'ɪnlət/ n. [schmale] Bucht

'inmate n. Insasse, der/Insassin, die

inn /ɪn/ n. (hotel) Gasthof, der; (pub) Wirtshaus, das

innate /ɪ'neɪt/ adj. angeboren

inner /'ɪnə(r)/ adj. inner...; Innen‹hof, -tür, -fläche, -seite usw.›; ∼ **tube** Schlauch, der

inner 'city n. Innenstadt, die; ∼ **areas** Innenbezirke

innermost /'ɪnəməʊst/ adj. innerst...

'innkeeper n. [Gast]wirt, der/-wirtin, die

innocence /'ɪnəsəns/ n. (a) Unschuld, die (b) (naivety) Naivität, die

innocent /'ɪnəsənt/ adj. (a) unschuldig (**of** an + Dat.) (b) (naïve) naiv

innocuous /ɪ'nɒkjʊəs/ adj. harmlos

innovation /ɪnə'veɪʃn/ n. Innovation, die; (thing, change) Neuerung, die

innovative /'ɪnəvətɪv/ adj. innovativ

innuendo /ɪnju:'endəʊ/ n., pl. ∼**es** or ∼**s** versteckte Andeutung

innumerable /ɪ'nju:mərəbl/ adj. unzählig

innumeracy /ɪ'nju:mərəsɪ/ n. Nicht-Rechnen-Können, das

innumerate /ɪ'nju:mərət/ adj. **be** ∼: nicht rechnen können

inoculate /ɪ'nɒkjʊleɪt/ v.t. impfen

inoculation /ɪnɒkjʊ'leɪʃn/ n. Impfung, die

inof'fensive adj. harmlos

inoperable /ɪn'ɒpərəbl/ adj. (Surg.) inoperabel (fachspr.)

inoperative /ɪn'ɒpərətɪv/ adj. ungültig

in'opportune adj. unpassend; unangebracht ‹Bemerkung›

inordinate /ɪ'nɔ:dɪnət/ adj. unmäßig; ungeheuer ‹Menge›

inor'ganic adj. anorganisch

'inpatient n. stationär behandelter Patient/behandelte Patientin

'input n. Input, der od. das

inquest /'ɪŋkwest/ n. gerichtliche Untersuchung der Todesursache

inquire, inquiry ▸ ENQUIR-

inquisitive /ɪn'kwɪzɪtɪv/ adj. neugierig

'inroad n. Eingriff, der (**on, into** in + Akk.); **make** ∼**s into sb.'s savings** jmds. Ersparnisse angreifen

in'sane adj. geisteskrank

in'sanitary adj. unhygienisch

in'sanity n. Geisteskrankheit, die

insatiable /ɪn'seɪʃəbl/ adj. unersättlich; unstillbar ‹Verlangen›

inscribe /ɪn'skraɪb/ v.t. schreiben; (on stone, rock) einmeißeln; mit einer Inschrift versehen ‹Denkmal, Grabstein›

inscription /ɪn'skrɪpʃn/ n. Inschrift, die; (on coin) Aufschrift, die

inscrutable /ɪn'skru:təbl/ adj. unergründlich; undurchdringlich ‹Miene›

insect /'ɪnsekt/ n. Insekt, das

insect: ∼ **bite** n. Insektenstich, der; ∼**-borne** adj. durch Insekten übertragen ‹Krankheit›

insecticide /ɪn'sektɪsaɪd/ n. Insektizid, das

'**insect repellent** *n.* Insektenschutzmittel, *das*

inse'cure *adj.* unsicher

inse'curity *n.* Unsicherheit, *die*

insemination /ɪnsemɪˈneɪʃn/ *n.* (of woman) Befruchtung, *die;* (of animal) Besamung, *die*

in'sensitive *adj.* (a) gefühllos ⟨Person, Art⟩; (unappreciative) unempfänglich (**to** für) (b) (physically) unempfindlich (**to** gegen)

in'separable *adj.* untrennbar; (fig.) unzertrennlich

insert /ɪnˈsɜːt/ *v.t.* (a) einlegen ⟨Film⟩; einwerfen ⟨Münze⟩; hineinstecken ⟨Schlüssel⟩; einstechen ⟨Nadel⟩ (b) (Comp.) einfügen; ∼ **key** Einfügetaste, *die*

insertion /ɪnˈsɜːʃn/ *n.* ▸ INSERT: Einlegen, *das;* Einwerfen, *das;* Hineinstecken, *das;* Einstechen, *das;* Einfügen, *das*

'**inset** *n.* (small map) Nebenkarte, *die;* (small photograph, diagram) Nebenbild, *das*

inside ☐1 /-'-, '--/ *n.* (a) (internal side) Innenseite, *die;* **on the** ∼: innen; **to/from the** ∼: nach/von innen (b) (inner part) Innere, *das* ☐2 /'--/ *adj.* inner...; Innen⟨wand, -einrichtung, -ansicht⟩; (fig.) intern ☐3 /-'-/ *adv.* (on or in the ∼) innen; (to the ∼) nach innen hinein/herein; (indoors) drinnen; **come** ∼: hereinkommen; **take a look** ∼: hineinsehen; **go** ∼: [ins Haus] hineingehen; **turn a jacket** ∼ **out** eine Jacke nach links wenden; **know sth.** ∼ **out** etw. in- und auswendig kennen ☐4 /-'-/ *prep.* (position) in (+ *Dat.*); (direction) in (+ *Akk.*) hinein

inside-'leg *adj.* ∼ **measurement** Schrittlänge, *die*

insidious /ɪnˈsɪdɪəs/ *adj.* heimtückisch

'**insight** *n.* (discernment) Verständnis, *das;* **gain an** ∼ **into sth.** Einblick in etw. (*Akk.*) gewinnen

insig'nificant *adj.* unbedeutend; geringfügig ⟨Summe⟩

insin'cere *adj.* unaufrichtig

insin'cerity *n.* Unaufrichtigkeit, *die*

insinuate /ɪnˈsɪnjʊeɪt/ *v.t.* andeuten (**to sb.** jmdm. gegenüber)

insinuation /ɪnsɪnjʊˈeɪʃn/ *n.* Anspielung, *die* (**about** auf + *Akk.*)

insipid /ɪnˈsɪpɪd/ *adj.* fade

insist /ɪnˈsɪst/ *v.i.* bestehen ([up]on auf + *Dat.*); ∼ **on doing sth./on sb.'s doing sth.** darauf bestehen, etw. zu tun/dass jmd. etw. tut; **if you** ∼: wenn du darauf bestehst

insistence /ɪnˈsɪstəns/ *n.* Bestehen, *das* (**on** auf + *Dat.*)

insistent /ɪnˈsɪstənt/ *adj.* **be** ∼ **that** ...: darauf bestehen, dass ...

insolence /ˈɪnsələns/ *n.* Unverschämtheit, *die;* Frechheit, *die*

insolent /ˈɪnsələnt/ *adj.*, '**insolently** *adv.* unverschämt; frech

in'soluble *adj.* (a) (esp. Chem.) unlöslich (b) (not solvable) unlösbar

insolvency /ɪnˈsɒlvənsɪ/ *n.* Zahlungsunfähigkeit, *die*

in'solvent *adj.* zahlungsunfähig

insomnia /ɪnˈsɒmnɪə/ *n.* Schlaflosigkeit, *die*

insomniac /ɪnˈsɒmnɪæk/ *n.* **be an** ∼: an Schlaflosigkeit leiden

inspect /ɪnˈspekt/ *v.t.* prüfend betrachten; (examine officially) überprüfen; kontrollieren ⟨Räumlichkeiten⟩

inspection /ɪnˈspekʃn/ *n.* Überprüfung, *die;* (of premises) Kontrolle, *die;* Inspektion, *die;* **on [closer]** ∼: bei näherer Betrachtung

inspector /ɪnˈspektə(r)/ *n.* (a) (on bus, train, etc.) Kontrolleur, *der*/Kontrolleurin, *die* (b) (Brit.) ≈ Polizeiinspektor, *der*

inspiration /ɪnspəˈreɪʃn/ *n.* Inspiration, *die* (geh.)

inspire /ɪnˈspaɪə(r)/ *v.t.* (a) inspirieren (geh.) ⟨Person⟩ (b) (instil) einflößen (**in** *Dat.*)

inspiring /ɪnˈspaɪərɪŋ/ *adj.* inspirierend (geh.)

insta'bility *n.* Instabilität, *die;* (of person) Labilität, *die*

install /ɪnˈstɔːl/ *v.t.* installieren; einbauen ⟨Badezimmer⟩; anschließen ⟨Telefon, Herd⟩; ∼ **oneself** sich installieren

installation /ɪnstəˈleɪʃn/ *n.* (a) Installation, *die;* (of bathroom) Einbau, *der;* (of telephone, cooker) Anschluss, *der* (b) (apparatus etc. installed) Anlage, *die*

instalment (*Amer.:* **installment**) /ɪnˈstɔːlmənt/ *n.* (a) (part payment) Rate, *die;* **pay by** *or* **in** ∼s in Raten zahlen (b) (of serial, novel) Fortsetzung, *die;* (Radio, Telev.) Folge, *die*

instance /ˈɪnstəns/ *n.* (example) Beispiel, *das* (**of** für); **for** ∼: zum Beispiel; **in many** ∼s (cases) in vielen Fällen; **in the first** ∼: zunächst einmal

instant /ˈɪnstənt/ ☐1 *adj.* unmittelbar; sofortig ⟨Wirkung, Linderung, Ergebnis⟩; ∼ **coffee/tea** Pulverkaffee/Instanttee, *der;* ∼ **potatoes** fertiger Kartoffelbrei ☐2 *n.* Augenblick, *der;* **at that very** ∼: genau in dem Augenblick; **come here this** ∼: komm sofort her; **in an** ∼: augenblicklich

instantaneous /ɪnstənˈteɪnɪəs/ *adj.* unmittelbar; **his reaction was** ∼: er reagierte sofort

'**instantly** *adv.* sofort

instead /ɪnˈsted/ *adv.* stattdessen; ∼ **of doing sth.** [an]statt etw. zu tun; ∼ **of sth.** anstelle einer Sache (*Gen.*); **I will go** ∼ **of you** ich gehe an deiner Stelle

'**instep** *n.* (of foot) Spann, *der;* Fußrücken, *der;* (of shoe) Blatt, *das*

instigate /ˈɪnstɪgeɪt/ *v.t.* anstiften (**to** zu); initiieren (geh.) ⟨Reformen, Projekt usw.⟩

instigation /ɪnstɪˈgeɪʃn/ n. Anstiftung, *die;* (of reforms, project, etc.) Initiierung, *die;* **at sb.'s ~:** auf jmds. Betreiben (*Akk.*)

instil (*Amer.:* **instill**) /ɪnˈstɪl/ v.t., -ll- einflößen (**in** *Dat.*); beibringen ⟨*gutes Benehmen, Wissen*⟩ (**in** *Dat.*)

instinct /ˈɪnstɪŋkt/ n. Instinkt, *der*

instinctive /ɪnˈstɪŋktɪv/ adj., **in'stinctively** adv. instinktiv

institute /ˈɪnstɪtjuːt/ ① n. Institut, *das* ② v.t. einführen; einleiten ⟨*Suche, Verfahren*⟩; anstrengen ⟨*Prozess*⟩

institution /ɪnstɪˈtjuːʃn/ n. Institution, *die;* (home) Heim, *das;* Anstalt, *die*

instruct /ɪnˈstrʌkt/ v.t. **(a)** (teach) unterrichten ⟨*Klasse, Fach*⟩ **(b)** (direct, command) anweisen

instruction /ɪnˈstrʌkʃn/ n. **(a)** (teaching) Unterricht, *der* **(b)** *esp. in pl.* (direction, order) Anweisung, *die;* **~ manual/~s for use** Gebrauchsanleitung, *die*

instructive /ɪnˈstrʌktɪv/ adj. aufschlussreich; lehrreich ⟨*Erfahrung, Buch*⟩

instructor /ɪnˈstrʌktə(r)/ n. Lehrer, *der*/Lehrerin, *die;* (Mil.) Ausbilder, *der*

instrument /ˈɪnstrʊmənt/ n. Instrument, *das*

instrumental /ɪnstrəˈmentl/ adj. **(a)** (Mus.) Instrumental- **(b)** (helpful) dienlich (**to** *Dat.*); **he was ~ in finding me a job** er hat mir zu einer Stelle verholfen

instrumentalist /ɪnstrʊˈmentəlɪst/ n. Instrumentalist, *der*/Instrumentalistin, *die*

insubordinate /ɪnsəˈbɔːdɪnət/ adj. aufsässig

insubordination /ɪnsəbɔːdɪˈneɪʃn/ n. Aufsässigkeit, *die*

insubstantial /ɪnsəbˈstænʃl/ adj. wenig substanziell (geh.)

insufferable /ɪnˈsʌfərəbl/ adj. (unbearably arrogant) unausstehlich

insuf'ficient adj. nicht genügend; unzulänglich ⟨*Beweise*⟩; unzureichend ⟨*Versorgung, Beleuchtung*⟩

insuf'ficiently adv. ungenügend

insular /ˈɪnsjʊlə(r)/ adj. **(a)** Insel-; insular (fachspr.) **(b)** (fig.: narrow-minded) provinziell (abwertend)

insulate /ˈɪnsjʊleɪt/ v.t. isolieren (**against, from** gegen); **insulating tape** Isolierband, *das*

insulation /ɪnsjʊˈleɪʃn/ n. Isolierung, *die*

insulin /ˈɪnsjʊlɪn/ n. Insulin, *das*

insult ① /ˈɪnsʌlt/ n. Beleidigung, *die* (**to** *Gen.*) ② /ɪnˈsʌlt/ v.t. beleidigen

insulting /ɪnˈsʌltɪŋ/ adj. beleidigend

insuperable /ɪnˈsuːpərəbl/ adj. unüberwindlich

insupportable /ɪnsəˈpɔːtəbl/ adj. (unendurable) unerträglich

insurance /ɪnˈʃʊərəns/ n. Versicherung, *die;* (fig.) Sicherheit, *die;* **take out ~ against/ on sth.** eine Versicherung gegen etw. abschließen/etw. versichern lassen; **travel ~:** Reisegepäck- und -unfallversicherung, *die*

insurance: ~ agent n. Versicherungsvertreter, *der*/-vertreterin, *die;* **~ broker** n. Versicherungsmakler, *der*/-maklerin, *die;* **~ claim** n. Versicherungsanspruch, *der;* **~ company** n. Versicherungsgesellschaft, *die;* **~ stamp** n. (Brit.) Versicherungsmarke, *die*

insure /ɪnˈʃʊə(r)/ v.t. versichern ⟨*Person*⟩; versichern lassen ⟨*Gepäck, Gemälde usw.*⟩; **~ oneself against sth.** [sich] gegen etw. versichern

insurer /ɪnˈʃʊərə(r)/ n. Versicherer, *der*

insurmountable /ɪnsəˈmaʊntəbl/ adj. unüberwindlich

intact /ɪnˈtækt/ adj. **(a)** (entire) unbeschädigt; intakt ⟨*Uhr, Maschine usw.*⟩ **(b)** (unimpaired) unversehrt

'intake n. **(a)** (action) Aufnahme, *die* **(b)** (persons, things) Neuzugänge *Pl.;* (amount) aufgenommene Menge

in'tangible adj. nicht greifbar; (mentally) unbestimmbar

integral /ˈɪntɪgrl/ adj. **(a)** wesentlich ⟨*Bestandteil*⟩ **(b)** (whole) vollständig

integrate /ˈɪntɪgreɪt/ v.t. integrieren (**into** in + *Akk.*)

integration /ɪntɪˈgreɪʃn/ n. Integration, *die* (**into** in + *Akk.*)

integrity /ɪnˈtegrɪti/ n. Redlichkeit, *die*

intellect /ˈɪntəlekt/ n. Verstand, *der;* Intellekt, *der*

intellectual /ɪntəˈlektjʊəl/ ① adj. intellektuell; geistig anspruchsvoll ⟨*Person, Publikum*⟩ ② n. Intellektuelle, *der/die*

intellectual 'property n., no pl. (Law) geistiges Eigentum; attrib. **~ rights** gewerblicher Rechtsschutz und Urheberrecht

intelligence /ɪnˈtelɪdʒəns/ n. **(a)** Intelligenz, *die* **(b)** (information) Informationen *Pl.* **(c) military ~** (organization) militärischer Geheimdienst

intelligence: ~ quotient n. Intelligenzquotient, *der;* **~ test** n. Intelligenztest, *der*

intelligent /ɪnˈtelɪdʒənt/ adj. intelligent

intelligible /ɪnˈtelɪdʒɪbl/ adj. verständlich (**to** für)

intend /ɪnˈtend/ v.t. beabsichtigen; **it was ~ed as a joke** das sollte ein Witz sein

in'tended adj. beabsichtigt ⟨*Wirkung*⟩; **be ~ for sb./sth.** für jmdn./etw. gedacht sein

intense /ın'tens/ adj. (a) intensiv; groß ⟨Hitze, Belastung, Interesse⟩; stark ⟨Schmerzen⟩ (b) (earnest) ernst

in'tensely adv. äußerst; intensiv ⟨studieren, fühlen⟩

intensify /ın'tensıfaı/ **1** v.t. intensivieren **2** v.i. zunehmen

intensity /ın'tensıtı/ n. ▶ INTENSE A: Intensität, die; Größe, die; Stärke, die

intensive /ın'tensıv/ adj. intensiv; Intensiv⟨kurs⟩; be in ~ care auf der Intensivstation sein

in'tensively adv. intensiv

intent /ın'tent/ **1** n. Absicht, die; to all ~s and purposes im Grunde **2** adj. be ~ on achieving sth. etw. unbedingt erreichen wollen

intention /ın'tenʃn/ n. Absicht, die

intentional /ın'tenʃənl/ adj., **in'tentionally** adv. absichtlich

in'tently adv. aufmerksam

interact /ıntər'ækt/ v.i. interagieren

interaction /ıntər'ækʃn/ n. Interaktion, die

interactive /ıntər'æktıv/ adj. (Sociol., Psych., Comp.) interaktiv; ~ television interaktives Fernsehen

intercede /ıntə'si:d/ v.i. sich einsetzen (with bei; for, on behalf of für)

intercept /ıntə'sept/ v.t. abfangen

interchange **1** /'ıntətʃeındʒ/ n. (a) Austausch, der (b) (road junction) [Autobahn]kreuz, das **2** /ıntə'tʃeındʒ/ v.t. austauschen

interchangeable /ıntə'tʃeındʒəbl/ adj. austauschbar

inter-city /ıntə'sıtı/ adj. Intercity-; ~ train Intercity[-Zug], der

intercom /'ıntəkɒm/ n. (coll.) Gegensprechanlage, die

interconnect /ıntəkə'nekt/ **1** v.t. miteinander verbinden **2** v.i. miteinander in Zusammenhang stehen

intercontinental /ıntəkɒntı'nentl/ adj. interkontinental

intercourse /'ıntəkɔ:s/ n. (sexual) [Geschlechts]verkehr, der

interest /'ıntrəst/ **1** n. (a) Interesse, das; take or have an ~ in sb./sth. sich für jmdn./etw. interessieren; [just] for or out of ~: [nur] interessehalber; with ~: interessiert; act in one's own/sb.'s ~[s] im eigenen/in jmds. Interesse handeln; be of ~: interessant sein (to für) (b) (Finance) Zinsen Pl. **2** v.t. interessieren; be ~ed sich interessieren (in für)

interest-'free adj., adv. unverzinslich ⟨Schuldverschreibung⟩; zinsfrei ⟨Darlehen⟩

'interesting adj. interessant

'interest rate n. Zinssatz, der; Zinsfuß, der

interface /'ıntəfeıs/ n. (Comp.) Schnittstelle, die

interfere /ıntə'fıə(r)/ v.i. sich einmischen (in in + Akk.); ~ with sth. sich (Dat.) an etw. (Dat.) zu schaffen machen

interference /ıntə'fıərəns/ n. (a) (interfering) Einmischung, die (b) (Radio, Telev.) Störung, die

interim /'ıntərım/ **1** n. in the ~: in der Zwischenzeit **2** adj. vorläufig

interior /ın'tıərıə(r)/ **1** adj. inner...; Innen⟨fläche, -wand⟩ **2** n. Innere, das

interior: ~ **deco'ration** n. Raumgestaltung, die; ~ **'decorator** n. Raumgestalter, der/-gestalterin, die; ~ **de'sign** n. Innenarchitektur, die; ~ **de'signer** n. Innenarchitekt, der/-architektin, die

interject /ıntə'dʒekt/ v.t. einwerfen

interjection /ıntə'dʒekʃn/ n. Ausruf, der

interloper /'ıntələʊpə(r)/ n. Eindringling, der

interlude /'ıntəlu:d/ n. Pause, die; (music) Zwischenspiel, das

intermediary /ıntə'mi:dıərı/ n. Vermittler, der/Vermittlerin, die

intermediate /ıntə'mi:djət/ adj. Zwischen-

interminable /ın'tɜ:mınəbl/ adj. endlos

intermingle /ıntə'mıŋgl/ v.i. sich vermischen

intermission /ıntə'mıʃn/ n. Pause, die

intermittent /ıntə'mıtənt/ adj. in Abständen auftretend

inter'mittently adv. in Abständen

intern /ın'tɜ:n/ v.t. gefangen halten

internal /ın'tɜ:nl/ adj. inner...; Innen⟨fläche, -abmessungen⟩

internalize (internalise) /ın'tɜ:nəlaız/ v.t. (Psych.) verinnerlichen

internally /ın'tɜ:nəlı/ adv. innerlich

international /ıntə'næʃənl/ **1** adj. international **2** n. (a) (Sport) (contest) Länderspiel, das (b) (participant) Nationalspieler, der/-spielerin, die

international: ~ **call** n. Auslandsgespräch, das; ~ **'law** n. Völkerrecht, das

inter'nationally adv. international

International 'Monetary Fund n. Internationaler Währungsfonds

internee /ıntɜ:'ni:/ n. Internierte, der/die

Internet /'ıntənet/ n. the ~ das Internet; on the ~: im Internet

Internet: ~ **ac'cess** n., no pl. Internetzugang, der; ~ **'cafe** n.

Internetcafé, *das;* ~ **'service provider**
n. Internetprovider, *der;* ~ **site** *n.*
Internetseite, *die*

in'ternment *n.* Internierung, *die*

interplay /'ɪntəpleɪ/ *n.* Zusammenspiel,
das

interpret /ɪn'tɜ:prɪt/ **1** *v.t.*
(a) interpretieren; deuten ‹*Traum, Zeichen*›
(b) (between languages) dolmetschen
2 *v.i.* dolmetschen

interpretation /ɪntɜ:prɪ'teɪʃn/ *n.*
Interpretation, *die;* (of dream, symptoms)
Deutung, *die*

in'terpreter *n.* Dolmetscher, *der/*
Dolmetscherin, *die*

interrogate /ɪn'terəgeɪt/ *v.t.* verhören;
ausfragen ‹*Freund, Kind usw.*›

interrogation /ɪnterə'geɪʃn/ *n.* Verhör,
das

interrogative /ɪntə'rɒgətɪv/ *adj.* (Ling.)
Interrogativ-

interrogator /ɪn'terəgeɪtə(r)/ *n.*
Vernehmer, *der*

interrupt /ɪntə'rʌpt/ **1** *v.t.* unterbrechen;
don't ~ **me when I'm busy** stör mich nicht,
wenn ich zu tun habe
2 *v.i.* unterbrechen; stören

interruption /ɪntə'rʌpʃn/ *n.*
Unterbrechung, *die;* Störung, *die*

intersect /ɪntə'sekt/ *v.i.* (a) ‹*Straßen:*›
sich kreuzen
(b) (Geom.) sich schneiden

intersection /ɪntə'sekʃn/ *n.* (a) (road
junction) Kreuzung, *die*
(b) (Geom.) Schnittpunkt, *der*

intersperse /ɪntə'spɜ:s/ *v.t.* **be** ~**d with**
durchsetzt sein mit

interval /'ɪntəvl/ *n.* (a) [Zeit]abstand, *der;*
at ~**s** in Abständen
(b) (break; also Brit. Theatre etc.) Pause, *die;*
sunny ~**s** Aufheiterungen *Pl.*

intervene /ɪntə'vi:n/ *v.i.* (a) [vermittelnd]
eingreifen (**in** in + *Akk.*)
(b) **the intervening years** die
dazwischenliegenden Jahre

intervention /ɪntə'venʃn/ *n.* Eingreifen,
das; Intervention, *die* (bes. Politik)

interview /'ɪntəvju:/ **1** *n.* (a) (for job)
Vorstellungsgespräch, *das*
(b) (Journ., Radio, Telev.) Interview, *das*
2 *v.t.* ein Vorstellungsgespräch führen mit;
interviewen ‹*Politiker, Filmstar usw.*›

'interviewer *n.* Interviewer, *der/*
Interviewerin, *die*

intestine /ɪn'testɪn/ *n.* Darm, *der*

intimacy /'ɪntɪməsɪ/ *n.* (a) Vertrautheit,
die
(b) (sexual) Intimität, *die*

intimate **1** /'ɪntɪmət/ *adj.* (a) eng
‹*Freund, Verhältnis*›; genau, (geh.) intim
‹*Kenntnis*›
(b) (sexually) intim

2 /'ɪntɪmeɪt/ *v.t.* (imply) andeuten

intimately /'ɪntɪmətlɪ/ *adv.* genau[estens]
‹*kennen*›; eng ‹*verbinden*›

intimidate /ɪn'tɪmɪdeɪt/ *v.t.*
einschüchtern

intimidation /ɪntɪmɪ'deɪʃn/ *n.*
Einschüchterung, *die*

into /*before vowel* 'ɪntʊ, *before consonant*
'ɪntə/ *prep.* in (+ *Akk.*); (against) gegen; **I went
out** ~ **the street** ich ging auf die Straße
hinaus; **translate sth.** ~ **English** etw. ins
Englische übersetzen

in'tolerable *adj.* unerträglich

in'tolerance *n.* Intoleranz, *die*

in'tolerant *adj.* intolerant (**of** gegenüber)

intonation /ɪntə'neɪʃn/ *n.* Intonation, *die*

intoxicant /ɪn'tɒksɪkənt/ *n.*
Rauschmittel, *das*

intoxicate /ɪn'tɒksɪkeɪt/ *v.t.* betrunken
machen

intoxication /ɪntɒksɪ'keɪʃn/ *n.* Rausch,
der

intractable /ɪn'træktəbl/ *adj.* hartnäckig
‹*Problem*›

intransigent /ɪn'trænsɪdʒənt/ *adj.*
unnachgiebig

in'transitive *adj.* (Ling.) intransitiv

intra-uterine /ɪntrə'ju:təraɪn/ *adj.*
(Med.) intrauterin; ~ **[contraceptive] device**
Intrauterinpessar, *das*

intravenous /ɪntrə'vi:nəs/ *adj.* (Med.)
intravenös

'in-tray *n.* Eingangskorb, *der*

intrepid /ɪn'trepɪd/ *adj.* unerschrocken

intricacy /'ɪntrɪkəsɪ/ *n.* Kompliziertheit,
die

intricate /'ɪntrɪkət/ *adj.* kompliziert

intrigue /ɪn'tri:g/ *v.t.* faszinieren

intriguing /ɪn'tri:gɪŋ/ *adj.* faszinierend

intrinsic /ɪn'trɪnsɪk/ *adj.* innewohnend;
inner...; ~ **value** innerer Wert

intrinsically /ɪn'trɪnsɪkəlɪ/ *adv.* im
Wesentlichen

intro /'ɪntrəʊ/ *n., pl.* ~**s** (coll.) (presentation)
Vorstellung, *die;* (Mus.) Einleitung, *die*

introduce /ɪntrə'dju:s/ *v.t.* einführen;
~ **oneself/sb.** [**to sb.**] sich/jmdn. [jmdm.]
vorstellen

introduction /ɪntrə'dʌkʃn/ *n.* Einführen,
das; Einführung, *die;* (to person) Vorstellung,
die; (to book) Einleitung, *die*

intro'duction agency *n.* Partnervermi
ttlung[sagentur], *die*

introductory /ɪntrə'dʌktərɪ/ *adj.*
einleitend; Einführungs‹*kurs, -vortrag*›

introspective /ɪntrə'spektɪv/ *adj.* in sich
‹*Akk.*› gerichtet

introvert /'ɪntrəvɜ:t/ **1** *n.* Introvertierte,
der/die; **be an** ~: introvertiert sein
2 *adj.* introvertiert

introverted /ˈɪntrəvɜːtɪd/ *adj.* introvertiert
intrude /ɪnˈtruːd/ *v.i.* stören
in'truder *n.* Eindringling, *der*
in'truder alarm *n.*
Einbruchmeldeanlage, *die*
intrusion /ɪnˈtruːʒn/ *n.* Störung, *die*
intrusive /ɪnˈtruːsɪv/ *adj.* aufdringlich
intuition /ɪntjuːˈɪʃn/ *n.* Intuition, *die*
intuitive /ɪnˈtjuːɪtɪv/ *adj.*, **in'tuitively**
adv. intuitiv
inundate /ˈɪnəndeɪt/ *v.t.* überschwemmen
inure /ɪˈnjʊə(r)/ *v.t.* gewöhnen (**to an**
+ *Akk.*)
invade /ɪnˈveɪd/ *v.t.* einfallen in (+ *Akk.*)
in'vader *n.* Angreifer, *der*
invalid[1] /ˈɪnvəlɪd/ (Brit.) [1] *n.* Kranke,
der/die; (disabled) Körperbehinderte, *der/die*
[2] *adj.* körperbehindert
invalid[2] /ɪnˈvælɪd/ *adj.* nicht schlüssig
⟨*Argument, Theorie*⟩; ungültig ⟨*Fahrkarte,
Garantie, Vertrag*⟩
invalidate /ɪnˈvælɪdeɪt/ *v.t.* aufheben;
widerlegen ⟨*Theorie, These*⟩
in'valuable *adj.* unersetzlich ⟨*Person*⟩;
unschätzbar ⟨*Dienst, Hilfe*⟩; außerordentlich
wichtig ⟨*Rolle*⟩
in'variable *adj.* unveränderlich
invariably /ɪnˈveərɪəblɪ/ *adv.* immer;
ausnahmslos ⟨*falsch, richtig*⟩
invasion /ɪnˈveɪʒn/ *n.* Invasion, *die*
invective /ɪnˈvektɪv/ *n.* Beschimpfungen
Pl.
invent /ɪnˈvent/ *v.t.* erfinden
invention /ɪnˈvenʃn/ *n.* Erfindung, *die*
inventive /ɪnˈventɪv/ *adj.* (a) schöpferisch
⟨*Person, Begabung*⟩
(b) (original) originell
inventor /ɪnˈventə(r)/ *n.* Erfinder,
der/Erfinderin, *die*
inventory /ˈɪnvəntərɪ/ *n.* Bestandsliste,
die; **make** *or* **take an** ~ **of sth.** von etw. ein
Inventar aufstellen
inverse /ˈɪnvɜːs/ *adj.* umgekehrt
invert /ɪnˈvɜːt/ *v.t.* umstülpen
in'vertebrate *n.* wirbelloses Tier
inverted 'commas *n. pl.* (Brit.)
Anführungszeichen *Pl.*
invest /ɪnˈvest/ *v.t.* (a) (Finance) anlegen (**in**
in + *Dat.*); investieren (**in** in + *Dat. od. Akk.*)
(b) (fig.) investieren; ~ **sb. with sth.** jmdm.
etw. übertragen; ~ **sth. with sth.** einer
Sache (*Dat.*) etw. verleihen
investigate /ɪnˈvestɪɡeɪt/ *v.t.*
untersuchen
investigation /ɪnvestɪˈɡeɪʃn/ *n.*
Untersuchung, *die*
investigative /ɪnˈvestɪɡətɪv/
adj. detektivisch; ~ **journalism**
Enthüllungsjournalismus, *der*
investigator /ɪnˈvestɪɡeɪtə(r)/ *n.* [private]
~: [Privat]detektiv, *der*/-detektivin, *die*

in'vestment *n.* Investition, *die;* (money
invested) angelegtes Geld; **be a good** ~ (fig.)
sich bezahlt machen
investor /ɪnˈvestə(r)/ *n.* [Kapital]anleger,
der/-anlegerin, *die*
inveterate /ɪnˈvetərət/ *adj.* eingefleischt
⟨*Trinker, Raucher*⟩; unverbesserlich
⟨*Lügner*⟩
invigilate /ɪnˈvɪdʒɪleɪt/ *v.i.* (Brit.: in
examination) Aufsicht führen
invigilator /ɪnˈvɪdʒɪleɪtə(r)/ *n.* (Brit.)
Aufsichtsperson, *die*
invigorate /ɪnˈvɪɡəreɪt/ *v.t.* stärken;
(physically) kräftigen
invigorating /ɪnˈvɪɡəreɪtɪŋ/ *adj.*
kräftigend ⟨*Getränk, Klima*⟩
invincible /ɪnˈvɪnsɪbl/ *adj.* unbesiegbar
in'visible *adj.* unsichtbar
invitation /ɪnvɪˈteɪʃn/ *n.* Einladung, *die;* **at
sb.'s** ~: auf jmds. Einladung (*Akk.*)
invite /ɪnˈvaɪt/ *v.t.* (a) (request to come)
einladen
(b) (request to do sth.) auffordern
(c) (bring on) herausfordern ⟨*Kritik,
Verhängnis*⟩
inviting /ɪnˈvaɪtɪŋ/ *adj.* einladend;
verlockend ⟨*Gedanke, Vorstellung*⟩
in-vitro fertili'zation /ɪnˈviːtrəʊ
fɜːtɪlaɪˈzeɪʃn/ *n.* künstliche Befruchtung
[im Reagenzglas]; In-vitro-Fertilisation, *die*
(fachspr.)
invoice /ˈɪnvɔɪs/ [1] *n.* (bill) Rechnung, *die*
[2] *v.t.* ~ **sb.** jmdm. eine Rechnung
schicken; ~ **sb. for sth.** jmdm. etw. in
Rechnung stellen
invoke /ɪnˈvəʊk/ *v.t.* anrufen
in'voluntarily *adv.*, **in'voluntary** *adj.*
unwillkürlich
involve /ɪnˈvɒlv/ *v.t.* (a) (implicate)
verwickeln
(b) become *or* get ~**d in a fight** in eine
Schlägerei verwickelt werden; **get** ~**d with
sb.** sich mit jmdm. einlassen
(c) (entail) mit sich bringen
involved /ɪnˈvɒlvd/ *adj.* verwickelt;
(complicated) kompliziert
invulnerable /ɪnˈvʌlnərəbl/ *adj.*
unverwundbar; (fig.) unantastbar
inward /ˈɪnwəd/ [1] *adj.* inner...
[2] *adv.* einwärts ⟨*gerichtet, gebogen*⟩; **open**
~: nach innen öffnen
'inwardly *adv.* im Inneren; innerlich
inwards /ˈɪnwədz/ ▶ INWARD 2
iodine /ˈaɪədiːn/ *n.* Jod, *das*
ion /ˈaɪən/ *n.* Ion, *das*
iota /aɪˈəʊtə/ *n.* **not one** *or* **an** ~: nicht ein
Jota (geh.)
IOU /aɪəʊˈjuː/ *n.* Schuldschein, *der*
IQ *abbr.* = **intelligence quotient** IQ,
der; **IQ-test** IQ-Test, *der*
IRA *abbr.* = **Irish Republican Army**
IRA, *die*

Iran /ɪˈrɑːn/ *pr. n.* Iran, *der od.* (*das*)

Iraq /ɪˈrɑːk/ *pr. n.* Irak, *der od.* (*das*)

Iraq 'War *n.* Irakkrieg, *der*

irate /aɪˈreɪt/ *adj.* wütend

Ireland /ˈaɪələnd/ *pr. n.* Irland (*das*)

iris /ˈaɪərɪs/ *n.* (Bot., Anat.) Iris, *die*

Irish /ˈaɪərɪʃ/ ☐1 *adj.* irisch; **sb. is ∼:** jmd. ist Ire/Irin

  ☐2 *n.* (a) (language) Irisch, *das; see also* ENGLISH 2A

  (b) *constr. as pl.* the ∼: die Iren *Pl.*

Irish: ∼man /ˈaɪərɪʃmən/ *n., pl.* ∼men /ˈaɪərɪʃmen/ Ire, *der;* ∼ **Re'public** *pr. n.* Irische Republik; ∼ **'Sea** *pr. n.* Irische See; **∼woman** *n.* Irin, *die*

irk /ɜːk/ *v.t.* ärgern

irksome /ˈɜːksəm/ *adj.* lästig

iron /ˈaɪən/ ☐1 *n.* (a) (metal) Eisen, *das*

  (b) (for smoothing) Bügeleisen, *das*

  ☐2 *attrib. adj.* eisern; Eisen⟨platte usw.⟩

  ☐3 *v.t. & i.* bügeln

■ **iron 'out** *v.t.* herausbügeln; (fig.) aus dem Weg räumen

Iron 'Curtain *n.* (Hist.) Eiserner Vorhang

ironic /aɪˈrɒnɪk/, **ironical** /aɪˈrɒnɪkl/ *adj.* ironisch

ironing /ˈaɪənɪŋ/ *n.* Bügeln, *das;* (items) Bügelwäsche, *die;* **do the ∼:** bügeln

'ironing board *n.* Bügelbrett, *das*

ironmonger /ˈaɪənmʌŋgə(r)/ *n.* (Brit.) Eisenwarenhändler, *der*/-händlerin, *die*

irony /ˈaɪrənɪ/ *n.* Ironie, *die;* **the ∼ was that ...:** die Ironie lag darin, dass ...

irradiate /ɪˈreɪdɪeɪt/ *v.t.* bestrahlen

irrational /ɪˈræʃənl/ *adj.* irrational

irreconcilable /ɪˈrekənsaɪləbl/ *adj.* (incompatible) unvereinbar

irrefutable /ɪrɪˈfjuːtəbl/ *adj.* unwiderlegbar

irregular /ɪˈregjʊlə(r)/ *adj.* unregelmäßig; unkorrekt ⟨Verhalten, Handlung usw.⟩

irregularity /ɪregjʊˈlærɪtɪ/ *n.*

  ▶ IRREGULAR: Unregelmäßigkeit, *die;* Unkorrektheit, *die*

irrelevance /ɪˈrelɪvəns/, **irrelevancy** /ɪˈrelɪvənsɪ/ *ns.* Belanglosigkeit, *die;* Irrelevanz, *die* (geh.)

irrelevant /ɪˈrelɪvənt/ *adj.* belanglos; irrelevant (geh.)

irreparable /ɪˈrepərəbl/ *adj.* nicht wieder gutzumachend *nicht präd.;* irreparabel (geh., Med.)

irreplaceable /ɪrɪˈpleɪsəbl/ *adj.* unersetzlich

irrepressible /ɪrɪˈpresɪbl/ *adj.* nicht zu unterdrücken *nicht präd.;* **she is ∼:** sie ist nicht unterzukriegen (ugs.)

irreproachable /ɪrɪˈprəʊtʃəbl/ *adj.* untadelig

irresistible /ɪrɪˈzɪstɪbl/ *adj.* unwiderstehlich; bestechend ⟨Argument⟩

irresolute /ɪˈrezəluːt/ *adj.* unentschlossen

irrespective /ɪrɪˈspektɪv/ *adj.* ∼ **of** ungeachtet (+ *Gen.*)

irresponsible /ɪrɪˈspɒnsɪbl/ *adj.* verantwortungslos ⟨Person⟩; unverantwortlich ⟨Benehmen⟩

irretrievable /ɪrɪˈtriːvəbl/ *adj.* nicht mehr wiederzubekommen *nicht attr.*

irreverence /ɪˈrevərəns/ *n.* Respektlosigkeit, *die*

irreverent /ɪˈrevərənt/ *adj.* respektlos

irreversible /ɪrɪˈvɜːsɪbl/, **irrevocable** /ɪˈrevəkəbl/ *adjs.* unwiderruflich

irrigate /ˈɪrɪgeɪt/ *v.t.* bewässern

irrigation /ɪrɪˈgeɪʃn/ *n.* Bewässerung, *die*

irritable /ˈɪrɪtəbl/ *adj.* (quick to anger) reizbar; (temporarily) gereizt

irritant /ˈɪrɪtənt/ *n.* Reizstoff, *der*

irritate /ˈɪrɪteɪt/ *v.t.* (a) ärgern; **get ∼d** ärgerlich werden; **be ∼d by sth.** sich über etw. (*Akk.*) ärgern

  (b) (Med.) reizen

irritating /ˈɪrɪteɪtɪŋ/ *adj.* lästig

irritation /ɪrɪˈteɪʃn/ *n.* (a) Ärger, *der*

  (b) (Med.) Reizung, *die*

is ▶ BE

Islam /ˈɪzlɑːm/ *n.* Islam, *der*

Islamist /ˈɪzlæmɪst/ ☐1 *n.* Islamist, *der*/Islamistin, *die*

  ☐2 *adj.* islamistisch

island /ˈaɪlənd/ *n.* Insel, *die*

'islander *n.* Inselbewohner, *der*/-bewohnerin, *die*

island: ∼-hop *v.i.* go ∼-hopping eine Inselhoppingtour machen; **∼-hopping** *n.* Inselhopping, *das*

isle /aɪl/ *n.* Insel, *die*

isn't /ˈɪznt/ (coll.) = is not; ▶ BE

isolate /ˈaɪsəleɪt/ *v.t.* isolieren

isolated /ˈaɪsəleɪtɪd/ *adj.* (a) (single) einzeln; ∼ **cases/instances** Einzelfälle

  (b) (remote) abgelegen

isolation /aɪsəˈleɪʃn/ *n.* (a) (act) Isolierung, *die*

  (b) (state) Isolation, *die*

ISP *abbr.* = **Internet service provider** ISP

Israel /ˈɪzreɪl/ *pr. n.* Israel (*das*)

Israeli /ɪzˈreɪlɪ/ ☐1 *adj.* israelisch; **sb. is ∼:** jmd. ist Israeli

  ☐2 *n.* Israeli, *der*/die

issue /ˈɪʃuː, ˈɪsjuː/ ☐1 *n.* (a) (point in question) Frage, *die;* **make an ∼ of sth.** etw. aufbauschen; **evade** *or* **dodge the ∼:** ausweichen

  (b) (of magazine etc.) Ausgabe, *die*

  (c) (result, outcome) Ergebnis, *das*

  ☐2 *v.t.* (a) (give out) ausgeben; ausstellen ⟨Pass⟩; erteilen ⟨Lizenz, Befehl⟩; ∼ **sb. with sth.** etw. an jmdn. austeilen

  (b) (publish) herausgeben ⟨Publikation⟩

it /ɪt/ *pron.* **(a)** es; **I can't cope with it any
more** ich halte das nicht mehr länger aus;
what is it? was ist los?
(b) (the thing, animal, young child previously
mentioned) er/sie/es; *as direct obj.* ihn/sie/es;
as indirect obj. ihm/ihr/ihm
(c) (the person in question) **who is it?** wer ist
da?; **it was the children** es waren die Kinder;
is it you, Dad? bist du es, Vater?

IT *abbr.* = **information technology**
IT

Italian /ɪ'tæljən/ 1 *adj.* italienisch; **sb. is
~:** jmd. ist Italiener/Italienerin
2 *n.* **(a)** (person) Italiener, *der*/Italienerin,
die
(b) (language) Italienisch, *das; see also*
ENGLISH 2A

italic /ɪ'tælɪk/ 1 *adj.* kursiv
2 *n. in pl.* Kursivschrift, *die;* **in ~s** kursiv

Italy /'ɪtəlɪ/ *pr. n.* Italien (*das*)

itch /ɪtʃ/ 1 *n.* Juckreiz, *der;* **I have an ~:** es
juckt mich
2 *v.i.* **(a)** einen Juckreiz haben; **it ~es** es
juckt
(b) **~ or be ~ing to do sth.** darauf brennen,

etw. zu tun

'itchy *adj.* kratzig; **be ~** ⟨*Körperteil:*⟩
jucken

it'd /'ɪtəd/ (coll.) **(a)** = **it had**
(b) = **it would**

item /'aɪtəm/ *n.* **(a)** Ding, *das;* Sache, *die;*
(in shop, catalogue) Artikel, *der;* (on radio, TV)
Nummer, *die;* **~ of clothing** Kleidungsstück,
das
(b) **~ [of news]** Nachricht, *die*

itemize /'aɪtəmaɪz/ *v.t.* einzeln aufführen

itinerary /aɪ'tɪnərərɪ/ *n.* Reiseroute, *die*

it'll /ɪtl/ (coll.) = **it will**

its /ɪts/ *poss. pron. attrib.* sein/ihr/sein

it's /ɪts/ **(a)** = **it is**
(b) = **it has**

itself /ɪt'self/ *pron.* **(a)** *emphat.* selbst
(b) *refl.* sich

IUD *abbr.* = **intrauterine device** IUD

I've /aɪv/ = **I have**

IVF *abbr.* = **in-vitro fertilization** IVF

ivory /'aɪvərɪ/ *n.* Elfenbein, *das; attrib.*
elfenbeinern; Elfenbein-

ivy /'aɪvɪ/ *n.* Efeu, *der*

··

Jj

··

J, j /dʒeɪ/ *n.* J, j, *das*

jab /dʒæb/ 1 *v.t.,* **-bb-** stoßen
2 *n.* **(a)** Stoß, *der;* (with needle) Stich, *der*
(b) (Brit. coll.: injection) Spritze, *die*

jabber /'dʒæbə(r)/ *v.i.* plappern (ugs.)

jack /dʒæk/ *n.* **(a)** (for car) Wagenheber, *der*
(b) (Cards) Bube, *der*

jackal /'dʒækl/ *n.* Schakal, *der*

jackdaw /'dʒækdɔː/ *n.* Dohle, *die*

jacket /'dʒækɪt/ *n.* **(a)** Jacke, *die;* (of suit)
Jackett, *das;* **sports ~:** Sakko, *der*
(b) (of book) Schutzumschlag, *der*
(c) **~ potatoes** in der Schale gebackene
Kartoffeln

jack: **~-knife** *v.i.* **the lorry ~-knifed** der
Anhänger des Lastwagens stellte sich quer;
~pot *n.* Jackpot, *der;* **hit the ~pot** (fig.) das
große Los ziehen

jacuzzi (*Amer.:* ®) /dʒə'kuːzɪ/ *n.* ≈
Whirlpool, *der*

jaded /'dʒeɪdɪd/ *adj.* abgespannt

jagged /'dʒægɪd/ *adj.* gezackt

jaguar /'dʒægjʊə(r)/ *n.* Jaguar, *der*

jail /dʒeɪl/ 1 *n.* Gefängnis, *das*
2 *v.t.* ins Gefängnis bringen

jail: **~bird** Knastbruder, *der* (ugs.);
~break *n.* Gefängnisausbruch, *der*

jailer, jailor /'dʒeɪlə(r)/ *n.*
Gefängniswärter, *der*/-wärterin, *die*

jam¹ /dʒæm/ 1 *v.t.,* **-mm-:** **(a)** (between two
surfaces) einklemmen
(b) (make immovable) blockieren; (fig.) lähmen
2 *v.i.,* **-mm-:** **(a)** (become wedged) sich
verklemmen
(b) ⟨*Maschine:*⟩ klemmen
3 *n.* **(a)** (crush, stoppage) Blockierung, *die*
(b) (coll.: dilemma) **be in a ~:** in der Klemme
stecken (ugs.)
■ **jam 'on** *v.t.* **~ the brakes [full] on** [voll]
auf die Bremse steigen (ugs.)

jam² *n.* Marmelade, *die*

Jamaica /dʒə'meɪkə/ *pr. n.* Jamaika (*das*)

jamb /dʒæm/ *n.* (of doorway, window) Pfosten,
der

'jam-packed *adj.* (coll.) knallvoll (ugs.),
proppenvoll (ugs.) (**with** von)

Jan. *abbr.* = **January** Jan.

jangle /'dʒæŋgl/ 1 *v.i.* klimpern;
⟨*Klingel:*⟩ bimmeln
2 *v.t.* rasseln mit

janitor /'dʒænɪtə(r)/ *n.* Hausmeister, *der*

January /'dʒænjʊərɪ/ *n.* Januar, *der; see
also* AUGUST

Japan /dʒə'pæn/ *n.* Japan (*das*)

Japanese /dʒæpə'niːz/ 1 *adj.* japanisch;

sb. is ~: jmd. ist Japaner/Japanerin
2 *n., pl. same* **(a)** (person) Japaner,
der/Japanerin, *die*
(b) (language) Japanisch, *das; see also*
ENGLISH 2A

jar¹ /dʒɑː(r)/ **1** *v.i.*, **-rr-** quietschen; (fig.)
~ **on sb./sb.'s nerves** jmdm. auf die Nerven
gehen
2 *v.t.*, **-rr-** erschüttern

jar² *n.* Topf, *der;* (glass ~) Glas, *das*

jargon /'dʒɑːgən/ *n.* Jargon, *der*

jasmin[e] /'dʒæsmɪn/ *n.* Jasmin, *der*

jaundice /'dʒɔːndɪs/ *n.* (Med.) Gelbsucht,
die

jaundiced /'dʒɔːndɪst/ *adj.* (fig.) verbittert

jaunt /dʒɔːnt/ *n.* Ausflug, *der*

jaunty /'dʒɔːntɪ/ *adj.* unbeschwert; keck
⟨*Hut*⟩; **he wore his hat at a** ~ **angle** er hatte
sich (*Dat.*) den Hut keck aufs Ohr gesetzt

javelin /'dʒævlɪn/ *n.* **(a)** Speer, *der*
(b) (Sport: event) Speerwerfen, *das*

jaw /dʒɔː/ Kiefer, *der*

'jawbone *n.* Kieferknochen, *der*

jay /dʒeɪ/ *n.* Eichelhäher, *der*

'jay-walk *v.i.* als Fußgänger im
Straßenverkehr unachtsam sein

jazz /dʒæz/ **1** *n.* Jazz, *der; attrib.* Jazz-
2 *v.t.* ~ **up** aufpeppen (ugs.)

jazz: ~ **band** *n.* Jazzband, *die;* ~ **dance**
n. Jazztanz, *der;* ~ **'rock** *n.* Jazzrock, *der*

jazzy /'dʒæzɪ/ *adj.* poppig; **a** ~ **sports car**
ein aufgemotzter Sportwagen (ugs.)

jealous /'dʒeləs/ *adj.* eifersüchtig (**of** auf
+ *Akk.*)

'jealousy *n.* Eifersucht, *die*

jeans /dʒiːnz/ *n. pl.* Jeans *Pl.*

Jeep ® /dʒiːp/ *n.* Jeep ⓦ, *der*

jeer /dʒɪə(r)/ *v.i.* höhnen (geh.); ~ **at sb.**
jmdn. verhöhnen

jelly /'dʒelɪ/ *n.* Gelee, *das;* (dessert)
Götterspeise, *die*

'jellyfish *n.* Qualle, *die*

jeopardize /'dʒepədaɪz/ *v.t.* gefährden

jeopardy /'dʒepədɪ/ *n.* **in** ~: in Gefahr;
gefährdet

jerk /dʒɜːk/ **1** *n.* Ruck, *der*
2 *v.t.* reißen an (+ *Dat.*)
3 *v.i.* zucken

jersey /'dʒɜːzɪ/ *n.* Pullover, *der;* (Sport)
Trikot, *das*

jest /dʒest/ **1** *n.* Scherz, *der;* **in** ~: im
Scherz
2 *v.i.* scherzen

Jesus /'dʒiːzəs/ *pr. n.* Jesus (*der*)

jet /dʒet/ *n.* **(a)** (stream) Strahl, *der*
(b) (nozzle) Düse, *die*
(c) (aircraft) Düsenflugzeug, *das;* Jet, *der*

jet: ~**-black** *adj.* pechschwarz;
~ **engine** *n.* Düsentriebwerk, *das;*
~**foil** *n.* [Jetfoil-]Tragflügelboot, *das;*
~ **lag** *n.* Jetlag, *der;* ~**-lagged** *adj.*

sb. is ~**-lagged** jmdm. macht der Jetlag
zu schaffen; ~ **plane** *n.* Düsenflugzeug,
das; ~**-propelled** *adj.* düsengetrieben;
~ **pro'pulsion** *n.* Düsen- *od.*
Strahlantrieb, *der*

jetsam /'dʒetsəm/ *n.* ▶ FLOTSAM

jet: ~ **set** *n.* Jet-set, *der;* ~ **ski** *n.* Jetski,
der

jettison /'dʒetɪsən/ *v.t.* über Bord werfen;
(discard) wegwerfen

jetty /'dʒetɪ/ *n.* Landungsbrücke, *die*

Jew /dʒuː/ *n.* Jude, *der*/Jüdin, *die*

jewel /'dʒuːəl/ *n.* Juwel, *das od. der*

'jewel box, 'jewel case *ns.*
Schmuckkasten, *der*

jeweller (*Amer.:* **jeweler**) /'dʒuːələ(r)/ *n.*
Juwelier, *der*

jewellery (Brit.), **jewelry** /'dʒuːəlrɪ/ *n.*
Schmuck, *der*

Jewish /'dʒuːɪʃ/ *adj.* jüdisch; **he/she is**
~: er ist Jude/sie ist Jüdin

jib /dʒɪb/ *v.i.*, **-bb-** sich sträuben (**at** gegen)

jibe ▶ GIBE

jiffy /'dʒɪfɪ/ *n.* (coll.) **in a** ~: sofort

'Jiffy bag ® *n.* gefütterte Versandtasche

jig /dʒɪg/ *n.* Jig, *die*

'jigsaw *n.* **(a)** Dekupiersäge, *die;* (electric)
Stichsäge, *die*
(b) ~ **[puzzle]** Puzzle, *das*

jihad /dʒɪˈhæd/ *n.* Dschihad, *der*

jihadi /dʒɪˈhædɪ/ *n.* Dschihad-Kämpfer, *der*

jilt /dʒɪlt/ *v.t.* sitzenlassen (ugs.)

jingle /'dʒɪŋgl/ **1** *n.* (Commerc.)
Werbespruch, *der;* Jingle, *der* (Werbespr.)
2 *v.i.* klimpern; ⟨*Glöckchen:*⟩ bimmeln
3 *v.t.* klimpern mit ⟨*Münzen, Schlüsseln*⟩

jinx /dʒɪŋks/ (coll.) **1** *n.* Fluch, *der*
2 *v.t.* verhexen

jitters /'dʒɪtəz/ *n. pl.* (coll.) großes Zittern

jittery /'dʒɪtərɪ/ *adj.* (coll.) (nervous) nervös;
(frightened) verängstigt

job /dʒɒb/ *n.* **(a)** (piece of work) Arbeit, *die;*
I have a ~ **for you** ich habe eine Aufgabe
für dich
(b) (employment) Stelle, *die;* Job, *der* (ugs.)

job: ~ **advert** *n.* Stellenanzeige, *die;*
~**centre** *n.* (Brit.)
Arbeitsvermittlungsstelle, *die;*
~ **creation scheme** *n.*
Beschäftigungsprogramm, *das;*
Arbeitsbeschaffungsprogramm, *das;*
~ **description** *n.*
Arbeitsplatzbeschreibung, *die;*
~ **evaluation** *n.* Arbeitsbewertung, *die;*
~**-hunt** *v.i.* go/be ~**-hunting** auf Arbeits-
od. Stellensuche gehen/sein; ~**-hunter** *n.*
Stellen- *od.* Arbeitsuchende, *der/die;*
~**-hunting** *n.* Arbeitsuche, *die;*
Stellensuche, *die*

'jobless *adj.* arbeitslos

job: ~ **market** *n.* Arbeitsmarkt,
der; Stellenmarkt, *der;* ~ **offer** *n.*   ····>

Stellenangebot, *das;* ~ **satisfaction** *n.*
Arbeitszufriedenheit, *die;* ~ **security**
n. Arbeitsplatzsicherheit, *die;* **~-share**
1 *n.* geteilter Arbeitsplatz; 2 *v.i.* sich
(*Dat.*) einen Arbeitsplatz teilen (**with** mit);
~-sharing *n.* Jobsharing, *das*
jockey /'dʒɒkɪ/ *n.* Jockei, *der*
jockey shorts *n. pl.* (Amer.) Unterhose,
die; Unterhosen *Pl.*
jocular /'dʒɒkjʊlə(r)/ *adj.* lustig
jodhpurs /'dʒɒdpəz/ *n. pl.* Reithose, *die*
jog /dʒɒg/ 1 *v.t.,* -gg-: (a) (shake) rütteln
(b) (nudge) [an]stoßen
(c) ~ sb.'s memory jmds. Gedächtnis (*Dat.*)
auf die Sprünge helfen
2 *v.i.,* -gg-: (a) (up and down) auf und ab
hüpfen
(b) (trot) ⟨*Pferd*:⟩ [dahin]trotten
(c) (Sport) joggen
3 *n.* go for a ~: joggen gehen
jogger /'dʒɒgə(r)/ *n.* Jogger, *der*/Joggerin,
die
'**jogging** *n.* Jogging, *das*
'**jogtrot** *n.* (lit. or fig.) Trott, *der*
john /dʒɒn/ *n.* (Amer. coll.: lavatory) Lokus, *der*
(salopp)
join /dʒɔɪn/ 1 *v.t.* (a) (connect) verbinden
(**to** mit)
(b) (come into company of) sich gesellen zu
(c) eintreten in (+ *Akk.*) ⟨*Armee, Firma,*
Verein, Partei⟩
2 *v.i.* ⟨*Straßen*:⟩ zusammenlaufen
■ **join in** 1 /-'-'-/ *v.i.* mitmachen (**with** bei)
2 /'--/ *v.t.* mitmachen bei
■ **join 'up** 1 *v.i.* (Mil.) einrücken
2 *v.t.* miteinander verbinden
'**joiner** *n.* Tischler, *der*/Tischlerin, *die*
joinery /'dʒɔɪnərɪ/ *n., no art.* (craft)
Tischlerei, *die;* Tischlerhandwerk, *das*
joint /dʒɔɪnt/ 1 *n.* (a) (Building) Fuge, *die*
(b) (Anat.) Gelenk, *das*
(c) a ~ [of meat] ein Stück Fleisch; (for
roasting) ein Braten
(d) (coll.: place) Laden, *der*
(e) (sl.: marijuana cigarette) Joint, *der*
2 *adj.* (a) (of two or more) gemeinsam
(b) Mit⟨*autor, -erbe, -besitzer*⟩
'**jointly** *adv.* gemeinsam
joint 'venture *n.* (Commerc.) Jointventure,
das
joist /dʒɔɪst/ *n.* (Building) Deckenbalken, *der;*
(steel) [Decken]träger, *der*
joke /dʒəʊk/ 1 *n.* Witz, *der;* Scherz, *der*
2 *v.i.* scherzen, Witze machen (**about** über
+ *Akk.*); **joking apart** Scherz beiseite!
'**joker** *n.* (a) Spaßvogel, *der*
(b) (Cards) Joker, *der*
jollity /'dʒɒlɪtɪ/ *n.* Fröhlichkeit, *die;*
(merrymaking) Festlichkeit, *die*
jolly /'dʒɒlɪ/ 1 *adj.* fröhlich
2 *adv.* (Brit. coll.) ganz schön (ugs.); ~ good!
ausgezeichnet!
jolt /dʒəʊlt/ 1 *v.t.* ⟨*Fahrzeug*:⟩ durchrütteln

2 *v.i.* ⟨*Fahrzeug*:⟩ holpern
3 *n.* (a) (jerk) Stoß, *der;* Ruck, *der*
(b) (fig.: shock) Schock, *der*
Jordan /'dʒɔ:dn/ *pr. n.* Jordanien (*das*)
jostle /'dʒɒsl/ 1 *v.i.* ~ [against each other]
aneinander stoßen
2 *v.t.* stoßen
jot /dʒɒt/ *n.* [not] a ~: [k]ein bisschen.
■ **jot 'down** *v.t.* [rasch] aufschreiben
jotter /'dʒɒtə(r)/ *n.* Notizblock, *der*
journal /'dʒɜ:nl/ *n.* Zeitschrift, *die*
journalism /'dʒɜ:nəlɪzm/ *n.* Journalismus,
der
journalist /'dʒɜ:nəlɪst/ *n.* Journalist,
der/Journalistin, *die*
journey /'dʒɜ:nɪ/ *n.* (a) Reise, *die*
(b) (of vehicle) Fahrt, *die*
jovial /'dʒəʊvɪəl/ *adj.* herzlich ⟨*Gruß*⟩;
fröhlich ⟨*Person*⟩
jowl /dʒaʊl/ *n.* (jaw) Unterkiefer, *der;* (lower
part of face) Kinnbacken *Pl.;* (double chin)
Doppelkinn, *das*
joy /dʒɔɪ/ *n.* Freude, *die*
joyful /'dʒɔɪfl/ *adj.* froh [gestimmt]
⟨*Person*⟩; freudig ⟨*Blick, Ereignis, Gesang*⟩
joy: ~**ride** *n.* (coll.) Spritztour, *die* [im
gestohlenen Auto]; ~**stick** *n.* (a) (Aeronaut.)
Knüppel, *der;* (b) (on computer etc.) Hebel, *der;*
Joystick, *der*
JP *abbr.* = **Justice of the Peace**
jubilant /'dʒu:bɪlənt/ *adj.* jubelnd; be ~
⟨*Person*:⟩ frohlocken
jubilation /dʒu:bɪ'leɪʃn/ *n.* Jubel, *der*
jubilee /'dʒu:bɪli:/ *n.* Jubiläum, *das*
Judaism /'dʒu:deɪɪzm/ *n., no art.*
Judentum, *das;* Judaismus, *der*
judge /dʒʌdʒ/ 1 *n.* (a) Richter, *der*/
Richterin, *die*
(b) (in contest) Preisrichter, *der*/-richterin,
die
(c) (fig.: critic) Kenner, *der*/Kennerin, *die*
2 *v.t.* (a) (sentence) richten (geh.)
(b) (form opinion about) [be]urteilen
'**judg[e]ment** *n.* (a) Urteil, *das*
(b) (critical faculty) Urteilsvermögen, *das*
judicial /dʒu:'dɪʃl/ *adj.* gerichtlich
judiciary /dʒu:'dɪʃərɪ/ *n.* Richterschaft, *die*
judicious /dʒu:'dɪʃəs/ *adj.* klar blickend
judo /'dʒu:dəʊ/ *n.* Judo, *das*
jug /dʒʌg/ *n.* Krug, *der;* (with lid, water ~)
Kanne, *die*
juggernaut /'dʒʌgənɔ:t/ *n.* (Brit.: lorry)
schwerer Brummer (ugs.)
juggle /'dʒʌgl/ *v.i.* jonglieren
juggler /'dʒʌglə(r)/ *n.* Jongleur,
der/Jongleurin, *die*
juice /dʒu:s/ *n.* Saft, *der*
juicy /'dʒu:sɪ/ *adj.* saftig
jukebox /'dʒu:kbɒks/ *n.* Jukebox, *die;*
Musikbox, *die*
Jul. *abbr.* = **July** Jul.

July /dʒʊ'laɪ/ n. Juli, der; see also AUGUST

jumble /'dʒʌmbl/ ①v.t. ~ **up** durcheinander bringen ②n. Durcheinander, das

'**jumble sale** n. (Brit.) Trödelmarkt, der

jumbo jet /dʒʌmbəʊ 'dʒet/ n. Jumbojet, der

jump /dʒʌmp/ ①n. (a) Sprung, der (b) (in prices) sprunghafter Anstieg ②v.i. (a) springen; ~ **for joy** einen Freudensprung machen (b) ~ **to conclusions** voreilige Schlüsse ziehen ③v.t. (a) überspringen (b) ~ **the queue** (Brit.) sich vordrängeln ■ **jump a'bout, jump a'round** v.i. herumspringen (ugs.)
■ '**jump at** v.t. (fig.) sofort zugreifen bei ⟨Angebot, Gelegenheit⟩

jumped-up /'dʒʌmptʌp/ adj. (coll.) emporgekommen

'**jumper** n. Pullover, der

jump: ~ **jet** n. Senkrechtstarter, der; ~ **leads** n. pl. (Brit. Motor Veh.) Starthilfekabel Pl.; ~-**start** ①v.t. Starthilfe geben (+ Dat.) ⟨Auto⟩; (fig.) [wieder] in Gang bringen; [wieder] ankurbeln ⟨Wirtschaft, Industrie⟩; ②n. Start durch Starthilfe; (fig.) neuer Impuls od. Auftrieb; ~**suit** n. Overall, der

jumpy /'dʒʌmpɪ/ adj. nervös

Jun. abbr. = **June** Jun.

junction /'dʒʌŋkʃn/ n. (a) (of railway lines, roads) ≈ Einmündung, die (b) (crossroads) Kreuzung, die

'**junction box** n. (Electr.) Verteilerkasten, der

juncture /'dʒʌŋktʃə(r)/ n. **at this** ~: zu diesem Zeitpunkt

June /dʒuːn/ n. Juni, der; see also AUGUST

jungle /'dʒʌŋgl/ n. Dschungel, der

junior /'dʒuːnɪə(r)/ adj. (a) (in age) jünger; ~ **team** (Sport) Juniorenmannschaft, die (b) (in rank) rangniedriger ⟨Person⟩; niedriger ⟨Rang⟩

junior: ~ '**partner** n. Juniorpartner, der/-partnerin, die; ~ **school** n. (Brit.) Grundschule, die

junk /dʒʌŋk/ n. Trödel, der (ugs.); (trash) Ramsch, der (ugs.)

junk 'email n. Junkmail, die

'**junk food** n. minderwertige Kost

junkie /'dʒʌŋkɪ/ n. (sl.) Junkie, der (Drogenjargon)

junk: ~ **mail** n. Postwurfsendungen Pl.; Reklame, die; ~ **shop** n. Trödelladen, der (ugs.)

Jupiter /'dʒuːpɪtə(r)/ pr. n. (Astron.) Jupiter, der

jurisdiction /dʒʊərɪs'dɪkʃn/ n. Gerichtsbarkeit, die

juror /'dʒʊərə(r)/ n. Geschworene, der/die

jury /'dʒʊərɪ/ n. (a) (in court) **the** ~: die Geschworenen Pl. (b) (in competition) Jury, die

just /dʒʌst/ ①adj. (morally right) gerecht ②adv. (a) (exactly) genau; ~ **then/enough** gerade da/genug; ~ **as** (exactly as) genauso wie; (when) gerade, als; ~ **as you like** or **please** ganz wie Sie wünschen/du magst; ~ **as good** etc. genauso gut usw. (b) (barely) gerade [eben]; (with little time to spare) gerade noch; (no more than) nur; ~ **under £10** nicht ganz zehn Pfund (c) (at this moment) gerade; **not** ~ **now** im Moment nicht (d) (coll.) (simply) einfach; (only) nur; esp. with imper. mal [eben]; ~ **look at that!** guck dir das mal an!; ~ **a moment** einen Moment mal; ~ **in case** für alle Fälle

justice /'dʒʌstɪs/ n. (a) Gerechtigkeit, die (b) (magistrate) Schiedsrichter, der/-richterin, die; **J**~ **of the Peace** Friedensrichter, der/-richterin, die

justifiable /dʒʌstɪ'faɪəbl/ adj. berechtigt

justifiably /dʒʌstɪ'faɪəblɪ/ adv. zu Recht

justification /dʒʌstɪfɪ'keɪʃn/ n. Rechtfertigung, die

justify /'dʒʌstɪfaɪ/ v.t. rechtfertigen; **be justified in doing sth.** etw. zu Recht tun

jut /dʒʌt/ v.i., -tt-: ~ **[out]** [her]vorragen; herausragen

juvenile /'dʒuːvənaɪl/ ①adj. (a) jugendlich (b) (immature) kindisch ②n. Jugendliche, der/die

juvenile delinquency /dɪ'lɪŋkwənsɪ/ n. Jugendkriminalität, die

juvenile delinquent /dɪ'lɪŋkwənt/ n. jugendlicher Straftäter/jugendliche Straftäterin

juxtapose /dʒʌkstə'pəʊz/ v.t. nebeneinander stellen (**with, to** und)

juxtaposition /dʒʌkstəpə'zɪʃn/ n. Nebeneinanderstellung, die

Kk

K, k /keɪ/ n. K, k, das

kale /keɪl/ n. Grünkohl, der; Krauskohl, der

kaleidoscope /kə'laɪdəskəʊp/ n. Kaleidoskop, das

kangaroo /kæŋgə'ruː/ n. Känguru, das

karaoke /kærɪ'əʊkɪ/ n., no indef. art. Karaoke, das; attrib. Karaoke-

karate /kə'rɑːtɪ/ n. Karate, das

kebab /kɪ'bæb/ n. Kebab, der

keel /kiːl/ n. ① (Naut.) Kiel, der ② v.i. ~ **over** umstürzen; ‹Schiff:› kentern; ‹Person:› umkippen

keen /kiːn/ adj. **(a)** (sharp) scharf **(b)** (cold) schneidend ‹Wind, Kälte› **(c)** (eager) begeistert ‹Fußballfan, Sportler›; lebhaft ‹Interesse›; **be ~ to do sth.** darauf erpicht sein, etw. zu tun; **be ~ on doing sth.** etw. gern[e] tun **(d)** (sensitive) scharf ‹Augen›; fein ‹Sinne›

'keenly adv. **(a)** (sharply) scharf **(b)** (eagerly) eifrig; brennend ‹interessiert sein› **(c)** (acutely) **be ~ aware of sth.** sich (Dat.) einer Sache (Gen.) voll bewusst sein

keep /kiːp/ ① v.t., kept /kept/ **(a)** halten ‹Versprechen, Schwur, Sabbat, Fasten›; einhalten ‹Verabredung, Vereinbarung›; begehen, feiern ‹Fest› **(b)** (have charge of) aufbewahren **(c)** (retain) behalten; (not lose or destroy) aufheben ‹Quittung, Rechnung› **(d)** halten ‹Bienen, Hund usw.› **(e)** führen ‹Tagebuch, Geschäft, Ware› **(f)** (support) versorgen ‹Familie› **(g)** (detain) festhalten; **~ sb. waiting** jmdn. warten lassen; **what kept you?** wo bleibst du denn? **(h)** (reserve) aufheben ② v.i., kept **(a)** (remain) bleiben; **are you ~ing well?** gehts dir gut? **(b)** **~ [to the] left/right** sich links/rechts halten; **~ doing sth.** (repeatedly) etw. immer wieder tun; **~ talking/working** etc. **until** ...: weiterreden/-arbeiten usw., bis ... **(c)** (remain good) ‹Lebensmittel:› sich halten ③ n. **(a)** (maintenance) Unterhalt, der **(b) for ~s** (coll.) auf Dauer **(c)** (Hist.: tower) Bergfried, der

■ **keep 'back** ① v.i. zurückbleiben ② v.t. **(a)** (restrain) zurückhalten ‹Menschenmenge› **(b)** (withhold) verschweigen ‹Informationen, Tatsachen› (from Dat.)

■ **keep 'down** ① v.i. unten bleiben ② v.t. **(a)** niedrig halten ‹Steuern, Preise usw.›; **~ one's weight down** nicht zunehmen **(b)** **~ your voice down!** rede nicht so laut!

■ **keep 'off** ① v.i. ‹Person:› wegbleiben ② v.t. fern halten; **'~ off the grass'** „Betreten des Rasens verboten"

■ **keep 'on** v.i. weitermachen (with Akk.); **~ on doing sth.** etw. [immer] weiter tun; (repeatedly) etw. immer wieder tun

■ **keep 'out** ① v.i. **'~ out'** „Zutritt verboten" ② v.t. nicht hereinlassen

■ **keep 'up** ① v.i. **~ up with sb./sth.** mit jmdm./etw. Schritt halten ② v.t. aufrechterhalten ‹Freundschaft, jmds. Moral›; **~ one's strength up** sich bei Kräften halten; **~ it up!** weiter so!

keep-'fit n. Fitnesstraining, das

keep-'fit class n. Fitnessgruppe, die; **go to ~es** zu Fitnessübungen gehen

'keeping n. **be in ~ with sth.** einer Sache (Dat.) entsprechen

'keepsake n. Andenken, das

keg /keg/ n. [kleines] Fass

kelp /kelp/ n. [See]tang, der

kennel /'kenl/ n. Hundehütte, die

Kenya /'kenjə/ pr. n. Kenia (das)

kept ▶ KEEP 1, 2

kerb /kɜːb/ n. (Brit.) Bordstein, der

kerb: ~-crawling n. (Brit.) (langsames) Fahren auf dem Autostrich zur Kontaktaufnahme mit einer Prostituierten; **~stone** n. (Brit.) Bordstein, der

kernel /'kɜːnl/ n. Kern, der

kerosene, kerosine /'kerəsiːn/ n. (Amer., Austral., NZ/as tech. term) Paraffin[öl], das; (for jet engines) Kerosin, das

kestrel /'kestrəl/ n. Turmfalke, der

ketch /ketʃ/ n. Ketsch, die

ketchup /'ketʃʌp/ n. Ketschup, der od. das

kettle /'ketl/ n. [Wasser]kessel, der

key /kiː/ ① n. **(a)** Schlüssel, der **(b)** (on piano, typewriter, computer, etc.) Taste, die **(c)** (Mus.) Tonart, die ② v.t. (Comp.) eintasten

key: ~board n. (of piano etc.) Klaviatur, die; (of typewriter, computer, etc.) Tastatur, die; **~board operator** Taster, der/Tasterin, die; **~boarder** n. Taster, der/Tasterin, die; **~boarding** n. Tasten, das; **~boarding error** Tastfehler, der; **~ card** n. Schlüsselkarte, die; **~hole** n. Schlüsselloch, das; **~hole surgery** n. Schlüssellochchirurgie, die; Knopflochchirurgie, die

'keying ▶ KEYBOARDING

key: ~ring n. Schlüsselring, der; **~stone** n. (Archit.) Schlussstein, der; (fig.)

Grundpfeiler, *der;* ~**stroke** *n.* Anschlag,
der

kg. *abbr.* = **kilogram[s]** kg
khaki /'kɑːkɪ/ ⟨1⟩ *adj.* khakifarben
　⟨2⟩ *n.* (cloth) Khaki, *der*
kick /kɪk/ ⟨1⟩ *n.* (a) [Fuß]tritt, *der;* (Footb.)
Schuss, *der;* **give sb. a** ~: jmdm. einen Tritt
geben
　(b) (coll.: thrill) **do sth. for** ~**s** etw. zum Spaß
tun; **he gets a** ~ **out of it** er hat Spaß daran
　⟨2⟩ *v.i.* treten; ⟨*Pferd:*⟩ ausschlagen
　⟨3⟩ *v.t.* einen Tritt geben (+ *Dat.*) ⟨*Person,*
Hund⟩; treten gegen ⟨*Gegenstand*⟩; kicken
(ugs.), schießen ⟨*Ball*⟩
　∎ **kick a'bout, kick a'round** *v.t.* [in
der Gegend] herumkicken (ugs.)
　∎ **kick 'off** *v.i.* (Footb.) anstoßen
　∎ **kick 'up** *v.t.* (coll.) ~ **up a fuss/row** Krach
schlagen/anfangen (ugs.)
kick: ~**-off** *n.* (Footb.) Anstoß, *der;*
~**-start** ⟨1⟩ *n.* (a) Kickstarter, *der;* **(b)** (fig.)
[neuer] Auftrieb; ⟨2⟩ *v.t.* (a) [mit dem
Kickstarter] starten; **(b)** (fig.) ankurbeln
⟨*Industrie, Wirtschaft*⟩; vorantreiben,
forcieren ⟨*Friedensprozess, Entwicklung*⟩
kid /kɪd/ ⟨1⟩ *n.* (a) (young goat) Kitz, *das*
　(b) (coll.: child) Kind, *das*
　⟨2⟩ *v.t.,* **-dd-** (coll.) auf den Arm nehmen (ugs.);
~ **oneself** sich (*Dat.*) was vormachen
kiddie /'kɪdɪ/ *n.* (coll.) Kindchen, *das*
kid-'glove *adj.* sanft
kidnap /'kɪdnæp/ *v.t.,* (Brit.) **-pp-** entführen
'kidnapper *n.* Entführer, *der*/Entführerin,
die
kidnapping /'kɪdnæpɪŋ/ *n.* Entführung,
die
kidney /'kɪdnɪ/ *n.* Niere, *die*
kidney: ~ **bean** *n.* Gartenbohne, *die;*
(scarlet runner bean) Feuerbohne, *die;* **red**
~ **bean** Kidneybohne, *die;* ~ **machine**
n. künstliche Niere; ~**-shaped** *adj.*
nierenförmig
kill /kɪl/ *v.t.* (a) töten; (deliberately)
umbringen; **be** ~**ed in action** im Kampf
fallen; **be** ~**ed in a car crash** bei einem
Autounfall ums Leben kommen
　(b) ~ **time** die Zeit totschlagen
'killer *n.* Mörder, *der*/Mörderin, *die*
'killer whale *n.* Mörderwal, *der*
'killing *n.* (a) Töten, *das*
　(b) **make a** ~ (coll.: great profit) einen
[Mords]reibach machen (ugs.)
'killjoy *n.* Spielverderber, *der*/-verderberin,
die
kiln /kɪln/ *n.* Brennofen, *der*
kilo /'kiːləʊ/ *n., pl.* ~**s** Kilo, *das*
'kilobyte /'kɪləbaɪt/ *n.* (Comp.) Kilobyte, *das*
kilogram, kilogramme /'kɪləgræm/ *n.*
Kilogramm, *das*
kilometre (*Brit.; Amer.:* **kilometer**)
/'kɪləmiːtə(r) (Brit.), kɪ'lɒmɪtə(r)/ *n.*
Kilometer, *der*

kilowatt *n.* /'kɪləwɒt/ Kilowatt, *das*
kilt /kɪlt/ *n.* Kilt, *der*
kimono /kɪ'məʊnəʊ/ *n., pl.* ~**s** Kimono,
der
kin /kɪn/ *n.* (relatives) Verwandte *Pl.;* (relative)
Verwandte, *der/die*
kind[1] /kaɪnd/ *n.* (a) (class, sort) Art, *die;*
several ~**s of apples** mehrere Sorten
Äpfel; **all** ~**s of things/excuses** alles
Mögliche/alle möglichen Ausreden; **no** ...
of any ~: keinerlei ...; **what** ~ **is it?** was für
einer/eine/eins ist es?; **what** ~ **of [a] tree is
this?** was für ein Baum ist das?
　(b) (implying vagueness) **a** ~ **of** ...: [so] eine
Art ...; ~ **of cute** (coll.) irgendwie niedlich
(ugs.)
kind[2] *adj.* liebenswürdig; (showing friendliness)
freundlich; **be** ~ **to animals** gut zu Tieren
sein; **how** ~! wie nett [von ihm/Ihnen *usw.*]!
kindergarten /'kɪndəɡɑːtn/ *n.*
Kindergarten, *der*
kind-hearted /kaɪnd'hɑːtɪd/ *adj.*
gutherzig
kindle /'kɪndl/ (fig.) wecken
kindly /'kaɪndlɪ/ ⟨1⟩ *adv.* (a) freundlich;
nett
　(b) *in polite request etc.* freundlicherweise;
thank you ~: herzlichen Dank
　⟨2⟩ *adj.* freundlich; nett; (kind-hearted) gütig
'kindness *n.* (a) *no pl.* (kind nature)
Freundlichkeit, *die*
　(b) **do sb. a** ~ (kind act) jmdm. eine
Gefälligkeit erweisen
kindred /'kɪndrɪd/ *adj.* verwandt; ~ **'spirit**
Gleichgesinnte, *der/die*
king /kɪŋ/ *n.* König, *der*
kingdom /'kɪŋdəm/ *n.* Königreich, *das*
'kingfisher *n.* Eisvogel, *der*
'king-size[d] *adj.* extragroß; King-size-
⟨*Zigaretten*⟩
kink /kɪŋk/ *n.* (in pipe, wire, etc.) Knick, *der;* (in
hair, wool) Welle, *die*
'kinky *adj.* (coll.) spleenig; (sexually) abartig
kinsman /'kɪnzmən/ *n., pl.* **kinsmen**
/'kɪnzmən/ Verwandte, *der*
kinswoman /'kɪnzwʊmn/ *n.* Verwandte,
die
kiosk /'kiːɒsk/ *n.* (a) Kiosk, *der*
　(b) (telephone booth) [Telefon]zelle, *die*
kip /kɪp/ *n.* (Brit. coll.: sleep) **have a/get some**
~: eine Runde pennen (salopp)
kipper /'kɪpə(r)/ *n.* Kipper, *der*
kiss /kɪs/ ⟨1⟩ *n.* Kuss, *der*
　⟨2⟩ *v.t.* küssen; ~ **sb. good night/goodbye**
jmdm. einen Gutenacht-/Abschiedskuss
geben
　⟨3⟩ *v.i.* **they** ~**ed** sie küssten sich
kit /kɪt/ *n.* (a) (Brit.: set of items) Set, *das*
　(b) (Brit.: clothing etc.) **sports** ~: Sportzeug,
das; **riding/skiing** ~: Reit-/Skiausrüstung,
die
'kitbag *n.* Tornister, *der*

k

kitchen /'kɪtʃɪn/ *n.* Küche, *die; attrib.* Küchen-

kitchen: ~ **paper** *n.* Küchenkrepp, *der;* ~ **roll** *n.* Küchenrolle, *die;* (kitchen paper) Küchenkrepp, *der;* ~ **'sink** *n.* [Küchen]ausguss, *der;* ~ **unit** *n.* Küchenelement, *das;* ~ **units** Küchenmöbel *Pl.;* ~ **utensil** *n.* Küchengerät, *das;* ~**ware** *n.* Küchengeräte *Pl.*

kite /kaɪt/ *n.* Drachen, *der*

kith /kɪθ/ *n.* ~ **and kin** Freunde und Verwandte

kitten /'kɪtn/ *n.* Kätzchen, *das*

kitty /'kɪtɪ/ *n.* (money) Kasse, *die*

kleptomania /kleptə'meɪnɪə/ *n.* Kleptomanie, *die*

kleptomaniac /kleptə'meɪnɪæk/ *n.* Kleptomane, *der*/Kleptomanin, *die*

km. *abbr.* = **kilometre[s]** km

knack /næk/ *n.* Talent, *das;* **get the** ~ **[of doing sth.]** den Bogen rauskriegen [, wie man etw. macht] (ugs.); **have lost the** ~: es nicht mehr zustande bringen

knapsack /'næpsæk/ *n.* Rucksack, *der;* (Mil.) Tornister, *der*

knead /niːd/ *v.t.* kneten

knee /niː/ *n.* Knie, *das*

knee: ~**cap** *n.* Kniescheibe, *die;* ~**-deep** *adj.* knietief; ~**-high** *adj.* kniehoch; ~**-jerk reaction** *n.* (fig.) automatische Reaktion; ~ **joint** *n.* Kniegelenk, *das*

kneel /niːl/ *v.i.,* knelt /nelt/ *or* (esp. Amer.) kneeled knien; ~ **down** niederknien

'knee-length *adj.* knielang

knelt ▶ KNEEL

knew ▶ KNOW

knickers /'nɪkəz/ *n. pl.* (Brit.) [Damen]schlüpfer, *der*

knife /naɪf/ [1] *n., pl.* knives /naɪvz/ Messer, *das*

[2] *v.t.* (stab) einstechen auf (+ *Akk.*); (kill) erstechen

'knife-edge *n.* Schneide, *die;* **be [balanced] on a** ~ (fig.) auf des Messers Schneide stehen

knight /naɪt/ *n.* (a) (Hist.) Ritter, *der* (b) (Chess) Springer, *der*

'knighthood *n.* Ritterwürde, *die*

knit /nɪt/ *v.t.,* -tt- stricken; ~ **one's brow** die Stirn runzeln

'knitting *n.* Stricken, *das;* (work being knitted) Strickarbeit, *die*

'knitting needle *n.* Stricknadel, *die*

'knitwear *n.* Strickwaren *Pl.*

knives *pl. of* KNIFE 1

knob /nɒb/ *n.* (a) (on door, walking stick, etc.) Knauf, *der* (b) (control on radio etc.) Knopf, *der* (c) (of butter) Klümpchen, *das*

knock /nɒk/ [1] *v.t.* (a) (strike) (lightly) klopfen an (+ *Akk.*); (forcefully) schlagen gegen *od.* an (+ *Akk.*); ~ **a hole in sth.** ein Loch in etw. (*Akk.*) schlagen (b) (coll.: criticize) herziehen über (+ *Akk.*) (ugs.)

[2] *v.i.* klopfen (**at** an + *Akk.*)

[3] *n.* Klopfen, *das*

■ **knock 'down** *v.t.* (a) (in car) umfahren (b) (demolish) abreißen

■ **knock 'off** [1] *v.t.* (a) ~ **off work** (coll.: leave) Feierabend machen (b) (deduct) ~ **five pounds off the price** es fünf Pfund billiger machen (c) (coll.: do quickly) aus dem Ärmel schütteln (ugs.) (d) (coll.: steal) klauen (salopp)

[2] *v.i.* (coll.) Feierabend machen

■ **knock 'out** *v.t.* (a) (make unconscious) bewusstlos umfallen lassen (b) (Boxing) k.o. schlagen (c) (coll.: exhaust) kaputtmachen (ugs.)

■ **knock 'over** *v.t.* umstoßen; ⟨*Fahrer, Fahrzeug:*⟩ umfahren ⟨Person⟩

'knock-down *adj.* ~ **prices** Schleuderpreise

'knocker *n.* [Tür]klopfer, *der*

knock: ~**-kneed** /'nɒkniːd/ *adj.* x-beinig ⟨Person⟩; ~**out** *n.* (Boxing) K.-o.-Schlag, *der*

knot /nɒt/ [1] *n.* Knoten, *der*

[2] *v.t.,* -tt- knoten ⟨Seil, Faden usw.⟩

'knotty *adj.* (fig.: puzzling) verwickelt

know /nəʊ/ *v.t.,* knew /njuː/, known /nəʊn/ (a) (recognize) erkennen (**by** an + *Dat.,* **for** als + *Akk.*) (b) (be able to distinguish) ~ **sth. from sth.** etw. von etw. unterscheiden können (c) (be aware of) wissen (d) (have understanding of) können ⟨ABC, Einmaleins, Deutsch usw.⟩; ~ **how to mend fuses** wissen, wie man Sicherungen repariert; ~ **how to drive a car** Auto fahren können (e) kennen ⟨Person⟩

'know-all *n.* Neunmalkluge, *der*/*die*

'know-how *n.* praktisches Wissen; (technical expertise) Know-how, *das*

'knowing *adj.* (a) wissend ⟨Blick, Lächeln⟩ (b) (cunning) verschlagen

'knowingly *adv.* (a) (intentionally) wissentlich (b) viel sagend ⟨lächeln, anblicken⟩

knowledge /'nɒlɪdʒ/ *n.* (a) (familiarity) Kenntnisse *Pl.* (**of** in + *Dat.*) (b) (awareness) Wissen, *das;* **have no** ~ **of sth.** nichts von etw. wissen; keine Kenntnis von etw. haben (geh.) (c) [a] ~ **of languages/French** Sprach-/Französischkenntnisse *Pl.*

knowledgeable /'nɒlɪdʒəbl/ *adj.* **be** ~ **about** *or* **on sth.** viel über etw. (*Akk.*) wissen

known /nəʊn/ [1] ▶ KNOW

[2] *adj.* bekannt

knuckle /'nʌkl/ *n.* [Finger]knöchel, *der*

Koran /kɔː'rɑːn, kə'rɑːn/ *n.* Koran, *der*

Koranic /kə'rænɪk, -'rɑːnɪk/ *adj.*
koranisch

Korea /kə'rɪə/ *pr. n.* Korea (*das*)

Korean /kə'riːən/ ❶ *adj.* koreanisch; *sb.*
is ∼: jmd. ist Koreaner/Koreanerin
❷ *n.* **(a)** (person) Koreaner, *der*/Koreanerin,
die
(b) (language) Koreanisch, *das; see also*
ENGLISH 2A

kosher /'kəʊʃə(r)/ *adj.* koscher

Kosovan /'kɒsəvən/ ❶ *adj.*
∼ **town/immigrant** Stadt im Kosovo/
Einwanderer aus dem Kosovo; ∼ **Albanian**
Kosovoalbaner, *der*/-albanerin, *die;* **he/she**
is ∼: er ist Kosovarer/sie ist Kosovarin

❷ *n.* (person) Kosovare, *der*/Kosovarin, *die*

Kosovo /'kɒsəvə/ *pr. n.* Kosovo, *der od.*
das od. (*das*)

kudos /'kjuːdɒs/ *n.* Prestige, *das*

Kurd /kɜːd/ *n.* Kurde, *der*/Kurdin, *die*

Kurdish /'kɜːdɪʃ/ ❶ *adj.* kurdisch; *sb.* **is**
∼: jmd. ist Kurde/Kurdin
❷ *n.* (language) Kurdisch, *das*

Kurdistan /kɜːdɪ'stɑːn/ *pr. n.* Kurdistan
(*das*)

Kuwait /kʊ'weɪt/ *pr. n.* Kuwait (*das*)

Kuwaiti /kʊ'weɪtɪ/ ❶ *adj.* kuwaitisch; *sb.*
is ∼: jmd. ist Kuwaiti
❷ *n.* Kuwaiti, *der*/*die*

kW *abbr.* = **kilowatt[s]** kW

Ll

L, l /el/ *n.* L, l, *das*

l. *abbr.* = **litre[s]** l

lab /læb/ *n.* (coll.) Labor, *das*

label /'leɪbl/ ❶ *n.* Schildchen, *das;* (on
bottles, in clothes) Etikett, *das;* (tied/stuck to an
object) Anhänger/Aufkleber, *der*
❷ *v.t.,* (Brit.) **-ll-**: **(a)** etikettieren;
auszeichnen ‹*Waren*›; (write on) beschriften
(b) (fig.) ∼ **sb./sth. [as] sth.** jmdn./etw. als
etw. etikettieren

labor (Amer.) ▸ LABOUR

laboratory /lə'bɒrətərɪ/ *n.* Labor[atorium],
das; ∼ **animal** Versuchstier, *das*

labored, laborer (Amer.) ▸ LABOUR-

laborious /lə'bɔːrɪəs/ *adj.* mühsam

la'boriously *adv.* mühevoll

labour /'leɪbə(r)/ (Brit.) ❶ *n.* **(a)** Arbeit, *die*
(b) (workers) Arbeiterschaft, *die;* **immigrant**
∼: ausländische Arbeitskräfte *Pl.*
(c) L∼, the L∼ Party (Polit.) die Labour Party
(d) (childbirth) Wehen *Pl.;* **be in** ∼: in den
Wehen liegen
❷ *v.i.* hart arbeiten (**at, on** an + *Dat.*)
❸ *v.t.* ∼ **the point** sich lange darüber
verbreiten

laboured /'leɪbəd/ *adj.* (Brit.) mühsam;
schwerfällig ‹*Stil*›; **his breathing was** ∼: er
atmete schwer

'labourer *n.* (Brit.) Arbeiter, *der*/Arbeiterin,
die

labour: ∼ **pains** *n. pl.* Wehenschmerzen
Pl.; ∼**-saving** *adj.* arbeit[s]sparend

laburnum /lə'bɜːnəm/ *n.* (Bot.) Goldregen,
der

labyrinth /'læbərɪnθ/ *n.* Labyrinth, *das*

lace /leɪs/ ❶ *n.* **(a)** (for shoe) Schnürsenkel,
der

(b) (fabric) Spitze, *die; attrib.* Spitzen-
❷ *v.t.* ∼ **[up]** [zu]schnüren

lacerate /'læsəreɪt/ *v.t.* aufreißen

'lace-up ❶ *attrib. adj.* Schnür-
❷ *n.* Schnürschuh/-stiefel, *der*

lack /læk/ ❶ *n.* Mangel, *der* (**of** an + *Dat.*)
❷ *v.t.* **sb./sth.** ∼**s sth.** jmdm./einer Sache
fehlt es an etw. (*Dat.*)

lackey /'lækɪ/ *n.* Lakai, *der*

'lacking *adj.* **be** ∼: fehlen

laconic /lə'kɒnɪk/ *adj.* lakonisch

lacquer /'lækə(r)/ *n.* Lack, *der*

lacrosse /lə'krɒs/ *n.* Lacrosse, *das*

lacy /'leɪsɪ/ *adj.* Spitzen-

lad /læd/ *n.* Junge, *der*

ladder /'lædə(r)/ ❶ *n.* **(a)** Leiter, *die*
(b) (Brit.: in tights etc.) Laufmasche, *die*
❷ *v.i.* (Brit.) Laufmaschen/eine Laufmasche
bekommen
❸ *v.t.* (Brit.) Laufmaschen/eine Laufmasche
machen in (+ *Akk.*)

laden /'leɪdn/ beladen (**with** mit)

ladle /'leɪdl/ *n.* Schöpfkelle, *die*

lady /'leɪdɪ/ *n.* **(a)** Dame, *die;* ∼**-in-waiting**
(Brit.) Hofdame, *die*
(b) 'Ladies' (WC) „Damen"
(c) *as form of address* **Ladies** meine Damen
(d) (Brit.) *as title* **L∼:** Lady

lady: ∼**bird,** (Amer.) ∼**bug** *ns.*
Marienkäfer, *der;* ∼**like** *adj.* damenhaft

lag[1] /læg/ *v.i.,* **-gg-:** ∼ **[behind]**
zurückbleiben; (fig.) im Rückstand sein

lag[2] *v.t.,* **-gg-** (insulate) isolieren

lager /'lɑːgə(r)/ *n.* Lagerbier, *das*

'lager lout *n.* Bier trinkender Rüpel

'lagging *n.* Isolierung, *die*

lagoon /lə'guːn/ *n.* Lagune, *die*

laid ▶ LAY²
'laid-back *adj.* (coll.) gelassen
lain ▶ LIE²
lair /leər/ *n.* (of wild animal) Unterschlupf, *der;* (of pirates, bandits) Schlupfwinkel, *der*
lake /leɪk/ *n.* See, *der*
Lake Constance /leɪk 'kɒnstəns/ *pr. n.* der Bodensee
lama /'lɑːmə/ *n.* Lama, *der*
lamb /læm/ *n.* **(a)** Lamm, *das* **(b)** (meat) Lamm[fleisch], *das*
lamb 'chop *n.* Lammkotelett, *das*
lambswool /'læmzwʊl/ *n.* Lambswool, *die*
lame /leɪm/ *adj.,* **'lamely** *adv.* lahm
lament /lə'ment/ ① *n.* Klage, *die* (for um) ② *v.t.* ∼ **that** ...: beklagen, dass ... ③ *v.i.* klagen (geh.); ∼ **over sth.** etw. beklagen (geh.)
lamentable /'læməntəbl/ *adj.* beklagenswert
laminated /'læmɪneɪtɪd/ *adj.* lamelliert; ∼ **glass** Verbundglas, *das*
lamp /læmp/ *n.* Lampe, *die;* (in street) [Straßen]laterne, *die*
lamp: ∼ **post** *n.* Laternenpfahl, *der;* ∼**shade** *n.* Lampenschirm, *der*
lance /lɑːns/ ① *n.* Lanze, *die* ② *v.t.* (Med.) mit der Lanzette öffnen
lance 'corporal *n.* Obergefreite, *der*
land /lænd/ ① *n.* Land, *das;* **have** or **own** ∼: Grundbesitz haben ② *v.t.* **(a)** (set ashore) [an]landen **(b)** (Aeronaut.) landen **(c)** ∼ **oneself in trouble** sich in Schwierigkeiten bringen; ∼ **sb. with sth.,** ∼ **sth. on sb.** jmdm. etw. aufhalsen (ugs.) ③ *v.i.* **(a)** ⟨*Boot usw.:*⟩ anlegen, landen; ⟨*Passagier:*⟩ aussteigen (from aus); **we** ∼**ed at Dieppe** wir gingen in Dieppe an Land **(b)** (Aeronaut.) landen **(c)** ∼ **on one's feet** (fig.) [wieder] auf die Füße fallen
'landed *adj.* ∼ **gentry/aristrocracy** Landadel, *der*
'landing *n.* **(a)** (of ship, aircraft) Landung, *die* **(b)** (on stairs) Treppenabsatz, *der;* (passage) Treppenflur, *der*
landing: ∼ **card** *n.* Landekarte, *die;* ∼ **stage** *n.* Landesteg, *der*
land: ∼**lady** *n.* **(a)** (of rented property) Vermieterin, *die;* **(b)** (of public house) [Gast]wirtin, *die;* ∼**locked** *adj.* vom Land eingeschlossen ⟨*Bucht, Hafen*⟩; ⟨*Staat*⟩ ohne Zugang zum Meer; ∼**lord** *n.* **(a)** (of rented property) Vermieter, *der;* **(b)** (of public house) [Gast]wirt, *der;* ∼**mark** *n.* **(a)** Orientierungspunkt, *der;* **(b)** (fig.) Markstein, *der;* ∼ **mass** *n.* Landmasse, *die;* ∼**mine** *n.* Landmine, *die;* ∼**owner** *n.* Grundbesitzer, *der/*-besitzerin, *die;* ∼**scape** /'lændskeɪp/ *n.* Landschaft, *die;* ∼**scape architect** *n.*

Landschaftsarchitekt, *der/*-architektin, *die;* ∼**scape format** *n.* (also Comp.) Querformat, *das;* ∼**scape gardener** *n.* Landschaftsgärtner, *der/*-gärtnerin, *die;* ∼**scape gardening** *n.* Landschaftsgärtnerei, *die;* ∼**slide** *n.* Erdrutsch, *der;* **a** ∼**slide [victory]** (Polit.) ein Erdrutsch[wahl]sieg
lane /leɪn/ *n.* **(a)** (in the country) Landsträßchen, *das;* Weg, *der* **(b)** (in town) Gasse, *die* **(c)** (part of road) [Fahr]spur, *die;* **'get in** ∼**'** „bitte einordnen" **(d)** (Sport) Bahn, *die*
language /'læŋgwɪdʒ/ *n.* Sprache, *die;* (style) Ausdrucksweise, *die*
language: ∼ **course** *n.* Sprachkurs[us], *der;* ∼ **school** *n.* Sprachenschule; *die;* ∼ **teacher** *n.* Sprachlehrer, *der/*-lehrerin, *die*
languid /'læŋgwɪd/ *adj.* träge
languish /'læŋgwɪʃ/ *v.i.* **(a)** (lose vitality) ermatten (geh.) **(b)** ∼ **under sth.** unter etw. (*Dat.*) schmachten (geh.)
lank /læŋk/ *adj.* **(a)** hager **(b)** glatt herabhängend ⟨Haar⟩
lanky /'læŋkɪ/ *adj.* schlaksig (ugs.)
lantern /'læntən/ *n.* Laterne, *die*
lap¹ /læp/ *n.* (part of body) Schoß, *der*
lap² *n.* (Sport) Runde, *die*
lap³ ① *v.i.,* -pp- schlecken ② *v.t.,* -pp-: ∼ **[up]** [auf]schlecken ▪ **lap 'up** *v.t.* (fig.) schlucken
'lap belt *n.* Beckengurt, *der*
lapel /lə'pel/ *n.* Revers, *das*
Lapland /'læplænd/ *pr. n.* Lappland (*das*)
lapse /læps/ ① *n.* **(a)** (interval) **a/the** ∼ **of** ...: eine/die Zeitspanne von ... **(b)** (mistake) Fehler, *der;* ∼ **of memory** Gedächtnislücke, *die* ② *v.i.* **(a)** ⟨*Vertrag, usw.:*⟩ ungültig werden **(b)** ∼ **into** verfallen in (+ *Akk.*)
'laptop ① *adj.* tragbar, Laptop⟨*gerät, -PC*⟩ ② *n.* Laptop, *der;* tragbarer PC
larceny /'lɑːsənɪ/ *n.* Diebstahl, *der*
lard /lɑːd/ *n.* Schweineschmalz, *das*
larder /'lɑːdə(r)/ *n.* Speisekammer, *die*
large /lɑːdʒ/ ① *adj.* groß ② *n.* **at** ∼ (not in prison etc.) auf freiem Fuß ③ *adv.* ▶ BY 2D
'largely *adv.* weitgehend
larger-than-'life *attrib. adj.* überlebensgroß
large: ∼**-scale** *attrib. adj.* groß angelegt; groß ⟨*Erfolg, Misserfolg*⟩; ⟨*Katastrophe*⟩ großen Ausmaßes; ⟨*Modell*⟩ in großem Maßstab; ∼**-scale manufacture** Massenproduktion, *die;* ∼**-size[d]** *adj.* groß
lark¹ /lɑːk/ *n.* (Ornith.) Lerche, *die*
lark² (coll.) ① *n.* Jux, *der* (ugs.)

② *v.i.* ∼ [about *or* around] herumalbern (ugs.)

larva /ˈlɑːvə/ *n., pl.* ∼e /ˈlɑːviː/ Larve, *die*

laryngitis /lærɪnˈdʒaɪtɪs/ *n.* Kehlkopfentzündung, *die*

larynx /ˈlærɪŋks/ *n.* Kehlkopf, *der*

lascivious /ləˈsɪvɪəs/ *adj.* lüstern (geh.)

laser /ˈleɪzə(r)/ *n.* Laser, *der*

laser: ∼ **beam** *n.* Laserstrahl, *der;* ∼**disc** *n.* Laserplatte, *die;* ∼ **printer** *n.* Laserdrucker, *der*

lash /læʃ/ ① *n.* (a) (stroke) [Peitschen]hieb, *der*
(b) (on eyelid) Wimper, *die*
② *v.i.* ⟨*Welle, Regen:*⟩ peitschen (**against** gegen, on auf + *Akk.*)
③ *v.t.* (a) (fasten) festbinden (**to** an + *Dat.*)
(b) (as punishment) auspeitschen
■ **lash 'down** ① *v.t.* festbinden
② *v.i.* ⟨*Regen:*⟩ niederprasseln
■ **lash 'out** *v.i.* (a) (hit out) um sich schlagen; ∼ **out at sb.** nach jmdm. schlagen
(b) ∼ **out on sth.** (coll.: spend freely) sich (*Dat.*) etw. leisten

lashings /ˈlæʃɪŋz/ *n. pl.* ∼ **of sth.** Unmengen von etw.

lass /læs/ *n.* Mädchen, *das*

lasso /ləˈsuː/ Lasso, *das*

last[1] /lɑːst/ ① *adj.* letzt...; **be** ∼ **to arrive** als Letzter/Letzte ankommen; ∼ **night** gestern Nacht/Abend
② *adv.* (a) [ganz] zuletzt; als Letzter/Letzte ⟨*sprechen, ankommen*⟩
(b) (on ∼ previous occasion) das letzte Mal; zuletzt
③ *n.* (a) (person or thing) the ∼: der/die/das Letztere; *pl.* die Letzteren
(b) **at [long]** ∼: endlich

last[2] *v.i.* (a) (continue) dauern; ⟨*Wetter, Ärger:*⟩ anhalten
(b) (suffice) reichen

'last-ditch *adj.* ∼ **attempt** letzter verzweifelter Versuch

'lasting *adj.* bleibend; dauerhaft ⟨*Beziehung*⟩; nachhaltig ⟨*Eindruck, Wirkung*⟩

'lastly *adv.* schließlich

last: ∼**-minute** *attrib. adj.* in letzter Minute vorgebracht ⟨*Plan, Aufruf, Ergänzung, Gesuch, Bewerbung*⟩; ∼ **name** *n.* Zuname, *der;* Nachname, *der*

latch /lætʃ/ *n.* Riegel, *der;* **on the** ∼: nur eingeklinkt
■ **latch 'on to** *v.t.* (coll.: understand) kapieren (ugs.)

late /leɪt/ ① *adj.* (a) spät; **am I** ∼? komme ich zu spät?; **be** ∼ **for the train** den Zug verpassen; **the train is [an hour]** ∼: der Zug hat [eine Stunde] Verspätung; ∼ **shift** Spätschicht, *die;* ∼ **summer** Spätsommer, *der*
(b) (dead) verstorben
(c) (former) ehemalig. *See also* LATER 1; LATEST

② *adv.* (a) (after proper time) verspätet
(b) (at/till a ∼ hour) spät; **be up** ∼: bis spät in die Nacht aufbleiben; **work** ∼ **at the office** [abends] lange im Büro arbeiten; **[a bit]** ∼ **in the day** (fig. coll.) reichlich spät
③ *n.* **of** ∼: in letzter Zeit

latecomer /ˈleɪtkʌmə(r)/ *n.* Zuspätkommende, *der/die*

'lately *adv.* in letzter Zeit

'lateness *n.* (a) (delay) Verspätung, *die*
(b) **the** ∼ **of the performance** der späte Beginn der Vorstellung

'late-night *attrib. adj.* Spät⟨*programm, -vorstellung*⟩

latent /ˈleɪtənt/ *adj.* latent

later /ˈleɪtə(r)/ ① *adj.* ∼ **[on]** später
② *adj.* später; (more recent) neuer

lateral /ˈlætərl/ *adj.* seitlich (**to** von); ∼ **thinking** Querdenken, *das*

latest /ˈleɪtɪst/ *adj.* (a) (modern) neu[e]st...
(b) (most recent) letzt...
(c) **at [the]** ∼/**the very** ∼: spätestens/ allerspätestens

lathe /leɪð/ *n.* Drehbank, *die*

lather /ˈlɑːðə(r)/ ① *n.* [Seifen]schaum, *der*
② *v.t.* einschäumen

Latin /ˈlætɪn/ ① *adj.* lateinisch
② *n.* Latein, *das; see also* ENGLISH 2A

Latin A'merica *pr. n.* Lateinamerika (*das*)

Latin-A'merican *adj.* lateinamerikanisch

latitude /ˈlætɪtjuːd/ *n.* (a) (freedom) Freiheit, *die*
(b) (Geog.) Breite, *die*

latrine /ləˈtriːn/ *n.* Latrine, *die*

latter /ˈlætə(r)/ *attrib. adj.* letzter...; **the** ∼: der/die/das Letztere; *pl.* die Letzteren

'latterly *adv.* in letzter Zeit

lattice /ˈlætɪs/ *n.* Gitter, *das*

laudable /ˈlɔːdəbl/ *adj.* lobenswert

laugh /lɑːf/ ① *n.* Lachen, *das;* (continuous) Gelächter, *das*
② *v.i.* lachen; ∼ **out loud** laut auflachen; ∼ **at sb./sth.** über jmdn./etw. lachen; (jeer) jmdn. auslachen/etw. verlachen
■ **laugh 'off** *v.t.* mit einem Lachen abtun

laughable /ˈlɑːfəbl/ *adj.* lachhaft; lächerlich

'laughing *n.* **be no** ∼ **matter** nicht zum Lachen sein

laughing: ∼ **gas** *n.* Lachgas, *das;* ∼ **stock** *n.* **make sb. a** ∼ **stock, make a** ∼ **stock of sb.** jmdn. zum Gespött machen

laughter /ˈlɑːftə(r)/ *n.* Lachen, *das;* (continuous) Gelächter, *das*

'laughter lines *n. pl.* Lachfältchen *Pl.*

launch /lɔːntʃ/ *v.t.* (a) zu Wasser lassen ⟨*Boot*⟩; vom Stapel lassen ⟨*neues Schiff*⟩; abschießen ⟨*Harpune, Torpedo*⟩; schleudern ⟨*Speer*⟩
(b) (fig.) auf den Markt bringen ⟨*Produkt*⟩; vorstellen ⟨*Buch,*

Schallplatte, Sänger⟩; ~ **an attack** einen
Angriff durchführen
■ **launch 'out** *v.i.* (fig.) ~ **out into films/a
new career/on one's own** sich beim Film
versuchen/beruflich etwas ganz Neues
anfangen/sich selbstständig machen
'**launching pad, launch pad** *ns.*
[Raketen]abschussrampe, *die*
launder /'lɔːndə(r)/ *v.t.* waschen und
bügeln
launderette /lɔːndə'ret/, **laundrette**
/lɔːn'dret/, (Amer.) **laundromat**
/'lɔːndrəmæt/ *ns.* Waschsalon, *der*
laundry /'lɔːndrɪ/ *n.* (a) (place) Wäscherei,
die
(b) (clothes etc.) Wäsche, *die*
'**laundry basket** *n.* Wäschekorb, *der*
lava /'lɑːvə/ *n.* Lava, *die*
lavatory /'lævətərɪ/ *n.* Toilette, *die*
lavender /'lævɪndə(r)/ *n.* Lavendel, *der*
lavish /'lævɪʃ/ [1] *adj.* großzügig
[2] *v.t.* ~ **sth. on sb.** jmdn. mit etw.
überhäufen
law /lɔː/ *n.* (a) Gesetz, *das;* **break the
~:** gegen das Gesetz verstoßen; **take the
~ into one's own hands** (*Dat.*) selbst
Recht verschaffen; ~ **and order** Ruhe und
Ordnung
(b) (of game) Regel, *die*
(c) (as subject) Jura *o. Art.*
law: ~**abiding** /'lɔːəbaɪdɪŋ/ *adj.*
gesetzestreu; ~**court** *n.* Gerichtsgebäude,
das; (room) Gerichtssaal, *der;* ~ **firm** *n.*
(Amer.) Anwaltskanzlei, *die*
lawful /'lɔːfl/ *adj.* rechtmäßig ⟨Besitzer,
Erbe⟩; legal, gesetzmäßig ⟨Vorgehen,
Maßnahme⟩
'**lawless** *adj.* gesetzlos
lawn /lɔːn/ *n.* Rasen, *der*
lawn: ~**mower** *n.* Rasenmäher, *der;*
~ **sprinkler** *n.* Rasensprenger, *der;*
~ **tennis** *n.* Rasentennis, *das*
'**law suit** *n.* Prozess, *der*
lawyer /'lɔːjə(r)/ *n.* Rechtsanwalt,
der/Rechtsanwältin, *die*
lax /læks/ *adj.* lax; **be** ~ **about hygiene/
paying the rent** *etc.* es mit der Hygiene/der
Zahlung der Miete *usw.* nicht so genau
nehmen
laxative /'læksətɪv/ *n.* Abführmittel, *das*
laxity /'læksɪtɪ/, '**laxness** *ns.* Laxheit,
die
lay¹ /leɪ/ *adj.* Laien-
lay² *v.t.,* **laid** /leɪd/ (a) legen ⟨Teppichboden,
Rohr, Kabel⟩
(b) (impose) auferlegen ⟨Verantwortung,
Verpflichtung⟩ (**on** *Dat.*); verhängen ⟨Strafe⟩
(**on** über + *Akk.*)
(c) ~ **the table** den Tisch decken
(d) (Biol.) legen ⟨Ei⟩
■ **lay a'side** *v.t.* beiseite legen
■ **lay 'by** *v.t.* beiseite legen
■ **lay 'down** *v.t.* (a) hinlegen

(b) festlegen ⟨Regeln, Bedingungen⟩
■ **lay 'off** [1] *v.t.* (from work) vorübergehend
entlassen
[2] *v.i.* (coll.: stop) aufhören
■ **lay 'out** *v.t.* (a) (spread out) ausbreiten
(b) anlegen ⟨Garten⟩
■ **lay 'up** *v.t.* (a) (store) lagern
(b) **I was laid up in bed for a week** ich
musste eine Woche das Bett hüten
lay³ ▶ LIE²

lay: ~**about** *n.* (Brit.) Gammler, *der* (ugs.);
~**-by** *n., pl.* ~**-bys** (Brit.) Parkbucht, *die;*
Haltebucht, *die*
layer /'leɪə(r)/ *n.* Schicht, *die*
layette /leɪ'et/ *n.* [baby's]
~: Babyausstattung, *die*
lay: ~**man** /'leɪmən/ *n., pl.* ~**men**
/'leɪmən/ Laie, *der;* ~**out** *n.* (of garden,
park) Anlage, *die;* (of book, advertisement, etc.)
Layout, *das*
laze /leɪz/ *v.i.* faulenzen; ~ **around** *or* **about**
herumfaulenzen (ugs.)
lazily /'leɪzɪlɪ/ *adv.* faul
laziness /'leɪzɪnɪs/ *n.* Faulheit, *die*
lazy /'leɪzɪ/ *adj.* faul
'**lazybones** *n. sing.* Faulpelz, *der*
lb. *abbr.* = **pound[s]** ≈ Pfd.
LCD *abbr.* = **liquid crystal display**
LCD
lead¹ /led/ [1] *n.* (a) (metal) Blei, *das*
(b) (in pencil) [Bleistift]mine, *die*
[2] *attrib. adj.* Blei-
[3] *v.t.* (a) in Blei fassen ⟨Fenster⟩; ~ed
bleigefasst
(b) ~ed **petrol** bleihaltiges Benzin
lead² /liːd/ [1] *v.t.,* **led** /led/ (a) führen;
~ **sb. to do sth.** (fig.) jmdn. dazu bringen,
etw. zu tun
(b) (fig.: influence) ~ **sb. to do sth.** jmdn.
veranlassen, etw. zu tun; **be easily led** sich
leicht beeinflussen lassen; **he led me to
believe that ...:** er machte mich glauben,
dass ...
(c) (be first in) anführen
(d) (direct) anführen ⟨Bewegung,
Abordnung⟩; leiten ⟨Diskussion, Orchester⟩
[2] *v.i.,* led (a) ⟨Straße usw., Tür:⟩ führen
(b) (be first) führen; (go in front) vorangehen
[3] *n.* (a) (precedent) Beispiel, *das;* (clue)
Anhaltspunkt, *der;* **follow sb.'s** ~: jmds.
Beispiel (*Dat.*) folgen
(b) (first place) Führung, *die;* **be in the** ~: in
Führung liegen
(c) (distance ahead) Vorsprung, *der*
(d) (leash) Leine, *die;* **on a** ~: an der Leine
(e) (Electr.) Kabel, *das*
(f) (Theatre) Hauptrolle, *die*
■ **lead a'way** *v.t.* abführen ⟨Gefangenen,
Verbrecher⟩
■ **lead 'off** [1] *v.t.* abführen
[2] *v.i.* beginnen
■ **lead 'on** [1] *v.t.* ~ **sb. on** (entice) jmdn.
reizen; (deceive) jmdn. auf den Leim führen
[2] *v.i.* ~ **on to the next topic** *etc.* zum

nächsten Thema *usw.* führen
■ **lead 'up to** *v.t.* schließlich führen zu
'**leader** *n.* (a) Führer, *der*/Führerin, *die;* (of political party) Vorsitzende, *der*/*die;* (of expedition) Leiter, *der*/Leiterin, *die* (b) (Brit. Journ.) Leitartikel, *der*
'**leadership** *n.* Führung, *die*
'**leader writer** *n.* Leitartikelschreiber, *der*/-schreiberin, *die;* Leitartikler, *der*/ -artiklerin, *die* (Pressejargon)
lead-free /'ledfriː/ *adj.* bleifrei
leading /'liːdɪŋ/ *adj.* führend
leading: ∼ '**lady** *n.* Hauptdarstellerin, *die;* ∼ '**man** *n.* Hauptdarsteller, *der;* ∼ '**question** *n.* Suggestivfrage, *die;* ∼ '**role** *n.* Hauptrolle, *die;* (fig.) führende Rolle
lead: ∼ '**pencil** /led'pensl/ *n.* Bleistift, *der;* ∼ '**poisoning** /'led pɔɪzənɪŋ/ *n.* Bleivergiftung, *die;* ∼ '**singer** /liːd 'sɪŋə(r)/ *n.* Leadsänger *der*/-sängerin, *die;* ∼ '**story** /'liːd stɔːrɪ/ *n.* (Journ.) Titelgeschichte, *die;* ∼ '**time** /'liːd taɪm/ *n.* (Econ.) Entwicklungszeit, *die*
leaf /liːf/ *n., pl.* **leaves** /liːvz/ Blatt, *das;* (of table) Platte *die*
■ **leaf 'through** *v.t.* durchblättern
leaflet /'liːflɪt/ *n.* [Hand]zettel, *der;* (advertising) Reklamezettel, *der;* (political) Flugblatt, *das*
'**leafy** *adj.* belaubt
league /liːg/ *n.* (a) (agreement) Bündnis, *das;* **be in** ∼ **with sb.** mit jmdm. im Bunde sein (b) (Sport) Liga, *die*
league: ∼ '**football** *n.* Ligafußball, *der;* ∼ **match** *n.* Ligaspiel, *das;* ∼ **table** *n.* Tabelle, *die* (Sport); **be at the top/bottom of the** ∼ **table** an der Tabellenspitze/am Tabellenende sein (fig.); an der Spitze rangieren/das Schlusslicht bilden (ugs.) (**of** unter + *Dat.*)
leak /liːk/ **1** *n.* (a) (hole) Leck, *das;* (in roof, tent; also fig.) undichte Stelle (b) (escaping gas) durch ein Leck austretendes Gas **2** *v.i.* (a) (escape) austreten (**from** aus) (b) ⟨Fass, Tank, Schiff:⟩ lecken; ⟨Rohr, Leitung, Dach:⟩ undicht sein; ⟨Gefäß, Füller:⟩ auslaufen (c) (fig.) ∼ **[out]** durchsickern **3** *v.t.* ∼ **sth. to sb.** jmdm. etw. zuspielen
leakage /'liːkɪdʒ/ *n.* Auslaufen, *das;* (of fluid, gas) Ausströmen, *das;* (fig.: of information) Durchsickern, *das*
'**leaky** *adj.* undicht; leck ⟨Boot⟩
lean[1] /liːn/ **1** *adj.* mager **2** *n.* (meat) Magere, *das*
lean[2] **1** *v.i.,* **leaned** /liːnd/ **lent**/ *or* (Brit.) **leant** /lent/ (a) **sich beugen;** ∼ **against the door** sich gegen die Tür lehnen; ∼ **down/ forward** sich herab-/vorbeugen; ∼ **back** sich zurücklehnen

(b) (support oneself) ∼ **against/on sth.** sich gegen/an etw (*Akk.*) lehnen
(c) (be supported) lehnen (**against** an + *Dat.*)
(d) (fig.) ∼ **[up]on sb.** (rely) auf jmdn. bauen; ∼ **to[wards] sth.** (tend) zu etw. neigen
2 *v.t.,* **leaned** *or* (Brit.) **leant** lehnen (**against** gegen *od.* an + *Akk.*)
■ **lean 'over** *v.i.* sich hinüberbeugen
'**leaning** *n.* Neigung, *die*
leant ▸ LEAN[2]
leap /liːp/ **1** *v.i.,* **leaped** /liːpt, lept/ *or* **leapt** /lept/ (a) springen; ⟨Herz:⟩ hüpfen (b) (fig.) ∼ **at the chance** die Gelegenheit beim Schopf packen **2** *v.t.,* **leaped** *or* **leapt** überspringen **3** *n.* Sprung, *der;* **with** *or* **in one** ∼: mit einem Satz; **by** ∼**s and bounds** (fig.) mit Riesenschritten
'**leapfrog** **1** *n.* Bockspringen, *das* **2** *v.i.,* **-gg-** Bockspringen machen **3** *v.t.* (a) ∼**frog sb.** einen Bocksprung über jmdn. machen (b) (fig.) übertreffen ⟨Konkurrenz, Kollegen *usw.*⟩
leapt ▸ LEAP 1, 2
'**leap year** *n.* Schaltjahr, *das*
learn /lɜːn/ **1** *v.t.,* **learned** /lɜːnd, lɜːnt/ *or* **learnt** /lɜːnt/ (a) lernen; ∼ **to swim** schwimmen lernen (b) (find out) erfahren **2** *v.i.,* **learned** *or* **learnt** (a) lernen; ∼ **about sth.** etwas über etw. (*Akk.*) lernen (b) (get to know) erfahren (**of** von)
learned /'lɜːnɪd/ *adj.* gelehrt
'**learner** *n.* (beginner) Anfänger, *der*/ Anfängerin, *die;* ∼ **[driver]** Fahrschüler, *der*/-schülerin, *die*
'**learning** *n.* (of person) Gelehrsamkeit, *die*
'**learning:** ∼ **curve** *n.* Lernkurve, *die;* ∼ **difficulties** *n. pl.* Lernschwierigkeiten *Pl.;* ∼ **disability** *n.* Lernbehinderung, *die*
learnt ▸ LEARN
lease /liːs/ **1** *n.* (of land, business premises) Pachtvertrag, *der;* (of house, flat, office) Mietvertrag, *der* **2** *v.t.* (a) (grant ∼ on) verpachten ⟨Grundstück, Geschäft, Rechte⟩; vermieten ⟨Haus, Wohnung, Büro⟩ (b) (take ∼ on) pachten ⟨Grundstück, Geschäft⟩; mieten ⟨Haus, Wohnung, Büro⟩
'**leasehold** *n.* ▸ LEASE 2: **have the** ∼ **of** *or* **on sth.** etw. gepachtet/gemietet haben
leash /liːʃ/ *n.* Leine, *die*
least /liːst/ **1** *adj.* (smallest) kleinst...; (in quantity) wenigst...; (in status) geringst... **2** *n.* Geringste, *das;* **the** ∼ **I can do** das Mindeste, was ich tun kann; **at** ∼: mindestens; (anyway) wenigstens; **at the [very]** ∼: [aller]mindestens; **not [in] the** ∼: nicht im Geringsten **3** *adv.* am wenigsten
leather /'leðə(r)/ **1** *n.* Leder, *das*

2 *adj.* ledern; Leder⟨*jacke, -mantel*⟩
'**leather goods** *n. pl.* Lederwaren *Pl.*
'**leathery** *adj.* ledern
leave[1] /li:v/ *n.* (a) (permission) Erlaubnis, *die*
(b) (from duty or work) Urlaub, *der;* ~ [of absence] Urlaub, *der*
(c) take one's ~ sich verabschieden
leave[2] *v.t.,* left /left/ (a) (make or let remain) hinterlassen; ~ **sb. to do sth.** es jmdm. überlassen, etw. zu tun; (in will) ~ **sb. sth.,** ~ **sth. to sb.** jmdm. etw. hinterlassen
(b) (refrain from doing, using, etc.) stehen lassen ⟨*Abwasch, Essen*⟩
(c) (in given state) lassen; ~ **sb. alone** (allow to be alone) jmdn. allein lassen; (stop bothering) jmdn. in Ruhe lassen
(d) (refer, entrust) ~ **sth. to sb.**/sth. etw. jmdm./einer Sache überlassen
(e) (go away from, quit, desert) verlassen; ~ **home at 6 a.m.** um 6 Uhr früh von zu Hause weggehen/-fahren; ~ **Bonn at 6 p.m.** (by car, in train) um 18 Uhr von Bonn abfahren; (by plane) um 18 Uhr in Bonn abfliegen; *abs.* **the train** ~**s at 8.30 a.m.** der Zug fährt *od.* geht um 8.30 Uhr; ~ **on the 8 a.m. train/flight** mit dem Achtuhrzug fahren/der Achtuhrmaschine fliegen
■ **leave a'side** *v.t.* beiseite lassen
■ **leave be'hind** *v.t.* zurücklassen; (by mistake) vergessen; liegen lassen
■ **leave 'off** *v.t.* (stop) aufhören mit; *abs.* aufhören
■ **leave 'out** *v.t.* auslassen
■ **leave 'over** *v.t.* **be left over** übrig [geblieben] sein
leaves *pl. of* LEAF
Lebanon /'lebənən/ *pr. n.* **[the]** ~: [der] Libanon
lecherous /'letʃərəs/ *adj.* lüstern (geh.)
lecture /'lektʃə(r)/ 1 (a) *n.* Vortrag, *der;* (Univ.) Vorlesung, *die*
(b) (reprimand) Strafpredigt, *die* (ugs.)
2 *v.i.* ~ **[to sb.] [on sth.]** [vor jmdm.] einen Vortrag/(Univ.) eine Vorlesung [über etw. *(Akk.)*] halten
3 *v.t.* (scold) ~ **sb.** jmdm. eine Strafpredigt halten
'**lecture hall** *n.* Hörsaal, *der*
'**lecturer** *n.* Vortragende, *der/die;* **senior** ~: Dozent, *der*/Dozentin, *die*
'**lecture room** *n.* Vortragsraum, *der;* (Univ.) Vorlesungsraum, *der*
lectureship /'lektʃəʃɪp/ *n.* Dozentur, *die*
lecture: ~ **theatre** *n.* Hörsaal, *der;* ~ **tour** *n.* Vortragsreise, *die*
led ▸ LEAD[2] 1, 2
LED *abbr.* = **light-emitting diode** LED
ledge /ledʒ/ *n.* Sims, *der od. das;* (of rock) Vorsprung, *der*
ledger /'ledʒə(r)/ *n.* (Commerc.) Hauptbuch, *das*
lee /li:/ *n.* (a) (shelter) Schutz, *der*

(b) ~ **[side]** (Naut.) Leeseite, *die*
leech /li:tʃ/ *n.* [Blut]egel, *der*
leek /li:k/ *n.* Stange Porree *od.* Lauch; ~**s** Porree, *der;* Lauch, *der*
leek 'soup *n.* Lauch[creme]suppe, *die*
leer /lɪə(r)/ 1 *n.* anzüglicher/spöttischer Blick
2 *v.i.* ~ **at sb.** jmdm. einen anzüglichen/ spöttischen [Seiten]blick zuwerfen
leeward /'li:wəd/ 1 *adj.* **to/on the** ~ **side of the ship** nach/in Lee
2 *n.* Leeseite, *die;* **to** ~: leewärts
'**leeway** *n.* (a) (Naut.) Leeweg, *der;* Abdrift, *die*
(b) (fig.) Spielraum, *der*
left[1] ▸ LEAVE[2]
left[2] /left/ 1 *adj.* (a) link...; **on the** ~ **side** auf der linken Seite; links
(b) **L**~ (Polit.) link...
2 *adv.* nach links
3 *n.* (a) (~-hand side) linke Seite; **on** *or* **to the** ~ **[of sb./sth.]** links [von jmdm./etw.]
(b) (Polit.) **the L**~: die Linke
left: ~**-hand** *adj.* link...; ~**-'handed** 1 *adj.* linkshändig; ⟨*Werkzeug*⟩ für Linkshänder; **be** ~**-handed** Linkshänder/ Linkshänderin sein; 2 *adv.* linkshändig; ~ '**luggage [office]** *n.* (Brit. Railw.) Gepäckaufbewahrung, *die;* ~**overs** *n. pl.* Reste *Pl.;* ~ '**wing** *n.* linker Flügel; ~**-wing** *adj.* (Polit.) linksgerichtet; Links⟨*extremist, -intellektueller*⟩; ~**-'winger** *n.* (a) (Sport) Linksaußen, *der;*
(b) (Polit.) Angehöriger/Angehörige des linken Flügels
leg /leg/ *n.* (a) Bein, *das;* **pull sb.'s** ~ (fig.) jmdn. auf den Arm nehmen (ugs.); **stretch one's** ~**s** sich *(Dat.)* die Beine vertreten
(b) ~ **of lamb** Lammkeule, *die*
(c) (of journey) Etappe, *die*
legacy /'legəsɪ/ *n.* Vermächtnis, *das* (Rechtsspr.); Erbschaft, *die*
legal /'li:gl/ *adj.* (a) (concerning the law) juristisch; Rechts⟨*beratung, -streit, -experte, -schutz*⟩; gesetzlich ⟨*Vertreter*⟩; rechtlich ⟨*Gründe, Stellung*⟩; Gerichts⟨*kosten*⟩
(b) (required by law) gesetzlich ⟨*Verpflichtung*⟩; gesetzlich verankert ⟨*Recht*⟩
(c) (lawful) legal; rechtsgültig ⟨*Vertrag, Testament*⟩
legal: ~ '**action** *n.* Gerichtsverfahren, *das;* Prozess, *der;* **take** ~ **action against sb.** gerichtlich gegen jmdn. vorgehen; ~ '**aid** *n.* ≈ Prozesskostenhilfe, *die*
legality /lɪ'gælɪtɪ/ *n.* Legalität, *die*
legalization /li:gəlaɪ'zeɪʃn/ *n.* Legalisierung, *die*
legalize /'li:gəlaɪz/ *v.t.* legalisieren
legend /'ledʒənd/ *n.* Sage, *die;* (unfounded belief) Legende, *die*
legendary /'ledʒəndərɪ/ *adj.* legendär
leggings /'legɪŋz/ *n. pl.* Ledergamaschen *Pl.* (veralt.); (of baby) Strampelhose, *die*

legibility /ledʒɪ'bɪlɪtɪ/ n. Leserlichkeit, *die*

legible /'ledʒɪbl/ *adj.* leserlich; **easily/ scarcely** ~: leicht/kaum lesbar

legion /'liːdʒn/ n. Legion, *die*

legion'naires' disease n. (Med.) Legionärskrankheit, *die*

legislate /'ledʒɪsleɪt/ *v.i.* Gesetze verabschieden

legislation /ledʒɪs'leɪʃn/ n. **(a)** (laws) Gesetze *Pl.* **(b)** (legislating) Gesetzgebung, *die*

legislative /'ledʒɪslətɪv/ *adj.* gesetzgebend

legislator /'ledʒɪsleɪtə(r)/ n. Gesetzgeber, *der*

legislature /'ledʒɪsleɪtʃə(r)/ n. Legislative, *die*

legitimacy /lɪ'dʒɪtɪməsɪ/ n. **(a)** Rechtmäßigkeit, *die;* Legitimität, *die* **(b)** (of child) Ehelichkeit, *die*

legitimate /lɪ'dʒɪtɪmət/ *adj.* **(a)** (lawful) legitim; rechtmäßig ‹*Besitzer, Regierung*› **(b)** (valid) berechtigt **(c)** ehelich ‹*Kind*›

legitimatize (legitimatise) /lɪ'dʒɪtɪmətaɪz/, **legitimize (legitimise)** /lɪ'dʒɪtɪmaɪz/ *v.t.* legitimieren

leisure /'leʒə(r)/ n. Freizeit, *die; attrib.* Freizeit-

'leisurely *adj.* gemächlich

'leisurewear n., *no indef. art.* Freizeitkleidung, *die*

lemon /'lemən/ n. Zitrone, *die*

lemonade /lemə'neɪd/ n. [Zitronen]limonade, *die*

lend /lend/ *v.t.*, **lent** /lent/ leihen; ~ **sth. to sb.** jmdm. etw. leihen

'lender n. Verleiher, *der*/Verleiherin, *die*

length /leŋθ, leŋkθ/ n. **(a)** (also of time) Länge, *die;* **be six feet in** ~: sechs Fuß lang sein; **a short** ~ **of time** kurze Zeit **(b)** **at** ~ (for a long time) lange; (eventually) schließlich; **at [great]** ~ (in great detail) lang und breit; **at some** ~: ziemlich ausführlich **(c)** **go to any/great** ~**s** alles nur/alles Erdenkliche tun **(d)** (piece of material) Länge, *die;* Stück, *das*

lengthen /'leŋθən/ ① *v.i.* länger werden ② *v.t.* verlängern; länger machen ‹*Kleid*›

lengthways /'leŋθweɪz/ *adv.* der Länge nach; längs

'lengthy *adj.* überlang

lenient /'liːnɪənt/ *adj.* nachsichtig

lens /lenz/ n. Linse, *die;* (of spectacles) Glas, *das*

lens cap n. Objektivdeckel, *der*

lent ▶ LEND

Lent /lent/ n. Fastenzeit, *die*

lentil /'lentl/ n. Linse, *die*

Leo /'liːəʊ/ n., *pl.* ~**s** (Astrol., Astron.) der Löwe

leopard /'lepəd/ n. Leopard, *der*

leotard /'liːətɑːd/ n. Turnanzug, *der*

leper /'lepə(r)/ n. Leprakranke, *der*/*die*

leprosy /'leprəsɪ/ n. Lepra, *die*

lesbian /'lezbɪən/ ① n. Lesbierin, *die* ② *adj.* lesbisch

less /les/ ① *adj.* weniger; **of** ~ **value/ importance** weniger wertvoll/wichtig ② *adv.* weniger; ~ **and** ~: immer weniger; ~ **and** ~ **[often]** immer seltener ③ *n.* weniger ④ *prep.* (deducting) **ten** ~ **three** zehn weniger drei

lessee /le'siː/ n. Pächter, *der*/Pächterin, *die;* Mieter, *der*/Mieterin, *die*

lessen /'lesn/ ① *v.t.* verringern ② *v.i.* sich verringern

lesser /'lesə(r)/ *attrib. adj.* geringer…

lesson /'lesn/ n. **(a)** (class) [Unterrichts]stunde, *die* **(b)** (example, warning) Lehre, *die* **(c)** (Eccl.) Lesung, *die*

let /let/ ① *v.t.*, **-tt-**, **let (a)** (allow to) lassen; ~ **sb. do sth.** jmdn. etw. tun lassen; ~ **alone** (far less) geschweige denn **(b)** (cause to) ~ **sb. know** jmdn. wissen lassen **(c)** (Brit.: rent out) vermieten ② *v. aux.*, **-tt-**, **let** lassen; **Let's go to the cinema. – Yes, ~'s/No, ~'s not** Komm/ Kommt, wir gehen ins Kino. – Ja, gut/Nein, lieber nicht; ~ **them come in** sie sollen hereinkommen

■ **let 'down** *v.t.* **(a)** (lower) herunter-/ hinunterlassen **(b)** (Dressm.) auslassen **(c)** (disappoint, fail) im Stich lassen

■ **let 'in** *v.t.* **(a)** (admit) herein-/hineinlassen **(b)** ~ **oneself in for sth.** sich auf etw. (*Akk.*) einlassen **(c)** ~ **sb. in on a secret/plan** *etc.* jmdn. in ein Geheimnis/einen Plan *usw.* einweihen

■ **'let into** *v.t.* **(a)** (admit into) lassen in (+ *Akk.*) **(b)** (fig.: acquaint with) ~ **sb. into a secret** jmdn. in ein Geheimnis einweihen

■ **let 'off** *v.t.* **(a)** (excuse) laufen lassen (ugs.); ~ **sb. off sth.** jmdm. etw. erlassen **(b)** (allow to alight) aussteigen lassen **(c)** abbrennen ‹*Feuerwerk*›

■ **let 'on** (coll.) ① *v.i.* **don't** ~ **on!** nichts verraten! ② *v.t.* **sb.** ~ **on to me that** …: man hat mir gesteckt, dass … (ugs.)

■ **let 'out** *v.t.* **(a)** ~ **sb./an animal out** jmdn./ein Tier heraus-/hinauslassen **(b)** ausstoßen ‹*Schrei*›; ~ **out a groan** aufstöhnen **(c)** verraten ‹*Geheimnis*› **(d)** (Dressm.) auslassen **(e)** (Brit.: rent out) vermieten

■ **let 'through** *v.t.* durchlassen

■ **let 'up** *v.i.* (coll.) nachlassen

'**let-down** n. Enttäuschung, die

lethal /'li:θl/ adj. tödlich

lethargic /lɪ'θɑ:dʒɪk/ adj. träge; (apathetic) lethargisch

lethargy /'leθədʒɪ/ n. Trägheit, die; (apathy) Lethargie, die

letter /'letə(r)/ n. (a) Brief, der (to an + Akk.) (b) (of alphabet) Buchstabe, der

letter: ~ **bomb** n. Briefbombe, die; ~ **box** n. Briefkasten, der; ~**head**, ~**-heading** ns. Briefkopf, der

'**lettering** n. Typographie, die

letter: ~ **pad** n. Briefblock, der; ~**s page** n. Leserbriefseite, die

lettuce /'letɪs/ n. [Kopf]salat, der

leukaemia, (Amer.) **leukemia** /lu:'ki:mɪə/ n. Leukämie, die

level /'levl/ ☐1 n. (a) Höhe, die; (storey) Etage, die
(b) (fig.: steady state) Niveau, das; **be on a** ~ **[with sb./sth.]** auf dem gleichen Niveau sein [wie jmd./etw.]
(c) (of computer game) Level, der
☐2 adj. (a) waagerecht; eben ⟨Boden, Land⟩
(b) (on a ~) **be** ~ **[with sth./sb.]** auf gleicher Höhe [mit etw./jmdm.] sein
(c) (fig.) **keep a** ~ **head** einen kühlen Kopf bewahren; **do one's** ~ **best** (coll.) sein Möglichstes tun
☐3 v.t., (Brit.) -**ll**-: (a) (make ~) ebnen
(b) (aim) richten ⟨Blick, Gewehr⟩ (at auf + Akk.); (fig.) richten ⟨Kritik usw.⟩ (at gegen)

level: ~ '**crossing** n. (Brit. Railw.) [schienengleicher] Bahnübergang; ~**-'headed** adj. besonnen

lever /'li:və(r)/ ☐1 n. Hebel, der
☐2 v.t. ~ **sth. open** etw. aufhebeln

leverage /'li:vərɪdʒ/ n. Hebelwirkung, die

levity /'levɪtɪ/ n. (frivolity) Unernst, der

levy /'levɪ/ ☐1 n. (tax) Steuer, die
☐2 v.t. erheben

lewd /lju:d/ adj. geil; anzüglich ⟨Geste⟩; schlüpfrig ⟨Witz⟩

lexicon /'leksɪkən/ n. (a) (dictionary) Wörterbuch, das; Lexikon, das (veralt.)
(b) (vocabulary) Wortschatz, der

liability /laɪə'bɪlɪtɪ/ n. (a) Haftung, die
(b) (handicap) Belastung, die (to für)

liable /'laɪəbl/ pred. adj. (a) (legally bound) **be** ~ **for sth.** für etw. haftbar sein od. haften
(b) (prone) **be** ~ **to sth.** ⟨Person:⟩ zu etw. neigen; **be** ~ **to do sth.** ⟨Sache:⟩ leicht etw. tun; ⟨Person:⟩ dazu neigen, etw. zu tun

liaise /lɪ'eɪz/ v.i. eine Verbindung herstellen; ~ **on a project** bei einem Projekt zusammenarbeiten

liaison /lɪ'eɪzɒn/ n. (cooperation) Zusammenarbeit, die

liar /'laɪə(r)/ n. Lügner, der/Lügnerin, die

libel /'laɪbl/ ☐1 n. Verleumdung, die
☐2 v.t., (Brit.) -**ll**- verleumden

libellous (Amer.: **libelous**) /'laɪbələs/

adj. verleumderisch

liberal /'lɪbərl/ ☐1 adj. (a) großzügig
(b) (Polit.) liberal; **the L**~ **Democrats** (Brit.) die Liberaldemokraten
☐2 n. **L**~ (Polit.) Liberale, der/die

liberate /'lɪbəreɪt/ v.t. befreien (**from** aus); **a** ~**d woman** eine emanzipierte Frau

liberation /lɪbə'reɪʃn/ n. Befreiung, die; see also WOMEN'S LIBERATION

liberator /'lɪbəreɪtə(r)/ n. Befreier, der/Befreierin, die

liberty /'lɪbətɪ/ n. Freiheit, die; **take the** ~ **of doing sth.** (Dat.) die Freiheit nehmen, etw. zu tun; **take liberties with sb.** sich (Dat.) Freiheiten gegen jmdn. herausnehmen (ugs.)

Libra /'li:brə/ n. (Astrol., Astron.) die Waage

librarian /laɪ'breərɪən/ n. Bibliothekar, der/Bibliothekarin, die

library /'laɪbrərɪ/ n. Bibliothek, die; **public** ~: öffentliche Bücherei

library: ~ **book** n. Buch aus der Bibliothek; ~ **ticket** n. Lesekarte, die

Libya /'lɪbɪə/ pr. n. Libyen (das)

lice pl. of LOUSE

licence /'laɪsəns/ ☐1 n. [behördliche] Genehmigung; Lizenz, die; [driving] ~: Führerschein, der
☐2 v.t. ▶ LICENSE 1

'**licence fee** n. Lizenzgebühr, die

license /'laɪsəns/ ☐1 v.t. ermächtigen; **the restaurant is** ~**d to sell drinks** das Restaurant hat eine Schankerlaubnis od. -konzession; ~**d** ⟨Händler, Makler, Buchmacher⟩ mit [einer] Lizenz; **licensing laws** Schankgesetze; ~**d premises** Gaststätte mit Schankerlaubnis; **get a car** ~**d** ≈ die Kfz-Steuer für ein Auto bezahlen
☐2 n. (Amer.) ▶ LICENCE 1

'**license plate** n. (Amer.) Nummernschild, das

licentious /laɪ'senʃəs/ adj. zügellos ⟨Person⟩; unzüchtig ⟨Benehmen⟩

lichen /'laɪkn, 'lɪtʃn/ n. Flechte, die

lick /lɪk/ ☐1 v.t. (a) lecken
(b) (coll.: beat) verdreschen (ugs.)
☐2 n. Lecken, das

■ **lick 'off** v.t. ablecken

lid /lɪd/ n. (a) Deckel, der
(b) (eyelid) Lid, das

lido /'li:dəʊ/ n., pl. ~**s** Freibad, das

lie[1] /laɪ/ ☐1 n. Lüge, die; **tell** ~**s/a** ~: lügen
☐2 v.i., **lying** /'laɪɪŋ/ lügen; ~ **to sb.** jmdn. be- od. anlügen

lie[2] v.i., **lying** /'laɪɪŋ/, **lay** /leɪ/, **lain** /leɪn/
(a) liegen; (assume horizontal position) sich legen
(b) ~ **idle** ⟨Maschine, Fabrik:⟩ stillstehen

■ **lie a'bout, lie a'round** v.i. herumliegen (ugs.)

■ **lie 'back** v.i. sich zurücklegen; (sitting) sich zurücklehnen

■ **lie 'down** v.i. sich hinlegen

lie detector /'laɪdɪ'tektə(r)/ *n.*
Lügendetektor, *der*

'lie-in *n.* (coll.) **have a** ~: [sich] ausschlafen

lieu /lju:/ *n.* **in** ~ **of** sth. anstelle einer Sache
⟨*Gen.*⟩; **get holiday in** ~: stattdessen Urlaub
bekommen

lieutenant /lef'tenənt/ *n.* (Army)
Oberleutnant, *der*

life /laɪf/ *n., pl.* **lives** /laɪvz/ Leben, *das;*
for ~: lebenslänglich ⟨*inhaftiert*⟩; **true to**
~: wahrheitsgetreu; **get a** ~ (coll.) was aus
seinem Leben machen

life: ~**-and-death** *adj.* ⟨*Kampf*⟩ auf
Leben und Tod; (fig.) überaus wichtig
⟨*Frage, Brief*⟩; ~ **assurance** *n.* (Brit.)
Lebensversicherung, *die;* ~**belt** *n.*
Rettungsring, *der;* ~**boat** *n.* Rettungsboot,
das; ~**buoy** *n.* Rettungsring, *der;*
~ **cycle** *n.* Lebenszyklus, *der;*
~ **expectancy** *n.* Lebenserwartung,
die; ~**guard** *n.* Rettungsschwimmer,
der/-schwimmerin, *die;* ~ **insurance**
n. Lebensversicherung, *die;* ~ **jacket** *n.*
Schwimmweste, *die;* ~**less** *adj.* leblos; (fig.)
farblos; ~**like** *adj.* lebensecht; ~**line** *n.*
Rettungsleine, *die;* (fig.) Rettungsanker, *der;*
~**long** *adj.* lebenslang

lifer /'laɪfə(r)/ *n.* (coll.) Lebenslängliche,
der/die (ugs.)

life: ~**-saving** *n.* Rettungsschwimmen,
das; attrib. Rettungs-; ~ **sciences** *n. pl.*
Biowissenschaften *Pl.;* ~ **sentence** *n.*
lebenslängliche Freiheitsstrafe; ~**-size,**
~**-sized** *adj.* lebensgroß; in Lebensgröße
nachgestellt; ~**span** *n.* Lebenserwartung,
die; (Biol.) Lebensdauer, *die;* ~**style** *n.*
Lebensstil, *der;* ~**time** *n.* Lebenszeit, *die;*
during my ~**time** während meines Lebens;
once in a ~**time** einmal im Leben; ~ **vest**
n. Schwimmweste, *die*

lift /lɪft/ ☐1 *v.t.* heben; (fig.) erheben ⟨*Gemüt,
Geist*⟩
☐2 *n.* **(a)** (in vehicle) **get a** ~: mitgenommen
werden; **give sb. a** ~: jmdn. mitnehmen
(b) (Brit.: elevator) Aufzug, *der*
☐3 *v.i.* ⟨*Nebel:*⟩ sich auflösen
■ **'lift off** *v.t. & i.* abheben
■ **lift 'up** *v.t.* hochheben; heben ⟨*Kopf*⟩

'lift-off *n.* Abheben, *das*

ligament /'lɪgəmənt/ *n.* Band, *das*

light¹ /laɪt/ ☐1 *n.* **(a)** Licht, *das;* ~ **of day**
Tageslicht, *das*
(b) (lamp) Licht, *das;* (fitting) Lampe, *die*
(c) (signal to traffic) Ampel, *die;* **as far as the**
~**s** bis zur Ampel
(d) (to ignite) **have you got a** ~? haben Sie
Feuer? **set** ~ **to sth.** etw. anzünden
(e) bring sth. to ~: etw. ans [Tages]licht
bringen; **throw** *or* **shed** ~ **[up]on sth.** Licht
in etw. (*Akk.*) bringen
(f) (aspect) **in that** ~: aus dieser Sicht; **seen**
in this ~: so gesehen; **in the** ~ **of** angesichts
(+ *Gen.*); **show sb. in a bad** ~: ein schlechtes
Licht auf jmdn. werfen

☐2 *adj.* hell; ~**-blue/-brown** *etc.* hellblau/
-braun *usw.*
☐3 *v.t.,* lit /lɪt/ *or* **lighted (a)** (ignite) anzünden
(b) (illuminate) erhellen
■ **light 'up** ☐1 *v.i.* **(a)** (become lit) erleuchtet
werden
(b) (become bright) aufleuchten **(with** vor)
☐2 *v.t.* **(a)** (illuminate) erleuchten
(b) anzünden ⟨*Zigarette*⟩

light² ☐1 *adj.* leicht; (mild) mild ⟨*Strafe*⟩
☐2 *adv.* **travel** ~: mit wenig *od.* leichtem
Gepäck reisen

light: ~ **'aircraft** *n.* Leichtflugzeug, *das;*
~**bulb** *n.* Glühbirne, *die*

'lighted *adj.* brennend ⟨*Kerze, Zigarette*⟩;
angezündet ⟨*Streichholz*⟩

light-emitting 'diode /'daɪəʊd/ *n.*
Leuchtdiode, *die*

lighten¹ /'laɪtn/ *v.t.* (make less heavy, difficult)
leichter machen

lighten² ☐1 *v.t.* (make brighter) aufhellen;
heller machen ⟨*Raum*⟩
☐2 *v.i.* sich aufhellen

'lighter *n.* Feuerzeug, *das*

light: ~**'headed** *adj.* leicht benommen;
~**'hearted** *adj.* **(a)** (humorous)
unbeschwert; **(b)** (optimistic) unbekümmert;
~**house** *n.* Leuchtturm, *der;*
~ **'industry** *n.* Leichtindustrie, *die*

'lighting *n.* Beleuchtung, *die*

'lightly *adv.* **(a)** leicht
(b) (without serious consideration) leichtfertig
(c) (cheerfully) leichthin; **not treat sth.** ~: etw.
nicht auf die leichte Schulter nehmen
(d) get off ~: glimpflich davonkommen

'light meter *n.* Lichtmesser, *der;* (exposure
meter) Belichtungsmesser, *der*

'lightness¹ *n.* (of weight; also fig.)
Leichtigkeit, *die*

lightness² *n.* (of colour) Helligkeit, *die*

lightning /'laɪtnɪŋ/ *n.* Blitz, *der;* **flash of**
~: Blitz, *der*

lightning: ~ **conductor** *n.*
Blitzableiter, *der;* ~ **strike** *n.* Blitzschlag,
der

light: ~**weight** ☐1 *adj.* leicht; ☐2 *n.*
Leichtgewicht, *das;* ~ **year** *n.* Lichtjahr,
das

like¹ /laɪk/ ☐1 *adj.* **(a)** (resembling) wie; **your**
dress is ~ **mine** dein Kleid ist so ähnlich
wie meins; **in a case** ~ **that** in so einem Fall;
what is sb./sth. ~? wie ist jmd./etw.?
(b) (characteristic of) typisch für ⟨*dich, ihn*
usw.⟩
(c) (similar) ähnlich
☐2 *prep.* (in the manner of) wie; **[just]** ~ **that**
[einfach] so
☐3 *n.* **(a)** (equal) **his/her** ~: seines-/
ihresgleichen
(b) (similar things) **the** ~: so etwas; **and the**
~: und dergleichen

like² ☐1 *v.t.* (be fond of, wish for) mögen;
~ **vegetables** Gemüse mögen; gern   ⋯⟶

Gemüse essen; ∼ **doing sth.** etw. gern
tun; **would you** ∼ **a drink?** möchtest du
etwas trinken?; **would you** ∼ **me to do it?**
möchtest du, dass ich es tue?; **how do you**
∼ **it?** wie gefällt es dir?; **if you** ∼ *expr. assent*
wenn du willst
2 *n., in pl.* ∼**s and dislikes** Vorlieben und
Abneigungen
likeable /'laɪkəbl/ *adj.* nett; sympathisch
likelihood /'laɪklɪhʊd/ *n.*
Wahrscheinlichkeit, *die*
likely /'laɪklɪ/ **1** *adj.* wahrscheinlich;
there are ∼ **to be** [traffic] hold-ups man
muss mit [Verkehrs]staus rechnen; **they are**
[not] ∼ **to come** sie werden wahrscheinlich
[nicht] kommen; **is it** ∼ **to rain tomorrow?**
wird es morgen wohl regnen?; **this is not**
∼ **to happen** es ist unwahrscheinlich, dass
das geschieht
2 *adv.* wahrscheinlich; **as** ∼ **as not**
höchstwahrscheinlich; **not** ∼! (coll.) auf
keinen Fall!
'like-minded *adj.* gleich gesinnt
liken /'laɪkn/ *v.t.* ∼ **sth./sb. to sth./sb.**
etw./jmdn. mit etw./jmdm. vergleichen
'likeness *n.* Ähnlichkeit, *die* (**to** mit)
likewise /'laɪkwaɪz/ *adv.* ebenso
liking /'laɪkɪŋ/ *n.* Vorliebe, *die;* **take a** ∼ **to
sb./sth.** an jmdm./etw. Gefallen finden;
sth. is [not] **to sb.'s** ∼: etw. ist [nicht] nach
jmds. Geschmack
lilac /'laɪlək/ **1** *n.* (a) (Bot.) Flieder, *der*
(b) (colour) Zartlila, *das*
2 *adj.* zartlila; fliederfarben
Lilo ® /'laɪləʊ/ *n.* Luftmatratze, *die*
lily /'lɪlɪ/ *n.* Lilie, *die*
limb /lɪm/ *n.* (a) (Anat.) Glied, *das*
(b) **be out on a** ∼ (fig.) exponiert sein
limber up /lɪmbər 'ʌp/ *v.i.* (loosen up) die
Muskeln lockern
lime¹ /laɪm/ *n.* [quick]∼: [ungelöschter] Kalk
lime² *n.* (fruit) Limone, *die*
lime³ ▶ LIME TREE
'limelight *n.* **be in the** ∼: im Rampenlicht
[der Öffentlichkeit] stehen
limerick /'lɪmərɪk/ *n.* Limerick, *der*
lime: ∼**stone** *n.* Kalkstein, *der;* ∼ **tree**
n. Linde, *die*
limit /'lɪmɪt/ **1** *n.* (a) Grenze, *die;* **set** *or*
put a ∼ **on sth.** etw. begrenzen; **be over the**
∼ 〈*Autofahrer:*〉 zu viele Promille haben;
lower/upper ∼: Untergrenze/Höchstgrenze,
die; **without** ∼: unbegrenzt; **within** ∼**s**
innerhalb gewisser Grenzen
(b) (coll.) **this is the** ∼! das ist [doch] die
Höhe!; **he/she is the** [very] ∼: er/sie ist
[einfach] unmöglich
2 *v.t.* begrenzen (**to** auf + *Akk.*);
einschränken 〈*Freiheit*〉
limitation /lɪmɪ'teɪʃn/ *n.* Beschränkung,
die
'limited *adj.* (a) (restricted) begrenzt
(b) (intellectually narrow) beschränkt

'limitless *adj.* grenzenlos
limousine /'lɪmʊziːn/ *n.* Limousine, *die*
limp¹ /lɪmp/ **1** *v.i.* hinken
2 *n.* Hinken, *das*
limp² *adj.* schlaff
limpet /'lɪmpɪt/ *n.* (Zool.) Napfschnecke, *die*
limpid /'lɪmpɪd/ *adj.* klar
'limply *adv.* schlaff; (weakly) schwach
linctus /'lɪŋktəs/ *n.* Hustensaft, *der*
line¹ /laɪn/ **1** *n.* (a) (string, cord, rope, etc.)
Leine, *die*
(b) (telephone cable) Leitung, *die*
(c) (long mark; also Math., Phys.) Linie, *die*
(d) (row, series) Reihe, *die;* (Amer.: queue)
Schlange, *die;* **bring sb. into** ∼: dafür
sorgen, dass jmd. nicht aus der Reihe tanzt
(ugs.)
(e) (row of words on a page) Zeile, *die*
(f) (wrinkle) Falte, *die*
(g) (direction, course) Richtung, *die;* **on the** ∼**s
of** nach Art (+ *Gen.*); **be on the right/wrong**
∼**s** in die richtige/falsche Richtung gehen;
along *or* **on the same** ∼**s** in der gleichen
Richtung
(h) (Railw.) Bahnlinie, *die;* (track) Gleis, *das*
(i) (field of activity) Branche, *die*
(j) (Commerc.: product) Artikel, *der;* Linie, *die*
(fachspr.)
2 *v.t.* (a) linieren 〈*Papier*〉; **a** ∼**d face** ein
faltiges Gesicht
(b) säumen (geh.) 〈*Straße, Strecke*〉
∎ **line 'up** **1** *v.t.* antreten lassen
〈*Gefangene, Soldaten usw.*〉; [in einer Reihe]
aufstellen 〈*Gegenstände*〉
2 *v.i.* 〈*Gefangene, Soldaten:*〉 antreten;
(queue up) sich anstellen
line² *v.t.* füttern 〈*Kleidungsstück*〉;
ausschlagen 〈*Schublade usw.*〉
lineage /'lɪnɪdʒ/ *n.* Abstammung, *die*
linear /'lɪnɪə(r)/ *adj.* linear
line: ∼ **dance** **1** *n.* Linedance, *der;*
2 *v.i.* Linedance tanzen; ∼ **dancing**
n. Linedance-Tanzen, *das;* ∼ **manager**
n. [unmittelbarer] Vorgesetzter;
Linienmanager, *der*
linen /'lɪnɪn/ **1** *n.* (a) Leinen, *das*
(b) (shirts, sheets, etc.) Wäsche, *die*
2 *adj.* Leinen〈*faden, -bluse*〉; Lein〈*tuch*〉
linen: ∼ **basket** *n.* (Brit.) Wäschekorb,
der; ∼ **cupboard** *n.* Wäscheschrank, *der*
'line printer *n.* (Comp.) Zeilendrucker, *der*
liner /'laɪnə(r)/ *n.* Linienschiff, *das*
'line-up *n.* Aufstellung, *die*
linger /'lɪŋgə(r)/ *v.i.* verweilen (geh.);
bleiben
lingerie /'læʒərɪ/ *n.* [women's]
∼: Damenunterwäsche, *die*
lingo /'lɪŋgəʊ/ *n.* (coll.) Sprache, *die*
linguist /'lɪŋgwɪst/ *n.* Sprachkundige,
der/die
linguistic /lɪŋ'gwɪstɪk/ *adj.* (of ∼s)
linguistisch; (of language) sprachlich

linguistics /lɪŋ'gwɪstɪks/ n. Linguistik, die

lining /'laɪnɪŋ/ n. (of clothes) Futter, das; (of objects, machines, etc.) Auskleidung, die

'lining paper n. Schrankpapier, das

link /lɪŋk/ ① n. (a) (of chain) Glied, das
(b) (connection) Verbindung, die
② v.t. verbinden; ~ arms sich unterhaken
■ **link 'up** v.t. miteinander verbinden

links /lɪŋks/ n. [golf] ~: Golfplatz, der

lino /'laɪnəʊ/ n., pl. ~s Linoleum, das

linoleum /lɪ'nəʊlɪəm/ n. Linoleum, das

linseed /'lɪnsiːd/ n. Leinsamen, der

linseed 'oil n. Leinöl, das

lint /lɪnt/ n. Mull, der

lintel /'lɪntl/ n. (Archit.) Sturz, der

lion /'laɪən/ n. Löwe, der

lioness /'laɪənɪs/ n. Löwin, die

lip /lɪp/ n. (a) Lippe, die; **lower/upper**
~: Unter-/Oberlippe, die
(b) (of cup) [Gieß]rand, der; (of jug) Schnabel, der

liposuction /'laɪpəʊsʌkʃn, 'lɪpəʊsʌkʃn/ n. Fettabsaugung, die; Liposuktion, die

lip: ~**-read** v.i. von den Lippen lesen;
~**-reading** n. Lippenlesen, das;
~ **service** n. pay ~ service to sth. ein Lippenbekenntnis zu etw. ablegen; ~**stick** n. Lippenstift, der

liquefy /'lɪkwɪfaɪ/ ① v.t. verflüssigen
② v.i. sich verflüssigen

liqueur /lɪ'kjʊə(r)/ n. Likör, der

liquid /'lɪkwɪd/ ① adj. flüssig
② n. Flüssigkeit, die

liquidate /'lɪkwɪdeɪt/ v.t. (Commerc.) liquidieren

liquidation /lɪkwɪ'deɪʃn/ n. (Commerc.) Liquidation, die

liquid crystal di'splay n. Flüssigkristallanzeige, die

liquidize /'lɪkwɪdaɪz/ v.t. auflösen;
(Cookery) [im Mixer] pürieren

'liquidizer n. Mixer, der

liquid 'measure n. Flüssigkeitsmaß, das

liquor /'lɪkə(r)/ n. (drink) Alkohol, der

liquorice /'lɪkərɪs/ n. Lakritze, die

Lisbon /'lɪzbən/ pr. n. Lissabon (das)

lisp /lɪsp/ ① v.i. & t. lispeln
② n. Lispeln, das

list¹ /lɪst/ ① n. Liste, die
② v.t. aufführen; auflisten; (verbally) aufzählen

list² v.i. (Naut.) Schlagseite haben

listed 'building n. (Brit.) Gebäude unter Denkmalschutz

listen /'lɪsn/ v.i. zuhören; ~ to music/the radio Musik/Radio hören; they ~ed to his words sie hörten ihm zu

listener /'lɪsnə(r)/ n. Zuhörer, der/ Zuhörerin, die; (to radio) Hörer, der/Hörerin, die

listless /'lɪstlɪs/ adj. lustlos

'list price n. Katalogpreis, der

lit ▶ LIGHT¹ 3

litany /'lɪtənɪ/ n. Litanei, die

lite, Lite ® /laɪt/ ① adj. kalorienreduziert
⟨Bier, Käse etc.⟩
② n. Leichtbier, das

liter (Amer.) ▶ LITRE

literacy /'lɪtərəsɪ/ n. Lese- und Schreibfertigkeit, die

literal /'lɪtərl/ adj. (a) wörtlich
(b) (not exaggerated) buchstäblich

literally /'lɪtərəlɪ/ adv. (a) wörtlich
(b) (actually) buchstäblich
(c) (coll.: with some exaggeration) geradezu

literary /'lɪtərərɪ/ adj. literarisch

literary 'agent n. Literaturagent, der/ -agentin, die

literate /'lɪtərət/ adj. des Lesens und Schreibens kundig; (educated) gebildet

literature /'lɪtrətʃə(r)/ n. Literatur, die

lithe /laɪð/ adj. geschmeidig

litigation /lɪtɪ'geɪʃn/ n. Rechtsstreit, der

litre /'liːtə(r)/ n. (Brit.) Liter, der od. das

litter /'lɪtə(r)/ ① n. (a) (rubbish) Abfall, der
(b) (of animals) Wurf, der
② v.t. verstreuen

litter: ~ **basket** n. Abfallkorb, der;
~ **bin** n. Abfalleimer, der; ~**bug,** ~ **lout** ns. Schmutzfink, der (ugs.)

little /'lɪtl/ ① adj., ~r /'lɪtlə(r)/, ~st /'lɪtlɪst/ (Note: it is more common to use the compar. and superl. forms smaller, smallest)
(a) klein; a ~ way ein kurzes Stück; after a ~ while nach kurzer Zeit
(b) (not much) wenig; there is very ~ tea left es ist kaum noch Tee da; a ~ ... (a small quantity of) etwas ...; ein bisschen ...
② n. wenig; a ~ (a small quantity) etwas;
(somewhat) ein wenig; ~ by ~: nach und nach

little: ~ **'finger** n. kleiner Finger;
~**-known** adj. wenig bekannt

liturgy /'lɪtədʒɪ/ n. Liturgie, die

live¹ /laɪv/ ① adj. (a) attrib. (alive) lebend
(b) (Radio, Telev.) ~ **performance** Liveaufführung, die; ~ **broadcast** Livesendung, die
(c) (Electr.) Strom führend
② adv. (Radio, Telev.) live ⟨übertragen usw.⟩

live² /lɪv/ ① v.i. (a) leben
(b) (make permanent home) wohnen; leben
② v.t. leben
■ **live 'down** v.t. Gras wachsen lassen über (+ Akk.); he will never be able to ~ it down das wird ihm ewig anhängen
■ **live on** ① /'--/ v.t. leben von
② /-'-/ v.i. weiterleben
■ **live 'up to** v.t. gerecht werden (+ Dat.)

live-in /'lɪvɪn/ attrib. adj. im Haus wohnend ⟨Personal⟩

livelihood /'laɪvlɪhʊd/ n. Lebensunterhalt, der

liveliness /'laɪvlɪnɪs/ n. Lebhaftigkeit, *die*
lively /'laɪvlɪ/ adj. lebhaft; lebendig ⟨*Schilderung*⟩; rege ⟨*Handel*⟩
liven up /laɪvn 'ʌp/ 1 v.t. Leben bringen in (+ *Akk.*)
  2 v.i. ⟨*Person:*⟩ aufleben
liver /'lɪvə(r)/ n. Leber, *die*
livery /'lɪvərɪ/ n. Livree, *die*
lives pl. of LIFE
live /laɪv/: **~stock** n. pl. Vieh, *das*; **~ 'wire** n. (fig.) Energiebündel, *das* (ugs.)
livid /'lɪvɪd/ adj. (Brit. coll.) fuchtig (ugs.)
living /'lɪvɪŋ/ 1 n. (a) Leben, *das* (b) **make a ~**: seinen Lebensunterhalt verdienen
  (c) pl. **the ~**: die Lebenden Pl.
  2 adj. lebend; **within ~ memory** seit Menschengedenken
living: ~ room n. Wohnzimmer, *das*; **~ 'will** n. Patientenverfügung, *die*
lizard /'lɪzəd/ n. Eidechse, *die*
llama /'lɑːmə/ n. Lama, *das*
load /ləʊd/ 1 n. (burden, weight; also fig.) Last, *die;* (amount carried) Ladung, *die*
  2 v.t. (a) (put ~ on) beladen; (put as load) **~ sb. with work** (fig.) jmdm. Arbeit auftragen
  (b) laden ⟨*Gewehr*⟩; **~ a camera** einen Film [in einen Fotoapparat] einlegen
  ■ **load 'up** v.i. laden (with *Akk.*)
'loaded adj. **a ~ question** eine suggestive Frage; **be ~** (coll.: rich) [schwer] Kohle haben (salopp)
'loading bay n. Ladeplatz, *der*
loaf¹ /ləʊf/ n., pl. **loaves** /ləʊvz/ Brot, *das;* [Brot]laib, *der;* **a ~ of bread** ein Laib Brot
loaf² v.i. **~ round town/the house** in der Stadt/zu Hause herumlungern (ugs.)
loan /ləʊn/ 1 n. (a) (thing lent) Leihgabe, *die;* **be out on ~**: ausgeliehen sein; **have sth. on ~ [from sb.]** etw. [von jmdm.] geliehen haben
  (b) (money lent) Darlehen, *das*
  2 v.t. **~ sth. to sb.** jmdm. etw. leihen
loan shark n. (coll.) Kredithai, *der* (ugs.)
loath /ləʊθ/ pred. adj. **be ~ to do sth.** etw. ungern tun
loathe /ləʊð/ v.t. verabscheuen
loathing /'ləʊðɪŋ/ n. Abscheu, *der* (of, for vor + *Dat.*)
loathsome /'ləʊðsəm/ adj. abscheulich; widerlich
loaves pl. of LOAF¹
lobby /'lɒbɪ/ n. (a) (pressure group) Lobby, *die* (b) (of hotel) Eingangshalle, *die;* (of theatre) Foyer, *das*
lobe /ləʊb/ n. (ear~) Ohrläppchen, *das*
lobster /'lɒbstə(r)/ n. Hummer, *der*
'lobster pot n. Hummerkorb, *der*
local /'ləʊkl/ 1 adj. lokal (bes. Zeitungsw.); Kommunal⟨*wahl, -abgaben*⟩; (of this area) hiesig; (of that area) dortig; ortsansässig ⟨*Firma, Familie*⟩; ⟨*Wein, Produkt,*

Spezialität⟩ [aus] der Gegend; **she's a ~ girl** sie ist von hier/dort
  2 n. (a) (person) Einheimische, *der/die* (b) (Brit. coll.: pub) [Stamm]kneipe, *die*
local: ~ anaes'thetic n. Lokalanästhetikum, *das;* **~ au'thority** n. (Brit.) Kommunalverwaltung, *die;* **~ call** n. (Teleph.) Ortsgespräch, *das;* **~ 'government** n. Kommunalverwaltung, *die*
locality /ləʊ'kælɪtɪ/ n. Ort, *der*
localization /ləʊkəlaɪ'zeɪʃn/ n. (Comp.) Lokalisierung, *die*
'locally adv. im/am Ort
locate /ləʊ'keɪt/ v.t. (a) **be ~d** liegen (b) (determine position of) ausfindig machen
location /ləʊ'keɪʃn/ n. (a) Lage, *die* (b) (Cinemat.) Drehort, *der;* **be on ~**: bei Außenaufnahmen sein
loch /lɒx, lɒk/ n. (Scot.) See, *der*
lock¹ /lɒk/ n. (of hair) [Haar]strähne, *die*
lock² 1 n. (a) (of door etc.) Schloss, *das* (b) (on canal etc.) Schleuse, *die*
  2 v.t. zuschließen
  3 v.i. ⟨*Tür, Kasten usw.:*⟩ sich zuschließen lassen
  ■ **lock a'way** v.t. einschließen; einsperren ⟨*Person*⟩
  ■ **lock 'in** v.t. einschließen; (deliberately) einsperren
  ■ **lock 'out** v.t. aussperren (of aus); **~ oneself out** sich aussperren
  ■ **lock 'up** 1 v.i. abschließen
    2 v.t. (a) abschließen ⟨*Haus, Tür*⟩ (b) (imprison) einsperren
locker /'lɒkə(r)/ n. Schließfach, *das*
locket /'lɒkɪt/ n. Medaillon, *das*
lock: ~jaw n. (Med.) Kieferklemme, *die;* **~out** n. Aussperrung, *die;* **~smith** n. Schlosser, *der*
locomotive /ləʊkə'məʊtɪv/ n. Lokomotive, *die*
locust /'ləʊkəst/ n. Heuschrecke, *die*
lodge /lɒdʒ/ 1 n. (a) (cottage) Pförtner-/ Gärtnerhaus, *das* (b) (porter's room) [Pförtner]loge, *die*
  2 v.t. (a) einlegen ⟨*Beschwerde, Protest usw.*⟩
  (b) einreichen ⟨*Klage*⟩
  3 v.i. [zur Miete] wohnen
'lodger n. Untermieter, *der*/Untermieterin, *die*
lodging /'lɒdʒɪŋ/ n. [möbliertes] Zimmer
loft /lɒft/ n. (attic) [Dach]boden, *der*
lofty /'lɒftɪ/ adj. (a) (exalted) hoch (b) (haughty) hochmütig
log /lɒg/ n. (a) (timber) [geschlagener] Baumstamm; (as firewood) [Holz]scheit, *das* (b) **~[book]** (Naut.) Logbuch, *das*
  ■ **log 'in** ▶ LOG ON
  ■ **log 'off** v.i. (Comp.) sich abmelden
  ■ **log 'on** v.i. (Comp.) sich anmelden
  ■ **log 'out** ▶ LOG OFF

log: ∼ **'cabin** n. Blockhütte, die; ∼ **'fire**
n. Holzfeuer, das
loggerheads /'lɒgəhedz/ n. pl. **be at**
∼ **with sb.** mit jmdm. im Clinch liegen
logic /'lɒdʒɪk/ n. Logik, die
logical /'lɒdʒɪkl/ adj. logisch; **she has a**
∼ **mind** sie denkt logisch
logically /'lɒdʒɪkəlɪ/ adv. logisch
'login n. (Comp.) Log-in, das
logistics /lə'dʒɪstɪks/ n. pl. Logistik, die
logo /'ləʊgəʊ/ n., pl. ∼s Signet, das
loin /lɔɪn/ n. Lende, die
'loincloth n. Lendenschurz, der
loiter /'lɔɪtə(r)/ v.i. trödeln; (linger
suspiciously) herumlungern
loll /lɒl/ v.i. sich lümmeln (ugs.)
lollipop /'lɒlɪpɒp/ n. Lutscher, der
London /'lʌndən/ ①_n._ London (das)
②_attrib. adj._ Londoner
'Londoner pr. n. Londoner, der/
Londonerin, die
lone /ləʊn/ attrib. adj. einsam
loneliness /'ləʊnlɪnɪs/ n. Einsamkeit, die
lonely /'ləʊnlɪ/ adj. einsam
lone 'parent n. allein erziehender
Elternteil; **she/he is a** ∼: sie/er ist allein
erziehend
loner /'ləʊnə(r)/ n. Einzelgänger, der/
-gängerin, die
lonesome /'ləʊnsəm/ adj. einsam
long¹ /lɒŋ/ ①_adj._, ∼er /'lɒŋgə(r)/, ∼est
/'lɒŋgɪst/ (a) lang; weit ⟨Reise, Weg⟩
(b) (elongated) länglich; schmal
(c) in the '∼ **run** auf die Dauer
②_n._ (∼ interval) **take** ∼: lange dauern; **for**
∼: lange; (since ∼ ago) seit langem; **before**
∼: bald
③_adv._, ∼er, ∼est (a) lang[e]; as or so ∼ as
solange; **you should have finished** ∼ **before**
now du hättest schon längst fertig sein
sollen; **much** ∼er viel länger
(b) as or **so** ∼ **as** (provided that) solange;
wenn
long² v.i. ∼ **for sb./sth.** sich nach jmdm./
etw. sehnen; ∼ **to do sth.** sich danach
sehnen, etw. zu tun
long-distance ① /'---/ adj.
Fern⟨gespräch, -verkehr usw.⟩;
Langstrecken⟨läufer, -flug usw.⟩
②/-'-'-/ adv. **phone** ∼: ein Ferngespräch
führen
longevity /lɒn'dʒevɪtɪ/ n. Langlebigkeit,
die
long: ∼**-haired** adj. langhaarig;
Langhaar⟨dackel, -katze⟩; ∼**-hand** n.
Langschrift, die; ∼**-haul** adj. Fern⟨verkehr,
-lastwagen⟩; Langstrecken⟨flug]verkehr⟩
'longing ①_n._ Sehnsucht, die
②_adj._ sehnsüchtig
'longingly adv. sehnsüchtig
longitude /'lɒŋgɪtjuːd/ n. (Geog.) Länge,
die

long: ∼ **jump** n. (Brit. Sport) Weitsprung,
der; ∼**-lasting** adj. langandauernd;
dauerhaft ⟨Beziehung, Freundschaft⟩;
∼**-legged** adj. langbeinig; ∼ **'lens** n.
Fernobjektiv, das; ∼**-life** adj. haltbar
[gemacht]; ∼**-life battery** Batterie mit langer
Lebensdauer; ∼**-life milk** H-Milch, die;
∼**-lived** /'lɒŋlɪvd/ adj. langlebig;
∼**-playing 'record** n. Langspielplatte,
die; ∼**-range** adj. (a) Langstrecken
⟨flugzeug, -rakete usw.⟩; **(b)** (relating to time)
langfristig; ∼**-sighted** /lɒŋ'saɪtɪd/ adj.
weitsichtig; (fig.) weitblickend; ∼**-sleeved**
/'lɒŋsliːvd/ adj. langärmelig; ∼**-standing**
attrib. adj. seit langem bestehend; alt
⟨Schulden, Streit⟩; ∼**-suffering** adj.
schwer geprüft; ∼**-term** adj. langfristig;
∼ **wave** n. (Radio) Langwelle, die;
∼**-winded** /lɒŋ'wɪndɪd/ adj. langatmig
loo /luː/ n. (Brit. coll.) Klo, das (ugs.)
look /lʊk/ ①_v.i._ (a) sehen; gucken (ugs.)
(b) (search) nachsehen
(c) (face) zugewandt sein (**to**[**wards**] Dat.)
(d) (appear) aussehen; ∼ **well/ill** gut/schlecht
aussehen
②_n._ (a) Blick, der; **have** or **take a** ∼ **at**
sb./sth. sich ⟨Dat.⟩ jmdn./etw. ansehen
(b) (appearance) Aussehen, das
▪ **look 'after** v.t. (care for) sorgen für
▪ **look a'head** v.i. (fig.) an die Zukunft
denken
▪ **'look at** v.t. (a) (regard) ansehen
(b) (consider) betrachten
▪ **look 'back** v.i. (a) sich umsehen
(b) ∼ **back on** or **to sth.** an etw. (Akk.)
zurückdenken
▪ **look 'down [up]on** v.t. (a) herunter-/
hinuntersehen auf (+ Akk.)
(b) (fig.: despise) herabsehen auf (+ Akk.)
▪ **'look for** v.t. (a) (seek) suchen nach
(b) (expect) erwarten
▪ **look 'out** v.i. (a) hinaus-/heraussehen
(**of** aus)
(b) (take care) aufpassen
(c) ∼ **out on sth.** ⟨Zimmer, Wohnung usw.:⟩
zu etw. hin liegen
▪ **look 'out for** v.t. (be prepared for)
achten auf (+ Akk.); (keep watching for)
Ausschau halten nach ⟨Arbeit, Gelegenheit,
Sammelobjekt usw.⟩
▪ **look 'over** v.t. (a) sehen über (+ Akk.)
(b) (survey) sich (Dat.) ansehen ⟨Haus⟩
▪ **look 'round** v.i. sich umsehen
▪ **'look through** v.t. (a) ∼ **through sth.**
durch etw. [hindurch] sehen
(b) (inspect) durchsehen ⟨Papiere⟩
▪ **'look to** v.t. (rely on) ∼ **to sb./sth. for sth.**
etw. von jmdm./etw. erwarten
▪ **look 'up** ①_v.i._ (a) aufblicken
(b) (improve) besser werden
②_v.t._ nachschlagen ⟨Wort⟩; heraussuchen
⟨Telefonnummer, Zugverbindung usw.⟩
▪ **look 'up to** v.t. ∼ **up to sb.** zu jmdm.
aufsehen

'**look-alike** n. Doppelgänger, der/
-gängerin, die

looker-'on n. Zuschauer, der/
Zuschauerin, die

'**looking glass** n. Spiegel, der

'**lookout** n., pl. ~s (a) (observation post)
Ausguck, der
(b) (person) Wache, die
(c) (Brit. fig.) **that's a bad** ~: das sind
schlechte Aussichten; **that's his** ~: das ist
sein Problem
(d) **keep a** ~ **[for sb./sth.]** [nach jmdm./etw.]
Ausschau halten

loom¹ /luːm/ n. (Weaving) Webstuhl, der

loom² v.i. auftauchen

loop /luːp/ ① n. (a) Schleife, die
(b) (cord) Schlaufe, die
② v.t. zu einer Schlaufe formen

'**loophole** n. (fig.) Lücke, die

'**loopy** /'luːpɪ/ adj. (coll.) verrückt (ugs.)

loose /luːs/ adj. (a) (not firm) locker ⟨Zahn,
Schraube, Knopf⟩
(b) (not fixed) lose ⟨Knopf, Buchseite, Brett,
Stein⟩; offen ⟨Haar⟩
(c) **be at a** ~ **end** (fig.) nichts zu tun haben
(d) (inexact) ungenau

loose: ~-**fitting** adj. bequem
geschnitten; ~-**leaf** adj. Loseblatt-; ~-**leaf
file** Ringbuch, das; ~-**limbed** adj. gelenkig

'**loosely** adv. locker; lose
⟨zusammenhängen⟩; frei ⟨übersetzen⟩

loosen /'luːsn/ v.t. lockern

■ **loosen 'up** v.i. sich auflockern; (relax)
auftauen

'**looseness** n. Lockerheit, die

loot /luːt/ ① v.t. plündern
② n. Beute, die

'**looter** n. Plünderer, der

lop /lɒp/ v.t. ~ **sth. [off** or **away]** etw.
abbauen od. abhacken

lopsided /lɒp'saɪdɪd/ adj. schief

loquacious /lə'kweɪʃəs/ adj. redselig

lord /lɔːd/ ① n. (a) (master) Herr, der
(b) L~ (Relig.) Herr, der
(c) (Brit.: as title) Lord, der; **the House of L~s**
(Brit.) das Oberhaus
② int. (coll.) Gott; **oh/good L~!** du lieber
Himmel!

'**lordship** n. Lordschaft, die

lore /lɔː(r)/ n. Überlieferung, die

lorry /'lɒrɪ/ n. (Brit.) Lastwagen, der; Lkw,
der

'**lorry driver** n. (Brit.) Lastwagenfahrer,
der; Lkw-Fahrer, der

lose /luːz/ ① v.t., **lost** /lɒst/ (a) verlieren;
~ **one's way** sich verlaufen/verfahren
(b) ⟨Uhr:⟩ nachgehen
(c) (waste) vertun ⟨Zeit⟩; (miss) versäumen
⟨Gelegenheit⟩
(d) ~ **weight** abnehmen
② v.i., **lost** (a) (in match, contest) verlieren
(b) ⟨Uhr:⟩ nachgehen

'**loser** n. Verlierer, der/Verliererin, die

loss /lɒs/ n. (a) Verlust, der (of Gen.); **sell at
a** ~: mit Verlust verkaufen
(b) **be at a** ~: nicht [mehr] weiterwissen; **be
at a** ~ **for words** um Worte verlegen sein; **be
at a** ~ **what to do** nicht wissen, was zu tun
ist

loss: ~ **adjuster** n. (Finance)
Schaden[s]regulierer, der/-reguliererin, die;
~-**making** adj. mit Verlust arbeitend

lost /lɒst/ ① ▶ LOSE
② adj. (a) verloren; **get** ~ ⟨Person:⟩ sich
verlaufen/verfahren; **get** ~! (coll.) verdufte!
(salopp); ~ **cause** aussichtslose Sache
(b) (wasted) vertan ⟨Zeit⟩; (missed) versäumt
⟨Gelegenheit⟩

lot /lɒt/ n. (a) (destiny) Los, das
(b) (set of persons) Haufen, der; **the** ~: [sie]
alle
(c) (set of things) Menge, die; **the** ~: alle/alles
(d) (coll.: large quantity) ~s or **a** ~ **of money**
etc. viel od. eine Menge Geld usw.; **a** ~ of
~: viel singen usw.; **like sth. a** ~: etw. sehr
mögen; **have** ~s **to do** viel zu tun haben
(e) (for choosing) Los, das; **draw/cast/throw**
~s **[for sth.]** um etw. losen

lotion /'ləʊʃn/ n. Lotion, die

lottery /'lɒtərɪ/ n. Lotterie, die

'**lottery number** n. Lottozahl, die

loud /laʊd/ ① adj. (a) laut; lautstark
⟨Protest, Kritik⟩
(b) (flashy, conspicuous) aufdringlich; grell
⟨Farbe⟩
② adv. laut; **laugh out** ~: laut auflachen;
say sth. out ~: etw. aussprechen

loud'hailer n. Megaphon, das

'**loudly** adv. laut

loud: ~**mouth** n. Großmaul, das;
~-**mouthed** /'laʊdmaʊðd/ adj.
großmäulig (ugs.)

'**loudness** n. Lautstärke, die

loud'speaker n. Lautsprecher, der

lounge /laʊndʒ/ ① v.i. ~ **[about** or **around]**
[faul] herumliegen/-sitzen/-stehen
② n. (a) (in hotel) [Hotel]halle, die; (at airport)
Wartehalle, die
(b) (sitting room) Wohnzimmer, das

lounger /'laʊndʒə(r)/ n. (sunbed) Liege, die

'**lounge suit** n. (Brit.) Straßenanzug, der

louse /laʊs/ n., pl. **lice** /laɪs/ Laus, die

lousy /'laʊzɪ/ adj. (coll.) (a) (disgusting)
ekelhaft
(b) (very poor) lausig (ugs.); **feel** ~: sich mies
(ugs.) fühlen

lout /laʊt/ n. Rüpel, der; Flegel, der

loutish /'laʊtɪʃ/ adj. rüpelhaft; flegelhaft

louver, louvre /'luːvə(r)/ n. ~ **window**
Jalousiefenster, das; ~ **door** Jalousietür, die

lovable /'lʌvəbl/ adj. liebenswert

love /lʌv/ ① n. (a) Liebe, die (of, for zu);
in ~ **[with]** verliebt [in (+ Akk.)]; **fall in**
~ **[with]** sich verlieben [in (+ Akk.)]; **for** ~:

aus Liebe; ⁓ **from Beth** (in letter) herzliche Grüße von Beth; **send one's ⁓ to sb.** jmdn. grüßen lassen
(b) (sweetheart) Geliebte, *der/die;* **[my]** ⁓ (coll.: form of address) [mein] Liebling *od.* Schatz
(c) (Tennis) **fifteen/thirty** ⁓: fünfzehn/dreißig null
2 *v.t.* **(a)** lieben; **our/their** ⁓**d ones** unsere/ihre Lieben
(b) (like) **I'd** ⁓ **a cigarette** ich hätte sehr gerne eine Zigarette; ⁓ **to do** *or* ⁓ **doing sth.** etw. gern tun
love: ⁓ **affair** *n.* Liebesverhältnis, *das;* ⁓ **letter** *n.* Liebesbrief, *der;* ⁓ **life** *n.* Liebesleben, *das*
loveliness /'lʌvlɪnɪs/ *n.* Schönheit, *die*
lovely /'lʌvlɪ/ *adj.* [wunder]schön; herrlich ⟨*Tag, Essen*⟩
lover /'lʌvə(r)/ *n.* **(a)** Liebhaber, *der;* Geliebte, *der;* (woman) Geliebte, *die;* **be** ⁓**s** ein Liebespaar sein
(b) (person who likes sth.) Freund, *der/* Freundin, *die*
love: ⁓**sick** *adj.* an Liebeskummer leidend; liebeskrank (geh.); ⁓ **song** *n.* Liebeslied, *das;* ⁓ **story** *n.* Liebesgeschichte, *die*
loving /'lʌvɪŋ/ *adj.* **(a)** (affectionate) liebend
(b) (expressing love) liebevoll
'**lovingly** *adv.* liebevoll
low /ləʊ/ 1 *adj.* **(a)** niedrig; tief ausgeschnitten ⟨*Kleid*⟩; tief ⟨*Ausschnitt*⟩; tief liegend ⟨*Grund*⟩
(b) (of humble rank) nieder...; niedrig
(c) (inferior) niedrig; gering ⟨*Intelligenz, Bildung*⟩
(d) (in pitch) tief; (in loudness) leise
2 *adv.* **(a)** (to a ⁓ position) tief
(b) (not loudly) leise
(c) lie ⁓ (hide) untertauchen
low: ⁓**-alcohol** *adj.* alkoholarm ⟨*Getränk*⟩; ⁓**brow** *adj.* schlicht ⟨*Person*⟩; [geistig] anspruchslos ⟨*Buch, Programm*⟩; ⁓**-budget** *adj.* Lowbudget-, Billig⟨*film, -produktion usw.*⟩; ⁓**-calorie** *adj.* kalorienarm ⟨*Kost, Getränk*⟩; ⁓**-cost** *adj.* preiswert; ⁓**-cut** *adj.* [tief] ausgeschnitten ⟨*Kleid*⟩; ⁓**-cut neck** tiefer Ausschnitt; ⁓**-cut shoes** Halbschuhe
lower[1] /'ləʊə(r)/ *v.t.* **(a)** herab-/hinablassen
(b) senken ⟨*Blick*⟩; auslassen ⟨*Saum*⟩; senken ⟨*Preis, Miete, Zins usw.*⟩; ⁓ **one's voice** leiser sprechen
lower[2] 1 *compar. adj.* unter...; Unter⟨*grenze, -arm, -lippe usw.*⟩
2 *compar. adv.* tiefer
lower 'case 1 *n.* Kleinbuchstaben *Pl.;*
2 *adj.* klein ⟨*Buchstabe*⟩
low: ⁓**-fat** *adj.* fettarm; ⁓**-flying** *adj.* tief fliegend; ⁓**-flying aircraft** Tiefflieger, *der;* ⁓ '**frequency** *n.* Niederfrequenz, *die;* ⁓**-grade** *adj.* minderwertig; ⁓**-income** *adj.* einkommenschwach; ⁓**-income families** Familien mit niedrigem Einkommen;

⁓**-key** *adj.* zurückhaltend; unaufdringlich ⟨*Beleuchtung, Unterhaltung*⟩; unauffällig ⟨*Einsatz*⟩; ⁓**land** /'ləʊlənd/ *n.* Tiefland, *das*
lowly /'ləʊlɪ/ *adj.* (modest) bescheiden
low: ⁓**-lying** *adj.* tief liegend; ⁓**-nicotine** *adj.* nikotinarm; ⁓**-paid** *adj.* niedrig bezahlt; ⁓**-paid families** Familien mit geringem Einkommen; ⁓ **point** *n.* Tiefpunkt, *der;* ⁓ **pressure** *n.* (Meteorol.) Tiefdruck, *der;* ⁓**-priced** *adj.* preisgünstig; ⁓ **season** *n.* Nebensaison, *die;* ⁓**-tech** *adj.* Lowtech ⟨*system, -ausrüstung etc.*⟩; ⁓**-voltage** *adj.* Niederspannungs-; ⁓**-wage** *attrib. adj.* schlecht bezahlt; Niedriglohn⟨*land*⟩
loyal /'lɔɪəl/ *adj.* treu
loyalty /'lɔɪəltɪ/ *n.* Treue, *die*
'**loyalty card** *n.* Treuekarte, *die* ⟨*für Kunden*⟩
lozenge /'lɒzɪndʒ/ *n.* Pastille, *die*
LP *abbr.* = **long-playing record** LP, *die*
'**L-plate** *n.* (Brit.) 'L'-Schild, *das;* ≈ „Fahrschule"-Schild, *das*
Ltd. *abbr.* = **Limited** GmbH
lubricant /'lu:brɪkənt/ *n.* Schmiermittel, *das*
lubricate /'lu:brɪkeɪt/ *v.t.* schmieren
lubrication /lu:brɪ'keɪʃn/ *n.* Schmierung, *die; attrib.* Schmier⟨*system, -vorrichtung*⟩
lucid /'lu:sɪd/ *adj.* klar
lucidity /lu:'sɪdɪtɪ/ *n.* Klarheit, *die*
luck /lʌk/ *n.* Glück, *das;* **good** ⁓: Glück, *das;* **bad** *or* **hard** ⁓: Pech, *das;* **good** ⁓**!** viel Glück!; **be in/out of** ⁓: Glück/kein Glück haben; **no such** ⁓: schön wärs
luckily /'lʌkɪlɪ/ *adv.* glücklicherweise
lucky /'lʌkɪ/ *adj.* **(a)** glücklich; **be** ⁓: Glück haben
(b) (bringing good luck) Glücks⟨*zahl, -tag usw.*⟩; ⁓ **charm** Glücksbringer, *der*
lucrative /'lu:krətɪv/ *adj.* einträglich; lukrativ
ludicrous /'lu:dɪkrəs/ *adj.* lächerlich; lachhaft ⟨*Angebot, Ausrede*⟩
lug /lʌg/ *v.t.,* **-gg-** (drag) schleppen
luggage /'lʌgɪdʒ/ *n.* Gepäck, *das*
luggage: ⁓ **locker** *n.* [Gepäck]schließfach, *das;* ⁓ **rack** *n.* Gepäckablage, *die*
lugubrious /lu:'gu:brɪəs/ *adj.* (mournful) kummervoll; (dismal) düster
lukewarm /'lu:kwɔ:m/ *adj.* lauwarm
lull /lʌl/ 1 *v.t.* **(a)** (soothe) lullen
(b) (fig.) einlullen; ⁓ **sb. into a false sense of security** jmdn. in einer trügerischen Sicherheit wiegen
2 *n.* Pause, *die*
lullaby /'lʌləbaɪ/ *n.* Schlaflied, *das*
lumbago /lʌm'beɪgəʊ/ *n., pl.* ⁓**s** (Med.) Hexenschuss, *der*
lumber /'lʌmbə(r)/ 1 *n.* **(a)** (furniture) Gerümpel, *das* ⋯⟶

(b) (useless material) Kram, *der* (ugs.)
(c) (Amer.: timber) [Bau]holz, *das*
2 *v.t.* ~ sb. with sth./sb. jmdm. etw./jmdn. aufhalsen (ugs.)
'lumbering *adj.* schwerfällig
lumberjack /'lʌmbədʒæk/ *n.* (Amer.) Holzfäller, *der*
luminous /'lu:mɪnəs/ *adj.* [hell] leuchtend; Leucht⟨*anzeige, -zeiger usw.*⟩
lump /lʌmp/ **1** *n.* **(a)** Klumpen, *der;* (of sugar, butter, etc.) Stück, *das;* (of wood) Klotz, *der;* (of dough) Kloß, *der;* (of bread) Brocken, *der*
(b) (swelling) Beule, *die*
2 *v.t.* ~ sth. with sth. etw. und etw. zusammentun
lump: ~ **'payment** *n.* einmalige Zahlung [einer größeren Summe]; ~ **'sum** *n.* Pauschalsumme, *die*
'lumpy *adj.* klumpig ⟨*Brei*⟩; ⟨*Kissen, Matratze*⟩ mit klumpiger Füllung
lunacy /'lu:nəsɪ/ *n.* Wahnsinn, *der*
lunar /'lu:nə(r)/ *adj.* Mond-
lunatic /'lu:nətɪk/ **1** *adj.* wahnsinnig
2 *n.* Wahnsinnige, *der/die;* Irre, *der/die*
'lunatic asylum *n.* (Hist.) Irrenanstalt, *die* (veralt., ugs.)
lunch /lʌntʃ/ **1** *n.* Mittagessen, *das;* **have** *or* **eat [one's]** ~: zu Mittag essen
2 *v.i.* zu Mittag essen
lunch: ~ **box** *n.* Lunchbox, *die;* ~ **break** ▶ ~ HOUR
luncheon: ~ **meat** *n.* Frühstücksfleisch, *das;* ~ **voucher** *n.* (Brit.) Essenmarke, *die*
lunch: ~ **hour** *n.* Mittagspause, *die;* ~**time** *n.* Mittagszeit, *die;* **at** ~**time** mittags
lung /lʌŋ/ *n.* (right or left) Lungenflügel, *der;* ~**s** Lunge, *die*
'lung cancer *n.* Lungenkrebs, *der*
lunge /lʌndʒ/ **1** *n.* Sprung nach vorn
2 *v.i.* ~ at sb. with a knife jmdm. mit einem Messer angreifen
lurch[1] /lɜ:tʃ/ *n.* **leave sb. in the** ~: jmdn. im Stich lassen

lurch[2] **1** *n.* Rucken, *das*
2 *v.i.* rucken; ⟨*Betrunkener:*⟩ torkeln
lure /ljʊə(r), lʊə(r)/ **1** *v.t.* locken
2 *n.* Lockmittel, *das*
lurid /'ljʊərɪd, 'lʊərɪd/ *adj.* **(a)** (in colour) grell
(b) (sensational) reißerisch
lurk /lɜ:k/ *v.i.* lauern
lurker /lɜ:kə(r)/ *n.* (Comp. sl.) Lurker, *der*/Lurkerin, *die*
luscious /'lʌʃəs/ *adj.* köstlich [süß]; saftig [süß] ⟨*Obst*⟩
lush /lʌʃ/ *adj.* saftig ⟨*Wiese*⟩; grün ⟨*Tal*⟩; üppig ⟨*Vegetation*⟩
lust /lʌst/ **1** *n.* **(a)** (sexual) Sinnenlust, *die*
(b) (strong desire) Gier, *die* (**for** nach)
2 *v.i.* ~ **after** [lustvoll] begehren (geh.)
lustful /'lʌstfl/ *adj.* lüstern (geh.)
lustily /'lʌstɪlɪ/ *adv.* kräftig; aus voller Kehle ⟨*rufen, singen*⟩
lustre /'lʌstə(r)/ *n.* (Brit.) **(a)** Schimmer, *der*
(b) (fig.: splendour) Glanz, *der*
lusty /'lʌstɪ/ *adj.* kräftig
Luxembourg, Luxemburg /'lʌksəmbɜ:g/ *pr. n.* Luxemburg (*das*)
luxuriant /lʌg'zjʊərɪənt/ *adj.* üppig
luxuriate /lʌg'zjʊərɪeɪt/ *v.i.* ~ **in** sich aalen in (+ *Dat.*)
luxurious /lʌg'zjʊərɪəs/ *adj.* luxuriös
luxury /'lʌkʃərɪ/ *n.* **(a)** Luxus, *der; attrib.* Luxus-
(b) (article) Luxusgegenstand, *der;* **luxuries** Luxus, *der*
LW *abbr.* (Radio) = **long wave** LW
lying /'laɪɪŋ/ *adj.* verlogen ⟨*Person*⟩. *See also* LIE[1] 2
lymph gland *n.* Lymphknoten, *der*
lynch /lɪntʃ/ *v.t.* lynchen
lynx /lɪŋks/ *n.* Luchs, *der*
lyre /'laɪə(r)/ *n.* Lyra, *die*
lyric /'lɪrɪk/ **1** *adj.* lyrisch; ~ **poetry** Lyrik, *die*
2 *n. in pl.* (of song) Text, *der*
lyrical /'lɪrɪkl/ *adj.* **(a)** lyrisch
(b) (coll.: enthusiastic) gefühlvoll

Mm

M, m /em/ *n.* M, m, *das*
m. *abbr.* **(a)** = **masculine** m.
(b) = **metre[s]** m
(c) = **million[s]** Mill.
(d) = **minute[s]** Min.
MA *abbr.* = **Master of Arts** M.A.
mac /mæk/ *n.* (Brit. coll.) Regenmantel, *der*

macaroni /mækə'rəʊnɪ/ *n.* Makkaroni Pl.
Macedonia /mæsɪ'dəʊnɪə/ *pr. n.* Makedonien (*das*)
machine /mə'ʃi:n/ *n.* Maschine, *die*
machine: ~ **gun** *n.* Maschinengewehr, *das;* ~**-made** *adj.* maschinell hergestellt; ~ **operator** *n.* [Maschinen]bediener,

der/-bedienerin, *die;* **∼-readable** *adj.* (Comp.) maschinenlesbar

machinery /məˈʃiːnərɪ/ *n.* **(a)** (machines) Maschinen *Pl.*
(b) (mechanism) Mechanismus, *der*

machine: ∼ tool *n.* Werkzeugmaschine, *die;* **∼-wash** *v.t.* in der Waschmaschine waschen; **∼-washable** *adj.* waschmaschinenfest

machinist /məˈʃiːnɪst/ *n.* Maschinist, *der*/Maschinistin, *die;* **[sewing]** ∼: [Maschinen]näherin, *die*/-näher, *der*

machismo /məˈtʃɪzməʊ, məˈkɪzməʊ/ *n.* Machismo, *der;* Männlichkeitswahn, *der*

macho /ˈmætʃəʊ/ *adj.* Macho-; **he is ∼:** er ist ein Macho

mackerel /ˈmækərl/ *n., pl. same or* ∼**s** Makrele, *die*

mackintosh /ˈmækɪntɒʃ/ *n.* Regenmantel, *der*

macro /ˈmækrəʊ/ *n.* (Comp.) Makro, *das*

macrobiotic /mækrəʊbaɪˈɒtɪk/ *adj.* makrobiotisch

mad /mæd/ *adj.* **(a)** (insane) geisteskrank
(b) (frenzied) wahnsinnig; **drive sb. mad** jmdn. um den Verstand bringen
(c) (foolish) verrückt (ugs.)
(d) (very enthusiastic) **be ∼ about** *or* **on sb.**/**sth.** auf jmdn./etw. wild sein (ugs.)
(e) (coll.: annoyed) ∼ **[with** *or* **at sb.]** sauer [auf jmdn.] (ugs.)
(f) (with rabies) toll[wütig]; **[run** *etc.*] **like ∼** (coll.) wie wild [laufen *usw.*]

madam /ˈmædəm/ *n.* gnädige Frau; **Dear M∼** (in letter) Sehr geehrte Dame

mad 'cow disease *n.* (coll.) Rinderwahnsinn, *der*

madden /ˈmædn/ *v.t.* (irritate) [ver]ärgern

maddening /ˈmædənɪŋ/ *adj.* (irritating) [äußerst] ärgerlich

made ▶ MAKE 1

made-to-'measure *attrib. adj.* Maß-

'madly *adv.* (coll.) wahnsinnig (ugs.)

madman /ˈmædmən/ *n., pl.* **madmen** /ˈmædmən/ *n.* Wahnsinnige, *der*

'madness *n.* Wahnsinn, *der*

magazine /mægəˈziːn/ *n.* **(a)** Zeitschrift, *die*
(b) (of firearm) Magazin, *das*

maggot /ˈmægət/ *n.* Made, *die*

magic /ˈmædʒɪk/ **1** *n.* **(a)** Magie, *die;* **work like ∼:** wie ein Wunder wirken
(b) (conjuring) Zauberei, *die*
2 *adj.* **(a)** magisch; Zauber⟨trank, -baum⟩
(b) (fig.) wunderbar

magical /ˈmædʒɪkl/ *adj.* zauberhaft

magician /məˈdʒɪʃn/ *n.* Magier, *der*/Magierin, *die;* (conjurer) Zauberer, *der*/Zauberin, *die*

magic 'wand *n.* Zauberstab, *der*

magistrate /ˈmædʒɪstreɪt/ *n.* Friedensrichter, *der*/-richterin, *die*

maglev /ˈmæglev/ *n.* ∼ **[system]/train** Magnetschwebebahn, *die*

magnanimity /mægnəˈnɪmɪtɪ/ *n.* Großmut, *die*

magnanimous /mægˈnænɪməs/ *adj.* großmütig **(towards** gegen)

magnate /ˈmægneɪt/ *n.* Magnat, *der*/Magnatin, *die*

magnesium /mægˈniːzɪəm/ *n.* Magnesium, *das*

magnet /ˈmægnɪt/ *n.* Magnet, *der*

magnetic /mægˈnetɪk/ *adj.* magnetisch

magnetic: ∼ 'north magnetisch Nord, *das;* ∼ **'tape** *n.* Magnetband, *das*

magnetism /ˈmægnɪtɪzm/ *n.* **(a)** (force, lit. or fig.) Magnetismus, *der*
(b) (fig.: charm) Anziehungskraft, *die*

magnetize /ˈmægnɪtaɪz/ *v.t.* magnetisieren

magnification /mægnɪfɪˈkeɪʃn/ *n.* Vergrößerung, *die*

magnificence /mægˈnɪfɪsəns/ *n.* Pracht, *die;* (beauty) Herrlichkeit, *die;* (lavishness) Üppigkeit, *die*

magnificent /mægˈnɪfɪsənt/ *adj.*
(a) prächtig; herrlich ⟨Garten, Kunstwerk, Wetter⟩; (lavish) üppig ⟨Mahl⟩
(b) (coll.: excellent) fabelhaft (ugs.)

magnifier /ˈmægnɪfaɪə(r)/ *n.* (Optics) Lupe, *die*

magnify /ˈmægnɪfaɪ/ *v.t.* **(a)** vergrößern
(b) (exaggerate) aufbauschen

'magnifying glass *n.* Lupe, *die*

magnitude /ˈmægnɪtjuːd/ *n.* **(a)** (size) Größe, *die*
(b) (importance) Wichtigkeit, *die*

magnolia /mægˈnəʊlɪə/ *n.* Magnolie, *die*

magnum /ˈmægnəm/ *n.* (bottle) Magnum, *die*

magpie /ˈmægpaɪ/ *n.* Elster, *die*

mahogany /məˈhɒgənɪ/ *n.* Mahagoni[holz], *das; attrib.* Mahagoni-

maid /meɪd/ *n.* Dienstmädchen, *das*

maiden /ˈmeɪdn/ **1** *n.* Jungfrau, *die*
2 *adj.* **(a)** (unmarried) unverheiratet
(b) (first) ∼ **voyage/speech** Jungfernfahrt/ -rede, *die*

'maiden name *n.* Mädchenname, *der*

mail /meɪl/ **1** *n.* ▶ POST² 1
2 *v.t.* abschicken

mail: ∼bag *n.* Postsack, *der;* ∼**box** *n.* (Amer.) Briefkasten, *der;* ∼**ing address** *n.* Postanschrift, *die;* ∼**ing list** *n.* Adressenliste, *die;* ∼**man** *n.* (Amer.) Briefträger, *der;* ∼ **order** *n.* Bestellung per Post; ∼ **order catalogue** *n.* Versandhauskatalog, *der;* ∼ **order firm** *n.* Versandhaus, *das;* ∼ **room** *n.* Poststelle, *die*

maim /meɪm/ *v.t.* verstümmeln

main /meɪn/ **1** *n.* **(a)** (channel, pipe) Hauptleitung, *die;* ∼**s** (Electr.) Stromnetz, *das* ⋯⟶

(b) in the ∼: im Großen und Ganzen
2 *attrib. adj.* Haupt-; the ∼ thing is that ...:
die Hauptsache ist, dass ...
main: ∼ **beam** *n.* (Motor Veh.) **on** ∼ **beam**
aufgeblendet; ∼ **course** *n.* Hauptgang,
der; Hauptgericht, *das;* ∼**frame** *n.* (Comp.)
Großrechner, *der;* ∼**land** /'meɪnlənd/
n. Festland, *das;* ∼ **'line** *n.* (Railw.)
Hauptstrecke, *die;* ∼-line station/train
Fernbahnhof/-zug, *der*
'mainly *adv.* hauptsächlich
main: ∼ **'road** *n.* Hauptstraße, *die;*
∼**stay** *n.* [wichtigste] Stütze; ∼ **street**
/Brit. '-'-, Amer. '--/ *n.* Hauptstraße, *die*
maintain /meɪn'teɪn/ *v.t.* **(a)** (keep up)
aufrechterhalten
(b) (provide for) ∼ sb. für jmds. Unterhalt
aufkommen
(c) (preserve) instand halten; warten
⟨*Maschine*⟩
(d) ∼ that ...: behaupten, dass ...
maintenance /'meɪntənəns/ *n.*
(a) (keeping up) Aufrechterhaltung, *die*
(b) (preservation) Instandhaltung, *die;* (of
machinery) Wartung, *die*
(c) (Law: money paid to support sb.) Unterhalt,
der
maintenance-'free *adj.* wartungsfrei
maison[n]ette /meɪzə'net/ *n.*
[zweistöckige] Wohnung
maize /meɪz/ *n.* Mais, *der*
majestic /mə'dʒestɪk/ *adj.,*
majestically /mə'dʒestɪkəlɪ/ *adv.*
majestätisch
majesty /'mædʒɪstɪ/ *n.* Majestät, *die* (geh.);
Your/Her *etc.* **M**∼: Eure/Seine *usw.* Majestät
major /'meɪdʒə(r)/ **1** *adj.* **(a)** *attrib.*
(greater) größer...
(b) *attrib.* (important) bedeutend...; (serious)
schwer; ∼ **road** Hauptverkehrsstraße, *die*
(c) (Mus.) Dur-; **C** ∼: C-Dur
2 *n.* (Mil.) Major, *der*
3 *v.i.* (Amer. Univ.) ∼ **in** sth. etw. als
Hauptfach haben
Majorca /mə'jɔːkə/ *pr. n.* Mallorca *(das)*
majority /mə'dʒɒrɪtɪ/ *n.* Mehrheit, *die;* **be**
in the ∼: in der Mehrzahl sein
majority 'rule *n.* Mehrheitsregierung, *die*
make /meɪk/ **1** *v.t.,* made /meɪd/
(a) machen (of aus); bauen ⟨*Straße,*
Flugzeug⟩; anlegen ⟨*Teich, Weg usw.*⟩;
zimmern ⟨*Tisch, Regal*⟩; basteln ⟨*Spielzeug,*
Vogelhäuschen usw.⟩; nähen ⟨*Kleider*⟩;
(manufacture) herstellen; (prepare) zubereiten
⟨*Mahlzeit*⟩; machen, kochen ⟨*Kaffee, Tee*⟩;
backen ⟨*Brot, Kuchen*⟩
(b) (establish, enact) treffen ⟨*Unterscheidung,*
Übereinkommen⟩; ziehen ⟨*Vergleich*⟩;
erlassen ⟨*Gesetz*⟩; aufstellen ⟨*Regeln,*
Behauptung⟩; stellen ⟨*Forderung*⟩; geben
⟨*Bericht*⟩; vornehmen ⟨*Zahlung*⟩; erheben
⟨*Protest, Beschwerde*⟩
(c) (cause to be or become) ∼ **happy/known**
etc. glücklich/bekannt *usw.* machen; ∼ **sb.**

captain jmdn. zum Kapitän machen
(d) ∼ **sb. do sth.** (cause) jmdn. dazu bringen,
etw. zu tun; (compel) jmdn. zwingen, etw. zu
tun; **be made to do sth.** etw. tun müssen
(e) (earn) machen ⟨*Profit, Verlust*⟩;
verdienen ⟨*Lebensunterhalt*⟩
(f) **what do you** ∼ **of him?** was hältst du von
ihm?
(g) (arrive at) erreichen; **make it** (succeed in
arriving) es schaffen
(h) ∼ **'do** vorlieb nehmen; ∼ **'do with/**
without sth. mit/ohne etw. auskommen
2 *n.* (brand) Marke, *die*
∎ **'make for** *v.t.* zusteuern auf (+ *Akk.*)
∎ **make 'off** *v.i.* sich davonmachen
∎ **make 'off with** *v.t.* ∼ off with sb./sth.
sich mit jmdm./etw. auf und davon machen
∎ **make 'out** **1** *v.t.* **(a)** (write) ausstellen;
∼ **out a cheque to sb.** einen Scheck auf
jmdn. ausstellen
(b) (claim) behaupten
(c) (manage to see or hear) ausmachen; (manage
to read) entziffern
(d) (pretend) vorgeben
2 *v.i.* (coll.) zurechtkommen (**at** bei)
∎ **make 'over** *v.t.* überschreiben (**to** auf
+ *Akk.*)
∎ **make 'up** **1** *v.t.* **(a)** (assemble)
zusammenstellen
(b) (invent) erfinden
(c) (constitute) bilden; **be made up of** ...:
bestehen aus ...
(d) (apply cosmetics to) schminken; ∼ **up one's**
face sich schminken
2 *v.i.* (be reconciled) sich wieder vertragen
∎ **make 'up for** *v.t.* wieder gutmachen;
∼ **up for lost time** Versäumtes nachholen
make: ∼**believe** **1** *n.* it's only
∼-**believe** das ist bloß Fantasie; **2** *adj.*
nicht echt; ∼-**or-'break** *attrib. adj.*
alles entscheidend; ∼**over** *n.* (of a person's
appearance) [grundlegende] Verwandlung; (of
a building) Umbau, *der*
'maker *n.* (manufacturer) Hersteller, *der*
make: ∼**shift** *adj.* behelfsmäßig; ∼**up**
n. Make-up, *das;* ∼**up bag** Kosmetiktasche,
die
making /'meɪkɪŋ/ *n.* **in the** ∼: im
Entstehen; **have the** ∼**s of a leader** das Zeug
zum Führer haben (ugs.)
maladjusted /mælə'dʒʌstɪd/ *adj.*
verhaltensgestört
malady /'mælədɪ/ *n.* Leiden, *das*
malaise /mə'leɪz/ *n.* Unbehagen, *das*
malaria /mə'leərɪə/ *n.* Malaria, *die*
Malaysia /mə'leɪzɪə/ *pr. n.* Malaysia *(das)*
male /meɪl/ **1** *adj.* männlich;
Männer⟨*stimme, -chor, -verein*⟩; ∼ **doctor/**
nurse Arzt, *der*/Krankenpfleger, *der*
2 *n.* (person) Mann, *der;* (animal) Männchen,
das
'male-dominated *adj.* von Männern
dominiert

m

malevolence /mə'levələns/ n.
Boshaftigkeit, die
malevolent /mə'levələnt/ adj. boshaft
malfunction /mæl'fʌŋkʃn/ **1** n. Störung,
die; (Med.) Funktionsstörung, die
2 v.i. nicht richtig funktionieren
malice /'mælɪs/ n. Bosheit, die
malicious /mə'lɪʃəs/ adj. böse
malign /mə'laɪn/ v.t. verleumden
malignant /mə'lɪgnənt/ adj. bösartig
malinger /mə'lɪŋgə(r)/ v.i. simulieren
ma'lingerer n. Simulant, der/Simulantin,
die
malleable /'mælɪəbl/ adj. formbar
mallet /'mælɪt/ n. Holzhammer, der
malnourished /mæl'nʌrɪʃt/ adj.
unterernährt
malnutrition /mælnjuː'trɪʃn/ n.
Unterernährung, die
malpractice /mæl'præktɪs/ n. (Law, Med.)
Kunstfehler, der
malt /mɔːlt/ n. Malz, das
Malta /'mɔːltə/ pr. n. Malta (das)
maltreat /mæl'triːt/ v.t. misshandeln
mal'treatment n. Misshandlung, die
malt 'whisky n. Malzwhisky, der
mammal /'mæml/ n. Säugetier, das
mammoth /'mæməθ/ **1** n. Mammut, das
2 adj. Mammut-; gigantisch ⟨Vorhaben⟩
man /mæn/ **1** n. (a) pl. **men** [men] Mann,
der
(b) (human race) der Mensch
2 v.t., **-nn-** bemannen ⟨Schiff⟩; besetzen
⟨Büro, Stelle usw.⟩; bedienen ⟨Telefon,
Geschütz⟩
manacle /'mænəkl/ **1** n., usu. in pl.
[Hand]fessel, die
2 v.t. Handfesseln anlegen (+ Dat.)
manage /'mænɪdʒ/ **1** v.t. (a) leiten
⟨Geschäft⟩
(b) (Sport) betreuen ⟨Mannschaft⟩
(c) (cope with) schaffen
(d) ~ to do sth. es fertig bringen, etw. zu
tun; he ~d to do it es gelang ihm, es zu tun
2 v.i. zurechtkommen; ~ without sth. ohne
etw. auskommen; I can ~: es geht
manageable /'mænɪdʒəbl/ adj. leicht
frisierbar ⟨Haar⟩; fügsam ⟨Person, Tier⟩;
überschaubar ⟨Größe, Menge⟩
'management n. (a) (of a business)
Leitung, die
(b) (managers) the ~: die Geschäftsleitung
management: ~ **consultancy**
n. Unternehmensberatung, die;
~ **consultant** n. Unternehmensberater,
der/-beraterin, die
'manager n. (of shop or bank) Filialleiter,
der/-leiterin, die; (of football team)
[Chef]trainer, der/-trainerin, die; (of
restaurant, shop, hotel) Geschäftsführer, der/
-führerin, die

manageress /mænɪdʒə'res/ n.
Geschäftsführerin, die
managerial /mænə'dʒɪərɪəl/ adj.
führend, leitend ⟨Stellung⟩; ~ skills
Führungsqualitäten
managing /'mænɪdʒɪŋ/ adj. ~ director
Geschäftsführer, der/-führerin, die
mandarin¹ /'mændərɪn/ n. ~ **[orange]**
Mandarine, die
mandarin² n. (bureaucrat) Bürokrat,
der/Bürokratin, die
mandarine /'mændəriːn/ n. ▶ MANDARIN¹
mandate /'mændeɪt/ n. Mandat, das
mandatory /'mændətərɪ/ adj.
obligatorisch
mandolin[e] /mændə'lɪn/ n. Mandoline,
die
mane /meɪn/ n. Mähne, die
maneuver[able] (Amer.) ▶ MANŒUVR-
manful /'mænfl/ adj., **manfully**
/'mænfəlɪ/ adv. mannhaft
manger /'meɪndʒə(r)/ n. Krippe, die
mangetout /mɑ̃ʒ'tuː/ n. Zuckererbse, die
mangle /'mæŋgl/ v.t. verstümmeln
⟨Person⟩; demolieren ⟨Sache⟩
mango /'mæŋgəʊ/ n., pl. ~**es** or ~**s** (fruit)
Mango[frucht], die
mangy /'meɪndʒɪ/ adj. (a) (Vet. Med.) räudig
(b) (shabby) schäbig
man: ~**handle** v.t. (a) von Hand bewegen
⟨Gegenstand⟩; (b) grob behandeln ⟨Person⟩;
~**hole** n. Mannloch, das
'manhood n. Mannesalter, das
man: ~**-hour** n. Arbeitsstunde, die;
~**hunt** n. Verbrecherjagd, die
mania /'meɪnɪə/ n. Manie, die
maniacal /mə'naɪəkl/ adj. wahnsinnig
manicure /'mænɪkjʊə(r)/ **1** n. Maniküre,
die
2 v.t. maniküren
manifest /'mænɪfest/ **1** adj. offenkundig
2 v.t. (reveal) offenbaren
'manifestly adv. offenkundig
manifesto /mænɪ'festəʊ/ n., pl. ~**s**
Manifest, das
manifold /'mænɪfəʊld/ adj. (literary)
mannigfaltig (geh.)
manipulate /mə'nɪpjʊleɪt/ v.t.
(a) manipulieren
(b) (handle) handhaben
manipulation /mənɪpjʊ'leɪʃn/ n.
(a) Manipulation, die
(b) (handling) Handhabung, die
manipulative /mə'nɪpjʊlətɪv/ adj.
manipulativ
mankind /mæn'kaɪnd/ n. Menschheit, die
manly /'mænlɪ/ adj. männlich
'man-made adj. künstlich; (synthetic)
Kunst⟨faser, -stoff⟩
manned /mænd/ adj. bemannt

manner /'mænə(r)/ n. **(a)** Art, die; Weise, die; **in this** ~: auf diese Art und Weise **(b)** (general behaviour) Art, die **(c)** in pl. Manieren Pl.

mannerism /'mænərɪzm/ n. Eigenart, die

manœuvrable /mə'nu:vrəbl/ adj. (Brit.) manövrierfähig

manœuvre /mə'nu:və(r)/ (Brit.) ① n. Manöver, das ② v.t. & i. manövrieren

manor /'mænə(r)/ n. **(a)** (land) [Land]gut, das **(b)** ▶ MANOR HOUSE

'manor house n. Herrenhaus, das

'manpower n. Arbeitskräfte Pl.

mansion /'mænʃn/ n. Herrenhaus, das

manslaughter /'mænslɔ:tə(r)/ n. Totschlag, der

mantel: ~**piece** /'mæntlpi:s/ n. **(a)** (above fireplace) Kaminsims, der od. das; **(b)** (around fireplace) Kamineinfassung, die; ~**shelf** ▶ ~PIECE A

mantle /'mæntl/ n. Umhang, der

manual /'mænjʊəl/ ① adj. **(a)** manuell; ~ **work** Handarbeit; ~ **worker** Handarbeiter, der/-arbeiterin, die **(b)** (not automatic) handbetrieben; ⟨Bedienung, Schaltung⟩ von Hand ② n. Handbuch, das

manually /'mænjʊəlɪ/ adv. manuell; **a** ~ **operated machine** eine handbetriebene Maschine

manufacture /mænjʊ'fæktʃə(r)/ ① n. Herstellung, die ② v.t. herstellen

manu'facturer n. Hersteller, der

manure /mə'njʊə(r)/ ① n. Dung, der ② v.t. düngen

manuscript /'mænjʊskrɪpt/ n. Manuskript, das

many /'menɪ/ ① adj. viele; **how** ~ **people/ books?** wie viele od. wie viel Leute/Bücher? ② n. viele [Leute]; ~ **of us** viele von uns; **a good/great** ~: eine Menge

map /mæp/ ① n. [Land]karte, die; (street plan) Stadtplan, der ② v.t., **-pp-** kartographieren

■ **map 'out** v.t. im Einzelnen festlegen

maple /'meɪpl/ n. Ahorn, der

'map-reading n. Kartenlesen, das

mar /mɑ:(r)/ v.t. verderben

marathon /'mærəθən/ n. **(a)** Marathon[lauf], der **(b)** (fig.) Marathon, das

marauder /mə'rɔ:də(r)/ n. Plünderer, der

marble /'mɑ:bl/ n. **(a)** (stone) Marmor, der **(b)** (toy) Murmel, die; [game of] ~s Murmelspiel, das

march ① n. Marsch, der; [protest] ~: Protestmarsch, der ② v.i. marschieren

■ **march 'off** ① v.i. losmarschieren

② v.t. abführen

■ **march 'past** v.i. vorbeimarschieren

March /mɑ:tʃ/ n. März, der; see also AUGUST

'marcher n. [protest] ~: Demonstrant, der/Demonstrantin, die

mare /meə(r)/ n. Stute, die

margarine /mɑ:dʒə'ri:n/, (coll.) **marge** /mɑ:dʒ/ ns. Margarine, die

margin /'mɑ:dʒɪn/ n. **(a)** (of page) Rand, der **(b)** (extra amount) Spielraum, der; [profit] ~: [Gewinn]spanne, die; **by a narrow** ~: knapp

marginal /'mɑ:dʒɪnl/ adj. adv. unwesentlich

marginalize /'mɑ:dʒɪnəlaɪz/ v.t. marginalisieren

marginally /'mɑ:dʒɪnəlɪ/ adv. unwesentlich

marigold /'mærɪgəʊld/ n. Ringelblume, die

marijuana /mærɪjʊ'ɑ:nə/ n. Marihuana, das

marina /mə'ri:nə/ n. Jachthafen, der

marinade /mærɪ'neɪd/ ① n. Marinade, die ② ▶ MARINATE

marinate /'mærɪneɪt/ v.t. marinieren

marine /mə'ri:n/ ① adj. Meeres-; See⟨versicherung, -recht usw.⟩; Schiffs⟨ausrüstung, -turbine usw.⟩ ② n. (person) Marineinfanterist, der

mariner /'mærɪnə(r)/ n. Seemann, der

marionette /mærɪə'net/ n. Marionette, die

marital /'mærɪtl/ adj. ehelich; ~ **status** Familienstand, der

maritime /'mærɪtaɪm/ adj. See-

mark¹ /mɑ:k/ ① n. **(a)** (trace) Spur, die; (stain etc.) Fleck, der; (scratch) Kratzer, der **(b)** (sign) Zeichen, das **(c)** (Sch.) Note, die **(d)** (target) Ziel, das ② v.t. **(a)** (dirty) schmutzig machen; (scratch) zerkratzen **(b)** (put distinguishing ~ on) kennzeichnen, markieren (**with** mit) **(c)** (Sch.) (correct) korrigieren; (grade) benoten **(d)** ~ **time** auf der Stelle treten

■ **mark 'off** v.t. abgrenzen (**from** von, gegen)

■ **mark 'out** v.t. markieren

mark² n. (monetary unit) Mark, die

marked /mɑ:kt/ adj., **markedly** /'mɑ:kɪdlɪ/ adv. deutlich

'marker n. Markierung, die

'marker pen n. Markierstift, der

market /'mɑ:kɪt/ ① n. Markt, der ② v.t. vermarkten

market: ~ **day** n. Markttag, der; ~ **e'conomy** n. Marktwirtschaft, die; ~ **'forces** n. pl. Kräfte des freien Marktes; ~ **'gardening** n. (Brit.) Gemüseanbau, der

'marketing n. Marketing, das

market: ~ **'leader** n. (company, brand) Marktführer, der; (product) meistverkaufte

Produkt; **the company is the ~ leader in its field** die Firma ist marktführend auf ihrem Gebiet; **~ place** n. Marktplatz, der; (fig.) Markt, der; **~ 'price** n. Marktpreis, der; **~ 'research** n. Marktforschung, die; **~ share** n. Marktanteil, der; **~ town** n. Marktort, der; **~ 'value** n. Marktwert, der

'marking n. (a) Markierung, die (b) (on animal) Zeichnung, die

marksman /'mɑːksmən/ n., pl. **marksmen** /'mɑːksmən/ Scharfschütze, der

marmalade /'mɑːməleɪd/ n. [orange] **~:** Orangenmarmelade, die

maroon¹ /mə'ruːn/ ⃞1 adj. kastanienbraun ⃞2 n. Kastanienbraun, das

maroon² v.t. (a) (Naut.: put ashore) aussetzen (b) ⟨Flut, Hochwasser:⟩ von der Außenwelt abschneiden

marquee /mɑː'kiː/ n. Festzelt, das

marquess, marquis /'mɑːkwɪs/ n. Marquis, der

marquetry /'mɑːkɪtrɪ/ n. Marketerie, die

marriage /'mærɪdʒ/ n. (a) Ehe, die (to mit) (b) (wedding) Hochzeit, die

marriage: ~ broker n. Heiratsvermittler, der/-vermittlerin, die; **~ bureau** n. Eheanbahnungs- od. Ehevermittlungsinstitut, das; **~ certificate** n. Trauschein, der; (record of civil marriage also) Heiratsurkunde, die; **~ 'guidance** n. Eheberatung, die; **~ licence** n. Heirats- od. Eheerlaubnis, die

married /'mærɪd/ adj. (a) verheiratet; **~ couple** Ehepaar, das (b) (marital) Ehe⟨leben, -name⟩

marrow /'mærəʊ/ n. (a) [vegetable] **~:** Speisekürbis, der (b) (Anat.) [Knochen]mark, das

marry /'mærɪ/ ⃞1 v.t. (a) heiraten (b) (join) trauen; **they were** or **got/have got married** sie haben geheiratet ⃞2 v.i. heiraten

Mars /mɑːz/ pr. n. (Astron.) Mars, der

marsh /mɑːʃ/ n. Sumpf, der

marshal /'mɑːʃl/ ⃞1 n. (a) (officer in army) Marschall, der (b) (Sport) Ordner, der ⃞2 v.t., (Brit.) -ll- aufstellen ⟨Truppen⟩; ordnen ⟨Fakten⟩

'marshalling yard n. Rangierbahnhof, der

marshmallow /mɑːʃ'mæləʊ/ n. (sweet) ≈ Mohrenkopf, der

'marshy adj. sumpfig

marsupial /mɑː'sjuːpɪəl/ n. Beuteltier, das

martial /'mɑːʃl/ adj. kriegerisch

martial 'law n. Kriegsrecht, das

martyr /'mɑːtə(r)/ ⃞1 n. Märtyrer, der/Märtyrerin, die ⃞2 v.t. **be ~ed** den Märtyrertod sterben

marvel /'mɑːvl/ ⃞1 n. Wunder, das ⃞2 v.i., (Brit.) -ll- (literary) **~ at sth.** über etw (Akk.) staunen

marvellous /'mɑːvələs/ adj., **'marvellously** adv. wunderbar

marvelous[ly] (Amer.) ▶ MARVELLOUS[LY]

Marxism /'mɑːksɪzm/ n. Marxismus, der

Marxist /'mɑːksɪst/ ⃞1 n. Marxist, der/Marxistin, die ⃞2 adj. marxistisch

marzipan /'mɑːzɪpæn/ n. Marzipan, das

mascara /mæ'skɑːrə/ n. Mascara, das

mascot /'mæskɒt/ n. Maskottchen, das

masculine /'mæskjʊlɪn/ adj. männlich

masculinity /mæskju'lɪnɪtɪ/ n. Männlichkeit, die

mash /mæʃ/ ⃞1 n. (a) Brei, der (b) (Brit. coll.: ~ed potatoes) Kartoffelbrei, der ⃞2 v.t. zerdrücken; **~ed potatoes** Kartoffelbrei, der

mask /mɑːsk/ ⃞1 n. Maske, die ⃞2 v.t. maskieren

'masking tape n. Abklebeband, das

masochism /'mæsəkɪzm/ n. Masochismus, der

masochist /'mæsəkɪst/ n. Masochist, der/Masochistin, die

masochistic /mæsə'kɪstɪk/ adj. masochistisch

mason /'meɪsn/ n. (a) Steinmetz, der (b) M**~** (Free**~**) [Frei]maurer, der

Masonic /mə'sɒnɪk/ adj. [frei]maurerisch; **~ lodge** [Frei]maurerloge, die

masonry /'meɪsnrɪ/ n. Mauerwerk, das

masquerade /mæskə'reɪd, mɑːskə'reɪd/ ⃞1 n. Maskerade, die ⃞2 v.i. **~ as sb./sth.** sich als jmd./etw. ausgeben

mass¹ /mæs/ n. (Eccl.) Messe, die

mass² ⃞1 n. (a) Masse, der (b) **a ~ of ...:** eine Unmenge von ... (c) attrib. (for many people) Massen- ⃞2 v.t. anhäufen ⃞3 v.i. sich ansammeln; ⟨Truppen:⟩ sich massieren

massacre /'mæsəkə(r)/ ⃞1 n. Massaker, das ⃞2 v.t. massakrieren

massage /'mæsɑːʒ/ ⃞1 n. Massage, die ⃞2 v.t. massieren

mass communi'cations n. pl. Massenkommunikation, die

masseur /mæ'sɜː(r)/ n. Masseur, der

masseuse /mæ'sɜːz/ n. fem. Masseurin, die

mass hy'steria n. Massenhysterie, die

massive /'mæsɪv/ adj. massiv; gewaltig ⟨Aufgabe⟩; enorm ⟨Schulden⟩

mass: ~ market attrib. adj. für den Massenmarkt nachgestellt; **~ 'media** n. pl. Massenmedien Pl.; ⋯✥

~ **'murderer** n. Massenmörder, der/-mörderin, die; ~**pro'duced** adj. serienmäßig produziert; ~ **pro'duction** n. Massenproduktion, die

mast /mɑːst/ n. Mast, der

mastectomy /mæ'stektəmɪ/ n. (Med.) Mastektomie, die

master /'mɑːstə(r)/ ① n. (a) Herr, der (b) (of dog) Herrchen, das; (of ship) Kapitän, der (c) (Sch.: teacher) Lehrer, der (d) (expert, great artist) Meister, der (at in + Dat.) (e) M~ of Arts/Science Magister Artium/ rerum naturalium ② adj. Haupt- ③ v.t. (learn) erlernen; have ~ed a language eine Sprache beherrschen

masterful /'mɑːstəfl/ adj. (masterly) meisterhaft

'master key n. Hauptschlüssel, der

masterly /'mɑːstəlɪ/ adj. meisterhaft

master: ~**mind** ① n. führender Kopf; ② v.t. ~mind the plot der Kopf des Komplotts sein; ~**piece** n. (work of art) Meisterwerk, das; ~ **stroke** n. Geniestreich, der; be a ~ stroke genial sein; ~ **switch** n. Hauptschalter, der

mastery /'mɑːstərɪ/ n. (a) (skill) Meisterschaft, die (b) (knowledge) Beherrschung, die (of Gen.)

masturbate /'mæstəbeɪt/ v.i. & t. masturbieren

masturbation /mæstə'beɪʃn/ n. Masturbation, die

mat /mæt/ n. (a) Matte, die (b) (to protect table etc.) Untersetzer, der

matador /'mætədɔː(r)/ n. Matador, der

match¹ /mætʃ/ ① n. (a) be no ~ for sb. sich mit jmdm. nicht messen können; meet one's ~: seinen Meister finden (b) be a [good etc.] ~ for sth. [gut usw.] zu etw. passen (c) (Sport) Spiel, das; (Boxing) Kampf, der ② v.t. (a) (equal) ~ sb. at chess es mit jmdm. im Schach aufnehmen [können] (b) (harmonize with) passen zu; a handbag and ~ing shoes eine Handtasche und [dazu] passende Schuhe; ~ each other zueinander passen ③ v.i. zusammenpassen

match² n. (~stick) Streichholz, das

'matchbox n. Streichholzschachtel, die

'matchless adj. unvergleichlich

match: ~**maker** n. Ehestifter, der/ Ehestifterin, die; ~**stick** n. Streichholz, das

mate¹ /meɪt/ ① n. (a) Kumpel, der (ugs.); look or listen, ~, ...: jetzt hör [mir] mal gut zu, Freundchen, ... (b) (Naut.) ≈ Kapitänleutnant, der (c) (workman's assistant) Gehilfe, der (d) (Zool.) (male) Männchen, das; (female)

Weibchen, das ② v.i. sich paaren ③ v.t. paaren ⟨Tiere⟩

mate² (Chess) ▶ CHECKMATE

material /mə'tɪərɪəl/ ① adj. (a) materiell (b) (relevant) wesentlich ② n. (a) ~[s] Material, das; building/writing ~s Bau-/Schreibmaterial, das (b) (cloth) Stoff, der

materialism /mə'tɪərɪəlɪzm/ n. Materialismus, der

materialistic /mətɪərɪə'lɪstɪk/ adj. materialistisch

materialize /mə'tɪərɪəlaɪz/ v.i. ⟨Plan, Idee:⟩ sich verwirklichen; ⟨Treffen:⟩ zustande kommen

maternal /mə'tɜːnl/ adj. mütterlich; Mutter⟨instinkt⟩

maternity /mə'tɜːnɪtɪ/ n. Mutterschaft, die

maternity: ~ **benefit** n. Mutterschaftsgeld, das; ~ **dress** n. Umstandskleid, das; ~ **hospital** n. Entbindungsheim, das; ~ **leave** n. Mutterschaftsurlaub, der; ~ **nurse** n. Hebamme, die; ~ **pay** n. Mutterschaftsgeld, das; ~ **unit,** ~ **ward** ns. Entbindungsstation, die; ~ **wear** n. Umstandskleidung, die

matey /'meɪtɪ/ adj., **matier** /'meɪtɪə(r)/, **matiest** /'meɪtɪɪst/ (Brit. coll.) kameradschaftlich

math /mæθ/ (Amer. coll.) ▶ MATHS

mathematical /mæθɪ'mætɪkl/ adj., **mathematically** /mæθɪ'mætɪkəlɪ/ adv. mathematisch

mathematician /mæθɪmə'tɪʃn/ n. Mathematiker, der/Mathematikerin, die

mathematics /mæθɪ'mætɪks/ n. Mathematik, die

maths /mæθs/ n. (Brit. coll.) Mathe, die (Schülerspr.)

matinée /'mætɪneɪ/ n. Nachmittagsvorstellung, die

matriarchal /meɪtrɪ'ɑːkl/ adj. matriarchalisch

matriarchy /'meɪtrɪɑːkɪ/ n. Matriarchat, das

matrices pl. of MATRIX

matriculate /mə'trɪkjʊleɪt/ ① v.t. immatrikulieren (in an + Dat.) ② v.i. sich immatrikulieren

matriculation /mətrɪkjʊ'leɪʃn/ n. Immatrikulation, die

matrimonial /mætrɪ'məʊnɪəl/ adj. Ehe-

matrimony /'mætrɪmənɪ/ n. Ehestand, der

matrix /'meɪtrɪks/ n., pl. **matrices** /'meɪtrɪsiːz/ or ~**es** Matrix, die

matron /'meɪtrən/ n. (in school) ≈ Hausmutter, die; (in hospital) Oberschwester, die

matt /mæt/ adj. matt

'matted *adj.* verfilzt
matter /'mætə(r)/ **1** *n.* (a) (affair) Angelegenheit, *die;* ~s die Dinge; **money** ~s Geldangelegenheiten
(b) **it's a** ~ **of taste** das ist Geschmackssache; **[only] a** ~ **of time** [nur noch] eine Frage der Zeit
(c) **what's the** ~? was ist [los]?
(d) (physical material) Materie, *die*
2 *v.i.* etwas ausmachen; **what does it** ~? was macht das schon?; **[it] doesn't** ~: [das] macht nichts (ugs.)
'matter-of-fact *adj.* sachlich
mattress /'mætrɪs/ *n.* Matratze, *die*
mature /mə'tjʊə(r)/ **1** *adj.* reif; ausgereift ‹Stil, Käse, Portwein, Sherry›
2 *v.t.* reifen lassen
3 *v.i.* reifen
maturity /mə'tjʊərɪtɪ/ *n.* Reife, *die*
Maundy Thursday /mɔːndɪ 'θɜːzdɪ/ *n.* Gründonnerstag, *der*
mausoleum /mɔːsə'liːəm/ *n.* Mausoleum, *das*
mauve /məʊv/ *adj.* mauve
mawkish /'mɔːkɪʃ/ *adj.* rührselig
max. *abbr.* = **maximum** *(adj.)* max., *(n.)* Max.
maxim /'mæksɪm/ *n.* Maxime, *die*
maximum /'mæksɪməm/ **1** *n., pl.* maxima /'mæksɪmə/ Maximum, *das*
2 *adj.* maximal; Maximal-; ~ **speed/ temperature** Höchstgeschwindigkeit, *die/* -temperatur, *die*
'maximum-security *attrib. adj.* Hochsicherheits‹[gefängnis]trakt›
may *v. aux., only in pres.* **may,** *neg.* (coll.) **mayn't** /meɪnt,/ *past* **might** /maɪt,/ *neg.* (coll.) **mightn't** /'maɪtnt/ (a) (expr. possibility) können; **it** ~ **be true** das kann stimmen; **I** ~ **be wrong** vielleicht irre ich mich; **it** ~ **not be possible** das wird vielleicht nicht möglich sein; **he** ~ **have missed his train** vielleicht hat er seinen Zug verpasst; **it** ~ *or* **might rain** es könnte regnen; **we** ~ *or* **might as well go** wir könnten eigentlich ebenso gut [auch] gehen
(b) (expr. permission) dürfen
(c) (expr. wish) mögen; ~ **the best man win!** auf dass der Beste gewinnt!
May /meɪ/ *n.* Mai, *der; see also* AUGUST
maybe /'meɪbiː, 'meɪbɪ/ *adv.* vielleicht
'May Day *n.* der Erste Mai; **the** ~ **holiday** der Maifeiertag
'mayfly *n.* Eintagsfliege, *die*
mayhem /'meɪhem/ *n.* Chaos, *das*
mayn't /meɪnt/ (coll.) = **may not;** ▸ MAY
mayonnaise /meɪə'neɪz/ *n.* Mayonnaise, *die*
mayor /meə(r)/ *n.* Bürgermeister, *der*
mayoress /'meərɪs/ *n.* (woman mayor) Bürgermeisterin, *die;* (mayor's wife) [Ehe]frau des Bürgermeisters

maze /meɪz/ *n.* Labyrinth, *das*
MBA *abbr.* = **Master of Business Administration** Diplom in Betriebswirtschaft
me /mɪ, *stressed* miː/ *pron.* mich; *as indirect object* mir; **who, me?** wer, ich?; **not me** ich nicht; **it's me** ich bins
ME *abbr.* (Med.) = **myalgic encephalomyelitis**
meadow /'medəʊ/ *n.* Wiese, *die*
meagre /'miːgə(r)/ *adj.* dürftig
meal /miːl/ *n.* Mahlzeit, *die;* **go out for a** ~: essen gehen; **enjoy your** ~: guten Appetit!; ~**s on wheels** (Brit.) Essen auf Rädern
meal: ~ **ticket** *n.* Essenmarke, *die;* (fig. coll.) melkende Kuh (ugs.); ~**time** *n.* Essenszeit, *die;* ~ **voucher** *n.* Essenmarke, *die*
mean¹ /miːn/ *n.* (a) Mittelweg, *der*
(b) (Math.) Mittelwert, *der*
mean² *adj.* (a) (miserly) geizig
(b) (unkind) gemein
(c) (shabby) schäbig
mean³ *v.t.,* meant /ment/ (a) (intend) beabsichtigen; ~ **to do sth.** etw. tun wollen
(b) (design, destine) **be** ~**t to do sth.** etw. tun sollen
(c) (intend to convey) meinen; **I [really]** ~ **it** ich meine das ernst; **what do you** ~ **by that?** was hast du damit gemeint?
(d) (signify) bedeuten
meander /mɪ'ændə(r)/ *v.i.* (a) ‹Fluss:› sich winden
(b) ‹Person:› schlendern
'meaning *n.* Bedeutung, *die;* (of text etc., life) Sinn, *der*
meaningful /'miːnɪŋfl/ *adj.* bedeutungsvoll ‹Blick, Ergebnis›; sinnvoll ‹Aufgabe, Gespräch›
'meaningless *adj.* ‹Wort, Gespräch:› ohne Sinn; sinnlos ‹Aktivität›
means /miːnz/ *n.* (a) Möglichkeit, *die;* [Art und] Weise; **by this** ~: hierdurch; ~ **of transport** Transportmittel, *das*
(b) *pl.* (resources) Mittel *Pl.;* **live within/ beyond one's** ~: seinen Verhältnissen entsprechend/über seine Verhältnisse leben
(c) **by all** ~! selbstverständlich!; **by no [manner of]** ~: ganz und gar nicht; **by** ~ **of** durch; mit [Hilfe von]
'means test *n.* Überprüfung der Bedürftigkeit
meant ▸ MEAN³
mean: ~**time 1** *n.* **in the** ~**time** inzwischen; **2** *adv.* inzwischen; ~**while** *adv.* inzwischen
measles /'miːzlz/ *n.* Masern *Pl.*
measly /'mɪːzlɪ/ *adj.* (coll.) pop[e]lig (ugs.)
measurable /'meʒərəbl/ *adj.* messbar
measure /'meʒə(r)/ **1** *n.* (a) Maß, *das;* **for good** ~: sicherheitshalber; (as an extra) zusätzlich; **made to** ~: maßgeschneidert ⋯⧠

(b) (degree) **in some/large** ∼: in gewisser
Hinsicht/ in hohem Maße
(c) (for measuring) Maß, *das*
(d) (step) Maßnahme, *die;* **take** ∼**s**
Maßnahmen treffen
2 *v.t.* messen ⟨*Größe, Menge usw.*⟩;
ausmessen ⟨*Raum*⟩
3 *v.i.* messen
■ **measure 'up to** *v.t.* entsprechen
(+ *Dat.*)
'measured /'meʒəd/ *adj.* gemessen
⟨*Schritt, Worte*⟩
'measurement *n.* **(a)** Messung, *die*
(b) (dimension) Maß, *das*
'measuring tape *n.* Bandmaß, *das*
meat /miːt/ *n.* Fleisch, *das*
'meaty *adj.* **(a)** fleischig
(b) (fig.) gehaltvoll
mechanic /mɪˈkænɪk/ *n.* Mechaniker,
der/Mechanikerin, *die*
mechanical /mɪˈkænɪkl/ *adj.*
mechanisch
mechanical engi'neering *n.*
Maschinenbau, *der*
me'chanically *adv.* mechanisch
mechanical 'pencil *n.* (Amer.)
Drehbleistift, *der*
me'chanics *n.* **(a)** Mechanik, *die*
(b) *pl.* (mechanism) Mechanismus, *der*
mechanism /'mekənɪzm/ *n.*
Mechanismus, *der*
mechanization /mekənaɪˈzeɪʃn/ *n.*
Mechanisierung, *die*
mechanize /'mekənaɪz/ *v.t.*
mechanisieren
medal /'medl/ *n.* Medaille, *die;* (decoration)
Orden, *der*
medallion /mɪˈdæljən/ *n.* [große] Medaille
medallist /'medəlɪst/ *n.*
Medaillengewinner, *der*/-gewinnerin, *die*
meddle /'medl/ *v.i.* ∼ **with sth.** sich (*Dat.*)
an etw. (*Dat.*) zu schaffen machen; ∼ **in sth.**
sich in etw. (*Akk.*) einmischen
media /'miːdɪə/ ▶ MASS MEDIA; MEDIUM 1
mediaeval ▶ MEDIEVAL
'media studies *n. sing.*
Medienwissenschaft, *die;* (school subject)
Medienkunde, *die*
mediate /'miːdɪeɪt/ *v.i.* vermitteln
mediator /'miːdɪeɪtə(r)/ *n.* Vermittler,
der/Vermittlerin, *die*
medical /'medɪkl/ *adj.* medizinisch;
ärztlich ⟨*Behandlung, Untersuchung*⟩
medical: ∼ **certificate** *n.* Attest,
das; ∼ **exami'nation** *n.* ärztliche
Untersuchung; ∼ **'history** *n.* (of person)
Krankengeschichte, *die;* ∼ **insurance**
n. Krankenversicherung, *die;* **have**
∼ **insurance** krankenversichert sein;
∼ **prac'titioner** *n.* praktischer
Arzt/praktische Ärztin; ∼ **report** *n.*
medizinisches Gutachten; ∼ **school** *n.*

medizinische Hochschule; ∼ **student** *n.*
Medizinstudent, *der*/-studentin *die*
medicament /mɪˈdɪkəmənt,
'medɪkəmənt/ *n.* Medikament, *das*
Medicare /'medɪkeə(r)/ *n.*
(Amer.) *[bundes]staatliches
Krankenversicherungssystem für Personen
über 65 Jahre*
medicated /'medɪkeɪtɪd/ *adj.* medizinisch
medication /medɪˈkeɪʃn/ *n.* (medicine)
Medikament, *das*
medicinal /mɪˈdɪsɪnl/ *adj.* medizinisch
medicine /'medsən, 'medɪsɪn/ *n.*
(a) (science) Medizin, *die*
(b) (preparation) Medikament, *das*
'medicine chest *n.*
Medikamentenschränkchen, *das;* (in home)
Hausapotheke, *die*
medieval /medɪˈiːvl/ *adj.* mittelalterlich
mediocre /miːdɪˈəʊkə(r)/ *adj.*
mittelmäßig
mediocrity /miːdɪˈɒkrɪtɪ/ *n.*
Mittelmäßigkeit, *die*
meditate /'medɪteɪt/ *v.i.* nachdenken, (esp.
Relig.) meditieren ([up]on über + *Akk.*)
meditation /medɪˈteɪʃn/ *n.* **(a)** (act)
Nachdenken, *das*
(b) (Relig.) Meditation, *die*
Mediterranean /medɪtəˈreɪnɪən/ *pr. n.*
the ∼: das Mittelmeer
medium /'miːdɪəm/ **1** *n., pl.* media
/'miːdɪə/ *or* ∼**s (a)** (substance) Medium, *das*
(b) (means) Mittel, *das;* **by** *or* **through the**
∼ **of** durch
(c) *pl.* ∼**s** (Spiritualism) Medium, *das*
(d) *in pl.* media (mass media) Medien *Pl.*
2 *adj.* mittler ...; medium *nur präd.* ⟨*Steak*⟩
medium: ∼**-range** *adj.*
Mittelstrecken-⟨*flugzeug, -rakete*⟩;
∼**-size[d]** *adj.* mittelgroß
medley /'medlɪ/ *n.* **(a)** buntes Gemisch
(b) (Mus.) Potpourri, *das*
meek /miːk/ *adj.* **(a)** (humble) sanftmütig
(b) (submissive) zu nachgiebig
meet /miːt/ **1** *v.t.,* met /met/ **(a)** treffen;
(collect) abholen
(b) (make the acquaintance of) kennen lernen;
pleased to ∼ **you** [sehr] angenehm
(c) (experience) stoßen auf (+ *Akk.*)
⟨*Widerstand, Problem*⟩
(d) (satisfy) entsprechen (+ *Dat.*) ⟨*Wunsch,
Bedürfnis, Kritik*⟩; einhalten ⟨*Termin,
Zeitplan*⟩
(e) (pay) decken ⟨*Kosten*⟩; bezahlen
⟨*Rechnung*⟩
2 *v.i.,* met **(a)** (by chance) sich (*Dat.*)
begegnen; (by arrangement) sich treffen; **we've
met before wir kennen uns bereits**
(b) ⟨*Komitee, Ausschuss usw.*⟩ tagen
■ **meet 'up** *v.i.* sich treffen; ∼ **up with sb.**
(coll.) sich treffen
■ **'meet with** *v.t.* **(a)** begegnen (+ *Dat.*)
(b) (experience) haben ⟨*Erfolg, Unfall*⟩; stoßen

m

auf (+ *Akk*.) ⟨*Widerstand*⟩

'**meeting** *n*. **(a)** Begegnung, *die;* (by arrangement) Treffen, *das* **(b)** (assembly) Versammlung, *die;* (of committee etc.) Sitzung, *die*

'**meeting place** *n*. Treffpunkt, *der*

mega /'megə/ (coll.) **1** *adj*. **(a)** (enormous) Mega- (Jugendspr.) **(b)** (excellent) geil (Jugendspr.) **2** *adv*. äußerst; **be ~ rich** super- *od*. (Jugendspr.) megareich sein

'**megabyte** *n*. (Comp.) Megabyte, *das*

megalomania /megələ'meɪnɪə/ *n*. Größenwahn, *der*

megaphone /'megəfəʊn/ *n*. Megaphon, *das*

melancholic /melən'kɒlɪk/ *adj*. melancholisch

melancholy /'melənkəlɪ/ **1** *n*. Melancholie, *die* **2** *adj*. melancholisch

mellow /'meləʊ/ **1** *adj*. **(a)** (softened by age or experience) abgeklärt **(b)** (ripe, well-matured) reif **2** *v.i.* reifen

melodic /mɪ'lɒdɪk/, **melodious** /mɪ'ləʊdɪəs/ *adjs.*, **me'lodiously** *adv*. melodisch

melodrama /'melədrɑːmə/ *n*. Melodrama, *das*

melodramatic /melədrə'mætɪk/ *adj*. melodramatisch

melody /'melədɪ/ *n*. Melodie, *die*

melon /'melən/ *n*. Melone, *die*

melt /melt/ **1** *v.i.* schmelzen **2** *v.t.* schmelzen; zerlassen ⟨*Butter*⟩ ■ **melt a'way** *v.i.* [weg]schmelzen ■ **melt 'down 1** *v.i.* schmelzen **2** *v.t.* einschmelzen

'**meltdown** *n*. **(a)** Schmelzen, *das* **(b)** (Finance) Einbruch, *der*

melting: ~ point *n*. Schmelzpunkt, *der;* **~ pot** *n*. (fig.) Schmelztiegel, *der*

member /'membə(r)/ *n*. **(a)** Mitglied, *das;* **be a ~:** Mitglied sein; **~ of a/the family** Familienangehörige, *der/die* **(b)** M~ **[of Parliament]** (Brit.) Abgeordnete [des Unterhauses], *der/die*

'**membership** *n*. **(a)** Mitgliedschaft, *die* (of in + *Dat*.) **(b)** (number of members) Mitgliederzahl, *die* **(c)** (members) Mitglieder *Pl*.

'**member state** *n*. Mitglied[s]staat, *der*

membrane /'membreɪn/ *n*. (Biol.) Membran, *die*

memento /mɪ'mentəʊ/ *n*., *pl*. ~**es** *or* ~**s** Andenken, *das* (of an + *Akk*.)

memo /'meməʊ/ *n*., *pl*. ~**s** (coll.) ▶ MEMORANDUM

memoirs /'memwɑːz/ *n. pl*. Memoiren *Pl*.

memorable /'memərəbl/ *adj*. denkwürdig ⟨*Ereignis, Tag*⟩; unvergesslich ⟨*Film, Buch,*

Aufführung⟩

memorandum /memə'rændəm/ *n*., *pl*. **memoranda** /memə'rændə/ *or* ~**s** Mitteilung, *die*

memorial /mɪ'mɔːrɪəl/ **1** *adj*. Gedenk- **2** *n*. Denkmal, *das* (**to** für)

memorize /'meməraɪz/ *v.t.* sich (*Dat*.) merken *od*. einprägen; (learn by heart) auswendig lernen

memory /'memərɪ/ *n*. **(a)** Gedächtnis, *das* **(b)** (thing remembered, act of remembering) Erinnerung, *die* (**of** an + *Akk*.); **from ~:** aus dem Gedächtnis; **in ~ of** zur Erinnerung an (+ *Akk*.) **(c)** (Comp.) Speicher, *der*

memory: ~ bank *n*. Speicherbank, *die;* **~ stick** *n*. (Comp.) Memorystick, *der;* Speicherstab, *der*

men *pl. of* MAN

menace /'menəs/ **1** *v.t.* bedrohen **2** *n*. Plage, *die*

menacing /'menəsɪŋ/ *adj*. drohend

mend /mend/ **1** *v.t.* reparieren; ausbessern ⟨*Kleidung*⟩; kleben ⟨*Glas, Porzellan*⟩ **2** *v.i.* ⟨*Knochen, Bein usw.:*⟩ heilen **3** *n*. **be on the ~:** auf dem Wege der Besserung sein

'**menfolk** *n. pl*. Männer *Pl*.

menial /'miːnɪəl/ *adj*. niedrig; untergeordnet ⟨*Aufgabe*⟩

meningitis /menɪn'dʒaɪtɪs/ *n*. Hirnhautentzündung, *die*

menopause /'menəpɔːz/ *n*. Wechseljahre *Pl*.

menstrual /'menstrʊəl/ *adj*. menstrual (fachspr.)

menstruate /'menstrʊeɪt/ *v.i.* menstruieren

menstruation /menstrʊ'eɪʃn/ *n*. Menstruation, *die*

menswear /'menzweə(r)/ *n*. Herrenbekleidung, *die*

mental /'mentl/ *adj*. **(a)** (of the mind) geistig; Geistes⟨*zustand, -störung*⟩ **(b)** (Brit. coll.: mad) verrückt (salopp)

mental: ~ a'rithmetic *n*. Kopfrechnen, *das;* **~ 'health** *n*. seelische Gesundheit; **~ hospital** *n*. Nervenklinik, *die* (ugs.); **~ 'illness** *n*. Geisteskrankheit, *die*

mentality /men'tælɪtɪ/ *n*. Mentalität, *die*

'**mentally** *adv*. geistig

mention /'menʃn/ **1** *n*. Erwähnung, *die* **2** *v.t.* erwähnen (**to** gegenüber); **don't ~ it** keine Ursache

menu /'menjuː/ *n*. **(a)** [Speise]karte, *die* **(b)** (Comp., Telev.) Menü, *das*

'**menu bar** *n*. (Comp.) Menüleiste, *die*

mercenary /'mɜːsɪnərɪ/ **1** *adj*. gewinnsüchtig **2** *n*. Söldner, *der*

merchandise /'mɜːtʃəndaɪz/ *n*. [Handels]ware, *die*

merchant /'mɜːtʃənt/ n. Kaufmann, der
merchant: ∼ 'bank n. Handelsbank,
die; ∼ 'navy n. (Brit.) Handelsmarine, die
merciful /'mɜːsɪfl/ adj. gnädig
mercifully /'mɜːsɪfəlɪ/ adv. (fortunately)
glücklicherweise
merciless /'mɜːsɪlɪs/ adj.,
'**mercilessly** adv. gnadenlos
mercury /'mɜːkjʊrɪ/ 1 n. Quecksilber,
das
2 pr. n. M∼ (Astron.) Merkur, der
mercy /'mɜːsɪ/ n. Erbarmen, das (on
mit); show sb. [no] ∼: mit jmdm. [kein]
Erbarmen haben; be at the ∼ of sb./sth.
jmdm./einer Sache [auf Gedeih und
Verderb] ausgeliefert sein
mere /mɪə(r)/ adj., '**merely** adv. bloß
merge /mɜːdʒ/ 1 v.t. (a) (combine)
zusammenschließen
(b) (blend gradually) verschmelzen (with mit)
2 v.i. (a) (combine) fusionieren (with mit)
(b) ⟨Straße:⟩ zusammenlaufen (with mit)
merger /'mɜːdʒə(r)/ n. Fusion, die
meringue /mə'ræŋ/ n. Meringe, die;
Baiser, das
merit /'merɪt/ 1 n. (a) (worth) Verdienst,
das
(b) (good feature) Vorzug, der
2 v.t. verdienen
mermaid /'mɜːmeɪd/ n. Nixe, die
merrily /'merɪlɪ/ adv. munter
merriment /'merɪmənt/ n. Fröhlichkeit,
die
merry /'merɪ/ adj. fröhlich; ∼ Christmas!
frohe od. fröhliche Weihnachten!
'**merry-go-round** n. Karussell, das
'**merrymaking** n. Feiern, das
mesh /meʃ/ n. (a) Masche, die
(b) (netting; also fig.: network) Geflecht, das; wire
∼: Maschendraht, der
mesmerize /'mezməraɪz/ v.t. faszinieren
mess /mes/ n. (a) (dirty/untidy state) [be]
a ∼ or in a ∼: schmutzig/unaufgeräumt
[sein]; what a ∼! was für ein Dreck
(ugs.)/Durcheinander!
(b) (bad state) be [in] a ∼: sich in einem
schlimmen Zustand befinden; ⟨Person:⟩
schlimm dran sein; get into a ∼: in
Schwierigkeiten geraten; make a ∼ of
verpfuschen (ugs.) ⟨Arbeit, Leben⟩
(c) (Mil.) Kasino, das
■ **mess a'bout, mess a'round**
1 v.i. (potter) herumwerken; (fool about)
herumalbern
2 v.t. ∼ sb. about or around mit jmdm.
nach Belieben umspringen
■ **mess 'up** v.t. (a) (make dirty) schmutzig
machen; (make untidy) in Unordnung bringen
(b) (bungle) ∼ it/things up Mist bauen (ugs.)
message /'mesɪdʒ/ n. Nachricht, die; give
sb. a ∼: jmdm. etwas ausrichten

messenger /'mesɪndʒə(r)/ n. Bote,
der/Botin, die
Messiah /mɪ'saɪə/ n. Messias, der
Messrs /'mesəz/ n. pl. (a) (in name of firm)
≈ Fa.
(b) pl. of MR; (in list of names) ∼ A and B die
Herren A und B
'**messy** adj. (dirty) schmutzig; (untidy)
unordentlich
met ▸ MEET
metabolism /mɪ'tæbəlɪzm/ n.
Stoffwechsel, der
metal /'metl/ 1 n. Metall, das
2 adj. Metall-
'**metal detector** n. Metallsuchgerät, das
metallic /mɪ'tælɪk/ adj. metallisch; have a
∼ taste nach Metall schmecken
metallurgy /mɪ'tælədʒɪ/ n. Metallurgie,
die
'**metalwork** n. (products) Metallarbeiten Pl.
metamorphosis /metə'mɔːfəsɪs/
n., pl. **metamorphoses** /metə'mɔːfəsiːz/
Metamorphose, die
metaphor /'metəfə(r)/ n. Metapher, die
metaphorical /metə'fɒrɪkl/ adj.,
metaphorically /metə'fɒrɪkəlɪ/ adv.
metaphorisch
meteor /'miːtɪə(r)/ n. Meteor, der
meteoric /miːtɪ'ɒrɪk/ adj. (fig.)
kometenhaft
meteorological /miːtɪərə'lɒdʒɪkl/ adj.
meteorologisch ⟨Instrument⟩; Wetter⟨ballon,
-bericht⟩
meteorologist /miːtɪə'rɒlədʒɪst/ n.
Meteorologe, der/Meteorologin, die
meteorology /miːtɪə'rɒlədʒɪ/ n.
Meteorologie, die
meter[1] /'miːtə(r)/ n. (a) Zähler, der; (for
coins) Münzzähler, der
(b) (parking ∼) Parkuhr, die
meter[2] (Amer.) ▸ METRE[1, 2]
methane /'miːθeɪn/ n. Methan, das
method /'meθəd/ n. Methode, die
methodical /mɪ'θɒdɪkl/ adj.,
me'thodically adv. systematisch
Methodist /'meθədɪst/ n. Methodist,
der/Methodistin, die
meths /meθs/ n. (Brit. coll.) [Brenn]spiritus,
der
methylated spirit[s] /meθɪleɪtɪd
'spɪrɪt(s)/ n. [pl.] Brennspiritus, der
meticulous /mɪ'tɪkjʊləs/ adj.,
me'ticulously adv. (scrupulous[ly])
sorgfältig; (overscrupulous[ly]) übergenau
metre[1] /'miːtə/ n. (Brit.: poetic rhythm)
Metrum, das
metre[2] n. (Brit.: unit) Meter, der od. das
metric /'metrɪk/ adj. metrisch; ∼ system
metrisches System
metrication /metrɪ'keɪʃn/ n. Umstellung
auf das metrische System

metro /'metrəʊ/ n., pl. ~s U-Bahn, die; the Paris M~ die [Pariser] Metro

metronome /'metrənəʊm/ n. Metronom, das

metropolis /mɪ'trɒpəlɪs/ n. Metropole, die

metropolitan /metrə'pɒlɪtən/ adj. ~ New York der Großraum New York; ~ London Großlondon (das)

Mexican /'meksɪkən/ [1] adj. mexikanisch; **sb. is** ~: jmd. ist Mexikaner/ Mexikanerin
[2] n. Mexikaner, der/Mexikanerin, die

Mexico /'meksɪkəʊ/ pr. n. Mexiko (das)

miaow /mɪ'aʊ/ [1] v.i. miauen
[2] n. Miauen, das

mice pl. of MOUSE

microbe /'maɪkrəʊb/ n. Mikrobe, die

micro /'maɪkrəʊ/: ~**chip** n. Mikrochip, der; ~**computer** n. Mikrocomputer, der; ~**dot** n. Mikrat, das; ~**fibre** n. Mikrofaser, die; ~**fiche** n. Mikrofiche, das od. der; ~**film** [1] n. Mikrofilm, der; [2] v.t. auf Mikrofilm aufnehmen; ~**light** ['aircraft] n. Ultraleichtflugzeug, das

microphone /'maɪkrəfəʊn/ n. Mikrofon, das

microprocessor /maɪkrəʊ'prəʊsesə(r)/ n. Mikroprozessor, der

microscope /'maɪkrəskəʊp/ n. Mikroskop, das

microscopic /maɪkrə'skɒpɪk/ adj. mikroskopisch; (fig.: very small) winzig

'**microwave** n. Mikrowelle, die; ~ [oven] Mikrowellenherd, der

mid- /mɪd/ in comb. in ~-air in der Luft; in ~-sentence mitten im Satz; ~-July Mitte Juli; the ~-60s die Mitte der Sechzigerjahre; a man in his ~-fifties ein Mittfünfziger; be in one's ~-thirties Mitte dreißig sein

midday /'mɪddeɪ, mɪd'deɪ/ n. (a) (noon) zwölf Uhr
(b) (middle of day) Mittag, der; attrib. Mittags-

middle /'mɪdl/ [1] attrib. adj. mittler...
[2] n. (a) Mitte, die; in the ~ of the forest/ night mitten im Wald/in der Nacht
(b) (waist) Taille, die

middle: ~ '**age** n. mittleres [Lebens]alter; ~-**aged** /'mɪdleɪdʒd/ adj. mittleren Alters nachgestellt; **M~** '**Ages** n. pl. the M~ Ages das Mittelalter; ~ '**class** n. Mittelstand, der; ~-**class** adj. bürgerlich; **M~** '**East** pr. n. the M~ East der Nahe [und Mittlere] Osten; **M~** '**Eastern** adj. nahöstlich; ~**man** n. (Commerc.) Zwischenhändler, der/-händlerin, die; (fig.) Vermittler, der/Vermittlerin, die; ~ '**management** n. mittleres Management; ~ **name** n. zweiter Vorname

middling /'mɪdlɪŋ/ adj. mittelmäßig

'**midfield** n. (Footb.) Mittelfeld, das

midge /mɪdʒ/ n. Stechmücke, die

midget /'mɪdʒɪt/ [1] n. Liliputaner, der/Liliputanerin, die
[2] adj. winzig

Midlands /'mɪdləndz/ n. pl. the ~ (Brit.) Mittelengland, das

midlife crisis /mɪdlaɪf 'kraɪsɪs/ n. Midlifecrisis, die

'**midnight** n. Mitternacht, die

'**midpoint** n. Mitte, die

midriff /'mɪdrɪf/ n. Bauch, der

midst /mɪdst/ n. in the ~ of sth. mitten in einer Sache; in our/their/your ~: in unserer/ihrer/eurer Mitte

midsummer /'---, -'--/ n. die [Zeit der] Sommersonnenwende

midway /'--, -'-/ adv. auf halbem Weg[e] ⟨sich treffen, sich befinden⟩

midweek /'mɪdwiːk, mɪd'wiːk/ n. in ~: in der Wochenmitte

'**midwife** n., pl. '**midwives** Hebamme, die

midwifery /'mɪdwɪfrɪ, mɪd'wɪfərɪ/ n., no art. Geburtshilfe, die

mid'winter n. die [Zeit der] Wintersonnenwende

might¹ ▶ MAY

might² /maɪt/ n. (a) (force) Gewalt, die
(b) (power) Macht, die

mightn't /'maɪtnt/ (coll.) = might not; ▶ MAY

mighty /'maɪtɪ/ [1] adj. mächtig
[2] adv. (coll.) verdammt (ugs.)

migraine /'miːɡreɪn/ n. Migräne, die

migrant /'maɪɡrənt/ n. (a) Auswanderer, der/Auswanderin, die
(b) (bird) Zugvogel, der

migrate /maɪ'ɡreɪt/ v.i. (a) (to a town) abwandern; (to another country) auswandern
(b) ⟨Vogel:⟩ fortziehen

migration /maɪ'ɡreɪʃn/ n. (a) (to a town) Abwandern, das; (to another country) Auswandern, das
(b) (of birds) Zug, der

migratory /maɪ'ɡreɪtərɪ/ adj. ~ bird/fish Zugvogel, der/Wanderfisch, der

mike /maɪk/ n. (coll.) Mikro, das

Milan /mɪ'læn/ pr. n. Mailand (das)

mild /maɪld/ adj. mild; sanft ⟨Person⟩

mildew /'mɪldjuː/ n. (a) Schimmel, der
(b) (on plant) Mehltau, der

'**mildly** adv. (a) (gently) mild[e]
(b) (slightly) ein bisschen
(c) **to put it** ~: gelinde gesagt

mile /maɪl/ n. (a) Meile, die
(b) (fig. coll.) ~s better/too big tausendmal besser/viel zu groß; be ~s ahead of sb. jmdm. weit voraus sein

mileage /'maɪlɪdʒ/ n. [Anzahl der] Meilen Pl.; a low ~: ein niedriger Meilenstand

'**milestone** n. Meilenstein, der

militant /'mɪlɪtənt/ [1] adj. militant
[2] n. Militante, der/die

militaristic /mɪlɪtə'rɪstɪk/ *adj.*
militaristisch

military /'mɪlɪtərɪ/ **1** *adj.* militärisch;
Militär⟨regierung, -akademie, -uniform,
-parade⟩; ~ **service** Militärdienst, *der*
2 *n.* the ~: das Militär

militate /'mɪlɪteɪt/ *v.i.* ~ **against/in favour
of** sth. [deutlich] gegen/für etw. sprechen

militia /mɪ'lɪʃə/ *n.* Miliz, *die*

milk /mɪlk/ **1** *n.* Milch, *die*
2 *v.t.* melken

milk: ~ **bottle** *n.* Milchflasche, *die;*
~ **'chocolate** *n.* Milchschokolade, *die;*
~ **float** *n.* (Brit.) Milchwagen, *der*

milking /'mɪlkɪŋ/ *n.* Melken, *das*

milk: ~ **jug** *n.* Milchkännchen,
das; ~**man** /'mɪlkmən/ *n., pl.* ~**men**
/'mɪlkmən/ Milchmann, *der;* ~ **shake** *n.*
Milchshake, *der;* ~ **tooth** *n.* Milchzahn,
der

'milky *adj.* milchig

Milky 'Way *n.* Milchstraße, *die*

mill /mɪl/ **1** *n.* (a) Mühle, *die*
(b) (factory) Fabrik, *die*
2 *v.t.* (a) mahlen ⟨Getreide⟩
(b) fräsen ⟨Metallgegenstand⟩

mill a'bout (Brit.), **mill a'round** *v.i.*
durcheinander laufen

millennium /mɪ'lenɪəm/ *n., pl.* ~**s** or
millennia /mɪ'lenɪə/ Jahrtausend, *das;*
Millennium, *das*

mil'lennium bug *n.* (Comp.)
Jahrtausendvirus, *der od. das*

'miller *n.* Müller, *der*

millet /'mɪlɪt/ *n.* Hirse, *die*

milligram /'mɪlɪgræm/ *n.* Milligramm, *das*

millilitre (*Brit.; Amer.:* **milliliter**)
/'mɪlɪliːtə(r)/ *n.* Milliliter, *der od. das*

millimetre (*Brit.; Amer.:* **millimeter**)
/'mɪlɪmiːtə(r)/ *n.* Millimeter, *der*

milliner /'mɪlɪnə(r)/ *n.* Modist, *der/*
Modistin, *die*

'millinery *n.* Hutmacherei, *die*

million /'mɪljən/ **1** *adj.* a or one/two
~: eine Million/zwei Millionen; **half a**
~: eine halbe Million
2 *n.* (a) Million, *die*
(b) (indefinite amount) ~**s of people** eine
Unmenge Leute

millionaire /mɪljə'neə(r)/ *n.* Millionär,
*der/*Millionärin, *die*

millionth /'mɪljənθ/ **1** *adj.* millionst...
2 *n.* (fraction) Millionstel, *das*

'millstone *n.* Mühlstein, *der*

mime /maɪm/ **1** *n.* (a) (performance)
Pantomime, *die*
(b) (art) Pantomimik, *die*
2 *v.i.* pantomimisch agieren
3 *v.t.* pantomimisch darstellen

mimic /'mɪmɪk/ **1** *n.* Imitator, *der*
2 *v.t.*, -**ck**- nachahmen

min. *abbr.* (a) = **minute[s]** Min.

(b) = **minimum** (*adj.*) mind., (*n.*) Min.

mince /mɪns/ **1** *n.* Hackfleisch, *das*
2 *v.t.* durch den [Fleisch]wolf drehen
⟨Fleisch⟩

'mincemeat *n.* (a) Hackfleisch, *das*
(b) (sweet) *süße Pastetenfüllung aus Obst,
Rosinen, Gewürzen, Nierenfett usw.*

mince 'pie *n.: mit süßem „mincemeat"
gefüllte Pastete*

'mincer *n.* Fleischwolf, *der*

mind /maɪnd/ **1** *n.* (a) Geist, *der*
(b) (remembrance) **bear** or **keep** sth. **in** ~: an
etw. (*Akk.*) denken; **have [got]** sb./sth. **in**
~: an jmdn./etw. denken
(c) (opinion) **give** sb. **a piece of one's**
~: jmdm. gründlich die Meinung sagen; **to
my** ~: meiner Meinung *od.* Ansicht nach;
change one's ~: seine Meinung ändern;
I have a good ~ **to do that** ich hätte große
Lust, das zu tun; **make up one's** ~, **make
one's** ~ **up** sich entscheiden
(d) ([normal] mental powers) Verstand, *der;*
be out of one's ~: den Verstand verloren
haben
(e) frame of ~: [seelische] Verfassung
2 *v.t.* (a) **I can't afford a bicycle, never
** ~ **a car** ich kann mir kein Fahrrad leisten,
geschweige denn ein Auto; **we've got some
decorations up, - not many,** ~ **you** wir
haben etwas dekoriert, allerdings nicht viel
(b) *usu. neg. or interrog.* (object to) **would you
** ~ **opening the door?** würdest du bitte die
Tür öffnen?; **I wouldn't** ~ **a walk** ich hätte
nichts gegen einen Spaziergang
(c) (take care) ~ **you don't go too near the
cliff edge!** pass auf, dass du nicht zu nah an
den Felsenrand gehst!; ~ **how you go!** pass
auf!
(d) (have charge of) aufpassen auf (+ *Akk.*)
3 *v.i.* (a) ~! Vorsicht!; Achtung!
(b) (care, object) **do you** ~ **if I smoke?** stört es
Sie, wenn ich rauche?
(c) never ~ (it's not important) macht nichts
■ **mind 'out** *v.i.* aufpassen (**for** auf + *Akk.*);
~ **out!** Vorsicht!

mind: ~-**bending**, (coll.) ~-**blowing**
adjs. bewusstseinsverändernd;
~-**boggling** /'maɪndbɒglɪŋ/ *adj.* (coll.)
wahnsinnig (ugs.)

'minded *adj.* **mechanically** ~: technisch
veranlagt; **not politically** ~: unpolitisch

minder /'maɪndə(r)/ *n.* (a) (for child)
we need a ~ **for the child** wir brauchen
jemanden, der auf das Kind aufpasst *od.* das
Kind betreut
(b) (sl.: protector of criminal) Gorilla, *der* (salopp)

mindful /'maɪndfl/ *adj.* **be** ~ **of** sth. etw.
berücksichtigen

'mindless *adj.* geistlos ⟨Person⟩; sinnlos
⟨Gewalt⟩

mine¹ /maɪn/ *n.* (a) Bergwerk, *das*
(b) (explosive) Mine, *die*

mine² *poss. pron. pred.* meiner/meine/
mein[e]s; *see also* HERS

mine: ~**-detector** *n.* Minensuchgerät, *das;* ~**field** *n.* Minenfeld, *das*

'**miner** *n.* Bergmann, *der*

mineral /'mɪnərl/ ① *adj.* mineralisch; Mineral‹*salz, -quelle*›
② *n.* (a) Mineral, *das*
(b) (Brit.: soft drink) Erfrischungsgetränk, *das*

'**mineral water** *n.* Mineralwasser, *das*

minesweeper /'maɪnswiːpə(r)/ *n.* Minensuchboot, *das*

mingle /'mɪŋgl/ ① *v.t.* [ver]mischen
② *v.i.* sich [ver]mischen (**with** mit)

mini /'mɪnɪ/ *n.* (coll.) (a) (car) M~ ® Mini, *der*
(b) (skirt) Mini, *der* (ugs.)

mini- /'mɪnɪ/ *in comb.* Mini-; Klein‹*bus, -wagen, -taxi*›

miniature /'mɪnɪtʃə(r)/ ① *n.* (picture) Miniatur, *die*
② *adj.* Miniatur-

mini: ~**bus** *n.* Kleinbus, *der;* ~**cab** *n.* Minicar, *das*

minim /'mɪnɪm/ *n.* (Brit. Mus.) halbe Note

minimal /'mɪnɪml/ *adj.* minimal

minimize /'mɪnɪmaɪz/ *v.t.* (a) (reduce) auf ein Mindestmaß reduzieren
(b) (understate) bagatellisieren

minimum /'mɪnɪməm/ ① *n., pl.* **minima** /'mɪnɪmə/ Minimum, *das* (**of** an + *Dat.*)
② *attrib. adj.* Mindest-

minimum: ~ '**lending rate** *n.:* Mindestausleihsatz [*der Bank von England*]; ≈ Mindestdiskontsatz, *der;* ~ '**wage** *n.* Mindestlohn, *der*

mining /'maɪnɪŋ/ *n.* Bergbau, *der;* attrib. Bergbau-

mining: ~ **industry** *n.* Bergbau, *der;* ~ **town** *n.* Bergbaustadt, *die*

minion /'mɪnjən/ *n.* Lakai, *der*

mini: ~ **roundabout** *n.* (Brit.) sehr kleiner, oft nur aufs Pflaster aufgezeichneter Kreisverkehr; ~**skirt** *n.* Minirock, *der*

minister /'mɪnɪstə(r)/ ① *n.* (a) (Polit.) Minister, *der*/Ministerin, *die*
(b) (Eccl.) Geistliche, *der*/*die;* Pfarrer, *der*/Pfarrerin, *die*
② *v.i.* ~ **to sb.** sich um jmdn. kümmern

ministerial /mɪnɪ'stɪərɪəl/ *adj.* (Polit.) Minister-; ministeriell

ministry /'mɪnɪstrɪ/ *n.* (a) (Polit.) Ministerium, *das*
(b) (Eccl.) geistliches Amt

mink /mɪŋk/ *n.* Nerz, *der*

minnow /'mɪnəʊ/ *n.* Elritze, *die*

minor /'maɪnə(r)/ ① *adj.* (a) (lesser) kleiner…
(b) (unimportant) weniger bedeutend; (not serious) leicht; ~ **road** kleine Straße
(c) (Mus.) Moll-; **A** ~: a-Moll
② *n.* Minderjährige, *der*/*die*

minority /maɪ'nɒrɪtɪ, mɪ'nɒrɪtɪ/ *n.* Minderheit, *die;* **in the** ~: in der Minderheit

minstrel /'mɪnstrl/ *n.* fahrender Sänger

mint[1] /mɪnt/ ① *n.* (place) Münzanstalt, *die*
② *adj.* funkelnagelneu (ugs.); **in** ~ **condition** in tadellosem Zustand
③ *v.t.* prägen

mint[2] *n.* (a) (plant) Minze, *die*
(b) (peppermint) Pfefferminz, *das; attrib.* Pfefferminz-

mint 'sauce *n.* Minzsoße, *die*

minuet /mɪnjʊ'et/ *n.* Menuett, *das*

minus /'maɪnəs/ *prep.* minus; weniger; (without) abzüglich (+ *Gen.*)

minuscule /'mɪnəskjuːl/ *adj.* winzig

minute[1] /'mɪnɪt/ *n.* (a) Minute, *die;* (moment) Moment, *der*
(b) ~**s** (of meeting) Protokoll, *das;* **take the** ~**s of a meeting** bei einer Sitzung [das] Protokoll führen

minute[2] /maɪ'njuːt/ *adj.* (tiny) winzig

minute hand /'mɪnɪthænd/ *n.* Minutenzeiger, *der;* großer Zeiger

minutiae /maɪ'njuːʃiː, mɪ'njuːʃiː/ *n. pl.* Details *Pl.*

miracle /'mɪrəkl/ *n.* Wunder, *das*

miraculous /mɪ'rækjʊləs/ *adj.* wunderbar

mirage /'mɪrɑːʒ/ *n.* Fata Morgana, *die*

mire /maɪə(r)/ *n.* Morast, *der*

mirror /'mɪrə(r)/ ① *n.* Spiegel, *der*
② *v.t.* [wider]spiegeln

mirror 'image *n.* Spiegelbild, *das*

misadventure /mɪsəd'ventʃə(r)/ *n.* Missgeschick, *das*

misanthropist /mɪ'zænθrəpɪst/ *ns.* Misanthrop, *der* (geh.); Menschenfeind, *der*

misanthropy /mɪ'zænθrəpɪ/ *n.* Menschenfeindlichkeit, *die*

misapprehension /mɪsæprɪ'henʃn/ *n.* Missverständnis, *das;* **be under a** ~: einem Irrtum unterliegen

misbehave /mɪsbɪ'heɪv/ *v.i. & refl.* sich schlecht benehmen

misbehaviour (*Amer.:* **misbehavior**) /mɪsbɪ'heɪvjə(r)/ *n.* schlechtes Benehmen

miscalculate /mɪs'kælkjʊleɪt/
① *v.t.* falsch berechnen; (misjudge) falsch einschätzen
② *v.i.* sich verrechnen

miscalculation /mɪskælkjʊ'leɪʃn/ *n.* Rechenfehler, *der;* (misjudgement) Fehleinschätzung, *die*

miscarriage /mɪs'kærɪdʒ/ *n.*
(a) Fehlgeburt, *die*
(b) ~ **of justice** Justizirrtum, *der*

miscarry /mɪs'kærɪ/ *v.i.* (a) (Med.) eine Fehlgeburt haben
(b) ‹*Plan, Vorhaben usw.*› fehlschlagen

miscellaneous /mɪsə'leɪnɪəs/ *adj.*
(a) [kunter]bunt
(b) *with pl. n.* verschieden

miscellany /mɪ'selənɪ/ *n.* [bunte] Sammlung; [buntes] Gemisch

mischief /'mɪstʃɪf/ n. (a) Unfug, der; get up to ∼: etwas anstellen
(b) (harm) Schaden, der
mischievous /'mɪstʃɪvəs/ adj. spitzbübisch; schelmisch
misconception /mɪskən'sepʃn/ n. falsche Vorstellung (about von); be [labouring] under a ∼ about sth. sich (Dat.) eine falsche Vorstellung von etw. machen
misconduct /mɪs'kɒndʌkt/ n. unkorrektes Verhalten
misconstrue /mɪskən'stru:/ v.t. missverstehen
miscount /mɪs'kaʊnt/ 1 v.i. sich verzählen
2 v.t. falsch zählen
misdeed /mɪs'di:d/ n. Missetat, die (veralt., scherzh.)
misdemeanour ⟨Amer.: **misdemeanor**⟩ /mɪsdɪ'mi:ne(r)/ n. Missetat, die (veralt., scherzh.)
misdirect /mɪsdɪ'rekt, mɪsdaɪ'rekt/ v.t. falsch adressieren ⟨Brief⟩; in die falsche Richtung schicken ⟨Person⟩
miser /'maɪzə(r)/ n. Geizhals, der
miserable /'mɪzərəbl/ adj.
(a) unglücklich; feel ∼: sich elend fühlen
(b) trist ⟨Wetter, Urlaub⟩
miserably /'mɪzərəblɪ/ adv. unglücklich; jämmerlich ⟨versagen⟩; ∼ poor bettelarm
miserly /'maɪzəlɪ/ adj. geizig
misery /'mɪzərɪ/ n. (a) Elend, das
(b) (coll.: discontented person) ∼ [guts] Miesepeter, der (ugs.)
misfire /mɪs'faɪə(r)/ v.i. (a) ⟨Motor:⟩ Fehlzündungen haben
(b) ⟨Plan, Versuch:⟩ fehlschlagen; ⟨Streich, Witz:⟩ danebengehen
misfit /'mɪsfɪt/ n. Außenseiter, der/ Außenseiterin, die
misfortune /mɪs'fɔ:tʃu:n/ n. Missgeschick, das
misgiving /mɪs'gɪvɪŋ/ n. ∼[s] Bedenken Pl.
misguided /mɪs'gaɪdɪd/ adj. töricht
mishandle /mɪs'hændl/ v.t. falsch behandeln
mishap /'mɪshæp/ n. Missgeschick, das
mishear /mɪs'hɪə(r)/ 1 v.i., misheard /mɪs'hɜ:d/ sich verhören
2 v.t., misheard falsch verstehen
mishit 1 /'mɪshɪt/ n. Fehlschlag, der
2 /mɪs'hɪt/ v.t., -tt-, mishit verschlagen
mishmash /'mɪʃmæʃ/ n. Mischmasch, der (ugs.) (of aus)
misinform /mɪsɪn'fɔ:m/ v.t. falsch informieren
misinterpret /mɪsɪn'tɜ:prɪt/ v.t. (make wrong inference from) falsch deuten; missdeuten
misinterpretation /mɪsɪntɜ:prɪ'teɪʃn/ n. be open to ∼: leicht missdeutet werden

können
misjudge /mɪs'dʒʌdʒ/ v.t. falsch einschätzen; falsch beurteilen ⟨Person⟩
misjudgement, misjudgment /mɪs'dʒʌdʒmənt/ n. Fehleinschätzung, die; (of person) falsche Beurteilung
mislay /mɪs'leɪ/ v.t., mislaid /mɪs'leɪd/ verlegen
mislead /mɪs'li:d/ v.t., misled /mɪs'led/ irreführen
mis'leading adj. irreführend
mismanage /mɪs'mænɪdʒ/ v.t. schlecht abwickeln ⟨Geschäft, Projekt⟩
mismanagement /mɪs'mænɪdʒmənt/ n. schlechte Abwicklung
misnomer /mɪs'nəʊmə(r)/ n. unzutreffende Bezeichnung
misogynist /mɪ'sɒdʒɪnɪst/ n. Frauenhasser, der
misplace /mɪs'pleɪs/ v.t. an den falschen Platz stellen/legen/setzen usw.
misprint 1 /'mɪsprɪnt/ n. Druckfehler, der
2 /mɪs'prɪnt/ v.t. verdrucken
mispronounce /mɪsprə'naʊns/ v.t. falsch aussprechen
misquote /mɪs'kwəʊt/ v.t. falsch zitieren; he was ∼d as saying that ...: man unterstellte ihm, gesagt zu haben, dass ...
misread /mɪs'ri:d/ v.t., misread /mɪs'red/ falsch lesen
misrepresent /mɪsreprɪ'zent/ v.t. falsch darstellen
misrepresentation /mɪsreprɪzen'teɪʃn/ n. falsche Darstellung
miss 1 n. Fehlschlag, der; (shot) Fehlschuss, der; (throw) Fehlwurf, der
2 v.t. (a) (fail to hit) verfehlen
(b) (let slip) verpassen; ∼ an opportunity sich (Dat.) eine Gelegenheit entgehen lassen
(c) (fail to catch) verpassen ⟨Zug⟩
(d) (fail to take part in) versäumen; ∼ school in der Schule fehlen
(e) (fail to see) übersehen; (fail to hear) nicht mitbekommen
(f) (feel the absence of) vermissen; she ∼es him er fehlt ihr
3 v.i. (not hit sth.) danebentreffen
■ miss 'out 1 v.t. weglassen
2 v.t. ∼ out on sth. (coll.) sich (Dat.) etw. entgehen lassen
Miss /mɪs/ n. ∼ Brown (unmarried woman) Frau Brown; Fräulein Brown (veralt.); (girl) Fräulein Brown
misshapen /mɪs'ʃeɪpn/ adj. missgebildet
missile /'mɪsaɪl/ n. (a) (thrown) [Wurf]geschoss, das
(b) (Mil.) Rakete, die
'missile base, 'missile site ns. Raketenbasis, die
'missing adj. fehlend; be ∼: fehlen; ⟨Person:⟩ (Mil. etc.) vermisst werden; (not present) fehlen; ∼ person Vermisste, der/die

mission /'mɪʃn/ *n.* **(a)** Mission, *die*
(b) (planned operation) Einsatz, *der*
missionary /'mɪʃənərɪ/ *n.* Missionar,
der/Missionarin, *die*
'mission statement *n.*
Unternehmensleitbild, *das*
misspell /mɪs'spel/ *v.t., forms as* SPELL¹
falsch schreiben
mist /mɪst/ *n.* (fog) Nebel, *der;* (haze) Dunst,
der; (on windscreen etc.) Beschlag, *der*
■ **mist 'up** *v.i.* [sich] beschlagen
mistake /mɪ'steɪk/ ⟦1⟧ *n.* Fehler, *der;* **by**
~: versehentlich
⟦2⟧ *v.t., forms as* TAKE 1: **(a)** falsch verstehen
(b) ~ x for y x mit y verwechseln
mistaken /mɪ'steɪkn/ *adj.* **be ~:** sich
täuschen; **a case of** ~ **identity** eine
Verwechslung
mi'stakenly *adv.* irrtümlicherweise
mistletoe /'mɪsltəʊ/ *n.* Mistel, *die*
mistook ▶ MISTAKE 2
mistranslate /mɪstræns'leɪt/ *v.t.* falsch
übersetzen
mistreat /mɪs'tri:t/ *v.t.* schlecht
behandeln; (violently) misshandeln
mistreatment /mɪs'tri:tmənt/
n. schlechte Behandlung; (violent)
Misshandlung, *die*
mistress /'mɪstrɪs/ *n.* **(a)** (Brit. Sch.: teacher)
Lehrerin, *die*
(b) (lover) Geliebte, *die*
mistrust /mɪs'trʌst/ ⟦1⟧ *v.t.* misstrauen
(+ *Dat.*)
⟦2⟧ *n.* Misstrauen, *das* (**of** gegenüber + *Dat.*)
mistrustful /mɪs'trʌstfl/ *adj.*
misstrauisch (**of** gegenüber)
'misty *adj.* dunstig
misunderstand /mɪsʌndə'stænd/ *v.t.,*
forms as UNDERSTAND: missverstehen
misunder'standing *n.* Missverständnis,
das
misuse ⟦1⟧ /mɪs'ju:z/ *v.t.* missbrauchen
⟦2⟧ /mɪs'ju:s/ *n.* Missbrauch, *der*
mite /maɪt/ *n.* **(a)** (Zool.) Milbe, *die*
(b) (small child) Würmchen, *das* (fam.); **poor**
little ~: armes Kleines
miter (Amer.) ▶ MITRE
mitigate /'mɪtɪgeɪt/ *v.t.* **(a)** (reduce) lindern
(b) (make less severe) mildern; **mitigating**
circumstances mildernde Umstände
mitre /'maɪtə(r)/ *n.* (Brit. Eccl.) Mitra, *die*
mitten /'mɪtn/ *n.* Fausthandschuh, *der*
mix /mɪks/ ⟦1⟧ *v.t.* [ver]mischen; verrühren
⟨Zutaten⟩
⟦2⟧ *v.i.* **(a)** (become ~ed) sich vermischen
(b) (be sociable, participate) Umgang mit
anderen [Menschen] haben; ~ **with** Umgang
haben mit; ~ **well** kontaktfreudig sein
⟦3⟧ *n.* (coll.) Mischung, *die;* **[cake]**
~: Backmischung, *die*
■ **mix 'up** *v.t.* **(a)** vermischen
(b) (muddle) durcheinander bringen; (confuse)

verwechseln
(c) be/get ~ed up in sth. in etw. (*Akk.*)
verwickelt sein/werden
mixed /mɪkst/ *adj.* **(a)** gemischt
(b) (diverse) unterschiedlich
mixed: ~ **'bag** *n.* bunte Mischung;
~ **'blessing** *n.* be a ~ blessing nicht
nur Vorteile haben; ~ **'grill** *n.* Mixedgrill,
der (Gastr.); gemischte Grillplatte;
~ **'marriage** *n.* Mischehe, *die;* ~ **'up**
adj. (fig. coll.) verwirrt, konfus ⟨Person⟩;
be/feel very ~ up völlig durcheinander sein
'mixer *n.* (for food) Küchenmaschine *die;*
hand ~: Handrührgerät, *das*
mixture /'mɪkstʃə(r)/ *n.* **(a)** Mischung, *die*
(of aus)
(b) (Med.) Mixtur, *die*
'mix-up *n.* Durcheinander, *das;*
(misunderstanding) Missverständnis, *das*
mm. *abbr.* = **millimetre[s]** mm
moan /məʊn/ ⟦1⟧ *n.* **(a)** Stöhnen, *das*
(b) have a ~ (complain) jammern
⟦2⟧ *v.i.* **(a)** stöhnen (**with** vor + *Dat.*)
(b) (complain) jammern (**about** über + *Akk.*)
⟦3⟧ *v.t.* stöhnen
moat /məʊt/ *n.* **[castle]** ~: Burggraben, *der*
mob /mɒb/ ⟦1⟧ *n.* **(a)** (rabble) Mob, *der*
(b) (coll.: group) **Peter and his** ~: Peter und
seine ganze Blase (salopp)
⟦2⟧ *v.t.,* **-bb-** belagern (ugs.) ⟨Star⟩
mobile /'məʊbaɪl/ ⟦1⟧ *adj.* beweglich;
(on wheels) fahrbar; **upwardly** ~: sozial
aufsteigend
⟦2⟧ *n.* Mobile, *das;* (~ phone) Handy, *das*
mobile: ~ **'home** *n.* transportable
Wohneinheit; ~ **'phone** *n.* Mobiltelefon,
das
mobility /mə'bɪlɪtɪ/ *n.* Beweglichkeit, *die*
mobilization /məʊbɪlaɪ'zeɪʃn/ *n.*
Mobilisierung, *die*
mobilize /'məʊbɪlaɪz/ *v.t.* mobilisieren
moccasin /'mɒkəsɪn/ *n.* Mokassin, *der*
mocha /'mɒkə/ *n.* Mokka, *der*
mock /mɒk/ ⟦1⟧ *v.t.* sich lustig machen
über (+ *Akk.*)
⟦2⟧ *v.i.* sich lustig machen (**at** über + *Akk.*)
⟦3⟧ *adj.* Schein⟨kampf, -angriff, -ehe⟩
mockery /'mɒkərɪ/ *n.* Spott, *der;* **make a**
~ **of sth.** etw. zur Farce machen
'mock-up *n.* Modell [in Originalgröße]
mode /məʊd/ *n.* **(a)** Art [und Weise], *die*
(b) (fashion) Mode, *die*
model /'mɒdl/ ⟦1⟧ *n.* **(a)** Modell, *das*
(b) (example to be imitated) Vorbild, *das*
(c) (Art) Modell, *das;* (Fashion) Mannequin,
das; (male) Dressman, *der*
⟦2⟧ *adj.* **(a)** (exemplary) Muster-
(b) (miniature) Modell-
⟦3⟧ *v.t.,* (Brit.) **-ll-: (a)** modellieren; ~ **sth.**
after *or* **[up]on sth.** etw. einer Sache (*Dat.*)
nachbilden
(b) (Fashion) vorführen
⟦4⟧ *v.i.* (Fashion) als Mannequin/ ⋯⟶

Dressman arbeiten; (Art) Modell stehen/sitzen

modem /'məʊdəm/ *n.* Modem, *der*

moderate ① /'mɒdərət/ *adj.*
(a) gemäßigt ‹*Ansichten*›; maßvoll ‹*Trinker, Forderungen*›
(b) mittler... ‹*Größe, Menge, Wert*›; (reasonable) angemessen ‹*Preis, Summe*›
② /'mɒdərət/ *n.* Gemäßigte, *der/die*
③ /'mɒdəreɪt/ *v.t.* mäßigen
④ *v.i.* nachlassen

moderately /'mɒdərətlɪ/ *adv.*
einigermaßen; mäßig ‹*begeistert, groß, begabt*›

moderation /mɒdə'reɪʃn/ *n.* Mäßigkeit, *die*; **in ~:** mit Maßen

modern /'mɒdn/ *adj.* modern; heutig ‹*Zeit[alter], Welt, Mensch*›; ~ **art/music** moderne Kunst/Musik; ~ **history** neuere Geschichte; ~ **languages** neuere Sprachen

modernize /'mɒdənaɪz/ *v.t.* modernisieren

modest /'mɒdɪst/ *adj.* bescheiden; einfach ‹*Haus, Kleidung*›

'**modestly** *adv.* bescheiden

'**modesty** *n.* Bescheidenheit, *die*

modification /mɒdɪfɪ'keɪʃn/ *n.* [Ab]änderung, *die*

modify /'mɒdɪfaɪ/ *v.t.* [ab]ändern

modulate /'mɒdjʊleɪt/ *v.t. & i.* modulieren

modulation /mɒdjʊ'leɪʃn/ *n.* Modulation, *die*

module /'mɒdjuːl/ *n.* (a) Bauelement, *das*
(b) (Astronaut.) **command ~:** Kommandoeinheit, *die*
(c) (Educ.) Unterrichtseinheit, *die*

mohair /'məʊheə(r)/ *n.* Mohair, *der*

moist /mɔɪst/ *adj.* feucht (**with** von)

moisten /'mɔɪsn/ *v.t.* anfeuchten

moisture /'mɔɪstʃə(r)/ *n.* Feuchtigkeit, *die*

moisturize /'mɔɪstjʊraɪz, 'mɔɪstʃəraɪz/ *v.t.* befeuchten; ~ **the skin** der Haut (*Dat.*) Feuchtigkeit zuführen; ‹*Creme:*› der Haut (*Dat.*) Feuchtigkeit verleihen

moisturizer /'mɔɪstʃəraɪzə(r)/, **moisturizing cream** /'mɔɪstʃəraɪzɪŋ kriːm/ *ns.* Feuchtigkeitscreme, *die*

molar /'məʊlə(r)/ *n.* Backenzahn, *der*

molasses /mə'læsɪz/ *n.* Melasse, *die*

mold (Amer.) ▶ MOULD[1, 2]

molder, molding, moldy (Amer.) ▶ MOULD-

mole[1] /məʊl/ *n.* (on skin) Leberfleck, *der*

mole[2] *n.* (animal) Maulwurf, *der*

molecular /mə'lekjʊlə(r)/ *adj.* molekular

molecule /'mɒlɪkjuːl/ *n.* Molekül, *das*

'**molehill** *n.* Maulwurfshügel, *der*

molest /mə'lest/ *v.t.* belästigen

mollify /'mɒlɪfaɪ/ *v.t.* besänftigen

mollusc, (Amer.) **mollusk** /'mɒləsk/ *n.* Weichtier, *das*

mollycoddle /'mɒlɪkɒdl/ *v.t.* [ver]hätscheln

molt (Amer.) ▶ MOULT

molten /'məʊltn/ *adj.* geschmolzen

mom /mɒm/ (Amer. coll.) ▶ MUM[2]

moment /'məʊmənt/ *n.* Augenblick, *der;* **at any ~,** (coll.) **any ~:** jeden Augenblick; **one or just a or wait a ~!** einen Augenblick!; **in a ~** (very soon) sofort; **at the ~:** im Augenblick; **the ~ of truth** die Stunde der Wahrheit

momentarily /'məʊməntərɪlɪ/ *adv.* einen Augenblick lang

momentary /'məʊməntərɪ/ *adj.* kurz

momentous /mə'mentəs/ *adj.* (important) bedeutsam; (of consequence) folgenschwer

momentum /mə'mentəm/ *n.* Schwung, *der*

Mon. *abbr.* = **Monday** Mo.

monarch /'mɒnək/ *n.* Monarch, *der*/Monarchin, *die*

'**monarchy** *n.* Monarchie, *die*

monastery /'mɒnəstrɪ/ *n.* Kloster, *das*

monastic /mə'næstɪk/ *adj.* mönchisch

Monday /'mʌndeɪ, 'mʌndɪ/ *n.* Montag, *der; see also* FRIDAY

monetary /'mʌnɪtərɪ/ *adj.* (a) (of currency) monetär; Währungs‹*politik, -system*›; ~ **union** Währungsunion, *die*
(b) (of money) finanziell

money /'mʌnɪ/ *n.* Geld, *das;* **make ~** ‹*Person:*› [viel] Geld verdienen; ‹*Geschäft:*› etwas einbringen; **for 'my ~:** wenn man mich fragt

money: ~ **bag** *n.* Geldsack, *der;* ~ **belt** *n.* Geldgürtel, *der;* ~ **box** *n.* Sparbüchse, *die;* ~**making** *adj.* Gewinn bringend; ~ **order** *n.* Postanweisung, *die*

Mongolia /mɒŋ'gəʊlɪə/ *pr. n.* Mongolei, *die*

Mongolian /mɒŋ'gəʊlɪən/ ① *adj.* mongolisch; **sb. is ~:** jmd. ist Mongole/ Mongolin
② *n.* (person) Mongole, *der*/Mongolin, *die* ~

mongrel /'mʌŋgrəl/ *n.* ~ [**dog**] Promenadenmischung, *die*

monitor /'mɒnɪtə(r)/ ① *n.* (a) (Sch.) Aufsichtsschüler, *der*/-schülerin, *die*
(b) (Med., Telev., Comp.) Monitor, *der*
② *v.t.* beobachten ‹*Wetter, Flugzeug*›; abhören ‹*Sendung, Telefongespräch*›

monk /mʌŋk/ *n.* Mönch, *der*

monkey /'mʌŋkɪ/ *n.* Affe, *der*

monkey: ~ **business** *n.* (coll.: mischief) Schabernack, *der;* ~ **nut** *n.* Erdnuss, *die;* ~ **wrench** *n.* Universalschraubenschlüssel, *der*

mono /'mɒnəʊ/ *adj.* Mono‹*platte[nspieler], -wiedergabe*›

monochrome /'mɒnəkrəʊm/ *adj.* monochrom (fachspr.); einfarbig; Schwarzweiß- (Ferns.)

monocle /'mɒnəkl/ *n.* Monokel, *das*

monogamous /mə'nɒgəməs/ *adj.* monogam

monogamy /mə'nɒɡəmɪ/ *n.* Monogamie, *die;* Einehe, *die*

monogram /'mɒnəɡræm/ *n.* Monogramm, *das*

monogrammed /'mɒnəɡræmd/ *adj.* monogrammiert; ⟨*Taschentuch usw.:*⟩ mit Monogramm

monologue (*Amer.:* **monolog**) /'mɒnəlɒɡ/ *n.* Monolog, *der*

monopolize /mə'nɒpəlaɪz/ *v.t.* (Econ.) monopolisieren; (fig.) mit Beschlag belegen; ∼ **the conversation** den/die anderen nicht zu Wort kommen lassen

monopoly /mə'nɒpəlɪ/ *n.* **(a)** (Econ.) Monopol, *das* (of auf + *Akk.*)
(b) (exclusive possession) alleiniger Besitz

monotone /'mɒnətəʊn/ *n.* gleich bleibender Ton

monotonous /mə'nɒtənəs/ *adj.*, **mo'notonously** *adv.* eintönig

monotony /mə'nɒtənɪ/ *n.* Eintönigkeit, *die*

monsoon /mɒn'suːn/ *n.* Monsun, *der*

monster /'mɒnstə(r)/ *n.* **(a)** (creature) Ungeheuer, *das;* (huge thing) Ungetüm, *das*
(b) (inhuman person) Unmensch, *der*

monstrosity /mɒn'strɒsɪtɪ/ *n.*
(a) (outrageous thing) Ungeheuerlichkeit, *die*
(b) (hideous building etc.) Ungetüm, *das*

monstrous /'mɒnstrəs/ *adj.* **(a)** (huge) riesig
(b) (outrageous) ungeheuerlich
(c) (atrocious) scheußlich

month /mʌnθ/ *n.* Monat, *der;* **for a** ∼/∼s einen Monat [lang]/monatelang

'monthly ⟨1⟩ *adj.* monatlich; Monats⟨*einkommen, -gehalt*⟩
⟨2⟩ *adv.* einmal im Monat
⟨3⟩ *n.* Monatsschrift, *die*

monument /'mɒnjʊmənt/ *n.* Denkmal, *das*

monumental /mɒnjʊ'mentl/ *adj.*
(a) (massive) monumental
(b) gewaltig ⟨*Misserfolg, Irrtum*⟩

moo /muː/ ⟨1⟩ *n.* Muhen, *das*
⟨2⟩ *v.i.* muhen

mooch /muːtʃ/ *v.i.* (coll.) ∼ **about** *or* **around/along** herumschleichen (ugs.)/ zockeln (ugs.)

mood /muːd/ *n.* **(a)** Stimmung, *die;* **be in a good/bad** ∼**:** [bei] guter/schlechter Laune sein; **I'm not in the** ∼**:** ich hab keine Lust dazu
(b) (bad ∼) Verstimmung, *die*

'moody *adj.* **(a)** (sullen) missmutig
(b) (subject to moods) launenhaft

moon /muːn/ *n.* Mond, *der*

moon: ∼**beam** *n.* Mondstrahl, *der;*
∼**light** ⟨1⟩ *n.* Mondlicht, *das;* Mondschein, *der;* ⟨2⟩ *v.i.* (coll.) nebenberuflich abends arbeiten; ∼**lit** *adj.* mondbeschienen (geh.)

moor¹ /mʊə(r), mɔː(r)/ *n.* (Geog.) [Hoch]moor, *das*

moor² *v.t. & i.* festmachen; vertäuen

'moorhen *n.* [Grünfüßiges] Teichhuhn

mooring *n.* ∼**[s]** Anlegestelle, *die*

'mooring post *n.* Pfahl, *der;* ≈ Duckdalben, *der*

moorland /'mʊələnd, 'mɔːlənd/ *n.* Moorland, *das*

moose /muːs/ *n., pl. same* Amerikanischer Elch

moot /muːt/ ⟨1⟩ *adj.* umstritten; offen ⟨*Frage*⟩; strittig ⟨*Punkt*⟩
⟨2⟩ *v.t.* erörtern ⟨*Frage, Punkt*⟩

mop /mɒp/ ⟨1⟩ *n.* **(a)** Mopp, *der*
(b) ∼ **[of hair]** Wuschelkopf, *der*
⟨2⟩ *v.t.,* **-pp-** moppen ⟨*Fußboden*⟩; (wipe) abwischen ⟨*Träne, Schweiß, Stirn*⟩
■ **mop 'up** *v.t.* aufwischen

mope /məʊp/ *v.i.* Trübsal blasen

moped /'məʊped/ *n.* Moped, *das*

moral /'mɒrl/ ⟨1⟩ *adj.* **(a)** moralisch; sittlich ⟨*Wert*⟩; Moral⟨*begriff, -prinzip*⟩
(b) (virtuous) moralisch ⟨*Leben, Person*⟩
⟨2⟩ *n.* **(a)** Moral, *die*
(b) *in pl.* (habits) Moral, *die*

morale /mə'rɑːl/ *n.* Moral, *die;* **low/high** ∼**:** schlechte/gute Moral

mo'rale-booster *n.* be a *or* act as a ∼ for sb. jds. Moral heben *od.* stärken

morality /mə'rælɪtɪ/ *n.* Moral, *die*

moral sup'port *n.* moralische Unterstützung

morbid /'mɔːbɪd/ *adj.* krankhaft; morbid (geh.) ⟨*Faszination, Neigung*⟩

more /mɔː(r)/ ⟨1⟩ *adj.* mehr; any *or* some ∼ (apples, books, etc.) noch welche; any *or* some ∼ (tea, paper, etc.) noch etwas; any *or* some ∼ **apples/tea** noch Äpfel/Tee; **I haven't any** ∼ **[apples/tea]** ich habe keine [Äpfel]/ keinen [Tee] mehr; ∼ **and** ∼**:** immer mehr
⟨2⟩ *n.* mehr; ∼ **and** ∼**:** immer mehr; **six or** ∼**:** mindestens sechs
⟨3⟩ *adv.* **(a)** mehr; ∼ **interesting** interessanter
(b) (nearer, rather) eher
(c) (again) wieder; **no** ∼**, not any** ∼**:** nicht mehr; **once** ∼**:** noch einmal
(d) ∼ **and** ∼**:** immer mehr; ∼ **and** ∼ **absurd** immer absurder
(e) ∼ **or less** (fairly) mehr oder weniger; (approximately) annähernd

moreish /'mɔːrɪʃ/ *adj.* (coll.) lecker

more'over *adv.* und außerdem

morgue /mɔːɡ/ ▶ MORTUARY

morning /'mɔːnɪŋ/ *n.* Morgen, *der;* (not afternoon) Vormittag, *der; attrib.* morgendlich; Morgen-; **this** ∼**:** heute Morgen; **tomorrow** ∼**,** (coll.) **in the** ∼**:** morgen früh; **[early] in the** ∼**:** am [frühen] Morgen; (regularly) [früh]morgens

morning: ∼ **'after,** ∼**-'after [feeling]** (coll.: hangover) Katzenjammer, *der;* ∼**-'after pill** *n.* Pille [für den Morgen] danach; ∼ **'star** *n.* Morgenstern, *der*

Moroccan /məˈrɒkən/ **1** adj.
marokkanisch; **sb. is** ∼: jmd. ist
Marokkaner/Marokkanerin
2 n. Marokkaner, der/Marokkanerin, die
Morocco /məˈrɒkəʊ/ pr. n. Marokko (das)
moron /ˈmɔːrɒn/ n. (coll.) Schwachkopf,
der (ugs.)
morose /məˈrəʊs/ adj. verdrießlich
morphine /ˈmɔːfiːn/ n. Morphin, das
Morse [code] /mɔːs ('kəʊd)/ n.
Morsealphabet, das
morsel /ˈmɔːsl/ n. (of food) Bissen, der
mortal /ˈmɔːtl/ **1** adj. **(a)** sterblich
(b) (fatal) tödlich **(to** für)
2 n. Sterbliche, der/die
mortality /mɔːˈtælɪtɪ/ n. **(a)** Sterblichkeit,
die
(b) ∼ **[rate]** Sterblichkeitsrate, die
mortally adv. tödlich
mortar /ˈmɔːtə(r)/ n. **(a)** Mörtel, der
(b) (vessel) Mörser, der
(c) (weapon) Minenwerfer, der; Mörser, der
mortgage /ˈmɔːgɪdʒ/ **1** n. Hypothek, die
2 v.t. mit einer Hypothek belasten
mortuary /ˈmɔːtjʊərɪ/ n. (building)
Leichenschauhaus, das; (room)
Leichenkammer, die
mosaic /məʊˈzeɪɪk/ n. Mosaik, das
Moscow /ˈmɒskəʊ/ pr. n. Moskau (das)
Moselle /məʊˈzel/ pr. n. Mosel, die
Moslem /ˈmɒzləm/ ▶ MUSLIM
mosque /mɒsk/ n. Moschee, die
mosquito /mɒsˈkiːtəʊ/ n., pl. ∼es
Stechmücke, die; (in tropics) Moskito, der
mosˈquito net n. Moskitonetz, das
moss /mɒs/ n. Moos, das
mossy adj. moosig
most /məʊst/ **1** adj. (in number, majority
of) die meisten; (in amount) meist…; **make
the** ∼ **mistakes/the** ∼ **noise** die meisten
Fehler/den größten Lärm machen; **for the**
∼ **part** größtenteils
2 n. **(a)** (greatest amount) **the** ∼ **it will cost is**
£10 es wird höchstens zehn Pfund kosten;
pay the ∼: am meisten bezahlen
(b) (greater part) ∼ **of the girls** die meisten
Mädchen; ∼ **of his friends** die meisten
seiner Freunde; ∼ **of the poem** der größte
Teil des Gedichts; ∼ **of the time** die meiste
Zeit
(c) (on ∼ occasions) meistens
3 adv. **(a)** am meisten; **the** ∼ **interesting**
book das interessanteste Buch; ∼ **often** am
häufigsten
(b) (exceedingly) äußerst
mostly adv. (most of the time) meistens;
(mainly) größtenteils
MOT ▶ MOT TEST
motel /məʊˈtel/ n. Motel, das
moth /mɒθ/ n. Nachtfalter, der; (in clothes)
Motte, die
moth: ∼**ball** n. Mottenkugel, die;

∼-**eaten** adj. von Motten zerfressen
mother /ˈmʌðə(r)/ **1** n. Mutter, die
2 v.t. (over-protect) bemuttern
motherboard n. (Comp.) Mutterplatine,
die
motherhood n. Mutterschaft, die
Mothering Sunday /ˈmʌðərɪŋ sʌndɪ/
(Brit. Eccl.) ▶ MOTHER'S DAY
mother: ∼-**in-law** n., pl. ∼s-in-law
Schwiegermutter, die; ∼**land** n. Vaterland,
das
motherly /ˈmʌðəlɪ/ adj. mütterlich; ∼ **love**
Mutterliebe, die
mother: ∼-**of-ˈpearl** n. Perlmutt, das;
M-∼**'s Day** n. Muttertag, der; ∼ **ˈtongue**
n. Muttersprache, die
moth: ∼ **hole** n. Mottenloch, das;
∼**proof** adj. mottenfest
motif /məʊˈtiːf/ n. Motiv, das
motion /ˈməʊʃn/ **1** n. **(a)** Bewegung, die
(b) (proposal) Antrag, der
2 v.t. & i. ∼ **[to]** sb. to do sth. jmdm.
bedeuten (geh.), etw. zu tun
motionless adj. bewegungslos
motivate /ˈməʊtɪveɪt/ v.t. motivieren
motivation /məʊtɪˈveɪʃn/ n. Motivation,
die
motive /ˈməʊtɪv/ n. Beweggrund, der; **the**
∼ **for the crime** das Tatmotiv
motley /ˈmɒtlɪ/ adj. bunt gemischt
motor /ˈməʊtə(r)/ **1** n. **(a)** Motor, der
(b) (Brit.: ∼ car) Auto, das
2 adj. Motor⟨mäher, -jacht usw.⟩
3 v.i. (Brit.) [mit dem Auto] fahren
motor: ∼**bike** n. (coll.) Motorrad, das;
∼ **boat** n. Motorboot, das
motorcade /ˈməʊtəkeɪd/ n. Fahrzeug- od.
Wagenkolonne, die
motor: ∼ **car** n. (Brit.) Kraftfahrzeug, das;
∼ **cycle** n. Motorrad, das; ∼**cyclist** n.
Motorradfahrer, der/-fahrerin, die
motoring n. (Brit.) Autofahren, das
motorist n. Autofahrer, der/-fahrerin, die
motorize /ˈməʊtəraɪz/ v.t. motorisieren
motor: ∼ **racing** n. Autorennsport, der;
∼ **show** n. Auto[mobil]ausstellung, die;
∼ **vehicle** n. Kraftfahrzeug, das; ∼**way**
n. (Brit.) Autobahn, die
MOT test n. (Brit.) ≈ TÜV, der
mottled /ˈmɒtld/ adj. gesprenkelt
motto /ˈmɒtəʊ/ n., pl. ∼es Motto, das
mould¹ /məʊld/ **1** n. (hollow container)
Form, die
2 v.t. formen **(out of, from** aus)
mould² n. (Bot.) Schimmel, der
moulder /ˈməʊldə(r)/ v.i. ∼ **[away]**
[ver]modern
moulding n. **(a)** Formteil, das **(of, in** aus);
(Archit.) Zierleiste, die
(b) (wooden) Leiste, die
mouldy adj. schimmlig; **go** ∼: schimmeln

moult /məʊlt/ *v.i.* ⟨*Vogel:*⟩ sich mausern; ⟨*Hund, Katze:*⟩ sich haaren

mound /maʊnd/ *n.* **(a)** (of earth) Hügel, *der*
(b) (heap) Haufen, *der*

mount /maʊnt/ ☐1 *n.* **(a)** M∼ Vesuvius/ Everest der Vesuv/der Mount Everest
(b) (animal) Reittier, *das;* (horse) Pferd, *das*
(c) (of picture, photograph) Passepartout, *das*
(d) (for gem) Fassung, *die*
☐2 *v.t.* **(a)** hinaufsteigen ⟨*Treppe*⟩; steigen auf (+ *Akk.*) ⟨*Plattform, Reittier, Fahrzeug*⟩
(b) aufziehen ⟨*Bild*⟩; einfassen ⟨*Edelstein usw.*⟩
(c) inszenieren ⟨*Stück, Oper*⟩; organisieren ⟨*Ausstellung*⟩; durchführen ⟨*Angriff, Operation*⟩
☐3 *v.i.* ∼ **[up]** (increase) steigen (**to** auf + *Akk.*)

mountain /'maʊntɪn/ *n.* Berg, *der;* **in the** ∼s im Gebirge

mountain: ∼ **bike** *n.* Mountainbike, *das;* ∼ **chain** *n.* Gebirgszug, *der*

mountaineer /maʊntɪ'nɪə(r)/ *n.* Bergsteiger, *der*/Bergsteigerin, *die*

mountai'neering *n.* Bergsteigen, *das*

mountainous /'maʊntɪnəs/ *adj.*
(a) gebirgig
(b) (huge) riesig

mountain: ∼ **'range** *n.* Gebirgszug, *der;* ∼**side** *n.* [Berg][ab]hang, *der;* ∼ **top** *n.* Berggipfel, *der*

mourn /mɔːn/ ☐1 *v.i.* trauern; ∼ **for** *or* **over** trauern um ⟨*Toten*⟩
☐2 *v.t.* betrauern

'mourner *n.* Trauernde, *der*/*die*

mournful /'mɔːnfl/ *adj.* klagend ⟨*Stimme, Ton, Schrei*⟩; trauervoll (geh.) ⟨*Person*⟩

'mourning *n.* Trauer, *die;* **be in**/**go into** ∼: Trauer tragen/anlegen

mouse /maʊs/ *n., pl.* **mice** /maɪs/ Maus, *die*

mouse: ∼ **button** *n.* (Comp.) Maustaste, *die;* ∼ **click** *n.* (Comp.) Mausklick, *der;* ∼ **mat** *n.* (Comp.) Mauspad, *das;* ∼ **pointer** *n.* (Comp.) Mauszeiger, *der;* ∼**trap** *n.* Mausefalle, *die*

mousse /muːs/ *n.* Mousse, *die*

moustache /mə'stɑːʃ/ *n.* Schnurrbart, *der*

mousy /'maʊsɪ/ *adj.* **(a)** mattbraun ⟨*Haar*⟩
(b) (timid) scheu

mouth ☐1 /maʊθ/ *n.* **(a)** (of person) Mund, *der;* (of animal) Maul, *das;* **with one's** ∼ **open**/**full** mit offenem/vollem Mund
(b) (harbour entrance) [Hafen]einfahrt, *die;* (of tunnel, cave) Eingang, *der;* (of river) Mündung, *die*
☐2 /maʊð/ *v.t.* mit Lippenbewegungen sagen

mouthful /'maʊθfʊl/ *n.* Mundvoll, *der*

mouth: ∼ **organ** *n.* Mundharmonika, *die;* ∼**piece** *n.* **(a)** Mundstück, *das;*
(b) (fig.) Sprachrohr, *das*

movable /'muːvəbl/ *adj.* beweglich

move /muːv/ ☐1 *n.* **(a)** (change of home) Umzug, *der*
(b) (action taken) Schritt, *der;* (Footb. etc.) Spielzug, *der*
(c) (turn in game) Zug, *der;* **make a** ∼: ziehen; **it's your** ∼: du bist am Zug
(d) **be on the** ∼ ⟨*Person:*⟩ unterwegs sein
(e) **make a** ∼ (do sth.) etwas tun; (coll.: leave) losziehen (ugs.)
(f) **get a** ∼ **on** (coll.) einen Zahn zulegen (ugs.); **get a** ∼ **on!** (coll.) [mach] Tempo! (ugs.)
☐2 *v.t.* **(a)** (change position of) bewegen; wegräumen ⟨*Hindernis, Schutt*⟩; (transport) befördern; ∼ **sth. to a new position** etw. an einen neuen Platz bringen; ∼ **house** umziehen
(b) (in game) ziehen
(c) (affect) bewegen; ∼ **sb. to tears** jmdn. zu Tränen rühren; **be** ∼**d by sth.** über etw. (*Akk.*) gerührt sein
(d) (prompt) ∼ **sb. to do sth.** jmdn. dazu bewegen, etw. zu tun
(e) (propose) beantragen
☐3 *v.i.* **(a)** sich bewegen; (in vehicle) fahren
(b) (in games) ziehen
(c) (do sth.) handeln
(d) (change home) umziehen (**to** nach); ∼ **into a flat** in eine Wohnung einziehen; ∼ **out of a flat** aus einer Wohnung ausziehen; ∼ **to London** nach London ziehen
(e) (change posture or state) sich bewegen; **don't** ∼**!** keine Bewegung!

■ **move a'bout** ☐1 *v.i.* zugange sein; (travel) unterwegs sein
☐2 *v.t.* herumräumen

■ **move a'long** ☐1 *v.i.* **(a)** gehen/fahren
(b) ∼ **along, please!** gehen/fahren Sie bitte weiter!
☐2 *v.t.* zum Weitergehen/-fahren auffordern

■ **move 'in** ☐1 *v.i.* **(a)** (to home etc.) einziehen
(b) ∼ **in on** ⟨*Truppen, Polizeikräfte:*⟩ vorrücken gegen
☐2 *v.t.* hineinbringen

■ **move 'off** *v.i.* sich in Bewegung setzen

■ **move 'on** ☐1 *v.i.* weitergehen/-fahren; ∼ **on to another question** (fig.) zu einer anderen Frage übergehen
☐2 *v.t.* zum Weitergehen/-fahren auffordern

■ **move 'out** *v.t.* ausziehen (**of** aus)

■ **move 'over** *v.i.* rücken

■ **move 'up** *v.i.* **(a)** rücken
(b) (in queue, hierarchy) aufrücken

'movement *n.* **(a)** Bewegung, *die;* (trend, tendency) Tendenz, *die* (**towards** zu)
(b) *in pl.* Aktivitäten *Pl.*
(c) (Mus.) Satz, *der*

movie /'muːvɪ/ *n.* (Amer. coll.) Film, *der;* **the** ∼s der Film; **go to the** ∼s ins Kino gehen

moving /'muːvɪŋ/ *adj.* **(a)** beweglich
(b) (affecting) ergreifend

mow /məʊ/ *v.t./v.i., p.p.* **mown** /məʊn/ *or* **mowed** /məʊd/ mähen

■ **mow 'down** *v.t.* (shoot) niedermähen ⟨*Menschen*⟩   ⋯⋗

'**mower** n. Rasenmäher, der

mown ▸ MOW

MP abbr. = **Member of Parliament**

m.p.g. abbr. = **miles per gallon**

m.p.h. abbr. = **miles per hour**

MPV abbr. = **multi-purpose vehicle**

Mr /'mɪstə(r)/ n. Herr; (in an address) Herrn

Mrs /'mɪsɪz/ n. Frau

Ms /mɪz/ n. Frau

MS abbr. (Med.) = **multiple sclerosis** MS

Mt. abbr. = **Mount**

much /mʌtʃ/ ①️ adj., more /mɔː(r)/, most /məʊst/ viel; **too** ~: zu viel indekl

②️ n. vieles; ~ **of the day** der Großteil des Tages; **not be** ~ **to look at** nicht sehr ansehnlich sein

③️ adv., **more, most (a)** viel ⟨besser, schöner usw.⟩; ~ **more lively/attractive** viel lebhafter/attraktiver

(b) mit Abstand ⟨der/die/das Beste, Klügste usw.⟩

(c) (greatly) sehr ⟨lieben, genießen usw.⟩; (for ~ of the time) viel ⟨lesen, spielen usw.⟩; (often) oft ⟨sehen, besuchen usw.⟩

(d) [pretty or very] ~ **the same** fast [genau] der-/die-/dasselbe

muck /mʌk/ n. **(a)** (coll.: something disgusting) Dreck, der (ugs.)

(b) (coll.: nonsense) Mist, der (ugs.)

■ **muck a'bout, muck a'round** (Brit. coll.) v.i. **(a)** herumalbern (ugs.)

(b) (tinker) herumfummeln (with an + Dat.)

■ **muck 'in** v.i. (coll.) mit anpacken (with bei)

■ **muck 'up** v.t. **(a)** (Brit. coll.: bungle) vermurksen (ugs.)

(b) (make dirty) dreckig machen (ugs.)

(c) (coll.: spoil) vermasseln (salopp)

'**mucky** adj. dreckig (ugs.)

mucus /'mjuːkəs/ n. Schleim, der

mud /mʌd/ n. Schlamm, der

muddle /'mʌdl/ ①️ n. Durcheinander, das

②️ v.t. ~ **[up]** durcheinander bringen; ~ **up** (mix up) verwechseln (with mit)

■ **muddle a'long, muddle 'on** v.i. vor sich (Akk.) hin wursteln (ugs.)

■ **muddle 'through** v.i. sich durchwursteln (ugs.)

muddy /'mʌdɪ/ adj. schlammig; **get** or **become** ~: verschlammen

'**mudguard** n. Schutzblech, das; (of car) Kotflügel, der

muesli /'mjuːzlɪ/ n. Müsli, das

muff[1] /mʌf/ n. Muff, der

muff[2] v.t. verpatzen (ugs.)

muffin /'mʌfɪn/ n. Muffin, der

muffle /'mʌfl/ v.t. **(a)** (envelop) ~ **[up]** einhüllen

(b) dämpfen ⟨Geräusch⟩

'**muffler** n. **(a)** (wrap, scarf) Schal, der

(b) (Amer. Motor Veh.) Schalldämpfer, der

mug /mʌg/ ①️ n. **(a)** Becher, der (meist mit Henkel); (for beer etc.) Krug, der

(b) (coll.: face, mouth) Visage, die (salopp)

(c) (Brit. coll.: gullible person) Trottel, der (ugs.)

②️ v.t., **-gg-** (rob) überfallen und berauben

'**mugger** n. Straßenräuber, der/-räuberin, die

'**mugging** n. Straßenraub, der

muggy /'mʌgɪ/ adj. schwül

mule /mjuːl/ n. Maultier, das

multi: ~**coloured** (Brit.; Amer.: ~colored) adj. mehrfarbig; bunt ⟨Stoff, Kleid⟩; ~'**cultural** adj. multikulturell; ~**function button** n. Multifunktionstaste, die; ~**media** n. sing. Multimedia, das; ~**millio'naire** n. Multimillionär, der/-millionärin, die; ~**national** /mʌltɪ'næʃənl/ ①️ adj. multinational; ②️ n. multinationaler Konzern, der; Multi, der (ugs.)

multiple /'mʌltɪpl/ adj. mehrfach

multiple: ~'**choice** adj. Multiplechoice⟨-test, -frage⟩; ~ '**store** n. (Brit.) Kettenladen, der

multiplication /mʌltɪplɪ'keɪʃn/ n. Multiplikation, die

multiply /'mʌltɪplaɪ/ ①️ v.t. multiplizieren, malnehmen (by mit)

②️ v.i. sich vermehren

multi: ~**purpose** adj. Mehrzweck-; ~**purpose 'vehicle** n. Großraumlimousine, die; '~**-storey** adj. mehrstöckig; mehrgeschossig; ~**-storey car park/block of flats** Parkhaus/ Wohnhochhaus, das; ~**track** adj. mehrspurig; Mehrspur⟨aufnahme, -ton, -tonbandgerät⟩

multitude /'mʌltɪtjuːd/ n. (crowd) Menge, die; (great number) Vielzahl, die

mum[1] /mʌm/ ①️ int. ~'**s the word** nicht weitersagen!

②️ adj. **keep** ~: den Mund halten (ugs.)

mum[2] n. (Brit. coll.: mother) Mama, die (fam.)

mumble /'mʌmbl/ v.i. & t. nuscheln (ugs.)

mummy[1] n. (Brit. coll.: mother) Mutti, die (fam.)

mummy[2] /'mʌmɪ/ n. Mumie, die

mumps /mʌmps/ n. Mumps, der

munch /mʌntʃ/ v.t. & i. ~ **[one's food]** mampfen (salopp)

mundane /mʌn'deɪn/ adj. **(a)** (dull) banal

(b) (worldly) weltlich

Munich /'mjuːnɪk/ pr. n. München (das)

municipal /mjʊ'nɪsɪpl/ adj. kommunal; Kommunal⟨politik, -verwaltung⟩

munition /mjuː'nɪʃn/ n., usu. in pl. Kriegsmaterial, das; ~**[s] factory** Rüstungsbetrieb, der

mural /'mjʊərl/ n. Wandbild, das

murder /'mɜːdə(r)/ ①️ n. Mord, der (**of an** + Dat.)

②️ v.t. ermorden

'murderer *n.* Mörder, *der*/Mörderin, *die*

murderess /'mɜːdərəs/ *n.* Mörderin, *die*

murderous /'mɜːdərəs/ *adj.* tödlich; Mord⟨*absicht, -drohung*⟩; mörderisch (ugs.) ⟨*Kampf*⟩

murk /mɜːk/ *n.* Dunkelheit, *die*

'murky *adj.* **(a)** (dark) düster **(b)** (dirty) schmutzig-trüb ⟨*Wasser*⟩

murmur /'mɜːmə(r)/ 1 *n.* **(a)** (subdued sound) Rauschen, *das* **(b)** (expression of discontent) Murren, *das* **(c)** (soft speech) Murmeln, *das* 2 *v.t.* murmeln 3 *v.i.* ⟨*Person:*⟩ murmeln; (complain) murren

muscle /'mʌsl/ *n.* Muskel, *der*

muscular /'mʌskjʊlə(r)/ *adj.* **(a)** (Anat.) Muskel- **(b)** (strong) muskulös

muse /mjuːz/ (literary) *v.i.* [nach]sinnen (geh.) (**on, over** über + *Akk.*)

museum /mjuː'ziːəm/ *n.* Museum, *das*

mush /mʌʃ/ *n.* Brei, *der*

mushroom /'mʌʃrʊm, 'mʌʃruːm/ 1 *n.* Pilz, *der;* (cultivated) Champignon, *der* 2 *v.i.* wie Pilze aus dem Boden schießen

'mushroom cloud *n.* Rauchpilz, *der;* (after nuclear explosion) Atompilz, *der*

'mushy *adj.* breiig

music /'mjuːzɪk/ *n.* **(a)** Musik, *die;* piece of ∼: Musikstück, *das;* set sth. to ∼: etw. vertonen **(b)** (score) Noten *Pl.*

musical /'mjuːzɪkl/ 1 *adj.* musikalisch; Musik⟨*instrument, -verständnis, -notation, -abend*⟩ 2 *n.* Musical, *das*

'musical box *n.* (Brit.) Spieldose, *die*

musician /mjuː'zɪʃn/ *n.* Musiker, *der*/Musikerin, *die*

music: ∼ lesson *n.* Musikstunde, *die;* ∼ **room** *n.* Musiksaal, *der;* ∼ **stand** *n.* Notenständer, *der;* ∼ **teacher** *n.* Musiklehrer, *der*/-lehrerin, *die;* ∼ **video** *n.* Musikvideo, *das*

Muslim /'mʊslɪm, 'mʌzlɪm/ 1 *adj.* moslemisch 2 *n.* Moslem, *der*/Moslime, *die*

muslin /'mʌzlɪn/ *n.* Musselin, *der*

mussel /'mʌsl/ *n.* Muschel, *die*

must /məst, *stressed* mʌst/ 1 *v. aux., only in pres., neg.* (coll.) mustn't /'mʌsnt/ müssen; *with neg.* dürfen 2 *n.* (coll.) Muss, *das*

mustache ▶ MOUSTACHE

mustard /'mʌstəd/ *n.* Senf, *der*

muster /'mʌstə(r)/ 1 *n.* **pass** ∼: akzeptabel sein 2 *v.t.* versammeln; (Mil., Naut.) [zum Appell] antreten lassen; (fig.) zusammennehmen ⟨*Kraft, Mut, Verstand*⟩ 3 *v.i.* sich [ver]sammeln ■ **muster 'up** *v.t.* aufbringen

mustn't /'mʌsnt/ (coll.) = must not; ▶ MUST 1

musty /'mʌsti/ *adj.* muffig

mutant /'mjuːtənt/ 1 *adj.* mutiert 2 *n.* Mutante, *die*

mutation /mjuː'teɪʃn/ *n.* Mutation, *die*

mute /mjuːt/ 1 *adj.* stumm 2 *n.* Stumme, *der*/*die*

'muted *adj.* gedämpft

mutilate /'mjuːtɪleɪt/ *v.t.* verstümmeln

mutilation /mjuːtɪ'leɪʃn/ *n.* Verstümmelung, *die*

mutinous /'mjuːtɪnəs/ *adj.* meuternd

mutiny /'mjuːtɪnɪ/ 1 *n.* Meuterei, *die* 2 *v.i.* meutern

mutter /'mʌtə(r)/ *v.i. & t.* murmeln

'muttering *n.* Gemurmel, *das*

mutton /'mʌtn/ *n.* Hammelfleisch, *das*

mutual /'mjuːtjʊəl/ *adj.* **(a)** gegenseitig **(b)** (coll.: shared) gemeinsam

'mutually *adv.* **(a)** gegenseitig; be ∼ **exclusive** sich [gegenseitig] ausschließen **(b)** (in common) gemeinsam

muzak /'mjuːzæk/ *n.* (often derog.) Hintergrundmusik, *die*

muzzle /'mʌzl/ 1 *n.* **(a)** (of dog) Schnauze, *die;* (of horse, cattle) Maul, *das* **(b)** (of gun) Mündung, *die* **(c)** (put over animal's mouth) Maulkorb, *der* 2 *v.t.* **(a)** einen Maulkorb anlegen (+ *Dat.*) ⟨*Hund*⟩ **(b)** (fig.) mundtot machen (ugs.) (+ *Dat.*)

muzzy /'mʌzɪ/ *adj.* verschwommen; feel ∼: ein dumpfes Gefühl haben

MW *abbr.* (Radio) = **medium wave** MW

my /maɪ/ *poss. pron. attrib.* mein; my[, my]!, [my] oh my! [ach du] meine Güte! (ugs.)

myalgic encephalomyelitis /maɪældʒɪk ensefələʊmaɪə'laɪtɪs/ *n.* (Med.) myalgische Enzephalomyelitis

myopia /maɪ'əʊpɪə/ *n.* Kurzsichtigkeit, *die* (auch fig.)

myopic /maɪ'ɒpɪk/ *adj.* kurzsichtig (auch fig.)

myself /maɪ'self/ *pron.* **(a)** *emphat.* selbst; I thought so ∼: das habe ich auch gedacht **(b)** *refl.* mich/mir. See also HERSELF

mysterious /mɪ'stɪərɪəs/ *adj.* rätselhaft; geheimnisvoll ⟨*Fremder, Orient*⟩

my'steriously *adv.* auf rätselhafte Weise; geheimnisvoll ⟨*lächeln usw.*⟩

mystery /'mɪstərɪ/ *n.* **(a)** Rätsel, *das* **(b)** (secrecy) Geheimnis, *das*

mystery: ∼ tour *n.* Fahrt ins Blaue (ugs.); ∼ **writer** Kriminalschriftsteller, *der*/-schriftstellerin, *die*

mystic /'mɪstɪk/ 1 *adj.* mystisch 2 *n.* Mystiker, *der*/Mystikerin, *die*

mystical /'mɪstɪkl/ *adj.* mystisch

mysticism /'mɪstɪsɪzm/ *n.* Mystik, *die*

mystify /'mɪstɪfaɪ/ *v.t.* verwirren

myth /mɪθ/ *n.* Mythos, *der*
mythical /'mɪθɪkl/ *adj.* **(a)** (based on myth)
mythisch
  (b) (invented) fiktiv

mythological /mɪθə'lɒdʒɪkl/ *adj.*
mythologisch
mythology /mɪ'θɒlədʒɪ/ *n.* Mythologie, *die*

Nn

N, n /en/ *n.* N, n, *das*
N. *abbr.* **(a)** = **north** N
  (b) = **northern** n.
NAAFI /'næfɪ/ *abbr.* (Brit.) = **Navy, Army
and Air Force Institutes** *Kaufhaus
für Angehörige der britischen Truppen*
nab /næb/ *v.t.,* **-bb-** (coll.) **(a)** (arrest)
schnappen (ugs.)
  (b) (seize) sich (*Dat.*) schnappen
nag /næg/ *v.i. & t.* **-gg-:** ~ **[at] sb.** an jmdm.
herumnörgeln; ~ **[at] sb. to do sth.** jmdm.
zusetzen (ugs.), dass er etw. tut
'**nagging** ⬜1 *adj.* (persistent) quälend;
bohrend ‹*Schmerz*›
  ⬜2 *n.* Genörgel, *das*
nail /neɪl/ ⬜1 *n.* Nagel, *der;* **hit the ~ on the
head** (fig.) den Nagel auf den Kopf treffen
(ugs.)
  ⬜2 *v.t.* nageln (**to** an + *Akk.*)
■ **nail** '**down** *v.t.* festnageln; zunageln
‹*Kiste*›
nail: ~ **brush** *n.* Nagelbürste, *die;*
  ~ **clippers** *n. pl.* [pair of] ~ clippers
Nagelknipser, *der;* ~ **file** *n.* Nagelfeile,
die; ~ **polish** *n.* Nagellack, *der;* ~ **polish
remover** Nagellackentferner, *der;*
  ~ **scissors** *n. pl.* [pair of] ~ scissors
Nagelschere, *die;* ~ **varnish** (Brit.)
  ▶ ~ POLISH
naive, naïve /naɪ'iːv/ *adj.,* **na'ively,
na'ively** *adv.* naiv
naked /'neɪkɪd/ *adj.* nackt; **visible to**
or **with the ~ eye** mit bloßem Auge zu
erkennen
'**nakedness** *n.* Nacktheit, *die*
name /neɪm/ ⬜1 *n.* **(a)** Name, *der;* **what's
your ~/the ~ of this place?** wie heißt
du/dieser Ort?; **my ~ is Jack** ich heiße Jack;
last ~: Nachname, *der;* **by ~:** namentlich
‹*erwähnen, aufrufen usw.*›; **know sb. by
~:** jmdn. mit Namen kennen
  (b) (reputation) Ruf, *der;* **make a ~ for oneself**
sich (*Dat.*) einen Namen machen
  (c) call sb. ~s jmdn. beschimpfen
  ⬜2 *v.t.* **(a)** (give ~ to) einen Namen geben
(+ *Dat.*); ~ **sb. John** jmdn. John nennen;
~ **sb./sth. after** *or* (Amer.) **for sb.** jmdn./etw.
nach jmdm. benennen; **be ~d John** John
heißen; **a man ~d Smith** ein Mann namens
Smith

  (b) (call by right ~) benennen
  (c) (nominate) ~ **sb. [as] sth.** jmdn. zu etw.
ernennen
'**name-drop** *v.i.* [scheinbar beiläufig]
bekannte Namen fallen lassen
'**nameless** *adj.* namenlos
'**namely** *adv.* nämlich
'**namesake** *n.* Namensvetter, *der/*
-schwester, *die*
nanny /'nænɪ/ *n.* (Brit.) Kindermädchen, *das*
nanny: ~ **goat** *n.* Ziege, *die;* ~ '**state** *n.*
(derog.) Versorgungsstaat, *der*
nap /næp/ ⬜1 *n.* Nickerchen, *das* (fam.);
have a ~: ein Nickerchen halten
  ⬜2 *v.i.,* **-pp-** dösen (ugs.); **catch sb. ~ping**
(fig.) jmdn. überrumpeln
nape /neɪp/ *n.* ~ **[of the neck]** Nacken, *der;*
Genick, *das*
napkin /'næpkɪn/ *n.* Serviette, *die*
Naples /'neɪplz/ *pr. n.* Neapel (*das*)
nappy /'næpɪ/ *n.* (Brit.) Windel, *die*
narcissistic /nɑːsɪ'sɪstɪk/ *adj.*
narzisstisch
narcissus /nɑː'sɪsəs/ *n., pl.* **narcissi**
/nɑː'sɪsaɪ/ *or* ~**es** Narzisse, *die*
narcotic /nɑː'kɒtɪk/ ⬜1 *n.* **(a)** (drug)
Rauschgift, *das*
  (b) (active ingredient) Betäubungsmittel, *das*
  ⬜2 *adj.* **(a)** narkotisch; ~ **drug** Rauschgift,
das
  (b) (causing drowsiness) einschläfernd
narrate /nə'reɪt/ *v.t.* erzählen;
kommentieren ‹*Film*›
narration /nə'reɪʃn/ *n.* Erzählung, *die*
narrative /'nærətɪv/ ⬜1 *n.* Erzählung, *die*
  ⬜2 *adj.* erzählend
narrator /nə'reɪtə(r)/ *n.* Erzähler,
*der/*Erzählerin, *die*
narrow /'nærəʊ/ ⬜1 *adj.* **(a)** schmal;
schmal geschnitten ‹*Rock, Hose, Ärmel
usw.*›; eng ‹*Tal, Gasse*›
  (b) (limited) eng; begrenzt ‹*Auswahl*›
  (c) knapp ‹*Sieg, Mehrheit*›; **have a ~ escape**
mit knapper Not entkommen (**from** *Dat.*)
  (d) (not tolerant) engstirnig
  ⬜2 *v.i.* sich verschmälern; ‹*Tal:*› sich
verengen
  ⬜3 *v.t.* verschmälern; (fig.) einengen

■ **narrow 'down** *v.t.* einengen (**to** auf
+ *Akk.*)
narrow-'minded *adj.* engstirnig
nasal /'neɪzl/ *adj.* (a) (Anat.) Nasen-
(b) näselnd; **speak in a** ~ **voice** näseln
nastily /'nɑːstɪlɪ/ *adv.* (a) (unpleasantly)
scheußlich
(b) (ill-naturedly) gemein; **behave** ~: hässlich
sein
nasty /'nɑːstɪ/ *adj.* (a) (unpleasant)
scheußlich ⟨*Geruch, Geschmack*⟩; gemein
⟨*Trick, Person*⟩; hässlich ⟨*Angewohnheit*⟩;
that was a ~ **thing to say/do** das war gemein
(b) (ill-natured) böse; **be** ~ **to sb.** hässlich zu
jmdm. sein
(c) (serious) übel; schlimm ⟨*Krankheit,
Husten, Verletzung*⟩; **she had a** ~ **fall** sie ist
übel gefallen
nation /'neɪʃn/ *n.* Nation, *die;* (people) Volk,
das
national /'næʃənl/ ⟦1⟧ *adj.* national;
National⟨*flagge, -held, -theater, -gericht,
-charakter*⟩; Staats⟨*sicherheit, -religion*⟩;
überregional ⟨*Rundfunkstation, Zeitung*⟩;
landesweit ⟨*Streik*⟩
⟦2⟧ *n.* (citizen) Staatsbürger, *der*/-bürgerin,
die; **foreign** ~: Ausländer, *der*/Ausländerin,
die
national: ~ **'anthem** *n.*
Nationalhymne, *die;* ~ **call** *n.* (Brit. Teleph.)
Inlandsgespräch, *das;* ~ **'costume**
n. Nationaltracht, *die;* **N**~ **'Health
[Service]** *n.* (Brit.) staatlicher
Gesundheitsdienst; **N**~ **Health doctor/
patient/spectacles** ≈ Kassenarzt, *der*/
-patient, *der*/-brille, *die;* **N**~ **In'surance**
n. (Brit.) Sozialversicherung, *die*
nationalism /'næʃənəlɪzm/ *n.*
Nationalismus, *der*
nationalist /'næʃənəlɪst/ ⟦1⟧ *n.*
Nationalist, *der*/Nationalistin, *die*
⟦2⟧ *adj.* nationalistisch
nationality /næʃə'nælɪtɪ/ *n.*
Staatsangehörigkeit, *die;* **what's his** ~?
welche Staatsangehörigkeit hat er?
nationalization /næʃənəlaɪ'zeɪʃn/ *n.*
Verstaatlichung, *die*
nationalize /'næʃənəlaɪz/ *v.t.*
verstaatlichen
'nationally *adv.* landesweit
National: **n**~ **'park** *n.* Nationalpark,
der; ~ **'Savings** *n. pl.* (Brit.)
Staatsschuldverschreibungen *Pl.;*
~ **Savings certificate** Sparkassengutschein,
der; öffentlicher Sparbrief; **n**~ **'service**
n. (Brit.) Wehrdienst, *der;* **do n**~ **service**
seinen Wehrdienst ableisten;
~ **'Socialist** *n.* Nationalsozialist, *der*/
-sozialistin, *die; attrib.* nationalsozialistisch;
~ **Vo'cational Qualification** *n.* (Brit.)
staatliches Berufsausbildungsprogramm
native /'neɪtɪv/ ⟦1⟧ *n.* (a) (of specified place)
a ~ **of Britain** ein gebürtiger Brite/eine

gebürtige Britin
(b) (person born in a place) Eingeborene,
der/*die*
(c) (local inhabitant) Einheimische, *der*/*die*
⟦2⟧ *adj.* eingeboren; einheimisch ⟨*Pflanze,
Tier*⟩; ~ **inhabitant** Eingeborene/
Einheimische, *der*/*die;* ~ **land** Geburts-
od. Heimatland, *das;* ~ **language**
Muttersprache, *die*
nativity /nə'tɪvɪtɪ/ *n.* **the N**~ [**of Christ**] die
Geburt Christi
na'tivity play *n.* Krippenspiel, *das*
NATO, Nato /'neɪtəʊ/ *abbr.* = **North
Atlantic Treaty Organization**
NATO, *die*
natter /'nætə(r)/ (Brit. coll.) ⟦1⟧ *v.i.*
quatschen (ugs.)
⟦2⟧ *n.* **have a** ~: quatschen (ugs.)
natural /'nætʃrəl/ *adj.* natürlich;
Natur⟨*zustand, -seide, -gewalt*⟩
natural: ~ **'childbirth** *n.* natürliche
Geburt; ~ **'gas** *n.* Erdgas, *das;*
~ **'history** *n.* Naturkunde, *die*
naturalism /'nætʃrəlɪzm/ *n.*
Naturalismus, *der*
naturalist /'nætʃrəlɪst/ *n.* Naturforscher,
der/-forscherin, *die*
naturalization /nætʃrəlaɪ'zeɪʃn/ *n.*
Einbürgerung, *die*
naturalize /'nætʃrəlaɪz/ *v.t.* einbürgern
'naturally *adv.* (a) (by nature) von Natur
aus ⟨*blass, fleißig usw.*⟩; (in a true-to-life way)
naturgetreu
(b) (of course) natürlich
'naturalness Natürlichkeit, *die*
nature /'neɪtʃə(r)/ *n.* (a) Natur, *die*
(b) (essential qualities) Beschaffenheit, *die;* **in
the** ~ **of things** naturgemäß
(c) (kind) Art, *die;* **things of this**
~: derartiges
(d) (character) Wesen, *das;* **be proud/friendly
etc. by** ~: ein stolzes/freundliches *usw.*
Wesen haben
nature: ~ **conservation** *n.*
Naturschutz, *der;* ~ **lover** *n.* Naturfreund,
der/-freundin, *die;* ~ **reserve** *n.*
Naturschutzgebiet, *das;* ~ **study** *n.*
Naturkunde, *die;* ~ **trail** *n.* Naturlehrpfad,
der
naturist /'neɪtʃərɪst/ *n.* (nudist) Naturist,
der/Naturistin, *die;* FKK-Anhänger,
der/FKK-Anhängerin, *die*
naught /nɔːt/ *n.* (arch./dial.) **come to**
~: zunichte werden
naughtily /'nɔːtɪlɪ/ *adv.* ungezogen
naughtiness /'nɔːtɪnɪs/ *n.*
Ungezogenheit, *die*
naughty /'nɔːtɪ/ *adj.* ungezogen; **you**
~ **boy/dog** du böser Junge/Hund
nausea /'nɔːzɪə/ *n.* Übelkeit, *die*
nauseate /'nɔːzɪeɪt/ *v.t.* (disgust) anwidern
'nauseating *adj.* (disgusting) widerlich

nauseous /'nɔːzɪəs/ adj. sb. is or feels ~: jmdm. ist übel

nautical /'nɔːtɪkl/ adj. nautisch

nautical 'mile n. Seemeile, die

naval /'neɪvl/ adj. Marine-; See⟨schlacht, -macht, -streitkräfte⟩; ~ **ship** Kriegsschiff, das

naval: ~ **base** n. Flottenstützpunkt, der; ~ **officer** n. Marineoffizier, der

nave /neɪv/ n. [Mittel]schiff, das

navel /'neɪvl/ n. Nabel, der

navigate /'nævɪgeɪt/ v.t. (a) navigieren ⟨Schiff, Flugzeug⟩ (b) befahren ⟨Fluss usw.⟩

navigation /nævɪ'geɪʃn/ n. Navigation, die

navigator /'nævɪgeɪtə(r)/ n. Navigator, der/Navigatorin, die

navy /'neɪvɪ/ 1 n. (a) [Kriegs]marine, die (b) ▶ NAVY BLUE 2 adj. ▶ NAVY-BLUE

navy: ~ **'blue** n. Marineblau, das; ~**-blue** adj. marineblau

Nazi /'nɑːtsɪ/ 1 n. Nazi, der 2 adj. nazistisch; Nazi-

NB abbr. = **nota bene** NB

NCO abbr. = **non-commissioned officer** Uffz.

NE abbr. = **north-east** NO

near /nɪə(r)/ 1 adv. nah[e]; **stand/live [quite]** ~: [ganz] in der Nähe stehen/ wohnen; **come** or **draw** ~/~**er** ⟨Tag, Zeitpunkt:⟩ nahen/näher rücken; **get** ~**er together** näher zusammenrücken; ~ **at hand** in Reichweite (Dat.); ⟨Ort⟩ ganz in der Nähe; ~ **to** = 2
2 prep. (a) (position) nahe an/bei (+ Dat.); (fig.) in der Nähe (+ Gen.); **keep** ~ **me** halte dich in meiner Nähe; **it's** ~ **here** es ist hier in der Nähe (b) (motion) nahe an (+ Akk.); (fig.) in der Nähe (+ Gen.); **don't come** ~ **me** komm mir nicht zu nahe
3 adj. (a) (in space or time) nahe; **in the** ~ **future** in nächster Zukunft; **the** ~**est man** der am nächsten stehende Mann (b) (in nature) **£30** or ~/~**est offer** 30 Pfund oder nächstbestes Angebot; ~ **escape** Entkommen mit knapper Not; **that was a** ~ **miss/thing!** das war knapp!
4 v.t. sich nähern (+ Dat.); **the building is** ~**ing completion** das Gebäude steht kurz vor seiner Vollendung
5 v.i. ⟨Zeitpunkt:⟩ näher rücken

'nearby adj. nahe gelegen

'nearly adv. fast; **be** ~ **in tears** den Tränen nahe sein; **it is** ~ **six o'clock** es ist kurz vor sechs Uhr; **are you** ~ **ready?** bist du bald fertig?

'nearness n. Nähe, die

'near-sighted adj. (Amer.) kurzsichtig

neat /niːt/ adj. (a) (tidy) ordentlich (b) (undiluted) pur

(c) (smart) gepflegt ⟨Erscheinung, Kleidung⟩ (d) (deft) geschickt

'neatly adv. ▶ NEAT A, C, D: ordentlich; gepflegt; geschickt

'neatness n. ▶ NEAT A, C, D: Ordentlichkeit, die; Gepflegtheit, die; Geschicktheit, die

necessarily /nesɪ'serɪlɪ/ adv. zwangsläufig; **it is not** ~ **true** es muss nicht [unbedingt] stimmen

necessary /'nesɪsərɪ/ 1 adj. nötig; notwendig; **do everything** ~: das Nötige od. Notwendige tun 2 n. **the necessaries of life** das Lebensnotwendige

necessitate /nɪ'sesɪteɪt/ v.t. erforderlich machen

necessity /nɪ'sesɪtɪ/ n. (a) (need, necessary thing) Notwendigkeit, die; **do sth. out of** or **from** ~: etw. notgedrungen tun; **of** ~: notwendigerweise (b) (want) Not, der (c) (thing) Bedürfnis, das 2 v.t. (a) (require) brauchen; **sth. that urgently** ~**s doing** etw., was dringend gemacht werden muss; **it** ~**s a coat of paint** es muss gestrichen werden (b) (expr. necessity) müssen; **I** ~ **to do it** ich muss es tun; **it** ~**s/doesn't** ~ **to be done** es muss getan werden/es braucht nicht getan zu werden (c) pres. **he** ~, neg. ~ **not** or (coll.) ~**n't** /'niːdnt/ (expr. desirability) müssen; with neg. brauchen zu

neck /nek/ n. (a) Hals, der; **be a pain in the** ~ (coll.) jmdm. auf die Nerven gehen (ugs.); **break one's** ~ (fig. coll.) sich den Hals brechen; ~ **and** ~: Kopf an Kopf (b) (of garment) Kragen, der

neck: ~**lace** /'neklɪs/ n. [Hals]kette, die; (with jewels) Kollier, das; ~**line** n. [Hals]ausschnitt, der; ~**tie** n. Krawatte, die

nectar /'nektə(r)/ n. Nektar, der

née (Amer.: **nee**) /neɪ/ adj. geborene

need /niːd/ 1 n. (a) Notwendigkeit, die (for, of Gen.); (demand) Bedarf, der (for, of an + Dat.); **as the** ~ **arises** nach Bedarf; **if** ~ **be** nötigenfalls; **there's no** ~ **for that** [das ist] nicht nötig; **there's no** ~ **to do sth.** es ist nicht nötig, etw. zu tun; **be in** ~ **of sth.** etw. brauchen; **there's no** ~ **for you to come** du brauchst nicht zu kommen (b) no pl. (emergency) Not, die; **in case of** ~: im Notfall

needle /'niːdl/ 1 n. Nadel, die 2 v.t. (coll.) nerven (ugs.)

needle: ~**cord** n. (Textiles) Feinkord, der; ~**craft** n. Nadelarbeit, die

needless /'niːdlɪs/ adj. unnötig; ~ **to add** or **say**, ...: überflüssig zu sagen, dass ...

'needlessly adv. unnötig

'needlework n. Handarbeit, die; **do** ~: handarbeiten

needn't /'niːdnt/ (coll.) = need not;
▶ NEED 2C

'needy *adj.* notleidend; bedürftig

negation /nɪ'geɪʃn/ *n.* Verneinung, *die*

negative /'negətɪv/ ① *adj.* negativ
② *n.* **(a)** (Photog.) Negativ, *das*
(b) (∼ statement) negative Aussage; (answer)
Nein, *das*

negative 'equity *n.* Negativwert, *der*

'negatively *adv.* negativ

neglect /nɪ'glekt/ ① *v.t.* vernachlässigen;
she ∼ed to write sie hat es versäumt zu
schreiben
② *n.* Vernachlässigung, *die;* be in a state of
∼ ⟨Gebäude:⟩ verwahrlost sein

neglectful /nɪ'glektfl/ *adj.* gleichgültig
(of gegenüber); be ∼ of sich nicht kümmern
um

negligence /'neglɪdʒəns/ *n.*
Nachlässigkeit, *die;* (Law, Insurance, etc.)
Fahrlässigkeit, *die*

negligent /'neglɪdʒənt/ *adj.* nachlässig; be
∼ about sth. sich um etw. nicht kümmern

negligible /'neglɪdʒɪbl/ *adj.* unerheblich

negotiable /nɪ'gəʊʃəbl/ *adj.*
(a) verhandlungsfähig ⟨Forderung,
Bedingungen⟩
(b) passierbar ⟨Straße, Fluss⟩

negotiate /nɪ'gəʊʃɪeɪt/ ① *v.i.* verhandeln
(for, on, about über + *Akk.*)
② *v.t.* **(a)** (arrange) aushandeln
(b) überwinden ⟨Hindernis⟩; passieren
⟨Straße, Fluss⟩; nehmen ⟨Kurve⟩

negotiation /nɪgəʊʃɪ'eɪʃn/ *n.*
Verhandlung, *die*

negotiator /nɪ'gəʊʃɪeɪtə(r)/ *n.*
Unterhändler, *der*/-händlerin, *die*

Negress /'niːgrɪs/ *n.* (dated/offensive)
Negerin, *die*

Negro /'niːgrəʊ/ ① *n., pl.* ∼es (dated/
offensive) Neger, *der*
② *adj.* Neger-

neigh /neɪ/ ① *v.i.* wiehern
② *n.* Wiehern, *das*

neighbor *etc.* (Amer.) ▶ NEIGHBOUR *etc.*

neighbour /'neɪbə(r)/ ① *n.* Nachbar,
der/Nachbarin, *die;* my next-door ∼s meine
Nachbarn von nebenan
② *v.t. & i.* ∼ [upon] grenzen an (+ *Akk.*)

'neighbourhood *n.* (district) Gegend, *die;*
(neighbours) Nachbarschaft, *die;* [somewhere]
in the ∼ of £100 [so] um [die] 100 Pfund

'neighbourhood watch *n.:* Programm
zur Verhütung von Straftaten, bes. von
Wohnungseinbrüchen, durch erhöhte
Wachsamkeit aller in einem Wohngebiet
lebenden Menschen

'neighbouring *adj.* Nachbar-; angrenzend
⟨Felder⟩

neighbourly /'neɪbəlɪ/ *adj.*
(a) (characteristic of neighbours)
[gut]nachbarlich

(b) (friendly) freundlich

neither /'naɪðə(r), niːðə(r)/ ① *adj.*
keiner/keine/keins der beiden
② *pron.* keiner/keine/keins von *od.* der
beiden
③ *adv.* (also not) auch nicht; ∼ am I, (coll.) me
∼: ich auch nicht
④ *conj.* (not either) weder; ∼ ... nor ...: weder
... noch ...

neo'classical *adj.* klassizistisch

neo'conservative ① *adj.*
neokonservativ;
② *n.* Neokonservative, *die/die*

neo'fascist *adj.* neofaszistisch

neon /'niːɒn/ *n.* Neon, *das*

neo-'nazi ① *n.* Neonazi, *der*
② *adj.* neonazistisch; a ∼ group eine
Neonazigruppe

neon: ∼ 'lamp, ∼ 'light *ns.* Neonlampe,
die; ∼ 'sign *n.* Neonreklame, *die*

nephew /'nevjuː, 'nefjuː/ *n.* Neffe, *der*

nepotism /'nepətɪzm/ *n.*
Vetternwirtschaft, *die*

Neptune /'neptjuːn/ *pr. n.* (Astron.) Neptun,
der

nerve /nɜːv/ *n.* Nerv, *der;* get on sb.'s ∼s
jmdm. auf die Nerven gehen (ugs.); lose
one's ∼: die Nerven verlieren; what [a] ∼!
[so eine] Frechheit!

nerve: ∼ **cell** *n.* Nervenzelle, *die;*
∼ **centre** *n.* (fig.) Schaltzentrale, *die;*
∼ **gas** *n.* Nervengas, *das;* ∼-**racking**
adj. nervenaufreibend

nervous /'nɜːvəs/ *adj.* **(a)** (Anat.,
Med.) Nerven-; ∼ **breakdown**
Nervenzusammenbruch, *der*
(b) (having delicate nerves) nervös; be a
∼ **wreck** mit den Nerven völlig am Ende
sein
(c) (Brit.: timid) be ∼ of *or* about Angst haben
vor (+ *Dat.*); be a ∼ **person** ängstlich sein

'nervously *adv.* nervös

'nervousness *n.* Ängstlichkeit, *die*

nervy /'nɜːvɪ/ *adj.* **(a)** nervös
(b) (Amer. coll.: impudent) unverschämt

nest ① *n.* Nest, *das*
② *v.i.* nisten

'nest egg *n.* (fig.) Notgroschen, *der*

nestle /'nesl/ *v.i.* **(a)** sich schmiegen (to, up
against an + *Akk.*)
(b) (lie half hidden) eingebettet sein

net¹ /net/ ① *n.* **(a)** Netz, *das*
(b) the Net (Comp.) das Netz
② *v.t.,* **-tt-** [mit einem Netz] fangen

net² *adj.* **(a)** netto; Netto⟨einkommen,
-[verkaufs]preis usw.⟩; ∼ **weight**
Nettogewicht, *das*
(b) (ultimate) End⟨ergebnis, -effekt⟩

net: ∼**ball** *n.* Netzball, *der;* ∼ 'curtain
n. Store, *der*

Netherlands /'neðələndz/ *pr. n. sing. or*
pl. Niederlande *Pl.*

net 'profit n. Reingewinn, der
'netspeak n. Internetjargon, der
nett ▸ NET² A
'netting n. ([piece of] net) Netz, das; wire
~: Maschendraht, der
nettle /'netl/ n. Nessel, die
'network n. Netz, das; (Comp.) Netzwerk,
das
'network provider n. (Comp.)
Netzanbieter, der
neuralgia /njʊə'rældʒə/ n. Neuralgie, die
neurological /njʊərə'lɒdʒɪkl/ adj.
neurologisch
neurologist /njʊə'rɒlədʒɪst/ n.
Neurologe, der/Neurologin, die
neurology /njʊə'rɒlədʒɪ/ n. Neurologie,
die
neurosis /njʊə'rəʊsɪs/ n., pl. **neuroses**
/njʊə'rəʊsiːz/ Neurose, die
neurotic /njʊə'rɒtɪk/ adj. (a) nervenkrank
(b) (coll.) neurotisch
neuter /'njuːtə(r)/ adj. sächlich
neutral /'njuːtrl/ **1** adj. neutral
2 n. (~ gear) Leerlauf, der
neutrality /njuː'trælɪtɪ/ n. Neutralität, die
neutralize /'njuːtrəlaɪz/ v.t.
neutralisieren
neutron /'njuːtrɒn/ n. Neutron, das
never /'nevə(r)/ adv. (a) nie; ~-ending
endlos
(b) (coll.) you ~ believed that, did you? du
hast das doch wohl nicht geglaubt?; well, I
~ [did]! [na] so was!
neverthe'less adv. trotzdem
new /njuː/ adj. neu
new: New Age n. Newage, das; attrib.
Newage-; ~**-born** adj. neugeboren;
~ **build** n. Neubau, der; ~**comer**
/'njuːkʌmə(r)/ n. Neuankömmling, der;
~**fangled** /'njuːfæŋgld/ adj. neumodisch;
~**-found** adj. neu; ~**-laid** adj. frisch
[gelegt]; **New 'Left** n. neue Linke;
~ **'look** n. (coll.) neuer Stil
'newly adv. (recently) neu; ~ married seit
kurzem verheiratet
'newly-wed n. Jungverheiratete, der/die
new: New 'Man n. der neue Mann;
~ **'moon** n. Neumond, der
'newness n. Neuheit, die
news /njuːz/ n. (a) Nachricht, die; be in
the ~: Schlagzeilen machen; good/bad
~: schlechte/gute Nachrichten Pl.
(b) (Radio, Telev.) Nachrichten Pl.
news: ~ **agency** n.
Nachrichtenagentur, die; ~**agent** n.
Zeitungshändler, der/-händlerin, die;
~ **bulletin** n. Nachrichten Pl.; ~**cast**
n. Nachrichtensendung, die; ~**caster**
n. Nachrichtensprecher, der/-sprecherin,
die; ~ **desk** n. Nachrichtenredaktion,
die; this is Joe Smith at the ~ desk
(Radio) hier ist Joe Smith mit den

Nachrichten; ~**flash** n. Kurzmeldung,
die; ~**group** n. (Comp.) Newsgroup,
die; ~ **'headline** n. Schlagzeile, die;
~**letter** n. Rundschreiben, das; ~**paper**
n. (a) Zeitung, die; ~**paper boy/girl**
Zeitungsausträger, der/-austrägerin, die;
(b) (material) Zeitungspapier, das; ~**reader**
n. Nachrichtensprecher, der/-sprecherin,
die; ~**reel** n. Wochenschau, die; ~**room**
n. Nachrichtenredaktion, die; ~**-sheet**
n. Informationsblatt, das; ~**stand**
n. Zeitungskiosk, der; Zeitungsstand, der;
~ **summary** n. Kurznachrichten Pl.;
~ **vendor** n. Zeitungsverkäufer, der/
-verkäuferin, die; ~**worthy** adj. [für die
Medien] interessant
newt /njuːt/ n. [Wasser]molch, der
New: new town n.: mit Unterstützung
der Regierung völlig neu entstandene
Ansiedlung; **new 'year** n. Neujahr, das;
over the new year über Neujahr; a Happy
New Year ein glückliches od. gutes neues
Jahr. ~ **'Year's** (Amer.), ~ **Year's 'Day**
ns. Neujahrstag, der; ~ **Year's 'Eve**
n. Silvester, der od. das; ~ **Zealand**
/- 'ziːlənd/ pr. n. Neuseeland (das);
~ **'Zealander** n. Neuseeländer, der/
-länderin, die
next /nekst/ **1** adj. nächst...; the ~ but
one der/die/das Übernächste; ~ to
(fig.: almost) fast; nahezu; [the] ~ time
das nächste Mal; the ~ best der/die/das
Nächstbeste; am I ~? komme ich jetzt dran?
2 adv. (in the ~ place) als Nächstes; (on the
~ occasion) das nächste Mal; it's my turn
~: ich komme als Nächster dran; sit/stand
~ to sb. neben jmdm. stehen/sitzen; place
sth. ~ to sb./sth. etw. neben jmdn./etw.
stellen
3 n. (a) the week after ~: [die] übernächste
Woche
(b) (person) ~ of kin nächster/nächste
Angehörige; ~, please! der Nächste, bitte!
'next-door adj. gleich nebenan
nachgestellt
NHS abbr. (Brit.) = **National Health
Service**
nib /nɪb/ n. Feder, die
nibble /'nɪbl/ v.t. & i. knabbern (at, on an
+ Dat.)
nice /naɪs/ adj. nett; angenehm ⟨Stimme⟩;
schön ⟨Wetter⟩; (iron.: disgraceful, difficult) schön;
~ [and] warm/fast schön warm/schnell;
~**-looking** gut aussehend
'nicely adv. (coll.) (a) (well) nett; gut
⟨arbeiten, sich benehmen, platziert sein⟩
(b) (all right) gut; that will do ~: das reicht
völlig
niceties /'naɪsɪtɪz/ n. pl. Feinheiten Pl.
niche /nɪtʃ, niːʃ/ n. (a) (in wall) Nische, die
(b) (fig.: suitable place) Platz, der
nick **1** n. (a) (notch) Kerbe, die
(b) (sl. prison) Knast, der (salopp)
(c) (Brit.: police station) Wache, die

(d) in good/poor ∼ (coll.) gut/nicht gut im Schuss (ugs.)
(e) in the ∼ **of time** gerade noch rechtzeitig
2 *v.t.* **(a)** einkerben
(b) (Brit. coll.: arrest) einlochen (salopp)
(c) (Brit. coll.: steal) klauen (salopp)
nickel /'nɪkl/ *n.* **(a)** Nickel, *das*
(b) (Amer. coll.: coin) Fünfcentstück, *das*
nickname /'nɪkneɪm/ *n.* Spitzname, *der;* (affectionate) Koseform, *die*
nicotine /'nɪkəti:n/ *n.* Nikotin, *das*
'nicotine patch *n.* Nikotinpflaster, *das*
niece /ni:s/ *n.* Nichte, *die*
Nigeria /naɪ'dʒɪərɪə/ *pr. n.* Nigeria (*das*)
niggardly /'nɪɡədlɪ/ *adj.* knaus[e]rig (ugs.)
niggling /'nɪɡlɪŋ/ *adj.* **(a)** (petty) belanglos
(b) (trivial) nichts sagend
(c) (nagging) nagend
night /naɪt/ *n.* Nacht, *die;* (evening) Abend, *der;* **the following** ∼: die Nacht/der Abend darauf; **the previous** ∼: die vorausgegangene Nacht/der vorausgegangene Abend; **on Sunday** ∼: Sonntagnacht/[am] Sonntagabend; **for the** ∼: über Nacht; **at** ∼: nachts/abends; **late at** ∼: spätabends
night: ∼**bird** *n.* (person) Nachteule, *die* (ugs. scherzh.); ∼ **blindness** *n.* Nachtblindheit, *die;* ∼**cap** *n.* (drink) Schlaftrunk, *der;* ∼**clothes** *n. pl.* Nachtwäsche, *die;* ∼**club** *n.* Nachtklub, *der;* ∼**dress** *n.* Nachthemd, *das;* ∼ **duty** *n.* Nachtdienst, *der;* **be on** ∼ **duty** Nachtdienst haben; ∼**fall** *n.* Einbruch der Dunkelheit
nightie /'naɪtɪ/ *n.* (coll.) Nachthemd, *das*
nightingale /'naɪtɪŋɡeɪl/ *n.* Nachtigall, *die*
'nightlife *n.* Nachtleben, *das*
nightly /'naɪtlɪ/ 1 *adj.* (happening every night/evening) allnächtlich/allabendlich
2 *adv.* (every night) jede Nacht; (every evening) jeden Abend
night: ∼**mare** *n.* Albtraum, *der;* ∼**marish** /'naɪtmeərɪʃ/ *adj.* albtraumhaft; ∼ **owl** *n.* **(a)** (Ornith.) Eule, *die;* **(b)** (coll.: person) Nachteule, *die* (ugs. scherzh.); ∼ **porter** *n.* Nachtportier, *der;* ∼ **safe** *n.* Nachttresor, *der;* ∼ **school** *n.* Abendschule, *die;* ∼ **shelter** *n.* Nachtasyl, *das;* ∼ **shift** *n.* Nachtschicht, *die;* ∼ **sky** *n.* Nachthimmel, *der;* ∼ **'storage heater** *n.* Nachtspeicherofen, *der;* ∼**-time** *n.* Nacht, *die;* **in the** *or* **at** ∼**-time** nachts; ∼**'watchman** *n.* Nachtwächter, *der;* ∼**wear** *n. sing.* ▸ NIGHTCLOTHES
nihilistic /naɪ'lɪstɪk, nɪhɪ'lɪstɪk/ *adj.* nihilistisch
nil /nɪl/ *n.* null
Nile /naɪl/ *pr. n.* Nil, *der*
nimble /'nɪmbl/ *adj.,* **nimbly** /'nɪmblɪ/ *adv.* flink
nine /naɪn/ 1 *adj.* neun
2 *n.* Neun, *die.* See also EIGHT

nineteen /naɪn'ti:n/ 1 *adj.* neunzehn
2 *n.* Neunzehn, *die.* See also EIGHT
nineteenth /naɪn'ti:nθ/ 1 *adj.* neunzehnt...
2 *n.* (fraction) Neunzehntel, *das.* See also EIGHTH
ninetieth /'naɪntɪɪθ/ *adj.* neunzigst...
ninety /'naɪntɪ/ 1 *adj.* neunzig
2 *n.* Neunzig, *die.* See also EIGHT; EIGHTY 2
ninth /naɪnθ/ 1 *adj.* neunt...
2 *n.* (in sequence, rank) Neunte, *der/die/das;* (fraction) Neuntel, *das.* See also EIGHTH
nip 1 *v.t.,* -pp- zwicken
2 *v.i.,* -pp- (Brit. coll.) ∼ **in** hinein-/ hereinflitzen (ugs.); ∼ **out** hinaus-/ herausflitzen (ugs.)
3 *n.* (pinch, squeeze) Kniff, *der;* (bite) Biss, *der*
'nipper *n.* (Brit. coll.: child) Balg, *das* (ugs.)
nipple /'nɪpl/ *n.* **(a)** Brustwarze, *die*
(b) (of feeding bottle) Sauger, *die*
niqab /nɪ'kɑ:b/ *n.* Niqab, *der*
nitrate /'naɪtreɪt/ *n.* **(a)** (salt) Nitrat, *das*
(b) (fertilizer) Nitratdünger, *der*
nitric acid /'naɪtrɪk æsɪd/ *n.* Salpetersäure, *die*
nitrogen /'naɪtrədʒən/ *n.* Stickstoff, *der*
'nitrogen cycle *n.* Stickstoffkreislauf, *der*
nitwit /'nɪtwɪt/ *n.* (coll.) Trottel, *der* (ugs.)
no /nəʊ/ 1 *adj.* kein
2 *adv.* **(a)** (by no amount) nicht; **no less [than]** nicht weniger [als]; **no more wine?** keinen Wein mehr?
(b) (as answer) nein
3 *n., pl.* **noes** /nəʊz/ Nein, *das*
No. *abbr.* = **number** Nr.
Noah's ark /nəʊəz 'ɑ:k/ *n.* die Arche Noah
Nobel prize /nəʊbel 'praɪz/ *n.* Nobelpreis, *der*
nobility /nə'bɪlɪtɪ/ *n.* Adel, *der;* **many of the** ∼: viele Adlige
noble /'nəʊbl/ 1 *adj.* ad[e]lig; edel ‹*Gedanken, Gefühle*›
2 *n.* Adlige, *der/die*
nobleman /'nəʊblmən/ *n., pl.* **noblemen** /'nəʊblmən/ Adlige, *der*
nobly /'nəʊblɪ/ *adv.* **(a)** edel [gesinnt]
(b) (generously) edelmütig (geh.)
nobody /'nəʊbədɪ/ *n. & pron.* niemand; keiner; (person of no importance) Niemand, *der*
no-brainer /nəʊ'breɪnə(r)/ *n.* (coll.: simple decision/idea) nahe liegende Sache
no-'claim[s] bonus *n.* (Insurance) Schadenfreiheitsrabatt, *der*
nocturnal /nɒk'tɜ:nl/ *adj.* nächtlich; ∼ **animal/bird** Nachttier, *das/*-vogel, *der*
nod /nɒd/ 1 *v.i.,* -dd- nicken
2 *v.t.,* -dd-: ∼ **one's head [in greeting]** [zum Gruß] mit dem Kopf nicken
3 *n.* [Kopf]nicken, *das*
■ **nod 'off** *v.i.* einnicken (ugs.)

nodule /'nɒdju:l/ n. (a) Klümpchen, das
(b) (Bot.) Knötchen, das

no-'fly zone n. Flugverbotszone, die

no-'go adj. Sperr⟨gebiet, -zone⟩

'no-good adj. (coll.) nichtsnutzig (abwertend)

no-hoper /nəʊ'həʊpə(r)/ n. absoluter
Außenseiter; **be a ~**: keine Chance haben

nohow /'nəʊhaʊ/ adv. (Amer. coll.) in keiner
Weise

noise /nɔɪz/ n. Geräusch, das; (loud, harsh,
unwanted) Lärm, der

'noise abatement n. Lärmbekämpfung,
die

'noiseless adj., **'noiselessly** adv.
lautlos

noise: ~ level n. Geräuschpegel,
der; (of unpleasant noise) Lärmpegel, der;
~ pollution n. Lärmbelästigung, die

noisily /'nɔɪzɪlɪ/ adv., **noisy** /'nɔɪzɪ/ adj.
laut

nomad /'nəʊmæd/ n. Nomade, der

nomadic /nəʊ'mædɪk/ adj. nomadisch;
~ tribe Nomadenstamm, der

'no man's land n. Niemandsland, das

nominal /'nɒmɪnl/ adj. (a) (in name only)
nominell
(b) (virtually nothing) äußerst gering

nominally /'nɒmɪnəlɪ/ adv. namentlich

nominate /'nɒmɪneɪt/ v.t. (a) (propose)
nominieren
(b) (appoint) ernennen

nomination /nɒmɪ'neɪʃn/ n.
▶ NOMINATE: Nominierung, die; Ernennung,
die

nominative /'nɒmɪnətɪv/ adj. & n.
~ [case] Nominativ, der

nominee /nɒmɪ'niː/ n. (candidate) Kandidat,
der/Kandidatin, die

non- /nɒn/ pref. nicht-

non-alco'holic adj. alkoholfrei

nonchalant /'nɒnʃələnt/ adj.
unbekümmert

non-commissioned 'officer n.
Unteroffizier, der

non-committal /nɒnkə'mɪtl/ adj.
unverbindlich; **he was ~**: er hat sich nicht
klar geäußert

noncon'formist n. Nonkonformist,
der/Nonkonformistin, die

non-con'tributory adj. beitragsfrei

nondescript /'nɒndɪskrɪpt/ adj.
unscheinbar; undefinierbar ⟨Farbe⟩

'non-drip adj. nicht tropfend ⟨Farbe⟩

non-'driver n. Nicht[auto]fahrer, der

none /nʌn/ ① pron. kein...; **~ of them**
keiner/keine/keines von ihnen; **~ of this**
nichts davon
② adv. keineswegs; **I'm ~ the wiser now**
jetzt bin ich um nichts klüger; **~ the less**
nichtsdestoweniger

nonentity /nɒ'nentɪtɪ/ n. Nichts, das

non-existent /nɒnɪg'zɪstənt/ adj. nicht
vorhanden

non-'fiction n. Sachliteratur, die

non-'iron adj. bügelfrei

non-'member n. Nichtmitglied, das

'no-no n., pl. **~es** (coll.) **be a ~**: nicht
infrage kommen (ugs.)

no-'notice account (Bankw.)
Tagesgeldkonto, das

non-'payment n. Nichtzahlung, die

nonplus /nɒn'plʌs/ v.t., **-ss-** verblüffen

non-'profit[-making] adj. nicht auf
Gewinn ausgerichtet

non-prolife'ration n. Nichtverbreitung
von Atomwaffen; **~ treaty** Atom[waffen]spe
rrvertrag, der

non-re'cyclable adj. nicht recycelbar

non-'resident n. (outside of a country)
Nichtansässige, der/die; **the bar is open to
~s** die Bar ist auch für Gäste geöffnet, die
nicht im Hotel wohnen

nonsense /'nɒnsəns/ ① n. Unsinn, der
② int. Unsinn

nonsensical /nɒn'sensɪkl/ adj. unsinnig

non sequitur /nɒn 'sekwɪtə(r)/ n.
unlogische Folgerung

non-'smoker n. (a) (person) Nichtraucher,
der/-raucherin, die
(b) (train compartment) Nichtraucherabteil,
das

non-'starter n. (fig. coll.) Reinfall, der (ugs.)

non-'stick adj. **~ frying pan** etc.
Bratpfanne usw. mit Antihaftbeschichtung

non-stop ① /'--/ adj. durchgehend ⟨Zug,
Busverbindung⟩; Nonstop⟨flug, -revue⟩
② /-'-/ adv. ohne Unterbrechung ⟨tanzen,
reden, reisen, senden⟩; nonstop ⟨fliegen,
tanzen, fahren⟩

'non-toxic adj. ungiftig

noodle /'nuːdl/ n., usu. pl. Nudel, die

nook /nʊk/ n. Winkel, der; Ecke, die

noon /nuːn/ n. Mittag, der; zwölf Uhr
[mittags]; **at/before ~**: um/vor zwölf [Uhr
mittags]

'no one pron. ▶ NOBODY

noose /nuːs/ n. Schlinge, die

nor /nɔ(r), stressed nɔː(r)/ conj. noch;
neither/not ... ~ ...: weder ... noch ...

norm /nɔːm/ n. Norm, die

normal /'nɔːml/ ① adj. normal
② n. (a) (~ value) Normalwert, der
(b) (usual state) normaler Stand; **everything
is back to** or **has returned to ~**: es hat sich
wieder alles normalisiert

normality /nɔː'mælɪtɪ/ Normalität, die

'normally adv. (a) (in normal way) normal
(b) (ordinarily) normalerweise

north /nɔːθ/ ① n. (a) Norden, der; **in/
to[wards]/from the ~**: im/nach/von Norden;
to the ~ of nördlich von
(b) usu. **N~** (Geog., Polit.) Norden, der

2 *adj.* nördlich; Nord⟨wind, -küste, -grenze⟩

3 *adj.* nach Norden; ∼ of nördlich von

north: N∼ 'Africa *pr. n.* Nordafrika (*das*); **N∼ A'merica** *pr. n.* Nordamerika (*das*); **N∼ A'merican** 1 *adj.* nordamerikanisch; 2 *n.* Nordamerikaner, *der/*-amerikanerin, *die;* ∼**bound** *adj.* ⟨Zug, Verkehr usw.⟩ in Richtung Norden; ∼-'**east** 1 *n.* Nordosten, *der;* 2 *adj.* nordöstlich; Nordost⟨wind, -küste⟩; 3 *adv.* nordostwärts; nach Nordosten; ∼-'**eastern** *adj.* nordöstlich

northerly /'nɔːðəlɪ/ *adj.* nördlich; ⟨Wind⟩ aus nördlichen Richtungen

northern /'nɔːðən/ *adj.* nördlich; Nord⟨grenze, -hälfte, -seite⟩

northern: N∼ 'Ireland *pr. n.* Nordirland (*das*); ∼ '**lights** *n. pl.* Nordlicht, *das*

North: ∼ 'Germany *pr. n.* Norddeutschland (*das*); ∼ '**Pole** *pr. n.* Nordpol, *der;* ∼ '**Sea** *pr. n.* Nordsee, *die*

northward[s] /'nɔːθwəd(z)/ *adv.* nordwärts

north: ∼-'west 1 *n.* Nordwesten, *der;* 2 *adj.* nordwestlich; Nordwest⟨wind, -küste⟩; 3 *adv.* nordwestwärts; nach Nordwesten; ∼-'**western** *adj.* nordwestlich

Norway /'nɔːweɪ/ *pr. n.* Norwegen (*das*)

Norwegian /nɔː'wiːdʒn/ 1 *adj.* norwegisch; **sb. is ∼:** jmd. ist Norweger/ Norwegerin

2 *n.* (a) (person) Norweger, *der/*Norwegerin, *die*

(b) (language) Norwegisch, *das; see also* ENGLISH 2A

Nos. *abbr.* = **numbers** Nrn.

nose /nəʊz/ 1 *n.* Nase, *die*

2 *v.t.* ∼ **one's way** sich (*Dat.*) vorsichtig seinen Weg bahnen

3 *v.i.* sich vorsichtig bewegen

■ **nose a'bout, nose a'round** *v.i.* (coll.) herumschnüffeln (ugs.)

nose: ∼bleed *n.* Nasenbluten, *das;* ∼**dive** 1 *n.* Sturzflug, *der;* 2 *v.i.* im Sturzflug hinuntergehen

nosey ▶ NOSY

nostalgia /nɒ'stældʒə/ *n.* Nostalgie, *die;* ∼ **for sth.** Sehnsucht nach etw.

nostalgic /nɒ'stældʒɪk/ *adj.* nostalgisch

nostril /'nɒstrɪl/ *n.* Nasenloch, *das;* (of horse) Nüster, *die*

nosy /'nəʊzɪ/ *adj.* (coll.) neugierig

not /nɒt/ *adv.* nicht; **he is ∼ a doctor** er ist kein Arzt; ∼ **at all** überhaupt nicht; ∼ ... **but ...:** nicht ..., sondern ...; ∼ **a thing** gar nichts

notable /'nəʊtəbl/ *adj.* bemerkenswert; **be ∼ for sth.** für etw. bekannt sein

notably /'nəʊtəblɪ/ *adv.* besonders

notation /nəʊ'teɪʃn/ *n.* Notierung, *die*

notch /nɒtʃ/ 1 *n.* Kerbe, *die*

2 *v.t.* kerben

■ **notch 'up** *v.t.* erreichen

note /nəʊt/ 1 *n.* (a) (Mus.) (sign) Note, *die;* (key of piano) Taste, *die;* (sound) Ton, *der*

(b) (jotting) Notiz, *die;* **take** *or* **make ∼s** sich (*Dat.*) Notizen machen; **take** *or* **make a ∼ of sth.** sich (*Dat.*) etw. notieren

(c) (comment, footnote) Anmerkung, *die*

(d) (short letter) [kurzer] Brief

(e) (importance) **a person/something of ∼:** eine bedeutende Persönlichkeit/etwas Bedeutendes; **be of ∼:** bedeutend sein

2 *v.t.* (a) (pay attention to) beachten

(b) (notice) bemerken

(c) (write) ∼ **[down]** [sich (*Dat.*)] notieren

'**notebook** *n.* (a) Notizbuch, *das;* (for lecture notes) Kollegheft, *das*

(b) ∼**book [computer]** Notebook, *das*

'**noted** *adj.* bekannt (**for** für, wegen)

note: ∼pad *n.* Notizblock, *der;* ∼**paper** *n.* Briefpapier, *das;* ∼**worthy** *adj.* bemerkenswert

nothing /'nʌθɪŋ/ *n.* nichts; ∼ **interesting** nichts Interessantes; ∼ **much** nichts Besonderes; ∼ **more than** nur; ∼ **more,** ∼ **less** nicht mehr, nicht weniger; **next to ∼:** so gut wie nichts; **have [got]** *or* **be ∼ to do with sb./sth.** (not concern) nichts zu tun haben mit jmdm./etw.; **have ∼ to do with sb.** (avoid) jmdm. aus dem Weg gehen

notice /'nəʊtɪs/ 1 *n.* (a) Anschlag, *der;* (in newspaper) Anzeige, *die*

(b) (warning) **at short/a moment's ∼:** kurzfristig/von einem Augenblick zum andern

(c) (formal notification) Ankündigung, *die;* **until further ∼:** bis auf weiteres

(d) (ending an agreement) Kündigung, *die;* **give sb. a month's ∼:** jmdm. mit einer Frist von einem Monat kündigen; **hand in one's ∼,** **give ∼** (Brit.), **give one's ∼** (Amer.) kündigen

(e) (attention) **bring sb./sth. to sb.'s ∼:** jmdn. auf jmdn./etw. aufmerksam machen; **take no ∼ of sb./sth.** (disregard) keine Notiz von jmdm./etw. nehmen; **take no ∼:** sich nicht darum kümmern

2 *v.t.* bemerken

noticeable /'nəʊtɪsəbl/ *adj.* wahrnehmbar ⟨Fleck, Schaden, Geruch⟩; merklich ⟨Verbesserung⟩; spürbar ⟨Mangel⟩

noticeably /'nəʊtɪsəblɪ/ *adv.* sichtlich ⟨größer, kleiner⟩; merklich ⟨verändern⟩; spürbar ⟨kälter⟩

'**noticeboard** *n.* (Brit.) Anschlagbrett, *das;* schwarzes Brett

notifiable /'nəʊtɪfaɪəbl/ *adj.* meldepflichtig ⟨Krankheit⟩

notification /nəʊtɪfɪ'keɪʃn/ *n.* Mitteilung, *die* (**of sth.** über etw. [Akk.])

notify /'nəʊtɪfaɪ/ *v.t.* (a) (make known) ankündigen

(b) (inform) benachrichtigen (**of** über + *Akk.*)

notion /'nəʊʃn/ *n.* Vorstellung, *die;* **not have the faintest/least ∼ of how/what** ⋯▷

etc. nicht die blasseste/geringste Ahnung haben, wie/was *usw.*

notoriety /nəʊtə'raɪətɪ/ *n.* traurige Berühmtheit

notorious /nə'tɔːrɪəs/ *adj.* berüchtigt (**for** wegen); notorisch ⟨*Lügner*⟩

nougat /'nuːgɑː/ *n.* Nougat, *das od. der*

nought /nɔːt/ *n.* Null, *die*

noun /naʊn/ *n.* (Ling.) Substantiv, *das*

nourish /'nʌrɪʃ/ *v.t.* ernähren (**on** mit)

'nourishing *adj.* nahrhaft

'nourishment *n.* Nahrung, *die*

Nov. *abbr.* = **November** Nov.

novel /'nɒvl/ 1 *n.* Roman, *der*
2 *adj.* neuartig

novelist /'nɒvəlɪst/ *n.* Romanautor, *der*/-autorin, *die*

novella /nə'velə/ *n.* Novelle, *die*

novelty /'nɒvltɪ/ *n.* (a) **be a/no** ~: etwas/nichts Neues sein
(b) (newness) Neuheit, *die*
(c) (gadget) Überraschung, *die*

November /nə'vembə(r)/ *n.* November, *der; see also* AUGUST

novice /'nɒvɪs/ *n.* Anfänger, *der*/Anfängerin, *die*

now /naʊ/ 1 *adv.* jetzt; (nowadays) heutzutage; (immediately) [jetzt] sofort; **just** ~ (very recently) gerade eben; **[every]** ~ **and then** *or* **again** hin und wieder; **well** ~: also; ~, ~: na, na; ~ **then** na (ugs.)
2 *conj.* ~ **[that]** …: jetzt, wo …
3 *n.* **before** ~: früher; **by** ~: inzwischen; **a week from** ~: [heute] in einer Woche

nowadays /'naʊədeɪz/ *adv.* heutzutage

nowhere /'nəʊweə(r)/ *adv.* nirgends; nirgendwo; (to no place) nirgendwohin

no-'win *attrib. adj.* Verlierer-

noxious /'nɒkʃəs/ *adj.* giftig

nozzle /'nɒzl/ *n.* Düse, *die*

nuance /'njuːɑ̃s/ *n.* Nuance, *die*

nuclear /'njuːklɪə(r)/ *adj.* Atom-; Kern⟨*explosion*⟩; atomar ⟨*Antrieb, Gefechtskopf, Wettrüsten, Abrüstung*⟩; nuklear ⟨*Sprengkörper*⟩; atomgetrieben ⟨*Unterseeboot*⟩

nuclear: ~ **'bomb** *n.* Atombombe, *die;* ~ **capa'bility** *n.* nukleares Potenzial; **a missile with** ~ **capability** eine nuklearfähige Rakete; **have** ~ **capability** nuklearfähig sein; ~ **de'terrent** *n.* atomare *od.* nukleare Abschreckung; ~ **'energy** *n.* Atom- *od.* Kernenergie, *die;* ~ **'family** *n.* Kernfamilie, *die;* ~**-free** *adj.* atomwaffenfrei ⟨*Zone*⟩; ~ **'fuel** *n.* Kernbrennstoff, *der;* ~ **'physics** *n.* Kernphysik, *die;* ~ **'power** *n.* (a) Atom-*od.* Kernkraft, *die;* (b) (country) Atom-*od.* Nuklearmacht, *die;* ~**-'powered** *adj.* atomgetrieben; ~ **'power station** *n.* Atom- *od.* Kernkraftwerk, *das;* ~ **'test** *n.* Atom[waffen]test, *der;* ~ **'testing**

n. Atomversuche *Pl.;* ~ **'warfare** *n.* Atomkrieg, *der;* ~ **'waste** *n.* Atommüll, *der*

nucleus /'njuːklɪəs/ *n., pl.* **nuclei** /'njuːklɪaɪ/ Kern, *der*

nude /njuːd/ 1 *adj.* nackt
2 *n.* (a) (figure) Akt, *der*
(b) **in the** ~: nackt

nudge /nʌdʒ/ 1 *v.t.* anstoßen
2 *n.* Stoß, *der*

nudism /'njuːdɪzm/ *n.* Nudismus, *der;* Freikörperkultur, *die*

nudist /'njuːdɪst/ *n.* Nudist, *der*/Nudistin, *die; attrib.* Nudisten-

nudity /'njuːdɪtɪ/ *n.* Nacktheit, *die*

nugget /'nʌgɪt/ *n.* Klumpen, *der;* (of gold) Goldklumpen, *der;* (fig.) ~**s of wisdom** goldene Weisheiten

nuisance /'njuːsns/ *n.* Ärgernis, *das;* **what a** ~! so etwas Dummes!

null /nʌl/ *adj.* ~ **and void** null und nichtig

numb /nʌm/ 1 *adj.* gefühllos, taub (**with** vor + *Dat.*); (without emotion) benommen
2 *v.t.* betäuben

number /'nʌmbə(r)/ 1 *n.* (a) (in series) Nummer, *die;* **you've got the wrong** ~ (Teleph.) Sie sind falsch verbunden; **dial a wrong** ~: sich verwählen (ugs.)
(b) (esp. Math.: numeral) Zahl, *die*
(c) (sum, total, quantity) [An]zahl, *die;* **a** ~ **of people/things** einige Leute/Dinge; **a** ~ **of times** mehrmals
2 *v.t.* (a) (assign ~ to) nummerieren
(b) (amount to, comprise) zählen
(c) (include) zählen (**among, with** zu)
(d) **sb.'s days are** ~**ed** jmds. Tage sind gezählt

'numbering *n.* Nummerierung, *die*

'numberless *adj.* unzählig; zahllos

'number plate *n.* Nummernschild, *das*

numeracy /'njuːmərəsɪ/ *n.* rechnerische Fähigkeiten *Pl.*

numeral /'njuːmərl/ *n.* Ziffer, *die*

numerate /njuːmərət/ *adj.* **be** ~: rechnen können

numerical /njuː'merɪkl/ *adj.* numerisch; Zahlen⟨*wert, -folge*⟩; zahlenmäßig ⟨*Stärke, Überlegenheit*⟩

numerically /njuː'merɪkəlɪ/ *adv.* numerisch

numerous /'njuːmərəs/ *adj.* zahlreich

nun /nʌn/ *n.* Nonne, *die*

nurse /nɜːs/ 1 *n.* Krankenschwester, *die;* [male] ~: Krankenpfleger, *der*
2 *v.t.* (a) pflegen ⟨*Kranke*⟩
(b) (fig.) hegen (geh.) ⟨*Gefühl, Groll*⟩

'nursemaid *n.* (lit. or fig.) Kindermädchen, *das*

nursery /'nɜːsərɪ/ *n.* (a) (room) Kinderzimmer, *das*
(b) (crèche) Kindertagesstätte, *die*
(c) ▸ NURSERY SCHOOL

(d) (for plants) Gärtnerei, *die*
nursery: ∼ **rhyme** *n.* Kinderreim,
der; ∼ **school** *n.* Kindergarten,
der; ∼**-school teacher** *n.* (female)
Kindergärtnerin, *die;* Erzieherin, *die;* (male)
Erzieher, *der;* ∼ **slopes** *n. pl.* (Skiing)
Idiotenhügel, *der* (ugs. scherzh.)
nursing /'nɜːsɪŋ/ *n.* Krankenpflege, *die;*
attrib. Pflege⟨*personal, -beruf*⟩
'nursing home *n.* Pflegeheim, *das*
nurture /'nɜːtʃə(r)/ *v.t.* (rear) aufziehen;
(fig.) nähren
nut /nʌt/ *n.* **(a)** Nuss, *die*
(b) (Mech. Engin.) [Schrauben]mutter, *die*
(c) (crazy person) Verrückte, *der/die* (ugs.)
nut: ∼ **case** *n.* (coll.) Verrückte, *der/die*
(ugs.); ∼**crackers** *n. pl.* Nussknacker,
der
nutmeg /'nʌtmeg/ *n.* Muskat, *der*
nutrient /'njuːtrɪənt/ *n.* Nährstoff, *der*
nutrition /njuːˈtrɪʃn/ *n.* Ernährung, *die;*
(food) Nahrung, *die*

nutritional /njuːˈtrɪʃənl/ *adj.* nahrhaft;
∼ **value** Nährwert, *der*
nutritionist /njuːˈtrɪʃənɪst/ *n.*
Ernährungswissenschaftler, *der/*
-wissenschaftlerin, *die*
nutritious /njuːˈtrɪʃəs/ *adj.* nahrhaft
'nutshell *n.* Nussschale, *die;* **in a** ∼ (fig.)
kurz [gesagt]
nutty /'nʌtɪ/ *adj.* **(a)** (in taste) nussig
(b) (coll.: crazy) verrückt (ugs.)
nuzzle /'nʌzl/ *v.i.* sich kuscheln (**up to,**
against an + *Akk.*)
NVQ *abbr.* (Brit.) = **National**
Vocational Qualification
NW *abbr.* = **north-west** NW
nylon /'naɪlɒn/ *n.* **(a)** Nylon, *das; attrib.*
Nylon-
(b) *in pl.* (stockings) Nylonstrümpfe *Pl.*
nymph /nɪmf/ *n.* Nymphe, *die*
nymphomaniac /nɪmfəˈmeɪnɪæk/ *n.*
Nymphomanin, *die*
NZ *abbr.* = **New Zealand**

Oo

O, o /əʊ/ *n.* O, o, *das*
oaf /əʊf/ *n.* Stoffel, *der* (ugs.)
oak /əʊk/ *n.* Eiche, *die*
'oak tree *n.* Eiche, *die*
OAP *abbr.* (Brit.) = **old-age pensioner**
Rentner, *der*/Rentnerin, *die*
oar /ɔː(r)/ *n.* Ruder, *das*
oarsman /'ɔːzmən/ *n.*, *pl.* oarsmen
/'ɔːzmən/ Ruderer, *der*
oasis /əʊˈeɪsɪs/ *n.*, *pl.* oases /əʊˈeɪsiːz/
Oase, *die*
oat /əʊt/ *n.* ∼**s** Hafer, *der*
'oatcake *n.* [flacher] Haferkuchen
oath /əʊθ/ *n.* **(a)** Eid, *der;* Schwur, *der;* **take**
or **swear an** ∼: einen Eid schwören
(b) (swear word) Fluch, *der*
'oatmeal *n.* Hafermehl, *das*
obedience /əˈbiːdɪəns/ *n.* Gehorsam, *der*
obedient /əˈbiːdɪənt/ *adj.* gehorsam; **be**
∼ **to sb./sth.** jmdm./einer Sache gehorchen
o'bediently *adv.* gehorsam
obelisk /'ɒbəlɪsk/ *n.* Obelisk, *der*
obese /əʊˈbiːs/ *adj.* fettleibig
obesity /əʊˈbiːsɪtɪ/ *n.* Fettleibigkeit, *die*
obey /əˈbeɪ/ ⨞**1** *v.t.* gehorchen (+ *Dat.*);
sich halten an (+ *Akk.*) ⟨*Vorschrift, Regel*⟩;
befolgen ⟨*Befehl*⟩
⨞**2** *v.i.* gehorchen

obituary /əˈbɪtjʊərɪ/ *n.* Nachruf, *der* (**to, of**
auf + *Akk.*)
object ⨞**1** /'ɒbdʒɪkt/ *n.* **(a)** (thing)
Gegenstand, *der*
(b) (purpose) Ziel, *das*
(c) (obstacle) **money/time** *etc.* **is no** ∼: Geld/
Zeit *usw.* spielt keine Rolle
(d) (Ling.) Objekt, *das*
⨞**2** /əbˈdʒekt/ *v.i.* **(a)** Einwände/einen
Einwand erheben (**to** gegen)
(b) (have objection or dislike) etwas dagegen
haben; ∼ **to sb./sth.** etwas gegen jmdn./etw.
haben
⨞**3** /əbˈdʒekt/ *v.t.* einwenden
objection /əbˈdʒekʃn/ *n.* **(a)** Einwand,
der; **raise** *or* **make an** ∼ [**to sth.**] einen
Einwand [gegen etw.] erheben
(b) (dislike) Abneigung, *die;* **have an/no** ∼ **to**
sb./sth. etw./nichts gegen jmdn./etw. haben;
have no ∼**s** nichts dagegen haben
objectionable /əbˈdʒekʃənəbl/ *adj.*
unangenehm ⟨*Anblick, Geruch*⟩; anstößig
⟨*Bemerkung, Wort, Benehmen*⟩
objective /əbˈdʒektɪv/ ⨞**1** *adj.* objektiv
⨞**2** *n.* (goal) Ziel, *das*
ob'jectively *adv.* objektiv
objectivity /ɒbdʒekˈtɪvɪtɪ/ *n.* Objektivität,
die
obligation /ɒblɪˈɡeɪʃn/ *n.* Verpflichtung,
die; **be under an** ∼ **to sb.** jmdm. verpflichtet
sein; **without** ∼: unverbindlich

obligatory /əˈblɪɡətərɪ/ *adj.* obligatorisch; **it has become ~ to ...**: es ist jetzt Pflicht, zu ...

oblige /əˈblaɪdʒ/ *v.t.* **(a)** (be binding on) **~ sb. to do sth.** jmdm. vorschreiben, etw. zu tun **(b)** (compel) zwingen; **be ~d to do sth.** gezwungen sein, etw. zu tun; **feel ~d to do sth.** sich verpflichtet fühlen, etw. zu tun **(c)** (be kind to) **~ sb. by doing sth.** jmdm. den Gefallen tun und etw. tun **(d)** (grateful) **be much/greatly ~d to sb.** [for sth.] jmdm. [für etw.] sehr verbunden sein; **much ~d!** besten Dank!

obliging /əˈblaɪdʒɪŋ/ *adj.* entgegenkommend

oblique /əˈbliːk/ *adj.* schief ‹*Gerade, Winkel*›; (fig.) indirekt

obliterate /əˈblɪtəreɪt/ *v.t.* auslöschen

oblivion /əˈblɪvɪən/ *n.* Vergessenheit, *die;* **sink** *or* **fall into ~**: in Vergessenheit geraten

oblivious /əˈblɪvɪəs/ *adj.* **be ~ to** *or* **of sth.** sich (*Dat.*) einer Sache (*Gen.*) nicht bewusst sein

oblong /ˈɒblɒŋ/ [1] *adj.* rechteckig [2] *n.* Rechteck, *das*

obnoxious /əbˈnɒkʃəs/ *adj.* widerlich

oboe /ˈəʊbəʊ/ *n.* Oboe, *die*

obscene /əbˈsiːn/ *adj.* obszön

obscenity /əbˈsenɪtɪ/ *n.* Obszönität, *die*

obscure /əbˈskjʊə(r)/ [1] *adj.* **(a)** (unexplained) dunkel **(b)** (hard to understand) schwer verständlich ‹*Argument, Dichtung, Autor, Stil*› **(c)** (unknown) unbekannt [2] *v.t.* **(a)** (make indistinct) verdunkeln; versperren ‹*Aussicht*› **(b)** (make unintelligible) unverständlich machen

obsequious /əbˈsiːkwɪəs/ *adj.* unterwürfig

observance /əbˈzɜːvəns/ *n.* Einhaltung, *die*

observant /əbˈzɜːvənt/ *adj.* aufmerksam

observation /ɒbzəˈveɪʃn/ *n.* **(a)** Beobachtung, *die;* **be [kept] under ~**: beobachtet werden; (by police) überwacht werden **(b)** (remark) Bemerkung, *die* **(on** über + *Akk.*)

obser'vation post *n.* Beobachtungsposten, *der*

observatory /əbˈzɜːvətərɪ/ *n.* (Astron.) Sternwarte, *die*

observe /əbˈzɜːv/ *v.t.* **(a)** (watch) beobachten; (perceive) bemerken **(b)** (abide by, keep) einhalten **(c)** (say) bemerken

ob'server *n.* Beobachter, *der/* Beobachterin, *die*

obsess /əbˈses/ *v.t.* **~ sb.** von jmdm. Besitz ergreifen (fig.); **be/become ~ed with** *or* **by sb./sth.** von jmdm./etw. besessen sein/werden

obsession /əbˈseʃn/ *n.* Zwangsvorstellung, *die*

obsessive /əbˈsesɪv/ *adj.* zwanghaft; **be ~ about sth.** von etw. besessen sein

obsolescent /ɒbsəˈlesənt/ *adj.* veraltend

obsolete /ˈɒbsəliːt/ *adj.* veraltet

obstacle /ˈɒbstəkl/ *n.* Hindernis, *das* (**to** für)

obstacle: ~ course *n.* Hindernisparcours, *der;* **~ race** *n.* Hindernisrennen, *das*

obstetrics /ɒbˈstetrɪks/ *n.* (Med.) Obstetrik, *die* (fachspr.)

obstinacy /ˈɒbstɪnəsɪ/ *n.* ▶ OBSTINATE: Starrsinn, *der;* Hartnäckigkeit, *die*

obstinate /ˈɒbstɪnət/ *adj.* starrsinnig; (adhering to particular course of action) hartnäckig

obstruct /əbˈstrʌkt/ *v.t.* **(a)** (block) blockieren; behindern ‹*Verkehr*›; **~ sb.'s view** jmdm. die Sicht versperren **(b)** (fig.: impede; also Sport) behindern

obstruction /əbˈstrʌkʃn/ *n.* Blockierung, *die;* (of progress; also Sport) Behinderung, *die*

obstructive /əbˈstrʌktɪv/ *adj.* hinderlich; obstruktiv ‹*Politik, Taktik*›; **be ~** ‹*Person:*› sich quer legen (ugs.)

obtain /əbˈteɪn/ *v.t.* bekommen; erzielen ‹*Resultat, Wirkung*›

obtainable /əbˈteɪnəbl/ *adj.* erhältlich

obtrusive /əbˈtruːsɪv/ *adj.* aufdringlich; (conspicuous) auffällig

obtuse /əbˈtjuːs/ *adj.* **(a)** stumpf ‹*Winkel*› **(b)** (stupid) begriffsstutzig

obvious /ˈɒbvɪəs/ *adj.* offenkundig; (easily seen) augenfällig; **be ~ [to sb.] that ...**: [jmdm.] klar sein, dass ...

'obviously *adv.* offenkundig; sichtlich ‹*enttäuschen, überraschen usw.*›

occasion /əˈkeɪʒn/ [1] *n.* **(a)** Gelegenheit, *die;* **rise to the ~**: sich der Situation gewachsen zeigen; **on several ~s** bei mehreren Gelegenheiten; **on ~[s]** gelegentlich **(b)** (special occurrence) Anlass, *der;* **it was quite an ~**: es war ein Ereignis **(c)** (reason) Grund, *der* (**for** zu) [2] *v.t.* verursachen

occasional /əˈkeɪʒənl/ *adj.* gelegentlich; vereinzelt ‹*Regenschauer*›

oc'casionally *adv.* gelegentlich; **[only] very ~**: gelegentlich einmal

occult /ɒˈkʌlt, ˈɒkʌlt/ *adj.* okkult; **the ~**: das Okkulte

occupant /ˈɒkjʊpənt/ *n.* Bewohner, *der/*Bewohnerin, *die;* (of car, bus, etc.) Insasse, *der/*Insassin, *die*

occupation /ɒkjʊˈpeɪʃn/ *n.* **(a)** (Mil.) Besetzung, *die;* (period) Besatzungszeit, *die* **(b)** (activity) Beschäftigung, *die* **(c)** (profession) Beruf, *der*

occupational /ɒkjʊˈpeɪʃənl/ *adj.*

Berufs⟨*beratung, -risiko*⟩; ~ **therapy**
Beschäftigungstherapie, *die;* ~ **therapist**
Beschäftigungstherapeut, *der*/-therapeutin,
die

occupier /'ɒkjʊpaɪə(r)/ *n.* (Brit.) Besitzer,
der/Besitzerin, *die;* (tenant) Bewohner,
der/Bewohnerin, *die*

occupy /'ɒkjʊpaɪ/ *v.t.* **(a)** (Mil.; as
demonstration) besetzen
(b) (live in) bewohnen
(c) (take up, fill) einnehmen; belegen
⟨*Zimmer*⟩; in Anspruch nehmen ⟨*Zeit,
Aufmerksamkeit*⟩
(d) (busy, employ) beschäftigen

occur /ə'kɜ:(r)/ *v.i.,* -rr-: **(a)** (be met with)
vorkommen; ⟨*Gelegenheit:*⟩ sich bieten;
⟨*Problem:*⟩ auftreten
(b) (happen) ⟨*Veränderung:*⟩ eintreten;
⟨*Unfall, Vorfall:*⟩ sich ereignen
(c) ~ **to sb.** (be thought of) jmdm. in den Sinn
kommen; ⟨*Idee:*⟩ jmdm. kommen

occurrence /ə'kʌrəns/ *n.* **(a)** (incident)
Ereignis, *das;* Begebenheit, *die*
(b) (occurring) Vorkommen, *das*

ocean /'əʊʃn/ *n.* Ozean, *der;* Meer, *das*

o'clock /ə'klɒk/ *adv.* **it is two/six** ~: es
ist zwei/sechs Uhr; **at two/six** ~: um
zwei/sechs Uhr; **six** ~ *attrib.* Sechsuhr⟨*zug,
-maschine, -nachrichten*⟩

Oct. *abbr.* = **October** Okt.

octagon /'ɒktəgən/ *n.* Achteck, *das*

octane /'ɒkteɪn/ *n.* Oktan, *das*

octave /'ɒktɪv/ *n.* Oktave, *die*

October /ɒk'təʊbə(r)/ *n.* Oktober, *der; see
also* AUGUST

octopus /'ɒktəpəs/ *n.* Tintenfisch, *der*

odd /ɒd/ *adj.* **(a)** (surplus, spare) übrig ⟨*Stück,
Silbergeld*⟩; **£25 and a few** ~ **pence** 25 Pfund
und ein paar Pence
(b) (occasional) gelegentlich; ~ **job**/~-**job
man** Gelegenheitsarbeit, *die*/-arbeiter, *der*
(c) (one of pair or group) einzeln; ~ **socks** nicht
zusammengehörende Socken; **be the** ~ **man
out** ⟨*Gegenstand:*⟩ nicht dazu passen
(d) (uneven) ungerade ⟨*Zahl, Seite,
Hausnummer*⟩
(e) (plus something) **forty** ~: über vierzig;
twelve pounds ~: etwas mehr als zwölf Pfund
(f) (strange, eccentric) seltsam

oddity /'ɒdɪtɪ/ *n.* (object, event) Kuriosität, *die*

'oddly *adv.* seltsam; ~ **enough**
seltsamerweise

odd 'man *n.* ~ **out** Außenseiter,
der/Außenseiterin, *die;* **be the** ~ **out** (extra
person) überzählig sein

'odd-numbered *adj.* ungerade

odds /ɒdz/ *n. pl.* **(a)** (Betting) Odds *Pl.*
(b) [the] ~ **are that she did it**
wahrscheinlich hat sie es getan; **the**
~ **are against/in favour of sb./sth.** jmds.
Aussichten/die Aussichten für etw. sind
gering/gut
(c) ~ **and ends** Kleinigkeiten; (of food) Reste

(d) be at ~ **with sb. over sth.** mit jmdm. in
etw. (*Dat.*) uneinig sein
(e) it makes no/little ~ [**whether** ...] es ist
völlig/ziemlich gleichgültig[, ob ...]

'odds-on ⓵ *adj.* gut ⟨*Chance, Aussicht*⟩;
hoch, klar ⟨*Favorit*⟩
⓶ *adv.* wahrscheinlich

odious /'əʊdɪəs/ *adj.* widerwärtig

odor *etc.* (*Amer.*) ▶ ODOUR *etc.*

odour /'əʊdə(r)/ *n.* Geruch, *der*

'odourless *adj.* geruchlos

oedema /ɪ'di:mə/ *n.* Ödem, *das*

oestrogen /'i:strədʒən/ *n.* Östrogen, *das*

œuvre /ɜ:vr/ *n.* Œuvre, *das* (geh.); Werk, *das*

of /əv, *stressed* ɒv/ *prep.* von; (indicating
material, substance) aus; **articles of clothing**
Kleidungsstücke; **a friend of mine** ein
Freund von mir; **where's that pencil of
mine?** wo ist mein Bleistift?; **it was clever
of you to do that** es war klug von dir, das zu
tun; **the approval of sb.** jmds. Zustimmung;
the works of Shakespeare Shakespeares
Werke; **be made of** ...: aus ... [hergestellt]
sein; **the fifth of January** der fünfte Januar;
his love of his father seine Liebe zu seinem
Vater; **person of extreme views** Mensch
mit extremen Ansichten; **a boy of 14 years**
ein vierzehnjähriger Junge; **the five of us**
wir fünf

Ofcom /'ɒfkɒm/ *abbr.* (Brit.) = **Office of
Communications** Regulierungsbehörde
für Kommunikation

off /ɒf/ ⓵ *adv.* **(a)** (away) **be a few miles**
~: wenige Meilen entfernt sein; **the lake is
not far** ~: der See ist nicht weit [weg]; **I'm**
~ **now** ich gehe jetzt; ~ **we go!** los gehts!
(b) (not on or attached or supported) ab; **get the
lid** ~: den Deckel abbekommen
(c) be ~ (switched or turned ~) ⟨*Wasser, Gas,
Strom:*⟩ abgestellt sein; **the light/radio** *etc.* **is**
~: das Licht/Radio *usw.* ist aus
(d) the meat *etc.* **is** ~: das Fleisch *usw.* ist
schlecht [geworden]
(e) be ~ (cancelled) abgesagt sein;
⟨*Verlobung:*⟩ [auf]gelöst sein; ~ **and on**
immer mal wieder (ugs.)
(f) (not at work) frei; **on my day** ~: an meinem
freien Tag; **have a week** ~: eine Woche
Urlaub bekommen
(g) (no longer available) [**the] soup** *etc.* **is** ~: es
gibt keine Suppe *usw.* mehr
(h) (situated as regards money etc.) **he is badly**
etc. ~: er ist *usw.* gestellt
⓶ *prep.* von; **be** ~ **school/work** in der
Schule/am Arbeitsplatz fehlen; **be** ~ **one's
food** keinen Appetit haben; **just** ~ **the
square** ganz in der Nähe des Platzes

offal /'ɒfl/ *n.* Innereien *Pl.*

off: ~**beat** *adj.* (fig.: eccentric)
unkonventionell; ~'**centre** *adv.* nicht
[genau] in der Mitte; ~ **'colour** *adj.*
unwohl; ~**cut** *n.* Rest, *der;* ~-**duty** *attrib.
adj.* Freizeit-; ⟨*Polizist usw.*⟩, der dienstfrei
hat

offence /əˈfens/ n. (Brit.) **(a)** (hurting of sb.'s feelings) Kränkung, die; **I meant no ~:** ich wollte Sie/ihn usw. nicht kränken **(b)** (annoyance) **give ~:** Missfallen erregen; **take ~:** verärgert sein **(c)** (crime) Straftat, die; **criminal ~:** strafbare Handlung

offend /əˈfend/ **1** v.i. verstoßen (**against** gegen) **2** v.t. **~ sb.** bei jmdm. Anstoß erregen; (hurt feelings of) jmdn. kränken

ofˈfender n. Straffällige, der/die

offense (Amer.) ▶ OFFENCE

offensive /əˈfensɪv/ **1** adj. **(a)** (aggressive) offensiv; Angriffs⟨waffe⟩ **(b)** (giving offence) ungehörig; (indecent) anstößig **2** n. Offensive, die; **take** or **go on the ~:** in die od. zur Offensive übergehen

offer /ˈɒfə(r)/ **1** v.t. anbieten; vorbringen ⟨Entschuldigung⟩; bieten ⟨Chance⟩; aussprechen ⟨Beileid⟩; **~ to help** seine Hilfe anbieten; **~ resistance** Widerstand leisten **2** n. Angebot, das; **[have/be] on ~:** im Angebot [haben/sein]

ˈoffering n. (thing) Angebot, das; (to a deity) Opfer, das

offˈhand **1** adv. **(a)** (without preparation) auf Anhieb ⟨sagen, wissen⟩; spontan ⟨beschließen, entscheiden⟩ **(b)** (casually) leichthin **2** adj. **(a)** (without preparation) spontan **(b)** (casual) beiläufig; **be ~ with sb.** zu jmdm. kurz angebunden sein

office /ˈɒfɪs/ n. **(a)** Büro, das **(b)** (branch) Zweigstelle, die **(c)** (position) Amt, das; **hold ~:** amtieren

office: ~ block n. Bürogebäude, das; **~ hours** n. pl. Dienststunden Pl.; **~ job** n. Bürotätigkeit, die

officer /ˈɒfɪsə(r)/ n. **(a)** (Army etc.) Offizier, der **(b)** (official) Beamte, der/Beamtin, die **(c)** (constable) Polizeibeamte, der/-beamtin, die

office: ~ technology n. Bürotechnik, die; **~ worker** n. Büroangestellte, der/die

official /əˈfɪʃl/ **1** adj. offiziell; amtlich ⟨Verlautbarung⟩; regulär ⟨Streik⟩ **2** n. Beamte, der/Beamtin, die; (party, union, or sports ~) Funktionär, der/Funktionärin, die

officialdom /əˈfɪʃldəm/ n., no art. Beamtentum, das; Bürokratie, die

ofˈficially adv. offiziell

officious /əˈfɪʃəs/ adj. übereifrig

offing /ˈɒfɪŋ/ n. **be in the ~:** bevorstehen; ⟨Gewitter:⟩ aufziehen

off: ~-licence n. (Brit.) ≈ Wein- und Spirituosenladen, der; **~-line** (Comp.) **1** /ˈ--/ adj. Offline-; **2** /-ˈ-/ adv. offline; **~-load** v.t. abladen; **~-peak** attrib. adj. during **~-peak hours** außerhalb der

Spitzenlastzeiten; **~-peak power** or **electricity** Nachtstrom, der; **~-print** n. Sonderdruck, der; **~-putting** /ˈɒfpʊtɪŋ/ adj. (Brit.) abstoßend; **~-road** attrib. adj. Gelände-, Offroad⟨fahrzeug, -fahrrad, -wagen, -fahrt, -einsatz⟩; **~-road driving** Fahren im Gelände; **~set** /ˈ--, -ˈ-/ v.t., forms as SET: ausgleichen; **~ season** n. Nebensaison, die; **~-shore** adj. küstennah; **~side** adj. Abseits-; **be ~-side** abseits sein; **~spring** n., pl. same Nachkommenschaft, die; (of animal) Junge Pl.; **~-the-peg** attrib. adj. Konfektions-; **~-the-shoulder** attrib. adj. schulterfrei ⟨Kleid⟩; **~-the-wall** attrib. adj. (esp. Amer. coll.) ausgeflippt (ugs.); **~-ˈwhite** adj. gebrochen weiß

often /ˈɒfn, ˈɒftn/ adv. oft; **every so ~:** gelegentlich

Ofwat /ˈɒfwɒt/ abbr. (Brit.) = **Office of Water Services** Regulierungsbehörde für Wasserwirtschaft

oh /əʊ/ int. oh; ⟨expr. pain⟩ au

OHP abbr. (Brit.) = **overhead projector** OHP

oil /ɔɪl/ **1** n. Öl, das **2** v.t. ölen

oil: ~-burner n. Ölbrenner, der; **~-can** n. Ölkanne, die; **~ change** n. (Motor Veh.) Ölwechsel, der; **~ drum** n. Ölfass, das; **~field** n. Ölfeld, das; **~ lamp** n. Öllampe, die; **~ painting** n. Ölgemälde, das; **~-producing** adj. [Erd]öl fördernd ⟨Land⟩; **~ refinery** n. [Erd]ölraffinerie, die; **~ rig** ▶ RIG¹ 1; **~skins** n. pl. Ölzeug, das; **~ slick** n. Ölteppich, der; **~ tanker** n. Öltanker, der; **~ well** n. Ölquelle, die

oily /ˈɔɪlɪ/ adj. ölig; ölverschmiert ⟨Gesicht, Hände⟩

ointment /ˈɔɪntmənt/ n. Salbe, die

OK /əʊˈkeɪ/ (coll.) **1** adj. in Ordnung; okay (ugs.) **2** adv. gut **3** int. okay (ugs.) **4** v.t. (approve) zustimmen (+ Dat.); **be OK'd by sb.** von jmdm. das Okay bekommen (ugs.)

okay /əʊˈkeɪ/ ▶ OK

old /əʊld/ adj. alt; **be [more than] 30 years ~:** [über] 30 Jahre alt sein

old: ~ 'age n. [fortgeschrittenes] Alter; **~-age** attrib. adj. Alters⟨rente, -ruhegeld⟩; **~-age pensioner** Rentner, der/Rentnerin, die; **~-fashioned** /əʊldˈfæʃnd/ adj. altmodisch; **~ 'people's home** n. Altenheim, das; Altersheim, das; **~ 'wives' tale** n. Ammenmärchen, das

oligarch /ˈɒlɪɡɑːk/ n. (Polit.) Oligarch, der/Oligarchin, die

olive /ˈɒlɪv/ n. Olive, die

olive 'oil n. Olivenöl, das

Olympic /əˈlɪmpɪk/ adj. olympisch; **~ Games** Olympische Spiele

Olympics /əˈlɪmpɪks/ n. pl. Olympiade, die; **Winter ~:** Winterolympiade, die

omelette (omelet) /'ɒmlɪt/ *n*. Omelett, *das*

omen /'əʊmən/ *n*. Vorzeichen, *das*

ominous /'ɒmɪnəs/ *adj*. (of evil omen) ominös; (worrying) beunruhigend

omission /ə'mɪʃn/ *n*. Auslassung, *die;* (failure to act) Unterlassung, *die*

omit /ə'mɪt/ *v.t.*, **-tt-** weglassen; **~ to do sth.** es versäumen, etw. zu tun

omnipotence /ɒm'nɪpətəns/ *n*. Allmacht, *die* (geh.)

omnipotent /ɒm'nɪpətənt/ *adj*. allmächtig

on /ɒn/ **1** *prep*. auf (*position:* + *Dat.; direction:* + *Akk.*); (attached to) an (+ *Dat./ Akk.*); (concerning, about) über (+ *Akk.*); (in expressions of time) an ⟨*einem Abend, Tag usw.*⟩; **write sth. on the wall** etw. an die Wand schreiben; **be hanging on the wall** an der Wand hängen; **have sth. on one** etw. bei sich haben; **on the bus/train** im Bus/Zug; (by bus/train) mit dem Bus/Zug; **on Oxford 556767** unter der Nummer Oxford 556767; **on Sundays** sonntags; **on [his] arrival** bei seiner Ankunft; **on entering the room** …: beim Betreten des Zimmers …; **it's just on 9** es ist fast 9 Uhr; **the drinks are on me** (coll.) die Getränke gehen auf mich **2** *adv*. **with/without a hat/coat on** mit/ohne Hut/Mantel; **have a hat on** einen Hut aufhaben; **on and on** immer weiter; **speak/ wait/work** *etc.* **on** weiterreden/-warten/ -arbeiten *usw.;* **from now on** von jetzt an; **the light/radio** *etc.* **is on** das Licht/Radio *usw.* ist an; **is Sunday's picnic on?** findet das Picknick am Sonntag statt?; **what's on at the cinema?** was läuft im Kino?; **on and off** immer mal wieder (ugs.); **on to, onto** auf (+ *Akk.*)

once /wʌns/ **1** *adv*. **(a)** einmal; **~ a week/ month/year** einmal die Woche/im Monat/im Jahr; **~ again** *or* **more** noch einmal; **~ [and] for all** ein für alle Mal; **never/not ~:** nicht ein einziges Mal **(b)** (multiplied by one) ein mal **(c)** (formerly) früher einmal; **~ upon a time there lived a king** es war einmal ein König **(d)** at **~** (immediately) sofort; (at the same time) gleichzeitig; **all at ~** (suddenly) plötzlich; (simultaneously) alle[s] zugleich **2** *conj*. wenn; (with past tense) als **3** *n*. **[just** *or* **only] this ~:** [nur] dieses eine Mal

'oncoming *adj*. entgegenkommend ⟨*Fahrzeug, Verkehr*⟩

one /wʌn/ **1** *adj*. ein; *see also* ЕIGHT 1; (single, only) einzig; **no/not ~:** kein; **the ~ thing** das Einzige; **at ~ time** einmal; **~ morning/night** eines Morgens/Nachts **2** *n*. **(a)** eins **(b)** (number, symbol) Eins, *die* **(c)** (unit) **in ~s** einzeln **3** *pron*. **(a)** ein… (of + *Gen.*); **big ~s and little ~s** Große und Kleine; **the older/**

younger **~:** der/die/das Ältere/Jüngere; **this ~:** dieser/diese/dieses [da]; **that ~:** der/die/das [da]; **which ~?** welcher/ welche/welches?; **which ~s?** welche?; **~ by ~:** einzeln; **love/hate ~ another** sich lieben/hassen; **be kind to ~ another** nett zueinander sein **(b)** (people in general; coll.: I, we) man; *as indirect object* einem; *as direct object* einen; **~'s** sein

one: ~-night 'stand *n*. (coll.) [sexuelles] Abenteuer für eine Nacht; **~-off** (Brit.) **1** *n*. (article) Einzelstück, *das;* **2** *adj*. einmalig; **~-parent family** *n*. Einelternfamilie, *die*

onerous /'əʊnərəs/ *adj*. schwer

one: ~'self *pron*. **(a)** *emphat*. selbst; **be ~self** man selbst sein; **(b)** *refl*. sich; *see also* HERSELF; **~-sided** *adj*. einseitig; **~-stop shopping** *n*. Einkaufen in einem Einkaufszentrum [mit Komplettangebot]; **~-storey** *adj*. eingeschossig; **~-touch** *adj*. **~-touch dialling** Zielwahl, *die;* **~-track** *adj*. eingleisig; **have a ~-track mind** (be obsessed) nur eins im Kopf haben; **~-upmanship** /wʌn'ʌpmənʃɪp/ *n.*, *no indef. art*. die Kunst, den anderen immer um eine Nasenlänge voraus zu sein; **~-way** *adj*. **(a)** in einer Richtung *nachgestellt;* Einbahn⟨*straße, -verkehr*⟩; **(b)** einfach ⟨*Fahrpreis, Flug*⟩

'ongoing *adj*. aktuell ⟨*Problem, Debatte*⟩; andauernd ⟨*Situation*⟩

onion /'ʌnjən/ *n*. Zwiebel, *die*

onion: ~ skin *n*. Zwiebelschale, *die;* **~ 'soup** *n*. Zwiebelsuppe, *die*

online (Comp.) **1** /'--/ *adj*. Online- **2** /-'-/ *adv*. online

'onlooker *n*. Zuschauer, *der*/Zuschauerin, *die*

only /'əʊnlɪ/ **1** *attrib. adj*. einzig…; **the ~ person** der/die Einzige; **an ~ child** ein Einzelkind **2** *adv*. nur; **we had been waiting ~ 5 minutes when** …: wir hatten erst 5 Minuten gewartet, als …; **it's ~/~ just 6 o'clock** es ist erst 6 Uhr/gerade erst 6 Uhr vorbei; **he ~ just made it** er hat es gerade noch geschafft; **~ if** nur [dann] …, wenn; **~ the other day/week** erst neulich

on-screen *adj*. (Comp., TV) Bildschirm-

'onset *n*. (of winter) Einbruch, *der;* (of disease) Ausbruch, *der*

onslaught /'ɒnslɔːt/ *n*. [heftige] Attacke (fig.)

'on-target *attrib. adj*. **~ earnings £50,000** Verdienst bei erfolgreicher Tätigkeit 50 000 Pfund

onto ▸ ON 2

onus /'əʊnəs/ *n*. **the ~ is on him to do it** es ist seine Sache, es zu tun

onward[s] /'ɒnwədz/ *adv*. (in space) vorwärts; **from X ~:** von X an; **from that day ~:** von diesem Tag an

onyx /'ɒnɪks/ n. Onyx, der

ooze /uːz/ ① v.i. sickern (**from** aus) ② v.t. triefen von od. vor (+ Dat.); (fig.) ausstrahlen

op /ɒp/ n. (coll.) Operation, die

opaque /əʊ'peɪk/ adj. lichtundurchlässig; opak (fachspr.)

open /'əʊpn/ ① adj. (a) offen; (not blocked or obstructed) frei; (available) frei ⟨Stelle⟩; **in the** ∼ **air** im Freien; **be** ∼ ⟨Laden, Museum, Bank usw.:⟩ geöffnet sein; **have an** ∼ **mind about** or **on sth.** einer Sache gegenüber aufgeschlossen sein
(b) unverhohlen ⟨Bewunderung, Hass, Verachtung⟩
(c) (frank, communicative) offen ⟨Wesen, Streit, Abstimmung, Regierungsstil⟩; (not secret) öffentlich ⟨Wahl⟩
(d) geöffnet ⟨Regenschirm⟩; aufgeblüht ⟨Blume, Knospe⟩; aufgeschlagen ⟨Zeitung, Landkarte⟩
② n. **in the** ∼ (outdoors) unter freiem Himmel; **[out] in the** ∼ (fig.) öffentlich bekannt
③ v.t. (a) öffnen
(b) eröffnen ⟨Konferenz, Diskussion, Laden⟩; beginnen ⟨Verhandlungen, Spiel⟩
(c) (unfold, spread out) aufschlagen ⟨Zeitung, Buch, Landkarte⟩; öffnen ⟨Schirm⟩
④ v.i. (a) sich öffnen; ∼ **into/on to sth.** zu etw. führen
(b) (become ∼ to customers) öffnen; (start trading etc.) eröffnet werden
(c) (start) beginnen; ⟨Ausstellung:⟩ eröffnet werden; ⟨Theaterstück:⟩ Premiere haben
■ **open 'up** ① v.t. öffnen; (establish) eröffnen
② v.i. sich öffnen; ⟨Filiale:⟩ eröffnet werden; ⟨Firma:⟩ sich niederlassen

open: ∼**-air** attrib. adj. Openair⟨konzert⟩; ∼**-air [swimming] pool** Freibad, das; ∼**-and-'shut case** n. (coll.) klarer Fall; ∼ **day** n. Tag der offenen Tür

'opener n. Öffner, der

'opening ① n. (a) Öffnen, das; (becoming open) Sichöffnen, das; (of exhibition, new centre) Eröffnen, das
(b) (establishment, ceremony) Eröffnung, die
(c) (initial part) Anfang, der
(d) (gap, aperture) Öffnung, die
(e) (opportunity) Möglichkeit, die; (vacancy) freie Stelle
② adj. einleitend

opening: ∼ **hours** n. pl. Öffnungszeiten Pl.; ∼ **time** n. Öffnungszeit, die

'openly adv. (a) (publicly) in der Öffentlichkeit; öffentlich ⟨zugeben, verurteilen⟩
(b) (frankly) offen

open: ∼ **'market** n. offener od. freier Markt; ∼**-'minded** adj. aufgeschlossen

openness /'əʊpnnɪs/ n. (frankness) Offenheit, die

open: ∼**-'plan** adj. ∼-plan office

Großraumbüro, das; ∼ **'prison** n. offene Anstalt; ∼ **'sandwich** n. belegtes Brot

opera /'ɒpərə/ n. Oper, die

opera: ∼ **glasses** n. pl. Opernglas, das; ∼ **house** n. Opernhaus, das; ∼ **singer** n. Opernsänger, der/-sängerin, die

operate /'ɒpəreɪt/ ① v.i. (a) (be in action) in Betrieb sein; ⟨Bus, Zug usw.:⟩ verkehren
(b) (function) arbeiten; **the torch** ∼**s on batteries** die Taschenlampe arbeitet mit Batterien
(c) ∼ **[on sb.]** (Med.) [jmdn.] operieren
② v.t. bedienen ⟨Maschine⟩; unterhalten ⟨Busverbindung, Telefondienst⟩; betätigen ⟨Hebel, Bremse⟩

operating: ∼ **system** n. (Comp.) Betriebssystem, das; ∼ **theatre** n. (Brit. Med.) Operationssaal, der

operation /ɒpə'reɪʃn/ n. (a) (causing to work) (of machine) Bedienung, die; (of bus service, telephone service, etc.) Unterhaltung, die; (of lever, brake) Betätigung, die
(b) **come into** ∼ ⟨Gesetz, Gebühr usw.:⟩ in Kraft treten; **be in/out of** ∼ ⟨Maschine, Gerät usw.:⟩ in/außer Betrieb sein
(c) (Med.) Operation, die; **have an** ∼**:** operiert werden

operational /ɒpə'reɪʃənl/ adj. (esp. Mil.: ready to function) einsatzbereit

operative /'ɒpərətɪv/ adj. **become** ∼ ⟨Gesetz:⟩ in Kraft treten; **the scheme is** ∼**:** das Programm läuft

operator /'ɒpəreɪtə(r)/ n. [Maschinen]bediener, der/-bedienerin, die; (Teleph.) (at exchange) Vermittlung, die; (at switchboard) Telefonist, der/Telefonistin, die

ophthalmic op'tician /ɒf'θælmɪk/ n. (Brit.) Augenoptiker, der/-optikerin, die

opinion /ə'pɪnjən/ n. Meinung, die (**on** über + Akk., zu); **have a high/low** ∼ **of sb.** eine/keine hohe Meinung von jmdm. haben; **in my** ∼**:** meiner Meinung nach

opinionated /ə'pɪnjəneɪtɪd/ adj. rechthaberisch

o'pinion poll n. Meinungsumfrage, die

opium /'əʊpɪəm/ n. Opium, das

opponent /ə'pəʊnənt/ n. Gegner, der/Gegnerin, die

opportune /'ɒpətjuːn/ adj. (a) (favourable) günstig
(b) (well-timed) zur rechten Zeit nachgestellt

opportunism /ɒpə'tjuːnɪzm/ n. Opportunismus, der

opportunist /ɒpə'tjuːnɪst/ n. Opportunist, der/Opportunistin, die

opportunity /ɒpə'tjuːnɪtɪ/ n. Gelegenheit, die

oppose /ə'pəʊz/ ① v.t. sich wenden gegen
② v.i. **the opposing team** die gegnerische Mannschaft

opposed /ə'pəʊzd/ adj. **as** ∼ **to** im Gegensatz zu; **be** ∼ **to sth.** ⟨Person:⟩ gegen etw. sein

opposite /'ɒpəzɪt/ **1** *adj.*
gegenüberliegend ⟨*Straßenseite, Ufer*⟩;
entgegengesetzt ⟨*Ende, Weg, Richtung*⟩; the
~ **sex** das andere Geschlecht
2 *n.* Gegenteil, *das* (**of** von)
3 *adv.* gegenüber
4 *prep.* gegenüber

opposite 'number *n.* (fig.) Pendant, *das*

opposition /ɒpə'zɪʃn/ *n.* (**a**) Opposition,
die; (resistance) Widerstand, *der* (**to** gegen); **in**
~ **to** entgegen
(**b**) (Brit. Polit.) **the O~**: die Opposition

oppress /ə'pres/ *v.t.* unterdrücken; (fig.)
⟨*Gefühl:*⟩ bedrücken

oppression /ə'preʃn/ *n.* Unterdrückung,
die

oppressive /ə'presɪv/ *adj.* repressiv; (fig.)
bedrückend ⟨*Ängste, Atmosphäre*⟩; (hot and
close) drückend ⟨*Wetter, Klima, Tag*⟩

opt /ɒpt/ *v.i.* sich entscheiden (**for** für); ~ **to**
do sth. sich dafür entscheiden, etw. zu tun;
~ **out** nicht mitmachen/(stop taking part) nicht
länger mitmachen (**of** bei)

optic /'ɒptɪk/ **1** *adj.* (Anat.) Seh⟨*nerv,*
-bahn⟩
2 *n. or* **O~** ® (Brit.: for spirits) Portionierer,
der

optical /'ɒptɪkl/ *adj.* optisch

optical 'character reader *n.* (Comp.)
Klarschriftleser, *der*

optician /ɒp'tɪʃn/ *n.* Optiker, *der/*
Optikerin, *die*

optics /'ɒptɪks/ *n.* Optik, *die*

optima *pl. of* OPTIMUM

optimise ▸ OPTIMIZE

optimism /'ɒptɪmɪzm/ *n.* Optimismus, *der*

optimist /'ɒptɪmɪst/ *n.* Optimist,
*der/*Optimistin, *die*

optimistic /ɒptɪ'mɪstɪk/ *adj.* optimistisch

optimize /'ɒptɪmaɪz/ *v.t.* (make the most of)
das Beste machen aus

optimum /'ɒptɪməm/ **1** *n., pl.* **optima**
/'ɒptɪmə/ Optimum, *das*
2 *adj.* optimal

option /'ɒpʃn/ *n.* (choice) Wahl, *die;* (thing)
Wahlmöglichkeit, *die*

optional /'ɒpʃənl/ *adj.* nicht zwingend;
~ **subject** Wahlfach, *das*

opulence /'ɒpjʊləns/ *n.* Wohlstand, *der*

opulent /'ɒpjʊlənt/ *adj.* wohlhabend;
feudal ⟨*Auto, Haus usw.*⟩

or /ɔ(r), *stressed* ɔː(r)/ *conj.* (**a**) oder; **he**
cannot read or write er kann weder lesen
noch schreiben; **without food or water** ohne
Essen und Wasser; **15 or 20 minutes** 15 bis 20
Minuten; **in a day or two** in ein, zwei Tagen
(**b**) (introducing explanation) das heißt; **or rather**
beziehungsweise

oracle /'ɒrəkl/ *n.* Orakel, *das*

oral /'ɔːrəl/ *adj.* mündlich; (Med.) oral

orally /'ɔːrəlɪ/ *adv.* **take** ~: einnehmen

orange /'ɒrɪndʒ/ **1** *n.* (**a**) (fruit) Orange,

die; Apfelsine, *die*
(**b**) (colour) Orange, *das*
2 *adj.* orange[farben]

orange: ~ **juice** *n.* Orangensaft,
der; ~ **peel** *n.* Orangenschale, *die;*
~ **'squash** *n.* Orangensaftgetränk, *das*

orator /'ɒrətə(r)/ *n.* Redner, *der/*Rednerin,
die

oratory /'ɒrətərɪ/ *n.* Redekunst, *die*

orb /ɔːb/ *n.* Kugel, *die*

orbit /'ɔːbɪt/ **1** *n.* (Astron.) [Umlauf]bahn,
die
2 *v.i.* kreisen
3 *v.t.* umkreisen

orbital /'ɔːbɪtl/ *adj.* ~ **road** Ringstraße, *die*

orchard /'ɔːtʃəd/ *n.* Obstgarten, *der;*
(commercial) Obstplantage, *die*

orchestra /'ɔːkɪstrə/ *n.* Orchester, *das*

orchestral /ɔː'kestrl/ *adj.* Orchester-

orchestrate /'ɔːkɪstreɪt/ *v.t.*
orchestrieren

orchid /'ɔːkɪd/ *n.* Orchidee, *die*

ordain /ɔː'deɪn/ *v.t.* (**a**) (Eccl.) ordinieren
(**b**) (decree) verfügen

ordeal /ɔː'diːl/ *n.* Qual, *die*

order /'ɔːdə(r)/ **1** *n.* (**a**) (sequence)
Reihenfolge, *die;* **out of** ~: durcheinander
(**b**) (regular arrangement, normal state) Ordnung,
die; **be/not be in** ~: in Ordnung/nicht in
Ordnung sein (ugs.); **be out of/in** ~ (not
in/in working condition) nicht funktionieren/
funktionieren; **'out of** ~' „außer Betrieb"; **in**
good/bad ~: in gutem/schlechtem Zustand
(**c**) (command) Anweisung, *die;* (Mil.) Befehl,
der
(**d**) **in** ~ **to do sth.** um etw. zu tun
(**e**) (Commerc.) Auftrag, *der* (**for** über + *Akk.*);
(to waiter, ~**ed goods**) Bestellung, *die*
(**f**) **keep** ~: Ordnung [be]wahren; *see also*
LAW B
(**g**) (religious ~) Orden, *der*
2 *v.t.* (**a**) (command) befehlen; ⟨*Richter:*⟩
verfügen; ~ **sb. to do sth.** jmdn. anweisen/
(Milit.) jmdm. befehlen, etw. zu tun
(**b**) (Commerc.) bestellen (**from** bei)
(**c**) (arrange) ordnen
■ **order a'bout, order a'round** *v.t.*
herumkommandieren

'order form *n.* Bestellformular, *das*

orderly /'ɔːdəlɪ/ **1** *adj.* friedlich;
diszipliniert ⟨*Menge*⟩; (methodical)
methodisch; (tidy) ordentlich
2 *n.* (**a**) (Mil.) [Offiziers]bursche, *der*
(**b**) **medical** ~: ≈ Krankenpflegehelfer, *der*

ordinal /'ɔːdɪnl/ *adj. & n.* **[number]**
Ordinalzahl, *die*

ordinarily /'ɔːdɪnərɪlɪ/ *adv.*
normalerweise; gewöhnlich

ordinary /'ɔːdɪnərɪ/ *adj.* (normal) normal
⟨*Gebrauch*⟩; üblich ⟨*Verfahren*⟩; (not
exceptional) gewöhnlich

ordination /ɔːdɪ'neɪʃn/ *n.* (Eccl.)
Ordination, *die;* Ordinierung, *die*

O

ordnance 'survey /'ɔ:dnəns/ *n.* (Brit.)
amtliche Landesvermessung; ~ **survey map**
amtliche topographische Karte

ore /ɔ:(r)/ *n.* Erz, *das*

organ /'ɔ:gən/ *n.* **(a)** (Mus.) Orgel, *die*
(b) (Biol.) Organ, *das*

'organ donor *n.* Organspender,
der/-spenderin, *die;* ~ **card**
Organspende[r]ausweis, *der*

organic /ɔ:'gænɪk/ *adj.* organisch;
biologisch, biodynamisch ‹*Nahrungsmittel*›;
biologisch-dynamisch ‹*Ackerbau*›; ~ **farmer**
Biobauer, *der*/-bäuerin, *die;* ~ **waste**
Biomüll, *der*

organically /ɔ:'gænɪkəlɪ/ *adv.* **(a)** (also
Med.) organisch
(b) (without chemicals) biologisch

organism /'ɔ:gənɪzm/ *n.* Organismus, *der*

organist /'ɔ:gənɪst/ *n.* Organist,
der/Organistin, *die*

organization /ɔ:gənaɪ'zeɪʃn/ *n.*
Organisation, *die;* ~ **of time/work** Zeit-/
Arbeitseinteilung, *die*

organize /'ɔ:gənaɪz/ *v.t.* organisieren;
einteilen ‹*Arbeit, Zeit*›; veranstalten
‹*Konferenz, Festival*›; ~ **into groups** in
Gruppen einteilen

organized /'ɔ:gənaɪzd/ *adj.* organisiert

'organizer *n.* Organisator, *der*/
Organisatorin, *die;* (of event, festival)
Veranstalter, *der*/Veranstalterin, *die*

'organ transplant *n.*
Organverpflanzung, *die*

orgasm /'ɔ:gæzm/ *n.* Orgasmus, *der*

orgy /'ɔ:dʒɪ/ *n.* Orgie, *die*

orient ⟦1⟧ /'ɔ:rɪənt/ *n.* **the O~:** der Orient
⟦2⟧ /'ɔrɪent/ *v.t.* ausrichten (**towards** nach);
~ **oneself** sich orientieren

oriental /ɒrɪ'entl/ ⟦1⟧ *adj.* orientalisch
⟦2⟧ *n.* Asiat, *der*/Asiatin, *die*

orientate /'ɒrɪənteɪt/ ▶ ORIENT 2

orientation /ɒrɪən'teɪʃn/ *n.* Orientierung,
die

orienteering /ɒrɪən'tɪərɪŋ/ *n.* (Brit.)
Orientierungslauf *der*

orifice /'ɒrɪfɪs/ *n.* Öffnung, *die*

origin /'ɒrɪdʒɪn/ *n.* (derivation) Herkunft, *die;*
(beginnings) Anfänge *Pl.;* (source) Ursprung,
der; **country of** ~: Herkunftsland, *das;* **have
its** ~ **in** sth. seinen Ursprung in etw. (*Dat.*)
haben

original /ə'rɪdʒɪnl/ ⟦1⟧ *adj.* ursprünglich;
Ur‹*text, -fassung*›; eigenständig
‹*Forschung*›; (inventive) originell; **an**
~ **painting** ein Original
⟦2⟧ *n.* Original, *das*

original 'gravity *n.* Stammwürze, *die*

originality /ərɪdʒɪ'nælɪtɪ/ *n.* Originalität,
die

originally /ə'rɪdʒɪnəlɪ/ *adv.*
(a) ursprünglich
(b) originell ‹*schreiben usw.*›

originate /ə'rɪdʒɪneɪt/ *v.i.* ~ **from**
entstehen aus; ~ **in** seinen Ursprung haben
in (+ *Dat.*)

ornament /'ɔ:nəmənt/ *n.* Ziergegenstand,
der

ornamental /ɔ:nə'mentl/ *adj.* dekorativ;
Zier‹*pflanze, -naht usw.*›

ornate /ɔ:'neɪt/ *adj.* reich verziert;
prunkvoll ‹*Dekoration*›

ornithologist /ɔ:nɪ'θɒlədʒɪst/ *n..*
Ornithologe, *der*/Ornithologin, *die*

ornithology /ɔ:nɪ'θɒlədʒɪ/ *n.*
Ornithologie, *die*

orphan /'ɔ:fn/ ⟦1⟧ *n.* Waise, *die*
⟦2⟧ *v.t.* **be ~ed** [zur] Waise werden

orphanage /'ɔ:fənɪdʒ/ *n.* Waisenhaus, *das*

orthodox /'ɔ:θədɒks/ *adj.* orthodox

orthopaedic /ɔ:θə'pi:dɪk/ *adj.*
orthopädisch

orthopaedics /ɔ:θə'pi:dɪks/ *n.*
Orthopädie, *die*

oscillate /'ɒsɪleɪt/ *v.i.* schwingen

oscillation /ɒsɪ'leɪʃn/ *n.* Schwingen, *das;*
(single ~) Schwingung, *die*

osmosis /ɒz'məʊsɪs/ *n.*, *pl.* **osmoses**
/ɒz'məʊsi:z/ Osmose, *die*

ostensible /ɒ'stensɪbl/ *adj.* vorgeschoben

ostensibly /ɒ'stensɪblɪ/ *adv.* vorgeblich

ostentatious /ɒsten'teɪʃəs/ *adj.*
prunkhaft ‹*Kleidung, Schmuck*›; prahlerisch
‹*Art*›

osteopath /'ɒstɪəpæθ/ *n.* Osteopath,
der/Osteopathin, *die*

osteoporosis /ɒstɪəʊpə'rəʊsɪs/ *n.*
Osteoporose, *die*

ostrich /'ɒstrɪtʃ/ *n.* Strauß, *der*

other /'ʌðə(r)/ ⟦1⟧ *adj.* **(a)** (not the same)
ander…; **the** ~ **two/three** *etc.* (the remaining)
die beiden/drei *usw.* anderen; **the** ~ **one**
der/die/das andere; **some** ~ **time** ein
andermal
(b) (further) **one** ~ **thing** noch eins; **some/six**
~ **people** noch ein paar/noch sechs [andere
od. weitere] Leute; **no** ~ **questions** keine
weiteren Fragen
(c) ~ **than** (different from) anders als; (except)
außer
(d) the ~ **day/evening** neulich/neulich
abends
⟦2⟧ *n.* anderer/andere/anderes; **there are
six** ~**s** es sind noch sechs andere da; **any**
~: irgendein anderer/-eine andere/-ein
anderes; **not any** ~: kein anderer/keine
andere/kein anderes; **one after the** ~: einer/
eine/eins nach dem/der/dem anderen
⟦3⟧ *adv.* anders; ~ **than that,** …: abgesehen
davon, …

otherwise /'ʌðəwaɪz/ ⟦1⟧ *adv.* **(a)** (in a
different way) anders
(b) (or else) anderenfalls
(c) (in other respects) im Übrigen
⟦2⟧ *pred. adj.* anders

O

otter /ˈɒtə(r)/ n. [Fisch]otter, der

ouch /aʊtʃ/ int. autsch

ought /ɔːt/ v. aux. only in pres. and past ought, neg. (coll.) oughtn't /ˈɔːtnt/ **I ~ to do/have done it** (expr. moral duty) ich müsste es tun/hätte es tun müssen; (expr. desirability) ich sollte es tun/hätte es tun sollen; **~ not** or **~n't you to have left by now?** müsstest du nicht schon weg sein?; **one ~ not to do it** man sollte es nicht tun; **he ~ to be hanged/in hospital** er gehört an den Galgen/ins Krankenhaus; **that ~ to be enough** das dürfte reichen; **he ~ to win** er müsste [eigentlich] gewinnen

oughtn't /ˈɔːtnt/ (coll.) = ought not

ounce /aʊns/ n. (measure) Unze, die

our /ˈaʊə(r)/ poss. pron. attrib. unser

ours /ˈaʊəz/ poss. pron. pred. unserer/ unsere/unseres; see also HERS

ourselves /aʊəˈselvz/ pron. (a) emphat. selbst

(b) refl. uns. See also HERSELF

oust /aʊst/ v.t. verdrängen; **~ sb. from his job/from power** jmdn. von seinem Arbeitsplatz vertreiben/jmdn. entmachten

out /aʊt/ adv. (a) (away from place) **~ here/there** hier/da draußen; **be ~ in the garden** draußen im Garten sein; **what's it like ~?** wie ist es draußen?; **go ~ shopping** etc. einkaufen usw. gehen; **be ~** (not at home, not in one's office, etc.) nicht da sein; **she was ~ all night** sie war eine/die ganze Nacht weg; **have a day ~ in London** einen Tag in London verbringen; **row ~ to …:** hinaus-/ herausrudern zu …; **be ~ at sea** auf See sein

(b) (Sport, Games) **be ~** ⟨Ball:⟩ aus od. im Aus sein; ⟨Mitspieler:⟩ ausscheiden; ⟨Schlagmann:⟩ aus[geschlagen] sein; **not ~:** nicht aus

(c) be ~ (asleep) weg sein (ugs.); (unconscious) bewusstlos sein

(d) (no longer burning) aus[gegangen]

(e) (in error) **be 3% ~ in one's calculations** sich um 3% verrechnet haben; **this is £5 ~:** das stimmt um 5 Pfund nicht

(f) (not in fashion) passee (ugs.); out (ugs.)

(g) say it ~ loud es laut sagen; **~ with it!** heraus mit der Sprache; **their secret is ~:** ihr Geheimnis ist bekannt geworden; **[the] truth will ~:** die Wahrheit wird an den Tag kommen; **the sun/moon is ~:** die Sonne/der Mond scheint; **the third volume is just ~:** der dritte Band ist soeben erschienen; **the roses are ~:** die Rosen blühen

(h) be ~ for sth./to do sth. auf etw. (Akk.) aus sein/darauf aus sein, etw. zu tun; **be ~ for trouble** Streit suchen

(i) (to or at an end) **before the day/month was ~:** am selben Tag/vor Ende des Monats. See also OUT OF

out: ~back n. (esp. Austral.) Hinterland, das; **~'bid** v.t., **~bid** überbieten; **~board**

adj. **~board motor** Außenbordmotor, der; **~break** n. Ausbruch, der; **at the ~break of war** bei Kriegsausbruch; **an ~break of flu** eine Grippeepidemie; **~building** n. Nebengebäude, das; **~burst** n. Ausbruch, der; **an ~burst of weeping/laughter** ein Weinkrampf/Lachanfall; **an ~burst of temper** ein Wutanfall; **~cast** n. Ausgestoßene, der/die; **a social ~cast** ein Geächteter/eine Geächtete; **~come** n. Ergebnis, das; Resultat, das; **~cry** n. [Aufschrei der] Empörung; **~'dated** adj. überholt; **~'do** v.t., forms as DO: überbieten (in an + Dat.); **~door** adj. **~door shoes/ things** Straßenschuhe/-kleidung, die; **~door games/pursuits** Spiele/Beschäftigungen im Freien; **~door swimming pool** Freibad, das; **~'doors** **1** adv. draußen; **go ~doors** nach draußen gehen; **2** n. **the [great] ~doors** die freie Natur

outer /ˈaʊtə(r)/ adj. äußer…; Außen⟨fläche, -seite, -wand, -tür⟩

outer 'space n. Weltraum, der

out: ~fit n. (a) (clothes) Kleider Pl.; **(b)** (equipment) Ausrüstung, die; **(c)** (coll.: organization) Laden, der (ugs.); **~'going 1** adj. (a) [aus dem Amt] scheidend ⟨Regierung, Präsident⟩; **(b)** (friendly) kontaktfreudig ⟨Person⟩; **2** n., in pl. **~s** (expenditure) Ausgaben Pl.; **~'grow** v.t., forms as GROW: herauswachsen aus ⟨Kleider⟩; (leave behind) entwachsen (+ Dat.); **~growth** n. Auswuchs, der; **~house** n. Nebengebäude, das

'outing n. Ausflug, der

out: ~landish /aʊtˈlændɪʃ/ adj. ausgefallen; **~last** v.t. überdauern; überleben ⟨Person, Jahrhundert⟩; **~law 1** n. Bandit, der/Banditin, die; **2** v.t. verbieten; **~lay** n. Ausgaben Pl. (on für); **~let** /ˈaʊtlet, ˈaʊtlɪt/ n. (a) Ablauf, Abfluss, der; Auslauf, Auslass, der; **(b)** (fig.) Ventil, das; **(c)** (market) Absatzmarkt, der; (shop) Verkaufsstelle, die; **~line 1** n. (a) in sing. or pl. Umriss, der; **(b)** (short account) Grundriss, der; (of topic) Übersicht, die (of über + Akk.); **2** v.t. (describe) umreißen; **~live** /aʊtˈlɪv/ v.t. überleben; **~look** n. (a) (view) Aussicht, die (over über + Akk., on to auf + Akk.); (fig.; Meteorol.) Aussichten Pl.; **(b)** (mental attitude) Einstellung, die (on zu); **~lying** adj. entlegen; **~ma'nœuvre** v.t. überlisten ⟨Truppen⟩; **~moded** /aʊtˈməʊdɪd/ adj. antiquiert; **~'number** v.t. zahlenmäßig überlegen sein (+ Dat.)

'out of prep. (a) (from within) aus; **go ~ the door** zur Tür hinausgehen

(b) (not within) **be ~ the country** im Ausland sein; **be ~ town/the room** nicht in der Stadt/im Zimmer sein; **feel ~ it** or **things** sich ausgeschlossen fühlen

(c) (from among) **one ~ every three smokers** jeder dritte Raucher; **58 ~ every 100** 58 von hundert

(d) (beyond range of) außer ⟨*Reich-/Hörweite, Sicht, Kontrolle*⟩

(e) (from) aus; **get money** ~ **sb.** Geld aus jmdm. herausholen; **do well** ~ **sb./sth.** von jmdm./etw. profitieren

(f) aus ⟨*Mitleid, Furcht, Neugier usw.*⟩

(g) (without) ~ **money** ohne Geld; **we're** ~ **tea** wir haben keinen Tee mehr

(h) (away from) von … entfernt; **ten miles** ~ **London** 10 Meilen außerhalb von London

out: ~**-of-court settlement** *n.* (Law) (agreement) außergerichtlicher Vergleich; (payment) Vergleichssumme, *die;* ~**-of-'date** *attrib. adj.* veraltet; (expired) ungültig ⟨*Karte*⟩; ~**-of-'pocket** *attrib. adj.* Bar⟨*auslagen*⟩; ~**-of-print** *attrib. adj.* vergriffen; ~**-of-work** *attrib. adj.* arbeitslos; ~**patient** *n.* ambulanter Patient/ambulante Patientin; ~**patients** [' **department**] Poliklinik, *die;* ~**play** *v.t.* (Sport) besser spielen als; ~**post** *n.* Außenposten, *der;* (of civilization etc.; also Mil.) Vorposten, *der;* ~**pouring** *n., usu. in pl.* Gefühlsäußerung, *die;* ~**put** *n.* **(a)** Produktion, *die;* (of liquid, electricity, etc.) Leistung, *die;* **(b)** (Comp.) Ausgabe, *die*

outrage [1] /'aʊtreɪdʒ/ *n.* **(a)** (deed) Verbrechen, *das;* (during war) Gräueltat, *die;* (against decency) grober Verstoß

(b) (strong resentment) Empörung, *die* (**at** gegen)

[2] /aʊt'reɪdʒ/ *v.t.* empören

outrageous /aʊt'reɪdʒəs/ *adj.* unverschämt; unverschämt hoch ⟨*Preis*⟩; unerhört ⟨*Frechheit, Skandal*⟩

out: ~**right** [1] /-'-/ *adv.* **(a)** ganz, komplett ⟨*kaufen, verkaufen*⟩; **(b)** (openly) freiheraus ⟨*erzählen, sagen, lachen*⟩; [2] /'--/ *adj.* ausgemacht ⟨*Unehrlichkeit*⟩; glatt (ugs.) ⟨*Ablehnung, Absage, Lüge*⟩; klar ⟨*Sieg, Niederlage, Sieger*⟩; ~**set** *n.* Anfang, *der;* **at the** ~**set** zu Anfang; **from the** ~**set** von Anfang an; ~'**shine** *v.t.,* ~**shone** /aʊt'ʃɒn/ (fig.) in den Schatten stellen

outside [1] /-'-, '--/ *n.* **(a)** Außenseite, *die;* **on the** ~: außen; **to/from the** ~: nach/von außen; ~ **lane** Überholspur, *die*

(b) (external appearance) Äußere, *das*

(c) at the [very] ~ äußerstenfalls; höchstens [2] /'--/ *adj.* **(a)** äußer…; Außen⟨*wand, -antenne, -kajüte, -toilette, -durchmesser*⟩; ~ **lane** Überholspur, *die*

(b) have only an ~ **chance** nur eine sehr geringe Chance haben

[3] /-'-/ *adv.* (on the ~) draußen; (to the ~)

[4] /-'-/ *prep.* **(a)** (position) außerhalb (+ *Gen.*); ~ **the door** vor der Tür

(b) (to the ~ of) aus … hinaus; **go** ~ **the house** nach draußen gehen

out'sider *n.* (Sport; also fig.) Außenseiter, *der*

out: ~**size** *adj.* überdimensional; ~**size clothes** Kleidung in Übergröße; ~**skirts** *n. pl.* Stadtrand, *der;* **the** ~**skirts of the town** die Außenbezirke der Stadt; ~**'smart**

v.t. (coll.) ausschmieren (ugs.); ~**source** *v.t.* extern vergeben ⟨*Arbeit, Aufträge*⟩; ~**sourcing** *n.* /'aʊtsɔːsɪŋ/ Outsourcing, *das* (fachspr.); Fremdbezug, *der* (fachspr.); ~'**spoken** *adj.* freimütig; **be** ~**spoken about sth.** sich freimütig über etw. äußern; ~'**standing** *adj.* **(a)** (exceptional) hervorragend; überragend ⟨*Bedeutung*⟩; außergewöhnlich ⟨*Person, Mut, Fähigkeit*⟩;

(b) (not yet settled) ausstehend ⟨*Schuld, Geldsumme*⟩; unbezahlt ⟨*Rechnung*⟩; ungelöst ⟨*Problem*⟩; ~'**standingly** *adv.* außergewöhnlich; ~**stretched** *adj.* ausgestreckt; (spread out) ausgebreitet; ~'**strip** *v.t.* (pass in running) überholen; (in competition) überflügeln; ~**tray** *n.* Ablage für Ausgänge; ~'**vote** *v.t.* überstimmen

outward /'aʊtwəd/ [1] *adj.* **(a)** (external, apparent) [rein] äußerlich; äußer… ⟨*Erscheinung, Bedingung*⟩

(b) Hin⟨*reise, -fracht*⟩

[2] *adv.* nach außen ⟨*aufgehen, richten*⟩

'**outwardly** *adv.* nach außen hin ⟨*Gefühle zeigen*⟩; öffentlich ⟨*Loyalität erklären*⟩

'**outwards** ▸ OUTWARD 2

out: ~'**weigh** *v.t.* schwerer wiegen als; überwiegen ⟨*Nachteile*⟩; ~'**wit** *v.t., -tt-* überlisten; ~'**worn** *adj.* veraltet

oval /'əʊvl/ [1] *adj.* oval

[2] *n.* Oval, *das*

ovary /'əʊvərɪ/ *n.* (Anat.) Eierstock, *der*

ovation /əʊ'veɪʃn/ *n.* Ovation, *die;* **a standing** ~: stehende Ovationen *Pl.*

oven /'ʌvn/ *n.* [Back]ofen, *der*

oven: ~ **cloth** *n.* Topflappen, *der;* ~ **glove** *n.* Topfhandschuh, *der;* ~**proof** *adj.* feuerfest; ~**-ready** *adj.* backfertig ⟨*Pommes frites, Pastete*⟩; bratfertig ⟨*Geflügel*⟩; ~**ware** *n.* feuerfestes Geschirr

over /'əʊvə(r)/ [1] *adv.* **(a)** (outward and downward) hinüber; **climb/look/jump** ~: hinüber- *od.* (ugs.) rüberklettern/-sehen/ -springen

(b) (so as to cover surface) **board/cover** ~: zunageln/-decken

(c) (across a space) hinüber; (towards speaker) herüber; **he swam** ~ **to us/the other side** er schwamm zu uns herüber/hinüber zur anderen Seite; ~ **here/there** (direction) hier herüber/dort hinüber; (location) hier/dort; **[come in, please,]** ~ (Radio) übernehmen Sie bitte; ~ **and out** (Radio) Ende

(d) (in excess etc.) **children of 12 and** ~: Kinder im Alter von zwölf Jahren und darüber; **be [left]** ~: übrig [geblieben] sein

(e) (from beginning to end) von Anfang bis Ende; **say sth. twice** ~: etw. zweimal sagen; **[all]** ~ **again**, (Amer.) ~: noch einmal [ganz von vorn]; ~ **and** ~ **[again]** immer wieder

(f) (at an end) vorbei; vorüber; **be** ~: vorbei sein; ⟨*Aufführung:*⟩ zu Ende sein; **get sth.** ~ **with** etw. hinter sich (*Akk.*) bringen; **be** ~ **and done with** erledigt sein

(g) all ~ (completely finished) aus [und vorbei];

I ache all ~: mir tut alles weh; **be shaking all** ~: am ganzen Körper zittern ② *prep.* **(a)** (above, on, round about) über (*position: + Dat.; direction: + Akk.*); (across) über (+ *Akk.*); **look** ~ **a wall** über eine Mauer sehen; **fall** ~ **a cliff** von einem Felsen stürzen; **the pub** ~ **the road** die Wirtschaft gegenüber; **hit sb.** ~ **the head** jmdm. auf den Kopf schlagen; ~ **the page** auf der nächsten Seite **(b)** (in or across every part of) [überall] in (+ *Dat.*); (to and fro upon) über (+ *Akk.*); (all through) durch; **all** ~ (in or on all parts of) überall in (+ *Dat.*); **travel all** ~ **the country** das ganze Land bereisen; **all** ~ **Spain** in ganz Spanien; **all** ~ **the world** in der ganzen Welt **(c)** (on account of) wegen **(d)** (engaged with) bei; **take trouble** ~ **sth.** sich (*Dat.*) mit etw. Mühe geben; **be a long time** ~ **sth.** lange für etw. brauchen; ~ **work/dinner** bei der Arbeit/beim Essen **(e)** (superior to, in charge of) über (+ *Akk.*); **have command/authority** ~ **sb.** Befehlsgewalt über jmdn./Weisungsbefugnis gegenüber jmdm. haben; **be** ~ **sb.** (in rank) über jmdm. stehen **(f)** (beyond, more than) über (+ *Akk.*); ~ **and above** zusätzlich zu **(g)** (throughout, during) über (+ *Akk.*); ~ **the weekend/summer** übers Wochenende/den Sommer über; ~ **the past years** in den letzten Jahren

over: ~'**active** *adj.* hyperaktiv; ~**all** ① *n.* (Brit.: garment) Arbeitskittel, *der;* ② *adj.* **(a)** Gesamt⟨*breite, -einsparung, -abmessung*⟩; **have an** ~**all majority** die absolute Mehrheit haben; **(b)** (general) allgemein; ③ /'---, --'-/ *adv.* **(a)** (in all parts) insgesamt; **(b)** (taken as a whole) im Großen und Ganzen; ~'**anxious** *adj.* **be** ~**anxious to do sth.** etw. unbedingt tun wollen; ~'**awe** *v.t.* Ehrfurcht einflößen (+ *Dat.*); ~'**balance** *v.i.* das Gleichgewicht verlieren; ~'**bearing** *adj.* herrisch; ~'**blown** *adj.* (past its prime, lit. or fig.) verblühend; ~**board** *adv.* über Bord; **fall** ~**board** über Bord gehen; ~**cast** *adj.* trübe; bewölkt ⟨*Himmel*⟩; ~'**charge** *v.t.* **(a)** (beyond reasonable price) zu viel abverlangen (+ *Dat.*); **(b)** (beyond right price) zu viel berechnen (+ *Dat.*); ~**coat** *n.* Mantel, *der;* ~'**come** *v.t., forms as* COME: **(a)** überwinden; bezwingen ⟨*Feind*⟩; ⟨*Dämpfe:*⟩ betäuben; **(b) he was** ~**come by grief/with emotion** Kummer/Rührung überwältigte ihn; ~'**confidence** *n.* übersteigertes Selbstvertrauen; ~'**confident** *adj.* übertrieben zuversichtlich; ~'**cooked** *adj.* verkocht; ~'**critical** *adj.* zu kritisch; ~'**crowded** *adj.* überfüllt; ~'**crowding** *n.* (of room, bus, train) Überfüllung, *die;* (of city) Übervölkerung, *die;* ~'**do** *v.t., forms as* DO: (carry to excess) übertreiben; ~**do it** *or*

things (work too hard) sich übernehmen; ~'**done** *adj.* **(a)** (exaggerated) übertrieben; **(b)** (~cooked) verkocht; verbraten ⟨*Fleisch*⟩; ~**dose** ① *n.* Überdosis, *die;* ② *v.i.* ~**dose on heroin** eine Überdosis Heroin einnehmen; ~**draft** *n.* Kontoüberziehung, *die;* **have an** ~**draft of £50** sein Konto um 50 Pfund überzogen haben; ~'**draw** *v.t., forms as* DRAW 1: überziehen ⟨*Konto*⟩; ~'**drawn** *adj.* überzogen ⟨*Konto*⟩; **I am** ~**drawn [at the bank]** mein Konto ist überzogen; ~**drive** *n.* Schongang, *der;* ~'**due** *adj.* überfällig; **the train is 15 minutes** ~**due** der Zug hat schon 15 Minuten Verspätung; ~'**eager** *adj.* übereifrig; ~'**eat** *v.i., forms as* EAT: zu viel essen; ~**estimate** ① /-'estmeɪt/ *v.t.* überschätzen; ② /-'estɪmət/ *n.* zu hohe Schätzung; ~**ex'ert** *v. refl.* sich überanstrengen; ~**ex'pose** *v.t.* (Photog.) überbelichten; ~'**fill** *v.t.* zu voll machen; ~ '**fish** *v.t.* überfischen; ~**flow** ① /--'-/ *v.t.* laufen über (+ *Akk.*) ⟨*Rand*⟩; (flow over brim of) überlaufen aus; ~**flow its banks** ⟨*Fluss:*⟩ über die Ufer treten; ② /--'-/ *v.i.* überlaufen; ③ /'---/ *n.* ~**flow [pipe]** Überlauf, *der;* ~**flow car park** Ausweichparkplatz, *der;* ~'**full** *adj.* zu voll; übervoll; ~**grown** *adj.* überwachsen (with von); ~**hang** ① /--'-/ *v.t.,* ~**hung** /əʊvə'hʌŋ/ ⟨*Felsen, Stockwerk:*⟩ hinausragen über (+ *Akk.*); ② /'---/ *n.* Überhang, *der;* ~'**hanging** *adj.* überhängend; ~**haul** ① /--'-/ *v.t.* überholen; überprüfen ⟨*System*⟩; ② /'---/ *n.* Überholung, *die;* ~**head** ① /--'-/ *adv.* über mir/ihm/uns *usw.;* ② /'---/ *adj.* ~**head wires** Oberleitung, *die;* ~**head lighting** Deckenbeleuchtung, *die;* ③ /'---/ *n.* ~**heads,** (Amer.) ~**head** (Commerc.) Gemeinkosten *Pl.;* ~'**hear** *v.t., forms as* HEAR 1 (accidentally) zufällig [mit]hören; (intentionally) belauschen; ~'**heat** *v.i.* zu heiß werden; ⟨*Maschine, Lager:*⟩ heißlaufen; ~**in'dulge** *v.i.* es übertreiben; ~**indulge in food and drink** sich an Essen und Trinken mehr als gütlich tun; ~**in'dulgence** *n.* übermäßiger Genuss (**in** von); (towards a person) zu große Nachgiebigkeit; ~**in'dulgent** *adj.* unmäßig; (towards a person) zu nachgiebig

overjoyed /əʊvə'dʒɔɪd/ *adj.* überglücklich (**at** über + *Akk.*)

over: ~'**land** /--'-/ *adv.* auf dem Landweg; ~**lap** ① /--'-/ *v.t.* überlappen; ② /--'-/ *v.i.* ⟨*Flächen, Dachziegel:*⟩ sich überlappen; ⟨*Aufgaben:*⟩ sich überschneiden; ③ *n.* Überlappung, *die;* ~'**leaf** *adv.* auf der Rückseite; ~'**load** *v.t.* überladen; ~'**look** *v.t.* **(a)** ⟨*Hotel, Zimmer, Haus:*⟩ Aussicht bieten auf (+ *Akk.*); **(b)** (ignore, not see) übersehen; (allow to go unpunished) hinwegsehen über (+ *Akk.*)

'**overly** *adv.* allzu

over: ~'**man** *v.t.* überbesetzen; ~'**manning** *n.* [personelle] Überbesetzung; ~'**modest** *adj.* zu ····⟶

bescheiden; ~**'much** 1 adj. allzu viel;
2 adv. allzu sehr; ~**night** 1 /--'-/
adv. (also fig.: suddenly) über Nacht; **stay**
~ **night** übernachten; 2 /'---/ adj. ~**night**
stay Übernachtung, die; **be an** ~**night**
success (fig.) über Nacht Erfolg haben;
~'**pay** v.t., forms as PAY 2: überbezahlen;
~'**populated** adj. überbevölkert;
~**popu'lation** n. Übervölkerung,
die; ~'**power** v.t. überwältigen;
~'**powering** adj. überwältigend;
durchdringend ⟨Geruch⟩; ~'**priced** adj. zu
teuer; ~'**qualified** adj. überqualifiziert;
~'**rate** v.t. überschätzen; ~**re'act** v.i.
unangemessen heftig reagieren (**to auf**
+ Akk.); ~**re'action** n. Überreaktion,
die (**to auf** + Akk.); ~'**ride** v.t. forms as
RIDE 3: sich hinwegsetzen über (+ Akk.);
~'**riding** adj. vorrangig; **be of** ~**riding**
importance wichtiger als alles andere sein;
~**ripe** adj. überreif; ~'**rule** v.t. aufheben
⟨Entscheidung⟩; zurückweisen ⟨Einwand,
Argument⟩; ~**rule sb.** jmds. Vorschlag
ablehnen; ~'**run** v.t., forms as RUN 3: **be**
~**run with** überlaufen sein von ⟨Touristen⟩;
überwuchert sein von ⟨Unkraut⟩; ~**seas**
1 /--'-/ adv. in Übersee ⟨leben, sein⟩; nach
Übersee ⟨gehen⟩; 2 /'---/ adj. Übersee-;
~'**see** v.t., forms as SEE 1: überwachen;
(manage) leiten ⟨Abteilung⟩; ~'**sensitive**
adj. überempfindlich; ~**sexed**
/əʊvə'sekst/ adj. sexbesessen; ~'**shadow**
v.t. überschatten; ~'**shoot** v.t., forms as
SHOOT 2: hinausschießen über (+ Akk.);
~**shoot [the runway]** ⟨Pilot, Flugzeug:⟩
zu weit kommen; ~**sight** n. Versehen,
das; ~**simplifi'cation** n. zu starke
Vereinfachung; ~'**simplify** v.t. zu
stark vereinfachen; ~'**sleep** v.i., forms
as SLEEP 2: verschlafen; ~'**spend** v.i.,
forms as SPEND: zu viel [Geld] ausgeben;
~**statement** n. Übertreibung, die;
~'**stay** v.t. überziehen ⟨Urlaub⟩; ~'**step**
v.t. überschreiten; ~'**stretch** v.t.
überdehnen; (fig.) überfordern

overt /əʊ'vɜːt/ adj. unverhohlen
over: ~'**take** v.t., forms as
TAKE: überholen; **'no** ~**taking'** (Brit.)
„Überholen verboten"; ~**-the-top** adj.
überzogen; ~'**throw** 1 /--'-/ v.t., forms
as THROW 1: stürzen; 2 /'---/ n. Sturz, der;
~**time** 1 n. Überstunden Pl.; 2 adv. **work**
~**time** Überstunden machen; ~'**tire** v.t.
übermüden; ~**tire oneself** sich übernehmen
od. überanstrengen

overtly /'əʊvətlɪ, əʊ'vɜːtlɪ/ adv.
unverhohlen
'**overtone** n. (fig.) Unterton, der
overture /'əʊvətjʊə(r)/ n. (Mus.)

Ouvertüre, die
over: ~'**turn** 1 v.t. umstoßen; 2 v.i.
⟨Auto, Boot:⟩ umkippen; ⟨Boot:⟩ kentern;
~**use** /əʊvə'juːz/ v.t. zu oft verwenden
overweening /əʊvə'wiːnɪŋ/ adj. maßlos
⟨Ehrgeiz, Gier, Stolz⟩
'**overweight** adj. übergewichtig ⟨Person⟩;
be ~**weight** Übergewicht haben
overwhelm /əʊvə'welm/ v.t.
überwältigen
over'whelming adj. überwältigend
over: ~'**work** 1 v.t. mit Arbeit
überlasten; 2 v.i. sich überarbeiten;
~'**wrought** adj. überreizt
ovulate /'ɒvjʊleɪt/ v.i. (Physiol.) ovulieren
ovulation /ɒvjʊ'leɪʃn/ n. Ovulation, die
owe /əʊ/ v.t., owing /'əʊɪŋ/ schulden; ~ **sb.**
sth., ~ **sth. to sb.** jmdm. etw. schulden; (fig.)
jmdm. etw. verdanken
owing /'əʊɪŋ/ pred. adj. ausstehend; **be**
~: ausstehen
'**owing to** prep. wegen
owl /aʊl/ n. Eule, die
own /əʊn/ 1 adj. eigen; **be sb.'s**
~ **[property]** jmdm. selbst gehören; **a house/**
ideas of one's ~: ein eigenes Haus/eigene
Ideen; **on one's/its** ~: allein
2 v.t. besitzen; **be** ~**ed by sb.** jmdm.
gehören
■ **own 'up** v.i. gestehen; ~ **up to sth.** etw.
zugeben
'**own-brand**, '**own-label** 1 attrib. adjs.
Eigenmarken-
2 n. Hausmarke, die
'**owner** n. Besitzer, der/Besitzerin, die; (of
shop, hotel, firm, etc.) Inhaber, der/Inhaberin,
die
owner-'occupier n. (Brit.)
Eigenheimbesitzer, der/-besitzerin, die
'**ownership** n. Besitz, der
own 'goal n. (lit. or fig.) Eigentor, das
ox /ɒks/ n., pl. **oxen** /'ɒksn/ Ochse, der
oxidize (oxidise) /'ɒksɪdaɪz/ v.t. & i.
(Chem.) oxidieren; oxydieren (fachspr.)
oxtail 'soup n. Ochsenschwanzsuppe, die
oxygen /'ɒksɪdʒən/ n. Sauerstoff, der
'**oxygen mask** n. Sauerstoffmaske, die
oyster /'ɔɪstə(r)/ n. Auster, die
oz. abbr. = **ounce[s]**
ozone /'əʊzəʊn/ n. Ozon, das
ozone: ~ **depletion** n. Ozonabbau, der;
~**-friendly** adj. ozonsicher; (not using CFCs)
FCKW-frei; ~ **hole** n. Ozonloch, das (ugs.;)
~ **layer** n. Ozonschicht, die

Pp

P, p /piː/ n. P, p, das
p. abbr. **(a)** = **page** S.
(b) (Brit.) = **penny**/**pence** p
pace /peɪs/ 1 n. **(a)** (step) Schritt, der
(b) (speed) Tempo, das; **keep ∼ with** Schritt
halten mit
2 v.i. **∼ up and down** auf und ab gehen
3 v.t. auf und ab gehen in (+ Dat.)
'pacemaker n. (Sport, Med.)
Schrittmacher, der
Pacific /pə'sɪfɪk/ 1 adj. (Geog.) **∼ Ocean**
Pazifischer od. Stiller Ozean
2 n. **the ∼:** der Pazifik
pacifier /'pæsɪfaɪə(r)/ n. (Amer.: dummy)
Schnuller, der
pacifism /'pæsɪfɪzm/ n. Pazifismus, der
pacifist /'pæsɪfɪst/ 1 n. Pazifist,
der/Pazifistin, die
2 adj. pazifistisch
pacify /'pæsɪfaɪ/ v.t. besänftigen
pack /pæk/ 1 n. **(a)** (bundle) Bündel, das;
(Mil.) Tornister, der; (rucksack) Rucksack, der
(b) (derog.: lot) (people) Bande, die; **a ∼ of
lies**/**nonsense** ein Sack voll Lügen/eine
Menge Unsinn
(c) (Brit.) **∼ [of cards]** [Karten]spiel, das
(d) (of wolves, wild dogs) Rudel, das; (of hounds)
Meute, die
(e) (packet) Packung, die
2 v.t. **(a)** einpacken; (fill) packen; **∼ one's
bags** seine Koffer packen
(b) (cram) voll stopfen (ugs.)
(c) (wrap) voll verpacken (in in + Dat. od. Akk.)
3 v.i. packen; **send sb. ∼ing** (fig.) jmdn.
rausschmeißen (ugs.)
∎ **pack 'up** 1 v.t. zusammenpacken
⟨Sachen, Werkzeug⟩; packen ⟨Paket⟩
2 v.i. (coll.: stop) aufhören
package /'pækɪdʒ/ 1 n. Paket, das
2 v.t. verpacken
package: ∼ deal n. Paket, das;
∼ holiday, ∼ tour ns. Pauschalreise,
die
packaging /'pækɪdʒɪŋ/ n. (material)
Verpackung, die
packed /pækt/ adj. **(a)** gepackt; **∼ lunch**
Lunchpaket, das
(b) (crowded) [über]voll; **∼ out** gerammelt
voll (ugs.)
packet /'pækɪt/ n. Päckchen, das; (box)
Schachtel, die; **a ∼ of cigarettes** ein
Päckchen/eine Schachtel Zigaretten; **cost**/
earn a ∼: ein Heidengeld kosten (ugs.)/ein
Schweinegeld verdienen (ugs.)
packet 'soup n. Instantsuppe, die
'packing n. (material) Verpackungsmaterial,

das; **postage and ∼:** Porto und Verpackung
'packing case n. [Pack]kiste, die
pact /pækt/ n. Pakt, der
pad¹ /pæd/ 1 n. Polster, das; (block of paper)
Block, der
2 v.t., -dd- polstern ⟨Jacke, Schulter⟩
∎ **pad 'out** v.t. (fig.) auswalzen
pad² v.i., -dd- tappen
padded /'pædɪd/ adj. gepolstert
padded 'envelope n. wattierter
Umschlag
padding /'pædɪŋ/ n., no indef. art.
Polsterung, die; (fig.) Füllsel, das
paddle¹ /'pædl/ 1 n. [Stech]paddel, das
2 v.t. & i. paddeln
paddle² 1 v.i. (with feet) planschen
2 n. **have a/go for a ∼:** ein bisschen
planschen/planschen gehen
paddling pool /'pædlɪŋpuːl/ n.
Planschbecken, das
paddock /'pædək/ n. Koppel, die
'padlock 1 n. Vorhängeschloss, das
2 v.t. [mit einem Vorhängeschloss]
verschließen
paediatrician /piːdɪə'trɪʃn/ n.
Kinderarzt, der/-ärztin, die
paediatrics /piːdɪ'ætrɪks/ n. Pädiatrie,
die (fachspr.); Kinderheilkunde, die
paedophile /'piːdəfaɪl/ 1 n. Pädophile,
der
2 adj. pädophil
pagan /'peɪgən/ 1 n. Heide, der/Heidin,
die
2 adj. heidnisch
page¹ /peɪdʒ/ n. (boy) Page, der
page² n. (of book etc.) Seite, die
pageant /'pædʒənt/ n. (spectacle)
Schauspiel, das
pageantry /'pædʒəntrɪ/ n. Prunk, der
page: ∼ break n. (Comp.) Seitenbruch,
der; **∼ number** n. Seitenzahl, die
pager /'peɪdʒə(r)/ n. Piepser, der (ugs.)
paginate /'pædʒɪneɪt/ v.t. paginieren
pagination /pædʒɪ'neɪʃn/ n. Paginierung,
die
'paging device ▶ PAGER
paid /peɪd/ 1 ▶ PAY 2, 3
2 adj. **(a)** bezahlt ⟨Urlaub, Arbeit⟩
(b) put a ∼ to (Brit. coll.) zunichte machen;
kurzen Prozess machen mit (ugs.) ⟨Person⟩
pail /peɪl/ n. Eimer, der
pain /peɪn/ n. **(a)** (suffering) Schmerzen Pl.;
(mental ∼) Qualen Pl.; **be in
∼:** Schmerzen haben ⋯→

(b) (instance) Schmerz, *der;* **I have a** ∼ **in my knee/stomach** mein Knie/Magen tut weh
(c) *in pl.* (trouble taken) Mühe, *die;* **take** ∼**s** sich (*Dat.*) Mühe geben (**over** mit, bei)

painful /ˈpeɪnfl/ *adj.* **(a)** schmerzhaft; **be** ∼ ⟨*Körperteil:*⟩ wehtun
(b) (distressing) schmerzlich ⟨*Gedanke, Erinnerung*⟩; traurig ⟨*Pflicht*⟩

'**painkiller** *n.* schmerzstillendes Mittel

'**painless** *adj.* schmerzlos; (fig.) unproblematisch

painstaking /ˈpeɪnzteɪkɪŋ/ *adj.* gewissenhaft

paint /peɪnt/ ①*n.* Farbe, *die;* (on car) Lack, *der*
②*v.t.* (cover, colour) [an]streichen; (make picture of, make by ∼ing) malen; bemalen ⟨*Wand, Vase, Decke*⟩

paint: ∼**box** *n.* Malkasten, *der;* ∼**brush** *n.* Pinsel, *der*

'**painter** *n.* Maler, *der*/Malerin, *die*

'**painting** *n.* (art) Malerei, *die;* (picture) Gemälde, *das;* Bild, *das*

'**painting book** *n.* Malbuch, *das*

paint: ∼ **stripper** *n.* Abbeizer, *der;* ∼**work** *n.* (on walls etc.) Anstrich, *der;* (of car) Lack, *der*

pair /peə(r)/ ①*n.* Paar, *das;* **a** ∼ **of gloves/socks/shoes** *etc.* ein Paar Handschuhe/Socken/Schuhe *usw.;* **in** ∼**s** paarweise; **a** ∼ **of trousers/jeans** eine Hose/Jeans
②*v.t.* paaren
■ **pair** '**off** *v.i.* Zweiergruppen bilden

pajamas /pəˈdʒɑːməz/ (Amer.) ▶ PYJAMAS

Pakistan /pɑːkɪˈstɑːn/ *pr. n.* Pakistan (*das*)

Pakistani /pɑːkɪˈstɑːnɪ/ ①*adj.* pakistanisch; **sb. is** ∼: jmd. ist Pakistani
②*n.* Pakistani, *der*/*die*

pal /pæl/ *n.* (coll.) Kumpel, *der* (ugs.)

palace /ˈpælɪs/ *n.* Palast, *der*

palate /ˈpælət/ *n.* Gaumen, *der*

palatial /pəˈleɪʃl/ *adj.* palastartig

pale¹ /peɪl/ *adj.* blass, (nearly white) bleich ⟨*Gesichtsfarbe, Haut, Gesicht*⟩; blass ⟨*Farbe*⟩; fahl ⟨*Licht*⟩; **go** ∼: blass/bleich werden; (fig.) ∼ **imitation** schlechte Nachahmung

pale² *n.* **beyond the** ∼: unmöglich

Palestine /ˈpælɪstaɪn/ *pr. n.* Palästina (*das*)

Palestinian /pælɪˈstɪnɪən/ ①*adj.* palästinensisch; **sb. is** ∼ jmd. ist Palästinenser/Palästinenserin
②*n.* Palästinenser, *der*/Palästinenserin, *die*

palette /ˈpælɪt/ *n.* Palette, *die*

pall¹ /pɔːl/ *n.* **(a)** (over coffin) Sargtuch, *das*
(b) (fig.) Schleier, *der*

pall² *v.i.* ∼ **[on sb.]** [jmdm.] langweilig werden

pallor /ˈpælə(r)/ *n.* Blässe, *die*

palm¹ /pɑːm/ *n.* (tree) Palme, *die*

palm² *n.* Handteller, *der*
■ **palm** '**off** *v.t.* ∼ **sth. off on sb.,** ∼ **sb. off with sth.** jmdm. etw. andrehen (ugs.)

palmistry /ˈpɑːmɪstrɪ/ *n.* Handlesekunst, *die*

palm: P∼ '**Sunday** *n.* Palmsonntag, *der;* ∼**top** *n.* ∼**top [computer]** Palmtop, *der;* ∼ **tree** *n.* Palme, *die*

palpitation /pælpɪˈteɪʃn/ *n. in pl.* (Med.: of heart) Palpitation, *die* (fachspr.); **suffer from** ∼**s** Herzklopfen haben

paltry /ˈpɔːltrɪ, ˈpɒltrɪ/ *adj.* schäbig

pamper /ˈpæmpə/ *v.t.* verhätscheln; ∼ **oneself** sich verwöhnen

pamphlet /ˈpæmflɪt/ *n.* (leaflet) Prospekt, *der;* (booklet) Broschüre, *die*

pan /pæn/ *n.* [Koch]topf, *der;* (for frying) Pfanne, *die*

panacea /pænəˈsɪə/ *n.* Allheilmittel, *das*

Panama /pænəˈmɑː/ *pr. n.* Panama (*das*); ∼ **Ca'nal** Panamakanal, *der*

'**pancake** *n.* Pfannkuchen, *der*

pancreas /ˈpæŋkrɪəs/ *n.* Bauchspeicheldrüse, *die*

panda /ˈpændə/ *n.* Panda, *der*

pandemonium /pændɪˈməʊnɪəm/ *n.* Chaos, *das;* (uproar) Tumult, *der*

pander /ˈpændə(r)/ *v.i.* ∼ **to** allzu sehr entgegenkommen (+ *Dat.*)

pane /peɪn/ *n.* Scheibe, *die*

panel /ˈpænl/ *n.* **(a)** Paneel, *das*
(b) (esp. Telev., Radio, etc.) (quiz team) Rateteam, *das;* (in public discussion) Podium, *das*

panelling /ˈpænəlɪŋ/ *n.* Täfelung, *die*

panellist /ˈpænəlɪst/ *n.* (Telev., Radio) (on quiz programme) Mitglied des Rateteams; (on discussion panel) Diskussionsteilnehmer, *der*/-teilnehmerin, *die*

'**pan-fry** *v.t.* [in der Pfanne] braten

pang /pæŋ/ *n.* (of pain) Stich, *der;* **feel** ∼**s of conscience/guilt** Gewissensbisse haben; ∼**[s] of hunger** quälender Hunger

panic /ˈpænɪk/ ①*n.* Panik, *die;* **hit the** ∼ **button** (fig. coll.) Alarm schlagen; (∼) durchdrehen (ugs.)
②*v.i.,* -ck- in Panik (*Akk.*) geraten; **don't** ∼! nur keine Panik!

panic: ∼ **attack** *n.* Angstanfall, *der;* ∼**-stricken,** ∼**-struck** *adjs.* von Panik erfasst

panorama /pænəˈrɑːmə/ *n.* Panorama, *das*

pansy /ˈpænzɪ/ *n.* Stiefmütterchen, *das*

pant /pænt/ *v.i.* keuchen; ⟨*Hund:*⟩ hecheln

panther /ˈpænθə(r)/ *n.* Panther, *der*

panties /ˈpæntɪz/ *n. pl.* (coll.) **[pair of]** ∼: Schlüpfer, *der*

pantomime /ˈpæntəmaɪm/ *n.* (Brit.) *Märchenspiel im Varieteestil, das um Weihnachten aufgeführt wird*

pantry /'pæntrɪ/ n. Speisekammer, die
pants /pænts/ n. pl. (a) (esp. Amer.
coll.: trousers) **[pair of]** ∼: Hose, die
(b) (Brit. coll.: underpants) Unterhose, die
paparazzo /pæpæ'rɑːtsəʊ/ n., pl.
paparazzi /pæpæ'rɑːtsi/ Paparazzo, der
paper /'peɪpə(r)/ 1 n. (a) (material) Papier,
das
(b) in pl. (documents) Unterlagen Pl.; (to prove
identity etc.) Papiere Pl.
(c) (in examination) (Univ.) Klausur, die; (Sch.)
Arbeit, die
(d) (newspaper) Zeitung, die
(e) (learned article) Referat, das
2 adj. aus Papier nachgestellt;
Papier⟨mütze, -taschentuch⟩
3 v.t. tapezieren
paper: ∼**back** 1 n. Paperback,
das; 2 adj. ∼**back book** Paperback,
das; ∼ **'bag** n. Papiertüte, die;
∼ **boy** n. Zeitungsjunge, der;
∼ **clip** n. Büroklammer, die; (larger)
Aktenklammer, die; ∼ **'handkerchief**
n. Papiertaschentuch, das; ∼ **mill** n.
Papierfabrik od. -mühle, die; ∼ **money**
n. Papiergeld, das; ∼ **'napkin** n.
Papierserviette, die; ∼ **round** n.
Zeitungenaustragen, das; ∼ **servi'ette**
▶ ∼ NAPKIN; ∼ **'towel** n. Papierhandtuch,
das; ∼**weight** n. Briefbeschwerer, der;
∼**work** n. Schreibarbeit, die
par /pɑː(r)/ n. **feel below** ∼: nicht ganz
auf dem Posten sein (ugs.); **be on a** ∼ **with
sb./sth.** jmdm./einer Sache gleichkommen
parable /'pærəbl/ n. Gleichnis, das
parachute /'pærəʃuːt/ 1 n. Fallschirm, der
2 v.i. ⟨Truppen:⟩ abspringen (**into** über
+ Dat.)
parade /pə'reɪd/ 1 n. (a) (display)
Zurschaustellung, die
(b) (Mil.) Appell, der
(c) (procession) Umzug, der; (of troops) Parade,
die
2 v.t. zur Schau stellen
3 v.i. paradieren
pa'rade ground n. Exerzierplatz, der
paradise /'pærədaɪs/ n. Paradies, das
paradox /'pærədɒks/ n. Paradox[on], das
paradoxical /pærə'dɒksɪkl/ adj. paradox
paraffin /'pærəfɪn/ n. Paraffin, das;
(Brit.: fuel) Petroleum, das
paragliding /'pærəglaɪdɪŋ/ n.
Paragliding, das
paragon /'pærəgən/ Muster, das (**of** an
+ Dat.); ∼ **of virtue** Tugendheld, der/-heldin,
die
paragraph /'pærəgrɑːf/ n. Absatz, der
parallel /'pærəlel/ 1 adj. parallel;
(fig.: similar) vergleichbar; ∼ **bars** Barren, der
2 n. Parallele, die; ∼ **[of latitude]**
Breitenkreis, der
Paralympian /pærə'lɪmpɪən/ 1 adj.
paralympisch

2 n. Paralympiker, der/Paralympikerin,
die
Paralympic /pærə'lɪmpɪk/ adj.
paralympisch; **the** ∼ **Games, the** ∼**s** die
Paralympischen Spiele
paralyse /'pærəlaɪz/ v.t. lähmen; (fig.)
lahm legen ⟨Verkehr, Industrie⟩
paralysis /pə'rælɪsɪs/ n. Lähmung, die
paralyze (Amer.) ▶ PARALYSE
paramedic /pærə'medɪk/ n. medizinische
Hilfskraft; (ambulance worker) Sanitäter,
der/Sanitäterin, die
parameter /pə'ræmɪtə(r)/ n. Faktor, der
paramilitary /pærə'mɪlɪtərɪ/ adj.
paramilitärisch
paramount /'pærəmaʊnt/ adj. größt...
⟨Wichtigkeit⟩; Haupt⟨überlegung⟩; **be**
∼: Vorrang haben
paranoia /pærə'nɔɪə/ n. Paranoia, die
(Med.); (tendency) Verfolgungswahn, der
paranoid /'pærənɔɪd/ adj. **be** ∼ ⟨Person:⟩
an Verfolgungswahn leiden
parapet /'pærəpɪt/ n. Brüstung, die
paraphernalia /pærəfə'neɪlɪə/ n. sing.
Apparat, der
paraphrase /'pærəfreɪz/ 1 n.
Umschreibung, die
2 v.t. umschreiben
paraplegic /pærə'pliːdʒɪk/ 1 adj.
doppelseitig gelähmt
2 n. doppelseitig Gelähmter/Gelähmte
parasite /'pærəsaɪt/ n. Schmarotzer, der
parasitic /pærə'sɪtɪk/ adj. (a) (Biol.)
parasitisch
(b) (fig.) schmarotzerhaft
parasol /'pærəsɒl/ n. Sonnenschirm, der
paratroops /'pærətruːps/ n. pl.
Fallschirmjäger Pl.
parcel /'pɑːsl/ n. Paket, das
parched /pɑːtʃt/ adj. ausgedörrt; trocken
⟨Lippen⟩
parchment /'pɑːtʃmənt/ n. Pergament,
das
pardon /'pɑːdn/ 1 n. Verzeihung, die; **beg
sb.'s** ∼: jmdn. um Entschuldigung bitten;
I beg your ∼: entschuldigen Sie bitte
2 v.t. (a) ∼ **sb. [for] sth.** jmdm. etw.
verzeihen
(b) (excuse) entschuldigen
pardonable /'pɑːdənəbl/ adj. verzeihlich
pare /peə(r)/ v.t. (trim) schneiden; (peel)
schälen
parent /'peərənt/ n. Elternteil, der; ∼**s**
Eltern Pl.
parental /pə'rentl/ adj. Eltern⟨pflicht,
-haus, -liebe⟩
parenthesis /pə'renθɪsɪs/ n., pl.
parentheses /pə'renθɪsiːz/ (bracket) runde
Klammer
'parents' evening n. Elternabend, der
'parents-in-law pl. Schwiegereltern Pl.

Paris /'pærɪs/ *pr. n.* Paris (*das*)

parish /'pærɪʃ/ *n.* Gemeinde, *die*

parish: ~ **'church** *n.* Pfarrkirche, *die;* ~ **'council** *n.* (Brit.) Gemeinderat, *der*

parishioner /pə'rɪʃənə(r)/ *n.* Gemeinde[mit]glied, *das*

parish 'priest *n.* Gemeindepfarrer, *der*

park /pɑːk/ 1 *n.* Park, *der*
2 *v.i.* parken
3 *v.t.* abstellen; parken ⟨*Kfz*⟩; a ~ed car ein parkendes Auto

park-and-'ride *n.* Park-and-ride-System, *das;* (place) Park-and-ride-Parkplatz, *der*

'parking *n.* Parken, *das;* 'no ~' „Parken verboten"

parking: ~ **fine** *n.* Geldbuße für falsches Parken; ~ **light** *n.* Parkleuchte, *die;* ~ **lot** *n.* (Amer.) Parkplatz, *der;* ~ **meter** *n.* Parkuhr, *die;* ~ **offence** *n.* Verstoß gegen das Parkverbot; ~ **space** *n.* (a) *no pl.* Parkraum, *der;* (b) (single space) Parkplatz, *der;* ~ **ticket** *n.* Strafzettel [für falsches Parken]

'park-keeper *n.* Parkwächter, *der/* -wächterin, *die*

parliament /'pɑːləmənt/ *n.* Parlament, *das;* [Houses of] P~ (Brit.) Parlament, *das*

parliamentary /pɑːlə'mentərɪ/ *adj.* parlamentarisch; Parlaments⟨*geschäfte, -wahlen, -reform*⟩

parlour (*Brit.; Amer.:* **parlor**) /'pɑːlə(r)/ *n.* (dated) Wohnzimmer, *das*

parochial /pə'rəʊkɪəl/ *adj.* krähwinklig

parody /'pærədɪ/ 1 *n.* Parodie, *die* (of auf + *Akk.*)
2 *v.t.* parodieren

parole /pə'rəʊl/ *n.* bedingter Straferlass (Rechtsw.); on ~: auf Bewährung

paroxysm /'pærəksɪzm/ *n.* Krampf, *der;* (fit, convulsion) Anfall, *der* (of von)

parquet /'pɑːkɪ, 'pɑːkeɪ/ *n.* ~ [floor/ flooring] Parkett, *das*

parrot /'pærət/ *n.* Papagei, *der*

parry /'pærɪ/ *v.t.* abwehren ⟨*Faustschlag*⟩; (Fencing; also fig.) parieren

parsley /'pɑːslɪ/ *n.* Petersilie, *die*

parsnip /'pɑːsnɪp/ *n.* Gemeiner Pastinak, *der*

parson /'pɑːsn/ *n.* Pfarrer, *der*

part /pɑːt/ 1 *n.* (a) Teil, *der;* the greater ~: der größte Teil; der Großteil; for the most ~: größtenteils; in ~: teilweise; in large ~: groß[en]teils; in ~s zum Teil
(b) (of machine) [Einzel]teil, *das*
(c) (share) Anteil, *der*
(d) (Theatre) Rolle, *die*
(e) (Mus.) Part, *der;* Stimme, *die*
(f) *usu. in pl.* (region) Gegend, *die;* (of continent, world) Teil, *der*
(g) (side) Partei, *die;* take sb.'s ~: jmds. od. für jmdn. Partei ergreifen
(h) take [no] ~ [in sth.] sich [an etw. (*Dat.*)] [nicht] beteiligen
(i) take sth. in good ~: etw. nicht übel nehmen
2 *adv.* teils
3 *v.t.* (a) (divide into ~s) teilen; scheiteln ⟨*Haar*⟩
(b) (separate) trennen
4 *v.i.* ⟨*Seil, Tau, Kette:*⟩ reißen; ⟨*Wege, Personen:*⟩ sich trennen; ~ with sich trennen von ⟨*Besitz, Geld*⟩

part ex'change *n.* accept sth. in ~ for sth. etw. für etw. in Zahlung nehmen; sell sth. in ~: etw. in Zahlung geben

partial /'pɑːʃl/ *adj.* (a) (biased) voreingenommen
(b) be/not be ~ to sth. eine Schwäche/keine besondere Vorliebe für etw. haben
(c) partiell ⟨*Lähmung, Sonnenfinsternis*⟩; a ~ success ein Teilerfolg

'partially *adv.* teilweise

participant /pɑː'tɪsɪpənt/ *n.* Beteiligte, *der/die* (in an + *Dat.*)

participate /pɑː'tɪsɪpeɪt/ *v.i.* sich beteiligen (in an + *Dat.*); (in arranged event) teilnehmen (in an + *Dat.*)

participation /pɑːtɪsɪ'peɪʃn/ *n.* Beteiligung, *die* (in an + *Dat.*); (in arranged event) Teilnahme, *die* (in bei an + *Dat.*)

participle /'pɑːtɪsɪpl/ *n.* Partizip, *das*

particle /'pɑːtɪkl/ *n.* Teilchen, *das*

particular /pə'tɪkjʊlə(r)/ 1 *adj.*
(a) besonder…; here in ~: besonders hier; nothing/anything [in] ~: nichts/irgendetwas Besonderes
(b) (fastidious) genau; I am not ~: es ist mir gleich; be ~ about sth. es mit etw. genau nehmen
2 *n., in pl.* Einzelheiten *Pl.;* (of person) Personalien *Pl.*

par'ticularly *adv.* besonders

'parting 1 *n.* (a) [final] ~: Abschied, *der*
(b) (Brit.: in hair) Scheitel, *der*
2 *attrib. adj.* Abschieds-

partisan /'pɑːtɪzæn/ *n.* Partisan, *der/*Partisanin, *die*

partition /pɑː'tɪʃn/ 1 *n.* (a) (Polit.) Teilung, *die*
(b) (room divider) Trennwand, *die*
2 *v.t.* (a) (divide) aufteilen ⟨*Land, Zimmer*⟩
(b) (Polit.) teilen ⟨*Land*⟩
■ **partition 'off** *v.t.* abteilen

'partly *adv.* zum Teil; teilweise

partner /'pɑːtnə(r)/ *n.* Partner, *der/* Partnerin, *die*

'partnership *n.* Partnerschaft, *die;* business ~: [Personen]gesellschaft, *die*

'part-owner *n.* Mitbesitzer, *der/* -besitzerin, *die*

partridge /'pɑːtrɪdʒ/ *n., pl. same or* ~s Rebhuhn, *das*

part: ~**time** 1 /'--/ *adj.* Teilzeit⟨*arbeit, -arbeiter*⟩; 2 /·'·/ *adv.* stundenweise, halbtags ⟨*arbeiten, studieren*⟩; ~**'timer**

n. Teilzeitkraft, *die;* **study as a ~-timer**
halbtags *od.* stundenweise studieren
party /'pɑːtɪ/ *n.* **(a)** (Polit., Law) Partei, *die;*
attrib. Partei-
(b) (group) Gruppe, *die*
(c) (social gathering) Party, *die*
party: ~ po'litical *adj.* parteipolitisch;
~ 'politics *n.* Parteipolitik, *die;* **~ wall**
n. Mauer zum Nachbargrundstück/-gebäude
pass /pɑːs/ ① *n.* **(a)** (passing of an
examination) bestandene Prüfung; '**~**' (mark)
Ausreichend, *das;* **get a ~ in maths** die
Mathematikprüfung bestehen
(b) (written permission) Ausweis, *der*
(c) (Footb.) Pass, *der* (fachspr.); Ballabgabe,
die
(d) (in mountains) Pass, *der*
② *v.i.* **(a)** (go by) ⟨*Fußgänger:*⟩ vorbeigehen;
⟨*Fahrer, Fahrzeug:*⟩ vorbeifahren; ⟨*Zeit,
Sekunde:*⟩ vergehen; (by chance) ⟨*Person,
Fahrzeug:*⟩ vorbeikommen
(b) (come to an end) vorbeigehen; ⟨*Gewitter,
Unwetter:*⟩ vorüberziehen
(c) (be accepted) durchgehen (**as** als, **for** für)
(d) (in exam) bestehen
③ *v.t.* **(a)** ⟨*Fußgänger:*⟩ vorbeigehen an
(+ *Dat.*); ⟨*Fahrer, Fahrzeug:*⟩ vorbeifahren
an (+ *Dat.*); (by chance) ⟨*Person, Fahrzeug:*⟩
vorbeikommen an (+ *Dat.*)
(b) (overtake) vorbeifahren an (+ *Dat.*)
(c) bestehen ⟨*Prüfung*⟩
(d) (approve) verabschieden ⟨*Gesetzentwurf*⟩;
annehmen ⟨*Vorschlag*⟩; bestehen lassen
⟨*Prüfungskandidaten*⟩
(e) (Footb. etc.) abgeben (**to** an + *Akk.*)
(f) (spend) verbringen ⟨*Leben, Zeit, Tag*⟩
(g) (hand) **~ sb. sth.** jmdm. etw. reichen *od.*
geben
(h) fällen ⟨*Urteil*⟩; machen ⟨*Bemerkung*⟩
(i) **~ water** Wasser lassen
∎ **pass a'way** *v.i.* (euphem.) verscheiden
(geh.)
∎ **pass 'off** *v.t.* **~ sth. off as sth.** etw. als
etw. ausgeben
∎ **pass 'on** *v.t.* weitergeben (**to** an + *Akk.*)
∎ **pass 'out** *v.i.* ohnmächtig werden
∎ **pass 'up** *v.t.* entgehen lassen
⟨*Gelegenheit*⟩; ablehnen ⟨*Angebot*⟩
passable /'pɑːsəbl/ *adj.* **(a)** (acceptable)
passabel
(b) befahrbar ⟨*Straße*⟩
passage /'pæsɪdʒ/ *n.* **(a)** (voyage)
Überfahrt, *die*
(b) (way) Durchgang, *der;* (corridor) Korridor,
der
(c) (part of book etc.) Textstelle, *die;* (Mus.)
Stelle, *die*
'passageway *n.* Gang, *der;* (between
houses) Durchgang, *der*
passenger /'pæsɪndʒə(r)/ *n.* Passagier,
der; (on train) Reisende, *der/die;* (on bus, in
taxi) Fahrgast, *der;* (in car, on motor cycle)
Mitfahrer, *der*/Mitfahrerin, *die;* (in front seat
of car) Beifahrer, *der*/Beifahrerin, *die*

passenger: ~ aircraft *n.*
Passagierflugzeug, *das;* **~ door**
n. Beifahrertür, *die;* **~ lounge**
n. Warteraum, *der;* **~ plane** *n.*
Passagierflugzeug, *das;* **~ seat** *n.*
Beifahrersitz, *der;* **~ service** *n.* (train)
Personenzugverbindung, *die;* (ferry)
Personenfährverbindung, *die*
passer-by /pɑːsə'baɪ/ *n.* Passant,
der/Passantin, *die*
'passing ① *n.* (of time, years) Lauf, *der;* **in
~**: beiläufig ⟨*bemerken usw.*⟩
② *adj.* **(a)** vorbeifahrend ⟨*Zug, Auto*⟩;
vorbeikommend ⟨*Person*⟩
(b) flüchtig ⟨*Blick*⟩; vorübergehend ⟨*Mode,
Interesse*⟩; flüchtig ⟨*Bekanntschaft*⟩
'passing place *n.* Ausweichstelle, *die*
passion /'pæʃn/ *n.* Leidenschaft, *die;*
(enthusiasm) leidenschaftliche Begeisterung;
he has a ~ for steam engines Dampfloks
sind seine Leidenschaft
passionate /'pæʃənət/ *adj.*
leidenschaftlich; heftig ⟨*Verlangen*⟩
passive /'pæsɪv/ ① *adj.* **(a)** passiv;
~ smoker Passivraucher, *der*/-raucherin,
die; **~ smoking** passives Rauchen
(b) (Ling.) Passiv-
② *n.* (Ling.) Passiv, *das*
pass: ~ key *n.* (master key)
Hauptschlüssel, *der;* **~ mark** *n.*
Mindestpunktzahl, *die;* **~port** *n.*
(a) [Reise]pass, *der; attrib.* Pass-; **~port
control** Passkontrolle, *die;* **(b)** (fig.)
Schlüssel, *der* (**to** zu); **~word** *n.* **(a)** Parole,
die; Losung, *die;* **(b)** (Comp.) Passwort, *das;*
~word-protected passwortgeschützt
past /pɑːst/ ① *adj.* **(a)** *pred.* (over) vorbei
(b) *attrib.* (previous) früher; vergangen;
ehemalig ⟨*Präsident, Vorsitzende usw.*⟩
(c) *attrib.* (just gone by) letzt...; vergangen; **in
the ~ few days** während der letzten Tage
(d) (Ling.) **~ tense** Vergangenheit, *die*
② *n.* Vergangenheit, *die;* **in the ~**: früher;
in der Vergangenheit ⟨*leben*⟩; **be a thing of
the ~**: der Vergangenheit angehören
③ *prep.* (in time) nach; (in place) hinter
(+ *Dat.*); **half ~ three** halb vier; **five
[minutes] ~ two** fünf [Minuten] nach
zwei; **gaze/walk ~ sb./sth.** an jmdm./etw.
vorbeiblicken/vorbeigehen; **~ repair** nicht
mehr zu reparieren
④ *adv.* vorbei; **hurry ~**: vorübereilen
pasta /'pæstə/ *n.* Teigwaren *Pl.*
paste /peɪst/ ① *n.* **(a)** Brei, *der*
(b) (glue) Kleister, *der*
(c) (of meat, fish, etc.) Paste, *die*
② *v.t.* **(a)** kleben; **~ sth. into sth.** etw. in
etw. ⟨*Akk.*⟩ einkleben
(b) (Comp.) einfügen (**into** in + *Akk.*); *see also*
CUT 1E
pastel /'pæstl/ ① *n.* (crayon) Pastellstift,
der
② *adj.* pastellfarben; Pastell⟨*farben, -töne,
-zeichnung*⟩

pasteurize /'pɑːstʃəraɪz/ v.t.
pasteurisieren

pastille /'pæstɪl/ n. Pastille, die

pastime /'pɑːstaɪm/ n. Zeitvertreib, der;
(person's specific ∼) Hobby, das

past 'master n. (fig.) Meister, der

pastor /'pɑːstə(r)/ n. Pfarrer, der/
Pfarrerin, die; Pastor, der/Pastorin, die

pastoral /'pɑːstərl/ adj. Weide-; ländlich
⟨Reiz, Idylle, Umgebung⟩

pastry /'peɪstrɪ/ n. Teig, der; (article of
food) Gebäckstück, das; **pastries** collect.
[Fein]gebäck, das

pasture /'pɑːstʃə(r)/ n. Weide, die

'pastureland n. Weideland, das

pasty /'pæstɪ/ n. Pastete, die

pat¹ /pæt/ ① n. **(a)** (tap) Klaps, der
(b) (of butter) Stückchen, das
② v.t., **-tt-** leicht klopfen auf (+ Akk.);
tätscheln, (once) einen Klaps geben (+ Dat.)
⟨Person, Hund, Pferd⟩; ∼ **sb. on the
arm/head** jmdm. den Arm/Kopf tätscheln

pat² adv. **have sth. off** ∼: etw. parat haben

patch /pætʃ/ ① n. **(a)** Stelle, die; **fog** ∼**es**
Nebelfelder
(b) (on worn garment) Flicken, der; **be not a**
∼ **on sth.** (fig. coll.) nichts gegen etw. sein
② v.t. flicken
■ **patch 'up** v.t. reparieren; (fig.) beilegen
⟨Streit⟩

patchwork n. Patchwork, das

patchy /'pætʃɪ/ adj. uneinheitlich
⟨Qualität⟩; ungleichmäßig ⟨Arbeit⟩; sehr
lückenhaft ⟨Wissen⟩

pâté /'pæteɪ/ n. Pastete, die

patent /'peɪtənt, 'pætənt/ ① adj. (obvious)
offenkundig
② n. Patent, das
③ v.t. patentieren lassen

patent 'leather n. Lackleder, das;
∼ **shoes** Lackschuhe Pl.

'patently adv. offenkundig; ∼ **obvious**
ganz offenkundig

paternal /pə'tɜːnl/ adj. väterlich

paternity /pə'tɜːnɪtɪ/ n. (fatherhood)
Vaterschaft, die

pa'ternity leave n. Vaterschaftsurlaub,
der

path /pɑːθ/ n. Weg, der; (line of motion) Bahn,
die

pathetic /pə'θetɪk/ adj. **(a)** (pitiful) Mitleid
erregend
(b) (contemptible) armselig ⟨Entschuldigung⟩;
erbärmlich ⟨Person, Leistung⟩

pathogen /'pæθədʒən/ n.
[Krankheits]erreger, der

pathological /pæθə'lɒdʒɪkl/ adj.
(a) pathologisch
(b) (fig.: obsessive) krankhaft

pathologist /pə'θɒlədʒɪst/ n. Pathologe,
der/Pathologin, die

pathology /pə'θɒlədʒɪ/ n. Pathologie, die;
the ∼ **of a disease** das Krankheitsbild

'pathway n. Weg, der

patience /'peɪʃəns/ n. Geduld, die

patient /'peɪʃənt/ ① adj. geduldig
② n. Patient, der/Patientin, die

'patiently adv. geduldig

patio /'pætɪəʊ/ n., pl. ∼**s** Veranda, die;
Terrasse, die

patio 'door n. große Glasschiebetür (zum
Garten)

patriarch /'peɪtrɪɑːk/ n. (of family)
Familienoberhaupt, das

patriarchal /peɪtrɪ'ɑːkl/ adj.
patriarchalisch

patriot /'peɪtrɪət/ n. Patriot, der/Patriotin,
die

patriotic /peɪtrɪ'ɒtɪk/ adj. patriotisch

patriotism /'peɪtrɪətɪzm/ n. Patriotismus,
der

patrol /pə'trəʊl/ ① n. (Police) Streife, die;
(Mil.) Patrouille, die; **be on** ∼: patrouillieren
② v.i., **-ll-** patrouillieren; ⟨Polizei:⟩ Streife
laufen/fahren
③ v.t., **-ll-** patrouillieren durch (+ Akk.);
abpatrouillieren ⟨Straßen, Gegend, Lager⟩;
patrouillieren vor (+ Dat.) ⟨Küste, Grenze⟩;
⟨Polizei:⟩ Streife laufen/fahren in (+ Dat.)
⟨Straßen, Stadtteil⟩

patrol: ∼ **boat** n. Patrouillenboot, das;
∼ **car** n. Streifenwagen, der

patron /'peɪtrən/ n. **(a)** Gönner,
der/Gönnerin, die; (of institution, campaign)
Schirmherr, der/Schirmherrin, die
(b) (customer) (of shop) Kunde, der/Kundin,
die; (of restaurant, hotel) Gast, der; (of theatre,
cinema) Besucher, der/Besucherin, die
(c) ∼ **[saint]** Schutzheilige, der/die

patronage /'pætrənɪdʒ/ n. Gönnerschaft,
die; (for campaign, institution) Schirmherrschaft,
die

patronize /'pætrənaɪz/ v.t. **(a)** (frequent)
besuchen
(b) (condescend to) ∼ **sb.** jmdn. herablassend
behandeln

patronizing /'pætrənaɪzɪŋ/ adj.
gönnerhaft; herablassend

patter /'pætə(r)/ ① n. (of rain) Prasseln,
das; (of feet) Trappeln, das
② v.i. ⟨Regen:⟩ prasseln

pattern /'pætən/ n. Muster, das; (model)
Vorlage, die; (for sewing) Schnittmuster, das;
(for knitting) Strickmuster, das

paunch /pɔːntʃ/ n. Bauch, der

pauper /'pɔːpə(r)/ n. Arme, der/die

pause /pɔːz/ ① n. Pause, die
② v.i. eine Pause machen; ⟨Redner:⟩
innehalten; (hesitate) zögern

pave /peɪv/ v.t. befestigen; (with stones)
pflastern; ∼ **the way for sth.** (fig.) einer
Sache (Dat.) den Weg ebnen

'**pavement** *n*. (a) (Brit.: footway)
Bürgersteig, *der*
(b) (Amer.: roadway) Fahrbahn, *die*
'**pavement café** *n*. Straßencafé, *das*
pavilion /pə'vɪljən/ *n*. Pavillon, *der;* (Brit.
Sport) Klubhaus, *das*
'**paving stone** *n*. Platte, *die;* Pflasterstein,
der
paw /pɔː/ *n*. Pfote, *die;* (of bear, lion, tiger)
Pranke, *die*
pawn¹ /pɔːn/ *n*. (Chess) Bauer, *der;* (fig.)
Schachfigur, *die*
pawn² 1 *n*. Pfand, *das; in* ∼: verpfändet
2 *v.t.* verpfänden
pawn: ∼**broker** *n*. Pfandleiher, *der/*
-leiherin, *die;* ∼**shop** *n*. Leihhaus, *das*
pay /peɪ/ 1 *n*. (wages) Lohn, *der;* (salary)
Gehalt, *das; be in the* ∼ *of sb./sth.* für
jmdn./etw. arbeiten
2 *v.t.*, paid /peɪd/ bezahlen; zahlen ⟨Geld⟩;
∼ sb. to do sth. jmdn. dafür bezahlen, dass
er etw. tut; ∼ sb. £10 jmdm. 10 Pfund zahlen
3 *v.i.*, pegud (a) zahlen; ∼ for sth./sb.
etw./für jmdn. bezahlen; **sth.** ∼**s for itself**
etw. macht sich bezahlt
(b) (be profitable) sich lohnen; ⟨Geschäft:⟩
rentabel sein; **it** ∼**s to be careful** es lohnt
sich, vorsichtig zu sein. *See also* PAID
■ **pay 'back** *v.t.* zurückzahlen; **I'll** ∼ **you**
back later ich gebe dir das Geld später
zurück
■ **pay 'in** *v.t.* einzahlen
■ **pay 'off** *v.t.* auszahlen ⟨Arbeiter⟩;
abbezahlen ⟨Schulden⟩; ablösen ⟨Hypothek⟩;
befriedigen ⟨Gläubiger⟩
■ **pay 'out** *v.t.* auszahlen; (spend) ausgeben
■ **pay 'up** *v.i.* zahlen
payable /'peɪəbl/ *adj.* zahlbar; **be** ∼ **to**
sb. an jmdn. zu zahlen sein; **make a cheque**
∼ **to the Post Office/to sb.** einen Scheck auf
die Post/auf jmds. Namen ausstellen
pay: ∼ **and display** 1 *n*. Parken mit
Parkschein; *attrib.* Parkschein-; 2 *n*.
∼ **and display car park** Parkplatz mit
Parkscheinautomat; ∼ **cheque** *n*. Lohn-/
Gehaltsscheck, *der;* ∼ **claim** *n*. Lohn-/
Gehaltsforderung, *die;* ∼ **day** *n*. Zahltag, *der*
payee /peɪ'iː/ *n*. Zahlungsempfänger, *der/*
-empfängerin, *die*
'**pay increase** ▶ PAY RISE
paying /'peɪɪŋ/: ∼ '**guest** *n*. zahlender
Gast; ∼-'**in slip** *n*. (Brit. Banking)
Einzahlungsschein, *der*
'**payment** *n*. (a) (of sum, bill, debt, fine)
Bezahlung, *die;* (of interest, instalment, tax, fee)
Zahlung, *die; in* ∼ **[for sth.]** als Bezahlung
[für etw.]
(b) (amount) Zahlung, *die*
pay: ∼ **packet** *n*. (Brit.) Lohntüte, *die;*
∼ **phone** *n*. Münzfernsprecher, *der;*
∼ **rise** *n*. Lohn-/Gehaltserhöhung, *die;*
∼**roll** *n*. Lohnliste, *die; be on sb.'s* ∼**roll**
für jmdn. arbeiten; ∼**slip** *n*. Lohnstreifen,

*der/*Gehaltszettel, *der;* ∼ **station** *n*. (Amer.)
▶ ∼ PHONE
p.c. *abbr.* = **per cent** *v*. H.
PC *abbr.* (a) (Brit.) = **police constable**
Wachtm.
(b) = **personal computer** PC
(c) = **politically correct** politisch
korrekt
PE *abbr.* = **physical education**
pea /piː/ *n*. Erbse, *die*
peace /piːs/ *n*. Frieden, *der;* (tranquillity)
Ruhe, *die;* ∼ **of mind** Seelenfrieden, *der*
peaceable /'piːsəbl/ *adj.* friedfertig; (calm)
friedlich
peaceful /'piːsfl/ *adj.* friedlich; friedfertig
⟨Person, Volk⟩
'**peacefully** *adv.* friedlich; **die** ∼: sanft
entschlafen
peace: ∼**keeper** *n*. Friedenswächter,
der; ∼**keeping force** Friedenstruppe,
die; ∼**maker** *n*. Friedensstifter,
der/-stifterin, *die;* ∼ **movement** *n*.
Friedensbewegung, *die;* ∼ **process**
n. Friedensprozess, *der* ∼ **treaty** *n*.
Friedensvertrag, *der*
peach /piːtʃ/ *n*. Pfirsich, *der*
'**peacock** *n*. Pfau, *der*
'**pea-green** *adj.* erbsengrün; maigrün
peak /piːk/ 1 *n*. (a) (of cap) Schirm, *der*
(b) (of mountain) Gipfel, *der;* (fig.) Höhepunkt,
der
2 *attrib. adj.* Höchst-, Spitzen⟨preise,
-werte⟩; ∼**-hour traffic** Stoßverkehr, *der*
peaked /piːkt/ *adj.* ∼ **cap** Schirmmütze, *die*
'**peak season** *n*. Hochsaison, *die*
peal /piːl/ *n*. Läuten, *das;* ∼ **of bells**
Glockenläuten, *das;* **a** ∼/∼**s of laughter**
schallendes Gelächter
peanut /'piːnʌt/ *n*. Erdnuss, *die;* ∼ **butter**
Erdnussbutter, *die;* ∼**s** (coll.: little money) ein
paar Kröten (salopp)
pear /peə(r)/ *n*. Birne, *die*
pearl /pɜːl/ *n*. Perle, *die*
pear: ∼**-shaped** *adj.* birnenförmig;
∼ **tree** *n*. Birnbaum, *der*
peasant /'pezənt/ *n*. [armer] Bauer, *der;*
Landarbeiter, *der*
pea 'soup Erbsensuppe, *die*
peat /piːt/ *n*. Torf, *der*
pebble /'pebl/ *n*. Kiesel[stein], *der*
peck /pek/ 1 *v.t.* hacken; picken ⟨Körner⟩
2 *v.i.* picken (at nach); ∼ **at one's food** im
Essen herumstochern
3 *n*. (kiss) flüchtiger Kuss
'**pecking order** *n*. Hackordnung, *die*
peckish /'pekɪʃ/ *adj.* (coll.) **feel/get**
∼: Hunger haben/bekommen
peculiar /pɪ'kjuːlɪə(r)/ *adj.* (a) (strange)
seltsam; **I feel [slightly]** ∼: mir ist [etwas]
komisch
(b) (especial) besonder...
(c) (belonging exclusively) eigentümlich (**to** *Dat.*)

p

peculiarity /pɪkjuːlɪˈærɪtɪ/ n. **(a)** (odd trait) Eigentümlichkeit, *die*
(b) (distinguishing characteristic) [charakteristisches] Merkmal
pe'culiarly adv. **(a)** (strangely) seltsam
(b) (especially) besonders
pedal /ˈpedl/ ① n. Pedal, *das*
② v.i., (Brit.) **-ll-** in die Pedale treten
'pedal bin n. Treteimer, *der*
pedalo /ˈpedələʊ/ n., pl. ∼s Tretboot, *das*
pedant /ˈpedənt/ n. Pedant, *der*/Pedantin, *die*
pedantic /pɪˈdæntɪk/ adj. pedantisch
peddle /ˈpedl/ v.t. auf der Straße verkaufen; (door to door) hausieren mit
pedestal /ˈpedɪstl/ n. Sockel, *der*
pedestrian /pɪˈdestrɪən/ ① adj. (uninspired) trocken; langweilig
② n. Fußgänger, *der*/-gängerin, *die*
pedestrian 'crossing n. Fußgängerüberweg, *der*
pedestrianize (pedestrianise) /pɪˈdestrɪənaɪz/ v.t. zur Fußgängerzone machen; ∼d zone Fußgängerzone, *die*
pedestrian 'precinct ▶ PRECINCT A
pediatrician etc. ▶ PAEDIATRICIAN etc.
pedicure /ˈpedɪkjʊə(r)/ n., no art. Pediküre, *die*
pedigree /ˈpedɪgriː/ ① n. Stammbaum, *der*
② adj. mit Stammbaum *nachgestellt*
pedlar /ˈpedlə(r)/ n. Straßenhändler, *der*/-händlerin, *die*; (door to door) Hausierer, *der*/Hausiererin, *die*
pee /piː/ (coll.) ① v.i. pinkeln (salopp); Pipi machen (Kinderspr.)
② n. **(a)** have a ∼: pinkeln (salopp)
(b) (urine) Pipi, *das* (Kinderspr.)
peek /piːk/ ▶ PEEP²
peel /piːl/ ① v.t. schälen
② v.i. ⟨Person, Haut:⟩ sich schälen; ⟨Farbe:⟩ abblättern
③ n. Schale, *die*
'peelings n. pl. Schalen *Pl.*
peep¹ /piːp/ ① v.i. ⟨Maus, Vogel:⟩ piep[s]en
② n. Piepsen, *das;* (coll.: remark etc.) Piep[s], *der*
peep² ① v.i. gucken (ugs.); (furtively) verstohlen gucken (ugs.)
② n. kurzer/verstohlener Blick
peep: ∼**hole** n. Guckloch, *das;* ∼**ing 'Tom** n. Spanner, *der* (ugs.)
peer¹ /pɪə(r)/ n. Peer, *der;* (equal) Gleichgestellte, *der/die*
peer² v.i. forschend schauen; (with difficulty) angestrengt schauen; ∼ at sth./sb. [sich (Dat.)] etw. genau ansehen/jmdn. forschend ansehen; (with difficulty) [sich (Dat.)] etw./jmdn. angestrengt ansehen
peerage /ˈpɪərɪdʒ/ n. Peerswürde, *die*
'peer pressure n. Gruppenzwang, *der*

peevish /ˈpiːvɪʃ/ adj. nörgelig
peg /peg/ n. **(a)** (for holding together) Stift, *der;* (for tying things to) Pflock, *der;* (for hanging things on) Haken, *der;* (clothes ∼) Wäscheklammer, *die;* (tent ∼) Hering, *der;* off the ∼ (Brit.: ready-made) von der Stange (ugs.)
pejorative /pɪˈdʒɒrətɪv/ adj., **pe'joratively** adv. abwertend
pelican /ˈpelɪkən/ n. Pelikan, *der*
'pelican crossing n. (Brit.) Ampelübergang, *der*
pellet /ˈpelɪt/ n. Kügelchen, *das*
pelmet /ˈpelmɪt/ n. Blende, *die*
pelt¹ /pelt/ n. Fell, *das*
pelt² ① v.t. ∼ sb. with sth. jmdn. mit etw. bewerfen
② v.i. **(a)** it was ∼ing down [with rain] es goss wie aus Kübeln (ugs.)
(b) (run fast) rasen (ugs.)
pelvic /ˈpelvɪk/ adj. Becken-
pelvis /ˈpelvɪs/ n., pl. **pelves** /ˈpelviːz/ or ∼**es** (Anat.) Becken, *das*
pen¹ /pen/ ① n. (enclosure) Pferch, *der*
② v.t., **-nn-:** ∼ sb. in a corner jmdn. in eine Ecke drängen
■ **pen 'in** v.t. einpferchen
pen² ① n. Federhalter, *der;* (fountain ∼) Füller, *der;* (ball ∼) Kugelschreiber, *der;* (felt-tip ∼) Filzstift, *der*
② v.t., **-nn-** schreiben
penal /ˈpiːnl/ adj. Straf-
penalize /ˈpiːnəlaɪz/ v.t. bestrafen; (Sport) eine Strafe verhängen gegen
penalty /ˈpenltɪ/ n. **(a)** Strafe, *die;* pay the ∼/the ∼ for or of sth. dafür/für etw. büßen [müssen]
(b) (Footb.) Elfmeter, *der*
penalty: ∼ **box** n. (Footb.) Strafraum, *der;* (Ice Hockey) Strafbank, *die;* ∼ **kick** n. (Footb.) Strafstoß, *der*
penance /ˈpenəns/ n. Buße, *die;* act of ∼: Bußwerk, *das;* do ∼: Buße tun
pence ▶ PENNY
pencil /ˈpensl/ ① n. Bleistift, *der;* red/coloured ∼: Rot-/Buntstift, *der*
② v.t., (Brit.) **-ll-** mit einem Bleistift/Farbstift schreiben
pencil: ∼ **case** n. Griffelkasten, *der;* (of soft material) Federmäppchen, *das;* ∼ **sharpener** n. Bleistiftspitzer, *der*
pendant /ˈpendənt/ n. Anhänger, *der*
pending /ˈpendɪŋ/ ① adj. unentschieden ⟨Angelegenheit, Sache⟩; schwebend ⟨Verfahren⟩
② prep. ∼ his return bis zu seiner Rückkehr
pendulum /ˈpendjʊləm/ n. Pendel, *das*
penetrate /ˈpenɪtreɪt/ v.t. eindringen in (+ Akk.); (pass through) durchdringen
penetrating /ˈpenɪtreɪtɪŋ/ adj. durchdringend
penetration /penɪˈtreɪʃn/ n. Eindringen, *das* (of in + Akk.); (passing through)

Durchdringen, *das*

'**penfriend** *n.* Brieffreund, *der*/-freundin, *die*

penguin /'peŋgwɪn/ *n.* Pinguin, *der*

penicillin /penɪ'sɪlɪn/ *n.* Penizillin, *das*

peninsula /pɪ'nɪnsjʊlə/ *n.* Halbinsel, *die*

penis /'piːnɪs/ *n.* Penis, *der*

penitence /'penɪtəns/ *n.* Reue, *die*

penitent /'penɪtənt/ *adj.* reuevoll (geh.); reuig (geh.) ⟨*Sünder*⟩

penitentiary /penɪ'tenʃərɪ/ *n.* (Amer.) Straf[vollzugs]anstalt, *die*

pen: ~knife *n.* Taschenmesser, *das;* **~ light** *n.* [Mini]stablampe, *die*

pennant /'penənt/ *n.* Wimpel, *der;* (on official car etc.) Stander, *der*

penniless /'penɪlɪs/ *adj.* mittellos

penny /'penɪ/ *n., pl. usu.* **pennies** /'penɪz/ (for separate coins), **pence** /pens/ (for sum of money) Penny, *der;* **fifty pence** fünfzig Pence; **two**/**fifty pence [piece]** Zwei-/ Fünfzigpencestück, *das*

pension /'penʃn/ *n.* Rente, *die;* (payment to retired civil servant) Pension, *die;* **widow's ~**: Witwenrente, *die*/-pension, *die;* **be on a ~**: eine Rente beziehen

■ **pension 'off** *v.t.* berenten (Amtsspr.); auf Rente setzen (ugs.); pensionieren ⟨*Lehrer, Beamten*⟩

'**pensioner** *n.* Rentner, *der*/Rentnerin, *die;* (retired civil servant) Pensionär, *der*/ Pensionärin, *die*

pensive /'pensɪv/ *adj.* nachdenklich

pentagon /'pentəgən/ *n.* Fünfeck, *das;* **the P~** (Amer. Polit.) das Pentagon

Pentecost /'pentɪkɒst/ *n.* Pfingsten, *das*

pent: ~house *n.* Penthaus, *das;* **~-up** *adj.* angestaut ⟨*Ärger, Wut*⟩; unterdrückt ⟨*Sehnsucht, Gefühle*⟩

penultimate /pe'nʌltɪmət/ *adj.* vorletzt…

people /'piːpl/ *n.* (a) *constr. as pl.* Leute *Pl.;* Menschen *Pl.;* (as opposed to animals) Menschen *Pl.;* **city**/**country ~** (inhabitants) Stadt-/Landbewohner *Pl.;* **local ~**: Einheimische *Pl.;* **working ~**: arbeitende Menschen; **coloured**/**white ~**: Farbige/ Weiße *Pl.;* **~ say …**: man sagt …; **a crowd of ~**: eine Menschenmenge (b) (nation) Volk, *das*

pepper /'pepə(r)/ ① *n.* (a) Pfeffer, *der* (b) (vegetable) Paprikaschote, *die;* **red**/**green ~**: roter/grüner Paprika ② *v.t.* (a) pfeffern (b) (pelt) bombardieren (ugs.)

pepper: ~corn *n.* Pfefferkorn, *das;* **~ mill** *n.* Pfeffermühle, *die;* **~mint** *n.* (sweet) Pfefferminz, *das;* **~ pot** *n.* Pfefferstreuer, *der*

peppery /'pepərɪ/ *adj.* pfeff[e]rig; (spicy) scharf

per /pə(r), *stressed* pɜː(r)/ *prep.* pro

perceive /pə'siːv/ *v.t.* wahrnehmen;

(with the mind) spüren; **~d** vermeintlich ⟨*Bedrohung, Gefahr, Wert*⟩

per cent (*Brit.; Amer.:* **percent**) /pə'sent/ ① *adv.* ninety **~ effective** zu 90 Prozent wirksam ② *adj.* **a 5 ~ increase** ein Zuwachs von 5 Prozent ③ *n.* (a) Prozent, *das* (b) ▶ PERCENTAGE

percentage /pə'sentɪdʒ/ *n.* Prozentsatz, *der*

per'centage sign *n.* Prozentzeichen, *das*

perceptible /pə'septɪbl/ *adj.* wahrnehmbar

perception /pə'sepʃn/ *n.* (act) Wahrnehmung, *die;* (result) Erkenntnis, *die;* (faculty) Wahrnehmungsvermögen, *das*

perceptive /pə'septɪv/ *adj.* einfühlsam ⟨*Person, Bemerkung*⟩

perch /pɜːtʃ/ ① *n.* Sitzstange, *die* ② *v.i.* (a) sich niederlassen (b) (be supported) sitzen ③ *v.t.* setzen/stellen/legen

percolate /'pɜːkəleɪt/ *v.i.* [durch]sickern

percolator /'pɜːkəleɪtə(r)/ *n.* Kaffeemaschine, *die*

percussion /pə'kʌʃn/ *n.* (Mus.) Schlagzeug, *das;* **~ instrument** Schlaginstrument, *das*

perennial /pə'renjəl/ ① *adj.* (a) (Bot.) ausdauernd (b) immer wieder auftretend ⟨*Problem*⟩ ② *n.* (Bot.) ausdauernde Pflanze

perfect ① /'pɜːfɪkt/ *adj.* vollkommen; perfekt ⟨*Englisch, Timing*⟩; tadellos ⟨*Zustand*⟩; (coll.: unmitigated) absolut; **a ~ stranger** ein völlig Fremder ② /pə'fekt/ *v.t.* vervollkommnen

perfection /pə'fekʃn/ *n.* Perfektion, *die;* **to ~**: perfekt

perfectionism /pə'fekʃənɪzm/ *n.* Perfektionismus, *der*

perfectionist /pə'fekʃənɪst/ *n.* Perfektionist, *der*/Perfektionistin, *die*

'**perfectly** *adv.* (a) (completely) vollkommen; **be ~ entitled to do sth.** durchaus berechtigt sein, etw. zu tun (b) (faultlessly) perfekt; tadellos ⟨*sich verhalten*⟩

perfect 'pitch *n.* (Mus.) absolutes Gehör

perforate /'pɜːfəreɪt/ *v.t.* perforieren; (make opening into) durchlöchern

perforation /pɜːfə'reɪʃn/ *n.* (a) (hole) Loch, *das* (b) *in pl.* **~s** Perforation, *die;* (in sheets of stamps) Zähnung, *die*

perform /pə'fɔːm/ ① *v.t.* ausführen ⟨*Arbeit, Operation*⟩; erfüllen ⟨*Pflicht, Aufgabe*⟩; vollbringen ⟨*[Helden]tat, Leistung*⟩; ausfüllen ⟨*Funktion*⟩; vollbringen ⟨*Wunder*⟩; anstellen ⟨*Berechnungen*⟩; durchführen ⟨*Experiment, Sektion*⟩; ···⫶

vorführen ‹Trick›; aufführen ‹Theaterstück, Scharade›; vortragen ‹Lied, Sonate usw.›
2 v.i. eine Vorführung geben; (sing) singen; (play) spielen

performance /pə'fɔːməns/ n. **(a)** (of duty, task) Erfüllung, die
(b) ([notable] achievement; Motor Veh.) Leistung, die
(c) (at theatre, cinema, etc.) Vorstellung, die; her ~ as Desdemona ihre Darstellung der Desdemona; the ~ of a play/opera die Aufführung eines Theaterstücks/einer Oper

performance: ~ art n. Performance-Art, die; ~ **artist** n. Performancekünstler, der/-künstlerin, die; ~**-enhancing** adj. ~-enhancing drug/substance leistungsfördernde od. -steigernde Droge/Substanz

per'former n. Künstler, der/Künstlerin, die

per'forming attrib. adj. dressiert ‹Tier›

performing 'arts n. pl. darstellende Künste

perfume /'pɜːfjuːm/ n. Duft, der; (fluid) Parfüm, das

perfunctory /pə'fʌŋktərɪ/ adj. oberflächlich ‹Arbeit, Überprüfung›; flüchtig ‹Erkundigung, Bemerkung›

perhaps /pə'hæps/ adv. vielleicht

peril /'perəl/ n. Gefahr, die

perilous /'perələs/ adj. gefahrvoll; be ~: gefährlich sein

perimeter /pə'rɪmɪtə(r)/ n. [äußere] Begrenzung; Grenze, die

period /'pɪərɪəd/ **1** n. **(a)** (of history or life) Periode, die; Zeit, die; (any portion of time) Zeitraum, der; the Classical/Romantic ~: die Klassik/Romantik
(b) (Sch.) Stunde, die; chemistry/English ~: Chemie-/Englischstunde, die
(c) (menstruation) Periode, die
(d) (punctuation mark) Punkt, der
2 adj. zeitgenössisch ‹Tracht, Kostüm›; antik ‹Möbel›

periodic /pɪərɪ'ɒdɪk/ adj. regelmäßig; (intermittent) gelegentlich

periodical /pɪərɪ'ɒdɪkl/ **1** adj. ▶ PERIODIC
2 n. Zeitschrift, die; weekly/monthly ~: Wochenzeitschrift/Monatsschrift, die

peri'odically adv. regelmäßig; (intermittently) gelegentlich

peripheral /pə'rɪfərl/ **1** adj. peripher (geh.); Rand‹problem, -erscheinung›
2 n. (Comp.) Peripheriegerät, das

periphery /pə'rɪfərɪ/ n. Peripherie, die

periscope /'perɪskəʊp/ n. Periskop, das

perish /'perɪʃ/ v.i. **(a)** (die) umkommen
(b) (rot) verderben; ‹Gummi:› altern

perishable /'perɪʃəbl/ adj. [leicht] verderblich

'perishing (coll.) **1** adj. mörderisch ‹Kälte›; it's/I'm ~: es ist bitterkalt/ich komme um vor Kälte (ugs.)

2 adv. mörderisch ‹kalt›

perjury /'pɜːdʒərɪ/ n. Meineid, der; commit ~: einen Meineid leisten

perk¹ /pɜːk/ (coll.) **1** v.i. ~ up munter werden
2 v.t. ~ up aufmuntern

perk² n. (Brit. coll.) [Sonder]vergünstigung, die

perky /'pɜːkɪ/ adj. lebhaft; munter

perm /pɜːm/ **1** n. Dauerwelle, die
2 v.t. have one's hair ~ed sich (Dat.) eine Dauerwelle machen lassen

permanence /'pɜːmənəns/ n. Dauerhaftigkeit, die

permanent /'pɜːmənənt/ adj. fest ‹Sitz, Bestandteil, Mitglied›; ständig ‹Wohnsitz, Adresse, Kampf›; Dauer‹stellung, -visum›; bleibend ‹Schaden›

'permanently adv. dauernd; auf Dauer ‹verhindern, bleiben›

permanent 'wave n. Dauerwelle, die

permeable /'pɜːmɪəbl/ adj. durchlässig; be ~ to sth. etw. durchlassen

permeate /'pɜːmɪeɪt/ **1** v.t. dringen durch; be ~d with or by sth. (fig.) von etw. durchdrungen sein
2 v.i. ~ through sth. etw. durchdringen

permissible /pə'mɪsɪbl/ adj. zulässig; be ~ to or for sb. jmdm. erlaubt sein

permission /pə'mɪʃn/ n. Erlaubnis, die; (given by official body) Genehmigung, die; give sb. ~ to do sth. jmdm. erlauben, etw. zu tun

permissive /pə'mɪsɪv/ adj. the ~ society die permissive Gesellschaft

permit 1 /pə'mɪt/ v.t., -tt- zulassen ‹Berufung, Einspruch usw.›; ~ sb. sth. jmdm. etw. erlauben; sb. is ~ted to do sth. es ist jmdm. erlaubt, etw. zu tun
2 v.i., -tt- es zulassen
3 /'pɜːmɪt/ n. Genehmigung, die

pernicious /pə'nɪʃəs/ adj. verderblich; bösartig ‹Krankheit›

peroxide /pə'rɒksaɪd/ n. Peroxid, das; ~ blonde Wasserstoffblondine, die

perpendicular /pɜːpən'dɪkjʊlə(r)/ adj. senkrecht

perpetrate /'pɜːpɪtreɪt/ v.t. begehen; verüben ‹Gräuel›

perpetual /pə'petjʊəl/ adj. **(a)** (eternal) ewig
(b) (continuous; coll.: repeated) ständig

per'petually adv. **(a)** (eternally) ewig
(b) (continuously; coll.: repeatedly) ständig

perpetuate /pə'petjʊeɪt/ v.t. aufrechterhalten

perplex /pə'pleks/ v.t. verwirren

perplexed /pə'plekst/ adj. verwirrt; (puzzled) ratlos

perplexity /pə'pleksɪtɪ/ n. Verwirrung, die; (puzzlement) Ratlosigkeit, die

persecute /'pɜːsɪkjuːt/ v.t. verfolgen

persecution /pɜːsɪ'kjuːʃn/ n. Verfolgung, die

persecutor /'pɜːsɪkjuːtə(r)/ n. Verfolger, der/Verfolgerin, die

perseverance /pɜːsɪ'vɪərəns/ n. Beharrlichkeit, die; Ausdauer, die

persevere /pɜːsɪ'vɪə(r)/ v.i. ausharren; ∼ with or at or in sth. bei etw. dabeibleiben

Persian /'pɜːʃn/ adj. persisch; Perser⟨katze, -teppich⟩

persist /pə'sɪst/ v.i. (a) nicht nachgeben; ∼ in doing sth. etw. weiterhin [beharrlich] tun
(b) (continue to exist) anhalten

persistence /pə'sɪstəns/ Hartnäckigkeit, die

persistent /pə'sɪstənt/ adj. (a) hartnäckig (b) (constantly repeated) dauernd; hartnäckig ⟨Gerüchte⟩

per'sistently adv. hartnäckig

person /'pɜːsn/ n. Mensch, der; in ∼: persönlich; selbst

personal /'pɜːsənl/ adj. persönlich; Privat⟨angelegenheit, -leben⟩; ∼ computer Personalcomputer, der; ∼ stereo Walkman, der; ∼ hygiene Körperpflege, die

personal: ∼ ad n. Privatanzeige, die; (seeking friendship, romance) Kontaktanzeige, die; ∼ as'sistant n. persönlicher Referent/persönliche Referentin, die; ∼ 'best n. (Sport) persönliche Bestleistung; ∼ call n. (Brit. Teleph.) Anruf mit Voranmeldung; ∼ column n. Rubrik für private [Klein]anzeigen; ∼ identifi'cation number n. persönliche Identifikationsnummer; Geheimnummer, die

personality /pɜːsə'nælɪtɪ/ n. Persönlichkeit, die

'personal loan n. Personal- od. Privatdarlehen, das; Personal- od. Privatkredit, der

'personally adv. persönlich

personal: ∼ 'organizer n. Terminplaner, der; ∼ 'pension plan n. persönlicher Renten[vorsorge]plan; ∼ 'property n. persönliches Eigentum

personification /pəsɒnɪfɪ'keɪʃn/ n. Verkörperung, die

personify /pə'sɒnɪfaɪ/ v.t. verkörpern; be kindness personified die Freundlichkeit in Person sein

personnel /pɜːsə'nel/ n. Belegschaft, die; (of shop, restaurant, etc.) Personal, das; attrib. Personal-; ∼ department Personalabteilung, die

person-to-'person adj. (Amer. Teleph.) ∼ call Anruf mit Voranmeldung

perspective /pə'spektɪv/ n. Perspektive, die; (fig.) Blickwinkel, der

perspiration /pɜːspɪ'reɪʃn/ n. Schweiß, der

perspire /pə'spaɪə(r)/ v.i. schwitzen

persuade /pə'sweɪd/ v.t. (a) (convince) überzeugen (of von); ∼ oneself [that] ...:

sich (Dat.) einreden, dass ...
(b) (induce) überreden

persuasion /pə'sweɪʒn/ n. Überzeugung, die; it didn't take much ∼: es brauchte nicht viel Überredungskunst

persuasive /pə'sweɪsɪv/ adj., **per'suasively** adv. überzeugend

pert /pɜːt/ adj. keck

pertinent /'pɜːtɪmənt/ adj. relevant (to für)

perturb /pə'tɜːb/ v.t. beunruhigen

Peru /pə'ruː/ pr. n. Peru (das)

peruse /pə'ruːz/ v.t. genau durchlesen; (fig.: examine) untersuchen

Peruvian /pə'ruːvɪən/ ① adj. peruanisch; sb. is ∼: jmd. ist Peruaner/Peruanerin ② n. Peruaner, der/Peruanerin, die

pervade /pə'veɪd/ v.t. durchdringen

pervasive /pə'veɪsɪv/ adj. durchdringend ⟨Geruch, Kälte⟩; weit verbreitet ⟨Ansicht⟩; sich ausbreitend ⟨Gefühl⟩

perverse /pə'vɜːs/ adj. starrköpfig

perversion /pə'vɜːʃn/ n. (a) (sexual) Perversion, die
(b) ∼ of justice Rechtsbeugung, die

pervert ① /pə'vɜːt/ v.t. (morally) verderben ② /'pɜːvɜːt/ n. perverser Mensch

perverted /pə'vɜːtɪd/ adj. (sexually) pervers

pessimism /'pesɪmɪzm/ n. Pessimismus, der

pessimist /'pesɪmɪst/ n. Pessimist, der/Pessimistin, die

pessimistic /pesɪ'mɪstɪk/ adj. pessimistisch

pest /pest/ n. (thing) Ärgernis, das; (person) Nervensäge, die (ugs.); (animal) Schädling, der

pester /'pestə(r)/ v.t. belästigen; nerven (ugs.); ∼ sb. for sth. jmdm. wegen etw. in den Ohren liegen

pesticide /'pestɪsaɪd/ n. Pestizid, das

pestle /'pesl/ n. Stößel, das

pet /pet/ ① n. (a) (animal) Haustier, das (b) (as term of endearment) Schatz, der ② adj. (favourite) Lieblings- ③ v.i., -tt- knutschen (ugs.)

petal /'petl/ n. Blütenblatt, das

peter /'piːtə(r)/ v.i. ∼ out [allmählich] zu Ende gehen; ⟨Weg:⟩ sich verlieren

'pet food n. Tierfutter, das

petite /pə'tiːt/ adj. zierlich

petition /pə'tɪʃn/ ① n. Petition, die; Eingabe, die ② v.t. eine Eingabe richten an (+ Akk.)

petitioner /pə'tɪʃənə(r)/ n. Antragsteller, der/Antragstellerin, die

'pet owner n. Tierhalter, der/-halterin, die

petrify /'petrɪfaɪ/ v.t. be petrified with fear/shock starr vor Angst/Schrecken sein

petrol /'petrl/ n. (Brit.) Benzin, das

petrol: ∼ bomb n. Benzinbombe, die; ∼ can n. (Brit.) Benzinkanister, der; ⋯⋗

∼ **cap** n. (Brit.) Tankverschluss, der
petroleum /pɪ'trəʊlɪəm/ n. Erdöl, das
petroleum 'jelly n. Vaseline, die
petrol: ∼ **pump** n. (Brit.) Zapfsäule, die; ∼ **station** n. (Brit.) Tankstelle, die; ∼ **tank** n. (Brit.) Benzintank, der; ∼ **tanker** n. (Brit.) Benzintankwagen, der
'**pet shop** n. Tierhandlung, die
petticoat /'petɪkəʊt/ n. Unterrock, der
petty /'petɪ/ adj. kleinlich ⟨Vorschrift, Einwand⟩; belanglos ⟨Detail, Sorgen⟩; ∼ **criminal** Kleinkriminelle, der/die; ∼ **theft** Bagatelldiebstahl, der; ∼ **thief** kleiner Dieb/kleine Diebin
petty 'cash n. kleine Kasse; Portokasse, die
petulance /'petjʊləns/ n. Bockigkeit, die
petulant /'petjʊlənt/ adj. bockig
pew /pju:/ n. Kirchenbank, die
pewter /'pju:tə(r)/ n. Zinn, das
phallic /'fælɪk/ adj. phallisch; ∼ **symbol** Phallussymbol, das
phantom /'fæntəm/ n. Phantom, das
pharmacist /'fɑ:məsɪst/ n. Apotheker, der/Apothekerin, die
pharmacy /'fɑ:məsɪ/ n. (dispensary) Apotheke, die
phase /feɪz/ n. Phase, die
■ **phase 'in** v.t. stufenweise einführen
■ **phase 'out** v.t. allmählich abschaffen ⟨Verfahrensweise, Methode⟩; (stop producing) [langsam] auslaufen lassen
Ph.D. /pi:eɪtʃ'di:/ abbr. = **Doctor of Philosophy** Dr. phil.
pheasant /'fezənt/ n. Fasan, der
phenomenal /fɪ'nɒmɪnl/ adj., **phenomenally** /fɪ'nɒmɪnəlɪ/ adv. phänomenal
phenomenon /fɪ'nɒmɪnən/ n., pl. **phenomena** /fɪ'nɒmɪnə/ Phänomen, das
phew /fju:/ int. puh
philanderer /fɪ'lændərə(r)/ n. Schürzenjäger, der (spött.)
philanthropist /fɪ'lænθrəpɪst/ n. Philanthrop, der/Philanthropin, die (geh.)
philanthropy /fɪ'lænθrəpɪ/ n. Philanthropie, die (geh.)
Philippines /'fɪlɪpi:nz/ pr. n. pl. Philippinen Pl.
philistine /'fɪlɪstaɪn/ n. Banause, der/Banausin, die
Phillips /'fɪlɪps/ n. ∼ **screw** ® Kreuz[schlitz]schraube, die; ∼ **screwdriver** ® Kreuz[schlitz]schraubenzieher, der
philosopher /fɪ'lɒsəfə(r)/ n. Philosoph, der/Philosophin, die
philosophical /fɪlə'sɒfɪkl/ adj.
(a) philosophisch
(b) (resigned) abgeklärt
philosophize (philosophise) /fɪ'lɒsəfaɪz/ v.i. philosophieren (**about, on**

über + Akk.)
philosophy /fɪ'lɒsəfɪ/ n. Philosophie, die
phishing /'fɪʃɪŋ/ n., no pl. Phishing, das
phlegm /flem/ n. Schleim, der
phobia /'fəʊbɪə/ n. Phobie, die
phobic /'fəʊbɪk/ adj. phobisch
phone /fəʊn/ (coll.) 1 n. Telefon, das; **by** ∼: telefonisch; **be on the** ∼: Telefon haben; (be phoning) telefonieren
2 v.t. & i. anrufen
■ **phone 'back** v.t. & i. zurückrufen; (make further call) wieder anrufen
■ **phone 'up** v.t. & i. anrufen
phone: ∼ **book** n. Telefonbuch, das; ∼ **booth,** ∼ **box** ns. Telefonzelle, die; ∼ **call** n. Anruf, der; ∼ **card** n. Telefonkarte, die; ∼**-in** ∼-in [programme] (Radio) Hörersendung, die; (Telev.) Phone-in-Sendung, die (Jargon); ∼ **number** n. Telefonnummer, die
phonetic /fə'netɪk/ adj. phonetisch
phonetics /fə'netɪks/ n. Phonetik, die
phoney /'fəʊnɪ/ adj. (coll.) (sham) falsch; gefälscht ⟨Brief, Dokument⟩
phonograph /'fəʊnəɡrɑ:f/ n. (Amer.) Plattenspieler, der
phony ▸ PHONEY
phosphate /'fɒsfeɪt/ n. Phosphat, das
phosphorus /'fɒsfərəs/ n. Phosphor, der
photo /'fəʊtəʊ/ n., pl. ∼**s** Foto, das
photo: ∼ **album** n. Fotoalbum, das; ∼**call** n. Fototermin, der; ∼**copier** n. Fotokopiergerät, das; ∼**copy** 1 n. Fotokopie, die; 2 v.t. fotokopieren
photogenic /fəʊtə'dʒi:nɪk/ adj. fotogen
photograph /'fəʊtəɡrɑ:f/ 1 n. Fotografie, die; Foto, das; **take a** ∼ [**of sb./sth.**] [jmdn./etw.] fotografieren
2 v.t. & i. fotografieren
'**photograph album** n. Fotoalbum, das
photographer /fə'tɒɡrəfə(r)/ n. Fotograf, der/Fotografin, die
photographic /fəʊtə'ɡræfɪk/ adj. fotografisch; Foto⟨ausrüstung, -apparat, -ausstellung⟩
photography /fə'tɒɡrəfɪ/ n. Fotografie, die
photo: ∼ **session,** ∼ **shoot** ns. Shooting, das; ∼'**synthesis** n. Photosynthese, die
phrase /freɪz/ 1 n. [Rede]wendung, die
2 v.t. formulieren
'**phrase book** n. Sprachführer, der
physical /'fɪzɪkl/ adj. (a) physisch ⟨Gewalt⟩; dinglich ⟨Welt, Universum⟩
(b) (of physics) physikalisch
(c) (bodily) körperlich
physical edu'cation n. (Sch.) Sport, der
'**physically** adv. (relating to the body) körperlich
physical 'training n. Sport, der; (Sch.) Sport[unterricht], der

physician /fɪˈzɪʃn/ n. Arzt, der/Ärztin, die
physicist /ˈfɪzɪsɪst/ n. Physiker, der/Physikerin, die
physics /ˈfɪzɪks/ n. Physik, die
physiology /fɪzɪˈblədʒɪ/ n. Physiologie, die
physiotherapist /fɪzɪəʊˈθerəpɪst/ n. Physiotherapeut, der/-therapeutin, die
physiotherapy /fɪzɪəʊˈθerəpɪ/ n. Physiotherapie, die
physique /fɪˈziːk/ n. Körperbau, der
pianist /ˈpiːənɪst/ n. Pianist, der/Pianistin, die
piano /pɪˈænəʊ/ n., pl. ~s (upright) Klavier, das; (grand) Flügel, der
piano: ~ acˈcordion n. Akkordeon, das; ~ **music** n. Klaviermusik, die; ~ **player** n. Klavierspieler, der/-spielerin, die; ~ **stool** n. Klavierschemel, der; ~ **tuner** n. Klavierstimmer, der/-stimmerin, die
pick¹ /pɪk/ n. (tool) Spitzhacke, die
pick² ① n. (a) (choice) Wahl, die; take your ~: du hast die Wahl (b) (best part) Elite, die; the ~ of the fruit die besten Früchte ② v.t. (a) pflücken ⟨Blumen, Äpfel usw.⟩; lesen ⟨Trauben⟩ (b) (select) auswählen; ~ one's way sich (Dat.) vorsichtig [s]einen Weg suchen (c) ~ one's nose in der Nase bohren (d) ~ sb.'s pocket jmdn. bestehlen; he had his pocket ~ed er wurde von einem Taschendieb bestohlen (e) ~ a lock ein Schloss knacken (salopp) ③ v.i. ~ and choose wählerisch sein ■ ˈpick at v.t. herumstochern in (+ Dat.) ⟨Essen⟩ ■ ˈpick on v.t. (victimize) es abgesehen haben auf (+ Akk.) ■ pick ˈout v.t. (a) (choose) auswählen; (for oneself) sich (Dat.) aussuchen (b) (distinguish) entdecken ⟨Detail, jmds. Gesicht in der Menge⟩ ■ pick up ① /ˈ--/ v.t. (a) [in die Hand] nehmen; hochnehmen ⟨Baby⟩; (after dropping) aufheben; aufnehmen ⟨Masche⟩; ~ up the telephone den [Telefon]hörer abnehmen (b) (collect) mitnehmen; (by arrangement) abholen (at, from von); (obtain) holen (c) (become infected by) sich (Dat.) holen (ugs.) ⟨Virus, Grippe⟩ (d) ⟨Bus, Autofahrer:⟩ mitnehmen (e) (rescue from the sea) [aus Seenot] bergen (f) empfangen ⟨Signal, Funkspruch usw.⟩ (g) (coll.: make acquaintance of) aufreißen (ugs.) ② /ˈ-ˈ-/ v.i. (a) sich bessern (b) ⟨Wind:⟩ auffrischen
ˈpickaxe (Amer.: **ˈpickax**) ▶ PICK¹
picket /ˈpɪkɪt/ ① n. Streikposten, der ② v.i. Streikposten stehen ③ v.t. Streikposten stellen vor (+ Dat.)
ˈpicket fence n. Palisadenzaun, der
ˈpicketing /ˈpɪkɪtɪŋ/ n. Aufstellen von Streikposten

ˈpicket line n. Streikpostenkette, die
pickle /ˈpɪkl/ ① n., usu. in pl. (food) Mixedpickles Pl. ② v.t. einlegen ⟨Gurken, Zwiebeln, Eier⟩; marinieren ⟨Hering⟩
pick: ~-me-up n. Stärkungsmittel, das; ~pocket n. Taschendieb, der/-diebin, die; ~up n. (a) ~up [truck] Kleinlastwagen, der; (b) (of record player, guitar) Tonabnehmer, der
picnic /ˈpɪknɪk/ ① n. Picknick, das; go for or on/have a ~: ein Picknick machen ② v.i., -ck- picknicken; Picknick machen
picnic: ~ **basket** n. Picknickkorb, der; ~ **site** n. Picknickplatz, der
pictorial /pɪkˈtɔːrɪəl/ adj. illustriert ⟨Bericht, Zeitschrift⟩; bildlich ⟨Darstellung⟩
picture /ˈpɪktʃə(r)/ ① n. (a) Bild, das; get the ~ (coll.) verstehen[, worum es geht]; put sb. in the ~: jmdn. ins Bild setzen (b) (film) Film, der (c) in pl. (Brit.: cinema) Kino, das; go to the ~s ins Kino gehen; what's on at the ~s? was läuft im Kino? ② v.t. ~ [to oneself] sich (Dat.) vorstellen
picture: ~ **book** n. Bilderbuch, das; ~ **frame** n. Bilderrahmen, der; ~ ˈpostcard n. Ansichtskarte, die
picturesque /pɪktʃəˈresk/ adj. malerisch
pidgin /ˈpɪdʒɪn/ n. Pidgin, das
pidgin ˈEnglish n. Pidginenglisch, das
pie /paɪ/ n. (of meat, fish, etc.) Pastete, die; (of fruit etc.) ~ Obstkuchen, der
piece /piːs/ ① n. (a) Stück, das; (of broken glass or pottery) Scherbe, die; (of jigsaw puzzle, crashed aircraft, etc.) Teil, der; (Amer.: distance) [kleines] Stück; a ~ of meat/cake ein Stück Fleisch/Kuchen; ~ of furniture/luggage Möbel-/Gepäckstück, das; a three-~ suite eine dreiteilige Sitzgarnitur; ~ of luck Glücksfall, der; ~ of news/gossip/information Nachricht, die/Klatsch, der/Information, die (b) (Chess) Figur, die (c) (coin) gold ~: Goldstück, das; a 10p ~: ein 10-Pence-Stück (d) (literary or musical composition) Stück, das; ~ of music Musikstück, das ② v.t. ~ toˈgether zusammenfügen (from aus)
piece: ~meal adv., adj. stückweise; ~work n. Akkordarbeit, die
pie: ~ **chart** n. Kreisdiagramm, das; ~crust n. Teigmantel, der
pier /pɪə(r)/ n. (at seaside) Pier, der
pierce /pɪəs/ v.t. (prick) durchstechen; (penetrate) [ein]dringen in (+ Akk.) ⟨Körper, Fleisch, Herz⟩; ~ a hole in sth. ein Loch in etw. (Akk.) stechen
piercing /ˈpɪəsɪŋ/ adj. durchdringend ⟨Stimme, Schrei, Blick⟩
piety /ˈpaɪətɪ/ n. Frömmigkeit, die

pig /pɪg/ n. (a) Schwein, das; ~s might fly (iron.) da müsste schon ein Wunder geschehen (b) (coll.: greedy person) Vielfraß, der (ugs.)

pigeon /'pɪdʒɪn/ n. Taube, die

pigeonhole n. [Ablage]fach, das; (for letters) Postfach, das

piggy /'pɪgɪ/: ~**back** n. give sb. a ~back jmdn. huckepack nehmen; ~ **bank** n. Sparschwein[chen], das

pig'headed adj. dickschädelig (ugs.)

piglet /'pɪglɪt/ n. Ferkel, das

pigment /'pɪgmənt/ n. Pigment, das

pigmentation /pɪgmən'teɪʃn/ n. Pigmentierung, die

pig's 'ear n. (Brit. coll.) make a ~'s ear of sth. etw. verpfuschen od. (ugs.) vermurksen

pig: ~**sty** n. (lit. or fig.) Schweinestall, der; ~**tail** n. (plaited) Zopf, der; ~tails (at either side of head) Rattenschwänzchen Pl. (ugs.)

pike /paɪk/ n., pl. same Hecht, der

pilchard /'pɪltʃəd/ n. Sardine, die

pile[1] /paɪl/ [1] n. (a) (of dishes, plates) Stapel, der; (of paper, books, letters) Stoß, der; (of clothes) Haufen, der (b) (coll.: large quantity) Haufen, der (ugs.) [2] v.t. (a) (load) [voll] beladen (b) (heap up) aufstapeln ⟨Holz, Steine⟩; aufhäufen ⟨Abfall, Schnee⟩

■ **pile 'in** v.i. (seen from outside) hineindrängen; (seen from inside) hereindrängen

■ **pile into** v.t. sich zwängen in (+ Akk.) ⟨Auto, Zimmer, Zugabteil⟩

■ **pile 'on** [1] v.i. ▶ PILE IN [2] v.t. (fig.) ~ on the pressure Druck machen

■ **pile on to** v.t. drängen in (+ Akk.) ⟨Bus usw.⟩

■ **pile 'out** v.i. nach draußen drängen

■ **pile 'up** [1] v.i. (a) ⟨Waren, Post, Arbeit, Schnee:⟩ sich auftürmen; ⟨Verkehr:⟩ sich stauen (b) (crash) aufeinander auffahren [2] v.t. aufstapeln ⟨Steine, Bücher usw.⟩; aufhäufen ⟨Abfall, Schnee⟩

pile[2] n. (of fabric etc.) Flor, der

pile[3] n. (stake) Pfahl, der

'piledriver n. [Pfahl]ramme, die

piles /paɪlz/ n. pl. (Med.) Hämorrhoiden Pl.

'pile-up n. Massenkarambolage, die

pilfer /'pɪlfə(r)/ v.t. stehlen

pilgrim /'pɪlgrɪm/ n. Pilger, der/Pilgerin, die

pilgrimage /'pɪlgrɪmɪdʒ/ n. Pilgerfahrt, die

pill /pɪl/ n. (a) Tablette, die; Pille, die (ugs.) (b) (coll.: contraceptive) the ~ or P~: die Pille (ugs.); be on the ~: die Pille nehmen (ugs.)

pillage /'pɪlɪdʒ/ v.t. [aus]plündern

pillar /'pɪlə(r)/ n. Säule, die

'pillar box n. (Brit.) Briefkasten, der

'pillbox n. Pillenschachtel, die

pillion /'pɪljən/ n. Beifahrersitz, der; ride ~: als Beifahrer/Beifahrerin mitfahren

pillow /'pɪləʊ/ n. [Kopf]kissen, das

'pillowcase, 'pillowslip ns. [Kopf]kissenbezug, der

'pill-popping n. (coll.) Pillenschluckerei, die (ugs.)

pilot /'paɪlət/ [1] n. (a) (Aeronaut.) Pilot, der/Pilotin, die (b) (Naut.) Lotse, der [2] adj. Pilot⟨programm, -studie, -projekt usw.⟩ [3] v.t. (a) (Aeronaut.) fliegen (b) (Naut.; fig.) lotsen

'pilot light n. Zündflamme, die

pimp /pɪmp/ n. Zuhälter, der

pimple /'pɪmpl/ n. Pickel, der

pimply /'pɪmplɪ/ adj. pick[e]lig

pin [1] n. (a) Stecknadel, die; ~s and needles (fig.) Kribbeln, das (b) (peg) Stift, der (c) (Electr.) a two-/three-~ plug ein zwei-/dreipoliger Stecker [2] v.t., -nn-: (a) nageln ⟨Knochen, Bein⟩; ~ a badge to one's lapel sich (Dat.) ein Abzeichen ans Revers stecken (b) (fig.) ~ one's hopes on sb./sth. seine [ganze] Hoffnung auf jmdn./etw. setzen; ~ the blame for sth. on sb. jmdm. die Schuld an etw. (Dat.) zuschieben (c) ~ sb. against the wall jmdn. an die Wand drängen

■ **pin 'down** v.t. (a) (fig.) festnageln (to or on auf + Akk.) (b) (trap) festhalten

■ **pin 'up** v.t. aufhängen ⟨Bild, Foto⟩; anschlagen ⟨Bekanntmachung, Liste⟩; aufstecken ⟨Haar⟩; abstecken ⟨Saum⟩

PIN /pɪn/ abbr. = **PIN [number]** ▶ PERSONAL IDENTIFICATION NUMBER

pinafore /'pɪnəfɔː(r)/ n. Schürze, die (mit Oberteil)

pincers /'pɪnsəz/ n. pl. (a) [pair of] ~: Beißzange, die (b) (of crab etc.) Schere, die

pinch /pɪntʃ/ [1] n. (a) (squeezing) Kniff, der; give sb. a ~ on the arm/cheek jmdn. od. jmdm. in den Arm/die Backe kneifen (b) (fig.) feel the ~: knapp bei Kasse sein (ugs.); at a ~: zur Not (c) (small amount) Prise, die [2] v.t. (a) kneifen; ~ sb.'s cheek/bottom jmdn. in die Wange/den Hintern (ugs.) kneifen (b) (coll.: steal) klauen (salopp)

'pincushion n. Nadelkissen, das

pine[1] /paɪn/ n. (tree) Kiefer, die

pine[2] v.i. sich [vor Kummer] verzehren (geh.)

■ **pine a'way** v.i. dahinkümmern

pineapple /'paɪnæpl/ n. Ananas, die

'pine tree n. Kiefer, die

ping-pong (*Amer.*: **Ping-Pong** ®) /'pɪŋpɒŋ/ *n.* Tischtennis, *das*

pinhole 'camera *n.* Lochkamera, *die;* Camera obscura, *die*

pink /pɪŋk/ **1** *n.* Rosa, *das* **2** *adj.* rosa

pinkie /'pɪŋkɪ/ *n.* (Amer., Scot.) kleiner Finger

'pin money *n.* Taschengeld, *das*

pinnacle /'pɪnəkl/ *n.* Gipfel, *der;* (fig.) Höhepunkt, *der*

pin: ∼point *v.t.* genau festlegen; **∼prick** *n.* Nadelstich, *der;* **∼stripe** *n.* Nadelstreifen, *der;* **∼stripe suit** Nadelstreifenanzug, *der*

pint /paɪnt/ *n.* Pint, *das;* ≈ halber Liter

pint 'mug *n.* ≈ Halbliterglas, *das od.* -humpen, *der*

'pin-up (coll.) *n.* Pin-up-Girl, *das;* (picture) (of beautiful girl) Pin-up[-Foto], *das;* (of sports, film or pop star) Starfoto, *das*

pioneer /paɪə'nɪə(r)/ **1** *n.* Pionier, *der* **2** *v.t.* Pionierarbeit leisten für

pious /'paɪəs/ *adj.* fromm

pip /pɪp/ *n.* (seed) Kern, *der*

pipe /paɪp/ **1** *n.* (a) (tube) Rohr, *das* (b) (Mus.) Pfeife, *die* (c) [tobacco] ∼: [Tabaks]pfeife, *die* **2** *v.t.* [durch ein Rohr/durch Rohre] leiten
■ **pipe 'down** *v.i.* (coll.) ruhig sein
■ **pipe 'up** *v.i.* (coll.) etwas sagen

pipe: ∼ dream *n.* Wunschtraum, *der;* Hirngespinst, *das* (abwertend); **∼line** *n.* Pipeline, *die;* **in the ∼line** (fig.) in Vorbereitung

piper /'paɪpə(r)/ *n.* Pfeifer, *der*/Pfeiferin, *die;* (bagpiper) Dudelsackspieler, *der*/ -spielerin, *die*

piping hot /'paɪpɪŋ hɒt/ *adj.* kochend heiß

piquant /'pi:kənt/ *adj.* pikant

pique /pi:k/ *n.* **in a [fit of]** ∼: verstimmt

piracy /'paɪrəsɪ/ *n.* Seeräuberei, *die*

piranha /pɪ'rɑ:nə, pɪ'rɑ:njə/ *n.* Piranha, *der*

pirate /'paɪrət/ *n.* (a) Pirat, *der;* Seeräuber, *der* (b) (Radio) ∼ **radio station** Piratensender, *der*

Pisces /'paɪsi:z/ *n.* (Astrol., Astron.) Fische *Pl.*

piss /pɪs/ (coarse) **1** *n.* (a) (urine) Pisse, *die* (derb) (b) **have a/go for a** ∼: pissen/pissen gehen (derb) **2** *v.i.* pissen (derb)
■ **'piss down** *v.i.* (sl.) ∼ **down [with rain]** schiffen (salopp)
■ **piss 'off** (Brit. sl.) **1** *v.i.* sich verpissen (salopp) **2** *v.t.* ankotzen (derb)

pissed /pɪst/ *adj.* (sl.) (a) (drunk) voll (salopp) (b) (Amer.: angry) [stock]sauer (**with** auf + *Akk.*) (salopp)

pissed 'off *adj.* (sl.) stocksauer (**with** auf + *Akk.*) (salopp)

'piss-up *n.* (sl.) Sauferei, *die* (salopp)

pistol /'pɪstl/ *n.* Pistole, *die*

piston /'pɪstən/ *n.* Kolben, *der*

pit /pɪt/ **1** *n.* (hole, mine) Grube, *die;* (natural) Vertiefung, *die* **2** *v.t.*, **-tt-:** ∼ **one's wits/skill** *etc.* **against sth.** seinen Verstand/sein Können *usw.* an etw. (*Dat.*) messen

'pit bull terrier *n.* Pitbullterrier, *der*

pitch[1] /pɪtʃ/ **1** *n.* (a) (Brit.: usual place) [Stand]platz, *der;* (Sport: playing area) Feld, *das;* Platz, *der* (b) (Mus.) Tonhöhe, *die* (c) (slope) Neigung, *die* **2** *v.t.* (a) (erect) aufschlagen; ∼ **camp** ein/das Lager aufschlagen (b) (throw) werfen **3** *v.i.* stürzen; ⟨*Schiff:*⟩ stampfen; ∼ **forward** vornüberstürzen

pitch[2] *n.* (substance) Pech, *das*

pitch: ∼-'black *adj.* pechschwarz; stockdunkel (ugs.) ⟨*Nacht*⟩; **∼-'dark** *adj.* stockdunkel (ugs.)

pitcher /'pɪtʃə(r)/ *n.* [Henkel]krug, *der*

'pitchfork *n.* Heugabel, *die*

'pitfall *n.* Fallstrick, *der*

pith /pɪθ/ *n.* (a) (of orange etc.) weiße Haut (b) (fig.) Kern, *der*

'pith helmet *n.* Tropenhelm, *der*

'pithy *adj.* (fig.) prägnant

pitiable /'pɪtɪəbl/, **pitiful** /'pɪtɪfl/ *adjs.* (a) Mitleid erregend (b) (contemptible) jämmerlich

pitifully /'pɪtɪfəlɪ/ *adv.* erbärmlich; jämmerlich

'pitiless *adj.* unbarmherzig

'pit stop *n.* (Motor racing) Boxenstopp, *der*

pittance /'pɪtəns/ *n.* Hungerlohn, *der*

pity /'pɪtɪ/ **1** *n.* Mitleid, *das;* **feel** ∼ **for sb.** Mitgefühl für jmdn. empfinden; **have/take** ∼ **on sb.** Erbarmen mit jmdm. haben; **[what a]** ∼! [wie] schade! **2** *v.t.* bemitleiden; **I** ∼ **you** du tust mir leid

pivot /'pɪvət/ **1** *n.* [Dreh]zapfen, *der* **2** *v.i.* sich drehen

pivotal /'pɪvətl/ *adj.* (fig.: crucial) zentral

pixel /'pɪksel/ *n.* (Comp. etc.) Bildpunkt, *der;* Pixel, *das*

pixie /'pɪksɪ/ *n.* Kobold, *der*

pizza /'pi:tsə/ *n.* Pizza, *die*

pizzeria /pi:tsə'ri:ə/ *n.* Pizzeria, *die*

placard /'plækɑ:d/ *n.* Plakat, *das*

placate /plə'keɪt/ *v.t.* beschwichtigen

place /pleɪs/ **1** *n.* (a) Ort, *der;* (spot) Stelle, *die;* **a [good]** ∼ **to park/to stop** ein [guter] Platz zum Parken/eine [gute] Stelle zum Halten; **do you know a good/cheap** ∼ **to eat?** weißt du, wo man gut/billig essen kann?; ∼ **of worship** Andachtsort, *der;* ⋯❖

all over the ∼: überall; (coll.: in a mess) ganz
durcheinander (ugs.)
(b) (rank, position) Stellung, *die;* **put sb. in his**
∼: jmdn. in seine Schranken weisen
(c) (country, town) Ort, *der;* ∼ **of birth**
Geburtsort, *der;* ∼ **of residence** Wohnort,
der; '**go** ∼**s** (coll.: fig.) es [im Leben] zu was
bringen (ugs.)
(d) (coll.: premises) Bude, *die* (ugs.)**; she is at
his** ∼: sie ist bei ihm
(e) (seat etc.) [Sitz]platz, *der;* **change** ∼**s
[with sb.]** [mit jmdm.] die Plätze tauschen;
(fig.) [mit jmdm.] tauschen
(f) (step, stage) **in the first** ∼: zuerst; **why
didn't you say so in the first** ∼? warum hast
du das nicht gleich gesagt?
(g) (proper ∼) Platz, *der;* **everything fell into**
∼ (fig.) alles wurde klar; **out of** ∼: nicht am
richtigen Platz; (several things) in Unordnung
(h) (position in competition) Platz, *der*
2 *v.t.* **(a)** (vertically) stellen; (horizontally) legen
(b) *in p.p.* (situated) gelegen
(c) (find situation or home for) unterbringen
(with bei)
(d) (class) einordnen; einstufen; **be** ∼**d
second in the race** im Rennen den zweiten
Platz belegen

placebo /plə'siːbəʊ/ *n., pl.* ∼**s** Placebo, *das*
'**place mat** *n.* Set, *der od. das*
placement /'pleɪsmənt/ *n.* Platzierung, *die*
'**place name** *n.* Ortsname, *der*
placenta /plə'sentə/ *n., pl.* ∼**e** /plə'sentiː/
or ∼**s** Plazenta, *die*
'**place setting** *n.* Gedeck, *das*
placid /'plæsɪd/ *adj.* ruhig
plagiarism /'pleɪdʒərɪzm/ *n.* Plagiat, *das*
plagiarize /'pleɪdʒəraɪz/ *v.t.* plagiieren
plague /pleɪg/ 1 *n.* **(a)** (esp. Hist.: epidemic)
Seuche, *die;* **the** ∼ (bubonic) die Pest
(b) (infestation) ∼ **of rats** Rattenplage, *die*
2 *v.t.* plagen; ∼**d with** *or* **by sth.** von etw.
geplagt
plaice /pleɪs/ *n., pl. same* Scholle, *die*
plain /pleɪn/ 1 *adj.* **(a)** (clear) klar; (obvious)
offensichtlich
(b) (frank) offen; schlicht ⟨*Wahrheit*⟩; **be**
∼ **sailing** (fig.) [ganz] einfach sein
(c) (unsophisticated) einfach; schlicht
⟨*Kleidung*⟩; unliniert ⟨*Papier*⟩; ⟨*Stoff*⟩ ohne
Muster
(d) (not attractive) ⟨*Mädchen*⟩
2 *adv.* **(a)** (clearly) deutlich
(b) (simply) einfach
3 *n.* Ebene, *die*
plain: ∼ '**chocolate** *n.* halbbittere
Schokolade; ∼ '**clothes** *n. pl.* **in**
∼ **clothes** in Zivil
'**plainly** *adv.* **(a)** (clearly) deutlich
(b) (obviously) offensichtlich; (undoubtedly)
eindeutig
(c) (frankly) offen
(d) (simply) schlicht
plaintiff /'pleɪntɪf/ *n.* Kläger, *der*/Klägerin,
die

plaintive /'pleɪntɪv/ *adj.* klagend
plait /plæt/ 1 *n.* Zopf, *der*
2 *v.t.* flechten
plan /plæn/ 1 *n.* Plan, *der;* **[go] according
to** ∼: nach Plan [gehen]; planmäßig
[verlaufen]
2 *v.t.,* -nn- planen; (design) entwerfen
3 *v.i.,* -nn- planen
plane¹ /pleɪn/ *n.* ∼ **[tree]** Platane, *die*
plane² 1 *n.* (tool) Hobel, *der*
2 *v.t.* hobeln
plane³ *n.* **(a)** (Geom.: fig.) Ebene, *die*
(b) (aircraft) Flugzeug, *das;* Maschine, *die*
(ugs.)
'**planeload** *n.* Flugzeugladung, *die*
planet /'plænɪt/ *n.* Planet, *der*
planetarium /plænɪ'teərɪəm/ *n., pl.* ∼**s** *or*
planetaria /plænɪ'teərɪə/ Planetarium, *das*
planetary /'plænɪtərɪ/ *adj.* planetarisch
plank /plæŋk/ *n.* Brett, *das;* (thicker) Bohle,
die; (on ship) Planke, *die*
plankton /'plæŋktən/ *n.* Plankton, *das*
planned e'conomy *n.* Planwirtschaft,
die
'**planner** *n.* Planer, *der*/Planerin, *die*
'**planning** *n.* Planen, *das;* Planung, *die*
plant /plɑːnt/ 1 *n.* **(a)** (Bot.) Pflanze, *die*
(b) *no indef. art.* (machinery) Maschinen *Pl.*
(c) (factory) Fabrik, *die;* Werk, *das*
2 *v.t.* **(a)** pflanzen
(b) (coll.: conceal) anbringen ⟨*Wanze*⟩;
legen ⟨*Bombe*⟩; ∼ **sth. on sb.** jmdm. etw.
unterschieben
plantation /plɑːn'teɪʃn/ *n.* Plantage, *die*
planter /'plɑːntə(r)/ *n.* (container)
Pflanzgefäß, *das*
'**plant food** *n.* Pflanzennahrung, *die*
plaque /plɑːk, plæk/ *n.* **(a)** Platte, *die;*
(commemorating sb.) [Gedenk]tafel, *die*
(b) (Dent.) Zahnbelag, *der*
plasma /'plæzmə/ *n.* Plasma, *das*
plaster /'plɑːstə(r)/ 1 *n.* **(a)** (for walls etc.)
[Ver]putz, *der*
(b) ∼ **[of Paris]** Gips, *der;* **have one's leg in**
∼: ein Gipsbein haben
(c) ▶ STICKING PLASTER
2 *v.t.* **(a)** verputzen ⟨*Wand*⟩
(b) (daub) ∼ **sth. on sth.** etw. dick auf etw.
(*Akk.*) auftragen
plaster: ∼**board** *n.* Gipsplatte, *die;*
∼ **cast** *n.* (Med.) Gipsverband, *der*
plastered /'plɑːstəd/ *adj.* (sl.: drunk) voll
(salopp)**; get** ∼: sich voll laufen lassen
(salopp)
'**plasterer** *n.* Gipser, *der*
plastic /'plæstɪk/ 1 *n.* **(a)** Plastik, *das;*
Kunststoff, *der*
(b) (coll.: credit cards etc.) Plastikgeld, *das*
2 *adj.* aus Plastik od. Kunststoff
nachgestellt; ∼ **bag** Plastiktüte, *die;*
∼ **money** (joc.) Kreditkarten *Pl.*
plastic 'bullet *n.* Plastikgeschoss, *das*

Plasticine ® /'plæstɪsiːn/ *n.* Plastilin, *das*
plastic: ∼ 'surgeon *n.* Facharzt für
plastische Chirurgie; ∼ **'surgery** *n.*
plastische Chirurgie
plate /pleɪt/ 1 *n.* (a) Teller, *der;* (serving ∼)
Platte, *die*
(b) (metal ∼ with name etc.) Schild, *das*
(c) (for printing) Platte, *die;* (illustration)
[Bild]tafel, *die*
2 *v.t.* ∼ sth. [with gold/silver] etw.
vergolden/versilbern
plateau /'plætəʊ/ *n., pl.* ∼x /'plætəʊz/ *or*
∼s Hochebene, *die;* Plateau, *das*
plate: ∼ 'glass *n.* Flachglas, *das;*
∼ **rack** *n.* (Brit.) Abtropfständer, *der;*
Geschirrablage, *die*
platform /'plætfɔːm/ *n.* (a) (Brit. Railw.)
Bahnsteig, *der;* ∼ 4 Gleis 4
(b) (stage) Podium, *das*
platinum /'plætɪnəm/ *n.* Platin, *das*
platitude /'plætɪtjuːd/ *n.* Plattitüde, *die*
(geh.); Gemeinplatz, *der*
platonic /plə'tɒnɪk/ *adj.* platonisch ⟨Liebe,
Freundschaft⟩
platoon /plə'tuːn/ *n.* (Mil.) Zug, *der*
plausible /'plɔːzɪbl/ *adj.* plausibel;
einleuchtend
play /pleɪ/ 1 *n.* (a) (Theatre) [Theater]stück,
das; television ∼: Fernsehspiel, *das*
(b) (recreation) Spielen, *das;* Spiel, *das;* ∼ on
words Wortspiel, *das*
(c) (Sport) Spiel, *das*
(d) come into ∼, be brought *or* called into
∼: ins Spiel kommen
2 *v.i.* (a) spielen; ∼ safe sichergehen;
∼ for time Zeit gewinnen wollen
(b) (Mus.) spielen (on auf + *Dat.*)
3 *v.t.* (also Sport, Theatre, Cards, Mus.) spielen;
abspielen ⟨Schallplatte, Tonband⟩; schlagen
⟨Ball⟩; spielen gegen ⟨Mannschaft, Gegner⟩;
∼ the violin *etc.* Geige *usw.* spielen;
∼ a trick/joke on sb. jmdn. hereinlegen
(ugs.)/jmdm. einen Streich spielen; ∼ one's
cards right (fig.) es richtig anfassen (fig.)
■ **play a'bout, play a'round** *v.i.*
spielen; **stop** ∼ing about *or* around hör doch
auf mit dem Unsinn!
■ **play a'long** *v.i.* mitspielen
■ **play 'back** *v.t.* abspielen ⟨Tonband⟩
■ **play 'down** *v.t.* herunterspielen
■ **play 'up** 1 *v.i.* (coll.) ⟨Kinder:⟩ nichts als
Ärger machen
2 *v.t.* (coll.: annoy) ärgern
play: ∼-acting *n.* Theater, *das* (ugs.);
∼ **area** *n.* Spielplatz, *der;* ∼**back** *n.*
Wiedergabe, *die;* **listen to the** ∼**back** die
Aufnahme anhören; ∼**boy** *n.* Playboy, *der*
'player *n.* Spieler, *der*/Spielerin, *die*
playful /'pleɪfl/ *adj.* spielerisch; (frolicsome)
verspielt
play: ∼ground *n.* Spielplatz, *der;* (Sch.)
Schulhof, *der;* ∼ **group** *n.* Spielgruppe, *die*
playing: ∼ area *n.* (Sport) Spielfeld, *das;*

∼ **card** *n.* Spielkarte, *die;* ∼ **field** *n.*
Sportplatz, *der*
play: ∼mate *n.* Spielkamerad,
der/-kameradin, *die;* ∼**off** *n.*
Entscheidungsspiel, *das;* ∼**pen** Laufgitter,
das; ∼ **school** *n.* Kindergarten, *der;*
∼**thing** *n.* Spielzeug, *das;* ∼**wright**
/'pleɪraɪt/ *n.* Dramatiker, *der*/Dramatikerin,
die
PLC, plc *abbr.* (Brit.) = **public limited
company** ≈ GmbH
plea /pliː/ *n.* Bitte, *die;* (public appeal) Appell,
der (for zu)
plead /pliːd/ 1 *v.i.* (a) inständig bitten (for
um); (imploringly) flehen (for um); ∼ with sb.
for sth. jmdn. inständig um etw. bitten
(b) (Law; also fig.) plädieren
2 *v.t.* (a) inständig bitten; (imploringly) flehen
(b) (Law) ∼ guilty/not guilty sich schuldig/
nicht schuldig bekennen
'pleading *adj.* flehend
pleasant /'plezənt/ *adj.* angenehm
pleasantry /'plezəntrɪ/ *n.* Nettigkeit, *die*
please /pliːz/ 1 *v.t.* gefallen (+ *Dat.*);
∼ oneself tun, was man will; ∼ yourself
ganz wie du willst
2 *v.i.* I come and go as I ∼: ich komme
und gehe, wie es mir gefällt; if you ∼: bitte
schön
3 *int.* bitte; ∼ do! aber bitte *od.* gern!
pleased /pliːzd/ *adj.* (satisfied) zufrieden
(by mit); (happy) erfreut (by über + *Akk.*);
be ∼ at or about sth. sich über etw. (*Akk.*)
freuen
pleasing /'pliːzɪŋ/ *adj.* gefällig
pleasure /'pleʒə(r)/ *n.* (joy) Freude, *die;*
(enjoyment) Vergnügen, *das;* have the ∼ of
doing sth. das Vergnügen haben, etw. zu
tun; with ∼: mit Vergnügen
'pleasure cruise *n.* Vergnügungsfahrt,
die
pleat /pliːt/ *n.* Falte, *die*
'pleated *adj.* gefältelt; Falten⟨rock⟩
plebiscite /'plebɪsɪt, 'plebɪsaɪt/ *n.*
Plebiszit, *das*
pledge /pledʒ/ 1 *n.* Versprechen, *das*
2 *v.t.* versprechen; geloben ⟨Treue⟩
plentiful /'plentɪfl/ *adj.* reichlich; be
∼: reichlich vorhanden sein
plenty /'plentɪ/ *n.* ∼ of viel; eine Menge;
(coll.: enough) genug
pleurisy /'plʊərɪsɪ/ *n.* Pleuritis, *die;*
Brustfellentzündung, *die*
pliable /'plaɪəbl/ *adj.* biegsam
plied ▸ PLY
pliers /'plaɪəz/ *n. pl.* [pair of] ∼: Zange, *die*
plight /plaɪt/ *n.* Notlage, *die*
plimsoll /'plɪmsl/ *n.* (Brit.) Turnschuh, *der*
plinth /plɪnθ/ *n.* Sockel, *der*
plod /plɒd/ *v.i.,* -dd- trotten
■ **plod 'on** *v.i.* (fig.) sich weiterkämpfen
plonk /plɒŋk/ *n.* (coll.) [billiger] Wein

plot /plɒt/ ① n. (a) (conspiracy)
Verschwörung, die
(b) (of play, novel) Handlung, die
(c) (of ground) Stück Land
② v.t., -tt-: (a) [heimlich] planen
(b) (mark on map) einzeichnen
③ v.i., -tt-: ~ against sb. sich gegen jmdn.
verschwören

'**plotter** n. Verschwörer, der/
Verschwörerin, die

plough /plaʊ/ ① n. Pflug, der
② v.t. pflügen
■ **plough** '**back** v.t. (Finance)
reinvestieren

plow (Amer./arch.) ▶ PLOUGH

ploy /plɔɪ/ n. Trick, der

pluck /plʌk/ ① v.t. (a) pflücken ⟨Obst⟩;
~ [out] auszupfen ⟨Federn, Haare⟩
(b) (pull at) zupfen an (+ Dat.)
(c) (strip of feathers) rupfen
② v.i. ~ at sth. an etw. (Dat.) zupfen
③ n. Mut, der
■ **pluck** '**up** v.t. ~ up [one's] courage all
seinen Mut zusammennehmen

pluckily /'plʌkɪlɪ/ adv., '**plucky** adj.
tapfer

plug /plʌg/ ① n. (a) (filling hole) Pfropfen,
der; (in cask) Spund, der; (for basin etc.) Stöpsel,
der
(b) (Electr.) Stecker, der
② v.t., -gg-: (a) ~ [up] zustopfen ⟨Loch
usw.⟩
(b) (coll.: advertise) Schleichwerbung machen
für
■ **plug** '**in** v.t. anschließen

'**plughole** n. Abfluss, der

plum /plʌm/ n. (a) Pflaume, die
(b) (fig.) Leckerbissen, der; a ~ job ein
Traumjob (ugs.)

plumage /'plu:mɪdʒ/ n. Gefieder, das

plumb¹ /plʌm/ ① v.t. [aus]loten
② adv. (a) lotrecht
(b) (fig.) genau

plumb² v.t. ~ in fest anschließen

plumber /'plʌmə(r)/ n. Klempner, der

plumbing /'plʌmɪŋ/ n.
(a) Klempnerarbeiten Pl.
(b) (waterpipes) Wasserleitungen Pl.

'**plumb line** n. Lot, das

plume /plu:m/ n. Feder, die; (ornamental
bunch) Federbusch, der

plummet /'plʌmɪt/ v.i. stürzen

plump /plʌmp/ adj. mollig; rundlich
■ '**plump for** v.t. sich entscheiden für

plunder /'plʌndə(r)/ ① v.t. [aus]plündern
⟨Gebäude, Gebiet⟩
② n. Plünderung, die; (booty) Beute, die

plunge /plʌndʒ/ ① v.t. stecken; (into liquid)
tauchen
② v.i. (a) ~ into sth. in etw. (Akk.) stürzen
(b) ⟨Straße usw.:⟩ steil abfallen
③ n. Sprung, der; take the ~ (fig. coll.) den
Sprung wagen

plunger /'plʌndʒə(r)/ n. (suction cup)
Stampfer, der

plural /'plʊərl/ ① adj. pluralisch; Plural-;
~ noun Substantiv im Plural
② n. Mehrzahl, die; Plural, der

pluralism /'plʊərəlɪzm/ n. Pluralismus,
der

plus /plʌs/ ① prep. plus (+ Dat.)
② n. (advantage) Pluspunkt, der

plush /plʌʃ/ ① n. Plüsch, der
② adj. (coll.) feudal (ugs.)

Pluto /'plu:təʊ/ pr. n. (Astron.) Pluto, der

plutonium /plu:'təʊnɪəm/ n. Plutonium,
das

ply /plaɪ/ ① v.t. (a) (use) gebrauchen
(b) nachgehen (+ Dat.) ⟨Handwerk, Arbeit⟩
(c) (supply) ~ sb. with sth. jmdn. mit etw.
versorgen
(d) (assail) überhäufen
② v.i. ~ between zwischen ⟨Orten⟩ [hin-
und her]pendeln

'**plywood** n. Sperrholz, das

p.m. /pi:'em/ adv. nachmittags; one ~: ein
Uhr mittags

PM abbr. = **Prime Minister**

PMT abbr. = **premenstrual tension**
PMS

pneumatic /nju:'mætɪk/ adj.
pneumatisch

pneumatic '**drill** n. Pressluftbohrer, der

pneumonia /nju:'məʊnɪə/ n.
Lungenentzündung, die

PO abbr. (a) = **postal order** PA
(b) = **Post Office** PA

poach¹ /pəʊtʃ/ v.t. (a) (catch illegally)
wildern; illegal fangen ⟨Fische⟩
(b) stehlen, (ugs.) klauen ⟨Idee⟩

poach² v.t. (Cookery) pochieren ⟨Ei⟩;
dünsten ⟨Fisch, Fleisch, Gemüse⟩; ~ed eggs
verlorene Eier

'**poacher** n. Wilderer, der

PO box ▶ POST OFFICE BOX

pocket /'pɒkɪt/ ① n. (a) Tasche, die
(b) (fig.) be in ~: Geld verdient haben; be
out of ~: draufgelegt haben
② adj. Taschen⟨rechner, -uhr, -ausgabe⟩
③ v.t. (a) einstecken
(b) (steal) in die eigene Tasche stecken (ugs.)

pocket: ~**book** n. (wallet) Brieftasche,
die; (notebook) Notizbuch, das;
~ '**handkerchief** n. Taschentuch,
das; ~ **knife** n. Taschenmesser,
das; ~ **money** n. Taschengeld, das;
~-**size[d]** adj. im Taschenformat
nachgestellt

'**pockmarked** adj. (a) pockennarbig
⟨Gesicht, Haut⟩
(b) a wall ~ with bullets eine mit
Einschüssen übersäte Wand

pod /pɒd/ n. Hülse, die; (of pea) Schote, die

podgy /'pɒdʒɪ/ adj. dicklich

poem /'pəʊɪm/ n. Gedicht, das

poet /'pəʊɪt/ n. Dichter, der/Dichterin, die
poetic /pəʊ'etɪk/ adj. dichterisch
poetry /'pəʊɪtrɪ/ n. [Vers]dichtung, die; Lyrik, die
pogrom /'pɒgrəm/ n. Pogrom, das od. der
poignant /'pɔɪnjənt/ adj. tief ⟨Bedauern, Trauer⟩; ergreifend ⟨Anblick⟩
point /pɔɪnt/ ① n. (a) (tiny mark, dot) Punkt, der
(b) (of tool, pencil, etc.) Spitze, die
(c) (single item; unit of scoring) Punkt, der
(d) (stage, degree) **up to a ~**: bis zu einem gewissen Grad; **he gave up at this ~**: an diesem Punkt gab er auf
(e) (moment) Zeitpunkt, der; **be on the ~ of doing sth.** etw. gerade tun wollen
(f) (distinctive trait) Seite, die; **best/strong ~**: starke Seite; Stärke, die
(g) (thing to be discussed) **come to** or **get to the ~**: zum Thema kommen; **be beside the ~**: keine Rolle spielen; **make a ~ of doing sth.** [großen] Wert darauf legen, etw. zu tun
(h) (of story, joke, remark) Pointe, die
(i) (purpose) Zweck, der; Sinn, der; **there's no ~ in protesting** es hat keinen Sinn od. Zweck zu protestieren
(j) (precise place, spot) Punkt, der; Stelle, die; **~ of view** (fig.) Standpunkt, der
(k) (Brit.) **[power** or **electric] ~**: Steckdose, die
(l) usu in pl. (Brit. Railw.) Weiche, die
② v.i. (a) zeigen, weisen (**to, at** auf + Akk.)
(b) **~ towards** or **to** (fig.) [hin]deuten auf (+ Akk.)
③ v.t. richten ⟨Waffe, Kamera⟩ (**at** auf + Akk.); **~ one's finger at sth./sb.** mit dem Finger auf etw./jmdn. zeigen
■ **point 'out** v.t. hinweisen auf (+ Akk.); **~ sth./sb. out to sb.** jmdn. auf etw./jmdn. hinweisen
point-'blank ① adj. (lit. or fig.) direkt; glatt ⟨Weigerung⟩; **~ range** kürzeste Entfernung ② adv. (at very close range) aus kürzester Entfernung
'**pointed** adj. (a) spitz
(b) (fig.) unmissverständlich
'**pointer** n. (a) Zeiger, der; (rod) Zeigestock, der
(b) (coll.: indication) Hinweis, der (**to** auf + Akk.)
'**pointless** adj. sinnlos; belanglos ⟨Bemerkung, Geschichte⟩
poise /pɔɪz/ n. (composure) Haltung, die; (self-confidence) Selbstvertrauen, das
poised /pɔɪzd/ adj. selbstsicher
poison /'pɔɪzn/ ① n. Gift, das ② v.t. vergiften
'**poisoning** n. Vergiftung, die
poisonous /'pɔɪzənəs/ adj. giftig
poke /pəʊk/ ① v.t. (a) **~ sth. [with sth.]** [mit etw.] gegen etw. stoßen; **~ sth. into sth.** etw. in etw. (Akk.) stoßen; **~ the fire** das Feuer schüren

(b) stecken ⟨Kopf⟩
② v.i. (a) [herum]stochern (**at, in, among** in + Dat.)
(b) (pry) schnüffeln (ugs.)
③ n. (thrust) Stoß, der; **give sb. a ~ [in the ribs]** jmdm. einen [Rippen]stoß versetzen; **give the fire a ~**: das Feuer [an]schüren
■ **poke a'bout, poke a'round** v.i. herumschnüffeln (ugs.)
'**poker**¹ n. Schüreisen, das
'**poker**² n. (Cards) Poker, das od. der
'**poker-faced** adj. mit unbewegter Miene nachgestellt
poky /'pəʊkɪ/ adj. winzig
Poland /'pəʊlənd/ pr. n. Polen (das)
polar /'pəʊlə(r)/ adj. polar ⟨Kaltluft, Gewässer⟩; Polar⟨eis, -gebiet, -fuchs⟩
polar: ~ 'bear n. Eisbär, der; **~ 'cap** n. Polkappe, die
pole¹ n. (support) Stange, die; **drive sb. up the ~** (Brit. coll.) jmdn. zum Wahnsinn treiben (ugs.)
pole² n. (Astron., Geog., Magn., Electr., fig.) Pol, der
Pole /pəʊl/ n. Pole, der/Polin, die
pole: ~ star n. Polarstern, der; **~-vault** n. Stabhochsprung, der; **~ vaulter** n. Stabhochspringer, der/-springerin, die
police /pə'liːs/ ① n. pl. Polizei, die; (members) Polizisten Pl.; attrib. Polizei-
② v.t. [polizeilich] überwachen ⟨Fußballspiel⟩; kontrollieren ⟨Gebiet⟩
police: ~ force n. the **~ force** die Polizei; **~man** /pə'liːsmən/ n., pl. -men /pə'liːsmən/ Polizist, der; **~ officer** n. Polizeibeamte, der/-beamtin, die; **~ state** n. Polizeistaat, der; **~ station** n. Polizeirevier, das; **~woman** n. Polizistin, die
policy¹ /'pɒlɪsɪ/ n. Politik, die
policy² n. (Insurance) Police, die
'**policy holder** n. Versicherte, der/die
polio /'pəʊlɪəʊ/ n., no art. Polio, die; [spinale] Kinderlähmung
polish /'pɒlɪʃ/ ① v.t. (a) polieren; bohnern ⟨Fußboden⟩; putzen ⟨Schuhe⟩
(b) (fig.) ausfeilen ⟨Text, Theorie, Stil⟩
② n. (a) (smoothness) Glanz, der
(b) (substance) Politur, die
(c) (fig.) Schliff, der
■ **polish 'off** v.t. (coll.) (a) (consume) verdrücken (ugs.)
(b) (complete quickly) durchziehen (ugs.)
■ **polish 'up** v.t. (a) polieren
(b) ausfeilen ⟨Stil⟩; aufpolieren ⟨Kenntnisse⟩
Polish /'pəʊlɪʃ/ ① adj. polnisch; **sb. is ~**: jmd. ist Pole/Polin ② n. Polnisch, das; see also ENGLISH 2A
polite /pə'laɪt/ adj., **~r** /pə'laɪtə(r)/, **~st** /pə'laɪtɪst/ höflich
po'liteness n. Höflichkeit, die
political /pə'lɪtɪkl/ adj. politisch

politically /pə'lɪtɪkəlɪ/ *adv.* politisch; ∼ **correct** politisch korrekt

political 'prisoner *n.* politischer Gefangener/politische Gefangene

politician /pɒlɪ'tɪʃn/ *n.* Politiker, *der*/Politikerin, *die*

politicize (politicise) /pə'lɪtɪsaɪz/ *v.t.* politisieren

politics /'pɒlɪtɪks/ *n.* Politik, *die;* (of individual) politische Einstellung

polka /'pɒlkə, 'pəʊlkə/ *n.* Polka, *die*

'polka dot *n.* [großer] Tupfen

poll /pəʊl/ ① *n.* (a) (voting) Abstimmung, *die;* (to elect sb.) Wahl, *die;* **go to the** ∼**s** zur Wahl gehen
(b) (opinion ∼) Umfrage, *die*
② *v.t.* (a) (take vote[s] of) abstimmen/wählen lassen
(b) (take opinion of) befragen

pollen /'pɒlən/ *n.* Pollen, *der;* Blütenstaub, *der*

'pollen count *n.* Pollenmenge, *die*

pollinate /'pɒlɪneɪt/ *v.t.* bestäuben

pollination /pɒlɪ'neɪʃn/ *n.* Bestäubung, *die*

polling /'pəʊlɪŋ/: ∼ **booth** *n.* Wahlkabine, *die;* ∼ **station** *n.* (Brit.) Wahllokal, *das*

'poll tax *n.* Kopfsteuer, *die*

pollutant /pə'luːtənt/ *n.* [Umwelt]schadstoff, *der*

pollute /pə'luːt/ *v.t.* verschmutzen ⟨*Luft, Boden, Wasser*⟩

pollution /pə'luːʃn/ *n.* [**environmental**] ∼: [Umwelt]verschmutzung, *die;* **noise** ∼: Lärmbelästigung, *die*

polo /'pəʊləʊ/ *n.* Polo, *das*

polo: ∼ **neck** *n.* Rollkragen, *der;* ∼ **shirt** *n.* Polohemd, *das*

poly /'pɒlɪ/ *n.*, *pl.* ∼**s** (coll.) Polytechnikum, *das;* ≈ TH, *die*

polyester /pɒlɪ'estə(r)/ *n.* Polyester, *der*

polygamy /pə'lɪgəmɪ/ *n.* Polygamie, *die*

polystyrene /pɒlɪ'staɪriːn/ *n.* Polystyrol, *das;* ∼ **foam** Styropor ⓌⓏ, *das*

polytechnic /pɒlɪ'teknɪk/ *n.* (Brit.) ≈ technische Hochschule

polythene /'pɒlɪθiːn/ *n.* Polyäthylen, *das;* ∼ **bag** Plastikbeutel, *der*

polyunsaturated /pɒlɪʌn'sætʃəreɪtɪd/ *adj.* mehrfach ungesättigt

polyunsaturates /pɒlɪʌn'sætjʊrəts/ *n. pl.* mehrfach ungesättigte Fettsäuren *Pl.*

pomegranate /'pɒmɪgrænɪt/ *n.* Granatapfel, *der*

'pommel horse *n.* Seitpferd, *das*

pomp /pɒmp/ *n.* Pomp, *der*

pompom /'pɒmpɒm/ *n.* Pompon, *der;* ∼ **hat** Pudelmütze, *die*

pompous /'pɒmpəs/ *adj.* großspurig; gespreizt ⟨*Sprache*⟩

pond /pɒnd/ *n.* Teich, *der*

ponder /'pɒndə(r)/ ① *v.t.* nachdenken über (+ *Akk.*) ⟨*Frage, Ereignis*⟩; abwägen ⟨*Vorteile, Worte*⟩
② *v.i.* nachdenken (**over, on** über + *Akk.*)

ponderous /'pɒndərəs/ *adj.* schwer

pong /pɒŋ/ (Brit. coll.) ① *n.* Mief, *der* (ugs.)
② *v.i.* miefen (ugs.)

pony /'pəʊnɪ/ *n.* Pony, *das*

pony: ∼**tail** *n.* Pferdeschwanz, *der;* ∼**-trekking** /'pəʊnɪtrekɪŋ/ *n.* (Brit.) Ponyreiten, *das*

poodle /'puːdl/ *n.* Pudel, *der*

pool¹ /puːl/ *n.* (a) Tümpel, *der*
(b) (temporary) Lache, *die;* ∼ **of blood** Blutlache, *die*
(c) (swimming ∼) Schwimmbecken, *das;* (public) Schwimmbad, *das;* (in house or garden) Pool, *der*

pool² ① *n.* (a) (Gambling) [gemeinsame Spiel]kasse; **the** ∼**s** (Brit.) das Toto
(b) (common supply) Topf, *der;* **a** ∼ **of experience** ein Erfahrungsschatz
(c) (game) Pool[billard], *das*
② *v.t.* zusammenlegen ⟨*Geld, Ersparnisse*⟩; bündeln ⟨*Anstrengungen*⟩

'pool table *n.* Pool[billard]tisch, *der*

poor /pʊə(r)/ ① *adj.* (a) arm
(b) (inadequate) schlecht; schwach ⟨*Spiel, Gesundheit, Leistung, Rede*⟩; dürftig ⟨*Kleidung, Essen, Unterkunft*⟩; **of** ∼ **quality** minderer Qualität
(c) (paltry) schwach ⟨*Trost*⟩; schlecht ⟨*Aussichten*⟩
(d) (unfortunate) arm (auch iron.)
(e) karg ⟨*Boden*⟩
(f) (deficient) arm (**in** an + *Dat.*); ∼ **in vitamins** vitaminarm
② *n. pl.* **the** ∼: die Armen *Pl.*

poorly /'pʊəlɪ/ *adv.*, *pred. adj.* schlecht

pop¹ /pɒp/ ① *v.i.*, **-pp-:** (a) (make sound) knallen
(b) (coll.: go quickly) **let's** ∼ **round to Fred's** komm, wir gehen kurz bei Fred vorbei (ugs.)
② *v.t.*, **-pp-:** (a) (coll.: put) ∼ **the meat in the fridge** das Fleisch in den Kühlschrank tun
(b) platzen ⟨*Luftballon*⟩
③ *n.* (a) Knall, *der;* Knallen, *das*
(b) (coll.: drink) Brause, *die* (ugs.)
④ *adv.* **go** ∼: knallen
▪ **pop 'out** *v.i.* hervorschießen; ∼ **out to the shops** schnell einkaufen gehen

pop² (coll.) ① *n.* Popmusik, *die;* Pop, *der*
② *adj.* Pop⟨*star, -musik usw.*⟩

'popcorn *n.* Popcorn, *das*

pope /pəʊp/ *n.* Papst, *der*/Päpstin, *die*

poplar /'pɒplə(r)/ *n.* Pappel, *die*

'pop music *n.* Popmusik, *die*

popper /'pɒpə(r)/ *n.* (Brit. coll.) Druckknopf, *der*

poppy /'pɒpɪ/ *n.* Mohn, *der*

popular /'pɒpjʊlə(r)/ *adj.* (a) (well liked) beliebt; populär ⟨*Entscheidung, Maßnahme*⟩;

∼ **music** Unterhaltungsmusik, *die*
(b) verbreitet ⟨*Aberglaube, Irrtum, Meinung*⟩; allgemein ⟨*Wahl, Unterstützung*⟩
popularity /pɒpjʊ'lærɪtɪ/ *n.* Beliebtheit, *die;* (of decision, measure) Popularität, *die*
popularize /'pɒpjʊləraɪz/ *v.t.* **(a)** (make popular) populär machen
(b) (make understandable) breiteren Kreisen zugänglich machen
'**popularly** *adv.* allgemein
populate /'pɒpjʊleɪt/ *v.t.* bevölkern; bewohnen ⟨*Insel*⟩
population /pɒpjʊ'leɪʃn/ *n.* Bevölkerung, *die;* **Britain has a** ∼ **of 56 million** Großbritannien hat 56 Millionen Einwohner; ∼ **density** Bevölkerungsdichte, *die*
popu'lation explosion *n.* Bevölkerungsexplosion, *die*
'**pop-up** *adj.* Stehauf⟨*buch, -illustration*⟩; ∼ **toaster** Toaster mit Auswerfmechanismus; ∼ **menu** (Comp.) Pop-up-Menü, *das;* ∼ **window** (Comp.) Pop-up-Fenster, *das*
porcelain /'pɔːslɪn/ *n.* Porzellan, *das*
porch /pɔːtʃ/ *n.* Vordach, *das;* (with side walls) Vorbau, *der;* (enclosed) Windfang, *der*
porcupine /'pɔːkjʊpaɪn/ *n.* Stachelschwein, *das*
pore[1] /pɔː(r)/ *n.* Pore, *die*
pore[2] *v.i.* ∼ **over sth.** etw. [genau] studieren
pork /pɔːk/ *n.* Schweinefleisch, *das; attrib.* Schweine-
pork: ∼ '**chop** *n.* Schweinekotelett, *das;* ∼ '**pie** *n.* Schweinepastete, *die*
porn /pɔːn/ *n.* (coll.) Pornographie, *die;* Pornos *Pl.* (ugs.)
pornographic /pɔːnə'græfɪk/ *adj.* pornographisch; Porno- (ugs.)
pornography /pɔː'nɒgrəfɪ/ *n.* Pornographie, *die*
porous /'pɔːrəs/ *adj.* porös
porridge /'pɒrɪdʒ/ *n.* [Hafer]brei, *der*
port[1] /pɔːt/ [1] *n.* **(a)** Hafen, *der*
(b) (Naut., Aeronaut.: left side) Backbord, *das* [2] *adj.* (Naut., Aeronaut.: left) Backbord-; backbordseitig
port[2] *n.* (wine) Portwein, *der*
portable /'pɔːtəbl/ *adj.* tragbar
port au'thority *n.* Hafenbehörde, *die*
porter[1] /'pɔːtə(r)/ *n.* (Brit.: doorman) Pförtner, *der;* (of hotel) Portier, *der*
porter[2] *n.* [Gepäck]träger, *der/*-trägerin, *die;* (in hotel) Hausdiener, *der*
portfolio /pɔːt'fəʊlɪəʊ/ *n. pl.* ∼**s (a)** (Polit.) Geschäftsbereich, *der*
(b) (case, contents) Mappe, *die*
porthole /'pɔːthəʊl/ *n.* (Naut.) Seitenfenster, *das;* (round) Bullauge, *das*
portion /'pɔːʃn/ *n.* **(a)** (part) Teil, *der;* (of ticket) Abschnitt, *der*
(b) (of food) Portion, *die*

portly /'pɔːtlɪ/ *adj.* beleibt
portrait /'pɔːtrɪt/ *n.* Porträt, *das*
'**portrait format** *n.* (also Comp.) Hochformat, *das*
portray /pɔː'treɪ/ *v.t.* darstellen; (make likeness of) porträtieren
Portugal /'pɔːtjʊgl/ *pr. n.* Portugal (*das*)
Portuguese /pɔːtjʊ'giːz/ [1] *adj.* portugiesisch; **sb. is** ∼: jmd. ist Portugiese/ Portugiesin [2] *n., pl. same* **(a)** (person) Portugiese, *der/*Portugiesin, *die*
(b) (language) Portugiesisch, *das; see also* ENGLISH 2A
pose /pəʊz/ [1] *v.t.* aufwerfen ⟨*Frage, Problem*⟩; darstellen ⟨*Bedrohung*⟩; mit sich bringen ⟨*Schwierigkeiten*⟩ [2] *v.i.* **(a)** (assume attitude) posieren; (fig.) sich geziert benehmen
(b) ∼ **as** sich geben als [3] *n.* Pose, *die;* **strike a** ∼: eine Pose einnehmen
poser /'pəʊzə(r)/ *n.* (question) knifflige Frage
posh /pɒʃ/ *adj.* (coll.) vornehm; nobel (spött.); stinkvornehm (salopp)
position /pə'zɪʃn/ [1] *n.* **(a)** (place occupied) Platz, *der;* (of player in team, of plane, ship, etc.) Position, *die;* (of hands of clock, words, stars) Stellung, *die;* (of building) Lage, *die;* **be in/out of** ∼: an seinem Platz/nicht an seinem Platz sein
(b) (Mil.) Stellung, *die*
(c) (fig.: mental attitude) Standpunkt, *der*
(d) (fig.: situation) **be in a good** ∼ **[financially]** [finanziell] gut gestellt sein; **be in a** ∼ **of strength** eine starke Position haben
(e) (rank) Stellung, *die*
(f) (job) Stelle, *die*
(g) (posture) Haltung, *die* [2] *v.t.* platzieren; postieren ⟨*Polizisten, Wachen*⟩; ∼ **oneself** sich stellen/(sit) setzen
positive /'pɒzɪtɪv/ *adj.* **(a)** (also Math.) positiv; konstruktiv ⟨*Vorschlag*⟩; (definite) eindeutig; (convinced) sicher; **I'm** ∼ **of it** ich bin [mir] [dessen] ganz sicher
(b) (Electr.) positiv ⟨*Elektrode, Ladung*⟩; Plus⟨*platte, -leiter*⟩
(c) *as intensifier* (coll.) echt
positive: ∼ **discrimi'nation** *n.* positive Diskriminierung; ∼ **'vetting** *n., no indef. art.* (Brit.) Sicherheitsüberprüfung, *die*
possess /pə'zes/ *v.t.* besitzen; (as faculty or quality) haben; ⟨*Furcht usw.:*⟩ ergreifen; **what** ∼**ed you?** was ist in dich gefahren?
possessed /pə'zest/ *adj.* besessen
possession /pə'zeʃn/ *n.* **(a)** (thing possessed) Besitz, *der;* **some of my** ∼**s** einige meiner Sachen
(b) *in pl.* (property) Besitz, *der*
(c) (possessing) Besitz, *der;* **be in** ∼ **of sth.** im Besitz einer Sache (*Gen.*) sein; **take** ∼ **of** in Besitz nehmen; beziehen ⟨*Haus, Wohnung*⟩

possessive /pə'zesɪv/ *adj.*
(a) besitzergreifend; be ∼ **about sth./sb.**
etw. eifersüchtig hüten/an jmdn.
Besitzansprüche stellen
(b) (Ling.) possessiv; Possessiv⟨*pronomen*⟩

possessor /pə'zesə(r)/ *n.* Besitzer,
der/Besitzerin, *die*

possibility /pɒsɪ'bɪlɪtɪ/ *n.* Möglichkeit, *die*

possible /'pɒsɪbl/ *adj.* möglich; (likely)
[gut] möglich; **if** ∼: wenn möglich; **as ... as**
∼: so ... wie möglich; möglichst ...

possibly /'pɒsɪblɪ/ *adv.* (a) as often as
I ∼ **can** sooft ich irgend kann; **I cannot**
∼ **commit myself** ich kann mich unmöglich
festlegen
(b) (perhaps) möglicherweise

post¹ /pəʊst/ *n.* (a) (as support) Pfosten, *der*
(b) (stake) Pfahl, *der*
(c) (starting/finishing ∼) Start-/Zielpfosten, *der*

post² ☐1 *n.* (a) (Brit.: one dispatch/delivery of
letters) Postausgang, *der*/Post[zustellung],
die; **by return of** ∼: postwendend
(b) *no indef. art.* (Brit.: official conveying) Post,
die; **by** ∼: mit der Post; per Post
(c) (∼ office) Post, *die*
☐2 *v.t.* (a) abschicken
(b) (fig. coll.) **keep sb.** ∼**ed** jmdn. auf dem
Laufenden halten

post³ ☐1 *n.* (a) (job) Stelle, *die;* Posten, *der*
(b) (Mil.; also fig.) Posten, *der*
☐2 *v.t.* postieren; aufstellen

postage /'pəʊstɪdʒ/ *n.* Porto, *das;* ∼ **paid**
freigemacht; frankiert; Frei⟨*umschlag*⟩

'**postage stamp** *n.* Briefmarke, *die*

postal /'pəʊstl/ *adj.* Post-; postalisch
⟨*Aufgabe, Einrichtung*⟩; (by post) per Post
nachgestellt

'**postal order** *n.* ≈ Postanweisung, *die*

post: ∼**box** *n.* (Brit.) Briefkasten, *der;*
∼**card** *n.* Postkarte, *die;* ∼**code** *n.* (Brit.)
Postleitzahl, *die;* ∼'**date** *v.t.* (give later date
to) vordatieren

poster /'pəʊstə(r)/ *n.* Plakat, *das*

poste restante /pəʊst re'stãt/ *n.*
Abteilung/Schalter für postlagernde
Sendungen; **write to sb. [at the]** ∼ **in Rome**
jmdm. postlagernd nach Rom schreiben

posterior /pɒ'stɪərɪə(r)/ *n.* (joc.) Hinterteil,
das (ugs.)

posterity /pɒ'sterɪtɪ/ *n., no art.* Nachwelt,
die

postgrad /pəʊst'græd/ (coll.),
post'graduate ☐1 *adj.* Graduierten-
☐2 *n.* Graduierte, *der*/*die*

posthumous /'pɒstjʊməs/ *adj.* postum

post: ∼**man** /'pəʊstmən/, *pl.* ∼**men**
/'pəʊstmən/ *n.* Briefträger, *der;*
∼**mark** ☐1 *n.* Poststempel, *der;* ☐2 *v.t.*
abstempeln; ∼'**modern** ▸ → MODERN 1;
∼'**modernist** ☐1 *adj.* postmodernistisch;
☐2 *n.* Postmodernist, *der*/Postmodernistin,
die

postmortem /pəʊst'mɔːtəm/ *n.*
Obduktion, *die*

post: ∼ **office** *n.* (a) (organization) the
P∼ Office die Post; (b) (place) Postamt, *das;*
Post, *die;* ∼ **office box** *n.* Postfach, *das*

postpone /pə'spəʊn/ *v.t.* verschieben; (for
an indefinite period) aufschieben

post'ponement *n.* Verschiebung,
die/Aufschub, *der*

'**post room** *n.* Poststelle, *die*

postscript /'pəʊskrɪpt/ *n.* Nachschrift,
die; (fig.) Nachtrag, *der*

posture /'pɒstʃə(r)/ *n.* [Körper]haltung,
die

'**post-war** *adj.* Nachkriegs-; der
Nachkriegszeit *nachgestellt*

posy /'pəʊzɪ/ *n.* Sträußchen, *das*

pot¹ /pɒt/ ☐1 *n.* (a) [Koch]topf, *der;* go to ∼
(coll.) den Bach runtergehen (ugs.)
(b) (container, contents) Topf, *der;* (teapot, coffee
pot) Kanne, *die*
(c) (coll.: large sum) **a** ∼ **of/**∼**s of** massenweise
☐2 *v.t.* ∼ **[up]** eintopfen ⟨*Pflanze*⟩

pot² *n.* (sl.: marijuana) Pot, *das* (Jargon)

potassium /pə'tæsɪəm/ *n.* Kalium, *das*

potato /pə'teɪtəʊ/ *n., pl.* ∼**es** Kartoffel, *die*

potato 'salad *n.* Kartoffelsalat, *der*

pot: ∼**belly** *n.* Schmerbauch, *der* (ugs.);
∼**boiler** *n.* (derog.) Fließbandprodukt, *das*

potent /'pəʊtənt/ *adj.* [hoch]wirksam
⟨*Droge*⟩; stark ⟨*Schnaps usw.*⟩; schlagkräftig
⟨*Waffe*⟩

potential /pə'tenʃl/ ☐1 *adj.* potenziell
(geh.); möglich
☐2 *n.* Potenzial, *das* (geh.); Möglichkeiten *Pl.*

potentially /pə'tenʃəlɪ/ *adv.* potenziell
(geh.); **he's** ∼ **dangerous** er kann gefährlich
werden; **a** ∼ **rich country** ein Land, das
reich sein könnte

pot: ∼**hole** *n.* (a) Schlagloch, *das;*
(b) (cave) [tiefe] Höhle; ∼**holer** *n.*
Höhlenforscher, *der*/-forscherin, *die;*
∼ **plant** *n.* Topfpflanze, *die*

potpourri /pəʊpʊə'riː/ *n.* Duftmischung,
die

pot: ∼ **roast** *n.* Schmorbraten, *der;*
∼**shot** *n.* take a ∼**shot [at sb./sth.]** aufs
Geratewohl [auf jmdn./etw.] schießen

'**potted** *adj.* (a) (planted) Topf-
(b) (abridged) kurz [gefasst]

'**potter¹** *n.* Töpfer, *der*/Töpferin, *die*

'**potter²** *v.i.* ∼ **[about]** [he]rumwerkeln
(ugs.)

pottery /'pɒtərɪ/ *n.* (a) Töpferware, *die*
(b) (workshop, craft) Töpferei, *die*

potty¹ /'pɒtɪ/ *adj.* (Brit. coll.) verrückt (ugs.)
(about, on nach)

potty² *n.* (Brit. coll.) Töpfchen, *das*

pouch /paʊtʃ/ *n.* Beutel, *der*

pouffe /puːf/ *n.* Sitzpolster, *das*

poultry /'pəʊltrɪ/ *n.* Geflügel, *das*

pounce /paʊns/ v.i. **(a)** sich auf sein Opfer stürzen; ⟨Raubvogel:⟩ herabstoßen auf (+ Akk.)
(b) (fig.) ~ [up]on/at sich stürzen auf (+ Akk.)

pound[1] /paʊnd/ n. **(a)** (unit of weight) [britisches] Pfund (453,6 Gramm); **two ~[s] of apples** 2 Pfund Äpfel
(b) (unit of currency) Pfund, das

pound[2] n. (enclosure) Pferch, der; (for stray dogs) Zwinger Pl.; (for cars) Abstellplatz, der

pound[3] ⟦1⟧ v.t. (crush) zerstoßen
⟦2⟧ v.i. **(a)** (make one's way heavily) stampfen
(b) ⟨Herz:⟩ heftig schlagen

'pound[s] sign n. Pfundzeichen, das

pour /pɔː(r)/ ⟦1⟧ v.t. gießen; (into cup, glass) einschenken
⟦2⟧ v.i. **(a)** (flow) strömen; ⟨Rauch:⟩ hervorquellen (from aus); ~ **[with rain]** in Strömen regnen
(b) (fig.) strömen; ~ **in** herein-/hineinströmen; ~ **out** heraus-/hinausströmen
■ **pour 'down** v.i. **it's ~ing down** es gießt [in Strömen] (ugs.)

pout /paʊt/ ⟦1⟧ v.i. einen Schmollmund machen
⟦2⟧ v.t. aufwerfen ⟨Lippen⟩

poverty /'pɒvətɪ/ n. Armut, die

poverty: ~ **line** n. Armutsgrenze, die; **be on the ~ line** an der Armutsgrenze liegen; **live below the ~ line** unterhalb der Armutsgrenze leben; **~-stricken** adj. Not leidend

powder /'paʊdə(r)/ ⟦1⟧ n. **(a)** Pulver, das
(b) (cosmetic) Puder, der
⟦2⟧ v.t. **(a)** pudern
(b) (reduce to ~) pulverisieren; **~ed milk** Milchpulver, das

'powdery adj. pulv[e]rig

power /'paʊə(r)/ ⟦1⟧ n. **(a)** (ability) Kraft, die; **do all in one's ~ to help sb.** alles in seiner Macht Stehende tun, um jmdm. zu helfen
(b) (faculty) Fähigkeit, die
(c) (strength, intensity) Kraft, die; (of blow) Wucht, die
(d) (authority, political ~) Macht, die (**over** über + Akk.); **come into ~:** an die Macht kommen
(e) (authorization) Vollmacht, die
(f) (State) Macht, die
(g) (Math.) Potenz, die
(h) (Mech., Electr.) Kraft, die; (electric current) Strom, der
⟦2⟧ v.t. ⟨Treibstoff, Strom:⟩ antreiben; ⟨Batterie:⟩ mit Energie versorgen

power: **~-assisted** adj. **~-assisted steering/brakes** Servolenkung, die/-bremsen Pl.; ~ **brakes** n. pl. Servobremsen Pl.; ~ **cable** n. Hochspannungsleitung, die; ~ **cut** n. Stromsperre, die; ~ **dressing** n.: das Tragen betont streng wirkender Kleidung; ~ **failure** n. Stromausfall, der

powerful /'paʊəfl/ adj. **(a)** (strong) stark; kräftig ⟨Tritt, Schlag, Tier⟩; heftig ⟨Gefühl,

Empfindung⟩; hell, strahlend ⟨Licht⟩
(b) mächtig ⟨Clique, Person, Herrscher⟩

'powerless adj. machtlos

power: ~ **plant** ▸ ~ STATION; ~ **point** n. (Brit.) Steckdose, die; ~ **station** n. Kraftwerk, das; ~ **steering** n. Servolenkung, die; ~ **supply** n. Energieversorgung, die (**to** Gen.)

pp. abbr. = **pages**

p.p. /piː'piː/ abbr. = **by proxy** pp[a].

practicable /'præktɪkəbl/ adj. durchführbar ⟨Projekt, Plan⟩

practical /'præktɪkl/ adj. **(a)** praktisch; praktisch veranlagt ⟨Person⟩
(b) (virtual) tatsächlich
(c) (feasible) möglich

practical 'joke n. Streich, der

'practically adv. praktisch; (almost) so gut wie; praktisch (ugs.)

practice[1] /'præktɪs/ n. **(a)** (repeated exercise) Übung, die; **be out of ~:** außer Übung sein
(b) (session) Übungen Pl.; **piano ~:** Klavierüben, das
(c) (of doctor, lawyer, etc.) Praxis, die
(d) (action) **put sth. into ~:** etw. in die Praxis umsetzen
(e) (custom) Gewohnheit, die; **regular ~:** Brauch, der

practice[2], **practiced, practicing** (Amer.) ▸ PRACTIS-

practise /'præktɪs/ ⟦1⟧ v.t. **(a)** (apply) anwenden; praktizieren
(b) ausüben ⟨Beruf, Religion⟩
(c) trainieren in (+ Dat.) ⟨Sportart⟩; ~ **the piano/flute** Klavier/Flöte üben
⟦2⟧ v.i. üben

practised /'præktɪst/ adj. geübt

practising /'præktɪsɪŋ/ adj. praktizierend ⟨Arzt, Katholik usw.⟩

practitioner /præk'tɪʃənə(r)/ n. Fachmann, der; see also GENERAL PRACTITIONER

pragmatic /præg'mætɪk/ adj. pragmatisch

Prague /prɑːg/ pr. n. Prag (das)

prairie /'preərɪ/ n. Grassteppe, die; (in North America) Prärie, die

praise /preɪz/ ⟦1⟧ v.t. loben; (more strongly) rühmen
⟦2⟧ n. Lob, das

'praiseworthy adj. lobenswert

pram /præm/ n. (Brit.) Kinderwagen, der

prance /prɑːns/ v.i. **(a)** ⟨Pferd:⟩ tänzeln
(b) (fig.) stolzieren; ~ **about** or **around** herumhüpfen

prank /præŋk/ n. Streich, der

prattle /'prætl/ ⟦1⟧ v.i. plappern (ugs.)
⟦2⟧ n. Geplapper, das (ugs.)

prawn /prɔːn/ n. Garnele, die

prawn 'cocktail n. Krabbencocktail, der

pray /preɪ/ v.i. beten (**for** um)

prayer /preə(r)/ n. (a) Gebet, das
(b) no art. (praying) Beten, das
'prayer book n. Gebetbuch, das
preach /priːtʃ/ ① v.i. predigen (to zu, vor
+ Dat.; on über + Akk.)
② v.t. halten ⟨Predigt⟩; predigen
⟨Evangelium, Botschaft⟩
'preacher n. Prediger, der/Predigerin, die
pre-arrange /priːəˈreɪndʒ/ v.t. vorher
absprechen; vorher ausmachen ⟨Treffpunkt,
Zeichen⟩
precarious /prɪˈkeərɪəs/ adj. (a) (uncertain)
labil; prekär; **make a** ∼ **living** eine
unsichere Existenz haben
(b) (insecure, dangerous) gefährlich
precaution /prɪˈkɔːʃn/ n. Vorsichts-,
Schutzmaßnahme, die; **as a** ∼:
vorsichtshalber
precede /prɪˈsiːd/ v.t. (in order or time)
vorangehen (+ Dat.)
precedence /ˈpresɪdəns/ n. Priorität, die
(geh.), Vorrang, der (over vor + Dat.)
precedent /ˈpresɪdənt/ n. Präzedenzfall,
der
precinct /ˈpriːsɪŋkt/ n. (a) [pedestrian]
∼: Fußgängerzone, die
(b) (Amer.: district) Bezirk, der
precious /ˈpreʃəs/ ① adj. (a) kostbar
⟨Schmuckstück, Zeit⟩; Edel⟨metall, -stein⟩
(b) (beloved) lieb
(c) (affected) affektiert
② adv. (coll.) herzlich ⟨wenig, wenige⟩
precipice /ˈpresɪpɪs/ n. Abgrund, der
precipitate ① /prɪˈsɪpɪtət/ adj. eilig
⟨Flucht⟩; übereilt ⟨Entschluss⟩
② /prɪˈsɪpɪteɪt/ v.t. (hasten) beschleunigen;
(trigger) auslösen
precipitation /prɪsɪpɪˈteɪʃn/ n. (Meteorol.)
Niederschlag, der
precipitous /prɪˈsɪpɪtəs/ adj. (a) (steep)
sehr steil
(b) ▶ PRECIPITATE 1
précis /ˈpreɪsiː/ n., pl. same /ˈpreɪsiːz/
Zusammenfassung, die
precise /prɪˈsaɪs/ adj. genau; präzise;
fein ⟨Instrument⟩; förmlich ⟨Art⟩; **be [more]**
∼: sich präzise[r] ausdrücken
pre'cisely adv. genau
precision /prɪˈsɪʒn/ n. Genauigkeit, die
precision 'instrument n.
Präzisions[mess]gerät, das
preclude /prɪˈkluːd/ v.t. ausschließen
precocious /prɪˈkəʊʃəs/ adj. frühreif
⟨Kind⟩; altklug ⟨Äußerung⟩
preconceived /priːkənˈsiːvd/ adj.
vorgefasst ⟨Ansicht, Vorstellung⟩
preconception /priːkənˈsepʃn/ n.
vorgefasste Meinung (of über + Akk.)
precondition /priːkənˈdɪʃn/ n.
Vorbedingung, die (of für)
pre-cooked /priːˈkʊkt/ adj. vorgekocht
precursor /priːˈkɜːsə(r)/ n. Wegbereiter,

der/-bereiterin, die
predator /ˈpredətə(r)/ n. Raubtier, das;
(fish) Raubfisch, der
'predatory adj. räuberisch; ∼ **animal**
Raubtier, das
predecessor /ˈpriːdɪsesə(r)/ n.
Vorgänger, der/-gängerin, die
predestine /priːˈdestɪn/ v.t. von
vornherein bestimmen (to zu)
predicament /prɪˈdɪkəmənt/ n.
Dilemma, das
predicate /ˈpredɪkət/ n. (Ling.) Prädikat,
das
predicative /prɪˈdɪkətɪv/ adj. (Ling.)
prädikativ
predict /prɪˈdɪkt/ v.t. voraus-,
vorhersagen; vorhersehen ⟨Folgen⟩
predictable /prɪˈdɪktəbl/ adj.
voraussagbar; vorhersehbar ⟨Ereignis,
Reaktion⟩; berechenbar ⟨Person⟩
prediction /prɪˈdɪkʃn/ n. Vorhersage, die
predominance /prɪˈdɒmɪnəns/ n.
(a) (control) Vorherrschaft, die (over über
+ Akk.)
(b) (majority) Überzahl, die (of von)
predominant /prɪˈdɒmɪnənt/ adj.
(having more power) dominierend; (prevailing)
vorherrschend
pre'dominantly adv. überwiegend
predominate /prɪˈdɒmɪneɪt/ v.i. (be more
powerful) dominierend sein; (be more important)
vorherrschen
pre-eminent /priːˈemɪnənt/ adj.
herausragend
pre-empt /priːˈempt/ v.t. zuvorkommen
(+ Dat.)
preen /priːn/ v.t. putzen ⟨Federn⟩
prefab /ˈpriːfæb/ n. (coll.) Fertighaus, das
prefabricated /priːˈfæbrɪkeɪtɪd/ adj.
vorgefertigt
preface /ˈprefəs/ ① n. Vorwort, das (to
Gen.)
② v.t. (introduce) einleiten
prefect /ˈpriːfekt/ n. (Sch.) die Aufsicht
führender älterer Schüler/führende ältere
Schülerin
prefer /prɪˈfɜː(r)/ v.t., -rr- vorziehen; ∼ **to
do sth.** etw. lieber tun; ∼ **sth. to sth.** etw.
einer Sache (Dat.) vorziehen
preferable /ˈprefərəbl/ adj. vorzuziehen
präd.; vorzuziehend attr.; besser (to als)
preferably /ˈprefərəblɪ/ adv. am besten;
(as best liked) am liebsten; **Wine or beer?**
– Wine, ∼**!** Wein oder Bier? – Lieber Wein!
preference /ˈprefərəns/ n. (a) (greater
liking) Vorliebe, die; **for** ∼ ▶ PREFERABLY;
have a ∼ **for sth. [over sth.]** etw. [einer
Sache (Dat.)] vorziehen; **do sth. in** ∼ **to sth.
else** etw. lieber als etw. anderes tun
(b) (thing preferred) **what are your** ∼**s?** was
wäre dir am liebsten?
(c) **give** ∼ **to sb.** jmdn. bevorzugen

preferential /prefə'renʃl/ adj. bevorzugt ⟨Behandlung⟩

preferred /prɪ'fɜːd/ adj. bevorzugt; **my ~ solution** etc. die Lösung (usw.), der ich den Vorzug gebe

prefix /'priːfɪks/ n. Präfix, das

pregnancy /'pregnənsɪ/ n. (of woman) Schwangerschaft, die; (of animal) Trächtigkeit, die

'pregnancy test n. Schwangerschaftstest, der

pregnant /'pregnənt/ adj. schwanger ⟨Frau⟩; trächtig ⟨Tier⟩

preheat /priː'hiːt/ v.t. vorheizen ⟨Backofen⟩; vorwärmen ⟨Geschirr, Essen⟩

prehistoric /priːhɪ'stɒrɪk/ adj. prähistorisch

prehistory /priː'hɪstərɪ/ Vorgeschichte, die

prejudge /priː'dʒʌdʒ/ v.t. vorschnell urteilen über (+ Akk.)

prejudice /'predʒʊdɪs/ ① n. Vorurteil, das
② v.t. beeinflussen

prejudiced /'predʒʊdɪst/ adj. voreingenommen (**about** gegenüber, **against** gegen)

preliminary /prɪ'lɪmɪnərɪ/ ① adj. Vor-; vorbereitend ⟨Forschung, Maßnahme⟩
② n., usu. in pl. **preliminaries** Präliminarien Pl.; **as a ~ to sth.** als Vorbereitung auf etw. (Akk.)

prelude /'preljuːd/ n. (a) (introduction) Anfang, der (**to** Gen.)
(b) (Theatre, Mus.) Vorspiel, das

premature /'premətjʊə(r)/ adj. (a) (hasty) übereilt
(b) (early) vorzeitig ⟨Altern, Ankunft⟩; verfrüht ⟨Bericht, Eile⟩; **~ baby** Frühgeburt, die

prema'turely adv. (early) vorzeitig; zu früh ⟨geboren werden⟩; (hastily) übereilt

premeditated /priː'medɪteɪtɪd/ adj. vorsätzlich

premeditation /priːmedɪ'teɪʃn/ n. Vorsatz, der

premenstrual /priː'menstrʊəl/ adj. prämenstruell; **~ tension** prämenstruelles Syndrom

premier /'premɪə(r)/ n. Premier[minister], der/Premierministerin, die

première /'premjeə(r)/ n. Premiere, die; Erstaufführung, die

premise /'premɪs/ n. (a) **~s** pl. (building) Gebäude, das; (buildings and land) Gelände, das; (rooms) Räumlichkeiten Pl.
(b) ▸ PREMISS

premiss /'premɪs/ n. Prämisse, die

premium /'priːmɪəm/ n. Prämie, die; **be at a ~** (fig.) sehr gefragt sein

'Premium Bond n. (Brit.) Prämienanleihe, die; Losanleihe, die

premonition /premə'nɪʃn/ n. Vorahnung, die

pre-natal /priː'neɪtl/ adj. pränatal (fachspr.); **~ care** Schwangerschaftsfürsorge, die

preoccupation /prɪɒkjʊ'peɪʃn/ n. Sorge, die (**with** um)

preoccupied /prɪ'ɒkjʊpaɪd/ adj. (lost in thought) gedankenverloren; (concerned) besorgt (**with** um)

pre-'packed adj. abgepackt

prepaid /priː'peɪd/ adj. **~ envelope** frankierter Umschlag

preparation /prepə'reɪʃn/ n. Vorbereitung, die; **~s** pl. Vorbereitungen Pl. (**for** für)

preparatory /prɪ'pærətərɪ/ ① adj. vorbereitend ⟨Maßnahme, Schritt⟩; **~ work** Vorarbeiten Pl.
② adv. **~ to sth.** vor etw. (Dat.)

prepare /prɪ'peə(r)/ ① v.t.
(a) vorbereiten; ausarbeiten ⟨Plan, Rede⟩; vorbereiten ⟨Person⟩ (**for** auf + Akk.); **be ~d to do sth.** (be willing) bereit sein, etw. zu tun
(b) herstellen ⟨Chemikalie usw.⟩; zubereiten ⟨Essen⟩
② v.i. sich vorbereiten (**for** auf + Akk.)

preponderance /prɪ'pɒndərəns/ n. Überlegenheit, die (**over** über + Akk.)

preposition /prepə'zɪʃn/ n. (Ling.) Präposition, die

prepossessing /priːpə'zesɪŋ/ adj. einnehmend

preposterous /prɪ'pɒstərəs/ adj. absurd; grotesk ⟨Äußeres, Kleidung⟩

'pre-program v.t., **-mm-** [vor]programmieren

prerequisite /priː'rekwɪzɪt/ ① n. [Grund]voraussetzung, die
② adj. unbedingt erforderlich

prerogative /prɪ'rɒgətɪv/ n. Privileg, das; Vorrecht, das

Presbyterian /prezbɪ'tɪərɪən/ ① adj. presbyterianisch
② n. Presbyterianer, der/Presbyterianerin, die

prescribe /prɪ'skraɪb/ v.t. (a) (impose) vorschreiben
(b) (Med.; also fig.) verschreiben

prescription /prɪ'skrɪpʃn/ n.
(a) Vorschreiben, das
(b) (Med.) Rezept, das

pre'scription charge n. Rezeptgebühr, die

presence /'prezəns/ n. (a) (of person) Anwesenheit, die; (of things) Vorhandensein, das; **in the ~ of** in Anwesenheit (+ Gen.)
(b) **~ of mind** Geistesgegenwart, die

present[1] /'prezənt/ ① adj. (a) anwesend (**at** bei); **all those ~:** alle Anwesenden
(b) (existing now) gegenwärtig; jetzig ⟨Bischof, Chef usw.⟩ ····❯

(c) (Ling.) ∼ **tense** Präsens, *das;* Gegenwart, *die*

2 *n.* **(a) the** ∼: die Gegenwart; **at** ∼: zurzeit; **for the** ∼: vorläufig

(b) (Ling.) Präsens, *das;* Gegenwart, *die*

present² 1 /'prezənt/ *n.* (gift) Geschenk, *das*

2 /prɪ'zent/ *v.t.* **(a)** schenken; überreichen ⟨*Preis, Medaille, Geschenk*⟩; ∼ **sth. to sb.** *or* **sb. with sth.** jmdm. etw. schenken/ überreichen; ∼ **sb. with difficulties/a problem** jmdn. vor Schwierigkeiten/ein Problem stellen

(b) überreichen ⟨*Gesuch*⟩ (**to** bei); vorlegen ⟨*Scheck, Bericht, Rechnung*⟩ (**to** *Dat.*); ∼ **one's case** seinen Fall darlegen

(c) (exhibit) zeigen; bereiten ⟨*Schwierigkeit*⟩

(d) (introduce) vorstellen (**to** *Dat.*); vorlegen ⟨*Abhandlung*⟩; moderieren ⟨*Sendung*⟩

3 *v. refl.* ⟨*Problem:*⟩ auftreten; ⟨*Möglichkeit:*⟩ sich ergeben; ∼ **oneself for an interview** zu einem Gespräch erscheinen

presentable /prɪ'zentəbl/ *adj.* ansehnlich; **I'm not** ∼: ich kann mich nicht so zeigen

presentation /prezən'teɪʃn/ *n.* **(a)** (giving) Schenkung, *die;* (of prize, medal) Überreichung, *die*

(b) (ceremony) Verleihung, *die*

(c) (of petition) Überreichung, *die;* (of cheque, report, account) Vorlage, *die;* (of case) Darlegung, *die*

present-day /'prezənt'deɪ/ *adj.* heutig

presenter /prɪ'zentə(r)/ *n.* (Radio, Telev.) Moderator, *der*/Moderatorin, *die*

presentiment /prɪ'zentɪmənt/ *n.* Vorahnung, *die*

presently /'prezntlɪ/ *adv.* bald; (Amer., Scot.: now) zurzeit

preservation /prezə'veɪʃn/ *n.* Erhaltung, *die;* (of leather, wood, etc.) Konservierung, *die*

preservative /prɪ'zɜːvətɪv/ *n.* Konservierungsmittel, *das*

preserve /prɪ'zɜːv/ 1 *n.* **(a)** *in sing. or pl.* (fruit) Eingemachte, *das*

(b) (fig.: special sphere) Domäne, *die* (geh.)

(c) **wildlife/game** ∼: Tierschutzgebiet, *das*/Wildpark, *der*

2 *v.t.* **(a)** (keep safe) schützen (**from** vor + *Dat.*)

(b) bewahren ⟨*Brauch*⟩; wahren ⟨*Anschein, Reputation*⟩

(c) (keep from decay) konservieren; einmachen ⟨*Obst, Gemüse*⟩

(d) (protect) hegen ⟨*Tierart, Wald*⟩

preside /prɪ'zaɪd/ *v.i.* präsidieren, vorsitzen (**over** *Dat.*); (at meeting etc.) den Vorsitz haben (**at** bei)

presidency /'prezɪdənsɪ/ *n.* **(a)** Präsidentschaft, *die*

(b) (of society) Vorsitz, *der*

president /'prezɪdənt/ *n.* **(a)** Präsident, *der*/Präsidentin, *die*

(b) (of society) Vorsitzende, *der*/*die*

presidential /prezɪ'denʃl/ *adj.* Präsidenten-

press¹ /pres/ 1 *n.* **(a)** (newspapers etc.) Presse, *die; attrib.* Presse-

(b) ▶ PRINTING PRESS

(c) (for flattening, compressing, etc.) Presse, *die*

2 *v.t.* **(a)** drücken; drücken auf (+ *Akk.*) ⟨*Klingel, Knopf*⟩; treten auf (+ *Akk.*) ⟨*Gas-, Brems-, Kupplungspedal usw.*⟩

(b) (urge) drängen ⟨*Person*⟩; (force) aufdrängen (**[up]on** *Dat.*); nachdrücklich vorbringen ⟨*Forderung, Argument*⟩; **he did not** ∼ **the point** er ließ die Sache auf sich beruhen

(c) (compress) pressen; auspressen ⟨*Orangen, Saft*⟩; keltern ⟨*Trauben, Äpfel*⟩

(d) (iron) bügeln

(e) **be** ∼ **for time/money** zu wenig Zeit/Geld haben

3 *v.i.* **(a)** (exert pressure) drücken

(b) (be urgent) drängen

(c) (make demand) ∼ **for sth.** auf etw. (*Akk.*) drängen

▪ **press a'head, press 'on** *v.i.* (continue) [zügig] weitermachen; (continue travelling) [zügig] weitergehen/-fahren; ∼ **on with one's work** sich mit der Arbeit ranhalten (ugs.)

press² *v.t.* ∼ **into service/use** in Dienst nehmen; einsetzen

press: ∼ **agent** *n.* Presseagent, *der*/-agentin, *die;* ∼ **conference** *n.* Pressekonferenz, *die;* ∼ **coverage** *n.* Berichterstattung in der Presse; ∼ **cutting** *n.* (Brit.) Zeitungsausschnitt, *der*

'pressing *adj.* (urgent) dringend

press: ∼ **man** *n.* (Brit.: journalist) Journalist, *der;* ∼ **release** *n.* Presseinformation, *die;* ∼ **stud** *n.* (Brit.) Druckknopf, *der;* ∼**-up** *n.* Liegestütz, *der*

pressure /'preʃə(r)/ 1 *n.* Druck, *der;* **put** ∼ **on sb.** jmdn. unter Druck setzen; **atmospheric** ∼: Luftdruck, *der*

2 *v.t.* unter Druck setzen ⟨*Person*⟩; ∼ **sb. into doing sth.** jmdn. [dazu] drängen, etw. zu tun

pressure: ∼ **cooker** *n.* Schnellkochtopf, *der;* ∼ **group** *n.* Pressuregroup, *die*

pressurize /'preʃəraɪz/ *v.t.* **(a)** ▶ PRESSURE 2

(b) ∼**d cabin** Druckkabine, *die*

prestige /pre'stiːʒ/ *n.* Prestige, *das*

prestigious /pre'stɪdʒəs/ *adj.* angesehen

presumably /prɪ'zjuːməblɪ/ *adv.* vermutlich

presume /prɪ'zjuːm/ 1 *v.t.* **(a)** ∼ **to do sth.** sich (*Dat.*) anmaßen, etw. zu tun; (take the liberty) sich (*Dat.*) erlauben, etw. zu tun

(b) (suppose) annehmen

2 *v.i.* **[up]on sth.** etw. ausnützen

presumption /prɪ'zʌmpʃn/ *n.* **(a)** (arrogance) Anmaßung, *die*

(b) (assumption) Annahme, *die*

presumptuous /prɪˈzʌmptjʊəs/ *adj.*
anmaßend
presuppose /priːsəˈpəʊz/ *v.t.*
voraussetzen
pre-teen /ˈpriːtiːn/ *adj.* ≈ zehn- bis
zwölfjährig
pretence /prɪˈtens/ *n.* (Brit.) **(a)** (pretext)
Vorwand, *der*
(b) *no art.* (make-believe, insincere behaviour)
Verstellung, *die*; **it is all** *or* **just a** ∼: das ist
alles nicht echt
pretend /prɪˈtend/ 1 *v.t.* **(a)** vorgeben;
she ∼**ed to be asleep** sie tat, als ob sie
schlief[e]
(b) (imagine in play) ∼ **to be sth.** so tun, als ob
man etw. sei
2 *v.i.* sich verstellen; **she's only** ∼**ing** sie
tut nur so
pretense (Amer.) ▸ PRETENCE
pretension /prɪˈtenʃn/ *n.* **(a)** Anspruch,
der (**to** auf + *Akk.*)
(b) (pretentiousness) Überheblichkeit, *die*
pretentious /prɪˈtenʃəs/ *adj.*
hochgestochen; wichtigtuerisch ⟨*Person*⟩;
(ostentatious) großspurig
pretext /ˈpriːtekst/ *n.* Vorwand, *der*;
[up]on *or* **under the** ∼ **of doing sth.** unter
dem Vorwand, etw. tun zu wollen
prettily /ˈprɪtɪlɪ/ *adv.* hübsch; sehr schön
⟨*singen, tanzen*⟩
pretty /ˈprɪtɪ/ 1 *adj.* (also iron.) hübsch
2 *adv.* ziemlich; **I am** ∼ **well** es geht mir
ganz gut
prevail /prɪˈveɪl/ *v.i.* **(a)** die Oberhand
gewinnen (**against, over** über + *Akk.*);
∼ **[up]on sb. to do sth.** jmdn. dazu bewegen,
etw. zu tun
(b) (predominate) ⟨*Zustand, Bedingung:*⟩
vorherrschen
(c) (be current) herrschen
prevalence /ˈprevələns/ *n.*
Vorherrschen, *das*
prevalent /ˈprevələnt/ *adj.* **(a)** (existing)
herrschend; weit verbreitet ⟨*Krankheit*⟩
(b) (predominant) vorherrschend
prevent /prɪˈvent/ *v.t.* (hinder) verhindern;
(forestall) vorbeugen; ∼ **sb. from doing sth.,**
∼ **sb.'s doing sth.,** (coll.) ∼ **sb. doing sth.**
jmdn. daran hindern, etw. zu tun
preventable /prɪˈventəbl/ *adj.*
vermeidbar
prevention /prɪˈvenʃn/ *n.* Verhinderung,
die; (forestalling) Vorbeugung, *die*
preventive /prɪˈventɪv/ *adj.* vorbeugend;
Präventiv⟨*maßnahme*⟩
preventive 'medicine *n.*
Präventivmedizin, *die*
preview /ˈpriːvjuː/ *n.* (of film, play)
Voraufführung, *die;* (of exhibition) Vernissage,
die (geh.)
previous /ˈpriːvɪəs/ 1 *adj.* **(a)** früher
⟨*Anstellung, Gelegenheit*⟩; vorherig ⟨*Abend*⟩;
vorig ⟨*Besitzer, Wohnsitz*⟩; **the** ∼ **page** die

Seite davor
(b) (prior) ∼ **to** vor (+ *Dat.*)
2 *adv.* ∼ **to** vor (+ *Dat.*)
'previously *adv.* vorher
pre-war /ˈpriːwɔː(r)/ *adj.* Vorkriegs-
prey /preɪ/ 1 *n., pl. same* **(a)** (animal[s])
Beute, *die;* **beast/bird of** ∼: Raubtier, *das/*
-vogel, *der*
(b) (victim) Opfer, *das*
2 *v.i.* ∼ **[up]on** ⟨*Raubtier, Raubvogel:*⟩
schlagen; (plunder) ausplündern ⟨*Person*⟩;
Jagd machen auf (+ *Akk.*); ∼ **[up]on sb.'s
mind** jmdm. keine Ruhe lassen
price /praɪs/ *n.* (lit. or fig.) Preis, *der;* **at
a** ∼ **of** zum Preis von; **what is the** ∼ **of
this?** was kostet das?; **at/not at any** ∼: um
jeden/keinen Preis
price: ∼ **bracket** ▸ ∼ RANGE; ∼ **cut**
n. Preissenkung, *die;* ∼**-cutting** *n.*
Preisschleuderei, *die;* ∼ **increase** *n.*
Preiserhöhung, *die*
'priceless *adj.* **(a)** (invaluable) unbezahlbar
(b) (coll.: amusing) köstlich
price: ∼ **list** *n.* Preisliste, *die;* ∼ **range**
n. Preisspanne, *die;* ∼ **rise** *n.* Preisanstieg,
der; ∼ **tag** *n.* Preisschild, *das;* ∼ **war** *n.*
Preiskrieg, *der*
pricey /ˈpraɪsɪ/ *adj.* (Brit. coll.) teuer
prick /prɪk/ 1 *v.t.* stechen; stechen in
⟨*Ballon*⟩; aufstechen ⟨*Blase*⟩
2 *v.i.* stechen
3 *n.* Stich, *der*
∎ **'prick up** *v.t.* aufrichten ⟨*Ohren*⟩; ∼ **up
one's/its ears** die Ohren spitzen
prickle /ˈprɪkl/ 1 *n.* **(a)** Dorn, *der*
(b) (Zool., Bot.) Stachel, *der*
2 *v.i.* kratzen
prickly /ˈprɪklɪ/ *adj.* dornig; stachelig; (fig.)
empfindlich
pride /praɪd/ 1 *n.* **(a)** Stolz, *der;* (arrogance)
Hochmut, *der;* **take [a]** ∼ **in sb./sth.** auf
jmdn./etw. stolz sein; **sb's** ∼ **and joy** jmds.
ganzer Stolz
(b) (of lions) Rudel, *das*
2 *v. refl.* ∼ **oneself [up]on sth.** auf etw.
(*Akk.*) stolz sein
pried ▸ PRY
priest /priːst/ *n.* Priester, *der*
'priesthood *n.* geistliches Amt
prig /prɪg/ *n.* Tugendbold, *der* (ugs., iron.)
priggish /ˈprɪgɪʃ/ *adj.* übertrieben
tugendhaft
prim /prɪm/ *adj.* spröde; (prudish) zimperlich
primarily /ˈpraɪmərɪlɪ/ *adv.* in erster Linie
primary /ˈpraɪmərɪ/ 1 *adj.* **(a)** (first)
primär (geh.); grundlegend
(b) (chief) Haupt⟨*rolle, -ziel, -zweck*⟩
2 *n.* (Amer.: election) Vorwahl, *die*
'primary school *n.* Grundschule, *die*
primate /ˈpraɪmeɪt/ *n.* **(a)** (Eccl.) Primas,
der
(b) (Zool.) Primat, *der*

prime¹ /praɪm/ ① *n.* Höhepunkt, *der;* **be in one's ~:** in den besten Jahren sein ② *adj.* **(a)** Haupt-; hauptsächlich **(b)** (excellent) erstklassig; vortrefflich ⟨*Beispiel*⟩

prime² *v.t.* **(a)** (equip) vorbereiten; **~ sb. with information/advice** jmdn. instruieren/ jmdm. Ratschläge erteilen **(b)** grundieren ⟨*Wand, Decke*⟩ **(c)** schärfen ⟨*Sprengkörper*⟩

prime: ~ 'minister *n.* Premierminister, *der/*-ministerin, *die;* **~ 'number** *n.* (Math.) Primzahl, *die*

'primer *n.* **(a)** (explosive) Zündvorrichtung, *die* **(b)** (paint) Grundierlack, *der*

'prime time *n.* Hauptsendezeit, *die;* **~-time** TV Hauptsendezeit im Fernsehen

primeval /praɪ'miːvl/ *adj.* urzeitlich; Ur⟨*zeiten, -wälder*⟩

primitive /'prɪmɪtɪv/ *adj.* primitiv; (prehistoric) urzeitlich ⟨*Mensch*⟩

primrose /'prɪmrəʊz/ *n.* gelbe Schlüsselblume

Primus ® /'praɪməs/ *n.* **~ [stove]** Primuskocher, *der*

prince /prɪns/ *n.* Prinz, *der*

'princely *adj.* fürstlich

princess /prɪn'ses/ *n.* Prinzessin, *die*

principal /'prɪnsɪpl/ ① *adj.* Haupt-; (most important) wichtigst... ② *n.* (of college) Rektor, *der/*Rektorin, *die*

principality /prɪnsɪ'pælɪtɪ/ *n.* Fürstentum, *das*

'principally *adv.* in erster Linie

principle /'prɪnsɪpl/ *n.* Prinzip, *das;* **on the ~ that ...:** nach dem Grundsatz, dass ...; **in ~:** im Prinzip; **do sth. on ~** *or* **as a matter of ~:** etw. prinzipiell *od.* aus Prinzip tun

print /prɪnt/ ① *n.* **(a)** (impression) Abdruck, *der;* (finger~) Fingerabdruck, *der* **(b)** (~ed lettering) Gedruckte, *das;* (typeface) Druck, *der* **(c) be in/out of ~** ⟨*Buch:*⟩ erhältlich/ vergriffen sein **(d)** (~ed picture or design) Druck, *der* **(e)** (Photog.) Abzug, *der* ② *v.t.* **(a)** drucken ⟨*Buch, Zeitschrift usw.*⟩ **(b)** (write) in Druckschrift schreiben ■ **print 'out** *v.t.* (Comp.) ausdrucken

'printed *adj.* **(a)** gedruckt **(b)** (published) veröffentlicht

'printed matter *n.* (Post) Drucksachen *Pl.*

'printer *n.* **(a)** (worker) Drucker, *der/* Druckerin, *die;* (firm) Druckerei, *die* **(b)** (Comp.) Drucker, *der*

'printing *n.* **(a)** Drucken, *das* **(b)** (writing like print) Druckschrift, *die* **(c)** (edition) Auflage, *die*

'printing press *n.* Druckerpresse, *die*

print: ~out *n.* (Comp.) Ausdruck, *der;*

~ run *n.* (Publishing) Auflage, *die;* **what is the ~ run?** wie hoch ist die Auflage?

prion /'priːɒn/ *n.* (Biol.) Prion, *das*

prior /'praɪə(r)/ ① *adj.* vorherig ⟨*Warnung, Zustimmung usw.*⟩; früher ⟨*Verabredung*⟩; Vor⟨*geschichte, -kenntnis*⟩ ② *adv.* **~ to** vor (+ *Dat.*); **~ to doing sth.** bevor man etw. tut/tat; **~ to that** vorher

priority /praɪ'ɒrɪtɪ/ *n.* **(a)** (precedence) Vorrang, *der; attrib.* vorrangig; **have** *or* **take ~:** Vorrang haben (**over** vor + *Dat.*); **have ~** (on road) Vorfahrt haben; **give ~ to sb./sth.** jmdm./einer Sache den Vorrang geben; **give top ~ to sth.** einer Sache (*Dat.*) höchste Priorität einräumen **(b)** (matter) vordringliche Angelegenheit

prioritize (prioritise) /praɪ'ɒrɪtaɪz/ *v.t.* nach Vordringlichkeit ordnen

prism /'prɪzm/ *n.* Prisma, *das*

prison /'prɪzn/ *n.* **(a)** Gefängnis, *das; attrib.* Gefängnis- **(b)** (custody) Haft, *die;* **in ~:** im Gefängnis; **go to ~:** ins Gefängnis gehen

'prison camp *n.* Gefangenenlager, *das*

'prisoner *n.* Gefangene, *der/die;* **take sb. ~:** jmdn. gefangen nehmen

prisoner of 'war *n.* Kriegsgefangene, *der/die*

prison: ~ sentence *n.* Gefängnisstrafe, *die;* **~ service** *n.* Strafvollzugsbehörde, *die*

pristine /'prɪstiːn/ *adj.* unberührt; **in ~ condition** in tadellosem Zustand

privacy /'prɪvəsɪ/ *n.* Privatsphäre, *die;* (being undisturbed) Ungestörtheit, *die;* **invasion of ~:** Eindringen in die Privatsphäre; **in the strictest ~:** unter strengster Geheimhaltung

private /'praɪvət/ ① *adj.* **(a)** (outside State system) privat; Privat⟨*schule, -industrie, -klinik usw.*⟩ **(b)** persönlich ⟨*Dinge, Meinung, Interesse*⟩; nichtöffentlich ⟨*Versammlung, Sitzung*⟩; privat ⟨*Telefongespräch, Vereinbarung*⟩; Privat⟨*strand, -parkplatz, -leben*⟩; geheim ⟨*Verhandlung, Geschäft*⟩; persönlich ⟨*Gründe*⟩; (confidential) vertraulich ② *n.* **(a)** (Brit. Mil.) einfacher Soldat **(b) in ~:** privat; in kleinem Kreis ⟨*feiern*⟩; (confidentially) ganz im Vertrauen

private: ~ de'tective *n.* [Privat]detektiv, *der/*-detektivin, *die;* **~ 'enterprise** *n.* das freie Unternehmertum; **[spirit of] ~ enterprise** (fig.) Unternehmungsgeist, *der;* **~ 'income** *n.* private Einkünfte *Pl.;* **~ investigator** *n.* Privatdetektiv, *der/*-detektivin, *die*

'privately *adv.* privat ⟨*erziehen, zugeben*⟩; vertraulich ⟨*jmdn. sprechen*⟩; insgeheim ⟨*denken, glauben*⟩; **~ owned** in Privatbesitz

private: ~ 'parts *n. pl.* Geschlechtsteile *Pl.;* **~ 'practice** *n.* (Med.) Privatpraxis, *die;* **~ 'property** *n.* Privateigentum, *das;* **~ 'view[ing]** *n.* (Art) Vernissage, *die*

privation /praɪ'veɪʃn/ n. Not, die; **suffer many ~s** viele Entbehrungen erleiden

privatize /'praɪvətaɪz/ v.t. privatisieren

privet /'prɪvɪt/ n. Liguster, der

privilege /'prɪvɪlɪdʒ/ n. (right, immunity) Privileg, das; (special benefit) Sonderrecht, das; (honour) Ehre, die

'privileged adj. privilegiert

privy /'prɪvɪ/ adj. **be ~ to sth.** in etw. (Akk.) eingeweiht sein

prize¹ /praɪz/ ① n. (a) (reward, money) Preis, der; **win** or **take first ~:** den ersten Preis gewinnen
(b) (in lottery) Gewinn, der
② v.t. **~ sth. [highly]** etw. hoch schätzen

prize² v.t. **~ [open]** aufstemmen

prize: **~-giving** n. Preisverleihung, die; **~ money** n. Geldpreis, der; (Sport) Preisgeld, das; **~winner** n. Preisträger, der/-trägerin, die; (in lottery) Gewinner, der/Gewinnerin, die

pro /prəʊ/ n. in pl. **the ~s and cons** das Pro und Kontra

proactive /prəʊ'æktɪv/ adj. aktiv ⟨Haltung, Rolle⟩; **be ~** ⟨Person:⟩ [selbst] die Initiative ergreifen

probability /prɒbə'bɪlɪtɪ/ n. Wahrscheinlichkeit, die; **in all ~:** aller Wahrscheinlichkeit nach

probable /'prɒbəbl/ adj. wahrscheinlich; **highly ~:** höchstwahrscheinlich

probably /'prɒbəblɪ/ adv. wahrscheinlich

probation /prə'beɪʃn/ n. (a) Probezeit, die (b) (Law) Bewährung, die; **on ~:** auf Bewährung

probationary /prə'beɪʃənərɪ/ adj. Probe-; **~ period** Probezeit, die

pro'bation officer n. Bewährungshelfer, der/-helferin, die

probe /prəʊb/ ① n. (a) Untersuchung, die (into Gen.)
(b) (Med., Astron.) Sonde, die
② v.t. untersuchen

problem /'prɒbləm/ n. Problem, das; (puzzle) Rätsel, das; **what's the ~?** (coll.) wo fehlts denn?; **the ~ about** or **with sb./sth.** das Problem mit jmdm./bei etw.

problematic /prɒblə'mætɪk/, **problematical** /prɒblə'mætɪkl/ adj. problematisch

procedure /prə'si:djə(r)/ n. Verfahren, das

proceed /prə'si:d/ v.i. (formal) (a) (on foot) gehen; (as or by vehicle) fahren; (after interruption) weitergehen/-fahren
(b) (begin and carry on) beginnen; (after interruption) fortfahren; **~ in** or **with sth.** (begin) [mit] etw. beginnen; (continue) etw. fortsetzen
(c) (be under way) ⟨Verfahren:⟩ laufen; (be continued after interruption) fortgesetzt werden

pro'ceedings n. pl. (a) (events) Vorgänge Pl.

(b) (Law) Verfahren, das; **legal ~:** Gerichtsverfahren, das; **start/take [legal] ~:** gerichtlich vorgehen (**against** gegen)

proceeds /'prəʊsi:dz/ n. pl. Erlös, der (from aus)

process¹ /'prəʊses/ ① n. (a) (of time or history) Lauf, der; **he learnt a lot in the ~:** er lernte eine Menge dabei; **be in the ~ of doing sth.** gerade etw. tun
(b) (proceeding, natural operation) Vorgang, der
(c) (method) Verfahren, das
② v.t. verarbeiten ⟨Rohstoff, Signal, Daten⟩; bearbeiten ⟨Antrag, Akte⟩; (Photog.) entwickeln ⟨Film⟩

process² /prə'ses/ v.i. ziehen

'process cheese (Amer.), **'processed cheese** ns. Schmelzkäse, der

procession /prə'seʃn/ n. Zug, der; (religious) Prozession, die; (festive) Umzug, der; **go/march in ~:** ziehen

proclaim /prə'kleɪm/ v.t. erklären ⟨Absicht⟩; geltend machen ⟨Recht, Anspruch⟩; verkünden ⟨Amnestie⟩; ausrufen ⟨Republik⟩

proclamation /prɒklə'meɪʃn/ n. (a) (proclaiming) Verkündung, die
(b) (notice) Bekanntmachung, die; (decree) Erlass, der

procreation /prəʊkrɪ'eɪʃn/ n. Fortpflanzung, die

procure /prə'kjʊə(r)/ v.t. beschaffen

prod /prɒd/ ① v.t., **-dd-** (poke) stupsen (ugs.); stoßen mit ⟨Stock, Finger usw.⟩; **~ sb. gently** jmdn. anstupsen
② n. Stupser, der; **give sb. a ~:** jmdm. einen Stupser geben

prodigal /'prɒdɪgl/ adj. verschwenderisch; **~ son** verlorener Sohn

prodigious /prə'dɪdʒəs/ adj. ungeheuer

prodigy /'prɒdɪdʒɪ/ n. [außergewöhnliches] Talent; **child ~:** Wunderkind, das

produce ① /'prɒdju:s/ n. Produkte Pl.; Erzeugnisse Pl.
② /prə'dju:s/ v.t. (a) vorzeigen ⟨Pass, Fahrkarte⟩
(b) produzieren ⟨Show, Film⟩; inszenieren ⟨Theaterstück, Hörspiel⟩; herausgeben ⟨Schallplatte, Buch⟩
(c) (manufacture) herstellen; (in nature; Agric.) produzieren
(d) (cause) hervorrufen; bewirken ⟨Änderung⟩
(e) (bring into being) erzeugen; führen zu ⟨Situation⟩
(f) (yield) geben ⟨Milch⟩; legen ⟨Eier⟩
(g) ⟨Baum, Blume:⟩ tragen ⟨Früchte, Blüten⟩; entwickeln ⟨Triebe⟩; bilden ⟨Keime⟩

producer /prə'dju:sə(r)/ n. (a) (Cinemat., Theatre, Radio, Telev.) Produzent, der/Produzentin, die
(b) (Brit. Theatre/Radio/Telev.) Regisseur, der/Regisseurin, die

product /'prɒdʌkt/ n. (a) Produkt, das; (of industrial process) Erzeugnis, das; (of art or intellect) Werk, das
(b) (result) Folge, die
(c) (Math.) Produkt, das (of aus)

production /prə'dʌkʃn/ n. (a) (Cinemat.) Produktion, die; (Theatre) Inszenierung, die; (of record, book) Herausgabe, die
(b) (making) Produktion, die; (manufacturing) Herstellung, die; (thing produced) Produkt, das; (thing created) Werk, das
(c) (yielding) Produktion, die; (yield) Ertrag, der

production: ~ **line** n. Fertigungsstraße, die; ~ **manager** n. Produktionsleiter, der/-leiterin, die

productive /prə'dʌktɪv/ adj. leistungsfähig ⟨Betrieb, Bauernhof⟩; fruchtbar ⟨Gespräch, Verhandlungen⟩

productivity /prɒdʌk'tɪvɪtɪ/ n. Produktivität, die

'product range n. Produktpalette, die

Prof. /prɒf/ abbr. = **Professor** Prof.

profane /prə'feɪn/ adj. (a) (irreligious) gotteslästerlich
(b) (secular) weltlich
(c) (irreverent) respektlos ⟨Bemerkung⟩; profan ⟨Sprache⟩

profess /prə'fes/ v.t. (a) (declare openly) bekunden ⟨Vorliebe, Abneigung⟩; ~ **to be/do** sth. erklären, etw. zu sein/tun
(b) (claim) vorgeben; ~ **to be/do** sth. behaupten, etw. zu sein/tun

profession /prə'feʃn/ n. (a) Beruf, der; **be a pilot by** ~: von Beruf Pilot sein
(b) (body of people) Berufsstand, der

professional /prə'feʃənl/ [1] adj.
(a) Berufs⟨ausbildung, -leben⟩; beruflich ⟨Qualifikation⟩
(b) (worthy of profession) (in technical expertise) fachmännisch; (in attitude) professionell; (in experience) routiniert
(c) ~ **people** Angehörige Pl. hoch qualifizierter Berufe
(d) (by profession) gelernt; (not amateur) Berufs⟨musiker, -sportler⟩; Profi⟨sportler⟩
(e) (paid) Profi⟨sport, -boxen⟩
[2] n. (trained person) Fachmann, der/Fachfrau, die; (non-amateur; also Sport) Profi, der

professor /prə'fesə(r)/ n. (a) (Univ.) Professor, der/Professorin, die (of für)
(b) (Amer.: teacher at university) Dozent, der/Dozentin, die

proficiency /prə'fɪʃənsɪ/ n. Können, das

proficient /prə'fɪʃənt/ adj. fähig; gut ⟨Pianist, Reiter usw.⟩; geschickt ⟨Radfahrer, Handwerker⟩; **be** ~ **at** or **in maths** viel von Mathematik verstehen

profile /'prəʊfaɪl/ n. (a) (side aspect) Profil, das
(b) (biographical sketch) Porträt, das
(c) (fig.) **keep a low** ~: sich zurückhalten

profit /'prɒfɪt/ n. Gewinn, der; Profit, der; **make a** ~ **from** or **out of** sth. mit etw. Geld verdienen; **make [a few pence]** ~ **on** sth. [ein paar Pfennige] an etw. (Dat.) verdienen; ~ **and loss** Gewinn und Verlust; ~**-and-loss account** Gewinn-und-Verlust-Rechnung, die
■ **'profit by** v.t. profitieren von; Nutzen ziehen aus ⟨Fehler, Erfahrung⟩
■ **'profit from** v.t. profitieren von

profitable /'prɒfɪtəbl/ adj. rentabel; einträglich; (fruitful) nützlich

profiteer /prɒfɪ'tɪə(r)/ [1] n. Profitmacher, der/-macherin, die
[2] v.i. sich bereichern

profi'teering n. Wucher, der

profit: ~ **margin** n. Gewinnspanne, die; ~**-sharing** n. Gewinnbeteiligung, die

profligate /'prɒflɪgət/ adj. verschwenderisch; **be** ~ **of** or **with sth.** verschwenderisch umgehen mit etw.

profound /prə'faʊnd/ adj. tief; nachhaltig ⟨Wirkung, Einfluss⟩; tief greifend ⟨Wandel, Veränderung⟩; tief empfunden ⟨Beileid, Mitgefühl⟩; tief sitzend ⟨Misstrauen⟩

prognosis /prɒg'nəʊsɪs/ n., pl. **prognoses** /prɒg'nəʊsiːz/ Prognose, die

program /'prəʊgræm/ [1] n. (a) (Amer.)
▶ PROGRAMME 1
(b) (Comp.) Programm, das; ~ **file** Programmdata, die
[2] v.t., **-mm-** (Comp.) programmieren

programme /'prəʊgræm/ n. (a) ([notice of] events) Programm, das
(b) (Radio, Telev.) Sendung, die
(c) (plan, instructions for machine) Programm, das

programmer /'prəʊgræmə(r)/ n. (Comp.) Programmierer, der/Programmiererin, die

progress [1] /'prəʊgres/ n. (a) no pl., no indef. art. (onward movement) [Vorwärts]bewegung, die
(b) (advance) Fortschritt, der; **make** ~: vorankommen; ⟨Student, Patient:⟩ Fortschritte machen; **in** ~: im Gange
[2] /prə'gres/ v.i. (a) (move forward) vorankommen
(b) (be carried on, develop) Fortschritte machen

progression /prə'greʃn/ n.
(a) (development) Fortschritt, der
(b) (succession) Folge, die

progressive /prə'gresɪv/ adj.
(a) fortschreitend ⟨Verbesserung, Verschlechterung⟩; schrittweise ⟨Reform⟩; allmählich ⟨Veränderung⟩
(b) (favouring reform; in culture) fortschrittlich; progressiv

pro'gressively adv. immer ⟨schlechter, weiter⟩

prohibit /prə'hɪbɪt/ v.t. (forbid) verbieten; ~ **sb.'s doing sth.,** ~ **sb. from doing sth.** jmdm. verbieten, etw. zu tun

prohibition /prəʊhɪ'bɪʃn, prəʊɪ'bɪʃn/ n.
Verbot, das
prohibitive /prə'hɪbɪtɪv/ adj.
unerschwinglich ⟨Preis, Miete⟩; untragbar
⟨Kosten⟩
project [1] /prə'dʒekt/ v.t. werfen ⟨Schein⟩;
senden ⟨Strahl⟩; (Cinemat.) projizieren
[2] /prə'dʒekt/ v.i. (jut out) ⟨Felsen:⟩
vorspringen; ⟨Zähne, Brauen:⟩ vorstehen
[3] /'prɒdʒekt/ n. Projekt, das
projectile /prə'dʒektaɪl/ n. Geschoss, das
projection /prə'dʒekʃn/ n. (a) (protruding
thing) Vorsprung, der
(b) (estimate) Hochrechnung, die; (forecast)
Voraussage, die
projectionist /prə'dʒekʃənɪst/ n.
(Cinemat.) Filmvorführer, der/-vorführerin,
die
pro'jection room n. (Cinemat.)
Vorführraum, der
projector /prə'dʒektə(r)/ n. Projektor, der
proletarian /prəʊlɪ'teərɪən/ [1] adj.
proletarisch
[2] n. Proletarier, der/Proletarierin, die
'pro-life adj. Lebensschutz-
'pro-lifer n. Verfechter, der/Verfechterin,
die des Rechts auf Leben
proliferate /prə'lɪfəreɪt/ v.i. (increase) sich
ausbreiten
proliferation /prəlɪfə'reɪʃn/ n. starke
Zunahme
prolific /prə'lɪfɪk/ adj. (a) (fertile) fruchtbar
(b) (productive) produktiv
prologue (Amer.: **prolog**) /'prəʊlɒg/ n.
Prolog, der (to zu)
prolong /prə'lɒŋ/ v.t. verlängern
prolonged /prə'lɒŋd/ adj. lang; lang
anhaltend ⟨Beifall⟩
promenade /prɒmə'nɑːd/ n. Promenade,
die
prominence /'prɒmɪnəns/ n.
(a) (conspicuousness) Auffälligkeit, die
(b) (distinction) Bekanntheit, die
prominent /'prɒmɪnənt/ adj.
(a) (conspicuous) auffallend
(b) (foremost) herausragend; **he was ~ in
politics** er war ein prominenter Politiker
(c) (projecting) vorspringend; vorstehend
⟨Backenknochen, Brauen⟩
promiscuity /prɒmɪ'skjuːɪtɪ/ n.
Promiskuität, die (geh.)
promiscuous /prə'mɪskjʊəs/ adj.
promiskuitiv (geh.); **a ~ man** ein Mann, der
häufig die Partnerin wechselt
promise /'prɒmɪs/ [1] n. (a) Versprechen,
das; **sb.'s ~s** jmds. Versprechungen; **give** or
make a ~ [to sb.] [jmdm.] ein Versprechen
geben; **give** or **make a ~ [to sb.] to do sth.**
[jmdm.] versprechen, etw. zu tun
(b) (fig.: reason for expectation) Hoffnung,
die; **a painter of** or **with ~:** ein viel
versprechender Maler

[2] v.t. (a) versprechen; **~ sth. to sb.**, **~ sb.
sth.** jmdm. etw. versprechen
(b) (fig.: give reason for expectation of) verheißen
(geh.); **~ sb. sth.** jmdm. etw. in Aussicht
stellen
[3] v.i. **~ well** or **favourably** viel
versprechend sein; **I can't ~:** ich kann es
nicht versprechen
promising /'prɒmɪsɪŋ/ adj. viel
versprechend
promote /prə'məʊt/ v.t. (a) (to more senior
job) befördern
(b) (encourage) fördern
(c) (publicize) Werbung machen für
(d) (Footb.) **be ~d** aufsteigen
pro'moter n. Veranstalter, der/
Veranstalterin, die
promotion /prə'məʊʃn/ n.
(a) Beförderung, die; **win** or **gain
~:** befördert werden
(b) (furtherance) Förderung, die
(c) (publicization) Werbung, die; (instance)
Werbekampagne, die
(d) (Footb.) Aufstieg, der
promotional /prə'məʊʃənl/ adj.
Werbe⟨kampagne, -broschüre usw.⟩
prompt /prɒmpt/ [1] adj. (a) (ready to act)
bereitwillig; **be ~ in doing sth.** or **to do sth.**
etw. unverzüglich tun
(b) (done readily) sofortig; **her ~ answer** ihre
prompte Antwort; **take ~ action** sofort
handeln
(c) (punctual) pünktlich
[2] adv. pünktlich; **at 6 o'clock ~:** Punkt 6
Uhr
[3] v.t. (a) (incite) veranlassen
(b) (supply with words) soufflieren (+ Dat.); (give
suggestion to) weiterhelfen (+ Dat.)
(c) hervorrufen ⟨Kritik⟩; provozieren
⟨Antwort⟩
'promptly adv. (a) (quickly) prompt
(b) (punctually) pünktlich
prone /prəʊn/ adj. (liable) **be ~ to** anfällig
sein für ⟨Krankheiten⟩; **be ~ to do sth.** dazu
neigen, etw. zu tun
prong /prɒŋ/ n. (of fork) Zinke, die
pronoun /'prəʊnaʊn/ n. (Ling.) Pronomen,
das/ Fürwort, das
pronounce /prə'naʊns/ [1] v.t. (a) (declare)
verkünden; **~ sb./sth. [to be] sth.** jmdn./
etw. für etw. erklären; **~ sb. fit for work**
jmdn. für arbeitsfähig erklären
(b) aussprechen ⟨Wort, Buchstaben usw.⟩
[2] v.i. **~ on sth.** zu etw. Stellung nehmen;
~ for or **in favour of/against sth.** sich
für/gegen etw. aussprechen
pronounced /prə'naʊnst/ adj. (marked)
ausgeprägt
pro'nouncement n. Erklärung, die;
make a ~ [about sth.] eine Erklärung [zu
etw.] abgeben
pronunciation /prənʌnsɪ'eɪʃn/ n.
Aussprache, die; **what is the ~ of this word?**
wie wird dieses Wort ausgesprochen?

p

proof /pru:f/ ① *n.* (a) (fact, evidence) Beweis, *der*
(b) *no indef. art.* (Law) Beweismaterial, *das*
(c) (proving) **in** ~ **of** zum Beweis (+ *Gen.*)
(d) *no art.* (standard of strength) Proof *o. Art.;* **100°** ~ (Brit.), **128°** ~ (Amer.) 64 Vol.-% Alkohol
(e) (Printing) [korrektur]abzug, *der*
② *adj.* (a) **be** ~ **against sth.** unempfindlich gegen etw. sein; (fig.) gegen etw. immun sein
(b) *in comb.* ⟨kugel-, einbruch-, idioten⟩sicher; ⟨schall-, wasser⟩dicht; **flame-** ~: nicht brennbar
proof ~**-read** *v.t.* Korrektur lesen; ~**-reader** *n.* Korrektor, *der*/Korrektorin, *die*
prop¹ /prɒp/ ① *n.* Stütze, *die;* (Mining) Strebe, *die*
② *v.t.,* **-pp-** stützen; **the ladder was** ~**ped against the house** die Leiter war gegen das Haus gelehnt
■ **prop 'up** *v.t.* stützen; (fig.) vor dem Konkurs bewahren ⟨Firma⟩; stützen ⟨Regierung⟩
prop² *n.* (Theatre, Cinemat.: also fig.) Requisit, *das*
propaganda /prɒpə'gændə/ *n.* Propaganda, *die*
propagate /'prɒpəgeɪt/ ① *v.t.* (a) (Hort., Agric.) vermehren (**from, by** durch)
(b) (spread) verbreiten
② *v.i.* (a) (Bot.) sich vermehren
(b) (spread) sich ausbreiten
propagation /prɒpə'geɪʃn/ *n.* (a) (Hort., Agric.) Züchtung, *die*
(b) (Bot.) Vermehrung, *die*
(c) (spreading) Verbreitung, *die*
propel /prə'pel/ *v.t.,* **-ll-** antreiben
propellant /prə'pelənt/ *n.* (a) Treibstoff, *der*
(b) (of aerosol spray) Treibgas, *das*
pro'peller *n.* Propeller, *der*
propelling 'pencil *n.* (Brit.) Drehbleistift, *der*
propensity /prə'pensɪtɪ/ *n.* **have a** ~ **to do sth.** *or* **for doing sth.** dazu neigen, etw. zu tun
proper /'prɒpə(r)/ *adj.* (a) (accurate) richtig; zutreffend ⟨Beschreibung⟩; eigentlich ⟨Wortbedeutung⟩
(b) *postpos.* (strictly so called) im engeren Sinn *nachgestellt;* **in London** ~: in London selbst
(c) (genuine) echt; richtig ⟨Wirbelsturm, Schauspieler⟩
(d) (satisfactory) richtig; zufrieden stellend ⟨Antwort⟩
(e) (suitable) angemessen; (morally fitting) gebührend; **do sth. the** ~ **way** etw. richtig machen
(f) *attrib.* (coll.: thorough) richtig
'properly *adv.* richtig; (rightly) zu Recht; ~ **speaking** genau genommen
proper 'name, proper 'noun *ns.* (Ling.) Eigenname, *der*

property /'prɒpətɪ/ *n.* (a) (possession[s]) Eigentum, *das;* **lost** ~ **[department** *or* **office]** Fundbüro, *das*
(b) (estate) Besitz, *der;* Immobilie, *die* (fachspr.)
(c) (attribute) Eigenschaft, *die;* (effect, special power) Wirkung, *die*
'property developer *n.* ≈ Bauunternehmer, *der*/-unternehmerin, *die*
prophecy /'prɒfɪsɪ/ *n.* (prediction) Vorhersage, *die;* (prophetic utterance) Propheseiung, *die*
prophesy /'prɒfɪsaɪ/ *v.t.* (predict) vorhersagen; (fig.) prophezeien ⟨Unglück⟩; (as fortune teller) weissagen
prophet /'prɒfɪt/ *n.* Prophet, *der*
prophetic /prə'fetɪk/ *adj.* prophetisch
proportion /prə'pɔ:ʃn/ ① *n.* (a) (portion) Teil, *der*
(b) (ratio) Verhältnis, *das;* **the** ~ **of sth. to sth.** das Verhältnis von etw. zu etw.
(c) (correct relation; Math.) Proportion, *die;* **be in** ~ **[to** *or* **with sth.]** im richtigen Verhältnis [zu *od.* mit etw.] stehen; **keep things in** ~ (fig.) die Dinge im richtigen Licht sehen; **be out of** ~**/all** *or* **any** ~ **[to** *or* **with sth.]** in keinem/keinerlei Verhältnis zu etw. stehen
(d) *in pl.* (size) Dimensionen *Pl.*
② *v.t.* proportionieren
proportional /prə'pɔ:ʃənl/ *adj.* (a) (in proportion) entsprechend; **be** ~ **to sth.** einer Sache (*Dat.*) entsprechen
(b) (Math.) **be directly/indirectly** ~ **to sth.** einer Sache (*Dat.*) direkt/umgekehrt proportional sein
proportionate /prə'pɔ:ʃənət/
▶ PROPORTIONAL A
proposal /prə'pəʊzl/ *n.* Vorschlag, *der;* (offer) Angebot, *das;* ~ **[of marriage]** [Heirats]antrag, *der*
propose /prə'pəʊz/ ① *v.t.* (a) vorschlagen; ~ **sth. to sb.** jmdm. etw. vorschlagen; ~ **marriage [to sb.]** [jmdm.] einen Heiratsantrag machen
(b) (nominate) ~ **sb. as/for sth.** jmdn. als/für etw. vorschlagen
(c) (intend) ~ **doing** *or* **to do sth.** beabsichtigen, etw. zu tun
② *v.i.* (offer marriage) ~ **[to sb.]** jmdm. einen Heiratsantrag machen
proposition /prɒpə'zɪʃn/ *n.* (a) (proposal) Vorschlag, *der;* **make** *or* **put a** ~ **to sb.** jmdm. einen Vorschlag machen
(b) (statement; Logic) Aussage, *die*
propound /prə'paʊnd/ *v.t.* darlegen
proprietary /prə'praɪətərɪ/ *adj.* ~ **name** *or* **term** Markenname, *der*
proprietor /prə'praɪətə(r)/ *n.* Inhaber, *der*/Inhaberin, *die*
propriety /prə'praɪətɪ/ *n.* Anstand, *der;* **breach of** ~: Verstoß gegen die guten Sitten
propulsion /prə'pʌlʃn/ *n.* Antrieb, *der*
prosaic /prə'zeɪɪk/ *adj.* prosaisch (geh.); nüchtern

proscribe /prə'skraɪb/ *v.t.* verbieten

prose /prəʊz/ *n.* Prosa, *die; attrib.* Prosa⟨*werk, -stil*⟩

prosecute /'prɒsɪkjuːt/ ☐ *v.t.* strafrechtlich verfolgen; ∼ **sb. for sth.**/ **doing sth.** jmdn. wegen etw. strafrechtlich verfolgen/jmdn. strafrechtlich verfolgen, weil er etw. tut/getan hat

☐ *v.i.* Anzeige erstatten

prosecution /prɒsɪ'kjuːʃn/ *n.* (bringing to trial) [strafrechtliche] Verfolgung; (court procedure) Anklage, *die;* (prosecuting party) Anklage[vertretung], *die;* **the** ∼**:** die Anklage

prosecutor /'prɒsɪkjuːtə(r)/ *n.* Ankläger, *der*/Anklägerin, *die;* **public** ∼ ≈ Generalstaatsanwalt, *der*/-anwältin, *die*

prospect ☐ /'prɒspekt/ *n.* (a) (expectation) Erwartung, *die* (**of** hinsichtlich); ∼ **of sth.**/**doing sth.** [bei der] Aussicht auf etw. (*Akk.*)/[darauf], etw. zu tun

(b) *in pl.* (hope of success) Zukunftsaussichten *Pl.* **a man with [good]** ∼**s** ein Mann mit Zukunft; **sb.'s** ∼**s of sth.**/**doing sth.** jmds. Chancen auf etw. (*Akk.*)/darauf, etw. zu tun; **the** ∼**s for sb.**/**sth.** die Aussichten für jmdn./etw

☐ /prə'spekt/ *v.i.* nach Bodenschätzen suchen

prospective /prə'spektɪv/ *adj.* voraussichtlich; zukünftig ⟨*Erbe, Braut*⟩; potenziell ⟨*Käufer, Kandidat*⟩

prospector /prə'spektə(r)/ *n.* Prospektor, *der;* (for gold) Goldsucher, *der*

prospectus /prə'spektəs/ *n.* Prospekt, *der;* (Brit. Univ.) Studienführer, *der*

prosper /'prɒspə(r)/ *v.i.* gedeihen; ⟨*Geschäft:*⟩ florieren; ⟨*Berufstätiger:*⟩ Erfolg haben

prosperity /prɒ'sperɪtɪ/ *n.* Wohlstand, *der*

prosperous /'prɒspərəs/ *adj.* wohlhabend; florierend ⟨*Unternehmen*⟩

prostitute /'prɒstɪtjuːt/ *n.* Prostituierte, *die*

prostitution /prɒstɪ'tjuːʃn/ *n.* Prostitution, *die*

prostrate ☐ /'prɒstreɪt/ *adj.* [auf dem Bauch] ausgestreckt

☐ /prə'streɪt/ *v. refl.* ∼ **oneself [at sth.**/**before sb.]** sich [vor etw./jmdm.] niederwerfen

protagonist /prəʊ'tægənɪst/ *n.* (Lit.) Protagonist, *der*/Protagonistin, *die*

protect /prə'tekt/ *v.t.* (a) schützen (**from** vor + *Dat.,* **against** gegen)

(b) (preserve) unter [Natur]schutz stellen ⟨*Pflanze, Tier*⟩

protection /prə'tekʃn/ *n.* Schutz, *der* (**from** vor + *Dat.,* **against** gegen)

protective /prə'tektɪv/ *adj.* schützend; Schutz⟨*hülle, -anstrich, -vorrichtung, -maske*⟩; **be** ∼ **towards sb.** fürsorglich gegenüber jmdm. sein

protein /'prəʊtiːn/ *n.* Protein, *das* (fachspr.); Eiweiß, *das*

protest ☐ /'prəʊtest/ *n.* (a) Beschwerde, *die;* **make** *or* **lodge a** ∼ **[against sb.**/**sth.]** eine Beschwerde [gegen jmdn./etw.] einreichen

(b) (gesture of disapproval) ∼**[s]** Protest, *der;* **under** ∼**:** unter Protest; **in** ∼ **[against sth.]** aus Protest [gegen etw.]

(c) *no art.* (dissent) Protest, *der*

☐ /prə'test/ *v.t.* (affirm) beteuern

☐ /prə'test/ *v.i.* protestieren (**about** gegen); (make written or formal ∼) Protest einlegen (**to** bei)

Protestant /'prɒtɪstənt/ ☐ *n.* Protestant, *der*/Protestantin, *die*

☐ *adj.* protestantisch; evangelisch

Protestantism /'prɒtɪstəntɪzm/ *n., no art.* Protestantismus, *der*

pro'tester *n.* Protestierende, *der*/*die;* (at demonstration) Demonstrant, *der*/ Demonstrantin, *die*

protocol /'prəʊtəkɒl/ *n.* Protokoll, *das*

proton /'prəʊtɒn/ *n.* Proton, *das*

prototype /'prəʊtətaɪp/ *n.* Prototyp, *der*

protract /prə'trækt/ *v.t.* verlängern

protractor /prə'træktə(r)/ *n.* (Geom.) Winkelmesser, *der*

protrude /prə'truːd/ *v.i.* herausragen (**from** aus); ⟨*Zähne:*⟩ vorstehen

protuberance /prə'tjuːbərəns/ *n.* Auswuchs, *der*

proud /praʊd/ ☐ *adj.* (a) stolz; ∼ **to do sth.** *or* **to be doing sth.** stolz darauf, etw. zu tun; ∼ **of sb.**/**sth.**/**doing sth.** stolz auf jmdn./etw./ darauf, etw. zu tun

(b) (arrogant) hochmütig

☐ *adv.* (Brit. coll.) **do sb.** ∼**:** jmdn. verwöhnen

'proudly *adv.* (a) stolz

(b) (arrogantly) hochmütig

provable /'pruːvəbl/ *adj.* beweisbar

prove /pruːv/ ☐ *v.t., p.p.* ∼**d** *or* **proven** /'pruːvn/ beweisen; nachweisen ⟨*Identität*⟩; ∼ **one's ability** sein Können unter Beweis stellen; ∼ **sb. right**/**wrong** ⟨*Ereignis:*⟩ jmdm. recht/unrecht geben; **be** ∼**d wrong** *or* **to be false** ⟨*Theorie:*⟩ widerlegt werden; ∼ **one's**/**sb.'s case** *or* **point** beweisen, dass man recht hat/jmdm. recht geben

☐ *v. refl., p. p.* **proved** *or* **proven:** ∼ **oneself** sich bewähren

☐ *v.i., p. p.* **proved** *or* **proven:** ∼ **[to be]** sich erweisen als

proven ▶ PROVE

proverb /'prɒvɜːb/ *n.* Sprichwort, *das*

proverbial /prə'vɜːbɪəl/ *adj.* sprichwörtlich

provide /prə'vaɪd/ *v.t.* (a) besorgen; liefern ⟨*Beweis*⟩; bereitstellen ⟨*Dienst, Geld*⟩; ∼ **a home**/**a car for sb.** jmdm. Unterkunft/ein Auto [zur Verfügung] stellen

(b) ⟨*Vertrag, Gesetz:*⟩ vorsehen ⋯⟩

■ **pro'vide for** *v.t.* (a) (make provision for) vorsorgen für; ⟨*Plan, Gesetz:*⟩ vorsehen
(b) (maintain) sorgen für, versorgen ⟨*Familie, Kind*⟩

pro'vided *conj.* ~ **[that]** ...: vorausgesetzt, [dass] ...

providence /'prɒvɪdəns/ *n.* (a) **[divine]** ~: die [göttliche] Vorsehung
(b) **P**~ (God) der Himmel

province /'prɒvɪns/ *n.* (a) Provinz, *die*
(b) the ~s (regions outside capital) die Provinz
(c) (sphere of action) [Tätigkeits]bereich, *der;* (area of responsibility) Zuständigkeitsbereich, *der*

provincial /prə'vɪnʃl/ *adj.* Provinz-

provision /prə'vɪʒn/ *n.* (a) (providing) Bereitstellung, *die;* make ~ for vorsorgen *od.* Vorsorge treffen für ⟨*Notfall*⟩
(b) ~s *pl.* (food) Lebensmittel *Pl.*

provisional /prə'vɪʒənl/ *adj.*, **provisionally** /prə'vɪʒənəlɪ/ *adv.* vorläufig; provisorisch

proviso /prə'vaɪzəʊ/ *n., pl.* ~s Vorbehalt, *der*

provocation /prɒvə'keɪʃn/ *n.* Provokation, *die.*

provocative /prə'vɒkətɪv/ *adj.* provozierend; (sexually) aufreizend

provoke /prə'vəʊk/ *v.t.* (a) provozieren ⟨*Person*⟩; reizen ⟨*Person, Tier*⟩; ~ sb. into doing sth. jmdn. so sehr provozieren, dass er etw. tut
(b) (give rise to) hervorrufen; erregen

prow /praʊ/ *n.* (Naut.) Bug, *der*

prowl /praʊl/ ①*v.i.* streifen
②*v.t.* durchstreifen
③*n.* be on the ~: auf einem Streifzug sein

proximity /prɒk'sɪmɪtɪ/ *n.* Nähe, *die*

proxy /'prɒksɪ/ *n.* by ~: durch einen Bevollmächtigten/eine Bevollmächtigte

prude /pruːd/ *n.* prüder Mensch

prudence /'pruːdəns/ *n.* Besonnenheit, *die*

prudent /'pruːdənt/ *adj.* (a) (careful) besonnen
(b) (circumspect) vorsichtig

prudish /'pruːdɪʃ/ *adj.* prüde

prune¹ /pruːn/ *n.* Backpflaume, *die*

prune² *v.t.* (a) (trim) [be]schneiden
(b) (fig.) reduzieren

pry /praɪ/ *v.i.* neugierig sein
■ **'pry into** *v.t.* seine Nase stecken in (+ *Akk.*) (ugs.) ⟨*Angelegenheit*⟩

PS *abbr.* = **postscript** PS

psalm /sɑːm/ *n.* Psalm, *der*

pseudo /'sjuːdəʊ/ ①*adj.* (a) (sham) unecht
(b) (insincere) verlogen
②*n., pl.* ~s (pretentious person) Möchtegern, *der* (ugs. spött.)

pseudonym /'sjuːdənɪm/ *n.* Pseudonym, *das*

psychiatric /saɪkɪ'ætrɪk/ *adj.* psychiatrisch

psychiatrist /saɪ'kaɪətrɪst/ *n.* Psychiater, *der*/Psychiaterin, *die*

psychiatry /saɪ'kaɪətrɪ/ *n.* Psychiatrie, *die*

psychic /'saɪkɪk/ *adj.* be ~: übernatürliche Fähigkeiten haben

psychoanalyse /saɪkəʊ'ænəlaɪz/ *v.t.* psychoanalysieren

psychoa'nalysis *n.* Psychoanalyse, *die*

psycho'analyst *n.* Psychoanalytiker, *der*/-analytikerin, *die*

psychological /saɪkə'lɒdʒɪkl/ *adj.* psychologisch; psychisch ⟨*Problem*⟩

psychologist /saɪ'kɒlədʒɪst/ *n.* Psychologe, *der*/Psychologin, *die*

psychology /saɪ'kɒlədʒɪ/ *n.* Psychologie, *die*

psychopath /'saɪkəpæθ/ *n.* Psychopath, *der*/Psychopathin, *die*

psychopathic /saɪkə'pæθɪk/ *adj.* psychopathisch

psychosis /saɪ'kəʊsɪs/ *n., pl.* **psychoses** /saɪ'kəʊsiːz/ Psychose, *die*

psychotherapist /saɪkəʊ'θerəpɪst/ *n.* Psychotherapeut, *der*/-therapeutin, *die*

psycho'therapy *n.* Psychotherapie, *die*

psychotic /saɪ'kɒtɪk/ *adj.* psychotisch

PTO *abbr.* = **please turn over** b.w.

pub /pʌb/ *n.* (Brit. coll.) Kneipe, *die* (ugs.)

'pub crawl *n.* (Brit. coll.) Zechtour, *die* (ugs.)

puberty /'pjuːbətɪ/ *n., no art.* Pubertät, *die*

'pub grub *n.* (Brit. coll.) Kneipenessen, *das* (ugs.)

pubic /'pjuːbɪk/ *adj.* Scham-

public /'pʌblɪk/ ①*adj.* öffentlich; make sth. ~: etw. bekannt machen
②*n., sing. or pl.* (a) (the people) Öffentlichkeit, *die*
(b) (section of community) Publikum, *das*
(c) in ~: öffentlich

publican /'pʌblɪkən/ *n.* (Brit.) [Gast]wirt, *der*/-wirtin, *die*

publication /pʌblɪ'keɪʃn/ *n.* Veröffentlichung, *die*

public: ~ **'building** *n.* öffentliches Gebäude; ~ **con'venience** *n.* öffentliche Toilette; ~ **'figure** *n.* Persönlichkeit des öffentlichen Lebens; ~ **'footpath** *n.* öffentlicher Fußweg; ~ **'holiday** *n.* gesetzlicher Feiertag; ~ **'house** *n.* (Brit.) Gastwirtschaft, *die;* Gaststätte, *die*

publicity /pʌb'lɪsɪtɪ/ *n.* Publicity, *die;* (advertising) Werbung, *die;* ~ **campaign** Werbekampagne, *die*

pub'licity agent *n.* Publicitymanager, *der*/-managerin, *die*

publicize /'pʌblɪsaɪz/ *v.t.* publik machen ⟨*Ungerechtigkeit*⟩; werben für, Reklame machen für ⟨*Produkt*⟩

public: ~ **'library** *n.* öffentliche Bücherei; ~ **limited company** *n.* (Brit.) ≈ Aktiengesellschaft, *die*

'publicly *adv.* öffentlich; ~ **owned**
staatseigen
public: ~ **property** *n.* Staatsbesitz,
der; ~ **re'lations** *n., sing. or pl.*
Publicrelations *Pl.;* ~ **school** *n.* (a) (Brit.)
Privatschule, *die;* (b) (Scot., Amer.) staatliche
od. öffentliche Schule; ~ **'servant** *n.*
Inhaber/Inhaberin eines öffentlichen
Amtes; ~ **'transport** *n.* öffentlicher
Personenverkehr
publish /'pʌblɪʃ/ *v.t.* ⟨*Verlag:*⟩ verlegen
⟨*Buch, Zeitschrift, Musik usw.*⟩; ⟨*Autor:*⟩
veröffentlichen ⟨*Text*⟩
'publisher *n.* Verleger, *der*/Verlegerin,
die; ~**[s]** (company) Verlag, *der*
'publishing *n., no art.* Verlagswesen, *das*
puck /pʌk/ *n.* (Ice Hockey) Puck, *der*
pucker /'pʌkə(r)/ **1** *v.t.* ~ **[up]** runzeln
⟨*Brauen, Stirn*⟩; kräuseln ⟨*Lippen*⟩
2 *v.i.* ~ **[up]** ⟨*Stoff:*⟩ sich kräuseln
pudding /'pʊdɪŋ/ *n.* (a) Pudding, *der*
(b) (dessert) süße Nachspeise
puddle /'pʌdl/ *n.* Pfütze, *die*
puerile /'pjʊəraɪl/ *adj.* kindisch
puff /pʌf/ **1** *n.* (a) Stoß, *der;* ~ **of breath/**
wind Atem-/Windstoß, *der*
(b) ~ **of smoke** Rauchstoß, *der*
(c) (pastry) Blätterteigteilchen, *das*
2 *v.i.* (a) ~ **[and blow]** schnaufen [und
keuchen]
(b) (~ cigarette smoke etc.) paffen (ugs.) (**at** an
+ *Dat.*)
(c) ⟨*Person:*⟩ keuchen; ⟨*Zug, Lokomotive*⟩
schnaufend fahren
3 *v.t.* blasen ⟨*Rauch*⟩; stäuben ⟨*Puder*⟩
■ **puff 'out** *v.t.* (a) bauschen ⟨*Segel*⟩
(b) (put out of breath) außer Atem bringen
⟨*Person*⟩; **be ~ed [out]** außer Atem sein
puff 'pastry *n.* Blätterteig, *der*
puffy /'pʌfɪ/ *adj.* verschwollen
pugnacious /pʌg'neɪʃəs/ *adj.* kampflustig
puke /pjuːk/ (coarse) **1** *v.i.* kotzen (salopp)
2 *n.* Kotze, *die* (salopp)
pull /pʊl/ **1** *v.t.* (a) (draw, tug) ziehen an
(+ *Dat.*); ziehen ⟨*Hebel*⟩; ~ **sb.'s** or **sb.**
by the hair/ears/sleeve jmdn. an den
Haaren/Ohren/am Ärmel ziehen; ~ **sth.**
over one's ears/head sich (*Dat.*) etw. über
die Ohren/den Kopf ziehen; ~ **to pieces** in
Stücke reißen; (fig.) zerpflücken ⟨*Argument*
usw.⟩
(b) (extract) [her]ausziehen; [heraus]ziehen
⟨*Zahn*⟩
(c) (strain) sich (*Dat.*) zerren ⟨*Muskel*⟩
2 *v.i.* (a) ziehen; **'P~'** „Ziehen"
(b) ~ **[to the left/right]** ⟨*Auto, Boot:*⟩ [nach
links/rechts] ziehen
(c) (pluck) ~ **at** ziehen an (+ *Dat.*); ~ **at sb.'s**
sleeve jmdn. am Ärmel ziehen
3 *n.* (a) Zug, *der*
(b) (influence) Einfluss, *der* (**with** auf + *Akk.,*
bei)
■ **pull a'part** *v.t.* (a) (take to pieces)

auseinander nehmen
(b) (fig.: criticize) zerpflücken; verreißen
⟨*Buch, [literarisches] Werk*⟩
■ **pull 'down** *v.t.* (a) herunterziehen
(b) (demolish) abreißen
■ **pull 'in** **1** *v.t.* hereinziehen
2 *v.i.* (a) ⟨*Zug:*⟩ einfahren
(b) (move to side of road) an die Seite fahren;
(stop) anhalten
■ **pull 'off** *v.t.* (a) (remove) abziehen;
(violently) abreißen
(b) (accomplish) an Land ziehen (ugs.)
■ **pull 'out** **1** *v.t.* herausziehen
2 *v.i.* (a) (depart) abfahren
(b) (away from roadside) ausscheren
■ **pull 'through** *v.i.* ⟨*Patient:*⟩
durchkommen
■ **pull to'gether** *v. refl.* sich
zusammennehmen
■ **pull 'up** **1** *v.t.* (a) hochziehen
(b) [he]rausziehen ⟨*Unkraut, Pflanze*⟩
(c) (reprimand) zurechtweisen
2 *v.i.* (stop) anhalten
'pull-down menu *n.* (Comp.) Pull-down-
Menü, *das*
pulley /'pʊlɪ/ *n.* Rolle, *die*
pullover /'pʊləʊvə(r)/ *n.* Pullover, *der*
pulp /pʌlp/ **1** *n.* Brei, *der*
2 *v.t.* zerdrücken ⟨*Rübe*⟩; einstampfen
⟨*Druckerzeugnis*⟩
pulpit /'pʊlpɪt/ *n.* Kanzel, *die*
pulsate /pʌl'seɪt/ *v.i.* pulsieren
pulse¹ /pʌls/ *n.* Puls, *der;* (single beat)
Pulsschlag, *der*
pulse² *n.* (Cookery) Hülsenfrucht, *die*
'pulse rate *n.* Pulsfrequenz, *die*
pulverize /'pʌlvəraɪz/ *v.t.* pulverisieren
puma /'pjuːmə/ *n.* Puma, *der*
pumice /'pʌmɪs/ *n.* ~ **[stone]** Bimsstein,
der
pummel /'pʌml/ *v.t., (Brit)* **-ll-** einschlagen
auf (+ *Akk.*)
pump /pʌmp/ **1** *n.* Pumpe, *die*
2 *v.i.* pumpen
3 *v.t.* pumpen; ~ **sth. dry** etw. leer pumpen;
~ **sb. for information** Auskünfte aus jmdm.
herausholen; ~ **up** aufpumpen
'pump-action *adj.* ~ **spray** Pumpspray,
das od. der
pumpkin /'pʌmpkɪn/ *n.* Kürbis, *der*
pun /pʌn/ *n.* Wortspiel, *das*
punch¹ **1** *v.t.* (a) (with fist) boxen
(b) (pierce) lochen; ~ **a hole** ein Loch
stanzen; ~ **a hole/holes in sth.** etw. lochen
2 *n.* (a) (blow) Faustschlag, *der*
(b) (for making holes) (in leather, tickets)
Lochzange, *die;* (in paper) Locher, *der*
punch² *n.* (drink) Punsch, *der*
punch: ~ **line** *n.* Pointe, *die;* ~**-up** *n.*
(Brit. coll.) Prügelei, *die*
punctual /'pʌŋktjʊəl/ *adj.* pünktlich

punctuality /pʌŋktjʊ'ælɪtɪ/ n.
Pünktlichkeit, die
'**punctually** adv. pünktlich
punctuate /'pʌŋktjʊeɪt/ v.t. mit
Satzzeichen versehen
punctuation /pʌŋktjʊ'eɪʃn/ n.
Zeichensetzung, die
punctu'ation mark n. Satzzeichen, das
puncture /'pʌŋktʃə(r)/ 1 n. (a) (flat tyre)
Reifenpanne, die
(b) (hole) Loch, das
2 v.t. durchstechen; **be ~d** ⟨Reifen:⟩ platt
sein
pundit /'pʌndɪt/ n. Experte, der/Expertin,
die
pungent /'pʌndʒənt/ adj. beißend, ätzend
⟨Rauch⟩; scharf ⟨Soße⟩; stechend riechend
⟨Gas⟩
punish /'pʌnɪʃ/ v.t. bestrafen
punishable /'pʌnɪʃəbl/ adj. strafbar
'**punishment** n. (a) (punishing) Bestrafung,
die
(b) (penalty) Strafe, die
punitive /'pjuːnɪtɪv/ adj. (a) (penal) Straf-
(b) (severe) [allzu] rigoros
punk /pʌŋk/ n. (a) (Amer. sl.: worthless person)
Dreckskerl, der (salopp)
(b) (admirer of ~ rock) Punk, der; (performer)
Punk[rock]er, der/-[rock]erin, die
(c) (music) Punkrock, der
punnet /'pʌnɪt/ n. (Brit.) Körbchen, das
punt /pʌnt/ n. Stechkahn, der
punter n. (coll.) **the ~s** (customers) die
Leutchen (ugs.)
puny /'pjuːnɪ/ adj. (a) (undersized) zu klein
⟨Baby, Junge⟩
(b) (feeble) gering ⟨Kraft⟩; schwach ⟨Waffe,
Person⟩
pup /pʌp/ n. Welpe, der
pupa /'pjuːpə/ n., pl. ~e /'pjuːpiː/ Puppe,
die
pupate /pjuː'peɪt/ v.i. sich verpuppen
pupil /'pjuːpɪl/ n. (a) Schüler, der/
Schülerin, die
(b) (Anat.) Pupille, die
puppet /'pʌpɪt/ n. Puppe, die; (marionette;
also fig.) Marionette, die
puppy /'pʌpɪ/ n. Hundejunge, das; Welpe,
der
puppy: ~ fat n. (Brit.) Babyspeck, der;
~ love n. Jugendschwärmerei, die
purchase /'pɜːtʃəs/ 1 n. (a) Kauf, der;
make a ~: etwas kaufen
(b) (hold) Halt, der; (leverage) Hebelwirkung,
die
2 v.t. kaufen
'**purchase price** n. Kaufpreis, der
'**purchaser** n. Käufer, der/Käuferin, die
'**purchasing power** n. Kaufkraft, die
pure /pjʊə(r)/ adj. rein
purée /'pjʊəreɪ/ n. Püree, das

'**purely** adv. (a) (solely) rein
(b) (merely) lediglich
purgatory /'pɜːgətərɪ/ n. **it was ~** (fig.) es
war eine Strafe
purge /pɜːdʒ/ 1 v.t. (a) (cleanse) reinigen
(of von)
(b) (remove) entfernen
(c) (rid) säubern ⟨Partei⟩ (of von)
2 n. Säuberung[saktion], die
purification /pjʊərɪfɪ'keɪʃn/ n.
Reinigung, die
purify /'pjʊərɪfaɪ/ v.t. reinigen
purist /'pjʊərɪst/ n. Purist, der/Puristin, die
puritan, (Hist.) **Puritan** /'pjʊərɪtn/ n.
Puritaner, der/Puritanerin, die
puritanical /pjʊərɪ'tænɪkl/ adj.
puritanisch
purity /'pjʊərɪtɪ/ n. Reinheit, die
purl /pɜːl/ 1 n. linke Masche
2 v.t. links stricken; **~ three [stitches]** drei
linke Maschen stricken
purple /'pɜːpl/ 1 adj. lila; violett
2 n. Lila, das; Violett, das
purport /pə'pɔːt/ v.t. **~ to do sth.** (profess)
[von sich] behaupten, etw. zu tun; (be
intended to seem) den Anschein erwecken
sollen, etw. zu tun
purpose /'pɜːpəs/ n. (a) (object) Zweck, der;
(intention) Absicht, die; **what is the ~ of doing
that?** was hat es für einen Zweck, das zu
tun?; **on ~:** mit Absicht; absichtlich
(b) (effect) **to no ~:** ohne Erfolg; **to some/
good ~:** mit einigem/gutem Erfolg
(c) (determination) Entschlossenheit, die
'**purpose-built** adj. [eigens] zu diesem
Zweck errichtet ⟨Gebäude⟩
purposeful /'pɜːpəsfl/ adj. zielstrebig;
(with specific aim) entschlossen
'**purposely** adv. absichtlich
'**purpose-made** adj. spezialgefertigt
purr /pɜː(r)/ 1 v.i. schnurren
2 n. Schnurren, das
purse /pɜːs/ 1 n. Portemonnaie, das
2 v.t. kräuseln ⟨Lippen⟩
purser /'pɜːsə(r)/ n. Zahlmeister, der/
-meisterin, die
pursue /pə'sjuː/ v.t. (a) (chase) verfolgen
(b) (look into) nachgehen (+ Dat.)
(c) (engage in) betreiben
pursuer /pə'sjuːə(r)/ n. Verfolger,
der/Verfolgerin, die
pursuit /pə'sjuːt/ n. (a) Verfolgung, die; (of
knowledge, truth, etc.) Streben, das (of nach); **in
~ of** auf der Jagd nach ⟨Wild, Dieb usw.⟩; in
Ausführung (+ Gen.) ⟨Beschäftigung⟩; **with
the police in [full] ~:** mit der Polizei [dicht]
auf den Fersen
(b) (pastime) Beschäftigung, die
pus /pʌs/ n. Eiter, der
push /pʊʃ/ 1 v.t. (a) schieben; (make fall)
stoßen; drücken gegen ⟨Tür⟩; **~ one's way
through/into/on to** etc. sth. sich (Dat.) einen

Weg durch/in/auf *usw.* etw. (*Akk.*) bahnen
(b) (fig.: impel) drängen
(c) (tax) ~ **sb. [hard]** jmdn. [stark] fordern;
be ~ed for sth. (coll.: find it difficult to provide sth.)
mit etw. knapp sein; **be ~ed for money** *or*
cash knapp bei Kasse sein (ugs.)
(d) (sell illegally, esp. drugs) pushen
(Drogenjargon)
2 *v.i.* **(a)** schieben; (in queue) drängeln; (at
door) drücken; ~ **and shove** schubsen und
drängeln
(b) (make demands) ~ **for sth.** etw. fordern
(c) (make one's way) **he ~ed between us** er
drängte sich zwischen uns; ~ **through the
crowd** sich durch die Menge drängeln
3 *n.* **(a)** Stoß, *der;* **give sth. a ~:** etw.
schieben
(b) (effort) Anstrengungen *Pl.;* (Mil.: attack)
Vorstoß, *der*
(c) (crisis) **when it comes to the ~,** (Amer. coll.)
when ~ comes to shove wenn es ernst wird
(d) (Brit. coll.: dismissal) **get the ~:** rausfliegen
(ugs.)
■ **push a'head** *v.i.* ~ **ahead with sth.** etw.
vorantreiben
■ **push 'in** *v.i.* sich hineindrängen
■ **push 'off** *v.i.* **(a)** (Boating) abstoßen
(b) (coll.: leave) abhauen (salopp)
■ **push 'on** 1 *v.i.* (with plans etc.)
weitermachen
2 *v.t.* draufdrücken ⟨*Deckel usw.*⟩
■ **push 'up** *v.t.* hochschieben; (fig.)
hochtreiben
push: ~**bike** *n.* (Brit. coll.) Fahrrad, *das;*
~-**button** *n.* [Druck]knopf, *der;*
Drucktaste, *die;* ~**chair** *n.* (Brit.)
Sportwagen, *der*
pusher /'pʊʃə(r)/ *n.* (seller of drugs) Dealer,
der/Dealerin, *die*
'**pushover** *n.* (coll.) Kinderspiel, *das*
pushy /'pʊʃɪ/ *adj.* (coll.) [übermäßig]
ehrgeizig ⟨*Person*⟩
pussy /'pʊsɪ/ *n.* (child lang.: cat) Miezekatze,
die (fam.)
put /pʊt/ 1 *v.t.,* -tt-, put **(a)** (place) tun;
(vertically) stellen; (horizontally) legen; ~ **plates
on the table** Teller auf den Tisch stellen; ~ **a
stamp on the letter** eine Briefmarke auf den
Brief kleben; ~ **the letter in an envelope/the
letter box** den Brief in einen Umschlag/in
den Briefkasten stecken; ~ **sth. in one's
pocket** etw. in die Tasche stecken; ~ **petrol
in the tank** Benzin in den Tank füllen; ~ **the
car in[to] the garage** das Auto in die Garage
stellen; ~ **the plug in the socket** den Stecker
in die Steckdose stecken; ~ **one's hands
over one's eyes** sich (*Dat.*) die Hände auf die
Augen legen; **where shall I ~ it?** wo soll ich
es hintun (ugs.)/-stellen/-legen *usw.*?; (fig.) **be
~ in a difficult position** in eine schwierige
Lage geraten; ~ **sb. on to sth.** jmdn. auf
etw. (*Akk.*) hinweisen; ~ **sb. to work** jmdn.
arbeiten lassen; ~ **sb. on antibiotics** jmdn.
auf Antibiotika setzen; ~ **oneself in sb.'s
place** *or* **situation** sich in jmds. Lage (*Akk.*)

versetzen
(b) (submit) unterbreiten ⟨*Vorschlag, Plan*⟩
(**to** *Dat.*)
(c) (express) ausdrücken; **let's ~ it like
this:** ...: sagen wir so: ...; ~ **sth. into English**
etc. etw. ins Englische *usw.* übertragen;
~ **sth. into words** etw. in Worte fassen
(d) (write) schreiben; ~ **one's name on the
list** seinen Namen auf die Liste setzen;
~ **sth. on the bill** etw. auf die Rechnung
setzen
(e) (stake) setzen (**on** auf + *Akk.*)
(f) (estimate) ~ **sb./sth. at** jmdn./etw.
schätzen auf (+ *Akk.*)
2 *v.i.* -tt-, put (Naut.) ~ **[out] to sea** in See
stechen
■ **put a'cross** *v.t.* **(a)** (communicate)
vermitteln (**to** *Dat.*)
(b) (make acceptable) ankommen mit
■ **put a'way** *v.t.* **(a)** wegräumen;
reinstellen ⟨*Auto*⟩; (in file) abheften
(b) (save) beiseite legen
(c) (coll.) (eat) verdrücken (ugs.); (drink)
runterkippen (ugs.)
(d) (coll.: confine) einsperren (ugs.)
■ **put 'back** *v.t.* **(a)** ~ **the book back** das
Buch zurücktun
(b) ~ **the clock back** die Uhr zurückstellen
(c) (postpone) verschieben
■ **put 'down** *v.t.* **(a)** (set down) (vertically)
hinstellen; (horizontally) hinlegen; auflegen
⟨*Hörer*⟩
(b) (suppress) niederwerfen
(c) (humiliate) herabsetzen
(d) (kill) töten
(e) (write) notieren
(f) (attribute) ~ **sth. down to sth.** etw. auf etw.
(*Akk.*) zurückführen
■ **put 'forward** *v.t.* **(a)** (propose) aufwarten
mit
(b) (nominate) vorschlagen
(c) ~ **the clock forward** die Uhr vorstellen
■ **put 'in** 1 *v.t.* **(a)** (install) einbauen
(b) (submit) stellen ⟨*Forderung*⟩; einreichen
⟨*Bewerbung*⟩
(c) (devote) aufwenden ⟨*Mühe*⟩; (perform)
einlegen ⟨*Sonderschicht, Überstunden*⟩
2 *v.i.* ~ **in for** sich bewerben um ⟨*Stellung*⟩;
beantragen ⟨*Urlaub*⟩
■ **put 'off** *v.t.* **(a)** (postpone) verschieben
(**until** auf + *Akk.*); (postpone engagement with)
vertrösten (**until** auf + *Akk.*)
(b) (switch off) ausmachen
(c) (repel) abstoßen; ~ **sb. off sth.** jmdm.
etw. verleiden
(d) (distract) stören
(e) (dissuade) ~ **sb. off doing sth.** jmdn.
davon abbringen, etw. zu tun
■ **put 'on** *v.t.* **(a)** anziehen ⟨*Kleidung, Hose
usw.*⟩; aufsetzen ⟨*Hut, Brille*⟩; draufsetzen
⟨*Deckel*⟩; ~ **it on** (coll.) [nur] Schau machen
(ugs.)
(b) anmachen ⟨*Radio, Licht*⟩; aufsetzen
⟨*Wasser, Kessel*⟩
(c) (gain) ~ **on weight** zunehmen
(d) (stage) spielen ⟨*Stück*⟩; zeigen ⟨*Film*⟩ ···⟩

■ **put 'out** *v.t.* **(a)** rausbringen
(b) ausmachen ⟨*Licht*⟩; löschen ⟨*Feuer*⟩
(c) (inconvenience) in Verlegenheit bringen
■ **put 'through** *v.t.* **(a)** (carry out)
durchführen ⟨*Plan, Programm*⟩
(b) (Teleph.) verbinden (**to** mit)
■ **put 'up** ① *v.t.* **(a)** heben ⟨*Hand*⟩;
errichten ⟨*Gebäude, Denkmal*⟩; aufstellen
⟨*Gerüst*⟩
(b) (display) aushängen
(c) hochnehmen ⟨*Fäuste*⟩; leisten
⟨*Widerstand, Gegenwehr*⟩
(d) (propose) vorschlagen; (nominate)
aufstellen
(e) (incite) ∼ **sb. up to sth.** jmdn. zu etw.
anstiften
(f) (accommodate) unterbringen
(g) (increase) [he]raufsetzen ⟨*Preis, Miete*⟩
② *v.i.* (lodge) übernachten
■ **put 'up with** *v.t.* sich (*Dat.*) bieten
lassen ⟨*Beleidigung, Benehmen*⟩; sich
abfinden mit ⟨*Lärm, Elend*⟩; sich abgeben
mit ⟨*Person*⟩
'**put-down** *n.* Herabsetzung, *die;* (snub)
Abfuhr, *die*
putrefaction /pju:trɪ'fækʃn/ *n., no indef.
art.* Zersetzung, *die*

putrefy /'pju:trɪfaɪ/ *v.i.* sich zersetzen
putrid /'pju:trɪd/ *adj.* (rotten) faul; ∼ **smell**
Fäulnisgeruch, *der*
putt /pʌt/ (Golf) ① *v.i. & t.* putten
② *n.* Putt, *der*
'**putter** *n.* Putter, *der*
putty /'pʌtɪ/ *n.* Kitt, *der*
'**put-up** *adj.* **a** ∼ **job** ein abgekartetes Spiel
(ugs.)
puzzle /'pʌzl/ ① *n.* (problem, enigma) Rätsel,
das; (toy) Geduldsspiel, *das*
② *v.t.* rätselhaft *od.* ein Rätsel sein (+ *Dat.*)
③ *v.i.* ∼ **over** *or* **about sth.** sich (*Dat.*) über
etw. den Kopf zerbrechen
puzzled /'pʌzld/ *adj.* ratlos
puzzling /'pʌzlɪŋ/ *adj.* rätselhaft
PVC *abbr.* = **polyvinyl chloride** PVC,
das
pygmy /'pɪgmɪ/ *n.* Pygmäe, *der*
pyjamas /pɪ'dʒɑ:məz/ *n. pl.* **[pair of]**
∼: Schlafanzug, *der*
pylon /'paɪlən/ *n.* Mast, *der*
pyramid /'pɪrəmɪd/ *n.* Pyramide, *die*
Pyrenees /pɪrə'ni:z/ *pr. n. pl.* **the** ∼: die
Pyrenäen
python /'paɪθən/ *n.* Python, *der*

Qq

Q, q /kju:/ *n.* Q, q, *das*
quack /kwæk/ ① *v.i.* ⟨*Ente:*⟩ quaken
② *n.* Quaken, *das*
quadrangle /'kwɒdræŋgl/ *n.*
[viereckiger] Innenhof
quadruped /'kwɒdrʊped/ *n.* Vierfüßler,
der
quadruple /'kwɒdrʊpl/ ① *adj.* vierfach
② *v.t.* vervierfachen
③ *v.i.* sich vervierfachen
quagmire /'kwægmaɪə(r)/ *n.* Sumpf, *der;*
Morast, *der*
quail[1] /kweɪl/ *n.* (Ornith.) Wachtel, *die*
quail[2] *v.i.* ⟨*Person:*⟩ [ver]zagen
quaint /kweɪnt/ *adj.* drollig ⟨*Häuschen,
Einrichtung*⟩; malerisch ⟨*Ort*⟩; (odd) kurios
⟨*Bräuche, Anblick*⟩
quake /kweɪk/ ① *n.* (coll.) [Erd]beben, *das*
② *v.i.* beben; ∼ **with fear** vor Angst zittern
Quaker /'kweɪkə(r)/ *n.* Quäker,
der/Quäkerin, *die*
qualification /kwɒlɪfɪ'keɪʃn/
n. **(a)** Qualifikation, *die;* (condition)
Voraussetzung, *die*
(b) (limitation) Vorbehalt, *der;* **without**
∼: vorbehaltlos

qualified /'kwɒlɪfaɪd/ *adj.* **(a)** qualifiziert;
(by training) ausgebildet
(b) (restricted) nicht uneingeschränkt; **a**
∼ **success** kein voller Erfolg; ∼ **acceptance**
bedingte Annahme
qualify /'kwɒlɪfaɪ/ ① *v.t.* **(a)** (make
competent) berechtigen (**for** zu)
(b) (modify) einschränken
② *v.i.* **(a)** ∼ **in law/medicine** seinen
[Studien]abschluss in Jura/Medizin
machen; ∼ **as a doctor/lawyer** sein Examen
als Arzt/Anwalt machen
(b) (fulfil a condition) in Frage kommen (**for**
für)
(c) (Sport) sich qualifizieren
qualifying /'kwɒlɪfaɪɪŋ/ *adj.* (Sport)
∼ **match** Qualifikationsspiel, *das*
quality /'kwɒlɪtɪ/ ① *n.* **(a)** Qualität, *die*
(b) (characteristic) Eigenschaft, *die*
② *adj.* Qualitäts-
quality: ∼ **control** *n.*
Qualitätskontrolle, *die;* ∼ **time** *n.: ganz
dem Miteinander gewidmete Zeit*
qualm /kwɑ:m/ *n.* Bedenken, *das* (**over,
about** gegen)
quandary /'kwɒndərɪ/ *n.* Dilemma, *das*

quantify /'kwɒntɪfaɪ/ *v.t.* quantifizieren

quantity /'kwɒntɪtɪ/ *n.* **(a)** Quantität, *die*
(b) (amount, sum) Menge, *die*

'quantity surveyor *n.*
Baukostenkalkulator, *der*/-kalkulatorin, *die*

quantum: ~ jump, ~ leap *ns.*
(Phys.; also fig.) Quantensprung, *der;*
~ me'chanics *n.* Quantenmechanik, *die*

quarantine /'kwɒrənti:n/ *n.* Quarantäne,
die; **be in ~:** unter Quarantäne stehen

quarrel /'kwɒrl/ [1] *n.* **(a)** Streit, *der;*
have/pick a ~ with sb. [about/over sth.] sich
mit jmdm. [über etw. (*Akk.*)] streiten/mit
jmdm. [wegen etw.] Streit anfangen
(b) (cause of complaint) Einwand, *der* (with
gegen)
[2] *v.i.,* (Brit.) **-ll-** [sich] streiten (over um,
about über + *Akk.*); **~ with each other**
[sich] [miteinander] streiten; (fall out) sich
[zer]streiten (over um, about über + *Akk.*)

quarrelsome /'kwɒrlsəm/ *adj.*
streitsüchtig

quarry¹ /'kwɒrɪ/ *n.* Steinbruch, *der*

quarry² *n.* (prey) Beute, *die*

quart /kwɔ:t/ *n.* Quart, *das*

quarter /'kwɔ:tə(r)/ [1] *n.* **(a)** Viertel, *das;*
a *or* **one ~ of** ein Viertel (+ *Gen.*); **a ~ of a
mile/an hour** eine Viertelmeile/-stunde
(b) (of year) Quartal, *das;* Vierteljahr, *das*
(c) **[a] ~ to/past six** Viertel vor/nach sechs
(d) (direction) Richtung, *die*
(e) (area of town) [Stadt]viertel, *das*
(f) **~s** *pl.* (lodgings) Quartier, *das* (bes. Milit.);
Unterkunft, *die*
(g) (Amer. coin) Vierteldollar, *der*
[2] *v.t.* **(a)** (divide) vierteln
(b) (lodge) einquartieren ‹Soldaten›

quarter-'final *n.* Viertelfinale, *das*

'quarterly [1] *adj.* vierteljährlich
[2] *n.* Vierteljahr[e]sschrift, *die*

quarter-'pounder *n.* Viertelpfünder, *der*

quartet /kwɔ:'tet/ *n.* Quartett, *das*

quartz /kwɔ:ts/ *n.* Quarz, *der*

quash /kwɒʃ/ *v.t.* **(a)** (annul) aufheben
(b) (suppress) niederschlagen

quaver /'kweɪvə(r)/ [1] *n.* (Brit. Mus.)
Achtelnote, *die*
[2] *v.i.* (vibrate) zittern

quay /ki:/, **'quayside** *ns.* Kai, *der*

queasy /'kwi:zɪ/ *adj.* unwohl

queen /kwi:n/ *n.* **(a)** Königin, *die*
(b) (Chess, Cards) Dame, *die*

queen: ~ 'bee *n.* Bienenkönigin, *die;*
~ 'mother *n.* Königinmutter, *die*

queer /kwɪə(r)/ [1] *adj.* **(a)** (strange)
sonderbar; (eccentric) verschroben
(b) (shady) merkwürdig
(c) (Brit. coll. dated: out of sorts) unwohl
(d) (sl. derog.: homosexual) schwul (ugs.)
[2] *n.* (sl. derog.: homosexual) Schwule, *der*
(ugs.)

quell /kwel/ *v.t.* (literary) niederschlagen

‹Aufstand›; zügeln ‹Furcht›

quench /kwentʃ/ *v.t.* löschen

query /'kwɪərɪ/ [1] *n.* Frage, *die*
[2] *v.t.* in Frage stellen ‹Anweisung,
Glaubwürdigkeit›; beanstanden ‹Rechnung›

quest /kwest/ *n.* Suche, *die* (for nach)

question /'kwestʃn/ [1] *n.* **(a)** Frage, *die;*
ask sb. a ~: jmdm. eine Frage stellen
(b) (doubt, objection) Zweifel, *der* (about an
+ *Dat.*); **there is no ~ about sth.** es besteht
kein Zweifel an etw. (*Dat.*); **beyond all** *or*
without ~: ohne Frage
(c) (problem, concern) Frage, *die;* **sth./it is only
a ~ of time** etw./es ist [nur] eine Frage der
Zeit; **it is [only] a ~ of doing sth.** es geht
[nur] darum, etw. zu tun; **the person/thing
in ~:** die fragliche Person/Sache; **sth./it is
out of the ~:** etw./es ist ausgeschlossen
[2] *v.t.* **(a)** befragen; ‹Polizei, Gericht usw.:›
vernehmen
(b) (throw doubt upon, raise objections to)
bezweifeln

questionable /'kwestʃənəbl/ *adj.*
fragwürdig

'question mark *n.* Fragezeichen, *das*

questionnaire /kwestʃə'neə(r)/ *n.*
Fragebogen, *der*

queue /kju:/ [1] *n.* Schlange, *die;* **join the
~:** sich anstellen
[2] *v.i.* **~ [up]** Schlange stehen

'queue-jumping *n.* (Brit.) Vordrängen,
das

quibble /'kwɪbl/ [1] *n.* Spitzfindigkeit, *die*
[2] *v.i.* streiten

quibbling /'kwɪblɪŋ/ *adj.* spitzfindig

quiche /ki:ʃ/ *n.* Quiche, *die*

quick /kwɪk/ [1] *adj.* schnell; kurz ‹Rede,
Pause›; flüchtig ‹Kuss, Blick›; **be ~!** mach
schnell! (ugs.); **be ~ to do sth.** etw. schnell
tun; **a ~ temper** ein aufbrausendes Wesen
[2] *adv.* schnell
[3] *n.* empfindliches Fleisch; **be cut to the ~**
(fig.) tief getroffen sein

quicken /'kwɪkn/ [1] *v.t.* beschleunigen
[2] *v.i.* sich beschleunigen

'quickly *adv.* schnell

'quickness *n.* **(a)** (speed) Schnelligkeit, *die*
(b) (~ of perception) Schärfe, *die*

quick: ~sand *n.* Treibsand, *der;*
~-tempered /-'tempəd/ *adj.* hitzig; **be
~-tempered** leicht aufbrausen; **~-witted**
adj. geistesgegenwärtig

quid /kwɪd/ *n., pl. same* (Brit. coll.) Pfund, *das*

quiet /'kwaɪət/ [1] *adj.,* **~er** /'kwaɪətə(r)/,
~est /'kwaɪətɪst/ **(a)** (silent) still; (not loud)
leise; **keep ~ about sth.** (fig.) etw. geheim
halten
(b) (peaceful, not busy) ruhig
(c) (not overt) versteckt; **on the ~:** still und
heimlich
[2] *n.* Ruhe, *die;* (silence, stillness) Stille, *die*

quieten /'kwaɪətn/ *v.t.* beruhigen
■ **quieten 'down** *v.i.* sich beruhigen

q

'quietly *adv.* **(a)** (silently) still; (not loudly) leise
(b) (peacefully) ruhig
'quietness *n.* (absence of noise) Stille, *die;* (peacefulness) Ruhe, *die*
quill /kwɪl/ *n.* (feather) Kielfeder, *die;* (of porcupine) Stachel, *der*
quilt /kwɪlt/ **1** *n.* Schlafdecke, *die* **2** *v.t.* wattieren
quince /kwɪns/ *n.* Quitte, *die*
quintessential /kwɪntɪ'senʃl/ *adj.* typisch; wesentlich
quintet /kwɪn'tet/ *n.* Quintett, *das*
quip /kwɪp/ **1** *n.* Witzelei, *die* **2** *v.i.,* **-pp-** witzeln (at über + *Akk.*)
quirk /kwɜːk/ *n.* Marotte, *die;* a ~ of fate eine Laune des Schicksals
quirky /'kwɜːkɪ/ *adj.* schrullig (ugs.)
quit /kwɪt/ *v.t.,* **-tt-**, (Amer.) quit **(a)** (give up) aufgeben; (stop) aufhören mit; ~ **doing sth.** aufhören, etw. zu tun; **they were given notice to** ~ **[the flat]** ihnen wurde [die Wohnung] gekündigt
(b) (Comp.) beenden
quite /kwaɪt/ *adv.* **(a)** (entirely) ganz; völlig; fest ⟨*entschlossen*⟩; ~ **[so]!** [ja,] genau! **(b)** (to some extent) ziemlich; ganz ⟨*gern*⟩; ~ **a few** ziemlich viele
quits /kwɪts/ *pred. adj.* be ~ **[with sb.]** [mit jmdm.] quitt sein (ugs.)

quiver¹ /'kwɪvə(r)/ *v.i.* zittern **(with** vor + *Dat.*); ⟨*Stimme, Lippen:*⟩ beben (geh.); ⟨*Lid:*⟩ zucken
quiver² *n.* (for arrows) Köcher, *der*
quiz /kwɪz/ **1** *n., pl.* ~zes Quiz, *das* **2** *v.t.,* **-zz-** ausfragen **(about** sth. nach etw., about sb. über jmdn.)
'quiz programme, 'quiz show *ns.* (Radio, Telev.) Quizsendung, *die*
quizzical /'kwɪzɪkl/ *adj.* fragend
quoit /kɔɪt/ *n.* [Gummi]ring, *der*
quorum /'kwɔːrəm/ *n.* Quorum, *das*
quota /'kwəʊtə/ *n.* **(a)** (share) Anteil, *der* **(b)** (goods to be produced) Produktionsmindestquote, *die* **(c)** (maximum number) Höchstquote, *die*
quotation /kwəʊ'teɪʃn/ *n.* **(a)** Zitieren, *das;* (passage) Zitat, *das* **(b)** (estimate) Kosten[vor]anschlag, *der*
quo'tation marks *n. pl.* Anführungszeichen *Pl.*
quote /kwəʊt/ **1** *v.t. also abs.* zitieren **(from** aus); zitieren aus ⟨*Buch, Text*⟩; (mention) anführen; nennen ⟨*Preis*⟩ **2** *n.* (coll.) **(a)** (passage) Zitat, *das* **(b)** (estimate) Kosten[vor]anschlag, *der* **(c)** *usu. in pl.* (quotation mark) Anführungszeichen, *das*
quotient /'kwəʊʃnt/ *n.* (Math.) Quotient, *der; see also* INTELLIGENCE QUOTIENT

Rr

R, r /ɑː(r)/ *n.* R, r, *das*
R. *abbr.* = **River** Fl.
rabbi /'ræbaɪ/ *n.* Rabbi[ner], *der;* (as title) Rabbi, *der*
rabbit /'ræbɪt/ *n.* Kaninchen, *das*
rabbit: ~ **burrow** *n.* Kaninchenbau, *der;* ~ **hutch** *n.* (also fig.) Kaninchenstall, *der;* ~ **warren** *n.* Kaninchengehege, *das;* (fig.) Labyrinth, *das*
rabble /'ræbl/ *n.* Mob, *der*
rabid /'ræbɪd/ *adj.* **(a)** tollwütig **(b)** (extreme) fanatisch
rabies /'reɪbiːz/ *n.* Tollwut, *die*
race¹ /reɪs/ **1** *n.* Rennen, *das;* (fig.) a ~ **against time** ein Wettlauf mit der Zeit **2** *v.i.* **(a)** (in swimming, running, etc.) um die Wette schwimmen/laufen *usw.* **(with, against** mit) **(b)** ⟨*Motor:*⟩ durchdrehen; ⟨*Puls:*⟩ jagen **(c)** (rush) sich sehr beeilen; ~ **after sb.** jmdn. hinterherhetzen **3** *v.t.* um die Wette schwimmen/laufen

usw. mit
race² *n.* (Anthrop., Biol.) Rasse, *die;* **the human** ~: die Menschheit
race: ~**course** *n.* Rennbahn, *die;* ~ **hatred** *n.* Rassenhass, *der;* ~**horse** *n.* Rennpferd, *das;* ~ **meeting** *n.* Renntag, *der;* (on successive days) Renntage *Pl.* ~ **relations** *n. pl.* Beziehung zwischen den Rassen; ~ **riot** *n.* Rassenkrawall, *der;* ~**track** *n.* Rennbahn, *die*
racial /'reɪʃl/ *adj.* Rassen⟨*diskriminierung, -konflikt, -gleichheit, -spannung, -vorurteil*⟩; rassisch ⟨*Gruppe, Minderheit*⟩
racialism /'reɪʃəlɪzm/ *n.* Rassismus, *der*
racialist /'reɪʃəlɪst/ **1** *n.* Rassist, *der*/Rassistin, *die* **2** *adj.* rassistisch
racially /'reɪʃəlɪ/ *adv.* rassisch; be ~ **prejudiced** Rassenvorurteile haben
racing /'reɪsɪŋ/ *n.* Rennsport, *der;* (with horses) Pferdesport, *der*
racing: ~ **bicycle** *n.* Rennrad, *das;*

Rennmaschine, *die;* ~ **car** *n.* Rennwagen, *der;* ~ **driver** *n.* Rennfahrer, *der/*-fahrerin, *die*

racism /'reɪsɪzm/ *n.* Rassismus, *der*

racist /'reɪsɪst/ ⟦1⟧ *n.* Rassist, *der/* Rassistin, *die*
⟦2⟧ *adj.* rassistisch

rack /ræk/ ⟦1⟧ *n.* (for luggage) Ablage, *die;* (for toast, plates) Ständer, *der;* (on bicycle, motor cycle) Gepäckträger, *der*
⟦2⟧ *v.t.* ~ one's brain[s] (fig.) sich (*Dat.*) den Kopf zerbrechen (ugs.)

racket¹ /'rækɪt/ *n.* Schläger, *der*

racket² *n.* (a) (disturbance) Lärm, *der;* Krach, *der*
(b) (scheme) Schwindelgeschäft, *das* (ugs.)

racketeer /rækɪ'tɪə(r)/ *n.* Ganove, *der;* (profiteer) Wucherer, *der*

racketeering /rækɪ'tɪərɪŋ/ *n.* kriminelle Geschäfte *Pl.*

racoon /rə'ku:n/ *n.* Waschbär, *der*

racy /'reɪsɪ/ *adj.* flott (ugs.) ⟨*Stil*⟩

radar /'reɪdɑ:(r)/ *n.* Radar, *das od. der*

'radar screen *n.* Radarschirm, *der*

radiant /'reɪdɪənt/ *adj.* strahlend; fröhlich ⟨*Stimmung*⟩; be ~: strahlen (with vor + *Dat.*)

radiate /'reɪdɪeɪt/ ⟦1⟧ *v.i.* (a) ⟨*Hitze, Wärme:*⟩ ausstrahlen; ⟨*Schein, Wellen:*⟩ ausgehen (from von)
(b) (from central point) strahlenförmig ausgehen (from von)
⟦2⟧ *v.t.* ausstrahlen ⟨*Licht, Wärme; Glück, Liebe*⟩; aussenden ⟨*Strahlen, Wellen*⟩

radiation /reɪdɪ'eɪʃn/ *n.* (of energy) Emission, *die;* (of signals) Ausstrahlung, *die;* (energy transmitted) Strahlung, *die*

radiator /'reɪdɪeɪtə(r)/ *n.* (a) (for heating) Heizkörper, *der*
(b) (Motor Veh.) Kühler, *der*

'radiator cap *n.* Kühlverschraubung, *die*

radical /'rædɪkl/ *adj.* ⟦1⟧ (a) (thorough; also Polit.) radikal; drastisch ⟨*Maßnahme*⟩
(b) (progressive) radikal
(c) (fundamental) grundlegend
⟦2⟧ *n.* (Polit.) Radikale, *der/die*

radicalize /'rædɪkəlaɪz/ *v.t.* (Polit., Soziol.) radikalisieren

radio /'reɪdɪəʊ/ ⟦1⟧ *n., pl.* ~s (a) *no indef. art.* Funk, *der;* (for private communication) Sprechfunk, *der*
(b) *no indef. art.* (Broadcasting) Rundfunk, *der;* on the ~: im Radio
(c) (apparatus) Radio, *das*
⟦2⟧ *attrib. adj.* (Broadcasting) Rundfunk-; Radio⟨*welle, -teleskop*⟩; Funk⟨*mast, -turm, -taxi*⟩
⟦3⟧ *v.t.* funken

radio: ~'**active** *adj.* radioaktiv; ~**ac'tivity** *n.* Radioaktivität, *die;* ~ **cas'sette player** *n.* Kassettenradio, *das;* Radio mit Kassettenteil; ~**con'trolled** *adj.* funkgesteuert;

~ **frequency** *n.* Hochfrequenz, *die;* *attrib.* ~-frequency Hochfrequenz-;
~ **play** *n.* Hörspiel, *das;* ~ **station** *n.* Rundfunkstation, *die;* Rundfunk- *od.* Radiosender, *der;* ~ '**telescope** *n.* Radioteleskop, *das;* ~'**therapy** *n.* Strahlentherapie, *die*

radish /'rædɪʃ/ *n.* Rettich, *der;* (small, red) Radieschen, *das*

radius /'reɪdɪəs/ *n., pl.* radii /'reɪdɪaɪ/ *or* ~es (Math.) Radius, *der;* (fig.) Umkreis, *der*

RAF /ɑːreɪ'ef, (coll.) ræf/ *abbr.* = **Royal Air Force**

raffle /'ræfl/ ⟦1⟧ *n.* Tombola, *die;* ~ ticket Los, *das*
⟦2⟧ *v.t.* ~ [off] verlosen

raft /rɑ:ft/ *n.* Floß, *das*

rafter /'rɑ:ftə(r)/ *n.* Sparren, *der*

rag¹ /ræg/ *n.* (a) [Stoff]fetzen, *der*
(b) *in pl.* (old and torn clothes) Lumpen *Pl.*
(c) (derog.: newspaper) Käseblatt, *das* (salopp)

rag² *v.t.,* -gg- (tease) aufziehen

rag: ~**bag** *n.* (fig.) Sammelsurium, *das;* ~ **doll** *n.* Stoffpuppe, *die*

rage /reɪdʒ/ ⟦1⟧ *n.* (a) (violent anger) Wut, *die;* (fit of anger) Wutausbruch, *der*
(b) sth. is [all] the ~: etw. ist [ganz] groß in Mode
⟦2⟧ *v.i.* (a) (rave) toben; ~ at *or* against sth./sb. gegen etw./jmdn. wüten
(b) (be violent, unchecked) toben; ⟨*Krankheit:*⟩ wüten

ragged /'rægɪd/ *adj.* zerrissen

'rag trade *n.* (coll.) Modebranche, *die* (ugs.)

raid /reɪd/ ⟦1⟧ *n.* Einfall, *der;* Überfall, *der;* (Mil.) Überraschungsangriff, *der;* (by police) Razzia, *die* (on in + *Dat.*)
⟦2⟧ *v.t.* ⟨*Polizei:*⟩ eine Razzia machen auf (+ *Akk.*); ⟨*Räuber, Soldaten:*⟩ überfallen

'raider *n.* Angreifer, *der/*Räuberin, *die*

rail /reɪl/ *n.* (a) Stange, *die;* (on ship) Reling, *die;* (as protection against contact) Barriere, *die*
(b) (Railw.: of track) Schiene, *die*
(c) (~way) [Eisen]bahn, *die; attrib.* Bahn-; by ~: mit der Bahn

'rail card *n.* Bahnkarte, *die*

railing /'reɪlɪŋ/ *n.* (round park) Zaun, *der;* (on staircase) Geländer, *die*

rail: ~**road** (Amer.) ▶ ~WAY; ~ **traffic** *n., no pl.* Schienenverkehr, *der;* ~**way** *n.* (a) (track) Bahnlinie, *die;* Bahnstrecke, *die;*
(b) (system) [Eisen]bahn, *die*

railway: ~ **carriage** *n.* Eisenbahnwagen, *der;* ~ **crossing** *n.* Bahnübergang, *der;* ~ **engine** *n.* Lokomotive, *die;* ~ **line** *n.* [Eisen]bahnlinie, *die;* ~ **station** *n.* Bahnhof, *der;* ~ **worker** *n.* Bahnarbeiter, *der/*-arbeiterin, *die*

rain /reɪn/ ⟦1⟧ *n.* (a) Regen, *der*
(b) (fig.: of arrows, blows, etc.) Hagel, *der*
⟦2⟧ *v.i. impers.* it is ~ing es regnet
⟦3⟧ *v.t.* hageln lassen ⟨*Schläge, Hiebe*⟩ ⋯⟩

rain: **~bow** /'reɪnbəʊ/ n. Regenbogen, der; ~ **check** n. (Amer. fig.) take a ~ check on sth. auf etw. (Akk.) später wieder zurückkommen; ~ **cloud** n. Regenwolke, die; ~**coat** n. Regenmantel, der; ~**fall** n. Niederschlag, der; ~**forest** n. Regenwald, der; ~**proof** adj. regendicht; ~**water** n. Regenwasser, das; ~**wear** n. Regenkleidung, die

'**rainy** adj. regnerisch ‹Tag, Wetter›; regenreich ‹Gebiet, Sommer›; ~ **season** Regenzeit, die; keep sth. for a ~ day (fig.) sich (Dat.) etw. für schlechte Zeiten aufheben

raise /reɪz/ v.t. (a) (lift up) heben; erhöhen ‹Temperatur, Miete, Gehalt›; hochziehen ‹Fahne›; aufziehen ‹Vorhang›; hochheben ‹Arm›; ~ one's glass to sb. das Glas auf jmdn. erheben

(b) (set upright) aufrichten; erheben ‹Banner›; ~ sb.'s spirits jmds. Stimmung heben

(c) erheben ‹Forderungen, Einwände›; aufwerfen ‹Frage›; zur Sprache bringen ‹Thema, Problem›

(d) aufziehen ‹Vieh, [Haus]tiere›; großziehen ‹Familie, Kinder›

(e) aufbringen ‹Geld, Betrag›

(f) aufheben ‹Belagerung, Blockade, Embargo, Verbot›

raisin /'reɪzn/ n. Rosine, die

rake /reɪk/ **1** n. Rechen, der; Harke, die **2** v.t. (a) harken

(b) ~ the fire die Asche entfernen

(c) (with eyes, shots) bestreichen

■ **rake 'in** v.t. (coll.) scheffeln (ugs.)

■ **rake 'up** v.t. zusammenharken; (fig.) wieder ausgraben

'**rake-off** n. (coll.) [Gewinn]anteil, der

rakish /'reɪkɪʃ/ adj. flott; kess

rally /'rælɪ/ **1** v.i. (regain health) sich wieder [ein wenig] erholen

2 v.t. (a) (reassemble) wieder zusammenrufen

(b) einigen ‹Partei, Kräfte›; sammeln ‹Anhänger›

3 n. (a) (mass meeting) Versammlung, die

(b) [motor] ~: Rallye, die

(c) (Tennis) Ballwechsel, der

ram /ræm/ **1** n. (Zool.) Schafbock, der; Widder, der

2 v.t., -mm-: (a) (force) stopfen; ~ a post into the ground einen Pfosten in die Erde rammen; ~ sth. home to sb. jmdm. etw. deutlich vor Augen führen

(b) (collide with) rammen

RAM /ræm/ abbr. (Comp.) = **random access memory** RAM

ramble /'ræmbl/ **1** n. [nature] ~: Wanderung, die

2 v.i. (a) (walk) umherstreifen (through, in in + Dat.)

(b) (in talk) zusammenhangloses Zeug reden; keep rambling on about sth. sich endlos über etw. (Akk.) auslassen

rambler /'ræmblə(r)/ n. Wanderer, der/Wanderin, die

rambling /'ræmblɪŋ/ **1** n. Wandern, das **2** adj. (a) (irregularly arranged) verschachtelt; verwinkelt ‹Straßen›

(b) (incoherent) unzusammenhängend ‹Erklärung›

(c) ~ rose Kletterrose, die

ramp /ræmp/ n. Rampe, die

rampage 1 /'ræmpeɪdʒ/ n. Randale, die (ugs.); be/go on the ~ (coll.) randalieren **2** /ræm'peɪdʒ/ v.i. randalieren

rampant /'ræmpənt/ adj. zügellos ‹Gewalt, Rassismus›; steil ansteigend ‹Inflation›; üppig ‹Wachstum›

rampart /'ræmpɑːt/ n. Wehrgang, der

ram: ~ **raid 1** v.t. [durch Rammen mit einem Fahrzeug] einbrechen in (+ Akk.); **2** n. [durch Rammen eines Gebäudes verübter] Einbruch; ~**raider** n.: Einbrecher, der sich durch Einrammen bes. eines Schaufensters mit einem Fahrzeug Zutritt verschafft

'**ramshackle** adj. klapprig ‹Auto›; verkommen ‹Gebäude›

ran ▶ RUN 2, 3

ranch /rɑːntʃ/ n. Ranch, die

'**ranch hand** n. Farmarbeiter, der/ -arbeiterin, die

rancid /'rænsɪd/ adj. ranzig

rancour (Brit.; Amer.: **rancor**) /'ræŋkə(r)/ n. [tiefe] Verbitterung

R&B abbr. = **rhythm and blues** R&B

R&D abbr. = **research and development** F&E

random /'rændəm/ **1** n. at ~: wahllos; willkürlich; (aimlessly) ziellos; choose at ~: aufs Geratewohl wählen

2 adj. willkürlich

random 'access memory n. (Comp.) Schreib-Lese-Speicher, der

randy /'rændɪ/ adj. geil; scharf (ugs.)

rang ▶ RING² 2, 3

range /reɪndʒ/ **1** n. (a) ~ of mountains Bergkette, die

(b) (of subjects) Palette, die; (of knowledge, voice) Umfang, der

(c) (of missile etc.) Reichweite, die; at a ~ of 200 metres auf eine Entfernung von 200 Metern

(d) (series, selection) Kollektion, die

(e) (stove) Herd, der

2 v.i. ‹Preise, Temperaturen:› schwanken, sich bewegen (from ... to zwischen [+ Dat.] ... und)

'**ranger** n. Förster, der/Försterin, die

rank¹ /ræŋk/ **1** n. (a) (position in hierarchy) Rang, der; (Mil. also) Dienstgrad, der

(b) (social position) [soziale] Stellung

(c) (row) Reihe, die; the ~ and file (fig.) die breite Masse; the ~s (enlisted men) die Mannschaften und Unteroffiziere

2 *v.t.* ~ **among** zählen zu
3 *v.i.* ~ **among** zählen zu
rank² *adj.* **(a)** krass ⟨*Außenseiter*⟩
(b) ~ **weeds** [wild]wucherndes Unkraut
rankings /'ræŋkɪŋz/ *n. pl.* (Sport)
Rangliste, *die;* **the team has fallen in the**
~: die Mannschaft ist in der Tabelle nach
unten gerutscht
ransack /'rænsæk/ *v.t.* **(a)** (search)
durchsuchen **(for** nach)
(b) (pillage) plündern
ransom /'rænsəm/ *n.* ~ **[money]** Lösegeld,
das; **hold to** ~: als Geisel festhalten
rant /rænt/ *v.i.* ~ **[and rave]** wettern (ugs.)
(about über + *Akk.*)
rap /ræp/ 1 *n.* [energisches] Klopfen
2 *v.t.,* **-pp-** klopfen
3 *v.i.,* **-pp-** klopfen **(on** an + *Akk.*)
rape¹ /reɪp/ 1 *n.* Vergewaltigung, *die*
2 *v.t.* vergewaltigen
rape² *n.* (Bot., Agric.) Raps, *der*
rape: ~**seed** *n.* Rapssamen, *der;* ~**seed**
oil *n.* Rapsöl, *das*
rapid /'ræpɪd/ 1 *adj.* schnell ⟨*Bewegung,*
Wachstum, Puls⟩; rasch ⟨*Fortschritt,*
Ausbreitung⟩
2 *n. in pl.* Stromschnellen *Pl.*
rapid-'fire *adj.* Schnellfeuer⟨*waffe,*
-schießen⟩; (fig.) schnell aufeinander folgend
⟨*Wiederholung*⟩; Schnellfeuer⟨*witze, -fragen*⟩
rapidity /rə'pɪdɪtɪ/ *n.* Schnelligkeit, *die*
'rapidly *adv.* schnell
rapist /'reɪpɪst/ *n.* Vergewaltiger, *der*
rapport /ræ'pɔː(r)/ *n.* [harmonisches]
Verhältnis
rapt /ræpt/ *adj.* gespannt ⟨*Miene*⟩
rapture /'ræptʃə(r)/ *n.* **[state of]**
~: Verzückung, *die*
rapturous /'ræptʃərəs/ *adj.* begeistert
rare¹ /reə(r)/ *adj.,* **'rarely** *adv.* selten
rare² *adj.* (Cookery) englisch gebraten
rarefied /'reərɪfaɪd/ *adj.* dünn ⟨*Luft*⟩; (fig.)
exklusiv
rarity /'reərɪtɪ/ *n.* Seltenheit, *die*
rash¹ /ræʃ/ *n.* [Haut]ausschlag, *der*
rash² *adj.* voreilig ⟨*Urteil, Entscheidung*⟩;
überstürzt ⟨*Versprechung*⟩
rasher /'ræʃə(r)/ *n.* Speckscheibe, *die*
'rashly *adv.* voreilig
rasp /rɑːsp/ 1 *n.* (tool) Raspel, *die*
2 *v.t.* (say gratingly) schnarren
raspberry /'rɑːzbərɪ/ *n.* Himbeere, *die*
rat /ræt/ *n.* **(a)** Ratte, *die;* **smell a** ~ (fig.)
Lunte riechen (ugs.)
(b) (coll. derog.: person) Ratte, *die* (derb)
ratchet /'rætʃɪt/ *n.* **(a)** (Mech. Engin.) (set of
teeth) Zahnkranz, *der*
(b) ~ **[wheel]** Klinkenrad, *das*
'ratchet screwdriver *n.*
Drillschraubenzieher, *der*

rate /reɪt/ 1 *n.* **(a)** (proportion) Rate, *die;*
~ **of inflation** Inflationsrate, *die*
(b) (tariff) Satz, *der;* ~ **[of pay]** Lohnsatz, *der*
(c) (speed) Geschwindigkeit, *die;* Tempo, *das*
(d) (Brit.: levy) **[local** *or* **council]** ~s
Gemeindeabgaben *Pl.*
(e) (coll.) **at any** ~ (at least) zumindest;
wenigstens; (whatever happens) auf jeden Fall;
at this ~ **we won't get any work done so**
kriegen wir gar nichts fertig (ugs.)
2 *v.t.* **(a)** einschätzen ⟨*Intelligenz,*
Leistung⟩
(b) (consider) betrachten; rechnen **(among**
zu)
3 *v.i.* ~ **as** gelten als
'ratepayer *n.* (Brit.) Realsteuerpflichtige,
der/die
rather /'rɑːðə(r)/ *adv.* **(a)** (by preference)
lieber
(b) (somewhat) ziemlich; **I** ~ **think that** …: ich
bin ziemlich sicher, dass …
(c) (more truly) vielmehr; **or**
~: beziehungsweise
ratification /rætɪfɪ'keɪʃn/ *n.*
Ratifizierung, *die*
ratify /'rætɪfaɪ/ *v.t.* ratifizieren
rating /'reɪtɪŋ/ *n.* **(a)** (estimated standing)
Einschätzung, *die*
(b) (Radio, Telev.) **[popularity]** ~:
Einschaltquote, *die*
(c) (Brit. Navy) Matrose, *der*
ratio /'reɪʃɪəʊ/ *n., pl.* ~**s** Verhältnis, *das*
ration /'ræʃn/ 1 *n.* ~**[s]** Ration, *die* **(of**
an + *Dat.*)
2 *v.t.* rationieren ⟨*Benzin, Zucker usw.*⟩
rational /'ræʃənl/ *adj.* (having reason)
rational ⟨*Wesen*⟩; (sensible) vernünftig
⟨*Person, Art usw.*⟩
rationalist /'ræʃənəlɪst/ *n.* Rationalist,
der/Rationalistin, *die*
rationalize /'ræʃənəlaɪz/ *v.t.*
rationalisieren
rationing /'ræʃənɪŋ/ *n.* Rationierung, *die*
rat: ~ **poison** *n.* Rattengift, *das;* ~ **race**
n. erbarmungsloser Konkurrenzkampf;
~ **run** *n.* (Brit. coll.) Schleichweg, *der*
rattle /'rætl/ 1 *v.i.* ⟨*Wagen:*⟩
klappern; ⟨*Flaschen:*⟩ klirren; ⟨*Kette:*⟩
rasseln
(b) ⟨*Zug, Bus:*⟩ rattern
2 *v.t.* **(a)** klappern mit ⟨*Würfel, Geschirr*⟩;
klirren lassen ⟨*Fenster[scheiben]*⟩; rasseln
mit ⟨*Kette*⟩
(b) (coll.: disconcert) ~ **sb., get sb.** ~**d** jmdn.
durcheinander bringen
3 *n.* **(a)** (of baby) Rassel, *die*
(b) (sound) Klappern, *das*
■ **rattle 'off** *v.t.* (coll.) herunterrasseln
(ugs.)
'rattlesnake *n.* Klapperschlange, *die*
raucous /'rɔːkəs/ *adj.* rau
raunchy /'rɔːntʃɪ/ *adj.* (lewd) vulgär;
(suggestive) scharf (salopp)

ravage /'rævɪdʒ/ 1 *v.t.* heimsuchen ⟨*Gebiet, Stadt*⟩
2 *n. in pl.* verheerende Wirkung
rave /reɪv/ 1 *v.i.* (a) (talk wildly) irrereden
(b) (speak admiringly) schwärmen (**about** von)
2 *attrib. adj.* (coll.) begeistert ⟨*Kritik*⟩
3 *n.* (coll.: dancing party) Rave, *der od. das*
raven /'reɪvn/ *n.* Rabe, *der*
ravenous /'rævənəs/ *adj.* **I'm ~:** ich habe einen Bärenhunger (ugs.)
'rave-up *n.* (Brit. coll.) [wilde] Fete (ugs.)
ravine /rə'viːn/ *n.* Schlucht, *die*
raving /'reɪvɪŋ/ 1 *adj.* irreredend ⟨*Idiot*⟩
2 *adv.* **be ~ mad** völlig verrückt sein (ugs.)
ravish /'rævɪʃ/ *v.t.* (charm) entzücken
'ravishing *adj.* bildschön ⟨*Anblick, Person*⟩; hinreißend ⟨*Schönheit*⟩
raw /rɔː/ *adj.* (a) (uncooked) roh
(b) (inexperienced) unerfahren
(c) (stripped of skin) blutig ⟨*Fleisch*⟩; offen ⟨*Wunde*⟩
(d) (chilly) nasskalt
Rawlplug ® /'rɔːlplʌg/ *n.* Dübel, *der*
raw ma'terial *n.* Rohstoff, *der*
ray /reɪ/ *n.* Strahl, *der;* **~ of sunshine/light** Sonnen-/Lichtstrahl, *der*
raze /reɪz/ *v.t.* **~ to the ground** dem Erdboden gleichmachen
razor /'reɪzə(r)/ *n.* Rasiermesser, *das;* [electric] **~:** [elektrischer] Rasierapparat
razor: ~ blade *n.* Rasierklinge, *die;*
~-sharp *adj.* sehr scharf ⟨*Messer*⟩; (fig.) messerscharf ⟨*Verstand, Intellekt*⟩; scharfsinnig ⟨*Person*⟩
RC *abbr.* = **Roman Catholic** r.-k.; röm.-kath.
Rd. *abbr.* = **Road** Str.
re /riː/ *prep.* (Commerc.) betreffs
RE *abbr.* (Brit.) = **Religious Education** Religionslehre, *die*
reach /riːtʃ/ 1 *v.t.* (a) (arrive at) erreichen; ankommen in (+ *Dat.*) ⟨*Stadt, Land*⟩; erzielen ⟨*Übereinstimmung*⟩; kommen zu ⟨*Entscheidung; Ausgang, Eingang*⟩; **you can ~ her at this number** du kannst sie unter dieser Nummer erreichen
(b) (extend to) ⟨*Straße:*⟩ führen bis zu; ⟨*Leiter, Haar:*⟩ reichen bis zu
2 *v.i.* (a) (stretch out hand) **~ for sth.** nach etw. greifen; **~ across the table** über den Tisch langen
(b) (be long/tall enough) **sth. will/won't ~:** etw. ist/ist nicht lang genug; **I can't ~:** ich komme nicht daran
(c) (go as far as) ⟨*Wasser, Gebäude, Besitz:*⟩ reichen (**[up] to** bis [hinauf] zu)
3 *n.* Reichweite, *die;* **be within easy ~** ⟨*Ort:*⟩ leicht erreichbar sein; **be out of ~** ⟨*Ort:*⟩ nicht erreichbar sein; ⟨*Gegenstand:*⟩ außer Reichweite sein
■ **reach 'out** *v.i.* die Hand ausstrecken (**for** nach)
react /rɪ'ækt/ *v.i.* reagieren (**to** auf + *Akk.*)

reaction /rɪ'ækʃn/ *n.* Reaktion, *die* (**to** auf + *Akk.*)
reactionary /rɪ'ækʃənərɪ/ (Polit.) 1 *adj.* reaktionär
2 *n.* Reaktionär, *der*/Reaktionärin, *die*
reactor /rɪ'æktə(r)/ *n.* **[nuclear] ~:** Kernreaktor, *der*
read /riːd/ 1 *v.t.,* read /red/ (a) lesen; **~ sb. sth., ~ sth. to sb.** jmdm. etwas vorlesen; **~ the gas meter** das Gas ablesen
(b) (interpret) deuten; **~ between the lines** zwischen den Zeilen lesen
(c) (study) studieren
2 *v.i.,* read (a) lesen; **~ to sb.** jmdm. vorlesen
(b) (convey meaning) lauten; **the contract ~s as follows** der Vertrag hat folgenden Wortlaut
■ **read 'out** *v.t.* laut vorlesen
■ **read 'over, read 'through** *v.t.* durchlesen
■ **read 'up** *v.t.* sich informieren (**on** über + *Akk.*)
readable /'riːdəbl/ *adj.* (a) (pleasant to read) lesenswert
(b) (legible) leserlich
'reader *n.* (a) Leser, *der*/Leserin, *die*
(b) (book) Lesebuch, *das*
'readership *n.* Leserschaft, *die*
readily /'redɪlɪ/ *adv.* (a) (willingly) bereitwillig
(b) (easily) ohne weiteres
readiness /'redɪnɪs/ *n.* Bereitschaft, *die;* **be in ~:** bereit sein (**for** für)
'reading *n.* (a) Lesen, *das*
(b) (figure shown) Anzeige, *die*
(c) (recital) Lesung, *die* (**from** aus)
(d) (Parl.) Lesung, *die*
reading: ~ glasses *n. pl.* Lesebrille, *die;* **~ lamp, ~ light** *ns.* Leselampe, *die;* **~ matter** *n.* Lesestoff, *der;* Lektüre, *die*
readjust /riːə'dʒʌst/ 1 *v.t.* neu einstellen; neu anpassen ⟨*Gehalt, Zinssatz*⟩
2 *v. refl. & i.* **~ [oneself] to** sich wieder gewöhnen an (+ *Akk.*)
read /riːd/: **~-'only memory** *n.* (Comp.) Fest[wert]speicher, *der;* **~-out** *n.* (Comp.) Ausgabe, *die;* **~-write** *n. attrib.* (Comp.) Schreib-Lese-; **~-write head** Schreib-Lese-Kopf, *der*
ready /'redɪ/ 1 *adj.* (a) (prepared) fertig; **be ~ to do sth.** bereit sein, etw. zu tun; **get ~:** sich fertig machen
(b) (willing) bereit
(c) (within reach) griffbereit
2 *adv.* fertig
3 *n.* **at the ~** ⟨*Schusswaffe*⟩ im Anschlag
ready: ~ 'cash ► MONEY;
~-cooked *adj.* vorgekocht; **~-cooked meal** Fertiggericht, *das;* Fertigmahlzeit, *die;* **~-'made** *adj.* (a) Konfektions⟨*anzug, -kleidung*⟩; (b) (fig.) vorgefertigt;
~ 'money *n.* Bargeld, *das;* **~-to-eat** *adj.* Fertig⟨*mahlzeit, -dessert*⟩;

∼-to-serve adj. tischfertig; **∼-to-wear** adj. Konfektions⟨anzug, -kleidung⟩

real /rɪəl/ adj. (a) (actually existing) real ⟨Ereignis, Lebewesen⟩; wirklich ⟨Macht⟩ (b) (genuine) echt ⟨Interesse, Gold, Seide⟩ (c) (complete) total (ugs.) ⟨Desaster, Enttäuschung⟩ (d) (true) wahr ⟨Grund, Name, Glück⟩; echt ⟨Mitleid, Sieg⟩; **the ∼ thing** der/die/das Echte (e) **be for ∼** (coll.) echt sein

'real estate n. (Amer.) Immobilien Pl.

realism /'rɪəlɪzm/ n. Realismus, der

'realist n. Realist, der/Realistin, die

realistic /rɪə'lɪstɪk/ adj. realistisch

reality /rɪ'ælɪtɪ/ n. Realität, die; **in ∼:** in Wirklichkeit

reality T'V n. Reality-TV, das

realization /rɪəlaɪ'zeɪʃn/ n. Erkenntnis, die

realize /'rɪəlaɪz/ v.t. (a) (be aware of) bemerken; erkennen ⟨Fehler⟩; **I didn't ∼** abs. ich habe es nicht gewusst; **∼ [that] …:** merken, dass … (b) (make happen) verwirklichen (c) erbringen ⟨Summe, Preis⟩

real-life attrib. adj. real

really /'rɪəlɪ/ adv. wirklich; **not ∼:** eigentlich nicht; **[well,] ∼!** [also] so was!

realm /relm/ n. Reich, das

realtor /'rɪəltə(r)/ (Amer.) Grundstücksmakler, der

reap /riːp/ v.t. (cut) schneiden ⟨Getreide⟩; (gather in) einfahren ⟨Getreide, Ernte⟩

reappear /riːə'pɪə(r)/ v.i. wieder auftauchen; (come back) [wieder] zurückkommen

rear¹ /rɪə(r)/ ① n. (a) (back part) hinterer Teil (b) (back) Rückseite, die (c) (Mil.) Rücken, der ② adj. hinter…; **∼ axle** Hinterachse, die

rear² ① v.t. großziehen ⟨Kind, Familie⟩; halten ⟨Vieh⟩ ② v.i. ⟨Pferd:⟩ sich aufbäumen

rear: ∼guard n. (Mil.) Nachhut, die; **∼ light** n. Rücklicht, das; **∼-wheel drive** ① n. Hinterradantrieb, der; ② adj. **a ∼-wheel drive vehicle** ein Fahrzeug mit Hinterradantrieb

rearm /riː'ɑːm/ v.i. & t. wieder aufrüsten

rearrange /riːə'reɪndʒ/ v.t. umräumen ⟨Möbel⟩; verlegen ⟨Spiel⟩ (for auf + Akk.); ändern ⟨Programm⟩

rear-view 'mirror n. Rückspiegel, der

reason /'riːzn/ ① n. (a) (cause) Grund, der; **have no ∼ to complain** sich nicht beklagen können; **for that [very] ∼:** aus [eben] diesem Grund (b) (power to understand; sense) Vernunft, die; (power to think) Verstand, der; **in** or **within ∼:** innerhalb eines vernünftigen Rahmens;

it stands to ∼ that …: es ist unzweifelhaft, dass … ② v.i. (a) schlussfolgern (from aus) (b) **∼ with** diskutieren mit (about, on über + Akk.); **you can't ∼ with her** mit ihr kann man nicht vernünftig reden ③ v.t. schlussfolgern

reasonable /'riːzənəbl/ adj. (a) vernünftig (b) (inexpensive) günstig

reasonably /'riːzənəblɪ/ adv. (a) (within reason) vernünftig (b) (fairly) ganz ⟨gut⟩; ziemlich ⟨gesund⟩

reasoned /'riːznd/ adj. durchdacht

reasoning /'riːzənɪŋ/ n. logisches Denken

reassurance /riːə'ʃʊərəns/ n. (a) (calming) give sb. **∼:** jmdn. beruhigen (b) (confirmation) Bestätigung, die

reassure /riːə'ʃʊə(r)/ v.t. beruhigen; **∼ sb. about his health.** jmdm. versichern, dass er gesund ist

reassuring /riːə'ʃʊərɪŋ/ adj. beruhigend

rebate /'riːbeɪt/ n. (a) (refund) Rückzahlung, die (b) (discount) Preisnachlass, der (on auf + Akk.)

rebel ① /'rebl/ n. Rebell, der/Rebellin, die ② attrib. adj. Rebellen- ③ /rɪ'bel/ v.i., **-ll-** rebellieren

rebellion /rɪ'beljən/ n. Rebellion, die

rebellious /rɪ'beljəs/ adj. rebellisch

rebirth /riː'bɜːθ/ n. (revival) Wiederaufleben, das

reboot /riː'buːt/ (Comp.) v.t. & i. neu booten.

rebound ① /rɪ'baʊnd/ v.i. (a) (spring back) abprallen (from von) (b) (fig.) zurückfallen (upon auf + Akk.) ② /'riːbaʊnd/ n. Abprall, der

rebuff /rɪ'bʌf/ ① n. [schroffe] Abweisung ② v.t. [schroff] zurückweisen

rebuild /riː'bɪld/ v.t., **rebuilt** /riː'bɪlt/ wieder aufbauen

rebuke /rɪ'bjuːk/ ① v.t. tadeln, rügen (for wegen) ② n. Rüge, die

recall ① /rɪ'kɔːl/ v.t. (a) (remember) sich erinnern an (+ Akk.) (b) (serve as reminder of) erinnern an (+ Akk.) (c) abberufen ⟨Botschafter⟩ ② /rɪ'kɔːl, 'riːkɔːl/ n. (a) **[powers of] ∼:** Gedächtnis, das (b) **beyond ∼:** unwiderruflich

recant /rɪ'kænt/ v.i. [öffentlich] widerrufen

recap /'riːkæp/ v.t. & i., **-pp-** (coll.) rekapitulieren

recapitulate /riːkə'pɪtjʊleɪt/ v.t. & i. rekapitulieren

recapture /riː'kæptʃə(r)/ v.t. wieder ergreifen ⟨Gefangenen⟩; wieder einfangen ⟨Tier⟩

r

recede /rɪ'siːd/ *v.i.* ⟨*Hochwasser, Flut:*⟩ zurückgehen; ~ **[into the distance]** in der Ferne verschwinden

receding /rɪ'siːdɪŋ/ *adj.* fliehend ⟨*Kinn, Stirn*⟩

receipt /rɪ'siːt/ *n.* **(a)** (receiving) Empfang, *der* **(b)** (written acknowledgement) Quittung, *die* **(c)** *in pl.* (amount received) Einnahmen *Pl.* (from aus)

receive /rɪ'siːv/ *v.t.* **(a)** (get) erhalten; beziehen ⟨*Gehalt, Rente*⟩ **(b)** (accept) entgegennehmen ⟨*Strauß, Lieferung*⟩ **(c)** (entertain) empfangen ⟨*Gast*⟩

re'ceiver *n.* **(a)** Empfänger, *der*/ Empfängerin, *die* **(b)** (Teleph.) [Telefon]hörer, *der* **(c)** (of stolen goods) Hehler, *der*/Hehlerin, *die*

recent /'riːsənt/ *adj.* jüngst… ⟨*Ereignisse, Vergangenheit usw.*⟩; **the ~ closure of the factory** die kürzlich erfolgte Schließung der Fabrik

'recently *adv.* (a short time ago) vor kurzem; (in the recent past) in der letzten Zeit

receptacle /rɪ'septəkl/ *n.* Behälter, *der*; Gefäß, *das*

reception /rɪ'sepʃn/ *n.* **(a)** (welcome) Aufnahme, *die* **(b)** (party) Empfang, *der* **(c)** (Brit.: foyer) die Rezeption

reception: ~ com'mittee *n.* Empfangskomitee, *das*; **~ desk** *n.* Rezeption, *die*

re'ceptionist *n* (in hotel) Empfangschef, *der*/-dame, *die*; (at doctor's, dentist's) Sprechstundenhilfe, *die*

receptive /rɪ'septɪv/ *adj.* aufgeschlossen, empfänglich (**to** für)

recess /rɪ'ses, 'riːses/ *n.* **(a)** (alcove) Nische, *die* **(b)** (Brit. Parl.; Amer.: short vacation) Ferien *Pl.*; (Amer. Sch.; between classes) Pause, *die*

recession /rɪ'seʃn/ *n.* (Econ.) Rezession, *die* (fachspr.); Konjunkturrückgang, *der*

recharge /riː'tʃɑːdʒ/ *v.t.* aufladen ⟨*Batterie*⟩

rechargeable /riː'tʃɑːdʒəbl/ *adj.* wieder aufladbar

recipe /'resɪpɪ/ *n.* Rezept, *das*

recipient /rɪ'sɪpɪənt/ *n.* Empfänger, *der*/Empfängerin, *die*

reciprocal /rɪ'sɪprəkl/ *adj.* gegenseitig ⟨*Abkommen, Zuneigung*⟩

reciprocate /rɪ'sɪprəkeɪt/ *v.t.* erwidern

recital /rɪ'saɪtl/ *n.* (performance) [Solisten]konzert, *das*; (of literature also) Rezitation, *die*

recitation /resɪ'teɪʃn/ *n.* Rezitation, *die*

recite /rɪ'saɪt/ *v.t.* **(a)** rezitieren ⟨*Gedicht*⟩ **(b)** (list) aufzählen

reckless /'reklɪs/ *adj.* unbesonnen; rücksichtslos ⟨*Fahrweise*⟩; **~ of the**

dangers/consequences ungeachtet der Gefahren/Folgen

reckon /'rekn/ *v.t.* **(a)** (work out) ausrechnen ⟨*Kosten*⟩; bestimmen ⟨*Position*⟩ **(b)** (consider) halten (**as** für) **(c)** (estimate) schätzen

■ **'reckon on** *v.t.* **(a)** (rely on) zählen auf (+ *Akk.*) **(b)** (expect) rechnen mit

■ **'reckon with** *v.i.* rechnen mit

'reckoning *n.* Berechnung, *die*; **by my ~:** nach meiner Rechnung

reclaim /rɪ'kleɪm/ *v.t.* **(a)** zurückbekommen ⟨*Steuern*⟩ **(b)** urbar machen ⟨*Land*⟩

recline /rɪ'klaɪn/ *v.i.* liegen; **reclining seat** Liegesitz, *der*

recluse /rɪ'kluːs/ *n.* Einsiedler, *der*/Einsiedlerin, *die*

recognition /rekəg'nɪʃn/ *n.* **(a)** Wiedererkennen, *das*; **be beyond all ~:** nicht wieder zu erkennen sein **(b)** (acknowledgement) Anerkennung, *die*; **in ~ of** als Anerkennung für

recognize /'rekəgnaɪz/ *v.t.* **(a)** (know again) wieder erkennen (**by an** + *Dat.*, **from** durch) **(b)** (acknowledge) erkennen; anerkennen ⟨*Gültigkeit, Land*⟩; **be ~d as** gelten als

recoil ① /rɪ'kɔɪl/ *v.i.* zurückfahren ② /'riːkɔɪl, rɪ'kɔɪl/ *n.* Rückstoß, *der*

recollect /rekə'lekt/ ① *v.t.* sich erinnern an (+ *Akk.*) ② *v.i.* sich erinnern

recollection /rekə'lekʃn/ *n.* Erinnerung, *die*

recommend /rekə'mend/ *v.t.* empfehlen

recommendation /rekəmen'deɪʃn/ *n.* Empfehlung, *die*; **on sb.'s ~:** auf jmds. Empfehlung (*Akk.*)

recompense /'rekəmpens/ ① *v.t.* entschädigen ② *n.* Entschädigung, *die*

reconcile /'rekənsaɪl/ *v.t.* **(a)** (restore to friendship) versöhnen **(b)** **~ oneself to sth.** sich mit etw. versöhnen

reconciliation /rekənsɪlɪ'eɪʃn/ *n.* Versöhnung, *die*

recondition /riːkən'dɪʃn/ *v.t.* [general]überholen; **~ed engine** Austauschmotor, *der*

reconnaissance /rɪ'kɒnɪsəns/ *n.* (Mil.) Aufklärung, *die*

reconnoitre (Brit.; Amer.: **reconnoiter**) /rekə'nɔɪtə(r)/ *v.i.* auf Erkundung [aus]gehen

reconsider /riːkən'sɪdə(r)/ *v.t.* [noch einmal] überdenken

reconstruct /riːkən'strʌkt/ *v.t.* wieder aufbauen; (fig.) rekonstruieren

reconstruction /riːkən'strʌkʃn/ *n.* Wiederaufbau, *der*; (thing reconstructed) Rekonstruktion, *die*

record ☐1 /rɪˈkɔːd/ *v.t.* **(a)** aufzeichnen;
∼ **a new CD** eine neue CD aufnehmen
(b) (register officially) dokumentieren;
protokollieren ⟨*Verhandlung*⟩
☐2 /ˈrekɔːd/ *n.* **(a) be on** ∼ ⟨*Prozess,
Verhandlung, Besprechung:*⟩ protokolliert
sein; **have sth. on** ∼: etw. dokumentiert
haben
(b) (report) Protokoll, *das*
(c) (document) Dokument, *das;* **[strictly] off
the** ∼: [ganz] inoffiziell
(d) (for ∼ player) [Schall]platte, *die*
(e) have a [criminal/police] ∼: vorbestraft
sein
(f) (Sport) Rekord, *der*
record /ˈrekɔːd/: ∼**-breaking** *adj.*
Rekord-; ∼ **deck** *n.* Plattenspieler, *der*
recorded /rɪˈkɔːdɪd/ *adj.* aufgezeichnet
⟨*Konzert, Rede*⟩; ∼ **music** Musikaufnahmen
Pl.
recorded deˈlivery *n.* (Brit. Post.)
eingeschriebene Sendung (ohne Versicherung)
recorder /rɪˈkɔːdə(r)/ *n.* (Mus.) Blockflöte,
die
ˈ**record holder** *n.* (Sport) Rekordhalter,
der/-halterin, *die*
recording /rɪˈkɔːdɪŋ/ *n.* **(a)** (process)
Aufzeichnung, *die*
(b) (what is recorded) Aufnahme, *die*
recording: ∼ **head** *n.* Aufnahmekopf,
der; ∼ **studio** *n.* Tonstudio, *das*
record /ˈrekɔːd/: ∼ **player** *n.*
Plattenspieler, *der;* ∼ **sleeve** *n.*
Plattenhülle, *die;* ∼ **token** *n.* [Schall]platt
engutschein, *der*
re-count ☐1 /riːˈkaʊnt/ *v.t.* [noch einmal]
nachzählen
☐2 /ˈriːkaʊnt/ *n.* Nachzählung, *die*
recoup /rɪˈkuːp/ *v.t.* [wieder]
hereinbekommen ⟨*[Geld]einsatz*⟩
recourse /rɪˈkɔːs/ *n.* **have** ∼ **to sb./sth.** bei
jmdm./zu etw. Zuflucht nehmen
recover /rɪˈkʌvə(r)/ ☐1 *v.t.*
zurückbekommen
☐2 *v.i.* ∼ **from sth.** sich von etw.
[wieder] erholen; **be [fully]** ∼**ed** [völlig]
wiederhergestellt sein
recovery /rɪˈkʌvərɪ/ *n.* Erholung, *die;*
make a quick/good ∼: sich schnell/gut
erholen
recovery: ∼ **position** *n.* (Med.)
stabile Seitenlage; ∼ **vehicle** *n.*
Bergungsfahrzeug, *das*
recreation /rekrɪˈeɪʃn/ *n.*
Freizeitbeschäftigung, *die;* Hobby, *das*
recreational /rekrɪˈeɪʃənl/ *adj.* Freizeit-
recreational: ∼ ˈ**drug** *n.*
Freizeitdroge, *die;* ∼ ˈ**vehicle** *n.* (Amer.)
Wohnmobil, *das*
recreˈation centre *n.* Freizeitzentrum,
das
recrimination /rɪkrɪmɪˈneɪʃn/ *n.*
Gegenbeschuldigung, *die*

recruit /rɪˈkruːt/ ☐1 *n.* **(a)** (Mil.) Rekrut, *der*
(b) (new member) neues Mitglied
☐2 *v.t.* (Mil.: enlist) anwerben; (into party
etc.) werben ⟨*Mitglied*⟩; einstellen ⟨*neuen
Mitarbeiter*⟩
reˈcruitment *n.* (Mil.) Anwerbung, *die;* (of
new staff) Neueinstellung, *die;* ∼ **of members**
Mitgliederwerbung, *die*
rectangle /ˈrektæŋgl/ *n.* Rechteck, *das*
rectangular /rekˈtæŋgjʊlə(r)/ *adj.*
rechteckig
rector /ˈrektə(r)/ *n.* **(a)** Pfarrer, *der*
(b) (Univ.) Rektor, *der*/Rektorin, *die*
rectory /ˈrektərɪ/ *n.* Pfarrhaus, *das*
recuperate /rɪˈkjuːpəreɪt/ *v.i.* sich
erholen
recuperation /rɪkjuːpəˈreɪʃn/ *n.*
Erholung, *die*
recur /rɪˈkɜː(r)/ *v.i.,* **-rr-** sich wiederholen;
⟨*Krankheit:*⟩ wiederkehren; ⟨*Symptom:*⟩
wieder auftreten
recurrence /rɪˈkʌrəns/ *n.* Wiederholung,
die; (of illness, thought, feeling) Wiederkehr, *die;*
(of symptom) Wiederauftreten, *das*
recurrent /rɪˈkʌrənt/ *adj.* immer
wiederkehrend
recyclable /riːˈsaɪkləbl/ *adj.* recycelbar
recycle /riːˈsaɪkl/ *v.t.* wieder verwerten;
∼**d paper** Recyclingpapier, *das*
recycling /riːˈsaɪklɪŋ/ *n.* Recycling, *das*
red /red/ ☐1 *adj.* rot
☐2 *n.* **(a)** Rot, *das*
(b) (debt) **[be] in the** ∼: in den roten Zahlen
[sein]
red: ∼ ˈ**card** *n.* (Footb.) rote Karte, *die;*
Red ˈCrescent *n.* Roter Halbmond;
Red ˈCross *n.* Rotes Kreuz; ∼ˈ**currant**
n. [rote] Johannisbeere
redden /ˈredn/ *v.i.* ⟨*Gesicht, Himmel:*⟩ sich
röten; ⟨*Person:*⟩ rot werden
reddish /ˈredɪʃ/ *adj.* rötlich
redecorate /riːˈdekəreɪt/ *v.t.* renovieren;
(with wallpaper) neu tapezieren; (with paint) neu
streichen
redeem /rɪˈdiːm/ *v.t.* **(a)** [wieder] einlösen
⟨*Pfand*⟩; einlösen ⟨*Gutschein, Coupon*⟩
(b) (save) retten
redemption /rɪˈdempʃn/ *n.* (from sin)
Erlösung, *die*
redeploy /riːdɪˈplɔɪ/ *v.t.* woanders
einsetzen ⟨*Arbeitskräfte*⟩
red: ∼**-ˈhanded** *adj.* **catch sb.**
∼**-handed** jmdn. auf frischer Tat ertappen;
∼ ˈ**herring** *n.* (fig.) Ablenkungsmanöver,
das; ∼**-hot** *adj.* [rot] glühend
redial ☐1 /riːˈdaɪəl/ *v.t.* noch einmal
wählen ⟨*Telefonnummer*⟩
☐2 /ˈriːdaɪəl/ *n.* Wahlwiederholung, *die;*
∼ **button** Wahlwiederholungstaste, *die*
Red ˈIndian (Brit. dated) ☐1 *n.* Indianer,
der/Indianerin, *die;*
☐2 *adj.* Indianer-   ····⟩

redirect /riːdaɪˈrekt/ *v.t.* nachsenden ⟨*Post, Brief usw.*⟩; umleiten ⟨*Verkehr*⟩

rediscover /riːdɪˈskʌvə(r)/ *v.t.* wieder entdecken

redistribute /riːdɪˈstrɪbjuːt/ *v.t.* umverteilen ⟨*Besitz, Einkommen*⟩

redistribution /riːdɪstrɪˈbjuːʃn/ *n.* (of land, wealth) Umverteilung, *die*

red: ∼-'**letter day** *n.* großer Tag; ∼ '**light** *n.* rotes Warnlicht; (traffic light) rote Ampel; **drive through a** ∼ **light** bei Rot über die Ampel fahren; ∼-'**light district** *n.* Strich, *der* (salopp); ∼ **meat** *n.* dunkles Fleisch (*z.B. vom Rind*)

redo /riːˈduː/ *v.t. forms as* DO: noch einmal machen ⟨*Bett, Hausaufgabe*⟩; neu frisieren ⟨*Haare*⟩

redouble /riːˈdʌbl/ *v.t.* verdoppeln

red 'pepper *n.* rote Paprika[schote]

redress /rɪˈdres/ **1** *n.* Entschädigung, *die* **2** *v.t.* wieder gutmachen; ∼ **the balance** das Gleichgewicht wiederherstellen

red 'tape *n.* (fig.) [unnötige] Bürokratie

reduce /rɪˈdjuːs/ *v.t.* **(a)** senken ⟨*Preis, Gebühr, Fieber, Aufwendungen, Blutdruck usw.*⟩; reduzieren ⟨*Geschwindigkeit, Gewicht*⟩; **at** ∼**d prices** zu herabgesetzten Preisen
(b) ∼ **to silence/tears** verstummen lassen/zum Weinen bringen

reduction /rɪˈdʌkʃn/ *n.* (in price, costs, speed, etc.) Senkung, *die* (in *Gen.*); ∼ **in wages/weight** Lohnsenkung, *die*/ Gewichtsabnahme, *die*

redundancy /rɪˈdʌndənsɪ/ *n.* (Brit.) Arbeitslosigkeit, *die;* **redundancies** Entlassungen *Pl.;* **take** *or* **accept voluntary** ∼: seiner betriebsbedingten Kündigung zustimmen; ∼ **payment** Abfindung, *die*

redundant /rɪˈdʌndənt/ *adj.* (Brit.) arbeitslos; **be made** ∼: den Arbeitsplatz verlieren; **make** ∼: entlassen

red 'wine *n.* Rotwein, *der*

reed /riːd/ *n.* Schilf[rohr], *das*

re-educate /riːˈedjʊkeɪt/ *v.t.* umerziehen

reef /riːf/ *n.* Riff, *das*

'**reef knot** *n.* Kreuzknoten, *der*

reek /riːk/ *v.i.* stinken (**of** nach)

reel /riːl/ **1** *n.* ⟨*Garn-, Angel*⟩rolle, *die;* ⟨*Film-, Tonband*⟩spule, *die* **2** *v.i.* **(a)** (be in a whirl) sich drehen **(b)** (sway) torkeln

re-establish /riːɪˈstæblɪʃ/ *v.t.* wiederherstellen

re-examine /riːɪgˈzæmɪn/ *v.t.* (scrutinize) erneut überprüfen

ref /ref/ *n.* (Sport coll.) Schiri, *der* (Sportjargon)

ref. *abbr.* = **reference** Verw.; **your/our ref.** Ihr/unser Zeichen

refashion /riːˈfæʃn/ *v.t.* umgestalten

refectory /rɪˈfektərɪ/ *n.* Mensa, *die*

refer /rɪˈfɜː(r)/ **1** *v.i.*, **-rr-:** **(a)** ∼ **to** (allude to) sich beziehen auf (+ *Akk.*) ⟨*Buch, Person usw.*⟩; (speak of) sprechen von ⟨*Person, Problem usw.*⟩
(b) ∼ **to** (apply to, relate to) betreffen
(c) ∼ **to** (consult, cite as proof) nachsehen in (+ *Dat.*)
2 *v.t.*, **-rr-:** ∼ **sb./sth. to sb./sth.** an jmdn./auf etw. (*Akk.*) verweisen

referee /refəˈriː/ (Sport) **1** *n.* (umpire) Schiedsrichter, *der*/-richterin, *die;* (Boxing) Ringrichter, *der*
2 *v.t.* als Schiedsrichter/-richterin leiten

reference /ˈrefrəns/ *n.* **(a)** (allusion) Hinweis, *der* (**to** auf + *Akk.*); **make no** ∼ **to sth.** etw. nicht ansprechen
(b) (testimonial) Zeugnis, *das*

reference: ∼ **book** *n.* Nachschlagewerk, *das;* ∼ **number** *n.* [Kenn]nummer, *die;* ∼ **point** *n.* Bezugspunkt, *der*

referendum /refəˈrendəm/ *n.* Volksentscheid, *der*

refill 1 /riːˈfɪl/ *v.t.* nachfüllen; ∼ **the glasses** nachschenken
2 /ˈriːfɪl/ *n.* (for ball pen) Ersatzmine, *die*

refine /rɪˈfaɪn/ *v.t.* **(a)** (purify) raffinieren
(b) (make cultured) kultivieren
(c) (improve) verbessern; verfeinern ⟨*Stil, Technik*⟩

refined /rɪˈfaɪnd/ *adj.* kultiviert

re'finement *n.* Kultiviertheit, *die;* (improvement) Verbesserung, *die*

refinery /rɪˈfaɪnərɪ/ *n.* Raffinerie, *die*

reflate /riːˈfleɪt/ *v.t.* (Econ.) ankurbeln

reflation /riːˈfleɪʃn/ *n.* (Econ.) Reflation, *die*

reflect /rɪˈflekt/ *v.t.* **(a)** reflektieren
(b) (fig.) widerspiegeln ⟨*Ansichten*⟩
(c) (contemplate) nachdenken über (+ *Akk.*); ∼ **what/how …:** überlegen, was/wie …
▪ **re'flect [up]on** *v.t.* **(a)** (consider) nachdenken über (+ *Akk.*)
(b) ∼ **badly [up]on sb./sth.** auf jmdn./etw. ein schlechtes Licht werfen

reflection /rɪˈflekʃn/ *n.* **(a)** Reflexion, *die;* (by surface of water) Spiegelung, *die*
(b) (image) Spiegelbild, *das*
(c) (consideration) Nachdenken, *das* (**upon** über + *Akk.*); **on** ∼: bei weiterem Nachdenken

reflective /rɪˈflektɪv/ *adj.*
(a) reflektierend
(b) (thoughtful) nachdenklich

reflector /rɪˈflektə(r)/ *n.* Rückstrahler, *der*

reflex /ˈriːfleks/ **1** *n.* Reflex, *der* **2** *adj.* ∼ **action** Reflexhandlung, *die*

reflexive /rɪˈfleksɪv/ *adj.* (Ling.) reflexiv

reforestation /riːfɒrɪˈsteɪʃn/ *n.* Wiederaufforstung, *die*

reform /rɪˈfɔːm/ **1** *v.t.* (make better) bessern ⟨*Person*⟩; reformieren ⟨*Institution*⟩
2 *n.* Reform, *die* (**in** *Gen.*)

reformation /refə'meɪʃn/ *n.* (of character) Wandlung, *die;* the R~ (Hist.) die Reformation

re'former *n.* [political] ~: Reformpolitiker, *der*/-politikerin, *die*

refract /rɪ'frækt/ *v.t.* (Phys.) brechen

refrain¹ /rɪ'freɪn/ *n.* Refrain, *der*

refrain² *v.i.* ~ from doing sth. es unterlassen, etw. zu tun

refresh /rɪ'freʃ/ *v.t.* erfrischen

re'fresher course *n.* Auffrischungskurs, *der*

re'freshing *adj.* erfrischend; wohltuend ⟨Abwechslung⟩

re'freshment *n.* Erfrischung, *die*

refrigerate /rɪ'frɪdʒəreɪt/ *v.t.* (a) kühl lagern ⟨Lebensmittel⟩
(b) (chill) kühlen; (freeze) einfrieren

refrigeration /rɪfrɪdʒə'reɪʃn/ *n.* kühle Lagerung; (chilling) Kühlung, *die;* (freezing) Einfrieren, *das*

refrigerator /rɪ'frɪdʒəreɪtə(r)/ *n.* Kühlschrank, *der*

refuel /ri:'fju:əl/, (Brit.) -ll-: ① *v.t.* auftanken
② *v.i.* [auf]tanken

refuge /'refju:dʒ/ *n.* Zuflucht, *die;* take ~ in Schutz *od.* Zuflucht suchen in (+ *Dat.*) (from vor + *Dat.*); women's ~: Frauenhaus, *das*

refugee /refjʊ'dʒi:/ *n.* Flüchtling, *der*

refu'gee camp *n.* Flüchtlingslager, *das*

refund ① /ri:'fʌnd/ *v.t.* (pay back) zurückzahlen ⟨Geld⟩; erstatten ⟨Kosten⟩
② /'ri:fʌnd/ *n.* Rückzahlung, *die;* (of expenses) [Rück]erstattung, *die*

refundable /ri:'fʌndəbl/ *adj.* be ~: zurückerstattet werden

refurbish /ri:'fɜ:bɪʃ/ *v.t.* renovieren ⟨Haus⟩

refurnish /ri:'fɜ:nɪʃ/ *v.t.* neu einrichten

refusal /rɪ'fju:zl/ *n.* Ablehnung, *die;* (after a period of time) Absage, *die;* ~ to do sth. Weigerung, etw. zu tun

refuse¹ /rɪ'fju:z/ ① *v.t.* ablehnen; verweigern ⟨Zutritt, Einreise, Erlaubnis⟩; ~ sb. admittance/entry/permission jmdm. den Zutritt/die Einreise/die Erlaubnis verweigern; ~ to do sth. sich weigern, etw. zu tun
② *v.i.* ablehnen; (after request) sich weigern

refuse² /'refju:s/ *n.* Abfall, *der*

refuse /'refju:s/: ~ **collection** *n.* Müllabfuhr, *die;* ~ **collector** *n.* Müllwerker, *der;* ~ **disposal** *n.* Abfallbeseitigung, *die*

refute /rɪ'fju:t/ *v.t.* widerlegen

regain /rɪ'geɪn/ *v.t.* zurückgewinnen ⟨Zuversicht, Vertrauen, Augenlicht⟩; ~ one's strength wieder zu Kräften kommen

regal /'ri:gl/ *adj.* majestätisch

regalia /rɪ'geɪlɪə/ *n. pl.* (of royalty) Krönungsinsignien *Pl.*

regard /rɪ'gɑ:d/ ① *v.t.* (a) (look at) betrachten
(b) (give heed to) beachten
(c) (fig.: look upon, contemplate) betrachten; ~ sb. as a friend/fool/genius jmdn. als Freund betrachten/für einen Dummkopf/ ein Genie halten; be ~ed as gelten als
(d) (concern, have relation to) betreffen; as ~s sb./sth., ~ing sb./sth. was jmdn./etw. angeht *od.* betrifft
② *n.* (a) (attention) pay *or* have ~ to sb./sth. jmdm./etw. Beachtung schenken; without ~ to ohne Rücksicht auf (+ *Akk.*)
(b) (esteem) Achtung, *die;* hold sb./sth. in high ~: jmdn./etw. sehr schätzen
(c) *in pl.* Grüße *Pl.* give her my ~s grüße sie von mir; with kind[est] ~s mit herzlich[st]en Grüßen

re'gardless *adj.* ohne Rücksicht (of auf + *Akk.*)

regatta /rɪ'gætə/ *n.* Regatta, *die*

regenerate /rɪ'dʒenəreɪt/ *v.t.* erneuern

reggae /'regeɪ/ *n.* Reggae, *der*

regime, régime /reɪ'ʒi:m/ *n.* [Regierungs]system, *das*

re'gime change *n., no pl.* Regimewechsel, *der*

regiment /'redʒɪmənt/ *n.* Regiment, *das*

regimental /redʒɪ'mentl/ *adj.* Regiments-

region /'ri:dʒn/ *n.* (a) (area) Gebiet, *das*
(b) (administrative division) Bezirk, *der;* in the ~ of (fig.) ungefähr

regional /'ri:dʒənl/ *adj.* regional

regionalism /'ri:dʒənəlɪzm/ *n.* (Polit., Ling.) Regionalismus, *der*

regionalize /'ri:dʒənəlaɪz/ *v.t.* regionalisieren

register /'redʒɪstə(r)/ ① *n.* Register, *das;* (at school) Klassenbuch, *das*
② *v.t.* (a) (enter) registrieren; (cause to be entered) registrieren lassen; anmelden ⟨Auto, Patent⟩; (at airport) einchecken ⟨Gepäck⟩; *abs.* (at hotel) sich ins Fremdenbuch eintragen; ~ with the police sich polizeilich anmelden
(b) (enrol) anmelden; (Univ.) sich einschreiben
(c) zum Ausdruck bringen ⟨Überraschung⟩; ~ a protest Protest anmelden

registered /'redʒɪstəd/ *adj.* eingetragen ⟨Firma⟩; eingeschrieben ⟨Student, Brief⟩; ~ trade mark eingetragenes Warenzeichen; by ~ post per Einschreiben

registrar /'redʒɪstrɑ:(r)/ *n.* Standesbeamte, *der*/-beamtin, *die*

registration /redʒɪ'streɪʃn/ *n.* Registrierung, *die;* (enrolment) Anmeldung, *die;* (of students) Einschreibung, *die*

registration: ~ **document** *n.* (Brit.) Kraftfahrzeugbrief, *der;* ~ **form** *n.* Anmeldeformular, *das;* ~ **number** *n.* amtliches Kennzeichen; ~ **plate** *n.* (Motor Veh.) Nummernschild, *das*

r

registry /'redʒɪstrɪ/ n. ~ [office]
Standesamt, das
regret /rɪ'gret/ ① v.t., -tt- bedauern; I ~ to
say that ...: ich muss leider sagen, dass ...
② n. Bedauern, das; have no ~s nichts
bereuen
regretfully /rɪ'gretfəlɪ/ adv. mit Bedauern
regrettable /rɪ'gretəbl/ adj. bedauerlich
regrettably /rɪ'gretəblɪ/ adv.
bedauerlicherweise
regroup /ri:'gru:p/ ① v.t. umgruppieren
② v.i. (a) (form new group) sich neu
gruppieren
(b) (Mil.) sich neu formieren
regular /'regjʊlə(r)/ ① adj. regelmäßig;
geregelt ⟨Arbeit⟩; fest ⟨Anstellung⟩;
~ customer Stammkunde, der/-kundin, die;
~ army reguläre Armee
② n. (coll.: ~ customer) Stammkunde, der/
-kundin, die; (in pub) Stammgast, der
regularity /regjʊ'lærɪtɪ/ n.
Regelmäßigkeit, die
'regularly adv. regelmäßig
regulate /'regjʊleɪt/ v.t. (control) regeln;
(restrict) begrenzen; (adjust) regulieren
regulation /regjʊ'leɪʃn/ n.
(a) ▶ REGULATE: Regelung, die; Begrenzung,
die; Regulierung, die
(b) (rule) Vorschrift, die
rehabilitate /ri:hə'bɪlɪteɪt/ v.t.
rehabilitieren; ~ [back into society] wieder
[in die Gesellschaft] eingliedern
rehabilitation /ri:həbɪlɪ'teɪʃn/ n. ~ [in
society] Wiedereingliederung, die [in die
Gesellschaft]
rehash ① /ri:'hæʃ/ v.t. aufwärmen
② /'ri:hæʃ/ n. Aufguss, der
rehearsal /rɪ'hɜːsl/ n. Probe, die
rehearse /rɪ'hɜːs/ v.t. proben
reheat /ri:'hiːt/ v.t. wieder erwärmen;
aufwärmen ⟨Essen⟩
rehouse /ri:'haʊz/ v.t. umquartieren
reign /reɪn/ ① n. Herrschaft, die
② v.i. herrschen (over über + Akk.)
reimburse /ri:ɪm'bɜːs/ v.t.
[zurück]erstatten ⟨[Un]kosten, Spesen⟩;
entschädigen ⟨Person⟩
rein /reɪn/ n. Zügel, der
reincarnation /ri:ɪnkɑː'neɪʃn/ n. (Relig.)
Reinkarnation, die
reindeer /'reɪndɪə(r)/ n., pl. same
Ren[tier], das
reinforce /ri:ɪn'fɔːs/ v.t. verstärken; ~d
concrete Stahlbeton, der
rein'forcement n. Verstärkung, die;
~[s] (additional men etc.) Verstärkung, die
reinstate /ri:ɪn'steɪt/ v.t. (in job) wieder
einstellen
reintegrate /ri:'ɪntɪgreɪt/ ① v.t. wieder
eingliedern (into in + Akk.)
② v. refl. sich wieder eingliedern (into in
+ Akk.)

reintegration /ri:ɪntɪ'greɪʃn/ n.
Wiedereingliederung, die (into in + Akk.)
reinvigorate /ri:ɪn'vɪgəreɪt/ v.t. neu
beleben; feel ~d sich gestärkt fühlen
reissue /ri:'ɪʃuː/ v.t. neu herausbringen
reiterate /ri:'ɪtəreɪt/ v.t. wiederholen
reject ① /rɪ'dʒekt/ v.t. ablehnen;
zurückweisen ⟨Bitte, Annäherungsversuch⟩
② /'ri:dʒekt/ (thing) Ausschuss, der
rejection /rɪ'dʒekʃn/ n. Ablehnung,
die/Zurückweisung, die
re'jection slip n. Absage, die
rejoice /rɪ'dʒɔɪs/ v.i. sich freuen (over, at
über + Akk.)
rejoin¹ /rɪ'dʒɔɪn/ v.t. (reply) erwidern (to
auf + Akk.)
rejoin² /ri:'dʒɔɪn/ v.t. wieder eintreten in
(+ Akk.) ⟨Partei, Verein⟩
rejoinder /rɪ'dʒɔɪndə(r)/ n. Erwiderung,
die (to auf + Akk.)
rejuvenate /rɪ'dʒuːvəneɪt/ v.t. verjüngen
rekindle /ri:'kɪndl/ v.t. wieder anfachen;
wieder aufleben lassen ⟨Verlangen,
Hoffnungen⟩
relapse /rɪ'læps/ ① v.i. ⟨Kranker:⟩ einen
Rückfall bekommen
② n. Rückfall, der
relate /rɪ'leɪt/ ① v.t. (a) erzählen
⟨Geschichte⟩; erzählen von ⟨Abenteuer⟩
(b) (bring into relation) in Zusammenhang
bringen (to, with mit)
② v.i. (a) ~ to (have reference to) in
Zusammenhang stehen mit; betreffen
⟨Person⟩
(b) ~ to (feel involved with) eine Beziehung
haben zu
re'lated adj. verwandt (to mit)
relation /rɪ'leɪʃn/ n. (a) (connection)
Beziehung, die, Zusammenhang, der (of ...
and zwischen ... und); in or with ~ to in
Bezug auf (+ Akk.)
(b) in pl. (dealings) Verhältnis, das (with zu)
(c) (relative) Verwandte, der/die
re'lationship n. (a) (mutual tie) Beziehung,
die (with zu)
(b) (kinship) Verwandtschaftsverhältnis, das
(c) (connection) Beziehung, die; (between cause
and effect) Zusammenhang, der
(d) (sexual) Verhältnis, das
relative /'relətɪv/ ① n. Verwandte,
der/die
② adj. relativ; Relativ⟨satz, -pronomen⟩
'relatively adv. relativ; verhältnismäßig
relative 'pronoun n. (Ling.)
Relativpronomen, das
relax /rɪ'læks/ ① v.t. (a) entspannen
⟨Muskel, Körper[teil]⟩; lockern ⟨Griff⟩
(b) (make less strict) lockern ⟨Gesetz,
Disziplin⟩
② v.i. sich entspannen
relaxation /ri:læk'seɪʃn/ n. Entspannung,
die; for ~: zur Entspannung

relaxed /rɪˈlækst/ *adj.* entspannt, gelöst ⟨*Atmosphäre, Person*⟩

reˈlaxing *adj.* entspannend

relay ① /ˈriːleɪ/ *n.* **(a)** (race) Staffel, *die* **(b)** (gang) Schicht, *die;* **work in ~s** schichtweise arbeiten **(c)** (Electr.) Relais, *das* ② /riːˈleɪ/ *v.t.* **(a)** weiterleiten **(b)** (Radio, Telev.) übertragen

ˈrelay race *n.* Staffellauf, *der;* (Swimming) Staffelschwimmen, *das*

release /rɪˈliːs/ ① *v.t.* **(a)** (free) freilassen ⟨*Tier, Häftling, Sklaven*⟩; (from jail) entlassen **(from** aus) **(b)** (let go) loslassen; lösen ⟨*Handbremse*⟩ **(c)** (make known) veröffentlichen ⟨*Erklärung, Nachricht*⟩; (issue) herausbringen ⟨*Film, Schallplatte*⟩ ② *n.* **(a)** ▶ 1A: Freilassung, *die;* Entlassung, *die* **(b)** (of published item) Veröffentlichung, *die* **(c)** (handle, lever, button) Auslöser, *der*

relegate /ˈrelɪɡeɪt/ *v.t.* **(a)** **~ sb. to the position of …:** jmdn. zu … degradieren **(b)** (Sport) absteigen lassen; **be ~d** absteigen **(to** in + *Akk.*)

relegation /relɪˈɡeɪʃn/ *n.* (Sport) Abstieg, *der*

relent /rɪˈlent/ *v.i.* nachgeben

reˈlentless *adj.,* **reˈlentlessly** *adv.* unerbittlich

relevance /ˈrelɪvəns/ *n.* Relevanz, *die* **(to** für)

relevant /ˈrelɪvənt/ *adj.* relevant **(to** für); wichtig ⟨*Information*⟩

reliability /rɪlaɪəˈbɪlɪtɪ/ *n.* Zuverlässigkeit, *die*

reliable /rɪˈlaɪəbl/ *adj.,* **reliably** /rɪˈlaɪəblɪ/ *adv.* zuverlässig

reliance /rɪˈlaɪəns/ *n.* Abhängigkeit, *die* **(on** von)

reliant /rɪˈlaɪənt/ *adj.* **be ~ on sb./sth.** auf jmdn./etw. angewiesen sein

relief[1] /rɪˈliːf/ *n.* **(a)** Erleichterung, *die;* **give [sb.] ~ [from pain]** [jmdm.] [Schmerz]linderung verschaffen; **what a ~!, that's a ~!** da bin ich aber erleichtert! **(b)** (assistance) Hilfe, *die*

relief[2] *n.* (Art) Relief, *das*

relief: ~ bus *n.* Entlastungsbus, *der;* (as replacement) Ersatzbus, *der;* **~ map** *n.* Reliefkarte, *die;* **~ road** *n.* Entlastungsstraße, *die;* **~ worker** *n.* Helfer, *der*

relieve /rɪˈliːv/ *v.t.* **(a)** erleichtern; unterbrechen ⟨*Eintönigkeit*⟩; abbauen ⟨*Anspannung*⟩; stillen ⟨*Schmerzen*⟩; **I am** *or* **feel ~d to hear that …:** es erleichtert mich zu hören, dass … **(b)** ablösen ⟨*Wache, Truppen*⟩

religion /rɪˈlɪdʒn/ *n.* Religion, *die*

religious /rɪˈlɪdʒəs/ *adj.* religiös; Religions⟨*freiheit, -unterricht*⟩

reˈligiously *adv.* (conscientiously) gewissenhaft

relinquish /rɪˈlɪŋkwɪʃ/ *v.t.* **(a)** (give up) aufgeben **(b)** **~ one's hold** *or* **grip on sb./sth.** jmdn./etw. loslassen

relish /ˈrelɪʃ/ ① *n.* **(a)** (liking) Vorliebe, *die;* **do sth. with [great] ~:** etw. mit [großem] Genuss tun **(b)** (condiment) Relish, *das* ② *v.t.* genießen

relive /riːˈlɪv/ *v.t.* noch einmal durchleben

reload /riːˈləʊd/ *v.t.* nachladen ⟨*Schusswaffe*⟩

relocate /riːləˈkeɪt/ ① *v.t.* verlegen ⟨*Fabrik, Büro*⟩; versetzen ⟨*Angestellten*⟩ ② *v.i.* (settle) sich niederlassen

relocation /riːləˈkeɪʃn/ *n.* (of factory, office) Verlegung, *die;* (of employee) Versetzung, *die;* **~ expenses** Umzugskosten *Pl.*

reluctance /rɪˈlʌktəns/ *n.* Widerwille, *der;* **have a [great] ~ to do sth.** etw. nur mit Widerwillen tun

reluctant /rɪˈlʌktənt/ *adj.* unwillig; **be ~ to do sth.** etw. nur ungern tun

reˈluctantly *adv.* nur ungern

rely /rɪˈlaɪ/ *v.i.* (have trust) sich verlassen/(be dependent) angewiesen sein ([up]on auf + *Akk.*)

remain /rɪˈmeɪn/ *v.i.* **(a)** (be left over) übrigbleiben **(b)** (stay) bleiben; **~ behind** noch dableiben **(c)** (continue to be) bleiben; **it ~s to be seen** es wird sich zeigen

remainder /rɪˈmeɪndə(r)/ *n.* Rest, *der*

reˈmaining *adj.* restlich

reˈmains *n. pl.* **(a)** Reste *Pl.* **(b)** (human) sterbliche [Über]reste *Pl.* (verhüll.)

remand /rɪˈmɑːnd/ ① *v.t.* **~ sb. [in custody]** jmdn. in Untersuchungshaft behalten ② *n.* **on ~:** in Untersuchungshaft

remark /rɪˈmɑːk/ ① *v.t.* bemerken **(to** gegenüber) ② *v.i.* eine Bemerkung machen ([up]on zu, über + *Akk.*) ③ *n.* Bemerkung, *die* **(on** über + *Akk.*)

remarkable /rɪˈmɑːkəbl/ *adj.* **(a)** (notable) bemerkenswert **(b)** (extraordinary) außergewöhnlich

remarkably /rɪˈmɑːkəblɪ/ *adv.* **(a)** (notably) bemerkenswert **(b)** (exceptionally) außergewöhnlich

remarry /riːˈmærɪ/ *v.i. & t.* wieder heiraten

remedy /ˈremɪdɪ/ ① *n.* [Heil]mittel, *das* **(for** gegen) ② *v.t.* beheben ⟨*Problem*⟩; retten ⟨*Situation*⟩

remember /rɪˈmembə(r)/ *v.t.* **(a)** sich erinnern an (+ *Akk.*); **I ~ed to bring the book** ich habe daran gedacht, das Buch mitzubringen; **an evening to ~:** ein unvergesslicher Abend ⋯⟶

(b) (convey greetings) ~ me to them grüße sie von mir

remembrance /rɪ'membrəns/ n. Gedenken, *das;* in ~ of sb. zu jmds. Gedächtnis

Remembrance Day, Remembrance Sunday ns. (Brit.) ≈ Volkstrauertag, *der*

remind /rɪ'maɪnd/ v.t. erinnern (of an + *Akk.*); ~ sb. to do sth. jmdn. daran erinnern, etw. zu tun; **that ~s me, …:** dabei fällt mir ein, …

re'minder n. Erinnerung, *die* (of an + *Akk.*); (letter) Mahnung, *die;* Mahnbrief, *der*

reminisce /remɪ'nɪs/ v.i. sich in Erinnerungen (*Dat.*) ergehen (about an + *Akk.*)

reminiscences /remɪ'nɪsənsɪz/ n. pl. Erinnerungen Pl. (memoirs) [Lebens]erinnerungen Pl.

reminiscent /remɪ'nɪsənt/ adj. be ~ of sth. an etw. (*Akk.*) erinnern

remiss /rɪ'mɪs/ adj. nachlässig (of von)

remission /rɪ'mɪʃn/ n. **(a)** (of debt, punishment) Erlass, *der* **(b)** (of prison sentence) Straferlass, *der*

remit /rɪ'mɪt/ v.t., **-tt-** (send) überweisen ⟨*Geld*⟩

remittance /rɪ'mɪtəns/ n. Überweisung, *die*

remnant /'remnənt/ n. Rest, *der*

remonstrate /'remənstreɪt/ v.i. protestieren (against gegen); ~ with sb. jmdm. Vorhaltungen machen (about, on wegen)

remorse /rɪ'mɔːs/ n. Reue, *die* (for, about über + *Akk.*)

re'morseful /rɪ'mɔːsfl/ adj. reumütig

re'morseless adj. unerbittlich

remote /rɪ'məʊt/ adj., ~r /rɪ'məʊtə(r)/, ~st /rɪ'məʊtɪst/ **(a)** fern ⟨*Vergangenheit, Zukunft, Zeit*⟩; abgelegen ⟨*Ort, Gebiet*⟩; ~ from weit entfernt von **(b)** (slight) gering ⟨*Chance*⟩

remote: ~ **con'trol** n. (of vehicle) Fernlenkung, *die;* (for TV set) Fernbedienung, *die;* ~-**con'trol[led]** adj. ferngelenkt; fernbedient ⟨*Anlage*⟩

re'motely adv. entfernt ⟨*verwandt*⟩; **they are not ~ alike** sie haben nicht die entfernteste Ähnlichkeit miteinander

removable /rɪ'muːvəbl/ adj. abnehmbar; entfernbar ⟨*Trennwand*⟩; herausnehmbar ⟨*Futter*⟩

removal /rɪ'muːvl/ n. **(a)** Entfernung, *die;* (of obstacle, problem) Beseitigung, *die* **(b)** (transfer of furniture) Umzug, *der*

removal: ~ **expenses** n. pl. Umzugskosten Pl.; ~ **firm** n. Spedition, *die;* ~ **man** n. Möbelpacker, *der;* ~ **van** n. Möbelwagen, *der*

remove /rɪ'muːv/ v.t. entfernen; beseitigen

⟨*Spur, Hindernis*⟩; (take off) abnehmen; ausziehen ⟨*Kleidungsstück*⟩; ~ **a book from the shelf** ein Buch vom Regal nehmen

re'mover n. **(a)** (of paint/varnish/hair/rust) Farb-/Lack-/Haar-/Rostentferner, *der* **(b)** (man) Möbelpacker, *der;* **[firm of]** ~s Spedition[sfirma], *die*

remunerate /rɪ'mjuːnəreit/ v.t. bezahlen

remuneration /rɪmjuːnə'reɪʃn/ n. Bezahlung, *die*

Renaissance /rə'neɪsəns, rɪ'neɪsəns/ n. (Hist.) Renaissance, *die*

rename /riː'neɪm/ v.t. umbenennen

render /'rendə(r)/ v.t. **(a)** (make) machen **(b)** erweisen ⟨*Dienst*⟩ **(c)** (translate) übersetzen (by mit)

'rendering n. (translation) Übersetzung, *die*

rendezvous /'rɒndeɪvuː/ n., pl. same /'rɒndeɪvuːz/ **(a)** (meeting place) Treffpunkt, *der* **(b)** (meeting) Verabredung, *die*

renegade /'renɪgeɪd/ **1** n. Abtrünnige, *der/die* **2** adj. abtrünnig

renegotiate /riːnɪ'gəʊʃieɪt/ v.t. neu aushandeln

renew /rɪ'njuː/ v.t. erneuern; fortsetzen ⟨*Angriff, Bemühungen*⟩; (extend) erneuern ⟨*Vertrag, Ausweis usw.*⟩; ~ **a library book** ⟨*Bibliothekar/Benutzer:*⟩ ein Buch [aus der Bücherei] verlängern/verlängern lassen

re'newable /rɪ'njuːəbl/ adj. regenerationsfähig ⟨*Energiequelle*⟩; verlängerbar ⟨*Vertrag, Genehmigung, Ausweis*⟩

renewal /rɪ'njuːəl/ n. Erneuerung, *die*

renounce /rɪ'naʊns/ v.t. verzichten auf (+ *Akk.*); verstoßen ⟨*Person*⟩; ~ **the devil/one's faith** dem Teufel/seinem Glauben abschwören

renovate /'renəveit/ v.t. renovieren ⟨*Gebäude*⟩; restaurieren ⟨*Möbel usw.*⟩

renovation /renə'veɪʃn/ n. ▶ RENOVATE: Renovierung, *die;* Restaurierung, *die*

renown /rɪ'naʊn/ n. Renommee, *das*

renowned /rɪ'naʊnd/ adj. berühmt (for wegen, für)

rent /rent/ **1** n. (for house etc.) Miete, *die;* (for land) Pacht, *die* **2** v.t. **(a)** (use) mieten ⟨*Haus, Wohnung usw.*⟩; pachten ⟨*Land*⟩; mieten ⟨*Auto*⟩ **(b)** (let) vermieten ⟨*Haus, Auto usw.*⟩ (to Dat., an + Akk.); verpachten ⟨*Land*⟩ (to Dat., an + Akk.)

■ **rent 'out** v.t. ▶ RENT 2B

rental /'rentl/ n. Miete, *die*

rent: ~ **boy** n. (coll.) Strichjunge, *der* (salopp); ~ **rebate** n. Mietermäßigung, *die;* ~ **tribunal** n. Mietgericht, *das*

renunciation /rɪnʌnsɪ'eɪʃn/ n. ▶ RENOUNCE: Verzicht, *der;* Verstoßung, *die*

reopen /riː'əʊpn/ ① *v.t.* wieder öffnen; wieder aufmachen; wieder eröffnen ⟨*Geschäft, Lokal usw.*⟩; wieder aufnehmen ⟨*Diskussion, Verhandlung*⟩
② *v.i.* ⟨*Geschäft, Lokal usw.:*⟩ wieder öffnen

reorder /riː'ɔːdə(r)/ *v.t.* **(a)** (Commerc.) nachbestellen ⟨*Ware*⟩
(b) (rearrange) umordnen

reorganization /riːɔːgənaɪ'zeɪʃn/ *n.* Umorganisation, *die;* (of time, work) Neueinteilung, *die*

reorganize /riː'ɔːgənaɪz/ *v.t.* umorganisieren; neu einteilen ⟨*Zeit, Arbeit*⟩

rep /rep/ *n.* (coll.: representative) Vertreter, *der*/Vertreterin, *die*

repaid ▶ REPAY

repair /rɪ'peə(r)/ ① *v.t.* (mend) reparieren; ausbessern ⟨*Kleidung, Straße*⟩
② *n.* Reparatur, *die;* **be in good/bad ~:** in gutem/schlechtem Zustand sein

repair: ~ man *n.* Mechaniker, *der;* (in house) Handwerker, *der;* **~ shop** *n.* Reparaturwerkstatt, *die*

repaper /riː'peɪpə(r)/ *v.t.* neu tapezieren

repatriate /riː'pætrɪeɪt/ *v.t.* repatriieren

repatriation /riːpætrɪ'eɪʃn/ *n.* Repatriierung, *die*

repay /riː'peɪ/ *v.t.,* **repaid** /riː'peɪd/ zurückzahlen ⟨*Schulden usw.*⟩; erwidern ⟨*Besuch, Gruß, Freundlichkeit*⟩; **~ sb. for sth.** jmdm. etw. vergelten

re'payment *n.* Rückzahlung, *die*

re'payment mortgage *n.* Tilgungshypothek, *die*

repeal /rɪ'piːl/ ① *v.t.* aufheben ⟨*Gesetz, Erlass usw.*⟩
② *n.* Aufhebung, *die*

repeat /rɪ'piːt/ ① *n.* Wiederholung, *die*
② *v.t.* wiederholen; **please ~ after me:** ...: sprich/sprecht/sprechen Sie mir bitte nach: ...

re'peated *adj.* wiederholt; (several) mehrere; **make ~ efforts to** ...: wiederholt *od.* mehrfach versuchen, ...zu...

re'peatedly *adv.* mehrmals

repel /rɪ'pel/ *v.t.,* **-ll-: (a)** (drive back) abwehren
(b) (be repulsive to) abstoßen

repellent /rɪ'pelənt/ ① *adj.* abstoßend
② *n.* **[insect] ~:** Insektenschutzmittel, *das*

repent /rɪ'pent/ *v.i.* bereuen (**of** *Akk.*)

repentance /rɪ'pentəns/ *n.* Reue, *die*

repentant /rɪ'pentənt/ *adj.* reuig

repercussion /riːpə'kʌʃn/ *n.,* usu. in pl. Auswirkung, *die* (**[up]on** auf + *Akk.*)

repertoire /'repətwɑː(r)/ *n.* Repertoire, *das*

repertory /'repətərɪ/ *n.* (Theatre) Repertoiretheater, *das*

'repertory company *n.* Repertoiretheater, *das*

repetition /repɪ'tɪʃn/ *n.* Wiederholung, *die*

repetitious /repɪ'tɪʃəs/ *adj.* sich immer wiederholend *attr.*

repetitive /rɪ'petɪtɪv/ *adj.* eintönig

repetitive 'strain injury *n.* chronisches Überlastungssyndrom

rephrase /riː'freɪz/ *v.t.* umformulieren; **I'll ~ that** ich will es anders ausdrücken

replace /rɪ'pleɪs/ *v.t.* **(a)** (vertically) zurückstellen; (horizontally) zurücklegen
(b) (take place of) ersetzen; **~ A with** *or* **by B** A durch B ersetzen
(c) (exchange) austauschen, auswechseln ⟨*Maschinen[teile] usw.*⟩

re'placement *n.*
(a) ▶ REPLACE A: Zurückstellen, *das;* Zurücklegen, *das*
(b) (provision of substitute for) Ersatz, *der; attrib.* Ersatz-
(c) (substitute) Ersatz, *der;* **~ [part]** Ersatzteil, *das*

replay ① /riː'pleɪ/ *v.t.* wiederholen ⟨*Spiel*⟩; nochmals abspielen ⟨*Tonband usw.*⟩
② /'riːpleɪ/ *n.* Wiederholung, *die;* (match) Wiederholungsspiel, *das*

replenish /rɪ'plenɪʃ/ *v.t.* auffüllen

replica /'replɪkə/ *n.* Nachbildung, *die*

reply /rɪ'plaɪ/ ① *v.i.* **~ [to sb./sth.]** [jmdm./auf etw. (*Akk.*)] antworten
② *v.t.* **~ that** ...: antworten, dass ...
③ *n.* Antwort, *die* (**to** auf + *Akk.*)

re'ply-paid *adj.* **~-paid telegram** RP-Telegramm, *das;* **~-paid envelope** Freiumschlag, *der*

repopulate /riː'pɒpjʊleɪt/ *v.t.* neu besiedeln

report /rɪ'pɔːt/ ① *v.t.* **(a)** (relate) berichten/ (in writing) einen Bericht schreiben über (+ *Akk.*); (state formally also) melden
(b) (name to authorities) melden (**to** *Dat.*); (for prosecution) anzeigen (**to** bei)
② *v.i.* **(a)** Bericht erstatten (**on** über + *Akk.*); berichten (**on** über + *Akk.*)
(b) (present oneself) sich melden (**to** bei)
③ *n.* **(a)** (account) Bericht, *der* (**on, about** über + *Akk.*)
(b) (Sch.) Zeugnis, *das*
(c) (of gun) Knall, *der*

reportedly /rɪ'pɔːtɪdlɪ/ *adv.* wie verlautet

reported 'speech *n.* indirekte Rede

re'porter *n.* Reporter, *der*/Reporterin, *die*

repossess /riːpə'zes/ *v.t.* wieder in Besitz nehmen

reprehensible /reprɪ'hensɪbl/ *adj.* tadelnswert

represent /reprɪ'zent/ *v.t.* **(a)** darstellen (**as** als)
(b) (act for) vertreten

representation /reprɪzen'teɪʃn/ *n.*
(a) (depicting, image) Darstellung, *die*
(b) (acting for sb.) Vertretung, *die*
(c) **make ~s to sb.** bei jmdm. Protest einlegen

representative /reprɪ'zentətɪv/ ① n.
(a) (Commerc.) Vertreter, der/Vertreterin, die
(b) R~ (Amer. Polit.) Abgeordnete, der/die
② adj. (typical) repräsentativ (of für)
repress /rɪ'pres/ v.t. (a) unterdrücken
⟨Aufruhr, Gefühle, Lachen usw.⟩
(b) (Psych.) verdrängen ⟨Gefühle⟩ (from aus)
repressed /rɪ'prest/ adj. unterdrückt;
(Psych.) verdrängt
repression /rɪ'preʃn/ n. Unterdrückung,
die
repressive /rɪ'presɪv/ adj. repressiv
reprieve /rɪ'priːv/ ① v.t. ~ sb. (postpone
execution) jmdm. Strafaufschub gewähren;
(remit execution) jmdn. begnadigen
② n. Strafaufschub, der (of für)/
Begnadigung, die; (fig.) Gnadenfrist, die
reprimand /'reprɪmɑːnd/ ① n. Tadel, der
② v.t. tadeln
reprint ① /riː'prɪnt/ v.t. wieder abdrucken
② /'riːprɪnt/ n. Nachdruck, der
reprisal /rɪ'praɪzl/ n. Vergeltungsakt, der
(for gegen)
reproach /rɪ'prəʊtʃ/ ① v.t. ~ sb. jmdm.
Vorwürfe machen
② n. Vorwurf, der
reproachful /rɪ'prəʊtʃfl/ adj. vorwurfsvoll
reproduce /riːprə'djuːs/ ① v.t.
wiedergeben
② v.i. (multiply) sich fortpflanzen
reproduction /riːprə'dʌkʃn/ n.
(a) Wiedergabe, die
(b) (producing offspring) Fortpflanzung, die
(c) (copy) Reproduktion, die
reproductive /riːprə'dʌktɪv/ adj.
Fortpflanzungs-
reprove /rɪ'pruːv/ v.t. tadeln
reptile /'reptaɪl/ n. Reptil, das
republic /rɪ'pʌblɪk/ n. Republik, die
republican /rɪ'pʌblɪkən/ ① adj.
republikanisch
② n. R~ (Amer. Polit.) Republikaner,
der/Republikanerin, die
repudiate /rɪ'pjuːdɪeɪt/ v.t. zurückweisen
repugnance /rɪ'pʌgnəns/ n. Abscheu, der
(to[wards] vor + Dat.)
repugnant /rɪ'pʌgnənt/ adj. widerlich
(to Dat.)
repulse /rɪ'pʌls/ v.t. abwehren
repulsion /rɪ'pʌlʃn/ n. (disgust) Widerwille,
der (towards gegen)
repulsive /rɪ'pʌlsɪv/ adj. abstoßend
reputable /'repjʊtəbl/ adj. angesehen
⟨Person, Beruf, Zeitung usw.⟩; anständig
⟨Verhalten⟩; seriös ⟨Firma⟩
reputably /'repjʊtəblɪ/ adv. anständig
reputation /repjʊ'teɪʃn/ n. (a) Ruf, der;
have a ~ for or of doing/being sth. in dem
Ruf stehen, etw. zu tun/sein
(b) (good name) Name, der
repute /rɪ'pjuːt/ ① v.t. in pass. be ~d [to
be] sth. als etw. gelten; she is ~d to have/

make ...: man sagt, dass sie ... hat/macht
② n. Ruf, der
reputed /rɪ'pjuːtɪd/ adj., **re'putedly**
adv. angeblich
request /rɪ'kwest/ ① v.t. bitten; ~ sth. of
or from sb. jmdn. um etw. bitten
② n. Bitte, die (for um); at sb.'s ~: auf jmds.
Bitte (Akk.) [hin]
re'quest stop n. (Brit.) Bedarfshaltestelle,
die
require /rɪ'kwaɪə(r)/ v.t. (a) (need)
brauchen
(b) (order, demand) verlangen (of von); be ~d
to do sth. etw. tun müssen
re'quirement n. (a) (need) Bedarf, der
(b) (condition) Erfordernis, das
requisite /'rekwɪzɪt/ ① adj. notwendig
(to, for für)
② n. in pl. **toilet/travel** ~s Toiletten-/
Reiseartikel Pl.
requisition /rekwɪ'zɪʃn/ ① n. (order for
sth.) Anforderung, die (for Gen.)
② v.t. anfordern
rescind /rɪ'sɪnd/ v.t. für ungültig erklären
rescue /'reskjuː/ ① v.t. retten (from aus)
② n. Rettung, die; attrib. Rettungs⟨dienst,
-mannschaft⟩; go/come to the/sb.'s
~: jmdm. zu Hilfe kommen
rescuer /'reskjuːə(r)/ n. Retter,
der/Retterin, die
'rescue worker n. [Einsatz]helfer, der/
-helferin, die
research /rɪ'sɜːtʃ, 'riːsɜːtʃ/ ① n.
Forschung, die (into, on über + Akk.)
② v.i. forschen; ~ into sth. etw. erforschen
research as'sistant n.
wissenschaftlicher Assistent/
wissenschaftliche Assistentin
researcher /-'--, '---/ n. Forscher,
der/Forscherin, die
research: ~ student n. ≈ Doktorand,
der/Doktorandin, die; ~ **work** n.
Recherchen Pl.; (medical, scientific)
Forschungsarbeit, die; ~ **worker** n.
≈ Rechercheur, der/Rechercheurin, die;
(medical, scientific) Forscher, der/Forscherin,
die
resell /riː'sel/ v.t., **resold** /riː'səʊld/
weiterverkaufen (to an + Akk.)
resemblance /rɪ'zembləns/ n.
Ähnlichkeit, die (to mit)
resemble /rɪ'zembl/ v.t. ähneln, gleichen
(+ Dat.)
resent /rɪ'zent/ v.t. übel nehmen
resentful /rɪ'zentfl/ adj. übelnehmerisch,
nachtragend ⟨Person, Art⟩; be ~ of or feel
~ about sth. etw. übel nehmen
re'sentment n. Groll, der (geh.); feel
~ towards or against sb. einen Groll auf
jmdn. haben
reservation /rezə'veɪʃn/ n.
(a) Reservierung, die; have a ~ [for a room]
ein Zimmer reserviert haben

(b) (doubt) Vorbehalt, *der* **(about** gegen); Bedenken **(about** bezüglich + *Gen.*); **without** ∼: ohne Vorbehalt

reserve /rɪ'zɜːv/ **1** *v.t.* reservieren lassen ⟨*Zimmer, Tisch, Platz*⟩; (set aside) reservieren; ∼ **the right to do sth.** sich (*Dat.*) [das Recht] vorbehalten, etw. zu tun **2** *n.* **(a)** (extra amount) Reserve, *die* **(of an** + *Dat.*) **have/hold** *or* **keep sth. in** ∼: etw. in Reserve haben/halten

(b) (place set apart) Reservat, *das*

(c) (Sport) Reservespieler, *der/*-spielerin, *die;* **the R**∼**s** die Reserve

(d) (reticence) Zurückhaltung, *die*

reserved /rɪ'zɜːvd/ *adj.* (reticent) reserviert

reservoir /'rezəvwɑː(r)/ *n.* ([artificial] lake) Reservoir, *das*

reshape /riː'ʃeɪp/ *v.t.* umgestalten

reshuffle /riː'ʃʌfl/ **1** *v.t.* **(a)** umbilden ⟨*Kabinett*⟩

(b) (Cards) neu mischen

2 *n.* Umbildung, *die*

reside /rɪ'zaɪd/ *v.i.* (formal) wohnen; wohnhaft sein (Amtsspr.)

residence /'rezɪdəns/ *n.* **(a)** (abode) Wohnsitz, *der;* (of ambassador etc.) Residenz, *die*

(b) (stay) Aufenthalt, *der*

'residence permit *n.* Aufenthaltsgenehmigung, *die*

resident /'rezɪdənt/ **1** *adj.* wohnhaft; **be** ∼ **in England** seinen Wohnsitz in England haben

2 *n.* (inhabitant) Bewohner, *der/*Bewohnerin, *die;* (at hotel) Hotelgast, *der*

residential /rezɪ'denʃl/ *adj.* Wohn⟨*gebiet, -siedlung, -straße*⟩; ∼ **hotel** Hotel für Dauergäste

residential 'care *n.* stationäre Pflege

resident's 'parking *n.* Parken nur für Anlieger

residual /rɪ'zɪdjʊəl/ *adj.* zurückgeblieben

residue /'rezɪdjuː/ *n.* **(a)** Rest, *der*

(b) (Chem.) Rückstand, *der*

resign /rɪ'zaɪn/ **1** *v.t.* zurücktreten von ⟨*Amt*⟩

2 *v. refl.* ∼ **oneself to sth./to doing sth.** sich mit etw. abfinden/sich damit abfinden, etw. zu tun

3 *v.i.* ⟨*Arbeitnehmer:*⟩ kündigen; ⟨*Regierungsbeamter:*⟩ zurücktreten **(from** von)

resignation /rezɪg'neɪʃn/ *n.*
(a) ▶ RESIGN 3: Kündigung, *die;* Rücktritt, *der;* **tender one's** ∼: seine Kündigung/seinen Rücktritt einreichen

(b) (being resigned) Resignation, *die;* **with** ∼: resigniert

resigned /rɪ'zaɪnd/ *adj.* resigniert; **be** ∼ **to sth.** sich mit etw. abgefunden haben

resilience /rɪ'zɪlɪəns/ *n.* **(a)** Elastizität, *die*

(b) (fig.) Unverwüstlichkeit, *die*

resilient /rɪ'zɪlɪənt/ *adj.* elastisch; (fig.) unverwüstlich

resin /'rezɪn/ *n.* Harz, *das*

resist /rɪ'zɪst/ **1** *v.t.* **(a)** standhalten (+ *Dat.*) ⟨*Frost, Hitze, Feuchtigkeit usw.*⟩

(b) (oppose) sich widersetzen (+ *Dat.*); widerstehen (+ *Dat.*) ⟨*Versuchung*⟩

2 *v.i.* ▶ 1B: sich widersetzen; widerstehen

resistance /rɪ'zɪstəns/ *n.* Widerstand, *der* **(to** gegen)

re'sistance movement *n.* Widerstandsbewegung, *die*

resistant /rɪ'zɪstənt/ *adj.* **(a)** (opposed) be ∼ **to** sich widersetzen (+ *Dat.*)

(b) (having power to resist) widerstandsfähig **(to** gegen)

reskill /riː'skɪl/ *v.t.* fort- *od.* weiterbilden; umschulen ⟨*Arbeitslose*⟩

resold ▶ RESELL

resolute /'rezəluːt/ *adj.* resolut, energisch ⟨*Person*⟩; entschlossen ⟨*Tat*⟩

resolution /rezə'luːʃn/ *n.* **(a)** (firmness) Entschlossenheit, *die*

(b) (decision) Entschließung, *die;* (Polit. also) Resolution, *die*

(c) (resolve) Vorsatz, *der;* **make a** ∼: einen Vorsatz fassen

resolve /rɪ'zɒlv/ **1** *v.t.* **(a)** lösen ⟨*Problem, Rätsel*⟩; ausräumen ⟨*Schwierigkeit*⟩

(b) (decide) beschließen

(c) (settle) beilegen ⟨*Streit*⟩; regeln ⟨*Angelegenheit*⟩

2 *n.* **(a)** Vorsatz, *der*

(b) (resoluteness) Entschlossenheit, *die*

resolved /rɪ'zɒlvd/ *adj.* ∼ **[to do sth.]** entschlossen[, etw. zu tun]

resonant /'rezənənt/ *adj.* hallend ⟨*Ton, Klang*⟩

resort /rɪ'zɔːt/ **1** *n.* **(a)** (place) Aufenthalt[sort], *der;* **[holiday]** ∼: Ferienort, *der;* **ski** ∼: Skiurlaubsort, *der;* **seaside** ∼: Seebad, *das*

(b) (recourse) **as a last** ∼: als letzter Ausweg **2** *v.i.* ∼ **to sth./sb.** zu etw. greifen/sich an jmdn. wenden **(for** um)

resound /rɪ'zaʊnd/ *v.i.* widerhallen

re'sounding *adj.* hallend ⟨*Lärm*⟩; überwältigend ⟨*Sieg, Erfolg*⟩

resource /rɪ'sɔːs, rɪ'zɔːs/ *n. usu. in pl.* (stock) Mittel *Pl.;* Ressource, *die*

resourceful /rɪ'sɔːsfl, rɪ'zɔːsfl/ *adj.* findig ⟨*Person*⟩

respect /rɪ'spekt/ **1** *n.* **(a)** (esteem) Respekt, *der,* Achtung, *die* **(for** vor + *Dat.*); **show** ∼ **for sb./sth.** Respekt vor jmdm./etw. zeigen

(b) (aspect) Hinsicht, *die;* **in some** ∼**s** in mancher Hinsicht

(c) with ∼ **to …:** in Bezug auf … (*Akk.*); was … [an]betrifft

2 *v.t.* respektieren; achten

respectable /rɪ'spektəbl/ *adj.* angesehen ⟨*Bürger usw.*⟩; ehrenwert ⟨*Motive*⟩; (decent) ehrbar (geh.) ⟨*Leute,* ⋯⟶

Kaufmann⟩; anständig, respektabel
⟨*Beschäftigung usw.*⟩
respectful /rɪ'spektfl/ *adj.* respektvoll
(**to[wards]** gegenüber)
re'spectfully *adv.* respektvoll
respective /rɪ'spektɪv/ *adj.* jeweilig
re'spectively *adv.* beziehungsweise
respiration /respɪ'reɪʃn/ *n.* Atmung, *die*
respiratory /'respərətərɪ/ *adj.*
Atmungs⟨*system, -organ, -funktion*⟩
respite /'respaɪt/ *n.* Ruhepause, *die;* (delay)
Aufschub, *der;* **without** ∼: ohne Pause
resplendent /rɪ'splendənt/ *adj.* prächtig
respond /rɪ'spɒnd/ **1** *v.i.* (a) (answer)
antworten (**to** auf + *Akk.*)
(b) (react) reagieren (**to** auf + *Akk.*); ⟨*Patient,
Bremsen:*⟩ ansprechen (**to** auf + *Akk.*)
2 *v.t.* antworten; erwidern
response /rɪ'spɒns/ *n.* (a) (answer)
Antwort, *die* (**to** auf + *Akk.*); **in** ∼ **[to]** als
Antwort [auf (+ *Akk.*)]
(b) (reaction) Reaktion, *die*
responsibility /rɪspɒnsɪ'bɪlɪtɪ/ *n.*
(a) (being responsible) Verantwortung, *die*
(b) (duty) Verpflichtung, *die*
responsible /rɪ'spɒnsɪbl/ *adj.*
(a) verantwortlich; **be** ∼ **to sb.** jmdm.
gegenüber verantwortlich sein (**for** für)
(b) (trustworthy) verantwortungsvoll
responsibly /rɪ'spɒnsɪblɪ/ *adv.*
verantwortungsbewusst
responsive /rɪ'spɒnsɪv/ *adj.*
aufgeschlossen ⟨*Person*⟩; **be** ∼ **to sth.** auf
etw. (*Akk.*) reagieren
rest¹ /rest/ **1** *v.i.* ruhen; ∼ **on** ruhen
auf (+ *Dat.*); ∼ **from sth.** sich von etw.
ausruhen; ∼ **assured that** ...: seien
Sie versichert, dass ...; ∼ **with sb.**
⟨*Verantwortung:*⟩ bei jmdm. liegen
2 *v.t.* (a) ∼ **sth. against sth.** etw. an etw.
(*Akk.*) lehnen
(b) ausruhen ⟨*Augen*⟩
3 *n.* (a) (repose) Ruhe, *die*
(b) (break, relaxation) Ruhe[pause], *die;*
Erholung, *die* (**from** von); **take a** ∼: sich
ausruhen (**from** von); **give it a** ∼! (coll.) hör
jetzt mal auf damit!
(c) (pause) **have a** ∼: [eine] Pause machen;
∼ **period** [Ruhe]pause, *die*
rest² *n.* **the** ∼: der Rest; **we'll do the**
∼: alles Übrige erledigen wir
restaurant /'restərɒnt/ *n.* Restaurant, *das*
'restaurant car *n.* (Brit. Railw.)
Speisewagen, *der*
rest: ∼ **cure** *n.* Erholungskur, *die;*
∼ **day** *n.* Ruhetag, *der*
'rested *adj.* ausgeruht
restful /'restfl/ *adj.* ruhig ⟨*Tag, Woche*⟩
'rest home *n.* Pflegeheim, *das*
restive /'restɪv/ *adj.* unruhig
'restless *adj.* unruhig ⟨*Nacht, Schlaf,
Bewegung*⟩; ruhelos ⟨*Person*⟩

restoration /restə'reɪʃn/ *n.* (a) (of peace,
health) Wiederherstellung, *die;* (of work of art,
building) Restaurierung, *die*
(b) **the R**∼ (Brit. Hist.) die Restauration
restore /rɪ'stɔː(r)/ *v.t.* (a) (give back)
zurückgeben
(b) restaurieren ⟨*Bauwerk, Kunstwerk
usw.*⟩; ∼ **sb. to health** jmdn.
wiederherstellen
(c) wiederherstellen ⟨*Ordnung, Ruhe*⟩
restrain /rɪ'streɪn/ *v.t.* zurückhalten
⟨*Gefühl, Lachen, Person*⟩; bändigen
⟨*unartiges Kind, Tier*⟩; ∼ **sb./oneself from
doing sth.** jmdn. davon abhalten/sich
zurückhalten, etw. zu tun
restrained /rɪ'streɪnd/ *adj.*
zurückhaltend ⟨*Wesen, Kritik*⟩; beherrscht
⟨*Reaktion, Worte*⟩
restraint /rɪ'streɪnt/ *n.* (a) (restriction)
Einschränkung, *die*
(b) (reserve) Zurückhaltung, *die*
(c) (self-control) Selbstbeherrschung, *die*
restrict /rɪ'strɪkt/ *v.t.* beschränken (**to** auf
+ *Akk.*)
re'stricted *adj.* beschränkt
restriction /rɪ'strɪkʃn/ *n.* Beschränkung,
die (**on** *Gen.*)
restrictive /rɪ'strɪktɪv/ *adj.* restriktiv
'rest room *n.* (esp. Amer.) Toilette, *die*
restyle /riː'staɪl/ *v.t.* neu stylen; ∼ **sb.'s
hair** jmdm. eine neue Frisur machen
result /rɪ'zʌlt/ **1** *v.i.* (a) (follow) ∼ **from sth.**
die Folge einer Sache (*Gen.*) sein
(b) (end) ∼ **in sth.** in etw. (*Dat.*) resultieren
2 *n.* Ergebnis, *das;* **be the** ∼ **of sth.** die
Folge einer Sache (*Gen.*) sein; **as a** ∼ **[of
this]** infolgedessen
re'sultant /rɪ'zʌltənt/ *attrib. adj.* daraus
resultierend
resume /rɪ'zjuːm/ *v.t.* wieder aufnehmen;
fortsetzen ⟨*Reise*⟩
résumé /'rezʊmeɪ/ *n.*
(a) Zusammenfassung, *die*
(b) (Amer.: curriculum vitae) Lebenslauf, *der*
resumption /rɪ'zʌmpʃn/ *n.*
Wiederaufnahme, *die*
resurface /riː'sɜːfɪs/ **1** *v.t.* ∼ **a road** den
Belag einer Straße erneuern
2 *v.i.* (lit. or fig.) wieder auftauchen
resurgence /rɪ'sɜːdʒəns/ *n.*
Wiederaufleben, *das*
resurrection /rezə'rekʃn/ *n.*
Auferstehung, *die*
resuscitate /rɪ'sʌsɪteɪt/ *v.t.* wieder beleben
resuscitation /rɪsʌsɪ'teɪʃn/ *n.*
Wiederbelebung, *die*
retail /'riːteɪl/ **1** *adj.* Einzel⟨*handel*⟩;
Einzelhandels⟨*geschäft, -preis*⟩
2 *adv.* **buy/sell** ∼: en détail kaufen/
verkaufen
'retailer *n.* Einzelhändler, *der*/-händlerin,
die

'retailing /'ri:teɪlɪŋ/ *n., no art.*
Einzelhandel, *der*

retail 'price index *n.* (Brit.) Preisindex
des Einzelhandels

retain /rɪ'teɪn/ *v.t.* behalten; ein-,
zurückbehalten ⟨*Gelder*⟩

retaining: ∼ **fee** *n.* Honorarvorschuss,
der; ∼ **wall** *n.* Böschungsmauer, *die*

retaliate /rɪ'tælɪeɪt/ *v.i.* Vergeltung üben
(**against** an + *Dat.*)

retaliation /rɪtælɪ'eɪʃn/ *n.* Vergeltung,
die; **in** ∼ **for** als Vergeltung für

retarded /rɪ'tɑːdɪd/ *adj.* **[mentally]**
∼: [geistig] zurückgeblieben

retch /retʃ/ *v.i.* würgen

retentive /rɪ'tentɪv/ *adj.* gut ⟨*Gedächtnis*⟩

rethink /ri:'θɪŋk/ *v.t.*, **rethought** /ri:'θɔːt/
noch einmal überdenken

reticence /'retɪsəns/ *n.* Zurückhaltung,
die

reticent /'retɪsənt/ *adj.* zurückhaltend
(**on, about** in Bezug auf + *Akk.*)

retina /'retɪnə/ *n.* Netzhaut, *die*

retinue /'retɪnjuː/ *n.* Gefolge, *das*

retire /rɪ'taɪə(r)/ *v.i.* **(a)** ⟨*Angestellter,
Arbeiter:*⟩ in Rente (*Akk.*) gehen; ⟨*Beamter,
Militär:*⟩ in Pension *od.* den Ruhestand
gehen
(b) (withdraw) sich zurückziehen (**to** in
+ *Akk.*)

retired /rɪ'taɪəd/ *adj.* aus dem Berufsleben
ausgeschieden; ⟨*Beamter, Soldat*⟩ im
Ruhestand, pensioniert

re'tirement *n.* Ruhestand, *der;* **take early**
∼ ⟨*Selbstständiger:*⟩ sich vorzeitig zur Ruhe
setzen; ⟨*Angestellter, Arbeiter:*⟩ vorzeitig in
Rente (*Akk.*) gehen; ⟨*Beamter, Militär:*⟩ sich
vorzeitig pensionieren lassen

retirement: ∼ **age** *n.* Altersgrenze,
die; ∼ **home** *n.* **(a)** (house, flat) Alters- *od.*
Ruhesitz, *der;* **(b)** (institution) Alters- *od.*
Altenheim, *das;* ∼ **pay,** ∼ **pension** *ns.*
[Alters]rente, *die*

retiring /rɪ'taɪərɪŋ/ *adj.* (shy)
zurückhaltend

retort /rɪ'tɔːt/ **1** *n.* Entgegnung, *die* (**to**
auf + *Akk.*)
2 *v.t.* entgegnen

retrace /rɪ'treɪs/ *v.t.* zurückverfolgen;
∼ **one's steps** denselben Weg noch einmal
zurückgehen

retract /rɪ'trækt/ *v.t.* zurücknehmen

retrain /ri:'treɪn/ **1** *v.i.* [sich] umschulen
[lassen]
2 *v.t.* umschulen

re'training *n.* Umschulung, *die*

retreat /rɪ'triːt/ **1** *n.* **(a)** (withdrawal)
Rückzug, *der;* **beat a** ∼ (fig.) das Feld räumen
(b) (place) Zufluchtsort, *der*
2 *v.i.* sich zurückziehen

retribution /retrɪ'bjuːʃn/ *n.* Vergeltung,
die

retrieval /rɪ'triːvl/ *n.* **(a)** (of
situation) Rettung, *die;* **beyond** *or* **past**
∼: hoffnungslos
(b) (rescue) Rettung, *die;* (from wreckage)
Bergung, *die*

retrieve /rɪ'triːv/ *v.t.* **(a)** (rescue) retten
(**from** aus); (from wreckage) bergen (**from** aus)
(b) (recover) zurückholen ⟨*Brief*⟩;
wiederholen ⟨*Ball*⟩; wiederbekommen
⟨*Geld*⟩
(c) (Comp.) wieder auffinden ⟨*Informationen*⟩
(d) ⟨*Hund:*⟩ apportieren
(e) retten ⟨*Situation*⟩

re'triever *n.* Apportierhund, *der;* (breed)
Retriever, *der*

retrospect /'retrəspekt/ *n.* **in** ∼: im
Nachhinein

retrospective /retrə'spektɪv/ **1** *adj.*
retrospektiv (geh.)
2 *n.* (Art) Retrospektive, *die* (geh.)

retrovirus /'retrəʊvaɪrəs/ *n.* Retrovirus,
das od. der

returf /ri:'tɜːf/ *v.t.* neuen Rasen verlegen
auf (+ *Dat.*)

return /rɪ'tɜːn/ **1** *v.i.* (come back)
zurückkommen; (go back) zurückgehen; (by
vehicle) zurückfahren
2 *v.t.* **(a)** (bring back) zurückbringen;
zurückgeben ⟨*geliehenen/gestohlenen
Gegenstand*⟩; ∼**ed with thanks** mit Dank
zurück
(b) erwidern ⟨*Besuch, Gruß, Liebe*⟩; sich
revanchieren für (ugs.) ⟨*Freundlichkeit,
Gefallen*⟩
(c) (elect) wählen ⟨*Kandidaten*⟩
(d) ∼ **a verdict of guilty/not guilty**
⟨*Geschworene:*⟩ auf „schuldig"/„nicht
schuldig" erkennen
3 *n.* **(a)** Rückkehr, *die;* **many happy** ∼**s
[of the day]!** herzlichen Glückwunsch [zum
Geburtstag]!
(b) by ∼ **[of post]** postwendend
(c) (ticket) Rückfahrkarte, *die;* (for flight)
Rückflugschein, *der*
(d) ∼**[s]** (proceeds) Gewinn, *der* (**on, from**
aus)
(e) (bringing back) Zurückbringen, *das;* (of
property, goods, book) Rückgabe, *die* (**to** an
+ *Akk.*); **receive/get sth. in** ∼ **[for sth.]** etw.
[für etw.] bekommen

returnable /rɪ'tɜːnəbl/ *adj.*
Mehrweg⟨*behälter, -flasche usw.*⟩;
rückzahlbar ⟨*Gebühr, Kaution*⟩; ∼ **bottle**
Pfandflasche, *die;* ∼ **deposit** Pfand, *der*

return: ∼ **'fare** *n.* Preis für eine
Rückfahrkarte/(for flight) einen
Rückflugschein; ∼ **'flight** *n.* Rückflug,
der; ∼ **'journey** *n.* Rückreise, *die;*
Rückfahrt, *die;* ∼ **'match** *n.* Rückspiel,
das; ∼ **'ticket** *n.* (Brit.) Rückfahrkarte, *die;*
(for flight) Rückflugschein, *der;* ∼ **'trip** *n.*
(a) (trip back) Rückweg, *der;* Rückfahrt, *die;*
(b) (trip out and back) Hin- und Rückfahrt, *die;*
Hin- und Rückreise, *die*

retype /riː'taɪp/ v.t. neu tippen

reunification /riːjuːnɪfɪ'keɪʃn/ n. Wiedervereinigung, die

reunify /riːjuːnɪfaɪ/ v.t. wieder vereinigen

reunion /riː'juːnjən/ n. (gathering) Treffen, das

reunite /riːjʊ'naɪt/ v.t. wieder zusammenführen

reusable /riː'juːzəbl/ adj. wieder verwendbar

reuse ① /riː'juːz/ v.t. wieder verwenden
② /riː'juːs/ n. Wiederverwendung, die

rev /rev/ (coll.) ① n., usu. in pl. Umdrehung, die
② v.i., -vv- hochtourig laufen
③ v.t., -vv- aufheulen lassen
∎ **rev 'up** v.t. aufheulen lassen

Rev. /'revərənd, (coll.) rev/ abbr. = **Reverend** Rev.

reveal /rɪ'viːl/ v.t. enthüllen (geh.); be ⁓ed ⟨Wahrheit:⟩ ans Licht kommen

re'vealing adj. aufschlussreich

revel /'revl/ v.i., (Brit.) -ll- genießen (in Akk.); ⁓ in doing sth. es [richtig] genießen, etw. zu tun

revelation /revə'leɪʃn/ n. (a) Enthüllung, die (geh.); be a ⁓: einem die Augen öffnen
(b) (Relig.) Offenbarung, die

reveller /'revələ(r)/ n. Feiernde, der/die

revelry /'revəlrɪ/ n. Feiern, das

revenge /rɪ'vendʒ/ ① v.t. rächen ⟨Person, Tat⟩
② n. (action) Rache, die; take ⁓ or have one's ⁓ [on sb.] [for sth.] Rache [an jmdm.] [für etw.] nehmen; in ⁓ for sth. als Rache für etw

revengeful /rɪ'vendʒfl/ adj. rachsüchtig (geh.)

revenue /'revənjuː/ n. ⁓[s] Einnahmen Pl.

revere /rɪ'vɪə(r)/ v.t. verehren

reverence /'revərəns/ n. Ehrfurcht, die

Reverend /'revərənd/ adj. the ⁓ John Wilson Hochwürden John Wilson

reverent /'revərənt/ adj. ehrfürchtig

reverie /'revərɪ/ n. Träumerei, die

reversal /rɪ'vɜːsl/ n. Umkehrung, die

reverse /rɪ'vɜːs/ ① adj. entgegengesetzt ⟨Richtung⟩; Rück⟨seite⟩; umgekehrt ⟨Reihenfolge⟩
② n. (a) (contrary) Gegenteil, das
(b) (Motor Veh.) Rückwärtsgang, der; put the car into ⁓, go into ⁓: den Rückwärtsgang einlegen
③ v.t. (a) umkehren ⟨Reihenfolge⟩; ⁓ the charge[s] (Brit.) ein R-Gespräch anmelden
(b) zurücksetzen ⟨Fahrzeug⟩
④ v.i. zurücksetzen; rückwärts fahren

reverse: ⁓-'charge adj. (Brit.) make a ⁓-charge call ein R-Gespräch führen; ⁓ 'gear n. (Motor Veh.) Rückwärtsgang, der; see also GEAR 1A

reversible /rɪ'vɜːsɪbl/ adj. beidseitig tragbar ⟨Kleidungsstück⟩; Wende⟨mantel, -jacke⟩

re'versing light n. Rückfahrscheinwerfer, der

revert /rɪ'vɜːt/ v.i. ⁓ to zurückkommen auf (+ Akk.) ⟨Thema, Frage⟩; ⁓ to savagery in den Zustand der Wildheit zurückfallen

review /rɪ'vjuː/ ① n. (a) (survey) Überblick, der (of über + Akk.)
(b) (re-examination) [nochmalige] Überprüfung
(c) (of book, play, etc.) Kritik, die; Rezension, die
② v.t. (a) (survey) untersuchen; prüfen
(b) (re-examine) überprüfen
(c) (Mil.) inspizieren
(d) (write a criticism of) rezensieren

re'viewer n. Rezensent, der/Rezensentin, die

revile /rɪ'vaɪl/ v.t. schmähen (geh.)

revise /rɪ'vaɪz/ v.t. (a) (check over) durchsehen ⟨Manuskript⟩
(b) (for exam) wiederholen; abs. lernen

revision /rɪ'vɪʒn/ n. (a) (checking over) Durchsicht, die
(b) (amended version) revidierte Fassung
(c) (for exam) Wiederholung, die

revisit /riː'vɪzɪt/ v.t. wieder besuchen

revitalize /riː'vaɪtəlaɪz/ v.t. neu beleben

revival /rɪ'vaɪvl/ n. Neubelebung, die

revive /rɪ'vaɪv/ ① v.i. (come back to consciousness) wieder zu sich kommen; (be reinvigorated) zu neuem Leben erwachen
② v.t. (a) (restore to consciousness) wieder beleben; (reinvigorate) wieder zu Kräften kommen lassen
(b) wieder wecken ⟨Lebensgeister, Interesse⟩

revoke /rɪ'vəʊk/ v.t. aufheben ⟨Entscheidung⟩; widerrufen ⟨Befehl, Erlaubnis, Genehmigung⟩

revolt /rɪ'vəʊlt/ ① v.i. revoltieren (against gegen)
② v.t. mit Abscheu erfüllen
③ n. Revolte, die (auch fig.); Aufstand, der

re'volting adj. abscheulich; (unpleasant) widerlich

revolution /revə'luːʃn/ n. Revolution, die

revolutionary /revə'luːʃənərɪ/ ① adj. revolutionär
② n. Revolutionär, der/Revolutionärin, die

revolve /rɪ'vɒlv/ ① v.t. drehen
② v.i. sich drehen (round, about, on um)

revolver /rɪ'vɒlvə(r)/ n. [Trommel]revolver, der

revolving /rɪ'vɒlvɪŋ/ attrib. adj. Dreh⟨bühne, -tür⟩

revue /rɪ'vjuː/ n. Kabarett, das; (musical show) Revue, die

revulsion /rɪ'vʌlʃn/ n. Abscheu, der (at vor + Dat., gegen)

reward /rɪ'wɔːd/ ① n. Belohnung, die
② v.t. belohnen

re'warding *adj.* lohnend; **be** ∼**/financially** ∼: sich lohnen/einträglich sein

rewind /riːˈwaɪnd/ *v.t.*, **rewound** /riːˈwaʊnd/ **(a)** wieder aufziehen ⟨*Uhr*⟩ **(b)** zurückspulen ⟨*Film, Band*⟩

'rewind button *n.* (on camera) Rückspulknopf, *der;* (on cassette recorder etc.) Rücklauftaste, *die*

reword /riːˈwɜːd/ *v.t.* umformulieren

rewrite /riːˈraɪt/ *v.t.*, **rewrote** /riːˈrəʊt/, **rewritten** /riːˈrɪtn/ noch einmal [neu] schreiben; (write differently) umschreiben

rhetoric /ˈretərɪk/ *n.* [art of] ∼: Redekunst, *die;* Rhetorik, *die*

rhetorical /rɪˈtɒrɪkl/ *adj.* rhetorisch

rheumatic /ruːˈmætɪk/ *adj.* rheumatisch

rheumatism /ˈruːmətɪzm/ *n.* Rheumatismus, *der;* Rheuma, *das* (ugs.)

Rhine /raɪn/ *pr. n.* Rhein, *der*

rhino /ˈraɪnəʊ/ *n., pl.* **same** *or* ∼**s** (coll.), **rhinoceros** /raɪˈnɒsərəs/ *n., pl.* **same** *or* ∼**es** Nashorn, *das;* Rhinozeros, *das*

rhododendron /rəʊdəˈdendrən/ *n.* Rhododendron, *der*

rhubarb /ˈruːbɑːb/ *n.* Rhabarber, *der*

rhyme /raɪm/ ① *n.* Reim, *der;* **without** ∼ **or reason** ohne Sinn und Verstand
② *v.i.* sich reimen (**with** auf + *Akk.*)

rhythm /ˈrɪðm/ *n.* Rhythmus, *der*

rhythmic /ˈrɪðmɪk/, **rhythmical** /ˈrɪðmɪkl/ *adj.* rhythmisch

rib /rɪb/ ① *n.* Rippe, *die*
② *v.t.*, **-bb-** (coll.) aufziehen (ugs.)

ribald /ˈrɪbəld/ *adj.* zotig

ribbon /ˈrɪbn/ *n.* Band, *das;* (on typewriter) [Farb]band, *das*

'ribcage *n.* Brustkorb, *der*

rice /raɪs/ *n.* Reis, *der*

rice: ∼ **'pudding** *n.* Milchreis, *der;* ∼ **wine** *n.* Reiswein, *der*

rich /rɪtʃ/ ① *adj.* **(a)** reich (**in** an + *Dat.*); (fertile) fruchtbar ⟨*Land, Boden*⟩ **(b)** (splendid) prachtvoll **(c)** (containing much fat, oil, eggs, etc.) gehaltvoll **(d)** (deep, full) voll[tönend] ⟨*Stimme*⟩; voll ⟨*Ton*⟩; satt ⟨*Farbe, Farbton*⟩
② *n. pl.* **the** ∼: die Reichen *Pl.;* ∼ **and poor** Arm und Reich

riches /ˈrɪtʃɪz/ *n. pl.* Reichtum, *der*

'richly *adv.* **(a)** (splendidly) reich; üppig ⟨*ausgestattet*⟩; prächtig ⟨*gekleidet*⟩ **(b)** (fully) voll und ganz; ∼ **deserved** wohlverdient

'richness *n.* **(a)** (of food) Reichhaltigkeit, *die* **(b)** (of voice) voller Klang; (of colour) Sattheit, *die*

rickets /ˈrɪkɪts/ *n.* Rachitis, *die*

rickety /ˈrɪkɪti/ *adj.* wack[e]lig

ricochet /ˈrɪkəʃeɪ/ ① *n.* **(a)** Abprallen, *das* **(b)** (hit) Abpraller, *der*

② *v.i.*, ∼**ed** /ˈrɪkəʃeɪd/ abprallen (**off** von)

rid /rɪd/ *v.t.*, **-dd-**, **rid:** ∼ **sth. of sth.** etw. von etw. befreien; ∼ **oneself of sb./sth.** sich von jmdm./etw. befreien; **be** ∼ **of sb./sth.** jmdn./etw. los sein (ugs.); **get** ∼ **of sb./sth.** jmdn./etw. loswerden

riddance /ˈrɪdəns/ *n.* **good** ∼! Gott sei Dank ist er/es *usw.* weg!

ridden ▸ RIDE 2, 3

riddle¹ /ˈrɪdl/ *n.* Rätsel, *das*

riddle² *v.t.* durchlöchern; ∼**d with bullets** von Kugeln durchsiebt

ride /raɪd/ ① *n.* (on horseback) [Aus]ritt, *der;* (in vehicle, at fair) Fahrt, die; ∼ **in a train/coach** Zug-/Busfahrt, *die;* **go for a** ∼: ausreiten; **go for a [bi]cycle** ∼: Rad fahren; **go for a** ∼ **[in the car]** [mit dem Auto] wegfahren; **take sb. for a** ∼ (fig. coll.: deceive) jmdn. reinlegen (ugs.)
② *v.i.*, **rode** /rəʊd/, **ridden** /ˈrɪdn/ (on horse) reiten; (on bicycle, in vehicle) fahren; ∼ **to town on one's bike/in one's car/on the train** mit dem Rad/Auto/Zug in die Stadt fahren
③ *v.t.*, **rode**, **ridden** reiten ⟨*Pferd usw.*⟩; fahren mit ⟨*Fahrrad*⟩

▪ **ride a'way**, **ride 'off** *v.i.* wegreiten/-fahren

'rider *n.* **(a)** Reiter, *der*/Reiterin, *die;* (of cycle) Fahrer, *der*/Fahrerin, *die* **(b)** (addition) Zusatz, *der*

ridge /rɪdʒ/ *n.* **(a)** (of roof) First, *der* **(b)** (long hilltop) Grat, *der;* Kamm, *der* **(c)** (Meteorol.) ∼ **[of high pressure]** lang gestrecktes Hoch

ridicule /ˈrɪdɪkjuːl/ ① *n.* Spott, *der*
② *v.t.* verspotten

ridiculous /rɪˈdɪkjʊləs/ *adj.* lächerlich

riding /ˈraɪdɪŋ/ *n.* Reiten, *das*

riding: ∼ **lesson** *n.* Reitstunde, *die;* ∼ **school** *n.* Reitschule, *die*

rife /raɪf/ *pred. adj.* weit verbreitet

riff-raff /ˈrɪfræf/ *n.* Gesindel, *das*

rifle /ˈraɪfl/ ① *n.* Gewehr, *das*
② *v.t.* durchwühlen
③ *v.i.* ∼ **through sth.** etw. durchwühlen

rift /rɪft/ *n.* Unstimmigkeit, *die*

rig¹ /rɪɡ/ *n.* (for oil well) [Öl]förderturm, *der;* (off shore) Förderinsel, *die*

▪ **rig 'out** *v.t.* ausstaffieren

▪ **rig 'up** *v.t.* aufbauen

rig² *v.t.*, **-gg-** manipulieren ⟨*[Wahl]ergebnis*⟩; fälschen ⟨*Wahl*⟩

rigging /ˈrɪɡɪŋ/ *n.* Takelung, *die*

right /raɪt/ ① *adj.* **(a)** (just, morally good, sound) richtig **(b)** (correct, true) richtig; **you're [quite]** ∼: du hast [völlig] recht; **be** ∼ **in sth.** Recht mit etw. haben; **is that clock** ∼? geht die Uhr da richtig?; **put** *or* **set** ∼: richtig stellen ⟨*Irrtum, Behauptung*⟩; wieder gutmachen ⟨*Unrecht*⟩; berichtigen ⟨*Fehler*⟩; richtig stellen ⟨*Uhr*⟩; **put** *or* **set sb.** ∼: jmdn. berichtigen; **that's** ∼: ja[wohl]; so ist ⋯▸

es; **is that** ~**?** stimmt das?; (indeed?) aha!;
[**am I**] ~**?** nicht [wahr]?
(c) (preferable, most suitable) richtig; recht; **do
sth. the** ~ **way** etw. richtig machen
(d) (opposite of left) recht…; **on the** ~ **side**
rechts
(e) R~ (Polit.) recht…
2 v.t. aus der Welt schaffen ⟨*Unrecht*⟩
3 n. **(a)** (fair claim, authority) Recht, *das;* **have
a/no** ~ **to sth.** ein/kein Anrecht *od.* Recht
auf etw. (*Akk.*) haben; **in one's own** ~**:** aus
eigenem Recht; ~ **of way** Vorfahrtsrecht,
das; **have** ~ **of way** Vorfahrt haben
(b) (what is just) Recht, *das;* **by** ~[**s**] von
Rechts wegen; **in the** ~**:** im Recht
(c) (~-hand side) rechte Seite; **on** *or* **to the**
~ [**of sb./sth.**] rechts [von jmdm./etw.]
(d) (Polit.) **the R**~**:** die Rechte
4 adv. **(a)** (correctly) richtig
(b) (to the ~-hand side) nach rechts
(c) (completely) ganz
(d) (exactly) genau; ~ **'now** im Moment; jetzt
sofort ⟨*handeln*⟩
(e) (straight) direkt
'right angle n. rechter Winkel; **at** ~**s to
sth.** rechtwinklig zu etw.
righteous /'raɪtʃəs/ adj. rechtschaffen
rightful /'raɪtfl/ adj. rechtmäßig ⟨*Besitzer,
Herrscher*⟩
right: ~-**hand** adj. recht…; ~-**'handed**
1 adj. rechtshändig; ⟨*Werkzeug*⟩ für
Rechtshänder; **be** ~-**handed** ⟨*Person:*⟩
Rechtshänder/Rechtshänderin sein; **2** adv.
rechtshändig; ~-**hand 'man** n. rechte
Hand
'rightly adv. zu Recht
right: ~-**'minded** adj. gerecht denkend;
~-**to-'life** attrib. adj. Recht-auf-Leben-;
~ **'wing** n. rechter Flügel; ~-**wing** adj.
(Polit.) rechtsgerichtet; Rechts⟨*extremist,
-intellektueller*⟩; ~-**'winger** n. **(a)** (Sport)
Rechtsaußen, *der;* **(b)** (Polit.) Rechte, *der/die*
rigid /'rɪdʒɪd/ adj. **(a)** starr; (stiff) steif
(b) (strict) streng; unbeugsam ⟨*System*⟩
rigidity /rɪ'dʒɪtɪ/ n. ▶ RIGID: Starrheit, *die;*
Steifheit, *die;* Strenge, *die*
rigmarole /'rɪgmərəʊl/ n. **(a)** (talk)
langatmiges Geschwafel (ugs.)
(b) (procedure) Zirkus, *der*
rigor /'rɪgə(r)/ (Amer.) ▶ RIGOUR
rigor mortis /rɪgə 'mɔːtɪs/ n. Totenstarre,
die
rigorous /'rɪgərəs/ adj. streng
rigour /'rɪgə(r)/ n. (Brit.) Strenge, *die*
rile /raɪl/ v.t. (coll.) ärgern
rim /rɪm/ n. Rand, *der;* (of wheel) Felge, *die*
rind /raɪnd/ n. (of fruit) Schale, *die;* (of cheese)
Rinde, *die;* (of bacon) Schwarte, *die*
ring¹ /rɪŋ/ **1** n. **(a)** Ring, *der*
(b) (Boxing) Ring, *der;* (in circus) Manege, *die*
2 v.t. (surround) umringen; einkreisen ⟨*Wort
usw.*⟩
ring² **1** n. **(a)** (act of sounding bell) Läuten,

das; Klingeln, *das*
(b) (Brit. coll.: telephone call) Anruf, *der;* **give sb.
a** ~**:** jmdn. anrufen
(c) (fig.: impression) **have the** ~ **of truth** [about
it] glaubhaft klingen
2 v.i., rang /ræŋ/, rung /rʌŋ/ **(a)** (sound
clearly) [er]schallen; ⟨*Hammer:*⟩
[er]dröhnen
(b) (be sounded) ⟨*Glocke, Klingel, Telefon:*⟩
läuten; ⟨*Wecker, Telefon, Kasse:*⟩ klingeln;
the doorbell rang es klingelte
(c) (~ bell) läuten (**for** nach)
(d) (Brit.: make telephone call) anrufen
3 v.t., rang, rung **(a)** läuten ⟨*Glocke*⟩; ~ **the
[door]bell** läuten; klingeln; **it** ~**s a bell** (fig.
coll.) es kommt mir [irgendwie] bekannt vor
(b) (Brit.: telephone) anrufen
■ **ring 'back** (Brit.) v.t. & i. **(a)** (again)
wieder anrufen
(b) (in return) zurückrufen
■ **ring 'off** v.i. (Brit.) auflegen
■ **ring 'out** v.i. ertönen
■ **ring 'up** v.t. (Brit.: telephone) anrufen
ring: ~ **binder** n. Ringbuch, *das;*
~ **finger** n. Ringfinger, *der*
ringing /'rɪŋɪŋ/ n. Läuten, *das;* (Brit. Teleph.)
~ **tone** Freiton, *der*
'ringleader n. Anführer, *der*/Anführerin,
die
ringlet /'rɪŋlɪt/ n. [Ringel]löckchen, *das*
ring: ~ **road** n. Ringstraße, *die;* ~**tone**
n. Klingelton, *der*
rink /rɪŋk/ n. (for ice skating) Eisbahn, *die;* (for
roller skating) Rollschuhbahn, *die*
rinse /rɪns/ **1** v.t. **(a)** (wash out) ausspülen
⟨*Mund, Gefäß usw.*⟩
(b) [aus]spülen ⟨*Wäsche usw.*⟩; abspülen
⟨*Hände, Geschirr*⟩
2 n. Spülen, *das;* **give sth. a** [good/quick]
~**:** etw. [gut/schnell] ausspülen/abspülen/
spülen
■ **rinse 'out** v.t. ausspülen
riot /'raɪət/ **1** n. Aufruhr, *der;* ~**s** Unruhen
Pl.; **run** ~**:** randalieren
2 v.i. randalieren
'rioter n. Randalierer, *der*
'riot gear n. Schutzkleidung *od.*
-ausrüstung
riotous /'raɪətəs/ adj. **(a)** gewalttätig
(b) (unrestrained) wild
rip /rɪp/ **1** n. Riss, *der*
2 v.t., -**pp**- zerreißen; ~ **open** aufreißen
■ **rip 'off** v.t. **(a)** (remove from) reißen von;
(remove) abreißen
(b) (coll.: defraud) übers Ohr hauen (ugs.)
■ **rip 'out** v.t. herausreißen (**of** aus)
RIP abbr. = **rest in peace** R.I.P.
'ripcord n. Reißleine, *die*
ripe /raɪp/ adj. reif (**for** zu)
ripen /'raɪpn/ **1** v.t. zur Reife bringen
2 v.i. reifen
'ripeness n. Reife, *die*
'rip-off n. (coll.) Nepp, *der* (ugs.)

riposte /rɪ'pɒst/ ☐1 *n.* (retort) [rasche] Entgegnung
☐2 *v.i.* [rasch] antworten
ripple /'rɪpl/ ☐1 *n.* kleine Welle
☐2 *v.i.* ⟨*See:*⟩ sich kräuseln; ⟨*Welle:*⟩ plätschern
☐3 *v.t.* kräuseln
rise /raɪz/ ☐1 *n.* (a) (advancement) Aufstieg, *der*
(b) (in value, price, cost) Steigerung, *die;* (in population, temperature) Zunahme, *die*
(c) (Brit.) [**pay**] ~ (in wages) Lohnerhöhung, *die;* (in salary) Gehaltserhöhung, *die*
(d) (hill) Anhöhe, *die*
(e) **give ~ to** führen zu; Anlass geben zu ⟨*Spekulation*⟩
☐2 *v.i.,* **rose** /rəʊz/, **risen** /'rɪzn/ (a) (go up) aufsteigen
(b) ⟨*Sonne, Mond:*⟩ aufgehen
(c) (increase, reach higher level) steigen
(d) (advance) ⟨*Person:*⟩ aufsteigen
(e) ⟨*Teig, Kuchen:*⟩ aufgehen
(f) (Theatre) ⟨*Vorhang:*⟩ aufgehen
(g) ⟨*Fluss:*⟩ entspringen
■ **rise 'up** *v.i.* (a) ~ **up** [**in revolt**] aufbegehren (geh.)
(b) ⟨*Berg:*⟩ aufragen
risen ▶ RISE 2
'**riser** *n.* **early ~:** Frühaufsteher, *der*/Frühaufsteherin, *die*
rising /'raɪzɪŋ/ ☐1 *n.* (of sun, moon, etc.) Aufgang, *der*
☐2 *adj.* (a) aufgehend ⟨*Sonne, Mond usw.*⟩
(b) steigend ⟨*Kosten, Temperatur, Wasser, Flut*⟩
(c) (sloping upwards) ansteigend
risk /rɪsk/ ☐1 *n.* Gefahr, *die;* (chance taken) Risiko, *das;* **at one's own ~:** auf eigene Gefahr *od.* eigenes Risiko; **take the ~ of doing sth.** es riskieren, etw. zu tun; **be at ~** ⟨*Zukunft, Plan:*⟩ gefährdet sein
☐2 *v.t.* riskieren; **I'll ~ it** ich lasse es darauf ankommen
'**risky** *adj.* gefährlich; gewagt ⟨*Experiment, Projekt*⟩
risotto /rɪ'zɒtəʊ/ *n., pl.* ~**s** Risotto, *der od. das*
risqué /'rɪskeɪ/ *adj.* gewagt
rissole /'rɪsəʊl/ *n.* Frikadelle, *die*
rite /raɪt/ *n.* Ritus, *der*
ritual /'rɪtʃʊəl/ ☐1 *adj.* rituell; Ritual⟨*mord, -tötung*⟩
☐2 *n.* Ritual, *das*
rival /'raɪvl/ ☐1 *n.* (competitor) Rivale, *der*/Rivalin, *die;* **business ~s** Konkurrenten *Pl.;*
☐2 *v.t.,* (Brit.) -**ll**- nicht nachstehen (+ *Dat.*)
rivalry /'raɪvlrɪ/ *n.* Rivalität, *die* (geh.)
river /'rɪvə(r)/ *n.* Fluss, *das*
river: ~ **bank** Flussufer, *der;* ~ **basin** *n.* Stromgebiet, *das;* ~ **bed** *n.* Flussbett, *das* ~**side** ☐1 *n.* Flussufer, *das;* ☐2 *attrib. adj.* am Fluss gelegen; am Fluss *nachgestellt*

rivet /'rɪvɪt/ ☐1 *n.* Niete, *die*
☐2 *v.t.* (a) [ver]nieten
(b) (fig.) fesseln
'**riveting** *adj.* fesselnd
rivulet /'rɪvjʊlɪt/ *n.* Bach, *der*
RN *abbr.* (Brit.) = **Royal Navy** Königl. Mar.
road /rəʊd/ *n.* Straße, *die;* **across** *or* **over the ~** [**from us**] [bei uns] gegenüber; **by ~** (by car/bus/lorry) per Auto/Bus/Lkw; **be on the ~:** auf Reisen *od.* unterwegs sein; ⟨*Theaterensemble usw.:*⟩ auf Tournee *od.* Tour sein
road: ~ **accident** *n.* Verkehrsunfall, *der;* ~ **atlas** *n.* Autoatlas, *der;* ~**block** *n.* Straßensperre, *die;* ~ **bridge** *n.* Straßenbrücke, *die;* ~ **haulage** *n.* Gütertransport auf der Straße; ~ **hog** *n.* Verkehrsrowdy, *der;* ~ **hump** ▶ SPEED BUMP
roadie /'rəʊdɪ/ *n.* (coll.) Roadie, *der*
road: ~ **manager** *n.* Roadmanager, *der;* ~ **map** *n.* Straßenkarte, *die;* ~**mender** *n.* Straßen[bau]arbeiter, *der*/-arbeiterin, *die;* ~ **rage** *n.: häufig zu gewalttätigen Ausbrüchen führende Wut eines Autofahrers;* ~ **safety** *n.* Verkehrssicherheit, *die;* ~ **sense** *n.* Gespür für Verkehrssituationen; ~**side** *n.* Straßenrand, *der;* **at** *or* **by/along the ~side an** Straßenrand; ~ **sign** *n.* Verkehrszeichen, *das;* Straßenschild, *das* (ugs.); ~ **sweeper** *n.* Straßenkehrer, *der*/-kehrerin, *die;* ~ **tax** *n.* (Brit.) Kraftfahrzeugsteuer, *die;* Kfz-Steuer, *die;* ~ **transport** *n.* Personen- und Güterbeförderung auf der Straße; **form of ~ transport** Verkehrsmittel der Straße; ~ **user** *n.* Verkehrsteilnehmer, *der*/-teilnehmerin, *die;* ~**way** *n.* Fahrbahn, *die;* ~**works** *n. pl.* Straßenbauarbeiten *Pl.;* ~**worthy** *adj.* fahrtüchtig
roam /rəʊm/ ☐1 *v.i.* umherstreifen
☐2 *v.t.* streifen durch
roaming /'rəʊmɪŋ/ *n.* (Teleph.) Roaming, *das*
roar /rɔː(r)/ ☐1 *n.* (of wild beast) Gebrüll, *das;* (of applause) Tosen, *das;* (of engine, traffic) Dröhnen, *das;* ~**s/a ~** [**of laughter**] dröhnendes Gelächter
☐2 *v.i.* brüllen (**with** vor + *Dat.*); ⟨*Motor:*⟩ dröhnen
'**roaring** *adj.* (a) bullernd (ugs.) ⟨*Feuer*⟩
(b) **a ~ success** ein Bombenerfolg; **do a ~ trade** ein Bombengeschäft machen
roast /rəʊst/ ☐1 *v.t.* braten; rösten ⟨*Kaffeebohnen, Kastanien*⟩
☐2 *attrib. adj.* gebraten ⟨*Fleisch, Ente usw.*⟩; Brat⟨*hähnchen, -kartoffeln*⟩; Röst⟨*kastanien*⟩; ~ **beef** (sirloin) Roastbeef, *das*
☐3 *n.* Braten, *der*
rob /rɒb/ *v.t.,* -**bb**- ausrauben ⟨*Bank, Safe, Kasse*⟩; berauben ⟨*Person*⟩

robber /'rɒbə(r)/ n. Räuber, der/Räuberin, die

robbery /'rɒbərɪ/ n. Raub, der; **robberies** Raubüberfälle Pl.

robe /rəʊb/ n. Gewand, das (geh.); (of judge, vicar) Talar, der

robin /'rɒbɪn/ n. ~ [redbreast] Rotkehlchen, das

robot /'rəʊbɒt/ n. Roboter, der

robotics /rəʊ'bɒtɪks/ n. Robotertechnik, die; Robotik, die

robust /rəʊ'bʌst/ adj. robust

rock¹ /rɒk/ n. (a) (piece of ~) Fels, der
(b) (large ~, hill) Felsen, der
(c) (substance) Fels, der; (esp. Geol.) Gestein, das
(d) (boulder) Felsbrocken, der; (Amer.: stone) Stein, der
(e) stick of ~: Zuckerstange, die
(f) be on the ~s (fig. coll.) ⟨Ehe, Firma:⟩ kaputt sein (ugs.)

rock² **1** v.t. wiegen; (in cradle) schaukeln **2** v.i. (a) schaukeln
(b) (sway) schwanken
3 n. (Mus.) Rock, der; attrib. Rock-; ~ and or 'n' roll [music] Rock and Roll, der

rock: ~-'bottom (coll.) **1** adj. ~-bottom prices Schleuderpreise Pl. (ugs.); **2** n. reach or touch ~-bottom ⟨Handel, Preis:⟩ in den Keller fallen (ugs.); her spirits reached ~-bottom ihre Stimmung war auf dem Tiefpunkt; ~ **climber** n. Kletterer, der/Kletterin, die; ~ **climbing** n. [Fels]klettern, das

rocker /'rɒkə(r)/ n. be off one's ~ (fig. coll.) übergeschnappt od. durchgedreht sein (ugs.)

rockery /'rɒkərɪ/ n. Steingarten, der

rocket /'rɒkɪt/ **1** n. Rakete, die **2** v.i. ⟨Preise:⟩ in die Höhe schnellen

rocket: ~ **base** n. (Mil.) Raketen[abschuss]basis, die; ~ **launcher** n. Raketenwerfer, der; ~-**propelled** adj. raketengetrieben

rock: ~ **face** n. Felswand, die; ~**fall** n. Steinschlag, der; ~ **formation** n. Gesteinsformation, die; ~ **garden** n. Steingarten, der; ~-**hard** adj. steinhart

rocking: ~ **chair** n. Schaukelstuhl, der; ~ **horse** n. Schaukelpferd, das

rock: ~ **plant** n. Felsenpflanze, die; (Hort.) Steingartengewächs, das; ~ **salt** n. Steinsalz, das

'rocky adj. (a) felsig
(b) (coll.: unsteady) wackelig (ugs.)

rod /rɒd/ n. Stange, die; (for punishing) Rute, die; (for fishing) [Angel]rute, die

rode ▶ RIDE 2, 3

rodent /'rəʊdənt/ n. Nagetier, das

rodeo /'rəʊdɪəʊ, rəʊ'deɪəʊ/ n., pl. ~s Rodeo, der od. das

roe¹ /rəʊ/ n. (of fish) [hard] ~: Rogen, der; [soft] ~: Milch, die

roe² n. ~ [deer] Reh, das

rogue /rəʊg/ n. Gauner, der

'rogue state n. Schurkenstaat, der

role, rôle /rəʊl/ n. Rolle, die

role: ~ **model** n. Leitbild, das; ~ **playing** n. Rollenspiel, das; ~ **reversal** n. Rollentausch, der

roll¹ /rəʊl/ n. (a) Rolle, die; (of cloth etc.) Ballen, der; ~ of film Rolle Film
(b) [bread] ~: Brötchen, das
(c) be on a ~ (coll.) eine Glückssträhne haben

roll² **1** n. (of drum) Wirbel, der
2 v.t. (a) rollen; (between surfaces) drehen
(b) (shape by ~ing) rollen; drehen ⟨Zigarette⟩
(c) walzen ⟨Rasen, Metall usw.⟩; ausrollen ⟨Teig⟩
3 v.i. (a) rollen
(b) ⟨Maschine:⟩ laufen; get sth. ~ing (fig.) etw. ins Rollen bringen
(c) be ~ing in money or in it (coll.) im Geld schwimmen (ugs.)
■ **roll a'bout** v.i. herumrollen; ⟨Schiff:⟩ schlingern; ⟨Kind, Hund:⟩ sich wälzen
■ **roll 'back** v.t. zurückrollen
■ **roll 'by** v.i. ⟨Zeit:⟩ vergehen
■ **roll 'in** v.i. (coll.) ⟨Briefe, Geldbeträge:⟩ eingehen
■ **roll 'out** v.t. ausrollen ⟨Teig, Teppich⟩
■ **roll 'over** v.i. ⟨Person:⟩ sich umdrehen, (to make room) sich zur Seite rollen.
■ **roll 'up** **1** v.t. aufrollen ⟨Teppich⟩; zusammenrollen ⟨Landkarte, Dokument usw.⟩; hochkrempeln ⟨Ärmel⟩
2 v.i. (coll.: arrive) aufkreuzen (salopp)

'roll-call n. Ausrufen aller Namen; (Mil.) Zählappell, der

rolled 'oats n. pl. Haferflocken Pl.

'roller n. (a) Rolle, die; (for lawn, road, etc.) Walze, die
(b) (for hair) Lockenwickler, der

roller: R~**blade** ® n. Rollerblade, der; Inliner, der; ~**blade** v.i. Rollerblades fahren; ~ **blind** n. Rouleau, das; ~ **coaster** n. Achterbahn, die; ~ **skate** n. Rollschuh, der; ~-**skate** v.i. Rollschuh laufen; ~ **skating** n. Rollschuhlaufen, das

'roll film n. Rollfilm, der

'rolling adj. wellig ⟨Gelände⟩; ~ **hills** sanfte Hügel Pl.

rolling: ~ **pin** n. Teigrolle, die; ~ **stock** n. (Brit. Railw.) Fahrzeugbestand, der

roll: ~-**neck** **1** n. Rollkragen, der; **2** adj. Rollkragen-; ~-**on** ~-**off** adj. ~-on ~-off ship/ferry Roll-on-roll-off-Schiff, das/-Fähre, die; ~**over** n. ⟨von Auslosung zu Auslosung⟩ aufgesteckter Jackpot; ~-**up** (Brit. coll.), ~-**your-own** (esp. Amer. coll.) ns. Selbstgedrehte, die

ROM /rɒm/ abbr. (Comp.) = **read only memory** ROM

Roman /'rəʊmən/ **1** n. Römer, der/Römerin, die

2 *adj.* römisch
Roman 'Catholic 1 *adj.* römisch-katholisch
2 *n.* Katholik, *der*/Katholikin, *die;* **sb. is a ~:** jmd. ist römisch-katholisch

romance /rə'mæns/ *n.* **(a)** (love affair) Romanze, *die*
(b) (love story) [romantische] Liebesgeschichte

Romania /rəʊ'meɪnɪə/ *pr. n.* Rumänien *(das)*

Romanian /rəʊ'meɪnɪən/ 1 *adj.* rumänisch; **sb. is ~:** jmd. ist Romäne/Romänin
2 *n.* **(a)** (person) Rumäne, *der*/Rumänin, *die*
(b) (language) Rumänisch, *das; see also* ENGLISH 2A

Roman 'numeral *n.* römische Ziffer

romantic /rəʊ'mæntɪk/ *adj.* romantisch

romanticism /rəʊ'mæntɪsɪzm/ *n.* (Lit., Art., Mus.) Romantik, *die*

romanticize /rəʊ'mæntɪsaɪz/ *v.t.* romantisieren

'roman type *n.* (Printing) Antiquaschrift, *die*

Romany /'rəʊmənɪ/ 1 **(a)** (person) Rom, *der*
(b) (language) Romani, *das*
2 *adj.* Roma-; (Ling.) Romani-

Rome /rəʊm/ *pr. n.* Rom *(das)*

romp /rɒmp/ 1 *v.i.* **(a)** [herum]tollen
(b) ~ **home** *or* **in** (coll.: win easily) spielend gewinnen
2 *n.* Tollerei, *die*

rompers /'rɒmpəz/ *n. pl.* Spielhöschen, *das*

roof /ru:f/ 1 *n.* **(a)** Dach, *das*
(b) ~ **of the mouth** Gaumen, *der*
2 *v.t.* bedachen

'roof garden *n.* Dachgarten, *der*

'roofing *n.* (material) Deckung, *die*

roof: ~ **rack** *n.* Dachgepäckträger, *der;* ~**top** *n.* Dach, *das*

rook¹ /rʊk/ *n.* (Ornith.) Saatkrähe, *die*

rook² *n.* (Chess) Turm, *der*

rookery /'rʊkərɪ/ *n.* Saatkrähenkolonie, *die*

room /ru:m, rʊm/ *n.* **(a)** (in building) Zimmer, *das;* (for function) Saal, *der*
(b) (space) Platz, *der;* **make ~ [for sb./sth.]** [jmdm./einer Sache] Platz machen; **there is still ~ for improvement in his work** seine Arbeit ist noch verbesserungsfähig

room: ~**mate** *n.* Zimmergenosse, *der*/-genossin, *die;* ~ **service** *n.* Zimmerservice, *der;* ~ **temperature** *n.* Zimmertemperatur, *die*

roomy /'ru:mɪ/ *adj.* geräumig

roost /ru:st/ 1 *n.* [Sitz]stange, *die*
2 *v.i.* ⟨*Vogel:*⟩ sich [zum Schlafen] niederlassen

root¹ /ru:t/ 1 *n.* Wurzel, *die;* **put down**

~**s/take ~:** Wurzeln schlagen
2 *v.i.* ⟨*Pflanze:*⟩ wurzeln
3 *v.t.* **stand ~ed to the spot** wie angewurzelt dastehen
■ **root 'out** *v.t.* ausrotten

root² *v.i.* **(a)** (turn up ground) wühlen **(for** nach)
(b) (coll.) ~ **for** (cheer) anfeuern

'root crop[s] *n. [pl.]* Hackfrüchte *Pl.*

'rooted *adj.* eingewurzelt

'rootless *adj.* wurzellos

'root vegetable *n.* Wurzelgemüse, *das*

rope /rəʊp/ 1 *n.* **(a)** (cord) Seil, *das*
(b) **know the ~s** sich auskennen
2 *v.t.* festbinden
■ **rope 'in** *v.t.* (fig.) einspannen (ugs.)

rope 'ladder *n.* Strickleiter, *die*

ro-ro /'rəʊrəʊ/ *adj.* Ro-Ro-⟨*Schiff, Fähre*⟩

rosary /'rəʊzərɪ/ *n.* Rosenkranz, *der*

rose¹ /rəʊz/ *n.* **(a)** (plant, flower) Rose, *die*
(b) (colour) Rosa, *das*

rose² ▶ RISE 2

rosé /rəʊ'zeɪ, 'rəʊzeɪ/ *n.* Rosé, *der*

rose: ~ **bed** *n.* Rosenbeet, *das;* ~**bud** *n.* Rosenknospe, *die;* ~ **bush** *n.* Rosenstrauch, *der;* ~ **hip** *n.* Hagebutte, *die*

rosemary /'rəʊzmərɪ/ *n.* Rosmarin, *der*

'rose petal *n.* Rosen[blüten]blatt, *das*

rosette /rəʊ'zet/ *n.* Rosette, *die*

roster /'rɒstə(r)/ *n.* Dienstplan, *der*

rostrum /'rɒstrəm/ *n., pl.* **rostra** /'rɒstrə/ *or* ~**s** Podium, *das*

rosy /'rəʊzɪ/ *adj.* rosig

rot /rɒt/ 1 *n.* **(a)** ▶ 2: Verrottung, *die;* Fäulnis, *die;* (fig.: deterioration) Verfall, *der;* **stop the ~** (fig.) dem Verfall Einhalt gebieten
(b) (coll.: nonsense) Quark, *der* (salopp)
2 *v.i.,* **-tt-** verrotten; ⟨*Fleisch, Gemüse, Obst:*⟩ verfaulen
3 *v.t.,* **-tt-** verrotten lassen; verfaulen lassen ⟨*Fleisch, Gemüse, Obst*⟩; zerstören ⟨*Zähne*⟩

rota /'rəʊtə/ *n.* (Brit.) (order of rotation) Turnus, *der;* (list) Arbeitsplan, *der*

rotary /'rəʊtərɪ/ *adj.* rotierend

rotate /rəʊ'teɪt/ 1 *v.i.* (revolve) rotieren; sich drehen
2 *v.t.* in Rotation versetzen

rotation /rəʊ'teɪʃn/ *n.* **(a)** Rotation, *die,* Drehung, *die* **(about** um)
(b) (succession) turnusmäßiger Wechsel; **in** *or* **by ~:** im Turnus

rote /rəʊt/ *n.* **by ~:** auswendig

rotten /'rɒtn/ *adj.,* ~**er** /'rɒtənə(r),/ ~**est** /'rɒtənɪst/ **(a)** (decayed) verrottet; verfault ⟨*Obst, Gemüse*⟩; faul ⟨*Ei, Holz, Zähne*⟩; ~ **to the core** (fig.) verdorben bis ins Mark
(b) (corrupt) verdorben
(c) (coll.: bad) mies (ugs.)

rotund /rəʊ'tʌnd/ *adj.* **(a)** (round) rund
(b) (plump) rundlich

rouble /'ru:bl/ *n.* Rubel, *der*

rouge /ru:ʒ/ n. Rouge, das

rough /rʌf/ **1** adj. **(a)** (coarse, uneven) rau; holp[e]rig ‹Straße usw.›; uneben ‹Gelände›; unruhig ‹Überfahrt›

(b) (violent) grob ‹Person, Worte, Behandlung›

(c) (trying) hart; **this is ~ on him** das ist hart für ihn; **sth. is ~ going** etw. ist nicht einfach

(d) (approximate) grob ‹Skizze, Schätzung›; vag ‹Vorstellung›; **~ paper/notebook** Konzeptpapier, das/Kladde, die

(e) (coll.: ill) angeschlagen (ugs.)

2 n. **[be] in ~:** [sich] im Rohzustand [befinden]

3 adv. rau ‹spielen›; **sleep ~:** im Freien schlafen

4 v.t. **~ it** primitiv leben

■ **rough 'out** v.t. grob entwerfen

■ **rough 'up** v.t. (coll.) zusammenschlagen

roughage /'rʌfɪdʒ/ n. Ballaststoffe Pl.

rough: **~-and-ready** adj. provisorisch; **~ and 'tumble** n. [milde] Rauferei; **~ copy, ~ draft** ns. grobe Skizze; grober Entwurf; **~ 'diamond** n. (fig.) ungehobelter, aber guter Mensch

roughen /'rʌfn/ v.t. aufrauen

rough: **~ 'justice** n. ziemlich willkürliche Urteile Pl.; **~ 'luck** n. Pech, das

'roughly adv. **(a)** (violently) roh; grob

(b) (crudely) leidlich; grob ‹skizzieren, bearbeiten, bauen›

(c) (approximately) ungefähr; grob ‹geschätzt›

'roughness n. **(a)** Rauheit, die; (unevenness) Unebenheit, die

(b) (violence) Rohheit, die

'roughshod adj. **ride ~ over sb./sth.** jmdn./etw. mit Füßen treten

roulette /ru:'let/ n. Roulette, das

round /raʊnd/ **1** adj. rund; **in ~ figures** rund gerechnet

2 n. **(a)** (recurring series) Serie, die; **~ of talks/negotiations** Gesprächs-/Verhandlungsrunde, die; **the daily ~:** der Alltag

(b) (of ammunition) Ladung, die; **50 ~s [of ammunition]** 50 Schuss Munition

(c) (of game or contest) Runde, die

(d) (burst) **~ of applause** Beifallssturm, der

(e) **~ [of drinks]** Runde, die

(f) (regular calls) Runde, die; Tour, die; **go [on] or make one's ~s** seine Runden machen

(g) **a ~ of toast/sandwiches** eine Scheibe Toast/eine Portion Sandwiches

3 adv. **(a)** **all the year ~:** das ganze Jahr hindurch; **the third time ~:** beim dritten Mal; **have a look ~:** sich umsehen; **ask sb. ~ [for a drink]** jmdn. [zu einem Gläschen zu sich] einladen

(b) (by indirect way) herum; **walk ~:** außen herum gehen

(c) (here) hier; (there) dort; **I'll go ~ tomorrow** ich gehe morgen hin

4 prep. **(a)** um [... herum]; **travel ~ England** durch England reisen; **run ~ the streets** durch die Straßen rennen; **walk ~ and ~ sth.** immer wieder um etw. herumgehen

(b) (in various directions from) um [... herum]; rund um ‹einen Ort›

5 v.t. **~ a bend** um eine Kurve fahren/gehen/kommen usw.

■ **round 'off** v.t. abrunden

■ **round 'up** v.t. verhaften ‹Verdächtige›; zusammentreiben ‹Vieh›

round: **~ a'bout** adv. (on all sides) ringsum; **~about 1** n. **(a)** (Brit.: merry-go-round) Karussell, das; **(b)** (Brit.: road junction) Kreisverkehr, der. **2** adj. umständlich; **~ 'brackets** n. pl. runde Klammern Pl.

rounded /'raʊndɪd/ adj. **(a)** rund

(b) harmonisch ‹Person›

rounders /'raʊndəz/ n. sing. (Brit.) Rounders, das; ≈ Schlagball, der

round: **~ 'number** n. runde Zahl; **~ 'robin** n. Petition, die; **~-shouldered** /raʊnd'ʃəʊldəd/ adj. ‹Person› mit einem Rundrücken; **~-the-'clock** adj. rund um die Uhr nachgestellt; **~ 'trip** n. Rundreise, die; **~-up** n. **(a)** (of animals) Zusammentreiben, das; **(b)** (summary) Zusammenfassung, die

rouse /raʊz/ v.t. wecken (from aus)

rousing /'raʊzɪŋ/ adj. mitreißend ‹Lied›; leidenschaftlich ‹Rede›

rout /raʊt/ **1** n. [wilde] Flucht; (defeat) verheerende Niederlage

2 v.t. aufreiben ‹Feind, Truppen›; vernichtend schlagen ‹Gegner›

route /ru:t/ n. Route, die; Weg, der

'route march n. (Mil.) Übungsmarsch, der

router[1] /'raʊtə(r)/ n. (tool) Nuthobel, der

router[2] /'ru:tə(r)/ n. (Comp.) Router, der

routine /ru:'ti:n/ **1** n. **(a)** Routine, die

(b) (coll.: set speech) Platte, die (ugs.)

(c) (Theatre) Nummer, die; (Dancing, Skating) Figur, die

2 adj. routinemäßig; Routine‹arbeit›

roux /ru:/ n. Mehlschwitze, die

row[1] /raʊ/ **1** (coll.) n. **(a)** (noise) Krach, der; **make a ~:** Krach machen

(b) (quarrel) Krach, der (ugs.); **have/start a ~:** Krach haben/anfangen (ugs.)

2 v.i. sich streiten

row[2] /rəʊ/ n. Reihe, die; **in a ~:** in einer Reihe

row[3] /rəʊ/ v.i. & t. (with oars) rudern

rowan /'rəʊən/ n. **~ [tree]** Eberesche, die

rowboat /'rəʊbəʊt/ n. (Amer.) Ruderboot, das

rowdy /'raʊdɪ/ **1** adj. rowdyhaft; **the party was ~:** auf der Party ging es laut zu

2 n. Krawallmacher, der

rower /'rəʊə(r)/ n. Ruderer, der/Ruderin, die

rowing /'rəʊɪŋ/ n. Rudern, das

rowing: ~ **boat** *n.* (Brit.) Ruderboot, *das;*
~ **machine** *n.* Rudergerät, *das*
royal /'rɔɪəl/ *adj.* königlich
royal: R~ 'Air Force *n.* (Brit.)
Königliche Luftwaffe; ~ **'blue** *n.* (Brit.)
Königsblau, *das;* ~ **'family** *n.* königliche
Familie; **R~ 'Navy** *n.* (Brit.) Königliche
Kriegsmarine
royalty /'rɔɪəltɪ/ *n.* (a) (payment) Tantieme,
die (**on** für)
(b) *collect.* (royal persons) Mitglieder *Pl.* des
Königshauses
RSI *abbr.* = **repetitive strain injury**
RSPCA *abbr.* (Brit.) = **Royal Society
for the Prevention of Cruelty to
Animals** *britischer Tierschutzverein*
rub /rʌb/ **1** *v.t.,* **-bb-** reiben (**on, against** an
+ *Dat.*); (to remove dirt etc.) abreiben; (to dry)
trockenreiben; ~ **sth. off sth.** etw. von etw.
[ab]reiben
2 *v.i.,* **-bb-** reiben ([up]**on, against** an
+ *Dat.*)
3 *n.* **give it a** ~: reib es ab; **there's the** ~
(fig.) da liegt der Haken [dabei] (ugs.)
■ **rub 'down** *v.t.* abreiben
■ **rub 'in** *v.t.* einreiben; **there's no need
to** *or* **don't** ~ **it in** (fig.) reib es mir nicht
[dauernd] unter die Nase
■ **rub 'off** *v.t.* wegreiben; wegwischen
■ **rub 'out** **1** *v.t.* ausreiben; (using eraser)
ausradieren
2 *v.i.* sich ausreiben/sich ausradieren
lassen
rubber /'rʌbə(r)/ *n.* (a) Gummi, *das od. der*
(b) (eraser) Radiergummi, *der*
rubber: ~ **'band** *n.* Gummiband, *das;*
~ **'glove** *n.* Gummihandschuh, *der;*
~ **plant** *n.* Gummibaum, *der;* ~ **'stamp**
n. Gummistempel, *der;* ~**-stamp** *v.t.* (fig.)
absegnen (ugs.)
rubbery /'rʌbərɪ/ *adj.* gummiartig; (tough)
zäh
rubbish /'rʌbɪʃ/ **1** *n.* (a) (refuse) Abfall,
der; (to be collected and dumped) Müll, *der*
(b) (worthless material) Plunder, *der* (ugs.); **be**
~: nichts taugen
(c) (nonsense) Quatsch, *der* (ugs.)
2 *int.* Quatsch (ugs.)
rubbish: ~ **bin** *n.* Abfall-/Mülleimer, *der;*
(in factory) Abfall-/Mülltonne, *die;* ~ **chute**
n. Müllschlucker, *der;* ~ **collection** *n.*
Müllabfuhr, *die;* ~ **dump** *n.* Müllkippe,
die; ~ **heap** *n.* Müllhaufen, *der;* ~ **tip** *n.*
Müllabladeplatz, *der*
rubbishy /'rʌbɪʃɪ/ *adj.* mies (ugs.)
rubble /'rʌbl/ *n.* Trümmer *Pl.*
rubella /rʊ'belə/ *n.* (Med.) Röteln *Pl.*
ruby /'ruːbɪ/ *n.* Rubin, *der*
ruby 'wedding *n.* Rubinhochzeit, *die*
rucksack /'rʌksæk, 'rʊksæk/ *n.*
Rucksack, *der*
rudder /'rʌdə(r)/ *n.* [Steuer]ruder, *das*
ruddy /'rʌdɪ/ *adj.* (a) (reddish) rötlich

(b) (Brit. coll.: bloody) verdammt (salopp)
rude /ruːd/ *adj.* (a) (impolite; stronger)
rüde; **be** ~ **to sb.** zu jmdm. grob unhöflich
sein/jmdn. rüde behandeln
(b) (abrupt) unsanft; ~ **awakening** böses
Erwachen
'rudely *adv.* (a) (impolitely) unhöflich; rüde
(b) (abruptly) jäh (geh.)
'rudeness *n.* (bad manners) ungehöriges
Benehmen
rudimentary /ruːdɪ'mentərɪ/ elementar;
primitiv ‹*Gebäude*›
rudiments /'ruːdɪmənts/ *n. pl.*
Grundlagen *Pl.*
rueful /'ruːfl/ *adj.* reumütig
ruffian /'rʌfɪən/ *n.* Rohling, *der*
ruffle /'rʌfl/ *v.t.* (a) kräuseln; ~ **sb.'s hair**
jmdm. durch die Haare fahren
(b) (upset) aus der Fassung bringen
rug /rʌg/ *n.* [kleiner, dicker] Teppich;
Persian ~: Perserbrücke, *die*
Rugby /'rʌgbɪ/ *n.* Rugby, *das*
Rugby: ~ **ball** *n.* Rugbyball, *der;*
~ **tackle** *n.* tiefes Fassen; **the policeman
brought him down with a** ~ **tackle** der
Polizist warf sich auf ihn und riss ihn zu
Boden
rugged /'rʌgɪd/ *adj.* (a) (uneven) zerklüftet;
unwegsam ‹*Land*›; zerfurcht ‹*Gesicht*›
(b) (sturdy) robust
ruin /'ruːɪn/ **1** *n.* (a) *in sing. or pl.* (remains)
Ruine, *die;* **in** ~**s** in Trümmern
(b) (downfall) Ruin, *der*
2 *v.t.* ruinieren; verderben ‹*Urlaub,
Abend*›; ~**ed** (reduced to ruins) verfallen; **a**
~**ed castle/church** eine Burg-/Kirchenruine
ruinous /'ruːɪnəs/ *adj.* ruinös
rule /ruːl/ **1** *n.* (a) Regel, *die;* **the** ~**s of
the game** die Spielregeln; **be against the** ~**s**
regelwidrig sein; (fig.) gegen die Spielregeln
verstoßen; **as a** ~: in der Regel; ~ **of thumb**
Faustregel, *die*
(b) *no pl.* (government) Herrschaft, *die* (**over**
über + *Akk.*)
2 *v.t.* (a) (control) beherrschen
(b) (be the ruler of) regieren; ‹*Monarch,
Diktator usw.*› herrschen über (+ *Akk.*)
3 *v.i.* (govern) herrschen
(b) (decide) entscheiden (**against** gegen; **in
favour of** für)
■ **rule 'out** *v.t.* ausschließen; (prevent)
unmöglich machen
'rule book *n.* Regeln
ruled /ruːld/ *adj.* liniert ‹*Papier*›
ruler /'ruːlə(r)/ *n.* (a) (person) Herrscher,
der/Herrscherin, *die*
(b) (for measuring) Lineal, *das*
ruling /'ruːlɪŋ/ **1** *adj.* herrschend ‹*Klasse*›;
regierend ‹*Partei*›
2 *n.* Entscheidung, *die*
rum /rʌm/ *n.* Rum, *der*
Rumania etc. /ruː'meɪnɪə/ ► ROMANIA etc.
rumble /'rʌmbl/ **1** *n.* Grollen, *das* ⋯⟫

2 *v.i.* (a) grollen; ⟨*Magen:*⟩ knurren
(b) ⟨*Fahrzeug:*⟩ rumpeln (ugs.)

ruminate /'ruːmɪneɪt/ *v.i.* ∼ **on** *or* **over**
sth. über etw. (*Akk.*) grübeln

rummage /'rʌmɪdʒ/ *v.i.* wühlen;
∼ **through sth.** etw. durchwühlen (ugs.)

rummy /'rʌmɪ/ *n.* Rommé, *das*

rumour (*Brit.; Amer.:* **rumor**) /'ruːmə(r)/
1 *n.* Gerücht, *das;* **there is a** ∼ **that** ...: es
geht das Gerücht, dass ...
2 *v.t.* **it is** ∼**ed that** ...: es geht das Gerücht,
dass ...

rump /rʌmp/ *n.* (a) (buttocks) Hinterteil,
das (ugs.)
(b) (remnant) Rest, *der*

rumple /'rʌmpl/ *v.t.* (a) (crease) zerknittern
(b) (tousle) zerzausen

'**rump steak** *n.* Rumpsteak, *das*

rumpus /'rʌmpəs/ *n.* (coll.) Krach, *der*
(ugs.); **kick up** *or* **make a** ∼: einen Spektakel
veranstalten (ugs.)

'**rumpus room** *n.* (Amer.) Spielzimmer,
das

run /rʌn/ 1 *n.* (a) (continuous stretch) Lauf, *der;* **go for a**
∼: laufen gehen; **on the** ∼ (fleeing) auf der
Flucht
(b) (trip in vehicle) Fahrt, *die;* (for pleasure)
Ausflug, *der*
(c) (continuous stretch) Länge, *die*
(d) (spell) **she has had a long** ∼ **of success**
sie war lange [Zeit] erfolgreich; **have a**
long ∼ ⟨*Stück, Show:*⟩ viele Aufführungen
erleben
(e) (succession) Serie, *die;* (Cards) Sequenz,
die; **a** ∼ **of victories** eine Siegesserie
(f) (use) **have the** ∼ **of sth.** etw. zu seiner
freien Verfügung haben
(g) (enclosure) Auslauf, *der*
(h) (in stocking etc.) Laufmasche, *die*
2 *v.i.,* **-nn-, ran** /ræn/, **run** (a) laufen; ∼ **for**
the bus laufen, um den Bus zu kriegen (ugs.);
∼ **to help sb.** jmdm. zu Hilfe eilen
(b) (roll, slide) laufen; ⟨*Ball, Kugel:*⟩ rollen,
laufen; ⟨*Schlitten, [Schiebe]tür:*⟩ gleiten
(c) ⟨*Rad, Maschine:*⟩ laufen
(d) (operate on a schedule) fahren; ∼ **between**
two places ⟨*Zug, Bus:*⟩ zwischen zwei Orten
verkehren
(e) (flow) laufen; ⟨*Fluss:*⟩ fließen; ⟨*Augen:*⟩
tränen; **his nose was** ∼**ning** ihm lief die
Nase
(f) ⟨*Vertrag, Theaterstück:*⟩ laufen
(g) (have wording) lauten; ⟨*Geschichte:*⟩ gehen
(fig.)
(h) ⟨*Butter, Eis:*⟩ zerlaufen; ⟨*Farben:*⟩
auslaufen
(i) (in election) kandidieren
3 *v.t.,* **-nn-, ran, run** (a) laufen lassen; (drive)
fahren; ∼ **one's hand/fingers through/along**
or **over sth.** mit der Hand/den Fingern
durch etw. fahren/über etw. (*Akk.*)
streichen; ∼ **an** *or* **one's eye along** *or* **down**
or **over sth.** (fig.) etw. überfliegen
(b) (cause to flow) [ein]laufen lassen; ∼ **a bath**

ein Bad einlaufen lassen
(c) (organize, manage) führen, leiten ⟨*Geschäft*
usw.⟩; veranstalten ⟨*Wettbewerb*⟩
(d) (operate) bedienen ⟨*Maschine*⟩; verkehren
lassen ⟨*Verkehrsmittel*⟩; einsetzen
⟨*Sonderbus, -zug*⟩; laufen lassen ⟨*Motor*⟩
(e) (own and use) sich (*Dat.*) halten ⟨*Auto*⟩
(f) ∼ **sb. into town** etc. jmdn. in die Stadt
usw. fahren

■ **run a'cross** *v.t.* ∼ **across sb./sth.** jmdn.
treffen/auf etw. (*Akk.*) stoßen

■ **run a'way** *v.i.* (a) (flee) weglaufen;
fortlaufen
(b) (abscond) ∼ **away [from home]** [von zu
Hause] weglaufen

■ **run 'down** 1 *v.t.* (a) (collide with)
überfahren
(b) (criticize) heruntermachen (ugs.)
(c) (reduce) abbauen
2 *v.i.* (a) hin-/herunterlaufen
(b) (decline) sich verringern
(c) ⟨*Uhr, Spielzeug:*⟩ ablaufen; ⟨*Batterie*⟩
leer werden

■ '**run into** *v.t.* (a) ∼ **into a tree** gegen
einen Baum fahren
(b) (meet) ∼ **into sb.** jmdm. in die Arme
laufen (ugs.)
(c) stoßen auf (+ *Akk.*) ⟨*Schwierigkeiten,*
Widerstand usw.⟩
(d) (amount to) ∼ **into thousands** in die
tausende gehen

■ **run 'off** 1 *v.i.* weglaufen
2 *v.t.* abziehen ⟨*Kopien*⟩

■ **run 'out** *v.i.* (a) hin-/herauslaufen
(b) ⟨*Vorräte, Bestände:*⟩ zu Ende gehen

■ **run 'out of** *v.t.* ∼ **sb.** ∼**s out of sth.** jmdm.
geht etw. aus; **I'm** ∼**ning out of patience**
meine Geduld geht zu Ende

■ **run 'over** 1 /'---/ *v.t.* (knock down)
überfahren
2 /-'--/ *v.i.* überlaufen

■ **run 'through** *v.t.* durchspielen
⟨*Theaterstück*⟩; durchgehen ⟨*Plan*⟩

■ '**run to** *v.t.* (a) (amount to) sich belaufen
auf (*Akk.*)
(b) (be sufficient for) **sth. will** ∼ **to sth.** etw.
reicht für etw.

■ **run 'up** 1 *v.i.* hinlaufen; **come** ∼**ning up**
hingelaufen kommen
2 *v.t.* (a) rasch nähen ⟨*Kleidungsstück*⟩
(b) zusammenkommen lassen ⟨*Schulden,*
Rechnung⟩

■ **run 'up against** *v.t.* stoßen auf (+ *Akk.*)
⟨*Probleme, Widerstand usw.*⟩

run: ∼**about** *n.* (coll.) [little] ∼**about**
Kleinwagen, *der;* ∼**around** *n.* (coll.)
give sb. the ∼**around** jmdn. an der Nase
herumführen (ugs.); ∼**away** 1 *n.*
Ausreißer, *der*/Ausreißerin, *die* (ugs.);
2 *attrib. adj.* durchgegangen ⟨*Pferd*⟩;
außer Kontrolle geraten ⟨*Fahrzeug, Preise*⟩;
galoppierend ⟨*Inflation*⟩; ∼**down** /'--/ *n.*
(coll.: briefing) Übersicht, *die* (**on** über + *Akk.*);
∼**-down** /-'-/ *adj.* (tired) mitgenommen

rung[1] /rʌŋ/ *n.* Sprosse, *die*

rung² ▸ RING² 2, 3
'runner *n.* **(a)** Läufer, *der*/Läuferin, *die*
  (b) (Bot.) Ausläufer, *der*
  (c) (on sledge) Kufe, *die*
'runner bean *n.* (Brit.) Stangenbohne, *die*
runner-'up *n.* Zweite, *der*/*die;* the runners-up die Platzierten *Pl.*
'running 1 *n.* **(a)** (management) Leitung, *die*
  (b) (action) Laufen, *das;* in/out of the
  ~: im/aus dem Rennen
  2 *adj.* (in succession) hintereinander; win
  for the third year ~: schon drei Jahre
  hintereinander gewinnen
running: ~ **'commentary** *n.*
  (Broadcasting; also fig.) Livekommentar,
  der; ~ **costs** *n. pl.* Betriebskosten *Pl.;*
  ~ **shoe** *n.* Rennschuh, *der;* ~ **'total**
  n. fortlaufende Summe; ~ **track** *n.*
  Aschenbahn, *die;* ~ **'water** *n.* hot and
  cold ~ **water** fließendes kaltes und warmes
  Wasser
runny /'rʌnɪ/ *adj.* **(a)** laufend ‹Nase›
  (b) zu dünn ‹Farbe, Marmelade›
run: ~**-off** *n.* (election) Stichwahl, *die;* (race)
  Entscheidungslauf, *der;* ~**-of-the-'mill**
  adj. ganz gewöhnlich; ~**-up** *n.* **(a)** during
  or in the ~**-up to an event** im Vorfeld eines
  Ereignisses; **(b)** (Sport) Anlauf, *der;* ~**way**
  n. (for take-off) Startbahn, *die;* (for landing)
  Landebahn, *die*
rupture /'rʌptʃə(r)/ 1 *n.* Bruch, *der*
  2 *v.t.* ~ **oneself** sich (*Dat.*) einen Bruch
  zuziehen
rural /'rʊərl/ *adj.* ländlich
ruse /ruːz/ *n.* List, *die*
rush¹ /rʌʃ/ *n.* (Bot.) Binse, *die*
rush² 1 *n.* **(a)** (hurry) Eile, *die;* what's all the
  ~? wozu diese Hast?; be in a [great] ~: in
  [großer] Eile sein
  (b) (period of great activity) Hochbetrieb, *der;*
  (~ hour) Stoßzeit, *die*
  (c) make a ~ for sth. sich auf etw. (*Akk.*)

stürzen
  2 *v.t.* **(a)** ~ sb./sth. somewhere jmdn./etw.
  auf schnellstem Wege irgendwohin bringen;
  be ~ed (have to hurry) in Eile sein; ~ sb. into
  doing sth. jmdn. dazu drängen, etw. zu tun
  (b) (perform quickly) auf die Schnelle
  erledigen; ~ it zu schnell machen
  3 *v.i.* **(a)** (move quickly) eilen; ‹Hund, Pferd:›
  laufen; ~ to help sb. jmdm. zu Hilfe eilen
  (b) (hurry unduly) sich zu sehr beeilen; don't
  ~! nur keine Eile!
  ∎ **rush a'bout, rush a'round** *v.i.*
  herumhetzen
rush: ~ **hour** *n.* Stoßzeit, *die;* ~ **job** *n.*
  eilige Arbeit
rusk /rʌsk/ *n.* Zwieback, *der*
Russia /'rʌʃə/ *pr. n.* Russland (*das*)
Russian /'rʌʃn/ 1 *adj.* russisch; sb. is
  ~: jmd. ist Russe/Russin
  2 *n.* **(a)** (person) Russe, *der*/Russin, *die*
  (b) (language) Russisch, *das;* see also
  ENGLISH 2A
rust /rʌst/ 1 *n.* Rost, *der*
  2 *v.i.* rosten
rustic /'rʌstɪk/ *adj.* **(a)** ländlich
  (b) rustikal ‹Mobiliar›
rustle /'rʌsl/ 1 *n.* Rascheln, *das*
  2 *v.i.* rascheln
  3 *v.t.* **(a)** rascheln lassen
  (b) (Amer.: steal) stehlen
  ∎ **rustle 'up** *v.t.* zusammenzaubern
  ‹Mahlzeit›
'rustproof *adj.* rostfrei
'rusty *adj.* rostig
rut /rʌt/ *n.* Spurrille, *die;* be in a ~
  (fig.) aus dem [Alltags]trott nicht mehr
  herauskommen
ruthless /'ruːθlɪs/ *adj.* rücksichtslos
RV *abbr.* (Amer.) = **recreational
  vehicle**
rye /raɪ/ *n.* Roggen, *der*
'rye bread *n.* Roggenbrot, *das*

r

s

Ss

S, s /es/ *n.* S, s, *das*
S. *abbr.* **(a)** = **south** S
  (b) = **southern** s.
sabbath /'sæbəθ/ *n.* Sabbat, *der*
sabbatical /sə'bætɪkl/ 1 *adj.* ~ **term/
  year** Forschungssemester/-jahr, *das*
  2 *n.* Forschungsurlaub, *der*
sabotage /'sæbətɑːʒ/ 1 *n.* Sabotage, *die*
  2 *v.t.* einen Sabotageakt verüben auf
  (+ *Akk.*); (fig.) sabotieren
saboteur /sæbə'tɜː(r)/ *n.* Saboteur, *der*

saccharin /'sækərɪn/ *n.* Saccharin, *das*
sachet /'sæʃeɪ/ *n.* Beutel, *der;* (cushion-shaped) Kissen, *das*
sack /sæk/ 1 *n.* **(a)** Sack, *der*
  (b) (coll.: dismissal) Rausschmiss, *der* (ugs.);
  get the ~: rausgeschmissen werden (ugs.);
  give sb. the ~: jmdn. rausschmeißen (ugs.)
  2 *v.t.* (coll.) rausschmeißen (ugs.) (for
  wegen)
sacking /'sækɪŋ/ *n.* **(a)** (coll.: dismissal)
  Rausschmiss, *der* (ugs.)   ⋯⟶

(b) (coarse fabric) Sackleinen, *das*

sacrament /'sækrəmənt/ *n.* Sakrament, *das*

sacred /'seɪkrɪd/ *adj.* heilig

sacrifice /'sækrɪfaɪs/ ① *n.* Opfer, *das* ② *v.t.* opfern

sacrilege /'sækrɪlɪdʒ/ *n.* [act of] ~: Sakrileg, *das*

sad /sæd/ *adj.* traurig (**at, about** über + *Akk.*); schmerzlich ⟨*Tod, Verlust*⟩; **feel** ~: traurig sein

sadden /'sædn/ *v.t.* traurig stimmen

SAD *abbr.* = **seasonal affective disorder**

saddle /'sædl/ ① *n.* Sattel, *der* ② *v.t.* (a) satteln ⟨*Pferd usw.*⟩ (b) (fig.) ~ sb. with sth. jmdm. etw. aufbürden (geh.)

'**saddlebag** *n.* Satteltasche, *die*

sadism /'seɪdɪzm/ *n.* Sadismus, *der*

sadist /'seɪdɪst/ *n.* Sadist, *der*/Sadistin, *die*

sadistic /sə'dɪstɪk/ *adj.*, **sa'distically** *adv.* sadistisch

'**sadly** *adv.* (a) (with sorrow) traurig (b) (unfortunately) leider

'**sadness** *n.* Traurigkeit, *die*

sadomasochism /seɪdəʊ'mæsəkɪzm/ *n.* Sadomasochismus, *der*

s.a.e. /eseɪ'iː/ *abbr.* = **stamped addressed envelope** adressierter Freiumschlag

safari /sə'fɑːrɪ/ *n.* Safari, *die;* **on** ~: auf Safari

safe /seɪf/ ① *n.* Safe, *der;* Geldschrank, *der* ② *adj.* (a) (out of danger) sicher (**from** vor + *Dat.*); **he's** ~: er ist in Sicherheit; ~ **and sound** sicher und wohlbehalten (b) (free from danger) ungefährlich; sicher ⟨*Ort, Hafen*⟩; **wish sb. a** ~ **journey** jmdm. eine gute Reise wünschen; **to be on the** ~ **side** zur Sicherheit (c) (reliable) sicher ⟨*Methode, Investition*⟩

safe: ~**guard** ① *n.* Schutz, *der;* ② *v.t.* schützen; ~ '**haven** *n.* (a) (safe place) Zuflucht, *die;* (b) (Polit.) Schutzzone, *die*

safely /'seɪflɪ/ *adv.* sicher; **did the parcel arrive** ~? ist das Paket heil angekommen?

safe 'sex Safersex, *der*

safety: ~ **belt** *n.* Sicherheitsgurt, *der;* ~ **catch** *n.* (of gun) Sicherungshebel, *der;* ~ **helmet** *n.* Schutzhelm, *der;* ~ **margin** *n.* Spielraum, *der;* ~ **pin** *n.* Sicherheitsnadel, *die;* ~ **valve** *n.* Sicherheitsventil, *das;* (fig.) Ventil, *das*

'**safe zone** *n.* (Polit.) Schutzzone, *die*

saffron /'sæfrən/ *n.* Safran, *der*

sag /sæg/ *v.i.,* **-gg-** durchhängen; (sink) sich senken

saga /'sɑːgə/ *n.* (a) (story of adventure) Heldenepos, *das;* (medieval narrative) Saga, *die* (b) (long involved story) [ganzer] Roman (fig.)

sage¹ /seɪdʒ/ *n.* (Bot.) Salbei, *der od. die*

sage² ① *adj.* weise ② *n.* Weise, *der*

Sagittarius /sædʒɪ'teərɪəs/ *n.* (Astrol., Astron.) der Schütze

Sahara /sə'hɑːrə/ *pr. n.* **the** ~ [Desert] die [Wüste] Sahara

said ▶ SAY 1

sail /seɪl/ ① *n.* (a) Segelfahrt, *die* (b) (piece of canvas) Segel, *das* ② *v.i.* (a) (travel on water) fahren; (in sailing boat) segeln (b) (start voyage) auslaufen (**for** nach) ③ *v.t.* (a) steuern ⟨*Boot, Schiff*⟩; segeln mit ⟨*Segeljacht, -schiff*⟩ (b) durchfahren/⟨*Segelschiff:*⟩ durchsegeln ⟨*Meer*⟩

sail: ~**board** *n.* Surfbrett, *das* (*zum Windsurfen*); ~**boarding** *n.* Windsurfen, *das;* ~**boat** *n.* (Amer.) Segelboot, *das*

'**sailing** *n.* Segeln, *das*

'**sailing:** ~ **boat** *n.* Segelboot, *das;* ~ **ship** *n.* Segelschiff, *das*

sailor /'seɪlə(r)/ *n.* Seemann, *der;* (in navy) Matrose, *der*

saint ① /sənt/ *adj.* **S**~ **Michael** der heilige Michael; Sankt Michael ② /seɪnt/ *n.* Heilige, *der/die*

'**saintly** /'seɪntlɪ/ *adj.* heilig

sake /seɪk/ *n.* **for the** ~ **of** um … (*Gen.*) willen; **for my** *etc.* ~: um meinetwillen *usw.;* mir *usw.* zuliebe

salad /'sæləd/ *n.* Salat, *der*

salad: ~ **cream** *n.* ≈ Mayonnaise, *die;* ~ **dressing** *n.* Salatsoße, *die;* ~ **servers** *n. pl.* Salatbesteck, *das*

salary /'sælərɪ/ *n.* Gehalt, *das*

sale /seɪl/ *n.* (a) Verkauf, *der;* (at reduced prices) Ausverkauf, *der;* (at end of season) Schlußverkauf, *der;* [**up] for** ~: zu verkaufen (b) ~**s** (amount sold) Verkaufszahlen *Pl.* (**of** für); Absatz, *der* (c) [**jumble** *or* **rummage**] ~: [Wohltätigkeits]basar, *der*

'**sale price** *n.* (a) (retail price) Verkaufspreis, *der* (b) (price in sale) Ausverkaufspreis, *der*

sales: ~ **assistant** (Brit.), ~ **clerk** (Amer.) *ns.* Verkäufer, *der*/Verkäuferin, *die;* ~**man** /'seɪlzmən/ *n., pl.* ~**men** /'seɪlzmən/ Verkäufer, *der*

'**salesmanship** *n.* Kunst des Verkaufens

sales: ~ **rep** (coll.), ~ **representative** *ns.* [Handels]vertreter, *der*/-vertreterin, *die;* ~**woman** *n.* Verkäuferin, *die*

salient /'seɪlɪənt/ *adj.* auffallend

saliva /sə'laɪvə/ *n.* Speichel, *der*

sallow /'sæləʊ/ *adj.* blassgelb

salmon /'sæmən/ *n.* Lachs, *der*

saloon /sə'luːn/ *n.* (a) (Brit.) ~ [bar] *separater Teil eines Pubs mit mehr Komfort* (b) (Brit.) ~ [car] Limousine, *die*

salt /sɔːlt, sɒlt/ ⟨1⟩ *n.* **[common]**
~: [Koch]salz, *das*
⟨2⟩ *adj.* (containing or tasting of ~) salzig;
(preserved with ~) gepökelt ⟨*Fleisch*⟩; gesalzen
⟨*Butter*⟩
⟨3⟩ *v.t.* **(a)** salzen
(b) (cure) [ein]pökeln
(c) ~ **the roads** Salz auf die Straßen streuen
salt: ~ **cellar** *n.* Salzfässchen, *das;*
~ **'water** *n.* Salzwasser, *das*
'salty *adj.* salzig
salute /sə'luːt/ ⟨1⟩ *v.t.* grüßen
⟨2⟩ *v.i.* (Mil., Navy) [militärisch] grüßen
⟨3⟩ *n.* Salut, *der;* militärischer Gruß
salvage /'sælvɪdʒ/ ⟨1⟩ *n.* Bergung, *die*
⟨2⟩ *v.t.* bergen
salvation /sæl'veɪʃn/ *n.* Erlösung, *die*
Salvation 'Army *n.* Heilsarmee, *die*
salvo /'sælvəʊ/ *n.* Salve, *die*
Samaritan /sə'mærɪtən/ *n.* **good
~:** [barmherziger] Samariter; **the ~s**
(organization) ≈ die Telefonseelsorge
same /seɪm/ ⟨1⟩ *adj.* **the ~: der/die/das
gleiche; the ~ [thing]** (identical) der-/die-/
dasselbe
⟨2⟩ *adv.* **all** *or* **just the ~:** trotzdem
sample /'sɑːmpl/ ⟨1⟩ *n.* (example)
[Muster]beispiel, *das;* (specimen) Probe, *die;*
[commercial] ~: Muster, *das*
⟨2⟩ *v.t.* probieren
'sample letter *n.* Musterbrief, *der*
sampler /'sɑːmplə(r)/ *n.* (trial pack)
Probe[packung], *die*
sanatorium /sænə'tɔːrɪəm/ *n.*
Sanatorium, *das*
sanctify /'sæŋktɪfaɪ/ *v.t.* heiligen
sanctimonious /sæŋktɪ'məʊnɪəs/ *adj.*
scheinheilig
sanction /'sæŋkʃn/ ⟨1⟩ *n.* Sanktion, *die*
⟨2⟩ *v.t.* sanktionieren
sanctity /'sæŋktɪtɪ/ *n.* Heiligkeit, *die*
sanctuary /'sæŋktʃʊərɪ/ *n.* **(a)** (holy place)
Heiligtum, *das*
(b) (refuge) Zufluchtsort, *der*
(c) (for animals) Naturschutzgebiet, *das*
sand /sænd/ ⟨1⟩ *n.* Sand, *der*
⟨2⟩ *v.t.* ~ **sth. [down]** etw. [ab]schmirgeln
sandal /'sændl/ *n.* Sandale, *die*
sandalwood *n.* Sandelholz, *das*
sand: ~**bag** ⟨1⟩ *n.* Sandsack, *der;* ⟨2⟩ *v.
t.* mit Sandsäcken schützen; ~**bank** *n.*
Sandbank, *die;* ~ **dune** *n.* Düne, *die;* ~**paper** ⟨1⟩ *n.*
Sandpapier, *das;* ⟨2⟩ *v.t.* [mit Sandpapier]
[ab]schmirgeln; ~**pit** *n.* Sandkasten, *der;*
~**stone** *n.* Sandstein, *der*
sandwich /'sænwɪdʒ/ ⟨1⟩ *n.* Sandwich, *der*
od. das; ≈ [zusammengeklapptes] belegtes
Brot; **cheese** ~: Käsebrot, *das*
⟨2⟩ *v.t.* einschieben (**between** zwischen
+ *Akk.;* **into** in + *Akk.*)
'sandy *adj.* **(a)** sandig; Sand⟨*boden,
-strand*⟩
(b) rotblond ⟨*Haar*⟩
sane /seɪn/ *adj.* **(a)** geistig gesund
(b) (sensible) vernünftig
sang ▶ SING
sanitary /'sænɪtərɪ/ *adj.* sanitär
⟨*Verhältnisse, Anlagen*⟩
'sanitary napkin (Amer.), **'sanitary
towel** (Brit.) *ns.* Damenbinde, *die*
sanitation /sænɪ'teɪʃn/ *n.* Kanalisation
und Abfallbeseitigung
sanitize (sanitise) /'sænɪtaɪz/ *v.t.* (fig.)
entschärfen
sanity /'sænɪtɪ/ *n.* geistige Gesundheit;
lose one's ~: den Verstand verlieren
sank ▶ SINK 2, 3
Santa Claus /'sæntə klɔːz/ *n.* der
Weihnachtsmann
sap /sæp/ ⟨1⟩ *n.* Saft, *der*
⟨2⟩ *v.t.,* **-pp-** zehren an (+ *Dat.*)
sapling /'sæplɪŋ/ *n.* junger Baum
sapphire /'sæfaɪə(r)/ *n.* Saphir, *der*
sarcasm /'sɑːkæzm/ *n.* Sarkasmus, *der*
sarcastic /sɑː'kæstɪk/ *adj.* sarkastisch
sardine /sɑː'diːn/ *n.* Sardine, *die*
Sardinia /sɑː'dɪnɪə/ *pr. n.* Sardinien (*das*)
sardonic /sɑː'dɒnɪk/ *adj.* höhnisch;
sardonisch ⟨*Lächeln*⟩
SARS /sɑːz/ *n.* SARS, *das*
sash /sæʃ/ *n.* Schärpe, *die*
sash 'window *n.* Schiebefenster, *das*
sat ▶ SIT
Sat. *abbr.* = **Saturday** Sa.
Satan /'seɪtən/ *pr. n.* Satan, *der*
satanic /sə'tænɪk/ *adj.* satanisch
satchel /'sætʃl/ *n.* [Schul]ranzen, *der*
satellite /'sætəlaɪt/ *n.* Satellit, *der*
satellite: ~ **'broadcasting**
n. Satellitenfunk, *der;* ~ **dish** *n.*
Satellitenschüssel, *die;* ~ **navi'gation** *n.*
Satellitennavigation, *die;* ~ **receiver** *n.*
Satellitenempfänger, *der;* ~ **technology**
n. Satellitentechnik, *die;* ~ **'television**
n. Satellitenfernsehen, *das;* ~ **town** *n.*
Satelliten- *od.* Trabantenstadt, *die*
satin /'sætɪn/ *n.* Satin, *der*
satire /'sætaɪə(r)/ *n.* Satire, *die* (**on** auf
+ *Akk.*)
satirical /sə'tɪrɪkl/ *adj.* satirisch
satisfaction /sætɪs'fækʃn/ *n.*
Befriedigung, *die* (**at, with** über + *Akk.*);
meet with sb.'s [complete] ~: jmdn. [in
jeder Weise] zufrieden stellen
satisfactory /sætɪs'fæktərɪ/ *adj.*
zufrieden stellend
satisfied /'sætɪsfaɪd/ *adj.* **(a)** (contented)
zufrieden
(b) (convinced) überzeugt (**of** von)
satisfy /'sætɪsfaɪ/ *v.t.* **(a)** befriedigen;
zufrieden stellen ⟨*Kunden*⟩; stillen
⟨*Hunger, Durst*⟩   ⋯⟶

S

(b) (convince) ∼ sb. [of sth.] jmdn. [von etw.] überzeugen

'**satisfying** adj. befriedigend; sättigend ⟨Gericht, Speise⟩

satnav /'sætnæv/ n. (coll.) Satelliten-Navigationsgerät, das; Navi, das (ugs.)

satphone /'sætfəʊn/ n. Satellitentelefon, das

saturate /'sætʃəreɪt/ v.t. durchnässen; [mit Feuchtigkeit durch]tränken ⟨Boden, Erde⟩

saturated /'sætʃəreɪtɪd/ adj. durchnässt

saturation /sætʃə'reɪʃn/ n. Durchnässung, die

Saturday /'sætədeɪ, 'sætədɪ/ n. Samstag, der; see also FRIDAY

'**Saturday job** n. Samstagsjob, der (ugs.)

Saturn /'sætən/ pr. n. (Astron.) Saturn, der

sauce /sɔːs/ n. (a) Soße, die (b) (impudence) Frechheit, die

sauce: ∼ **boat** n. Sauciere, die; ∼**pan** /'sɔːspən/ n. Kochtopf, der; (with straight handle) [Stiel]kasserolle, die

saucer /'sɔːsə(r)/ n. Untertasse, die

saucy /'sɔːsɪ/ adj. (a) (rude) frech (b) (pert, jaunty) keck

Saudi Arabia /saʊdɪ ə'reɪbɪə/ pr. n. Saudi-Arabien (das)

sauna /'sɔːnə, 'saʊnə/ n. Sauna, die

saunter /'sɔːntə(r)/ v.i. schlendern

sausage /'sɒsɪdʒ/ n. Wurst, die

sausage: ∼ **meat** n. Wurstmasse, die; ∼ '**roll** n.: Blätterteig mit Wurstfüllung

savage /'sævɪdʒ/ 1 adj. (a) (uncivilized) primitiv; wild ⟨Volksstamm⟩; unzivilisiert ⟨Land⟩ (b) (fierce) brutal; wild ⟨Tier⟩ 2 n. Wilde, der/die (veralt.)

savagery /'sævɪdʒrɪ/ n. Brutalität, die

save /seɪv/ 1 v.t. (a) (rescue) retten (from vor + Dat.); ∼ oneself from falling sich [beim Hinfallen] fangen (b) (put aside) aufheben; sparen ⟨Geld⟩; sammeln ⟨Briefmarken usw.⟩; (conserve) sparsam umgehen mit (c) (make unnecessary) sparen ⟨Geld, Zeit, Energie⟩; ∼ sb./oneself sth. jmdm./sich etw. ersparen (d) (Sport) abwehren ⟨Schuss, Ball;⟩ (e) (Comp.) speichern; sichern; ∼ sth. on [to] a disk etw. auf Diskette abspeichern 2 v.i. sparen (on Akk.) 3 n. (Sport) Abwehr, die
■ **save** '**up** 1 v.t. sparen 2 v.i. sparen (for für, auf + Akk.)

'**saver** n. Sparer, der/Sparerin, die

saving /'seɪvɪŋ/ 1 n. in pl. Ersparnisse Pl. 2 adj. ⟨kosten-, benzin⟩sparend

savings: ∼ **account** n. Sparkonto, das; ∼ **bank** n. Sparkasse, die

saviour /'seɪvjə(r)/ n. (a) Retter, der/Retterin, die

(b) (Relig.) **the S**∼: der Heiland

savor etc. (Amer.) ▸ SAVOUR etc.

savour /'seɪvə(r)/ (Brit.) 1 n. (flavour) Geschmack, der 2 v.t. genießen

savoury /'seɪvərɪ/ (Brit.) 1 adj. (a) pikant; salzig (b) (appetizing) appetitanregend 2 n. [pikantes] Häppchen

saw[1] /sɔː/ 1 n. Säge, die 2 v.t., p.p. sawn /sɔːn/ or sawed [zer]sägen; ∼ in half in der Mitte durchsägen 3 v.i., p.p. sawn or sawed sägen; ∼ through sth. etw. durchsägen

saw[2] ▸ SEE

saw: ∼**dust** n. Sägemehl, das; ∼**mill** n. Sägemühle, die

sawn ▸ SAW[1] 2, 3

'**sawn-off** adj. (Brit.) ⟨Gewehr⟩ mit abgesägtem Lauf

saxophone /'sæksəfəʊn/ n. Saxophon, das

saxophonist /sæk'sɒfənɪst/ n. Saxophonist, der/Saxophonistin, die

say /seɪ/ 1 v.t. pres. t. he says /sez/, p.t. & p.p. said /sed/ (a) sagen; that is to ∼: das heißt; do as or what I ∼: tun Sie, was ich sage; when all is said and done letzten Endes; go without ∼ing sich von selbst verstehen; she is said to be clever/to have done it man sagt, sie sei klug/habe es getan (b) (recite) sprechen ⟨Gebet, Text⟩ (c) (have specified wording or reading) sagen; ⟨Zeitung:⟩ schreiben; ⟨Uhr:⟩ zeigen ⟨Uhrzeit⟩; what does it ∼ here? was steht hier? 2 n. have a or some ∼: ein Mitspracherecht haben (in bei); have no ∼: nichts zu sagen haben; have one's ∼: seine Meinung sagen

'**saying** n. Redensart, die

scab /skæb/ n. [Wund]schorf, der

scaffold /'skæfəld/ n. Schafott, das

'**scaffolding** n. Gerüst, das

'**scaffolding pole** n. Gerüststange, die

scald /skɔːld, skɒld/ 1 n. Verbrühung, die 2 v.t. verbrühen

scale[1] /skeɪl/ n. (a) (of fish, reptile, etc.) Schuppe, die (b) (in kettle etc.) Kesselstein, der; (on teeth) Zahnstein, der

scale[2] n. (a) in sing. or pl. (weighing instrument) ∼[s] Waage, die (b) (dish of balance) Waagschale, die

scale[3] 1 n. (a) (series of degrees) Skala, die (b) (Mus.) Tonleiter, die (c) (dimensions) Ausmaß, das; be on a small ∼: bescheidenen Umfang haben (d) (ratio of reduction) Maßstab, der; what is the ∼ of the map? welchen Maßstab hat diese Karte? (e) (indication) (on map) Maßstab, der; (on thermometer) [Anzeige]skala, die 2 v.t. ersteigen ⟨Mauer, Leiter, Gipfel⟩

■ **scale 'down** *v.t.* [entsprechend] drosseln ⟨*Produktion*⟩; Abstriche machen bei ⟨*Planungen*⟩

scalp /skælp/ *n.* Kopfhaut, *die*

scalpel /'skælpl/ *n.* Skalpell, *das*

scam /skæm/ *n.* (coll.) Masche, *die* (ugs.)

scamper /'skæmpə(r)/ *v.i.* ⟨*Person:*⟩ flitzen; ⟨*Tier:*⟩ huschen

scampi /'skæmpɪ/ *n. pl.* Scampi *Pl.*

scan /skæn/ ① *v.t.,* **-nn-: (a)** (search thoroughly) absuchen (**for** nach)
(b) (look over cursorily) flüchtig ansehen; überfliegen ⟨*Zeitung, Liste usw.*⟩ (**for** auf der Suche nach)
(c) (Med.) szintigraphisch untersuchen
(d) (Comp.) scannen
② *v.i.,* **-nn-** ⟨*Vers[zeile]:*⟩ das richtige Versmaß haben
③ *n.* (Med.) szintigraphische Untersuchung, *die;* (image) szintigramm, *das*

scandal /'skændl/ *n.* **(a)** Skandal, *der* (**about/of** um); (story) Skandalgeschichte, *die*
(b) (outrage) Empörung, *die*
(c) (gossip) Klatsch, *der* (ugs.)

scandalize /'skændəlaɪz/ *v.t.* schockieren

scandalous /'skændələs/ *adj.* skandalös; schockierend ⟨*Bemerkung*⟩

Scandinavia /skændɪ'neɪvɪə/ *pr. n.* Skandinavien ⟨*das*⟩

Scandinavian /skændɪ'neɪvɪən/ ① *adj.* skandinavisch; **sb. is ~:** jmd. ist Skandinavier/Skandinavierin
② *n.* **(a)** (person) Skandinavier, *der/* Skandinavierin, *die*
(b) (Ling.) skandinavische Sprachen *Pl.*

scanner /'skænə(r)/ *n.* **(a)** (to detect radioactivity) Geigerzähler, *der*
(b) (radar aerial) Radarantenne, *die*
(c) (Comp., Med.) Scanner, *der*

scant /skænt/ *adj.* wenig

scanty /'skæntɪ/ *adj.* spärlich; knapp ⟨*Bikini*⟩

scapegoat /'skeɪpɡəʊt/ *n.* Sündenbock, *der;* **make sb. a ~:** jmdn. zum Sündenbock machen

scar /skɑː(r)/ ① *n.* Narbe, *die*
② *v.t.,* **-rr-:** **~ sb./sb.'s face** bei jmdm./in jmds. Gesicht (*Dat.*) Narben hinterlassen

scarce /skeəs/ *adj.* **(a)** (insufficient) knapp
(b) (rare) selten; **make oneself ~** (coll.) sich aus dem Staub machen (ugs.)

'**scarcely** *adv.* kaum

scarcity /'skeəsɪtɪ/ *n.* Knappheit, *die* (**of** an + *Dat.*)

scare /skeə(r)/ ① *n.* **(a)** (sensation of fear) Schreck[en], *der;* **give sb. a ~:** jmdm. einen Schreck[en] einjagen
(b) (general alarm) [allgemeine] Hysterie; **bomb ~:** Bombendrohung, *die*
② *v.t.* (frighten) Angst machen (+ *Dat.*); (startle) erschrecken

■ **scare a'way, scare 'off** *v.t.* verscheuchen

'**scarecrow** *n.* Vogelscheuche, *die*

scared /skeəd/ *adj.* **be ~ of sb./sth.** vor jmdm./etw. Angst haben; **be ~ of doing/to do sth.** sich nicht [ge]trauen, etw. zu tun

scaremongering /'skeəmʌŋɡərɪŋ/ *n.* Panikmache, *die*

scarf /skɑːf/ *n., pl.* **~s** or **scarves** /skɑːvz/ Schal, *der;* (square) Halstuch, *das;* (worn over hair) Kopftuch, *das*

scarlet /'skɑːlɪt/ ① *n.* Scharlach, *der*
② *adj.* scharlachrot

scarlet 'fever *n.* Scharlach, *der*

scarves ▶ SCARF

scary /'skeərɪ/ *adj.* Furcht erregend ⟨*Anblick*⟩; schaurig ⟨*Film, Geschichte*⟩

scathing /'skeɪðɪŋ/ *adj.* bissig ⟨*Person, Humor, Bemerkung*⟩

scatter /'skætə(r)/ ① *v.t.* **(a)** vertreiben; auseinander treiben ⟨*Menge*⟩
(b) (distribute irregularly) verstreuen
② *v.i.* sich auflösen; ⟨*Menge:*⟩ sich zerstreuen; (in fear) auseinander stieben

scattered /'skætəd/ *adj.* verstreut; vereinzelt ⟨*Regenschauer*⟩

scatty /'skætɪ/ *adj.* (Brit. coll.) dusslig (salopp)

scavenge /'skævɪndʒ/ *v.i.* **~ for sth.** nach etw. suchen

'**scavenger** *n.* (animal) Aasfresser, *der;* (fig. derog.: person) Aasgeier, *der* (ugs.)

scenario /sɪ'nɑːrɪəʊ/ *n., pl.* **~s** Szenario, *das*

scene /siːn/ *n.* **(a)** (place of event) Schauplatz, *der;* **~ of the crime** Tatort, *der*
(b) (division of act) Auftritt, *der*
(c) (view) Anblick, *der*
(d) behind the **~s** hinter den Kulissen
(e) the political/drug/artistic **~:** die politische/Drogen-/Kunstszene

scenery /'siːnərɪ/ *n.* **(a)** Landschaft, *die*
(b) (Theatre) Bühnenbild, *das*

scenic /'siːnɪk/ *adj.* landschaftlich schön

scent /sent/ ① *n.* **(a)** (smell) Duft, *der*
(b) (Hunting; also fig.: trail) Fährte, *die;* **be on the ~ of sb./sth.** (fig.) jmdm./einer Sache auf der Spur sein
(c) (Brit.: perfume) Parfüm, *das*
② *v.t.* wittern

scented /'sentɪd/ *adj.* **(a)** (having smell) duftend
(b) (perfumed) parfümiert

sceptic /'skeptɪk/ *n.* Skeptiker, *der/*Skeptikerin, *die*

sceptical /'skeptɪkl/ *adj.* skeptisch; **be ~ about** or **of sb./sth.** jmdm./einer Sache skeptisch gegenüberstehen

scepticism /'skeptɪsɪzm/ *n.* Skepsis, *die*

schedule /'ʃedjuːl/ ① *n.* **(a)** (list) Tabelle, *die;* (for event) Programm, *das*
(b) (of work) Zeitplan, *der*
(c) **on ~:** plangemäß
② *v.t.* zeitlich planen

S

'scheduled flight n. Linienflug, der
scheme /ski:m/ n. (a) (arrangement)
Anordnung, die
(b) (plan) Programm, das; (project) Projekt,
das
(c) (dishonest plan) Intrige, die
schizophrenia /skɪtsə'fri:nɪə/ n.
Schizophrenie, die
schizophrenic /skɪtsə'frenɪk,
skɪtsə'fri:nɪk/ adj. schizophren
scholar /'skɒlə(r)/ n. Gelehrte, der/die
'scholarly adj. wissenschaftlich; gelehrt
⟨Person⟩
'scholarship n. (a) (award) Stipendium,
das
(b) (scholarly work) Gelehrsamkeit, die
school /sku:l/ n. Schule, die; (Amer.: college)
Hochschule, die; **be at** or **in** ∼: in der Schule
sein; (attend ∼) zur Schule gehen; **go to**
∼: zur Schule gehen; ∼ **holidays/exchange**
Schulferien Pl./Schüleraustausch, der
school: ∼ **age** n. Schulalter, das;
∼**bag** n. Schultasche, die; ∼**boy** n.
Schüler, der; ∼**child** n. Schulkind, das;
∼ **friend** n. Schulfreund, der/-freundin,
die; ∼**girl** n. Schülerin, die; ∼ **'governor**
n.: ≈ Mitglied des Schulbeirats; ∼**kid** n.
(coll.) Schulkind, das; ∼ **leaver** n. (Brit.)
Schulabgänger, der/-abgängerin, die;
∼**master** n. Lehrer, der; ∼**mistress** n.
Lehrerin, die; ∼ **'rule** n. Schulvorschrift,
die; Schulregel, die; **it is a** ∼ **rule that** ...:
an der Schule ist es Vorschrift, dass ...;
∼**teacher** n. Lehrer, der/Lehrerin,
die; ∼ **'uniform** n. Schuluniform, die;
∼ **work** n. Schularbeiten Pl.; ∼ **'year** n.
Schuljahr, das
sciatica /saɪ'ætɪkə/ n. Ischias, der od. das
science /'saɪəns/ n. Wissenschaft, die
science 'fiction n. Sciencefiction, die
scientific /saɪən'tɪfɪk/ adj.
wissenschaftlich
scientist /'saɪəntɪst/ n. Wissenschaftler,
der/Wissenschaftlerin, die
sci-fi /'saɪfaɪ/ n. (coll.) Sciencefiction, die
scintillating /'sɪntɪleɪtɪŋ/ adj. (fig.)
geistsprühend
scissors /'sɪzəz/ n. pl. **[pair of]** ∼: Schere,
die
scoff[1] /skɒf/ v.i. (mock) spotten; ∼ **at** sich
lustig machen über (+ Akk.)
scoff[2] v.t. (coll.: eat greedily) verschlingen
scold /skəʊld/ v.t. ausschimpfen (**for**
wegen); **she** ∼**ed him for being late** sie
schimpfte ihn aus, weil er zu spät kam
scone /skɒn, skəʊn/ n.: weicher, oft zum
Tee gegessener kleiner Kuchen
scoop /sku:p/ **1** n. (a) Schaufel, die; (for ice
cream etc.) Portionierer, der
(b) (Journ.) Knüller, der (ugs.)
2 v.t. schaufeln ⟨Kohlen, Zucker⟩; schöpfen
⟨Flüssigkeit⟩
■ **scoop 'out** v.t. (a) (hollow out) aushöhlen;

schaufeln ⟨Loch, Graben⟩
(b) [her]ausschöpfen ⟨Flüssigkeit⟩;
auslöffeln ⟨Fruchtfleisch⟩; (with a knife)
herausschneiden ⟨Gehäuse, Fruchtfleisch⟩
■ **scoop 'up** v.t. schöpfen ⟨Flüssigkeit,
Suppe⟩; schaufeln ⟨Erde⟩
scooter /'sku:tə(r)/ n. (a) (toy) Roller, der
(b) [motor] ∼: [Motor]roller, der
scope /skəʊp/ n. (a) Bereich, der; (of
discussion etc.) Rahmen, der
(b) (opportunity) Entfaltungsmöglichkeiten Pl.
scorch /skɔːtʃ/ v.t. versengen
scorched 'earth policy n. Politik der
verbrannten Erde
scorching /'skɔːtʃɪŋ/ adj. glühend heiß
score /skɔː(r)/ **1** n. (a) (points)
[Spiel]stand, der; (made by one player)
Punktzahl, die; **keep [the]** ∼: zählen
(b) (Mus.) Partitur, die; (Cinemat.)
[Film]musik, die
(c) pl. same or ∼**s** (group of 20) zwanzig
(d) in pl. (great numbers) ∼**s [and** ∼**s] of** zig
(ugs.); Dutzende [von]
(e) **on that** ∼: was das betrifft
(f) **pay off** or **settle an old** ∼ (fig.) eine alte
Rechnung begleichen
2 v.t. erzielen ⟨Erfolg, Punkt usw.⟩; ∼ **a**
goal ein Tor schießen
3 v.i. (a) (make ∼) Punkte/einen Punkt
erzielen; (∼ goal/goals) ein Tor/Tore
schießen/werfen
(b) (keep ∼) aufschreiben
'scoreboard n. Anzeigetafel, die
'scorer n. (a) (recorder) Anschreiber,
der/Anschreiberin, die
(b) (Footb.) Torschütze, der/-schützin, die
'scoresheet n. Anschreibebogen, der
scorn /skɔːn/ **1** n. Verachtung, die
2 v.t. verachten; in den Wind schlagen
⟨Rat⟩; ausschlagen ⟨Angebot⟩
scornful /'skɔːnfl/ adj. verächtlich
⟨Lächeln, Blick⟩; **be** ∼ **of sth.** für etw. nur
Verachtung haben
Scorpio /'skɔːpɪəʊ/ n. (Astrol., Astron.) der
Skorpion
scorpion /'skɔːpɪən/ n. Skorpion, der
Scot /skɒt/ n. Schotte, der/Schottin, die
scotch v.t. den Boden entziehen (+ Dat.)
⟨Gerücht⟩; zunichte machen ⟨Plan⟩
Scotch /skɒtʃ/ **1** adj. ▶ SCOTTISH
2 n. Scotch, der; schottischer Whisky
Scotch: ∼ **'egg** n.: hart gekochtes Ei in
Wurstbrät; ∼ **'whisky** n. schottischer
Whisky
scot-'free adj. **[get off/go]** ∼:
ungeschoren [davonkommen od. bleiben]
Scotland /'skɒtlənd/ pr. n. Schottland
(das)
Scots /skɒts/ **1** adj. (esp. Scot.) schottisch;
sb. is ∼: jmd. ist Schotte/Schottin
2 n. (dialect) Schottisch, das
Scotsman /'skɒtsmən/ n., pl. **Scotsmen**
/'skɒtsmən/ Schotte, der

'Scotswoman n. Schottin, die
Scottish /'skɒtɪʃ/ adj. schottisch; **sb.** is
~: jmd. ist Schotte/Schottin
scoundrel /'skaʊndrl/ n. Schuft, der
scour[1] /skaʊə(r)/ v.t. (search)
durchkämmen (**for** nach)
scour[2] v.t. scheuern ⟨Topf, Metall⟩
'scourer n. Topfreiniger, der
scourge /skɜːdʒ/ n. Geißel, die
scout /skaʊt/ [1] n. (a) [Boy]
S~: Pfadfinder, der
(b) (Mil.) Späher, der
[2] v.i. ~ **for** Ausschau halten nach
scowl /skaʊl/ [1] v.i. ein mürrisches
Gesicht machen
[2] n. mürrischer [Gesichts]ausdruck
scram /skræm/ v.i., **-mm-** (coll.) abhauen
(salopp)
scramble /'skræmbl/ [1] v.i. (a) (clamber)
klettern; ~ **through a hedge** sich durch eine
Hecke zwängen
(b) (move hastily) rennen (ugs.); ~ **for sth.** um
etw. rangeln
[2] v.t. (Teleph., Radio) verschlüsseln
scrambled 'egg n. Rührei, das
scrap[1] /skræp/ [1] n. (a) (of paper) Fetzen,
der; (of food) Bissen, der
(b) in pl. (odds and ends) (of food) Reste Pl.
(c) (smallest amount) **not a** ~ **of** kein bisschen;
(of sympathy, truth also) nicht ein Fünkchen;
not a ~ **of evidence** nicht die Spur eines
Beweises
(d) ~ **[metal]** Schrott, der; ~ **iron** Alteisen,
das
[2] v.t., **-pp-** wegwerfen; (send for ~)
verschrotten; (fig.) aufgeben
scrap[2] (coll.) [1] n. (fight) Rauferei, die
[2] v.i., **-pp-** sich raufen
'scrapbook n. [Sammel]album, das
scrape /skreɪp/ [1] v.t. (a) (make smooth)
schaben ⟨Häute, Möhren, Kartoffeln usw.⟩;
abziehen ⟨Holz⟩; (damage) verschrammen
⟨Fußboden, Auto⟩
(b) (remove) [ab]kratzen ⟨Farbe, Schmutz,
Rost⟩ (**off, from** von)
(c) (draw along) schleifen
(d) ~ **together** (raise) zusammenkratzen
(ugs.); (save up) zusammensparen
[2] v.i. (a) (move with sound) schleifen
(b) (emit scraping noise) ein schabendes
Geräusch machen
(c) (rub) streifen (**against, over** Akk.)
[3] n. (a) (act, sound) Kratzen, das (**against an**
+ Dat.)
(b) (predicament) Schwulitäten Pl. (ugs.)
■ **scrape 'by** v.i. (fig.) sich über Wasser
halten (**on** mit)
■ **scrape 'out** v.t. (a) (excavate) buddeln
(ugs.); scharren
(b) (clean) auskratzen
■ **scrape through** [1] /'--/ v.t. sich
zwängen durch; (fig.) mit Hängen und
Würgen kommen durch ⟨Prüfung⟩

[2] /-'-/ v.i. sich durchzwängen; (fig.: in
examination) mit Hängen und Würgen
durchkommen
'scraper n. (for shoes) Kratzeisen, das;
(grid) Abtreter, der; (tool, kitchen utensil)
Schaber, der; (for removing ice from car windows)
[Eis]kratzer, der
scrap: ~ **heap** n. Schrotthaufen,
der; ~ **merchant** n. Schrotthändler,
der/-händlerin, die; ~ **'paper** n.
Schmierpapier, das
scrappy /'skræpɪ/ adj. lückenhaft
'scrapyard n. Schrottplatz, der
scratch /skrætʃ/ [1] v.t. (a) (score surface of)
zerkratzen; (score skin of) kratzen
(b) (get scratch[es] on) ~ **oneself/one's hands**
etc. sich schrammen/sich (Dat.) die Hände
usw. zerkratzen
(c) (scrape without marking) kratzen; kratzen
an (+ Dat.) ⟨Insektenstich usw.⟩; ~ **oneself/**
one's arm sich kratzen/sich (Dat.) den Arm
od. am Arm kratzen
[2] v.i. kratzen; (~ oneself) sich kratzen
[3] n. (a) (mark, wound) Kratzer, der (ugs.);
Schramme, die
(b) (sound) Kratzen, das
(c) **have a [good]** ~: sich [ordentlich]
kratzen
(d) **start from** ~: bei Null anfangen (ugs.);
be up to ~ ⟨Arbeit, Leistung:⟩ nichts zu
wünschen übrig lassen; ⟨Person:⟩ den
Anforderungen genügen
■ **scratch a'bout, scratch a'round**
v.i. scharren; (fig.: search) suchen (**for** nach)
'scratch card n. Rubbellos, das
scrawl /skrɔːl/ [1] v.t. hinkritzeln
[2] v.i. kritzeln
[3] n. Gekritzel, das; (handwriting) Klaue, die
(salopp)
scrawny /'skrɔːnɪ/ adj. hager; dürr
scream /skriːm/ [1] v.i. schreien (**with** vor
+ Dat.)
[2] v.t. schreien
[3] n. Schrei, der; (of jet engine) Heulen, das;
~**s of pain** Schmerzensschreie Pl.
screech /skriːtʃ/ [1] v.i. & t. kreischen
[2] n. Kreischen, das
screen /skriːn/ [1] n. (a) (partition)
Trennwand, die; (piece of furniture)
Wandschirm, der
(b) (of trees, persons, fog) Wand, die
(c) (Cinemat.) Leinwand, die; [TV] ~:
Bildschirm, der
[2] v.t. (a) (shelter) schützen (**from** vor
+ Dat.); (conceal) verdecken
(b) vorführen ⟨Film⟩
(c) (for disease) untersuchen
screening /'skriːnɪŋ/ n. (a) (in cinema)
Vorführung, die; (on TV) Sendung, die
(b) (Med.) Untersuchung, die
screen: ~**play** n. Drehbuch, das;
~ **saver** n. (Comp.) Bildschirmschoner,
der; ~**writer** n. Filmautor, der/-autorin,
die

S

screw /skru:/ ① *n.* Schraube, *die;* **he has a**
~ **loose** (coll. joc.) bei ihm ist eine Schraube
locker *od.* lose (salopp)
② *v.t.* (a) schrauben (**to** an + *Akk.*);
~ **together** zusammenschrauben; ~ **down**
festschrauben
(b) ~ **you!** (coarse) leck mich am Arsch!
(salopp)
■ **screw 'up** *v.t.* (a) (crumple up)
zusammenknüllen ⟨*Blatt Papier*⟩
(b) verziehen ⟨*Gesicht*⟩; zusammenkneifen
⟨*Augen, Mund*⟩
(c) (sl.: bungle) vermurksen (salopp);
~ **it/things up** Mist bauen (salopp)
screw: ~ **cap** *n.* Schraubverschluss, *der;*
~**driver** *n.* Schraubenzieher, *der*
'**screwed-up** *adj.* (fig. coll.) neurotisch
'**screw top** ▶ ~ CAP
screwy /'skru:ɪ/ *adj.* (coll.) spinnig (ugs.)
scribble /'skrɪbl/ ① *v.t.* hinkritzeln
② *v.i.* kritzeln
③ *n.* Gekritzel, *das*
script /skrɪpt/ *n.* (a) (handwriting)
Handschrift, *die*
(b) (of play) Regiebuch, *das;* (of film)
[Dreh]buch, *das*
(c) (for broadcaster) Manuskript, *das*
scripture /'skrɪptʃə(r)/ *n.* (a) [Holy] S~,
the [Holy] S~s die [Heilige] Schrift
(b) (Sch.) Religion, *die*
'**scriptwriter** *n.* (of film) Drehbuchautor,
der/-autorin, *die*
scroll /skrəʊl/ ① *n.* (roll) Rolle, *die*
② *v.t.* (Comp.) scrollen
■ **scroll 'down** *v.i.* (Comp.) runterscrollen
■ **scroll 'up** *v.i.* (Comp.) hochscrollen
scrollable /'skrəʊləbl/ *adj.* (Comp.)
scrollbar
'**scroll bar** *n.* (Comp.) Rollbalken, *der*
scrounge /'skraʊndʒ/ (coll.) ① *v.t.*
schnorren (ugs.) (**off, from** von)
② *v.i.* schnorren (ugs.) (**from** bei)
'**scrounger** *n.* (coll.) Schnorrer,
*der/*Schnorrerin, *die* (ugs.)
scrub¹ /skrʌb/ ① *v.t.,* **-bb-:** (a) schrubben
(ugs.); scheuern
(b) (coll.: cancel) zurücknehmen ⟨*Befehl*⟩;
sausen lassen (ugs.) ⟨*Plan*⟩
② *v.i.,* **-bb-** schrubben (ugs.); scheuern
③ *n.* give sth. a ~: etw. schrubben (ugs.) *od.*
scheuern
scrub² *n.* (brushwood) Buschwerk, *das;* (area)
Buschland, *das*
scruff¹ /skrʌf/ *n.* by the ~ of the neck beim
Genick
scruff² *n.* (Brit. coll.) (man) vergammelter Typ
(ugs.); (woman, girl) Schlampe, *die*
'**scruffy** *adj.* vergammelt (ugs.)
scrum /skrʌm/ *n.* Gedränge, *das*
scruple /'skru:pl/ *n.* Skrupel, *der;* **have no**
~**s about doing sth.** keine Skrupel haben,
etw. zu tun
scrupulous /'skru:pjʊləs/ *adj.*

gewissenhaft ⟨*Person*⟩; unbedingt
⟨*Ehrlichkeit*⟩; peinlich ⟨*Sorgfalt*⟩
scrutinize /'skru:tɪnaɪz/ *v.t.* [genau]
untersuchen ⟨*[Forschungs]gegenstand*⟩;
[über]prüfen ⟨*Rechnung, Pass, Fahrkarte*⟩;
mustern ⟨*Person*⟩
scrutiny /'skru:tɪnɪ/ *n.* (a) (critical gaze)
musternder Blick
(b) (examination) (of recruit) Musterung, *die;* (of
bill, passport, ticket) [Über]prüfung, *die*
scuff /skʌf/ ① *v.t.* streifen; verschrammen
⟨*Schuhe, Fußboden*⟩
② *n.* Schramme, *die*
scuffle /'skʌfl/ ① *n.* Handgreiflichkeiten
Pl.
② *v.i.* handgreiflich werden (**with** gegen)
scullery /'skʌlərɪ/ *n.* Spülküche, *die*
sculptor /'skʌlptə(r)/ *n.* Bildhauer, *der/*
-hauerin, *die*
sculpture /'skʌlptʃə(r)/ *n.* (a) (art)
Bildhauerei, *die*
(b) (piece of work) Skulptur, *die;* Plastik, *die;*
(pieces collectively) Skulpturen *Pl.*
scum /skʌm/ *n.* (a) Schmutzschicht, *die;*
(film) Schmutzfilm, *der*
(b) (fig. derog.) Abschaum, *der*
'**scumbag** *n.* (sl. derog.) Schwein, *das*
(salopp)
scurry /'skʌrɪ/ *v.i.* huschen
scuttle¹ /'skʌtl/ *n.* Kohlenfüller, *der*
scuttle² (Naut.) *v.t.* versenken
scuttle³ *v.i.* rennen; flitzen (ugs.); ⟨*Maus,
Krabbe:*⟩ huschen
scythe /saɪð/ *n.* Sense, *die*
SE *abbr.* = **south-east** SO
sea /si:/ *n.* (a) Meer, *das;* **the** ~: das Meer;
die See; **by** ~: mit dem Schiff; **by the** ~: am
Meer; **at** ~: auf See (*Dat.*); **be all at** ~ (fig.)
nicht mehr weiter wissen; **put [out] to** ~: in
See (*Akk.*) gehen
(b) (specific tract of water) Meer, *das*
sea: ~ '**air** *n.* Seeluft, *die;* ~'**bed** *n.*
Meeresboden, *der;* ~**bird** *n.* Seevogel, *der;*
~ **breeze** *n.* Seewind, *der;* ~**food** *n.*
Meeresfrüchte *Pl.; attrib.* Fisch⟨*restaurant*⟩;
~**gull** *n.* [See]möwe, *die*
seal¹ /si:l/ *n.* (Zool.) Robbe, *die;* [**common]**
~: [Gemeiner] Seehund
seal² ① *n.* (wax etc., stamp, impression) Siegel,
das
② *v.t.* (a) (stamp, affix ~ to) siegeln
⟨*Dokument*⟩; (fasten with ~) verplomben ⟨*Tür,
Stromzähler*⟩
(b) (close securely) abdichten ⟨*Behälter, Rohr
usw.*⟩; zukleben ⟨*Umschlag, Paket*⟩
(c) (stop up) verschließen; abdichten ⟨*Leck*⟩;
verschmieren ⟨*Riss*⟩
■ **seal 'off** *v.t.* abriegeln
sea: ~ **lane** *n.* See⟨schifffahrts]straße,
die; ~ **legs** *n. pl.* Seebeine *Pl.*
(Seemannsspr.); **get** *or* **find one's** ~ **legs** sich
(*Dat.*) Seebeine wachsen lassen; ~ **level** *n.*
Meeresspiegel, *der*

'sealing wax n. Siegellack, der

'sea lion n. Seelöwe, der

seam /si:m/ n. **(a)** Naht, die **(b)** (of coal) Flöz, das

sea: ~man /'si:mən/ n., pl. ~men /'si:mən/ Matrose, der; ~ **mist** n. Küstennebel, der

'seamless adj. nahtlos

'seamy adj. the ~ side [of life etc.] (fig.) die Schattenseite[n] [des Lebens usw.]

seance /'seɪəns/, **séance** /'seɪɑ̃s/ n. Séance, die

sea: ~plane n. Wasserflugzeug, das; ~**port** n. Seehafen, der; ~ **power** n. Seemacht, die

sear /'sɪə(r)/ v.t. versengen

search /sɜːtʃ/ **1** v.t. durchsuchen (for nach); absuchen ⟨Gebiet, Fläche⟩ (for nach); (fig.: probe) erforschen ⟨Herz, Gewissen⟩; suchen in (+ Dat.) ⟨Gedächtnis⟩ (for nach) **2** v.i. suchen (for nach) **3** n. Suche, die (for nach); (of building, room, etc.) Durchsuchung, die; in ~ of sb./sth. auf der Suche nach jmdm./etw

searchable /'sɜːtʃəbl/ adj. durchsuchbar

'searching adj. prüfend, forschend ⟨Blick⟩; bohrend ⟨Frage⟩

'search engine n. (Comp.) Suchmaschine, die

search: ~light n. Suchscheinwerfer, der; ~ **party** n. Suchtrupp, der; ~ **warrant** n. Durchsuchungsbefehl, der

sea: ~ salt n. Meersalz, das; Seesalz, das; ~**shore** n. [Meeres]küste, die; (beach) Strand, der; ~**sick** adj. seekrank; ~**sickness** n. Seekrankheit, die; ~**side** n. [Meeres]küste, die; by/to/at the ~side am/ans/am Meer; ~side town Seestadt, die

season /'si:zn/ **1** n. **(a)** Jahreszeit, die; nesting ~: Nistzeit, die **(b)** (period of social activity) [opera/football] ~: [Opern-/Fußball]saison, die; holiday or (Amer.) vacation ~: Urlaubszeit, die; tourist ~: Reisezeit, die **(c)** raspberries are in/out of or not in ~: jetzt ist die/nicht die Saison od. Zeit für Himbeeren; be in ~ (on heat) brünstig sein **(d)** ▶ SEASON TICKET **2** v.t. würzen ⟨Fleisch, Rede⟩

seasonable /'si:zənəbl/ adj. der Jahreszeit gemäß

seasonal /'si:zənl/ adj. Saison⟨arbeit, -geschäft⟩; saisonabhängig ⟨Preise⟩

seasonal af'fective disorder /si:zənl ə'fektɪv dɪsɔ:də(r)/ n. (Med.) saisonabhängige Depression

'seasoned adj. (fig.) erfahren

'seasoning n. Gewürze Pl.; Würze, die

'season ticket n. Dauerkarte, die

seat /si:t/ **1** n. **(a)** Sitzgelegenheit, die; (in vehicle, cinema, etc.) Sitz, der; (of toilet) [Klosett]brille, die (ugs.)

(b) (place) Platz, der; (in vehicle) [Sitz]platz, der; have or take a ~: sich [hin]setzen **(c)** (part of chair) Sitzfläche, die **(d)** (buttocks) Gesäß, das; (part of clothing) Gesäßpartie, die; (of trousers) Sitz, der **2** v.t. **(a)** (cause to sit) setzen; ⟨Platzanweiser:⟩ einen Platz anweisen (+ Dat.); ~ oneself sich setzen **(b)** (have ~s for) Sitzplätze bieten (+ Dat.); ~ 500 people 500 Sitzplätze haben

'seat belt n. Sicherheitsgurt, der

'seat-belt tensioner /'tenʃnə(r)/n. Gurtstraffer, der

'seated adj. sitzend; remain ~: sitzen bleiben

'seating n. Sitzplätze Pl.; attrib. Sitz⟨ordnung, -plan⟩

sea: ~ urchin n. Seeigel, der; ~ **wall** n. Strandmauer, die; ~ **water** n. Meerwasser, das; ~**weed** n. [See]tang, der; ~**worthy** adj. seetüchtig

secateurs /sekə'tɜ:z/ n. pl. (Brit.) Gartenschere, die

secluded /sɪ'klu:dɪd/ adj. (hidden) versteckt; (isolated) abgelegen; zurückgezogen ⟨Leben⟩

seclusion /sɪ'klu:ʒn/ n. (remoteness) Abgelegenheit, die; (privacy) Zurückgezogenheit, die

second¹ /'sekənd/ **1** adj. zweit...; ~ largest/highest etc. zweitgrößt.../ -höchst... usw.; come/be ~: Zweiter/Zweite werden/sein

2 n. **(a)** (unit of time or angle) Sekunde, die **(b)** (coll.: moment) Sekunde, die (ugs.); wait a few ~s einen Moment warten; in a ~ (immediately) sofort (ugs.); (very quickly) im Nu (ugs.); just a ~! (coll.) einen Moment! **(c)** the ~ (in sequence, rank) der/die/das Zweite **(d)** in pl. (helping of food) zweite Portion **3** v.t. (support) unterstützen

second² /sɪ'kɒnd/ v.t. (transfer) vorübergehend versetzen

secondary /'sekəndərɪ/ adj. (of less importance) zweitrangig; Neben⟨sache⟩; be ~ to sth. einer Sache (Dat.) untergeordnet sein

'secondary school n. höhere Schule

second: ~-best **1** /'---/ adj. zweitbest...; **2** /--'-/ n. Zweitbeste, der/die/das; ~**-class** **1** /'---/ adj. (of lower class) zweiter Klasse nachgestellt; Zweite[r]-Klasse- ⟨Fahrkarte, Abteil, Post, Brief usw.⟩; ~**-class** stamp Briefmarke für einen Zweiter-Klasse-Brief; **2** /--'-/ adv. zweiter Klasse ⟨fahren⟩; ~ **'floor** ▶ FLOOR 1B; ~ **hand** n. Sekundenzeiger, der; ~**-hand** **1** /'---/ adj. **(a)** gebraucht ⟨Kleidung, Auto usw.⟩; antiquarisch ⟨Buch⟩; **(b)** (selling used goods) Gebrauchtwaren-; Secondhand⟨laden⟩; **(c)** ⟨Nachrichten, Bericht⟩ aus zweiter Hand; **2** /--'-/ adv. aus zweiter Hand; ~ **'home** n. Zweitwohnung, die

'secondly *adv.* zweitens

second: ~ **name** *n.* Nachname, *der;* ~**-'rate** *adj.* zweitklassig; ~ **'thoughts** *n. pl.* **have** ~ **thoughts** es sich (*Dat.*) anders überlegen (**about** mit); **we've had** ~ **thoughts about buying it** wir wollen es nun doch nicht kaufen; **but on** ~ **thoughts** ...: wenn ich's mir [noch mal] überlege, ...

secrecy /'si:krɪsɪ/ *n.* **(a)** (keeping of secret) Geheimhaltung, *die*
(b) (secretiveness) Heimlichtuerei, *die*
(c) **in** ~: im Geheimen

secret /'si:krɪt/ **1** *adj.* geheim; Geheim⟨fach, -tür, -abkommen, -kode⟩; heimlich ⟨Trinker, Liebhaber⟩; **keep sth.** ~: etw. geheim halten (**from** vor + *Dat.*)
2 *n.* **(a)** Geheimnis, *das;* **make no** ~ **of sth.** kein Geheimnis aus etw. machen; (fig.) keinen Hehl aus etw. machen; **keep** ~**s/ a** ~: schweigen (fig.)
(b) in ~: im Geheimen

secret 'agent *n.* Geheimagent, *der/*-agentin, *die*

secretarial /sekrə'teərɪəl/ *adj.* Sekretärinnen⟨kursus, -tätigkeit⟩; ⟨Arbeit⟩ als Sekretärin

secretary /'sekrətərɪ/ *n.* Sekretär, *der/*Sekretärin, *die*

secret 'ballot *n.* geheime Abstimmung

secretive /'si:krɪtɪv/ *adj.* verschlossen ⟨Person⟩: **be** ~: geheimnisvoll tun (**about** mit)

'secretly *adv.* heimlich; insgeheim ⟨etw. glauben⟩

sect /sekt/ *n.* Sekte, *die*

section /'sekʃn/ *n.* **(a)** (part cut off) Abschnitt, *der;* Stück, *das;* (part of divided whole) Teil, *der*
(b) (of firm) Abteilung, *die;* (of organization) Sektion, *die*
(c) (of chapter, book) Abschnitt, *der;* (of statute etc.) Paragraph, *der*

sector /'sektə(r)/ *n.* Sektor, *der*

secular /'sekjʊlə(r)/ *adj.* weltlich

secure /sɪ'kjʊə(r)/ **1** *adj.* sicher; (firmly fastened) fest; ~ **against burglars** gegen Einbruch geschützt
2 *v.t.* **(a)** sichern (**for** *Dat.*); beschaffen ⟨Auftrag⟩ (**for** *Dat.*); (for oneself) sich (*Dat.*) sichern
(b) (fasten) sichern

se'curely *adv.* (firmly) fest ⟨verriegeln, zumachen⟩; sicher ⟨befestigen, untergebracht sein⟩

security /sɪ'kjʊərɪtɪ/ *n.* **(a)** Sicherheit, *die;* ~ **[measures]** Sicherheitsmaßnahmen *Pl.*
(b) (Finance) **securities** *pl.* Wertpapiere *Pl.*

security: ~ **check** *n.* Sicherheitskontrolle, *die;* ~ **forces** *n. pl.* Sicherheitskräfte *Pl.;* ~ **guard** *n.* Wächter, *der/*Wächterin, *die;* ~ **risk** *n.* Sicherheitsrisiko, *das;* ~ **van** *n.* gepanzerter Transporter; (for money)

Geldtransporter, *der*

sedan /sɪ'dæn/ *n.* (Amer. Motor Veh.) Limousine, *die*

sedate /sɪ'deɪt/ **1** *adj.* bedächtig; gesetzt ⟨alte Dame⟩; gemächlich ⟨Tempo, Leben⟩
2 *v.t.* sedieren

sedation /sɪ'deɪʃn/ *n.* Sedation, *die;* **be under** ~: sediert sein

sedative /'sedətɪv/ **1** *n.* Beruhigungsmittel, *das*
2 *adj.* sedativ

sedentary /'sedəntərɪ/ *adj.* sitzend

sediment /'sedɪmənt/ *n.* Ablagerung, *die;* (of tea, coffee, etc.) Bodensatz, *der*

seduce /sɪ'dju:s/ *v.t.* verführen

seduction /sɪ'dʌkʃn/ *n.* Verführung, *die*

seductive /sɪ'dʌktɪv/ *adj.* verführerisch; verlockend ⟨Angebot⟩

see /si:/ **1** *v.t.,* **saw** /sɔ:/, **seen** /si:n/ **(a)** sehen; **I can** ~ **it's hard for you** ich verstehe, dass es nicht leicht für dich ist; **I** ~ **what you mean** ich verstehe[, was du meinst]
(b) (meet [with]) sehen; treffen; (meet socially) sich treffen mit; **I'll** ~ **you there/at five** wir sehen uns dort/um fünf; ~ **you!, [I'll] be** ~**ing you!** (coll.) bis bald! (ugs.)
(c) (speak to) sprechen ⟨Person⟩ (**about** wegen); (visit) gehen zu ⟨Arzt, Anwalt usw.⟩; (receive) empfangen
(d) (find out) feststellen; (by looking) nachsehen
(e) (make sure) ~ **[that]** ...: darauf achten, dass ...
(f) (imagine) sich (*Dat.*) vorstellen
(g) (escort) begleiten
2 *v.i.,* **saw, seen (a)** sehen
(b) (make sure) nachsehen
(c) **I** ~: ich verstehe; **you** ~: weißt du/wisst ihr/wissen Sie
■ **'see about** *v.t.* sich kümmern um
■ **see 'off** *v.t.* **(a)** (say goodbye to) verabschieden
(b) (chase away) vertreiben
■ **see 'out** *v.t.* (escort) hinausbegleiten (**of** aus); ~ **oneself out** allein hinausfinden
■ **see through** *v.t.* **(a)** /'--/ hindurchsehen durch; (fig.) durchschauen
(b) /-'-/ (not abandon) zu Ende bringen
■ **'see to** *v.t.* sich kümmern um

seed /si:d/ **1** *n.* **(a)** Samen, *der;* (of grape etc.) Kern, *der*
(b) no pl., no indef. art. (~s collectively) Samen[körner] *Pl.;* (as collected for sowing) Saatgut, *das;* (for birds) Körner *Pl.;* **go** *or* **run to** ~: Samen bilden; (fig.) herunterkommen (ugs.)
(c) (Sport) gesetzter Spieler/gesetzte Spielerin
2 *v.t.* **(a)** (place ~s in) besäen
(b) (Sport) setzen ⟨Spieler⟩; **be** ~**ed number one** als Nummer eins gesetzt werden/sein

'seed bed *n.* [Saat]beet, *das*

'seedless *adj.* kernlos

seedling /'si:dlɪŋ/ *n.* Sämling, *der*

'seedy *adj.* **(a)** (coll.: unwell) feel ∼: sich [leicht] angeschlagen fühlen **(b)** (shabby) schäbig, (ugs.) vergammelt ⟨*Aussehen*⟩; heruntergekommen ⟨*Stadtteil*⟩ **(c)** (disreputable) zweifelhaft

'seeing *conj.* ∼ [that] ...: in Anbetracht dessen, dass ...

seek /siːk/ *v.t.*, sought /sɔːt/ suchen; anstreben ⟨*Posten, Amt*⟩; sich bemühen um ⟨*Anerkennung, Interview, Einstellung*⟩; (try to reach) aufsuchen

seem /siːm/ *v.i.* scheinen; you ∼ tired du wirkst müde; she ∼s nice sie scheint nett zu sein

'seeming *adj.* scheinbar

'seemingly *adv.* **(a)** (evidently) offensichtlich **(b)** (to outward appearance) scheinbar

seemly /'siːmlɪ/ *adj.* schicklich

seen ▶ SEE

seep /siːp/ *v.i.* ∼ [away] [ab]sickern

'see-saw *n.* Wippe, *die*

seethe /siːe/ *v.i.* **(a)** ∼ [with anger/ inwardly] vor Wut/innerlich schäumen **(b)** ⟨*Straßen usw.*:⟩ wimmeln (**with** von)

'see-through *adj.* durchsichtig

segment /'segmənt/ *n.* (of orange, pineapple, etc.) Scheibe, *die*

segregate /'segrɪgeɪt/ *v.t.* trennen; (racially) absondern

segregation /segrɪ'geɪʃn/ *n.* Trennung, *die;* [racial] ∼: Rassentrennung, *die*

seismic /'saɪzmɪk/ *adj.* seismisch

seize /siːz/ ① *v.t.* **(a)** ergreifen; ∼ power die Macht ergreifen; ∼ sb. by the arm/collar jmdn. am Arm/Kragen packen; ∼ the opportunity [to do sth.] die Gelegenheit ergreifen [und etw. tun]; ∼ any/a or the chance [to do sth.] jede/die Gelegenheit nutzen[, um etw. zu tun]; be ∼d with remorse/panic von Gewissensbissen geplagt/von Panik ergriffen werden **(b)** (capture) gefangen nehmen ⟨*Person*⟩; kapern ⟨*Schiff*⟩; mit Gewalt übernehmen ⟨*Flugzeug, Gebäude*⟩; einnehmen ⟨*Festung, Brücke*⟩ **(c)** (confiscate) beschlagnahmen ② *v.i.* ▶ ∼ UP

■ **'seize on** *v.t.* sich (*Dat.*) vornehmen ⟨*Einzelheit, Aspekt, Schwachpunkt*⟩; aufgreifen ⟨*Idee, Vorschlag*⟩

■ **seize 'up** *v.i.* sich festfressen

seizure /'siːʒə(r)/ *n.* **(a)** ▶ SEIZE 1B, C: Gefangennahme, *die;* Kapern, *das;* Übernahme, *die;* Einnahme, *die;* Beschlagnahme, *die* **(b)** (Med.) Anfall, *der*

seldom /'seldəm/ *adv.* selten

select /sɪ'lekt/ ① *adj.* ausgewählt ② *v.t.* auswählen

selection /sɪ'lekʃn/ *n.* **(a)** (what is selected [from]) Auswahl, *die* (**of** an + *Dat.*, **from** aus) **(b)** (act of choosing) [Aus]wahl, *die*

selective /sɪ'lektɪv/ *adj.* (using selection) selektiv; (careful in one's choice) wählerisch

self /self/ *n.*, *pl.* **selves** [selvz] Selbst, *das* (geh.); Ich, *das*

self- *pref.* selbst-/Selbst-

self: ∼-**ab'sorbed** *adj.* mit sich selbst beschäftigt; ∼-**ad'dressed** *adj.* ∼-**addressed envelope** adressierter Rückumschlag; ∼-**ad'hesive** *adj.* selbstklebend; ∼-**ap'pointed** *adj.* selbst ernannt; ∼-**as'surance** *n.* Selbstsicherheit, *die;* ∼-**as'sured** *adj.* selbstsicher; ∼-**a'wareness** *n.* Selbsterkenntnis, *die;* ∼-**'catering** ① *adj.* mit Selbstversorgung *nachgestellt;* ② *n.* Selbstversorgung, *die;* ∼-**'centred** *adj.* egozentrisch; ∼-**con'fessed** *adj.* erklärt; ∼-**'confidence** *n.* Selbstbewusstsein, *das;* ∼-**'confident** *adj.* selbstbewusst; ∼-**'conscious** *adj.* unsicher; ∼-**'consciousness** *n.* Unsicherheit, *die;* ∼-**con'tained** *adj.* abgeschlossen ⟨*Wohnung*⟩; ∼-**'control** *n.* Selbstbeherrschung, *die;* ∼-**con'trolled** *adj.* voller Selbstbeherrschung *nachgestellt;* ∼-**'critical** *adj.* selbstkritisch; ∼-**de'ception** *n.* Selbsttäuschung, *die;* ∼-**de'feating** *adj.* unsinnig; ∼-**de'fence** *n.* Notwehr, *die;* in ∼-**defence** aus Notwehr; ∼-**de'lusion** *n.* Selbsttäuschung, *die;* ∼-**de'nial** *n.* Selbstverleugnung, *die;* ∼-**de'structive** *adj.* selbstzerstörerisch; ∼-**'discipline** *n.* Selbstdisziplin, *die;* ∼-**'drive** *adj.* ∼-**drive hire [company]** Autovermietung, *die;* ∼-**drive vehicle** Mietwagen, *der;* ∼-**em'ployed** *adj.* selbstständig; ∼-**e'steem** *n.* Selbstachtung, *die;* ∼-**'evident** *adj.* offenkundig; ∼-**ex'planatory** *adj.* ohne weiteres verständlich; be ∼-**explanatory** für sich selbst sprechen; ∼-**ful'filling** *adj.* zur eigenen Bestätigung mit beitragend; ∼-**'help** *n.* Selbsthilfe, *die;* ∼-**im'portant** *adj.* eingebildet; ∼-**in'dulgent** *adj.* maßlos; ∼-**in'flicted** *adj.* selbst beigebracht ⟨*Wunde*⟩; selbst auferlegt ⟨*Strafe*⟩; ∼-**'interest** *n.* Eigeninteresse, *das*

'selfish *adj.,* **'selfishly** *adv.* selbstsüchtig

'selfishness *n.* Selbstsucht, *die*

self-'knowledge *n.* Selbsterkenntnis, *die*

selfless /'selflɪs/ *adj.* selbstlos

self: ∼-**'motivated** *adj.* von sich aus motiviert; ∼-**ob'sessed** *adj.* ichbesessen; ∼-**o'pinionated** *adj.* eingebildet; ∼-**'pity** *n.* Selbstmitleid, *das;* ∼-**'portrait** *n.* Selbstporträt, *das;* ∼-**pos'sessed** *adj.* selbstbeherrscht; ∼-**preser'vation** *n.* Selbsterhaltung, *die;* ∼-**'raising flour** *n.* (Brit.) mit Backpulver versetztes Mehl; ∼-**re'liant** *adj.* selbstbewusst; ∼-**re'spect** *n.* Selbstachtung, *die;* ∼-**re'specting** *adj.* no ∼-**respecting** ⋯❖

S

person ...: niemand, der etwas auf sich hält, ...; ~-'**righteous** *adj.* selbstgerecht; ~-'**sacrifice** *n.* Selbstaufopferung, *die;* ~-'**satisfied** *adj.* selbstzufrieden; (smug) selbstgefällig; ~-'**service** *n.* Selbstbedienung, *die; attrib.* Selbstbedienungs-; ~-**suf'ficient** *adj.* unabhängig; selbstständig ⟨*Person*⟩; ~-'**taught** *adj.* autodidaktisch; ~-**taught person** Autodidakt, *der*/Autodidaktin, *die;* ~-'**willed** *adj.* eigenwillig

sell /sel/ ⊡ *v.t.,* sold /səʊld/ ~ sth. to sb., ~ sb. sth. jmdm. etw. verkaufen; be sold out ausverkauft sein ⊡ *v.i.,* sold sich verkaufen; ⟨*Person:*⟩ verkaufen

■ **sell 'off** *v.t.* verkaufen

■ **sell 'out** ⊡ *v.t.* (a) ausverkaufen (b) (coll.: betray) verraten ⊡ *v.i.* we have *or* are sold out wir sind ausverkauft

'**sell-by date** *n.* ≈ Mindesthaltbarkeitsdatum, *das*

'**seller** *n.* (a) Verkäufer, *der*/Verkäuferin, *die* (b) (product) be a good/slow ~: sich gut/nur langsam verkaufen

'**selling point** *n.* a [good] ~ point (fig.) ein Pluspunkt

'**sellotape** *v.t.* mit Tesafilm kleben

Sellotape ® /'seləteɪp/ *n.* ≈ Tesafilm, *der* (W)

'**sell-out** *n.* be a ~: ausverkauft sein; (coll.: betrayal) Verrat sein

selves *pl. of* SELF

semaphore /'seməfɔ:(r)/ ⊡ *n.* (system) Winken, *das* ⊡ *v.i.* ~ to sb. jmdm. ein Winksignal übermitteln

semblance /'sembləns/ *n.* Anschein, *der*

semen /'si:mən/ *n.* Samen, *der*

semester /sɪ'mestə(r)/ *n.* Semester, *das*

semi- /semi/ *pref.* halb-/Halb-

semi- ~**bold** *adj.* (Printing) halbfett; ~**breve** *n.* (Brit. Mus.) ganze Note; ~**circle** *n.* Halbkreis, *der;* ~'**circular** *adj.* halbkreisförmig; ~'**colon** *n.* Semikolon, *das;* ~-**de'tached** *adj. & n.* ~-**detached** [house] Doppelhaushälfte, *die;* ~-'**final** *n.* Halbfinale, *das*

seminar /'semɪnɑ:(r)/ *n.* Seminar, *das*

semi- ~'**precious** *adj.* ~**precious stone** Halbedelstein, *der;* ~-**skimmed** ⊡ *adj.* teilentrahmt; ⊡ *n.* teilentrahmte Milch; ~**tone** *n.* (Mus.) Halbton, *der*

semolina /semə'li:nə/ *n.* Grieß, *der*

senate /'senət/ *n.* Senat, *der*

senator /'senətə(r)/ *n.* Senator, *der*

send /send/ *v.t.,* sent [sent] schicken; senden (geh.)

■ **send a'way** ⊡ *v.t.* wegschicken ⊡ *v.i.* ~ away [to sb.] for sth. etw. [bei jmdm.] anfordern

■ **send 'back** *v.t.* zurückschicken

■ '**send for** *v.t.* (a) (tell to come) holen lassen; rufen ⟨*Polizei, Arzt usw.*⟩ (b) (order from elsewhere) anfordern

■ **send 'off** *v.t.* ⊡ (a) (dispatch) abschicken ⟨*Sache*⟩ (b) (Sport) vom Platz stellen ⊡ *v.i.* ▸ SEND AWAY 2

■ **send 'up** *v.t.* (Brit. coll.: parody) parodieren

'**sender** *n.* Absender, *der*

'**send-off** *n.* Verabschiedung, *die*

senile /'si:naɪl/ *adj.* senil

senile de'mentia *n.* senile Demenz

senility /sɪ'nɪlɪti/ *n.* Senilität, *die*

senior /'si:nɪə(r)/ ⊡ *adj.* (a) (older) älter (b) höher ⟨*Rang, Beamter, Stellung*⟩; leitend ⟨*Angestellter, Stellung*⟩; ~ **manager** obere Führungskraft; ~ **management** oberer Führungskreis ⊡ *n.* (older) Ältere, *der*/*die;* (of higher rank) Vorgesetzte, *der*/*die*

senior 'citizen *n.* Senior, *der*/Seniorin, *die*

seniority /si:nɪ'ɒrɪti/ *n.* (greater length of service) höheres Dienstalter; (higher rank) höherer Rang

senior 'partner *n.* Seniorpartner, *der* /-partnerin, *die*

sensation /sen'seɪʃn/ *n.* (a) (feeling) Gefühl, *das* (b) (person, event, etc.) Sensation, *die*

sensational /sen'seɪʃnl/ *adj.* sensationell

sensationalise ▸ SENSATIONALIZE

sensationalism /sen'seɪʃənəlɪzm/ *n.* Sensationshascherei, *die*

sensationalist /sen'seɪʃənəlɪst/ *adj.* sensationslüstern

sensationalize /sen'seɪʃənəlaɪz/ *v.t.* ~ sth. etw. zur Sensation aufbauschen

sense /sens/ ⊡ *n.* (a) (faculty) Sinn, *der;* ~ **of smell/touch/taste** Geruchs-/Tast-/Geschmackssinn, *der;* **come to one's** ~s das Bewusstsein wiedererlangen (b) *in pl.* (normal state of mind) Verstand, *der;* **have taken leave of one's** ~s den Verstand verloren haben (c) (consciousness) Gefühl, *das;* ~ **of responsibility/guilt** Verantwortungs-/Schuldgefühl, *das* (d) (practical wisdom) Verstand, *der;* **sound** *or* **good** ~: [gesunder Menschen]verstand; **not have the** ~ **to do sth.** nicht so schlau sein, etw. zu tun; **there is no** ~ **in doing that** es hat keinen Sinn, das zu tun (e) (meaning) Sinn, *der;* (of word) Bedeutung, *die;* **make** ~: einen Sinn ergeben; **in a** *or* **one** ~: in gewisser Hinsicht; **make** ~ **of sth.** etw. verstehen ⊡ *v.t.* spüren

'**senseless** *adj.* (a) (unconscious) bewusstlos (b) (purposeless) sinnlos

sensible /'sensɪbl/ adj. (a) (reasonable) vernünftig
(b) (practical) zweckmäßig
sensibly /'sensɪblɪ/ adv. (a) (reasonably) vernünftig
(b) (practically) zweckmäßig
sensitive /'sensɪtɪv/ adj. empfindlich; **be ∼ to sth.** empfindlich auf etw. (Akk.) reagieren
sensitivity /sensɪ'tɪvɪtɪ/ n. Empfindlichkeit, die
sensory /'sensərɪ/ adj. Sinnes-
sensual /'sensjʊəl/ adj. sinnlich
sensuous /'sensjʊəs/ adj. sinnlich
sent ▸ SEND
sentence /'sentəns/ ①n. (a) (Law) [Straf]urteil, das
(b) (Ling.) Satz, der
② v.t. verurteilen (to zu)
sentiment /'sentɪmənt/ n. (a) Gefühl, das
(b) (sentimentality) Sentimentalität, die
(c) (thought) Gedanke, der
sentimental /sentɪ'mentl/ adj. sentimental
sentimentality /sentɪmen'tælɪtɪ/ n. Sentimentalität, die
sentimentalize /sentɪ'mentəlaɪz/ v.t. sentimental darstellen
sentry /'sentrɪ/ n. Wache, die
separable /'sepərəbl/ adj. trennbar
separate ① /'sepərət/ adj. verschieden ⟨Fragen, Probleme, Gelegenheiten⟩; gesondert ⟨Teil⟩; separat ⟨Eingang, Toilette, Blatt Papier, Abteil⟩; (one's own, individual) eigen ⟨Zimmer, Identität, Organisation⟩; **keep two things ∼:** zwei Dinge auseinander halten
② /'sepəreɪt/ v.t. trennen; **they are ∼d** (no longer live together) sie leben getrennt
③ v.i. (a) (disperse) sich trennen
(b) ⟨Ehepaar:⟩ sich trennen
separately /'sepərətlɪ/ adv. getrennt
separation /sepə'reɪʃn/ n. Trennung, die
Sept. abbr. = **September** Sept.
September /sep'tembə(r)/ n. September, der; see also AUGUST
septic /'septɪk/ adj. septisch; **go ∼:** eitrig werden
sequel /'si:kwl/ n. (a) (consequence; result) Folge, die (to von)
(b) (continuation) Fortsetzung, die
sequence /'si:kwəns/ n. (a) Reihenfolge, die
(b) (part of film) Sequenz, die
sequin /'si:kwɪn/ n. Paillette, die
Serbia /'sɜ:bɪə/ pr. n. Serbien, das
Serbian /'sɜ:bɪən/ ① adj. serbisch; **sb. is ∼:** jmd. ist Serbe/Serbin
② n. (a) (Ling.) serbischer Dialekt
(b) (person) Serbe, der/Serbin, die. See also ENGLISH 2A
serenade /serə'neɪd/ ① n. Ständchen, das

② v.t. ∼ **sb.** jmdm. ein Ständchen bringen
serene /sɪ'ri:n/ adj. gelassen
serenity /sɪ'renɪtɪ/ n. Gelassenheit, die
sergeant /'sɑ:dʒənt/ n. (Mil.) Unteroffizier, der; (police officer) ≈ Polizeimeister, der
sergeant 'major n. ≈ [Ober]stabsfeldwebel, der
serial /'sɪərɪəl/ n. Fortsetzungsgeschichte, die; (Radio, Telev.) Serie, die
serialize /'sɪərɪəlaɪz/ v.t. in Fortsetzungen veröffentlichen; (Radio, Telev.) in Fortsetzungen senden
'serial killer n. Serienmörder, der
series /'sɪəri:z, 'sɪərɪz/ n., pl. same
(a) (sequence) Reihe, die; (of events, misfortunes) Folge, die
(b) (set of successive issues) Serie, die; **radio/TV ∼:** Hörfunkreihe/Fernsehserie, die
(c) (set of books) Reihe, die
serious /'sɪərɪəs/ adj. (a) (earnest) ernst
(b) (important, grave) ernst ⟨Angelegenheit, Lage, Problem, Zustand⟩; ernsthaft ⟨Frage, Einwand, Kandidat⟩; schwer ⟨Krankheit, Unfall, Fehler, Niederlage⟩; ernst zu nehmend ⟨Rivale⟩; ernstlich ⟨Gefahr, Bedrohung⟩; bedenklich ⟨Mangel⟩
'seriously adv. (a) (earnestly) ernst; **take sth./sb. ∼:** etw./jmdn. ernst nehmen
(b) (severely) ernstlich; schwer ⟨verletzt⟩
'seriousness n. Ernst, der; **in all ∼:** ganz im Ernst
sermon /'sɜ:mən/ n. Predigt, die
serpent /'sɜ:pənt/ n. Schlange, die
serrated /se'reɪtɪd/ adj. gezackt; **∼ knife** Sägemesser, das
serum /'sɪərəm/ n. Serum, das
servant /'sɜ:vənt/ n. Diener, der/Dienerin, die
serve /sɜ:v/ ① v.t. (a) (work for) dienen (+ Dat.)
(b) (be useful to) dienlich sein (+ Dat.)
(c) (meet needs of) nutzen (+ Dat.); **∼ a/no purpose** einen Zweck erfüllen/keinen Zweck haben
(d) durchlaufen ⟨Lehre⟩; verbüßen ⟨Haftstrafe⟩
(e) (dish up) servieren; (pour out) einschenken (to Dat.)
(f) **∼[s]** or **it ∼s him right!** [das] geschieht ihm recht!
② v.i. (a) dienen; **∼ as chairman** das Amt des Vorsitzenden innehaben; **∼ as a Member of Parliament** Mitglied des Parlaments sein; **∼ on a jury** Geschworener/Geschworene sein
(b) (be of use) **∼ to do sth.** dazu dienen, etw. zu tun; **∼ to show sth.** etw. zeigen; **∼ for** or **as** dienen als
(c) (Sport) aufschlagen
③ n. ▸ SERVICE 1G
■ **serve 'up** v.t. (a) servieren
(b) (offer for consideration) auftischen (ugs.)
server /'sɜ:və(r)/ n. (Comp.) Server, der

service /'sɜːvɪs/ ① *n.* **(a)** Dienst, *der;* **do sb. a** ~: jmdm. einen guten Dienst erweisen **(b)** (Eccl.) Gottesdienst, *der* **(c)** (attending to customer) Service, *der;* (in shop, garage, etc.) Bedienung, *die* **(d)** (system of transport) Verbindung, *die;* **there is no [bus]** ~ **on Sundays** sonntags verkehren keine Busse **(e)** (provision of maintenance) **[after-sale]** ~: Kundendienst, *der;* **take one's car in for a** ~: sein Auto zur Inspektion bringen **(f)** (operation) Betrieb, *der;* **out of** ~: außer Betrieb **(g)** (Sport) Aufschlag, *der;* **whose** ~ **is it?** wer hat Aufschlag? **(h)** (crockery set) Service, *das* **(i)** (assistance) **can I be of** ~ **[to you]?** kann ich Ihnen behilflich sein?; **I'm at your** ~: ich stehe zu Ihren Diensten **(j)** (Mil.) **the [armed** *or* **fighting]** ~**s** die Streitkräfte *Pl.;* **in the** ~**s** beim Militär **(k)** **[motorway]** ~**s** [Autobahn]raststätte, *die* ② *v.t.* warten ⟨*Wagen, Waschmaschine, Heizung*⟩

serviceable /'sɜːvɪsəbl/ *adj.* **(a)** (useful) nützlich **(b)** (durable) haltbar

service: ~ **area** *n.* Raststätte, *die;* ~ **charge** *n.* Bedienungsgeld, *das;* ~ **hatch** *n.* Durchreiche, *die;* ~ **industry** *n.* Dienstleistungsbetrieb, *der;* ~**man** /'sɜːvɪsmən/ *n. pl.* ~**men** /'sɜːvɪsmən/ Militärangehörige, *der;* ~ **provider** *n.* (Comp.) Provider, *der;* **Internet** ~ **provider** Internetanbieter, *der;* ~ **station** *n.* Tankstelle, *die*

serviette /sɜːvɪ'et/ *n.* (Brit.) Serviette, *die*

servile /'sɜːvaɪl/ *adj.* unterwürfig

servility /sɜːʹvɪlɪtɪ/ *n.* Unterwürfigkeit, *die*

serving /'sɜːvɪŋ/ *n.* Portion, *die*

'serving spoon *n.* Vorlegelöffel, *der*

servitude /'sɜːvɪtjuːd/ *n.* Knechtschaft, *die*

sesame /'sesəmɪ/ *n.* ~ **[seed]** Sesamkorn, *das*

session /'seʃn/ *n.* (meeting) Sitzung, *die;* **be in** ~: tagen

set /set/ ① *v.t.,* -tt-, **set** **(a)** (put) (horizontally) legen; (vertically) stellen; ~ **sb. ashore** jmdn. an Land setzen; ~ **sth./things right** *or* **in order** etw./die Dinge in Ordnung bringen **(b)** (apply) setzen; ~ **a match to sth.** ein Streichholz an etw. (*Akk.*) halten; *see also* FIRE 1A; LIGHT¹ 1D **(c)** (adjust) einstellen (**at** auf + *Akk.*); aufstellen ⟨*Falle*⟩; stellen ⟨*Uhr*⟩; ~ **the alarm for 5.30 a.m.** den Wecker auf 5.30 Uhr stellen **(d)** **be** ~ ⟨*Buch, Film*⟩ spielen (**in** in + *Dat.*) **(e)** (specify) festlegen ⟨*Bedingungen*⟩; festsetzen ⟨*Termin, Ort usw.*⟩ (**for** auf + *Akk.*); ~ **limits** Grenzen setzen **(f)** ~ **sb. thinking that ...:** jmdn. auf den Gedanken bringen, dass ... **(g)** (put forward) stellen ⟨*Frage, Aufgabe*⟩; aufgeben ⟨*Hausaufgabe*⟩; aufstellen

⟨*Rekord*⟩; (compose) zusammenstellen ⟨*Rätsel, Fragen*⟩; ~ **sb. an example,** ~ **an example to sb.** jmdm. ein Beispiel geben; ~ **sb. a task/problem** jmdm. eine Aufgabe stellen/jmdn. vor ein Problem stellen; ~ **[sb./oneself] a target** [jmdm./sich] ein Ziel setzen **(h)** (Med.: put into place) [ein]richten; einrenken ⟨*verrenktes Gelenk*⟩ **(i)** legen ⟨*Haare*⟩ **(j)** decken ⟨*Tisch*⟩; auflegen ⟨*Gedeck*⟩ **(k)** fassen ⟨*Edelstein*⟩ ② *v.i.,* -tt-, **set** **(a)** (solidify) fest werden **(b)** (go down) ⟨*Sonne, Mond:*⟩ untergehen ③ *n.* **(a)** (group) Satz, *der;* ~ **[of two]** Paar, *das;* **a** ~ **of chairs** eine Sitzgruppe **(b)** (radio, TV) Gerät, *das* **(c)** (Tennis) Satz, *der* **(d)** (of hair) Legen, *das* **(e)** (Theatre: scenery) Bühnenbild, *das;* ⟨*area of performance*⟩ (*of film*) Drehort, *der;* (of play) Bühne, *die* **(f)** (of people) Kreis, *der* **(g)** (Math.) Menge, *die* ④ *adj.* **(a)** (fixed) fest ⟨*Absichten, Zielvorstellungen, Zeitpunkt*⟩; **be** ~ **in one's ways** *or* **habits** in seinen Gewohnheiten festgefahren sein; ~ **meal** *or* **menu** Menü, *das* **(b)** vorgeschrieben ⟨*Buch, Lektüre*⟩ **(c)** (ready) **be [all]** ~ **for sth.** zu etw. bereit sein; **be [all]** ~ **to do sth.** bereit sein, etw. zu tun **(d)** (determined) **be** ~ **on sth./doing sth.** zu etw. entschlossen sein/entschlossen sein, etw. zu tun

■ **'set about** *v.t.* ~ **about sth.** sich an etw. (*Akk.*) machen; ~ **about doing sth.** sich daranmachen, etw. zu tun

■ **set a'side** *v.t.* **(a)** beiseite legen **(b)** aufheben ⟨*Urteil, Entscheidung*⟩

■ **set 'back** *v.t.* **(a)** aufhalten ⟨*Entwicklung*⟩; zurückwerfen ⟨*Projekt, Programm*⟩ **(b)** (coll.: cost) kosten ⟨*Person*⟩ **(c)** (place at a distance) zurücksetzen

■ **set 'down** *v.t.* **(a)** absetzen ⟨*Fahrgast*⟩ **(b)** (record) niederschreiben

■ **set 'off** ① *v.i.* (begin journey) aufbrechen; (start to move) loslaufen; ⟨*Fahrzeug:*⟩ losfahren ② *v.t.* **(a)** (cause to explode) explodieren lassen; abbrennen ⟨*Feuerwerk*⟩ **(b)** auslösen ⟨*Reaktion, Alarmanlage*⟩

■ **set 'out** ① *v.i.* **(a)** (begin journey) aufbrechen (**for** nach/zu) **(b)** ~ **out to do sth.** sich (*Dat.*) vornehmen, etw. zu tun ② *v.t.* darlegen

■ **set 'up** ① *v.t.* **(a)** errichten ⟨*Straßensperre, Denkmal*⟩; aufbauen ⟨*Zelt, Klapptisch*⟩ **(b)** (establish) gründen ⟨*Firma, Organisation*⟩; einrichten ⟨*Büro*⟩ ② *v.i.* ~ **up in business** ein Geschäft aufmachen

'setback n. Rückschlag, der

settee /se'tiː/ n. Sofa, das

'setting n. **(a)** (Mus.) Vertonung, die
(b) (surroundings) Rahmen, der; (of novel etc.)
Schauplatz, der

'setting lotion n. Haarfestiger, der

settle /'setl/ **1** v.t. **(a)** (horizontally)
[sorgfältig] legen; (vertically) [sorgfältig]
stellen; (at an angle) [sorgfältig] lehnen
(b) (determine, resolve) sich einigen
auf ⟨Preis⟩; beilegen ⟨Streit, Konflikt,
Meinungsverschiedenheit⟩; entscheiden
⟨Frage, Spiel⟩
(c) bezahlen ⟨Rechnung, Betrag⟩; erfüllen
⟨Forderung, Anspruch⟩; ausgleichen ⟨Konto⟩
2 v.i. **(a)** (become established) sich
niederlassen; (as colonist) sich ansiedeln
(b) (pay) abrechnen
(c) (in chair, in front of fire, etc.) sich
niederlassen; (to work etc.) sich konzentrieren
(**to** auf + Akk.); (into way of life, retirement, etc.)
sich gewöhnen (**into** an + Akk.)
(d) (subside) ⟨Haus, Fundament, Boden:⟩ sich
senken
(e) ⟨Schnee:⟩ liegen bleiben
■ **settle 'down** **1** v.i. **(a)** (make oneself
comfortable) sich niederlassen (**in** in + Dat.)
(b) (in town or house) heimisch werden
2 v.t. **(a)** ~ **oneself down** sich [gemütlich]
hinsetzen
(b) (calm down) beruhigen
■ **'settle for** v.t. (agree to) sich zufrieden
geben mit
■ **'settle 'in** v.i. (in new home) sich einleben
■ **'settle on** v.t. (decide on) sich
entscheiden für
■ **settle 'up** v.i. abrechnen; ~ **up with the**
waiter beim Kellner bezahlen

'settlement n. **(a)** (of argument, conflict,
dispute, differences) Beilegung, die; (of question)
Klärung, die; (of bill, account) Bezahlung, die;
(of court case) Vergleich, der
(b) (colony) Siedlung, die

settler /'setlə(r)/ n. Siedler, der/Siedlerin,
die

set: ~**-to** n., pl. ~**-tos:** have a ~**-to** Streit
haben; (with fists) sich prügeln; ~**-up** n.
System, das

seven /'sevn/ **1** adj. sieben
2 n. Sieben, die. See also EIGHT

seventeen /sevn'tiːn/ **1** adj. siebzehn
2 n. Siebzehn, die. See also EIGHT

seventeenth /sevn'tiːnθ/ **1** adj.
siebzehnt...
2 n. (fraction) Siebzehntel, das. See also
EIGHTH

seventh /'sevnθ/ **1** adj. sieb[en]t...
2 n. (in sequence, rank) Sieb[en]te, der/die/
das; (fraction) Sieb[en]tel, das. See also EIGHTH

seventieth /'sevntɪɪθ/ adj. siebzigst...

seventy /'sevntɪ/ **1** adj. siebzig
2 n. Siebzig, die. See also EIGHT; EIGHTY 2

sever /'sevə(r)/ v.t. **(a)** (cut) durchtrennen;
(fig.) abbrechen ⟨Beziehungen⟩

(b) (separate) abtrennen; (with axe etc.)
abhacken

several /'sevrl/ **1** adv. mehrere; einige;
~ **times** mehrmals
2 pron. einige; ~ **of us** einige von uns;
~ **of the buildings** einige od. mehrere [der]
Gebäude

severe /sɪ'vɪə(r)/ adj., ~**r** /sɪ'vɪərə(r)/, ~**st**
/sɪ'vɪərɪst/ hart ⟨Urteil, Strafe, Kritik, Test,
Prüfung⟩; streng ⟨Frost, Stil, Schönheit⟩;
schwer ⟨Dürre, Verlust, Behinderung,
Verletzung, Krankheit⟩; rau ⟨Wetter⟩; heftig
⟨Anfall, Schmerz⟩; bedrohlich ⟨Mangel,
Knappheit⟩; stark ⟨Blutung⟩

se'verely adv. hart; schwer ⟨verletzt,
behindert⟩

severity /sɪ'verɪtɪ/ n. Strenge, die; (of
drought, shortage) großes Ausmaß; (of criticism)
Schärfe, die

sew /səʊ/ v.t. & i., p.p. **sewn** /səʊn/ or
sewed /səʊd/ nähen
■ **sew 'on** v.t. annähen ⟨Knopf⟩; aufnähen
⟨Abzeichen, Band⟩
■ **sew 'up** v.t. nähen ⟨Saum, Naht, Wunde⟩

sewage /'sjuːɪdʒ/ n. Abwasser, das

'sewage disposal n.
Abwasserbeseitigung, die

sewer /'sjuːə(r), 'suːə(r)/ n. (tunnel)
Abwasserkanal, der; (pipe) Abwasserleitung,
die

'sewing n. Näharbeit, die

'sewing machine n. Nähmaschine, die

sewn ▶ SEW

sex /seks/ n. **(a)** Geschlecht, das
(b) (sexuality; coll.: intercourse) Sex, der (ugs.);
have ~ **with sb.** (coll.) mit jmdm. schlafen;
Sex mit jmdm. haben (salopp)

sex: ~ **appeal** n. Sexappeal, der;
~ **change** n. Geschlechtsumwandlung,
die; ~ **discrimination** n. sexuelle
Diskriminierung; ~ **education** n.
Sexualerziehung, die

sexism /'seksɪzm/ n. Sexismus, der

sexist /'seksɪst/ adj. sexistisch

sex: ~ **life** n. Geschlechtsleben,
das; Sexualleben, das; ~ **maniac** n.
Triebverbrecher, der; **you** ~ **maniac!** (coll.)
du geiler Bock! (ugs.); ~ **offender** n.
Sexual[straf]täter, der/-täterin, die

sexploitation /seksplɔɪ'teɪʃn/ n.
[kommerzielle] Ausbeutung der Sexualität

sex: ~ **shop** n. Sexshop, der; ~ **symbol**
n. Sexidol, das

sexual /'sekʃʊəl/ adj. sexuell

sexual: ~ **a'buse** n. sexueller
Missbrauch; ~ **'harassment** n.
sexuelle Belästigung; ~ **'intercourse** n.
Geschlechtsverkehr, der

sexuality /sekʃʊ'ælɪtɪ/ n. Sexualität, die

sexual: ~ **'organs** n. pl.
Geschlechtsorgane Pl.; ~ **'partner** n.
Sexualpartner, der/-partnerin, die

S

'sexy *adj.* sexy (ugs.)

sh /ʃ/ *int.* sch; pst

shabbily /'ʃæbɪlɪ/ *adv.*, **shabby** /'ʃæbɪ/ *adj.* schäbig

shack /ʃæk/ *n.* [armselige] Hütte

shackle /'ʃækl/ [1] *n., usu. in pl.* Fessel, *die*
[2] *v.t.* anketten (**to** an + *Akk.*)

shade /ʃeɪd/ [1] *n.* (a) Schatten, *der*
(b) (colour) Ton, *der;* (fig.) Schattierung, *die*
(c) (lamp‿) [Lampen]schirm, *der*
[2] *v.t.* (a) (screen) beschatten
(b) (darken with lines) ‿ [in] [ab]schattieren
[3] *v.i.* übergehen (**into** in + *Akk.*)

shadow /'ʃædəʊ/ [1] *n.* Schatten, *der*
[2] *v.t.* (follow) beschatten

'shadowy *adj.* (indistinct) schattenhaft

shady /'ʃeɪdɪ/ *adj.* (a) schattig
(b) (disreputable) zwielichtig

shaft /ʃɑːft/ *n.* (a) (of tool, golf club) Schaft, *der*
(b) (Mech. Engin.) Welle, *die*
(c) (of mine, lift) Schacht, *der*
(d) (of light, lightning) Strahl, *der*

shaggy /'ʃægɪ/ *adj.* zottelig

shake /ʃeɪk/ [1] *n.* Schütteln, *das;* **give sb./sth. a** ‿: jmdn./etw. schütteln
[2] *v.t.*, **shook** /ʃʊk/, **shaken** /'ʃeɪkn/
(a) (move violently) schütteln; ‿ **one's fist/a stick at sb.** jmdm. mit der Faust/einem Stock drohen; ‿ **hands** sich (*Dat.*) die Hand geben
(b) (cause to tremble) erschüttern (*Gebäude usw.*); ‿ **one's head** den Kopf schütteln
(c) (shock) erschüttern
[3] *v.i.*, **shook, shaken** wackeln; (*Boden, Stimme:*) beben; (*Hand:*) zittern
■ **shake 'off** *v.t.* abschütteln
■ **shake 'up** *v.t.* (a) (upset, shock) einen Schrecken einjagen (+ *Dat.*)
(b) (reorganize) umkrempeln (ugs.)

shaken ▶ SHAKE 2, 3

shaky /'ʃeɪkɪ/ *adj.* wack[e]lig (*Möbelstück, Leiter*); zittrig (*Hand, Stimme, Greis*); **feel** ‿: sich zittrig fühlen

shall /ʃl, *stressed* ʃæl/ *v. aux. only in pres.* shall, *neg.* (coll.) **shan't** /ʃɑːnt/, *past* **should** /ʃəd, *stressed* ʃʊd/, *neg.* (coll.) **shouldn't** /'ʃʊdnt/ (a) (*expr. simple future*) werden
(b) **should** (*expr. conditional*) würde/ würdest/würden/würdet; **I should have been killed if I had let go** ich wäre getötet worden, wenn ich losgelassen hätte; **if we should be defeated** falls wir unterliegen [sollten]
(c) (*expr. will or intention*) **what** ‿ **we do?** was sollen wir tun?; **let's go in,** ‿ **we?** gehen wir doch hinein, oder?; **we should be safe by now** jetzt dürften wir in Sicherheit sein; **he shouldn't do things like that!** er sollte so etwas nicht tun!

shallot /ʃə'lɒt/ *n.* Schalotte, *die*

shallow /'ʃæləʊ/ *adj.* seicht (*Wasser, Fluss*); flach (*Schüssel, Teller, Wasser*); (fig.) flach (*Person*)

sham /ʃæm/ [1] *adj.* unecht; imitiert (*Leder, Holz, Pelz*)
[2] *n.* (pretence) Heuchelei, *die;* (person) Heuchler, *der*/Heuchlerin, *die*
[3] *v.t.*, **-mm-** vortäuschen
[4] *v.i.*, **-mm-** simulieren

shambles /'ʃæmblz/ *n.* (coll.) Chaos, *das;* **the room was a** ‿: das Zimmer glich einem Schlachtfeld

shambolic /ʃæm'bɒlɪk/ *adj.* (coll.) chaotisch

shame /ʃeɪm/ *n.* (a) Scham, *die*
(b) (state of disgrace) Schande, *die;* **put sb./sth. to** ‿: jmdn. beschämen/etw. in den Schatten stellen
(c) **what a** ‿! wie schade!

'shamefaced *adj.* betreten

shameful /'ʃeɪmfl/ *adj.* beschämend

'shameless *adj.* schamlos

shampoo /ʃæm'puː/ [1] *v.t.* schamponieren
[2] *n.* Shampoo[n], *das*

shamrock /'ʃæmrɒk/ *n.* Klee, *der*

shandy /'ʃændɪ/ *n.* Bier mit Limonade; Radlermaß, *die* (bes. südd.)

shan't /ʃɑːnt/ (coll.) = shall not

shanty[1] /'ʃæntɪ/ *n.* (hut) [armselige] Hütte

shanty[2] *n.* (song) Shanty, *das*

'shanty town *n.* Elendsviertel, *das*

shape /ʃeɪp/ [1] *v.t.* formen; bearbeiten (*Holz, Stein*) (**into** zu)
[2] *n.* Form, *die;* **take** ‿: Gestalt annehmen
■ **shape 'up** *v.i.* sich entwickeln

'shapeless *adj.* formlos; unförmig (*Kleid, Person*)

shapely /'ʃeɪplɪ/ *adj.* wohlgeformt (*Beine, Busen*); gut (*Figur*)

share /ʃeə(r)/ [1] *n.* (a) (portion) Teil, *der od. das;* [fair] ‿: fair ‿s gerechte Teile; **do more than one's [fair]** ‿ **of the work** mehr als seinen Teil zur Arbeit beitragen
(b) (Commerc.) Aktie, *die*
[2] *v.t.* teilen; gemeinsam tragen (*Verantwortung*)
[3] *v.i.* ‿ **in** teilnehmen an (+ *Dat.*); beteiligt sein an (+ *Dat.*) (*Gewinn*); teilen (*Freude, Erfahrung*)
■ **share 'out** *v.t.* aufteilen (**among** unter + *Akk.*)

share: ‿ **certificate** *n.* Aktienurkunde, *die;* ‿**holder** *n.* Aktionär, *der*/Aktionärin, *die;* ‿ **index** *n.* Aktienindex, *der;* ‿**-out** *n.* Aufteilung, *die;* ‿**ware** *n.* (Comp.) Shareware, *die*

shark /ʃɑːk/ *n.* Hai[fisch], *der*

sharp /ʃɑːp/ [1] *adj.* (a) scharf; spitz (*Nadel, Bleistift, Gipfel, Winkel*); deutlich (*Unterscheidung*); sauer (*Apfel*); herb (*Wein*); (shrill, piercing) schrill (*Schrei, Pfiff*); heftig (*Schmerz, Krampf, Kampf*); begabt

⟨*Schüler, Student*⟩
(b) (derog.: dishonest) gerissen
(c) (Mus.) [um einen Halbton] erhöht ⟨*Note*⟩
2 *adv.* **(a)** (punctually) **at six o'clock**
∼: Punkt sechs Uhr
(b) turn ∼ right/left scharf nach rechts/links
abbiegen
(c) look ∼! halt dich ran! (ugs.)
(d) (Mus.) zu hoch ⟨*singen, spielen*⟩
sharpen /ˈʃɑːpn/ *v.t.* schärfen; [an]spitzen
⟨*Bleistift*⟩
'sharpener *n.* (for pencils) Spitzer, *der* (ugs.)
'sharp-eyed *adj.* scharfäugig; **be**
∼: scharfe Augen haben
'sharpish *adv.* (coll.) (quickly) rasch;
(promptly) unverzüglich; sofort
'sharply *adv.* scharf; in scharfem Ton
⟨*antworten*⟩
'sharpness *n.* Schärfe, *die;* (fineness of point)
Spitzheit, *die*
'sharp-witted *adj.* scharfsinnig
shatter /ˈʃætə(r)/ **1** *v.t.* zertrümmern;
zerbrechen ⟨*Glas, Fenster*⟩; zerschlagen
⟨*Hoffnungen*⟩
2 *v.i.* zerbrechen
shattered /ˈʃætəd/ *adj.* **(a)** zerbrochen
⟨*Glas, Fenster*⟩; (fig.) zerstört ⟨*Hoffnungen*⟩;
zerrüttet ⟨*Nerven*⟩
(b) (coll.: greatly upset) **she was ∼ by the news**
die Nachricht hat sie schwer mitgenommen;
I'm ∼! ich bin ganz erschüttert!; (Brit.
coll.: exhausted) ich bin kaputt! (ugs.)
'shattering *adj.* verheerend ⟨*Wirkung*⟩;
vernichtend ⟨*Schlag, Niederlage*⟩
shave /ʃeɪv/ **1** *v.t.* rasieren; abrasieren
⟨*Haare*⟩
2 *v.i.* sich rasieren
3 *n.* Rasur, *die;* **have a ∼:** sich rasieren
■ **shave 'off** *v.t.* abrasieren
'shaven /ˈʃeɪvn/ *adj.* rasiert; [kahl]
geschoren ⟨*Kopf*⟩
'shaver *n.* Rasierapparat, *der*
'shaver point *n.* Anschluss, *der* für den
Rasierapparat
shaving /ˈʃeɪvɪŋ/ *n.* **(a)** Rasieren, *das*
(b) *in pl.* (of wood, metal, etc.) Späne *Pl.*
shaving: ∼ brush *n.* Rasierpinsel, *der;*
∼ cream *n.* Rasiercreme, *die;* **∼ foam** *n.*
Rasierschaum, *der* **∼ soap** *n.* Rasierseife,
die; **∼ stick** *n.* Stangenrasierseife, *die*
shawl /ʃɔːl/ *n.* Schultertuch, *das*
she /ʃɪ, *stressed* ʃiː/ *pron.* sie
sheaf /ʃiːf/ *n., pl.* **sheaves** /ʃiːvz/ (of corn
etc.) Garbe, *die;* (of paper, arrows, etc.) Bündel,
das
shear /ʃɪə(r)/ *v.t., p.p.* **shorn** /ʃɔːn/ *or*
sheared (clip) scheren
shears /ʃɪəz/ *n. pl.* **[pair of] ∼:** Schere, *die;*
garden ∼: Gartenschere, *die*
sheath /ʃiːθ/ *n., pl.* **∼s** /ʃiːz, ʃiːθs/ **(a)** (for
knife, sword, etc.) Scheide, *die*
(b) (condom) Gummischutz, *der*

sheaves *pl. of* SHEAF
shebang /ʃɪˈbæŋ/ *n.* (Amer. coll.) **the whole**
∼: der ganze Kram (ugs.)
shed[1] /ʃed/ *v.t.,* **-dd-,** **shed** **(a)** verlieren;
abwerfen ⟨*Laub, Geweih*⟩
(b) vergießen ⟨*Blut, Tränen*⟩
(c) verbreiten ⟨*Licht*⟩
shed[2] *n.* Schuppen, *der*
she'd /ʃɪd, *stressed* ʃiːd/ **(a)** = **she had;**
(b) = **she would**
sheen /ʃiːn/ *n.* Glanz, *der*
sheep /ʃiːp/ *n., pl. same* Schaf, *das*
sheep: ∼ dip *n.* Desinfektionsbad
für Schafe; **∼dog** *n.* Hütehund, *der;*
Schäferhund, *der;* **Old English S∼dog**
Bobtail, *der*
sheepish /ˈʃiːpɪʃ/ *adj.* verlegen
sheep: ∼ shearer /ˈʃiːp ʃɪərə(r)/
n. Schafscherer, *der;* **∼shearing** *n.*
Schafschur, *die;* **∼skin** *n.* Schaffell, *das*
sheer /ʃɪə(r)/ *adj.* **(a)** rein; blank ⟨*Unsinn,*
Gewalt⟩; **by ∼ chance** rein zufällig
(b) schroff ⟨*Felsen, Abfall*⟩
sheet /ʃiːt/ *n.* **(a)** Laken, *das*
(b) (of thin metal or plastic) Folie, *die;* (of iron,
tin) Blech, *das;* (of glass) Platte, *die;* (of paper)
Bogen, *der;* Blatt, *das*
(c) ⟨*Eis-, Nebel-*⟩decke, *die*
sheet: ∼ lightning *n.* Flächenblitz, *der;*
∼ music *n.* Notenblätter *Pl.*
sheik[h] /ʃeɪk, ʃiːk/ *n.* Scheich, *der*
shelf /ʃelf/ *n., pl.* **shelves** /ʃelvz/ Brett, *das;*
bord, *das;* **shelves** (set) Regal, *das*
'shelf life *n.* Lagerfähigkeit, *die*
shell /ʃel/ **1** *n.* **(a)** (shield) Schale, *die;* (of snail)
Haus, *das;* (of turtle, tortoise) Panzer, *der;* (on
beach) Muschel, *die*
(b) (Mil.) (bomb) Granate, *die*
2 *v.t.* **(a)** (take out of ∼) schälen
(b) (Mil.) [mit Artillerie] beschießen
■ **shell 'out** *v.t. & i.* (coll.) blechen (ugs.)
(on für)
she'll /ʃɪl, *stressed* ʃiːl/ = **she will**
shell: ∼fish *n., pl. same* **(a)** Schal[en]tier,
das; (oyster, clam) Muschel, *die;*
(crustacean) Krebstier, *das;* **(b)** *in pl.*
(Gastr.) Meeresfrüchte *Pl.;* **∼ shock**
n. Kriegsneurose, *die;* **∼ suit** *n.*
Trilobalanzug, *der*
shelter /ˈʃeltə(r)/ **1** *n.* **(a)** (shield) Schutz,
der (**against** vor + *Dat.*, gegen); **bomb** or
air-raid ∼: Luftschutzraum, *der;* **get under**
∼: sich unterstellen
(b) *no pl.* (place of safety) Zuflucht, *die*
2 *v.t.* schützen (**from** vor + *Dat.*);
Unterschlupf gewähren (+ *Dat.*) ⟨*Flüchtling*⟩
3 *v.i.* Schutz suchen (**from** vor + *Dat.*)
'sheltered /ˈʃeltəd/ *adj.* geschützt;
behütet ⟨*Leben;*⟩ **live in ∼ housing** in einer
Altenwohnung/in Altenwohnungen leben
shelve /ʃelv/ **1** *v.t.* (defer) auf Eis legen
(ugs.)
2 *v.i.* (slope) abfallen

S

shelves *pl. of* SHELF

'**shelving** *n.* Regale *Pl.*

shepherd /'ʃepəd/ ① *n.* Schäfer, *der*
　② *v.t.* führen

'**shepherdess** *n.* Schäferin, *die*

shepherd: ~'s 'crook *n.* Schäferstock,
der; **~'s 'pie** *n.*: Auflauf aus Hackfleisch
mit einer Schicht Kartoffelbrei darüber

sheriff /'ʃerɪf/ *n.* Sheriff, *der*

sherry /'ʃerɪ/ *n.* Sherry, *der*

she's /ʃɪz, *stressed* ʃiːz/ (a) = she is;
　(b) = she has

Shia(h) /'ʃiːə/ *n.* (Muslim Relig.) Shia, *die*

shield /ʃiːld/ ① *n.* Schild, *der*
　② *v.t.* schützen (**from** vor + *Dat.*)

shift /ʃɪft/ ① *v.t.* (a) (move) umstellen
⟨Möbel⟩; wegnehmen ⟨Arm, Hand, Fuß⟩;
wegräumen ⟨Schutt⟩; entfernen ⟨Schmutz,
Fleck⟩; **~ the responsibility/blame on to
sb.** die Verantwortung/Schuld auf jmdn.
schieben
　(b) (Amer. Motor Veh.) **~ gears** schalten
　② *v.i.* (a) ⟨Wind:⟩ drehen (**to** nach);
⟨Ladung:⟩ verrutschen
　(b) (coll.: move quickly) rasen
　③ *n.* (a) a **~ in emphasis** eine Verlagerung
des Akzents; **a ~ in public opinion** ein
Umschwung der öffentlichen Meinung
　(b) (for work) Schicht, *die;* **eight-hour/late
~:** Achtstunden-/Spätschicht, *die;* **do** *or*
work the late ~: Spätschicht haben

'**shift work** *n.* Schichtarbeit, *die*

shifty /'ʃɪftɪ/ *adj.* verschlagen

Shiite /'ʃiːaɪt/ (Muslim Relig.) ① *n.* Schiit,
der/Schiitin, *die;*
　② *adj.* schiitisch

shilling /'ʃɪlɪŋ/ *n.* (Hist.) Shilling, *der*

shilly-shally /'ʃɪlɪʃælɪ/ *v.i.* zaudern; **stop
~ing!** entschließ dich endlich!

shimmer /'ʃɪmə(r)/ ① *v.i.* schimmern
　② *n.* Schimmer, *der*

shin /ʃɪn/ ① *n.* Schienbein, *das*
　② *v.i.*, -nn-: **~ up/down a tree** *etc.* einen
Baum *usw.* hinauf-/hinunterklettern

'**shin bone** *n.* Schienbein, *das*

shine /ʃaɪn/ ① *v.i.*, shone /ʃɒn/ ⟨Lampe,
Licht, Stern:⟩ leuchten; ⟨Sonne, Mond:⟩
scheinen; (reflect light) glänzen
　② *v.t.*, shone: **~ a light on sth./in sb.'s
eyes** etw. anleuchten/jmdm. in die Augen
leuchten
　③ *n.* Glanz, *der*

shingle /'ʃɪŋgl/ *n.* (pebbles) Kies, *der*

'**shingles** *n.* (Med.) Gürtelrose, *die*

shin: ~ guard, ~ pad *ns.*
Schienbeinschutz, *der*

shiny /'ʃaɪnɪ/ *adj.* glänzend

ship /ʃɪp/ ① *n.* Schiff, *das*
　② *v.t.*, -pp- (transport by sea) verschiffen; (send
by road, train, or air) verschicken ⟨Waren⟩

'**shipbuilding** *n.* Schiffbau, *der*

'**shipment** *n.* (a) Versand, *der;* (by sea)
Verschiffung, *die*
　(b) (amount) Sendung, *die*

'**shipowner** *n.* Schiffseigentümer, *der*/
-eigentümerin, *die;* (of several ships) Reeder,
der/Reederin, *die*

'**shipper** *n.* Spediteur, *der*/Spediteurin, *die;*
(company) Spedition, *die*

'**shipping** *n.* (a) (ships) Schiffe *Pl.;* (traffic)
Schifffahrt, *die*
　(b) (transporting) Versand, *der*

shipping: ~ agent *n.* Schiffsagent, *der;*
~ forecast *n.* Seewetterbericht, *der;*
~ lane *n.* Schifffahrtsweg, *der*

ship: ~shape *adj.* in bester Ordnung;
~wreck ① *n.* Schiffbruch, *der* ② *v.t.* **be
~wrecked** Schiffbruch erleiden; **~yard** *n.*
[Schiffs]werft, *die*

shirk /ʃɜːk/ *v.t.* sich drücken vor (+ *Dat.*)

'**shirker** *n.* Drückeberger, *der*/
Drückebergerin, *die* (ugs.)

shirt /ʃɜːt/ *n.* [man's] **~:** [Herren- *od.*
Ober]hemd, *das;* [woman's] **~:** Hemdbluse,
die

'**shirtsleeve** *n.* Hemdsärmel, *der;* **in ~s** in
Hemdsärmeln

shit /ʃɪt/ (coarse) ① *v.i.*, -tt-, shitted *or* shit
scheißen (derb)
　② *n.* (a) Scheiße, *die* (derb); **have** (Brit.) *or*
(Amer.) **take a ~:** scheißen (derb)
　(b) (person) Scheißkerl, *der* (derb)
　(c) (nonsense) Scheiß, *der* (salopp)

shiver /'ʃɪvə(r)/ ① *v.i.* zittern (**with** vor
+ *Dat.*)
　② *n.* Schau[d]er, *der* (geh.)

shoal /ʃəʊl/ *n.* (of fish) Schwarm, *der*

shock /ʃɒk/ ① *n.* (a) Schock, *der;* **give sb.
a ~:** jmdm. einen Schock versetzen
　(b) (violent impact) Erschütterung, *die* (of
durch)
　(c) (Electr.) Schlag, *der*
　(d) (Med.) Schock, *der*
　② *v.t.* **~ sb. [deeply]** ein [schwerer] Schock
für jmdn. sein; (scandalize) jmdn. schockieren

'**shock absorber** *n.* Stoßdämpfer, *der*

'**shocking** *adj.* (a) schockierend
　(b) (coll.: very bad) fürchterlich (ugs.)

shock: ~ jock *n.* (coll.) Skandal-DJ,
der; **~proof** *adj.* stoßfest; **~ wave** *n.*
Druckwelle, *die* (from *Gen.*); (of earthquake)
Erschütterungswelle, *die* (from *Gen.*)

shod ▸ SHOE 2

shoddy /'ʃɒdɪ/ *adj.* schäbig; minderwertig
⟨Arbeit, Stoff, Artikel⟩

shoe /ʃuː/ ① *n.* Schuh, *der;* (of horse)
[Huf]eisen, *das;* **put oneself into sb.'s ~s**
(fig.) sich in jmds. Lage (*Akk.*) versetzen
　② *v.t.*, **~ing, shod** /ʃɒd/ beschlagen ⟨Pferd⟩

shoe: ~cream *n.* Schuhcreme, *die;*
~horn *n.* Schuhlöffel, *der;* **~lace**
n. Schnürsenkel, *der;* **~maker**
n. Schuhmacher, *der;* **~ polish**
n. Schuhcreme, *die;* **~ shop** *n.*
Schuhgeschäft, *das;* **~string** *n.* **on a**

~string (coll.) mit ganz wenig Geld

shone ▸ SHINE 1, 2

shoo /ʃuː/ **1** *int.* sch
2 *v.t.* scheuchen; ~ **away** fortscheuchen

shook ▸ SHAKE 2, 3

shoot /ʃuːt/ **1** *v.i.*, **shot** /ʃɒt/ **(a)** schießen
(**at** auf + *Akk.*)
(b) (move rapidly) schießen (ugs.)
2 *v.t.*, **shot (a)** (wound) anschießen; (kill)
erschießen; (hunt) schießen; ~ **sb. dead**
jmdn. erschießen
(b) schießen mit ⟨*Bogen, Munition, Pistole*⟩;
abschießen ⟨*Pfeil, Kugel*⟩ (**at** auf + *Akk.*)
(c) (Cinemat.) drehen ⟨*Film, Szene*⟩
3 *n.* (Bot.) Trieb, *der*
■ **shoot 'down** *v.t.* niederschießen
⟨*Person*⟩; abschießen ⟨*Flugzeug*⟩
■ **shoot 'out** *v.i.* hervorschießen
■ **shoot 'up** *v.i.* in die Höhe schießen;
⟨*Preise, Kosten, Temperatur*⟩ in die Höhe
schnellen

shooting: ~ **range** *n.* Schießstand, *der*
~ **'star** *n.* Sternschnuppe, *die;* ~ **stick** *n.*
Jagdstock, *der;*
'shoot-out *n.* Schießerei, *die*

shop /ʃɒp/ **1** *n.* Laden, *der;* Geschäft,
das; **go to the** ~**s** einkaufen gehen; **talk**
~: fachsimpeln (ugs.)
2 *v.i.*, **-pp-** einkaufen; **go** ~**ping** einkaufen
gehen
■ **shop a'round** *v.i.* sich umsehen (**for**
nach)

shopaholic /ˈʃɒpəhɒlɪk/ *n.* Kaufsüchtige,
der/die

shop: ~ **assistant** *n.* (Brit.) Verkäufer,
*der/*Verkäuferin, *die;* ~**front** *n.*
Schaufensterfront, *die;* ~**keeper** *n.*
Ladenbesitzer, *der/*-besitzerin, *die;* ~**lifter**
n. Ladendieb, *der/*-diebin, *die;* ~**lifting** *n.*
Ladendiebstahl, *der;* ~**owner** ▸ ~KEEPER
'shopper *n.* Käufer, *der/*Käuferin, *die*
'shopping *n.* **(a)** Einkaufen, *das;* **do**
the/one's ~: einkaufen/[seine] Einkäufe
machen
(b) (items bought) Einkäufe *Pl.*
shopping: ~ **bag** *n.* Einkaufstasche,
die; ~ **basket** *n.* Einkaufskorb,
der; ~ **centre** *n.* Einkaufszentrum,
das; ~ **list** *n.* Einkaufszettel, *der;*
~ **mall** /-mæl/ *n.* Einkaufszentrum,
das; ~ **precinct** *n.* Einkaufs- *od.*
Geschäftsviertel, *das;* ~ **trolley** *n.* (in
supermarket) Einkaufswagen, *der;* (personal)
Einhaufsroller, *der*
shop: ~**-soiled** *adj.* (Brit.) (slightly damaged)
leicht beschädigt; (slightly dirty) angeschmutzt;
~ **steward** *n.* [gewerkschaftlicher]
Vertrauensmann; ~ **'window** *n.*
Schaufenster, *das*

shore /ʃɔː(r)/ *n.* Ufer, *das;* (beach) Strand,
der
■ **shore 'up** *v.t.* abstützen ⟨*Mauer, Haus*⟩;
(fig.) stützen

shorn ▸ SHEAR

short /ʃɔːt/ **1** *adj.* **(a)** kurz; **in a** ~ **time** *or*
while (soon) bald; in Kürze; **a** ~ **time** *or* **while**
ago/later vor kurzem/kurze Zeit später; **in**
~, ...: kurz, ...
(b) klein ⟨*Person, Wuchs*⟩
(c) (deficient, scanty) knapp; **go** ~ [**of sth.**]
[an etw. (*Dat.*)] Mangel leiden; **sb. is** ~ **of**
sth. jmdm. fehlt es an etw. (*Dat.*); **time is**
getting/is ~: die Zeit wird/ist knapp; **be in**
~ **supply** knapp sein; **be** ~ [**of cash**] knapp
[bei Kasse] sein (ugs.)
2 *adv.* **(a)** (abruptly) plötzlich; **stop**
~: plötzlich abbrechen; **stop sb.** ~: jmdm.
ins Wort fallen
(b) **stop** ~ **of doing sth.** nicht so weit gehen,
etw. zu tun

shortage /ˈʃɔːtɪdʒ/ *n.* Mangel, *der* (**of** an
+ *Dat.*); ~ **of fruit/teachers** Obstknappheit,
*die/*Lehrermangel, *der*

short: ~**bread** *n.* Shortbread, *das;* Kekse
aus Butterteig; ~ **'circuit** *n.* (Electr.)
Kurzschluss, *der;* ~**coming** *n., usu.*
in pl. Unzulänglichkeit, *die;* ~ **'cut** *n.*
(a) Abkürzung, *die;* **take a** ~ **cut** den Weg
abkürzen; **(b)** (Comp.) [**keyboard**] ~ **cut**
Shortcut, *der*

shorten /ˈʃɔːtn/ **1** *v.i.* kürzer werden
2 *v.t.* kürzen; verkürzen ⟨*Besuch,*
Wartezeit⟩

short: ~**fall** *n.* Fehlmenge, *die;*
~**-haired** *adj.* kurzhaarig;
Kurzhaar⟨*dackel, -katze*⟩; ~**hand** *n.*
Stenografie, *die;* ~**hand typist** Stenotypist,
der/-typistin, *die;* ~ **list** *n.* (Brit.) engere
Auswahl; **be on/put sb. on the** ~ **list** in der
engeren Auswahl sein/jmdn. in die engere
Auswahl nehmen; ~**list** *v.t.* in die engere
Auswahl nehmen; ~**-lived** *adj.* kurzlebig
'shortly *adv.* in Kürze; demnächst;
~ **before/after sth.** kurz vor/nach etw.
short: ~ **'pastry** *n.* Mürbeteig, *der;*
~**-range** *adj.* **(a)** Kurzstrecken⟨*flugzeug,*
-rakete usw.⟩; **(b)** (relating to time) kurzfristig

shorts /ʃɔːts/ *n. pl.* **(a)** (trousers) kurze
Hose[n *Pl.*]; Shorts *Pl.*
(b) (Amer.: underpants) Unterhose, *die*

short: ~**-'sighted** *adj.* kurzsichtig;
~**-sleeved** /-ˈsliːvd/ *adj.* kurzärm[e]lig;
~**-staffed** /-ˈstaːft/ *adj.* **be [very]**
~**-staffed** [viel] zu wenig Personal
haben; ~ **'story** *n.* Kurzgeschichte,
die; ~**-'tempered** *adj.* aufbrausend;
~**-term** *adj.* kurzfristig; (provisional)
vorläufig ⟨*Lösung*⟩; befristet ⟨*Vertrag*⟩;
~ **'trousers** *n. pl.* kurze Hose[n *Pl.*];
~ **wave** *n.* (Radio) Kurzwelle, *die*

shot /ʃɒt/ **1** *n.* **(a)** Schuss, *der;* **fire a**
~: einen Schuss abgeben (**at** auf + *Akk.*);
like a ~ (fig.) wie der Blitz (ugs.); **I'd do it like**
a ~: ich würde es auf der Stelle tun
(b) (Athletics) **put the** ~: die Kugel stoßen;
[**putting**] **the** ~: Kugelstoßen, *das*
(c) (Sport: stroke, kick, throw) Schuss, *der* ⋯▸

S

(d) (Photog.) Aufnahme, *die;* (Cinemat.) Einstellung, *die*
2 ▸ SHOOT 1, 2
3 *adj.* **be/get ~ of** (coll.) los sein/loswerden
'**shotgun** *n.* [Schrot]flinte, *die*
should ▸ SHALL
shoulder /'ʃəʊldə(r)/ 1 *n.* Schulter, *die*
2 *v.t.* schultern; (fig.) übernehmen
shoulder: ~ bag *n.* Umhängetasche, *die;*
~ blade *n.* Schulterblatt, *das;* **~ joint** *n.* Schultergelenk, *das;* **~-length** *adj.* schulterlang; **~ pad** *n.* Schulterpolster, *das;* **~ strap** *n.* (on garment) Schulterklappe, *die;* (on bag) Tragriemen, *der*
shouldn't /'ʃʊdnt/ (coll.) = **should not;**
▸ SHALL
shout /ʃaʊt/ 1 *n.* Ruf, *der;* (inarticulate) Schrei, *der*
2 *v.i. & t.* schreien
■ **shout 'down** *v.t.* niederschreien
■ **shout 'out** 1 *v.i.* aufschreien
2 *v.t.* [laut] rufen
'**shouting** *n.* Geschrei, *das*
shove /ʃʌv/ 1 *n.* Stoß, *der*
2 *v.t.* stoßen; schubsen (ugs.); (coll.: put) tun
■ **shove a'way** *v.t.* (coll.) wegschubsen (ugs.)
■ **shove 'off** *v.i.* (coll.: leave) abschieben (ugs.)
shovel /'ʃʌvl/ 1 *n.* Schaufel, *die*
2 *v.t.,* (Brit.) **-ll-** schaufeln
show /ʃəʊ/ 1 *n.* **(a)** (entertainment, performance) Show, *die;* (Theatre) Vorstellung, *die;* (Radio, Telev.) [Unterhaltungs]sendung, *die*
(b) (exhibition) Ausstellung, *die;* Schau, *die;* **put sth. on ~:** etw. ausstellen; **be on ~:** ausgestellt sein
(c) (appearance) Anschein, *der;* **be for ~:** reine Angeberei sein (ugs.)
2 *v.t., p.p.* **shown** /ʃəʊn/ **(a)** zeigen; vorzeigen ‹Pass, Fahrschein usw.›; **~ sb. sth., ~ sth. to sb.** jmdm. etw. zeigen
(b) beweisen ‹Mut, Urteilsvermögen usw.›; **~ sb. that ...:** jmdm. beweisen, dass ...; **~ [sb.] kindness/mercy** freundlich [zu jmdm.] sein/Erbarmen [mit jmdm.] haben
(c) ‹Thermometer, Uhr usw.:› zeigen
(d) (exhibit in a show) ausstellen; zeigen ‹Film›
3 *v.i., p.p.* **shown (a)** (be visible) sichtbar *od.* zu sehen sein; (come into sight) sich zeigen
(b) (be ~n) ‹Film:› laufen; ‹Künstler:› ausstellen
■ **show 'in** *v.t.* hinein-/hereinführen
■ **show 'off** *v.i.* angeben (ugs.); prahlen
■ **show 'out** *v.t.* hinausführen
■ **show 'round** *v.t.* herumführen
■ **show 'through** *v.i.* durchscheinen
■ **show 'up** 1 *v.t.* **(a)** (make visible) [deutlich] sichtbar machen
(b) (coll.: embarrass) blamieren
2 *v.i.* **(a)** (be visible) [deutlich] zu sehen sein
(b) (coll.: arrive) sich blicken lassen (ugs.)

show: ~ biz (coll.), **~ business** *ns., no art.* Schaugeschäft, *das;* **~ case** *n.* Vitrine, *die;* (fig.) Schaufenster, *das;* **~ down** *n.* (fig.) Kraftprobe, *die;* **have a ~down [with sb.]** sich [mit jmdm.] auseinander setzen
shower /'ʃaʊə(r)/ 1 *n.* **(a)** Schauer, *der;* **~ of rain/hail** Regen-/Hagelschauer, *der*
(b) (for washing) Dusche, *die;* **have** *or* **take a [cold/quick] ~:** [kalt/schnell] duschen
2 *v.t.* (lavish) **~ sth. [up]on sb., ~ sb. with sth.** jmdn. mit etw. überhäufen
3 *v.i.* (have a **~**) duschen
shower: ~ cap *n.* Duschhaube, *die;*
~ curtain *n.* Duschvorhang, *der;* **~ gel** *n.* Duschgel, *das;* **~proof** *adj.* [bedingt] regendicht
'**showery** *adj.* **it is ~:** es gibt immer wieder kurze Schauer; **a ~ day** ein Tag mit Schauerwetter
'**showjumping** *n.* Springreiten, *das*
shown ▸ SHOW 2, 3
show: ~-off *n.* (coll.) Angeber, *der*/Angeberin, *die;* **~piece** *n.* (of exhibition, collection) Schaustück, *das;* (highlight) Paradestück, *das;* **~room** *n.* Ausstellungsraum, *der;* **~ trial** *n.* Schauprozess, *der*
'**showy** *adj.* protzig (ugs.)
shrank ▸ SHRINK
shred /ʃred/ 1 *n.* Fetzen, *der;* (fig.) Spur, *die;* **tear sth. to ~s** etw. zerfetzen; (fig.) etw. zerpflücken
2 *v.t.,* **-dd-** [im Reißwolf] zerkleinern
shredder /'ʃredə(r)/ *n.* (for paper) Reißwolf, *der*
shrew /ʃruː/ *n.* (Zool.) Spitzmaus, *die*
shrewd /ʃruːd/ *adj.* klug; genau ‹[Ein]schätzung›
shriek /ʃriːk/ 1 *n.* [Auf]schrei, *der*
2 *v.i.* [auf]schreien
3 *v.t.* schreien
shrift /ʃrɪft/ *n.* **give sb. short ~:** jmdn. kurz abfertigen (ugs.); **get short ~** kurz abgefertigt werden (ugs.)
shrill /ʃrɪl/ *adj.* schrill
shrimp /ʃrɪmp/ *n.* Garnele, *die*
shrine /ʃraɪn/ *n.* (tomb) Grab, *das*
shrink /ʃrɪŋk/ 1 *v.i.,* **shrank** /ʃræŋk/, **shrunk** /ʃrʌŋk/ **(a)** schrumpfen; ‹Kleidung, Stoff:› einlaufen; ‹Metall, Holz:› sich zusammenziehen
(b) (recoil) **~ from sb./sth.** vor jmdm. zurückweichen/vor etw. (Dat.) zurückschrecken; **~ from doing sth.** sich scheuen, etw. zu tun
2 *v.t.,* **shrank, shrunk** einlaufen lassen ‹Textilien›
shrinkage /'ʃrɪŋkɪdʒ/ *n.* (of clothing) Einlaufen, *das*
shrink: ~-proof, ~-resistant *adjs.* schrumpffrei; **be ~-proof** nicht einlaufen; **~-wrap** *v.t.* in einer Schrumpffolie verpacken

shrivel /'ʃrɪvl/ v.i., (Brit.) **-ll-:** ~ **[up]** verschrumpeln; ⟨Pflanze, Blume:⟩ welk werden

shroud /ʃraʊd/ ①️ n. Leichentuch, das ②️ v.t. ~ sth. in sth. etw. in etw. (Akk.) hüllen

Shrove 'Tuesday /ʃrəʊv/ n. Fastnachtsdienstag, der

shrub /ʃrʌb/ n. Strauch, der

shrubbery /'ʃrʌbərɪ/ n. Gesträuch, das

shrug /ʃrʌɡ/ ①️ v.t. & i., **-gg-:** ~ **[one's shoulders]** die Achseln zucken ②️ n. ~ **[of one's or the shoulders]** Achselzucken, das
■ **shrug 'off** v.t. in den Wind schlagen

shrunk ▶ SHRINK

shrunken /'ʃrʌŋkn/ adj. verhutzelt (ugs.) ⟨Person⟩; schrump[e]lig ⟨Apfel⟩

shudder /'ʃʌdə(r)/ ①️ v.i. zittern (**with** vor + Dat.) ②️ n. Zittern, das

shuffle /'ʃʌfl/ ①️ n. (a) Schlurfen, das; **walk with a** ~: schlurfen (b) (Cards) Mischen, das; **give the cards a [good]** ~: die Karten [gut] mischen ②️ v.t. (a) (Cards) mischen (b) ~ **one's feet** von einem Fuß auf den anderen treten

shun /ʃʌn/ v.t., **-nn-** meiden

shunt /ʃʌnt/ v.t. (Railw.) rangieren

shush /ʃʊʃ/ int. still

shut /ʃʌt/ ①️ v.t., **-tt-,** shut zumachen; schließen; zusammenklappen ⟨Klappmesser, Fächer⟩; ~ **one's finger in the door** sich (Dat.) den Finger in der Tür einklemmen ②️ v.i., **-tt-,** shut schließen; ⟨Blüte:⟩ sich schließen
■ **shut 'down** ①️ v.t. (a) schließen, zumachen ⟨Deckel⟩ (b) stilllegen ⟨Fabrik⟩; abschalten ⟨Kernreaktor⟩ ②️ v.i. ⟨Laden, Fabrik:⟩ geschlossen werden
■ **shut 'out** v.t. aussperren
■ **shut 'up** ①️ v.t. abschließen; einsperren ⟨Tier, Person⟩ ②️ v.i. (coll.: be quiet) den Mund halten

shutter /'ʃʌtə(r)/ n. (a) [Fenster]laden, der (b) (Photog.) Verschluss, der; ~ **release** Auslöser, der; ~ **speed** Verschlusszeit, die

shuttle /'ʃʌtl/ ①️ n. (in loom) Schiffchen, das ②️ v.i. pendeln

shuttle: ~**cock** n. Federball, der; ~ **service** n. Pendelverkehr, der

shy /ʃaɪ/ adj., ~**er** or **shier** /'ʃaɪə(r)/, ~**est** or **shiest** /'ʃaɪɪst/ scheu; (diffident) schüchtern
■ **shy a'way** v.i. ~ **away from sth./doing sth.** etw. scheuen/sich scheuen, etw. zu tun

'shyness n. Scheuheit, die; (diffidence) Schüchternheit, die

Siamese /saɪə'miːz/ ~ **'cat** n. Siamkatze, die; ~ **'twins** n. pl. siamesische Zwillinge Pl.

Siberia /saɪ'bɪərɪə/ pr. n. Sibirien (das)

sibling /'sɪblɪŋ/ n. (male) Bruder, der; (female) Schwester, die; in pl. Geschwister Pl.

Sicily /'sɪsɪlɪ/ pr. n. Sizilien (das)

sick /sɪk/ ①️ adj. (a) (ill) krank; **be off** ~: krank [gemeldet] sein (b) (Brit.: vomiting or about to vomit) **be** ~: sich erbrechen; **I'm going to be** ~: ich muss mich erbrechen; **sb. gets/feels** ~: jmdm. wird/ist [es] übel od. schlecht; **be/get** ~ **of sb./sth.** (fig.) jmdn./etw. satt haben/ allmählich satt haben; **make sb.** ~ (disgust) jmdn. anekeln ②️ n. pl. **the** ~: die Kranken Pl.

sick 'building syndrome n. Sickbuildingsyndrom, das

'sicken /'sɪkn/ ①️ v.i. **be** ~**ing for sth.** (Brit.) krank werden; etw. ausbrüten (ugs.) ②️ v.t. (disgust) anwidern

'sickening adj. Ekel erregend, widerlich ⟨Anblick, Geruch⟩

sickle /'sɪkl/ n. Sichel, die

sick: ~ **leave** n. Urlaub wegen Krankheit; **be on** ~ ≈ krank geschrieben sein; ~ **list** n. Liste der Kranken, die; **on the** ~ **list:** krank [gemeldet/geschrieben]

'sickly adj. kränklich

'sickness n. Krankheit, die; (nausea) Übelkeit, die

sick: ~ **pay** n. Entgeltfortzahlung im Krankheitsfalle; (paid by insurance) Krankengeld, das; ~**room** n. Krankenzimmer, das

side /saɪd/ ①️ n. (a) Seite, die; ~ **of beef** Rinderhälfte, die; ~ **of bacon** Speckseite, die; **walk/stand** ~ **by** ~: nebeneinander gehen/stehen; **work/fight** ~ **by** ~ **[with sb.]** Seite an Seite [mit jmdm.] arbeiten/ kämpfen; **live** ~ **by** ~ **[with sb.]** in [jmds.] unmittelbarer Nachbarschaft leben; **to one** ~: zur Seite; **on one** ~: an der Seite; **on the** ~ (as ~line) nebenbei; **take** ~**s [with/against sb.]** [für/gegen jmdn.] Partei ergreifen (b) (Sport: team) Mannschaft, die ②️ v.i. ~ **with sb.** sich auf jmds. Seite (Akk.) stellen ③️ adj. Seiten-

side: ~**board** n. Anrichte, die; ~**boards** (coll.), ~**burns** ns. pl. (on cheeks) Backenbart, der; (in front of the ears) Koteletten Pl.; ~**car** n. Beiwagen, der; ~ **dish** n. Beilage, die; ~ **door** n. Seitentür, die; ~ **effect** n. Nebenwirkung, die; ~ **entrance** n. Seiteneingang, der; ~ **exit** n. Seitenausgang, der; ~ **issue** n. Randproblem, das; ~**kick** n. (coll.) Kumpan, der; ~**light** n. Begrenzungsleuchte, die; **drive on** ~**lights** mit Standlicht fahren; ~**line** n. (occupation) Nebenbeschäftigung, die; ~**long** adj. **a** ~**long look/glance** ein Seitenblick; ~ **plate** n. kleiner Teller (neben dem Teller für das Hauptgericht); ~ **road** n. Seitenstraße, die; ~**-saddle** adv. ride ⋯⋗

~-saddle im Damensitz reiten; ~ **salad** *n.* Salat [als Beilage]; **steak with chips and a** ~ **salad** Steak mit Pommes frites und dazu ein Salat; ~**show** *n.* Nebenattraktion, *die;* ~**step** 1 *n.* Schritt zur Seite; 2 *v.t.* ausweichen (+ *Dat.*); ~ **street** *n.* Seitenstraße, *die;* ~ **table** *n.* Beistelltisch, *der;* ~**track** *v.t.* get ~tracked abgelenkt werden; ~**walk** *n.* (Amer.) Bürgersteig, *der;* ~**ways** /'saɪdweɪz/ 1 *adv.* look at sb./sth. ~ways jmdn./etw. von der Seite ansehen; 2 *adj.* seitlich; ~ **wind** *n.* Seitenwind, *der*

siding /'saɪdɪŋ/ *n.* Abstellgleis, *das*

sidle /'saɪdl/ *v.i.* schleichen [up to zu]

siege /siːdʒ/ *n.* Belagerung, *die;* (by police) Umstellung, *die;* lay ~ to sth. etw. belagern

siesta /sɪ'estə/ *n.* Siesta, *die*

sieve /sɪv/ 1 *n.* Sieb, *das* 2 *v.t.* sieben

sift /sɪft/ *v.t.* sieben; ~ sth. from sth. etw. von etw. trennen

∎ **sift 'out** *v.t.* aussieben

sigh /saɪ/ 1 *n.* Seufzer, *der;* breathe or give or heave a ~: einen Seufzer ausstoßen; ~ of relief/contentment Seufzer der Erleichterung/Zufriedenheit 2 *v.i.* seufzen; ~ with relief/despair erleichtert/verzweifelt seufzen

sight /saɪt/ 1 *n.* (a) (faculty) Sehvermögen, *das;* know sb. by ~: jmdn. vom Sehen kennen (b) (act of seeing; spectacle) Anblick, *der;* catch/lose ~ of sb./sth. jmdn./etw. erblicken/aus dem Auge verlieren; at first ~: auf den ersten Blick (c) *in pl.* ~s (places of interest) Sehenswürdigkeiten *Pl.;* see the ~s die Sehenswürdigkeiten besichtigen (d) (range) Sichtweite, *die;* in ~: in Sicht; within *or* in ~ of sb./sth. (able to see) in jmds. Sichtweite (*Dat.*)/in Sichtweite einer Sache; out of ~: außer Sicht (e) (of gun) Visier, *das;* set/have [set] one's ~s on sth. (fig.) etw. anpeilen 2 *v.t.* sichten ⟨*Land, Schiff, Flugzeug*⟩; sehen ⟨*Entflohenen, Vermissten*⟩

sighted /'saɪtɪd/ *adj.* sehend; partially ~: [hochgradig] sehbehindert

'sighting *n.* Beobachtung, *die*

sight-read (Mus.) *v.t. & i.* ⟨*Pianist usw.:*⟩ vom Blatt spielen; ⟨*Sänger:*⟩ vom Blatt singen

'sightseeing *n.* go ~: Besichtigungen machen

sightseer /'saɪtsiːə(r)/ *n.* Tourist (*der die Sehenswürdigkeiten besichtigt*)

sign /saɪn/ 1 *n.* (a) (symbol, signal, indication) Zeichen, *das;* (of future event) Anzeichen, *das;* as a ~ of als Zeichen (+ *Gen.*) (b) (Astrol.) ~ [of the zodiac] Sternzeichen, *das* (c) (notice; on shop etc.) Schild, *das* 2 *v.t. & i.* unterschreiben; ~ one's name [mit seinem Namen] unterschreiben

∎ **sign 'on** *v.i.* (as unemployed) sich arbeitslos melden

∎ **sign 'up** *v.i.* sich [vertraglich] verpflichten (with bei); (for course) sich einschreiben

signal /'sɪgnl/ 1 *n.* Signal, *das;* a ~ for sth./to sb. ein Zeichen zu etw./für jmdn 2 *v.i.*, (Brit.) **-ll-** signalisieren; Signale geben; ⟨*Kraftfahrer:*⟩ blinken; (with hand) anzeigen; ~ to sb. [to do sth.] jmdm. ein Zeichen geben[, etw. zu tun]

signal: ~ **box** *n.* Stellwerk, *das;* ~**man** /-mən/ *n* Bahnwärter, *der*

signature /'sɪgnətʃə(r)/ *n.* Unterschrift, *die;* (on painting) Signatur, *die*

'signature tune *n.* Erkennungsmelodie, *die*

'signboard *n.* Schild, *das*

signet ring /'sɪgnɪt rɪŋ/ *n.* Siegelring, *der*

significance /sɪg'nɪfɪkəns/ *n.* Bedeutung, *die;* be of [no] ~: [nicht] von Bedeutung sein

significant /sɪg'nɪfɪkənt/ *adj.* (a) (noteworthy, important) bedeutend (b) (full of meaning) bedeutsam

sig'nificantly *adv.* (a) (meaningfully) bedeutungsvoll; ~ [enough] bedeutsamerweise (b) (notably) bedeutend

signify /'sɪgnɪfaɪ/ *v.t.* bedeuten

sign: ~ **language** *n.* Zeichensprache, *die;* ~**post** *n.* Wegweiser, *der;* ~**writer** *n.* Schildermaler, *der*

Sikh /siːk, sɪk/ *n.* Sikh, *der*

silence /'saɪləns/ 1 *n.* Schweigen, *das;* (keeping a secret) Verschwiegenheit, *die;* (stillness) Stille, *die;* there was ~: es herrschte Schweigen/Stille; in ~: schweigend 2 *v.t.* zum Schweigen bringen; (fig.) ersticken ⟨*Proteste*⟩; mundtot machen ⟨*Gegner*⟩

'silencer *n.* (on gun; Brit. Motor Veh.) Schalldämpfer, *der*

silent /'saɪlənt/ *adj.* stumm; (noiseless) unhörbar; (still) still; be ~ (say nothing) schweigen; ~ film Stummfilm, *der*

'silently *adv.* schweigend; stumm ⟨*weinen, beten*⟩; (noiselessly) lautlos

silent ma'jority *n.* schweigende Mehrheit

silhouette /sɪlʊ'et/ 1 *n.* (a) (picture) Schattenriss, *der* (b) (appearance against the light) Silhouette, *die* 2 *v.t.* be ~d against sth. sich als Silhouette gegen etw. abheben

silicon /'sɪlɪkən/ *n.* Silicium, *das;* ~ chip Siliciumchip, *der*

silicone /'sɪlɪkəʊn/ *n.* Silikon, *das;* ~ [breast] implant Silikon[brust]implantat, *das*

silk /sɪlk/ 1 *n.* Seide, *die* 2 *attrib. adj.* seiden; Seiden-

'silkworm n. Seidenraupe, *die*

'silky adj. seidig

sill /sɪl/ n. (of door) [Tür]schwelle, *die;* (of window) Fensterbank, *die*

silly /'sɪlɪ/ adj. dumm; (imprudent, unwise) töricht; (childish) albern

silo /'saɪləʊ/ n., pl. ~s Silo, *der*

silt /sɪlt/ n. Schlamm, *der;* Schlick, *der*

silver /'sɪlvə(r)/ ① n. Silber, *das*
② attrib. adj. silbern; Silber⟨pokal, -münze⟩

silver: ~ **'jubilee** n. silbernes Jubiläum; ~ **'medal** n. Silbermedaille, *die;* ~ **'paper** n. Silberpapier, *das;* ~**-plated** adj. versilbert; ~**smith** n. Silberschmied, *der*/-schmiedin, *die;* ~ **'wedding** n. Silberhochzeit, *die*

SIM card /'sɪm kɑ:d/ n. Sim-Karte, *die*

similar /'sɪmɪlə(r)/ adj. ähnlich (**to** Dat.)

similarity /sɪmɪ'lærɪtɪ/ n. Ähnlichkeit, *die* (**to** mit)

'similarly adv. ähnlich; (in exactly the same way) ebenso

simile /'sɪmɪlɪ/ n. Vergleich, *der*

simmer /'sɪmə(r)/ ① v.i. ⟨Flüssigkeit:⟩ sieden; ziehen
② v.t. köcheln od. ziehen lassen
■ **simmer 'down** v.i. sich abregen (ugs.)

simper /'sɪmpə(r)/ v.i. affektiert od. gekünstelt lächeln

simple /'sɪmpl/ adj. einfach; (unsophisticated, not elaborate) schlicht ⟨Mobiliar, Schönheit, Kunstwerk, Kleidung⟩; **it was a** ~ **misunderstanding** es war [ganz] einfach ein Missverständnis

'simple-minded adj. (a) (unsophisticated) schlicht
(b) (unintelligent) beschränkt

simpleton /'sɪmpltən/ n. Einfaltspinsel, *der* (ugs.)

simplicity /sɪm'plɪsɪtɪ/ n. Einfachheit, *die;* (unpretentiousness, lack of sophistication) Schlichtheit, *die*

simplification /sɪmplɪfɪ'keɪʃn/ n. Vereinfachung, *die*

simplify /'sɪmplɪfaɪ/ v.t. vereinfachen

simplistic /sɪm'plɪstɪk/ adj. [all]zu simpel

simply /'sɪmplɪ/ adv. einfach; (in an unsophisticated manner) schlicht; (merely) nur; **it isn't true** es ist einfach nicht wahr; **I was** ~ **trying to help** ich wollte nur helfen

simulate /'sɪmjʊleɪt/ v.t. (a) (feign) vortäuschen
(b) simulieren ⟨Bedingungen, Wetter usw.⟩

simulation /sɪmjʊ'leɪʃn/ n. (a) (feigning) Vortäuschung, *die*
(b) (imitation of conditions) Simulation, *die*
(c) (simulated object) Imitation, *die*

simulator /'sɪmjʊleɪtə(r)/ n. Simulator, *der*

simultaneous /sɪml'teɪnɪəs/ adj., **simul'taneously** adv. gleichzeitig

sin /sɪn/ ① n. Sünde, *die*
② v.i., **-nn-** sündigen

since /sɪns/ ① adv. seitdem
② prep. seit; **I have/had been waiting** ~ **8 o'clock** ich warte/wartete [schon] seit 8 Uhr; **he has lived here** ~ **his childhood** er wohnt seit seiner Kindheit hier; ~ **seeing you …**: seit ich dich gesehen habe; ~ **then/that time** inzwischen
③ conj. (a) (from the time when) seit; **it is a long time/so long/not so long** ~ **…**: es ist lange/so lange/gar nicht lange her, dass …
(b) (seeing that, as) da

sincere /sɪn'sɪə(r)/ adj., ~**r** /sɪn'sɪərə(r)/, ~**st** /sɪn'sɪərɪst/ aufrichtig; herzlich ⟨Grüße, Glückwünsche usw.⟩

sin'cerely adv. aufrichtig; **yours** ~: mit freundlichen Grüßen

sincerity /sɪn'serɪtɪ/ n. Aufrichtigkeit, *die*

sinew /'sɪnju:/ n. Sehne, *die*

sinful /'sɪnfl/ adj. sündig; (reprehensible) sündhaft; **it is** ~ **to …**: es ist eine Sünde, zu …

sing /sɪŋ/ v.i. & t., **sang** /sæŋ/, **sung** /sʌŋ/ singen
■ **sing 'up** v.i. lauter singen

singe /sɪndʒ/ v.t. & i., ~**ing** versengen

singer /'sɪŋə(r)/ n. Sänger, *der*/Sängerin, *die*

single /'sɪŋgl/ ① adj. (a) einfach; (sole) einzig; (separate, individual, isolated) einzeln; **not a** ~ **one** kein Einziger/keine Einzige/kein Einziges; **every** ~ **one** jeder/jede/jedes Einzelne; **every** ~ **day** jeden Tag; ~ **ticket** (Brit.) einfache Fahrkarte
(b) (for one person) Einzel⟨bett, -zimmer⟩
(c) (unmarried) ledig; **a** ~ **man/woman** ein Lediger/eine Ledige; ~ **people** Ledige Pl.; ~ **parent** allein erziehender Elternteil; ~ **mother** allein erziehende od. stehende Mutter
② n. (a) (Brit.: ticket) einfache Fahrkarte; **[a]** ~/**two** ~**s to Manchester, please** einmal/zweimal einfach nach Manchester, bitte
(b) (record) Single, *die*
(c) in pl. (Tennis etc.) Einzel, *das*
■ **single 'out** v.t. ~ **sb./sth. out as/for sth.** jmdn./etw. als/für etw. auswählen

single: ~ **cream** n. [einfache] Sahne; ~ **'currency** n. Einheitswährung, *die;* ~**-decker** ① n. Bus/Straßenbahn mit nur einem deck; **be a** ~**-decker** ⟨Bus, Straßenbahn:⟩ nur ein Deck haben; ② adj. ~**-decker bus/tram** Bus/Straßenbahn mit nur einem Deck; ~ **[European] market** n. [europäischer] Binnenmarkt; ~**-'handed** adv. allein; ~**-lens 'reflex camera** n. (Photog.) einäugige Spiegelreflexkamera; ~**-minded** adj. zielstrebig; ~**-mindedly** /sɪŋgl'maɪndɪdlɪ/ adv. zielstrebig

'singles bar n. Singlekneipe, *die*

single: ~**-sex** adj. ~ **school** reine Mädchen-/Jungenschule; ~**-storey** adj. eingeschossig

singlet /'sɪŋglɪt/ n. (Brit.) (vest) Unterhemd, *das;* (Sport) Trikot, *das*

singly /'sɪŋglɪ/ adv. einzeln

singular /'sɪŋgjʊlə(r)/ ① adj. (a) (Ling.) singularisch; Singular-; ~ **noun** Substantiv im Singular
(b) (extraordinary) einmalig
② n. (Ling.) Einzahl, *die;* Singular, *der*

'singularly adv. (extraordinarily) außerordentlich

sinister /'sɪnɪstə(r)/ adj. finster; (of evil omen) Unheil verkündend

sink /sɪŋk/ ① n. Spülbecken, *das*
② v.i., sank /sæŋk/ or sunk /sʌŋk,/ sunk sinken
③ v.t., sank or sunk, sunk (a) versenken ⟨*Schiff*⟩
(b) niederbringen ⟨*Schacht*⟩
■ **sink 'in** v.i. (fig.) jmdm. ins Bewusstsein dringen; ⟨*Warnung, Lektion:*⟩ verstanden werden

'sink unit n. Spüle, *die*

'sinner n. Sünder, *der/*Sünderin, *die*

sinus /'saɪnəs/ n. Nebenhöhle, *die*

sinusitis /saɪnə'saɪtɪs/ n. Nebenhöhlenentzündung, *die*

sip /sɪp/ ① v.t., **-pp-**: ~ [up] schlürfen
② v.i., **-pp-**: ~ at/from sth. an etw. (*Dat.*) nippen
③ n. Schlückchen, *das*

siphon /'saɪfn/ ① n. Siphon, *der*
② v.t. [durch einen Saugheber] laufen lassen

sir /sɜː(r)/ n. (a) (formal address) der Herr; (to teacher) Herr Meier/Schmidt *usw.*
(b) (in letter) **Dear Sir** Sehr geehrter Herr; **Dear Sirs** Sehr geehrte [Damen und] Herren; **Dear Sir or Madam** Sehr geehrte Dame/Sehr geehrter Herr
(c) **Sir** /sə(r)/ (title of knight etc.) Sir

siren /'saɪrən/ n. Sirene, *die*

sirloin /'sɜːlɔɪn/ n. (a) (Brit.) Roastbeef, *das;* ~ **steak** Rumpsteak, *das*
(b) (Amer.) Rumpsteak, *das*

sissy /'sɪsɪ/ ① n. Waschlappen, *der*
② adj. feige

sister /'sɪstə(r)/ n. (a) Schwester, *die*
(b) (Brit.: nurse) Oberschwester, *die*

'sister-in-law n., pl. **sisters-in-law** Schwägerin, *die*

sisterly /'sɪstəlɪ/ adj. schwesterlich

sit /sɪt/ ① v.i., **-tt-**, sat /sæt/ (a) (become seated) sich setzen; ~ on or in a chair/in an armchair sich auf einen Stuhl/in einen Sessel setzen
(b) (be seated) sitzen
② v.t., **-tt-**, sat (a) setzen
(b) (Brit.) machen ⟨*Prüfung*⟩
■ **sit 'back** v.i. sich zurücklehnen; (fig.) sich im Sessel zurücklehnen
■ **sit 'down** v.i. (a) (become seated) sich setzen (**on/in** auf/in + *Akk.*)
(b) (be seated) sitzen

■ **sit 'up** ① v.i. (a) (rise) sich aufsetzen
(b) (be sitting erect) [aufrecht] sitzen
(c) (stay up) aufbleiben
② v.t. aufsetzen

sitcom /'sɪtkɒm/ (coll.) ▶ SITUATION COMEDY

site /saɪt/ ① n. (a) (land) Grundstück, *das*
(b) (location) Sitz, *der;* (of new factory etc.) Standort, *der*
② v.t. stationieren ⟨*Raketen*⟩; ~ **a factory in London** London als Standort einer Fabrik wählen; **be** ~**d** gelegen sein

siting /'saɪtɪŋ/ n. Standortwahl, *die* (**of** für); (position) Lage, *die*

sitter /'sɪtə(r)/ ▶ BABYSITTER

'sitting n. Sitzung, *die;* **the first** ~ [for lunch] der erste Schub [zum Mittagessen]

sitting: ~ **'duck** n. (fig.) leichtes Ziel; ~ **room** n. Wohnzimmer, *das;* ~ **'target** ▶ ~ DUCK

situate /'sɪtjʊeɪt/ v.t. legen

'situated adj. gelegen; **be** ~: liegen

situation /sɪtjʊ'eɪʃn/ n. (a) (location) Lage, *die*
(b) (circumstances) Situation, *die*
(c) (job) Stelle, *die*

situation 'comedy n. Situationskomödie, *die*

six /sɪks/ ① adj. sechs
② n. Sechs, *die.* See also EIGHT

six: ~**-'footer** n. (person) Zweimetermann, *der/*-frau, *die;* ~**-pack** n. Sechserpack, *der*

sixteen /sɪks'tiːn/ ① adj. sechzehn
② n. Sechzehn, *die.* See also EIGHT

sixteenth /sɪks'tiːnθ/ ① adj. sechzehnt...
② n. (fraction) Sechzehntel, *das.* See also EIGHTH

sixth /sɪksθ/ ① adj. sechst...
② n. (in sequence, rank) Sechste, *der/die/das;* (fraction) Sechstel, *das.* See also EIGHTH

sixth: ~ **form** n. (Brit. Sch.) ≈ zwölfte/ dreizehnte Klasse; ~**-form college** n. (Brit. Sch.) ≈ Oberstufenzentrum, *das; College, das nur Schüler der zwölften/ dreizehnten Klasse aufnimmt;* ~**-former** n. (Brit. Sch.) Schüler/Schülerin der zwölften/ dreizehnten Klasse; ~ **'sense** n. sechster Sinn

sixtieth /'sɪkstɪɪθ/ adj. sechzigst...

sixty /'sɪkstɪ/ ① adj. sechzig
② n. Sechzig, *die.* See also EIGHT; EIGHTY 2

size /saɪz/ n. Größe, *die;* (of paper) Format, *das;* **be twice the** ~ **of sth.** zweimal so groß wie etw. sein; **a** ~ **8 dress** ein Kleid [in] Größe 8; **be** ~ **8** ⟨*Person:*⟩ Größe 8 haben
■ **size 'up** v.t. taxieren ⟨*Lage*⟩

sizeable /'saɪzəbl/ adj. ziemlich groß; beträchtlich ⟨*Summe, Einfluss*⟩

sizzle /'sɪzl/ v.i. zischen

skate ① n. (ice ~) Schlittschuh, *der;* (roller ~) Rollschuh, *der*
② v.i. (ice-~) Schlittschuh laufen; (roller-~) Rollschuh laufen

841

skateboard ···> skyline ····

'skateboard [1] *n.* Skateboard, *das;* Rollerbrett, *das*
[2] *v.i.* Skateboard fahren
'skateboarder *n.* Skateboardfahrer, *der*/-fahrerin, *die*
'skateboarding *n.* Skateboardfahren, *das*
'skater *n.* (ice ~) Eisläufer, *der*/-läuferin, *die;* (roller ~) Rollschuhläufer, *der*/-läuferin, *die*
skating /'skeItIŋ/ *n.* (ice ~) Schlittschuhlaufen, *das;* (roller ~) Rollschuhlaufen, *das*
'skating rink *n.* (ice) Eisbahn, *die;* (for roller skating) Rollschuhbahn, *die*
skeleton /'skelItn/ *n.* Skelett, *das*
skeleton: ~ **'key** *n.* Dietrich, *der;* ~ **'staff** *n.* Minimalbesetzung, *die*
skeptic *etc.* (Amer.) ▶ SCEPTIC *etc.*
sketch /sketʃ/ [1] *n.* (a) (drawing) Skizze, *die*
(b) (play) Sketch, *der*
[2] *v.t.* skizzieren
sketch: ~**book** *n.* Skizzenbuch, *das;* ~ **map** *n.* Faustskizze, *die*
'sketchy *adj.* skizzenhaft; lückenhaft ⟨*Informationen, Bericht*⟩
skew /skju:/ [1] *adj.* schräg
[2] *n.* on the ~: schief
skewer /'skju:ə(r)/ [1] *n.* Bratspieß, *der*
[2] *v.t.* aufspießen
ski /ski:/ [1] *n.* (a) Ski, *der*
(b) (on vehicle) Kufe, *die*
[2] *v.i.* Ski laufen *od.* fahren
'ski boot *n.* Skistiefel, *der*
skid /skId/ [1] *v.i.*, **-dd-** schlittern; (from one side to the other; spinning round) schleudern
[2] *n.* Schlittern/Schleudern, *das*
'skid marks *n. pl.* Schleuderspur, *die*
skier /'ski:ə(r)/ *n.* Skiläufer, *der*/-läuferin, *die*
skiing /'ski:ŋ/ *n.* Skilaufen, *das;* (Sport) Skisport, *der*
'ski jumping *n.* Skispringen, *das*
skilful /'skIlfl/ *adj.* geschickt; gewandt ⟨*Redner*⟩; gut ⟨*Beobachter, Lehrer*⟩
'ski lift *n.* Skilift, *der*
skill /skIl/ *n.* (a) (expertness) Geschick, *das;* (of artist) Können, *das*
(b) (technique) Fertigkeit, *die;* (of weaving, bricklaying) Technik, *die*
skilled /'skIld/ *adj.* (a) ▶ SKILFUL
(b) qualifiziert ⟨*Arbeit, Tätigkeit*⟩; ~ **trade** Ausbildungsberuf, *der*
(c) (trained) ausgebildet
'skillful (Amer.) ▶ SKILFUL
skim /skIm/ *v.t.*, **-mm-:** (a) (remove) abschöpfen
(b) abrahmen ⟨*Milch*⟩
(c) ▶ ~ THROUGH
■ **skim 'off** *v.t.* abschöpfen
■ **'skim through** *v.t.* überfliegen ⟨*Buch, Zeitung*⟩

skimmed 'milk *n.* entrahmte Milch
skimp /skImp/ [1] *v.t.* sparen an (+ *Dat.*)
[2] *v.i.* sparen (**with, on** an + *Dat.*)
'skimpy *adj.* winzig ⟨*Badeanzug*⟩; spärlich ⟨*Wissen*⟩
skin /skIn/ [1] *n.* (a) Haut, *die*
(b) (fur) Fell, *das*
(c) (peel) Schale, *die*
[2] *v.t.*, **-nn-** häuten; schälen ⟨*Frucht*⟩
skin: ~ **cancer** *n.* Hautkrebs, *der;* ~ **colour** *n.* Hautfarbe, *die;* ~ **cream** *n.* Hautcreme, *die;* ~-'**deep** *adj.* (fig.) oberflächlich; ~ **disease** *n.* Hautkrankheit, *die;* ~ **diver** *n.* Taucher, *der*/Taucherin, *die;* ~ **diving** *n.* Tauchen, *das;* ~**flint** *n.* Geizhals, *der;* ~ **graft** *n.* Hauttransplantation, *die;* ~**head** *n.* Skinhead, *der*
skinny /'skInI/ *adj.* mager
skint /skInt/ *adj.* (Brit. coll.) **be** ~: blank *od.* pleite sein (ugs.)
'skin-tight *adj.* hauteng
skip¹ /skIp/ [1] *v.i.*, **-pp-:** (a) hüpfen
(b) (with skipping rope) seilspringen
[2] *v.t.*, **-pp-** (omit) überspringen; ~ **breakfast/lunch** das Frühstück/ Mittagessen auslassen
[3] *n.* Hüpfer, *der*
skip² *n.* (Building) Container, *der*
ski: ~ **pass** *n.* Skipass, *der;* ~ **pole** *n.* Skistock, *der*
skipper /'skIpə(r)/ *n.* Kapitän, *der*
'skipping rope (Brit.), **'skip rope** (Amer.) *ns.* Sprungseil, *das*
'ski resort *n.* Skiurlaubsort, *der*
skirmish /'skɜ:mIʃ/ *n.* (Mil.) Gefecht, *das*
skirt /skɜ:t/ [1] *n.* Rock, *der*
[2] *v.t.* herumgehen um
■ **skirt 'round** *v.t.* herumgehen um; (fig.) umgehen
'skirting *n.* ~ [**board**] (Brit.) Fußleiste, *die*
ski: ~ **run** *n.* Skihang, *der;* (prepared) [Ski]piste, *die;* ~**stick** *n.* Skistock, *der*
skittle /'skItl/ *n.* (a) Kegel, *der*
(b) ~**s** *sing.* (game) Kegeln, *das*
skive /skaIv/ *v.i.* (Brit. coll.) sich drücken (ugs.)
■ **skive 'off** (Brit. coll.) [1] *v.i.* sich verdrücken (ugs.)
[2] *v.t.* schwänzen (ugs.)
skulk /skʌlk/ *v.i.* lauern
skull /skʌl/ *n.* Schädel, *der*
skunk /skʌŋk/ *n.* Stinktier, *das*
sky /skaI/ *n.* Himmel, *der;* **in the** ~: am Himmel
sky: ~**diving** *n.* Fallschirmspringen, *das* (als Sport); Fallschirmsport, *der;* ~**high** [1] *adj.* himmelhoch; astronomisch (ugs.) ⟨*Preise usw.*⟩; [2] *adv.* **go** ~**-high** ⟨*Preise usw.*⟩ in astronomische Höhen klettern (ugs.); ~**light** *n.* Dachfenster, *das;* ~**line** *n.* Silhouette, *die;* (characteristic of ···>

certain town) Skyline, *die;* ~ **marshal**
n. Skymarshal, *der;* ~**scraper** *n.*
Wolkenkratzer, *der*

slab /slæb/ *n.* **(a)** (flat stone etc.) Platte, *die*
(b) (thick slice) [dicke] Scheibe; (of cake)
[dickes] Stück; (of chocolate, toffee) Tafel, *die*

slack /slæk/ ① *adj.* **(a)** (lax) nachlässig;
schlampig (ugs.)
(b) (loose) schlaff; locker ‹*Verband*›
② *n.* take in *or* up the ~: das Seil/die
Schnur *usw.* straffen
③ *v.i.* (coll.) bummeln (ugs.)

slacken /'slækn/ ① *v.i.* **(a)** (loosen) sich
lockern
(b) (diminish) nachlassen; ‹*Geschwindigkeit:*›
sich verringern
② *v.t.* **(a)** (loosen) lockern
(b) (diminish) verringern

slacker /'slækə(r)/ *n.* (derog.) Faulenzer,
*der/*Faulenzerin, *die*

slacks /slæks/ *n. pl.* **[pair of]** ~: lange
Hose; Slacks *Pl.*

slag /slæg/ *n.* Schlacke, *die*

slain ▸ SLAY

slake /sleɪk/ *v.t.* löschen, stillen ‹*Durst*›

slam /slæm/ ① *v.t.*, **-mm-: (a)** (shut)
zuschlagen
(b) (put violently) knallen (ugs.)
② *v.i.*, **-mm-** zuschlagen

slander /'slɑːndə(r)/ ① *n.* Verleumdung,
die (on *Gen.*)
② *v.t.* verleumden

slanderous /'slɑːndərəs/ *adj.*
verleumderisch

slang /slæŋ/ *n.* Slang, *der;* ‹*Theater-,
Soldaten-, Juristen*›jargon, *der; attrib.*
Slang‹*wort, -ausdruck*›

'**slanging match** *n.* gegenseitige
[lautstarke] Beschimpfung

slangy /'slæŋɪ/ *adj.* Slang‹*ausdruck,
-wort*›; salopp ‹*Wortwahl, Redeweise*›

slant /slɑːnt/ ① *v.i.* ‹*Fläche:*› sich neigen;
‹*Linie:*› schräg verlaufen
② *v.t.* **(a)** abschrägen
(b) (fig.: bias) [so] hinbiegen (ugs.) ‹*Meldung,
Bemerkung*›
③ *n.* Schräge, *die;* on the *or* a ~: schräg

slanting /'slɑːntɪŋ/ *adj.* schräg

slap /slæp/ ① *v.t.*, **-pp-: (a)** schlagen
(b) (put) knallen (ugs.)
② *v.i.*, **-pp-** schlagen; klatschen
③ *n.* Schlag, *der*
④ *adv.* voll; ~ **in the middle** genau in der
Mitte

'**slapdash** *adj.* schludrig (ugs.)

'**slap-up** *attrib. adj.* (coll.) ‹*Essen*› mit allen
Schikanen (ugs.)

slash /slæʃ/ ① *v.t.* **(a)** aufschlitzen
(b) (fig.) [drastisch] reduzieren; [drastisch]
kürzen ‹*Gehalt, Umfang*›
② *n.* **(a)** (slit) Schlitz, *die*
(b) (~ing stroke) Hieb, *der*

slat /slæt/ *n.* Latte, *die*

slate /sleɪt/ ① *n.* **(a)** (Geol.) Schiefer, *der*
(b) (Building) Schieferplatte, *die*
② *v.t.* (Brit. coll.: criticize) in der Luft zerreißen
(ugs.)

slaughter /'slɔːtə(r)/ ① *n.* Schlachten,
das; (massacre) Gemetzel, *das*
② *v.t.* schlachten; (massacre) abschlachten

slave /sleɪv/ ① *n.* Sklave, *der/*Sklavin, *die*
② *v.i.* ~ **[away]** schuften (ugs.); sich
abplagen (at mit)

'**slave driver** *n.* (fig.) Sklaventreiber, *der/*
-treiberin, *die*

slavery /'sleɪvərɪ/ *n.* Sklaverei, *die*

slavish /'sleɪvɪʃ/ *adj.* sklavisch

slay /sleɪ/ *v.t.*, slew /sluː/, slain /sleɪn/
(literary) ermorden

sleaze /sliːz/ *n.* (derog.) Korruption, *die*

'**sleazebag,** '**sleazeball** *ns.* (sl. derog.)
Drecksack, *der* (derb abwertend)

sleazy /'sliːzɪ/ *adj.* schäbig; (disreputable)
anrüchig

sled /sled/, **sledge** /sledʒ/ *ns.* Schlitten, *der*

'**sledgehammer** *n.* Vorschlaghammer,
der

sleek /sliːk/ *adj.* (glossy) seidig

sleep /sliːp/ ① *n.* Schlaf, *der;* **get/go to** ~:
einschlafen; **put to** ~: einschläfern ‹*Tier*›
② *v.i.,* slept /slept/ schlafen
③ *v.t.* slept: the hotel ~s 80 das Hotel hat
80 Betten
■ **sleep a'round** *v.i.* (coll.) herumschlafen
(ugs.)
■ **sleep 'in** *v.i.* im Bett bleiben
■ **sleep 'off** *v.t.* ausschlafen; ~ it off
seinen Rausch ausschlafen
■ **sleep 'over** *v.i.* [auswärts]
übernachten; our cousin was ~ing over
unser Cousin übernachtete bei uns
■ **sleep together** *v.i.* (also coll. euphem.)
miteinander schlafen
■ **sleep with** *v.t.* ~ with sb. (coll. euphem.)
mit jmdm. schlafen

'**sleeper** *n.* **(a)** be a heavy/light ~: einen
tiefen/leichten Schlaf haben
(b) (Brit. Railw.: support) Schwelle, *die*
(c) (Railw.) (coach) Schlafwagen, *der;* (train)
[night] ~: Nachtzug mit Schlafwagen

sleeping: ~ **accommodation** *n.*
Übernachtungsmöglichkeit, *die;* ~ **bag** *n.*
Schlafsack, *der;* ~ **car** *n.* Schlafwagen, *der;*
~ '**partner** *n.* (Commerc.) stiller Teilhaber;
~ **pill,** ~ **tablet** *ns.* Schlaftablette, *die*

sleep: ~**less** *adj.* schlaflos

'**sleepover** *n.* Übernachtung außer Haus
od. bei anderen Leuten

sleep: ~**walk** *v.i.* schlafwandeln;
~**walker** *n.* Schlafwandler, *der/*
-wandlerin, *die*

'**sleepy** *adj.* schläfrig

sleet /sliːt/ ① *n.* Schneeregen, *der*
② *v.i. impers.* it is ~ing es gibt Schneeregen

sleeve /sliːv/ *n.* **(a)** Ärmel, *der;* (fig.) **have
sth. up one's** ~: etw. in petto haben (ugs.);

roll up one's ∼s die Ärmel hochkrempeln (ugs.)
(b) (for record) Hülle, *die*
'sleeveless *adj.* ärmellos
sleigh /sleɪ/ *n.* Schlitten, *der*
sleight of 'hand /slaɪt/ *n.* Fingerfertigkeit, *die*
slender /'slendə(r)/ *adj.* **(a)** (slim) schlank; schmal ⟨*Buch, Band*⟩
(b) gering ⟨*Chance, Mittel, Hoffnung*⟩
slept ▸ SLEEP 2, 3
sleuth /sluːθ/ *n.* Detektiv, *der*
slew¹ /sluː/ *v.i. & t.* schwenken
slew² ▸ SLAY
slice /slaɪs/ ☐1 *n.* Scheibe, *die;* (of apple, melon, peach, cake, pie) Stück, *das;* **a** ∼ **of cake** ein Stück Kuchen
☐2 *v.t.* in Scheiben schneiden; in Stücke schneiden ⟨*Bohnen, Apfel, Kuchen usw.*⟩; ∼d **bread** Schnittbrot, *das*
slick /slɪk/ ☐1 *adj.* **(a)** (dexterous) professionell
(b) (pretentiously dexterous) clever (ugs.)
☐2 *n.* **[oil]** ∼: Ölteppich, *der*
slid ▸ SLIDE 1, 2
slide /slaɪd/ ☐1 *v.i.,* **slid** /slɪd/ rutschen; ⟨*Kolben, Schublade, Feder:*⟩ gleiten
☐2 *v.t.,* **slid** schieben
☐3 *n.* **(a)** (children's ∼) Rutschbahn, *die*
(b) (Photog.) Dia[positiv], *das*
slide: ∼ **film** *n.* Diafilm, *der;*
∼ **projector** *n.* Diaprojektor, *der;*
∼ **show** *n.* Diashow, *die*
sliding door /'slaɪdɪŋ/ *n.* Schiebetür, *die*
slight /slaɪt/ ☐1 *adj.* leicht; schwach ⟨*Hoffnung, Aussichten, Wirkung*⟩; **not in the** ∼**est** nicht im Geringsten
☐2 *n.* Verunglimpfung, *die* (on *Gen.*); (lack of courtesy) Affront, *der* (on gegen)
'slightly *adv.* ein bisschen; leicht ⟨*verletzen, riechen nach, gewürzt sein, ansteigen*⟩; flüchtig ⟨*jmdn. kennen*⟩; oberflächlich ⟨*etw. kennen*⟩
slim /slɪm/ ☐1 *adj.* schlank; schmal ⟨*Band, Buch*⟩; schwach ⟨*Aussicht, Hoffnung*⟩; gering ⟨*Gewinn, Chancen*⟩
☐2 *v.i.,* **-mm-** abnehmen
slime /slaɪm/ *n.* Schleim, *der*
slimmer /'slɪmə(r)/ *n.* (Brit.) *jmd., der etwas für die schlanke Linie tut;* **advice/a diet for** ∼**s** Ratschläge *Pl.*/eine Diät zum Abnehmen
slimming /'slɪmɪŋ/ ☐1 *n.* Abnehmen, *das; attrib.* Schlankheits-
☐2 *adj.* schlank machend
slimy /'slaɪmɪ/ *adj.* schleimig
sling /slɪŋ/ ☐1 *n.* (Med.) Schlinge, *die*
☐2 *v.t.,* **slung** /slʌŋ/ (coll.: throw) schmeißen (ugs.)
■ **sling 'out** *v.t.* (coll.) wegschmeißen (ugs.); ∼ **sb. out** jmdn. rausschmeißen (ugs.)
slink /slɪŋk/ *v.i.,* **slunk** /slʌŋk/ schleichen
■ **slink a'way, slink 'off** *v.i.*

davonschleichen
slip /slɪp/ ☐1 *v.i.,* **-pp-: (a)** (slide) rutschen; ⟨*Messer:*⟩ abrutschen; (and fall) ausrutschen
(b) (escape) schlüpfen
(c) (go) ∼ **to the butcher's** *etc.* [rasch] zum Fleischer *usw.* rüberspringen (ugs.)
☐2 *v.t.,* **-pp-: (a)** stecken; ∼ **the dress over one's head** das Kleid über den Kopf streifen
(b) ∼ **sb.'s mind** *or* **memory** jmdm. entfallen
☐3 *n.* **(a)** (fall) **after his** ∼: nachdem er ausgerutscht [und gestürzt] war
(b) (mistake) Versehen, *das;* ∼ **of the tongue** Versprecher, *der*
(c) (underwear) Unterrock, *der*
(d) (piece of paper) Zettel, *der*
(e) give sb. the ∼: jmdm. entwischen (ugs.)
■ **slip a'way** *v.i.* **(a)** ⟨*Person:*⟩ sich fortschleichen
(b) ⟨*Zeit:*⟩ verfliegen
■ **slip 'down** *v.i.* runterrutschen (ugs.)
■ **slip 'in** *v.i.* ⟨*Person:*⟩ sich hineinschleichen
■ **'slip into** *v.t.* schlüpfen in (+ *Akk.*) ⟨*Kleidungsstück*⟩
■ **slip 'off** ☐1 *v.i.* **(a)** runterrutschen (ugs.)
(b) ▸ SLIP AWAY A.
☐2 *v.t.* abstreifen ⟨*Schmuck, Handschuh*⟩; schlüpfen aus ⟨*Kleid, Schuh*⟩
■ **slip 'on** *v.t.* überstreifen ⟨*Handschuh, Ring*⟩; schlüpfen in (+ *Akk.*) ⟨*Kleid, Schuh*⟩
■ **slip 'out** *v.i.* ⟨*Person:*⟩ sich hinausschleichen
■ **slip 'over** *v.i.* (fall) ausrutschen
■ **slip 'up** *v.i.* (coll.) einen Schnitzer machen (ugs.)
slipped 'disc /slɪpt/ *n.* Bandscheibenvorfall, *der*
'slipper *n.* Hausschuh, *der*
slippery /'slɪpərɪ/ *adj.* schlüpfrig
slippy /'slɪpɪ/ (coll.) ▸ SLIPPERY
slip: ∼ **road** *n.* (Brit.) (to motorway) Auffahrt, *die;* (from motorway) Ausfahrt, *die;* ∼**shod** *adj.* schludrig (ugs.); ∼**-up** *n.* (coll.) Schnitzer, *der*
slit /slɪt/ ☐1 *n.* Schlitz, *der*
☐2 *v.t.,* **-tt-,** **slit** aufschlitzen; ∼ **sb.'s throat** jmdm. die Kehle durchschneiden
slither /'slɪðə(r)/ *v.i.* rutschen
sliver /'slɪvə(r)/ *n.* Splitter, *der*
slob /slɒb/ *n.* (coll.) Schwein, *das* (derb)
slobber /'slɒbə(r)/ *v.i.* sabbern (ugs.)
slog /slɒɡ/ ☐1 *v.t.,* **-gg-** (in boxing, fight) voll treffen
☐2 *v.i.,* **-gg-** (work) schuften (ugs.)
☐3 *n.* **(a)** (hit) wuchtiger Schlag
(b) (work) Plackerei, *die* (ugs.)
slogan /'sləʊɡən/ *n.* Slogan, *der;* (advertising ∼) Werbeslogan, *der*
slop /slɒp/ ☐1 *v.i.* schwappen (out of, from aus)
☐2 *v.t.* schwappen; (intentionally) kippen
■ **slop 'over** *v.i.* überschwappen
slope /sləʊp/ ☐1 *n.* **(a)** (slant) Neigung, *die*
(b) (slanting ground) Hang, *der* ┈┈╍┊

2 *v.i.* (slant) sich neigen; ⟨*Boden, Garten:*⟩
abschüssig sein; ~ **downwards/upwards**
⟨*Straße:*⟩ abfallen/ansteigen
■ **slope a'way** *v.i.* abfallen
■ **slope 'off** *v.i.* (coll.) sich verdrücken
(ugs.)
sloppy /'slɒpɪ/ *adj.* schludrig (ugs.)
slosh /slɒʃ/ **1** *v.i.* platschen (ugs.);
⟨*Flüssigkeit:*⟩ schwappen
2 *v.t.* (coll.: pour clumsily) schwappen
sloshed /slɒʃt/ *adj.* (Brit. coll.) blau (ugs.)
slot /slɒt/ **1** *n.* **(a)** (hole) Schlitz, *der*
(b) (groove) Nut, *die*
2 *v.t.*, **-tt-:** ~ **sth. into place/sth.** etw.
einfügen/in etw. (*Akk.*) einfügen
■ **slot 'in 1** *v.t.* einfügen
2 *v.i.* sich einfügen
■ **slot to'gether 1** *v.t.* zusammenfügen
2 *v.i.* (lit. or fig.) sich zusammenfügen
sloth /sləʊθ/ *n.* **(a)** (lethargy) Trägheit, *die*
(b) (Zool.) Faultier, *das*
'slot machine *n.* Automat, *der;* (for
gambling) Spielautomat, *der*
slouch /slaʊtʃ/ *v.i.* sich schlecht halten
Slovak /'sləʊvæk/ **1** *adj.* slowakisch; **sb.**
is ~: jmd. ist Slowake/Slowakin
2 *n.* **(a)** (person) Slowake, *der*/Slowakin, *die*
(b) (language) Slowakisch, *das; see also*
ENGLISH 2A
Slovakia /slə'vɑːkɪə/ *pr. n.* Slowakei, *die*
Slovene /'sləʊviːn/ **1** *adj.* slowenisch; **sb.**
is ~: jmd. ist Slowene/Slowenin
2 *n.* **(a)** (person) Slowene, *der*/Slowenin, *die*
(b) (language) Slowenisch, *das*
Slovenia /slə'viːnɪə/ *pr. n.* Slowenien (*das*)
Slovenian /slə'viːnɪən/ ▶ SLOVENE
slovenly /'slʌvnlɪ/ *adj.* schlampig (ugs.)
slow /sləʊ/ **1** *adj.* langsam; langwierig
⟨*Arbeit*⟩; **be [ten minutes]** ~ ⟨*Uhr:*⟩ [zehn
Minuten] nachgehen
2 *adv.* langsam
3 *v.i.* langsamer werden; ~ **to a halt**
anhalten
■ **slow 'down, slow 'up** *v.i.* langsamer
werden
'slowcoach *n.* Trödler, *der*/Trödlerin,
die (ugs.)
'slowly *adv.* langsam
slow 'motion *n.* **in** ~: in Zeitlupe
slowness *n.* Langsamkeit, *die*
slow: ~ **'puncture** *n.* winziges Loch;
~ **train** *n.* Bummelzug, *der* (ugs.);
~**-witted** /sləʊ'wɪtɪd/ *adj.* [geistig]
schwerfällig
sludge /slʌdʒ/ *n.* Schlamm, *der*
slug /slʌg/ *n.* Nacktschnecke, *die*
sluggish /'slʌgɪʃ/ *adj.* träge; schleppend
⟨*Nachfrage*⟩
sluice /sluːs/ **1** *n.* Schütz, *das*
2 *v.t.* ~ **[down]** abspritzen
'sluice gate *n.* Schütz, *das*
slum /slʌm/ *n.* Slum, *der;* (single house or

apartment) Elendsquartier, *das*
slumber /'slʌmbə(r)/ (poet./rhet.) **1** *n.* ~**[s]**
Schlummer, *der* (geh.)
2 *v.i.* schlummern (geh.)
slump /slʌmp/ **1** *n.* Sturz, *der* (fig.);
(in demand, investment, sales) starker
Rückgang (in *Gen.*); (economic depression)
Depression, *die*
2 *v.i.* **(a)** (Commerc.) stark zurückgehen;
⟨*Preise, Kurse:*⟩ stürzen
(b) (collapse) ⟨*Person:*⟩ fallen; ~**ed in a chair**
in einem Sessel zusammengesunken
slung ▶ SLING 2
slunk ▶ SLINK
slur /slɜː(r)/ **1** *v.t.*, **-rr-:** ~ **one's words/**
speech undeutlich sprechen
2 *n.* Beleidigung, *die* (on für)
slurp /slɜːp/ (coll.) **1** *v.t.* ~ **[up]** schlürfen
2 *n.* Schlürfen, *das*
slush /slʌʃ/ *n.* Schneematsch, *der*
'slush fund *n.* Fonds, *der* für
Bestechungsgelder
'slushy *adj.* **(a)** matschig
(b) (sloppy) sentimental
slut /slʌt/ *n.* Schlampe, *die* (ugs.)
sly /slaɪ/ **1** *adj.* schlau; gerissen (ugs.)
⟨*Geschäftsmann, Trick*⟩; verschlagen ⟨*Blick*⟩
2 *n.* **on the** ~: heimlich
smack[1] /smæk/ **1** *n.* **(a)** (sound) Klatsch,
der
(b) (blow) Schlag, *der;* (on child's bottom) Klaps,
der (ugs.)
2 *v.t.* **(a)** [mit der flachen Hand] schlagen
(b) ~ **one's lips** [mit den Lippen] schmatzen
3 *adv.* (coll.) direkt
smack[2] *v.i.* ~ **of** schmecken nach; (fig.)
riechen nach (ugs.)
small /smɔːl/ **1** *adj.* klein; gering
⟨*Wirkung, Appetit, Fähigkeit*⟩; schmal
⟨*Taille*⟩; dünn ⟨*Stimme*⟩; **make sb. feel**
~: jmdn. beschämen
2 *n.* ~ **of the back** Kreuz, *das*
3 *adv.* klein
small: ~ **ad** *n.* (coll.) Kleinanzeige, *die;*
~ **'change** *n.* Kleingeld, *das;* ~**holding**
n. landwirtschaftlicher Kleinbetrieb;
~**-'minded** *adj.* kleinlich; ~**pox**
n. Pocken *Pl.;* ~ **'print** *n.* (lit. or fig.)
Kleingedruckte, *das*
smalls /smɔːlz/ *n. pl.* (Brit. coll.)
Unterwäsche, *die*
small: ~ **'screen** *n.* (Telev.) Bildschirm,
der; ~ **talk** *n.* leichte Unterhaltung; (at
parties) Smalltalk, *der;* **make** ~ **talk [with sb.]**
[mit jmdm.] Konversation machen
smarmy /'smɑːmɪ/ *adj.* (coll.) kriecherisch
smart /smɑːt/ **1** *adj.* **(a)** (clever) clever;
(ingenious) raffiniert
(b) (neat) schick; schön ⟨*Haus, Garten, Auto*⟩
(c) *attrib.* (fashionable) elegant; smart
2 *v.i.* schmerzen
smart: ~ **alec[k]** /smɑːt 'ælɪk/ *n.* (coll.)
Besserwisser, *der*/Besserwisserin, *die;*

~ **bomb** *n.* intelligente Bombe; ~ **card** *n.* Chipkarte, *die;* ~ **drug** *n.* Nootropikum, *das*

smarten /'smɑːtn/ *v.t.* herrichten; ~ oneself [up] auf sein Äußeres achten

'**smartly** *adv.* (a) (cleverly) clever (b) (neatly) schmuck ⟨[an]gestrichen⟩; smart, flott ⟨gekleidet, geschnitten⟩

'**smart money** *n.* the ~ is on … Experten setzen auf …

smash /smæʃ/ ① *v.t.* (a) zerschlagen (b) ~ sb. in the face/mouth jmdm. [hart] ins Gesicht/auf den Mund schlagen (c) (Tennis etc.) schmettern ② *v.i.* (a) zerbrechen (b) (crash) krachen (into gegen) ③ *n.* (a) (sound) Krachen, *das* (b) ▶ SMASH-UP (c) (Tennis) Schmetterball, *der* ▪ **smash 'in** *v.t.* zerschmettern; einschlagen ⟨Tür, Schädel⟩ ▪ **smash 'up** *v.t.* zertrümmern

smash-and-'grab [raid] *n.* (coll.) Schaufenstereinbruch, *der*

smashed /smæʃt/ *adj.* (sl.) (a) (drunk) get ~ on sth. von etw. besoffen werden (derb); be ~ out of one's head *or* mind *or* brains sturzbetrunken (ugs.) *od.* (derb) sturzbesoffen sein (b) (on drugs) stoned (Drogenjargon)

'**smashing** *adj.* (coll.) toll (ugs.)

'**smash-up** *n.* schwerer Zusammenstoß

smattering /'smætərɪŋ/ *n.* [have] a ~ of German *etc.* ein paar Brocken Deutsch *usw.* [können]

smear /smɪə(r)/ ① *v.t.* (a) (daub) beschmieren; (put on *or* over) schmieren (b) (smudge) verwischen (c) (fig.) in den Schmutz ziehen ② *n.* (a) (blotch) [Schmutz]fleck, *der* (b) (fig.) Beschmutzung, *die* (on *Gen.*)

smear: ~ campaign *n.* Schmutzkampagne, *die;* ~ **tactics** *n. pl.* schmutzige Mittel *Pl.;* ~ **test** *n.* (Med.) Abstrich, *der*

smell /smel/ ① *n.* (a) have a good/bad sense of ~: einen guten/schlechten Geruchssinn haben (b) (odour) Geruch, *der* (of nach); (pleasant also) Duft, *der* (of nach); a ~ of burning/gas ein Brand-/Gasgeruch (c) (stink) Gestank, *der* ② *v.t.*, smelt /smelt/ *or* smelled /smeld/ (a) (perceive) riechen (b) (inhale ~ of) riechen an (+ *Dat.*) ③ *v.i.*, smelt *or* smelled (a) (emit ~) riechen; (pleasantly also) duften (b) ~ of sth. (lit. or fig.) nach etw. riechen (c) (stink) riechen

'**smelly** *adj.* stinkend; be ~: stinken

smelt ▶ SMELL 2, 3

smile /smaɪl/ ① *n.* Lächeln, *das;* give sb. a ~: jmdn. anlächeln

② *v.i.* lächeln; ~ at sb./sth. jmdn. anlächeln/über etw. (*Akk.*) lächeln

smirk /smɜːk/ ① *v.t.* grinsen ② *n.* Grinsen, *das*

smith /smɪθ/ *n.* Schmied, *der*

smithereens /smɪðə'riːnz/ *n. pl.* blow/ smash sth. to ~: etw. in tausend Stücke sprengen/schlagen

smock /smɒk/ *n.* Kittel, *der*

smog /smɒg/ *n.* Smog, *der*

smoke /sməʊk/ ① *n.* Rauch, *der* ② *v.i. & t.* rauchen

smoked /sməʊkt/ *adj.* (Cookery) geräuchert

'**smoke detector** *n.* Rauchmelder, *der*

'**smoke-free** *adj.* rauchfrei

'**smokeless** *adj.* rauchlos; rauchfrei ⟨Zone⟩

smoker /'sməʊkə(r)/ *n.* (a) Raucher, *der/* Raucherin, *die;* ~'s cough Raucherhusten, *der* (b) (Railw.) Raucherabteil, *das*

'**smokescreen** *n.* [künstliche] Nebelwand; (fig.) Vernebelung *die* (for *Gen.*)

smoking /'sməʊkɪŋ/ *n.* (a) Rauchen, *das;* 'no ~' „Rauchen verboten" (b) (seating area) [do you want to sit in] ~ or non-~? möchten Sie für Raucher oder Nichtraucher?

'**smoking compartment** *n.* (Railw.) Raucherabteil, *das*

smoky /'sməʊkɪ/ *adj.* (emitting smoke) rauchend; (smoke-filled) verräuchert

smooth /smuːð/ ① *adj.* (a) (even) glatt; eben ⟨Straße, Weg⟩ (b) (mild) weich (c) (not jerky) geschmeidig ⟨Bewegung⟩; ruhig ⟨Fahrt, Flug⟩; weich ⟨Landung⟩ (d) (without problems) reibungslos ② *v.t.* glätten

smoothie /'smuːðɪ/ *n.* (coll. derog.) aalglatter Typ (ugs.)

'**smoothly** *adv.* (a) (evenly) glatt (b) (not jerkily) geschmeidig ⟨sich bewegen⟩; weich ⟨landen⟩; reibungslos ⟨funktionieren⟩

smother /'smʌðə(r)/ *v.t.* ersticken; (fig.) unterdrücken ⟨Gähnen⟩; ersticken ⟨Gelächter, Schreie⟩

smoulder /'sməʊldə(r)/ *v.i.* schwelen; she was ~ing with rage Zorn schwelte in ihr

smudge /smʌdʒ/ ① *v.t.* verwischen ② *v.i.* schmieren ③ *n.* Fleck, *der*

smug /smʌg/ *adj.* selbstgefällig

smuggle /'smʌgl/ *v.t.* schmuggeln ▪ **smuggle 'in** *v.t.* einschmuggeln; hinein-/ hereinschmuggeln ⟨Person⟩ ▪ **smuggle 'out** *v.t.* hinaus-/ herausschmuggeln

smuggler /'smʌglə(r)/ *n.* Schmuggler, *der*/Schmugglerin, *die*

smuggling /'smʌglɪŋ/ *n.* Schmuggel, *der*

smutty /'smʌtɪ/ *adj.* (lewd) schmutzig

snack /snæk/ *n.* Imbiss, *der*

'snackbar *n.* Schnellimbiss, *der*

snag /snæg/ *n.* (problem) Haken, *der;* what's the ~? wo klemmt es? (ugs.)

snail /sneɪl/ *n.* Schnecke, *die;* at [a] ~'s pace im Schneckentempo (ugs.)

'snail mail *n.* (coll. joc.) Schneckenpost, *die*

snake /sneɪk/ *n.* Schlange, *die*

snap /snæp/ ① *v.t.,* **-pp-: (a)** (break) zerbrechen; ~ **sth. in two** *or* **in half** etw. in zwei Stücke brechen
(b) ~ **one's fingers** mit den Fingern schnalzen
(c) ~ **sth. home** *or* **into place** etw. einschnappen lassen; ~ **shut** zuschnappen lassen ‹Portemonnaie, Schloss›; zuklappen ‹Buch, Etui›; ~ **sth. open** etw. aufschnappen lassen
(d) (take photograph of) knipsen
(e) (say sharply) fauchen; (speak crisply or curtly) bellen
② *v.i.,* **-pp-: (a)** (break) brechen
(b) (fig.: give way under strain) ausrasten (ugs.); **my patience has finally ~ped** nun ist mir der Geduldsfaden aber gerissen
③ *n.* (Photog.) Schnappschuss, *der*
■ **'snap at** *v.t.* (speak sharply to) anfauchen (ugs.)
■ **snap 'off** *v.t. & i.* abbrechen
■ **snap 'up** *v.t.* (fig. coll.) [sich (*Dat.*)] schnappen (ugs.)

'snapshot *n.* Schnappschuss, *der*

snare /sneə(r)/ ① *n.* Schlinge, *die*
② *v.t.* [in einer Schlinge] fangen

snarl¹ /snɑːl/ ① *v.i.* knurren
② *n.* Knurren, *das*

snarl² *n.* (tangle) Knoten, *der*
■ **snarl 'up** *v.t.* (bring to a halt) zum Erliegen bringen; **get ~ed up in the traffic** im Verkehr stecken bleiben

'snarl-up *n.* Stau, *der*

snatch /snætʃ/ ① *v.t.* **(a)** (grab) schnappen; ~ **sth. from sb.** jmdm. etw. wegreißen; ~ **some sleep** ein bisschen schlafen
(b) (steal) klauen (ugs.)
② *v.i.* einfach zugreifen
③ *n.* ~**es of talk/conversation** Gesprächsfetzen *Pl.*

snazzy /'snæzɪ/ *adj.* (coll.) [super]schick (ugs.)

sneak /sniːk/ ① *v.t.* schmuggeln; ~ **a look at** schielen nach
② *v.i.* **(a)** schleichen
(b) (Brit. Sch. coll.: tell tales) petzen (Schülerspr.)
③ *n.* (Brit. Sch. coll.) Petze, *die* (Schülerspr.)
■ **sneak 'out** *v.i.* [sich] hinausschleichen

'sneaker (Amer.) Turnschuh, *der*

'sneaking *attrib. adj.* heimlich; leise ‹Verdacht›

'sneak thief *n.* Einschleichdieb, *der*

'sneaky *adj.* **(a)** (underhand) hinterhältig
(b) have a ~ feeling that ...: so ein leises Gefühl haben, dass ...

sneer /snɪə(r)/ *v.i.* höhnisch lächeln/grinsen

■ **'sneer at** *v.t.* höhnisch anlächeln/angrinsen; (scorn) verhöhnen

sneeze /sniːz/ ① *v.i.* niesen
② *n.* Niesen, *das*

snicker /'snɪkə(r)/ ▸ SNIGGER

snide /snaɪd/ *adj.* abfällig

sniff /snɪf/ ① *n.* Schnuppern, *das;* (with running nose, while crying) Schniefen, *das*
② *v.i.* schniefen; (to detect a smell) schnuppern
③ *v.t.* riechen *od.* schnuppern an (+ *Dat.*); ~ **glue/cocaine** Klebstoff schnüffeln/Kokain sniffen (Drogenjargon)
■ **'sniff at** *v.t.* **(a)** ▸ SNIFF 3
(b) (show contempt for) die Nase rümpfen über

sniffer dog /'snɪfə dɒg/ *n.* Spürhund, *der*

snigger /'snɪgə(r)/ ① *v.i.* [boshaft] kichern
② *n.* [boshaftes] Kichern

snip /snɪp/ ① *v.t.,* **-pp-** schnippeln (ugs.), schneiden ‹Loch›; schnippeln (ugs.) *od.* schneiden an (+ *Dat.*) ‹Tuch, Haaren, Hecke›; (cut off) abschnippeln (ugs.); abschneiden
② *n.* (cut) Schnitt, *der;* Schnipser, *der* (ugs.)

snipe /snaɪp/ *v.i.* ~ **at** aus dem Hinterhalt beschießen

'sniper *n.* Heckenschütze, *der*

snippet /'snɪpɪt/ *n.* (of information in newspaper) Notiz, *die;* (of conversation) Gesprächsfetzen, *der;* **useful ~s of information** nützliche Hinweise

snivel /'snɪvl/ *v.i.,* (Brit.) **-ll-** schniefen

'snivelling (*Amer.:* **sniveling**) (fig.) *attrib. adj.* heulend

snob /snɒb/ *n.* Snob, *der*

snobbery /'snɒbərɪ/ *n.* Snobismus, *der*

snobbish /'snɒbɪʃ/ *adj.* snobistisch

snog /snɒg/ (Brit. coll.) ① *v.i.,* **-gg-** knutschen (ugs.)
② *n.* Knutschen, *das* (ugs.)

snooker /'snuːkə(r)/ *n.* Snooker, *das*

snoop /snuːp/ *v.i.* schnüffeln (ugs.)

snooty /'snuːtɪ/ *adj.* (coll.) hochnäsig (ugs.)

snooze /snuːz/ (coll.) ① *v.i.* dösen (ugs.)
② *n.* Nickerchen, *das* (fam.)

'snooze button *n.* Schlummertaste, *die*

snore /snɔː(r)/ ① *v.i.* schnarchen
② *n.* Schnarcher, *der* (ugs.); ~**s** Schnarchen, *das*

snorkel /'snɔːkl/ *n.* Schnorchel, *der*

snort /snɔːt/ *v.i.* schnauben (**with, in** vor + *Dat.*); (sl.: take) ~ **[coke]** [Koks] sniffen (Drogenjargon)

snot /snɒt/ *n.* (sl.) Rotz, *der* (derb)

snotty *adj.* rotznäsig (salopp); ~ **child/nose** Rotznase, *die* (salopp)

snout /snaʊt/ *n.* Schnauze, *die;* (of pig) Rüssel, *der*

snow /snəʊ/ ① *n.* Schnee, *der*
② *v.i. impers.* **it ~s/is ~ing** es schneit
■ **snow 'in** *v.t.* **they are ~ed in** sie sind eingeschneit

■ **snow 'under** *v.t.* be ∼ed under (with work) erdrückt werden; (with gifts, mail) überschüttet werden

snow: ∼**ball** 1 *n.* Schneeball, *der;* 2 *v.i.* (fig.) lawinenartig zunehmen; ∼ **blindness** *n.* Schneeblindheit, *die;* ∼**board** 1 *n.* Snowboard, *das;* 2 *v.i.* Snowboard fahren; ∼**boarder** *n.* Snowboarder, *der/*Snowboarderin, *die;* ∼**boarding** *n.* Snowboardfahren, *das;* Snowboarden, *das;* ∼**bound** *adj.* eingeschneit; ∼**-capped** *adj.* schneebedeckt; ∼ **chains** *n. pl.* Schneeketten *Pl.;* ∼**drift** *n.* Schneewehe, *die;* ∼**drop** *n.* Schneeglöckchen, *das;* ∼**fall** *n.* Schneefall, *der;* ∼**flake** *n.* Schneeflocke, *die;* ∼**man** *n.* Schneemann, *der;* ∼**plough** *n.* Schneepflug, *der;* ∼**storm** *n.* Schneesturm, *der*

'**snowy** *adj.* schneereich ⟨*Gegend*⟩; schneebedeckt ⟨*Berge*⟩

snub /snʌb/ 1 *v.t.* -bb-: **(a)** (rebuff) brüskieren
(b) (reject) ablehnen
2 *n.* Abfuhr, *die*

snub-'nosed *adj.* stupsnasig

snuff¹ /snʌf/ *n.* Schnupftabak, *der;* **take a pinch of** ∼: eine Prise schnupfen

snuff² *v.t.* ∼ [out] löschen ⟨*Kerze*⟩

snuffle /'snʌfl/ *v.i.* schnüffeln

snug /snʌg/ *adj.* gemütlich; behaglich; **be a** ∼ **fit** genau passen

snuggle /'snʌgl/ *v.i.* ∼ **up to sb.** sich an jmdn. kuscheln; ∼ **together** sich aneinander kuscheln; ∼ **up** *or* **down in bed** sich ins Bett kuscheln

so /səʊ/ 1 *adv.* **(a)** so; **as winter draws near, so it gets darker** je näher der Winter rückt, desto dunkler wird es; **so … as** so … wie; **so far** bis hierher; (until now) bisher; (to such a distance) so weit; **so much the better** um so besser; **so long!** bis dann! (ugs.); **and so on** [and so forth] und so weiter [und so fort]; **so as to** um … zu; **so [that]** damit; **I'm so glad/tired!** ich bin ja so froh/müde!; **It's a rainbow! – So it is!** Es ist ein Regenbogen! – Ja, wirklich!; '**You suggested it. – So I did** Du hast es vorgeschlagen. – Das stimmt; **is that so?** so? (ugs.); wirklich?; **so am/have/ would/could/will/do I** ich auch
(b) *pron.* he suggested that I take the train, **and if I had done so,** …: er riet mir, den Zug zu nehmen, und wenn ich es getan hätte, …; **I'm afraid so** leider ja; **I told you so** ich habe es dir [ja] gesagt; **a week or so** etwa eine Woche; **very much so** in der Tat
2 *conj.* (therefore) daher; **so there you 'are!** ich habe also recht!; **so 'there!** [und] fertig!; **so?** na und?; **so you see** …: du siehst also …; **so where have you been?** wo warst du denn?

soak /səʊk/ 1 *v.t.* **(a)** einweichen ⟨*Wäsche in Lauge*⟩; eintauchen ⟨*Brot in Milch*⟩
(b) (wet) nass machen

2 *v.i.* **(a)** (steep) put sth. in sth. to ∼: etw. in etw. (*Dat.*) einweichen
(b) (drain) ⟨*Feuchtigkeit, Nässe:*⟩ sickern

'**soaking** *adj. & adv.* ∼ [wet] völlig durchnässt

'**so-and-so** *n., pl.* ∼'**s (a)** (person not named) [Herr/Frau] Soundso
(b) (coll.: disliked person) Biest, *das* (ugs.)

soap /səʊp/ *n.* **(a)** Seife, *die;* **with** ∼ **and water** mit Wasser und Seife
(b) (coll.) ▶ SOAP OPERA.

soap: ∼ **flakes** *n. pl.* Seifenflocken *Pl.;* ∼ **opera** *n.* Seifenoper, *die* (ugs.); ∼ **powder** *n.* Seifenpulver, *das;* ∼**suds** *n. pl.* Seifenschaum, *der*

'**soapy** *adj.* seifig; ∼ **water** Seifenlauge, *die*

soar /sɔː(r)/ *v.i.* aufsteigen; (fig.) ⟨*Preise, Kosten usw.:*⟩ in die Höhe schießen (ugs.)

sob /sɒb/ 1 *v.i.,* -bb- schluchzen (with vor + *Dat.*)
2 *n.* Schluchzer, *der*

sober /'səʊbə(r)/ *adj.* **(a)** (not drunk) nüchtern
(b) (serious) ernst

■ **sober 'up** 1 *v.i.* nüchtern werden
2 *v.t.* ausnüchtern

'**sobering** *adj.* ernüchternd

so-called /'səʊkɔːld/ *adj.* so genannt; (alleged) angeblich

soccer /'sɒkə(r)/ *n.* Fußball, *der*

sociable /'səʊʃəbl/ *adj.* gesellig

social /'səʊʃl/ *adj.* **(a)** sozial; gesellschaftlich
(b) (of ∼ life) gesellschaftlich; gesellig ⟨*Abend, Beisammensein*⟩

'**social club** *n.* Klub für gesellliges Beisammensein

socialism /'səʊʃəlɪzm/ *n.* Sozialismus, *der*

socialist /'səʊʃəlɪst/ 1 *n.* Sozialist, *der/*Sozialistin, *die*
2 *adj.* sozialistisch

socialize /'səʊʃəlaɪz/ *v.i.* gesellligen Umgang pflegen; ∼ **with sb.** (chat) sich mit jmdm. unterhalten

'**social life** *n.* gesellschaftliches Leben; **not have much** ∼ ⟨*Person:*⟩ nicht viel ausgehen

'**socially** *adv.* **meet** ∼: sich privat treffen; ∼ **deprived** sozial benachteiligt

social: ∼ '**networking site** *n.* soziales Netzwerk; ∼ '**science** *n.* Sozialwissenschaften *Pl.;* Gesellschaftswissenschaften *Pl.;* ∼ **se'curity** *n.* **(a)** (Brit.: benefit) Sozialhilfe, *die;* **(b)** (system) soziale Sicherheit; ∼ '**service** *n.* staatliche Sozialleistung; ∼ '**services** *n. pl.* Sozialdienste *Pl.;* ∼ **work** *n.* Sozialarbeit, *die;* ∼ **worker** *n.* Sozialarbeiter, *der/*-arbeiterin, *die*

society /sə'saɪətɪ/ *n.* **(a)** Gesellschaft, *die;* **high** ∼: Highsociety, *die*
(b) (club, association) Verein, *der*

socio-eco'nomic *adj.* sozioökonomisch

sociological /səʊsɪə'lɒdʒɪkl/ *adj.* soziologisch

sociologist /səʊsɪ'ɒlədʒɪst/ *n.* Soziologe, *der*/Soziologin, *die*

sociology /səʊsɪ'ɒlədʒɪ/ *n.* Soziologie, *die*

sock[1] /sɒk/ *n.* Socke, *die*

sock[2] *v.t.* (coll.: hit) hauen (ugs.)

socket /'sɒkɪt/ *n.* (a) (Anat.) (of eye) Höhle, *die;* (of joint) Pfanne, *die*
(b) (Electr.) Steckdose, *die*

soda /'səʊdə/ *n.* Soda, *das*

'soda water *n.* Soda[wasser], *das*

sodden /'sɒdn/ *adj.* durchnässt (with von)

sodium /'səʊdɪəm/ *n.* Natrium, *das*

sodium: ~ **bi'carbonate** *n.* doppeltkohlensaures Natrium; Natriumhydrogenkarbonat, *das;*
~ **'chloride** *n.* Natriumchlorid, *das*

sofa /'səʊfə/ *n.* Sofa, *das*

soft /sɒft/ *adj.* weich; (quiet) leise; (gentle) sanft; **have a** ~ **spot for sb.** eine Vorliebe für jmdn. haben

soft: ~**-boiled** *adj.* weich gekocht ⟨*Ei*⟩; ~**-centred** *adj.* ⟨*Praline usw.*⟩ mit weicher Füllung; ~ **copy** *n.* (Comp.) Softcopy, *die;* ~ **cover** *n.* book with a ~ cover Buch mit einem Softcover (Verlagsw.) *od.* mit einem flexiblen Einband; ~ **drink** *n.* alkoholfreies Getränk; ~ **drug** *n.* weiche Droge

soften /'sɒfn/ [1] *v.i.* weicher werden [2] *v.t.* aufweichen ⟨*Boden*⟩; enthärten ⟨*Wasser*⟩; mildern ⟨*Farbe*⟩

soft: ~ **'furnishings** *n. pl.* (Brit.) Raumtextilien *Pl.;* ~**'hearted** /sɒft'hɑːtɪd/ *adj.* weichherzig

'softly *adv.* (quietly) leise; (gently) sanft

soft: ~ **option** *n.* Weg des geringsten Widerstandes; ~ **'porn** (coll.), ~ **por'nography** *ns.* Softpornographie, *die;* ~**-spoken** *adj.* leise sprechend ⟨*Person*⟩; ~ **top** *n.* (a) (roof) Stoffverdeck, *das;* (b) (car) Cabrio, *das;* ~ **'toy** *n.* Stoffspielzeug, *das;* (toy animal) Stofftier, *das;* ~ **verge** *n.* (Brit.) Grünstreifen, *der;* ~**ware** *n.* (Comp.) Software, *die*

soggy /'sɒgɪ/ *adj.* aufgeweicht

soil[1] /sɔɪl/ *n.* Erde, *die;* Boden, *der*

soil[2] *v.t.* beschmutzen

solace /'sɒləs/ *n.* Trost, *der;* **take** *or* **find** ~ **in sth.** Trost in etw. (*Dat.*) finden

solar /'səʊlə(r)/ *adj.* Sonnen-

solar: ~ **e'clipse** *n.* Sonnenfinsternis, *die;* ~ **'energy** *n.* Sonnenenergie, *die;* ~ **'panel** *n.* Sonnenkollektor, *der;* (on satellite) Sonnensegel, *das;* ~**-powered** *adj.* mit Sonnenenergie betrieben; ~ **system** *n.* Sonnensystem, *das*

sold ▸ SELL

solder /'səʊldə(r)/ [1] *n.* Lot, *das* [2] *v.t.* löten

soldering iron /'səʊldərɪŋaɪən/ *n.* Lötkolben, *der*

soldier /'səʊldʒə(r)/ *n.* Soldat, *der*

sole[1] /səʊl/ *n.* (of foot/shoe) Sohle, *die*

sole[2] *adj.* einzig; alleinig ⟨*Verantwortung, Recht*⟩; Allein⟨*erbe, -eigentümer*⟩

'solely *adv.* einzig und allein

solemn /'sɒləm/ *adj.* feierlich; ernst ⟨*Anlass, Gespräch*⟩

solicitor /sə'lɪsɪtə/ *n.* (Brit.: lawyer) Rechtsanwalt, *der*/-anwältin, *die*

solid /'sɒlɪd/ [1] *adj.* (a) (rigid) fest
(b) (of the same substance all through) massiv
(c) (well-built) stabil; solide gebaut ⟨*Haus, Mauer usw.*⟩
(d) (complete) ganz; **a good** ~ **meal** eine kräftige Mahlzeit
[2] *n.* fester Körper

solidarity /sɒlɪ'dærɪtɪ/ *n.* Solidarität, *die*

solid: ~ **'fuel** *n.* fester Brennstoff; ~**-'fuel** *attrib. adj.* Festbrennstoff-; ~**-fuel rocket** Feststoffrakete, *die*

solidify /sə'lɪdɪfaɪ/ *v.i.* fest werden

solitary /'sɒlɪtərɪ/ *adj.* (a) einsam; ~ **confinement** Einzelhaft, *die*
(b) (sole) einzig

solitude /'sɒlɪtjuːd/ *n.* Einsamkeit, *die*

solo /'səʊləʊ/ [1] *n., pl.* ~**s** (Mus.) Solo, *das*
[2] *adj.* (a) (Mus.) Solo-
(b) ~ **flight** Alleinflug, *der*
[3] *adv.* (a) (Mus.) solo
(b) **go/fly** ~ (Aeronaut.) einen Alleinflug machen

soloist /'səʊləʊɪst/ *n.* (Mus.) Solist, *der*/Solistin, *die*

solstice /'sɒlstɪs/ *n.* Sonnenwende, *die*

soluble /'sɒljʊbl/ *adj.* (a) (esp. Chem.) löslich
(b) (solvable) lösbar

solution /sə'luːʃn/ *n.* (a) (esp. Chem.) Lösung, *die*
(b) ([result of] solving) Lösung, *die* (to *Gen.*); **find a** ~ **to sth.** eine Lösung für etw. finden; etw. lösen

solvable /'sɒlvəbl/ *adj.* lösbar

solve /sɒlv/ *v.t.* lösen

solvent /'sɒlvənt/ [1] *adj.* (a) (esp. Chem.) lösend
(b) (Finance) solvent
[2] *n.* Lösungsmittel, *das*

sombre (*Amer.:* **somber**) /'sɒmbə(r)/ *adj.* dunkel; düster ⟨*Stimmung, Atmosphäre*⟩

some /səm, *stressed* sʌm/ [1] *adj.* (a) (one or other) [irgend]ein; ~ **day** eines Tages
(b) (a considerable quantity of) einig...
(c) (a small quantity of) ein bisschen; **would you like** ~ **wine/cherries?** möchten Sie [etwas] Wein/[ein paar] Kirschen?; **do** ~ **shopping/reading** einkaufen/lesen
(d) (to a certain extent) ~ **guide** eine gewisse Orientierungshilfe

2 *pron.* einig...; **would you like ~?** möchtest du etwas/(plural) welche?; **~ ..., others ...:** manche ..., andere ...

somebody /'sʌmbədɪ/ *n. & pron.* jemand; **~ or other** irgendjemand

'somehow *adv.* **~ [or other]** irgendwie

someone /'sʌmwʌn/ ▶ SOMEBODY

somersault /'sʌməsɔːlt/ *n.* Purzelbaum, *der* (ugs.); Salto, *der* (Sport); **turn a ~:** einen Purzelbaum schlagen (ugs.)/einen Salto springen

'something *n. & pron.* etwas; **~ new** etwas Neues; **~ or other** irgendetwas; **see ~ of sb.** jmdn. sehen

'sometime **1** *adj.* ehemalig **2** *adv.* irgendwann

'sometimes *adv.* manchmal

'somewhat *adv.* ziemlich

'somewhere **1** *adv.* **(a)** (in a place) irgendwo
(b) (to a place) irgendwohin
2 *n.* **look for ~ to stay** sich nach einer Unterkunft umsehen

son /sʌn/ *n.* Sohn, *der*

sonata /sə'nɑːtə/ *n.* Sonate, *die*

song /sɒŋ/ *n.* **(a)** Lied, *das*
(b) (bird cry) Gesang, *der*

song: ~bird *n.* Singvogel, *der;* **~book** *n.* Liederbuch, *das*

sonic /'sɒnɪk/ *attrib. adj.* Schall-; **~ bang** *or* **boom** Überschallknall, *der*

'son-in-law *n., pl.* **sons-in-law** Schwiegersohn, *der*

soon /suːn/ *adv.* **(a)** bald; (quickly) schnell
(b) (early) früh; **none too ~:** keinen Augenblick zu früh; **~er or later** früher oder später
(c) we'll set off as ~ as he arrives sobald er ankommt, machen wir uns auf den Weg; **as ~ as possible** so bald wie möglich
(d) (willingly) **just as ~ [as ...]** genauso gern [wie ...]; **she would ~er die than ...:** sie würde lieber sterben, als ...

soot /sʊt/ *n.* Ruß, *der*

soothe /suːe/ *v.t.* **(a)** (calm) beruhigen
(b) lindern ⟨*Schmerz*⟩

soothing /'suːeɪŋ/ *adj.* beruhigend; wohltuend ⟨*Bad, Creme, Massage*⟩

'sooty *adj.* verrußt; rußig

sophisticated /sə'fɪstɪkeɪtɪd/ *adj.*
(a) (cultured) kultiviert
(b) (elaborate, complex) hoch entwickelt; subtil ⟨*Argument, System*⟩

soporific /sɒpə'rɪfɪk/ *adj.* einschläfernd

sopping /'sɒpɪŋ/ *adj. & adv.* **~ [WET]** völlig durchnässt

soppy /'sɒpɪ/ *adj.* (Brit. coll.) rührselig; sentimental ⟨*Person*⟩

soprano /sə'prɑːnəʊ/ *n.* Sopran, *der;* (female also) Sopranistin, *die*

sorbet /'sɔːbɪt, 'sɔːbeɪ/ *n.* Sorbet, *das*

sorcerer /'sɔːsərə(r)/ *n.* Zauberer, *der*

sorcery /'sɔːsərɪ/ *n.* Zauberei, *die*

sordid /'sɔːdɪd/ *adj.* dreckig; unerfreulich ⟨*Detail, Geschichte*⟩

sore /sɔː(r)/ **1** *adj.* weh; (inflamed or injured) wund; **a ~ throat** Halsschmerzen *Pl.;* **sb. has a ~ back/foot** *etc.* jmdm. tut der Rücken/Fuß *usw.* weh
2 *n.* wunde Stelle

'sorely *adv.* sehr; dringend ⟨*nötig*⟩; **~ tempted** stark versucht

sorrow /'sɒrəʊ/ *n.* Kummer, *der*

sorry /'sɒrɪ/ *adj.* **(a) sb. is ~ that ...:** es tut jmdm. Leid, dass ...; **sb. is ~ about sth.** jmdm. tut etwas Leid; **I am** *or* **feel ~ for him** er tut mir Leid; **sb. is** *or* **feels ~ for sth.** jmd. bedauert etw.; **~!** Entschuldigung!; **~?** wie bitte?; **I'm ~ to say** leider; **you'll be ~!** das wird dir noch Leid tun
(b) (wretched) traurig

sort /sɔːt/ **1** *n.* **(a)** Art, *die;* (type) Sorte, *die;* **a new ~ of bicycle** ein neuartiges Fahrrad; **all ~s of ...:** alle möglichen ...; **there are all ~s of things to do** es gibt alles Mögliche *od.* allerlei zu tun; **~ of** (coll.: more or less) mehr oder weniger; **nothing of the ~:** nichts dergleichen
(b) be out of ~s nicht in Form sein
2 *v.t.* sortieren
■ **sort 'out** *v.t.* **(a)** (settle) klären; schlichten ⟨*Streit*⟩; beenden ⟨*Verwirrung*⟩
(b) (select) aussuchen

'sort code *n.* Bankleitzahl, *die*

sortie /'sɔːtɪ/ *n.* Ausfall, *der;* (flight) Einsatz, *der*

'sorting office *n.* Postverteilstelle, *die*

SOS *n.* SOS, *das*

'so so, 'so-so *adj., adv.* so lala (ugs.)

soufflé /'suːfleɪ/ *n.* Soufflé, *das*

sought ▶ SEEK

soul /səʊl/ *n.* Seele, *die;* **not a ~:** keine Menschenseele

'soul-destroying *adj.* **(a)** (boring) nervtötend
(b) (depressing) deprimierend

soulful /'səʊlfl/ *adj.* gefühlvoll; (sad) schwermütig

soul: ~ mate *n.* Seelenverwandte, *der/ die;* **~-searching** *n.* Gewissenskampf, *der*

sound¹ /saʊnd/ **1** *adj.* **(a)** (healthy) gesund; intakt ⟨*Gebäude, Mauerwerk*⟩; **of ~ mind** im Vollbesitz seiner geistigen Kräfte
(b) (well-founded) vernünftig ⟨*Argument, Rat*⟩; klug ⟨*Wahl*⟩; **it makes ~ sense** es ist sehr vernünftig
(c) (Finance: secure) gesund, solide ⟨*Basis*⟩; klug ⟨*Investition*⟩
2 *adv.* fest, tief ⟨*schlafen*⟩

sound² **1** *n.* **(a)** (Phys.) Schall, der
(b) (noise) Laut, *der;* (of wind, sea, car, footsteps, breaking glass or twigs) Geräusch, *das;* (of voices, laughter, bell) Klang, *der;* **do sth. without a ~:** etw. lautlos tun ⋯▷

(c) (Radio, Telev., Cinemat.) Ton, *der*
(d) (fig.: impression) **I like the ~ of your plan**
ich finde, Ihr Plan hört sich gut an; **I don't
like the ~ of this** das hört sich nicht gut an
2 *v.i.* klingen; **it ~s as if .../like ...:** es
klingt, als .../wie ...; **that ~s a good idea
to me** ich finde, die Idee hört sich gut an;
that ~s odd to me das hört sich seltsam an,
finde ich; **~s good to me!** klingt gut! (ugs.)
3 *v.t.* **(a)** ertönen lassen
(b) (utter) **~ a note of caution** zur Vorsicht
mahnen
■ **sound 'off** *v.i.* tönen (ugs.),
schwadronieren (**on, about, of**)
■ **sound 'out** *v.i.* ausfragen ⟨*Person*⟩;
~ sb. out on sth. bei jmdm. wegen etw.
vorfühlen
sound: ~ barrier *n.* Schallmauer,
die; **~ bite** *n.* kurzes, prägnantes
Zitat; **~ card** *n.* (Comp.) Soundkarte,
die; **~ effect** *n.* Geräuscheffekt, *der;*
~ engineer *n.* Toningenieur, *der/*
-ingenieurin, *die*
'sounding board *n.* **(a)** (Mus.) Decke, *die*
(b) (fig.: trial audience) ≈ Testgruppe, *die*
'soundless *adj.* lautlos
'soundly *adv.* **(a)** (solidly) stabil, solide
⟨*bauen*⟩
(b) (deeply) tief, fest ⟨*schlafen*⟩
(c) (thoroughly) ordentlich (ugs.) ⟨*verhauen*⟩;
vernichtend ⟨*schlagen, besiegen*⟩
sound: ~proof **1** *adj.* schalldicht; **2** *v.t.*
schalldicht machen; **~ system** *n.*
Tonanlage, *die;* **~track** *n.* Soundtrack,
der; **~ wave** *n.* Schallwelle, *die*
soup /suːp/ *n.* Suppe, *die;* **be/land in the ~**
(fig. coll.) in der Patsche sitzen/landen (ugs.)
souped-up /'suːptʌp/ *attrib. adj.* (Motor
Veh. coll.) frisiert (ugs.)
soup: ~ plate *n.* Suppenteller, *der;*
~ spoon *n.* Suppenlöffel, *der*
sour /'saʊə(r)/ *adj.* **(a)** sauer
(b) (morose) griesgrämig; säuerlich ⟨*Blick*⟩
(c) (unpleasant) bitter
source /sɔːs/ *n.* Quelle, *die;* **~ of
income/infection** Einkommensquelle,
*die/*Infektionsherd, *der;* **at ~:** an der Quelle
sour 'cream *n.* saure Sahne; Sauerrahm,
der
south /saʊθ/ **1** *n.* **(a)** Süden, *der;* **in/
to[wards]/from the ~:** im/nach/von Süden;
to the ~ of südlich von
(b) *usu.* **S~** (Geog., Polit.) Süden, *der*
2 *adj.* südlich; Süd⟨*küste, -wind, -grenze*⟩
3 *adv.* nach Süden; **~ of** südlich von
South: ~ 'Africa *pr. n.* Südafrika
(*das*); **~ 'African** *adj.* südafrikanisch;
~ A'merica *pr. n.* Südamerika (*das*);
~ A'merican *adj.* südamerikanisch;
s~bound *adj.* ⟨*Zug, Verkehr usw.*⟩ in
Richtung Süden; **s~-'east** **1** *n.* Südosten,
der; **2** *adj.* südöstlich; Südost⟨*wind, -küste*⟩;
3 *adv.* südostwärts; nach Südosten;
s~-'eastern *adj.* südöstlich

southerly /'sʌðəlɪ/ *adj.* südlich; ⟨*Wind*⟩
aus südlichen Richtungen
southern /'sʌðən/ *adj.* südlich;
Süd⟨*grenze, -hälfte, -seite*⟩
Southern Europe *pr. n.* Südeuropa
(*das*)
South: ~ 'Germany *pr. n.*
Süddeutschland (*das*); **~ 'Pole** *pr. n.*
Südpol, *der*
southward[s] /'saʊθwəd(s)/ *adv.*
südwärts
south: ~-'west **1** *n.* Südwesten, *der;*
2 *adj.* südwestlich; Südwest⟨*wind, -küste*⟩;
3 *adv.* südwestwärts; nach Südwesten;
~-'western *adj.* südwestlich
souvenir /suːvə'nɪə(r)/ *n.* Souvenir, *das*
(of aus); Andenken, *das*
sovereign /'sɒvrɪn/ *n.* (ruler) Souverän, *der*
sovereignty /'sɒvrɪntɪ/ *n.* Souveränität,
die
Soviet /'səʊvɪət, 'sɒvɪət/ *adj.* (Hist.)
sowjetisch; Sowjet⟨*bürger, -literatur*⟩
Soviet 'Union *pr. n.* (Hist.) Sowjetunion,
die
sow[1] /səʊ/ *v.t., p.p.* **sown** /səʊn/ *or* **sowed**
/səʊd/ **(a)** (plant) [aus]säen
(b) einsäen ⟨*Feld, Boden*⟩
sow[2] /saʊ/ *n.* (female pig) Sau, *die*
sown ▶ **sow**[1]
soya [bean] /'sɔɪə (biːn)/ *n.* Sojabohne,
die
soy sauce /'sɔɪ sɔːs/ *n.* Sojasoße, *die*
sozzled /'sɒzld/ *adj.* (coll.) voll (ugs.)
spa /spɑː/ *n.* **(a)** (place) Bad, *das;* Badeort,
der
(b) (spring) Mineralquelle, *die*
space /speɪs/ *n.* **(a)** Raum, *der*
(b) (interval between points) Platz, *der;* **clear a
~:** Platz schaffen
(c) the wide open ~s das weite, flache Land
(d) (Astron.) Weltraum, *der*
(e) (blank between words) Zwischenraum, *der*
(f) (interval of time) Zeitraum, *der;* **in the ~ of a
minute/an hour** innerhalb einer Minute/
Stunde; **in a short ~ of time he was back**
nach kurzer Zeit war er zurück
■ **space 'out** *v.t.* verteilen
space: ~ age *n.* [Welt]raumzeitalter,
das; **~ bar** *n.* Leertaste, *die;* **~craft**
n. Raumfahrzeug, *das;* **~-saving** *adj.*
Platz sparend; **~ship** *n.* Raumschiff, *das;*
~suit *n.* Raumanzug, *der;* **~ travel** *n.*
Raumfahrt, *die*
spacious /'speɪʃəs/ *adj.* geräumig
spade /speɪd/ *n.* **(a)** Spaten, *der*
(b) (Cards) Pik, *das; see also* CLUB 1C
spaghetti /spə'getɪ/ *n.* Spaghetti *Pl.*
Spain /speɪn/ *pr. n.* Spanien (*das*)
spam /spæm/ *n.* (Comput.) Spam, *der*
span /spæn/ **1** *n.* **(a)** Spanne, *die;*
Zeitspanne, *die*
(b) (of bridge) Spannweite, *die*

2 *v.t.*, **-nn-** überspannen ⟨*Fluss*⟩; umfassen ⟨*Zeitraum*⟩

Spaniard /'spænjəd/ *n.* Spanier, *der*/Spanierin, *die*

Spanish /'spænɪʃ/ 1 *adj.* spanisch; **sb. is ~:** jmd. ist Spanier/Spanierin
2 *n.* **(a)** (language) Spanisch, *das; see also* ENGLISH 2A
(b) the **~** *pl.* die Spanier *Pl.*

spank /spæŋk/ 1 *n.* ≈ Klaps, *der* (ugs.)
2 *v.t.* **~ sb.** jmdm. einen Klaps geben (ugs.)

spanner /'spænə(r)/ *n.* (Brit.) Schraubenschlüssel, *der*

spar /spɑː(r)/ *v.i.*, **-rr-: (a)** (Boxing) sparren
(b) (fig.: argue) [sich] zanken

spare /speə(r)/ 1 *adj.* **(a)** (not in use) übrig; **~ time/moment** Freizeit, *die*/freier Augenblick; **there is one ~ seat** ein Platz ist noch frei
(b) (for use when needed) zusätzlich, Extra⟨*bett, -tasse*⟩; **~ room** Gästezimmer, *das*
2 *n.* Ersatzteil, *das*/-reifen, *der usw.*
3 *v.t.* **(a)** entbehren; **we arrived with ten minutes to ~:** wir kamen zehn Minuten früher an
(b) (not inflict on) **~ sb. sth.** jmdm. etw. ersparen
(c) (not hurt) [ver]schonen
(d) (fail to use) **not ~ any expense/pains** *or* **efforts** keine Kosten/Mühe scheuen; **no expense ~d** an nichts gespart

spare: ~ 'part *n.* Ersatzteil, *das;* **~ 'tyre** *n.* Reserve-, Ersatzreifen, *der;* **~ 'wheel** *n.* Ersatzrad, *das*

sparing /'speərɪŋ/ *adj.*, **sparingly** *adv.* sparsam

spark /spɑːk/ 1 *n.* **(a)** Funke, *der;* (fig.) **a ~ of generosity/decency** ein Funke[n] Großzügigkeit/Anstand
(b) **a bright ~** (coll.: person, also iron.) ein schlauer Kopf
2 *v.t.* **~ [off]** zünden; (fig.) auslösen

sparkle /'spɑːkl/ 1 *v.i.* **(a)** ⟨*Diamant:*⟩ glitzern; ⟨*Augen:*⟩ funkeln
(b) (be lively) sprühen (**with** vor + *Dat.*)
2 *n.* Funkeln, *das*

sparkling /'spɑːklɪŋ/ *adj.* glitzernd ⟨*Diamant*⟩; funkelnd ⟨*Augen*⟩

sparkling 'wine *n.* Schaumwein, *der*

'spark plug *n.* Zündkerze, *die*

sparrow /'spærəʊ/ *n.* Spatz, *der*

sparse /spɑːs/ *adj.* spärlich; dünn ⟨*Besiedlung*⟩

spasm /'spæzm/ *n.* Krampf, *der*

spasmodic /spæz'mɒdɪk/ *adj.* **(a)** (marked by spasms) krampfartig
(b) (intermittent) sporadisch

spastic /'spæstɪk/ 1 *n.* Spastiker, *der*/Spastikerin, *die*
2 *adj.* spastisch

spat ▶ SPIT 1, 2

spate /speɪt/ *n.* **(a) the river is in [full]**

~: der Fluss führt Hochwasser
(b) (fig.) **a ~ of sth.** eine Flut von etw.; **a ~ of burglaries** eine Einbruchsserie

spatial /'speɪʃl/ *adj.* räumlich

spatter /'spætə(r)/ *v.t.* spritzen; **~ sb./sth. with sth.** jmdn./etw. mit etw. bespritzen

spatula /'spætjʊlə/ *n.* Spachtel, *der od. die*

spawn /spɔːn/ 1 *v.t.* (fig.) hervorbringen
2 *v.i.* (Zool.) laichen
3 *n.* (Zool.) Laich, *der*

speak /spiːk/ 1 *v.i.*, **spoke** /spəʊk/, **spoken** /'spəʊkn/ **(a)** sprechen; **~ [with sb.] on** *or* **about sth.** [mit jmdm.] über etw. (*Akk.*) sprechen; **~ for/against sth.** sich für/gegen etw. aussprechen
(b) (on telephone) **Is Mr Grant there? – S~ing!** Ist Mister Grant da? – Am Apparat!; **who is ~ing, please?** wer ist am Apparat, bitte?
2 *v.t.*, **spoke, spoken** sprechen ⟨*Satz, Wort, Sprache*⟩; sagen ⟨*Wahrheit*⟩; **~ one's mind** sagen, was man denkt
■ **'speak for** *v.t.* sprechen für; **sth. is spoken for** (reserved) etw. ist schon vergeben
■ **'speak of** *v.t.* sprechen von; **~ing of Mary** da wir gerade von Mary sprechen; **nothing to ~ of** nichts Besonderes
■ **'speak to** *v.t.* sprechen *od.* reden mit
■ **speak 'up** *v.i.* lauter sprechen

'speaker *n.* **(a)** (in public) Redner, *der*/Rednerin, *die*
(b) (of a language) Sprecher *der*/Sprecherin, *die;* **be a 'French ~:** Französisch sprechen
(c) (loudspeaker) Lautsprecher, *der*

'speaking 1 *n.* Sprechen, *das; ~* **clock** (Brit.) telefonische Zeitansage
2 *adv.* **strictly/generally ~:** genau genommen/im Allgemeinen

spear /spɪə(r)/ *n.* Speer, *der*

'spearhead 1 *n.* (fig.) Speerspitze, *die*
2 *v.t.* (fig.) anführen

'spearmint *n.* Grüne Minze; **~ chewing gum** Pfefferminzkaugummi, *der od. das*

spec¹ /spek/ (coll.) ▶ SPECIFICATION

spec² /spek/ *n.* (coll.: speculation) **on ~:** auf gut Glück; auf Verdacht (ugs.)

special /'speʃl/ *adj.* speziell; besonder…; **nobody ~:** niemand Besonderes

special de'livery *n.* (Post) Eilzustellung, *die*

special ef'fects *n. pl.* (Cinemat.) Special effects *Pl.*

specialist /'speʃəlɪst/ *n.* **(a)** Spezialist, *der*/Spezialistin, *die* (**in** für)
(b) (Med.) Facharzt, *der*/-ärztin, *die*

speciality /speʃɪ'ælɪti/ *n.* Spezialität, *die*

specialization /speʃəlaɪ'zeɪʃn/ *n.* Spezialisierung, *die*

specialize /'speʃəlaɪz/ *v.i.* sich spezialisieren (**in** auf + *Akk.*)

specialized /'speʃəlaɪzd/ *adj.*
(a) (requiring detailed knowledge) speziell; Spezial⟨*kenntnisse, -gebiet*⟩
(b) (concentrating on small area) spezialisiert

'specially *adv.* **(a)** speziell; **make sth.
∼:** etw. speziell *od.* extra anfertigen
(b) (especially) besonders

special: ∼ **'needs** *n.* **children
with** ∼ **needs** Kinder, die besonders
betreut werden müssen; ∼ **needs
teacher** Förderlehrer, *der*/-lehrerin, *die;*
∼ **'offer** *n.* Sonderangebot, *das;* **on**
∼ **offer** im Sonderangebot; ∼ **school** *n.*
Sonderschule, *die*

specialty /'speʃltɪ/ (esp. Amer.)
▶ SPECIALITY

species /'spiːʃiːz/ *n., pl. same* Art,
die; ∼ **barrier** (Biol.) Artenbarriere, *die;*
Artengrenze, *die*

specific /spɪ'sɪfɪk/ *adj.* bestimmt; **could
you be more** ∼? kannst du dich genauer
ausdrücken?

specifically /spɪ'sɪfɪkəli/ *adv.*
ausdrücklich; eigens; extra (ugs.)

specification /spesɪfɪ'keɪʃn/ *n., often
pl.* (details) technische Daten *Pl.;* (for building)
Baubeschreibung, *die*

specify /'spesɪfaɪ/ *v.t.* ausdrücklich sagen;
unless otherwise specified wenn nicht
anders angegeben

specimen /'spesɪmən/ *n.* **(a)** (example)
Exemplar, *das*
(b) (sample) Probe, *die*

speck /spek/ *n.* **(a)** (spot) Fleck, *der*
(b) (particle) Teilchen, *das;* ∼ **of** soot/dust
Rußflocke, *die*/Staubkörnchen, *das*

specs /speks/ *n. pl.* (coll.: spectacles) Brille,
die

spectacle /'spektəkl/ *n.* **(a)** *in pl.* **[pair of]**
∼**s** Brille, *die*
(b) (public show) Spektakel, *das*
(c) (object of attention) Anblick, *der*

'spectacle case *n.* Brillenetui, *das*

spectacular /spek'tækjʊlə(r)/ *adj.*
spektakulär

spectator /spek'teɪtə(r)/ *n.* Zuschauer,
der/Zuschauerin, *die*

spec'tator sport *n.* Publikumssport, *der*

specter (Amer.) ▶ SPECTRE

spectra *pl. of* SPECTRUM

spectre /'spektə(r)/ *n.* (Brit.) **(a)** (ghost)
Gespenst, *das*
(b) (fig.) Schreckgespenst, *das*

spectrum /'spektrəm/ *n., pl.* **spectra**
/'spektrə/ Spektrum, *das*

speculate /'spekjʊleɪt/ *v.i.* spekulieren
(about, on über + *Akk.*)

speculation /spekjʊ'leɪʃn/ *n.*
Spekulation, *die* **(over** über + *Akk.*)

speculative /'spekjʊlətɪv/ *adj.* spekulativ

speculator /'spekjʊleɪtə(r)/ *n.* Spekulant,
der/Spekulantin, *die*

sped ▶ SPEED 2

speech /spiːtʃ/ *n.* **(a)** (public address) Rede,
die; **make** *or* **deliver** *or* **give a** ∼: eine Rede
halten

(b) (faculty or manner of speaking) Sprache, *die*

'speechless *adj.* sprachlos **(with** vor
+ *Dat.*)

speed /spiːd/ ⓵ *n.* Geschwindigkeit, *die;*
Schnelligkeit, *die;* **at a** ∼ **of** …: mit einer
Geschwindigkeit von …
⓶ *v.i.* **(a)** *p.t. & p.p.* **sped** /sped/ *or* **speeded**
schnell fahren; rasen (ugs.)
(b) *p.t.&p.p.* **speeded** (go too fast) zu schnell
fahren; rasen (ugs.)

speed: ∼**boat** *n.* Rennboot,
das; ∼ **bump** *n.* Bodenschwelle,
die; ∼ **camera** *n.*
Geschwindigkeitsüberwachungskamera,
die; ∼ **dating** *n.* Speeddating, *das*

'speeding *n.*
Geschwindigkeitsüberschreitung, *die*

'speed limit *n.*
Geschwindigkeitsbeschränkung, *die*

speedo /'spiːdəʊ/ *n., pl.* ∼**s** (Brit. coll.)
Tacho, *der* (ugs.)

speedometer /spiːˈdɒmɪtə(r)/ *n.*
Tachometer, *der od. das*

speed: ∼ **ramp** *n.* Bodenschwelle, *die;*
∼**way** *n.* Speedwayrennen, *das*

'speedy *adj.* schnell; umgehend, prompt
⟨Antwort⟩

spell¹ /spel/ ⓵ *v.t.,* **spelt** /spelt/ (Brit.) *or*
spelled (a) schreiben; (aloud) buchstabieren
(b) (fig.: mean) bedeuten
⓶ *v.i.,* **spelt** (Brit.) *or* **spelled** (say)
buchstabieren; (write) richtig schreiben

spell² *n.* (period) Weile, *die;* **a cold** ∼: eine
Kälteperiode

spell³ *n.* **(a)** (magic charm) Zauberspruch,
der; **cast a** ∼ **on sb.** jmdn. verzaubern
(b) (fascination) Zauber, *der;* **break the** ∼: den
Bann brechen

'spellbound *adj.* verzaubert

'spell checker ▶ SPELLING CHECKER

'spelling *n.* Rechtschreibung, *die*

spelling: ∼ **checker** *n.*
Rechtschreibprogramm, *das;* ∼ **mistake**
n. Rechtschreibfehler, *der*

spelt ▶ SPELL¹

spend /spend/ *v.t.,* **spent** /spent/ **(a)** (pay
out) ausgeben; ∼ **a penny** (fig. coll.) mal
verschwinden (ugs.)
(b) verbringen ⟨Zeit⟩

'spendthrift *n.* Verschwender,
der/Verschwenderin, *die*

spent ⓵ ▶ SPEND
⓶ *adj.* **(a)** (used up) verbraucht
(b) (drained of energy) erschöpft

sperm /'spɜːm/ *n. pl* ∼**s** *or same* Sperma,
der

sperm: ∼ **bank** *n.* Samenbank, *die;*
∼ **count** *n.* Spermienzahl, *die*

spew /spjuː/ *v.t.* spucken

sphere /sfɪə(r)/ *n.* **(a)** (field of action)
Bereich, *der;* Sphäre, *die* (geh.)
(b) (Geom.) Kugel, *die*

spherical /'sferɪkl/ *adj.* kugelförmig
spice /spaɪs/ ⓵ *n.* Gewürz, *das;* (fig.)
Würze, *die*
⓶ *v.t.* würzen
'**spice rack** *n.* Gewürzregal, *das*
spicy /'spaɪsɪ/ *adj.* pikant; würzig
spider /'spaɪdə(r)/ *n.* Spinne, *die*
spider: ~ **plant** *n.* Grünlilie, *die;* ~'s
web (*Amer.:* ~ **web**) Spinnennetz, *das;*
(fig.) Netz, *das*
spike /spaɪk/ *n.* Stachel, *der*
spiky /'spaɪkɪ/ *adj.* stachelig
spill /spɪl/ ⓵ *v.t.*, spilt /spɪlt/ *or* spilled
verschütten ⟨*Flüssigkeit*⟩; ~ **sth. on** sth.
etw. auf etw. (*Akk.*) schütten; ~ **the beans**
aus der Schule plaudern
⓶ *v.i.*, spilt *or* spilled überlaufen
spilt ▸ SPILL
spin /spɪn/ ⓵ *v.t.*, -nn-, spun /spʌn/
(a) spinnen; ~ **yarn** Garn spinnen
(b) (in washing machine etc.) schleudern
⓶ *v.i.*, -nn-, spun sich drehen; **my head is**
~**ning** (fig.) mir schwirrt der Kopf
■ **spin** '**out** *v.t.* (prolong) in die Länge ziehen
spinach /'spɪnɪdʒ/ *n.* Spinat, *der*
spinal /'spaɪnl/ *adj.* Wirbelsäulen-;
Rückgrat[s]-
spinal: ~ '**column** *n.* Wirbelsäule, *die;*
~ '**cord** *n.* Rückenmark, *das*
spindle /'spɪndl/ *n.* Spindel, *die*
spindly /'spɪndlɪ/ *adj.* spindeldürr
spin: ~ **doctor** *n.* (coll.) Spin-Doktor, *der;*
~ '**drier** *n.* Wäscheschleuder, *die;* ~-**dry**
v.t. schleudern
spine /spaɪn/ *n.* (a) (backbone) Wirbelsäule,
die
(b) (Bot., Zool.) Stachel, *der*
'**spineless** *adj.* (fig.) rückgratlos
'**spin-off** *n.* Nebenprodukt, *das*
spinster /'spɪnstə(r)/ *n.* ledige Frau
spiny /'spaɪnɪ/ *adj.* stachelig
spiral /'spaɪrl/ ⓵ *adj.* spiralförmig
⓶ *n.* Spirale, *die*
⓷ *v.i.*, (Brit.) -ll- ⟨*Weg:*⟩ sich hochwinden;
⟨*Kosten:*⟩ in die Höhe klettern; ⟨*Rauch:*⟩ in
einer Spirale aufsteigen
spiral '**staircase** *n.* Wendeltreppe, *die*
spire /spaɪə(r)/ *n.* Turmspitze, *die*
spirit /'spɪrɪt/ *n.* (a) *in pl.* (distilled liquor)
Spirituosen *Pl.*
(b) (mental attitude) Geisteshaltung, *die;* **in the**
right/wrong ~: mit der richtigen/falschen
Einstellung; **take sth. in the wrong** ~: etw.
falsch auffassen
(c) (courage) Mut, *der*
(d) (mental tendency) Geist, *der;* **high** ~s
gehobene Stimmung; **in poor** *or* **low** ~s
niedergedrückt
'**spirited** *adj.* beherzt
'**spirit level** *n.* Wasserwaage, *die*
spiritual /'spɪrɪtʃʊəl/ *adj.* spirituell (geh.)

spit /spɪt/ ⓵ *v.i.*, -tt-, spat /spæt/ *or* spit
spucken
⓶ *v.t.*, -tt-, spat *or* spit spucken
⓷ *n.* Spucke, *die*
■ **spit** '**out** *v.t.* ausspucken
spite /spaɪt/ ⓵ *n.* (a) Boshaftigkeit, *die*
(b) **in** ~ **of** trotz; **in** ~ **of oneself** obwohl
man es eigentlich nicht will
⓶ *v.t.* ärgern
spiteful /'spaɪtfl/ *adj.* gehässig
spitting '**image** *n.* **be the** ~ **of sb.** jmdm.
wie aus dem Gesicht geschnitten sein
spittle /'spɪtl/ *n.* Spucke, *die*
splash /splæʃ/ ⓵ *v.t.* spritzen; ~ **sth. on**
[**to**] *or* **over sb./sth.** jmdn./etw. mit etw.
bespritzen
⓶ *v.i.* (a) spritzen
(b) (in water) platschen (ugs.)
⓷ *n.* (a) (liquid) Spritzer, *der*
(b) (noise) Plätschern, *das*
■ **splash** '**out** *v.i.* (coll.) ~ **out on sth.** für
etw. unbekümmert Geld ausgeben
splendid /'splendɪd/ *adj.* (excellent)
großartig; (magnificent) prächtig
splendour (*Brit.; Amer.:* **splendor**)
/'splendə(r)/ *n.* Pracht, *die*
splint /splɪnt/ *n.* Schiene, *die*
splinter /'splɪntə(r)/ *n.* Splitter, *der*
split /splɪt/ ⓵ *n.* (a) (tear) Riss, *der*
(b) (division into parts) [Auf]teilung, *die;* (fig.)
Spaltung, *die*
⓶ *adj.* gespalten; **be** ~ **on a question** [sich
(*Dat.*] in einer Frage uneins sein
⓷ *v.t.*, -tt-, split (a) (tear) zerreißen
(b) (divide) teilen
⓸ *v.i.*, -tt-, split (a) ⟨*Holz:*⟩ splittern; ⟨*Stoff,*
Seil:⟩ reißen; ~ **apart** zersplittern
(b) (divide into parts) sich teilen
■ **split** '**up** ⓵ *v.t.* aufteilen
⓶ *v.i.* (coll.) sich trennen; ~ **up with sb.** sich
von jmdm. trennen
split: ~-**level** *adj.* mit Zwischengeschoss
nachgestellt; auf zwei Ebenen *nachgestellt;*
a ~-**level lounge** ein Wohnraum auf zwei
Ebenen; ~-**level cooker** *Einbauherd, bei*
dem Kochplatten und Backofen getrennt
sind; ~ '**pea** *n.* getrocknete [halbe]
Erbse; ~ **perso'nality** *n.* gespaltene
Persönlichkeit; ~ '**second** *n.* **in a**
~ **second** im Bruchteil einer Sekunde;
~-**second timing** [zeitliche] Abstimmung
auf die Sekunde genau
splitting /'splɪtɪŋ/ *adj.* **a** ~ **headache**
rasende Kopfschmerzen *Pl.*
splutter /'splʌtə(r)/ *v.i.* ⟨*Person:*⟩ prusten;
⟨*Motor:*⟩ stottern
spoil /spɔɪl/ ⓵ *v.t.*, spoilt /spɔɪlt/ *or* spoiled
(a) (impair) verderben
(b) (pamper) verwöhnen; **be** ~**t for choice** die
Qual der Wahl haben
⓶ *v.i.*, spoilt *or* spoiled (a) verderben
(b) **be** ~**ing for a fight** Streit suchen
⓷ *n.* ~[**s** *pl.*] Beute, *die*

S

'spoiler n. (of car, aircraft) Spoiler, der

'spoilsport n. Spielverderber, der/
-verderberin, die

spoilt ▶ SPOIL 1, 2

spoke¹ /spəʊk/ n. Speiche, die

spoke², spoken ▶ SPEAK

spokesman /'spəʊksmən/ n., pl.
spokesmen /'spəʊksmən/ Sprecher, der

sponge /spʌndʒ/ ① n. Schwamm, der
② v.t. mit einem Schwamm waschen
■ **'sponge on** v.t. ~ **on sb.** bei od. von
jmdm. schnorren (ugs.)

sponge: ~ **bag** n. (Brit.) Kulturbeutel,
der; ~ **cake** n. Biskuitkuchen, der

sponger /'spʌndʒə(r)/ n. Schmarotzer,
der/Schmarotzerin, die

spongy /'spʌndʒɪ/ adj. schwammig

sponsor /'spɒnsə(r)/ ① n. Sponsor, der
② v.t. (a) sponsern
(b) (Polit.) ~ **sb.** jmds. Kandidatur
unterstützen

spontaneity /spɒntə'ni:ɪtɪ/ n.
Spontaneität, die

spontaneous /spɒn'teɪnɪəs/ adj. spontan

spooky /'spu:kɪ/ adj. gespenstisch

spool /spu:l/ n. Spule, die

spoon /spu:n/ n. (a) Löffel, der
(b) (amount) ▶ SPOONFUL

'spoon-feed v.t. (fig.) ~ **sb.** jmdm. alles
vorkauen (ugs.)

spoonful /'spu:nfʊl/ n. a ~ **of sugar** ein
Löffel [voll] Zucker

sporadic /spə'rædɪk/ adj. sporadisch

sporadically /spə'rædɪkəlɪ/ adv. hin und
wieder

spore /spɔ:(r)/ n. Spore, die

sport /spɔ:t/ ① n. (a) Sport, der; ~**s**
Sportarten Pl.; **water/indoor** ~: Wasser-/
Hallensport, der
(b) (fun) Spaß, der
(c) **be a [real]** ~ (coll.) ein prima Kerl sein
(ugs.); **be a** ~**!** sei kein Spielverderber!
② v.t. stolz tragen

'sporting adj. (a) sportlich
(b) **give sb. a** ~ **chance** jmdm. eine [faire]
Chance geben

sports: ~ **bra** n. Sport-BH, der;
~ **car** n. Sportwagen, der; ~ **centre**
n. Sportzentrum, das; ~ **channel** n.
Sportkanal, der; ~ **commentator** n.
Sportberichterstatter, der/
-berichterstatterin, die; ~ **complex** n.
Sportzentrum, das; ~ **field** n. Sportplatz,
der; ~ **hall** n. Sporthalle, die; ~ **jacket**
n. sportlicher Sakko; ~**man** /'spɔ:tsmən/
n., pl. ~**men** /'spɔ:tsmən/ Sportler,
der; ~**manship** /'spɔ:tsmənʃɪp/ n.
(fairness) [sportliche] Fairness; ~ **page**
n. (Journ.) Sportseite, die; ~ **section**
n. (Journ.) Sportteil, der; ~**wear** n.
Sport[be]kleidung, die; ~**woman** n.
Sportlerin, die

'sporty adj. sportlich

spot /spɒt/ ① n. (a) (precise place) Stelle,
die; **on this** ~: an dieser Stelle; **be in a tight**
~ (fig. coll.) in der Klemme sitzen (ugs.); **put**
sb. on the ~ (fig. coll.) jmdn. in Verlegenheit
bringen
(b) (suitable area) Platz, der
(c) (dot) Tupfen, der
(d) (stain) ~ **[of blood/grease/ink]** [Blut-/
Fett-/Tinten]fleck, der
(e) (Brit. coll.: small amount) **do a** ~ **of work/**
sewing ein bisschen arbeiten/nähen
(f) (drop) **a** ~ **or a few** ~**s of rain** ein paar
Regentropfen
(g) (Med.) Pickel, der
② v.t., **-tt-** (detect) entdecken; erkennen
⟨Gefahr⟩

spot: ~ '**check** n. Stichprobe, die;
~**less** adj. fleckenlos; **her house is**
absolutely ~**less** (fig.) ihr Haus ist makellos
sauber; ~**light** n. Scheinwerfer, der; **be in**
the ~**light** (fig.) im Rampenlicht stehen

spotted /'spɒtɪd/ adj. gepunktet

'spotty adj. (pimply) picklig

spouse /spaʊs/ n. [Ehe]gatte, der/-gattin,
die

spout /spaʊt/ ① n. Schnabel, der; (of tap)
Ausflussrohr, das
② v.i. (gush) schießen (**from** aus)

sprain /spreɪn/ ① v.t. verstauchen
② n. Verstauchung, die

sprang ▶ SPRING 2, 3

sprawl /sprɔ:l/ v.i. (a) sich ausstrecken;
(fall) der Länge nach hinfallen
(b) (straggle) sich ausbreiten

'sprawling attrib. adj. wuchernd
⟨Großstadt⟩

spray¹ /spreɪ/ (bouquet) Strauß, der

spray² ① v.t. spritzen; sprühen ⟨Parfüm⟩;
besprühen ⟨Haar, Pflanze⟩
② n. (a) (drops) Sprühnebel, der
(b) (liquid) Spray, der od. das

spray: ~ **can** ▶ AEROSOL A; ~ **gun** n.
Spritzpistole, die

spread /spred/ ① v.t., **spread**
(a) ausbreiten ⟨Tuch, Landkarte⟩ (**on**
auf + Dat.); streichen ⟨Butter, Farbe,
Marmelade⟩
(b) (extend range of) verbreiten
(c) (distribute) verteilen
② v.i., **spread** sich ausbreiten
③ n. (a) Verbreitung, die; (of city, poverty)
Ausbreitung, die
(b) (coll.: meal) Festessen, das
(c) (paste) Brotaufstrich, der
(d) (Printing) **the advertisement was a full-**
page/double-page ~: die Anzeige war
ganzseitig/doppelseitig
■ **spread 'out** ① v.t. ausbreiten
② v.i. sich verteilen

'spreadsheet n. (Comp.) Arbeitsblatt, das

spree /spri:/ n. **go on a shopping** ~: ganz
groß einkaufen gehen

spree killer ⋯▸ squeeze ⋯⋯

'spree killer *n.* Amokläufer, *der*

sprig /sprɪg/ *n.* Zweig, *der*

sprightly /'spraɪtlɪ/ *adj.* munter

spring /sprɪŋ/ **1** *n.* **(a)** (season) Frühling, *der;* **in [the]** ∼: im Frühling *od.* Frühjahr
(b) (water) Quelle, *die*
(c) (Mech.) Feder, *die*
(d) (jump) Sprung, *der*
2 *v.i.,* **sprang** /spræŋ/ *or* (Amer.) **sprung** /sprʌŋ/*,* **sprung (a)** (jump) springen; ∼ **to life** (fig.) [plötzlich] zum Leben erwachen
(b) (arise) entspringen **(from** *Dat.*)
3 *v.t.,* **sprang** *or* (Amer.) **sprung, sprung:** ∼ **sth. on sb.** jmdn. mit etw. überfallen

spring: ∼**board** *n.* Sprungbrett, *das;* ∼ **'chicken** *n.* **be no** ∼ **chicken** nicht mehr der/die Jüngste sein (ugs.); ∼**'clean** **1** *n.* Frühjahrsputz, *der;* **2** *v.t.* Frühjahrsputz machen in (+ *Dat.*); ∼**loaded** *adj.* mit Sprungfeder *nachgestellt;* ∼ **'onion** *n.* Frühlingszwiebel, *die;* ∼**time** *n.* Frühling, *der*

springy /'sprɪŋɪ/ *adj.* elastisch; federnd ‹Schritt, Brett, Boden›

sprinkle /'sprɪŋkl/ *v.t.* streuen; sprengen ‹Flüssigkeit›

sprinkler /'sprɪŋklə(r)/ *n.* (Hort.) Sprinkler, *der*

sprinkling /'sprɪŋklɪŋ/ *n.* **a** ∼ **of snow/sugar/dust** eine dünne Schneedecke/Zucker-/Staubschicht

sprint /sprɪnt/ **1** *v.t. & i.* rennen; sprinten (bes. Sport)
2 *n.* Sprint, *der*

sprout /spraʊt/ **1** *n.* **(a) Brussels** ∼**s** Rosenkohl, *der*
(b) (Bot.) Trieb, *der*
2 *v.i.* sprießen (geh.)

spruce /spruːs/ **1** *adj.* gepflegt
2 *n.* Fichte, *die*

sprung /sprʌŋ/ **1** ▶ SPRING 2, 3
2 *attrib. adj.* gefedert

spry /spraɪ/ *adj.* rege

spud /spʌd/ *n.* (coll.) Kartoffel, *die*

spun ▶ SPIN

spunk /spʌŋk/ *n.* (coll.: courage) Mumm, *der* (ugs.)

spur /spɜː(r)/ **1** *n.* Sporn, *der;* (fig.) Ansporn, *der;* **on the** ∼ **of the moment** ganz spontan
2 *v.t.,* **-rr-** (fig.) anspornen

spurious /'spjʊərɪəs/ *adj.* gespielt ‹Interesse›; unberechtigt ‹Anspruch, Anklage›

spurn /spɜːn/ *v.t.* zurückweisen

spurt¹ /spɜːt/ *n.* Spurt, *der;* **put on a** ∼: einen Spurt einlegen

spurt² /spɜːt/ **1** *v.i.* ∼ **out [from** *or* **of]** herausspritzen [aus]
2 *n.* Strahl, *der*

spy /spaɪ/ **1** *n.* Spion, *der*/Spionin, *die*

2 *v.i.* spionieren; ∼ **on sb.** jmdm. nachspionieren

spy: ∼**master** *n.* Chef, *der* eines Spionagerings; ∼ **ring** *n.* Spionagering, *der;* ∼ **story** *n.* Spionagegeschichte, *die*

squabble /'skwɒbl/ **1** *n.* Streit, *der*
2 *v.i.* sich zanken **(over, about** wegen)

squad /skwɒd/ *n.* **(a)** (Mil.) Gruppe, *die*
(b) (group) Mannschaft, *die*

squadron /'skwɒdrən/ *n.* **(a)** (Navy) Geschwader, *das*
(b) (Air Force) Staffel, *die*

squalid /'skwɒlɪd/ *adj.* **(a)** (dirty) schmutzig
(b) (poor) schäbig

squall /skwɔːl/ *n.* (gust) Bö, *die*

squalor /'skwɒlə(r)/ *n.* Schmutz, *der*

squander /'skwɒndə(r)/ *v.t.* vergeuden

square /skweə(r)/ **1** *n.* **(a)** (Geom.) Quadrat, *das*
(b) (open area) Platz, *der*
2 *adj.* **(a)** quadratisch
(b) a ∼ **metre/mile** ein Quadratmeter/eine Quadratmeile
(c) be all ∼: [völlig] quitt sein (ugs.)
3 *v.t.* **(a)** (Math.) quadrieren
(b) ∼ **it with sb.** es mit jmdm. klären
4 *v.i.* (agree) übereinstimmen
■ **square 'up** *v.i.* (settle up) abrechnen

square: ∼ **'brackets** *n. pl.* eckige Klammern *Pl.;* ∼ **'meal** *n.* anständige Mahlzeit (ugs.); ∼ **'root** *n.* Quadratwurzel, *die*

squash /skwɒʃ/ **1** *v.t.* (crush) zerquetschen; ∼ **sth. flat** etw. platt drücken
2 *n.* **(a)** Fruchtsaftgetränk, *das*
(b) (Sport) Squash, *das*

squash: ∼ **court** *n.* Squashfeld, *das;* ∼ **racket** *n.* Squashschläger, *der*

squat /skwɒt/ *v.i.,* **-tt-:** **(a)** (crouch) hocken
(b) ∼ **in a house** ein Haus besetzen

'squatter *n.* Hausbesetzer, *der*/-besetzerin, *die*

squawk /skwɔːk/ *v.i.* ‹Krähe:› krähen; ‹Huhn:› kreischen

squeak /skwiːk/ **1** *n.* **(a)** (of animal) Quieken, *das*
(b) (of brakes, hinge, etc.) Quietschen, *das*
2 *v.i.* **(a)** ‹Tier:› quieken
(b) ‹Scharnier, Tür, Bremse, Schuh usw.:› quietschen

squeaky /'skwiːkɪ/ *adj.* quietschend

squeal /skwiːl/ **1** *v.i.* **(a)** ∼ **with pain/in fear** ‹Person:› vor Schmerz/Angst aufschreien; ‹Tier:› vor Schmerz/Angst laut quieken
(b) ‹Bremsen, Räder:› kreischen; ‹Reifen:› quietschen
2 *n.* Kreischen, *das;* (of tyres) Quietschen, *das;* (of animal) Quieken, *das*

squeamish /'skwiːmɪʃ/ *adj.* **be** ∼: zart besaitet sein

squeeze /skwiːz/ **1** *n.* Druck, *der;* **give sth. a small** ∼: etw. [leicht] drücken ⋯▸

S

2 *v.t.* **(a)** (press) drücken; drücken auf (+ *Akk.*) 〈*Tube, Plastikflasche*〉; (to get juice) auspressen
(b) (extract) drücken (**out** of aus); ~ **out** sth. etw. herausdrücken
(c) (force) zwängen

squelch /skweltʃ/ *v.i.* quatschen (ugs.)

squid /skwɪd/ *n.* Kalmar, *der*

squiggle /'skwɪgl/ *n.* Schnörkel, *der*

squint /skwɪnt/ 1 *n.* Schielen, *das*
2 *v.i.* **(a)** (Med.) schielen
(b) (with half-closed eyes) blinzeln

squire /'skwaɪə(r)/ *n.* ≈ Gutsherr, *der*

squirm /skwɜːm/ *v.i.* sich winden (**with** vor + *Dat.*)

squirrel /'skwɪrl/ *n.* Eichhörnchen, *das*

squirt /skwɜːt/ 1 *v.t.* spritzen; sprühen 〈*Spray, Puder*〉; ~ sth. at sb. jmdn. mit etw. bespritzen/besprühen
2 *v.i.* spritzen
3 *n.* Spritzer, *der*

st. *abbr.* (Brit.: unit of weight) = **stone**

St *abbr.* = **Saint** St.

St. *abbr.* = **Street** Str.

stab /stæb/ 1 *v.t.*, **-bb-** stechen; ~ sb. **in the chest** jmdm. in die Brust stechen
2 *v.i.*, **-bb-** stechen
3 *n.* **(a)** Stich, *der*
(b) (coll.: attempt) **make** *or* **have a** ~ **[at it]** [es] probieren

stability /stə'bɪlɪtɪ/ *n.* Stabilität, *die*

stabilize /'steɪbɪlaɪz/ 1 *v.t.* stabilisieren
2 *v.i.* sich stabilisieren

stable[1] /'steɪbl/ *adj.* stabil; gefestigt 〈*Person*〉

stable[2] *n.* Stall, *der*

stack /stæk/ 1 *n.* **(a)** (pile) Stoß, *der;* Stapel, *der*
(b) (coll.: large amount) Haufen, *der* (ugs.)
(c) [chimney] ~: Schornstein, *der*
2 *v.t.* ~ **[up]** [auf]stapeln

stadium /'steɪdɪəm/ *n.* Stadion, *das*

staff /stɑːf/ 1 *n.* **(a)** (stick) Stock, *der*
(b) (personnel) Personal, *das;* (of school) Lehrerkollegium, *das*
2 *v.t.* mit Personal ausstatten

staff: ~ **meeting** *n.* [Lehrer]konferenz, *die;* ~**room** *n.* Lehrerzimmer, *das*

stag /stæg/ *n.* Hirsch, *der*

stage /steɪdʒ/ 1 *n.* **(a)** (Theatre) Bühne, *die*
(b) (part of process) Stadium, *das;* **at this** ~: in diesem Stadium; **do sth. by** ~s etw. abschnittsweise tun; **in the final** ~**s** in der Schlussphase
(c) (distance) Etappe, *die*
2 *v.t.* **(a)** (present) inszenieren
(b) (arrange) veranstalten

stage: ~**coach** *n.* Postkutsche, *die;* ~ **door** *n.* Bühneneingang, *der;* ~ **effect** *n.* Bühneneffekt, *der;* ~ **fright** *n.* Lampenfieber, *das;* ~**hand** *n.* Bühnenarbeiter, *der*/-arbeiterin, *die;*

~-**manage** *v.t.* (fig.) veranstalten; ~ **name** *n.* Künstlername, *der*

stagger /'stægə(r)/ 1 *v.i.* schwanken
2 *v.t.* (astonish) die Sprache verschlagen (+ *Dat.*)

stagnant /'stægnənt/ *adj.* **(a)** stehend 〈*Gewässer*〉
(b) (Econ.) stagnierend

stagnate /stæg'neɪt/ *v.i.* **(a)** 〈*Wasser:*〉 abstehen
(b) 〈*Wirtschaft, Geschäft:*〉 stagnieren; 〈*Person:*〉 abstumpfen

stagnation /stæg'neɪʃn/ *n.* **(a)** (of water) Stehen, *das*
(b) (Econ.) Stagnation, *die*

stag: ~ **night** *n.*: *Zechabend des Bräutigams mit seinen Freunden kurz vor seiner Hochzeit;* ~ **party** *n.* Herrenabend, *der*

staid /steɪd/ *adj.* gesetzt

stain /steɪn/ 1 *v.t.* **(a)** verfärben; (make ~s on) Flecken hinterlassen auf (+ *Dat.*)
(b) (colour) beizen 〈*Holz*〉
2 *n.* Fleck, *der*

stained 'glass *n.* farbiges Glas; ~ 'window Fenster mit Glasmalerei

'stainless *adj.* fleckenlos

stainless 'steel *n.* Edelstahl, *der*

'stain remover *n.* Fleck[en]entferner, *der*

stair /steə(r)/ *n.* (step) [Treppen]stufe, *die;* ~s Treppe, *die*

stair: ~**case** *n.* Treppenhaus, *das;* ~**way** *n.* Treppe, *die*

stake /steɪk/ *n.* **(a)** (pointed stick) Pfahl, *der*
(b) (wager) Einsatz, *der;* **be at** ~: auf dem Spiel stehen

stale /steɪl/ *adj.* alt; muffig; abgestanden 〈*Luft*〉; alt[backen] 〈*Brot*〉; schal 〈*Bier, Wein usw.*〉

'stalemate *n.* Patt, *das*

stalk[1] /stɔːk/ *v.t.* **(a)** sich heranpirschen an (+ *Akk.*)
(b) (follow obsessively) ~ sb. jmdm. nachstellen

stalk[2] *n.* (Bot.) (main stem) Stängel, *der;* (of leaf, flower, fruit) Stiel, *der*

stalker /'stɔːkə(r)/ *n.* (obsessive pursuer) [lästiger] Verfolger

stall /stɔːl/ 1 *n.* **(a)** Stand, *der*
(b) (Brit. Theatre) ~s Parkett, *das*
2 *v.t.* abwürgen (ugs.) 〈*Motor*〉
3 *v.i.* 〈*Motor:*〉 stehen bleiben

'stallholder *n.* Standinhaber, *der*/ -inhaberin, *die*

stallion /'stæljən/ *n.* Hengst, *der*

stalwart /'stɔːlwət/ *adj.* (determined) entschieden; (loyal) treu

stamen /'steɪmen/ *n.* Staubblatt, *das*

stamina /'stæmɪnə/ *n.* Ausdauer, *die*

stammer /'stæmə(r)/ 1 *v.i.* stottern
2 *v.t.* stammeln

|3| *n.* Stottern, *das*

stamp /stæmp/ |1| *v.t.* **(a)** (impress, imprint sth. on) [ab]stempeln
(b) ~ one's foot mit dem Fuß stampfen
(c) (put postage ~ on) frankieren; ~ed addressed envelope frankierter Rückumschlag
(d) become *or* be ~ed on sb.'s memory *or* mind sich jmdm. fest einprägen
|2| *v.i.* aufstampfen
|3| *n.* Marke, *die;* (postage ~) Briefmarke, *die;* (instrument for ~ing) Stempel, *der*
■ **'stamp on** *v.t.* **(a)** zertreten ⟨Insekt⟩; ~ on sb's foot jmdm. auf den Fuß treten
(b) (suppress) durchgreifen gegen
■ **stamp 'out** *v.t.* [aus]stanzen; (fig.) ausmerzen

stamp: ~ **album** *n.* Briefmarkenalbum, *das;* ~ **collecting** *n.* Briefmarkensammeln, *das;* ~ **collection** *n.* Briefmarkensammlung, *die;* ~ **duty** *n.* Stempelsteuer, *die*

stampede /stæm'pi:d/ *n.* Stampede, *die*

stance /stɑːns/ *n.* (posture; fig.: attitude) Haltung, *die*

stanch /stɑːnʃ/ *v.t.* stillen ⟨Blut⟩; abbinden ⟨Wunde⟩

stand /stænd/ |1| *v.i.,* stood /stʊd/
(a) stehen
(b) my offer/promise still ~s mein Angebot/Versprechen gilt nach wie vor; as it ~s, as things ~: wie die Dinge [jetzt] liegen; I'd like to know where I ~ (fig.) ich möchte wissen, wo ich dran bin
(c) (be candidate) kandidieren
(d) [not] ~ in sb.'s way (fig.) jmdm. [keine] Steine in den Weg legen
(e) (be likely) ~ to win *or* gain/lose sth. etw. gewinnen/verlieren können
|2| *v.t.,* stood **(a)** (set in position) stellen
(b) (endure) ertragen; I cannot ~ [the sight of] him/her ich kann ihn/sie nicht ausstehen; he can't ~ the pressure/strain er ist dem Druck/den Strapazen nicht gewachsen; I can't ~ it any longer! ich halte es nicht mehr aus!
(c) (buy) ~ sb. sth. jmdm. etw. spendieren
|3| *n.* **(a)** (support) Ständer, *der*
(b) (stall; at exhibition) Stand, *der*
(c) (raised structure) Tribüne, *die*
■ **stand a'bout, stand a'round** *v.i.* herumstehen
■ **stand a'side** *v.i.* zur Seite treten
■ **stand 'back** *v.i.* **(a)** ~ [well] back [from sth.] [ein gutes Stück] [von etw.] entfernt stehen
(b) (fig.: distance oneself) zurücktreten
■ **'stand between** *v.t.* sth. ~s between sb. and sth. (fig.) etw. steht jmdm. bei etw. im Wege
■ **stand by** |1| /'--/ *v.i.* **(a)** (be near) daneben stehen
(b) (be ready) sich zur Verfügung halten
|2| /'--/ *v.t.* **(a)** (support) ~ by sb./one another jmdm./sich [gegenseitig] beistehen

(b) (adhere to) ~ by sth. zu etw. stehen
■ **stand 'down** *v.i.* verzichten
■ **'stand for** *v.t.* **(a)** (signify) bedeuten
(b) (coll.: tolerate) sich ⟨Dat.⟩ bieten lassen
■ **stand 'in** *v.i.* aushelfen; ~ in for sb. für jmdn. einspringen
■ **stand 'out** *v.i.* (be prominent) herausragen; ~ out a mile (fig.) nicht zu übersehen sein
■ **'stand over** *v.t.* beaufsichtigen
■ **stand 'up** *v.i.* **(a)** aufstehen; ~ up straight sich aufrecht hinstellen
(b) ~ up well [in comparison with sb./sth.] [im Vergleich zu jmdm./etw.] gut abschneiden; ~ up for sb./sth. für jmdn./etw. Partei ergreifen; ~ up to sb. sich jmdm. entgegenstellen

stand-alone /stændə'ləʊn/ *adj.* (Comp.) selbstständig

standard /'stændəd/ |1| *n.* **(a)** Maßstab, *der;* safety ~s Sicherheitsnormen *Pl.;* above/below/up to ~: überdurchschnittlich [gut]/unter dem Durchschnitt/der Norm entsprechend
(b) (degree) Niveau, *das;* ~ of living Lebensstandard, *der*
(c) ~s (morals) Prinzipien *Pl.*
(d) (flag) Standarte, *die*
|2| *adj.* Standard-; be ~ practice allgemein üblich sein

standardize /'stændədaɪz/ *v.t.* standardisieren

'standard lamp *n.* Stehlampe, *die*

stand: ~-by |1| *n.* be on ~-by einsatzbereit sein; |2| *adj.* Ersatz-; ~-in |1| *n.* Ersatz, *der;* |2| *adj.* Ersatz-

'standing |1| *n.* **(a)** (repute) Ansehen, *das*
(b) (duration) of long/short ~: von langer/kurzer Dauer
|2| *adj.* **(a)** (erect) stehend
(b) fest ⟨Regel, Brauch⟩

standing: ~ **'order** *n.* Dauerauftrag, *der;* ~ o'vation *n.* stürmischer Beifall; ~ **room** *n.* Stehplätze *Pl.*

stand-offish /stænd'ɒfɪʃ/ *adj.* reserviert

stand: ~pipe *n.* Standrohr, *das;* ~point *n.* (fig.) Standpunkt, *der;* ~still *n.* Stillstand, *der;* be at a ~still stillstehen; come to a ~still zum Stehen kommen

stank ▶ STINK 1

staple[1] /'steɪpl/ |1| *n.* [Heft]klammer, *die*
|2| *v.t.* heften (on to an + *Akk.*)

staple[2] |1| *attrib. adj.* **(a)** Grund-; a ~ diet ein Grundnahrungsmittel
(b) (Commerc.) grundlegend; ~ goods Haupthandelsartikel *Pl.*
|2| *n.* (Commerc.: major item) Haupterzeugnis, *das*

stapler /'steɪplə(r)/ *n.* [Draht]hefter, *der*

star /stɑː(r)/ |1| *n.* **(a)** Stern, *der*
(b) (prominent person) Star, *der*
|2| *v.i.* ~ in a film in einem Film die Hauptrolle spielen

starboard /'stɑːbəd/ *n.* Steuerbord, *das*

starch /stɑːtʃ/ n. Stärke, die

starchy /'stɑːtʃɪ/ adj. stärkehaltig ⟨Nahrungsmittel⟩; (fig.: prim) steif

stardom /'stɑːdəm/ n. Starruhm, der

stare /steə(r)/ v.i. starren; ~ at sb./sth. jmdn./etw. anstarren

'**starfish** n. Seestern, der

stark /stɑːk/ **1** adj. scharf ⟨Kontrast, Umriss⟩
2 adv. völlig; ~ naked splitternackt (ugs.)

'**starless** adj. stern[en]los

starlet /'stɑːlɪt/ n. Starlet[t], das

starling /'stɑːlɪŋ/ n. Star, der

'**starlit** adj. sternhell

starry /'stɑːrɪ/ adj. sternklar

star: ~ **sign** n. Sternzeichen, das; ~-**studded** adj. ⟨Show, Film, Besetzung⟩ mit großem Staraufgebot

start /stɑːt/ **1** v.i. (a) (begin) anfangen; ~ on sth. etw. beginnen
(b) (set out) aufbrechen
(c) (begin to function) anlaufen; ⟨Auto, Motor usw.:⟩ anspringen
2 v.t. (a) (begin) beginnen [mit]; ~ doing or to do sth. [damit] anfangen, etw. zu tun
(b) (cause) auslösen; anfangen ⟨Streit, Schlägerei⟩; legen/(accidentally) verursachen ⟨Brand⟩
(c) (set up) ins Leben rufen ⟨Organisation, Projekt⟩
(d) (switch on) einschalten; anlassen ⟨Motor, Auto⟩
3 n. (a) Anfang, der; Beginn, der; (of race) Start, der; from the ~: von Anfang an; from ~ to finish von Anfang bis Ende; make a ~: anfangen (on mit); (on journey) aufbrechen
(b) (Sport: ~ing place) Start, der

'**starter** n. (a) (food) Vorspeise, die
(b) (Sport) Starter, der

starting /'stɑːtɪŋ/: ~ **point** n. (lit. or fig.) Ausgangspunkt, der; ~ **post** n. (Sport) Startpfosten, der; ~ **salary** n. Anfangsgehalt, das

startle /'stɑːtl/ v.t. erschrecken; be ~d by sth. über etw. (Akk.) erschrecken

startling /'stɑːtlɪŋ/ adj. erstaunlich

starvation /stɑː'veɪʃn/ n. Verhungern, das

starve /stɑːv/ v.i. ~ [to death] verhungern

stash /stæʃ/ (coll.) **1** v.t. ~ [away] verstecken
2 n. [geheimes] Lager

state /steɪt/ **1** n. (a) (condition) Zustand, der
(b) (nation) Staat, der
(c) be in a ~: aufgeregt sein
(d) lie in ~: aufgebahrt sein
2 v.t. (express) erklären; angeben ⟨Alter usw.⟩

stately /'steɪtlɪ/ adj. majestätisch; stattlich ⟨Körperbau, Gebäude⟩

stately '**home** n. Herrensitz, der

'**statement** n. (a) (stating, account) Aussage, die; (declaration) Erklärung, die
(b) [bank] ~: Kontoauszug, der

state: ~-**of-the-**'**art** adj. auf dem neuesten Stand der Technik nachgestellt; ~-**owned** adj. staatlich; ~ **school** n. (Brit.) staatliche Schule

statesman /'steɪtsmən/ n., pl. **statesmen** /'steɪtsmən/ Staatsmann, der

static /'stætɪk/ adj. statisch

static elec'tricity n. statische Elektrizität

station /'steɪʃn/ **1** n. (a) ▶ RAILWAY STATION
(b) (status) Rang, der
2 v.t. aufstellen ⟨Wache⟩

stationary /'steɪʃənərɪ/ adj. stehend; be ~: stehen

stationer /'steɪʃənə(r)/ n. ~'s [shop] Schreibwarengeschäft, das

stationery /'steɪʃənərɪ/ n. (a) (writing materials) Schreibwaren Pl.
(b) (writing paper) Briefpapier, das

'**station wagon** n. (Amer.) Kombiwagen, der

statistic /stə'tɪstɪk/ n. statistische Tatsache

statistical /stə'tɪstɪkl/ attrib. adj., **statistically** /stə'tɪstɪkəlɪ/ adv. statistisch

statistics /stə'tɪstɪks/ n. Statistik, die

statue /'stætʃuː, 'stætjuː/ n. Statue, die

statuesque /stætjʊ'esk/ adj. statuenhaft; (imposing) stattlich

stature /'stætʃə(r)/ n. Statur, die; (fig.) Format, das

status /'steɪtəs/ n. Rang, der; social ~: [gesellschaftlicher] Status

'**status symbol** n. Statussymbol, das

statute /'stætjuːt/ n. Gesetz, das

statutory /'stætjʊtərɪ/ adj. gesetzlich

staunch /stɔːntʃ/ adj. treu ⟨Freund⟩; überzeugt ⟨Katholik usw.⟩

stave /steɪv/ v.t. ~ 'off abwenden; stillen ⟨Hunger⟩

stay /steɪ/ **1** n. Aufenthalt, der; (visit) Besuch, der; come/go for a short ~ with sb. jmdn. kurz besuchen
2 v.i. bleiben; ~ put (coll.) ⟨Person:⟩ bleiben[, wo man ist]; ~ the night in a hotel die Nacht in einem Hotel verbringen
3 v.t. ~ the course (fig.) durchhalten
■ **stay a'head** v.i. die Führung halten
■ **stay a'way** v.i. wegbleiben
■ **stay be'hind** v.i. zurückbleiben
■ **stay 'in** v.i. zu Hause bleiben
■ **stay 'out** v.i. (a) (not go home) wegbleiben (ugs.)
(b) (remain outside) draußen bleiben
■ **stay 'over** v.i. (coll.) über Nacht bleiben
■ **stay 'up** v.i. aufbleiben

'**staying power** n. Durchhaltevermögen, das

stead /sted/ n. (a) in sb.'s ~: an jmds. Stelle (Dat.)

(b) stand sb. in good ∼: jmdm. zustatten kommen

steadfast /'stedfɑːst/ *adj.* standhaft; zuverlässig ⟨*Freund*⟩

steadily /'stedɪlɪ/ *adv.* **(a)** (stably) fest **(b)** (continuously) stetig

steady /'stedɪ/ **1** *adj.* **(a)** (stable) stabil; (not wobbling) standfest
(b) (still) ruhig
(c) (regular, constant) stetig; gleichmäßig ⟨*Arbeit, Tempo*⟩; stabil ⟨*Preis, Lohn*⟩; gleich bleibend ⟨*Temperatur*⟩; **we had** ∼ **rain/drizzle** wir hatten Dauerregen/es nieselte [bei uns] ständig
(d) a ∼ **job** eine feste Stelle; **a** ∼ **boyfriend** ein fester Freund
2 *v.t.* festhalten ⟨*Leiter*⟩; beruhigen ⟨*Nerven*⟩

steak /steɪk/ *n.* Steak, *das*

'steak knife *n.* Messer mit Sägezahnung

steal /stiːl/ **1** *v.t.*, **stole** /stəʊl/, **stolen** /'stəʊln/ stehlen (**from** *Dat.*)
2 *v.i.*, **stole, stolen (a)** stehlen; ∼ **from sb.** jmdn. bestehlen
(b) ∼ **in/out** sich hinein-/hinausstehlen

stealth /stelθ/ *n.* Heimlichkeit, *die;* **by** ∼: heimlich

stealthy /'stelθɪ/ *adj.* heimlich

steam /stiːm/ **1** *n.* Dampf, *der;* **let off** ∼ (fig.) Dampf ablassen (ugs.); **run out of** ∼ (fig.) den Schwung verlieren; **under one's own** ∼ (fig.) aus eigener Kraft
2 *v.t.* (Cookery) dämpfen; dünsten
3 *v.i.* dämpfen; ∼**ing hot** dampfend heiß
■ **steam a'head** *v.i.* (fig. coll.) rasche Fortschritte machen
■ **steam 'up** *v.i.* beschlagen

steam: ∼**boat** *n.* Dampfschiff, *das;* (small) Dampfboot, *das;* ∼ **engine** *n.* Dampflok[omotive], *die;* (stationary) Dampfmaschine, *die*

'steamer *n.* Dämpfer, *der*

steam: ∼ **iron** *n.* Dampfbügeleisen, *das;* ∼**roller** *n.* Dampfwalze, *die;* ∼ **train** *n.* Dampfzug, *der*

'steamy *adj.* dunstig; beschlagen ⟨*Glas*⟩

steel /stiːl/ **1** *n.* Stahl, *der*
2 *attrib. adj.* stählern; Stahl⟨*helm, -block, -platte*⟩
3 *v.t.* ∼ **oneself for/against sth.** sich für/gegen etw. wappnen (geh.); ∼ **oneself to do sth.** allen Mut zusammennehmen, um etw. zu tun

steel: ∼ **'band** *n.* (Mus.) Steelband, *die;* ∼ **'drum** *n.* (Mus.) Steeldrum, *die;* ∼ **industry** *n.* Stahlindustrie, *die;* ∼ **'wool** *n.* Stahlwolle, *die;* ∼**works** *n. sing. or pl.* Stahlwerk, *das*

steep¹ /stiːp/ *adj.* **(a)** steil
(b) (coll.: excessive) happig (ugs.); **the bill is [a bit]** ∼: die Rechnung ist [ziemlich] gesalzen (ugs.)

steep² *v.t.* (soak) einweichen

steeped /stiːpt/ *adj.* durchdrungen (**in** von)

steeple /'stiːpl/ *n.* Kirchturm, *der*

steer /stɪə(r)/ **1** *v.t.* steuern; lenken
2 *v.i.* steuern; ∼ **clear of sb./sth.** (fig. coll.) jmdm./einer Sache aus dem Weg[e] gehen

'steering *n.* (Motor Veh.) Lenkung, *die*

steering: ∼ **column** *n.* Lenksäule, *die;* ∼ **lock** *n.* Lenkradschloss, *das;* ∼ **wheel** *n.* Lenkrad, *das*

stem¹ /stem/ **1** *n.* **(a)** (Bot.) Stiel, *der*
(b) (Ling.) Stamm, *der*
2 *v.i.*, **-mm-:** ∼ **from sth.** auf etw. (*Akk.*) zurückzuführen sein

stem² *v.t.*, **-mm-** (check, dam up) aufhalten; eindämmen ⟨*Flut*⟩; stillen ⟨*Blutung*⟩

'stem cell *n.* (Biol.) Stammzelle, *die; attrib.* ∼ **research** Stammzellenforschung, *die*

stench /stentʃ/ *n.* Gestank, *der*

stencil /'stensl/ *n.* Schablone, *die;* (for duplicating) Matrize, *die*

step /step/ **1** *n.* **(a)** (stride) Schritt, *der;* **take a** ∼ **back/forwards** einen Schritt zurücktreten/nach vorn treten
(b) (stair) Stufe, *die;* **a flight of** ∼**s** eine Treppe; **[pair of]** ∼**s** (ladder) Stehleiter, *die*
(c) be in ∼: im Schritt sein; (with music) im Takt sein
(d) take ∼**s to do sth.** Schritte unternehmen, um etw. zu tun
(e) (stage) ∼ **by** ∼: Schritt für Schritt; **what is the next** ∼? wie geht es weiter?
(f) (grade) Stufe, *die*
2 *v.i.*, **-pp-** treten; ∼ **inside** eintreten; ∼ **into sb's shoes** (fig.) an jmds. Stelle treten; ∼ **over sb./sth.** über jmdn./etw. steigen
■ **step 'back** *v.i.* zurücktreten
■ **step 'in** *v.i.* **(a)** eintreten
(b) (fig.) (take sb.'s place) einspringen; (intervene) eingreifen
■ **step 'up** **1** *v.i.* (ascend) hinaufsteigen
2 *v.t.* erhöhen; verstärken ⟨*Anstrengungen*⟩

step: ∼ **aerobics** *n.* Stepaerobic, *das;* ∼**child** *n.* Stiefkind, *das;* ∼**daughter** *n.* Stieftochter, *die;* ∼**father** *n.* Stiefvater, *der;* ∼**ladder** *n.* Stehleiter, *die;* ∼**mother** *n.* Stiefmutter, *die*

'stepping stone *n.* Trittstein, *der;* (fig.) Sprungbrett, das (**to** für)

stereo /'sterɪəʊ/ **1** *n.* Stereo, *das;* (equipment) Stereoanlage, *die*
2 *adj.* stereo; Stereo⟨*aufnahme, -platte*⟩

stereophonic /sterɪə'fɒnɪk/ *adj.* stereophon

stereotype /'sterɪətaɪp/ **1** *n.* Stereotyp, *das*
2 *v.t.* in ein Klischee zwängen; ∼**d** stereotyp

sterile /'steraɪl/ *adj.* steril

sterility /stə'rɪlɪtɪ/ *n.* Sterilität, *die*

sterilization /sterɪlaɪ'zeɪʃn/ *n.* Sterilisation, *die*

sterilize /'sterɪlaɪz/ *v.t.* sterilisieren

sterling /'stɜːlɪŋ/ ① n. Sterling, der; in
~: in Pfund [Sterling]
② attrib. adj. (a) ~ silver Sterlingsilber, das
(b) (fig.) gediegen

stern¹ /stɜːn/ adj. streng; ernst ⟨Warnung⟩

stern² n. (Naut.) Heck, das

'sternly adv. streng

steroid /'steroɪd/ n. Steroid, das

stethoscope /'steθəskəʊp/ n.
Stethoskop, das

stew /stjuː/ ① n. Eintopf, der
② v.t. schmoren [lassen]

steward /'stjuːəd/ n. (a) (on ship, plane)
Steward, der
(b) (at public meeting etc.) Ordner, der

'stewardess n. Stewardess, die

stewed /stjuːd/ adj. (Cookery) geschmort

'stewing steak n.
[Rinder]schmorfleisch, das

stick /stɪk/ ① v.t., stuck /stʌk/ (a) (thrust
point of) stecken; ~ sth. in[to] sth. mit etw. in
etw. (Akk.) stechen
(b) (coll.: put) stecken; ~ a picture on the
wall/a vase on the shelf ein Bild an die
Wand hängen/eine Vase aufs Regal stellen;
~ sth. in the kitchen etw. in die Küche tun
(ugs.)
(c) (with glue etc.) kleben
(d) the car is stuck in the mud das Auto ist
im Schlamm stecken geblieben; the door is
stuck die Tür klemmt [fest]
② v.i., stuck (a) (be fixed by point) stecken
(b) (adhere) kleben; ~ to sth. an etw. (Dat.)
kleben
(c) (become immobile) ⟨Auto, Räder:⟩ stecken
bleiben; ⟨Schublade, Tür, Griff, Bremse:⟩
klemmen; ⟨Schlüssel:⟩ feststecken
③ n. Stock, der; a ~ of chalk ein Stück
Kreide; a ~ of celery/rhubarb eine Stange
Sellerie/Rhabarber
■ **stick a'bout, stick a'round** v.i.
(coll.) dableiben; (wait) warten
■ **'stick by** v.t. (fig.) stehen zu
■ **stick 'on** v.t. (glue on) aufkleben
■ **stick 'out** ① v.t. (a) herausstrecken
⟨Zunge⟩
(b) ~ it out (coll.) durchhalten
② v.i. (a) ⟨Bauch:⟩ vorstehen; his ears
~ out er hat abstehende Ohren
(b) (fig.: be obvious) sich abheben; ~ out a
mile (coll.) [klar] auf der Hand liegen; ~ out
like a sore thumb (coll.) ins Auge springen
■ **'stick to** v.t. (a) (be faithful to) halten
⟨Versprechen⟩; bleiben bei ⟨Entscheidung⟩
(b) ~ to the point beim Thema bleiben
■ **stick to'gether** v.i. zusammenkleben;
(fig.) zusammenhalten.
■ **stick 'up** ① v.t. (a) (coll.) anschlagen
⟨Poster⟩; ~ up one's hand die Hand heben
(b) (seal) zukleben
② v.i. ~ up for sb./sth. für jmdn./etw.
eintreten; ~ up for yourself! setz dich zur
Wehr!

stick de'odorant n. Deo[dorant]stift, der

'sticker n. Aufkleber, der

'sticking plaster n. Heftpflaster, das

stickler /'stɪklə(r)/ n. be a ~ for tidiness/
authority es mit der Sauberkeit sehr genau
nehmen/in puncto Autorität keinen Spaß
verstehen

'stick-up n. (coll.) bewaffneter Raubüberfall

'sticky adj. (a) klebrig; ~ label Aufkleber,
der
(b) (humid) schwül ⟨Klima, Luft⟩

stiff /stɪf/ adj. (a) (rigid) steif; hart ⟨Bürste,
Stock⟩; be frozen ~: steif vor Kälte sein
(b) (intense, severe) hartnäckig
(c) (formal) steif
(d) (difficult) hart ⟨Test⟩; schwer ⟨Frage,
Prüfung⟩
(e) (coll.) be bored/scared ~: sich zu Tode
langweilen/eine wahnsinnige Angst haben
(ugs.)

stiffen /'stɪfn/ ① v.t. steif machen
② v.i. steifer werden; ⟨Person:⟩ erstarren

'stiffness n. Steifheit, die

stifle /'staɪfl/ ① v.t. ersticken; (fig.)
unterdrücken
② v.i. ersticken

stifling /'staɪflɪŋ/ adj. stickig; drückend
⟨Hitze⟩

stigma /'stɪgmə/ n. Stigma, das (geh.)

stile /staɪl/ n. Zauntritt, der

stiletto /stɪ'letəʊ/ n. ~ [heel]
Stöckelabsatz, der

still¹ /stɪl/ ① pred. adj. still; be ~: [still]
stehen; hold sth. ~: etw. ruhig halten; keep
or stay ~: stillhalten; stand ~: stillstehen
② adv. (a) (without change) noch; expr.
surprise or annoyance immer noch
(b) (nevertheless) trotzdem
(c) with comparative (even) noch

still² n. Destillierapparat, der

still: ~ **birth** n. Totgeburt, die; ~**born** adj.
tot geboren; ~ **'life** n. (Art) Stillleben, das

stilt /stɪlt/ n. Stelze, die

'stilted adj. gestelzt

stimulant /'stɪmjʊlənt/ n. Stimulans, das

stimulate /'stɪmjʊleɪt/ v.t. anregen

stimulation /stɪmjʊ'leɪʃn/ n. Anregung, die

stimulus /'stɪmjʊləs/ n., pl. stimuli
/'stɪmjʊlaɪ/ Ansporn, der

sting /stɪŋ/ ① n. (a) (wounding) Stich, der;
(by jellyfish, nettles) Verbrennung, die
(b) (from ointment, wind) Brennen, das
② v.t., stung /stʌŋ/ stechen
③ v.i., stung brennen

'stinging nettle n. Brennnessel, die

stingy /'stɪndʒɪ/ adj. geizig; knaus[e]rig
(ugs.)

stink /stɪŋk/ ① v.i., stank /stæŋk/ or stunk
/stʌŋk/, stunk stinken (of nach)
② n. Gestank, der

'stink bomb n. Stinkbombe, die

stint /stɪnt/ ① v.i. ~ on sth. an etw. (Dat.)
sparen

2 n. [Arbeits]pensum, *das*

stipulate /'stɪpjʊleɪt/ v.t. (demand) fordern; (lay down) festlegen

stipulation /stɪpjʊ'leɪʃn/ n. (condition) Bedingung, *die*

stir /stɜː(r)/ **1** v.t., -rr-: (a) (mix) rühren; umrühren ‹Tee, Kaffee›
(b) (move) bewegen
2 v.i., -rr- (move) sich rühren
3 n. Aufregung, *die*
■ **stir 'in** v.t. einrühren
■ **stir 'up** v.t. (a) (disturb) aufrühren
(b) (fig.: arouse) wecken ‹Interesse, Leidenschaft›

stirring /'stɜːrɪŋ/ adj. bewegend ‹Musik, Poesie›; mitreißend ‹Rede›

stirrup /'stɪrəp/ n. Steigbügel, *der*

stitch /stɪtʃ/ **1** n. (a) (Sewing) Stich, *der;* (Knitting) Masche, *die*
(b) (pain) have a ∼: Seitenstechen haben
2 v.t. nähen
■ **stitch 'up** v.t. (a) nähen; vernähen ‹Loch, Riss, Wunde›
(b) (Brit. fig. coll.: betray, cheat) reinlegen (ugs.); linken (salopp)

stoat /stəʊt/ n. Hermelin, *das*

stock /stɒk/ **1** n. (a) (origin, family, breed) Abstammung, *die*
(b) (supply, store) Vorrat, *der;* (in shop etc.) Warenbestand, *der;* be in/out of ∼ ‹Ware:› vorrätig/nicht vorrätig sein; have sth. in ∼: etw. auf Lager haben; take ∼ of sth. (fig.) über etw. (Akk.) Bilanz ziehen
(c) (Cookery) Brühe, *die*
2 v.t. (a) (supply with ∼) beliefern
(b) (Commerc.: keep in ∼) auf Lager haben
3 attrib. adj. Standard-

stock: ∼**broker** Effektenmakler, *der/* -maklerin, *die;* ∼ **cube** n. Brühwürfel, *der;* ∼ **exchange** n. Börse, *die.*

stocking /'stɒkɪŋ/ n. Strumpf, *der*

'**stockist** n. Fachhändler, *der/*-händlerin, *die*

stock: ∼ **market** n. (a) Börse, *die;*
(b) (trading) Börsengeschäft, *das;* ∼ **market crash** Börsenkrach, *der;* ∼**pile** **1** n. Vorrat, *der;* (weapons) Arsenal, *das;* **2** v.t. horten; anhäufen ‹Waffen›; ∼**pot** n. Suppentopf, *der;* ∼**room** n. Lager, *das;* ∼-'**still** pred. adj. bewegungslos; ∼**taking** n. Inventur, *die*

stocky /'stɒkɪ/ adj. stämmig

stodgy /'stɒdʒɪ/ adj. pappig

stoical /'stəʊɪkl/ adj. stoisch

stoicism /'stəʊɪsɪzm/ n. Stoizismus, *der*

stoke /stəʊk/ v.t. heizen ‹Ofen, Kessel›; unterhalten ‹Feuer›

stole ▶ STEAL

stolen /'stəʊln/ **1** ▶ STEAL
2 attrib. adj. heimlich ‹Vergnügen, Kuss›

stolid /'stɒlɪd/ adj. stur (ugs.)

stomach /'stʌmək/ **1** n. (a) Magen, *der*

(b) (abdomen) Bauch, *der*
2 v.t. (fig.: tolerate) ausstehen

stomach: ∼ **ache** n. Magenschmerzen Pl.; have a ∼ ache Magenschmerzen haben; ∼ **upset** n. Magenverstimmung, *die*

stone /stəʊn/ **1** n. (a) Stein, *der;* a ∼'s throw [away] (fig.) nur einen Steinwurf weit entfernt; be written or carved or set in ∼ (fig.) unverrückbar sein
(b) (Brit.: weight unit) Gewicht von 6,35 kg
2 adj. steinern; Stein‹mauer, -brücke›
3 v.t. mit Steinen bewerfen

stone: **S∼ Age** n. Steinzeit, *die;* ∼-**cold** adj. eiskalt

stoned /stəʊnd/ adj. (sl.) stoned (Drogenjargon); (drunk) voll zu (salopp)

stone: ∼-'**dead** pred. adj. mausetot (fam.); kill sth. ∼-dead (fig.) etw. völlig zunichte machen; ∼-'**deaf** adj. stocktaub (ugs.); ∼**mason** n. Steinmetz, *der;* ∼'**wall** (Brit.) v.i. mauern (fig.); ∼**ware** n., no pl. Steingut, *das; attrib.* ‹Krug, Vase› aus Steingut; ∼**washed** adj. mit Steinen ausgewaschen; ∼**work** n. Mauerwerk, *das*

stony /'stəʊnɪ/ adj. steinig

stood ▶ STAND 1, 2

stool /stuːl/ n. Hocker, *der*

stoop /stuːp/ **1** v.i. ∼ [down] sich bücken
2 n. walk with a ∼: gebeugt gehen

stop /stɒp/ **1** v.t., -pp-: (a) anhalten ‹Person, Fahrzeug›; aufhalten ‹Fortschritt, Verkehr, Feind›
(b) (not let continue) unterbrechen ‹Redner, Spiel, Gespräch›; beenden ‹Krieg, Arbeit›; stoppen ‹Produktion, Uhr›; einstellen ‹Zahlung, Lieferung›; ∼ that! hör damit auf!; ∼ smoking/crying aufhören zu rauchen/weinen
(c) (not let happen) verhindern ‹Verbrechen, Unfall›; ∼ sth. [from] happening verhindern, dass etw. geschieht
(d) (switch off) abstellen ‹Maschine›
(e) (block up) zustopfen ‹Loch›; verschließen ‹Wasserhahn, Flasche›
(f) ∼ a cheque einen Scheck sperren lassen
2 v.i., -pp-: (a) (not extend further) aufhören; ‹Zahlungen, Lieferungen:› eingestellt werden
(b) (not move further) ‹Fahrzeug, Fahrer:› halten; ‹Maschine, Motor:› stillstehen; ‹Uhr, Fußgänger, Herz:› stehen bleiben
3 n. (a) (halt) Halt, *der;* bring to a ∼: zum Stehen bringen ‹Fahrzeug›; zum Erliegen bringen ‹Verkehr›; unterbrechen ‹Arbeit›; come to a ∼: stehen bleiben; ‹Fahrzeug:› zum Stehen kommen; ‹Arbeit, Verkehr:› zum Erliegen kommen; put a ∼ to abstellen ‹Missstände, Unsinn›
(b) (place) Haltestelle, *die*
■ **stop 'by** v.i. (Amer.) vorbeischauen (ugs.)
■ **stop 'out** v.i. (coll.) draußen bleiben
■ **stop 'over** v.i. (coll.) übernachten (at bei)
■ **stop 'up** **1** v.t. zustopfen ‹Loch, Öffnung›
2 v.i. (coll.) ▶ STAY UP ┈┈╌>

S

stop: ∼ **button** n. Stopptaste, die; ∼**cock** n. Abstellhahn, der; ∼**gap** n. Notlösung, die; ∼ **light** n. (traffic light) rotes Licht; ∼**over** n. Stopover, der

stoppage /'stɒpɪdʒ/ n. (a) (halt) Stillstand, der; (strike) Streik, der (b) (deduction) Abzug, der

'**stoppage time** n., no pl. (Sport) Nachspielzeit, die

stopper /'stɒpə(r)/ n. Stöpsel, der

stopping /'stɒpɪŋ/: ∼ **distance** n. Anhalteweg, der; ∼ **place,** ∼ **point** ns. Station, die

stop: ∼**press** n. letzte Meldung/ Meldungen Pl.; ∼ **sign** n. Stoppschild, das; ∼ **signal** n. Haltesignal, das; ∼**watch** n. Stoppuhr, die

storage /'stɔːrɪdʒ/ n. Lagerung, die; (of films, books, documents) Aufbewahrung, die; (of data, water, electricity) Speicherung, die

storage: ∼ **capacity** n. (Comp.) Speicherkapazität, die; ∼ **device** n. (Comp.) Speichermedium, das; ∼ **heater** n. [Nacht]speicherofen, der; ∼ **space** n. Lagerraum, der; (in house) Platz [zum Aufbewahren]; ∼ **tank** n. Sammelbehälter, der

store /stɔː(r)/ ① n. (a) (Amer.: shop) Laden, der (b) (Brit.: large general shop) Kaufhaus, das (c) (warehouse) Lager, das; put sth. in ∼: etw. einlagern (d) (stock) Vorrat, der (of an + Dat.); be or lie in ∼ for sb. jmdn. erwarten (e) set [great] ∼ by or on sth. [großen] Wert auf etw. (Akk.) legen ② v.t. einlagern; speichern ⟨Getreide, Energie, Wissen, Daten⟩ ■ **store** '**up** v.t. speichern; ∼ up provisions sich (Dat.) Vorräte anlegen

store: ∼ **detective** n. Kaufhausdetektiv, der; ∼**house** n. Lager[haus], das; ∼**keeper** n. (Amer.: shopkeeper) Besitzer eines Einzelhandelsgeschäftes; ∼**room** n. Lagerraum, der

storey /'stɔːrɪ/ n. Stockwerk, das

stork /stɔːk/ n. Storch, der

storm /stɔːm/ ① n. Unwetter, das; (thunder∼) Gewitter, das ② v.t. & i. stürmen

'**storm damage** n. Sturmschaden, der (meist Pl.)

'**stormy** adj. stürmisch

story[1] /'stɔːrɪ/ n. (a) Geschichte, die (b) (news item) Bericht, der (c) (coll.: lie) Märchen, das

story[2] (Amer.) ▶ STOREY

'**story book** n. Geschichtenbuch, das; (with fairy tales) Märchenbuch, das

stout /staʊt/ adj. (a) (strong) fest (b) (fat) beleibt

stove /stəʊv/ n. Ofen, der; (for cooking) Herd, der

stow /stəʊ/ v.t. verstauen (into in + Dat.)

■ **stow a**'**way** ① v.t. verwahren ② v.i. als blinder Passagier reisen

straddle /'strædl/ v.t. ∼ a fence/chair rittlings auf einem Zaun/Stuhl sitzen

straggle /'strægl/ v.i. ∼ [along] behind the others den anderen hinterherzockeln (ugs.)

straggler /'stræglə(r)/ n. Nachzügler, der

straggly /'stræglɪ/ zottig ⟨Haar, Bart⟩

straight /streɪt/ ① adj. (a) gerade; glatt ⟨Haar⟩; in a ∼ line in gerader Linie (b) (undiluted) drink whisky ∼: Whisky pur trinken (c) (direct) direkt ⟨Blick, Schuss, Weg⟩; be ∼ with sb. zu jmdm. offen sein; get sth. ∼ (fig.) etw. genau verstehen; put or set the record ∼: die Sache richtig stellen ② adv. (a) gerade (b) (directly) geradewegs; ∼ after sofort nach; come ∼ to the point direkt zur Sache kommen; look sb. ∼ in the eye jmdm. direkt in die Augen blicken; ∼ ahead or on immer geradeaus (c) (frankly) aufrichtig (d) (clearly) klar ⟨sehen, denken⟩

straight a'**way** adv. sofort

straighten /'streɪtn/ ① v.t. (a) gerade ziehen ⟨Teppich⟩; glätten ⟨Kleidung, Haare⟩ (b) (put in order) aufräumen ② v.i. gerade werden ■ **straighten** '**out** ① v.t. (a) gerade biegen; glätten ⟨Decke, Teppich⟩ (b) (clear up) klären ② v.i. gerade werden ■ **straighten** '**up** ① v.t. ▶ TIDY UP ② v.i. sich aufrichten

straight: ∼ '**face** n. with a ∼ face ohne eine Miene zu verziehen; keep a ∼ face keine Miene verziehen; ∼**-faced** adj. mit unbewegter Miene nachgestellt; ∼'**forward** adj. (a) (frank) freimütig; schlicht ⟨Stil, Sprache, Bericht⟩; klar ⟨Anweisung, Vorstellungen⟩; (b) (simple) einfach

strain /streɪn/ ① n. (a) (pull) Belastung, die; (on rope) Spannung, die (b) (tension) Stress, der; be under [a great deal of] ∼: unter großem Stress stehen (c) (person, thing) be a ∼ on sb./sth. jmdn./ etw. belasten (d) (muscular injury) Zerrung, die ② v.t. (a) (overexert) überanstrengen; zerren ⟨Muskel⟩ (b) (stretch tightly) [fest] spannen (c) (filter) durchseihen; seihen (through durch) ③ v.i. (strive intensely) sich anstrengen

strained /streɪnd/ adj. gezwungen ⟨Lächeln⟩; ∼ relations gespannte Beziehungen Pl.

'**strainer** n. Sieb, das

strait /streɪt/ n. (a) in sing. or pl. (Geog.) Meerenge, die (b) usu. in pl. (distress, difficulty)

Schwierigkeiten *Pl.*

strait: ~**jacket** *n.* Zwangsjacke, *die;* ~**-laced** /streɪt'leɪst/ *adj.* puritanisch

strand[1] /strænd/ *n.* (thread) Faden, *der;* (of beads) Kette, *die;* (of hair) Strähne, *die;* (of rope) Strang, *der*

strand[2] *v.t.* (leave behind) trockensetzen; **be [left]** ~**ed** festsitzen (fig.) seinem Schicksal überlassen sein

strange /streɪndʒ/ *adj.* (peculiar) seltsam; sonderbar; ~ **to say** seltsamerweise; **feel** ~: sich komisch fühlen

strangely /'streɪndʒlɪ/ *adv.* seltsam

stranger /'streɪndʒə(r)/ *n.* Fremde, *der/die;* **he is a** ~ **here/to the town** er ist hier/in der Stadt fremd; **be a/no** ~ **to sth.** etw. nicht gewöhnt/etw. gewöhnt sein

strangle /'stræŋgl/ *v.t.* erwürgen

stranglehold *n.* Würgegriff, *der*

strangulation /stræŋgjʊ'leɪʃn/ *n.* Erwürgen, *das*

strap /stræp/ [1] *n.* **(a)** (leather) Riemen, *der;* (textile) Band, *das;* (shoulder ~) Träger, *der;* (for watch) Armband, *das* **(b)** (to grasp in vehicle) Halteriemen, *der* [2] *v.t.,* -**pp**-: ~ **[into position]/down** festschnallen; ~ **oneself in** sich anschnallen

strapless *adj.* trägerlos

strapping /'stræpɪŋ/ *adj.* stramm

strata *pl. of* STRATUM

strategic /strə'tiːdʒɪk/ *adj.* strategisch

strategically /strə'tiːdʒɪkəlɪ/ *adv.* strategisch

strategist /'strætɪdʒɪst/ *n.* Stratege, *der*/Strategin, *die*

strategy /'strætɪdʒɪ/ *n.* Strategie, *die*

stratosphere /'strætəsfɪə(r)/ *n.* Stratosphäre, *die*

stratum /'strɑːtəm/ *n.,* *pl.* **strata** /'strɑːtə/ Schicht, *die*

straw /strɔː/ *n.* **(a)** *no pl.* Stroh, *das* **(b)** (single stalk) Strohhalm, *der;* **that's the last or final** ~: jetzt reichts aber **(c)** [drinking] ~: Strohhalm, *der*

strawberry /'strɔːbərɪ/ *n.* Erdbeere, *die*

stray /streɪ/ [1] *v.i.* **(a)** (wander) streunen **(b)** (deviate) abweichen **(from** von) [2] *n.* (animal) streunendes Tier [3] *adj.* **(a)** streunend **(b)** (occasional) vereinzelt

streak /striːk/ *n.* Streifen, *der;* (in hair) Strähne, *die;* **have a jealous/cruel** ~: zur Eifersucht/Grausamkeit neigen

streaky *adj.* streifig; ~ **bacon** durchwachsener Speck

stream /striːm/ [1] *n.* (of water) Wasserlauf, *der;* (brook) Bach, *der* [2] *v.i.* strömen; (Sonnenlicht:) fluten; **have a** ~**ing cold** einem schlimmen Schnupfen haben

streamer /'striːmə(r)/ *n.* (ribbon) Band, *das;* (of paper) Luftschlange, *die*

streamline *v.t.* [eine] Stromlinienform geben (+ *Dat.*); **be** ~**lined** eine Stromlinienform haben

street /striːt/ *n.* Straße, *die;* **in the** ~: auf der Straße; **in** (Brit.) *or* **on ... Street** in der ...straße

street: ~**car** *n.* (Amer.) Straßenbahn, *die;* ~ **cred** /'striːt kred/ (coll.), ~ **credibility** *ns.* [glaubwürdiges] Image; ~ **crime** *n.,* *no indef. art.* Straßenkriminalität, *die;* ~ **lamp** *n.* Straßenlaterne, *die;* ~ **lighting** *n.* Straßenbeleuchtung, *die;* ~ **map** *n.* Stadtplan, *der;* ~ **market** *n.* Straßenmarkt, *der;* ~ **plan** *n.* Stadtplan, *der;* ~ **sweeper** *n.* **(a)** (person) Straßenfeger, *der*/-fegerin, *die* (bes. nordd.); Straßenkehrer, *der*/-kehrerin, *die* (bes. südd.); **(b)** (vehicle) Straßenkehrmaschine, *die;* ~ **vendor** *n.* Straßenhändler, *der*/-händlerin, *die;* ~**-wise** *adj.* (coll.) **be** ~**-wise** wissen, wo es langgeht

strength /streŋθ/ *n.* (power) Kraft, *die;* (strong point, force, intensity, amount of ingredient) Stärke, *die;* (of poison, medicine) Wirksamkeit, *die;* **not know one's own** ~: nicht wissen, wie stark man ist; **give sb.** ~: jmdn. stärken; **go from** ~ **to** ~: immer erfolgreicher werden; **on the** ~ **of sth./that** aufgrund einer Sache (*Gen.*)/dessen; **in full** ~: in voller Stärke; **the police were there in** ~: ein starkes Polizeiaufgebot war da

strengthen /'streŋθən/ *v.t.* stärken; (reinforce, intensify) verstärken

strenuous /'strenjʊəs/ *adj.* **(a)** (energetic) energisch; gewaltig (Anstrengung) **(b)** (requiring exertion) anstrengend

stress /stres/ [1] *n.* **(a)** (strain) Stress, *der;* **be under** ~: unter Stress (*Dat.*) stehen **(b)** (emphasis) Betonung, *die* [2] *v.t.* (emphasize) betonen

stressed out *adj.* (coll.) [völlig] gestresst

stressful /'stresfl/ *adj.* anstrengend

stress: ~ **mark** *n.* Betonungszeichen, *das;* ~**-related** *adj.* stressbedingt

stretch /stretʃ/ [1] *v.t.* **(a)** (lengthen) strecken (Arm, Hand); recken (Hals); dehnen (Gummiband); (tighten) spannen **(b)** (widen) dehnen [2] **(a)** *v.i.* (extend in length) sich dehnen **(b)** ~ **to sth.** (be sufficient for) für etw. reichen [3] *v. refl.* sich strecken [4] *n.* **(a)** **have a** ~: sich strecken **(b)** **at a** ~ (fig.) wenn es sein muss **(c)** (expanse) Abschnitt, *der;* **a** ~ **of road** ein Stück Straße **(d)** (period) **a four-hour** ~: eine [Zeit]spanne von vier Stunden; **at a** ~: ohne Unterbrechung [5] *adj.* Stretch(hose, -gewebe)

stretcher /'stretʃə(r)/ *n.* [Trag]bahre, *die*

stretch: ~ **marks** *n. pl.* Schwangerschaftsstreifen *Pl.;* ~ **pants** *n. pl.* Stretchhose, *die*

S

stretchy /'stretʃɪ/ *adj.* (coll.) dehnbar
strew /struː/ *v.t., p.p.* **strewed** /struːd/ *or*
strewn /struːn/ streuen
stricken /'strɪkn/ *adj.* (afflicted)
heimgesucht; havariert ⟨*Schiff*⟩; be ∼ with
fear/grief angsterfüllt/gramgebeugt
strict /strɪkt/ *adj.* (a) (firm) streng; in
∼ **confidence** streng vertraulich
(b) (precise) streng
'strictly *adv.* streng; ∼ **[speaking]** streng
genommen
stride /straɪd/ **1** *n.* Schritt, *der;* put sb. off
his ∼ (fig.) jmdn. aus dem Konzept bringen;
take sth. in one's ∼ (fig.) mit etw. gut fertig
werden
2 *v.i.,* **strode** /strəʊd/, **stridden** /'strɪdn/
[mit großen Schritten] gehen
strident /'straɪdənt/ *adj.* schrill
strife /straɪf/ *n.* Streit, *der*
strike /straɪk/ **1** *n.* (Industry) Streik, *der;*
Ausstand, *der;* be on/go [out] *or* come out
on ∼: in den Streik getreten sein/in den
Streik treten
2 *v.t.,* **struck** /strʌk/ (a) (hit) schlagen;
⟨*Schlag, Geschoss:*⟩ treffen; ⟨*Blitz:*⟩
[ein]schlagen in (+ *Akk.*)
(b) (delete) streichen (**from, off** aus)
(c) (ignite) anzünden ⟨*Streichholz*⟩
(d) (chime) schlagen
(e) (impress) beeindrucken; ∼ sb. as [being]
silly jmdm. dumm erscheinen; it ∼s sb.
that …: es scheint jmdm., dass …
(f) (occur to) einfallen (+ *Dat.*)
3 *v.i.,* **struck** (a) (deliver a blow) zuschlagen;
⟨*Blitz:*⟩ einschlagen; ⟨*Unheil, Katastrophe:*⟩
hereinbrechen (geh.); (hit) schlagen (**against**
gegen, **[up]on** auf + *Akk.*)
(b) (ignite) zünden
(c) (chime) schlagen
(d) (Industry) streiken
■ **strike 'back** *v.i.* zurückschlagen
■ **strike 'off** *v.t.* (∼ off list) streichen
⟨*Namen*⟩; (from professional body) die
Zulassung entziehen (+ *Dat.*)
■ **'strike through** *v.t.* durchstreichen
⟨*Wort*⟩; (on list also) ausstreichen
■ **'strike up** *v.t.* beginnen ⟨*Unterhaltung*⟩;
schließen ⟨*Freundschaft*⟩
strike: ∼ **action** *n.* Streikaktionen *Pl.;*
∼ **pay** *n.* Streikgeld, *das*
'striker *n.* (a) (worker on strike) Streikende,
der/die
(b) (Footb.) Stürmer, *der*/Stürmerin, *die*
striking /'straɪkɪŋ/ *adj.* auffallend;
erstaunlich ⟨*Ähnlichkeit*⟩; schlagend
⟨*Beispiel*⟩
'striking distance *n.* Reichweite, *die*
string /strɪŋ/ **1** *n.* (a) (thin cord) Schnur,
die; (to tie up parcels etc. also) Bindfaden,
der; pull [a few *or* some] ∼s (fig.) seine
Beziehungen spielen lassen; with no ∼s
attached ohne Bedingung[en]
(b) (of bow) Sehne, *die;* (of racket, musical
instrument) Saite, *die*

2 *v.t.,* **strung** /strʌŋ/ (thread) auffädeln
■ **string a'long** *v.t.* (deceive) an der Nase
herumführen (ugs.)
■ **string to'gether** *v.t.* auffädeln;
miteinander verknüpfen ⟨*Wörter*⟩
■ **string 'up** *v.t.* aufhängen
string: ∼ **bag** *n.* [Einkaufs]netz, *das;*
∼ **'bean** *n.* (Amer.) Stangenbohne, *die*
stringed /strɪŋd/ *attrib. adj.* (Mus.) Saiten-
stringent /'strɪndʒənt/ *adj.* streng
string 'vest *n.* Netzhemd, *das*
strip[1] /strɪp/ **1** *v.t.,* **-pp-** ausziehen
⟨*Person*⟩
2 *v.i.,* **-pp-** sich ausziehen
strip[2] *n.* (narrow piece) Streifen, *der*
strip: ∼ **cartoon** *n.* Comic[strip], *der;*
∼ **club** *n.* Stripteaselokal, *das*
stripe /straɪp/ *n.* Streifen, *der*
striped /straɪpt/ *adj.* gestreift
strip: ∼ **light** *n.* Neonröhre, *die;*
∼ **lighting** *n.* Neonbeleuchtung, *die*
stripped pine /strɪpt 'paɪn/ *n.* abgebeizte
Kiefer
stripper /'strɪpə(r)/ *n.* Stripper,
der/Stripperin, *die* (ugs.)
strip'tease *n.* Striptease, *der*
stripy /'straɪpɪ/ *adj.* gestreift;
Streifen⟨*muster*⟩
strive /straɪv/ *v.i.,* **strove** /strəʊv/, **striven**
/'strɪvn/ sich bemühen; ∼ **after** *or* **for sth.**
nach etw. streben
strode ▸ STRIDE 2
stroke[1] /strəʊk/ *n.* (a) (act of striking) Schlag,
der
(b) (Med.) Schlaganfall, *der*
(c) (sudden impact) ∼ **of lightning** Blitzschlag,
der; ∼ **of [good] luck** Glücksfall, *der*
(d) at *a or* one ∼: auf einen Schlag; not do a
∼ **[of work]** keinen [Hand]schlag tun; ∼ of
genius genialer Einfall
(e) (in swimming) Zug, *der*
(f) (of clock) Schlag, *der;* on the ∼ of nine
Punkt neun [Uhr]
stroke[2] **1** *v.t.* streicheln
2 *n.* give sb./sth. a ∼: jmdn./etw.
streicheln
stroll /strəʊl/ **1** *v.i.* spazieren gehen
2 *n.* go for a ∼: einen Spaziergang machen
strong /strɒŋ/ *adj.,* ∼**er** /'strɒŋə(r)/,
∼**est** /'strɒŋɪst/ stark; fest ⟨*Fundament,
Schuhe*⟩; robust ⟨*Konstitution, Magen*⟩;
kräftig ⟨*Arme, Muskeln, Tritt, Zähne*⟩;
leistungsfähig ⟨*Wirtschaft*⟩; gut, handfest
⟨*Grund, Beispiel, Argument*⟩; glühend
⟨*Anhänger*⟩; kräftig ⟨*Geruch, Geschmack,
Stimme*⟩; there is a ∼ **possibility that** …: es
ist sehr wahrscheinlich, dass …; take
∼ **measures/action** energisch vorgehen
strong: ∼**hold** *n.* Festung, *die;* (fig.)
Hochburg, *die;* ∼ **'language** *n.* derbe
Ausdrucksweise
'strongly *adv.* stark; solide ⟨*gearbeitet*⟩;
energisch ⟨*protestieren, bestreiten*⟩;

nachdrücklich ⟨*unterstützen*⟩; dringend
⟨*raten*⟩; fest ⟨*glauben*⟩

strong: ∼**man** *n.* Muskelmann, *der* (ugs.);
∼-'**minded** *adj.* willensstark; ∼**room**
n. Tresorraum, *der;* ∼-'**willed** *adj.*
willensstark

stroppy /'strɒpɪ/ *adj.* (Brit. coll.) pampig
(salopp)

strove ▶ STRIVE

struck ▶ STRIKE 2, 3

structural /'strʌktʃərl/ *adj.* baulich

structure /'strʌktʃə(r)/ *n.* (a) Struktur,
die
(b) (something constructed) Konstruktion, *die;*
(building) Bauwerk, *das*

structured /'strʌktʃəd/ *adj.* strukturiert;
geregelt ⟨*Leben*⟩

struggle /'strʌgl/ ① *v.i.* kämpfen; ∼ **to do**
sth. sich abmühen, etw. zu tun; ∼ **against**
or **with sb./sth.** mit jmdm./etw. *od.* gegen
jmdn./etw. kämpfen; ∼ **with sth.** (try to cope)
mit etw. kämpfen
② *n.* Kampf, *der*

strum /strʌm/ ① *v.i.,* -mm- klimpern (ugs.)
(**on** auf + *Dat.*)
② *v.t.,* -mm- klimpern (ugs.) auf (+ *Dat.*)

strung ▶ STRING 2

strut[1] /strʌt/ ① *v.i.,* -tt- stolzieren
② *n.* stolzierender Gang

strut[2] *n.* (support) Strebe, *die*

stub /stʌb/ ① *n.* (a) (remaining portion)
Stummel, *der;* (of cigarette) Kippe, *die*
(b) (counterfoil) Abschnitt, *der*
② *v.t.,* -bb-: (a) ∼ **one's toe** [**against** *or* **on**
sth.] sich (*Dat.*) den Zeh [an etw. (*Dat.*)]
stoßen
(b) ausdrücken ⟨*Zigarette*⟩
◼ **stub 'out** *v.t.* ausdrücken

stubble /'stʌbl/ *n.* Stoppeln *Pl.*

stubbly /'stʌblɪ/ *adj.* stopp[e]lig

stubborn /'stʌbən/ *adj.* (a) (obstinate)
starrköpfig; störrisch ⟨*Tier, Gesicht,*
Haltung⟩
(b) (resolute) hartnäckig

'**stubbornness** *n.* ▶ STUBBORN:
Starrköpfigkeit, *die;* Hartnäckigkeit, *die*

stuck ▶ STICK 1, 2

'**stuck up** *adj.* (conceited) eingebildet

student /'stju:dənt/ *n.* Student, *der/*
Studentin, *die;* (in school or training establishment)
Schüler, *der/*Schülerin, *die;* **be a** ∼ **of sth.**
etw. studieren

studio /'stju:dɪəʊ/ *n., pl.* ∼s (a) (workroom)
Atelier, *das*
(b) (Cinemat., Radio, Telev.) Studio, *das*

studio: ∼ **apartment** (Amer.) ▶ ∼ FLAT;
∼ '**audience** *n.* (Radio, Telev.) Publikum
im Studio; ∼ **flat** *n.* (Brit.) (a) Atelier, *das;*
(b) (one-room flat) Einzimmerwohnung, *die*

studious /'stju:dɪəs/ *adj.* lerneifrig

study /'stʌdɪ/ ① *n.* (a) Studium, *das*
(b) (room) Arbeitszimmer, *das*

② *v.t.* studieren; sich (*Dat.*) [sorgfältig]
durchlesen ⟨*Prüfungsfragen, Bericht*⟩

'**study group** *n.* Arbeitsgruppe, *die*

stuff /stʌf/ ① *n.* (material[s]) Zeug, *das* (ugs.)
② *v.t.* (a) stopfen; zustopfen ⟨*Loch, Ohren*⟩;
(Cookery) füllen; ∼ **sth. with** *or* **full of sth.**
etw. mit etw. voll stopfen (ugs.)
(b) (sl.) ∼ **him!** zum Teufel mit ihm!

stuffed 'shirt *n.* (coll. derog.) Spießer, *der*
(ugs. abwertend)

'**stuffing** *n.* (a) (material) Füllmaterial, *das*
(b) (Cookery) Füllung, *die*

stuffy /'stʌfɪ/ *adj.* stickig

stumble /'stʌmbl/ *v.i.* stolpern (**over** über
+ *Akk.*)

stumbling block /'stʌmblɪŋblɒk/ *n.*
Stolperstein, *der*

stump /stʌmp/ ① *n.* (of tree, branch, tooth)
Stumpf, *der;* (of cigar, pencil) Stummel, *der*
② *v.t.* verwirren; **be** ∼**ed** ratlos sein

'**stumpy** *adj.* gedrungen; ∼ **tail**
Stummelschwanz, *der*

stun /stʌn/ *v.t.,* -nn- (knock senseless)
betäuben; **be** ∼**ned at** *or* **by sth.** (fig.) von
etw. wie betäubt sein

stung ▶ STING 2, 3

stunk ▶ STINK 1

stunner /'stʌnə(r)/ *n.* (coll.) **be a** ∼: Spitze
sein (ugs.)

stunning /'stʌnɪŋ/ *adj.* (coll.) (a) (splendid)
hinreißend
(b) (shocking) bestürzend ⟨*Nachricht*⟩;
(amazing) sensationell

stunt[1] /stʌnt/ *v.t.* hemmen

stunt[2] *n.* halsbrecherisches Kunststück;
(Cinemat.) Stunt, *der*

'**stunt man** *n.* Stuntman, *der*

stupefying /'stju:pɪfaɪɪŋ/ *adj.* die Sinne
betäubend ⟨*Hitze*⟩; (fig.: astonishing) unfassbar

stupendous /stju:'pendəs/ *adj.* gewaltig

stupid /'stju:pɪd/ *adj.* dumm; (ridiculous)
lächerlich; **it would be** ∼ **to do sth.** es wäre
töricht, etw. zu tun

stupidity /stju:'pɪdɪtɪ/ *n.* Dummheit, *die*

'**stupidly** *adv.* dumm

stupor /'stju:pə(r)/ *n.* Benommenheit, *die;*
in a drunken ∼: sinnlos betrunken

sturdy /'stɜ:dɪ/ *adj.* kräftig; stämmig
⟨*Beine, Arme*⟩

stutter /'stʌtə(r)/ ① *v.i.* stottern
② *n.* Stottern, *das*

sty[1] /staɪ/ ▶ PIGSTY

sty[2]**, stye** /staɪ/ *n.* (Med.) Gerstenkorn, *das*

style /staɪl/ *n.* Stil, *der;* [hair]∼: Frisur,
die; **dress in the latest** ∼: sich nach der
neuesten Mode kleiden

styli *pl. of* STYLUS

stylish /'staɪlɪʃ/ *adj.* stilvoll; elegant
⟨*Kleidung, Auto, Person*⟩

stylist /'staɪlɪst/ *n.* (hair∼) Haarstilist, *der/*
-stilistin, *die*

S

stylus /'staɪləs/ n., pl. **styli** /'staɪlaɪ/ or ~**es** [Abtast]nadel, die

suave /swɑːv/ adj. gewandt

sub- /sʌb/ pref. unter-; sub-

sub'conscious ⟦1⟧ adj. unterbewusst ⟦2⟧ n. Unterbewusstsein, das

sub'continent n. Subkontinent, der

'**subcontract** v.t. an einen Subunternehmer vergeben

subcon'tractor n. Subunternehmer, der/-unternehmerin, die

'**subculture** n. Subkultur, die

subdivide /'---, --'-/ v.t. unterteilen

subdue /səb'djuː/ v.t. bändigen ⟨Kind, Tier⟩; dämpfen ⟨Zorn, Lärm, Licht⟩

subdued /səb'djuːd/ adj. gedämpft

'**subgroup** n. Untergruppe, die

'**subheading** n. Untertitel, der

sub'human adj. unmenschlich

subject ⟦1⟧ /'sʌbdʒɪkt/ n. (a) Staatsbürger, der/-bürgerin, die; (to monarch) Untertan, der/Untertanin, die

(b) (topic) Thema, das; (of study) Fach, das; **change the** ~: das Thema wechseln

⟦2⟧ /'sʌbdʒɪkt/ adj. **be** ~ **to sth.** von etw. abhängen

⟦3⟧ /səb'dʒekt/ v.t. unterwerfen (**to** Dat.); (expose) ~ **sb./sth. to sth.** jmdn./etw. einer Sache (Dat.) aussetzen

subjective /səb'dʒektɪv/ adj., **sub'jectively** adv. subjektiv

'**subject matter** n., no indef. art. Gegenstand, der

subjugate /'sʌbdʒʊgeɪt/ v.t. unterjochen (**to** unter + Akk.)

subjugation /sʌbdʒʊ'geɪʃn/ n. Unterjochung, die

subjunctive /səb'dʒʌŋktɪv/ n. Konjunktiv, der

sub'let v.t., -tt-, **sublet** untervermieten

sublime /sə'blaɪm/ adj. erhaben

submarine /sʌbmə'riːn/ n. Unterseeboot, das; U-Boot, das

submerge /səb'mɜːdʒ/ v.t. (a) ~ **sth.** [**in the water**] etw. eintauchen

(b) (flood) ⟨Wasser:⟩ überschwemmen; **be** ~**d in water** unter Wasser stehen

submerged /səb'mɜːdʒd/ adj. versunken

submission /səb'mɪʃn/ n. (a) (surrender, meekness) Unterwerfung, die

(b) (presentation) Einreichung, die (**to** bei)

submissive /səb'mɪsɪv/ adj. gehorsam

submit /səb'mɪt/ v.t., -tt- (present) einreichen; vorbringen ⟨Vorschlag⟩; ~ **sth. to sb.** jmdm. etw. vorlegen

subordinate ⟦1⟧ /sə'bɔːdɪnət/ adj. untergeordnet

⟦2⟧ /sə'bɔːdɪnət/ n. Untergebene, der/die

⟦3⟧ /sə'bɔːdɪneɪt/ v.t. unterordnen (**to** Dat.)

subprime /'sʌbpraɪm/ adj. zweitklassig

subscribe /səb'skraɪb/ v.i. (a) (support) ~ **to sth.** sich einer Sache anschließen

(b) (make contribution) ~ **to sth.** eine Spende für etw. zusichern

(c) ~ **to a newspaper** eine Zeitung abonnieren

sub'scriber n. (to newspaper etc.) Abonnent, der/Abonnentin, die (**to** Gen.)

subscription /səb'skrɪpʃn/ n. (membership fee) Mitgliedsbeitrag, der (**to** für); (to newspaper etc.) Abonnement, das

subsequent /'sʌbsɪkwənt/ adj. folgend; später ⟨Gelegenheit⟩

'**subsequently** adv. später; danach

subservient /səb'sɜːvɪənt/ adj. untergeordnet (**to** Dat.); (servile) unterwürfig

subside /səb'saɪd/ v.i. (a) (sink lower) ⟨Flut, Fluss:⟩ sinken; ⟨Boden, Haus:⟩ sich senken

(b) (abate) nachlassen

subsidence /səb'saɪdəns/ n. (of ground, structure) Senkung, die

subsidiary /səb'sɪdɪərɪ/ ⟦1⟧ adj. untergeordnet ⟨Funktion, Stellung⟩; Neben⟨fach, -aspekt⟩

⟦2⟧ n. (Commerc.) Tochtergesellschaft, die

subsidize /'sʌbsɪdaɪz/ v.t. subventionieren

subsidy /'sʌbsɪdɪ/ n. Subvention, die

subsist /səb'sɪst/ v.i. ~ **on sth.** von etw. leben

subsistence /səb'sɪstəns/ n. [Über]leben, das

'**subsoil** n. Untergrund, der

substance /'sʌbstəns/ n. (a) Stoff, der

(b) (solidity) Substanz, die

(c) (content) Inhalt, der

'**substance abuse** n. Drogen- und Genussmittelmissbrauch, der

sub'standard adj. unzulänglich

substantial /səb'stænʃl/ adj.

(a) (considerable) beträchtlich

(b) gehaltvoll ⟨Essen⟩

(c) (solid) solide ⟨Möbel, Haus⟩; wesentlich ⟨Unterschied⟩

sub'stantially adv. (a) (considerably) wesentlich

(b) (solidly) solide

(c) (essentially) im Wesentlichen

substitute /'sʌbstɪtjuːt/ ⟦1⟧ n. ~[**s** pl.] Ersatz, der

(b) (Sport) Ersatzspieler, der/-spielerin, die

⟦2⟧ v.t. ~ **A for B** B durch A ersetzen

substitution /sʌbstɪ'tjuːʃn/ n. Ersetzung, die; **make a** ~ (Sport) [einen Spieler] auswechseln

subterfuge /'sʌbtəfjuːdʒ/ n. Täuschungsmanöver Pl.

'**subtitle** n. Untertitel, der

subtle /'sʌtl/ adj. subtil (geh.); zart ⟨Duft, Parfüm, Hinweis⟩; fein ⟨Geschmack, Unterschied, Humor⟩

'**subtotal** n. Zwischensumme, die

subtract /səb'trækt/ v.t. abziehen

subtraction ⋯⟩ suffocate ⋯⟩

subtraction /səb'trækʃn/ *n.* Subtraktion, *die*

sub'tropical *adj.* subtropisch

suburb /'sʌbɜːb/ *n.* Vorort, *der*

suburban /sə'bɜːbən/ *adj.* Vorort-; ‹*Leben, Haus*› am Stadtrand

suburbia /sə'bɜːbɪə/ *n.* (derog.) die [eintönigen] Vororte *Pl.*

subversive /səb'vɜːsɪv/ *adj.* subversiv

'subway *n.* **(a)** (passage) Unterführung, *die*
(b) (Amer.: railway) Untergrundbahn, *die;* U-Bahn, *die*

sub-'zero *adj.* ~ temperatures/conditions Temperaturen unter Null

succeed /sək'siːd/ ① *v.i.* **(a)** Erfolg haben; **sb. ~s in sth.** jmdm. gelingt etw.; jmd. schafft etw.; **sb. ~s in doing sth.** es gelingt jmdm., etw. zu tun; jmd. schafft es, etw. zu tun; ~ **in business/college** geschäftlich/im Studium erfolgreich sein; **I did not ~ in doing it** ich habe es nicht geschafft
(b) (come next) die Nachfolge antreten
② *v.t.* (take place of) ablösen

success /sək'ses/ *n.* Erfolg, *der;* **make a ~ of sth.** bei etw. Erfolg haben

successful /sək'sesfl/ *adj.* erfolgreich; **be ~ in sth./doing sth.** Erfolg bei etw. haben/dabei haben, etw. zu tun

suc'cessfully *adv.* erfolgreich

succession /sək'seʃn/ *n.* **(a)** Folge, *die;* **in ~:** hintereinander
(b) (series) Serie, *die*
(c) (to throne) Erbfolge, *die*

successive /sək'sesɪv/ *adj.* aufeinander folgend

suc'cessively *adv.* hintereinander

successor /sək'sesə(r)/ *n.* Nachfolger, *der*/Nachfolgerin, *die*

suc'cess story *n.* Erfolgsstory, *die* (ugs.)

succinct /sək'sɪŋkt/ *adj.* **(a)** (terse) knapp
(b) (clear) prägnant

succulent /'sʌkjʊlənt/ *adj.* saftig

succumb /sə'kʌm/ *v.i.* unterliegen; ~ **to sth.** einer Sache (*Dat.*) erliegen

such /sʌtʃ/ ① *adj.* **(a)** (of that kind) solch...; ~ **a person** ein solcher Mensch; ~ **a book** ein solches Buch; ~ **people** solche Leute; ~ **things** so etwas; **I said no ~ thing** ich habe nichts dergleichen gesagt; **there is no ~ bird** einen solchen Vogel gibt es nicht; **or some ~ thing** oder so etwas; **you'll do no ~ thing** das wirst du nicht tun; **experiences ~ as these** solche Erfahrungen
(b) (so great) solch...; derartig; **I got ~ a fright that ...:** ich bekam einen derartigen *od.* (ugs.) so einen Schrecken, dass ...; ~ **was the force of the explosion that ...:** die Explosion war so stark, dass ...; **to ~ an extent** dermaßen
(c) *with adj.* so; ~ **a big house** ein so großes Haus; ~ **a long time** so lange
② *pron.* **as ~:** als solcher/solche/solches;

(strictly speaking) im Grunde genommen; an sich; ~ **as** wie [zum Beispiel]; ~ **is life** so ist das Leben

such-and-such /'sʌtʃənsʌtʃ/ *adj.* **at ~ a time** um die und die Zeit

'suchlike *pron.* derlei

suck /sʌk/ ① *v.t.* saugen (**out of** aus); lutschen ‹*Bonbon*›
② *v.i.* ~**s** (esp. Amer. sl.) etw. ist Scheiße (derb)
■ **suck 'up** ① *v.t.* aufsaugen
② *v.i.* ~ **up to sb.** (coll.) jmdm. in den Hintern kriechen (salopp)

'sucker *n.* **(a)** (suction pad) Saugfuß, *der;* (Zool.) Saugnapf, *der*
(b) (coll.: dupe) Dumme, *der/die*

suckle /'sʌkl/ *v.t.* säugen

suction /'sʌkʃn/ *n.* Saugwirkung, *die*

Sudan /suːˈdɑːn/ *pr. n.* **[the] ~:** [der] Sudan

sudden /'sʌdn/ ① *adj.* **(a)** (unexpected) plötzlich
(b) (abrupt) jäh ‹*Abgrund, Übergang, Ruck*›; **there was a ~ bend in the road** plötzlich machte die Straße eine Biegung
② *n.* **all of a ~:** plötzlich

'suddenly *adv.* plötzlich

'suddenness *n.* Plötzlichkeit, *die*

suds /sʌdz/ *n. pl.* **[soap]~:** [Seifen]lauge, *die;* (froth) Schaum, *der*

sue /suː/ ① *v.t.* verklagen (**for** auf + *Akk.*)
② *v.i.* klagen (**for** auf + *Akk.*)

suede /sweɪd/ *n.* Wildleder, *das*

suet /'suːɪt/ *n.* Talg, *der*

Suez /'suːɪz, 'sjuːɪz/ *pr. n.* Suez (*das*); ~ **Canal** Suez-Kanal, *der*

suffer /'sʌfə(r)/ ① *v.t.* erleiden; durchmachen ‹*Schweres, Kummer*›; dulden ‹*Unverschämtheit*›
② *v.i.* leiden
■ **'suffer from** *v.t.* leiden unter (+ *Dat.*); leiden an (+ *Dat.*) ‹*Krankheit*›

sufferance /'sʌfərəns/ *n.* Duldung, *die;* **he remains here on ~ only** er ist hier bloß geduldet

'suffering *n.* Leiden, *das*

suffice /sə'faɪs/ ① *v.i.* genügen; ~ **it to say ...:** nur so viel sei gesagt: ...
② *v.t.* genügen (+ *Dat.*)

sufficiency /sə'fɪʃənsɪ/ *n.* Zulänglichkeit, *die*

sufficient /sə'fɪʃənt/ *adj.* genug; ~ **money/food** genug Geld/genug zu essen; **be ~:** genügen; ~ **reason** Grund genug; **have you had ~?** (food, drink) haben Sie schon genug?

suf'ficiently *adv.* genug; (adequately) ausreichend; ~ **large** groß genug; **a ~ large number** eine genügend große Zahl

suffix /'sʌfɪks/ *n.* Nachsilbe, *die*

suffocate /'sʌfəkeɪt/ ① *v.t.* ersticken; **he was ~d by the smoke** der Rauch ⋯⟩

S

erstickte ihn
2 *v.i.* ersticken

suffocation /sʌfə'keɪʃn/ *n.* Erstickung, *die;* a feeling of ∼: das Gefühl, zu ersticken

sugar /'ʃʊgə(r)/ 1 *n.* Zucker, *der;* two ∼s, please (lumps) zwei Stück Zucker, bitte; (spoonfuls) zwei Löffel Zucker, bitte
2 *v.t.* zuckern

sugar: ∼ **basin** ▶ ∼ BOWL; ∼ **beet** *n.* Zuckerrübe, *die;* ∼ **bowl** *n.* Zuckerschale, *die;* (covered) Zuckerdose, *die;* ∼ **cane** *n.* Zuckerrohr, *das;* ∼**-coated** *adj.* gezuckert; mit Zucker überzogen ⟨Dragee usw.⟩; ∼ **daddy** *n.* (coll.) *spendabler älterer Mann, der ein junges Mädchen aushält;* ∼ **lump** *n.* Zuckerstück, *das;* (when counted) Stück Zucker; ∼ **tongs** *n. pl.* Zuckerzange, *die*

'**sugary** *adj.* süß; (fig.) süßlich

suggest /sə'dʒest/ *v.t.* (a) (propose) vorschlagen; ∼ sth. to sb. jmdm. etw. vorschlagen; he ∼ed going to the cinema er schlug vor, ins Kino zu gehen
(b) (assert) are you trying to ∼ that he is lying wollen Sie damit sagen, dass er lügt?
(c) (make one think of) suggerieren; ⟨Symptome, Tatsachen:⟩ schließen lassen auf (+ *Akk.*)

suggestion /sə'dʒestʃn/ *n.* (a) Vorschlag, *der;* at *or* on sb.'s ∼: auf jmds. Vorschlag (*Akk.*)
(b) (insinuation) Andeutungen *Pl.*
(c) (fig.: trace) Spur, *die*

suggestive /sə'dʒestɪv/ *adj.* (a) be ∼ of sth. auf etw. (*Akk.*) schließen lassen
(b) (indecent) anzüglich

suicidal /su:ɪ'saɪdl/ *adj.* selbstmörderisch; I felt *or* was quite ∼: ich hätte mich am liebsten gleich umgebracht

suicide /'su:ɪsaɪd/ *n.* Selbstmord, *der*

suicide: ∼ **attempt** *n.* Selbstmordversuch, *der;* ∼ **attack** *n.* Selbstmordanschlag, *der*

suit /su:t/ 1 *n.* (a) (for men) Anzug, *der;* (for women) Kostüm, *das*
(b) (Law) ∼ [at law] Prozess, *der*
(c) (Cards) Farbe, *die;* follow ∼ (fig.) das Gleiche tun
2 *v.t.* (a) anpassen (to *Dat.*)
(b) be ∼ed [to sth./one another] [zu etw./zueinander] passen
(c) (satisfy needs of) passen (+ *Dat.*); will Monday ∼ you? passt Ihnen Montag?; does the climate ∼ you? bekommt Ihnen das Klima?
(d) (go well with) passen zu; does this hat ∼ me? steht mir dieser Hut?; black ∼s her Schwarz steht ihr gut
3 *v. refl.* ∼ oneself tun, was man will; ∼ yourself! [ganz] wie du willst!

suitability /su:tə'bɪlɪtɪ/ *n.* Eignung, *die* (for für)

suitable /'su:təbl/ *adj.* geeignet; angemessen ⟨Kleidung⟩; (convenient) passend;

∼ for children für Kinder geeignet; **Monday is the most** ∼ **day [for me]** Montag passt [mir] am besten

suitably /'su:təblɪ/ *adv.* angemessen; entsprechend ⟨gekleidet⟩

'**suitcase** *n.* Koffer, *der*

suite /swiːt/ *n.* (a) (of furniture) Garnitur, *die;* three-piece ∼: Polstergarnitur, *die*
(b) (of rooms) Suite, *die*

suitor /'su:tə(r)/ *n.* Freier, *der*

sulfur, sulfuric (Amer.) ▶ SULPH-

sulk /sʌlk/ *v.i.* schmollen

'**sulky** *adj.* schmollend; eingeschnappt (ugs.)

sullen /'sʌlən/ *adj.* mürrisch

sulphur /'sʌlfə(r)/ *n.* Schwefel, *der*

sulphuric /sʌl'fjʊərɪk/ *adj.* ∼ acid Schwefelsäure, *die*

sultan /'sʌltən/ *n.* Sultan, *der*

sultana /sʌl'tɑːnə/ *n.* Sultanine, *die*

sultry /'sʌltrɪ/ *adj.* schwül

sum /sʌm/ *n.* (a) Summe, *die* (of aus); ∼ [total] Ergebnis, *das*
(b) (Arithmetic) Rechenaufgabe, *die;* do ∼s rechnen; she is good at ∼s sie kann gut rechnen

■ **sum 'up** 1 *v.t.* (a) zusammenfassen
(b) (Brit.: assess) einschätzen
2 *v.i.* ein Fazit ziehen

summarily /'sʌmərɪlɪ/ *adv.* summarisch; ∼ dismissed fristlos entlassen

summarize /'sʌməraɪz/ *v.t.* zusammenfassen

summary /'sʌmərɪ/ 1 *adj.* summarisch; fristlos ⟨Entlassung⟩
2 *n.* Zusammenfassung, *die*

summer /'sʌmə(r)/ *n.* Sommer, *der;* in [the] ∼: im Sommer

summer: ∼ **house** *n.* [Garten]laube, *die;* ∼ **school** *n.* Sommerkurs, *der;* ∼ **term** *n.* Sommerhalbjahr, *das;* ∼**time** *n.* Sommer, *der*

'**summery** *adj.* sommerlich

summing 'up *n.* Zusammenfassung, *die*

summit /'sʌmɪt/ *n.* Gipfel, *der;* ∼ **conference/meeting** Gipfelkonferenz, *die*/-treffen, *das*

summon /'sʌmən/ *v.t.* (a) rufen (to zu); holen ⟨Hilfe⟩
(b) (Law) vorladen

■ **summon 'up** *v.t.* aufbringen

summons /'sʌmənz/ *n.* Vorladung, *die*

sump /sʌmp/ *n.* Ölwanne, *die*

sumptuous /'sʌmptjʊəs/ *adj.* üppig; luxuriös ⟨Möbel, Kleidung⟩

sun /sʌn/ 1 *n.* Sonne, *die;* catch the ∼ (be in sunny position) viel Sonne abbekommen; (get ∼burnt) einen Sonnenbrand bekommen
2 *v. refl.* **-nn-** sich sonnen

Sun. *abbr.* = **Sunday** So.

sun: ∼**baked** *adj.* an der Sonne getrocknet ⟨Ziegel⟩; ausgedörrt ⟨Landschaft,

Prärie usw.›; ~**bathe** *v.i.* sonnenbaden; ~**bathing** *n.* Sonnenbaden, *das;* ~**beam** *n.* Sonnenstrahl, *der;* ~**bed** *n.* (with UV lamp) Sonnenbank, *die;* (in garden) Gartenliege, *die;* ~**block** *n.* Sonnenschutzcreme, *die* [mit hohem Lichtschutzfaktor]; ~**burn** *n.* Sonnenbrand, *der;* ~**burnt** *adj.* be/get ~burnt einen Sonnenbrand haben/ bekommen; ~**cream** *n.* Sonnencreme, *die*

sundae /'sʌndeɪ/ *n.* [ice cream] ~: Eisbecher, *der*

Sunday /'sʌndeɪ, 'sʌndɪ/ *n.* Sonntag, *der;* ~ opening die sonntägliche Öffnung; ~ trading sonntägliche Ladenöffnung; *see also* FRIDAY

sun: ~**deck** *n.* Sonnendeck, *das;* ~**dial** *n.* Sonnenuhr, *die;* ~**-drenched** *adj.* sonnenüberflutet (geh.); ~**dress** *n.* Strand- od. Sonnenkleid, *das;* ~**-dried** *adj.* an der Sonne getrocknet

sundry /'sʌndrɪ/ [1] *adj.* verschieden [2] *n. in pl.* Verschiedenes

'sunflower *n.* Sonnenblume, *die*

sung ▸ SING

sun: ~**glasses** *n. pl.* Sonnenbrille, *die;* ~**hat** *n.* Sonnenhut, *der*

sunk ▸ SINK 2, 3

sun: ~**lamp** *n.* Höhensonne, *die;* ~**light** *n.* Sonnenlicht, *das;* ~**lit** *adj.* sonnenbeschienen

Sunni /'sʌnɪ/ *n.* (Muslim Relig.) Sunnit, *der*/Sunnitin, *die; attrib.* sunnitisch

sunny /'sʌnɪ/ *adj.* sonnig; ~ intervals Aufheiterungen

sun: ~ **protection factor** *n.* Lichtschutzfaktor, *der;* ~**ray** *n.* Sonnenstrahl, *der;* ~**rise** *n.* Sonnenaufgang, *der;* ~**roof** *n.* (Motor Veh.) Schiebedach, *das;* ~**set** *n.* Sonnenuntergang, *der;* ~**shade** *n.* Sonnenschirm, *der;* ~**shine** *n.* Sonnenschein, *der;* ~**stroke** *n.* Sonnenstich, *der;* ~**tan** *n.* [Sonnen]bräune, *die;* get a ~tan braun werden; ~**tan lotion** *n.* Sonnencreme, *die;* ~**tanned** *adj.* braun [gebrannt]; ~**tan oil** *n.* Sonnenöl, *das;* ~**trap** *n.* sonniges Plätzchen; ~ **worshipper** *n.* (lit./joc.) Sonnenanbeter, *der*/-anbeterin, *die*

super /'su:pə(r)/ *adj.* (coll.) super (ugs.)

superb /su:'pɜ:b/ *adj.* einzigartig; erstklassig ‹*Essen*›

superbug /'su:pəbʌg/ *n.* multiresistenter Erreger

supercilious /su:pə'sɪlɪəs/ *adj.* hochnäsig

supercomputer /'su:pəkəmpju:tə(r)/ *n.* Supercomputer, *der*

superficial /su:pə'fɪʃl/ *adj.* oberflächlich

superficiality /su:pəfɪʃɪ'ælɪtɪ/ *n.* Oberflächlichkeit, *die*

superfluous /su'pɜːfluəs/ *adj.* überflüssig

super: ~**glue** *n.* Sekundenkleber, *der;* ~**highway** *n.* (a) (Amer.) Autobahn, *die;*

(b) (Comp.) Datenautobahn, *die;* ~**human** *adj.* übermenschlich

superintendent /su:pərɪn'tendənt/ *n.* (Brit. Police) Kommissar, *der*/Kommissarin, *die*

superior /su:'pɪərɪə(r)/ [1] *adj.* (a) (of higher quality) besonders gut ‹*Restaurant, Qualität, Stoff*›; überlegen ‹*Technik, Intelligenz*›; he thinks he is ~ to us er hält sich für besser als wir

(b) (having higher rank) höher…; be ~ to sb. einen höheren Rang als jmd. haben [2] *n.* Vorgesetzte, *der*/*die*

superiority /su:pɪərɪ'ɒrɪtɪ/ *n.* Überlegenheit, *die* (to über + *Akk.*)

superlative /su:'pɜːlətɪv/ [1] *adj.* (a) unübertrefflich (b) (Ling.) a ~ adjective/adverb ein Adjektiv/ Adverb im Superlativ [2] *n.* (Ling.) Superlativ, *der*

super: ~**market** *n.* Supermarkt, *der;* ~**model** *n.* Supermodel, *das;* ~**natural** *adj.* übernatürlich; ~**power** *n.* (Polit.) Supermacht, *die*

supersede /su:pə'si:d/ *v.t.* ablösen (by durch)

supersonic /su:pə'sɒnɪk/ *adj.* Überschall-

superstar /'su:pəstɑ:(r)/ *n.* Superstar, *der*

superstition /su:pə'stɪʃn/ *n.* Aberglaube, *der*

superstitious /su:pə'stɪʃəs/ *adj.* abergläubisch

superstore /'su:pəstɔ:(r)/ *n.* Großmarkt, *der*

supervise /'su:pəvaɪz/ *v.t.* beaufsichtigen

supervision /su:pə'vɪʒn/ *n.* Aufsicht, *die*

supervisor /'su:pəvaɪzə(r)/ *n.* Aufseher, *der*/Aufseherin, *die*

supper /'sʌpə(r)/ *n.* Abendessen, *das;* have [one's] ~: zu Abend essen

'suppertime *n.* Abendbrotzeit, *die;* it's ~: es ist Zeit zum Abendessen

supplant /sə'plɑ:nt/ *v.t.* ablösen, ersetzen (by durch)

supple /'sʌpl/ *adj.* geschmeidig

supplement /'sʌplɪmənt/ [1] *n.* (a) Ergänzung, *die* (to + *Gen.*); (addition) Zusatz, *der* (b) (of book) Nachtrag, *der;* (of newspaper) Beilage, *die* (c) (to fare) Zuschlag, *der* [2] *v.t.* ergänzen

supplementary /sʌplɪ'mentərɪ/ *adj.* zusätzlich; ~ fare/charge Zuschlag, *der*

supplier /sə'plaɪə(r)/ *n.* (Commerc.) Lieferant, *der*/Lieferantin, *die*

supply /sə'plaɪ/ [1] *v.t.* liefern ‹*Waren usw.*›; beliefern ‹*Kunden, Geschäft*›; ~ sth. to sb., ~ sb. with sth. jmdn. mit etw. versorgen/(Commerc.) beliefern [2] *n.* Vorräte *Pl.;* military/medical supplies militärischer/medizinischer Nachschub;

S

∼ **and demand** (Econ.) Angebot und Nachfrage

sup'ply teacher *n.* Vertretung, *die*

support /sə'pɔːt/ [1] *v.t.* **(a)** (hold up) stützen ⟨*Mauer, Verletzten*⟩; (bear weight of) tragen **(b)** unterstützen ⟨*Politik, Verein*⟩; (Footb.) ∼ **Spurs** Spurs-Fan sein **(c)** (provide for) ernähren ⟨*Familie, sich selbst*⟩ **(d)** (speak in favour of) befürworten [2] *n.* **(a)** Unterstützung, *die;* **in** ∼**:** zur Unterstützung; **speak in** ∼ **of sb./sth.** jmdn. unterstützen/etw. befürworten **(b)** (money) Unterhalt, *der* **(c)** (sb./sth. that ∼s) Stütze, *die*

sup'porter *n.* Anhänger, *der*/Anhängerin, *die;* **football** ∼**:** Fußballfan, *der*

sup'porting *adj.* (Cinemat., Theatre) ∼ **role** Nebenrolle, *die;* ∼ **actor/actress** Schauspieler/-spielerin in einer Nebenrolle; ∼ **film** Vorfilm, *der*

supportive /sə'pɔːtɪv/ *adj.* hilfreich; **be very** ∼ **[to sb.]** [jmdm.] eine große Hilfe *od.* Stütze sein

suppose /sə'pəʊz/ *v.t.* **(a)** (assume) annehmen; ∼ *or* **supposing [that] he ...:** angenommen, [dass] er ... **(b)** (presume) vermuten; **I** ∼ **so** (doubtfully) ja, vermutlich; (more confidently) ich glaube schon **(c) be** ∼**d to do/be sth.** (be generally believed to do/be sth.) etw. tun/sein sollen **(d)** (allow) **you are not** ∼**d to do that** das darfst du eigentlich nicht; **I'm not** ∼**d to be here** ich dürfte eigentlich gar nicht hier sein

supposed /sə'pəʊzd/ *attrib. adj.* mutmaßlich

supposedly /sə'pəʊzɪdlɪ/ *adv.* angeblich

supposition /sʌpə'zɪʃn/ *n.* Annahme, *die;* Vermutung, *die*

suppress /sə'pres/ *v.t.* unterdrücken

suppression /sə'preʃn/ *n.* Unterdrückung, *die*

supremacy /suː'preməsɪ/ *n.* **(a)** (supreme authority) Souveränität, *die* **(b)** (superiority) Überlegenheit, *die*

supreme /suː'priːm/ *adj.* höchst...

Supt. *abbr.* = **Superintendent**

surcharge /'sɜːtʃɑːdʒ/ *n.* Zuschlag, *der*

sure /ʃʊə(r)/ [1] *adj.* sicher; **be** ∼ **of sth.** sich (*Dat.*) einer Sache (*Gen.*) sicher sein; ∼ **of oneself** selbstsicher; **don't be too** ∼**:** da wäre ich mir nicht so sicher; **there is** ∼ **to be a petrol station** es gibt bestimmt eine Tankstelle; **don't worry, it's** ∼ **to turn out well** keine Sorge, es wird schon alles gut gehen; **for** ∼ (coll.) auf jeden Fall; **make** ∼ **[of sth.]** sich [einer Sache] vergewissern; **make** *or* **be** ∼ **you do it, be** ∼ **to do it** (do not fail to do it) sieh zu, dass du es tust; (do not forget) vergiss nicht, es zu tun; **a** ∼ **winner** ein todsicherer Tipp (ugs.) [2] *adv.* ∼ **enough** tatsächlich [3] *int.* ∼**!,** ∼ **thing!** (Amer.) na klar! (ugs.)

sure: ∼**-fire** *attrib. adj.* (Amer. coll.)

todsicher; ∼**-footed** *adj.* trittsicher

'surely [1] *adv.* **(a)** *as sentence-modifier* doch; ∼ **we've met before?** wir kennen uns doch, oder? **(b)** (steadily) sicher; **slowly but** ∼**:** langsam, aber sicher **(c)** (certainly) sicherlich [2] *int.* (Amer.) natürlich

surf /sɜːf/ [1] Brandung, *die* [2] *v.i.* **(a)** surfen **(b)** (Comp.) surfen; (TV) zappen (ugs.) [3] *v.t.* (Comp., TV) ∼ **the Internet** im Internet surfen; ∼ **the channels** sich durch die Kanäle zappen (ugs.)

surface /'sɜːfɪs/ [1] *n.* Oberfläche, *die;* **outer** ∼**:** Außenfläche, *die;* **the earth's** ∼**:** die Erdoberfläche; **on the** ∼**:** an der Oberfläche; (fig.) oberflächlich betrachtet [2] *v.i.* auftauchen; (fig.) hochkommen

surface: ∼ **area** *n.* Oberfläche, *die;* ∼ **mail** *n.* gewöhnliche Post

'surfboard *n.* Surfbrett, *das*

surfeit /'sɜːfɪt/ *n.* Übermaß, *das*

'surfer *n.* Surfer, *der*/Surferin, *die*

'surfing *n.* Surfen, *das*

surge /sɜːdʒ/ *v.i.* ⟨*Wellen:*⟩ branden; **the crowd** ∼**d forward** die Menschenmenge drängte nach vorn

surgeon /'sɜːdʒən/ *n.* Chirurg, *der*/ Chirurgin, *die*

surgery /'sɜːdʒərɪ/ *n.* **(a)** Chirurgie, *die;* **undergo** ∼**:** sich einer Operation (*Dat.*) unterziehen **(b)** (Brit.: place) Praxis, *die;* **doctor's/dental** ∼**:** Arzt-/Zahnarztpraxis, *die* **(c)** (Brit.: time) Sprechstunde, *die*

surgical /'sɜːdʒɪkl/ *adj.* chirurgisch; ∼ **treatment** Operation, *die*/Operationen *Pl.*

surly /'sɜːlɪ/ *adj.* mürrisch

surmise /sə'maɪz/ [1] *n.* Vermutung, *die* [2] *v.t.* mutmaßen

surmount /sə'maʊnt/ *v.t.* überwinden

surmountable /sə'maʊntəbl/ *adj.* überwindbar

surname /'sɜːneɪm/ *n.* Nachname, *der;* Zuname, *der*

surpass /sə'pɑːs/ *v.t.* übertreffen; ∼ **oneself** sich selbst übertreffen

surplus /'sɜːpləs/ [1] *n.* Überschuss, *der* (**of** an + *Dat.*) [2] *adj.* überschüssig; **be** ∼ **to sb.'s requirements** von jmdm. nicht benötigt werden

surprise /sə'praɪz/ [1] *n.* **(a)** Überraschung, *die;* **take sb. by** ∼**:** jmdn. überrumpeln; **to my great** ∼**, much to my** ∼**:** zu meiner großen Überraschung; **it came as a** ∼ **to us** es war für uns eine Überraschung **(b)** *attrib.* überraschend, unerwartet ⟨*Besuch*⟩; **a** ∼ **attack** ein Überraschungsangriff [2] *v.t.* überraschen; überrumpeln ⟨*Feind*⟩; **I**

shouldn't be ∼d if ...: es würde mich nicht
wundern, wenn ...; **be** ∼**d at sb./sth.** sich
über jmdn./etw. wundern
surprising /sə'praɪzɪŋ/ *adj.* überraschend
'surprisingly *adv.* überraschend;
∼ **[enough], he was ...:**
überraschenderweise war er ...
surreal /sə'riːəl/ *adj.* surrealistisch
surrealism /sə'riːəlɪzm/ *n.* Surrealismus,
der
surrender /sə'rendə(r)/ **1** *n.* (to enemy)
Kapitulation, *die;* (of possession) Aufgabe, *die*
2 *v.i.* kapitulieren
3 *v.t.* aufgeben
surreptitious /sʌrəp'tɪʃəs/ *adj.* heimlich;
verstohlen ⟨*Blick*⟩
surrogate /'sʌrəgət/ *n.* Ersatz, *der*
surrogate 'mother *n.* Leihmutter, *die*
surround /sə'raʊnd/ *v.t.* **(a)** (come or
be all round) umringen ⟨*Truppen, Heer:*⟩
umzingeln ⟨*Stadt, Feind*⟩
(b) (encircle) umgeben; **be** ∼**ed by** *or* **with sth.**
von etw. umgeben sein
sur'rounding *adj.* umliegend; **the**
∼ **countryside** die [Landschaft in der]
Umgebung
sur'roundings *n. pl.* Umgebung, *die*
surveillance /sə'veɪləns/ *n.*
Überwachung, *die;* **be under** ∼: überwacht
werden
survey **1** /sə'veɪ/ *v.t.* betrachten;
überblicken ⟨*Landschaft*⟩; inspizieren
⟨*Gebäude*⟩; bewerten ⟨*Situation*⟩
2 /'sɜːveɪ/ *n.* Überblick, *der* (of über + *Akk.*);
(poll) Umfrage, *die;* (Surv.) Vermessung, *die*
surveyor /sə'veɪə(r)/ *n.* (of building)
Gutachter, *der/*Gutachterin, *die;* (of land)
Landvermesser, *der/*-vermesserin, *die*
survival /sə'vaɪvl/ *n.* Überleben, *das;* **fight**
for ∼: Existenzkampf, *der*
sur'vival kit *n.* Notausrüstung, *die*
survive /sə'vaɪv/ **1** *v.t.* überleben
2 *v.i.* ⟨*Person:*⟩ überleben; ⟨*Schriften,*
Traditionen:⟩ erhalten bleiben
survivor /sə'vaɪvə(r)/ *n.* Überlebende,
der/die
sus /sʌs/ (Brit. coll.) *v.t.,* **-ss-** spitzkriegen
(ugs.); **get sb.** ∼**sed** jmdn. durchschauen
■ **sus 'out** *v.t.* (coll.) checken (ugs.);
spannen (ugs.)
susceptible /sə'septɪbl/ *adj.* empfänglich
(to für); (to illness) anfällig **(to** für)
suspect **1** /sə'spekt/ *v.t.* **(a)** (imagine to be
likely) vermuten; ∼ **the worst** das Schlimmste
befürchten; ∼ **sb. to be sth.,** ∼ **that sb. is**
sth. glauben *od.* vermuten, dass jmd. etw. ist
(b) (mentally accuse) verdächtigen; ∼ **sb.**
of sth./of doing sth. jmdn. einer Sache
verdächtigen/jmdn. verdächtigen, etw. zu
tun
2 /'sʌspekt/ *adj.* fragwürdig; verdächtig
⟨*Stoff, Paket*⟩
3 /'sʌspekt/ *n.* Verdächtige, *der/die*

suspend /sə'spend/ *v.t.* **(a)** (hang up)
[auf]hängen
(b) (stop) suspendieren
(c) (from work) ausschließen **(from** von);
sperren ⟨*Sportler*⟩
suspended 'sentence *n.* (Law) Strafe
mit Bewährung
suspender belt /sə'spendə belt/ *n.* (Brit.)
Strumpfbandgürtel, *der*
suspenders /sə'spendəz/ *n. pl.* **(a)** (Brit.: for
stockings) Strumpfbänder *Pl.*
(b) (Amer.: for trousers) Hosenträger *Pl.*
suspense /sə'spens/ *n.* Spannung, *die;*
keep sb. in ∼: jmdn. auf die Folter spannen
suspension /sə'spenʃn/ *n.* (Motor Veh.)
Federung, *die*
suspension: ∼ **bridge** *n.* Hängebrücke,
die; ∼ **forks** *n. pl.* Federgabel, *die*
suspicion /sə'spɪʃn/ *n.* **(a)** (uneasy feeling)
Misstrauen, *das* (of gegenüber); (unconfirmed
belief) Verdacht, *der;* **have a** ∼ **that ...:** den
Verdacht haben, dass ...
(b) (suspecting) Verdacht, *der* (of auf + *Akk.*);
on ∼ **of murder** wegen Mordverdachts; **be**
under ∼: verdächtigt werden
suspicious /sə'spɪʃəs/ *adj.* **(a)** (tending to
suspect) misstrauisch (of gegenüber); **be** ∼ **of**
sb./sth. jmdm./einer Sache misstrauen
(b) (arousing suspicion) verdächtig
sustain /sə'steɪn/ *v.t.* **(a)** (support) tragen
⟨*Gewicht*⟩; (fig.) aufrechterhalten
(b) erleiden ⟨*Verlust, Verletzung*⟩
sustainable /sʌ'steɪnəbl/ *adj.* (Ecology)
nachhaltig
sustenance /'sʌstɪnəns/ *n.* Nahrung, *die*
SW *abbr.* **(a)** = **south-west** SW
(b) (Radio) = **short wave** KW
swab /swɒb/ *n.* (Med.: pad) Tupfer, *der*
swagger /'swægə(r)/ *v.i.* großspurig
stolzieren
swallow[1] /'swɒləʊ/ **1** *v.t.* schlucken; (by
mistake) verschlucken
2 *v.i.* schlucken
3 *n.* Schluck, *der*
■ **swallow 'up** *v.t.* verschlucken
swallow[2] *n.* Schwalbe, *die*
swam ▸ SWIM 1
swamp /swɒmp/ **1** *n.* Sumpf, *der*
2 *v.t.* überschwemmen
'swampy *adj.* sumpfig
swan /swɒn/ *n.* Schwan, *der*
'swansong *n.* (fig.) Schwanengesang, *der*
swap /swɒp/ **1** *v.t.,* **-pp-** tauschen **(for**
gegen)
2 *v.i.,* **-pp-** tauschen
3 *n.* Tausch, *der*
swarm /swɔːm/ **1** *n.* Schwarm, *der*
2 *v.i.* schwärmen; (teem) wimmeln **(with** von)
swarthy /'swɔːeɪ/ *adj.* dunkel
swastika /'swɒstɪkə/ *n.* Hakenkreuz, *das*
swat /swɒt/ *v.t.,* **-tt-** totschlagen
sway /sweɪ/ **1** *v.i.* [hin und her] ⋯⟫

S

schwanken; (gently) sich wiegen
2 v.t. (a) wiegen
(b) (influence) beeinflussen
3 n. (fig.) Herrschaft, die; hold ∼ over sb. über jmdn. herrschen
swear /sweə(r)/ 1 v.t., swore /swɔː(r)/, sworn /swɔːn/ schwören ⟨Eid usw.⟩
2 v.i., swore, sworn (a) fluchen
(b) ∼ to sth. etw. beschwören
■ '**swear at** v.t. beschimpfen
■ '**swear by** v.t. (coll.) schwören auf (+ Akk.)
'**swear word** n. Kraftausdruck, der
sweat /swet/ 1 n. Schweiß, der
2 v.i. schwitzen
'**sweatband** n. Schweißband, das
sweater /'swetə(r)/ n. Pullover, der
sweat: ∼**shirt** n. Sweatshirt, das; ∼**shop** n. ausbeuterische [kleine] Klitsche (ugs.)
'**sweaty** adj. schweißig
swede n. Kohlrübe, die
Swede /swiːd/ n. Schwede, der/Schwedin, die
Sweden /'swiːdn/ pr. n. Schweden (das)
Swedish /'swiːdɪʃ/ 1 adj. schwedisch; sb. is ∼: jmd. ist Schwede/Schwedin
2 n. Schwedisch, das; see also ENGLISH 2A
sweep /swiːp/ 1 v.t., swept /swept/
(a) fegen; kehren
(b) ∼ the country ⟨Epidemie, Mode:⟩ das Land überrollen
2 v.i., swept (a) fegen; kehren
(b) (go fast) ⟨Person, Auto:⟩ rauschen; ⟨Wind usw.:⟩ fegen
3 n. (a) give sth. a ∼: etw. fegen od. kehren
(b) (curve) Bogen, der
■ **sweep** '**up** v.t. zusammenfegen; zusammenkehren
'**sweeping** adj. pauschal; weit reichend ⟨Einsparung⟩; umwälzend ⟨Veränderung⟩
sweet /swiːt/ 1 adj. süß; reizend ⟨Wesen, Gesicht, Mädchen⟩; have a ∼ tooth gern Süßes mögen; how ∼ of you! wie nett od. lieb von dir!
2 n. (Brit.) (a) (candy) Bonbon, das od. der
(b) (dessert) Nachtisch, der
sweet: ∼**-and-**'**sour** attrib. adj. süßsauer; ∼ **corn** n. Zuckermais, der
sweeten /'swiːtn/ v.t. süßen
'**sweetener** n. Süßstoff, der
'**sweetheart** n. Schatz, der
'**sweetness** n. Süße, die
sweet: ∼ '**pea** n. Wicke, die; ∼ **po**'**tato** n. Batate, die; ∼**shop** n. (Brit.) Süßwarengeschäft, das; ∼ **talk** (Amer.) n. Süßholzgeraspel, das (ugs.); ∼**-talk** v.t. ∼-talk sb. [into doing sth.] jmdn. beschwatzen[, etw. zu tun]
swell /swel/ 1 v.t., swelled, swollen /'swəʊlən/ or swelled anschwellen lassen
2 v.i., swelled, swollen or swelled
(a) (expand) ⟨Körperteil:⟩ anschwellen;

⟨Segel:⟩ sich blähen; ⟨Material:⟩ aufquellen
(b) ⟨Anzahl:⟩ zunehmen
'**swelling** n. Schwellung, die
swelter /'sweltə(r)/ v.i. ∼ in the heat in der Hitze schmoren (ugs.); ∼ing glühend heiß ⟨Tag, Wetter⟩; ∼ing heat Bruthitze, die
swept ▶ SWEEP 1, 2
swerve /swɜːv/ 1 v.i. einen Bogen machen; ∼ to the right/left nach rechts/links [aus]schwenken
2 n. Bogen, der
swift /swɪft/ 1 adj. schnell
2 n. Mauersegler, der
'**swiftly** adv. schnell
swig /swɪg/ (coll.) Schluck, der
swill /swɪl/ v.t. ∼ [out] [aus]spülen
swim /swɪm/ 1 v.i., -mm-, swam /swæm/, swum /swʌm/ schwimmen; my head was ∼ming mir war schwindelig
2 n. have a/go for a ∼: schwimmen/ schwimmen gehen
'**swimmer** n. Schwimmer, der/ Schwimmerin, die; be a good/poor ∼: gut/schlecht schwimmen können
'**swimming** n. Schwimmen, das
swimming: ∼ **baths** n. pl. Schwimmbad, das; ∼ **costume** n. Badeanzug, der; ∼ **lesson** n. Schwimmstunde, die; ∼ **lessons** Schwimmunterricht, der; ∼ **pool** n. Schwimmbecken, das; (building) Schwimmbad, das; ∼ **trunks** n. pl. Badehose, die
'**swimsuit** n. Badeanzug, der
swindle /'swɪndl/ 1 v.t. betrügen; ∼ sb. out of sth. jmdn. um etw. betrügen
2 n. Schwindel, der; Betrug, der
swindler /'swɪndlə(r)/ n. Schwindler, der/Schwindlerin, die
swine /swaɪn/ n. Schwein, das
swing /swɪŋ/ 1 n. (a) Schaukel, die
(b) (∼ing) Schaukeln, das; in full ∼ (fig.) in vollem Gang[e]
2 v.i., swung /swʌŋ/ (a) schwingen; (in wind) schaukeln
(b) (go in sweeping curve) schwenken
3 v.t., swung schwingen
swing: ∼**bin** n. Schwingdeckel[müll]eimer, der; ∼ '**door** n. Pendeltür, die
swipe /swaɪp/ (coll.) 1 v.t. (a) (hit) knallen (ugs.)
(b) (coll.: steal) klauen (ugs.)
(c) ∼ the card through the swipe reader die Karte durch das [Karten]lesegerät ziehen
2 n. (device) ∼ [reader] [Karten]lesegerät, das
'**swipe card** n. Magnetkarte, die
swirl /swɜːl/ 1 v.i. wirbeln
2 v.t. umherwirbeln
3 n. Spirale, die
swish /swɪʃ/ 1 v.i. zischen
2 n. Zischen, das
3 adj. (coll.) schick (ugs.)

Swiss /swɪs/ ① *adj.* Schweizer; schweizerisch; **sb. is** ∼: jmd. ist Schweizer/ Schweizerin
② *n.* Schweizer, *der*/Schweizerin, *die;* **the** ∼ *pl.* die Schweizer *Pl.*
Swiss 'roll *n.* Biskuitrolle, *die*
switch /swɪtʃ/ ① *n.* **(a)** (esp. Electr.) Schalter, *der*
(b) (change) Wechsel, *der*
② *v.t.* **(a)** (change) ∼ sth. **[over] to** sth. etw. auf etw. (*Akk.*) umstellen *od.* (Electr.) umschalten
(b) (exchange) tauschen
③ *v.i.* wechseln; ∼ **[over] to** sth. auf etw. (*Akk.*) umstellen *od.* (Electr.) umschalten
■ **switch 'off** *v.t. & i.* ausschalten; (also fig. coll.) abschalten
■ **switch 'on** ① *v.t.* einschalten; anschalten
② *v.i.* sich anschalten
switch: ∼**back** *n.* Achterbahn, *die;* ∼**blade** *n.* Springmesser, *das;* ∼**board** *n.* [Telefon]zentrale, *die*
Switzerland /'swɪtsələnd/ *pr. n.* die Schweiz
swivel /'swɪvl/ ① *v.i.*, **-ll-** sich drehen
② *v.t.*, **-ll-** drehen
'swivel chair *n.* Drehstuhl, *der*
swollen /'swəʊlən/ ① ▸ SWELL
② *adj.* geschwollen; angeschwollen ⟨*Fluss*⟩
swoon /swuːn/ (literary) *v.i.* ohnmächtig werden
swoop /swuːp/ ① *n.* **(a)** Sturzflug, *der*
(b) (coll.: raid) Razzia, *die*
② *v.i.* herabstoßen; ∼ **on sb.** sich auf jmdn. stürzen
swop ▸ SWAP
sword /sɔːd/ *n.* Schwert, *das*
'swordfish *n.* Schwertfisch, *der*
swore, sworn ▸ SWEAR
swot /swɒt/ (Brit. coll.) ① *n.* Streber, *der*/Streberin, *die*
② *v.i.*, **-tt-** büffeln (ugs.)
swum ▸ SWIM 1
swung ▸ SWING 2, 3
'swung dash *n.* Tilde, *die*
sycamore /'sɪkəmɔː(r)/ *n.* Bergahorn, *der*
sycophant /'sɪkəfænt/ *n.* Kriecher, *der*
syllable /'sɪləbl/ *n.* Silbe, *die*
syllabus /'sɪləbəs/ *n.* Lehrplan, *der;* (for exam) Studienplan, *der*
symbol /'sɪmbl/ *n.* Symbol, *das* **(of** für)
symbolic /sɪm'bɒlɪk/, **symbolical** /sɪm'bɒlɪkl/ *adj.* symbolisch
symbolism /'sɪmbəlɪzm/ *n.* Symbolik, *die*
symbolize /'sɪmbəlaɪz/ *v.t.* symbolisieren
symmetrical /sɪ'metrɪkl/ *adj.* symmetrisch
symmetry /'sɪmɪtrɪ/ *n.* Symmetrie, *die*
sympathetic /sɪmpə'θetɪk/ *adj.* mitfühlend

sympathize /'sɪmpəθaɪz/ *v.i.* **(a)** ∼ **with sb.** mit jmdm. [mit]fühlen
(b) ∼ **with** (understand) Verständnis haben für
sympathy /'sɪmpəθɪ/ *n.* Mitgefühl, *das;* **in deepest** ∼: mit aufrichtigem Beileid
symphonic /sɪm'fɒnɪk/ *adj.* sinfonisch
symphony /'sɪmfənɪ/ *n.* Sinfonie, *die*
'symphony orchestra *n.* Sinfonieorchester, *das*
symposium /sɪm'pəʊzɪəm/ *n., pl.* symposia /sɪm'pəʊzɪə/ Symposion, *das*
symptom /'sɪmptəm/ *n.* Symptom, *das*
symptomatic /sɪmptə'mætɪk/ *adj.* symptomatisch **(of** für)
synagogue (*Amer.:* **synagog**) /'sɪnəgɒg/ *n.* Synagoge, *die*
sync /sɪŋk/ (coll.) *n.* **be in** ∼/**out of** ∼: harmonieren/nicht harmonieren **(with** mit)
synchromesh /'sɪŋkrəmeʃ/ *n.* (Motor Veh.) Synchrongetriebe, *das*
synchronize /'sɪŋkrənaɪz/ *v.t.* synchronisieren; gleichstellen ⟨*Uhren*⟩
syndicate /'sɪndɪkət/ *n.* Syndikat, *das*
syndrome /'sɪndrəʊm/ *n.* Syndrom, *das*
synonym /'sɪnənɪm/ *n.* Synonym, *das*
synonymous /sɪ'nɒnɪməs/ *adj.* **(a)** (Ling.) synonym **(with** mit)
(b) ∼ **with** (fig.) gleichbedeutend mit
synopsis /sɪ'nɒpsɪs/ *n., pl.* synopses /sɪ'nɒpsiːz/ Inhaltsangabe, *die*
syntactic /sɪn'tæktɪk/ *adj.* syntaktisch
syntax /'sɪntæks/ *n.* Syntax, *die*
synthesis /'sɪnθɪsɪs/ *n., pl.* syntheses /'sɪnθɪsiːz/ Synthese, *die*
synthesize /'sɪnθɪsaɪz/ *v.t.* zur Synthese bringen; (Chem.) synthetisieren
synthesizer /'sɪnθɪsaɪzə(r)/ *n.* (Mus.) Synthesizer, *der*
synthetic /sɪn'θetɪk/ *adj.* synthetisch
syphilis /'sɪfɪlɪs/ *n.* Syphilis, *die*
syphon ▸ SIPHON
Syria /'sɪrɪə/ *pr. n.* Syrien (*das*)
syringe /sɪ'rɪndʒ/ ① *n.* Spritze, *die*
② *v.t.* spritzen; ausspritzen ⟨*Ohr*⟩
syrup /'sɪrəp/ *n.* Sirup, *der*
system /'sɪstəm/ *n.* System, *das*
systematic /sɪstə'mætɪk/ *adj.*, **systematically** /sɪstə'mætɪkəlɪ/ *adv.* systematisch
systematize /'sɪstəmətaɪz/ *v.t.* systematisieren
system: ∼ **disk** *n.* (Comp.) Systemdiskette, *die;* ∼ **error** *n.* (Comp.) Systemfehler, *der;* ∼**s analyst** *n.* Systemanalytiker, *der*/-analytikerin, *die;* ∼ **software** *n.* (Comp.) Systemsoftware, *die*

S

Tt

T, t /tiː/ n. T, t, das; **to a T** ganz genau;
T-junction Einmündung, die; **T-bone steak**
T-Bone-Steak, das; **T-shirt** T-Shirt, das
ta /tɑː/ int. (Brit. coll.) danke
tab /tæb/ **1** n. (a) (projecting flap) Zunge,
die; (on clothing) Etikett, das; (with name)
Namensschild, das
(b) **pick up the** ~ (Amer. coll.) die Zeche
bezahlen
(c) **keep** ~s or **a** ~ **on** (watch) [genau]
beobachten
(d) (Comp.) Tabulator, der
2 v.t. (Comp.) tabellarisieren
tabby /'tæbɪ/ n. ~ **[cat]** Tigerkatze, die
'**tab key** n. (Comp.) Tabulatortaste, die
table /'teɪbl/ **1** n. (a) Tisch, der
(b) (list) Tabelle, die; ~ **of contents**
Inhaltsverzeichnis, das
2 v.t. einbringen
tableau /'tæbləʊ/ n., pl. ~x /'tæbləʊz/
Tableau, das
table: ~**cloth** n. Tischdecke, die; ~ **leg**
n. Tischbein, das; ~ **linen** n. Tischwäsche,
die; ~ **manners** n. pl. Tischmanieren Pl.;
~ **mat** n. Set, das; ~ **salt** n. Tafelsalz,
das; ~**spoon** n. Servierlöffel, der;
~**spoonful** n. Servierlöffel [voll]
tablet /'tæblɪt/ n. (a) Tablette, die
(b) (of soap) Stück, das
table: ~ **tennis** n. Tischtennis, das;
~ **tennis bat** Tischtennisschläger, der;
~ **wine** n. Tischwein, der
tabloid /'tæblɔɪd/ n. Boulevardzeitung,
die; **the** ~**s** (derog.) die Boulevardpresse;
~ **journalism** Sensationsjournalismus, der
taboo, tabu /tə'buː/ **1** n. Tabu, das
2 adj. Tabu⟨wort⟩; **be** ~: tabu sein
tabulate /'tæbjʊleɪt/ v.t. tabellarisch
darstellen
tabulator /'tæbjʊleɪtə(r)/ n. Tabulator,
der
tacit /'tæsɪt/ adj., '**tacitly** adv.
stillschweigend
taciturn /'tæsɪtɜːn/ adj. schweigsam;
wortkarg
tack /tæk/ **1** n. (a) (nail) kleiner Nagel
(b) (stitch) Heftstich, der
(c) (Naut., also fig.) Kurs, der
2 v.t. (a) (nail) festnageln
(b) (stitch) heften
3 v.i. (Naut.) kreuzen
tackle /'tækl/ **1** v.t. (a) angehen ⟨Problem
usw.⟩; ~ **sb. about/on/over sth.** jmdn. auf
etw. (Akk.) ansprechen; (ask for sth.) jmdn.
um etw. angehen
(b) (Sport) angreifen ⟨Spieler⟩; (Amer. Footb.;

Rugby) fassen
2 n. (a) (equipment) Ausrüstung, die
(b) (Sport) Angriff, der; (sliding ~) Tackling,
das; (Amer. Footb.; Rugby) Fassen und Halten
tacky /'tækɪ/ adj. (a) (sticky) klebrig
(b) (coll. derog.: tasteless) geschmacklos
tact /tækt/ n. Takt, der; **he has no** ~: er hat
kein Taktgefühl
tactful /'tæktfl/ adj., '**tactfully** adv.
taktvoll
tactical /'tæktɪkl/ adj. taktisch
tactics /'tæktɪks/ n. pl. Taktik, die
'**tactless** adj., '**tactlessly** adv. taktlos
tadpole /'tædpəʊl/ n. Kaulquappe, die
tag¹ /tæg/ **1** n. (a) Schild, das
(b) (electronic device) (on person) elektronische
Fessel; (on goods) Sicherungsetikett, das
(c) (Comp.) Tag, das; Markierung, die
2 v.t., **-gg-**: (Comp.) taggen; markieren
■ **tag a'long** v.i. mitkommen
tag² n. (game) Fangen, das
tail /teɪl/ **1** n. (a) Schwanz, der
(b) in pl. (on coin) ~s **[it is]** Zahl
2 v.t. (coll.: follow) beschatten
■ **tail 'back** v.i. sich stauen
■ **tail 'off** v.i. (a) zurückgehen
(b) (into silence) verstummen
tail: ~**back** n. (Brit.) Rückstau, der;
~ **end** n. Ende, das; ~**gate** **1** n. (Motor
Veh.) Heckklappe, die; **2** v.i. zu dicht
auffahren; ~ **light** n. Rücklicht, das
tailor /'teɪlə(r)/ n. Schneider, der/
Schneiderin, die
tailored /'teɪləd/, '**tailor-made** adjs.
maßgeschneidert
'**tail wind** n. Rückenwind, der
taint /teɪnt/ v.t. verderben; **be** ~**ed with sth.**
mit etw. behaftet sein (geh.)
Taiwan /taɪ'wɑːn/ pr. n. Taiwan (das)
take /teɪk/ **1** v.t., **took** /tʊk/, **taken** /'teɪkn/
(a) (get hold of, grasp, seize) nehmen
(b) (capture) einnehmen ⟨Stadt, Festung⟩;
machen ⟨Gefangenen⟩
(c) (gain, earn) ⟨Laden:⟩ einbringen; ⟨Person:⟩
einnehmen; ⟨Film, Stück:⟩ einspielen; (win)
gewinnen ⟨Satz, Spiel, Preis, Titel⟩
(d) (~ away with one) mitnehmen; (steal)
mitnehmen (verhüll.); ~ **place** stattfinden;
(spontaneously) sich ereignen; ⟨Wandlung:⟩
sich vollziehen
(e) (avail oneself of, use) nehmen; machen
⟨Pause, Ferien, Nickerchen⟩; ~ **the**
opportunity to do/of doing sth. die
Gelegenheit dazu benutzen, etw. zu tun
(f) (carry, guide, convey) bringen; ~ **sb. to visit**
sb. jmdn. zu Besuch bei jmdm. mitnehmen;

~ **home** mit nach Hause nehmen; (earn) nach Hause bringen ‹*Geld*›; (accompany) nach Hause bringen

(g) (remove) nehmen; (deduct) abziehen; ~ **sth./sb. from sb.** jmdm. etw./jmdm. wegnehmen

(h) (make) machen ‹*Foto, Kopie*›; (photograph) aufnehmen; aufnehmen ‹*Brief, Diktat*›; machen ‹*Prüfung, Sprung, Spaziergang, Reise*›; ablegen ‹*Gelübde, Eid*›; treffen ‹*Entscheidung*›

(i) (conduct) halten ‹*Gottesdienst, Unterricht*›; **Ms X ~s us for maths** in Mathe haben wir Frau X

(j) (eat, drink) nehmen ‹*Zucker, Milch, Tabletten, Überdosis*›; trinken ‹*Tee, Kaffee, Kognak usw.*›

(k) (need, require) brauchen ‹*Platz, Zeit*›; haben ‹*Objekt, Plural-s*›; gebraucht werden mit ‹*Kasus*›; **sth. ~s an hour/a year/all day** etw. dauert eine Stunde/ein Jahr/einen ganzen Tag

(l) (ascertain and record) notieren ‹*Namen, Adresse, Autonummer usw.*›; fühlen ‹*Puls*›; messen ‹*Temperatur, Größe usw.*›

(m) (assume) ~ **it [that]** …: annehmen, dass …; ~ **sb./sth. for/to be sth.** jmdn./etw. für etw. halten

(n) (react to) aufnehmen; ~ **sth. well/badly** etw. gut/nur schwer verkraften; ~ **sth. calmly** *or* **coolly** etw. gelassen [auf]nehmen

(o) (accept) annehmen

(p) (adopt, choose) ergreifen ‹*Maßnahmen*›; unternehmen ‹*Schritte*›; ~ **the wrong road** die falsche Straße fahren/gehen

(q) be ~n ill krank werden

(r) ~ **sth. to bits** *or* **pieces** etw. auseinander nehmen

2 *v.i.*, **took, taken (a)** ‹*Transplantat:*› vom Körper angenommen werden; ‹*Sämling, Pflanze:*› angehen

(b) (detract) ~ **from sth.** etw. schmälern

■ **take after** *v.t.* ~ **after sb.** (resemble) jmdm. ähnlich sein; (~ **as one's example**) es jmdm. gleichtun

■ **take a'way** *v.t.* **(a)** (remove) wegnehmen; (to a distance) mitnehmen; ~ **sth. away from sb.** jmdm. etw. abnehmen; **to** ~ **away** ‹*Pizza, Snack usw.*› zum Mitnehmen

(b) (Math.: deduct) abziehen

■ **take a'way from** *v.t.* schmälern

■ **take 'back** *v.t.* zurücknehmen; (return) zurückbringen

■ **take 'down** *v.t.* **(a)** (carry or lead down) hinunterbringen

(b) abnehmen ‹*Bild, Ankündigung, Weihnachtsschmuck*›; herunterziehen ‹*Hose*›; ~ **sth. down from a shelf** etw. von einem Regal herunternehmen

(c) (write down) aufnehmen

■ **take 'in** *v.t.* **(a)** hineinbringen; (bring indoors) hereinholen

(b) enger machen ‹*Kleidungsstück*›

(c) (understand) begreifen

(d) (cheat) hereinlegen (ugs.); (deceive) täuschen

■ **take 'off** **1** *v.t.* **(a)** abnehmen ‹*Deckel, Hut, Tischtuch, Verband*›; abziehen ‹*Kissenbezug*›; ausziehen ‹*Schuhe, Handschuhe*›; ablegen ‹*Mantel, Schmuck*›

(b) (deduct) abziehen; ~ **sth. off sth.** etw. von etw. abziehen

(c) ~ **a day** *etc.* **off** sich (*Dat.*) einen Tag *usw.* frei nehmen (ugs.)

(d) (mimic) nachahmen

2 *v.i.* (Aeronaut.) starten

■ **take 'on** *v.t.* **(a)** (undertake) übernehmen; auf sich (*Akk.*) nehmen ‹*Bürde*›

(b) (employ) einstellen

(c) (as opponent) es aufnehmen mit; (Sport: meet) antreten gegen

■ **take 'out** *v.t.* **(a)** (remove) herausnehmen; ziehen ‹*Zahn*›; ~ **sth. out of sth.** etw. aus etw. [heraus]nehmen

(b) (withdraw) abheben ‹*Geld*›

(c) (go out with) ~ **sb. out** mit jmdm. ausgehen; ~ **sb. out to** *or* **for lunch** jmdn. zum Mittagessen einladen

(d) (get issued) abschließen ‹*Versicherung*›; ausleihen ‹*Bücher*›; ~ **out a subscription to sth.** etw. abonnieren

(e) ~ **it out on sb.** seine Wut an jmdm. auslassen

■ **take 'over** **1** *v.t.* übernehmen

2 *v.i.* übernehmen; ‹*Manager, Firmenleiter:*› die Geschäfte übernehmen; ‹*Regierung, Präsident:*› die Amtsgeschäfte übernehmen; ~ **over from sb.** jmdn. ersetzen; (temporarily) jmdn. vertreten

■ **'take to** *v.t.* **(a)** (get into habit of) ~ **to doing sth.** es sich (*Dat.*) angewöhnen, etw. zu tun

(b) (like) sich hingezogen fühlen zu ‹*Person*›; sich erwärmen für ‹*Sache*›

■ **take 'up** **1** *v.t.* **(a)** (lift up) hochheben; (pick up) aufheben; herausreißen ‹*Dielen*›; aufreißen ‹*Straße*›

(b) (carry or lead up) hinaufbringen

(c) in Anspruch nehmen ‹*Zeit*›; brauchen/ (undesirably) wegnehmen ‹*Platz*›

(d) (start) ergreifen ‹*Beruf*›; anfangen ‹*Tennis, Schach, Gitarre usw.*›; aufnehmen ‹*Arbeit, Kampf*›; antreten ‹*Stelle*›; ~ **up a hobby** sich (*Dat.*) ein Hobby zulegen

(e) (pursue further) ~ **sth. up with sb.** sich in einer Sache an jmdn. wenden

2 *v.i.* ~ **up with sb.** (coll.) sich mit jmdm. einlassen

'takeaway *n.* (meal) Essen zum Mitnehmen; (restaurant) Restaurant mit Straßenverkauf

taken ▶ TAKE

take: ~**-off** *n.* **(a)** (Aeronaut.) Start, *der;* **(b)** (coll.: caricature) Parodie, *die;* ~**over** *n.* Übernahme, *die*

takings /ˈteɪkɪŋz/ *n. pl.* Einnahmen *Pl.*

talc /tælk/ *n.* Talkum, *das*

talcum /ˈtælkəm/ *n.* ~ **[powder]** Körperpuder, *der*

tale /teɪl/ *n.* Erzählung, *die;* Geschichte, *die* (of von, about über + *Akk.*)

talent /'tælənt/ n. Talent, *das;* **have [great/no** *etc.*] ~ **[for sth.]** [viel/kein *usw.*] Talent [zu *od.* für etw.] haben

'**talented** *adj.* talentiert

'**talent-spotting** n. Talentsuche, *die*

talk /tɔ:k/ [1] n. **(a)** (discussion) Gespräch, *das;* **have a** ~ **[with sb.] [about sth.]** [mit jmdm.] [über etw. (*Akk.*)] sprechen; **have** *or* **hold** ~**s [with sb.]** [mit jmdm.] Gespräche führen; **there is [much/some]** ~ **of ...:** man hört [häufig/öfter] von ...
(b) (speech, lecture) Vortrag, *der*
[2] v.i. sprechen (**with, to** mit); (lecture) sprechen; (converse) sich unterhalten; (have ~s) Gespräche führen; (gossip) reden; ~ **on the phone** telefonieren
[3] v.t. reden; ~ **sb. into/out of sth.** jmdn. zu etw. überreden/jmdm. etw. ausreden
■ **talk** '**over** v.t. besprechen
■ **talk** '**round** v.t. ~ **sb. round** jmdn. überreden

talkative /'tɔ:kətɪv/ *adj.* gesprächig

talking: ~ **point** n. Gesprächsthema, *das;* ~**-to** n. (coll.) Standpauke, *die* (ugs.)

'**talk show** n. Talkshow, *die*

tall /tɔ:l/ *adj.* hoch; groß ⟨*Person, Tier*⟩; **that's a** ~ **order** das ist ziemlich viel verlangt; ~ **story** unglaubliche Geschichte

tally /'tælɪ/ [1] n. **keep a** ~ **of sth.** über etw. (*Akk.*) Buch führen
[2] v.i. übereinstimmen

talon /'tælən/ n. Klaue, *die*

tambourine /tæmbə'ri:n/ n. Tamburin, *das*

tame /teɪm/ [1] *adj.* zahm; (fig.: spiritless) lahm (ugs.)
[2] v.t. zähmen

tamper /'tæmpə(r)/ v.i. ~ **with** sich (*Dat.*) zu schaffen machen an (+ *Dat.*)

tampon /'tæmpɒn/ n. Tampon, *der*

tan /tæn/ [1] v.t., **-nn-** gerben ⟨*Tierhaut, Fell*⟩
[2] v.i., **-nn-** braun werden
[3] n. **(a)** (colour) Gelbbraun, *das*
(b) (sun~) Bräune, *die;* **have/get a** ~: braun sein/werden
[4] *adj.* gelbbraun

tandem /'tændəm/ n. ~ **[bicycle]** Tandem, *das*

tang /tæŋ/ n. (taste) Geschmack, *der;* (smell) Geruch, *der*

tangent /'tændʒənt/ n. Tangente, *die;* **go off at a** ~ (fig.) plötzlich vom Thema abschweifen

tangerine /tændʒə'ri:n/ n. (fruit) ~ **[orange]** Tangerine, *die*

tangible /'tændʒɪbl/ *adj.* greifbar; spürbar ⟨*Unterschied, Verbesserung*⟩; handfest ⟨*Beweis*⟩

tangle /'tæŋgl/ [1] n. Gewirr, *das;* (in hair) Verfilzung, *die*
[2] v.t. verheddern (ugs.); verfilzen ⟨*Haar*⟩
■ **tangle** '**up** v.t. verheddern (ugs.)

tango /'tæŋgəʊ/ n., pl. ~**s** Tango, *der*

tank /tæŋk/ n. **(a)** Tank, *der*
(b) (Mil.) Panzer, *der*

tankard /'tæŋkəd/ n. Krug, *der*

tanker /'tæŋkə(r)/ n. (ship) Tanker, *der;* (vehicle) Tank[last]wagen, *der*

tanned /tænd/ *adj.* braun gebrannt

tantalize /'tæntəlaɪz/ v.t. reizen

tantalizing /'tæntəlaɪzɪŋ/ *adj.* verlockend

tantamount /'tæntəmaʊnt/ *adj.* **be** ~ **to sth.** gleichbedeutend mit etw. sein

tantrum /'tæntrəm/ n. Wutanfall, *der;* (of child) Trotzanfall, *der;* **throw a** ~**:** einen Wutanfall/Trotzanfall bekommen

tap[1] /tæp/ [1] n. Hahn, *der;* **hot/cold[-water]** ~**:** Warm-/Kaltwasserhahn, *der;* **be on** ~ (fig.) zur Verfügung stehen
[2] v.t., **-pp-: (a)** erschließen ⟨*Reserven, Markt*⟩
(b) (Teleph.) abhören; anzapfen (ugs.)

tap[2] [1] v.t., **-pp-** klopfen an (+ *Akk.*); (on upper surface) klopfen auf (+ *Akk.*)
[2] v.i., **-pp-:** ~ **at/on sth.** an etw. (*Akk.*) klopfen; (on upper surface) auf etw. (*Akk.*) klopfen
[3] n. Klopfen, *das*

'**tap dance** [1] n. Stepp[tanz], *der*
[2] v.i. Stepptanzen; steppen

tape /teɪp/ [1] n. **(a)** Band, *das;* **adhesive** *or* (coll.) **sticky** ~**:** Klebeband, *das*
(b) (for recording) [Ton]band, *das* (**of** mit); **make a** ~ **of sth.** etw. auf Band aufnehmen
[2] v.t. **(a)** (record on ~) [auf Band] aufnehmen
(b) (bind with ~) [mit Klebeband] zukleben
(c) **have got sb./sth.** ~**d** (coll.) jmdn. durchschaut haben/etw. im Griff haben

tape: ~ **cassette** n. Tonbandkassette, *die;* ~ **deck** n. Tapedeck, *das;* ~ **measure** n. Bandmaß, *das*

taper /'teɪpə(r)/ [1] v.i. sich verjüngen; ~ **[to a point]** spitz zulaufen
[2] n. [wax] ~: Wachsstock, *der*

tape: ~ **recorder** n. Tonbandgerät, *das;* ~ **recording** n. Tonbandaufnahme, *die*

tapestry /'tæpɪstrɪ/ n. Gobelingewebe, *das;* (wall-hanging) Bildteppich, *der*

'**tapeworm** n. Bandwurm, *der*

'**tap water** n. Leitungswasser, *das*

tar /tɑ:(r)/ [1] n. Teer, *der;* **high-**~/**low-**~ **cigarette** Zigarette mit hohem/niedrigem Teergehalt
[2] v.t., **-rr-** teeren

target /'tɑ:gɪt/ [1] n. **(a)** Ziel, *das;* **hit/miss the/its** ~**:** [das Ziel] treffen/das Ziel verfehlen; **production/export/savings** ~**:** Produktions-/Export-/Sparziel, *das;* **be above/below** ~ (fig.) das Ziel über-/unterschritten haben
(b) (Sport) Zielscheibe, *die*
[2] v.t. (fig.) zielen auf ⟨*Käufergruppe*⟩

target: ~ **date** n. vorgesehener Termin; ~ **figure** n. (esp. Commerc.) Ziel, *das*

tariff /'tærɪf/ n. (a) (tax) Zoll, der
(b) (list of charges) Tarif, der

tarnish /'tɑːnɪʃ/ ① v.t. stumpf werden
lassen ⟨Metall⟩; (fig.) beflecken ⟨Ruf⟩
② v.i. stumpf werden

tarpaulin /tɑː'pɔːlɪn/ n. Plane, die

tart¹ /tɑːt/ adj. herb; sauer ⟨Obst⟩; (fig.)
scharfzüngig

tart² n. (a) (Brit.) (filled pie) ≈ Obstkuchen,
der; (small pastry) Obsttörtchen, das
(b) (sl.: prostitute) Nutte, die (salopp)
■ **tart 'up** v.t. (Brit. coll.) ~ oneself up, get
~ed up sich auftakeln (ugs.)

tartan /'tɑːtən/ ① n. Schotten[stoff], der
② adj. Schotten⟨rock, -jacke⟩

tartar /'tɑːtə(r)/ n. Zahnstein, der

tartar sauce /'tɑːtə 'sɔːs/ n.
Remoulade[nsoße], die

task /tɑːsk/ n. Aufgabe, die; take sb. to
~: jmdm. eine Lektion erteilen

task: ~bar n. (Comp.) Taskleiste, die;
~ **force** n. Sonderkommando, das

tassel /'tæsl/ n. Quaste, die

taste /teɪst/ ① v.t. (a) schmecken; (try a
little) probieren
(b) (recognize flavour of) [heraus]schmecken
② v.i. schmecken (of nach); not ~ of
anything nach nichts schmecken
③ n. (a) (flavour) Geschmack, der; [sense of]
~: Geschmack[ssinn], der
(b) (discernment) Geschmack, der
(c) (sample) Kostprobe, die

tasteful /'teɪstfl/ adj., **'tastefully** adv.
geschmackvoll

tasteless adj. geschmacklos

tasty /'teɪstɪ/ adj. lecker

tat /tæt/ n. ▶ TIT²

tattered /'tætəd/ adj. zerlumpt
⟨Kleidung⟩; zerfleddert ⟨Buch⟩

tatters /'tætəz/ n. pl. Fetzen Pl.; be in
~: in Fetzen sein; (fig.) ruiniert sein

tattoo /tə'tuː/ ① v.t. tätowieren
② n. Tätowierung, die

tattooer /tə'tuːə(r)/, **tattooist** /tə'tuːɪst/
ns. Tätowierer, der/Tätowiererin, die

tatty /'tætɪ/ adj. (coll.) schäbig

taught ▶ TEACH

taunt /tɔːnt/ ① v.t. verspotten (about
wegen)
② n. spöttische Bemerkung

Taurus /'tɔːrəs/ n. (Astrol., Astron.) der Stier

taut /tɔːt/ adj. straff ⟨Seil, Kabel⟩; gespannt
⟨Muskel⟩

tavern /'tævən/ n. Schenke, die

tawny /'tɔːnɪ/ adj. gelbbraun

tax /tæks/ ① n. Steuer, die; before/after
~: vor Steuern/nach Abzug der Steuern; for
~ reasons aus steuerlichen Gründen
② v.t. (a) besteuern; versteuern
⟨Einkommen⟩
(b) (fig.) strapazieren ⟨Kräfte, Geduld⟩

taxable /'tæksəbl/ adj. steuerpflichtig

tax: ~ **allowance** n. Steuerfreibetrag,
der; ~ **assessment** n. Steuerbescheid,
der

taxation /tæk'seɪʃn/ n. Besteuerung, die;
(taxes payable) Steuern Pl.

tax: ~ **avoidance** n. Steuerumgehung,
die; ~ **bill** n. Steuerbescheid, der; (amount)
Steuerschuld, die; ~ **bracket** n. Stufe
im Steuertarif; ~**-deductible** adj.
steuerabzugsfähig; [steuerlich] absetzbar;
~ **demand** n. Steuerforderung, die;
~ **disc** n. (Motor Veh.) Steuerplakette, die;
~ **evasion** n. Steuerhinterziehung, die;
~ **exile** n. (person) Steuerflüchtling, der;
~ **form** n. Steuerformular, das; ~**-free**
adj. steuerfrei; ~ **haven** n. Steueroase,
die (ugs.)

taxi /'tæksɪ/ ① n. Taxi, das
② v.i. ~ing or taxying ⟨Flugzeug:⟩ rollen

'taxi driver n. Taxifahrer, der/-fahrerin,
die

tax: ~ **incentive** n. steuerlicher Anreiz;
~ **inspector** n. Steuerinspektor, der/
-inspektorin, die

taxi: ~ **rank** (Brit.), ~ **stand** (Amer.) ns.
Taxistand, der

tax: ~**man** n. (coll.) Finanzbeamte, der/
-beamtin, die; ~ **office** n. Finanzamt, das
~**payer** n. Steuerzahler, der/-zahlerin,
die; ~ **relief** n. Steuererleichterung,
die; ~ **return** n. Steuererklärung, die;
~ **year** n. Steuerjahr, das

TB abbr. = **tuberculosis** Tb, die

tbsp. abbr., pl. same or ~s:
= **tablespoon**

tea /tiː/ n. (a) Tee, der
(b) (meal) [high] ~: Abendessen, das

tea: ~ **bag** n. Teebeutel, der; ~ **break**
n. (Brit.) Teepause, die; ~ **caddy** n.
Teebüchse, die

teach /tiːtʃ/ ① v.t., taught /tɔːt/
unterrichten; (at university) lehren; ~ sb./
oneself/an animal sth. jmdm./sich/einem
Tier etw. beibringen; ~ sb. to ride jmdm.
das Reiten beibringen
② v.i., taught unterrichten

'teacher n. Lehrer, der/Lehrerin, die

teacher: ~ **training** n.
Lehrerausbildung, die; ~**-training
college** n. ≈ pädagogische Hochschule

'teaching profession n. Lehrberuf, der

tea: ~ **cloth** n. Geschirrtuch, das;
~ **cosy** n. Teewärmer, der; ~**cup** n.
Teetasse, die

teak /tiːk/ n. Teak[holz], das

'tea leaf n. Teeblatt, das

team /tiːm/ n. Team, das; (Sport also)
Mannschaft, die
■ **team 'up** v.i. sich zusammentun (ugs.)

team: ~ **effort** n. Team- od.
Gemeinschaftsarbeit, die; ~ **game** n.
Mannschaftsspiel, das; ~ **leader** n.
Gruppenleiter, der/-leiterin, die; ⋯⋗

⁓**mate** n. Mannschaftskamerad, der/
-kameradin, die; ⁓ **'spirit** n. Teamgeist,
der; (Sport also) Mannschaftsgeist, der;
⁓**work** n. Teamarbeit, die

'**teapot** n. Teekanne, die

tear¹ /teə(r)/ ① n. Riss, der
② v.t., tore /tɔː(r)/, torn /tɔːn/ (a) (rip)
zerreißen; (pull apart) auseinander reißen;
(damage) aufreißen; ⁓ **open** aufreißen ‹Brief,
Paket›
(b) ⁓ sth. out of sb.'s hands jmdm. etw. aus
der Hand reißen
③ v.i., tore, torn (a) (rip) [zer]reißen
(b) (move hurriedly) rasen (ugs.)
■ **tear a'way** v.t. wegreißen; ⁓ oneself
away (fig.) sich losreißen
■ **tear 'up** v.t. zerreißen

tear² /tɪə(r)/ n. Träne, die

'**tear drop** /tɪə(r)/ n. Träne, die

tearful /'tɪəfl/ adj. weinend

'**tear gas** /tɪə(r)/ n. Tränengas, das

tease /tiːz/ ① v.t. necken (about wegen);
aufziehen (ugs.) (about mit)
② v.i. seine Späße machen

tea: ⁓ **service,** ⁓**set** ns. Teeservice,
das; ⁓ **shop** n. (Brit.) ≈ Café, das;
⁓**spoon** n. Teelöffel, der; ⁓ **strainer** n.
Teesieb, das

teat /tiːt/ n. (a) Zitze, die
(b) (of rubber or plastic) Sauger, der

tea: ⁓**time** n. Teezeit, die; ⁓ **towel** n.
Geschirrtuch, das; ⁓ **trolley** n. Teewagen,
der; ⁓ **urn** n. Teebehälter, der

techie /'tekɪ/ n. (coll.) Technikfreak, der;
(computer expert) Computerfreak, der

technical /'teknɪkl/ adj. technisch
‹Problem, Daten, Fortschritt›; Fach‹kenntnis, -sprache, -begriff, -wörterbuch›;
⁓ **college** Fachhochschule, die; ⁓ **term**
Fachbegriff, der; Fachausdruck, der

technicality /teknɪ'kælɪtɪ/ n. technisches
Detail

technician /tek'nɪʃn/ n. Techniker,
der/Technikerin, die

technique /tek'niːk/ n. Technik, die;
(procedure) Methode, die

techno ① adj. Techno-
② n. Techno, der od. das

technological /teknə'lɒdʒɪkl/ adj.
technisch; technologisch

technology /tek'nɒlədʒɪ/ n. Technik, die;
(application of science) Technologie, die

technophobe /'teknəʊfəʊb/ n. Mensch
mit einer Technikphobie

tectonic /tek'tɒnɪk/ (Geol.) ① adj.
tektonisch; ⁓ **plate** tektonische Platte
② n., in pl. Tektonik, die; plate ⁓s
Plattentektonik, die

teddy /'tedɪ/ n. ⁓ **[bear]** Teddy[bär], der

tedious /'tiːdɪəs/ adj. langwierig ‹Reise,
Arbeit›; (uninteresting) langweilig

tee /tiː/ n. (Golf) Tee, das

teem /tiːm/ v.i. wimmeln (**with** von)

teen /tiːn/ adj. Teenager-

teenage[d] /'tiːneɪdʒ(d)/ attrib. adj. im
Teenageralter nachgestellt

teenager /'tiːneɪdʒə(r)/ n. Teenager, der;
(loosely) Jugendliche, der/die

teens /tiːnz/ n. pl. Teenagerjahre Pl.

'**tee shirt** n. T-Shirt, das

teeter /'tiːtə(r)/ v.i. wanken; ⁓ **on the edge
of sth.** schwankend am Rande einer Sache
(Gen.) stehen

teeth pl. of TOOTH

teething troubles /'tiːðɪŋ trʌblz/ n. pl.
have ⁓ (fig.) Anfangsschwierigkeiten haben

teetotal /tiː'təʊtl/ adj. abstinent lebend

teetotaller /tiː'təʊtələ(r)/ n. Abstinenzler,
der/Abstinenzlerin, die

TEFL /'tefl/ abbr. = **teaching of
English as a foreign language**

Teflon ® /'teflɒn/ n. Teflon ⓌⓏ, das

Tel., tel. abbr. = **telephone** Tel.

telebanking /'telɪbæŋkɪŋ/ n.
Telebanking, das

telecommunications
/telɪkəmjuːnɪ'keɪʃnz/ n. pl. Fernmelde- od.
Nachrichtentechnik, die

telecommute /'telɪkəmjuːt/ v.i.
Telearbeit verrichten

telecommuting /'telɪkəmjuːtɪŋ/ n.
Telearbeit, die

teleconference /'telɪkɒnfərəns/ n.
Telekonferenz, die

telecottage /'telɪkɒtɪdʒ/ n.: jedermann
zugängliche Einrichtung, die bes.
Telearbeitern Zugang zu einem ans Internet
angeschlossenen Computer bietet

telegram /'telɪgræm/ n. Telegramm, das

telegraph /'telɪgrɑːf/ n. Telegraf, der;
⁓ **pole** Telegrafenmast, der

telemarketing /'telɪmɑːkɪtɪŋ/ n.
Telefonmarketing, das

telepathy /tɪ'lepəθɪ/ n. Telepathie, die

telephone /'telɪfəʊn/ ① n. Telefon, das;
attrib. Telefon-; **answer the** ⁓: Anrufe
entgegennehmen; (on one occasion) ans
Telefon gehen; (speak) sich melden; **be
on the** ⁓: Telefon haben; (be speaking)
telefonieren (**to** mit)
② v.t. anrufen
③ v.i. anrufen; ⁓ **for a taxi** nach einem Taxi
telefonieren

telephone: ⁓ **'answering
machine** n. Anrufbeantworter, der;
⁓ **'banking** n. Telefonbanking, das;
⁓ **book** n. Telefonbuch, das; ⁓ **booth,**
(Brit.) ⁓ **box** ns. Telefonzelle, die; ⁓ **call**
n. Telefongespräch, das; ⁓ **connection**
n. Telefonverbindung, die; ⁓ **directory**
n. Telefonverzeichnis, das; ⁓ **exchange**
n. Fernmeldeamt, das; ⁓ **number** n.
Telefonnummer, die; ⁓ **operator** n.
Telefonist, der/Telefonistin, die

telephonist /tɪ'lefənɪst/ n. Telefonist, der/Telefonistin, die

telephoto /telɪ'fəʊtəʊ/ adj. ~ **lens** 'Teleobjektiv, das

teleprinter /'telɪprɪntə(r)/ n. Fernschreiber, der

'telesales n. pl. Telefonverkauf, der; Verkauf per Telefon

telescope /'telɪskəʊp/ n. Teleskop, das; Fernrohr, das

telescopic /telɪ'skɒpɪk/ adj. (collapsible) ausziehbar; Teleskop⟨antenne⟩

Teletex ® /'telɪteks/ n. Teletex, das

teletext /'telɪtekst/ n. Teletext, der

televise /'telɪvaɪz/ v.t. im Fernsehen senden od. übertragen

television /'telɪvɪʒn, telɪ'vɪʒn/ n. **(a)** no art. das Fernsehen; **on** ~: im Fernsehen; **watch** ~: fernsehen

(b) (~ set) Fernsehapparat, der; Fernseher, der (ugs.)

television: ~ **aerial** n. Fernsehantenne, die; ~ **channel** n. [Fernseh]kanal, der; ~ **coverage** n. Fernsehberichterstattung, die; ~ **licence** n. (Brit.) Fernsehgenehmigung, die ⟨die jährlich gegen Zahlen der Gebühren erneuert wird⟩; ~ **licence fee** Fernsehgebühren Pl.; ~ **lounge** n. Fernsehraum, der; ~ **personality** n. Fernsehgröße, die (ugs.); ~ **picture** n. Fernsehbild, das; ~ **programme** n. Fernsehsendung, die; ~ **screen** n. Bildschirm, der; ~ **serial** n. Fernsehserie, die; ~ **set** n. Fernsehgerät, das; ~ **studio** n. Fernsehstudio, das; ~ **viewer** n. Fernsehzuschauer, der/-zuschauerin, die

teleworking /'telɪwɜːkɪŋ/ n. Telearbeit, die

telex /'teleks/ ① n. Telex, das
② v.t. ein Telex schicken (+ Dat.); telexen ⟨Nachricht⟩

tell /tel/ ① v.t., **told** /təʊld/ **(a)** (relate) erzählen; (make known) sagen ⟨Name, Adresse⟩; anvertrauen ⟨Geheimnis⟩; ~ **sb. sth.** or **sth. to sb.** jmdm. etw. erzählen/sagen/anvertrauen; ~ **sb. the way to the station** jmdm. den Weg zum Bahnhof beschreiben; ~ **sb. the time** jmdm. die Uhrzeit sagen; ~ **tales** (lie) Lügengeschichten erzählen; (gossip) tratschen (ugs.)

(b) (instruct) sagen; ~ **sb. [not] to do sth.** jmdm. sagen, er soll[e] etw. [nicht] tun

(c) (determine) feststellen; (see, recognize) erkennen (**by an** + Dat.); (with reference to the future) [vorher]sagen

(d) (distinguish) unterscheiden

(e) **all told** insgesamt

② v.i., **told (a)** (determine) **how can you** ~? wie kann man das feststellen od. wissen?; **you never can** ~: man kann nie wissen

(b) (give information) erzählen (**of, about** von)

(c) (reveal secret) es verraten; **time will** ~: das wird sich zeigen

(d) (produce an effect) sich auswirken

■ **tell a'part** v.t. auseinander halten

■ **tell 'off** v.t. (coll.) ~ **sb. off** [**for sth.**] jmdn. [für od. wegen etw.] ausschimpfen

teller /'telə(r)/ n. **(a)** (in bank) ▶ CASHIER
(b) (counting votes) Stimmenzähler, der/-zählerin, die

telly /'telɪ/ n. (Brit. coll.) Fernseher, der (ugs.); **on** ~: im Fernsehen; **watch** ~: Fernsehen gucken (ugs.)

temp /temp/ n. (Brit. coll.) Zeitarbeitskraft, die

temper /'tempə(r)/ ① n. **(a)** Naturell, das; **be in a good/bad** ~: gute/schlechte Laune haben; **keep/lose one's** ~: sich beherrschen/die Beherrschung verlieren
(b) (anger) **fit of** ~: Wutanfall, der; **have a** ~: jähzornig sein
② v.t. mäßigen; mildern ⟨Kritik⟩

temperament /'temprəmənt/ n. (nature) Veranlagung, die; Natur, die; (disposition) Temperament, das

temperamental /temprə'mentl/ adj. launenhaft

temperate /'tempərət/ adj. gemäßigt

temperature /'temprɪtʃə(r)/ n. Temperatur, die; **have** or **run a** ~ (coll.) Temperatur od. Fieber haben

template /'templɪt/ n. **(a)** Schablone, die
(b) (Comp.) Schablone, die; Template, das

temple¹ /'templ/ n. Tempel, der

temple² n. (Anat.) Schläfe, die

tempo /'tempəʊ/ n., pl. ~**s** or **tempi** /'tempiː/ Tempo, das

temporarily /'tempərərɪlɪ/ adv. vorübergehend

temporary /'tempərərɪ/ ① adj. vorübergehend; provisorisch ⟨Gebäude, Büro⟩; ~ **job** Aushilfstätigkeit, die
② n. Aushilfe, die; Aushilfskraft, die

tempt /tempt/ v.t. **(a)** ~ **sb. to do sth.** jmdn. geneigt machen, etw. zu tun; **be** ~**ed to do sth.** versucht sein, etw. zu tun; ~ **sb. out** jmdn. hinauslocken
(b) (provoke) herausfordern; ~ **fate** das Schicksal herausfordern

temptation /temp'teɪʃn/ n. **(a)** no pl. (attracting) Verlockung, die; (being attracted) Versuchung, die
(b) (thing) Verlockung, die

'tempting adj. verlockend

ten /ten/ ① adj. zehn
② n. Zehn, die. See also EIGHT

tenable /'tenəbl/ adj. haltbar ⟨Theorie⟩; vertretbar ⟨Standpunkt⟩

tenacious /tɪ'neɪʃəs/ adj. hartnäckig

tenacity /tɪ'næsɪtɪ/ n. Hartnäckigkeit, die

tenant /'tenənt/ n. (of flat, residential building) Mieter, der/Mieterin, die; (of farm, shop) Pächter, der/Pächterin, die

tend¹ /tend/ v.i. ~ **to do sth.** dazu neigen od. tendieren, etw. zu tun;

∼ to sth. zu etw. neigen; **he** ∼**s to get upset if ...**: er regt sich leicht auf, wenn ...
tend² *v.t.* sich kümmern um; hüten ⟨*Schafe*⟩; bedienen ⟨*Maschine*⟩
tendency /'tendənsı/ *n.* (inclination) Tendenz, *die;* **have a** ∼ **to do sth.** dazu neigen, etw. zu tun
tender¹ /'tendə(r)/ *adj.* (a) (not tough) zart
(b) (loving) zärtlich
(c) (sensitive) empfindlich
tender² 1 *v.t.* (a) (present) einreichen ⟨*Rücktritt*⟩; vorbringen ⟨*Entschuldigung*⟩
(b) (offer as payment) anbieten
2 *n.* Angebot, *das*
'**tenderly** *adv.* (gently) behutsam; (lovingly) zärtlich
'**tenderness** *n.* ▸ TENDER¹: Zartheit, *die;* Zärtlichkeit, *die;* Empfindlichkeit, *die*
tendon /'tendən/ *n.* (Anat.) Sehne, *die*
tenement /'tenımənt/ *n.* Mietshaus, *das*
tenet /'tenıt/ *n.* Grundsatz, *der*
tenner /'tenə(r)/ *n.* (Brit. coll.) Zehnpfundschein, *der*
tennis /'tenıs/ *n.* Tennis, *das*
tennis: ∼ **ball** *n.* Tennisball, *der;* ∼ **club** *n.* Tennisverein, *der;* ∼ **court** *n.* (for lawn ∼) Tennisplatz, *der;* (indoor) Tennishalle, *die;* ∼ '**elbow** *n., no art.* (Med.) Tennisell[en]bogen, *der;* ∼ **match** *n.* Tennismatch, *das;* Tennisspiel, *das;* ∼ **racket** *n.* Tennisschläger, *der;* ∼ **shoe** *n.* Tennisschuh, *der*
tenor /'tenə(r)/ *n.* (Mus.) Tenor, *der*
tense¹ /tens/ *n.* (Ling.) Zeit, *die;* **in the present/future** *etc.* ∼: im Präsens/Futur *usw.*
tense² 1 *adj.* gespannt
2 *v.i.* **sb.** ∼**s** jmds. Muskeln spannen sich an
3 *v.t.* anspannen
tension /'tenʃn/ *n.* (a) Spannung, *die*
(b) (mental strain) Anspannung, *die*
tent /tent/ *n.* Zelt, *das*
tentacle /'tentəkl/ *n.* Tentakel, *der od. das*
tentative /'tentətıv/ *adj.* (a) (not definite) vorläufig
(b) (hesitant) zaghaft
tenterhooks /'tentəhʊks/ *n. pl.* **be on** ∼: [wie] auf glühenden Kohlen sitzen
tenth /tenθ/ 1 *adj.* zehnt...
2 *n.* (in sequence, rank) Zehnte, *der/die/das;* (fraction) Zehntel, *das. See also* EIGHTH
tent: ∼ **peg** *n.* Zeltpflock, *der;* ∼ **pole** *n.* Zeltstange, *die*
tenuous /'tenjʊəs/ *adj.* dünn ⟨*Atmosphäre*⟩; dürftig ⟨*Argument*⟩; unbegründet ⟨*Anspruch*⟩
tepid /'tepıd/ *adj.* lauwarm
term /tɜːm/ *n.* (a) [Fach]begriff, *der*
(b) *in pl.* (conditions) Bedingungen *Pl.;* **come to** ∼**s with sth.** mit etw. zurechtkommen; (resign oneself to sth.) sich mit etw. abfinden

(c) *in pl.* (charges) Konditionen *Pl.*
(d) in the short/long/medium ∼: kurz-/lang-/mittelfristig
(e) (Sch.) Halbjahr, *das;* (Univ.: one of two/three divisions per year) Semester, *das*/Trimester, *das*
(f) (limited period) Zeitraum, *der;* ∼ **[of office]** Amtszeit, *die*
(g) *in pl.* (mode of expression) Worte *Pl.*
(h) *in pl.* (relations) **be on good/bad** ∼**s with sb.** mit jmdm. auf gutem/schlechtem Fuß stehen
2 *v.t.* nennen
terminal /'tɜːmınl/ 1 *n.* (a) (for train or bus) Bahnhof, *der;* (for airline passengers) Terminal, *der od. das*
(b) (Teleph., Comp.) Terminal, *das*
2 *adj.* (Med.) unheilbar
terminally /'tɜːmınəlı/ *adv.* ∼ **ill** unheilbar krank
terminate /'tɜːmıneıt/ *v.t.* (a) beenden; lösen ⟨*Vertrag*⟩
(b) (Med.) unterbrechen ⟨*Schwangerschaft*⟩
termination /tɜːmı'neıʃn/ *n.* (a) *no pl.* Beendigung, *die;* (of lease) Ablauf, *der*
(b) (Med.) Schwangerschaftsabbruch, *der*
termini *pl. of* TERMINUS
terminology /tɜːmı'nɒlədʒı/ *n.* Terminologie, *die*
terminus /'tɜːmınəs/ *n., pl.* ∼**es** *or* termini /'tɜːmınaı/ Endstation, *die*
terrace /'terəs, 'terıs/ *n.* Terrasse, *die;* (row of houses) Häuserreihe, *die*
terraced house /'terəst haʊs, 'terıst haʊs/ *n.* Reihenhaus, *das*
terracotta /terə'kɒtə/ *n., no indef. art.* Terrakotta, *die*
terrain /te'reın/ *n.* Gelände, *das*
terrestrial /tə'restrıəl/ *adj.* terrestrisch ⟨*Raumschiff, Fernsehen, Bevölkerung*⟩; Erd⟨*satellit, -bevölkerung*⟩
terrible /'terıbl/ *adj.* (a) (coll.: very great or bad) schrecklich (ugs.)
(b) (coll.: incompetent) schlecht
(c) (causing terror) furchtbar
terribly /'terıblı/ *adv.* (a) (coll.: very) unheimlich (ugs.)
(b) (coll.: appallingly) furchtbar (ugs.)
(c) (coll.: incompetently) schlecht
(d) (fearfully) auf erschreckende Weise
terrier /'terıə(r)/ *n.* Terrier, *der*
terrific /tə'rıfık/ *adj.* (coll.) (a) (great, intense) irrsinnig (ugs.)
(b) (magnificent) sagenhaft (ugs.)
(c) (highly expert) klasse (ugs.)
terrify /'terıfaı/ *v.t.* (a) Angst machen (+ *Dat.*); **be terrified that ...**: Angst haben, dass ...
(b) (scare) Angst einjagen (+ *Dat.*)
'**terrifying** *adj.* entsetzlich ⟨*Erlebnis, Buch*⟩; Furcht erregend ⟨*Anblick*⟩; beängstigend ⟨*Geschwindigkeit*⟩
terrine /tə'riːn/ *n.* (a) (dish) Steinguttopf, *der*

(b) (Gastr.) Terrine, *die*

territorial /terɪ'tɔːrɪəl/ *adj.* territorial; Gebiets⟨*anspruch usw.*⟩

territory /'terɪtrɪ/ *n.* Gebiet, *das*

terror /'terə(r)/ *n.* [panische] Angst; Schrecken, *das*

terrorism /'terərɪzm/ *n.* Terrorismus, *der;* (terrorist acts) Terror, *der*

'terrorist *n.* Terrorist, *der*/Terroristin, *die; attrib.* Terror⟨*gruppe, -organisation, -angriff, -netzwerk, -zelle*⟩;

terrorize /'terəraɪz/ *v.t.* **(a)** (frighten) in [Angst und] Schrecken versetzen
(b) (coerce) terrorisieren

terse /tɜːs/ *adj.* **(a)** (concise) kurz und bündig
(b) (curt) knapp

test /test/ ① *n.* **(a)** (Sch.) Klassenarbeit, *die;* (Univ.) Klausur, *die;* **put sb./sth. to the** ~: jmdn./etw. erproben
(b) (analysis) Test, *der*
② *v.t.* untersuchen ⟨*Wasser, Augen*⟩; testen ⟨*Gehör, Augen*⟩; prüfen ⟨*Schüler*⟩; ~ **sb. for Aids** jmdn. auf Aids untersuchen
■ **'test out** *v.t.* ausprobieren ⟨*Produkte*⟩ (**on** an + *Dat.*); erproben ⟨*Theorie, Idee*⟩

Testament /'testəmənt/ *n.* **Old/New** ~ (Bibl.) Altes/Neues Testament

test: ~ **ban** *n.* Atom[waffen]teststopp, *der;* ~ **ban treaty** *n.* [Atom]teststopp-Abkommen, *das;* ~ **drive** *n.* Probefahrt, *die;* ~**-drive** *v.t.* Probe fahren

testicle /'testɪkl/ *n.* Testikel, *der* (fachspr.); Hoden, *der*

testicular /tes'tɪkjʊlə(r)/ *adj.* testikulär (fachspr.); Hoden⟨*krebs, -tumor*⟩

testify /'testɪfaɪ/ ① *v.i.* **(a)** ~ **to sth.** etw. bezeugen
(b) (Law) ~ **against sb.** gegen jmdn. aussagen
② *v.t.* bestätigen

testimonial /testɪ'məʊnɪəl/ *n.* Zeugnis, *das;* Referenz, *die*

testimony /'testɪmənɪ/ *n.* Aussage, *die*

test: ~ **pilot** *n.* Testpilot, *der*/-pilotin, *die;* ~ **tube** *n.* Reagenzglas, *das;* ~**-tube baby** *n.* (coll.) Retortenbaby, *das* (ugs.)

testy /'testɪ/ *adj.* leicht reizbar ⟨*Person*⟩; gereizt ⟨*Antwort*⟩

tetanus /'tetənəs/ *n.* Tetanus, *der*

tetchy /'tetʃɪ/ *adj.* leicht reizbar; gereizt

tether /'teðə(r)/ ① *n.* **be at the end of one's** ~: am Ende [seiner Kraft] sein
② *v.t.* anbinden (**to** an + *Dat. od. Akk.*)

text /tekst/ ① *n.* Text, *der;*
② *v.t.* ~ **sb.** jmdm. eine [Text]nachricht schicken
③ *v.i.* eine Textnachricht [ver]schicken; (to mobile phone) eine SMS [ver]schicken; simsen (ugs.)

text: ~**book** *n.* Lehrbuch, *das;* ~**book case** Paradefall, *der;* ~ **file** *n.* (Comp.) Textdatei, *die*

textile /'tekstaɪl/ *n.* Stoff, *der;* ~**s** Textilien *Pl.*

'textphone *n.* Texttelefon, *das*

'text processing *n.* (Comp.) Textverarbeitung, *die*

texture /'tekstʃə(r)/ *n.* Beschaffenheit, *die;* (of fabric) Struktur, *die*

Thai /taɪ/ ① *adj.* thailändisch; **sb. is** ~: jmd. ist Thai
② *n.* **(a)** *pl. same or* ~**s** Thai, *der*/*die*
(b) (language) Thai, *das*

Thailand /'taɪlænd/ *pr. n.* Thailand (*das*)

Thames /temz/ *pr. n.* Themse, *die*

than /ðən, *stressed* ðæn/ *conj.* als; **I know you better** ~ **[I do]** him ich kenne dich besser als ihn

thank /θæŋk/ *v.t.* ~ **sb. [for sth.]** jmdm. [für etw.] danken; ~ **God** *or* **goodness** *or* **heaven[s]** Gott sei Dank; **[I]** ~ **you** danke; **no,** ~ **you** nein, danke; **yes,** ~ **you** ja, bitte; ~ **you very much** vielen herzlichen Dank

thankful /'θæŋkfl/ *adj.* dankbar

thankfully /'θæŋkfəlɪ/ *adv.* **(a)** (gratefully) dankbar
(b) (as sentence-modifier: fortunately) glücklicherweise

'thankless *adj.* undankbar

thanks /θæŋks/ *n. pl.* **(a)** (gratitude) Dank, *der;* ~ **to** (with the help of) dank; (on account of the bad influence of) wegen
(b) (formula expr. gratitude) danke; **no,** ~: nein, danke; **yes,** ~: ja, bitte; **many** ~ (coll.) vielen Dank

thanksgiving /'θæŋksgɪvɪŋ/ *n.* **T~ [Day]** (Amer.) [amerikanisches] Erntedankfest; Thanksgiving Day, *der*

'thank-you *n.* (coll.) Dankeschön, *das*

that ① /ðæt/ *adj., pl.* **those** /ðəʊz/
(a) dieser/diese/dieses
(b) (coupled or contrasted with 'this') der/die/das
② /ðæt/ *pron., pl.* **those (a)** der/die/das; **what bird is** ~? was für ein Vogel ist das?; **like** ~: so; **[just] like** ~ (without effort, thought) einfach so; ~**'s right!** gut *od.* recht so; (iron.) nur so weiter!; ~ **will do** das reicht
(b) (Brit.) **who is** ~? wer ist da?; (on telephone) wer ist am Apparat?
③ /ðət/ *rel. pron., pl. same* der/die/das; **everyone** ~ **I know** jeder, den ich kenne; **this is all [the money]** ~ **I have** das ist alles [Geld], was ich habe
④ /ðæt/ *adv.* (coll.) so
⑤ /ðæt/ *rel. adv.* der/die/das; **the day** ~ **I first met her** der Tag, an dem ich sie zum ersten Mal sah
⑥ /ðæt, *stressed* ðæt/ *conj.* dass; **[in order]** ~: damit

thatch /θætʃ/ *n.* (of straw) Strohdach, *das;* (of reeds) Schilfdach, *das;* (roofing) Dachbedeckung, *die*

thatched /θætʃt/ *adj.* stroh-/schilfgedeckt

thaw /θɔː/ ① *n.* Tauwetter, *das*
② *v.i.* **(a)** tauen ⋯❯

(b) (melt) auftauen
3 *v.t.* auftauen
■ **thaw 'out** ▶ THAW 2, 3
the /*before vowel* ðɪ, *before consonant* ðə, *when stressed* ðiː/ **1** *def. art.* der/die/das
2 *adv.* ~ **more I practise** ~ **better I play** je mehr ich übe, desto *od.* umso besser spiele ich; **so much** ~ **worse for sb./sth.** umso schlimmer für jmdn./etw
theatre (*Amer.:* **theater**) /'θɪətə(r)/ *n.*
(a) Theater, *das*
(b) (lecture ~) Hörsaal, *der*
(c) (Brit. Med.) ▶ OPERATING THEATRE
theatrical /θɪ'ætrɪkl/ *adj.*
(a) schauspielerisch
(b) (showy) theatralisch
theft /θeft/ *n.* Diebstahl, *der*
their /ðeə(r)/ *poss. pron. attrib.* ihr
theirs /ðeəz/ *poss. pron. pred.* ihrer/ihre/ ihres
them /ðəm, *stressed* ðem/ *pron.* sie; (as indirect object) ihnen; *see also* HER¹
theme /θiːm/ *n.* Thema, *das*
theme: ~ **music** *n.* Titelmelodie, *die;* ~ **park** *n.:* *Freizeitpark, dessen Attraktionen und Einrichtungen auf ein bestimmtes Thema bezogen sind;* ~ **song** *n.* Erkennungssong, *der;* ~ **tune** Erkennungsmelodie, *die*
themselves /ðəm'selvz/ *pron.*
(a) *emphat.* selbst
(b) *refl.* sich ⟨*waschen usw.*⟩; sich selbst ⟨*die Schuld geben, regieren*⟩. *See also* HERSELF
then /ðen/ **1** *adv.* **(a)** (at that time) damals; ~ **and there** auf der Stelle
(b) (after that) dann; ~ **[again]** (and also) außerdem; **but** ~ (after all) aber schließlich
(c) (in that case) dann; **but** ~ **again** aber andererseits
2 *n.* **before** ~: vorher; davor; **from** ~ **on** von da an; **since** ~: seitdem
3 *adj.* damalig
theological /θiːə'lɒdʒɪkl/ *adj.* theologisch; Theologie⟨*student*⟩
theology /θɪ'ɒlədʒɪ/ *n.* Theologie, *die*
theoretical /θɪə'retɪkl/ *adj.* theoretisch
theory /'θɪərɪ/ *n.* Theorie, *die;* **in** ~: theoretisch
therapeutic /θerə'pjuːtɪk/ *adj.* therapeutisch
therapist /'θerəpɪst/ *n.* Therapeut, *der*/Therapeutin, *die*
therapy /'θerəpɪ/ *n.* Therapie, *die*
there /ðeə(r)/ **1** *adv.* **(a)** (in/at that place) da; dort; (fairly close) da; **be down/in/up** ~: da unten/drin/oben sein
(b) (calling attention) **hello** *or* **hi** ~! hallo!; **you** ~! Sie da!
(c) (in that respect) da; **so** ~: und damit basta (ugs.)
(d) (to that place) dahin, dorthin ⟨*gehen, fahren, rücken*⟩; **down/up** ~: dort hinunter/ hinauf

(e) /ðə(r), *stressed* ðeə(r)/ **was** ~ **anything in it?** war da irgendwas drin?; ~ **was once es** war einmal; ~ **is enough food** es gibt genug zu essen
2 *int.* ~, ~: na, na (ugs.); ~ **[you are]!** da, siehst du!
3 *n.* da; dort; **near** ~: da *od.* dort in der Nähe
thereabouts /'ðeərəbaʊts/ *adv.* **(a)** da [in der Nähe]
(b) (near that number) ungefähr
therefore /'ðeəfɔː(r)/ *adv.* deshalb; also
thermal /'θɜːml/ *adj.* thermisch; ~ **underwear** kälteisolierende Unterwäsche
thermal imaging /θɜːml 'ɪmɪdʒɪŋ/ *n.* Thermographie, *die*
thermometer /θə'mɒmɪtə(r)/ *n.* Thermometer, *das*
Thermos, thermos ® /'θɜːməs/ *n.* ~ **[flask/jug/bottle]** Thermosflasche, *die* ⓦ
thermostat /'θɜːməstæt/ *n.* Thermostat, *der*
these *pl. of* THIS
thesis /'θiːsɪs/ *n., pl.* **theses** /'θiːsiːz/
(a) (proposition) These, *die*
(b) (dissertation) Dissertation, *die* (**on** über + *Akk.*)
they /ðeɪ/ *pron.* **(a)** sie
(b) (people in general) man
they'd /ðeɪd/ **(a)** = they would
(b) = they had
they'll /ðeɪl/ = they will
they're /ðeə(r)/ = they are
they've /ðeɪv/ = they have
thick /θɪk/ **1** *adj.* **(a)** dick; **a rope two inches** ~, **a two-inch** ~ **rope** ein zwei Zoll starkes *od.* dickes Seil
(b) (dense) dicht ⟨*Haar, Nebel, Wolken usw.*⟩
(c) (filled) ~ **with** voll von
(d) dickflüssig ⟨*Sahne*⟩; dick ⟨*Suppe, Schlamm, Kleister*⟩
(e) (stupid) dumm
2 *n.* **in the** ~ **of** mitten in (+ *Dat.*)
thick 'ear *n.* **give sb. a** ~ (Brit. coll.) jmdm. ein paar hinter die Ohren geben (ugs.)
thicken /'θɪkn/ **1** *v.t.* dicker machen; eindicken ⟨*Sauce*⟩
2 *v.i.* **(a)** dicker werden
(b) ⟨*Nebel:*⟩ dichter werden
(c) the plot ~**s** die Sache wird kompliziert
'thickly *adv.* **(a)** (in a thick layer) dick
(b) (densely) dicht
'thickness *n.* **(a)** Dicke, *die;* **be two metres in** ~: zwei Meter dick sein
(b) (denseness) Dichte, *die*
thick: ~**set** *adj.* gedrungen; ~**-skinned** *adj.* (fig.) dickfellig (ugs.)
thief /θiːf/ *n., pl.* **thieves** /θiːvz/ Dieb, *der*/Diebin, *die*
thieve /θiːv/ *v.i.* stehlen
thieves *pl. of* THIEF
thigh /θaɪ/ *n.* Oberschenkel, *der*

thimble /'θɪmbl/ *n.* Fingerhut, *der*

thin /θɪn/ **1** *adj.* (a) dünn; **a tall, ~ man** ein großer, hagerer Mann
(b) (sparse) dünn, schütter ⟨Haar⟩
2 *adv.* dünn
3 *v.t.,* **-nn-:** (a) dünner machen
(b) (dilute) verdünnen
■ **thin 'out** *v.i.* ⟨Menschenmenge:⟩ sich verlaufen; ⟨Verkehr:⟩ abnehmen

thing /θɪŋ/ *n.* (a) Sache, *die;* Ding, *das;* **what's that ~ in your hand?** was hast du da in der Hand?; **be a rare ~:** etwas Seltenes sein
(b) (action) **it was the right ~ to do** es war das einzig Richtige; **that was a foolish/friendly ~ to do** das war eine große Dummheit/das war sehr freundlich
(c) (fact) [Tat]sache, *die;* **it's a strange ~ that ...:** es ist seltsam, dass ...; **the best/worst ~ about her** das Beste/Schlimmste an ihr
(d) (idea) **say the first ~ that comes into one's head** das sagen, was einem gerade so einfällt; **what a ~ to say!** wie kann man nur so etwas sagen!
(e) (task) **she has a reputation for getting ~s done** sie ist für ihre Tatkraft bekannt; **a big ~ to undertake** ein großes Unterfangen
(f) (affair) Sache, *die;* Angelegenheit, *die*
(g) (circumstance) **take ~s too seriously** alles zu ernst nehmen; **how are ~s?** wie gehts [dir]?
(h) (individual, creature) Ding, *das*
(i) *in pl.* (personal belongings, clothes) Sachen *Pl.*
(j) (product of work) Sache, *die;* **the latest ~:** der letzte Schrei
(k) (what is important or proper) das Richtige; **the ~ is ...** (question) die Frage ist ...

thingamy /'θɪŋəmɪ/, **thingumabob** /'θɪŋəməbɒb/, **thingumajig** /'θɪŋəmədʒɪɡ/, **thingummy** /'θɪŋəmɪ/, **thingy** /'θɪŋɪ/ *ns.* (coll.) Dings, *der/die/das* (salopp); Dingsbums, *der/die/das* (ugs.)

think /θɪŋk/ **1** *v.t.,* **thought** /θɔːt/ (a) (consider) meinen; **we ~ [that] he will come** wir denken *od.* glauben, dass er kommt; **what do you ~?** was meinst du? **do you really ~ so?** findest du wirklich?; **what do you ~ of him/it?** was hältst du von ihm/davon?; ..., **don't you ~?** ..., findest *od.* meinst du nicht auch?; **I ~ so/not** ich glaube schon/nicht; **I ~ I'll try** ich glaube, ich werde es versuchen
(b) (imagine) sich (*Dat.*) vorstellen
2 *v.i.,* **thought** [nach]denken; **I need time to ~:** ich muss es mir erst überlegen; **I've been ~ing** ich habe nachgedacht; **~ twice** es sich (*Dat.*) zweimal überlegen
■ **'think of** *v.t.* (a) denken an (+ *Akk.*); **he ~s of everything** er denkt einfach an alles
(b) (have as idea) **we'll ~ of something** wir werden uns etwas einfallen lassen; **can you ~ of anyone who ...?** fällt dir jemand ein, der ...?
(c) (remember) sich erinnern an (+ *Akk.*); **I just can't ~ of her name** ich komme einfach

nicht auf ihren Namen
(d) **~ little/nothing of sb./sth.** (consider contemptible) wenig/nichts von jmdm./etw. halten; **not ~ much of sb./sth.** nicht viel von jmdm./etw. halten
■ **think 'over** *v.t.* sich (*Dat.*) überlegen
■ **think 'through** *v.t.* [gründlich] durchdenken
■ **think 'up** *v.t.* (coll.) sich (*Dat.*) ausdenken

'thinker *n.* Denker, *der/*Denkerin, *die*

'think tank *n.* Beraterstab, *der*

'thin-skinned *adj.* (fig.) empfindlich; dünnhäutig (geh.)

third /θɜːd/ **1** *adj.* dritt...
2 *n.* (in sequence, rank) Dritte, *der/die/das;* (fraction) Drittel, *das. See also* EIGHTH

'thirdly *adv.* drittens

third: ~ 'party *n. attrib.* **~-party insurance** Haftpflichtversicherung, *die;* **~-rate** *adj.* drittklassig; **T~ 'World** *n.* Dritte Welt; **countries of the T~ World,** **T~ World countries** Länder der Dritten Welt

thirst /θɜːst/ **1** *n.* Durst, *der;* **die of ~:** verdursten
2 *v.i.* **~ for revenge/knowledge** nach Rache/Wissen dürsten (geh.)

'thirsty *adj.* durstig; **be ~:** Durst haben

thirteen /θɜː'tiːn/ **1** *adj.* dreizehn
2 *n.* Dreizehn, *die. See also* EIGHT

thirteenth /θɜː'tiːnθ/ *adj.* dreizehnt... *See also* EIGHTH

thirtieth /'θɜːtɪɪθ/ **1** *adj.* dreißigst...
2 *n.* (fraction) Dreißigstel, *das. See also* EIGHTH

thirty /'θɜːtɪ/ **1** *adj.* dreißig
2 *n.* Dreißig, *die. See also* EIGHT; EIGHTY 2

'thirty-something **1** *adj.* **be ~** in den Dreißigern sein
2 *n.* Dreißiger, *der/*-in, *die*

this /ðɪs/ **1** *adj., pl.* **these** /ðiːz/ dieser/diese/dieses; (with less emphasis) der/die/das; **at ~ time** zu dieser Zeit; **by ~ time** inzwischen; mittlerweile; **these days** heut[zutag]e; **before ~ time** vorher; zuvor; **all ~ week** die[se] ganze Woche; **~ morning/evening** *etc.* heute Morgen/Abend *usw.;* **these last three weeks** die letzten drei Wochen; **~ Monday** (to come) nächsten Montag
2 *pron., pl.* **these** (a) **what's ~?** was ist [denn] das?; **fold it like ~:** falte es so!
(b) (the present) **before ~:** bis jetzt
(c) (Brit. Teleph.: person speaking) **~ is Andy** hier [spricht *od.* ist] Andy; (Amer. Teleph.) **who did you say ~ was?** wer ist am Apparat?
(d) **~ and that** dies und das

thistle /'θɪsl/ *n.* Distel, *die*

thorn /θɔːn/ *n.* (a) (part of plant) Dorn, *der*
(b) (plant) Dornenstrauch, *der*

'thorny *adj.* (a) dornig
(b) (fig.) heikel

thorough /'θʌrə/ *adj.* gründlich ⋯⟩

thorough: ∼**bred** n. reinrassiges Tier; (horse) Rassepferd, das; ∼**fare** n. Durchfahrtsstraße, die; 'no ∼**fare**' „Durchfahrt verboten"; (on foot) „kein Durchgang"

'**thoroughly** adv. gründlich ‹untersuchen›; gehörig ‹erschöpft›; so richtig ‹genießen›; zutiefst ‹beschämt›; total ‹verdorben, verwöhnt›; **be** ∼ **fed up with sth.** (coll.) von etw. die Nase gestrichen voll haben (ugs.)

'**thoroughness** n. Gründlichkeit, die

those ▸ THAT 1, 2

though /ðəʊ/ ① conj. **(a)** (despite the fact that) obwohl; **late** ∼ **it was** obwohl es so spät war; **the car,** ∼ **powerful, is also economical** der Wagen ist zwar stark, aber [zugleich] auch wirtschaftlich
(b) (but nevertheless) aber; **a slow** ∼ **certain method** eine langsame, aber od. wenn auch sichere Methode
(c) (even if) **[even]** ∼: auch wenn
(d) (and yet) ∼ **you never know** obwohl man nie weiß
② adv. (coll.) trotzdem

thought /θɔːt/ ① ▸ THINK
② n. **(a)** no pl. Denken, das
(b) no pl., no art. (reflection) Überlegung, die; Nachdenken, das
(c) (consideration) Rücksicht, die (**for** auf + Akk.)
(d) (idea, conception) Gedanke, der; **it's the** ∼ **that counts** der gute Wille zählt; **give up all** ∼**[s] of sth.** sich (Dat.) etw. aus dem Kopf schlagen

thoughtful /'θɔːtfl/ adj. **(a)** nachdenklich
(b) (considerate) rücksichtsvoll; (helpful) aufmerksam

'**thoughtfully** adv. **(a)** nachdenklich
(b) (considerately) rücksichtsvollerweise

'**thoughtless** adj. **(a)** gedankenlos
(b) (inconsiderate) rücksichtslos

'**thoughtlessly** adv. **(a)** gedankenlos
(b) (inconsiderately) aus Rücksichtslosigkeit

thought: ∼ **process** n. Denkprozess, der; ∼**-provoking** adj. nachdenklich stimmend; **be** ∼**-provoking** nachdenklich stimmen

thousand /'θaʊznd/ ① adj. **(a)** tausend; **a** or **one** ∼: eintausend; **two/several** ∼: zweitausend/mehrere tausend; **a** or **one** ∼ **and one** [ein]tausend[und]eins
(b) a ∼ **[and one]** (fig.: innumerable) tausend (ugs.)
② n. **(a)** (number) tausend; **a** or **one/two** ∼: ein-/zweitausend
(b) (written figure; group) Tausend, das
(c) (indefinite amount) ∼**s** tausende

thousandth /'θaʊzndθ/ ① adj. tausendst...
② n. (fraction) Tausendstel, das; (in sequence) Tausendste, der/die/das

thrash /θræʃ/ v.t. **(a)** verprügeln
(b) (defeat) vernichtend schlagen
∎ **thrash 'out** v.t. ausdiskutieren

thrashing /'θræʃɪŋ/ n. (beating) Prügel Pl.; **give sb. a** ∼: jmdm. eine Tracht Prügel verpassen (ugs.)

thread /θred/ ① n. **(a)** Faden, der
(b) (of screw) Gewinde, das
② v.t. **(a)** einfädeln; auffädeln ‹Perlen›
(b) ∼ **one's way through sth.** sich durch etw. schlängeln

'**threadbare** adj. abgenutzt; abgetragen ‹Kleidung›; (fig.) abgedroschen ‹Argument›

threat /θret/ n. Drohung, die

threaten /'θretn/ v.t. **(a)** bedrohen; ∼ **sb. with sth.** jmdm. etw. androhen
(b) ∼ **to do sth.** damit drohen, etw. zu tun
(c) drohen mit ‹Gewalt, Rache usw.›

threatening /'θretnɪŋ/ adj. drohend

three /θriː/ ① adj. drei
② n. Drei, die. See also EIGHT

three: ∼**-dimensional** /θriːdɪˈmenʃənl/ adj. dreidimensional; ∼**fold** adj., adv. dreifach; **a** ∼**fold increase** ein Anstieg auf das Dreifache; ∼**-lane** adj. dreispurig; ∼**-pin** ▸ PIN 1 C; ∼**-quarters** ① n. drei Viertel pl. (**of** + Gen.); ∼**-quarters of an hour** eine Dreiviertelstunde; ② adv. drei viertel ‹voll›; ∼**some** /'θriːsəm/ n. Dreigespann, das; Trio, das

thresh /θreʃ/ v.t. dreschen

threshold /'θreʃəʊld/ n. Schwelle, die

threw ▸ THROW 1

thrift /θrɪft/ n. Sparsamkeit, die

'**thrifty** adj. sparsam

thrill /θrɪl/ ① v.t. **(a)** (excite) faszinieren
(b) (delight) begeistern
② n. **(a)** Erregung, die
(b) (exciting experience) aufregendes Erlebnis

'**thriller** n. Thriller, der

'**thrilling** adj. aufregend; spannend ‹Buch, Film›

thrive /θraɪv/ v.i., **thrived** or **throve** /θrəʊv/, **thrived** or **thriven** /'θrɪvn/ adj. ‹Pflanze:› wachsen und gedeihen
(b) (prosper) aufblühen (**on** bei)

throat /θrəʊt/ n. Hals, der; (esp. inside) Kehle, die; **a [sore]** ∼: Halsschmerzen Pl.

throb /θrɒb/ ① v.i., **-bb-** pochen; ‹Motor:› dröhnen
② n. Pochen, das; (of engine) Dröhnen, das

throes /θrəʊz/ n. pl. Qual, die; **be in the** ∼ **of sth.** (fig.) mitten in etw. (Dat.) stecken (ugs.)

thrombosis /θrɒmˈbəʊsɪs/ n., pl. **thromboses** /θrɒmˈbəʊsiːz/ Thrombose, die

throne /θrəʊn/ n. Thron, der

throng /θrɒŋ/ n. [Menschen]menge, die

throttle /'θrɒtl/ v.t. erdrosseln

through /θruː/ ① prep. **(a)** durch
(b) (Amer.: up to and including) bis [einschließlich]
(c) (by reason of) durch; infolge von ‹Vernachlässigung, Einflüssen›
② adv. **(a) let sb.** ∼: jmdn. durchlassen

(b) (Teleph.) **be** ∼: durch sein (ugs.); **be** ∼ **to sb.** mit jmdm. verbunden sein
3 *attrib. adj.* durchgehend ⟨*Zug*⟩

through'out **1** *prep.* ∼ **the war/period** den ganzen Krieg/die ganze Zeit hindurch; ∼ **the country** im ganzen Land
2 *adv.* (entirely) ganz; (always) stets; die ganze Zeit [hindurch]

throve ▶ THRIVE

throw /θrəʊ/ **1** *v.t.,* **threw** /θruː/, **thrown** /θrəʊn/ **(a)** werfen; ∼ **sth. to sb.** jmdm. etw. zuwerfen; ∼ **sth. at sb.** etw. nach jmdm. werfen
(b) (bring to the ground) zu Boden werfen; abwerfen ⟨*Reiter*⟩
(c) (coll.: disconcert) ⟨*Frage:*⟩ aus der Fassung bringen
2 *n.* Wurf, *der*

■ **throw a'way** *v.t.* **(a)** wegwerfen
(b) (lose by neglect) verschenken ⟨*Vorteil, Spiel usw.*⟩

■ **throw 'up** **1** *v.t.* **(a)** hochwerfen ⟨*Arme, Hände*⟩
(b) (produce) hervorbringen ⟨*Ideen usw.*⟩
2 *v.i.* (coll.) brechen (ugs.)

'throwaway *adj.* **(a)** Wegwerf-; Einweg-
(b) beiläufig ⟨*Bemerkung*⟩

thrown ▶ THROW 1

thrush /θrʌʃ/ *n.* (Ornith.) Drossel, *die*

thrust /θrʌst/ **1** *v.t.,* **thrust** stoßen; ∼ **aside** (fig.) beiseite schieben
2 *n.* Stoß, *der*

thud /θʌd/ *n.* dumpfer Schlag

thug /θʌg/ *n.* Schläger, *der;* **football** ∼**s** Fußballrowdys *Pl.*

thuggish /'θʌgɪʃ/ *adj.* aggressiv ⟨*Verhalten, Fußballfan*⟩

thumb /θʌm/ **1** *n.* Daumen, *der;* **get the** ∼**s up** ⟨*Person, Projekt:*⟩ akzeptiert werden; **be under sb.'s** ∼: unter jmds. Fuchtel stehen
2 *v.t.* ∼ **a lift** per Anhalter fahren
■ **'thumb through** *v.t.* durchblättern

thumb: ∼ **index** *n.* Daumenregister, *das;* ∼**nail** *n.* Daumennagel, *der;* ∼**tack** *n.* (Amer.) Reißzwecke, *die*

thump /θʌmp/ **1** *v.t.* [mit Wucht] schlagen
2 *v.i.* **(a)** hämmern (**at, on** gegen)
(b) ⟨*Herz:*⟩ heftig pochen
3 *n.* (blow) Schlag, *der;* (sound) Bums, *der* (ugs.); dumpfer Schlag

thunder /'θʌndə(r)/ **1** *n.* Donner, *der*
2 *v.i.* donnern

thunder: ∼**clap** *n.* Donnerschlag, *der;* ∼**storm** *n.* Gewitter, *das*

thundery /'θʌndərɪ/ *adj.* gewittrig

Thurs. *abbr.* = **Thursday** Do.

Thursday /'θɜːzdeɪ, 'θɜːzdɪ/ *n.* Donnerstag, *der; see also* FRIDAY

thus /ðʌs/ *adv.* so

thwart /θwɔːt/ *v.t.* durchkreuzen ⟨*Pläne*⟩; vereiteln ⟨*Versuch*⟩; ∼ **sb.** jmdm. einen Strich durch die Rechnung machen

thyme /taɪm/ *n.* Thymian, *der*

thyroid /'θaɪrɔɪd/ *n.* Schilddrüse, *die*

tiara /tɪ'ɑːrə/ *n.* Diadem, *das*

tick /tɪk/ **1** *v.i.* ticken
2 *v.t.* **(a)** mit einem Häkchen versehen
(b) ▶ ∼ OFF A
3 *n.* **(a)** (of clock etc.) Ticken, *das*
(b) (mark) Häkchen, *das*
■ **tick 'off** *v.t.* **(a)** (cross off) abhaken
(b) (coll.: reprimand) rüffeln (ugs.)

ticket /'tɪkɪt/ *n.* Karte, *die;* (for bus, train) Fahrschein, *der;* (for aeroplane) Flugschein, *der;* (for lottery, raffle) Los, *das;* (for library) Ausweis, *der;* **price** ∼: Preisschild, *das*

ticket: ∼ **agency** *n.* Kartenvorverkaufsstelle, *die;* ∼ **agent** *n.* Inhaber/Inhaberin einer Kartenvorverkaufsstelle; ∼ **collector** *n.* (on train) Schaffner, *der/*Schaffnerin, *die;* (on station) Fahrkartenkontrolleur, *der/*-kontrolleurin, *die;* ∼ **dispenser** *n.* Kartenautomat, *der;* (for train etc.) Fahrschein- od. Fahrkartenautomat, *der;* ∼ **holder** *n.* Besitzer/Besitzerin einer Eintrittskarte; ∼ **machine** ▶ ∼ DISPENSER; ∼ **office** *n.* Fahrkartenschalter, *der;* (for advance booking) Kartenvorverkaufsstelle, *die*

tickle /'tɪkl/ *v.t. & i.* kitzeln.

ticklish /'tɪklɪʃ/ *adj.* kitzlig

tidal /'taɪdl/ *adj.* Gezeiten-

'tidal wave *n.* Flutwelle, *die*

tiddlywinks /'tɪdlɪwɪŋks/ *n. sing.* (game) Flohhüpfen, *das*

tide /taɪd/ **1** *n.* Tide, *die* (nordd.); **high** ∼: Flut, *die;* **low** ∼: Ebbe, *die;* **the** ∼**s** die Gezeiten; **the** ∼ **is in/out** es ist Flut/Ebbe
2 *v.t.* ∼ **sb. over** jmdm. über die Runden helfen (ugs.)

tidiness /'taɪdɪnɪs/ *n.* Ordentlichkeit, *die*

tidy /'taɪdɪ/ **1** *adj.* ordentlich; aufgeräumt ⟨*Zimmer, Schreibtisch*⟩
2 *v.t.* aufräumen; ∼ **oneself** sich zurechtmachen
■ **tidy 'up** *v.i.* aufräumen

tie /taɪ/ **1** *v.t.,* **tying** /'taɪɪŋ/ binden (**to an** + *Akk.,* **into** zu); ∼ **a knot** einen Knoten machen; (Sport) ∼ **the match** unentschieden spielen
2 *v.i.,* **tying (a)** (be fastened) **it** ∼**s at the back** es wird hinten gebunden
(b) (have equal scores) ∼ **for second place** mit gleicher Punktzahl den zweiten Platz erreichen
3 *n.* **(a)** Krawatte, *die*
(b) (bond) Band, *das;* (restriction) Bindung, *die*
(c) (equality of scores) Punktgleichheit, *die*
(d) (Sport: match) Begegnung, *die*
■ **tie 'in** *v.i.* ∼ **in with sth.** zu etw. passen
■ **tie 'up** *v.t.* **(a)** festbinden; ∼ **up a parcel** ein Paket verschnüren
(b) (keep busy) beschäftigen

tier /tɪə(r)/ *n.* **(a)** Rang, *der*
(b) (unit) Stufe, *die*

⋯⋯▹

tiger /'taɪgə(r)/ *n.* Tiger, *der*

tiger e'conomy *n.* Tigerstaat, *der*

tight /taɪt/ **1** *adj.* **(a)** (firm) fest; fest angezogen ⟨*Schraube, Mutter*⟩; fest sitzend ⟨*Deckel*⟩
(b) (close-fitting) eng ⟨*Kleid, Schuh usw.*⟩
(c) (impermeable) ~ **seal/joint** dichter Verschluss/dichte Fuge
(d) (taut) straff
(e) (difficult to negotiate) a ~ **corner** eine enge Kurve; **be in a ~ corner** (fig.) in der Klemme sein (ugs.)
(f) (strict) streng ⟨*Kontrolle, Disziplin*⟩
(g) (coll.: stingy) knauserig (ugs.)
(h) (coll.: drunk) voll (salopp)
2 *adv.* fest; **hold ~!** halt dich fest!
3 *n. in pl.* **(a)** (Brit.) **[pair of]** ~s Strumpfhose, *die*
(b) (of dancer etc.) Trikothose, *die*

tighten /'taɪtn/ **1** *v.t.* **(a)** [fest] anziehen ⟨*Knoten, Schraube*⟩; straff ziehen ⟨*Seil*⟩
(b) verschärfen ⟨*Kontrolle*⟩
2 *v.i.* sich spannen

tight-fisted /taɪt'fɪstɪd/ *adj.* geizig

'tightrope *n.* Drahtseil, *das*

tile /taɪl/ **1** *n.* (on roof) Ziegel, *der;* (on floor) Fliese, *die;* (on wall) Kachel, *die*
2 *v.t.* [mit Ziegeln] decken ⟨*Dach*⟩; fliesen ⟨*Fußboden*⟩; kacheln ⟨*Wand*⟩

till¹ /tɪl/ **1** *prep.* bis; (followed by article + noun) bis zu; **not [...] ~:** erst
2 *conj.* bis

till² *n.* Kasse, *die*

'till receipt *n.* Kassenzettel, *der*

tilt /tɪlt/ **1** *v.i.* kippen
2 *v.t.* kippen; neigen ⟨*Kopf*⟩
3 *n.* **(a)** Schräglage, *die;* **a 45° ~:** eine Neigung von 45°
(b) **[at] full ~:** mit voller Wucht

timber /'tɪmbə(r)/ *n.* [Bau]holz, *das*

time /taɪm/ **1** *n.* **(a)** Zeit, *die;* **in [the course of]** ~, **as ~ goes on/went on** mit der Zeit; im Laufe der Zeit; **in ~, with ~** (sooner or later) mit der Zeit; **in [good] ~** (not late) rechtzeitig; **all the** *or* **this ~:** die ganze Zeit; (without ceasing) ständig; **a short ~ ago** vor kurzem; ~ **off** *or* **out** freie Zeit; **in 'no ~:** im Handumdrehen; **in a week's/year's ~:** in einer Woche/in einem Jahr; **harvest/Christmas ~:** Ernte-/Weihnachtszeit, *die;* **on ~** (punctually) pünktlich; **ahead of ~:** zu früh ⟨*ankommen*⟩; vorzeitig ⟨*fertig werden*⟩; **have a good ~:** sich amüsieren; Spaß haben (ugs.); **have no ~ for sb./sth.** (fig.) für jmdn./etw. ist einem seine Zeit zu schade
(b) (occasion) Mal, *das;* **for the first ~:** zum ersten Mal; **at ~s** gelegentlich; ~ **and again,** ~ **after** ~: immer [und immer] wieder; **at one ~, at [one and] the same** ~ (simultaneously) gleichzeitig; **one at a** ~: einzeln; **two at a ~:** zwei zwei
(c) (point in day etc.) [Uhr]zeit, *die;* **tell the ~:** die Uhr lesen; **what ~ is it?, what is the ~?** wie spät ist es?; **by this/that ~:** inzwischen; **by**

the ~ [that] we arrived bis wir hinkamen; **T~!** (Brit.: in pub) Feierabend!; ~, **[ladies and] gentlemen, please!** wir machen Feierabend, meine [Damen und] Herren!
(d) (multiplication) mal; **three ~s four** drei mal vier
(e) (Mus.) Takt, *der;* **in ~:** im Takt
2 *v.t.* **(a)** zeitlich abstimmen; **be well ~d** zur richtigen Zeit kommen
(b) (set to operate at correct ~) einstellen
(c) (measure ~ taken by) stoppen

time: ~ **bomb** *n.* Zeitbombe, *die;* ~**-consuming** *adj.* **(a)** (taking ~) zeitaufwendig; **(b)** (wasteful of ~) zeitraubend; ~ **lag** *n.* zeitliche Verzögerung

timeless /'taɪmlɪs/ *adj.* zeitlos

'time limit *n.* Frist, *die*

timely /'taɪmlɪ/ *adj.* rechtzeitig

time: ~**scale** *n.* Zeitskala, *die;* ~ **sheet** *n.* Stundenzettel, *der;* ~ **switch** *n.* Zeitschalter, *der;* ~**table** *n.* **(a)** (scheme of work) Zeitplan, *der;* (Educ.) Stundenplan, *der;* **(b)** (Transport) Fahrplan, *der;* ~ **warp** *n.* Verwerfung im Raum-Zeit-Kontinuum; ~ **zone** *n.* Zeitzone, *die*

timid /'tɪmɪd/ *adj.* **(a)** scheu ⟨*Tier*⟩
(b) zaghaft ⟨*Mensch*⟩; (shy) schüchtern

timing /'taɪmɪŋ/ *n.* **(a)** that was perfect ~! du kommst gerade im richtigen Augenblick!
(b) (Theatre, Sport) Timing, *das*

tin /tɪn/ **1** *n.* **(a)** (metal) Zinn, *das;* ~**[plate]** Weißblech, *das*
(b) (Brit.: for preserving) [Konserven]dose, *die*
2 *v.t.,* **-nn-** (Brit.) zu Konserven verarbeiten

tin 'foil *n.* Stanniol, *das;* Alufolie, *die*

tinge /tɪndʒ/ **1** *v.t.,* ~**ing** /'tɪndʒɪŋ/ tönen
2 *n.* [leichte] Färbung; (fig.) Hauch, *der*

tingle /'tɪŋgl/ *v.i.* kribbeln

tinker /'tɪŋkə(r)/ **1** *n.* Kesselflicker, *der*
2 *v.i.* ~ **with sth.** an etw. (*Dat.*) herumbasteln (ugs.)

tinkle /'tɪŋkl/ **1** *n.* Klingeln, *das*
2 *v.i.* klingeln

tinned /tɪnd/ *adj.* (Brit.) Dosen-

tin: ~**-opener** *n.* (Brit.) Dosenöffner, *der;* ~**pot** *attrib. adj.* (derog.) schäbig

tinsel /'tɪnsl/ *n.* Lametta, *das*

tint /tɪnt/ **1** *n.* Farbton, *der*
2 *v.t.* tönen; kolorieren ⟨*Zeichnung*⟩

tiny /'taɪnɪ/ *adj.* winzig

tip¹ /tɪp/ *n.* (end, point) Spitze, *die*

tip² **1** *v.i.,* **-pp-** (lean, fall) kippen; ~ **over** umkippen
2 *v.t.,* **-pp-:** **(a)** (make tilt) kippen
(b) (make overturn) umkippen; (Brit.: discharge) kippen
(c) voraussagen ⟨*Sieger*⟩; ~ **sb. to win** auf jmds. Sieg tippen
(d) (reward) ~ **sb.** jmdm. Trinkgeld geben
3 *n.* **(a)** (money) Trinkgeld, *das*
(b) (special information) Hinweis, *der;* Tipp, *der* (ugs.)

(c) (Brit.) Müllkippe, *die*
■ **tip 'off** *v.t.* ~ **sb. off** jmdm. einen Hinweis *od.* (ugs.) Tipp geben
'tip-off *n.* Hinweis, *der*
tipsy /'tɪpsɪ/ *adj.* (coll.) angeheitert; beschwipst (ugs.)
tip: ~**toe** ⓵ *v.i.* auf Zehenspitzen gehen; ⓶ *n.* on ~**toe[s]** auf Zehenspitzen; ~**top** *adj.* tipptopp (ugs.)
tire¹ /'taɪə(r)/ (Amer.) ▶ TYRE
tire² ⓵ *v.t.* ermüden
⓶ *v.i.* müde werden; ermüden; ~ **of sth.**/ **doing sth.** einer Sache (*Gen.*) überdrüssig werden
■ **tire 'out** *v.t.* erschöpfen; ~ **oneself out doing sth.** etw. bis zur Erschöpfung tun
tired /'taɪəd/ *adj.* **(a)** (weary) müde
(b) (fed up) be ~ **of sth.**/**doing sth.** etw. satt haben/es satt haben, etw. zu tun
tiredness /'taɪədnɪs/ *n.* Müdigkeit, *die*
'tireless *adj.* unermüdlich
tiresome /'taɪəsəm/ *adj.* **(a)** (wearisome) mühsam
(b) (annoying) lästig
tiring /'taɪərɪŋ/ *adj.* ermüdend
tissue /'tɪʃuː, 'tɪsjuː/ *n.* **(a)** (material) Gewebe, *das*
(b) [paper] ~: Papiertuch, *das;* (handkerchief) Papiertaschentuch, *das*
(c) ~ [paper] Seidenpapier, *das*
tit¹ /tɪt/ *n.* (Ornith.) Meise, *die*
tit² *n.* it's ~ **for tat** wie du mir, so ich dir
'titbit *n.* **(a)** (food) Häppchen, *das* (ugs.)
(b) (piece of news) Neuigkeit, *die*
titchy /'tɪtʃɪ/ *adj.* (coll.) klitzeklein (ugs.)
titillate /'tɪtɪleɪt/ *v.t.* erregen
titillation /tɪtɪ'leɪʃn/ *n.* Kitzel, *der*
title /'taɪtl/ *n.* Titel, *der*
title: ~ **deed** *n.* (Law) Eigentumsurkunde, *die;* ~**-holder** *n.* (Sport) Titelhalter, *der*/ -halterin, *die;* ~ **page** *n.* Titelseite, *die;* ~ **role** *n.* Titelrolle, *die*
tittle-tattle /'tɪtltætl/ *n.* Klatsch, *der* (ugs.)
'T-junction *n.* Einmündung, *die*
to ⓵ /*before vowel* tʊ, *before consonant* tə, *stressed* tuː/ *prep.* **(a)** (in the direction of and reaching) zu; (with name of place) nach; **go to work**/**to the theatre** zur Arbeit/ins Theater gehen; **to France** nach Frankreich
(b) (as far as) bis zu; **from London to Edinburgh** von London [bis] nach Edinburgh; **increase from 10% to 20%** von 10% auf 20% steigen
(c) (*introducing relationship or indirect object*) **to sb.**/**sth.** jmdm./einer Sache (*Dat.*); **lend**/**explain** *etc.* **to sb.** jmdm. etw. leihen/erklären *usw.;* **speak to sb.** mit jmdm. sprechen; **that's all there is to it** mehr ist dazu nicht zu sagen; **what's that to you?** was geht das dich an?; **to me** (in my opinion) meiner Meinung nach; **14 miles to the gallon** 14 Meilen auf eine Gallone
(d) (until) bis; **to the end** bis zum Ende; **to this day** bis heute; **five [minutes] to eight** fünf

[Minuten] vor acht
(e) (*with infinitive of a verb*) zu; (*expr. purpose, or after*) TOO um [...] zu; **want to know** wissen wollen; **do sth. to annoy sb.** etw. tun, um jmdn. zu ärgern; **too hot to drink** zu heiß zum Trinken; **he would have phoned but forgot to** er hätte angerufen, aber er vergaß es
⓶ *adv.* /tuː/ **to and fro** hin und her
toad /təʊd/ *n.* (also fig. derog.) Kröte, *die*
'toadstool *n.* Giftpilz, *der*
toast /təʊst/ ⓵ *n.* **(a)** no pl. Toast, *der;* **a piece of** ~: eine Scheibe Toast
(b) (call to drink) Toast, *der;* **drink a** ~ **to sb.**/**sth.** auf jmdn./etw. trinken
⓶ *v.t.* **(a)** rösten; toasten ⟨Brot⟩
(b) (drink to) trinken auf (+ *Akk.*)
'toaster *n.* Toaster, *der*
'toast rack *n.* Toastständer, *der*
tobacco /tə'bækəʊ/ *n., pl.* ~**s** Tabak, *der*
tobacconist /tə'bækənɪst/ *n.* Tabak[waren]händler, *der*/-händlerin, *die*
toboggan /tə'bɒgən/ ⓵ *n.* Schlitten, *der*
⓶ *v.i.* Schlitten fahren
tod /tɒd/ *n.* (Brit. coll.) **on one's** ~: [ganz] allein
today /tə'deɪ/ ⓵ *n.* heute; ~**'s newspaper** die Zeitung von heute
⓶ *adv.* heute
toddler /'tɒdlə(r)/ *n.* ≈ Kleinkind, *das*
to-do /tə'duː/ *n.* Getue, *das* (ugs.)
toe /təʊ/ ⓵ *n.* Zeh, *der;* Zehe, *die;* (of footwear) Spitze, *die*
⓶ *v.t.*, ~**ing** (fig.) ~ **the line** *or* (Amer.) **mark** sich einordnen
'toenail *n.* Zeh[en]nagel, *der*
toffee /'tɒfɪ/ *n.* Karamell, *der;* (Brit.: piece) Toffee, *das;* Sahnebonbon, *das*
'toffee apple *n.* mit Karamell überzogener Apfel am Stiel
tofu /'təʊfuː/ *n., no indef. art.* Tofu, *der*
together /tə'geðə(r)/ *adv.* **(a)** (in or into company) zusammen
(b) (simultaneously) gleichzeitig
(c) (one with another) miteinander
toggle /'tɒgl/ ⓵ *n.* **(a)** (button) Knebelknopf, *der*
(b) (Comp.) [Kipp]schalter, *der;* Umschalttaste, *die*
⓶ *v.i.* (Comp.) [hin und her] schalten
toil /tɔɪl/ ⓵ *v.i.* schwer arbeiten
⓶ *n.* [harte] Arbeit
toilet /'tɔɪlɪt/ *n.* Toilette, *die;* **go to the** ~: auf die Toilette gehen
toilet: ~ **bag** *n.* Kulturbeutel, *der;* ~ **brush** *n.* Klosettbürste, *die;* ~ **paper** *n.* Toilettenpapier, *das*
toiletries /'tɔɪlɪtrɪz/ *n. pl.* Körperpflegemittel *Pl.;* Toilettenartikel *Pl.*
toilet: ~ **roll** *n.* Rolle Toilettenpapier; ~ **seat** *n.* Klosettbrille, *die* (ugs.); Toilettensitz, *der;* ~ **tissue** ┈┈┊

▶ ~ PAPER; ~ **water** n. Toilettenwasser, das; Eau de Toilette, das

token /'təʊkn/ ① n. (a) (voucher) Gutschein, der
(b) (counter, disc) Marke, die
(c) (sign) Zeichen, das
② attrib. adj. symbolisch ⟨Preis⟩

Tokyo /'təʊkjəʊ/ pr. n. Tokio (das)

told ▶ TELL

tolerable /'tɒlərəbl/ adj. (a) (endurable) erträglich (**to, for** für)
(b) (fairly good) leidlich; annehmbar

tolerance /'tɒlərəns/ n. Toleranz, die

tolerant /'tɒlərənt/ adj. tolerant (**of, towards** gegen[über])

tolerate /'tɒləreɪt/ v.t. dulden; (bear) ertragen ⟨Schmerzen⟩

toleration /tɒlə'reɪʃn/ n. Tolerierung, die (geh.)

toll¹ /təʊl/ n. (a) (tax, duty) Gebühr, die
(b) (damage etc.) Aufwand, der; **take its ~ of sth.** einen Tribut an etw. (Dat.) fordern (fig.)

toll² v.i. ⟨Glocke:⟩ läuten

toll: ~ **bridge** n. gebührenpflichtige Brücke; ~**road** n. gebührenpflichtige Straße; Mautstraße, die (bes. österr.)

tom /tɒm/ n. (cat) Kater, der

tomato /tə'mɑːtəʊ/ n., pl. ~es Tomate, die

tomato: ~ **juice** n. Tomatensaft, der; ~ **ketchup** n. Tomatenketschup, der od. das; ~ **'purée** n. Tomatenmark, das

tomb /tuːm/ n. Grab, das; (monument) Grabmal, das

'tomboy n. Wildfang, der

'tombstone n. Grabstein, der

'tomcat n. Kater, der

tome /təʊm/ n. dicker Band; Wälzer, der (ugs.)

tomfoolery /tɒm'fuːlərɪ/ n. Blödsinn, der (ugs.)

tomorrow /tə'mɒrəʊ/ ① n. morgen; ~ **morning/afternoon/evening/night** morgen früh od. Vormittag/Nachmittag/Abend/Nacht; ~**'s newspaper** die morgige Zeitung ② adv. morgen; **see you ~!** (coll.) bis morgen!; **the day after ~:** übermorgen

ton /tʌn/ n. Tonne, die

tone /təʊn/ ① n. (a) (sound) Klang, der; (Teleph.) Ton, der
(b) (style of speaking) Ton, der
(c) (tint, shade) [Farb]ton, der
(d) (fig.: character) **lower/raise the ~ of sth.** das Niveau einer Sache (Gen.) senken/erhöhen; **set the ~:** den Ton angeben ② v.t. tönen; abtönen ⟨Farbe⟩
■ **tone 'down** v.t. [ab]dämpfen ⟨Farbe⟩; (fig.) mäßigen ⟨Sprache⟩

tone: ~**'deaf** adj. ohne musikalisches Gehör; ~ **dialling** (Teleph.) n. Tonwahl, die

tongs /tɒŋz/ n. pl. **[pair of]** ~: Zange, die

tongue /tʌŋ/ n. Zunge, die; **bite one's ~** (lit. or fig.) sich auf die Zunge beißen; **find one's ~:** seine Sprache wieder finden; **hold one's ~:** stillschweigen; **he made the remark ~ in cheek** (fig.) er meinte die Bemerkung nicht ernst

tongue: ~**-tied** adj. schüchtern; ~**-twister** n. Zungenbrecher, der (ugs.)

tonic /'tɒnɪk/ ① n. (a) (Med.) Tonikum, das
(b) (fig.: invigorating influence) Wohltat, die (geh.)
(c) (~ water) Tonic, das
② attrib. adj. kräftigend; (fig.) wohltuend ⟨Wirkung⟩

'tonic water n. Tonic[wasser], das

tonight /tə'naɪt/ ① n. (a) (this evening) heute Abend; ~**'s performance** die heutige [Abend]vorstellung
(b) (this or the coming night) heute Nacht
② adv. (a) (this evening) heute Abend
(b) (during this or the coming night) heute Nacht; **[I'll] see you ~!** bis heute Abend!

tonne /tʌn/ n. [metrische] Tonne

tonsil /'tɒnsl/ n. [Gaumen]mandel, die; **have one's ~s out** sich (Dat.) die Mandeln herausnehmen lassen

tonsillitis /tɒnsə'laɪtɪs/ n. Mandelentzündung, die

too /tuː/ adv. (a) (excessively) zu; ~ **difficult a task** eine zu schwierige Aufgabe
(b) (also) auch
(c) (coll.: very) besonders; **not ~ pleased** nicht gerade erfreut

took ▶ TAKE

tool /tuːl/ n. (a) Werkzeug, das; (garden ~) Gerät, das; **[set of]** ~s Werkzeug, das
(b) (Comp.) Tool, das; Werkzeug, das
(c) (fig.: means) [Hilfs]mittel, das

tool: ~**bar** n. (Comp.) Werkzeugleiste, die; ~**box** n. Werkzeugkasten, der; ~ **kit** n. Werkzeug, das

toot /tuːt/ ① v.i. (on car etc. horn) hupen ② n. Tuten, das

tooth /tuːθ/ n., pl. **teeth** /tiːθ/ (a) Zahn, der
(b) (of rake, fork, comb) Zinke, die; (of cogwheel, saw) Zahn, der

tooth: ~**ache** n. Zahnschmerzen Pl.; ~**brush** n. Zahnbürste, die; ~ **decay** n. Zahnverfall, der; ~**glass** n. Zahnputzglas, das; ~ **mug** n. Zahnputzbecher, der; ~**paste** n. Zahnpasta, die; ~**pick** n. Zahnstocher, der; ~ **powder** n. Zahnpulver, das

top¹ /tɒp/ ① n. (a) (highest part) Spitze, die; (of table) Platte, die; (~ end) oberes Ende; (of tree) Wipfel, der; (~ floor) oberstes Stockwerk; (rim of glass) Rand, der; **on ~ of one another** aufeinander; **on ~ of sth.** (fig.: in addition) zusätzlich zu etw.; **from ~ to bottom** von oben bis unten; **at the ~:** oben; **at the ~ of the building/hill/pile/stairs** oben im Gebäude/[oben] auf dem Hügel/[oben] auf dem Stapel/oben an der Treppe
(b) (highest rank) Spitze, die; ~ **of the table** (Sport) Tabellenspitze, die; **be [at the] ~ of the class** der/die Klassenbeste sein
(c) (upper surface) Oberfläche, die; (of cupboard,

chest) Oberseite, *die;* **on** ~ **of sth.** [oben] auf
etw. (*position: Dat.; direction: Akk.*)
(d) (folding roof) Verdeck, *das*
(e) (upper deck of bus) Oberdeck, *das*
(f) (cap of pen) [Verschluss]kappe, *die*
(g) (upper garment) Oberteil, *das*
(h) (lid) Deckel, *der;* (of bottle) Stöpsel, *der*
[2] *adj.* oberst...; höchst... ⟨*Ton, Preis*⟩;
~ **end** oberes Ende; **the** ~ **pupil** der
beste Schüler; ~ **speed** Spitzen- *od.*
Höchstgeschwindigkeit, *die*
[3] *v.t.* **(a)** (be taller than) überragen
(b) (surpass) übertreffen
■ **top 'up** (Brit. coll.) *v.t.* auffüllen ⟨*Tank,
Flasche, Glas*⟩

top² *n.* (toy) Kreisel, *der*

top: ~**-flight** *attrib. adj.* erstrangig;
Spitzen⟨*sportler, -politiker*⟩; ~ **'hat**
n. Zylinder[hut], *der;* ~**-heavy** *adj.*
oberlastig

topic /'tɒpɪk/ *n.* Thema, *das*

topical /'tɒpɪkl/ *adj.* aktuell

'topless *adj.* **a** ~ **dress/swimsuit**
ein busenfreies Kleid/ein Oben-ohne-
Badeanzug; **go/bathe** ~: oben ohne
gehen/baden

top-level *attrib. adj.* Gipfel⟨*treffen,
-konferenz*⟩; ~**-level negotiations/deals**
Verhandlungen/Vereinbarungen auf
höchster Ebene

topmost /'tɒpməʊst, 'tɒpməst/ *adj.*
oberst...; höchst... ⟨*Gipfel, Note*⟩

top-'notch *adj.* (coll.) fantastisch (ugs.)

topple /'tɒpl/ [1] *v.i.* fallen
[2] *v.t.* stürzen
■ **topple 'down** *v.i.* hinab-/herabfallen.
■ **topple 'over** *v.i.* umfallen

top: ~**-quality** *adj.* [qualitativ]
hochwertig; ~**-ranking** *attrib. adj.*
Spitzen⟨*funktionär, -beamter, -politiker,
-sportler*⟩; hochrangig ⟨*Offizier*⟩;
~ **'secret** *adj.* streng geheim; ~**soil** *n.*
Mutterboden, *der*

topsy-turvy /tɒpsɪ'tɜːvɪ/ *adv.*
verkehrtrum (ugs.); **turn sth.** ~: etw. auf den
Kopf stellen (ugs.)

'top-up *n.* (coll.) Auffüllung, *die;* **I need a**
~: ich muss mir noch mal nachgießen/
nachgießen lassen; ~ **card** (for mobile phone)
Aufladekarte, *die*

torch /tɔːtʃ/ *n.* (Brit.) Taschenlampe, *die*

'torchlight *n.* Licht der/einer
Taschenlampe; **by** ~**light** im Schein einer
Taschenlampe

tore, torn ► TEAR¹ 2, 3

torment [1] /'tɔːment/ *n.* Qual, *die*
[2] /tɔː'ment/ *v.t.* quälen

tornado /tɔː'neɪdəʊ/ *n., pl.* ~es
Wirbelsturm, *der;* (in North America) Tornado,
der

torpedo /tɔː'piːdəʊ/ [1] *n., pl.* ~es
Torpedo, *der*
[2] *v.t.* torpedieren

torrent /'tɒrənt/ *n.* reißender Bach; (fig.)
Flut, *die*

torrential /tə'renʃl/ *adj.*
wolkenbruchartig ⟨*Regen*⟩

torso /'tɔːsəʊ/ *n., pl.* ~**s** Rumpf, *der;* **bare**
~: nackter Oberkörper

tortoise /'tɔːtəs/ *n.* Schildkröte, *die*

tortoiseshell /'tɔːtəsʃel/ *n.* Schildpatt,
das

tortuous /'tɔːtjʊəs/ *adj.* verschlungen; (fig.)
umständlich

torture /'tɔːtʃə(r)/ [1] *n.* Folter, *die*
[2] *v.t.* foltern; (fig.) quälen

Tory /'tɔːrɪ/ (Brit. Polit. coll.) *n.* Tory, *der*

toss /tɒs/ [1] *v.t.* **(a)** (throw upwards)
hochwerfen; ~ **a pancake** einen
Pfannkuchen [durch Hochwerfen] wenden
(b) (throw casually) werfen; schmeißen (ugs.)
(c) ~ **a coin** eine Münze werfen
(d) (Cookery: mix) wenden; mischen ⟨*Salat*⟩
[2] *v.i.* **(a)** ~ **and turn** sich [schlaflos] im Bett
wälzen
(b) ⟨*Schiff:*⟩ hin und her geworfen werden
(c) (~ coin) eine Münze werfen; ~ **for sth.**
mit einer Münze um etw. losen
[3] *n.* **(a)** ~ **of a coin** Hochwerfen einer
Münze
(b) (throw) Wurf, *der*
(c) **I couldn't give a** ~ (fig. Brit. sl.) es ist mir
scheißegal (salopp)
■ **toss 'up** *v.i.* eine Münze werfen; ~ **up**
for sth. mit einer Münze um etw. losen

tot¹ /tɒt/ *n.* (coll.) **(a)** kleines Kind
(b) (of liquor) Gläschen, *das*

tot² (coll.) *v.t., -tt-:* ~ **'up** zusammenziehen
(ugs.)

total /'təʊtl/ [1] *adj.* **(a)** gesamt;
Gesamt⟨*gewicht, -wert, usw.*⟩
(b) (absolute) völlig *nicht präd.;* **a** ~ **beginner**
ein absoluter Anfänger
[2] *n.* (number) Gesamtzahl, *die;* (amount)
Gesamtbetrag, *der;* (result of addition)
Summe, *die;* **a** ~ **of 200** insgesamt 200; **in**
~: insgesamt
[3] *v.t.,* (Brit.) **-ll-: (a)** addieren,
zusammenzählen ⟨*Zahlen*⟩
(b) (amount to) [insgesamt] betragen

total e'clipse *n.* (Astron.) totale Finsternis

totalitarian /təʊtælɪ'teərɪən/ *adj.*
totalitär

'totally *adv.* völlig

totter /'tɒtə(r)/ *v.i.* wanken; taumeln

touch /tʌtʃ/ [1] *v.t.* **(a)** berühren
(b) (harm) anrühren
(c) (fig.: rival) ~ **sth.** an etw. (*Akk.*)
heranreichen
(d) (affect emotionally) rühren
[2] *v.i.* sich berühren; **don't** ~! nicht
anfassen!
[3] *n.* **(a)** Berührung, *die*
(b) *no art.* (faculty) **[sense of]** ~: Tastsinn,
der
(c) (small amount) **a** ~ **of salt/pepper** ⋯⫶

etc. eine Spur Salz/Pfeffer *usw.;* a ~ **of irony**
etc. ein Anflug von Ironie *usw.*
(d) (fig.) Detail, *das*
(e) (communication) be in/out of ~ [with sb.]
[mit jmdm.] Kontakt/keinen Kontakt haben;
get in ~: mit jmdm. Kontakt aufnehmen
■ **touch 'down** *v.i.* ⟨Flugzeug:⟩ landen
■ **touch on** *v.t.* (mention) ansprechen
■ **touch 'up** *v.t.* (improve) ausbessern
'touch: ~-and-go *adj.* it is ~-and-go
[whether…] es steht auf des Messers
Schneide [, ob…]; **~down** *n.* (Aeronaut.)
Landung, *die*

'touching *adj.* rührend

touch: ~line *n.* (Footb., Rugby) Seitenlinie,
die; **~paper** *n.* Zündpapier, *das;* (on
firework) Papierlunte, *die;* **~-tone** *adj.*
a ~-tone **telephone** ein Telefon mit
Mehrfrequenzwahl; **~-type** *v.i.* blind
schreiben; **~-typing** *n.* Blindschreiben,
das

touchy /'tʌtʃɪ/ *adj.* empfindlich; heikel
⟨Thema⟩

tough /tʌf/ *adj.* **(a)** fest ⟨Material, Stoff⟩;
zäh ⟨Fleisch; fachspr.: Werkstoff, Metall⟩;
widerstandsfähig ⟨Belag, Glas, Haut⟩;
strapazierfähig ⟨Kleidung⟩
(b) (hardy) zäh ⟨Person⟩
(c) (difficult) schwierig
(d) (severe, harsh) hart
(e) (coll.) ~ **luck** Pech, *das*

toughen /'tʌfn/ *v.t.* ~ [up] abhärten
⟨Person⟩; verschärfen ⟨Gesetz⟩

toupee, toupet /'tu:peɪ/ *n.* Toupet, *das*

tour /tʊə(r)/ **1** *n.* **(a)** [Rund]reise, *die;*
Tour, *die* (ugs.)
(b) (Theatre, Sport) Tournee, *die*
(c) (of house etc.) Besichtigung, *die*
(d) ~ **[of duty]** Dienstzeit, *die*
2 *v.i.* **(a)** ~/go ~ing in *or* through a
country eine Reise *od.* (ugs.) Tour durch ein
Land machen
(b) (Theatre, Sport) eine Tournee machen
3 *v.t.* **(a)** besichtigen ⟨Stadt, Gebäude⟩; ~ a
country/region eine Reise *od.* (ugs.) Tour
durch ein Land/Gebiet machen
(b) (Theatre, Sport) ~ a country/the provinces
eine Tournee durch das Land/die Provinz
machen

tour de force /tʊə də 'fɔ:s/ *n., pl.* **tours de
force** /tʊə də 'fɔ:s/ Glanzleistung, *die*

'tour guide *n.* Reiseführer, *der*/
Reiseführerin, *die;* (book) Reiseführer, *der*
(to, of von)

'touring holiday *n.* have a ~ in a
country in den Ferien/im Urlaub durch ein
Land fahren

tourism /'tʊərɪzm/ *n.* **(a)** Tourismus, *der*
(b) (operation of tours) Touristik, *die*

tourist /'tʊərɪst/ **1** *n.* Tourist, *der*/
Touristin, *die*
2 *attrib. adj.* Touristen-

tourist: ~ agency *n.* Reisebüro, *das;*
~ **attraction** *n.* Touristenattraktion,

die; ~ **board** *n.* (Brit.) Amt für
Fremdenverkehrswesen; ~ **class**
n. Touristenklasse, *die;* ~ **hotel** *n.*
Touristenhotel, *das;* ~ **industry**
n. Tourismusindustrie, *die;*
~ **infor'mation centre,** ~ **office**
ns. Fremdenverkehrsbüro, *das;*
Touristeninformation, *die* (ugs.); ~ **season**
n. Touristensaison, *die;* ~ **trade**
▶ ~ INDUSTRY

touristy /'tʊərɪstɪ/ *adj.* (derog.) auf
Tourismus getrimmt (ugs.); Touristen⟨stadt,
-nest, -gegend⟩ (ugs. abwertend)

'tour leader *n.* Reiseleiter, *der*/-leiterin,
die

tournament /'tʊənəmənt/ *n.* (Hist.; Sport)
Turnier, *das*

tourniquet /'tʊənɪkeɪ/ *n.* (Med.)
Tourniquet, *das*

'tour operator *n.* Reiseveranstalter, *der*/
-veranstalterin, *die*

tousle /'taʊzl/ *v.t.* zerzausen

tout /taʊt/ **1** *v.i.* ~ **for customers** Kunden
anreißen (ugs.) *od.* werben
2 *n.* Anreißer, *der*/Anreißerin, *die* (ugs.);
ticket ~: Kartenschwarzhändler, *der*/
-händlerin, *die*

tow /təʊ/ **1** *v.t.* schleppen; ziehen
⟨Anhänger, Wasserskiläufer⟩
2 *n.* Schleppen, *das;* **give a car a** ~: einen
Wagen schleppen; **on** ~: im Schlepp[tau]
■ **tow a'way** *v.t.* abschleppen

toward /tə'wɔ:d/, **towards** /tə'wɔ:dz/
prep. **(a)** (in direction of) ~ sb./sth. auf
jmdn./etw. zu; **turn** ~ sb. sich zu jmdm.
umdrehen
(b) (in relation to) gegenüber; **feel sth.** ~ sb.
jmdm. gegenüber etw. empfinden
(c) (for) a **contribution** ~ sth. ein Beitrag
zu etw.; **proposals** ~ **solving a problem**
Vorschläge zur Lösung eines Problems
(d) (near) gegen; ~ **the end of May** [gegen]
Ende Mai

'tow bar *n.* (Motor Veh.) Anhängerkupplung,
die

towel /'taʊəl/ *n.* Handtuch, *das*

towelling (*Amer.:* **toweling**) /'taʊəlɪŋ/
n., no indef. art. Frottierware, *die*

'towel rail *n.* Handtuchhalter, *der*

tower /'taʊə(r)/ **1** *n.* Turm, *der*
2 *v.i.* in die Höhe ragen
■ **'tower above** *v.t.* ~ **above sb./sth.**
jmdn./etw. überragen

'tower block *n.* Hochhaus, *das*

'towering *attrib. adj.* hoch aufragend; (fig.)
herausragend ⟨Leistung⟩

town /taʊn/ *n.* Stadt, *die;* **the** ~ **of Cambridge**
die Stadt Cambridge; **in [the]** ~: in der Stadt;
the ~ (people) die Stadt; **be in/out of** ~: in der
Stadt/nicht in der Stadt sein

town: ~ 'centre *n.* Stadtmitte, *die;*
Stadtzentrum, *das;* ~ **'council** *n.* (Brit.)
Stadtrat, *der;* ~ **'councillor** *n.* (Brit.)

Stadtrat, *der*/-rätin, *die;* ~ **'hall** *n.* Rathaus, *das;* ~ **house** *n.* (residence in ~) Stadthaus, *das;* (terrace house) Reihenhaus, *das*

townie /'taʊnɪ/ *n.* Stadtmensch, *der*

town: ~ **'planner** *n.* Stadtplaner, *der*/-planerin, *die;* ~ **'planning** *n.* Stadtplanung, *die*

tow: ~**path** *n.* Leinpfad, *der;* ~ **rope** *n.* Abschleppseil, *das*

toxic /'tɒksɪk/ *adj.* giftig

toxicity /tɒk'sɪsɪtɪ/ *n.* Giftigkeit, *die*

toxic 'waste *n.* Giftmüll *der;* ~ **tip** or **dump** Giftmülldeponie, *die*

toxin /'tɒksɪn/ *n.* Toxin, *das*

toy /tɔɪ/ [1] *n.* Spielzeug, *das;* ~s Spielzeug, *das* [2] *adj.* Spielzeug- [3] *v.i.* ~ **with the idea of doing sth.** mit dem Gedanken spielen, etw. zu tun

toy: ~ **boy** *n.* (coll.) Gespiele, *der* (scherzh.); ~**shop** *n.* Spielwarengeschäft, *das*

trace /treɪs/ [1] *v.t.* **(a)** (copy) durchpausen; abpausen **(b)** zeichnen ‹Linie› **(c)** (follow track of) folgen (+ *Dat.*); verfolgen **(d)** (find) finden [2] *n.* Spur, *die*

'trace element *n.* (Chem.) Spurenelement, *das*

'tracing paper /'treɪsɪŋ peɪpə(r)/ *n.* Pauspapier, *das*

track /træk/ [1] *n.* **(a)** Spur, *die;* (of wild animal) Fährte, *die;* ~s (footprints) [Fuß]spuren; (of animal also) Fährte, *die;* **keep** ~ **of sb./sth.** jmdn./etw. im Auge behalten **(b)** (path) Weg, *der;* (footpath) Pfad, *der* **(c)** (Sport) Bahn, *die;* **cycling/greyhound** ~: Radrennbahn, *die*/Windhundrennbahn, *die* **(d)** (Railw.) Gleis, *das* **(e)** (course taken) Route, *die;* (of rocket, satellite) Bahn, *die* [2] *v.t.* ~ **an animal** die Spur/Fährte eines Tieres verfolgen; **the police** ~**ed him [to Paris]** die Polizei folgte seiner Spur [bis nach Paris] ■ **track 'down** *v.t.* aufspüren

'trackball, 'tracker ball *ns.* (Comp.) Rollball, *der*

'track events *n. pl.* Laufwettbewerbe *Pl.*

'tracking station *n.* (Astronaut.) Bahnverfolgungsstation, *die*

track: ~ **shoe** *n.* Rennschuh, *der;* ~**suit** *n.* Trainingsanzug, *der*

tract[1] /trækt/ *n.* (area) Gebiet, *das*

tract[2] *n.* (pamphlet) [Flug]schrift, *die*

tractor /'træktə(r)/ *n.* Traktor, *der*

trad /træd/ (Mus. coll.) *adj.* traditional (Jargon); ~ **jazz** Traditional Jazz, *der*

trade /treɪd/ [1] *n.* **(a)** (line of business) Gewerbe, *das;* **he's a butcher/lawyer** *etc.* **by** ~: er ist von Beruf Metzger/Rechtsanwalt *usw.*

(b) *no indef. art* (commerce) Handel, *der* **(c)** (craft) Handwerk, *das* [2] *v.i.* (buy and sell) Handel treiben [3] *v.t.* tauschen; austauschen ‹Waren, Grüße›; sich (*Dat.*) sagen ‹Beleidigungen›; ~ **sth. for sth.** etw. gegen etw. tauschen ■ **trade 'in** *v.t.* in Zahlung geben ■ **trade 'up** *v.i.* sich verbessern

trade: ~ **balance** *n.* Handelsbilanz, *die;* ~ **deficit** *n.* passive Handelsbilanz; Handelsbilanzdefizit, *das;* ~ **'discount** *n.* Branchenrabatt, *der;* ~ **fair** *n.* [Fach]messe, *die;* ~ **journal** *n.* Fachzeitschrift, *die;* ~ **mark** *n.* Warenzeichen, *das;* **leave one's** ~ **mark on sth.** (fig.) einer Sache (*Dat.*) seinen Stempel aufdrücken; ~ **name** *n.* Fachbezeichnung, *die;* (proprietary name) Markenname, *der;* ~ **price** *n.* Einkaufspreis, *der*

'trader *n.* Händler, *der*/Händlerin, *die*

trade: ~ **'secret** *n.* Geschäftsgeheimnis, *das;* ~**sman** /'treɪdzmən/ *n., pl.* ~**smen** /'treɪdzmən/ (shopkeeper) [Einzel]händler, *der;* (craftsman) Handwerker, *der;* ~ **'union** *n.* Gewerkschaft, *die; attrib.* Gewerkschafts-; ~ **'unionist** *n.* Gewerkschaft[l]er, *der*/Gewerkschaft[l]erin, *die*

trading /'treɪdɪŋ/ *n.* Handel, *der*

trading: ~ **estate** *n.* (Brit.) Gewerbegebiet, *das;* ~ **hours** *n. pl.* Geschäftszeit, *die;* **during/outside** ~ **hours** während/außerhalb der Geschäftszeit; **'Trading hours: …'** „Geschäftszeiten: …"; ~ **partner** *n.* Handelspartner, *der*

tradition /trə'dɪʃn/ *n.* Tradition, *die*

traditional /trə'dɪʃənl/ *adj.* traditionell; herkömmlich ‹Erziehung, Methode›

tra'ditionally *adv.* traditionell

traffic /'træfɪk/ [1] *n.* **(a)** *no indef. art.* Verkehr, *der* **(b)** (trade) Handel, *der* [2] *v.i.,* -ck-: ~ **in sth.** mit etw. handeln

traffic: ~ **calming** *n.* Verkehrsberuhigung, *die;* ~ **circle** *n.* (Amer.) Kreisverkehr, *der;* ~ **cone** *n.* Pylon, *der;* Leitkegel, *der;* ~ **island** *n.* Verkehrsinsel, *die;* ~ **jam** *n.* [Verkehrs]stau, *der*

trafficker /'træfɪkə(r)/ *n.* Händler, *der*/Händlerin, *die;* ~ **in drugs:** Drogenhändler, *der*/-händlerin, *die*

traffic: ~ **lights** *n. pl.* [Verkehrs]ampel, *die;* ~ **police** *n.* Verkehrspolizei, *die;* ~ **report** *n.* Verkehrsübersicht, *die;* (on radio) Verkehrsservice, *der;* ~ **sign** *n.* Verkehrszeichen, *das;* ~ **signals** ▶ ~ LIGHTS; ~ **warden** *n.* (Brit.) Hilfspolizist, *der;* (woman) Hilfspolizistin, *die;* Politesse, *die*

tragedy /'trædʒɪdɪ/ *n.* Tragödie, *die*

tragic /'trædʒɪk/ *adj.* tragisch

trail /treɪl/ [1] *n.* **(a)** Spur, *die;* ~ **of smoke/dust** Rauch-/Staubfahne, *die* **(b)** (Hunting) Spur, *die;* Fährte, *die*

(c) (path) Pfad, *der;* Weg, *der*
⚁ *v.t.* **(a)** (pursue) verfolgen
(b) (drag) ~ **sth.** [after *or* behind one] etw. hinter sich (*Dat.*) herziehen
⚂ *v.i.* **(a)** (be dragged) schleifen
(b) (lag) hinterhertrotten
(c) ⟨*Pflanze:*⟩ kriechen

trailer /'treɪlə(r)/ *n.* **(a)** Anhänger, *der;* (Amer.: caravan) Wohnanhänger, *der*
(b) (Cinemat., Telev.) Trailer, *der*

train /treɪn/ ⚀ *v.t.* **(a)** ausbilden (in in + *Dat.*); erziehen ⟨*Kind*⟩; abrichten ⟨*Hund*⟩; dressieren ⟨*Tier*⟩
(b) (Sport) trainieren
(c) (Hort.) ziehen
⚁ *v.i.* **(a)** eine Ausbildung machen; **he is ~ing as** *or* **to be a doctor/engineer** er macht eine Arzt-/Ingenieurausbildung
(b) (Sport) trainieren
⚂ *n.* **(a)** (Railw.) Zug, *der;* **on the ~:** im Zug
(b) (of skirt etc.) Schleppe, *die*
(c) ~ **of thought** Gedankengang, *der*

'train driver *n.* Lokomotivführer, *der/* -führerin, *die*

trained /treɪnd/ *adj.* ausgebildet ⟨*Arbeiter, Lehrer, Arzt, Stimme*⟩; abgerichtet ⟨*Hund*⟩; dressiert ⟨*Tier*⟩; geschult ⟨*Geist, Auge, Ohr*⟩

trainee /treɪ'niː/ *n.* Auszubildende, *der/die*

'trainer *n.* [Konditions]trainer, *der/* -trainerin, *die*

'train fare *n.* Fahrpreis, *der*

'training *n.* **(a)** Ausbildung, *die*
(b) (Sport) Training, *das*

training: ~ **camp** *n.* (Sport) Trainingslager, *das;* ~ **college** *n.* berufsbildende Schule; ~ **course** *n.* Lehrgang, *der;* ~ **scheme** *n.* Ausbildungsprogramm, *das;* ~ **shoes** *n. pl.* Trainingsschuhe *Pl.*

train: ~ **journey** *n.* Bahnfahrt, *die;* (long) Bahnreise, *die;* ~ **service** *n.* Zugverbindung, *die;* ~ **set** *n.* [Modell]eisenbahn, *die;* ~**spotting** *n.:* das Aufschreiben von Lokomotivnummern als Hobby; ~ **station** *n.* (Amer.) Bahnhof, *der*

traipse /treɪps/ *v.i.* (coll.) latschen (salopp)
■ **traipse about, traipse around** *v.i.* rumlatschen (salopp)

trait /treɪt/ *n.* Eigenschaft, *die*

traitor /'treɪtə(r)/ *n.* Verräter, *der/* Verräterin, *die*

traitorous /'treɪtərəs/ *adj.* verräterisch

trajectory /trə'dʒektərɪ/ *n.* [Flug-]bahn, *die*

tram /træm/ *n.* (Brit.) Straßenbahn, *die;* ~**lines** Straßenbahnschienen *Pl.*

tramp /træmp/ ⚀ *n.* Landstreicher, *der/*-streicherin, *die;* (in city) Stadtstreicher, *der/*-streicherin, *die*
⚁ *v.i.* **(a)** (tread heavily) trampeln
(b) (walk) marschieren

trample /'træmpl/ ⚀ *v.t.* zertrampeln
⚁ *v.i.* trampeln

■ **'trample on** *v.t.* herumtrampeln auf (+ *Dat.*)

trampoline /'træmpəliːn/ *n.* Trampolin, *das*

'tram stop *n.* Straßenbahnhaltestelle, *die*

trance /trɑːns/ *n.* Trance, *die;* **be in a ~:** in Trance sein

tranquil /'træŋkwɪl/ *adj.* ruhig

tranquillity /træŋ'kwɪlɪtɪ/ Ruhe, *die*

tranquillizer /'træŋkwɪlaɪzə(r)/ *n.* Beruhigungsmittel, *das*

transact /træn'zækt/ *v.t.* ~ **business** Geschäfte tätigen

transaction /træn'zækʃn/ *n.* Geschäft, *das;* (financial) Transaktion, *die*

transatlantic /trænsət'læntɪk/ *adj.* transatlantisch

transcend /træn'send/ *v.t.* übersteigen

transcript /'trænskrɪpt/ *n.* Abschrift, *die;* (of trial) Protokoll, *das*

transfer ⚀ /træns'fɜː(r)/ *v.t.,* -rr-:
(a) (move) verlegen (**to** nach); überweisen ⟨*Geld*⟩ (**to** auf + *Akk.*); übertragen ⟨*Befugnis, Macht*⟩ (**to** *Dat.*)
(b) übereignen ⟨*Gegenstand, Grundbesitz*⟩ (**to** *Dat.*)
(c) versetzen ⟨*Arbeiter, Angestellte*⟩; (Footb.) transferieren
⚁ /træns'fɜː(r)/ *v.i.,* -rr-: **(a)** (when travelling) umsteigen
(b) (change job etc.) wechseln
⚂ /'trænsfɜː(r)/ *n.* **(a)** (moving) Verlegung, *die;* (of powers) Übertragung, *die* (**to** an + *Akk.*); (of money) Überweisung, *die*
(b) (of employee etc.) Versetzung, *die;* (Footb.) Transfer, *der*
(c) (picture) Abziehbild, *das*

transferable /træns'fɜːrəbl/ *adj.* übertragbar

'transfer: ~ **fee** *n.* (Footb.) Ablösesumme, *die;* Transfersumme, *die* (fachspr.); ~ **list** *n.* (Footb.) Transferliste, *die*

transform /træns'fɔːm/ *v.t.* verwandeln

transformation /trænsfə'meɪʃn/ *n.* Verwandlung, *die*

trans'former *n.* (Electr.) Transformator, *der*

transfusion /træns'fjuːʒn/ *n.* (Med.) Transfusion, *die*

transient /'trænzɪənt/ *adj.* kurzlebig; vergänglich

transistor /træn'zɪstə(r)/ *n.* Transistor, *der*

transit /'trænsɪt/ *n.* **in ~:** auf der Durchreise; ⟨*Waren*⟩ auf dem Transport; **passengers in ~:** Transitreisende *Pl.*

transition /træn'sɪʒn, træn'zɪʃn/ *n.* Übergang, *der;* Wechsel, *der*

transitional /træn'zɪʃənl/ *adj.* Übergangs-

transitive /'trænsɪtɪv/ *adj.* (Ling.) transitiv

'transit lounge *n.* Transithalle, *die*

transitory /'trænsɪtərɪ/ *adj.* vergänglich; (fleeting) flüchtig

'transit passenger *n.* Transitpassagier, *der*

translate /træns'leɪt/ *v.t.* übersetzen

translation /træns'leɪʃn/ *n.* Übersetzung, *die*

translator /træns'leɪtə(r)/ *n.* Übersetzer, *der*/Übersetzerin, *die*

translucent /træns'luːsənt/ *adj.* durchscheinend

transmission /træns'mɪʃn/ *n.*
(a) Übertragung, *die*
(b) (Motor Veh.) Antrieb, *der;* (gearbox) Getriebe, *das*

transmit /træns'mɪt/ *v.t.,* -tt-: (a) (pass on) übersenden; übertragen
(b) durchlassen ⟨*Licht*⟩; leiten ⟨*Wärme*⟩

trans'mitter *n.* Sender, *der*

transparency /træns'pærənsɪ/ *n.*
(a) Durchsichtigkeit, *die*
(b) (Photog.) Transparent, *das;* (slide) Dia, *das*

transparent /træns'pærənt/ *adj.* durchsichtig

transparently /træns'pærəntlɪ/ *adv.* offenkundig; ～ **obvious** ganz offenkundig

transpire /træn'spaɪə(r)/ *v.i.* sich herausstellen; (coll.: happen) passieren

transplant ⟨1⟩ /træns'plɑːnt/ *v.t.*
(a) verpflanzen ⟨*Organ*⟩
(b) (plant in another place) umpflanzen
⟨2⟩ /'trænsplɑːnt/ *n.* (Med.) Transplantation, *die;* Verpflanzung, *die*

transport ⟨1⟩ /træns'pɔːt/ *v.t.* transportieren; befördern
⟨2⟩ /'trænspɔːt/ *n.* (a) Transport, *der;* Beförderung, *die; attrib.* Beförderungs-
(b) (means of conveyance) Verkehrsmittel, *das;* **be without** ～: kein [eigenes] Fahrzeug haben

'transport café *n.* (Brit.) Fernfahrerlokal, *das*

transpose /træns'pəʊz/ *v.t.* vertauschen; umstellen

transsexual /træns'seksjʊəl/ ⟨1⟩ *adj.* transsexuell
⟨2⟩ *n.* Transsexuelle, *der*/*die*

transvestite /træns'vestaɪt/ *n.* Transvestit, *der*

trap /træp/ ⟨1⟩ *n.* (a) Falle, *die;* **set** *or* **lay a** ～ **for an animal** eine Falle für ein Tier legen *od.* aufstellen; **set** *or* **lay a** ～ **for sb.** (fig.) jmdm. eine Falle stellen; **fall into a/sb.'s** ～ (fig.) in die/jmdm. in die Falle gehen
(b) (sl.: mouth) Klappe, *die* (salopp)
⟨2⟩ *v.t.,* -pp-: (a) [in *od.* mit einer Falle] fangen ⟨*Tier*⟩; (fig.) in eine Falle locken ⟨*Person*⟩; **be** ～**ped** (fig.) in eine Falle gehen/ in der Falle sitzen; **be** ～**ped in a cave/by the tide** in einer Höhle festsitzen/von der Flut abgeschnitten sein
(b) (confine) einschließen; einklemmen ⟨*Körperteil*⟩

trap'door *n.* Falltür, *die*

trapeze /trə'piːz/ *n.* Trapez, *das*

tra'peze artist *n.* Trapezkünstler, *der*/ -künstlerin, *die*

trash /træʃ/ *n.* (a) (rubbish) Abfall, *der*
(b) (badly made thing) Mist, *der* (ugs.); (bad literature) Schund, *der* (ugs.)

trauma /'trɔːmə/ *n., pl.* ～**ta** /'trɔːmətə/ *or* ～**s** Trauma, *das*

traumatic /trɔː'mætɪk/ *adj.* traumatisch

traumatize /'trɔːmətaɪz/ *v.t.* traumatisieren

travel /'trævl/ ⟨1⟩ *n.* Reisen, *das; attrib.* Reise-
⟨2⟩ *v.i.,* (Brit.) -ll- reisen; (go in vehicle) fahren
⟨3⟩ *v.t.,* (Brit.) -ll- zurücklegen ⟨*Strecke, Entfernung*⟩; benutzen ⟨*Weg, Straße*⟩; **we had** ～**led 10 miles** wir waren 10 Meilen gefahren

■ **travel a'bout, travel a'round** *v.i.* umherreisen

travel: ～ **agency** *n.* Reisebüro, *das;* ～ **agent** *n.* Reisebürokaufmann, *der*/-kauffrau, *die;* ～ **brochure** *n.* Reiseprospekt, *der;* ～ **bureau** *n.* Reisebüro, *das*

traveler, traveling (Amer.) ▶ TRAVELL-

'travel insurance *n.* Reiseversicherung, *die*

traveller /'trævlə(r)/ *n.* (Brit.) (a) Reisende, *der*/*die*
(b) *in pl.* (gypsies etc.) fahrendes Volk

'traveller's cheque *n.* Reisescheck, *der*

travelling /'trævlɪŋ/ *attrib. adj.* (Brit.) Wander⟨*zirkus, -ausstellung*⟩

travelling: ～ **clock** *n.* Reisewecker, *der;* ～ **'salesman** *n.* Vertreter, *der*

travel: ～**-sick** *adj.* reisekrank; ～**-sickness** *n.* Reisekrankheit, *die;* ～**-sickness pill** *n.* Tablette gegen Reisekrankheit

trawler /'trɔːlə(r)/ *n.* [Fisch]trawler, *der*

tray /treɪ/ *n.* Tablett, *das;* (for correspondence) Ablagekorb, *der*

treacherous /'tretʃərəs/ *adj.* (a) treulos ⟨*Person*⟩
(b) (deceptive) tückisch

treachery /'tretʃərɪ/ *n.* Verrat, *der*

treacle /'triːkl/ *n.* (Brit.) Sirup, *der*

tread /tred/ ⟨1⟩ *n.* (a) (of tyre, boot, etc.) Lauffläche, *die;* **2 millimetres of** ～ **on a tyre** 2 Millimeter Profil auf einem Reifen
(b) (sound of walking) Schritt, *der*
⟨2⟩ *v.i.,* trod /trɒd/, trodden /'trɒdn/ *or* trod treten (in/on in/auf + *Akk.*); (walk) gehen
⟨3⟩ *v.t.,* trod, trodden *or* trod treten auf (+ *Akk.*); stampfen ⟨*Weintrauben*⟩

'treadmill *n.* (lit. or fig.) Tretmühle, *die*

treason /'triːzn/ *n.* [high] ～: Hochverrat, *der*

treasure /'treʒə(r)/ ⟨1⟩ *n.* Schatz, *der;* Kostbarkeit, *die;* **art** ～**s** Kunstschätze. Pl.
⟨2⟩ *v.t.* in Ehren halten ⋯⭢

treasure: ~ **house** *n.* [wahre] Fundgrube; ~ **hunt** *n.* Schatzsuche, *die*

treasurer /'treʒərə(r)/ *n.* Kassenwart, *der*/-wartin, *die*

treasury /'treʒərɪ/ *n.* **the T~:** das Finanzministerium

treat /triːt/ ☐ *n.* **(a)** [besonderes] Vergnügen
(b) (entertainment) *Vergnügen, für dessen Kosten jmd. anderes aufkommt;* **lay on a special ~ for sb.** jmdm. etwas Besonderes bieten; **it's my ~:** ich lade ein
② *v.t.* **(a)** behandeln; ~ **sth. as a joke** etw. als Witz nehmen; ~ **sth. with contempt** für etw. nur Verachtung haben
(b) (Med.) behandeln; ~ **sb. for sth.** jmdn. wegen etw. behandeln; (before confirmation of diagnosis) jmdn. auf etw. (*Akk.*) behandeln
(c) klären ⟨*Abwässer*⟩
(d) (provide with at own expense) einladen; ~ **sb. to sth.** jmdm. etw. spendieren; ~ **oneself to a new hat** sich (*Dat.*) einen neuen Hut leisten

treatise /'triːtɪs, 'triːtɪz/ *n.* Abhandlung, *die*

'**treatment** *n.* Behandlung, *die*

treaty /'triːtɪ/ *n.* [Staats]vertrag, *der*

treble /'trebl/ ☐ *adj.* **(a)** dreifach
(b) (Brit. Mus.) ~ **voice** Sopranstimme, *die*
② *n.* **(a)** (~ quantity) Dreifache, *das*
(b) (Mus.) **he is a ~:** er singt Sopran
③ *v.t.* verdreifachen
④ *v.i.* sich verdreifachen

'**treble clef** *n.* (Mus.) Violinschlüssel, *der*

tree /triː/ *n.* Baum, *der*

'**tree house** *n.* Baumhaus, *das*

'**treeless** *adj.* baumlos

tree: ~-**lined** *adj.* von Bäumen gesäumt; ~ **surgeon** *n.* Baumchirurg, *der;* ~ **surgery** *n.* Baumchirurgie, *die;* ~**top** *n.* [Baum]wipfel, *der;* ~ **trunk** *n.* Baumstamm, *der*

trek /trek/ ☐ *v.i.*, -kk- ziehen (across durch)
② *n.* [schwierige] Reise

trellis /'trelɪs/ *n.* Gitter, *das;* (for plants) Spalier, *das*

tremble /'trembl/ *v.i.* zittern (with vor + *Dat.*)

trembling /'tremblɪŋ/ ☐ *adj.* zitternd
② *n.* Zittern, *das*

tremendous /trɪ'mendəs/ *adj.* gewaltig; (coll.: wonderful) großartig

tremor /'tremə(r)/ *n.* **(a)** Zittern, *das*
(b) [earth] ~: leichtes Erdbeben

trench /trentʃ/ *n.* Graben, *der;* (Mil.) Schützengraben, *der*

trench 'warfare *n.* Grabenkrieg, *der*

trend /trend/ *n.* **(a)** Trend, *der;* **upward** ~: steigende Tendenz
(b) (fashion) Mode, *die;* [Mode]trend, *der*

trendiness *n.* (Brit. coll.) modische Art

'**trendsetter** *n.* Trendsetter, *der*

'**trendy** *adj.* (Brit. coll.) modisch; Schickimicki⟨*kneipe*⟩ (ugs.)

trepidation /trepɪ'deɪʃn/ *n.* Beklommenheit, *die*

trespass /'trespəs/ *v.i.* ~ **on** unerlaubt betreten ⟨*Grundstück*⟩

'**trespasser** *n.* Unbefugte, *der*/*die*

trial /'traɪəl/ *n.* **(a)** (Law) [Gerichts]verfahren, *das;* **be on ~** [for murder] [wegen Mordes] vor Gericht stehen
(b) (testing) Test, *der;* **employ sb. on ~:** jmdn. probeweise einstellen; **[by] ~ and error** [durch] Ausprobieren
(c) (trouble) Problem, *das*
(d) (Sport) (competition) Prüfung, *die;* (for selection) Testspiel, *das*

trial 'run *n.* (of car) Testfahrt, *die;* (fig.) Probelauf, *der*

triangle /'traɪæŋgl/ *n.* **(a)** Dreieck, *das*
(b) (Mus.) Triangel, *der od. das*

triangular /traɪ'æŋgjʊlə(r)/ *adj.* dreieckig

tribal /'traɪbl/ *adj.* Stammes-

tribalism /'traɪbəlɪzm/ *n.* Tribalismus, *der* (fachspr.)

tribe /traɪb/ *n.* Stamm, *der*

tribulation /trɪbjʊ'leɪʃn/ *n.* Kummer, *der*

tribunal /traɪ'bjuːnl/ *n.* Schiedsgericht, *das*

tributary /'trɪbjʊtərɪ/ *n.* Nebenfluss, *der*

tribute /'trɪbjuːt/ *n.* Tribut, *der* (to an + *Akk.*); **pay ~ to sb./sth.** jmdm./einer Sache den schuldigen Tribut zollen (geh.)

trice /traɪs/ *n.* **in a ~:** im Handumdrehen

trick /trɪk/ ☐ *n.* **(a)** Trick, *der;* **it was all a ~:** das war [alles] nur Bluff
(b) (feat of skill etc.) Kunststück, *das;* **that should do the ~** (coll.) damit dürfte es klappen (ugs.)
(c) (knack) **get** *or* **find the ~** [of doing sth.] den Dreh finden[, wie man etw. tut]
(d) (prank) Streich, *der;* **play a ~ on sb.** jmdm. einen Streich spielen
(e) (Cards) Stich, *der*
② *v.t.* täuschen; hereinlegen; ~ **sb. out of/into sth.** jmdm. etw. ablisten
③ *adj.* ~ **photograph** Trickaufnahme, *die;* ~ **question** Fangfrage, *die*

trickery /'trɪkərɪ/ *n.* [Hinter]list, *die*

trickle /'trɪkl/ *v.i.* rinnen; (in drops) tröpfeln

trickster /'trɪkstə(r)/ *n.* Schwindler, *der*/Schwindlerin, *die*

'**tricky** *adj.* verzwickt (ugs.)

tricycle /'traɪsɪkl/ *n.* Dreirad, *das*

tried ▸ TRY 2, 3

trifle /'traɪfl/ *n.* **(a)** (Brit. Gastron.) Trifle, *das*
(b) (thing of slight value) Kleinigkeit, *die*

trifling /'traɪflɪŋ/ *adj.* unbedeutend ⟨*Angelegenheit*⟩; gering ⟨*Wert*⟩

trigger /'trɪgə(r)/ ☐ *n.* **(a)** (of gun) Abzug, *der;* (of machine) Drücker, *der*
(b) (fig.) Auslöser, *der*

2 *v.t.* ~ [off] auslösen
trigonometry /trɪgə'nɒmɪtrɪ/ *n.* Trigonometrie, *die*
trilingual /traɪ'lɪŋgwəl/ *adj.* dreisprachig
trill /trɪl/ 1 *n.* Trillern, *das;* (Mus.) Triller, *der*
2 *v.i.* trillern
trillion /'trɪljən/ *n.* (million million) Billion, *die*
trilogy /'trɪlədʒɪ/ *n.* Trilogie, *die*
trim /trɪm/ 1 *v.t.,* -mm-: (a) schneiden ‹Hecke›; [nach]schneiden ‹Haar›; beschneiden ‹Papier, Hecke, Budget›
(b) (ornament) besetzen (with mit)
2 *adj.* proper; gepflegt ‹Garten›
3 *n.* (a) be in ~ (healthy) in Form *od.* fit sein
(b) (cut) Nachschneiden, *das*
'**trimming** *n.* (a) (decorations) Verzierung, *die*
(b) *in pl.* (coll.: accompaniments) Beilagen *Pl.;* with all the ~s mit allem Drum und Dran (ugs.)
Trinity /'trɪnɪtɪ/ *n.* (Theol.) the [Holy] ~: die Heilige Dreieinigkeit
trinket /'trɪŋkɪt/ *n.* kleines, billiges Schmuckstück
trio /'triːəʊ/ *n., pl.* ~s Trio, *das*
trip /trɪp/ 1 *n.* (a) Reise, *die;* (shorter) Ausflug, *der*
(b) (coll.: drug-induced hallucinations) Trip, *der*
2 *v.i.,* -pp- stolpern (on über + *Akk.*)
■ **trip 'over** *v.t.* stolpern über (+ *Akk.*)
■ **trip 'up** 1 *v.i.* (a) stolpern
(b) (fig.) einen Fehler machen
2 *v.t.* (a) stolpern lassen
(b) (fig.) aufs Glatteis führen (fig.)
tripe /traɪp/ *n.* (a) Kaldaunen *Pl.*
(b) (coll.: rubbish) Quatsch, *der* (ugs.)
triple /'trɪpl/ 1 *adj.* (a) (threefold) dreifach
(b) (three times greater than) ~ the ...: der/die/das dreifache ...
2 *n.* Dreifache, *das*
3 *v.i.* sich verdreifachen
4 *v.t.* verdreifachen
'**triple jump** *n.* (Sport) Dreisprung, *der*
triplet /'trɪplɪt/ *n.* Drilling, *der*
triplicate /'trɪplɪkət/ *n.* in ~: in dreifacher Ausfertigung
trip 'mileage recorder *n.* (Motor Veh.) Tageskilometerzähler, *der*
tripod /'traɪpɒd/ *n.* Dreibein, *das*
'**tripper** *n.* (Brit.) Ausflügler, *der*/Ausflüglerin, *die*
'**tripwire** *n.* Stolperdraht, *der*
trite /traɪt/ *adj.* banal
triumph /'traɪəmf, 'traɪʌmf/ 1 *n.* Triumph, *der* (over über + *Akk.*)
2 *v.i.* triumphieren (over über + *Akk.*)
triumphant /traɪ'ʌmfənt/ *adj.*
(a) siegreich
(b) triumphierend ‹Blick›
trivia /'trɪvɪə/ *n. pl.* Belanglosigkeiten *Pl.*
trivial /'trɪvɪəl/ *adj.* belanglos

triviality /trɪvɪ'ælɪtɪ/ *n.* Belanglosigkeit, *die*
trivialize /'trɪvɪəlaɪz/ *v.t.* auf eine belanglose Ebene bringen
trod, trodden ▸ TREAD 2, 3
trolley /'trɒlɪ/ *n.* (a) (for serving food) Servierwagen, *der*
(b) [supermarket] ~: Einkaufswagen, *der*
trombone /trɒm'bəʊn/ *n.* Posaune, *die*
troop /truːp/ 1 *n.* (a) *in pl.* Truppen *Pl.*
(b) (fig.) Schar, *die*
2 *v.i.* ~ in/out hinein-/hinausströmen
troop: ~ **carrier** *n.* Truppentransporter, *der;* ~**ship** *n.* Truppentransporter, *der*
trophy /'trəʊfɪ/ *n.* Trophäe, *die*
tropic /'trɒpɪk/ *n.* the T~s (Geog.) die Tropen; the ~ of Cancer/Capricorn (Astron., Geog.) der Wendekreis des Krebses/Steinbocks
tropical /'trɒpɪkl/ *adj.* tropisch; Tropen‹krankheit, -kleidung›
tropical: ~ '**medicine** *n.* Tropenmedizin, *die;* ~ '**rainforest** *n.* tropischer Regenwald
trot /trɒt/ 1 *n.* (coll.) on the ~: hintereinander; be on the ~: auf Trab sein (ugs.)
2 *v.i.,* -tt- traben
trouble /'trʌbl/ 1 *n.* (a) Ärger, *der;* Schwierigkeiten *Pl.;* there'll be ~ [if ...] es wird Ärger geben, [wenn ...]; what's the ~? was ist denn?
(b) engine/brake ~: Probleme mit dem Motor/der Bremse; suffer from heart/liver ~: herz-/leberkrank sein
(c) (inconvenience) Mühe, *die;* take a lot of ~: sich (*Dat.*) sehr viel Mühe geben; it's more ~ than it's worth es lohnt sich nicht
(d) *in sing. or pl.* (unrest) Unruhen *Pl.*
2 *v.t.* (a) (agitate) beunruhigen; don't let it ~ you mach dir deswegen keine Sorgen
(b) (inconvenience) stören
3 *v.i.* (make an effort) sich bemühen
troubled /'trʌbld/ *adj.* (a) (worried) besorgt
(b) (restless) unruhig
trouble: ~**free** *adj.* problemlos; ~**maker** *n.* Unruhestifter, *der*/-stifterin, *die*
troublesome /'trʌblsəm/ *adj.* schwierig; lästig ‹Krankheit›
trough /trɒf/ *n.* Trog, *der*
troupe /truːp/ *n.* Truppe, *die*
trouser /'traʊzə/: ~ **leg** *n.* Hosenbein, *das;* ~ **press** *n.* Bügelpresse, *die;* Hosenbügler, *der*
trousers /'traʊzəz/ *n. pl.* [pair of] ~: Hose, *die*
'**trouser suit** *n.* (Brit.) Hosenanzug, *der*
trousseau /'truːsəʊ/ *n., pl.* ~s *or* ~x /'truːsəʊz/ Aussteuer, *die*
trout /traʊt/ *n., pl.* same Forelle, *die*
trout: ~ **farm** *n.* Forellenzuchtbetrieb, *der;* ~**fishing** *n.* Forellenfang, *der* ⋯▸

trowel /'trauəl/ n. Kelle, die; (Hort.)
Pflanzkelle, die

truant /'tru:ənt/ n. **play ~:** [die Schule]
schwänzen (ugs.)

truce /tru:s/ n. Waffenstillstand, der

truck /trʌk/ n. **(a)** Last[kraft]wagen, der;
Lkw, der
(b) (Brit. Railw.) offener Güterwagen

'truck driver, trucker /'trʌkə(r)/ ns.
Lastwagenfahrer, der/-fahrerin, die; (long-
distance) Fernfahrer, der/-fahrerin, die

truculent /'trʌkjʊlənt/ adj. aufsässig

trudge /trʌdʒ/ v.i. trotten; (through snow etc.)
stapfen

true /tru:/ adj., **~r** /'tru:ə(r),/ **~st** /'tru:ɪst/
(a) wahr; wahrheitsgetreu ⟨Bericht⟩; richtig
⟨Vorteil⟩; (rightly so called) eigentlich; echt,
wahr ⟨Freund⟩; **is it ~ that ...?** stimmt es,
dass ...?; **~ to life** lebensecht
(b) (loyal) treu

truffle /'trʌfl/ n. Trüffel, die od. (ugs.) der

truism /'tru:ɪzm/ n. Binsenweisheit, die

truly /'tru:lɪ/ adv. **(a)** wirklich
(b) (accurately) zutreffend; **yours ~:** mit
freundlichen Grüßen

trump /trʌmp/ (Cards) **1** n. Trumpf, der
2 v.t. übertrumpfen

'trump card n. (lit. or fig.) Trumpf, der

trumped up /'trʌmpt ʌp/ adj. falsch
⟨Beschuldigung usw.⟩

trumpet /'trʌmpɪt/ n. Trompete, die

'trumpeter n. Trompeter, der/
Trompeterin, die

truncheon /'trʌntʃn/ n. Schlagstock, der

trundle /'trʌndl/ v.t. & i. rollen

trunk /trʌŋk/ n. **(a)** (of elephant etc.) Rüssel,
der
(b) (large box) Schrankkoffer, der
(c) (of tree) Stamm, der
(d) (of body) Rumpf, der
(e) (Amer.: of car) Kofferraum, der
(f) in pl. (Brit.) **[swimming] ~s** Badehose, die

truss /trʌs/ n. (Med.) Bruchband, das

trust /trʌst/ **1** n. **(a)** Vertrauen, das; **place**
or put one's ~ in sb./sth. sein Vertrauen
auf od. in jmdn./etw. setzen; **take sth. on**
~: etw. einfach glauben
(b) (organization managed by trustees)
Treuhandgesellschaft, die; **[charitable]**
~: Stiftung, die; (association of companies)
Trust, der
(c) (Law) **hold in ~:** treuhänderisch
verwalten
2 v.t. (rely on) trauen (+ Dat.); vertrauen
(+ Dat.) ⟨Person⟩; **~ sb. with sth.** jmdm. etw.
anvertrauen
3 v.i. **(a) ~ to** sich verlassen auf (+ Akk.)
(b) (believe) **~ in sb./sth.** auf jmdn./etw.
vertrauen

trustee /trʌ'sti:/ n. Treuhänder,
der/Treuhänderin, die

trustful /'trʌstfl/, **'trusting** adjs.

trust: ~ fund n. Treuhandvermögen, das;
~worthy adj. vertrauenswürdig

truth /tru:θ/ n., pl. **~s** /tru:ðz, tru:θs/
Wahrheit, die; **tell the [whole] ~:** die [ganze]
Wahrheit sagen

truthful /'tru:θfl/ adj. ehrlich

try /traɪ/ **1** n. Versuch, der; **have a ~ at**
sth./doing sth. etw. versuchen/versuchen,
etw. zu tun; **give it a ~, have a ~:** es
versuchen
2 v.t. **(a)** (attempt) versuchen
(b) (test usefulness of) probieren
(c) (test) auf die Probe stellen ⟨Fähigkeit,
Kraft, Geduld⟩
(d) (Law.: take to trial) **~ a case** einen Fall
verhandeln; **~ sb. [for sth.]** jmdn. [wegen
einer Sache] vor Gericht stellen
3 v.i. es versuchen; **~ hard/harder** sich
(Dat.) viel/mehr Mühe geben
■ **try 'on** v.t. anprobieren ⟨Kleidungsstück⟩
■ **try 'out** v.t. ausprobieren

'trying adj. **(a)** (testing) schwierig
(b) (difficult to endure) anstrengend

tsar /zɑ:(r)/ n. (Hist.) Zar, der

'T-shirt n. T-Shirt, das

tub /tʌb/ n. Kübel, der; (for ice cream etc.)
Becher, der

tuba /'tju:bə/ n. (Mus.) Tuba, die

tubby /'tʌbɪ/ adj. rundlich

tube /tju:b/ n. **(a)** (for conveying liquids etc.)
Rohr, das
(b) (small cylinder) Tube, die; (for sweets, tablets)
Röhrchen, das
(c) (Anat., Zool.) Röhre, die
(d) (of TV etc.) Röhre, die
(e) (Brit. coll.: underground railway) U-Bahn, die

tuber /'tju:bə(r)/ n. (Bot.) Knolle, die

tuberculosis /tju:bɜ:kjʊ'ləʊsɪs/ n.
Tuberkulose, die

tube: ~ station n. (Brit. coll.) U-Bahnhof,
der; **~ train** n. (Brit. coll.) U-bahn-Zug, der

tubing /'tju:bɪŋ/ n. Rohre Pl.

tubular /'tju:bjʊlə(r)/ adj. röhrenförmig

tuck /tʌk/ **1** v.t. stecken
2 n. (in fabric) (for decoration) Biese, die; (to
tighten) Abnäher, der
■ **tuck 'in 1** v.t. hineinstecken
2 v.i. (coll.) zulangen (ugs.)
■ **tuck 'up** v.t. **(a)** hochkrempeln ⟨Ärmel,
Hose⟩; hochnehmen ⟨Rock⟩
(b) (cover snugly) zudecken

Tue., Tues. abbrs. = **Tuesday** Di.

Tuesday /'tju:zdeɪ, 'tju:zdɪ/ n. Dienstag,
der; see also FRIDAY

tuft /tʌft/ n. Büschel, das

tug /tʌg/ **1** n. **(a)** Ruck, der; **~ of war**
Tauziehen, das
(b) ~ [boat] Schlepper, der
2 v.t. **-gg-** ziehen
3 v.i. **-gg-** zerren (**at** an + Dat.)

tuition /tju:'ɪʃn/ n. Unterricht, der

897

tulip ⋯✦ turn ⋯ ⋯

tulip /'tju:lɪp/ n. Tulpe, *die*
tumble /'tʌmbl/ ⟨1⟩ v.i. stürzen; fallen
⟨2⟩ n. Sturz, *der*
tumble: ~down adj. verfallen; **~-drier**
n. Wäschetrockner, *der;* **~-dry** v.t. im
Automaten trocknen
tumbler /'tʌmblə(r)/ n. (short) Whiskyglas,
das; (long) Wasserglas, *das*
tummy /'tʌmi/ n. (child lang./coll.) Bäuchlein,
das
tummy: ~ ache n. (child lang./coll.)
Bauchweh, *das;* **~ button** n. (child
lang./coll.) Bauchnabel, *der;* **~ upset** n.
(child lang./coll.) Magenverstimmung, *die*
tumour (*Brit.; Amer.:* **tumor**) /'tju:mə(r)/
n. Tumor, *der*
tumult /'tju:mʌlt/ n. Tumult, *der*
tuna /'tju:nə/ n., pl. same or ~s Thunfisch,
der
tune /tju:n/ ⟨1⟩ n. (a) (melody) Melodie, *die;*
change one's ~ (fig.) sein Verhalten ändern;
call the ~: den Ton angeben
(b) (correct pitch) **sing in/out of ~:** richtig/
falsch singen; **be in/out of ~** ⟨*Instrument:*⟩
richtig gestimmt/verstimmt sein
⟨2⟩ v.t. (a) (Mus.: put in ~) stimmen
(b) (Radio, Telev.) einstellen (**to** auf + *Akk.*)
(c) einstellen ⟨*Motor, Vergaser*⟩
tune 'in v.i. (Radio, Telev.) ~ **to a station**
einen Sender einstellen
tuneful /'tju:nfl/ adj. melodisch
tuner /'tju:nə(r)/ n. (a) (Mus.) Stimmer,
der/Stimmerin, *die*
(b) (radio) Tuner, *der*
tunic /'tju:nɪk/ n. (of soldier) Uniformjacke,
die; (of schoolgirl) Kittel, *der*
'tuning fork /'tju:nɪŋfɔ:k/ n. Stimmgabel,
die
Tunisia /tju:'nɪzɪə/ pr. n. Tunesien (*das*)
tunnel /'tʌnl/ ⟨1⟩ n. Tunnel, *der;* (dug by
animal) Gang, *der*
⟨2⟩ v.i., (Brit.) -II- einen Tunnel graben
turban /'tɜ:bən/ n. Turban, *der*
turbine /'tɜ:baɪn/ n. Turbine, *die*
turbocharged /'tɜ:bəʊtʃɑ:dʒd/ adj. mit
Turbolader *nachgestellt*
turbot /'tɜ:bət/ n. Steinbutt, *der*
turbulence /'tɜ:bjʊləns/ n.
(a) Aufgewühltheit, *die;* (fig.) Aufruhr, *der*
(b) (Phys.) Turbulenz, *die*
turbulent /'tɜ:bjʊlənt/ adj. (a) aufgewühlt
(b) (Phys.) turbulent
turd /tɜ:d/ n. (coarse) Scheißhaufen, *der*
(derb)
tureen /tjʊə'ri:n/ n. Terrine, *die*
turf /tɜ:f/ n., pl. ~s or turves /tɜ:vz/ (a) no
pl. Rasen, *der*
(b) (segment) Rasenstück, *das*
■ **turf 'out** v.t. (coll.) rausschmeißen (ugs.)
Turk /tɜ:k/ n. Türke, *der*/Türkin, *die*
turkey n. Truthahn, *der*/Truthenne, *die;*
(esp. as food) Puter, *der*/Pute, *die*

Turkey /'tɜ:kɪ/ pr. n. die Türkei
Turkish /'tɜ:kɪʃ/ ⟨1⟩ adj. türkisch; **sb. is
~:** jmd. ist Türke/Türkin
⟨2⟩ n. Türkisch, *das; see also* ENGLISH 2A
turmoil /'tɜ:mɔɪl/ n. Aufruhr, *der*
turn /tɜ:n/ ⟨1⟩ n. (a) **it is sb.'s ~ to do sth.**
jmd. ist an der Reihe, etw. zu tun; **it's your
~ [next]** du bist als Nächster/Nächste dran
(ugs.) od. an der Reihe; **out of ~:** außer der
Reihe; (fig.) an der falschen Stelle ⟨*lachen*⟩;
take [it in] ~s sich abwechseln
(b) (rotary motion) Drehung, *die*
(c) (change of direction) Wende, *die;* **take a ~ to
the right/left, do** or **take a right/left ~:** nach
rechts/links abbiegen; (fig.) **take a favourable
~** sich zum Guten wenden; **the ~ of the
year/century** die Jahres-/Jahrhundertwende
(d) (bend) Kurve, *die;* (corner) Ecke, *die*
(e) (short performance) Nummer, *die*
(f) (service) **do sb. a good ~:** jmdm. einen
guten Dienst erweisen
(g) (coll.: fright) **give sb. quite a ~:** jmdm.
einen gehörigen Schrecken einjagen (ugs.)
⟨2⟩ v.t. (a) (make revolve) drehen
(b) (reverse) umdrehen; wenden
⟨*Pfannkuchen, Auto, Heu*⟩; **~ sth. upside
down** or **on its head** (lit. or fig.) etw. auf den
Kopf stellen; **~ the page** umblättern
(c) (give new direction to) drehen, wenden
⟨*Kopf*⟩; **~ a hose/gun on sb./sth.** einen
Schlauch/ein Gewehr auf jmdn./etw.
richten; **~ one's attention/mind to sth.**
sich/seine Gedanken einer Sache (*Dat.*)
zuwenden
(d) ~ sb. loose on sb./sth. jmdn. auf
jmdn./etw. loslassen
(e) (cause to become) verwandeln; **~ the
lights [down] low** das Licht dämpfen; **~ a
play/book into a film** ein Theaterstück/Buch
verfilmen
(f) (shape in lathe) drechseln ⟨*Holz*⟩; drehen
⟨*Metall*⟩
(g) drehen ⟨*Pirouette*⟩; schlagen
⟨*Purzelbaum*⟩
⟨3⟩ v.i. (a) (revolve) sich drehen
(b) (reverse direction) ⟨*Person:*⟩ sich
herumdrehen; ⟨*Auto:*⟩ wenden
(c) (take new direction) sich wenden; (**~ round**)
sich umdrehen; **~ to the left/right** nach
links/rechts abbiegen
(d) (become) werden; **~ [in]to sth.** zu etw.
werden; (be transformed) sich in etw. (*Akk.*)
verwandeln
(e) (become sour) ⟨*Milch:*⟩ sauer werden
■ **turn a'way** ⟨1⟩ v.i. sich abwenden
⟨2⟩ v.t. (a) (avert) abwenden
(b) (send away) wegschicken
■ **turn 'down** v.t. (a) herunterschlagen
⟨*Kragen*⟩
(b) niedriger stellen ⟨*Heizung*⟩;
herunterdrehen ⟨*Gas*⟩; leiser stellen ⟨*Ton,
Radio, Fernseher*⟩
(c) (reject) ablehnen; abweisen ⟨*Kandidaten
usw.*⟩
■ **turn 'in** ⟨1⟩ v.t. (a) nach innen drehen ⋯✦

(b) (hand in) abgeben
2 *v.i.* (a) (enter) einbiegen
(b) (coll.: go to bed) in die Falle gehen (salopp)
■ **turn 'off** **1** *v.t.* abschalten; abstellen ‹*Wasser, Gas*›; zudrehen ‹*Wasserhahn*›
2 *v.i.* abbiegen
■ **turn on** *v.t.* (a) /-'-/ anschalten; aufdrehen ‹*Wasserhahn, Gas*›
(b) /'--/ (attack) angreifen
■ **turn 'out** **1** *v.t.* (a) (expel) hinauswerfen (ugs.)
(b) (switch off) ausschalten; abdrehen ‹*Gas*›
(c) (produce) produzieren
(d) (Brit.) (empty) ausräumen; leeren; (get rid of) wegwerfen
2 *v.i.* (a) (prove to be) sb./sth. ~s out to be sth. jmd./etw. stellt sich als jmd./etw. heraus; everything ~ed out well/all right in the end alles endete gut
(b) (appear) ‹*Fans usw.*:› erscheinen
■ **turn 'over** **1** *v.t.* umdrehen
2 *v.i.* (a) (tip over) umkippen; ‹*Boot*:› kentern; ‹*Auto, Flugzeug*:› sich überschlagen
(b) (from one side to the other) sich umdrehen
(c) (~ a page) umblättern
■ **turn 'round** *v.i.* sich umdrehen
■ **'turn to** *v.t.* (fig.) ~ to sb. sich an jmdn. wenden; ~ to sb. for help/advice bei jmdm. Hilfe/Rat suchen; ~ to drink sich in den Alkohol flüchten
■ **turn 'up** **1** *v.i.* (a) ‹*Person*:› erscheinen
(b) (present itself) auftauchen; ‹*Gelegenheit*:› sich bieten
2 *v.t.* (a) hochschlagen ‹*Kragen*›
(b) lauter stellen ‹*Ton, Radio, Fernseher*›; aufdrehen ‹*Heizung, Gas*›; heller machen ‹*Licht*›
'turnaround *n.* (a) (change) [Kehrt]wende, *die*
(b) (of aircraft, ship, vehicle) Abfertigung, *die*
turned-up /'tɜ:ndʌp/ *adj.* ~ nose Stupsnase, *die* (ugs.)
'turning *n.* Abzweigung, *die*
'turning point *n.* Wendepunkt, *der*
turnip /'tɜ:nɪp/ *n.* [weiße] Rübe, *die*
turn: ~**out** *n.* (of people) Beteiligung, *die* (for an + *Dat.*); ~**over** *n.* (a) (Commerc.) Umsatz, *der;* (of stock) Umschlag, *der;* (b) (of staff) Fluktuation, *die;* ~**pike** *n.* (Amer.) gebührenpflichtige Autobahn; ~**stile** *n.* Drehkreuz, *das;* ~**table** *n.* Plattenteller, *der;* ~**up** *n.* (Brit. Fashion) Aufschlag, *der*
turpentine /'tɜ:pntaɪn/ *n.* Terpentin, *das*
turps /tɜ:ps/ *n.* (coll.) Terpentin, *das* (ugs.)
turquoise /'tɜ:kwɔɪz/ **1** *n.* (a) Türkis, *der*
(b) (colour) Türkis, *das*
2 *adj.* türkis[farben]
turret /'tʌrɪt/ *n.* Türmchen, *das*
turreted /'tʌrɪtɪd/ *adj.* ‹*Schloss*› mit Mauertürmchen
turtle /'tɜ:tl/ *n.* (a) Meeresschildkröte, *die*
(b) (Amer.: freshwater reptile) Wasserschildkröte, *die*

'turtleneck *n.* ~neck pullover Pullover mit Stehbund
turves ▸ TURF B
tusk /tʌsk/ *n.* Stoßzahn, *der*
tussle /'tʌsl/ **1** *n.* Gerangel, *das* (ugs.)
2 *v.i.* sich balgen
tutor /'tju:tə(r)/ *n.* [private] ~: [Privat]lehrer, *der*/-lehrerin, *die*
tut[-tut] /tʌt('tʌt)/ **1** *int.* na[, na]
2 *v.i.*, -tt-: ~ [with disapproval] [missbilligend] „na, na!" sagen
tutu /'tu:tu:/ *n.* Tutu, *das*
tuxedo /tʌk'si:dəʊ/ *n., pl.* ~s *or* ~es (Amer.) Smoking, *der*
TV /ti:'vi:/ *n.* (a) Fernsehen, *das*
(b) (television set) Fernseher, *der* (ugs.)
twaddle /'twɒdl/ *n.* Gewäsch, *das* (ugs.)
twang /twæŋ/ **1** *v.t.* zupfen ‹*Saite*›
2 *n.* [nasal] ~: Näseln, *das*
tweed /twi:d/ *n.* Tweed, *der*
tweezers /'twi:zəz/ *n. pl.* [pair of] ~: Pinzette, *die*
twelfth /twelfθ/ **1** *adj.* zwölft...
2 *n.* (fraction) Zwölftel, *das*. See also EIGHTH
twelve /twelv/ **1** *adj.* zwölf
2 *n.* Zwölf, *die*. See also EIGHT
twentieth /'twentɪɪθ/ **1** *adj.* zwanzigst...
2 *n.* (fraction) Zwanzigstel, *das*. See also EIGHTH
twenty /'twentɪ/ **1** *adj.* zwanzig
2 *n.* Zwanzig, *die*. See also EIGHT; EIGHTY 2
twice /twaɪs/ *adv.* (a) zweimal
(b) (doubly) doppelt
twiddle /'twɪdl/ *v.t.* herumdrehen an (+ *Dat.*) (ugs.); ~ one's thumbs (lit. or fig.) Däumchen drehen
twig¹ /twɪg/ *n.* Zweig, *der*
twig² (coll.) **1** *v.t.*, -gg- kapieren (ugs.)
2 *v.i.*, -gg- es kapieren (ugs.)
twilight /'twaɪlaɪt/ *n.* (a) (evening light) Dämmerlicht, *das*
(b) (period of half-light) Dämmerung, *die*
twin /twɪn/ **1** *attrib. adj.* (a) Zwillings-
(b) (forming a pair) Doppel-
2 *n.* Zwilling, *der*
3 *v.t.* Bottrop is ~ned with Blackpool Bottrop und Blackpool sind Partnerstädte
twin 'beds *n. pl.* zwei Einzelbetten *Pl.*
twine /twaɪn/ **1** *n.* Bindfaden, *der*
2 *v.i.* sich winden (about, around um)
twinge /twɪndʒ/ *n.* Stechen, *das;* ~[s] of conscience (fig.) Gewissensbisse *Pl.*
twinkle /'twɪŋkl/ **1** *v.i.* funkeln (with vor + *Dat.*)
2 *n.* Funkeln, *das*
twinkling /'twɪŋklɪŋ/ *n.* in a ~, in the ~ of an eye im Handumdrehen
'twin town *n.* (Brit.) Partnerstadt, *die*
twirl /twɜ:l/ **1** *v.t.* [schnell] drehen
2 *v.i.* wirbeln (around über + *Akk.*)

twist /twɪst/ **1** *v.t.* **(a)** verdrehen ⟨*Worte, Bedeutung*⟩; ~ **one's ankle** sich (*Dat.*) den Knöchel verrenken; ~ **sb.'s arm** jmdm. den Arm umdrehen; (fig.) jmdm. [die] Daumenschrauben anlegen
(b) (rotate) drehen
2 *v.i.* sich winden
3 *n.* **(a)** (motion) Drehung, *die*
(b) (unexpected occurrence) überraschende Wendung

'twisted *adj.* verbogen; (fig.) verdreht (ugs. abwertend) ⟨*Geist*⟩; verquer ⟨*Humor*⟩

twit /twɪt/ *n.* (Brit. coll.) Trottel, *der* (ugs.)

twitch /twɪtʃ/ **1** *v.i.* ⟨*Mund, Lippe*⟩ zucken
2 *n.* Zucken, *das*

twitter /'twɪtə(r)/ **1** *n.* Zwitschern, *das*
2 *v.i.* zwitschern

two /tu:/ **1** *adj.* zwei
2 *n.* Zwei, *die.* See also EIGHT

two: ~**-bit** *adj.* (Amer.) (of poor quality) mies (ugs.); ~**-faced** /'tu:feɪst/ *adj.* (fig.) falsch; ~**fold** *adj., adv.* zweifach; **a** ~**fold increase** ein Anstieg auf das Doppelte; ~**-lane** *adj.* zweispurig; ~**-piece** **1** *n.* Zweiteiler, *der;* **2** *adj.* zweiteilig; ~**-seater** /-'--/ *n.* Zweisitzer, *der;* ~**some** /'tu:səm/ *n.* Paar, *das;* ~**-storey** *adj.* zweigeschossig; ~**-tone** *adj.* zweifarbig; ~**-up** ~**-down** *n.* kleines [Reihen]haus; ~**-way** *adj.* **(a)** zweibahnig (Verkehrsw.); '~**-way traffic ahead'** „Achtung Gegenverkehr"; **(b)** ~**-way mirror** Einwegspiegel, *der*

tycoon /taɪ'ku:n/ *n.* Magnat, *der*

tying ▶ TIE 1, 2

type /taɪp/ **1** *n.* **(a)** Art, *die;* (person) Typ, *der;* **what** ~ **of car** ...? was für ein Auto ...?
(b) (Printing) Drucktype, *die*
2 *v.t.* [mit der Maschine] schreiben; tippen (ugs.)
3 *v.i.* Maschine schreiben
■ **type 'out** *v.t.* [mit der Schreibmaschine] abschreiben; abtippen (ugs.)

type: ~**cast** *v.t.* [auf eine bestimmte Rolle] festlegen; ~**face** *n.* Schriftbild, *das;* ~**script** *n.* maschine[n]geschriebene Fassung; ~**setter** *n.* [Schrift]setzer, *der*/-setzerin, *die;* ~**setting** *n.* [Schrift]setzen, *das;* ~**writer** *n.* Schreibmaschine, *die;* ~**written** *adj.* maschine[n]geschrieben

typhoid /'taɪfɔɪd/ *n.* ~ **[fever]** Typhus, *der*

typhoon /taɪ'fu:n/ *n.* Taifun, *der*

typical /'tɪpɪkl/ *adj.* typisch (**of** für)

typify /'tɪpɪfaɪ/ *v.t.* ~ **sth.** als typisches Beispiel für etw. dienen

typing /'taɪpɪŋ/ *n.* Maschineschreiben, *das*

'typing error *n.* Tippfehler, *der*

typist /'taɪpɪst/ *n.* Schreibkraft, *die*

typography /taɪ'pɒgrəfɪ/ *n.* Typographie, *die*

tyrannical /tɪ'rænɪkl/ *adj.* tyrannisch

tyranny /'tɪrənɪ/ *n.* Tyrannei, *die*

tyrant /'taɪərənt/ *n.* Tyrann, *der*

tyre /'taɪə(r)/ *n.* Reifen, *der*

'tyre pressure *n.* Reifendruck, *der*

tzar *etc.* ▶ TSAR *etc.*

Uu

U, u /ju:/ *n.* U, u, *das*

'U-bend *n.* U-Rohr, *das*

ubiquitous /ju:'bɪkwɪtəs/ *adj.* allgegenwärtig

udder /'ʌdə(r)/ *n.* Euter, *das*

UFO /'ju:fəʊ/ *n., pl.* ~**s** Ufo, *das*

ugh /ʌh, ʊh, ɜ:h/ *int.* bah

ugliness /'ʌglɪnɪs/ *n.* Hässlichkeit, *die*

ugly /'ʌglɪ/ *adj.* **(a)** hässlich
(b) (nasty) übel ⟨*Wunde, Laune usw.*⟩

UHF *abbr.* = **ultra-high frequency** UHF

UHT *abbr.* = **ultra heat-treated** ultrahoch erhitzt

UK *abbr.* = **United Kingdom**

Ukraine /ju:'kreɪn/ *pr. n.* Ukraine, *die*

Ukrainian /ju:'kreɪnɪən/ **1** *adj.* ukrainisch; **sb. is** ~: jmd. ist Ukrainer/ Ukrainerin

2 *n.* **(a)** (person) Ukrainer, *der*/Ukrainerin, *die*
(b) (language) Ukrainisch, *das; see also* ENGLISH 2 A

ulcer /'ʌlsə(r)/ *n.* Geschwür, *das*

ulterior /ʌl'tɪərɪə(r)/ *adj.* hintergründig; ~ **motive** Hintergedanke, *der*

ultimate /'ʌltɪmət/ **1** *attrib. adj.* **(a)** (final) letzt...; (eventual) endgültig ⟨*Sieg*⟩
(b) (fundamental) tiefst...
2 *n.* **the** ~ **in comfort/luxury** der Gipfel an Bequemlichkeit/Luxus

'ultimately *adv.* **(a)** (in the end) schließlich
(b) (in the last analysis) letzten Endes

ultimatum /ʌltɪ'meɪtəm/ *n., pl.* ~**s** or ultimata /ʌltɪ'meɪtə/ Ultimatum, *das*

ultra'sound *n.* Ultraschall, *der*

ultra'violet *adj.* (Phys.) ultraviolett; UV- ⟨*Lampe, Filter*⟩

umbilical cord /ʌmˈbɪlɪkl kɔːd/ *n.* Nabelschnur, *die*

umbrage /ˈʌmbrɪdʒ/ *n.* take ∼ [at sth.] [an etw. (+ *Dat.*)] Anstoß nehmen

umbrella /ʌmˈbrelə/ *n.* [Regen]schirm, *der*

um'brella stand *n.* Schirmständer, *der*

umpire /ˈʌmpaɪə(r)/ *n.* Schiedsrichter, *der*/-richterin, *die*

umpteen /ʌmpˈtiːn/ *adj.* (coll.) zig (ugs.); x (ugs.)

unabashed /ʌnəˈbæʃt/ *adj.* ungeniert

unable /ʌnˈeɪbl/ *pred. adj.* be ∼ to do sth. etw. nicht tun können

unabridged /ʌnəˈbrɪdʒd/ *adj.* ungekürzt

unac'ceptable *adj.* unannehmbar

unaccompanied /ʌnəˈkʌmpənɪd/ *adj.* ohne Begleitung *nachgestellt*

unac'countable *adj.* unerklärlich

unaccountably /ʌnəˈkaʊntəblɪ/ *adv.* unerklärlicherweise

unac'customed *adj.* ungewohnt; be ∼ to sth. etw. (*Akk.*) nicht gewöhnt sein

unadulterated /ʌnəˈdʌltəreɪtɪd/ *adj.*
(a) (pure) unverfälscht
(b) (utter) völlig

unadventurous /ʌnədˈventʃərəs/ *adj.* bieder ⟨*Person*⟩; ereignislos ⟨*Leben*⟩

unafraid /ʌnəˈfreɪd/ *adj.* be ∼ [of sb./sth.] keine Angst [vor jmdm./etw.] haben

unaided /ʌnˈeɪdɪd/ *adj.* ohne fremde Hilfe

unalike /ʌnəˈlaɪk/ *pred. adj.* unähnlich

unambiguous /ʌnæmˈbɪɡjʊəs/ *adj.* unzweideutig

unambitious /ʌnæmˈbɪʃəs/ *adj.* ⟨*Person*⟩ ohne Ehrgeiz

unanimity /juːnəˈnɪmɪtɪ/ *n.* Einmütigkeit, *die*

unanimous /juːˈnænɪməs/ *adj.* einstimmig; be ∼ in doing sth. etw. einmütig tun

u'nanimously *adv.* einstimmig

unannounced /ʌnəˈnaʊnst/ *adj.* unangemeldet

unappetizing /ʌnˈæpɪtaɪzɪŋ/ *adj.* unappetitlich

unarmed /ʌnˈɑːmd/ *adj.* unbewaffnet; ∼ combat Kampf ohne Waffen

unassuming /ʌnəˈsjuːmɪŋ/ *adj.* bescheiden

unattached /ʌnəˈtætʃt/ *adj.* (a) nicht befestigt
(b) (without a partner) ungebunden

unat'tended *adj.* (a) ∼ to (not dealt with) unerledigt; nicht bedient ⟨*Kunde*⟩; nicht behandelt ⟨*Patient*⟩
(b) (not supervised) unbewacht ⟨*Parkplatz, Gepäck*⟩

unat'tractive *adj.* unattraktiv

unauthorized /ʌnˈɔːθəraɪzd/ *adj.* unbefugt; no entry for ∼ persons Zutritt für Unbefugte verboten

una'vailable *adj.* nicht erhältlich ⟨*Ware*⟩; be ∼ for comment zur Stellungnahme nicht zur Verfügung stehen

una'voidable *adj.* unvermeidlich

unaware /ʌnəˈweə(r)/ *adj.* be ∼ of sth. sich (*Dat.*) einer Sache (*Gen.*) nicht bewusst sein

unawares /ʌnəˈweəz/ *adv.* catch sb. ∼: jmdn. überraschen

unbalanced /ʌnˈbælənst/ *adj.*
(a) unausgewogen
(b) (mentally ∼) unausgeglichen

un'bearable *adj.*, **unbearably** /ʌnˈbeərəblɪ/ *adv.* unerträglich

unbeatable /ʌnˈbiːtəbl/ *adj.* unschlagbar (ugs.)

un'beaten *adj.* (a) ungeschlagen
(b) (not surpassed) unerreicht; ungebrochen ⟨*Rekord*⟩

unbe'lievable *adj.* (a) unglaublich
(b) (tremendous) unwahrscheinlich

unbiased, unbiassed /ʌnˈbaɪəst/ *adj.* unvoreingenommen

unblemished /ʌnˈblemɪʃt/ *adj.* makellos ⟨*Haut, Ruf*⟩

un'block *v.t.* frei machen

un'bolt *v.t.* aufriegeln ⟨*Tür*⟩

unborn /ʌnˈbɔːn, *attrib.* ˈʌnbɔːn/ *adj.* ungeboren

un'breakable *adj.* unzerbrechlich

unburden /ʌnˈbɜːdn/ *v.t.* ∼ oneself sein Herz ausschütten

un'button *v.t.* aufknöpfen

uncalled-for /ʌnˈkɔːldfɔː(r)/ *adj.* unangebracht

uncanny /ʌnˈkænɪ/ *adj.* unheimlich

uncared-for /ʌnˈkeədfɔː(r)/ *adj.* vernachlässigt

uncaring /ʌnˈkeərɪŋ/ *adj.* gleichgültig

unceasing /ʌnˈsiːsɪŋ/ *adj.* unaufhörlich

unceremonious /ʌnserɪˈməʊnɪəs/ *adj.*
(a) (informal) formlos
(b) (abrupt) brüsk

uncere'moniously *adv.* ohne Umschweife

un'certain *adj.* (a) (not sure) be ∼ [whether ...] sich (*Dat.*) nicht sicher sein[, ob ...]
(b) (not clear) ungewiss ⟨*Ergebnis, Zukunft*⟩; of ∼ age/origin unbestimmten Alters/ unbestimmter Herkunft
(c) (ambiguous) vage; in no ∼ terms ganz eindeutig

uncertainty /ʌnˈsɜːtntɪ/ *n.*
(a) Ungewissheit, *die*
(b) (hesitation) Unsicherheit, *die*

unchanged /ʌnˈtʃeɪndʒd/ *adj.* unverändert

uncharacteristic /ʌnkærɪktəˈrɪstɪk/ *adj.* uncharakteristisch (of für)

un'charitable *adj.*, **uncharitably** /ʌnˈtʃærɪtəblɪ/ *adv.* lieblos

un'civil *adj.* unhöflich
uncle /'ʌŋkl/ *n.* Onkel, *der*
un'comfortable *adj.* **(a)** unbequem
(b) (feeling discomfort) **be ~:** sich unbehaglich fühlen
(c) (uneasy, disconcerting) unangenehm; peinlich ⟨*Stille*⟩
un'comfortably *adv.* unbequem; **be ~ aware of sth.** sich (*Dat.*) einer Sache peinlich bewusst sein
un'common *adj.* ungewöhnlich
uncompli'mentary *adj.* wenig schmeichelhaft
uncompromising /ʌn'kɒmprəmaɪzɪŋ/ *adj.* kompromisslos
uncon'ditional *adj.* bedingungslos ⟨*Kapitulation*⟩; kategorisch ⟨*Ablehnung*⟩; ⟨*Versprechen*⟩ ohne Vorbehalte
unconfirmed /ʌnkən'fɜ:md/ *adj.* unbestätigt
un'conscious [1] *adj.* **(a)** (Med.) bewusstlos
(b) (unaware) **be ~ of sth.** sich einer Sache (*Gen.*) nicht bewusst sein
(c) (not intended; Psych.) unbewusst
[2] *n.* Unbewusste, *das*
un'consciously *adv.* unbewusst
uncontrollable /ʌnkən'trəʊləbl/ *adj.* unkontrollierbar; **the child is ~:** das Kind ist nicht zu bändigen
uncon'ventional *adj.*, **uncon'ventionally** *adv.* unkonventionell
unconvinced /ʌnkən'vɪnst/ *adj.* nicht überzeugt; **remain ~:** sich nicht überzeugen lassen
uncooked /ʌn'kʊkt/ *adj.* roh
unco'operative *adj.* unkooperativ; (unhelpful) wenig hilfsbereit
uncoordinated /ʌnkəʊ'ɔ:dɪneɪtɪd/ *adj.* unkoordiniert
un'cork *v.t.* entkorken
uncouth /ʌn'ku:θ/ *adj.* ungehobelt ⟨*Person, Benehmen*⟩; grob ⟨*Bemerkung*⟩
un'cover *v.t.* aufdecken
undaunted /ʌn'dɔ:ntɪd/ *adj.* unverzagt
undecided /ʌndɪ'saɪdɪd/ *adj.* **(a)** (not settled) nicht entschieden
(b) (hesitant) unentschlossen
undeclared /ʌndɪ'kleəd/ *adj.* **~ income** (for tax) nicht angegebenes Einkommen
'undelete *v.t.* (Comp.) wiederherstellen
undemanding /ʌndɪ'mɑ:ndɪŋ/ *adj.* anspruchslos
unde'niable *adj.*, **undeniably** /ʌndɪ'naɪəblɪ/ *adv.* unbestreitbar
under /'ʌndə(r)/ [1] *prep.* **(a)** (underneath, below) unter (*position:* + *Dat.; motion:* + *Akk.*); **from ~ the table/bed** unter dem Tisch/Bett hervor
(b) (undergoing) **~ treatment** in Behandlung;

~ repair in Reparatur; **~ construction** im Bau
(c) (in conditions of) bei ⟨*Stress, hohen Temperaturen usw.*⟩
(d) (subject to) unter (+ *Dat.*); **~ the terms of the contract** nach den Bestimmungen des Vertrags
(e) (with the use of) unter (+ *Dat.*); **~ an assumed name** unter falschem Namen
(f) (less than) unter (+ *Dat.*)
[2] *adv.* **(a)** (in or to a lower or subordinate position) darunter
(b) (in/into a state of unconsciousness) **be ~/put sb. ~:** in Narkose liegen/jmdn. in Narkose versetzen
under: ~a'chieve *v.i.* unter dem erreichbaren Leistungsniveau bleiben; **~-age** *adj.* minderjährig; **~carriage** *n.* Fahrwerk, *das;* **~clothes** *n. pl.,* **~clothing** *n.* ▸ UNDERWEAR; **~coat** *n.* (layer of paint) Grundierung, *die;* (paint) Grundierfarbe, *die;* **~'cover** *adj.* (disguised) getarnt; (secret) verdeckt; **~cover agent** Geheimagent, *der;* **~current** *n.* Unterströmung, *die;* (fig.) Unterton, *der;* **~'cut** *v.t.,* **~cut** unterbieten; **~dog** *n.* **(a)** (in fight) Unterlegene, *der/die;* **(b)** (fig.) Benachteiligte, *der/die;* **~'done** *adj.* halb gar; **~estimate** /ʌndər'estɪmeɪt/ [1] *v.t.* unterschätzen; [2] /ʌndər'estɪmət/ *n.* Unterschätzung, *die;* **~'fed** *adj.* unterernährt; **~'foot** *adv.* am Boden; **be trampled ~foot** mit Füßen zertrampelt werden; **~'funding** *n.* Unterfinanzierung, *die;* **~'go** *v.t., forms as* GO 1: durchmachen; **~go treatment** sich einer Behandlung unterziehen; **~go a change** sich verändern; **~'graduate** *n.* **~graduate [student]** Student/Studentin vor der ersten Prüfung; **~ground** [1] /--'-/ *adv.* **(a)** unter der Erde; (Mining) unter Tage; **(b)** (fig.) (in hiding) im Untergrund; (into hiding) in den Untergrund; [2] /'---/ *adj.* unterirdisch ⟨*Höhle, See*⟩; **~ground railway** Untergrundbahn, *die;* U-Bahn, *die;* **~ground car park** Tiefgarage, *die;* [3] /'---/ *n.* (railway) U-Bahn, *die;* **~ground station/train** U-Bahnhof, *der*/U-Bahn-Zug, *der;* **~growth** *n.* Unterholz, *das;* **~hand, ~'handed** *adj.* **(a)** (secret) heimlich; **(b)** (crafty) hinterhältig; **~lay** *n.* Unterlage, *die;* **~'lie** *v.t., forms as* LIE²: **~lie sth.** (fig.) einer Sache (*Dat.*) zugrunde liegen; **~lying cause** eigentliche Ursache; **~'line** *v.t.* unterstreichen
underling /'ʌndəlɪŋ/ *n.* Untergebene, *der/die*
under: ~'lying ▸ UNDERLIE; **~'mine** *v.t.* **(a)** unterhöhlen; **(b)** (fig.) untergraben; unterminieren ⟨*Autorität*⟩
underneath /ʌndə'ni:θ/ [1] *prep.* unter (*position:* + *Dat.; motion:* + *Akk.*)
[2] *adv.* darunter
under: ~'nourished *adj.* unterernährt; **~'paid** *adj.* unterbezahlt; **~pants** *n. pl.* Unterhose, *die;* **~pass** *n.* ⋯⋗

Unterführung, *die;* ~**'play** *v.t.*
herunterspielen; ~**'privileged**
adj. unterprivilegiert; ~**'rate**
v.t. unterschätzen; ~**seal** *n.*
Unterbodenschutz, *der;* ~**signed**
/ʌndə'saɪnd/ *adj.* unterzeichnet; **the** ~**signed** der/
die Unterzeichnete/(pl.) die Unterzeichneten
(Papierdt.); ~**'staffed** *adj.* unterbesetzt; **be**
~**staffed** an Personalmangel leiden
understand /ʌndə'stænd/ [1] *v.t.,*
understood /ʌndə'stʊd/ **(a)** verstehen;
make oneself understood sich verständlich
machen
(b) (have heard) gehört haben
(c) (take as implied) **it was understood that …:**
es wurde allgemein angenommen, dass …
[2] *v.i.,* **understood (a)** verstehen
(b) (gather, hear) **if I** ~ **correctly** wenn ich
mich nicht irre; **he is, I** ~**, no longer here** er
ist, wie ich höre, nicht mehr hier
understandable /ʌndə'stændəbl/ *adj.*
verständlich
understandably /ʌndə'stændəblɪ/ *adv.*
verständlicherweise
under'standing [1] *adj.* verständnisvoll
[2] *n.* **(a)** (agreement) Verständigung,
die; **reach an** ~ **with sb.** sich mit jmdm.
verständigen; **on the** ~ **that …:** unter der
Voraussetzung, dass …
(b) (intelligence) Verstand, *der*
(c) (insight) Verständnis, *das* (**of, for** für)
under: ~**statement** *n.* Untertreibung,
die; ~**study** *n.* Ersatzspieler, *der/*
-spielerin, *die;* ~**'take** *v.t., forms as*
TAKE 1: unternehmen; ~**take a task** eine
Aufgabe übernehmen; ~**take to do sth.**
sich verpflichten, etw. zu tun; ~**taker**
n. Leichenbestatter, *der/*-bestatterin,
die; ~**'taking** *n.* **(a)** (task) Aufgabe, *die;*
(b) (pledge) Versprechen, *das;* ~**tone** *n.*
in ~**tones** *or an* ~**tone** mit gedämpfter
Stimme; ~**tone of criticism** kritischer
Unterton; ~**tow** *n.* Unterströmung, *die;*
~**'value** *v.t.* unterbewerten; ~**water**
[1] /'----/ *attrib. adj.* Unterwasser-;
[2] /--'--/ *adv.* unter Wasser; ~**wear**
n. Unterwäsche, *die;* ~**'weight** *adj.*
untergewichtig; ~**world** *n.* Unterwelt, *die*
undeserved /ʌndɪ'zɜːvd/ *adj.* unverdient
unde'sirable *adj.* unerwünscht; **it is**
~ **that …:** es ist nicht wünschenswert,
dass …
undeveloped /ʌndɪ'veləpt/ *adj.*
(a) (immature) nicht voll ausgebildet
(b) (not built on) nicht bebaut
undies /'ʌndɪz/ *n. pl.* (coll.) Unterwäsche,
die
un'dignified *adj.* blamabel
undisciplined /ʌn'dɪsɪplɪnd/ *adj.*
undiszipliniert
undiscovered /ʌndɪ'skʌvəd/ *adj.*
unentdeckt
undisguised /ʌndɪs'ɡaɪzd/ *adj.*
unverhohlen

undisturbed /ʌndɪ'stɜːbd/ *adj.* (not
interrupted) ungestört
undo /ʌn'duː/ *v.t.,* **undoes** /ʌn'dʌz/,
undoing /ʌn'duːɪŋ/, **undid** /ʌn'dɪd/, **undone**
/ʌn'dʌn/ (unfasten) aufmachen
un'done *adj.* **(a)** (not accomplished)
unerledigt
(b) (not fastened) offen
undoubted /ʌn'daʊtɪd/ *adj.* unzweifelhaft
un'doubtedly *adv.* zweifellos
un'dress [1] *v.t.* ausziehen; **get** ~**ed** sich
ausziehen
[2] *v.i.* sich ausziehen
undrinkable /ʌn'drɪŋkəbl/ *adj.* nicht
trinkbar; ungenießbar
un'due *attrib. adj.* übertrieben; übermäßig
undulating /'ʌndjʊleɪtɪŋ/ *adj.*
Wellen⟨*linie*⟩; ~ **country** sanfte
Hügellandschaft
unduly /ʌn'djuːlɪ/ *adv.* übermäßig
undying /ʌn'daɪɪŋ/ *adj.* ewig; unsterblich
⟨*Ruhm*⟩
unearth /ʌn'ɜːθ/ *v.t.* **(a)** ausgraben
(b) (fig.: discover) aufdecken
unearthly /ʌn'ɜːθlɪ/ *adj.* unheimlich; **at an**
~ **hour** in aller Herrgottsfrühe
un'easy *adj.* **(a)** (anxious) besorgt; **he felt**
~**:** ihm war unbehaglich zumute
(b) (restless) unruhig
uneatable /ʌn'iːtəbl/ *adj.* ungenießbar
uneco'nomic *adj.* unrentabel
uneco'nomical *adj.* ~ **[to run]**
unwirtschaftlich
uneducated /ʌn'edjʊkeɪtɪd/ *adj.*
ungebildet
unemotional /ʌnɪ'məʊʃənl/ *adj.*
emotionslos; nüchtern
unemployed /ʌnɪm'plɔɪd/ [1] *adj.*
arbeitslos
[2] *n. pl.* **the** ~**:** die Arbeitslosen *Pl.*
unem'ployment *n.* Arbeitslosigkeit, *die*
unem'ployment benefit *n.*
Arbeitslosengeld, *das*
un'ending *adj.* endlos
un'equal *adj.* unterschiedlich; ungleich
⟨*Kampf*⟩; **be** ~ **to sth.** einer Sache (*Dat.*)
nicht gewachsen sein
unequalled (*Amer.:* **unequaled**)
/ʌn'iːkwld/ *adj.* unerreicht
une'quivocal *adj.* eindeutig
unerring /ʌn'ɜːrɪŋ/ *adj.* unfehlbar
un'ethical *adj.* unmoralisch
un'even *adj.* **(a)** (not smooth) uneben
(b) (not uniform) ungleichmäßig
(c) (odd) ungerade ⟨*Zahl*⟩
un'evenly *adv.* ungleichmäßig
uneventful /ʌnɪ'ventfl/ *adj.* ereignislos
unexciting /ʌnɪk'saɪtɪŋ/ *adj.* wenig
aufregend; (boring) langweilig
unex'pected *adj.* unerwartet

unexplained /ˌʌnɪk'spleɪnd/ *adj.*
ungeklärt

un'fair *adj.* unfair; ungerecht

un'fairly *adv.* (a) (unjustly) ungerecht;
unfair ⟨*spielen*⟩
(b) (unreasonably) zu Unrecht

un'fairness *n.* Ungerechtigkeit, *die*

un'faithful *adj.* untreu

unfa'miliar *adj.* (a) (strange) unbekannt;
ungewohnt ⟨*Arbeit*⟩
(b) be ∼ with sth. sich mit etw. nicht
auskennen

un'fasten *v.t.* (a) öffnen
(b) (detach) lösen

un'favourable *adj.* ungünstig

un'favourably *adv.* ungünstig; be
∼ disposed towards sb./sth. jmdm./etw.
gegenüber ablehnend eingestellt sein

un'feeling *adj.* gefühllos

unfinished /ʌn'fɪnɪʃt/ *adj.* unvollendet
⟨*Werk*⟩; unerledigt ⟨*Arbeit*⟩

un'fit *adj.* (a) ungeeignet
(b) (not physically fit) nicht fit (ugs.); ∼ for
military service [wehrdienst]untauglich

un'flattering *adj.* wenig schmeichelhaft

un'flinching *adj.* unerschrocken

un'fold ⟦1⟧ *v.t.* entfalten; ausbreiten
⟨*Zeitung, Landkarte*⟩
⟦2⟧ *v.i.* sich entfalten; (develop) sich
entwickeln

unfore'seen *adj.* unvorhergesehen

unforgettable /ʌnfə'ɡetəbl/ *adj.*
unvergesslich

unforgivable /ʌnfə'ɡɪvəbl/ *adj.*
unverzeihlich

un'fortunate *adj.* unglücklich

un'fortunately *adv.* leider

un'founded *adj.* (fig.) unbegründet

un'freeze *v.t.* & *i.*, **unfroze** /ʌn'frəʊz/,
unfrozen /ʌn'frəʊzn/ auftauen

un'friendly *adj.* unfreundlich; feindlich
⟨*Staat*⟩

unfulfilled /ʌnfʊl'fɪld/ *adj.* unerfüllt
⟨*Person*⟩

un'furl ⟦1⟧ *v.t.* aufrollen; losmachen ⟨*Segel*⟩
⟦2⟧ *v.i.* sich aufrollen

un'furnished *adj.* unmöbliert

ungainly /ʌn'ɡeɪnlɪ/ *adj.* unbeholfen

ungram'matical *adj.* ungrammatisch

un'grateful *adj.* undankbar

un'happily *adv.* (a) unglücklich
(b) (unfortunately) leider

un'happiness *n.* Bekümmertheit, *die*

un'happy *adj.* unglücklich; (not content)
unzufrieden (about with); be *or* feel ∼ about
doing sth. Bedenken haben, etw. zu tun

un'harmed *adj.* unbeschädigt; (uninjured)
unverletzt

un'healthy *adj.* ungesund

unheard-of /ʌn'hɜːdɒv/ *adj.* (unknown)
[gänzlich] unbekannt; (unprecedented)

beispiellos; (outrageous) unerhört

un'helpful *adj.* wenig hilfsbereit ⟨*Person*⟩;
⟨*Bemerkung, Kritik*⟩ die einem nicht
weiterhilft

un'hook *v.t.* vom Haken nehmen; aufhaken
⟨*Kleid*⟩

un'hurt *adj.* unverletzt

unhy'gienic *adj.* unhygienisch

unicorn /'juːnɪkɔːn/ *n.* Einhorn, *das*

uni'dentified *adj.* nicht identifiziert;
∼ flying object unbekanntes Flugobjekt

unification /juːnɪfɪ'keɪʃn/ *n.* Einigung,
die

uniform /'juːnɪfɔːm/ ⟦1⟧ *adj.* einheitlich;
be ∼ in shape/size die gleiche Form/Größe
haben
⟦2⟧ *n.* Uniform, *die;* in/out of ∼: in/ohne
Uniform

uniformity /juːnɪ'fɔːmɪtɪ/ *n.*
Einheitlichkeit, *die*

'uniformly *adv.* einheitlich

unify /'juːnɪfaɪ/ *v.t.* einigen

unilateral /juːnɪ'lætərl/ *adj.* einseitig

uni'maginable *adj.* unvorstellbar

uni'maginative *adj.* fantasielos

unim'portant *adj.* unwichtig;
bedeutungslos

unimpressed /ʌnɪm'prest/ *adj.* nicht
beeindruckt

unin'habitable *adj.* unbewohnbar

unin'habited *adj.* unbewohnt

un'injured *adj.* unverletzt

uninspired /ʌnɪn'spaɪəd/ *adj.* einfallslos;
I am/feel ∼: mir fehlt die Inspiration

uninspiring /ʌnɪn'spaɪərɪŋ/ *adj.*
langweilig

unin'telligent *adj.* nicht intelligent

unin'telligible *adj.* unverständlich

unin'tended *adj.* unbeabsichtigt

unin'tentional *adj.*, **unin'tentionally**
adv. unabsichtlich

un'interested *adj.* desinteressiert (in an
+ *Dat.*)

un'interesting *adj.* uninteressant

uninterrupted /ʌnɪntə'rʌptɪd/ *adj.*
ununterbrochen

uninvited /ʌnɪm'vaɪtɪd/ *adj.* ungeladen

union /'juːnɪən/ *n.* (a) (trade ∼)
Gewerkschaft, *die*
(b) (Polit.) Union, *die*

Union 'Jack *n.* (Brit.) Union Jack, *der*

unique /juː'niːk/ *adj.* einzigartig

unisex /'juːnɪseks/ *adj.* Unisex⟨*mantel,
-kleidung*⟩; ∼ hairdresser Damen-und-
Herren-Frisör, *der*

unison /'juːnɪsən/ *n.* Unisono, *das;* in
∼: einstimmig; act in ∼ (fig.) vereint handeln

unit /'juːnɪt/ *n.* (a) (also Mil., Math.) Einheit,
die; ∼ of length/monetary ∼: Längen-/
Währungseinheit, *die*
(b) (piece of furniture) Element, *das;* kitchen

~: Küchenelement, *das*

unite /ju:'naɪt/ **1** *v.t.* vereinigen; einen, einigen ⟨*Partei, Mitglieder*⟩ **2** *v.i.* sich vereinigen

u'nited *adj.* (a) (harmonious) einig (b) (combined) gemeinsam

United: ~ **'Kingdom** *pr. n.* Vereinigtes Königreich [Großbritannien und Nordirland]; ~ **'Nations** *pr. n. sing.* Vereinte Nationen *Pl.;* ~ **States [of A'merica]** *pr. n. sing.* Vereinigte Staaten [von Amerika] *Pl.*

unit 'price *n.* Stückpreis, *der*

unity /'ju:nɪtɪ/ *n.* Einheit, *die*

universal /ju:nɪ'vɜ:sl/ *adj.*, **uni'versally** *adv.* allgemein

universe /'ju:nɪvɜ:s/ *n.* Universum, *das*

university /ju:nɪ'vɜ:sɪtɪ/ *n.* Universität, *die; attrib.* Universitäts-

uni'versity place *n.* Studienplatz, *der*

un'just *adj.* ungerecht

unjustified /ʌn'dʒʌstɪfaɪd/ *adj.* ungerechtfertigt

unkempt /ʌn'kempt/ *adj.* ungepflegt

un'kind *adj.*, **un'kindly** *adv.* unfreundlich

un'kindness *n.* Unfreundlichkeit, *die*

un'known **1** *adj.* unbekannt **2** *adv.* ~ to sb. ohne dass jmd. davon weiß/wusste

un'lawful *adj.* ungesetzlich

unleaded /ʌn'ledɪd/ *adj.* bleifrei ⟨*Benzin*⟩

unless /ən'les/ *conj.* es sei denn; wenn … nicht

un'like **1** *adj.* nicht ähnlich **2** *prep.* be ~ sb./sth. jmdm./einer Sache nicht ähnlich sein; ~ him, …: im Gegensatz zu ihm …

un'likely *adj.* unwahrscheinlich; be ~ to do sth. etw. wahrscheinlich nicht tun

un'limited *adj.* unbegrenzt

un'load *v.t.* entladen ⟨*Lastwagen, Waggon*⟩; löschen ⟨*Schiff, Schiffsladung*⟩; ausladen ⟨*Gepäck*⟩

un'lock *v.t.* aufschließen

un'lucky *adj.* (a) unglücklich; (not successful) glücklos; be [very] ~: [großes] Pech haben (b) (bringing bad luck) an ~ number eine Unglückszahl; be ~: Unglück bringen

unmanageable /ʌn'mænɪdʒbl/ *adj.* widerspenstig ⟨*Kind, Pferd*⟩; unkontrollierbar ⟨*Situation*⟩

un'manned *adj.* unbemannt

un'married *adj.* unverheiratet; ledig

un'mask *v.t.* (fig.) entlarven

unmi'stakable /ʌnmɪ'steɪkəbl/ *adj.* deutlich; unverwechselbar ⟨*Handschrift, Stimme*⟩

unmistakably /ʌnmɪ'steɪkəblɪ/ *adv.* unverkennbar

un'mitigated *adj.* vollkommen; be an ~ disaster (coll.) eine einzige Katastrophe

sein

unmotivated /ʌn'məʊtɪveɪtɪd/ *adj.* unmotiviert

un'natural *adj.*, **un'naturally** *adv.* unnatürlich; (abnormal) nicht normal

un'necessarily *adv.*, **un'necessary** *adj.* unnötig

unnerve /ʌn'nɜ:v/ *v.t.* entnerven

unnerving /ʌn'nɜ:vɪŋ/ *adj.* entnervend

unnoticed /ʌn'nəʊtɪst/ *adj.* unbemerkt

unobservant /ʌnəb'zɜ:vənt/ *adj.* unaufmerksam

unobserved /ʌnəb'zɜ:vd/ *adj.* unbeobachtet

unob'tainable *adj.* nicht erhältlich; number ~ (Teleph.) kein Anschluss unter dieser Nummer

unof'ficial *adj.*, **unof'ficially** *adv.* inoffiziell

un'pack *v.t. & i.* auspacken

un'paid *adj.* unbezahlt; nicht bezahlt; ~ for nicht bezahlt

unpalatable /ʌn'pælətəbl/ *adj.* ungenießbar

un'paralleled *adj.* beispiellos

un'pardonable *adj.* unverzeihlich

un'pleasant *adj.*, **un'pleasantly** *adv.* unangenehm

un'pleasantness *n.* (bad feeling) Verstimmung, *die*

un'plug *v.t.*, -gg-: ~ a lamp den Stecker einer Lampe herausziehen

un'popular *adj.* unbeliebt ⟨*Lehrer, Regierung usw.*⟩; unpopulär ⟨*Maßnahme, Politik*⟩ (with bei)

un'precedented *adj.* beispiellos

unpre'dictable *adj.* unberechenbar

unpre'pared *adj.* unvorbereitet

unprepos'sessing *adj.* wenig attraktiv

unpre'tentious *adj.* einfach ⟨*Wein, Stil, Haus*⟩; bescheiden ⟨*Person*⟩

unprincipled /ʌn'prɪnsɪpld/ *adj.* skrupellos

unprintable /ʌn'prɪntəbl/ *adj.* nicht druckreif

unpro'ductive *adj.* fruchtlos ⟨*Diskussion, Nachforschung*⟩; unproduktiv ⟨*Zeit, Arbeit*⟩

unpro'fessional *adj.* (contrary to standards) standeswidrig

un'profitable *adj.* unrentabel

un'promising *adj.* nicht sehr viel versprechend

unpublished /ʌn'pʌblɪʃt/ *adj.* unveröffentlicht

un'qualified *adj.* (a) unqualifiziert (b) (absolute) uneingeschränkt; voll ⟨*Erfolg*⟩

un'questionable *adj.* unbezweifelbar ⟨*Tatsache*⟩; unbestreitbar ⟨*Recht, Ehrlichkeit*⟩

unquestionably /ʌn'kwestʃənəblɪ/ *adv.* ohne Frage

unquote /ʌn'kwəʊt/ *v.i.* ..., quote, ...,
~: ..., Zitat, ..., Ende des Zitats
unravel /ʌn'rævl/ ① *v.t.*, (Brit.) -ll-
entwirren; (undo) aufziehen; (fig.) ~ a
mystery/the truth ein Geheimnis enträtseln/
die Wahrheit aufdecken
② *v.i.*, (Brit.) -ll- sich aufziehen
un'real *adj.* unwirklich
unrea'listic *adj.* unrealistisch
un'reasonable *adj.* unvernünftig;
übertrieben ‹Ansprüche, Forderung, Preis,
Kosten›
unrecognizable /ʌn'rekəgnaɪzəbl/ *adj.*
be [absolutely or quite] ~: [überhaupt]
nicht wieder zu erkennen sein
unre'lated *adj.* be ~: nicht miteinander
zusammenhängen; (by family) nicht verwandt
sein
unrelenting /ʌnrɪ'lentɪŋ/ *adj.*
unvermindert, nicht nachlassend ‹Hitze,
Kälte›
unre'liable *adj.* unzuverlässig
unrequited /ʌnrɪ'kwaɪtɪd/ *adj.*
unerwidert
unreservedly /ʌnrɪ'zɜːvɪdlɪ/ *adv.*
uneingeschränkt
unresolved /ʌnrɪ'zɒlvd/ *adj.* (a) (not
solved) ungelöst
(b) (undecided) be ~: sich [noch] nicht
entschieden haben
un'rest *n.* Unruhen *Pl.*
unre'stricted *adj.* unbeschränkt;
uneingeschränkt
un'ripe *adj.* unreif
un'rivalled (Amer.: **un'rivaled**) *adj.*
unübertroffen
un'roll ① *v.t.* aufrollen
② *v.i.* sich aufrollen
unromantic /ʌnrə'mæntɪk/ *adj.*
unromantisch
unruly /ʌn'ruːlɪ/ *adj.* ungebärdig
un'safe *adj.* nicht sicher; feel ~: sich
unsicher fühlen
un'said *adj.* ungesagt
un'salted *adj.* ungesalzen
unsatis'factory *adj.* unbefriedigend
unsatisfying /ʌn'sætɪsfaɪɪŋ/ *adj.*
unbefriedigend
un'savoury (Amer.: **un'savory**) *adj.*
unangenehm; zweifelhaft ‹Angelegenheit›;
unerfreulich ‹Einzelheiten›
unscathed /ʌn'skeɪðd/ *adj.* unversehrt
unscented /ʌn'sentɪd/ *adj.* nicht
parfümiert ‹Seife, Shampoo›
un'screw ① *v.t.* abschrauben
② *v.i.* sich abschrauben lassen
un'scrupulous *adj.* skrupellos
unsecured /ʌnsɪ'kjʊəd/ *adj.* (Finance)
ohne Sicherheit[en] *nachgestellt*
un'seemly *adj.* unschicklich
unself'conscious *adj.* unbefangen

un'selfish *adj.* selbstlos
un'selfishness *n.* Selbstlosigkeit, *die*
un'settled *adj.* (changeable) wechselhaft;
(fig.) ruheloos ‹Leben›; unruhig ‹Zeit, Land›
un'settling *adj.* störend
unshak[e]able /ʌn'ʃeɪkəbl/ *adj.*
unerschütterlich
un'shaven *adj.* unrasiert
un'sightly *adj.* unschön
un'skilled *adj.* ungelernt ‹Arbeiter›
un'skimmed *adj.* ~ milk Vollmilch, *die*
un'sociable *adj.* ungesellig
unsolved /ʌn'sɒlvd/ *adj.* unaufgeklärt
‹Verbrechen›
unso'phisticated *adj.* einfach
un'sound *adj.* (a) (diseased) nicht gesund;
krank
(b) baufällig ‹Gebäude›
(c) (ill-founded) wenig stichhaltig; nicht
vertretbar ‹Ansicht, Methode›
(d) of ~ mind unzurechnungsfähig
unspeakable /ʌn'spiːkəbl/ *adj.*
unbeschreiblich; (very bad) unsäglich
unspecified /ʌn'spesɪfaɪd/ *adj.* nicht
näher bezeichnet
unspoken /ʌn'spəʊkn/ *adj.* ungesagt
un'stable *adj.* nicht stabil; [mentally/
emotionally] ~: [psychisch] labil
un'steadily *adv.* unsicher
un'steady *adj.* unsicher; wackelig ‹Leiter,
Tisch›
unstoppable /ʌn'stɒpəbl/ *adj.* unhaltbar
‹Schuss aufs Fußballtor›; (fig.) unaufhaltsam
un'stuck *adj.* come ~: sich lösen; (fig. coll.:
fail) ‹Person:› baden gehen (ugs.) (over mit)
unsuc'cessful *adj.* erfolglos; be
~: keinen Erfolg haben
unsuc'cessfully *adv.* erfolglos
un'suitable *adj.* ungeeignet
unsu'specting *adj.* nichtsahnend
un'sweetened *adj.* ungesüßt
unsympa'thetic *adj.* wenig mitfühlend;
be ~: kein Mitgefühl zeigen
untalented /ʌn'tæləntɪd/ *adj.* untalentiert
untenable /ʌn'tenəbl/ *adj.* unhaltbar
unthinkable /ʌn'θɪŋkəbl/ *adj.*
unvorstellbar
unthinking /ʌn'θɪŋkɪŋ/ *adj.*,
un'thinkingly *adv.* gedankenlos
un'tidily *adv.* unordentlich
un'tidiness *n.* ▶ UNTIDY: Ungepflegtheit,
die; Unaufgeräumtheit, *die*
un'tidy *adj.* ungepflegt ‹Äußeres, Person,
Garten›; unaufgeräumt ‹Zimmer›
un'tie *v.t.*, untying aufknüpfen ‹Seil, Paket›;
aufbinden ‹Knoten›; losbinden ‹Pferd, Boot›
until /ən'tɪl/ ① *prep.* bis; ~ [the] evening
bis zum Abend; ~ then bis dahin;
not ~ [Christmas/the summer] erst
[Weihnachten/im Sommer]
② *conj.* bis

U

un'timely adj. (a) ungelegen (b) (premature) vorzeitig

un'tiring adj. unermüdlich

un'told adj. unbeschreiblich; unermesslich ⟨Reichtümer, Anzahl⟩

untoward /ˌʌntə'wɔːd, ʌn'təʊəd/ adj. ungünstig; **nothing** ~ **happened** es gab keine Schwierigkeiten

untranslatable /ˌʌntræns'leɪtəbl/ adj. unübersetzbar

untreated /ʌn'triːtɪd/ adj. unbehandelt

un'true adj. unwahr; **that's** ~: das ist nicht wahr

un'trustworthy adj. unzuverlässig

un'truth n. Unwahrheit, die

un'truthful adj. verlogen

un'typical adj. untypisch (of für)

unusable /ʌn'juːzəbl/ adj. unbrauchbar

unused[1] /ʌn'juːzd/ adj. (new, fresh) unbenutzt; (not utilized) ungenutzt

unused[2] /ʌn'juːst/ adj. (unaccustomed) **be** ~ **to sth./doing sth.** etw. (Akk.) nicht gewohnt sein/nicht gewohnt sein, etw. zu tun

un'usual adj., **un'usually** adv. ungewöhnlich

unvarnished /ʌn'vɑːnɪʃt/ adj. unlackiert; (fig.) ungeschminkt ⟨Wahrheit⟩

un'veil v.t. enthüllen; (fig.) vorstellen ⟨Produkt⟩; enthüllen ⟨Plan⟩

un'versed adj. nicht bewandert (in in + Dat.)

un'wanted adj. unerwünscht

un'warranted adj. ungerechtfertigt

un'welcome adj. unwillkommen

un'well adj. unwohl; **look** ~: nicht wohl od. gut aussehen; **he feels** ~ (poorly) er fühlt sich nicht wohl

un'wholesome adj. (lit. or fig.) ungesund

unwieldy /ʌn'wiːldɪ/ adj. sperrig

un'willing adj. widerwillig; **be** ~ **to do sth.** etw. nicht tun wollen

un'willingly adv. widerwillig

unwind /ʌn'waɪnd/ [1] v.t., **unwound** /ʌn'waʊnd/ abwickeln
[2] v.i., **unwound (a)** sich abwickeln (b) (coll.: relax) sich entspannen

un'wise adj. unklug

unwitting /ʌn'wɪtɪŋ/ adj., **un'wittingly** adv. unwissentlich

un'workable adj. undurchführbar ⟨Plan⟩

un'worthy adj. unwürdig; **be** ~ **of sth.** einer Sache (Gen.) nicht würdig sein; **be** ~ **of sb./sth.** (Verhalten:) einer Person/ Sache (Gen.) unwürdig sein

un'wrap v.t., **-pp-** auswickeln

un'written adj. ungeschrieben

un'zip v.t., **-pp-: (a)** ~ **a dress/bag** etc. den Reißverschluss eines Kleides/einer Tasche usw. öffnen
(b) (Comp.) entpacken ⟨Datei⟩

up /ʌp/ [1] adv. (a) (to higher place) nach oben; (in lift) aufwärts; **the bird flew up to the roof** der Vogel flog aufs Dach [hinauf]; **up into the air** in die Luft [hinauf]; **up here/there** hier herauf/dort hinauf; **higher/a little way up** höher/ein kurzes Stück hinauf; **come on up!** komm [hier/weiter] herauf!
(b) (to upstairs) herauf/hinauf; nach oben
(c) (in higher place, upstairs) oben; **up here/there** hier/da oben; **the next floor up** ein Stockwerk höher
(d) (out of bed) **be up** auf sein
(e) (in price, value, amount) **prices have gone up/are up** die Preise sind gestiegen; **butter is up [by …]** Butter ist […] teurer
(f) (as far as) **up to sth.** bis zu etw.; **up to here/there** bis hier[hin]/bis dorthin
(g) [not] **be/feel up to sth.** (capable of sth.) einer Sache (Dat.) [nicht] gewachsen sein/ sich einer Sache (Dat.) [nicht] gewachsen fühlen; [not] **be/feel up to doing sth.** [nicht] in der Lage sein/sich [nicht] in der Lage fühlen, etw. zu tun
(h) **be up to sth.** (doing) etw. anstellen (ugs.); **it is [not] up to sb. to do sth.** (sb.'s duty) es ist [nicht] jmds. Sache, etw. zu tun
(i) **be three points/games up** mit drei Punkten/Spielen vorn liegen
(j) **walk up and down** auf und ab gehen
(k) **time is up** die Zeit ist abgelaufen
[2] prep. herauf/hinauf; **walk up the hill/road** den Berg/die Straße hinaufgehen; **walk up and down the platform** auf dem Bahnsteig auf und ab gehen; **further up the ladder/ coast** weiter oben auf der Leiter/an der Küste; **live just up the road** ein Stück weiter oben in der Straße wohnen
[3] adj. (coll.: amiss) **what's up?** was ist los? (ugs.); **something is up** irgendwas ist los (ugs.)
[4] v.t., **-pp-** (coll.: increase) erhöhen

'up-and-coming adj. (coll.) aufstrebend

'up-and-up n. (coll.) **be on the** ~: auf dem aufsteigenden Ast sein (ugs.)

'upbeat [1] n. (Mus.) Auftakt, der
[2] adj. (coll.) (optimistic) optimistisch; (cheerful) fröhlich

'upbringing n. Erziehung, die

up'date v.t. auf den aktuellen Stand bringen

up 'front adv. (coll.: as down payment) im Voraus

upgrade [1] /-'-/ v.t. (a) aufwerten ⟨Stellung⟩
(b) (improve) verbessern
(c) (Comp.) aufrüsten, nachrüsten ⟨Computer⟩
[2] /'--/ n. (Comp.) (act of upgrading) Nachrüsten, die; Erweiterung, die; (upgraded version) erweiterte Version; Upgrade, der (fachspr.)

upheaval /ʌp'hiːvl/ n. Aufruhr, der; (disturbance) Durcheinander, das

up'hill [1] adj. (fig.) **an** ~ **task/struggle** eine

mühselige Aufgabe/ein harter Kampf
[2] *adv.* bergauf

uphold *v.t.,* **upheld** unterstützen; wahren
⟨*Tradition*⟩

upholster /ʌp'həʊlstə(r)/ *v.t.* polstern

up'holsterer *n.* Polsterer, *der*/Polsterin,
die

up'holstery *n.* **(a)** (craft)
Polster[er]handwerk, *das*
(b) (padding) Polsterung, *die*

'upkeep *n.* Unterhalt, *der*

up'lifting *adj.* erhebend

'uplighter *n.* Deckenfluter, *der*

up'load *v.t.* (Comp.) hinaufladen ⟨*Datei,
Daten*⟩

'upmarket *adj.* exklusiv

upon /ə'pɒn/ *prep.* auf (*direction:* + *Akk.;
position:* + *Dat.*)

upper /'ʌpə(r)/ [1] *compar. adj.* ober…;
Ober⟨*grenze, -lippe, -arm usw.*⟩; ~ **circle**
oberer Rang; ~ **class[es]** Oberschicht, *die;*
have/get/gain the ~ hand die Oberhand
haben/gewinnen/erhalten
[2] *n.* Oberteil, *das*

upper 'deck *n.* Oberdeck, *das*

'uppermost [1] *adj.* oberst…
[2] *adv.* ganz oben

'upright *adj.* aufrecht

'uprising *n.* Aufstand, *der*

'uproar *n.* Aufruhr, *der*

up'root *v.t.* [her]ausreißen; ⟨*Sturm:*⟩
entwurzeln

upset [1] /ʌp'set/ *v.t.,* **-tt-, upset (a)** (overturn)
umkippen; (accidentally) umstoßen ⟨*Tasse,
Milch usw.*⟩
(b) (distress) erschüttern; (make angry)
aufregen; **don't let it ~ you** nimm es nicht so
schwer
(c) (make ill) **sth. ~s sb.** etw. bekommt jmdm.
nicht
(d) durcheinander bringen ⟨*Plan*⟩
[2] *v.i.,* **-tt-, upset** umkippen
[3] *adj.* (distressed) bestürzt; (agitated)
aufgeregt; **get ~ [about/over sth.]** sich [über
etw. (*Akk.*)] aufregen
[4] /'ʌpset/ *n.* **(a)** (agitation) Aufregung, *die;*
(annoyance) Verärgerung, *die*
(b) stomach ~: Magenverstimmung, *die*
(c) (upheaval) Aufruhr, *der*

up'setting *adj.* erschütternd; (sad) traurig;
(annoying) ärgerlich

'upshot *n.* Ergebnis, *das*

upside 'down [1] *adv.* verkehrt herum;
turn sth. ~: etw. auf den Kopf stellen
[2] *adj.* auf dem Kopf stehend ⟨*Bild*⟩; **be
~:** auf dem Kopf stehen

upstairs [1] /-'-/ *adv.* nach oben ⟨*gehen,
kommen*⟩; oben ⟨*sein, wohnen*⟩
[2] /'--/ *adj.* im Obergeschoss *nachgestellt*

'upstart *n.* Emporkömmling, *der*

up'stream *adv.* flussaufwärts

'uptake *n.* **be quick/slow on the ~** (coll.)

schnell begreifen/schwer von Begriff sein
(ugs.)

uptight /-'-, '--/ *adj.* (coll.: tense) nervös
(about wegen)

up to 'date *adj.* **be/keep ~:** auf dem
neuesten Stand sein/bleiben; **bring sth.
~:** etw. auf den neuesten Stand bringen

up-to-'date *attrib. adj.* (current) aktuell;
(modern) modern

up-to-the-'minute *adj.* hochaktuell

'upturn *n.* Aufschwung, *der* (**in** *Gen.*)

upturned /'ʌptɜːnd/ *adj.* umgedreht;
~ **nose** Stupsnase, *die*

upward /'ʌpwəd/ [1] *adj.* nach oben
gerichtet
[2] *adv.* aufwärts ⟨*sich bewegen*⟩; nach oben
⟨*sehen, gehen*⟩

upwards /'ʌpwədz/ *adv.* **(a)** ▶ UPWARD 2
(b) ~ **of** über (+ *Akk.*)

uranium /jʊə'reɪnɪəm/ *n.* Uran, *das*

Uranus /'jʊərənəs, jʊə'reɪnəs/ *pr. n.*
(Astron.) Uranus, *der*

urban /'ɜːbn/ *adj.* städtisch; Stadt⟨*gebiet,
-bevölkerung, -planung*⟩

urbane /ɜː'beɪn/ *adj.* weltmännisch

urchin /'ɜːtʃɪn/ *n.* Strolch, *der*

urge /ɜːdʒ/ [1] *v.t.* ~ **sb. to do sth.** jmdn.
drängen, etw. zu tun
[2] *n.* Trieb, *der*

■ **urge 'on** *v.t.* antreiben; (encourage)
anfeuern

urgency /'ɜːdʒənsɪ/ *n.* Dringlichkeit, *die*

urgent /'ɜːdʒənt/ *adj.* dringend; (to be dealt
with immediately) eilig; **be in ~ need of sth.**
etw. dringend brauchen

'urgently *adv.* dringend; (immediately) eilig

urinal /jʊə'raɪnl/ *n.* **[public] ~:** [öffentliche]
Herrentoilette; Pissoir, *das*

urinary /'jʊərɪnərɪ/ *adj.* Harn-

urinate /'jʊərɪneɪt/ *v.i.* urinieren

urine /'jʊərɪn/ *n.* Urin, *der;* Harn, *der*

URL *abbr.* (Comp.) = **uniform resource
locator** URL, *der*

urn /ɜːn/ *n.* **(a) tea/coffee ~:** Tee-/
Kaffeemaschine, *die*
(b) (vessel) Urne, *die*

Uruguay /'jʊərəgwaɪ/ *pr. n.* Uruguay (*das*)

us /əs, *stressed* ʌs/ *pron.* uns; **it's us** wir
sind s (ugs.)

US *abbr.* = **United States** USA

USA *abbr.* = **United States of
America** USA

usage /'juːzɪdʒ, 'juːsɪdʒ/ *n.* **(a)** Brauch, *der*
(b) (Ling.) Sprachgebrauch, *der*

use [1] /juːs/ *n.* **(a)** Gebrauch, *der;* (of
dictionary, calculator, room) Benutzung, *die;* (of
word, pesticide, spice) Verwendung, *die;* **[not]
be in ~:** [nicht] in Gebrauch sein; **be no
longer in ~:** nicht mehr verwendet werden;
make ~ of sb./sth. jmdn./etw. gebrauchen/
(exploit) ausnutzen; **make good ~ of,
turn** *or* **put to good ~:** gut nutzen ⟨*Zeit,* ⋯▸

Talent, Geld); **put sth. to** ∼: etw. verwenden
(b) (usefulness) Nutzen, *der;* **is it of [any]** ∼?
ist das [irgendwie] von Nutzen?; **be [of]**
no ∼ **[to sb.]** [jmdm.] nicht nützen; **it's no**
∼ **[doing that]** es hat keinen Sinn[, das zu
tun]
(c) (purpose) Verwendung, *die;* **have/find a**
∼ **for sth./sb.** für etw./sb. Verwendung
haben/finden; **have no/not much** ∼ **for**
sth./sb. etw./jmdn. nicht/kaum brauchen
2 /juːz/ *v.t.* **(a)** benutzen; nutzen
⟨*Gelegenheit*⟩; anwenden ⟨*Gewalt*⟩; in
Anspruch nehmen ⟨*Firma, Dienstleistung*⟩;
nutzen ⟨*Zeit, Gelegenheit*⟩; verwenden
⟨*Kraftstoff, Butter, Wort*⟩
(b) ∼**d to** /ˈjuːst tə/ **: /ˌaɪ** ∼**d to live in London**
früher habe ich in London gelebt
■ **use 'up** *v.t.* aufbrauchen; verbrauchen
⟨*Geld, Energie*⟩
use-by date /ˈjuːzbaɪ/ *n.* (esp. Brit.)
[Mindest]haltbarkeitsdatum, *das*
used **1** *adj.* **(a)** /juːzd/ gebraucht;
gestempelt ⟨*Briefmarke*⟩; ∼ **car**
Gebrauchtwagen, *der*
(b) /juːst/ ∼ **to sth.** [an] etw. (*Akk.*) gewöhnt
2 /juːst/ ▶ USE 2B
useful /ˈjuːsfl/ *adj.* nützlich; praktisch
⟨*Werkzeug*⟩; hilfreich ⟨*Rat, Idee*⟩
'usefulness *n.* Nützlichkeit, *die*
useless /ˈjuːslɪs/ *adj.* unbrauchbar
⟨*Werkzeug, Rat, Idee*⟩; nutzlos ⟨*Wissen,*
Information, Protest, Anstrengung, Kampf⟩;
zwecklos ⟨*Widerstand, Protest*⟩
user /ˈjuːzə(r)/ *n.* Benutzer, *der*/Benutzerin,
die
user: ∼**-friendly** *adj.*
benutzerfreundlich; ∼ **group** *n.*
Benutzergruppe, *die;* ∼ **interface** *n.*
(Comp.) Benutzerschnittstelle, *die;* ∼ **name**
n. (Comp.) Benutzername, *der*
usher /ˈʌʃə(r)/ **1** *n.* (in court)

Gerichtsdiener, *der;* (at cinema, church)
Platzanweiser, *der*
2 *v.t.* führen
■ **usher 'in** *v.t.* hineinführen; (fig.) einläuten
usherette /ʌʃəˈret/ *n.* Platzanweiserin, *die*
USSR *abbr.* (Hist.) = **Union of Soviet**
Socialist Republics UdSSR, *die*
usual /ˈjuːʒʊəl/ *adj.* üblich
usually /ˈjuːʒʊəlɪ/ *adv.* gewöhnlich
usurp /juːˈzɜːp/ *v.t.* sich (*Dat.*)
widerrechtlich aneignen
utensil /juːˈtensɪl/ *n.* Utensil, *das;* **writing**
∼**s** Schreibutensilien *Pl.;* **kitchen** ∼**s**
Küchengeräte *Pl.*
uterus /ˈjuːtərəs/ *n.* Gebärmutter, *die*
utilitarian /juːtɪlɪˈteərɪən/ *adj.* funktionell
utility /juːˈtɪlɪtɪ/ *n.* **(a)** Nutzen, *der*
(b) [public] ∼: öffentlicher
Versorgungsbetrieb
u'tility room *n.: Raum, in dem [größere]*
Haushaltsgeräte (z.B. Waschmaschine)
installiert sind
utilize /ˈjuːtɪlaɪz/ *v.t.* nutzen
utmost /ˈʌtməʊst/ **1** *adj.* äußerst...;
größt... ⟨*Höflichkeit, Eleganz, Einfachheit,*
Geschwindigkeit⟩
2 *n.* Äußerste, *das;* **do or try one's** ∼ **to do**
sth. mit allen Mitteln versuchen, etw. zu tun
utter[1] /ˈʌtə(r)/ *adj.* völlig; vollkommen;
∼ **fool** Vollidiot, *der* (ugs.)
utter[2] *v.t.* **(a)** von sich geben ⟨*Schrei,*
Seufzer⟩
(b) (say) sagen
utterance /ˈʌtərəns/ *n.* Worte *Pl.*
'utterly *adv.* völlig; vollkommen; äußerst
⟨*dumm, lächerlich*⟩
'U-turn *n.* Wende [um 180°]; (fig.)
Kehrtwendung, *die;* **make a** ∼: wenden; **'No**
∼**s'** „Wenden verboten"
UV *abbr.* = **ultraviolet** UV

Vv

V[1]**, v** /viː/ *n.* V, v, *das*
V[2] *abbr.* = **volt[s]** V
v. *abbr.* = **versus** gg.
vacancy /ˈveɪkənsɪ/ *n.* **(a)** (job) freie Stelle
(b) (room) freies Zimmer; **'vacancies'**
„Zimmer frei"; **'no vacancies'** „belegt"
vacant /ˈveɪkənt/ *adj.* **(a)** frei; **'situations**
∼**'** „Stellenangebote"
(b) (mentally) leer
vacate /vəˈkeɪt/ *v.t.* räumen
vacation /vəˈkeɪʃn/ *n.* **(a)** (Brit. Univ.)
Ferien *Pl.*

(b) (Amer.) ▶ HOLIDAY B
vaccinate /ˈvæksɪneɪt/ *v.t.* impfen
vaccination /væksɪˈneɪʃn/ *n.* Impfung,
die; **have a** ∼: geimpft werden
vaccine /ˈvæksiːn/ *n.* Impfstoff, *der*
vacillate /ˈvæsɪleɪt/ *v.i.* schwanken
vacuum /ˈvækjʊəm/ **1** *n.* **(a)** Vakuum,
das; **live in a** ∼: im luftleeren Raum leben
(b) (coll.: ∼ cleaner) Staubsauger, *der* (ugs.)
2 *v.t. & i.* [staub]saugen
vacuum: ∼ **cleaner** *n.* Staubsauger,
der; ∼ **flask** *n.* (Brit.) Thermosflasche, *die;*

~**-packed** *adj.* vakuumverpackt

vagaries /'veɪgərɪz/ *n. pl.* Launen *Pl.*

vagina /və'dʒaɪnə/ *n.* Scheide, *die*

vagrant /'veɪgrənt/ *n.* Landstreicher, *der*/-streicherin, *die;* (in cities) Stadtstreicher, *der*/-tstreicherin, *die*

vague /veɪg/ *adj.* vage; verschwommen ⟨*Form, Umriss*⟩; (absent-minded) geistesabwesend; **not have the** ~**st idea** *or* **notion** nicht die blasseste *od.* leiseste Ahnung haben

'**vaguely** *adv.* vage; entfernt ⟨*bekannt sein, erinnern an*⟩; schwach ⟨*sich erinnern*⟩

vain /veɪn/ *adj.* (a) (conceited) eitel (b) (useless) leer; vergeblich ⟨*Hoffnung, Versuch*⟩; **in** ~: vergeblich

'**vainly** *adv.* vergebens

vale /veɪl/ *n.* (arch./poet.) Tal, *das*

valentine /'væləntaɪn/ *n.* ~ **[card]** Grußkarte zum Valentinstag; **St. V**~**'s Day** Valentinstag, *der*

valet /'væleɪ/ *n.* Kammerdiener, *der*

valiant /'vælɪənt/ *adj.*, '**valiantly** *adv.* tapfer

valid /'vælɪd/ *adj.* (a) (legally acceptable) gültig; berechtigt ⟨*Anspruch*⟩ (b) (justifiable) stichhaltig ⟨*Argument*⟩; triftig ⟨*Grund*⟩; begründet ⟨*Einwand, Entschuldigung*⟩

validate /'vælɪdeɪt/ *v.t.* rechtskräftig machen

validity /və'lɪdɪtɪ/ *n.* Gültigkeit, *die*

valley /'vælɪ/ *n.* Tal, *das*

valour (*Amer.:* **valor**) /'vælə(r)/ *n.* Tapferkeit, *die*

valuable /'væljʊəbl/ 1 *adj.* wertvoll; **be** ~ **to sb.** für jmdn. wertvoll sein 2 *n.* ~**s** Wertsachen *Pl.*

valuation /væljʊ'eɪʃn/ *n.* Schätzung, *die*

value /'væljuː/ 1 *n.* Wert, *der;* **be of great/little/some/no** ~ **[to sb.]** [für jmdn.] von großem/geringem/einigem/keinerlei Nutzen sein; **know the** ~ **of sth.** wissen, was etw. wert ist; **something/nothing of** ~: etwas/nichts Wertvolles 2 *v.t.* schätzen

value added '**tax** *n.* Mehrwertsteuer, *die*

valued /'væljuːd/ *adj.* geschätzt

'**value judgement** *n.* Werturteil, *das*

'**valueless** *adj.* wertlos

valuer /'væljʊə(r)/ *n.* Schätzer, *der;* Taxator, *der*

valve /vælv/ *n.* (a) Ventil, *das* (b) (Anat.) Klappe, *die*

vampire /'væmpaɪə(r)/ *n.* Vampir, *der*

van /væn/ *n.* **[delivery]** ~: Lieferwagen, *der*

vandal /'vændl/ *n.* Rowdy, *der*

vandalism /'vændəlɪzm/ *n.* Wandalismus, *der*

vandalize /'vændəlaɪz/ *v.t.* [mutwillig] beschädigen

vanilla /və'nɪlə/ 1 *n.* Vanille, *die* 2 *adj.* Vanille-

vanish /'vænɪʃ/ *v.i.* verschwinden

vanity /'vænɪtɪ/ *n.* Eitelkeit, *die*

'**vanity bag** *n.* Kosmetiktäschchen, *das*

'**vantage point** /'vɑːntɪdʒ pɔɪnt/ *n.* Aussichtspunkt, *der*

vapour (*Brit.; Amer.:* **vapor**) /'veɪpə(r)/ *n.* Dampf, *der*

'**vapour trail** *n.* (Aeronaut.) Kondensstreifen, *der*

variable /'veərɪəbl/ *adj.* (a) (alterable) veränderbar; **be** ~: verändert werden können (b) (inconsistent) unbeständig ⟨*Wetter, Wind, Leistung*⟩; wechselhaft ⟨*Wetter, Launen, Qualität*⟩

variance /'veərɪəns/ *n.* **be at** ~ **[with sth.]** [mit etw.] nicht übereinstimmen

variant /'veərɪənt/ *n.* Variante, *die*

variation /veərɪ'eɪʃn/ *n.* (a) (varying) Veränderung, *die;* (difference) Unterschied, *der* (b) (variant) Variante, *die* (of, on *Gen.*)

varicose vein /værɪkəʊs 'veɪn/ *n.* Krampfader, *die*

varied /'veərɪd/ *adj.* unterschiedlich; abwechslungsreich ⟨*Diät, Leben*⟩

variety /və'raɪətɪ/ *n.* (a) (diversity) Vielfältigkeit, *die;* (in diet, routine) Abwechslung, *die;* **add** *or* **give** ~ **to sth.** etw. abwechslungsreicher gestalten (b) (assortment) Auswahl, *die* (of an + *Dat.*, von); **for a** ~ **of reasons** aus verschiedenen Gründen (c) (Theatre) Varietee, *das* (d) (form) Art, *die;* (of fruit, vegetable) Sorte, *die;* (cultivated) Züchtung, *die*

various /'veərɪəs/ *adj.* (a) *pred.* (different) verschieden; unterschiedlich (b) *attrib.* (several) verschiedene; **at** ~ **times** mehrere Male

'**variously** *adv.* unterschiedlich

varnish /'vɑːnɪʃ/ 1 *n.* Lasur, *die* 2 *v.t.* lasieren

vary /'veərɪ/ 1 *v.t.* verändern; ändern ⟨*Bestimmungen, Programm, Methode, Route*⟩; (add variety to) abwechslungsreicher gestalten 2 *v.i.* (become different) sich ändern; ⟨*Preis, Qualität:*⟩ schwanken; (be different) unterschiedlich sein

'**varying** *adj.* wechselnd; (different) unterschiedlich

vase /vɑːz/ *n.* Vase, *die*

vast /vɑːst/ *adj.* (a) (huge) riesig; weit ⟨*Fläche, Meer*⟩ (b) (coll.: great) enorm; Riesen⟨*menge, -summe*⟩

'**vastly** *adv.* (coll.) enorm; weitaus ⟨*besser*⟩; weit ⟨*überlegen, unterlegen*⟩

v

vat /væt/ n. Bottich, der

VAT /viːeɪˈtiː, væt/ abbr. = **value added tax** MwSt.

Vatican /ˈvætɪkən/ pr. n. Vatikan, der

vault¹ /vɔːlt, vɒlt/ n. (a) (Archit.) Gewölbe, das
(b) (in bank) Tresorraum, der
(c) (tomb) Gruft, die

vault² ① v.i. sich schwingen
② v.t. sich schwingen über (+ Akk.)
③ n. Sprung, der

VD n. Geschlechtskrankheit, die

VDU abbr. = **visual display unit**

veal /viːl/ n. Kalb[fleisch], das; attrib. Kalbs-

veer /vɪə(r)/ v.i. ⟨Auto:⟩ ausscheren
■ **veer a'way, veer 'off** v.i. ⟨Auto:⟩ ausscheren; ⟨Fahrer, Straße:⟩ abbiegen

veg /vedʒ/ n., pl. same (coll.) Gemüse, das

vegan /ˈviːgən/ ① n. Veganer, der/ Veganerin, die
② adj. vegan

vegetable /ˈvedʒɪtəbl/ n. Gemüse, das; fresh ~s frisches Gemüse; attrib. Gemüse⟨suppe, -extrakt, -garten⟩

'vegetable oil n. Pflanzenöl, das

vegetarian /vedʒɪˈteərɪən/ ① n. Vegetarier, der/Vegetarierin, die
② adj. vegetarisch; sb. is ~: jmd. ist Vegetarier/Vegetarierin; eat ~ [food] vegetarisch essen

vegetarianism /vedʒɪˈteərɪənɪzm/ n. Vegetarismus, der

vegetate /ˈvedʒɪteɪt/ v.i. nur noch [dahin]vegetieren

vegetation /vedʒɪˈteɪʃn/ n. Vegetation, die

veggie /ˈvedʒɪ/ (coll.) ① adj. vegetarisch; ~ burger Bratling, der
② n. Vegetarier, der/Vegetarierin, die

vehement /ˈviːəmənt/ adj., **'vehemently** adv. heftig

vehicle /ˈviːɪkl/ n. (a) Fahrzeug, das
(b) (fig.: medium) Vehikel, das

vehicular /vɪˈhɪkjʊlə(r)/ adj. Fahrzeug-

veil /veɪl/ ① n. Schleier, der
② v.t. verschleiern

veiled /veɪld/ adj. verschleiert; (fig.) versteckt

vein /veɪn/ n. (a) Vene, die; (any blood vessel) Ader, die
(b) (fig.: mood) Stimmung, die; in a similar ~: vergleichbarer Art

Velcro ® /ˈvelkrəʊ/ n. Klettverschluss, der ⟨Wz⟩

velocity /vɪˈlɒsɪtɪ/ n. Geschwindigkeit, die

velvet /ˈvelvɪt/ ① n. Samt, der
② adj. aus Samt nachgestellt; Samt-

'velvety adj. samtig

vendetta /venˈdetə/ n. Hetzkampagne, die; (feud) Fehde, die

vending machine /ˈvendɪŋ məʃiːn/ n. [Verkaufs]automat, der

vendor /ˈvendə(r)/ n. Verkäufer, der/Verkäuferin, die

veneer /vɪˈnɪə(r)/ n. Furnier, das

venerable /ˈvenərəbl/ adj. ehrwürdig

venerate /ˈvenəreɪt/ v.t. verehren

ve'nereal disease n. (Med.) Geschlechtskrankheit, die

venetian blind /vɪˈniːʃn blaɪnd/ n. Jalousie, die

Venezuela /venɪˈzweɪlə/ pr. n. Venezuela (das)

vengeance /ˈvendʒəns/ n. (a) Rache, die; take ~ [up]on sb. [for sth.] sich an jmdm. [für etw.] rächen
(b) with a ~ (coll.) gewaltig (ugs.)

Venice /ˈvenɪs/ pr. n. Venedig (das)

venison /ˈvenɪsn, ˈvenɪzn/ n. Hirsch, der; Hirschfleisch, das; (roe deer) Reh[fleisch], das

venom /ˈvenəm/ n. Gift, das

venomous /ˈvenəməs/ adj. giftig

vent¹ /vent/ ① n. (a) Öffnung, die
(b) (fig.) Ventil, das (fig.); give ~ to Luft machen (+ Dat.)
② v.t. (fig.) Luft machen (+ Dat.)

vent² n. (in garment) Schlitz, der

ventilate /ˈventɪleɪt/ v.t. belüften

ventilation /ventɪˈleɪʃn/ n. Belüftung, die

ventilator /ˈventɪleɪtə(r)/ n.
(a) Ventilator, der
(b) (Med.) Beatmungsgerät, das

ventriloquist /venˈtrɪləkwɪst/ n. Bauchredner, der/-rednerin, die

venture /ˈventʃə(r)/ ① n. Unternehmung, die
② v.i. (a) (dare) wagen
(b) (dare to go) sich wagen
③ v.t. wagen
■ **venture 'out** v.i. sich hinauswagen

venue /ˈvenjuː/ n. (Sport) [Austragungs]ort, der; (Mus., Theatre) [Veranstaltungs]ort, der; (meeting place) Treffpunkt, der

Venus /ˈviːnəs/ pr. n. (Astron.) Venus, die

veranda[h] /vəˈrændə/ n. Veranda, die

verb /vɜːb/ n. Verb, das

verbal /ˈvɜːbl/ adj., **verbally** /ˈvɜːbəlɪ/ adv. (a) (relating to words) sprachlich
(b) (oral[ly]) mündlich

verbatim /vəˈbeɪtɪm/ adj., adv. [wort]wörtlich

verbose /vəˈbəʊs/ adj. weitschweifig ⟨Roman, Autor⟩; langatmig ⟨Rede, Redner⟩

verdict /ˈvɜːdɪkt/ n. Urteil, das; ~ of guilty/not guilty Schuld-/Freispruch, der; reach a ~: zu einem Urteil kommen

verge /vɜːdʒ/ n. (a) Rasensaum, der; (on road) Bankette, die
(b) (fig.) be on the ~ of war/tears am Rande des Krieges stehen/den Tränen nahe sein; be on the ~ of doing sth. kurz davor stehen, etw. zu tun

■ **'verge on** *v.t.* [an]grenzen an (+ *Akk.*)

verger /'vɜːdʒə(r)/ *n.* Küster, *der*

verifiable /'verɪfaɪəbl/ *adj.* nachprüfbar

verification /verɪfɪ'keɪʃn/ *n.* **(a)** (check) Überprüfung, *die*
(b) (confirmation) Bestätigung, *die*

verify /'verɪfaɪ/ *v.t.* **(a)** (check) überprüfen
(b) (confirm) bestätigen

veritable /'verɪtəbl/ *adj.* richtig

vermin /'vɜːmɪn/ *n.* Ungeziefer, *das*

vermouth /'vɜːməθ/ *n.* Wermut[wein], *der*

vernacular /və'nækjʊlə(r)/ *n.* Landessprache, *die*

versatile /'vɜːsətaɪl/ *adj.* vielseitig; (having many uses) vielseitig verwendbar

versatility /vɜːsə'tɪlɪtɪ/ *n.* Vielseitigkeit, *die*

verse /vɜːs/ *n.* **(a)** (stanza) Strophe, *die*
(b) (poetry) Lyrik, *die;* write some ~: einige Verse schreiben; piece of ~: Gedicht, *das;* written in ~: in Versform
(c) (in Bible) Vers, *der*

versed /vɜːst/ *adj.* be [well] ~ in sth. sich in etw. (*Dat.*) [gut] auskennen

version /'vɜːʃn/ *n.* Version, *die;* (in another language) Übersetzung, *die;* (of vehicle, machine, tool) Modell, *das*

versus /'vɜːsəs/ *prep.* gegen

vertebra /'vɜːtɪbrə/ *n., pl.* ~e /'vɜːtɪbriː/ Wirbel, *der*

vertebrate /'vɜːtɪbrət/ *n.* Wirbeltier, *das*

vertical /'vɜːtɪkl/ *adj.* senkrecht; be ~: senkrecht stehen

vertically /'vɜːtɪkəlɪ/ *adv.* senkrecht

vertigo /'vɜːtɪɡəʊ/ *n.* Schwindel, *der*

verve /vɜːv/ *n.* Schwung, *der*

very /'verɪ/ **1** *attrib. adj.* **(a)** (precise, exact) genau; you're the ~ person I wanted to see genau dich wollte ich sehen; at the ~ moment when …: im selben Augenblick, als …; at the ~ centre genau in der Mitte; the ~ thing genau das Richtige
(b) (extreme) at the ~ back/front ganz hinten/vorn; at the ~ end/beginning ganz am Ende/Anfang; from the ~ beginning von Anfang an; only a ~ little nur ein ganz kleines bisschen
(c) (mere) bloß ⟨*Gedanke*⟩
(d) (absolute) absolut ⟨*Minimum, Maximum*⟩; the ~ most I can offer is …: ich kann allerhöchstens … anbieten; for the ~ last time zum allerletzten Mal
(e) *emphat.* before their ~ eyes vor ihren Augen
2 *adv.* **(a)** (extremely) sehr; it's ~ near es ist ganz in der Nähe; ~ probably höchstwahrscheinlich; not ~ much nicht sehr; ~ little [nur] sehr wenig ⟨*verstehen, essen*⟩; thank you [~,] ~ much [vielen,] vielen Dank
(b) (absolutely) aller⟨*best…, -letzt…, -leichtest…*⟩; at the ~ latest allerspätestens
(c) (precisely) the ~ same one genau der-/

die-/dasselbe

vessel /'vesl/ *n.* **(a)** (receptacle) Gefäß, *das;* [drinking] ~: Trinkgefäß, *das*
(b) (Naut.) Schiff, *das*

vest /vest/ **1** *n.* **(a)** (Brit.) Unterhemd, *das*
(b) (Amer.: waistcoat) Weste, *die*
2 *v.t.* ~ sb. with sth., ~ sth. in sb. jmdm. etw. verleihen

'vested *adj.* have a ~ interest in sth. ein persönliches Interesse an etw. (*Dat.*) haben

vestige /'vestɪdʒ/ *n.* Spur, *die;* not a ~ of truth kein Fünkchen Wahrheit

vestment /'vestmənt/ *n.* [Priester]gewand, *das*

vestry /'vestrɪ/ *n.* Sakristei, *die*

vet /vet/ **1** *n.* Tierarzt, *der*/-ärztin, *die*
2 *v.t.*, -tt- überprüfen

veteran /'vetərən/ *n.* Veteran, *der*/ Veteranin, *die*

veteran 'car *n.* (Brit.) Veteran, *der*

veterinarian /vetərɪ'neərɪən/ *n.* (Amer.) Tierarzt, *der*/-ärztin, *die*

veterinary /'vetərɪnərɪ/ *adj.* tiermedizinisch

veterinary 'surgeon *n.* (Brit.) Tierarzt, *der*/-ärztin, *die*

veto /'viːtəʊ/ **1** *n., pl.* ~es Veto, *das*
2 *v.t.* sein Veto einlegen gegen

vex /veks/ *v.t.* [ver]ärgern; (cause to worry) beunruhigen; be ~ed with sb. sich über jmdn. ärgern

vexation /vek'seɪʃn/ *n.* Verärgerung, *die*

vexed /vekst/ *adj.* **(a)** verärgert
(b) ~ question viel diskutierte Frage

VHF *abbr.* = **Very High Frequency** UKW

via /'vaɪə/ *prep.* über (+ *Akk.*) ⟨*Ort, Sender, Telefon*⟩; durch ⟨*Eingang, Schornstein, Person*⟩; per ⟨*Post*⟩

viability /vaɪə'bɪlɪtɪ/ *n.* (feasibility) Realisierbarkeit, *die*

viable /'vaɪəbl/ *adj.* (feasible) realisierbar

viaduct /'vaɪədʌkt/ *n.* Viadukt, *die* od. *der*

Viagra ® /vaɪ'æɡrə/ *n.* Viagra, *das* ⟨Wz⟩

vibrant /'vaɪbrənt/ *adj.* lebensprühend ⟨*Atmosphäre*⟩; lebhaft ⟨*Farbe*⟩

vibrate /vaɪ'breɪt/ **1** *v.i.* vibrieren; (under strong impact) beben
2 *v.t.* vibrieren lassen

vibration /vaɪ'breɪʃn/ *n.* Vibrieren, *das;* (under strong impact) Beben, *das*

vicar /'vɪkə(r)/ *n.* Pfarrer, *der*

vicarage /'vɪkərɪdʒ/ *n.* Pfarrhaus, *das*

vicarious /vɪ'keərɪəs/ *adj.* nachempfunden

vice[1] /vaɪs/ *n.* Laster, *das*

vice[2] *n.* (Brit.: tool) Schraubstock, *der*

vice: ~'chairman *n.* stellvertretender Vorsitzender; ~'president *n.* Vizepräsident, *der*/-präsidentin, *die;* ~ squad *n.* Sittenpolizei, *die*

vice versa /vaɪsɪ 'vɜːsə/ adv. umgekehrt

vicinity /vɪ'sɪnɪtɪ/ n. Umgebung, die; **in the ~ [of a place]** in der Nähe [eines Ortes]

vicious /'vɪʃəs/ adj. **(a)** (malicious) böse; bösartig ‹Tier›

(b) (violent) brutal

vicious 'circle n. Teufelskreis, der

'viciously adv. **(a)** (maliciously) boshaft

(b) (violently) brutal

victim /'vɪktɪm/ n. Opfer, das; (of sarcasm, abuse) Zielscheibe, die (fig.).

victimization /vɪktɪmaɪ'zeɪʃn/ n. Schikanierung, die

victimize /'vɪktɪmaɪz/ v.t. schikanieren

victor /'vɪktə(r)/ n. Sieger, der/Siegerin, die

victorious /vɪk'tɔːrɪəs/ adj. siegreich

victory /'vɪktərɪ/ n. Sieg, der (**over** über + Akk.); attrib. Sieges-

video /'vɪdɪəʊ/ ① adj. Video-

② n., pl. ~s (~ recorder) Videorekorder, der; (~tape, ~ recording) Video, das (ugs.)

③ v.t. ▶ VIDEOTAPE 2

video: ~ camera n. Videokamera, die; **~ cas'sette** n. Videokassette, die; **~ cas'sette recorder** n. Videokassettenrekorder, der; **~ clip** n. Videoclip, der; **~conference** n. Videokonferenz, die; **~ film** n. Videofilm, der; **~ game** n. Videospiel, das; **~ library** n. Videothek, die; **~ machine** n. Videogerät, das; **~ 'nasty** n. Horrorvideo, das; **~-on-demand** n. Video-on-Demand, das; **~ player** n. Video-Player, der; **~ recorder** n. Videorekorder, der; **~ recording** n. Videoaufnahme, die; **~tape** ① n. Videoband, das; ② v.t. [auf Videoband (Akk.)] aufnehmen

vie /vaɪ/ v.i., vying /'vaɪɪŋ/ **~ [with sb.] for sth.** [mit jmdm.] um etw. wetteifern

Vienna /vɪ'enə/ ① pr. n. Wien (das)

② attrib. adj. Wiener

Viennese /vɪə'niːz/ ① adj. Wiener

② n., pl. same Wiener, der/Wienerin, die

Vietnam /vɪet'næm/ pr. n. Vietnam (das)

Vietnamese /vɪetnə'miːz/ ① adj. vietnamesisch; **sb. is ~** : jmd. ist Vietnamese/Vietnamesin

② n., pl. same **(a)** (person) Vietnamese, der/Vietnamesin, die

(b) (language) Vietnamesisch, das

view /vjuː/ ① n. **(a)** (range of vision) Sicht, die; **be out of/in ~** : nicht zu sehen/zu sehen sein

(b) (what is seen) Aussicht, die

(c) (picture) Ansicht, die

(d) (opinion) Ansicht, die; **what is your ~** or **are your ~s on this?** was meinst du dazu?; **hold** or **take the ~ that ...:** der Ansicht sein, dass ...; **in my ~:** meiner Ansicht nach

(e) be on ~: besichtigt werden können; **in ~ of sth.** (fig.) angesichts einer Sache; **with a**

~ to doing sth. in der Absicht, etw. zu tun

② v.t. **(a)** (look at) sich (Dat.) ansehen

(b) (consider) betrachten

(c) (inspect) besichtigen

③ v.i. (Telev.) fernsehen

viewdata /'vjuː.deɪtə/ n. (Teleph.) Bildschirmtextsystem, das

'viewer n. **(a)** (Telev.) [Fernseh]zuschauer, der/-zuschauerin, die

(b) (for slides) Diabetrachter, der

'viewfinder n. Sucher, der

'viewing n. (Telev.) Fernsehen, das; **~ figures** Einschaltquoten Pl.; **at peak ~ time** zur besten Sendezeit

'viewpoint n. Standpunkt, der

vigil /'vɪdʒɪl/ n. Wachen, das; **keep ~:** wachen

vigilance /'vɪdʒɪləns/ n. Wachsamkeit, die

vigilant /'vɪdʒɪlənt/ adj. wachsam

vigilante /vɪdʒɪ'læntɪ/ n. Mitglied einer/der Bürgerwehr

vigor (Amer.) ▶ VIGOUR

vigorous /'vɪɡərəs/ adj. kräftig; heftig ‹Attacke, Protest›; energisch ‹Versuch, Anstrengung, Leugnen, Maßnahme›

'vigorously adv. heftig; kräftig ‹schrubben, drücken›

vigour /'vɪɡə(r)/ n. (Brit.) (of person) Vitalität, die; (of body) Kraft, die; (of protest, attack) Heftigkeit, die

vile /vaɪl/ adj. gemein ‹Verleumdung›; vulgär ‹Sprache›; (repulsive) widerwärtig; (coll.: very unpleasant) scheußlich (ugs.)

villa /'vɪlə/ n. **(a)** [holiday] ~: Ferienhaus, das

(b) [country] ~: Landhaus, das

village /'vɪlɪdʒ/ n. Dorf, das; attrib. Dorf-

village: ~ 'green n. Dorfwiese, die; **~ 'hall** n. Dorfgemeinschaftshaus, das

villager /'vɪlɪdʒə(r)/ n. Dorfbewohner, der/-bewohnerin, die

villain /'vɪlən/ n. **(a)** Verbrecher, der

(b) (Theatre) Bösewicht, der

villainous /'vɪlənəs/ adj. gemein

vindicate /'vɪndɪkeɪt/ v.t. **(a)** (justify) rechtfertigen

(b) (clear) rehabilitieren

vindication /vɪndɪ'keɪʃn/ n.

(a) (justification) Rechtfertigung, die

(b) (clearing) Rehabilitierung, die

vindictive /vɪn'dɪktɪv/ adj. nachtragend

vine /vaɪn/ n. Weinrebe, die

vinegar /'vɪnɪɡə(r)/ n. Essig, der

vinegary /'vɪnɪɡərɪ/ adj. sauer

vineyard /'vɪnjɑːd, 'vɪnjəd/ n. Weinberg, der

vintage /'vɪntɪdʒ/ ① n. Jahrgang, der

② adj. erlesen ‹Wein›

vintage 'car n. (Brit.) Oldtimer, der

vintner /'vɪntnə(r)/ n. Weinhändler, der/-händlerin, die

vinyl /'vaɪnɪl/ n. Vinyl, das

viola /vɪ'əʊlə/ n. Bratsche, die

violate /'vaɪəleɪt/ v.t. (a) verletzen; brechen ‹Vertrag, Versprechen, Gesetz› (b) (profane, rape) schänden

violation /vaɪə'leɪʃn/ n. ▸ VIOLATE: Verletzung, die; Bruch, der; Schändung, die

violence /'vaɪələns/ n. (a) (force) Heftigkeit, die; (of blow) Wucht, die (b) (brutality) Gewalt, die; (at public event) Gewalttätigkeiten Pl.; **resort to** or **use** ∼: Gewalt anwenden

violent /'vaɪələnt/ adj. gewalttätig; (fig.) heftig; wuchtig ‹Schlag, Stoß›; Gewalt‹verbrecher, -tat›

'**violently** adv. brutal; (fig.) heftig

violet /'vaɪələt/ 1 n. (a) Veilchen, das (b) (colour) Violett, das 2 adj. violett

violin /vaɪə'lɪn/ n. Violine, die; Geige, die

vio'linist n. Geiger, der/Geigerin, die

VIP /viː'aɪ'piː/ n. Prominente, der/die; **the** ∼**s** die Prominenz

viper /'vaɪpə(r)/ n. Viper, die

virgin /'vɜːdʒɪn/ 1 n. (a) Jungfrau, die (b) **the [Blessed] V**∼ **[Mary]** die [Heilige] Jungfrau [Maria] 2 adj. (unspoiled) unberührt; ∼ **olive oil** natives Olivenöl

virginity /və'dʒɪnɪtɪ/ n. Unschuld, die

Virgo /'vɜːgəʊ/ n., pl. ∼**s** (Astrol., Astron.) die Jungfrau

virile /'vɪraɪl/ adj. männlich

virility /vɪ'rɪlɪtɪ/ n. Männlichkeit, die

virology /vaɪə'rɒlədʒɪ/ n. Virologie, die

virtual /'vɜːtjʊəl/ adj. **a** ∼ ...: so gut wie ein/eine ...; **the traffic came to a** ∼ **standstill** der Verkehr kam praktisch zum Stillstand (ugs.)

'**virtually** adv. so gut wie; praktisch (ugs.)

virtual re'ality n. (Comp.) virtuelle Realität

virtue /'vɜːtjuː/ n. (a) (moral excellence) Tugend, die (b) (advantage) Vorteil, der (c) **by** ∼ **of** aufgrund (+ Gen.)

virtuoso /vɜːtjʊ'əʊzəʊ/ n., pl. **virtuosi** /vɜːtjʊ'əʊziː/ or ∼**s** Virtuose, der/Virtuosin, die

virtuous /'vɜːtjʊəs/ adj. rechtschaffen ‹Person›; tugendhaft ‹Leben›

virulent /'vɪrʊlənt/ adj. (a) (Med.) virulent; stark wirkend ‹Gift› (b) (fig.) heftig; scharf ‹Angriff›

virus /'vaɪərəs/ n. (a) Virus, der (b) (Comp.) [Computer]virus, das od. der

visa /'viːzə/ n. Visum, das

vis-à-vis /viːzɑː'viː/ prep. (in relation to) bezüglich (+ Gen.)

viscosity /vɪs'kɒsɪtɪ/ n. Dickflüssigkeit, die

viscount /'vaɪkaʊnt/ n. Viscount, der

viscous /'vɪskəs/ adj. dickflüssig

visibility /vɪzɪ'bɪlɪtɪ/ n. (a) Sichtbarkeit, die (b) (range of vision) Sicht, die; (Meteorol.) Sichtweite, die

visible /'vɪzɪbl/ adj. sichtbar

'**visibly** adv. sichtlich

vision /'vɪʒn/ n. (a) (sight) Sehkraft, die (b) (dream) Vision, die (c) usu. pl. (imaginings) Fantasien Pl. (d) (insight, foresight) Weitblick, der

visit /'vɪzɪt/ 1 v.t. besuchen; aufsuchen ‹Arzt› 2 v.i. einen Besuch/Besuche machen 3 n. Besuch, der; **pay** or **make a** ∼ **to sb.**, **pay sb. a** ∼: jmdm. einen Besuch abstatten (geh.)

'**visiting:** ∼ **card** n. Visitenkarte, die; ∼ **hours** n. pl. Besuchszeiten Pl.

visitor /'vɪzɪtə(r)/ n. Besucher, der/Besucherin, die; (to hotel) Gast, der; **have** ∼**s/a** ∼: Besuch haben

'**visitors' book** n. Gästebuch, das; **sign the** ∼: sich ins Gästebuch eintragen

visual /'vɪzjʊəl, 'vɪʒjʊəl/ adj. visuell; optisch ‹Eindruck, Darstellung›

visual: ∼ **aids** n. pl. Anschauungsmaterial, das; ∼ **dis'play unit** n. Bildschirmgerät, das

visualization /vɪzjʊəlaɪ'zeɪʃn/ n. Veranschaulichung, die; (imagining) Sichvorstellen, das

visualize /'vɪzjʊəlaɪz, 'vɪʒjʊəlaɪz/ v.t. (a) (imagine) sich (Dat.) vorstellen (b) (envisage) voraussehen

'**visually** adv. bildlich

vital /'vaɪtl/ adj. (a) (essential to life) lebenswichtig (b) (essential) unbedingt notwendig (c) (crucial) entscheidend (to für); **it is** ∼ **that you** ...: es ist von entscheidender Bedeutung, dass Sie ...

vitality /vaɪ'tælɪtɪ/ n. Vitalität, die

'**vitally** adv. ∼ **important** von allergrößter Wichtigkeit; (crucial) von entscheidender Bedeutung

vitamin /'vɪtəmɪn, 'vaɪtəmɪn/ n. Vitamin, das

vitamin pill n. Vitamintablette, die

vitriolic /vɪtrɪ'ɒlɪk/ adj. ätzend

vivacious /vɪ'veɪʃəs/ adj. lebhaft

vivacity /vɪ'væsɪtɪ/ n. Lebhaftigkeit, die

vivid /'vɪvɪd/ adj. lebhaft ‹Farbe, Erinnerung›; lebendig ‹Schilderung›

'**vividly** adv. lebhaft ‹beschreiben›; **remember sth.** ∼: sich lebhaft an etw. (Akk.) erinnern

vixen /'vɪksn/ n. Füchsin, die

vocabulary /və'kæbjʊlərɪ/ n. (a) (list) Vokabelverzeichnis, das; **learn** ∼: Vokabeln lernen ⋯⬧

(b) (range of language) Wortschatz, *der*
vocal /'vəʊkl/ *adj.* **(a)** (concerned with voice) stimmlich
(b) lautstark ⟨*Minderheit, Protest*⟩
'**vocal cords** *n. pl.* Stimmbänder *Pl.*
vocalist /'vəʊkəlɪst/ *n.* Sänger, *der*/Sängerin, *die*
vocation /və'keɪʃn/ *n.* Berufung, *die*
vocational /və'keɪʃənl/ *adj.* berufsbezogen
vocational: ~ **college** *n.* Berufsschule, *die;* ~ **guidance** *n.* Berufsberatung, *die;* ~ **training** *n.* berufliche Bildung
vociferous /və'sɪfərəs/ *adj.* laut; lautstark ⟨*Forderung, Protest*⟩
vodka /'vɒdkə/ *n.* Wodka, *der*
vogue /vəʊg/ *n.* Mode, *die;* **be in/come into** ~: in Mode sein/kommen
voice /vɔɪs/ ⟨1⟩ *n.* Stimme, *die;* **in a firm/loud/soft** ~: mit fester/lauter/sanfter Stimme
⟨2⟩ *v.t.* zum Ausdruck bringen
voice: ~**mail** *n.* Voicemail, *die;* ~**-over** *n.* Begleitkommentar, *der;* ~ **recognition** *n.* (Comp.) Spracherkennung, *die*
void /vɔɪd/ ⟨1⟩ *adj.* **(a)** (empty) leer
(b) (invalid) ungültig
(c) ~ **of** ohne [jeden/jedes/jede]
⟨2⟩ *n.* Nichts, *das*
vol. *abbr.* = **volume** Bd.
volatile /'vɒlətaɪl/ *adj.* **(a)** (Chem.) flüchtig
(b) (fig.) impulsiv; brisant ⟨*Lage*⟩
volcanic /vɒl'kænɪk/ *adj.* vulkanisch
volcano /vɒl'keɪnəʊ/ *n., pl.* ~**es** Vulkan, *der*
vole /vəʊl/ *n.* Wühlmaus, *die*
volition /və'lɪʃn/ *n.* Wille, *der;* **of one's own** ~: aus eigenem Willen
volley /'vɒlɪ/ *n.* **(a)** (of missiles) Salve, *die;* **a** ~ **of arrows** ein Hagel von Pfeilen
(b) (Tennis) Volley, *der*
'**volleyball** *n.* Volleyball, *der*
volt /vəʊlt/ *n.* Volt, *das*
voltage /'vəʊltɪdʒ/ *n.* Spannung, *die*
voluble /'vɒljʊbl/ *adj.* redselig
volume /'vɒljuːm/ *n.* **(a)** (book) Band, *der*
(b) (loudness) Lautstärke, *die;* (of voice) Volumen, *das*
(c) (space) Rauminhalt, *der;* (amount of substance) Teil, *der*
'**volume control** *n.* Lautstärkeregler, *der*
voluntarily /'vɒləntərɪlɪ/ *adv.*,
voluntary /'vɒləntərɪ/ *adj.* freiwillig
volunteer /vɒlən'tɪə(r)/ ⟨1⟩ *n.* Freiwillige, *der/die*
⟨2⟩ *v.t.* anbieten ⟨*Hilfe, Dienste*⟩; herausrücken mit ⟨*Informationen*⟩
⟨3⟩ *v.i.* sich [freiwillig] melden; ~ **to do** *or*

~ **for the shopping** sich zum Einkaufen bereit erklären
voluptuous /və'lʌptjʊəs/ *adj.* üppig
vomit /'vɒmɪt/ ⟨1⟩ *v.t.* erbrechen
⟨2⟩ *v.i.* sich übergeben
⟨3⟩ *n.* Erbrochene, *das*
voodoo /'vuːduː/ *n.* Wodu, *der*
voracious /və'reɪʃəs/ *adj.* gefräßig ⟨*Person*⟩; unbändig ⟨*Appetit*⟩
vote /vəʊt/ ⟨1⟩ *n.* **(a)** (individual ~) Stimme, *die*
(b) (act of voting) Abstimmung, *die;* **take a** ~ **on sth.** über etw. (*Akk.*) abstimmen
(c) (right to ~) Stimmrecht, *das*
⟨2⟩ *v.i.* abstimmen; (in election) wählen; ~ **for/against** stimmen für/gegen; ~ **to do sth.** beschließen, etw. zu tun; ~ **Labour/Conservative** *etc.* Labour/die Konservativen *usw.* wählen
⟨3⟩ *v.t.* ~ **sb. Chairman/President** *etc.* jmdn. zum Vorsitzenden/Präsidenten *usw.* wählen
■ **vote 'in** *v.t.* wählen
'**vote-catching** *n.* Stimmenfang, *der*
'**voter** *n.* Wähler, *der*/Wählerin, *die*
voting /'vəʊtɪŋ/ *n.* Abstimmen, *das;* (in election) Wählen, *das*
voting: ~ **age** *n.* Wahlalter, *das;* ~ **slip** *n.* Wahlzettel, *der;* Stimmzettel, *der;* ~ **system** *n.* Wahlsystem, *das*
vouch /vaʊtʃ/ ⟨1⟩ *v.t.* ~ **that** …: sich dafür verbürgen, dass …
⟨2⟩ *v.i.* ~ **for sb./sth.** sich für jmdn./etw. verbürgen
'**voucher** *n.* Gutschein, *der*
vow /vaʊ/ ⟨1⟩ *n.* Gelöbnis, *das;* (Relig.) Gelübde, *das*
⟨2⟩ *v.t.* geloben
vowel /'vaʊəl/ *n.* Vokal, *der*
voyage /'vɔɪɪdʒ/ ⟨1⟩ *n.* Reise, *die* (sea ~) Seereise, *die;* **outward/homeward** ~, ~ **out/home** Hin-/Rückreise, *die;* **a** ~ **to the moon** ein Mondflug
⟨2⟩ *v.i.* (literary) reisen
voyeur /vwɑː'jɜː(r)/ *n.* Voyeur, *der*
voyeurism /vwɑː'jɜːrɪzm/ *n.* Voyeurismus, *der*
vulgar /'vʌlgə(r)/ *adj.* vulgär; ordinär ⟨*Person, Benehmen, Witz*⟩
vulgarity /vʌl'gærɪtɪ/ *n.* Vulgarität, *die*
vulnerable /'vʌlnərəbl/ *adj.* **(a)** (exposed to danger) angreifbar; **be** ~ **to sth.** für etw. anfällig sein; **be** ~ **to attack/in a** ~ **position** leicht angreifbar sein
(b) (without protection) schutzlos
vulture /'vʌltʃə(r)/ *n.* Geier, *der*
vying ▶ VIE

Ww

W¹, w /'dʌblju:/ *n.* W, w, *das*

W² *abbr.* = **watt[s]** W

W. *abbr.* (a) = **west** W.
(b) = **western** w.

wad /wɒd/ *n.* (a) Knäuel, *das;* (smaller) Pfropfen, *der*
(b) (of papers) Bündel, *das*

wadding /'wɒdɪŋ/ *n.* Futter, *das*

waddle /'wɒdl/ ① *v.i.* watscheln
② *n.* watschelnder Gang

wade /weɪd/ *v.i.* waten
■ 'wade through *v.t.* (fig. coll.) durchackern (ugs.) ⟨*Buch*⟩

wafer /'weɪfə(r)/ *n.* Waffel, *die*

'**wafer-thin** *adj.* hauchdünn

waffle¹ /'wɒfl/ *n.* (Gastr.) Waffel, *die*

waffle² (Brit. coll.: talk) ① *v.i.* schwafeln (ugs.)
② *n.* Geschwafel, *das* (ugs.)

waft /wɒft, wɑ:ft/ ① *v.t.* wehen
② *v.i.* ziehen

wag /wæg/ ① *v.t.,* **-gg-** ⟨*Hund:*⟩ wedeln mit ⟨*Schwanz*⟩; ~ **one's finger at sb.** jmdm. mit dem Finger drohen
② *v.i.,* **-gg-** ⟨*Schwanz:*⟩ wedeln

wage /weɪdʒ/ ① *n. in sing. or pl.* Lohn, *der*
② *v.t.* führen ⟨*Krieg*⟩

wage: ~ **claim** *n.* Lohnforderung, *die;* ~ **earner** *n.* Lohnempfänger, *der/*-empfängerin, *die;* **be the** ~ **earner of the family** der Ernährer/die Ernährerin der Familie sein; ~ **freeze** *n.* Lohnstopp, *der;* ~ **increase** *n.* Lohnerhöhung, *die;* ~ **packet** *n.* Lohntüte, *die*

wager /'weɪdʒə(r)/ (dated/formal) ① *n.* Wette, *die;* **lay a** ~ **on sth.** auf etw. (*Akk.*) wetten
② *v.t. & i.* wetten

wage: ~ **rise** *n.* Lohnerhöhung, *die;* ~ **scale** *n.* Tarif, *der;* ~ **slave** *n.* Lohnsklave, *der*

waggle /'wægl/ (coll.) ① *v.t.* ~ **its tail** ⟨*Hund:*⟩ mit dem Schwanz wedeln
② *v.i.* hin und her schlagen

waggon (Brit.), **wagon** /'wægən/ *n.* Wagen, *der*

waif /weɪf/ *n.* (child) verlassenes Kind

wail /weɪl/ ① *v.i.* klagen (geh.) (**for** um); ⟨*Kind:*⟩ heulen
② *n.* klagender Schrei; ~s Geheul, *das*

waist /weɪst/ *n.* Taille, *die;* **tight round the** ~: eng in der Taille

'**waistband** *n.* Gürtelbund, *der;* (of trousers) [Hosen]bund, *der;* (of skirt) [Rock]bund, *der*

waistcoat /'weɪskəʊt/ *n.* (Brit.) Weste, *die*

'**waistline** *n.* Taille, *die;* **be bad for the** ~: schlecht für die schlanke Linie sein

wait /weɪt/ ① *v.i.* (a) warten; ~ **[for] an hour** eine Stunde warten; ~ **a moment** Moment mal; **keep sb.** ~**ing, make sb.** ~: jmdn. warten lassen
(b) ~ **at table** servieren
② *v.t.* (await) warten auf (+ *Akk.*); ~ **one's turn** warten, bis man drankommt
③ *n.* (a) **after a long/short** ~: nach langer/kurzer Wartezeit
(b) **lie in** ~ **for sb./sth.** jmdm./einer Sache auflauern
■ **wait be'hind** *v.i.* noch dableiben
■ '**wait for** *v.t.* warten auf (+ *Akk.*); ~ **for sb. to do sth.** darauf warten, dass jmd. etw. tut; ~ **for the rain to stop** warten, bis der Regen aufhört
■ '**wait on** *v.t.* (serve) bedienen
■ **wait 'up** *v.i.* aufbleiben (**for** wegen)

'**waiter** *n.* Kellner, *der;* ~! Herr Ober!

'**waiting:** ~ **list** *n.* Warteliste, *die;* ~ **room** *n.* Wartezimmer, *das;* (Railw.) Warteraum, *der*

waitress /'weɪtrɪs/ *n.* Serviererin, *die;* ~! Fräulein! (veralt.)

waive /weɪv/ *v.t.* verzichten auf (+ *Akk.*)

wake¹ /weɪk/ ① *v.i.,* woke /wəʊk/, woken /'wəʊkn/ aufwachen
② *v.t.,* woke, woken wecken
③ *n.* (by corpse) Totenwache, *die*
■ **wake 'up** ① *v.i.* aufwachen; ~ **up to sth.** (fig.: realize) etw. erkennen
② *v.t.* (a) wecken
(b) (fig.: enliven) wachrütteln

wake² *n.* Kielwasser, *das;* **in the** ~ **of sth.** (fig.) im Gefolge von etw.

waken /'weɪkn/ ① *v.t.* wecken
② *v.i.* aufwachen

'**wake-up call** (esp. Amer.) ▶ ALARM CALL

Wales /weɪlz/ *pr. n.* Wales (*das*)

walk /wɔ:k/ ① *v.i.* (a) laufen; (not run) gehen; (not drive) zu Fuß gehen; **learn to** ~: laufen lernen
(b) (exercise) gehen
② *v.t.* (a) (lead) führen; ausführen ⟨*Hund*⟩
(b) (accompany) bringen
③ *n.* (a) Spaziergang, *der;* **go [out] for** *or* **take** *or* **have a** ~: einen Spaziergang machen; **ten minutes'** ~ **from here** zehn Minuten zu Fuß von hier
(b) (gait) Gang, *der*
(c) (path) [Spazier]weg, *der*
■ **walk a'way with** *v.t.* (coll.: win easily) spielend leicht gewinnen
■ '**walk into** *v.t.* (hit by accident) laufen gegen ⟨*Pfosten, Laternenpfahl*⟩; ~ **sb.** mit jmdm. zusammenstoßen; ~ **into a trap** in eine Falle gehen ⋯⋙

■ **walk 'off with** *v.t.* sich davonmachen mit

■ **walk 'out** *v.i.* (a) (leave in protest) aus Protest den Saal verlassen (b) (go on strike) in den Streik treten

■ **walk 'out of** *v.t.* (leave in protest) aus Protest verlassen

■ **walk 'out on** *v.t.* verlassen

'**walker** *n.* (a) Spaziergänger, *der/* -gängerin, *die;* (rambler) Wanderer, *der/*Wanderin, *die* (b) (baby-~) Laufstuhl, *der*

walkie-talkie /wɔ:kɪ'tɔ:kɪ/ *n.* Walkie-Talkie, *das*

'**walking** *n.* [Spazieren]gehen, *das;* at ~ pace im Schritttempo; be within ~ distance zu Fuß zu erreichen sein

walking: ~ **frame** *n.* Gehbock, *der;* Gehgestell, *das;* ~ **holiday** *n.* Wanderurlaub, *der;* ~ **shoe** *n.* Wanderschuh, *der;* ~ **stick** *n.* Spazierstock, *der;* ~ **tour** *n.* Wanderung, *die*

Walkman ® /'wɔ:kmən/ *n., pl.* **Walkmans** Walkman, *der* Ⓦ

walk: ~**out** *n.* Arbeitsniederlegung, *die;* ~**over** *n.* (fig.: easy victory) Spaziergang, *der* (ugs.); ~**way** *n.* Fußweg, *der;* (over machinery etc.) Laufsteg, *der*

wall /wɔ:l/ *n.* Wand, *die;* (freestanding) Mauer, *die;* **drive sb. up the** ~ (fig. coll.) jmdn. auf die Palme bringen (ugs.); **go to the** ~ (fig.) an die Wand gedrückt werden

■ **wall 'up** *v.t.* zumauern

wall: ~**chart** *n.* Schautafel, *die;* ~ **cupboard** *n.* Hängeschrank, *der*

wallet /'wɒlɪt/ *n.* Brieftasche, *die*

wall: ~**flower** *n.* Goldlack, *der;* ~ **hanging** *n.* Wandbehang, *der;* ~ **light** *n.* Wandlampe, *die*

wallop /'wɒləp/ (coll.) ⒈ *v.t.* schlagen ⒉ *n.* Schlag, *der*

wallow /'wɒləʊ/ *v.i.* (a) sich wälzen (b) (fig.) schwelgen (in in + *Dat.*)

wall: ~ **painting** *n.* Wandgemälde, *das;* ~**paper** ⒈ *n.* (a) Tapete, *die;* (b) (Comp.) Hintergrund, *der;* (pattern) Hintergrundmuster, *das;* ⒉ *v.t.* tapezieren; ~**-to-**~ *adj.* ~**-to-** ~ **carpeting** Teppichboden, *der;* ~ **unit** *n.* Hängeelement, *das*

walnut /'wɔ:lnʌt/ *n.* Walnuss, *die*

walrus /'wɔ:lrəs/ *n.* Walross, *das*

waltz /wɔ:lts, wɔ:ls/ ⒈ *n.* Walzer, *der* ⒉ *v.i.* Walzer tanzen

wan /wɒn/ *adj.* bleich

wand /wɒnd/ *n.* Stab, *der*

wander /'wɒndə(r)/ ⒈ *v.i.* (go aimlessly) umherirren; (walk slowly) bummeln ⒉ *v.t.* wandern durch ⒊ *n.* (coll.) Spaziergang, *der*

■ **wander a'bout** *v.i.* sich herumtreiben

■ **wander 'off** *v.i.* (stray) weggehen

wane /weɪn/ *v.i.* abnehmen

wangle /'wæŋgl/ *v.t.* (coll.) organisieren (ugs.)

wannabe /'wɒnəbɪ/ *n.* (coll. derog.) Möchtegern, *der; attrib.* Möchtegern-

want /wɒnt/ ⒈ *v.t.* (a) (desire) wollen; ~ to do sth. etw. tun wollen; I ~ it done by tonight ich will, dass es bis heute Abend fertig wird (b) (require, need) brauchen; '**W**~ed – **cook**' „Koch/Köchin gesucht"; you're ~ed on the phone du wirst am Telefon verlangt; the windows ~ painting die Fenster müssten gestrichen werden; you ~ to be [more] careful du solltest vorsichtig[er] sein (c) ~ed [by the police] [polizeilich] gesucht ⒉ *n.* (a) (lack) Mangel, *der* (of an + *Dat.*); for ~ of sth. aus Mangel an etw. (*Dat.*) (b) (need) Not, *der* (c) (desire) Bedürfnis, *das*

■ '**want for** *v.t.* sb. ~s for nothing or doesn't ~ for anything jmdm. fehlt es an nichts

'**wanting** *adj.* be ~: fehlen; sb./sth. is ~ in sth. jmdm./einer Sache fehlt es an etw. (*Dat.*); be found ~: für unzureichend befunden werden

wanton /'wɒntən/ *adj.*, '**wantonly** *adv.* mutwillig

war /wɔ:(r)/ *n.* Krieg, *der;* between the ~s zwischen den Weltkriegen; **declare** ~: den Krieg erklären (on *Dat.*); **be at** ~: sich im Krieg befinden; **make** ~: Krieg führen (on gegen)

warble /'wɔ:bl/ *v.t. & i.* trällern

war: ~ **correspondent** *n.* Kriegsberichterstatter, *der/* -berichterstatterin, *die;* ~ **crime** *n.* Kriegsverbrechen, *das;* ~ **criminal** *n.* Kriegsverbrecher, *der/*-verbrecherin, *die*

ward /wɔ:d/ *n.* (a) (in hospital) Station, *die;* she's in W~ 3 sie liegt auf Station 3 (b) (child) Mündel, *das od. die* (c) (electoral division) Wahlbezirk, *der*

■ **ward 'off** *v.t.* abwehren

'**war damage** *n.* Kriegsschäden *Pl.*

warden /'wɔ:dn/ *n.* (a) (of hostel) Heimleiter, *der/*-leiterin, *die;* (of youth hostel) Herbergsvater, *der/*-mutter, *die* (b) (supervisor) Aufseher, *der/*Aufseherin, *die*

'**warder** *n.* (Brit.) Wärter, *der*

wardrobe /'wɔ:drəʊb/ *n.* (a) Kleiderschrank, *der* (b) (clothes) Garderobe, *die*

warehouse /'weəhaʊs/ *n.* Lagerhaus, *das;* (part of building) Lager, *das*

wares /weəz/ *n. pl.* Ware, *die*

warfare /'wɔ:feə(r)/ *n.* Krieg, *der*

war: ~ **game** *n.* Kriegsspiel, *das;* ~ **grave** *n.* Kriegs- od. Soldatengrab, *das;* ~**head** *n.* Sprengkopf, *der*

warily /'weərɪlɪ/ *adv.* vorsichtig; (suspiciously) misstrauisch

'**warlike** *adj.* kriegerisch

warm /wɔːm/ **1** *adj.* (a) warm; **I am [very]** ∼: mir ist [sehr] warm
(b) (enthusiastic) herzlich ⟨*Grüße, Dank*⟩
2 *v.t.* wärmen; warm machen ⟨*Flüssigkeit*⟩; ∼ **one's hands** sich (*Dat.*) die Hände wärmen
3 *v.i.* ∼ **to sb./sth.** (come to like) sich für jmdn./etw. erwärmen
■ **warm 'up** **1** *v.i.* warm werden; ⟨*Sportler:*⟩ sich aufwärmen
2 *v.t.* aufwärmen ⟨*Speisen*⟩; erwärmen ⟨*Raum, Zimmer*⟩

warm-blooded /'wɔːmblʌdɪd/ *adj.* warmblütig

'**war memorial** *n.* Kriegerdenkmal, *das*

warm-hearted /'wɔːmhɑːtɪd/ *adj.* warmherzig ⟨*Person*⟩

'**warmly** *adv.* (a) warm
(b) (fig.) herzlich ⟨*willkommen heißen, gratulieren, begrüßen, grüßen, danken*⟩

warmonger /'wɔːmʌŋgə(r)/ *n.* Kriegshetzer, *der*/-hetzerin, *die*

warmth /wɔːmθ/ *n.* (a) Wärme, *die*
(b) (fig.) Herzlichkeit, *die*

'**warm-up** *n.* have a ∼ (Sport) sich aufwärmen; ∼ **[lap]** (Motor Racing) Aufwärmrunde, *die*

warn /wɔːn/ *v.t.* (a) (inform, give notice) warnen (**against, of, about** vor + *Dat.*); ∼ **sb. that** ...: jmdn. darauf hinweisen, dass ...; ∼ **sb. not to do sth.** jmdn. davor warnen, etw. zu tun
(b) (admonish) ermahnen; (officially) abmahnen

warning **1** *n.* (a) (advance notice) Vorwarnung, *die*
(b) (lesson) **let that be a ∼ to you** lass dir das eine Warnung sein
(c) (caution) Verwarnung, *die;* (less official) Warnung, *die*
2 *adj.* Warn⟨*schild, -signal usw.*⟩

'**warning triangle** *n.* Warndreieck, *das*

warp /wɔːp/ **1** *v.i.* sich verbiegen; ⟨*Holz, Schallplatte:*⟩ sich verziehen
2 *v.t.* (a) verbiegen
(b) (fig.) **a ∼ed sense of humour** ein abartiger Humor

war: ∼**path** *n.* **be on the** ∼**path** (fig.) in Rage sein; ∼**plane** *n.* Kampfflugzeug, *das*

warrant /'wɒrənt/ **1** *n.* (for sb.'s arrest) Haftbefehl, *der;* **[search]** ∼: Durchsuchungsbefehl, *der*
2 *v.t.* (a) (justify) rechtfertigen
(b) (guarantee) garantieren

'**warranty** *n.* Garantie, *die*

warrior /'wɒrɪə(r)/ *n.* (esp. literary) Krieger, *der* (geh.)

Warsaw /'wɔːsɔː/ **1** *pr. n.* Warschau (*das*)
2 *attrib. adj.* Warschauer; ∼ **Pact** (Hist.) Warschauer Pakt

'**warship** *n.* Kriegsschiff, *das*

wart /wɔːt/ *n.* Warze, *die*

war: ∼**time** *n.* (a) Kriegszeit, *die;* **in**

or during ∼**time**: im Krieg; (b) *attrib.* Kriegs⟨*rationierung, -evakuierung usw.*⟩
∼**-torn** *adj.* kriegsgeschunden

wary /'weərɪ/ *adj.* vorsichtig; (suspicious) misstrauisch (**of** gegenüber); **be** ∼ **of sb./sth.** sich vor jmdm./etw. in Acht nehmen

'**war zone** *n.* Kriegsgebiet, *das*

was ▸ BE

wash /wɒʃ/ **1** *v.t.* (a) waschen; ∼ **oneself** sich waschen; ∼ **one's hands/face/hair** sich (*Dat.*) die Hände/das Gesicht/die Haare waschen; ∼ **the clothes** Wäsche waschen; ∼ **the dishes** [Geschirr] spülen; ∼ **the floor** den Fußboden aufwischen
(b) (remove) waschen ⟨*Fleck*⟩ (**out of** aus); abwaschen ⟨*Schmutz*⟩ (**off** von)
(c) (carry along) spülen
2 *v.i.* (a) sich waschen
(b) ⟨*Stoff, Kleidungsstück:*⟩ sich waschen lassen
3 *n.* (a) **give sb./sth. a [good]** ∼: jmdn./ etw. [gründlich] waschen
(b) (laundering) Wäsche, *die*
(c) (of ship) Sog, *der*
■ **wash 'down** *v.t.* abspritzen ⟨*Auto, Deck, Hof*⟩
■ **wash 'off** **1** *v.t.* ∼ sth. off etw. abwaschen
2 *v.i.* abgehen; (from fabric etc.) herausgehen
■ **wash 'out** *v.t.* ausscheuern ⟨*Topf*⟩; ausspülen ⟨*Mund*⟩; ∼ **dirt/marks out of clothes** Schmutz/Flecken aus Kleidern [her]auswaschen
■ **wash 'up** **1** *v.t.* (Brit.) ∼ **the dishes** up das Geschirr spülen
2 *v.i.* abwaschen; spülen

washable /'wɒʃəbl/ *adj.* waschbar

'**washbasin** *n.* Waschbecken, *das*

washed-'out *adj.* verwaschen (fig.: exhausted) abgespannt

washed-'up *adj.* (coll.) kaputt (ugs.)

washer /'wɒʃə(r)/ *n.* (of tap) Dichtungsring, *der*

'**washing** *n.* Wäsche, *die;* **do the** ∼: waschen

washing: ∼ **machine** *n.* Waschmaschine, *die;* ∼ **powder** *n.* Waschpulver, *das;* ∼**-'up** *n.* (Brit.) Abwasch, *der;* **do the** ∼**-up** abwaschen; spülen; ∼**-'up liquid** *n.* Spülmittel, *das*

'**washtub** *n.* Waschbottich, *der*

wasn't /'wɒznt/ (coll.) = **was not**; ▸ BE

wasp *n.* Wespe, *die*

waste /weɪst/ **1** *n.* (a) (useless remains) Abfall, *der;* **kitchen** ∼: Küchenabfälle *Pl.*
(b) (extravagant use) Verschwendung, *die;* **it's a** ∼ **of time/money/energy** das ist Zeit-/Geld-/ Energieverschwendung
2 *v.t.* (squander) verschwenden; **all his efforts were** ∼**d** all seine Mühe war umsonst; **don't** ∼ **my time!** stehlen Sie mir nicht die Zeit!
3 *adj.* (a) ∼ **material** Abfall, *der* ····⟫

(b) lay sth. ∼: etw. verwüsten
■ **waste a'way** *v.i.* immer mehr abmagern
waste: ∼**basket** ▶ WASTE-PAPER BASKET;
∼ **disposal** *n.* Abfallbeseitigung, *die;*
∼ **disposal site** *n.* [Müll]deponie *die;*
∼ **disposal unit** *n.* Müllzerkleinerer, *der*
wasteful /'weɪstfl/ *adj.* **(a)** (extravagant) verschwenderisch
(b) (causing waste) unwirtschaftlich
waste: ∼**land** *n.* Ödland, *das;*
∼ **management** *n.* Abfallmanagement, *das;* Müllmanagement, *das;* ∼ '**paper** *n.* Papierabfall, *der;* ∼-'**paper basket** *n.* Papierkorb, *der;* ∼ **pipe** *n.* Abflussrohr, *das;* ∼ **reduction** *n.* Abfallverminderung, *die;* Müllreduzierung, *die*
watch /wɒtʃ/ [1] *n.* **(a)** [wrist/pocket] ∼: [Armband-/Taschen]uhr, *die*
(b) keep ∼: Wache halten; keep [a] ∼ for sb./sth. auf jmdn./etw. achten
(c) (Naut.) Wache, *die*
[2] *v.i.* ∼ for sb./sth. auf jmdn./etw. warten
[3] *v.t.* **(a)** (observe) sich (*Dat.*) ansehen ⟨*Sportveranstaltung, Fernsehsendung*⟩;
∼ [the] television *or* TV fernsehen; ∼ sb. do *or* doing sth. zusehen, wie jmd. etw. tut; we are being ∼ed wir werden beobachtet
(b) (be careful of, look after) achten auf (+ *Akk.*)
■ **watch 'out** *v.i.* **(a)** (be careful) aufpassen; ∼ out! Vorsicht!
(b) (look out) ∼ out for sb./sth. auf jmdn./etw. achten
'**watchdog** *n.* Wachhund, *der;* (fig.) **[public]** ∼: *[Leiter/Leiterin einer] Aufsichtsbehörde*
watchful /'wɒtʃfl/ *adj.* wachsam
watch: ∼**maker** *n.* Uhrmacher, *der/*-macherin, *die;* ∼**man** /'wɒtʃmən/ *n.,* *pl.* ∼**men** /'wɒtʃmən/ Wachmann, *der;*
∼ **strap** *n.* [Uhr]armband, *das;* ∼**tower** *n.* Wachturm, *der*
water /'wɔːtə(r)/ [1] *n.* **(a)** Wasser, *das*
(b) *in pl.* (part of the sea etc.) Gewässer *Pl.*
[2] *v.t.* **(a)** bewässern ⟨*Land*⟩; wässern ⟨*Pflanzen*⟩; ∼ the flowers die Blumen [be]gießen
(b) verwässern ⟨*Bier usw.*⟩
(c) tränken ⟨*Tier*⟩
[3] *v.i.* ⟨*Augen:*⟩ tränen; my mouth was ∼ing mir lief das Wasser im Munde zusammen
■ **water 'down** *v.t.* verwässern
water: ∼**bed** *n.* Wasserbett, *das;*
∼ **birth** *n.* Unterwassergeburt, *die;*
∼ **biscuit** *n.* Cracker, *der;* ∼ **bottle** *n.* Wasserflasche, *die;* ∼ **butt** *n.* Regentonne, *die;* ∼ **closet** *n.* Toilette, *die;* WC, *das;* Wasserklosett, *das* (veralt.); ∼**colour** *n.* **(a)** (paint) Wasserfarbe, *die;* **(b)** (picture) Aquarell, *das;* ∼**cress** *n.* Brunnenkresse, *die;* ∼**fall** *n.* Wasserfall, *der;* ∼**front** *n.* Ufer, *das;* a ∼front location eine Gegend am Wasser; ∼ **heater** *n.* Heißwassergerät, *das;* ∼**hole** *n.* Wasserloch, *das*

watering: ∼ **can** *n.* Gießkanne, *die;*
∼ **place** *n.* (for animals) Wasserstelle, *die*
water: ∼ **level** *n.* Wasserstand, *der;*
∼**lily** *n.* Seerose, *die;* ∼**line** *n.* (Naut.) Wasserlinie, *die;* ∼**logged** /'wɔːtəlɒgd/ *adj.* nass ⟨*Boden*⟩; aufgeweicht ⟨*Sportplatz*⟩;
∼ **main** *n.* Hauptwasserleitung, *die;*
∼**mark** *n.* Wasserzeichen, *das;* ∼**melon** *n.* Wassermelone, *die;* ∼ **meter** *n.* Wasseruhr, *die;* ∼ **pipe** *n.* Wasserrohr, *das;* ∼ **pistol** *n.* Wasserpistole, *die;*
∼ **polo** *n.* Wasserball, *der;* ∼**proof**
[1] *adj.* wasserdicht; wasserfest ⟨*Farbe*⟩;
[2] *v.t.* wasserdicht machen; imprägnieren ⟨*Stoff*⟩; ∼ **rates** *n. pl.* the ∼ rates die Wassergebühren *Pl.;* ∼**repellent** *adj.* Wasser abstoßend; ∼**resistant** *adj.* wasserundurchlässig; wasserfest ⟨*Farbe*⟩;
∼**shed** *n.* (fig.) Wendepunkt, *der;* ∼**ski**
[1] *n.* Wasserski, *der;* [2] *v.i.* Wasserski laufen; ∼**skiing** *n.* Wasserskilaufen, *das;* ∼ **softener** /'sɒfənə(r)/ *n.* Wasserenthärter, *der;* ∼**-soluble** *adj.* wasserlöslich; ∼ **supply** *n.* Wasserversorgung, *die;* ∼ **table** *n.* Grundwasserspiegel, *der;* ∼ **tap** *n.* Wasserhahn, *der;* ∼**tight** *adj.* wasserdicht; ∼ **tower** *n.* Wasserturm, *der;*
∼ **vapour** *n.* Wasserdampf, *der;* ∼**way** *n.* Wasserstraße, *die;* ∼**works** *n. sing., pl. same* (establishment) Wasserwerk, *das;* (system) Wasserversorgungssystem, *das*
'**watery** *adj.* wässrig
watt /wɒt/ *n.* Watt, *das*
wattage /'wɒtɪdʒ/ *n.* Wattzahl, *die*
wave /weɪv/ [1] *n.* **(a)** Welle, *die*
(b) (gesture) give sb. a ∼: jmdm. zuwinken; with a ∼ of one's hand mit einem Winken
[2] *v.i.* **(a)** ⟨*Fahne, Flagge, Wimpel:*⟩ wehen; ⟨*Baum, Gras, Korn:*⟩ sich wiegen
(b) (with hand) winken; ∼ at *or* to sb. jmdm. zuwinken
[3] *v.t.* schwenken; schwingen ⟨*Schwert*⟩;
∼ one's hand at *or* to sb. jmdm. zuwinken;
∼ goodbye to sb. jmdm. zum Abschied zuwinken
■ **wave a'side** *v.t.* **(a)** abtun ⟨*Zweifel, Einwand*⟩
(b) (signal to move) ∼ sb. aside [jmdm.] abwinken
wave: ∼**band** *n.* Wellenbereich, *der;* ∼**farm** *n.* Wellenkraftwerk, *das;*
∼**length** *n.* Wellenlänge, *die*
waver /'weɪvə(r)/ *v.i.* schwanken
wavy /'weɪvɪ/ *adj.* wellig; ∼ line Schlangenlinie, *die*
wax¹ /wæks/ [1] *n.* **(a)** Wachs, *das*
(b) (in ear) Schmalz, *das*
[2] *v.t.* wachsen
wax² *v.i.* **(a)** ⟨*Mond:*⟩ zunehmen
(b) (become) werden
wax 'crayon *n.* Wachsmalstift, *der*
waxed /wækst/ *adj.* gewachst; ∼ **paper** Wachspapier, *das*

w

wax: ~work *n.* Wachsfigur, *die;*
~works *n. sing., pl. same*
Wachsfigurenkabinett, *das*
'waxy *adj.* wachsweich
way /weɪ/ 1 *n.* (a) Weg, *der;* **ask the** *or*
one's ~: nach dem Weg fragen; **'W~ In/Out'**
„Ein-/Ausgang"; **by ~ of Switzerland** über
die Schweiz; **lead the ~:** vorausgehen; **go
out of one's ~:** einen Umweg machen; (fig.)
keine Mühe scheuen
(b) (method) Art und Weise, *die;* **do it this
~:** mach es so
(c) (distance) Stück, *das;* **it's a long ~ off** *or*
a long ~ from here es ist weit weg von hier;
all the ~: den ganzen Weg
(d) (direction) Richtung, *die;* **she went
this/that/the other ~:** sie ist in diese/die/die
andere Richtung gegangen; **stand sth. the
right/wrong ~ up** etw. richtig/falsch herum
stellen
(e) (respect) **in [exactly] the same ~:** [ganz]
genauso; **in some ~s** in gewisser Hinsicht;
in one ~: auf eine Art; **in every ~:** in jeder
Hinsicht; **in a ~:** auf eine Art
(f) (custom) Art, *die*
(g) get *or* **have one's [own] ~, have it one's
[own] ~:** seinen Willen kriegen; **be in sb.'s**
or **the ~:** [jmdm.] im Weg sein; **make ~ for
sth.** für etw. Platz machen; (fig.) einer Sache
(*Dat.*) Platz machen; **in a bad ~:** schlecht;
either ~: so oder so; **by the ~:** übrigens
2 *adv.* weit; **~ back** (coll.) vor langer Zeit
way: ~bill *n.* Frachtbrief, *der;* **~'lay** *v.t.,
forms as* LAY² 1: **(a)** (ambush) überfallen;
(b) (stop for conversation) abfangen; **~'out**
adj. (coll.) extrem; verrückt; **~side** *n.*
Wegrand, *der;* **fall by the ~side** (fig.) auf der
Strecke bleiben (ugs.)
wayward /'weɪwəd/ *adj.* eigenwillig
WC *abbr.* = **water closet** WC, *das*
we /wɪ, *stressed* wiː/ *pl. pron.* wir
weak /wiːk/ *adj.* **(a)** schwach; (easily led)
labil ⟨*Charakter, Person*⟩
(b) dünn ⟨*Getränk*⟩
weaken /'wiːkn/ 1 *v.t.* schwächen;
beeinträchtigen ⟨*Augen*⟩
2 *v.i.* ⟨*Entschlossenheit, Kraft:*⟩ nachlassen
weak-kneed /'wiːkniːd/ *adj.* (fig.) feige
weakling /'wiːklɪŋ/ *n.* Schwächling, *der*
'weakly *adv.* schwach
'weakness *n.* Schwäche, *die*
'weak-willed *adj.* willensschwach
wealth /welθ/ *n.* **(a)** (abundance) Fülle, *die*
(b) (riches, being rich) Reichtum, *der*
'wealth tax *n.* Vermögenssteuer, *die*
'wealthy 1 *adj.* reich
2 *n. pl.* **the ~:** die Reichen *Pl.*
wean /wiːn/ *v.t.* abstillen; **~ sb. [away]
from sth.** (fig.) jmdm. etw. abgewöhnen
weapon /'wepən/ *n.* Waffe, *die;* **~ of mass
destruction** Massenvernichtungswaffe, *die*
weaponry /'wepənrɪ/ *n.* Waffen *Pl.*
wear /weə(r)/ 1 *n.* **(a)** ~ **[and tear]**

Abnutzung, *die*
(b) (clothes) Kleidung, *die*
2 *v.t.,* wore /wɔː(r)/, worn /wɔːn/ **(a)** (have
on) tragen ⟨*Schmuck, Brille, Kleidung,
Perücke*⟩; **I haven't a thing to ~:** ich habe
überhaupt nichts anzuziehen
(b) (rub) abtragen ⟨*Kleidungsstück*⟩;
abnutzen ⟨*Teppich*⟩; **a [badly] worn tyre** ein
[stark] abgefahrener Reifen
3 *v.i.,* wore, worn **(a)** ⟨*Kleider:*⟩ sich
durchscheuern; ⟨*Absätze:*⟩ sich ablaufen;
⟨*Teppich:*⟩ sich abnutzen
(b) (endure rubbing) halten; **~ well/badly** sich
gut/schlecht tragen
■ **wear a'way** 1 *v.t.* abschleifen
2 *v.i.* sich abnutzen
■ **wear 'down** *v.t.* (fig.) zermürben
■ **wear 'off** *v.i.* ⟨*Schicht:*⟩ abgehen;
⟨*Wirkung, Schmerz:*⟩ nachlassen
■ **wear 'out** 1 *v.t.* **(a)** aufbrauchen;
auftragen ⟨*Kleidungsstück*⟩
(b) (fig.: exhaust) kaputtmachen (ugs.); **be
worn out** kaputt sein (ugs.)
2 *v.i.* kaputtgehen (ugs.)
■ **wear 'through** 1 *v.i.* sich
durchscheuern
2 *v.t.* durchscheuern
wearable /'weərəbl/ *adj.* **sth. is [not]
~:** man kann etw. [nicht] anziehen
wearer /'weərə(r)/ *n.* Träger, *der/*
Trägerin, *die*
wearily /'wɪərɪlɪ/ *adv.* müde
wearing /'weərɪŋ/ *adj.* ermüdend
wearisome /'wɪərɪsəm/ *adj.* ermüdend
weary /'wɪərɪ/ 1 *adj.* **(a)** (tired) müde
(b) be ~ of sth. einer Sache (*Gen.*)
überdrüssig sein
2 *v.t.* **be wearied by sth.** durch etw.
erschöpft sein
3 *v.i.* **~ of sth./sb.** einer Sache/jmds.
überdrüssig werden
weasel /'wiːzl/ *n.* Wiesel, *das*
weather /'weðə(r)/ 1 *n.* Wetter, *das;*
what's the ~ like? wie ist das Wetter?; **in all
~s** bei jedem Wetter; **he is feeling under the
~** (fig.) er ist [zur Zeit] nicht ganz auf dem
Posten
2 *v.t.* abwettern ⟨*Sturm*⟩; (fig.) durchstehen
⟨*schwere Zeit*⟩
weather: ~beaten *adj.* wettergegerbt
⟨*Gesicht*⟩; verwittert ⟨*Felsen, Gebäude*⟩;
~ chart *n.* Wetterkarte, *die;* **~cock** *n.*
Wetterhahn, *der;* **~ conditions** *n. pl.*
Witterungsverhältnisse *Pl.;* **~ forecast**
n. Wettervorhersage, *die*
weathering /'weðərɪŋ/ *n., no indef. art.*
Verwitterung, *die*
weather: ~man *n.* Meteorologe, *der;*
~ map *n.* Wetterkarte, *die;* **~proof** *adj.*
wetterfest; **~ report** *n.* Wetterbericht, *der;*
~ vane *n.* Wetterfahne, *die*
weave¹ /wiːv/ 1 *n.* Bindung, *die*
2 *v.t.,* wove /wəʊv/, woven /'wəʊvn/
(a) weben; flechten ⟨*Korb, Kranz*⟩ ····⊱

(b) (fig.) einflechten ‹*Thema usw.*› **(into** in + *Akk.*)

weave² *v.i.* (take intricate course) sich schlängeln

'weaver *n.* Weber, *der*/Weberin, *die*

web /web/ *n.* **(a)** Netz, *das;* **spider's** ∼: Spinnennetz, *das*
(b) the web (Comp.) das Web (fachspr.); das Netz

'web authoring *n.* Webauthoring, *das* (fachspr.); *attrib.* Webauthoring-‹*Programm, Software usw.*›

webbed feet /webd 'fi:t/ *n. pl.* Schwimmfüße *Pl.*

web: ∼ **browser** *n.* (Comp.) Web-Browser, *der;* ∼ **designer** *n.* Webdesigner, *der*/-designerin, *die;* ∼ **page** *n.* (Comp.) Webseite, *die;* ∼**site** *n.* (Comp.) Website, *die*

we'd /wɪd, *stressed* wi:d/ **(a)** = we had; **(b)** = we would

Wed. *abbr.* = **Wednesday** Mi.

wedding /'wedɪŋ/ *n.* Hochzeit, *die*

wedding: ∼ **anniversary** *n.* Hochzeitstag, *der;* ∼ **cake** *n.* Hochzeitskuchen, *der;* ∼ **day** *n.* Hochzeitstag, *der;* ∼ **dress** *n.* Brautkleid, *das;* ∼ **present** *n.* Hochzeitsgeschenk, *das;* ∼ **ring** *n.* Ehering, *der*

wedge /wedʒ/ **1** *n.* Keil, *der* **2** *v.t.* verkeilen; ∼ **a door/window open** eine Tür/ein Fenster festklemmen, damit sie/es offen bleibt

'wedge-shaped *adj.* keilförmig

wedlock /'wedlɒk/ *n.* **born in/out of** ∼: ehelich/unehelich geboren

Wednesday /'wenzdeɪ, 'wenzdɪ/ *n.* Mittwoch, *der; see also* FRIDAY

wee¹ /wi:/ *adj.* (child lang./Scot.) klein

wee² ▶ WEE-WEE

weed /wi:d/ **1** *n.* ∼**[s]** Unkraut, *das* **2** *v.t.* jäten
■ **weed 'out** *v.t.* (fig.) aussieben

'weedkiller *n.* Unkrautvertilgungsmittel, *das*

'weedy *adj.* spillerig (ugs.) ‹*Person*›

week /wi:k/ *n.* Woche, *die;* **for several** ∼**s** mehrere Wochen lang; **once a** ∼, **every** ∼: einmal in der Woche; **three times a** ∼: dreimal in der Woche; **a two-**∼ **visit** ein zweiwöchiger Besuch; **a** ∼ **today/tomorrow** heute/morgen in einer Woche; **a** ∼ **on Monday, Monday** ∼: Montag in einer Woche

'weekday *n.* Wochentag, *der*

weekend /-'-, '--/ *n.* Wochenende, *das;* **at the** ∼: am Wochenende; **go away for the** ∼: übers Wochenende wegfahren

weekly /'wi:klɪ/ **1** *adj.* wöchentlich; Wochen‹*zeitung, -zeitschrift, -lohn*› **2** *adv.* wöchentlich **3** *n.* (newspaper) Wochenzeitung, *die;* (magazine) Wochenzeitschrift, *die*

weep /wi:p/ *v.i. & t.,* **wept** /wept/ weinen

weepie /'wi:pɪ/ *n.* (coll.) Schmachtfetzen, *der* (salopp)

weeping 'willow *n.* Trauerweide, *die*

weepy /'wi:pɪ/ **1** *adj.* weinerlich **2** *n.* ▶ WEEPIE

'wee-wee (coll.) **1** *n.* Pipi, *das* (ugs.); **do a** ∼: Pipi machen (ugs.) **2** *v.i.* Pipi machen (ugs.)

weigh /weɪ/ *v.t. & i.* wiegen
■ **weigh 'down** *v.t.* (fig.: depress) niederdrücken
■ **weigh 'up** *v.t.* abwägen

'weighing machine *n.* Waage, *die*

weight /weɪt/ *n.* Gewicht, *das;* **what is your** ∼? wie viel wiegen Sie?; **be under/over** ∼: zu wenig/zu viel wiegen

'weighting *n.* Zulage, *die*

'weightlessness *n.* Schwerelosigkeit, *die*

weight: ∼**lifter** *n.* Gewichtheber, *der*/-heberin, *die;* ∼**lifting** *n.* Gewichtheben, *das* ∼**-train** *v.i.* mit Hanteln trainieren; ∼ **training** *n.* Hanteltraining, *das;* ∼**-watcher** *n.* Schlankheitsbewusste, *der*/*die*

'weighty *adj.* **(a)** (heavy) schwer **(b)** (important) gewichtig

weir /wɪə(r)/ *n.* Wehr, *das*

weird /wɪəd/ *adj.* (coll.: odd) bizarr

weirdie /'wɪədɪ/ *n.* (coll.) Freak, *der* (ugs.)

weirdo /'wɪədəʊ/ *n., pl.* ∼**s** ▶ WEIRDIE

welcome /'welkəm/ **1** *int.* willkommen; ∼ **home/to England!** willkommen zu Hause/in England! **2** *n.* **(a)** Willkommen, *das* **(b)** (reception) Empfang, *der* **3** *v.t.* begrüßen **4** *adj.* **(a)** willkommen; gefällig ‹*Anblick*› **(b)** *pred.* **you are** ∼ **to take it** du kannst es gern nehmen; **you're** ∼: gern geschehen!

welcoming /'welkəmɪŋ/ *adj.* einladend

weld /weld/ *v.t.* (join) verschweißen; (repair, make, attach) schweißen (**[on] to** an + *Akk.*)

'welder *n.* Schweißer, *der*/Schweißerin, *die*

'welding *n.* Schweißen, *das*

welfare /'welfeə(r)/ *n.* **(a)** (health and prosperity) Wohl, *das* **(b)** (social work; payments etc.) Sozialhilfe, *die;* **be on** ∼ (Amer.) Sozialhilfe bekommen

welfare: **W**∼ **'State** *n.* Wohlfahrtsstaat, *der;* ∼ **work** *n.* Sozialarbeit, *die;* ∼ **worker** *n.* Sozialarbeiter, *der*/-arbeiterin, *die*

well¹ /wel/ *n.* **(a)** Brunnen, *der* **(b)** ▶ OIL WELL **(c)** (stair∼) Treppenloch, *das*

well² **1** *int.* ∼! meine Güte!; ∼, **let's forget that** na ja, lassen wir das; ∼, **who was it?** nun *od.* und, wer war's?; **oh** ∼[, **never mind**] na ja[, macht nichts]; ∼? na? **2** *adv.,* **better** /'betə(r)/, **best** /best/

gut; gründlich ‹*trocknen, schütteln*›; **the business/patient is doing** ~: das Geschäft geht gut/dem Patienten geht es gut; ~ **done!** großartig!; **he is** ~ **over forty** er ist weit über vierzig; **as** ~ (in addition) auch; **A as** ~ **as B** B und auch [noch] A

3 *adj.* (in good health) **How are you feeling now? – Quite** ~**, thank you** Wie fühlen Sie sich jetzt? – Ganz gut, danke; **look** ~: gut aussehen; **feel** ~: sich wohl fühlen; **he isn't [very]** ~: es geht ihm nicht [sehr] gut; **get** ~ **soon!** gute Besserung!; **make sb.** ~: jmdn. gesund machen

we'll /wɪl, *stressed* wiːl/ = **we will**

well: ~**-aimed** *adj.* gezielt; ~**-balanced** *adj.* ausgeglichen ‹*Person*›; ~**-behaved** ▸ BEHAVE 1; ~**-being** *n.* Wohl, *das;* ~**-bred** *adj.* anständig; ~**-built** *adj.* ‹*Person*› mit guter Figur; **be** ~**-built** eine gute Figur haben; ~**-chosen** *adj.* wohlgesetzt ‹*Worte*›; ~**-connected** *adj.* ‹*Person*› mit guten Beziehungen; ~ **done** *adj.* (Cookery) durchgebraten; ~**-dressed** *adj.* gut gekleidet; ~**-educated** *adj.* gebildet; ~**-fed** *adj.* wohlgenährt; ~**-founded** *adj.* [wohl] fundiert; ~**-heeled** *adj.* (coll.) gut betucht (ugs.)

wellington /'welɪŋtən/ *n.* ~ **[boot]** Gummistiefel, *der*

well: ~**-intentioned** /'welɪntenʃənd/ *adj.* gut gemeint; ~**-known** *adj.* bekannt; ~ **made** *adj.* gut [gearbeitet]; ~**-mannered** *adj.* ‹*Person*› mit guten Manieren; **be** ~**-mannered** gute Manieren haben; ~**-meaning** *adj.* wohlmeinend; **be** ~**-meaning** es gut meinen; ~**-meant** *adj.* gut gemeint; ~ **off** *adj.* wohlhabend; **sb. is** ~ **off** jmdm. geht es [finanziell] gut; ~ **paid** *adj.* gut bezahlt; ~**-read** /'welred/ *adj.* belesen; ~**-spoken** *adj.* sprachlich gewandt; ~**-timed** *adj.* zeitlich gut gewählt; ~**-to-do** *adj.* wohlhabend; ~**-tried** *adj.* bewährt; ~**-wisher** *n.* Sympathisant, *der*/Sympathisantin, *die*

Welsh /welʃ/ **1** *adj.* walisisch; **sb. is** ~: jmd. ist Waliser/Waliserin
2 *n.* **(a)** (language) Walisisch, *das; see also* ENGLISH 2A
(b) *pl.* **the** ~: die Waliser *Pl.*

Welsh: ~**man** /'welʃmən/ *n., pl.* ~**men** /'welʃmən/ Waliser, *der;* ~ **'rabbit,** ~ **'rarebit** /'reəbɪt/ *ns.* Käsetoast, *der*

went ▸ GO 1

wept ▸ WEEP

were ▸ BE

we're /wɪə(r)/ = **we are;** ▸ BE

weren't (coll.) = were not; ▸ BE

west /west/ **1** *n.* **(a)** Westen, *der;* **in/ to[wards]/from the** ~: im/nach/von Westen; **to the** ~ **of** westlich von **(b)** *usu.* **W**~ (Geog., Polit.) Westen, *der* **2** *adj.* westlich; West‹*küste, -wind, -grenze, -tor*›

3 *adv.* nach Westen; ~ **of** westlich von

West: ~ **Ber'lin** *pr. n.* (Hist.) West-Berlin (*das*); **w**~**bound** *adj.* ‹*Zug, Verkehr usw.*› in Richtung Westen; ~ **Country** *n.* (Brit.) Westengland, *das;* ~ **'End** *n.* (Brit.) Westend, *das*

westerly /'westəlɪ/ *adj.* westlich; ‹*Wind*› aus westlichen Richtungen

western /'westən/ **1** *adj.* westlich; West‹*grenze, -hälfte, -seite*›; ~ **Germany** Westdeutschland, *das* **2** *n.* Western, *der*

Western 'Europe *pr. n.* Westeuropa (*das*)

West: ~ **'German** (Hist.) **1** *adj.* westdeutsch; **he/she is** ~ **German** er ist Westdeutscher/sie ist Westdeutsche; **2** *n.* Westdeutsche, *der/die;* ~ **'Germany** *pr. n.* (Hist.) Westdeutschland (*das*); ~ **'Indian 1** *adj.* westindisch; **sb. is** ~ **Indian** jmd. ist Westinder/-inderin; **2** *n.* Westinder, *der/*-inderin, *die;* ~ **'Indies** *pr. n. pl.* Westindische Inseln *Pl.*

westward[s] /'westwəd(z)/ *adv.* westwärts

wet /wet/ **1** *adj.* **(a)** nass **(b)** (rainy) regnerisch; feucht ‹*Klima*› **(c)** frisch ‹*Farbe*›; '~ **paint**„frisch gestrichen" **(d)** (coll.: feeble) schlapp (ugs.) **2** *v.t.,* **wet** *or* **wetted** befeuchten **3** *n.* **(a)** (moisture) Feuchtigkeit, *die* **(b) in the** ~: im Regen

'wetness *n.* Nässe, *die*

'wet suit *n.* Tauchanzug, *der*

we've /wɪv, *stressed* wiːv/ = **we have**

whack /wæk/ (coll.) **1** *v.t.* hauen (ugs.) **2** *n.* Schlag, *der*

whacked /wækt/ *adj.* (Brit. coll.: tired out) erledigt (ugs.); kaputt (ugs.)

whale /weɪl/ *n.* **(a)** Wal, *der* **(b)** (coll.) **we had a** ~ **of a [good] time** wir haben uns bombig (ugs.) amüsiert

'whalebone *n.* Fischbein, *das*

whaler /'weɪlə(r)/ *n.* Walfänger, *der*

whaling /'weɪlɪŋ/ *n.* Walfang, *die*

wharf /wɔːf/ *n., pl.* **wharves** /wɔːvz/ *or* ~**s** Kai, *der*

what /wɒt/ **1** *adj.* welch...; ~ **book?** welches Buch?; ~ **time does it start?** um wie viel Uhr fängt es an?; ~ **kind of man is he?** was für ein Mensch ist er?; ~ **a fool you are!** was für ein Dummkopf du doch bist!; ~ **cheek/luck!** was für eine Frechheit/ein Glück!; **I will give you** ~ **help I can** ich werde dir helfen, so gut ich kann **2** *adv.* ~ **do I care?** was kümmerts mich?; ~ **does it matter?** was macht's? **3** *pron.* was; ~**?** wie?; was? (ugs.); ~ **is your name?** wie heißt du/heißen Sie?; ~ **about ...?** (~ **will become of ...**)? was ist mit ...?; ~ **about a game of chess?** wie wärs mit einer Partie Schach?; ~**'s-his/-her/** ⋯▷

-its-name wie heißt er/sie/es noch; ∼ for? wozu?; ∼ is it like? wie ist es?; so ∼? na und?; do ∼ I tell you tu, was ich dir sage

whatever /wɒt'evə(r)/ ① *adj.* ∼ problems you have was für Probleme Sie auch haben; nothing ∼: absolut nichts

② *pron.* do ∼ you like mach, was du willst; ∼ happens, ...: was auch geschieht, ...; or ∼: oder was auch immer; ∼ does he want? (coll.) was will er nur?

whatsit /'wɒtsɪt/ *n.* (coll.) (thing) Dingsbums, *das* (ugs.); (person) Dingsda, *der* (ugs.)

wheat /wiːt/ *n.* Weizen, *der*

wheedle /'wiːdl/ *v.t.* ∼ sb. into doing sth. jmdm. so lange gut zureden, bis er etw. tut; ∼ sth. out of sb. jmdm. etw. abschwatzen (ugs.)

wheel /wiːl/ ① *n.* (a) Rad, *das*; [potter's] ∼: Töpferscheibe, *die*
(b) (steering ∼) Lenkrad, *das*; (ship's ∼) Steuerrad, *das*; at *or* behind the ∼ (of car) am Steuer
② *v.t.* (push) schieben
③ *v.i.* (a) (turn round) kehrtmachen
(b) (circle) kreisen

wheel: ∼barrow *n.* Schubkarre, *die*; ∼ brace *n.* Radschlüssel, *der*; ∼chair *n.* Rollstuhl, *der*; ∼ clamp *n.* Parkkralle, *die*

wheeler-dealer /wiːlə'diːlə(r)/ *n.* Mauschler, *der*/Mauschlerin, *die*; (financial) Geschäftemacher, *der*/-macherin, *die*

'**wheelie bin** *n.* (Brit. coll.) Müllcontainer, *der* auf Rollen

'**wheel reflector** (on bicycle) *n.* Speichenreflektor, *der*

wheeze /wiːz/ *v.t.* schnaufen

whelk /welk/ *n.* Wellhornschnecke, *die*

when /wen/ ① *adv.* wann; the time ∼ ...: die Zeit, zu der/(with past tense) als ...; the day ∼ ...: der Tag, an dem/(with past tense) als ...
② *conj.* (a) (at the time that) als; (with present or future tense) wenn; ∼ reading [a newspaper] beim Lesen [einer Zeitung]
(b) (whereas) why do you go abroad ∼ it's cheaper here? warum fährst du ins Ausland, wo es doch hier billiger ist?
③ *pron.* by/till ∼ ...?; bis wann ...?; since ∼ ...? seit wann ...?

whence /wens/ *adv., conj.* (arch./literary) woher

whenever /wen'evə(r)/ ① *adv.* wann immer; or ∼: oder wann immer; ∼ did he do it? (coll.) wann hat er es nur getan?
② *conj.* jedes Mal wenn

where /weə(r)/ ① *adv.* (a) (position) wo; ∼ shall we sit? wohin wollen wir uns setzen?
(b) (to ∼) wohin
② *conj.* wo
③ *pron.* near/not far from ∼ it happened nahe der Stelle/nicht weit von der Stelle, wo es passiert ist

whereabouts ① /weərə'baʊts/ *adv.* (where) wo; (to where) wohin
② /'weərəbaʊts/ *n., sing. or pl.* (of thing) Verbleib, *der*; (of person) Aufenthalt[sort], *der*

where: ∼'as *conj.* während; he is very quiet, ∼as she is an extrovert er ist sehr ruhig, sie dagegen ist eher extravertiert; ∼'by *adv.* mit dem/der/denen; ∼upon /weərə'pɒn/ *adv.* worauf

wherever /weər'evə(r)/ ① *adv.* (a) (position) überall [da], wo; ∼ possible wo *od.* wenn [irgend] möglich
(b) (direction) wohin auch; ∼ he went wohin er auch ging
② *conj.* (a) (position) überall [da], wo; ∼ possible wo *od.* wenn [irgend] möglich
(b) (direction) wohin auch; ∼ he went wohin er auch ging

wherewithal /'weəwɪðɔːl/ *n.* (coll.) the ∼: das nötige Kleingeld (ugs.)

whet /wet/ *v.t.*, -tt-: (a) (sharpen) wetzen
(b) (fig.) anregen ⟨Appetit⟩

whether /'weðə(r)/ *conj.* ob; I don't know ∼ to go [or not] ich weiß nicht, ob ich gehen soll [oder nicht]

which /wɪtʃ/ ① *adj.* welch...; ∼ one welcher/welche/welches; ∼ ones welche; ∼ way (how) wie; (in ∼ direction) wohin
② *pron.* (a) *interrog.* welcher/welche/welches; ∼ of you? wer von euch?
(b) *rel.* der/die/das; of ∼: dessen/deren; after ∼: worauf[hin]

whichever /wɪtʃ'evə(r)/ ① *adj.* welcher/welche/welches ... auch
② *pron.* (a) welcher/welche/welches ... auch
(b) (coll.) ∼ could it be? welcher/welche/welches könnte das nur sein?

whiff /wɪf/ *n.* (puff; fig.: trace) Hauch, *der*; (smell) leichter Geruch

while /waɪl/ ① *n.* Weile, *die*; [for] a ∼: eine Weile; a long ∼: lange; for a little *or* short ∼: eine kleine Weile; [only] a little *or* short ∼ ago [erst] kürzlich *od.* vor kurzem; be worth sb.'s ∼: sich [für jmdn.] lohnen
② *conj.* (a) während; (as long as) solange
(b) (although) obgleich
(c) (whereas) während
■ **while a'way** *v.t.* ∼ away the time sich (*Dat.*) die Zeit vertreiben (by, with mit)

whilst /waɪlst/ (Brit.) ▶ WHILE 2

whim /wɪm/ *n.* Laune, *die*

whimper /'wɪmpə(r)/ ① *n.* ∼[s] Wimmern, *das*; (of dog etc.) Winseln, *das*
② *v.i.* wimmern; ⟨Hund:⟩ winseln

whimsical /'wɪmzɪkl/ *adj.* launenhaft; (odd, fanciful) spleenig

whine /waɪn/ ① *v.i.* (a) heulen; ⟨Hund:⟩ jaulen
(b) (complain) jammern
② *n.* (a) Heulen, *das*; (of dog) Jaulen, *das*

(b) (complaint) ~[s] Gejammer, *das*

whip /wɪp/ **1** *n.* **(a)** Peitsche, *die*
(b) (Brit. Parl.) Fraktionsgeschäftsführer,
der/-führerin, *die*
2 *v.t.,* **-pp-: (a)** peitschen
(b) (Cookery) schlagen
(c) (move quickly) reißen
(d) (coll.: steal) klauen (ugs.)
■ **whip 'out** *v.t.* [blitzschnell]
herausziehen
■ **whip 'up** *v.t.* **(a)** (arouse) anheizen (ugs.)
(b) (coll.: make quickly) schnell hinzaubern
⟨Gericht, Essen⟩

whiplash *n.* ~lash [injury]
Peitschenschlagverletzung, *die*

whipped 'cream *n.* Schlagsahne, *die*

'whipping cream *n.* [flüssige]
Schlagsahne

'whip-round *n.* (Brit. coll.) Sammlung, *die*

whirl /wɜːl/ **1** *v.t.* [im Kreis]
herumwirbeln
2 *v.i.* wirbeln
3 *n.* **(a)** Wirbeln, *das;* she was *or* her
thoughts were in a ~ (fig.) ihr schwirrte der
Kopf
(b) (bustle) Trubel, *der*
■ **whirl 'round** **1** *v.t.* [im Kreis]
herumwirbeln
2 *v.i.* [im Kreis] herumwirbeln; ⟨Rad,
Rotor:⟩ wirbeln

whirl: ~**pool** *n.* Strudel, *der;* (bathing pool)
Whirlpool, *der;* ~**wind** *n.* Wirbelwind, *der*

whirr /wɜː(r)/ **1** *v.i.* surren
2 *n.* Surren, *das*

whisk /wɪsk/ **1** *n.* (Cookery) Schneebesen,
der; (part of mixer) Rührbesen, *der*
2 *v.t.* **(a)** (Cookery) [mit dem Schnee-/
Rührbesen] schlagen
(b) (convey rapidly) in Windeseile bringen
■ **whisk a'way** *v.t.* **(a)** (remove suddenly)
~ **sth. away [from sb.]** [jmdm.] etw.
[plötzlich] wegreißen
(b) (convey rapidly) in Windeseile wegbringen

whisker /'wɪskə(r)/ *n.* **(a)** ~s (on man's
cheek) Backenbart, *der*
(b) (of cat, mouse, rat) Schnurrhaar, *das*

whiskey (Amer., Ir.), **whisky** /'wɪskɪ/ *n.*
Whisky, *der;* (American or Irish) Whiskey, *der*

whisper /'wɪspə(r)/ **1** *v.i.* flüstern; ~ **to**
sb. jmdm. etwas zuflüstern
2 *v.t.* flüstern; ~ **sth. to sb.** jmdm. etw.
zuflüstern
3 *n.* **(a)** Flüstern, *das;* in a ~, in ~s im
Flüsterton
(b) (rumour) Gerücht, *das*

whistle /'wɪsl/ **1** *v.i.* pfeifen; ~ **at sb.** (in
disapproval) jmdn. auspfeifen
2 *v.t.* pfeifen
3 *n.* **(a)** (sound) Pfiff, *der;* (whistling) Pfeifen,
das
(b) (instrument) Pfeife, *die;* blow a/one's
~: pfeifen

whistling 'kettle *n.* Pfeifkessel, *der*

white /waɪt/ **1** *adj.* weiß

2 *n.* **(a)** (colour) Weiß, *das*
(b) (of egg) Eiweiß, *das*
(c) W~ (person) Weiße, *der*/*die*

white: ~ **bread** *n.* Weißbrot, *das;*
~ **cell** *n.* weißes Blutkörperchen;
~ '**coffee** *n.* (Brit.) Kaffee mit Milch;
~-'**collar worker** *n.* Angestellte,
der/*die;* ~ **corpuscle** ▶ ~ CELL;
~ '**elephant** ▶ ELEPHANT; **W**~ **House**
pr. n. (Amer. Polit.) the W~ House das Weiße
Haus; ~-**knuckle ride** *n.* Fahr mit
äußerstem Nervenkitzel; ~ '**lie** ▶ LIE[1] 1;
~ '**meat** *n.* weißes Fleisch [und Geflügel]

whiten /'waɪtn/ **1** *v.t.* weiß machen;
weißen ⟨Wand, Schuhe⟩
2 *v.i.* weiß werden

'whiteness *n.* Weiß, *das*

white: **W**~ '**Paper** *n.* (Brit.) *öffentliches*
Diskussionspapier über Vorhaben der
Regierung; ~ '**sauce** *n.* weiße *od.* helle
Soße; ~ '**wash** **1** *n.* [weiße] Tünche; (fig.)
Schönfärberei, *die;* **2** *v.t.* [weiß] tünchen;
~ '**wedding** *n.* Hochzeit, *die* in Weiß;
~ '**wine** *n.* Weißwein, *der*

Whit 'Monday /wɪt/ *n.* Pfingstmontag,
der

Whitsun /'wɪtsn/ *n.* Pfingsten, *das od. Pl.;*
at ~: zu *od.* an Pfingsten

whittle /'wɪtl/: ~ **a'way** *v.t.* ~ away
sb.'s rights/power jmdm. nach und nach
alle Rechte/Macht nehmen; ~ '**down** *v.t.*
allmählich reduzieren ⟨Anzahl, Gewinn⟩;
verkürzen ⟨Liste⟩

whiz, whizz /wɪz/ **1** *v.i.,* **-zz-** zischen
2 *n.* Zischen, *das*

'whiz[z]-kid *n.* (coll.) Senkrechtstarter, *der*

who /huː, *stressed* huː/ *pron.* **(a)** *interrog.*
wer; (coll.: whom) wen; (coll.: to whom) wem
(b) *rel.* der/die/das; *pl.* die; (coll.: whom)
den/die/das; (coll.: to whom) dem/der/denen;
anyone/those ~ ...: wer ...; **everybody** ~ ...:
jeder, der ...

whoa /wəʊ/ *int.* brr

who'd /huːd, *stressed* huːd/ **(a)** = who had;
(b) = who would

whoever /huːˈevə(r)/ *pron.* **(a)** wer
[immer]
(b) (no matter who) wer ... auch
(c) (coll.) ~ could it be? wer könnte das nur
sein?

whole /həʊl/ **1** *adj.* ganz; the ~ lot [of
them] [sie] alle
2 *n.* Ganze, *das;* the ~: das Ganze; the ~ of
my money/the village/London mein ganzes
Geld/das ganze Dorf/ganz London; as a
~: als Ganzes; on the ~: im Großen und
Ganzen

whole: ~**food** *n.* Vollwertkost,
die; ~**hearted** /həʊlˈhɑːtɪd/ *adj.*
herzlich ⟨Dank[barkeit]⟩; rückhaltlos
⟨Unterstützung⟩; ~**meal** *adj.* Vollkorn-;
~ '**milk** *n.* Vollmilch, *die;* ~ **note** *n.*
(Amer. Mus.) ganze Note; ~ '**number**
n. ganze Zahl; ~**sale** **1** *adj.* ⸱⸱⸱>

W

(a) Großhandels-; **(b)** (fig.: on a large scale) massenhaft; Massen-; **2** adv. **(a)** en gros; **(b)** (fig.: on a large scale) massenweise; **~saler** /'həʊlseɪlə(r)/ n. Großhändler, der/-händlerin, die

wholesome /'həʊlsəm/ adj. gesund

who'll /hʊl, stressed huːl/ = who will

wholly /'həʊllɪ/ adv. völlig

whom /huːm/ pron. **(a)** interrog. wen; as indirect object wem
(b) rel. den/die/das; pl. die; as indirect object dem/der/dem; pl. denen

whooping cough /'huːpɪŋ kɒf/ n. Keuchhusten, der

whopper /'wɒpə(r)/ n. (coll.) **(a)** Riese, der **(b)** (lie) faustdicke Lüge

whopping /'wɒpɪŋ/ adj. (coll.) riesig; Riesen- (ugs.); faustdick ⟨Lüge⟩

whore /hɔː(r)/ n. Hure, die

who's /huːz/ **(a)** = who is
(b) = who has

whose /huːz/ pron. **(a)** interrog. wessen; ~ [book] is that? wem gehört das [Buch]?
(b) rel. dessen/deren/dessen; pl. deren

who've /huːv/ stressed huːv/ = who have

why /waɪ/ **1** adv. **(a)** (for what reason) warum; (for what purpose) wozu; ~ is that? warum das?
(b) (on account of which) the reason ~ he did it der Grund, warum er es tat
2 int. ~, certainly/of course! aber sicher!

wick /wɪk/ n. Docht, der

wicked /'wɪkɪd/ adj. böse

'wickedness n. Bosheit, die

wicker /'wɪkə(r)/ n. Korbgeflecht, das; attrib. Korb⟨waren, -stuhl⟩

'wickerwork n. **(a)** (material) Korbgeflecht, das
(b) (articles) Korbwaren Pl.

wicket /'wɪkɪt/ n. (Cricket) Tor, das

'wicketkeeper n. (Cricket) Torwächter, der/-wächterin, die

wide /waɪd/ **1** adj. **(a)** (broad) breit; groß ⟨Abstand, Winkel⟩; three feet ~: drei Fuß breit
(b) (extensive) weit; umfassend ⟨Lektüre, Wissen, Kenntnisse⟩; reichhaltig ⟨Auswahl, Sortiment⟩
(c) (off target) be ~ of sth. etw. verfehlen
2 adv. **(a)** ~ awake hellwach
(b) (off target) shoot ~: danebenschießen; go ~: das Ziel verfehlen

wide: ~-angle 'lens n. (Photog.) Weitwinkelobjektiv, das; ~-eyed adj. (surprised) mit großen Augen nachgestellt

'widely adv. **(a)** (over a wide area) weit ⟨verbreitet, gestreut⟩
(b) (by many people) weithin ⟨bekannt, akzeptiert⟩; a ~ held view eine weit verbreitete Ansicht
(c) (greatly) erheblich ⟨sich unterscheiden⟩

widen /'waɪdn/ **1** v.t. verbreitern

2 v.i. sich verbreitern

wide: ~-open attrib. adj., ~ 'open pred. adj. weit geöffnet ⟨Fenster, Tür⟩; weit aufgerissen ⟨Mund, Augen⟩; be ~ open ⟨Fenster, Tür⟩ weit offen stehen;
~-ranging /'waɪdreɪndʒɪŋ/ adj. weit gehend ⟨Maßnahme, Veränderung⟩; ausführlich ⟨Diskussion, Gespräch⟩;
~ 'screen n. Breitwand, die; ~screen television, ~screen TV ns. Breitwandfernsehen, das; ~spread adj. weit verbreitet

widow /'wɪdəʊ/ n. Witwe, die

widowed /'wɪdəʊd/ adj. verwitwet

widower /'wɪdəʊə(r)/ n. Witwer, der

width /wɪdθ/ n. Breite, die; (of garment) Weite, die

wield /wiːld/ v.t. schwingen; (fig.) ausüben ⟨Macht, Einfluss⟩

wife /waɪf/ n., pl. wives /waɪvz/ Frau, die

'wife battering n. Misshandlung der [Ehe]frau

wig /wɪg/ n. Perücke, die

wiggle /'wɪgl/ (coll.) **1** v.t. hin und her bewegen
2 v.i. wackeln

wild /waɪld/ **1** adj. **(a)** wild lebend ⟨Tier⟩; wild wachsend ⟨Pflanze⟩
(b) wild ⟨Landschaft⟩
(c) (unrestrained) wild ⟨Erregung⟩; run ~ ⟨Pferd, Hund:⟩ frei herumlaufen; ⟨Kind:⟩ herumtoben; send or drive sb. ~: jmdn. rasend vor Erregung machen
(d) (coll.: very keen) be ~ about sb./sth. wild auf jmdn./etw. sein
2 n. the ~[s] die Wildnis; see an animal in the ~: ein Tier in freier Wildbahn sehen

wild: ~ 'boar n. Wildschwein, das; ~ card n. wilde Karte; ~cat n. Wildkatze, die

wilderness /'wɪldənɪs/ n. Wildnis, die; (desert) Wüste, die

wild: ~ 'goose chase n. (fig.) aussichtslose Suche; ~life n. die Tier- und Pflanzenwelt; ~life park/reserve/sanctuary Naturpark, der/-reservat, das/-schutzgebiet, das

'wildly adv. wild; be ~ excited about sth. über etw. (Akk.) ganz aus dem Häuschen sein (ugs.); ~ inaccurate völlig ungenau

wilful /'wɪlfl/ adj., **wilfully** /'wɪlfəlɪ/ adv. **(a)** (deliberate[ly]) vorsätzlich
(b) (obstinate[ly]) starrsinnig

will[1] /wɪl/ v. aux., only in: pres. will, neg. (coll.) won't /wəʊnt/, past would /wʊd/, neg. (coll.) wouldn't /'wʊdnt/ He won't help me. W~/Would you? Er will mir nicht helfen. Bist du bereit?; the car won't start das Auto springt nicht an; ~/would you pass the salt, please? gibst du bitte mal das Salz rüber?/würdest du bitte mal das Salz rübergeben?; ~ you be quiet! willst du wohl ruhig sein!; he ~ sit there hour after hour er pflegt dort stundenlang zu sitzen; **he '∼ insist on doing it** er besteht unbedingt darauf, es zu tun; **∼ you have some more cake?** möchtest *od.* willst du noch etwas Kuchen?; **the box ∼ hold 5 lb.** of tea in die Kiste gehen 5 Pfund Tee; **tomorrow he ∼ be in Oxford** morgen ist er in Oxford; **I promise I won't do it again** ich verspreche, ich mach's nicht noch mal; **if he tried, he would succeed** wenn er es versuchen würde, würde er es schaffen; **∼ you please tidy up** würdest du bitte aufräumen?

will² *n.* **(a)** (faculty) Wille, *der*
(b) (Law: testament) Testament, *das*
(c) (desire) **at ∼:** nach Belieben; **∼ to live** Lebenswille, *der;* **against one's/sb.'s ∼:** gegen seinen/jmds. Willen

'willing *adj.* willig; **ready and ∼; be ∼ to do sth.** bereit sein, etw. zu tun

'willingly *adv.* **(a)** (with pleasure) gern[e]
(b) (voluntarily) freiwillig

'willingness *n.* Bereitschaft, *die*

willow /'wɪləʊ/ *n.* Weide, *die*

willowy /'wɪləʊɪ/ *adj.* gertenschlank

'will power *n.* Willenskraft, *die*

willy-nilly /wɪlɪ'nɪlɪ/ *adv.* wohl oder übel ⟨*etw. tun müssen*⟩

wilt /wɪlt/ *v.i.* ⟨*Pflanze, Blumen:*⟩ welk werden, welken

wily /'waɪlɪ/ *adj.* listig; gewieft ⟨*Person*⟩

wimp /wɪmp/ *n.* (coll.) Schlappschwanz, *der* (ugs.)

wimpish /wɪmpɪʃ/ *adj.* (coll.) lahm (ugs.)

win /wɪn/ ① *v.t.,* **-nn-, won** /wʌn/ gewinnen; bekommen ⟨*Stipendium, Vertrag, Recht*⟩; **∼ sb. sth.** jmdm. etw. einbringen
② *v.i.,* **-nn-, won** gewinnen
③ *n.* Sieg, *der;* **have a ∼:** gewinnen
■ **win 'over, win 'round** *v.t.* bekehren; (to one's side) auf seine Seite bringen; (convince) überzeugen
■ **win 'through** *v.i.* Erfolg haben

wince /wɪns/ *v.i.* zusammenzucken (**at** bei)

winch /wɪntʃ/ ① *n.* Winde, *die*
② *v.t.* winden; **∼ up** hochwinden

wind¹ /wɪnd/ ① *n.* Wind, *der;* (Med.) Blähungen *Pl.;* **get ∼ of sth.** (fig.) Wind von etw. bekommen; **be in the ∼** (fig.) in der Luft liegen; **get/have the ∼ up** (coll.) Manschetten (ugs.) kriegen/haben
② *v.t.* **the blow ∼ed him** der Schlag nahm ihm den Atem

wind² /waɪnd/ ① *v.i.,* **wound** /waʊnd/
(a) (curve) sich winden; (move) sich schlängeln
(b) (coil) sich wickeln
② *v.t.,* **wound (a)** (coil) wickeln; **∼ sth. on [to] sth.** etw. auf etw. (*Akk.*) [auf]wickeln
(b) aufziehen ⟨*Uhr*⟩
■ **wind 'down** *v.t.* **(a)** herunterdrehen ⟨*Autofenster*⟩
(b) (fig.: reduce gradually) einschränken
■ **wind 'up** ① *v.t.* **(a)** hochdrehen

⟨*Autofenster*⟩
(b) (coil) aufwickeln
(c) aufziehen ⟨*Uhr*⟩
(d) (coll.: annoy deliberately) auf die Palme bringen (ugs.)
(e) beschließen ⟨*Debatte*⟩
(f) (Finance, Law) auflösen
② *v.i.* **(a)** (conclude) schließen
(b) (coll.: end up) **∼ up in prison/hospital** [zum Schluss] im Gefängnis/Krankenhaus landen (ugs.)

wind /wɪnd/: **∼-blown** *adj.* vom Wind zerzaust ⟨*Haar*⟩; **∼break** *n.* Windschutz, *der;* **∼breaker** (Amer.), **∼cheater** (Brit.) *ns.* Windjacke, *die;* **∼ chill factor** *n.* Wind-chill-Index, *der*

winded /'wɪndɪd/ *adj.* **be ∼:** außer Atem sein

winder /'waɪndə(r)/ *n.* (of watch) Krone, *die;* (of clock, toy) Aufziehschraube, *die*

wind /wɪnd/: **∼fall** *n.* **(a)** (fruit) **∼falls** Fallobst, *das;* **(b)** (fig.) warmer Regen (ugs.); **∼fall tax** *(einmalige) Sondersteuer auf Privatisierungsgewinne;* **∼ farm** *n.* Windpark, *der;* **∼ force** *n.* Windstärke, *die;* **∼ instrument** *n.* Blasinstrument, *das;* **∼mill** *n.* Windmühle, *die*

window /'wɪndəʊ/ *n.* (also Comp.) Fenster, *das;* (shop **∼**) [Schau]fenster, *das;* **break a ∼:** eine Fensterscheibe zerbrechen

window: **∼ box** *n.* Blumenkasten, *der;* **∼ cleaner** *n.* Fensterputzer, *der*/-putzerin, *die;* **∼ cleaning** *n.* Fensterputzen, *das;* **∼ display** *n.* Schaufensterauslage, *die;* **∼ dresser** *n.* Schaufensterdekorateur, *der*/-dekorateurin, *die;* **∼ dressing** *n.* (fig.) Schönfärberei, *die;* **∼ frame** *n.* Fensterrahmen, *der;* **∼ ledge** *n.* (inside) Fensterbank, *die;* (outside) Fenstersims, *der od. das;* **∼ pane** *n.* Fensterscheibe, *die;* **∼ shopping** *n.* Schaufensterbummeln, *das;* **go ∼ shopping** einen Schaufensterbummel machen; **∼ sill** *n.* (inside) Fensterbank, *die;* (outside) Fenstersims, *der od. das*

wind /wɪnd/: **∼pipe** *n.* (Anat.) Luftröhre, *die;* **∼ power** *n.* Windkraft, *die;* **∼proof** *adj.* windabweisend; **∼proof jacket** Windjacke, *die;* **∼screen,** (Amer.) **∼shield** *ns.* Windschutzscheibe, *die;* **∼screen/∼shield wiper** Scheibenwischer, *der;* **∼screen/∼shield washer** Scheibenwaschanlage, *die;* **∼surfer** *n.* Windsurfer, *der;* **∼surfing** *n.* Windsurfing, *das;* **∼swept** *adj.* windgepeitscht; vom Wind zerzaust ⟨*Person, Haare*⟩; **∼ tunnel** *n.* Windkanal, *der*

windward /'wɪndwəd/ *adj.* **∼ side** Windseite, *die*

'windy *adj.* windig

wine /waɪn/ *n.* Wein, *der*

wine: **∼ bar** *n.* Weinstube, *die;* **∼ bottle** *n.* Weinflasche, *die;* **∼ cellar** *n.* [Wein]keller, *das;* **∼ cooler** *n.* ⋯⋯⟶

Weinkühler, *der;* ~**glass** *n.* Weinglas, *das;* ~**grower** *n.* Winzer, *der*/Winzerin, *die;* ~**growing** ⟨1⟩ *n.* Weinbau, *der;* ⟨2⟩ *adj.* ~-**growing area** Weingegend, *die;* ~ **list** *n.* Weinkarte, *die;* ~ **merchant** *n.* Weinhändler, *der*/-händlerin, *die;* ~ **merchants** (business) Weinhandlung, *die;* ~ **tasting** /'waɪnteɪstɪŋ/ *n.* Weinprobe, *die;* ~ **vault** *n.* Weinkeller, *der;* ~ '**vinegar** *n.* Weinessig, *der*

wing /wɪŋ/ *n.* **(a)** (Ornith., Archit., Sport) Flügel, *der*
(b) (Aeronaut.) Tragfläche, *die*
(c) (Brit. Motor. Veh.) Kotflügel, *der*

winged /wɪŋd/ *adj.* geflügelt

winger /'wɪŋə(r)/ *n.* (Sport) Außenstürmer, *der*/-stürmerin, *die*

wing: ~ **mirror** *n.* (Brit. Motor Veh.) Außenspiegel, *der;* ~**span** *n.* [Flügel]spannweite, *die;* ~ **tip** *n.* Flügelspitze, *die*

wink /wɪŋk/ ⟨1⟩ *v.i.* **(a)** blinzeln; (as signal) zwinkern; ~ **at sb.** jmdm. zuzwinkern
(b) (flash) blinken
⟨2⟩ *n.* **(a)** Blinzeln, *das;* (signal) Zwinkern, *das;* **give sb. a** ~: jmdm. zuzwinkern
(b) not sleep a ~: kein Auge zutun

'**winner** *n.* Sieger, *der*/Siegerin, *die;* (of competition or prize) Gewinner, *der*/Gewinnerin, *die*

'**winning** *adj.* **(a)** *attrib.* siegreich; ~ **number** Gewinnzahl, *die*
(b) (charming) einnehmend; gewinnend ⟨*Lächeln*⟩

'**winning post** *n.* Zielpfosten, *der*

'**winnings** *n. pl.* Gewinn, *der*

winter /'wɪntə(r)/ *n.* Winter, *der;* **in [the]** ~: im Winter

winter 'sports *n. pl.* Wintersport, *der*

wintry /'wɪntrɪ/ *adj.* winterlich; ~ **shower** Schneegestöber, *das*

wipe /waɪp/ ⟨1⟩ *v.t.* **(a)** abwischen; [auf]wischen ⟨*Fußboden*⟩; (dry) abtrocknen; ~ **one's mouth/eyes/nose** sich (*Dat.*) den Mund/die Tränen/die Nase abwischen; ~ **one's feet/shoes** [sich (*Dat.*)] die Füße/Schuhe abtreten
(b) (get rid of) [ab]wischen; ~ **one's/sb.'s tears** sich/jmdm. die Tränen abwischen
⟨2⟩ *n.* **give sth. a** ~: etw. abwischen
■ **wipe 'down** *v.t.* abwischen; (dry) abtrocknen
■ **wipe 'off** *v.t.* **(a)** (remove) wegwischen; löschen ⟨*Bandaufnahme*⟩
(b) (pay off) zurückzahlen ⟨*Schulden*⟩
■ **wipe 'out** *v.t.* **(a)** (remove) wegwischen; (erase) auslöschen
(b) (cancel) tilgen; zunichte machen ⟨*Vorteil, Gewinn usw.*⟩
(c) (destroy) ausrotten ⟨*Rasse, Tierart, Feinde*⟩; ausmerzen ⟨*Seuche, Korruption*⟩
■ **wipe 'up** *v.t.* **(a)** aufwischen
(b) (dry) abtrocknen

'**wiper** *n.* (Motor Veh.) Wischer, *der*

wire /'waɪə(r)/ ⟨1⟩ *n.* **(a)** Draht, *der*
(b) (Electr., Teleph.) Leitung, *die*
(c) (coll.: telegram) Telegramm, *das*
⟨2⟩ *v.t.* **(a)** (fasten) ~ **sth. together** etw. mit Draht verbinden
(b) (Electr.) ~ **sth. to sth.** etw. an etw. (*Akk.*) anschließen; ~ **a house** in einem Haus die Stromleitungen legen

wire: ~ '**brush** *n.* Drahtbürste, *die;* ~ **cutters** *n. pl.* Drahtschneider, *der*

'**wireless** ⟨1⟩ *adj.* (Comp.) drahtlos; ⟨2⟩ *n.* (Brit. dated) Radio, *das*

wire: ~ '**netting** *n.* Maschendraht, *der;* ~ **strippers** *n. pl.* Abisolierzange, *die;* ~ '**wool** *n.* Stahlwolle, *die*

wiring /'waɪərɪŋ/ *n.* [elektrische] Leitungen *Pl.*

wisdom /'wɪzdəm/ *n.* **(a)** Weisheit, *die*
(b) (prudence) Klugheit, *die*

'**wisdom tooth** *n.* Weisheitszahn, *der*

wise /waɪz/ *adj.* **(a)** weise; vernünftig ⟨*Meinung*⟩
(b) (prudent) klug
(c) be none the ~**r** kein bisschen klüger als vorher sein

wise: ~**crack** *n.* (coll.) witzige Bemerkung; ~ **guy** *n.* (coll.) Klugscheißer, *der* (salopp)

'**wisely** *adv.* weise; (prudently) klug

wish /wɪʃ/ ⟨1⟩ *v.t.* wünschen; **I** ~ **I was** *or* **were rich** ich wollte, ich wäre reich; **I** ~ **to go** ich möchte gehen; ~ **sb. luck/success** *etc.* jmdm. Glück/Erfolg *usw.* wünschen; ~ **sb. well** jmdm. alles Gute wünschen
⟨2⟩ *v.i.* wünschen; ~ **for sth.** sich (*Dat.*) etw. wünschen
⟨3⟩ *n.* Wunsch, *der;* **make a** ~: sich (*Dat.*) etwas wünschen; **get** *or* **have one's** ~: seinen Wunsch erfüllt bekommen

wishful thinking /wɪʃfl 'θɪŋkɪŋ/ *n.* Wunschdenken, *das*

'**wishing well** *n.* Wunschbrunnen, *der*

wishy-washy /'wɪʃɪwɒʃɪ/ *adj.* labberig (ugs.); (fig.) lasch

wisp /wɪsp/ *n.* (of straw) Büschel, *das;* ~ **of hair** Haarsträhne, *die;* ~ **of cloud/smoke** Wolkenfetzen, *der*/Rauchfahne, *die*

wistful /'wɪstfl/ *adj.,* '**wistfully** *adv.* wehmütig

wit /wɪt/ *n.* **(a)** (humour) Witz, *der*
(b) (intelligence) Geist, *der;* **be at one's** ~'**s** *or* ~**s' end** sich (*Dat.*) keinen Rat mehr wissen; **be frightened** *or* **scared out of one's** ~**s** Todesangst haben; **have/keep one's** ~**s about one** auf Draht (ugs.) sein/nicht den Kopf verlieren
(c) (person) geistreicher Mensch

witch /wɪtʃ/ *n.* Hexe, *die*

witch: ~**craft** *n.* Hexerei, *die;* ~ **doctor** *n.* Medizinmann, *der;* ~-**hunt** *n.* Hexenjagd, *die* (for auf + *Akk.*)

with /wɪð/ *prep.* mit; **put sth.** ~ **sth.** etw. zu etw. stellen/legen; **have nothing to write**

~: nichts zum Schreiben haben; **I'm not '~ you** (coll.) ich komme nicht mit; **tremble ~ fear** vor Angst zittern; **I have no money ~ me** ich habe kein Geld dabei *od.* bei mir; **sleep ~ the window open** bei offenem Fenster schlafen

with'draw 1 *v.t., forms as* DRAW 1: zurückziehen; abziehen ⟨*Truppen*⟩; **~ sth. from an account** etw. von einem Konto abheben

2 *v.i., forms as* DRAW 1: sich zurückziehen

withdrawal /wɪð'drɔːəl/ *n.*
(a) Zurücknahme, *die;* (of troops) Abzug, *der;* (of money) Abhebung, *die*
(b) (from drugs) Entzug, *der;* **~ symptoms** Entzugserscheinungen *Pl.*

with'drawn *adj.* (unsociable) verschlossen

wither /'wɪðə(r)/ 1 *v.t.* verdorren lassen
2 *v.i.* [ver]welken

■ **wither a'way** *v.i.* dahinwelken (geh.)

withered /'wɪðəd/ *adj.* verwelkt ⟨*Gras, Pflanze*⟩; verkrüppelt ⟨*Gliedmaße*⟩

withering /'wɪðərɪŋ/ *adj.* vernichtend ⟨*Blick*⟩

with'hold *v.t., forms as* HOLD²: **~ sth. from sb.** jmdm. etw. vorenthalten

within /wɪ'ðɪn/ *prep.* innerhalb; **stay/be ~ the law** den Boden des Gesetzes nicht verlassen; **~ eight miles of sth.** acht Meilen im Umkreis von etw.

without /wɪ'ðaʊt/ *prep.* ohne; **~ doing sth.** ohne etw. zu tun; **~ his knowing** ohne dass er davon weiß/wusste

with'stand *v.t.*, with'stood standhalten (+ *Dat.*); aushalten ⟨*Beanspruchung, hohe Temperaturen*⟩

witness /'wɪtnɪs/ 1 *n.* Zeuge, *der*/Zeugin, *die* (of, to *Gen.*)
2 *v.t.* **(a)** (see) **~ sth.** Zeuge/Zeugin einer Sache (*Gen.*) sein
(b) bestätigen ⟨*Unterschrift*⟩

'witness box (Brit.), **'witness stand** (Amer.) *ns.* Zeugenstand, *der*

witticism /'wɪtɪsɪzm/ *n.* Witzelei, *die*

wittingly /'wɪtɪŋlɪ/ *adv.* wissentlich

witty /'wɪtɪ/ *adj.* witzig; geistreich ⟨*Person*⟩

wives *pl. of* WIFE

wizard /'wɪzəd/ *n.* Zauberer, *der*

wizardry /'wɪzədrɪ/ *n.* Zauberei, *die*

wizened /'wɪzənd/ *adj.* runz[e]lig

WMD *abbr.* = **weapon of mass destruction** MVW

wobble /'wɒbl/ *v.i.* wackeln

wobbly /'wɒblɪ/ *adj.* wack[e]lig

woe /wəʊ/ *n.* (arch./literary/joc.) **~[s]** Jammer, *der;* **~ betide you!** wehe dir!

woebegone /'wəʊbɪɡɒn/ *adj.* jammervoll

woeful /'wəʊfl/ *adj.* (deplorable) beklagenswert; (distressed) jammervoll

wok /wɒk/ *n.* (Cookery) Wok, *der*

woke, woken ▶ WAKE¹ 1, 2

wolf /wʊlf/ 1 *n., pl.* **wolves** /wʊlvz/ Wolf, *der*
2 *v.t.* **~ [down]** verschlingen

woman /'wʊmən/ *n., pl.* **women** /'wɪmɪn/ Frau, *die;* **~ doctor** Ärztin, *die;* **~ friend** Freundin, *die*

womanize /'wʊmənaɪz/ *v.i.* den Frauen nachstellen

womanizer /'wʊmənaɪzə(r)/ *n.* Schürzenjäger, *der*

'womanly *adj.* fraulich

womb /wuːm/ *n.* Gebärmutter, *die*

women *pl. of* WOMAN

women: ~folk *n. pl.* Frauen *Pl.;* **W~'s 'Lib** (coll.), **W~'s Libe'ration** *ns.* die Frauenbewegung; **~'s movement** *n.* Frauenbewegung, *die;* **~'s 'prison** *n.* Frauengefängnis, *das;* **~'s 'refuge** *n.* Frauenhaus, *das;* **~'s 'rights** *n. pl.* die Rechte der Frau

won ▶ WIN 1, 2

wonder /'wʌndə(r)/ 1 *n.* **(a)** (thing) Wunder, *das*
(b) (feeling) Staunen, *das*
2 *adj.* Wunder-
3 *v.i.* sich wundern; staunen (**at** über + *Akk.*)
4 *v.t.* sich fragen; **I ~ what the time is** wie viel Uhr mag es wohl sein?; **I ~ whether I might open the window** dürfte ich vielleicht das Fenster öffnen?

wonderful /'wʌndəfl/ *adj.*, **wonderfully** /'wʌndəfəlɪ/ *adv.* wunderbar

wondering /'wʌndərɪŋ/ *adj.*, **wonderingly** /'wʌndərɪŋlɪ/ *adv.* staunend

won't /wəʊnt/ (coll.) = **will not;** ▶ WILL¹

woo /wuː/ *v.t.* **(a)** (literary: court) **~ sb.** um jmdn. werben (geh.)
(b) umwerben ⟨*Kunden, Wähler*⟩

wood /wʊd/ *n.* **(a)** Holz, *das;* **touch ~** (Brit.), **knock on ~** (Amer.) unberufen!
(b) (trees) Wald, *der*

wood: ~ carving *n.* (object) Holzschnitzerei, *die;* **~craft** *n.* (~work) Holzschnitzerei, *die;* **~cut** *n.* Holzschnitt, *der;* **~cutter** *n.* Holzfäller, *der*

'wooded *adj.* bewaldet

wooden /'wʊdn/ *adj.* **(a)** hölzern; Holz-
(b) (fig.: stiff) hölzern

wood: ~land /'wʊdlənd/ *n.* Waldland, *das;* **~pecker** *n.* Specht, *der;* **~ pigeon** *n.* Ringeltaube, *die;* **~shed** *n.* Holzschuppen, *der;* **~wind** *n.* the **~wind [section]** die Holzbläser *Pl.;* **~wind instrument** Holzblasinstrument, *das;* **~work** *n.* **(a)** (craft) Arbeiten mit Holz; **(b)** (things) Holzarbeit[en *Pl.*]; **~worm** *n.* Holzwurm, *der;* **it's got ~worm** da ist der Holzwurm drin (ugs.)

'woody *adj.* **(a)** (wooded) waldreich
(b) (consisting of wood) holzig

w

wool /wʊl/ n. Wolle, die; attrib. Woll-
woollen (Amer.: **woolen**) /'wʊlən/
⊞ adj. wollen
⊡ n. ～s Wollsachen Pl.
'**woolly** adj. (a) wollig; Woll⟨pullover, -mütze⟩
(b) (confused) verschwommen
woozy /'wuːzɪ/ adj. (coll.) (a) (dizzy) duselig (ugs.)
(b) (drunk) angeduselt (salopp)
word /wɜːd/ ⊞ n. Wort, das; ～s (of song or actor) Text, der; in other ～s mit anderen Worten; ～ for ～: Wort für Wort; too funny etc. for ～s unsagbar komisch usw.; have ～s einen Wortwechsel haben; have a ～ [with sb.] about sth. [mit jmdm.] über etw. (Akk.) sprechen; could I have a ～ [with you]? kann ich dich mal sprechen?; say a few ～s ein paar Worte sprechen; keep/break one's ～: sein Wort halten/brechen; by ～ of mouth durch mündliche Mitteilung; send ～ that ...: Nachricht geben, dass ...
⊡ v.t. formulieren
'**wording** n. Formulierung, die
word: ～ **order** n. Wortstellung, die; ～**play** n. Wortspiel, das; ～ **processing** n. Textverarbeitung, die; ～ **processor** n. Textverarbeitungssystem, das
wordy /'wɜːdɪ/ adj. weitschweifig
wore ▸ WEAR 2, 3
work /wɜːk/ ⊞ n. (a) Arbeit, die; at ～ (engaged in ～ing) bei der Arbeit; (fig.: operating) am Werk; (at job) auf der Arbeit; out of ～: arbeitslos; be in ～: eine Stelle haben; set to ～ ⟨Person:⟩ sich an die Arbeit machen; go out to ～: arbeiten gehen
(b) ～s sing. or pl. (factory) Werk, das
(c) ～s pl. (～ing parts) Werk, das; (operations) Arbeiten Pl.
(d) (thing made or achieved) Werk, das; a ～ of art/literature ein Kunstwerk/literarisches Werk
⊡ v.i. (a) arbeiten
(b) (function effectively) funktionieren; make the television ～: den Fernsehapparat in Ordnung bringen
(c) (have an effect) wirken (on auf + Akk.)
(d) ～ loose sich lockern
⊟ v.t. (a) bedienen ⟨Maschine⟩; betätigen ⟨Bremse⟩
(b) (get labour from) arbeiten lassen
(c) ausbeuten ⟨Steinbruch, Grube⟩
(d) (cause to go gradually) führen; ～ one's way up/into sth. sich hocharbeiten/in etw. hineinarbeiten
∎ **work 'off** v.t. (a) (get rid of) loswerden; abreagieren ⟨Wut⟩
(b) abarbeiten ⟨Schuld⟩
∎ '**work on** v.t. (a) ～ on sth. an etw. (Dat.) arbeiten
(b) (try to persuade) ～ on sb. jmdn. bearbeiten (ugs.)
∎ **work 'out** ⊞ v.t. (a) (calculate) ausrechnen

(b) (solve) lösen
(c) (devise) ausarbeiten
⊡ v.i. (a) sth. ～s out at £2 etw. ergibt 2 Pfund
(b) (have result) laufen; things ～ed out [well] in the end es ist schließlich doch alles gut gegangen
∎ **work 'up** ⊞ v.t. (excite) aufpeitschen ⟨Menge⟩; get ～ed up sich aufregen
⊡ v.i. ～ up to sth. ⟨Musik:⟩ sich zu etw. steigern; ⟨Geschichte, Film:⟩ auf etw. (Akk.) zusteuern
workable /'wɜːkəbl/ adj. (feasible) durchführbar
workaholic /wɜːkə'hɒlɪk/ n. (coll.) arbeitswütiger Mensch
work: ～**bench** n. Werkbank, die; ～**day** n. Werktag, der
'**worker** n. Arbeiter, der/Arbeiterin, die
'**worker bee** n. Arbeiterbiene, die
work: ～ **ethic** n. Arbeitsethos, das; ～ **experience** n. (for schoolchildren) Praktikum, das; ～**force** n. Belegschaft, die;
'**working** adj. (a) (in work) werktätig
(b) ～ model funktionsfähiges Modell
working: ～ '**capital** n. Betriebskapital, das; ～ '**class** n. Arbeiterklasse, die; ～**-class** adj. der Arbeiterklasse nachgestellt; sb. is ～-class jmd. gehört zur Arbeiterklasse; ～ **clothes** n. pl. Arbeitskleidung, die; ～ '**day** n. (a) (portion of day) Arbeitstag, der; (b) (day when work is done) Werktag, der; ～ '**hours** n. pl. Arbeitszeit, die; ～ '**knowledge** n. ausreichende Kenntnisse (of in + Dat.); ～ '**mother** n. berufstätige Mutter; ～ '**order** n. be in [good] ～ order betriebsbereit sein; ⟨Auto:⟩ fahrbereit sein; ～'-**over** n. (sl.) Abreibung, die (ugs.); ～ '**week** n. Arbeitswoche, die; a 35-hour ～ week eine 35-Stunden-Woche; ～ '**wife** n. berufstätige Ehefrau
work: ～**load** n. Arbeitslast, die; ～**man** /'wɜːkmən/ n., pl. ～**men** /'wɜːkmən/ Arbeiter, der; ～**manship** /'wɜːkmənʃɪp/ n. (quality) Kunstfertigkeit, die; ～**out** n. [Fitness]training, das; ～ **permit** n. Arbeitserlaubnis, die; ～**sheet** n. (a) (recording work done) Arbeitszettel, der; (b) (for student) Formular mit Prüfungsfragen; ～**shop** n. (a) (room) Werkstatt, die; (b) (building) Werk, das; ～**station** n. (Comp.) Workstation, die; ～ **table** n. Arbeitstisch, der; ～**-to-'rule** n. Dienst nach Vorschrift
world /wɜːld/ n. (a) Welt, die; in the ～: auf der Welt; the tallest building in the ～: das höchste Gebäude der Welt; all over the ～: in od. auf der ganzen Welt
(b) (vast amount) it will do him a or the ～ of good es wird ihm unendlich gut tun; a ～ of difference ein weltweiter Unterschied
world: W～ '**Bank** n. Weltbank, die;

~ **'champion** n. Weltmeister, der/-meisterin, die; **W~ 'Cup** n. Worldcup, der; **~-famous** adj. weltberühmt

'worldly adj. weltlich; weltlich eingestellt ⟨Person⟩

worldly 'wise adj. weltklug

world: ~ **'music** n. Weltmusik, die; ~ **'power** n. Weltmacht, die; ~ **'record** n. Weltrekord, der; **~-record holder** Weltrekordhalter, der/-halterin, die; **~-shaking** adj. welterschütternd; **W~ Trade organization** n. Welthandelsorganisation, die; ~ **view** n. Weltsicht, die; ~ **'war** n. Weltkrieg, der; **the First/Second W~ War, W~ War I/II** der Erste/Zweite Weltkrieg; der 1./2. Weltkrieg; **~wide** /'--/ adj. weltweit nicht präd.; **W~ Wide 'Web** n. (Comp.) World Wide Web, das

worm /wɜːm/ 1 n. Wurm, der 2 v.t. (a) ~ oneself into sb.'s favour sich in jmds. Gunst (Akk.) schleichen (b) ~ sth. out of sb. etw. aus jmdm. herausbringen (ugs.)

'worm-eaten adj. wurmstichig

worn ▶ WEAR 2, 3

'worn-out adj. (a) abgetragen ⟨Kleidungsstück⟩; abgenutzt ⟨Teppich⟩ (b) erschöpft ⟨Person⟩

worried /'wʌrɪd/ adj. besorgt

worry /'wʌrɪ/ 1 v.t. (a) beunruhigen (b) (bother) stören 2 v.i. sich (Dat.) Sorgen machen 3 n. Sorge, die; **sth. is the least of sb.'s worries** etw. ist jmds. geringste Sorge

'worrying adj. (a) (causing worry) beunruhigend (b) (full of worry) sorgenvoll ⟨Zeit, Woche⟩

worse /wɜːs/ 1 adj. schlechter; schlimmer ⟨Schmerz, Krankheit, Benehmen⟩ 2 adv. schlechter; schlimmer, schlechter ⟨sich benehmen⟩ 3 n. Schlimmeres

worsen /'wɜːsn/ 1 v.t. verschlechtern 2 v.i. sich verschlechtern

worship /'wɜːʃɪp/ 1 v.t., (Brit.) -pp-: (a) anbeten (b) (idolize) abgöttisch verehren 2 v.i., (Brit.) -pp- am Gottesdienst teilnehmen 3 n. (a) Anbetung, die; (service) Gottesdienst, der (b) Your/His W~: ≈ Euer/seine Ehren

'worshipper ⟨Amer.: **worshiper**⟩ n. Gottesdienstbesucher, der/-besucherin, die

worst /wɜːst/ 1 adj. schlechtest...; schlimmst... ⟨Schmerz, Krankheit, Benehmen⟩ 2 adv. am schlechtesten/schlimmsten 3 n. (a) **the ~:** der/die/das Schlimmste; **get** or **have the ~ of it** (suffer the most) am meisten zu leiden haben; **if the ~ comes to the ~:** wenn es zum Schlimmsten kommt

(b) (poorest in quality) Schlechteste, der/die/das

worsted /'wʊstɪd/ n. Kammgarn, das

worth /wɜːθ/ 1 adj. wert; **it's ~ £80** es ist 80 Pfund wert; **is it ~ hearing/the effort?** ist es hörenswert/der Mühe wert?; **is it ~ doing?** lohnt es sich?; **it isn't ~ it** es lohnt sich nicht 2 n. Wert, der; **ten pounds' ~ of petrol** Benzin für zehn Pfund

'worthless adj. (a) (valueless) wertlos (b) (having bad qualities) nichtswürdig

'worthwhile adj. lohnend

worthy /'wɜːðɪ/ adj. würdig

wouldn't /'wʊdnt/ (coll.) = would not; ▶ WILL[1]

wound[1] /wuːnd/ 1 n. Wunde, die 2 v.t. verwunden; (fig.) verletzen

wound[2] ▶ WIND[2]

wove, woven ▶ WEAVE[1] 2

wrangle /'ræŋgl/ 1 v.i. [sich] streiten 2 n. Streit, der

wrap /ræp/ 1 v.t., -pp- einwickeln; (fig.) hüllen; **~ped** abgepackt ⟨Brot usw.⟩; ~ **sth. [a]round sth.** etw. um etw. wickeln 2 n. Umschlag[e]tuch, das

■ **wrap 'up** v.t. (a) einwickeln (b) (conclude) abschließen (c) **be ~ped up in one's work** in seine Arbeit völlig versunken sein

'wrapper n. (a) sweet/toffee ~[s] Bonbonpapier, das (b) (of book) Schutzumschlag, der

'wrapping n. Verpackung, die

'wrapping paper n. (strong) Packpapier, das; (decorative) Geschenkpapier, das

wrath /rɒθ/ n. Zorn, der

wreak /riːk/ v.t. (a) (cause) anrichten (b) ~ **vengeance on sb.** an jmdm. Rache nehmen

wreath /riːθ/ n., pl. **wreaths** /riːðz, riːθs/ Kranz, der

wreck /rek/ 1 n. (a) Wrack, das (b) (destruction of ship) Schiffbruch, der 2 v.t. (a) (destroy) ruinieren; zu Schrott fahren ⟨Auto⟩; **be ~ed** (shipwrecked) Schiffbruch erleiden (b) (fig.: ruin) zerstören; ruinieren ⟨Gesundheit, Urlaub⟩

wreckage /'rekɪdʒ/ n. Wrackteile Pl.; (fig.) Trümmer Pl.

wren n. Zaunkönig, der

wrench /rentʃ/ 1 n. (a) (esp. Amer.: spanner) Schraubenschlüssel, der (b) (violent twist) Verrenkung, die (c) (fig.) **be a great ~ [for sb.]** sehr schmerzhaft für jmdn. sein 2 v.t. (a) reißen; ~ **sth. from sb.** jmdm. etw. entreißen (b) ~ **one's ankle** sich (Dat.) den Knöchel verrenken

wrest /rest/ v.t. ~ **sth. from sb.** jmdm. etw. entreißen

wrestle /'resl/ *v.i.* ringen
wrestler /'reslə(r)/ *n.* Ringer, *der*/ Ringerin, *die*
wrestling /'reslɪŋ/ *n.* Ringen, *das*
wretch /retʃ/ *n.* Kreatur, *die*
wretched /'retʃɪd/ *adj.* **(a)** (miserable) unglücklich
(b) (coll.: damned) elend
(c) (very bad) erbärmlich
wriggle /'rɪgl/ *v.i.* **(a)** sich winden; ‹*Fisch:*› zappeln
(b) (move) sich schlängeln
2 *v.t.* ~ one's way sich schlängeln
3 *n.* Windung, *die*
wring /rɪŋ/ *v.t.*, wrung /rʌŋ/ **(a)** wringen; ~ out auswringen
(b) ~ sb.'s hand jmdm. fest die Hand drücken; ~ the neck of an animal einem Tier den Hals umdrehen
(c) ~ sth. from *or* out of sb. (fig.) jmdm. etw. abpressen
wringing 'wet *adj.* tropfnass
wrinkle /'rɪŋkl/ **1** *n.* Falte, *die;* (in paper) Knick, *der*
2 *v.t.* falten
3 *v.i.* sich in Falten legen
wrinkled /'rɪŋkld/ *adjs.* runz[e]lig
wrinkly /'rɪŋklɪ/ **1** *adj.* runz[e]lig
2 *n.* (coll.) Grufti, *der* (ugs.)
wrist /rɪst/ *n.* Handgelenk, *das*
'**wristwatch** *n.* Armbanduhr, *die*
writ /rɪt/ *n.* (Law) Verfügung, *die*
write /raɪt/ **1** *v.i.*, wrote /rəʊt/, written /'rɪtn/ schreiben; ~ to sb./a firm jmdm./an eine Firma schreiben
2 *v.t.*, wrote, written schreiben; ausschreiben ‹*Scheck*›; the written language die Schriftsprache; written applications schriftliche Anträge *Pl.*
■ **write** 'back *v.i.* zurückschreiben
■ **write** '**down** *v.t.* aufschreiben
■ **write** '**off** **1** *v.t.* **(a)** abschreiben ‹*Schulden, Verlust*›
(b) (destroy) zu Schrott fahren
2 *v.i.* ~ off for sth. etw. [schriftlich] anfordern
'**write-off** *n.* Totalschaden, *der*

write-pro'**tect** *v.t.* (Comp.) shreibschützen; mit einem Shreibschutz versehen
writer /'raɪtə(r)/ *n.* Schriftsteller, *der*/Schriftstellerin, *die;* (of letter, article) Verfasser, *der*/Verfasserin, *die*
'**write-up** *n.* (by critic) Kritik, *die*
writhe /raɪð/ *v.i.* sich winden
writing /'raɪtɪŋ/ *n.* **(a)** Schreiben, *das;* put sth. in ~: etw. schriftlich machen (ugs.)
(b) (handwriting, something written) Schrift, *die*
'**writing paper** *n.* Schreibpapier, *das*
written ▶ WRITE
wrong /rɒŋ/ **1** *adj.* **(a)** (morally bad) unrecht (geh.); (unfair) ungerecht
(b) (mistaken) falsch; be ~ ‹*Person:*› sich irren; the clock is ~: die Uhr geht falsch
(c) (not suitable) falsch; give the ~ answer eine falsche Antwort geben; [the] ~ way round verkehrt herum
(d) (out of order) nicht in Ordnung; what's ~? was ist los?
2 *adv.* falsch
3 *n.* Unrecht, *das;* do ~: Unrecht tun
4 *v.t.* ~ sb. jmdn. ungerecht behandeln
'**wrongdoer** *n.* Übeltäter, *der*/-täterin, *die;* Missetäter, *der*/-täterin, *die* (geh.)
'**wrongdoing** *n.* no indef. art. Missetaten *Pl.* (geh.)
wrongful /'rɒŋfl/ *adj.* **(a)** (unfair) unrecht (geh.)
(b) (unlawful) rechtswidrig
'**wrongfully** *adv.* **(a)** (unfairly) unrecht (geh.) ‹*handeln*›; zu Unrecht ‹*beschuldigen*›
(b) (unlawfully) rechtswidrig
'**wrongly** *adv.* **(a)** falsch
(b) (mistakenly) zu Unrecht
(c) ▶ WRONGFULLY A
wrote ▶ WRITE
wrought iron /rɔːt 'aɪən/ *n.* Schmiedeeisen, *das; attrib.* schmiedeeisern
wrung ▶ WRING
wry /raɪ/ *adj.*, ~er *or* wrier /'raɪə(r)/, ~est *or* wriest /'raɪɪst/ ironisch ‹*Blick*›; fein ‹*Humor, Witz*›
WTO *abbr.* ▶ WORLD TRADE ORGANIZATION
WWW *abbr.* = **World Wide Web** WWW

Xx

X, x /eks/ *n.* X, x, *das*
xenophobia /zenə'fəʊbɪə/ *n.* Fremdenfeindlichkeit, *die*
xenophobic /zenə'fəʊbɪk/ *adj.* fremdenfeindlich
Xerox ®, **xerox** /'zɪərɒks/ **1** *n.* (copy)

Xerokopie, *die*
2 **xerox** *v.t.* xerokopieren
Xmas /'krɪsməs, 'eksməs/ *n.* (coll.) Weihnachten, *das*
'**X-ray** **1** *n.* (picture) Röntgenaufnahme, *die*
2 *v.t.* röntgen; durchleuchten ‹*Gepäck*›

Yy

Y, y /waɪ/ *n.* Y, y, *das*

yacht /jɒt/ *n.* **(a)** (for racing) Segeljacht, *die* **(b)** (for pleasure) Jacht, *die*

'yachting *n.* Segeln, *das*

yachtsman /'jɒtsmən/ *n., pl.* **yachtsmen** /'jɒtsmən/ Segler, *der*

yank (coll.) **1** *v.t.* reißen an (+ *Dat.*) **2** *n.* Reißen, *das*

Yank /jæŋk/ *n.* (Brit. coll.: American) Ami, *der* (ugs.)

yap /jæp/ *v.i.,* -pp- kläffen

yard[1] /jɑːd/ *n.* (measure) Yard, *das*

yard[2] *n.* **(a)** (attached to building) Hof, *der;* in the ~: auf dem Hof **(b)** (for storage) Lager, *das* **(c)** (Amer.: garden) Garten, *der*

'yardstick *n.* (fig.) Maßstab, *der*

yarn /jɑːn/ *n.* **(a)** (thread) Garn, *das* **(b)** (coll.: story) Geschichte, *die*

yawn /jɔːn/ **1** *n.* Gähnen, *das* **2** *v.i.* gähnen

'yawning *adj.* gähnend

year /jɪə(r)/ *n.* **(a)** Jahr, *das; for* [many] ~s jahrelang; once a ~, every ~: einmal im Jahr; a ten-~-old ein Zehnjähriger/eine Zehnjährige **(b)** (group of students, vintage of wine) Jahrgang, *der*

'yearbook *n.* Jahrbuch, *das*

'yearly **1** *adj.* jährlich; Einjahres⟨*abonnement*⟩ **2** *adv.* jährlich

yearn /jɜːn/ *v.i.* ~ for *or* after sth./for sb. sich nach etw./jmdm. sehnen; ~ to do sth. sich danach sehnen, etw. zu tun

'yearning *n.* Sehnsucht, *die*

yeast /jiːst/ *n.* Hefe, *die*

yell /jel/ **1** *n.* gellender Schrei **2** *v.t. & i.* [gellend] schreien

yellow /'jeləʊ/ **1** *adj.* gelb **2** *n.* Gelb, *das*

yellow: ~ **'card** *n.* (Footb.) gelbe Karte; ~ **'fever** *n.* Gelbfieber, *das*

yellowish /'jeləʊɪʃ/ *adj.* gelblich

Yellow 'Pages ® *n. pl.* gelbe Seiten *Pl.*

yelp /jelp/ **1** *v.i.* jaulen **2** *n.* Jaulen, *das*

yen /jen/ *n.* (coll.: longing) **sb. has a** ~ **to do sth.** es drängt jmdn. danach, etw. zu tun

yes /jes/ **1** *adv.* ja; (in contradiction) doch **2** *n., pl.* ~es Ja, *das*

'yes-man *n.* (coll. derog.) Jasager, *der* (abwertend)

yesterday /'jestədeɪ, 'jestədɪ/ **1** *n.* gestern; **the day before** ~: vorgestern; ~'s **paper** die gestrige Zeitung **2** *adv.* gestern; **the day before** ~: vorgestern

yet /jet/ **1** *adv.* **(a)** (still) noch; ~ **again** noch einmal **(b)** (hitherto) bisher; **his best** ~: sein bisher bestes **(c)** *neg.* **not [just]** ~: [jetzt] noch nicht **(d)** (before all is over) doch noch; **he could win** ~: er könnte noch gewinnen **(e)** *with compar.* (even) noch **(f)** (nevertheless) doch **2** *conj.* doch

yew /juː/ *n.* ~ **[tree]** Eibe, *die*

Yiddish /'jɪdɪʃ/ **1** *adj.* jiddisch **2** *n.* Jiddisch, *das; see also* ENGLISH 2A

yield /jiːld/ **1** *v.t.* (give) bringen; hervorbringen ⟨*Ernte*⟩; abwerfen ⟨*Gewinn*⟩ **2** *v.i.* **(a)** sich unterwerfen **(b)** (give right of way) Vorfahrt gewähren **3** *n.* Ertrag, *der*

yob /jɒb/ *n.* (Brit. coll.) Rowdy, *der*

yobbish /'jɒbɪʃ/ *adj.* (Brit. coll.) rowdyhaft

yobbo /'jɒbəʊ/ *n. pl.* ~s ▸ YOB

yodel /'jəʊdl/ *v.i. & t.,* (Brit.) -ll- jodeln

yoga /'jəʊgə/ *n.* Joga, *der od. das*

yoghurt, yogurt /'jɒgət/ *n.* Joghurt, *der od. das*

yoke /jəʊk/ *n.* Joch, *das*

yokel /'jəʊkl/ *n.* [Bauern]tölpel, *der*

yolk /jəʊk/ *n.* Dotter, *der od. das;* Eigelb, *das*

yonder /'jɒndə(r)/ (literary) **1** *adj.* ~ **tree** jener Baum dort (geh.) **2** *adv.* dort drüben

Yorkshire 'pudding *n.* Yorkshirepudding, *der*

you /jʊ, stressed juː/ *pron.* **(a)** *sing./pl.* du/ihr; (polite) *sing. or pl.* Sie; *as direct object* dich/euch/Sie; *as indirect object* dir/euch/ Ihnen; *refl.* dich/dir/euch; (polite) sich; **it was** ~: du warst/ihr wart/Sie waren es **(b)** (one) man

you'd /jʊd, stressed juːd/ **(a)** = you had **(b)** = you would

you'll /jʊl, stressed juːl/ **(a)** = you will **(b)** = you shall

young /jʌŋ/ **1** *adj.,* ~**er** /'jʌŋgə(r)/, ~**est** /'jʌŋgɪst/ jung **2** *n. pl.* (of animals) Junge *Pl.;* **the** ~ (~ people) die jungen Leute

youngish *adj.* ziemlich jung

youngster /'jʌŋstə(r)/ *n.* **(a)** (child) Kleine, *der/die/das* ⋯⟶

(b) (young person) Jugendliche, *der/die*

your /jə(r), *stressed* jʊə(r), jɔː(r)/ *poss. pron.* *attrib.: sing.* dein; *pl.* euer; (polite) *sing. or pl.* Ihr

you're /jə(r), *stressed* jʊə(r), jɔː(r)/ = **you are**

yours /jʊəz, jɔːz/ *poss. pron. pred.: sing.* deiner/deine/dein[e]s; *pl.* eurer/eure/eures; (polite) *sing. or pl.* Ihrer/Ihre/Ihr[e]s; *see also* HERS

yourself /jə'self, jʊə'self, jɔː'self/ *pron.* **(a)** *emphat.* selbst **(b)** *refl.* dich/dir/(polite) sich. *See also* HERSELF

yourselves /jə'selvz, jʊə'selvz, jɔː'selvz/ *pron.* **(a)** *emphat.* selbst **(b)** *refl.* euch/(polite) sich. *See also* HERSELF

youth /juːθ/ *n.* **(a)** Jugend, *die* **(b)** *pl.* ~s /juːðz/ (young man) Jugendliche, *der*

youth: ~ **centre** *n.* Jugendzentrum, *das;* ~ **club** *n.* Jugendklub, *der*

youthful /'juːθfl/ *adj.* jugendlich

'youth hostel *n.* Jugendherberge, *die*

you've /jʊv, *stressed* juːv/ = **you have**

yo-yo ® /'jəʊjəʊ/ *n., pl.* ~s Jo-Jo, *das*

Yugoslav /'juːɡəslɑːv/ ▶ YUGOSLAVIAN

Yugoslavia /juːɡə'slɑːvɪə/ *pr. n.* Jugoslawien (*das*); **ex-**~: Ex-Jugoslawien (*das*)

Yugoslavian /juːɡə'slɑːvɪən/ [1] *adj.* jugoslawisch; **sb. is** ~: jmd. ist Jugoslawe/Jugoslawin [2] *n.* Jugoslawe, *der*/Jugoslawin, *die*

yuk /jʌk/ *int.* (coll.) bäh

yummy /'jʌmɪ/ (coll.) *int.* lecker

yuppie /'jʌpɪ/ *n.* (coll.) Yuppie, *der*

yuppie 'flu *n.* (coll.) Yuppie-Grippe, *die*

Zz

Z, z /zed, (Amer.) ziː/ *n.* Z, z, *das*

Zaire /zɑː'ɪə(r)/ *pr. n.* Zaire (*das*)

Zambia /'zæmbɪə/ *pr. n.* Sambia (*das*)

zany /'zeɪnɪ/ *adj.* irre komisch (ugs.); Wahnsinns⟨*humor, -komiker*⟩

zap /zæp/ (coll.) *v.i.* **-pp-** (Telev. coll.) zappen (ugs.)

zapper /'zæpə(r)/ *n.* (Telev. coll.) Drücker, *der* (ugs.)

zeal /ziːl/ *n.* Eifer, *der*

zealous /'zeləs/ *adj.* eifrig

zebra /'zebrə, 'ziːbrə/ *n.* Zebra, *das*

zebra 'crossing *n.* (Brit.) Zebrastreifen, *der*

zenith /'zenɪθ/ *n.* Zenit, *der*

zero /'zɪərəʊ/ *n., pl.* ~s Null, *die*

zero: ~-'**rated** *adj.* ~-rated goods nicht mehrwertsteuerpflichtige Güter; ~ '**tolerance** *n.* Nulltoleranz, *die* (**for, to, of** gegenüber)

zest /zest/ *n.* (enthusiasm) Begeisterung, *die;* ~ **for living** Lebenslust, *die*

zigzag /'zɪɡzæɡ/ [1] *adj.* zickzackförmig; Zickzack⟨*muster, -anordnung*⟩ [2] *n.* Zickzacklinie, *die*

Zimbabwe /zɪm'bɑːbwɪ/ *pr. n.* Simbabwe (*das*)

zinc /zɪŋk/ *n.* Zink, *das*

zip /zɪp/ [1] *n.* Reißverschluss, *der* [2] *v.t.,* **-pp-:** **(a)** ~ [up] sth. den Reißverschluss an etw. (*Dat.*) zuziehen **(b)** (Comp.) ~ [up] packen (*Datei*)

'zip bag *n.* Tasche, *die* mit Reißverschluss

'Zip code *n.* (Amer.) Postleitzahl, *die*

zip fastener ▶ ZIP 1

zipper /'zɪpə(r)/ ▶ ZIP 1

zither /'zɪðə(r)/ *n.* Zither, *die*

zodiac /'zəʊdɪæk/ *n.* Tierkreis, *der;* **sign of the** ~: Tierkreiszeichen, *das*

zombie (*Amer.:* **zombi**) /'zɒmbɪ/ *n.* Zombie, *der*

zone /zəʊn/ *n.* Zone, *die*

zoo /zuː/ *n.* Zoo, *der*

'zookeeper *n.* Zoowärter, *der*/-wärterin, *die*

zoological /zuːə'lɒdʒɪkl/ *adj.* zoologisch

zoologist /zuː'ɒlədʒɪst/ *n.* Zoologe, *der*/Zoologin, *die*

zoology /zuː'ɒlədʒɪ/ *n.* Zoologie, *die*

zoom /zuːm/ *v.i.* rauschen ■ **zoom 'in on** *v.t.* zoomen auf (+ *Akk.*)

'zoom lens *n.* Zoomobjektiv, *das*

zucchini /zʊ'kiːnɪ/ *n., pl. same or* ~s (esp. Amer.) Zucchino, *der*

Glossary of grammatical terms

Abbreviation A shortened form of a word or phrase: **etc.** = **usw.**

Absolute use The use of a transitive verb without an expressed object, as in: **I didn't** *realize*

Accusative The case of a direct object; some German prepositions take the accusative

Active In the active form the subject of the verb performs the action: **he asked** = **er hat gefragt**

Adjective A word describing a noun: **a** *red* **pencil** = **ein** *roter* **Stift**

Adverb A word that describes or changes the meaning of a verb, an adjective, or another adverb: **she sings** *beautifully* = **sie singt** *schön*

Article The definite article, **the** = **der/die/das**, and indefinite article, **a/an** = **ein/eine/ein**, used in front of a noun

Attributive An adjective or noun is attributive when it is used directly before a noun: **the** *black* **dog** = **der** *schwarze* **Hund**; *farewell* **speech** = **Abschiedsrede**

Auxiliary verb One of the verbs – as German **haben, sein, werden** - used to form the perfect or future tense: **I** *will* **help** = **ich** *werde* **helfen**

Cardinal number A whole number representing a quantity: **one/two/three** = **eins/zwei/drei**

Case The form of a noun, pronoun, adjective, or article that shows the part it plays in a sentence; there are four cases in German - nominative, accusative, genitive, and dative

Clause A self-contained section of a sentence that contains a subject and a verb

Collective noun A noun that is singular in form but refers to a group of individual persons or things, e.g. **royalty, grain**

Collocate A word that regularly occurs with another; in German, **Buch** is a typical collocate of the verb **lesen**.

Comparative The form of an adjective or adverb that makes it "more": **smaller** = **kleiner, more clearly** = **klarer**

Compound adjective An adjective formed from two or more separate words: **selbstbewusst (selbst + bewusst)** = **self-confident**

Compound noun A noun formed from two or more separate words: **der Flughafen (Flug+ Hafen)** = **airport**

Compound verb A verb formed by adding a prefix to a simple verb; in German, some compound verbs are separable **(an|fangen)**, and some are inseparable **(verlassen)**

Conditional tense A tense of a verb that expresses what might happen if something else occurred: **he would go** = **er würde gehen**

Conjugation Variation of the form of a verb to show tense, person, mood, etc.

Conjunction A word used to join clauses together: **and** = **und, because** = **weil**

Consonant In German, all the letters of the alphabet other than a, e, i, o, u, ä, ö, ü

Copula A verb, such as **be** or **become**, which links a **subject** and **predicate**

Dative The case of an indirect object; many German prepositions take the dative

Declension The form of a noun, pronoun, or adjective that corresponds to a particular case, number, or gender; some German nouns decline like adjectives, e.g. **Beamte, Taube**

Definite article: the = **der/die/das**

Demonstrative adjective: an adjective indicating the person or thing referred to; *this* **table** = *dieser* **Tisch**

Demonstrative pronoun A pronoun indicating the person or thing referred to; *this* **is my bicycle** = *das* **ist mein Fahrrad**

Direct object The noun or pronoun directly affected by the verb: **he caught** *the ball* = **er fing** *den Ball*

Direct speech A speaker's actual words or the use of these in writing

Elliptical Having a word or words omitted, especially where the sense can be guessed from the context

Ending Letters added to the stem of verbs, as well as to nouns and adjectives, according to tense, case, etc.

Feminine One of the three noun genders in German: **die Frau** = **the woman**

Future tense The tense of a verb that refers to something that will happen in the future: **I will go** = **ich werde gehen**

Glossary of grammatical terms

Gender One of the three groups of nouns, pronouns, and adjectives in German: masculine, feminine, or neuter

Genitive The case that shows possession; some prepositions in German take the genitive

Imperative A form of a verb that expresses a command: **go away! = geh weg!**

Imperfect tense The tense of a verb that refers to an uncompleted or a habitual action in the past: **I went there every Friday = ich ging jeden Freitag dorthin**

Impersonal verb A verb in English used only with 'it', and in German only with 'es': **it is raining = es regnet**

Indeclinable adjective An adjective that has no inflected forms, as German **klasse, Moskauer**

Indefinite article: a/an = **ein/eine/ein**

Indefinite pronoun A pronoun that does not identify a specific person or object: **one = man, something = etwas**

Indicative form The form of a verb used when making a statement of fact or asking questions of fact: **he is just coming = er kommt gleich**

Indirect object The noun or pronoun indirectly affected by the verb, at which the direct object is aimed: **I gave *him* the book = ich gab *ihm* das Buch**

Indirect speech A report of what someone has said which does not reproduce the exact words

Infinitive The basic part of a verb: **to play = spielen**

Inflect To change the ending or form of a word to show its tense or its grammatical relation to other words: **gehe** and **gehst** are inflected forms of the verb **gehen**

Inseparable verb A verb with a prefix that can never be separated from it: **verstehen, ich verstehe**

Interjection A sound, word, or remark expressing a strong feeling such as anger, fear, or joy: **oh! = ach!**

Interrogative pronoun A pronoun that asks a question: **who? = wer?**

Intransitive verb A verb that does not have a direct object: **he died suddenly = er ist plötzlich gestorben**

Irregular verb A verb that does not follow one of the set patterns and has its own individual forms

Masculine One of the three noun genders in German: **der Mann = the man, der Stuhl = the chair**

Modal verb A verb that is used with another verb (not a modal) to express permission, obligation, possibility, etc., as German **können, sollen**, English **might, should**

Negative expressing refusal or denial; **there aren't any = es gibt keine**

Neuter One of the three noun genders in German: **das Buch = the book, das Kind = the child**

Nominative The case of the subject of a sentence; in sentences with **sein** and **werden** the noun after the verb is in the nominative: **that is my car = das ist mein Auto**

Noun A word that names a person or a thing

Number The state of being either singular or plural

Object The word or words naming the person or thing acted upon by a verb or preposition, as 'Buch' in **er las das Buch** or 'ihm' in **ich traue ihm**

Ordinal number A number that shows a person's or thing's position in a series: **the *twenty-first* century = das *einundzwanzigste* Jahrhundert, the *second* door on the left = die *zweite* Tür links**

Part of speech A grammatical term for the function of a word; noun, verb, adjective, etc., are parts of speech.

Passive In the passive form the subject of the verb experiences the action rather than performs it: **he was asked = er wurde gefragt**

Past participle The part of a verb used to form past tenses: **she had gone, er hat gelogen**

Perfect tense The tense of a verb that refers to a completed action in the past or an action that started in the past and is still going on: **I have already eaten = ich habe schon gegessen; I have been reading all day = ich habe den ganzen Tag gelesen**

Person Any of the three groups of personal pronouns and forms taken by verbs; the **first person** (e.g. **I/ich**) refers to the person(s) speaking, the **second person** (e.g. **you/du**) refers to the person(s) spoken to; the **third person** (e.g. **he/er**) refers to the persons spoken about

Personal pronoun A pronoun that refers to a person or thing: **he/she/it = er/sie/es**

Phrasal verb A verb in English combined with a preposition or an adverb to have a particular meaning: **run away = weglaufen**

Phrase A self-contained section of a sentence that does not contain a full verb

Pluperfect tense The tense of a verb that refers to something that happened before a particular point in the past: **als ich ankam, war er schon** *losgefahren* = **when I arrived, he** *had* already *left*

Plural Of nouns etc., referring to more than one: **the trees = die Bäume**

Possessive adjective An adjective that shows possession, belonging to someone or something; **my = mein/meine/mein**

Possessive pronoun A pronoun that shows possession, belonging to someone or something: **mine = meiner/meine/meins**

Postpositive Placed after the word to which it relates, as **in stock** in the phrase **items in stock**

Predicate The part of a sentence that says something about the subject, e.g. **went home** in **John went home**

Predicative An adjective is predicative when it comes after a verb such as **be** or **become** in English, or after **sein** or **werden** in German: **she is beautiful = sie ist schön**

Prefix A letter or group of letters added to the beginning of a word to change its meaning; in German, the prefix can move from separable verbs (**an|fangen**), but stays fixed to inseparable verbs (**verlassen**)

Preposition A word that stands in front of a noun or pronoun, relating it to the rest of the sentence; in German prepositions are always followed by a particular case, usually either the accusative or dative, but occasionally the genitive: **with = mit (+ dative), for = für (+ accusative), because of = wegen (+ genitive)**

Present participle The part of a verb that in English ends in –ing, and in German adds –d to the infinitive: **asking = fragend**

Present tense The tense of a verb that refers to something happening now: **I make = ich mache**

Pronoun A word that stands instead of a noun: **he = er, she = sie, mine = meiner/meine/meins**

Proper noun A name of a person, place, institution, etc., in English written with a capital letter at the start; **Germany**, the **Atlantic**, **Karl**, **Europa** are all proper nouns

Reflexive pronoun A pronoun that goes with a reflexive verb: in German **mich, dich, sich, uns, euch, sich**

Reflexive verb A verb whose object is the same as its subject; in German, it is used with a reflexive pronoun: **du sollst dich waschen = you should wash yourself**

Regular verb A verb that follows a set pattern in its different forms

Relative pronoun A pronoun that introduces a subordinate clause, relating to a person or thing mentioned in the main clause: **the man** *who* **visited us = der Mann,** *der* **uns besucht hat**

Reported Speech Another name for **Indirect speech**

Root The part of a word to which inflections are added; **fahr-** is the root of the verb **fahren**

Sentence A sequence of words, with a subject and a verb, that can stand on their own to make a statement, ask a question, or give a command

Separable verb A verb with a prefix that can be separated from it in some tenses: **anfangen, anzufangen, angefangen**, but **ich fange an, du fingst an**

Singular Of nouns etc., referring to just one: **the tree = der Baum**

Stem The part of a verb to which endings are added; **fahr-** is the stem of **fahren**

Subject In a clause or sentence, the noun or pronoun that causes the action of the verb: *he* **caught the ball =** *er* **fing den Ball**

Subjunctive A verb form that is used to express doubt or unlikelihood: **if I were to tell you that ... = wenn ich dir sagen würde, dass ...**

Subordinate clause A clause which adds information to the main clause of a sentence but cannot be used as a sentence by itself

Suffix A letter or group of letters joined to the end of a word to make another word, as **-heit** in **Schönheit**

Superlative The form of an adjective or adverb that makes it "most": **the** *smallest* **house = das** *kleinste* **Haus, most clearly = am klarsten**

Syllable A division of a word that contains a vowel sound that is pronounced as a single unit: **Helikopter** has four syllables, he-li-kop-ter

Tense The form of a verb that tells when the action takes place: present, future, imperfect, perfect, pluperfect

Transitive verb A verb that is used with a direct object: **she read the book = sie las das Buch**

Verb A word or group of words that describes an action: **the children** *are playing* **= die Kinder** *spielen*

Vowel In German, one of the following letters: **a, e, i, o, u, ä, ö, ü**

Summary of German grammar

1 Verbs

1.1 Regular verbs

Most German verbs are regular and add the same endings to their stem. You find the stem by taking away the **-en** (or sometimes just **-n**) from the end of the infinitive. The infinitive of the verb, for example the regular verb **machen**, is the form you look up in the dictionary. The stem of **machen** is **mach-**. There are six endings for each tense, to go with the different pronouns:

ich = *I*   du = *you*   er/sie/es = *he/she/it*
wir = *we*   ihr = *you*   sie/Sie = *they/you* (*polite form*).

1.2 Irregular verbs

Some German verbs are irregular and change their stem or add different endings. All the irregular verbs that appear in the dictionary are given in the following section, *German irregular verbs*.

1.3 Present tense

For example, *I make, I am making,* or *I do make*:

infinitive	ich	du	er/sie/es	wir	ihr	sie/Sie
machen	mache	machst	macht	machen	macht	machen

1.4 Imperfect tense

For example, *I made, I was making,* or *I used to make*:

infinitive	ich	du	er/sie/es	wir	ihr	sie/Sie
machen	machte	machtest	machte	machten	machtet	machten

1.5 Future tense

For example, *I will make* or *I shall make*. The future is formed by using the present tense of **werden**, which is the equivalent of *will* or *shall*, with the infinitive of the main verb: **ich werde machen**.

infinitive	ich	du	er/sie/es	wir	ihr	sie/Sie
werden	werde	wirst	wird	werden	werdet	werden

1.6 Perfect tense

For example, *I made* or *I have made*. Most German verbs form the perfect tense with the present tense of **haben**, which is the equivalent of *have*, plus the past participle: **ich habe gemacht**. Some verbs form the perfect tense with **sein** instead of **haben**, and these are all marked (*sein*) in the dictionary. They are either verbs expressing motion and involving a change of place:

> er ist heute nach Berlin gefahren = *he drove to Berlin today*
> *he went out* = er ist hinausgegangen

or, they express a change of state, and this includes verbs meaning to happen (**geschehen, passieren, vorkommen**):

> er ist aufgewacht = *he woke up*
> sie ist gestern gestorben = *she died yesterday*

infinitive	ich	du	er/sie/es	wir	ihr	sie/Sie
haben	habe	hast	hat	haben	habt	haben
sein	bin	bist	ist	sind	seid	sind

1.7 The subjunctive

This is a form of the verb that is used to express speculation, hope, and doubt, and in reported speech. (It is rarely used in English; one example is: *if I were you*, instead of *if I was you*.) The subjunctive is used in both written and spoken German.

> es könnte wahr sein = *it could be true*
> wenn ich du wäre, … = *if I were you*, …
> er sagt, dass er selten in die Stadt gehe = *he says he seldom goes into town*

Present subjunctive

infinitive	ich	du	er/sie/es	wir	ihr	sie/Sie
machen	mache	machest	mache	machen	machet	machen
sein	sei	sei(e)st	sei	seien	seid	seien

Imperfect subjunctive

For regular verbs this is the same as the normal imperfect forms, but irregular verbs vary.

infinitive	ich	du	er/sie/es	wir	ihr	sie/Sie
machen	machte	machtest	machte	machten	machtet	machten
werden	würde	würdest	würde	würden	würdet	würden
sein	wäre	wär(e)st	wäre	wären	wär(e)t	wären

1.8 Conditional tense

The conditional tense expresses what would happen if something else occurred. The imperfect subjunctive of **werden** (**würde, würdest**, etc) is used with the infinitive to form the conditional tense.

> er würde gehen = *he would go*
> das würde ich nicht machen = *I wouldn't do that*

1.9 Reflexive verbs

The object of a reflexive verb is the same as its subject. In German, the object is a reflexive pronoun. This is usually in the accusative (**ich wasche mich** = *I wash myself*). The reflexive pronouns of some verbs are in the dative (**ich stelle mir vor** = *I imagine*), and these are marked in both halves of the dictionary with the label (*Dat*).

infinitive	ich	du	er/sie/es	wir	ihr	sie/Sie
sich waschen	wasche mich	wäschst dich	wäscht sich	waschen uns	wascht euch	waschen sich
sich vorstellen	stelle mir vor	stellst dir vor	stellt sich vor	stellen uns vor	stellt euch vor	stellen sich vor

1.10 The passive

In the passive, the subject of the verb experiences the action rather than performs it: **er wurde gefragt** = *he was asked*. In German, the passive is formed as follows:

PRESENT PASSIVE	es wird gemacht (present tense of **werden** + past participle)	*it is done*
IMPERFECT PASSIVE	es wurde gemacht (imperfect tense of **werden** + past participle)	*it was done*
FUTURE PASSIVE	es wird gemacht werden (present tense of **werden** + past participle + **werden**)	*it will be done*
PERFECT PASSIVE	es ist gemacht worden (present tense of **sein** + past participle + **worden**)	*it has been done*

When forming the perfect passive, note that the past participle of **werden** used is **worden** rather than **geworden**.

1.11 Separable verbs

Some German verbs have stressed separable prefixes, such as **ab-, an-, aus, her-, hin-, nach-, vor-, zu-**. These prefixes become detached from the main verb in the simple tenses: **hinausgehen: ich gehe hinaus**, **sie ging hinaus**. In compound tenses formed with the past participle, for example the perfect tense, the **ge-** of the past participle comes between the prefix and the verb:

er/sie/es hat angefangen = *he/she/it has begun*
er/sie/es ist angekommen = *he/she/it has arrived*

1.12 Inseparable verbs

The following unstressed prefixes are never separated from their verb in either simple or compound tenses and do not take **ge-** in the past participle:

be-, emp-, ent-, er-, ge-, ver-, zer-.
er begleitet seinen Bruder = *he is accompanying his brother*
er wurde nicht begleitet = *he was not accompanied*

2 Articles

The definite article (*the*) can be translated in the nominative case by **der**, **die** or **das** in German. Similarly the indefinite article (*a*) can be translated by **ein**, **eine**, or **ein**.

Summary of German grammar

There are three genders of nouns in German: masculine (**der Mann** = *the man*), feminine (**die Frau** = *the woman*), and neuter (**das Buch** = *the book*). There are two forms of number: singular (**der Baum** = *the tree*) and plural (**die Bäume** = *the trees*). And there are four cases, which show the part a noun plays in a sentence: nominative (for the subject), accusative (for the object), genitive (to show possession), and dative (for the indirect object). The plural forms of the definite article are the same for all three genders. More information on gender is given below.

2.1 Definite article: der/die/das, (*plural*) die = *the*

	SINGULAR masculine	feminine	neuter	PLURAL all genders
NOMINATIVE	**der** Mann	**die** Frau	**das** Buch	**die** Bäume
ACCUSATIVE	**den** Mann	**die** Frau	**das** Buch	**die** Bäume
GENITIVE	**des** Mannes	**der** Frau	**des** Buches	**der** Bäume
DATIVE	**dem** Mann	**der** Frau	**dem** Buch	**den** Bäumen

2.2 Indefinite article

ein/eine/ein = *a* or *an*. This article can only be singular.

	masculine	feminine	neuter
NOMINATIVE	**ein** Mann	**eine** Frau	**ein** Buch
ACCUSATIVE	**einen** Mann	**eine** Frau	**ein** Buch
GENITIVE	**eines** Mannes	**einer** Frau	**eines** Buches
DATIVE	**einem** Mann	**einer** Frau	**einem** Buch

3 Nouns

In German, all nouns take an initial capital letter wherever they appear in a sentence: **der Baum**, **die Schule**, **das Buch**.

3.1 Gender

All German nouns belong to one of the three genders: masculine (**der Mann** = *the man*), feminine (**die Frau** = *the woman*), and neuter (**das Buch** = *the book*). These three examples are logical, with masculine for a male person, feminine for a female person, and neuter for an object. But genders of German nouns do not always follow logic. For example, **der Fluss** (= *the river*), **die Menge** (= *the quantity/crowd*), **das Haus** (= *the house*). **Das Mädchen** (= *the girl*) is neuter and not feminine, because the ending -**chen** is always neuter.

The gender of German nouns is given in both sides of the dictionary by adding **der**, **die**, or **das** after each noun. There are some general rules regarding the gender of groups of nouns, but these cover only a small proportion of them and in many cases a noun's gender can only be established by looking it up.

. . . .

3.2 Masculine nouns

■ male persons and animals: **der Arbeiter** = *worker*; **der Bär** = *bear*

■ 'doers' and 'doing' instruments ending in **-er** in German: **der Gärtner** = *gardener*; **der Computer** = *computer*

■ days, months, and seasons: **(der) Montag** = *Monday*; **(der) März** = *March*; **der Frühling** = *spring*

■ words ending in **-ich**, **-ig**, and **-ling**: **der Strich** = line; **der Honig** = *honey*; **der Lehrling** = *apprentice*

■ words ending in **-ismus**, **-ist**, and **-ant**: **der Kapitalismus** = *capitalism*; **der Kriminalist** = *detective*; **der Diamant** = *diamond*

3.3 Feminine nouns

■ female persons and animals: **die Schauspielerin** = *actress*; **die Henne** = *hen*. The feminine form of professions and animals is made by adding **-in** to the masculine: **der Schauspieler/die Schauspielerin** = *actor/ actress*

■ nouns ending in **-ei**, **-ie**, **-ik**, **-in**, **-ion**, **-heit**, **-keit**, **-schaft**, **-tät**, **-ung**, **-ur**: **die Gärtnerei** = *gardening*; **die Energie** = *energy*; **die Million** = *million*; **die Freiheit** = *freedom*; **die Freundlichkeit** = *friendliness*; **die Feindschaft** = *enmity*; **die Universität** = *university*; **die Verwaltung** = *management*; **die Natur** = *nature*

■ many nouns ending in **-e**: **die Blume** = *flower*. Note that there are many common exceptions, including **der Name** = *name*; **der Käse** = *cheese*; **das Ende** = *end*

3.4 Neuter nouns

■ names of continents, most countries, and towns: **(das) Europa** = *Europe*; **(das) Deutschland** = *Germany*; **(das) Köln** = *Cologne*

■ nouns ending in **-chen** and **-lein** (diminutive suffixes): **das Mädchen**, **das Fräulein** = *girl*

■ most (but not all) nouns beginning with **Ge-** or ending in **-nis**, **-tel**, or **-um**: **das Geheimnis** = *secret*; **das Viertel** = *quarter*; **das Zentrum** = *centre*

■ infinitives of verbs used as nouns: **das Lachen** = *laughter*; **das Essen** = *food*

3.5 Compound nouns

When two nouns combine to make a compound noun, the gender of the compound is that of the second noun:

der Brief + die Marke = die Briefmarke (= *stamp*).

. . . .

3.6 Plural

There are no hard and fast rules for the the formation of plural nouns in German. An ending is generally added. Masculine nouns frequently add **-e (der Freund, die Freunde)**. When the vowels **-a-** or **-u-** appear in the stem of a noun, they may add an umlaut to give: **-ä-, -ü-** as in: (**der Gast, die Gäste; das Haus, die Häuser**). Feminine words ending in **-heit**, **-keit**, and **-ung** always add **-en** to make the plural (**die Abbildung, die Abbildungen**).

The plurals of all nouns are shown in the German-English part of the dictionary.

3.7 Case

There are four cases, which show the part a noun plays in a sentence: nominative, accusative, genitive, and dative. The noun's article changes according to the case, and the ending of the noun changes in some cases:

| | SINGULAR | | |
	masculine	**feminine**	**neuter**
NOMINATIVE	der Mann	die Frau	das Buch
ACCUSATIVE	den Mann	die Frau	das Buch
GENITIVE	des **Mann(e)s**	der Frau	des **Buch(e)s**
DATIVE	dem Mann	der Frau	dem Buch

| | PLURAL | | |
	masculine	**feminine**	**neuter**
NOMINATIVE	die Männer	die Frauen	die Bücher
ACCUSATIVE	die Männer	die Frauen	die Bücher
GENITIVE	der Männer	der Frauen	der Bücher
DATIVE	den **Männern**	den Frauen	den **Büchern**

The nominative is used for the subject of a sentence. It is important to note that in sentences with **sein** (*to be*) and **werden** (*to become*), the noun after the verb is in the nominative.

der Hund bellte = *the dog barked*
das ist mein Wagen = *that is my car*

The accusative is used for the direct object and after some prepositions (listed in section 7, *Prepositions*, below):

sie hat einen Sohn = *she has a son*

The genitive shows possession, and is also used after some prepositions (listed in section 7, *Prepositions*, below):

der Hund meines Mannes = *my husband's dog*

The dative is used for the indirect object. Some German verbs, such as **helfen**, take the dative when you might have expected the accusative. This information is given in both halves of the dictionary. The dative is also used after some prepositions (listed in section 7, *Prepositions*, below):

sie gab den Kindern die Bücher = *she gave the books to the children*
er hilft der Frau = *he is helping the woman*

The following sentence combines all four cases:

der Mann gibt der Frau den Bleistift = *the man gives the woman the girl's pencil*
des Mädchens

der Mann *is the subject* (*in the nominative*)
gibt *is the verb*
der Frau *is the indirect object* (*in the dative*)
den Bleistift *is the direct object* (*in the accusative*)
des Mädchens *is in the genitive* (*showing possession*).

4 Adjectives

An adjective is a word qualifying a noun. In German, an adjective in front of a noun adds endings that vary with the noun's gender, number, and case. Adjectives that come after a noun do not add endings.

4.1 Adjectives following the definite article **der**, **die**, **das** take the following endings:

	SINGULAR			PLURAL
	masculine	**feminine**	**neuter**	**all genders**
NOMINATIVE	der rote Hut	die rote Lampe	das rote Buch	die roten Autos
ACCUSATIVE	den roten Hut	die rote Lampe	das rote Buch	die roten Autos
GENITIVE	des roten Hutes	der roten Lampe	des roten Buches	der roten Autos
DATIVE	dem roten Hut	der roten Lampe	dem roten Buch	den roten Autos

4.2 German demonstrative adjectives follow the pattern of the definite article, and adjectives after them change their endings in the same way as after **der/die/das**. For example, **dieser/diese/dieses** (= *this*):

	SINGULAR			PLURAL
	masculine	**feminine**	**neuter**	**all genders**
NOMINATIVE	dieser	diese	dieses	diese
ACCUSATIVE	diesen	diese	dieses	diese
GENITIVE	dieses	dieser	dieses	dieser
DATIVE	diesem	dieser	diesem	diesen

Other adjectives of this type are:

jeder, jede, jedes = *every, each*
jener, jene, jenes = *that*
mancher, manche, manches = *many a, some*

solcher, solche, solches = *such*
welcher, welche, welches = *which*

4.3 Adjectives following the indefinite article **ein**, **eine**, **ein** take the following endings:

| | SINGULAR | | |
	masculine	feminine	neuter
NOMINATIVE	ein roter Hut	eine rote Lampe	ein rotes Buch
ACCUSATIVE	einen roten Hut	eine rote Lampe	ein rotes Buch
GENITIVE	eines roten Hutes	einer roten Lampe	eines roten Buches
DATIVE	einem roten Hut	einer roten Lampe	einem roten Buch

Other German adjectives that follow the pattern of the indefinite article, and take the same endings as **ein**, **eine**, **ein**, are:

dein = *your*	ihr = *her/their*	mein = *my*	kein = *no*
euer = *your*	sein = *his/its*	unser = *our*	
Ihr = *your*			

These adjectives can also be used in the plural: **keine Autos** = *no cars*; **deine Eltern** = *your parents*; **unsere Lehrer** = *our teachers*, etc. The endings of adjectives that follow them are the same in the plural regardless of gender:

| | PLURAL |
	all genders
NOMINATIVE	keine roten Autos
ACCUSATIVE	keine roten Autos
GENITIVE	keiner roten Autos
DATIVE	keinen roten Autos

4.4 Adjectives in front of a noun, without an article, take the following endings:

| | SINGULAR | | | PLURAL |
	masculine	feminine	neuter	all genders
NOMINATIVE	guter Wein	frische Milch	kaltes Bier	alte Leute
ACCUSATIVE	guten Wein	frische Milch	kaltes Bier	alte Leute
GENITIVE	guten Weins	frischer Milch	kalten Biers	alter Leute
DATIVE	gutem Wein	frischer Milch	kaltem Bier	alten Leuten

4.5 Adjectives as nouns

In German, adjectives can be used as nouns, spelt with a capital letter: **alt** = *old*, **ein Alter** = *an old man*, **eine Alte** = *an old woman*.

With the definite article (**der**, **die**, **das**), these nouns take the following endings:

| | SINGULAR | | | PLURAL |
	masculine	feminine	neuter	all genders
NOMINATIVE	der Alte	die Alte	das Alte	die Alten
ACCUSATIVE	den Alten	die Alte	das Alte	die Alten
GENITIVE	des Alten	der Alten	des Alten	der Alten
DATIVE	dem Alten	der Alten	dem Alten	den Alten

Adjectives can be used in this way in the neuter, usually to express an abstract concept: **das Gute** = *the good* (nominative and accusative), **des Guten** (genitive), **dem Guten** (dative).

With the indefinite article (**ein, eine, ein**), these nouns take the following endings:

	SINGULAR masculine	feminine	neuter	PLURAL all genders without an article
NOMINATIVE	ein Alter	eine Alte	ein Altes	Alte
ACCUSATIVE	einen Alten	eine Alte	ein Altes	Alte
GENITIVE	eines Alten	einer Alten	eines Alten	Alter
DATIVE	einem Alten	einer Alten	einem Alten	Alten

4.6 Comparatives and superlatives of adjectives

In English, the comparative of the adjective *small* is *smaller*, and of *difficult* is *more difficult*. The superlatives are *smallest* and *most difficult*. In German, there is just one way to form the comparative and superlative: by adding the endings **-er** and **-(e)st**:

klein, kleiner, der/die/das kleinste = *small, smaller, smallest*

Many adjectives whose stem vowel is **-a-**, **-o-**, or **-u-** take an umlaut to become **-ä-**, **-ö-** or **-ü-**, in the comparative and superlative:

kalt, kälter, der/die/das kälteste = *cold, colder, coldest*
grob, gröber, der/die/das gröbste = *rude, ruder, rudest*
jung, jünger, der/die/das jüngste = *young, younger, youngest*

Some important adjectives are irregular:

groß, größer, der/die/das größte = *big, bigger, biggest*
gut, besser, der/die/das beste = *good, better, best*
hoch, höher, der/die/das höchste = *high, higher, highest*
viel, mehr, der/die/das meiste = *much, more, most*
nah, näher, der/die/das nächste = *near, nearer, nearest*

Comparative and superlative adjectives take the same endings as basic adjectives:

ein kleineres Kind = *a smaller child*
ein billigerer Hut = *a cheaper hat*
der kälteste Monat = *the coldest month*
die nächste Bushaltestelle = *the nearest bus stop*

5 Adverbs

5.1 In German almost all adjectives can also be used as adverbs. Adverbs can modify a verb, an adjective, or another adverb.

sie singt schön (adverb: schön + verb: singt) = *she sings beautifully*
sie war schnell fertig (adverb: schnell + adjective: fertig) = *she was ready quickly*
er fährt sehr langsam (adverb: sehr + adverb: langsam) = *he drives very slowly*

The following important adverbs are invariable: **auch** = *also*, **fast** = *almost*, **immer** = *always*, **sehr** = *very*, **leider** = *unfortunately*

sie ist sehr klug = *she is very clever*

Summary of German grammar

5.2 Comparatives and superlatives of adverbs

The comparative is formed by adding **-er** to the basic adverb, and the superlative by adding the ending **-(e)sten** to the basic adverb and putting **am** in front:

> klar, klarer, am klarsten = *clearly, more clearly, most clearly*

Some important adverbs are irregular:

> bald, früher, am frühesten = *soon, earlier, at the earliest*
> gut, besser, am besten = *well, better, best*
> gern, lieber, am liebsten = *willingly, more willingly, most willingly*

5.3 Adverbs of time

There are many adverbs and adverbial expressions of time. They are invariable. Some common ones are:

> morgens = *in the morning*   wochenlang, jahrelang *etc* = *for weeks, for years etc*
> nachmittags = *in the afternoon*   montags, dienstags *etc* = *on Mondays, Tuesdays etc*
> nachts = *in the night*
>
> bald = *soon*   jetzt = *now*
> endlich = *in the end*   kürzlich = *recently*
> immer, stets = *always*   wieder = *again*

5.4 Adverbs of order

The use of adverbs and adverbial expressions to convey order is frequent in German. Here are some common patterns of usage:

> erstens = *firstly*   zum ersten Mal = *for the first time*
> zweitens = *secondly*   zum zweiten Mal = *for the second time*
> drittens = *thirdly*   zum dritten Mal = *for the third time*

6 Pronouns

Pronouns are words that can replace a noun. Examples in English are: *I, you, he, she, it, which, theirs, mine, yours.*

6.1 Personal pronouns

These pronouns, such as **er**, **sie**, **es** = *he/she/it*, refer to people or things.

	I	you	he/it	she/it	it	we	you	they	you
NOMINATIVE	ich	du	er	sie	es	wir	ihr	sie	Sie
	me	you	him/it	her/it	it	us	you	them	you
ACCUSATIVE	mich	dich	ihn	sie	es	uns	euch	sie	Sie
DATIVE	mir	dir	ihm	ihr	ihm	uns	euch	ihnen	Ihnen

The genitive form is not given, because it is so rarely used.

Summary of German grammar

In German there are two forms for *you*, **du** and **Sie**. **Du** (plural **ihr**) is informal and is used when speaking to a child, a member of your family, or someone you know well. When speaking to a person or a group of people you do not know very well, use the polite form, **Sie**.

German pronouns agree in gender with the noun they refer to. In the nominative case, *it* can be be translated by **er** or **sie**, as well as **es**:

er (der Bleistift) ist rot = *it (the pencil) is red*
sie (die Rose) ist schön = *it (the rose) is beautiful*
es (das Auto) ist teuer = *it (the car) is expensive*

6.2 Possessive pronouns

The possessive pronouns are:

meiner/meine/mein(e)s = *mine*
deiner/deine/dein(e)s = *yours*
(informal singular)
seiner/seine/sein(e)s = *his*
ihrer/ihre/ihr(e)s = *hers*
seiner/seine/sein(e)s = *its*

unserer/unsere/unser(e)s = *ours*
eurer/eure/eures = *yours*
(informal plural)
ihrer/ihre/ihr(e)s = *theirs*
Ihrer, Ihre, Ihr(e)s = *yours* (polite)

They all take endings like **meiner/meine/mein(e)s**, as follows:

	SINGULAR			PLURAL
	masculine	feminine	neuter	all genders
NOMINATIVE	meiner	meine	mein(e)s	meine
ACCUSATIVE	meinen	meine	mein(e)s	meine
GENITIVE	meines	meiner	meines	meine
DATIVE	meinem	meiner	meinem	meinen

As can be seen in the table, in the neuter form an **-e-** can be added (making **meines**). This applies to all the possessive pronouns, but the extra **-e-** is rare.

6.3 Relative pronouns

Relative pronouns link a main clause to a subordinate clause. In English they are *who*, *which*, *that*, and *what*. In German they are **der**, **die**, or **das**, depending on the noun referred to:

	SINGULAR			PLURAL
	masculine	feminine	neuter	all genders
NOMINATIVE	der	die	das	die
ACCUSATIVE	den	die	das	die
GENITIVE	dessen	deren	dessen	deren
DATIVE	dem	der	dem	denen

Relative pronouns can be left out in English, but never in German:

das Buch, das ich lese = *the book (that) I'm reading*

They agree in gender and number with the noun they refer back to:

der Mann, der uns besucht hat = *the man who visited us*

(**der** is masculine singular)

• •

der Mann, dessen Frau den Wagen   =   *the man, whose wife had rented the car,*
vermietet hatte, wusste es nicht   *did not know about it*

The case of the pronoun depends on its function in the clause it introduces:

der Bleistift, den ich gestern gekauft habe = *the pencil I bought yesterday*

(**den** is masculine singular, and accusative, because it is the object of the clause it introduces)

6.4 Interrogative pronouns

These pronouns are used to ask questions:

wer? = *who?*   was? = *what?*   welcher/welche/welches? = *which?*

Wer changes as follows:

NOMINATIVE wer?   ACCUSATIVE wen?   GENITIVE wessen?   DATIVE wem?

wer sprach? = *who was speaking?*
wen trafst du? = *who (whom) did you meet?*
wessen Buch ist das? = *whose book is that?*
mit wem spricht er? = *who is he talking to?*

Was? is invariable.

was ist das? = *what is that?*

Welcher: The forms are the same as those given for dieser on page 934.

welche Zeitung hast du gekauft? = *which newspaper have you bought?*

Was für ein ... ? This expression means 'what kind or sort of ...?' **Ein** takes the endings according to whether the noun qualified is the subject, object, or indirect object.

was für ein Mann/eine Frau ist das? (subject) = *what sort of a man/woman is that?*

was für ein Geschenk bekam er? (object) = *what sort of a present did he get?*
was für Zeitungen haben Sie? (plural object) = *what sort of newspapers do you have?*

6.5 Reflexive pronouns

The object of a reflexive verb is the same as its subject. In German, the object is a reflexive pronoun. This is usually in the accusative (**ich wasche mich** = *I wash myself*). The reflexive pronouns of some verbs are in the dative (**ich stelle mir vor** = *I imagine*).

The following table shows which accusative reflexive pronoun corresponds to the normal (nominative) personal pronoun.

ich	mich	wir	uns
du	dich	ihr	euch
er, sie, es, man	sich	sie, Sie	sich

sie erinneren sich daran = *they remember it*
es bewegt sich = *it's moving*

The dative forms are the same as the above, except for the **ich** and **du** forms: **ich**: **mir**; **du**: **dir**.

. . . .

6.6 Indefinite pronouns

Some of these pronouns take endings according to whether they are the subject, object, or indirect object in the sentence. Among those that do are: **jemand** = *someone* or *somebody*, **niemand** = *no one* or *nobody*, **irgend jemand** = *anyone* or *anybody*.

	someone	no one	anyone
NOMINATIVE	jemand	niemand	irgend jemand
ACCUSATIVE	jemanden	niemanden	irgend jemanden
DATIVE	jemandem	niemandem	irgend jemandem

jemand hat mein Fahrrad genommen = *someone has taken my bicycle*
sie sah niemanden = *she saw no one*
er gab es jemandem = *he gave it to someone*

The genitive case is rarely used.

6.7 One

The pronoun *one* is translated by **einer**, **eine**, **eines** or **eins**, which take the endings already given in section 6.2 for singular possessive pronouns, according to their function in the sentence.

trinken wir ein(e)s? (ein Bier) = *shall we have one?* (*a beer*)
einer von uns muss es tun = *one of us must do it*

Similarly **keiner**, **keine**, **keines** or **keins** = *no one* or *nobody*, *nothing* (neuter) take the endings according to their function in the sentence.

keiner will ihn begleiten = *no one wants to go with him*

Indefinite pronouns which are invariable are:

something = etwas; *everything* = alles; *nothing* = nichts
gefällt noch etwas? = *would you like something else?*
sie nahm alles = *she took everything*
er weisst nichts = *he knows nothing*

Note that *something/everything/nothing good* is translated by **etwas/alles/nichts Gutes**

something good has happened = etwas Gutes ist geschehen

. . . .

7 Prepositions

Prepositions are words like *above*, *in*, *under* that convey the idea of place and come in front of a noun or pronoun. In German, the noun following a preposition always has to be in one of three cases: dative, accusative, or genitive.

Prepositions can also be prefixes and form separable verbs:

die Straße entlanggehen = *to walk along the street*
er geht die Straße entlang = *he is walking along the street*

In the dictionary, the case governed by a preposition is given as follows:

> **mit 1** *Präp mit Dat.*

This means that **mit** always takes the dative case.

The following prepositions always take the dative:

> aus bei mit nach seit von zu

The following prepositions always take the accusative:

> bis durch entlang für gegen ohne um

The following prepositions always take the genitive:

> anstatt während trotz wegen

There is a group of prepositions that can take the dative or the accusative, depending on the sense of the sentence.

They are:

> an auf außer hinter in unter neben vor über zwischen

If the speaker wishes to convey the idea that someone or something is stationary, the dative case is used:

> sie saß in der Küche = *she sat in the kitchen*
> es liegt auf dem Tisch = *it's lying on the table*

But if the speaker wishes to convey the idea of movement the accusative case is used:

> sie ging in die Küche = *she went into the kitchen*
> er legte den Beutel auf den Tisch = *he put the bag on the table*

Note the expressions **nach Hause** and **zu Hause**: **nach Hause** = *home* (*homewards*), and **zu Hause** = *at home*.

Some forms of the definite article are usually shortened when used with certain prepositions:

> **am** (an dem); **ans** (an das); **aufs** (auf das); **beim** (bei dem)
> **durchs** (durch das); **fürs** (für das); **im** (in dem); **ins** (in das)
> **ums** (um das); **vom** (von dem); **zum** (zu dem); **zur** (zu der)

8 Conjunctions

Conjunctions are words, such as **und** = *and*, **aber** = *but*, which link clauses in a sentence.

Some common conjunctions are:

> aber = *but* denn = *for* oder = *or* sondern = *but* (*on the contrary*) und = *and*

These conjunctions do not change normal word order in the two clauses:

> ich gehe und er kommt auch = *I am going and he is coming too*

This is because the clauses are of equal weight or importance.

Summary of German grammar

Conjunctions which introduce a subordinate clause make the verb in the subordinate clause appear at the end:

als = *when*, = *as*	bevor = *before*	bis = *until*	da = *since*	dass = *that*
ob = *whether*	während = *while*	wenn = *when, = if*	weil = *because*	

als er das erfuhr, wollte er nicht mitkommen	= *when he found out, he didn't want to come*
er konnte nicht in die Schule gehen, weil er krank war	= *he couldn't go to school, because he was ill*
wenn sie in die Stadt geht, nimmt sie immer ihre Handtasche	= *when she goes to town, she always takes her handbag*

9 Word order

The basic rule for German word order is that the verb comes second in a sentence. The subject of the sentence usually comes before the verb:

meine Mutter fährt am Freitag nach Köln = *my mother is going to Cologne on Friday*

When the verb used is in a compound tense, such as the perfect and the future tenses, the auxiliary verb comes second in the sentence, while the past participle (in the perfect) or infinitive (in the future tense) goes to the end:

wir haben sehr lang gewartet = *we waited a very long time*
sie wird sicher bald kommen = *she is sure to come soon*

Infinitives go to the end in other sentences too, as when used with modal verbs or the verb **lassen**:

ich kann dieses Lied nicht leiden = *I can't stand this song*
du musst hier bleiben = *you must stay here*
ich lasse mir die Haare schneiden = *I'm going to have my hair cut*

In questions the normal order of the subject and the verb is inverted, as in English:

kommst du heute Abend? = *are you coming this evening?*

In commands the verb is placed first:

komm schnell rein! = *come in quickly!*

Subordinate clauses

A speaker or writer may start a sentence with a subordinate clause in order to introduce variety or for effect. In this case the verb stays in second place, after the subordinate clause, and the subject of the main clause follows the verb; **blieb** in the example below:

da ich kein Geld hatte, blieb ich zu Hause = *since I had no money, I stayed at home*

In the subordinate clause itself, the verb goes to the end; *cf.* **hatte** in the previous example and **war** in the following one:

er konnte nicht in die Schule gehen, weil er krank war

The relative pronouns **der**, **die**, and **das**, as well as conjunctions such as **als** = *when*, **dass** = *that*, **weil** = *because*, introduce subordinate clauses and therefore cause the verb to go to the end of the subordinate clause.

(See the section on Conjunctions for more examples.)

der Junge, der hier wohnt, ist in der Schule	=	*the boy, who lives here, is at school*
die Soldaten, die gestern hier waren, haben nicht bezahlt	=	*the soldiers, who were here yesterday, did not pay*

When separable verbs separate, the prefix goes to the end:

der Film fängt um acht Uhr an	=	*the film starts at 8 o'clock*
wann kommt der Zug an?	=	*when does the train arrive?*

When there are a number of phrases in a sentence, the usual order for the different elements is: 1 time, 2 manner, 3 place:

wir fahren heute mit dem Auto nach München = *we are driving to Munich today*

(*time* = heute; *manner* = mit dem Auto; *place* = nach München)

German irregular verbs / Deutsche unregelmäßige Verben

1st, 2nd, and 3rd person present and imperative forms are given after the infinitive, and preterite subjunctive forms after the preterite indicative, where they take an umlaut, change *e* to *i*, etc.

Compound verbs (including verbs with prefixes) are only given if a) they do not take the same forms as the corresponding simple verb, e.g. *befehlen*, or b) there is no corresponding simple verb, e.g. *bewegen*.

An asterisk (*) indicates a verb which is also conjugated regularly.

Infinitive *Infinitiv*	Preterite *Präteritum*	Past Participle *2. Partizip*
abwägen	wog (wöge) ab	abgewogen
backen (du bäckst, er bäckt; *auch:* du backst, er backt)	backte, *älter:* buk (büke)	gebacken
befehlen (du befiehlst, er befiehlt; befiehl!)	befahl (beföhle, befähle)	befohlen
beginnen	begann (begänne, *seltener:* begönne)	begonnen
beißen	biss	gebissen
bergen (du birgst, er birgt; birg!)	barg (bärge)	geborgen
bersten (du birst, er birst; birst!)	barst (bärste)	geborsten
besinnen	besann (besänne)	besonnen
bewegen[2]	bewog (bewöge)	bewogen
biegen	bog (böge)	gebogen
bieten	bot (böte)	geboten

German irregular verbs

Infinitive *Infinitiv*	Preterite *Präteritum*	Past Participle *2. Partizip*
binden	band (bände)	gebunden
bitten	bat (bäte)	gebeten
blasen (du bläst, er bläst)	blies	geblasen
bleiben	blieb	geblieben
bleichen*	blich	geblichen
braten (du brätst, er brät)	briet	gebraten
brechen (du brichst, er bricht; brich!)	brach (bräche)	gebrochen
brennen	brannte (brennte)	gebrannt
bringen	brachte (brächte)	gebracht
denken	dachte (dächte)	gedacht
dreschen (du drischst, er drischt; drisch!)	drosch (drösche)	gedroschen
dringen	drang (dränge)	gedrungen
dürfen (ich darf, du darfst, er darf)	durfte (dürfte)	gedurft
empfehlen (du empfiehlst, er empfiehlt, empfiehl!)	empfahl (empföhle, *seltener:* empfähle)	empfohlen
erklimmen	erklomm (erklömme)	erklommen
erlöschen (du erlischst, er erlischt; erlisch!)	erlosch (erlösche)	erloschen
erschallen*	erscholl (erschölle)	erschollen
erschrecken[1,3] (du erschrickst, er erschrickt; erschrick!)	erschrak (erschäke)	erschrocken
erwägen	erwog (erwöge)	erwogen
essen (du isst, er isst; iss!)	aß (äße)	gegessen
fahren (du fährst, er fährt)	fuhr (führe)	gefahren
fallen (du fällst, er fällt)	fiel	gefallen
fangen (du fängst, er fängt)	fing	gefangen
fechten (du fichtst, er ficht; ficht!)	focht (föchte)	gefochten
finden	fand (fände)	gefunden
flechten (du flichtst, er flicht; flicht!)	flocht (flöchte)	geflochten
fliegen	flog (flöge)	geflogen
fliehen	floh (flöhe)	geflohen
fließen	floss (flösse)	geflossen
fressen (du frisst, er frisst; friss!)	fraß (fräße)	gefressen
frieren	fror (fröre)	gefroren
gären*	gor (gäre)	gegoren
gebären (*geh.:* du gebierst, sie gebiert; gebier!)	gebar (gebäre)	geboren
geben (du gibst, er gibt; gib!)	gab (gäbe)	gegeben
gedeihen	gedieh	gediehen
gehen	ging	gegangen
gelingen	gelang (gelänge)	gelungen
gelten (du giltst, er gilt; gilt!)	galt (gölte, gälte)	gegolten
genesen	genas (genäse)	genesen
genießen	genoss (genösse)	genossen
geschehen (es geschieht)	geschah (geschähe)	geschehen
gewinnen	gewann (gewönne, gewänne)	gewonnen
gießen	goss (gösse)	gegossen
gleichen	glich	geglichen
gleiten	glitt	geglitten
glimmen	glomm (glömme)	geglommen
graben (du gräbst, er gräbt)	grub (grübe)	gegraben
greifen	griff	gegriffen
haben (du hast, er hat)	hatte (hätte)	gehabt
halten (du hältst, er hält)	hielt	gehalten
hängen[1]	hing	gehangen
hauen	haute, *geh.:* hieb	gehauen
heben	hob (höbe)	gehoben

Infinitive	Preterite	Past Participle
Infinitiv	*Präteritum*	*2. Partizip*
heißen	hieß	geheißen
helfen (du hilfst, er hilft; hilf!)	half (hülfe, *selten*: hälfe)	geholfen
kennen	kannte (kennte)	gekannt
klingen	klang (klänge)	geklungen
kneifen	kniff	gekniffen
kommen	kam (käme)	gekommen
können (ich kann, du kannst, er... kann)	konnte (könnte)	gekonnt
laden[1,2] (du lädst, er lädt)	lud (lüde)	geladen
lassen (du lässt, er lässt)	ließ	gelassen
laufen (du läufst, er läuft)	lief	gelaufen
leiden	litt	gelitten
leihen	lieh	geliehen
lesen[1,2] (du liest, er liest; lies!)	las (läse)	gelesen
liegen	lag (läge)	gelegen
lügen	log (löge)	gelogen
mahlen	mahlte	gemahlen
meiden	mied	gemieden
melken* (du milkst, er milkt; milk!; du melkst, er melkt; melke!)	molk (mölke)	gemolken
messen (du misst, er misst; miss!)	maß (mäße)	gemessen
misslingen	misslang (misslänge)	misslungen
mögen (ich mag, du magst, er... mag)	mochte (möchte)	gemocht
müssen (ich muss, du musst, er... muss)	musste (müsste)	gemusst
nehmen (du nimmst, er nimmt; nimm!)	nahm (nähme)	genommen
nennen	nannte (nennte)	genannt
pfeifen	pfiff	gepfiffen
preisen	pries	gepriesen
quellen (du quillst, er quillt; quill!)	quoll (quölle)	gequollen
raten (du rätst, er rät)	riet	geraten
reiben	rieb	gerieben
reißen	riss	gerissen
reiten	ritt	geritten
rennen	rannte (rennte)	gerannt
riechen	roch (röche)	gerochen
ringen	rang (ränge)	gerungen
rinnen	rann (ränne, *seltener:* rönne)	geronnen
rufen	rief	gerufen
salzen*	salzte	gesalzen
saufen (du säufst, er säuft)	soff (söffe)	gesoffen
saugen*	sog (söge)	gesogen
schaffen*	schuf (schüfe)	geschaffen
schallen*	scholl (schölle)	geschallt
scheiden	schied	geschieden
scheinen	schien	geschienen
scheißen	schiss	geschissen
schelten (du schiltst, er schilt; schilt!)	schalt (schölte)	gescholten
scheren[1]	schor (schöre)	geschoren
schieben	schob (schöbe)	geschoben
schießen	schoss (schösse)	geschossen
schinden	schindete	geschunden
schlafen (du schläfst, er schläft)	schlief	geschlafen
schlagen (du schlägst, er schlägt)	schlug (schlüge)	geschlagen

German irregular verbs

● ●

Infinitive *Infinitiv*	Preterite *Präteritum*	Past Participle *2. Partizip*
schleichen	schlich	geschlichen
schleifen[1]	schliff	geschliffen
schließen	schloss (schlösse)	geschlossen
schlingen	schlang (schlänge)	geschlungen
schmeißen	schmiss	geschmissen
schmelzen (du schmilzt, er schmilzt; schmilz!)	schmolz	geschmolzen
schneiden	schnitt	geschnitten
schrecken* (du schrickst, er schrickt; schrick!)	schrak (schräke)	geschreckt
schreiben	schrieb	geschrieben
schreien	schrie	geschrie[e]n
schreiten	schritt	geschritten
schweigen	schwieg	geschwiegen
schwellen (du schwillst, er schwillt; schwill!)	schwoll (schwölle)	geschwollen
schwimmen	schwamm (schwömme, *seltener:* schwämme)	geschwommen
schwinden	schwand (schwände)	geschwunden
schwingen	schwang (schwänge)	geschwungen
schwören	schwor (schwüre)	geschworen
sehen (du siehst, er sieht; sieh[e]!)	sah (sähe)	gesehen
sein (ich bin, du bist, er ist, wir sind, ihr seid, sie sind; sei!)	war (wäre)	gewesen
senden*	sandte (sendete)	gesandt
sieden*	sott (sötte)	gesotten
singen	sang (sänge)	gesungen
sinken	sank (sänke)	gesunken
sitzen	saß (säße)	gesessen
sollen (ich soll, du sollst, er soll)	sollte	gesollt
spalten*	spaltete	gespalten
speien	spie	gespie[e]n
spinnen	spann (spönne, spänne)	gesponnen
sprechen (du sprichst, er spricht; sprich!)	sprach (spräche)	gesprochen
sprießen	spross (sprösse)	gesprossen
springen	sprang	gesprungen
stechen (du stichst, er sticht; stich!)	stach (stäche)	gestochen
stehen	stand (stünde, *auch:* stände)	gestanden
stehlen (du stiehlst, er stiehlt; stiehl!)	stahl (stähle, *seltener:* stöhle)	gestohlen
steigen	stieg	gestiegen
sterben (du stirbst, er stirbt; stirb!)	starb (stürbe)	gestorben
stinken	stank (stänke)	gestunken
stoßen (du stößt, er stößt)	stieß	gestoßen
streichen	strich	gestrichen
streiten	stritt	gestritten
tragen (du trägst, er trägt)	trug (trüge)	getragen
treffen (du triffst, er trifft; triff!)	traf (träfe)	getroffen
treiben	trieb	getrieben
treten (du trittst, er tritt; tritt!)	trat (träte)	getreten
triefen*	troff (tröffe)	getroffen
trinken	trank (tränke)	getrunken
trügen	trog (tröge)	getrogen
tun	tat (täte)	getan
verderben (du verdirbst, er verdirbt; verdirb!)	verdarb (verdürbe)	verdorben
verdrießen	verdross (verdrösse)	verdrossen

German irregular verbs

Infinitive	Preterite	Past Participle
Infinitiv	*Präteritum*	*2. Partizip*
vergessen (du vergisst, er vergisst, ... vergiss!)	vergaß (vergäße)	vergessen
verlieren	verlor (verlöre).	verloren
verschleißen*	verschliss	verschlissen
verzeihen	verzieh...........................	verziehen
wachsen[1] (du wächst, er wächst)	wuchs (wüchse)	gewachsen
waschen (du wäschst, er wäschst)	wusch (wüsche)	gewaschen
weichen...............................	wich	gewichen
weisen	wies	gewiesen
wenden[2]*****	wandte (wendete).	gewandt
werben (du wirbst, er wirbt; .... wirb!)	warb (würbe)	geworben
werden (du wirst, er wird; .... werde!)	wurde, *dichter.:* ward .... (würde)	geworden; *als Hilfsv.:* worden
werfen (du wirfst, er wirft; wirf!)........	warf (würfe)......................	geworfen
wiegen[1]	wog (wöge)	gewogen
winden...............................	wand (wände).....................	gewunden
wissen (ich weiß, du weißt, er .... weiß)	wusste (wüsste)	gewusst
wollen (ich will, du willst, er .... will)	wollte............................	gewollt
wringen..............................	wrang (wränge)	gewrungen
ziehen...............................	zog (zöge)........................	gezogen
zwingen..............................	zwang (zwänge)	gezwungen

English irregular verbs / Englische unregelmäßige Verben

Ein Sternchen (*) weist darauf hin, dass die korrekte Form von der jeweiligen Bedeutung abhängt.

Infinitive	Past Tense	Past Participle	Infinitive	Past Tense	Past Participle
Infinitiv	*Präteritum*	*2. Partizip*	*Infinitiv*	*Präteritum*	*2. Partizip*
arise	arose	arisen	**bid**..........	*bade, bid	*bidden, bid
awake.......	awoke.........	awoken	**bind**.........	bound..........	bound
be...........	was *sing.*, ... were *pl.*	been	**bite**.........	bit..............	bitten
bear.........	bore	borne	**bleed**........	bled............	bled
beat.........	beat...........	beaten	**blow**	blew	blown
become......	became	become	**break**	broke	broken
begin	began.........	begun	**breed**	bred	bred
bend	bent	bent	**bring**........	brought	brought
bet..........	bet, betted	bet, betted	**broadcast** ...	broadcast	broadcast
			build........	built	built

English irregular verbs

Infinitive *Infinitiv*	Past Tense *Präteritum*	Past Participle *2. Partizip*
burn	burnt, burned	burnt, burned
burst	burst	burst
bust	bust, busted	bust, busted
buy	bought	bought
cast	cast	cast
catch	caught	caught
choose	chose	chosen
cling	clung	clung
come	came	come
cost	*cost, costed	*cost, costed
creep	crept	crept
cut	cut	cut
deal	dealt	dealt
dig	dug	dug
dive	dived,	dived
	(Amer.) dove	
do	did	done
draw	drew	drawn
dream	dreamt,	dreamt,
	dreamed	dreamed
drink	drank	drunk
drive	drove	driven
dwell	dwelt	dwelt
eat	ate	eaten
fall	fell	fallen
feed	fed	fed
feel	felt	felt
fight	fought	fought
find	found	found
flee	fled	fled
fling	flung	flung
floodlight	floodlit	floodlit
fly	flew	flown
forbid	forbade,	forbidden
	forbad	
forecast	forecast,	forecast,
	forecasted	forecasted
foretell	foretold	foretold
forget	forgot	forgotten
forgive	forgave	forgiven
forsake	forsook	forsaken
freeze	froze	frozen
get	got	got, *(Amer.)*
		gotten
give	gave	given
go	went	gone
grind	ground	ground
grow	grew	grown
hang	*hung,	*hung,
	hanged	hanged
have	had	had
hear	heard	heard
hew	hewed	hewn, hewed
hide	hid	hidden
hit	hit	hit
hold	held	held
hurt	hurt	hurt
keep	kept	kept

Infinitive *Infinitiv*	Past Tense *Präteritum*	Past Participle *2. Partizip*
kneel	knelt,	knelt,
	(esp. Amer.)	*(esp. Amer.)*
	kneeled	kneeled
know	knew	known
lay	laid	laid
lead	led	led
lean	leaned,	leaned,
	(Brit.) leant	*(Brit.)* leant
leap	leapt, leaped	leapt, leaped
learn	learnt,	learnt,
	learned	learned
leave	left	left
lend	lent	lent
let	let	let
lie[a]	lay	lain
light	lit, lighted	lit, lighted
lose	lost	lost
make	made	made
mean	meant	meant
meet	met	met
mow	mowed	mown, mowed
overhang	overhung	overhung
pay	paid	paid
prove	proved	proved, proven
put	put	put
quit	quitted,	quitted,
	(Amer.) quit	*(Amer.)* quit
read /riːd/	read /red/	read /red/
rid	rid	rid
ride	rode	ridden
ring	rang	rung
rise	rose	risen
run	ran	run
saw	sawed	sawn, sawed
say	said	said
see	saw	seen
seek	sought	sought
sell	sold	sold
send	sent	sent
set	set	set
sew	sewed	sewn, sewed
shake	shook	shaken
shear	sheared	shorn,
		sheared
shed	shed	shed
shine	shone	shone
shit	shitted, shit	shitted, shit
shoe	shod	shod
shoot	shot	shot
show	showed	shown
shrink	shrank	shrunk
shut	shut	shut
sing	sang	sung
sink	sank, sunk	sunk
sit	sat	sat
slay	slew	slain
sleep	slept	slept

Infinitive *Infinitiv*	Past Tense *Präteritum*	Past Participle *2. Partizip*
slide	slid	slid
sling	slung	slung
slink	slunk	slunk
slit	slit	slit
smell	smelt, smelled	smelt, smelled
sow	sowed	sown, sowed
speak	spoke	spoken
speed	*sped, speeded	*sped, speeded
spell	spelled, (*Brit.*) spelt	spelled, (*Brit.*) spelt
spend	spent	spent
spill	spilt, spilled	spilt, spilled
spin	spun	spun
spit	spat, spit	spat, spit
split	split	split
spoil	spoilt, spoiled	spoilt, spoiled
spread	spread	spread
spring	sprang, (*Amer.*) sprung	sprung
stand	stood	stood
steal	stole	stolen
stick	stuck	stuck
sting	stung	stung
stink	stank, stunk	stunk
strew	strewed	strewed, strewn
stride	strode	stridden
strike	struck	struck
string	strung	strung

Infinitive *Infinitiv*	Past Tense *Präteritum*	Past Participle *2. Partizip*
strive	strove	striven
sublet	sublet	sublet
swear	swore	sworn
sweep	swept	swept
swell	swelled	swollen, swelled
swim	swam	swum
swing	swung	swung
take	took	taken
teach	taught	taught
tear	tore	torn
tell	told	told
think	thought	thought
thrive	thrived, throve	thrived, thriven
throw	threw	thrown
thrust	thrust	thrust
tread	trod	trodden, trod
understand	understood	understood
undo	undid	undone
wake	woke	woken
wear	wore	worn
weave[1]	wove	woven
weep	wept	wept
wet	wet, wetted	wet, wetted
win	won	won
wind[2] /waɪnd/	wound /waʊnd/	wound /waʊnd/
wring	wrung	wrung
write	wrote	written

Numbers / Zahlen

Cardinal numbers		*Kardinalzahlen*		Ordinal numbers		*Ordinalzahlen*
1	one	1	eins, ein...	1st	first	1. erst...
2	two	2	zwei	2nd	second	2. zweit...
3	three	3	drei	3rd	third	3. dritt...
4	four	4	vier	4th	fourth	4. viert...
5	five	5	fünf	5th	fifth	5. fünft...
6	six	6	sechs	6th	sixth	6. sechst...
7	seven	7	sieben	7th	seventh	7. siebt..., siebent...
8	eight	8	acht	8th	eighth	8. acht...
9	nine	9	neun	9th	ninth	9. neunt...
10	ten	10	zehn	10th	tenth	10. zehnt...
11	eleven	11	elf	11th	eleventh	11. elft...
12	twelve	12	zwölf	12th	twelfth	12. zwölft...
13	thirteen	13	dreizehn	13th	thirteenth	13. dreizehnt...
14	fourteen	14	vierzehn	14th	fourteenth	14. vierzehnt...
15	fifteen	15	fünfzehn	15th	fifteenth	15. fünfzehnt...

Numbers / Zahlen

Cardinal numbers	*Kardinalzahlen*	Ordinal numbers	*Ordinalzahlen*
16 sixteen	16 sechzehn	16th sixteenth	16. sechzehnt...
17 seventeen	17 siebzehn	17th seventeenth	17. siebzehnt...
18 eighteen	18 achtzehn	18th eighteenth	18. achtzehnt...
19 nineteen	19 neunzehn	19th nineteenth	19. neunzehnt...
20 twenty	20 zwanzig	20th twentieth	20. zwanzigst...
21 twenty-one	21 einundzwanzig	21st twenty-first	21. einundzwanzigst...
30 thirty	30 dreißig	30th thirtieth	30. dreißigst...
40 forty	40 vierzig	40th fortieth	40. vierzigst...
50 fifty	50 fünfzig	50th fiftieth	50. fünfzigst...
60 sixty	60 sechzig	60th sixtieth	60. sechzigst...
70 seventy	70 siebzig	70th seventieth	70. siebzigst...
80 eighty	80 achtzig	80th eightieth	80. achtzigst...
90 ninety	90 neunzig	90th ninetieth	90. neunzigst...
100 one hundred	100 [ein]hundert	100th [one] hundredth	100. [ein]hundertst...
101 one hundred and one	101 [ein]hundert-[und]eins	101st [one] hundred and first	101. [ein]hundert-[und]erst...
1,000 one thousand	1 000 [ein]tausend	1,000th [one] thousandth	1 000. [ein]tausendst...
1,001 one thousand and one	1 001 [ein]tausend-[und]eins	1,001st one thousand and first	1 001. [ein]tausend-[und]erst...
10,000 ten thousand	10 000 zehntausend	10,000th ten thousandth	10 000. zehntausendst...
13,438 thirteen thousand, four hundred and thirty-eight	13 438 dreizehntausendvierhundert-[und]achtunddreißig	13,438th thirteen thousand, four hundred and thirty-eighth	13 438. dreizehntausendvierhundert-[und]achtunddreißigst...
100 000 one hundred thousand	100 000 [ein]hunderttausend	100,000th [one] hundred thousandth	100 000. [ein]hunderttausendst...
1,000,000 one million	1 000 000 eine Million	1,000,000th [one] millionth	1 000 000. millionst...
2,000,000 two million	2 000 000 zwei Millionen	2,000,000th two millionth	2 000 000. zweimillionst...
1,000,000,000 one billion	1 000 000 000 eine Milliarde	1,000,000,000th one billionth	1 000 000 000. milliardst...

Vulgar fractions and mixed numbers / Brüche (gemeine Brüche) und gemischte Zahlen

in figures *in Zahlen*	in words	*in Worten*	in figures *in Zahlen*	in words	*in Worten*
1/2	a/one half	*ein halb*	1/1	one over one	*ein eintel*
1/3	a/one third	*ein drittel*	4/1	four over one	*vier eintel*
1/4	a/one quarter	*ein viertel*	m/n	m over n	*m n-tel*
1/10	a/one tenth	*ein zehntel*	x/6	x over six	*x sechstel*
2/3	two-thirds	*zwei drittel*	1 1/2	one and a half	*ein[und]einhalb*

Decimal numbers / Dezimalzahlen

written as	*geschrieben*	spoken as	*gesprochen*
0.1	*0,1*	nought point one	*null Komma eins*
0.015	*0,015*	nought point nought one five	*null Komma null eins fünf*
1.40	*1,40*	one point four o /əʊ/	*eins Komma vier null*